LET US KNOW WHAT YOU THINK:

In order to produce a directory that can better serve you, we ask that you take the time to fill out this short questionnaire. Thank you for your continued support. PLEASE FEEL FREE TO PHOTOCOPY THIS FORM!

Is this the first time you have purchased the *Conservation Directory*?   ❏ Yes ❏ No

If no, how long have you been purchasing the *Conservation Directory*? _____

How would you categorize yourself (please check one)
- ❏ Environmental Professional
- ❏ College or University Library
- ❏ Career Center
- ❏ Public Library
- ❏ Environmental Activist
- ❏ Business or Corporation
- ❏ Environmental Lawyer
- ❏ Conservation Organization
- ❏ Educator
- ❏ Student
- ❏ Scientist
- ❏ Other _____

What resources would you like to see added to the *Conservation Directory*?
_____
_____

What resources would you like to see removed from the *Conservation Directory*?
_____
_____

Are you pleased with the format of the **1999** *Conservation Directory*?   ❏ Yes ❏ No

If no, what suggestions do you have for the future organization of the 2000 *Conservation Directory*_____
_____
_____

Which index is most useful to you?
- ❏ Geographic Index
- ❏ Staff Name Index
- ❏ Keyword Index
- ❏ Organization Name Index
- ❏ I do not use the indices

If organization listings contained less information would the directory still be as useful? ❏Yes ❏No

Would you be interested in purchasing the *Conservation Directory* on CD-ROM?   ❏Yes ❏No

Would you be interested in an online version of the *Conservation Directory*?   ❏Yes ❏No

Additional Comments:
_____
_____

There are forms in the back of this book to update information and suggest new organizations

**Return to: National Wildlife Federation
ATTN: Rue Gordon, 8925 Leesburg Pike, Vienna, VA 22184.**

1999 Conservation Directory

44TH EDITION

A Guide To Worldwide
Environmental Organizations

Rue E. Gordon, *Editor*

Jamie N. Anderson, *Assistant Editor*

Published annually by the
National Wildlife Federation

NATIONAL WILDLIFE FEDERATION®
8925 Leesburg Pike•Vienna•Virginia 22184-0001
www.nwf.org

The mission of the National Wildlife Federation is to educate, inspire, and assist individuals and organizations of diverse cultures to conserve wildlife and other natural resources, and to protect the Earth's environment in order to achieve a peaceful, equitable, and sustainable future.

Printed on recycled paper containing a minimum of 10% post consumer fiber. The balance is pre-consumer fiber.

Copyright 1999, National Wildlife Federation
Library of Congress Catalog Card Number 70-10646
ISSN 0069-911X
ISBN 1-55821-920-X
The Library of Congress-in-Publication Data is available on file.

CELEBRATING THE 25TH ANNIVERSARY OF THE ENDANGERED SPECIES ACT

The *Conservation Directory* is published as a public service. Organizations are included on the basis of their stated objectives and other information provided. Inclusion does not imply confirmation of the information nor does it imply any endorsement of the organizations listed by the National Wildlife Federation.

The *Conservation Directory* may be purchased by calling (800) 836-0510.

If you have any general questions about the *Conservation Directory*, please call (703) 790-4100

LETTER FROM THE EDITORS

To Our Loyal Subscribers:

Every year as we begin the process of publishing a new edition of the *Conservation Directory*, we look closely at the previous editions and take very seriously the comments and suggestions we have received. This year upon careful consideration of these comments, we have decided to use a slightly different formatting for the **1999** *Conservation Directory.* What you will find in this book is a new setup combining past years' formats with new ideas. We hope that this year's *Conservation Directory* will prove to be the most useful source of information you possess in the most easy to use format.

Along with new formatting of the *Conservation Directory*, we would also like to remind everyone that every effort was made to ensure that all information is as accurate as possible. However, this is not always possible due to circumstances out of our control, such as elections that occur after our printing date or the inability to know or gain relevant listing changes from organizations. We are sorry for any inconveniences that arise from errors. Additionally, there are two forms in the back of this edition of the Directory for organizations to update their listing and for anyone to recommend a new organization for listing. We encourage everyone to use these forms.

Finally, we would like to welcome any comments you have on this edition of the Directory, as well as any further suggestions you may have as to how we can make the Directory even better next year. **To make this easier we have included a short questionnaire in the front of the book and ask that you take the time to complete and return it to the address printed on the back**. Thank you.

Sincerely,

Rue E. Gordon
Editor and Coordinator

Jamie N. Anderson
Assistant Editor

ABOUT THE COVER

The Cover of the *1999 Conservation Directory* is a celebration of the 25th anniversary of the Endangered Species Act, one of our nation's premier wildlife protection laws. NWF is using this occasion to launch an ambitious multiple year campaign celebrating endangered species conservation successes, analyzing existing challenges, and educating the nation about endangered species issues. The campaign has been titled *Save Endangered Species: Keep the Wild Alive.* ™ It will combine public awareness, media, and legislative components to heighten national awareness of endangered species and galvanize concrete, on-the-ground conservation action. Twenty-five specific endangered species have been selected as a reoccurring theme used to show the very real animal faces of imperiled species. Each species was carefully chosen to represent broader messages of threats relevant to a wide array of endangered species. We have chosen to feature seven of the 25 species on the *Conservation Directory* cover. NWF believes this campaign will make a significant impact in the way people understand, and go about saving endangered species.

ENDANGERED SPECIES FEATURED ON THE COVER:

#1, GRAY WOLF (*Canis lupus*): Once wolves were everywhere across most of North America, they played an important role in a variety of ecosystems, hunting large mammals and keeping the ungulate herds strong by eliminating sick and old individuals. But with widespread human development, wolves were ruthlessly exterminated from most of the United States. Now, gray, or timber, wolves are found in abundance only in the Arctic, Canada, and Alaska, with smaller populations in some upper Midwest and Northern Rockies states.

#2, ROSY PERIWINKLE (*Catharanthus roseus*): The Rosy Periwinkle is an attractive foot-high plant with deep green, shiny leaves. It has given modern medicine an effective treatment for two deadly types of cancer: Alkaloids from the plant have produced effective agents for fighting childhood leukemia and Hodgkin's disease. The Rosy Periwinkle comes from Madagascar, an African Island with incredible biodiversity, but threatened by deforestation and local agricultural practices.

#3, CANADA LYNX (*Lynx canadensis*): Secretive and solitary, the lynx once prowled the snowy evergreen forests of North America in large numbers. But while lynx populations are still healthy in Canada and Alaska, the animals have almost disappeared in the United States. Snowshoe hares are its chief prey, and populations of both species fluctuate together every seven to ten years. The lynx depends on dense, mature forests with many snags (hollow trees) or windfallen logs for dens. Its decline is an indication of the loss of such ecosystems to forest clearing.

#4 KARNER BLUE BUTTERFLY (*Lycaeides melissa samuelis*): The Karner blue butterfly survives in scattered areas of grassy sandplain, oak savanna, and pine barrens from the upper Midwest to the East Coast and Canada. This one-inch endangered insect shares its habitat with many other rare species, such as the frosted elfin butterfly, Blanding's turtle, and loggerhead shrike.

#5 UTAH PRAIRIE DOG (*Cynomys parvidens*): The squirrel-sized Utah prairie dog lives in the high country of eastern Utah's open mountain valleys. It is one of three distinct prairie dog subspecies found in the United States. These roly-poly creatures spend their days tumbling in play, grazing on grass, and calling to each other. To survive fierce winter storms and escape predators such as raptors, coyotes, and badgers, they create the only available shelter on their treeless habitat by digging extensive burrows. Inhabited or empty, these burrows are then adopted by rabbits, snakes, mice, salamanders, and other species. Thus, the prairie dog is one of nature's great architects.

#6 DESERT TORTOISE (*Gopherus agassizzi*): The desert tortoise has adapted to the most scorching deserts in America, including the Mojave and Death Valley. These threatened tortoises dig shallow, sandy burrows to escape the worst daytime heat underground, emerging at night to graze on cacti and other plants. They can survive as long as 100 years under these harsh conditions.

Back Cover, KEMP'S RIDLEY SEA TURTLE (*Lepidochelys kempii*): Kemp's Ridley sea turtles range the Atlantic Basin and Gulf of Mexico, from the open ocean surface to rocky near-shore feeding areas all along the Gulf and East Coasts. The entire population nests on a single sandy beach in Mexico, where eggs and young are highly vulnerable to predators that include coyotes and people. Other threats include pollution from offshore oil wells, consumption of carelessly discarded plastic bags that the turtles mistake for jellyfish, and shrimp trawler nets. Kemp's Ridley sea turtles are the most seriously endangered of all sea turtle species.

HOW YOU CAN HELP:
- Join and support conservation organizations that help protect endangered species.
- Help save species by protecting local habitats.
- Never buy endangered species or products made from endangered species.
- Spread the word to others about endangered species and their plight.
- Join the National Wildlife Federation's *Endangered Species Activist Network* at no cost. We send network members e-mail alerts and updates on endangered species issues, as well as important action alerts and informative newsletters. To sign up or to find out more about conservation activities in your region, send your name, address, e-mail address and fax number to: Endangered Species, National Wildlife Federation, 1400 16th Street, NW, Washington, DC 20036, or visit out website at www.nwf.org

GET INVOLVED – ENDANGERED SPECIES NEED YOU!

KEEP THE WILD ALIVE™

National Wildlife Federation's Senior Leadership

Mark Van Putten, *President & Chief Executive Officer*
Eileen Morgan Johnson, *General Counsel*
Lawrence J. Amon, *Vice President for Finance and Administration & Chief Financial Officer*
Natalie S. Waugh, *Senior Vice President, Constituent Programs*
R. Montgomery Fischer, *Vice President & Coordinator, Conservation Programs*

Vice Presidents: Barbara J. Bramble, Robert S. Ertter, J. Scott Feierabend, John H. Giesecke, Philip B. Kavits, James S. Lyon (Acting), Jaime Berman Matyas, Steven J. Shimberg, Bob Strohm, Carolyn Waldron; Chief Information Technology Officer: Kenneth Herman

National Wildlife Productions: Christopher N. Palmer, *President & CEO*

Past Presidents: Thomas L. Kimball, Jay D. Hair

Conservation Directory Staff

Rue S. Gordon
Editor/Project Coordinator

Jamie N. Anderson
Assistant Editor

James S. Lyon
Acting Vice President, Educational Outreach

Furey Design/Kathleen Furey
Cover Design

Cover Photo Credits:

Back Cover: Kemp's Ridley Sea Turtle, by Susan Middleton and David Liittschwager ©1994
Front Cover and Left Column, first picture: Gray Wolf, by Joe McDonald
Front Cover, Left Colunm, second picture: Rosy Periwinkle, by Richard Shiell, Earth Scenes
Front Cover, Left Column, third picture: Canada Lynx, by Art Wolfe
Front Cover, Left Column, fourth picture: Karner Blue Butterfly, by Ken Cole, Animals Animals
Front Cover, Left Column, fifth picture: Utah Prairie Dog, by Jeff Vanuga
Front Cover, Left Column, sixth picture: Desert Tortoise, by Susan Middleton and David Liittschwager ©1994

NATIONAL
WILDLIFE
FEDERATION®

TABLE OF CONTENTS

Introduction
Acknowledgements
User's Guide
National Wildlife Federation Affiliate Organizations
National Wildlife Federation
1997 National Conservation Achievement Awards
1998 Goldman Environmental Awards

U. S. CONGRESS, COMMITTEES, AND SUBCOMMITTEES 1

U. S. FEDERAL AND INTERNATIONAL GOVERNMENT AGENCIES 7
Includes Departments of the Executive Branch, Independent Agencies, Commissions, Canadian Federal Government Agencies, and other International Government Agencies.

STATE AND PROVINCE GOVERNMENT AGENCIES 39
Includes State and Provincial Government Agencies.

NON-GOVERNMENTAL ORGANIZATIONS 133
Consists of United States and International Organizations not affiliated with government agencies.

EDUCATIONAL INSTITUTIONS 366
Includes two and four year colleges and universities with conservation programs.

CONSERVATION INFORMATION RESOURCES 394
Fish and Wildlife Commissioners and Directors 394
State Agency Coordinators for Environmental Education 396
Periodicals and Directories 397
Sources of Audio-Visual Materials 401
Natural Heritage Programs 402
Environmental Databases and Services 406

FEDERALLY PROTECTED AREAS 414
National Forests 414
National Marine Sanctuaries 416
National Parks 417
National Seashores 418
National Grasslands 419
Bureau of Land Management Districts 419
National Wildlife Refuges 421

INDICES
ORGANIZATION NAME INDEX 427
KEYWORD INDEX 445
STAFF NAME INDEX 495
GEOGRAPHIC INDEX 523

INTRODUCTION

This is the forty-fourth edition of the National Wildlife Federation's *Conservation Directory*. It has been published every year since 1955. Our first Directory listed only the National Wildlife Federation state affiliate organizations. Expansion of the Directory began in 1960 with the inclusion of the U.S. government agencies, international, national, regional organizations and commissions, Canadian government agencies and U.S. and Canadian citizen's groups. The 1999 Directory has over 3,000 entries, an expansion of more than 100 new organizations from the previous edition. It also includes the winners of the Goldman Environmental Prize and the National Wildlife Federation Conservation Achievement awards.

Listings now include:
- United States Congressional Members, Committees, and Subcommittees
- Federal Government Agencies (United States, Canadian, and International)
- State Government Agencies (United States and Canadian)
- Non-Governmental Organizations (United States, Canadian, and International)
- Educational Institutions (Colleges and Universities with Conservation Programs)
- Conservation Information Resources (Periodicals and Databases)
- Federally Protected Conservation Areas
- And pages and pages more of essential information you will use throughout the year.

ACKNOWLEDGEMENTS

We would like to take the time to thank the many people who have taken part in the production of this book. It is an enormous undertaking each year, and one that would be impossible without the help and support of our colleagues. Their advice and assistance throughout production is the only way we have been able to bring you this extraordinary resource. From the beautiful cover to the wisely organized information on its pages, these people have allowed us to once again bring to the public the best directory of conservation organizations. Thanks to all who made it possible to produce a quality publication.

Many thanks to **Jim Lyon**, Acting Vice President for the Educational Outreach Department, **Ian Mishalove**, WEB Manager, **Jeff Flocken** and **Sara Barth**, Endangered Species Campaign Coordinators, **Kathleen Furey**, Cover Designer, **Don Worthley**, Technical Consultant, **Kay Lybrand**, Staff Assistant for Communications, **Loren Magruder**, Staff Assistant for Educational Outreach, **Stephanie Bisulco**, Administrative Assistant for Community-Based Programs, and special thanks to **Roy Geiger**, Manager of our Education Center, and **Sharon Levy,** our dedicated librarian. Their tiresome dedication to the publication of the Directory is greatly appreciated. We would also like to acknowledge our **Information Systems and Fulfillment Services** staff. Without their help, it would have been impossible to produce this Directory.

Also, many thanks to all of the organizations listed and to the individuals involved for their cooperation in providing the information that was included in this Directory. We commend all of these organizations for their continuing work to protect and defend our natural world.

Rue E. Gordon, Editor and Coordinator
Conservation Directory
National Wildlife Federation
8925 Leesburg Pike
Vienna, VA 22184-0001
Phone (703) 790-4402; Fax (703) 790-4468
Email: gordon@nwf.org

THE *CONSERVATION DIRECTORY* IS DIVIDED INTO THREE PARTS:

●Part One: Table of Contents
An excellent resource for beginning a search. Lists all of the sections headings with the page numbers they begin.

●Part Two: Descriptive Listings
Entries are arranged alphabetically according to sections:

- *U. S. Congress, Committees, and Subcommittees*
- *U. S. Federal and International Government Agencies*: Consists of Executive Branch Organizations, Government Independent Agencies, Commissions, and International Government Agencies.
- *State and Province Government Agencies*: Organized by State, consists of State Environmental Agencies.
- *Non-Governmental Organizations*: Consists of United States and International organizations that are not affiliated with any state or government agency whose mission is to help protect, preserve, and defend the natural world. Listed in alphabetical order.
- *Educational Institutions*: Colleges and Universities with Conservation Programs and Research Centers. Organized by State.
- *Conservation Information Resources*: Includes Fish and Wildlife Commissioners and Directors, State Agency Coordinators for Environmental Education, Periodicals and Directories, Audio-Visual Materials, Natural Heritage Programs, and Environmental Databases.
- *Federally Protected Areas*: Consists of National Forests, National Marine Sanctuaries, National Parks, National Seashores, National Grasslands, Bureau of Land Management Districts, and National Wildlife Refuges.

National Wildlife Federation affiliates are listed in the Non-Governmental Organizations section. Governors are listed first in the State Government Section. Entries include name, address, phone and fax number, e-mail and WWW address, founding date, membership (where appropriate), senior staff by name and title, and description of the organization's primary goals and mission.

●Part Three: Indices

Organization Index
This is a quick and easy way to locate an organization. The index includes the name of every organization included in the Directory in alphabetical order with the corresponding page number.

Keyword Index
This useful reference tool lists various subject areas and gives the name of those organizations whose work is related to that keyword. Index citations contain page numbers.

Staff Name Index
This directory is helpful if you know the name of an individual involved with an organization but do not know the specific name of the organization. The index lists all individuals listed in the *Conservation Directory*. Each citation contains the individual's name and page numbers where it appears.

Geographic Index
This index lists the Congressional Committees, U.S. Federal and Canadian Government Agencies, State and Province Government Agencies, and U.S. Non-Governmental Organizations by geographic regions. It is a great way to find out what organizations can be found in a certain state or province.

NATIONAL WILDLIFE FEDERATION AFFILIATES

National Wildlife Federation affiliates are autonomous, state-wide organizations which support the purposes and objectives of the National Wildlife Federation. Each affiliate is governed by its own board of directors and develops its own membership on a local level. There are currently 46 affiliates, including the Virgin Islands. Affiliates provide NWF with an organized grassroots network nationwide. The elected delegates from the state affiliates determine the conservation policy for NWF through a resolution process at the NWF Annual Meeting. The delegates also elect NWF's Chair, Vice Chairs, and 13 Regional Directors.

ALABAMA WILDLIFE FEDERATION
46 Commerce St., P.O. Box 2102,
Montgomery, AL 36104
Phone: 334-832-9453; fax: 334-832-9454
E-mail: alabamawf@mindspring.com

WILDLIFE FEDERATION OF ALASKA
750 West Second Ave., Suite 200-B
Anchorage, AK 99501
Phone: 907-274-3388; fax: 907-258-4811
E-mail: wfa@micronet.net
WWW: www.micronet.net/users/~wfa/default.html

ARIZONA WILDLIFE FEDERATION
644 N. Country Club, Suite E
Mesa, AZ 85201-4991
Phone: 602-644-0077; fax: 602-644-0078
E-mail: awf@primenet.com; WWW: www.primenet.com/~awf

ARKANSAS WILDLIFE FEDERATION
7509 Cantrell Rd., # 104
Little Rock, AR 72207
Phone: 50l-663-7255; fax: 501-664-7397

COLORADO WILDLIFE FEDERATION
445 Union Blvd., #302
Lakewood, CO 80228-1243
Phone: 303-987-0400; fax: 303-987-0200
E-mail: cwfed@aol.com

CONNECTICUT FOREST AND PARK ASSOCIATION
Middlefield, 16 Meriden Rd.
Rockfall, CT 06481-2961
Phone: 860-346-2372; fax: 860-347-7463
E-mail: conn.forest.assoc@asnet.net;
WWW: www.ctwoodlands.org

DELAWARE NATURE SOCIETY
Box 700, Hockessin, DE 19707
Phone: 302-239-2334; fax: 302-239-2473
E-mail: Ashland@DCA.net
WWW: www.dca.net/naturesociety

FLORIDA WILDLIFE FEDERATION
P.O. Box 6870
Tallahassee, FL 32314-6870
Phone: 850-656-7113; fax: 850-942-4431
E-mail: wildfed@aol.com
WWW: www.ssnow.com/fwf/org.htm

GEORGIA WILDLIFE FEDERATION
1930 Iris Dr.
Conyers, GA 30094-5046
Phone: 770-929-3350; fax: 770-929-3534
E-mail: gwf@gwf.org; WWW: www.gwf.org

CONSERVATION COUNCIL FOR HAWAII
250 Ward Avenue, Suite 217
Honolulu, HI 96814
Phone: 808-236-2234; Fax: 808-247-2551
Email: sagerw00l@hawaii.rr.com
WWW: www.planet-hawaii.com/~cch

IDAHO WILDLIFE FEDERATION
P.O. Box 6426
Boise, ID 83707
Phone: 208-342-7055; fax: 208-342-7097
E-mail: IWFBOI@cyberhighway.net
WWW: www.buytheworld.com/norest/iwf/iwf/htm

INDIANA WILDLIFE FEDERATION
950 North Rangeline Rd., Suite A
Carmel, IN 46032-1315
Phone: 317-571-1220, 1-800-347-3445;
Fax: 317-571-1223, call first
E-mail: iwf@indy.net

IOWA WILDLIFE FEDERATION
3125 Douglas, Suite 103
Des Moines, IA 50310
Phone: 515-279-0655

KANSAS WILDLIFE FEDERATION
4840 W. 15th St., Suite 1000
Lawrence, KS 66049-3876
Phone: 785-843-7786; fax: 785-843-7555
E-mail: kwf@kswildlife.org
WWW: www.kswildlife.org

LEAGUE OF KENTUCKY SPORTSMEN, INC.
P.O. Box 406, 4776 U.S. 27 S.
Alexandria, KY 41075
Phone/fax: 606- 635-8896;
E-mail: ksportsmen@fuse.net; WWW: www.loks.org

LOUISIANA WILDLIFE FEDERATION, INC.
P.O. Box 65239, 337 S. Acadian Thruway
Baton Rouge, LA 70896-5239
Phone/fax: 504-344-6707

NATURAL RESOURCES COUNCIL OF MAINE
3 Wade Street,
Augusta, ME 04330
Phone: 207-622-3101; fax: 207-622-4343
E-mail: nrcm@nrcm.org

MICHIGAN UNITED CONSERVATION CLUBS, INC.
2101 Wood S.
Lansing, MI 48912-3728
Phone: 517-371-1041; fax: 517-371-1505
E-mail: mucc@mucc.org
WWW: www.mucc.org

MINNESOTA CONSERVATION FEDERATION
551 S. Snelling Ave., #B
St. Paul, MN 55116-1525
Phone/fax: 6l2-690-3077
E-mail: mncf@mtn.org

MISSISSIPPI WILDLIFE FEDERATION
P.O. Box 1814
Jackson, MS 39215-1814
Phone: 601- 353-6922; fax: 601-352-3437
E-mail: mwf@netdoor.com

CONSERVATION FEDERATION OF MISSOURI
728 W. Main St.
Jefferson City, MO 65101-1159
Phone: 573-634-2322; fax: 573-634-8205
E-mail: modfed@sockets.net

MONTANA WILDLIFE FEDERATION
P.O. Box 1175
Helena, MT 59601
Phone: 406-449-7604; fax: 406- 449-8946
E-mail: mwf@desktop.org
WWW: www.montanawildlife.com

NEBRASKA WILDLIFE FEDERATION, INC.
P.O. Box 81437
Lincoln, NE 68501-1437
Phone: 402- 476-908; fax: 402-994-2001

NEVADA WILDLIFE FEDERATION
P.O. Box 71238, Reno, NV 89570
Phone: 702-645-5423; Fax: 702-885-0405
E-mail: dupree@pyramid.net
WWW: www.nvwf.org

NEW HAMPSHIRE WILDLIFE FEDERATION
P.O. Box 239, 54 Portsmouth St.
Concord, NH 03302
Phone: 603-224-5953; fax: 603-228-0423
E-mail: nhwf@aol.com
WWW: www.nhwf.org/

NEW MEXICO WILDLIFE FEDERATION
3240-D Juan Tabo NE, Suite 204
Albuquerque, NM 87111
Phone: 505-299-5404

ENVIRONMENTAL ADVOCATES
353 Hamilton St.
Albany, NY 12210
Phone: 518-462-5526; fax: 518-427-0381
E-mail: info@envadocates.org
WWW: www.envadvocates.org

NORTH CAROLINA WILDLIFE FEDERATION
Box 10626
Raleigh, NC 27605
Phone: 919-833-1923; fax: 919-829-1192

NORTH DAKOTA WILDLIFE FEDERATION
P.O. Box 7248
Bismarck, ND 58507-7248
Phone: 701-222-2557; fax: 701-222-0334

LEAGUE OF OHIO SPORTSMEN
3953 Indianola Ave.
Columbus, OH 43214
Phone: 614-268-9924

OKLAHOMA WILDLIFE FEDERATION
P.O. Box 60126
Oklahoma City, OK 73118
Phone: 405-524-7009; fax: 405-521-9270

PENNSYLVANIA FEDERATION OF SPORTSMEN'S CLUBS
2426 N. Second St.
Harrisburg, PA 17110
Phone: 717-232-3480; fax: 717-231-3524
E-mail: pawild@paonline.com

PLANNING AND CONSERVATION LEAGUE
926 J Street, Suite 612
Sacramento, CA 95814
Phone: 916-444-8726; fax: 916-448-1789
E-mail: pclmail@pcl.org, WWW: www.pcl.org/pcl

ENVIRONMENT COUNCIL OF RHODE ISLAND
P.O. Box 9061
Providence, RI 02940
Phone/fax: 401-621-8048
E-mail: ecri@studentweb.providence.edu

SOUTH CAROLINA WILDLIFE FEDERATION
2711 Middleburg Dr., Suite 104
Columbia, SC 29204
Phone: 803-256-0670; fax: 803-256-0690
E-mail: mail@scwf.org; WWW: www.scwf.org

SOUTH DAKOTA WILDLIFE FEDERATION
P.O. Box 7075, Pierre, SD 57501
Phone/fax: 605-224-7524
E-mail: sdwf@cam-walnet.com; WWW: www.sdwf.org

TENNESSEE CONSERVATION LEAGUE
300 Orlando Ave.
Nashville, TN 37209-3257
Phone: 615-353-1133; fax: 615-353-0083
E-mail: conserve.tcl@nashville.com

TEXAS COMMITTEE ON NATURAL RESOURCES
601 Westlake Dr.
Austin, TX 78746
Phone: 512-327-4119; fax: 512-328-3399
E-mail: tconr@eden.com; WWW: www.eden.com/tconr

UTAH WILDLIFE FEDERATION
Box 526367
Salt Lake City, UT 84152-6367
Phone: 801-487-1946; fax: 801-486-0611

VERMONT NATURAL RESOURCES COUNCIL
9 Bailey Ave., Montpelier, VT 05602
Phone: 802-223-2328; fax: 802-223-0287
E-Mail: vnrc@together.net

VIRGIN ISLANDS CONSERVATION SOCIETY, INC.
Arawak Bldg., Suite 3, Gallows Bay
Christiansted, VI 00820
Phone: 340-773-1989; fax: 340-773-7545
E-mail: sea@viaccess.net
WWW: www.ecani.com/environassoc

VIRGINIA WILDLIFE FEDERATION
1001 East Broad St.
1928 Richmond, VA 23219
Phone: 804-648-3136; fax: 804-648-8010

WASHINGTON WILDLIFE FEDERATION
P.O Box 1966
Olympia, WA 98507-1966
Phone: 360-705-1903
WWW: www.washingtonwildlife.org

WEST VIRGINIA WILDLIFE FEDERATION, INC.
P.O. Box 275
Paden City, WV 26159
Phone: 304782-3685; E-mail: pleinback@aol.com

WISCONSIN WILDLIFE FEDERATION, INC.
P.O. Box 2504, 242 Keoller Ave.
Oshkosh, WI 54901
Phone: 414-235-9136; fax: 414-235-6030
E-mail: wwf@POP.prodigy.net
WWW: www.easy-axcess.com/wwf

WYOMING WILDLIFE FEDERATION
P.O. Box 106, Cheyenne, WY 82003
Phone: 307-637-5433; fax: 307-637-6629
E-mail: admin@wyomingwildlife.org
WWW: www.wyomingwildlife.org

WHO WE ARE:

The National Wildlife Federation is the nation's oldest and largest member-supported conservation organization, working with individuals, communities, organizations, businesses, and governments to protect wildlife, wild places, and the environment upon which we all depend. Through our grass-roots members, 46 state affiliate organizations, and 10 field offices nationwide, we educate, assist, and inspire people from all walks of life to conserve wildlife and other natural resources. Our common-sense approach to environmental protection balances the demands of a healthy economy with the need for a healthy environment, ensuring a brighter future for people and wildlife everywhere.

NATIONAL WILDLIFE FEDERATION REGIONAL AND PROJECT OFFICES

- **Headquarters** in Vienna, Virginia; Phone (703) 790-4000
- **The Alaska Project Office** in Anchorage, Alaska; Phone: (970) 258-4800
- **Everglades Project Office** in Naples, Florida; Phone: (941) 643-4111
- **Great Lakes Natural Resource Center** in Ann Arbor, Michigan; Phone: (734) 769-3351
- **Gulf States Natural Resource Center** in Austin, Texas; Phone: (512) 346-3934
- **Northeastern Natural Resource Center** in Montpelier, Vermont; Phone: (802) 229-0650
- **Northern Rockies Natural Resource Center** in Missoula, Montana; Phone: (406) 721-6705
- **Office of Federal and International Affairs (OFIA)** in Washington, DC; Phone: (202) 797-6800
- **Rocky Mountain's Natural Resource Center** in Boulder, Colorado; Phone: (303) 786-8001
- **Southeastern Natural Resource Center** in Atlanta, Georgia; Phone: (404) 876-8733
- **Western Natural Resource Center** in Portland, Oregon; Phone: (503) 230-0421

Detailed descriptions of these offices can be found in their listings in the Non-Governmental Organization Section.

OUR MISSION:

The mission of the National Wildlife Federation is to educate, inspire, and assist individuals and organizations of diverse cultures to conserve wildlife and other natural resources, and to protect the Earth's environment in order to achieve a peaceful, equitable, and sustainable future.

WHAT WE DO:

NWF focuses its efforts on five core issue areas (*Endangered Habitats, Water Quality, Land Stewardship, Wetlands, and Sustainable Communities*) and pursues a diverse range of education and advocacy based on programs within these core areas.

EDUCATIONAL PROGRAMS: Education is at the heart of the NWF's mission. NWF offers a variety of educational programs that reach thousands of people of all ages, teaching them about nature and wildlife and their importance to human survival. These programs include:

- **ANIMAL TRACKS®** is our environmental education program that trains elementary and middle school teachers. The program offers both on-line and printed conservation education materials to assist teachers.
- **BACKYARD WILDLIFE HABITAT™** is a program that encourages people to plan their landscaping with the needs of wildlife in mind. Since 1973, NWF has officially certified over 22,000 Backyard Wildlife Habitats. NWF also promotes a **SCHOOLYARD HABITAT®** project to educate children about wildlife habitats on school grounds.
- **CAMPUS ECOLOGY®** assists students, faculty, and administrators in transforming colleges and universities into learning and teaching models of environmental sustainability by providing factual resources, organizing tools, one-on-one consultation, and training clinics.
- **CONSERVATION SUMMITS®** offer a fun, week-long adult and family learning experience that builds environmental awareness and appreciation through hands-on classes, outdoor activities, and field trips to some of America's most spectacular sites.
- **EARTH TOMORROW®** is a conservation leadership education program for high-school aged students. The program is currently piloted in Detroit through the Great Lakes Center.
- **EARTH SAVERS®** is a club program for children (ages 6-13) who care about the Earth and want to help.
- **NATURE LINK®** program connects youth and families to nature through outdoor education. It builds an awareness of the natural world and encourages families to adopt an environmentally-friendly lifestyle.
- **NATIONAL WILDLIFE WEEK,** celebrated each April, is a program that brings free conservation curriculum materials to more than 620,000 educators who reach more than 20 million students.

ACTIVISM, ADVOCACY, AND LITIGATION: NWF's activism begins at the grassroots level by providing our members with the resources they need to make a difference. Through advocacy efforts at the local, state, federal, and international level, we bring common sense discussion of conservation policies to the American public. Finally, we ensure the development and enforcement of effective conservation policies that protect people, wildlife, and natural resources.

Some of the current NWF programs within the five core areas include the following:

ENDANGERED HABITATS
- Keep the Wild Alive Campaign
- Endangered Species Act
- Climate Change and Wildlife
- Takings

LAND STEWARDSHIP
- Fire Away
- Northern Forest Restoration Project
- Wildlife on the Prairie
- Grazing and Grasslands

WATER QUALITY
- Saving our Watersheds
- Toxic Pollution
- Coastal Waters and Estuaries

WETLANDS
- Florida Everglades
- Okefenokee Swamp
- Alaska Copper River Delta
- Gulf States Wetlands
- Alaska Wetlands Watch
- National Wetlands Protection

SUSTAINABLE COMMUNITIES
- Population and the Environment
- Trade and the Environment
- Banking and the Environment
- Sustainable Communities Pilot Projects
- Flood Plain Management

NATIONAL WILDLIFE PRODUCTIONS: National Wildlife Productions (NWP) is the not-for-profit television, film, and multimedia arm of the National Wildlife Federation. NWP's mission is to produce films, television programs, and other media that entertain people while opening their eyes to the importance of conserving natural resources for the needs of both people and wildlife. NWP produces NWF documentaries for TBS Superstation, The Disney Channel, Animal Planet, Home and Garden Television, the Outdoor Life Network, and public television. NWP also produces giant-screen films for IMAX theaters.

NWF's PUBLICATIONS: NWF's award-winning magazines celebrate wildlife in all its wondrous diversity. *National Wildlife* and *International Wildlife* use riveting text and captivating images to educate readers about conservation issues and to explore the latest discoveries affecting the natural world. *Ranger Rick*, for children ages 7 to 12, and *Your Big Backyard*, for kids ages 3 to 6, combine colorful photographs, funny drawings and exciting stories to turn readers on to nature, outdoor adventure, and helping the environment.

FOR MORE INFORMATION ABOUT THESE AND OTHER NWF PROGRAMS, PLEASE CALL (800) 822-9919 OR CHECK OUT OUR WEB SITE AT www.nwf.org

Established in 1965 through funds donated by Sears, Roebuck & Company, the **National Conservation Achievement Awards** are presented annually by the National Wildlife Federation, to recognize people and organizations whose work has helped to safeguard wildlife and our natural resources. Recipients, who are chosen through a nomination process, represent a wide variety of ongoing environmental work. The 1997 awards were presented at our 1998 Annual Meeting, in the following categories: *Affiliate of the Year, Communications, Corporate Leadership, Education, Government, International, Legal/Legislative, Organization, Science, Youth, and Special Achievement*.

RECIPIENTS:

VIRGIN ISLANDS CONSERVATION SOCIETY, INC.
Affiliate of the Year
Box 3839, Christiansted, St. Croix, V.I. 00822
(340) 773-2785; Fax (340) 773-5427
coralbrief@virgin.usvi.net

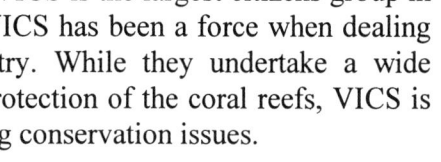

Divided into two chapters, the St. Croix Environmental Association (SEA), and the Environmental Association of St. Thomas (EAST), VICS is the largest citizens group in the Virgin Islands. Through volunteer leadership, VICS has been a force when dealing with government officials, developers, and industry. While they undertake a wide variety of issues from solid waste disposal to the protection of the coral reefs, VICS is deeply committed to educating the public on pressing conservation issues.

MARTIN KRATT AND CHRIS KRATT
Communications
Kratts' Creatures
Paragon Entertainment Corporation
119 Spadina Ave., Suite 900
Toronto, Ontario, Canada M5V2L1
(416) 977-2929; Fax (416) 977-8247

For two years the "Kratt Brothers" as they are known, have been an inspiration to children from ages 6-11 with their award winning television show *Kratts' Creatures*. The show, which they created and host, is an adventure for kids into the natural world. Martin and Chris have also developed conservation field projects, published scientific articles, and won several awards for their children's educational programs. Their mission is to empower children as future custodians of the planet.

ANNHEUSER-BUSCH COMPANIES, INC.
Corporate Leadership
ANNHEUSER-BUSCH COMPANIES, INC.
One Busch Place, St. Louis, MO 63118
(314) 577-0674

Annheuser-Busch has made education their driving force having established formal education programs at Sea World and Busch Gardens. They are also the world's leader in using bio-energy recovery technology. Additionally, Anheuser-Busch is a leader in protecting wildlife and wildlife habitat through its Busch Garden parks.

DR. STEPHEN R. KELLERT
Education
STEPHEN R. KELLERT
Yale University School of Forestry and Environmental Studies
205 Prospect Street, New Haven, CT 06511
(203) 432-5114; Fax (203) 432-3817
stephen.kellert@yale.edu

A professor at Yale University School of Forestry and Environmental Studies, Stephen Kellert has advanced the cause of environmental education through twenty years of original research and writing. Kellert is renowned for the Biophilia hypothesis, which he developed with biologist E.O. Wilson. This hypothesis explores the relationship humans have with the natural world.

VALDAS V. ADAMKUS
Government
President of Lithuania
Vilnius, Lithuania

The current president of Lithuania, Valdas V. Adamkus has spent his life working for a clean environment in the former Soviet Union and the United States. During his time in the United States he was the longest serving senior executive in the U.S. Environmental Protection Agency. He has led efforts to develop Great Lakes protection agreements with Canada and exposed EPA officials and Congress for their attempts to cover up negative reports on dioxin emissions.

AMBASSADOR RAZALI ISMAIL
International
Permanent Mission of Malaysia to the United Nations
313 East 43rd Street, New York, NY 10017
(212) 986-6310; Fax (212) 983-4891

As a permanent representative of Malaysia to the United Nations, Ambassador Ismail was effective in helping the international community make progress on achieving globally sustainable development. Through his efforts at the Rio Earth Summit, he was able to bridge the differences between countries of the North and South, helping the world to reach a definition of sustainable development.

THE HONORABLE ELIZABETH FURSE
Legal/Legislative
Former Member of Congress of the United States

Having just completed her final term as a United States Representative from Oregon, the Honorable Elizabeth Furse has been a voice for the environment, not only in the Pacific Northwest, but also in the halls of Congress. Throughout her tenure she championed the Endangered Species Act and was the sponsor of a bill to repeal salvage timber riders.

NATIONAL CONSERVATION ACHIEVEMENT AWARDS

LOS ANGELES CONSERVATION CORPS
Organization
P.O. Box 15868
Los Angeles, CA 90015
(213) 362-9000

The Los Angeles Conservation Corps has brought conservation ideas to an inner city setting and has given its youth on the job training in a conservation related setting. For over 10 years they have worked diligently to fight against graffiti, vandalism, trash, traffic, and developments. They have planted over 15,000 trees and recycled close to 250 tons of debris. The Corps has taken their message to community members where they stress the importance of preventing the dumping of toxins down household and storm drains.

DR. JOANN BURKHOLDER
Science
North Carolina State University
P.O. Box 7612, Raleigh, NC 27695-7612
(919) 515-2726; Fax (919) 515-3436
joann_burkholder@ncsu.edu

As an aquatic biologist, Dr. Burkholder is best known for her work in codiscovering the deadly bacteria *pfiesteria*. She is currently sharing her knowledge of *pfiesteria* through education and advocacy efforts across the country.

LA'MOYNE D. WILLIAMS
Youth
Xavier University of Louisiana
7325 Palmetto Street, New Orleans, LA 70125
(504) 483-7506; Fax (504) 887-7643
williams@xavier.xula.edu

La'Moyne Williams' conservation efforts stem back to when he was a student at Xavier University of Louisiana where he was the founder and three time president of their campus environmental organization. He is currently the Assisting Director for Environmental Programs at Xavier where he is responsible for promoting environmental awareness on campus.

J. DAVID BAMBERGER
Special Achievement
Selah, Bamberger Ranch
Route #1, P.O. Box 102, Johnson City, TX 78636
(830) 868-7303; Fax (830) 868-4639

A rancher from Texas, J. David Bamberger is a conservationist who transformed 5,000 acres of barren, desolate land into a productive ranch and education center. *Selah*, his ranch, is the largest restoration project on private land including a wildlife reserve and several endangered plants species. Through these achievements, Bamberger has realized his childhood dream of becoming a good steward of the land.

ALDEN E. LIND
Special Achievement
Director, Conservation Legacy Alliance
4130 McCulloch Street, Duluth, MN 55804
(218) 525-2692; Fax (218) 525-2692
alind@d.umn.edu
Alden E. Lind is a grassroots organizer whose efforts were instrumental in saving Lake Superior. He is responsible for the ground-breaking environmental court case against Reserve Mining Company that resulted in the prohibition of asbestos dumping in Lake Superior. Lind has also developed and directed the Conservation Legacy Alliance, formed to combat the so-called "wise use" movement in Minnesota.

LORRIE OTTO
Special Achievement
9701 North Lake Drive
Milwaukee, WI 53217-6103
(414) 258-6731
As an advocate for natural landscaping for 40 years, Lorrie Otto has made a great impact in backyards across America. Beginning with her backyard, Otto began turning landscapes into habitats for wildlife and greatly spread the growth of NWF's Backyard Wildlife Habitat™ certification program. Earlier, she lobbied for the ban of DDT and successfully saved 20 acres of woodland near her home in Wisconsin.

1998 GOLDMAN ENVIRONMENTAL PRIZE

The Internationally renowned *Goldman Environmental Prize* is a project of the Goldman Environmental Foundation, established in 1989 by *Richard N. Goldman* and his late wife *Rhoda H. Goldman*. Richard N. Goldman is Chairman of Goldman Insurance Services, an independent insurance brokerage firm based in San Francisco. Rhoda H. Goldman was a descendant of Levi Strauss, the founder of the worldwide clothing company that bears his name. For further information on the awards and past recipients, please call (415) 788-9090 or email gef@igc.apc.org. Additional information can be obtained from the website at www.goldmanprize.org/goldman/.

1998 RECIPIENTS:

AFRICA:
Sven "Bobby" Peek
South Africa

A native of South Africa's highly industrial South Durban area, Bobby Peek lives adjacent to a refinery producing 60 tons of sulfur dioxide a day. As a youth he suffered from respiratory illness so severe that he had to be sent away from his home. Now a tireless champion of environmental justice, Peek has united his racially divided community, which last year succeeded in closing an illegal toxic dump.

ASIA:
Hirofumi Yamashita
Japan

Hirofumi Yamashita has dedicated more than 25 years to fighting a land reclamation project planned for Isahaya Bay, one of the richest wetlands in the world. Due to Yamashita's efforts, the scale of the project was reduced substantially. Nonetheless a dike completed in 1997 created much public concern about this and other destructive public works schemes in Japan. Yamashita is now leading a crusade to force a thorough review of the project with the aim of opening the gates to the Bay and restoring the ecosystem.

EUROPE:
Anna Maria Giordano
Italy

Located between the Italian mainland and the island of Sicily, the Messina Strait is one of the world's busiest flyways for migratory birds. As a high school student in the 1980s, Anna Maria Giordano launched a campaign in defense of raptors, traditionally shot for sport by poachers. Although she narrowly escaped irate hunters who firebombed her car, Giordano persevered. As a result, the number of birds killed each spring has dropped dramatically.

ISLAND NATIONS:
Atherton Martin
Dominica

Atherton Martin overcame strong governmental opposition and stopped a proposed copper mine in Dominica through extensive local and international organizing. The destructive mining operation would have covered ten percent of the island nation, which is mostly covered with primary tropical rainforests. Known as "the Nature Isle," Dominica contains some of the greatest biodiversity in the Caribbean.

NORTH AMERICA:
Kory Johnson
U.S.A.

Kory Johnson was 11 years old in 1989, when her older sister died of a heart ailment her mother believed to be caused by contaminated water she drank during her pregnancy. Johnson reacted by founding Children for a Safe Environment. In addition to organizing a successful youth campaign that helped stop a proposed incinerator in Phoenix, Arizona, Johnson has led efforts on a variety of environmental health issues affecting children, especially in low-income communities.

SOUTHCENTRAL AMERICA:
Berito KuwarU'wa (Roberto Cobaría)
Colombia

Designated by the indigenous U'wa as their spokesperson to the outside world, Berito KuwarU'wa has waged an international campaign imploring multinational oil companies not to drill in the U'wa's oil-rich homeland. The U'wa, a highly traditional and unacculturated people, believe that oil is the blood of the earth and that to extract it is equivalent to committing matricide.

U.S. CONGRESS, COMMITTEES, AND SUBCOMMITTEES

UNITED STATES CONGRESSIONAL MEMEBERS

Listings are by state, with Senators first and then, by District, Representatives. One may contact a Senator by writing: The Honorable _____, U.S. Senate, Washington, DC 20510. One may contact a member of the House of Representatives by writing: The Honorable _____, U.S. House of Representatives, Washington, DC 20515. **NOTE: Listings as of November 3, 1998**. Contact the Clerk for changes: House: (D): (202, 225-7330), (R): (202, 225-7350); Senate: (D): (202, 224-4691), (R): (202, 224-6391). The White House Office: 1600 Pennsylvania Ave., NW, Washington, DC 20500 (202, 456-1414; E-mail: Internet: president@whitehouse.gov)

President of the United States: WILLIAM J. CLINTON
Vice President of the United States: ALBERT GORE, JR.

ALABAMA
Senators: JEFF SESSIONS; RICHARD C. SHELBY
Representatives: 1st, SONNY CALLAHAN; 2nd, TERRY EVERETT; 3rd, BOB RILEY; 4th, ROBERT ADERHOLT; 5th, ROBERT E. CRAMER, JR.; 6th, SPENCER BACHUS; 7th, EARL HILLIARD

ALASKA
Senators: TED STEVENS; FRANK H. MURKOWSKI
Representative: At-Large, DON YOUNG

ARIZONA
Senators: JON KYL; JOHN McCAIN
Representatives: 1st, MATT SALMON; 2nd, ED PASTER; 3rd, BOB STUMP; 4th, JOHN SHADEGG; 5th, JIM KOLBE; 6th, J.D. HAYWORTH

ARKANSAS
Senators: BLANCHE LAMBERT LINCOLN; TIM HUTCHINSON
Representatives: 1st, MARION BERRY; 2nd, VIC SNYDER; 3rd, ASA HUTCHINSON; 4th, JAY DICKEY

CALIFORNIA
Senators: DIANNE FEINSTEIN; BARBARA BOXER
Representatives: 1st, MIKE THOMPSON; 2nd, WALLY HERGER; 3rd, DOUGALS OSE; 4th, JOHN DOOLITTLE 5th, ROBERT T. MATSUI; 6th, LYNN WOOLSEY; 7th, GEORGE MILLER; 8th, NANCY PELOSI; 9th, BARBARA LEE; 10th, ELLEN TAUSCHER; 11th, RICHARD POMBO; 12th, TOM LANTOS; 13th, FORTNEY H. STARK; 14th, ANNE ESHOO; 15th, TOM CAMPBELL; 16th, ZOE LOFGREN; 17th, SAM FARR; 18th, GARY CONDIT; 19th, GEORGE RADANOVICH; 20th, CALVIN DOOLEY; 21st, BILL THOMAS; 22nd, LOIS CAPPS; 23rd, ELTON GALLEGLY; 24th, BRAD SHERMAN; 25th, HOWARD McKEON; 26th, HOWARD L. BERMAN; 27th, JAMES ROGAN; 28th, DAVID DREIER; 29th, HENRY A. WAXMAN; 30th, XAVIER BECERRA; 31st, MATTHEW G. MARTINEZ; 32nd, JULIAN C. DIXON; 33rd, LUCILLE ROYBAL-ALLARD; 34th, GRACE NAPOLITANO; 35th, MAXINE WATERS; 36th, STEVEN KUYKENDALL; 37th, J. M. McDONALD; 38th, STEVE HORN; 39th, EDWARD ROYCE; 40th, JERRY LEWIS; 41st, GARY MILLER; 42nd, GEORGE BROWN; 43rd, KEN CALVERT; 44th, MARY BONO; 45th, DANA ROHRABACHER; 46th, LORETTA SANCHEZ; 47th, CHRISTOPHER COX; 48th, RON PACKARD; 49th, BRIAN BILBRAY; 50th, BOB FILNER; 51st, RANDY CUNNINGHAM; 52nd, DUNCAN HUNTER

COLORADO
Senators: WAYNE ALLARD; BEN N. CAMPBELL
Representatives: 1st, DIANA DeGETTE; 2nd, MARK UDALL; 3rd, SCOTT McINNIS; 4th, ROBERT SCHAFFER; 5th, JOEL HEFLEY; 6th, TOM TANCREDO

CONNECTICUT
Senators: JOE I. LIEBERMAN; CHRISTOPHER J. DODD
Representatives: 1st, JOHN LARSON; 2nd, SAM GEJDENSON; 3rd, ROSA L. DeLAURO; 4th, CHRISTOPHER SHAYS; 5th, JAMES MALONEY; 6th, NANCY L. JOHNSON

DELAWARE
Senators: WILLIAM V. ROTH, JR.; JOSEPH R. BIDEN, JR.
Representative: At-Large, MICHAEL CASTLE

FLORIDA
Senators: CONNIE MACK; BOB GRAHAM
Representatives: 1st, JOE SCARBOROUGH; 2nd, ALLEN BOYD; 3rd, CORRINE BROWN; 4th, TILLIE FOWLER; 5th, KAREN THURMAN; 6th, CLIFFORD STEARNS; 7th, JOHN MICA; 8th, BILL McCOLLUM; 9th, MICHAEL BILIRAKIS; 10th, BILL YOUNG; 11th, JIM DAVIS; 12th, CHARLES CANADY; 13th, DAN MILLER; 14th, PORTER J. GOSS; 15th, DAVE WELDON; 16th, MARK FOLEY; 17th, CARRIE MEEK; 18th, ILEANA ROS-LEHTINEN; 19th, ROBERT WEXLER; 20th, PETER DEUTSCH; 21th, LINCOLN DIAZ-BALART; 22nd, E. CLAY SHAW, JR.; 23rd, ALCEE HASTINGS

GEORGIA
Senators: MAX CLELAND; PAUL COVERDELL
Representatives: 1st, JACK KINGSTON; 2nd, SANFORD BISHOP; 3rd, MICHAEL COLLINS; 4th, CYNTHIA McKINNEY; 5th, JOHN LEWIS; 6th, NEWT GINGRICH; 7th, BOB BARR; 8th, SAXBY CHAMBLISS; 9th, NATHAN DEAL; 10th, CHARLIE NORWOOD; 11th, JOHN LINDER

HAWAII
Senators: DANIEL K. INOUYE; DANIEL K. AKAKA
Representatives: 1st, NEIL ABERCROMBIE; 2nd, PATSY T. MINK

IDAHO

Senators: LARRY E. CRAIG; MICHAEL D. CRAPO
Representatives: 1st, HELEN CHENOWETH; 2nd, MIKE SIMPSOM

ILLINOIS

Senators: PETER G. FITZGERALD; RICHARD DURBIN
Representatives: 1st, BOBBY RUSH; 2nd, JESSE JACKSON, JR.; 3rd, WILLIAM LIPINSKI; 4th, LUIS GUTIERREZ; 5th, ROD BLAGOJEVICH; 6th, HENRY J. HYDE; 7th, DANNY DAVIS; 8th, PHILIP M. CRANE; 9th, JANICE SCHAKOWSKY; 10th, JOHN PORTER; 11th, JERRY WELLER; 12th, JERRY COSTELLO; 13th, JUDY BIGGERT; 14th, DENNIS HASTERT; 15th, THOMAS W. EWING; 16th, DONALD MANZULLO; 17th, LANE EVANS; 18th, RAY LaHOOD; 19th, DAVID PHELPS; 20th, JOHN SHIMKUS

INDIANA

Senators: EVAN BAYH; RICHARD G. LUGAR
Representatives: 1st, PETER J. VISCLOSKY; 2nd, DAVID McINTOSH; 3rd, TIM ROEMER; 4th, MARK SOUDER; 5th, STEVE BUYER; 6th, DAN BURTON; 7th, EDWARD PEASE; 8th, JOHN HOSTETTLER; 9th, BARON HILL; 10th, JULIA CARSON

IOWA

Senators: CHUCK GRASSLEY; TOM HARKIN
Representatives: 1st, JIM LEACH; 2nd, JIM NUSSLE; 3rd, LEONARD BOSWELL; 4th, GREG GANSKE; 5th, TOM LATHAM

KANSAS

Senators: SAM BROWNBACK; PAT ROBERTS
Representatives: 1st, JERRY MORAN; 2nd, JIM RYUN; 3rd, DENNIS MOORE; 4th, TODD TIAHRT

KENTUCKY

Senators: JIM BUNNING; MITCH McCONNELL
Representatives: 1st, EDWARD WHITFIELD; 2nd, RON LEWIS; 3rd, ANNE NORTHUP; 4th, KENNETH LUCAS; 5th, HAROLD ROGERS; 6th, ERNIE FLETCHER

LOUISIANA

Senators: JOHN B. BREAUX; MARY LANDRIEU
Representatives: 1st, ROBERT LIVINGSTON, JR.; 2nd, WILLIAM J. JEFFERSON; 3rd, W.J. TAUZIN; 4th, JIM McCRERY; 5th, JOHN COOKSEY; 6th, RICHARD H. BAKER; 7th, CHRIS JOHN

MAINE

Senators: SUSAN MARGARET COLLINS; OLYMPIA SNOWE
Representatives: 1st, THOMAS ALLEN; 2nd, JOHN BALDACCI

MARYLAND

Senators: PAUL S. SARBANES; BARBARA A. MIKULSKI
Representatives: 1st, WAYNE T. GILCHREST; 2nd, ROBERT EHRLICH; 3rd, BENJAMIN L. CARDIN; 4th, ALBERT WYNN; 5th, STENY H. HOYER; 6th, ROSCOE BARTLETT; 7th, ELIJAH CUMMINGS; 8th, CONSTANCE MORELLA

MASSACHUSETTS

Senators: EDWARD M. KENNEDY; JOHN F. KERRY
Representatives: 1st, JOHN W. OLVER; 2nd, RICHARD E. NEAL; 3rd, JAMES McGOVERN; 4th, BARNEY FRANK; 5th, MARTIN MEEHAN; 6th, MICHAEL CAPUANO; 7th, EDWARD J. MARKEY; 8th, MICHAEL CAPUANO, II; 9th, JOE MOAKLEY; 10th, WILLIAM DELAHUNT

MICHIGAN

Senators: SPENCER ABRAHAM; CARL LEVIN
Representatives: 1st, BART STUPAK; 2nd, PETER HOEKSTRA; 3rd, VERNON EHLERS; 4th, DAVE CAMP; 5th, JAMES BARCIA; 6th, FRED UPTON; 7th, NICK SMITH; 8th, DEBBIE STABENOW; 9th, DALE KILDEE; 10th, DAVID BONIOR; 11th, JOSEPH KNOLLENBERG; 12th, SANDER LEVIN; 13th, LYNN RIVERS; 14th, JOHN CONYERS, JR.; 15th, CAROLYN KILPATRICK; 16th, JOHN D. DINGELL

MINNESOTA

Senators: ROD GRAMS; PAUL DAVID WELLSTONE
Representatives: 1st, GIL GUTKNECHT; 2nd, DAVID MINGE; 3rd, JIM RAMSTAD; 4th, BRUCE F. VENTO; 5th, MARTIN SABO; 6th, WILLIAM LUTHER; 7th, COLLIN C. PETERSON; 8th, JAMES L. OBERSTAR

MISSISSIPPI

Senators: TRENT LOTT; THAD COCHRAN
Representatives: 1st, ROGER WICKER; 2nd, BENNIE THOMPSON; 3rd, CHARLES PICKERING; 4th, RONNIE SHAWS; 5th, GENE TAYLOR

MISSOURI

Senators: JOHN ASHCROFT; CHRISTOPHER S. BOND
Representatives: 1st, WILLIAM CLAY, SR.; 2nd, JAMES TALENT; 3rd, RICHARD A. GEPHARDT; 4th, IKE SKELTON; 5th, KAREN McCARTHY; 6th, PAT DANNER; 7th, ROY BLUNT; 8th, JO ANN EMERSON; 9th, KENNY HULSHOF

MONTANA

Senators: CONRAD R. BURNS; MAX BAUCUS
Representative: At-Large, RICK HILL

NEBRASKA

Senators: CHUCK HAGEL; J. ROBERT KERREY
Representatives: 1st, DOUG BEREUTER; 2nd, LEE TERRY; 3rd, BILL BARRETT

NEVADA

Senators: RICHARD H. BRYAN; HARRY REID
Representatives: 1st, SHELLY BERKLEY; 2nd, JIM GIBBONS

U.S. CONGRESS, COMMITTEES, AND SUBCOMMITTEES

NEW HAMPSHIRE

Senators: ROBERT C. SMITH; JUDD GREGG
Representatives: 1st, JOHN E. SUNUNU; 2nd, CHARLES BASS

NEW JERSEY

Senators: ROBERT TORRICELLI; FRANK R. LAUTENBERG
Representatives: 1st, ROBERT E. ANDREWS; 2nd, FRANK LoBIONDO; 3rd, JIM SAXTON; 4th, C. SMITH; 5th, MARGE ROUKEMA; 6th, FRANK PALLONE, JR.; 7th, BOB FRANKS; 8th, WILLIAM PASCRELL; 9th, STEVEN ROTHMAN; 10th, DONALD M. PAYNE; 11th, RODNEY FRELINGHUYSEN; 12th, RUSH HOLT; 13th, ROBERT MENENDEZ

NEW MEXICO

Senators: PETE V. DOMENICI; JEFF BINGAMAN
Representatives: 1st, HEATHER WILSON; 2nd, JOE SKEEN; 3rd, THOMAS UDALL

NEW YORK

Senators: DANIEL P. MOYNIHAN; CHARLES E. SCHUMER
Representatives: 1st, MICHAEL FORBES; 2nd, RICK LAZIO; 3rd, PETER KING; 4th, CAROLYN McCARTHY; 5th, GARY L. ACKERMAN; 6th, GREGORY MEEK; 7th, JOSEPH CROWLEY; 8th, JERROLD NADLER; 9th, ANTHONY WEINER; 10th, EDOLPHUS TOWNS; 11th, MAJOR R. OWENS; 12th, NYDIA VELAZQUEZ; 13th, VITO FOSSELLA; 14th, CAROLYN MALONEY; 15th, CHARLES B. RANGEL; 16th, JOSE SERRANO; 17th, ELIOT L. ENGEL; 18th, NITA M. LOWEY; 19th, SUE KELLY; 20th, BENJAMIN A. GILMAN; 21st, MICHAEL R. McNULTY; 22nd, JOHN SWEENEY; 23rd, SHERWOOD L. BOEHLERT; 24th, JOHN McHUGH; 25th, JAMES T. WALSH; 26th, MAURICE HINCHEY; 27th, THOMAS REYNOLDS; 28th, LOUISE M. SLAUGHTER; 29th, JOHN J. LaFALCE; 30th, JACK QUINN; 31st, AMO HOUGHTON, JR.

NORTH CAROLINA

Senators: JESSE HELMS; JOHN EDWARDS
Representatives: 1st, EVA CLAYTON; 2nd, BOB ETHERIDGE; 3rd, WALTER JONES, JR.; 4th, DAVID PRICE; 5th, RICHARD BURR; 6th, HOWARD COBLE; 7th, MIKE McINTYRE; 8th, ROBIN HAYES; 9th, SUE MYRICK; 10th, CASS BALLENGER; 11th, CHARLES H. TAYLOR; 12th, MELVIN WATT

NORTH DAKOTA

Senators: KENT CONRAD; BYRON DORGAN
Representative: At-Large, EARL POMEROY

OHIO

Senators: GEORGE V. VOINOVICH; MIKE DeWINE
Representatives: 1st, STEVE CHABOT; 2nd, ROB PORTMAN; 3rd, TONY P. HALL; 4th, MICHAEL G. OXLEY; 5th, PAUL GILLMORE; 6th, TED STRICKLAND; 7th, DAVID L. HOBSON; 8th, JOHN A. BOEHNER; 9th, MARCY KAPTUR; 10th, DENNIS KUCINICH; 11th, STEPHANIE TUBBS JONES; 12th, JOHN R. KASICH; 13th, SHERROD BROWN; 14th, THOMAS C. SAWYER; 15th, DEBORAH PRYCE; 16th, RALPH REGULA; 17th, JAMES A. TRAFICANT, JR.; 18th, BOB NEY; 19th, STEVEN LaTOURETTE

OKLAHOMA

Senators: JAMES INHOFE; DON NICKLES
Representatives: 1st, STEVE LARGENT; 2nd, TOM COBURN; 3rd, WES WATKINS; 4th, J.C. WATTS; 5th, ERNEST ISTOOK; 6th, FRANK LUCAS

OREGON

Senators: GORDON SMITH ; RON WYDEN
Representatives: 1st, DAVID WU; 2nd, GREG WALDEN; 3rd, EARL BLUMENAUER; 4th, PETER A. DeFAZIO; 5th, DARLENE HOOLEY

PENNSYLVANIA

Senators: RICK SANTORUM; ARLEN SPECTER
Representatives: 1st, ROBERT BRADY; 2nd, CHAKA FATTAH; 3rd, ROBERT BORSKI; 4th, RON KLINK; 5th, JOHN PETERSON; 6th, TIM HOLDEN; 7th, CURT WELDON; 8th, JIM GREENWOOD; 9th, BUD SHUSTER; 10th, DONALD SHERWOOD; 11th, PAUL E. KANJORSKI; 12th, JOHN P. MURTHA; 13th, JOSEPH HOEFFEL; 14th, WILLIAM J. COYNE; 15th, PATRICH TOOMEY; 16th, JOSEPH PITTS; 17th, GEORGE W. GEKAS; 18th, MICHAEL DOYLE; 19th, WILLIAM F. GOODLING; 20th, FRANK MASCARA; 21st, PHILIP ENGLISH

RHODE ISLAND

Senators: JACK REED; JOHN H. CHAFEE
Representatives: 1st, PATRICK KENNEDY; 2nd, ROBERT WEYGAND

SOUTH CAROLINA

Senators: STROM THURMOND; ERNEST F. HOLLINGS
Representatives: 1st, MARK SANFORD; 2nd, FLOYD SPENCE; 3rd, LINDSEY GRAHAM; 4th, JAMES DEMINT; 5th, JOHN SPRATT, JR.; 6th, JAMES CLYBURN

SOUTH DAKOTA

Senators: TIM JOHNSON;THOMAS A. DASCHLE
Representative: At-Large, JOHN THUNE

TENNESSEE

Senators: BILL FRIST; FRED THOMPSON
Representatives: 1st, WILLIAM JENKINS; 2nd, JOHN J. DUNCAN, JR; 3rd, ZACH WAMP; 4th, VAN HILLEARY; 5th, BOB CLEMENT; 6th, BART GORDON; 7th, ED BRYANT; 8th, JOHN S. TANNER; 9th, HAROLD FORD, JR.

TEXAS

Senators: KAY B. HUTCHISON; PHIL GRAMM
Representatives: 1st, MAX SANDLIN; 2nd, JIM TURNER; 3rd, SAM JOHNSON; 4th, RALPH M. HALL; 5th, PETE SESSIONS; 6th, JOE BARTON; 7th, BILL ARCHER; 8th, KEVIN BRADY; 9th, NICK LAMPSON; 10th, LLOYD DOGGETT; 11th, CHET EDWARDS; 12th, KAY GRANGER; 13th, MAC THORNBERRY; 14th, RON PAUL; 15th, RUBEN HINOJOSA; 16th, SILVESTRE REYES; 17th, CHARLES W. STENHOLM; 18th, SHEILA JACKSON-LEE; 19th, LARRY COMBEST; 20th, CHARLIE GONZALEZ; 21st, LAMAR S.

SMITH; 22nd, TOM DeLAY; 23rd, HENRY BONILLA; 24th, MARTIN FROST; 25th, KEN BENTSEN; 26th, RICHARD ARMEY; 27th, SOLOMON P. ORTIZ; 28th, CIRO D. RODRIGUEZ; 29th, GENE GREEN; 30th, EDDIE B. JOHNSON

UTAH

Senators: ROBERT BENNETT; ORRIN G. HATCH
Representatives: 1st, JAMES V. HANSEN; 2nd, MERRILL COOK; 3rd, C. CANNON

VERMONT

Senators: JAMES M. JEFFORDS; PATRICK J. LEAHY
Representative: At-Large, BERNIE SANDERS

VIRGINIA

Senators: JOHN WARNER; CHARLES S. ROBB
Representatives: 1st, HERBERT H. BATEMAN; 2nd, OWEN B. PICKETT; 3rd, ROBERT SCOTT; 4th, NORMAN SISISKY; 5th, VIRGIL GOODE; 6th, ROBERT GOODLATTE; 7th, THOMAS J. BLILEY, JR.; 8th, JAMES P. MORAN; 9th, FREDERICK BOUCHER; 10th, FRANK R. WOLF; 11th, THOMAS DAVIS, III

WASHINGTON

Senators: SLADE GORTON; PATTY MURRAY
Representatives: 1st, JAY INSLEE; 2nd, JACK METCALF; 3rd, BRIAN BAIRD; 4th, DOC HASTINGS; 5th, GEORGE NETHERCUTT; 6th, NORMAN D. DICKS; 7th, JIM McDERMOTT; 8th, JENNIFER DUNN; 9th, ADAM SMITH

WEST VIRGINIA

Senators: ROBERT C. BYRD; JOHN D. ROCKEFELLER, IV
Representatives: 1st, ALAN B. MOLLOHAN; 2nd, BOB WISE, JR.; 3rd, NICK J. RAHALL, II

WISCONSIN

Senators: HERBERT KOHL; RUSSELL FEINGOLD
Representatives: 1st, PAUL RYAN; 2nd, TAMMY BALDWIN; 3rd, RON KIND; 4th, GERALD D. KLECZKA; 5th, THOMAS BARRETT; 6th, THOMAS E. PETRI; 7th, DAVID R. OBEY; 8th, MARK GREEN; 9th, JIM SENSENBRENNER

WYOMING

Senators: CRAIG THOMAS; MICHAEL ENZI
Representative: At-Large, BARBARA CUBIN

DISTRICT OF COLUMBIA

Delegate: ELEANOR HOLMES NORTON

GUAM

Delegate: ROBERT A. UNDERWOOD

PUERTO RICO

Resident Commissioner: CARLOS A. ROMERO-BARCELO

VIRGIN ISLANDS

Delegate: DONNA M. CHRISTIAN-GREEN

AMERICAN SAMOA

Delegate: ENI F.H. FALEOMAVAEGA

HOUSE COMMITTEES

HOUSE COMMITTEE ON RESOURCES
Rm. 1324 Longworth House Office Bldg., Washington, 31 20515
Phone: 202-225-2761
Description: Consists of 46 members: Forest reserves and national parks created from the public domain; national parks lands; forfeiture of land grants and alien ownership, including alien ownership of mineral lands; geological survey; interstate compacts relating to apportionment of waters for irrigation purposes; irrigation and reclamation, including water supply for reclamation projects, and easements on public lands for irrigation projects, and acquisition of private lands when necessary to complete irrigation projects; measures relating to the care and management of Indians, including the care and allotment of Indian lands and general and special measures relating to Indian claims; measures (including funding measures) relating generally to the U.S. territories, commonwealths, and successor governments of the Trust Territory of the Pacific Islands, except measures concerning the federal tax system and federal appropriations; military parks and battlefields; national cemeteries administered by the Secretary of the Interior, and parks within the District of Columbia; mineral land laws and claims and entries thereunder; mineral resources of the public lands; mining interests generally; mining schools and experimental stations; petroleum conservation on the public lands and conservation of the radium supply in the U.S.; preservation of prehistoric ruins and objects of interest on the public domain; public lands generally, including entry, easements, and grazing thereon; relations of the U.S. with the Indians and the Indian tribes; regulation of the domestic nuclear energy industry, including regulation of research and development of reactors and nuclear regulatory research. Also special oversight functions with respect to all programs affecting Indians and nonmilitary nuclear energy and research and development, including the disposal of nuclear waste.
Contact(s):
Chair: DON YOUNG

HOUSE COMMITTEE ON AGRICULTURE
Rm. 1301, Longworth House Office Bldg., Washington, 31 20515
Phone: 202-225-2171
Founded: 1820
Description: Adulteration of seeds, insect pests, and protection of birds and animals in forest reserves; agriculture generally; agricultural and industrial chemistry; agricultural colleges and experiment stations; agricultural economics and research; agricultural education extension services; agricultural production and marketing and stabilization of prices of agricultural products; animal industry and diseases of animals; crop insurance and soil conservation; dairy industry; entomology and plant quarantine; extension of farm credit and farm security; forestry in general, and forest reserves other than those created from the public domain; human nutrition and home economics; inspection of livestock and

U.S. CONGRESS, COMMITTEES, AND SUBCOMMITTEES

meat products; plant industry, soils, and agricultural engineering; rural electrification; commodities exchanges and rural development.
Contact(s):
Chair: BOB SMITH
Subcommittees: Environment, Credit, and Rural Development; Foreign Agriculture and Hunger; General Farm Commodities; Specialty Crops and Natural Resources; Livestock; Department Operations and Nutrition.

HOUSE COMMITTEE ON APPROPRIATIONS
Rm. H-218, Capitol Bldg., Washington, 31 20515
Phone: 202-225-2771
Description: Consists of 60 members: Appropriation of the revenue for the support of the government, rescissions of appropriations contained in appropriation acts, and transfers of unexpended balances.
Contact(s):
Chair: BILL YOUNG
Subcommittees: Agriculture, Rural Development, Food and Drug Administration; Commerce, Justice, State, and Judiciary; District of Columbia; Energy and Water Development; Foreign Operations, Export Financing, and Related Programs; Interior; Labor, Health and Human Services, and Education; Legislative; Military Construction; National Security; Transportation; Treasury, Postal Service, and General Government; VA, HUD, and Independent Agencies.

HOUSE COMMITTEE ON COMMERCE
2125 Rayburn House Office Bldg., Washington, 31 20515
Phone: 202-225-2927
Description: Jurisdiction: Interstate and foreign commerce generally; national energy policy generally; measures relating to the exploration, production, storage, supply, marketing, pricing, and regulation of energy resources, including all fossil fuels, solar energy, and other unconventional or renewable energy resources; measures relating to the conservation of energy resources; measures relating to the commercial application of energy technology; measures relating to energy information generally; measures relating to: (A) the generation and marketing of power (except by federally chartered or federal regional power marketing authorities), (B) the reliability and interstate transmission of, and ratemaking for, all power, and (C) the siting of generation facilities (except the installation of interconnections between government waterpower projects); interstate energy compacts; measures relating to general management of the Department of Energy, and the management and all functions of the Federal Energy Regulatory Commission; regulation of interstate and foreign communications; securities and exchanges; consumer affairs and consumer protection; travel and tourism; public health and quarantine; health and health facilities, except health care supported by payroll deductions; and biomedical research and development. The committee shall have the same jurisdiction with respect to regulation of nuclear facilities and of use of nuclear energy as it has with respect to regulation of non-nuclear facilities and of use of non-nuclear energy.
Contact(s):
Chair: THOMAS BLILEY
Chief of Staff: JAMES DERDERIAN
General Counsel: JAMES BARNETTE
Subcommittees: Telecommunications, Trade, and Consumer Protection; Finance and Hazardous Materials; Health and Environment; Energy and Power; Oversight and Investigations.

HOUSE COMMITTEE ON EDUCATION AND THE WORKFORCE
2181 Rayburn House Office Bldg., Washington, 31 20515
Phone: 202-225-4527
Description: Jurisdiction: Measures relating to education or labor generally; child labor; Gallaudet College; Howard University; convict labor and the entry of goods made by convicts into interstate commerce; labor standards; labor statistics; mediation and arbitration of labor disputes; regulation or prevention of importation of foreign laborers under contract; food programs for children in schools; United States Employees' Compensation Commission; vocational rehabilitation; wages and hours of labor; welfare of miners; and work incentive programs.
Contact(s):
Chair: BILL GOODLING
Subcommittees: Elementary, Secondary, and Vocational Education; Postsecondary Education and Training; Labor Standards, Occupational Health and Safety; Labor-Management Relations; Human Resources; and Select Education and Civil Rights.

HOUSE COMMITTEE ON INTERNATIONAL RELATIONS
2170 Rayburn House Office Bldg., Washington, 31 20515
Phone: 202-225-5021
Description: Jurisdiction: Foreign policy; international economic and environmental policy; international conferences and congresses; United Nations organizations; fishing agreements; nuclear export policy.
Contact(s):
Chair: BENJAMIN A. GILMAN
Subcommittees: Africa; Asia and the Pacific; the Western Hemisphere; International Economic Policy and Trade; International Operations and Human Rights.

HOUSE COMMITTEE ON RULES
Rm. H-312 Capitol Bldg., Washington, 31 20515
Phone: 202-225-9486
Description: Consists of 13 members: Grants rules outlining conditions for floor debate on legislation reported by regular standing committees, which includes granting emergency waivers under the Congressional Budget Act of 1974; also has legislative authority to create committees, change the rules of the House, and provide order of business of the House.
Contact(s):
Chair: GERALD SOLOMON

HOUSE COMMITTEE ON TRANSPORTATION AND INFRASTRUCTURE
Rm. 216 Rayburn House Office Bldg., Washington, 31 20515
Phone: 202-225-4472; Fax: 202-226-0921
Description: Consists of 73 members.
Contact(s):
Chairman: BUD SHUSTER
Subcommittees: Coast Guard and Maritime Transportation; Public Buildings and Economic Development; Railroade; Surface Transportation; Water Resources; and Environment.

SENATE COMMITTEES

SENATE COMMITTEE ON AGRICULTURE, NUTRITION, AND FORESTRY
Rm. 328-A, Russell Bldg, Washington, 31 20510
Phone: 202-224-2035
Description: Concerned with agriculture and agricultural commodities; inspection of livestock, meat, and agricultural products; animal industry and diseases; pests and pesticides; agricultural extension services and experiment stations; forestry in general and forest reserves and wilderness areas other than those created from the public domain; agricultural economics and research; human nutrition; home economics; farm credit and farm security; rural development, rural electrification and watersheds; agricultural production, marketing, and stabilization of prices; crop insurance and soil conservation; school nutrition programs; food stamp programs; food from fresh waters; plant industry, soils, and agricultural engineering. Such committee shall also study and review, on a comprehensive basis, matters relating to food, nutrition, and hunger, both in the United States and foreign countries, and rural affairs and report thereon from time to time.
Contact(s):
Chair: RICHARD LUGAR
Chief Clerk: ROBERT STURM

U.S. CONGRESS, COMMITTEES, AND SUBCOMMITTEES

Chief Counsel: DAVID JOHNSON
Minority Staff Director: DAN SMITH
Ranking Minority Member: TOM HARKIN
Staff Director: RANDY GREEN
Subcommittees: Production and Price Competitiveness; Marketing, Inspection, and Product Promotion; Forestry, Conservation, and Rural Revitalization; Research, Nutrition, and General Legislation.

SENATE COMMITTEE ON APPROPRIATIONS
SD-128, Capitol Bldg., Washington, 31 20510
Phone: 202-224-3471
Description: Concerned with all proposed legislation, messages, petitions, memorials, and other matters relating to appropriation of the revenue for the support of the federal government.
Contact(s):
Chair: TED STEVENS

SENATE COMMITTEE ON COMMERCE SCIENCE AND TRANSPORTATION
U.S. Senate SD508, Washington, 31 20510
Phone: 202-224-5115
Description: Concerned with interstate commerce; transportation; regulation of interstate common carriers, including railroads, buses, trucks, vessels, pipelines, and civil aviation; merchant marine and navigation; marine and ocean navigation, safety and transportation, including navigational aspects of deepwater ports; Coast Guard; inland waterways, except construction; communications; regulation of consumer products and services, except for credit, financial services, and housing; the Panama Canal, except for maintenance, operation, administration, sanitation, and government, and interoceanic canals generally; standards and measurements; highway safety; science, engineering and technology research, and development and policy; nonmilitary aeronautical and space sciences; transportation and commerce aspects of Outer Continental Shelf lands; marine fisheries; coastal zone management; oceans, weather, and atmospheric activities; sports.
Contact(s):
Chair: JOHN McCAIN
Subcommittees: Aviation; Communications; Consumer Affairs, Foreign Commerce and Tourism; Science, Technology, and Space; Surface Transportation and Merchant Marine; Oceans and Fisheries.

SENATE COMMITTEE ON ENERGY AND NATURAL RESOURCES
Rm. SD-364 Dirksen Bldg., Washington, 31 20510
Phone: 202-224-4971
Description: Concerned with the comprehensive study and review of matters relating to energy and resources development. Jursdiction: Coal production, distribution, and utilization; energy policy; energy regulation and conservation; energy related aspects of deepwater ports; energy research and development; extraction of minerals from oceans and Outer Continental Shelf lands; hydroelectric power, irrigation, and reclamation; mining education and research; mining, mineral lands, mining claims, and mineral conservation; national parks, recreation areas, wilderness areas, wild and scenic rivers, historical sites, military parks and battlefields, and on the public domain, preservation of prehistoric ruins and objects of interest; naval petroleum reserves in Alaska; nonmilitary development of nuclear energy; oil and gas production and distribution; public lands and forests, including farming and grazing thereon, and mineral extraction therefrom; solar energy systems; and territorial possessions of the United States, including trusteeships.
Contact(s):
Chair: FRANK MURKOWSI

SENATE COMMITTEE ON ENVIRONMENT AND PUBLIC WORKS
Rm. SD-410 Dirksen Bldg., Washington, 31 20510
Phone: 202-224-6176
Description: Committee on Environment and Public Works, to which shall be referred all proposed legislation, messages, petitions, memorials, and other matters relating to the following subjects: environmental policy; environmental research and development; ocean dumping; fisheries and wildlife; environmental aspects of Outer Continental Shelf lands; solid waste disposal and recycling; environmental effects of toxic substances, other than pesticides; water resources; flood control and improvements of rivers and harbors, including environmental aspects of deepwater ports; public works, bridges, and dams; water pollution; air pollution; noise pollution; nonmilitary environmental regulation and control of nuclear energy; regional economic development; construction and maintenance of highways; public buildings and improved grounds of the United States generally, including federal buildings in the District of Columbia. Such committee shall also study and review on a comprehensive basis matters relating to environmental protection and resource utilization and conservation, and report thereon from time to time.
Contact(s):
Chair: JOHN H. CHAFEE
Minority Staff Director: J. THOMAS SLITER
Staff Director: JIMMIE POWELL
Subcommittees: Transportation and Infrastructure; Superfund; Waste Control and Risk Assesment; Clean Air, Wetlands, Private Property, and Nuclear Safety; Drinking Water, Fisheries, and Wildlife.

SENATE COMMITTEE ON FOREIGN RELATIONS
Washington, 31 20510-6225
Phone: 202-224-4651
Description: Jurisdiction: Foreign and national security policy; international treaties, conferences, and congresses; World Bank and International Monetary Fund; oceans and international environmental and scientific affairs; humanitarian assistance and hunger; and United Nations and its affiliated organizations.
Contact(s):
Chair: JESSE HELMS
Subcommittees: African Affairs; East Asian and Pacific Affairs; European Afffairs; International Economic Policy, Trade, Oceans, and Environment; Near Eastern and South Asian Affairs; Terrorism, Narcotics, and International Operations; Western Hemisphere and Peace Corps

SENATE COMMITTEE ON LABOR AND HUMAN RESOURCES
SD-428 Dirksen Bldg., Washington, 31 20510
Phone: 202-224-5375
Contact(s):
Chair: JAMES JEFFORDS
Subcommittees: Aging; Children, Family, Drugs, and Alcoholism; Education, Arts, and Humanities; Employment and Productivity; Handicapped; Labor.

U.S. FEDERDAL AND INTERNATIONAL GOVERNMENT AGENCIES

COMMISSIONS

APPALACHIAN REGIONAL COMMISSION
1666 Connecticut Ave., NW, Washington, DC 20235
Phone: 202-884-7700
Founded: 1965
Description: To promote the economic and social development of the region and to provide a framework for joint federal and state efforts. Includes Alabama, Georgia, Kentucky, Maryland, Mississippi, New York, North Carolina, Ohio, Pennsylvania, South Carolina, Tennessee, Virginia, West Virginia.
Contact(s):
Executive Director: TOM HUNTER; Phone: 202-884-7700
Federal Co-Chairman: JESSE L. WHITE JR.; Phone: 202-884-7660
Public Information: MICHAEL KIERNAN; Phone: 202-884-7771
States' Co-Chairman: GOV. D. KIRK FORDICE
States' Washington Representative: BILL WALKER; Phone: 202-884-7746

ATLANTIC STATES MARINE FISHERIES COMMISSION
1444 Eye St., NW, 6th Fl., Washington, DC 20005
Phone: 202-289-6400; Fax: 202-289-6051; Email: Compuserve 74107,2632
Founded: 1942
Description: The Commission was established by the Atlantic States Marine Fisheries Compact to promote better utilization of the fisheries, marine, and shell of the 15 Atlantic seaboard states, Maine to Florida, through the development of a joint program for the promotion and protection of such fisheries, and by the prevention of physical waste of the fisheries from any cause.
Contact(s):
Chairman: PAUL A. SANDIFER
Vice Chairman: DAVID V.D. BORDEN
Executive Director: JOHN H. DUNNIGAN

COLUMBIA RIVER INTER-TRIBAL FISH COMMISSION
729 NE Oregon, Suite 200, Portland, OR 97232
Phone: 503-238-0667
Founded: 1977
Description: The Commission was formed to return salmon to Columbia basin rivers and to protect the Indian tribes' treaty-reserved fishing rights.
Contact(s):
Executive Director: TED STRONG

DELAWARE RIVER BASIN COMMISSION
P.O. Box 7360, West Trenton, NJ 08628
Phone: 609-883-9500; Fax: 609-883-9522; Email: drbc@drbc.state.nj.us
Founded: 1961
Description: The Delaware River Basin Compact created the Delaware River Basin Commission to develop and implement plans, policies, and projects relating to the water resources of the Delaware River Basin. The Commission is responsible for adopting and promoting "uniform and coordinated policies for water conservation, control, use, and management in the basin."
Contact(s):
2nd Vice Chair: GOV. THOMAS R. CARPER
Chair: GOV. CHRISTINE TODD WHITMAN
Executive Director: CAROL R. COLLIER
Public Information Officer: CHRISTOPHER M. ROBERTS
Vice Chair: GOV. GEORGE E. PATAKI
Publication(s): *Delaware River Basic Compact; Annual Report; Water Resources Program; Administrative Manual and Water Code*

GREAT LAKES FISHERY COMMISSION
2100 Commonwealth Blvd., Suite 209, Ann Arbor, MI 49105-1563
Phone: 734-662-3209; Fax: 734-741-2010; WWW: www.glfc.org
Description: The 1955 Canada-U.S. Convention on Great Lakes Fisheries established the Commission to advise governments on ways to improve the fisheries, to develop and coordinate fishery research programs, to develop measures and implement programs to manage sea lamprey, and to improve and perpetuate fishery resources.
Contact(s):
Executive Secretary: CHRIS GODDARD
Publication(s): *Economics of Great Lakes Fisheries: A 1985 Assessment; Fish Community Objectives for Lake Superior, The State of Lake Superior in 1992; Fish-Community Objectives for Lake Huron.*

GREAT LAKES INDIAN FISH AND WILDLIFE COMMISSION
P.O. Box 9, Odanah, WI 54861
Phone: 715-682-6619; Fax: 715-682-9294
Founded: 1983
Description: Provide biological, enforcement, and legal services to our member tribes in matters related to off-reservation treaty gathering rights in Wisconsin, Michigan, and Minnesota.
Contact(s):
Chairman of the Board: TOM MAULSON
Deputy Administrator: GERALD DePERRY
Executive Administrator: JAMES H. SCHLENDER
Publication(s): *Masinaigan; Technical reports*

GULF STATES MARINE FISHERIES COMMISSION
P.O. Box 726, Ocean Springs, MS 39566-0726
Phone: 228-875-5912; Fax: 228-875-6604; Email: lsimpson@gsmfc.org; WWW: www:\\gsmfc.org
Founded: 1949
Description: The GSMFC is an interstate compact of the states of Alabama, Florida, Louisiana, Mississippi, and Texas. The compact was authorized by the U.S. Congress. The Commission has 15 commissioners. The purpose of the Commission is to promote better utilization of the fisheries, marine, shell, and anadromous, of the seaboard of the Gulf of Mexico by cooperative programs for the promotion and protection of such fisheries and the prevention of the physical waste of the fisheries from any cause.
Contact(s):
Assistant Director: RONALD R. LUKENS
Executive Director: LARRY B. SIMPSON
Chairman: GEORGE SEKUL

HELSINKI COMMISSION/ BALTIC MARINE ENVIRONMENT PROTECTION COMMISSION
Katajanokanlaituri 6 B FIN- 00160, Helsinki 00160 Finland
Phone: 358-9-6220220; Fax: 358-9-62202239; Email: helcom@helcom.fi)
Founded: 1980
Description: To protect the marine environment of the Baltic Sea against pollution from all sources.
Contact(s):
Executive Secretary: TAPANI KOHONEN
Administrative Officer: RITVA KOSTAKOW-KAMPE
Environment Secretary: KJCU GRIP
Maritime Secretary: ANNE CHRISTINE BRUSENDORFF
Programme Implementation Coordinator: ULRICH KREMSER
Technological Secretary: AIN LOANE
Publication(s): *Baltic Sea Environment Proceedings (BSEP); HELCOM News*

INTER-AMERICAN TROPICAL TUNA COMMISSION
c/o Scripps Institution of Oceanography 8604 La Jolla Shores Dr., La Jolla, CA 92037-1508
Phone: 619-546-7100
Founded: 1949
Description: Charged with the investigation and conservation of the tuna and dolphin resources of the eastern Pacific Ocean. Member nations: U.S., Costa Rica, El Salvador, Ecuador, France, Japan, Nicaragua, Panama, Vanuatu, and Venezuela. Established by convention between the U.S. and Costa Rica.
Contact(s):
Director: JAMES JOSEPH; Phone: 619-546-7019
Editor: WILLIAM H. BAYLIFF; Phone: 619-546-7025
Publication(s): Bulletin of the Inter-American Tropical Tuna Commission; Annual Report; Special Report of the Inter-American Tropical Tuna Commission

INTERNATIONAL JOINT COMMISSION (Canada Office)
100 Metcalfe St., 18th Fl., Ottawa, Ontario K1P 5M1
Phone: 613-995-2984

INTERNATIONAL JOINT COMMISSION (Great Lakes Regional Office)
8th Fl. 100 Ouellette Ave., Windsor, Ontario N9A 6T3
Phone: 519-257-6700; Fax: 313-226-2170

INTERNATIONAL JOINT COMMISSION (Headquarters)
1250 23rd St., NW, Suite 100, Washington, DC 20440
Phone: 202-736-9000
Description: Established by the Boundary Waters Treaty of 1909 to prevent and resolve disputes regarding the use of the waters on the U.S.- Canadian Boundary, and to act as an independent advisor on issues referred by both countries. Regional office monitors, evaluates, and reports on compliance with the Great Lakes Water Quality Agreement of November 22, 1978. Commission functions in quasi-judicial, investigative, and coordination capacities.
Contact(s):
Canadian Section Secretary: MURRAY CLAMEN; Phone: 613-995-2984
Director, Regional Office: THOMAS BEHLEN; Phone: 519-257-6700; Fax: 313-226-2170
Editor: JENNIFER DAY; Fax: 519-257-6740; Email: DayJ@ijc.wincom.net
Editor: FRANK BEVACQUA; Fax: 202-736-9015; Email: bevacquaF@ijc.org.inter.net
Publication(s): Focus

INTERNATIONAL PACIFIC HALIBUT COMMISSION
P.O. Box 95009, Seattle, WA 98145-2009
Phone: 206-634-1838; Fax: 206-632-2983
Founded: 1923
Description: Scientific investigation and management of the Pacific halibut resource. Established by a convention between Canada and the United States.
Contact(s):
Director: BRUCE M LEAMAN

INTERNATIONAL WHALING COMMISSION
The Red House 135 Station Rd., Histon, Cambridge+I32 CB4 4NP
Phone: 01223-233971; Fax: 01223-232876; Email: iwcoffice@compuserve.com
Founded: 1946
Description: Established under the International Convention for the Regulation of Whaling in 1946 to provide for the conservation of whale stocks and the orderly development of the whaling industry. Member Nations: USA, Antigua and Barbuda, Argentina, Australia, Austria, Brazil, Chile, People's Republic of China, Costa Rica, Denmark, Dominica, Finland, France, Germany, Grenada, India, Ireland, Italy, Japan, Kenya, Republic of Korea, Mexico, Monaco, Netherlands, New Zealand, Norway, Oman, Peru, Russia Federation, Saint Kitts and Nevis, Saint Lucia, Saint Vincent and the Grenadines, Senegal, Solomon Islands, South Africa, Spain, Sweden, Switzerland, United Kingdom, and Venezuela.
Contact(s):
Chairman (Ireland): M. CANNY
Executive Officer (Cambridge): M. HARVEY
Secretary (Cambridge): DR. R. GAMBELL
U.S. Commissioner: DR. J. BAKER, U.S. Department of Commerce, Rm. 5128, Herbert C. Hoover Bldg., 14th and Constitution Ave., NW, Washington, DC 20230
Vice Chairman (Sweden): PROF BO FERNHOLM
Publication(s): Annual reports of the Commission (including reports and papers of the Scientific Committee); Special Issues Series on specialist cetacean subjects; Interntaional Journal of Cetacean Research and Management

INTERSTATE COMMISSION ON THE POTOMAC RIVER BASIN
6110 Executive Blvd., Suite 300, Rockville, MD 20852-3903
Phone: 301-984-1908
Founded: 1940
Description: Interstate compact, established by Maryland, Pennsylvania, Virginia, West Virginia, and the District of Columbia. Coordinates tabulates, and summarizes existing data on condition of streams in Potomac Watershed; promotes uniform legislation; disseminates information; cooperates in studies; promotes coordination of program in Basin states. Areas of interest are water quality, water supply, and land resources associated with the Potomac and its tributaries.
Contact(s):
Acting Executive Director: ROBERT L. BOLLE
Administrative Assistant: SUSAN M. JACKSON
Associate Director of Living Resources: JAMES D. CUMMINS
Associate Director, Technical Services: CARLTON HAYWOOD
Associate Director, Water Resources: DR. ROLAND C. STEINER
Public Affairs Officer: CURTIS DALPRA
Publication(s): Potomac Basin Reporter; In the Anacostia Watershed

MARINE MAMMAL COMMISSION
4340 East-West Highway, Rm. 905, Bethesda, MD 20814
Phone: 301-504-0087; Fax: 301-504-0099; Email: firstinitialandlastname@mmc.gov
Founded: 1972
Description: Established by the Marine Mammal Protection Act of 1972, P.L. 92-522, the Marine Mammal Commission, in consultation with its Committee of Scientific Advisors on Marine Mammals, periodically reviews the status of marine mammal populations; manages a research program concerned with their conservation; and develops, reviews, and makes recommendations on federal activities and policies which affect the protection and conservation of marine mammals.
Contact(s):
Executive Director: JOHN R. TWISS JR.
General Counsel: MICHAEL L. GOSLINER
Policy and Program Analyst: DAVID W. LAIST
Scientific Program Director: DR. ROBERT J. HOFMAN
Publication(s): Annual Report; Research Reports

MIGRATORY BIRD CONSERVATION COMMISSION
Interior Bldg., Washington, DC 20240
Phone: 703-358-1716
Founded: 1929
Description: Considers, passes upon, and fixes the prices for lands recommended by the Secretary of the Interior for purchase or lease by him under the Migratory Bird Conservation Act of February 18, 1929, as amended, as migratory bird refuges in the National Wildlife Refuge System.
Contact(s):
Secretary: JEFFERY M. DONAHOE; Phone: 703-358-1716; Fax: 703-358-2223
Chairman: BRUCE BABBITT, Secretary of the Interior, ; Phone: 202-208-7351; Fax: 202-208-6956

U.S. FEDERAL AND INTERNATIONAL GOVERNMENT AGENCIES - COMMISSIONS

MINNESOTA-WISCONSIN BOUNDARY AREA COMMISSION
619 2nd St., Hudson, WI 54016
Phone: 651-436-7131; Fax: 715-386-9571; Email: mwbac@mwvac.state.wi.us
Founded: 1965
Description: To conduct studies, develop recommendations, and coordinate planning for protection, use, and development in the public interest of lands, river valleys, and waters that form the boundary between Minnesota and Wisconsin, principally on the St. Croix and Mississippi rivers.
Contact(s):
Secretary: JESSIE MESCHIEVITZ
Executive Director: BUCK MALICK
Office Manager: ROSETTA M. HERRICKS
Public Affairs Director: JAMES M. HARRISON
Technical Director: ERIC J. MACBETH

NEW ENGLAND INTERSTATE WATER POLLUTION CONTROL COMMISSION
Boot Mills South, 100 Foot of John St., Lowell, MA 01852-1124
Phone: 978-323-7929
Founded: 1947
Description: The Commission provides a forum for interstate communication on high priority water-related environmental issues; provides training opportunities for state environmental staff and wastewater treatment plant operators; and provides the public with outreach and training materials on a wide range of environmental issues.
Contact(s):
Executive Director: RONALD F. POLTAK
Publication(s): *Water Connection (newsletter); LUSTLine (bulletin on tanks); Annual Report; NEI Environmental Information Catalog; Water Source (newsletter)*

NORTH AMERICAN WETLANDS CONSERVATION COUNCIL
4401 North Fairfax Dr., Suite 110, Arlington, VA 22203
Phone: 703-358-1784; Fax: 703-358-2282; Email: r9arw_nawwo@mail.fws.gov; WWW: www.fws.gov/~r9nawwo/nawcahp.html
Founded: 1989
Description: The North American Wetlands Conservation Council encourages public-private partnerships to conserve wetland ecosystems for waterfowl, other migratory birds, fish, and wildlife. Grant projects with a 1-1 match are funded to acquire, restore, and enhance wetlands and associated habitats in Canada, the U.S., and Mexico.
Contact(s):
Coordinator: DAVID A. SMITH
Publication(s): *North American Wetlands Conservation Act Progress Report for 1994-1995 and 1996-1997; North American Wetlands Conservation Act Grant Application Instructions*
Keyword(s): Aquatic Habitats, Birds, Coasts, Grants, Waterfowl, Wetlands

NORTH PACIFIC ANADROMOUS FISH COMMISSION
Suite 502, 889 W. Pender St., Vancouver, British Columbia V6C 3B2 Canada
Phone: 604-775-5550; Fax: 604-775-5577
Founded: 1993
Description: Established by a Convention between Canada, Japan, Russia, and the U.S. for the conservation of the anadromous fish resources of the North Pacific Ocean.
Contact(s):
Executive Director: DR. IRINA SHESTAKOVA
President (Japan): K. IMAMURA
Vice President (Canada): D. BEVAN

NORTHEAST ATLANTIC FISHERIES COMMISSION
Rm. 425, Nobel House 17 Smith Square, London SW1P 3JR
Phone: 071-238 5920; Fax: 071-238-5721
Founded: 1980
Description: To promote the conservation and optimum utilization of the fishery resources of the northeast Atlantic, within a framework appropriate to the regime of extended coastal state jurisdiction over fisheries, and to encourage international cooperation and consultation with respect to these resources.
Contact(s):
Secretary: S. C. WHITEHEAD, 427 Nobel House, 17 Smith Square, London, SW1P 3JR U.K.
President: O. TOUGAARD
Vice President: E. LEMCHE
Vice President: V. ZILANOV
Publication(s): *Annual Report; Handbook of Basic Texts*

NORTHEASTERN FOREST FIRE PROTECTION COMMISSION
36 Roslyn Ave., Warner, NH 03278-4021
Phone: 603-456-3474
Description: International forest fire protection mutual aid organization composed of three commissioners each from CT, ME, MA, NH, RI, VT, NY, and the Canadian Provinces of Quebec, New Brunswick, and Nova Scotia plus New England national forests (Green Mountain and While Mountain). Uniform fire organization planning and suppression technique training carried out annually by the members. The Northeastern Interstate Forest Fire Protection Compact is the governing document that established the organization.
Contact(s):
Executive Director: CLARK M. DAVIS, 36 Roslyn Ave., Warner, NH 03278-4021; Phone: 603-456-3474

OHIO RIVER VALLEY WATER SANITATION COMMISSION
5735 Kellogg Ave., Cincinnati, OH 45228-1112
Phone: 513-231-7719
Founded: 1948
Description: An interstate agency representing Illinois, Indiana, Kentucky, New York, Ohio, Pennsylvania, Virginia, and West Virginia for control of water pollution in the Ohio River Valley Compact District.
Contact(s):
Chairman (IL): PHILLIP MORGAN
Editor: KAREL FRASER
Editor: JEANNE JAHNIGEN ISON
Executive Director and Chief Engineer: ALAN H. VICORY JR.
Secretary and Treasurer (KY): VASILIKI KERAMIDA
Vice Chairman (KY): ROY MUNDY JR
Publication(s): *ORSANCO Quality Monitor; Annual Report; publications of general or technical interest, such as Ohio River fish populations, trace chemicals, and monitoring programs.*

PACIFIC SALMON COMMISSION
1155 Robson St., Suite 600, Vancouver, British Columbia V6E 1B5
Phone: 604-684-8081
Description: Charged with implementation of the Pacific Salmon Treaty signed by Canada and the United States in 1985, the Commission provides regulatory advice and recommendations to the U.S. and Canada relative to their management of salmon originating in one country, but subject to interception by the other. The Commission is also charged with conserving Pacific Salmon stocks in order to achieve optimum production, and dividing salmon harvests so each nation receives benefits equivalent to salmon produced in its waters. Each nation appoints four commissioners and four alternates to serve on the Commission. The Commission is the body through which the U.S. and Canada can work to resolve complex salmon management problems.
Contact(s):
Executive Secretary: IAN TODD

PACIFIC STATES MARINE FISHERIES COMMISSION
45 SE 82nd Dr., Suite 100, Gladstone, OR 97027-2522
Phone: 503-650-5400; Fax: 503-650-5426
Founded: 1947
Description: The Commission serves the Pacific states of Alaska, California, Idaho, Oregon, and Washington to promote conservation, development, and management of marine and anadromous fisheries of mutual concern through a coordinated regional approach to

fisheries research, monitoring, and utilization. Activities focus on marine debris, saving fisheries habitat, and marine mammal/fishery interactions.
Contact(s):
Executive Director: RANDY FISHER

ST. CROIX INTERNATIONAL WATERWAY COMMISSION
Box 610, Calais, ME 04619
Phone: 506-466-7550; Fax: 506-466-7551
Description: A commission of the state of Maine and province of New Brunswick to help implement a cooperative international management plan for the St. Croix River system, which forms 110 miles of the U.S. and Canada border.
Contact(s):
Executive Director: LEE SOCHASKY
Co-Chairman: DON OLMSTEAD
Co-Chairman: KEN GORDON
Publication(s): *Management Plan for the St. Croix International Waterway; Annual Report; St. Croix Heritage Brochure*

ST. CROIX INTERNATIONAL WATERWAY COMMISSION (Canadian Office)
#8 - #1 Highway, St. Stephen, New Brunswick E3L 2Y7

SUSQUEHANNA RIVER BASIN COMMISSION
1721 N. Front St., Harrisburg, PA 17102
Phone: 717-238-0422
Description: Conservation and development of water resources and water-related resources in the river basin, comprising parts of Maryland, New York, and Pennsylvania.
Contact(s):
Executive Director: PAUL O. SWARTZ, 1721 N. Front St., Harrisburg, PA 17102; Phone: 717-238-0422
Publication(s): *Annual Report; Susquehanna guardian (newsletter)*

UPPER COLORADO RIVER COMMISSION
355 S. 4th East St., Salt Lake City, UT 84111
Phone: 801-531-1150
Founded: 1949
Description: An administrative agency composed of commissioners appointed by the states of the Upper Division of the Colorado River - Colorado, New Mexico, Utah, and Wyoming, and by the President of the U.S.
Contact(s):
Chairman: FRANK E. MAYNES, P.O. Drawer 2717, Durango, CO 81501
Executive Director and Secretary: WAYNE E. COOK

EXECUTIVE BRANCH

COUNCIL ON ENVIRONMENTAL QUALITY
722 Jackson Pl., NW, Washington, DC 20503
Phone: 202-456-6224 or 202-395-5750
Founded: 1970
Description: CEQ serves as the source of environmental expertise and policy analysis for the President and other organizations within the Executive Office of the President, and provides for coordination between departments and agencies. It is also charged with implementing statutory or regulatory requirements and programs.
Contact(s):
Acting Chair: GEORGE T. FRAMPTON JR.
Administrative Officer: CAROLYN MOSLEY
Associate Director for Communications: ELLIOT DIRINGER
Associate Director for Global Environment: DAVID SANDALOW
Associate Director for Natural Resources: SALLY ERICSSON
Associate Director for NEPA: RAY CLARK
Associate Director for Public Liason: BETH A. VIOLA
Associate Director for Sustainable Development: KEITH LAUGHLIN
Associate Director for Toxics and Environmental Protection: BRAD CAMPBELL

multistate databases, interjurisdiction fishery management plans, Associate Director for Transportation and Land Management: LINDA LANCE
Associate General Counsel: ELISABETH BLAUG
Chief of Staff: WESLEY WARREN
Congressional Liason: JUDY JABLOW
General Counsel: DINAH BEAR
Special Assistant for Outreach and Commications: MICHAEL TERRELL
Special Assistant to the Chair: NANCY MARLOWE
Special Assistant to the Chair: PETER UMHOFER
Publication(s): *CEQ Annual Report*

ENVIRONMENTAL PROTECTION AGENCY
401 M St., SW, Washington, DC 20460
Phone: 202-260-2090; WWW: www.epa.gov
Description: The Environmental Protection Agency (EPA) was established as an independent agency in the Executive Branch of the U.S. Government, pursuant to Reorganization Plan No. 3 of 1970, effective December 2, 1970. EPA endeavors to achieve systematic control and abatement of pollution, by properly administering and integrating a variety of research, monitoring, standard-setting, and enforcement activities.
Contact(s):
Administrator: CAROL BROWNER; Phone: 202-260-4700
Deputy Administrator (Acting): PETER D. ROBERTSON
Associate Administrator for Communications, Education, and Media Relations: LORETTA M. UCELLI; Phone: 202-260-9828
Associate Administrator for Congressional and Intergovernmental Relations: JOSEPH R. CRAPA; Phone: 202-260-5200
Associate Administrator for Reinvention (Acting): JAY BENFORADO; Phone: 202-260-1849
Civil Rights Director: ANN E GOODE
Science Advisory Board Director: DONALD G. BARNES; Phone: 202-260-4125
Small and Disadvantaged Business Utilization Director: JEANETTE L. BROWN; Phone: 202-260-4100
Chief Financial Officer (Acting): SALLYANNE HARPER; Phone: 202-260-1151
Comptroller: W. S. RYAN; Phone: 202-260-9674
General Counsel (Acting): SCOTT C. FULTON; Phone: 202-260-8064
Inspector General (Acting): NIKKI I. TINSLEY; Phone: 202-260-3137

Administration and Resources Management
Contact(s):
Assistant Administrator (Acting): ALVIN M. PESACHOWITZ; Phone: 202-260-4600
Director of Administration and Resources Management, Research Triangle Park, NC: WILLIAM LAXTON; Phone: 919-541-2258
Director of Administration, Cincinnati, OH: WILLIAM M. HENDERSON; Phone: 513-569-7910
Director of Information Resources Management (Acting): MARK DAY; Phone: 202-260-4465
Human Resources and Organizational Services Director: DAVID J. O'CONNOR; Phone: 202-260-4467

Air and Radiation
Contact(s):
Assistant Administrator: ROBERT PERCIASEPE; Phone: 202-260-7400
Deputy Administrator: RICHARD D. WILSON; Phone: 202-260-7400
Air Quality Planning and Standards Director: JOHN S. SEITZ; Phone: 919-541-5504
Atmospheric Programs Director: PAUL M. STOPLMAN; Phone: 202-564-9150
Mobile Sources Director: MARGO T. OGE; Phone: 202-233-7645
Radiation and Indoor Air Director (Acting): LAWRENCE G. WEINSTOCK; Phone: 202-564-9370

U.S. FEDERAL AND INTERNATIONAL GOVERNMENT AGENCIES - EXECUTIVE BRANCH

Enforcement and Compliance
Contact(s):
Assurance Administrator: STEVEN A. HERMAN; Phone: 202-564-2440
Compliance Director: ELAINE G. STANLEY; Phone: 202-564-2280
Criminal Enforcement, Forensics, and Training Director: EARL E. DEVANEY; Phone: 202-564-2480
Environmental Justice Director (Acting): ROBERT J. KNOX; Phone: 202-564-2515
Federal Activities Director: RICHARD E. SANDERSON; Phone: 202-564-2400
Regulatory Enforcement Director: ERIC V. SCHAFFER; Phone: 202-564-2220
Site Remediation Enforcement Director: BARRY N. BREEN; Phone: 202-564-5110

Policy
Contact(s):
Assistant Administrator: DAVID M. GARDINER; Phone: 202-260-4332
Economy and Environment Director: ALBERT M. MCGARLAND; Phone: 202-260-3354
Program Support and Resource Management Director: PAMELA P STERLING; Phone: 202-260-4335
Regulatory management and Information Director: THOMAS E. KELLY; Phone: 202-260-4335
Sustainable Ecosystems and Communities Director (Acting): LEONARD J. FLECKENSTEIN; Phone: 202-260-4002

Prevention, Pesticides, and Toxic Substances
Contact(s):
Assistant Administrator: LYNN R. GOLDMAN; Phone: 202-260-2902
Pesticide Programs Director: MARCIA E. MULKEY; Phone: 703-305-7090
Pollution Prevention and Toxics Director: WILLIAM H. SANDERS III; Phone: 202-260-3810

Region I (CT, ME, MA, NH, RI, VT)
John F. Kennedy Federal Building, Boston 02203-0001
Phone: 617-918-1111; WWW: www.epa.gov/region01
Contact(s):
Regional Administrator: JOHN P. DEVILLARS; Phone: 617-918-1010

Region II (NJ, NY, PR, VI)
290 Broadway, New York, NY 10007-1866
Phone: 212-637-3000; WWW: www.epa.gov/region02/
Contact(s):
Regional Administrator: JEANNE M. FOX; Phone: 212-637-5000

Region III (DE, DC, MD, PA, VA, WV)
1650 Arch St., Philadelphia, PA 19103
Phone: 215-814-5000; WWW: www.epa.gov/region03/
Contact(s):
Regional Administrator: MICHAEL MCCABE; Phone: 215-814-2900

Region IV (AL, FL, GA, KY, MS, NC, SC, TN)
61 Forsyth St., S.W., Atlanta, GA 30303
Phone: 404-562-9900; WWW: www.epa.gov/region04
Contact(s):
Regional Administrator: JOHN H. HANKINSON JR.; Phone: 404-562-8357

Region IX (GU, AS, NV, HI, CA, AZ)
75 Hawthorne St., San Francisco, CA 94105
Phone: 415-744-1702; WWW: www.epa.gov/region09/
Contact(s):
Regional Administrator: FELICIA A. MARCUS; Phone: 415-744-1001

Region V (IL, IN, MI, NM, OH, WI)
77 West Jackson Blvd., Chicago, IL 60604-3507
Phone: 312-353-2000; WWW: www.epa.gov/region5/
Contact(s):
Regional Administrator (Acting): DAVID A. ULRICH; Phone: 312-886-3000

Region VI (AR, LA, NM, OK, TX)
Fountain Place, 12th Fl., Suite 1200, 1445 Ross Ave., Dallas, TX 75202-2733
Phone: 214-665-6444; WWW: www.epa.gov/regiono6/
Contact(s):
Regional Adminstrator: GREGG COOKE; Phone: 214-665-2100

Region VII (IA, KS, MO, NE)
726 Minnesota Ave., Kansas City, KS 66101
Phone: 913-551-7000; WWW: www.epa.gov/region07/
Contact(s):
Regional Administrator: DENNIS D. GRAMS; Phone: 913-551-7006

Region VIII (CO, MT, ND, SD, UT, WY)
999 18th St., Suite 500, Denver, CO 80202-2466
Phone: 303-312-6312; WWW: www.epa.gov/region08/
Contact(s):
Regional Administrator: WILLIAM P. YELLOWTAIL JR.; Phone: 303-312-6308

Region X (WA, OR, ID, AK)
1200 Sixth Ave., Seattle, WA 98101
Phone: 206-553-1200; Email: epa-seattle@epamail.epa.gov; WWW: www.epa.gov/region10/
Contact(s):
Regional Administrator: CHARLES C. CLARKE; Phone: 206-553-1234

Research and Development
Contact(s):
Assistant Administrator: HENRY L. LONGEST II; Phone: 202-564-6620
Science Policy Directory: DOROTHY E. PATTON; Phone: 202-564-6705
National Center for Environmental Assessment: WILLIAM H. FARLAND; Phone: 202-564-3322
National Center for Environmental Research and Quality Assurance: PETER W. PREUSS; Phone: 202-564-6825
National Exposure Research Laboratory Director: GARY J. FOLEY Ph.D.; Phone: 919-541-2106
National Health and Environmental Effects Director: LAWERNCE W. REITER Ph.D.; Phone: 919-541-2281
Associate Director for Ecology: GILMAN D. VEITH Ph.D.; Phone: 919-541-2283
Associate Director for Health: HAROLD ZENICH Ph.D.; Phone: 919-541-2283
National Risk Management Research Laboratory Director: TIMOTHY OPPELT; Phone: 513-569-7418

Solid Waste and Emergency Response
Contact(s):
Assistant Administrator (Acting): TIMOTHY FIELDS JR.; Phone: 202-260-4610
Chief Preparedness and Prevention Director: JAMES L. MAKRIS; Phone: 202-260-8600
Emergency and Remedial Response (Superfund/Oil Programs) Director: STEPHEN D. LUFTIG; Phone: 703-603-8960
Solid Waste Director (Acting): ELIZABETH COTSWORTH; Phone: 703-308-8895
Technology Innovation Director: WALTER W. KOVALICK JR.; Phone: 703-603-9910

Water
Contact(s):
Assistant Adminitrator (Acting): JONHATHAN C. FOX; Phone: 202-260-5700

American Indian Environmental Directory: KATHY GOROSPE; Phone: 202-260-7939
Ground Water and Drinking Water Director: CYNTHIA C. DOUGHERTY; Phone: 202-260-5543
Science and Technology Director: TUDOR T. DAVIES; Phone: 202-260-5400
Wastewater Management Director: MICHAEL B. COOK; Phone: 202-260-5850
Wetlands, Oceans, and Watersheds Director: ROBERT H. WAYLAND III; Phone: 202-260-7166

DEPARTMENT OF COMMERCE
Herbert C. Hoover Bldg., Rm. 5610, 15th St. and Constitution Ave., NW, Washington, DC 20230
Phone: 202-219-3605; WWW: www.doc.gov
Description: The Department of Commerce promotes job creation, economic growth, sustainable development, and improved living standards for all Americans, by working in partnership with business, universities, communities, and workers.
Contact(s):
Secretary: WILLIAM M. DALEY; Phone: 202-482-2112
Deputy Secretary: ROBERT L. MALLETT

ECONOMIC DEVELOPMENT ADMINISTRATION
Department of Commerce, Herbert C. Hoover Bldg., 14th St. and Constitution Ave., NW, Washington, DC 20230
Phone: 202-482-5081
Description: Conducts programs to help stimulate private enterprise and create permanent jobs in economically distressed areas of the Nation. Provides public works grants and planning and technical assistance in areas with high unemployment or low median family income.
Contact(s):
Assistant Secretary: PHILLIP A. SINGERMAN; Phone: 202-482-5081; Fax: 202-273-4781; Email: Psingerm@doc.gov

NATIONAL OCEANIC AND ATMOSPHERIC ADMINISTRATION
Department of Commerce, Herbert C. Hoover Bldg., Rm. 5128, 14th and Constitution Ave., NW, Washington, DC 20230
Phone: 202-482-3384
Founded: 1970
Description: NOAA was created within the Department of Commerce to promote global environmental stewardship and to describe and predict changes in the Earth's environment. NOAA conducts oceanic and atmospheric research; maintains environmental databases and disseminates environmental information products; manages living marine resources and the marine environment; and operates environmental satellites, ships, aircraft, and buoys. NOAA provides the environmental information, science, technology, and resource management expertise necessary for our nation to build a future sustained by both environmental stewardship and economic growth.
Contact(s):
Under Secretary for Oceans and Atmosphere of Administrator of NOAA: DR. D. JAMES BAKER; Phone: 202-482-3436
Assistant Administrator of National Environmental Satellite Data and Information Service: ROBERT S. WINOKUR JR.; Phone: 301-457-5115
Assistant Administrator of National Marine Fisheries Service: ROLLAND A. SCHMITTEN; Phone: 301-713-2239
Assistant Administrator of National Ocean Service: NANCY FOSTER Ph.D.; Phone: 301-713-3074
Assistant Administrator of National Weather Service: JOHN J. KELLY JR.; Phone: 301-713-0689
Assistant Administrator of Oceanic and Atmospheric Research: DAVID L. EVANS; Phone: 301-713-2458
Assistant Secretary for Oceans and Atmosphere of Deputy Administrator of NOAA (Acting): TERRY D. GARCIA; Phone: 202-482-3567
Associate Deputy Under Secretary: JOHN CAREY; Phone: 202-482-3565
Deputy Under Secretary for Oceans and Atmosphere: SCOTT B. GUDES; Phone: 202-482-4569

National Environmental Satellite, Data, and Information Service
Federal Bldg. #4, Rm. 2069, Suitland and Silver Hill Roads, Suitland, MD 20746
Phone: 301-457-5115
Description: A component of the National Oceanic and Atmospheric Administration. Manages satellites which observe the natural variability of the global Earth systems - the ocean, atmosphere, features of the solid earth, and the near-space system.
Contact(s):
Assistant Administrator: ROBERT S. WINOKUR; Phone: 301-457-5115301-457-5115
Public Affairs Officer: PAT VIETS; Phone: 301-457-5005

National Marine Fisheries Service (NMFS)
Silver Spring Metro Center 3, 1315 East-West Hwy., Silver Spring, MD 20910
Phone: 301-713-2239
Description: A component of the National Oceanic and Atmospheric Administration. Provides management, research, and services for the protection and rational use of living marine resources for their aesthetic, economic, and recreational value. Determines the consequences of the natural environment and human activities on living marine resources and provides knowledge and services to achieve efficient and judicious domestic and international management, use, and conservation of the resources.
Contact(s):
Assistant Administrator for Fisheries and Director of NMFS: ROLLAND A. SCHMITTEN; Phone: 301-713-2239
Deputy Assistant Administrator: DR. ANDREW A. ROSENBERG; Phone: 301-713-2239
Public Affairs Officer: SCOTT SMULLEN; Phone: 301-713-2370

National Ocean Service NOS
Rm. 13609, 1305 East-West Highway, Silver Spring, MD 20910
Phone: 301-713-3074
Description: A component of the National Oceanic and Atmospheric Administration. Administers the National Geodetic Survey, Nautical and Aeronautical Charting, National Estuarine Research Reserves, National Marine Sanctuaries, Coastal Zone Management, Marine Assessments, and Coastal Ocean Programs.
Contact(s):
Assistant Administrator for National Ocean Service: NANCY FOSTER Ph.D.; Phone: 301-713-3074
Public Affairs Officer of Ocean Services: DAN DEWELL; Phone: 301-713-3070

National Weather Service
Silver Spring Metro Center 2, 1325 East-West Hwy., Silver Spring, MD 20910
Phone: 301-713-0689
Description: A component of the National Oceanic and Atmospheric Administration. Observes, describes, and predicts the natural variability of the atmosphere, and to some extent, the ocean and the earth, in order to protect life and property and enhance the national economy.
Contact(s):
Deputy Assistant Administrator for Modernization: LOUIS J. BOEZI; Phone: 301-713-0397
Deputy Assistant Administrator for Operations: DR. SUSAN ZEVIN; Phone: 301-713-0711
Director and Assistant Administrator for Weather Service: DR. JOHN J. KELLY JR.; Phone: 301-713-0689
Director of National Centers for Environmental Prediction: DR. RONALD D. McPHERSON; Phone: 301-713-8016
Director of National Data Buoy Center: DR. JERRY C. McCALL; Phone: 601-688-2800
Director of National Hurricane Center: DR. ROBERT BURPEE; Phone: 305-229-4470

U.S. FEDERAL AND INTERNATIONAL GOVERNMENT AGENCIES - EXECUTIVE BRANCH

Director of Severe Storm Forecast Center: FREDERICK P. OSTBY; Phone: 816-426-5922
National Weather Service Alaska Region: RICHARD J. HUTCHEON; Phone: 907-271-5136
National Weather Service Central Region: RICHARD P. AUGULIS; Phone: 816-426-5400
National Weather Service Eastern Region: JOHN FORSING; Phone: 516-244-0100
National Weather Service Pacific Region: RICHARD H. HAGEMEYER; Phone: 808-541-1641
National Weather Service Western Region: DR. THOMAS D. POTTER; Phone: 801-524-5122
Public Affairs Officer of Weather: RANDEE EXTER; Phone: 301-713-0622
Southern Region: HARRY S. HASSEL; Phone: 817-334-2651

Office of Global Program
1100 Wayne Ave., Suite 1225, Silver Spring, MD 20910
Phone: 301-427-2089
Description: A component of the National Oceanic and Atmospheric Administration. Manages, coordinates, and integrates NOAA's Climate and Global Change Program. Provides the primary focus for coordination with national and international scientific communities in the areas of global warming, Tropical Oceans and Global Atmosphere Project, and worldwide climate research.
Contact(s):
Director of Office of Global Programs: DR. J. MICHAEL HALL; Phone: 301-427-2089

Office of Oceanic and Atmospheric Research (OAR)
Silver Spring Metro Center 3, 1315 East-West Hwy., Silver Spring, MD 20910
Phone: 301-713-2458
Description: A component of the National Oceanic and Atmospheric Administration. Conducts environmental research in the oceans, atmosphere, and space. Administers the National Sea Grant College Program, which provides grants to academic institutions for research, education, and advisory/extension services in the marine environment.
Contact(s):
Assistant Administrator for Oceanic and Atmospheric Research (Acting): DAVID L. EVANS; Phone: 301-713-2458
Deputy Assistant Administrator: LOUISA KOCH; Phone: 301-713-2458
Director of Environmental Research Laboratories: DR. JAMES L. RASMUSSEN; Phone: 301-713-2458
Director of National Sea Grant College Program of Extension Service (Acting): RONALD C. BAIRD; Phone: 301-713-2448
Director of National Undersea Research Program (Acting): DR. BARBARA MOORE; Phone: 301-713-2427
Public Affairs Officer of OAR: DANE KONOP; Phone: 301-713-2483
Resource Management: MARYANN WHITCOMB; Phone: 301-713-2454

DEPARTMENT OF DEFENSE
The Pentagon, Office of the Secretary, 3400 Defense Pentagon, Washington, DC 20301-3400
WWW: www.denir.asd.mil
Description: Responsible for the security of the U.S. by establishing policies and procedures relating to national defense. The Department of Defense conducts programs to prevent pollution, enhance the environment, and conserve the natural and cultural resources on military lands.
Contact(s):
Secretary: WILLIAM COHEN; Phone: 703-695-5261
Deputy Under Secretary of Environmental Security: SHERRI W. GOODMAN; Phone: 703-695-6639
Director of Conservation: L. PETER BOICE; Phone: 703-604-0524; Fax: 703-607-4237; Email: boicepl@acq.osd.mil
Executive Director of Armed Forces Pest Management Board: COL DONALD DRIGGERS; Phone: 301-295-7476; Fax: 301-295-7473; Email: driggersdp@acq.osd.mil
Principal Assistant Deputy Under Secretary of Environmental Security: GARY VEST; Phone: 703-695-7011
Publication(s): *Natural Resources in the Department of Defense; Cultural Resources in the Department of Defense; Legacy Resource Management Program Report to Congress; DOD Commanders' Guide to Biodiversity; Coral Reef Conservation Guide for Military; Chesapeake Bay Watershed Access Guide*

DEPARTMENT OF EDUCATION
400 Maryland Ave., SW, Washington, DC 20202-0498
Phone: 1-800-USA-LEARN; WWW: www.ed.gov
Contact(s):
Secretary: RICHARD W. RILEY; Phone: 202-401-3000
Deputy Secretary: MARSHALL SMITH
Director of Public Affairs: DAVID FRANK; Phone: 202-401-3026
Assistant Secretary of Civil Rights: NORMA V. CANTU; Phone: 202-401-1000
Assistant Secretary of Educational Research and Improvement: SHARON ROBINSON
Assistant Secretary of Elementary and Secondary Education: DR. THOMAS PAYZANT
Assistant Secretary of Human Resources and Administration: ROD McCOWAN
Assistant Secretary of Intergovernmental and Interagency Affairs (Designee): MARIO MORENO
Assistant Secretary of Legislation and Congressional Affairs: KAY L. CASSTEVENS
Assistant Secretary of Office of Adult and Vocational Education: AGUSTA KAPPNER
Assistant Secretary of Postsecondary Education: DAVID LONGANECKER
Assistant Secretary of Special Education and Rehabilitative Services: JUDITH HEUMANN; Phone: 202-205-5465
Chief Financial Officer of Management and Budget/Services: DON WURTZ
Chief of Staff: BILLY WEBSTER
Director (Acting) of Bilingual Education and Minority Languages Affairs: EUGENE GARCIA
Director of Policy and Planning: ALAN L. GINSBURG
Executive Secretariat Director: PHILIP S. LINK
General Counsel: JANNIENNE S. STUDLEY; Phone: 202-401-6000
Inspector General: JAMES B. THOMAS JR.

DEPARTMENT OF ENERGY
Forrestal Bldg., 1000 Independence Ave., SW, Washington, DC 20585
WWW: www.doe.gov
Description: Provides the framework for a comprehensive and balanced national energy strategy through the coordination and administration of the energy functions of the federal government. The department is responsible for research, development, and demonstration of energy technology; the marketing of federal power; energy conservation programs; the nuclear weapons program; energy regulatory programs; and a central energy data collection and analysis program. Established by the Department of Energy Organization Action: 1977.
Contact(s):
Secretary: BILL RICHARDSON; Phone: 202-586-6210
Acting Assistant Secretary of Environment, Safety of and Health: PETER N. BRUSH; Phone: 202-586-5430
Acting Assistant Secretary of Environmental Restoration and Waste Management: JAMES M. OWENDOFS; Phone: 202-586-7710
Acting Assistant Secretary of Fossil Energy: ROBERT S. KRIPOWITCZ; Phone: 202-586-5506
Administrator of Energy Information Administration: JAY E. HAKES; Phone: 202-586-4361
Assistant Secretary of Congressional and Intergovernmental Affairs: JOHN M. ANGELL, III, ; Phone: 202-586-5450
Assistant Secretary of Energy Efficiency and Renewable Energy: DAN W. REICHER; Phone: 202-586-9220
Director of Office of Public Affairs: BROOK D. ANDERSON; Phone: 202-586-5823

Publication(s): *National Energy Strategy; National Energy Strategy: One Year Later; Report to the Congress of the United States: Limiting New Greenhouse Gas Emissions in the United States; Assessment of Costs and Benefits of Flexible and Alternative Fuel Use in the United States Transportation Sector*

CARBON DIOXIDE INFORMATION ANALYSIS CENTER
Oak Ridge National Laboratory, P.O. Box 2008 MS-6335, Oak Ridge, TN 37831-6335
Phone: 423-574-0390; WWW: cdiac.esd.ornl.gov
Founded: 1982
Description: The Carbon Dioxide Information Analysis Center (CDIAC) provides data and information support for the United States Department of Energy's global change research program and makes these data and information products available to a multidisciplinary community of researchers, policymakers, and educators at no cost.
Contact(s):
Director: ROBERT M. CUSHMAN; Phone: 423-574-4791
User Services: SONJA B. JONES; Phone: 423-574-3645
Publication(s): *Trends Online; CDIAC Communications*

FEDERAL ENERGY REGULATORY COMMISSION
888 First St., NE, Washington, DC 20426
Description: Established October 1, 1977, pursuant to the Department of Energy Organization Act of 1977, the Federal Energy Regulatory Commission regulates the interstate aspects of the electric power and natural gas industries and establishes rates for transporting oil by pipeline. The Commission issues and enforces licenses for construction and operation of nonfederal hydroelectric power projects. The FERC also advises federal agencies on the merits of proposed federal multiple-purpose water development projects.
Contact(s):
Secretary: DAVID P. BOERGERS; Phone: 202-208-0400
Chair: JAMES HOECKER; Phone: 202-208-0000
Chief Administrative Law Judge: CURTIS J. WAGNER JR.; Phone: 202-219-2500
Chief Information Officer: KATHLEEN M. HIRNING; Phone: 202-208-1055
Commisioner: CURTIS L. HERBERT JR.; Phone: 202-208-0601
Commissioner: WILLIAM L. MASSEY; Phone: 202-208-0366
Commissioner: LINDA K. BREATHITT; Phone: 202-208-0377
Commissioner: VICKY A. BAILEY; Phone: 202-208-0388
Director of Economic Policy: RICHARD P. O'NEILL; Phone: 202-208-0100
Director of Electric Power Regulation: SHELTON M. CANNON; Phone: 202-208-1200
Director of Hydropower Licensing: CAROL L. SAMPSON; Phone: 202-219-2700
Director of Office of External Affairs: REBECCA F. SCHAFFER; Phone: 202-208-0004
Director of Pipeline Regulation: KEVIN P. MADDEN; Phone: 202-208-0700
Executive Director and Chief Financial Officer: CHRISTIE L. McGUE; Phone: 202-208-0300
General Counsel: DOUGLAS W. SMITH; Phone: 202-208-1000
Office of Chief Accountant: DEBBIE L. CLARK; Phone: 202-219-2600

DEPARTMENT OF HEALTH AND HUMAN SERVICES
200 Independence Ave., SW, Washington, DC 20201
WWW: www.hhs.gov
Description: The Department of Health and Human Services is the United States government's principal agency for protecting the health of all Americans and providing essential human services, especially for those who are least able to help themselves.
Contact(s):
Secretary: DONNA SHALALA; Phone: 202-690-7000
Acting Principal Deputy Assistant Secretary for Health: DR. JOHN M. EISENBERG; Phone: 202-690-7694
Administration for Aging: WILLIAM F. BENSON; Phone: 202-401-4634
Administration for Children and Families: OLIVIA GOLDEN; Phone: 202-401-2337
Administrator of Health Care Financing Administration: BRUCE C. VLADECK; Phone: 202-690-6726
Assistant Secretary for Legislation: RICHARD TARPLIN; Phone: 202-690-7627
Assistant Secretary for Management and Budget (Acting): JOHN J. CALLAHAN; Phone: 202-690-6396
Assistant Secretary for Planning and Evaluation: DR. MARGARET HAMBURG; Phone: 202-690-7858
Assistant Secretary for Public Affairs (Acting): MELISSA SKOLFIELD; Phone: 202-690-7850
Chief of Staff: WILLIAM CORR; Phone: 202-690-7431
Counselor to the Secretary: ANN ROSEWATER; Phone: 202-690-8157
Deputy Secretary: KEVIN THURM; Phone: 202-690-6133
Office of Civil Rights: DENNIS W. HAYASHI; Phone: 202-619-0403
Office of Consumer Affairs: LESLIE BYRNE; Phone: 202-565-0040
Office of Inspector General: JUNE G. BROWN; Phone: 202-619-3148
Office of the General Counsel: HARRIET S. RABB; Phone: 202-690-7741

FOOD AND DRUG ADMINISTRATION
5600 Fishers Ln., Rockville, MD 20857
Phone: 410-433-1544; WWW: www.fda.gov
Description: Protects the health of American consumers by enforcing federal laws which require that foods must be safe, pure, and wholesome; human and veterinary drugs, biologies, and therapeutic devices must be safe and effective; cosmetics and radiation-emitting products must be harmless; and that all these products must be honestly and informatively labeled and packaged.
Contact(s):
Director: D. BRUCE BURLINGTON; Phone: 410-443-4690
Director: RICHARD H. TESKE; Phone: 410-594-1740
Director: BERNARD A. SCHWETZ; Phone: 501-543-7517
Director: GERALD F. MEYER; Phone: 410-443-2894
Director: DR. FRED R. SHANK; Phone: 202-205-4850
Director: KATHRYN C. ZOON; Phone: 410-496-3556
Director: DR. MARY ANN DANELLO; Phone: 410-443-1565
Associate Commissioner for Consumer Affairs: R. ALEXANDER GRANT; Phone: 410-443-5006
Associate Commissioner for Health Affairs: DR. STUART L. NIGHTINGALE; Phone: 410-433-6143
Associate Commissioner for Legislative Affairs: DIANNE E. THOMPSON; Phone: 410-443-3793
Associate Commissioner for Management and Operations: SHARON SMITH HOLSTON; Phone: 410-443-3370
Associate Commissioner for Planning and Evaluation: PAUL L. COPPINGER; Phone: 410-433-4230
Associate Commissioner for Public Affairs: JAMES A. O'HARA, III, ; Phone: 410-443-1130
Associate Commissioner for Regulatory Affairs: RONALD G. CHESEMORE; Phone: 410-433-1594
Chief Counsel for Office of General Counsel: MARY JANE PORTER; Phone: 410-443-4370
Deputy Commissioner for External Affairs: CAROL SCHEMAN; Phone: 410-443-2400
Deputy Commissioner for Management and Systems: MARY JO VEVERKA; Phone: 410-443-1263
Deputy Commissioner for Operations: JANE HENNEY; Phone: 410-433-2400
Deputy Commissioner for Policy: MICHAEL R. TAYLOR; Phone: 410-443-2854
Director of AIDS Coordination Staff: DR. RANDOLPH WYKOFF
Director of Office of Biotechnology: DR. HENRY MILLER; Phone: 410-443-7573
Director of Office of Equal Employment and Civil Rights: ROSAMELIA de la ROCHA; Phone: 410-443-5541

U.S. FEDERAL AND INTERNATIONAL GOVERNMENT AGENCIES - EXECUTIVE BRANCH

Director of Office of Executive Operations: JOSEPH A. LEVITT; Phone: 410-443-5004
Director of Office of Orphan Products Development: DR. MARLENE HAFFNER
Director of Press Relations for Staff of Office of Public Affairs: BETSY ADAMS; Phone: 410-443-4177
Ombudsman: AMANDA PEDERSEN; Phone: 410-443-1306
Special Assistant to the Commissioner for Program Policy: JACK W. MARTIN; Phone: 410-443-6776

DEPARTMENT OF HOUSING AND URBAN DEVELOPMENT
HUD Bldg., 451 7th St., SW, Washington, DC 20410
Phone: 202-755-5111; WWW: www.hud.gov
Contact(s):
Secretary: ANDREW M. CUOMO; Phone: 202-708-0417
Acting Assistant Deputy Secretary for Field Policy and Management: DEBORAH WILLIAMS; Phone: 202-708-2426
Assistant Secretary for Administration (Acting): JOSEPH SMITH; Phone: 202-708-0940
Assistant Secretary for Community Planning and Development: SAUL RAMIREZ; Phone: 202-708-0123
Assistant Secretary of Housing FHA Commissioner: DESIGNEE BILL APGAR; Phone: 202-708-3600
Deputy Assistant Secretary for Research, Eval., and Monitoring: XAVIER de-SOUZA BRIGGS; Phone: 202-708-1600
Deputy Chief of Staff for Policy and Programs: JACQUIE LAWING; Phone: 202-708-2236
Director of Office of Environment and Energy: RICHARD BROUN; Phone: 202-708-2894
Inspector General: SUSAN GAFFNEY; Phone: 202-708-0430
Senior Advisor to the Secretary: CARDELL COOPER; Phone: 202-708-2690
Senior Advisor to the Secretary of Public and Indian Housing: HAROLD LUCAS; Phone: 202-708-0950

DEPARTMENT OF JUSTICE
Environment and Natural Resources Division, Rm. 2143, 10th St. and Constitution Ave., NW, Washington, DC 20530
Phone: 202-514-2701
Description: The Environment and Natural Resources Division handles litigation involving American's pollution control laws; central resources laws, the protection and enhancement of the American environment and wildlife resources; the acquisition, administration, and disposition of public land, water, and mineral resources; and the safeguarding of Indian rights and property.
Contact(s):
Attorney General: JANET RENO; Phone: 202-514-2001
Appellate Section Chief: JAMES KILBOURNE; Phone: 202-514-2748
Assistant Attorney General: LOIS J. SCHIFFER; Phone: 202-514-2701
Deputy Assistant Attorney General: JAMES F. SIMON; Phone: 202-514-3370
Deputy Assistant Attorney General: PETER D. COPPELMAN; Phone: 202-514-4760
Environmental Crimes Section Chief: STEVEN SOLOW; Phone: 202-272-9877
Environmental Defense Section Chief: LETITIA J. GRISHAW; Phone: 202-514-2219
Environmental Enforcement Section Chief: JOEL GROSS; Phone: 202-514-1604
Executive Assistant (Acting): ROBERT BRUFFY; Phone: 202-616-3147
General Litigation Section Chief: WILLIAM M. COHEN; Phone: 202-272-6851
Indian Resources Section Chief (Acting): JAMES J. CLEAR; Phone: 202-272-4111
Land Acquisition Section Chief: WILLIAM J. KOLLINS; Phone: 202-272-6776
Policy of Legislation and Special Litigation Section Chief: PAULINE H. MILIUS; Phone: 202-514-2586
Wildlife and Marine Resources Section Chief: EILEEN SOBECK; Phone: 202-272-4421

DEPARTMENT OF LABOR
200 Constitution Ave., NW, Washington, DC 20210
Phone: 202-219-5000; WWW: www.dol.gov
Contact(s):
Secretary: ALEXIS M. HERMAN; Phone: 202-219-8271
Deputy Secretary: THOMAS P. GLYNN; Phone: 202-219-6151
Mine Safety and Health Administrator: J. DAVITT McATEER; Phone: 703-235-1385

JOB CORPS
Department of Labor, Employment and Training Administration, Frances Perkins Bldg., 200 Constitution Ave., NW, Washington, DC 20210
Phone: 202-219-8550
Description: Authorized by the Job Training Partnership Act, the program includes conservation centers known as Civilian Conservation Centers, located primarily in rural areas and operated for the Department of Labor by the departments of Agriculture and Interior conservation agencies. In addition to providing training and other assistance to young people, the programs of work experience, training, and remedial education are focused upon activities to conserve, develop, or manage public resources or public recreational areas or to assist in developing community projects in the public interest.
Contact(s):
Director: MARY H. SILVA; Phone: 202-219-8550

MINE SAFETY AND HEALTH ADMINISTRATION
Department of Labor, Ballston Tower 3, 4015 Wilson Blvd., Arlington, VA 22203
Phone: 703-235-1452
Description: Objectives are to administer the Federal Mine Safety and Health Act, thereby promoting safety and health in the mining industry, preventing disasters, and protecting the health and safety of the nation's miners.
Contact(s):
Acting Director of Educational Policy and Development: FRANK SCHWAMBERGER; Phone: 703-235-1515
Administrator of Coal Mine Health and Safety: ROBERT ELAM; Phone: 703-235-9423
Administrator of Metal and Nonmetal Mine Health and Safety: EDWARD HUGLER; Phone: 703-235-1565
Assistant Secretary: J. DAVITT McATEER; Phone: 703-235-1385
Deputy Assistant Secretary: MARVIN NICHOLS; Phone: 703-235-2600
Director of Administration and Management: PATRICIA SILVEY; Phone: 703-235-1383
Office of Congressional and Legislative Affairs: SYLVIA MILANESE; Phone: 703-235-1392
Office of Information and Public Affairs Acting Director: KATHARINE SNYDER; Phone: 703-235-1452
Office of Standards of Regulations and Variances of Director: CAROL JONES; Phone: 703-235-1910

DEPARTMENT OF STATE
Main State Department Bldg., 2201 C St., NW, Washington, DC 20520
Phone: 202-647-4000; Fax: 202-736-7720
Contact(s):
Secretary: MADELINE ALBRIGHT
Acting Under Secretary for Global Affairs: C. WENDY SHERMAN

BUREAU OF OCEANS AND INTERNATIONAL ENVIRONMENTAL AND SCIENTIFIC AFFAIRS
Department of State, 2201 C St., NW, Washington, DC 20520
Description: OES has the principal responsibility for formulating and implementing U.S. policies for oceans, environmental, scientific, and technological aspects of U.S. relations with other governmental and multilateral institutions. The Bureau's activities cover a broad

range of foreign policy issues relating to environment, pollution, tropical forests, biological diversity, wildlife, oceans policy, fisheries, global climate change, atmospheric ozone-depletion, space, and advanced technologies.
Contact(s):
Acting Assistant Secretary: MELINDA L. KIMBLE; Phone: 202-647-1554
Deputy Assistant Secretary of Environment and Development (OES/E): RAFE POMERANCE; Phone: 202-647-2232
Deputy Assistant Secretary of Oceans, Fisheries and Space (OES/O): MARY BETH WEST; Phone: 202-647-2396
Executive Assistant/Executive Director of Administration: STEPHANIE KINNEY; Phone: 202-647-3622
Office of Ecology and Terrestrial Conservation (OES/ETC) Director: MARY MCLEAD; Phone: 202-647-2418
Office of Emerging Infectious Diseases (OES/EID) Director: NANCY CARTER FOSTER; Phone: 202-647-2435
Office of Environment Policy (OES/ENV) Director: MICHAEL D. MTELITS; Phone: 202-647-9266
Office of Global Change (OES/EGC) Director: DANIEL A. REIFSNYDER; Phone: 202-647-4069
Office of Marine Conservation (OES/OMC) Director: DAVID A. BALTON; Phone: 202-647-2335
Office of Oceans Affairs (OES/OA) Director: R. TUCKER SCULLY; Phone: 202-647-3262
Office of Science and Environmental Initiative (OES/SCI) Director: LESLIE GERSON; Phone: 202-647-3625
Office of Space and Advanced Technology (OES/SAT) Director: RALPH BRAIBANTI; Phone: 202-647-2433
Principle Department Assisting Secretary: MELINDA L. KIMBLE
Special Negotiator: AMB. MARK HAMBLEY
U.S. Man and the Biosphere Program (MAB) Director: ROGER E. SOLES; Phone: 703-235-2948

UNITED STATES MAN AND THE BIOSPHERE PROGRAM (U.S. MAB)
U.S. MAB Secretariat, OES/ETC/MAB SA-44C 1st Fl. Dept. of State, Washington, DC 20522-4401
Description: The mission of the United States Man and the Biosphere Program (U.S. MAB) is to explore, demonstrate, promote, and encourage harmonious relationships between people and their environments, building on the MAB network of Biosphere Reserves and interdisciplinary research. The long-term goal of the U.S. MAB Program is to contribute to achieving a sustainable society early in the 21st century. The MAB mission and long-term goal will be implemented, in the U.S. and internationally, through public-private partnerships and interdisciplinary research, experimentation, education, and information exchange on options by which societies can achieve sustainability.
Contact(s):
Chairman of U.S. MAB National Committee: DAVID HALES
Executive Director of U.S. MAB: DR. ROGER E. SOLES; Phone: 202-776-8318
Publication(s): *U.S. MAB Bulletin; research reports from U.S. MAB; proceedings of symposia, conferences, and workshops; directories and bibliographies*

DEPARTMENT OF THE AIR FORCE
Environmental Division, HQ USAF/ILEV, 1260 Air Force Pentagon, Washington, DC 20330-1260
Description: A comprehensive natural resources conservation program focusing on fish and wildlife management, forestry, outdoor recreation, and soil and water conservation has been conducted on Air Force lands since the mid-1950's. Current policy requires all installations with significant land and water resources to develop integrated natural resource management plans as part of the base comprehensive planning process.

Air Force Center For Environmental Excellence
3207 North Rd., Brooks AFB, TX 78235-5363
Phone: 210-536-5630
Contact(s):
Chief of Resources Conservation (AFCEE/ECR): LT. COL ROBERT KULL JR.

Air Force Civil Engineering Support Agency
139 Barnes Dr., Tyndall AFB, FL 32403-5319
Phone: 904-283-6465
Contact(s):
Management Agronomist (AFCESA/CEM): WAYNE FORDHAM

Bird Aircraft Strike Hazard (BASH) Team
9700 Avenue G, Bld. 24499, Kirtland AFB, NM 87117-5671
Phone: 505-846-0698
Contact(s):
Chief, BASH Team (HQ AFSA/SEFW): MAJ. DAVID ARRINGTON

Office of the Civil Engineer
1260 Air Force Pentagon, Washington, DC 20330-1260
Phone: 703-604-0632
Contact(s):
Chief of Cultural Resources Team (AF/ILEVP): STEPHANIE STEVENSON, 1260 Air Force Pentagon, Washington, DC 20330-1260; Phone: 703-604-0551
Chief of Environmental Division (AF/ILEV): TERESA POHLMAN, 1260 Air Force Pentagon, Washington, DC 20330-1260; Phone: 703-604-0650
Chief of Environmetnal Planning (AF/ILEVP): KENNETH REINERTSON, 1260 Air Force Pentagon, Washington, DC 20330-1260; Phone: 703-607-0221
Chief of Natural Resources Team (AF/ILEVP): J. DOUGLAS RIPLEY, 1260 Air Force Pentagon, Washington, DC 20330-1260; Phone: 703-604-0632

MAJOR AIR COMMANDS

Air Combat Command
129 Andrews St., Suite 102, Langley AFB, VA 23665-2769
Phone: 757-764-9338
Contact(s):
Natural Resources Manager (HQ ACC/CEVA): ROY BARKER

Air Education and Training Command
266 F St., West, Bldg. 901, Randolph AFB, TX 78150-4321
Phone: 210-652-3959
Contact(s):
Natural Resources Manager (HQ AETC/CEV): CARL W. LAHSHER

Air Force Base Conversion Agency (AFBCA)
Contact(s):
Convservation Manger (HQ AFBCA/EV): JERRY CLEAVER, 1700 N. Moore St., Suite 2300, Arlington, VA 22209-2802; Phone: 703-696-5536

Air Force District of Washington
3700 Brookley Ave., Washington, DC 20332
Phone: 202-767-8600
Contact(s):
Chief of Environmental Planning Branch (HQ 11WG/CEV): AYODELE MCCLENNEY

Air Force Material Command
4225 Logistics Ave., Suite 8, Wright Patterson, OH 45433-5747
Phone: 937-656-1409
Contact(s):
Natural Resource Manager (HQ AFRES/CEVP): MICHAEL CORNELIUS

U.S. FEDERAL AND INTERNATIONAL GOVERNMENT AGENCIES - EXECUTIVE BRANCH

Air Force Reserves (AFRES)
155 2nd St., Robins AFB, GA 31098-1635
Phone: 912-327-1072
Contact(s):
Natural Resource Manager (HQ AFRES/CEVP): THOMAS PILCHER

Air Force Space Command (AFSPC)
150 Vandenberg St., Suite 1105, Peterson AFB, CO 80914-4150
Phone: 719-554-9895
Contact(s):
Chief of Environmental Planning Branch (HQ AFSPC/CEVP): LINDA KELLY

Air Force Special Operations Command HQ/AFSOC/CEV
100 Bartley St., Suite 218E, Hurlburt Field, FL 32544-5273
Phone: 850-884-2260
Contact(s):
Natural Resource Manager and Entomologist: MICHAEL APPLEGATE; Phone: 904-884-2260

Air Mobility Command (AMC)
507 A St., Scott AFB, IL 62225-5022
Phone: 618-256-5764
Contact(s):
Natural Resources Manager (HQ AMC/CEVP): WILLIAM J. SUMMERS

Air National Guard (ANG)
3500 Fetchet Ave., Andrews AFB, MD 20331-5157
Phone: 301-836-8065
Contact(s):
Natural Resources Manager (HQ ANG/CEVP): RICHARD MASSE, 3500 Fetchet Ave., Andrews AFB, MD 20331-5157; Phone: 301-836-8065 ext 8142

Pacific Air Forces (PACAF)
25 E St., Suite D-306, Hickman AFB, HI 96853-5412
Phone: 808-449-9695
Contact(s):
Natural Resources Manager (HQ PACAF/CEVEP): ARTHUR BUCKMAN

U.S. Air Force Academy
8120 Edgerton Dr., Suite 40, USAF Academy, CO 80840-2400
Phone: 719-333-3336
Contact(s):
Natural Resource Manager (HQ USAFA/CEVP): DANA GREEN

U.S. Air Forces Europe (USAFE)
Unit 3050, Box 10, Ramstein AB/APO AE 09094 Germany
Phone: 011-49-6371-47-6482
Contact(s):
Natural Resources Manager (HQ USAFE/CEV): JAMIE AGUDLO

MAJOR U.S. INSTALLATIONS

Alaskan Remote Sites (611 Support Group)
Contact(s):
Natural Resources Manager: GENE AUGUSTINE; Phone: 907-552-0788

Altus AFB, OK
Contact(s):
Natural Resources Manager: JIM BELLON; Phone: 405-481-7606

Anderson AFB, Guam
Contact(s):
Natural Resources Manager: HEIDI HIRSH; Phone: 671-366-2549

Andrews AFB, MD
Contact(s):
Natural Resources Manager: BRIAN LAFLAMME; Phone: 301-981-2348

Arnold AFB, TN
Contact(s):
Natural Resources Manager: MARK MORAN; Phone: 615-454-4066

Avon Park AFB, FL
Contact(s):
Chief of Conservation Programs: PAUL EBERSBACH; Phone: 914-452-4119 ext 301

Barksdale AFB, LA
Contact(s):
Natural Resources Manager: BRUCE HOLLAND; Phone: 318-456-1981

Beale AFB, CA
Contact(s):
Natural Resouces Manager: BRUCE REINHARDT; Phone: 916-634-2643

Bolling AFB, Washington, DC
Contact(s):
Natural Resources Manager: PETER DROTTAR; Phone: 202-404-7003

Brooks AFB, TX
Contact(s):
Natural Resources Manager: HAMID KAMALPOUR; Phone: 210-536-6703

Cannon AFB, NM
Contact(s):
Natural Resources Manager: RICK CROW; Phone: 505-784-6383

Charleston AFB, SC
Contact(s):
Natural Resource Manager: AL URRUTIA; Phone: 803-963-4978

Columbus AFB, MS
Contact(s):
Natural Resources Manager: LT. CHIN SU; Phone: 601-434-7958

Davis-Monthan AFB, AZ
Contact(s):
Natural Resources Manager: GWEN LISA; Phone: 520-228-3215

Dover AFB, DE
Contact(s):
Natural Resources Manager: MILTON BECK; Phone: 302-677-6850

Dyes AFB, TX
Contact(s):
Natural Resources Manager: DON PITTS; Phone: 915-696-5049

Edwards AFB, CA
Contact(s):
Natural Resources Manager: MARK HAGAN; Phone: 805-277-1418

Edwards AFB, FL

Eglin AFB, FL
Contact(s):
Natural Resources Manager: RICK MCWHITE; Phone: 904-882-4164

Eielson AFB, AK
Contact(s):
Natural Resources Manager: GERALD VON RUEDEN; Phone: 907-377-4210

Ellsworth AFB, SD
Contact(s):
Natural Resources Manager: CHRIS LEONARD; Phone: 605-385-6629

Elmendorf AFB, AK
Contact(s):
Natural Resources Manager: ALAN RICHMOND; Phone: 907-552-2282

F.E. Warren AFB, WY
Contact(s):
Natural Resources Manager: TOM SMITH; Phone: 307-775-4357

Fairchild, AFB, AK
Contact(s):
Natural Resources Manager: GERALD JOHNSON; Phone: 509-247-5847

Goodfellow AFB, TX
Contact(s):
Natural Resources Manager: LYNDAL FISHER; Phone: 915-657-3470

Grand Forks AFB, ND
Contact(s):
Natural Resources Manager: WAYNE C. KOOP; Phone: 701-747-4590

Hanscom AFB, MA
Contact(s):
Natural Resources Manager: DON MORRIS; Phone: 615-377-4667

Hickam AFB, HI
Contact(s):
Natural Resources Manager: LT. DAWN WAGNER; Phone: 808-449-1584 ext 205

Hill AFB, UT
Contact(s):
Natural Resources Manager: MARCUS BLOOD; Phone: 801-777-4618

Holloman AFB, NM
Contact(s):
Natural Resources Manager: HILDY REISER; Phone: 505-479-3931

Howard AFB, Panama
Contact(s):
Natural Resources Manager: JIMMY CHAVERS; Phone: 011-50-7284-5165

Hurlburt Field, FL
Contact(s):
Natural Resources Manager: PHILIP PRUIT; Phone: 850-884-4651

Keesler AFB, MS
Contact(s):
Natural Resources Manager: MARGARET SARTAR; Phone: 505-844-2489

Kelly AFB, TX
Contact(s):
Natural Resources Manager: ROBIN DEVINE; Phone: 210-925-3100 ext. 215

Kirtland AFB, NM
Contact(s):
Natural Resources Manager: BOB DOW; Phone: 505-846-0042

Lackland AFB, TX
Contact(s):
Natural Resources Manager: GABRIEL GONZALES; Phone: 512-671-4843

Langley AFB, VA
Contact(s):
Natural Resources Manager: TOM WITTKAMP; Phone: 804-764-1135

Laughlin AFB, TX
Contact(s):
Natural Resources Manager: JULIE WILLIS; Phone: 830-298-4298

Little Rock AFB, AR
Contact(s):
Natural Resources Manager: JAMES POPHAM; Phone: 501-988-6809

Luke AFB (and the Barry M. Goldwater AFR), AZ
Contact(s):
Chief of Conservation Programs: ROBERT BARRY; Phone: 602-856-3823, ext 242

MacDill AFB, FL
Contact(s):
Natural Resources Manager: BOB HOFFMAN; Phone: 813-828-2567

Malstrom AFB, MT
Contact(s):
Natural Resources Manager: TIM NEU; Phone: 406-731-6437

Maxwell AFB, AL
Contact(s):
Natural Resources Manager: DENNIS TATES; Phone: 334-953-3892

McChord AFB, WA
Contact(s):
Natural Resources Manager: CHERY L. DUNNING; Phone: 253-984-3913

McClellan AFB, CA
Contact(s):
Natural Resources Manager: DIANE ARREOLA; Phone: 919-643-0836

McConnell AFB, KS
Contact(s):
Natural Resources Manager: JAY ZIMMERMAN; Phone: 316-652-3927

McGuire AFB, NJ
Contact(s):
Natural Resources Manager: KING MAK; Phone: 609-724-2096

Moody AFB, GA
Contact(s):
Natural Resources Manager: TIMOTHY BOTTOMLEY; Phone: 912-257-4980

Mountain Home AFB, ID
Contact(s):
Natural Resources Manager: NATHAN ROWLAND; Phone: 208-828-4297

Nellis AFB, NV (and Nellis Air Force Range)
Contact(s):
Natural Resources Manager: ERIC WATKINS; Phone: 702-652-3173

U.S. FEDERAL AND INTERNATIONAL GOVERNMENT AGENCIES - EXECUTIVE BRANCH

New Boston AFB, NH
Contact(s):
Natural Resources Manager: STEPHEN NAJJAR; Phone: 603-471-2426

Offut AFB, NE
Contact(s):
Natural Resource Manager: GENE SVENSEN; Phone: 402-232-5891

Patrick AFB, FL
Contact(s):
Natural Resources Manager: CLAY GORDON; Phone: 407-494-2905

Peterson AFB, CO
Contact(s):
Natural Resources Manager: DAN RODRIGUEZ; Phone: 719-556-1459

Pope AFB, SC
Contact(s):
Natural Resources Manager: PAMELA MORGAN; Phone: 910-394-1638

Randolph AFB, TX
Contact(s):
Natural Resources Manager: JOHN WILDIE; Phone: 512-652-4668

Scott AFB, IL
Contact(s):
Natural Resources Manager: WILLIAM CALVERT; Phone: 618-256-2092

Seymour Johnson AFB (and Dare County AFR) NC
Contact(s):
Natural Resources Manager: BRIAN HENDERSON; Phone: 919-736-6501

Shaw AFB, SC
Contact(s):
Natural Resources Manager: TERRY MADEWELL; Phone: 803-668-9977

Sheppard AFB, TX
Contact(s):
Natural Resources Manager: TIM HUNTER; Phone: 940-283-5698

Shriever AFB, CO
Contact(s):
Natural Resources Manager: RALPH MITCHELL; Phone: 719-567-2075

Tinker AFB, OK
Contact(s):
Natural Resources Manager: JOHN KRUPOVAGE; Phone: 405-734-4100

Travis AFB, CA
Contact(s):
Natural Resources Manager: ROBERT HOLMES; Phone: 707-424-3897

Tyndall AFB, FL
Contact(s):
Natural Resources Manager: BOB BATES; Phone: 850-283-2641

Vance AFB, OK
Contact(s):
Natural Resources Manager: SHANNON ELLEDGE; Phone: 580-249-6244

Vandenberg AFB, CA
Contact(s):
Natural Resources Manager: ALLAN NAYDOL; Phone: 805-866-9687

Whiteman AFB, MO
Contact(s):
Natural Resources Manager: DON MEUSCHKE; Phone: 816-687-1227

Wright-Patterson AFB, OH
Contact(s):
Natural Resources Planner: TERRI LUCAS; Phone: 513-257-5535

DEPARTMENT OF THE ARMY
Pentagon, Washington, DC 20310
Contact(s):
Assistant for Conservation: PHIL HUBER; Phone: 703-614-9555
Deputy Assistant Secretary of the Army (Environment of Safety of and Occupational Health): RAYMOND J. FATZ; Phone: 703-695-7824

ARMY TRAINING AND DOCTRINE COMMAND
Department of the Army, HQ TRADOC, ATBO-SE, Environmental Division, Fort Monroe, VA 23651
Description: Manages conservation programs for 2 million acres at 16 Army installations nationwide. It also provides for compliance with federal, state, and local environmental regulations.
Contact(s):
Conservation and Analysis Branch: SHAWN HOLSINGER; Phone: 757-727-3045
General/Technical Libraries of HQ TRADOC (ATBO-NT) of Director: FRANCES DOYLE, Ft. Monroe, VA 23651
Natural Resources Specialist: ROBERT ANDERSON; Phone: 757-727-2077
NEPA Consultant: JOHN ESSON; Phone: 757-727-3335
NEPA Consultant: JIM WHITE; Phone: 757-727-5896
NEPA Consultant: DR. JACK DAMRON; Phone: 757-727-4135
Publication(s): *Historic Preservation Sourcebook; Army Leader's Guide to NEPA; Endangered Species Law Sourcebook*

HEADQUARTERS, U.S. ARMY TRAINING AND DOCTRINE COMMAND
ATBO-SE, Fort Monroe, VA 23651
Contact(s):
Agronomist of Fort Dix: ROGER SMITH; Phone: 609-562-2040
Agronomist of Fort Leonard Wood: MARVIN MYERS; Phone: 314-596-0871
Agronomist of Fort Rucker: DELARIE PARMER; Phone: 205-255-9363
Agronomist of Health Services Command, Academy of Health Sciences: WILLIAM PITTMAN; Phone: 512-221-4411
Agronomist of Schofield Barracks: PATRICK CHING; Phone: 808-655-6383
Agronomist of U.S. Army Military District of Washington: JAMES MURPHY; Phone: 202-696-3815
Agronomist of U.S. Military Academy, Natural Resources Branch: ROBERT JONES; Phone: 914-938-3467
Archeologist: DR. MARIE COTTRELL; Phone: 804-727-2389
Archeologist of Fort Bliss: PAUL LUKOWSKI; Phone: 915-568-6999
Archeologist of Fort Bliss: GLEN DeGARMO; Phone: 915-568-5140
Biological Tech./Game Warden of Fort Sill: KEVIN McCURDY; Phone: 405-351-4324
Biologist of DA Headquarters: JAMES McCRACKEN; Phone: 803-751-4622
Biologist of Fort Lee: JAMES LOEWEN; Phone: 804-734-5080
Chief (Acting) of Environmental and Natural Resources Division of Fort Belvoir: DOROTHY KEOUGH; Phone: 703-806-4007
Chief Environment Branch of Fort Chaffee: BOB COLEMAN; Phone: 501-484-2516
Chief Environmental Management Division of Fort Knox: AL FREELAND; Phone: 502-624-3629

U.S. FEDERAL AND INTERNATIONAL GOVERNMENT AGENCIES - EXECUTIVE BRANCH

Chief Natural Resources Manager of Fort Benning: CHARLES FORD; Phone: 706-544-7319
Chief Natural Resources Section of Fort Chaffee: JERRY STURDY; Phone: 501-484-2231
Chief of Environment of Fort Benjamin Harrison: THOMAS SHAFER; Phone: 317-549-5386
Chief of Environmental and Natural Resources of Fort Gordon: STEVE WILLARD; Phone: 706-791-2403
Chief of Environmental Resources Management of Army National Guard Bureau: LTC. ROBERT McGUIRE; Phone: 703-756-5794
Chief of Natural Resources of DA Headquarters: MARK DUTTON; Phone: 803-751-4103
Chief of Natural Resources of U.S. Military Academy, Natural Resources Branch: JOE DESCHENES; Phone: 914-938-2314
Chief of Natural/Environmental Resources of Fort Sill: GENE STOUT; Phone: 405-351-4324
Director of Environment of Fort McClellan: RON LEVY; Phone: 205-848-3539
Ecologist of Fort Bliss: KEVIN VON FINGER; Phone: 915-568-7031
Entomologist: DONALD TEIG; Phone: 804-727-2366
Entomologist of Fort Benning: CHRIS DUNN; Phone: 706-545-3224
Entomologist of Fort Eustis: JOHN SCHENCK; Phone: 804-878-2585
Entomologist of Fort Rucker: ROBERT TURNBOW; Phone: 205-255-3710
Entomologist of Headquarters of U.S. Army Pacific: STUART HAYASHI; Phone: 808-438-2180
Entomologist of U.S. Army Military District of Washington: JOE TARNOPOL; Phone: 202-475-1003
Environmental Officer of U.S. Army Military District of Washington: EDNA BARBER; Phone: 202-696-3815
Environmental Protection Specialist of Fort Greely: JOYCE BEELMAN; Phone: 907-451-2141
Environmental Protection Specialist of Fort Greely: BRAD FRISTOE; Phone: 907-451-2159
Environmental Protection Specialist of Fort Greely: DOUG DASHER; Phone: 907-451-2172
Environmental Protection Specialist of Headquarters of U.S. Army Pacific: LAWRENCE HIRAI; Phone: 808-438-8997
Environmental Protection Specialist of Schofield Barracks: MARK SALLEY; Phone: 808-656-2878
Environmental Specialist of Fort Richardson: BILL QUIRK; Phone: 907-384-3021
Fish and Wildlife Administrator of Fort Sill: GLEN WAMPLER; Phone: 405-442-8111
Forester of Fort Belvoir: MIKE HUDSON; Phone: 703-806-4007
Forester of Fort Benning: JACK GREENLEE; Phone: 706-544-7319
Forester of Fort Eustis: TONY RIZZIO; Phone: 804-878-4152
Forester of Fort Gordon: ALLEN BRASWELL; Phone: 706-791-2327
Forester of Fort Knox: DAVE APSLEY; Phone: 502-624-8147
Forester of Fort Leavenworth: MATT NOWAK; Phone: 913-684-2749
Forester of Fort Leonard Wood: STEVE THURMAN; Phone: 314-596-0871
Forester of Fort McClellan: BILL GARLAND; Phone: 205-848-3758
Forester of Fort Rucker: BOB SHUFFIELD; Phone: 205-255-9368
Forester of Information Systems Command: JOHN MILLER; Phone: 602-533-7083
Forester of Military Traffic Management Command, Military Ocean Terminal: HERSHEL GAW; Phone: 919-457-8292
Natural Resources Manager of Army National Guard Bureau: MARK IMLAY; Phone: 703-756-5794
Natural Resources Manager of Camp Atterbury: RONALD MOORE; Phone: 812-526-1250
Natural Resources Manager of Navajo Depot Activity: SSG. DON HACK; Phone: 602-774-7161 ext. 274
Natural Resources Specialist: BOB ANDERSON; Phone: 804-727-2077
Natural Resources Specialist of Fort Chaffee: WAYNE JOHNDROWN; Phone: 501-484-2231
Natural Resources Specialist of Fort McClellan: LUTHER OWEN; Phone: 205-848-5663
Natural Resources Team of U.S. Army Environmental Center: JERRY WILLIAMSON; Phone: 410-612-6833
Natural Resources Team of U.S. Army Environmental Center: SCOTT BELFIT; Phone: 410-612-6831
Natural Resources Team of U.S. Army Environmental Center: ERIC SEABORN; Phone: 410-612-6833
Natural Resources Team of U.S. Army Environmental Center: PAMELA KLINGER; Phone: 410-612-6832
Natural Resources Team of U.S. Army Environmental Center: WILLIAM HERB; Phone: 410-671-1234
Natural Resources Team of U.S. Army Environmental Center: BOB DECKER; Phone: 410-612-6831
Natural Resources Team of U.S. Army Environmental Center: STEVE SEKSCIENSKI; Phone: 410-612-6832
Wildlife Biologist of DA Headquarters: BILL GATES; Phone: 803-751-4793
Wildlife Biologist of Fort Benning: ROBERT KING; Phone: 706-544-7319
Wildlife Biologist of Fort Chaffee: CLARK REAMES; Phone: 501-484-2231
Wildlife Biologist of Fort Dix: ROGER MEYERS; Phone: 609-562-2040
Wildlife Biologist of Fort Gordon: KENNETH BOYD; Phone: 706-791-2403
Wildlife Biologist of Fort Leonard Wood: TOM GLUECK; Phone: 314-596-0871
Wildlife Biologist of Fort Richardson: WILLIAM GOSSWEILER; Phone: 907-384-3017
Wildlife Biologist of Information Systems Command: SHERIDAN STONE; Phone: 602-538-7340
Wildlife Biologist Tech. of Fort Knox: DONALD SHEROAN; Phone: 502-624-7373

HQ ARMY MATERIAL COMMAND, INSTALLATIONS AND SERVICES ACTIVITY
ATTN: AMXEN-U, Rock Island, IL 61299-7190
Contact(s):
Agronomist of Red River Army Depot: TOM COLEMAN; Phone: 903-334-2385
Agronomist of U.S. Army Research Laboratory: BOB WARDWELL; Phone: 301-394-1060
Archeologist of White Sands Missile Range: ROBERT BURTON; Phone: 505-678-8731
Chief of Conservation and Preservation of Dugway Proving Ground: JOHN MARTIN; Phone: 801-831-2986
Entomologist of U.S. Army Aberdeen Proving Ground Support Activities: ABDUL SHIEK, ATTN STEAP-FE-G, Bldg. 5110, Aberdeen Proving Ground, MD 21005-5001; Phone: 410-278-3303
Environmental Protection Specialist of U.S. Army Aberdeen Proving Ground Support Activities: STEVE WAMPLER, Directorate of Safety Health and Environment, ATTN STEAP-SH-E, Aberdeen Proving Ground, MD 21010; Phone: 410-671-4843
Environmental Protection Specialist of U.S. Army Aberdeen Proving Ground Support Activities: TIMOTHY McNAMARA, Directorate of Safety Health and Environment, ATTN STEAP-SH-E, Aberdeen Proving Ground, MD 21005-4001; Phone: 410-278-5622
Forester: TOM VORAC; Phone: 309-782-4062
Forester of Anniston Army Depot: WILLIAM BURNS; Phone: 205-235-4217
Forester of Red River Army Depot: TERRY RUTH; Phone: 903-334-2379
Forester of Redstone Arsenal Support Activity: JESSE HORTON; Phone: 205-876-3122
Forester of U.S. Army Aberdeen Proving Ground Support Activities: ROGER STOFLET; Phone: 410-278-4915
Forester, Chief LM of Red River Army Depot: BENNIE MURRAY; Phone: 903-334-2379

U.S. FEDERAL AND INTERNATIONAL GOVERNMENT AGENCIES - EXECUTIVE BRANCH

GIS Manager of Dugway Proving Ground: JAMES MIKKELSEN; Phone: 801-831-2189
Land Manager of Blue-Grass Army Depot: MS. BILLYE HASLETT; Phone: 606-625-6669
Natural Resources Manager of Jefferson Proving Ground: KEN KNOUF; Phone: 812-273-7436
Natural Resources Manager of Letterkenny Army Depot: RANDY QUINN; Phone: 717-267-8438
Natural Resources Manager of Savanna Army Depot: BOB SPEAKER; Phone: 815-273-8533
Natural Resources Specialist: RICHARD CLEWELL; Phone: 309-782-8252
Project Engineer of Tooele Army Depot: MASON WALKER; Phone: 801-833-2891
Wildlife Biologist of Dugway Proving Ground: SCOTT BATES; Phone: 801-831-2157
Wildlife Biologist of U.S. Army Aberdeen Proving Ground Support Activities: JAMES POTTIE, Directorate of Safety Health and Environment, ATTN, STEAP-SH-BR, Aberdeen Proving Ground, MD 21005-5001; Phone: 410-278-6772
Wildlife Biologist of U.S. Army Aberdeen Proving Ground Support Activities: JAMES BAILEY, ATTN STEAP-FE-G, Bldg. 5110, Aberdeen Proving Ground, MD 21005-5001; Phone: 410-278-6748
Wildlife Biologist of White Sands Missile Range: DAISAN TAYLOR; Phone: 505-678-6140
Wildlife Biologist of White Sands Missile Range: PATRICK MORROW; Phone: 505-678-7095
Wildlife Biologist of Yuma Proving Ground: VALERIE MORRILL; Phone: 602-328-2244
Wildlife Biologist of Yuma Proving Ground: JUNIOR KERNS; Phone: 602-328-2148

U.S. ARMY CONSTRUCTION ENGINEERING RESEARCH LABORATORIES CERL

P.O. Box 9005, Champaign, IL 61826-9005
Phone: 217-352-6511
Founded: 1969
Description: CERL conducts research on infrastructure and environmental problems facing the operations of military facilities. CERL also conducts research on innovative materials and engineering procedures; energy reduction measures and equipment; management systems; air and water pollution; environmental compliance; and natural resource management.
Contact(s):
Director: DR. MICHAEL O'CONNOR
Chief of Public Affairs: DANA FINNEY
Commander: COL. JAMES A. WALTER
Publication(s): *CERL Abstracts; Index to Publications; The Cutting Edge*

U.S. ARMY CORPS OF ENGINEERS

20 Massachusetts Ave., NW, Washington, DC 20314-1000
Description: The mission of the Corps of Engineers is to provide quality, responsive engineering and environmental services to the nation. The Corps plans, designs, builds, and operates water resources and other civil works projects. The Corps designs and manages the construction of military facilities and activities for the Army and Air Force and provides design and construction management support for other defense and federal agencies. In addition to military and civilian engineers, the Corps has a diverse workforce of biologists, geologists, hydrologists, natural resource managers and other professionals.
Contact(s):
Chief of Engineers: LT. GEN. JOE N. BALLARD; Phone: 202-761-0001
Chief, Environmental Compliance: JAMES E. WOLCOTT; Phone: 202-761-0200
Chief, Natural Resources: DARRELL L. LEWIS; Phone: 202-761-0247
Chief, Office of Environmental Policy: DR. ROBERT F. SOOTS JR.; Phone: 703-428-6491
Chief, Public Affairs: COL. ROBERT N. MIRELSON; Phone: 202-761-0010
Chief, Regulatory: JOHN STUDT; Phone: 202-761-1785
Cultural Resources Coordinator: PAUL D. RUBENSTEIN; Phone: 202-761-1257
Deputy Chief of Engineers: MAJ. GEN. ALBERT J. GENETTI JR.; Phone: 202-761-0002
Director of Civil Works: MAJ. GEN RUSSEL FUHRMAN; Phone: 202-761-0099
Endangered Species/NEPA Coordinator: JOHN BELLINGER; Phone: 202-761-0166
Executive Secretary, Environmental Advisory Board: LLOYD SAUNDERS; Phone: 202-761-8731
Fish and Wildlife Coordinator: TIMOTHY R. TOPLISEK; Phone: 202-761-1789

U.S. Army Cold Regions Research and Engineering Laboratory
72 Lyme Road, Hanover, NH 03755-1290
Phone: 603-646-4386

U.S. Army Construction Engineering Research Laboratories
P.O. Box 9005, Champaign, IL 61826-9005
Phone: 217-373-6714

U.S. Army Corps of Engineers Water Resources Support Center
7701 Telegraph Road, Alexandria, VA 22315-3868
Phone: 703-428-7250

U.S. Army Engineer District, Alaska
P.O. Box 898, Anchorage, AK 99506-0898
Phone: 907-753-2520

U.S. Army Engineer District, Albuquerque
4101 Jefferson Plaza NE, Albuquerque, NM 87109
Phone: 505-342-3171

U.S. Army Engineer District, Baltimore
P.O. Box 1715, Baltimore, MD 21203-1715
Phone: 410-962-2809

U.S. Army Engineer District, Buffalo
1766 Niagara Street, Buffalo, NY 14207-3199
Phone: 716-879-4200

U.S. Army Engineer District, Charleston
P.O. Box 919, Charleston, SC 29401-0919
Phone: 803-727-4201

U.S. Army Engineer District, Chicago
111 N. Canal Street, Suite 600, Chicago, IL 60606-7206
Phone: 312-353-6400

U.S. Army Engineer District, Detroit
P.O. Box 1027, Detroit, MI 48231-1027
Phone: 313-226-4680

U.S. Army Engineer District, Fort Worth
P.O. Box 17300, Forth Worth, TX 76102-0300
Phone: 817-978-2196

U.S. Army Engineer District, Galveston
Jadwin Building, 2000 Fort Point Road, Galveston, TX 77550
Phone: 409-766-3049

U.S. Army Engineer District, Honolulu
Building 230, Fort Shafter, HI 96858-5440
Phone: 808-438-9862

U.S. Army Engineer District, Huntington
502 8th Street, Huntington, WV 25701-2070
Phone: 304-529-5453

U.S. Army Engineer District, Jacksonville
P.O. Box 4970, Jacksonville, FL 32232-0019
Phone: 904-232-2235

U.S. Army Engineer District, Kansas City
601 E. 12th Street, Kansas City, MO 64106-2896
Phone: 816-983-5241

U.S. Army Engineer District, Little Rock
P.O. Box 867, Little Rock, AR 72203-0867
Phone: 501-324-5551

U.S. Army Engineer District, Los Angeles
P.O. Box 2711, Los Angeles, CA 90053-2325
Phone: 213-452-3921

U.S. Army Engineer District, Louisville
P.O. Box 59, Louisville, KY 40201-0059
Phone: 502-582-5736

U.S. Army Engineer District, Memphis
167 N. Main Street, Room B202, Memphis, TN 38103-1894
Phone: 901-544-3348

U.S. Army Engineer District, Mobile
P.O. Box 2288, Mobile, AL 36628-0001
Phone: 334-690-2505

U.S. Army Engineer District, Nashville
P.O. Box 1070, Nashville, TN 37202-1070
Phone: 615-736-7161

U.S. Army Engineer District, New England
696 Virginia Rd., Concord, MA 01742-2751
Phone: 978-318-8237

U.S. Army Engineer District, New Orleans
P.O. Box 60167, New Orleans, LA 70160-0267
Phone: 504-862-2201

U.S. Army Engineer District, New York
Jacob K. Javits Federal Building, 26 Federal Plaza, New York, NY 10278-0090
Phone: 212-264-5818

U.S. Army Engineer District, Norfolk
803 Front Street, Norfolk, VA 23510-1096
Phone: 757-441-7606

U.S. Army Engineer District, Philadelphia
Wanamaker Building, 100 Penn Square East, Philadelphia, PA 19107-3390
Phone: 215-656-6500

U.S. Army Engineer District, Pittsburg
Rm. 1828, William S. Moorhead Federal Building, 1000 Liberty Avenue, Pittsburgh, PA 15222-4186
Phone: 412-395-7501

U.S. Army Engineer District, Portland
P.O. Box 2946, Portland, OR 97208-2946
Phone: 503-808-4510

U.S. Army Engineer District, Rock Island
P.O. Box 2004, Rock Island, IL 61204-2004
Phone: 309-794-5900

U.S. Army Engineer District, Sacramento
1325 J Street, Sacramento, CA 95814-2922
Phone: 916-557-7461

U.S. Army Engineer District, San Francisco
333 Market Street, San Francisco, CA 94105-2195
Phone: 415-977-8658

U.S. Army Engineer District, Savannah
P.O. Box 889, Savannah, GA 31402-0889
Phone: 912-652-5279

U.S. Army Engineer District, Seattle
P.O. Box 3755, Seattle, WA 98124-3755
Phone: 206-764-3769

U.S. Army Engineer District, St. Louis
1222 Spruce Street, St. Louis, MO 63103-2833
Phone: 314-331-8010

U.S. Army Engineer District, St. Paul
Army Corps of Engineers Centre, 190 East 5th Street, St. Paul, MN 55101-1638
Phone: 612-290-5201

U.S. FEDERAL AND INTERNATIONAL GOVERNMENT AGENCIES - EXECUTIVE BRANCH

U.S. Army Engineer District, Tulsa
P.O. Box 61, Tulsa, OK 74121-0061
Phone: 918-669-7366

U.S. Army Engineer District, Vicksburg
4155 Clay Street, Vicksburg, MS 39180-3435
Phone: 601-631-5052

U.S. Army Engineer District, Walla Walla
201 North 3rd Avenue, Walla Walla, WA 99362-1876
Phone: 509-527-7020

U.S. Army Engineer District, Wilmington
P.O. Box 1890, Wilmington, NC 28402-1890
Phone: 910-251-4626

U.S. Army Engineer Division, Great Lakes and Ohio
Regional Headquarters, P.O. Box 1159, Cincinnati, OH 45201-1159
Phone: 513-684-3010

U.S. Army Engineer Division, Great Lakes and Ohio River
Regional Headquarters, 111 North Canal Street, Chicago, IL 60606-7205
Phone: 312-353-6317

U.S. Army Engineer Division, Mississippi Valley
P.O. Box 80, Vicksburg, MS 39181-0080
Phone: 601-634-5757

U.S. Army Engineer Division, North Atlantic
Fort Hamilton Military Community, General Lee Ave., Guilding 302, Brooklyn, NY 11252
Phone: 718-491-8707

U.S. Army Engineer Division, Northwestern
Regional Headquarters, P.O. Box 2870, Portland, OR 97208-2870
Phone: 503-808-3710
Regional Headquarters, 12565 West Center Road, Omaha, NE 68144-3869
Phone: 401-697-2600

U.S. Army Engineer Division, Pacific Ocean
Building 230, Fort Shafter, HI 96858-5440
Phone: 808-438-9862

U.S. Army Engineer Division, South Atlantic
Room 322, 77 Forsyth Street, SW, Atlanta, GA 30303-3490
Phone: 404-331-7444

U.S. Army Engineer Division, South Pacific
333 Market Street, San Francisco, CA 94105-2195
Phone: 415-977-8221

U.S. Army Engineer Division, Southwestern
1114 Commerce Street, Dallas, TX 75242-0216
Phone: 214-767-2510

U.S. Army Engineer Waterways Experiment Station
3909 Halls Ferry Road, Vicksburg, MS 39180-6199
Phone: 601-634-2504

U.S. Army Topographic Engineering Center
7701 Telegraph Rd., Alexandria, VA 22315-3864
Phone: 703-428-6634

U.S. ARMY FORCES COMMAND
Forester, HQ FORSCOM, Attn: AFPI-ENE, Fort McPherson, GA 30330-1062
Phone: 404-464-5762; Fax: 404-669-7827; Email: cannons@forscom.army.mil
Contact(s):
Forester: STUART M. CANNON
Wildlife Biologist: DR. ALBERT E. BIVINGS; Email: bivingsb@forscom.army.mil

U.S. MILITARY ACADEMY

Natural Resources Branch
DHPW, West Point, NY 10996-1592
Phone: 914-938-2314; Fax: 914-938-2324
Contact(s):
Agronomist for Fish and Wildlife: ROBERT JONES; Phone: 914-938-6789
Biologist for ITAM Program: JAMES BEEMER
Branch Chief and Forester: JOE DESCHENES
Manager: CATHERINE COLEMAN; Phone: 914-938-5939

DEPARTMENT OF THE ARMY CONSERVATION DIVISION

ASSISTANT CHIEF OF STAFF FOR INSTALLATION MANAGEMENT
ATTN: DAIM-ED-N, 600 Army Pentagon, Washington, DC 20310-0600
Description: Natural and cultural resources professionals are responsible for the management of approximately 12 million acres of land on Army military installations. Management objectives include: Compliance with environmental laws, conservation and protection of resources, support to the military mission uses of the land, and contributions to programs which support the public needs. Resources managed include: Land, forest, wildlife, soils, vegetation, and historical and archaeological sites.
Contact(s):
Agronomist: VIC DIERSING; Phone: 703-696-8813
Archaeologist: MARY ANNE WOODS; Phone: 703-696-8813
Associate Director: DONALD BANDEL; Phone: 703-696-8813; Fax: 703-696-8821
Entomologist: RAUL MARROQUIN; Phone: 703-696-8813
Fish and Wildlife Administrator: PHILLIP PIERCE; Phone: 703-696-8813
Forester: DONALD COLE; Phone: 703-696-8813
Historic Preservation Officer: CONSTANCE RAMIREZ; Phone: 703-696-8813
Natural Resource Specialist: CHUCK WRIGHT; Phone: 703-696-8813
Natural Resources Specialist: PETE WAAS; Phone: 703-696-8813

DEPARTMENT OF THE INTERIOR
Interior Bldg., 1849 C St., NW, Washington, DC 20240
Phone: 202-208-3100; WWW: www.doi.gov
Description: The mission of the Department of the Interior is to protect and provide access to our Nation's natural and cultural heritage and honor our trust responsibilities to tribes.
Contact(s):
Secretary: BRUCE BABBITT; Phone: 202-208-7351
Assistant Secretary of Fish of Wildlife of and Parks: DONALD J. BARRY
Assistant Secretary of Indian Affairs: KEVIN GOVER
Assistant Secretary of Land and Minerals Management: BOB ARMSTRONG
Assistant Secretary of Policy of Management of and Budget: JOHN BERRY
Assistant Secretary of Water and Science: PATRICIA BENEKE
Assistant to the Secretary and Director of Office of Communications: MICHAEL GAULDIN
Assistant to the Secretary and Director of Office of Congressional and Legislative Affairs: MELANIE BELLER
Associate Solicitor of Audit and Inspections: THOMAS E. ROBINSON
Associate Solicitor of Conservation and Wildlife: BARRY HILL
Associate Solicitor of General Law: KAREN MALOY SPRECHER
Associate Solicitor of Indian Affairs: DERRIL B. JORDAN
Associate Solicitor of Surface Mining: GLENDA OWENS
Chief of Staff: ANNE SHIELDS

Commissioner of Bureau of Reclamation: ELVID L. MARTINEZ
Deputy Assistant Secretary - Budget and Finance: ROBERT L. LAMB
Deputy Commissioner of Bureau of Indian Affairs: HILDA MANUEL
Deputy Solicitor: EDWARD COHEN
Director (Acting) of Economic Development: DOM NESSI
Director (Acting) of Office of Surface Mining Reclamation and Enforcement: KATHERINE KARPAN
Director (Acting) of United States Fish and Wildlife Service: JAMIE RAPPAPORT CLARK
Director of Acquisition and Property Management: DEBRA E. SONDERMAN
Director of Bureau of Land Management: PATRICK SHEA
Director of Geological Survey: THOMAS CASADEVALL
Director of Minerals Management Service: CYNTHIA QUARTERMAN
Director of National Park Service: ROBERT G. STANTON
Director of Office for Equal Opportunity: E. MELODEE STITH
Director of Office Information Resources Management: DARYL W. WHITE
Director of Office of Budget: MARY ANN LAWLER
Director of Office of Environmental Policy and Compliance: WILLIE TAYLOR
Director of Office of Hearings and Appeals: BOB BAUM
Director of Office of Personnel: MARI BARR
Director of Office of Policy Analysis: JAMES PIPKEN
Director of Tribal Government Services: BETTIE RUSHING
Director of Trust: TERRY VIRDER
Director Office of Aircraft Services: ELMER HURD
Director, Interior Service Center: TIMOTHY G. VIGOTSKY
Inspector General: RICHARD REBACK
Solicitor: JOHN D. LESHY

BUREAU OF INDIAN AFFAIRS
1849 C St., NW, Washington, DC 20240
Phone: 202-208-5116
Founded: 1824
Description: An agency charged with carrying out the major portion of the trust responsibility of the United States to Indian tribes. This trust includes the protection and enhancement of Indian lands and the conservation and development of natural resources, including fish, wildlife, and outdoor recreation resources.
Contact(s):
Assistant Secretary: KEVIN GOVER; Phone: 202-208-7163
Chief of Branch of Fish, Wildlife and Recreation: GARY L. RANKEL; Phone: 202-208-4088
Deputy Commissioner: HILDA A. MANUEL; Phone: 202-208-5116
Director of Office of Trust Responsibilities: TERRY VIRDEN; Phone: 202-208-5831

BUREAU OF LAND MANAGEMENT
1849 C. St., NW, LSB-204, Washington, DC 20240
Phone: 202-208-3801
Founded: 1946
Description: Administers the public lands which are located primarily in the Western states and which amount to about 48 percent over 272 million acres of all federally owned lands. These lands and resources are managed under multiple-use principles, including outdoor recreation, fish and wildlife production, livestock grazing, timber, industrial development, watershed protection, and onshore mineral production.
Contact(s):
Deputy Director: NINA ROSE HATFIELD
Director: PATRICK SHEA; Phone: 202-208-3801
Acting Assistant Director of Business and Fiscal Services: PETER NIEBAUGER; Phone: 202-208-4864
Acting Assistant Director of Communications: GWEN MASON; Phone: 202-208-6913
Assistant Director of Human Resources: WARREN JOHNSON; Phone: 202-501-6723
Assistant Director of Information Resources Management: GAYLE GORDON; Phone: 202-208-7701
Assistant Director of Minerals, Realty, & Resource Protection: PETE CULP; Phone: 202-208-4201
Assistant Director of Renewable Resources & Planning: HENRI BISSON; Phone: 202-208-4896
Special Assistant: TOM FRY; Phone: 202-208-3801

National Applied Resource Center
Denver Federal Center, Bldg. 50, Denver, CO 80225
Phone: 303-236-6454
Contact(s):
Director: LEE BARKOW
AK State Director: TOM ALLEN, 222 W. 7th Ave., #13, Anchorage, AK 99513; Phone: 907-271-5076
AZ State Director: DENISE MEREDITH, 222 North Central Avenue, Phoenix, AZ 85004; Phone: 602-417-9500
CA State Director: EDWARD L. HASTEY, 2135 Butano Drive, Sacramento, CA 95825; Phone: 916-978-4600
CO State Director: ANN MORGAN, 2850 Youngfield St., Lakewood, CO 80215; Phone: 303-239-3700
Eastern States Director: W. HORD TIPTON, 7450 Boston Blvd., Springfield, VA 22153; Phone: 703-440-1700
Group Manager for Fish, Wildlife, and Forests: CHRISTINE JAUHOLA; Phone: 202-452-7761
ID State Director: MARTHA G. HAHN, 1387 S. Vinnell Way, Boise, ID 83709-1657; Phone: 208-373-4001
MT State Director: LARRY E. HAMILTON, 222 N. 32nd St., Billings, MT 59101; Phone: 406-255-2904
NM State Director: WILLIAM CALKINS, 1474 Rodeo Rd., Santa Fe, NM 87504; Phone: 505-438-7501
NV State Director: ROBERT ABBEY, 1340 Financial Blvd, Reno, NV 89502-7147; Phone: 702-861-6590
OR State Director: ELAINE ZIELINSKI, 1515 SW 5th Ave., Portland, OR 97208; Phone: 503-952-6024
UT State Director: BILL LAMB, 324 S. State St., Salt Lake City, UT 84145-0155; Phone: 801-539-4010
WY State Director: AL PIERSON, 5353 Yellowstone Rd., Cheyenne, WY 82003; Phone: 307-775-6001

National Interagency Fire Center
3833 S. Development Ave., Boise, ID 83705
Phone: 208-387-5512
Contact(s):
Director: LESTER ROSENKRANCE

BUREAU OF RECLAMATION
U.S. Department of the Interior 1849 C St., NW, Washington, DC 20240
Description: The U.S. Department of the Interior's Bureau of Reclamation was created by the Reclamation Act of 1902 to reclaim arid lands in the 17 Western states. This has been accomplished by the development of a system of works for the storage, diversion, and development of water. Reclamation's future role entails a shift in emphasis from development to total resource management and more effective use of existing facilities. Nonstructural means of meeting future water and power needs is now being emphasized.
Contact(s):
Commissioner: ELUID L. MARTINEZ; Phone: 202-208-4157
Chief Issue Managers Group: SHANNON CUNNIFF; Phone: 202-208-5007
Chief of Public Affairs Division: PAUL BLEDSOE; Phone: 202-208-4662
Director of Operations: STEPHEN MAGNUSSEN; Phone: 202-208-4081
Director of Policy and External Affairs: STEVEN RICHARDSON; Phone: 202-208-4081
Manager of Washington Adminstration and Performance Review Initiatives: CARMEN R. MAYMI

U.S. FEDERAL AND INTERNATIONAL GOVERNMENT AGENCIES - EXECUTIVE BRANCH

Denver Office
Bldg. 67, Denver Federal Center, P.O. Box 25007, Denver, CO 80225
Contact(s):
Deputy Director of Program Analysis Office: WAYNE O. DEASON; Phone: 303-236-3292
Director of Human Resources: MARGARET SIBLEY; Phone: 303-236-7464
Director of Management Services: KATHY GORDON; Phone: 303-236-0005
Director of Program Analysis Office: J. AUSTIN BURKE; Phone: 303-236-3292
Director of Reclamation Service Center: NEAL STESSMAN; Phone: 303-236-9208
Director of Technical Service Center: FELIX W. COOK; Phone: 303-236-6985

Great Plains Region
P.O. Box 36900, Billings, MT 59107-6900
Phone: 406-247-7600
Contact(s):
Director: MARYANNE BACH, P.O. Box 36900, Billings, MT 59107-6900; Phone: 406-247-7600
Director of Public Affairs Officer: RODNEY J. OTTENBREIT; Phone: 406-657-7608
Environmental Specialist: JOHN BOEHMKE; Phone: 406-247-7715

Lower Colorado Region
P.O. Box 61470, Boulder City, NV 89006-1470
Phone: 702-293-8411
Contact(s):
Director of Public Affairs Officer: BOB WALSH, P.O. Box 61470, Boulder City, NV 89006-1470; Phone: 702-293-8421

Mid Pacific Region: Federal Office Bldg.
Federal Office Bldg, 2800 Cottage Way, Sacramento, CA 95825
Phone: 916-978-5580
Contact(s):
Director: ROGER G. PATTERSON, Federal Office Bldg., 2800 Cottage Way, Sacramento, CA 95825; Phone: 916-979-2200
Public Affairs Officer: JEFFREY S. McCRACKEN; Phone: 916-978-5101
Regional Environmental Officer: FRANK MICHNY; Phone: 916-978-5025

Pacific Northwest Region
1150 N. Curtis Rd., Boise, ID 83706-1234
Phone: 208-378-5012
Contact(s):
Environmental Officer: MONTY MCCLENDON; Phone: 208-378-5036
Public Affairs Officer: DIANA CROSS; Phone: 208-378-5020

Upper Colorado Region
125 South State St., Salt Lake City, UT 84138
Phone: 801-524-3785
Contact(s):
Chief of Environmental Resources Group: CHRISTINE KARAS; Phone: 801-524-3679
Public Affairs Officer: BARRY WIRTH; Phone: 801-524-3774
Regional Director: CHARLES CALHOUN, P.O. Box 11568, Salt Lake City, UT 84147; Phone: 801-524-3600

NATIONAL PARK SERVICE
U.S. Department of the Interior, 1849 C St., NW, Washington, DC 20240
Phone: 202-208-4747
Description: Administers parks, monuments, and other administrative classifications of national significance for their recreational, historic, and natural values. Manages landmarks programs for natural and historic properties; coordinates Wild and Scenic Rivers System and National Trail System; administers study and grants programs.
Contact(s):
Director: ROBERT G. STANTON; Phone: 202-208-4621
Deputy Director: DENIS GALVIN; Phone: 202-208-3818
Deputy Director: JACQUELINE LOWEY; Phone: 202-208-6741
Acting Associate Director of Professional Services: DAVID MOOREHOUSE; Phone: 202-208-3264
Alaska Regional Director: ROBERT BARBEE, 2525 Gambell St., Anchorage, AK 99503-2892; Phone: 907-257-2690
Associate Director of Budget and Administration: SUE MASICA; Phone: 202-208-6953
Associate Director of Cultural Resources: KATE STEVENSON; Phone: 202-208-7625
Associate Director of Natural Resources: MICHAEL SOUKUP; Phone: 202-208-3884
Associate Director of Park Operations: MAUREEN FINNERTY; Phone: 202-208-5651
Chief of Office of Communications: DAVID BARNA; Phone: 202-208-6843
Comptroller: C. BRUCE SHEAFFER; Phone: 202-208-4566
Intermountain Regional Director: JOHN COOK, P.O. Box 25287, Denver, CO 80225; Phone: 303-969-2503
Manager of Denver Service Center: CHARLES CLAPPER; Phone: 303-969-2100
Manager of Harpers Ferry Center: GARY CUMMINS; Phone: 304-535-6211
Midwest Regional Director: WILLIAM SCHENK, 1709 Jackson St., Omaha, NE 68102; Phone: 402-221-3431
National Capital Regional Director: TERRY CARLSTROM, 1100 Ohio Dr., SW, Washington, DC 20242; Phone: 202-619-7005
Northeast Region: MARIE RUST, U.S. Customs House, 3rd Fl., 200 Chestnut Street, Philadelphia, PA 19106; Phone: 215-597-7013
Office of Legislative and Congressional Affairs: KITTY ROBERTS; Phone: 202-208-5656
Pacific West: JOHN REYNOLDS, 600 Harrison St., Suite 600, San Francisco, CA 94107; Phone: 415-427-1304
Southeast Regional Director: JERRY BELSON, 100 Alabama St., NW 1924 Bldg, Atlanta, GA 30303; Phone: 404-331-4998

OFFICE OF SURFACE MINING RECLAMATION AND ENFORCEMENT
Department of Interior, Interior South Bldg., 1951 Constitution Ave., NW, Washington, DC 20240
Phone: 202-208-2565
Description: Established by the Surface Mining Control and Reclamation Act of 1977 to administer the nationwide program to protect society and the environment from adverse side effects of coal mining operations, to establish national standards for regulating the surface environmental effects of coal mining, to support state implementation of such regulatory programs, and to promote reclamation of previously mined areas.
Contact(s):
Director: KATHY KARPAN; Phone: 202-208-4006
Acting Deputy Director: ROBERT J. EWING; Phone: 202-028-2560
Assistant Director of Finance and Administration: ROBERT EWING; Phone: 202-208-2560
Assistant Director of Program Support: MARY JOSIE BLANCHARD; Phone: 202-208-4264
Chief of Staff: MARGY WHITE; Phone: 202-208-4006
Office of Communications: NANCY SMITH; Phone: 202-208-2565

U.S. GEOLOGICAL SURVEY
U.S. National Center, Reston, VA 22092
Phone: 703-648-4000
Founded: 1879
Description: This research agency of the Interior Department publishes and distributes maps and reports covering our nation's physical features and its mineral, fuel, and water resources. Responsibilities include activities in topographic mapping, geology, water, energy and mineral resources, and natural hazards. Personnel are stationed in Reston, VA, and at more than 300 field

offices and two major regional centers in Denver, CO, and Menlo Park, CA.
Contact(s):
Associate Director of Operations: BARBARA RYAN; Phone: 703-648-7413
Associate Director of Programs: BONNIE McGREGOR; Phone: 703-648-7412
Director (Acting): THOMAS J. CASADEVALL; Phone: 703-648-7411
Public Affairs Officer: TRUDY HARLOW; Phone: 703-648-4460

U.S. GEOLOGICAL SURVEY BIOLOGICAL RESOURCES DIVISION
12201 Sunrise Valley Dr., MS-300, Reston, VA 20192
Phone: 703-648-4050
Description: The Biological Resources Division works with others to provide the scientific understanding and technologies needed to manage the Nation's biological resources.
Contact(s):
Central Regional Chief Biologist: J. LARRY LUDKE; Phone: 303-236-2730/222
Chief Biologist: DENNIS B. FENN; Phone: 703-648-4050
Chief of International Affairs: BILL GREGG; Phone: 703-648-4067
Deputy Chief Biologist for Science: SUSAN HASELTINE; Phone: 703-648-4060
Eastern Regional Chief Biologist: DR. SUZETTE KIMBALL; Phone: 304-724-4500
Western Regional Chief Biologist: JOHN D. BUFFINGTON; Phone: 206-220-4600

UNITED STATES FISH AND WILDLIFE SERVICE
Department of Interior, 1849 C. St., Rm 3012, Washington, DC 20240
WWW: www.fws.gov
Description: Effective July 1, 1974, an act of Congress (Public Law 93-271, April 22, 1974 renamed the Bureau of Sport Fisheries and Wildlife, the United States Fish and Wildlife Service, under the Assistant Secretary for Fish and Wildlife and Parks. The Service is the lead federal agency in the conservation of the nation's migratory birds, threatened and endangered species, certain marine mammals, and sport fishing. This includes the management of national wildlife refuges and fish hatcheries; management of migratory birds through habitat conservation and hunting regulations; listing and recovery actions for endangered species; conservation and enhancement of wetlands; biological review of the environmental impacts of some kind of development projects; and enforcement of federal wildlife laws such as the Endangered Species Act, the Lacey Act, the Marine Mammal Protection Act, and the Migratory Bird Treaty Act. The Service administers fish and wildlife restoration grant programs to state governments, provides technical assistance to state and foreign governments, serves as lead federal agency in international conventions on wildlife conservation, and operates a program of public affairs and education to enhance the public's understanding and appreciation of America's fish and wildlife resources.
Contact(s):
Director: JAMIE RAPPAPORT CLARK; Phone: 202-208-4717
Chief of Division of Endangered Species: LAVERNE SMITH; Phone: 703-358-2171
Chief of Division of Engineering: PAUL J. CAMP; Phone: 303-275-2300
Chief of Division of Environmental Contaminants: FRANK DeLUISE; Phone: 703-358-2148
Chief of Division of Finance: DAVID HOLLAND; Phone: 703-358-1742
Chief of Division of Fish and Wildlife Management Assistance: HANNIBAL BOLTON; Phone: 703-358-1718
Chief of Division of Habitat Conservation: STEVE FORSYTHE; Phone: 703-358-2161
Chief of Division of Information Resources Management: WILLIAM T. BROOKS; Phone: 703-358-1729
Chief of Division of Law Enforcement: THOMAS L. STRIEGLER; Phone: 703-358-1949
Chief of Division of National Fish Hatcheries: WILLIAM KNAPP; Phone: 703-358-1715
Chief of Division of Personnel Management: KENT BAUM; Phone: 202-208-6104
Deputy Director: JOHN G. ROGERS JR.; Phone: 202-208-4545
Chief of Division of Realty: JEFFERY M. DONAHOE; Phone: 703-358-1713
Chief of Division of Refuge Management: ROBERT SHALLENBERGER; Phone: 703-358-1744
Chief of FWS Finance Center: ARTHUR FORD, Denver Federal Center, P.O. Box 25207, Denver, CO 80225-0207
Chief of Office for Human Resources: NATE BROWN; Phone: 202-208-1724
Chief of Office of Congressional and Legislative Services: ALEXANDRA PITTS; Phone: 202-208-5403
Chief of Office of Federal Aid: ROBERT LANGE; Phone: 703-358-2156
Chief of Office of International Affairs: HERBERT A. RAFFAELE; Phone: 703-358-1754
Chief of Office of Management Authority: KENNETH B. STANSELL; Phone: 703-358-2093
Chief of Office of Migratory Bird Management: PAUL SCHMIDT; Phone: 703-358-1714
Assistant Director (Acting) of Policy, Budget, and Administration: PAUL W. HENNE; Phone: 202-208-4888
Chief of Office of Public Affairs: PHIL MILLION; Phone: 202-208-4131
Assistant Director of Ecological Services: JAMIE R. CLARK; Phone: 202-208-4646
Assistant Director of External Affairs: THOMAS O. MELIVS; Phone: 202-208-4500
Assistant Director of Fisheries: GARY B. EDWARDS; Phone: 202-208-6394
Assistant Director of International Affairs: MARSHALL JONES; Phone: 202-208-6393
Assistant of Refuges and Wildlife: DANIEL M. ASHE; Phone: 202-208-5333
Chief of Division of Contracting and General Services: JOEL G. GREENSTEIN; Phone: 703-358-1901
Program Manager of Federal Duck Stamp Program: ROBERT C. LESINO; Phone: 202-208-4354

Alaska Regional Office 7
1011 E. Tudor Rd., Anchorage, AK 99503
Contact(s):
Regional Director: DAVID B. ALLEN; Phone: 907-786-3542

California-Nevada Operations
3310 El Camino Ave., Suite 120, Sacramento, CA 95821-6340
Phone: 916-979-2034; Fax: 916-979-2056
Contact(s):
Manager: MICHAEL J. SPEAR

Delaware Estuary Project
R.R. 1 Box 146-A, Smyrna, DE 19977
Phone: 302-653-9152
Description: The Delaware Estuary Project was established to coordinate, complement, and support existing U.S. Fish and Wildlife Service programs, focusing on important natural resource issues in the Delaware River watershed. The office provides technical assistance to the EPA's National Estuary Program for the Delaware Bay and Delaware's Inland Bays Estuary programs (started in 1988.

Great Lakes-Big Rivers Regional Office 3
1 Federal Dr., Federal Bldg., Fort Snelling, MN 55111
Contact(s):
Regional Director: WILLIAM F. HARTWIG; Phone: 612-713-3563
Deputy Regional Director: MARVIN E. MORIARTY; Phone: 612-713-3503
Assistant Regional Director of External Affairs: SUSAN DREIBAND; Phone: 612-713-3520

U.S. FEDERAL AND INTERNATIONAL GOVERNMENT AGENCIES - EXECUTIVE BRANCH

Mountain-Prairie Regional Office 6
134 Union Blvd., P.O. Box 25486, Denver, CO 80225
Contact(s):
Regional Director: RALPH MORGENWECK; Phone: 303-236-7920
Regional Director of External Affairs: TERRY SEXSTON; Phone: 303-236-7905; Fax: 303-236-3815

National Fish and Wildlife Forensics Laboratory
1490 East Main St., Ashland, OR 97520
Phone: 503-482-4191; Fax: 503-482-4989
Description: The mission of the Laboratory is to provide forensic crime lab, support for wildlife law enforcement investigations at the federal, state, and international levels.
Contact(s):
Director: KEN GODDARD

Northeast Regional Office 5
300 Westgate Center Dr., Hadley, MA 01035
Phone: 413-253-8200
Contact(s):
Regional Director: RONALD E. LAMBERTSON; Phone: 413-253-8300

Pacific Regional Office 1
Eastside Federal Complex, 911 NE 11th Ave., Portland, OR 97232-4181
Contact(s):
Regional Director: ANN BADAKY; Phone: 503-231-6118
Chief Officer of Public Affairs: JOAN JEWETT; Phone: 503-231-6121

Southeast Regional Office 4
1875 Century Blvd., Atlanta, GA 30345
Contact(s):
Regional Director: SAM HAMILTON; Phone: 404-679-4000

Southwest Regional Office 2
500 Gold Ave., SW, Rm. 3018, Albuquerque, NM 87102
Contact(s):
Regional Director: NANCY KAUFMAN; Phone: 505-248-6282
Assistant Director of External Affairs: TOM BAUER; Phone: 505-248-6911; Fax: 404-248-6915

DEPARTMENT OF THE NAVY
1000 Navy Pentagon, Department of the Navy, Washington, DC 20350-1000
WWW: www.navy.mil
Description: The mission of the Navy is to maintain, train, and equip combat-ready Naval forces capable of winning wars, deterring aggression and maintaining freedom of the seas.
Contact(s):
Secretary of the Navy: HON. RICHARD DANZIG
Undersecretary of the Navy: HON. JERRY MACARTHUR HULTIN

U.S. MARINE CORPS
Headquarters, U.S. Marine Corps, 2 Navy Annex, Washington, DC 20380-4775
Phone: 703-695-8332
Description: The Marine Corps, as America's premier crisis response force, trains as it fights. Accordingly, Marine Corps cultural and natural resources managers provide and maintain a variety of landscapes to support military training, while protecting and preserving the cultural and natural resources the American people cherish for their intrinsic value.
Contact(s):
Head of Natural Resources Section: JIM OMANS; Phone: 703-695-8232

Marine Corps Installations
Contact(s):
MCAGCC Twentynine Plams, CA: Head of Natural Resources Branch: ROY MADDEN; Phone: 619-830-5719
MCAS Beufort, SC: Head of Environmental Management Department: ALICE HOWARD; Phone: 803-522-7370
MCAS Cherry Point, NC: Head of Environmental Department: MAJOR MARK BRANNAN
MCAS Yuma, AZ: Head of Natural Resources Branch: RON PEARCE; Phone: 802-341-3318
MCB Camp Lejeune, NC: Head of Environmental Management Department: BOB WARREN; Phone: 910-451-5003
MCB Camp Pendleton, CA: Head of Environmental Management Department: LUPE ARMAS; Phone: 619-725-3561
MCCDC Quantico, VA: Head of Environmental Management Department: BRUCE FRIZZELL; Phone: 703-640-4030
MCLB Albany, GA: Head of Environmental Management Department: JERRY PALMER; Phone: 912-439-6261
MCLB Barstow, CA: Head of Environmental Management Department: JACK STORMO; Phone: 619-577-6111
MCRD Parris Island, SC: Head of Environmental Management Department: JOHNSIE NABORS; Phone: 803-525-2779

DEPARTMENT OF TRANSPORTATION
Nassif Bldg., 400 7th St., SW, Washington, DC 20590
Phone: 202-366-4000; WWW: www.dot.gov
Founded: 1967
Description: Composed of these main elements: The United States Coast Guard, Federal Aviation Administration, Federal Highway Administration, Federal Railroad Administration, Maritime Administration, St. Lawrence Seaway Development Corporation, National Highway Traffic Safety Administration, Federal Transit Administration, and Research and Special Programs Administration. Major objectives are to develop and improve a coordinated national transportation system consistent with other national objectives, such as environmental protection, and to stimulate technological advances in the industry, preserving the nation's free enterprise transportation network.
Contact(s):
Secretary: RODNEY SLATER; Phone: 202-366-1111
Deputy Secretary: MORTIMER L. DOWNEY; Phone: 202-366-4220
Assistant to the Secretary and Director of Public Affairs: STEVEN AKEY
Publication(s): *Public Roads (Federal Highway Administration); Merchant Vessels of the United States (United States Coast Guard)*

FEDERAL AVIATION ADMINISTRATION
FOB 10A 800 Independence Ave., SW, Washington, DC 20591
Phone: 202-267-3484
Description: Charged with regulating air commerce to foster aviation safety; promoting civil aviation and a national system of airports; achieving efficient use of navigable airspace; and developing and operating a common system of air traffic control and air navigation for both civilian and military aircraft.
Contact(s):
Administrator: JANE GARVEY; Phone: 202-267-3111
Deputy Administrator: MONTE BELGER; Phone: 202-267-8111
Director (Acting) of Environment and Energy: JAMES ERIKSON; Phone: 202-267-3576

FEDERAL HIGHWAY ADMINISTRATION
Washington Headquarters, 400 7th St., SW, Washington, DC 20590
Description: Charged with carrying out the Department of the Transportation responsibilities concerned with the highway mode of land transport, has the primary missions of ensuring that the Nation's highway transportation system is safe, economic, and efficient with respect to the movement of people and goods, while giving full consideration to the highway's impact on the environment and social and economic conditions.
Contact(s):
Executive Director: ANTHONY R. KANE; Phone: 202-366-2242
Administrator: KENNETH R. WYKLE; Phone: 202-366-0650
Associate Administrator for Administration: GEORGE S. MOORE JR.; Phone: 202-366-0604

Associate Administrator for Motor Carriers: GEORGE L. REAGLE; Phone: 202-366-2519
Associate Administrator for Program Development: THOMAS J. PTAK; Phone: 202-366-0371
Associate Administrator for Research and Development: ROBERT J. BETSOLD; Phone: 703-285-2051
Associate Administrator for Safety and System Applications: DENNIS C. JUDYCKI; Phone: 202-366-2149
Deputy Administrator: GLORIA J. JEFF; Phone: 202-366-2240
Deputy Chief Counsel: EDWARD V.A. KUSSY; Phone: 202-366-0740
Director of External Communications of Office of Public Affairs (Acting): JAMES PINKELMAN; Phone: 202-366-0660
Director of Intelligent Transportation Systems Joint Program Office: CHRISTINE M. JOHNSON; Phone: 202-366-9536
Director of Office of Civil Rights: EDWARD W. MORRIS JR.; Phone: 202-366-0693
Director of Office of Program Quality Coordination: FRED J. HEMPEL; Phone: 202-366-9393
Federal Lands Highway Program Administrator: ALLEN BURDEN; Phone: 202-366-9486
Keyword(s): Engineering, Historic Preservation, Planning Management, Transportation

FEDERAL RAILROAD ADMINISTRATION
400 7th St., SW, Stop 5, Washington, DC 20590
Phone: 202-366-4000
Founded: 1967
Description: The Federal Railroad Administration (FRA became a separate operating component of the Department of Transportation in 1972. The FRA promulgates and enforces rail safety regulations, administers financial assistance programs for designated railroads, conducts research and development in support of improved railroad safety and national rail transportation policy, as well as monitors rail passenger service nationwide, and consolidates government support of rail transportation activities.
Contact(s):
Administrator: JOLENE M. MOLITORIS
Associate Administrator for Safety: JANET T. SCHULTZ
Chief Counsel: S. MARK LINDSEY
Deputy Administrator: DONALD M. ITZKOFF
Director of Office Public Affairs: DAVID A. BOLGER

FEDERAL TRANSIT ADMINISTRATION
400 7th St., SW, Washington, DC 20590
Phone: 202-366-4043
Description: Seeks to improve the environmental standards of American cities through grant programs which extend and modernize existing urban mass transit equipment and facilities and which study, develop, and test new equipment and concepts in urban mass transit applications and operations.
Contact(s):
Administrator of Office of The Administrator: GORDON J. LINTON; Phone: 202-366-4040
Associate Administrator of Office of Administration: DORRIE ALDRICH; Phone: 202-366-4007
Associate Administrator of Office of Budget and Policy: MICHAEL WINTER; Phone: 202-366-4050
Associate Administrator of Office of Grants Management: HIRAM J. WALKER; Phone: 202-366-4020
Associate Administrator of Office of Technical Assistance and Safety: EDWARD L. THOMAS; Phone: 202-366-4052
Chief Counsel: PATRICK REILLY; Phone: 202-366-4063
Deputy Administrator of Office of the Administrator: NURIA FERNANDEZ; Phone: 202-366-4325
Deputy Associate Administrator: JOHN W. SPENCER; Phone: 202-366-4050
Deputy Chief Counsel: GREGORY B. McBRIDE; Phone: 202-366-4063
Director of Office of Civil Rights: ARTHUR LOPEZ; Phone: 202-366-4018
Director of Office of Public Affairs: BRUCE C. FRAME; Phone: 202-366-4319
Executive Information Officer of Office of Public Affairs: MARY F. KNAPP; Phone: 202-366-9788

NATIONAL HIGHWAY TRAFFIC SAFETY ADMINISTRATION
Nassif Bldg., 400 7th St., SW, Washington, DC 20590
Phone: 202-366-9550
Contact(s):
Deputy Director: PHILIP R. RECHT; Phone: 202-366-2775
Executive Director: DONALD C. BISCHOFF; Phone: 202-366-2111
Administrator: RICARDO MARTINEZ; Phone: 202-366-1836
Associate Administrator for Administration (Acting): HERMAN L. SIMMS; Phone: 202-366-1788
Associate Administrator for Plans and Policy: WILLIAM WALSH; Phone: 202-366-2550
Associate Administrator for Research and Development: RAYMOND OWINGS; Phone: 202-366-1537
Associate Administrator for Safety Assurance: KENNETH WEINSTEIN; Phone: 202-366-9700
Associate Administrator for Safety Performance Standards: L. ROBERT SHELTON; Phone: 202-366-1810
Associate Administrator for Traffic Safety Programs (Acting): JAMES NICHOLS; Phone: 202-366-1755
Chief Counsel: FRANK SEALES JR.; Phone: 202-366-9511

SAINT LAWRENCE SEAWAY DEVELOPMENT CORPORATION
U.S. Department of Transportation, 400 7th St. SW, Suite 5424, Washington, DC 20590
Phone: 202-366-0091
Contact(s):
Administrator (Acting): DAVID G. SANDERS; Phone: 202-366-0091
Deputy Director of Office of Congressional and Public Affairs: DENNIS E. DEUSCHL, P.O. Box 44090, Washington, DC 20026-4090; Phone: 202-366-0110

U.S. COAST GUARD
2100 2nd St., SW, Washington, DC 20593-0001
Phone: 202-267-2229
Contact(s):
Chief of Staff: RADM. K. H. WILLIAMS; Phone: 202-267-1642

U.S. DEPARTMENT OF AGRICULTURE
14th St. and Independence Ave., SW, Washington, DC 20250
Phone: 202-720-8732
Founded: 1862
Description: Created by Congress to acquire and disperse "useful" information on subjects connected with agriculture in the most general and comprehensive sense of that word, and to procure, propagate, and distribute among the people new and valuable seeds and plants. Today, in addition to managing the national forests and grasslands, USDA manages a variety of research, regulatory, domestic and foreign marketing, food and nutrition, and many other programs.
Contact(s):
Secretary: DAN GLICKMAN; Phone: 202-720-3631
Under Secretary (Acting) for Food Safety: DR. CATHY WOTEKI; Phone: 202-720-7025
Under Secretary (Acting) for Research Education and Economics: MILEY GONZALEZ; Phone: 202-720-5923
Under Secretary for Farm and Foreign Agricultural Services: AUGUST SCHUMACHER; Phone: 202-720-3111
Under Secretary for Food Nutrition and Consumer Services: SHIRLEY WATKINS; Phone: 202-720-7711
Under Secretary for Natural Resources and Environment: JAMES LYONS; Phone: 202-720-7173
Under Secretary for Rural Development: JILL LONG-THOMPSON; Phone: 202-720-4581
Assistant Secretary for Administration: BRAD PITTMAN-EVANS; Phone: 202-720-3291
Assistant Secretary for Congressional Relations: DAVE CARLIN; Phone: 202-720-7095

U.S. FEDERAL AND INTERNATIONAL GOVERNMENT AGENCIES - EXECUTIVE BRANCH

Assistant Secretary for Marketing and Regulatory Programs: MIKE DUNN; Phone: 202-720-4256
Chief Economist: KEITH COLLINS; Phone: 202-720-4164
Deputy Secretary: RICHARD ROMINGER; Phone: 202-720-6158
Director (Acting) of Communications: TOM AMONTREE; Phone: 202-720-4623

ANIMAL AND PLANT HEALTH INSPECTION SERVICE
U.S. Dept. of Agri., P.O. Box 96464, Washington, DC 20090-6464
Contact(s):
Chief of Staff: RICK CERTO
Director of Western Region: MIKE WORTHEN, 12345 W. Alameda Parkway, Suite 204, Lakewood, CO 80228; Phone: 303-969-6560
Deputy Administrator for International Services: ANGEL CIELO; Phone: 202-720-7021
Deputy Administrator of Animal Damage Control: BOBBY R. ACORD; Phone: 202-720-2054
Deputy Director of Legislative and Public Affairs: LINDA SWACINA; Phone: 202-720-3981
Director of Denver Wildlife Research Center: RICHARD D. CURNOW, P.O. Box 25266, Bldg. 16, Federal Center, Denver, CO 80225-0266; Phone: 303-236-7820
Director of Eastern Region: GARY E. LARSON, Suite 301, 3322 West End Avenue, Nashville, TN 37027; Phone: 615-736-2007
Director of Legislative and Public Affairs: PATRICK COLLINS; Phone: 202-720-2511
Director of Operational Support Staff: ROBERT BOKMA; Phone: 301-734-8892
Director of Trade Support Team: JOHN GREIFER; Phone: 202-720-7677
Administrator: DR. ISI SIDDIQUI; Phone: 202-720-3668
Assistant Director for Executive Correspondence: LYNN QUARLES; Phone: 301-734-7776
Assistant Director for Public Affairs: RICK McNANEY; Phone: 301-734-7799
Associate Deputy Administrator for International Services: CARL CASTLETON; Phone: 202-720-7021
Associate Deputy Administrator of Animal Damage Control: WILLIAM H. CLAY; Phone: 202-720-2054
Associate Deputy Administrator of International Services: DAN SHEESLEY; Phone: 202-720-7593
Freedom of Information Act Officer: MICHAEL MARQUIS; Phone: 301-734-8296
Publication(s): *Careers in APHIS*

Animal Care
Description: Investigates and prosecutes violations of federal laws governing the movement of animals and plants between states or into and out of the United States and regulates the humane care and treatment of warmblooded animals used for purposes of research or exhibiition, for sale as pets at the wholesale level, or transported in commerce.
Contact(s):
Acting Deputy Administrator for Regulatory Enforcement and Animal Care: RON DEHAVEN; Phone: 301-734-4980
Assistant Deputy Administrator (Acting) for Animal Care: WM. RON COOK; Phone: 301-734-4981

Animal Care Eastern Regional Office
2568A Riva Rd., Suite 302, Annapolis, MD 21401-7400
Contact(s):
Regional Director: ELIZABETH GOLDENTYER; Phone: 410-571-8692

Animal Care Regional Central Office
501 Felix St., Bldg. 11, Ft. Worth, TX 76115
Contact(s):
Regional Director: WALTER A. CHRISTENSEN

Animal Care Western Regional Office
9580 Micron Ave., Suite. J, Sacramento, CA 95827-2623
Contact(s):
Regional Director: ROBERT M. GIBBONS; Phone: 916-857-6205

International Services Central America, Caribbean & Panama Office
USDA-APHIS-IS, American Embassy, Guatemala, Unit 3319, APO 34024-3319
Phone: 011-502-331-2036
Contact(s):
Assistant Director of Operational Support: MARY NEAL; Phone: 301-734-8261
Associate Deputy Administrator: CHARLES SCHWALBE; Phone: 202-720-4441
Chief Operations Officer for Biological Assessment and Taxonomic Support: REBECCA BECH; Phone: 301-734-8896
Deputy Administrator (Acting) for Plant Protection and Quarantine: AL ELDER; Phone: 202-720-5601
Director of Central Region: ROBERT L. WILLIAMSON, 3505 Boca Chica Blvd, Suite. 360, Brownsville, TX 78521-4065; Phone: 210-504-4150
Director of National Biological Control Institute: MICHAEL J. ORAZE; Phone: 301-734-4329
Director of Northeastern Region: PAUL EGGERT, Blason II, 1st Fl., 505 S. Lenola Rd., Moorestown, NJ 08057; Phone: 609-968-4960
Director of Southeastern: JERRY FOWLER, 3505 25th Ave., Bldg. 1, North Gulfport, MS 39501; Phone: 601-863-1813
Director of Western Region: JAMES R. REYNOLDS, 9580 Micron Ave., Suite. 1, Sacramento, CA 95827; Phone: 916-857-6065
Phytosanitary Issues Management Team: ROBERT SPAIDE; Phone: 301-734-8262
Program Coordinator of Boll Weevil: GARY CUNNINGHAM; Phone: 301-734-8676
Regional Director: FAROUK HAMDY

International Services Europe, Africa, Russia, Near East Office
USDA-APHIS-IS FAS-USEU, PSC 82, Box 002, APO 09724
Phone: 011-322-508-2762
Contact(s):
Regional Director: ALEX B. THIERMANN

International Services Mexico Office
USDA-APHIS-IS, P.O. Box 3087, Laredo, TX 78044
Phone: 011-525-520-6892
Contact(s):
Regional Director: PETER FERNANDEZ

International Services Screwworm Eradication Program Office
USDA-APHIS-IS, P.O. Box 3087, Laredo, TX 78044
Phone: 011-525-520-4222
Contact(s):
Regional Director: JOHN WYSS

International Services South America Office: USDA/APHSIS
American Embassy Santiago, Unit 4113, APO, NY 34033
Phone: 011-562-638-1989
Contact(s):
Regional Director: JAMES MACKLEY

International Servies Asia and Pacific Office
USDA-APHIS-IS, Unit 66, 4700 River Rd., Riverdale, MD 20737
Phone: 301-734-8292
Contact(s):
Regional Director: ROBERT T. TANAKA

Plant Protection and Quarantine
Description: Regulates the importation of plants, plant products, and animal products from foreign countries. Regulates the movement of such products between U.S. possessions and the mainland and the importation and interstate movement of plant

pests. Inspects and certifies plants and plant products for export. Administers cooperative programs with states to control and eradicate insects, diseases, weeds, and nematodes of economic importance. Enforces the Convention on International Trade in Endangered Species of Flora and Fauna (CITES) for plants.

Regulatory Enforcement Eastern Regional Office
2568A Riva Rd., Suite 302, Annapolis, MD 21401-7400
Contact(s):
Regional Director: JOHN S. KINSELLA

Veterinary Services
Description: Regulates the importation of animals, animal semen, embryos, and animal products from foreign countries and the interstate movement of animals. Inspects and certifies animals for export. Administers cooperative federal-state programs to control and eradicate animal pests and diseases. Provides laboratory support for animal health programs and diagnostic referral assistance for private and state laboratories.
Contact(s):
Chief of Foreign Animal Disease Diagnostic Laboratory: ALFONSO TORRES, P.O. Box 848, Greenport Long Island, NY 11844-0848; Phone: 516-323-2506
Chief of Veterinary Services National Center for Import and Export: GARY S. COLGROVE; Phone: 301-734-6954
Deputy Administrator for Veterinary Services: JOAN M. ARNOLDI; Phone: 202-720-5193
Director (Acting) of Veterinary Services Operations Support Staff: RICHARD L. RISSLER; Phone: 301-734-8097
Director of Central Region: RUBE HARRINGTON, 100 W. Pioneer Pkwy., Suite. 100, Arlington, TX 76010; Phone: 817-885-7850
Director of National Veterinary Services Laboratories: JAMES PEARSON, P.O. Box 844, 1800 Dayton Rd., Ames, IA 50010; Phone: 515-239-8301
Director of Northern Region: WILLIAM W. BUISCH, One Winners Cir., Suite. 100, Albany, NY 12203; Phone: 518-453-0103
Director of Southeastern Region: CHESTER GIPSON, 501 E. Polk St., Suite. 880, Tampa, FL 33602-3945; Phone: 813-228-2952
Director of Western Region: ROBERT M. NERVIG, 384 Inverness Dr. S., Englewood, CO 80112; Phone: 303-784-6201
National Animal Health Programs Staff: MICHAEL GILSDORF; Phone: 301-734-6954
Veterinary Services Brucellosis Eradication Staff: GRANVILLE H. FRYE; Phone: 301-734-8711
Veterinary Services Emergency Programs: JOSEPH ANNELLI; Phone: 301-734-7767
Veterinary Services Trade Negotiator for National Center for Import and Export: ROBERT F. KAHRS; Phone: 301-734-3294

ECONOMIC RESEARCH SERVICE
1301 New York Ave., NW, Rm. 1226, Washington, DC 20005-4788
Phone: 202-219-0300
Description: Provides a program of agricultural, economic, and social research and analysis, statistical programs, technical consultation, planning assistance, and associated services. Conducts research and staff work relating to natural resources and environmental quality, including supplies, uses, and projected future requirements for land and water; effects of environmental quality improvement measures on agricultural production and agricultural resource use; achievement of environmental goals in rural areas; ownership and control of land and water resources; methods for natural resource planning; and evaluation of natural resource plans and projects.
Contact(s):
Administrator: SUSAN OFFUTT
Director of Natural Resources and Environment Division: MARGOT ANDERSON
Information Services Division: BRUCE GREENSHIELDS
Publication Services Branch: ADRIE CUSTER

Publication(s): *Various research monographs on natural resources use, pest control, agricultural inputs, conservation, food, rural issues, commodities, and U.S. trade.*

FARM SERVICE AGENCY (FSA), FORMERLY AGRICULTURAL STABILIZATION AND CONSERVATION SERVICE
1400 Independence Ave., SW, Washington, DC 20013
Phone: 202-720-6221
Description: Administers the following nationwide or regional programs: Conservation Reserve Program, Emergency Conservation Program, Livestock Feed Program, and various commodity loan programs, production flexibility contracts, and various farm loan and disaster assistance programs.
Contact(s):
Deputy Director: ROBERT STEPHENSON
Administrator: KEITH KELLY
Conservation Programs Branch Chief: CHERYL LAVODNY
Director (Acting) of Public Affairs: MARLYN AYCOCK
Director of Conservation and Environmental Protection Division: GEORGE T. DENLEY
Environmental Activities Chief: MICHAEL LINSENBIGLER
Planning Evaluation and Automation: LARRY L. HOWARD

NATURAL RESOURCES CONSERVATION SERVICE (formerly Soil Conservation Service)
USDA, 14th and Independence Ave., SW, P.O. Box 2890, Washington, DC 20013
Phone: 202-720-3210
Founded: 1935
Description: NRCS has national responsibility for helping America's farmers, ranchers, and other private landowners develop and carry out voluntary efforts to conserve and protect our natural resources. NRCS is the technical delivery arm for conservation of the United States Department of Agriculture. It provides technical assistance and conservation programs through a unique partnership with America's soil and water conservation districts and state conservation agencies.
Contact(s):
Director, Conservation Communications Staff: DAVID C. WHITE, Rm. 6123-s, Washington, DC 20013; Phone: 202-720-3210; Fax: 202-720-1564; Email: dave.white@usda.gov
Program Assistant: JOYCE HAWKINS, Rm. 6123-s, Washington, DC 20013; Phone: 202-720-3210; Fax: 202-720-1564; Email: joyce.hawkins@usda.gov
Public Affairs Specialist: MARY CRESSEL, Rm. 6123-s, Washington, DC 20013; Phone: 202-690-0547; Fax: 202-720-1564; Email: mary.cressel@usda.gov
AK Public Affairs Spcialist: VACANT , 949 E. 36th Ave., Suite 400, Achorage, AK 99508-4362; Phone: 907-271-2424; Fax: 907-271-3951
AL Public Affairs Specialist: JOAN SMITH, 665 Opelika Rd., Auburn, AL 36830-0311; Phone: 334-887-4530; Fax: 334-887-4551; Email: jismith@al.nrcs.usda.gov
AR Public Affairs Specialist: SUZANNE PUGH, Federal Office Bldg., Rm. 5404, 700 W. Capitol Ave., Little Rock, AR 72201-3228; Phone: 501-324-5464; Fax: 501-324-6138; Email: mpugh@ar.nrcs.usda.gov
AZ Public Affairs Specialist: MARY ANN MCQUINN, 3003 N. Central Ave., Suite 800, Phoenix, AZ 85012-2945; Phone: 602-280-8778; Fax: 602-280-8809; Email: mmcquinn@az.nrcs.usda.gov
CA Public Affairs Specialist: ANITA BROWN, 2121-C 2nd St., Suite 102, Davis, CA 95616-5475; Phone: 530-757-8241; Fax: 530-757-8217; Email: abrown@ca.nrcs.usda.gov
CO Public Affairs Specialist: PETRA BARNES, 655 Parfet St., Rm. E 200C, Lakewood, CO 80215-5517; Phone: 303-236-2886; Fax: 303-236-2896; Email: pbarnes@co.nrcs.usda.gov
CT Public Affairs Specialist, Acting: CAROLYN MILLER, 16 Professional Park Rd., Storrs, CT 06268-1299; Phone: 860-487-4029; Fax: 860-487-4054; Email: cmiller@ct.nrcs.usda.gov
DE Public Affairs Specialist: PAUL PETRICHENKO, 1203 College Park Dr., Suite 101, Dover, DE 19904-8713; Phone: 302-678-

U.S. FEDERAL AND INTERNATIONAL GOVERNMENT AGENCIES - EXECUTIVE BRANCH

4178; Fax: 302-678-0843; Email: ppetrichencko@de.nrcs.usda.gov

FL Public Affairs Specialist: DOROTHY STALEY, 2614 NW, 43rd St., Gainesville, FL 32606-6611; Phone: 352-338-9565; Fax: 352-338-9574; Email: dstaley@fl.nrcs.usda.gob

GA Public Affairs Specialist: ART GREENBERG, Federal Bldg., Box 13, 355 E. Hancock Ave., Athens, GA 30601-2769; Phone: 706-546-2273; Fax: 706-546-2276; Email: art@ga.nrcs.usda.gov

HI Public Affairs Specialist: JOLENE LAU, 300 Ala Moana Blvd., Rm. 4316, Honolulu, HI 96850-0002; Phone: 808-541-2600; Fax: 808-541-2652; Email: lau@hi.nrcs.usda.gov

IA Public Affairs Specialist: LYNN BETTS, 693 Federal Bldg., 210 Walnut St., Des Moines, IA 50309-2180; Phone: 515-284-4262; Fax: 515-284-4394; Email: lynn.betts@ia.nrcs.usda.gov

IA Public Affairs Speicialist: SHARON NORRIS, 3244 Elder St., Rm 124, Boise, ID 83705-4711; Phone: 208-378-5725; Fax: 208-378-5735; Email: snorris@id.nrcs.usda.gov

IL Public Affairs Specialist: PAIGE MITHCHELL, 1902 Fox Dr., Champaign, IL 61820-7335; Phone: 630-505-7808; Fax: 630-505-7992; Email: paige.mitchell@il.nrcs.usda.gov

IN Public Affairs Specialist: MICHAEL MCGOVERN, 6013 Lakeside Blvd., Indianapolis, IN 46278-2933; Phone: 317-290-3222; Fax: 317-290-3225; Email: mmcgovern@in.nrcs.usda.gov

KS Public Affairs Specialist: VACANT , 760 S. Broadway, Salina, KS 67401; Phone: 785-823-4570; Fax: 785-823-4540

KY Public Affairs Specialist: LOIS JACKSON, 771 Corporate Dr., Suite 110, Lexington, KY 40503-5479; Phone: 606-224-7372; Fax: 606-224-7393; Email: ljackson@kcc.fsa.usda.gov

LA Public Affairs Specialist: HERB BOURQUE, 3737 Government St., Alexandria, LA 71302-3727; Phone: 318-473-7762; Fax: 318-473-7771; Email: hbourque@la.nrcs.usda.gov

MA Public Affairs Specialist: ALYSSA ALDRICH, 451 West St., Amherst, MA 01002-2995; Phone: 978-692-1904; Fax: 978-392-1305; Email: aaldrich@ma.nrcs.usda.gov

MD Public Affairs Specialist: CAROL HOLLINGSWORTH, John Hanson Business Center, 339 Busch's Frontage Rd., Suite 30, Annapolis, MD 21401-5534; Phone: 410-757-0861; Fax: 410-757-0687; Email: chollingsworth@md.nrcs.usda.gov

ME Public Affairs Specialist: ELAINE TREMBLE, 5 Godfrey Dr., Orono, ME 04473; Phone: 207-866-7241; Fax: 207-866-7264; Email: etremble@me.nrcs.usda.gov

MI Public Affairs Specialist: CHRISTINA COULON, 1405 S. Harrison Rd., Rm. 101, East Lansing, MI 48823-5243; Phone: 517-337-6701; Fax: 517-337-6905; Email: ccoulon@miso.mi.nrcs.usda.gov

MN Public Affairs Specialist: SYLVIA RAINFORD, 600 Farm Credit Services Bldg., 375 Jackson St., St. Paul, MN 55101-1854; Phone: 612-602-7859; Fax: 612-602-7914; Email: str@mn.nrcs.usda.gov

MO Public Affairs Specialist: NORM KLPFENSTEIN, Parkade Center, Suite 250, 601 Business Loop, 70 West, Columbia, MO 65203-2546; Phone: 573-876-0901; Fax: 573-876-0913; Email: normk@mo.nrcs.usda.gov

MS Public Affairs Specialist: JEANINE MAY, Federal Bldg., Suite 1321, 100 W. Capitol St., Jackson, MS 39269-1399; Phone: 601-965-4337; Fax: 601-965-4536; Email: jbm@ms.nrcs.usda.gov

MT Public Affairs Specialist: LORI VALDEZ, Federal Bldg., Rm 443, 10 E. Babcock St., Bozeman, MT 59715-4704; Phone: 406-587-6842; Fax: 406-587-6761; Email: lvaladez@mr.nrcs.usda.gov

NC Public Affairs Specialist: ANDREW SMITH, 4405 Bland Rd., Suite 205, Raleigh, NC 27609-6293; Phone: 919-873-2107; Fax: 919-873-2156; Email: asmith@nc.nrcs.usda.gov

ND Public Affairs Specialist: ARLENE DEUTSCHER, Federal Bldg., 220 E. Rosser Ave., Rm. 278, 220 E. Rosser Ave., Bismarck, ND 58502-1458; Phone: 701-250-4768; Fax: 701-250-4778; Email: ajd@nd.nrcs.usda.gov

NE Public Affairs Specialist: PAT MCGRANE, Federal Bldg., Rm. 152, 100 Centennial Mall, N., Lincoln, NE 68508-3866; Phone: 402-437-5328; Fax: 402-437-5327; Email: pat.mcgrane@ne.nrcs.usda.gov

NH Public Affairs Specialist: LYNN HOWELL, Federal Bldg., 2 Madbury Rd., Durham, NH 03824; Phone: 603-868-7581; Fax: 603-868-5301; Email: lhl@nh.nrcs.usda.gov

NJ Public Affairs Specialist: IRENE LIEBERMAN, 1370 Hamilton St., Somerset, NJ 08873-3157; Phone: 732-246-1171; Fax: 732-246-2358; Email: ilieberman@nj.nrcs.usda.gov

NM Public Affairs Specialist: REBECCA de la TORRE, 6200 Jefferson St., NE, Suite 305, Albuquerque, NM 87109-3734; Phone: 505-761-4404; Fax: 505-761-4463; Email: rdelatorre@nm.nrcs.usda.gov

NV Public Affairs Specialist: LIZ WARNER, 5301 Langley Ln., Bldg. F, Suite 201, Reno, NV 89511; Phone: 702-784-5288; Fax: 702-784-5939; Email: lwarner@nv.nrcs.usda.gov

NY Public Affairs Specialist: CYNTHIA PORTALATIN VALLES, 441 S. Salina St., Suite 354, Syracuse, NY 13202-2450; Phone: 315-477-6550; Fax: 315-477-6550; Email: cvalles@ny.nrcs.usda.gov

OH Public Affairs Specialist: LATAWNYA DIA, 200 North High St., Rm., Columbus, OH 43215-2748; Phone: 614-469-6962; Fax: 614-469-2083; Email: l atawnya.dia@oh.nrcs.usda.gov

OK Public Affairs Specialist: DWAIN PHILLIPS, 100 USDA Agriculture Center Bldg., Suite 203, Stillwater, OK 74074-2624; Phone: 405-742-1243; Fax: 405-742-1201; Email: dphillips@ok.nrcs.usda.gov

OR Public Affairs Specialist: GAYLE NORMAN, 101 SW Main Street, Suite 1300, Portland, OR 97204-3221; Phone: 503-414-3236; Fax: 503-414-3101; Email: pacbas@ite.net

PA Public Affairs Specialist: STACY MITCHELL, One Credit Union Pl., Suite 340, Harrisburg, PA 17110-2993; Phone: 717-237-2200; Fax: 717-237-2238; Email: smitchell@pa.nrcs.usda.gov

Puerto Rico Public Affairs Specialist: BECKY FRATICELLI, IBM Bldg., 6th Flr., 654 Munoz Rivera Ave., Hato Rey, PR 00918-7013; Phone: 787-766-5206; Fax: 787-766-5987; Email: becky@pr.nrcs.usda.gov

RI Public Affairs Specialist: VACANT , 60 Quaker Ln., Suite 46, Warwick, RI 02886-0111; Phone: 401-828-1300; Fax: 401-828-0433

SC Public Affairs Specialist: PERDITA BELK, Strom Thurmond Federal Bldg., 1835 Assembly St., Rm. 950, Columbia, SC 29201-2489; Phone: 803-765-5402; Fax: 803-253-3670; Email: pbelk@sc.nrcs.usda.gov

SD Public Affairs Specialist: JOYCE WATKINS, 200 4th St., SW, Federal Bldg., Huron, SD 57350-2475; Phone: 605-352-1227; Fax: 605-352-1261; Email: joyce.watkins@sd.nrcs.usda.gov

TN Public Affairs Specialist: LARRY BLICK, 675 U.S. Courthouse, 801 Broadway St., Nashville, TN 37203-3878; Phone: 615-736-5490; Fax: 615-736-7764; Email: lblick@tn.nrcs.usda.gov

TX Public Affairs Specialist: HAROLD BRYANT, W.R. Poage Federal Bldg., 101 S. Main St., Temple, TX 76501-7682; Phone: 254-742-9811; Fax: 254-298-1388; Email: hbryant@tx.nrcs.usda.gov

UT Public Affairs Specialist: RON NICHOLS, Wallace F. Bennett FB, 125 South State Street, Rm 4402, Salt Lake City, UT 84138-0350; Phone: 801-524-5050; Fax: 801-524-4403; Email: rnichols@ut.nrcs.usda.gov

VA Public Affairs Specialist: PAT PAUL, Culpeper Bldg, 1606 Santa Rosa Rd., Suite 209, Richmond, VA 23229-5014; Phone: 804-287-1681; Fax: 804-287-1737; Email: ppaul@va.nrcs.usda.gov

VT Public Affairs Specialist: ANNE HILLARD, 69 Union St., Winooski, VT 05404-1999; Phone: 802-951-6796; Fax: 802-951-6327; Email: ahillard@vt.nrcs.usda.gov

WA Public Affairs Specialist: CHIRS BIEKER, Rock Pointe Tower 2, Suite 450, West 316 Boone Ave., Spokane, WA 99201-2348; Phone: 509-323-2912; Fax: 509-323-2909; Email: cbieker@wa.nrcs.usda.gov

WI Public Affairs Specialist: RENAE ANDERSON, 6515 Watts Rd., Suite 200, Madison, WI 53719-2726; Phone: 608-264-5341; Fax: 608-264-5483; Email: randerson@wi.nrcs.usda.gov

WV Public Affairs Specialist: PEG REESE, 75 High St., Rm. 301, Morgantown, WV 26505; Phone: 304-291-4152; Fax: 304-291-4628; Email: preese@wv.nrcs.usda.gov

WY Public Affairs Specialist: NANCY ATKINSON, Federal Office Bldg., 100 East B St., Room 3124, Casper, WY 82601; Phone:

307-261-6482; Fax: 307-261-6490; Email: nla@wy.nrcs.usda.gov

RESEARCH EDUCATION AND ECONOMICS
Rm. 217-W 14th & Independence Ave. SW, Washington, DC 20250
Phone: 202-720-5923
Contact(s):
Under Secretary: I. MILEY GONZALEZ

Agricultural Research Service
REE, Washington, DC 20250
Description: Conducts research in natural resources, plant sciences, animal sciences, food sciences and human nutrition.
Contact(s):
Administrator: FLOYD P. HORN; Phone: 202-720-3656
Associate Administrator: EDWARD KNIPLINS; Phone: 202-720-3658
Associate Deputy Administrator (Acting) for Animal Sciences (NPS): ROGER GERRITS; Phone: 301-504-7050
Associate Deputy Administrator for Natural Resources and Systems (NPS): ALAN DEDRICK; Phone: 301-504-7987
Associate Deputy Administrator of Agriproducts and Human Nutrition Sciences (NPS): WILDA MARTINEZ
Associate Deputy Administrator of Plant Sciences (NPS): JOHN JUDITY ST. JOHN; Phone: 301-504-6252
Deputy Administrator (NPS): E. B. KNIPLING; Phone: 301-504-5084

Beltsville Office: USDA-ARS
Rm. 223, B-003 BARC-West, Beltsville, MD 20705
Phone: 301-504-6078
Contact(s):
Area Director: K. D. MURRELL

Cooperative State Research, Education, and Extension Service
Washington, DC 20250
Description: The Cooperative State Research, Education, and Extension Service links the research and education resources and programs of the U.S. Department of Agriculture and works with land-grant institutions in each state, territory, and the District of Columbia.
Contact(s):
Administrator (Acting): COLIEN HEFFERAN; Phone: 202-720-4423
Associate Administrator: COLIEN HEFFERAN; Phone: 202-720-7441
Deputy Administrator for Communications Technology and Distance Education: BARBARA WHITE; Phone: 202-720-2597
Deputy Administrator for Competitive Research Grants and Awards Management: SARAH ROCKEY; Phone: 202-401-1761
Deputy Administrator for Families 4-H and Nutrition: ALMA HOBBS; Phone: 202-720-2908
Deputy Administrator for Natural Resources and Environment: RALPH OTTO; Phone: 202-401-4555
Deputy Administrator for Partnerships: GEORGE STAPER; Phone: 202-720-5623
Deputy Administrator for Rural Economic and Social Development: ROBERT KOOPMAN; Phone: 202-720-7947
Deputy Administrator for Science and Education Resources Development: JANE COULTER; Phone: 202-720-3377
Deputy Administrator of Plant and Animal Production Protection and Processing: EDWARD M. WILSON; Phone: 202-401-4329

Mid South: USDA-ARS
P.O. Box 225, Stoneville, MS 38776
Phone: 601-686-5265
Contact(s):
Area Director: THOMAS J. ARMY

Midwest: USDA-ARS
1815 N. University St., Peoria, IL 61604
Phone: 309-681-6602
Contact(s):
Area Director: RICHARD DUNKLE

North Atlantic Office
USDA-ARS, 600 E. Mermaid Ln., Wynmoor, PA 19038
Phone: 489-6593/215; Fax: 489-233-6593
Contact(s):
Area Director: DR. HERBERT L. ROTHBART

Northern Plains: USDA-ARS
1201 Oakridge Rd. Suite 150, Fort Collins, CO 80525
Phone: 303-229-5557
Contact(s):
Area Director: WILBERT BLACKBURN

Pacific West: USDA-ARS
800 Buchanan St., Albany, CA 94710
Phone: 510-559-6060
Contact(s):
Area Director:

South Atlantic Office: USDA-ARS
Russell Agr. Res. Center, P.O. Box 5677, College Station Rd., Athens, GA 30604-5677
Phone: 706-546-3311
Contact(s):
Area Director: ROGER BREEZE

Southern Plains: USDA-ARS
7607 Eastmark Dr., Ste. 230, College Station, TX 77840
Phone: 409-260-9346
Contact(s):
Area Director: CHARLES ONSTAD

UNITED STATES FOREST SERVICE
P.O. Box 96090, Washington, DC 20090-6090
Phone: 202-205-8333; WWW: www.fs.fed.us
Description: Administers National Forests and National Grasslands and is responsible for the management of their resources. Cooperates with federal and state officials in the enforcement of game laws on the National Forests and in the development and maintenance of wildlife resources; cooperates with the state and private owners in the application of sound forest management practices, in protection of forest lands against fire, insects, diseases, and in the distribution of planting stock. Conducts research in the entire field of forestry and wildland management.
Contact(s):
Chief: MIKE DOMBECK; Phone: 202-205-1661
Chief Operating Officer: FRANCIS PANDOLFI; Phone: 202-205-1661
Director of Office Communications: GEORGE D. LENNON; Phone: 202-205-1760
Civil Rights Director (Acting): THELMA FLOYD; Phone: 202-205-1585
Law Enforcement and Investigations: BILL WASLEY; Phone: 703-605-4690
International Programs: VALDIS MEZAINIS; Phone: 202-205-1650
Chief Financial Officer: VINCETTE GOERL; Phone: 202-205-1784
Deputy Operations: CLYDE THOMPSON; Phone: 202-205-1707
Deputy Operations (PD&B): RONALD STEWART; Phone: 202-205-1663
Deputy Research and Development: ROBERT LEWIS; Phone: 202-205-1665
Associate Deputy Research and Development: BARBARA WEBER; Phone: 202-205-1702
Deputy National Forest System: ROBERT JOSLIN; Phone: 202-205-1523
Associate Deputy National Forest System: PAUL BROUHA; Phone: 202-205-1465
Associate Deputy National Forest System: GLORIA MANNING; Phone: 202-205-1465
Director WFRP: HARV FORSGREN; Phone: 202-205-1205
Deputy State and Private Forestry: PHIL JANIK; Phone: 202-205-4657
Associate Deputy State and Private Forestry: LARRY PAYNE; Phone: 202-205-1602

U.S. FEDERAL AND INTERNATIONAL GOVERNMENT AGENCIES - EXECUTIVE BRANCH

Associate Deputy State and Private Forestry: JANICE MCDOUGLE;
Phone: 202-205-1331

Forest Products Laboratory Station
One Gifford Pinchot Dr., Madison, WI 53705-2398
Phone: 608-231-9200
Contact(s):
Director: THOMAS E. HAMILTON

North Central Forest Experiment Station
1992 Folwell Ave., St. Paul, MN 55108
Phone: 612-649-5249
Contact(s):
Director: LINDA R. DONAGHUE

Northeastern Area State and Private Forestry
100 Matsonford Rd., 5 Radnor Corporate Center, Suite 200, Radnor, PA 19087-4585
Phone: 610-975-4103
Contact(s):
Area Director: MICHAEL T. RAINS

Northeastern Research Station
100 Matsonford Rd., 5 Ranor Corporate Center, Suite 200, Radnor, PA 19087-4585
Phone: 610-975-4017
Contact(s):
Director: BOV B EAV

Pacific Northwest Research Station
333 SW 1st Ave., P.O. Box 3890, Portland, OR 97208-3890
Phone: 503-808-2100
Contact(s):
Director: THOMAS J. MILLS

Pacific Southwest Research Station
800 Buchanan St., West Building, Albany, CA 94710-0011
Phone: 510-559-6310
Contact(s):
Director: HAL SALWASSER

Region 1 Northern Region
Federal Bldg., P.O. Box 7669, Missoula, MT 59807
Phone: 406-329-3316
Contact(s):
Regional Forester: DALE BOSWORTH

Region 10 Alaska Region
709 W. 9th St., P.O. Box 21628, Juneau, AK 99802-1628
Phone: 907-586-8863

Region 2 Rocky Mountain Region
P.O. Box 25127, Lakewood, CO 80225
Phone: 303-275-5450
Contact(s):
Regional Forester: LYLE LAVERTY

Region 3 Southwestern Region
517 Gold Ave., SW, Albuquerque, NM 87102
Phone: 505-476-3300
Contact(s):
Regional Forester: ELEANOR S. TOWNS

Region 4 Intermountain Region
Federal Office Bldg. 324, 25th St., Ogden, UT 84401
Phone: 801-625-5605
Contact(s):
Regional Forester: JACK A. BLACKWELL

Region 5 Pacific Southwest Region
630 Sansome St., San Francisco, CA 94111
Phone: 415-705-2870
Contact(s):
Regional Forester: LYNN SPRAGUE

Region 6 Pacific Northwest Region
333 SW 1st Ave., P.O. Box 3523, Portland, OR 97208
Phone: 503-808-2200
Contact(s):
Regional Forester: ROBERT W. WILLIAMS

Region 8 Southern Region
1720 Peachtree Rd., NW, Atlanta, GA 30367
Phone: 404-347-4177
Contact(s):
Regional Forester: ELIZABETH ESTILL

Region 9 Eastern Region
310 W. Wisconsin Ave., Rm. 500, Milwaukee, WI 53203
Phone: 414-297-3600
Contact(s):
Regional Forester: ROBERT T. JACOBS

Rocky Mountain Research Station
240 W. Prospect St., Ft. Collins, CO 80526-2098
Phone: 303-498-1126
Contact(s):
Director: DENVER P. BURNS

Southern Research Station
200 Weaver Blvd., P.O. Box 2680, Asheville, NC 28802
Phone: 704-257-4300
Contact(s):
Director: PETER J. ROUSSOPOULOS

U.S. TREASURY DEPARTMENT
1500 Pennsylvania Ave., NW, Washington, DC 20220
Phone: 202-622-2000; Fax: 202-622-6415; WWW: www.ustreas.gov
Description: The basic functions of the Department of the Treasury include: economic and fiscal policy; government accounting, cash, and debt management; international economic policy; and enforcement of customs and trade laws.
Contact(s):
Secretary: ROBERT E. RUBIN; Phone: 202-622-2000
Deputy Secretary: LAWRENCE H. SUMMERS

U.S CUSTOMS SERVICE

Southeast
909 SE 1st Ave., Miami, FL 33131
Phone: 305-536-5283
Contact(s):
Director: HOWARD COOPERMAN

U.S. CUSTOMS SERVICE
1301 Pennsylvania Ave., NW, Rm. 5316, Washington, DC 20229
Phone: 202-927-1770; Fax: 202-927-1208
Description: The United States Customs Service is responsible for the enforcement of the U.S. laws regarding the importation and exportation of injurious and endangered species.
Contact(s):
Commissioner: RAYMOND W. KELLY
Assistant Commissioner (Acting) for Investigations: BONNI G. TISCHLER
Assistant Commissioner for Office of Field Operations: ROBERT TROTTER
Special Agent in Charge: GARY W. WAUGH, Detroit, MI 48226-2568
Special Agent in Charge: JOHN VARRONE, New York, NY 11430
Special Agent in Charge: JOHN HENSLEY, Terminal Island, CA 90731
Special Agent in Charge: EDWARD W. LOGAN, San Diego, CA 92101
Special Agent In Charge: CHARLIE SIMONSEN, San Francisco, CA 94111

Special Agent in Charge: SHELLEY ALTENSTADTER, Seattle, WA 98104-1048
Special Agent in Charge: GARY HILLBERRY, Denver, CO 80294-3609
Special Agent in Charge: P. JEFFREY CASEY, Baltimore, MD 21202
Special Agent in Charge: JEREMIAH J. SULLIVAN, Buffalo, NY 14202
Special Agent in Charge: LINWOOD ROUNDTREE, Atlanta, GA 30354
Special Agent in Charge: RAPHAEL LOPEZ, Miami, FL 33166
Special Agent in Charge: STEVEN J. TRENT, Tampa, FL 33607
Special Agent in Charge: FRANK FIGUEROA, Old San Juan, PR 00902-0431
Special Agent in Charge: LEONARD C. LINDHEIM, San Antonio, TX 78216
Special Agent in Charge: STEVEN DeVAUGHN, Chicago, IL 60607
Special Agent in Charge (Acting): AWILDA VILLAFANE, 555 E. River Rd., Tucson, AZ 85704
Special Agent in Charge (Acting): JOE WEBBER, El Paso, TX 75202

New York Office
6 World Trade Center, New York, NY 10048
Phone: 212-466-4500
Contact(s):
Director: JEFFREY MARGALIT

North Central Office
55 East Monroe St., Chicago, IL 60603
Phone: 312-353-4745
Contact(s):
Director: HENRY RISTIC

Northeast Office
10 Causeway St., Boston, MA 02222
Phone: 617-565-6321
Contact(s):
Director: JOE WILSON

Pacific Office
One World Trade Center, Long Beach, CA 90831
Phone: 310-980-3200
Contact(s):
Director: AILEEN COLON

South Central Office
423 Canal St., New Orleans, LA 70130
Phone: 504-589-6479
Contact(s):
Director: LEWELLYN ROBISON

Southwest Office
5850 San Felipe St., Houston, TX 77050
Phone: 713-985-0500
Contact(s):
Director: DONNA DE LA TORRE

INDEPENDENT AGENCIES

ADVISORY COUNCIL ON HISTORIC PRESERVATION
1100 Pennsylvania Ave., NW, #809, The Old Post Office Bldg., Washington, DC 20004
Phone: 202-606-8503
Description: An independent federal agency, the Council is the primary policy advisor to the President and Congress on historic preservation matters and guides, and other federal agencies to ensure their actions do not result in unnecessary harm to the nation's historic,properties. The Council was established by the National Historic Preservation Act of 1966, is made up of the heads of seven federal departments whose actions regularly affect historic properties; eight members, a governor and a mayor appointed by the President; and representatives of the National Trust for Historic Preservation and the National Conference of State Historic Preservation Officers. The Council is supported by a small professional staff. Offices are in Washington, DC and Denver.
Contact(s):
Executive Director: JOHN FOWLER
Keyword(s): Environmental Preservation, Public Health Protection, Solid Waste Management, Toxic Substances

GENERAL SERVICES ADMINISTRATION
GSA Bldg., 1800 F St., NW, Washington, DC 20405
Phone: 202-501-1231
Description: Concerned with the conveyance of surplus real property for wildlife conservation purposes to the,,Secretary of Interior or to a state, pursuant to Public Law 537, 80th Congress.
Contact(s):
Administrator (Acting): DAVID BARRAM
Program Development and Outreach Director: RONALD L. RICE; Phone: 202-501-0052
Redeployment Services Division Director: JOHN Q. MARTIN; Phone: 202-501-4671

NATIONAL SCIENCE FOUNDATION
4201 Wilson Blvd., Arlington, VA 22230
Phone: 703-306-1234
Founded: 1950
Description: Responsible for the support of science and engineering research and the development of science,education programs. Policy is set by the National Science Board, which is composed of 24 part-time members appointed by the President, with the consent of the Senate, and includes the,Director of the Foundation.
Contact(s):
Director: DR. RITA COLWELL; Phone: 703-306-1000
Chairman of National Science Board: DR. EAMON A. KELLY; Phone: 703-306-2000
Deputy Director (Acting): DR. JOSEPH BORDOGNA; Phone: 703-306-1000
Director of Office of Legislative and Public Affairs: JULIA A. MOORE; Phone: 703-306-1070
Head Librarian: STEPHANIE BIANCHI; Phone: 703-306-0658
Publication(s): *Guide to Programs; Grant Proposal Guide; NSF in a Changing World; The National Science Foundation Strategic Plan; About the National Science Foundation*

NATIONAL TRANSPORTATION SAFETY BOARD
490 L'Enfant Plaza East, SW, Washington, DC 20594
Phone: 202-314-6000
Description: The Safety Board is an independent federal accident investigation agency. The Board's mission is,to determine the "probable cause" of transportation accidents and to formulate safety recommendations to improve transportation safety.
Contact(s):
Chairman: JAMES HALL
Chief Financial Officer: CRAIG KELLER
Director of Office of General Counsel: DANIEL D. CAMPBELL
Director of Office of Government, Public, and Family Affairs: JAMIE FINCH
Managing Director: PETER GOELZ
Vice Chairman: ROBERT T. FRANCIS II

NUCLEAR REGULATORY COMMISSION
Washington, DC 20555
Phone: 301-415-7000
Founded: 1975
Description: Five-member commission responsible for regulating all commercial uses of nuclear energy to,protect the health and safety of the public and the environment.
Contact(s):
Deputy Director: JAMES F. McDERMOTT; Phone: 301-415-7516
Deputy Director: ROGER A. FORTUNA; Phone: 301-415-3476

U.S. FEDERAL AND INTERNATIONAL GOVERNMENT AGENCIES - INDEPENDENT AGENCIES

Deputy Director: MALCOLM R. KNAPP; Phone: 301-415-8468
Deputy Director: DENWOOD F. ROSS; Phone: 301-415-7473
Deputy Director: ELIZABETH A. HAYDEN; Phone: 301-415-8200
Deputy Director: THEMIS P. SPEIS; Phone: 301-415-6802
Executive Director: JOHN T. LARKINS; Phone: 301-415-7360
Executive Director: JOHN T. LARKINS; Phone: 301-415-7360
Director: BRIAN K. GRIMES; Phone: 301-415-1193
Director: PAUL H. LOHAUS; Phone: 301-415-2326
Acting Deputy Director: ASHOK C. HADAN; Phone: 301-415-1272
Acting Director of Office of Commission Appellate Adjudication: JOHN F. CORDES JR.; Phone: 301-415-1600
Acting Director of Office of Nuclear Reactor Regulation: FRANK MIRAGLIA; Phone: 301-415-1270
Associate Director: LINDA E. PORTNER; Phone: 301-415-1776
Associate Director of Contract, Security, F01 and Publications: EDWARD L. HALMAN; Phone: 301-415-7305
Associate Director of Facilities and Property Management: MICHAEL L. SPRINGER; Phone: 301-415-8080
Associate Director of Office of Administration: PATRICIA G. NORRY; Phone: 301-415-7443
Associate Director of Projects: ROY P. ZIMMERMAN; Phone: 301-415-1284
Associate Director, Insp. and Tech. Review: ASHOK C. THADANI; Phone: 301-415-1274
Associate General Counsel for Hearing, Enforcement, and Administration: STEPHEN G. BURNS; Phone: 301-415-1740
Chairman: SHIRLEY ANN JACKSON; Phone: 301-415-1820
Chairman of Advisory Committee on Nuclear Waste: MARTIN J. STEINDLER; Phone: 301- 415-7360
Chief Administrative Judge and Chairman of Atomic Safety and Licensing Board Panel: B. PAUL COTTER JR.; Phone: 301-415-7450
Commissioner: KENNETH C. ROGERS; Phone: 301-415-1855
Commissioner: GRETA J. DIRUS; Phone: 301-415-1820
Deputy: ARTHUR B. BEACH; Phone: 708-829-9658
Deputy: SAMUEL J. COLLINS; Phone: 817-860-8226
Deputy: LUIS A. REYES; Phone: 404-331-5610
Deputy: WILLIAM F. KANE; Phone: 610-337-5340
Deputy Chief Administrative Judge: FREDERICK J. SHON; Phone: 301-415-7468
Deputy Chief Financial Officer/Controller: RONALD M. SCROGGINS; Phone: 301-415-7501;
Deputy Controller: JESSE L. FUNCHES; Phone: 301-415-7322
Deputy Director of Division of Reactor Programs: THOMAS T. MARTIAN; Phone: 301-415-1199
Deputy Director of Licensing Support Systems Administrator: ARNOLD E. LEVIN; Phone: 301-415-7458
Deputy Director of Office of State Programs: RICHARD L. BANGART; Phone: 301-415-3340
Deputy Executive Director for Nuclear Materials, Safety, Safeguards, and Operations Support: HUGH L. THOMPSON JR.; Phone: 301-504-1713
Deputy Executive Director for Nuclear Reactor Regulation, Regional Operations and Research: JAMES L. MILHOAN; Phone: 301-415-1705
Deputy General Counsel: MARTIN G. MALSCH; Phone: 301-415-1740
Director of Division of Engineering: BRIAN SHERON; Phone: 301-415-2722
Director of Division of Engineering Technology: LAWRENCE C. SHAO; Phone: 301-415-5678
Director of Division of Fuel Cycle Safety and Safeguards: ELIZABETH Q. TENEYCK; Phone: 301-415-7212
Director of Division of Industrial and Medical Nuclear Safety: DONALD A. COOL; Phone: 301-415-7197
Director of Division of Inspection and Support Programs: FRANCIS P. GILLESPIE; Phone: 301-415-1275
Director of Division of Reactor Controls and Human Factors: BRUCE A. BOGER; Phone: 301-415-1004
Director of Division of Regulatory Applications: BILL M. MORRIS; Phone: 301-415-6207
Director of Division of Systems Safety and Analysis: GARY M. HOLAHAN; Phone: 301-415-2884
Director of Division of Systems Technology: M. WAYNE HODGES; Phone: 301-415-5728
Director of Division of Waste Management: JOHN T. GREEVES; Phone: 301-415-7358
Director of Financial Management, Procurement, and Administration Staff: LLOYD J. DONNELLY; Phone: 301-415-5828
Director of Incident Response Division: FRANK CONGEL; Phone: 301-415-7476
Director of Office for Analysis and Evaluation of Operational Data: EDWARD L. JORDAN; Phone: 301-415-7472
Director of Office of Congressional Affairs: DENNIS K. RATHBUN; Phone: 301-415-1776
Director of Office of Enforcement: JAMES LIEBERMAN; Phone: 301-415-2741
Director of Office of Information Resources Management: GERALD F. CRANFORD; Phone: 301-415-7585
Director of Office of International Programs: CARLTON R. STOIBER; Phone: 301-415-1780
Director of Office of Investigations: GUY P. CAPUTO; Phone: 301-415-2373
Director of Office of Nuclear Material Safety and Safeguards: CARL J. PAPERIELLO; Phone: 301-415-7800
Director of Office of Nuclear Regulatory Research: DAVID L. MORRISON; Phone: 301-415-6641;
Director of Office of Personnel: PAUL E. BIRD; Phone: 301-415-7516
Director of Office of Public Affairs: WILLIAM M. BEECHER; Phone: 301-415-8200
Director of Office of Small Business and Civil Rights: IRENE LITTLE; Phone: 301-415-7380
Director of Program Management, Policy Development, and Analysis Staff: JOHN J. LINEHAN; Phone: 301-415-7780
Director of Safety Programs Division: C. E. ROSSI; Phone: 301-415-7499
Director of Spent Fuel Project Office: WILLIAM D. TRAVERS; Phone: 301-415-8500
Director of Technical Training Division: KENNETH A. RAGLIN; Phone: 423-855-6500
Executive Director for Operations: JAMES M. TAYLOR; Phone: 301-415-1700
General Counsel: KAREN D. CYR; Phone: 301-415-1743
Inspector General: HUBERT BELL; Phone: 301-415-5930
Licensing and Regulation: WILLIAM J. OLMSTEAD; Phone: 301-415-1740
Regional Administrator, Region 1: HUBERT J. MILLER, 475 Allendale Rd., King of Prussia, PA 19406-1415; Phone: 610-337-5299
Regional Administrator, Region 2: STEWART D. EBNETER, 101 Marietta St., Suite. 2900, Atlanta, GA 30323-0199; Phone: 404-331-5500
Regional Administrator, Region 3: ARTHUR B. BEACH, 801 Warrenville Rd., Lisle, IL 60532-4351; Phone: 708-829-9500
Regional Administrator, Region 4: LEONARD J. CALLAN, 611 Ryan Plaza Dr., Suite. 4000, Arlington, TX 76011-8064; Phone: 817-860-8225
Secretary of the Commission: JOHN C. HOYLE; Phone: 301-415-1969
Vice Chairman: PAUL W. POMEROY; Phone: 301-415-7360
Vice Chairman: ROBERT L. SEALE; Phone: 301-415-7360
Keyword(s): Energy

PEACE CORPS OF THE UNITED STATES
1111 20th St., NW, Washington, DC 20526
Phone: 202-692-2100; WWW: www.peacecorps.gov
Founded: 1961
Description: The Peace Corps was established by President John F. Kennedy to promote world peace and friendship. Since 1961, more than 148,000 Americans have joined the Peace Corps and have served in 132 countries around the world. The Peace Corpos has three goals: to provide volunteers who contribute to the social, economic, and human development of interested countries; to promote a better understanding of Americans among the people whom Peace Corps volunteers serve; and to strengthen Americans'

understanding of the other peoples and cultures--to help bring the world back home.
Contact(s):
Deputy Director: CHARLES BACQUET III; Phone: 202-606-3970
Director: MARK GEARAN; Phone: 202-606-3970
Publication(s): *Peace Corps Times, The*

TENNESSEE VALLEY AUTHORITY
400 W. Summit Hill Dr., Knoxville, TN 37902
Phone: 423-632-2101
Founded: 1933
Description: TVA was created by an Act of Congress for the regional development of the Tennessee Valley, Region, in Tennessee, Kentucky, Mississippi, Alabama, Virginia, Georgia, and North Carolina.,In 1964, TVA opened Land Between the Lakes as a national demonstration project for outdoor recreation, environmental education, and resource management.
Contact(s):
Director: JOHNNY H. HAYES
Director: WILLIAM H. KENNOY
Chairman of the Board: CRAVEN CROWELL
Chief Administrative Officer: NORMAN A. ZIGROSSI
Executive Vice President and Chief Financial Officer: DAVID N. SMITH
Executive Vice President of Resource Group: KATHRYN J. JACKSON
Executive Vice President/Chief Officer and Nuclear Officer of TVA Nuclear: JOHN A. SCALICE
President and Chief Operating Officer: OSWALD ZERINGUE
Senior Vice President and General Counsel: EDWARD S. CHRISTENBURY
Senior Vice President for Strategic Initiatives: PEYTON T. HARRISTON JR.
Publication(s): *RiverPulse; Recreation on TVA Lakes; various others on different subjects*

KNOXVILLE AND CHATTANOOGA CORPORATE LIBRARY
400 W. Summit Hill Dr., ET PC, Knoxville, TN 37902-1499
Phone: 423-632-3464; Fax: 423-632-4475

MUSCLE SHOALS TECHNICAL LIBRARY
CTR 1E, Muscle Shoals, AL 35660
Phone: 205-386-2417; Fax: 205-386-2453

INTERNATIONAL

CONSERVATION COUNCIL OF WESTERN AUSTRALIA, INC.
79 Stirling St., Perth 6000 Australia
Phone: 08-9220-0652; Fax: 08-9220-0653
Description: To promote the cause of conservation and environmentalism throughout the state of Western Australia; and to serve as a liaison to other bodies dealing with conservation and environmental issues.
Contact(s):
Contact: RACHEL SIEWERT

DEPARTMENT FOR ENVIRONMENT, HERITAGE AND ABORIGINAL AFFAIRS
Level 9, Chesser House, 91-97 Grenfell Street, Adelaide 5000 Australia
Phone: 08-8204-9322; Fax: 08-8204-9321
Contact(s):
Chief Executive: JOHN SCANLON

DEPARTMENT OF CANADIAN HERITAGE

CORPORATE SERVICE
Contact(s):
Assistant Deputy Minister: PETER HOMULAS; Phone: 819-994-3046

DEPARTMENT OF FISHERIES AND OCEANS
200 Kent St., Ottawa, Ontario K1A 0E6
Description: The Department of Fisheries and Oceans is responsible for fisheries development and management on both coasts, fisheries research, oceanography, hydrography, and the administration of small craft harbours.
Contact(s):
Assistant Deputy Minister of Corporate Services: CAROL BEAL; Phone: 613-993-0868
Assistant Deputy Minister of Fisheries Management: PAT CHAMUT; Phone: 613-990-9867
Assistant Deputy Minister of Oceans: SCOTT PARSONS; Phone: 613-993-0850
Assistant Deputy Minister of Science: SCOTT PARSONS; Phone: 619-993-0880
Assistant Deputy Minister Policy: ; Phone: 613-993-1808
Deputy Minister: WAYNE WOUTERS; Phone: 613-993-2200
Director General of Communications Directorate: PAUL SCHUBERT; Phone: 613-993-0989
Director General of Fisheries and Oceans Science Directorate: BILL DOUBLEDAY; Phone: 613-990-0271
Director General of International Directorate: EARL WISEMAN; Phone: 613-998-2644
Director General of Marine Environment and Habitat: GERRY SWANSON; Phone: 613-991-1280
Director General of Oceans Directorate: KATHRYN BRUCE; Phone: 613-993-0802
Director General of Resource Management: JACQUE ROBICHAUD; Phone: 613-990-0189
Director General of Small Craft Harbours Branch: ROBERT BERGERON; Phone: 613-993-1937; Fax: 613-952-6788
Dominion Hydrographer: ANTHONY O'CONNOR; Phone: 613-995-4413; Fax: 613-996-9053
Minister: HON. DAVID ANDERSON; Phone: 613-992-3474

ENVIRONMENTAL CONSERVATION SERVICE

ATLANTIC REGION ENVIRONMENT CANADA
63 E. Main St., Box 1590, Sackville, New Brunswick E0A 3C0 Canada
Phone: 506-364-5044; Fax: 506-364-5062
Contact(s):
Regional Director: GEORGE FINNEY

CANADIAN WILDLIFE SERVICE
3rd Fl., Place Vincent Massey, 351 St. Joseph Blvd., Hull, Quebec K1A 0H3 Canada
Contact(s):
Director General: DAVID BRACKETT; Phone: 819-997-1301; Fax: 819-953-7177

ECOSYSTEM AND ENVIRONMENTAL RESOURCES DIRECTORATE
6th Fl., Place Vincent Massey, 351 St. Joseph Blvd., Hull, Quebec K1A 0H3 Canada
Contact(s):
Director General: JENNIFER MOORE; Phone: 819-997-5674; Fax: 819-994-2541

ECOSYSTEM SCIENCE DIRECTORATE
7th Fl., Place Vincent Massey, 351 St. Joseph Blvd., Hull, Quebec K1A 0H3 Canada
Contact(s):
Director General: KEN SOTO; Phone: 819-953-8056; Fax: 819-994-2724

ENVIRONMENTAL CONSERVATION SERVICE
15th Fl., Place Vincent Massey, 351 St. Joseph Blvd., Hull, Quebec K1A OH3 Canada
Description: In Environmental Conservation Service (ECS) our goal is to ensure that future generations of Canadians inherit a natural environment as rich as the one we enjoy today. We work with many partners--individual Canadians, environmental and community

groups, Aboriginal peoples, industry, other levels of government, and international organizations. We provide information on the natural environment to Canadians.
Contact(s):
Assistant Deputy Minister: KAREN BROWN; Phone: 819-997-2161; Fax: 819-997-1541

ONTARIO REGION ENVIRONMENT CANADA
4905 Dufferin St., Dawnsview, Ontario M3H 5T4 Canada
Phone: 416-739-5839; Fax: 416-739-5845
Contact(s):
Regional Director: SIMON LLEWELLYN

PACIFIC AND YUKON REGION: ENVIRONMENT CANADA
Suite 700, 1200 West 73rd Avenue, Vancouver, British Columbia V4K 3Y3 Canada
Phone: 604-664-4065; Fax: 604-664-4068
Contact(s):
Regional Director: VIC NIEMELA

PRAIRIE AND NORTHERN REGION
Environment Canada, Rm. 210, Twin Atria Bldg. #2, 4999-98th Ave., Edmonton, Alberta T6B 2X3 Canada
Phone: 403-951-8853; Fax: 403-495-2615
Contact(s):
Regional Director: GERALD McKEATING

QUEBEC REGION ENVIRONNEMENT CANADA
1141 Rte. de l'eglise, 9ieme etage, C.P. 10100, Ste-Foy, Quebec G1V 4H5 Canada
Phone: 418-648-7808; Fax: 418-649-6591
Contact(s):
Regional Director: MICHEL LAMONTAGNE

ENVIRONMENTAL PROTECTION SERVICE
Place Vincent Massey, 351 Blvd. St. Joseph, Hull, Quebec, Ontario K1A 0H3 Canada
Description: Purpose is to formulate and take action to meet threats to environment arising through adverse impacts of human activities. Priority responsibilities include toxic chemicals, acid rain ozone depletion, urban smog, and the ongoing management of concerns such as hazardous wastes.
Contact(s):
Assistant Deputy Minister: H. A. CLARKE; Phone: 819-997-1575
Assistant Director General of Regulatory Affairs and Program Integration: J. MOORE; Phone: 819-997-5674
Chief of Operations: B. SCHACKER; Phone: 819-953-1706
Director General of Special Projects: G. ALLARD; Phone: 819-994-3408
Director of Finance and Administration Branch: D. BOWIE; Phone: 819-997-3391
Director of Personnel Branch: C. LANGLOIS; Phone: 819-953-1183
Executive Assistant: C. GRAHAM; Phone: 819-997-1575

AIR POLLUTION PREVENTION DIRECTORATE
Contact(s):
Assistant Director of Transboundary Air Issues Branch: WAYNE DRAPER; Phone: 819-953-8441; Fax: 819-953-9547
Director General: D. EGAR, Place Vincent Massey, 11e et., 351, Blvd., St. Joseph Hull, Quebec K1A 0H3 Canada; Phone: 819-997-1298; Fax: 819-953-9547
Director of Global Air Issues Branch: A. MacKENZIE; Phone: 819-994-1924; Fax: 819-994-0549

ENVIRONMENTAL CONSERVATION SERVICE
15th Fl., Place Vincent Massey, 351 St. Joseph Blvd., Hull, Quebec K1A OH3 Canada
Contact(s):
Director General: KAREN BROWN, Place Vincent Massey, 7e et., 351, Blvd., St. Joseph Hull, Quebec K1A 0H3 Canada; Phone: 819-953-3009

ENVIRONMENTAL TECHNOLOGY ADVANCEMENT DIRECTORATE
Contact(s):
Director General: ED NORRENA; Phone: 819-953-3160; Fax: 819-953-9029

NATIONAL PROGRAMS DIRECTORATE
Contact(s):
Assistant Director General: R. BOULDEN; Phone: 819-997-2019; Fax: 819-997-0086
Assistant Director of Environmental Assessment: B. STACEY; Phone: 819-953-1690
Director of Environmental Emergencies: M. TAYLOR; Phone: 819-953-0607
Director of Office of Enforcement: D. KIMMETT; Phone: 819-953-1523; Fax: 819-997-0086

TOXICS POLLUTION PREVENTION DIRECTORATE
Contact(s):
Director General: V. SHANTORA, Place Vincent Massey, 11e et., 351, Blvd., St. Joseph Hull, Quebec K1A 0H3 Canada; Phone: 819-953-1114; Fax: 819-953-5371
Director of Commercial Chemicals Evaluation Branch: J. BUCCINI; Phone: 819-997-1499; Fax: 819-953-4936
Director of Hazardous Waste Management Branch: G. CORNWALL; Phone: 819-953-1712; Fax: 819-953-7643
Director of National Office of Pollution Prevention: J. RIORDAN; Phone: 819-953-3353; Fax: 819-953-7970

INSTITUTO NACIONAL DE BIODIVERSIDAD (INBIO)
Apdo. #22-3100, Santo Domingo Costa Rica
Phone: 506-244-0690; Fax: 506-244-2816; Email: askinbio@quercus.inbio.ac.cr
Founded: 1989
Description: INBIO is conducting a biodiversity inventory in Costa Rica's protected areas. Through this knowledge, society will be able to appreciate and value the resources contained in the wildlands, and use this information in a sustainable manner.
Contact(s):
Deputy Director: DR. ALFIO PIVA
Biodiversity Education: SONIA ROJAS
Biodiversity Garden: NATALIA ZAMORA
Biodiversity Inventory: CARLOS MARIO RODRIGUEZ
Biodiversity Prospecting Coordinator: DR. NICOLAS MATEO
Communication: ANA GLENA VALDEZ
Director General: DR. RODRIGO GAMEZ
Information Management Coordinator: DR. ERIC MATA
Publications: MARIA LOURDES GONZOLEZ
Publication(s): *Biodiversity Prospecting; Biodiversidad de Costa Rica: Lecturas para Ecoturistas; Guia de Aves de Costa Rica; Mariposas Heliconius de Costa Rica.*

MINISTRY OF THE ENVIRONMENT OF THE CZECH REPUBLIC
Vrsovicka 65, 100 10 Praha Czech Republic
Phone: 420-2-6712-2769; Fax: 420-2-73 94 11; Email: roundna@env.cz
Contact(s):
Chairman: PROF. MILAN STRASKRABA; Phone: 420-2-67122218; Fax: 420-2-739411; Email: alex@env.cz
Minister: JIRI SKALICKY; Phone: 420-2-67122048; Fax: 420-2-67311096; Email: roth@env.cz

ENVIRONMENTAL COMMISSION
Academy of Sciences of The Czech Republic, Narodni 3, 111 42 Praha 1 Czech Republic
Phone: 420-2-2420538; Fax: 420-2-24220944

NATURAL RESOURCES CANADA, CANADIAN FOREST SERVICE
580 Booth St., Ottawa, Ontario K1A 0E4 Canada
WWW: www.NRCan.gc.ca/cfs
Description: The mission of the Canadian Forest Service (CFS) is: "To promote the sustainable development of Canada's forests and

competitiveness of the Canadian forest sector for the well-being of present and future generations of Canadians." In an effort to increase understanding of the complexity of forest ecosystems, the CFS evaluates approaches to forest management, monitors forest health conditions and conducts research on issues of national and international significance such as biodiversity and the impact of atmospheric change on forests and climate change. Equipped with scientific and technical expertise, the CFS plays a strong policy role in addressing national and international issues affecting the sustainable development of Canada's forests. To this end, the CFS brings together various stakeholders to develop common strategies and arrive at national consensus on forestry issues. The CFS also establishes links with other federal departments, provinces, industry, and non-governmental organizations to better address issues such as international trade, market access and the sustainable management of forests world-wide.

Contact(s):
Assistant Deputy Minister of Canadian Forest Service: YVAN HARDY; Phone: 613-947-7400; Fax: 613-947-7395
Assistant Director General of Science Branch: GORDON MILLER; Phone: 613-947-8984; Fax: 613-947-9090
Assistant Director of Management Services: BRUCE MANION; Phone: 613-947-7334; Fax: 613-947-7396
Deputy Minister: JEAN C. McLOSKEY; Phone: 613-992-3456; Fax: 613-992-3828
Director General: HAP OLDHAM, P.O. Box 4000, Regent St., Fredericton, New Brunswick E3B 5P7 Canada; Phone: 506-452-3508; Fax: 506-452-3140
Director General: NORMAND LAFRENIERE, 1055 du P.E.P.S. St., P.O. Box 3800, Sainte-Foy, Quebec G1V-4C7 Canada; Phone: 418-648-3957; Fax: 418-648-7317
Director General: ED KONDO, P.O. Box 490, 1219 Queen St. East, Sault Ste. Marie, Ontario P6A 5M7 Canada; Phone: 705-949-9461/Ext. 2039; Fax: 705-759-5714
Director General: BOYD CASE, 5320 122 St., Edmonton, Alberta T6H 3S5 Canada; Phone: 403-435-7202; Fax: 403-435-7396
Director General: CARL WINGET, 506 West Burnside Rd., Victoria, British Columbia V8Z 1M5 Canada; Phone: 604-363-0608; Fax: 604-363-6088
Director General for Industry of Economics and Programs Branch (IEPB): JACQUES CARETTE; Phone: 613-947-9052; Fax: 613-947-9038
Director General of Policy, Planning and International Affairs Branch (PPIAB): JACQUES CARETTE; Phone: 613-947-9100; Fax: 613-947-9038
Director of Communications and Executive Services: SYLVIE LETELLIER; Phone: 613-947-7404; Fax: 613-947-7396
Manager of Sector Human Resources Unit: SYLVIA FREHNER; Phone: 613-947-7386; Fax: 613-947-7409
Minister: ANNE McLELLAN; Phone: 613-996-2007; Fax: 613-996-4516

Keyword(s): Agriculture, Biodiversity, Conservation of Protected Areas, Developing Countries, Environment, Fisheries, Forest Management, Internships, Land Use Planning, Research, Rural Development, Sustainable Development

UNITED NATIONS RESEARCH INSTITUTE FOR SOCIAL DEVELOPMENT (UNRISD)
Palais des Nations, CH 1211, Geneva 10 Switzerland
Phone: 41-22-798-8400, 798-5850; Fax: 41-22-740-0791; Email: info@UNRISD.org; WWW: www.unrisd.org
Founded: 1963
Description: UNRISD is an autonomous agency that researches the social dimensions of contemporary development problems. The Institute provides governments, development agencies, grassroots organizations, and scholars with a better understanding of how development policies and processes of economic, social, and environmental change affect different social groups. UNRISD promotes original research and strengthens research capacity in developing countries.
Contact(s):
Director: DHARAM GHAI
Publication(s): *UNRISD News; The Challenge of Peace; Focus on Integrating Gender into The Politics of Development; Discussion Papers; Occasional Papers; Briefing Papers; Conference Reports; Monographs; Co-publications.*

STATE AND PROVINCE GOVERNMENT AGENCIES

UNITED STATES

ALABAMA

GOVERNOR OF ALABAMA, DONALD SIEGELMAN
State Capitol, 600 Dexter Ave., Montgomery, AL 36130
Phone: 334-242-7100

ALABAMA COOPERATIVE EXTENSION SYSTEM
109 Duncan Hall, Auburn, AL 36849-5612
Phone: 334-844-4444
Founded: 1914
Description: The extension system (Alabama A&M and Auburn Universities), through its statewide network of County Extension Offices, conducts informal education programs using research-based knowledge and techniques. Programs are offered in agriculture and forestry profitability; developing, conserving, and managing natural resources; enhancing family and individual well being; developing human resources; and community development.
Contact(s):
Extension Director: STEPHEN B. JONES
Publication(s): *Contact Extension Communications*
Keyword(s): Agriculture, Fisheries, Forests and Forestry, Gardening and Horticulture, Wildlife Management

ALABAMA COOPERATIVE FISH AND WILDLIFE RESEARCH UNIT (USDI)
331 Funchess Hall, Auburn University, Auburn, AL 36849
Phone: 334-844-4796
Founded: 1935
Description: The unit is sponsored by the Biological Resources Division, U.S. Geological Survey; Alabama Department of Conservation and Natural Resources, Division of Game and Fish; Auburn University; and the Wildlife Management Institute. Fish and wildlife research, graduate education, and technical assistance are the unit's primary purposes.
Contact(s):
Assistant Leader of Fisheries: DR. ELISE R. IRWIN
Leader: DR. JAMES B. GRAND
Keyword(s): Biodiversity, Endangered and Threatened Species, Fisheries, Wildlife and Wildlife Habitat, Wildlife Management

ALABAMA DEPARTMENT OF AGRICULTURE AND INDUSTRIES
The Richard Beard Bldg., P.O. Box 3336, Montgomery, AL 36193
Phone: 334-242-2650
Description: The Alabama Department of Agriculture and Industries is responsible for enforcing the laws of Alabama relating to agriculture. It also works to provide agribusiness assistance such as marketing, loan mediation, and trade information. The department strives to ensure consumer safety and to promote all of Alabama agriculture.
Contact(s):
Commissioner: JACK THOMPSON

ALABAMA DEPARTMENT OF CONSERVATION AND NATURAL RESOURCES
64 N. Union St., Montgomery, AL 36130
Phone: 334-242-3486; Fax: 334-242-3489
Contact(s):
Acting Director of Division of State Parks: DON COOLEY; Phone: 334-242-3334
Assistant Commissioner: BOB MACRORY; Phone: 334-242-3487
Chief of Accounting: SUSAN MIMS; Phone: 334-242-3260
Chief of Engineering: TERRY BOYD; Phone: 334-242-3476
Chief of Film and Video Section: DENNIS HOLT, P.O. Box 278, Pelham, AL 35124; Phone: 205-663-7938
Chief of Information: DAN BROTHERS; Phone: 334-242-3151/800-262-3151
Chief of Personnel and Payroll: JEFF GREENE; Phone: 334-242-3502
Commissioner: JAMES D. MARTIN; Phone: 334-242-3486
Director of Division of Game and Fish: CHARLES D. KELLEY; Phone: 334-242-3465
Director of Division of Marine Police: WILLIAM B. GARNER; Phone: 334-242-3673
Director of Division of Marine Resources: R. VERNON MINTON, P.O. Box 189, DauphinIsland, AL 36528; Phone: 334-861-2882
Director of Division of State Lands: JAMES H. GRIGGS; Phone: 334-242-3484
Editor: CINDY THOMPSON; Phone: 334-242-3151/1-800-262-3151; Fax: 334-242-1880
Property Inventory Manager: JOHN F. DAVIS; Phone: 334-242-2574
Publication(s): *Outdoor Alabama*

ALABAMA DEPARTMENT OF ECONOMIC AND COMMUNITY AFFAIRS, COASTAL PROGRAMS (ADECA)
1208 Main St., Daphne, AL 36526
Phone: 334-626-0042; Fax: 334-626-3503; Email: ala-coastal@surf.nos.noaa.gov
Founded: 1979
Description: The program goal of the Alabama Coastal Area Management Program is to protect and, where possible, enhance or restore our coastal resources for this and succeeding generations.
Contact(s):
Chief: GIL GILDER; Phone: 334-242-5502
Manager: PHILLIP HINELSLY; Phone: 334-626-0042; Fax: 334-626-3503; Email: phinesley@surfnos.noaa.gov
Publication(s): *Alabama's Coastal Connection; Research Roundup; Various Program Brochures*
Keyword(s): Coasts, Conservation, Planning Management

ALABAMA DEPARTMENT OF ENVIRONMENTAL MANAGEMENT
P.O. Box 301463, Montgomery, AL 36130-1463
Phone: 205-271-7700; Fax: 205-271-7950
Founded: 1982
Description: To respond in an efficient, comprehensive, and coordinated manner to environmental problems, thereby assuring a safe, healthful, and productive environment. Encompasses water quality, public water supply, underground injection control, solid waste, hazardous waste, air pollution control, well water standards, operator certification, and coastal area functions.
Contact(s):
Deputy Director: RICHARD GRUSNICK
Director: JAMES W. WARR
Office of General Counsel: OLIVIA JENKINS
Staf of Air Division: RON GORE
Staff of Field Operations: E. JOHN WILLIFORD
Staff of Land Division: JOHN POOLE
Staff of Office of Education and Outreach: SUE ROBERTSON
Staff of Permits and Services: MARILYN ELLIOTT
Staff of Public Affairs: CLARK BRUNER
Staff of Water Division: CHARLES HORN
Publication(s): *Environmental Update*
Keyword(s): Air Quality and Pollution, Coasts, Solid Waste Management, Water Pollution Management, Wetlands

ALABAMA FORESTRY COMMISSION
513 Madison Ave., Montgomery, AL 36130
Phone: 334-240-9300; Fax: 334-240-9390
Description: The FC was created by the 1969 regular session of the Alabama Legislature and is charged by law to protect, conserve, and increase the timber and forest resources of this state. A seven-member board is the policymaking body of the Commission. The State Forester is Chief Administrative Officer. Fire prevention and suppression, educational programs and materials, and free forest

management assistance are some of the services which the Commission offers to the general public.
Contact(s):
Chairman: JAMES D. SPEARS
Assistant State Forester: RICHARD H. CUMBIE; Phone: 334-240-9367
Director of Administration Division: JOHN C. KUMMEL; Phone: 334-240-9333
Director of Forest Programs Division: DAVID FREDERICK; Phone: 334-240-9335
Editor: KIM GILLILAND; Phone: 334-240-9355
State Forester: TIMOTHY C. BOYCE; Phone: 334-240-9304
Publication(s): *Alabama's TREASURED Forests*
Keyword(s): Environmental and Conservation Education, Forest Management, Forests and Forestry, Renewable Resources, Sustainable Development, Urban Forestry

ALABAMA SEA GRANT PROGRAM
Mississippi and Alabama Sea Grant Consortium, Caylor Bldg., Gulf Coast Research Lab., P.O. Box 7000, Ocean Springs, AL 39566-7000
Phone: 228-875-9341; Fax: 228-875-0528
Contact(s):
Coordinator and Marine Economist: DR. WILLIAM HOSKING, Alabama Sea Grant Extension Program: 4170 Commanders Dr., Mobile, AL 36615; Phone: 334-438-5690; Fax: 334-438-5670
Head: DR. C. DAVID VEAL, Mississippi Sea Grant Advisory Service 2710 W. Beach Blvd. Suite 1-E, Biloxi, MS 39531; Phone: 228-388-4710; Fax: 228-388-1375

ALABAMA SOIL AND WATER CONSERVATION COMMITTEE
Exe. Dir., P.O. Box 304800, Montgomery, AL 36130
Contact(s):
Chair: CHARLES W. RITTENOUR JR., 1144 Meriwether Rd., Pike Road, AL 36064; Phone: 334-284-5320
Executive Director: STEPHEN M. CAUTHEN, P.O. Box 304800, Montgomery, AL 36130-4800; Phone: 334-242-2681; Fax: 334-242-0551; Email: scauthen@dsmd.dsmd.state.al.us

ALASKA

GOVERNOR OF ALASKA, TONY KNOWLES
P.O. Box 110001, Juneau, AK 99811-0001
Phone: 907-465-3500

ALASKA COOPERATIVE FISH AND WILDLIFE RESEARCH UNIT
209 Irving I Bldg., P.O. Box 757020, University of Alaska Fairbanks, Fairbanks, AK 99775-7020
Phone: 907-474-7661
Founded: 1978
Description: Sponsored jointly by the U.S. Geological Service, Alaska Department of Fish and Game, University of Alaska Fairbanks, and Wildlife Management Institute, the Unit conducts graduate education and research programs on the ecology and management of Alaskan fish and wildlife, and their habitats.
Contact(s):
Assistant Leader of Ecology: DR. A. DAVID McGUIRE
Assistant Leader of Fisheries: DR. JACQUELINE D. LAPERRIERE
Assistant Leader of Wildlife: DR. BRAD GRIFFITH
Leader: DR. JAMES B. REYNOLDS
Keyword(s): Aquatic Habitats, Ecology, Fisheries, Wildlife and Wildlife Habitat, Wildlife Management

ALASKA DEPARTMENT OF ENVIRONMENTAL CONSERVATION
410 Willoughby Ave., Juneau, AK 99801-1795
Phone: 907-465-5000
Founded: 1971
Description: Created by the Seventh Alaska Legislature to protect the quality of the state's natural resources and the health and quality of life of its people. The department has broad regulatory authority in the areas of water quality, drinking water, air quality, solid waste disposal, oil spills, subsurface pollution, pesticides, food safety, seafood wholesomeness, sanitation, and radiation. The department also has programs for construction of water, sewer, and solid waste facilities in Alaskan cities and villages.
Contact(s):
Commissioner: MICHELE BROWN; Phone: 907-465-5050
Deputy Commissioner: AL EWING; Phone: 907-465-5050
Director of Division of Administrative Services: BARBARA FRANK; Phone: 907-465-5010
Director of Division of Air and Water Quality: MIKE CONWAY; Phone: 907-465-5260
Director of Division of Environmental Health: JANICE ADAIR; Phone: 907-269-7644
Director of Division of Facilities Construction and Operations: KEITH KELTON; Phone: 907-465-5180
Director of Spill Prevention and Response: KURT FREDRIKSSON; Phone: 907-465-5250
Director of Statewide Public Service: MARIANNE SEE; Phone: 907-269-7634
Public Information: JOE FERGUSON; Phone: 907-465-5060
Keyword(s): Air Quality and Pollution, Environmental Health, Environmental Planning, Environmental Protection, Public Health Protection, Solid Waste Management, Water Pollution Management, Water Quality

ALASKA DEPARTMENT OF FISH AND GAME
P.O. Box 25526, Juneau, AK 99802
Phone: 907-465-4100
Description: A research and management agency whose mission is to develop and organize its technical, human, and fiscal assets to maintain, rehabilitate, and enhance the fish and wildlife resources of the state, and to provide for their sustained optimum use consistent with the social, cultural, environmental, and economic needs of the public.
Contact(s):
Board of Fisheries Chairman: DR. JOHN R. WHITE, Bering Sea Dental Center, P.O. Box 190, Bethel, AK 99559
Board of Fisheries Vice Chair: DAN J. COFFEY, 207 E. Northern Lights Blvd., Suite 200, Anchorate, AK 99503
Board of Game Chair: LORI QUAKENBUSH, P.O. Box 82391, Faibankes, AK 99708
Board of Game Vice Chairman: WALTER SAMPSON, P.O. Box 49, Kotzebue, AK 99752
Commissioner: DAVID BENTON
Commissioner: FRANK RUE
Deputy Commissioner: ROBERT BOSWORTH
Director of Commercial Fisheries Management and Development Division: BOB CLASBY; Phone: 907-465-4210
Director of Division of Administration: KEVIN BROOKS; Phone: 907-465-5999
Director of Division of Sport Fish: KEVIN DELANEY; Phone: 907-465-4180
Director of Division of Subsistence: MARY PETE; Phone: 907-465-4147
Director of Division of Wildlife Conservation: WAYNE REGELIN; Phone: 907-465-4190
Director of Habitat and Restoration Division: JANET KOWALSKI; Phone: 907-465-4105
Executive Director of Board of Fish: LAIRD JONES; Phone: 907-465-6098
Executive Director of Board of Game: DIANA COTE; Phone: 907-465-6095
Public Communications Section: DIANE REGAN; Phone: 907-465-6167
Special Assistant for Legislative Liaision: GERON BRUCE; Phone: 907-465-6143
State and Federal Relations: JAY NELSON; Phone: 907-465-6139
Keyword(s): Fisheries, Hunting, Renewable Resources, Sport Fishing, Wildlife and Wildlife Habitat

STATE AND PROVINCE GOVERNMENT AGENCIES - AMERICAN SAMOA

ALASKA DEPARTMENT OF NATURAL RESOURCES
400 Willoughby, 5th Fl., Juneau, AK 99801
Phone: 907-465-2400
Contact(s):
Commissioner: JOHN SHIVELY
Director (Acting) of Division of Geological and Geophysical Surveys: MILTON WILTSE, 794 University Ave. Suite 200, Fairbanks, AK 99709-3654; Phone: 907-451-5000
Director of Division of Agriculture: JAY KERTULLA, 1800 Glenn Hwy. Suite 12: P.O. Box 949, Palmer, AK 99645-0949; Phone: 907-745-7200
Director of Division of Land: JANE ANGVIK, 3601 C St. Suite 1122, Anchorage, AK 99503-5947; Phone: 907-269-8503
Director of Division of Mining and Water Management: JULES TILESTON, 3601 C St., Anchorage, AK 99503-5935; Phone: 907-269-8600
Director of Division of Oil and Gas: KEN BOYD, 3601 C St. Suite 1380, Anchorage, AK 99503-5948; Phone: 907-269-8800
Director of Division of Parks and Outdoor Recreation: JIM STRATTON, 3601 C St. Suite 1200, Anchorage, AK 99503-5921; Phone: 907-269-8700
State Forester of Division of Forestry: TOM BOUTIN, 3601 C St. Suite 1030, Anchorage, AK 99503; Phone: 907-269-8463
Keyword(s): Agriculture, Forests and Forestry, Land Use Planning, Public Lands, Renewable Resources

ALASKA HEALTH PROJECT
218 East 4th Avenue, Anchorage, AK 99501
Phone: 907-276-2864; Fax: 907-279-3089
Founded: 1980
Description: To provide information and advocacy on occupational and environmental health issues in Alaska, the Pacific Northwest, and Canada.
Contact(s):
Executive Director: DANIEL MIDDAUGH
Instructor: R. J. GRYDER
Publication(s): Involve waste management and worker health, and are inclusive of a 22 edition list.
Keyword(s): Communications, Engineering, Environmental and Conservation Education, Solid Waste, Training

ALASKA SEA GRANT COLLEGE PROGRAM
University of Alaska, P.O. Box 755040, Fairbanks, AK 99775-5040
Phone: 907-474-7086; Fax: 907-474-6285; Email: fnrkd@uaf.edu; WWW: www.uaf.edu/seagrant/
Description: A state/federal partnership administered by the National Oceanic and Atmospheric Administration and the University of Alaska that sponsors and conducts marine research, graduate education, marine industry advisory services, and formal and nonformal public education aimed at promoting the wise use and conservation of Alaska's coastal and marine resources.
Contact(s):
Director: RONALD K. DEARBORN; Email: fnrkd@uaf.edu
Communications Manager: KURT BYERS, Alaska Sea Grant College Program:University of Alaska: P.O. Box 755040, Fairbanks, AK 99775-5040; Phone: 907-474-6702; Email: fnkmb1@uaf.edu
Leader of Marine Advisory Program: DONALD E. KRAMER, University of Alaska Carlton Trust Bldg.: Suite 110: 2221 E. Northern Lights Blvd., Anchorage, AK 99508-4140; Phone: 907-274-9691; Fax: 907-277-5242; Email: afdek@uaa.alaska.edu
Publications Manager: SUE KELLER, P.O. Box 755040, Fairbanks, AK 99775-5040; Phone: 907-474-6703; Email: fnsk@uaf.edu
Publication(s): Guide to Marine Mammals of Alaska; Management Strategies for Exploited Fish Populations; Biennial Program Report; SeaWeek Curriculum Series; posters, videos; free catalog
Keyword(s): Coasts, Environmental and Conservation Education, Fisheries, Marine Mammals, Oceanography

ALASKA STATE EXTENSION SERVICES
Alaska Cooperative Extension, P.O. Box 756180, University of Alaska, Fairbanks, AK 99775-6180
Phone: 907-474-7246
Contact(s):
Chairman of Land Resources and Community Development: ROBERT F. GORMAN

DEPARTMENT OF PUBLIC SAFETY
P.O. Box 111200, Juneau, AK 99811
Phone: 907-465-4322
Description: Responsible for enforcing all of the Fish and Game laws and regulations of the state.
Contact(s):
Commissioner: RONALD L. OTTE
Director of Fish and Wildlife Protection: COL. JOHN D. GLASS
Enforcement Commander: MAJ. JOSEPH S. D'AMICO
Operations Commander: CAPT. ALAN G. CAIN
Keyword(s): Hunting, Resource Law Enforcement, Sport Fishing, Trapping, Wildlife Management

Division of Fish and Wildlife Protection
5700 E. Tudor Rd., Anchorage, AK 99507
Phone: 907-269-5509

AMERICAN SAMOA

GOVERNOR OF AMERICAN SAMOA, TAUESE P.F. SUNIA
American Samoa Government,, Pago Pago, American Samoa 96799
Phone: 011-684-699-9272

AMERICAN SAMOA DEPARTMENT OF AGRICULTURE
American Samoa Government, Pago Pago, American Samoa 96799 American Samoa
Phone: 011-684-699-9272; Fax: 011-684-699-4031
Contact(s):
Director: PHILO F. MALUIA

ARIZONA

GOVERNOR OF ARIZONA, JANE DEE HULL
State House, 1700 W. Washington, Phoenix, AZ 85007
Phone: 602-542-4331

ARIZONA COOPERATIVE FISH AND WILDLIFE RESEARCH UNIT (USDI)
Rm. 104 Biological Sciences East, University of Arizona, Tucson, AZ 85721
Phone: 520-621-1959; Fax: 520-621-8801
Description: The Unit is a cooperative effort by the U.S. Department of Interior, the Arizona Game and Fish Department, the University of Arizona, and the Wildlife Management Institute. The Unit conducts research on fish and wildlife questions for client agencies.
Contact(s):
Assistant Leader: STEPHEN DeSTEFANO
Assistant Leader: CAROLE C. McIVOR
Leader: O. EUGENE MAUGHAN

ARIZONA DEPARTMENT OF AGRICULTURE
1688 W. Adams, Phoenix, AZ 85007
Phone: 602-542-4373; Fax: 602-542-5420
Description: The ADA is responsible for ensuring that the public consumes wholesome food of good quality and is provided with readily useable fiber. Consumables for which ADA is responsible include fruits, vegetables, meat, milk and eggs and associated products, plant and plant products, and commercial feed. The department is charged with promoting the economic vitality of Arizona's agricultural industry.

STATE AND PROVINCE GOVERNMENT AGENCIES - ARIZONA

Contact(s):
Director: SHELDON R. JONES; Phone: 602-542-0998

Animal Services Division
1688 W. Adams, Phoenix, AZ 85007
Description: The Animal Services Division is responsible for the protection of livestock from theft and disease and for the regulation of the state's aquaculture, dairy, egg, and slaughtering and meat-processing industries.
Contact(s):
Associate Director of Animal ServicesDivision: JOE LANE; Phone: 602-542-6309

Environmental Services Division
Description: The Environmental Services Division is responsible for regulating the agricultural industry to ensure the safe use of pesticides, and to ensure the quality of feed, fertilizer, and pesticide formulations.
Contact(s):
Assistant Director of State Agricultural Laboratory (Animal Services Division): DWIGHT HARDER; Phone: 602-542-1920
Associate Director of Environmental Services Division: JACK E. PETERSON; Phone: 602-542-3579

Integrated Pest Management (IPM)
Contact(s):
Fruit and Vegetable State Standardization and Federal State Grade Inspection (Integrated Pest Management): AL DAVIS
Native Plant Program Manager of Integrated Pest Management: JIM McGINNIS
Non-Program Manager of Integrated Pest Management: JOE FRIESEN
Port of Entry Program Manager of Integrated Pest Management: DONNA DIAZ
Seed and Hay Program Manager of Integrated Pest Management: KATHLEEN WILLEY
Survey and Detection Program Manager of Integrated Pest Management: DR. AHMED NASSER
Keyword(s): Agriculture, Pesticides

Plant Services Division
Phone: 602-542-0996; Fax: 602-542-0999
Description: The Plant Services Division is responsible for enforcement of state plant regulatory statutes, state agricultural industry plants, and plant health service programs.
Contact(s):
Associate Director of Plant Services Division: KEN BOYD

ARIZONA DEPARTMENT OF ENVIRONMENTAL QUALITY
3033 N. Central Ave., Phoenix, AZ 85012
Phone: 602-207-2300
Founded: 1987
Description: The Arizona Department of Environmental Quality shall preserve, protect, and enhance the environment and the public health, and shall be a leader in the development of public policy to maintain and improve the quality of Arizona's air, land, and water resources.
Contact(s):
Deputy Director: JOHN F. HAGEN; Phone: 602-207-2204
Director: RUSSELL F. RHOADES; Phone: 602-207-2203
Director of Administration Division: JOHN F. TIMKO
Director of Air Quality Division: NANCY C. WRONA; Phone: 602-207-2308
Director of Waste Programs Division: JEAN A. CALHOUN; Phone: 602-207-2381
Director of Water Quality Division: KAREN L. SMITH; Phone: 602-207-2306
Keyword(s): Air Quality and Pollution, Environmental and Conservation Education, Environmental Protection, Pollution Prevention, Solid Waste Management, Toxic Substances, Water Pollution, Water Quality

ARIZONA GAME AND FISH DEPARTMENT
2221 W. Greenway Rd., Phoenix, AZ 85023-4312
Phone: 602-942-3000
Description: The mission of the Arizona Game and Fish Department is to conserve, enhance, and restore Arizona's diverse wildlife resources and habitats through aggressive protection and management programs, and to provide wildlife resources and safe watercraft and off-highway vehicle recreation for the enjoyment, appreciation, and use by present and future generations.
Contact(s):
Deputy Director: THOMAS W. SPALDING
Director: DUANE L. SHROUFE
Administrative Officer: G. PATRICK O'BRIEN
Assistant Director of Field Operations Division: STEVE FERRELL
Assistant Director of Information and Education Division: DAVE DAUGHTRY
Assistant Director of Special Services Division: JIM BURTON
Assistant Director of Wildlife Management Division: BRUCE TAUBERT
Commissioner Chair: HERB GUENTER
Funds and Contracts: LARRY RILEY
Heritage Program Coordinator: TOM OHMART
Personnel Manager: PAMELA TENNEY
Planner: SHERRY CROUCH
Publications Editor: ROBERTA A. DOBOLEK
Regional Coordinator: MIKE SENN
Publication(s): *Arizona Wildlife Views*
Keyword(s): Environmental and Conservation Education, Nongame Wildlife, Sport Fishing, Wildlife and Wildlife Habitat, Wildlife Management

ARIZONA GEOLOGICAL SURVEY
416 W. Congress St., Suite 100, Tucson, AZ 85701
Phone: 520-770-3500
Founded: 1881-1912
Description: Develops, maintains, and disseminates information related to the geologic framework, geological hazards and limitations, and mineral and energy resources. Provides staff support for the Arizona Oil and Gas Conservation Commission, which regulates the drilling and production of oil, gas, geothermal, and helium resources.
Contact(s):
Director and State Geologist: DR. LARRY D. FELLOWS; Phone: 520-770-3500
Publication(s): *Arizona Geology; circulars; special papers; bulletins; maps; open-file reports; miscellaneous maps; contributed maps and reports*
Keyword(s): Energy, Engineering, Environmental and Conservation Education, Geology, Land Use Planning, Mineral Resources, Public Information, Research, Water Resources

ARIZONA LAND DEPARTMENT
1616 W. Adams St., Phoenix, AZ 85007
Phone: 602-542-4621; Fax: 602-542-2590
Founded: 1915
Description: The purpose of the Arizona State Land Department is to manage 9.4 million acres of Trust lands, through leasing and sale, in order to generate revenue for 14 state institutions. Resource protection and preservation is an integral part of trust land management.
Contact(s):
Commissioner of State Land: J. DENNIS WELLS
Deputy Commissioner of State Land: MICHAEL E. ANABLE
Director of Administration and Resource Analysis Division: LYNN LARSON; Phone: 602-542-4621
Director of Fire Management Division: KIRK ROWDABAUGH; Phone: 602-255-4059
Director of Forestry Division: T. MIKE HART; Phone: 602-542-4627
Director of Natural Resources Division: ROBERT E. YOUNT; Phone: 602-542-4625
Director of Operations Division: RICHARD B. OXFORD; Phone: 602-542-4602

STATE AND PROVINCE GOVERNMENT AGENCIES - ARKANSAS

Director of Planning and Land Disposition Division: BILL FOSTER; Phone: 602-542-1704
NRCD Administrator: BILL WARSKOW; Phone: 602-542-2699; Fax: 602-524-4688; Email: wwarskow@lnd.state.az.us
Keyword(s): Land Use Planning, Public Lands, Renewable Resources, Sustainable Development, Water Resources

ARIZONA STATE EXTENSION SERVICES
University of Arizona, Tucson, AZ 85721
Phone: 520-621-7209
Contact(s):
Aquaculture Specialist: KEVIN FITZSIMMONS, Soil, Water, and Environmental Science, ERL-Shantz 429, Bio Sci E 207, University of Arizona, Tucson, AZ 85721; Phone: 520-741-1990
Director of Cooperative Extension: DR. JAMES A. CHRISTENSON, Forbes Bldg., Rom 301, University of Arizona, Tucson, AZ 85721; Phone: 520-621-7209
Extension Range Management Specialist: DR. GEORGE RUYLE, School of Renewable Natural Resources: College of Agriculture, Bio Sci E 302, University of Arizona, Tucson, AZ 85721; Phone: 520-621-1384
Natural Resources Specialist: LARRY SULLIVAN, School of Renewable Natural Resources: College of Agriculture, Bio Sci E 309, University of Arizona, Tucson, AZ 85721; Phone: 520-621-7998
Range Management Assistant Specialist: LARRY HOWERY, School of Renewable Natural Resources: College of Agriculture, Bio Sci E 301B, University of Arizona, Tucson, AZ 85721; Phone: 520-621-7277
Range Management Specialist: DR. LAMAR SMITH, School of Renewable Natural Resources, College of Agriculture, Bio Sci E 301 E, University of Arizona, Tucson, AZ 85721; Phone: 520-621-3803
Watershed Management Specialist: DR. RICHARD HAWKINS, School of Renewable Natural Resources, College of Agriculture, Bio Sci E 207, University of Arizona, Tucson, AZ 85721; Phone: 520-621-7273

ARIZONA STATE PARKS BOARD
1300 W. Washington Ave., Phoenix, AZ 85007
Phone: 602-542-4174; Fax: 602-542-4188; WWW: www.pr.state.az.us
Founded: 1957
Description: The purposes and objectives of the Arizona State Parks Board are to select, acquire, preserve, establish, and maintain areas of natural features, scenic beauty, historical and scientific interest, zoos, and botanical gardens, for the education, pleasure, recreation, and health of the people. Programs include: Resource Stewardship with the Trails Program, Natural Areas Program, Off-Highway Vehicle Program, and Environmental Education Program. Also, State Historic Preservation Office with Registry Programs for National and State Registers of Historic Places. In addition, grants and planning statewide programs award funds for development and rehabilitation of recreational facilities using Arizona Heritage Funds, Land and Water Conservation Funds, and State Lake Improvement Funds. Planners in this section are also responsible for the creation of the Statewide Outdoor Recreation Plan.
Contact(s):
Deputy Director: CHARLES R. EATHERLY
Executive Director: KENNETH E. TRAVOUS
Chairperson: JOSEPH HOLMWOOD
Public Information Officer: ELLEN BILBREY; Phone: 602-542-1996
Publication(s): *Arizona Rivers and Streams Guide; Arizona State Trails Guides; Arizona Wildlife Viewing Guides; Access Arizona (disabled/seniors)*
Keyword(s): Botanical Gardens, Cultural Preservation, Natural Areas, Nongame Wildlife, Outdoor Recreation

ARKANSAS

GOVERNOR OF ARKANSAS, MIKE HUCKABEE
Governor of Arkansas, 250 State Capitol, LittleRock, AR 72201
Phone: 501-682-2345

ARKANSAS COOPERATIVE RESEARCH UNIT
Department of Interior, U.S. Geological Survey, Biological Sciences SCEN 617, University of Arkansas, Fayetteville, AR 72701
Phone: 501-575-6709; Fax: 501-575-3330
Founded: 1988
Description: Primary purpose is field research, graduate research training in fisheries and wildlife resources, technical assistance, and extension activities. Areas of research include habitat selection, species coexistence, life history and demographics, endangered species conservation, ecology, animal behavior, and fisheries biology. Supported cooperatively by the U.S. Geological Survey, University of Arkansas, Arkansas Game and Fish Commission, and the Wildlife Management Institute.
Contact(s):
Assistant Leader of Fisheries: DR. THOMAS J. KWAK
Unit Leader: DR. JAMES E. JOHNSON
Publication(s): *Transactions of the American Fisheries Society; North American Journal of Fisheries Management; Southwestern Naturalist; Ecology of Freshwater Fish*
Keyword(s): Ecology, Endangered and Threatened Species, Fisheries, Research, Wildlife Management

ARKANSAS DEPARTMENT OF PARKS AND TOURISM
One Capitol Mall, Little Rock, AR 72201
Phone: 501-682-7777; Fax: 501-682-1364
Description: Develop, maintain and operate 50 state parks and four museums; advertise and promote all the state's recreation and travel potentials; provide information to attract retirees and others wanting to relocate; assist communities in establishing local litter prevention and recycling projects; provide accurate information on the state's scenic, recreational, cultural, historic attractions, and trails; manage the state's archives; provide interpretive services; provide technical assistance and grants to museums throughout the state; administration of the Land and Water Conservation Fund; and preparation and implementation of the Statewide Comprehensive Outdoor Recreation Plan.
Contact(s):
Executive Director: RICHARD W. DAVIES; Phone: 501-682-2535
Director of Administration: R.L. CARGILE; Phone: 501-682-2039
Director of Great River Rd. Division: NANCY CLARK; Phone: 501-682-1120
Director of Historical Resources and Museum Services Section: PATRICIA M. MURPHY; Phone: 501-682-3603
Director of History Commission: DR. JOHN L. FERGUSON; Phone: 501-682-6900
Director of Parks Division: G. GREG BUTTS; Phone: 501-682-7743
Director of Tourism Division: JOE DAVID RICE; Phone: 501-682-1088
Keep Arkansas Beautiful: ROBERT PHELPS; Phone: 501-682-3507
Outdoor Recreation Grants: BRYAN KELLAR; Phone: 501-682-1301
Keyword(s): Cultural Preservation, Environmental and Conservation Education, Environmental Preservation, Historic Preservation, Outdoor Recreation

ARKANSAS GAME AND FISH COMMISSION
#2 Natural Resources Dr., Little Rock, AR 72205
Phone: 501-223-6300
Founded: 1915
Description: The mission of the Arkansas Game and Fish Commission is to wisely manage the fish and wildlife resources of Arkansas while providing maximum enjoyment for the people.
Contact(s):
Chairman: RICK EVANS; Phone: 501-748-2411
Assistant Director: SCOTT HENDERSON; Phone: 501-223-6309; Fax: 501-223-6448; Email: shenderson@agfc.state.ar.us

Assistant Director: SCOTT C. YAICH; Phone: 501-223-6307; Fax: 501-223-6448; Email: syaich@agfc.state.ar.us
Director: STEVE N. WILSON; Phone: 501-223-6305; Fax: 501-223-6448; Email: snw001@agfc.state.ar.us
Acting Chief of Wildlife Management: DONNY HARRIS; Phone: 501-223-6359
Chief of Computer Services: BILL ROBINSON; Phone: 501-223-6368
Chief of Educational Services: MARC KILBURN; Phone: 501-223-6402
Chief of Enforcement: LOREN HITCHCOCK; Phone: 501-223-6384
Chief of Fiscal Services: RAY SEBREN; Phone: 501-223-6341
Chief of Fisheries Management: ALLEN CARTER; Phone: 501-223-6371
Chief of Human Resources: MARY GRACE SMITH; Phone: 501-223-6317
Editor: KEITH SUTTON; Phone: 501-223-6406
Editor: JIM SPENCER; Phone: 501-223-6336
Legal Counsel: JIM GOOHART; Phone: 501-223-6327
Operational Services: BILL WHITE; Phone: 501-223-6355
Public Affairs Coordinator: STEPHEN R. WILSON; Phone: 501-223-6408
Publication(s): *Arkansas Game and Fish Magazine; Arkansas Outdoors Newsletter*

ARKANSAS STATE EXTENSION SERVICES
Head, P.O. Box 391, Little Rock, AR 72203
Description: An off-campus education organization with faculty and offices in each county with the basic mission to disseminate and encourage the application of research-generated knowledge and leadership techniques to individuals, families, and communities. The county faculty is backed by subject matter specialists and their research counterparts.
Contact(s):
Assistant Extension Specialist, Natural Resources: KELLY LOFTIN, P.O. Box 391, LittleRock, AR 72203; Phone: 501-671-2361; Email: kloftin@uaex.edu
Assistant Extension Specialist, Wildlife: REX R. ROBERG, P.O. Box 391, LittleRock, AR 72203; Phone: 501-671-2334; Email: rrobert@uaex.edu
Assistant Professor: ANDREW GOODWIN, P.O. Box 4990: UAPB, PineBluff, AR 71611; Phone: 870-543-8150; Email: goodwin@seark.net
Associate Vice President for Agriculture-Extension: DAVID E. FOSTER, P.O. Box 391, LittleRock, AR 72203; Phone: 501-671-2001; Email: dfoster@uaex.edu
Chair, Department of Aquaculture and Fisheries: CAROLE R. ENGLE, 1890 Research and Extension: UAPB: Box 4990, PineBluff, AR 71611; Phone: 501-543-8537; Email: engle_c@vx4500.uapb.edu
Environmental Management Specialist of Agriculture: MICHAEL B. DANIELS, P.O. Box 391, LittleRock, AR 72203; Phone: 501-671-2281; Email: mdaniels@uaex.edu
Estension Forester: FRANK A. ROTH II, Rt. 3 Box 258, Hope, AR 71801; Phone: 501-777-1549; Email: froth@uaex.edu
Extension Fisheries Specialist: NATHAN M. STONE, P.O. Box 4966: UAPB, PineBluff, AR 71611; Phone: 870-543-8141; Email: stone_n@vx4500.uapb.edu
Extension Fisheries Specialist: JOSEPH MARET, P.O. Drawer D, Lonoke, AR 72086; Phone: 501-676-3124; Email: jmaret@lonoke.uaex.edu
Extension Fisheries Specialist: H. STEVEN KILLIAN, 405 Suite A: Highway 65+82, LakeVillage, AR 71653; Phone: 870-265-8055; Email: skillian@uaexsun.uaex.edu
Extension Fisheries Specialist: DAVID HEIKES, P.O. Box 4912: UAPB, PineBluff, AR 71611; Phone: 870-543-8537; Email: heikes_d@vx4500.uapb.edu
Extension Forester: TAMARA L. WALKINGSTICK, P.O. Box 3468, Monticello, AR 71655; Phone: 870-460-1549; Email: walkingstick@uamont.edu
Extension Natural Resources Assistant Specialist: DONNA R. SHANKLIN, P.O. Box 391, LittleRock, AR 72203; Phone: 870-460-4893; Email: shanklin@uamont.edu
Extension Specialist, Wildlife: REBECCA J. STOUT, P.O. Box 391, LittleRock, AR 72203; Phone: 501-671-2285; Email: rstout@uaex.edu
Extension Waste Management Specialist: SUZANNE SMITH HIRREL, P.O. Box 391, LittleRock, AR 72203; Phone: 501-671-2288; Email: shirrel@uaex.edu
Head of Extension Forester: BOB BLACKMON, School of Forestry, University of Arkansas-Monticello, P.O. Box 3468, Monticello, AR 71665; Phone: 870-460-1049; Email: blackmon@uamont.edu
Leader of Environmental and Natural Resources Section: TOM L. RILEY JR., P.O. Box 391, LittleRock, AR 72203; Phone: 501-671-2080; Email: triley@uaex.edu
Keyword(s): Agriculture, Forests and Forestry, Gardening and Horticulture, Renewable Resources, Wildlife and Wildlife Habitat

DEPARTMENT OF ENVIRONMENTAL QUALITY (ARKANSAS)
8001 National Dr., P.O. Box 8913, Little Rock, AR 72219-8913
Phone: 501-682-0744; WWW: www.adeq.state.ar.us
Founded: 1949
Description: To prevent, abate, and control all types of pollution and maintain the state's natural environment.
Contact(s):
Chairman: THOMAS SCHUECK
Deputy Director: LARRY WILSON
Deputy Director: JIM SHIRRELL
Director: RANDALL MATHIS
Administrator of Management Services: DR. ED MORRIS
Chief of Air Division: KEITH MICHAELS
Chief of Computer Services Division: ROBERT GAGE
Chief of Construction Assistance Division: MIKE CHANDLER
Chief of Customer Service Division: JAMES GILSON
Chief of Environmental Preservation Division: GREGG PATTERSON
Chief of Fiscal Division: ROBIN MORRISSEY
Chief of Hazardous Waste Division: MIKE BATES
Chief of Legal Division: AL ECKERT
Chief of Mining Division: FLOYD DURHAM
Chief of Regulated Storage Tank Division: JIM SHELL
Chief of Solid Waste Division: DENNIS BURKS
Chief of Technical Services Division: RICHARD CASSAT
Chief of Water Division: CHUCK BENNETT
Vice Chairman: JULIA PECK MOBLEY
Publication(s): *Arkansas Waste Line*
Keyword(s): Air Quality and Pollution, Ecology, Environmental Protection, Solid Waste, Water Pollution

FORESTRY COMMISSION (ARKANSAS)
3821 W. Roosevelt Rd., Little Rock, AR 72204-6395
Phone: 501-296-1940; Fax: 501-296-1949
Description: To prevent and suppress forest fires; control forest insects and diseases; grow and distribute forest planting stock; and collect and disseminate information concerning growth, utilization, and renewal of forests.
Contact(s):
Baucum Nursery: ALAN MURRAY; Phone: 501-945-3345
Commission Chairman: TOM R. CURTNER
Deputy State Forester: ROBERT J. McFARLAND
Fire Control: JOHN V. BURTON
Fiscal Department: BOB C. CHAPMAN
Forest Management: LARRY NANEE
Information and Education: JAMES E. GRANT JR.
State Forester: JOHN T. SHANNON

STATE AND PROVINCE GOVERNMENT AGENCIES - CALIFORNIA

NATURAL AND SCENIC RIVERS COMMISSION (ARKANSAS)
1500 Tower Bldg., 323 Center St., Little Rock, AR 72201
Phone: 501-324-9159; Fax: 501-324-9154; Email: info@dah.state.ar.us
Founded: 1979
Description: The purpose of the Natural and Scenic Rivers Commission is to prepare surveys and recommendations to the governor and the legislature for the preservation of selected rivers in the state of Arkansas possessing outstanding natural, scenic, educational, geological, recreational, historic, fish and wildlife, scientific, and cultural values of great present and future benefit to the people.
Contact(s):
Director: JANE JONES
Publication(s): *Arkansas Landowners Guide to Stream Bank Management; Arkansas Floater's Kit; Arkansas River - Resource in Criis - What Are the Limits? How Do We Share? (Poster 28 x 40)*
Keyword(s): Environmental and Conservation Education, Environmental Planning, Rivers, Water Pollution Management, Water Resources

NATURAL HERITAGE COMMISSION (ARKANSAS)
1500 Tower Bldg., 323 Center St., Little Rock, AR 72201
Phone: 501-324-9619; Fax: 501-324-9618; WWW: www.heritage.state.ar.us/nhc
Founded: 1973
Description: Responsible for system of natural areas; acquires and holds both lands and interests in land; maintains a registry of natural areas in other ownerships; maintains a Heritage Inventory System and environmental review and information sharing program; and defends natural areas from adverse influences.
Contact(s):
Chairman: HURLON RAY
Deputy Director: MINA MARSH; Email: mina@dah.state.ar.us
Executive Director: HAROLD K. GRIMMETT; Email: harold@dah.state.ar.us
Chief of Research: TOM FOTI; Email: tom@dah.state.ar.us
Coordinator of Environmental Applications: WILLIAM M. SHEPHERD; Email: bills@dah.state.ar.us
Coordinator of Stewardship: JOHN BENEKE; Email: johnb@dah.state.ar.us
Keyword(s): Biodiversity, Endangered and Threatened Species, Environmental Preservation, Land Purchase, Natural Areas, Rivers, Sustainable Ecosystems

PINE BLUFF COOPERATIVE FISHERY RESEARCH PROJECT
USGS-BRG-University of Arkansas, Ag. Exp. Station, 1200 N. University, P.O. Box 4005, Pine Bluff, AR 71611
Phone: 501-543-8136
Description: The Pine Bluff Cooperative Fishery Research Project is a cooperative educational effort between the U. S. Geological Survey-Biological Resources Division, Cooperative Research Units Division, and the University of Arkansas - Pine Bluff. The project provides undergraduate training in fisheries science and biology and conducts research on environmental problems, fisheries, and related topics.
Contact(s):
Project Leader: DR. WILLIAM G. LAYHER
Keyword(s): Endangered and Threatened Species, Environmental and Conservation Education, Environmental Law, Environmental Protection, Fisheries, Research, Rivers

STATE PLANT BOARD (ARKANSAS)
1 Natural Resources Dr., P.O. Box 1069, Little Rock, AR 72203
Phone: 501-225-1598
Contact(s):
Chairman: SHERMAN D. CULLUM
Director: GERALD KING

CALIFORNIA

GOVERNOR OF CALIFORNIA, GRAY DAVIS
State Capitol, Sacramento, CA 95814
Phone: 916-445-2841

CA DEPARTMENT OF EDUCATION, OFFICE OF ENVIRONMENTAL EDUCATION
721 Capitol Mall, P.O. Box 944272, Sacramento, CA 94244-2720
Founded: 1970
Description: The California Department of Education provides technical assistance and curriculum leadership in environmental education for counties and schools in California. The department offers an annual competitive grant program and provides curriculum and other publications related to environmental education in California.
Contact(s):
Environmental Education Consultant: BILL ANDREWS; Phone: 916-657-5374; Fax: 916-657-3682
Publication(s): *Endangered Species Resource Guide; Environmental Education Compendia on Air Quality, Energy Resources, Human Communities, Integrated Waste Management, Natural Communities, and Water Resources; A Child's Place in the Environment; Greatest Hits of Environmental Education*
Keyword(s): Air Quality and Pollution, Endangered and Threatened Species, Environmental and Conservation Education, Scholarships and Grants

CALIFORNIA ACADEMY OF SCIENCES

California Academy of Sciences Library
Golden Gate Park, San Francisco, CA 94118
Phone: 415-750-7102, 415-750-7361; Fax: 415-750-7106; Email: library@calacademy.org
Description: Library holdings included in: OCLC, University of California MELVYL on-line catalog, and California Union List of Periodicals. Noncirculating, closed-stack collection open to the public. Reference requests accepted by mail, phone, fax, or e-mail. Interlibrary loan requests accepted via OCLC, phone, mail, fax, or e-mail. Some pictoral items in Special Collections available for loan or duplication.
Contact(s):
Librarian: THOMAS D. MORITZ

CALIFORNIA COOPERATIVE FISHERY RESEARCH UNIT (USGS)
Fisheries Department, Humboldt State University, Arcata, CA 95521
Phone: 707-826-3268
Contact(s):
Leader: DR. WALTER G. DUFFY

CALIFORNIA ENVIRONMENTAL PROTECTION AGENCY
555 Capitol Mall, Suite 525, Sacramento, CA 95814
Founded: 1991
Description: The Secretary for Environmental Protection, a member of the Governor's Cabinet, serves as the Governor's principal advisor on environmental protection issues and oversees the activities of the Air Resources Board, Water Resources Control Board, and Integrated Waste Management Board, The Department of Toxic Substances Control, the Office of Environmental Health Hazard Assessment, and the Department of Pesticide Regulation.
Contact(s):
Secretary: PETER M. ROONEY; Phone: 916-445-3846
Deputy Secretary: CRAWFORD M. TUTTLE; Phone: 916-322-5844
Deputy Secretary of External Affairs: LOU SMALLWOOD; Phone: 916-323-2520
Deputy Secretary of Law Enforcement and Counsel: GERALD G. JOHNSTON; Phone: 916-327-2064
Deputy Secretary of Policy Development: ENRIQUE G. FARIAS; Phone: 916-324-8124

Director of Communications: JAMES SPAGNOLE; Phone: 916-324-9670
Director of Legislative: CHRIS REYNOLDS; Phone: 916-322-7315
Undersecretary: B. B. BLEVINS

California Air Resources Board
P.O. Box 2815, Sacramento, CA 95812
Phone: 916-322-2990
Founded: 1968
Description: The California Air Resources Board is responsible for the adoption and enforcement of the state's ambient air quality standards, rules, and regulations for the control of vehicular air pollution and toxic air contaminants throughout the state. Oversees the efforts of 34 air pollution control districts that regulate emissions from industrial facilities. Conducts studies of the causes of air pollution and evaluates its effort upon human, plant, and animal life. The Board is comprised of 11 members.
Contact(s):
Chairman of California Air Resources Board: JOHN D. DUNLAP III
Administrative Services Division Chief of the California Air Resources Board: LARRY MORRIS; Phone: 916-322-8198
Assistant Executive Officer of the California Air Resources Board: LYNN TERRY; Phone: 916-322-2739
Chief Deputy Executive Officer of the California Air Resources Board: TOM CACKETTE; Phone: 916-322-2892
Compliance Division Chief of the California Air Resources Board: JAMES J. MORGESTER; Phone: 916-322-6022
Deputy Executive Officer of the California Air Resources Board: MICHAEL SCHEIBLE; Phone: 916-322-2890
Executive Officer of the California Air Resources Board: MICHAEL P. KENNY; Phone: 916-445-4383
Legislative Office Chief of the California Air Resources Board: RON OGLESBY; Phone: 916-322-2896
Mobile Source Division Chief the California Air Resources Board: BOB CROSS; Phone: 818-575-6820
Monitoring and Laboratory Division Chief of the California Air Resources Board: WILLIAM V. LOSCUTOFF; Phone: 916-445-3742
Office of Legal Affairs General Counsel of the California Air Resources Board: KATHLEEN WALSH; Phone: 916-322-2884
Office of Ombudsman Chief of the California Air Resources Board: JIM SCHONING; Phone: 916-323-6791
Public Information Officer of the California Air Resources Board: JERRY MARTIN; Phone: 916-322-2990
Research Division Chief of the California Air Resources Board: DR. JOHN R. HOLMES; Phone: 916-445-0753
Stationary Source Division Chief of theCalifornia Air Resources Board: PETER D. VENTURINI; Phone: 916-445-0650
Technical Support Division Chief of the California Air Resources Board: TERRY W. McGUIRE; Phone: 916-322-5350

Department of Pesticide Regulation
830 K. St., Exec Office, Rm 307, Sacramento, CA 95814-3510
Phone: 916-445-4300
Description: The Department of Pesticide Regulation regulates all aspects of pesticides sales and use, recognizing the need to control pests, while protecting public health and the environment and fostering reduced-risk pest management strategies.
Contact(s):
Director: JAMES W. WELLS; Phone: 916-445-4000
Keyword(s): Air Quality and Pollution, Pesticides, Solid Waste Management, Toxic Substances, Water Pollution Management

Department of Toxic Substances Control
400 P St., 4th Fl., Sacramento, CA 95814
Phone: 916-323-9723
Description: Responsible for overseeing the cleanup of hazardous waste sites; monitoring and regulatory management of hazardous waste transportation, treatment, storage and disposal; and promotion of hazardous waste reduction in California.
Contact(s):
Deputy Director: SUE SIMS; Phone: 916-322-0449

Integrated Waste Management Board, IWMB
8800 Cal Center Dr., Sacramento, CA 95826
Founded: 1990
Description: The CIWMB is comprised of six members; four appointed by the governor and two by the legislature. CIWMB's goal is to protect the public's health and safety and the environment through waste prevention, waste diversion, and safe waste processing and disposal. Also, minimizing waste generation and disposal in California while facilitating the development of industries that use recyclable materials, will be realized by establishing sustainable markets for recyclable materials, reducing reliance on land disposal, and effectively educating the public.
Contact(s):
Assistant Director: JOHN FRITA; Phone: 916-255-2296

Office of Environmental Health Hazard Assessment
301 Capital Mall, Rm 205, Sacramento, CA 95815-4327
Phone: 916-324-7572
Description: The Office of Environmental Health Hazard Assessment is charged with assessing human health risks posed by chemicals in the environment. The office is also the lead agency for implementation of the Safe Drinking Water and Toxic Enforcement Act of 1986 (Proposition 65).
Contact(s):
Director: DR. JOAN E. DENPON

Water Resources Control Board
901 P St., P.O. Box 100, Sacramento, CA 95812-0100
Phone: 916-657-1247
Description: To protect water quality and allocate water rights. These objectives are achieved through two action programs: water quality and water rights.
Contact(s):
Deputy Director: DALE CLAYPOOLE
Executive Director: WALT PETTIT
Regional Executive Officer of the Central Coast Region: ROGER BRIGGS; Phone: 805-549-3147
Regional Executive Officer of the Central Valley Region: GARY CARLTON; Phone: 916-255-3000
Regional Executive Officer of the Colorado River Basin Region: PHIL GRUENBERG; Phone: 619-346-7491
Regional Executive Officer of the Lahonton Region: HAROLD SINGER; Phone: 916-542-5400
Regional Executive Officer of the Los Angeles Region: DENNIS DICKERSON; Phone: 213-266-7500
Regional Executive Officer of the North Coast Region: LEE MICHLIN; Phone: 707-576-2220
Regional Executive Officer of the San Diego Region: JOHN ROBERTUS; Phone: 619-467-2952
Regional Executive Officer of the San Francisco bay Region: LORETTA BARSAMILAN; Phone: 510-286-1255
Regional Executive Officer of the Santa Ana Region: GERALD THIBEAULT; Phone: 909-782-4130

CALIFORNIA SEA GRANT COLLEGE SYSTEM
California Sea Grant College, University of California, 9500 Gilman Dr., La Jolla, CA 92093-0232
Phone: 619-534-4440
Description: A multiuniversity program of marine research, extension services, and education that contributes to the growing body of knowledge about coastal and oceanic resources and helps solve contemporary problems in the marine sphere.
Contact(s):
Director: DR. JAMES J. SULLIVAN, California Sea Grant College System, University of California, 9500 Gilman Drive, La Jolla, CA 92093-0232; Phone: 619-534-4440; Fax: 619-534-2231
Coordinator of Sea Grant Extension Program: DR. CHRISTOPHER DEWEES, Cooperative Extension: University of California, Davis, CA 95616; Phone: 530-752-1497
Director of USC Sea Grant Program: DR. DOUGLAS SHERMAN, University of Southern California: University Park, LosAngeles, CA 90089-0373; Phone: 213-740-1961; Fax: 213-740-5936

STATE AND PROVINCE GOVERNMENT AGENCIES - CALIFORNIA

Leader of USC Sea Grant Marine Advisory Program and Associate Director of USC Sea Grant Program: DR. SUSAN YODER, USC Sea Grant Program Marine Advisory Service: University of Southern California: University Park, LosAngeles, CA 90089-0373; Phone: 213-740-1965; Fax: 213-740-5936
Publication(s): *Sea Grant in Brief*
Keyword(s): Biotechnology, Coasts, Fisheries, Water Resources, Wetlands

CALIFORNIA STATE EXTENSION SERVICES
Cooperative Extension and Agricultural Experiment Station, University of California, 300 Lakeside Dr., 6th Fl., Oakland, CA 94612-3560
Phone: 415-987-0060
Contact(s):
Vice President: W. R. GOMES, Agricultural and Natural Resources, Director, Cooperative Extension and Agricultural Experiment Station, Unversity of California, 300 Lakeside Drive, 6th Floor, Oakland, CA 94612-3560; Phone: 415-987-0060
Director: TERRELL P. SALMON, Associate Director CE Programs, Northern Region, University of California, Davis, CA 95616; Phone: 916-754-8491
Director: ALLYN D. SMITH, Associate Director CE Programs, Southern Region, 125 Highlander Hall, University of California, Riverside, CA 92521; Phone: 714-787-3321
Director: A. CHARLES CRABB, Associate Director CE Programs, South Central Region, Kearney Agricultural Center, 9240 S. Riverbend Ave., Parlier, CA 93648; Phone: 209-891-2566
Director: NICELMA J. KING, Associate Director CE, North Central Region, University of California, Davis, CA 95616; Phone: 916-754-8509
Associate Vice President and ANR Programs Associate Director: HENRY J. VAUX JR., Cooperative Extension and Agricultural Experiment Station: University of California: 300 Lakeside Dr.: 6th Fl., Oakland, CA 94612-3560; Phone: 415-987-0026
Dean: BENNIE OSBURN, Veterinary Medicine, University of California, Davis, CA 95616; Phone: 916-752-1360
Dean: BARBARA O. SCHNEEMAN, College of Agricultural and Environmental Sciences, Associate Director of AES Programs, University of California, Davis, CA 95616; Phone: 916-752-1605
Dean: GORDON C. RAUSSER, College of Natural Resources: Associate Director: AES Programs: University of California, Berkeley, CA 94720; Phone: 15-642-7171
Interim Dean: MICHAEL T. CLEGG, College of Natural and Agricultural Sciences, University of California, Riverside, CA 92521; Phone: 714-787-3101

DEPARTMENT OF FOOD AND AGRICULTURE (CALIFORNIA)
P.O. Box 942871, 1220 N St., Sacramento, CA 94271-0001
Phone: 916-654-0466
Description: To assure public health, safety, and welfare; protects agriculture by administering, directing and enforcing the state's agricultural laws and regulations.
Contact(s):
Secretary: ANN M. VENEMAN; Phone: 916-654-0433
Chief Counsel: FRANCINE KAMMEYER; Phone: 916-654-1393
Deputy Secretary: DARRELL GUENSLER; Phone: 916-654-0321
Director of Animal Industry: RICHARD BREITMEYER; Phone: 916-654-0881
Director of Fairs and Expositions: SHARON JENSEN; Phone: 916-263-2952
Director of Inspection Services: ROBERT WYNN; Phone: 916-654-0792
Director of Marketing Services: KELLY KRUG; Phone: 916-654-1240
Director of Measurement Standards: BARBARA BLOCH; Phone: 916-229-3000
Director of Plant Industry: ISI SIDDIQUI; Phone: 916-654-0317
Legislative Director: GREG HARNER; Phone: 916-654-0326
Policy and Planning Assistant Secretary: NITA VAIL; Phone: 916-653-7643
Public Affairs Assistant Secretary: KEVIN HERGLOTZ; Phone: 916-654-0462
Undersecretary: A. J. YATES; Phone: 916-654-0321

GOVERNOR'S OFFICE OF PLANNING AND RESEARCH (CALIFORNIA)
1400 10th St., Sacramento, CA 95814
Phone: 916-322-2318
Founded: 1970
Description: Primary areas of concentration are the development of environmental and related land use goals and policies; growth management; evaluation of state plans and programs; and preparation of statewide environmental goals and policies statements.
Contact(s):
Acting Director: PAUL F. MINER
Keyword(s): Environmental Planning, Geography, Land Use Planning, Planning Management, Population Growth

RESOURCES AGENCY, THE
1416 9th St., Rm. 1311, Sacramento, CA 95814
Phone: 916-653-5656
Description: Responsible for ensuring an adequate and properly balanced management of government functions related to California's natural environment.
Contact(s):
Assistant Secretary of Administration and Finance: DON WALLACE
Assistant Secretary of Conservation Programs: DEBBIE DRAKE
Deputy Assistant of Communications: SANTANA GARCIA
Deputy Secretary for Legislative Affairs: JULIE MacDONALD
Deputy Secretary for Operations: JIM YOUNGSON
General Counsel: MAUREEN GORSEN
Secretary of Resources: DOUGLAS P. WHEELER
Under Secretary of Resources: MICHAEL A. MANTELL

California Coastal Commission
45 Fremont St., Suites 1900 and 2000, San Francisco, CA 94105-2219
Phone: 415-904-5200; Fax: 415-904-5400
Description: A coastal management agency which carries out mandated policies on coastal conservation and development through regulation and planning programs. These policies deal with public access to the coast, coastal recreation, the California marine environment, coastal land resources, and coastal development of various types, including power plant and other energy installation.
Contact(s):
Executive Director: PETER DOUGLAS
Assistant Deputy Director of Land Use: STEVE SCHOLL
Chief of Administrative Services Division: LANE YEE
Chief of Deputy Director: JAMES W. BURNS
Chief of Staff Counsel: RALPH FAUST
Deputy Director of Energy and Ocean Resources and Technical Services Division: SUSAN HANSCH
Legislative Liaison of Sacramento: CA: JEFF STUMP; Phone: 916-445-6067
Public Education and Activities Coordinator: CHRISTIANE PARRY

California Coastal Conservancy
1330 Broadway, Suite 1100, Oakland, CA 94612
Phone: 510-286-1015; Fax: 510-286-0470
Description: A state agency using planning, land-use conflict resolution, acquisition, and development techniques in the restoration, enhancement, and preservation of coastal resources. Program areas include agricultural preservation, lot consolidation, urban waterfront restoration, coastal resource enhancement, the reservation of significant resource sites, provision of public access, and assistance to nonprofit organizations.
Contact(s):
Interim Executive Officer: STEVE HORN
Publication(s): *Coast and Ocean*

STATE AND PROVINCE GOVERNMENT AGENCIES - CALIFORNIA

California Conservation Corps
1530 Capitol Ave., Sacramento, CA 95814
Phone: 916-445-0307
Founded: 1976
Description: The CCC was created with a dual mission: the employment and development of the state's youth, and the protection and enhancement of California's natural resources. Some 42 million hours of public service conservation work and emergency assistance have been provided by the Corps in its twenty years of existence.
Contact(s):
Director: AL ARAMBURU
Deputy Director of External Affairs: JOHN COLEMAN
Deputy Director of Program Support: KAREN MEYRELES
Regional Deputy Director: WALT HUGHES
Regional Deputy Director: PAUL CARRILLO
Regional Deputy Director: TOM POWERS
Regional Deputy Director: STEW OGBURN
Special Assistant to the Director: CRAIG MILLER

California Energy Commission
1516 9th St., Sacramento, CA 95814
Phone: 916-654-4287; Fax: 916-654-4420
Founded: 1975
Description: To ensure continuation of a reliable and affordable supply of energy for California at a level consistent with the state's needs.
Contact(s):
Chairman: CHARLES R. IMBRECHT; Phone: 916-654-5000
Deputy Director (Acting) of Administrative Services: CYNTHIA HOBSON; Phone: 916-654-5204; Fax: 916-654-4423
Deputy Director of Energy Efficiency Division: ROSS DETER; Phone: 916-654-5013; Fax: 916-654-4304
Deputy Director of Energy Facilities Siting and Environmental Protection Division: ROBERT L. THERKELSEN; Phone: 916-654-3924; Fax: 916-654-3882
Deputy Director of Energy Forecasting Resource Assessment Division: DAN NIX; Phone: 916-654-4861; Fax: 916-654-4559
Deputy Director of Energy Technology Division: NANCY DELLER; Phone: 916-654-4628; Fax: 916-654-4676
Executive Director (Acting): KENT SMITH; Phone: 916-654-4996
Vice Chair: DAVID A. ROHY; Phone: 916-654-4930
Vice Chair: JANANNE SHARPLESS; Phone: 916-654-5036
Vice Chair: SALLY RAKOW; Phone: 916-654-3992

California Water Commission
1416 9th St., Rm. 1148, Sacramento, CA 95814
Phone: 916-653-5958; Fax: 916-653-9745
Founded: 1913
Description: Serves as a policy advisory body to the Director of Water Resources on matters within the Department's jurisdiction and coordinates state and local views on federal appropriations for water projects in California. The commission also conducts public hearings and investigations statewide for the department and provides an open forum for interested citizens to voice their opinion on water development issues.
Contact(s):
Executive Officer: RAYMOND E. BARSCH
Keyword(s): Fisheries, Flood Control, Rivers, Water Resources, Watersheds, Wetlands

Colorado River Board of California
770 Fairmont Ave., Suite 100, Glendale, CA 91203-1035
Phone: 818-543-4676
Founded: 1937
Description: The board was established to represent California, its agencies, and citizens in matters concerning the water and power resources provided by the Colorado River and its tributaries. Working with federal and state agencies, Congress, courts, and other Colorado River Basin states, the board analyzes engineering, legal, and economic matters concerning the use of Colorado River resources within the United States.
Contact(s):
Executive Director: GERALD R. ZIMMERMAN

Department of Boating and Waterways
1629 S St., Sacramento, CA 95814
Phone: 916-445-6281; Fax: 916-327-7250
Description: Makes loans to public agencies and small businesses for small craft harbor development and grants to public agencies for boat-launching facilities, floating restrooms, and vessel waste disposal equipment; licenses yacht and ship brokers and for-hire vessel operators; conducts programs of boating safety, education, and regulation; and grants funds to local entities for boating law enforcement activities. Participates with the Corps of Engineers and local agencies in the construction of beach erosion control projects, assists local jurisdictions in obtaining the greatest benefits available from federal beach erosion programs, and conducts an aquatic pest control program in the Sacramento-San Joaquin Delta.
Contact(s):
Director: CHARLES F. RAYSBROOK
Chief of Administrative Services Division: DEBRA DeVERTER; Phone: 916-445-2671
Chief of Boating Facilities Division: DON WALTZ; Phone: 916-322-1801
Chief of Boating Operations Division: DOLORES FARRELL; Phone: 916-322-1826
Keyword(s): Coasts, Grants, Lakes, Oceanography, Outdoor Recreation

Department of Conservation
801 K St., MS 24-01, Sacramento, CA 95814
Phone: 916-322-1080; Fax: 916-445-0732
Description: The department acts as a steward and guardian of California's earth resources through the promotion of conservation and wise use of the state's land, energy, and mineral resources.
Contact(s):
Deputy Director: PAT MEEHAN
Director: LAWRENCE GOLDZBAND; Email: goldzban@www.consrv.ca.gov
Chief Deputy Director: B. B. BLEVNS

Department of Fish and Game
1416 9th St., Sacramento, CA 95814
Phone: 916-653-7664; Fax: 916-653-1856
Description: Responsible for the protection and management of fish and wildlife and threatened native plants in California. Enforces the laws pertaining to fish and game and threatened native plants enacted by the legislature and the regulations of the Fish and Game Commission.
Contact(s):
Director: JACQUELINE E. SCHAFER; Phone: 916-653-7667
Chief Deputy Director: RYAN BRODDRICK; Phone: 916-653-7556
Deputy Director of Administration: R. A. BERNHEIMER; Phone: 916-653-4633
Deputy Director of Habitat Conservation Division: RYAN BRODDRICK; Phone: 916-653-4207
Central Valley Bay-Delta-Chief: PERRY HERRGESELL; Phone: 209-948-7800
Habitat Conservation Planning-Chief: RON REMPEL; Phone: 562-590-5113
Water & Aquatic Habitat Conservation-Chief: JIM STEELE; Phone: 916-653-2459
Watershed Restoration-Chief: TIM FARLEY; Phone: 916-653-6194
General Counsel: LINUS MASOUREDIS; Phone: 916-653-6194
Deputy Director of Legislation and Intergoverernmental Affairs: KASSANDRA GOUGH; Phone: 916-653-4633
Intergovernmental Affairs Representative: L. B. BOYDSTUN; Phone: 916-653-3136
Legislative Representative: JULIE E. OLTMANN; Phone: 916-653-5581
Administrator for Spill Prevention and Response Division: PETE BONTADELLI; Phone: 916-445-9338

STATE AND PROVINCE GOVERNMENT AGENCIES - CALIFORNIA

Deputy Director of Wildlife and Inland Fisheries Division: TERRY MANSFIELD; Phone: 916-653-6184
Conservation Education & Enforcement-Chief: RICH ELLIOTT; Phone: 916-653-4094
Fisheries Programs-Chief: GENE FLEMING; Phone: 916-653-4280
Lands & Facilities-Chief: RON PELZMAN; Phone: 916-653-4899
Wildlife Programs-Chief: DAVE ZEZULAK; Phone: 916-653-7203

Department of Forestry and Fire Protection
1416 9th St., P.O. Box 944246, Sacramento, CA 94244-2460
Phone: 916-653-5121

Description: The CDF is responsible for the fire protection, fire prevention, maintenance, and enhancement of the state's forest, range, and brushland resources, including enforcement of the Z'berg-Nejedly Forest Practice Act and other related forest and fire laws, forest pest control, contract fire protection, associated emergency services, and assistance in civil disasters and other nonfire emergencies. The CDF is also responsible for the administration of forest practice rules, forest advisory services, and underwriting forest and fire research programs.

Contact(s):
Director: RICHARD A. WILSON; Phone: 916-653-7772
Chief Deputy Director and State Fire Marshall: RONNY J. COLEMAN; Phone: 916-653-7097
Deputy of Fire Protection: JAMES E. OWEN; Phone: 916-653-9424
Deputy of Public Affairs, Public Education, and Legislation (Acting): JOHN B. ALLARD II; Phone: 916-653-1586
Deputy of Resource Management and Management Services: CRAIG E. ANTHONY; Phone: 916-653-4298

Department of Parks and Recreation
1416 9th St., P.O. Box 942896, Sacramento, CA 94296-0001
Phone: 916-653-8380

Description: Responsible for the acquisition, preservation, development, interpretation, and operation of the state park system; also responsible for the administration of grants for recreation to local government and for development of the California Outdoor Recreation Resources Plan.

Contact(s):
Director: PATRICIA J. MEGASON; Phone: 916-653-8380
Chief of Environmental Design Division: ROBERT D. CATES; Phone: 916-653-7475
Chief of Northern Division: CARL CHAVEZ; Phone: 916-657-4042
Chief of Park Services Division: TED CRANE; Phone: 916-653-2021
Chief of Resource Management Division: RICHARD G. RAYBURN; Phone: 916-653-6745
Chief of Southern Division: DICK TROY; Phone: 916-657-4042
Deputy Director of Administration: DENZIL VERARDO; Phone: 916-653-0528
Deputy Director of Historic Preservation Office: CHERILYN E. WIDELL; Phone: 916-653-6624
Deputy Director of Marketing and Revenue Generation: KAREN COLLINS
Deputy Director of Off Highway Motor Vehicle Recreation: CLIFFORD GLIDDEN; Phone: 916-324-4442
Deputy Director of Park Stewardship: KEN JONES; Phone: 916-653-8288
Deputy Director of Public Policy and Legislation: CINDY SHAMROCK; Phone: 916-653-6887
Human Resources: RAY ANN WATSON; Phone: 916-653-9990
Legal Office: TIM LAFRANCH; Phone: 916-653-6884

Department of Water Resources
1416 9th St., P.O. Box 942836, Sacramento, CA 94236-0001
Phone: 916-653-5791

Description: To manage the water resources of California in cooperation with other agencies, to benefit the state's people, and to protect, restore, and enhance the natural and human environments.

Contact(s):
Deputy Director: STEPHEN L. KASHIWADA; Phone: 916-653-7092
Director: DAVID N. KENNEDY; Phone: 916-653-7007
Assistant Director of Legislation: L. LUCINDA CHIPPONERI; Phone: 196-653-0488
Chief Counsel: SUSAN N. WEBER; Phone: 916-653-6186
Chief Deputy Director: ROBERT G. POTTER; Phone: 916-653-6055
District Chief of Central (Acting): KARL P. WINKLER; Phone: 916-227-7550
District Chief of Northern: WILLIAM J. BENNETT; Phone: 916-529-7342
District Chief of San Joanquin: LOUIS A. BECK; Phone: 209-445-5222
District Chief of Southern: CHARLES R. WHITE; Phone: 818-543-4600
Division of Engineering: ARNOLD W. JOHNSON; Phone: 916-653-3927
Division of Fiscal Services: CHESTER M. WINN; Phone: 916-653-4413
Division of Flood Management: GEORGE QUALLEY; Phone: 916-653-7572
Division of Land and Right of Way: FRANK CONTI; Phone: 916-653-7891
Division of Local Assistance: RAY HART, 1020 9th St., Sacramento, CA 95814; Phone: 916-327-1646
Division of Management Services: WILLIAM H. FRYE; Phone: 916-653-6743
Division of Operations and Maintenance: EDWARD F. HUNTLEY; Phone: 916-653-8583
Division of Planning: KATHLIN R. JOHNSON; Phone: 916-653-1099
Division of Safety of Dams: VERNON H. PERSSON; Phone: 916-445-7606
Environmental Services Office: RANDALL L. BROWN, 3252 S St., Sacramento, CA 95816; Phone: 916-227-7531
Office of Water Education: ANITA GARCIA-FANTE; Phone: 196-653-7431

Fish and Game Commission
1416 9th St., Rm. 1320, P.O. Box 944209, Sacramento, CA 94244-2090
Phone: 916-653-4899

Founded: 1870

Description: Adopts fish, game, and plant regulations as authorized by the Fish and Game Code and sets policies for the Department of Fish and Game.

Contact(s):
President: RICHARD T. THIEROIT
Executive Director: ROBERT R. TREANOR

Native American Heritage Commission
915 Capitol Mall, Rm. 364, Sacramento, CA 95814
Phone: 916-653-4082

Contact(s):
Executive Secretary: LARRY MYERS

San Francisco Bay Conservation and Development Commission
30 Van Ness Ave., Suite 2011, San Francisco, CA 94102
Phone: 415-557-3686

Founded: 1965

Description: To implement a planning and regulatory program designed to conserve and use beneficially the environmental, economic, social, and aesthetic values of San Francisco Bay through carefully considered and democratically determined policies. Composed of 27 commissioners, representing the public and state, federal, and local governmental agencies.

Contact(s):
Chairman: ROBERT TUFTS
Deputy Director: STEVE McADAM
Executive Director: WILL TRAVIS
Chief Planner: JEFFRY BLANCHFIELD

State Reclamation Board
1416 9th St., Rm. 1148, Sacramento, CA 95814
Phone: 916-653-5434; Fax: 916-653-5434

Founded: 1911

Description: Agency provides flood protection along the Sacramento and San Joaquin Rivers and their tributaries by

planning, constructing, operating, and maintaining flood control projects in cooperation with local, state, and federal agencies, and by implementing nonstructural flood control measures.
Contact(s):
President: FRANK DAL GALLO
Vice President: BARBARA LeVAKE
Secretary: BRENDA JAHNS
General Manager: PETER D. RABBON

Wildlife Conservation Board
801 K St., Suite 806, Sacramento, CA 95814
Phone: 916-445-8448; Fax: 916-323-0280
Founded: 1947
Description: In concert with the Department of Fish and Game, the board authorizes the acquisition, restoration, and enhancement of land and water for wildlife conservation and related recreational purposes. The board also administers the Inland Wetlands Conservation Program and the California Riparian Habitat Conservation Program to protect, restore, and enhance wetland and riparian habitats.
Contact(s):
Executive Director: W. JOHN SCHMIDT
Assistant Executive Director of Development Program: GEORGIA LIPPHARDT
Assistant Executive Director of Land Acquisition: JAMES V. SARRO

STATE LANDS COMMISSION (CALIFORNIA)
100 Howe Ave., Suite 100 S., Sacramento, CA 95825
Phone: 916-574-1800
Description: Jurisdiction over and management responsibility for state-owned sovereign and congressional grant lands. Handles related land leases, exchanges, and transactions. Conducts oil, gas, geothermal, and other mineral leasing programs. Related activity involves boundary and ownership determination, granted lands administration, and maintaining land information system.
Contact(s):
Assistant Executive Officer: GARY GREGORY; Phone: 916-574-1800
Assistant Executive Officer: PAUL THAYER; Phone: 916-574-1800
Chief Counsel: JACK RUMP; Phone: 916-574-1850
Chief of Division of Environmental Planning and Management: DWIGHT E. SANDERS; Phone: 916-574-1890
Chief of Division of Land Management and Conservation: ROBERT LYNCH; Phone: 916-574-1940
Chief of Mineral Resources Division: PAUL MOUNT, 200 Oceangate: 12th Fl., LongBeach, CA 90802; Phone: 310-590-5205
Executive Officer: ROBERT C. HIGHT; Phone: 916-574-1800
Legislative Liaison: WILLIAM V. MORRISON; Phone: 916-574-1800
Lieutenant Governor of Finance: GRAY DAVIS
State Controller: KATHLEEN CONNELL
State Director of Finance: CRAIG L. BROWN
Keyword(s): Public Lands

COLORADO

GOVERNOR OF COLORADO, BILL OWENS
Governor of Colorado, 136 State Capitol, Denver, CO 80203
Phone: 303-866-2471

COLORADO COOPERATIVE FISH AND WILDLIFE RESEARCH UNIT (USDI)
201 Wagar Bldg., Dept. of Fishery and Wildlife Biology, Colorado State University, Ft. Collins, CO 80523-1484
Phone: 970-491-5396
Founded: 1947
Description: Offers expertise and training facilities in fish and wildlife population ecology, aquatic habitat analysis, conservation biology, sampling and analysis theory, and biostatistics.
Contact(s):
Assistant Leader: DR. KENNETH P. BURNHAM
Assistant Leader: DR. ERIC P. BERGERSEN
Leader: DR. DAVID R. ANDERSON
Keyword(s): Birds, Endangered and Threatened Species, Fish Wildlife Management, Fisheries, Nongame Wildlife, Whirling Disease

COLORADO DEPARTMENT OF AGRICULTURE
700 Kipling St., Suite 4000, Lakewood, CO 80215
Phone: 303-239-4100
Founded: 1949
Description: Strives to meet the increasingly complex needs of agriculture through work on marketing problems, technological changes in pest and insect control, and rapidly changing patterns in crop and livestock operations.
Contact(s):
Brand Commissioner of Board of Stock Inspection Division: GARY SHOUN
Commission Chairman: DALE DE JACAMO
Commissioner: THOMAS A. KOURLIS
Deputy Commissioner: ROBERT G. McLAVEY
Director of Animal Industry Division: JOHN GERHARDT
Director of Division of Inspection and Consumer Services: RONALD TURNER
Director of Markets Development Division: JIM RUBINGH
Director of Plant Industry Division: JOHN GERHARDT
Resource Analyst: DAVID CARLSON
Keyword(s): Agriculture, Environmental and Conservation Education, Pesticides, Public Lands, Toxicology

COLORADO DEPARTMENT OF EDUCATION
201 E. Colfax Ave., State Office Bldg., Denver, CO 80203
Phone: 303-866-6787; Fax: 303-866-6836
Description: Conservation Education Services, jointly with the Division of Wildlife.
Contact(s):
Environmental Education Consultant: DON HOLLUMS; Phone: 303-866-6787
Keyword(s): Environmental and Conservation Education, Environmental Ethics, Pollution Prevention, Urban Environment, Wildlife and Wildlife Habitat

COLORADO DEPARTMENT OF NATURAL RESOURCES
1313 Sherman, Rm. 718, Denver, CO 80203
Phone: 303-866-3311; Fax: 303-866-2115
Founded: 1968
Description: Responsible for mineral and energy, land, water, wildlife, and park resources management for the state. Also responsible for major environmental conservation and management programs.
Contact(s):
Deputy Director: RONALD W. CATTANY
Executive Director: JAMES S. LOCHHEAD
Human Resources Director: CINDY HORIUCHI

Colorado Geologic Survey
1313 Sherman St., Rm. 715, Denver, CO 80203
Phone: 303-866-2611; Fax: 303-866-2461
Contact(s):
State Geologist: VICKI COWART

Division of Minerals and Geology
1313 Sherman St., Rm. 215, Denver, CO 80203
Phone: 303-866-3567; Fax: 303-832-8106
Contact(s):
Director: MICHAEL B. LONG

Division of Parks and Outdoor Recreation
1313 Sherman St., Rm. 618, Denver, CO 80203
Phone: 303-866-3437; Fax: 303-866-3206
Contact(s):
Director: LAURIE MATHEWS

STATE AND PROVINCE GOVERNMENT AGENCIES - CONNECTICUT

Division of Water Resources
1313 Sherman St., Rm. 818, Denver, CO 80203
Phone: 303-866-3581; Fax: 303-866-3589
Contact(s):
State Engineer: HAROLD SIMPSON

Division of Wildlife
6060 Broadway, Denver, CO 80216
Phone: 303-297-1192; Fax: 303-294-0894
Contact(s):
Director: JOHN MUMMA

Oil and Gas Conservation Commission
1120 Lincoln St., Suite 801, Denver, CO 80203
Phone: 303-894- 2100; Fax: 303-894-2109
Contact(s):
Director: RICHARD GRIEBLING

Soil Conservation Board
1313 Sherman St., Rm. 219, Denver, CO 80203-2243
Phone: 303-866-3351; Fax: 303-832-8106
Contact(s):
President: HARLEY ERNST, 2860 Rd QQ, Flagler, CO 80815; Phone: 970-357-4258
Director: MAX VEZZANI; Email: maxvezzani@state.co.us

State Board of Land
1313 Sherman St., Rm. 620, Denver, CO 80203
Phone: 303-866-3454; Fax: 303-866-3152
Contact(s):
President: MAXINE STEWART
Director: MAX VEZZANT

Water Conservation Board
1313 Sherman St., Rm. 721, Denver, CO 80203
Phone: 303-866-3441; Fax: 303-866-4474
Contact(s):
Director: DARIES LILE
Keyword(s): Environmental and Conservation Education, Outdoor Recreation, Public Lands, Water Resources, Wildlife Management

COLORADO DEPARTMENT OF PUBLIC HEALTH AND ENVIRONMENT
4300 Cherry Creek Dr., S., Denver, CO 80246-1530
Phone: 303-692-2000
Description: The Colorado Department of Public Health and Environment has the responsibility for improving and protecting the health and environment for Colorado's citizens by: assuring a healthy working and living environment, protecting people against exposure to diseases, establishing preventive health services, and providing a quality environment through air, waste, water, radiation, and other environmental protection activities.
Contact(s):
Executive Director: PATTI SHWAYDER

COLORADO STATE COOPERATIVE EXTENSION
1 Administration Bldg., Colorado State University, Ft. Collins, CO 80523
Phone: 970-491-6281
Founded: 1915
Description: A branch of Colorado State University. Conducts statewide noncredit educational programs off campus.
Contact(s):
Associate Director of Programs: DR. MARY McPHAIL GRAY, 1 Administration Bldg.: Colorado State University, Ft.Collins, CO 80523; Phone: 970-491-6281
Director of Cooperative Extension: MILAN A. REWERTS
Extension Agent-Natural Resources: NANCY ZUSCHLAG, 15200 W. Sixth Ave., Golden, CO 80401; Phone: 303-271-6620
Extension Wildlife Specialist: Animal Damage Control: DR. WILLIAM F. ANDELT, Dept. of Fishery and Wildlife Biology: 109 Wagar: Colorado State University, Ft.Collins, CO 80523; Phone: 970-491-7093
Extension Wildlife Specialist: Wildlife Management: DR. DELWIN E. BENSON, Dept. of Fishery and Wildlife Biology: 109 Wagar: Colorado State University, Ft.Collins, CO 80523; Phone: 970-491-6411
Keyword(s): Agriculture, Biotechnology, Environmental and Conservation Education, Gardening and Horticulture, Health and Nutrition, Hunting, Outdoor Recreation, Pesticides, Precision Farming, Renewable Resources, Rural Development, Solid Waste Management, Sustainable Development, Sustainable Ecosystems, Urban Environment

COLORADO STATE FOREST SERVICE
Forestry Bldg., Colorado State University, Ft. Collins, CO 80523
Phone: 970-491-6303; Fax: 970-491-7736
Founded: 1885
Description: The mission of the State Forest Service is to achieve stewardship of Colorado's environment through forestry outreach and service.
Contact(s):
Assistant State Forester: BILL WILCOX
Community Forestry: PHIL HOEFER
Conservation Education: BOB STURTEVANT
Forest Management: PHIL SCHWOLERT
State Forester: JAMES E. HUBBARD
Wildfire Protection: RICH HOMANN
Keyword(s): Environmental and Conservation Education, Forests and Forestry, Land Use Planning, Sustainable Ecosystems, Urban Forestry

GOVERNOR'S OFFICE OF ENERGY CONSERVATION (COLORADO)
1675 Broadway Suite 1300, Denver, CO 80202-4613
Phone: 303-620-4288; Email: oec@c5n.net; WWW: www.state.co.u5/gov_dir/energy_gov.html
Founded: 1977
Description: OEC's mission includes leading the citizens of Colorado by promoting the efficient use of energy and resources. OEC develops, implements, and monitors energy conservation programs and offers services for individuals, community organizations, institutions, businesses, and government. Those services are designed to reduce energy consumption and increase awareness of the environmental, economic, and personal benefit to efficient energy use.
Contact(s):
Deputy Director: SHEILA TON
Deputy Director: TOM BROTHERTON
Director: WADE BUCHANAN
ROB DESOTO
Publication(s): *Recycle Colorado Bulletin*
Keyword(s): Energy, Environmental and Conservation Education, Renewable Resources, Solar Energy, Solid Waste Management

CONNECTICUT

GOVERNOR OF CONNECTICUT, JOHN G. ROWLAND
210 Capitol Ave., Hartford, CT 06106
Phone: 203-566-4840

CONNECTICUT DEPARTMENT OF AGRICULTURE
165 Capitol Ave., Rm. 273, State Office Bldg., Hartford, CT 6106
Phone: 203-566-4667
Contact(s):
Commissioner: SHIRLEY FERRIS
Deputy Director: Marketing and Technology: FRANK A. INTINO; Phone: 860-566-2683
Deputy Director: Regulation and Inspection: GABRIEL F. MOQUIN; Phone: 860-566-5894
Director: Administration: DAWN L. CASSADA; Phone: 860-566-5972

Director: Aquaculture Division: JOHN VOLK, P.O. Box 97, Milford, CT 06460; Phone: 860-874-2855
Director: Farmland Preservation: JOSEPH J. DIPPEL; Phone: 860-566-3227
Director: Marketing and Technology: ROBERT R. PELLEGRINO; Phone: 860-566-4845
Director: Personnel: EMILIE M. ANDREWS; Phone: 860-566-1911
Director: Regulation and Inspection: DR. BRUCE A. SHERMAN; Phone: 860-566-4268
Executive Director: Connecticut Marketing Authority: ROBERT BADAL, 101 Reserve Rd., Hartford, CT 06106; Phone: 860-566-3699
State Veterinarian: DR. JACK MEISTER; Phone: 860-566-4616

COUNCIL ON ENVIRONMENTAL QUALITY (CONNECTICUT)
79 Elm Street, Hartford, CT 6106
Phone: 860-424-4000; Fax: 860-424-4070; Email: karl.wagener@po.state.ct.us
Founded: 1971
Description: Prepares annual reports to the Governor on the status of Connecticut's environment; receives and investigates citizen complaints pertaining to the environment; and reviews environmental assessments of construction activities of state agencies. The council is composed of nine appointed members who serve without compensation.
Contact(s):
Chairman: DONAL C. O'BRIEN JR.
Executive Director: KARL J. WAGENER
Publication(s): *Environmental Quality in Connecticut (Annual Report)*
Keyword(s): Environment, Environmental Planning, Environmental Protection, Land Use Planning

DEPARTMENT OF ENVIRONMENTAL PROTECTION (CONNECTICUT)
79 Elm St., Hartford, CT 06106-5127
Description: Created by the Connecticut General Assembly to conserve, protect, and improve the state's environment and to manage the basic resources of air, water, and land for the benefit of present and future generations.
Contact(s):
Assistant Commissioner, Air, Water and Waste: JANE STAHL; Phone: 860-424-3009
Assistant Commissioner, Environemental Conservations: DAVID K. LEFF; Phone: 860-424-3005
Chief: Bureau of Air Management: CARMINE N. DIBATTISTA; Phone: 860-424-3026
Chief: Bureau of Natural Resources: EDWARD C. PARKER; Phone: 860-424-3010
Chief: Bureau of Outdoor Recreation: RICHARD K. CLIFFORD; Phone: 860-424-3014
Chief: Bureau of Waste Management: RICHARD J. BARLOW; Phone: 860-424-3021
Chief: Bureau of Water Management: ROBERT L. SMITH; Phone: 860-424-3704
Commissioner: ARTHUR J. ROCQUE JR; Phone: 860-424-3001
Director: Communications: Education: and Publications: MICHELE SULLIVAN; Phone: 860-424-4100
Director: Fisheries Division: ERNEST E. BECKWITH; Phone: 860-424-3474
Director: Forestry Division: DONALD H. SMITH; Phone: 860-424-3630
Director: Land Acquisition and Management: CHARLES J. REED; Phone: 860-424-3016
Director: Law Enforcement Division: GEORGE J. BARONE JR.; Phone: 860-424-3012
Director: Natural Resources Center: STEVEN O. FISH; Phone: 860-424-3642
Director: Parks Division: PAMELA A. ADAMS; Phone: 860-424-3200
Director: Wildlife Division: DALE W. MAY; Phone: 860-424-3011
Staff: DALE MAY; Phone: 860-424-3011
Publication(s): *Connecticut Wildlife*

UNIVERSITY OF CONNECTICUT COOPERATIVE EXTENSION
College of Agriculture and Natural Resources, Box U-66, 1376 Storrs Rd., Univesity of Connecticut, Storrs, CT 06269-4066
Description: Natural resource components includes forest management, forest stewardship, urban forestry, water resources, and wildlife managment.
Contact(s):
Extension Educator: Forest Managment: STEPHEN BRODERICK, 139 Wolf Den Rd., Brooklyn, CT 06234; Phone: 203-774-9600
Extension Specialist: Water Resources: DR. GLENN WARNER, Natural Resources Managment and Engineering: Box U-87: University of Connecticut, Storrs, CT 06269-4087; Phone: 203-486-2840
Extension Specialist: Wildlife: DR. JOHN S. BARCLAY, Natural Resources Management and Engineering: Box U-87: University of Connecticut, Storrs, CT 06269-4087; Phone: 203-486-2840
Program Leader: Marine Advisory Program: NORMAN BENDER, University of CT-MAS: 1084 Shennecossett Rd., Groton, CT 06340-6097; Phone: 203-445-8664
State Climatologist: DR. DAVID R. MILLER, Natural Resources Management and Engineering: Box U-87: University of Connecticut, Storrs, CT 06269-4087; Phone: 203-486-2840

DELAWARE

GOVERNOR OF DELAWARE, THOMAS R. CARPER
Tatnall Bldg., William Penn St., Dover, DE 19901
Phone: 302-739-4101

DELAWARE DEPARTMENT OF AGRICULTURE
2320 S. DuPont Highway, Dover, DE 19901-5515
Phone: 302-739-4811
Description: The DDA works to provide mandated services which protect the health and welfare of Delaware consumers and to advertise those services; to promote the sound utilization of resources, especially agricultural lands; and to advance the economic viability of the food, fiber, and agricultural industries of Delaware.
Contact(s):
Secretary: JOHN F. TARBURTON: JR.
Agriculture Compliance Laboratory: TERESA CRENSHAW
Community Relations Officer: ANNE FITZGERALD
Deputy Secretary: SUSAN STUCHLIK-EDWARDS
Executive Assistant: DAVE HILL
Keyword(s): Agriculture, Forests and Forestry, Land Use Planning, Pesticides, Urban Forestry

DELAWARE DEPARTMENT OF NATURAL RESOURCES AND ENVIRONMENTAL CONTROL
89 Kings Highway, Dover, DE 19901
Founded: 1970
Description: The mission of the Delaware Department of Natural Resources and Environmental Control is to protect and manage the state's natural resources, protect public health and safety, provide quality outdoor recreation and to serve and educate the citizens of Delaware to promote the wise use, conservation, and enhancement of Delaware's environment.
Contact(s):
Secretary: CHRISTOPHE A.G. TULOU; Phone: 302-739-4403
Deputy Secretary: MARY McKENZIE; Phone: 302-739-4403
Editor: KATHLEEN JAMISON; Phone: 302-739-4506
Office of Information and Education: DAVID SMALL; Phone: 302-739-4506
Publication(s): *Outdoor Delaware*

Division of Air and Waste Management
89 Kings Hwy., P.O. Box 1401, Dover, DE 19903
Contact(s):
Director: NICHOLAS DiPASQUALE; Phone: 302-739-4764
Administrator: Air Resources: DARRYL TYLER; Phone: 302-739-4791

STATE AND PROVINCE GOVERNMENT AGENCIES - DISTRICT OF COLUMBIA

Program Manager: Hazardous Waste Branch: NANCY MARKER; Phone: 302-739-3689

Division of Fish and Wildlife
89 Kings Hwy., P.O. Box 1401, Dover, DE 19903
Contact(s):
Director: ANDREW T. MANUS; Phone: 302-739-5295
Administrator: Enforcement: JAMES GRAYBEAL; Phone: 302-739-3440
Administrator: Fisheries: CHARLES A. LESSER; Phone: 302-739-3441
Administrator: Mosquito Control: CHESTER J. STACHECKI; Phone: 302-739-3493
Administrator: Wildlife: H. LLOYD ALEXANDER JR.; Phone: 302-739-5297
Federal Aid Coordinator and Senior Planner: LYNN HERMAN; Phone: 302-739-5296
Manager: Acquisition/Construction: LACY NICHOLS; Phone: 302-739-3441

Division of Parks and Recreation
89 Kings Hwy., P.O. Box 1401, Dover, DE 19903
Contact(s):
Director: CHARLES SALKIN; Phone: 302-739-4401
Manager: Cultural & Recreation Services: JAMES O'NEILL; Phone: 302-739-4413
Manager: Park Operations: CLYDE SHIPMAN; Phone: 302-739-4406
Manager: Planning: Preservation and Development: MARK R. CHURA; Phone: 302-739-5285

Division of Soil and Water Conservation
Phone: 302-739-4411; Fax: 302-739-6724
Contact(s):
Director: JOHN A. HUGHES; Email: jhughes@dnrec.state.de.us
Administrator: Conservation Districts: KEVIN DONNELLY
Administrator: Delaware Coastal Management Program: SARAH COOKSEY; Phone: 302-739-3451
Administrator: Drainage Operations: RICHARD T. SMITH; Phone: 302-856-5488
Administrator: Shoreline and Waterway Management: ROBERT D. HENRY
Keyword(s): Air Quality and Pollution, Environmental and Conservation Education, Soil Conservation, Water Pollution Management, Wildlife Management

Division of Water Resources
Contact(s):
Director: GERARD L. ESPOSITO; Phone: 302-739-4860
Manager: Wetlands: WILLIAM F. MOYER; Phone: 302-739-4691
Program Manager Environmental Services Section: KATHY KNOWLES; Phone: 302-739-4771
Program Manager: Ground Water Discharge Section: RODNEY WYATT; Phone: 302-739-4762

DELAWARE GEOLOGICAL SURVEY
DGS Bldg., University of Delaware, Newark, DE 19716
Phone: 302-831-2833; Fax: 302-831-3579; Email: DGS@mvs.udel.edu
Founded: 1951
Description: The survey was formed to study the geology, water, and other earth resources of Delaware; also to prepare reports, maps, and otherwise disseminate its findings, and to provide assistance in its area to other agencies and individuals.
Contact(s):
Associate Director: JOHN H. TALLEY
Librarian: DOROTHY C. WINDISH
State Geologist and Director: ROBERT R. JORDAN
Keyword(s): Geology, Research, Water Resources

DELAWARE SEA GRANT PROGRAM
University of Delaware, Newark, DE 19716
Phone: 302-831-2841
Contact(s):
Executive Director: RICHARD TARPLEY, University of Delaware, Newark, DE 19716; Phone: 302-831-2855
DR. CAROLYN THOROUGHGOOD

DELAWARE SOLID WASTE AUTHORITY
1128 S. Bradford St., P.O. Box 455, Dover, DE 19903
Phone: 302-739-5361; Fax: 302-739-4287
Founded: 1975
Description: To define, develop, and implement cost-effective plans and programs for solid waste management which best serve Delaware and protect our public health and enviroment.
Contact(s):
Chief Executive Officer (P.E., DEE): N. C. VASUKI
Chief of Administrative/ Services Officer (P.E.): THOMAS E. HOUSKA II
Chief Operating Officer (P.E., DEE): PASQUALE S. CANZANO
Publication(s): *Statewide Solid Waste Management Plan and Executive Summary; Great Waste Mystery Curriculum, The; Marketing Research Findings and Executive Summary; Trash Tracks (DSWA Newsletter)*
Keyword(s): Environmental and Conservation Education, Environmental Planning, Public Health Protection, Research, Solid Waste Management

DELAWARE STATE EXTENSION SERVICE
Delaware Cooperative Extension, Townsend Hall, University of Delaware, Newark, DE 19717-1303
Phone: 302-831-2501; Fax: 302-831-6758; WWW: www.bluehen.ags.udel.edu
Contact(s):
Associate Dean for Extension and Outreach: DR. PATRICIA S. BARBER
Keyword(s): Agriculture, Conservation Tillage, Energy Conservation, Engineering, Environmental and Conservation Education, Environmental Protection, Flowers, Plants, and Trees, Forest Management, Gardening and Horticulture, Health and Nutrition, Insects and Butterflies, Land Use Planning, Pesticides, Precision Farming, Public Health Protection

DISTRICT OF COLUMBIA

DEPARTMENT OF HEALTH, Environmental Health Administration, (District of Columbia)
c/o Hamid Karimi, 2100 Martin Luther King Jr. Ave., SE, Suite 203, Washington, DC 20020
Contact(s):
Acting Program Manager for Soils Quality Division: HAMID KARIMI, 2100 Martin Luther King Jr. Avenue SE, Suite 203, Washington, DC 20020; Phone: 202-645-6617; Fax: 202-645-6622

DEPARTMENT OF PUBLIC WORKS
2000 14th St., NW, Washington, DC 20009
Contact(s):
Director: LARRY KING; Phone: Administrator: Public Space Maintenance Administration: LESLIE HOTALING; Phone: 202-645-7044
Administrator: Water and Sewer Utility Administration: LARRY KING; Phone: 202-645-6160
Keyword(s): Pedestrian Environment, Solid Waste, Transportation, Urban Environment, Water Pollution

DISTRICT OF COLUMBIA STATE EXTENSION SERVICES
University of the District of Columbia, 4200 Connecticut Ave. N.W., Suite 3009, Washington, DC 20008
Phone: 202-274-6470
Contact(s):
Associate Director for Programs: DR. MAURICE W. DORSEY, University of the District of Columbia, Cooperative Extension Service, 901 Newton St., NE, Washington, DC 20017; Phone: 202-274-6908
Director of Cooperative Extension Service: DR. CLINTON V. TURNER
State Program Leader: Agriculture and Natural Resources: DR. MOHAMID KAHN, DC Cooperative Extension Service, 901 Newton St., NE, Washington, DC 20017; Phone: 202-274-6907

FLORIDA

GOVERNOR OF FLORIDA, JEB BUSH
State Capitol, Tallahassee, FL 32399-0001
Phone: 850-488-2272

FLORIDA COOPERATIVE FISH AND WILDLIFE RESEARCH UNIT (USDI)
P.O. Box 110450, 117 Newins-Ziegler Hall, University of Florida, Gainesville, FL 32611-0450
Phone: 904-392-1861
Founded: 1979
Description: Established by cooperative agreement among the National Biological Survey, Florida Game and Fresh Water Fish Commission, and the University of Florida. Primary purpose is research, graduate education, and extension activities integrating fish and wildlife ecology and management in Florida's unique ecosystems, particularly wetlands.
Contact(s):
Assistant Unit Leader of Fisheries:
Assistant Unit Leader: Wildlife: DR. H. FRANKLIN PERCIVAL
Unit Leader: DR. WILEY M. KITCHENS
Keyword(s): Aquatic Habitats, Biodiversity, Endangered and Threatened Species, Reptiles and Amphibians, Wetlands

FLORIDA DEPARTMENT OF AGRICULTURE AND CONSUMER SERVICES
The Capitol, PL10, Tallahassee, FL 32399-0800
Contact(s):
Commissioner: BOB CRAWFORD; Phone: 850-488-3022

Division of Forestry
Founded: 1927
Description: To protect and manage Florida's forest resources through a stewardship ethic to assure these resources will be available for future generations. Current number of employees: 1,100.
Contact(s):
Assistant Director: MIKE C. LONG; Phone: 850-414-9967
Director: L. EARL PETERSON; Phone: 850-922-0135
Chief of Fire Control: LARRY F. WOOD; Phone: 850-488-6595
Chief of Forest Management: C. CHARLES MAYNARD; Phone: 850-488-6611
Chief of Planning and Support Services: ROBERT B. McDONALD; Phone: 850-414-0843
Chief: Field Operations: RAYMOND K. GEIGER; Phone: 850-414-9969

Office of Agricultural Water Policy
B-41 Administration Bldg., 3125 Conner Blvd., Tallahassee, FL 32399-1650
Phone: 904-488-6249
Description: Provides administrative, legislative, and promotional assistance to 61 Soil and Water Conservation Districts in Florida.
Contact(s):
Director: CHUCK ALLER

Council Chairman: TIM FORD; Phone: 850-488-6249
Soil and Water Conservation Administrator: DAVID VOGEL; Phone: 850-488-6249

Soil and Water Conservation Board
Contact(s):
Chair: LYNN HARRISON, Rt. 2 Box 715, Arcadia, FL 33821; Phone: 813-322-1188
SWC Administrator: DAVID VOGEL, 3125 Conner Blvd., Rm. B-41, Conner Bldg, Tallahassee, FL 32399; Phone: 904-488-6249; Fax: 904-488-2164

FLORIDA DEPARTMENT OF ENVIRONMENTAL PROTECTION
3900 Commonwealth Blvd., Tallahassee, FL 32399-3000
Contact(s):
Secretary: VIRGINIA B. WETHERELL; Phone: 904-488-1554/904-488-4805
Communications Director: CATHERINE ARNOLD; Phone: 904-488-1073
Deputy Secretary: KIRBY GREEN III; Phone: 904-488-7131
Director for Air Resources Management Division: HOWARD RHODES; Phone: 850-488-0114
Director for Division of Administrative and Technical Services: NEVIN SMITH; Phone: 850-488-2955
Director for Division of Administrative Services: MYRA WILLIAMS; Phone: 850-488-0878
Director for Division of Law Enforcement: MICKEY WATSON; Phone: 850-488-5600
Director for Division of Recreation and Parks: FRAN MAINELLA; Phone: 850-488-6131
Director for Division of State Lands: PETE MALLISON; Phone: 850-488-2725
Director for Division of Waste Management: JOHN M. RUDDELL; Phone: 850-487-3299
Director for Division of Water Facilities: MIMI DREW; Phone: 852-487-1855
Director for Ecosystem Management Division: PAM McVETY; Phone: 850-488-7454
Director for Marine Resources Division: ED CONKLIN; Phone: 850-488-6058
General Counsel: PERRY ODOM; Phone: 904-488-9735
General Counsel: PERRY ODOM; Phone: 850-488-9730
Inspector General: PINKY HALL; Phone: 904-488-2287
Special Assistant: MOLLIE PALMER; Phone: 904-488-1554

Air Resources Management Division
3900 Commonwealth Blvd., Tallahassee, FL 32399
Contact(s):
Staff: HOWARD RHODES; Phone: 904-488-0114
Staff of Air Monitoring and Assessment: DOTTY DILTZ; Phone: 904-488-6140
Staff of Air Regulation: CLAIR FANCY; Phone: 904-488-1344

Beaches and Shores Division
3900 Commonwealth Blvd., Tallahassee, FL 32399-3000
Contact(s):
Staff: KIRBY GREEN; Phone: 904-487-4469
Staff of Coastal Data Acquisition: HAROLD BEAN; Phone: 904-487-4471
Staff of Coastal Engineering and Regulation: AL DEVEREAUX; Phone: 904-488-3181
Staff ofBeach Management: LONNIE RYDER; Phone: 904-487-1262

Ecosytem Management Division
Contact(s):
Ecosytem Planning and Coordination: ZRNIE BARNETT; Phone: 904-487-4892
Executive Coordinator: PAM McVETY; Phone: 904-488-7454
Staff of Environmental Education: JIM LEWIS; Phone: 904-488-7326/9334
Staff of Intergovernmental Programs: DEBBIE PAZZISH; Phone: 904-487-2231

STATE AND PROVINCE GOVERNMENT AGENCIES - FLORIDA

Staff of Water Policy/SWIM: JANET LLEWELLYZ; Phone: 904-488-0784

Environmental Resource Permitting Division
Contact(s):
Staff: JEREMY CRAFT; Phone: 904-488-3177
Staff of Surface Water Management: ; Phone: 904-488-6221

Law Enforcement Division
Contact(s):
Staff: MICKEY WATSON; Phone: 904-488-5757
Staff of Coastal Protection: DEBBIE PREBBLE; Phone: 904-487-2974
Staff of Vessel Titling and Registration: ELAYNE HUEBNER; Phone: 904-488-1195
Staff of Technical Services: HENRY NASH; Phone: 904-488-5600

Legislative and Cabinet Affairs Division
Contact(s):
Executive Services Director: NEVIN SMITH; Phone: 904-488-2955
Staff: DIANE HADI; Phone: 904-487-2916
Staff of General Services: JOHN CHERRY; Phone: 904-488-1309
Staff of Information Systems: JOHN WILLMOTT; Phone: 904-488-0892
Staff of Administrative Services: MYRA WILLIAMS; Phone: 904-488-8587
Staff of Budget: JAMIE DELOACH; Phone: 904-488-8587
Staff of Finance and Accounting: JACK DULL; Phone: 904-488-1093
Staff of Human Resource Services: ALYCE PARMER; Phone: 904-488-2996
Staff of Laboratories: JERRY BROOKS; Phone: 904-488-2790
Staff of Management Systems: MANNY MUNOZ; Phone: 904-922-4146
Staff of Quality Assurance: SYLVIA LABIE; Phone: 904-488-2796
Staff of Systems Support: RICK MITCHELL; Phone: 904-488-4883/904-487-1841

Marine Resource Division
Contact(s):
Staff: ED CONKLIN; Phone: 904-488-6058
Staff of Fisheries Management and Assistance: VIRGINIA VAIL; Phone: 904-922-4340
Staff of Florida Marine Research Institute (St. Petersburg): KEN HADDAD; Phone: 813-896-8626
Staff of Marine Resources Regulation and Development: DAVID HELL; Phone: 904-488-5471
Staff of Protected Species Management: PAT ROSE; Phone: 904-922-3456
Staff of Sanctuaries and Research Reserves: DANNY RILEY; Phone: 904-488-3456

Recreation and Parks division
Contact(s):
Staff: FRAN MAINELLA; Phone: 904-488-6131
Staff of Aquatic Plant Management: TOM BROWN; Phone: 904-488-5631
Staff of Design and Construction Division: MIKE BULLOCK; Phone: 904-488-2191
Staff of Geology: WALTER SCHMIDT; Phone: 904-488-4191
Staff of Local Recreational Services: DON GERTEISEN; Phone: 904-488-7896
Staff of Mine Reclamation: JOE BAKKER; Phone: 904-488-8217
Staff of Natural and Cultural Resources: DANA BRYANT; Phone: 904-488-8666
Staff of Operational Services: JOHN BAUST; Phone: 904-488-3300
Staff of Park Planning: ALBERT GREGORY; Phone: 904-488-2200

State Lands Division
Contact(s):
Deputy Director of Land Acquisition: DIANA DARTLAND; Phone: 904-488-3797
Staff: PETE MALLISON; Phone: 904-488-2725
Staff of Appraisal: JOHN SANTANGINI; Phone: 904-488-9025
Staff of Conservation and Recreation Lands Program (CARL): GREG BROCK; Phone: 904-487-1750
Staff of Land Acquisition: ED KUESTER; Phone: 904-488-2351
Staff of Land Management Services: DAN CRABB; Phone: 904-488-2291
Staff of Submerged Lands and Preserves: MIKE ASHEY; Phone: 904-488-2297
Staff of Survey and Mapping: TERRY WILKINSON; Phone: 904-488-2427

Waste Management Division
Contact(s):
Staff: JOHN RUDDELL; Phone: 904-487-3299
Staff of Solid and Hazardous Waste: BILL HINKLEY; Phone: 904-488-0300
Staff of Waste Cleanup: DOUG JONES; Phone: 904-488-0190

Water Facilities Division
Contact(s):
Staff: MIMI DREW; Phone: 904-487-1855
Staff of Drinking Water and Ground Water Resources: MARY WILLIAMS; Phone: 904-488-3601
Staff of Local Government Wastewater Financial Assistance: DON BERRYHILL; Phone: 904-488-8163
Staff of Water Facilities Planning and Regulation: RICHARD DREW; Phone: 904-487-0563

FLORIDA GAME AND FRESH WATER FISH COMMISSION
620 S. Meridian St., Tallahassee, FL 32399-1600
Phone: 850-487-3796
Contact(s):
Executive Director: DR. ALLAN L. EGBERT; Phone: 850-488-2975
Assistant Executive Director: VICTOR J. HELLER; Phone: 850-488-3084
Director: Division of Administrative Services: SANDRA PORTER; Phone: 850-488-6551
Director: Division of Fisheries: EDWIN J. MOGER; Phone: 850-488-0331
Director: Division of Law Enforcement: ROBERT L. EDWARDS; Phone: 850-488-6251
Director: Division of Wildlife: FRANK MONTALBANO III; Phone: 850-488-3831
Director: Office of Environmental Services: BRAD HARTMAN; Phone: 850-488-6662
Director: Office of Informational Services: L. ROSS MORRELL; Phone: 850-488-4676
Editor: DICK SUBLETTE; Phone: 850-488-5564
General Counsel: JAMES V. ANTISTA; Phone: 850-487-1764
Publication(s): *FLORIDA WILDLIFE*
Keyword(s): Aquatic Habitats, Birds, Endangered and Threatened Species, Environment, Fisheries, Hunting, Lakes, Outdoor Recreation, Sport Fishing, Wildlife and Wildlife Habitat, Wildlife Management

FLORIDA SEA GRANT COLLEGE
Florida Sea Grant College Program, Bldg. 803, Rm. 4, P.O. Box 110400, University of Florida, Gainesville, FL 32611-0400
Phone: 904-392-5870
Description: A statewide university-based program of coastal and ocean research, education, and public service to enhance productivity, conservation, and long-term use and management of marine systems and resources.
Contact(s):
Assistant Dean and Coordinator: Sea Grant Extension Program: DR. MARION L. CLARKE, Bldg. 803, Rm. 5, P.O. Box 110405, University of Florida, Gainesville, FL 32611-0405; Phone: 904-392-1837
Associate Director: Florida Sea Grant College Program: DR. WILLIAM SEAMAN, Bldg. 803, Rm. 4, P.O. Box 110400, University of Florida, Gainesville, FL 32611-0400; Phone: 904-392-5870
Director: Florida Sea Grant College Program: DR. JAMES C. CATO

Editor: JAY HUMPHREYS, University of Florida, Bldg. 803, Rm. 5, P.O. Box 110409, Gainesville, FL 32611-0409; Phone: 904-392-2801
Publication(s): *Fathom Magazine; Florida Sea Grant SGEB-5; listing of various publications available*
Keyword(s): Coasts, Environmental and Conservation Education, Fisheries

FLORIDA STATE COOPERATIVE EXTENSION SERVICE
1038 McCarty Hall, P.O. Box 110210, University of Florida, Gainesville, FL 32611-0210
Contact(s):
Coordinator of Sea Grant Science Programs: DR. MARION L. CLARKE, Bldg. 803, Rm. 7, University of Florida, Gainesville, FL 32611-0405; Phone: 904-392-1837
Dean of Extension: DR. CHRISTINE WADDILL, 1038 McCarty Hall, P.O. Box 110210, University of Florida, Gainesville, FL 32611-0210; Phone: 352-392-1761
Director for Center for Natural Resources Programs: DR. P. S. RAO, 1051 McCarty Hall, P.O Box 110230, University of Florida, Gainesville, FL 32611-0335; Phone: 352-392-7622
Extension Environmental Education: DR. MARTHA C. MONROE, 347 Newins-Ziegler Hall, P.O. Box 110410, School of Forest Resources and Conservation, University of Florida, Gainsesville, FL 32611-0410; Phone: 352-846-0878
Extension Fisheries: DR. CHARLES CICHRA, Fisheries and Aquaculture, 7922 NW 71st St., Gainesville, FL 32606; Phone: 904-392-9617
Extension Forestry: DR. MICHAEL G. JACOBSON, Newins-Ziegler Hall, P.O. Box 110410, School of Forest Resources and Consesrvation, Univeristy of Florida, Gainesville, FL 32611-0420; Phone: 352-846-0849
Extension Forestry: DR. ALAN J. LONG, Newins-Ziegler Hall, P.O. Box 110410, School of Forest Resources and Consesrvation, Univeristy of Florida, Gainesville, FL 32611-0420; Phone: 352-846-0849
Extension Forestry: DR. MARY L DURYEA, Newins-Ziegler Hall, P.O. Box 110410, School of Forest Resources and Consesrvation, Univeristy of Florida, Gainesville, FL 32611-0420; Phone: 352-846-0849
Keyword(s): Environmental and Conservation Education, Fisheries, Forests and Forestry, Lakes, Wildlife Management

FLORIDA STATE DEPARTMENT OF HEALTH
State Health Office, 2020 Capital Circle SE, BIN # AOO, Tallahassee, FL 32399-1701
Phone: 904-487-2945
Contact(s):
Deputy State Health Officer for Prevention and Control Programs: RICHARD G. HUNTER; Phone: 850-487-2945
Division Director of Environmental Health: SHARON HEBER; Phone: 850-487-2945
Environmental Hazards: ROGER INMAN; Phone: 850-488-3385
Environmental Programs: BART BIBLER; Phone: 850-488-4070
Environmental Programs: ERIC GRIMM; Phone: 850-487-0004
Epidemiology Programs: BRIAN HUGHES; Phone: 850-488-3370
Keyword(s): Public Health Protection, Toxic Substances, Toxicology

LEE COUNTY PARKS AND RECREATION SERVICES
Regional Park Program Office, 7330 Gladiolus Dr., Fort Myers, FL 33908
Phone: 941-432-2004; Fax: 941-432-2032
Founded: 1990
Description: To promote and develop environmental awareness in Southwest Florida by conducting educational programs which teach ecological concepts and outdoor skills, and by coordinating informational events which alert citizens and community leaders of environmental concerns.
Contact(s):
Biologist: ROGER CLARK; Email: rogersclark@juno.com
Environmental Educator: JOHN KISEDA; Email: lpecoman@juno.com
Interpretive Naturalist: MARY RUDE
Outdoor Recreation Specialist: NANCY MacPHEE; Email: lpnanmac@juno.com
Publication(s): *Elements Newsletter; Explorers Companion Brochure*
Keyword(s): Biodiversity, Birds, Conservation of Protected Areas, EcoAction, Endangered and Threatened Species, Energy Conservation, Environmental and Conservation Education, Environmental Preservation, Environmental Protection, Land Preservation, Nature Preservation, Outdoor Recreation, Public Lands, Wetlands, Wildlife and Wildlife Habitat

MARINE LABORATORY (FLORIDA)
Florida State University, Rt. 1, Box 219A, Sopchoppy, FL 32358
Phone: 904-697-4095; Fax: 904-697-4098
Description: Includes studies on the biology, chemistry, and geology of coastal communities, physical oceanography of near-shore waters, aquatic and terrestrial ecosystems, and aquaculture.
Contact(s):
Director: NANCY H. MARCUS
Keyword(s): Aquatic Habitats, Biology, Coasts, Fisheries, Oceanography

SOUTH FLORIDA WATER MANAGEMENT DISTRICT
3301 Gun Club Rd., P.O. Box 24680, West Palm Beach, FL 33416-4680
Phone: 561-686-8800
Description: Responsible for local cooperation in the Federal-State Central and Southern Florida flood Control Project. Goals include: Flood control, water supply, water quality, and environmental protection for sixteen counties in south Florida. Additional benefits are preservation of natural conditions in the Everglades, land purchases under Save Our Rivers program, and enhancement of wetlands, fish, wildlife, and waterfowl and public recreation.
Contact(s):
Executive Director: SAMUEL POOLE
Deputy Executive Director: MIKE SLAYTON
Director of Water Resource Evaluation: LESLIE WEDDERBURN
Director: Construction and Land Management: WILLIAM MALONE
Director: Ecosystem Director: Enterprise Engineering and Chief Information Officer: TREVOR CAMPBELL
Director: Everglades Construction Project: JOE SCHWERGART
Director: Government and Public Affairs: KATHY COPELAND
Director: Inspector General: ALLEN VANN
Director: Management Services: JILL WONKLE
Director: Office of Budget: JOE MOORE
Director: Operations and Maintenance: JEANNE HALL
Director: Planning: DAN CARY
Director: Regulation: TERRIE BATES
General Counsel: BARBARA MARKHAM
Technical Reference Librarian: CYNTHIA PLOCKELMAN

SOUTHWEST FLORIDA WATER MANAGEMENT DISTRICT (SWFWMD)
2379 Broad St., U.S. 41 South, Brooksville, FL 34609-6899
Phone: 352-796-7211; Fax: 352-754-6885
Founded: 1961
Description: A governmental agency dedicated to resource protection conservation programs, which are supported through regulatory and nonregulatory initiatives and cooperative funding projects.
Contact(s):
Manager of Water Conservation: LOU KAVOURAS
Water Resource Analyst and Secretary of the Florida Water Wise Council: KATHY FOLEY
Publication(s): *Fifty Ways to Turn it Off; Hydroscope; Plant Guide and associated technical bulletins; list of vendors and manufacturers of water conservation devices and services;Residential and Commercial Water Conservation Education*

STATE AND PROVINCE GOVERNMENT AGENCIES - GEORGIA

Keyword(s): Environmental and Conservation Education, Environmental Planning, Natural Systems, Rivers, Water Conservation, Water Quality, Water Resources, Wetlands

GEORGIA

GOVERNOR OF GEORGIA, ROY BARNES
203 State Capitol, Atlanta, GA 30334
Phone: 404-656-1776

GEORGIA COOPERATIVE FISH AND WILDLIFE RESEARCH UNIT (USDI)
Warnell School of Forest Resources, University of Georgia, Athens, GA 30602-2152
Phone: 706-542-5260
Founded: 1984
Description: The Unit is supported by the Biological Resources Division, USGS; Georgia Department of Natural Resources; and the Wildlife Management Institute; and the University of Georgia. Fisheries and wildlife research, graduate education and training, technical assistance, and extension are the main missions of the Unit.
Contact(s):
Assistant Leader: Wildlife: MICHAEL J. CONROY
Unit Leader: CECIL A. JENNINGS
Keyword(s): Aquatic Habitats, Environmental Preservation, Fisheries, Wildlife and Wildlife Habitat, Wildlife Management

GEORGIA DEPARTMENT OF AGRICULTURE
Agricu. Bldg., 19 Martin Luther King Dr., Capitol Sq., Atlanta, GA 30334
Phone: 404-656-3600
Founded: 1874
Description: The department serves farmers and consumers in the state by verifying and enforcing the accuracy and quality of both products and services in many areas including food products, seed, fertilizers, pesticides, fuel, weights and measures, and bedding, and by overseeing the health and well-being of Georgia's livestock, poultry, and commercial pet industry.
Contact(s):
Assistant Commissioner for Consumer Protection Field Forces: CAMERON SMOAK; Phone: 404-656-3627
Assistant Commissioner for Entomology and Pesticides: RON CONLEY; Phone: 404-656-0437
Assistant Commissioner for Fuel and Measures: BILL TRUBY; Phone: 404-656-3605
Assistant Commissioner of Administration: EARL HARRIS; Phone: 404-656-3608
Assistant Commissioner of Animal Industry: DR. LEE MEYERS; Phone: 404-656-3671
Assistant Commissioner of Finance: PHIL KEA; Phone: 404-656-3608
Assistant Commissioner of Marketing: DON ROGERS; Phone: 404-656-3368
Commissioner of Agriculture: TOMMY IRVIN
Publication(s): *Farmers and Consumers Market Bulletin; Georgia Agricultural Facts; Georgia Poultry Facts;*
Keyword(s): Agriculture, Consumer Protection, Consumer Services, Food Safety, Pesticides

Consumers Services Library
Agriculture Bldg., Rm. 224, Capitol Square, Atlanta, GA 30334
Phone: 404-656-3685; Fax: 404-651-7957

GEORGIA DEPARTMENT OF EDUCATION
1952 Twin Towers East, Atlanta, GA 30334-5040
Phone: 404-656-2685
Contact(s):
Science Coordinator: KATHLEEN B. VARNELL

GEORGIA DEPARTMENT OF NATURAL RESOURCES
205 Butler St., SE, East Tower, Atlanta, GA 30334
Phone: 404-656-3500
Contact(s):
Commissioner: LONICE C. BARRETT

Coastal Resources Division
205 Butler St., SE Tower, Altanta, GA 30334
Contact(s):
Director: DUANE HARRIS; Phone: 912-264-7218

Environmental Protection Division
Contact(s):
Assistant Director: DAVID WORD
Director: HAROLD REHEIS; Phone: 404-656-4713
Assistant Branch Chief: MARK SMITH
Chief: Air Protection Branch: RON METHIER
Chief: Hazardous Waste Branch: JENNIFER KADUCK
Chief: Land Protection Branch: JOHN TAYLOR
Chief: Program Coordination Branch: JIM SETSER
Chief: Water Protection Branch: ALAN HALLUM
Chief: Water Resources Branch: NOLTON JOHNSON

Historic Preservation Division
Contact(s):
Director: MARK EDWARDS; Phone: 404-656-2840

Parks, Recreation and Historic Sites Division
Contact(s):
Director: BURT WEERTS; Phone: 404-656-2770
Chief: Maintenance and Construction Section: DAVID FREEDMAN
Chief: Parks Operation Section: WAYNE ESCOE

Pollution Prevention Assistance Division
Contact(s):
Director: BOB KERR; Phone: 404-651-5120

Program Support Division
Contact(s):
Director: PAUL BURKHALTER; Phone: 404-656-7559

Wildlife Resources Division
2070 U.S. Highway 278, SE, Social Cir., GA 30025
Phone: 770-918-6400
Contact(s):
Director: DAVID WALLER
Chief: Fisheries Management: MIKE GENNINGS; Phone: 770-918-6406
Chief: Game Management: TODD HOLBROOK; Phone: 770-918-6404
Chief: Nongame Wildlife/Natural Heritage: MIKE HARRIS; Phone: 770-761-3035

GEORGIA FORESTRY COMMISSION
P.O. Box 819, Macon, GA 31202-0819
Phone: 912-751-3500
Founded: 1925
Description: To foster, improve, and encourage reforestation; to engage in research and other projects for better forestry practices; to inform the public of the values and benefits of forestry; and to detect, prevent, and combat forest fires.
Contact(s):
Deputy Director: WILLIAM R. LAZENBY; Phone: 912-751-3480
Director: J. FRED ALLEN; Phone: 912-751-3480
Board of Commissioner Chairman: JIM L. GILLIS JR.
Chief of Forest Administration: GARLAND NELSON; Phone: 912-751-3464
Chief of Forest Management: LYNN HOOVEN; Phone: 912-751-3458
Chief of Forest Products Utilization, Marketing, and Development: TOMMY LOGGINS; Phone: 912-751-3521
Chief of Forest Protection: WESLEY WELLS; Phone: 912-751-3488

Chief of Information and Education: SHARON DOLLIVER; Phone: 912-751-3530
Chief of Reforestation: JOHNNY BRANAN; Phone: 912-751-3530
Editor: TOMMY LOGGINS; Phone: 912-751-3521
Editor: LYNN WALTON; Phone: 912-751-3530
Personnel Officer: RANDALL PERRY; Phone: 404-298-4949
Publication(s): *Georgia Forestry; Wood Using Industries*

GEORGIA SEA GRANT COLLEGE PROGRAM
The University of Georgia, Marine Sciences Bldg., Athens, GA 30602-3636
Phone: 706-542-6009
Founded: 1971
Description: A part of the National Sea Grant College Program, the Georgia program fosters the sustainable development and environmental stewardship of the nation's marine resources. It is a competitive grant program funding, applied marine research, education, and advisory service projects at universities in Georgia.
Contact(s):
Director: DR. WILLIAM GRAY POTTER; Phone: 706-542-0621
Associate Director: Collections and Public Services: DR. JOHN R. YELVERTON; Phone: 706-542-0626
Director: Sea Grant College Program: DR. MAC RAWSON JR.
Leader of Marine Advisory Service Communicator: DAVID BRYANT
Leader: Education Program: EDITH SCHMIDT
Leader: Marine Advisory Service: KEITH GATES
Keyword(s): Coasts, Environmental and Conservation Education, Oceanography, Renewable Resources, Sustainable Development

GEORGIA STATE EXTENSION SERVICES
College of Agricultural and Environmental Sciences, The University of Georgia, Athens, GA 30602-7501
Phone: 706-542-3924
Contact(s):
Aquaculture and Fisheries Specialist: DR. GEORGE W. LEWIS; Phone: 706-542-1924
Associate Dean for Extension: DR. ROBERT A. ISAAC, Cooperative Extension Service, The University of Georgia, Athens, GA 30602-7504; Phone: 706-542-3824; Fax: 706-542-8815; Email: risaac@arches.uga.edu
Dean and Director: DR. GALE A. BUCHANAN; Phone: 706-542-3924
Extension Coordinator for Forest Resources Unit: DR. BEN D. JACKSON; Phone: 706-542-3446
Wildlife Specialist: DR. JEFFERY J. JACKSON; Phone: 706-542-9054

STATE SOIL AND WATER CONSERVATION COMMISSION (GEORGIA)
P.O. Box 8024, Athens, GA 30603
Phone: 706-542-3065
Founded: 1937
Description: Established under the Soil Conservation Districts Act to work with and assist the 40 Soil and Water Conservation Districts and their 370 District Supervisors throughout Georgia.
Contact(s):
Chairman: J. M. PLEMONS; Phone: 706-935-4324
Executive Director: F. GRAHAM LILES JR.; Phone: 706-542-3065; Fax: 706-542-4242
Editor: DENNIS HOPPER
Publication(s): *Conservation Commission; Conservation Contact*
Keyword(s): Agriculture, Soil Conservation, Urban Environment, Water Resources, Wetlands

GUAM

GOVERNOR OF GUAM, CARL T.C. GUTIERREZ
Executive Chambers, P.O. Box 2950, Agana, Guam 96932
Phone: 011-671-472-8931

DEPARTMENT OF PARKS AND RECREATION (GUAM)
P.O. Box 2950, Agana, Guam 96910
Phone: 671-475-6296/7; Fax: 671-472-9626
Contact(s):
Deputy Director: FRANKLIN J. GUTIERREZ
Director: A. J. SHELTON
Keyword(s): Historic Preservation, Nature Preservation, Outdoor Recreation

DIVISION OF FORESTRY AND SOIL RESOURCES (GUAM)
192 Dairy Road; Mangilao, Guam 96923
Phone: 671-735-3949; Fax: 671-734-0111
Founded: 1953
Description: The DFSR was formed for the management, protection, and enhancement of the territory's forest and land resources to produce ample amounts of water, wood, fiber, and recreation to benefit the most number of people.
Contact(s):
Chief: DAVID T. LIMTIACO; Email: DLIMITI@ns.gu
Forester I: LOUANN C. GUZMAN
Forester I: BELMINA I. SOLIVA
Management Forester: RODOLFO L. ANDO
Urban and Community Forester: JOSEPH L.M. ACFALLE
Keyword(s): Afforestation, Environmental and Conservation Education, Fire Prevention, Forest Management, Forest Stewardship, Urban Forestry

GUAM COASTAL MANAGEMENT PROGRAM
Bureau of Planning, P.O. Box 2950, Agana, Guam 96932
Phone: 671-472-4201; Fax: 671-477-1812
Founded: 1979
Contact(s):
Administrator: Guam Coastal Management Program: MICHAEL L. HAM
Director: Bureau of Planning: VINCENT P. ARRIOLA
Library Services: Bureau of Planning: Supervisor: SUSAN M. HAM
Publication(s): *Public Television Show: Man, Land, and Sea (Guam only); List of publications, posters, and fliers available upon request.*
Keyword(s): Coasts, Coral Reefs, Planning Management, Sustainable Development, Sustainable Ecosystems

GUAM DEPARTMENT OF AGRICULTURE
192 Dairy Rd., Mangilao, Guam 96923
Phone: 671-734-3941/42/43; Fax: 671-734-6569
Founded: 1950
Description: Charged with responsibility for the conservation and management of Guam's fish, wildlife, soil, and forestry resources, together with development of agricultural and fishery production for food purposes.
Contact(s):
Deputy Director: JOSEPH G. SABLAN
Director: MICHAEL W. KUHLMANN, 192 Dairy Rd., Mangilao, GU 96923; Phone: 671-734-3942; Fax: 671-734-6569

Division of Aquatic and Wildlife Resources
192 Dairy Rd., Mangilao, Guam 96923
Phone: 671-734-3944/45; Fax: 671-734-6570
Contact(s):
Administrative Officer: ALAN G. VAN AKEN
Chief: ROBERT D. ANDERSON

STATE AND PROVINCE GOVERNMENT AGENCIES - HAWAII

GUAM ENVIRONMENTAL PROTECTION AGENCY
P.O. Box 22439, Guam Main Facility, Barrigada, Guam 96921
Phone: 671-472-8863
Founded: 1973
Description: Activities include: land-use planning; review of environmental impact assessments and environmental protection plans; supervision, planning, and regulation of all new or modified wastewater sources; and the development and protection of potable water supplies; solid and hazardous waste management, pesticides importation, distribution, and use; and air pollution sources. Provide field and laboratory support for the agency's water, air, and land regulatory programs.
Contact(s):
Administrative Services Officer Administrative Services: ROSALIE A. LANCERO
Administrator: JESUS T. SALAS
Administrator: Air and Land Programs Division: CONCHITA S.N. TAITANO
Assistant to the Administrator: BEN MACHOL
Board of Directors Chairman: ALBERT W.C. WONG
Board of Directors Vice Chairwoman: JOSEPHINE B. COAD
Chief Engineer: Water Programs Division: NARCISO G. CUSTODIO P.E.
Chief Planner: Environmental Planning and Review: JORDAN KAYE
Chief: Analysis Section: MILA P. PADOR
Chief: Surveillance: MELVIN B. BORJA
Deputy Administrator:
Director: Air Pollution Control Program: JOAQUIN Q. CRUZ
Director: Drinking Water Program: ANGEL B. MARQUEZ
Director: Pesticides Enforcement Program: VIRGILIO L. OBIAS
Director: Solid and Hazardous Waste Program: FRANCIS P. DAMIAN
Director: Water Pollution Control Program: DOMINGO S. CABUSAO
Director: Water Resources Management Program: MARILOU B. YAMANAKA
Legal Counsel: ELISABETH T. CRUZ
Public Information Officer: GRACE OMEGA GARCES
Special Assistant to the Administrator: MARK PETERSEN
Territorial Hydrogeologist: H. VICTOR WUERCH
Publication(s): Annual Report; list available on request.

GUAM EXTENSION SERVICE
College of Agriculture and Life Sciences, University of Guam, 303 University Dr., University of Guam Station, Mangilao, Guam 96923
Phone: 671-734-6842; Email: jbarcina@uog.edu
Contact(s):
4-H and Youth Program Leader: ANTHONY ARTERO
Agricultural and Natural Resources Program Leader: FRANK CRUZ
Agricultural Engineer: DR. PREM SINGH
Animal Science: DR. FAROUQ G. ABAWI
Associate Dean: Extension Service: VICTOR T. ARTERO
Associate Director of the Agricultural Experiment Station: DR. JOHN W. BROWN
Community Resource Development Program Leader: DR. RANDALL WORKMAN
Consumer and Family Sciences Program Leader: DR. ERLINDA DEMETERIO
Dean and Director of Extension Service and Agricultural Experiment Station: JEFF BARCINAS
Entomology: DR. ROSS H. MILLER
Horticulture: DR. MARI MARUTANI
Ornamental Horticulture: DR. JAMES McCONNELL
Plant Pathology: DR. GEORGE WALL
Pomology: DR. E. MARLER
Soil Science: DR. PETER MOTAVALLI
Turfgrass Management: DR. GREG WIECKO

GUAM SEA GRANT PROGRAM
University of Hawaii, 1000 Pope Rd., Rm. 222, Honolulu, Guam 96822
Phone: 808-956-7031; Fax: 808-956-3014
Description: The University of Hawaii Sea Grant College Program supports research projects in marine-related areas. Its extension arm has agents and specialists located in Honolulu, the Big Island of Hawaii, Guam, Pohnpei (Federated States of Micronesia) and soon Saipana (Commonwealth of the Northern Mariana Islands). Agents help marine users benefit from the Sea Grant-supported research, especially in the areas of commercial and recreational fishing, aquaculture, marine recreation and tourism development, marine education and conservation, and global climate change.
Contact(s):
Aquaculture Extension Agent: RICHARD BAILEY, 1000 Pope Rd., Rm. 209, Honolulu, HI 96822; Phone: 808-956-2873; Fax: 808-956-2858
Aquaculture Extension Specialist: CLYDE TAMARU, 1000 Pope Rd., Rm. 210, Honolulu, HI 96822; Phone: 808-956-2869; Fax: 808-956-2858
Associate Director: ROSE T. PFUND
Coastal Recreation & Tourism Extension Agent: CHRISTINE WOOLAWAY, 1000 Pope Rd., Rm. 217, Honolulu, HI 96822; Phone: 808-956-2872; Fax: 808-956-2858
Coastal Recreation & Tourism Extension Agent: RAYMOND S. TABATA, 1000 Pope Rd., Rm. 230, Honolulu, HI 96822; Phone: 808-956-2866; Fax: 808-956-2858
Coastal Resource Management Extension Agent: PETER J. RAPPA, 1000 Pope Rd., Rm. 208, Honolulu, HI 96822; Phone: 808-956-2868; Fax: 808-956-2858
Director of Communications Program: PRISCILLA P. BILLIG, 1000 Pope Rd., Rm. 200, Honolulu, HI 96822; Phone: 808-956-2414; Fax: 808-956-2880
Director of Sea Grant Extension Service: BRUCE J. MILLER, 1000 Pope Rd., Rm. 227, Honolulu, HI 96822; Phone: 808-956-8645; Fax: 808-956-2858
Director: Sea Grant College Program: DR. CHARLES HELSLEY
Education Coordinator for Hanauma Bay Educational Program: JOHN CULLINEY, 1000 Pope Rd., Rm. 226, Honolulu, HI 96822; Phone: 808-956-8645; Fax: 808-956-2858
Fisheries Extension Agent: ALAN KAM, 1000 Pope Rd., Rm. 204, Honolulu, HI 96822; Phone: 808-956-2865; Fax: 808-956-2858
Fisheries Extension Agent: RICHARD E. BROCK, 1000 Pope Rd., Rm. 204, Honolulu, HI 96822; Phone: 808-956-2859; Fax: 808-956-2858
Hanauma Bay Educational Program Volunteer Coordinator: JEFF KUWABARA, 1000 Pope Rd., Rm. 226, Honolulu, HI 96822; Phone: 808-956-8645; Fax: 808-956-2858
Pacific Region Environmental Education Specialist: ELIZABETH KUMABE, 1000 Pope Rd., Rm. 225, Honolulu, HI 96822; Phone: 808-956-2860; Fax: 808-956-2858
Pacific Region Sustainable Development Agent: ANNE M. ORCUTT-BAILEY, 1000 Pope Rd., Rm. 208, Honolulu, HI 96822; Phone: 808-956-2862; Fax: 808-956-2858

HAWAII

GOVERNOR OF HAWAII, BENJAMIN CAYETANO
235 S. Beretania St., State Capitol, Honolulu, HI 96813
Phone: 808-586-0034

DEPARTMENT OF LAND AND NATURAL RESOURCES

Division of Boating and Ocean Recreation (DOBOR
333 Queen Street, Room 300, Honolulu, HI 96813
Phone: 808-587-1963

Division of Water Resource Management,
P.O. Box 621, Honolulu, HI 96809
Phone: 808-587-0215
Contact(s):
Deputy: RAE M. LOUI

Keyword(s): Environmental Protection, Fisheries, Land Preservation, Water Resources, Wildlife Management

DEPARTMENT OF LAND AND NATURAL RESOURCES (HAWAII)
Box 621, Honolulu, HI 96809
Phone: 808-587-0400
Contact(s):
Chairman: Commission on Water Resources Management: MICHAEL D. WILSON
Chairperson: MICHAEL D. WILSON; Phone: 808-587-0041
Deputy to Chairperson: RAE M. LOUI
Deputy to Chairperson: GILBERT S. COLOMA-AGARAN
Manager: Aquaculture Development Program (ADP): JOHN S. CORBIN

Division of Aquatic Resources
1151 Punchbowl St., Honolulu, HI 96813
Phone: 808-587-0100
Contact(s):
Administrator (Acting): WILLIAM DEVICK
Program Manager: Commercial Fisheries Aquaculture Branch: ERIC W. ONIZUICA

Division of Conservation and Resources Enforcement
1151 Punchbowl St., Honolulu, HI 96813
Phone: 808-587-0077
Contact(s):
Administrator (Acting): GARY MONIZ
Manager: Hunter Education Program: WENDELL W.S. KAM; Phone: 808-587-0200

Division of Forestry and Wildlife
1151 Punchbowl St., Honolulu, HI 96813
Phone: 808-587-0166
Contact(s):
Administrator: MICHAEL G. BUCK
Manager: Forestry Program: CARL T. MASAKI

Division of Historic Preservation
33 S. King St., 6th Fl., Honolulu, HI 96809
Contact(s):
Administrator: DON HIBBARD; Phone: 808-587-0045

Division of State Parks
P.O. Box 621, Honolulu, HI 96809
Phone: 808-587-0300
Contact(s):
Administrator: State Parks: RALSTON H. NAGATA

Land Division
P.O. Box 621, Honolulu, HI 96809
Phone: 808-587-0432
Contact(s):
Administrator: DEAN UCHIDA

ENVIRONMENTAL CENTER
Water Resource Research Center, University of HI, 2550 Campus Rd., Honolulu, HI 2550
Phone: 808-956-7361; Fax: 808-956-3980
Founded: 1970
Description: To stimulate, expand, and coordinate education, research, and service efforts of the university related to ecological relationships, natural resources, and environmental quality, with special relation to human needs and social institutions, particularly with regard to the state. For information on Liberal Studies BA Degree in Environmental Studies, check the University of Hawaii website: www.hawaii.edu/catalog/special-pgms-files/inter-progs.html#es
Contact(s):
Director: ROGER FUJIOKA
Associate Environmental Coordinator: JACQUELIN N. MILLER; Email: jackiem@hawaii.edu
Environmental Coordinator: JOHN T. HARRISON; Email: jth@hawaii.edu
Keyword(s): Environmental and Conservation Education, Environmental Law, Research, Water Quality

HAWAII COOPERATIVE FISHERY RESEARCH UNIT (USDI)
2538 The Mall, University of Hawaii, Honolulu, HI 96822
Phone: 808-956-8350; Fax: 808-956-9812; Email: jparrish@zoogate.zoo.hawaii.edu
Description: Activities include research, graduate program teaching, and public service regarding inshore marine and inland waters with emphasis on native fishes and invertebrates.
Contact(s):
Leader: DR. JAMES D. PARRISH
Keyword(s): Aquatic Habitats, Fisheries, Islands, Oceanography, Sustainable Ecosystems

HAWAII DEPARTMENT OF AGRICULTURE
P.O. Box 22159, Honolulu, HI 96823-2159
Description: Promotes the best use of Hawaii's agricultural resources. Concerned with the protection of agricultural lands and water and diversification of the state's agricultural economy. Functions include agricultural planning, agricultural credit, product promotion and market development, plant and animal quarantine, plant and animal disease and pest control, milk control, livestock and market reporting service, commodities grading, pesticide use enforcement, and enforcement of weights and measures standards.
Contact(s):
Chairperson: JAMES NAKATANI; Phone: 808-973-9551
Chief: Administrative Services: ELAINE T. ABE; Phone: 808-973-9606
Deputy to the Chairperson: LETITIA N. UYEHARA; Phone: 808-973-9553
Head: Agricultural Loan Division: DOREEN K. SHISHIDO; Phone: 808-973-9460
Head: Agricultural Resource Management Division: PAUL T. MATSUO; Phone: 808-973-9475
Head: Agriculture Development Division: SAMUEL CAMP; Phone: 808-973-9566
Head: Animal Industry Division: CALVIN W.S. LUM; Phone: 808-483-7111
Head: Plant Industry Division: DR. LYLE WONG; Phone: 808-973-9535
Head: Quality Assurance Division: SAMUEL CAMP; Phone: 808-586-0870

HAWAII DEPARTMENT OF HEALTH
Office of Environmental Quality Control, 235 S. Beretania St., Suite 702, Honolulu, HI 96813
Phone: 808-586-4185
Description: OEQC advises the Governor on environmental quality control matters; implements Hawaii's EIS law; reviews all documents required by Hawaii's EIS process; and informs the public of proposed actions through The Environmental Notice (OEQC Bulletin). The director of OEQC is also responsible for environmental education projects, and proposing and encouraging legislation supporting the preservation of environmental resources.
Contact(s):
Director: GARY GILL
Publication(s): *A Guidebook for the Hawaii State Environmental Review Process; OEQC Bulletin; Annual Report--Environmental Indicators and Report Card*
Keyword(s): Environmental and Conservation Education, Environmental Law

INSTITUTE OF MARINE BIOLOGY
University of Hawaii, P.O. Box 1346, Kaneohe, HI 96744-1346
Phone: 808-236-7401
Description: Concerned with research in tropical marine biology and oceanography with emphasis on coral reef biology, aquaculture, fish endocrinology, and behavior of reef organisms. Provides

STATE AND PROVINCE GOVERNMENT AGENCIES - IDAHO

research facilities for investigations in tropical marine biology. Offers annual summer program in selected topics for graduate students.
Contact(s):
Director: PHILIP HELFRICH

INSTITUTE OF TROPICAL AGRICULTURE AND HUMAN RESOURCES
College of Tropical Agriculture and Human Resources, University of Hawaii, 3050 Maile Way, Honolulu, HI 96822
Phone: 808-956-8131
Founded: 1978
Description: Plan and implement research and extension in agriculture, natural resources, and human resources relevant to Hawaii and the tropics, with emphasis on the Pacific and Asia.
Contact(s):
Acting Director: H. MICHAEL HARRINGTON
Publication(s): *Various research and extension* **Keyword(s):** Agriculture, Biotechnology, Chemical Pollution Control, Conservation Tillage, Engineering, Environment, Flowers, Plants, and Trees, Gardening and Horticulture, Health and Nutrition, Insects and Butterflies, Landscape Architecture, Pesticides, Public Health Protection, Renewable Resources

WATER RESOURCES RESEARCH CENTER
University of Hawaii, Holmes Hall 283, 2540 Dole St., Honolulu, HI 96822
Phone: 808-956-7847
Founded: 1964
Description: To initiate, coordinate, and conduct research in hydrology, hydrogeology, hydrometeorology and agrohydrology, hydraulic and sanitary engineering, water quality and pollution, environmental aspects, and water-related socioeconomics and law for the university and the state.
Contact(s):
Assistant Director: JAMES E.T. MONCUR
Director: DR. ROGER S. FUJIOKA
Communications Coordinator: PHILIP S. MORAVCIK
Publication(s): *Technical Report; Technical Memorandum Report; Annual Report; Cooperative Report; Publications List; Project Reports and Special Publications*
Keyword(s): Aquatic Habitats, Oceanography, Public Health Protection, Water Pollution Management, Water Resources

IDAHO

GOVERNOR OF IDAHO, DIRK KEMPTHORNE
700 West Jefferson, Boise, ID 83720-0034
Phone: 208-334-2100

DEPARTMENT OF LANDS (IDAHO)
P.O. Box 83720, 954 West Jefferson Street, Boise, ID 83720-0500
Phone: 208-334-0200
Description: The State Board of Land Commissioners is a constitutional board charged with administering the trust under which endowment lands are held. These lands were granted to the state at the time of statehood for the financial support of nine beneficiaries, the largest being the common schools.
Contact(s):
Attorney General: ALAN G. LANCE; Phone: 208-334-2400
Secretary of State: PETE T. CENARRUSA; Phone: 208-334-2300
Secretary to the Board and Director of the Idaho Department of Lands: STANLEY F. HAMILTON; Phone: 208-334-0200
State Board of Land Commissioner President: GOV. PHILIP E. BATT; Phone: 208-334-2100
State Contorller: J. D. WILLIAMS; Phone: 208-334-3100
Superintendent of Public Instruction: DR. ANNE C. FOX; Phone: 208-332-6800

DEPARTMENT OF WATER RESOURCES (IDAHO)
Statehouse, Boise, ID 83720
Description: Administration of State Water Plan and Energy Plan; allocation and planning of water resources and energy programs and projects; permit and license procedures for water rights, dams, and mine tailing impoundment structures, well construction, injection wells, and stream channel alterations.
Contact(s):
Director: KARL J. DREHER; Phone: 208-327-7910
Administrator of Energy Division: ROBERT W. HOPPIE; Phone: 208-327-7910
Administrator of Policy and Planning Division: WAYNE T. HAAS; Phone: 208-327-7910
Administrator of Resources Administration Division: NORMAN C. YOUNG; Phone: 208-327-7910
Chairman of the Board: CLARENCE FARR; Phone: 208-678-8620
Publication(s): *Water and Energy Information Bulletins; Rules; State Water Plan, and Newsletter*

IDAHO COOPERATIVE EXTENSION
University of Idaho, Cooperative Extension System, Moscow, ID 83843
Phone: 208-885-6356
Contact(s):
Extension Forester: RONALD MAHONEY

IDAHO COOPERATIVE FISH AND WILDLIFE RESEARCH UNIT (USDI)
College of Forestry, Wildlife and Range Sciences, University of Idaho, Moscow, ID 83844-1141
Phone: 208-885-6336
Founded: 1963
Description: An interagency organization which conducts research, graduate level training, and extension in the fields of fish, wildlife, and conservation biology.
Contact(s):
Assistant Leader: DR. R. GERALD WRIGHT
Assistant Leader: DR. JAMES L. CONGLETON
Assistant Leader: DR. THEODORE C. BJORNN
Leader: DR. J. MICHAEL SCOTT
Keyword(s): Biodiversity, Birds, Endangered and Threatened Species, Fisheries, Wildlife and Wildlife Habitat

IDAHO DEPARTMENT OF PARKS AND RECREATION
P. O. Box 83720, Boise, ID 83720-0065
Phone: 208-334-4199
Founded: 1965
Description: To formulate and put into execution a long-range program for the acquisition, planning, protection, operation, maintenance, development, and wise use of parks; and to provide state leadership in recreation.
Contact(s):
Deputy Director: DR. FRANKLIN E. BOTELER
Director: YVONNE FERRELL
Chairman of the Board: MONTE LATER; Phone: 208-624-3852
Keyword(s): Cultural Preservation, Environmental and Conservation Education, Environmental Preservation, Outdoor Recreation, Rivers

IDAHO FISH AND GAME DEPARTMENT
600 S. Walnut, Box 25, Boise, ID 83707
Phone: 208-334-3700; Fax: 208-334-2114; WWW: www.state.id.us/fishgame
Founded: 1938
Description: To preserve, protect, perpetuate, and manage all wildlife within the state of Idaho; to make and declare such rules and regulations, and to employ personnel necessary to administer and enforce the harvest of wildlife.
Contact(s):
Assistant Director: JERRY MALLET; Phone: 208-334-3771
Assistant Director: KENNETH D. NORRIE; Phone: 208-334-3613
Director: STEPHEN P. MEALEY; Phone: 208-334-5159

Bureau Chief of Administration: STEPHEN BARTON; Phone: 208-334-3782
Chief of DP Management: BOB ROYCE; Phone: 208-334-3700
Chief of Enforcement: AL NICHOLSON; Phone: 208-334-3736
Chief of Engineering: PHIL JEPPSON; Phone: 208-334-3730
Chief of Fisheries: VIRGIL K. MOORE; Phone: 208-334-3791
Chief of Information and Education: JOHN GAHL; Phone: 208-334-3746/x257
Chief of Natural Resources Policy: TRACEY TRENT; Phone: 208-334-2595
Chief of Wildlife: STEVE HUFFAKER; Phone: 208-334-2920
Editor: JACK TRUEBLOOD; Phone: 208-334-3746
Publication(s): *Idaho Fish & Game News*
Keyword(s): Environmental and Conservation Education, Fisheries, Hunting, Sport Fishing, Wildlife Management

IDAHO FISH AND WILDLIFE FOUNDATION
P.O. Box 2254, Boise, ID 83701
Phone: 208-334-2648; Fax: 208-334-2148; Email: kfreuden@idfg.state.id.us
Founded: 1990
Description: To facilitate the organization and funding of natural resource projects: fish, wildlife, habitat, and education. Work with Idaho Department of Fish and Game and other entities to build public and private partnerships for wildlife projects.
Contact(s):
Executive Director: KIT FREUDENBERG
Publication(s): *Steelhead Fishing Economic Survey (1996); Steelhead Fishing Economic Values brochure; Salmon Fishing Economic Survey (1998).*
Keyword(s): Environmental and Conservation Education, Fisheries, Natural Areas, Nature Centers, Wildlife and Wildlife Habitat

IDAHO GEOLOGICAL SURVEY
Morrill Hall, Third Floor, University of Idaho, Moscow, ID 83844-3014
Phone: 208-885-7991
Founded: 1919
Description: The Survey is the lead state agency for the collection, interpretation, and dissemination of all geologic and mineral data for Idaho. Conducts field investigations and laboratory studies; assists in preparation of geologic maps, derivative land-use planning, and geologic hazards maps; provides expertise to individuals and governmental and private groups in planning land use.
Contact(s):
Director: EARL H. BENNETT; Phone: 208-885-7991
Associate Director: KURT L. OTHBERG
Associate Director: ROY M BRECKENRIDGE; Phone: 208-885-7991

IDAHO STATE DEPARTMENT OF AGRICULTURE
P.O. Box 790, Boise, ID 83701
Phone: 208-334-3240
Contact(s):
Director: PATRICK A. TAKASUGI
Division of Agricultural Inspections Administrator: LANE JOLLIFFE; Phone: 208-332-8666
Division of Agricultural Resources, Marketing, and Development: MIKE EVERETT; Phone: 208-332-8531
Division of Animal Industries Administrator: DR. BOB HILLMAN; Phone: 208-332-8541
Division of Plant Industries and Labs Administrator: DR. ROGER R. VEGA; Phone: 208-332-8627
Keyword(s): Agriculture, Biotechnology, Chemical Pollution Control, Endangered and Threatened Species, Land Preservation, Land Use Planning, Pesticides, Public Health Protection, Soil Conservation, Solid Waste Management, Toxic Substances, Water Pollution, Water Quality, Watersheds

STATE OF IDAHO, DIVISION OF ENVIRONMENTAL QUALITY
1410 N. Hilton St., Boise, ID 83706-1255
Phone: 208-373-0502; Fax: 208-373-0417
Description: Administers and directs programs designed to protect and enhance the environment and public health. Emphasis is placed on monitoring, technical assistance, and environmental education at the community level. The agency is additionally responsible for all permitting and permit review functions.
Contact(s):
Administrator of Division of Environmental Quality: WALLACE N. CORY; Phone: 208-373-5840
Assistant Administrator for Air and Hazardous Waste: ORVILLE GREEN; Phone: 208-373-0440
Assistant Administrator for Regional Services: JIM JOHNSTON; Phone: 208-528-2650
Assistant Administrator for Water Quality and Remediation: LARRY KOENIG; Phone: 208-373-0407
Publication(s): *Hazardous Waste Report; Drinking Water Report; Goundwater Report; Strategic Plan; State of the Environment Report; Performance Partnership Agreement*
Keyword(s): Air Quality and Pollution, Environmental Planning, Environmental Protection, Water Quality

STATE SOIL CONSERVATION COMMISSION (IDAHO)
P.O. Box 790, Boise, ID 83701-0790
Phone: 208-332-8650
Founded: 1939
Description: Coordinates programs and activities of Soil Conservation Districts in Idaho. Concerned with overall leadership and administration of districts in development, wise use, and conservation of soil and water and other closely related resources. Participates in the National Cooperative Soil Survey Program through employment of soil scientists and has been designated the state water quality management agency for private and state agricultural lands. Administers low-interest loan program for conservation improvements on private and public lands.
Contact(s):
Chairman: ROBERT GRIFFEL, 1000N 4301 E., Ashton, ID 83420; Phone: 208-653-3388; Fax: 208-652-7817
Administrator: JERRY NICOLESCU; Phone: 208-332-8649; Fax: 508-334-2386
Keyword(s): Agriculture, Environmental and Conservation Education, Renewable Resources, Soil Conservation, Water Resources

ILLINOIS

GOVERNOR OF ILLINOIS, GEORGE RYAN
State Capitol, Rm. 207, Springfield, IL 62706
Phone: 217-782-6830/TDD800-526-0884

ILLINOIS DEPARTMENT OF AGRICULTURE
State Fairgrounds, P.O. Box 19281, Springfield, IL 62794-9281
Phone: 217-782-9272
Founded: 1917
Description: The Illinois Department of Agriculture protects and promotes the state's agricultural and natural resources. The agency provides services that benefit consumers, farmers, and agribusinesses.
Contact(s):
Director: BECKY DOYLE
Deputy Director for Natural Resource and Agri-Industry Regulation: CHET BORUFF
Executive Office: Assistant Director: DAVE BENDER
Superintendent for Fairs and Promotions: JIM REYNOLDS
Publication(s): *Illinois Agricultural Guide; Illinois Agricultural Organizations Directory; Illinois Grain and Livestock Market News; Illinois Food Products*
Keyword(s): Agriculture, Land Use Planning, Pesticides, Renewable Resources, Soil Conservation

STATE AND PROVINCE GOVERNMENT AGENCIES - INDIANA

Soil and Water Conservation Districts Advisory Board
P.O. Box 19281, Springfield, IL 62794-9281
Phone: 217-782-6297; Fax: 217-524-4882
Contact(s):
Bureau Chief: TERRY DONOHUE

ILLINOIS DEPARTMENT OF NATURAL RESOURCES
524 S. 2nd St., Rm. 400 LTP, Springfield, IL 62701-1787
Phone: 217-782-6302
Description: The mission of the Illinois Department of Natural Resources is to promote an understanding and appreciation of the state's natural resources and work with the people of Illinois to protect and manage those resources to ensure a high quality of life for present and future generations.
Contact(s):
Deputy Director: BRUCE CLAY
Director: BRENT MANNING
Chief Fiscal Officer: JOHN BANDY; Phone: 217-785-8552
Chief Legal Cousel: ROBERT LAWLEY; Phone: 217-782-1809
Chief of Law Enforcement Office: LARRY CLOSSON; Phone: 217-782-6431
Conservation Foundation Executive Director: JOHN SCHMITT; Phone: 312-814-7237
Director of Legislation and Constituency Services: DIANE HENDREN; Phone: 217-785-0073
Director of Office Mines and Minerals: RICHARD MOTTERSHAW; Phone: 217-782-0031
Director of Office of Administration: KEVIN SRONCE; Phone: 217-782-0179
Director of Office of Capital Development: BRUCE CLARK; Phone: 217-782-1807
Director of Office of Land Management and Education: JERRY BEVERLIN; Phone: 217-782-6752
Director of Public Affairs Office: CAROL KNOWLES; Phone: 217-785-0970
Director of Public Services Office: JIM FULGENZI; Phone: 217-782-7454
Director of Realty and Environmental Planning Office: TOM FLATTERY; Phone: 217-782-7940
Director of Resource Conservation Office: KIRBY COTTRELL; Phone: 217-785-8547
Director of Scientific Research and Analysis Office: KAREN WITTER; Phone: 217-524-9506
Director of Water Resources Office: DON VONNAHME; Phone: 217-782-2152
Division Manager of Internal Audit Office: BRAD HAMMOND; Phone: 217-785-0853
Equal Employment Opportunity Officer: THERESA CUMMINGS; Phone: 217-785-0067
Publication(s): *Digest of Hunting and Trapping Regulations; Illinois Fishing Information Book; State Park Magazine; Outdoor Illinois Magazine*
Keyword(s): Biodiversity, Biology, Conservation of Protected Areas, Endangered and Threatened Species, Environmental and Conservation Education

ILLINOIS DEPARTMENT OF TRANSPORTATION
2300 S. Dirksen Pkwy., Springfield, IL 62764
Phone: 217-782-5597
Contact(s):
Secretary: KIRK BROWN; Phone: 217-782-6828
Chief of Environment: PETER J. FRANTZ; Phone: 217-782-4770; Fax: 217-524-9356
Chief: Bureau of Design and Environment: WILLIAM T. SUNLEY; Phone: 217-782-7526; Fax: 217-524-0989
Director: Division of Highways: JAMES C. SLIFER; Phone: 217-782-2151; Fax: 217-524-2972
Keyword(s): Transportation

ILLINOIS ENVIRONMENTAL PROTECTION AGENCY
2200 Churchill Rd., Springfield, IL 62794
Phone: 217-782-3397; Fax: 217-782-9039
Founded: 1970
Description: Responsible for implementing the environmental program for the state of Illinois. Administers a variety of programs to protect the air, land, and water.
Contact(s):
Deputy Director: BERNARD P. KILLIAN
Director: MARY A. GADE
Chief: Bureau of Air: BHARAT MATHUR; Phone: 217-785-4140
Chief: Bureau of Land: WILLIAM CHILD; Phone: 217-785-9407
Chief: Bureau of Water: JAMES PARK; Phone: 217-782-1654
Editor: JOAN MURARO; Phone: 217-785-7209
Head Librarian: NANCY SIMPSON, 1021 N. Grand Ave. E., P.O. Box 19276, Springfield, ILq62794-9276 ; Phone: 217-782-9691
Manager: Public Information: DENNIS McMURRAY
Publication(s): *Digester/Over the Spillway; Environmental Progress*
Keyword(s): Air Quality and Pollution, Environmental Law, Environmental Preservation, Toxic Substances, Water Pollution

NATURE PRESERVES COMMISSION
524 S. Second St., Lincoln Tower Plaza, Springfield, IL 62701-1787
Phone: 217-785-8686
Founded: 1963
Description: The mission of the Illinois Nature Preserves Commission (INPC) is to assist private and public landowners in protecting high quality natural areas and habitats of endangered and threatened species in perpetuity, through voluntary dedication of such lands into the Illinois Nature Preserves System. The commission promotes the preservation of these significant lands, and once dedicated as nature preserves, oversees their stewardship, management, and protection.
Contact(s):
Secretary: DON PIERCE, P.O. Box 1866, FairviewHeights, IL 62208
Director: CAROLYN TAFT GROSBOLL
Chairperson: THOMAS DONNELLEY II, 77 W. Wacker Dr., 17th Fl., Chicago, IL 60601-1696
Deputy Director and Legal Counsel: CAROLYN T. GROSBOLL
Deputy Director for Protection: DON McFALL
Deputy Director for Stewardship: RANKY HEIDORN
Vice Chairperson: VICTORIA POST RANNEY, 18202 W. Casey Rd., Grayslake, IL 60030
Keyword(s): Environmental Preservation, Land Preservation, Nature Preservation

INDIANA

GOVERNOR OF INDIANA, FRANK O'BANNON
Rm. 206, Statehouse, Indianapolis, IN 46204
Phone: 317-232-4567

INDIANA DEPARTMENT OF ENVIRONMENTAL MANAGEMENT
P.O. Box 6015, Indianapolis, IN 46206
Phone: 317-232-8603
Description: The Indiana Department of Environmental Management is dedicated to conserving, protecting, enhancing, restoring, and managing Indiana's environment. We strive to fairly but vigorously enforce laws and standards; promulgate regulations consistent with the law and public policy; and promote conservation, pollution prevention, and a healthy and sustainable ecosystem. We are committed to making Indiana a cleaner, healthier place to live.
Contact(s):
Acting Assistant Commissioner for Solid and Hazardous Waste: BRUCE PALIN; Phone: 317-232-3210
Assistant Commissioner for Environmental Response: MARY BETH TUOHY; Phone: 317-308-3006
Assistant Commissioner for Office of Pollution Prevention: THOMAS NELTNER; Phone: 317-232-8172

Assistant Commissioner for Water Management: MATHEW RUEFF; Phone: 317-232-8476
Assistant Commissioner of Enforcement: FELICIA GEORGE; Phone: 317-233-5523
Assistant Commissioner Results and Chief Counsel: DAVE HENSEL; Phone: 317-233-0942
Assistant Commissioner: Air Management: JANET MCCABE; Phone: 317-233-6861
Commissioner: JOHN M. HAMILTON; Phone: 317-232-8611
Deputy Commissioner for Environmental and Regulatory Affairs: TIMOTHY METHOD; Phone: 317-233-3706
Deputy Commissioner for Operations: CAROLE CASTO BRUBAKER; Phone: 317-232-8180
Director of Business & Legislative Relations: ERICKA SEYDEL; Phone: 317-232-8598
Director of Investigations: LEON GRIFFITH; Phone: 317-232-8128
Director of Media & Communication Services: PETE BLUM; Phone: 317-232-8560
Director of Northcentral Office: JUDY DIOUS THOMANN; Phone: 812-436-2570
Director of Northwest Regional Office: DAVID ROZ MANICH; Phone: 219-881-6712
Director of Planning & Assessment: LARRY WILSON; Phone: 317-233-6645

INDIANA DEPARTMENT OF NATURAL RESOURCES
402 W. Washington St., Rm. W255B, Indianapolis, IN 46204-2748
Phone: 317-232-4200
Description: The DNR administers more than 100 properties throughout Indiana, comprising more than 400,000 acres. The DNR provides recreational opportunities for millions of Hoosiers and out-of-state visitors annually at its state parks, forests, reservoirs, and fish and wildlife areas. The DNR also has wide-ranging responsibilities for various programs such as maintaining the Indiana State Museum and more than a dozen historic sites throughout the state; ensuring that coal mining and reclamation of those mines take place in a manner that is in the best interests of the citizens of Indiana, and making sure that proper use is made of, and adequate protection is given to, the state's natural resources such as water, soil, forests, wildlife and historic resources.
Contact(s):
Director: PATRICK R. RALSTON; Phone: 317-232-4020
Chairman: Lands and Cultural Resources Advisory Council: JERRY MILLER; Phone: 317-232-4020
Chairman: Natural Resources Commission: MICHAEL KILEY; Phone: 317-232-4020
Chairman: Water and Resource Regulation Advisory Council: JOSEPH SIENER; Phone: 317-232-4020
Chief Counsel: LORI KAPLAN; Phone: 317-232-4020
Chief Hearings Officer: STEVEN LUCAS; Phone: 317-232-0156
Controller: JAMES VAUGHN; Phone: 317-232-4020
Deputy Director: Bureau of Lands and Cultural Resources: JOHN T. COSTELLO; Phone: 317-232-4020
Deputy Director: Bureau of Mine Reclamation: PAUL EHRET; Phone: 317-232-4020
Deputy Director: Bureau of Water and Resource Regulation: DAVID L. HERBST; Phone: 317-232-4020
Deputy Director: Law Enforcement and Administration: DAVID VICE; Phone: 317-232-4020
Director: Division of Accounting: THOMAS BARTON; Phone: 317-232-4041
Director: Division of Budget and Support Services: RICHARD LEKENS; Phone: 317-232-4036
Director: Division of Fish and Wildlife: GARY DOXTATER; Phone: 317-232-4080
Director: Division of Historic Preservation and Archaeology: DANIEL J. FOGERTY; Phone: 317-232-1646
Director: Division of Human Resources: S. FRANCES MILLER; Phone: 317-232-4031
Director: Division of Internal Audit: JAMES LIVERETT; Phone: 317-232-8092
Director: Division of Land Acquisition: JOHN DAVIS; Phone: 317-232-4050
Director: Division of Law Enforcement: COL. CHARLES; Phone: 317-232-4010
Director: Division of Nature Preserves: JOHN BACONE; Phone: 317-232-4052
Director: Division of Oil and Gas: JIM SLUTZ; Phone: 317-232-4055
Director: Division of Outdoor Recreation (Administers Land and Water Conservation Fund): EMILY KRESS; Phone: 317-232-4070
Director: Division of Public Information and Education: STEPHEN SELLERS; Phone: 317-232-4200
Director: Division of Reclamation: MIKE SPONSLER; Phone: 812-665-2207
Director: Division of Reservoir Management: J. BLAKE TAYLOR; Phone: 317-232-4060
Director: Division of Safety & Training: PHILIP WAGNER; Phone: 317-232-4145
Director: Division of Safety and Training: PHILIP WAGNER; Phone: 317-232-4145
Director: Division of Soil Conservation: HARRY NIKIDES; Phone: 317-233-3880
Director: Division of State Museum and Historical Sites: DR. RICHARD GANTZ; Phone: 317-232-1637
Director: Division of State Parks: GERALD PAGAC; Phone: 317-232-4124
Director: Division of Water: JOHN SIMPSON; Phone: 317-232-4160
Director: Internal Audit: JIM LIVERETT; Phone: 317-232-8092
Director: Management Information Systems: MIKE QUIGLEY; Phone: 317-232-4007
Editor: STEPHEN SELLERS
Head Chief Engineer: Division of Engineering: TOM HOHMAN; Phone: 317-232-4150
State Entomologist Director: Division of Entomology and Plant Pathology: DR. ROBERT WALTZ; Phone: 317-232-4120
State Forester: Head: Division of Forestry: DR. BURNELL FISCHER; Phone: 317-232-4105
Publication(s): Outdoor Indiana
Keyword(s): Forests and Forestry, Historic Preservation, Outdoor Recreation, Water Resources, Wildlife Management

Division of Soil Conservation
402 W. Washington St., Rm. W265, Indianapolis, IN 46204-2739
Phone: 317-233-3870; WWW: www.dnr.state.in.us/soilcons/index.htm
Description: The Division's mission is to facilitate the protection, wise use, and enhancement of Indiana's soil and water resources by: coordinating implementation of the state's T-by-2000 soil conservation/water quality protection program and providing assistance to local soil and water conservation districts.
Contact(s):
Director: HARRY S. NIKIDES; Phone: 317-233-3880; Fax: 317-233-3882; Email: harry_nikides_at_dnrlan@ima.isd.state.in.us
Chairman of the Board: PETER A. HIPPENSTEEL
Vice Chairman: DAVID L. AVERY
Publication(s): Indiana Handbook for Erosion Control in Developing Areas*; Topsoil; Lake and River Enhancement Program; Urban Conservation Program; Use of Sand or Pea Gravel in Underwater Beach Construction; Who We Are and What We Do*; Erosion Control for the Home Builder; Wetland Conservation Guidelines; Your Resource Guide to Water Quality; Lakeshore Protection in Indiana (all publications except those noted with * are available on our website).
Keyword(s): Agriculture, Lakes, Rivers, Soil Conservation, Water Quality

INDIANA STATE DEPARTMENT OF HEALTH
Two North Meridian St., Indianapolis, IN 46204
Phone: 317-233-7400
Contact(s):
State Health Commissioner: DR. RICHARD D. FELDMAN

STATE AND PROVINCE GOVERNMENT AGENCIES - IOWA

Keyword(s): Health and Nutrition, Nuclear/Radiation, Public Health Protection, Toxic Substances, Toxicology

INDIANA STATE GEOLOGICAL SURVEY
Institute of Indiana University, 611 N. Walnut Grove, Bloomington, IN 47405
Phone: 812-855-7636
Founded: 1869
Description: Conducts basic and applied research in geology and disseminates geologic information as published reports and maps; consults with industry, academia, and the public on the geologic makeup, mineral and energy resources, and geologic hazards of the state.
Contact(s):
Assistant Director: JOHN R. HILL; Phone: 812-855-6067
Director and State Geologist: JOHN C. STENMETZ; Phone: 812-855-5067
Keyword(s): Environmental Planning, Geology, Mineral Resources

PURDUE UNIVERSITY EXTENSION SERVICES
1140 Agriculture Administration Bldg., Purdue University, West Lafayette, IN 47907-1140
Phone: 765-494-8489; Fax: 765-494-5876
Contact(s):
Assistant Director of Agriculture and Natural Resources Programs: DAVID C. PETRITZ, 1140 Agriculture Administration Bldg., Purdue University, West Lafayette, IN 47907-1140; Phone: 765-494-8494
Director of Extension Service: DR. HENRY A. WADSWORTH
Extension Wildlife Specialist: BRIAN K. MILLER, Dept. of Forestry and Natural Resources, Purdue University, West Lafayette, IN 47907; Phone: 765-494-3586

IOWA

GOVERNOR OF IOWA, TOM VILSACK
State Capitol, DesMoines, IA 50319
Phone: 515-281-5211

IOWA ASSOCIATION OF COUNTY CONSERVATION BOARDS
405 SW 3rd, Ste 1, Ankeny, IA 50021
Description: Promotes the objectives of Iowa's County Conservation Boards, board member education, information exchange, legislation, and public awareness.
Contact(s):
President: GENE OLSEN
Vice President: DAN HEISSEL
Secretary: STEVE LEKWA
Executive Secretary: DON BRAZELTON
Publication(s): *Iowa Board Member; IACCB Memo; IACCB Legislative Update; Outdoor Adventure Guide (Area Directory)*

IOWA COOPERATIVE FISH AND WILDLIFE RESEARCH UNIT
Animal Ecology Department 11 Science Hall II Iowa State University, Ames, IA 50011-3221
Phone: 515-294-3056; Fax: 515-294-5468
Founded: 1932
Contact(s):
Assistant Leader of Fisheries: CLAY L. PIERCE
Assistant Leader of Wildlife: ROLF R. KOFORD
Leader: DR. ERWIN E. KLAAS
Keyword(s): Biodiversity, Fisheries, Gap Analysis, Research, Sustainable Ecosystems, Wildlife and Wildlife Habitat

IOWA DEPARTMENT OF AGRICULTURE AND LAND STEWARDSHIP

Bureau of Field Services
E. 9th and Grand Ave., Wallace Bldg, Des Moines, IA 50319-0034
Contact(s):
JAMES GILLESPIE; Phone: 515-281-5258

Bureau of Financial Incentive Program
E. 9th and Grand Ave., Wallace Bldg, Des Moines, IA 50319-0034
Contact(s):
WILLIAM McGILL; Phone: 515-281-5851

Bureau of Mines and Minerals
E. 9th and Grand Ave., Wallace Bldg, Des Moines, IA 50319-0034
Contact(s):
KENNETH R. TOW; Phone: 515-281-6142

Bureau of Water Resources
E. 9th and Grand Ave., Wallace Bldg, Des Moines, IA 50319-0034
Contact(s):
DAN LINDQUIST; Phone: 515-281-5851

Division of Soil Conservation
Wallace State Office Bldg., Des Moines, IA 50319
Phone: 515-281-5851
Description: Administers soil and water conservation district laws. Allocates state appropriations to 100 soil and water conservation districts for personnel, commissioners' expense, and financial incentives for erosion control and water quality measures. Reviews watershed and RC & D project applications. Oversees erosion control law. Involved with water resources and nonpoint-source pollution control planning. Division licenses mine operations and administers federal surface mining and Abandoned Mine Land Program regulations.
Contact(s):
Assistant Director: KENNETH R. TOW; Phone: 515-281-6142
Director: JAMES B. GULLIFORD; Phone: 515-281-6146; Fax: 515-281-6170; Email: jgull@sela.osmre.gov
Chairperson: DIANE THOMPSON, 35530-125th Ave., ForestCity, IA 50436
Vice Chairperson: MARY ANN DRISH, 1373 Spruce Ave., Brighton, IA 52540

IOWA DEPARTMENT OF NATURAL RESOURCES
E. 9th and Grand Ave., Wallace Bldg., Des Moines, IA 50319-0034
Phone: 515-281-5145
Founded: 1986
Description: Established with the merging of the following state agencies: Iowa Conservation Commission, Department of Water, Air and Waste Management; Iowa Geological Survey; and the resources/conservation functions of the Energy Policy Council. The seven-member Natural Resources Commission is a policy and rule-setting authority over the Fish and Wildlife Division, Parks, Recreation, and Preserves Division, and the Forestry Division; the nine-member Environmental Protection Commission is the policy and rule-setting authority over the Environmental Protection Division and the Waste Management Division.
Contact(s):
Deputy Director: DONALD J. PAULIN
Director: LARRY J. WILSON
Chief of Information-Education Bureau: ROSS HARRISON
Editor of Iowa Conservationist: JULIE HOLMES SPARKS
Environmental Protection Commission Chair: WILLIAM EHM
Natural Resource Commision Chair: LAVONNE TROYNA
Keyword(s): Air Quality and Pollution, Aquatic Habitats, Birds, Chemical Pollution Control, Conservation of Protected Areas, Endangered and Threatened Species, Energy, Environment, Fisheries, Geology, Hunting, Lakes, Land Purchase, Natural Areas

Administrative Services Division
Des Moines, IA 50319
Contact(s):
Administrator: STAN KUHN
Chief of Administrative Support Bureau: SALLY JAGNANDAN
Chief of Budget and Finance Bureau: MARK SLATTERLY
Chief of Construction Services Bureau: BASIL NIMRY

Chief of Land Acquisition and Management Bureau: JOHN BEAMER
Chief of Licensing Bureau and Data Processing Bureau: JUDY PAWELL

Cooperative North American Shotgunning Education Program
Wallace State Office Bldg., Des Moines, IA 50319
Phone: 515-281-6156; Fax: 503-884-2974
Founded: 1982
Description: The Cooperative North American Shotgunning Program is a research, information, and education program designed to assist wildlife professionals, hunters, and sportsmen in making a successful transition from lead shot to nontoxic shot, as well as educating sportsmen on improving shooting skills and harvest efficiency, thereby reducing wounding losses.
Contact(s):
Chairman: RICHARD BISHOP, Wallace State Bldg., DesMoines, IA 50319; Phone: 515-281-6156
Admistrator: STAN KUHN
Chief: Administrative Support Bureau: SALLY JAGNANDAN
Chief: Budget and Finance Bureau: MARK SLATTERLY
Chief: Construction Services Bureau: BASIL NIMRY
Chief: Land Acquisition and Management Bureau: JOHN BEAMER
Chief: Licensing Bureau and Data Processing: JUDY PAWELL
Consultant: TOM ROSTER, 1190 Lynnewood Blvd., KlamathFalls, OR 97601; Phone: 503-884-2974
Contact for Atlantic Flyway: LLOYD ALEXANDER, 89 Kings Highway, P.O. Box 1401, Dover, DE ; Phone: 302-739-5287
Contact for Canadian Wildlife Service: BOB MCLEAN, 17th Fl., Place Vincent Massey, Ottawa, Ontario K1A 0H3 Canada; Phone: 819-997-2957
Contact for Central Flyway: GEORGE VANDEL, 445 E. Capitol, Pierre, SD ; Phone: 605-773-3381
Contact for Mississippi Flyway: RICHARD ELDEN, P.O. 30028, Lansing, MI ; Phone: 517-373-1263
Contact for Pacific Flyway: DON CHILDRESS, 1420 E. 6th, Box 20071, Helena, MT 59601; Phone: 406-444-2612
Publication(s): *CONSEP Newsletter; Periodic Ballistics Reports*
Keyword(s): Hunting, Waterfowl, Wildlife Management

Energy and Geological Resources Division
Contact(s):
Administrator: LARRY BEAN
Chief of Energy Bureau: SHARON TAHTINEN
Chief of Geological Survey Bureau: DON KOCH

Environmental Protection Division
Contact(s):
Administrator: ALLAN STOKES
Chief of Air Quality Bureau: PETE HAMLIN
Chief of Compliance & Enforcement Bureau: MIKE MURPHY
Chief of Land Quality Bureau: JOE OBR
Chief of Water Quality Bureau: DARRELL McALLISTER

Fish and Wildlife Division
Contact(s):
Administrator: ALLEN FARRIS
Chief of Fisheries Bureau: MARION CONOVER
Chief of Law Enforcement Bureau: RICK McGEOUGH
Chief of Wildlife Bureau: RICHARD BISHOP
Coordinator of Hunter Safety: SONNY SATRE

Forests and Forestry Division
Contact(s):
Administrator: BILL FARRIS
Chief of Forestry Services Bureau: MIKE BRANDRUP
Chief of State Forests Management Bureau: JIM BULMAN

Parks
Contact(s):
Administrator: MIKE CARRIER
Chief of Field Operations Bureau: STEPHEN PENNINGTON
Chief of Program Administration Bureau: ARNIE SOHN

Waste Management Division
Contact(s):
Administrator: ROYA STANLEY
Bureau Chief: SHERRY TIMMINS
Executive Officer: BRENT LANING

IOWA STATE EXTENSION SERVICES
Attn: Vice Provost of Extension Services, 218 Beardshear Hall, Iowa State University, Ames, IA 50011
Phone: 515-294-6192; Fax: 515-294-4715; Email: vpforext@exnet.iastate.edu
Description: ISU Extension is a client-centered organization that provides research-based, unbiased information and education to help people make better decisions in their personal, community, and professional lives.
Contact(s):
Extension Forester: PAUL H. WRAY, 251 Bessey Hall, Iowa State University, Ames, IA 50011; Phone: 515-294-1168
Extension Wildlife Conservationist: JAMES L. PEASE, 103 Science II, Iowa State University, Ames, IA 50011; Phone: 515-294-7429

KANSAS

GOVERNOR OF KANSAS, BILL GRAVES
State Capitol, 2nd Fl., Topeka, KS 66612-1590
Phone: 913-296-3232

KANSAS BIOLOGICAL SURVEY
2041 Constant Ave., Foley Hall, Lawrence, KS 66047-2906
Phone: 785-864-7725; Fax: 785-864-5093
Founded: 1959
Description: A research and development branch of the University of Kansas whose purpose is to survey and inventory the native plants and animals of Kansas, report on its findings, and develop and administer lands for the study and preservation of native animal and plant resources.
Contact(s):
Assistant Director: PAUL M. LIECHTI
Associate Director: DR. FRANK deNOYELLES
Director and State Biologist: DR. EDWARD MARTINKO
Keyword(s): Aquatic Habitats, Biodiversity, Endangered and Threatened Species, Prairies, Sustainable Ecosystems

KANSAS COOPERATIVE FISH AND WILDLIFE RESEARCH UNIT
205 Leasure Hall, Kansas State University, Manhattan, KS 66506-3501
Phone: 785-532-6070; Fax: 785-532-7159
Founded: 1991
Contact(s):
Assistant Leader of Fisheries: DR. CHRISTOPHER S. GUY
Assistant Leader of Wildlife: DR. JACK F. CULLY JR.
Leader: DR. PHILIP S. GIPSON

KANSAS DEPARTMENT OF AGRICULTURE
901 S. Kansas Ave., Topeka, KS 66612-1280
Contact(s):
Secretary: ALICE DEVINE
Chief Engineer and Director of Water Resources Division: DAVID L. POPE; Phone: 785-296-3717
Operations Manager for Water Resources Division: STEVE STANKIEWICZ
Water Appropriations Program Manager: TOM HUNTZINGER
Water Management Services Program Manager: MATT SCHERER
Keyword(s): Agriculture, Environmental and Conservation Education, Renewable Resources, Water Resources, Wetlands

STATE AND PROVINCE GOVERNMENT AGENCIES - KANSAS

KANSAS DEPARTMENT OF WILDLIFE AND PARKS
900 SW Jackson St., Suite 502, Topeka, KS 66612
Phone: 785-296-2281; Fax: 785-296-6953

Description: Charged with the conservation of state wildlife and fishery resources, provision of environmental services and habitat protection, and park development and management. Administers state boating law, hunter education programs, Land and Water Conservation Funds, and other related functions.

Contact(s):
Secretary: STEVEN A. WILLIAMS
Assistant Secretary for Administration: RICHARD KOERTH
Boating Education (Topeka Office): CHERYL SWAYNE
Commissioner Members Chairman: JOHN DYKES; Phone: 913-722-3985
Federal Aid Coordinator: TERRY DENKER

Keyword(s): Agriculture, Aquatic Habitats, Biodiversity, Biology, Birds, Communications, Conservation of Protected Areas, Conservation Tillage, Ecology, Endangered and Threatened Species, Environment, Fisheries, Hunting, Lakes

Operations Office
512 SE 25th Ave., Pratt, KS 67124-8174
Phone: 316-672-5911

Contact(s):
Administrative Services Division: MIKE THEURER
Assistant Secretary for Operations: ROB MANES
Coordinator of Hunter Education and Furharvester Education Sections: WAYNE DOYLE
Coordinator of Wildlife Education Service: ROLAND STEIN
Editor: MIKE MILLER
Fisheries and Wildlife Division: JOE KRAMER
Information and Education: BOB MATHEWS
Law Enforcement Division: STEVE STACKHOUSE
Parks Division: JEROLD HOVER
Public Information: BOB MATHEWS

Publication(s): *Kansas Wildlife and Parks*

Keyword(s): Fisheries, Outdoor Recreation, Public Lands, Sport Fishing

Region 1
P.O. Box 338, U.S. 183 Bypass, Hays, KS 67601
Phone: 785-628-8614

Publication(s): *Kansas Wildlife and Parks*

Region 2
3300 SW 29th St., Topeka, KS 66614
Phone: 785-273-6740

Region 3
1001 W. McArtor Rd., Dodge City, KS 67801
Phone: 316-227-8609

Region 4
6232 E. 29th St. N, Wichita, KS 67220
Phone: 316-683-8069

KANSAS DEPARTMENT OF WILDLIFE AND PARKS, Region 5
1500 W. 7th, P.O. Box 777, Chanute, KS 66720-0777
Phone: 316-431-0380

KANSAS FOREST SERVICE
2610 Claflin Rd., Manhattan, KS 66502-2798
Phone: 785-532-3300; Fax: 785-532-3305

Description: Provides technical forestry assistance to landowners, wood industries, and communities; conducts a tree distribution program, and a rural fire protection program.

Contact(s):
Conservation Forester: WILLIAM L. LOUCKS
Fire Manager: JAMES W. KUNKEL
Rural Forestry Coordinator: ROBERT L. ATCHISON
State Forester: RAYMOND G. ASLIN

Keyword(s): Environmental and Conservation Education, Forest Management, Forests and Forestry, Renewable Resources, Urban Forestry, Water Quality, Water Resources

KANSAS GEOLOGICAL SURVEY
1930 Constant Ave., Campus West, Kansas University, Lawrence, KS 66047
Phone: 785-864-3965

Founded: *1889*

Description: Purpose is to research and develop information about minerals, water resources, and geologic hazards of Kansas, and to publish reports on those subjects.

Contact(s):
Deputy Director: WILLIAM E. HARRISON
Chief: Geohydrology: DON WHITTEMORE
Chief: Geologic Investigations: PIETER BERENDSEN
Chief: Mathematical Geology: JOHN C. DAVIS
Chief: Petroleum Research: TIMOTHY CARR
Director and State Geologist: LEE C. GERHARD

Publication(s): *Bulletin; journals; maps; technical series; educational series; public information circulars.*

Keyword(s): Energy, Environmental and Conservation Education, Geology, Water Pollution, Water Resources

KANSAS STATE CONSERVATION COMMISSION
109 SW Ninth St., Suite 500, Topeka, KS 66612-1299
Phone: 785-296-3600; Fax: 785-296-6172; WWW: www.ink.org/public/kscc

Founded: *1937*

Description: The SCC administrative responsibility is to provide leadership, direction, and support to the conservation districts, watershed districts, and other special purpose districts for the protection and enhancement of Kansas' natural resources. It administers a total of ten programs: seven are financial assistance programs funded by appropriations from the Special Revenue Fund of the State Water Plan.

Contact(s):
Executive Director: TRACY D. STREETER; Phone: 913-296-3600; Fax: 913-296-6172

Keyword(s): Environmental and Conservation Education, Soil Conservation, Water Pollution, Water Quality, Water Resources, Watersheds, Wetlands

KANSAS STATE DEPARTMENT OF HEALTH AND ENVIRONMENT
Landon State Office Bldg., Rm. 620, Topeka, KS 66612-1290

Description: The Kansas Department of Health and Environment is responsible for administering a diverse collection of programs that enhance public health and state wildlife protection efforts. The path of the department is defined by strengthening programs and developing initatives on pollutant releases, spill cleanup, air and water quality, water resources, pollution prevention, waste management, and general health and environmental protection.

Contact(s):
Secretary: GARY R. MITCHELL; Phone: 785-296-0461
Director of Division of Health:
Director: Bureau of Environmental Field Services: THERESA HODGES; Phone: 785-296-6603
Director: Bureau of Environmental Health Services: STEVE PAIGE; Phone: 785-296-5600
Director: Bureau of Environmental Remediation: LARRY KNOCHE; Phone: 785-296-1660
Director: Bureau of Waste Management: BILL BIDER
Director: Bureau of Water: KARL MUELDENER; Phone: 785-296-5500
Director: Division of Environment: RON HAMMERSCHMIDT; Phone: 785-296-1535
Director: Office of Public Information: DON BROWN; Phone: 785-296-1529

Keyword(s): Air Quality and Pollution, Environment, Health and Nutrition, Pollution Prevention, Public Health Protection, Solid Waste, Water Quality, Water Resources

KANSAS STATE EXTENSION SERVICES
Wildlife Damage Control, Department of Animal Sciences and Industry, 127 Call Hall, Kansas State University, Manhattan, KS 66506
Phone: 785-532-5734
Founded: 1914
Contact(s):
Extension Specialist: CHARLES D. LEE
Keyword(s): Hunting, Predators, Trapping, Wetlands, Wildlife and Wildlife Habitat, Wildlife Management, Youth Organizations

KANSAS WATER OFFICE
109 SW Ninth St., Suite 300, Topeka, KS 66612-1249
Phone: 913-296-3185
Description: State water planning, policy, and coordination agency. Prepares state plan of water resources management; conservation; fish and, wildlife, and recreation and development reviews water laws, and recommends new or amendatory legislation. Administers the state water marketing program.
Contact(s):
Assistant Director: CLARK DUFFY
Director: AL LeDOUX
Keyword(s): Lakes, Planning Management, Rivers, Sustainable Development, Water Resources

KENTUCKY

GOVERNOR OF KENTUCKY, PAUL E. PATTON
State Capitol, 700 Capitol St., Frankfort, KY 40601
Phone: 502-564-2611

KENTUCKY DEPARTMENT OF AGRICULTURE
7th Fl., 500 Mero St., Frankfort, KY 40601
Phone: 502-564-4696
Founded: 1876
Description: The service, regulatory, and promotional agency for Kentucky's agriculture industry.
Contact(s):
Commissioner: BILLY RAY SMITH
Director: Division of Communications: MISTIANNA H. BARNES; Phone: 502-564-4696
Editor: STACEY GISH; Phone: 502-746-7030
Publication(s): *Kentucky Agricultural News*
Keyword(s): Agriculture, Environmental and Conservation Education, Pesticides, Soil Conservation, Wetlands

KENTUCKY DEPARTMENT OF FISH AND WILDLIFE RESOURCES
#1 Game Farm Rd., Frankfort, KY 40601
Phone: 502-564-3400; Fax: 502-564-6508; Email: username%gamefarm%fw%internet@msmail.state.ky.us
Founded: 1944
Description: We are stewards of Kentucky's fish and wildlife resources and their habitats. We manage for the perpetuation of these resources and their use by present and future generations. Through partnerships, we will enhance wildlife diversity and promote sustainable use, including hunting, fishing, boating, and other nature-related recreation.
Contact(s):
Commissioner: C. TOM BENNETT
Coordinator of Pittman-Robertson Section: DON WALKER; Phone: 502-564-4406
Coordinator of Sport Fish Restoration Section: JAMES AXON; Phone: 502-564-5448
Deputy Commissioner: THOMAS A. YOUNG
Director of Administrative Services Division: ROBERT M. BATES; Phone: 502-564-4224
Director of Division of Fisheries: PETER W. PFEIFFER; Phone: 502-564-3596
Director of Division of Information and Education: NANCY THEISS; Phone: 502-564-4762
Director of Division of Law Enforcement: DAVID LOVELESS; Phone: 502-564-3176
Director of Division of Wildlife: ROY GRIMES; Phone: 502-564-4406
Director of Engineering Division: CHARLES BUSH; Phone: 502-564-2468
Director of Public Affairs Division: LYNN GARRISON; Phone: 502-564-4338
District 1 Commissioner: MIKE BOATWRIGHT, 2601 N. 10th St., Paducah, KY 42001; Phone: 502-442-6784
District 2 Commissioner: TOM BAKER, 661 A U.S. 31 W. By-Pass, Bowling Green, KY 42101; Phone: 502-782-2250
District 3 Commissioner: ALLEN K. GAILOR, 730 W. Market, Louisville, KY 40202; Phone: 502-584-7217
District 4 Commissioner: CHARLES BALE, 855 Parkers Grove Rd., Hodgenville, KY 42748; Phone: 502-324-3211
District 5 Commissioner: JAMES RICH, 5975 Taylor Mill Rd., Covington, KY 41015; Phone: 606-356-9274
District 6 Commissioner: FRANK BROWN, 124 Lancaster Ave., Richmond, KY 40475; Phone: 606-624-0014; Fax: 606-624-0820
District 7 Commissioner: DOUG HENSLEY, P.O. Box 480, Hazard, KY 41701; Phone: 606-436-2321; Fax: 606-436-5180
District 8 Commissioner: DR. ROBERT C. WEBB, 45 Webb Circle, Grayson, KY 41143; Phone: 606-474-5149
District 9 Commissioner: DAVID GOLBY, P.O. Box 1277, Somerset, KY 42502; Phone: 606-677-0115; Fax: 606-677-0115
Regional Boating Supervisor: DENNIS WATSON, Route 1 Sand Knob, Falls of Rough, KY 40119; Phone: 502-257-8170
Regional Boating Supervisor: STEVE OWENS, 338 Candlelite Drive, Almo, KY 42020; Phone: 502-753-7432
Regional Boating Supervisor: REED SANDERS, 185 Gwinn Island Circle, Danville, KY 40422
Regional Boating Supervisor: K. R. HENDERSON, P.O. Box 131, Clarkson, KY 42726; Phone: 502-242-7331
Regional Law Enforcement Supervisor: GERALD ALEXANDER, 6575 Beech Grove Rd., Farmington, KY 42040
Superintendent of State Game Farm: JOHN AKERS; Phone: 502-564-2468
Publication(s): *Kentucky Wildlife Viewing Guide; Kentucky Afield Magazine; Kentucky Fish; Hunting and Fishing Regulation Guides*
Keyword(s): Biodiversity, Environmental and Conservation Education, Fisheries, Wildlife and Wildlife Habitat

KENTUCKY DEPARTMENT OF PARKS
10th Fl., Capital Plaza Tower, Frankfort, KY 40601
Phone: 502-564-2172
Contact(s):
Commissioner: KENNY RAPIER
Deputy Commissioner: BOB BENDER
Director of Resort Parks: JIM GOODMAN
Director: Rangers: DANNY REED
State Naturalist: CAREY TICHENOR
Keyword(s): Land Preservation, Outdoor Recreation, Public Lands

KENTUCKY GEOLOGICAL SURVEY
228 Mining and Mineral Resources Bldg., University of Kentucky, Lexington, KY 40506-0107
Phone: 606-257-5500
Founded: 1854
Description: Investigates the geology and mineral and water resources of Kentucky and makes this information available to the public. It is a research and service organization.
Contact(s):
Assistant State Geologist for Administration: JOHN D. KIEFER
Assistant State Geologist for Research and Head: Coal and Minerals Section: JAMES C. COBB
Director and State Geologist: DONALD C. HANEY
Head: Computer and Laboratory Services Section: STEVEN J. CORDIVIOLA
Head: Publications Section: DONALD W. HUTCHESON
Head: Stratigraphy and Petroleum Geology Section: JAMES DRAHOVZAL

STATE AND PROVINCE GOVERNMENT AGENCIES - LOUISIANA

Head: Water Resources Section: JAMES S. DINGER
Publication(s): *List available on request.*

KENTUCKY SOIL AND WATER CONSERVATION COMMISSION
663 Teton Trail, Frankfort, KY 40601
Contact(s):
Chair: DAVID GERREIN; Phone: 606-623-3960
Director of Division of Conservation: STEPHEN A. COLEMAN; Phone: 502-564-3080; Fax: 502-564-9195; Email: coleman@NREPC.NR.STATE.KY.US

KENTUCKY STATE EXTENSION SERVICES
University of Kentucky, Lexington, KY 40546
Phone: 606-257-4302; Fax: 606-323-1031
Contact(s):
Acting Chairman: Dept. of Forestry: DR. DON GRAVES, University of Kentucky, Lexington, KY 40546; Phone: 606-257-7596; Email: dgraves@ca.uky.edu
Assistant Extension Director of Agriculture: DR. CURTIS ABSHER, University of Kentucky, Lexington, KY 40546; Phone: 606-257-1846
Associate Dean and Associate Director of Extension Service: DR. WALTER J. WALLA
Extension Forestry: DR. JEFF STRINGER, University of Kentucky, Lexington, KY 40546; Phone: 606-257-5994
Wildlife Expert: DR. THOMAS G. BARNES, Dept. of Forestry, University of Kentucky, Lexington, KY 40546; Phone: 606-257-8633; Email: tbarnes@ca.uky.edu

KENTUCKY STATE NATURE PRESERVES COMMISSION
801 Schenkel Lane, Frankfort, KY 40601
Phone: 502-573-2886; Fax: 502-573-2355; Email: STMP:KSNpcemail@nqepc.nr.state.ky.us; WWW: www.state.ky.us\stb.htm
Founded: 1976
Description: KSNP's mission is to protect Kentucky's natural heritage by (1) identifying, acquiring, and managing natural areas that represent the best known occurrences of rare native species, natural communitites, and significant natural features in a statewide nature preserve system; (2) working with others to protect biological diveristy; and (3) educating Kentuckians as to the value and purpose of nature preserves and biodiversity conservation.
Contact(s):
Director: DONALD S. DOTT JR.; Phone: 502-573-2886; Fax: 502-573-2355; Email: ksnpcemail@nrepc.nr.state.ky.us
Chair of Commission: JUDITH MCCANDLESS; Phone: 502-895-5775; Email: judithmc@iglou.com
Secretary of Commission: KEN JACKSON; Phone: 506-734-4436

NATURAL RESOURCES AND ENVIRONMENTAL PROTECTION CABINET
5th Fl., Capital Plaza Tower, Frankfort, KY 40601
Phone: 502-564-3350; Fax: 502-564-3354
Contact(s):
Secretary: JAMES BICKFORD
Deputy Secretary: BRUCE WILLIAMS
General Counsel: Office of Legal Services: BARBARA FOSTER; Phone: 502-564-5576; Fax: 502-564-6131

Department for Environmental Protection
14 Reilly Rd., Frankfort, KY 40601
Phone: 502-564-2150; Fax: 502-564-9245
Contact(s):
Commissioner: ROBERT W. LOGAN
Deputy Commissioner: RALPH COLLINS
Director: Division for Air Quality: JOHN E. HORNBACK; Phone: 502-573-3382; Fax: 502-573-3787
Director: Division of Environmental Services: WILLIAM E. DAVIS; Phone: 502-564-6120; Fax: 502-564-8930
Director: Division of Waste Management: ROBERT DANIELL; Phone: 502-564-6716; Fax: 502-564-4049
Director: Division of Water: JACK A. WILSON; Phone: 502-564-3410; Fax: 502-564-4245

Department for Natural Resources
663 Teton Trail, Frankfort, KY 40601
Phone: 502-564-2184; Fax: 502-564-6193
Contact(s):
Commissioner: HUGH N. ARCHER
Director: Division of Conservation: STEVE COLEMAN; Phone: 502-564-3080; Fax: 502-564-7484
Director: Division of Energy: JOHN STAPLETON; Phone: 502-564-7192; Fax: 502-564-7484
Director: Division of Forestry: MARK MATUSZEWSKI; Phone: 502-564-4496; Fax: 502-564-6553

Department for Surface Mining Reclamation and Enforcement
#2 Hudson Hollow, Frankfort, KY 40601
Phone: 502-564-6940; Fax: 502-564-5698
Contact(s):
Commissioner: CARL CAMPBELL
Deputy Commissioner: ALLEN LUTTRELL
Director: Division of Abandoned Lands: STEPHEN HOHMANN; Phone: 502-564-2141; Fax: 502-564-6544
Director: Division of Field Services: MARK THOMPSON; Phone: 502-564-2340; Fax: 502-564-5848
Director: Division of Permits: VICKI PETTUS; Phone: 502-564-2320; Fax: 502-564-6764

Environmental Quality Commission
14 Reilly Rd., Frankfort, KY 40601
Phone: 502-564-2150; Fax: 502-567-4245
Contact(s):
Chair: ALOMA DEW
Executive Director: LESLIE COLE

Nature Preserves Commission
801 Schenkel Ln., Frankfort, KY 40601
Phone: 502-573-2886; Fax: 502-573-2355
Contact(s):
Chairman: JUDITH MCCANDLESS
Director: DON S. DOTT; Phone: 502-573-2355

LOUISIANA

GOVERNOR OF LOUISIANA, M. J. FOSTER, JR.
State Capitol, P.O. Box 94004, BatonRouge, LA 70804
Phone: 504-342-7015

LOUISIANA COOPERATIVE FISH AND WILDLIFE RESEARCH UNIT (USDI)
National Biological Survey, School of Forestry, Wildlife, and Fisheries, Rm. 124, Louisiana State University, Baton Rouge, LA 70803-6202
Phone: 504-388-4179
Contact(s):
Assistant Leader: ALAN D. AFTON
Leader: CHARLES F. BRYAN

LOUISIANA DEPARTMENT OF AGRICULTURE

Office of Forestry
P.O. Box 1628, Baton Rouge, LA 70821-1628
Phone: 225-925-4500
Founded: 1944
Description: Charged with: Detection and suppression of wildfire on forest lands; providing technical management assistance to forest landowners; and dissemination of materials and information for education of the public. Produces approximately 50 million seedlings annually (pine and hardwood) for Louisiana landowners, operates a,400-acre seed orchard that produces improved slash and loblolly pine seed that are genetically improved. Actively engaged in promoting urban forestry activities.
Contact(s):
Chairman: BURTON D. WEAVER JR.
Associate State Forester: CYRIL LeJEUNE

STATE AND PROVINCE GOVERNMENT AGENCIES - LOUISIANA

Chief: Forest Management: DONALD P. FEDUCCIA; Phone: 225-925-4500
Chief: Forest Protection: LOUIS HEATON III
Chief: Information: Education: and Urban Forestry: JAMES L. CULPEPPER; Phone: 225-925-4500
Chief:Reforestation: CHARLES MATHERNE; Phone: 225-925-4515
State Forester: PAUL D. FREY
Keyword(s): Environmental and Conservation Education, Forest Management, Outdoor Recreation, Renewable Resources, Sustainable Ecosystems, Urban Forestry

Office of Soil and Water Conservation, State Soil and Water Conservation Committee
P.O. Box 3554, Baton Rouge, LA 70821-3554
Phone: 504-922-1269
Founded: 1938
Description: To assist soil and water conservation districts in carrying out their conservation programs, to coordinate activities among districts, and to secure the cooperation and assistance of state and federal agencies in the work of such districts.
Contact(s):
Chairman: PEDRO ANGELLE, 4879 Main Hwy., St. Martinville, LA 70582; Phone: 318-332-2910; Fax: 318-332-6563
Executive Director: BRADLEY E. SPICER; Phone: 504-922-1269; Fax: 504-922-2577
Secretary and Treasurer: A. LEE ALLEE
Vice Chairman: THAD SPURLOCK

LOUISIANA DEPARTMENT OF AGRICULTURE AND FORESTRY
P.O. Box 631, Baton Rouge, LA 70821-0631
Phone: 504-922-1234
Contact(s):
Assistant Commissioner: Office of Management and Finance: SKIP RHORER
Commissioner: BOB ODOM
Deputy Commissioner: BUD COURSON; Phone: 504-922-1238; Fax: 504-922-1253

LOUISIANA DEPARTMENT OF WILDLIFE AND FISHERIES
P.O. Box 98000, Baton Rouge, LA 70898-9000
Phone: 225-765-2800
Founded: 1872
Description: Established as a part of state government to protect, conserve, and replenish the natural resources of the state, including wild game and nongame quadrupeds or animals, oysters, fish, and other aquatic life.
Contact(s):
Chairman: THOMAS GATTLE JR.
Secretary: JAMES H. JENKINS JR.; Phone: 225-765-2623
Administrator: Colonel: Law Enforcement Division: WINTON VIDRINE; Phone: 225-765-2989
Administrator: Fur & Refuge Division: BRANDT SAVIOE; Phone: 225-765-2811
Administrator: Inland Fisheries Division: BENNIE FONTENOT; Phone: 225-765-2330
Administrator: Marine Fisheries Division: KAREN FOOTE; Phone: 225-765-2384
Administrator: Wildlife Division: HUGH BATEMAN; Phone: 225-765-2346
Assistant Secretary: Office of Fisheries: JOHN ROUSSEL; Phone: 225-765-2801
Assistant Secretary:Office of Wildlife: PHIL BOWMAN; Phone: 225-765-2806
Deputy Secretary: CLYDE W. KIMBALL; Phone: 225-765-2957
Director: Information and Education Division: DR. LYLE M. SONIAT; Phone: 225-765-2916
Head: DR. LYLE M. SONIAT
Librarian: ROSALIND HOLLINS, Louisiana Department of Wildlife and Fisheries Library, P.O. Box 98000, Baton Rouge, LA 70898-9000; Phone: 504-765-2934
Undersecretary: Office of Management and Finance: JAMES L. PATTON; Phone: 225-765-2860
Vice Chairman: DANIEL J. BABIN
Publication(s): *Louisiana Conservationist*

LOUISIANA GEOLOGICAL SURVEY
P.O. Box G, University Sta., Baton Rouge, LA 70893
Founded: 1934
Description: Established by legislative act, the Louisiana Geological Survey is now a research unit of Lousiana State University. The Survey is charged with conducting geologic investigations and preparing technical reports that assist in finding and developing new reserves of natural resources in the state and in protecting the state's environment. Attention is focused on those matters that are most critical to the state and have the maximum human impact: oil and gas, lignite, groundwater, geothermal energy, and mineral, coastal, and environmental resources. Because it is not a regulatory organization, the Geological Survey is able to conduct studies from an objective viewpoint, thus ensuring that the results are valuable to both the public and private sectors.
Contact(s):
Director: CHACKO J. JOHN
Keyword(s): Coasts, Energy, Geology, Water Resources, Wetlands

LOUISIANA SEA GRANT COLLEGE PROGRAM
Louisiana State University, Baton Rouge, LA 70803
Phone: 225-388-6710; Fax: 225-388-6331
Founded: 1968
Description: The Louisiana Sea Grant College Program is a research, education, and public service organization supported by federal, state, and private sector funds. The Program provides the knowledge, trained personnel, and public awareness needed to wisely and effectively develop and manage coastal and marine areas and resources in a manner that will assure sustainable economic and societal benefits.
Contact(s):
Assistant Director: MICHAEL M. LIFFMANN
Executive Director: DR. JACK R. VANLOPIK, Louisiana State University, BatonRouge, LA 70803; Phone: 225-388-6710; Fax: 225-388-6331; Email: jvanlop@unix1.sncc.lsu.edu
Associate Director: RONALD E. BECKER, Sea Grant College Program, Louisiana State University, BatonRouge, LA 70803; Phone: 225-388-6345
Communications Coordinator: ELIZABETH B. COLEMAN, Louisiana Sea Grant College Program, Louisiana State University, BatonRouge, LA 70803; Phone: 225-388-6448/6449
Publication(s): *Coast and Sea: Marine and Coastal Research in Louisiana's Universities (Quarterly Louisiana Coastal Law)*
Keyword(s): Coasts, Environmental and Conservation Education, Renewable Resources, Sustainable Development, Wetlands

LOUISIANA STATE EXTENSION SERVICES
P.O. Box 25100, Baton Rouge, LA 70894-5100
Phone: 504-388-6083
Contact(s):
Area Agent for Wetland and Coastal Resources: PAUL D. COREIL; Phone: 504-388-2266; Fax: 504-388-2478; Email: pcoreil@agctr.lsu.edu
Assistant Specialist for Forestry: DR. TODD F. SHUPE; Phone: 504-388-2266; Fax: 504-388-2478; Email: tshupe@agctr.lsu.edu
Assistant Specialist for Forestry and Wildlife: DR. DONALD P. REED; Phone: 504-388-2145; Fax: 504-388-2478; Email: dreed@agctr.lsu.edu
Assistant Specialist of Aquaculture: DR. CHARLES G. LUTZ; Phone: 504-388-2152; Fax: 504-388-2478; Email: clutz@agctr.lsu.edu
Associate Area Agent: JIMMY L. AVERY; Phone: 504-388-2152; Fax: 504-388-2478; Email: javery@agctr.lsy.edu
Director of Extension Service: DR. JACK L. BAGENT
Project Leader of (Forestry and Wildlife) and Specialist of Wildlife: DR. JAMES F. FOWLER; Phone: 504-388-3659; Fax: 504-388-2478; Email: jfowler@agctr.lsu.edu
Project Leader of Aquaculture: Fisheries: Wetland & Coastal Management and Sea Grant and Specialist for Marine

STATE AND PROVINCE GOVERNMENT AGENCIES - MAINE

Resource Economics: DR. KENNETH J. ROBERTS; Phone: 504-388-2152; Fax: 504-388-2478; Email: kroberts@agctr.lsu.edu

Specialist for Seafood Technology: DR. MICHAEL W. MOODY; Phone: 504-388-2152; Fax: 504-388-2478; Email: mmoody@agctr.lsu.edu

Specialist: Forestry: DR. ROBERT H. MILLS; Phone: 504-388-4087; Fax: 504-388-2478; Email: bobm@agctr.lsu.edu

OFFICE OF STATE PARKS, DEPARTMENT OF CULTURE, RECREATION, AND TOURISM
P.O. Box 44426, Baton Rouge, LA 70804
Phone: 225-342-8111 or 1-888-677-1400; Email: parks@crt.state.la.us

Founded: 1934
Description: Created to plan, design, construct, operate, and maintain the state's parks, natural areas, recreational facilities, and commemorative sites. Office has 17 parks or recreational areas, 15 commemorative sites, and one preservation area open to the public. The Office is assisted by the Parks and Recreation Commission, an advisory board appointed by the Governor.
Contact(s):
Assistant Secretary: DWIGHT LANDRENEAU
Keyword(s): Cultural Preservation, Historic Preservation, Nature Preservation, Outdoor Recreation, Public Lands

STATE OFFICE OF CONSERVATION (LOUISIANA)
P.O. Box 94275, Capitol Sta., Baton Rouge, LA 70804-9275
Phone: 225-342-5540

Description: The State Office of Conservation is an oil and gas regulatory agency.
Contact(s):
Assistant Commissioner: JIM WELSH
Commissioner: PHILIP N. ASPERODITES
Keyword(s): Energy, Engineering, Geology, Pollution Prevention, Transportation

MAINE

GOVERNOR OF MAINE, ANGUS S. KING, JR.
State House, Station 1, Augusta, ME 04333
Phone: 207-287-3531

DEPARTMENT OF ENVIRONMENTAL PROTECTION (MAINE0
State House Station 17, Augusta, ME 04333
Phone: 207-287-7688; Fax: 207-287-7826

Founded: 1972
Description: DEP is charged with the protection and improvement of Maine's natural environment and acting in the best interests of the citizens' health and quality of life.
Contact(s):
Commissioner: EDWARD O. SULLIVAN
Deputy Commissioner: ERIKA MORGAN
Director: Bureau of Air Quality: JAMES BROOKS
Director: Bureau of Land and Water Quality: MARTHA KIRKPATRICK
Director: Bureau of Remediation and Waste Management: ALLAN BALL
Publication(s): *A Citizen's Guide to Lake Watershed Surveys; The Quality of Maine Waters--A Condensed Version on the 1996 Maine Water Quality Assessment; Watershed: An Action Guide to Improving Maine Waters; Planning Guides for Municipalities (series); Issue profiles and fact sheets on a variety of topics*
Keyword(s): Air Quality and Pollution, Environmental Protection, Pollution Prevention, Solid Waste Management, Water Quality

DEPARTMENT OF INLAND FISHERIES AND WILDLIFE
284 State St., Station #41, Augusta, ME 04333-0041
Phone: 207-287-8000

Founded: 1880
Contact(s):
Chief: Engineering and Realty Division: G. DONALD TAYLOR; Phone: 207-287-5210
Chief: Fishery Research and Management Division: PETER M. BOURQUE; Phone: 207-287-5261
Chief: Wildlife Research and Management Division: G. MARK STADLER; Phone: 207-287-5252
Colonel: Bureau of Warden Service: TIMOTHY PEABODY; Phone: 207-287-2766
Commissioner: LEE E. PERRY; Phone: 207-287-5202
Deputy Commissioner: FREDERICK B. HURLEY JR; Phone: 207-287-3371
Director: Bureau of Administrative Service: RICHARD RECORD; Phone: 207-287-5210
Director: Bureau of Resource Management: KENNETH D. ELOWE; Phone: 207-287-5252
Director: Licensing and Registration Division: VESTA C. BILLING; Phone: 207-287-5225
Rules and Regulations Officer: ANDREA L. ERSKINE; Phone: 207-287-5201
Publication(s): *Maine Fish and Wildlife*
Keyword(s): Endangered and Threatened Species, Fisheries, Hunting, Sport Fishing, Wildlife and Wildlife Habitat

DEPARTMENT OF MARINE RESOURCES
State House, Station #21, Augusta, ME 04333
Phone: 207-624-6550

Founded: 1867
Description: Responsible for research, development, promotion, planning, and enforcement of laws relating to conservation of Maine's marine resources. The Department of Marine Resources was established to conserve and develop marine and estuarine resources of the state of Maine by conducting and sponsoring scientific research, promoting and developing the Maine commercial fishing industry, and by advising agencies of government concerned with development or activity in coastal waters. Through the authority vested in its Commissioner, the Department of Marine Resources is empowered to conserve and develop the marine resources of the state, and to enforce the laws relating to marine resources. The Department of Marine Resources originated with the establishment of Commissioners of Fisheries in the 19th century.
Contact(s):
Chief of Bureau of Marine Patrol: JOSEPH E. FESSENDEN
Commissioner: ROBIN ALDEN
Deputy Commissioner: E. PENN ESTABROOK
Director of Bureau of Resource Management: DR. LINDA MERCER, WestBoothbayHarbor, ME 04575; Phone: 207-633-9500
Director of Division of Administrative Services: GILBERT M. BILODEAU
Keyword(s): Aquatic Habitats, Ecology, Environmental and Conservation Education, Fisheries, Public Health Protection

MAINE ATLANTIC SALMON AUTHORITY (formerly Maine Atlantic Sea Run Salmon Commission)
650 State St., Bangor, ME 04401-5654
Phone: 207-941-4449; Fax: 207-941-4443; WWW: www.state.me.us/ASA

Founded: 1948
Description: The Atlantic Salmon Authority was established for the purposes of undertaking research, planning, management, restoration, and propagation of the Atlantic sea run salmon in the state. The Authority has authority to adopt and amend regulations to promote the conservation and propagation of Atlantic salmon in all Maine waters.
Contact(s):
Commissioner of Inland Fisheries and Wildlife: LEE PERRY
Member at Large (Chairman): WILLIAM NICHOLS
Northern Maine Representative: JAMES BARRESI

Passamaquoddy Indian Tribe Representative: CLIRE DORE
Penobscot Indian Nation Representative: JOHN BANKS
Southern Maine Representative: URBAN PIERCE
Keyword(s): Atlantic Salmon, Biology, Endangered and Threatened Species, Fisheries, Rivers, Sport Fishing

MAINE COOPERATIVE FISH AND WILDLIFE RESEARCH UNIT (USDI)
USGS Biological Resources Division, 5755 Nutting Hall, University of Maine, Orono, ME 04469-5755
Phone: 207-581-2870
Founded: 1935
Description: Provide graduate training and research experience in wildlife and fish ecology and management. Supported cooperatively by the University of Maine in Orono, ME, Maine Department of Inland Fisheries and Wildlife, U.S. Geological Survey, and the Wildlife Management Institute.
Contact(s):
Assistant Leader: Fisheries: DR. JOHN R. MORING, 310 Murray Hall, University of Maine, Orono, ME 04469; Phone: 207-581-2582
Assistant Leader: Wildlife:
Leader: DR. WILLIAM B. KROHN, 258 Nutting Hall, University of Maine, Orono, ME 04469; Phone: 207-581-2870; Fax: 207-581-2858
Keyword(s): Aquatic Habitats, Biodiversity, Fisheries, Geographic Information Systems, Wildlife and Wildlife Habitat, Wildlife Management

MAINE DEPARTMENT OF AGRICULTURE, FOOD, AND RURAL RESOURCES
State House Station # 28, Augusta, ME 4333
Contact(s):
Director: PETER N. MOSHER; Phone: 207-287-1132; Fax: 207-287-7548; Email: peter.mosher@state.me.us
Commissioner: EDWARD McLAUGHLIN; Phone: 207-287-3871

MAINE DEPARTMENT OF CONSERVATION
22 State House Station, Augusta, ME 04333-0022
Phone: 207-287-2211
Founded: 1973
Description: To preserve, protect, and enhance the land resources of the State of Maine; to encourage the wise use of the scenic, mineral, and forest resources; to ensure that coordinated planning for the future allocation of lands for recreational, forest production, mining, and other public and private uses is effectively accomplished; and to provide for the effective management of public lands.
Contact(s):
Administrative Assistant: GALE ROSS
Commissioner: RONALD B. LOVAGLIO
Deputy Commissioner: DAWN GALLAGHER
Director of General Services: WILL HARRIS
Director of Public Information: SUSAN BENSON

Land Use Regulation Commission
State House, Station #22, Augusta, ME 04333
Phone: 207-287-2631, In-state toll free 1800-452-8711
Contact(s):
Director: JOHN WILLIAMS
Resource Administrator: ANDREW FISK

Maine Forest Service
22 State House Station, Augusta, ME 04333
Phone: 207-287-2791
Contact(s):
Director: CHUCK GADZIK
Forest Fire Control Supervisor: TOM PARENT
Forest Policy and Management: DON MANSIUS
Resource Administrator: PETER BERINGER
State Entomologist: DAVE STRUBLE

Natural Resource Information & Mapping
22 State House Station, Augusta, ME 04333
Phone: 207-287-2801
Contact(s):
Director, Applied Geology: TOM WEDDLE
Director, Maine Natural Areas: MOLLY DOCHERTY; Phone: 207-287-8045
Director, Resource Date Services: ROBERT TUCKER
State Geologist and Director: ROBERT MARVINNEY

MAINE DEPARTMENT OF CONSERVATION, Bureau of Parks and Lands)
22 State House Station, Augusta, ME 04333
Phone: 207-287-3821
Contact(s):
Deputy Director: HERB HARTMAN
Director: TOM MORRISON; Phone: 207-287-3821
Allagash Wilderness Waterwa: TIM CAVERLY
Boating Facilities: RICHARD SKINNER
Off-Road Vehicle Program: SCOTT RAMSAY
Planning & Land Use Acquisition: RALPH KNOLL
Resource Administrator: MARLENE BOWMAN

MAINE SEA GRANT PROGRAM
5715 Coburn Hall #14, University of Maine, Orono, ME 04469-5715
Phone: 207-581-1435
Contact(s):
Director: Ira C. Darling Center: DR. KEVIN ECKELBARGER; Phone: 207-563-3146
Director: School of Marine Sciences: DR. BRUCE SIDELL, University of Maine, 200 Libby Hall, Orono, ME 04469; Phone: 207-581-4381
Director: Sea Grant Marine Advisory Program: RON BEARD; Phone: 207-581-1442
Keyword(s): Aquatic Habitats, Coasts, Environmental and Conservation Education, Fisheries, Oceanography

UNIVERSITY OF MAINE COOPERATIVE EXTENSION
Attn:Prog. Admin., 5741 Libby Hall, U. of ME, Orono, ME 04469
Contact(s):
Forestry Specialist: JAMES F. PHILP, 261 Nutting Hall, University of Maine, Orono, ME 04469; Phone: 207-581-2885
Program Administrator: CATHERINE ELLIOTT, 5741 Libby Hall, University of Maine, Orono, ME 04469-5741; Phone: 207-581-2902

MARYLAND

GOVERNOR OF MARYLAND, PARRIS N. GLENDENING
State House, 100 State Cir., Annapolis, MD 21404
Phone: 410-974-3901

DEPARTMENT OF THE ENVIRONMENT
2500 Broening Highway, Baltimore, MD 21224
Phone: 410-631-3000
Founded: 1987
Description: The Department of the Environment is charged with protection of the state's land, air, and water resources, to ensure the long-term protection of public health and quality of life.
Contact(s):
Secretary: JANE T. NISHIDA; Phone: 410-631-3084
Assistant Secretary for Policy: J. CHARLES FOX; Phone: 410-631-4187
Deputy Secretary: ARTHUR W. RAY; Phone: 410-631-3086
Directo of Waste Management Administration: RICHARD W. COLLINS; Phone: 410-631-3304
Director of Administrative and Employee Services: LESLIE CHAMPBELL; Phone: 410-631-3116

STATE AND PROVINCE GOVERNMENT AGENCIES - MARYLAND

Director of Air and Radiation Management Administration: MERRYLIN ZAW-MON; Phone: 410-631-3255
Director of Office of Public Information and Community Assistance: VIOLA O. LEWIS; Phone: 410-631-3172
Director of Technical and Regulatory Services Administration: MICHAEL HAIRE; Phone: 410-631-3680
Director of Water Management Administration: J. L. HEARN; Phone: 410-631-3567
Librarian: DR. ETTA LYLES, 2500 Broening Hwy., Baltimore, MD 21224; Phone: 410-631-3818
Publication(s): *Regulatory Calendar; Annual Air Quality Data Report; Biennial Water Report; List of Potential Hazardous Waste Sites*
Keyword(s): Air Quality and Pollution, Environmental Protection, Pollution Prevention, Solid Waste Management, Water Pollution

MARYLAND DEPARTMENT OF AGRICULTURE
50 Harry S. Truman Pkwy., Annapolis, MD 21401
Phone: 410-841-5700
Founded: 1972
Description: Created as a cabinet-level state agency, the Department is charged with assisting soil conservation districts to protect state waters from agricultural nonpoint source pollution, overseeing numerous inspection, testing, grading, and marketing programs, mosquito control and gypsy moth control, and forest pest management under various laws. The department also has responsibility for regulatory functions, such as pesticide applicators, weights and measures, nursery inspection, seed and turf regulation, certification; and agricultural chemical and product registration.
Contact(s):
Secretary: LEWIS R. RILEY; Phone: 410-841-5880
Assistant Secretary: Marketing, Animal Industries and Consumer Services: BRAD POWERS; Phone: 410-841-5782
Assistant Secretary: Office of Plant Industries and Pest Management: DR. CHARLES W. PUFFINBERGER; Phone: 410-841-5870
Assistant Secretary: Office of Resource Conservation: ROYDEN POWELL; Phone: 410-841-5865
Counsel: CRAIG A. NIELSEN; Phone: 410-841-5883
Deputy Secretary: HENRY A. VIRTS; Phone: 410-841-5881
Editor: HAROLD KANAREK
State Veterinarian: DR. ROGER O. OLSON; Phone: 410-841-5810
Publication(s): *List on request.*

Agricultural Commission
50 Harry S. Truman Pkwy., Annapolis, MD 21401
Phone: 410-841-5882
Founded: 1961
Description: Established by law as the Agricultural Advisory Board to the Governor, the Maryland Agricultural Commission was renamed in 1968 and placed within the Department of Agriculture in 1973. The commission formulates and makes proposals for the advancement of Maryland agriculture by serving as an advisory body to the Secretary of Agriculture. Composed of 24 members, one member is the principal administrative officer for agricultural affairs at the University of Maryland; one appointee represents consumer interests and serves a three-year term; the remaining 22 members are appointed for three-year terms by the Governor from nominations submitted by commodity and agricultural organizations.
Contact(s):
Chairman: JIM STEELE
Executive Director: LAURIE J. ADELHARDT; Phone: 410-841-5882

State Soil Conservation Committee
50 Harry S. Truman Pkwy., Annapolis, MD 21401
Phone: 410-841-5863
Founded: 1937
Description: Established to organize soil conservation districts and to establish policy, resolve problems to give guidance and assistance to districts. The SSCC membership includes representatives from the Maryland Departments of Natural Resources, Agriculture, and Environment, Maryland Agricultural Commission, University of Maryland, Maryland Association of Soil Conservation Districts, and five soil conservation district supervisors. The committee is a unit of the Maryland Dept. of Agriculture.
Contact(s):
Chairman: JIM BEAVAN, Star Rt Box 14, Chaptico, MD 20621; Phone: 301-884-3376
Executive Secretary: LOUISE LAWRENCE; Phone: 410-841-5865; Fax: 410-841-5914
Assistant Secretary: ROYDEN POWELL; Phone: 410-841-5865; Fax: 410-841-5914
Publication(s): *SSCC Reporter Newsletter*
Keyword(s): Agriculture, Environmental and Conservation Education, Fisheries, Pesticides

MARYLAND DEPARTMENT OF NATURAL RESOURCES
Tawes State Office Bldg., Annapolis, MD 21401
Contact(s):
Secretary: JOHN R. GRIFFIN; Phone: 410-260-8101
Deputy Secretary: CAROLYN D. DAVIS; Phone: 410-260-8102
Director: Public Communications Office: LIZ KALINOWSKI; Phone: 410-260-8001
Legislative Officer: Intergovernmental and Community Relations: NITA SETTINA; Phone: 410-260-8110
Principal Counsel: JOSEPH P. GILL; Phone: 410-260-8350

Chesapeake Bay and Watershed Programs
Tawes State Office Bldg., Annapolis, MD 21401
Contact(s):
Assistant Secretary: VERNA E. HARRISON; Phone: 410-260-8116
Chief of Regional Chesapeake Bay Program: CAROLYN WATSON; Phone: 410-260-8729
Director of Chesapeake and Coastal Watershed Administration: DAVID BURKE; Phone: 410-260-8705
Director of Education, Bay Policy, and Growth Management: THERESA PEIRNO; Phone: 410-260-8715
Director of Resource Assessment Service: PAUL MASSICOT; Phone: 410-260-8680

Management Services
Contact(s):
Assistant Secretary: ALLEN W. CARTWRIGHT JR.; Phone: 410-260-8106
Director of Audit and Management Review: STEVE POWELL; Phone: 410-260-8383
Director of Chesapeake Bay Trust: DAVID A. MINGES; Phone: 410-974-2941
Director of Finance and Administrative Services: BONNIE MULIERI; Phone: 410-260-8032
Director of Human Resources Services: KATHRYN MARR; Phone: 410-260-8081
Director of Maryland Environmental Trust: JOHN BERNSTEIN; Phone: 410-514-7900
Keyword(s): Fisheries, Forests and Forestry, Public Lands, Watersheds, Wildlife Management

Public Lands Division
Contact(s):
Assistant Secretary: JAMES W. DUNMYER; Phone: 410-260-8108
Director of Engineering and Construction: ROBERT P. GAUDETTE; Phone: 410-260-8897
Director of Land and Water Conservation: MICHAEL J. NELSON; Phone: 410-260-8446
Director of Program Open Space: H. GRANT DeHART; Phone: 410-260-8425
Director of Resource Planning: GENE PIOTROWSKI; Phone: 410-260-8405
Superintendent of Natural Resources Police: COL. JOHN RHOADS; Phone: 410-260-8881
Superintendent of State Forest and Park Service: COL. RICK BARTON; Phone: 410-260-8186

Resource Management Services
Contact(s):
Assistant Secretary: DR. SARAH J. TAYLOR-ROGERS; Phone: 410-260-8113
Director of Environmental Review: RAY C. DINTAMAN JR.; Phone: 410-260-8331
Director of Fish, Heritage and Wildlife: ERIC C. SCHWAAB; Phone: 410-260-8582
Director of Fisheries: DOROTHY L. LEONARD; Phone: 410-260-8251
Director of Forest Service: JAMES MALLOW; Phone: 410-260-8501
Director of Licensing Registration Services: BRUCE GILMORE; Phone: 410-260-8233
Director of Wildlife and Natural Heritage: JOSH SANDT; Phone: 410-974-3195
Executive Director of Chesapeake Bay Critical Areas Commission: REN SEREY; Phone: 410-974-2426

MARYLAND SEA GRANT COLLEGE
Sea Grant College, University of Maryland, College Park, MD 20742
Phone: 301-405-6371; Fax: 301-314-9581
Founded: 1977
Description: Maryland Sea Grant supports marine research, education, and outreach activities, especially in connection with the Chesapeake Bay. It currently supports research at four of the region's marine laboratories, and on the campuses of the University System of Maryland, the Johns Hopkins University, and other institutions of higher learning.
Contact(s):
Assistant Director: GAIL B. MACKIERNAN; Phone: 301-405-6373
Assistant Director: JONATHAN G. KRAMER; Phone: 301-405-6377
Director: DR. CHRISTOPHER F. D'ELIA
Publication(s): *Maryland Marine Notes ; Watershed; Maryland Sea Grant Books and Videos*
Keyword(s): Aquatic Habitats, Biotechnology, Environmental and Conservation Education, Fisheries, Oceanography

MARYLAND STATE EXTENSION SERVICES
University of Maryland, 1104 Symons Hall, College Park, MD 20742
Phone: 301-405-2072
Contact(s):
Associate Dean and Associate Director of Cooperative Extension Service: DR. JAMES WADE, University of Maryland, Cooperative Extension Service, 1200 Symons Hall, College Park, MD 20742-5565; Phone: 301-405-2907; Fax: 301-405-2963
Coordinator: Sea Grant Extension Program: DR. DOUG LIPTON, University of Maryland, Cooperative Extension Service, 2218B Symons Hall, College Park, MD 20742; Phone: 301-405-1280
Dean and Director of Agricultural Experiment Station and Cooperative Extension Service: DR. THOMAS A. FRETZ; Fax: 301-314-9146
Program Leader and Assistant Director of Agriculture and Natural Resources Program: DR. JAMES HANSON, University of Maryland, Cooperative Extension Service, 1200 Symons Hall, College Park, MD 20742-5565; Phone: 301-405-7992; Fax: 301-405-2963
Regional Natural Resource Specialist: JONATHAN KAYS, University of Maryland, Cooperative Extension Service, Western Maryland Research and Education Center, 18330 Keedysville Road, Keedysville, MD 21756; Phone: 301-432-2735, ext. 323; Fax: 301-432-4089
Regional Natural Resource Specialist: BOB TJADEN, University of Maryland, Cooperative Extension Service, Wye Research and Education Center, P.O. box 169, Queenstown, MD 21658; Phone: 410-827-8056; Fax: 410-827-9039

MARYLAND-NATIONAL CAPITAL PARK AND PLANNING COMMISSION
6611 Kenilworth Ave., Riverdale, MD 20737
Phone: 301-454-1740
Founded: 1927
Description: Established by the General Assembly of the state of Maryland to provide for the orderly development of Montgomery and Prince George's counties; to provide a system of parks to serve the residents of this bi-county region; and to provide recreation programs and services in Prince George's county.
Contact(s):
Chairman: WILLIAM H. HUSSMANN, 787 Georgia Ave., SilverSpring, MD 20910; Phone: 301-495-4605
Executive Director: TRUDYE MORGAN JOHNSON; Phone: 301-454-1740
Acting General Counsel, Legal Department: ISAAC H. MARKS; Phone: 301-454-1670
Director of Montgomery County Department of Parks and Planning: RODNEY H. IRWIN; Phone: 301-495-4500
Director: Prince George's County Planning: FERN V. PIRET; Phone: 301-952-3595
Montgomery County Director: Parks: DONALD K. COCHRAN; Phone: 301-495-2500
Prince George's County Director of Parks and Recreation: MARY GODFREY; Phone: 301-699-2582
Secretary-Treasurer, Department of Finance: A. EDWARD NAVARRE; Phone: 301-454-1540
Vice Chairman: ELIZABETH HEWLETT, 14741 Governor Oden Bowie Dr., UpperMarlboro, MD 20772; Phone: 301-952-3560

MASSACHUSETTS

GOVERNOR OF MASSACHUSETTS, ARGEO PAUL CELLUCCI
State House, Rm. 360, Boston, MA 02133
Phone: 617-727-9173

COOPERATIVE EXTENSION SYSTEM (MASSACHUSETTS)
Univ of MA, Stockbridge Hall, Amherst, MA 01003
Contact(s):
Associate Director of Cooperative Extension: DR. JOHN M. GERBER, University of Massachusetts, Stockbridge Hall, Amherst, MA 01003; Phone: 413-545-4800
Extension Staff: SCOTT D. JACKSON, University of Massachusetts, Department of Forestry and Wildlife Management, Holdsworth Natural Resources Center, Amherst, MA 01003; Phone: 413-545-2665
Keyword(s): Fisheries, Forests and Forestry, Renewable Resources, Sustainable Ecosystems, Urban Forestry

EXECUTIVE OFFICE OF ENVIRONMENTAL AFFAIRS

Division of Fisheries and Wildlife
100 Cambridge St., Rm. 2103, Boston, MA 02202
Contact(s):
Director: WAYNE F. MacCALLUM; Phone: 617-727-3155
Director of Law Enforcement: RICHARD MURRAY
Director of Public Access Board: JACK SHEPPARD; Phone: 617-727-3190

EXECUTIVE OFFICE OF ENVIRONMENTAL AFFAIRS (MASSACHUSETTS)
Leverett Saltonstall Bldg., 100 Cambridge St., Rm. 2000, Boston, MA 02202
Phone: 617-727-9800
Description: The cabinet-level environmental agency in the state and includes within the secretariat all state environmental agencies.
Contact(s):
Secretary: TRUDY COXE
Director: Coastal Zone Management: PEG BRADY; Phone: 617-727-9530

STATE AND PROVINCE GOVERNMENT AGENCIES - MASSACHUSETTS

Director: Conservation Services: JOEL A. LERNER; Phone: 617-727-1552
Director: Impact Review Unit (MEPA): R. J. LYMAN; Phone: 617-727-5830
Under Secretary: Administration & Finance: GEORGE CROMBIE
Under Secretary: Policy: JAN REITSMA

Animal Health
Leverett Staltonstall Bldg., 100 Cambridge St., Rm 2000, Boston, MA 02202
Contact(s):
Program Coordinator: ROBERT BENNETT; Phone: 617-727-3018

Bureau of Land Use
Leverett Staltonstall Bldg., 100 Cambridge St., Rm 2000, Boston, MA 02202
Contact(s):
Chief: RICHARD HUBBARD; Phone: 617-727-0464

Bureau of Markets
Leverett Staltonstall Bldg., 100 Cambridge St., Rm 2000, Boston, MA 02202
Contact(s):
Chief: SUSAN BLACK; Phone: 617-727-3000

Bureau of Pesticides
Leverett Staltonstall Bldg., 100 Cambridge St., Rm 2000, Boston, MA 02202
Contact(s):
Chief: BRAD MITCHELL; Phone: 617-727-7712

Department of Environmental Management
100 Cambridge St., Rm. 1905, Boston, Boston, MA 02202
Phone: 617-727-3163
Contact(s):
Chief of Legal Services: KATE LEWIS; Phone: 617-727-3160
Commissioner: PETER WEBBER
Deputy Commissioner (Acting): Resource Conservation: RICHARD THIBEDEAU; Phone: 617-727-3267
Director of Engineering: RALPH SILVA; Phone: 617-727-3160
Director: Division of Forests and Parks: TODD FREDERICKS; Phone: 617-727-3180

Department of Environmental Protection
One Winter St., Boston, MA 02108
Phone: 617-292-5500
Contact(s):
Assistant Commissioner: Waste Prevention: KARL DIERKER; Phone: 617-292-5570
Commissioner: DAVID STRUHS
Director of Planning and Evaluation: BARBARA KWETZ; Phone: 617-292-5593

Department of Fisheries, Wildlife, and Environmental Law Enforcement
100 Cambridge St., Rm. 1901, Boston, MA 02202
Contact(s):
Assistant Commissioner: BOB AUSTIN
Commissioner: JOHN PHILLIPS; Phone: 617-727-1614
Director: Division of Marine Fisheries: PHILIP G. COATES; Phone: 617-727-3193

Department of Food and Agriculture
100 Cambridge St., Rm. 2103, Boston, MA 02202
Phone: 617-727-3000
Contact(s):
Commissioner: JONATHAN HEALY

Division of Agricultural Development
100 Cambridge St., Rm. 2103, Boston, MA 02202
Contact(s):
Director: JAMES HINES; Phone: 617-727-3018

Division of Regulatory Services
100 Cambridge St., Rm. 2103, Boston, MA 02202
Contact(s):
Director: DAVID SHELDON; Phone: 617-727-3020

Division of Wetlands and Waterways
One Winter St., Boston, MA 02108
Phone: 617-292-5695
Contact(s):
Director: CHRISTY FOOTE-SMITH

Metropolitan District Commission
20 Somerset St., Boston, MA 02108
Phone: 617-727-5114
Founded: 1919
Description: Operates and maintains 19 swimming pools, 17 salt water beaches, 3 fresh water beaches, 23 skating rinks, and various other recreational facilities; also maintains a network of parkways and main traffic roadways and a police force for protection of its property and people using its facilities.
Contact(s):
Commissioner: DAVID BALFOUR
Director: Division of Recreation: GARY DOAK; Phone: 617-727-9547
Director: Reservations and Historic Sites Unit: BRIAN BRODERICK; Phone: 617-727-2744

State Commission for Conservation of Soil, Water and Related Resources
Contact(s):
Executive Secretary: THOMAS C. ANDERSON, 100 Cambridge Street, Boston, MA 02202; Phone: 617-727-9800, ext. 232; Fax: 617-727-2630; Email: tanderson_EOE@state.ma.us
Contact: THOMAS QUINK, 67 Church Street, Gilbertville, MA 01031-9864; Phone: 413-477-8870

Watershed Division
Contact(s):
Director: JOSEPH McGINN

MASSACHUSETTS COOPERATIVE FISH AND WILDLIFE RESEARCH UNIT (USDI)
Box 34220, Holdsworth Natural Resources Ctr., University of Massachusetts, Amherst, MA 01003-4220
Phone: 413-545-0080
Founded: 1948
Description: Provides graduate training and research experience in fisheries and wildlife research management, ecology, habitat, population dynamics, and management. Supported cooperatively by the University of Massachusetts, Massachusetts Division of Fisheries and Wildlife, Massachusetts Division of Marine Fisheries, the U.S. Department of Interior, and the Wildlife Management Institute.
Contact(s):
Assistant Leader: Fisheries: MARTHA E. MATHER
Assistant Leader: Wildlife: REBECCA FIELD
Leader: JAY B. HESTBECK
Keyword(s): Biodiversity, Environmental and Conservation Education, Fisheries, Wildlife and Wildlife Habitat, Wildlife Management

MASSACHUSETTS HIGHWAY DEPARTMENT
10 Park Plaza, Boston, MA 02116
Phone: 617-973-7800
Description: The mission of the Massachusetts Highway Department is to provide a safe, efficient, quality highway system in a cost-effective and environmentally sensitive manner that continuously meets the diverse needs of its users.
Contact(s):
Chief Engineer: THOMAS F. BRODERICK; Phone: 617-973-7830
Commissioner: KEVIN J. SULLIVAN; Phone: 617-973-7800
Deputy Chief Engineer: Construction: DAVID ANDERSON; Phone: 817-973-7491

Deputy Chief Engineer: Environmental Division: GREGORY PRENDERGAST; Phone: 617-973-7484
Deputy Chief Engineer: Highway Engineering: JOHN BLUNDO; Phone: 617-973-7513
Deputy Chief Engineer: Operations: GORDON BROZ; Phone: 617-973-7741
Project Development: KEVIN WALSH; Phone: 617-973-7529
Supervisor: Cultural Resources Unit: JAMES ELLIOTT; Phone: 617-973-7494
Supervisor: Permitting and Regulatory Compliance: LISA RHODES; Phone: 617-973-7582
Supervisor: Wetlands and Water Resources: HENRY BARBARO; Phone: 617-973-7419
Keyword(s): Air Quality, Cultural Preservation, Environment, Hazardous Materials & Waste, Noise, Solid Waste, Transportation, Water Quality, Wetlands

WOODS HOLE OCEANOGRAPHIC INSITUTION (WHOI) SEA GRANT PROGRAM

Woods Hole Oceanographic Institution, 193 Oyster Pond Rd., MS #2, Woods Hole, MA 02543-1525
Phone: 508-289-2398; Fax: 508-457-2172; Email: seagrant@whoi.edu; WWW: www.whoi.edu/seagrant/

Founded: 1973

Description: The WHOI Sea Grant Program supports research, education, and advisory projects to promote the wise use and understanding of ocean and coastal resources for the public benefit. It is part of the National Sea Grant College Program of the National Oceanic and Atmospheric Administration, a network of 29 individual programs located in each of the coastal and Great Lakes states to foster cooperation among government, academia, and industry.

Contact(s):
Director: DR. JUDITH E. McDOWELL; Phone: 508-289-2557
Communicator: TRACEY I. CRAGO; Phone: 508-289-2665
Fisheries Aquaculture Specialist: DR. DALE F. LEAVITT; Phone: 508-289-2997
Program Assistant: SHERI D. DEROSA; Phone: 508-289-2398
Keyword(s): Aquaculture, Biodiversity, Coasts, Fisheries, Oceanography, Water Pollution

MICHIGAN

GOVERNOR OF MICHIGAN, JOHN ENGLER

State Capitol, P.O. Box 30013, Lansing, MI 48909
Phone: 517-373-3400

MICHIGAN DEPARTMENT OF AGRICULTURE

4th Fl., Ottawa Bldg., P.O. Box 30017, Lansing, MI 48909
Phone: 517-373-1052

Contact(s):
Director: DAN WYANT
Director of Environmental Stewardship Division: DR. KURT THELEN HENSINGER; Phone: 517-335-3400
Director of Marketing & Communications Division: MARGARET R. COOKE; Phone: 517-373-1104
Director of Pesticide & Plant Pest Management Division: KEN RAUSCHER; Phone: 517-373-1087
Keyword(s): Agriculture, Biodiversity, Flowers, Plants, and Trees, Pesticides, Soil Conservation

MICHIGAN DEPARTMENT OF ENVIRONMENTAL QUALITY

106 West Allegan Street, Hollister Building, 6th Floor, P.O. Box 30473, Lansing, MI 48090-7973
Phone: 517-373-7917; Fax: 517-241-7401; WWW: www.deq.state.mi.us

Founded: 1995

Description: Our mission is to drive improvements in environmental quality for the protection of public health and natural resources to benefit current and future generations. This will be accomplished through effective administration of agency programs, and providing for the use of innovative strategies, while helping to foster a strong and sustainable economy.

Contact(s):
Director: RUSSELL J. HARDING; Phone: 517-373-7917
Chief of Financial and Business Services Division: DENNIS FEDEWA; Phone: 517-241-7428; Fax: 517-241-7401
Deputy Director for Operations: GARY R. HUGHES; Phone: 517-241-7394; Fax: 517-241-7401
Deputy Director for Programs and Regulations: W. CHAD McINTOSH; Phone: 517-241-7392; Fax: 517-241-7401
Keyword(s): Air Quality and Pollution, Chemical Pollution Control, Coasts, Drinking Water Protection, Environmental and Conservation Education, Environmental Protection, Geology, Lakes, Mining, Pollution Prevention, Solid Waste Management, Toxic Substances, Toxicology, Water Pollution, Water Resources

MICHIGAN DEPARTMENT OF NATURAL RESOURCES

Box 30028, Lansing, MI 48909
Phone: 517-373-1214; WWW: www.dnr.states.mi.us

Founded: 1921

Description: State agency for administration, including enforcement of laws and regulations, regarding the state's natural resources; and for enhancing recreational opportunities and quality. Derived from the Department of Conservation.

Contact(s):
Director: K. L. COOL; Phone: 517-373-2329
Acting Chief of Wildlife: REBECCA HUMPHRIES; Phone: 517-373-1263
Acting Deputy for Resource Management: GEORGE E. BURGEYNE JUR.; Phone: 517-373-0046
Chief of Finance and Operations Bureau: ROB ABENT; Phone: 517-373-1750
Chief of Fisheries: KELLY SMITH; Phone: 517-373-1280
Chief of Forest Management: JOHN M. ROBERTSON; Phone: 517-373-1275
Chief of Human Resources: JAMES A. CARTER; Phone: 517-373-1207
Chief of Information Systems and Technology Division: DOUGLAS JESTER; Phone: 517-373-9510
Chief of Law Enforcement: HERBERT BURNS; Phone: 517-373-1230
Chief of Office of Internal Audit: THOMAS BENSON; Phone: 517-373-0755
Chief of Parks and Recreation: RODNEY STOKES; Phone: 517-373-9900
Chief of Real Estate: MINDY KOCH; Phone: 517-241-2438
Deputy for Administrative Services: KELLI SOBEL; Phone: 517-373-2425
Deputy Upper Peninsula Field Headquarters: JAMES EKDAHL; Phone: 906-228-6561
Equal Opportunity, Litigation and Legal Services: CORDREE McCONNELL; Phone: 517-373-3503
Executive Assistant: GUY GORDON; Phone: 517-373-2329
Executive Secretary to the Natural Resources Commission: TERESA GLODEN; Phone: 517-373-2352
Field and Investigative Studies: GERALD THIEDE; Phone: 517-335-4225
Information and Education: BRUCE MATTHEWS; Phone: 517-373-1214
Legislative Liaison: CAROL BAMBERY; Phone: 517-373-0023
Mackinac Island State Park Commission: CARL R. NOLD; Phone: 906-847-3328
Press Secretary: TIM ROBY; Phone: 517-373-1214
Keyword(s): Fisheries, Forests and Forestry, Outdoor Recreation, Public Lands, Wildlife Management

MICHIGAN DEPARTMENT OF PUBLIC HEALTH
3423 Martin Luther King, Jr. Blvd., Box 30195, Lansing, MI 48909
Phone: 517-335-8022
Founded: 1873
Description: Is the fifth-oldest state-health agency in the nation. The protection and improvement of the health of the people of Michigan is the statutory responsibility and purpose of the department. The state health department also serves as the coordinator for the control and prevention of disease in Michigan.
Contact(s):
Director: State Health: VERNICE DAVIS ANTHONY
Keyword(s): Public Health Protection

MICHIGAN SEA GRANT COLLEGE PROGRAM
University of Michigan, 2200 Bonisteel Blvd., Ann Arbor, MI 48109
Phone: 739-764-1138; Fax: 739-647-0768
Founded: 1969
Description: To promote the understanding and wise use of the Great Lakes through research, education, and extension.
Contact(s):
Assistant Director: PEGGY BRITT, Michigan Sea Grant College Program, University of Michigan, IST Bldg., Rm. 4111, 2200 Bonisteel Blvd., AnnArbor, MI 48109; Phone: 734-763-1437
Director: DR. RUSSEL MOLL, Michigan Sea Grant College Program, University of Michigan, I.S.T. Bldg., Rm. 4103, AnnArbor, MI 48109; Phone: 734-763-1437
Associate Director: DR. WILLIAM W. TAYLOR, Department of Fisheries and Wildlife, Michigan State University, 7 Natural Resources Bldg., East Lansing, MI 48824; Phone: 517-353-0647
Program Leader: Sea Grant Extension: JOHN D. SCHWARTZ, Michigan Sea Grant College Program, Michigan State University, 334 Natural Resources Bldg., East Lansing, MI 48824; Phone: 517-353-9568
Publications Assistant: BROOKE SCELZA, Sea Grant College Program, University of Michigan, 2200 Bonisteel Blvd., Ann Arbor, MI 48109; Phone: 734-764-1118
Senior Editor: JOYCE JAKUBIAK; Phone: 734-647-0766

MICHIGAN STATE UNIVERSITY EXTENSION
Bulletin Office, 10-B Agric. Hall, East Lansing, MI 48824
Phone: 517-355-0240
Description: Helps people improve their lives through an educational process that applies knowledge to critical issues, needs, and opportunities. Publications, instructional videos, and microcomputer software are listed in a catalogue which is available from: Bulletin Office, 10B Agriculture Hall, East Lansing, MI 48824-1039
Contact(s):
Assistant Vice Provost and Associate Director: DR. LEAH COX RITCHIE; Phone: 517-355-0265; Fax: 517-355-6473
Associate Vice Provost and Director: DR. ARLEN G. LEHOLM; Phone: 517-355-2308; Fax: 517-355-6473
Interim Assistant Vice Provost and Associate Director: DR. LARRY OLSEN; Phone: 517-355-0118; Fax: 517-355-6473
Keyword(s): Agriculture, Forests and Forestry, Pesticides, Water Resources, Wildlife Management

MINNESOTA

GOVERNOR OF MINNESOTA, JESSE VENTURA
130 State Capitol, 75 Constitution Ave., St.Paul, MN 55155
Phone: 612-296-3391

MINNESOTA BOARD OF WATER AND SOIL RESOURCES
One W. Water St., Suite 200, St. Paul, MN 55107
Phone: 612-296-3767
Founded: 1987
Description: Formed under M.S. chapter 103B to develop the capabilities of local governments in resource management. Works most often with soil and water conservation districts, watershed districts, watershed management organizations, and counties. Provides these local governments with financial and technical assistance. Administers programs focusing on erosion control and water quality.
Contact(s):
Chair: KATHLEEN ROER, Medina, MN
Director: RONALD D. HARNACK; Fax: 612-297-5615; Email: ron.harnack@bwsr.state.mn.us
Publication(s): *Conservation Mentor, The; Water BillBoard*
Keyword(s): Conservation Tillage, Lakes, Land Use Planning, Soil Conservation, Training, Water Quality, Water Resources, Watersheds, Wetlands

MINNESOTA COOPERATIVE FISH AND WILDLIFE RESEARCH UNIT
U.S. Geological Survey, Biological Resources Division, University of Minnesota, Department of Fisheries and Wildlife, 200 Hodson Hall, 1980 Folwell Ave., St. Paul, MN 55108
Phone: 612-624-3421
Founded: 1987
Description: The research mission of the Minnesota Cooperative Fish and Wildlife Research Unit (MNCFWRU) is to address the biological, social, and economic aspects of both game and nongame wildlife and fisheries management in the context of conservation of biological diversity, and integrity and sustainability of ecosystems.
Contact(s):
Assistant Leader: Fisheries: DR. BRUCE C. VONDRACEK
Assistant Leader: Wildlife: DR. DAVID C. FULTON
Librarian: LORALEE KERR, 375 Hodson Hall, 1980 Folwell Ave., St.Paul, MN 55108; Phone: 612-624-9288
Unit Leader: DR. DAVID E. ANDERSEN
Keyword(s): Aquatic Habitats, Fisheries, Nongame Wildlife, Toxicology, Wildlife and Wildlife Habitat

MINNESOTA DEPARTMENT OF AGRICULTURE
90 W. Plato Blvd., St. Paul, MN 55107
Phone: 612-297-2200
Founded: 1919
Description: Enforces laws to protect the public health, promote family farming and marketing of farm products, conserve soil and water, and prevent fraud and deception in the manufacture and distribution of foods, animal feeds, fertilizers, pesticides, seeds, and other items.
Contact(s):
Assistant Commissioner: PERRY AASNESS
Assistant Commissioner: TOM MASSO
Assistant Commissioner: SHARON CLARK
Commissioner: GENE HUGOSON
Deputy Commissioner: SHARON CLARK
Director (Acting): Dairy and Food: FRED MITCHELL; Phone: 612-296-1590
Director of Grain and Produce Inspection: DALE HEIMERMANN; Phone: 612-341-7190
Director: Administration and Personnel: HAROLD FRANK; Phone: 612-296-2323
Director: Agricultural Statistics: JIM HUNST; Phone: 612-296-3896
Director: Agriculture Certification: JAMES GRYNIEWSKI; Phone: 612-297-2230

Director: Agriculture Finance: JIM BOERBOOM; Phone: 612-297-3557
Director: Agriculture Marketing and Development: GERALD HEIL; Phone: 612-296-1486
Director: Agronomy and Plant Protection: GREG BUZICKY; Phone: 612-297-7121
Director: Information Services: KAREN NELSON; Phone: 612-296-4659
Director: Laboratory Services: WILLIAM KRUEGER; Phone: 612-296-3273
Keyword(s): Agriculture, Biodiversity, Pesticides, Sustainable Development, Water Pollution

MINNESOTA DEPARTMENT OF NATURAL RESOURCES
500 Lafayette Rd., St. Paul, MN 55155-4001
Phone: 612-296-6157
Founded: 1931
Description: The Department of Conservation was renamed the Department of Natural Resources (DNR) in 1971. The DNR's goal is to achieve optimum natural resources planning, protection, and development responsive to public need, consistent with resource potentials, and for the social and economic well-being of both present and future generations.
Contact(s):
Administrator: Bureau of Engineering: JOHN ERNSTER; Phone: 612-296-2119
Administrator: Bureau of Financial Management: PEGGY ADELMANN; Phone: 612-296-8340
Administrator: Bureau of Human Resources: MARY O'NEILL; Phone: 612-296-6493
Administrator: Bureau of Information and Education: MARCY DOWSE; Phone: 612-296-3336
Administrator: Bureau of Licenses: MARGARET WINKEL-DEIN; Phone: 612-296-4507
Administrator: Bureau of Management Information Services: HENRY MAY; Phone: 612-297-3906
Administrator: Bureau of Real Estate Management: JIM LAWLER; Phone: 612-296-4097
Administrator: Office of Planning: VONNY HAGEN; Phone: 612-296-0565
Administrator:Bureau of Field Service: NORM KORDELL; Phone: 612-297-3758
Assistant Commissioner: Human Resources and Legal Affairs: GAIL LEWELLAN; Phone: 612-296-9556
Assistant Commissioner: Operations: RAY HITCHCOCK; Phone: 612-296-5229
Chief: Ecological Services Section: LEE PFANNMULLER; Phone: 612-296-2835
Chief: Fisheries Section: JACK SKRYPEK; Phone: 612-296-3325
Chief: Wildlife Section: TIM BREMICKER; Phone: 612-296-3344
Commissioner: RODNEY W. SANDO; Phone: 612-296-2549
Deputy Commissioner: RONALD NARGANG; Phone: 612-296-2540
Director: Agricultural Policy: WAYNE EDGERTON; Phone: 612-297-8341
Director: Division of Enforcement: LEO HASEMAN; Phone: 612-297-2368
Director: Division of Fish and Wildlife: ROGER HOLMES; Phone: 612-297-1308
Director: Division of Forestry: GERALD ROSE; Phone: 612-296-4491
Director: Division of Minerals: WILLIAM BRICE; Phone: 612-296-4807
Director: Division of Parks and Recreation: WILLIAM MORRISSEY; Phone: 612-296-9223
Director: Division of Waters: KENT LOKKESMOE; Phone: 612-296-4800
Director: Regulatory and Legislative Services: PATTY BURKE; Phone: 612-296-0915
Director: Trails and Waterways Unit: DENNIS ASMUSSEN; Phone: 612-297-1151
Editor: KATHLEEN WEFLEN; Phone: 612-296-0900
Library Director: COLLEEN MLECOCH; Phone: 612-296-1305
Regional Administrator: KATHLEEN WALLACE; Phone: 612-772-7900
Regional Administrator: CHERYL HEIDE; Phone: 507-359-6000
Regional Administrator: PAUL SWENSON; Phone: 218-755-3955
Regional Administrator: LARRY NELSON; Phone: 507-285-7418
Regional Administrator: ROBERT HANCE; Phone: 218-828-2561
Regional Administrator: JOHN GUENTHER; Phone: 218-327-4455
Publication(s): *Minnesota Volunteer, The*

MINNESOTA ENVIRONMENTAL QUALITY BOARD
3rd Fl. Centennial Bldg., 658 Cedar St., St. Paul, MN 55155
Phone: 612-296-9027
Founded: 1973
Description: The EQB is Minnesota's principal forum for discussing environmental issues. The EQB provides an opportunity for the public to have direct input into the development of the state's environmental policy. The EQB is an independent decisionmaking body and is staffed by the Minnesota Office of Strategic and Long Range Planning.
Contact(s):
Executive Director: MICHAEL SULLIVAN, 3rd Fl. Centennial Bldg., 658 Cedar St., St.Paul, MN 55155; Phone: 612-296-9027
Commissioner: ROD SANDO, 3rd Fl. Centennial Bldg., 658 Cedar St., St.Paul, MN 55155; Phone: 612-297-1257
Publication(s): *EQB Monitor*
Keyword(s): Energy, Environmental Planning, Sustainable Development, Sustainable Ecosystems, Water Resources

MINNESOTA GEOLOGICAL SURVEY
University of Minnesota, 2642 University Ave., St. Paul, MN 55114
Phone: 612-627-4780
Founded: 1872
Description: Established as a Geological and Natural History Survey, reconstituted in 1911 as the Minnesota Geological Survey to investigate the geology of the state; describe, classify and map the geological formations and mineral and water resources; and investigate all aspects of the geology affecting the environment.
Contact(s):
Director: DAVID L. SOUTHWICK
Associate Director and Chief Geologist: GLENN B. MOREY
Publication(s): *List available on request.*
Keyword(s): Geology, Water Resources

MINNESOTA POLLUTION CONTROL AGENCY
520 Lafayette Rd., St. Paul, MN 55155
Phone: 612-296-6300
Founded: 1967
Description: Administers the state statutes covering water pollution, air pollution, and solid and hazardous waste control.
Contact(s):
Assistant Commissioner: GORDON WEGWART; Phone: 612-296-7319
Chairman of the Board and Commissioner: CHARLES W. WILLIAMS; Phone: 612-296-7301
Deputy Commissioner: PETER LARSON; Phone: 612-296-7305
Director: Division of Administrative Services: ELAINE JOHNSON; Phone: 612-296-7224
Director: Division of Air Quality: LISA J. THORVIG; Phone: 612-296-7331
Director: Division of Groundwater and Solid Waste: JAMES WARNER; Phone: 612-296-7777
Director: Division of Hazardous Waste: TIMOTHY K. SCHERKENBACH; Phone: 612-297-8502
Director: Division of Water Quality: PATRICIA M. BURKE; Phone: 612-296-7202

Brainerd, MN
1601 Minnesota St., Brainerd, MN 56401
Phone: 218-828-2492
Contact(s):
Director: LARRY SHAW

STATE AND PROVINCE GOVERNMENT AGENCIES - MISSISSIPPI

Detroit Lakes, MN
Lake Avenue Plaza 714 Lake Ave. Suite 220, Detroit Lakes, MN 56501
Phone: 218-847-1519
Contact(s):
Director: JEFF LEWIS

Duluth, MN
Duluth Government Svc. Ctr. Rm. 704 320 W. 2nd St., Duluth, MN 55802
Phone: 218-723-4660
Contact(s):
Director: WAYNE GOLLY

Marshall, MN
700 N. Seventh St., Marshall, MN 56258
Phone: 507-537-7146
Contact(s):
Director: MARK JACOBS

Rochester, MN
2116 Campus Dr. SE, Rochester, MN 55904
Phone: 507-285-7343
Contact(s):
Director: LARRY LANDHERR

MINNESOTA SEA GRANT COLLEGE PROGRAM
Univ. of MN, 2305 E. 5th St., Duluth, MN 55812
WWW: www.d.umn.edu/seagr/
Description: A statewide program that supports research, outreach, and educational programs related to Lake Superior and Minnesota's inland waters. Research areas include: water quality, fisheries, biotechnology, aquaculture, exotic species, and coastal tourism.
Contact(s):
Director: MICHAEL McDONALD, University of Minnesota, 2305 E. 5th St., Duluth, MN 55812; Phone: 218-726-8710; Fax: 218-726-6556; Email: seagr@d.umn.edu
Editor: MARIE SALES; Phone: 218-726-7677
Publication(s): *Seiche, The Newsletter*
Keyword(s): Aquatic Habitats, Biotechnology, Communications, Environment, Fisheries, Lakes, Sustainable Development, Sustainable Ecosystems, Water Pollution, Water Resources, Wildlife Management

MINNESOTA STATE EXTENSION SERVICES
University of Minnesota, 240 Coffey Hall, 1420 Eckles Ave., St. Paul, MN 55108
Phone: 612-625-3774
Contact(s):
Associate Dean and Collegiate Program Leader: STEVEN B. DALEY LAURSEN; Phone: 612-624-9298
Dean and Director of the University of Minnesota Extension Service: KATHERINE FENNELLY; Phone: 612-624-2703
Extension Specialist: Aquaculture: ANNE KAPUSCINSKI; Phone: 612-624-3019
Forest Resources Specialist: MELVIN J. BAUGHMAN; Phone: 612-624-0734
Housing Specialist: PATRICK HUELMAN; Phone: 612-624-1286
Public Policy Specialist: STEVEN TAFF; Phone: 612-625-3103
Sea Grant Extension and Fisheries Educator: JEFFREY GUNDERSON
Specialist: CARL E. VOGT; Phone: 612-624-3639
Specialist: FLOYD T. MILTON; Phone: 612-624-5307
Specialist: HARLAN D. PETERSEN; Phone: 612-624-3407
Specialist: GARY R. JOHNSON; Phone: 612-625-3765
Specialist: CHARLES R. BLINN; Phone: 612-624-3788
Tourism Educator Specialist: GLENN KREAG
Water Quality Educator Specialist: CYNTHIA HAGLEY
Wildlife Specialist: JAMES R. KITTS; Phone: 612-624-3298
Youth Specialist: STEPHAN CARLSON; Phone: 612-626-1259

MISSISSIPPI

GOVERNOR OF MISSISSIPPI, KIRK FORDICE
P.O. Box 139, Jackson, MS 39205
Phone: 601-359-3100; Fax: 601-359-3741

DEPARTMENT OF ENVIRONMENTAL QUALITY (MISSISSIPPI)
Office of Polluton Control, P.O. Box 10385, Jackson, MS 39289-0385
Phone: 601-961-5171
Contact(s):
Head: Office of Pollution Control: CHARLES H. CHISOLM

Office of Land and Water Resources
Southport Mall, P.O. Box 10631, Jackson, MS 39289
Phone: 601-961-5200
Founded: *1956*
Description: Administers Water Use Permitting Act of 1985, licensing of water well drillers, and the 1978 Dam Safety Act; inventories water resources; coordinates water and land resources planning; and conducts reviews of proposed water resources development.
Contact(s):
Chief: Division of Hydrologic Investigation and Reporting: PATRICIA A. PHILLIPS; Phone: 601-961-5213
Director: Bureau: CHARLES T. BRANCH

FORESTRY COMMISSION (MISSISSIPPI)
301 N. Lamar St., Suite 300, Jackson, MS 39201
Phone: 601-359-1386; Fax: 601-359-1349
Founded: *1926*
Description: Basic duties are forest protection against wildfire, insects, and disease; operation of tree-seedlings nurseries for reforestation; provision of forest resource management assistance to private landowners; and creation of interest in forestry.
Contact(s):
Deputy State Forester Services: JAMES MORDICA
Deputy State Forester: Management Chief: DON NEVELS
Deputy State Forester: Protection Chief: WILLIAM LAMBERT
Director: Information and Education: BILL COLVIN
Editor: KENT GRIZZARD
Editor: JOE McDONALD
Fiscal Officer: ROD SANDERS
State Forester: JAMES L. SLEDGE JR.
Publication(s): *Inside The Bark; Forestry Forum Magazine*
Keyword(s): Environmental and Conservation Education, Forests and Forestry, Public Lands, Renewable Resources, Urban Forestry

GULF COAST RESEARCH LABORATORY
P.O. Box 7000, Ocean Springs, MS 39566
Phone: 601-872-4200
Founded: *1947*
Description: Conducts research in marine biology, fisheries, geology, chemistry, and oceanography, and conducts an academic program in the marine sciences.
Contact(s):
Assistant Director: Research: WILLIAM W. WALKER
Editor: ROBERT T. VANALLER
Interim Director: ROBERT T. VANALLER
Publication(s): *Marine Briefs Newsletter; Gulf Research Reports-Scientific Journal*

MISSISSIPPI COOPERATIVE FISH AND WILDLIFE RESEARCH UNIT (USDI)
Mailstop 9691, Mississippi State University, Mississippi State, MS 39762
Phone: 601-325-2643
Founded: *1978*
Description: The Unit is sponsored by the U.S.G.S. Biological Resources Division; Mississippi Department of Wildlife, Fisheries, and Parks; Mississippi State University; and the Wildlife Management Institute. Fisheries and wildlife research, graduate

education, technical assistance, and extension are the Unit's main missions.
Contact(s):
Assistant Leader: Fisheries: L. E. MIRANDA
Assistant Leader: Wildlife: FRANCISCO J. VILELLA
Leader: HAROLD L. SCHRAMM JR.
Keyword(s): Endangered and Threatened Species, Fisheries, Nongame Wildlife, Rivers, Sport Fishing

MISSISSIPPI DEPARTMENT OF AGRICULTURE AND COMMERCE
P.O. Box 1609, Jackson, MS 39215-1609
Phone: 601-354-7050
Founded: 1906
Description: The department was created to foster and promote the business of agriculture. Duties include: Regulatory, consumer protection, marketing, and a wide range of service activities.
Contact(s):
Commissioner: DR. LESTER SPELL JR.
Deputy Commissioner: CHRIS SPARKMAN; Phone: 601-354-7056
Director of Board of Animal Health: DR. FRANK ROGERS; Phone: 601-354-6089
Director of Consumer Protection: JOHN TILLSON; Phone: 601-354-7075
Director of Farmers Market: BILLY CARTER; Phone: 601-354-6573
Director of Feed: Seed: & Fertilizer: JOHN HALL; Phone: 601-354-7072
Director of Fruit & Vegetable Inspections: DONNIS ROBERSON; Phone: 601-354-6608
Director of Grain Inspection: RALPH HOWELL; Phone: 601-762-8141
Director of Market Development: ROGER BARLOW; Phone: 601-354-7097
Director of Market News: BILLY CARTER; Phone: 601-354-6818
Director of Meat Inspection: DR. ROBERT WEST; Phone: 601-354-6581
Director of National Agricultural Statistics: TOMMY GREGORY; Phone: 601-965-4575
Director of Regulatory Services: JOE HARDY; Phone: 601-354-7063
Director of Weights and Measures: BILL ELDRIDGE; Phone: 601-354-7070
Editor: CLAUDE NASH; Phone: 601-354-7086
Personnel Officer: STELLA CESSNA; Phone: 601-354-7083
Publication(s): *Mississippi Market Bulletin*

MISSISSIPPI DEPARTMENT OF WILDLIFE, FISHERIES, AND PARKS
P.O. Box 451, Jackson, MS 39205
Phone: 601-362-9212
Description: The purpose of the MDWFP is to manage, conserve, develop, and protect Mississippi's outdoors, state parks, wildlife and marine resources, and their habitats; and to provide continuing recreational, economic, educational, ecological, aesthetic, social and scientific benefits for present and future generations.
Contact(s):
Executive Director: DR. SAM POLLES; Phone: 601-364-2000
Boating Enforcement: JIMMY LAIRD; Phone: 601-364-2182
Chief: Fisheries: RON GARAVELLI; Phone: 601-364-2202
Chief: Game: BILL THOMASON; Phone: 601-364-2212
Chief: Law Enforcement: RANDALL MILLER; Phone: 601-364-2232
Coordinator: Planning and Policy: TOMMY SHROPSHIRE; Phone: 601-364-2107
Deputy Administrator: BOB TYLER; Phone: 601-364-2010
Director of Marketing: ELLEN B. MORGAN; Phone: 601-364-2152
Director of Parks: LATTELLE ASHLEY; Phone: 601-364-2154
Director: Museum of Natural Science: LIBBY HARTFIELD; Phone: 601-354-7303
Director: Personnel: BETTY ASH; Phone: 601-364-2116
Director: Public Information: JIM WALKER; Phone: 601-364-2124
Director: Support Services Division: AL TUCK; Phone: 601-364-2046
Editor: DAVID L. WATTS; Phone: 601-364-2129
Executive Assistant: BILL QUISENBERRY; Phone: 601-364-2004
Head Librarian: MARY P. STEVENS, Museum of Natural Science, 111 N. Jefferson, Jackson, MS 39202-2897; Phone: 601-354-7303
Hunter Education: RICHARD CAIN; Phone: 601-364-2192
Outdoor Recreation Grants: JIMMY GRAVES; Phone: 601-364-2156
Parks Director: LATRELLE ASHLEY; Phone: 601-364-2154
Publication(s): *Mississippi Outdoors; Mississippi* **Keyword(s):** Endangered and Threatened Species, Fisheries, Outdoor Recreation, Wetlands, Wildlife Management

MISSISSIPPI SEA GRANT PROGRAM
Mississippi-Alabama Sea Grant Consortium, Caylor Bldg., Gulf Coast Research Laboratory, P.O. Box 7000, Ocean Springs, MS 39566-7000
Phone: 228-875-9341; Fax: 228-875-0528
Contact(s):
Coordinator and Marine Economist: DR. WILLIAM HOSKING, Alabama Sea Grant Extension Program, 4710 Commanders Dr., Mobile, AL 36615; Phone: 334-438-5690; Fax: 334-438-5670
Head: DR. C. DAVID VEAL, Mississippi Sea Grant Advisory Service, 2710 Beach Blvd., Suite 1-E, Biloxi, MS 39531; Phone: 228-388-4710; Fax: 228-388-1375

MISSISSIPPI SOIL AND WATER CONSERVATION COMMISSION
Soundings
Attn: Public Information Coordinator, P.O. Box 3005, Jackson, MS 39225
Founded: 1938
Description: Originally established as the state agency for the control of soil erosion. Current statutory responsibilities include assistance to local soil and water conservation districts in the areas of water and soil quality projects, qualifications and elections of Commisioners, and administration of programs. Other responsibilities include reviewing and commenting on surface mining reclamation efforts. Also serves as the state resource agency for agricultural nonpoint source pollution issues and projects by assisting individual landowners, operators and other organized groups through demonstrations and educational programs.
Contact(s):
Chairman: ROSS McGEHEE, 176 McGehee Road, Natchez, MS 39120
Executive Director: GALE MARTIN, P.O. Box 23005, Jackson, MS 39225-3005; Phone: 601-354-7645; Fax: 601-354-6628
Public Information: EMMA CERAMI, P.O. Box 23005, Jackson, MS 39225-3005
Publication(s): *Conservation Comments*
Keyword(s): Environmental and Conservation Education, Erosion Control, Nonpoint Source Pollution, Soil Conservation, Water Pollution, Water Quality, Water Resources

MISSISSIPPI STATE DEPARTMENT OF HEALTH
P.O. Box 1700, Jackson, MS 39215-1700
Contact(s):
Director: Division of Epidemiology: DR. F. E. THOMPSON; Phone: 601-960-7725
Director: Environmental Health: JOE D. BROWN; Phone: 601-960-7518
State Health Officer: DR. ALTON B. COBB; Phone: 601-960-7634

MISSISSIPPI STATE EXTENSION SERVICES
Mississippi State University, Mississippi State, MS 39762
Phone: 601-325-3036
Contact(s):
Area Extension Agent: Aquaculture: JAMES A. STEEBY, Delta Area, P.O. Box 239, Belzoni, MS 39038; Phone: 601-247-2915
Area Extension Forester: TIMOTHY A. TRAUGOTT, 1241 Mound St., Grenada, MS 38901; Phone: 601-226-6000
Director of Extension Service: DR. RONALD A. BROWN

STATE AND PROVINCE GOVERNMENT AGENCIES - MISSOURI

Extension Aquaculture Specialist: DR. DAVID WISE, Delta Research and Extension Center, P.O. Box 197, Stoneville, MS 38776; Phone: 601-686-9311/ext.239
Extension Forestry Specialist: DR. ROBERT A. DANIELS, Mississippi State University, Box 9681, Mississippi State, MS 39762; Phone: 601-325-3150; Fax: 601-325-0027
Extension Forestry Specialist: DR. ANDREW W. EZELL, Mississippi State University, Box 9681, Mississippi State, MS 39762; Phone: 601-325-3150; Fax: 601-325-0027
Extension Leader: Wildlife and Fisheries Department: DR. MARTIN W. BRUNSON, Box 9690, Mississippi State University, Mississippi State, MS 39762; Phone: 601-325-3174; Fax: 601-325-8726
Extension Wildlife Specialist: DEAN W. STEWART, Box 9690, Mississippi State University, Mississippi State, MS 39762; Phone: 601-325-8726
Head: Wildlife and Fisheries Department: DR. RANDALL ROBINETTE, Box 9690, Mississippi State University, Mississippi State, MS 39762; Phone: 601-325-3830
Leader: Extension Forestry: DR. THOMAS A. MONAGHAN, Box 9681, Mississippi State University, Mississippi State, MS 39762; Phone: 601-325-3905; Fax: 601-325-0027
Keyword(s): Environmental and Conservation Education, Fisheries, Forests and Forestry, Wildlife and Wildlife Habitat, Wildlife Management

MISSOURI

GOVERNOR OF MISSOURI, MEL CARNAHAN
State Capitol, P.O. Box 720, JeffersonCity, MO 65101
Phone: 573-751-3222

MISSOURI COOPERATIVE FISH AND WILDLIFE RESEARCH UNIT (USDI)
302 Anheuser-Busch Natural Resources Building, Fisheries and Wildlife, University of Missouri, Columbia, MO 65211-7240
Phone: 573-882-3634; Fax: 573-884-5070
Founded: 1985
Description: Established by cooperative agreement among the Biological Resources Division of the U.S. Geological Survey, Missouri Department of Conservation, University of Missouri, and Wildlife Management Institute. Primary purpose is research and graduate student education in wildlife conservation, aquatic ecology, and fisheries management areas.
Contact(s):
Administrative Officer: SANDY CLARK; Phone: 573-882-3634
Assistant Leader: Fisheries: DR. DAVID L. GALAT; Phone: 573-882-9426
Assistant Leader: Wildlife: DR. RONALD D. DROBNEY; Phone: 573-882-9420
Leader: DR. CHARLES F. RABENI; Phone: 573-882-3524
Keyword(s): Fisheries, Rivers, Waterfowl, Wetlands, Wildlife and Wildlife Habitat

MISSOURI DEPARTMENT OF AGRICULTURE
P.O. Box 630, 1616 Missouri Blvd., Jefferson City, MO 65101
Phone: 573-751-4211
Contact(s):
Deputy Director: KYLE VICKERS
Director: JOHN L. SAUNDERS
Public Information Officer: SALLY OXENHANDLER

MISSOURI DEPARTMENT OF CONSERVATION
P.O. Box 180, Jefferson City, MO 65102-0180
Phone: 573-751-4115; Fax: 573-751-4467
Founded: 1937
Contact(s):
Deputy Director: JOHN W. SMITH
Director: JERRY M. CONLEY
Assistant to Director: GERALD E. ROSS
Editor of Publications: THOMAS J. CWYNAR
General Counsel: JANE A. SMITH
Internal Auditor: ROBBIE B. BRISCOE
Publication(s): *Missouri Conservationist*

Fisheries Division
Contact(s):
Divisions Administrator: NORMAN P. STUCKY
Field Operations (Mississippi River Unit): STANLEY M. MICHAELSON
Field Operations (Missouri River Unit): LOUIS S. EDER
Field Operations (Ozark Unit): KEVIN R. RICHARDS
Research Chief: GARY D. NOVINGER

Forestry Division
Contact(s):
Division Administrator: MARVIN D. BROWN
Management Chief (Mississippi River Unit): LISA G. ALLEN
Management Chief (Missouri River Unit): THOMAS P. RONK
Management Chief (Ozark Unit): CARL E. HAUSER
Staff & Research Chief: MICHAEL R. HOFFMAN

Protection Division
Contact(s):
Division Administrator: RONALD L. GLOVER
Field Chief (Mississippi River Unit): JOHN D. HOSKINS
Field Chief (Missouri River Unit): ALLEN W. BRESHEARS
Field Chief (Ozark Unit): DENNIS W. STEWARD

Wildlife Division
Contact(s):
Divison Administrator: OLIVER A. TORGERSON
Management Chief (Mississippi River Unit): WAYNE R. PORATH
Management Chief (Missouri River Unit): NORBERT D. GIESSMAN
Management Chief (Ozark Unit): RUSSELL R. TITUS
Research Chief: DIANA L. HALLET

MISSOURI DEPARTMENT OF NATURAL RESOURCES
P.O. Box 176, Jefferson City, MO 65102
Phone: 314-751-4422; Fax: 1-800-334-6946
Description: The Missouri Department of Natural Resources is the state resource management agency that deals with the critical area of efficient energy management, helps develop mineral resources in an environmentally safe manner; protects Missouri's air, land, and water resources; and preserves the state's natural and cultural heritage while providing outdoor recreation.
Contact(s):
Director: STEPHEN M. MMAHFOOD, P.O. Box 176, Jefferson City, MO 65102-0176; Phone: 573-751-4732
Department Information Officer: NINA THOMPSON; Phone: 573-751-1010
Deputy Directoy: JEFF STAAKE; Phone: 573-522-8796
Director of Division of Environmental Improvement and Energy Resources Authority: THOMANS WELCH, P.O. Box 744, Jefferson City, MO 65102-0176; Phone: 573-751-4919
Director of Division of Administrative Support: GARY HEMERICKS; Phone: 573-751-7961
Director of Division of Energy: ANITA RANDOLPH; Phone: 573-751-2254
Director of Division of Environmental Quality: JOHN A. YOUNG; Phone: 573-751-0763
Director of Division of State Parks: DOUGLAS K. EIKEN; Phone: 573-751-9392
Director of Divison Geology and Land Survey: DR. JAMES HADLEY; Phone: 573-368-2102
Eastern Parks District Administrator: DAN PAIGE, 2901 Highway 61, Festus, MO 63028; Phone: 314-937-3697
Jefferson City Regional Office Administrator: ROBERT HENGTES, P.O. Box 176, Jefferson City, MO 65102-0176; Phone: 573-751-2729
Kansas City Regional Office Administrator: JIM MACY, 500 NE Colbern Rd., Lee's Summit, MO 667086-4710; Phone: 816-554-4100

Missouri River District: LARRY JOHNSON, P.O. Box 166, Boonville, MO 65233; Phone: 660-882-8196

North Hills District Administrator: FRANK ST. CLAIR, P.O. Box 314, Brookfield, MO 64628; Phone: 660-258-7496

Northeast Regional Office Administrator: STEVE DECKER, 1709 Prospect Dr., Macon, MO 63552-2602; Phone: 660-385-2129

Northern Missouri Historic District Administrator: JAMES REHARD, P.O. Box 314, Brookfield, MO 64628; Phone: 660-258-7496

Ozarks District Administrator: DENNY BOPP, P.O. Box 951, Lebanon, MO 65536; Phone: 417-532-7361

Southeast Regional Office Administrator: GARY GAINES, 948 Lester St., P.O. Box 1420, Poplar Bluff, MO 63901-1420; Phone: 573-840-9750

Southern Missouri Historic District: GARY WALRATH, 2901 Highway 61, Festus, MO 63028; Phone: 314-937-3697

Southwest Regional Office Administrator: BRUCE MARTIN, 2040 W. Woodland, Springfield, MO 65807-5912; Phone: 471-891-4300

St. Louis Regional Office Administrator: ROBERT ECK, 10805 Sunset Office Dr., St. Louis, MO 63127-1017; Phone: 314-301-7100

Publication(s): *Missouri Resources*
Keyword(s): Energy, Environmental Preservation, Geology, Outdoor Recreation, Public Lands

MISSOURI STATE EXTENSION SERVICES
University of Missouri, 309 University Hall, Columbia, MO 65211
Phone: 573-882-7754; Fax: 573-884-4204
Contact(s):
Director: Extension Service: DR. RONALD J. TURNER
Extension Fish and Wildlife Specialist: ROBERT A. PIERCE II, 302 Natural Resources Bldg., Columbia, MO 65211; Phone: 573-882-4337
Extension Forester: JOHN P. SLUSHER, 203 Natural Resources Bldg., Columbia, MO 65211; Phone: 573-882-4444; Fax: 573-882-1977

MONTANA

GOVERNOR OF MONTANA, MARC RACICOT
State Capitol, Helena, MT 59620
Phone: 406-444-3111

BUREAU OF MINES AND GEOLOGY
c/o Montana College of Mineral Science and Technology, Butte, MT 59701
Phone: 406-496-4167
Founded: 1919
Description: Established by law to aid the development and wise use of the state's mineral, energy, and groundwater resources by geologic and hydrogeologic studies of their occurrence and potential. Publishes formal reports and maps on Montana geology and groundwater.
Keyword(s): Energy, Geology, Water Resources

ENVIRONMENTAL QUALITY COUNCIL
State Capitol, P.O. Box 201704, Helena, MT 59620-1704
Phone: 406-444-3742
Contact(s):
Co-Chair: REPRESENTATIVE VICKI COCCHIARELLA
Co-Chair: SENATOR KEN MESAROS
Legislative Environmental Analyst: TODD EVERTS
Keyword(s): Air Quality and Pollution, Environmental Law, Land Use Planning, Water Quality, Water Resources

MONTANA COOPERATIVE FISHERY RESEARCH UNIT (USDI)
Dept. of Biology, Montana State University, P.O. Box 173460, Bozeman, MT 59717-3460
Phone: 406-994-4549; Fax: 406-994-7479
Contact(s):
Assistant Leader: DR. ALEXANDER ZALE; Phone: 406-994-4549
Leader: DR. ROBERT G. WHITE; Phone: 406-994-3491; Email: ubirw@montana.edu
Keyword(s): Aquatic Habitats, Endangered and Threatened Species, Fisheries, Research, Rivers

MONTANA COOPERATIVE WILDLIFE RESEARCH UNIT (USGS/BRD)
University of Montana, Missoula, MT 59812
Phone: 406-243-5372; Fax: 406-243-6064
Founded: 1950
Description: Conducts basic and applied research, trains graduate students in wildlife biology and management, and disseminates information. Research specialties include breeding productivity, nest predation, and habitat use by birds (particularly nongame and waterfowl species) in relation to land use practices, predator populations, and natural variation in the environment.
Contact(s):
Assistant Leader: DR. THOMAS E. MARTIN; Email: tmartin@selway.umt.edu
Leader: DR. I. J. BALL; Email: ball1@selway.umt.edu
Keyword(s): Birds, Forests and Forestry, Grasslands, Nongame Wildlife, Waterfowl, Wetlands

MONTANA DEPARTMENT OF AGRICULTURE
P.O. Box 200201, Helena, MT 59620-0201
Phone: 406-444-3144
Contact(s):
Director: W. RALPH PECK
Administrator: Agricultural Development Division: WILL KISSINGER; Phone: 406-444-2402
Administrator: Agricultural Sciences Division: GARY L. GINGERY; Phone: 406-444-2944
Keyword(s): Agriculture, Endangered and Threatened Species, Ground Water Protection, Pest Management, Pesticides

MONTANA DEPARTMENT OF FISH, WILDLIFE, AND PARKS
1420 E. 6th, P.O. Box 200701, Helena, MT 59620-0701
Phone: 406-444-3186; Fax: 406-444-4952
Contact(s):
Director: PATRICK J. GRAHAM; Phone: 406-444-3186
Administrator: Administration and Finance: DAVE MOTT; Phone: 406-444-4786
Administrator: Conservation Education: RON AASHEIM; Phone: 406-444-4038
Administrator: Enforcement: BEATA GALDA; Phone: 406-444-5657
Administrator: Field Services: RICH CLOUGH; Phone: 406-444-3196
Administrator: Wildlife: DON CHILDRESS; Phone: 406-444-2612
Administrator:Fisheries: LARRY PETERMAN; Phone: 406-444-2449
Chief of Operations: ARNOLD OLSEN; Phone: 406-444-3186
Chief of Staff: CHRISTINA SMITH; Phone: 406-444-3186
Editor: DAVE BOOKS; Phone: 406-444-2474
Publication(s): *Montana Outdoors*
Keyword(s): Environmental and Conservation Education, Hunting, Outdoor Recreation, Sport Fishing, Wildlife and Wildlife Habitat

MONTANA DEPARTMENT OF NATURAL RESOURCES AND CONSERVATION
1625 11th Ave. P.O. Box 201601, Helena, MT 59620-1601
Phone: 406-444-2074; Fax: 406-444-2684
Founded: 1971
Description: State government agency created by the Executive Reorganization Act of 1971. Administers state-owned water projects; plans, regulates, and coordinates the development and use of other water, land, and forest resources; water-right adjudication; floodplain management; supervision, assistance, and coordination for local

STATE AND PROVINCE GOVERNMENT AGENCIES - NEBRASKA

conservation and grazing districts; and regulation of oil and gas production.
Contact(s):
Director: BUD CLINCH; Phone: 406-444-2074
Administrator for Central Services Division: ANN BAUCHMAN; Phone: 406-444-6734
Administrator: Conservation and Resource Development Division: RAY BECK, 1520 E. 6th Ave., Helena, MT 59620; Phone: 406-444-6667; Fax: 406-444-6721; Email: rbeck@mt.gov
Administrator: Forestry Division: DON ARTLEY, 2705 Spurgin Rd., Missoula, MT 59801; Phone: 406-542-4300
Administrator: Trust Land Management Division: JEFF HAGENER; Phone: 406-444-4978
Administrator: Water Resources Division: GARY FRITZ, 1520 E. 6th Ave., Helena, MT 59620; Phone: 406-444-6605
Chief Legal Counsel: DONALD D. MacINTYRE; Phone: 406-444-6713
Chief: Technology Bureau: BOB AUER; Phone: 406-444-4948
Executive Secretary: Oil and Gas Conservation Division: DEE RICKMAN, 1520 E. 6th Ave., Helena, MT 59620; Phone: 406-444-6675
Personnel and EEO Officer: GLENNA McCLURE; Phone: 406-444-4942
Special Projects Coordinator: WAYNE WETZEL; Phone: 406-444-6722
Supervisor and Editor for Information Services: CAROLE MASSMAN; Phone: 406-444-6737
Keyword(s): Agriculture, Soil Conservation, Water Resources

MONTANA NATURAL HERITAGE PROGRAM
1515 E 6th Ave., Helena, MT 59620-1800
Phone: 406-444-3009; Fax: 406-444-0581; Email: mtnhp@nris.state.mt.us; WWW: www.nris.state.mt.us/mtnhp
Founded: 1985
Description: A centralized repository and clearinghouse of information on Montana's biodiversity, emphasizing features and species that are rare, threatened, endangered, or in need of further research.
Contact(s):
Director: SUSAN CRISPIN
Publication(s): *Montana Plant Species of Special Concern; Montana Animal Species of Special Concern; Montana Bird Distribution*
Keyword(s): Zoology

MONTANA STATE EXTENSION SERVICES
Director of Extension Service, Linfield Hall, Montana State University, Bozeman, MT 59717
Phone: 406-994-6647
Contact(s):
Extension Wildlife Specialist: JIM KNIGHT, Dept. of Animal and Range Science, Montana State University, Bozeman, MT 59717; Phone: 406-994-5579

NEBRASKA

GOVERNOR OF NEBRASKA, MIKE JOHANNS
P.O. Box 94848, Lincoln, NE 68509
Phone: 402-471-2244; Fax: 402-471-6031

DEPARTMENT OF ENVIRONMENTAL QUALITY (NEBRASKA)
Suite 400, The Atrium, 1200 N St., P.O. Box 98922, Lincoln, NE 68509-8922
Phone: 402-471-2186
Founded: 1971
Description: Created by the Nebraska Environmental Protection Act. Administers and enforces rules and regulations, and monitors the quality of the environment in Nebraska.
Contact(s):
Deputy Director: TOM LAMBERSON
Director: RANDOLPH WOOD
Assistant Director: Air & Waste Division: JOE FRANCIS
Assistant Director: Water Division: GALE HUTTON
Editor: BRIAN McMANUS
Public Information Officer: BRIAN McMANUS
Secretary: State Environmental Quality Council: RANDOLPH WOOD
Publication(s): *Environmental Update*

DEPARTMENT OF WATER RESOURCES (NEBRASKA)
State House Station, Box 94676, Lincoln, NE 68509
Phone: 402-471-2363
Description: Administers and enforces the state water laws and all matters pertaining to water rights; measuring and recording the flow of various streams and canals; approving plans and specifications for dam construction; inspection of dams; and registration of wells.
Contact(s):
Assistant Director: DONALD G. BLANKENAU
Director: J. MICHAEL JESS
Chief: Legal Counsel: DONALD G. BLANKENAU
Permits and Adjudications: SUSAN A. FRANCE
State Hydrologist: ANN SALOMON BLEED
Publication(s): *Channels Newsletter; Biennial Report; Hydrographic Report*
Keyword(s): Engineering, Lakes, Rivers, Water Resources

GAME AND PARKS COMMISSION
2200 N. 33rd St., P.O. Box 30370, Lincoln, NE 68503-0370
Phone: 402-471-0641
Description: The commission has sole charge of state parks, game and fish, and all things pertaining thereto; boating; and administration of the Land and Water Conservation Fund. Complete information on Game and Parks Commission facilities is available on the WWW at: www.ngpc.state.ne.us.
Contact(s):
Assistant Director: KIRK NELSON; Phone: 402-471-5537; Email: knelson@ngpsun.ngpc.state.ne.us
Assistant Director: ROGER KUHN; Phone: 402-471-5512
Assistant Director: NOELYN ISOM; Phone: 402-471-5537; Email: bisom@ngpsun.ngpc.state.ne.us
Chair: WILLIAM BERRYMAN
Director: REX AMACK; Phone: 402-471-5539; Email: ramack@ngpsun.ngpc.state.ne.us
Administrator: Engineering: JIM SHEFFIELD; Phone: 402-471-5557; Email: jsheff@ngpsun.ngpc.state.ne.us
Administrator: Administration: MARK BROHMAN; Phone: 402-471-5537; Email: mbrohman@hgpsun
Administrator: Budget and Fiscal: LARRY WITT; Phone: 402-471-5523
Administrator: Central Regional Parks Manager: JAMES CARNEY; Phone: 402-471-5547; Email: jcarney@ngpsun.ngpc.state.ne.us
Administrator: Fisheries: DON GABELHOUSE JR.; Phone: 402-471-5515; Email: gabel@ngpsun.ngpc.state.ne.us
Administrator: Information and Education: PAUL HORTON; Phone: 402-471-5481; Email: phorton@ngpsun.ngpc.state.ne.us
Administrator: Law Enforcement: DICK TURPIN; Phone: 402-471-5533
Administrator: Operations and Construction: EARL JOHNSON; Phone: 402-471-5525
Administrator: Parks: JAMES FULLER; Phone: 402-471-5550; Email: jfuller@ngpsun.ngpc.state.ne.us
Administrator: Planning and Development: DUANE WESTERHOLT; Phone: 402-471-5511; Email: dwester@ngpsun.ngpc.state.ne.us
Administrator: Realty: BRUCE SACKETT; Phone: 402-471-5536; Email: bsackett@ngpsun.ngpc.state.ne.us
Administrator: Wildlife: JAMES DOUGLAS; Phone: 402-471-5411; Email: jdouglas@ngpsun.ngpc.state.ne.us
Editor: DON CUNNINGHAM
Librarian: BARBARA VOELTZ, 2200 N 33rd St., P.O. Box 30370, Lincoln, NE 68503; Phone: 402-471-5587; Fax: 402-471-5528; Email: bvoeltz@ngpsun.ngpc.state.ne.us

STATE AND PROVINCE GOVERNMENT AGENCIES - NEVADA

Western Regional Parks Manager: STEVE KEMPER; Phone: 308-665-2900
Publication(s): *Nebraskaland Magazine*

Game and Parks Commission
1212 Deer Park Blvd, Omaha, NE 68108
Phone: 402-595-2144

GAME AND PARKS COMMISSION-NEBRASKA

AK-Sar-Ben Aquarium
21502,W. Hwy. 31, Gretna, NE 68028
Phone: 402-332-3901; Fax: 402-332-5853

NEBRASKA DEPARTMENT OF AGRICULTURE
301 Centennial Mall S., P.O. Box 94947, Lincoln, NE 68509
Phone: 402-471-2341
Contact(s):
Assistant Director: PATRICK PTACEK; Fax: Fax-402-471-2759
Director: LARRY SITZMAN

NEBRASKA GEOLOGICAL SURVEY
Conservation and Survey Division, University of Nebraska, Lincoln, NE 68588
Phone: 402-472-3471, 402-472-2410
Description: The CSD has responsibilities to survey and describe Nebraska's natural resources, including soil, water, geology, mineral resources, and climate. Additionally, the division publishes studies which describe operations and production of leading industries in the state. Staff members also provide educational talks and materials to citizens.
Contact(s):
Director: P. B. WIGLEY

NEBRASKA NATURAL RESOURCES COMMISSION
301 Centennial Mall S., 4th Fl., P.O. Box 94876, Lincoln, NE 68509-4876
Phone: 402-471-2081
Founded: 1937
Description: The state agency responsible for comprehensive water resources planning, flood plain management, administration of state financial assistance for water resources, flood control, and soil and water conservation. It also has advisory and administrative responsibility for Natural Resources Districts throughout the state.
Contact(s):
Director: DAYLE E. WILLIAMSON; Phone: 402-471-2081; Fax: 402-471-3132; Email: daylew@nrcdec.nrc.state.ne.us
Chairperson: VINCE KRAMPER, 498 190th St., Dakota City, NE 98731; Phone: 402-987-3560
Publication(s): *Nebraska Resources*
Keyword(s): Environmental and Conservation Education, Planning Management, Rivers, Soil Conservation, Water Resources

NEBRASKA STATE EXTENSION SERVICES
University of Nebraska, Lincoln, NE 68583-0703
Phone: 402-472-2966
Contact(s):
Dean and Director of Cooperative Extension: DR. KENNETH R. BOLEN
Environmental Education Specialist: DR. TOM SEIBERT, Department of Forestry, Fisheries and Wildlife, 202 Natural Resources Hall, University of Nebraska-Lincoln, Lincoln, NE 68583-0819; Phone: 402-472-8913
Extension Aquaculture Specialist: DR. TERRENCE B. KAYES, Department of Forestry, Fisheries and Wildlife, 12 Plant Industry, Institute of Agriculture and Natural Resources, University of Nebraska-Lincoln, Lincoln, NE 68583-0814; Phone: 402-472-8183
Extension Vertebrate Pest Specialist: DR. SCOTT E. HYGNSTROM, Department of Forestry, Fisheries and Wildlife, 202 Natural Resources Hall, University of Nebraska-Lincoln, Lincoln, NE 68583-0819; Phone: 402-472-6822
Extension Wildlife Specialist: DR. RON J. JOHNSON, Department of Forestry, Fisheries and Wildlife, 202 Natural Resources Hall, University of Nebraska-Lincoln, Lincoln, NE 68583-0819; Phone: 402-472-6823
State Forester: DR. GARY HERGENRADER, Department of Forestry, Fisheries and Wildlife, 102 Plant Industry Bldg., Institute of Agriculture and Natural Resources, Lincoln, NE 68583-0814; Phone: 402-472-1467
Keyword(s): Agriculture, Environmental and Conservation Education, Renewable Resources, Sustainable Ecosystems, Wildlife and Wildlife Habitat

NEVADA

GOVERNOR OF NEVADA, KENNY GUINN
State Capitol, CarsonCity, NV 89710
Phone: 702-687-5670

DIVISION OF AGRICULTURE
Division of Agriculture, 350 Capitol Hill Ave., Reno, NV 89502-2992
Phone: 775-688-1180; Fax: 775-688-1178
Contact(s):
Administrator: PAUL J. IVERSON
Chief: Bureau of Animal Industry: DAVID THAIN
Chief: Bureau of Plant Industry: ROBERT GRONOWSKI

NEVADA BUREAU OF MINES AND GEOLOGY
University of Nevada, Reno, NV 89557-0088
Phone: 702-784-6691
Description: Conducts research on Nevada geology and mineral resources. Collects and disseminates information (including published maps and reports) on Nevada geology, mineral resources, base maps, and airphotos.
Contact(s):
Director and State Geologist: JONATHAN G. PRICE
Keyword(s): Geography, Geology, Land Use Planning, Public Lands, Water Resources

NEVADA DEPARTMENT OF CONSERVATION AND NATURAL RESOURCES
Capitol Complex, 123 W. Nye Ln., Carson City, NV 89710
Phone: 702-687-4360
Contact(s):
Director: PETER G. MORROS
Administrator and State Land Registrar: PAMELA B. WILCOX; Phone: 702-687-4363
Administrator: Division of Conservation Districts: PAMELA B. WILCOX; Phone: 702-687-4363
Administrator: Division of Environmental Protection: LEWIS H. DODGION; Phone: 702-687-4670
Administrator: Division of State Parks: WAYNE PEROCK; Phone: 702-687-4384
Administrator: Division of Water Planning: NAOMI DUERR; Phone: 702-687-3600
Administrator: Division of Wildlife: WILLIE MOLINI; Phone: 702-688-1500
Assistant Administrator: TERRY CRAWFORTH
Chairman: State Environmental Commission: MELVIN D. CLOSE
Chief:Planning and Development: J. STEPHEN WEAVER
Deputy Administrator: RICHARD E. REAVIS
Deputy Administrator: VERNE L. ROSSE; Phone: 702-687-5872
Deputy State Engineer: CHRISTINE THIEL
Deputy State Engineer: HUGH H. RICCI
Executive Officer: LEWIS H. DODGION; Phone: 702-687-4670
Program Manager: Nevada Natural Heritage: GLENN CLEMMER; Phone: 702-687-4245
State Engineer: Division of Water Resources: R. MICHAEL TURNIPSEED; Phone: 702-687-4380
State Forester: Division of Forestry: ROY W. TRENOWETH; Phone: 702-687-4350

STATE AND PROVINCE GOVERNMENT AGENCIES - NEW HAMPSHIRE

State Conservation Commission
Contact(s):
Chair: EDDIE VENTURACCI, 441 Venturacci Lane, Fallon, NV 89406; Phone: 702-423-2472
Conservation Program Specialist: CHRIS FREEMAN, 333 W. Nye Lane, Room 118, Carson City, NV 89706; Phone: 702-687-6977; Fax: 702-687-3783

NEVADA DIVISION OF WILDLIFE
Box 10678, Reno, NV 89520
Phone: 775-688-1500; Fax: 775-688-1595
Description: A regulatory and policymaking body, administering laws, regulations, and policies. Mission is the protection, propagation, restoring, introduction, transplanting, and management of wildlife throughout the state.
Contact(s):
Administrator: TERRY R. CRAWFORTH
Board of Wildlife Commissioner Chairman: BILL BRADLEY
Board of Wildlife Commissioner Vice Chairman: BOYD SPRATLING
Chief: Enforcement: THOMAS ATKINSON
Chief: Fisheries: GENE WELLER
Chief: Game: GREGG TANNER
Chief: Habitat: ROBERT McQUIVEY
Chief:Conservation Education: DAVID K. RICE

NEVADA NATURAL HERITAGE PROGRAM
1550 E. College Parkway, Suite 145, Carson City, NV 89706-7921
Phone: 702-687-4245; Fax: 702-687-1288; WWW: www.heritage.tnc.org
Founded: 1986
Description: The program represents an ongoing effort to collect and standardize data on Nevada's sensitive biodiversity and share this information with developers, researchers, and decision-makers for environmentally wise planning.
Contact(s):
Program Manager: GLENN CLEMMER
Publication(s): *Nevada's Sensitive Species List; Scorecard-Highest Priority Conservation Sites; Endangered, Threatened, and Sensitive Vascular Plants of Nevada*
Keyword(s): Biodiversity, Conservation, Conservation of Protected Areas, Endangered and Threatened Species, Environmental Planning, Nongame Wildlife

NEVEDA COOPERATIVE EXTENSION
Universtiy of Neveda, 2345 Red Rock #330, Las Vegas, NV 89512
Phone: 702-251-7531
Contact(s):
Assistant Director: JANET USINGER-LESQUEREUX; Phone: 702-251-7531
Central Area Agronomy and Range Specialist: JASON DAVIDSON, Fallon, NV ; Phone: 702-428-0212
State Range Specialist: SHERMAN SWANSON; Phone: 702-784-4057
State Water Specialist: MARK WALKER; Phone: 702-784-1938
Western Area Natural Resources Specialist: ED SMITH, Garderville, NV ; Phone: 702-782-9960
Western Area Water Specialist: JOHN COBOURN, Incline Village, NV ; Phone: 702-832-4150
Keyword(s): Renewable Resources, Sustainable Ecosystems, Water Resources

NEW HAMPSHIRE

GOVERNOR OF NEW HAMPSHIRE, JEANNE SHAHEEN
State House, Rm. 208, Concord, NH 03301
Phone: 603-271-2121

COUNCIL ON RESOURCES AND DEVELOPMENT
c/o Office of State Planning, 2 1/2 Beacon St., Concord, NH 03301
Phone: 603-271-2155
Founded: 1963
Description: The ten members on the council represent the state's development and resource agencies. The council conducts studies and presents recommendations concerning problems in the fields of environmental protection, natural resources, and growth management; consults with, negotiates with, and obtains information from other state and federal agencies; offers guidance and recommendations to the Governor and Council or the General Court; recommends disposition or lease of state-owned surplus real property; and resolves differences or conflicts concerning development, resource management, and the implementation of the state policy.
Contact(s):
Chairman: JEFFREY H. TAYLOR

DEPARTMENT OF RESOURCES AND ECONOMIC DEVELOPMENT
P.O. Box 1856, 172 Pembroke Rd., Concord, NH 03302-1856
Contact(s):
Chief of Bureau of Off-Highway Recreational Vehicles: PAUL GRAY; Phone: 603-271-3254
Commissioner: GEORGE BALD; Phone: 603-271-2411
Director of Division of Economic Development: NORMAN STORRS; Phone: 603-271-2341
Director of Division of Forests and Lands: PHILIP A. BRYCE; Phone: 603-271-2214
Director of Division of Parks: RICHARD McLEOD; Phone: 603-271-3556
Urban Forester of Urban Forestry Center: J. B. CULLEN; Phone: 603-431-6774

NEW HAMPSHIRE DEPARTMENT OF AGRICULTURE, MARKETS, AND FOOD
P.O. Box 2042, Concord, NH 03302-2042
Founded: 1913
Description: The department is responsible for a broad range of activities, including protecting the environment, food safety, market integrity, animal and plant health, and the economic security of the New Hampshire agricultural industry.
Contact(s):
Commissioner: STEPHEN H. TAYLOR; Phone: 603-271-3551; Fax: 603-271-1109
Publication(s): *Weekly Market Bulletin*
Keyword(s): Agriculture, Environmental Justice, Land Protection, Rural Development, Sustainable Development

State Conservation Committee
P.O. Box 2042, Concord, NH 03302-2042
Phone: 603-271-3551
Founded: 1945
Description: The SCC consists of eleven members. Five members represent state agencies, five are appointed, and one represents the NH Association of Conservation Commissions. Duties are to offer assistance to supervisors of the ten conservation districts, keep supervisors of each district informed of other district activities, and coordinate the conservation of New Hampshire activities.
Contact(s):
Chair: PETER BLAKEMAN, P.O. Box 4, North Sutton, NH 03260; Phone: 603-927-4163; Fax: 603-224-8260
Coordinator: JOANNA PELLERIN, 118 North Rd., Brentwood, NH 03833-6614; Phone: 603-679-2790; Fax: 603-679-2860
Coordinator: Representing (NPS): ERIC WILLIAMS
Member: MARJORY SWOPE; Phone: 603-224-7867

Member: ROBERT VARNEY; Phone: 603-271-2358
Member: ROBB THOMSON; Phone: 603-271-2214
Member: STEPHEN H. TAYLOR; Phone: 603-271-3551
Member: DR. WILLIAM MAUTZ; Phone: 603-862-1450
Member: DR. PETER HORNE; Phone: 603-862-1520
Keyword(s): Agriculture, Environmental and Conservation Education, Soil Conservation, Water Resources, Wetlands

NEW HAMPSHIRE DEPARTMENT OF ENVIRONMENTAL SERVICES
6 Hazen Dr., P.O. Box 95, Concord, NH 03302-0095
Phone: 603-271-3503
Founded: 1987
Description: The DES is a result of a legislatively-mandated state environmental agency. The DES consists of three divisions: Water Division; Waste Management Division; and Air Resources Division.
Contact(s):
Assistant Commissioner: G. DANA BISBEE
Commissioner: ROBERT W. VARNEY
Director of Air Resources Division: KENNETH A. COLBURN, 64 N. Main St., Caller Box 2033, Concord, NH 03302; Phone: 603-271-1390; Fax: 603-271-1381
Director of Waste Management Division: DR. PHILIP J. O'BRIEN; Phone: 603-271-2900; Fax: 603-271-2456
Director of Water Division: HARRY T. STEWART; Phone: 603-271-2503; Fax: 603-271-2867
Keyword(s): Air Quality and Pollution, Solid Waste, Water Pollution, Water Resources, Wetlands

NEW HAMPSHIRE FISH AND GAME DEPARTMENT
2 Hazen Dr., Concord, NH 03301
Phone: 603-271-3422; Fax: 603-271-1438
Contact(s):
Executive Director: WAYNE E. VETTER
Business Administrator: RICHARD N. CUNNINGHAM
Chief: Access and Engineering Division: JOHN S. BOWYER JR.
Chief: Inland Fisheries: STEPHEN G. PERRY
Chief: Law Enforcement Division: MAJ. RONALD ALIE
Chief: Marine Fisheries Division: JOHN I. NELSON JR.
Chief: Public Affairs Division: JUDY STOKES
Chief: Wildlife Division: JAMES J. DISTEFANO
Commission Chairman: RICHARD MOQUIN
Commission Vice Chairman: ELLIS HATCH
Commissioner Secretary: JIM JONES
Keyword(s): Biology, Endangered and Threatened Species, Environmental and Conservation Education, Fisheries, Hunting, Internships, Nongame Wildlife, Sport Fishing, Trapping, Wildlife Management

NEW HAMPSHIRE NATURAL HERITAGE INVENTORY
P.O. Box 1856, Concord, NH 03302-1856
Phone: 603-271-3623; Fax: 603-271-2629
Founded: 1987
Description: New Hampshire Natural Heritage Inventory is responsible for finding, tracking, and providing information about the state's rare species and exemplary ecosystems.
Contact(s):
Coordinator: DAVID VAN LUVEN
Publication(s): *List of New Hampshire's Rare Plant Species; List of New Hampshire's Rare Animal Species; Checklist of New Hampshire's Vascular Plants*
Keyword(s): Biodiversity, Biology, Ecology, Endangered and Threatened Species, Flowers, Plants, and Trees, Terrestrial Habitats

NEW HAMPSHIRE SEA GRANT PROGRAM
Kingman Farm, University of New Hampshire, Durham, NH 03824
Phone: 603-749-1565
Contact(s):
Coordinator: Communication and Information: STEVE ADAMS, Kingman Farm, University of New Hampshire, Durham, NH 03824; Phone: 603-749-1565
Director of UM/UNH Joint Sea Grant College Program: ANN BUCKLIN; Phone: 603-862-0122
Program Leader: Sea Grant Extension Program: BRIAN DOYLE, Kingman Farm, University of New Hampshire, Durham, NH 03824; Phone: 603-749-1565
Keyword(s): Aquatic Habitats, Coasts, Environmental and Conservation Education, Fisheries, Marine Mammals, Oceanography, Renewable Resources, Research, Sea Grass, Sport Fishing, Sustainable Development, Sustainable Ecosystems, Water Pollution, Wetlands

UNIVERSITY OF NEW HAMPSHIRE COOPERATIVE EXTENSION
59 College Rd., Taylor Hall, Durham, NH 03824-2618
Founded: 1925 (Forestry Program)
Description: The natural resource components include Forest Stewardship, Community Forestry, Rural Economic Well-Being, Agriculture, and Natural Resource Conservation Education.
Contact(s):
Dean and Director of UNH Cooperative Extension: DR. JOHN PIKE, UNH, 59 College Rd., Taylor Hall, Durham, NH 03824-3587; Phone: 603-862-1520
Extension Specialist: Water Resources: FRANK S. MITCHELL, UNH Cooperative Extension, 55 College Rd., Pettee Hall, Durham, NH 03824-3599; Phone: 603-862-1067
Extension Specialist: Water Resources Lakes Lay Monitoring Program: JEFFREY SCHLOSS, UNH, 55 College Rd., Pettee Hall, Durham, NH 03824-3599; Phone: 603-862-3848
Forest Stewardship Coordinator: KAREN BENNETT, UNH Cooperative Extension, 55 College Rd., Pettee Hall, Durham, NH 03824-3599; Phone: 603-862-2512
Program Leader: Forestry/Wildlife: ROBERT LEE EDMONDS, UNH Cooperative Extension, 59 College Rd., Taylor Hall, Durham, NH 03824-3587; Phone: 603-862-2619
Wildlife Specialist: ELLEN SNYDER, UNH Cooperative Extension, 55 College Rd., Pettee Hall, Durham, NH 03824-3599; Phone: 603-862-3594
Keyword(s): Environmental and Conservation Education, Forests and Forestry, Lakes, Urban Forestry, Wildlife and Wildlife Habitat

NEW JERSEY

GOVERNOR OF NEW JERSEY, CHRISTINE T. WHITMAN
State House, 125 W. State St., Office of the Governor, CN-001, Trenton, NJ 08625
Phone: 609-292-6000

DEPARTMENT OF ENVIRONMENTAL PROTECTION (NEW JERSEY)
401 E. State St., P. O. 402, Trenton, NJ 08625-0402
Phone: 609-292-2885
Contact(s):
Assistant Cmmissioner: Policy and Planning: BOB TUDOR; Phone: 609-292-1254
Assistant Commissioner: Enforcement: MARLEN DOOLEY; Phone: 609-984-3285
Assistant Commissioner: Environmental Regulation: GARY SONDERMEYER; Phone: 609-292-2795
Assistant Commissioner: Land Use Mangement: RAY CANTOR, 401 E. State St., P.O. Box 439, ; Phone: 609-292-2178
Assistant Commissioner: Management and Budget: RONALD TUMINSKI; Phone: 609-292-2916
Assistant Commissioner: Natural and Historic Resources: JIM HALL; Phone: 609-292-3541

STATE AND PROVINCE GOVERNMENT AGENCIES - NEW JERSEY

Assistant Commissioner: Site Remediation: RICHARD GIMELLO; Phone: 609-292-1250
Commissioner: ROBERT C. SHINN JR.
Deputy Commissioner: JUDY JENGO; Phone: 609-292-9661
Deputy Commissioner: MARK SMITH; Phone: 609-292-2885
Director: Communications: PETER PAGE; Phone: 609-777-1344
Director: Division of Science and Research: LESLIE McGEORGE; Phone: 609-984-6070
Editor: DENISE MIKICS; Phone: 609-777-4182
Publication(s): *New Jersey Outdoors*

Division of Fish, Game, and Wildlife
P.O. Box 400, Trenton, NJ 08625-0400
Phone: 609-292-2965
Contact(s):
Director: ROBERT L. McDOWELL; Phone: 609-292-9410
Assistant Director:Central Services: ROBERT ITCHMONEY; Phone: 609-292-0891
Chief: Bureau of Marine Fisheries: TOM McCLOY; Phone: 609-984-5546
Chief: Freshwater Fisheries: ROBERT SOLDWEDEL; Phone: 609-292-8642
Chief: Lands Management: TONY PETRONGOLO; Phone: 609-292-1599
Chief: Law Enforcement: ROB WINKEL; Phone: 609-292-9430
Chief: Shell Fisheries: JIM JOSEPH; Phone: 609-984-5546
Chief: Wildlife Education: DAVID CHANDA; Phone: 609-292-9450
Chief: Wildlife Management: FRED CARLSON; Phone: 609-292-6685
Chief:Endangered and Nongame Species Program: LARRY NILES; Phone: 609-292-9101

Division of Parks and Forestry
P.O. Box 404, Trenton, NJ 08625-0404
Phone: 609-292-2733
Contact(s):
Deputy Director: CARL R. NORDSTROM; Phone: 609-292-5990
Director: GREGORY A. MARSHALL
Administrator: Office of Historic Preservation: DOROTHY P. GUZZO; Phone: 609-984-0176
Assistant Director: State Park Service: JAMES BARRESI; Phone: 609-292-2530
Assistant Director: State Park Service: RICHARD F. BARKER; Phone: 609-292-2772
Chief: Bureau of Forest Fire Management and State Firewarden: DAVID B. HARRISON; Phone: 609-292-2977
Chief: Bureau of Forest Management: State Forester: LES ALPAUGH; Phone: 609-292-2531
Communications Coordinator: AMY CRADICK; Phone: 609-984-1423
Education Coordinator: FRANK GALLAGHER; Phone: 609-292-8190

Division of Publicly Funded Site Remediation
401 E. State St., P.O. Box 402, Trenton, NJ 08625-0402
Phone: 609-984-2902
Contact(s):
Director: ANTHONY J. FARRO

Division of Solid and Hazardous Waste
P.O. Box 414, Trenton, NJ 08625-0414
Phone: 609-984-6880
Contact(s):
Director: JOHN CASRER

Geological Survey
P.O. Box 427, Trenton, NJ 08625-0427
Phone: 609-292-1185; Fax: 609-633-1004; WWW: www.state.nj.us/dep.njgs
Founded: 1835
Description: Formed to study, evaluate, and prepare maps and reports on New Jersey's resources. In addition to a geologic map and information on the mineral industry and water resources, the survey provides geologic and ground water reports, geologic and topographic maps, ground water monitoring, and other resource information.
Contact(s):
Chief of Bureau of Geology and Topography: RICHARD DALTON; Phone: 609-292-2576
Chief of Bureau of Ground Water Resource Evaluation: KARL MUESSIG; Phone: 609-984-6587
Editor: THOMAS SECKLER; Phone: 609-292-2576
State Geologist: HAIG KASABACH; Phone: 609-292-1185
Keyword(s): Geology, Water Resources

Green Acres and Recreation Program
P.O. Box 412, Trenton, NJ 08625-0412
Phone: 609-984-0500
Contact(s):
Administrator: THOMAS WELLS
Chief of Compliance: JEANNE DONLON; Phone: 609-984-0631
Chief of Office of Natural Resource Damages: MARTIN J. McHUGH; Phone: 609-984-5475
Chief of Outdoor Recreation Planning: ROBERT STOKES; Phone: 609-984-0495
Deputy Administrator: DENNIS DAVIDSON; Phone: 609-984-0555

NEW JERSEY DEPARTMENT OF AGRICULTURE
CN 330, Trenton, NJ 08625
Contact(s):
Assistant Secretary: SAMUEL GARRISON; Phone: 609-292-5530
Chief of Staff: CAROL SHIPP; Phone: 609-633-7794
Coordinator of Soil and Water Conservation Services: SAMUEL R. RACE; Phone: 609-292-5540
Director of Division of Administration: JOHN J. GALLAGHER JR.; Phone: 609-292-6931
Director of Division of Animal Health: DR. ERNEST ZIRKLE; Phone: 609-292-3965
Director of Division of Dairy and Commodity Regulation: DHUN B. PATEL; Phone: 609-292-5575
Director of Division of Markets: DR. H. VANCE YOUNG; Phone: 609-292-5536
Director of Division of Plant Industry: ROBERT J. BALAAM; Phone: 609-292-5441
Director of Division of Rural Resources: GEORGE HORZEPA; Phone: 609-292-5532
Executive Director of State Agriculture Development Committee: GREGORY ROMANO; Phone: 609-984-2504
Keyword(s): Agriculture

State Soil and Conservation Committee
P.O. Box 330, Trenton, NJ 08625
Phone: 609-292-5540
Founded: 1937
Description: A unit of state government administered by the state Dept. of Agriculture. Responsible for conservation of soil resources and control and prevention of soil erosion and nonpoint source pollution, prevention of damage by floodwater or sediment, and conservation of water for agricultural purposes. Provides direction, leadership, standards, rules, funding, and administrative assistance; coordinates local district conservation programs; and is interagency with 12 members.
Contact(s):
Chairman: ARTHUR R. BROWN JR.; Phone: 609-292-3976; Fax: 609-292-3978
Executive Secretary: SAMUEL R. RACE; Phone: 609-292-5540; Fax: 609-633-7229; Email: agurace@ag.state.nj.us
Publication(s): *On Land and Water; Standards for Soil Erosion and Sediment Control in New Jersey*
Keyword(s): Agriculture, Renewable Resources, Soil Conservation, Urban Environment, Water Pollution, Water Quality, Water Resources, Watersheds

NEW JERSEY PINELANDS COMMISSION

P.O Box 7, New Lisbon, NJ 08064
Phone: 609-894-9342; Fax: 606-894-0026; Email: tmoore@njpines.state.nj.us; WWW: www.state.nj.us/pinelands/

Founded: 1979

Description: State planning and regulatory agency with jurisdiction over land use and development in the million-acre Pinelands national reserve; 53 municipalities in the state Pinelands area have and revise local master plans and zoning ordinances to incorporate standards of regional conservation plan.

Contact(s):
Chairman: DANIEL L. KELLEHER
Executive Director: TERRENCE D. MOORE
Assistant Director of Development Review and Enforcement: WILLIAM F. HARRISON
Assistant Director of Planning and Management: JOHN C. STOKES
Editor of Publications: NANCY SOPER; Email: info@njpines.state.nj.us
Educational Coordinator: BETSY CARPENTER

Publication(s): *Pinelander, The Newsletter; a list of reports and studies is available upon request.*

Keyword(s): Environmental Preservation, Land Use Planning, Planning Management, Sustainable Ecosystems, Water Resources

NEW JERSEY SEA GRANT PROGRAM

New Jersey Marine Sciences Consortium, Ft. Hancock, NJ 07732
Phone: 908-872-1300

Description: The New Jersey Marine Sciences Consortium is an alliance of 33 institutions from New Jersey, New York, and Pennsylvania formed for the purposes of Conducting large-scale projects in marine and coastal science on technology through group action; and assembling material resources which lie beyond the capabilities of the individual member institutions. The consortium manages the Sea Grant College Program and the Sea Grant Marine Advisory Service in New Jersey, New York, and Pennsylvania.

Contact(s):
Director: GEORGE D. KLEIN
Marine Advisory Service Director: ALEX WYPYSZINSKI, P.O. Box 231, Rutgers University, Cook College, NewBrunswick, NJ 08903; Phone: 908-932-9636

NEW JERSEY STATE EXTENSION SERVICES

Rutgers Cooperative Extension, Zane R. Helsel-Director, 88 Lipman Drive, New Brunswick, NJ 08901-8525
Phone: 732-932-9306

Contact(s):
Specialist in Forest Resources: DR. MARK C. VODAK, Rutgers, The State University, Cook College, P.O. Box 231, NewBrunswick, NJ 08903; Phone: 732-932-8993
Specialist in Natural Resources: DR. ROGER LOCANDRO, Rutgers, The State University, Cook College, P.O. Box 231, NewBrunswick, NJ 08903; Phone: 732-932-8242

Keyword(s): Agriculture, Gardening and Horticulture, Pesticides, Solid Waste Management, Youth Organizations

NEW MEXICO

GOVERNOR OF NEW MEXICO, GARY JOHNSON

State Capitol, Suite 400, SantaFe, NM 087503
Phone: 505-827-3000

ENERGY, MINERALS, AND NATURAL RESOURCES DEPARTMENT

2040 Pacheco St., Santa Fe, NM 87505
Phone: 505-827-5950

Description: As the steward for New Mexico's natural resources, the department seeks to preserve the unique natural beauty of New Mexico and to facilitate the beneficial development and use of its resources in an environmentally responsible manner.

Contact(s):
Cabinet Secretary: JENNIFER SALISBURY, 2040 S. Pacheco, SantaFe, NM 87505; Phone: 505-827-5950

Administrative Services Division

2040 Pacheco St., Santa Fe, NM 87505
Phone: 505-827-5925

Description: Provides clerical, recordkeeping, and administrative support to the department in the areas of personnel, budget, procurement and contracting, and administration of federal and state grants.

Contact(s):
Director: JIM FIRKINS

Keyword(s): Energy, Environmental and Conservation Education, Environmental Preservation, Outdoor Recreation, Renewable Resources

Energy Conservation and Management Division

Villagra Bldg., 408 Galisteo St., Santa Fe, NM 87505
Phone: 505-827-5900

Description: Administers state and federally funded energy conservation and alternative energy technology programs to state agencies, political subdivisions, regional organizations, nonprofit community service agencies, and New Mexico energy consumers, by providing engineering and technical assistance, and informational, financial, and programmatic support.

Contact(s):
Director: DIANE CARON

Forestry and Resources Conservation Division

Villagra Bldg., 408 Galisteo St., Santa Fe, NM 87501
Phone: 505-827-5830

Description: Provides management and protection of New Mexico's renewable forest, rangeland, soil, and water resources through professional forest, pest, fire, and land management; provides law enforcement and administration, public education in conservation; and supports to enhance the environment and quality of resources to protect jobs and maintain social and economic benefits.

Contact(s):
State Forester: TOBY MARTINEZ

Mining and Minerals Division

2040 Pacheco St., Santa Fe, NM 87505
Phone: 505-827-5970

Description: Provides for the study, development, and optimum production of the mineral and energy resources within the state; the reduction of hazards associated with these processes consistent with the conservation of these resources; the protection of public health, safety, and the environment, and the economic well-being of the citizens.

Contact(s):
Director: KATHLEEN GARLAND

Oil Conservation Division

2040 S. Pacheco St., Santa Fe, NM 87505
Phone: 505-827-7131

Description: Regulates and sets standards for operations related to the drilling and production of crude oil, natural gas, and geothermal resources and promotes the development and conservation of these resources while ensuring the prevention of waste and protection. Cares for the prevention of loss and contamination of freshwater supplies.

Contact(s):
Director: BILL LeMAY

State Parks and Recreation Division

2040 S. Pacheco St., Santa Fe, NM 87505
Phone: 505-827-7465

Description: Provides and cares for the recreational resources, facilities, and opportunities, and promotes user safety on recreational land and water to benefit and enrich the lives of New Mexico residents and visitors alike.

STATE AND PROVINCE GOVERNMENT AGENCIES - NEW MEXICO

Contact(s):
Director: TOM TRUJILLO

NEW MEXICO BUREAU OF MINES AND MINERAL RESOURCES
Campus Station, Socorro, NM 87801
Phone: 505-835-5420; Fax: 505-835-6333

Founded: 1927

Description: Charged with investigating and reporting on all types of mineral resources and the geology of the state, including environmental geology, water resources, and geological hazards; responsible for conducting applied research on all aspects of geology and mineral resources.

Contact(s):
Director and State Geologist: DR. CHARLES E. CHAPIN; Phone: 505-835-5302
Editor: DR. JIRI ZIDEK
Environmental Geologist: DR. MICHAEL WHITWORTH; Phone: 505-835-5921
Environmental Geologist: DR. WILLIAM C. HANEBERG; Phone: 505-835-5808
Environmental Geologist: DR. DAVID W. LOVE; Phone: 505-835-5146
Manager of Geological Extension Service: SUSAN WELCH; Phone: 505-835-5112

Publication(s): *Bulletins; Circulars; Memoirs; Ground Water Reports; Geologic Maps; New Mexico Geology; Lite Geology; Scenic Trips to the Geologic Past; Databases on CD-ROM and home page*

Keyword(s): Chemistry, Energy, Geology, Natural History, Water Resources

Geological Information Center Library
Campus Station, Socorro, NM 87801
Phone: 505-835-5145; Fax: 505-835-6333; WWW: www.geoinfo.nmt.edu/

NEW MEXICO COOPERATIVE FISH AND WILDLIFE RESEARCH UNIT
P.O. Box 30003, MSC 4901, New Mexico State University, Las Cruces, NM 88003-0003
Phone: 505-646-6053

Founded: 1988

Description: Supported cooperatively by the U.S.G.S. Biological Resources Division, New Mexico State University, New Mexico Department of Game and Fish, and the Wildlife Management Institute, the New Mexico Fish and Wildlife Research Unit's primary purpose is research on management and conservation of fish and wildlife species and graduate research training in fisheries and wildlife resources.

Contact(s):
Assistant Leader for Fisheries: COLLEEN A. CALDWELL
Leader: BRUCE C. THOMPSON

Keyword(s): Aquatic Habitats, Arid Lands, Conservation Plannning, Endangered and Threatened Species, Toxic Substances, Wildlife and Wildlife Habitat

NEW MEXICO DEPARTMENT OF AGRICULTURE
P.O. Box 30005, Dept. 3189, Las Cruces, NM 88003-8005

Founded: 1955

Description: Organized to protect state agriculture from importation of plant diseases and insects and help control those that gain entrance; to ensure products offered for sale meet quality standards as advertised and labeled; maintain inspection of agricultural products for interstate shipping; laboratory analyses of animal diseases and deaths on fee basis; promote state agricultural commodities; provide market news; and conduct consumer and producer service activities designated by law.

Contact(s):
Assistant Director: JEFF M. WITTE; Phone: 505-646-3007
Director of Agricultural and Environmental Services Division: LARRY DOMINQUEZ; Phone: 505-646-3208
Director of Agricultural Programs and Resources Division: RONALD J. WHITE; Phone: 505-646-2642
Director of Marketing and Development Division: EDWARD AVALOS; Phone: 505-646-4929
Director of Standards and Consumer Services Division: GARY WEST; Phone: 505-646-1616
Director of Veterinary Diagnostic Services: DR. JOHN THILSTED; Phone: 505-841-2576
Directoy/Secretary: FRANK A. DUBOIS, P.O. Box 30005, Dept. 3189, LasCruces, NM 88003-8005; Phone: 505-646-3007
Head of Public Relations: LANA DICKSON; Phone: 505-646-3008
State Chemist of Laboratory: RICK JANECKA; Phone: 505-646-3318
State Seed Analyst of Laboratory: RICHARD KOCHEVAR; Phone: 505-646-3407

Publication(s): *Biennial Report; New Mexico Agricultural Statistics; New Mexico Agricultural Export Directory; Growing Season Data, Degree Day Data, and Design Temperatures*

NEW MEXICO DEPARTMENT OF GAME AND FISH
P.O. Box 25112, Santa Fe, NM 87504
Phone: 505-827-7911

Description: The State Game Commission and the Game and Fish Department are administratively attached to the Energy, Minerals, and Natural Resources Department. The responsibility of the State Game Commission is to develop policy for the Game and Fish Department.

Contact(s):
Director: JERRY MARACCHINI, P.O. Box 25112, SantaFe, NM 87504; Phone: 505-827-7899
Assistant Director of Field Operations: LARRY BELL; Phone: 505-827-7899
Assistant Director of Resourc Divisions: SCOTT BROWN; Phone: 505-827-7899
Cabinet Secretary of Energy, Minerals, and Natural Resources: JENNIFER SALISBURY
Chairman of State Game Commission: BILL BRININSTOOL
Chief of Administrative Services: JUDE GONZALES; Phone: 505-827-7920
Chief of Conservation Services: ANDREW SANDOVAL; Phone: 505-827-7882
Chief of Public Affairs: LUKE SHELBY; Phone: 505-827-7911
Chief of Fish Management: JACK KELLY; Phone: 505-827-7905
Chief of Law Enforcement: JOHN MILES; Phone: 505-827-7934
Chief of Wildlife Division: SANTIAGO GONZALES; Phone: 505-827-7893

Albuquerque NM Office
3481 Midway Pl. NE, Albuquerque, NM 87109
Phone: 505-841-8881

Contact(s):
Chief: TOD STEVENSON

Las Cruces NM Office
566 N. Telshor Blvd., Las Cruces, NM 88011
Phone: 505-522-9796

Contact(s):
Chief: STEVE HENRY

Raton NM Office
P.O. Box 1145, 215 York Canyon Rd., Raton, NM 87740
Phone: 505-445-2311

Contact(s):
Chief: JOANNA LACKEY

Roswell NM Office
1912 West 2nd St., Roswell, NM 88201
Phone: 505-624-6135

Contact(s):
Chief: MIKE BELL

NEW MEXICO ENVIRONMENT DEPARTMENT
1190 Saint Francis Dr., P.O. Box 26110, Santa Fe, NM 87502

Description: To preserve, protect, and perpetuate New Mexico's environment for present and future generations.

Contact(s):
Secretary: MARK E. WEIDLER; Phone: 505-827-2855
Chief of Department of Energy Oversight Bureau: JOHN PARKER; Phone: 505-827-4252
Chief of Solid Waste Bureau: ERALD SILVA; Phone: 505-827-0197
Chief of Air Quality Bureau: CECILIA WILLIAMS; Phone: 505-827-0042
Chief of Ground Water Protection and Remediation Bureau: MARCY LEAVITT; Phone: 505-827-2919
Chief of Hazardous & Radioactive Materials Bureau: BENITO GARCIA; Phone: 505-827-4358
Chief of Occupational Health and Safety Bureau: SAM ROGERS; Phone: 505-827-2877
Chief of Program Support Bureau: CLIFF HAWLEY; Phone: 505-827-2844
Chief of Underground Storage Tank Bureau: DAVID DURAN; Phone: 505-827-2932
Director of Administrative Services Division: ROBERT MENKE; Phone: 505-827-2774
Director of Environmental Protection Division: PETER MAGGIORE; Phone: 505-827-2855
Director of Field Operations Division: TITO MADRID; Phone: 505-827-2855
Director of Water and Waste Management Division: NATHAN ("ED") KELLY; Phone: 505-827-2855
Manager of District II: JAMES BEARZI; Phone: 505-474-4405
Manager of District III: KEN SMITH; Phone: 505-524-6300
Manager of District IV: GARY McCASLIN; Phone: 505-624-6046

NEW MEXICO SOIL AND WATER CONSERVATION COMMISSION
Chair, 11 McMillen Rd., Silver City, NM 88061
Contact(s):
Chair: DUTSON HUNT, 11 McMillen Rd, Silver City, NM 88061; Phone: 505-535-2420; Fax: 505-388-0376
Acting Bureau Chief: JEFF LEWIS, 530 S. Melendres, Las Cruces, NM 88005; Phone: 505-524-6210; Fax: 505-524-6211

NEW MEXICO STATE EXTENSION SERVICES
Box 30003, Campus Box 3AG, NM State University, Las Cruces, NM 88003
Phone: 505-646-3748
Contact(s):
Dean and Chief Administrative Officer: JERRY G. SCHECKEDANZ, Box 30003, Campus Box, NM State University, Las Cruces, NM 88003; Phone: 505-646-3748
Dean and Chief Administrative Officer: JERRY G. SCHICKEDANZ, NM State University, Box 3AE, LasCruces, NM 88003; Phone: 505-646-3015
Extension Department Head of Animal Resources: RON PARKER, Box 3AE, NM State University, LasCruces, NM 88003; Phone: 505-646-1709
Extension Department Head of Plant Sciences: RON BYFORD, Box 3AE, NM State University, LasCruces, NM 88003; Phone: 505-646-2458
Extension Range Management Specialist: CHRIS ALLISON, Box 3AE,NM State University, LasCruces, NM 88003; Phone: 505-646-1944
Extension Wildlife Specialist: JON BOREN, Box 3AE, NM State University, LasCruces, NM 88003; Phone: 505-646-1164

STATE ENGINEER OFFICE/INTERSTATE STREAM COMMISSION
Bataan Memorial Bldg., P.O. Box 25102, Santa Fe, NM 87504
Phone: 505-827-6175; Fax: 505-827-6188
Description: Administration, development, protection, and conservation of the water resources of the state of New Mexico.
Contact(s):
Chairman: J. PHELPS WHITE III, P.O. Box 874, Roswell, NM 88202-0874; Phone: 505-662-5701; Fax: 505-625-0227
Chief of Technical Division: DONALD T. LOPEZ
Chief of Water Rights Division: PAUL SAAVEDRA
General Counsel of Legal Services Division: TED APODACA
Interstate Stream Engineer: NORMAN GAUME; Phone: 505-827-6160; Fax: 505-827-6188
Librarian: BARBARA AUSTIN, State Engineer Office Library, P.O. Box 25102, Bataan Memorial Bldg., SantaFe, NM 87504; Phone: 505-827-6187; Fax: 505-827-6188
State Engineer and Secretary: THOMAS C. TURNEY; Phone: 505-827-6160
Vice Chairman: TRACY SEIDMAN HEPHNER, P.O. Box 277, Wagon Mound, NM 87752; Phone: 505-666-2497
Publication(s): *Water Line*
Keyword(s): Water Resources

NEW YORK

GOVERNOR OF NEW YORK, GEORGE E. PATAKI
State Capitol, 138 Eagle St., Albany, NY 12224
Phone: 518-474-7516

ADIRONDACK PARK AGENCY
P.O. Box 99, Ray Brook, NY 12977
Phone: 518-891-4050
Founded: 1971
Description: Created by state law and charged with developing a state Land Master Plan for the 40% of the park that is public land and a Private Land Use and Development Plan for the private lands within the six-million-acre Adirondack Park. The agency also administers the state's Wild, Scenic, and Recreational Rivers System Act for private lands within the park and the state's Freshwater Wetlands Act for both state and private lands within the park. The agency also operates two Adirondack Park Visitor Interpretive centers (nature education and tourism information centers) at Paul Smiths and Newcomb which are open year-round.
Contact(s):
Chairman: RICHARD LEFEBVRE
Deputy Director: KARYN B. RICHARDS
Executive Director: DANIEL T. FITTS
Director of Interpretive Programs: SANDRA BUREAU
Director of Planning: JOHN BANTA
Director of Regulatory Programs: WILLIAM J. CURRAN
Publication(s): *Adirondack Park, Land Use Planning for the Adirondack Park, Annual Report, The*; publications list available upon request.
Keyword(s): Environmental and Conservation Education, Lakes, Land Use Planning, Rivers, Wetlands

DEPARTMENT OF ENVIRONMENTAL CONSERVATION (NEW YORK)
50 Wolf Rd., Albany, NY 12233
Contact(s):
Director: JOHN IANNOTTI; Phone: 518-457-7267
50 Wolf Rd., Albany, NY 12233
Founded: 1970
Description: The mission of the New York State Department of Environmental Conservation is to conserve, improve, and protect its natural resources and environment, and control water, land and air pollution, in order to enhance the health, safety and welfare of the people of the state and their overall economic and social well-being.
Contact(s):
Acting General Counsel: FRANK BIFERA; Phone: 518-457-4415
Adirondacks: SANDY LeBARRON; Phone: 518-623-3671
Assistant Commissioner for Administrative Services: SUSAN TALUTO; Phone: 518-457-6533
Assistant Commissioner for External Affairs: GARY SHEFFER; Phone: 518-457-5400
Assistant Commissioner for Office of Bond Act: GLEN BRUENING; Phone: 518-457-6558
Assistant Commissioner for the Office of Public Protection: ANDY LIDDLE; Phone: 518-457-0331
Assistant Commissioner of Office of Hearings and Mediation Services: PETER BERGEN; Phone: 518-457-3468

STATE AND PROVINCE GOVERNMENT AGENCIES - NEW YORK

Assistant Commissioner of Office of Science and Technology: S. T. RAO; Phone: 518-457-3200
Commissioner: JOHN P. CAHILL; Phone: 518-457-1162
Deputy Commissioner for Environmental Quality and Pollution Prevention: DAVID STERMAN; Phone: 518-457-1415
Deputy Commissioner for Natural Resources: PETER DUNCAN; Phone: 518-457-0975
Director of Office of Internal Audit and Investigation: RANDY HINTON; Phone: 518-457-9160
Environmental Facilities Corporation: TERRY AGRISS; Phone: 518-457-4222
Fresh Kills: PAUL GALLAY; Phone: 718-482-4949
Hudson River: FRAN DUNWELL; Phone: 914-256-3017
Legislative Counsel: STEPHEN BOBARAKIS; Phone: 518-457-2239
Marine Resources: GORDON COLVIN; Phone: 516-444-0430
Natural Resources Planning: FRANCIS SHEEHAN; Phone: 518-457-4208
Salmon River: FRAN VERDOLIVA; Phone: 315-298-7605
Senior Deputy Commissioner: GAVIN DONOHUE; Phone: 518-457-2390
Special Assistant to the Commissioner: LINDA FRICK; Phone: 518-457-0904
Special Projects: JIM AUSTIN; Phone: 518-457-6610
Special Projects: TOM KUNKEL; Phone: 518-457-6610
Publication(s): *Environmental Notice Bulletin*

Divisin of Environmental Permits
50 Wolf Rd., Albany, NY 12233
Contact(s):
Director: JEFFREY SAMA; Phone: 518-457-7424

Division of Air Resources
50 Wolf Rd., Albany, NY 12233
Contact(s):
Acting Director: ROBERT WARLAND; Phone: 518-457-7230

Division of Environmental Enforcement
50 Wolf Rd., Albany, NY 12233
Contact(s):
Acting Director: CHARLES SULLIVAN; Phone: 518-457-4348

Division of Environmental Remediation
50 Wolf Rd., Albany, NY 12233
Contact(s):
Director: MICHAEL O'TOOLE; Phone: 518-457-5861

Division of Fish, Wildlife and Marine Resources
50 Wolf Rd., Albany, NY 12233
Contact(s):
Director: GERRY BARNHART; Phone: 518-457-5690

Division of Forest Protection & Fire Management
50 Wolf Rd., Albany, NY 12233
Contact(s):
Director: DAVE AMES; Phone: 518-457-5740

Division of in Mineral Resources
50 Wolf Rd., Albany, NY 12233
Contact(s):
Director: GREGORY SOVAS; Phone: 518-457-9337

Division of Information Services
50 Wolf Rd., Albany, NY 12233
Contact(s):
Director: HENRY S. VACEK; Phone: 518-457-6367

Division of Lands and Forests
50 Wofl Rd., Albany, NY 12233
Contact(s):
Director: FRANK DUNSTAN; Phone: 518-457-2475

Division of Law Enforcement
50 Wolf Rd., Albany, NY 12233
Contact(s):
Director: WAYNE BREWER; Phone: 518-457-5681

Division of Legal Affairs
50 Wolf Rd., Albany, NY 12233
Contact(s):
Acting Director: ALISON SMITH; Phone: 518-457-3551

Division of Management and Budget
50 Wolf Rd., Albany, NY 12233
Contact(s):
Director: RICHARD K. RANDLES; Phone: 518-457-1141

Division of Operations
50 Wolf Rd., Albany, NY 12233
Contact(s):
Director: ROBERT BARSHIELD; Phone: 518-457-6310

Division of Public Affairs and Education
50 Wolf Rd., Albany, NY 12233
Contact(s):
Director: LAUREL REMUS; Phone: 518-457-0840

Division of Solid & Hazardous Materials
50 Wolf Rd., Albany, NY 12233
Contact(s):
Director: STEPHEN HAMMOND; Phone: 518-457-6934

Division of Transportation Services
50 Wolf Rd., Albany, NY 12233
Contact(s):
Director: KARL RODENHAUSER; Phone: 518-457-7888

Division of Water
50 Wolf Rd., Albany, NY 12233
Contact(s):
Director: N. G. KAUL; Phone: 518-457-6674

Press Office
50 Wofl Rd., Albany, NY 12233
Contact(s):
Press Officer: GARY SHEFFER; Phone: 518-457-5400

Regional Directors
50 Wolf Rd., Albany, NY 12233
Contact(s):
Region 1: RAYMOND COWEN III, Bldg. 40, State University of New York, Stony Brook, NY 11794; Phone: 516-444-0345
Region 2: MARY ELLEN KRIS, Hunters Point Plaza, Long Island City, NY 11101; Phone: 718-482-4900
Region 3: MARC MORAN, 21 S. Putt Corners Rd., New Paltz, NY 12561; Phone: 914-256-3005
Region 4: STEVE SCHASSLER, 11 North Westcott Road, Schenectady, NY 12306; Phone: 518-357-2068
Region 5: STUART BUCHANAN, Route 86, P.O. Box 296, Ray Brook, NY 12977; Phone: 518-897-1211
Region 6: THOMAS BROWN, 317 Washington Street, Watertown, NY 13204; Phone: 315-785-2239
Region 7: KENNETH LYNCH, 615 Erie Blvd., W, Syracuse, NY 13204; Phone: 315-426-7400
Region 8: JOHN HICKS, 6274 E. Avon-Lima Road, Avon, NY 14414; Phone: 716-226-2466
Region 9: GERALD MIKOL, 270 Michigan Avenue, Buffalo, NY 14203; Phone: 716-851-7200

ENVIRONMENTAL PROTECTION BUREAU
Department of Law, State of New York, 120 Broadway, New York City, NY 10271
Description: Institutes legal actions on behalf of the people of the state in cases involving air and water pollution, protection of wildlife, waste site remediation, and protection of scenic and natural

resources. Has responsibility for enforcement of laws protecting endangered species of wildlife, as well as public nuisance actions to restrain pollution and other environmental damage.
Contact(s):
Assistant Attorney General in Charge: WILLIAM HELMER; Phone: 518-474-8096
Environmental Engineer: PETER SKINNER; Phone: 518-474-2432

MARINE SCIENCES RESEARCH CENTER (NEW YORK)
State University of New York, Stony Brook, NY 11794
Phone: 516-632-8700; Fax: 516-632-8915
Description: University-wide center to develop marine and atmospheric research, instructional programs, and facilities for the State University of New York. Ongoing research projects are directed toward coastal oceanographic processes, marine environmental problems and management, atmospheric sciences, and resources management. Among the Center's organized units are the Living Marine Resources Institute, the Waste Management Institute, the Coastal Ocean Action Strategies Institute, the Institute for Urban Ports and Harbors, the Institute for Planetary and Terrestrial Atmospheres, and the Flax Pond Laboratory.
Contact(s):
Associate Dean for Education: H. J. BOKUNIEWICZ; Phone: 516-632-8674
Associate Director: W. M. WISE; Phone: 516-632-8656
Dean and Director: J. KIRK COCHRAN; Phone: 516-632-8701
Graduate Programs: LAURA RICHARDSON; Phone: 516-632-8681
Publication(s): *Technical Report Series; Working Report Series; Special Report Series; Newsletter*
Keyword(s): Coasts, Greenhouse Effect/Global Warming, Oceanography, Solid Waste Management, Water Pollution Management

NEW YORK COOPERATIVE FISH AND WILDLIFE RESEARCH UNIT
Department of Natural Resources, Fernow Hall, Cornell University, Ithaca, NY 14853
Phone: 607-255-2839
Founded: *1961 (Wildlife Unit), 1963 (Fisheries Unit), 1984 Combined.*
Description: Primary purpose is field and laboratory research on management and conservation of a variety of fish and wildlife species, and graduate research training in fisheries and wildlife resources. Supported cooperatively by U.S. Geological Survey, Cornell University, New York State Department of Environmental Conservation, and the Wildlife Management Institute.
Contact(s):
Assistant Leader of Fisheries: DR. MARK B. BAIN; Phone: 607-255-2840
Assistant Leader of Wildlife: DR. RICHARD A. MALECKI; Phone: 607-255-2836
Leader: DR. MILO E. RICHMOND; Phone: 607-255-2151; Email: MER6@cornell.edu

NEW YORK DEPARTMENT OF AGRICULTURE AND MARKETS
1 Winners Cir., Albany, NY 12235
Phone: 518-457-3880
Founded: *1884*
Description: Promotes and regulates production, manufacturing, marketing, storing, and distribution of food. Supervises quality of plant materials, health of animals, and regulates dogs. Also, represents agricultural interests before NY Public Service Commission on siting of transmission lines and power plants.
Contact(s):
Commissioner: DONALD R. DAVIDSEN
Director of Division of Agricultural Protection and Support Services: KIM T. BLOT
Director of Division of Plant Industry: ROBERT MUNGARI
Public Information Officer: PETE GREGG
Keyword(s): Agriculture, Biotechnology, Flowers, Plants, and Trees, Pesticides, Soil Conservation

State Soil and Water Conservation Committee
Contact(s):
Chair: PHILIP GRIFFEN, 28 Spook Hollow Rd., Stillwater, NY 12170; Phone: 518-664-5038
Director: JOHN WILDEMAN; Phone: 518-457-3738; Fax: 518-457-1204

NEW YORK DEPARTMENT OF HEALTH
Tower Bldg., Empire State Plaza, Albany, NY 12237
Contact(s):
Director of Center for Environmental Health (P.E.): RONALD TRAMMONTANO; Phone: 518-458-6400

NEW YORK GEOLOGICAL SURVEY AND STATE MUSEUM
Cultural Education Center, Albany, NY 12230
Phone: 518-474-5816; Fax: 518-473-8497; Email: rfakundi@museum.nysed.gov
Founded: *1836*
Description: The Geological Survey and State Museum serves as a clearinghouse for information concerning bedrock and surficial geology within the state. The survey conducts regular mapping projects and investigations in basic, environmental, and applied geology and publishes maps and reports of investigations.
Contact(s):
Engineering and Environmental Geology: ROBERT H. FICKIES; Phone: 518-474-5810
Oil and Gas Office Director: RICHARD NYAHAY; Phone: 518-486-2161
State Geologist and Chief Scientist: ROBERT H. FAKUNDINY
State Seismologist: WALTER MITRONOVAS; Phone: 518-486-2014
Publication(s): *New York State Geogram; publications list of the New York State Geological Survey*
Keyword(s): Coasts, Energy, Geology, Land Use Planning, Water Resources

NEW YORK SEA GRANT
121 Discovery Hall, State University of New York at Stony Brook, Stony Brook, NY 11794-5001
Phone: 516-632-6905
Founded: *1971*
Description: A cooperative program of the State University of New York and Cornell University fostering the wise use and development of coastal resources through research grants, extension advisory services, education, training, and informational materials.
Contact(s):
Assistant Director of New York Sea Grant: CORNELIA G. SCHLENK, 121 Discovery Hall, SUNY at Stony Brook, Stony Brook, NY 11794-5001; Phone: 516-632-6905
Associate Director and Program Leader: DALE BAKER, New York Sea Grant, 348 Roberts Hall, Cornell University, Ithaca, NY 14853-4203; Phone: 607-255-2832
Director of New York Sea Grant Institute: DR. JACK S. MATTICE, New York Sea Grant, 121 Discovery Hall, SUNY at Stonybrook, Stony Brook, NY 11794-5001; Phone: 516-632-6905
Fiscal Officer of New York Sea Grant: STEPHANIE MASSUCCI, 121 Discovery Hall, SUNY at Stony Brook, Stony Brook, NY 11794-5001; Phone: 516-632-6905
Great Lakes Program Coordinator: DAVID WHITE, New York Sea Grant, 101 Rich Hall, SUNY College at Oswego, Oswego, NY 13126-3599; Phone: 315-341-3042
Marine Program Coordinator: ROBERT KENT, New York Sea Grant, Cornell University Lab, 3059 Sound Ave., Riverhead, NY 11901-1098; Phone: 516-727-3910
Keyword(s): Coasts, Environmental and Conservation Education, Research, Scholarships and Grants, Water Resources

STATE AND PROVINCE GOVERNMENT AGENCIES - NEW YORK

NEW YORK STATE COOPERATIVE EXTENSION
New York State College of Agriculture and Life Sciences, and Human Ecology, 365 Roberts Hall, Cornell University, Ithaca, NY 14853-4203
Phone: 607-255-2237
Contact(s):
Agriculture: R. DAVID SMITH
Chairman/Department Extension Leader: DR. JAMES P. LASSOIE, Department of Natural Resources, 118 Fernow Hall, Cornell University, Ithaca, NY 14853-3001; Phone: 607-255-2810
Director of Cooperative Extension: DR. D. MERRILL EWERT
Environmental/Conservation Youth Education: DR. MARIANNE E. KRASNY, Associate Professor, Dept. of Natural Resources, 16 Fernow Hall, Cornell University, Ithaca, NY 14853-3001; Phone: 607-255-2827
Forestry Resource Management: DR. PETER J. SMALLIDGE, Sr. Extension Associate, Dept. of Natural Resources, 116 Fernow Hall, Cornell University, Ithaca, NY 14853-3001; Phone: 607-255-4696
Forestry/Wildlife: GARY R. GOFF, Extension Associate/Director Master Forest Owners/COVERTS Volunteer Program, Dept. of Natural Resources, 104 Fernow Hall, Cornell University, Ithaca, NY 14853-3001; Phone: 607-255-2824
Human Dimensions Research Unit: TOMMY L. BROWN, Sr. Res. Assoc., Dept. of Natural Resources, 122B Fernow Hall, Cornell University, Ithaca, NY 14853-3001; Phone: 607-255-7695
Protected Area Planning and Management: DR. DAVID W. GROSS, Sr. Extension Associate & Environmental Program Leader, Department of Natural Resources, 112 Fernow Hall, Cornell University, Ithaca, NY 14853-3001; Phone: 607-255-2825
Sportfishing and Aquatic Resources Education (SAREP): STEVE BROWN, Director, Extension Associate, Dept. of Natural Resources, 120 Fernow Hall, Cornell University, Ithaca, NY 14853-3001; Phone: 607-255-9370
Wetlands: DR. REBECCA L. SCHNEIDER, Assistant Professor, Dept. of Natural Resources, 122C Fernow Hall, Cornell University, Ithaca, NY 14853-3001; Phone: 607-255-2110
Wildlife Management: DR. PAUL CURTIS, Sr. Extension Associate, Dept. of Natural Resources, 114 Fernow Hall, Cornell University, Ithaca, NY 14853-3001; Phone: 607-255-2835
Keyword(s): Agriculture, Environmental and Conservation Education, Fisheries, Forest Management, Planning Management, Renewable Resources, Solid Waste Management, Sustainable Ecosystems, Water Resources, Wetlands, Wildlife Management

NEW YORK STATE OFFICE OF PARKS, RECREATION AND HISTORIC PRESERVATION
The Governor Nelson A. Rockefeller Empire State Plaza, Agency Bldg. 1, Albany, NY 12238
Phone: 518-474-0456, TDD 518-486-1899; Fax: 518-474-4492
Description: Administers and operates 151 parks, park preserves, and recreational facilities, three arboretums, and 35 historic sites throughout the state; administers 15 heritage areas in partnership with local communities. Acquires and protects public lands and open space; coordinates athletic programs; develops environmental interpretive programs; maintains a field services bureau which oversees historic resources and National Historic Register entries; administers boating and snowmobiling laws.
Contact(s):
Chief Counsel: MEGAN LESSER LEVINE; Phone: 518-474-0447
Commissioner: BERNADETTE CASTRO; Phone: 518-474-0443
Deputy Commissioner for Administration: NANCY PALUMBO; Phone: 518-474-0430
Deputy Commissioner for Historic Preservation: WINTHROP J. ALDRICH; Phone: 518-473-5385
Deputy Commissioner for Land Management: ALBERT E. CACCESE; Phone: 518-474-0402
Deputy Commissioner for Operations, New York City/Long Island: EDWARD F. WANKEL; Phone: 516-669-1000
Deputy Commissioner for Operations, Saratoga/Taconic/Palisades: JULIA S. STOKES; Phone: 518-584-2000
Director of Communications: BRIAN R. VATTIMO; Phone: 518-486-1868
Director of Law Enforcemetn: TIMOTHY H. COWIN; Phone: 518-474-0402
Director of Marine, Coastal, and Legislative Program Development: DOMINIC JACANGELO; Phone: 518-474-7336
Publication(s): *New York State Operated Parks; Historic Sites and Their Programs; Exploring New York's Past; New York State Boater's Guide; New York State Boat Launching Sites*
Keyword(s): Cultural Preservation, Environmental and Conservation Education, Environmental Preservation, Historic Preservation, Outdoor Recreation

OFFICE OF ENERGY EFFICIENCY AND ENVIRONMENT
New York State Dept. of Public Service, 3 Empire State Plaza, Albany, NY 12223
Phone: 518-474-1677; Fax: 518-474-5026
Founded: 1970
Description: The Office of Energy Efficiency and Environment provides staff support in developing and administering policies that assure appropriate consideration of energy efficiency and environmental protection in utility regulation, management, and restructuring. The office also plays a major role in the development of systems and procedures necessary to introduce retail competition in the state.
Contact(s):
Director: DR. LAURENCE B. DEWITT; Phone: 518-474-1677
Keyword(s): Acid Rain, Energy, Environmental Planning, Land Use Planning, Renewable Resources

STATE FISH AND WILDLIFE MANAGEMENT BOARD (NEW YORK)
50 Wolf Rd, Albany, NY 12233
Founded: 1957
Description: Membership composed of sportsmen, landowners, and local government representatives. State and regional boards advise the Department of Environmental Conservation in programs designed to improve resource management by landowners and increase public access to private lands.
Contact(s):
Chairman: EMORY GREEN, 519 Rte 247, Rushville, NY 14544; Phone: 716-554-3362
Secretary: RANDALL STUMVOLL, 50 Wolf Rd., Albany, NY 2233-4750; Phone: 518-457-4480
Vice Chairman: LEWIS NAGY JR., RTE 1, Box 271-A1, Glenfield, NY 13343; Phone: 315-376-3389
Keyword(s): Hunting, Outdoor Recreation, Public Lands, Water Resources, Wildlife and Wildlife Habitat

Region 3
36 Cooper St, Accord, NY 12404
Phone: 914-626-0066
Contact(s):
Board Chairman: BOB KEAGLE

Region 4
Milford, NY 13807
Phone: 607-286-7601
Contact(s):
Board Chaiman: DEANE WINSOR

Region 5
149 White Head Rd., Crown Point, NY 12928
Phone: 518-962-8225
Contact(s):
Board Chairman: ED TUTHILL

Region 6
81 Miner St., Canton, NY 13617
Phone: 315-386-8345
Contact(s):
Board Chairman: EVERETT QUACKENBUSH

STATE AND PROVINCE GOVERNMENT AGENCIES - NORTH CAROLINA

Region 7
2365 Olanco Rd., Marietta, NY 13110
Phone: 315-636-8891
Contact(s):
Board Chairman: CRAIG TRYON

Region 8
947 NYS Rt. 96, Waterloo, NY 13165
Phone: 315-539-2820
Contact(s):
Board Chairman: JOHN ANDREWS

Region 9
7915 State Rd., Eden, NY 14057
Phone: 716-992-9668
Contact(s):
Board Chairman: JIM AGLE

TUG HILL COMMISSION
317 Washington St., Watertown, NY 13601
Phone: 315-785-2380; Fax: 315-785-2574; Email: tughill@tughill.org
Founded: 1972
Description: The Tug Hill Commission is a nonregulatory state agency charged with helping local governments, organizations, and citizens shape the future of this rural, 2,100 square mile region, especially its environment and economy.
Contact(s):
Executive Director: ROBERT QUINN
Publication(s): *Headwaters; Tug Hill Program, The; Cooperative Rural Planning; Issue Paper series*
Keyword(s): Environmental Planning, Historic Preservation, Outdoor Recreation, Planning Management, Rural Development

NORTH CAROLINA

GOVERNOR OF NORTH CAROLINA, JAMES B. HUNT, JR.
State Capitol, 116 W. Jones St., Raleigh, NC 27603-8001
Phone: 919-733-4240

COOPERATIVE EXTENSION SERVICE (NORTH CAROLINA)
North Carolina State University, Box 7602, Raleigh, NC 27695
Phone: 919-515-2811; Fax: 919-515-3135
Contact(s):
Aquaculture Specialist: HARRY V. DANIELS, Vernon James Research and Extension Center, 207 Research Station Rd., Plymouth, NC 27962; Phone: 919-793-4428
Aquaculture Specialist: THOMAS M. LOSORDO, Box 7646, North Carolina State University, Raleigh, NC 29695; Phone: 919-515-7587
Assistant Director and State Program Leader: DR. ROGER CRICKENBERGER, NCSU, Box 7602, Raleigh, NC 27695-7602; Phone: 919-515-3252; Fax: 919-515-5950
Director of Extension Service: DR. JON F. ORT
Extension Aquaculture Specialist: RONALD G. HODSON, Sea Grant, Box 8605, North Carolina State University, Raleigh, NC 27695; Phone: 919-515-2454
Extension Fisheries Specialist: JAMES A. RICE, Box 7617, North Carolina State University, Raleigh, NC 27695; Phone: 919-515-4592
Extension Trout Specialist: JEFFREY M. HINSHAW, Research and Extension Center, Box 9628, 2016 Fanning Bridge Rd., Fletcher, NC 28732-9216; Phone: 704-684-3562
Wildlife Specialist and Extension Leader: PETER T. BROMLEY, Zoology Dept., Box 7646, North Carolina State University, Raleigh, NC 27695; Phone: 919-515-7587; Fax: 919-515-4592
Wildlife Specialist and Extension Leader: CRAIG R. McKINLEY, North Carolina State University, Box 8003, Raleigh, NC 27695; Phone: 919-515-5576; Fax: 919-515-6883
Keyword(s): Agriculture, Environmental and Conservation Education, Fisheries, Wildlife Management, Youth Organizations

NORTH CAROLINA DEPARTMENT OF ENVIRONMENT AND NATURAL RESOURCES
P.O. Box 27687, Raleigh, NC 27611
Phone: 919-733-4984
Contact(s):
Secretary: WAYNE McDEVITT; Phone: 919-715-4101
Assistant Secretary for Environment: BILL HOLMAN; Phone: 919-715-4141
Dirctor of Division of Water Resources: JOHN MORRIS; Phone: 919-733-4064
Director of Coastal Management: DONNA MOFFITT; Phone: 919-733-2293
Director of Division of Marine Fisheries: PRESTON PATE; Phone: 919-726-7021
Director of Division of Radiation Protection: MEL FRYE; Phone: 919-571-4141
Director of Division of Solid Waste Management: BILL MEYER; Phone: 919-733-4996
Director of Environmental Water Quality: PRESTON HOWARD; Phone: 919-733-7015
Director of Forest Resources: STANFORD M. ADAMS; Phone: 919-733-2162
Director of Museum of Natural Sciences: DR. BETSY BENNETT; Phone: 919-733-7450
Director of North Carolina Aquariums: RHETT WHITE; Phone: 919-733-2290
Director of Office of Environmental Education: ANNE TAYLOR; Phone: 919-733-0711
Director of Office of Pollution Prevention and Environmental Assistance: GARY HUNT; Phone: 919-715-4100
Director of Public Affairs: DON REUTER; Phone: 919-715-4112
Director of Soil and Water Conservation: DEWEY BOTTS; Phone: 919-733-2302
Director of State Parks and Recreation: DR. PHIL McKNELLY; Phone: 919-733-4181
Director of Zoological Park: DR. DAVID JONES; Phone: 910-879-7102
Executive Director of Wildlife Resources Commission: CHARLES R. FULLWOOD, JR.; Phone: 919-733-3391
Land Resources Staff: CHARLES GARDNER; Phone: 919-733-3833
Librarian: FIONA CLEM

NORTH CAROLINA COOPERATIVE FISH AND WILDLIFE RESEARCH UNIT (USDI)
Box 7617, 4105 Gardner Hall, North Carolina State University, Raleigh, NC 27695
Phone: 919-515-2631
Contact(s):
Leader:

NORTH CAROLINA DEPARTMENT OF AGRICULTURE
P.O. Box 27647, Raleigh, NC 27611
Contact(s):
Commissioner: JAMES A. GRAHAM; Phone: 919-733-7125
Agronomic Services Staff: DR. DONALD EADDY; Phone: 919-733-2556
Aquaculture & Natural Resources Staff: TOM ELLIS; Phone: 919-733-7125
Food and Drug Protection Staff: ROBERT GORDON; Phone: 919-733-7366
Legal Staff: DAVID McLEOD; Phone: 919-733-7125
Pesticide Disposal Staff: WILLIAM McCLELLAND; Phone: 919-733-7366
Pesticide Section Staff: JOHN SMITH; Phone: 919-733-3556
Plant Conservation Program Staff: CECIL FROST; Phone: 919-733-3610
Plant Industry Division Staff: BILL DICKERSON; Phone: 919-733-3930
Public Affairs Staff: JIM KNIGHT; Phone: 919-733-4216
Research Stations Staff: PAT KELLEY; Phone: 919-733-3236

STATE AND PROVINCE GOVERNMENT AGENCIES - NORTH DAKOTA

Staff: RODNEY BARFIELD, 315 Front St., Beaufort, NC 28516; Phone: 919-728-7317
Structural Pest Staff: CARL FALCO; Phone: 919-733-6100
Veterinary Services Staff: GEORGE EDWARDS; Phone: 919-733-7601
Keyword(s): Agriculture, Health and Nutrition, Pesticides, Soil Conservation

NORTH CAROLINA DEPARTMENT OF ENVIRONMENT AND NATURAL RESOURCES

State Soil and Water Conservation Commission
Box 27606, Raleigh, NC 27611-7687
Phone: 919-733-2302
Founded: 1937
Description: A unit of state government administered by the Division of Soil and Water Conservation in the Department of Environment, Health, and Natural Resources. To organize soil and water conservation districts; grant funds for operations, technical assistance, and the NC Agriculture Cost-Share Program for Nonpoint Source Pollution Control--a water quality program; provide for control of soil erosion and improvement of water quality; accept PL566 Small Watershed applications. Support staff provided through the Division of Soil and Water Conservation Commission.
Contact(s):
Chairman: JAMES FERGUSON, 11571 Betsy Gap Rd., Clyde, NC 28721; Phone: 704-627-6458
Director: DEWEY BOTTS, 512 N. Salisbury St., Raleigh, NC 27611; Phone: 919-715-6097; Fax: 919-715-3559; Email: dewey_botts@mail.ehnr.state.nc.us

NORTH CAROLINA SEA GRANT PROGRAM
Box 8605, 100B 1911 Bldg., North Carolina State University, Raleigh, NC 27695-8605
Phone: 919-515-2454
Contact(s):
Director: DR. RONALD G. HODSON
Keyword(s): Aquaculture, Aquatic Habitats, Aquatic Species, Coasts, Estuaries, Fisheries, Harmful Algal Blooms, Oceanography, Seafood Technology, Water Pollution, Water Quality, Coastal Construction and Erosion

WILDLIFE RESOURCES COMMISSION
Archdale Bldg., 512 N. Salisbury St., Raleigh, NC 27604-1188
Phone: 919-733-3391; Fax: 919-733-7083
Founded: 1947
Description: The commission has the function, purpose, and duty to manage, restore, develop, cultivate, conserve, protect, and regulate the wildlife resources of the state, and to administer the laws relating to boating, hunting, fishing, and other wildlife resources, including nongame.
Contact(s):
Assistant Director: RICHARD B. HAMILTON
Executive Director: CHARLES R. FULLWOOD
Chief of Division of Administrative Services: CECILIA F. EDGAR; Phone: 919-733-4566
Chief of Division of Conservation Education: A. SIDNEY BAYNES; Phone: 919-733-7123
Chief of Division of Enforcement: COL. ROGER W. LeQUIRE; Phone: 919-733-7191
Chief of Division of Inland Fisheries: FRED HARRIS; Phone: 919-733-3633
Chief of Division of Wildlife Management: DAVID T. COBB; Phone: 919-733-7291
Commission Chairman: JIM BENNETT; Phone: 336-222-9258
Commission Vice Chairman: JOHN E. PECHMANN; Phone: 910-483-0107
Division of Engineering Services: GORDON MYERS; Phone: 919-715-3155
Head of Personnel Section: CAROL A. BATKER; Phone: 919-733-2241
Publications Coordinator and Editor: LARRY S. EARLEY; Phone: 919-733-7123
Publication(s): *Wildlife in North Carolina*
Keyword(s): Fisheries, Hunting, Nongame Wildlife, Wildlife and Wildlife Habitat, Wildlife Management

NORTH DAKOTA

GOVERNOR OF NORTH DAKOTA, EDWARD T. SCHAFFER
State Capitol, 600 E. Blvd. Ave., Bismarck, ND 58505-0001
Phone: 701-328-2200

INSTITUTE FOR ECOLOGICAL STUDIES
P.O. Box 7110, University of North Dakota, Grand Forks, ND 58202
Phone: 701-777-2851
Founded: 1965
Description: A nonprofit university research center devoted to ecology, policy analysis, and environmental biology. A interdisciplinary staff composed of university faculty, biologists, and associates conducts basic and applied research centering in the upper Midwest, and provides technical services for government and corporate agencies, and the public.
Contact(s):
Interim Director: RICHARD CRAWFORD
Publication(s): *Contributions; research reports*
Keyword(s): Biodiversity, Endangered and Threatened Species, Environmental and Conservation Education, Wetlands, Wildlife and Wildlife Habitat

NORTH DAKOTA DEPARTMENT OF AGRICULTURE
600 E. Blvd. Ave., 6th Fl., Bismarck, ND 58505-0020
Description: The North Dakota Department of Agriculture is the regulating and licensing agency for the agricultural industry in North Dakota.
Contact(s):
Commissioner: ROGER JOHNSON; Phone: 701-328-2231

NORTH DAKOTA DEPARTMENT OF HEALTH
600 East Blvd. Ave., Bismarck, ND 58505-0200
Description: State pollution control programs.
Contact(s):
Chief Environmental Health Section: FRANK SCHWINDT, P.O. Box 5520, Bismarck, ND 58506-5520; Phone: 701-328-5150; Fax: 701-328-5200
Director of Division of Environmental Engineering: DANA K. MOUNT, P.O. Box 5520, Bismarck, ND 58506-5520; Phone: 701-328-5188; Fax: 701-328-5200
Director of Division of Municipal Facilities: JACK LONG, P.O. Box 5520, Bismarck, ND 58506-5520; Phone: 701-328-5211; Fax: 701-328-5200
Director of Division of Waste Management: NEIL KNATTERUD, P.O. Box 5520, Bismarck, ND 58506-5520; Phone: 701-328-5166; Fax: 701-328-5200
Director of Division of Water Quality: DENNIS FEWLESS, P.O. Box 5520, Bismarck, ND 58506-5520; Phone: 701-328-5210; Fax: 701-328-5200
State Health Officer: MURRAY SAGSVEEN; Phone: 701-328-2372; Fax: 701-328-4727
Keyword(s): Air Quality and Pollution, Environmental Justice, Public Health Protection, Solid Waste Management, Water Quality

NORTH DAKOTA GAME AND FISH DEPARTMENT
100 N. Bismarck Expy., Bismarck, ND 58501
Phone: 701-328-6300; Fax: 701-328-6352
Contact(s):
Deputy Director: ROGER ROSTVET
Director: DEAN C. HILDEBRAND
Chief of Administrative Services: PAUL SCHADEWALD
Chief of Enforcement: RAY GOETZ
Chief of Fisheries: TERRY STEINWAND
Chief of Information and Education: TED UPGREN
Chief of Natural Resources: MIKE McKENNA

Chief of Wildlife: RANDY KREIL
Editor: HAROLD UMBER
Publication(s): *North Dakota Outdoors*
Keyword(s): Environmental and Conservation Education, Hunting, Nongame Wildlife, Sport Fishing, Wildlife Management

NORTH DAKOTA GEOLOGICAL SURVEY
600 E. Blvd., Bismarck, ND 58505-0840
Phone: 701-328-8000
Founded: 1895
Description: Responsible for collecting and disseminating geologic information.
Contact(s):
Editor: ANN FRITZ
State Geologist: JOHN P. BLUEMLE
Publication(s): *NDGS Newsletter*
Keyword(s): Energy, Environmental Preservation, Geology, Land Use Planning, Water Pollution

NORTH DAKOTA STATE EXTENSION SERVICE
North Dakota State University, Box 5437, Fargo, ND 58105
Phone: 701-231-7173
Contact(s):
Assistant Director of Agriculture and Natural Resources: DR. DARNELL LUNDSTROM, North Dakota State University, Box 5437, Fargo, ND 58105; Phone: 701-231-7173

NORTH DAKOTA STATE FOREST SERVICE
307 First St., Bottineau, ND 58318-1100
Phone: 701-228-5422
Founded: 1891
Description: Mission Statement: Caring for, protecting, and improving forest resources for future generations.
Contact(s):
Centennial Trees Coordinator: THOMAS CLAEYS, 307 First Street East, Bottineau, ND 58318-1100; Phone: 701-28-5446; Fax: 701-228-5448
Community Forestry Coordinator: W. L. JACKSON BIRD, 1511 E. Interstate Ave., Bismarck, ND 58501; Phone: 701-328-9945; Fax: 701-250-4454
Fire Management Coordinator: MAURE SAND, 511 E. Interstate Ave., Bismarck, ND 58501; Phone: 701-328-9946, Fax: 701-250-4454
Information and Education Coordinator: GLENDA FAUSKE; Phone: 701-228-5446
Staff Forester: THOMAS BERG; Phone: 701-228-5483
State Forester: LARRY KOTCHMAN; Phone: 701-228-5422
Towner Nursery Manager: ROY LAFRAMBOISE, 878 Nursery Road, Towner, ND 58788; Phone: 701-537-5636; Fax: 701-537-5680
Publication(s): *Prairie Forester, The*
Keyword(s): Environmental and Conservation Education, Flowers, Plants, and Trees, Forests and Forestry, Public Lands, Urban Forestry

NORTH DAKOTA STATE SOIL CONSERVATION COMMITTEE
4023 North State Street, Suite 30, Bismarck, ND 58501-0620
Phone: 701-328-3725; Fax: 701-328-5123
Founded: 1937
Description: To organize soil conservation districts and provide for control and prevention of soil erosion; represent the state in soil conservation matters; accept P.L. 566 Small Watershed applications and, assign planning priority; and administer the Surface Mining Reports Law; and soil conservation technician grants program.
Contact(s):
Chairperson: WILLIAM PIETSON
Soil Conservation Coordinator: SCOTT HOCHHALTER; Email: shochhal@ndsuext.nodak.edu
Keyword(s): Agriculture, Environmental and Conservation Education, Pesticides, Soil Conservation, Wetlands

NORTH DAKOTA WATER COMMISSION
900 E. Blvd., Bismarck, ND 58505-0850
Phone: 701-328-2750; Fax: 701-328-3696
Contact(s):
Secretary and State Engineer: DAVID A. SPRYNCZYNATYK

PARKS AND RECREATION DEPARTMENT (NORTH DAKOTA)
1835 Bismarck Expy., Bismarck, ND 58504
Phone: 701-328-5370
Founded: 1993
Description: Plan and coordinate government programs encouraging the full development and preservation of existing and future parks, outdoor recreation areas, nature preserves, rare plant and animal species, and unique natural communities.
Contact(s):
Director: DOUG PRCHAL
Coordinator of Nature Preserve/Natural Heritage Programs: KATHY DUTTENHEFNER
Coordinator of Planning and Natural Resources: JESSE HANSON
Publication(s): *Recreation Digest; Natural Areas Registry Newsletter*
Keyword(s): Biodiversity, Environmental Preservation, Historic Preservation, Land Preservation, Nature Preservation

OHIO

GOVERNOR OF OHIO, ROBERT TAFT
State House, 77 S. High St., 30th Fl., Columbus, OH 43266
Phone: 614-466-3555

ENVIRONMENTAL REVIEW APPEALS COMMISSION
236 E. Town St., Rm. 300, Columbus, OH 43215
Phone: 614-466-8950
Description: The Environmental Review Appeals Commission is an administrative commission designed to review the actions of the Ohio EPA, State Fire Marshal, and the various county boards of health charged with environmental jurisdiction in order to determine that the agencies' actions have been reasonable and lawful.
Contact(s):
Chairman: TONI E. MULRANE
Executive Secretary: MARY J. OXLEY
Member: JERRY HAMMOND
Vice Chairman: JULIANNA F. BULL

OHIO COOPERATIVE FISH AND WILDLIFE RESEARCH UNIT (USDI)
The Ohio State University, 1735 Neil Ave., Columbus, OH 43210
Phone: 614-292-6112; Fax: 614-469-7395; Email: rimmer@osu.edu
Founded: 1936
Description: The purpose of the unit is to conduct research and train graduate students in wildlife and fish biology and management. The unit is cooperatively supported by the Ohio Division of Wildlife, The Ohio State University, Biological Resources Division (USGS), and Wildlife Management Institute.
Contact(s):
Acting Unit Leader: DR. MARTIN STAPAUIDU
Keyword(s): Aquatic Habitats, Biodiversity, Birds, Conservation of Protected Areas, Ecology, Endangered and Threatened Species, Environment, Environmental and Conservation Education, Fisheries, Mammals, Nongame Wildlife, Prairies, Preservation and Protection, Renewable Resources, Research

OHIO DEPARTMENT OF AGRICULTURE
8995 E. Main Street, Reynoldsburg, OH 43068
Phone: 614-466-2732
Contact(s):
Director: FRED L. DAILEY
Communication Director: MARK ANTHONY; Phone: 614-752-4505

STATE AND PROVINCE GOVERNMENT AGENCIES - OHIO

OHIO DEPARTMENT OF NATURAL RESOURCES
Fountain Square, Columbus, OH 43224
Phone: 614-265-6565
Founded: 1949
Description: The mission of the Ohio Department of Natural Resources is to provide for the preservation, conservation, utilization, and enjoyment of our natural resources through the wise management, careful planning, efficient and effective delivery of services, and the collection and dissemination of data and information needed for environmental protection and natural resource management decisions. We recognize that these actions impact the social, recreational, and economic well-being of our citizens and that education is the key to the realization of an environmental ethic and the preservation of our natural and cultural hertiage.
Contact(s):
Assistant Director: J. WILLIAM MOODY; Phone: 614-265-6877
Deputy Director: JIM MORRIS; Phone: 614-265-6845
Deputy Director: KYME RENNICK; Phone: 614-265-6845
Director: DONALD C. ANDERSON; Phone: 614-265-6875
Acting Chief of Division of Engineering: JIM MORRIS; Phone: 614-265-6948
Acting Chief of Division of Oil and Gas: TOM TUGNED; Phone: 614-265-6917
Acting Chief of Division of Parks and Recreation: DAN WEST; Phone: 614-265-6561
Chief (Acting) of Division of Natural Areas and Preserves: GUY DENNY; Phone: 614-265-6453
Chief (Acting) of Office of Recycling and Litter Prevention: JENNI WORSTER; Phone: 614-265-6333
Chief of Division of Civilian Conservation: SALLY PROUTY; Phone: 614-265-6423
Chief of Division of Forestry: RONALD ABRAHAM; Phone: 614-265-6694
Chief of Division of Geological Survey: THOMAS BERG; Phone: 614-265-6576
Chief of Division of Real Estate and Land Management: WAYNE WARREN; Phone: 614-265-6395
Chief of Division of Reclamation: LISA MORRIS; Phone: 614-265-6633
Chief of Division of Soil and Water Conservation: LAWRENCE VANCE; Phone: 614-265-6610; Fax: 614-262-2064; Email: larry.vance@dnr.ohio.gov.us
Chief of Division of Water: MICHELE WILLIS; Phone: 614-265-6717
Chief of Division of Watercraft: JEFF HOEDT; Phone: 614-265-6480
Chief of Division of Wildlife: MICHAEL BUDZIK; Phone: 614-265-6300
Chief of Office of Administrative Services: BILL DEMIDOVICH; Phone: 614-265-6859
Chief of Office of Marketing Services: NANCY MANACKE; Phone: 614-265-6787
Keyword(s): Forests and Forestry, Outdoor Recreation, Soil Conservation, Water Resources, Wildlife Management

OHIO ENVIRONMENTAL PROTECTION AGENCY
1800 Watermark Dr., P.O. Box 163669, Columbus, OH 43216-3669
Phone: 614-644-3020
Founded: 1972
Description: State regulatory agency with jurisdiction covering air, waste water, drinking water, hazardous waste, and land pollution control; maintains central office in Columbus and has five district offices.
Contact(s):
Assistant Director: ; Phone: 614-644-2782
Director: DONALD SCHREGARDUS; Phone: 614-644-2782
Chief of Division of Air Pollution Control: ROBERT HODANBOSI; Phone: 614-644-2270
Chief of Division of Drinking and Ground Water: JOHN SADZEWICZ; Phone: 614-644-2752
Chief of Division of Emergency and Remedial Response: JAN CARLSON; Phone: 614-644-2924
Chief of Division of Environmental and Financial Assistance: GREG SMITH; Phone: 614-644-2798
Chief of Division of Environmental Services: GERRY IOANNIDES; Phone: 614-644-4247
Chief of Division of Hazardous Waste Management: LINDA WELCH; Phone: 614-644-2917
Chief of Division of Solid and Infectious Waste: BARBARA BRDICKA; Phone: 614-644-2621
Chief of Division of Surface Water: TOM BEHLEN; Phone: 614-644-2001
Chief of Environmental Education Fund: MICHELE MORRONE; Phone: 614-644-2873
Deputy Director of Administration: STEVE SCOLES; Phone: 614-644-2339
Deputy Director of Communications: PATRICIA MADIGAN; Phone: 614-644-2160
Deputy Director of Legal Affairs: JUDITH FRENCH; Phone: 614-644-2782
Deputy Director of Policy/Legislation: KATE BARTTER; Phone: 614-644-2782
Deputy Director Programs: JENNIFER TIELL; Phone: 614-644-2782
Keyword(s): Air Quality and Pollution, Environmental and Conservation Education, Solid Waste, Water Pollution, Wetlands

OHIO SEA GRANT COLLEGE PROGRAM, F.T. STONE LABORATORY, AND GREAT LAKES AQUATIC ECOSYSTEM RESEARCH CONSORTIUM (GLAERC)
Head, 2120 Fyffe Rd., Columbus, OH 43210
Description: The Ohio Sea Grant College Program is dedicated to the goal of promoting the understanding and management, development, utilization, and conservation of ocean, coastal, and Great Lakes resources, specifically Lake Erie, through research, education, outreach, and communications. The program is administrated by The Ohio State University. Stone Laboratory is Ohio's biological field station located on Gibraltar Island at Put-in-Bay, Ohio.
Contact(s):
Director: DR. JEFFREY M. REUTTER, Ohio Sea Grant College Program, 1314 Kinnear Rd., Columbus, OH 43212; Phone: 614-292-8949; Fax: 614-242-4364; Email: reutter.1@osu.edu
Assistant Director and Communications Coordinator: KAREN T. RICKER, Ohio Sea Grant College Program, 1314 Kinneus Rd., Columbus, OH 43212; Phone: 614-242-8949; Fax: 614-292-4364; Email: ricker.15@osu.edu
Publication(s): *Twine Line; bi-monthly newsletter*
Keyword(s): Aquatic Habitats, Aquatic Species, Environmental and Conservation Education, Fisheries, Lakes, Research, Toxicology, Water Pollution

OHIO STATE EXTENSION SERVICES
Ohio State University Extension, 2120 Fyffe Rd., Columbus, OH 43210
Phone: 614-292-4067; Fax: 614-688-3807; Email: smith.150@osu.edu
Description: To help people improve their lives through an educational process using scientific knowledge focused on identified issues and needs.
Contact(s):
Assistant Director of Agriculture and Natural Resources: DR. STEPHEN R. BAERTSCHE, Ohio State University Extension, 2120 Fyffe Rd., Columbus, OH 43210; Phone: 614-292-4077; Fax: 614-292-3747; Email: baertsche.1@osu.edu
Associate Director of Environmental Education: DR. ROBERT ROTH, School of Natural Resources, 2021 Coffey Rd., Columbus, OH 43210; Phone: 614-292-2265; Fax: 614-292-7432
Director of School of Natural Resources: DR. FRED MILLER, Ohio State University, 2021 Coffey Rd., Columbus, OH 43210; Phone: 614-292-8522; Fax: 614-292-7432; Email: miller.48@osu.edu
Extension Specialist of Forestry: RANDALL B. HEILIGMANN, Ohio State University, 2021 Coffey Rd., Columbus, OH 43210; Phone: 614-292-9838; Fax: 614-292-7432

Extension Specialist of Natural Resources: ERIC NORLAND, School of Natural Resources, 2021 Coffey Rd., Columbus, OH 43210; Phone: 614-292-6544; Fax: 614-292-7432; Email: norland.1@osu.edu
Head: MARY P. KEY, The Ohio State University, 2120 Fyffe Rd., Columbus, OH 43210; Phone: 614-292-6125
Leader of Environmental Science: DR. JOE E. HEIMLICH, 700 Ackerman Road, Suite 235, Columbus, OH 43202-1578; Phone: 614-292-6926; Fax: 614-292-7341

OKLAHOMA

GOVERNOR OF OKLAHOMA, FRANK KEATING
State Capitol Bldg., Suite 212, OklahomaCity, OK 73105
Phone: 405-521-2342

DEPARTMENT OF WILDLIFE CONSERVATION
1801 N. Lincoln, P.O. Box 53465, Oklahoma City, OK 73152
Phone: 405-521-3851; Fax: 405-521-6535
Founded: 1909
Contact(s):
Director: GREG D. DUFFY; Phone: 405-521-4660
Chief of Fisheries: KIM ERICKSON; Phone: 405-521-3721
Chief of Game: RICHARD HATCHER; Phone: 405-521-2739
Chief of Information-Education: DAVID WARREN; Phone: 405-521-3855
Chief of Law Enforcement: JOHN STREICH; Phone: 405-521-3719
Commission Chairman: WM. H. CRAWFORD
Commission Vice Chairman: HARLAND STONECIPHER
Commissioner Secretary: MARK PATTON
Editor: NELS RODEFELD; Phone: 405-521-4635
Employee Services and Communications Staff: HANK STOKES; Phone: 405-232-1569
Employee Services Property Staff: KEN RYEL; Phone: 405-521-4600
Fiscal Services Coordinator: ROBERT TAYLOR; Phone: 405-521-4665
Human Resources Staff: MELINDA STURGESS; Phone: 405-521-4640
Natural Resources Section Staff: RON SUTTLES; Phone: 405-521-4616
Publication(s): *Outdoor Oklahoma*
Keyword(s): Aquatic Habitats, Endangered and Threatened Species, Environmental and Conservation Education, Hunting, Sport Fishing

OKLAHOMA BIOLOGICAL SURVEY
111 E. Chesapeake St., University of Oklahoma, Norman, OK 73019
Phone: 405-325-4034; Fax: 405-325-7702
Founded: 1927
Description: State agency and organized research unit of university. Acquires information on biological resources and natural areas, conducts research on natural biota, jointly maintains Bebb Herbarium, has responsibility for Oklahoma Natural Heritage Inventory, and provides training for students. Jointly operates Oklahoma Fishery Research Laboratory with Oklahoma Department of Wildlife Conservation.
Contact(s):
Director: GARY D. SCHNELL; Phone: 405-325-4034; Email: gschnell@ou.edu
Coordinator of Oklahoma Natural Heritage Inventory: CARYN C. VAUGHN; Phone: 405-325-1985; Email: cvaugh@ou.edu
Curator of Bebb Herbarium: MIA MOLVRAY; Phone: 405-325-6443; Email: mmolvray@ou.edu
Executive Director of Sutton Avian Research Center: STEVE K. SHERROD; Phone: 918-336-7778; Email: gmsarc@aol.com
Keyword(s): Biodiversity, Biology, Botany, Conservation of Protected Areas, Ecology, Endangered and Threatened Species, Flowers, Plants, and Trees, Geographic Information Systems, Nongame Wildlife, Wildlife and Wildlife Habitat, Zoology

OKLAHOMA COOPERATIVE FISH AND WILDLIFE RESEARCH UNIT (USDI)
404 Life Sciences West Bldg., Oklahoma State University, Stillwater, OK 74078-3051
Phone: 405-744-6342
Contact(s):
Assistant Leader (Ecology): WILLIAM L. FISHER
Assistant Leader (Fisheries): DANA L. WINKLEMAN
Assistant Leaders of Fisheries:
Leader: DAVID M. LESLIE JR.
Keyword(s): Endangered and Threatened Species, Fisheries, Nongame Wildlife, Research, Wildlife and Wildlife Habitat

OKLAHOMA DEPARTMENT OF ENVIRONMENTAL QUALITY
1000 NE 10th St., Oklahoma City, OK 73117-1212
Phone: 405-271-8056
Description: The Department of Environmental Quality is dedicated to providing quality service to the people of Oklahoma through comprehensive environmental protection and management programs. Those programs are designed to assist the people of the state in sustaining a clean sound environment and in preserving and enhancing our natural surroundings.
Contact(s):
Executive Director: MARK S. COLEMAN; Phone: 405-271-8056
Deputy Executive Director: STEVEN A. THOMPSON; Phone: 405-271-8056
Director of Air Quality: LARRY BYRUM; Phone: 405-271-5220
Director of Complaints and Local Services: LARRY McKEE; Phone: 405-271-7363
Director of Customer Services: JUDY DUNCAN; Phone: 405-271-1400
Director of Public Information and Education: ELLEN BUSSERT; Phone: 405-271-8056
Director of Support Services: LAWRENCE A. GALES; Phone: 405-271-8062
Director of Waste Management: H.A. Caves; Phone: 405-271-5338
Director of Water Quality: JON CRAIG; Phone: 405-271-5205
General Counsel: BOB KELLOGG; Phone: 405-271-8056
Publication(s): *Clear View; Certified Operator News Letter (Waterworks and Wastewater); Superfund program Sites Status Report; Air Quality Annual Report*
Keyword(s): Air Quality and Pollution, Environmental Protection, Pollution Prevention, Solid Waste Management, Water Quality

OKLAHOMA GEOLOGICAL SURVEY
University of Oklahoma, Sarkeys Energy Center, 100 E. Boyd, Rm. N-131, Norman, OK 73019-0628
Phone: 405-325-3031; WWW: www.ou.edu/special/ogs-pttc
Founded: 1908
Description: To investigate and disseminate information on the geology of the state, with special reference to mineral resources and environmental issues. Investigations include: geologic mapping, evaluation of metallic and nonmetallic mineral deposits, and studies of earthquakes, groundwater, and fossil fuels, plus basic research and environmental studies.
Contact(s):
Director: CHARLES J. MANKIN
Associate Director: KENNETH S. JOHNSON
Librarian: CLAREN KIDD, 100 E. Boyd, Rm. 220, Norman, OK 73019-0628
Promotion and Information Specialist: CONNIE G. SMITH
Publication(s): *Oklahoma Geology Notes; bulletins, circulars, guidebooks, geologic map series, educational publications series, hydrologic atlases, special publications.*
Keyword(s): Energy, Environment, Geology, Land Use Planning, Mapping, Water Resources

OKLAHOMA STATE BOARD OF AGRICULTURE
2800 N. Lincoln Blvd., Oklahoma City, OK 73105
Phone: 405-521-3864
Description: The Oklahoma Department of Agriculture is principally a service agency, but it is also a promotional and cooperative

STATE AND PROVINCE GOVERNMENT AGENCIES - OKLAHOMA

agency for segments of agriculture and forestry. Major divisions of the department are forestry, animal industry, legal, plant industry, marketing, water quality, agriculture laboratory, and the federal-state cooperative programs of wildlife services and agricultural statistics.
Contact(s):
Administration Staff: DAVID LIGON; Phone: 405-521-3864/Ext.220
Assistant Commissioner: COY MORSE
Deputy Commissioner: DR. CHARLES FREEMAN; Phone: 405-521-3864/Ext.202
Director of Agricultural Laboratory: SUE CANNON; Phone: 405-521-3864
Director of Agricultural Statistics: BARRY BLOYD; Phone: 405-525-9226
Director of Animal Industry Services: DR. BURKE HEALEY; Phone: 405-521-3864
Director of Forestry Services: ROGER L. DAVIS; Phone: 405-521-3864
Director of Legal Services: DR MARK NEWMAN; Phone: 403-521-3864 Ext. 344
Director of Market Development 414 Services: RICK MALONEY
Director of Wildlife Services: DON HAWTHORNE; Phone: 405-521-4039
Information Officer: JACK CARSON; Phone: 405-521-3864/Ext.414
Secretary of Agriculture: DENNIS HOWARD
Keyword(s): Agriculture, Environmental Law, Forests and Forestry, Pesticides, Urban Environment

OKLAHOMA STATE CONSERVATION COMMISSION

2800 N. Lincoln Blvd., Suite 160, Oklahoma City, OK 73105
Phone: 405-521-2384; Fax: 405-521-6686; WWW: www.state.ok.us/-conscom
Founded: 1938
Description: To assist and supervise conservation districts in carrying out conservation practices of all renewable natural resources.
Contact(s):
Chairman: JAMES EDDIE PHILLIPS
Assistant Director: BEN POLLARD
Executive Director: MIKE THRAUS
Director of Abandoned Mine Land Reclamation Program: MIKE KASTL
Director of Water Quality Program: JOHN HASSELL
District Operations Director: DR. DAN A. SEBERT
Information Officer: MARK HARRISON
Publication(s): *Conservation Conversation Newsletter; Geographic Information Systems Newsletter*
Keyword(s): Abandoned Mine Land Reclamation, Environmental and Conservation Education, Nonpoint Source Pollution, Soil Conservation, Upstream Flood Prevention

OKLAHOMA STATE EXTENSION SERVICES

Oklahoma State University, Rm. 139, Agricultural Hall, Stillwater, OK 74078
Phone: 405-744-5398
Founded: 1946
Description: Extension Forestry and Wildlife are a unit of the Oklahoma Cooperative Extension Service and the Department of Forestry, Division of Agricultural Sciences and Natural Resources, Oklahoma State University. The Department of Forestry provides accredited education in forest resources management, conducts forestry research through the Oklahoma Agricultural Experiment Station, and brings forest resources education to the citizens of Oklahoma through its extension efforts.
Contact(s):
Assistant Extension Forester and Wildlife Specialist: CHAMPE GREEN, Oklahoma State University, Rm. 242, Agricultural Hall, Stillwater, OK 74078; Phone: 405-744-5445
Associate Director of Cooperative Extension Service: DR. R. E. CAMPBELL, Oklahoma State University, Rm. 139, Agricultural Hall, Stillwater, OK 74078; Phone: 405-744-5398
Dean of Libraries: EDWARD R. JOHNSON, OSU, Stillwater, OK 74078; Phone: 405-744-6321
Department Head of Forestry: DR. ED MILLER, Oklahoma State University, Rm. 012, Agricultural Hall, Stillwater, OK 74078; Phone: 405-744-5437/Ext.5284
Director of Cooperative Extension Service: DR. SAM E. CURL
Extension Wildlife Specialist: DR. RON MASTERS, Oklahoma State University, Rm. 240, Agricultural Hall, Stillwater, OK 74078; Phone: 405-744-6432/Ext.8065
Publication(s): *Oklahoma Renewable Resources newsletter; Oklahoma Forest Industry bulletin; Natural Resources Speakers Bureau*
Keyword(s): Endangered and Threatened Species, Environmental and Conservation Education, Forests and Forestry, Urban Forestry, Wildlife Management

OKLAHOMA TOURISM AND RECREATION DEPARTMENT

P.O. Box 52002, Capitol Post Office, Oklahoma City, OK 73105-4492
Phone: 405-521-2409
Founded: 1972
Description: To encourage residents and travelers to "Native America" as a vacation destination; and to develop human and natural resources for the purpose of promoting tourism, recreation, wildlife preservation, and environmental conservation. An annual industry conference is held each fall.
Contact(s):
Deputy Director: TOM RICH; Phone: 405-521-3793
Cabinet Secretary: EDWARD H. COOK; Phone: 405-521-2413
Director of State Parks: JOHN RESSMEYER; Phone: 405-521-4291
Division of Administration: DEBBIE SHARP; Phone: 405-521-2471
Division of Human Resources: AMOS MOSES; Phone: 405-522-4523
Division of Planning and Development: KRISTINA S. MAREK; Phone: 405-521-2973
Division of Travel and Tourism: KATHLEEN MARKS; Phone: 405-521-3981
Publisher: JOAN HENDERSON; Phone: 405-521-2496
Publication(s): *Oklahoma Today; Oklahoma Vacation* **Keyword(s):** Nature Preservation, Nongame Wildlife, Outdoor Recreation, Public Lands

OKLAHOMA WATER RESOURCES BOARD

3800 N. Classen Blvd., Oklahoma City, OK 73118
Phone: 405-530-8800; Fax: 405-530-8900
Founded: 1957
Description: Promulgates water quality standards for state; lead agency in Clean Lakes Program; investigates pollution complaints; assesses water quality, quantity of groundwater, and stream water; issues permits for water use; administers dam safety, floodplain management programs, and plans for adequate supplies of good quality water for all beneficial uses; updates plans; administers financial assistance programs for water and wastewater systems.
Contact(s):
Chairman: J. ROSS KIRTLEY
Executive Director: DUANE A. SMITH
Assistant to the Director: MICHAEL R. MELTON
Librarian: SUSAN BIRCHFIELD
Publication(s): *Oklahoma Water News*
Keyword(s): Environmental and Conservation Education, Lakes, Rivers, Water Quality, Water Resources

OREGON

GOVERNOR OF OREGON, JOHN A. KITZHABER
254 State Capitol, Salem, OR 97310
Phone: 503-378-3111

DEPARTMENT OF FISH AND WILDLIFE (OREGON)
2501 SW 1st Ave., Portland, OR 97207
Phone: 503-872-5310
Founded: 1975
Description: Responsibilities include management of fish and wildlife resources and regulation of commercial and recreational harvest.
Contact(s):
Deputy Director: STEVE WILLIAMS; Phone: 503-872-5272
Director: JIM GREER; Phone: 503-872-5272
Editor: PAT WRAY; Phone: 541-757-4206
Head of Administrative Services: RICHARD CORESON; Phone: 503-872-5270
Head of Fisheries: DOUG DEHART; Phone: 503-872-5252
Head of Habitat Conservation: JILL ZARNOWITZ; Phone: 503-872-5255
Head of Information and Education: KYLE WALKER; Phone: 503-872-5264
Head of Realty and Licensing: WAYNE RAWLINS; Phone: 503-872-5310
Head of Statistical Services: DALE CHRISTENSEN; Phone: 503-872-5267
Head of Wildlife: RICHARD BERRY; Phone: 503-872-5260
Human Resources: CAROL BROWN; Phone: 503-872-5262
Region 1 Acting Supervisor: DAVE L. ANDERSON; Phone: 541-757-4186
Region 2 Supervisor: BOB MULLEN; Phone: 541-440-3353
Region 3 Acting Supervisor: CLAIR KUNKEL; Phone: 541-388-6363
Region 4 Acting Supervisor: CRAIG ELY; Phone: 541-963-2138
Region 7 Supervisor: CHRIS WHEATON; Phone: 503-657-2000
Publication(s): *Oregon Wildlife*

DEPARTMENT OF GEOLOGY AND MINERAL INDUSTRIES
800 NE Oregon St., Suite 965, #28, Portland, OR 97232-2162
Phone: 503-731-4100
Contact(s):
Librarian: KLAUS NEVENDORF, 800 NE Oregon St., Suite 965, #28, Portland, OR 97232-2162
State Geologist: DONALD A. HULL
Publication(s): *List available on request from Nature of the Northwest Information Center, Suite 177, 800 NE Oregon St., #5, Portland, OR 97232-2162 503-872-2750,Fax: 503-731-4066*

DEPARTMENT OF TRANSPORTATION (OREGON)
Mgr. Of Envir., 1158 Chemeketa St., NE, Salem, OR 97310
Contact(s):
Manager of Environmental Services Section: EB ENGELMANN, Oregon Department of Transportation, 1158 Chemeketa St., NE, Salem, OR 97310; Phone: 503-986-3477
Keyword(s): Engineering, Environment, Environmental Planning, Research, Transportation

FISH AND WILDLIFE DIVISION/DEPARTMENT OF STATE POLICE
400 Public Service Bldg., Salem, OR 97310
Phone: 503-378-3720; Fax: 503-363-5475
Description: The Fish and Wildlife Division is charged with the enforcement of fish and game, commercial fish, shellfish, environmental protection laws, and all endangered species laws, rules, and regulations. Also provides general law enforcement services in rural areas. Provides law enforcement services on contract with the Oregon Department of Fish and Wildlife, the Department of Environmental Quality, and the Department of Forestry. Enforcement priorities for fish and wildlife resources cooperatively identified with ODFW.
Contact(s):
Aircraft Supervisor: LT. J. E. HUNSAKER; Phone: 503-378-3720
C & D Director (Captain): LINDSAY A. BALL; Phone: 503-378-3720
District I Supervisor of Portland, OR: LT. K. L. ALLISON; Phone: 503-731-3027
District II Supervisor of Salem, OR: LT. S. R. LANE; Phone: 503-378-2110
District III Supervisor of Medford, OR: LT. L. BELCHER; Phone: 503-776-6114
District IV Supervisor of Baker City, OR: LT. R. D. SCORBY; Phone: 503-523-5848
Special Investigations Unit Supervisor: SGT. W. D. MARKEE; Phone: 503-378-3387
Staff of Commercial Fisheries: LT. J. S. LARSON; Phone: 503-378-3720
Staff of Wildlife: LT. C. K. KOK; Phone: 503-378-3720
Keyword(s): Endangered and Threatened Species, Environmental Law, Fisheries, Hunting, Law Enforcement, Wildlife and Wildlife Habitat

OREGON COOPERATIVE FISH AND WILDLIFE RESEARCH UNIT (USDI)
Department of Fisheries and Wildlife, Oregon State University, Corvallis, OR 97331-3803
Phone: 503-737-4531
Description: Research focus on physiological, ecological, and genetic factors affecting production and performance of freshwater fishes. The staff consists of two permanent and two-three other Ph.D., level scientists, as well as graduate students and technicians.
Contact(s):
Assistant Leader: DR. HIRAM W. LI
Leader: DR. CARL B. SCHRECK
Keyword(s): Aquatic Habitats, Biodiversity, Environmental and Conservation Education, Fisheries, Wildlife Disease

OREGON COOPERATIVE FISH AND WILDLIFE RESEARCH UNIT (USDI)
104 Nash Hall, Oregon State University, Corvallis, OR 97331
Phone: 541-737-1938
Contact(s):
Wildlife Assistant Leader: DR. DANIEL D. ROBY
Wildlife Leader: DR. ROBERT G. ANTHONY
Keyword(s): Endangered and Threatened Species, Nongame Wildlife, Raptors, Wildlife and Wildlife Habitat, Wildlife Management

OREGON DEPARTMENT OF AGRICULTURE
Natural Resources Division, 635 Capitol St., NE, Salem, OR 97310-0110
Founded: 1939 (Department of Agriculture), 1989 (Natural Resources Division)
Description: Supervises the organization and operation of soil and water conservation districts, approves or disapproves all projects, practices, personnel, budgets, contracts, and regulations of Oregon's 45 districts. State administrative agency for nonpoint source water quality programs dealing with agricultural lands. Also responsible for managing the state's field burning weather monitoring program, the native plant species conservation program, and the weather modification program.
Contact(s):
Administrator: JOHN MELLOTT; Phone: 503-378-3810; Email: jmellott@oda.state.or.us
Advisory Member: ANDREW HASHIMOTO, Department of Agriculture Engineering, Oregon State University, Corvallis, OR 97331-2213; Phone: 503-737-2041
Advisory Member: JACK SAINSBURY, ASCS, 1220 SW 3rd. Ave., 15th Fl., Portland, OR 97204-2880; Phone: 503-326-2741
Advisory Member: BOB GRAHAM, SCS, 1220 SW 3rd Ave., 16th Fl., Portland, OR 97204-2881; Phone: 503-326-2751
Advisory Member: RAY LEDGERWOOD, NACD, NE 1615 Eastgate Blvd., Suite B, Pullman, WA 509-334-1823
Assistant Administrator: CHARLES CRAIG; Phone: 503-378-3810

STATE AND PROVINCE GOVERNMENT AGENCIES - OREGON

Soil and Water Conservation Commission Chairman: THOMAS STRAUGHAN, 1421 SW 45th Dr., Pendleton, OR 97801; Phone: 503-278-0218; Email: tstraugh@orednet.org

Soil and Water Conservation Commissioner Vice Chairman: JOE BRUMBACH, 4260 Buckhorn Rd., Roseburg, OR 97470; Phone: 503-673-3998

Publication(s): *Oregon Natural Resources Conservation News*

OREGON DEPARTMENT OF ENVIRONMENTAL QUALITY (DEQ)
811 SW 6th Ave., Portland, OR 97204
Phone: 503-229-5696

Founded: 1969

Description: Our mission is to be an active leader in restoring, maintaining, and enhancing the quality of Oregon's air, water, and land.

Contact(s):
Director: LANGDON MARSH; Phone: 503-229-5300
Air Quality Administrator: GREG GREEN; Phone: 503-229-5397
Eastern Region Administrator: STEPHANIE HALLOCK; Phone: 541-338-6146
Laboratory Administrator: RICK GATES; Phone: 503-229-5983
Northwest Region Administrator: NEIL MULLANE; Phone: 503-229-5372
Waste Management Cleanup Administrator: MARY WAHL; Phone: 503-229-5072
Water Quality Administrator: MICHAEL LLEWELYN; Phone: 503-229-5324
Western Region Administrator: STEVE GREENWOOD; Phone: 541-686-7838

Publication(s): *Recycling Newsletter; Beyond Waste; Tankline*

Keyword(s): Air Quality and Pollution, Environmental and Conservation Education, Environmental Cleanup, Solid Waste Management, Water Pollution Management

OREGON DEPARTMENT OF FORESTRY
2600 State St., Salem, OR 97310-1336
Phone: 503-945-7200; Fax: 503-945-7212

Founded: 1911

Description: Responsible for fire protection of 15.8 million acres of private and public forests; directs insect and disease management on 11 million acres of state and private forests; manages 789,000 acres of state-owned forests; provides forestry assistance to private forest landowners; enforces Oregon forest laws; provides forestry information to schools, organizations, and individuals; and advises Governor and State Legislature on forestry matters.

Contact(s):
Assistant State Forester of Administrative Services: STEVE JACKY; Phone: 503-945-7203
Assistant State Forester of Forest Management: RAY CRAIG; Phone: 503-945-7204
Assistant State Forester of Forest Protection: CHARLIE STONE; Phone: 503-945-7205
Assistant State Forster of Resource Policy: ANN HANUS; Phone: 503-945-7206
Deputy State Forester: J. MICHAEL BEYERLE; Phone: 503-945-7202
Director of Fire Prevention: RICK GIBSON; Phone: 503-945-7440
Director of Fire Protection: CLARK SEELY; Phone: 503-945-7435
Director of Forestry Assistance: WALLACE RUTLEDGE; Phone: 503-945-7392
Director of Public Affairs: CARY GREENWOOD; Phone: 503-945-7420
Director of State Forest Management: MIKE BORDELON; Phone: 503-945-7348
Eastern Orgon Director: CLIFF LIEDTKE, 3501 E 3rd St., Prineville, OR 97754; Phone: 541-447-5658; Fax: 541-447-1469
Forestry Member: DICK BALDWIN, 97 Constantine Place, Eugene, OR 97405; Phone: 541-343-3488
Forestry Member: BRAD WITT, 2110 State St., Salem, OR 97301; Phone: 503-585-6320
Forestry Member: WAYNE KRIEGER, 95702 Skyview Ranch Rd., GoldBeach, OR 97444; Phone: 541-247-7990
Forestry Member: SAM JOHNSON, 1449 SW Davenport St., Portland, OR 97201; Phone: 503-223-4772
Forestry Member: JANET NEUMAN, 10015 SW Terwilliger Blved, Portland, OR 97219; Phone: 503-768-6633
Forestry Member Chair: DAVID E. GILBERT
Northwest Oregon Director: ROY WOO, 801 Gales Creek Rd., ForestGrove, OR 97117-1199; Phone: 503-357-2191; Fax: 503-333357-4548
Southern Oregon Director: CRAIG ROYCE, 1758 NE Airport Rd., Roseburg, OR 97470-1499; Phone: 541-440-3412; Fax: 541-440-3424
State Board of Forestry Member: HOWARD SOHN, Box 1137, Roseburg, OR 97470; Phone: 541-673-0141
State Forester: JAMES E. BROWN; Phone: 503-945-7211

Publication(s): *Forest Log, The*

Keyword(s): Endangered and Threatened Species, Fisheries, Forests and Forestry, Urban Forestry

OREGON PARKS AND RECREATION DEPARTMENT
1115 Commercial St., NE, Salem, OR 97301-1002
Phone: 503-378-6305

Founded: 1921

Description: To provide and protect outstanding natural, scenic, cultural, historic, and recreational sites for the enjoyment and education of present and future generations.

Contact(s):
Deputy Director: NANCY ROCKWELL, 1115 Commercial St.. NE, Salem, OR 97301-1002; Phone: 503-378-6905
Director: BOB MEINEN, 1115 Commercial St., NE, Salem, OR 97301-1002; Phone: 503-378-5019

Publication(s): *Oregon Outdoors*

Keyword(s): Environmental and Conservation Education, Historic Preservation, Natural Areas, Ocean Conservation, Outdoor Recreation, Rivers

OREGON SEA GRANT PROGRAM
Administrative Services, A500, Oregon State University, Corvallis, OR 97331-2131
Phone: 541-737-2714; Fax: 503-737-2392

Description: Oregon Sea Grant takes an integrated approach to addressing the problems and opportunities of Oregon's marine resources through three related primary activities--research, education, and extension services. Oregon Sea Grant responds to the needs of ocean users.

Contact(s):
Director of Administrative Services: JOSEPH CONE, Communications, 402, Oregon State University, Corvallis, OR 97331; Phone: 541-737-2716
Director of Sea Grant College Program: ROBERT E. MALOUF
Interim Program Leader: ED KOLBE, Extension Sea Grant Program, Gilm 200, Oregon State University, Corvallis, OR 97331-3906; Phone: 541-737-0702; Fax: 541-737-4423

Publication(s): *Catalogue available upon request from Sea Grant Communications.*

Keyword(s): Biotechnology, Coasts, Communications, Fisheries, Oceanography

OREGON STATE EXTENSION SERVICES
Oregon State University, Corvallis, OR 97331
Phone: 541-737-2713

Contact(s):
Associate Director of Extension County Programs: PETER BLOOME, Extension Hall 102, Oregon State University, Corvalis, OR 97331; Phone: 541-737-2711
Extension Agriculture Program Leader: KELVIN KOONG, State Agriculture Hall, #126, Oregon State University, Corvallis, OR 97331; Phone: 541-737-2331
Extension Wildlife Specialist: DANIEL EDGE, Nash Hall 104E, Oregon State University, Corvallis, OR 97331; Phone: 541-737-1953
Head of Fisheries and Wildlife: ERIC FRITZELL, Nash Hall 104C, Oregon State University, Corvallis, OR 97331; Phone: 541-737-1952

Program Leader of Forestry Extension: A. SCOTT REED, Peavy Hall 121, Oregon State University, Corvallis, OR 97331; Phone: 541-737-3700
Regional Director: DEBORAH MADDY, Extension Hall 102, Oregon State University, Corvallis, OR 97331; Phone: 541-737-2711

STATE MARINE BOARD (OREGON)
P.O. Box 14145, Salem, OR 97309-5065
Phone: 503-378-8587
Contact(s):
Director: PAUL E. DONHEFFNER
Keyword(s): Outdoor Recreation, Recreational Boating, Water Quality

WATER RESOURCES DEPARTMENT
158 12th St., NE, Salem, OR 97310
Phone: 503-378-8455; Fax: 503-378-2496; WWW: www.wrd.state.or.us
Description: The Water Resources Department is the steward of the state's water resources. The agency enforces state water laws and policies; promotes actions that restore and protect streamflows and watersheds in order to ensure the long-term sustainability of Oregon's ecosystems, economy, and quality of life; addresses water supply needs; and increases the understanding of the resource and the demands on it.
Contact(s):
Deputy Director: GEOFF HUNTINGTON; Phone: 503-378-8455
Director: MARTHA O. PAGEL; Phone: 503-378-2982
Acting Administrator of Resource Management Division: DICK BAILEY; Phone: 503-378-8455
Acting Administrator of Water Rights Division: DWIGHT FRENCH; Phone: 503-378-8455
Administrator of Administrative Services Division: BRUCE MOYER; Phone: 503-378-8455
Administrator of Field and Technical Services Division: BARRY NORRIS; Phone: 503-378-8455

Water Resources Commission
Founded: 1985
Description: The Water Resources Commission was created to oversee policy and all rulemaking activity of the department.
Contact(s):
Chair, Commissioner, West Central Region: NANCY LEONARD; Phone: 541-265-4100
Commissioner, Eastern Region: JIM NAKANO; Phone: 541-889-6823
Commissioner, Eastside at Large: TYLER HANSELL; Phone: 541-567-8939
Commissioner, North Central Region: RON NELSON; Phone: 541-548-6047
Commissioner, Northwest Region: JOHN FREWLING; Phone: 503-227-1276
Commissioner, Southwest Region: DAN THORNDIKE; Phone: 541-857-8222
Vice Chair, Commissioner, Westdale at large: MIKE JEWETT; Phone: 541-265-4100
Keyword(s): Planning Management, Rivers, Sustainable Development, Sustainable Ecosystems, Water Resources

PENNSYLVANIA

GOVERNOR OF PENNSYLVANIA, TOM RIDGE
Rm. 225, Main Capitol Bldg., Harrisburg, PA 17120
Phone: 717-787-2500

DEPARTMENT OF ENVIRONMENTAL PROTECTION (PENNSYLVANIA)
Public Participation Coordinator, 16th Floor, Rachel Carson State Office Bldg., P.O. Box 2063, Harrisburg, PA 17105-2063
Phone: 717-783-7404; Email: To DEP staff, use: lastname.firstname@a1.dep.state.pa.us; WWW: www.dep.state.pa.us
Founded: 1971
Description: The Department of Environmental Protection's mission is to protect Pennsylvania's air, land, and water from pollution and to provide for the health and safety of its citizens through a cleaner environment. We will work as partners with individuals, organizations, governments, and businesses to prevent pollution and restore our natural resources.
Contact(s):
Secretary: JAMES M. SEIF; Phone: 717-787-2814
21st Century Environment Commission Executive Director: CAROL COLLIER; Phone: 717-772-4770
Chief Counsel: TERRY R. BOSSERT; Phone: 717-787-4449
Deputy Secretary for Air, Recycling and Radiation Protection: DENISE K. CHAMBERLAIN; Phone: 717-772-2724
Deputy Secretary for Federal/State Relations: DONALD S. WELSH; Phone: 717-783-1566
Deputy Secretary for Field Operations: TERRY R. FABIAN; Phone: 717-787-5028
Deputy Secretary for Management and Technical Services: KENWOOD GIFFHORN; Phone: 717-787-7116
Deputy Secretary for Mineral Resources Management: ROBERT C. DOLENCE; Phone: 717-783-5338
Deputy Secretary for Pollution Prevention and Compliance Assistance: STACEY A. RICHARDS; Phone: 717-783-0540
Deputy Secretary for Water Management: HUGH V. ARCHER; Phone: 717-787-4686
Director (Acting), Bureau of Water Quality Protection: GLENN E. MAURER; Phone: 717-787-2666
Director (Acting), Bureau of Water Supply Management: FREDERICK A. MARROCCO; Phone: 717-787-9035
Director of Environmental Education: HELEN OLENA; Phone: 717-772-1828
Director of Local Government Relations: DON HERSHEY; Phone: 717-787-9580
Director of Program Integration and Effectiveness: KIMBERLY NELSON; Phone: 717-787-9580
Director of Program Operations, Pollution Prevention and Compliance Assistance: MEREDITH L. HILL; Phone: 717-783-0540
Director, Bureau of Abandoned Mine Reclamation: ERNEST F. GIOVANNITTI; Phone: 717-783-2267
Director, Bureau of Air Quality: JAMES M. SALVAGGIO; Phone: 717-787-9702
Director, Bureau of Deep Mine Safety: RICHARD STRICKLER; Phone: 717-787-1376
Director, Bureau of Fiscal Management: RONALD K. FLORY; Phone: 717-787-1319
Director, Bureau of Human Resources: KAREN GOOD; Phone: 717-787-9313
Director, Bureau of Information Services: DARWIN AURAND; Phone: 717-772-5909
Director, Bureau of Investigations: GARY F. NILAND; Phone: 717-787-0453
Director, Bureau of Land Recycling and Waste Management: JAMES P. SNYDER; Phone: 717-783-2388
Director, Bureau of Mining and Reclamation: RODERICK FLETCHER; Phone: 717-787-5103
Director, Bureau of Office Systems and Services: JAMES S. TOOTHAKER; Phone: 717-787-4190

STATE AND PROVINCE GOVERNMENT AGENCIES - PENNSYLVANIA

Director, Bureau of Oil and Gas Management: JAMES E. ERB; Phone: 717-772-2199
Director, Bureau of Regulatory Counsel: RICHARD P. MATHER; Phone: 717-787-7060
Director, Bureau of Watershed Conservation: STUART I. GANSELL; Phone: 717-787-5267
Director, Bureau of Waterways Engineering: MICHAEL D. CONWAY; Phone: 717-787-3411
Director, District Mining Operations: JEFFREY D. JARRETT; Phone: 412-942-7283
Director, The Policy Office: BARBARA A. SEXTON; Phone: 717-783-8727
Economic Development Project Coordinator: MICHAEL WOLF; Phone: 717-787-9580
Executive Deputy Secretary: DAVID E. HESS; Phone: 717-772-1856
Executive Director, Citizens Advisory Council to DEP: SUSAN M. WILSON, 5th Floor, Rachel Carson State Office Building, P.O. Box 8459, Harrisburg, PA 17105-8459; Phone: 717-787-4527
Legislative Liaison: PAMELA A. WITMER; Phone: 717-783-8303
Office for River Basin Cooperation Executive Director: IRENE B. BROOKS; Phone: 717-772-4785
Press Secretary: CHRISTINA NOVAK; Phone: 717-787-1323
Public Participation Coordinator: CHRISTOPHER ALLEN; Phone: 717-783-7404
Senior Counselor to the Govenor: PATRICK J. SOLANO; Phone: 717-783-6387

Citizens Advisory Council to DEP
5th Fl., Rachel Carson State Office Bldg., P.O. Box 8459, Harrisburg, PA 17105-8459
Contact(s):
Executive Director: SUSAN M. WILSON
Publication(s): *PA Geology; Annual Report of Mining Activities; PA DER Publications*
Keyword(s): Environmental Preservation, Public Health Protection

FISH AND BOAT COMMISSION
P.O. Box 67000, Harrisburg, PA 17106-7000
Phone: 717-657-4518
Founded: 1866
Description: To conduct and support public education and information efforts related to aquatic resource protection, improvement, and management programs, and enhance public understanding of the wise and safe use of our fishing and boating resources.
Contact(s):
President: ENOCH S. MOORE
Vice President: DONALD K. ANDERSON
Executive Director: PETER A. COLANGELO; Phone: 717-657-4515
Art Director: TED R. WALKE; Phone: 717-564-6846
Deputy Executive Director/Chief Counsel: DENNIS T. GUISE; Phone: 717-657-4525
Director of Bureau of Administration Services: WASYL J. POLISCHUK, JR.; Phone: 717-657-4522
Director of Bureau of Boating and Education: JOHN F. SIMMONS; Phone: 717-657-4538
Director of Bureau of Engineering and Development: JAMES A. YOUNG; Phone: 814-359-5152
Director of Bureau of Fisheries: DELANO R. GRAFF; Phone: 814-359-5154
Director of Bureau of Law Enforcement: EDWARD W. MANHART; Phone: 717-657-4542
Editor: ARTHUR J. MICHAELS; Phone: 717-657-4520
Legislative Liaison: JOSEPH A. GREENE; Phone: 717-657-4517
Planning Coordinator: THOMAS P. FORD; Phone: 717-657-4394
Publication(s): *Pennsylvania Angler and Boater*
Keyword(s): Aquatic Habitats, Environmental and Conservation Education, Fisheries, Outdoor Recreation, Sport Fishing

Region 1 Northwest
1281 Otter St., Franklin, PA 16323
Phone: 814-437-5774
Contact(s):
Law Enforcement Supervisor: GARY E. DEIGER, 11528 State Highway 98, Meadville, PA 16335; Phone: 814-337-0444

Region 2 Southwest
R.R. 2, Box 39, Somerset, PA 15501
Phone: 814-445-8974
Contact(s):
Law Enforcement Supervisor: ANTHONY B. MURAWSKI, 236 Lake Road, Somerset, PA 15501; Phone: 814-445-8974

Region 3 Northeast
Box 88, Sweet Valley, PA 18656
Phone: 717-477-5717
Contact(s):
Law Enforcement Supervisor: KERRY L. MESSERLE

Region IV Southeast
Box 8, Elm, PA 17521
Phone: 717-626-0228
Contact(s):
Law Enforcement Supervisor: JEFFREY S. BRIDI

Region V North Central
P. O. Box 187, Fishing Creek Rd., Lamar, PA 16848
Phone: 717-726-6056
Contact(s):
Law Enforcement Supervisor: PAUL F. SWANSON

Region VI South Central
1704 Pine Rd., Newville, PA 17241
Phone: 717-486-7087
Contact(s):
WILLIAM E. HARTLE

GAME COMMISSION
2001 Elmerton Ave., Harrisburg, PA 17110-9797
Phone: 717-787-4250
Founded: 1895
Contact(s):
President: ROBERT J. GILFORD
Vice President: VERNON K. SHAFFER
Secretary: DR. NICHOLS SPOCK MD
Executive Director: DONALD C. MADL; Phone: 717-787-3633
Assistant Director of Bureau of Information and Education: J. CARL GRAYBILL, JR.; Phone: 717-787-6286
Associate Editor: ROBERT D'ANGELO; Phone: 717-787-3745
Chief of Audio-Visual Services Division: JOSEPH OSMAN; Phone: 717-787-1434
Chief of Hunter and Trapper Education Division: KEITH A. SNYDER; Phone: 717-787-7015
Chief of Public Information Division: F. BRUCE WHITMAN; Phone: 717-787-7015
Chief of Publications Division: ROBERT C. MITCHELL; Phone: 717-787-3745
Coordinator of Project Wild: THERESA ALBERICI; Phone: 717-783-4872
Deputy Executive Director of Administration: MICHAEL W. SCHMIT; Phone: 717-787-3633
Deputy Executive Director of Field Operations: DAVID SLOAN; Phone: 717-787-3633
Director of Bureau of Administration: THOMAS C. WYLIE; Phone: 717-787-5670
Director of Bureau of Automated Technology Services: ROBERT STRAILEY; Phone: 717-787-4076
Director of Bureau of Information and Education: LANTZ A. HOFFMAN; Phone: 717-787-6286
Director of Bureau of Land Management: GREGORY J. GRABOWICZ; Phone: 717-787-6818

STATE AND PROVINCE GOVERNMENT AGENCIES - PENNSYLVANIA

Director of Bureau of Law Enforcement: J. RICHARD FAGAN; Phone: 717-787-5743
Director of Bureau of Wildlife Management: CALVIN W. DuBROCK; Phone: 717-787-5529
Editor, Pennsylvania Game News: ROBERT C. MITCHELL; Phone: 717-787-3745
Legislative Liaison: WILLIAM D. SCHULTZ; Phone: 717-783-1076
Norhtcentral Regional Director: HENRY G. STANKEWICH; Phone: 717-398-4744
Northeast Regional Director: BARRY L. WARNER; Phone: 717-675-1143
Northwest Regional Director: HOWARD L. HARSHAW; Phone: 814-432-3187
Southcentral Regional Director: WILLIS A. SNEATH; Phone: 814-643-1831
Southeast Regional Director: BARRY K. MOORE; Phone: 610-926-3136
Southwest Regional Director: HARRY E. RICHARDS; Phone: 412-238-9523

Publication(s): *Pennsylvania Game News*
Keyword(s): Hunting, Public Lands, Trapping, Wildlife and Wildlife Habitat, Wildlife Management

PENNSYLVANIA COOPERATIVE FISH AND WILDLIFE RESEARCH UNIT

Merkle Bldg., Pennsylvania State University, University Park, PA 16802
Phone: 814-865-4511

Founded: 1938
Description: Established as a cooperative activity among Pennsylvania State University, Pennsylvania Fish and Boat Commission, Wildlife Management Institute, Pennsylvania Game Commission, and the Department of the Interior. Areas of research are: The effects of natural and manmade forces on aquatic and terrestrial ecosystems, animal-habitat interactions, acid precipitation effects, fish and wildlife management, and health profiles of game animals. Graduate training is also provided.
Contact(s):
Associate Leader of Wildlife: DR. GERALD L. STORM
Leader: DR. ROBERT F. CARLINE
Publication(s): *Annual Report available on request.*

PENNSYLVANIA DEPARTMENT OF AGRICULTURE

2301 N. Cameron St., Harrisburg, PA 17110-9408
Phone: 717-787-4737

Founded: 1895
Description: The Department of Agriculture was established as an administrative agency of the Executive Department of the Commonwealth. The Secretary of Agriculture is charged with "encouraging and promoting agriculture and related industries throughout the Commonwealth." The Department's mission is accomplished through three major programs: Consumer protection, property protection, and agribusiness development. Three deputies help determine policy, program development, and overall administration. The department provides a full range of services to farmers and consumers from Harrisburg through seven regional offices located around the state.
Contact(s):
Agricultural Development Bureau: CARL MULLER; Phone: 717-783-8460
Comptroller: ROSS E. STARNER; Phone: 717-772-7000
Deputy Secretary of Marketing of Promotion of and Program Services: RUSSELL C. REDDING; Phone: 717-787-3418
Deputy Secretary of Regulatory Programs: CHRISTIAN R. HERR; Phone: 717-787-4626
Deputy Secretary, Administrator: DR. ZOANN PARKER; Phone: 717-783-6985
Director of Administrative Services Bureau: ROBERT KORBONITS; Phone: 717-787-4854
Director of Animal Health and Diagnostic Service: MAX A. VANBUSKIRK, JR.; Phone: 717-783-6677
Director of Dog Law Enforcement Bureau: RICHARD HESS; Phone: 717-787-4833
Director of Farmland Protection Bureau: RAY PICKERING; Phone: 717-783-3167
Director of Food Safety Bureau: LEROY C. CORBIN; Phone: 717-787-4315
Director of Government Donated Food Bureau: BARRY SHUTT; Phone: 717-787-2940
Director of Market Development Bureau: WARREN MATHIAS; Phone: 717-787-6041
Director of Pennsylvania Agricultural Statistics Service: WALLACE EVANS; Phone: 717-787-3904
Director of Pennsylvania State Farm Show Bureau: DENNIS GRUMBINE; Phone: 717-787-5373
Director of Plant Industry Bureau: LYLE FORER; Phone: 717-787-4843
Director of Race Horse Testing Laboratory: DR. CORNELIUS E. UBOH; Phone: 610-436-3501
Director of Ride and Measurement Standards Bureau: CHARLES BRUCKNER; Phone: 717-787-6772
Director of Veterinary Diagnostic Laboratory: DR. FRED ROMMEL; Phone: 717-787-8808
Executive Assistant: ALLEN KIFER; Phone: 717-705-2122
Executive Secretary of Pennsylvania Harness Racing Commission: RICHARD SHARBAUGH; Phone: 717-787-5196
Executive Secretary of Pennsylvania Horse Racing Commission: BEN NOLT; Phone: 717-787-1942
Legal Counsel: GERALD OSBURN; Phone: 717-787-8744
Legal Office Staff: GERALD T. OSBURN; Phone: 717-787-8744
Office of Legislation: GWEN BOWER; Phone: 717-772-2854
Office of Policy: MARY BENDER; Phone: 717-783-2058
Press Office Staff: SALLY BAIR; Phone: 717-787-5085
Press Secretary: SALLY BAIR; Phone: 717-787-5085
Secretary of Agriculture: SAMUEL E. HAYES JR.; Phone: 717-772-2853

Publication(s): *Agriculture News*
Keyword(s): Agriculture, Flowers, Plants, and Trees, Land Preservation, Pesticides, Public Health Protection

Region I
R.D. 2, Box 825C, Meadville, PA
Phone: 814-332-6890
Contact(s):
Director: GEORGE GREGG

Region II
2130 County Farm Rd., Suite 2, Montowsville, PA 17754-9605
Phone: 717-433-2640
Contact(s):
Director: J. WAYNE YORKS

Region III
Rt. 92 South, Tunkhannock, PA 18657
Phone: 717-836-2181
Contact(s):
Director: RUSSELL GUNTON

Region IV
5349 William Flynn Hwy., Gibsonia, PA 15044
Phone: 412-443-1585
Contact(s):
Director: R. EDWIN NEHRIG

Region V
615 Howard Ave., Altoona, PA 16601
Phone: 814-946-7315
Contact(s):
Director: KENNETH MOWRY

STATE AND PROVINCE GOVERNMENT AGENCIES - PUERTO RICO

Region VI
P.O. Box 419, Summerdale, PA 17093
Phone: 717-787-3400
Contact(s):
Director: CAROLYN RUTTER

Region VII
Rt. 113, Creamery, PA 19420
Phone: 610-489-1003
Contact(s):
Director: FRANK STEARNS

State Conservation Commission
2301 N. Cameron St., Harrisburg, PA 17110
Phone: 717-787-8821
Founded: 1945
Description: To establish policy for Pennsylvania's 66 local conservation districts. Programs administered by the commission include: a $2,850,000 annual grant program, which provides funds to conservation districts for the employment of managerial and technical staff; a $5.2 million annual Chesapeake Bay Program, which provides technical and financial assistance to farmers to install soil conservation and nutrient management practices, and a $4,000,000 annual grant program; which provides funds to local municipalities for the maintenance of dirt and gravel roads.
Contact(s):
Chairman: JAMES M. SELF
Executive Secretary: KARL G. BROWN; Fax: 717-705-3778; Email: brown@pda.pa.state.us
Keyword(s): Agriculture, Environmental and Conservation Education, Soil Conservation

PENNSYLVANIA DEPARTMENT OF CONSERVATION AND NATURAL RESOURCES
P.O. Box 8767, Harrisburg, PA 17105-8767
Phone: 717-787-2869; Fax: 717-772-9106; WWW: www.dcnr.state.pa.us
Founded: 1995
Description: To maintain and preserve state parks; to manage state forest lands to assure their long-term health, sustainability and economic use; to provide information on Pennsylvania's ecological and geologic resources; and to administer grant and technical assistance programs that will benefit river conservation, trails and greenways, local recreation, regional heritage conservation and environmental education programs across Pennsylvania.
Contact(s):
Secretary: JOHN C. OLIVER
Publication(s): *Resource; PA State Park Recreation Guide; Penn's Woods; Become a Conservation Volunteer, Discover DCNR*
Keyword(s): Biodiversity, Conservation of Protected Areas, Environmental and Conservation Education, Forest Management, Land Preservation, Natural Areas, State Parks

PENNSYLVANIA FOREST STEWARDSHIP PROGRAM
DCNR, Bureau of Forestry, P.O. Box 8552, Harrisburg, PA 17105-8552
Phone: 717-787-2106
Founded: 1990
Description: To educate Pennsylvania forest landowners and citizens about the importance of sound forest management and the need to conserve our forest resources for future generations through wise use today. Works in conjunction with the Stewardship Incentive Program, which provides cost-share assistance to landowner's forest management practices.
Contact(s):
Director: DR. JAMES GRACE
Program Coordinator: GENE ODATO
Publication(s): *Forest Stewardship Bulletin Series (forest management information) for landowners: Pennsylvania Forest Stewardship-Our Link to the Past, Our Legacy for the Future; Sources of Information and Guidance for Forest Stewards; Teaching Youth About Forest Stewa*
Keyword(s): Biodiversity, Forests and Forestry, Sustainable Ecosystems, Water Resources, Wildlife and Wildlife Habitat

PENNSYLVANIA STATE EXTENSION SERVICES
201 Agricultural Administration Bldg., Pennsylvania State University, University Park, PA 16802-2600
Phone: 814-865-2541
Contact(s):
Associate Director of Extension: DR. DIANE V. BROWN, 217 Agricultural Administration Bldg., Pennsylvania State University, UniversityPark, PA 16802-2600; Phone: 814-863-3438
Interim Dean and Director of Extension: DR. THEODORE R. ALTER
Pesticides Coordinator: DR. WINAND K. HOCK, 114 Buckhout Laboratory, Pennsylvania State University, UniversityPark, PA 16802; Phone: 814-863-0263
Wildlife Resource Specialist: DR. MARGARET BRITTINGHAM, 320 Forest Resources Lab., Pennsylvania State University, UniversityPark, PA 16802; Phone: 814-863-8442

PUERTO RICO

GOVERNOR OF PUERTO RICO, PEDRO J. ROSSELLO
La Fortaleza, P.O. Box 82, SanJuan, PR 00901
Phone: 809-721-7000

COMITE DESPERTAR CIDRENO
Box 123, Cidra, PR 00739
Phone: 787-739-5492
Founded: 1987
Description: Primarily devoted to educate and organize communities in the east-central part of the island to deal with water pollution and wildlife habitat. Also deals with toxic waste problems.
Contact(s):
President: ELIEZER COLON RIVERO
Secretary: ROSA N. GUZMAN
Treasurer: JUANITA GARCIA
Publication(s): *Despertar Cidreno*
Keyword(s): Air Quality and Pollution, Endangered and Threatened Species, Environment, Lakes, Urban Environment

PUERTO RICO DEPARTMENT OF AGRICULTURE
Box 10163, Santurce, PR 00908-1163
Phone: 809-721-2120; Fax: 809-722-0291
Contact(s):
Executive Secretary: TEDDY MERCADO GALINDO

PUERTO RICO DEPARTMENT OF NATURAL AND ENVIRONMENTAL RESOURCES
P.O. Box 5887, Puerta de Tierra Sta., San Juan, PR 00906
Phone: 809-724-8774/809; Fax: 723-3090
Founded: 1973
Description: To develop, protect, manage, evaluate, and administer the natural resources of Puerto Rico; and to derive maximum public benefits.
Contact(s):
Secretary: PEDRO A. GELABERT; Phone: 809-723-3090
Keyword(s): Biodiversity, Environmental and Conservation Education, Fisheries, Forests and Forestry, Land Purchase

PUERTO RICO SEA GRANT PROGRAM
Marine Education Program, A. ORTIZ-SOTOMAYOR, Coordinator, Marine Education Center, Humacao University College, HUC Station, Humacao, PR 00791-4300
Phone: 787-850-9360; Fax: 787-850-0710
Founded: 1985
Description: Promote marine education activities among pre-college teachers and students. Faciliate interdisciplinary teaching and learning experience using the marine environment as a resource.

Contact(s):
Director of UPR Sea Grant College Program: DR. MANUEL VALDEZ-PIZZINI
Keyword(s): Aquatic Habitats, Biodiversity, Coasts, Coral Reefs, EcoAction, Endangered and Threatened Species, Environmental and Conservation Education, Fisheries, Geology, Islands, Mangrove Habitats, Marine Mammals, Natural Areas, Oceanography

PUERTO RICO STATE EXTENSION SERVICES
Puerto Rico Agricultural Extension Service, College Station, Mayaguez, PR 00681
Phone: 809-832-4040/Ext. 2181; Fax: 809-832-4220
Founded: 1934
Description: The Cooperative Extension Service helps people improve their lives through an educational process that uses scientific knowledge focused on issues and needs. It is a dynamic, ever-changing organization pledged to meet the country's needs for research, knowlege, and educational programs that will enable people to make practical decisions that can improve their lives.
Contact(s):
Associate Dean and Subdirector: PEDRO RODRIGUEZ, University of Puerto Rico, Mayaguez, PR 00681
Dean and Director: JOHN FERNANDEZ-VANCLEUS, University of Puerto Rico, Mayaguez, PR 00681; Phone: 809-832-4040/Ext.2181
Specialist Agricultural Programs: RAFAEL OLMEDA
Specialist of i/c 4-H Clubs and Youth: MARIA M. GAJIGAS
Specialist of i/c CRD Program: EMILIO VARGAS
Specialist of i/c Home Economics and Nutrition: GLORIA M. TORRES
Publication(s): *Related to Agriculture, Home Economics, Leadership, and Community Development*
Keyword(s): Agriculture, Environmental and Conservation Education, Health and Nutrition, Soil Conservation, Youth Organizations

SOIL CONSERVATION COMMITTEE OF PUERTO RICO
P.O. Box 10163, Santurce, PR 00908
Phone: 787-725-3040
Contact(s):
Executive Secretary: TEDDY MERCADO; Phone: 787-725-3040; Fax: 787-721-7350
Secretary of Agriculture: DR. MIGUEL MUNOZ; Phone: 787-721-2120; Fax: 787-722-2283

RHODE ISLAND

GOVERNOR OF RHODE ISLAND, LINCOLN ALMOND
222 State House, Providence, RI 02903
Phone: 401-277-2080

DEPARTMENT OF ENVIRONMENTAL MANAGEMENT (RHODE ISLAND)
235 Promenade St., Providence, RI 02908
Phone: 401-277-2774
Description: The Department of Environmental Management's top priorities include the preservation and protection of the environmental quality of Rhode Island. Air pollution, water pollution, and waste disposal problems are handled by the DEM. The DEM develops, administers, and enforces programs designed to preserve and manage Rhode Island's forests, parks, farms, wildlife, fisheries, and coastline. DEM is also responsible for providing, on the average, 750 full-time jobs for the people of Rhode Island.
Contact(s):
Director: ANDREW H. McLEOD, 235 Promenade St., Providence, RI 02908; Phone: 401-277-2771
Assistant Director of Water Resources: ALICIA M. GOOD, 235 Promenade St., Providence, RI 02908; Phone: 401-277-3961
Associate Director of Bureau of Environmental Protection: JAMES FESTER, 235 Promenade St., Providence, RI 02908; Phone: 401-277-2234
Associate Director of Bureau of Natural Resources: MALCOLM J. GRANT, 235 Promenade St., Providence, RI 02908; Phone: 401-277-6605
Associate Director of Bureau of Policy and Administration: FREDERICK J. VINCENT, 235 Promenade St., Providence, RI 02908; Phone: 401-277-2776
Associate Director of Bureau of Regualtions: EDWARD S. SZYMANSKI, 235 Promenade St., Providence, RI 02908; Phone: 401-277-3961
Chief Hearing Officer of Administrative Adjudication: KATHLEEN LANPHEAR, 235 Promenade, Providence, RI 02908; Phone: 401-277-1357
Chief of Agriculture: STEPHEN VOLPE, 83 Park St., Providence, RI 02903; Phone: 401-277-2781
Chief of Air Resources: STEPHEN MAJKUT, 235 Promenade St., Providence, RI 02908; Phone: 401-277-2808
Chief of Coastal Resources: JAMES T. BEATTIE, 83 Park St., Providence, RI 02903; Phone: 401-277-3429
Chief of Criminal Investigation Office: MARTIN A. CAPPELLI, 235 Promenade St., Providence, RI 02908; Phone: 401-277-6768
Chief of Enforcement: STEPHEN HALL, 83 Park St., Providence, RI 02903; Phone: 401-277-2284
Chief of Fish and Wildlife: JOHN STOLGITIS, Stedman Government Center, Wakefield, RI 02879; Phone: 401-277-3075
Chief of Forest Environment: THOMAS DUPREE, R.F.D. #2 Box 851, NorthScituate, RI 02859; Phone: 401-277-1414
Chief of Groundwater and Administrator, Permitting: RUSSELL J. CHATEAUNEUF, 235 Promenade St., Providence, RI 02908; Phone: 401-277-2306
Chief of Management Services: GELNN MILLER, 235 Promenade St., Providence, RI 02908; Phone: 401-277-6825
Chief of Office of Human Resources: MELANIE MOURADJIAN, 235 Promenade St., Providence, RI 02908; Phone: 401-277-2774
Chief of Parks and Recreation: LARRY MOURADJIAN, 2321 Hartford Ave., Johnston, RI 02919; Phone: 401-277-2632
Chief of Planning and Development: ROBERT SUTTON, 235 Promenade St., Providence, RI 02908; Phone: 401-277-2776
Chief of Strategic Planning and Policy: JANET KELLER, 235 Promenade St., Providence, RI 02908; Phone: 401-277-3434
Chief of Technical and Customer Assistance: RONALD GAGNON, 291 Promenade St., Providence, RI 02908; Phone: 401-277-2797
Chief of Waste Management: TERRENCE GRAY, 235 Promenade St., Providence, RI 02908; Phone: 401-277-2797
Chief of Watershed and Standards: SUSAN BUNDY, 235 Promenade St., Providence, RI 02908
Compliance and Inspection: DEAN ALBRO, 235 Promenade St., Providence, RI 02908; Phone: 401-277-6820

DEPARTMENT OF TRANSPORTATION (RHODE ISLAND)
Two Capitol Hill, Providence, RI 02903
Phone: 401-277-2481
Description: To provide a safe, efficient, effective, and environmentally responsible intermodal transportation system that supports economic development and improves our quality of life.
Contact(s):
Director: WILLIAM F. BUNDY
Keyword(s): Engineering, Transportation

RHODE ISLAND COOPERATIVE EXTENSION
Office of Director, University of Rhode Island, Kingston, RI 02881-0804
Phone: 401-874-2900; Fax: 401-874-2259
Contact(s):
Director: MARICA A. MORREIRA
Keyword(s): Agriculture, Pesticides, Water Pollution Management, Water Resources, Wetlands

STATE AND PROVINCE GOVERNMENT AGENCIES - SOUTH CAROLINA

RHODE ISLAND STATE CONSERVATION COMMITTEE
Chair, Sosnowski Farm, P.O. Box 722, W. Kingston, RI 02892
Contact(s):
Chair: HON. SUSNA. SOSNOWSKI, Sosnowski Farm, P.O. Box 722, W. Kington, RI 02892; Phone: 401-783-7704; Email: senmike@uriacc.uri.edu

STATE WATER RESOURCES BOARD (RHODE ISLAND)
265 Melrose St., Providence, RI 02907
Phone: 401-277-2217; Fax: 401-277-4707
Founded: 1967
Description: The Water Resources Board is the key agency in water-supply planning, financing, regulation, and development. The Board also plans for the future water needs of cities and towns.
Contact(s):
Chairman: DANIEL SCHATZ
General Manager and Secretary and Treasurer: M. PAUL SAMS
Vice Chairman: MAURICE TRUDEAU
Publication(s): *RI Public Water Supply; RI Fish and Wildlife; RI Industrial Water; RI Legal and Legislative Aspects of Water Supply*
Keyword(s): Land Use Planning, Public Health Protection, Renewable Resources, Water Quality, Water Resources

SOUTH CAROLINA

GOVERNOR OF SOUTH CAROLINA, JIM HODGES
P.O. Box 11369, Columbia, SC 29211
Phone: 803-734-9818
Keyword(s): Agriculture, Environmental Law, Forests and Forestry, Rivers, Wetlands

DEPARTMENT OF INTERIOR, U.S.G.S/B.R.D, SOUTH CAROLINA COOPERATIVE FISH AND WILDLIFE RESEARCH UNIT
G27 Lehotsky Hall, Clemson University, Clemson, SC 29634
Phone: 864-656-0168
Founded: 1988
Description: The Unit conducts ecological research of importance to its cooperators, i.e., the Department of Interior, Clemson University, and the state of South Carolina. Its mission also involves training of graduate students in fish and wildlife biology and related fields.
Contact(s):
Assistant Leader of Fisheries: J. JEFFREY ISELY
Assistant Leader of Wildlife: CRAIG R. ALLEN
Unit Leader: DAVID L. OTIS
Keyword(s): Birds, Endangered and Threatened Species, Fisheries, Hunting, Landscape Ecology, Nongame Wildlife, Research, Sport Fishing, Wetlands, Wildlife and Wildlife Habitat, Wildlife Management

DEPARTMENT OF PARKS, RECREATION, AND TOURISM
Edgar A. Brown Bldg., 1205 Pendleton St., Columbia, SC 29201
Phone: 803-734-0122
Contact(s):
Director: WILLIAM R. JENNINGS
Director of Business Development Office: ANN KIRKLEY
Director of Film Office: ISABEL HILL
Director of Finance Office: MANDY KIBLER
Director of Heritage Areas Tourism Development Office: CURT COTTLE
Director of Human Resource Management Office: ROGER DEATON
Director of International Marketing Office: ROBERT G. LIMING
Director of Office of Recreation, Planning, and Engineering: BETH McCLURE
Director of State Park Service: CHARLES W. HARRISON
Director of Tourism Sales Office: AMY DUFFY

FORESTRY COMMISSION (SOUTH CAROLINA)
Box 21707, Columbia, SC 29221-1707
Phone: 803-896-8800; Email: jrich@forestry.statesc.us
Founded: 1927
Description: Provides basic forest fire protection on all state and private forest lands in South Carolina; assists landowners in proper management and utilization of forest lands; promotes forest fire prevention and other forestry practices through an information and education program; and operates forest tree nursery, seed orchards, and state forests.
Contact(s):
Coastal Regional Forester: BILL BOYKIN; Phone: 803-538-3708
Commission Chairman: LAWRENCE J. BLOOMER, 404 Huntington Rd., Easley, SC 29642-1941; Phone: 803-859-3434
Commission Vice Chairman: ED MUCKENFUSS, P.O. Box 1950, Summerville, SC 29484; Phone: 803-871-5000
Deputy State Forester: WRAY FREEMAN; Phone: 803-896-8832
Director of Administration Division: JOE RICHBOURG; Phone: 803-896-8858
Director of Field Operations Support: TIM ADAMS; Phone: 803-896-8802
Executive Assistant to State Forester: JUDY J. WESTON; Phone: 803-896-8875
Pee Dee Regional Forester: STEVE SCOTT; Phone: 803-662-5571
Piedmont Regional Forester: CHARLES RAMSEY; Phone: 803-276-0205
State Forester: J. HUGH RYAN; Phone: 803-896-8800
Technical Assistant to the State Forester: C. DEAN CARSON; Phone: 803-896-8822
Keyword(s): Environmental and Conservation Education, Forests and Forestry, Rural Development, Urban Forestry, Wetlands

SAVANNAH RIVER ECOLOGY LABORATORY
University of Georgia, P.O. Drawer E, Aiken, SC 29802-1030
Phone: 803-725-2473; Fax: 803-725-3309; Email: Gibbons@srel.edu
Founded: 1951
Description: Learning and communicating ecological processes and principles is the mission of the University of Georgia's Savannah River Ecology Laboratory. The Lab accomplishes its mission through research, outreach and education, and service. Research is conducted in wetlands ecology, wildlife ecology and toxicology, and biogeochemical ecology, including radioecology. Outreach and education activities reach more than 120,000 people annually in Georgia and South Carolina.
Contact(s):
Director: DR. MICHAEL SMITH
Outreach and Education Director: DR. WHIT GIBBONS
Public Relations: ROSEMARY FORREST
Publication(s): *Forty Years and Beyond; SREL General Brochure; Snakes of Georgia and South Carolina; complete list of scientific reprints available upon request.*
Keyword(s): Biodiversity, Chemistry, Environmental and Conservation Education, Wetlands, Wildlife and Wildlife Habitat

SOUTH CAROLINA DEPARTMENT OF AGRICULTURE
Wade Hampton Office Bldg., P.O. Box 11280, Columbia, SC 29211
Phone: 803-734-2210
Founded: 1904
Description: Administers more than 30 state laws relating to agriculture and the consumer. Represents the farmer in national, regional, and state policy matters and is involved in local and international programs of commodity promotion. Enforces regulatory programs affecting the consumer on a statewide basis.
Contact(s):
Administrative Manager: DANIEL P. BREAZEALE SR.
Assistant Commissioner of Consumer Services: CAROL FULMER
Assistant Commissioner of Executive Affairs: DAVID L. TOMPKINS
Assistant Commissioner of Laboratory Services: WILLIAM BROOKS
Commissioner: D. LESLIE TINDAL
Director of Agribusiness Development: LARRY BOYLESTON
Director of Market Services: DICK JESSE

Director of Marketing and Promotions: WAYNE MACK
Director of Public Information: BECKY J. WALTON
Editor: HENRY W. SMITH
Executive Assistant to the Commissioner: KAY RIKE
Publication(s): *South Carolina Market, The*
Keyword(s): Agriculture, Chemistry, Gardening and Horticulture, Wetlands

SOUTH CAROLINA DEPARTMENT OF HEALTH AND ENVIRONMENTAL CONTROL
J. Marion Sims Bldg., 2600 Bull St., Columbia, SC 29201
Contact(s):
Bureau of Air Quality: JAMES A. JOY III; Phone: 803-734-4750
Commissioner: DOUGLAS E. BRYANT; Phone: 803-734-4880
Deputy Commissioner of Environmental Quality Control Office: R. LEWIS SHAW; Phone: 803-734-5360
Publication(s): *A General Guide to Environmental Permitting in South Carolina*
Keyword(s): Air Quality and Pollution, Public Health Protection, Solid Waste Management, Toxic Substances, Water Resources

Office of Ocean and Coastal Resource Management (OCRM)
Suite 400, 1362 McMillan Avenue, Charleston, SC 29405
Phone: 803-744-5838; Fax: 803-744-5847
Description: OCRM is a division of South Carolina's Department of Health and Environmental Control. OCRM has the dual responsibility of protecting the coastal environment while promoting responsible development within the eight coastal counties.
Contact(s):
Bureau Chief: CHRISTOPHER L. BROOKS
Director of Permitting: STEVE MOORE
Director of Planning: STEVE SNYDER
Publication(s): *Carolina Currents; Legislature Update*
Keyword(s): Coasts, Environmental Law, Environmental Planning, Environmental Preservation, Wetlands

SOUTH CAROLINA DEPARTMENT OF NATURAL RESOURCES
Rembert C. Dennis Bldg., P.O. Box 167, Columbia, SC 29202
Phone: 803-734-3888
Founded: 1994
Description: The Department was created by Act 181 of 1993 to provide for the conservation, management, utilization, and protection of the state's natural resources. It also administers the state's Heritage Trust Program for significant natural areas and historical sites. Five state agencies combined July 1, 1994, to form the SC Dept. of Natural Resources: the former Wildlife and Marine Resources Dept.; SC Geological Survey; Migratory Waterfowl Committee; and the non-regulatory portions of the Water Resources Commission, and the Land Resources Conservation Commission.
Contact(s):
Director: DR. PAUL A. SANDIFER; Phone: 803-734-4007
Associate Director: CARY D. CHAMBLEE; Phone: 803-734-9102
Board Chairman: GEORGE G. GRAHAM, Spartanburg, SC ; Phone: 864-585-1964
Deputy Director of Administrative Services Division: JOHN B. REEVES; Phone: 803-734-3883
Deputy Director of Conservation Education and Communications Division: PRESCOTT S. BAINES; Phone: 803-734-3948
Deputy Director of Land, Water and Conservation Division: ALFRED H. VANG, 1201 Main St., Suite 1100, Columbia, SC 29201; Phone: 803-737-0800
Deputy Director of Marine Resources Division: JOHN V. MIGLARESE, P.O. Box 12559, Charleston, SC 29422-2559; Phone: 843-762-5000
Deputy Director of Natural Resources Enforcement Division: COL. ALVIN WRIGHT; Phone: 803-734-4021
Deputy Director of Wildlife and Freshwater Fisheries Division: W. BROCK CONRAD, 803-734-3889
Director Emeritus: DR. JAMES A. TIMMERMAN JR.; Phone: 803-798-2858
Publication(s): *South Carolina Wildlife; Resource, The; South Carolina Geology; South Carolina Weekly Climate Summary*
Keyword(s): Endangered and Threatened Species, Fisheries, Hunting, Natural Areas, Wildlife Management

SOUTH CAROLINA ENERGY OFFICE
1201 Main St., Suite 820, Columbia, SC 29201
Phone: 803-737-8030; Fax: 803-737-9846; WWW: www.state.sc.us/energy/
Description: The SC Energy Office is responsible for the statewide promotion of energy conservation and cost effective use of new energy sources.
Contact(s):
Director: MITCH PERKINS
Public Information Coordinator: RENEE DAGGERHART; Email: rdaggerhart@gsl.state.sc.us/energy
Publication(s): *Energy Connection Newsletter, The; $aving Money in Your Manufactured Home Through Energy Efficiency--A Guide for South Carolinians; How to Reduce Your Energy Costs--A Guide for Business, Industry, Government, and Institutions; Twelve Easy Ways to Save Energy at Home; The Energy Factbook; Rebuilding Your Flooded Home: Guidelines for Incorporating Energy Efficiency (Note: This book is a great reference in any disaster, not just a flood. A must for homeowners.)*
Keyword(s): Energy, Renewable Resources, Solar Energy, Solid Waste, Transportation

SOUTH CAROLINA SEA GRANT CONSORTIUM
287 Meeting St., Charleston, SC 29401
Phone: 843-727-2078; Fax: 843-727-2080
Description: A Universtiy-based state agency that supports research, education and outreach to conserve coastal and marine reserves and provide economic oppurtunities for the cities of South Carolina and the region.
Contact(s):
Chairman: JAMES A. TIMMERMAN, S.C. Department of Natural Resources
Assistant Director: ELAINE KNIGHT; Email: knightel@musc.edu
Executive Director: M. RICHARD DEVOE; Email: devoemr@musc.edu
Director of Communications: LINDA BLACKWELL; Email: blackwlj@musc.edu
SGEP Coordinator: BOB BACON; Email: baconrh@musc.edu
Publication(s): *Coastal Heritage; Inside SeaGrant; extension materials; marine education publications and slide presentations; aquaculture handbooks; coastal hazard information.*
Keyword(s): Fisheries, Oceanography, Sustainable Development, Sustainable Ecosystems, Wetlands

SOUTH CAROLINA STATE EXTENSION SERVICES
Clemson University, Clemson, SC 29634-0310
Phone: 864-656-3382
Contact(s):
Assistant Director of School of Natural Resources: DR. ALLEN DUNN, 102 Barre Hall, Clemson University, Clemson, SC 29634; Phone: 864-656-3215; Email: ADUNN@clemson.edu
Director of Extension Service: DANIEL B. SMITH, 103 Barre Hall, Clemson University, Clemson, SC 29634-0310; Phone: 864-656-3382; Email: DBSMITH@Clemson.edu
Extension Entomologist: DR. P. M. HORTON, 111 Long Hall, Clemson University, Clemson, SC 29634-0365; Phone: 864-656-3113; Email: CSHLTS@clemson.edu
Extension Fish and Wildlife Specialist: DR. GREG YARROW; Phone: 864-656-7370; Email: GYARROW@clemson.edu
Extension Fish and Wildlife Specialist: JOHN R. SWEENEY, Department Head of Aquaculture, Fisheries, and Wildlife, Lehotsky Hall, Clemson University, Clemson, SC 29634-0362; Phone: 864-656-3117; Email: SWEEN@clemson.edu
Extension Forester: DR. LARRY NELSON, 272-E Lehotsky Hall, Clemson University, Clemson, SC 29634-1003; Phone: 864-656-4866; Email: LNELSON@clemson.edu

STATE AND PROVINCE GOVERNMENT AGENCIES - SOUTH DAKOTA

SOUTH DAKOTA

GOVERNOR OF SOUTH DAKOTA, WILLIAM J. JANKLOW
500 E. Capitol, Pierre, SD 57501
Phone: 605-773-3212

BOARD OF MINERALS AND ENVIRONMENT
Department of Environment and Natural Resources, 523 E. Capitol Avenue, Pierre, SD 57501
Founded: 1981
Description: The Board of Minerals and Environment promulgates rules and issues permits in the areas of air quality, solid waste, hazardous waste, mineral exploration and mining, and oil and gas exploration and production.
Contact(s):
Secretary of the Department: NETTIE H. MYERS; Phone: 605-773-5559

DEPARTMENT OF ENVIRONMENT AND NATURAL RESOURCES (SOUTH DAKOTA)
523 E. Capitol, Joe Foss Office Bldg., Pierre, SD 57501
Phone: 605-773-3151; Fax: 605-773-6035
Description: To provide environmental and natural resources assessment, financial assistance, and regulation in a customer service orientated manner which provides protection of public health, conservation of natural resources, preservation of the environment, and promotes development.
Contact(s):
Secretary: NETTIE H. MYERS
Director of Division of Environmental Services: STEVE PIRNER; Phone: 605-773-3153
Director of Division of Financial and Technical Assistance: DAVID TEMPLETON; Phone: 605-773-4216
Keyword(s): Air Quality and Pollution, Chemical Pollution Control, Environment, Environmental Protection, Grants, Lakes, Mining, Solid Waste, Solid Waste Management, Toxic Substances, Water Pollution, Water Quality, Water Resources, Watersheds

SOUTH DAKOTA COOPERATIVE FISH AND WILDLIFE RESEARCH UNIT (USDI)
Department of Wildlife and Fisheries Sciences, South Dakota State University, Brookings, SD 57007
Phone: 605-688-6121; Fax: 605-688-4515; Email: Longielj@mg.sdstate.edu
Description: Conducts fish and wildlife research and provides training for fishery and wildlife biologists. Cooperating Agents: South Dakota Department of Game, Fish and Parks, South Dakota State University, U.S. Geological Survey, U.S.D.I., Wildlife Management Institute.
Contact(s):
Assistant Leader of Wildlife: KENNETH F. HIGGINS
Leader: CHARLES R. BERRY JR.
Publication(s): *Annual Report*
Keyword(s): Endangered and Threatened Species, Fisheries, Prairies, Rivers, Wetlands

SOUTH DAKOTA DEPARTMENT OF AGRICULTURE
523 E. Capitol, Foss Bldg., Pierre, SD 57501-3182
Phone: 605-773-3375
Contact(s):
Secretary: DARRELL CRUEA
State Forester: RAYMOND A. SOWERS; Phone: 605-773-3623

Division of Resource Conservation and Forestry
523 E. Capitol Ave., Pierre, SD 57501-3182
Contact(s):
Director: RAYMON SOWERS; Phone: 605-773-3623

State Conservation Commission
523 E. Capitol Ave., Pierre, SD 57501-3182
Phone: 605-773-3623
Contact(s):
Chairman: BILL KEIRY

SOUTH DAKOTA GAME, FISH, AND PARKS DEPARTMENT
523 East Capitol, Pierre, SD 57501-3182
Phone: 605-773-3387
Contact(s):
Secretary: JOHN COOPER; Phone: 605-773-3387
Boating and Hunting Safety: WILLIAM SHATTUCK; Phone: 605-773-4506
Communications Manager: AL BAHE; Phone: 605-773-3485
Director of Administration Division: KEN ANDERSON; Phone: 605-773-3396
Director of Custer State Park Division: ROLLIE NOEM; Phone: 605-255-4515
Director of Parks and Recreation Division: DOUG HOFER; Phone: 605-773-3391
Director of Wildlife Division: DOUG HANSEN; Phone: 605-773-3381
Editor: BRUCE COONROD; Phone: 605-773-3485
Federal Aid Manager: WAYNE WINTER; Phone: 605-773-6228
Operations Assistant Director of Wildlife Division: EMMETT KEYSER; Phone: 605-773-4607
Specialist of Enforcement: RONALD CATLIN; Phone: 605-773-4505
Specialist of Environmental Review: JOHN KIRK; Phone: 605-773-4501
Specialist of Game: RON FOWLER; Phone: 605-773-4193
Specialist of Habitat: DAVE McGUIGAN; Phone: 605-773-4194
Staff Specialist of Fisheries: DENNIS UNKENHOLZ; Phone: 605-773-4508
Technical Services Assistant Director of Wildlife Division: GEORGE VANDEL; Phone: 605-773-4192
Turn in Poachers (TIPs) Training Coordinator: ROBERT SCHUURMANS; Phone: 605-773-5906
Publication(s): *South Dakota Conservation Digest*
Keyword(s): Aquatic Habitats, Fisheries, Outdoor Recreation, Terrestrial Habitats, Wildlife and Wildlife Habitat

SOUTH DAKOTA STATE EXTENSION SERVICES
South Dakota State University, AgH, P.O. Box 2207D, Brookings, SD 57007
Phone: 605-688-4792
Contact(s):
Extension Range Management Specialist: JAMES R. JOHNSON, West River Ag Center, South Dakota State University, 1905 Paza Blvd., Rapid City, SD 55702-9302; Phone: 605-394-2236
Interim Director of Extension: LARRY J. TIDEMAN
Range Management Extension Assistant: SCOTT KRONBERG, Animal & Range Sciences Dept., P.O. Box 2170, South Dakota State University, Brookings, SD 57007; Phone: 605-688-5412
Range Management Specialist: PATRICIA S. JOHNSON, West River Ag Center, South Dakota State University, 1905 Plaza Blvd., Rapid City, SD 57702-9302
Keyword(s): Agriculture, Environmental and Conservation Education, Pesticides, Renewable Resources, Water Resources

TENNESSEE

GOVERNOR OF TENNESSEE, DON SUNDQUIST
State Capitol, 1st Fl., Nashville, TN 37423-0001
Phone: 615-741-2001

DEPARTMENT OF ENVIRONMENT AND CONSERVATION (TENNESSEE)
401 Church St., Nashville, TN 37243
Phone: 615-532-0109
Description: To plan, promote, protect, and conserve this state's natural, cultural, recreational, and historical resources, and to enforce environmental laws and regulations which protect the state's land and water.
Contact(s):
Commissioner: MILTON H. HAMILTON JR.; Phone: 615-532-0109
Director of Air Pollution Control: JOHN WALTON; Phone: 615-532-0554

STATE AND PROVINCE GOVERNMENT AGENCIES - TEXAS

Director of Construction Grants and Loans: RON GRAHAM; Phone: 615-532-0445
Director of Geology: RON ZURAWSKI; Phone: 615-532-1500
Director of Groundwater Protection: KENT TAYLOR; Phone: 615-532-0762
Director of Historical Commission: HERBERT HARPER; Phone: 615-532-1550
Director of Indian Affairs: LUVENIA BUTLER
Director of Land Reclamation: TIM EAGLE; Phone: 615-594-6203
Director of Natural Heritage Division: REGGIE REEVES; Phone: 615-532-0434
Director of Pollution Prevention: ANGELA PITCOCK; Phone: 615-532-0760
Director of Radiological Health: MIKE MOBLEY; Phone: 615-532-0364
Director of Real Property Management: BOB WARD
Director of Recreation Services: JOYCE HOYLE; Phone: 615-742-6521
Director of Solid Waste Assistance: PAUL EVAN DAVIS; Phone: 615-532-0091
Director of Solid Waste Management: TOM TIESLER; Phone: 615-532-0780
Director of Superfund: JIM HAYNES; Phone: 615-532-0900
Director of Underground Storage Tanks: CHUCK HEAD; Phone: 615-532-0945
Director of Water Pollution Control: PAUL DAVIS; Phone: 615-532-0625
Director of Water Supply: DAVID DRAUGHON; Phone: 615-532-0191
State Archaeologist of Archaeology Division: NICK FIELDER; Phone: 615-741-1588

TENNESSEE COOPERATIVE FISHERY RESEARCH UNIT (USDI)
Tennessee Technological University, Box 5114, Cookeville, TN 38505
Phone: 615-372-3032/3094
Contact(s):
Leader (Acting): DR. JAMES B. LAYZER

TENNESSEE DEPARTMENT OF AGRICULTURE
P.O. Box 40627, Melrose Station, Ellington Agricultural Center, Nashville, TN 37204
Phone: 615-360-0103
Contact(s):
Commissioner: DAN WHEELER

State Soil Conservation Committee
Ellington Agriculture Center, P.O. Box 40627, Nashville, TN 37204
Phone: 615-360-0108
Contact(s):
Chair: BARRY LAKE, P.O. Box 107, Hickory Valley, TN 38042; Phone: 901-764-2909
Executive Secretary: JIM NANCE; Phone: 615-360-0108
Keyword(s): Agriculture, Environmental and Conservation Education, Pollution Prevention, Soil Conservation, Water Quality

TENNESSEE STATE EXTENSION SERVICES
Agricultural Extension Service, University of Tennessee, P.O. Box 1071, Knoxville, TN 37901-1071
Phone: 423-974-7114
Contact(s):
Dean of Extension Service: DR. BILLY G. HICKS
General Fish and Wildlife Specialist: DR. THOMAS K. HILL, Forestry, Wildlife & Fisheries, Agricultural Extension Service, P.O. Box 1071, University of Tennessee, Knoxville, TN 37901-1071; Phone: 423-974-7164; Fax: 423-974-4714
General Wildlife Specialist: DR. CRAIG HARPER, Forestry, Wildlife, & Fisheries, P.O. Box 1071, Knoxville, TN 37901; Phone: 423-974-7346; Fax: 423-974-4714
Professor and Head: DR. GEORGE M. HOPPER, Department of Forestry, Wildlife and Fisheries, P.O. Box 1071, Agricultural Extension Service, University of Tennessee, Knoxville, TN 37901-1071; Phone: 423-974-7126; Fax: 423-974-4714

WILDLIFE RESOURCES AGENCY
P.O. Box 40747, Ellington Agricultural Center, Nashville, TN 37204
Phone: 615-781-6500
Founded: 1949
Description: Created to have full and exclusive jurisdiction of the duties and functions relating to wildlife and boating and to the management, protection, propagation, and conservation of wildlife, including hunting and fishing.
Contact(s):
Executive Director: GARY T. MYERS; Phone: 615-781-6552
Assistant Director of Field Operations: RON FOX; Phone: 615-781-6557
Assistant Director of Staff Operations: ALLEN S. GEBHARDT; Phone: 615-781-6555
Chief of Administrative Services Division: KEN TARKINGTON; Phone: 615-781-6512
Chief of Boating Division: ED CARTER; Phone: 615-781-6682
Chief of Engineering Division: LES HAUN; Phone: 615-781-6545
Chief of Environmental Division: DAVID McKINNEY; Phone: 615-781-6643
Chief of Fish Management Division: BILL REEVES; Phone: 615-781-6575
Chief of Information & Education: DAVE WOODWARD; Phone: 615-781-6502
Chief of Law Enforcement Division: BOB HARMON; Phone: 615-781-6580
Chief of Management Systems: LOY FULFORD; Phone: 615-781-6528
Chief of Personnel: JIM DILLARD; Phone: 615-781-6594
Chief of Planning and Federal Aid: CLIFTON J. WHITEHEAD; Phone: 615-781-6599
Chief of Real Estate and Forestry Division: JOHN GREGORY; Phone: 615-781-6560
Chief of Wildlife Management Division: LARRY MARCUM; Phone: 615-781-6610
Commission Chairman: CURTIS KING
Commission Vice Chairman: JOHN SMOLKO
Editor: DAVE WOODWARD; Phone: 615-781-6502
Education Supervisor: NORMAN BATES; Phone: 615-781-6538
Manager of Nongame/Endangered Species: BOB HATCHER; Phone: 615-781-6670
Regional Manager of Cumberland Plateau: REID TATUM; Phone: 615-484-9571
Regional Manager of East Tennessee: BOB RIPLEY; Phone: 615-587-7037
Regional Manager of Middle Tennessee: STEVE PATRICK; Phone: 615-781-6622
Regional Manager of West Tennessee: HAROLD HURST; Phone: 901-423-5725
Staff Attorney: BROOKS GARLAND; Phone: 615-781-6606
Publication(s): *Tennessee Wildlife*
Keyword(s): Endangered and Threatened Species, Hunting, Nongame Wildlife, Sport Fishing, Wildlife Management

TEXAS

GOVERNOR OF TEXAS, GEORGE W. BUSH
P.O. Box 12428, Austin, TX 78711
Phone: 512-463-2000

AGRICULTURAL EXTENSION SERVICE
Texas A&M University, College Station, TX 77843-7101
Phone: 409-845-7967
Contact(s):
Associate Department Head and Extension Program Leader: DR. C. WAYNE HANSELKA, Rangeland Ecology and Management,

STATE AND PROVINCE GOVERNMENT AGENCIES - TEXAS

Rt. 2 Box 589, CorpusChristi, TX 78406-9704; Phone: Fax-512-265-9434; Email: C-hanselka@tamu.edu
Associate Department Head and Extension Program Leader: DR. DONNY W. STEINBACH, Department of Wildlife and Fisheries Sciences, Texas A&M University, CollegeStation, TX 77843; Phone: 409-845-7471; Fax: 409-845-7103; Email: d-steinbach@tamu.edu
Associate Department Head and Extension Program Leader: ALAN D. DREESEN, Department of Forest Science, 4390 FM 1488, Conroe, TX 77384-3905; Phone: 409-273-2120; Fax: 409-273-5233; Email: a-dreesen@tamu.edu
Associate Director for Agriculture Sciences: DR. B. L. HARRIS, Texas A&M University, CollegeStation, TX 77843-7101; Phone: 409-862-3932; Email: b-harris4@tamu.edu
Director of Extension Service: EDWARD A. HILER
Head of Forest Science Department: BOB MERRIFIELD, Texas A&M University, CollegeStation, TX 77843; Phone: 409-845-5000; Fax: 409-845-6049
Head of Rangeland Ecology and Management Department: DR. BOB WHITSON, Texas A&M University, CollegeStation, TX 77843; Phone: 409-845-5579; Fax: 409-845-6430; Email: R-Whitson@tamu.edu
Head of Recreation and Parks Department: DR. PETER A. WITT, Texas A&M University, CollegeStation, TX 77843-2261; Phone: 409-845-7324; Fax: 409-845-0871; Email: P-witt@tamu.edu
Head of Wildlife and Fisheries Sciences: DR. BOB BROWN, Texas A&M University, CollegeStation, TX 77843; Phone: 409-845-5777; Fax: 409-845-3786; Email: rdbrown@tamu.edu
Keyword(s): Agriculture, Environmental and Conservation Education, Forests and Forestry, Renewable Resources, Sustainable Development

BUREAU OF ECONOMIC GEOLOGY
University of Texas at Austin, University Station, Box X, Austin, TX 78713-7508
Phone: 512-471-1534
Founded: 1909
Description: Functions as a state geological survey. Program includes basic research; application of geology to resources, conservation, and engineering problems; and publication of varied reports and maps. Maintains an extensive environmental mapping program.
Contact(s):
Director: N. TYLER
Associate Director for Administration: D. C. RATCLIFF
Publication(s): *Publications, University of Texas Report of Investigations; geological circulars; special publications; environmental geologic atlases; Geological Atlas of Texas; geological quadrangle maps; guidebooks; handbooks; annual reports; mineral resource circula*
Keyword(s): Energy, Geology, Water Resources

FOREST SERVICE (Texas)
301 Tarrow, Suite 364, College Station, TX 77840
Phone: 409-845-2601
Founded: 1915
Description: To encourage and aid private landowners to practice multiple-use forestry; to protect private forest land against wildfire, insects, and diseases; and to inform the public of the contribution that forests make. Member of The Texas A&M University System.
Contact(s):
Assistant Director: TOM G. BOGGUS
Director: JAMES B. HULL
Associate Director of Forest Resource Development: EDWIN H. BARRON; Phone: 409-845-2641
Associate Director of Forest Resources Protection: BOBBY R. YOUNG; Phone: 409-639-8100
Head of Forest Products Department: I. DEWAYNE WELDON; Phone: 409-639-8180
Regional Forester of Northern Region: ERNEST H. SMITH, P.O. Box 3527, Longview, TX 75606-3527; Phone: 409-875-4400
Regional Forester of Southern Region: WILLIAM E. OATES, 1825 Sycamore, Huntsville, TX 77340; Phone: 409-564-9276
Regional Forester of West Texas: ROBERT F. FEWIN, Rt. 3 Box 216, Lubbock, TX 79401; Phone: 806-746-5801
Keyword(s): Flowers, Plants, and Trees, Forest Management, Forests and Forestry, Public Lands, Renewable Resources, Urban Forestry, Water Quality

GUADALUPE-BLANCO RIVER AUTHORITY
933 East Court, Seguin, TX 78155
Phone: 830-379-5822; Fax: 830-379-9718
Founded: 1935
Description: Responsibility to develop, conserve, and protect the water resources within its ten county service area and to aid in the prevention of soil erosion and flooding. Actively engaged in water supply, irrigation, hydroelectric power generation, water and wastewater treatment, and outdoor recreation operations.
Contact(s):
Chief Engineer: THOMAS D. HILL
Deputy General Manager: FRED BLUMBERG
Director of Accounting and Finance: ALVIN SCHUERG
Director of Administration and Economic Development: JAMES L. COOKSEY
Director of Project Development: DAVID WELSCH
Director of Water Quality: JAMES E. ARNST
General Manager: W. E. WEST JR.
Manager of Hydro Operations: LARRY MOLTZ
Manager of Utility Operations: JOHN SMITH
Manager of Water Resources Operations: BRYAN SEROLD

TEXAS COOPERATIVE FISH AND WILDLIFE RESEARCH UNIT
Texas Tech. University, Lubbock, TX 79409-2120
Phone: 806-742-2851; Fax: 806-742-2946; Email: nparksa@ttu.edu; WWW: www.teru.ttu.edu/teru
Founded: 1988
Description: To conduct research, train graduate students, and provide technical assistance in the maintenance and management of fish and wildlife biodiversity, wetland ecology, molecular (genetic) biology, aquatic and wildlife ecology, general and reproductive physiology, and fish culture using the technical expertise of three federal staff members and collaborators.
Contact(s):
Assistant Unit Leader of Fisheries: REYNALDO PATINO
Unit Leader: NICK C. PARKER
Keyword(s): Agriculture, Biodiversity, Biotechnology, Environment, Fisheries

TEXAS DEPARTMENT OF AGRICULTURE
P.O. Box 12847, Austin, TX 78711
Phone: 512-463-7476; Fax: 512-463-1104; WWW: www.agr.state.tx.us
Founded: 1904
Description: Our mission is to make Texas the nation's leader in agriculture while providing efficient and extraordinary service.
Contact(s):
Assistant Commissioner of Administrative Services: DIANE SMITH
Assistant Commissioner of Marketing and Agribusiness Development: MATT BROCKMAN
Assistant Commissioner of Communications: GENE ACUNA
Assistant Commissioner of Field Operations: DANNY PRESNAL
Assistant Commissioner of Human Resources: SARA JO SNODGRASS
Assistant Commissioner of Pesticide Division: DONNIE DIPPEL
Assistant Commissioner of Regulatory Division: WALDO MORGAN
Commissioner: RICK PERRY
Deputy Commissioner: LARRY SOWARD
Special Assistant of Producer Relations: KATIE DICKIE

TEXAS DEPARTMENT OF HEALTH
1100 W. 49th St., Austin, TX 78756
Phone: 512-458-7111
Founded: 1879
Description: Created to protect and promote the health of the people of Texas.

Contact(s):
Associate Commissioner (Acting) of Environmental and Consumer Health Protection: JOE FULLER; Phone: 512-458-7541
Chief of Bureau of Environmental Health (P.E.): JOHN JACOBI; Phone: 512-834-6640
Commissioner of Health: DR. WILLIAM R. ARCHER
Director of Shellfish Sanitation Control Division: RICHARD E. THOMPSON; Phone: 512-458-7510

Keyword(s): Health and Nutrition, Nuclear/Radiation, Toxic Substances, Toxicology

TEXAS GENERAL LAND OFFICE
Stephen F. Austin State Office Bldg., 1700 N. Congress Ave., Austin, TX 78701-1495

Description: Serves as the custodian of approximately 20.5 million acres of state-owned land including 4.25 million acres of submerged coastal land. Responsibilities include: administering state land sales, trades, and leases; issuing land patents; protecting state land from unlawful use; ensuring compliance for mining claims, gas and oil leases, pipeline easements, coastal easements, and various other permits; managing special projects which protect the state's natural resources, including public beaches; administering the Texas Coastal Management Program; and providing the public with information pertaining to the state's land resources.

Contact(s):
Commissioner: DAVID DEWHURST; Phone: 512-463-5256

Keyword(s): Coasts, Public Lands

TEXAS PARKS AND WILDLIFE DEPARTMENT
4200 Smith School Rd., Austin, TX 78744
Phone: 512-389-4800; WWW: **Description:** The agency manages and conserves natural and cultural resources of Texas for the use and enjoyment of future generations.

Contact(s):
Executive Director: ANDREW SANSOM; Phone: 512-389-4802
Chief Financial Officer: JAYNA BURGDORF; Phone: 512-389-4420
Chief of Staff: GENE McCORTY; Phone: 512-389-4651
Chief Operating Officer: ROBERT L. COOK; Phone: 512-389-4976
Commission Chairman: LEE M. BASS
Commission Vice Chairman: RICHARD HEATH
Director of Communications: LYDIA SALDANA; Phone: 512-389-4994
Director of Human Resources: ANNETTE DOMINGUEZ; Phone: 512-389-4809
Director of Infrastructure: DAN PATTON; Phone: 512-389-4995
Director of Inland Fisheries: PHIL DUROCHER; Phone: 512-389-8110
Director of Law Enforcement: JIM ROBERTSON; Phone: 512-389-4845
Director of Resource Protection: LARRY McKINNEY; Phone: 512-389-4864
Director of Wildlife: GARY GRAHM; Phone: 512-389-4971
Editor: SUSAN EBERT; Phone: 512-912-7000
Media and News Coordinator: TOM HARVEY; Phone: 512-389-4453

Publication(s): *Texas Parks and Wildlife Magazine*

TEXAS SEA GRANT PROGRAM
Sea Grant College Program, ROBERT R. STICKNEY, Texas A&M University, 1716 Briarcrest, S-702, Bryan, TX 77802
Phone: 409-845-3854; Fax: 409-845-7525; Email: stickne@unix.tamu.edu

Contact(s):
Director: ROBERT R. STICKNEY, Texas A&M University, 1716 Briarcrest 702, Bryan, TX 77802; Phone: 409-845-3854; Fax: 409-845-7525
Associate Director, Head and Editor: AMY BROUSSARD, Marine Information Service, Texas A&M University, 1716 Briarcrest, S-602, Bryan, TX 77802; Phone: 409-862-3769
Editor: JIM HINEY
Program Coordinator and Deputy Director: MIKE HIGHTOWER, Marine Advisory Program, 1716 Briarcrest, S-702, Bryan, TX 77802; Phone: 409-845-7524

Publication(s): *Texas Shores; Marine Education*

Keyword(s): Agriculture, Aquatic Habitats, Biology, Coasts, Communications, Conservation of Protected Areas, Coral Reefs, Ecology, Endangered and Threatened Species, Environment, Environmental and Conservation Education, Environmental Ethics, Environmental Law, Environmental Planning, Environmental Preservation

TEXAS STATE SOIL AND WATER CONSERVATION BOARD
P.O. Box 658, Temple, TX 76503
Phone: 817-773-2250

Description: The Texas State Soil and Water Conservation Board is a state agency established to administer and carry out Texas' soil and water conservation law. The Board is charged with the responsibility of administering and coordinating Texas' soil and water conservation program with the state's 216 local soil and water conservation districts. The Board is also the agency responsible for planning, implementing, and managing programs and practices for abating agricultural and silvicultural nonpoint source pollution within Texas.

Contact(s):
Executive Director: ROBERT G. BUCKLEY, 101 S. Main St., Temple, TX 76501-7682; Fax: 254-773-3311

Keyword(s): Agriculture, Environmental and Conservation Education, Renewable Resources, Soil Conservation, Water Resources

TEXAS WATER DEVELOPMENT BOARD
1700 N. Congress, Austin, TX 78701
Phone: 512-463-7847

Founded: 1957

Description: Texas Water Development Board provides loans to local governments for water supply projects; water quality projects, including wastewater treatment, municipal solid waste management, and nonpoint source pollution control; agricultural water conservation projects; and flood control projects. Provides water related research and planning and agricultural water conservation funding.

Contact(s):
Chairman: WILLIAM B. MADDEN
Border Project Management Division: FERNANDO ESCARCEGA; Phone: 512-475-2070
Deputy Executive Administrator for Office of Project Finance and Construction Assistance: J. KEVIN WARD; Phone: 512-463-0991
Deputy Executive Administrator for Planning: TOMMY KNOWLES; Phone: 512-463-8043
Director of Water Resources Information: RODDY SEEKINS; Phone: 512-463-8043
Executive Administrator: CRAIG D. PEDERSEN; Phone: 512-463-7850
General Counsel: SUZANNE SCHWARTZ; Phone: 512-463-7981
Northern Project Management Division: GEORGE GREEN; Phone: 512-463-7853
Special Assistant for Intergovernmental and External Customer Relations: LEONARD OLSON; Phone: 512-463-7931
Texas Natural Resource Information System: CHARLES PALMER; Phone: 512-475-8402
Vice Chairman: NOE FERNANDEZ

Publication(s): *Water For Texas - Today and Tomorrow; Texas Water Facts; ground water reports since 1957; bay and estuary reports since 1967*

Keyword(s): Aquatic Habitats, Environmental and Conservation Education, Planning Management, Rivers, Water Resources

UTAH

GOVERNOR OF UTAH, MIKE LEAVITT
210 State Capitol, SaltLakeCity, UT 84114
Phone: 801-538-1500

UTAH COOPERATIVE FISH AND WILDLIFE RESEARCH UNIT (USDI-USGS-BRD-CRU)
College of Natural Resources, Utah State University, Logan, UT 84322-5210
Phone: 435-797-2509/2509
Founded: 1935 (Wildlife), 1962 (Fisheries), 1985 (combined)
Description: The unit conducts research and training in all aspects of fishery and wildlife biology and management.
Contact(s):
Assistant Leader of Fisheries: DR. DAVID BEAUCHAMP; Phone: 435-797-2509
Assistant Leader of Wildlife: DR. THOMAS C. EDWARDS, JR.; Phone: 435-797-2509
Financial Assistant: BRYAN MEACHAM; Phone: 435-797-2558
Leader: DR. JOHN A. BISSONETTE; Phone: 435-797-2511
Keyword(s): Aquatic Habitats, Biodiversity, Birds, Ecology, Endangered and Threatened Species, Fisheries, Landscape Analysis, Mammals, Nongame Wildlife, Predators, Renewable Resources, Sport Fishing, Terrestrial Habitats, Wildlife and Wildlife Habitat

UTAH DEPARTMENT OF AGRICULTURE
350 N. Redwood Rd., Salt Lake City, UT 84116
Phone: 801-538-7100; Fax: 801-538-7126
Contact(s):
Commissioner: MILES FERRY
Deputy Commissioner: VAN BURGESS
Director of Administrative Services: RENEE MATSUURA
Director of Marketing: RANDY PARKER
Director of Plant Industry: G. RICHARD WILSON
Information Officer: EL SHAFFER
Staff of Agricultural Development and Conservation: JAMES CHRISTENSEN
Staff of Food and Dairy: KYLE STEPHENS
Staff of Weights and State Chemist: AHMAD SALARI
State Veterinarian: DR. MICHAEL MARSHALL

UTAH DEPARTMENT OF HEALTH
P.O. Box 16700, Salt Lake City, UT 84116-0700
Phone: 801-538-6111
Contact(s):
Department of Health Public Information Officer: ROSS MARTIN; Phone: 801-538-6339
Interim Executive Director: ROD BETIT
Keyword(s): Biotechnology, Health and Nutrition, Public Health Protection, Toxic Substances, Toxicology

UTAH STATE DEPARTMENT OF NATURAL RESOURCES
1594 W. North Temple, Suite 3710, P.O. Box 145610, Salt Lake City, UT 84114-5610
Phone: 801-538-7200; Fax: 801-538-7315
Contact(s):
Deputy Director: MARTY OH
Deputy Director: HOWARD RIGTRUP
Executive Director: KATHLEEN CLARKE
Legislative and Public Affairs Administrator: DOTTI BROCKBANK

Division of Forestry, Fire and State Lands
1594 W. North Temple, Suite 3520, P.O. Box 145703, Salt Lake City, UT 84114-5703
Phone: 801-538-5555; Fax: 801-533-4111
Description: Legislation enacted July 1994 dissolved the Division and Board of State Lands and Forestry and created the Division of Sovereign Lands and Forestry, and the Sovereign Lands and Forestry Advisory Council. Division and council names were legislatively changed to Division of Forestry, Fire and State Lands and Forestry, Fire and State Lands Advisory Council in July 1995.
Contact(s):
State Forester and Director: ARTHUR W. DUFAULT
Strategic Planner: KARL KAPPE

Division of Oil, Gas and Mining
1594 W. North Temple, Suite 1210, P.O. Box 145801, Salt Lake City, UT 84114-5801
Phone: 801-538-5340; Fax: 801-359-3940
Contact(s):
Acting Director: LOWELL BRAXTON

Division of Parks and Recreation
1594 W. North Temple, Suite 116, P.O. Box 146001, Salt Lake City, UT 84114-6001
Phone: 801-538-7220; Fax: 801-538-7378
Contact(s):
Deputy Director: MARY TULIUS
Deputy Director: DAVE MORROW
Director: COURTLAND NELSON
Boating Coordinator: TED WOOLLEY
Park Operations Coordinator: JAY CHRISTIANSON; Phone: 801-538-7220
Regional Manager of Northeast: DENNIS WEAVER; Phone: 801-533-5127
Regional Manager of Northwest: JIM HARLAND; Phone: 801-533-5127
Regional Manager of Southeast: MAX JENSEN; Phone: 435-259-8151
Regional Manager of Southwest: GORDON TOPHAM; Phone: 435-586-4497

Division of Water Rights
1594 W. North Temple, Suite 220, P.O. Box 146300, Salt Lake City, UT 84114-6300
Phone: 801-538-7240; Fax: 801-538-7240
Contact(s):
Assistant State Engineer: JERRY OLDS
Assistant State Engineer: KENT JONES
Assistant State Engineer: LEE H. SIM
Assistant State Engineer: RICHARD HALL
State Engineer and Director: ROBERT L. MORGAN

Division of Wildlife Resources
1594 W. North Temple, Suite 2110, P.O. Box 146301, Salt Lake City, UT 84114-6301
Phone: 801-538-4700; Fax: 801-538-4709
Contact(s):
Assistant Director: RALPH MILES
Assistant Director: KEVIN CONWAY
Chair: BRENDA FREEMAN
Director: JOHN KIMBALL
Board Member: MAX G. MORGAN
Board Member: J. COLIN ALLAN
Board Member: CONNIE BROOKS
Board Member: B. CURTIS DASTRUP
Board Member: RICK E. DANVIR
Board Member: RAYMOND V. HEATON

Office of Energy and Resource Planning
1594 W. North Temple, Suite 3610, P.O. Box 146480, Salt Lake City, UT 84114-6480
Phone: 801-538-5428; Fax: 801-521-0657
Contact(s):
Director: JEFFREY S. BURKS

Regional Supervisors
Contact(s):
Central Region: JORDAN PEDERSEN, 1115 N. Main Street, Springville, UT 84663; Phone: 435-489-5678; Fax: 435-7000
Northeast Region: WALT DONALDSON, 152 E. 100 North, Vernal, UT 84078; Phone: 435-789-3103; Fax: 435-789-8343
Northern Region: ROBERT HASENYAGER, 515 E. 5300 South, Ogden, UT 84405; Phone: 435-476-2740; Fax: 435-479-4010

Southeastern Region: MILES MORETTI, 475 W. Price River Dr., Ste C, Price, UT 84501; Phone: 435-636-0260; Fax: 435-637-7361
Southern Region: JIM GUYMON, P.O. Box 606, Cedar City, UT 84721; Phone: 435-865-6100; Fax: 435-586-2457

State Soil Conservation Committee
1594 W. North Temple, Suite 3110, P.O. Box 146100, Salt Lake City, UT 84114-6100
Phone: 801-537-3300; Fax: 801-537-3400
Contact(s):
State Geologist and Director: DR. M. LEE ALLISON

UTAH STATE DEPARTMENT OF NATURAL RESOURCES, Division of Water Resources
1594 W. North Temple, Suite 310, P.O. Box 146201, Salt Lake City, UT 84114-6201
Phone: 801-538-7230; Fax: 801-538-7279
Contact(s):
Director: D. LARRY ANDERSON

UTAH STATE EXTENSION SERVICES
Utah State University, Logan, UT 84322-4900
Phone: 801-797-2201
Contact(s):
Animal Damage Management Extension Specialist: DR. ROBERT SCHMIDT, College of Natural Resources, Utah State University, Logan, UT 84322; Phone: 801-797-2459
Coordinator of Extension and Outreach Education: DR. CHARLES W. GAY, College of Natural Resources, Utah State University, Logan, UT 84322; Phone: 801-797-2445
Dean: DR. F. E. BUSTY, College of Natural Resources, Utah State University, Logan, UT 84322-5200; Phone: 801-797-2445
Director of Extension Service: DR. ROBERT L. GILLILAND
Extension Fish and Wildlife Specialist: DR. TERRY A. MESSMER, College of Natural Resources, Utah State University, Logan, UT 84322; Phone: 801-797-2459
Extension Forester: DR. MIKE KUHNS, College of Natural Resources, Utah State University, Logan, UT 84322-5215; Phone: 801-797-4056
Extension Range Specialist: DR. G. ALLEN RASMUSSEN, College of Natural Resources, Utah State University, Logan, UT 84322; Phone: 801-797-2469
Extension Range Specialist: DR. ROGER E. BANNER, College of Natural Resources, Utah State University, Logan, UT 84322-5230; Phone: 801-797-2472
Outdoor Recreation Specialist: DR. DALE BLAHNA, College of Natural Resources, Utah State University, Logan, UT 84322; Phone: 801-797-2544
Utah Geographic Alliance: DR. CLIFFORD B. CRAIG, College of Natural Resources, Utah State University, Logan, UT 84322; Phone: 801-797-1790
Water Quality Extension Specialist: NANCY MESNER, College of Natural Resources Utah State University, Logan, UT 84322; Phone: 801-797-2465
Keyword(s): Forests and Forestry, Public Lands, Renewable Resources, Water Resources, Wetlands

UTAH STATE SOIL CONSERVATION COMMISSION
350 N. Redwood Rd., Salt Lake City, UT 84116
Phone: 801-538-7120
Founded: 1938
Description: Assists Utah's 39 soil conservation districts (SCD) in encouraging land operators to implement measures and practices; to prevent soil deterioration; restore depleted soil; prevent flood damage; improve irrigation water efficiency; and to encourage nonpoint water pollution control programs. The commission has 12 members; 5 ex-officio, and 7 governor-appointed SCD members with their alternates.
Contact(s):
Chairman: MILES FERRY
Executive: K. N. JACOBSON

Keyword(s): Agriculture, Environmental and Conservation Education, Renewable Resources, Soil Conservation, Sustainable Development

VERMONT

GOVERNOR OF VERMONT, HOWARD DEAN
Pavilion Office Bldg., Montpelier, VT 05609
Phone: 802-828-3333; Fax: 802-828-3339

AGENCY OF NATURAL RESOURCES
103 S. Main St., Waterbury, VT 05671
Phone: 802-241-3600
Founded: 1970
Description: The Agency's mission is to act as a steward of Vermont's natural resources. We work to manage Vermont's natural systems and to foster public understanding so that the integrity, vitality, and diversity of these natural systems are sustained or restored.
Contact(s):
Secretary: BARBARA G. RIPLEY; Phone: 802-241-3600
Deputy Secretary: JOHN KASSEL; Phone: 802-241-3600
Director of Media and Public Relations: JAMES E. BRESSOR; Phone: 802-241-3600
Director of Planning: STEPHEN B. SEASE; Phone: 802-241-3620
Enforcement: SALVATOR SPINOSA; Phone: 802-241-3820
Executing Special Assistant: BERNARD JOHNSON; Phone: 802-241-3601
General Counsel: MARK SINCLAIR

Department of Environmental Conservation
Waterbury Complex, 10 S., Waterbury, VT 05677
Contact(s):
Commissioner: CANUTE PALMASSE; Phone: 802-241-3800
Director of Air Quality: RICHARD A. VALENTINETTI; Phone: 802-241-3840
Director of Environmental Assistance: RICHARD PHILLIPS
Director of Facilities: LARRY FITCH; Phone: 802-241-3737
Director of Waste Management: P. HOWARD FLANDERS; Phone: 802-241-3888
Director of Wastewater: MARILYN DAVIS; Phone: 802-241-3822
Director of Water Quality: WALLACE McLEAN; Phone: 802-241-3770
Director of Water Supply: JAY RUTHERFORD; Phone: 802-241-3400

Department of Fish and Wildlife
103 S. Main, 10 South, Waterbury, VT 05671-0501
Phone: 802-241-3700
Contact(s):
Business Manager: SANDY BARTON
Chair of Fish and Wildlife Board: MONTGOMERY MOORE
Commissioner: ALLEN ELSER
Director of Fisheries: TIM HESS
Director of Law Enforcement: ROGER WHITCOMB
Director of Operations: ANGELO INCERPI
Director of Wildlife: RON REGAN
Information and Education: JOHN HALL
Keyword(s): Air Quality and Pollution, Fisheries, Solid Waste Management, Water Resources

Department of Forests, Parks, and Recreation
Commissioner's Office, 103 South Main St., Waterbury, VT 05671
Phone: 802-241-3670
Contact(s):
Chief of Forest Resource Management: M. BRIAN STONE
Chief of Forest Resource Protection: H. BRENTON TEILLON
Chief of Park Operations: CRAIG WHIPPLE
Commissioner: CONRAD MOTYKA
Director of Forests: DAVID STEVENS; Phone: 802-241-3678

STATE AND PROVINCE GOVERNMENT AGENCIES - VIRGIN ISLANDS

Director of State Parks: LARRY SIMINO; Phone: 802-241-3655
State Naturalist: CHARLES JOHNSON

Environmental Board
East State St., Montpelier, VT 05602
Phone: 802-828-3309
Contact(s):
Chairman: JOHN EWING
General Counsel: GEORGE GAY

Vermont Geological Survey
103 S. Main St., Center Bldg., Waterbury, VT 05671-0301
Phone: 801-241-3496
Founded: 1844
Description: The Vermont Geological Survey encompasses two divisions. The State Geologist provides surveys of the geology, mineral resources, topography and geological information services to citizens, industry, and state and federal agencies. The Radioactive Waste Management Program manages the disposal of low-level radioactive waste generated in Vermont.
Contact(s):
State Geologist: LAWRENCE R. BECKER
Publication(s): *Price list sent upon request or visit the website.*
Keyword(s): Communications, Environmental Preservation, Geology, Nuclear/Radiation, Toxic Substances

UNIVERSITY OF VERMONT EXTENSION
601 Main St., Burlington, VT 05401-3439
Phone: 802-656-2990
Founded: 1914
Description: UVM Extension is a system of nonformal education, bringing research information in a practical form to Vermonters. Extension with the specific expertise of our state university meets the needs of agriculture, communities, families, and youth. Programs are specifically focused on natural resource conservation, sustainable agriculture and rural development, health care in rural areas, resource distribution in communities, and the contemporary stresses on the American family.
Contact(s):
Director: LAWRENCE K. FORCIER
Director of Sustainable Agriculture Center: VERN GRUBINGER; Phone: 802-257-7967
Family and Community Resource and Economic Development: LOIS FREY; Phone: 802-223-2389
Natural Resources and Environmental Management: JOHN DONNELLY; Phone: 802-656-3258
Natural Resources and Environmental Management: BOB TOWNSEND; Phone: 802-257-7967
Nutrition, Food Safety, and Health: DALE STEEN; Phone: 802-748-8177
Nutrition, Food Safety, and Health: ROBERT TYZBIR; Phone: 802-656-3374
Program Leader of Agriculture: NEIL PELSUE; Phone: 802-257-7967
Keyword(s): Acid Rain, Health and Nutrition, Research, Sustainable Development, Youth Organizations

Publications Office
Communications and Technology Resources, Agricultural Engineering Bldg., Burlington, VT 05405-0004
Phone: 802-656-0301

VERMONT DEPARTMENT OF AGRICULTURE, FOOD, AND MARKETS
116 State St., Drawer 20, Montpelier, VT 05620-2901
Phone: 802-828-2500
Founded: 1908
Contact(s):
Business Manager of Administrative Services: RUDOLPH POLLI; Phone: 802-828-3567
Commissioner: LEON C. GRAVES; Phone: 802-828-2430
Deputy Commissioner of Administration: KENNETH BECKER

Director of Plant Industry of Laboratories of and Consumer Assurance: PHILIP R. BENEDICT; Phone: 802-828-2431
State Veterinarian: DR. SAMUEL HUTCHINS; Phone: 802-828-2421
Publication(s): *Agriview; list available on request.*

Natural Resources Conservation Council
116 State St., Montpelier, VT 05620-2901
Description: The Conservation Council is the administrative body for the 14 conservation districts in Vermont. The goal of conservation districts is to ensure the wise use, protection and enhancement of Vermont soil, water, and related natural resources; to foster public awareness and appreciation of the need for conservation; and to advance the concept that we are all stewards of the living earth.
Contact(s):
Executive Secretary: JON W. ANDERSON; Phone: 802-828-3529
Chairperson: TOM BUSHY, 116 State St., Montpelier, VT 05620-2901
Keyword(s): Agriculture, Environmental and Conservation Education, Environmental Preservation, Soil Conservation, Water Pollution

State Conservation Commission
Contact(s):
Chair: THOMAS BUSHEY; Phone: 802-985-2048; Fax: 802-951-6327
Executive Secretary: JON W. ANDERSON; Phone: 802-828-3529; Fax: 802-828-2361; Email: jwa@agr.state.vt.us

VERMONT DEPARTMENT OF HEALTH
P.O. Box 70, 108 Cherry St., Burlington, VT 05402
Phone: 802-863-7280
Contact(s):
Commissioner: DR. JAN K. CARNEY; Phone: 802-863-7280
Director of Health Protection: LARRY CRIST; Phone: 802-863-7223
Keyword(s): Air Quality and Pollution, Health and Nutrition, Pesticides, Toxic Substances, Toxicology

VIRGIN ISLANDS

GOVERNOR OF THE VIRGIN ISLANDS, ROY L. SCHNEIDER
Government House, St.Thomas, VI 00801
Phone: 809-774-0001

COOPERATIVE EXTENSION SERVICE (VIRGIN ISLANDS)
University of Virgin Islands, R.R. #2, Box 100, Kingshill, St. Croix, VI 00850
Phone: 809-778-0246; Fax: 809-778-6570
Contact(s):
Coordinator, Integrated Pest Management of Pesticide Impact Assessement Program Liaison: DR. JOZEF KEULARTS
Program Leader of Agriculture and Natural Resources: CLINTON GEORGE
Vice President of Research and Land Grant Affairs and Director of CES: DR. DARSHAN S. PADDA

DEPARTMENT OF PLANNING AND NATURAL RESOURCES
Suite 231, Nisky Center, St. Thomas, VI 00803
Phone: 809-774-3320
Founded: 1970
Description: Responsible for: Fish and wildlife; trees, vegetation and water resources; air and water pollution control; flood control; sewers and sewage disposal; culture and the arts; libraries and museums; minerals and other natural resources; historical preservation; submerged lands; earth change permits; and oil spill prevention and control.
Contact(s):
Chief of Environmental Education Bureau: RALF H. BOULON JR.
Chief of Fisheries Bureau: STEPHEN MEYERS
Chief of Wildlife Bureau: DAVID NELLIS
Commissioner: BEULAH DALMIDA-SMITH
Director of Coastal Zone Management: PAUL THOMAS

Director of Environmental Enforcement Division: ROBERT DANET
Director of Environmental Protection Division: ALEXANDER MOORHEAD
Director of Fish and Wildlife Division: BARBARA KOJIS; Phone: 809-775-6762

Publication(s): *Annual Report; Zone Management Notes (CZM Notes); Blue Book; Proceedings - Fisheries in Crisis Conference (Division of Fish and Wildlife; Wildlife Plant booklet; Natural History Atlas to the Cays of the Virgin Islands; Species Technical Bulletin (Bureau*

Keyword(s): Aquatic Habitats, Birds, Endangered and Threatened Species, Environmental and Conservation Education, Mammals

Division of Fish and Wildlife
6291 Estate Nazareth, 101, St. Thomas, VI 00802
Phone: 340-775-6762; Fax: 340-775-3972
Contact(s):
Acting Director: BARBARA KOJIS; Email: bkojis@mola.uvi.edu

VIRGIN ISLANDS SOIL AND WATER CONSERVATION DIVISION
Contact(s):
Commissioner: DR. ARTHUR PETERSON; Phone: 809-778-0997

VIRGINIA

GOVERNOR OF VIRGINIA, JAMES S. GILMORE II
State Capitol, Richmond, VA 23219
Phone: 804-786-2211
Contact(s):
Deputy Secretary of Natural Resources: THOMAS L. HOPKINS; Phone: 804-786-0044
Secretary of Natural Resources: JOHN PAUL WOODLEY JR.; Phone: 804-786-0044

DEPARTMENT OF FORESTRY
P.O. Box 3758, Fontaine Research Park, 900 Natural Resources Drive, Charlottesville, VA 22903-0758
Phone: 804-977-6555; Fax: 804-296-2369
Founded: 1914
Description: The mission of the Department of Forestry is to protect and develop healthy, sustainable forest resources for Virginians. The Department assists private landowners with the management and protection of forest resources. We also provide at-cost seedlings for reforestation of the state's forestlands, and management of public state forests and other state public forest lands.
Contact(s):
Deputy State Forester: BETTINA K. RING
Fiscal Director: FAYE E. DiFAZIO
Human Resources Director: ELLIE WHINNERY
State Forester: JAMES W. GARNER
Team Leader for Forest Management: JAMES D. STARR
Team Leader for General Services: RONALD S. JENKINS
Team Leader for Information Technology: JAMES A. COPONY
Team Leader for Resource Information: TIMOTHY C. TIGNER
Team Leader for Resource Protection: GREGORY L. SANDERS

DEPARTMENT OF GAME AND INLAND FISHERIES
4010 W. Broad St., P.O. Box 11104, Richmond, VA 23230
Phone: 804-367-1000; Email: dgifweb@dgif.state.va.us; WWW: www.dgif.state.va.us
Description: To provide for the management, conservation, restoration, and enhancement of the Commonwealth's fish and wildlife resources. The department shall also provide public informational and educational services related to wildlife resource use and appreciation.
Contact(s):
Director: WILLIAM L. WOODFIN JR.; Phone: 804-367-9231; Fax: 804-367-0405; Email: bwoodfin@dgif.state.va.us
Boating Law Administrator: NANCY JAMERSON; Phone: 804-367-1189; Email: njamerson@dgif.state.va.us
Capital Outlay Program Manager: PHIL LOWNES; Phone: 804-367-1253; Email: plownes@dgif.state.va.us
Chief of Wallop-Breaux: FRED D. LECKIE; Phone: 804-367-8629; Email: fleckie@dgif.state.va.us
Director for Boating and Facilities: LARRY G. HART; Phone: 804-367-1295; Email: lhart@dgif.state.va.us
Director of Administration: RAYMOND E. DAVIS; Phone: 804-367-2387; Email: rdavis@dgif.state.va.us
Director of Boating and Resource Education: CHARLES A. SLEDD; Phone: 804-367-6481; Email: csledd@dgif.state.va.us
Director of Fisheries: GARY F. MARTEL; Phone: 804-367-0509; Email: gmartel@dgif.state.va.us
Director of Hunter Safety: TERRY BRADBERY; Phone: 804-367-8704; Email: tbradbery@dgif.state.va.us
Director of Information Management Systems: VIRGIL E. KOPF; Phone: 804-367-0787; Email: vkopf@dgif.state.va.us
Director of Planning, Policy and Public Relations: DAVID K. WHITEHURST; Phone: 804-367-4335; Email: dwhitehurst@dgif.state.va.us
Director of Wildlife: ROBERT W. DUNCAN; Phone: 804-367-9588; Email: rduncan@dgif.state.va.us
Director of Wildlife Information and Enhancement: DAVID K. WHITEHURST; Phone: 804-367-4335; Email: dwhitehurst@dgif.state.va.us
Division Director of Law Enforcement: COL. JEFFERY A. UERZ; Phone: 804-367-0776; Email: juerz@dgif.state.va.us
Editor: LEE WALKER; Email: lwalker@dgif.state.va.us
Federal Aid Coordinator: FRED D. LECKIE; Phone: 804-367-8629; Email: fleckie@dgif.state.va.us
Federal Aid Coordinator: RICK BUSCH; Phone: 804-367-1215; Email: rbusch@dgif.state.va.us
Publication(s): *Virginia Wildlife*

Region I
5806 Mooretown Rd., Williamsburg, VA 23188
Phone: 757-253-7072

Region II
910 Thomas Jefferson Road, Forest, VA 24551-9223
Phone: 804-525-7522

Region III
1796 Highway Sixteen, Marion, VA 24354
Phone: 540-783-4860

Region IV
4725 Lee Highway, Verona, VA 24482
Phone: 540-248-9360

Region V
1320 Belman Rd., Fredericksburg, VA 22401
Phone: 540-899-4169

DEPARTMENT OF MINES, MINERALS AND ENERGY
Ninth St. Office Bldg., 8th Fl., 202 N. Ninth St., Richmond, VA 23219
Phone: 804-692-3200; Fax: 804-692-3237
Founded: 1985
Description: Committed to enhancing the development and conservation of energy and mineral resources in a safe and environmentally sound manner in order to support a more productive economy in Virginia. Six operating divisions: Division of Mined Land Reclamation regulates the operation of coal surface-mining activities, enforces the reclamation laws and regulations, and administers financial resources for reclaiming abandoned coal mining sites; Division of Mineral Resources provides information on Virginia's geology, mineral resources, and physical and cultural features; Division of Mines enforces the coal mining laws of the Commonwealth to promote the safety and health of coal miners; Division of Energy promotes the efficient use and conservation of energy and the use of alternative energy sources; Division of Mineral Mining regulates the operation of noncoal mining activities for environmental protection and worker safety; Division of Gas and

STATE AND PROVINCE GOVERNMENT AGENCIES - VIRGINIA

Oil regulates the operation and reclamation of gas and oil extractions.
Contact(s):
Director: O. GENE DISHNER

Division of Energy
9th St. Office Bldg., 8th Fl., 202 9th St., Richmond, VA 23219
Contact(s):
Director: STEPHEN A. WALZ, Ninth St. Office Bldg., 8th Fl., 202 N. Ninth St., Richmond, VA 23219; Phone: 540-692-3211

Division of Gas and Oil
9th St. Office Bldg., 8th Fl., 202 N. 9th St., Richmond, VA 23219
Contact(s):
Inspector: TOM FULMER, P.O. Box 1416, Abingdon, VA 24212; Phone: 540-676-5423

Division of Mined Land Reclamation
9th St. Office Bldg., 8th Fl., 202 N. 9th St., Richmond, VA 23219
Contact(s):
Commissioner: DANNY R. BROWN, Drawer 900, BigStoneGap, VA 24219; Phone: 540-523-8100

Division of Mineral Mining
9th St. Office Bldg., 8th Fl., 202 N. 9th St., Richmond, VA 23219
Contact(s):
Director: CONRAD T. SPANGLER III, P.O. Box 3727, Charlettesville, VA 22903; Phone: 804-961-5000

Division of Mineral Resources
9th St. Office Bldg., 8th Fl., 202 N. 9th St., Richmond, VA 23219
Contact(s):
State Geologist: STANLEY S. JOHNSON, Box 3667, Charlottesville, VA 22903; Phone: 804-293-5121

DEPARTMENT OF MINES, MINERALS, AND ENERGY

Division of Mines
Contact(s):
Chief: FRANK A. LINKOUS, P.O. Drawer 900, BigStoneGap, VA 24219; Phone: 540-523-8100

MARINE RESOURCES COMMISSION (VIRGINIA)
P.O. Box 756, Newport News, VA 23607
Phone: 804-247-2200
Founded: 1875
Description: This state agency holds regulatory jurisdiction over all commercial and sports fishing, marine fish, marine shellfish, and marine organisms in the tidal waters of Virginia. Holds permit jurisdiction on all projects involving use of state-owned submerged lands and authority over use or development in vegetated and nonvegetated tidal wetlands and coastal primary sand dunes.
Contact(s):
Chief of Administration and Finance: ROBERT D. CRAFT
Chief of Conservation and Replenishment: JIM WESSON
Chief of Fisheries Management: JACK G. TRAVELSTEAD
Chief of Law Enforcement: STEVEN G. BOWMAN
Chief of Management Information Systems: ERIK J. BARTH
Chief, Habitat Management: ROBERT W. GRABB
Commissioner: WILLIAM A. PRUITT
Publication(s): *Virginia Landings Bulletin*

NORTHERN VIRGINIA REGIONAL PARK AUTHORITY
5400 Ox Rd., Fairfax Station, VA 22039
Phone: 703-352-5900; Fax: 703-273-0905
Founded: 1959
Description: To preserve open and wooded areas and provide outdoor recreation to meet the needs of a growing population.
Contact(s):
Chairman: WALTER L. MESS
Executive Director: DAVID C. HOBSON
Publication(s): *Discover Your Regional Parks; Calendar of Events; Policy Plan; Washington and Old Dominion Railroad Regional Park Trail Guide*
Keyword(s): Botanical Gardens, Environmental and Conservation Education, Environmental Preservation, Flowers, Plants, and Trees, Outdoor Recreation

VIRGINIA COOPERATIVE FISH AND WILDLIFE RESEARCH UNIT (USDI)
106 Cheatham Hall, Virginia Polytechnic Institute and State University, Blacksburg, VA 24061
Phone: 540-231-5927
Founded: 1935
Description: Founded for training graduate students in fisheries and wildlife; with teaching and extension in fisheries and wildlife biology. Cooperatively supported by the Biological Resources Division of U.S.G.S., Department of Game and Inland Fisheries, and Virginia Polytechnic Institute and State University.
Contact(s):
Assistant Leader: DR. PAUL L. ANGERMEIER; Phone: 540-231-4501
Assistant Leader: DR. MICHAEL R. VAUGHAN; Phone: 540-231-5046
Leader: DR. RICHARD J. NEVES
Publication(s): *Annual reports; journal articles; research publications.*
Keyword(s): Aquatic Habitats, Endangered and Threatened Species, Fisheries, Wildlife and Wildlife Habitat, Wildlife Management

VIRGINIA DEPARTMENT OF AGRICULTURE AND CONSUMER SERVICES
P.O. Box 1163, Richmond, VA 23209
Phone: 804-786-3501; Fax: 804-371-2945
Founded: 1877
Description: To promote the economic growth and development of Virginia agriculture, encourage environmental stewardship, and provide consumer protection. Thirteen-member board appointed by Governor.
Contact(s):
Department Commissioner: J. CARLTON COURTER III; Phone: 804-786-3501
Director of Communication: ELAINE J. LIDHOLM; Phone: 804-786-7686
Director of Policy Planning and Research: ROY E. SEWARD; Phone: 804-786-3535
Editor: ELAINE J. LIDHOLM
Manager of Pesticides Services: DR. MARVIN A. LAWSON; Phone: 804-371-6558
Publication(s): *Bulletin*
Keyword(s): Agriculture, Endangered and Threatened Species, Pesticides

VIRGINIA DEPARTMENT OF CONSERVATION AND RECREATION
203 Governor St., Suite 302, Richmond, VA 23219
Phone: 804-786-6124
Description: The Department's mission is to conserve, protect, enhance, and advocate wise use of Virginia's natural, recreational, and scenic resources in order to maintain and improve the quality of life for present and future generations. The Department is responsible for administrative support of various state collegial bodies including: The Board of Conservation and Recreation, the Virginia Cave Board, the Virginia Soil and Water Conservation Board, the Breaks Interstate Park Commission, the Conservation and Development of Public Beaches Board, Chippokes Plantation Farm Foundation, Virginia State Parks Foundation, and 17 state Scenic River Boards and Committees.

STATE AND PROVINCE GOVERNMENT AGENCIES - VIRGINIA

Contact(s):
Director: DAVID G. BRINKLEY; Phone: 804-786-2123
Administrative Staff Assistant: LINDA J. COX
Conservation & Development Programs Supervisor: LEON E. APP

Board of Conservation and Recreation
203 Governor St., Suite 302, Richmond, VA 23219
Contact(s):
Chairman: W. BRUCE WINGO, 203 Governor St., Suite 302, Richmond, VA 23219

Breaks Interstate Park Commission
203 Governor St., Suite 302, Richmond, VA 23219
Contact(s):
Chairman: JACK C. SYKES, 101 Summitt Drive, Pikesville, KY 41501; Phone: 606-432-1447
Advisor: JOSEPH ELTON

Chippokes Plantation Farm Foundation
203 Governor St., Suite 302, Richmond, VA 23209
Contact(s):
Chairman: FREDERICK M. QUAYLE, Member, Senate of Virginia, 3808 Poplar Hill Road, Chesapeake, VA 23321
Advisor: KATHERINE R. WRIGHT

Conservation and Development of Public Beaches Board
203 Governor St., Suite 302, Richmond, VA 23209
Contact(s):
Chairman: DONALD O. CAMPEN JR., 7603 Hillside Avenue, Richmond, VA 23229
Advisor: CARLTON LEE HILL

Division of Administration
203 Governor St., Suite 302, Richmond, VA 23219
Contact(s):
Director: WILLIAM E. PRICE, 203 Governor St, Suite 204, Richmond, VA 23219; Phone: 804-786-0001
Director of ADP: DONALD H. BRYNE
Director of Finance: DEBORAH COURTNEY
Director of Human Resources: RONALD G. SHOWALTER

Division of Dam Safety
203 Governor St., Suite 302, Richmond, VA 23219
Contact(s):
Director: JOSEPH S. HAUGH, 203 Governor Street, Suite 423, Richmond, VA 23219; Phone: 804-786-1369

Division of Natural Heritage
203 Governor St., Suite 302, Richmond, VA 23219
Contact(s):
Director: THOMAS L. SMITH, 217 Governor St., 3rd Floor, Richmond, VA 23219; Phone: 804-786-7951

Division of Planning and Recreation Resources
203 Governor St., Suite 302, Richmond, VA 23219

Division of Soil and Water Conservation
Contact(s):
Director: JACK E. FRYE, 203 N. Governor St., Suite 206, Richmond, VA 23219; Phone: 804-786-6523; Email: dordswc@erols.com

Division of State Parks
Contact(s):
Director: JOSEPH ELTON, 203 Governor St., Suite 306, Richmond, VA 23219; Phone: 804-786-4375

Virginia Cave Board
Contact(s):
Chairman: BILL KEITH, Rt. 1 Box 17, Cleveland, VA 24225
Advisor: LAWRENCE R. SMITH

Virginia Soil and Water Conservation Board
Contact(s):
Chairman: CHARLES E. HORN, 203 Governor St., Suite 206, Richmond, VA 23219; Phone: 804-786-2064
Advisor: JACK E. FRYE

VIRGINIA DEPARTMENT OF ENVIRONMENTAL QUALITY
629 E. Main St., P.O. Box 10009, Richmond, VA 23240-0009
Founded: 1993
Description: The Department of Environmental Quality strives to provide efficient, cost-effective services that promote a proper balance between environmental improvement and economic vitality.
Contact(s):
Director: THOMAS L. HOPKINS
Keyword(s): Air Quality and Pollution, Environment, Solid Waste Management, Water Resources

VIRGINIA DEPARTMENT OF HEALTH
Commissioner's Office, Suite 214, Main St. Station, 1500 E. Main St., Richmond, VA 23219
Phone: 804-786-3561
Founded: 1872
Description: The Department carries out protective and preventive public health services for all citizens of the Commonwealth and provides public health care services to the indigent.
Contact(s):
Deputy Commissioner of Administration: C. GEORGE TULLI JR.; Phone: 804-786-3575
Deputy Commissioner of Public Health Programs: SUZANNE E. DANDOY; Phone: 804-786-3566
Director of Division of Dental Health: JOSEPH M. DOHERTY; Phone: 804-786-3556
Director of Medical Examiner Division: DAVID K. WIECKING; Phone: 804-786-3174
Director of Water Programs Division: ERIC BARTSCH; Phone: 804-786-1760
Health Commissioner (M.D., M.P.H.): ROBERT B. STROUBE
Publication(s): *Virginia's Health*

VIRGINIA MUSEUM OF NATURAL HISTORY
1001 Douglas Ave., Martinsville, VA 24112
Phone: 540-666-8000; Fax: 540-632-6487
Founded: 1988
Description: Preserves, studies, and interprets Virginia's natural and cultural heritage. Statewide system of museum facilities, research sites, and educational programs. The museum has more than one million specimens in collections.
Contact(s):
Executive Director: STEPHEN J. PIKE, Virginia Museum of Natural History, 1001 Douglas Ave., Martinsville, VA 24112; Phone: 540-666-8600; Email: spike@ngocomm.net
Staff: DR. JUDY WINSTON, Virginia Museum of Natural History, 1001 Douglas Ave., Martinsville, VA 24112; Phone: 540-666-8609; Email: jwinston@leo.vsla.edu
Publication(s): *Virginia Explorer, The; VMNH Newsletter; Books; Scientific Publication Series; Children's Activity Books*
Keyword(s): Biodiversity, Endangered and Threatened Species, Environmental and Conservation Education, Geology, Research

VIRGINIA OUTDOORS FOUNDATION
P.O. Box 322, Aldie, VA 20105
Phone: 703-327-6118; Fax: 703-327-6444
Description: To preserve Virginia's natural scenic, historic, scientific, open space, and recreational areas by means of private philanthropy. The Foundation accepts gifts of cash, stock, real property, or open spaces easements to achieve its purpose.
Contact(s):
Chairman: PAUL G. ZILUCA
Executive Director: TAMARA VANCE; Phone: 540-951-2822
Keyword(s): Conservation of Protected Areas, Land Preservation, Open Space

STATE AND PROVINCE GOVERNMENT AGENCIES - WASHINGTON

VIRGINIA SEA GRANT PROGRAM
Virginia Graduate Marine Science Consortium, 170 Rugby Rd., Madison House, University of Virginia, Charlottesville, VA 22903
Phone: 804-924-5965
Contact(s):
Director: DR. WILLIAM L. RICKARDS
Staff of Marine Advisory Program: DR. WILLIAM DuPAUL, Virginia Institute of Marine Science, GloucesterPoint, VA 23062; Phone: 804-684-7163
Keyword(s): Aquatic Habitats, Coasts, Environmental and Conservation Education, Renewable Resources, Wetlands

VIRGINIA STATE EXTENSION SERVICES
Virginia Polytechnic Institute and State University, Blacksburg, VA 24061-0402
Phone: 540-231-5299
Contact(s):
Director of Cooperative Extension: C. CLARK JONES
Extension Aquaculture Specialist: BRIAN L. NERRIE, Virginia State University, P.O. Box 9081, Petersburg, VA 23806; Phone: 804-524-5903
Extension Fisheries Specialist: DR. LOUIS A. HELFRICH, Department of Fisheries and Wildlife Sciences, Virginia Polytechnic Institute and State University, Blacksburg, VA 24061-0321; Phone: 540-231-5059
Extension Wildlife Specialist: DR. JAMES A. PARKHURST, Department of Fisheries & Wildlife Sciences, Virginia Polytechnic Institute and State University, Blacksburg, VA 24061-0321; Phone: 540-231-9283
Extension Wildlife Specialist: DR. GERALD H. CROSS, Department of Fisheries and Wildlife Sciences, Virginia Polytechnic Institute and State University, Blacksburg, VA 24061-0321; Phone: 540-231-8844
Project Leader of Forestry and Wildlife Extension: DR. JAMES E. JOHNSON, College of Forestry and Wildlife Resources, Virginia Polytechnic Institute and State University, Blacksburg, VA 24061-0324; Phone: 540-231-7679
Sea Grant Extension Seafood Technologist: DR. GEORGE J. FLICK JR., Dept. of Food Science and Technology, Virginia Polytechnic Institute and State University, Blacksburg, VA 24061-0418; Phone: 540-231-6965

WASHINGTON

GOVERNOR OF WASHINGTON, GARY LOCKE
Legislative Bldg., Olympia, WA 98504-0002
Phone: 360-753-6780

COLUMBIA RIVER GORGE COMMISSION
P.O. Box 730, White Salmon, WA 98672
Phone: 509-493-3323; Fax: 509-493-2229
Description: Established by the states of Oregon and Washington to implement the Columbia River Gorge National Scenic Area Act by developing a regional management plan, in cooperation with the U.S. Forest Service. The commission is composed of three members from Oregon, three from Washington, and one from each of the six local Gorge counties. A Secretary of Agriculture appointee is a thirteenth nonvoting member. Purpose of the National Scenic Area Act is to protect and enhance scenic, natural, cultural, and recreation resources, while encouraging economic development within 13 established urban areas.
Contact(s):
Chairman: BOB THOMPSON
Executive Director: JONATHAN DOHERTY
Vice Chairman: ANNE SQUIER
Keyword(s): Environmental Planning, Land Use Planning, Natural Areas, Outdoor Recreation, Wildlife and Wildlife Habitat

DEPARTMENT OF ECOLOGY
P.O. Box 47600, Olympia, WA 98504-7600
Phone: 360-407-6000
Founded: 1970
Description: Charged with programs of air quality control, water pollution control, solid waste management, management of water resources, hazardous waste management, reduction, and cleanup, shoreline management, coastal zone management, and State Environmental Policy Act (SEPA).
Contact(s):
Deputy Director: DAN SILVER; Phone: 360-407-7011
Director: TOM FITZSIMMONS; Phone: 360-407-7001
Administrative Services Manager: CAROL FLESKES; Phone: 360-407-7012
Assistant Director of Legislative & Intergovernmental Relations: BILL ALKIRE; Phone: 360-407-7003
Attorney General of Office of Attorney General: JAY MANNING; Phone: 360-459-6158
Chief Financial Officer: NANCY STEVENSON; Phone: 360-407-7005
Deputy Director for Water Issues: TERRY HUSSEMAN; Phone: 360-407-7002
Librarian: BARBARA CALQUHOUN; Phone: 206-407-6152

Central Regional Office
Contact(s):
Staff: PAT SPURGIN; Phone: 509-457-7120

Eastern Regional Office
Contact(s):
Staff: TONY GROVER; Phone: 509-456-6149

Northwest Regional Office
Contact(s):
Staff: MIKE RUNDLETT; Phone: 425-649-7010

Southwest Regional Office
Contact(s):
Staff: SUE MAUERMANN; Phone: 360-407-6307

DEPARTMENT OF FISH AND WILDLIFE (WASHINGTON)
600 Capitol Way, N., Olympia, WA 98501-1091
Phone: 360-902-2200; Fax: 360-902-2947
Founded: 1933
Contact(s):
Deputy Director: DIRK BRAZIL; Phone: 360-902-2232
Director: DR. BERNARD SHANKS; Phone: 360-902-2225
Assistant Director of Administrative Services: DAVE BRITTELL; Phone: 360-902-2206
Assistant Director of Enforcement Program: RON SWATFIGURE; Phone: 360-902-2927
Assistant Director of Fish Management Program: BRUCE CRAWFORD; Phone: 360-902-2325
Assistant Director of Habitat and Lands Services Program: ELYSE KANE; Phone: 360-902-2402
Assistant Director of Wildlife Management Program: DAVE BRITTELL; Phone: 360-902-2504
Regional Director: SARA LABORDE, 48 B Devonshire Rd., Montesona, WA 98563; Phone: 206-249-6522
Regional Director: LEE VAN TUSSENBROOK, 5405 NE Hazel Dell, Vancouver, WA 98663; Phone: 206-696-6211
Regional Director: BOB EVERITT, 16018 Mill Creek Blvd., MillCreek, WA 98012; Phone: 425-775-1311
Regional Director: DALE BAMBRICK, 1701 S. 24th Ave., Yakima, WA 98902-5720; Phone: 509-575-2740
Regional Director: JEFF TAYER, 1550 Alder St., NW, Ephrata, WA 98823; Phone: 509-754-4624
Regional Director: BRUCE SMITH, 8702 N. Division St., Spokane, WA 99218; Phone: 509-456-4082
Regional Director: MIKE KUTTEL, 600 Capital Way N., Olympia, WA 98501-1091; Phone: 360-902-2804
Keyword(s): Aquatic Habitats, Endangered and Threatened Species, Hunting, Sport Fishing, Wildlife and Wildlife Habitat

STATE AND PROVINCE GOVERNMENT AGENCIES - WASHINGTON

INTERAGENCY COMMITTEE FOR OUTDOOR RECREATION (IAC)
1111 Washington St., SE, P.O. Box 40917, Olympia, WA 98504-0917
Phone: 360-902-3000
Founded: 1965
Description: IAC administers grants and technical assistance programs for public recreation, open space, and conservation projects in Washington state. The agency assists local, state, federal, and nonprofit organizations in planning, acquiring, and developing recreation resources. IAC also writes the state's outdoor recreation and open space plan, as well as plans on trails and nonhighway off-road vehicle recreation.
Contact(s):
Director: LAURA ECKERT JOHNSON; Phone: 360-902-3003
Assistant Director of Management Services: DEBRA WILHELMI; Phone: 360-902-3005
Manager of Applied Planning: GREGORY W. LOVELADY; Phone: 360-902-3008
Manager of Project Services: ERIC JOHNSON; Phone: 360-902-3015
Special Assistant to the Director: JIM FOX; Phone: 360-902-3021
Keyword(s): Environmental Preservation, Land Purchase, Land Use Planning, Outdoor Recreation, Public Lands

STATE PARKS AND RECREATION COMMISSION (WASHINGTON)
7150 Cleanwater Ln., P.O. Box 42650, Olympia, WA 98504-2650
Founded: 1912
Description: To acquire, develop, improve, and maintain state parks and recreation areas. Involvement includes but is not limited to state parks, seashore conservation, water and boating safety, snowmobile safety, and natural and historic heritage interpretation.
Contact(s):
Deputy Director: FRANK BOTELER; Phone: 360-902-8502
Director: CLEVE PINNIX; Phone: 360-902-8501
Administrator of Public Affairs: SUSAN ZEMEK; Phone: 360-902-8562
Assistant Director of Administrative Services: RITA COOPER; Phone: 360-902-8525
Assistant Director of Operations: KATHY SMITH; Phone: 360-902-8594
Assistant Director of Resources Development: LARRY FAIRLEIGH; Phone: 360-902-8642
Chief Engineer: TOM BOYER; Phone: 360-902-8616
Chief of Boating Programs: JIM FRENCH; Phone: 360-902-8515
Chief of Budget Services: BETHANY MILLER; Phone: 360-902-8532
Chief of Employee Services: JUDY JOHNSON; Phone: 360-902-8568
Chief of Environmental Coordination: BILL JOLLY; Phone: 360-902-8636
Chief of Fiscal Services: SANDY REES; Phone: 360-902-8575
Chief of Information Processing: ART BROWN; Phone: 360-902-8585
Chief of Natural Resource Management: DAN INGMAN; Phone: 360-902-8592
Chief of Parks Maintenance: PAUL GEORGE; Phone: 360-902-8540
Chief of Programs Management: JAMES HORAN; Phone: 360-902-8580
Chief of Research and Long Range Planning: WILLIAM C. JOLLY; Phone: 360-902-8641
Chief of Site Planning: BILL KOSS; Phone: 360-902-8629
Chief of Visitor Protection and Law Enforcement: BILL GANSBERG; Phone: 360-902-8598
Chief of Visitor Services: PAM McCONKEY; Phone: 360-902-8595
Contracts Specialist: WAYNE McLAUGHLIN; Phone: 360-902-8599
Legislative Liaison: REX DERR; Phone: 306-902-8504
Keyword(s): Cultural Preservation, Nature Preservation, Open Space, Outdoor Recreation, Public Lands

Eastern Region
Contact(s):
Staff (Acting): JIM HARRIS, 2201 N. Duncan Dr., Wenatchee, WA 98801; Phone: 509-662-0420

Northwest Region
Contact(s):
Staff: TERRY DORAN, P.O. Box 487, Burlington, WA 98801-1007; Phone: 360-755-9231

Puget Sound Region
Contact(s):
Staff: DON SIMMONS, 1602 29th St., SE, Auburn, WA 98002; Phone: 206-931-3907

Southwest Region
Contact(s):
Staff: PAUL MALMBERG, 11838 Tilley Rd., S., Olympia, WA 98512-9167; Phone: 360-753-7143

WASHINGTON COOPERATIVE FISH AND WILDLIFE RESEARCH UNIT (USDI)
U.S. Geological Survey, School of Fisheries, Box 357980, University of Washington, Seattle, WA 98195
Phone: 206-543-6475; Fax: 206-616-9012
Founded: 1988
Description: The goals of the WCFWRU are: (1) conduct research in support of the Department of the Interior and Washington State; (2) train graduate students in fisheries and wildlife science through research support and by teaching; and (3) disseminate research results to the scientific community, management agencies, and the general public.
Contact(s):
Assistant Leader of Wildlife: GLENN R. VanBLARICOM
Leader: CHRISTIAN E. GRUE
Keyword(s): Aquatic Habitats, Biodiversity, Fisheries, Toxicology, Wildlife and Wildlife Habitat

WASHINGTON DEPARTMENT OF AGRICULTURE
P.O. Box 42560, Olympia, WA 98504-2560
Phone: 360-902-1800; WWW: www.wa.gov/agr/contact.htm
Contact(s):
Director: JIM JESERNIG; Phone: 360-902-1801
Assistant Director of Agency Operations: BILL BROOKRESON; Phone: 360-902-1810
Assistant Director of Commodity Inspection: BOB GORE; Phone: 360-902-1827
Assistant Director of Consumer and Producer Protection Division: JULIE SANDBERG; Phone: 360-902-1850
Assistant Director of Food Safety and Animal Health Division: CANDACE JACOBS; Phone: 360-902-1888
Assistant Director of Laboratory Services: MARY M. TOOHEY; Phone: 360-902-1907
Assistant Director of Pesticide Management Division: BOB ARRINGTON; Phone: 360-902-2011
Information Officer: LINDA WARING; Phone: 360-902-1815
State Veterinarian: DR. ROBERT MEAD; Phone: 360-902-1878
Keyword(s): Agriculture, Pesticides

WASHINGTON DEPARTMENT OF NATURAL RESOURCES
P.O. Box 47001, Olympia, WA 98504-7001
Phone: 360-902-1000
Contact(s):
Deputy Commissioner: KALEEN COTTINGHAM; Phone: 360-920-1003
Deputy Supervisor: JOHN DALY; Phone: 360-902-1006
Division Manager of Forest Resources: MICHAEL PEREZ-GIBSON; Phone: 360-902-1603
Executive Assistant: MICHELLE BENTON; Phone: 360-902-1004
Manager of Agriculture Division: LOREN STERN; Phone: 360-902-1101
Manager of Aquatic Lands: MARIA PEELER; Phone: 360-902-1101

STATE AND PROVINCE GOVERNMENT AGENCIES - WASHINGTON

Manager of Employee Services: JUDY BRUNNER; Phone: 360-902-1652
Manager of Engineering: TERRY KIRKPATRICK; Phone: 206-902-1199
Manager of Financial Services: PAT McLAIN; Phone: 360-902-1240
Manager of Forest Practices: JOHN EDWARDS; Phone: 360-902-1730
Manager of Geology and Earth Resources: RAYMOND LASMANIS; Phone: 360-902-1442
Manager of Geology Library: CONNIE MANSON; Phone: 360-902-1472
Manager of Information Management: AL BLOOMBERG; Phone: 360-902-1490
Manager of Resource Protection: RANDY ACKER; Phone: 360-902-1011
Publications: DAVE WORKMAN; Phone: 360-902-1023
Publication(s): *DNR News*

Central Region
Contact(s):
Staff: HOWARD THRONSON; Phone: 360-748-2383

Northeast Region
Contact(s):
Staff: WES CULP; Phone: 509-684-7474

Northwest Region
Contact(s):
Staff: BILL WALLACE; Phone: 360-856-3500

Olympic Region
Contact(s):
Staff: TOM ROBINSON; Phone: 360-374-6131

South Puget Sound Region
Contact(s):
Staff: BONNIE BUNNING; Phone: 360-825-1631

Southeast Region
Contact(s):
Staff: BILL BOYUM; Phone: 509-925-1631

Southwest Region
Contact(s):
Staff: RICK COOPER; Phone: 360-577-2025

WASHINGTON NATURAL HERITAGE PROGRAM
Forest Resources Division, Dept. of Natural Resources, Olympia, WA 98504-7016
Phone: 360-902-1682; Fax: 360-902-1783; WWW: www.wa.gov/dnr/htdocs/fr/nhp/wanhp.html
Founded: 1978
Description: Identify and evaluate native ecosystems and species, set conservation prioities, provide information to protect these irreplaceable resources for the benefit of current and future generations.
Contact(s):
Program Manager (Acting) and Botanist: JOHN GAMON; Phone: 360-902-1661
Publication(s): *State of Washington Natural Heritage Plan; Endangered, Threatened, and Sensitive Vascular Plants of Washington with working list of Rare Non-vascular Species*
Keyword(s): Biodiversity, Botany, Zoology

WASHINGTON SEA GRANT PROGRAM
Comm. Mgr., 3716 Brooklyn Ave., NE, Seattle, WA 98105
Description: Since 1968, Washington Sea Grant Program has supported research, advisory, and communication activities for the benefit of marine resources, users, and communities. It is part of a national network of universities meeting the changing environmental and economic needs of people in our coastal and Great Lakes regions.
Contact(s):
Director: LOUIE S. ECHOLS, University of Washington, 3716 Brooklyn Ave., NE, Seattle, WA 98105; Phone: 206-543-6600
Assistant Director of Advisory Services: MICHAEL S. SPRANGER, Marine Advisory Services, University of Washington, 3716 Brooklyn Ave., NE, Seattle, WA 98105; Phone: 206-685-9261
Assitant Director: ANDREA COPPING, 3716 Brooklyn Ave., NE, Seattle, WA 98105; Phone: 206-685-8209
Communications Manager: NANCY BLANTON, 3716 Brooklyn Ave., NE, Seattle, WA 98105; Phone: 206-685-9215
Publications Coordinator/Web Master: SUSAN COOK; Phone: 206-685-2606; Fax: 206-685-0380
Senior Program Associate: MEGAN BAILIFF, 3716 Brooklyn Ave., NE, Seattle, WA 98105; Phone: 206-685-1108
Publication(s): *El Nino North: Nino Effects in the Eastern Subarctic Pacific Ocean; Ocean Ecology of North Pacific Salmonids; Guide to Manila Clam Culture in Washington; Shape and Form of Puget Sound, The*
Keyword(s): Biotechnology, Fisheries, Oceanography, Sustainable Development, Wetlands

WASHINGTON STATE CONSERVATION COMMISSION
P.O. Box 47721, Olympia, WA 98504-7721
Phone: 206-407-6200; Fax: 206-407-6215
Founded: 1939
Description: Assists, guides, and coordinates the programs of 48 conservation districts and encourages the cooperation and collaboration of the federal, state, regional, interstate, and local public agencies which assist them; keeps the public informed of renewable natural resource conservation activities.
Contact(s):
Chair: RONALD JURIS, P.O. Box 157, Bickleton, WA 98322-0157
Executive Director: STEVEN R. MEYER; Phone: 206-407-6201; Fax: 360-407-6215; Email: smey461@ecy.wa.gov
Central WA Field Representative: CHUCK BAGLEY; Phone: 509-664-3154; Fax: 509-665-3366
Eastern WA Field Representative: WILLIAM C. BROUGHTON; Phone: 509-397-4740; Fax: 509-397-4921
Grants Officer: ROBERT P. BOTTMAN; Phone: 360-407-6204
Puget Sound Field Representative: STU TREFRY; Phone: 360-407-6211
Keyword(s): Agriculture, Environmental and Conservation Education, Renewable Resources, Soil Conservation, Water Resources

WASHINGTON STATE EXTENSION SERVICES
Director,WA State U., P.O. Box 646230, Pullman, WA 99164
Description: Washington State University Cooperative Extension helps people develop leadership skills and use research-based knowledge to improve their economic status and quality of life.
Contact(s):
Associate Dean and Associate Director of Extension Services: MICHAEL J. TATE, Washington State University, P.O. Box 646230, Pullman, WA 99164-6230; Phone: 509-335-2933
Extension Forester: DAVID M. BAUMGARTNER, Department of Natural Resource Sciences, P.O. Box 646410, Washington State University, Pullman, WA 99164-6410; Phone: 509-335-2964
Extension Forester: DONALD P. HANLEY, College of Forest Resources, University of Washington, Box 352100, Seattle, WA 98195-2100; Phone: 206-685-4960
Extension Urban and Community Forestry: VAN M. BOBBITT, Washington State University, Research and Extension Center, 7612 Pioneer Way E., Puyallup, WA 98371-4998; Phone: 253-445-4547
Program Leader: PHILLIP E. CRAWFORD, Washington State University Cooperative Extension, P.O. Box 646230, Pullman, WA 99164-6230; Phone: 509-335-2885; Fax: 509-335-2926; Email: crawford@wsu.edu
Keyword(s): Agriculture, Environmental and Conservation Education, Forests and Forestry, Renewable Resources, Sustainable Ecosystems

WASHINGTON STATE OFFICE OF ENVIRONMENTAL EDUCATION
Office of Superintendent of Public Instruction, 2800 NE 200th St., Seattle, WA 98155-1418
Phone: 206-365-3893; WWW: http://cisl.ospi.wednet.edu

Description: To provide curriculum resources and training for teachers in environmental education, and to evaluate these programs pursuant to improving content and effectiveness. The office is responsible for E.E. program coordination and cooperation as it applies to K-12 public school programs and to state mandate requiring E.E. K-12.

Contact(s):
Administrative Assistant: MICHELE HALFHILL
State Supervisor of Environmental Education: TONY ANGELL

Publication(s): *Clean Water, Streams and Fish: A Holistic View of Watersheds; Energy Food & You; Puget Sound Habitats Teachers Guide and Charts; Closing the Achievement Gap: using the Environment as an Integrating Context for Learning; Tools for Understanding:focus on Environmental Education*

Keyword(s): Environmental and Conservation Education, Solid Waste Management, Sustainable Ecosystems, Water Pollution Management, Wildlife and Wildlife Habitat

WEST VIRGINIA

GOVERNOR OF WEST VIRGINIA, CECIL UNDERWOOD
State Capitol Complex, Charleston, WV 25305-0370
Phone: 304-558-2000

DIVISION OF NATURAL RESOURCES
1900 Kanawha Blvd., East, Charleston, WV 25305
Phone: 304-558-2754; Fax: 304-558-2764

Description: The Division's objective is to provide a comprehensive program for the exploration, conservation, development, protection, enjoyment, and use of the natural resources of the state of West Virginia. The West Virginia Conservation Commission, formed in 1933, was the forerunner of the Department of Natural Resources, created by the legislature in 1961 and modified to the Division of Natural Resources in 1993.

Contact(s):
Deputy Director: TONY POLITINO
Executive Secretary: HARRY F. PRICE; Phone: 304-558-3315
Director: JOHN B. RADER
Assistant Chief of Coldwater Fisheries: MICHAEL V. SHINGLETON; Phone: 304-637-0245
Assistant Chief of Game Management: PAUL R. JOHANSEN; Phone: 304-558-2771
Assistant Chief of Special Projects: DONALD P. PHARES; Phone: 304-637-0245
Assistant Chief of Warmwater Fisheries: BERT E. PIERCE; Phone: 304-558-2771
Assistant Chief, Biometrics and Planning: WALT KORDEK; Phone: 304-637-0245
Chief of Law Enforcement: JAMES D. FIELDS; Phone: 304-558-2784
Chief of Parks & Recreation: CORDIE HUDKINS; Phone: 304-558-2764
Chief of Wildlife Resources: BERNARD F. DOWLER; Phone: 304-558-2771
Conservation Education/Litter Control: EMILY J. FLEMING; Phone: 304-558-3370
Deputy Chief of Wildlife Resources: GORDON C. ROBERTSON; Phone: 304-558-2771
Deputy Chief, Law Enforcement: W. B. DANIEL; Phone: 304-558-2784
Deputy Chief, Paks and Recreation: KEN CAPLINGER; Phone: 304-558-2764
District I Commissioner: DR. CHARLES P. CAPITO, Suite #3 2619 Pennsylvania Ave., Weirton, WV 36062; Phone: 304-723-3355
District I Commissioner: JEFFREY S. BOWERS, HC 70 Box 40 A, Sugar Grove, WV 26815; Phone: 304-358-3333
District II Commissioner: CARL E. GAINER, P.O. Box 670, Richwood, WV 26261; Phone: 304-846-6247
District Ii Commissioner: CHARLES R. HOOTEN, 1570 Summit Drive, Charleston, WV 25302; Phone: 304-346-0521
District II Commissioner: CARL FRISCHKORN, 1234 Upper Ridgeway Road, Charleston, WV 25314; Phone: 304-926-9036
District II Commissioner: DR. THOMAS R. HOMAN, 1410 Bedford Rd., Charleston, Wv 25314; Phone: 304-346-3330
District III Commissioner: DR. THOMAS W. JARRETT, 203 Brookshire Lane, Beckley, WV 25801; Phone: 304-255-0549
Editor: ARNOUT HYDE JR.; Phone: 304-558-9152
Public Information Officer: HOY MURPHY; Phone: 304-558-3380
Real Estate Management: JAMES JONES; Phone: 304-558-3225; Fax: 304-558-3680

Publication(s): *Wonderful West Virginia*

Keyword(s): Aquatic Habitats, Hunting, Nongame Wildlife, Sport Fishing, Wildlife Management

WEST VIRGINIA BUREAU OF ENVIRONMENT
Division of Environmental Protection, #10, McJunkin Rd., Nitro, WV 25143-2546
Phone: 304-759-0515

Founded: 1991

Description: The Division of Environmental Protection is charged with the protection of West Virginia's environment through the regulation and administration of the state's abandoned mine lands, air quality, mining & reclamation, oil & gas, waste management, and water resources programs.

Contact(s):
Director: MICHAEL P. MIANO
Chief Communications Officer: ANDY GALLAGHER; Phone: 304-759-0515
Chief of Administration: RANDY HUFFMAN; Phone: 304-759-0515
Chief of Air Quality: JOHN JOHNSTON; Phone: 304-558-4022
Chief of Legal Services: BILL ADAMS; Phone: 304-558-9160
Chief of Mining & Reclamation: JOHN AILES; Phone: 304-759-0510
Chief of Oil & Gas: TED STREIT; Phone: 304-759-0514
Chief of Waste Management: B. F. SMITH; Phone: 304-558-5929
Chief of Water Resources: BARBARA S. TAYLOR; Phone: 304-558-2107

WEST VIRGINIA COOPERATIVE FISH AND WILDLIFE RESEARCH UNIT
Division of Forestry, West Virginia University, P.O. Box 6125, Morgantown, WV 26506-6125
Phone: 304-293-3794 ext. 2430

Description: A cooperative research and graduate education organization sponsored by the Biological Resources Division of USGS, West Virginia Division of Natural Resources, West Virginia University, and Wildlife Management Institute. The role of the unit is to conduct natural resources research of state, regional, or national scope, and to train graduate-level researchers in natural resources.

Contact(s):
Assistant Leader of Wildlife: DR. PETRA BOHALL WOOD

Keyword(s): Aquatic Habitats, Fisheries, Nongame Wildlife, Rivers, Wildlife and Wildlife Habitat

WEST VIRGINIA DEPARTMENT OF AGRICULTURE
State Capitol, Rm. M-28, Charleston, WV 25305
Phone: 304-558-3550; Fax: 304-558-0451

Contact(s):
Assistant Commissioner: JANET L. FISHER
Commissioner: GUS R. DOUGLASS
Deputy Commissioner: DAVID E. MILLER
Director of Plant Industries Division: DR. CHARLES C. COFFMAN

Keyword(s): Agriculture, Pesticides, Public Health Protection, Soil Conservation, Water Resources

West Virginia State Soil Conservation Committee
Contact(s):
Executive Director: LANCE TABOR; Phone: 304-558-2204; Fax: 304-558-1635; Email: taborl@wvlc.wvnet.edu

STATE AND PROVINCE GOVERNMENT AGENCIES - WISCONSIN

WEST VIRGINIA GEOLOGICAL AND ECONOMIC SURVEY
Box 879, Morgantown, WV 26507-0879
Phone: 304-594-2331; Fax: 304-594-2575
Founded: 1897
Description: Charged with the responsibility of examining all geological formations and physical features of the state with particular emphasis on their economic importance, utilization, and conservation, and preparing reports and maps of the geology and natural resources of West Virginia.
Contact(s):
Associate State Geologist and Deputy Director: CARL J. SMITH; Phone: 304-594-2331
Deputy Director of Finance and Administration: JOHN D. MAY
Director and State Geologist: LARRY D. WOODFORK; Phone: 304-594-2331; Email: woodfork@geoserv.wvnet.edu
Editor: CHUCK GOVER; Phone: 304-594-2331
Program Manager for Coal: NICK FEDORKO III
Program Manager for Geologic Date: MARY C. BEHLING
Program Manager for Oil and Gas: KATHERINE LEE AVARY
Program Manager for Publications and Graphics Section: CHARLES H. GOVER
Program Manager for Service: STEVEN W. McCLELLAND
Publication(s): *Bulletins; reports of investigations; circulars; coal-geology bulletins; environmental geology bulletins; mineral resources series; river basin bulletins; basic data reports; county geologic reports; educational series; state park bulletins; field trip guide.*

WEST VIRGINIA STATE EXTENSION SERVICES
West Virginia University, 817 Knapp Hall, Morgantown, WV 26506
Phone: 304-293-5691
Contact(s):
Associate Director, Center for Agriculture and Natural Resources Development: EDMOND B. COLLINS, West Virginia University, 2080 Agriculural Sciences Bldg., P.O. Box 6108, Morgantown, WV 26506-6108; Phone: 304-293-6131; Email: ecollin@wvu.edu
Associate Provost for Extension and Public Service: DR. LAWRENCE S. COTE, West Virginia University, 817 Knapp Hall, P.O. Box 6031, Morgantown, WV 26506-6125; Phone: 304-293-5691; Email: lcote@wvu.edu
Director, Center for Agricultural and Natural Resources Development: DR. RICHARD ZIMMERMAN, West Virginia University, 2102 Agricultural Science Bldg., P.O. Box 6108, Morgantown, WV 26506-6108; Phone: 304-293-6131; Email: rzimmerman@wvu.edu
Extension Specialist of Crop Managment: THOMAS J. BASDEN, West Virginia University, 1058 Agricultural Sciences Bldg, P.O. Box 6108, Morgantown, WV 26506-6108; Phone: 304-293-6131; Email: tbasden2@wvu.edu
Extension Specialist of Land Reclamation: DR. JEFFREY G. SKOUSEN, West Virginia University, 1106 Agricultural Science Bldg., Morgantown, WV 26506-6108; Phone: 304-293-6131; Email: jskousen@wvu.edu
Extension Specialist of Soil and Water Resources: DR. D. K. BHUMBLA, West Virginia University, 1072 Agricultural Sciences Bldg., P.O. Box 6108, Morgantown, WV 26506-6108; Phone: 304-293-6131; Email: dbhumbla@wvu.edu
Extension Specialist of Wildlife: WILLIAM GRAFTON, West Virginia University, 311-B Percival Hall, P.O Box 6125, Morgantown, WV 26506-6125; Phone: 304-293-4797/Ext.2493; Email: wgrafton@wvu.edu
Program Specialist of Wildlife: WILLIAM GRAFTON, West Virginia University, 311-B, Percival Hall, P.O. Box 6125, Morgantown, WV 26506-6108; Phone: 304-293-4797; Email: wgrafton@wvu.edu
Keyword(s): Agriculture, Forests and Forestry, Pesticides, Renewable Resources, Water Resources

WISCONSIN

GOVERNOR OF WISCONSIN, TOMMY G. THOMPSON
State Capitol, Madison, WI 53707
Phone: 608-266-1212

WISCONSIN CONSERVATION CORPS
30 W. Mifflin, Suite 406, Madison, WI 53703-2558
Phone: 608-266-7730
Founded: 1983
Description: The WCC provides work experience and personal development opportunities to young adults ages 18-25, and valuable conservation and other services to Wisconsin communities. Approximately 550 corps members annually work at four dozen rotating project sites throughout the state. Government agencies and nonprofit organizations are eligible to apply for WCC assistance.
Contact(s):
Executive Director: BRIAN A. SCHIMMING
Publication(s): *On Corps! Newsletter; Biennial Report*
Keyword(s): Environmental and Conservation Education, Fisheries, Forests and Forestry, Outdoor Recreation, Water Resources

WISCONSIN COOPERATIVE FISHERY RESEARCH UNIT (USDI)
College of Natural Resources, University of Wisconsin, Stevens Point, WI 54481
Phone: 715-346-2178
Description: Interagency organization on the federal, state, and university levels. It carries out research, training, and extension in biology and management of freshwater fishery resources.
Contact(s):
Assistant Leader: DR. MICHAEL A. BOZEK
Leader: DR. DANIEL W. COBLE
Keyword(s): Aquatic Habitats, Fisheries, Lakes, Rivers, Sport Fishing

WISCONSIN COOPERATIVE WILDLIFE RESEARCH UNIT (USDI)
USGS, Department of Wildlife Ecology, 204 Russell Laboratories, University of Wisconsin, Madison, WI 53706-1598
Phone: 608-263-6882
Contact(s):
Leader: DR. DONALD H. RUSCH

WISCONSIN DEPARTMENT OF AGRICULTURE
Trade and Consumer Protection, P.O. Box 8911, 2811 Agriculture Drive, Madison, WI 53708-8911
Phone: 608-266-7100
Founded: 1916
Description: To assure the safety and quality of food; fair business practices for the buyer and seller; healthy animals and plants; efficient use of agricultural resources in a quality environment; and promotion of the interests of agriculture.
Contact(s):
Executive Assistant and Acting Secretary: JOSEPH E. TREGONING
Publication(s): *Biennial Report: Summary of Department Programs; Publications Directory; various consumer, legal, food, environmental, agricultural, and marketing publications*
Keyword(s): Agriculture, Environmental and Conservation Education, Pesticides, Renewable Resources, Sustainable Development

WISCONSIN DEPARTMENT OF AGRICULTURE (Land and Water Resources Bureau)
Trade and Consumer Protection, 2811 Agriculture Dr., P.O. Box 8911, Madison, WI 53708-8911
Phone: 608-224-4621
Description: Responsible for administering state soil and water conservation and farmland preservation programs.
Contact(s):
Acting Secretary: JOSEPH E. TREGONING
Bureau Director: DAVID JELINSKI; Phone: 608-224-4621; Fax: 608-224-4615

STATE AND PROVINCE GOVERNMENT AGENCIES - WISCONSIN

Keyword(s): Environment, Environmental Preservation, Land Preservation, Land Use Planning, Rural Development, Soil Conservation, Water Quality, Water Resources, Watersheds, Wetlands

WISCONSIN DEPARTMENT OF NATURAL RESOURCES
Box 7921, Madison, WI 53707
Phone: 608-266-2621

Description: Responsibilities include: Fisheries, wildlife, forest, parks management, endangered resources protection, forest fire control, air and water pollution control, solid and hazardous waste management, mining regulation, enforcement of conservation and environmental laws, flood plain and shoreland zoning, water management and regulation, lake rehabilitation, and long-range planning in the broad fields of outdoor recreation and natural resources.

Contact(s):
Secretary: GEORGE E. MEYER; Phone: 608-266-2121
Administrator of Administration and Technology Division: FRANCIS M. FENNESSY; Phone: 608-264-6133
Administrator of Air and Waste Division: JAY C. HOCHMUTH; Phone: 608-267-9521
Administrator of Customer Assistance and External Relations Division: CRAIG L. KARR; Phone: 608-266-5896
Administrator of Enforcement and Science Division: DAVID J. MEIER; Phone: 608-266-0015
Administrator of Land Division: STEVEN W. MILLER; Phone: 608-266-5782
Administrator of Water Division: SUSAN L. SYLVESTER; Phone: 608-266-1099
Bureau of Cooperative Environmental Assistance: LYNDA M. WEISE; Phone: 608-267-3125
Bureau of Enterprise Information Technology and Applications: SHARON L. MICHEL; Phone: 608-266-7547
Bureau of Watershed Management: ALLEN K. SHEA; Phone: 608-267-2759
Deputy Administrator of Air and Waste Division: MARY JO KOPECKY; Phone: 608-261-8448
Deputy Administrator of Bureau of Water: BRUCE J. BAKER; Phone: 608-266-1902
Deputy Secretary: DARRELL L. BAZZELL; Phone: 608-266-2252
Direcor of Bureau of Management and Habitat Protection: MICHAEL D. STAGGS; Phone: 608-267-0796
Director of Bureau of Administrative and Field Services: MARTIN M. HENERT; Phone: 608-266-9980
Director of Bureau of Air Management: LLOYD L. EAGAN; Phone: 608-266-0603
Director of Bureau of Communication and Education: LAUREL J. STEFFES; Phone: 608-266-8109
Director of Bureau of Community Financial Assistance: KATHRYN A. CURTNER; Phone: 608-266-0860
Director of Bureau of Drinking Water and Ground Water: ROBERT M. KRILL; Phone: 608-267-7651
Director of Bureau of Endangered Resources: CHARLES M. PILS; Phone: 608-266-2625
Director of Bureau of Facilities and Lands: ROBERT W. RODEN; Phone: 608-266-2197
Director of Bureau of Finance: HERBERT M. ZIMMERMAN; Phone: 608-266-0062
Director of Bureau of Forestry: CHARLES E. HIGGS; Phone: 608-266-0842
Director of Bureau of Human Resources: DEBRA K. MARTINELLI; Phone: 608-266-2048
Director of Bureau of Intergrated Science Services: JAMES T. ADDIS; Phone: 608-266-0837
Director of Bureau of Law Enforcement: THOMAS L. HARELSON; Phone: 608-266-1115
Director of Bureau of Legal Services: JAMES A. KURTZ; Phone: 608-266-3695
Director of Bureau of Management and Budget: JOSEPH P. POLASEK; Phone: 608-266-2794
Director of Bureau of Remediation and Redevelopment: MARK F. GIESFELDT; Phone: 608-267-7562
Director of Bureau of Waste Management: SUZANNE BANGERT; Phone: 608-266-0014
Director of Bureau of Wildlife Management: THOMAS M. HAUGE; Phone: 608-266-2193
Director of Customer Service and Licensing: MARILYN A. DAVIS; Phone: 608-267-7799
Editor, WI Natural Resources Magazine: LARRY SPERLING, Box 7921, Madison, WI 53707; Phone: 608-356-7711
Executive Assistant: HOWARD S. DRUCKENMILLER; Phone: 608-266-2136
Librarian: ERIN E. BAGGOTT; Phone: 608-267-7592
Natural Resources Board Chairman: TRYGVE A. SOLBERG; Phone: 608-356-7711
Natural Resources Board Secretary: NEAL W. SCHNEIDER; Phone: 608-754-4444
Natural Resources Board Vice-Chair: BETTY JO NELSEN
Northeast Regional Director: WILLIAM SELBIG, P.O. Box 10448, Green Bay, WI 54307; Phone: 920-492-5815
Northern Regional Director: WILLIAM H. SMITH, 810 W. Maple Street, Spooner, WI 54801; Phone: 715-635-4010
South Central Regional Director: RUTHE BADGER, 3911 Fish Hatchery Road, Madison, WI 53711; Phone: 608-275-3260
Southeast Regional Director: GLORIA L. McCUTCHEON, P.O. Box 12436, Milwaukee, WI 53212; Phone: 414-263-8510
West Central Regional Director: SCOTT HUMRICKHOUSE, P.O. Box 4001, Eau Claire, WI 54702; Phone: 715-839-3711

Publication(s): WI Natural Resources Magazine
Keyword(s): Air Quality and Pollution, Endangered Resources, Forests and Forestry, Land Management, Outdoor Recreation, Solid Waste, Water Resources

WISCONSIN DEPARTMENT OF PUBLIC INSTRUCTION
125 S. Webster St., P.O. Box 7841, Madison, WI 53707-7841
Phone: 800-441-4563; Fax: 608-267-9110

Description: A state government agency that promotes environmental education in public schools and supervises teacher preparation programs. Conducts workshops, and provides consultant services to elementary and secondary schools, colleges and universities. Produces publications to aid in program development.

Contact(s):
Environmental Education Consultant: SUE GRADY; Phone: 608-266-2364

Publication(s): A Guide to Curriculum Planning in Environmental Education; "Wisconsin's Model Academic Standards for Environmental Education"
Keyword(s): Environmental and Conservation Education

WISCONSIN ENVIRONMENTAL EDUCATION BOARD (WEEB)
P.O. Box 7841, Madison, WI 53707-7841
Phone: 608-266-3155

Founded: 1990
Description: Grants board providing $200,000 annually to environmental education (EE) initiative projects within the state of Wisconsin, with a maximum grant of $20,000 per project. The board priorities are further development of previously-funded WEEB projects.

Contact(s):
Chairperson: JACK FINSER
Program Assistant: RON RUECKERT

Publication(s): Annual Report; Grant Application **Keyword(s):** Environmental and Conservation Education, Scholarships and Grants

STATE AND PROVINCE GOVERNMENT AGENCIES - WYOMING

WISCONSIN GEOLOGICAL AND NATURAL HISTORY SURVEY
University of Wisconsin Extension, 3817 Mineral Point Rd., Madison, WI 53705
Phone: 608-262-1705
Founded: 1897
Description: Created by the legislature, with the responsibility to survey the state's geology, mineral, water, soil, plant, animal, and climate resources, and to coordinate topographic mapping.
Contact(s):
Assistant Director: RONALD HENNINGS; Phone: 608-263-7395
Budgeting Specialist: KATHLEEN ZWETTLER; Phone: 608-262-9418
State Geologist and Director: JAMES ROBERTSON; Phone: 608-263-7384
Keyword(s): Geology, Natural History, Soil Conservation, Water Resources

WISCONSIN SEA GRANT INSTITUTE
Dir., U of WI, 1800 Univ. Ave., Madison, WI 53705
Founded: 1968
Description: Represents a unique working partnership of federal, state, university, and private sectors. UW Sea Grant is a statewide program that supports university-based research, education, and public service activities related to the wise use and management of marine and Great Lakes resources.
Contact(s):
Director: DR. ANDERS W. ANDREN, University of Wisconsin, 1800 University Ave., Madison, WI 53705-4094; Phone: 608-262-0905
Assistant Director of Administration: MARY LOU REEB; Phone: 608-263-3296
Assistant Director of Advisory Services: ALLEN H. MILLER; Phone: 608-262-0644
Assistant Director of Communications: STEPHEN WITTMAN; Phone: 608-263-5371
Keyword(s): Aquatic Habitats, Biotechnology, Fisheries, Lakes, Water Pollution

WISCONSIN STATE EXTENSION SERVICES
University of Wisconsin Extension, 432 N. Lake St., Madison, WI 53706
Phone: 608-263-2775
Contact(s):
Dean and Director of Cooperative Extension: DR. CARL O'CONNOR
Extension Forester: DR. A. JEFF MARTIN, 111 Russell Laboratories, University of Wisconsin, Madison, WI 53706; Phone: 608-262-0134
Extension Wildlife Specialist: DR. ROBERT L. RUFF, 226 Russell Laboratories, University of Wisconsin, Madison, WI 53706; Phone: 608-263-2071
Statewide Program Leader: DR. PATRICK WALSH, Community of Natural Resource and Economic Development, University of Wisconsin-Extension, Rm. 625, 432 N. Lake St., Madison, WI 53706; Phone: 608-262-1748
Wildlife Specialist: DR. SCOTT CRAVEN, 215 Russell Laboratories, University of Wisconsin, Madison, WI 53706; Phone: 608-263-6325

WYOMING

GOVERNOR OF WYOMING, JIM GERINGER
State Capitol, Cheyenne, WY 82002
Phone: 307-777-7434

DEPARTMENT OF COMMERCE
Division of Economic and Community Development, Energy Section1st Floor, Herschler Bldg., Cheyenne, WY 82002
Phone: 307-777-7284; Fax: 307-777-5840
Founded: 1985
Description: To promote the enhancement of domestic fossil energy resources, as well as the production of sustainable/renewable energy, while fostering the conservation of current energy resources.
Contact(s):
Executive Director: JOHN F. NUNLEY III
Publication(s): *Wyoming Minerals Yearbook; Wyoming Recycling Directory*

ENVIRONMENTAL QUALITY DEPARTMENT
122 W. 25th St., Herschler Bldg., Cheyenne, WY 82002
Phone: 307-777-7937
Founded: 1973
Description: Established to plan the development, use, reclamation, preservation, and enhancement of the air, land, and water resources of the state.
Contact(s):
Director: DENNIS HEMMER; Phone: 307-777-7938
Administrator of Abandoned Mine Land: STAN BARNARD; Phone: 307-777-6145
Administrator of Air Quality: DAN OLSON; Phone: 307-777-7391
Administrator of Land Quality: RICHARD CHANCELLOR; Phone: 307-777-7756
Administrator of Management Services: JAMES UZZELL; Phone: 307-777-7937
Administrator of Water Quality: GARY BEACH; Phone: 307-777-7781
Manager of Solid Waste Program: DAVID A. FINLEY; Phone: 307-777-7752

GAME AND FISH DEPARTMENT
5400 Bishop Blvd., Cheyenne, WY 82006
Phone: 307-777-4600; Fax: 307-777-4610
Founded: 1939
Description: To provide an adequate and flexible system for the control, propagation, management, protection, and regulation of Wyoming wildlife for the public interest.
Contact(s):
Deputy Director: BILL WICHERS
Deputy Director: STEVE FACCIANI
Director: JOHN BAUGHMAN
Chief of Fiscal Division: LARRY GABRIELE; Phone: 307-777-4516
Chief of Fish Division: MIKE STONE; Phone: 307-777-4559
Chief of Services Division: ART REESE; Phone: 307-777-4563
Chief of Wildlife Division: JAY LAWSON; Phone: 307-777-4579
District Wildlife Supervisor: SCOTT TALBOTT, 3030 Energy Ln., Suite 100, Casper, WY 82604; Phone: 307-473-3400
District Wildlife Supervisor: KENT SCHMIDLIN, 260 Buena Vista, Lander, WY 82520; Phone: 307-332-2688
District Wildlife Supervisor: GREGG ARTHUR, 528 S. Adams, Laramie, WY 82070; Phone: 307-745-4046
District Wildlife Supervisor: STEVE DeCECCO, 351 Astle, GreenRiver, WY 82935; Phone: 307-875-3223
District Wildlife Supervisor: GARY SHORMA, Box 6249, Sheridan, WY 82801; Phone: 307-672-7418
District Wildlife Supervisor: GARY BROWN, 2820 State Highway 120, Cody, WY 82414; Phone: 307-527-7125
District Wildlife Supervisor: BERNIE HOLZ, Box 67, Jackson, WY 83001; Phone: 307-733-2321
Special Assistant for Policy: LARRY KRUCKENBERG; Phone: 307-777-4539
Publication(s): *Wyoming Wildlife*

Keyword(s): Environmental and Conservation Education, Fisheries, Hunting, Nongame Wildlife, Wildlife and Wildlife Habitat

INDUSTRIAL SITING DIVISION/DEPARTMENT OF ENVIRONMENTAL QUALITY
State of Wyoming 3rd Fl E Herschler Bldg., Cheyenne, WY 82002
Phone: 307-777-4369; Email: VFORSE@missc.state.wy.us
Founded: 1975
Description: Administers the Wyoming Industrial Development Information and Siting Act, which deals with the social, economic, and environmental impacts of large-scale industrial development. Responsibilities consist of investigating, reviewing, processing, and serving notice of permit applications.
Contact(s):
Administrator: GARY G. BEACH; Phone: 307-777-7369

STATE FORESTRY DIVISION (WYOMING)
1100 W. 22nd St., Cheyenne, WY 82002
Phone: 307-777-7586; Fax: 307-637-8726
Founded: 1952
Description: Has direction of all forestry matters within the jurisdiction of the state of Wyoming; manages of state-owned forest land; coordinates fire protection on twenty-nine million acres of state and private rural lands; assists landowners and communities in proper management of woody vegetation and forested lands; and provides forestry information to schools, organizations, and individuals.
Contact(s):
Assistant State Forester of Fire Management: RAY A. WEIDENHAFT
Assistant State Forester of Forest Management: HOWARD C. PICKERD
Deputy State Forester: DANIEL J. PERKO
State Forester: THOMAS W. OSTERMANN
Publication(s): *Wyoming State Forest Resource Program; Wyoming's Forest Wealth; Wyoming State Forest Resource Program (Executive Summary)*
Keyword(s): Diseases, Flowers, Plants, and Trees, Forests and Forestry, Insects and Butterflies, Renewable Resources, Urban Forestry, Wildlife Management

WYOMING COOPERATIVE FISH AND WILDLIFE RESEARCH UNIT (USDI)
University of Wyoming, Box 3166, Biological Sciences Bldg., Rm. 419, Laramie, WY 82071
Phone: 307-766-5415; Fax: 307-766-5400
Founded: 1980
Description: Conducts research under auspices of the USGS Biological Resources Division and Wyoming Game and Fish Department in the northern Rocky Mountain region.
Contact(s):
Assistant Leader of Fisheries: DR. WAYNE A. HUBERT
Assistnat Leader of Wildlife: DR. FRED G. LINZEY
Extension Range Management Specialist: KELLY CRANE, Box 579, Pinedale, WY 82941-0579; Phone: 307-367-4342
Extension Rangeland Habitat Specialist: RICH OLSON, University Station, P.O Box 3354, Laramie, WY 82071-3354; Phone: 307-766-6198
Manager of Wildlife: JIM YOUNG; Phone: 705-755-1925
Manger of Fisheries: EVAN THOMAS; Phone: 705-755-1906
Publication(s): *Journal articles; scientific abstracts; science monographs; research journals; bulletins; 4-H publications; regional publications*
Keyword(s): Agriculture, Environmental and Conservation Education, Sustainable Development, Water Resources, Wildlife Management

Leader: DR. STANLEY H. ANDERSON
Keyword(s): Endangered and Threatened Species, Fisheries, Nongame Wildlife, Wildlife and Wildlife Habitat, Wildlife Management

WYOMING DEPARTMENT OF AGRICULTURE
2219 Carey Ave., Cheyenne, WY 82002
Phone: 307-777-7321; Fax: 307-777-6593
Contact(s):
Deputy Director: JIM SCHWARTZ; Phone: 307-777-6591
Director: RON MICHELI; Phone: 307-777-6569; Fax: 307-777-6593; Email: rmiche@missc.state.wy.us
Natural Resource and Policy Manager: GRANT STUMBOUGH; Phone: 307-777-6579

WYOMING DEPARTMENT OF COMMERCE

Division of State Parks and Historic Sites
1st Floor, Herschler Bldg, Cheyenne, WY 82002
Phone: 307-777-5598
Founded: 1967
Description: Responsible for administering the state parks, state recreation areas, historic sites, petroglyph site, archaeological site, markers and monuments, snowmobile program, and state trails program.
Contact(s):
Director of Division of State Parks and Historic Sites: GARY THORSON; Phone: 307-777-5598; Fax: 307-777-6472
Manager of Field Operations: MIKE ABEL; Phone: 307-777-5598
Manager of Planning and Development: LARRY HOOTMAN; Phone: 307-777-5598
Keyword(s): Historic Preservation, Land Preservation, Nature Preservation, Outdoor Recreation, Public Lands

WYOMING STATE BOARD OF LAND COMMISSIONERS
Herschler Bldg., Cheyenne, WY 82002
Phone: 307-777-7331; Fax: 307-777-5400
Contact(s):
Chairman: JIM GERINGER
Secretary: JIM MAGAGNA
Keyword(s): Environment, Land Preservation, Public Lands, Renewable Resources

WYOMING STATE EXTENSION SERVICES
University Station, Box 3354, Laramie, WY 82071
Phone: 307-766-5124
Contact(s):
Director: ANDREW HOUSER; Phone: 705-755-1909
Director: GLEN WHIPPLE, University Station, Box 3354, Laramie, WY 82071-3354; Phone: 307-766-5124
Associate Director for Agriculture and Natural Resources: JOE HILLER, University Station, P.O. Box 3354, Laramie, WY 82071-3354; Phone: 307-766-3567

WYOMING STATE GEOLOGICAL SURVEY
Box 3008, Laramie, WY 82071
Phone: 307-766-2286; Fax: 307-766-2605; Email: wsgs@wsgs.uwyo.edu; sales@wsgs.uwyo.edu
Founded: 1933
Description: Activities include surface and subsurface geologic mapping; mineral, rock, and fossil investigations; natural resource and natural hazards investigations; and assistance in resources development.
Contact(s):
Coal Geologist: ROBERT M. LYMAN
Editor: RICHARD W. JONES
Geologic Hazards Geologist: JAMES C. CASE
Geologic Mapping Geologist: ALAN J. VERPLOEG
Industrial Minerals Geologist: RAY E. HARRIS
Petroleum Geologist: RODNEY H. DeBRUIN

Senior Economic Geologist of Metals and Precious Stones: W. DAN HAUSEL
State Geologist: GARY B. GLASS; Email: gglass@wsgs.uwyo.edu
Publication(s): *Memoirs; bulletins; reports of investigations; public information circulars; quarterly newsletter (Wyoming Geo-notes); list of publications sent on request.*
Keyword(s): Energy, Geology, Land Use Planning, Mineral Resources

INTERNATIONAL

ALBERTA

ALBERTA DEPARTMENT OF ENVIRONMENTAL PROTECTION
Main Fl., Petroleum Plaza, North Tower, 9945-108 St., Edmonton, Alberta T5K296 Canada
Phone: 403-427-7381
Founded: 1992
Description: The Department of Environmental Protection is responsible for protecting, enhancing, and ensuring the wise use of Alberta's environment. The services within the department work cooperatively to meet the needs of Albertans by protecting wildlife, forests, parks, and other natural resources through enforcement of provincial legislation and ensuring the sustainable management of all these resources.
Contact(s):
Contact for Information Centre: ; Phone: 403-944-0313
Contact for Library: ; Phone: 409-427-587; Fax: 403-422-0170
Minister: TY LUND; Phone: 403-427-2391
Publication(s): *State of Environment Report; Annual Regulation Guides to Sportfishing, Hunting, and Trapping; Timber Supply Report; State of Alberta's Wildlife Report*

Communications Division
9th Florr, Petroleum Plaza, S. Tower, 9945-108 St., Edmonton, Alberta T5K 2C6 Canada
Contact(s):
Director: BOB SCOTT; Phone: 403-427-8636

Corporate Management Service
9th Florr, Petroleum Plaza, S. Tower, 9945-108 St., Edmonton, Alberta T5K 2C6 Canada

Environmental Service
Contact(s):
Assistant Deputy Minister: DOUG TUPPER; Phone: 403-427-6247

Land and Forest Service
Contact(s):
Assistant Deputy Minister: CLIFF HENDERSON; Phone: 403-427-3542

Natural Resources Service
Contact(s):
Deputey Minister: MORLEY BARRET; Phone: 403-427-6749

BRITISH COLUMBIA

MINISTRY OF ENVIRONMENT, LANDS, AND PARKS
P.O. Box 9339 STN PROV GOVT, Victoria, British Columbia V8W 9M1 Canada
Phone: 604-387-9422
Description: The Ministry of Environment's mission is to provide leadership in building environmental principles into day-to-day decisions of governments, corporations, and private individuals; to monitor and report on the state of the environment, and to ensure that defensible environmental standards are set and complied with; and to manage natural habitats, fish, wildlife, and water resources for ecological diversity and the economic and recreational opportunities they provide.
Contact(s):
Assistant Deputy Minister, Corporate Services: GREG KOYL; Phone: 250-387-9888
Assistant Deputy Minister, Headquarters Division: DON FAST; Phone: 250-387-1280
Assistant Deputy Minister, Parks Division: DENIS O'GORMAN; Phone: 250-387-9997
Assistant Deputy Minister, Regions Division: JON O'RIORDAN; Phone: 250-387-9877
Deputy Minister: CASSIE DOYLE; Phone: 250-387-5429
Director of Resource Stewardship Branch: NANCY WILKIN; Phone: 250-387-9555
Director of Resources Inventory Branch: JIM MATTISON; Phone: 250-387-1112
Director of Wildlife: NANCY BIRCHER; Phone: 250-387-9731
Executive Director, Environment and Resources Management: KEN BAKER; Phone: 250-387-9990
Minster: HON CATHY MCGREGOR; Phone: 250-387-1187
Special Advisor, Land Use: JIM WALKER; Phone: 250-356-0139

MINISTRY OF FISHERIES
3rd Floor, 780 Blanshard St., Victoria, British Columbia V8V 1X4 Canada
Contact(s):
Director of Recreational Fisheries: JAMIE ALLEY; Phone: 250-387-9711
Minister: HON. DENNIS STREIFEL; Phone: 250-356-2735

MINISTRY OF SMALL BUSINESS TOURISM AND CULTURE
P.O. Box 9805, Stn. Prov. Govt., 1405 Douglas St., Victoria, British Columbia V8W 9W1 Canada
Contact(s):
Assistant Deputy Minister: Culture, Recreation, Heritage & Sport Division: DAVID RICHARDSON, P.O. Box 9817, Stn. Prov. Govt., 5th Floor, 800 Johson Street, Victoria, British Columbia V8W 9W3 Canada; Phone: 250-387-0106
Assistant Deputy Minister: Culture, Recreation, Heritage & Sport Division: DAVID RICHARDSON, P.O. Box 9804, Stn. Prov. Govt., 4th Floor, 1405 Douglas Street, Victoria, British Columbia V8W 9W1 Canada; Phone: 250-356-7363
Assistant Deputy Minister: Management Services Division: RHONDA HUNTER, P.O. Box 9802, Stn. Prov. Govt., 2nd Floor, 1405 Douglas Street, Victoria, British Columbia V8W 9W1 Canada; Phone: 250-356-1680
Assitant Deputy Minister: Government Agents, Small Business and Co-operatives Division: DEBORAH GEORGE, P.O. Box 9804, Stn. Prov. Govt., 4th Floor, 1405 Douglas St., Victoria, British Columbia V8W 9W1; Phone: 250-356-7363
Chief Executive Officer, Royal British Columbia Museum: BILL BARKLEY, P.O. Box 9815, Stn. Prov. Govt., 675 Belleville St., Victoria, British Columbia V8W 9W5 Canada; Phone: 250-387-3685
Deputy Minister: LYN TAIT, P.O. Box 9805 Stn. Prov. Govt., Victoria, British Columbia V8W 9W1 Canada; Phone: 250-356-2175
Director, British Columbia Film Commission: PETER MITCHELL, 601 West Cordova St., Vancouver, British Columbia V6B 1G1; Phone: 604-660-2732
Executive Director: Tourism and Corporate Policy Division: LYNELLE SPRING, P.O. Box 9806, Stn. Prov. Govt., 5th Floor, 1405 Douglas St., Victoria, British Columbia V8W 9W1 Canada; Phone: 250-387-8002
Minister: IAN G. WADDEL, Rm. 322, Parliament Buildings, Victoria, British Columbia V8V 1X4 Canada; Phone: 250-387-1683
President and Chief Executive Officer, Tourism British Columbia: ROD HARRIS, P.O. Box 9830, Stn. Prov. Govt., 300 - 1803 Douglas St., Victoria, British Columbia V8W 9W5 Canada; Phone: 250-356-2026

MANITOBA

DEPARTMENT OF INDUSTRY, TRADE AND TOURISM
Travel Manitoba, Department RH8, 7th Fl., 155 Carlton St., Winnipeg, Manitoba R3C3H8 Canada
Phone: 204-945-3777/ext. RH8/1800-665-0040/ext.RH8; Fax: 204-945-2302
Description: Coordinates visits to Manitoba by travel and outdoor editors; produces and distributes travel and outdoor literature and films.
Contact(s):
Assistant Deputy Minister of Tourism and Business Development: LORETTA CLARKE; Phone: 204-945-4204
Manager of Marketing and Promotions: DANITA SCHMIDTKE; Phone: 204-945-2392
Marketing Consultant: COLETTE FONTAINE; Phone: 204-945-4045

MANITOBA DEPARTMENT OF NATURAL RESOURCES
Rm. 333, Legislative Bldg., Winnipeg, Manitoba R3C0V8 Canada
Phone: 204-945-3730
Description: The purpose of Manitoba Natural Resources is to encourage wise use of Manitoba's natural resources and preserve them for future generations.
Contact(s):
Acting Director of Policy Coordination: BLAIR McTAOISH, Box 38, 200 Saulteaux Cres., Winnipeg, Manitoba R3J 3W3 Canada; Phone: 204-945-6658
Assistant Deputy Minister: HARVEY BOYLE, Box 80,200 Saulteaux, Winnipeg, ; Phone: 204-945-4842
Assistant Deputy Minister: DR. MERLIN SHOESMITH, Box 80, 200 Saulteaux Cres., Winnipeg, Manitoba R3J 3W3 Canada; Phone: 204-945-6829
Deputy Minister: DAVID TOMASSON, Rm. 327, Legislative Bldg., Winnipeg, Manitoba R3C 0V8 Canada; Phone: 204-945-3785
Director of Financial Services: PETER J. LOCKETT, Box 85,200 Saulteaux, Winnipeg, Manitoba Canada; Phone: 204-945-4187
Director of Fisheries Branch: JOE O'CONNOR, Box 20, 200 Saulteaux Cres., Winnipeg, Manitoba R3J 3W3 Canada; Phone: 204-945-7814
Director of Forestry: , Box 70, 200, Saulteaux Cres., Winnipeg, Manitoba R3J 3W3 Canada; Phone: 204-945-7998
Director of Forestry: RICHARD WESTWOOD
Director of Headquarters Operations: WAYNE FISHER, Box 44, 200 Saulteaux Cres., Winnipeg, Manitoba R3J 3W3 Canada; Phone: 204-945-6647
Director of Human Resources: LORRAINE METZ, 500-326 Broadway WPG MB, R3C 055 Canada; Phone: 204-945-2810
Director of Lands Branch: HARLEY JONASSON
Director of Lands Branch: , 123 Main St., W., Box 20000, Neepawa, Manitoba R0J 1H0 Canada; Phone: 204-476-3441
Director of Parks and Natural Areas: C. GORDON PROUSE, Box 50, 200 Saulteax Cres., Winnipeg, Manitoba R3J 3W3 Canada; Phone: 204-945-4362
Director of Resource Information Systems: KERRY POOLE, Box 90, 200 Saulteaux Cres., Winnipeg, Manitoba R3J 3W3 Canada; Phone: 204-945-2929
Director of Surveys and Mapping: WAYNE LEEMAN, 1007 Century St., Winnipeg, Manitoba R3H 0W4 Canada; Phone: 204-945-0011
Director of Water Resources Branch: STEVEN TOPPING, Box 11 200 Saulteaux, Winnipeg, Manitoba R3E 3J5 Canada; Phone: 204-945-7488
Director of Wildlife: BRIAN GILLESPIE, Box 24, 200 Salteaux Cres., Winnipeg, Manitoba R3J 3W3 Canada; Phone: 204-945-7761
Executive Director of Land Information Centre: JACK SCHREUDER, 1007 Century St., Winnipeg, Manitoba R3H 0W4 Canada; Phone: 204-945-6613
Executive Director of Management Services: W. J. PODOLSKY, Box 85,200 Saulteaux Cres., Winnipeg, Manitoba R3J 3W3 Canada; Phone: 204-945-4056
Minister: HON. J. GLEN CUMMINGS, Rm. 333, Legislative Bldg., Winnipeg, Manitoba, R3C 0V8 Canada; Phone: 204-945-3730
Special Assistant to the Minister: PETER CONNELLY; Phone: 204-945-1206

Central Region
Box 6000, Gimli, Manitoba R0C1B0 Canada
Phone: 204-642-6096
Contact(s):
Regional Director: WORTH HAYDEN
Regional Superintendent: SYD ROBAK

Eastern Region
Box 4000, Lac du Bonnet, Manitoba R0E1A0 Canada
Phone: 204-345-1433
Contact(s):
Regional Director: BOB ENNS
Regional Superintendent: BOB CAMERON

Northeastern Region
Box 28, 59 Elizabeth Rd., Thompson, Manitoba R8N1X4 Canada
Phone: 204-677-6628
Contact(s):
Regional Director: DON COOK
Regional Superintendent: STEVE KEARNEY

Northwestern Region
Box 2550, 3rd St. and Ross Ave., The Pas, Manitoba R9A1M4 Canada
Phone: 204-627-8261
Contact(s):
Regional Director: ALBERT D. KING
Regional Superintendent: ROB DEAN

Western Region
Box 488, 340-9th St., Brandon, Manitoba R7A5Z4 Canada
Phone: 204-726-6299
Contact(s):
Regional Director: BOB WOOLEY
Regional Superintendent: BLAIR BASTIAN

NEW BRUNSWICK

NEW BRUNSWICK DEPARTMENT OF NATURAL RESOURCES AND ENERGY
P.O. Box 6000, Fredericton, New Brunswick E3B5H1 Canada
Contact(s):
Deputy Minister: GEORGE D. BOUCHARD; Phone: 506-453-2501
Executive Director of Fish and Wildlife: DR. ARNOLD H. BOER, P.O. Box 6000, Fredericton, New Brunswick E3B 5H1 Canada; Phone: 506-453-2440
Minister: HON. ALAN R. GRAHAM; Phone: 506-453-2510

NEWFOUNDLAND

NEWFOUNDLAND DEPARTMENT OF FOREST RESOURCES AND AGRIFOODS
P.O. Box 8700, St. John's, Newfoundland A1B4J6 Canada
Contact(s):
Assistant Deputy Minister: MUHAMMAD NAZIR; Phone: 709-729-2704
Deputy Minister: ROBERT SMART; Phone: 709-729-4720
Minister: HON. KEVIN AYLWARD; Phone: 709-729-4715

Ecosystem Health Division
P.O. Box 8700, St. John's, Newfoundland A1B4J6 Canada
Contact(s):
Director: D. FONG; Phone: 709-729-1804

STATE AND PROVINCE GOVERNMENT AGENCIES - INTERNATIONAL

Senior Biologist (Endangered Species): J. BRAZIL; Phone: 709-729-3773
Senior Biologist (Environmental/Land Use): C. BUTLER; Phone: 709-729-2543

Inland Fish and Wildlife Division
Bldg. 810, Pleasantville, P.O. Box 8700, St. John's, Newfoundland A1B4J6 Canada
Description: Objective is to maintain diverse and abundant wildlife populations and wildlife habitat; provide for the safe and sustainable use of wildlife, both consumptive and nonconsumptive; and help create a social environment conducive to effective wildlife conservation.
Contact(s):
Director: J. HANCOCK; Phone: 709-729-2817
Chief of Inland Fish: K. CURNEW; Phone: 709-729-2540
Chief of Research and Inventory: S. MAHONEY; Phone: 709-729-3593
Chief of Wildlife Management Planning: M. CAHILL; Phone: 709-729-2548
Manager of Conservation Services: J. BLAKE; Phone: 709-729-3509
Manager of Salmonier Nature Park and Environmental Education: R. JARVIS; Phone: 709-729-6974
Senior Biologist (Inland Fish): M. VanZYLL de JONG; Phone: 709-729-4306
Senior Biologist (Small Game/Fur): M. McGRATH; Phone: 709-729-0748
Supervisor of Administration: L. CROKE; Phone: 709-729-2636
Supervisor of Licencing: R. GULLIVER; Phone: 709-729-2630
Publication(s): *Newfoundland and Labrador Hunting and Trapping Guide; Trappers Guide; Newfoundland and Labrador Hunter Education Manual (student and instructor editions); Trapper's Update; Endangered Species Poster and brochure series*

Legislation and Compliance Division
P.O. Box 8700, St. John's, Newfoundland A1B 4J6 Canada
Contact(s):
Director: R. WHITTEN; Phone: 709-729-2647

Regional Offices
Contact(s):
Eastern Director (Gander): E. BLACKMORE; Phone: 709-256-1451
Labrador Director (Goose Bay): K. COLBERT; Phone: 709-896-3405
Regional Comliance Manager: R. TRASK; Phone: 709-256-1461
Regional Compliance Manager: D. LeBOUBON; Phone: 709-896-2541
Regional Compliance Manager: M. PARSONS; Phone: 709-637-2918
Regional Ecologist: L. SOPER; Phone: 709-637-2399
Western Director (Corner Brook): A. MASTERS; Phone: 709-637-2370

NORTHWEST TERRITORIES

DEPARTMENT OF RESOURCES, WILDLIFE AND ECONOMIC DEVELOPMENT, GOVERNMENT OF THE NORTHWEST TERRITORIES
Scotia Centre Box 21, 600 5102 - 50 Ave., Yellowknife, Northwest Territories X1A3S8 Canada
Description: Has broad responsibility for wildlife and fisheries environmental protection, forest management, parks and tourism, trade and investment, and minerals, oil, and gas in the Northwest Territories, and provides assistance to people dependent on these resources to harvest wildlife in a manner which will ensure continued availability of the resource.
Contact(s):
Assistant Deputy Minister of Resources and Economic Development: DOUG DOAN; Phone: 867-873-7115; Fax: 867-873-0114
Assistant Deputy Minister of East: KATHERINE TRUMPER, Bag 1000, Iqaluit, Northwest Territories X0A 0H0 Canada; Phone: 819-979-5071; Fax: 819-979-6026
Deputy Minister: JOSEPH HANDLEY; Phone: 867-920-8048; Fax: 867-873-0563
Director of Community Economic Development Services: GERRY LEPRIEUR; Phone: 867-873-7838; Fax: 867-873-0434
Director of Corporate Service: JIM KENNEDY; Phone: 867-873-7532; Fax: 867-920-2756
Director of Diamond Projects: MARTIN IRVING; Phone: 867-920-3125; Fax: 867-873-0254
Director of Environmental Protection: EMERY PAQUIN; Phone: 867-873-7654; Fax: 867-873-0221
Director of Forest Management: ROBERT BAILEY, Box 7, Fort Smith, Northwest Territories X0E 0P0 Canada; Phone: 867-872-770; Fax: 867-872-2077
Director of Minerals, Oil and Gas: DOUG MATTHEWS; Phone: 867-920-3222; Fax: 867-920-0254
Director of Parks and Tourism: ROBIN REILLY; Phone: 867-873-7902; Fax: 867-873-0163
Director of Policy and Legislation: KATHRYN EMMETT; Phone: 867-920-8046; Fax: 867-873-0114
Director of Trade and Investment: OTTO OLAH; Phone: 867-873-7361; Fax: 867-920-0101
Director of Wildlife and Fisheries: DOUG STEWART; Phone: 867-920-8064; Fax: 867-873-0293
Librarian: ALISON WELCH, NWT Resources, Wildlife and Economic Development Library, Scotia Centre 5th Floor, 600 5102 - 50 Ave., Yellowknife, NT X1A 3S8 Canada; Phone: 867-920-8606/867- 873-0293
Minister: STEPHEN KAKFWI; Phone: 867-669-2366; Fax: 867-873-0169
Regional Superintendent for Baffin: KEN TONER, Bag 1000, Iqaluit, NT X0A0H0 Canada; Phone: 819-979-5012; Fax: 819-979-6791
Regional Superintendent for Deh Cho: PAUL KRAFT, Box 240, Fort Simpson, NT X0E0N0 Canada; Phone: 879-695-2231; Fax: 897-695-2442
Regional Superintendent for Inuvik: RON MORRISON, Bag 1, Inuvik, NT X0E0T0 Canada; Phone: 879-777-7286; Fax: 879-777-7238
Regional Superintendent for Keewatin: RON ROACH, Bag Service 2, Rankin Inlet, NT X0C0G0 Canada; Phone: 819-645-5067; Fax: 819-645-2346
Regional Superintendent for Kitikmeot: JOHN STEVENSON, Kugluktuk, NT X0E0E0 Canada; Phone: 879-982-7241; Fax: 879-982-3701
Regional Superintendent for North Slave: LARRY ADAMSON, Box 2668, Yellowknife, NT X1A2P9 Canada; Phone: 879-920-6134; Fax: 879-873-6230
Regional Superintendent for Sahtu: CELINA STROEDER, Box 130, Normal Wells, NT X0E 0V0 Canada; Phone: 879-587-2310; Fax: 879-587-2204
Regional Superintendent for South Slave: LLOYD JONES, Box 390, Fort Smith, NT X0E 0P0 Canada; Phone: 867-872-4242; Fax: 879-872-4250
Publication(s): *Safety in Bear Country; Summary of Hunting Regulations; NWT Explorers Guide; NWT Wildlife Sketches; Sport Fishing Guide*

NOVA SCOTIA

DEPARTMENT OF FISHERIES AND AQUACULTURE
P.O. Box 2223, Halifax, Nova Scotia B3J3C4 Canada
Phone: 902-424-4560
Description: The Department is involved in almost all aspects of the province's fishing industry. It has significant input into some of the policies and programs legislated and administered by the federal government, which has jurisdiction over much of the fishery. The department has jurisdictional responsibility for developing and regulating aquaculture and freshwater recreational fisheries. It is

also responsible for the licensing and inspection of fish processing plants. The department provides training, marketing, and loan assistance to the industry. Department goals include conservation development and enhancement of renewable fisheries resources for the benefit of all Nova Scotians.
Contact(s):
Deputy Minister: PETER UNDERWOOD; Phone: 902-424-0300
Director of Aquaculture: LEO MUISE; Phone: 902-424-3664
Director of Inland Fisheries: MURRAY HILL; Phone: 902-485-7021
Director of Loan Board: JIM SARTY; Phone: 902-424-0312
Director of Marketing: JANIS RAYMOND; Phone: 902-424-0330
Director of Policy, Planning and Coastal Resources: GREG ROACH; Phone: 902-424-0348
Director of Technology and Inspection: DAVE HANSEN; Phone: 902-424-0337
Director of Training & Field Services: BARB RILEY; Phone: 902-424-0328
Minister: KEITH COLWELL; Phone: 902-424-8953

DEPARTMENT OF NATURAL RESOURCES
P.O. Box 698, Halifax, Nova Scotia B3J2T9 Canada
Phone: 902-424-5935
Description: Charged with the administration of the Wildlife Act and various other statutes. Inherent in the legislation and incumbent upon the Department are responsibilities pertaining to the productivity of the forests generally, the supply of forest products, the conservation of wildlife, the development of mineral resources, the administration of Crown Lands, and the enhancement of recreational areas.
Contact(s):
Deputy Minister: DANIEL J. GRAHAM; Phone: 902-424-4121
Executive Assistant to Minister: HAROLD AUCOIN; Phone: 902-424-4047
Minister: KEN MACASKILL; Phone: 902-424-4037
Publication(s): *Natures Resources; Nova Scotia Trappers Newsletter*

NEW MEXICO DEPARTMENT OF NATURAL RESOURCES

Corporate Service Unit
2040 Pacheco St., Santa Fe, Nova Scotia 87505 Canada
Contact(s):
Director of Finance: FRANK DUNN; Phone: 902-424-3288
Information Officer: BLAIN HENSHAW; Phone: 902-424-5252
Information Officer: SUSAN MADER ZWICK; Phone: 902-424-2354

Land Services Division

Regional Services
Contact(s):
Executive Director: BRIAN GILBERT; Phone: 902-424-3949
Acting Director of Surveys: LEE JOHNSTON; Phone: 424-3145
Director of Crown Lands Management: DAN EIDT; Phone: 902-424-7594
Director of Extension Services: BILL SMITH; Phone: 902-424-4445
Director of Private Lands Management: ARDEN WHIDDEN; Phone: 902-424-5703
Manager of Enforcement: JOHN MOMBOURQUETTE; Phone: 902-424-5254

Renewable Resources
Contact(s):
Executive Director: ED MacAULAY; Phone: 902-424-4103
Acting Director of Forestry: NANCY McINNIS LEEK, P.O. Box 68, Truro, Nova Scotia B2N 5B8 Canada; Phone: 902-893-6102
Director of Parks and Recreation: , R.R. #1, Belmont, Colchester County, Nova Scotia B0M 1C0 Canada; Phone: 902-662-3030; Fax: 902-662-2160
Director of Wildlife Management: BARRY C. SABEAN, 136 Exhibition St., Kentville, Nova Scotia B4N 4E5 Canada; Phone: 902-679-6139; Fax: 902-679-6176
Supervisor of Wildlife Parks: BERT VISSERS, P.O. Box 299, Shubenacadie, Nova Scotia B0N 2H0 Canada; Phone: 902-758-2040

ONTARIO

MINISTRY OF NATURAL RESOURCES

Algonquin Forestry Authority
84-6 Isabella St., Huntsville, Ontario K8A5S5 Canada
Phone: 613-735-0173
Contact(s):
General Manager: B. A. CONNELLY

Corporate Services Division
Description: This division facilitates the delivery of ministry programs by providing leadership, strategic advice, and responsive results-oriented services to ministry clients. These services include business planning, audit and evaluation, financial, administrative, legal, and human resources. The division also develops corporate and administrative policies and gives advice on standards, guidelines, planning, and management. It is the primary liaison with the central agencies of government for corporate policy and the functions associated with the Chief Administrative Officer.
Contact(s):
Director of Corporate Affairs Branch: LARRY DOUGLAS; Phone: 416-314-1923
Director of Finance and Administration Branch: JOHN KENRICH; Phone: 705-755-2505
Director of Human Resources Branch: GEORGE ROSS; Phone: 705-755-3131
Director of Legal Services Branch: BARRY JONES; Phone: 416-314-2002

Field Services Division
Description: Delivering resource management programs for Ontario's fisheries, wildlife, forests and provincial lands is the responsibility of this division. It is also responsible for the Aviation, Flood, and Fire Management Branch and the Provincial Enforcement Section. The division's structure is highly decentralized with three regional offices, 25 district offices, and 17 area offices located across the province.
Contact(s):
Director of Aviation, Flood, and Fire Management: JACK McFADDEN; Phone: 705-945-5937
Director of Northwest Region: MIKE WILLICK; Phone: 807-475-1264
Director of South Central Region: DICK HUNTER; Phone: 705-755-3235
Manager of Enforcement Section: GUY WINTERON; Phone: 705-755-1750

Fish and Wildlife Branch
300 Water St., P.O. Box 7000, Peterborough, Ontario K9J8M5 Canada
Contact(s):
Director: ANDREW HOUSER; Phone: 705-755-1909
Manager of Fisheries: EVAN THOMAS; Phone: 705-755-1906
Manager of Wildlife: JIM YOUNG; Phone: 705-755-1925

Natural Resource Management Division
Description: The division is responsible for ensuring that natural resource programs are responsive to the needs of Ontarians and consistent with the ministry's vision of sustainable development and its mission of ecological sustainability. Its mandate covers lands, waters, forests, fish, wildlife, and parks, and includes fish hatcheries, tree nurseries, and the management of the Great Lakes.
Contact(s):
Director of Fish and Wildlife Branch: ANDREW HOUSER; Phone: 705-755-1909
Director of Forest Management Branch: BILL THORNTON; Phone: 705-945-6660

STATE AND PROVINCE GOVERNMENT AGENCIES - INTERNATIONAL

Director of Land Use Planning Branch: DAVE WATTON; Phone: 705-755-2369
Director of Lands and Natural Heritage Branch: BOB BEECHER; Phone: 705-755-1212
Director of Ontario Parks: NORM RICHARDS; Phone: 705-755-1702

Northeast Region
Ontario Government Complex, Highway 101 East, P.O. Bag 3020, South Porcupine, Ontario P0N 1H0 Canada
Phone: 705-235-1153
Contact(s):
Regional Director: BOB GALLOWAY

Northwest Region
Ontario Government Bldg., P.O. Box 5000, 435 James St., South, Thunder Bay, Ontario P7C5G6 Canada
Phone: 807-475-1261
Contact(s):
Regional Director: MIKE WILLICH

Ontario
Toronto, Ontario M7A1W3 Canada
Description: The ministry's business plan establishes the following as MNR's core businesses: natural resource management; Crown land management; public safety and enforcement; parks and protected areas; and geographic information. In pursuing these core businesses, the ministry contributes to the environmental, social, and economic well-being of Ontario through the biological features of provincial interest, and protects human life, the resource base, and physical property from the threats of forest fires, floods, and erosion.
Contact(s):
Assistant Deputy Minister for Corporate Services: PATRICIA E. MALCOLMSON; Phone: 416-314-1897
Assistant Deputy Minister for Field Services: CAMERON D. CLARK; Phone: 807-475-1438
Assistant Deputy Minister for Natural Resource Management: GAIL BEGGS; Phone: 416-314-6131
Assistant Deputy Minister for Science and Information Resources: DR. DAVID BALSILLIE; Phone: 416-314-1528
Commissioner of Mining and Lands: RUSSELL YURKOW, 700 Bay St., 24th Fl., Toronto, Ontario M5G1Z6 Canada; Phone: 416-314-2323
Deputy Minister: RON VRANCART; Phone: 416-314-2150
Director of Communications Services: JOHN McHUGH; Phone: 416-314-2119
Director of Communications Services Branch: JOAN KRANTZBERG; Phone: 416-314-2119
Minister: HON. CHRIS HODGSON; Phone: 416-314-2301
Parliamentary Assistant: TED CHUDLEIGH; Phone: 416-314-2193

Science and Information Resources Division
Description: Provides the ministry with leadership in the development and application of scientific knowledge, information management, and information technology. The division also plays a lead role in the provision of land-related information.
Contact(s):
Associate Director of Zimbabwe Natural Resource Management: COLLIN TURNPENNY; Phone: 416-314-1550
Director of Information Management and Systems Branch: GLENN HOLDER; Phone: 705-755-2139
Director of Information Technology Services Branch: DES McKEE; Phone: 705-755-1401
Director of Science Development and Transfer Branch: JIM MacLEAN; Phone: 705-755-1565

South Central Region
P.O. Box 9000, Brendale Square, Huntsville, Ontario P0A1K0 Canada
Phone: 705-789-9611
Contact(s):
Regional Director: ALLAN STEWART

NIAGARA ESCARPMENT COMMISSION
232 Guelph St., Georgetown, Ontario L7G4B1 Canada
Phone: 905-877-5191
Founded: 1973
Description: Maintains the Niagara Escarpment and land in its vicinity substantially as a continuous natural environment, and ensures that only such development occurs as is compatible with that natural environment. The commission was established under the Niagara Escarpment Planning and Development Act. In 1990, the Niagra Escarpment was designated a World Biosphere Reserve.
Contact(s):
Chair: DON SCOTT
Director: FRANK SHAW
Manager of Development Control: KEITH C. JORDAN
Manager of Public Affairs: RICHARD MURZIN
Public Affairs Officer: SUSAN POWELL

PRINCE EDWARD ISLAND

DEPARTMENT OF ENVIRONMENTAL RESOURCES (PRINCE EDWARD ISLAND)
P.O. Box 2000, Charlottetown, Prince Edward Island C1A7N8 Canada
Description: To work with individuals, businesses, groups and communities to protect, enhance and enjoy in a sustainable way the province's environment and natural resources.
Contact(s):
Deputy Minister: DIANE F. GRIFFIN; Phone: 902-368-5340
Director of Fish and Wildlife Division: ARTHUR SMITH; Phone: 902-368-6083
Firearm Safety Coordinator: CLARE J. BIRCH; Phone: 902-368-4686
Habitat and Natural Areas Biologist: ROSEMARY CURLEY; Phone: 902-368-4807
Head of Investigations and Enforcement: GERALD MacDOUGALL; Phone: 902-368-4808
Minister: BARRY HICKEN; Phone: 902-368-6410
Waterfowl and Furbearer Biologist: RANDALL DIBBLEE; Phone: 902-368-4666
Publication(s): *Tracks in the Snow; Patterns of the Pond; Wildlife Policy; The Bald Eagle in Prince Edward Island; Our Land and Water*

QUEBEC

DEPARTMENT OF ENVIRONMENT AND WILDLIFE (QUEBEC)
Edifice Marie-Guyart, 675, Blvd. Rene-Levesque Est, Quebec City, Quebec G1R5V7 Canada
Contact(s):
Assistant Deputy Minister for Sustainable Development: SUZANNE GIGUERE; Phone: 418-521-3860
Assistant Deputy Minister of Operations: NORMAN D. CARRIER; Phone: 418-521-3860
Assistant Deputy Minister of Recreation of Environment: DENYS JEAN; Phone: 418-521-3860
Assistant Deputy Minister of Wildlife and Natural Heritage: GEORGE ARSENAULT; Phone: 418-521-3860
Departmental Secretary: HERVE BOLDUC; Phone: 418-521-3860
Deputy Minister: DIANE GAUDET; Phone: 418-521-3860
Director General of Administration: ANDRE TAILLON; Phone: 418-521-3860
Director of Institutional Affairs and Communications: LUCIEN BEAUMONT; Phone: 418-521-3823
Director of Intergovernmental and Native Affairs: LUC POIRIER; Phone: 418-521-3828
Director of Quebec Aquarium: ANDRE MARTEL; Phone: 418-659-5266
Director of Quebec Parks: LUC BERTHIAUME; Phone: 418-644-9393

Director of Wildlife Territories, Regulations and Permits: CLAUDETTE BLAIS; Phone: 418-643-7674
Interim Director of Quebec Zoo: ANDRE MARTEL; Phone: 418-622-0313
Minister: PAUL BEGIN; Phone: 418-521-3911

SASKATCHEWAN

SASKATCHEWAN ENVIRONMENT AND RESOURCE MANAGEMENT
3211 Albert St., Regina, Saskatchewan S4S5W6 Canada
Founded: 1930
Description: To manage, enhance, and protect Saskatchewan's natural and environmental resources - fish, forests, parks, lands, wildlife, air and water for conservation, recreation, social, and economic purposes, all to be sustained for future generations.
Contact(s):
Deputy Minister: STUART KRAMER; Phone: 306-787-2931
Director of Communication Services: RICK BATES; Phone: 306-787-7034
Minister: HON. LORNE SCOTT, 43 Legislative Bldg., Regina, Saskatchewan S4S 0B3 Canada; Phone: 306-787-0393
Publication(s): *State of the Environment Report; Annual Reports*

Corporate Services
3211 Albert St., Regina, Saskatchewan S4S 5W6 Canada
Contact(s):
DAVE TULLOCH; Phone: 306-787-1095
AL PARENTEAU
Director of Cooperative Development: SUE MITTEN; Phone: 306-787-2336
Director of Information Mangement: MIKE DUMELIE; Phone: 306-787-3194
Director of Service Bureau: DONNA KELLSEY; Phone: 306-787-6121
Publication(s): *State of the Environment Report; Annual Reports*

East Boreal
Box 3003, Prince Albert, Saskatchewan S6V6G1 Canada
Phone: 306-953-2899
Contact(s):
Regional Director: RON ERICKSON

Enforcement and Compliance Branch
Contact(s):
Regional Director: DAVE HARVEY, Box 3003, Prince Albert, Saskatchewan S6V 6G1 Canada; Phone: 306-953-2993

Fire Management and Forest Protection Branch
Contact(s):
Regional Director: MURDOCH CARRIERRE, Box 3003, Prince Albert, Saskatchewan S6V 6G1 Canada; Phone: 306-953-2206

Grassland
350 Cheadle St. W., Swift Current, Saskatchewan S9H4G3 Canada
Phone: 306-778-8527
Contact(s):
Regional Director: SYD BARBER

Operations
Contact(s):
Assistant Deputy Minister: DAVE PHILLIPS; Phone: 306-787-9079
Director of Regional Services: HUGH HUNT; Phone: 306-787-9117

Parkland
112 Research Dr., Saskatoon, Saskatchewan S7K2H6 Canada
Phone: 306-933-6242
Contact(s):
Regional Director: MERV SWANSON

Policy and Assessment
Contact(s):
Executive Director: RON ZUKOWSKY; Phone: 306-787-6285
Acting Director of Policy and Legislation: SHARON COFFIN; Phone: 306-787-2323
Director of Ecosystems Management: LYNDA LANGFORD; Phone: 306-787-6868
Director of Environmental Assessment Branch: LARRY LECHNER; Phone: 306-787-5789
Director of Public Involvment and Aboriginal Affairs: JOE MULDOON; Phone: 306-787-7803

Programs
Contact(s):
Director of Environmental Protection Branch: BOB RUGGLES; Phone: 306-787-6178
Director of Fish and Wildlife Branch: DENNIS SHERRATT; Phone: 306-787-2309
Director of Forest Ecosystems Branch: AL WILCOCKS, Box 3003, Prince Albert, Saskatchewan S6V 6G1 Canada; Phone: 306-953-2486
Director of Parks and Special Places Branch: DON MacAULEY; Phone: 306-787-2846
Director of Sustainable Land Management Branch: DOUG MAZUR; Phone: 306-787-7024

Shield
Box 5000, La Ronge, Saskatchewan S0J1L0 Canada
Phone: 306-425-4231
Contact(s):
Regional Director: JOHN SCHISLER

West Boreal
201-2nd St. W, Meadow Lake, Saskatchewan S9X1C7 Canada
Phone: 306-236-7540
Contact(s):
Regional Director: TOM HARRISON

YUKON TERRITORY

DEPARTMENT OF RENEWABLE RESOURCES
Box 2703, Whitehorse, Yukon Territory Y1A 2C6 Canada
Contact(s):
Acting Assistant Deputy Minister: JIM CONNELL; Phone: 402-667-8955
Acting Director of Fish and Wildlife: DON TOEWS; Phone: 403-667-5715
Acting Director of Policy and Planning: KARYN ARMOUR; Phone: 403-667-5634
Deputy Minister: BILL OPPEN; Phone: 403-667-5460
Director of Agriculture: DAVE BECKMAN; Phone: 403-667-5838
Director of Environmental Protection and Assessment: JOE BALLANTYNE; Phone: 403-667-8177
Director of Finance and Administration: STAN MARINOSKE; Phone: 403-667-5197
Director of Parks and Outdoor Recreation: JIM MCINTYRE; Phone: 403-667-5261

NON-GOVERNMENTAL ORGANIZATIONS

1000 FRIENDS OF FLORIDA
P.O. Box 5948, Tallahassee, FL 32314-0000
Phone: 904-222-6277
Founded: 1986; Membership: 6,000
Scope: Statewide
Description: The mission of 1000 Friends of Florida is to advocate, through education, negotiation, and litigation, the implementation of growth management principles which successfully balance the social, economic, and environmental values which make up Florida's quality of life.
Contact(s):
Chairman: NATHANIEL P. REED, Box 375, 6 Riverview Rd., Hobe Sound, FL 33475-2325; Phone: 407-546-2666
President: JOHN DeGROVE, FAU University Tower 220 SE 2nd Ave., Ft. Lauderdale, FL 33301; Phone: 954-355-5255
Vice President: MARY A. KUMPE, 1564 Bay Point Dr., Sarasota, FL 34236; Phone: 813-955-4094
Treasurer: JERRY SOKOLOW, Sokolow and Burell, 1680 NE 135 St. Suite 102 W., Miami, FL 33181; Phone: 305-895-9955
Publication(s): *Foresight; Growth Bulletin; Vista*
Keyword(s): Environmental and Conservation Education, Environmental Law, Environmental Planning, Environmental Preservation, Land Preservation

A. E. HOWELL WILDLIFE CONSERVATION CENTER
HCR #61, Box 6, N. Amity, ME 04471-9601
Phone: 207-532-6880; Fax: 207-532-0910
Founded: 1981; Membership: 225
Scope: National
Description: The A.E.H.W.C.C., Inc. and Spruce Acres Refuge have combined to provide a 65+ acre Refuge Rehabilitation center for people from all the world to enjoy. The Conservation Center is a nonprofit organization established for the purpose of preserving our natural resources and providing educational programs to all people to encourage proper wildlife and natural resource management.
Contact(s):
Vice President: PENNY KERN
Chairman of the Board: MAXIM LANGSTAFF
Founder/President/Wildlife Rehabilitator: ARTHUR E. HOWELL JR.
Secretary and Treasurer: DOROTHY HOWELL
Publication(s): *Membership and Features; If You Care Please Leave Them There; Coyotes in Maine; Trees - Walk The Nature Trails; Planet Earth; American Wetlands*
Keyword(s): Environmental and Conservation Education, Mammals, Raptors, Wetlands, Wildlife Rehabilitation

A.B. ENVIRONMENTAL EDUCATION CENTER
Oglebay Institute, Oglebay Park, Wheeling, WV 26003
Phone: 304-242-6855; Fax: 304-242-4203
Scope: Statewide
Description: Oglebay Institute operates a variety of programs: Resident nature summer camps for adults and children; Ecotourism Club; resident environmental education programs; children's day camping; special workshops and weekends; exhibits; school programs; and also the A.B. Brooks Environmental Education Center and Speidel Observatory.
Contact(s):
Associate Director of Environmental Education: TISH SHERRIN
Associate Director of Environmental Education: JENNIFER SHELBURNE
Associate Director of Environmental Education: JEFF DONAHUE
Director of Nature and Environmental Education: FORD H. PARKER
Keyword(s): Aquatic Habitats, Fisheries, Renewable Resources, Water Pollution Management, Wetlands

ABUNDANT LIFE SEED FOUNDATION
P.O. Box 772, 930 Lawrence, Port Townsend, WA 98368
Phone: 360-385-5660; Fax: 360-385-7455; Email: abundant@olypen.com
Founded: 1975; Membership: 1,200
Scope: National
Description: Abundant Life Seed Foundation is a nonprofit, tax-exempt organization that propagates and preserves seeds of Northwest native plants and heritage (non-hybrid) vegetables, herbs, and flowers. The Foundation conducts the distribution of seeds (and related books) via a mail-order catalog. Also operates the World Seed Fund, donating seed internationally to those in need, both in the United States and internationally.
Contact(s):
President: LYNN MOSER
Manager: ALETA ANDERSON
Secretary and Treasurer: DAVE DAVISON
Publication(s): *Seed and Book Catalog; Seed Midden*
Keyword(s): Agriculture, Endangered and Threatened Species, Flowers, Plants, and Trees, Gardening and Horticulture

ACRES LAND TRUST
2000 N. Wells St., Fort Wayne, IN 46808-2474
Phone: 219-422-1004; Fax: 219-422-1004
Founded: 1960; Membership: 800
Scope: Statewide
Description: A nonprofit organization dedicated to the acquisition and permanent preservation of natural areas in northeastern Indiana. Conducts a guided field-trip program for children and adults. Organizes canoe trips, concerts and festivals for the membership and the public. Administers 40 nature preserves totaling more than 2,500 acres.
Contact(s):
President: DAVID GALL
Vice President: THEODORE H. HEEMSTRA
Vice President: JAMES D. HADDOCK
Vice President: ROBERT C. WEBER
Treasurer: RICHARD E. WALKER
Publication(s): *Acres Quarterly; Acres Brochure; Field*
Keyword(s): Biodiversity, Endangered and Threatened Species, Environmental and Conservation Education, Land Preservation, Wetlands

ACTION FOR NATURE, INC.
300 Broadway, Suite 28, San Francisco, CA 94133
Phone: 415-421-2640
Scope: National
Description: Action for Nature was organized to foster respect and affection for nature through personal environmental initiatives. AFN is a clearing-house and catalyst for personal action projects and publicizes young peoples' successful environmental initiatives through a newsletter and publication of a book of some of their stories.
Contact(s):
President: EVELYN BALLARD DE GHETALDI
Secretary: MARY MURRAY GRIFFIN-JONES
Treasurer: DAVID YAMAKAWA

ADIRONDACK COUNCIL, THE
P.O. Box D-2, Elizabethtown, NY 12932
Phone: 518-873-2240; Fax: 518-873-6675
Founded: 1975; Membership: 18,000
Scope: Statewide
Description: A nonprofit environmental organization working for protection and preservation of the six million acre Adirondack Park. Programs include monitoring and influencing state programs in the park, helping to promote understanding of the park and the need to protect its very special character, and supporting and advancing positive programs to enhance the park and benefit its people.

Contact(s):
Chairman: JOHN ERNST
Secretary: DEAN COOK
Treasurer: CURTIS WELLING
Executive Director: TIMOTHY BURKE
Vice Chairman: DAVID SKOVRON
Vice Chairman: THOMAS D. THACHER II
Publication(s): *Adirondack Council Newsletter; Adirondack Wildguide: A Natural History of The Adirondack Park; State of the Park*
Keyword(s): Acid Rain, Land Use Planning, Open Space, Sustainable Development, Wildlife and Wildlife Habitat

ADIRONDACK MOUNTAIN CLUB, INC., THE
814 Goggins Rd., Lake George, NY 12845-4117
Phone: 518-668-4447; Fax: 518-668-3746; Email: adkinfo@adk.org; WWW: www.adk.org
Founded: 1922; Membership: 24,000
Scope: Statewide
Description: The Adirondack Mountain Club is dedicated to the protection and responsible recreational use of the New York State Forest Preserve, parks, and other wild lands and waters. The Club is a member-directed organization committed to public service and stewardship. ADK employs a balanced approach to outdoor recreation, advocacy, environmental education, and natural resource conservation. ADK has 26 chapters in NY and NJ.
Contact(s):
President: CHARLES S. LAWRENCE III, c/o ADK 814 Goggins Rd., Lake George, NY 12845-4117
Executive Director: JO A. BENTON; Phone: 518-668-4447
Deputy Executive Director for Public and Legal Affairs: NEIL WOODWORTH; Phone: 518-449-3870; Email: neilwood@ix.netcom.com
Editor: NEAL BURDICK, 35 Woods Dr., Canton, NY 13617
North Country Director of Facilities: ROB BOND
North Country Director of Field Programs: TIMOTHY TIERNEY
Publication(s): *Adirondack Magazine; Guides to Adirondack and Catskill Trails; Adirondack Canoe Waters: North Flow; South and West Flow; Western and Central New York State*
Keyword(s): Conservation of Protected Areas, Environment, Environmental and Conservation Education, Environmental Law, Environmental Preservation, Environmental Protection, Forest Management, Land Preservation, Natural Areas, Natural History, Nongame Wildlife, Public Lands, Wilderness, Wildlands, Wildlands Management

ADIRONDACK NATURE CONSERVANCY/ADIRONDACK LAND TRUST, INC.
P.O. Box 65, Keene Valley, NY 12943
Phone: 518-576-2082
Founded: 1984
Scope: Statewide
Description: The Adirondack Nature Conservancy and Adirondack Land Trust are separate land conservation organizations that have acted in partnership since 1988, coordinating programs and staff. The Adirondack Nature Conservancy protects the plants, animals, and natural communities that represent the diversity of life in the Adirondacks by protecting the lands and waters they need to survive.
Contact(s):
Chairman: EDWARD McNEIL, 108 Burlingame Rd., Syracuse, NY 13202-1604
Secretary: FRANCISCA IRWIN, Rt. 1 Box 80, Essex, NY 12936
Treasurer: MEREDITH PRIME, Heather Hill, Lake Placid, NY 12946
Executive Director: TIMOTHY L. BARNETT
Publication(s): *Developing a Land Conservation Strategy: A Handbook for Land Trusts (1987)*
Keyword(s): Agriculture, Forests and Forestry, Land Preservation, Open Space, Sustainable Development

ADKINS ARBORETUM
P.O. Box 147, Hillsboro, MD 21641
Phone: 410-634-2847; Fax: 410-634-2878; Email: ealtman@shore.intercom.net; WWW: www.bluecrab.org/adkins
Founded: 1984; Membership: 100
Scope: Statewide
Description: The Arboretum is dedicated to the growth and display of native plants and plant communities of the Mid-Atlantic Coastal Plain, and to educate the public about these, and their horticultural uses and conservation.
Contact(s):
President: DEBBY BENNET; Phone: 410-479-2978; Fax: 410-479-1443
Vice President: K. MARC TEFFEAU; Phone: 410-827-8056; Fax: 410-827-9059
Secretary: CAROL STOCKLEY; Phone: 410-479-1750
Treasurer: JOHN ATWOOD; Phone: 410-822-4032
Executive Director: ELLIE ALTMAN; Phone: 410-634-2847; Fax: 410-634-2878; Email: ealtman@shore.intercom.net
Publication(s): *Native Seed*
Keyword(s): Biodiversity, Conservation of Protected Areas, Ecology, Endangered and Threatened Species, Environmental and Conservation Education, Flowers, Plants, and Trees, Landscape Architecture, Wetlands, Wildlife and Wildlife Habitat

ADOPT-A-STREAM FOUNDATION, THE
600-128th St., SE, Everett, WA 98208-6353
Phone: 425-316-8592; Fax: 425-338-1423; Email: aasf@streamkeeper.org; WWW: www.streamkeeper.org
Founded: 1985
Scope: National
Description: Adopt-A-Stream Foundation's mission is to empower people to become stewards of watersheds, wetlands, and streams. The Foundation's long term goal is to ensure that all streams are adopted by watershed residents. The current focus is in the Pacific Northwest. The Foundation conducts "Streamkeeper" workshops that train volunteers how to conduct watershed inventories, and monitor small streams.
Contact(s):
Vice President: TOM SASAKI
Secretary: DARRYL WILLIAMS
Treasurer: GRANT WOODFIELD
Executive Director: TOM MURDOCH
Board President: DICK WALSH
Publication(s): *Adopting a Stream: A Northwest Handbook; Adopting a Wetland: A Northwest Guide; A Streamkeeper's Field Guide: Watershed Inventory and Stream Monitoring Methods; Streamlines; Video: The Streamkeeper, featuring Bill Nye "The Science Guy."*
Keyword(s): Aquatic Habitats, Environmental and Conservation Education, Environmental Planning, Environmental Preservation, Environmental Protection, Fisheries, Lakes, Land Use Planning, Nature Preservation, Nongame Wildlife, Open Space, Raptors, Reptiles and Amphibians, Rivers, Urban Environment

AFRICAN WILDLIFE FOUNDATION
1400 16th St., NW, Suite 120, Washington, DC 20036
Phone: 202-939-3333; Fax: 202-939-3332; Email: awfwash@igc.apc.com; WWW: www.awf.org
Scope: National
Description: The African Wildlife Foundation recognizes that the wildlife and wild lands of Africa have no equal. We work with people-our supporters worldwide and our partners in Africa-to craft and deliver creative solutions for the long-term well-being of Africa's remarkable species, habitats, and the people who depend upon them.
Contact(s):
President: R. MICHAEL WRIGHT
Vice President: MARK STANLEY PRICE
Secretary: JANE W. GASTON
Treasurer: STUART T. SAUNDERS JR.

NON-GOVERNMENTAL ORGANIZATIONS

Assistant Secretary: SIEGLINDE FRIEDMAN
Assistant Treasurer: BARBARA DiPIETRO
Chairman of the Board: STUART SAUNDERS
Vice Chair of the Board: DAVID CHALLINOR
Publication(s): *African Wildlife News*
Keyword(s): Conservation of Protected Areas, Endangered and Threatened Species, International Conservation, Sustainable Development, Wildlife and Wildlife Habitat

AFRICAN WILDLIFE NEWS SERVICE
P.O. Box 546, Olympia, WA 98507-0546
Phone: 360-459-8862; Fax: 360-459-877; Email: awns@aol.com; WWW: www.africanwildlife.org
Founded: *1990*
Scope: *International*
Description: AWNS is a nonprofit, tax-exempt news agency dedicated to reporting the latest news and information on African wildlife.
Contact(s):
President: STEPHEN R. MISHKIN
Vice President: HANK KLEIN
Secretary: PAULA J. SCHWEICH
Treasurer: STEPHEN R. MISHKIN
Editor: STEPHEN R. MISHKIN
Publication(s): *African Wildlife Update*
Keyword(s): Conservation of Protected Areas, Endangered and Threatened Species, International Conservation, Wildlife and Wildlife Habitat, Wildlife Management

AIR AND WASTE MANAGEMENT ASSOCIATION
One Gateway Center, 3rd Fl., Pittsburgh, PA 15222
Phone: 412-232-3444; Fax: 412-232-3450
Founded: *1907;* **Membership:** *13,000*
Scope: *National*
Description: The Air and Waste Management Association is a nonprofit, technical, and environmental association that provides a neutral forum for discussing all sides of an environmental issue. The Association encourages environmental technology development, facilitates technology transfer, and improves environmental management and education. As a leading forum for discussing diverse views on environmental issues, it challenges leaders, professionals, and citizens worldwide to use dialogue for improving the quality of decisions affecting our environment.
Contact(s):
President: PAUL KING
Secretary: DENNIS MITCHELL
Treasurer: DOUGLAS BISSET
1st Vice President: ROBERT E. HALL
Immediate Past President: WILLIAM C. ZEGEL
Publication(s): *Journal of the Air & Waste Management Association; other publications include proceedings of specialty conferences and symposia, prints and videotapes; EM; A&WMA News, monthly newsletter*
Keyword(s): Air Quality and Pollution, Engineering, Environmental Law, Greenhouse Effect/Global Warming, Solid Waste Management

ALABAMA ASSOCIATION OF SOIL AND WATER CONSERVATION DISTRICTS
ATTN: Executive Director, P.O. Box 304800, Montgomery, AL 36130-4800
Scope: *Statewide*
Contact(s):
Executive Director: JEAN M. BALL, P.O. Box 304800, Montgomery, AL 36130-4800; Phone: 334-242-2622; Fax: 334-242-0551; Email: jball@dsmd.dsmd.state.al.us
1st Vice President: GEORGE ROBERTSON JR., 2181 Country Rd. 22, Waverly, AL 36879; Phone: 334-887-6070
2nd Vice President: JAKE HARPER, Rt 1 Box 468, Camden, AL 36726; Phone: 334-682-4463
Board Member: CHARLES A. HOLMES, Rt 1 Box 212, Marion, AL 36756; Phone: 334-683-6869; Fax: 334-583-6869

President/Alternate Board Member: BARNETT KING, Rt 2 Box 27, Luverne, AL 36049-9604; Phone: 334-335-3105; Fax: 334-335-5227
Secretary/Treasurer: CHARLES W. RITTENOUR JR., 1144 Meriwether Rd., Pike Road, AL 36064; Phone: 334-284-5320

ALABAMA B.A.S.S. CHAPTER FEDERATION
ATTN: President, P.O. Box 190, Notasulga, AL 36866
Phone: 334-257-1177
Scope: *Statewide*
Description: An organization of Bassmaster chapters, affiliated with the Bass Anglers Sportsman Society, organized to fight pollution, assist state and national conservation agencies in their efforts, and teach the young people of our country good conservation practices. Dedicated to the realistic conservation of our water resources.
Contact(s):
President: AL REDDING, P.O. Box 190, Notasulga, AL 36866; Phone: 334-257-1177; Fax: 334-257-4665; Email: alred@auburn.campus.mci.net
Conservation Director: BOB FOUNTAIN, 503 Stoney Brook Dr. SW, Jacksonville, AL 36265; Phone: 256-435-8400, 256-435-9127; Fax: 256-435-9005; Email: rfountj@aol.com

ALABAMA ENVIRONMENTAL COUNCIL
2717 7th Ave. S., Suite 207, Birmingham, AL 35233
Phone: 205-322-3126; Fax: 205-324-3784
Founded: *1967;* **Membership:** *1,500 individuals, 40 organizations*
Scope: *Statewide*
Description: Dedicated to the preservation of Alabama's environment on all fronts: air, water, land, and wildlife.
Contact(s):
President: JEFF deGRAFFENREID
Director of Recycling: LARRY CRENSHAW
Manager of Recycling: CRAIG UNDERWOOD; Phone: 205-252-5011
Vice President for Administration: LEILA NABORS
Publication(s): *State News*
Keyword(s): Endangered and Threatened Species, Environmental and Conservation Education, Forests and Forestry, Solid Waste, Water Pollution

ALABAMA NATURAL HERITAGE PROGRAM
The Nature Conservancy, 1500 E. Fairview Ave., Montgomery, AL 36106
Phone: 334-834-4519; Fax: 334-834-5439; Email: alnhp@wsnet.com; WWW: www.heritage.tnc.org/nhp/usal/
Founded: *1989*
Scope: *Regional*
Description: The mission of the Alabama Natural Heritage Program is to provide the best available scientific information on the biological diversity of Alabama, to guide conservation action and promote sound stewardship practices within the state and throughout the Southeast.
Contact(s):
President: JOHN C. SAWHILL; Phone: 703-841-5330; Fax: 703-841-1283
Director: JAREL HILTON
Publication(s): *Natural Heritage News; Inventory List of Rare Threatened and Endangered Plants, Animals, and Natural Communities of Alabama*
Keyword(s): Biodiversity, Conservation, Conservation of Protected Areas, Endangered and Threatened Species, Land Use Planning, Natural Areas, Natural History, Nature Preservation

ALABAMA WATERFOWL ASSOCIATION, INC. (AWA)
P.O. Box 67, Guntersville, AL 35768
Phone: 205-259-2509
Founded: *1987;* **Membership:** *1,276*
Scope: *Statewide*
Description: To protect, enhance, and create wetlands habitat for all wildlife species and other human values; and to enhance waterfowl population and protect our hunting heritage in Alabama.

Contact(s):
Executive Director: GARY BENEFIELD, P.O. Box 67, Guntersville, AL 35976; Phone: 205-593-7712
Chief Executive Officer: JERRY D. DAVIS, 1346 County Rd. 11, Scottsboro, AL 35768; Phone: 205-259-2509
Executive Treasurer: ROGER CROUCH, P.O. Box 67, Guntersville, AL 35976
Publication(s): *Wetlands and Waterfowl News*
Keyword(s): Historic Preservation, Hunting, Waterfowl, Wetlands, Wildlife and Wildlife Habitat

ALABAMA WILDLIFE FEDERATION
46 Commerce St., P.O. Box 2102, Montgomery, AL 36104
Phone: 334-832-9453; Fax: 334-832-9454; Email: alabamawf@mindspring.com
Founded: 1935
Scope: Statewide
Description: A representative statewide organization affiliated with the National Wildlife Federation, dedicated to the protection and enhancement of wildlife and its habitat through public education and government interaction.
Contact(s):
President: BO STARKE
Executive Director: TIM GOTHARD
Affiliate Representative: REBECCA PRITCHETT
Editor: APRIL LUPARDUS
Publication(s): *Alabama Wildlife Magazine*

ALASKA ASSOCIATION OF SOIL AND WATER CONSERVATION DISTRICTS
ATTN: President, P.O. Box 2376, Kodiak, AK 99615
Scope: Statewide
Contact(s):
President, Board Member: OMAR STRATMAN, P.O. Box 2376, Kodiak, AK 99615; Phone: 907-486-5578; Fax: 907-486-5578
Vice President: SHIRLEY SCHOLLENBERG, HC 67 Box 250, Anchor Point, AK 99556; Phone: 907-567-3467
1st Vice President: MERIBETH CRICK, P.O. Box 56505, North Pole, AK 56505; Phone: 907-488-2215
Alternate Board Member: MIKE CARLSON, P.O. Box 953, Delta Junction, AK 99737; Phone: 907-895-4819
Project Coordinator: DOUR WITT, 351 W. Parks Hwy #101, Wasilla, AK 99645; Phone: 907-373-6492; Fax: 907-373-7192
Secretary-Treasurer: MEG BURGETT, P.O. Box 874554, Wasilla, AK 99687; Phone: 907-373-0885; Email: asb@micronet.net

ALASKA AUDUBON SOCIETY
308 G. St., Suite 217, Anchorage, AK 99501
Phone: 907-276-7034; Fax: 907-276-5069; Email: jschoen@audubon.org
Membership: 2,400
Scope: Statewide
Description: The Alaska Audubon Society applies sound science and common sense to protect birds, other wildlife, and their habitats in Alaska. The staff works in cooperation with four local chapters to create a culture of conservation and an environmental ethic that supports a healthy, sustainable economy and a quality of life in harmony with Alaska's natural environment.
Contact(s):
Executive Director: DR. JOHN W. SCHOEN
Development Director: DIANE BLACK
Office Manager: CATHERINE DENNERLEIN
Keyword(s): Biodiversity, Biology, Birds, Conservation of Protected Areas, Endangered and Threatened Species, Environmental and Conservation Education, Forest Management, Nature Preservation, Public Lands, Sustainable Ecosystems, Wetlands, Wildlands, Wildlife and Wildlife Habitat

ALASKA CENTER FOR THE ENVIRONMENT
519 W. 8th, Suite 201, Anchorage, AK 99501
Phone: 907-274-3621; Fax: 907-274-8733; Email: akcenter@alaska.net
Founded: 1971
Scope: Statewide
Description: Nonprofit organization which functions as an advocacy and citizen organizing facility for Alaskan environmental activities. With a professional staff of twelve and a corps of volunteers, the center conducts policy analyses and encourages grassroots activism to conserve and protect Alaska's natural resources, particularly its wildlands.
Contact(s):
Executive Director: KEVIN HARUN
Alaska Rainforest Campaign Grassroots Organizer: SCOTT ANAYA
Director of Alaska Rainforest Issues: KAREN BUTTON
Director of Issues and State Lands Director: CLIFF EAMES
Director of Trailside Discovery Camp: TOM BUREK; Phone: 907-274-5437
Director of Transportation Project: CHERYL RICHARDSON
Director of Valley ACE: DORI McDANNOLD, 642 S. Alaska St., Suite 201, Palmer, AK 99645; Phone: 907-745-8223; Fax: 907-745-8223
Financial Director and Officer Manager: JENNY NORRIS
Membership Director and Volunteer Coordinator: PATTY BLISS
Project Coordinator of Potter Marsh Watershed: RANDY VIRGIN

ALASKA CONSERVATION ALLIANCE
750 West 2nd Ave., Suite 109, Anchorage, AK 99501
Phone: 907-258-6171; Fax: 907-258-6177; Email: unite@akvoice.org
Founded: 1997
Scope: National
Description: An alliance dedicated to strengthening environmental organizations and empowering individuals to protect Alaska's environment through public education, training, advocacy, communication, and strategy development, all with respect for communities and human dignity.
Contact(s):
President: CLAIRE HOLLAND
Secretary: PATTI SAUNDERS
Treasurer: BETH CARLSON
Executive Director: KAY BROWN
Field Organizer: PAULA PHILLIPS
Keyword(s): Air Quality and Pollution, Ancient Forests, Aquatic Habitats, Chemical Pollution Control, Cultural Preservation, EcoAction, Environment, Environmental and Conservation Education, Environmental Justice, Environmental Protection, Sustainable Development, Wetlands, Wilderness

ALASKA CONSERVATION FOUNDATION
750 W. 2nd Ave., Suite 104, Anchorage, AK 99501-2167
Phone: 907-276-1917; Fax: 907-274-4145; Email: acfinfo@akcf.org
Scope: Statewide
Description: A community foundation providing grants for environmental conservation in Alaska. It is not a membership organization. It lists its donors as "Circle of Friends."
Contact(s):
Chair: MATT KIRCHOFF
Executive Director: JAN KONIGSBERG
Honorary Chair: JIMMY CARTER
Program and Finance Director: CHRISTY McGRAW
Secretary and Treasurer: PEG TILESTON
Vice Chair of Alaska Trustees: CINDY ADAMS
Vice Chair of National Trustees: DAVID ROCKEFELLER JR.
Publication(s): *Alaska Conservation Directory; Dispatch; Annual Report; Grant Guidelines*
Keyword(s): Fisheries, Forests and Forestry, Sustainable Ecosystems, Water Resources, Wildlife and Wildlife Habitat

NON-GOVERNMENTAL ORGANIZATIONS

ALASKA CONSERVATION VOICE
750 West 2nd Ave., Suite 109, Anchorage, AK 99501
Phone: 907-258-6171; Fax: 907-258-6177; Email: unite@akvoice.org
Founded: 1997
Scope: Statewide
Description: An organization dedicated to protecting Alaska's environment through public education and advocacy in the Alaska state legislature, Congress and other forums.
Contact(s):
Assistant Director: PATTI SAUNDERS
President: SHANNON O'FALLON
Secretary: PATTI SAUNDERS
Treasurer: BETH CARLSON
Executive Director: KAY BROWN
Field Organizer: PAULA PHILLIPS
Office Assistant: MARLO SHEDLOCK
Organizer/Lobbyist: KIRSTEN SHELTON
Keyword(s): Air Quality and Pollution, Ancient Forests, Aquatic Habitats, Chemical Pollution Control, Cultural Preservation, EcoAction, Environment, Environmental and Conservation Education, Environmental Justice, Environmental Protection, Sustainable Development, Wetlands, Wilderness

ALASKA NATURAL RESOURCE AND OUTDOOR EDUCATION ASSOCIATION
P.O. Box 110536, Anchorage, AK 99511-0536
WWW: www.sfos.alaska.edu:8000/ANROE/ANROE_home.html
Founded: 1983; Membership: 85
Scope: Statewide
Description: ANROE is a statewide network of K-12 school teachers, state and federal agency staff, university faculty and staff, students, and other concerned citizens united to promote the development, delivery, and implementation of educational efforts that help people of all ages learn about and appreciate Alaska's natural resources.
Contact(s):
President: LAUREL DEVANEY; Phone: 907-456-0558; Fax: 907-456-0454; Email: laurel_devaney@fws.gov
Publication(s): *Flyways, Pathways, and Waterways* (newsletter); *ANROE Guide to Natural Resource Education Materials* (catalog)
Keyword(s): Environmental and Conservation Education, Natural History, Training

ALASKA RAINFOREST CAMPAIGN
406 G St., #209, Anchorage, AK 99501
Phone: 907-222-2552; Fax: 907-222-2598; Email: akrain@alaska.net; WWW: www.akrain.org
Founded: 1992; Membership: 14,000 in Alaska/2 million nationwide
Scope: Statewide
Description: Alaska Rainforest Campaign is a coalition of Alaska-based and national environmental organizations working to protect the coastal old-growth rainforests of Alaska, especially the Tongass and Chugach National Forests.
Contact(s):
Campaign Manager: MATTHEW ZENCEY
Director of Washington, DC Office: DIANA RHOADES, 320 Fourth St., NE, Washington, DC 20002; Phone: 202-544-0475; Fax: 202-544-5197; Email: akrain@boo.net
National Field Director: CORRIE BOSMAN
Keyword(s): Rainforests

ALASKA WILDLIFE ALLIANCE, THE
P.O. Box 202022, Anchorage, AK 99520
Phone: 907-277-0897; Fax: 907-277-7423; Email: awa@alaska.net
Founded: 1978
Scope: Statewide
Description: The Alliance is a nonprofit organization whose mission is the protection of Alask's natural wildlife and habitat diversity for its intrinsic value as well as for the benefit of present and future generations.
Contact(s):
Executive Director: DR. PAUL JOSLIN
Associate Director: KAREN DEATHERAGE

ALBERTA FISH AND GAME ASSOCIATION, THE
6924-104 St., Edmonton, Alberta T6H 2L7 Canada
Phone: 403-437-2342; Fax: 403-438-6872
Founded: 1908; Membership: 15,000
Scope: Statewide
Description: To promote through education, lobbying, and programs the conservation and utilization of fish and wildlife, and to protect and enhance the habitat they depend upon.
Contact(s):
President: DAVE POWELL
Editor: KEVIN ROLFE
Executive Vice Director: RON HOUSER
Publication(s): *Outdoor Edge, The*

ALBERTA TRAPPERS ASSOCIATION
#2 9919-106 St., Westlock, Alberta T7P 2K1 Canada
Phone: 403-349-6626
Founded: 1974; Membership: 1,700
Scope: Statewide
Description: Cooperates with all trappers associations and government agencies for a sensible conservation program.
Contact(s):
President: TED GANSKE, Box 6038, Bonnyville, Alberta T9N 2G7 Canada; Phone: 403-826-5026
1st Vice President: MARC McOUAT, Box 1898, High Level, Alberta T0H 1Z0 Canada; Phone: 403-926-2756
2nd Vice President: RON DeSMIT, Box 24, Bellis, Alberta T0A 0J0 Canada; Phone: 403-636-3543
Editor: LUISE VALENTINE
Editor: TED GANSKE
Executive Manager: LUISE VALENTINE
Publication(s): *Alberta Trapper, The*

ALBERTA WILDERNESS ASSOCIATION
Box 6398, Station D, Calgary, Alberta T2P 2E1 Canada
Phone: 403-283-2025; Fax: 403-270-2743; Email: awa@web.net
Founded: 1968; Membership: 2,500
Scope: Statewide
Description: A province-wide, non-profit, charitable organization with a mission to be an advocate for wild Alberta through awareness and action, and functioning on the values of ecocentredness, integrity, respectfulness, participation, tenacity, and passion. The AWA promotes sound ideas and policies for wilderness conservation, fosters appreciation and enjoyment of wilderness, and works with government, industry, organizations and individuals to encourage careful management of Alberta's natural lands and waters.
Contact(s):
President: GLENDA HANNA
Vice President: JENNIFER KLIMEK
Vice President: PETER SHERRINGTON
Secretary: COLIN YOUNG
Administrator: GLENDA HOLST
Conservation Director: DIANNE PACHAL
Editor: WENDY ADAMS
Editor: SHIRLEY BRAY
Past President: CLIFF WALLIS
Volunteer Coordinator: LEE TYMCHUK
Publication(s): *Wild Lands Advocate; Eastern Slopes Wildlands: Our Living Heritage; Landscapes of Southern Alberta; Wild Alberta- Our Last Best Hopes; Willmore Wilderness Park*; list of other publications upon request.
Keyword(s): Conservation of Protected Areas, Endangered and Threatened Species, Environmental Preservation, Nature

Preservation, Public Lands, Wilderness, Wildlands, Wildlife and Wildlife Habitat

ALLIANCE FOR THE CHESAPEAKE BAY
P.O. Box 1981, Richmond, VA 23218
Phone: 804-775-0951
Founded: 1971; Membership: 80 organizations and 900 individuals
Scope: Statewide
Description: To build, maintain, and serve the partnership among the general public, the private sector, and the government that is essential for establishing and sustaining policy, programs, and the political will to preserve and restore the resources of the Chesapeake Bay.
Contact(s):
President: JOHN T. KAUFFMAN; Phone: 610-774-5043
Secretary: TERRY HARWOOD; Phone: 301-380-3106
Treasurer: MICHAEL MARINO; Phone: 410-347-6201
Executive Director: FRANCES FLANIGAN, 6600 York Rd. Suite 100, Baltimore, MD 21212; Phone: 410-377-6270
Vice President, Maryland: JOSEPH A. TIERNAN; Phone: 410-234-5328
Vice President, Pennsylvania: WALTER L. POMEROY; Phone: 717-763-4985
Vice President, Virginia: SUSAN TAYLOR HANSEN; Phone: 757-397-3481
Publication(s): *Bay Journal*
Keyword(s): Environment, Environmental and Conservation Education, Environmental Protection, Fisheries, Pollution Prevention, Population Growth, Rivers, Sustainable Development, Toxic Substances, Water Pollution, Water Quality, Water Resources, Watersheds, Wetlands

Balitmore Office
6600 York Rd., Suite 100, Baltimore, MD 21212
Phone: 410-377-6270; Fax: 410-377-7144
Scope: Statewide
Keyword(s): Environmental and Conservation Education, Rivers, Water Pollution, Water Quality, Wetlands

CRIS Office
P.O. Box 1981, Richmond, VA 23218
Phone: 800-662-CRIS
Scope: Statewide

Harrisburg Office
225 Pine St., Harrisburg, PA 17101
Phone: 717-236-8825; Fax: 717-236-9019
Scope: Statewide

AMANAKA'A AMAZON NETWORK
60 E. 13th St., 5th Fl., New York, NY 10003
Phone: 212-253-9502; Fax: 212-253-9507
Founded: 1990
Scope: National
Description: The Amanaka's Amazon Network is a nonprofit environmental and social justice organization. Amanaka'a serves as a liaison between the peoples of the Amazon and their allies in the U.S. We work to educate the American public about the Amazon Rainforest and its peoples, and support grassroots organizations in the Amazon.
Contact(s):
President: ZEZE WEISS
Vice President: JOHN FRIEDE
Secretary: CHRISTINE HALVORSON
Executive Director (Acting): CHRISTINE HALVORSON
Publication(s): *Letters from the Amazon; series of booklets by people of the Amazon; Amanaka'a Update*
Keyword(s): Cultural Preservation, Environmental Protection, Human Rights, Indigenous People, Rainforests, Sustainable Development

AMERICA THE BEAUTIFUL FUND
1730 K. St., NW, Suite 1002, Washington, DC 20006
Phone: 202-638-1649
Founded: 1965
Scope: National
Description: America the Beautiful Fund gives recognition, technical support, small seed grants, gifts of free seeds and national recognition awards to volunteers and community groups to initiate new local action projects improving the quality of the environment, including design, land preservation, local food production, arts, historical and cultural preservation, and horticultural therapy.
Contact(s):
President: NANINE BILSKI, 1730 K St. Suite 1002, Washington, DC 20006
Vice President: KAY LAUTMAN, 1730 Rhode Island Ave., NW, Suite 700, Washington, DC 20036
Vice President: JEAN WALLACE DOUGLAS, 4733 Woodway Ln., NW, Washington, DC 20016
Secretary: PENNY PAGANO, 4701 Berkley Terr., NW, Washington, DC 20007
Treasurer: SUSAN ANDERSON, 235 Mason Dr., Manhasset, NY 11030
Chairman of the Board: THOMAS FARRELL, First Chicago, 153 W 51 St., New York, NY 10019
Publication(s): *Old Glory; Better Times; The Green Earth Guide*
Keyword(s): Agriculture, Biodiversity, Birds, Botanical Gardens, Conservation of Protected Areas, Conservation Tillage, Cultural Preservation, Culture, Ecology, Environmental and Conservation Education, Flowers, Plants, and Trees, Gardening and Horticulture, Grants, Health and Nutrition, Historic Preservation

AMERICAN ALLIANCE FOR HEALTH PHYSICAL EDUCATION AND RECREATION AND DANCE
1900 Association Dr., Reston, VA 22091
Phone: 703-476-3400
Membership: 30,000
Scope: National
Description: A voluntary professional organization for educators in the fields of physical education, sports and athletics, dance, health and safety, recreation, and outdoor and environmental education. Its purpose is the improvement of education through such professional services as consultation, periodicals and special publications, conferences and workshops, leadership development, determination of standards, and research.
Contact(s):
President: CAROL V. PERSSON, Westfield State College, Westfield, MA 01086
District Representative: MARY-MARGARET McHUGH, Illinois Benedictine College, 5700 College Rd., Lisle, IL 60532
District Representative: WILLIAM J. VINCENT, Department of Kinesiology, California State University, 18111 Nordhoff St., Northridge, CA 91330
District Representative: HELEN CHREST, Box 179, East Helena, MT 59635
District Representative: KATHY KINDERFATHER, 15 E. Jackson Rd., Webster Groves, MO 63119
District Representative: GLENN ROSWAL, Department of HPER, Jacksonville State University, Jacksonville, FL 32265
District Representative: JIM AGLI, PE Department, Southern Connecticut State University, New Haven, CT 06515
Editor: FRAN ROWAN
Executive Vice President: A. GILSON BROWN
President Elect: QUENTINE CHRISTIAN, 7000 Quill Leaf Cove, Austin, TX 78750
Publication(s): *Journal of Physical Education, Recreation and Dance; Health Education; AAHPERD Update; Strategies*

NON-GOVERNMENTAL ORGANIZATIONS

AMERICAN ASSOCIATION FOR LEISURE AND RECREATION (AALR)
1900 Association Dr., Reston, VA 20191
Phone: 703-476-3472
Founded: 1939; Membership: 3,500
Scope: National
Description: The AALR was formed to promote school, community, and national leisure and recreation programs; to communicate to society the importance of intelligent use of leisure time; and to provide for those working or interested in recreation and leisure the opportunity to network and to join together for mutual strength and benefit.
Contact(s):
President: DONNA THOMPSON, University of Northern Iowa, School of HPELS, National Program for Playground Safety, 209 WRC, Cedar Falls, IA 50614-0241; Phone: 800-554-7529; Fax: 319-273-7308
Past President: GALE WIEDOW, University of South Dakota, Dakota Dome Rm 221, Vermillion, SD 57069-2390; Phone: 605-677-5337; Fax: 605-677-5338/5438; Email: gwiedow@usd.edu
President Elect: RANDY SWEDBURG, Concordia University, 7141 Sherbrooke W., Montreal, Quebec H4B 1R6 Canada; Phone: 514-848-3331; Fax: 514-848-4200
Representative to the Board of Governors: NORMAN GILCHREST, Baylor University, HHPR Dept., Box 97313, Waco, TX 76798-7313; Phone: 254-710-3505; Fax: 254-710-3527; Email: buddy_gilchrest@baylor.edu
Publication(s): *Leisure Today; AALReporter*
Keyword(s): Family Recreation, Leisure, Outdoor Recreation

AMERICAN ASSOCIATION FOR THE ADVANCEMENT OF SCIENCE
1200 New York Ave., NW, Washington, DC 20005
Phone: 202-326-6400
Founded: 1848; Membership: 140,000
Scope: National
Description: Objectives are to further the work of scientists, to facilitate cooperation among them, to foster scientific freedom and responsibility, to improve the effectiveness of science in the promotion of human welfare, and to increase public understanding and appreciation of the importance and promise of the methods of science in human progress.
Contact(s):
President: M. R. GREENWOOD
Treasurer: WILLIAM T. GOLDEN; Phone: 212-425-0333
Chairman of the Board: RITA COLWELL
Editor-in-Chief: FLOYD E. BLOOM; Phone: 202-326-6505
Executive Officer: RICHARD S. NICHOLSON; Phone: 202-326-6639
Publication(s): *Science; Science Books and Films, Science's Next Wave*
Keyword(s): Biodiversity, Biology, Communications, Greenhouse Effect/Global Warming, Population Growth

AMERICAN ASSOCIATION OF BOTANICAL GARDENS AND ARBORETA, INC.
351 Longwood Rd., Kennett Square, PA 19348
Phone: 610-925-2500
Founded: 1940; Membership: 2,400
Scope: National
Description: AABGA is a nonprofit, membership organization serving North American botanical gardens, arboreta, and their professional staffs.
Contact(s):
President: GERARD T. DONNELLY, Executive Director of The Morton Arboretum, Rt. 53, Lisle, IL 60532
Vice President: ERIC TSCHANZ
Secretary: RICHARD DALEY, Director of Denver Botanic Gardens, 909 York St., Denver, CO 80206
Treasurer: JONATHAN SHAW, President of Bok Tower Gardens, P.O. Box 3810, Lake Wales, FL 33859-3810
Executive Director: NANCY MORIN
Director of Publications: JOSH BLUMENFELD
Past President: GEORGE BRIGGS, Director of The North Carolina Arboretum, P.O. Box 6617, Asheville, NC 28816
Publication(s): *Public Garden, The; AABGA Newsletter*
Keyword(s): Botanical Gardens, Flowers, Plants, and Trees, Gardening and Horticulture, Internships

AMERICAN ASSOCIATION OF FIELD BOTANISTS
P.O. Box 23542, Chattanooga, TN 37422
Founded: 1983; Membership: 200
Scope: National
Description: The American Association of Field Botanists is an organization of amateur and professional botanists dedicated to the protection of native plants and the preservation of their natural habitats, the exchange of information necessary to understand and maintain biodiversity, and the education of the public regarding threatened and endangered flora.
Contact(s):
President: CHARLES L. WILSON, 4201 Gann Store Rd., Hixson, TN 37343; Phone: 423-875-9625
Secretary: JOYCE S. MERRITT, 327 Guild Dr., Chattanooga, TN 37421
Treasurer: KURT A. EMMANUELE, Baylor School, Box 1337, Chattanooga, TN 37401
Publication(s): *American Association of Field Botanists Newsletter*
Keyword(s): Biodiversity, Conservation of Protected Areas, Ecology, Endangered and Threatened Species, Flowers, Plants, and Trees

AMERICAN ASSOCIATION OF ZOO KEEPERS, INC.
Administrative Offices, 635 SW Gage Blvd., Topeka, KS 66606
Phone: 785-273-1980; Fax: 785-273-1980
Founded: 1967; Membership: 2,800
Scope: National
Description: An international nonprofit organization of animal keepers and other persons interested in quality animal care and in promoting animal keeping as a profession. Chapters are active at zoos throughout North America. Promotes continuing education for keepers, national and international conservation projects, keeper-initiated zoo research, and educational publications.
Contact(s):
Administrative Secretary of Administrative Offices: BARBARA MANSPEAKER
Board of Directors: JAN REED-SMITH, JohnBall Zoo, 1300 W. Fulton St., Grand Rapids, MI 49504; Phone: 616-336-4301
Board of Directors: DAVID LUCE, Oklahoma City Zoological Park, 2101 NE 50th St., Oklahoma City, OK 73111; Phone: 405-424-3344
Board of Directors: LUCY SEGERSON, NC Zoo, 4401 Zoo Parkway, Asheboro, NC 27203-9416; Phone: 910-879-7672
Board of Directors: MARILYN COLE, Box 335, Pickering, Ontario L1V 2R6 Canada; Phone: 905-683-2116
Board of Directors: DIANE CALLAWAY, Omaha's Henry Doorly Zoo, 3702 S. 10th St., Omaha, NE 68107; Phone: 402-733-8401
Board of Directors: JACQUE BLESSINGTON, Kansas City Zoological Gardens, 6700 Zoo Dr., Kansas City, MO ; Phone: 816-871-5700
Board of Directors: SCOTT M. WRIGHT, Cleveland Metroparks Zoo, 3900 Brookside Park Dr., Cleveland, OH 44109; Phone: 216-661-6500
Editor: SUSAN CHAN
Executive Director of the Board: ED HANSEN, c/o AAZK Inc., 635 SW Gage Blvd., Topeka, KS 66606-2066; Phone: 785-273-1980
President of the Board: RIC URBAN, Houston Zoological Gardens, 1513 N. MacGregor Way, Houston, TX 77030; Phone: 713-284-8303
Publication(s): *Animal Keepers' Forum; Diet Notebook and Mammals vol. 1; Handbook of Zoonotic Diseases; Crisis Management Resource Notebook*

Keyword(s): Conservation of Protected Areas, Endangered and Threatened Species, International Conservation, Natural History, Wildlife Management, Zoology

AMERICAN BASS ASSOCIATION OF CONNECTICUT, THE
ATTN: President, 115 Summer St., Portland, CT 06480
Scope: Statewide
Description: An organization of the individual members and bass fishing clubs, affiliated with the American Bass Association, Inc. Dedicated to protecting and enhancing the state's fishery resources, to promote the sport of bass fishing, and to teach youngsters the fun of fishing and instill in them an appreciation of the life-giving waters of America.
Contact(s):
President: BRUCE E. THIVIERGE, 115 Summer St., Portland, CT 06480; Phone: 203-342-5249

AMERICAN BASS ASSOCIATION OF KENTUCKY, THE
3301 Hardeman Dr., Ashland, KY 41101
Phone: 606-324-4894
Scope: Statewide
Contact(s):
President: MARK BAYES, 3301 Hardeman Dr., Ashland, KY 41101; Phone: 606-324-4894

AMERICAN BASS ASSOCIATION OF MAINE, THE
ATTN: President, R.R. #2101, Munroe, ME 04951
Scope: Statewide
Contact(s):
President: BUTCH GREEN, R.R. #2101, Munroe, ME 04951; Phone: 207-525-3001

AMERICAN BASS ASSOCIATION OF MARYLAND, THE
ATTN: President, 15401 Wembrough St., Colesville, MD 20905
Founded: 1987
Scope: Statewide
Description: An organization of the individual members and bass fishing clubs, affiliated with the American Bass Association, Inc., dedicated to protecting and enhancing the state's fishery resources; to promote the sport of bass fishing; and to teach youngsters the fun of fishing and instill in them an appreciation of the life-giving waters of America. Meetings held in Cockeysville on the second Wednesday of every other month.
Contact(s):
President: EDWARD R. LOHR SR., 15401 Wembrough St., Colesville, MD 20905; Phone: 301-989-2507
Vice President: BOB JONES
Secretary: JIM BURKHART
Treasurer: CHUCK DUVALL
Publication(s): *Maryland ABA News*
Keyword(s): Environmental Preservation, Fisheries, Sport Fishing, Water Resources, Youth Organizations

AMERICAN BASS ASSOCIATION OF MASSACHUSETTS, THE
359 Providence Rd., South Grafton, MA 01560
Phone: 508-839-6008
Scope: Statewide
Contact(s):
President: STEVE LEMOINE

AMERICAN BASS ASSOCIATION OF NEW HAMPSHIRE, THE
ATTN: President, 235 Ridgeview Rd., Weare, NH 03281
Scope: Statewide
Description: An organization of the individual members and bass fishing clubs, affiliated with the American Bass Association, Inc., dedicated to protecting and enhancing the state's fishery resources; to promote the sport of bass fishing; and to teach youngsters the fun of fishing and instill in them an appreciation of the life-giving waters of America.
Contact(s):
President: JOHN COWAN, 235 Ridgeview Rd., Weare, NH 03281; Phone: 603-529-2642

AMERICAN BASS ASSOCIATION OF NEW JERSEY, THE
ATTN: President, 418 B Willow Turn, Mt. Laurel, NJ 08054
Scope: Statewide
Description: An organization of the individual members and bass fishing clubs, affiliated with the American Bass Association, Inc., dedicated to protecting and enhancing the state's fishery resources; to promote the sport of bass fishing; and to teach youngsters the fun of fishing and instill in them an appreciation of the life-giving waters of America.
Contact(s):
President: JOE ROBBINS, 418 B Willow Turn, Mt. Laurel, NJ 08054; Phone: 609-778-0383

AMERICAN BASS ASSOCIATION OF WEST VIRGINIA, THE
2620 Fairmont Ave., Suite 110, Fairmont, WV 26554
Phone: 304-366-8183
Scope: Statewide
Contact(s):
President: DENZIL COURTNEY
Keyword(s): Environmental and Conservation Education, Internships, Natural History, Outdoor Recreation

AMERICAN BASS ASSOCIATION, INC.
P.O Box 896, Gate City, VA 24251-0896
Phone: 540-386-2109; Fax: 540-386-9421; Email: aba@mounet.com
Founded: 1985; Membership: 20,000
Scope: National
Description: A nonprofit, tax-exempt national association dedicated to protecting and enhancing America's fishery resources; to promoting bass fishing as a major sport; and to teaching young people the fun of fishing and instilling in them an appreciation of the life-giving waters of America.
Contact(s):
President: BOB BARKER
Secretary: JOHN KEEGAN, 104 S. Cove Rd., Williamsburg, VA 23188; Phone: 757-564-0825
Director: AUDREY BARNETT, 1201 Bohmen, Pubelo, CO 81006
Director: WAYNE J. HOOD, 2909 N. Bayshore Dr., LaCrosse, WI 54603
Director of Eastern Region: PAUL NOECHEL, Rt. 2 Box 270, Lost Creek, WV 26385
Director-At-Large: ED METZGER, 710 Edgewater Dr., Inverness, FL 34450

AMERICAN BIRD CONSERVANCY
1250 24th St., NW, Suite 400, Washington, DC 20037
Phone: 202-778-9666; Fax: 202-778-9778; Email: abc@abcbirds.org
Founded: 1994
Scope: National
Description: American Bird Conservancy (ABC), is a U.S. based, nonprofit, membership organization dedicated to the conservation of wild birds and their habitats throughout the Americas. ABC supports the partners in flight initiative through the magazine Bird Conservation and programs such as the important Bird Area Program.
Contact(s):
Chairman: HOWARD P. BROKAW
President: DR. GEORGE H. FENWICK
Secretary: CRAIG S. HARRISON
Treasurer: STEPHEN ECCLES
Director of Important Bird Areas: DR. JEFF PRICE
Director of Internation Development: MIKE PARR
Vice Chair: CYNTHIA LENHART
Vice President of Government Relations: GERALD WINEGRAD
Vice President of Membership Development: MERRIE MORRISON
Vice Presient of Partners In Flight: DR. DAVID PASHLEY
Keyword(s): Birds, Conservation of Protected Areas, Endangered and Threatened Species, Environmental Planning, International Conservation

NON-GOVERNMENTAL ORGANIZATIONS

AMERICAN BIRDING ASSOCIATION
P.O. Box 6599, Colorado Springs, CO 80934
Phone: 719-578-1614
Founded: 1969; Membership: 20,000
Scope: National
Description: The American Birding Association provides leadership to field birders by increasing their knowledge, skills, and enjoyment of birding. The ABA supports the interests of birders of all ages and experience and actively encourages the conservation of birds and their habitats.
Contact(s):
President: ALLAN R. KEITH
Vice President: WAYNE R. PETERSEN
Secretary: BLAKE MAYBANK
Treasurer: GERARD ZIARNO
Executive Director: GREGORY S. BUTCHER
Editor: PAUL BAICICH
Editor: MATT PEUKAN
Editor: CAROL LAWSON
Editor: KENN KAUFMAN
Publication(s): *Birding; Winging It; Field Notes; ABA Checklist; ABA/Lane Series of Birdfinding Guides (15 titles); Volunteer Directory; Membership Directory*
Keyword(s): Biodiversity, Birds, Environmental and Conservation Education, Outdoor Recreation, Wildlife and Wildlife Habitat

AMERICAN CAMPING ASSOCIATION, INC.
5000 State Rd. 67N, Martinsville, IN 46151
Phone: 765-342-8456; Email: aca@aca-camps.org
Founded: 1910; Membership: 5,600
Scope: National
Description: The American Camping Association is a nonprofit and nonsectarian organization. Its mission is to enhance the quality of the experience for youths and adults in organized camping, to promote high professional practices in camp administration, and to interpret the values of organized camping to the public. Services are offered from the national office and through its 25 local sections.
Contact(s):
President: RODGER POPKIN
Director of Public Relations: BOB SCHULTZ
Executive Vice President: PEG SMITH
Publication(s): *Camping Magazine; Guide to Accredited Camps; various camp-related publications*
Keyword(s): Environmental and Conservation Education, Health and Nutrition, Internships, Outdoor Recreation, Youth Organizations

AMERICAN CANAL SOCIETY, INC.
840 Rinks Lane, Savannah, PA 38372-9704
Founded: 1972; Membership: 900
Scope: National
Description: A nonprofit organization dedicated to historic canal research, preservation, and canal parks.
Contact(s):
President: TERRY K. WOODS, 6939 Eastham Circle, Canton, OH 44708
Editor: DAVID ROSS, 840 Rinks Lane, Savannag, TN 38372-9704
Secretary and Treasurer: CHARLES W. DERR JR., 117 Main St., Freemansburg, PA 18017; Phone: 215-691-0956
Publication(s): *American Canals (Quarterly Bulletin), American Canal Guides #1, #2, #3, #4, #5; Best From American Canals #1, #2, #3, #4 #5, #6, #7, #8 Journal*

AMERICAN CAVE CONSERVATION ASSOCIATION
119 E. Main St., P.O. Box 409, Horse Cave, KY 42749
Phone: 502-786-1466
Founded: 1977
Scope: National
Description: The ACCA is a national organization formed to conserve caves and karstlands, and other resources associated with them. Primary objectives are to provide information, technical assistance, and public education and management training programs; and operation of the American Cave and Karst Center, a national environmental education center and museum.
Contact(s):
President: ROY POWERS JR.; Phone: 540-546-5386
Vice President: TOM ALEY; Phone: 417-785-4289
Executive Director: DAVID G. FOSTER; Phone: 502-786-1466
Publication(s): *American Caves Magazine*
Keyword(s): Cave, Endangered and Threatened Species, Environmental and Conservation Education, Geology, Land Use Planning, Museum, Water Resources

AMERICAN CETACEAN SOCIETY
P.O. Box 1391, San Pedro, CA 90733-0391
Phone: 310-548-6279; Fax: 310-548-6950; Email: acs@pobox.com; WWW: www.acsonline.org
Founded: 1967; Membership: 1,200
Scope: National
Description: A nonprofit organization that works in the areas of conservation, education, and research to protect marine mammals, especially whales, dolphins, and porpoises, and the oceans they live in.
Publication(s): *Whalewatcher: Journal of the American Cetacean Society; Spyhopper; ACS National Newsletter*
Keyword(s): Aquatic Habitats, Endangered and Threatened Species, Environmental and Conservation Education, Marine Mammals, Wildlife and Wildlife Habitat

AMERICAN CHESTNUT FOUNDATION, THE
469 Main St., P.O. Box 4044, Bennington, VT 05201-4044
Phone: 802-447-0110; Fax: 802-447-3712; Email: chestnut@acf.org; WWW: www.chestnut.acf.org
Founded: 1983; Membership: 2,800
Scope: National
Description: Funded by private contributions, the purpose of The American Chestnut Foundation is to promote the preservation and restoration of the American chestnut, an important wildlife and timber tree killed by a blight early in the Twentieth Century; to operate two research breeding farms in Meadowview, VA; to provide grants for cutting edge research; and to identify surviving trees and establish satellite research plantings.
Contact(s):
President: L. L. COULTER, P.O. Box 365, Central Lake, MI 49622
Secretary: DR. DENNIS FULBRIGHT, Dept. of Botany and Plant Pathology, 166 Plant Biology, Michigan State University, E.Lansing, MI 48824
Treasurer: DR. WILLIAM MacDONALD, College of Agriculture and Forestry, West Virginia University, P.O. Box 6057, Morgantown, WV 26506
Development Director: TAMMY L. CARPENTER, 469 Main St., P.O. Box 4044, Bennington, VT 05201-4044
Membership Director: KELLY GRUNDMAN, 469 Main St., P.O. Box 4044, Bennington, VT 05201-4044
Vice President of Development: FORREST MACGREGOR, TACF Asheville Office, 46 Haywood St., Suite 213, Ashevill, NC 28801
Vice President of Science: DR. J. HILL CRADDOCK, U of TN - Chattanooga, 615 McCallie Ave, Chattanooga, TN 37403-2598
Publication(s): *Bark, The; Journal of The American Chestnut Foundation*
Keyword(s): Biodiversity, Endangered and Threatened Species, Flowers, Plants, and Trees, Wildlife and Wildlife Habitat

AMERICAN CONSERVATION ASSOCIATION, INC.
1200 New York Ave., NW, Suite 400, Washington, DC 20005
Phone: 202-289-2431; Fax: 202-289-1396
Founded: 1958
Scope: National
Description: A nonmembership nonprofit, educational and scientific organization formed to advance knowledge and understanding of conservation, and to preserve and develop natural resources for public use.

Contact(s):
President: LAURANCE ROCKEFELLER
Secretary: R. SCOTT GREATHEAD
Treasurer: CARMEN REYES
Executive Director: CHARLES CLUSEN
Founder Honorary Trustee: LAURANCE S. ROCKEFELLER
Keyword(s): Air Quality and Pollution, Coasts, Environmental Law, Outdoor Recreation, Urban Environment

AMERICAN CONSERVATION ASSOCIATION, INC. (New York Office)
30 Rockefeller Plaza, Rm. 5402, New York, NY 10112
Phone: 212-649-5822
Scope: National

AMERICAN COUNCIL FOR AN ENERGY-EFFICIENT ECONOMY
1001 Connecticut Ave., NW, #801, Washington, DC 20036
Phone: 202-429-8873; Fax: 202-429-2248; Email: ace3pubs@ix.netcom.com
Founded: 1980
Scope: National
Description: Advancing energy efficiency as a means of promoting both economic prosperity and environmental protection. ACEEE conducts technical and policy assessments; advises governments and utilities; publishes books, conference proceedings and reports; organizes conferences and workshops; and informs consumers.
Contact(s):
Deputy Director: STEVE NADEL; Phone: 202-429-8873; Fax: 202-429-2248
President: CARL BLUMSTEIN; Phone: 202-429-8873; Fax: 202-429-2248
Executive Director: HOWARD GELLER; Phone: 202-429-8873; Fax: 202-429-2248
Publication(s): *Consumer Guide to Home Energy Savings: Guide to Energy-Efficient Office Equipment; Regulatory Incentives for Demand-Side Management; Transportation and Energy: Strategies for a Sustainable Transportation System; Using Consensus Building to Improve Utility Reulation; Energy Innovations: A Prosperous Path to a Clean Environment*
Keyword(s): Energy, Transportation

AMERICAN FARMLAND TRUST
1200 18th St., NW, Suite 800, Washington, DC 20036
Phone: 202-331-7300; Email: info@farmland.org
Founded: 1980; Membership: 30,000
Scope: National
Description: AFT is a nonprofit conservation organization working to stop the loss of productive farmland and to promote farming practices that lead to a healthy environment. Its programs include public education, technical assistance, policy development, and direct farmland-protection projects.
Contact(s):
President: RALPH E. GROSSI
Chairman of the Board: WILLIAM K. REILLY
Director for Farmland Advisory Services: JULIA FREEDGOOD
Director of Administration and Finance: SHARON PHENNEGER
Director of Center for Agriculture in the Environment: DR. ANN SORENSEN
Director of Farms: BRYAN PETRUCCI
Director of Field Operations: ROBERT WAGNER
Director of Land Protection: DENNIS BIDWELL
Director of Public Education: BERNADINE PRINCE
Executive Committee of the Board Chairman: ALFRED H. TAYLOR JR.
Senior Vice President for Public Policy: EDWARD THOMPSON JR.
Vice Chairman of the Board: EDWARD H. HARTE
Vice President for Marketing: JIMMY DAUKAS
Vice President for Programs: TIM WARMAN
Publication(s): *Your Land Is Your Legacy (1997); Saving American Farmland: What Works (1997); Farming on the Edge II (1997); Forging New Protections: Purchasing Development Rights to Save Farmland (1996); Living on the Edge:The Costs and Risks of Scatter Development (1998); Sharing the Responsibility: What Agricultural Landowners Think About Property Rights, Government Regulation, and the Environment (1998); American Farmland (Quarterly Magazine); Investing in the Future of Agriculture (1997)*
Keyword(s): Agriculture, Environmental and Conservation Education, Land Purchase, Land Use Planning, Wetlands

AMERICAN FEDERATION OF MINERALOGICAL SOCIETIES
Central Office, P.O. Box 26523, Oklahoma City, OK 73126-0523
Founded: 1945; Membership: 56,000
Scope: National
Description: To promote popular interest and education in the various earth sciences, in particular, the subjects of geology, mineralogy, paleontology, lapidary and other related subjects, and to sponsor and provide means of coordinating the work and efforts of all persons and groups interested therein; to sponsor and encourage the formation and international development of societies and regional federations, and by and through such means to strive toward greater international goodwill and fellowship.
Contact(s):
President: LEWIS ELROD, 2699 Lascassas Pike, Murfreesboro, TN 37230
Secretary: DAN McLENNAN, P.O. Box 26523, Oklahoma City, OK 73126-0523
Treasurer: TOBY COZENS, 4401 SW Hill St., Seattle, WA 98116-1924
Editor: MEL ALBRIGHT, Rt. 3 Box 8500, Bartlesville, OK 74003
Publication(s): *American Federation Newsletter; AFMS Safety Manual; AFMS Uniform Rules booklets*
Keyword(s): Environmental Preservation, Public Lands, Wilderness

AMERICAN FISHERIES SOCIETY
Headquarters, 5410 Grosvenor Ln., Suite 110, Bethesda, MD 20814
Phone: 301-897-8616; Fax: 301-897-8096; Email: main@fisheries.org; WWW: www.fisheries.org
Founded: 1870; Membership: 9,200
Scope: National
Description: A professional society to promote the conservation, development, and wise utilization of fisheries, both recreational and commercial.
Contact(s):
President: ROBERT F. CARLINE, 113 Merkle Bldg., University Park, PA 16802; Phone: 814-865-5611; Fax: 814-863-4710
Vice President: CHRISTINE M. MOFFITT, Department of Fish and Wildlife Resources, University of ID, Moscow, ID 83844; Phone: 208-885-7047; Fax: 208-885-9080
1st Vice President: CARL BURGER, USFWS, Abernathy Tech Center, 1440 Abernathy Rd., Longview, WA 98632; Phone: 360-425-6072; Fax: 360-636-1885
2nd Vice President: KENNETH BEAL, NMFS, 1 Blackburn Dr., Glouseter, MA 01930; Email: ken.beal@noaa.gov
Acting Executive Director: ROBERT KENALL
Director of Administration and Finance: BETSY FRITZ
Director of Publications: ROBERT KENDALL
Past President: WILLIAM W. TAYLOR, Department of Fish and Wildlife, MI State University, East Lansing, MI 48824; Phone: 517-353-0647; Fax: 517-432-1699
Publication(s): *Transactions of the American Fisheries Society; North American Journal of Fisheries Management; Progressive Fish-Culturist, The Journal of Aquatic Animal Health, Fisheries*
Keyword(s): Aquatic Habitats, Fisheries, Renewable Resources, Water Pollution, Wetlands

Bioengineering Section
R.R. 7 Box 422, Wellsboro, PA 16901
Phone: 717-724-3322; Fax: 717-724-2525
Scope: National
Contact(s):
President: JAMES W. MEADE

NON-GOVERNMENTAL ORGANIZATIONS

Canadian Aquatic Resources Section
ON Min Nat Resour, Glenora Fish Sta RR4, Picton, Manitoba K0K 2T0 Canada
Phone: 613-476-3287; Fax: 613-476-7131; Email: casselj@gov.on.ca
Scope: National
Contact(s):
President: JOHN CASSELMAN

Computer User Section
Michigan DNR - Fisheries Division, P.O. Box 241, Shaftsburg, MI 48882
Phone: 517-373-1280; Fax: 517-373-0381; Email: whelang@state.mi.us
Scope: National
Contact(s):
President: GARY E. WHELAN

Early Life History
NOAA - National Marine Fisheries Service, The Beaufort Laboratory, 101 Pivers Island Rd., Beufort, NC 28526
Phone: 919-728-8727; Fax: 919-728-8747; Email: jgovoni@hatteras.bea.nmfs.gov
Scope: National
Contact(s):
President: JEFF GOVONI

Education Section
MT Cooperative Fishery Research Unit, Dept. of Biol., MT State University, Bozeman, MT 59717
Phone: 406-994-2380; Fax: 406-994-7479
Scope: National
Contact(s):
President: ALEXANDER V. ZALE

Equal Opportunities Section
OR Department of Fish and Wildlife, 211 Inlow Hall, EOSC, La Grande, OR 97850
Phone: 541-962-3777; Fax: 541-962-3849
Scope: National
Contact(s):
President: MARY LOUISE KEEFE

Estuaries Section
NOAA/NMFS F/HP4 Off., Hab. Prot., 1315 East-West Highway, Silver Spring, MD 20910-3282
Phone: 301-713-2319; Fax: 301-713-1043
Scope: National
Contact(s):
President: STEPHEN M. WASTE

Fish Culture Section
Texas Parks & Wildlife Dept., P.O. Box 56, Staples, TX
Phone: 512-353-0313; Fax: 512-353-0629
Scope: National
Contact(s):
President: DON MacKINLAY

Fish Health Section
Clear Springs Food Inc., Resources Dept., P.O. Box 712, Buhl, ID 83316
Phone: 208-543-3456; Fax: 208-543-4146
Scope: National
Contact(s):
President: SCOTT LaPATRA

Fisheries Administrators Section
4200 Smith School Rd., Austin, TX 78744
Phone: 512-689-8100; Fax: 512-389-4388
Scope: National
Contact(s):
President: PHILIP P. DUROCHER

Fisheries History Section
8200 Pine Cross, Ann Arbor, MI 48103
Phone: 313-426-2975; Fax: 313-426-2975
Scope: National
Contact(s):
President: CARLOS FETTEROLF

Fisheries Law Section
1339 East Capitol, SE, Washington, DC 20003-1551
Phone: 202-547-3797; Fax: 202-547-4174
Scope: National
Contact(s):
President: DAVID L. ALLISON

Fisheries Management Section
OK Fish Res Lab, 500 E. Constellation, Norman, OK 73072
Phone: 405-325-7288; Fax: 405-325-7631
Scope: National
Contact(s):
President: STEPHEN FILIPEK

Genetics Section
Trout Unlimited, 1500 Wilson Blvd., Ste 310, Arlington, VA 22209
Phone: 703-284-9415; Fax: 703-284-9400; Email: jepifanio@tu.org
Scope: National
Contact(s):
President: JOHN M. EPIFANIO

International Fisheries Section
Dept. of Soc., 429 Berkey Hall, MI State University, East Lansing, MI 48824-1111
Phone: 517-355-5048; Fax: 517-432-2856
Scope: National
Contact(s):
President: CRAIG K. HARRIS

Introduced Fish Section
Dept. Fisheries & Wildlife Utah State Univ., Logan, UT 84322-5210
Phone: 801-797-0997; Fax: 801-797-1871; Email: toline@cc.usu.edu
Scope: National
Contact(s):
President: ANNA TOLING

Marine Fisheries Section
Hatfield Marine Science Center, Oregon State University, Newport, OR 98365
Phone: 503-867-0135; Fax: 503-867-0105
Scope: National
Contact(s):
President: MAX STOCKER

Native People Fisheries Section
USFWS, 4401 N. Fairfax Dr., Suite 840, Arlington, VA 22203
Phone: 703-358-1718; Fax: 703-358-2044; Email: hannibal_bolton@fws.gov
Scope: National
Contact(s):
President: HANNIBAL BOLTON

North Central Division
Il DNR Watershed Mgmt., 600 N. Grand Ave., West Springfield, IL 62701
Phone: 217-785-5935; Fax: 217-785-8262; Email: dausten@dnrmail.state.il.us
Scope: National
Contact(s):
President: DOUGLAS J. AUSTEN

Northeastern Division
NE Utilities Service CO, P.O. Box 270, Hartford, CT 06141-0270
Phone: 860-665-5448; Fax: 860-665-3777; Email: birelle@nu.com
Scope: National
Contact(s):
President: LINDA E. BIRELY

Physiology Section
Conte Anadromous Fish Res Ctr, Turn Falls, MA 01376
Phone: 413-863-8995; Fax: 413-863-9810; Email: mccormick@umext.umass.edu
Scope: National
Contact(s):
President: STEVE MCCORMICK

Socioeconomics Section
MIT Sea Grant, 292 Main St., E38-300, Cambridge, MA 02139
Phone: 617-253-9308; Fax: 617-252-1615
Scope: National
Contact(s):
President: MADELEINE HALL-ARBER

Southern Division
Horn Point Environmental Lab, Univ MD, Box 775, Cambridge, MD 21613
Phone: 410-221-8466; Fax: 410-221-8456; Email: harrell@hpl.umces.edu
Scope: National
Contact(s):
President: REGINAL M. HARRELL

Southern Ontario Chapter
ATTN: President, S. Ontario Chapter, Tarandus Assoc. Limited, 18 Rregan Rd. Unit 24, Brampton, Ontario L7A1CZ
Founded: 1988
Scope: National
Description: A professional society to promote the conservation, development, and wise utilization of fisheries, both recreational and commercial. Affiliated with American Fisheries Society Headquarters in Bethesda, Maryland.
Contact(s):
President: S. DEBROAH SPELLER, S. Ontario Chapter, Tarandus Assoc. Limited, 18 Rregan Rd. Unit 24, Brampton, ON L7A 1CZ Canada; Phone: 905-840-6563

Water Quality Section
OH River Valley Water San Comm, 5735 Kellog Ave., Cincinnati, OH 45228-1112
Phone: 513-231-7719; Fax: 513-231-7761
Scope: National
Contact(s):
President: GERRY G. SCHULTE

Western Division
Weyerhaeuser CO, Tech Ctr. 1A5, Tacoma, WA 98477
Phone: 253-924-6557; Fax: 253-924-6970; Email: bilbyb@wdni.com
Scope: National
Contact(s):
President: ROBERT E. BILBY

AMERICAN FISHERIES SOCIETY, ALABAMA CHAPTER
ATTN: President, Alabama Chapter, 3355 Audubon Rd., Montgomery, AL 36106-2404
Founded: 1991
Scope: Statewide
Description: A professional society to promote the conservation, development, and wise utilization of fisheries, both recreational and commerical. Affiliatted with American Fisheries Society Headquarters in Bethesda, Maryland.
Contact(s):
President: GREGORY M. LEIN, Alabama Chapter, 3355 Audubon Rd., Montgomery, AL 36106-2404; Phone: 334-844-9318
Keyword(s): Aquatic Habitats, Fisheries, Renewable Resources, Water Pollution Management, Wetlands

AMERICAN FISHERIES SOCIETY, ALASKA CHAPTER
ATTN: President Alaska Chapter, For Sci Lab, 2770 Sherwood Ln., Ste 2A, Juneau, AK 99801
Founded: 1973
Scope: Statewide
Description: A professional society to promote the conservation, development, and wise utilization of fisheries, both recreational and commerical. Affiliated with American Fisheries Society Headquarters in Bethesda, Maryland.
Contact(s):
President: MASON D. BRYANT, Alaska Chapter, For Sci Lab, 2770 Sherwood Ln, Ste 2A, Juneau, AK 99801; Phone: 907-586-8811
Keyword(s): Aquatic Habitats, Fisheries, Renewable Resources, Water Pollution Management, Wetlands

AMERICAN FISHERIES SOCIETY, ARIZONA-NEW MEXICO CHAPTER
ATTN: President, Arizona-New Mexico Chapter, NBS NMSU Coop Res Unit, Box 30003 4901, Las Cruces, AZ 88003-0003
Founded: 1967
Scope: Statewide
Description: A professional society to promote the conservation, development, and wise utilization of fisheries, both recreational and commerical. Affiliated with American Fisheries Society Headquarters in Bethesda, Maryland.
Contact(s):
President: COLLEEN A. CALDWELL, Arizona-New Mexico Chapter, NBS NMSU Coop Res Unit, Box 30003 4901, Las Cruces, AZ 88003-0003; Phone: 505-646-8126
Keyword(s): Aquatic Habitats, Fisheries, Renewable Resources, Water Pollution Management, Wetlands

AMERICAN FISHERIES SOCIETY, ARKANSAS CHAPTER
ATTN: President, Arkansas Chapter, 786 Belle Cove Rd., Mtn. Home, AR 72653
Founded: 1986
Scope: Statewide
Description: A professional society to promote the conservation, development, and wise utilization of fisheries, both recreational and commerical. Affiliated with American Fisheries Society Headquarters in Bethesda, MD.
Contact(s):
President: MARK L. OLIVER, Arkansas Chapter, 786 Belle Cove Rd., Mtn Home, AR 72653; Phone: 501-491-5750
Keyword(s): Aquatic Habitats, Fisheries, Renewable Resources, Water Pollution Management, Wetlands

AMERICAN FISHERIES SOCIETY, ATLANTIC INTERNATIONAL CHAPTER
ATTN: President, Atlantic Int'l Chapter, P.O. Box 2123, Concord, NH 03302
Founded: 1975
Scope: National
Description: A professional society to promote the conservation, development, and wise utilization of fisheries, both recreational and commercial. Affiliate with American Fisheries Society Headquarters in Bethesda, Maryland.
Contact(s):
President: JOSEPH F. MCKEON, Atlantic Int'l Chapter, P.O. Box 2123, Concord, NH 03302; Phone: 6003-528-8750

NON-GOVERNMENTAL ORGANIZATIONS

AMERICAN FISHERIES SOCIETY, AUBURN UNIVERSITY STUDENT CHAPTER
ATTN: President, Auburn University Student Chapter, 237 Gay St. #33A, Aubrn, AL 36830
Founded: 1974
Scope: Statewide
Description: A professional society to promote the conservation, development, and wise utilization of fisheries, both recreational and commerical. Affiliated with American Fisheries Society Headquarters in Bethesda, Maryland.
Contact(s):
President: THEODORE B. HENRY, Auburn University Student Chapter, 237 S. Gay St. #33A, Alburn, AL 36830; Phone: 334-844-9318
Keyword(s): Aquatic Habitats, Fisheries, Renewable Resources, Water Pollution Management, Wetlands

AMERICAN FISHERIES SOCIETY, BONNEVILLE CHAPTER
ATTN: President, Bonneville Chapter, 1594 W. N. Temple Ste 2110, Salt Lake Cityu, UT 84114-6301
Phone: 801-789-3103
Founded: 1963
Scope: Statewide
Description: A professional society to promote the conservation, development, and wise utilization of fisheries, both recreational and commerical. Affiliated with American Fisheries Society Headquarters in Bethesda, Maryland.
Contact(s):
President: WILLIMA A. BRADWISCH, Bonneville Chapter, 1594 W. North Temple Ste 2110, Salt Lake City, UT 84114-6301; Phone: 801-538-4866
Publication(s): *Quarterly newsletter; bulletins*
Keyword(s): Deserts, Endangered and Threatened Species, Environmental Preservation, Public Lands, Wilderness

AMERICAN FISHERIES SOCIETY, CALIFORNIA-NEVADA CHAPTER
ATTN: President CA-NV Chapter, 346 W. Le Roy Ave., Arcadia, CA 91007-6909
Founded: 1963
Scope: Statewide
Description: A professional society to promote the conservation, development, and wise utilization of fisheries, both recreational and commerical. Affiliated with American Fisheries Society Headquarters in Bethesda, Maryland.
Contact(s):
President: CAMM C. SWIFT, CA-NV Chapter, 346 W Le Roy Ave., Arcadia, CA 91007-6909; Phone: 310-338-5386
Keyword(s): Aquatic Habitats, Fisheries, Renewable Resources, Water Pollution Management, Wetlands

AMERICAN FISHERIES SOCIETY, COLLEGE OF ENVIRONMENTAL SCIENCE AND FORESTRY CHAPTER
ATTN: President, American Fisheries Society, Col. Environ. Sci & Forestry Chapter, SUNY Environ Science/Forestry, Syracuse, NY 13210
Founded: 1975
Scope: Statewide
Description: A professional society to promote the conservation, development, and wise utilization of fisheries, both recreational and commerical. Affiliated with American Fisheries Society Headquarters in Bethesda, Maryland.
Contact(s):
President: ROBERT COLOMBO, Col. Environ Sci. & For Chapter, SUNY Enviro Science/Forestry, American Fisheries Soc, Syracuse, NY 13210; Email: recolombo@mailbox.syr.edu
Keyword(s): Aquatic Habitats, Fisheries, Renewable Resources, Water Pollution Management, Wetlands

AMERICAN FISHERIES SOCIETY, COLORADO and WYOMING CHAPTER
ATTN: President, Colorado-Wyoming Chapter, Box 1078, Pinedale, WY 82941
Founded: 1966
Scope: Statewide
Description: A professional society to promote the conservation, development, and wise utilization of fisheries, both recreational and commerical. Affiliated with American Fisheries Society Headquarters in Bethesda, Maryland.
Contact(s):
President: RONALD REMMICK, Colorado-Wyoming Chapter, Box 1078, Pinedale, WY 82941; Phone: 307-367-4353
Keyword(s): Aquatic Habitats, Fisheries, Renewable Resources, Water Pollution Management, Wetlands

AMERICAN FISHERIES SOCIETY, DAKOTA CHAPTER
ATTN: President, Dakota Chapter, ND Game & Fish Dept. Box 506, Riverdale, ND 58565
Founded: 1964
Scope: Statewide
Description: A professional society to promote the conservation, development, and wise utilization of fisheries, both recreational and commerical. Affiliated with American Fisheries Society Headquarters in Bethesda, Maryland.
Contact(s):
President: JASON LEE, Dakota Chapter, ND Game & Fish Dept., Box 506, Riverdale, ND 58565; Phone: 701-654-7475
Publication(s): *ARI News Bulletin*

AMERICAN FISHERIES SOCIETY, FLORIDA CHAPTER
ATTN: President, Florida Chapter, 5920 1st St., SW, Vero Beach, FL 35968
Founded: 1981
Scope: Statewide
Description: A professional society to promote the conservation, development, and wise utilization of fisheries, both recreational and commerical. Affiliated with American Fisheries Society Headquarters in Bethesda, Maryland.
Contact(s):
President: R. GRANT GILMORE, Florida Chapter, 5920 1st St. SW, Vero Beach, FL 35968; Phone: 561-465-2400
Keyword(s): Aquatic Habitats, Fisheries, Renewable Resources, Water Pollution Management, Wetlands

AMERICAN FISHERIES SOCIETY, GEORGIA CHAPTER
ATTN: President, Georgia Chapter, WRD 2123 Hwy 278 Se, Social Circle, GA 30279
Founded: 1985
Scope: Statewide
Description: A professional society to promote the conservation, development, and wise utilization of fisheries, both recreational and commerical. Affiliated with American Fisheries Society Headquarters in Bethesda, Maryland.
Contact(s):
President: ALFRED C. MAULDIN, Georgia Chapter, WRD 2123 HWY 278 SE, Social Circle, GA 30279; Phone: 770-918-6418
Keyword(s): Aquatic Habitats, Fisheries, Renewable Resources, Water Pollution Management, Wetlands

AMERICAN FISHERIES SOCIETY, GREATER PORTLAND, OR CHAPTER
ATTN: President, 7059 SW Barbara Lane, Tigard, OR 97223
Phone: 503-245-9363
Founded: 1962
Scope: Statewide
Description: A professional society to promote the conservation, development, and wise utilization of fisheries, both recreational and commerical. Affiliated with American Fisheries Society Headquarters in Bethesda, Maryland.

Contact(s):
President: RICHARD B. TURNER, 7059 SW Barbara Lane, Tigard, OR 97223; Phone: 503-245-9363
Publication(s): *Audubon Warbler; Urban Naturalist, The; Familiar Birds of the Northwest; Protecting a Vanishing Ecosystem - The Ancient Forests of the Pacific Northwest*
Keyword(s): Biodiversity, Birds, Environmental and Conservation Education, Urban Environment, Wildlife and Wildlife Habitat

AMERICAN FISHERIES SOCIETY, HAWAII CHAPTER
ATTN: President, Hawaii Chapter, NMFS SW Fish Ctr Lab, 2570 Dole St., Honolulu, HI 96822-2396
Founded: *1982*
Scope: *Statewide*
Description: A professional society to promote the conservation, development, and wise utilization of fisheries, both recreational and commerical. Affiliated with American Fisheries Society Headquarters in Bethesda, Maryland.
Contact(s):
President: ROBERT A. SKILLMAN, Hawaii Chapter, NMFS SW Fish Ctr Lab, 2570 Dole St., Honolulu, HI 96822-2396; Phone: 808-943-1257
Keyword(s): Aquatic Habitats, Fisheries, Renewable Resources, Water Pollution Management, Wetlands

AMERICAN FISHERIES SOCIETY, HUMBOLDT CHAPTER
ATTN: President, Humbolt Chapter, 1165 H St. Apt F, Arcata, CA 95521
Founded: *1973*
Scope: *Statewide*
Description: A professional society to promote the conservation, development, and wise utilization of fisheries, both recreational and commerical. Affiliated with American Fisheries Society Headquarters in Bethesda, Maryland.
Contact(s):
President: SUSAN C. MCBRIDE, Humbolt Chapter, 1165 H. St Apt F, Arcata, CA 95521; Email: scmcbride@ucdavis.edu
Keyword(s): Aquatic Habitats, Fisheries, Renewable Resources, Water Pollution Management, Wetlands

AMERICAN FISHERIES SOCIETY, IDAHO CHAPTER
ATTN: President, Idaho Chapter, 2250 W. Buckhorn Ct., Eagle, ID 83616
Founded: *1963*
Scope: *Statewide*
Description: A professional society to promote the conservation, development, and wise utilization of fisheries, both recreational and commerical. Affiliated with American Fisheries Society Headquarters in Bethesda, Maryland.
Contact(s):
President: CINDY WILLIAMS, ID Chapter 2250 W. Buckhorn Ct., Eagle, ID 83616; Phone: 208-939-8697
Keyword(s): Aquatic Habitats, Fisheries, Renewable Resources, Water Pollution Management, Wetlands

AMERICAN FISHERIES SOCIETY, ILLINOIS CHAPTER
ATTN: President, Illinois Chapter, IL Nat. History Survey, 607 E. Peabody, Champaign, IL 61820
Phone: 309-968-6837; Fax: 309-968-6017
Founded: *1963*
Scope: *Statewide*
Description: A professional society to promote the conservation, development, and wise utilization of fisheries, both recreational and commerical. Affiliated with American Fisheries Society Headquarters in Bethesda, Maryland.
Contact(s):
President: JULIE E. CLAUSSEN, Illinois Chapter, IL Nat History Survey, 607 E. Peabody, Champaign, IL 61820; Phone: 217-244-5113
Keyword(s): Aquatic Habitats, Fisheries, Renewable Resources, Water Pollution Management, Wetlands

AMERICAN FISHERIES SOCIETY, INDIANA CHAPTER
ATTN: President, Indiana Chapter, Lake Michigan Investig, 100 W. Water St., Michigan City, IN 46360
Founded: *1970*
Scope: *Statewide*
Description: A professional society to promote the conservation, development, and wise utilization of fisheries, both recreational and commerical. Affiliated with American Fisheries Society Headquarters in Bethesda, Maryland.
Contact(s):
President: JAMES T. FRANCIS, Indiana Chapter, Lake Michigan Investig, 100 W. Water St., Michigan City, IN 46360; Phone: 219-874-6824
Keyword(s): Aquatic Habitats, Fisheries, Renewable Resources, Water Pollution Management, Wetlands

AMERICAN FISHERIES SOCIETY, IOWA CHAPTER
ATTN: President, Iowa Chapter, Dept. Animal Ecol. IA St. Univ., 124 Sci II, Ames, IA 50011
Founded: *1969*
Scope: *Statewide*
Description: A professional society to promote the conservation, development, and wise utilization of fisheries, both recreational and commerical. Affiliated with American Fisheries Society Headquarters in Bethesda, Maryland.
Contact(s):
President: JOSEPH E. MORRIS, Iowa Chapter, Dept. Animal Ecol IA St Univ., 124 Sci II, Ames, IA 50011; Phone: 515-294-4622
Keyword(s): Aquatic Habitats, Fisheries, Renewable Resources, Water Pollution Management, Wetlands

AMERICAN FISHERIES SOCIETY, KANSAS CHAPTER
ATTN: President Kansas Chapter, KS Coop Fish & Wildlife Res Unit, 205 Leasure Hall KS State Univ., Manhattan, KS 66506
Founded: *1975*
Scope: *Statewide*
Description: A professional society to promote the conservation, development, and wise utilization of fisheries, both recreational and commerical. Affiliated with American Fisheries Society Headquarters in Bethesda, Maryland.
Contact(s):
President: CHRISTOPHER GUY, KS Coop Fish & Wildlife Res Unit, 205 Leasure Hall KS State Univ., Manhattan, KS 66506; Phone: 785-532-6634
Keyword(s): Aquatic Habitats, Fisheries, Renewable Resources, Water Pollution Management, Wetlands

AMERICAN FISHERIES SOCIETY, KENTUCKY CHAPTER
ATTN: Kentucky Chapter, 5060 Louisville Rd., Frankfort, KY 40601
Founded: *1990*
Scope: *Statewide*
Description: A professional society to promote the conservation, development, and wise utilization of fisheries, both recreational and commerical. Affiliated with American Fisheries Society Headquarters in Bethesda, Maryland.
Contact(s):
President: KERRY W. PRATHER, Kentucky Chapter, 5060 Louisville Rd., Frankfort, KY 40601; Phone: 502-564-5448
Keyword(s): Aquatic Habitats, Fisheries, Renewable Resources, Water Pollution Management, Wetlands

AMERICAN FISHERIES SOCIETY, LOUISIANA CHAPTER
ATTN: President, LA Chapter, Coastal Fish Inst., LA State Univ., Baton Rouge, LA 70803
Phone: 504-388-6512; Fax: 504-388-6513
Founded: *1979*
Scope: *Statewide*
Description: A professional society to promote the conservation, development, and wise utilization of fisheries, both recreational and commerical. Affiliated with American Fisheries Society Headquarters in Bethesda, Maryland.

NON-GOVERNMENTAL ORGANIZATIONS

Contact(s):
President: DON BALTZ, LA Chapter, Coastal Fish Inst., LA State Univ., Baton Rouge, LA 70803; Phone: 504-388-6512
Keyword(s): Aquatic Habitats, Fisheries, Renewable Resources, Water Pollution Management, Wetlands

AMERICAN FISHERIES SOCIETY, MICHIGAN CHAPTER
ATTN: President, Michigan Chapter, Dept. of Fish & Wdlf, 13 Nat Resource Bldg. MSU, East Lansing, MI 48824
Founded: 1973
Scope: Statewide
Description: A professional society to promote the conservation, development, and wise utilization of fisheries, both recreational and commerical. Affiliated with American Fisheries Society Headquarters in Bethesda, Maryland.
Contact(s):
President: DANIEL B. HAYES, Michigan Chapter, Dept Fish & Wdlf, 13 Nat Resour Bldg MSU, East Lansing, MI 48824; Phone: 517-432-3781
Keyword(s): Aquatic Habitats, Fisheries, Renewable Resources, Water Pollution Management, Wetlands

AMERICAN FISHERIES SOCIETY, MID-ATLANTIC CHAPTER
ATTN: President, Mid-Atlantic Chapter, Nacote Creek Research Station, P.O. Box 418, Port Republic, NJ 08241
Founded: 1983
Scope: Statewide
Description: A professional society to promote the conservation, development, and wise utilization of fisheries, both recreational and commerical. Affiliated with American Fisheries Society Headquarters in Bethesda, Maryland.
Contact(s):
President: J. MCCLAIN, Mid-Atlantic Chapter, Nacote Creek Research Station, P.O. Box 418, Port Republic, NJ 08241; Phone: 609-748-2040
Keyword(s): Aquatic Habitats, Fisheries, Renewable Resources, Water Pollution Management, Wetlands

AMERICAN FISHERIES SOCIETY, MID-CANADA CHAPTER
ATTN: President, 19 Acadia Bay, Winnipeg, Alberta R3T3J1 Canada
Phone: 204-945-7791; Fax: 204-948-2308
Founded: 1986
Scope: National
Description: A professional society to promote the conservation, development, and wise utilization of fisheries, both recreational and commercial. Affiliate with American Fisheries Society Headquarters in Bethesda, Maryland.
Contact(s):
President: ARTHUR J. DERKSEN, 19 Acadia Bay, Winnipeg, Alberta R3T 3J1 Canada; Phone: 204-945-7791; Fax: 204-948-2308

AMERICAN FISHERIES SOCIETY, MINNESOTA CHAPTER
ATTN: President, Minnesota Chapter, MN Coop Fish & Wdlf Res Unit, Univ MN 1980 Folwell Ave., St. Paul, MN 55108
Founded: 1967
Scope: Statewide
Description: A professional society to promote the conservation, development, and wise utilization of fisheries, both recreational and commerical. Affiliated with American Fisheries Society Headquarters in Bethesda, Maryland.
Contact(s):
President: BRUCE VONDRACEK, Minnesota Chapter, MN Coop Fish & Wdlf Res Unit, Univ MN 1980 Folwell Ave., St Paul, MN 55108; Phone: 612-624-3421
Keyword(s): Aquatic Habitats, Fisheries, Renewable Resources, Water Pollution Management, Wetlands

AMERICAN FISHERIES SOCIETY, MISSISSIPPI CHAPTER
ATTN: President, Mississippi Chapter, MS Museum Nat. Sci., 111 N. Jefferson St., Jackson, MS 39202
Phone: 601-354-7303; Fax: 601-354-7227
Founded: 1975
Scope: Statewide
Description: A professional society to promote the conservation, development, and wise utilization of fisheries, both recreational and commerical. Affiliated with American Fisheries Society Headquarters in Bethesda, Maryland.
Contact(s):
President: CHARLES KNIGHT, MS Museum Nat. Sci., 111 N. Jefferson St., Jackson, MS 39202; Phone: 601-354-7303; Fax: 601-354-7227
Keyword(s): Aquatic Habitats, Fisheries, Renewable Resources, Water Pollution Management, Wetlands

AMERICAN FISHERIES SOCIETY, MISSOURI CHAPTER
c/o Devona Weirich, Chapter Secretary, 1110 S. College Ave., Columbia, MO 65201
Founded: 1963; Membership: 175
Scope: Statewide
Description: The Missouri Chapter of the American Fisheries Society promotes the scientific management of aquatic resources for the optimum use and enjoyment by the people of Missouri and North America.
Contact(s):
President: CHRISTOPHER VITELLO, Missouri Chapter, MO Dept. Conserv, 2630 N. Mayfair, Springfield, OH 65803; Phone: 417-895-680
Keyword(s): Aquatic Habitats, Fisheries

AMERICAN FISHERIES SOCIETY, MONTANA CHAPTER
ATTN: President, Montant Chapter, 10 Bridle Bit Rd., Clancy, MT 59634
Founded: 1998
Scope: Statewide
Contact(s):
President: MARK E. LERE, Montana Chapter, 10 Bridle Bit Rd., Clancy, MT 59634

AMERICAN FISHERIES SOCIETY, NEW MEXICO STATE UNIVERSITY STUDENT CHAPTER
ATTN: President, NM State Student Chapter, 3200 Del Rey Blvd #16, Las Cruces, NM 88012
Founded: 1972
Scope: Statewide
Description: A professional society to promote the conservation, development, and wise utilization of fisheries, both recreational and commerical. Affiliated with American Fisheries Society Headquarters in Bethesda, Maryland.
Contact(s):
President: NIKKOAL MCCLELLAND-DICTSON, NM State Univ Student Chapter, 3200 Del Rey Blvd #16, Las Cruces, NM 88012; Phone: 505-382-5160

AMERICAN FISHERIES SOCIETY, NEW YORK CHAPTER
ATTN: President, New York Chapter, 5000 Brittonfield Pkwy, P.O. Box 4873, Syracuse, NY 13221
Founded: 1968
Scope: Statewide
Description: A professional society to promote the conservation, development and wise utilization of fisheries, both recreational, and commerical. Affiliated with American Fisheries Society Headquarters in Bethesda, Maryland.
Contact(s):
President: MARGARET H. MURPHY, New York Chapter, 5000 Brittonfield Pkwy, P.O. Box 4873, Syracuse, NY 13221; Phone: 315-437-6100
Keyword(s): Aquatic Habitats, Fisheries, Renewable Resources, Water Pollution Management, Wetlands

AMERICAN FISHERIES SOCIETY, NORTH CAROLINA CHAPTER
ATTN: President, North Carolina Chapter, 57 Hilltop Rd., Asheville, NC 28803
Founded: 1990
Scope: Statewide
Description: A professional society to promote the conservation, development, and wise utilization of fisheries, both recreational and commerical. Affiliated with American Fisheries Society Headquarters in Bethesda, Maryland.
Contact(s):
President: DAVID LEE YOW, North Carolina Chapter, 57 Hilltop Rd., Asheville, NC 28803; Phone: 704-274-3646
Keyword(s): Aquatic Habitats, Fisheries, Renewable Resources, Water Pollution Management, Wetlands

AMERICAN FISHERIES SOCIETY, NORTH PACIFIC INTERNATIONAL CHAPTER
ATTN: President, N. Pacific Int'l Chapter, 1423 Craddock St., Victoria, British Columbia V9A5K3 Canada
Founded: 1978
Scope: National
Description: A professional society to promote the conservation, development, and wise utilization of fisheries, both recreational and commercial. Affiliate with American Fisheries Society Headquarters in Bethesda, Maryland.
Contact(s):
President: JUANITA PTOLEMY, N. Pacific Int'l Chapter, 1423 Craddock St., Victoria, BC V9A 5K3 Canada; Phone: 250-387-9586

AMERICAN FISHERIES SOCIETY, NORTHWESTERN ONTARIO CHAPTER
ATTN: Presdent, Northwester Ontario Chapter, RR 6, #4 Box 13, 138 McLaren Rd., Thunder Bay, Ontario P7C5N5 Canada
Founded: 1979
Scope: National
Description: A professional society promoting the conservation, development, and wise utilization of fisheries, both recreational and commercial. Affiliated with American Fisheries Society Headquarters in Bethesda, Maryland.
Contact(s):
President: DOMINIQUE M. HOUSTOUN, Northwestern Ontario Chapter, RR 6 #4 Box 13, 138 McLaren Rd., Thunder Bay, Ontario P7C 5N5 Canada

AMERICAN FISHERIES SOCIETY, OHIO CHAPTER
ATTN: President, Ohio Chapter, Fairport Fish Res. Unit, 421 High. St., Fairport Harbor, OH 44077
Founded: 1974
Scope: Statewide
Description: A professional society to promote the conservation, development, and wise utilization of fisheries, both recreational and commerical. Affiliated with American Fisheries Society Headquarters in Bethesda, Maryland.
Contact(s):
President: CAREY T. KNIGHT, Ohio Chapter, Fairport Fish Res Unit, 421 High St., Fairport Harbor, OH 44077; Phone: 216-352-6100
Keyword(s): Aquatic Habitats, Fisheries, Renewable Resources, Wetlands

AMERICAN FISHERIES SOCIETY, OKLAHOMA CHAPTER
ATTN: President, Oklahoma Chapter, 3108 Roses Run, Aiken, OK 29803
Founded: 1968
Scope: Statewide
Description: A professional society to promote the conservation, development, and wise utilization of fisheries, both recreational and commerical. Affiliated with American Fisheries Society Headquarters in Bethesda, Maryland.
Contact(s):
President: BRIAN T. BRISTOW, Oklahoma Chapter, 3108 Roses Run, Aiken, SC 29803; Email: brian_bristow@mail.fws.gov
Keyword(s): Aquatic Habitats, Fisheries, Renewable Resources, Water Pollution Management, Wetlands

AMERICAN FISHERIES SOCIETY, OREGON CHAPTER
ATTN: President, Oregon Chapter, OSU Sea Grant, 29 SE 2nd St., Newport, OR 97365
Founded: 1964
Scope: Statewide
Description: A professional society to promote the conservation, development, and wise utilization of fisheries, both recreational and commerical. Affiliated with American Fisheries Society Headquarters in Bethesda, Maryland.
Contact(s):
President: HAROLD J. WEEKS, Oregon Chapter, OSU Sea Grant, 29 SE 2nd St., Newport, OR 97365; Email: weeksha@ccmail.orst.edu
Keyword(s): Aquatic Habitats, Fisheries, Renewable Resources, Water Pollution Management, Wetlands

AMERICAN FISHERIES SOCIETY, PENNSYLVANIA CHAPTER
ATTN: President, PA Fish & Boat Commision, 1225 Shiloh Rd., State College, PA 16801
Founded: 1969
Scope: Statewide
Description: A professional society to promote the conservation, development, and wise utilization of fisheries, both recreational and commerical. Affiliated with American Fisheries Society Headquarters in Bethesda, Maryland.
Contact(s):
President: MICHAEL L. HENDRICKS, PA Fish & Boat Comm, 1225 Shiloh Rd., State College, PA 16801; Phone: 814-355-4837
Publication(s): *ACP Drummer*
Keyword(s): Birds, Environmental and Conservation Education, Environmental Protection, Wetlands, Wildlife and Wildlife Habitat

AMERICAN FISHERIES SOCIETY, POTOMAC CHAPTER
ATTN: President, Potomac Chapter, ASMFC, 1444 Eye St. NW 6th Fl., Washington, DC 20036
Founded: 1976
Scope: Statewide
Description: A professional society to promote the conservation, development, and wise utilization of fisheries, both recreational and commerical. Affiliated with American Fisheries Society Headquarters in Bethesda, Maryland.
Contact(s):
President: RICHARD T. CHRISTIAN, Potomac Chapter, ASMFC, 1444 Eye St. NW 6th Fl., Washington, DC 20036
Keyword(s): Aquatic Habitats, Fisheries, Renewable Resources, Water Pollution Management, Wetlands

AMERICAN FISHERIES SOCIETY, SOUTH CAROLINA CHAPTER
ATTN: President, South Carolina Chapter, Shealy Environmental Service, 106 Vantage Point Dr., Cayce, SC 29033
Phone: 803-791-9700; Fax: 803-791-9111
Founded: 1982
Scope: Statewide
Description: A professional society to promote the conservation, development, and wise utilization of fisheries, both recreational and commerical. Affiliated with American Fisheries Society Headquarters in Bethesda, Maryland.
Contact(s):
President: RICHARD SHEALY, Shealy Environmental Service, 106 Vantage Point Dr., Cayce, SC 29033; Phone: 803-791-9700; Fax: 803-791-9111

NON-GOVERNMENTAL ORGANIZATIONS

AMERICAN FISHERIES SOCIETY, SOUTHERN NEW ENGLAND CHAPTER
ATTN: President, S. New England Chapter, P.O. Box 218, West Kingston, RI 02892
Phone: 401-789-0281; Fax: 401-783-7490
Founded: 1967
Scope: Statewide
Description: A professional society to promote the conservation, development, and wise utilization of fisheries, both recreational and commerical. Affiliated with American Fisheries Society Headquarters in Bethesda, Maryland.
Contact(s):
President: CHRISTOPHER POWELL, S. New England Chapter, P.O. Box 218, West Kingston, RI 02892; Phone: 401-789-0281
Keyword(s): Aquatic Habitats, Fisheries, Renewable Resources, Water Pollution Management, Wetlands

AMERICAN FISHERIES SOCIETY, TENNESSEE CHAPTER
ATTN: President, 1123 Cooperwood Dr., Hixson, TN 37343-2346
Founded: 1977
Scope: Statewide
Description: A professional society to promote the conservation, development, and wise utilization of fisheries, both recreational and commerical. Affiliated with American Fisheries Society Headquarters in Bethesda, Maryland.
Contact(s):
President: ROBERT WALLUS, 1123 Cooperwood Dr., Hixson, TN 37343-2346; Phone: 423-751-7506; Fax: 423-751-7648

AMERICAN FISHERIES SOCIETY, TEXAS A&M CHAPTER
ATTN: President Texas A&M Student Chapter, TX A&M University, 210 Nagle Hall, College Station, TX 77843
Founded: 1969
Scope: Statewide
Description: A professional society to promote the conservation, development, and wise utilization of fisheries, both recreational and commerical. Affiliated with American Fisheries Society Headquarters in Bethesda, Maryland.
Contact(s):
President: SONER TARIM, Texas A&M Student Chapter, TX A&M University, 210 Nagle Hall, College Station, TX 77843; Phone: 409-776-6063
Keyword(s): Aquatic Habitats, Fisheries, Renewable Resources, Water Pollution Management, Wetlands

AMERICAN FISHERIES SOCIETY, TEXAS CHAPTER
ATTN: President, 11045 Spur 164, Tyler, TX 75709
Founded: 1976
Scope: Statewide
Description: A professional society to promote the conservation, development, and wise utilization of fisheries, both recreational and commerical. Affiliated with American Fisheries Society Headquarters in Bethesda, Maryland.
Contact(s):
President: KATHERINE RAMOS, 11045 Spur 164, Tyler, TX 75709; Email: tylerhat@ballistic.com

AMERICAN FISHERIES SOCIETY, TIDEWATER CHAPTER
ATTN: President Tidewater Chapter, E. Carolina Univ. Dept. of Biology, Inst. Coastal & Marine Resources, Greenville, VA 27858
Phone: 919-328-6718919-328-6718; Fax: 919-328-4178
Founded: 1986
Scope: Statewide
Description: A professional society to promote the conservation, development, and wise utilization of fisheries, both recreational and commerical. Affiliated with American Fisheries Society Headquarters in Bethesda, Maryland.
Contact(s):
President: JOSEPH J. LUCZKOVICH, East Carolina Univ. Dept. Biology; Inst Coastal & Mar Res, Greenville, NC 27858; Phone: 919-328-6718; Fax: 919-328-4178
Keyword(s): Aquatic Habitats, Fisheries, Renewable Resources, Water Pollution Management, Wetlands

AMERICAN FISHERIES SOCIETY, VIRGINIA CHAPTER
ATTN: President, VDGIF, P.O. Box 11104, Richmond, VA 23230
Phone: 804-367-8998
Founded: 1990
Scope: Statewide
Description: A professional society to promote the conservation, development, and wise utilization of fisheries, both recreational and commerical. Affiliated with American Fisheries Society Headquarters in Bethesda, Maryland.
Contact(s):
President: THOMAS F. WILCOX, VDGIF, P.O. Box 11104, Richmond, VA 23230; Phone: 804-367-8998

AMERICAN FISHERIES SOCIETY, VIRGINIA TECH CHAPTER
ATTN: President, Virginia Tech Chapter, 106 Cheatham Hall, VA Tech, Blacksburg, VA 24051-0321
Founded: 1972
Scope: Statewide
Description: A professional society to promote the conservation, development, and wise utilization of fisheries, both recreational and commerical. Affiliated with American Fisheries Society Headquarters in Bethesda, Maryland.
Contact(s):
President: TRAVIS O. BRENDEN, Virginia Tech Chapter, 106 Cheatham Hall, VA Tech, Blacksburg, VA 24051-0321; Phone: 540-231-3329; Fax: 540-231-7580
Publication(s): *Lab Notes*
Keyword(s): Environmental and Conservation Education, Environmental Preservation, Nature Preservation, Outdoor Recreation, Youth Organizations

AMERICAN FISHERIES SOCIETY, WEST VIRGINIA CHAPTER
ATTN: President, WV DNR, P.O. Box 67, Elkins, WV 26241
Phone: 304-637-0245; Fax: 304-637-0250
Founded: 1989
Scope: Statewide
Description: A professional society to promote the conservation, development, and wise utilization of fisheries, both recreational and commerical. Affiliated with American Fisheries Society Headquarters in Bethesda, Maryland.
Contact(s):
President: THOMAS E. OLDHAM, WV DNR, P.O. Box 67, Elkins, WV 26241; Phone: 304-637-0245; Fax: 304-637-0250

AMERICAN FISHERIES SOCIETY, WISCONSIN CHAPTER
ATTN: President Wisconsin Chapter, 15601 Butts Corners Rd., Evansville, WI 53536
Founded: 1972
Scope: Statewide
Description: A professional society to promote the conservation, development, and wise utilization of fisheries, both recreational and commerical. Affiliated with American Fisheries Society Headquarters in Bethesda, Maryland.
Contact(s):
President: DON FAGO, Wisconsin Chapter, 15601 Butts Corners Rd., Evansville, WI 53536; Phone: 608-221-6366
Publication(s): *CNRA Report, The; Wisconsin Roadsides*
Keyword(s): Endangered and Threatened Species, Environmental Preservation, Land Use Planning, Pesticides, Wetlands

AMERICAN FOREST FOUNDATION
1111 19th St., NW, Suite 780, Washington, DC 20036
Phone: 202-463-2462
Founded: 1981
Scope: National
Description: American Forest Foundation conducts charitable education and research programs. AFF supports American Tree Farm System -- 71,000 private landowners managing 95 million acres of forests -- and Project Learning Tree (PLT), award-winning pre K-12 environmental education curriculum and training program, active in U.S. and abroad. Nongrantmaking.
Contact(s):
President: LAURENCE D. WISEMAN
Vice President of American Tree Farm System: ROBERT SIMPSON
Vice President of Project Learning Tree: KATHY McGLAUFLIN
Publication(s): *Tree Farmer Magazine; PLT Branch*
Keyword(s): Communications, Environmental and Conservation Education, Forests and Forestry, Renewable Resources

AMERICAN FORESTS (formerly American Forestry Association)
P.O. Box 2000, Washington, DC 20013
Phone: 202-955-4500; Fax: 202-955-4588; Email: member@amfor.org; WWW: www.amfor.org
Founded: 1875
Scope: National
Description: Building on its rich history as the oldest national citizens' conservation organization in the U.S. and conservation movement pioneer, American Forests has several programs to address today's environmental challenges including Global ReLeaf 2000, the Urban Forestry Center, and the Forest Policy Center.
Contact(s):
Treasurer: RICHARD PORTERFIELD
Executive Director: DEBORAH GANGLOFF
Board Chair: JONATHAN SILVER
Editor: MICHELLE ROBBINS
Famous & Historic Tree Nursery: JEFF MEYER; Phone: 904-765-0727
Immediate Past Chair: JAMES HUBBARD
Regional Representative: JANE WESTENBERGER
Regional Representative: ZANE G. SMITH JR.
Regional Representative: NOEL K. SHELDON
Southeast Region Coordinator: NANCY MASTERSON; Phone: 305-372-6555
Vice President for Development: RICHARD J. CROUSE
Vice President of Communications: DANIEL C. SMITH
Vice President of Forest Policy Center: GERALD J. GRAY
Publication(s): *American Forests (quarterly magazine)*
Keyword(s): Environmental and Conservation Education, Forests and Forestry, Greenhouse Effect/Global Warming, Outdoor Recreation, Public Lands

AMERICAN GEOGRAPHICAL SOCIETY
120 Wall St., Suite 100, New York, NY 10005-3904
Phone: 212-422-5456; Fax: 212-422-5480; Email: amgeosoc@earthlink.net
Founded: 1851
Scope: National
Description: The AGS has sponsored research projects field work, and educational travel, held symposia and lectures, and published scientific and popular books, periodicals, and maps. Its publications bring accurate, up-to-date information on man and the land to more than 8,000 fellows and subscribers in over 100 countries.
Contact(s):
Chair: JOHN E. GOULD
President: DONALD LLOYD-JONES
Secretary: JOHN R. MATHER
Treasurer: JOHN J. McCABE
Executive Director: MARY LYNNE BIRD
Chair Emeritus: RICHARD H. NOLTE
Editor: PAUL STARRS, Geographical Review Dept. Geography, University of Neveda-Reno, Reno, NV 89557
Editor, Focus and Around the World: HILARY LAMBERT HOPPER, Dept. of Geography, University of Kentucky, Lexington, KY 40506
Editor, Ubique: PETER G. LEWIS
Publication(s): *Geographical Review; Focus; Ubique, Around the World Program*
Keyword(s): Environmental and Conservation Education, Greenhouse Effect/Global Warming, Land Use Planning, Sustainable Development, Urban Environment

AMERICAN GEOLOGICAL INSTITUTE
4220 King St., Alexandria, VA 22302-1502
Phone: 703-379-2480; Fax: 703-379-7563; Email: agi@agi.web.org
Founded: 1948
Scope: National
Description: AGI provides information services for earth scientists to be an advocate for the interests of the earth-science community; plays a major role in strengthening earth-science education; and increases public awareness of the role that earth sciences play in mankind's use of resources and interaction with the environment.
Contact(s):
Executive Director: DR. MARCUS E. MILLING
Publication(s): *Geotimes; Bibliography and Index of Geology; Glossary of Geology; Directory of Geoscience Departments*
Keyword(s): Geology

AMERICAN GROUND WATER TRUST
P.O. Box 1796, 16 Centre St., Concord, NH 03301
Phone: 603-228-5444; Fax: 603-228-6557; Email: agwtHQ@aol.com; WWW: www.agwt.org
Founded: 1987
Scope: National
Description: The American Ground Water Trust is an independent nonprofit, membership organization which promotes public awareness of the environmental and economic importance of ground water through public education programs. The Trust promotes opportunity, cooperation, and action among individuals, groups, and organizations throughout America.
Contact(s):
Chairman: RANDY LYNE
Secretary: JAMES NATTIER
Treasurer: MIKE LALLY
Executive Director: ANDREW W. STONE
Vice Chair: SAM DANIELS
Publication(s): *Ground Water information pamphlets; Ground Water and Wetlands in the United States; Ground Water Basics (video), Education Poster, Wellowner newletter subscription*
Keyword(s): Environmental and Conservation Education, Geology, Scholarships and Grants, Water Pollution, Water Resources

AMERICAN HIKING SOCIETY
1422 Fenwick Ln., Silver Spring, MD 20910
Phone: 301-565-6704
Founded: 1976
Scope: National
Description: American Hiking Society (AHS) is a national nonprofit organization working to cultivate a nation of hikers dedicated to establishing, protecting and maintaining foot trails in America. AHS is comprised of over 100 member trail clubs and 10,000 individual members. As much, American Hiking represents half a million outdoorspeople and serves as the voice of the American hiker. AHS encourages volunteerism in trail building and maintenance through work trips, "Volunteer Vacations;" a directory of volunteer opportunities on public lands, "HELPING OUT in the OUTDOORS;" and National Trails Day, a nationwide celebration of trails in America. AHS effectively lobbies to encourage funding for trails.
Contact(s):
President: DAVID LILLARD
Communications Director: GWYN HICKS
Conservation Director: MARY MARGARET SLOAN
Editor: GWYN HICKS

NON-GOVERNMENTAL ORGANIZATIONS

Publication(s): *American Hiker; Pathways Across America; Helping Out in the Outdoors*
Keyword(s): Environmental and Conservation Education, Forests and Forestry, Land Use Planning, Outdoor Recreation, Public Lands

AMERICAN HORSE PROTECTION ASSOCIATION
1000 29th St., NW, Suite T-100, Washington, DC 20007
Phone: 202-965-0500
Founded: 1966
Scope: National
Description: A national nonprofit, tax-exempt organization dedicated entirely to the welfare of horses, both wild and domestic. Works for the enforcement of all humane legislation for both wild and domestic horses.
Contact(s):
Vice President: MICHELE RYDELL
Executive Director: ROBIN C. LOHNES
President and Chairman of the Board of Directors: NANCY G. HARGRAVE
Secretary and Treasurer: NANCY A.. MURRAY
Publication(s): *Newsletter; Special Bulletins*
Keyword(s): Environmental Law, Land Use Planning, Mammals, Public Lands, Wildlife Management

AMERICAN HUMANE ASSOCIATION
63 Inverness Dr. East, Englewood, CO 80112
Phone: 303-792-9900
Founded: 1877
Scope: National
Description: A federation of more than 3,500 local humane organizations, representing approximately 350,000 individuals and serving as the central agency in the U.S. for collection and dissemination of humane materials and methods. Nationwide programs deal with problems of child abuse and neglect, and cruelty to animals. Maintains close liaison with related interest groups to protect small animals, livestock, and wildlife.
Contact(s):
President: DR. JOHN F. JONES, Dean of Graduate School of Social Work, University of Denver, 2148 S. High, Denver, CO 80208; Phone: 303-871-2203
Vice President: CHARLES M. GRANOSKI JR., 2626 N. Pearl, Tacoma, WA 98407; Phone: 206-752-7799
Treasurer: HAROLD F. DATES, General Manager of The Hamilton County SPCA, 3949 Colerain Ave., Cincinnati, OH 45223; Phone: 513-541-6100
Executive Director: LAWRENCE C. BROWN
Editor: JANE EHRHARDT
Publication(s): *Shoptalk; Advocate*

AMERICAN INSTITUTE OF BIOLOGICAL SCIENCES
1444 I St., NW, Washington, DC 20005
Phone: 202-628-1500; Fax: 202-628-1509
Founded: 1947; Membership: 8,000
Scope: National
Description: A national organization for biology and biologists, combining an individual membership organization with the federation principle. Operates educational, advisory, liaison, informational, publication and editorial programs to serve biologists, promote unity and effectiveness of effort, and apply knowledge of biology to human welfare.
Contact(s):
President: DR. GARY BARRETT, Inst. Of Ecollogy, Univ. of GA, Athens, GA 30602-2202; Phone: 706-542-2968; Fax: 706-542-4819; Email: gbarrett@sparrow.ecology.uga.edu
Executive Director: DR. RICHARD O'GRADY
Editor: DR. REBECCA CHASAN
Immediate Past President: DR. FRANCES C. JAMES, Dept. of Biological Sciences, FL State Univ., Tallahassee, FL 32306; Phone: 850-644-2217; Fax: 850-644-9829; Email: james@bio.fsu.edu
President-elect: DR. GREGORY J. ANDERSON, Ecology & Evolutionary Bio., University of CT, Storrs, CT 06269-3043;
Phone: 860-486-4555; Fax: 860-486-6364/4320; Email: ander@uconnvm.uconn.edu
Secretary and Treasurer: DR. JANE BROCKMANN, Professor of Zoology, University of Fl, Gainesville, FL 32611-8525; Phone: 352-392-1297; Fax: 352-392-3704; Email: hjb@zoo.ufl.edu
Publication(s): *BioScience*
Keyword(s): Biology, Grants, Sustainable Ecosystems, Zoology

AMERICAN INSTITUTE OF FISHERY RESEARCH BIOLOGISTS
c/o Dr. Clark Hubbs, University of Texas, Department of Zoology, Austin, TX 78712
Founded: 1957; Membership: 1,200
Scope: National
Description: The Institute was founded to advance the science of fishery biology and to promote conservation and proper use of fishery resources. It serves that goal primarily by being concerned with the professional development and performance of its members, and recognition of their competence and achievement.
Contact(s):
President: DR. CLARK HUBBS, University of Texas, Department of Zoology, Austin, TX 78712; Phone: 512-471-1176
Secretary: KATE MYERS, University of Washington Fish Research Inst., Box 357980, Seattle, WA 98195-7980; Phone: 206-543-1101
Treasurer: DR. J. W. RACHLIN
Editor: DR. OLIVER B. COPE, 15 Adamswood Rd., Asheville, NC 28803; Phone: 704-274-7773
Secretary of Membership: SAMMY RAY, Marine Biology Bldg., Texas A&M University, Fort Crockett, Galveston, TX 77550; Phone: 409-766-3325
Publication(s): *Briefs*
Keyword(s): Aquatic Habitats, Fisheries, Renewable Resources

AMERICAN LAND CONSERVANCY
456 Montgomery St., Suite 1450, San Francisco, CA 94104
Phone: 415-403-3850; Fax: 415-403-3856; Email: alc@econet.org; WWW: www.alcnet.org
Founded: 1990
Scope: National
Description: To preserve land for this and future generations; in particular, to preserve its scientific, historic, educational, ecological, geological, recreational, agricultural, and scenic features, and its native plant and animal life or biotic community.
Contact(s):
President: HARRIET BURGESS
Publication(s): *American Land Conservancy Newsletter; Statement of Opportunity Brochure; Fifty Wildflowers of Bear Valley*
Keyword(s): Coasts, Deserts, Forests and Forestry, Land Purchase, Public Lands

AMERICAN LANDS (formerly Western Ancient Forest Campaign)
726 7th St., SE, Washington, DC 20003
Phone: 202-547-9400; Fax: 202-547-9213; Email: wafcdc@AmericanLands.org
Founded: 1991
Scope: National
Description: The mission of American Lands is the protection and recovery of North American native forest, grassland, and aquatic ecosystems; the preservation of biological diversity; the restoration of watershed integrity; and the promotion of environmental justice in connection with these goals. This mission is accomplished by strengthening grassroots conservation networks; providing advocacy services and other assistance to local conservation groups; and helping to improve communications and coordination among these groups and other societal institutions.
Contact(s):
President: RANDI SPIVAK, K-2 Communications, 880 Apollo St. Suite 239, El Segundo, CA 90245; Phone: 310-563-2610
Treasurer: CHUCK WILLER, Coast Range Association, P.O. Box 2250, Corvallis, OR 97339; Phone: 541-758-0255
Executive Director: JIM JONTZ; Phone: 202-547-9095

Campaign Coordinator: STEVE HOLMER; Phone: 202-547-9105
Publication(s): *Report from Washington*
Keyword(s): Aquatic Habitats, Forests and Forestry, Public Lands

AMERICAN LEAGUE OF ANGLERS AND BOATERS
1225 New York Ave., NW, #450, Washington, DC 20005
Phone: 202-682-9530; Fax: 202-682-9529
Founded: 1985
Scope: National
Description: ALAB was formed to be a vigilant patron of the Sport Fishing and Boating Enhancement Act (PL 98-369 and the Aquatic Resources Trust Fund created by the Act. Composed of more than 30 organizations, ALAB is dedicated to this pioneering user-pays legislation which provides some $330 million annually in funding for U.S. Coast Guard recreational boating programs and in matching grants to the states for sportfish research and enhancement, as well as wetlands conservation, boating safety, and boating access improvements. Membership in ALAB is open to nonprofit organizations, businesses, corporations, and individuals seeking improvement in the scope and health of the nation's aquatic resources and expansions of opportunities for responsible utilization by the fishing and boating public.
Contact(s):
Treasurer: GEORGE STEWART; Phone: 302-678-9143
Co-chair: VERONICA FLOYD; Phone: 703-960-2223
Co-chair: DERRICK CRANDALL; Phone: 202-682-9530
Immediate Past Chair: PAUL BROUHA; Phone: 301-897-8616
Keyword(s): Fisheries, Outdoor Recreation, Sport Fishing, Water Resources

AMERICAN LITTORAL SOCIETY
Headquarters, Sandy Hook, Highlands, NJ 07732
Phone: 201-291-0055
Founded: 1961; Membership: 8,000
Scope: National
Description: A national organization of professionals and amateurs interested in the study and conservation of coastal habitat, barrier beaches, wetlands, estuaries, and near-shore waters, and their fish, shellfish, bird, and mammal resources. Publishes scientific and popular material. Conducts field trips, dive and study expeditions, and a fish tag-and-release program. Special activities for scuba divers.
Contact(s):
President: MICHAEL HUBER
Vice President: FRANK STEIMLE
Secretary: ANGELA CRISTINI
Treasurer: SHELDON ABRAMS
Executive Director: D. W. BENNETT
Publication(s): *Underwater Naturalist; Coastal Reporter*
Keyword(s): Aquatic Habitats, Coasts, Coral Reefs, Fisheries, Wetlands

AMERICAN LITTORAL SOCIETY (Coral Reef Conservation Center Office)
2809 Bird Ave., Suite 162, Miami, FL 33160
Phone: 305-358-4600
Scope: National
Contact(s):
Head: ALEXANDER STONE

AMERICAN LITTORAL SOCIETY (Delaware Riverkeeper Crossin)
P.O. Box 326, Washington Crossing, PA 18977
Phone: 215-369-1188
Scope: National
Contact(s):
Contact: MAYA VAN ROSSUM

AMERICAN LITTORAL SOCIETY (New York Office)
28 West 9th Rd., Broad Channel, NY 11693
Phone: 718-634-6467
Scope: National
Contact(s):
Contact: DONALD RIEPE

AMERICAN LIVESTOCK BREEDS CONSERVANCY
P.O. Box 477, 15 Hillsboro, Pittsboro, NC 27312
Phone: 919-542-5704
Founded: 1977; Membership: 4,000
Scope: National
Description: ALBC is a nonprofit membership organization working to protect genetic diversity in domestic animals through the conservation of nearly 100 rare breeds of livestock and poultry in America. ALBC does research on breed status and characteristics, operates a gene bank to preserve genetic materials for the future, and provides technical support on conservation breeding and animal use in sustainable, diversified agriculture.
Contact(s):
Chair: CLAUDE HUGHES
Secretary: ELAINE SHIRLEY
Treasurer: THOMAS WALVOORD
Executive Director: DR. DONALD BIXBY
Technical Coordinator: PHILLIP SPONENBERG
Vice Chair: DARMIN KELSEY
Publication(s): *ALBC News; Taking Stock: The North American Livestock Census, The; A Conservation Breeding Handbook; A Rare Breeds Album of American Livestock*
Keyword(s): Agriculture, Biodiversity, Endangered and Threatened Species, Historic Preservation, Sustainable Development

AMERICAN LUNG ASSOCIATION
1740 Broadway, New York, NY 10019-4374
Phone: 212-315-8700
Founded: 1904
Scope: National
Description: Formerly known as the National Tuberculosis and Respiratory Disease Association. The American Lung Association is a voluntary agency concerned with the conquest of lung disease and the promotion of lung health, which includes preventing and controlling air pollution. National Air Conservation Commission and local and state air conservation committees work with citizenry and other groups for effective air pollution control. Informational material available from national, state, and local lung associations.
Contact(s):
Director of National Health Programs: RONALD WHITE; Phone: 202-785-3355
Editor: ROBERT A. KLOCKE
Managing Director: JOHN R. GARRISON; Phone: 212-315-8701
Publication(s): *American Journal of Respiratory and Critical Care Medicine; American Journal of Respiratory Cell and Molecular Biology*
Keyword(s): Air Quality and Pollution

AMERICAN LUNG ASSOCIATION OF LOUISIANA, INC.
Suite 500, 333 St. Charles Ave., New Orleans, LA 70130
Phone: 504-523-LUNG
Founded: 1923
Scope: Statewide
Description: A nonprofit citizens' agency, serving as the Louisiana unit of the national ALA, the organization has the prevention and control of lung diseases as its primary goal. Devotes considerable time to public education, social action, advocacy, and coordination aimed at prevention and control of air pollution.
Contact(s):
Executive Director: BEN FONTAINE
Volunteer Officer/President: BETTY-LANE QUERBES
Volunteer Officer/Treasurer: BERNICE JACOBS
Volunteer Officer/Vice President: ROBERT McMULLEN

NON-GOVERNMENTAL ORGANIZATIONS

AMERICAN MUSEUM OF NATURAL HISTORY
Central Park West at 79th St., New York, NY 10024
Phone: 212-769-5000
Founded: 1869; Membership: 515,000
Scope: National
Description: Conducts research in anthropology, astronomy, entomology, herpetology, ichthyology, invertebrates, mammalogy, earth and planetary sciences, ornithology, and vertebrate and invertebrate paleontology using museum collections and field studies. Publishes scientific and popular material. Instructs the public, especially its over three million yearly visitors, in natural sciences, including living and extinct animals, ecological relationships, evolution of earth and life, development of human cultures, and astronomy.
Contact(s):
President: ELLEN V. FUTTER; Phone: 212-769-5997
Publication(s): *Natural History; Bulletin of the American Museum of Natural History; American Museum Novitates; Anthropological Papers of the American Museum of Natural History; Micropaleontology Press; Curator*
Keyword(s): Biodiversity, Endangered and Threatened Species, Geology, Natural History, Zoology

AMERICAN NATURE STUDY SOCIETY
c/o PEEC, R.D. Box 1010, Dingmans Ferry, PA 18328
Founded: 1908; Membership: 800
Scope: National
Description: Promotes environmental education and avocation by conducting meetings, workshops and field excursions, producing and distributing publications, and contributing to publications of other agencies; cooperates with organizations with allied interests, and, through membership in Alliance for Environmental Education, encourages members to contribute consultant services; assists in training nature lay leaders.
Contact(s):
President: STEVE MELCHER, 103 Kreag Rd., Fairport, NY 14450-363; Phone: 716-425-1059
Secretary: BETTY McKNIGHT, R.D. 3, Trumansburg, NY 14886
Treasurer: PAUL SPECTOR, Holden Arboretum, 9500 Sperry Rd., mentor, OH 44094; Phone: 216-256-1110
Editor: JANET HAWKES, 1420 Tanghannock Blvd., Ithaca, NY 14850; Phone: 607-273-6260
Editor: FLORENCE MAURO, PEEC, R.D. 2 Box 1010, Dingmans Ferry, PA 18328; Phone: 717-828-2319
Recording Secretary: FLO MAURO, PEEC, R.D. 2 Box 1010, Dingmans Ferry, PA 18328; Phone: 717-828-2319
Publication(s): *ANSS Newsletter; Nature Study, A Journal of Environmental Education and Interpretation*
Keyword(s): Environmental and Conservation Education, Natural History, Outdoor Recreation, Urban Environment, Youth Organizations

AMERICAN OCEANS CAMPAIGN
Headquarters, 725 Arizona Ave., Suite 102, Santa Monica, CA 90401
Phone: 310-576-6162; Fax: 310-576-6170; Email: aoc@earthlink.net; WWW: www.americanoceans.org
Founded: 1987; Membership: 22,000
Scope: National
Description: The well-being and sustainability of the Earth is dependent upon healthy oceans. The mission of American Oceans Campaign is to safeguard the vitality of the oceans and our coastal waters. AOC is committed to scientific information in advocating for sound public policy. We are equally committed to developing partnerships with all entities interested in protecting the environment. AOC seeks to ensure healthy sources of food and coastal recreation as well as to protect the ocean's grandeur for future generations.
Contact(s):
President: TED DANSON
Vice President: ANNETT WOLF
Treasurer: BARBARA KOHN
Executive Director: DAVID YOUNKMAN
Board Chair: JERRY KRAMER
Publication(s): *Splash; Esturaries on the Edge: The Vital Link Between Land and Sea; Chemical Contaminant Release Into the Santa Monica Bay: A Pilot Study; Drainage to the Oceans: The Effects of Stormwater Pollution on Coastal Waters*
Keyword(s): Aquatic Habitats, Beaches, Coasts, Estuaries, Fisheries, Marine Protected Areas, Pollution Prevention, Public Health Protection, Water Pollution, Water Quality

AMERICAN OCEANS CAMPAIGN (Washington DC Office)
600 Pennsylvania Ave., Suite 210, Washington, DC 20005
Phone: 202-544-3526; Fax: 202-544-5625; Email: aocdc@wizard.net
Scope: National

AMERICAN ORNITHOLOGISTS' UNION
National Museum of Natural History, MRC-116, Smithsonian Institution, Washington, DC 20560-0116
Phone: 202-357-2051; Fax: 202-633-8084; Email: aou@nmnh.si.edu
Founded: 1883; Membership: 4,500
Scope: National
Description: Aims to advance ornithological science through its publications, annual meetings, committees, and membership.
Contact(s):
President: FRANK GILL, National Audubon Society, 700 Broadway, New York, NY 10003; Phone: 212-979-3074
Vice President: JAMES KUSHLAN, USGS Patwxent Wildlife Research Center, 12100 Beach Forest Rd., Suite 4039, Laurel, MD 20708-4039
Secretary: MARY V. McDONALD, Lewis Science Center 129, University of Central Arkansas, Conway, AR 72035; Phone: 501-450-5924
Treasurer: FRED SHELDON, Museum of Natural Science, Louisiana State University, Baton Rouge, LA 70803; Phone: 504-388-2855; Fax: 504-388-3075
Chairman of the Conservation Committee: STEVEN BEISSINGER, Director of Ecosystem Science, 151 Hilgard Hall #3110, University of California, Berkeley, CA 94720-3110; Phone: 313-763-5945
Editor: THOMAS MARTIN, The Auk Editorial Office, Montana Cooperative Research Unit, NS 205, University of Montana, Missoula, MT 59812
Mongraphs Editor: DAVID WIEDENFELD, Sutton Avian Research Center, P.O. Box 2007, Bartlesville, OK 74005
Newsletter Editor: CHERYL TRINE, 3889 E. Valley View, Berrien Springs, MI 49103; Phone: 508-224-6521
President-Elect: JOHN FITZPATRICK, Cornell Laboratory of Ornithology, 159 Sapsucker Rd., Ithica, NY 14850
Publication(s): *Auk; Ornithological Monographs; Ornithological Newsletter*
Keyword(s): Birds

AMERICAN PIE (PUBLIC INFORMATION ON THE ENVIRONMENT)
124 High St., P.O. Box 340, South Glastonbury, CT 06073
Phone: 1-800-320-APIE; Fax: 860-633-5090; Email: info@americanpie.org; WWW: www.AmericanPIE.org
Founded: 1993; Membership: 310
Scope: National
Description: American PIE is a 501(c)(3 nonprofit group serving the nation with a 1-800 environmental information line. The organization offers action programs and uniquely accessible assistance to people who have environmental questions and concerns in a wide variety of subject areas ranging from drinking water safety to wetlands preservation. Trained staff answer the information line Monday-Friday, 8:30 - 5:00 Eastern time.
Contact(s):
Director: LAWRENCE R. BACON, 36 Carriage Dr., Farmington, CT 06032; Phone: 860-674-8442
President and Secretary: TONI BENNETT EASTERSON

Vice President and Treasurer: BRAD EASTERSON; Phone: 860-633-9786

Publication(s): *American PIE*

Keyword(s): Communications, EcoAction, Environmental and Conservation Education, Environmental Justice, Pesticides

AMERICAN PLANNING ASSOCIATION
1776 Massachusetts Ave., NW, Washington, DC 20036
Phone: 202-872-0611; Fax: 202-872-0643

Founded: 1909; Membership: 29,000

Scope: National

Description: Provides informational services, education, and research in city and regional planning. Includes the American Institute of Certified Planners which sets professional and ethical standards and participates in the accreditation of planning degree programs. Forty-six chapters include all of the states. Sixteen divisions address planning specialties and provide placement services and studies.

Contact(s):
President: ERIC DAMIAN KELLEY
Executive Director: FRANK SO; Phone: 202-872-0611
Editor: SYLVIA LEWIS
Immediate Past President: SAM CASELLA
Secretary and Treasurer: JAMES SHELBY

Publication(s): *PLANNING Magazine; Journal of The American Planning Association; Land Use Law and Zoning Digest; Environment and Development Newsletter*

Keyword(s): Environmental Law, Environmental Planning, Land Use Planning, Planning Management, Urban Environment

AMERICAN RECREATION COALITION
1225 New York Ave., NW, #450, Washington, DC 20005
Phone: 202-682-9530; Fax: 202-682-9529

Founded: 1979

Scope: National

Description: ARC is a national nonprofit, tax-exempt federation of more than 125 recreation-related trade associations, corporations, and enthusiasts' organizations that provides a unified voice for American recreation interests to ensure their full participation in government policy-making on such issues as energy and public lands and waters management. ARC also initiates and supports partnerships between public and private recreation providers and conducts meetings, seminars, and activities to improve public awareness of recreation opportunities.

Contact(s):
Chairman: DAVID J. HUMPHREYS, RVIA, 1896 Preston White Dr., Reston, VA 22090; Phone: 703-620-6003
President: DERRICK A. CRANDALL
Vice President of Member Services: CATHERINE A. AHERN

AMERICAN RESOURCES GROUP
Suite 210, Signet Bank Bldg., 374 Maple Ave. E., Vienna, VA 22180
Phone: 703-255-2700

Founded: 1981

Scope: National

Description: A conservation service organization engaged in education, monitoring, research, and related activities to promote the wise use of America's forest resources. Provides forestry, environmental inventory, conservation support services, and land acquisition assistance to conservation organizations, public agencies, and landowners. Programs include: Land Conservation Fund of America (land acquisition), National Forestry Network (referrals), National Historic Lookout Register, American Woodlands (demonstration forests and conservation easements), and National Forestry Association Forest Practice Certification.

Contact(s):
President: DR. KEITH A. ARGOW
Executive Secretary: DORIS H. WATERS
Coordinator of National Historic Lookout Register: WENDY BECKWITH II
Editor: DR. KEITH A. ARGOW
National Forestry Association: DAVID EDSON, Green Tag Forestry, ; Phone: 202-827-4456
Northeast Representative of National Historic Lookout Register: BOB SPEAR; Phone: 201-651-0466
Northwest Representative of National Historic Lookout Register: RAY KRESEK; Phone: 509-466-9171
Vice President of Forestry: DAVID A. TICE, 977 Seminole Trail #282, Charlottesville, VA 22901; Phone: 804-973-1703
Western Representative of National Historic Lookout Register: RON JOHNSON; Phone: 541-782-2311

Publication(s): *Conservation News Digest*

Keyword(s): Forests and Forestry, Land Purchase, Public Lands, Renewable Resources

AMERICAN RIVERS (formerly American Rivers Conservation Council)
1025 Vermont Ave., NW., Suite 720, Washington, DC 20005
Phone: 202-347-7550; Fax: 202-347-9240; Email: amrivers@amrivers.org; WWW: www.amrivers.org

Founded: 1973

Scope: National

Description: America's leading river conservation organization. Preserves and restores America's river systems and fosters a river stewardship ethic. River conservation goals focused on protecting wild rivers, restoring hometown rivers, and repairing big rivers. Conservation programs in wild/nationally significant rivers, hydropower reform, urban rivers, and floodplains. Three-part strategy: develop and demonstrate community-based solutions to protect and restore rivers; communicate river values and build a diverse nationwide constituency for river conservation; and advocate reform of national policies and practices to foster river health and restore river values.

Contact(s):
President: REBECCA R. WODDER
Administrative Director: WALT SISSON
Board of Directors 1st Vice Chair: RICHARD V. HOPPLE
Board of Directors 2nd Vice Chair: ANTHONY P. GRASSI
Board of Directors Chair: WHITNEY HATCH
Board of Directors Secretary: JOHN I. TAYLOR
Board of Directors Treasurer: DONALD B. AYER
Chair of Scientific and Technical Advisory Committee: DR. J. DAVID ALLAN
Director of Floodplain Programs: SCOTT FABER
Director of Hydorpower Programs: MARGARET BOWMAN
Director of Northwest Programs: KATHERINE RANSEL
Director of Southwest Programs: MARY ORTON
Director of Strategic Communications: CARRIE COLLINS
Director of Urban River Programs: VICTOR McMAHAN
General Counsel: THOMAS J CASSIDY JR.

Publication(s): *American Rivers Newsletter; Restoring Rivers Through Hydropower Dam Relicensing; Annual Report: America's Most Endangered Rivers; Mississippi Monitor; Missouri Monitor*

Keyword(s): Conservation, Environmental and Conservation Education, Rivers, Water Resources, Watersheds, Wetlands

AMERICAN SOCIETY FOR ENVIRONMENTAL HISTORY
701 Vickers Ave., Durham, NC 27701
Phone: 919-682-9319

Founded: 1976; Membership: 1,000

Scope: National

Description: A nonprofit international society that seeks understanding of human ecology through the perspectives of history and the humanities.

Contact(s):
President: DONALD J. PISANI, Department of History, University of OklahomaMissouri, Normal, OK 73019; Phone: 405-325-6001
Vice President: JEFFREY STINE, National Museum of American History, Smithsonian Institute, Washington, DC 20560; Phone: 202-357-2058
Secretary: LISA MIGHETTO, Historical Research Associates, 119 Pine St., Suite 207, Seattle, WA 98101
Treasurer: GAIL EVANS, 427 Grant St., Silverton, OR 97381

NON-GOVERNMENTAL ORGANIZATIONS

Book Review Editor: MARK HARVEY, Department of History, North Dakota State University, Su Station, P.O. Box 5075, Fargo, ND 58105-5075

Editor: HAL K. ROTHMAN, Department of History, University of Nevada-Las Vegas, Las Vegas, NV 89154; Phone: 702-739-3349

Publication(s): *Environmental History; newsletter*

Keyword(s): Environmental and Conservation Education, Environmental Law, Natural History, Public Lands, Water Resources

AMERICAN SOCIETY OF ICHTHYOLOGISTS AND HERPETOLOGISTS

Attn: Secretary, TX Natural History Collection, R4000, University of TX, Austin, TX 78712-11000
WWW: http://www.utexas.edu/depts/asih/

Founded: *1913;* **Membership:** *3,500*

Scope: *National*

Description: To advance the scientific study of fishes, amphibians, and reptiles.

Contact(s):

President: ALAN H. SAVITZKY, Dept. of Biological Sciences, Old Dominion University, Norfolk, VA 23529-0266

Secretary: DEAN HENDRICKSON, Texas Natural History Collection - R4000, University of Texas, Austin, TX 78712-1100; Phone: 512-471-9774

Treasurer: DR. LARRY M. PAGE, Center for Biodiversity, Illinois Natural History Survey, 607 E. Peabody, Champaign, IL 61820; Phone: 217-333-6847

Chairman of Committee on Environmental Quality: DR. MELVIN L. WARREN JR., USDA Forest Service, Hydrology Lab, P.O. Box 947, Oxford, MS 38655; Phone: 407-393-3331

Managing Editor: DR. MICHAEL E. DOUGLAS, Department of Zoology, Arizona State University, Tempe, AZ 85287-1501; Phone: 602-965-1752

Publication(s): *Copeia*

Keyword(s): Aquatic Habitats, Biology, Endangered and Threatened Species, Reptiles and Amphibians, Zoology

AMERICAN SOCIETY OF LANDSCAPE ARCHITECTS

636 Eye St., NW, Washington, DC 20001-3736
Phone: 202-686-ASLA

Founded: *1899;* **Membership:** *12,500*

Scope: *National*

Description: ASLA is a professional organization representing the landscape architecture profession in the United States. Landscape architicture, comprehensive by definition, is the art and science of analysis, planning, design, management, preservation, and rehabilitation of the land. ASLA works on issues such as land use planning, sustainable communities, transportation, public open space, and water conservation. The mission of ASLA is the advancement of the art and science of landscape architecture by leading and informing the public, by serving members, and by leading the profession in achieving quality in the natural and built environments.

Contact(s):

Director of Public Affairs: JIM TOLLIVER

Editor: ANNE POWELL

Executive Vice President: PETER KIRSCH

Publication(s): *Landscape Architecture Magazine; Landscape Architecture News Digest (LAND)*

Keyword(s): Land Use Planning, Landscape Architecture, Open Space, Public Lands, Urban Environment

AMERICAN SOCIETY OF LIMNOLOGY AND OCEANOGRAPHY

Attn: Susan C. Weiler, 200 Boyer Ave., Whitman College, Walla Walla, WA 99362
Phone: 509-527-5948; Fax: 509-527-5961; Email: weiler@whitman.edu

Founded: *1936;* **Membership:** *3,700*

Scope: *National*

Description: To promote the advancement of the various aquatic science diciplines through scientific and technical symposia, colloquia and meetings; promotion of scientific research; discussion, publication and education; and conducting special programs in response to community interest.

Contact(s):

President: THOMAS C. MALONE, Horn Point Lab., U. of MD Ctr. For Env. Sci., P.O. Box 775, Cambridge, MD 21613; Phone: 410-221-8406; Fax: 410-221-8473; Email: malone@hpl.umces.edu

Secretary: ASIT MAZUMDER, Sci. Biologiques, U. of Montreal, C.P. 6128, Succ A Quebec, Montreal, QUEBEC H3C 3J7 Canada; Phone: 514-343-2286; Fax: 514-343-2293; Email: mazumdea@ere.umontreal.ca

Treasurer: RUSSELL A. MOLL, MI Sea Grant Program, U. of MI, 2200 Bonisteel Blvd., Ann Arbor, MI 48109-2099; Phone: 734-763-1437; Fax: 734-647-0768; Email: rmoll@umich.edu

Executive Director: SUSAN C. WEILER

Editor-in-Chief: EVERETT J. FEE, 343 Lady MacDonald Crescent, Canmore, ALBERTA T1W 1H5 Canada; Phone: 403-609-2456; Fax: 403-609-2400; Email: efee@telusplanet.net

Past President: DIANE M. McKNIGHT, Inst. Of Artic & Alpine Research, U. of CO, 1500 30th St., Boulder, CO 80309-0450; Phone: 303- 492-4687; Fax: 303-492-6388; Email: mcknight@snobear.colorado.edu

President-elect: WILLIAM M. LEWIS JR., Rm. 318, CIRES, Main Campus, U. of CO, Boulder, CO 80309-0334; Phone: 303-492-6378; Fax: 303-492-0928; Email: lewis@spot.colorado.edu

Publication(s): *Limnology and Oceanography; Bulletin*

Keyword(s): Lakes, Ocean Conservation, Rivers, Streams, Wetlands

AMERICAN SOCIETY OF MAMMALOGISTS

ATTN: President American Society of Mammalogists, Dept. Of Biology, Texas Tech Univesity, Lubbock, TX 79409

Founded: *1919;* **Membership:** *3,600*

Scope: *National*

Description: Encourages research and learning in all phases of mammalogy and by holding annual meetings for presentation and discussion of the results of research dealing with mammals, through issuing periodicals and other publications, and by giving advice on matters pertaining to mammals, particularly conservation issues.

Contact(s):

President: ROBERT J. BAKER, Department of Biology, Texas Tech. University, Lubbock, TX 79409; Phone: 806-742-2702

1st Vice President: ALICIA V. LINZEY, Department of Biology, Indiana University of Pennsylvania, Indiana, PA 15705; Phone: 412-357-2352

2nd Vice President: SARAH B. GEORGE, Utah Museum of Natural History, University of Utah, Salt Lake City, UT 84112; Phone: 801-581-4889

Chairman of Committee on Conservation of Land Mammals: GORDON L. KIRKLAND JR., The Vertebrate Museum, Shippensburg University, Shippensburg, PA 17257

Chairman of Committee on Legislation and Regulations: WINSTON P. SMITH, Southern Forest Experimental Station, S. Hardwoods Laboratory, P.O. Box 227, Stoneville, MS 38776

Chairman of Committee on Marine Mammals: JOHN E. HAYNING, Natural History Museum of Los Angles CA, 900 Exposition Blvd., Los Angles, CA 90007; Phone: 213-746-2999

Managing Editor: TROY L. BEST, Department of Zoology, 331 Funchess Hall, Auburn University, AL 36849; Phone: 205-844-9260

Secretary and Treasurer: H. DUANE SMITH, Department of Zoology, Brigham Young University, Provo, UT 84602; Phone: 801-378-2492

Publication(s): *Journal of Mammalogy; Mammalian Species; Special Publications of American Society of Mammalogists*

Keyword(s): Endangered and Threatened Species, International Conservation, Mammals, Marine Mammals, Nongame Wildlife

AMERICAN SOCIETY OF ZOOLOGISTS
104 Sirius Cir., Thousand Oaks, CA 91360
Phone: 805-492-3585

Founded: 1890; Membership: 4,000
Scope: National
Description: The association of professional zoologists for the presentation, discussion and public dissemination of new or important facts and concepts in the area of animal biology. Supports the adoption of measures that will advance the zoological sciences.
Contact(s):
President: ALBERT F. BENNETT, School of Biological Sciences, University of California+I365, Irvine, CA 92717; Phone: 714-856-6930; Fax: 714-725-2181
Secretary: MARY ANN OTTINGER, Department of Poultry Science, University of Maryland, College Park, MD 20742; Phone: 301-405-5780; Fax: 301-314-9557
Treasurer: MARJORIE L. REAKA, Department of Zoology, University of Maryland, College Park, MD 20742; Phone: 301-454-0259
Business Manager: MARQUESA MILLS, 104 Sirius Cir., Thousand Oaks, CA 91360; Phone: 805-492-3585; Fax: 805-492-0370
Executive Officer: MARY ADAMS-WILEY, 104 Sirius Cir., Thousand Oaks, CA 91360; Phone: 805-492-3585; Fax: 805-492-0370
Managing Editor: MILTON FINGERMAN, Department of Biology, Tulane University, New Orleans, LA 70118; Phone: 504-865-5546
Publication(s): *American Zoologist, The*
Keyword(s): Biology, Insects and Butterflies, Mammals, Reptiles and Amphibians, Zoology

AMERICAN SPORTFISHING ASSOCIATION
1033 North Fairfax St., Suite 200, Alexandria, VA 22314
Phone: 703-519-9691; Fax: 703-519-1872; Email: info@asafishing.org; WWW: www.asafishing.org

Founded: 1994; Membership: 500
Scope: National
Description: ASA is a nonprofit industry association working to ensure healthy and sustainable fisheies resources and increase sportfishing participation through education, conservation, promotion, and marketing.
Contact(s):
Chairman: MARK MASTERSON
President and CEO: MIKE HAYDEN
Publication(s): *American Sportfishing*

AMERICAN WATER RESOURCES ASSOCIATION
950 Herndon Parkway, Suite 300, Herndon, VA 20170-5531
Phone: 703-904-1225; Fax: 703-904-1228

Founded: 1964; Membership: 3,500
Scope: National
Description: A nonprofit scientific organization which advances water resources research, planning, development, and management; establishes a common meeting ground for engineers and physical, biological, and social scientists concerned with water resources; disseminates information in the field of water resources policy, science, and technology through the publication of a scientific journal newsletter and symposium proceedings as well as two to three conferences and symposia per year.
Contact(s):
President: N. EARL SPANGENBERG
Secretary: GREGORY WESTFALL
Treasurer: JANET L. BOWERS
Editor: CHRISTOPHER LANT
Editor: N. EARL SPANGENBERG
Executive Vice President: KENNETH D. REID
President Elect: JOHN J. WARWICK
Publication(s): *Journal of the American Water Resources Assiciation; Hydata-News and Views; Symposium Proceedings*
Keyword(s): Environmental and Conservation Education, Renewable Resources, Rivers, Water Resources, Wetlands

AMERICAN WATER WORKS ASSOCIATION (AWWA)
6666 W. Quincy Ave., Denver, CO 80235
Phone: 303-794-7711; Fax: 303-795-1440; WWW: www.waterwiser.org, www.awwa.org

Founded: 1881; Membership: 55,000
Scope: National
Description: The AWWA advances the science, technology, consumer awareness management, government policies, and water use efficiencies related to public drinking water.
Contact(s):
Executive Director: JACK W. HOFFBUHR
Deputy Executive Director: ROBERT C. RENNER
Deputy Executive Director of Government Affairs Division: JOHN H. SULLIVAN, 1401 New York Ave. NW, Suite 640, Washington, DC 20005; Phone: 202-628-8303
Publication(s): *Main Stream; AWWA Journal; Opflow; WaterWiser - The Water Efficiency Clearinghouse (an on-line Internet Resource (http://www.waterwiser.org)*
Keyword(s): Planning Management, Pollution Prevention, Public Health Protection, Water Quality, Water Resources

AMERICAN WILDLANDS
6551 S. Revere Parkway, Suite 160, Englewood, CO 80111
Phone: 303-649-1211; Fax: 303-649-1221

Founded: 1977; Membership: 2,800
Scope: Regional
Description: A nonprofit conservation organization dedicated to ecologically sustainable use and protection of America's wildland resources in the Rocky Mountains West, including wilderness, wetlands, rangelands, free-flowing rivers, wildlife and fisheries, and forests.
Contact(s):
President: SALLY A. RANNEY
Executive Director: JEFF LARMER
Executive Editor: CLIFTON MERRITT
Secretary and Treasurer: CLIFTON MORRITT
Vice Chairman: WILLIAM CUNNINGHAM
Publication(s): *On The Wild Side; Forest Activist Green Papers; Policy Reports*
Keyword(s): Biodiversity, Forests and Forestry, Public Lands, Wildlands, Wildlife and Wildlife Habitat

AMERICAN WILDLIFE RESEARCH FOUNDATION, INC.
P.O. Box 902, Hartsdale, NY 10530-0902
Phone: 914-761-2653; Fax: 914-761-2653

Founded: 1911; Membership: 51
Scope: International
Description: AWRF uses the interest income of its funds to support research of wildlife and its habitats. Its mission is to enhance fish and wildlife resources and their habitats through research, education and conservation, ensuring that present and future generations can continue to use and enjoy them.
Contact(s):
President: PETER ROEMER; Phone: 914-677-8393; Fax: 914-677-9013
Vice President: STUART L. FREE; Phone: 518-861-5357; Fax: 518-452-6392
Secretary: WILLIAM M. SCHWERD; Phone: 518-885-8995; Fax: 518-885-9078
Treasurer: ROGER H. COLE; Phone: 914-761-2653; Fax: 518-761-2653
Contact for Moon Library at Syracuse University, College of ESF: DR. MAURICE M. ALEXANDER; Phone: 315-492-0032
Publication(s): *Newsletter*
Keyword(s): Grants, Research

NON-GOVERNMENTAL ORGANIZATIONS

AMERICAN ZOO AND AQUARIUM ASSOCIATION (AZA)
Executive Office and Conservation Center, 7970-D Old Georgetown Rd., Bethesda, MD 20814
Phone: 301-907-7777; Fax: 301-907-2980
Founded: 1924; Membership: 6,200
Scope: National
Description: Dedicated to the improvement of modern, professionally-managed zoological parks and aquariums through conservation, public education, scientific research, and membership services. Administers scientifically-managed captive breeding and field conservation programs for 134 threatened and endangered species through its Species Survival Plan Program.
Contact(s):
President: DR. TERRY MAPLE
Deputy Director and Director of Government Affairs: KRISTIN VEHRS
Director of Conservation and Science: DR. MICHAEL HUTCHINS
Director of Conservation Education: DR. BRUCE CARR
Director of Development and Marketing: ROBERT RAMIN
Director of Finance and Administration: LAURA BENSON
Director of Public Affairs: JANE BALLENTINE
Executive Director of Executive Office and Conservation Center: SYDNEY J. BUTLER
Publication(s): *COMMUNIQUE; Directory of Zoological Parks and Aquariums; Annual Report on Conservation and Science; Annual and Regional Conference Proceedings*
Keyword(s): Aquariums, Endangered and Threatened Species, International Conservation, Wildlife Management, Zoological Parks

AMERICANS FOR THE ENVIRONMENT
1400 16th St., NW, Box 24, Washington, DC 20036-2266
Phone: 202-797-6665; Fax: 202-797-6563; Email: afedc@AforE.org; WWW: www.AforE.org
Founded: 1982
Scope: National
Description: Americans for the Environment is a nonpartisan educational organization.
Contact(s):
Board of Directors Chair: STELLA KOCH
Board of Directors Member: JERALD WHITE
Board of Directors Member: JOHN ECHEVERRIA
Board of Directors Member: BETTY SPENCE
Board of Directors Member: CHUCK PAQUETTE
Board of Directors Member: JOY OAKES
Board of Directors Member: ROY HOAGLAND
Board of Directors Member: JONI BOSH
Board of Directors Member: MONTE BELOTE
Board of Directors Member: JOHANNAH BARRY
Board of Directors President: ROY MORGAN
Board of Directors Secretary: TENSIE WHELAN
Board of Directors Treasurer: ALICE WALKER
Board of Directors Vice Chair: CONNIE MAHER
Publication(s): *Lobbying Strategies; Opposition to Conservation Ballot Measures; Permissible Political Activities; Political Agenda of the "Wise Use" Movement, The; Taking the Initiative*
Keyword(s): Environment

ANACOSTIA WATERSHED SOCIETY
The George Washington House, 4302 Baltimore Ave., Bladensburg, MD 20710
Phone: 301-699-6204; Fax: 301-699-3317; Email: robert@anacostiaws.org; WWW: www.anacostiaws.org
Founded: 1989; Membership: 600
Scope: Statewide
Description: The Anacostia Watershed Society provides opportunities for volunteers to take part in local environmental restoration projects; and provides advocacy for environmental equity issues in the Anacostia-Washington region.
Contact(s):
President: ROBERT E. BOONE
Secretary: JAMES WADDELL
Treasurer: DAVID TIBBETTS
Executive Director: JAMES CONNOLLY
Publication(s): *Voice of the River*
Keyword(s): Environmental Protection, Pollution Prevention, Rivers, Watersheds

ANCIENT FOREST INTERNATIONAL
P.O. Box 1850, Redway, CA 95560
Phone: 707-923-3015; Fax: 707-923-3015
Founded: 1989
Scope: National
Description: An alliance of conservationists dedicated to helping preserve, study, and increase awareness of the Earth's few still-intact forest ecosystems. Old-growth forests of southern Chile, highland Mexico, Ecuador, and the north Pacific coast are current projects. Work is also underway to document the distribution of ancient rainforests worldwide and to promote their preservation.
Contact(s):
President: RICK KLEIN
Secretary: SUZELLE HUNT
Treasurer: ROSE MADRONE
Washington DC Representative: MARDA MAYO; Phone: 202-387-5854
Publication(s): *News of Old Growth; Chile's Native Forest: An Overview*
Keyword(s): Biodiversity, Endangered and Threatened Species, Forests and Forestry, International Conservation, Land Purchase

ANGLERS FOR CLEAN WATER
P.O. Box 17900, Montgomery, AL 36141
Phone: 205-272-9530
Founded: 1970
Scope: National
Description: A nonprofit organization dedicated to educating the American public on the conditions of pollution nationwide and to the danger of the failure to halt the pollution of the streams, rivers, and lakes of the United States and to promote, educate, and inform the American public of the need for conservation of our water and fisheries resources.
Contact(s):
President: HELEN SEVIER
Communications: ANN LEWIS
Conservation Director: BRUCE SHUPP
Editor: MATT VINCENT
Finance: KARL DABBS
Publication(s): *Living Waters*
Keyword(s): Aquatic Habitats, Communications, Environmental and Conservation Education, Fisheries, Water Resources

ANIMAL PROTECTION INSTITUTE
P.O. Box 22505, 2831 Fruitridge Rd., Sacramento, CA 95822
Phone: 916-731-5521; Fax: 916-731-4467; Email: onlineapi@aol.com; WWW: www.api4animals.org
Founded: 1968; Membership: 80,000
Scope: National
Description: The Animal Protection Institute is a national animal advocacy nonprofit organization dedicated to protecting animals against abuse through enforcement and legislative actions, investigations, advocacy campaigns, crisis intervention, public awareness, and education. Specific areas of concern are wildlife protection and habitat conservation, companion animals, marine mammals, domestic and farm animals, animals used in research, and humane ecucation.
Contact(s):
Executive Director: ALAN BERGER
Chairman of the Board: DUF FISCHER
Creative Services: BARBARA TUGAEFF
Editor: GIL LAMONT
Program Director: DENA JONES
Publication(s): *Animal Issues*
Keyword(s): Endangered and Threatened Species, Hunting, Mammals, Marine Mammals, Nongame Wildlife, Predators, Public Lands, Trapping, Wildlife and Wildlife Habitat

ANIMAL WELFARE INSTITUTE
P.O. Box 3650, Washington, DC 20007
Phone: 202-337-2332; Fax: 202-338-9478; WWW: www.animalwelfare.com
Founded: 1951; Membership: 15,000
Scope: National
Description: Active in improvement of conditions for laboratory animals and reducing the numbers used in research, protection of endangered species, Save the Whales campaign, ending use of steel jaw traps, stopping imports of wild birds for the pet trade, and humane education. Albert Schweitzer award is presented for outstanding contributions to animal welfare.
Contact(s):
President: CHRISTINE STEVENS; Phone: 202-337-2332
Vice President: CYNTHIA WILSON
Secretary: FREEBORN JEWETT
Treasurer: FRED HUTCHISON
Executive Director: CATHY LISS; Phone: 202-337-2332
Administrative Assistant: JENNIFER PIKE; Phone: 202-337-2332
Editor: CHRISTINE STEVENS
Mail Order Secretary: NELL NAUGHTON
Marine Mammal Research Analyst: BEN WHITE
Publications Coordinator: KELLY HANSEN; Phone: 202-337-2332
Research Associate: ADAM ROBERTS; Phone: 202-337-2332
Whale Campaign Coordinator: LYNNE HUTCHISON
Publication(s): *Animal Welfare Institute Quarterly; Animals and Their Legal Rights; Endangered Species Handbook; Alternative Traps*
Keyword(s): Endangered and Threatened Species, International Conservation, Mammals, Marine Mammals, Trapping

ANTARCTICA PROJECT
P.O. Box 76920, Washington, DC 20013
Phone: 202-544-0236; Fax: 202-544-8483; Email: antarctica@igc.org
Founded: 1982
Scope: National
Description: Works to preserve Antarctica by monitoring all activities to ensure minimal environmental impact and consulting with key users of Antarctica, including scientists, tourists, governments. Conducts legal and policy research and analysis; produces educational materials; focuses international scientific community on globally-significant research. Secretariat to Antarctic and Southern Ocean Coalition (ASOC), composed of 240 conservation groups in 50 nations.
Contact(s):
Director: BETH CLARK
Counsel: JIM BARNES
Publication(s): *ECO Newspaper (ASOC); Antarctica Project (Quarterly Newsletter);* publications and educational resources list on request
Keyword(s): Biodiversity, Conservation of Protected Areas, International Conservation, Wilderness

APPALACHIAN MOUNTAIN CLUB
5 Joy St., Boston, MA 02108
Phone: 617-523-0636; Fax: 617-523-0722
Founded: 1876; Membership: 74,000
Scope: Regional
Description: The AMC pursues a far-reaching conservation agenda while encouraging responsible recreation, based on the philosophy that successful, long-term conservation depends on firsthand experience and enjoyment of the natural environment. Areas of focus: Northern Forest, Sterling Forest, White Mountain N.F., NY and NJ Highlands, Berkshire and Taconics Region, Delaware Water Gap National Recreation Area, and Acadia National Park. Expertise: Conservation policy, advocacy; land, trail, river and greenway stewardship; environmental research, education, guidebook and outdoor leadership publishing.
Contact(s):
Deputy Director: WALTER GRAFF; Phone: 603-466-2721
President: JENNIFER HUNTINGTON
Executive Director: ANDREW J. FALENDER
Conservation Director: TOM STEINBACH; Phone: 617-523-0655/ext.358
Director of Conservation Programs: KEVIN KNOBLOCH; Phone: 617-523-0655/ext.365
Research Director: DR. KENNETH KIMBALL; Phone: 603-466-2721
Publication(s): *Appalachia Journal; AMC Outdoors; AMC guidebooks and maps*
Keyword(s): Air Quality and Pollution, Environmental and Conservation Education, Outdoor Recreation, Public Lands, Rivers

APPALACHIAN TRAIL CONFERENCE
P.O. Box 807, Harpers Ferry, WV 25425
Phone: 304-535-6331
Founded: 1925; Membership: 23,000
Scope: National
Description: Coordinates preservation and management of the Appalachian Trail, a 2,100-mile footpath and protective corridor generally following the crest of the Appalachian Mountains from Maine to Georgia. Prepares and distributes trail guidebooks and other user information.
Contact(s):
Chair: DAVID B. FIELD, 191 Emerson Mill Rd., Hampden, ME 04444; Phone: 207-862-3674
Secretary: SARA H. DAVIS, 25 Dycus Dr., Fairview, NC 28730; Phone: 704-628-4563
Treasurer: ARTHUR P. FOLEY, P.O. Box 18710, Asheville, NC 28814-0710; Phone: 704-687-0931
Executive Director: DAVID N. STARTZELL
Editor: ROBERT WILLIAMS
Editor: JOHN M. MORGAN
Editor: JUDY JENNER
Vice Chair: JAMES HUTCHINGS, 551 Windridge Parkway, Hardy, VA 24101; Phone: 540-427-4536
Vice Chair: DAVID N. BARR, 43 Walnut Tr., Carroll Valley, PA 17320; Phone: 717-642-8782
Vice Chair: BRIAN T. FITZGERALD, R.D. 1 Box 1360, Moretown, VT 05660; Phone: 802-496-7094
Publication(s): *Appalachian Trailway News; Register, The; Trail Lands; Inside ATC*
Keyword(s): Endangered and Threatened Species, Environmental and Conservation Education, Historic Preservation, Land Purchase, Outdoor Recreation

ARCHAEOLOGICAL CONSERVANCY
5301 Central Ave., NE, Suite 1218, Albuquerque, NM 87106
Phone: 505-266-1540
Founded: 1979
Scope: National
Description: National Nonprofit membership organization dedicated to the permanent preservation of the most significant archaeological sites in the United States, usually through acquisition. Cooperates with government, universities, museums, and private conservation organizations to acquire lands for permanent archaeological preserves.
Contact(s):
President: MARK MICHEL
Chairman of the Board: EARL GADBERY
Eastern Regional Director: ROB CRISELL, 1307 S. Glebe Rd., Arlington, VA 22204; Phone: 703-979-4410
Midwest Regional Office Director: PAUL GARDNER, 74 E. Jeffrey Pl., Columbus, OH 43214; Phone: 614-267-1100
Southeastern Regional Office Director: ALAN GRUBER, 5997 Cedar Crest Rd., Acworth, GA 30101; Phone: 770-975-4344
Southwest Regional Office Director: JAMES B. WALKER, 5301 Central Ave. NE, Suite 1218, Albuquerque, NM 87108; Phone: 505-266-1540
Western Regional Office Director: LYNN DUNBAR, 1217 23rd St., Sacramento, CA 95816-4917; Phone: 916-448-1892
Publication(s): *American Archaeology*
Keyword(s): Cultural Preservation, Historic Preservation, Land Purchase

NON-GOVERNMENTAL ORGANIZATIONS

ARCHBOLD BIOLOGICAL STATION
P.O. Box 2057, Lake Placid, FL 33862-2057
Phone: 941-465-2571; Fax: 941-699-1297; Email: archbold@archbold-station.org
Founded: 1941
Scope: Statewide
Description: The Station is an independent, nonprofit facility devoted to long-term ecological research and conservation. Primary focus is on organisms, including many endangered species, and environments of the unique Lake Wales Ridge and adjacent Florida.
Contact(s):
Executive Director: DR. HILARY SWAIN
Assistant Director for Agro-Ecology: DR. PATRICK BOLEN
Education Coordinator: NANCY DEYRUP
Internship Coordinator: DIANNE CUMMINGS
Librarian: FRED LOHRER
Publication(s): *Biennial Report*
Keyword(s): Ecology, Endangered and Threatened Species, Environmental and Conservation Education, Environmental Preservation, Research

ARCHERY MANUFACTURERS AND MERCHANTS ORGANIZATION (AMO)
4131 NW 28th Lane #7, Gainesville, FL 32606
Phone: 352-377-8262; Fax: 352-375-3961
Founded: 1953; Membership: 500
Scope: National
Description: Formed to promote and to protect the sports of target archery, field archery, and bowhunting. Programs also educate manufacturers, dealers, distributors, sales representatives, and the archery media.
Contact(s):
Director of Member Services: PAT WISEMAN SNIDER
Marketing Director: DOUG ENGH
President and CEO: DICK LATTIMER
Publication(s): *AMO Newsletter*
Keyword(s): Hunting, Outdoor Recreation, Wildlife and Wildlife Habitat, Wildlife Management, Youth Organizations

ARCTIC INSTITUTE OF NORTH AMERICA
University Library Tower, 2500 University Dr., NW, Calgary, Alberta T2N 1N4 Canada
Phone: 403-220-7515
Founded: 1945; Membership: 2,200
Scope: National
Description: A nonprofit research organization dedicated to acquisition, interpretation, and dissemination of knowledge of the polar regions. Sponsors research by its thirty-three research associates.
Contact(s):
Executive Director: MICHAEL ROBINSON
Business Manager: ANNE NAIL
Chairman of the AINA Board of Governors: CARL BENSON
Editor: KAREN McCULLOUGH
Publication(s): *Arctic Journal; Information North*

ARIZONA ASSOCIATION OF CONSERVATION DISTRICTS
ATTN: Executive Director, 3003 N. Central Ave., Suite 800, Phoenix, AZ 85012
Scope: Statewide
Contact(s):
Executive Director: LISA HAYES, 3003 N. Central Ave. Suite 800, Phoenix, AZ 85012; Phone: 602-280-8803; Fax: 602-280-8779
1st Vice President: FRANK MARTINEZ, Box 1152, Parker, AZ 85344; Phone: 520-669-8459
President and Board Member: SHARON REID, Rt. 1 Box 49-C, St. David, AZ 85630; Phone: 520-586-3347
Secretary/Treasurer: DAVE SCHOFIELD, 16251 W. Glendale Ave, Litchfield Park, AZ 85340; Phone: 602-935-2837; Fax: 602-935-1236
Vice President, Alternate Board Member: ROBERT AHKEAH, P.O. Box 550, Shiprock, NM 87416; Phone: 505-368-5430

ARIZONA B.A.S.S. CHAPTER FEDERATION
ATTN: President, 18210 N. 39th Ave., Glendale, AZ 85308
Phone: 602-547-2228
Scope: Statewide
Description: An organization of Bassmaster chapters, affiliated with the Bass Anglers Sportsman Society, organized to fight pollution, assist state and national conservation agencies in their efforts, and teach the young people of our country good conservation practices. Dedicated to the realistic conservation of our water resources.
Contact(s):
President: MIKE SEGELKE, 18210 N. 39th Ave., Glendale, AZ 85308; Phone: 602-547-2228
Conservation Director: DAVE COHEN, 839 S. Westwood #266, Mesa, AZ 85210; Phone: 602-962-9009

ARIZONA WILDLIFE FEDERATION
644 N. Country Club Dr., Suite E, Mesa, AZ 85201-4991
Phone: 602-644-0077; Fax: 602-644-0078; Email: awf@primenet.com; WWW: www.primenet.com/~awf
Founded: 1923
Scope: Statewide
Description: A representative statewide organization, affiliated with the National Wildlife Federation, dedicated to the protection and enhancement of wildlife and its habitat through public education and government interaction.
Contact(s):
President: DON FARMER
Affiliate Representative: JOHN CALKINS
Editor: STEVE GALIZIOLLI
Publication(s): *Arizona Wildlife News*

ARKANSAS ASSOCIATION OF CONSERVATION DISTRICTS
ATTN: President, Box 8004 State Line Plaza 18004, Texarkana, AR 75502
Scope: Statewide
Contact(s):
President: DON R. MITCHELL, Box 8004 State Line Plaza 18004, Texarkana, AR 75502; Phone: 870-773-1061
1st Vice President, Alternate Board Member: PAUL MAYFIELD, 783 Rio Vista Rd., Baid Knob, AR 72010; Phone: 501-724-5932; Email: mayfield@IPA.Net
2nd Vice President: BILL RAINWATER, P.O. Box 2245, Jonesboro, AR 72401; Phone: 870-935-1624
Board Member: TIM WHISENHUNT, Rt. 1 Box 12, Bradley, AR 71826; Phone: 870-894-3413; Fax: 870-894-3635
Executive Vice President: DON RICHARDSON, 101 E. Capitol Suite 350, Little Rock, AR 72201; Phone: 501-682-2915; Fax: 501-682-3991; Email: donrichar@aol.com
Secretary/Treasurer: ROY MAHLER, Rt. 2 Box 130, Elkins, AR 72727; Phone: 501-430-3385

ARKANSAS B.A.S.S. CHAPTER FEDERATION
ATTN: President, 119 Lilly St., Searcy, AR 72143
Phone: 501-268-6659
Scope: Statewide
Description: An organization of Bassmaster chapters, affiliated with the Bass Anglers Sportsman Society, organized to fight pollution, assist state and national conservation agencies in their efforts, and teach the young people of our country good conservation practices. Dedicated to the realistic conservation of our water resources.
Contact(s):
President: L. J. SCOGGIN JR., 119 Lilly St., Searcy, AR 72143; Phone: 501-268-6659
Conservation Director: GENE CARSON, Rt. 1 Box 225L, Branch, AR 72928; Phone: 501-635-5951

ARKANSAS ENVIRONMENTAL EDUCATION ASSOCIATION
P.O. Box 210, Hackett, AR 72937
Phone: 501-638-7151; Fax: 501-638-7123; Email: arkenved@aol.com
Founded: 1995; Membership: 100
Scope: Statewide
Description: The Association promotes environmental education and supports the work of environmental eucators in Arkansas.
Contact(s):
President: ROBERT McAFEE
Vice President: DORI BROWN; Phone: 501-444-1860; Fax: 501-444-1880
Secretary: BECKY HORTON; Phone: 870-257-9998
Treasurer: SUZANNE SMITH HIRREL; Phone: 501-671-2288; Fax: 501-671-2185; Email: shirrel@vavaex.edu
Publication(s): *Natural State, The; Membership Directory, Resource Directory*
Keyword(s): Environmental and Conservation Education

ARKANSAS WILDLIFE FEDERATION
7509 Cantrell Rd., #104, Little Rock, AR 72207
Phone: 501-663-7255; Fax: 501-664-7397
Founded: 1936
Scope: Statewide
Description: A representative statewide organization, affiliated with the National Wildlife Federation, dedicated to the protection and enhancement of wildlife and its habitat through public education and government interaction.
Contact(s):
President: HOWARD ROBINSON
Affiliate Representative: JIM WOOD
Publication(s): *Arkansas Out of Doors*

ARLINGTON OUTDOOR EDUCATION ASSOCIATION, INC.
P.O. Box 5646, Arlington, VA 22205
Phone: 540-347-2258
Founded: 1967; Membership: 1,200
Scope: Statewide
Description: AOEA's Outdoor Lab annually provides approximately 9,000 northern Virginia school children, in grades kindergarten through twelve, with enriching environmental and educational opportunities in a natural setting. In addition to daily classes during the school year, the lab conducts camps during the summer and astronomical observatory sessions throughout the year.
Contact(s):
President: CATHERINE REISING-JONES
Vice President: KATHLEEN DRENNAN
Secretary: LORI LOWE
Treasurer: SCOTT SMITH
Editor: KATHLEEN DRENNAN; Phone: 703-525-6284
Lab Director: NEIL HEINEKAMP
Keyword(s): Aquatic Habitats, Environmental and Conservation Education, Environmental Protection, Fisheries, Land Preservation

ASSOCIATION FOR CONSERVATION INFORMATION, INC.
ATTN: President, New Hampshire Fish and Game Department, 2 Hazen Dr., Concord, NH 33301
Founded: 1938
Scope: National
Description: Facilitates free exchange of ideas, materials, techniques, experiences, and procedures bearing on conservation information and education and establishes media furthering such exchange; promotes public understanding of basic conservation principles; informs states, territories, and provinces that do not have conservation education programs of their desirability and assists them in setting up conservation education, information and public relations programs.
Contact(s):
President: JUDY STOKES, New Hampshire Fish and Game Department, 2 Hazen Dr., Concord, NH 3301; Phone: 603-271-3211
Vice President: DAVID WARREN, Oklahoma Dept. of Wildlife Conservation, 1801 N. Lincoln, Oklahoma City, OK 73105; Phone: 405-521-3855
Secretary: JOAN GUILFOYLE, Region 3, US Fish & Wildlife Service, 1 Federal Dr., Federal Bldg, Fort Snelling, MN 55111; Phone: 612-725-3519
Treasurer: DAVID K. RICE, Nevada Department of Conservation and Natural Resources, P.O. Box 10678, Reno, NE 89520; Phone: 702-688-1550
Balance Wheel Editor: GARY THOMAS, Illinois Department of Conservation, 524 S. Second St., Springfield, IL 62701-1787; Phone: 217-782-7454
Immediate Past President: CHRIS CHAFFIN, Idaho Department of Fish and Game, P.O. Box 25, Boise, ID 83707; Phone: 208-334-3746
Publication(s): *Balance Wheel, The*

ASSOCIATION FOR FISH AND WILDLIFE ENFORCEMENT TRAINING
ATTN: President Alberta Fish and Wildlife, Main Fl. N. Tower, Petroleum Plaza 9945 - 108 St., Edmonton, Alberta T5K 2G6 Canada
Scope: National
Description: The goal of the association is to promote and enhance professional standards of training in fish and wildlife enforcement. The objectives are: (1 to promote officer safety and a safer working environment; (2 to promote uniform training standards and exchange training information; (3 to promote law enforcement research and development by determining training requirements, conducting training research, and developing training strategies; (4 to encourage cost-effective training programs; (5 to act as a repository for catalogue agency training personnel and materials; and (6 to host annual workshop to facilitate the exchange of training information. Open to Canadian and United States agencies.
Contact(s):
President: RED HASAY, Alberta Fish and Wildlife, Main Fl. North Tower, Petroleum Plaza 9945 - 108 St., Edmonton, Alberta T5K 2G6 Canada; Phone: 403-427-6735
Vice President: RUSS FILLMORE, Department of Renewable Resources, Box 2703, Whitehorse, Yukon Y1A 2C6 Canada; Phone: 403-667-5786
Secretary and Treasurer: JOHN C. SMITH, Conservation Officer Service, 2162 Esplanade, Victoria, British Columbia V8V 1X5 Canada; Phone: 604-387-9402

ASSOCIATION FOR THE PROTECTION OF THE ADIRONDACKS, THE
P.O. Box 951, Schenectady, NY 12301
Phone: 518-377-1452; Fax: 518-377-1452
Founded: 1901; Membership: 1,500
Scope: Statewide
Description: To protect the natural character of the state forest preserve lands in the Adirondacks and Catskills as water-holding and regulating forests which serve as a home for wildlife and as wilderness recreation areas, and to protect and enhance the natural resources of the Adirondack Park.
Contact(s):
President: THOMAS L. COBB, Box 454, Bear Mountain State Park, Bear Mountain, NY 10911
Vice President: HARVEY M. KELSEY JR.
Vice President: CLAIRE L BARNETT
Vice President: PAUL M. BRAY
Secretary: MARYDE KING
Treasurer: DAVID NEWHOUSE
Executive Director: DAVID H. GIBSON
Keyword(s): Biodiversity, Lakes, Land Use Planning, Public Lands, Sustainable Development

NON-GOVERNMENTAL ORGANIZATIONS

ASSOCIATION OF AMERICAN GEOGRAPHERS
1710 16th St., NW, Washington, DC 20009-3198
Phone: 202-234-1450; Email: gaia@aag.org; WWW: www.aag.org
Founded: 1904; Membership: 7,000
Scope: National
Description: To further professional investigations in geography and encourage the application of geographic findings in education, government, and business.
Contact(s):
President: WILLIAM L. GRAF, Dept. of Geography, AZ State University, Box 870104, Tempe, AZ 85286; Phone: 602-965-7533; Email: graf@asu.edu
Vice President: REGINALD G. GOLLEDGE, Dept. of Geography, University of CA, Santa Barbara, CA 93106-4060; Phone: 805-893-2731
Secretary: RICHARD A. MARSTON, Geography & Recreation Dept., University of WY, Laramie, WY 82071-3371; Phone: 307-766-3311; Email: marston@uwyo.edu
Treasurer: LIZBETH A. PYLE, Institutional Analysis & Planning, P.O. Box 6710, WV University, Morgantown, WV 26506-6710; Phone: 304-293-7664/4906; Email: lpyle@wvu.edu
Executive Director: RONALD F. ABLER
Editor of AAG Journal: JOHN PAUL JONES III, University of KY, Dept. of Geography, Lexington, KY 40506-0027; Phone: 606-257-6950
Editor of Newsletter: LINDA BRADSHAW
Past President: PATRICIA GOBER, Dept. of Geography, AZ State University, Box 870104, Tempe, AZ 85287-0104; Phone: 602-965-7533; Email: gober@asu.edu
Publication(s): *The Annals; Professional Geographer, The; AAG Newsletter*
Keyword(s): Agriculture, Geography, Land Use Planning, Urban Environment, Water Resources

ASSOCIATION OF AVIAN VETERINARIANS
Central Office, P.O. Box 811720, Boca Raton, FL 33481
Phone: 561-393-8901; Fax: 561-393-8902
Founded: 1980; Membership: 3,600
Scope: International
Description: The Association of Avian Veterinarians is a nonprofit international organization dedicated to advancing and promoting avian medicine and stewardship.
Contact(s):
President: GLENN H. OLSEN, Patuxent Environmental Science Center, 11510 American Holly Dr., Laurel, MD 20708
Coordinator of Publications: CATHY LYONS, Library AAV Publications Office, P.O. Box 618372, Orlando, FL 32861; Phone: 407-521-6401
Immediate Past President: DR. SUSAN E. OROSZ, Avian University of Tennesee, Department Comp. Animal Medicine, Knoxville, TN 37923
President-Elect: JERRY LABONDE, Avian and Exotic Animal Hospital, 6900 S. Holly Cir., Englewood, CO 80112
Publication(s): *Journal of the Association of Avian Veterinarians: Advancing and Promoting Avian Medicine and Stewardship; 1980-1996 Proceedings of the Annual Conference*
Keyword(s): Birds, Endangered and Threatened Species, Environmental and Conservation Education, International Conservation, Wildlife Rehabilitation

ASSOCIATION OF CONSERVATION ENGINEERS
Attn: President, IL Dept. of Nuclear Safety, 1035 Outer Park Dr., Springfield, IL 62704
Founded: 1961; Membership: 200
Scope: National
Description: To encourage and broaden the educational, social, and economic interests of conservation engineering practices; to promote recognition of the importance of sound engineering practices in fish, wildlife, and recreation development; to enable each member to take advantage of the experience of other states.
Contact(s):
President: GARY McCANDLESS, IL Dept. of Nuclear Safety, 1035 Outer Park Dr., Springfield, IL 62704; Phone: 217-782-1329; Fax: 217-524-6417
Secretary and Treasurer: JIM PRICE, AR Game & Fish Commission, #2 Natural Resources Dr., Little Rock, AR 72205; Phone: 501-219-4306; Fax: 501-219-4315
Publication(s): *A.C.E. Newsletter; handbook; conference proceedings; informational brochure*
Keyword(s): Engineering, Environmental and Conservation Education, Outdoor Recreation, Water Resources, Wildlife and Wildlife Habitat

ASSOCIATION OF CONSULTING FORESTERS OF AMERICA
723 North Washington St., Suite 4-A, Alexandria, VA 22314
Phone: 703-548-0990; Fax: 703-548-6395; Email: acf@igc.apc.org; WWW: www.acf-foresters.com
Founded: 1948; Membership: 500
Scope: National
Description: The Association of Consulting Foresters of America, Inc. represents interests of private consulting foresters. Administers a continuing education program, enforces a code of ethics, and promotes use of private consulting foresters.
Contact(s):
President: WILLIAM C. HUMPHRIES JR.
Executive Director: LOREN R. LARSON II
Administrative Director: LYNN C. WILSON
Gulf Director: J. MARVIN TAYLOR
Northern Director: MARK R. WEBB
Past President: RONALD E. STUNTZNER
President-Elect: DAVID C. PARKER
Southern Director: GERALD W. FRAZIER
Western Director: GEORGE D. GENTRY
Publication(s): *Consultant, The; Membership Specialization Directory*
Keyword(s): Environmental and Conservation Education, Forests and Forestry, Renewable Resources, Wildlife and Wildlife Habitat, Wildlife Management

ASSOCIATION OF FIELD ORNITHOLOGISTS
Attn: President, Inst. For Field Ornithology, Univ. of ME at Machias, 9 O'Brien Ave., Machias, ME 04654
Founded: 1922
Scope: National
Description: To promote the study of birds in their natural habitats throughout the new world and dissemination of the information obtained from this study.
Contact(s):
President: CHARLES D. DUNCAN, Inst. For Field Ornithology, Univ. of ME at Machias, Machias, ME 04654; Phone: 207-255-1358; Email: cduncan@acad.umm.maine.edu
Vice President: JEROME A. JACKSON, Dept. of Biology, MS State Univ., P.O. Box GY, Mississippi State, MS 39762; Phone: 601-325-3210; Email: picus@ra.msstate.edu
Secretary: RUSS McCLAIN, Department of Biology, University of Memphis Memphis, Memphis, TN 38152; Phone: 901-678-2581; Email: wrmcclain@msuvxi.memphis.edu
Treasurer: GEORGE B. MOCK, P.O. Box 393, Mattapoisett, MA 02739; Phone: 508-758-4408; Email: gmock@nyclubricants.com
Editor: DR. C. RAY CHANDLER, Dept. of Bio., GA Southern Univ., Statesboro, GA 30460-8042; Phone: 912-681-5657; Email: chandler@gasou.edu
Publication(s): *Journal of Field Ornithology*
Keyword(s): Biology, Birds, Conservation Biology, Research

ASSOCIATION OF GREAT LAKES OUTDOOR WRITERS
109 N. Broadway, Hartington, NE 67839
Phone: 402-254-3266
Founded: 1957; Membership: 320
Scope: Regional
Description: A nonprofit professional association of outdoor communicators dedicated to perpetuate the great outdoors through the judicious use of the written and spoken word.
Contact(s):
President: MARTIN JARANOWSKI, P.O. Box 604, Glenwood, IL 60425; Phone: 708-757-7522
Vice President: PEGGY BOEHMER, P.O. Box 96, Goose Lake, IA 52750; Phone: 319-242-3046
Treasurer: ELMER A. GUERRI, 8401 North Lakewood Pl., W. Terre Haute, IN 47885; Phone: 812-535-1230
Board of Directors Chairman: JACK SPAULDING, 5287 W. 1000 S., Milroy, IN 46156; Phone: 765-629-2493
Editor: BOB SCHMIDT, 5016 Argyle, Chicago, IL 60630; Phone: 773-283-7871
Publication(s): *AGLOW Horizons*

ASSOCIATION OF MIDWEST FISH AND GAME LAW ENFORCEMENT OFFICERS
Attn: Executive Secretary, CO Div. of Wildlife, Law Enforcement Section, 6060 Broadway, Denver, CO 80216
Phone: 303-291-7216; Email: dave.croonquist@state.co.us
Founded: 1944
Scope: National
Description: To promote law enforcement cooperation among members, develop efficient cooperative law enforcement practices, establish a medium for disseminating information relating to illegal game law practices, devise legislative or regulatory changes for improving and standardizing law enforcement, and encourage the highest possible standards and practices of law enforcement among member organizations.
Contact(s):
Executive Secretary: DAVE CROONQUIST
Keyword(s): Environmental Law, Fisheries, Outdoor Recreation, Renewable Resources, Wildlife Management

ASSOCIATION OF NEW JERSEY ENVIRONMENTAL COMMISSIONS
P.O. Box 157, Mendham, NJ 07945
Phone: 973-539-7547; Fax: 973-539-7713; Email: anjec@aol.com; WWW: www.members.aol.com/anjec
Founded: 1969; Membership: 2,100
Scope: Statewide
Description: Private, nonprofit environmental organization serving the state's municipal environmental commissions, environmental organizations, and individual members by providing training programs, publications, research, reference, and liaison services.
Contact(s):
President: JANET LARSON
Executive Director: SALLY DUDLEY
Director of ANJEC Resource Center (Library): JAMIE MAURER
Publication(s): *ANJEC Report; Environmental Manual for Municipal Officials; Freshwater Wetlands Protection in New Jersey: A Manual for Local Officials; Keeping Our Garden State Green: A Local Government Guide for Greenway and Open Space Planning; Environmental Commissioner's Handbook*
Keyword(s): Environmental Preservation, Environmental Protection, Open Space, Pollution Prevention, Rural Development, Sustainable Development, Training, Water Quality, Water Resources, Watersheds

ASSOCIATION OF STATE AND TERRITORIAL HEALTH OFFICIALS
1275 K St., NW, Suite 800, Washington, DC 20005
Phone: 202-371-9090; Fax: 202-371-9797
Founded: 1941
Scope: National
Description: ASTHO represents the directors of public health in each of the 50 states, the District of Columbia, and the U.S. Territories. Its purpose is to formulate and influence through collective action the establishment of sound national public health policy. ASTHO also assists and serves state health agencies in the development and implementation of state programs and policies in advancing the public health and prevention of disease.
Contact(s):
President: DR. DONALD E. WILLIAMSON; Phone: 334-206-5200
Executive Vice President: CHERYL A. BEVERSDORF
Publication(s): *Washington Report; Tobacco-Free Press; Environmental Health News; Astho Report; Shotime*
Keyword(s): Communications, Environment, Health and Nutrition, Public Health Protection

ATLANTIC CENTER FOR THE ENVIRONMENT
55 S. Main St., Ipswich, MA 01938-2396
Phone: 978-356-0038; Fax: 978-356-7322; WWW: www.qlf.org
Scope: Regional
Description: A regional community-based conservation organization promoting public involvement in resource management through year-round education, policy, and research programs in Atlantic Canada, Eastern Quebec, and New England (the Atlantic Region). As a technical assistance resource for local private and public agencies, the Atlantic Center provides resource assessments, conservation planning and strategy, policy analysis, and information services. It conducts many of its programs through an intern work force, which it recruits from colleges and universities across North America. The Atlantic Center also facilitates the exchange of ideas between its region and others. It has an active exchange program with organizations in Latin America and the Caribbean, the Middle East, and Europe. The Atlantic Center is a division of the Quebec-Labrador Foundation.
Contact(s):
President: LAWRENCE B. MORRIS
Administrative Assistant: LINDA R. MITTON
President of QLF Canada: KATHLEEN A. BLANCHARD
Vice President for International Programs: JESSICA BROWN
Vice President of Operations: THOMAS F. HORN
Publication(s): *Compass*
Keyword(s): Environmental and Conservation Education, International Conservation, Internships, Scholarships and Grants, Sustainable Development

ATLANTIC CENTER FOR THE ENVIRONMENT (New England Office)
P.O. Box 217, Montpelier, VT 05602
Phone: 802-229-0707; Fax: 802-229-1603
Scope: Regional
Contact(s):
Vice President: THOMAS F. HORN

NON-GOVERNMENTAL ORGANIZATIONS

ATLANTIC CENTER FOR THE ENVIRONMENT (QLF Canada Office)
 1253 McGill College Ave., Suite 680, Montreal, Quebec H3B 2Y5 Canada
 Phone: 514-395-6020; Fax: 514-395-4505
Scope: Regional

ATLANTIC SALMON FEDERATION
 International Headquarters, P.O. Box 429, St. Andrews, New Brunswick E0G 2X0 Canada
 Phone: 506-529-4581; Fax: 506-529-4438; Email: asf@nbnet.nb.ca
Founded: 1982; Membership: 40,000
Scope: International
Description: The largest international nonprofit organization dedicated to the preservation and wise management of the Atlantic salmon and its habitat. It was established upon consolidation of two leading salmon organizations, The Atlantic Salmon Association and The International Atlantic Salmon Foundation. ASF programs are directed toward research, conservation, education, and international cooperation. The Federation supports a network of regional groupings of local salmon conservation and other organizations which address a variety of salmon issues. ASF is totally dependent on contributions from individuals, foundations, and corporations in Canada, the United States, and overseas. Membership inquiries are welcomed.
Contact(s):
President: BILL TAYLOR
Chairman of Canada (Montreal) Office: JOHN HOUGHTON, 1435 St. Alexandre, Suite 1030, Montreal, P.Q. H3A2G4 Canada; Phone: 514-842-8059
Chairman of New York Office: DONALD C. O'BRIEN JR., Milbank,Tweed, Hadley, and McCloy, One Chase Manhattan Plaza, 54th Floor, New York, NY 10005-1413; Phone: 212-530-5818
Controller: BILL MALLORY
Editor: JIM GOURLAY, P.O. Box 429, St. Andrews, NewBrunswick E0G2X0 Canada; Phone: 506-529-4581
Executive Director of Communications and Public Policy: SUE SCOTT
Executive Director, Development: ROBERT BEATTY
President Emeritus: WILFRED M. CARTER
Vice President of Conservation Programs: JOHN ALBRIGHT
Vice President-Research and Environment: DR. FREDERICK WHORISKEY
Publication(s): *Atlantic Salmon Journal, The*
Keyword(s): Atlantic Salmon, Endangered and Threatened Species, Research, Wildlife and Wildlife Habitat, Wildlife Management

ATLANTIC STATES LEGAL FOUNDATION
 658 W. Onondaga St., Syracuse, NY 13204-3757
 Phone: 315-475-1170; Email: aslf@igc.apc.org
Founded: 1982; Membership: 8,250
Scope: National
Description: Atlantic States Legal Foundation, Inc., enforces environmental laws, engages in public education, conducts research and promotes environmental justice for the economically disadvantaged and people of color.
Contact(s):
President: SAMUEL H. SAGE
Executive Director: LOUCHES POWELL JR.
Administrative Assistant: LEE GECHAS
Research Associate: THEODORE NEWMAN
Publication(s): *Quarterly newsletter*
Keyword(s): Chemical Pollution Control, Developing Countries, Environmental and Conservation Education, Environmental Justice, Environmental Law, Lakes, Mining, People of Color in the Environment, Pollution Prevention, Public Health Protection, Renewable Resources, Solid Waste Management, Sustainable Development, Sustainable Ecosystems, Urban Environment

AUDUBON COUNCIL OF CONNECTICUT
 c/o Audubon Center in Greenwich, 613 Riversville Rd., Greenwich, CT 06831
 Phone: 203-629-1248
Founded: 1967; Membership: 24,000
Scope: Statewide
Description: The Audubon Council of Connecticut is a coalition of 16 chapters and affiliates of the National Audubon Society in Connecticut, representing close to 10,000 residents. The Council recognize humankind's dependence on the natural environment and appreciates the beauty and wondrous diversity of the natural world. The mission of the Council is, therefore, to protect and restore biodiversity in our state and on our planet.
Contact(s):
President: JANE-KERIN MOFFOT, 98 Valley Rd., #12, Cos Cob, CT 06807; Phone: 203-629-1248
Keyword(s): Birds, Environment, Natural Areas

AUDUBON COUNCIL OF ILLINOIS
 ATTN: President, 1631 N. Evergreen, Arlington Heights, IL 60004
Founded: 1973
Scope: Statewide
Description: Composed of representatives of 13 National Audubon Society chapters in Illinois, the Council's purpose is to coordinate efforts of the chapters on statewide environmental issues.
Contact(s):
President: BOB LIPPOLD, 1631 N. Evergreen, Arlington Heights, IL 60004; Phone: 847-870-0337
Vice President: MARIANNE HAHN, 18429 Gottschalk Ave., Homewood, IL 60430; Phone: 708-799-0249
Secretary: JILL VENSKUS, 109 W. Traube Ave., Downers Grove, IL 60515; Phone: 630-963-9258
Treasurer: ELEANOR SMITH, R.R. 1 Box 327, Homer, IL 61849; Phone: 217-896-2079
Keyword(s): Biodiversity, Birds, Environmental Preservation, Wetlands, Wildlife and Wildlife Habitat

AUDUBON INTERNATIONAL
 Headquarters, 46 Rarick Rd., Selkirk, NY 12158
 Phone: 518-767-9051; Fax: 518-767-9076; WWW: www.audubonint1.org
Founded: 1897; Membership: 2,500+ properties/395,534 associate members
Scope: International
Description: Audubon International is a nonprofit environmental organization that specializes in sustainable natural resource management. The mission of Audubon International is to improve the quality of life and the environment through research, education, and conservation assistance.
Contact(s):
Business Manager: PAULA DONNELLY
Director of Communications: MARY COLLEEN LIBURDI
Director of Environmental Education: JEAN MACKAY
Director of Environmental Planning: DR. MILES SMART; Phone: 919-380-9640
Director of Research: DR. LAWRENCE WOOLBRIGHT; Phone: 518-783-2440
Director of Sustainable Development Demonstration: NANCY RICHARDSON; Phone: 502-869-9419
Executive Assistant: MARY L. JACK
MIS: ERIC DODSON
President and CEO: RONALD G. DODSON
Publication(s): *ACSS Field Notes; Stewardship News; Landscape Restoration Handbook; Principles for Sustainable Resource Management; A Guide to Environmental Stewardship on the Golf Course*
Keyword(s): Biodiversity, Birds, Environmental and Conservation Education, Environmental Planning, Land Use Planning, Nongame Wildlife, Renewable Resources, Research, Sustainable Development, Water Quality, Wildlife and Wildlife Habitat

AUDUBON NATURALIST SOCIETY OF THE CENTRAL ATLANTIC STATES
8940 Jones Mill Rd., Chevy Chase, MD 20815
Phone: 301-652-9188; Fax: 301-951-7179; Email: audubonnaturalist.com

Founded: 1897; Membership: 11,000
Scope: Regional

Description: One of the original independent Audubon societies active in environmental education, conservation issues, sancturaries, and natural science studies in the greater Washington metropolitan area for 100 years. The ANS is headquartered at Woodend, a 40-acre Nature Preserve in suburban Maryland.

Contact(s):
President: JOHN BJERKE
Vice President: JEFF SMITH
Treasurer: FRANK REED
Executive Director: MIKE NELSON
Director of Conservation: NEAL FITZPATRICK
Director of Education: JANE HUFF
Director of Finance: MURIEL ROBINSON
Editor: LESLIE CRONIN

Publication(s): *Naturalist News*

Keyword(s): Birds, Environmental and Conservation Education, Natural History, Sustainable Development, Water Quality

AUDUBON SOCIETY OF MISSOURI
ATTN: President, 1001 SW 19th, Blue Springs, MO 64015
Phone: Rare Bird Hotline: 573-445-9115

Founded: 1901
Scope: Statewide

Description: A nonprofit statewide society affiliated with National Audubon Society. Dedicated to the preservation and protection of birds and all wildlife forms and habitat; to educate citizenry toward appreciation of the natural world; and to work for wise conservation practices related to people and wildlife.

Contact(s):
President: MIKE BECK, 1001 SW 19th, Blue Springs, MO 64015; Phone: 816-229-6811
Vice President: SUSAN HAZELWOOD, 3005 Chapel Hill Rd., Columbus, MO 65203; Phone: 573-445-9925
Secretary: SUSAN DORNFELD, 700 S. Weller, Springfield, MO 65208; Phone: 417-831-9702
Treasurer: JEAN GRAEBNER, 1800 S. Roby Farm Rd., Rocheport, MO 65279; Phone: 314-698-2855
Hotline Coordinator: JERRY & EDGE WADE, 1221 Bradshaw Ave., Columbia, MO 65203-0807; Phone: 573-445-6697

Publication(s): *Bluebird, The; Annotated Checklist of the Birds of Missouri; Guide to the Birding Areas of Missouri, A*

Keyword(s): Birds, Environmental and Conservation Education, Natural History, Wildlife and Wildlife Habitat

AUDUBON SOCIETY OF NEW HAMPSHIRE
3 Silk Farm Rd., Concord, NH 03301-8200
Phone: 603-224-9909

Founded: 1914; Membership: 7,000
Scope: Statewide

Description: Independent statewide nonprofit organization dedicated to the preservation, understanding, and appreciation of New Hampshire's wildlife and other natural resources.

Contact(s):
President: RICHARD MOORE
Secretary: LARRY SUNDERLAND, RFD 1 Box 179, Hillsboro, NH 03244
Treasurer: ANDREW KENDALL, 37 St. Mary's St., Newton, MA 02162
Chair of the Board of Trustees: TOM BURACK, Sheehan, Phinney, Bass, and Green, 1000 Elm St., Manchester, NH 03105-3701
Director for Membership: JENNIFER FOX
Director of Education: SCOTT FITZPATRICK
Director of Environmental Affairs: JULIAN ZELAZNY
Director of Loon Preservation Committee: HARRY VOGEL
Vice Chairperson: SUSAN McLANE, 203 Mountain Rd., Concord, NH 03301
Vice President for Conservation: RICHARD COOK

AUDUBON SOCIETY OF PORTLAND
5151 NW Cornell Rd., Portland, OR 97210
Phone: 503-292-6855; Fax: 503-292-1021; Email: general@audubon-pdx.org

Founded: 1902; Membership: 6,500
Scope: Statewide

Description: The Audubon Society of Portland is a nonprofit organization, dedicated to promoting understanding, enjoyment, and protection of the natural world, particularly native wildlife and its habitats.

Contact(s):
President: ARLAN MADSEN
Vice President: MARLI LINTNER
Secretary: SCOTT LUKENS
Treasurer: MARY CHRISTENSEN
Executive Director: DAVE ESHBAUGH
Director of Conservation: PAUL KETCHAM

Publication(s): *Audubon Warbler*

Keyword(s): Ancient Forests, Birds, Conservation, Endangered and Threatened Species, Environmental and Conservation Education, Environmental Protection, Natural History, Outdoor Recreation, Sustainable Development, Urban Environment, Wetlands, Wildlife Rehabilitation

AUDUBON SOCIETY OF RHODE ISLAND
12 Sanderson Rd., Smithfield, RI 02917-2600
Phone: 401-949-5454; Fax: 401-949-5788; Email: audubon_ri@ids.net

Founded: 1897; Membership: 4,500
Scope: Statewide

Description: To focus attention on critical natural resource problems, provide leadership when conservation action is necessary, carry out a broad program of public conservation education, and preserve examples of unique natural areas and native wildlife habitat.

Contact(s):
President: SAMUEL H. HALLOWELL JR.
Secretary: DR. JOSEPH D. DIMASE
Treasurer: DAVID M. MERCHANT
Executive Director: LEE C. SCHISLER JR.
1st Vice President: A. MAX KOHLENBERG
2nd Vice President: J. WILLIAM HARSCH
Caretaker of Fisherville Brook: JIM HAVENS
Caretaker of Ruecker Wildlife Refuge: BURKLEY C. WEILBURG
Caretaker of Touissat Marsh Wildlife Refuge: DANNY DUTRUMBLE
Caretakers of Parker Woodland: JIM/DONNA HAVE
Director of Development: WELLS PILE
Director of Education Program: WILLIAM E. TYLER
Director of Publications, Advocacy, and Research: EUGENIA S. MARKS
Editor: KEN WEBER
Editor: DAVID L. EMERSON
Education Specialist: TRACEY HALL
Education Specialist: ANNE DIMONTI
Education Specialist: KIM BUTELHO
Education Specialist: LAURA J. SMITH
Manager of Caratunk Wildlife Refuge: DARRYL K. SPEICHER
Manager of Eppley Wildlife Sanctuary: DAVID A. RODRIGUES
Manager of Fisherville Brook Wildlife Refuge: TARA S. NELSON
Manager of Powder Mill Ledges W.R.: DANNY DUTRUMBLE
Manager of Retail Sales: DORIS A. MATHURIN
Membership Secretary: DORIS THORPE

Publication(s): *Audubon Society of Rhode Island Report; Checklist of Rhode Island Birds; Fields Notes of Rhode Island Birds*

Keyword(s): Air Quality and Pollution, Birds, Coasts, Conservation of Protected Areas, Endangered and Threatened Species, Environment, Environmental and Conservation Education, Environmental Preservation, Fisheries, Flowers, Plants, and Trees,

NON-GOVERNMENTAL ORGANIZATIONS

Insects and Butterflies, Land Preservation, Open Space, Wildlife Management

AUDUBON SOCIETY OF WESTERN PENNSYLVANIA
Beechwood Farms Nature Reserve, 614 Dorseyville Rd., Pittsburgh, PA 15238-1618
Phone: 412-963-6100; Fax: 412-963-6761
Founded: 1916; Membership: 4,500
Scope: Statewide
Description: The mission of the Audubon Society of Western Pennsylvania is to inspire and educate people of southwestern Pennsylvania to be respectful and responsible stewards of the natural world.
Contact(s):
President: CAROLYN SANFORD
Vice President: WILLIAM DANCHUCK
Secretary: JIM WILKINSON
Secretary: MARIAN CROSSMAN
Publication(s): *Bulletin; Seasoning*
Keyword(s): Birds, Environmental and Conservation Education, Flowers, Plants, and Trees, Insects and Butterflies, Mammals, Native Plants, Natural History, Raptors, Reptiles and Amphibians, Waterfowl, Wildlife and Wildlife Habitat

AVSC INTERNATIONAL
79 Madison Ave., New York, NY 10016
Phone: 212-561-8000; Fax: 212-779-9439; Email: info@avsc.org; WWW: www.avsc.org
Founded: 1943; Membership: 5,500
Scope: National
Description: A nonprofit family planning and reproductive health organization. To ensure through education, research, and service, that men and women everywhere have access to reprroductive health care, including safe contraception. Special expertise in the areas of female sterilization, vasectomy, postpartum contraceptive care, postabortion contraceptive care, and reproductive health programs for men.
Contact(s):
Chair: LYMAN B. BRAINERD JR.
President: DR. AMY E. POLLACK
Chief of Operations and Vice President: TERRENCE W. JEZOWSKI
Director of Programs: LYNN BAKAMJIAN
Medical Director and Vice President: DR. VANNESSA COUINS
Publication(s): *AVSC News*
Keyword(s): Family Planning, Health and Nutrition, Population Growth

BARRIER ISLAND TRUST, INC.
P.O. Box 37310, Tallahassee, FL 32315
Founded: 1989; Membership: 200
Scope: Statewide
Description: To preserve the natural resources of Florida's barrier islands, initially focusing on Dog Island and Apalachicola Bay, hold and manage barrier island property to preserve it in its natural state, promote research on barrier island ecology, and translate research into educational programs and effective policies for protection of barrier islands.
Contact(s):
Board of Trustee Chair: GUY SMITH IV, 352 North St., Greenwich, CT 06830; Phone: 203-972-5504
Board of Trustee President: LEROY COLLINS III, 16 Davis Blvd. #12, Tampa, FL 33606; Phone: 813-259-9484
Board of Trustee Treasurer: MITCHELL SMITH, P.O. Box 1912, Albany, GA 31702
Board of Trustee Vice President: DIANNE MELLON, 1515 Country Club, Tallahassee, FL 32301; Phone: 850-877-3942
Keyword(s): Islands, Land Preservation

BASS ANGLERS SPORTSMAN SOCIETY (B.A.S.S, INC.)
5845 Carmichael Rd., Montgomery, AL 36117
Phone: 334-272-9530; WWW: www.bassmasters.com
Founded: 1968
Scope: National
Description: Organized to fight pollution, assist state and national conservation agencies in their efforts, and teach the young people of our country good conservation practices. Dedicated to the realistic conservation of our water resources.
Contact(s):
Chairman and CEO: HELEN SEVIER
National Conservation Director: BRUCE SHUPP
National Federation Director: DON K. CORKRAN
Publication(s): *Bassmaster Magazine; Guns and Gear; B.A.S.S. Times; Fishing Tackle Retailer; Television Show: The Bassmasters*

BASS RESEARCH FOUNDATION
1001 Market St., Chattanooga, TN 37402
Phone: 615-756-2514
Founded: 1973
Scope: National
Description: A nonprofit, tax-deductible, public foundation organized to promote and encourage results-oriented research aimed at improving both the quantity and quality of America's bass fishery resources. Works to provide the angler with a better understanding of scientific bass management and to provide the bass manager with a better understanding of the needs and desires of the angler.
Contact(s):
Executive Director: H. WILLIAM BUCHER
Board of Directors: RON PEDDERSON; Phone: 414-354-2322
Board of Directors: BARRY CARIS
Board of Directors: LOREN HILL
Board of Directors: LARRY BOST
Board of Directors: STU BELL
Coordinator of Chapter Services: ANN DAHL
Publication(s): *BRF Report; Bass Life*

BAT CONSERVATION INTERNATIONAL
P.O. Box 162603, Austin, TX 78716
Phone: 512-327-9721; WWW: www.batcon.org
Founded: 1982; Membership: 14,000
Scope: International
Description: A nonprofit organization with members in 71 countries. BCI's purpose is to document and publicize the values and conservation needs of bats, to promote bat conservation projects, and to assist with management initiatives worldwide.
Contact(s):
Chairman: MICHAEL L. COOK
Secretary: MRS. JOHN C. PHILLIPS
Treasurer: MARK RITTER
Founder and Executive Director: DR. MERLIN D. TUTTLE
Publication(s): *BATS(quarterly)*
Keyword(s): Biodiversity, Biology, Ecology, Endangered and Threatened Species, Environment, Environmental and Conservation Education, International Conservation, Mammals, Nongame Wildlife, Research, Scholarships, Wildlife and Wildlife Habitat

BERKSHIRE-LITCHFIELD ENVIRONMENTAL COUNCIL, INC.
P.O. Box 552, Lakeville, CT 06039
Phone: 203-435-2004
Founded: 1970; Membership: 1,000
Scope: Statewide
Description: Primarily concerned with energy, invasive transportation, and land use issues in the southern Berkshires and Litchfield Hills. Offers public programs and environmental education for all ages.
Contact(s):
President: STARLING W. CHILDS; Phone: 203-542-5569
Vice President: NIC OSBORN
Secretary: ELLERY W. SINCLAIR
Treasurer: PETER DOLAN

Executive Director: JUDY ISACOFF THOMAS
Counsel: WILLIAM F. MORRILL
Publication(s): *BLEC News*
Keyword(s): Agriculture, Biodiversity, Environmental and Conservation Education, Environmental Preservation, Wilderness

BIG BEND NATURAL HISTORY ASSOCIATION
P.O. Box 196, Big Bend National Park, TX 79834
Phone: 915-477-2236
Founded: 1956; Membership: 559
Scope: Statewide
Description: A private nonprofit organization whose main objectives are to facilitate popular interpretation of the scenic, scientific and historical values of Big Bend, and to encourage research related to those values. To accomplish these goals, the association is authorized by the National Park Service to publish, print, or otherwise provide books, maps, and illustrative material on the Big Bend region and to sponsor a Big Bend seminar program.
Contact(s):
Chairman: ROB DUNAGAN; Phone: 915-336-5274
Executive Director: MIKE BOREN
Editor: ALISA LYNCH
Publication(s): *Native Plant Society of Texas News*
Keyword(s): Environmental and Conservation Education, Flowers, Plants, and Trees, Gardening and Horticulture, Natural Areas, Nature Preservation

BILLFISH FOUNDATION
2419 E. Commercial Blvd., Suite 303, Ft. Lauderdale, FL 33308
Phone: 954-938-0150/800-438-8247; Fax: 954-938-5311
Scope: National
Description: The Billfish Foundation is a nonprofit organization dedicated to the conservation of billfish worldwide through scientific research, education, and advocacy. The research funded by The Billfish Foundation is specifically designed to provide scientific data that will allow for the development of an international management plan for billfish that will help to ensure the worldwide future of these important fish.
Contact(s):
Chairman of Trustees: WINTHROP P. ROCKEFELLER
Executive Director of Trustees: ELLEN PEEL
President of Trustees and Vice Chairman: MEL M. IMMERGUT
Treasurer of Trustees: BOBBY JONES
Vice Chairman of Trustees: RALPH VICENTE
Publication(s): *TBF News; Billfish*
Keyword(s): Billfish, Endangered and Threatened Species, Environmental and Conservation Education, Fisheries, International Conservation, Sport Fishing

BIO-INTEGRAL RESOURCE CENTER
P.O. Box 7414, Berkeley, CA 94707
Phone: 510-524-2567
Founded: 1979; Membership: 5,000
Scope: National
Description: A nonprofit educational organization dedicated to providing information on least-toxic pest control.
Contact(s):
Executive Director: SHEILA DAAR
Managing Editor of Publications: WILLIAM QUARLES
Project Director: HELGA OLKOWSKI
Technical Director: WILLIAM OLKOWSKI
Publication(s): *IPM Practitioner, The; Common Sense Pest Control; Least-toxic Pest Management for Fleas, Termites, Cockroaches, Raccoons, Ticks, and more*
Keyword(s): Agriculture, Gardening and Horticulture, Insects and Butterflies, Pesticides, Urban Environment

BIODIVERSITY LEGAL FOUNDATION
P.O. Box 18327, Boulder, CO 80308-1327
Phone: 303-442-3037; Email: blfrog@aol.com
Founded: 1991; Membership: 1,400
Scope: National
Description: The Biodiversity Legal Foundation is a nonprofit, science-based tax-exempt organization dedicated to the preservation of all native plants, animals, and naturally functioning ecosystems with a special emphasis on the Rocky Mountain Region. Through educational, administrative, and legal actions, we endeavor to encourage improved public attitudes for all living things.
Contact(s):
President: EDWARD W. MUDD JR.
Vice President: ROGER CANDEE
Director: JASPER CARLTON
Secretary and Treasurer: JOYCE HUDSON
Publication(s): *Administrative and Legal Update; How You Can Help Rare and Endangered Species within the Framework of Existing Conservation Law; Guidelines for the Preparation of Species Status Reviews and species conservation assessments*
Keyword(s): Biodiversity, Endangered and Threatened Species, Environmental Law, Fisheries, Nongame Wildlife, Prairies, Predators, Public Lands, Sustainable Ecosystems, Wildlife and Wildlife Habitat

BIOMASS USERS NETWORK
383 Franklin St., Bloomfield, NJ 07003
Phone: 201-680-9100
Founded: 1985; Membership: 51 countries
Scope: International
Description: To advance rural economic development in Third World countries in an environmentally sound manner, through the innovative production and efficient use of biomass resources.
Contact(s):
Chairman: DAVID MAZAMBANI
Publication(s): *Network News*
Keyword(s): Energy, Flowers, Plants, and Trees, Forests and Forestry, Soil Conservation, Sustainable Development

BIRDLIFE INTERNATIONAL
Canada Nature Federation,1 Nicholas St., Ste. 606, Ottawa, Ontario KIN 7B7 Canada
Phone: 613-562-3447; Fax: 613-562-3371; Email: cnf@cnf.ca; WWW: www.magna.cal~cnfgen
Scope: National
Description: Protection of birds and their habitats in Canada, in their winter quarters in North and South America, and off Canada's coasts are among major concerns.
Contact(s):
Contact: MICHAEL BRADSTREET, Bird Studies Canada, Box 160, Port Rowan, Ontario N0E 1M0 Canada; Phone: 519-586-3531; Fax: 519-586-3532
Contact: CAROLINE SCHULTZ
Keyword(s): Birds, Conservation of Protected Areas, Endangered and Threatened Species, Environmental Preservation, International Conservation, Nature Preservation, Wildlife and Wildlife Habitat

BLACK BASS FOUNDATION
260 Crest Rd., Edgefield, SC 29824
Phone: 803-637-3100; Fax: 803-637-3100
Founded: 1993; Membership: 15,000
Scope: International
Description: An international nonprofit conservation organization dedicated to the protection of bass habitat, the promotion of research, education, restoration, and conservation of the black bass fishery in North America. Supports annual grants-in-aid programs through the Black Bass Superfund and Kids' Fishin' Network.
Contact(s):
President: THOMAS F. RODGERS, P.O. Box 670, Edgefield, SC 29824; Phone: 803-637-3100
Editor: BOOK ELLIOTT
Publication(s): *The Black Bass Journal*

NON-GOVERNMENTAL ORGANIZATIONS

Keyword(s): Fisheries, Lakes, Rivers, Sport Fishing, Youth Organizations

BLUEBIRDS ACROSS VERMONT PROJECT
255 Sherman Hollow Rd., Hungtinton, VT 05462
Phone: 802-434-3068
Founded: 1987; Membership: 800
Scope: Statewide
Description: A project of the Vermont Audubon Council and Green Mountain Audubon, Bluebirds Across Vermont (BAV) was formed to help restore native eastern bluebird populations. BAV promotes the proper placement of correctly-built nestboxes by informed citizens who monitor them throughout the nesting season and send the data to BAV for yearly compilation.
Contact(s):
Contact: MARK LaBARR

BOONE AND CROCKETT CLUB
Old Milwaukee Depot, 250 Station Dr., Missoula, MT 59801
Phone: 406-542-1888; Fax: 406-542-0784; Email: bcclub@boone-crockett.org; WWW: www.boone-crockett.org
Founded: 1887
Scope: National
Description: A 501 (c) (3) organization. Established by Theodore Roosevelt and other concerned sportsmen to promote hunting ethics, foster the concept of Fair Chase, and help establish wildlife conservation practices which led to the recovery of big game animals in North America. The Club documents the records of North American big game and exhibits its National Collection of Heads and Horns in Cody, WY.
Contact(s):
President: DANIEL A. PEDROTTI; Phone: 512-884-2443
Secretary: GILBERT ADAMS; Phone: 409-835-3000
Treasurer: JOSEPH A. OSTERVICH; Phone: 608-486-2341
Associates Committee: GEORGE A. BETTAS; Phone: 509-335-4531
Conservation Committee: RICHARD A. GOODING; Phone: 505-884-4242
Director of North American Big Game Records: JACK RENEAU; Phone: 406-542-1888
Ethics Committee: WILLIAM O. BARRETT; Phone: 210-829-7831
Museum Committee: FREDERICK J. KING; Phone: 406-994-2654
Records of North American Big Game Committee: C. RANDALL BYERS; Phone: 208-885-7341
Publication(s): *FAIR CHASE; Records of North American Big Game; Records of North American Elk and Mule Deer; An American Crusade for Wildlife; Records of North American Whitetail Deer*
Keyword(s): Environmental and Conservation Education, Hunting, Public Lands, Scholarships and Grants, Wildlife and Wildlife Habitat

BOONE AND CROCKETT FOUNDATION
Old Milwaukee Depot, 250 Station Dr., Missoula, MT 59801
Phone: 406-542-1888; Fax: 406-542-0784; Email: bcclub@boone-crockett.org; WWW: www.boone-crockett.org
Scope: National
Description: The BCF owns and operates the 6,000 acre Theodore Roosevelt Memorial Ranch near Dupuyer, MT, as a working cattle ranch to support the program. BCF supports natural resource conservation research, education, and demonstration primarily through the Boone and Crockett wildlife conservation program in conjunction with the University of Montana.
Contact(s):
President: DANIEL A. PEDROTTI; Phone: 512-884-2443
Secretary: GILBERT ADAMS; Phone: 409-835-3000
Treasurer: JOSEPH A. OSTERVICH; Phone: 608-486-2341
TRMR Manager: ROBERT K. PEEBLES; Phone: 406-472-3380
Keyword(s): Hunting, Renewable Resources, Sustainable Development, Sustainable Ecosystems, Wildlife and Wildlife Habitat

BORDER ECOLOGY PROJECT (BEP)
Drawer CP, Bisbee, AZ 85603
Phone: 520-432-7456; Fax: 520-432-7473; Email: bep@primenet.com
Founded: 1983
Scope: National
Description: BEP advocates for solutions to environmental problems along the U.S. and Mexico border. Areas of focus include Right-to-Know, environmental pollution, international trade, mining, and hazardous materials trucking.
Contact(s):
Director: DICK KAMP
Publication(s): *Environmental and Health Conditions in the Interior of Mexico: Options for Transnational Safeguards; Environmental Protection within the Mexican Mining Sector and the Impact of the World Bank Loan #3359*
Keyword(s): Air Quality and Pollution, Rivers, Solid Waste Management, Toxic Substances, Water Pollution Management

BOTANICAL CLUB OF WISCONSIN
c/o Wisconsin Academy of Science, Arts, and Letters, 1922 University Ave., Madison, WI 53705
Phone: 608-262-2792; Fax: 608-262-7509
Founded: 1969; Membership: 185
Scope: Statewide
Description: Botanical Club of Wisconsin promotes preservation of Wisconsin's native plants and educates the public as to the value of plants. The Club also fosters research on plant biology and provides a means for fellowship and information exchange.
Contact(s):
President: EMMET J. JUDZIEWICZ; Phone: 920-842-4620
Vice President: JAMES P. BENNETT; Phone: 608-262-5489; Fax: 608-262-5489
Secretary: JUNE DOBBERPUHL; Phone: 608-267-5037; Fax: 608-266-2925
Treasurer: EDWARD N. GOLVER; Phone: 608-437-4578
Publication(s): *Wisconsin Flora; The Bulletin of the Botanical Club of Wisconsin*
Keyword(s): Environmental and Conservation Education, Flowers, Plants, and Trees, Nature Preservation

BOTANICAL SOCIETY OF WESTERN PENNSYLVANIA
5837 Nicholson St., Pittsburgh, PA 15217-2309
Phone: 412-521-9425; Email: yoree@sgi.net; WWW: www.home.kiski.net//~speedy/b1.html
Membership: 200
Scope: Statewide
Description: Botanical Society of Western Pennsylvania brings together those who are interested in botany and encourages the study of botany and knowledge of plants.
Contact(s):
President: DR. MARY JOY HAYWOOD; Phone: 412-578-6175
Secretary: LOREE SPEEDY
Treasurer: WALTER GARDILL; Phone: 412-364-5308
Publication(s): *Wildflowers*
Keyword(s): Conservation, Environmental and Conservation Education, Flowers, Plants, and Trees, Gardening and Horticulture

BOUNTY INFORMATION SERVICE
4849 E. St. Charles Rd., Columbia, MO 65201
Phone: 573-474-6967; Email: claun01@mail.coin.missouri.edu
Founded: 1966
Scope: National
Description: Promotes the removal of bounties in North America by publishing Bounty News and studies of the bounty system and by coordinating activities and legal aspects.
Contact(s):
Director and Editor: H. CHARLES LAUN
Publication(s): *Bounty News; A Guide to the Removal of Bounties*
Keyword(s): Environmental and Conservation Education, Mammals, Trapping, Wildlife and Wildlife Habitat, Wildlife Management

BOY SCOUTS OF AMERICA
National Office, P.O. Box 152079, 1325 West Walnut Hill Ln., Irving, TX 75015-2079
Phone: 214-580-2000

Founded: 1910
Scope: National
Description: Boy Scouts of America (BSA) was chartered by Congress in 1916 to provide an educational program for boys and young adults that builds character and develops responsibility, citizenship, and personal fitness. Community groups with goals compatible with BSA receive national charters to use the Scouting program as part of their own youth work.
Contact(s):
President: JOHN W. CREIGHTON JR.
Treasurer: MILTON H. WARD
Assistant Treasurer: E. W. WENDELL
Chief Scout Executive: JERE B. RATCLIFFE
Conservation Director: DAVID R. BATES
Regional Executive: ROY L. WILLIAMS, P.O. Box 22019, Tempe, AZ 85285-2019; Phone: 602-752-7000
Regional Executive: RON K. HEGWOOD, P.O. Box 3085, Naperville, IL 60566-7085; Phone: 708-983-6730
Regional Executive: PARVIN L. BISHOP, P.O. Box 440728, Kennesaw, GA 30144; Phone: 770-421-1601
Regional Executive of Northeast Region: KENNETH L. CONNELLY, P.O. Box 350, Dayton, NJ 08810-0350; Phone: 908-297-6500
Keyword(s): Environmental and Conservation Education, Outdoor Recreation, Youth Organizations

BRANDYWINE CONSERVANCY, INC.
P.O. Box 141, Chadds Ford, PA 19317
Phone: 610-388-2700; Fax: 610-388-1575

Founded: 1967; **Membership:** 4,122
Scope: Statewide
Description: A nonprofit organization providing model land use and environmental regulations for Pennsylvania municipalities, and land, water resources, and historic site conservation and management assistance to landowners and conservation,organizations, primarily in Pennsylvania and Delaware.
Contact(s):
Chairman: GEORGE A. WEYMOUTH
Executive Director: JAMES H. DUFF
Assistant Director of Administration (Environmental Management Center): PHILIP E. PYLE JR.
Associate Director of Design (Environmental Management Center): JOHN SNOOK
Associate Director of Municipal Assistance (Environmental Management Center): WESLEY R. HORNER
Associate of Director of Land Stewardships (Environmental Management Center): DAVID D. SHIELDS
Director of Environmental Management Center: H. WILLIAM SELLERS
Public Relations: HALSEY SPRUANCE
Publication(s): Catalyst, The; Environmental Currents; Environmental Management Handbook
Keyword(s): Environmental and Conservation Education, Environmental Protection, Pollution Prevention, Water Resources, Wetlands

BRITISH COLUMBIA FIELD ORNITHOLOGISTS
P.O. Box 8059, Victoria, British Columbia V8W 3R7 Canada

Founded: 1991; **Membership:** 250
Scope: Statewide
Description: To promote the study and enjoyment of birds in British Columbia; to disseminate knowledge and appreciation of birds by means of publications; to foster cooperation between amateur and professional ornithologists; and to promote conservation of birds and their habitats.
Contact(s):
President: TONY GREENFIELD, P.O. Box 319, Sechelt, British Columbia V0N 3A0 Canada; Phone: 250-885-5539
Vice President: BRYAN GATES, 3085 Uplands Rd., Victoria, British Columbia V8R 6B3 Canada; Phone: 250-598-7789
Treasurer: EVERAND MIYASAKI, 8587 Sentinel Place, Sidney, British Columbia V8L 4Z8 Canada; Phone: 250-656-8066
Editor: MARILYN BUHLER, 1132 Loenholm Rd., Victoria, British Columbia V8Z 2Z6 Canada; Phone: 250-744-2521
Editor: ANDY BUHLER, 1132 Loenholm Rd., Victoria, British Columbia V8Z 2Z6 Canada; Phone: 250-744-2521
Editor: MARTIN K. McNICHOLL, 4735 Canada Way, Burnaby, Columbia V5G 1L3 Canada; Phone: 250-294-9333
Publication(s): British Columbia Birds (journal); BC Birding (newsletter)
Keyword(s): Birds

BRITISH COLUMBIA WATERFOWL SOCIETY, THE
5191 Robertson Rd., Delta, British Columbia V4K 3N2 Canada
Phone: 604-946-6980

Membership: 2,426
Scope: Statewide
Description: The organization was set in 1963 on federal land leased for 30 years to be opened to the public as a bird viewing area at the mouth of the Fraser River, which supports one of the largest wintering populations of waterfowl in Canada. The organization attempts to promote awareness of all parts of the environment.
Contact(s):
President: KEN HALL
Vice President: JOHN BOWLES
Secretary: VARRI JOHNSON
Treasurer: JAMES MORRISON
Manager: JOHN IRELAND
Publication(s): Marsh Notes; BirdCheck List

BROOKS BIRD CLUB INC., THE
P.O. Box 4077, Wheeling, WV 26003

Founded: 1932; **Membership:** 1,000
Scope: National
Description: A nonprofit organization formed to encourage the study and conservation of birds and other phases of natural history. Members in thirty-eight states, Canada, and eight foreign countries. Named in honor of A.B. Brooks, naturalist.
Contact(s):
President: JAMES BULLARD, P.O. Box 137, Ashton, MD 20861
Vice President: FRED MCCULLOUGH
Secretary: VIRGINIA CRONENBERGER, Rt. 1 Box 37, Petroleum, WV 26161
Treasurer: GERALD A. DEVAUL, 17 Mozart Rd., Wheeling, WV 26003
Administrator: CARL A. SLATER, 57290 Mehlmen Rd., Bellaire, OH 43906
Immediate Past President: TOM FOX, Route L Box 420, Millstone, WV 25261
Mail-Bag Editor: WILLIAM MURRAY, P.O. Box 944, New Cumberland, WV 26047
Membership Chairman: CAROLYN CONRAD, 423 Warwood Ave., Wheeling, WV 26003
President-Elect: CINDY ELLIS, 103A Oakwood Estates, Scott Depot, WV 25560
Redstart-Editor: DR. A. R. BUCKELEW JR., Box J, Bethany, WV 26032
Publication(s): Redstart, The; Mail Bag, The
Keyword(s): Birds, Environmental and Conservation Education, Flowers, Plants, and Trees, Nature Preservation, Wildlife and Wildlife Habitat

BROTHERHOOD OF THE JUNGLE COCK, INC., THE
P.O. Box 576, Glen Burnie, MD 21061

Scope: National
Description: Seeks to teach youth the true meaning of conservation. Primary interest is the preservation of American game fishes, placing great emphasis on adult responsibility of personal instruction along those lines.

NON-GOVERNMENTAL ORGANIZATIONS

Contact(s):
President: GUS DAY
Secretary: EDWARD T. LITTLE, 6623 Kenwood Ave., Baltimore, MD 21237; Phone: 401-682-4631
Treasurer: M. H. DAY, 706 Orchard Way, Silver Spring, MD 20904
1st Vice President: WILLIAM SIMMS
Administrator: BOSLEY WRIGHT; Phone: 410-761-7727
Keyword(s): Endangered and Threatened Species, Environmental and Conservation Education, Fisheries, Water Pollution, Youth Organizations

CADDO LAKE INSTITUTE, INC.
P.O. Box 2710, Aspen, CO 81612
Phone: 970-925-2710; Fax: 970-923-4245; Email: ornitzb2@aol.com
Scope: National
Description: A non-profit organization whose purpose is environmental awareness. The program director is based near Caddo Lake, Texas. The director will coordinate college programs. Students are paid a stipend to collect samples and return to the student's laboratory for analysis; will also give seminars at secondary schools, all to promote environmental awareness.
Contact(s):
President: DWIGHT SHELLMAN; Email: 72007.165@compuserve.com
Vice President: SARA KNEIPP; Phone: 903-938-3545; Fax: 903-938-3545; Email: sjkneipp@aol.com
Publication(s): *Caddo Lake Institute Update*
Keyword(s): Ecology, Internships, Watersheds, Wetlands, Wildlife and Wildlife Habitat, Youth Organizations

CALIFORNIA ACADEMY OF SCIENCES
Golden Gate Park, San Francisco, CA 94118
Phone: 415-221-5100
Founded: 1853; Membership: 24,000
Scope: Statewide
Description: The Academy of Sciences' goal is the exploration and interpretation of natural history. Maintains research collections and operates a museum-aquarium-planetarium complex to which one and one-half million visitors come each year.
Contact(s):
Vice President: DR. JOHN S. PEARSE
Secretary: MARTHA KROPF
Director: DR. PATRICK KOCIOLEK
Biodiversity Resource Center Coordinator: ANNE MARIE MALLEY
Board of Trustees Chairman: W. RICHARD BINGHAM
Librarian: THOMAS D. MORITZ
Vice Chairman: SANDRA LINDER
Vice Chairman: MERVIN G. MORRIS
Publication(s): *Academy Newsletter; California Wild; Proceedings; Occasional Papers*
Keyword(s): Environment, Natural History, Nature Preservation, Reptiles and Amphibians, Research

CALIFORNIA ASSOCIATION OF RESOURCE CONSERVATION DISTRICTS
ATTN: President, P.O. Box 158, Rio Nido, CA 95471
Scope: Statewide
Contact(s):
President, Alternate Board Member: GLENDA HUMISTON, P.O. Box 158, Rio Nido, CA 95471; Phone: 707-869-9003; Fax: 707-869-9070; Email: gih@agrocate.com
Vice President: DONNA THOMAS, 8158 Panorama Trail, Inyokem, CA 93527; Phone: 760-377-4525; Fax: 760-377-45250
Executive Director: TOM WEHRI, 801 K St. Suite 1318, Sacramento, CA 95814; Phone: 916-447-7237; Fax: 916-447-2532; Email: carcd@ns.net
Board Member: CHUCK PRITCHARD, 9765 Carrisa Highway, Santa Margarita, CA 93453; Phone: 805-475-2386; Fax: 805-475-2533
Secretary-Treasurer: JOE FURTADO, 6 S Eldorado Ste 300, Stockton, CA 95202; Phone: 209-464-1185; Fax: 209-464-1183

CALIFORNIA B.A.S.S. CHAPTER FEDERATION
ATTN: President, 751 Melva Ave., Oakdale, CA 95361
Phone: 209-847-3272; WWW: www.californiabass.com
Scope: Statewide
Description: An organization of Bassmaster chapters, affiliated with the Bass Anglers Sportsman Society, organized to fight pollution, assist state and national conservation agencies in their efforts, and teach the young people of our country good conservation practice. Dedicated to the realistic conservation of our water resources.
Contact(s):
President: FRANK LASITER, 751 Melva Ave., Oakdale, CA 95361; Phone: 209-541-3673(W)/209-847-3272(H)
Conservation Director: EDWARD PETERSON, 1575 Wimbledon Dr., Auburn, CA 95603; Phone: 916-355-6281(W)/916-889-2902(H); Fax: 916-355-5025; Email: peterson_edward@aphub.aerojetpd.com

CALIFORNIA NATIVE PLANT SOCIETY (CNDS)
1722 J. St., #17, Sacramento, CA 95814
Phone: 916-447-2677; Fax: 916-447-2727; Email: cnps@cnps.org; WWW: www.cnps.org
Founded: 1965; Membership: 10,000
Scope: Statewide
Description: CNPS increases understanding and appreciation of California's native plants and works to preserve them in their natural habitat through scientific activities, education, and conservation.
Contact(s):
President: LORI HUBBART; Phone: 707-882-1655
Executive Director: ALLEN BARNES; Phone: 916-447-2677; Fax: 916-447-2727; Email: cnps@cnps.org
Publication(s): *Fremontia, CNPS Bulletin*
Keyword(s): Conservation, Endangered and Threatened Species, Plants

CALIFORNIA NATIVE PLANT SOCIETY, THE
1722 J St., Suite 17, Sacramento, CA 95814
Phone: 916-447-2677; Fax: 916-447-2727; Email: cnps@cnps.org
Founded: 1965
Scope: Statewide
Description: A statewide nonprofit organization of amateurs and professionals with a common interest in California's native plants. The society, working through its local chapters, seeks to increase understanding of California's native flora and to preserve the rich resource for future generations. Membership is open to all.
Contact(s):
President: LORI HUBBART
Executive Director: ALLEN BARNES
Editor: JOYCE HAWLEY
Editor: PHYLLIS FABER
Legal Advisor: SANDY McCOY
Recording Secretary: JAKE SIGG
Vice President for Administration: ROY WEST
Vice President for Chapter Relations: LINDA BELL
Vice President for Conservation: DAVID CHIPPING
Vice President for Education: CAROL BAIRD
Vice President for Educaton: LORRAE FUENTES
Vice President for Finance: STEVE HARTMAN
Vice President for Legislation: JOE WILLINGHAM
Vice President for Rare Plants: ANN DENNIS
Vice President of Publications: PHYLLIS FABER
Publication(s): *Fremontia; Bulletin; Conservation & Management of Rare and Endangered Plants; Terrestrial Vegetation of California; California's Changing Landscape; Inventory of Rare and Endangered Vascular Plants of California; Flora of San Bruno Mountain; Plant Communities of Marin County; Flowering Plants of Santa Monica Mountains; Chapter Newsletters*
Keyword(s): Biodiversity, Endangered and Threatened Species, Environmental and Conservation Education, Environmental Preservation, Wetlands

CALIFORNIA TRAPPERS ASSOCIATION
99 Poinsettia Gardens Dr., Ventura, CA 93004
Phone: 805-647-8903; Fax: 805-647-9970
Founded: 1969; Incorporated: 1973; Membership: 420
Scope: Statewide
Description: Dedicated to the encouragement of conservation, enhancement, and scientific management of all our natural resources, especially furbearing mammals. Promotes state and federal wildlife projects through volunteer skilled labor and financial contributions. Gives $500 to $1,000 grants each year to college students studying furbearing mammals.
Contact(s):
President: KEITH CARLY, P.O. Box 73, Elk Creek, CA 95939; Phone: 916-968-5038
Vice President: JOHN CLARK, 907 Holmes Flat Rd., Red Crest, CA 95569; Phone: 707-722-4259
Treasurer: TOM LAUSTALOT, 18907 Indian Creek Rd., Fort Jones, CA 96032; Phone: 916-468-2228
Executive Secretary: DONALD L. STEHSEL
Lobbyist: KATHY LYNCH; Phone: 916-537-7169
Publication(s): *Fur Facts; Legislative Alerts*
Keyword(s): Biology, Endangered and Threatened Species, Environmental and Conservation Education, Environmental Ethics, Environmental Planning, Environmental Preservation, Environmental Protection, Predators, Renewable Resources, Scholarships and Grants, Trapping, Wetlands, Wilderness, Wildlands, Wildlife and Wildlife Habitat

CALIFORNIA TROUT, INC.
870 Market St., #859, San Francisco, CA 94102
Phone: 415-392-8887
Founded: 1970; Membership: 4,000 individuals
Scope: Statewide
Description: Statewide organization of anglers dedicated to protection and restoration of wild trout, native steelhead, and their waters in California, and to the creation of high-quality angling adventures for the public to enjoy. Motto: "Keeper of the Streams."
Contact(s):
Executive Director: JIM EDMONDSON
Board Chairman: BILL HOOPER
Publication(s): *Streamkeepers Log*
Keyword(s): Fisheries, Forests and Forestry, Land Purchase, Outdoor Recreation, Sport Fishing, Trout, Water Conservation

CALIFORNIA WATERFOWL ASSOCIATION
4630 Northgate Blvd., Suite 150, Sacramento, CA 95834
Phone: 916-648-1406; Fax: 916-648-1665
Founded: 1945
Scope: Statewide
Description: A statewide nonprofit, public benefit corporation, whose principal objectives are the conservation, protection, and enhancement of California's waterfowl resources and the waterfowling opportunities which they provide. The association directly represents the interests of over 12,000 sportsmen and conservationists throughout the state and indirectly represents the interests of other Californians who are concerned with and benefit from these unique resources.
Contact(s):
Chairman: VICTOR GONELLA
Secretary: GEORGE KAMMERER
Treasurer: RAY BURMASTER
Chairman of the Board: JIM CALLENDER
Director of Waterfowl and Wetlands Programs: DR. ROBERT McLANDRESS
Editor: BECKY EASTER
First Vice Chairman: BOB BELL
Publication(s): *California Waterfowl Magazine*
Keyword(s): Environmental Preservation, Hunting, Water Resources, Waterfowl, Wetlands

CALIFORNIA WILDLIFE DEFENDERS
P.O. Box 2025, Hollywood, CA 90078
Phone: 213-663-1856
Scope: Statewide
Description: A nonprofit association whose purpose is to eradicate the prejudice toward predators, especially coyotes; authored an ordinance banning the feeding of coyotes in order to restrict hillside residents who unknowingly exacerbated the urban coyote problem; has been instrumental in its enactment in several California cities and counties; and in halting the use of steel-jawed leghold traps in the county of Los Angeles.
Contact(s):
Director: LILA BROOKS
Associate: JUDY GARCIA
Associate: ALBERTA BURKE
Associate: DR. SUZANNE ULMAN
Publication(s): *Wildlife Alerts*
Keyword(s): Nature Preservation, Nongame Wildlife, Predators, Trapping, Wildlife and Wildlife Habitat, Wildlife Management, Wildlife Rehabilitation

CALIFORNIA WILDLIFE FEDERATION
P.O. Box 1527, Sacramento, CA 95812-1527
Phone: 916-441-7563
Founded: 1952; Membership: 8,600 individuals
Scope: Statewide
Description: A nonprofit statewide organization of councils, clubs, and individual members dedicated to promote the conservation, enhancement, scientific management, and wise use of all our natural resources.
Contact(s):
President: RANDY WALKER, 4908 Sunset Dr,, Fresno, CA 93704; Phone: 209-225-9003
Vice President: KEITH RINGGENBERG, 933 W. Pontiac Way, Fresno, CA 93712; Phone: 209-225-6962
Treasurer: REID AITON, P.O. Box 84, Korbel, CA 95550; Phone: 707-668-5298
Editor: LAURIE MATTHEW, P.O. Box 197, Bella Vista, CA 96008; Phone: 530-549-5604
Publication(s): *California Wildlife*
Keyword(s): Biodiversity, Endangered and Threatened Species, Fisheries, Hunting, Wildlife and Wildlife Habitat

CALIFORNIANS FOR POPULATION STABILIZATION (CAPS)
926 J St., Suite 915, Sacramento, CA 95814
Phone: 916-446-1033; Email: caps@calweb.com; WWW: www.calweb.com/~caps
Founded: 1986; Membership: 3,000
Scope: Statewide
Description: CAPS is a nonprofit membership organization dedicated to stabilizing population in California to protect and preserve the state's environment, ecology, and resources. CAPS believes overpopulation is the ultimate environmental threat. Activities include: public education, media campaigns, public policy research and advocacy, and grassroots organizing.
Contact(s):
Executive Director: TOM MCMAHON
Board President: JIM FANDREM
Legislative Director: BETSEY L. BALLASH
Media Director: JOSEPH GUZZARDI
Publication(s): *CAPS Data Reports; CAPS NEWSLETTERS; action alerts; brochures and fact sheets*
Keyword(s): Environmental Preservation, Land Preservation, Land Use Planning, Open Space, Population Growth

CAMP FIRE BOYS AND GIRLS
4601 Madison Ave., Kansas City, MO 64112
Phone: 816-756-1950
Founded: 1910; Membership: 661,000
Scope: National
Description: Open to boys and girls from birth to 21 years of age, without regard to race, creed, ethnic origin, sex, or income level.

NON-GOVERNMENTAL ORGANIZATIONS

Provides a program of informal education that focuses on developing skills in interpersonal relationships, decision-making, leadership, creativity, citizenship, community service, and individual growth.
Contact(s):
Director of Program and Council Services: JUDY THOMPSON
National Executive Director and CEO: STEWART J. SMITH
National President: GRETCHEN L. BIENEMAN
Keyword(s): Air Quality and Pollution, Endangered and Threatened Species, Environmental and Conservation Education, Health and Nutrition, Outdoor Recreation

CAMP FIRE CLUB OF AMERICA, THE
230 Campfire Rd., Chappaqua, NY 10514
Phone: 914-941-0199; Fax: 914-923-0977
Founded: 1897
Scope: National
Description: Works to preserve forests and woodland; to protect and conserve the wildlife of our country; and to sponsor and support all reasonable measures to the end that present and future generations may continue to enjoy advantages and benefits of life outdoors.
Contact(s):
President: SCOTT T. SUTTON
Chairman of Committee on Conservation of Forests and Wildlife: LEONARD J. VALLENDER
Deputy Chairman of Committee on Conservation of Forests and Wildlife: EUGENE McCARDLE
Editor: STEVE BURNETT
Secretary of Committee on Conservation of Forests and Wildlife: THOMAS F. QUIRK
Publication(s): *Backlog, The*
Keyword(s): Forests and Forestry, Hunting, Sport Fishing, Wildlife and Wildlife Habitat, Wildlife Management

CAMP FIRE CONSERVATION FUND
230 Camp Fire Rd., Chappaqua, NY 10514
Phone: 914-941-9681
Founded: 1977
Scope: National
Description: A tax-exempt membership organization, dedicated to the preservation of wildlife and its habitat to coordinate the efforts of sportsmen's and conservation organizations; to inform the general public and governmental agencies with regard to intelligent use of our natural resources; and to support and promote conservation research.
Contact(s):
President: GEORGE R. LAMB
Secretary: HENRY F. AYRES JR.
Treasurer: MOTTELL D. PEEK
Keyword(s): Endangered and Threatened Species, Environmental and Conservation Education, Scholarships and Grants, Wildlife and Wildlife Habitat, Wildlife Management

CAMPAIGN FOR A PROSPEROUS GEORGIA
1083 Austin Ave., NE, Atlanta, GA 30307
Phone: 404-659-5675; Fax: 404-659-5676
Founded: 1983; *Membership:* 300
Scope: Statewide
Description: CPG is a nonprofit statewide organization protects the environment and improves the economy by changing the way energy is produced and consumed in Georgia through public education and advocacy.
Contact(s):
President: CAROL ANN DALTON
Vice President: NA`TAKI OSBORNE
Secretary: SUSAN ABRAMSON
Treasurer: MIKI DAVIS
Publication(s): *Plugging In;* technical reports
Keyword(s): Air Quality and Pollution, Energy, Sustainable Development

CANADA-UNITED STATES ENVIRONMENTAL COUNCIL (United States Office)
1101 14th St., NW, Suite 1400, Washington, DC 20005
Phone: 202-682-9400/243; Fax: 202-682-1331
Founded: 1974
Scope: International
Description: Nongovernmental organization sponsored by major Canadian and American conservation and environmental groups. Established to facilitate interchange of information and cooperative action on questions of concern in the two nations.
Contact(s):
Coordinating Committee Co-Chairman: JAMES G. DEANE, Defenders of Wildlife, 1101 14th St. NW, Suite 1400, Washington, DC 20005; Phone: 202-682-9400/ext.243; Fax: 202-682-1334
Coordinating Committee Co-Chairman: JULIE GELFAND, Canadian Nature Federation, Suite 606, 1 Nicholas St., Ottawa, Ontario K1N 7B7 Canada; Phone: 613-562-3447; Fax: 613-562-3371
Keyword(s): Air Quality and Pollution, Endangered and Threatened Species, Public Lands, Wildlife and Wildlife Habitat, Wildlife Management

CANADIAN ARCTIC RESOURCES COMMITTEE, INC.
7 Hinton Ave. N., Suite 200, Ottawa, Ontario K1Y 4P1 Canada
Phone: 613.759-4284; Fax: 613-722-3318
Founded: 1971
Scope: National
Description: To ensure that important social, environmental, and economic ramifications of northern development are studied and analyzed before major decisions relating to northern Canada are made; to exchange information and viewpoints among the public, government, and industry; to develop better perspectives on options available; and to inform the public.
Contact(s):
Executive Director: ROBBIE KEITH
Chairperson: NIGEL BANKES
Publication(s): *Northern Perspectives Member's Update;* list of books on request.

CANADIAN COOPERATIVE WILDLIFE HEALTH CENTRE
Dept. of Veterinary Pathology, WCVM, Univ. of Saskatchewan, 52 Campus Dr., Saskatoon, Saskatchewan S7N 5B4 Canada
Phone: 306-966-5099/800-567-2033; Fax: 306-966-7439; Email: ccwhc@sask.usask.ca
Founded: 1992
Scope: National
Description: The Canadian Cooperative Wildlife Health Centre is a national organization that provides diagnosis of disease, investigation of disease outbreaks, information, education, and consultation to wildlife managers, veterinarians, and members of the public on matters pertaining to the health of free-living wild animals in Canada.
Contact(s):
Co-Director: G. A. WOBESER; Phone: 306-966-7310
Co-Director: F. A. LEIGHTON; Phone: 306-966-7281
Contact for Atlantic Region: DR. PIERRE-YVES DAOUST; Phone: 902-566-0667
Contact for Ontario Region: DR. I. BARKER; Phone: 519-823-8800/4616
Contact for Quebec Region: DR. DANIEL MARTINEAU; Phone: 514-773-8521
Contact for West and North Region: DR. TRENT BOLLINGER; Phone: 306-966-5099
Publication(s): *Wildlife Health Centre Newsletter; Bulletin du Centre de la Sante de la Faune; Wildlife Disease Investigation Manual; Directory of Wildlife Health Expertise*
Keyword(s): Birds, Mammals, Reptiles and Amphibians, Research, Wildlife Disease

CANADIAN ENVIRONMENTAL LAW ASSOCIATION

517 College St., Ste. 401, Toronto, Ontario M6G 4A2 Canada
Phone: 416-960-2284; Fax: 416-960-9392; Email: cela@web.ner; WWW: www.web.net/cela

Founded: 1970
Scope: National

Description: Nonprofit, independent, public-interest legal group formed to use current environmental laws to protect the environment, and to promote better environmental legislation throughout Canada.

Contact(s):
Executive Director: PAUL MULDOON
Communications Coordinator: DAVID MCLARNMCLAREN
Coordinator: SARAH MILLER
Counsel: THERESA MCLENAGHAN
Counsel: RAMINI NADARAJAH
Counsel: RICHARD LINDGREN
Director of International Programs: MICHELLE SWENARCHUK
Librarian: LISA MCSHANE
Researcher: KATHY COOPER

Publication(s): *Newsletter; Intervenor, The*

CANADIAN FEDERATION OF HUMANE SOCIETIES

30 Concourse Gate, Ste. 102, Nepean, Ontario K2E 7V7 Canada
Phone: 613-224-8072; Fax: 613-723-0252; Email: cfhs@magi.com

Founded: 1957; Membership: 45
Scope: National

Description: CFHS is a national body comprised of animal welfare organizations and individuals whose purpose is to promote compassion and humane treatment for all animals.

Contact(s):
President: J. JOY RIPLEY
Executive Director: FRANCES RODENBURG
Editor: FRANCES RODENBURG
Editor: STEPHANIE BROWN

Publication(s): *Whalekind; Caring for Animals; Animal Welfare in Focus; The Humane Educator*

Keyword(s): Agriculture, Endangered and Threatened Species, Fisheries, Marine Mammals, Nongame Wildlife, Trapping, Wildlife and Wildlife Habitat, Wildlife Management

CANADIAN FORESTRY ASSOCIATION

185 Somerset St., W., Ste. 203, Ottawa, Ontario K2P 0J2 Canada
Phone: 613-232-1815; Fax: 613-232-4210; Email: cfa@cyberus.ca

Founded: 1900
Scope: National

Description: The Canadian Forestry Association is a federation of self-governing Provincial Forestry Associations across Canada. It is nongovernmental and nonindustrial. Its purpose is to develop public understanding and cooperation in the wise use, conservation, and sustainable development of Canada's forests and related resources of land, water, and wildlife.

Contact(s):
President: IVAN BALENOVIC, Daveluyville, Quebec Canada
Executive Director: GLEN BLOUIN, Cantley, Quebec Canada
1st Vice President: SUSAN GESNER, Winnipeg, Manitoba Canada
Immediate Past President: JOHN R. HRENO, Winnipeg, Manitoba Canada

Publication(s): *Forest Forum; Proceedings of National Forest Congress 1992; National Forest Education Resources Catalogue; Proceedings: Canadian Urban Forests Conference*

CANADIAN INSTITUTE FOR ENVIRONMENTAL LAW AND POLICY (CIELAP)

517 College St., Ste. 400, Toronto, Ontario M6G 4A2 Canada
Phone: 416-923-3529; Fax: 416-923-5949

Founded: 1970
Scope: National

Description: CIELAP is an independent, not-for-profit research and education institute providing environmental law and policy analysis. CIELAP provides leadership in the development of environmental law and policy which promotes the public interest and the principles of sustainability, including the protection of the health and well-being of present and future generations, and of the natural environment.

Contact(s):
President: ISOBEL HEATHCOTE
Executive Director: ANNE MITCHELL
Secretary and Treasurer: MICHAEL GRESSMANN

Publication(s): *Environment on Trial: A Guide to Ontario Environmental Law and Policy; A Carbon Dioxide Strategy for Ontario: A Discussion paper; Ontario's Environment and the "Common Sense Revolution"; Hazardous Waste Management in Ontario: A Report and Recommendation; Electricity Competition and Clean Air*

CANADIAN INSTITUTE OF FORESTRY/INSTITUT FORESTIER DU CANADA

151 Slater St., Ste. 606, Ottawa, Ontario K1P 5H3 Canada
Phone: 613-234-2242; Fax: 613-234-6181

Founded: 1908; Membership: 2,400
Scope: National

Description: Our mission is to advance the stewardship of Canada's forest resources through leadership, professional competence and public awareness. Our membership includes foresters, forest technicians, academics, scientists and others with a professional interest in Forestry. CIF/IFC represents the largest professional voice for forestry in Canada.

Contact(s):
President: EVELYNNE WRANGLER, Alberta Environmental Protection, Lands & Forests Service, 9th Floor, 9920 108th St., Edmonton AB, Alberta T5K 2M4 Canada; Phone: 403-422-4599; Fax: 403-427-0085; Email: ewrangle@env.gov.ab.ca
Executive Director: ROXANNE COMEAU, 151 Slater St., Suite 606, Ottawa, Ontario K1P 5H3 Canada; Phone: 613-234-2242; Fax: 613-234-6181; Email: cif@cif-ifc.org
Past President: RALPH ROBERTS, Senior Forestry Advisor, Canadian International Development Agency, 200 Promenade du Portage, Hull, PQ K1A 0G4 Canada; Phone: 819-997-6586; Fax: 819-953-3348; Email: ralph_roberts@ACDI-CIDA.GC.CA

Publication(s): *The Forestry Chronicle*

CANADIAN NATIONAL SPORTSMEN'S SHOWS

703 Evans Ave., Ste. 202, Toronto, Ontario M9C 5E9 Canada
Phone: 416-695-0311; Fax: 416-695-0381

Founded: 1948
Scope: National

Description: A national corporation presenting outdoor shows and events. Products relate to fishing, hiking, camping, boating, skiing, and the consumer shows are produced from Vancouver to Quebec City. All net proceeds are distributed to projects which encourage Canadians to appreciate, enjoy, and protect Canada's outdoor heritage.

Contact(s):
Chairman: WALTER G. OSTER
Executive

CANADIAN NATURE FEDERATION

1 Nicholas St., Suite 520, Ottawa, Ontario K1N 7B7 Canada
Phone: 613-562-3447; Fax: 613-562-3371

Founded: 1971
Scope: Statewide

Description: Canada's national naturalists' organization promotes protection of nature, its diversity and the processes that sustain it. The Federation was formed from the Canadian Audubon Society,

the CNF represents over 150 affiliated conservation groups and 40,000 individual supporters across the country.
Contact(s):
President: CLIFF WALLIS
Executive Director: JULIE GELFAND; Phone: 613-562-3447
Director of Conservation Programs: CAROLINE SCHULTZ
Editor: BARBARA STEVENSON
Publication(s): *Nature Canada Magazine; Nature Alert*

CANADIAN PARKS AND WILDERNESS SOCIETY
401 Richmond St. W., Suite 380, Toronto, Ontario M5V 3A8 Canada
Phone: 416-979-2720; Fax: 416-979-3155; Email: cpaws@web.net; WWW: www.cpaws.org
Founded: 1963
Scope: National
Description: A national, nonprofit advocacy organization dedicated to the protection of wilderness areas and the preservation and proper stewardship of Canada's national and provincial parks.
Contact(s):
President: DAVID THOMSON
Executive Director: MARY GRANSKOU; Phone: 416-979-2720
Manager of Membership Services: FRED HENDERSON
Publication(s): *Wilderness Activist, The*

CANADIAN SOCIETY OF ENVIRONMENTAL BIOLOGISTS
P.O. Box 962, Station F, Toronto, Ontario M4Y 2N9 Canada
Founded: 1959
Scope: National
Description: A Canada-wide society of environmental biologists whose primary goals are: the conservation of the natural resources of Canada; the prudent management of these resources so as to minimize adverse environmental effects; the interchange of ideas among environmental biologists; and maintaining high professional standards in education, research, and management related to natural resources and the environment.
Contact(s):
President: SEAN SHARPE
Publication(s): *Canadian Society of Environmental Biologists Newsletter*

CANADIAN WILDLIFE FEDERATION
2740 Queensview Dr., Ottawa, Ontario K2B 1A2 Canada
Phone: 613-721-2286; Fax: 613-721-2902
Founded: 1961; Membership: 250,000
Scope: National
Description: To foster understanding of natural processes so that people may live in harmony with the land and its resources for the long-term benefit and enrichment of society; to maintain a substantial program of information and education based on ecological principles; and to conduct or sponsor research and scientific investigation.
Contact(s):
President: YVES JEAN
Secretary: PAT DOYLE
Treasurer: NICHOLAS LAURIN
1st Vice President: NESTOR ROMANIUK
2nd Vice President: DERREK STANLEY
3rd Vice President: BOB BARTON
Executive Vice President: COLIN MAXWELL
Past President: CARL SHIER
Publication(s): *Wildlife Update; Canadian Wildlife; Wild Magazine; Your Big Backyard; Biosphere; You Can Do It*

CANVASBACK SOCIETY
P.O. Box 101, Gates Mills, OH 44040
Founded: 1975
Scope: National
Description: A nonprofit, tax-exempt organization established to conserve, restore, and promote the increase of the canvasback species of duck on the North American continent.
Contact(s):
Chairman of the Board: KEITH C. RUSSELL
President and Treasurer: OAKLEY V. ANDREWS; Phone: 216-621-0200
Keyword(s): Renewable Resources, Water Pollution Management, Water Resources, Waterfowl, Wetlands

CARIBBEAN CONSERVATION CORPORATION
P.O. Box 2866, Gainesville, FL 32602
Phone: 904-373-6441; Fax: 904-375-2449
Scope: International
Description: A nonprofit international membership organization founded in 1959 to support research and conservation of marine turtles in the Caribbean and throughout the world. In addition to conservation activities, it operates a research station at Tortuguero, Costa Rica--the site of the largest green turtle nesting colony in the Caribbean Sea--and maintains a semi-natural impoundment for sea turtles on Great Inagua Island in the Bahamas.
Contact(s):
President: ANTHONY D. KNERR, 891 Park Ave., New York, NY 10021
Secretary: CAROLINE P. MAYNARD, 219 Hudson St., Pelham Manor, NY 10803
Executive Director: DAVID CARR
Chairman of the Board of Directors: L. CLAY, 24 Federal St., Boston, MA 02110
Editor: SUSAN MARYNOWSKI
Publication(s): *Velador*

CARIBBEAN CONSERVATION CORPORATION (Costa Rica Office)
Apartado Postal 246 - 2050, San Pedro, San Pedro Costa Rica
Phone: 506-24-92-15
Scope: International
Keyword(s): Aquatic Habitats, Fisheries, International Conservation, Reptiles and Amphibians, Wildlife and Wildlife Habitat

CARIBBEAN NATURAL RESOURCES INSTITUTE
St. Lucia Office, P.O. Box VF 383 New Dock Rd., Vieux Fort, Vieux Fort St. Lucia
Phone: 758-454-6060; Fax: 758-454-5188; Email: canari@candw.lc
Founded: 1986
Scope: National
Description: To create avenues for the equitable participation and effective collaboration of Caribbean communities and institutions in managing the use of natural resources critical to development.
Contact(s):
Executive Director: YVES RENARD
Board of Directors Chair: DR. CAROL JAMES
Publication(s): *Caribbean Moss Bulletin; Community and the Environment: Lessons from the Caribbean; Canari Guidelines Series*
Keyword(s): Coral Reefs, Rural Development, Sustainable Development, Training

CAROLINA BIRD CLUB, INC.
P.O. Box 29555, Raleigh, NC 27626-0555
Founded: 1937; Membership: 1,050
Scope: Statewide
Description: Nonprofit, educational, and ornithological organization to promote bird study and conservation. Affiliated local chapters.
Contact(s):
President: BERT FISHER, 614 Chapel Dr., Box 90572, Durham, NC 27708-0572
Editor: CLYDE SMITH JR., 2615 Wells Ave., Raleigh, NC 27608; Phone: 919-781-2637
Editor: BOB WOOD, 2421 Owl Circle, West Columbia, NC 29169
Headquarters Secretary: TULLIE HOYLE JOHNSON, Raleigh, NC 27626; Phone: 919-733-7450
Publication(s): *Chat, The; CBC Newsletter*

CARRYING CAPACITY NETWORK
2000 P St., NW, Suite 240, Washington, DC 20036-5915
Phone: 202-296-4548; Fax: 202-296-4609; Email: ccn@us.net; WWW: www.carryingcapacity.org
Founded: 1989; Membership: 15,000
Scope: National
Description: CCN is a nonprofit network which mobilizes many diverse individuals and groups to meet the critical challenges facing our nation with solid information and analysis, effective advocacy tools, and targeted solutions. CCN's action-oriented initiatives focus on achieving national revitalization, population stabilization, immigration limitation, resource conservation, and economic sustainability.
Contact(s):
Vice President: VIRGINIA ABERNETHY
Network Coordinator: LEON KOLANKIEWICZ
President of the Board: DAVID F. DURHAM
Secretary and Treasurer: K. R. HAMMOND
Publication(s): *Network Bulletin; FOCUS*
Keyword(s): Agriculture, Environment, Population Growth, Renewable Resources, Sustainable Development, Wilderness

CASCADIA RESEARCH
218 1/2 W. 4th Ave., Olympia, WA 98501
Phone: 206-943-7325
Founded: 1979
Scope: National
Description: A nonprofit, tax-exempt organization established to conduct scientific research and education related to marine mammals and birds. Primary funding for research projects comes from federal and state agencies and environmental groups.
Contact(s):
President: GRETCHEN STEIGER
Vice President: JAMES CUBBAGE
Secretary and Treasurer: JOHN CALAMBOKIDIS
Keyword(s): Birds, Endangered and Threatened Species, Marine Mammals, Nongame Wildlife, Water Pollution

CATSKILL CENTER FOR CONSERVATION AND DEVELOPMENT, INC., THE
Route 28, Arkville, NY 12406-0504
Phone: 914-586-2611; Fax: 914-586-3044; Email: cccd@catskill.net; WWW: www.catskillcenter.org
Founded: 1969; Membership: 4,000
Scope: Statewide
Description: The Catskill Center is a non-for-profit membership organization concerned with increasing public awareness of and involvement with issues affecting human communities and the natrual environment of the Catskill Mountain Region. Its activities emphasize environmental education and regional planning advocacy, as well as development and support of programs relating to historic preservation, sustainable economic development and regional arts and culture in the Catskill.
Contact(s):
President: GEDDY SVEIKAUSKAS
Executive Director: DARLENE DOWNING
Secretary and Treasurer: PAUL T. SHULTZ
Publication(s): *Catskill Center News; Successful Catskill Communities; Catskill Environmental Monograph; Summary Guide to the Terms of the Watershed Agreement*
Keyword(s): Alternative Agriculture, Culture, Environmental and Conservation Education, Land Protection, Natural Resource Conservation, Rural Development, Sustainable Development

CATSKILL FOREST ASSOCIATION
P.O. Box 336, Arkville, NY 12406
Phone: 914-586-3054; Fax: 914-586-3044
Founded: 1982; Membership: 275
Scope: National
Description: Advocates of quality forest management practices to improve the health of the forest and prevent threats to the forest ecosystem, the Catskill Forest Association is an independent nonprofit regional organization that supports forest conservation efforts in the Catskill Mountains through the promotion of forest stewardship by landowners, foresters, timber harvesters, and the general public. Affiliated with the New York Forest Owners Association.
Contact(s):
President: JERRY GOTSCH
Vice President: DOUGLAS MURPHY
Secretary and Treasurer: ART ROTMAN
Executive Director: RICHARD D. SLOMAN
Director of Education: DONNA K. ROGLER
Publication(s): *CFA News*
Keyword(s): Biodiversity, Environmental and Conservation Education, Forests and Forestry, Sustainable Development, Sustainable Ecosystems

CAVE RESEARCH FOUNDATION
P.O. Box 126, Loiusville, KY 40201-0126
Phone: 502-637-2030
Founded: 1957
Scope: National
Description: The Foundation is a nonprofit organization that supports and promotes research, interpretation, and conservation activities in caves and karst areas. Permanent field operations are maintained within Mammoth Cave National Park, Carlsbad Caverns National Park, Sequoia and Kings Canyon National Parks, and Lava Beds National Monument. Approximately 800 joint-venturers participate in program.
Contact(s):
President: PHILIP DIBLASI; Phone: 502-852-6724; Fax: 502-852-6725; Email: pjdibl01@home.louisville.edu
Secretary: JOHN TINSLEY III; Phone: 415-327-2368
Treasurer: PAUL CANNALEY; Phone: 317-862-5618
Editor: RICHARD ZOPF, 1112 Xenia Ave., Yellow Springs, OH 45378-1101
Editor: PATRICIA KAMBESIS, 3473 Regalwoods Dr., Doraville, GA 30340
Publication(s): *Annual Report; CRF Newsletter; Cave* **Keyword(s):** Environmental Preservation, Geology, Historic Preservation, Public Lands, Scholarships and Grants

CENTER FOR ENVIRONMENT
1336 Bay Ave., Annapolis, DC 21403
Founded: 1985
Scope: National
Description: A nonprofit public interest organization dedicated to protecting the environment, enhancing the human ecology, and working to ensure the efficient use of natural resources. (CE)2's secondary mission is to provide opportunities for blacks and other minorities to participate in the environmental movement. Major areas of concern are: Air quality and pollution, water resources and pollution, energy, renewable resources, toxic substances, Africa and Third World environment, land use, internships, and urban environment.
Contact(s):
Chairman: CHARLES STEPHENSON
President: NORRIS McDONALD; Phone: 202-879-3183
Treasurer: JANNIE PITTMAN
Publication(s): *African American Environmentalist; A complete list of (CE)2's publications is available upon request.*

CENTER FOR ENVIRONMENTAL EDUCATION
c/o Antioch New England, 40 Avon St., Keene, NY 03431
Phone: 603-355-3251; Fax: 603-357-0781; Email: cee@antiochne.edu; WWW: www.cee_ane.org
Founded: 1989; Membership: 5,000
Scope: National
Description: A nonprofit environmental education resource center housing one of the nation's most comprehensive collections of environmental education materials. The library has over 10,000 materials--books, videos, curricula and resources that can be accessed in person, by phone, fax, or through the website.

NON-GOVERNMENTAL ORGANIZATIONS

Contact(s):
Co-Executive Director: CINDY THOMASHOW
Co-Executive Director: DAVID SOBEL
Founder: JAYNI CHASE
Publication(s): *Grapevine Newsletter; Blueprint for a Green School*
Keyword(s): Environmental and Conservation Education, Internships, Youth Organizations

CENTER FOR ENVIRONMENTAL INFORMATION
55 St. Paul St., Rochester, NY 14604-1314
Phone: 716-262-2870; Fax: 716-262-4156; WWW: www.awa.com/nature/cei

Founded: 1974
Scope: National

Description: Provides on-call reference and referral and current awareness and educational services to scientists, educators, government agency staff, policymakers, business and industry managers, and interested citizens. Maintains special library collection. Sponsors conferences and seminars.

Contact(s):
Executive Director: WILLIAM R. WAGNER
Editor: DR. FREDERICK M. O'HARA JR., P.O. Box 4273, Oak Ridge, TN 37831; Phone: 423-482-1447

Publication(s): *Global Climate Change Digest; Proceedings of Annual Conferences;*
Keyword(s): Acid Rain, Communications, Energy, Environmental and Conservation Education, Greenhouse Effect/Global Warming

CENTER FOR ENVIRONMENTAL PHILOSOPHY
EESAT Bldg., Rm. 370, Corner of Ave. C and Mulberry, University of North Texas, P.O. Box 310980, Denton, TX 76203-0980
Phone: 940-565-2727; Fax: 940-565-4439; Email: ee@unt.edu.; WWW: www.cep.unt.edu

Founded: 1980
Scope: National

Description: A nonprofit, tax-deductible organization. The Center promotes research and instruction in environmental ethics and its application in environmental policy and decision-making. The Center works with governmental and environmental organizations on conferences, workshops, and other educational projects.

Contact(s):
Vice President: J. BAIRD CALLICOTT, Dept. of Philosophy, Univ. of North TX, P.O. Box 310920, Denton, TX 76203-0920; Phone: 940-565-2255; Fax: 940-565-4448; Email: callicott@unt.edu
Executive Director: JAN DICKSON, Center for Environmental Philosophy, Univ. of North TX, P.O. Box 310980, Denton, TX 76203-0980; Phone: 940-565-2727; Fax: 940-565-4439; Email: jdickson@unt.edu
President, Editor and Publisher: EUGENE C. HARGROVE, Center for Environmental Philosophy, Univ. of North TX, P.O. Box 310980, Denton, TX 76203-0980; Phone: 940-565-2727; Fax: 940-565-4439; Email: hargrove@unt.edu
Secretary and Treasurer: MAX OELSCHLAEGER, Dept. Humanities, Arts & Religion, Northern Arizona, P.O. Box 6031, Flagstaff, AZ 86011-6031; Phone: 520-523-0389; Email: Max.Oelschlaeger@Nau.edu

Publication(s): *Environmental Ethics: An Interdisciplinary Journal Dedicated to the Philosophical Aspects of Environmental Problems*
Keyword(s): Environmental Ethics, Wilderness

CENTER FOR ENVIRONMENTAL STUDY
Grand Rapids Community College, 143 Bostwick NE, Grand Rapids, MI 49503
Phone: 616-771-3935; Fax: 616-771-4005; Email: ces1@iserv.net; WWW: www..cesmi.org/

Founded: 1969
Scope: National

Description: The Center for Environmental Study, a 501C (3) organization, has served its community as an independent, science-based environmental education and research authority. It provides curricula and conducts professional development workshops on a variety of subjects ranging from water and air quality to tropical forest and Great Lakes issues.

Contact(s):
Executive Director: DR. RICK SULLIVAN
Board Chair: PATRICK MULDOON
Founder: PETER M. WEGE

Publication(s): *Mahogany: A Research Bibliography of Swietenia; Field Guide to Ecosystems and Habitats of the Great Lakes Region (in prep.); The Great Lakes - An Interactive CD-ROM Game*
Keyword(s): Air Quality and Pollution, Communications, Ecology, Environmental and Conservation Education, Watersheds, Wildlife and Wildlife Habitat, Youth Organizations

CENTER FOR HEALTH, ENVIRONMENT, AND JUSTICE
P.O. Box 6806, Falls Church, VA 22040-6806
Phone: 703-237-2249; Fax: 703-237-8389; Email: CCHW@essential.org; WWW: www.essential.org/cchw or www.hoharm.org

Founded: 1981
Scope: National

Description: CHEJ provides assistance to more than 8,000 grassroots citizens groups fighting for environmental justice. CHEJ is a nonprofit organization dedicated to helping people nationwide by providing one-on-one assistance and information on how to organize politically, scientifically, and legally to prevent or clean up environmental catastrophies. Founded by Lois Marie Gibbs.

Contact(s):
Executive Director: LOIS MARIE GIBBS

Publication(s): *Everyone's Backyard; catalog of how-to guide books; Environmental Health Monthly; Dioxin Digest*
Keyword(s): Internships, People of Color in the Environment, Scholarships and Grants, Toxic Substances, Women in the Environment

CENTER FOR INTERNATIONAL ENVIRONMENTAL LAW (CIEL)
1367 Connecticut Ave., NW, Suite 300, Washington, DC 20036-1860
Phone: 202-785-8700; Fax: 202-785-8701; Email: cielus@igc.apc.org; WWW: www.econet.apc.org/ciel/

Founded: 1989
Scope: National

Description: The CIEL is a public interest environmental law organization founded to focus the energy and experience of the public interest environmental law movement on reforming international environmental law and institutions, and on forging stronger and more meaningful connection between the top down diplomatic approach of international law, and the bottom up participatory approach that has been the hallmark of the public interest environmental law movement.

Contact(s):
President: DURWOOD J. ZAELKE
Vice President and Secretary: BARBARA L. SHAW
Vice President for Programs: DAVID B. HUNTER

Publication(s): *International Environmental Law and Policy;Biodiversity in the Seas: Implementing the Convention on Biological Diversity in Marine and Coastal Habitats; A Citizen's Guide to the World Bank Inspection Panel; Trade and the Environment: Law, Economics, and Policy; Carbon Conservation: Climate Change, Forests and the Clear Development Mechanism; a complete list of CIEL's publications is available upon request on CIEL's home page.*
Keyword(s): Biodiversity, Environmental and Conservation Education, Environmental Law, Greenhouse Effect/Global Warming, International Trade and Environment

CENTER FOR MARINE CONSERVATION
1725 DeSales St., NW, Suite 600, Washington, DC 20036
Phone: 202-429-5609; Fax: 202-872-0619; Email: dccmc@ix.netcom.com; WWW: www.cmc-ocean.org

Founded: 1972; **Membership:** 120,000
Scope: National
Description: A nonprofit, scientific organization dedicated to protecting marine wildlife and its habitats, and to conserving coastal and ocean resources. The center's programs are conducted in five major areas: Fisheries and Wildlife Conservation, Ecosystem Protection, Biodiversity Conservation, International Initiatives, Citizen Monitoring, and Outreach. Program efforts focus on research, policy analysis, education, and public information and involvement.
Contact(s):
President: ROGER E. McMANUS
Chairman of the Board: E. U. BOHLEN
Director of Constituency Development: DAVID DIXON
Director of Ecosystems Programs: JACK SOBEL
Director of the Chesapeake Region: SEBA SHEAVLEY, 306A Buckroe Ave., Hampton, VA 23664; Phone: 804-851-6734
Director of the Gulf Coast Region: GERALD LEONARD, One Beach Dr. SE, #304, St. Petersburg, FL 33701; Phone: 813-895-2188
Director of the Pacific Coast Region: WARNER CHABOT, 580 Market St., Suite 550, San Francisco, CA 94104; Phone: 415-391-6204
Special Assistant to the President: CHARLOTTE MEYER
Vice President for Communications and Marketing: KRISHNA K. ROY
Vice President for Development: DAVID KNIGHT
Vice President for Finance and Administration: PETER JONES
Vice President for Marine Wildlife Conservation and General Counsel: WILLIAM ROBERT IRVIN
Vice President for Programs: LORI WILLIAMS
Publication(s): Marine Conservation News; Coastal Connection; list of additional publications on request.
Keyword(s): Biodiversity, Biology, Conservation of Protected Areas, Coral Reefs, Ecology, Endangered and Threatened Species, Environmental and Conservation Education, Fisheries, International Conservation, Marine Mammals, Pollution Prevention, Sustainable Ecosystems, Water Pollution, Watersheds, Wildlife Management

CENTER FOR PLANT CONSERVATION
P.O. Box 299, St. Louis, MO 63166
Phone: 314-577-9450; Fax: 314-577-9465; Email: cpc@mobot.org; WWW: www.mobot.org/cpc

Scope: National
Description: A national network of 28 botanical gardens and arboreta dedicated to the conservation and study of rare and endangered U.S. plants. The Center establishes conservation collections of endangered species in regional gardens and seed banks as a resource for conservation and research efforts: The National Collection of Endangered Plants.
Contact(s):
Executive Director: DR. BRIEN A. MEILLEUR
Publication(s): Plant Conservation (newsletter); Plant Conservation Directory; Restoring Diversity; Guidelines for the Manangent of Orthodox Seeds, Plants in Peril
Keyword(s): Biodiversity, Botanical Gardens, Endangered and Threatened Species, Environment, Environmental and Conservation Education, Environmental Preservation, Flowers, Plants, and Trees

CENTER FOR RESOURCE ECONOMICS
Island Press, 1718 Connecticut Ave., NW, Suite 300, Washington, DC 20009
Phone: 202-232-7933; Email: info@islandpress.org

Founded: 1978
Scope: National
Description: The Center for Resource Economics is a nonprofit organization that develops, publishes, markets and disseminates books and other information products essential for solving local and global environmental problems and planning for the future.
Contact(s):
Controller and Finance Manager: CHERI LEVY; Phone: 202-232-7933
Editor, Shearwater Books: LAURIE BURNHAM; Phone: 612-227-1722
Editor-in-Chief: DAN SAYRE; Phone: 202-232-7933
Marketing Director: SAMUEL DORRANCE; Phone: 202-232-7933
President and Publisher: CHARLES SAVITT; Phone: 202-232-7933
Publication(s): Island Press Book Distribution Center: Box 7, Covelo, CA 954281-800-828-1302; 707-983-6432; FAX: 707-983-6414
Keyword(s): Biodiversity, Energy, Sustainable Development, Sustainable Ecosystems, Wetlands

CENTER FOR RESOURCEFUL BUILDING TECHNOLOGY
P.O. Box 100, Missoula, MT 59806
Phone: 406-549-7678; Fax: 406-549-4100; Email: crbt@montana.com; WWW: www.montana.com/crbt

Founded: 1990
Scope: National
Description: The Center for Resourceful Building Technology (CRBT) is a non-profit corporation dedicated to promoting environmentally responsible practices in construction. Its mission is to serve as both catalyst and facilitator in encouraging building technologies which realize a sustainable and efficient use of resources.
Contact(s):
Chair: TIM MELLGREN, 151 Fairway Dr., Missoula, MT 59801; Phone: 406-728-6711
Founder: STEVE LOKEN, 2605 Lincoln Hills Dr., Missoula, MT 59802; Phone: 406-728-1412
Research Director: TRACY MUMMA
Technical Director: DALE McCORMICK
Publication(s): Guide to Resource Efficient Building Elements; Recraft 90 Handbook; Affordable Resource Efficiency: Reducing Construction and Demolition Waste; Building Our Children's Future
Keyword(s): Environmental and Conservation Education, Environmental Preservation, Forests and Forestry, Renewable Resources, Sustainable Development

CENTER FOR SCIENCE IN THE PUBLIC INTEREST
1875 Connecticut Ave., NW, Suite 300, Washington, DC 20009
Phone: 202-332-9110; Fax: 202-265-4954; Email: cspi@cspinet.org; WWW: www.cspinet.org

Founded: 1971; **Membership:** 1,000,000
Scope: National
Description: National consumer advocacy organization that focuses on health, nutrition, and alcohol issues. CSPI informs the public of its findings through a variety of publications, press releases, speeches, media appearances, and initiates legal actions. The Center has an intern program throughout the year.
Contact(s):
Executive Director: DR. MICHAEL F. JACOBSON
Publication(s): Nutrition Action Healthletter; reports, posters, books, and video
Keyword(s): Agriculture, Health and Nutrition, Internships, Pesticides, Toxicology

CENTER FOR SCIENCE INFORMATION
63 Homestead St., San Francisco, CA 94114
Phone: 415-824-3192; Fax: 415-824-0201

Founded: 1981
Scope: National
Description: The CSI educates decisionmakers and journalists on the environmental and public policy issues surrounding biotechnology; and publishes materials on specific topics in environmental, agricultural, and human biotechnology. CSI is a nonmembership, nonadvocate organization.
Contact(s):
President: STEVEN C. WITT
Publication(s): Biotechnology, Microbes and the Environment; Biotechnology and Genetic Diversity; Genetic Engineering of Plants

NON-GOVERNMENTAL ORGANIZATIONS

Keyword(s): Agriculture, Biodiversity, Communications, Environmental and Conservation Education

CENTER FOR THE STUDY OF TROPICAL BIRDS, INC. (Administative Office)
218 Conway, San Antonio, TX 78209-1716
Phone: 210-828-5306/1-800-858-CSTB; Fax: 210-828-9732
Founded: 1987
Scope: National
Description: A nonprofit organization devoted to the conservation of tropical birdlife through cooperative programs of scientific research, conservation and education. Current projects include development and distribution of Spanish language wildlife education materials, field research, organization of workshops on the conservation and management of various major avian families (eg. parrots, birds of prey, etc.), as well as assisting Latin American ornithologists in securing needed funds for avian conservation projects. CSTB currently has major programs in Mexico, Belize, and Honduras.
Contact(s):
Treasurer: MICHAEL GARTSIDE
Director: JACK CLINTON EITNIEAR
Mexico Program Coordinator: ALVARO ARAGON TAPIA
Keyword(s): Birds, Endangered and Threatened Species, Grants, International Conservation, Nongame Wildlife, Raptors, Research, Wildlife and Wildlife Habitat, Wildlife Management

CENTER FOR THE STUDY OF TROPICAL BIRDS, INC. (Field Office)
22 Cesar Lopez De Lara Y Carranza No. 553, Fovissste, Ciudad Victoria C.P. 87020 Mexico
Phone: 13-16-09-52
Scope: International

CENTER FOR WATERSHED PROTECTION
8737 Colesville Rd., Suite 300, Silver Spring, MD 20910
Phone: 301-589-1890; Fax: 301-589-8745; Email: MrRunnoff@usa.pipeline.com
Founded: 1992
Scope: National
Description: CWP is dedicated to new cooperative ways of protecting and restoring watersheds. CWP's mission is put into practice through four main functions; the professional journal Watershed Protection Techniques; nationwide training seminars and workshops; watershed protection manuals; and partnerships with local governments.
Contact(s):
Executive Director: THOMAS R. SCHUELER
Principal Engineer: RICHARD A. CLAYTOR, P.E.
Senior Environmental Analyst: WHITNEY E. BROWN
Publication(s): *Watershed Protection Techniques; Site Planning for Urban Stream Protection; Environmental Indicators to Assess Stormwater Control Programs and Practices*
Keyword(s): Environmental Planning, Land Use Planning, Urban Environment, Water Pollution Management, Watersheds

CENTER FOR WILDLIFE LAW
University of New Mexico, Institute of Public Law, 1117 Stanford NE, Albuquerque, NM 87131
Phone: 505-277-5006; Fax: 505-277-7064
Founded: 1990
Scope: National
Description: Through projects, publications, conferences, and training programs, the Center provides wildlife law and policy analysis and other educational information to legal and nonlegal communities. The Center also conducts a unique law-related wildlife education program. Staff have expertise in wildlife and environmental law and policy, biology, education, geographic information systems, publishing.
Contact(s):
Director: RUTH S. MUSGRAVE
Publication(s): *Federal Wildlife Laws Handbook with Related Laws; State Wildlife Laws Handbook; Wild Friends: A Wildlife Education Strategy for Youth and Elders; The Status of Poaching in the U.S.*

CENTRAL OHIO ANGLERS AND HUNTERS CLUB
P.O. Box 28224, Columbus, OH 43228
Scope: Statewide
Description: Promotion of conservation and conservation education in all their phases, with a particular reference to land, air, and water; to promote good fellowship and good citizenship; to inculcate regard for the rights of others and respect for the obedience to law; to support a safe and effective conservation program for and by the state and nation.
Contact(s):
Vice President: TERRY WILSON, 487 Townsend Ave., Columbus, OH 43223; Phone: 614-272-6023
Secretary: ROBERT L. GOSE, 287 Danbury Rd., West Jefferson, OH 43162; Phone: 614-879-6416
Treasurer: JERRY BANYOTS, 3543 Kroehler Dr., Hilliard, OH 43026; Phone: 614-876-7001
Director: JOE JOHNSON, 7370 Weldon Rd., Plain City, OH 43064
Director: DONNIE MARSH, 429 Branding Iron Dr., Galloway, OH 43119
Director: GARY WILSON, 4767 Waybridge Rd. Apt C, Columbus, OH 43220

CENTRAL STATES EDUCATION CENTER
809 S. Fifth, Champaign, IL 61820
Phone: 217-344-2371
Founded: 1968
Scope: Regional
Description: A regional conservation organization primarily concerned with rivers, water policy, and pollution prevention issues. Organizational and technical assistance is provided to persons and organizations in related activities.
Contact(s):
President: BRUCE M. HANNON; Phone: 217-352-3646
Treasurer: BILL JOHNSON; Phone: 317-523-2436
Executive Director: ROBERT MOORE; Phone: 217-344-2371; Email: robmoore@earthlink.net
Publication(s): *Rivers; Roads; Toxic Wastes; Solid Wastes*
Keyword(s): Nuclear/Radiation, Pollution Prevention, Solid Waste Management, Toxic Substances, Water Resources

CENTRO de INFORMACION, INVESTIGACION y EDUCACION SOCIAL (CIIES)
Condominium El Centro I, Ofic. 1404, San Juan, PR 00918
Phone: 787-759-8787/9116; Fax: 787-767-6757
Founded: 1989
Scope: Statewide
Description: CIIES was founded as a part of Servicios Cientificos y Tecnicos, a nonprofit organization dealing with natural resources, environmental health, and safety issues. It provides services in the form of seminars, workshops, and a resource center to students, teachers, journalists, communities, and workers.
Contact(s):
Secretary: JOSE SEPULVEDA
Treasurer: MARIA VILCHES
Director: DR. NEFTALI GARCIA MARTINEZ
Keyword(s): Biodiversity, Environmental and Conservation Education, Environmental Justice, Habitat Conservation, Pollution Prevention

CETACEAN SOCIETY INTERNATIONAL
P.O. Box 953, Georgetown, CT 06829
Phone: 203-544-8617; Fax: 203-544-8617; Email: 71322.1637@compuserve.com; WWW: elfi.com/cslhome.html
Founded: 1974; Membership: 500
Scope: National
Description: CSI is dedicated to the preservation and protection of all cetaceans (whales, dolphins, and porpoises) and the marine environment on a global basis. CSI is an all-volunteer, nonprofit conservation education and research organization with representatives in over 27 countries.

Contact(s):
President: WILLIAM W. ROSSITER, 21 Laurel Hill Rd., Ridgefield, CT 06877; Phone: 203-544-8902; Email: william_rossiter@compuserve.com
Vice President: BARBARA KILPATRICK, 15 Wood Pond Rd., West Hartford, CT 06107; Phone: 860-561-0187
Secretary: MARTHA FITZGERALD, 120 Retreat Ave. C-3, Hartford, CT 06106; Phone: 860-246-3143
Treasurer: ROBERT VICTOR, 57 Crossroads Ln., Glastonbury, CT 06033; Email: rfvictor@juno.com
Director Emeritus: DR. ROBBINS BARSTOW, 190 Stillwold Dr., Wethersfield, CT 06109; Phone: 860-563-2565; Email: robbinsb@aol.com
Publication(s): *Whales Alive (newsletter); Meet the Great Ones (book, English and Spanish); Several education packages.*
Keyword(s): Endangered and Threatened Species, Environmental Protection, International Conservation, Marine Mammals, Research

CHARLES A. AND ANNE MORROW LINDBERGH FOUNDATION, THE
708 S. Third St., Suite 110, Minneapolis, MN 55415-1141
Phone: 612-338-1703; Fax: 612-338-6826; Email: lindfdtn@mtn.org
Founded: 1977
Scope: National
Description: The Charles A. and Anne Morrow Lindbergh Foundation is a nonprofit organization, advancing Charles and Anne Morrow Lindbergh's vision of a balance between technological progress and environmental preservation by offering Lindbergh Grants to individuals for research and educational projects which will further this balance, presenting the Lindbergh Award for extraordinary contributions to the balance, and sponsoring other projects and programs. Associate membership information is available by writing the Foundation office.
Contact(s):
President: REEVE LINDBERGH
Vice President: BARBARA KAUFFMAN STOKES
Vice President: CLARE HALLWARD
Secretary: JAMES W. LLOYD
Treasurer: CHARLES J. KELLY JR.
Executive Director: GENE BRATSCH
Chairperson of Award Selection and Lecture Committee: BARBARA KAUFFMAN STOKES
Chairperson of Grants Selection Committee: CLARE HALLWARD
Editor: GENE BRATSCH
Publication(s): *Charles A. and Anne Morrow Lindbergh Foundation Newsletter, The*
Keyword(s): Agriculture, Environmental Preservation, Research Grants, Sustainable Development, Water Resources, Wildlife and Wildlife Habitat

CHELONIA INSTITUTE
P.O. Box 9174, Arlington, VA 22209
Phone: 703-516-2600
Founded: 1977
Scope: National
Description: A private operating foundation with ecological concerns focused primarily on the conservation of marine turtles. The Institute undertakes a broad range of programs including technical publications, land acquisition, and so on, and works cooperatively with other organizations.
Contact(s):
Assistant Director: MARY W. TRULAND
Director and Trustee: ROBERT W. TRULAND
Program Director: DR. PETER PRITCHARD

CHESAPEAKE BAY FOUNDATION, INC.
Headquarters, 162 Prince George St., Annapolis, MD 21401
Phone: 410-268-8816; WWW: www.savethebay.cbf.org
Founded: 1966; Membership: 80,000
Scope: National
Description: A nonprofit membership organization established to promote the environmental protection and restoration of Chesapeake Bay and its full watershed. CBF operates programs in environmental education and environmental protection and restoration.
Contact(s):
Chairman: WAYNE A. MILLS
President: WILLIAM C. BAKER
Vice President for Education: DONALD R. BAUGH
Vice President for Public Affairs: MICHAEL SHULTZ
Vice President for Resource Protection and Restoration: MICHAEL HIRSHFIELD
Publication(s): *Save the Bay; Megalops; Grassroots* **Keyword(s):** Environmental and Conservation Education, Environmental Protection, Restoration, Watersheds

CHESAPEAKE BAY FOUNDATION, INC. (Maryland Office)
111 Annapolis St., Annapolis, MD 21401
Phone: 410-268-8833; Fax: 410-280-3513
Founded: 1977; Membership: 83,000
Scope: Statewide
Description: The Chesapeake Bay Foundation conducts activities of the foundation specific to the state of Maryland and operates a field office in Laurel, MD and Delaware. (See listing for Chesapeake Bay Foundation under the International, National, and Regional section of the Directory
Contact(s):
Executive Director: TOM GRASSO
Keyword(s): Aquatic Habitats, Environmental and Conservation Education, Environmental Justice, Land Use Planning, Renewable Resources

CHESAPEAKE BAY FOUNDATION, INC. (Pennsylvania Office)
The Old Waterworks Bldg., 614 N. Front St., Suite G, Harrisburg, PA 17101
Phone: 717-234-5550; Fax: 717-234-9632
Founded: 1966; Membership: 83,000
Scope: Statewide
Description: The Foundation conducts activities and programs specific to the Commonwealth of Pennsylvania.
Contact(s):
Executive Director: JOLENE CHINCHILLI
Publication(s): *Fresh Air; Recycling Roll Call; Council in Action; Environmentalists for Public Transit Newsletter*
Keyword(s): Air Quality and Pollution, Energy, Solid Waste, Transportation

CHESAPEAKE BAY FOUNDATION, INC. (Virginia Office)
1001 E. Main St., Heritage Bldg., Suite 710, Richmond, VA 23219
Phone: 804-780-1392; Fax: 804-648-4011
Founded: 1967
Scope: Statewide
Description: The Chesapeake Bay Foundation conducts activities of the foundation in the Commonwealth of Virginia and operates field offices in Norfolk and Tappahannock, Virginia.
Contact(s):
Assistant Director: ROY HOAGLAND
Executive Director: JOSEPH MAROON
Keyword(s): Birds, Environmental and Conservation Education, Environmental Protection, Nature Preservation, Water Quality

NON-GOVERNMENTAL ORGANIZATIONS

CHESAPEAKE FARMS
7319 Remington Dr., Chestertown, MD 21620
Phone: 410-778-8400
Founded: 1956
Scope: National
Description: Operated by Dupont Agricultural Products to demonstrate, research, and promote sustainable farming and wildlife management practices. Provides a forum for exploring agricultural issues and interactions between environmental and economic sustainability. Agricultural project conducted by coalition of Dupont, universities, government and private organizations. Wildlife research conducted through graduate fellows.
Contact(s):
Manager: MARK C. CONNER

CHESAPEAKE WILDLIFE HERITAGE (CWH)
P.O. Box 1745, Easton, MD 21601
Phone: 410-822-5100; Fax: 410-822-4016; Email: cheswildlife@skipjack.bluecrab.org
Founded: 1980; Membership: 650
Scope: Regional
Description: A private, nonprofit conservation group working with private and public landowners to restore and protect wildlife habitat in the Chesapeake Bay watershed. CWH constructs and manages wetlands, warm season grass and wildflower meadows, nesting structures, marshes, and woodlands. CWH advises on and carries out sustainable farming techniques in order to benefit the Chesapeake Bay and its wildlife. CWH also conducts ecological research on plants and migratory birds.
Contact(s):
Board of Directors President: LARRY ALBRIGHT
Habitat Ecologist: MICHAEL ROBIN HAGGIE
Habitat Ecologist: JOHN E. GERBER
Secretary of Public Relations: DEBBIE COLLISON
Keyword(s): Wildlife and Wildlife Habitat

CHICAGO HERPETOLOGICAL SOCIETY
2060 N. Clark St., Chicago, IL 60614
Phone: 312-281-1800
Founded: 1966; Membership: 1,957
Scope: Statewide
Description: The Chicago Herpetological Society is a group of reptile and amphibian enthusiasts. Its goals are education, conservation, and the advancement of herpetology.
Contact(s):
President: STEVE SPITZER, 1939 W Lunt Ave., Chicago, IL 60626; Phone: 773-262-1847
Vice President: JACK SCHOENFELDER, c/o Ivy Tech College, 2401 Valley Dr., Valparaiso, IN 46383; Phone: 219-929-1525
Treasurer: GARY FOGEL, 4108 N. Damen Ave., Chicago, IL 60618; Phone: 312-935-6938
Publication(s): *Bulletin of the Chicago Herpetological* **Keyword(s):** Biology, Environmental and Conservation Education, Reptiles and Amphibians, Scholarships and Grants, Zoology

CHIHUAHUAN DESERT RESEARCH INSTITUTE
P.O. Box 905, Ft. Davis, TX 79734
Founded: 1974
Scope: National
Description: Nonprofit organization formed to promote human understanding and appreciation of the Chihuahuan Desert through scientific research and public education. Current studies include life history related studies, systematic zoology, systematic botany, desert ecology, anthropology, archeology, geology, and theoretical ecology.
Contact(s):
President: ROB DUNAGAN
Vice President: JAMES F. SCUDDAY
Secretary: THOMAS BRUNNER
Treasurer: LARRY BRYANT
Executive Director: DENNIS J. MILLER
Publication(s): *CDRI Contributions; Chihuahuan Desert Discovery, The; Chihuahaun Newsbriefs*
Keyword(s): Biology, Deserts, Endangered and Threatened Species, Geology, Natural History

CHINA REGION LAKES ALLIANCE
RR 1, Box 970, South China, ME 04358
Phone: 207-445-5021; Fax: 207-445-3208
Founded: 1994
Scope: Statewide
Description: To protect and improve water quality in 3 Culturally Eutrophic Maine Lakes, Threemile Pond, and Webber Pond and to benefit our local economy through integrated watershed management.
Contact(s):
President: DANIEL J. DUBORD; Phone: 207-872-2743; Fax: 207-872-2962
Executive Director: REBECCA MANTHEY
Publication(s): *Walk for a Rainy Day: What You Can Do For Your Camp Road; Vegetative Buffer Strips*
Keyword(s): Environmental and Conservation Education, Environmental Planning, Lakes, Pollution Prevention, Water Pollution, Water Quality, Water Resources, Watersheds

CHRISTINA CONSERVANCY, INC.
P.O. Box 1680, Wilmington, DE 19899-1680
Phone: 302-984-3801
Scope: Statewide
Description: The purpose of the Christina Conservancy, Inc. is to preserve, protect, and urge the wise use of the Christina River.
Contact(s):
President: EDWARD W. COOCH JR.
Keyword(s): Rivers

CIRCUMPOLAR CONSERVATION UNION
900 17th St., NW, 3rd Fl., Washington, DC 20006-2596
Phone: 202-429-7440; Fax: 202-429-7444; Email: circumpolar@igc.apc.org; WWW: www.circumpolar.org
Founded: 1993
Scope: National
Description: Circumpolar Conservation Union is a public interest initiative dedicated to protecting the ecological and culutural integrity of the Arctic for present and future generations. CCU works nationally and internationally through policy advocacy, public education, and by building links among diverse constituencies, to achieve comprehensive legal protection for the Arctic.
Contact(s):
Executive Director: EVELYN M. HURWICH
Office and Communications Manager: DAR RUDNYCKYI
Keyword(s): Arctic, Environmental Law, Indigenous People, Sustainable Development

CITIZENS ALLIANCE FOR SAVING THE ATMOSPHERE AND THE EARTH (CASA)
1-3-17-711 Tanimachi, Chuo-ku, Osaka 540-0012 Japan
Phone: 81-6-941-3745; Fax: 81-6-941-5699; Email: casa@netplus.ne.jp; WWW: www.netplus.ne.jp/-casa/
Founded: 1988
Scope: International
Description: CASA is committed to preserving both the local and global environment through solidarity with both Japanese and international environmental NGO's. CASA is composed of 50 NGO's and about 500 individuals, such as scientists, teachers, lawyers, farmers, grassroots activitists, artists, consumer group leaders, and others.
Contact(s):
Executive Director: YUJI NISHI
Managing Director: MITSUTOSHI HAYAKAWA
Representative Director: TSUNETOSHI YAMAMURA
Publication(s): *CASA Letter (Japanese)*

CITIZENS NATURAL RESOURCES ASSOCIATION OF WISCONSIN, INC.
Attn: President, 3805 Paunack St., Madison, WI 53711
Phone: 608-231-9721
Founded: 1951
Scope: Statewide
Description: To protect Wisconsin's natural resources through education, legislation, and the courts. The CNRA initiated and sponsored the action which resulted in the banning of DDT in Wisconsin and two years later in the United States. Recently, the CNRA has been concentrating on protecting and restoring native vegetation along Wisconsin's roads.
Contact(s):
President: KIRA HENSCHEL
Vice President: LORRIE OTTO, 9701 N. Lake Dr., Milwaukee, WI 53217; Phone: 414-352-0734
Secretary: LAURA ALLHANDS, N 5908 S. Center Rd., Beaver Dam, WI 53916; Phone: 920-885-9598
Treasurer: CHARLES STURM, J-1233 Mayfair Rd. Suite 125, Milwaukee, WI 53226
Editor: JAN SCALPONE, 2033 Menominee Dr., Oshkosh, WI 54901; Phone: 920-231-0063
Membership Chair: LOUISE COUMBE, 1028 Elmwood Ave., Oshkosh, WI 54901
Publication(s): *CNRA Report, The; Wisconsin Roadsides*

CITIZENS' NUCLEAR INFORMATION CENTER
1-59-14-302 Higashi-Nakano, Nakano-ku, Tokyo 164 Japan
Phone: 81-3-5330-9520; Fax: 81-3-5330-9530
Founded: 1975
Scope: International
Description: A nonprofit organization to collect and provide the public a broad range of information on nuclear power issues, and cooperate with individuals and other organizations concerned with nuclear proliferation in Japan and around the world. Information includes the Japanese government policy of plutonium utilization, effects of radioactive contamination, nuclear power plant accidents, economics, and other impacts on the local communities caused by construction of nuclear power plants.
Contact(s):
Executive Director: JINZABURO TAKAGI
International Relations Director: JINZABURO TAKAGI
Secretariat: HIDEYUKI BAN
Publication(s): *Citizens' Nuclear Information Center Report (Japanese); Nuke Info Tokyo (English)*

CLEAN OCEAN ACTION
P.O. Box 505, Sandy Hook, NJ 07732
Phone: 732-872-0111; Fax: 732-872-8041; WWW: www.cleanoceanaction.org
Founded: 1984
Scope: National
Description: A broad-based coalition of 175 conservation, fishing, diving, boating, real estate, student, and civic groups; over 300 businesses; and thousands of citizens concerned with the degraded waters off the New York and New Jersey coasts. COA uses education, research, and citizen action to pressure public officials to enact and enforce protective laws for our marine resources. Programs: Storm Drain Stenciling; 10 Tips Series; Regulatory Review; Contaminated Sediments; Non-Point Source Pollution.
Contact(s):
President: DERY BENNETT
Vice President: WILLIAM FEINBERG
Secretary: PAT SCHNEIDER
Treasurer: BEN FOREST
Executive Director: CINDY ZIPF
Publication(s): *Ocean Advocate*
Keyword(s): Coasts, Contaminated Sediments, Water Pollution

CLEAN WATER ACTION
4455 Connecticut Ave., NW, Suite A300, Washington, DC 20008-2328
Phone: 202-895-0420; Fax: 202-895-0438; Email: cleanwater@essential.org; WWW: www.cleanwateraction.org
Scope: National
Description: The national citizen's organization working full-time for clean safe water at an affordable cost, control of toxic chemicals, and protection of our natural resources.
Contact(s):
Development Associate: JIM PIERCE

CLEAN WATER FUND
4455 Connecticut Ave., NW, Suite A 300, Washington, DC 20008
Phone: 202-895-0420; Fax: 202-895-0438; Email: cleanwater@essential.org
Scope: National
Description: Clean Water Fund is a 501 © (3) research, training and educational organization that advances environmental and consumer protection with a special focus on water pollution, toxic hazards, solid waste management, and natural resources.
Contact(s):
Board of Directors, Executive Vice President: DAVID ZWICK
Board of Directors, President: PETER VAN LOCKWOOD
Board of Directors, Treasurer: KATHLEEN ATERNO
Development Associate: JIM PIERCE; Phone: 202-895-0432
Publication(s): *WATER: Riches for Clean Up, Pennies for Prevention, 1993; SOLID WASTE: Expanding Rhode Island's Market with RI War on Waste, 1993; TOXICS: If Its Broke, Fit it, 1993; TOXICS: Toxic Metals in Batteries, 1992*

CLEAN WATER NETWORK, THE
1200 New York Avenue, NW, Suite 400, Washington, DC 20005
Phone: 202-289-2395; Fax: 202-289-1060; Email: cleanwaternt@igc.org; WWW: www.cwn.org
Scope: National
Description: The Clean Water Network is a national alliance of over 1,000 organizations representing environmentalists, commercial fishers, anglers, surfers, family farmers, environmental justice advocates, faith communities, civic associations, boaters, labor unions, and recreational enthusiasts working together for cleaner waters.
Contact(s):
National Coordinator: KATHY NEMSICK; Phone: 202-289-2395
Outreach Coordinator: JODY THEUT; Phone: 202-289-2421

CLEVELAND MUSEUM OF NATURAL HISTORY, THE
1 Wade Oval Dr., University Cir., Cleveland, OH 44106
Phone: 216-231-4600/x219; Fax: 216-231-5919; Email: botany@cmnh.org
Founded: 1920; Membership: 9,000
Scope: Statewide
Description: To instill an understanding of and appreciation for nature and inspire responsibility for conservation and stewardship of natural diversity. The Museum program areas include exhibits, publications, education, collections, research, and natural areas. The Museum owns a system of seventeen sanctuaries.
Contact(s):
Director: DR. JAMES KING
Coordinator of Natural Areas: JAMES BISSELL
Publication(s): *Explorer; Kirtlandia*
Keyword(s): Environmental and Conservation Education, Research

CLIMATE INSTITUTE
324 4th St. NW, Washington, DC 20002
Phone: 202-547-0104; Fax: 202-547-0111
Founded: 1986; Membership: 1,500
Scope: National
Description: Designed to serve as a catalyst for international response and cooperation to address the threats posed by climate

NON-GOVERNMENTAL ORGANIZATIONS

change and depletion of the stratospheric ozone layer. The Climate Institute operates as a bridge between scientists and policymakers with the intent of expediting policy responses to the challenges posed by human-induced climate change.
Contact(s):
President: JOHN C. TOPPING JR., 324 4th St. NW, Washington, DC 20002; Phone: 202-547-0104
Vice President for Global Environmental Programs: DR. ATA QURESHI, 324 4th St. NW, Washington, DC 20002; Phone: 202-547-0104
Publication(s): *Climate Alert; Coping with Climate Change; Forests in a Changing Climate; Climate Change in Asia*
Keyword(s): Coasts, Energy, Sustainable Development, Urban Forestry

COALITION FOR CLEAN AIR
10780 Santa Monica Blvd., #210, Los Angeles, CA 90025
Phone: 310-441-1544
Founded: 1970; Membership: 2,000
Scope: Statewide
Description: A nonprofit, tax-exempt organization dedicated to restoring clean, healthful air to Southern California residents through a combination of efforts including outreach and education, litigation, research, and policy advocacy.
Contact(s):
President: GLADYS MEADE
Vice President: RALPH PERRY
Treasurer: DAVID ALLGOOD
Executive Director: LINDA WAADE
Policy Director: TIM CARMICHAEL
Publication(s): *Clearing the Air*
Keyword(s): Air Quality and Pollution, Environmental Protection, Pollution Prevention

COALITION FOR EDUCATION IN THE OUTDOORS
S.U.N.Y. at Cortland Box 2000, Cortland, NY 13045
Phone: 607-753-4971; Fax: 607-753-5982; Email: yaplec@snycorva.cortland.edu
Founded: 1986
Scope: National
Description: The Coalition is composed of more than 100 businesses, institutions, organizations, associations, centers, agencies, and individuals affiliated in support of communicating and networking concerning education in, for and about the outdoors. The Coalition's magazine is a critically acclaimed education resource.
Contact(s):
Executive Coordinator: DR. CHARLES H. YAPLE
Publication(s): *Taproot*
Keyword(s): Environmental and Conservation Education, Environmental Ethics, Nature Preservation, Outdoor Education, Outdoor Recreation, Wildlands

COALITION FOR NATURAL STREAM VALLEYS, INC.
430 Orchard Rd., Newark, DE 19711-5137
Phone: 302-366-8059
Membership: 50 individuals and 12 organizations
Scope: National
Description: The purpose of the Coalition for Natural Stream Valleys, Inc. is to promote the wise use of, and the preservation of natural stream valleys.
Contact(s):
Chairman: ROLAND R. ROTH

COAST ALLIANCE
215 Pennsylvania Ave., SE, Washington, DC 20003
Phone: 202-546-9554; Fax: 202-546-9609
Founded: 1979
Scope: National
Description: The Coast Alliance is a nonprofit public interest group dedicated to raising public awareness about our priceless coastal resources. Composed of concerned activists across the United States, the Coast Alliance provides information on activities affecting the nation's four coasts: the Atlantic, Pacific, Gulf of Mexico, and Great Lakes.
Contact(s):
Executive Director: JACQUELINE SAVITZ
Chairperson of the Board: DERY BENNETT
Treasurer and Secretary: TODD MILLER
Vice Chairperson: DAVID MILLER
Publication(s): *And Two If By Sea: Fighting The Attack on America's Coasts; Storm on The Horizon: The National Flood Insurance Program and America's Coasts; Using Common Sense to Protect The Coasts: The Need to Expand The Coastal Barrier Resources System; Getting to The Bottom of It*
Keyword(s): Aquatic Habitats, Coasts, Contaminated Sediments, Development, Environmental and Conservation Education, Land Use Planning, Runoff, Water Pollution

COASTAL CONSERVATION ASSOCIATION
4801 Woodway, Suite 220 West, Houston, TX 77056
Phone: 713-626-4234; Fax: 713-626-5852
Founded: 1977; Membership: 55,000
Scope: National
Description: A national nonprofit corporation organized exclusively for the purpose of promoting and advancing the preservation, conservation, and protection of the marine, animal, and plant life both onshore and offshore along the coastal areas of the United States for the benefit and enjoyment of the general public.
Contact(s):
President: ALEX JERNIGAN
Vice President: GUS SCHRAM III
Chairman of the Board: WALTER W. FONDREN III
Editor: DOUG PIKE
Executive Director of Alabama Regional Office: DAVID DEXTER, 144 Florence Place, Mobile, AL 36607; Phone: 334-478-3474; Fax: 334-476-5214
Executive Director of Connecticut Regional Office: RON DOMURAT, P.O. Box 290224, Wethersfield, CT 06129-0224; Phone: 860-529-7878
Executive Director of Florida Regional Office: TED FORSGREN, 905 East Park Ave., Tallahassee, FL 32301-2646; Phone: 904-224-3474; Fax: 904-224-5199
Executive Director of Georgia Regiona Office: BILL FORD, Varsity Plaza, 11418 Abercorn, Suite C, Savannah, GA 31419; Phone: 912-920-2300; Fax: 912-920-2313
Executive Director of Louisiana Regional Office: JEFF ANGERS, 8281 Goodwood, Suite B1, Baton Rouge, LA 70806; Phone: 504-952-9200; Fax: 504-952-9204
Executive Director of Maine Regional Office: PAT KELIHER, 40 Lafayette St., Yarmouth, ME 04096; Phone: 207-846-1015; Fax: 207-846-1168
Executive Director of Massachusetts Regiona Office: DAVID RIMMER, 4 Middle St., Suite 215, Newburyport, MA 01950; Phone: 978-499-4313; Fax: 978-499-4314
Executive Director of New York Regional Office: JOHN MCMURRAY, P.O. Box 1118, West Babylon, NY 11704; Phone: 516-422-4162
Executive Director of North Carolina Regional Office: DICK BRAME, 2030 Eastwood Rd., Suite 3, Wilmington, NC 28403; Phone: 910-256-0083; Fax: 910-256-6040
Executive Director of South Carolina Regional Office: BETH PIERCE, P.O. Box 1823, Mt. Pleasant, SC 29465; Phone: 843-852-7880; Fax: 843-852-9202
Executive Director of Texas Regional Office: KEVIN DANIELS, 4801 Woodway, Suite 220W, Houston, TX 77056; Phone: 713-626-4222; Fax: 713-961-3801
Executive Director of Virginia Regional Office: RICHARD WELTON, 2100 Marina Shores Dr., Suite 108, Virginia Beach, VA 23451; Phone: 757-481-1226; Fax: 757-481-6910
Secretary and Treasurer: DAVID G. CUMMINS
Vice Chairman: WILL OHMSTEDE
Publication(s): *Tide*
Keyword(s): Aquatic Habitats, Coasts, Fisheries, Sport Fishing, Water Quality, Water Resources, Wetlands

COASTAL SOCIETY, THE
P.O. Box 25408, Alexandria, VA 22313-5408
Phone: 703-768-1599; Fax: 703-768-1598
Founded: 1975
Scope: International
Description: An international nonprofit organization dedicated to promoting the understanding and responsible use of coastal environments. Through conferences, workshops, and publications, the society seeks to foster improved interdisciplinary communication, promote responsible use of resources consistent with natural processes, and further public understanding and knowledge of the coast.
Contact(s):
President: MEGAN D. BAILIFF
Secretary: LAURIE McGILVRAY, 7010 Woodland Ave., Takoma Park, MD 20912; Phone: 301-713-3155
Treasurer: TINA BERND-COHEN, 729 Power St., Helena, MT 59601; Phone: 406-442-4002
Executive Director: JUDY TUCKER
Editor: ROBERT BOYLES
Past President: MICHAEL K. ORBACH, Nicholas School for the Environment, Duke University, 135 Duke Marine Lab Rd., Beaufort, NC 28516-9720
Publication(s): *Coastal Society, The Bulletin;* conference proceedings
Keyword(s): Coasts, Environmental and Conservation Education, Sustainable Development, Water Pollution, Wetlands

COLORADO ASSOCIATION OF SOIL CONSERVATION DISTRICTS
ATTN: President, 18105 Enoch Rd., Colorado Springs, CO 80930
Scope: Statewide
Contact(s):
President, Alternate Board Member: ROBERT CORDOVA, 18105 Enoch Rd., Colorado Springs, CO 80930; Phone: 719-683-2126
Vice President: JIM ROSSI, P.O. Box 247, Oak Creek, CO 80467; Phone: 970-638-4459
Executive Director: GLEN ANDERSON, 3000 Youngfield St. Suite 163, Lakewood, CO 80215-6545; Phone: 303-232-6242; Fax: 303-232-1624
Board Member: JOHN FREZIERS, 1858 M Rd., Fruita, CO 81521; Phone: 970-858-7165
Executive Assistant: MARY KLEIN, 3000 Youngfield St., Suite 163, Lakewood, CO 80215-6545; Phone: 303-232-6242; Fax: 303-232-1624
Secretary and Treasurer: LEE CAMPBELL, 2666 W. 2nd Ave., Durango, CO 81301; Phone: 970-247-1496; Fax: 970-385-7910

COLORADO B.A.S.S. CHAPTER FEDERATION
ATTN: President, 2713 Garden Dr., Ft. Collins, CO 80526
Phone: 970-221-3608
Scope: Statewide
Description: An organization of Bassmaster chapters, affiliated with the Bass Anglers Sportsman Society, organized to fight pollution, assist state and national conservation agencies in their efforts, and teach the young people of our country good conservation practices. Dedicated to the realistic conservation of our water resources.
Contact(s):
President: JIM BLISS, 2713 Garden Dr., Ft. Collins, CO 80526; Phone: 970-221-3608
Conservation Director: PAT SNIDER, 4842 W. 9th St. Rd., Greeley, CO 80634; Phone: 970-353-5375

COLORADO ENVIRONMENTAL COALITION
1536 Wynkoop, #5C, Denver, CO 80202
Phone: 303-534-7066; Fax: 303-534-7063; Email: infocec@cecenviro.org; WWW: www.cecenviro.org
Founded: 1965; Membership: 50 organizations plus 2,300 individuals
Scope: Statewide
Description: The Colorado Environmental Coalition is the grass roots action arm of Colorado's environmental movement. The Coalition coordinates the conservation community and mobilizes citizen constituencies behind environmental campaigns to preserve wilderness, wildlife, and a sustainable way of life.
Contact(s):
President: JOHN POWERS
Executive Director: SUSAN TIXIER; Phone: 303-534-5533; Email: sjtix@cecenviro.org
Associate Director: TED FICKES; Phone: 303-534-7066; Email: fickes@cecenviro.org
Circuit Rider: TREY BECK; Phone: 303-534-1774; Email: trey@cecenviro.org
Field Director: JEFF WIDEN; Phone: 970-385-8509; Email: widen@cecenviro.org
Field Organizer: MONICA PIERGROSSI; Phone: 303-534-7492; Email: monica@cecenviro.org
Growth Management: LAUREN MARTENS; Phone: 303-534-5798; Email: martens@cecenviro.org
Membership Director: JODY KENNEDY; Phone: 303-534-7310; Email: jody@cecenviro.org
West Slope Field Organizer: PETE KOLBENSCHLAG, 1000 N 9th St., #29, Grand Junction, CO 81501; Phone: 970-243-0002; Email: pete@cecenviro.org
Publication(s): *Colorado Environmental Report; Colorado Environmental Handbook-State of the State; Conservationist's Wilderness Proposal for BLM Lands*
Keyword(s): Environmental Health, Public Lands, Sustainable Development, Wilderness, Wildlife and Wildlife Habitat

COLORADO FORESTRY ASSOCIATION
P.O. Box 270132, Ft. Collins, CO 80527
Phone: 970-491-6303
Founded: 1982; Membership: 650
Scope: Statewide
Description: A statewide organization affiliated with the National Woodland Owners Association, concerned with forest ecology and advocating a forest-perpetuating balance between preservation and harvest of Colorado forests.
Contact(s):
President: C.W. MILLER, Bellvue, CO
Vice President: KEN ASHLEY, Ft. Collins, CO
Secretary: BETTY DAY, Aurora, CO
Treasurer: ED OLMSTED, Northglen, CO
Editor: JOHN ORAM; Phone: 303-477-0552
Publication(s): *Colorado Forestry*
Keyword(s): Forests and Forestry

COLORADO NATURAL HERITAGE PROGRAM
254 General Services Bldg., Colorado State University, Ft. Collins, CO 80523
Phone: 970-491-1309; Fax: 970-491-3349; Email: heritage@lamar.colostate.edu; WWW: www.colostate.edu/orgs/CNHP/
Founded: 1979
Scope: Statewide
Description: The mission of the Colorado Natural Heritage Program is to empower the people of Colorado by providing the information that they need to make wise choices regarding the irreplacable biological resources that their actions may affect.
Contact(s):
Director: MARY KLEIN; Phone: 970-491-1309; Fax: 970-491-3349; Email: heritage@lamar.colostate.edu
Publication(s): *Rare and Imperiled Animals, Plants, and Plant Communities of Colorado; Colorado Rare Plant Guide*

NON-GOVERNMENTAL ORGANIZATIONS

Keyword(s): Biodiversity, Ecology, Land Use Planning, Planning Management

COLORADO TRAPPERS ASSOCIATION
P.O. Box 397, Empire, CO 80438
Founded: 1975; Membership: 500
Scope: Statewide
Description: Associate of Fur Takers of America and National Trappers Association. Dedicated to the wise conservation and management of furbearing animals, the education of fur harvesters and public about furbearer management and the preservation of America's rich heritage in the harvest of wild furs.
Contact(s):
President: AL DAVIDSON, Box 225, Gunnison, CO 81230; Phone: 970-641-4022
Vice President: MARVIN MILLER, 29156 Summit Ranch Dr., Golden, CO 80401; Phone: 303-526-9207
Secretary: DEBRA WATTS, P.O. Box 397, Empire, CO 80438; Phone: 303-569-2551
Treasurer: DEBORAH LINDAHL, 5109 Parkway Cir., W., Ft. Collins, CO 80525; Phone: 970-206-0309
Director of Public Relations: BILL ROGERS, Box 128, Brighton, CO 80601; Phone: 303-659-0773
Director of Publications: MAJ. L. BODDICKER
Editor: MAJ. L. BODDICKER
Publication(s): *Managing Rocky Mountain Furbearers; Fur Marketing and Trappers Supply Handbook*
Keyword(s): Agriculture, Hunting, Predators, Trapping, Wildlife Management

COLORADO WATER CONGRESS
1390 Logan St., Suite 312, Denver, CO 80203
Phone: 303-837-0812; Fax: 303-837-1607
Founded: 1958
Scope: Statewide
Description: To institute and advance programs for the conservation, development, protection, and efficient utilization of the water resources of Colorado.
Contact(s):
President: JIM HOKIT
Vice President: NEIL JAQUET
Executive Director: RICHARD D. MacRAVEY
Publication(s): *Colorado Water Rights; Colorado Water Almanac & Directory; Water Intelligence Report; Water Legal News; Water Legislative Report; Water Research News; Water Special Report; Water Quality News; Colorado Laws Enacted of Interest to Water Users*

COLORADO WILDLIFE FEDERATION
445 Union Blvd., #302, Lakewood, CO 80228-1243
Phone: 303-987-0400; Fax: 303-987-0200; Email: cwfed@aol.com
Founded: 1952
Scope: Statewide
Description: A representative statewide organization, affiliated with the National Wildlife Federation, dedicated to the protection and enhancement of wildlife and its habitat through public education and government interaction.
Contact(s):
Chairman: DENNIS BUECHLER
Affiliate Representative: CHARLES OLMSTED
Alternate Representative: COLLEEN GADD
Executive Director and Editor: DIANE GANSAUER
Publication(s): *Colorado Wildlife*

COLORADO WILDLIFE HERITAGE FOUNDATION
6060 Broadway, Denver, CO 80216
Phone: 303-291-7212
Founded: 1989; Membership: 300
Scope: Statewide
Description: The Colorado Wildlife Heritage Foundation has been endorsed by four Colorado governors. The foundation's objectives are threefold: (1) environmental education, (2) habitat acquistion and management, and (3) wildlife research. Where appropriate, the foundation pursues projects with the support and expertise of the Colorado Division of Wildlife.
Contact(s):
President: REBECCA L. FRANK, 2004 Wood Ct., Grand Junction, CO 81503; Phone: 303-243-1603
Vice President: TERRY COMBS, American Cargo Handling P.O. Box 17594, Denver, CO 80217; Phone: 303-398-2416
Treasurer: BUCK HUTCHISON, Hutchison Western P.O. Box 1158, Adams City, CO 80022; Phone: 303-287-2826
Executive Director: EDWARD J. ALEXANDER, Colorado Wildlife Heritage Foundation 6060 Broadway, Denver, CO 80216; Phone: 303-291-7416
Director: CHARLES L. WARREN, 333 Logan St., Denver, CO 80203; Phone: 303-778-7797
Chairman of the Board: DR. RUSSELL SCOTT JR., Scott Capital Corporation P.O. Box 280409, Lakewood, CO 80228; Phone: 303-274-8112
Vice Chairman: JAMES M. COWPERTHWAITE, 378 S. Pontiac Way, Denver, CO 80224; Phone: 303-355-3957
Publication(s): *Colorado Wildlife Heritage Today*
Keyword(s): Endangered and Threatened Species, Environmental and Conservation Education, Land Purchase, Sustainable Ecosystems, Wildlife and Wildlife Habitat

COLUMBIA BASIN FISH AND WILDLIFE AUTHORITY
2501 SW 1st Ave. Suite 200, Portland, OR 97201
Phone: 503-326-7031
Founded: 1982
Scope: National
Description: A regional association of all the fish and wildlife agencies (two federal, five state) and Indian tribes (13 in the Columbia River Basin (Idaho, Montana, Oregon, and Washington). Established to coordinate planning and implementation of the fish and wildlife provisions of the Pacific Northwest Electric Power Planning and Conservation Act and for oversight of fish and wildlife resource management under the Fish and Wildlife Coordination Act and other authorities. Current charter: 1987.
Contact(s):
Chairman: BERN SHANKS, WA Dept. of Fish and Wildlife, 600 Capitol Way, N., Olympia, WA 98501; Phone: 360-902-2225; Fax: 360-902-2947
Executive Director: DR. BRIAN J. ALLEE; Phone: 503-326-7031; Fax: 503-326-7033; Email: brian@cbfwf.org
Fish Passage Center Manager: MICHELE DeHART, 2501 SW 1st Ave., Suite 230, Portland, OR 97201-4752; Phone: 503-230-4288; Fax: 503-230-7559; Email: mdehart@fpc.org
Keyword(s): Fisheries, Wildlife and Wildlife Habitat, Wildlife Rehabilitation

COMMITTEE FOR NATIONAL ARBOR DAY
Attn: National Chairman, 63 Fitzrandolph Rd., West Orange, NJ 07052
Founded: 1936
Scope: National
Description: To establish a unified national observance date on the last Friday in April.
Contact(s):
Honorary National Chairman: MRS. EDWARD H. SCANLON, P.O. Box 38247, Olmsted Falls, OH 44138
National Chairman: HARRY J. BANKER, 63 Fitzrandolph Rd., West Orange, NJ 07052

COMMITTEE FOR THE NATIONAL INSTITUTE FOR THE ENVIRONMENT (CNIE)
1725 K Street NW, Suite 212, Washington, DC 20006
Phone: 202-530-5810; Fax: 202-628-4311; Email: cnie@access.digex.net
Founded: 1990
Scope: National
Description: The CNIE is a nonprofit organization of scientists, policymakers, environmentalists, business representatives, and other stakeholders in environmental policy. The CNIE's mission is to

improve the scientific basis for making decisions on environmental issues through the creation and successful operation of a National Institute for the Environment. The proposed institute would reform the relationship between science and environmental decision-making by establishing programs for environmental research, assessment, education and training, and a National Library for the Environment.
Contact(s):
Chair: STEPHEN P. HUBBELL, Professor of Biology and Butler Fellow, Princeton University Department of Ecology and Evolutionary Biology, Guyot Hall Rm. 101, Princeton, NJ 08544-1003; Phone: 609-258-6797; Fax: 609-258-1712
Executive Director: PETER D. SAUNDRY, Committee for the NIE, 1725 K Street NW, Ste. 212, Washington, DC 20006; Phone: 202-530-5810; Fax: 202-628-4311
Secretary and Treasurer: A. KARIM AHMED, Science and Policy Assoc., 1333 H St. NW, Ste 400, The West Tower, Washington, DC 20005; Phone: 202-789-1201; Fax: 202-789-1206
Vice Chair: HENRY F. HOWE, Professor and Ecology Coordinator, University of Illinois at Chicago, Biological Sciences, (M and C 066), 845 W. Taylor St., Chicago, IL 60607-7060; Phone: 312-413-0023; Fax: 312-996-2017
Publication(s): *A Proposal for a National Institute for the Environment; Federal Environmental Research and Development Programs; Environmental Justice: Breaking New Ground*
Keyword(s): Communications, Environmental and Conservation Education, Sustainable Development, Sustainable Ecosystems, Wildlife and Wildlife Habitat

COMMITTEE ON AGRICULTURAL SUSTAINABILITY FOR DEVELOPING COUNTRIES
1709 New York Ave. NW, Washington, DC 20006
Phone: 202-638-6300
Founded: 1987
Scope: National
Description: The Committee on Agricultural Sustainability aims to increase support for farmers in developing countries working to improve their living conditions and feed the world's expanding population without destroying the soil and water supplies on which agricultural productivity ultimately depends.
Contact(s):
Chairman: ROBERT O. BLAKE, 1709 New York Ave. NW, Washington, DC 20006
Keyword(s): Agriculture, Developing Countries, Soil Conservation, Sustainable Development

COMMUNITIES FOR A BETTER ENVIRONMENT
500 Howard St., Suite 506, San Francisco, CA 94105
Phone: 415-243-8373
Founded: 1971; Membership: 15,000
Scope: Statewide
Description: The CBE is a nonprofit, multiracial environmental health organization working to prevent public exposure to toxic chemical pollutants. CBE has over 19 years experience in the California environmental arena. CBE uses science-based research, legal tactics, and organizing strategies to prevent air and water pollution, to eliminate toxic hazards, and to improve the health of the people of California.
Contact(s):
Secretary: KEN FINNEY
Executive Director: MICHAEL BELLIVEAU
Board President: STEPHANIE PINCETL
Publication(s): *Environmental Review; Oil Rag*
Keyword(s): Air Quality and Pollution, Environmental Justice, Environmental Law, Internships, Water Pollution

COMMUNITY CONSERVATION CONSULTANTS/HOWLERS FOREVER, INC.
50542 Zintz Rd., Rt. 1 Box 96, Gays Mills, WI 54631
Phone: 608-735-4717; Fax: 608-735-4765; Email: ccc@mwt.net
Founded: 1989
Scope: National
Description: Specializing in catalyzing of community-based conservation initiatives and designing for their sustainability. Active in Wisconsin, Belize, and India. Coordination of volunteers for projects.
Contact(s):
Assistant Director: DR. JONATHAN LYON
Director: DR. ROB HORWICH
Keyword(s): Conservation, Local Resource Conservation

COMMUNITY ENVIRONMENTAL COUNCIL
930 Miramonte Dr., Santa Barbara, CA 93109
Phone: 805-963-0583
Founded: 1970; Membership: 600
Scope: National
Description: CEC's primary goal is to serve as a connecting institution linking government agencies, business and industry, universities and regulatory bodies, environmental organizations, and the community. Using Santa Barbara as its urban laboratory, CEC conducts research and develops local programs in recycling, hazardous waste, sustainable agriculture, and environmental education.
Contact(s):
President: CHARLES ECKBERG, 930 Miramonte Dr., Santa Barbara, CA 93109; Phone: 805-963-0583
Vice President: SUSAN VAN ATTA, 930 Miramonte Dr., Santa Barbara, CA 93209; Phone: 805-963-0583
Secretary: JERRY STURMER, 930 Miramonte Dr., Santa Barbara, CA 93109; Phone: 805-963-0583
Treasurer: BILL ADLER, 930 Miramonte Dr., Santa Barbara, CA 93109; Phone: 805-963-0583
Executive Director: JON CLARK, 930 Miramonte Dr., Santa Barbara, CA 93109; Phone: 805-963-0583
Publication(s): *Gildea Review; Manufacturing with Recyclables; A Question of Responsibility: Recycling Market Development*
Keyword(s): Gardening and Horticulture, Land Use Planning, Solid Waste Management, Sustainable Development, Toxic Substances

COMMUNITY RIGHTS COUNSEL
1726 M St., Suite 703, Washington, DC 20036-4524
Phone: 202-296-6889; Fax: 202-296-6895; Email: crc@communityrights.org; WWW: www.communityrights.org
Founded: 1997
Scope: Statewide
Description: CRC is a public interest law firm defending laws that make our communities healthier, more livable, and socially just.
Contact(s):
Program Director: F. G. COURTNEY
Keyword(s): Endangered and Threatened Species, Environmental Law, Environmental Planning, Land Preservation, Land Use Planning, Open Space, Planning Management, Sustainable Development, Urban Environment, Wetlands

CONCERN, INC.
1794 Columbia Rd. NW, Washington, DC 20009
Phone: 202-328-8160; Fax: 202-387-3378; Email: concern@igc.visit the sustainable communities; WWW: www.sustainable.org
Founded: 1970
Scope: National
Description: A nonprofit, tax-exempt organization which provides environmental information to individuals and groups. Concern's publications give an overview of the issue and include guidelines to encourage and aid citizen participation in the community and in policy decisions at the local, state, and federal levels of government.

NON-GOVERNMENTAL ORGANIZATIONS

Also are developing a community sustainability program which includes a database on sustainability.
Contact(s):
Chair: BURKS LAPHAM
Executive Director: SUSAN BOYD
Publication(s): *Community Action Guides on Pesticides, Drinking Water, Farmland, Waste, Household Waste, and Global Warming*
Keyword(s): Environmental and Conservation Education, Pesticides, Solid Waste Management, Sustainable Development, Water Resources

CONFEDERATED SALISH AND KOOTENAI TRIBES
P.O. Box 278, Pablo, MT 59855
Phone: 406-675-2700; Fax: 406-675-2806
Scope: Statewide
Description: The 1.25 million acre Flathead Indian Reservation was created in 1855 by the Treaty of the Hellgate as a homeland for the Salish, Kootenai, and Pend d' Oreille Tribes. The constitutional government of the Confederated Salish and Kootenai Tribes was formed in 1934 and approved by the Secretary of the Interior in 1935 to establish a more responsible organization, promote our general welfare, conserve and develop our land and resources, and secure to ourselves and our posterity the power to exercise certain rights of self-government. The Tribal Natural Resources Department includes the divisions of Water, Environmental Protection, Lands, and Fisheries, Wildlife, Recreation, and Conservation. The Tribal Forestry Department is responsible for forest management activities on the Reservation.
Contact(s):
Executive Secretary: JOSEPH E. DUPUIS
Forestry Department Head: RALPH GOODE
Natural Resources Department Head: SAM MORIGEAU
Tribal Chairman: MICHAEL T. PABLO
Publication(s): *Char-Koosta News*
Keyword(s): Cultural Preservation, Environmental Preservation, Land Use Planning, Renewable Resources, Wildlife Management

CONFERENCE OF NATIONAL PARK COOPERATING ASSOCIATIONS
8375 Jumpers Hole Rd. Suite 104, Millersville, MD 21108
Phone: 410-647-9001; Fax: 410-647-9003; Email: cnpca@nps.gov
Founded: 1977
Scope: National
Description: CNPCA is the official umbrella organization for nonprofit interpretive associations that operate bookstores and sales areas in national parks and in other federal, state, and municipal vistor centers. The Associations are the single largest contributors of donated funds for the support of education, vistor services, and research activities in our nation's parks ($17 million per year).
Contact(s):
Executive Director: PAULA DEGEN, 8375 Jumpers Hole Rd., Suite 104, Millersville, MD 21108; Phone: 410-647-9001
Publication(s): *Newswire; Exchange, The; Cooperating Association Directory*
Keyword(s): Natural Areas, Outdoor Recreation, Public Lands, Training

CONNECTICUT ASSOCIATION OF SOIL AND WATER CONSERVATION DISTRICTS, INC.
ATTN: President, 41 Millville Ave #108, Naugatuck, CT 06770
Scope: Statewide
Contact(s):
President: ANTHONY PESANELLI, 41 Millville Ave #108, Naugatuck, CT 06770; Phone: 203-729-9694
Vice President: THOMAS ODELL, 9 Cherry St., Westborrk, CT 06498; Phone: 860-399-7912; Fax: 860-345-9175
Alternate Board Member: NORMA O'LEARY, 62 O'Leary Place, Thompson, CT 06277; Phone: 860-923-2969; Fax: 860-923-9554
Board Member: JOHN BREAKELL, 54 Bear Hill Rd., Goshen, CT 06756; Phone: 860-491-2243
Secretary/Treasurer: JEFFREY FOLGER, 67 Burbank Rd., Ellington, CT 06029; Phone: 860-644-2511

CONNECTICUT AUDUBON SOCIETY, INC.
118 Oak St., Hartford, CT 06106
Phone: 860-527-8737
Founded: 1898; Membership: 8,500
Scope: Statewide
Description: Dedicated to environmental education to conserve natural resources. Sanctuary acquisition and management, legislative action, and wildlife and natural areas research.
Contact(s):
President: SHERMAN T. KENT; Phone: 860-527-8737
Vice President: PETER KUNKEL
Vice President: BRAD BELISLE
Vice President: BARBARA MILLER
Vice President: JUDITH RICHARDSON
Chairman of the Board: LESLIE CAROTHERS
Director of Development: ALISON OLIVIERI; Phone: 203-254-3315
Director of Environmental Affairs: LISA SANTACROCE; Phone: 860-527-8737
Editor: CATHY O'DONNELL; Phone: 203-254-1092
Teacher/Naturalist: LAURIE PARADIS-BRANT
Teacher/Naturalist: ANN F. GUION
Teacher/Naturalist: KASHA BREAU
Teacher/Naturalist: CHRIS KRUMPERMAN
Teacher/Naturalist: RICHARD JULIAN
Teacher/Naturalist: JEFF WEILER
Teacher/Naturalist: JAMES SIRCH
Vice President of Legal: W. BRADLEY MOREHOUSE
Keyword(s): Environmental and Conservation Education, Environmental Protection, Open Space, Sustainable Development, Wildlife and Wildlife Habitat

CONNECTICUT B.A.S.S. CHAPTER FEDERATION
ATTN: President, P.O. Box 763, Killingsworth, CT 06419
Phone: 860-663-1351
Scope: Statewide
Description: An organization of Bassmaster chapters, affiliated with the Bass Anglers Sportsman Society, organized to fight pollution, assist state and national conservation agencies in their efforts, and teach the young people of our country good conservation practices. Dedicated to the realistic conservation of our water resources.
Contact(s):
President: FRED PERRY, P.O. Box 763, Killingworth, CT 06419; Phone: 860-663-1351
Conservation Director: LEE JOHNSON, 155 Candlewood Lake Rd., North New Milford, CT 06776; Phone: 860-350-1368(H)/860-761-4169(W)

CONNECTICUT BOTANICAL SOCIETY
P.O. Box 208104, Yale University Herbarium, 165 Prospect St., New Haven, CT 06520-8104
Founded: 1903; Membership: 300
Scope: Statewide
Description: The Society increases knowledge of the state's flora accumulate and maintains specimens and records for a permanent botanical record. The Society also recommends botanically significant areas for protection and supports scholarly botanical research.
Contact(s):
President: CASPER J. ULTEE; Phone: 860-633-7557; Email: casperu@aol.com
Vice President: CAROL LEMMON; Phone: 203-488-7813
Secretary: KAREN SEXTON; Phone: 860-228-4647
Treasurer: EDWARD P. STAUTON; Phone: 203-888-6277
Publication(s): *Newsletter; Yearbook; The Vascular Flora of Southeastern Connecticut*
Keyword(s): Conservation, Endangered and Threatened Species, Environmental Protection, Flowers, Plants, and Trees, Nature Preservation, Wetlands

CONNECTICUT FOREST AND PARK ASSOCIATION
Middlefield, 16 Meriden Rd., Rockfall, CT 06481-2961
Phone: 860-346-2372; Fax: 860-347-7463; Email: conn.forest.assoc@snet.net; WWW: www.ctwoodlands.org
Scope: Statewide
Description: A representative statewide organization, affiliated with the National Wildlife Federation, dedicated to the protection and enhancement of wildlife and its habitat through public education and government interaction.
Contact(s):
President: RUSSELL BRENNEMAN
Executive Director: JOHN E. HIBBARD
Affiliate Representative: RUTH CUTLER
Alternate Representative and Editor: CAROL YOUELL
Publication(s): *Connecticut Woodlands; Connecticut Forest and Park Association Newsletter; Connecticut Walk Book, The; Forest Trees of Southern New England*

CONNECTICUT FUND FOR THE ENVIRONMENT
1032 Chapel St., 3rd Fl., New Haven, CT 06510
Phone: 203-787-0646
Membership: 3,000
Scope: Statewide
Description: CFE is a nonprofit group dedicated to protecting Connecticut's natural resources through legal action, education, and scientific investigation.
Contact(s):
President: DR. GORDON GEBALLE
Vice President: CAMPBELL HUDSON III
Secretary: BARBARA DAVID
Treasurer: THOMAS HOLLOWAY
Director: DONALD S. STRAIT
Publication(s): *Newsletter; Fact Sheets; Annual Reports*
Keyword(s): Air Quality and Pollution, Energy, Land Use Planning, Toxic Substances, Water Pollution

CONNECTICUT PUBLIC INTEREST RESEARCH GROUP (ConnPIRG)
41 S. Main, W. Hartford, CT 06107
Phone: 203-233-7554; Fax: 203-233-7574
Founded: 1972; Membership: 31,000
Scope: Statewide
Description: Works for concrete solutions to improve and protect our environment. Engaged in public education, study, and legislative action in many areas of the environment, including water and air pollution and solid waste.
Contact(s):
President: GENE KARPINSKI, 215 Pennsylvania Ave. SE, Washington, DC 20003; Phone: 202-546-9707
Treasurer: JAMES LEAHY, Fairfield Ave., Hartford, CT 06106; Phone: 203-247-2622
Secretary and Organizing Director: KIRSTEN DUNTON, 163 Park Rd. W., Hartford, CT 06107; Phone: 203-236-2321
Publication(s): *ConnPIRG Reports*
Keyword(s): Air Quality and Pollution, Endangered and Threatened Species, Solid Waste Management, Toxic Substances, Water Pollution Management

CONNECTICUT RIVER WATERSHED COUNCIL INC.
Headquarters One Ferry St., Easthampton, MA 01027
Phone: 413-529-9500; Fax: 413-529-9501; Email: crwc@crocker.com
Founded: 1952; Membership: 1,500
Scope: Regional
Description: A member-supported nonprofit organization, CRWC is a regional voice for improvement and protection of the Connecticut River and water resources throughout the 11,260 square-mile, four-state river basin of Vermont, New Hampshire, Massachusetts, and Connecticut. CRWC participates in relevant environmental and resource allocation issues through its land conservancy, water quality improvement, and watershed stewardship programs. Land conservancy revolving loan fund. Conservation education and research grant fund.
Contact(s):
Chairman: NEIL W. SHERIDAN
Secretary: NANCY ROGERS
Executive Director: WHITTY SANFORD
Vice Chair: ERLING HEISTAD
Vice Chair: NANCY ROGERS
Vice Chair: ANDY WIZNER
Publication(s): *Currents and Eddies; Complete Boating Guide to the Connecticut River*
Keyword(s): Environmental Protection, Land Use Planning, Rivers, Water Pollution, Water Quality, Watersheds, Wetlands

CONNECTICUT WATERFOWL ASSOCIATION, INC.
Attn: Treasurer, P.O. Box 74, Bozrah, CT 06334-0074
Phone: 860-663-2292
Founded: 1967; Membership: 300
Scope: Statewide
Description: To preserve, reclaim, and enhance wetland and wildlife habitat in the state of Connecticut in a manner that promotes the wise use of our natural resources and the progress of our society.
Contact(s):
President: PATRICIA HOCHMAN, 18 Langworthy Ave., Stonington, CT 06378; Phone: 203-838-8421
Vice President: PAUL ROTHBART, 177 Romulus Rd., Cheshire, CT 06410; Phone: 860-295-9523
Secretary: PATTI HOLMES, 17 Blake St., Norwalk, CT 06851; Phone: 203-846-8526
Treasurer: PAUL CAPOTOSTO, 23 Beechwood Rd., Oakdale, CT 06370; Phone: 860-642-7239
Publication(s): *Connecticut Waterfowl and Wetlands*
Keyword(s): Environmental and Conservation Education, Waterfowl, Wetlands, Wildlife and Wildlife Habitat, Wildlife Management

CONSERVANCY OF SOUTHWEST FLORIDA, THE
1450 Merrihue Drive, Naples, FL 34102
Phone: 941-262-0304; Fax: 941-262-0672; WWW: www.conservancy.org
Scope: Statewide
Description: The Conservancy is a nonprofit environmental organization supported by memebers and donors. Annual family memeberships begin at $35 and include admission to the nature center, educational publications and discounted rates for canoe rentals, special programs and purchases made in the nature stores.
Contact(s):
Director: MARAN BRAINARD HILGENDORF

CONSERVATION AND RESEARCH FOUNDATION, INC., THE
24 Schillhammer Rd., Jericho, VT 05465
Founded: 1953
Scope: National
Description: To promote the conservation of renewable natural resources; to encourage study and research in the biological sciences; and to deepen understanding of the intricate relationship between man and the environment that supports him.
Contact(s):
President: H. W. VOGELMANN, 24 Schillhammer Rd., Jericho, UT 05405
Secretary: RICHARD H. GOODWIN SR., Box 5264, Connecticut College, New London, CT 06320
Keyword(s): Air Quality and Pollution, Environmental Law, Population Growth, Renewable Resources, Wildlife and Wildlife Habitat

NON-GOVERNMENTAL ORGANIZATIONS

CONSERVATION COUNCIL FOR HAWAII
250 Ward Ave., Suite 217, Honolulu, HI 96814
Phone: 808-236-2234; Fax: 808-247-2551; Email: sagerw001@hawaii.rr.com; WWW: www.planet-hawaii.com/~cch
Scope: Statewide
Description: A representative statewide organization, affiliated with the National Wildlife Federation, dedicated to the protection and enhancement of wildlife and its habitat through public education and government interaction.
Contact(s):
Executive Director: BILL SAGER
Alternate Representative: KAREN BLUE
Chair and Affiliate Representative and Editor: KATE SCHUERCH
Publication(s): *The Hawai'I Conserver*

CONSERVATION COUNCIL OF NORTH CAROLINA
P.O. Box 12671, Raleigh, NC 27605
Phone: 919-832-8083; Fax: 919-829-1192; Email: ccnc@bellsouth.net
Founded: 1968; Membership: 750, 30+ member organizations
Scope: Statewide
Description: To initiate, participate in, and coordinate local, regional, state, and national action in environmental and energy matters and in conservation and environmental education.
Contact(s):
President: RICK JOHNSON, 600 Winding Creek, Carthage, NC 28327
Vice President: JANE SHARP, 307 Granville Rd., Chapel Hill, NC 27514
Editor: MAUREEN SULTON, 345 N. Page, Southern Pines, NC 28387
Lobbyist: NAT MUND, P.O. Box 12671, Raleigh, NC 27605
Publication(s): *Carolina Conservationist Newsletter; Legislative Bulletin*
Keyword(s): Air Quality and Pollution, Coasts, Nuclear/Radiation, Rivers, Solid Waste

CONSERVATION DISTRICTS FOUNDATION INC.
Davis Conservation Library, 408 E. Main, P.O. Box 855, League City, TX 77574-0855
Phone: 281-332-3402; Fax: 281-332-5259
Founded: 1962
Scope: National
Description: Directed by the Conservation Districts Foundation, Inc., an adjunct of the National Association of Conservation Districts. Collects various conservation and environmental education materials. Dedicated to the memory of Waters S. Davis, Past President of NACD.
Contact(s):
Chief Executive Officer: ERNEST SHEA, NACD, 509 Capitol Ct. NE, Washington, DC 20002; Phone: 202-547-6223
Director of Office of Public Affairs: RONALD G. FRANCIS; Phone: 281-332-3402/28; Email: ron-francis@nacdnet.org
Keyword(s): Environmental and Conservation Education, Soil Conservation, Water Resources, Wetlands, Wildlife Management

CONSERVATION FEDERATION OF MARYLAND/For A Rural Maryland (F.A.R.M.)
P.O. Box 455, Poolesville, MD 20837
Phone: 301-916-3510
Scope: Statewide
Description: The Conservation Federation of Maryland is devoted to the wise use, conservation, aesthetic appreciation, and restoration of wildlife and other natural resources. The Conservation Federation of Maryland was recently merged with For A Rural Maryland to help safeguard the dwindling supply of farmland and open space in the state of Maryland.
Contact(s):
President: DOLOLRES MILMORE, 18801 River Rd., Poolesville, MD 20837
Vice President: CAROLINE TAYLOR GOLDMAN, 15711Hughes Rd., Poolesville, MD 20837
Secretary: CATHY HALL, 17826 Walling Rd., Poolesville, MD 20837
Treasurer: MARILYN EMERY, 9713 Old Spring Dr., Kensington, MD
Keyword(s): Agriculture, Conservation of Protected Areas, Environmental Justice, Land Preservation, Sustainable Development

CONSERVATION FEDERATION OF MISSOURI
728 W. Main St., Jefferson City, MO 65101-1543
Phone: 573-634-2322; Fax: 573-634-8205; Email: modfed@sockets.net
Scope: Statewide
Description: A representative statewide organization, affiliated with the National Wildlife Federation, dedicated to the protection and enhancement of wildlife and its habitat through public education and government interaction.
Contact(s):
President: HOWARD FLEMING
Executive Director: DEIRDRE HIRNER
Affiliate Representative: ED STEGNER
Editor: CHARLES F. DAVIDSON
Publication(s): *Missouri Wildlife*

CONSERVATION FUND, THE
1800 North Kent St., Suite 1120, Arlington, VA 22209
Phone: 703-525-6300; Fax: 703-525-4610
Founded: 1985
Scope: National
Description: The Conservation Fund seeks sustainable conservation solutions for the 21st century, emphasizing the integration of economic and environmental goals. Through land conservation services, demonstration projects, education, and community-based activities, the Fund develops innovative measures to conserve land and water. The Fund forges partnerships to protect America's irreplaceable outdoor heritage and a tangible legacy for future generations. Programs: Land Conservation Services, Sustainable Programs, American Land Conservation Program, American Greenways, Freshwater Institute, Conservation Leadership Network, Civil War Battlefield Campaign. Awards: Alexander Calder Conservation Award, Cartledge Award for Excellence in Environmental Education, American Greenways DuPont, American Land Conservation, CF Industries National Watershed, Hastings National Park Leadership awards.
Contact(s):
Chairman: PATRICK F. NOONAN
Treasurer: HADLAI A. HULL
Conservation Leadership Network Liaison: MARK A. BENEDICT
Director for American Greenways Program: EDWARD T. McMAHON
Director of Aquaculture Programs: JOSEPH A. HANKINS
Director of Civil War Battlefield Program: FRANCES H. KENNEDY
Director of Conservation Leadership Network: MARK A. BENEDICT
Director of Development: ELIZABETH M. MADISON
Director of Finance: ROBERT J. WYDRA JR.
Director of Florida Office: ELIZABETH B. SHIELDS; Phone: 561-624-4927
Director of Georgia Office: REX BONER; Phone: 770-414-0211
Director of Great Lakes Office: ELIZABETH J. CISAR; Phone: 312-913-9305
Director of Midwest Office: MARGARET A. KOHRING; Phone: 612-521-1237
Director of Montana Office: KIKU A. HANES; Phone: 406-388-9733
Director of Science: ROBERT E. PUTZ
Director of Texas Office: DANIEL McNAMARA JR.; Phone: 512-477-1712
Director of Vermont Office: NANCY BELL; Phone: 802-492-3368
Editor: MIKE McQUEEN
President and CEO: JOHN F. TURNER
Representative of Alaska: BRAD MEIKLEJOHN
Representative of Maryland: JODI R. O'DAY
Representative of Midwest: MARGARET A. KOHRING
Representative of Montana: KIKU H. HANES

Representative of Northwest: MARK ELSBREE
Representative of Vermont: NANCY BELL
Secretary and Director of Administration: PAMELA A. GRAY
Vice President and Director fo Western Regional Office: SYDNEY S. MACY
Vice President and General Counsel: RICHARD L. ERDMANN
Vice President for Real Estate: DAVID M. SUTHERLAND
Vice President for Sustainable Programs: LAWRENCE A. SELZER
Vice President of Western Regional Office: SYDNEY S. MACY
Publication(s): *Common Ground*
Keyword(s): Environmental and Conservation Education, Land Purchase, Land Use Planning, Training, Water Resources

CONSERVATION INTERNATIONAL
2501 M Street NW, Ste 200, Washington, DC 20037
Phone: 202-429-5660; Fax: 202-887-5188; WWW: www.conservation.org
Founded: 1987; Membership: 4,000
Scope: International
Description: Conservation International (CI) is a private nonprofit organization dedicated to the preservation of tropical and temperate ecosystems. CI works in partnership with indigenous peoples and with organizations to sustain biological diversity and the ecological processes that support life on earth. CI has programs in Bolivia, Botswana, Brazil, Colombia, Costa Rica, Ecuador, Ghana, Guatemala, Guyana, Indonesia, Madagascar, Mexico, Papua, New Guinea, Panama, Peru, the Philippines, the Solomon Islands, and Suriname.
Contact(s):
President: RUSSELL MITTERMEIER
Chairman of the Board: PETER SELIGMANN
Vice President for Brazil Program: GUSTAVO FONSECA
Vice President for Communications and Development: KAREN ZIFFER
Vice President for Conservation Biology: JORGEN THOMSEN
Vice President for Conservation Planning and Technical Cooperation: SILVIO OLIVIERI
Vice President for Conservation Policy: IAN BOWLES
Vice President for New Mexico and Central America Programs: JAMES NATIONS
Vice President for the Andean Program: CLAUDIA SOBREVILLA
Keyword(s): Biodiversity, Endangered and Threatened Species, Environmental and Conservation Education, Forests and Forestry, International Conservation

CONSERVATION LAW FOUNDATION, INC. (CLF)
Headquarters, 62 Summer St., Boston, MA 02110
Phone: 617-350-0990; WWW: www.clf.org
Founded: 1966; Membership: 10,000
Scope: National
Description: CLF is a nonprofit, member-supported environmental law organization dedicated to improving resource management, environmental protection, and public health in New England. Work includes: Energy and water conservation, environmental health, transportation planning, water resources protection, land preservation, and marine resources protection.
Contact(s):
President: DOUGLAS I. FOY
Treasurer: GEORGE T. SHAW
Chairman of the Board: CHARLES CABOT JR.
Vice Chairman of the Board: PAULA W. GOLD
Vice Chairman of the Board: JOHN M. TEAL
Publication(s): *Take Back Your Streets (community transportation planning); Power to Spare I&II (energy conservation opportunities in New England); A Silent and Costly Epidemic (costs of childhood lead poisoning); TROUBLED WATERS (report on the environmental health of Casco Bay); Annual Report; Journal: Conservation Matters; Handbod of Local Pesticide Regulations for Massachusetts*
Keyword(s): Air Quality and Pollution, Energy, Environmental Law, Transportation, Water Pollution

CONSERVATION LAW FOUNDATION, INC. (CLF) (Maine Office)
120 Tillson Ave., Rockland, ME 04841
Phone: 207-594-8107
Scope: National

CONSERVATION LAW FOUNDATION, INC. (CLF) (Vermont Office)
21 E. State St., Montpelier, VT 05602
Phone: 802-223-5992
Scope: National

CONSERVATION TECHNOLOGY INFORMATION CENTER
1220 Potter Dr. Rm. 170, West Lafayette, IN 47906-1383
Phone: 765-494-9555; Fax: 765-494-5969
Founded: 1982; Membership: 70 Corporate, 34 Institutional, 7 Government Agencies, 20,000 individuals
Scope: National
Description: Conservation Technology Information Center (CTIC) is a nonprofit information and data transfer center. The national Center promotes environmentally and economically beneficial agricultural decision-making by: producing and circulating information, data, and contacts, coordinating national initiatives, and sponsoring interactive meetings and conferences. The Center is supported by members and participating governmental agencies.
Contact(s):
Chair: PAUL KINDINGER
Executive Director: JOHN HEBBLETHWAITE, 1220 Potter Dr. Rm. 170, West Lafayette, IN 47906-1383; Phone: 765-494-9555; Fax: 795-494-5969; Email: heb@ctic.purdue.edu
Chair, Board of Directors: PAUL KINDINGER, 11701 Boman Dr Ste 110, St. Louis, MO 63146; Phone: 314-567-6655; Fax: 314-567-6808
Natural Resources Specialist: LARISSA STOUFFER; Email: stouffer@ctic.purdue.edu
Office Manager: TAMMY TAYLOR
Past Chair: RAY BROWNFIELD
Project Manager: KAROL KEPPY
Vice Chair: RAY BROWNFIELD, Capital Agircultural Property Services, 801 Warrenville Rd., Ste 150, Lisle, IL 60532; Phone: 630-434-1820
Vice Chair: BRUNO ALESII, Monsonto 800 N. Lindbergh Blvd., C3NH, St. Louis, MO 63167
Vice Chair: BOB DITTMER, Dupont, 11711 N. Meridian St., Ste 210, Carmel, IN 46032
Water Quality Specialist: LYN KIRSHNER; Email: kirschnew@ctic.purdue.edu
Publication(s): *CTIC Partners Newsletter; Conservation Tillage: A Checklist for U.S. Farmers; Watershed Management; Nonpoint Source Water Quality Contacts Directory*
Keyword(s): Conservation Tillage, Precision Farming, Water Quality, Watersheds

CONSERVATION TREATY SUPPORT FUND
3705 Cardiff Rd., Chevy Chase, MD 20815
Phone: 301-654-3150; Fax: 301-652-6390; Email: ctsf@conservationtreaty.org; WWW: www.conservationtreaty.org
Founded: 1986
Scope: International
Description: CTSF provides direct support to major inter-governmental treaties, including CITES (the endangered species treaty), the wetlands and the migratory species treaty, through fund-raising and education.
Contact(s):
President: GEORGE A. FURNESS JR.; Phone: 301-652-6390; Fax: 301-652-6390
Vice President: FREDERICK E. MORRIS; Phone: 703-683-8512; Fax: 703-683-4622
Secretary: FAITH T. CAMPBELL; Phone: 202-861-2242; Fax: 202-861-4622
Treasurer: LAWRENCE N. MASON; Phone: 703-241-8896; Fax: 703-241-8896

NON-GOVERNMENTAL ORGANIZATIONS

Publication(s): *CITES Endangered Species Book; CITES Video (also Wetlands Video); Caribbean Buyer Beware Poster "Wild Treasures of the Caribbean"*
Keyword(s): Biodiversity, Habitat Conservation, International Conservation

CONSERVATION TRUST OF PUERTO RICO
P.O. Box 9023554, 155 Tetuan St., Old San Juan, PR 00902-3554
Phone: 787-722-5834; Email: rafael@fideicomiso.org
Founded: 1970
Scope: Statewide
Description: A private nonprofit institution created by the Governor of Puerto Rico and the U.S. Secretary of the Interior to preserve and enhance Puerto Rico's natural beauty and resources, primarily through land acquisition. Owns or manages over 11,000 acres representative of the island's major endangered habitats. It educates the public about environmental issues; manages a vast reforestation program; and finances conservation in Caribbean countries via debt-for-nature swaps. Puerto Rico's major conservation organization, the Trust acts as land acquisition agent for the Commonwealth Department of Natural Resources.
Contact(s):
Chairman: ANTONIO LUIS FERRE
Executive Director: FRANSISCO JAVIER BLANCO
Assistant Executive Director: JOSI L. BARRETO
Program and Properties Director: ALEXIS MOLINARES

COOK INLET KEEPER
P.O. Box 3269, Homer, AK 99603
Phone: 907-235-4068; Fax: 907-235-4069; Email: keeper@xy2.net; WWW: www.xy2/~keeper
Founded: 1995; Membership: 400
Scope: Statewide
Description: The mission of Cook Inlet Keeper is to protect the Cook Inlet Watershed and the life it sustains. Keeper relies on environmental monitoring, research, education, and advocacy to give citizens the tools they need to protect water quality.
Contact(s):
President: STEVE KOTEFF; Phone: 907-345-8302; Email: koteff@alaska.net
Vice President: DANIEL ZATE; Phone: 907-235-4102; Fax: 907-235-4202; Email: akraven1@aol.com
Secretary: PAMELA K. MILLER; Phone: 907-276-3337; Fax: 907-222-7715; Email: acat@akcf.org
Treasurer: JIM HEMMING; Phone: 907-235-2535; Fax: 907-235-2531
Executive Director: BOB SHAVELSON
Director: BRAD VAN APPEL
Publication(s): *State of the Inlet Report; Cook Inlet Watershed Directory; Cook Inlet GIS Atlas on CD-ROM*
Keyword(s): Environmental Law, Toxic Substances, Water Quality

COOPER ORNITHOLOGICAL SOCIETY
Department of Biology, University of California, Los Angeles, CA 90024-1606
Founded: 1893; Membership: 2,340
Scope: National
Description: Observation and cooperative study of birds; the spread of interest in bird study; the conservation of birds and wildlife in general; the publication of ornithological knowledge.
Contact(s):
President: DR. J. MICHAEL SCOTT, Department of Fish and Wildlife Resources, University of Idaho, Moscow, ID 83844-1141; Phone: 208-885-6960; Email: mscott@uidaho.edu
Secretary: DR. EILEEN KIRSCH, BRD/USGS, Upper Mississippi Science Center, P.O. Box 818, LaCrosse, WI 54602; Phone: 608-783-6451 ext226; Email: eileen_kirsch@usgs.gov
Treasurer: DR. ERICK CAMPBELL, 2114 NE 90th Ave, Vancouver, WA 98664; Phone: 503-952-6382; Email: ecampbel@or.blm.gov
Editor, Studies in Avian Biology: DR. JOHN T. ROTENBERRY, Department of Biology, University of California, Riverside, CA 92521; Phone: 909-787-3953; Email: rote@citrus.ucr.edu
Editor, The Condor: DR. WALTER KOENIG, Hastings Natural History Reservation, 38601 E. Carmel Valley Rd., Carmal Valley, CA 93924; Phone: 408-659-5981; Email: wicker@uclink.berkeley.edu
President-Elect: DR. GLENN E. WALSBERG, Department of Biology, Arizona State University, Tempe, AZ 85287-1501; Phone: 602-965-3543; Email: walsberg@asu.edu
Publication(s): *Condor, The; Studies in Avian Biology*

CORAL REEF ALLIANCE, THE (CORAL)
64 Shattuck Square, Suite 220, Berkeley, CA 94704
Phone: 510-848-0110; Fax: 510-848-3720; Email: coralmail@aol.com; WWW: www.coral.org/
Founded: 1994; Membership: 3,500
Scope: National
Description: The Coral Reef Alliance is a nonprofit organization that works with divers, government conservation organizations, and others to promote coral reef conservation around the the world. CORAL focuses primarily on helping local communities to establish their own marine protected area. CORAL also sponsors a number of educational programs and publications.
Contact(s):
Executive Director: STEPHEN COLWELL
Director of Education: CARLOS WESLEY
Managing Director: SHAWN REIFSTECK
Publication(s): *Coral News; Coral Reefs - The Vanishing Rainbow*
Keyword(s): Coasts, Conservation of Protected Areas, Coral Reefs, International Conservation

CORNELL LAB OF ORNITHOLOGY
159 Sapsucker Woods Rd., Ithaca, NY 14850
Phone: 607-254-2473; Email: www.ornith.cornell.edu
Founded: 1917; Membership: 23,000
Scope: National
Description: A membership institute dedicated to the study, appreciation, and conservation of birds world-wide. The Lab maintains programs in academic research, public education, and citizen involvement. The Lab promotes science to foster understanding about nature and the importance of the earth's biological diversity.
Contact(s):
Associate Director: SCOTT SUTCLIFFE; Phone: 607-254-2424
Associate Editor: LESLIE INTEMANN; Phone: 607-254-2451
Curator of Library of Natural Sounds: GREGORY BUDNEY; Phone: 607-254-2406
Curatorial Associate for Systematics and Collections: KEVIN McGOWAN; Phone: 607-257-8135
Director of Bioacoustics Research Program: CHRISTOPHER CLARK; Phone: 607-254-2405
Director of Bird Population Studies: ANDRE DHONDT; Phone: 607-254-2445
Director of Education Program: RICK BONNEY; Phone: 607-254-2440; Email: birdeducation@cornell.edu
Editor: TIM GALLAGHER; Phone: 607-254-2443
Louis Agassiz Fuertes Director: JOHN FITZPATRICK; Phone: 607-254-2410
Publication(s): *Living Bird; Birdscope; Bird Notes*
Keyword(s): Biodiversity, Birds, Environmental and Conservation Education, Natural History, Nongame Wildlife

COUNCIL FOR ENVIRONMENTAL EDUCATION
c/o Josetta Hawthorne, Executive Director, 5555 Morningside, Suite 212, Houston, TX 77005
Phone: 713-520-1936
Founded: 1970
Scope: National
Description: The Council for Environmental Education is a nonprofit educational organization founded in a unique effort to create a partnership and network between education and natural resource professionals. The specific and primary purpose of the Council is to

support environmental education programs, to publish and disseminate environmental education materials, and to facilitate the development and maintenance of partnerships for environmental education. The Council for Environmental Education co-sponsors Project WILD, Project Learning Tree, and Project WET (Water Education for Teachers), and administers Project WILD nationally.
Contact(s):
President: JIM WILSON, Missouri Dept. of Conservation, P.O. Box 180, Jefferson City, MO 65102
Executive Director: JOSETTA HAWTHORNE
Director of Project Learning Tree: KATHY McGLAUFLIN, 1250 Connecticut Ave. NW, Suite 320, Washington, DC 20036; Phone: 202-463-2455
Director of Project WILD: DONNA ASBURY, 707 Conservation Ln., Suite 305, Gaithersburg, MD 20878
Past President: ARVA JACKSON, Chair of EPA Environmetal Education Advisory Council, 11629 Regency Dr., Potomac, MD 20854
Keyword(s): Environmental and Conservation Education

COUNCIL FOR PLANNING AND CONSERVATION
Box 228, Beverly Hills, CA 90213
Phone: 310-276-2685; Email: esharris@earthlink.net
Scope: Statewide
Description: Serves as a clearinghouse for information and gives inexperienced groups ready access to advice and assistance. Provides a center through which opportunities for southern California's environmental protection and enhancement may be communicated.
Contact(s):
Vice President: BETTY H. HARRIS
President and Executive Director: ELLEN STERN HARRIS
Treasurer and Secretary: SAM WEISZ

COUSTEAU SOCIETY, INC., THE
Headquarters, 870 Greenbrier Cir., Suite 402, Chesapeake, VA 23320
Phone: 800-441-4395; Fax: 727-523-2747; Email: cousteau@infi.net; WWW: www.cousteau.org; dolphinlog.org
Founded: 1973; Membership: 200,000
Scope: National
Description: A nonprofit, membership-supported environmental education organization dedicated to environmental protection and the need to ensure ecological sustainability for present and future generations. Believing that an informed and alerted public can best make the choices that will promote global stability, it produces television films, research, lectures, books, and other publications.
Contact(s):
Vice President: FRANCINE COUSTEAU
Editor: ISABELLE ERARD
Vice President of Finance: ROBERT L. STEELE
Publication(s): *Calypso Log; Dolphin Log*
Keyword(s): Environmental and Conservation Education, Population Growth, Sustainable Development, Sustainable Ecosystems, Water Resources

COUSTEAU SOCIETY, INC., THE (France Office)
7 Rue de l'Amiral d'Estaing, Paris, Paris 75116 France
Phone: 1-53-67-77-77
Scope: National

COUSTEAU SOCIETY, INC., THE (New York Office)
777 United Nations Plaza, New York, NY 10017
Phone: 212-949-6290
Scope: National

CRAIGHEAD ENVIRONMENTAL RESEARCH INSTITUTE
Box 156, Moose, WY 83012
Phone: 307-733-3387
Founded: 1955
Scope: National
Description: A nonprofit professional organization of scientists, dedicated to exploring the cause-and-effect relationships of man and his environment. Activity includes research, education, and conservation, with emphasis on ecological studies and interdisciplinary approach. Originally the Outdoor Recreation Institute. Staff Members: 6.
Contact(s):
President: FRANK C. CRAIGHEAD JR.
Media Director: CHARLES S. CRAIGHEAD; Phone: 307-739-9527
Program Director: FRANK L. CRAIGHEAD
Keyword(s): Raptors, Rivers, Wildlife and Wildlife Habitat

CRAIGHEAD WILDLIFE-WILDLANDS INSTITUTE
5200 Upper Miller Creek Rd., Missoula, MT 59803
Phone: 406-251-3867; Fax: 406-251-5069; Email: cwwi@mssl.uswest.net
Founded: 1977
Scope: National
Description: A nonprofit, multidisciplinary research center in the Northern Rockies devoted to field-based ecological discovery and scientific activism. The Institute's mission is to generate new ecological information and concepts, widely communicate these insights, and influence public policy and individual behavior in directions that preserve regional biodiversity.
Contact(s):
President: DEREK J. CRAIGHEAD, P.O. Box 160, Kelly, WY 83011; Phone: 307-734-8862
Chairman of the Board: DR. JOHN J. CRAIGHEAD, 5125 Orchard Ln., Missoula, MT 59803; Phone: 406-251-3944
Director of Development and Finance: WILLIAM T. ZADER, 20002 King Rd., Florence, MT 59833; Phone: 406-273-2475
Director of Science: DR. JOHN T. HOGG, 194 McCalla Creek Dr., Stevensville, MT 59870; Phone: 406-642-3035
Publication(s): *The Grizzly Bears of Yellowstone, Their Ecology in the Yellowstone Ecosystem (1959, 1992, 1995); An Integrated Satellite Technique to Evaluate Grizzly Bear Habitat Use (1997); Mapping Arctic Vegetation in Northwest Alaska Using Landsat MSS Imagery (1998); Bia Newsletter*
Keyword(s): Biodiversity, Ecology, Endangered and Threatened Species, Research, Sustainable Ecosystems

CRESTON VALLEY WILDLIFE MANAGEMENT AUTHORITY
P.O. Box 640, Creston, British Columbia V0B 1G0 Canada
Phone: 250-428-3260
Founded: 1968
Scope: Statewide
Description: A unique joint provincial-private agency established in 1968 to conserve, develop, and manage remaining waterfowl habitat in a mountain valley. Broader purpose is to demonstrate cooperative wetland management in action. Operates a 17,000-acre wetland and upland complex, primarily as a waterfowl management area, with public recreation facilities (campground, trails, and visotr centre).
Contact(s):
Area Manager: BRIAN G. STUSHNOFF; Phone: 250-428-3260
Chairman of the Management Authority: STEVE BULLOCK; Phone: 250-428-2214
Publication(s): *Creston Valley Wildlife Management Area Annual*

NON-GOVERNMENTAL ORGANIZATIONS

DAWES ARBORETUM, THE
7770 Jacksontown Rd., SE, Newark, OH 43056-9380
Phone: 740-323-2355 / 1-800-44-DAWES; WWW: www.dawesarb.org
Founded: 1929
Scope: Statewide
Description: A not-for-profit organization that promotes the planting of forest and ornamental trees, and promotes increased love and knowledge of trees, shrubs, and related subjects through over 200 annually-offered classes and programs. The 1,149-acre grounds are open daily from dawn to dusk, free of charge.
Contact(s):
Director: DONALD R. HENDRICKS
Editor: LUKE E. MESSINGER
Horticulturist: MICHAEL E. ECKER
Natural Resource Specialist: TIMOTHY A. MASON
Naturalist and Educator: LORI A. TOTMAN
Researcher: ELAINE G. HENDRICKS
Publication(s): *Dawes Arboretum Newsletter, The*

DEEP-PORTAGE CONSERVATION RESERVE
Rt. 1 Box 129, Hackensack, MN 56452
Phone: 218-682-2325; Fax: 218-682-3121; WWW: www.deep-portage.org
Founded: 1975
Scope: Statewide
Description: Deep-Portage is a 6,100-acre demonstration working forest with a primary purpose of environmental education. The campus includes dormitories, classrooms, laboratory, theater, interpretive center, natural history museum, and thirty-seven miles of recreational trails. It is owned by Cass County and operated by the Deep-Portage Conservation Foundation, a nonprofit corporation.
Contact(s):
Executive Director: DALE YERGER
Foundation President: CLARENCE WESTIN
Publication(s): *Deep-Portage Log*
Keyword(s): Environmental and Conservation Education, Forests and Forestry, Internships, Water Resources, Wildlife and Wildlife Habitat

DEFENDERS OF WILDLIFE
1101 14th St., NW, Suite 1400, Washington, DC 20005
Phone: 202-682-9400; Fax: 202-682-1331; Email: information@defenders.org; WWW: www.defenders.org
Founded: 1947; Membership: 250,000
Scope: National
Description: Since 1947, Defenders of Wildlife has been one of the nation's most effective advocates for wildlife, endangered species, and habitat. Defenders works to protect and restore native species, habitats, ecosystems, and overall biological diversity. Defenders is a nonprofit, tax-exempt organization, supported by 250,000 members and activists across the country.
Contact(s):
President: RODGER SCHLICKEISEN
Secretary: ANN F. BOREN
Treasurer: ARTHUR C. MARTINEZ
Chairman of the Board: ALAN R. PILKINGTON
Director of Development: MARTHA SCHUMACHER
Director of Habitat Conservation Division: ROBERT DEWEY
Director of Legal Division: WILLIAM J. SNAPE III
Director of Media Relations: JOAN MOODY
Director of Membership: KATE MATHEWS
Director of Science Division: LAURA HOOD
Director of Species Conservation Division: ROBERT M. FERRIS
Director of West Coast: SARA VICKERMAN, 1637 Laurel St., Lake Oswego, OR 97034; Phone: 503-697-3222
Editor: HEIDI RIDGLEY
Editor: JAMES G. DEANE
Editor: MARIA W. CECIL
Regional Representative of Alaska: JOEL BENNETT, 15255 Point Louisa Rd., Juneau, AK 99801; Phone: 907-586-1255
Regional Representative of Arizona: CRAIG MILLER, 6020 S. Camino de la Tierra, Tucson, AZ 85746; Phone: 520-578-9334
Regional Representative of Florida: CHRISTINE SMALL, 31409 Prestwick Ave., Sorrento, FL 32776; Phone: 352-735-6909
Regional Representative of Florida: LAURIE MacDONALD, 103 Wildwood Ln., St. Petersburg, FL 33705; Phone: 813-821-9585
Regional Representative of New Mexico: SUSAN GEORGE, P.O. Box 40046, Albuquerque, NM 87196-0046; Phone: 505-255-5966
Regional Representative of New York: STEVE KENDROT, P.O. Box B2598, Plattsburgh, NY 12901; Phone: 518-563-9307
Regional Representative of Northern Rockies: HANK FISCHER, 1534 Mansfield Ave., Missoula, MT 59801; Phone: 406-549-0761
Regional Representative of Washington: GERRY RING ERICKSON, 2324 NE 103rd St., Seattle, WA 98125-7642; Phone: 206-522-5139/360-427-2887
Vice Chairman: WINSOME McINTOSH
Vice President for Communications: JAMES G. DEANE
Vice President for Operations: CHARLES J. ORASIN
Vice President for Program: MARK SHAFFER
Viewing Guide Program Manager: KATE DAVIES
Publication(s): *DEFENDERS*
Keyword(s): Biodiversity, Endangered and Threatened Species, Environment, Environmental and Conservation Education, Environmental Preservation, Environmental Protection, Nature Preservation, Predators, Wilderness, Wildlife and Wildlife Habitat, Wolves

DELAWARE ASSOCIATION OF CONSERVATION DISTRICTS
ATTN: President, 2138 Graves Rd., Hockessin, DE 19707
Founded: 1953
Scope: Statewide
Description: DACD is a voluntary nonprofit alliance that provides a forum for discussion and coordination among the Delaware Conservation Districts as they work to ensure the wise use and treatment of renewable resources.
Contact(s):
President and Board Member: DARIEL RAKESTRAW, 2138 Graves Rd., Hockessin, DE 19707; Phone: 302-239-2969
1st Vice President, Alternate Board Member: TERRY PEPPER, 104 Captain Davis Dr., Campden-Wyoming, DE 19934; Phone: 302-697-6176; Fax: 303-736-2040; Email: kentcol@aol.com
2nd Vice President: GREG MCCABE, Rd. Box 120A, Selbyville, DE 19975; Phone: 302-436-2171; Fax: 302-436-5597
Staff Assistant: SHIRLEY BOWDEN, P.O. Box 242, Dover, DE 19903-0242; Phone: 302-739-4411; Fax: 302-739-6724; Email: ShirleyW.Bowden@Soil@DNREC
Keyword(s): Agriculture, Land Use Planning, Soil Conservation, Urban Environment, Water Pollution Management

DELAWARE AUDUBON SOCIETY
P.O. Box 1713, Wilmington, DE 19899
Phone: 302-428-3959
Membership: 900
Scope: Statewide
Description: The Delaware Audubon Society is dedicated to the appreciation and wise use of our natural resources and natural beauties.
Contact(s):
Contact: ANN RYDGREN, 2705 Kenneth Ln., Wilmington, DE 19803

DELAWARE B.A.S.S. CHAPTER FEDERATION
ATTN: President, 3700 South State St., Camden, DE 19934
Phone: 302-698-9257
Scope: Statewide
Description: An organization of Bassmaster chapters, affiliated with the Bass Anglers Sportsman Society, organized to fight pollution, assist state and national conservation agencies in their efforts, and teach the young people of our country good conservation practices. Dedicated to the realistic conservation of our water resources.

Contact(s):
President: JIM FIELDS, 3700 South State St., Camden, DE 19934; Phone: 302-698-9257
Conservation Director: BUD FAIRCLOTH, 327 Beechwood Ave., Dover, DE 19901; Phone: 302-335-1725; Email: budfair@aol.com

DELAWARE FORESTRY ASSOCIATION
2320 S. DuPont Hwy., Dover, DE 19901
Phone: 302-739-4811
Founded: 1982; Membership: 315
Scope: Statewide
Description: A statewide organization affiliated with the National Woodland Owners Association, dedicated to promote good forest practices and multiple use of private forest lands in Delaware.
Contact(s):
President: W. ALLEN; Phone: 410-742-3163
Vice President: JIM BENNETT
Editor: W. ALLEN JONES; Phone: 410-546-9696
Publication(s): *DFA Newsletter*
Keyword(s): Forests and Forestry

DELAWARE GREENWAYS, INC.
P.O. Box 2095, Wilmington, DE 19899
Phone: 302-655-7275
Founded: 1989; Membership: 500
Scope: Statewide
Description: Preserve, enhance, and connect the ecological, scenic, historical, cultural, and recreational resources in Delaware.
Contact(s):
Executive Director: GAIL L. VAN GILDER
Keyword(s): Cultural Preservation, Environmental Preservation, Historic Preservation, Sustainable Development, Transportation

DELAWARE MUSEUM OF NATURAL HISTORY
P.O. Box 3937, Wilmington, DE 19807
Phone: 302-658-9111; Fax: 302-658-2610; WWW: www.delmnh.org
Founded: 1957; Membership: 630
Scope: Statewide
Description: To use all of the sciences to increase awareness and understanding of life on earth, past, present, and future. The major focuses of the museum will be continued leadership in research and collections in malacology and ornithology, and the ecology of the Delmarva Peninsula.
Contact(s):
Director: GEOFF HALFPENNY
Editor and Public Relations: LINDA GOULD
Librarian and Malacology: DR. TIM PEARCE
Librarian and Ornithology: GENE K. HESS
Publication(s): *Nemouria; Musenews*
Keyword(s): Birds, Natural History, Research

DELAWARE NATURE SOCIETY
P.O. Box 700, Hockessin, DE 19707
Phone: 302-239-2334; Fax: 302-239-2473; Email: Ashland@DCA.net; WWW: www.dca.net/naturesociety
Founded: 1964; Membership: 8,000
Scope: Statewide
Description: A representative statewide organization, affiliated with the National Wildlife Federation, dedicated to the protection and enhancement of wildlife and its habitat through public education and government interaction.
Contact(s):
President: PETER H. FLINT
Executive Director: MIKE RISKA
Affiliate Representative: BERNARD S. DEMPSEY
Alternate Representative: JUNE MacARTOR
Editor: JANICE TAYLOR
Publication(s): *Birds of Delaware; Butterflies of Delmarva*

Keyword(s): Air Quality and Pollution, Endangered and Threatened Species, Environmental and Conservation Education, Natural Areas, Wetlands

DELAWARE WILD LANDS, INC.
315 Main St., P.O. Box 505, Odessa, DE 19730-0505
Phone: 302-378-2736
Founded: 1961
Scope: Statewide
Description: A nonprofit charitable land conservancy actively engaged in acquiring areas on the Delmarva Peninsula for their natural resource values and for educational purposes; presently owns and manages approximately 20,000 acres. Produced two films, "The Endangered Shore" and "Swamp," now available on loan or for purchase.
Contact(s):
President: CHARLES F. GUMMEY JR.
Vice President: MRS. WILLIAM PRICKETT
Secretary: BLAINE T. PHILLIPS
Treasurer: ROBERT L. EDGELL
Executive Director: HOLGER H. HARVEY

DELMARVA ORNITHOLOGICAL SOCIETY
P.O. Box 4247, Greenville, DE 19807
Founded: 1963; Membership: 320
Scope: Statewide
Description: The purpose of this society shall be the promotion of the study of birds, the advancement and diffusion of ornithological knowledge, and the conservation of birds and their environment.
Contact(s):
President: JOHN P. JANOWSKI, 122 Pine Valley Dr., Middletown, DE 19709; Phone: 302-834-9710
Vice President: JIM WHITE, 3507 Barley Mill Rd., Hockessin, DE 19707; Phone: 302-239-7065
Editor: GENE K. HESS, P.O. Box 3937, Greenville, DE 19807; Phone: 302-378-9357
Editor: KAREN ZEITLER, 1307 Quincy Dr., Green Acres, Wilmington, DE 19803; Phone: 302-478-9173
Publication(s): *Delmarva Ornithologist; DOS Flyer*

DELTA WATERFOWL FOUNDATION
R.R. 1 Box 1, Portage la Prairie, Manitoba R1N 3A1 Canada
Phone: 204-239-1900
Scope: National
Description: Delta Waterfowl's primary mission is to support graduate student training and research on all aspects of waterfowl and wetlands ecology and management. Since 1938, Delta students have produced over 200 graduate theses and 600 scientific publications. In addition to graduate research, Delta is currently involved in several demonstration projects incuding Adopt-A-Pothole, a habitat easement program; Hen Houses, predator-resistant nesting structures, Voluntary Restraint, a hunter ethics program; and several policy initiatives.
Contact(s):
President: WILLIAM B. WEBSTER III
Vice President: STEPHEN D. BUSCH
Secretary: DONALD J. DOUGLAS
Treasurer: DANIEL C. HUGHES JR.
Executive Vice President: JONATHAN SCARTH
Keyword(s): Communications, Environmental and Conservation Education, International Conservation, Waterfowl, Wetlands

DELTA WILDLIFE FOUNDATION
P.O. Box 276, Stoneville, MS 38776
Phone: 601-686-4062; Fax: 601-686-4780
Founded: 1990; Membership: 2,000
Scope: Regional
Description: The Delta Wildlife Foundation will improve the quality of life in the Mississippi Delta by restoring and enhancing the region's wildlife resources. This will be accomplished by approaching the challenge from the standpoint of image, economics,

stewardship, and by involving all people concerned in a positive manner, with specific projects.

Contact(s):
President: JAMES L. CUMMINS JR., Leland, MS ; Phone: 601-686-3370; Fax: 601-686-4780
Vice President: JOHN SHARP HOWIE, Rt. 1, Benton, MS 39039; Phone: 601-746-5184
Treasurer: PEYTON SELF, 701 Peyton Cir., Marks, MS 38646; Phone: 601-326-2841
Director: J. TOL THOMAS, Egypt Planting Co., Rt. 1 Box 55, Cruger, MS 38924; Phone: 601-453-5761
Director: W. A. PERCY II, P.O. Box 189, Arcola, MS 38722; Phone: 601-827-2258
Director: HOWARD MILLER, 1709 Clay St., Vicksburg, MS 39180; Phone: 601-636-7551
Director: W. W. GRESHAM JR., P.O. Box 690, Indianola, MS 38751; Phone: 601-887-2160
Director: R.B. FLOWERS, P.O. Box 38, Tunica, MS 38676; Phone: 601-363-1121
Director: ROBROY FISHER, Rt. 1 Box 200, Glen Allan, MS 38744; Phone: 601-839-2641
Director: JAMES R. CARTER, P.O. Box 458, Rolling Fork, MS 39159; Phone: 601-873-4054

Publication(s): *Delta Wildlife Magazine*
Keyword(s): Agriculture, Communications, Environmental and Conservation Education, Wetlands, Wildlife and Wildlife Habitat

DESERT FISHES COUNCIL
P.O. Box 337, Bishop, CA 93514
Phone: 760-872-8751

Founded: 1969; Membership: 300
Scope: National

Description: A nationwide and international representation of state, federal, and university scientists and resource specialists and private conservation groups to provide for the exchange and transmittal of information on the status, protection, and management of the endemic fauna and flora of North American desert ecosystems.

Contact(s):
Executive Secretary: EDWIN P. PISTER, Desert Fishes Council, P.O. Box 337, Bishop, CA 93515; Phone: 760-872-8751; Email: phildesfish@telis.org
Chairman and Editor: GARY GARRETT, TX Parks and Wildlife, HC 7, Box 62, Ingram, TX 78025; Phone: 830-866-3356; Email: gpg@ktc.com

Publication(s): *Proceedings of the Desert Fishes Council*
Keyword(s): Aquatic Habitats, Conservation of Protected Areas, Deserts, Endangered and Threatened Species, Fisheries, Natural Areas, Sustainable Development, Water Resources, Zoology

DESERT TORTOISE COUNCIL
P.O. Box 1738, Palm Desert, CA 92261
Phone: 619-431-8449

Founded: 1975
Scope: National

Description: Formed to assure the continued survival of viable populations of the desert tortoise, Gopherus agassizi, which is endemic to Arizona, California, Nevada, and Utah.

Contact(s):
Secretary: ED LaRUE
Treasurer: MARE SAZAKI
Co-Chairman: KATHERINE ZODER
Co-Chairman: DANIEL PATTERSEN
Recording Secretary: ED LaRUE

Keyword(s): Biology, Conservation of Protected Areas, Deserts, Endangered and Threatened Species, Environment, Environmental Protection, Health and Nutrition, Land Preservation, Land Use Planning, Mining, Nature Preservation, Public Lands, Reptiles and Amphibians, Wildlife and Wildlife Habitat

DESERT TORTOISE PRESERVE COMMITTEE, INC.
P.O. Box 2910, San Bernardino, CA 92406

Founded: 1974
Scope: Regional

Description: A nonprofit organization formed to promote the welfare of the desert tortoise in the southwestern United States and to establish a preserve as a natural area in a portion of the Western Mojave Desert known to be ideal habitat.

Contact(s):
President: BOB BROOKS, 13711 East Gaylin St., Whittier, CA 90601
Corrsponding Secretary: JAMES ANDERSON, P.O. Box 2910, San Bernardino, CA 92406; Phone: 909-683-3872
Editor and Treasurer: KRISTIN BEARY, P.O. Box 2910, San Bernardino, CA 92406

Publication(s): *Newsletter; Tortoise T-R-A-C-K-S*
Keyword(s): Endangered and Threatened Species, Land Purchase, Nongame Wildlife, Wildlife and Wildlife Habitat, Wildlife Management

DISTRICT OF COLUMBIA SOIL AND WATER CONSERVATION DISTRICT
ATTN: Chair, 800 9th St. SW 3rd Fl., Washington, DC 20024

Scope: Statewide

Contact(s):
Chair: THEODORE GORDON, 800 9th St. SW 3rd Fl., Washington, DC 20024; Phone: 202-645-5556; Fax: 202-645-0526
Acting District Manager: ALEXANDER OKECHUKWU, 2100 Martin Luther King Jr. Ave. SE Suite 203, Washington, DC 20020; Phone: 202-645-6059, ext. 3060; Fax: 202-645-6063

DOGTOOTH GROUP
Waterloo-Wellington Chapter, Botany Department, University of Guelph, Guelph, Ontario N1G 2W1 Canada
Phone: 519-824-4120 ext 2730; Fax: 519-767-1991; WWW: www.vogvelph.ca/~mursic/dogtooth.htm

Founded: 1990; Membership: 65
Scope: National

Description: The Dogtooth Group is a non-profit organization based in Guelph, Ontario dedicated to the use and protection of native plants in parks, gardens and other open spaces.

Contact(s):
President: MARGOT URSIC, 296 Suffolk st. West, Guelph, Ontario N1H 2K3 Canada; Phone: 519-763-8101; Email: mKronick@uoguelph.ca
Vice President and Treasurer: CAROLE ANN LACROIX; Phone: 519-824-3807

Publication(s): *Dogtooth Group Newsletter*
Keyword(s): Environmental and Conservation Education, Flowers, Plants, and Trees, Nature Preservation

DRAGONFLY SOCIETY OF THE AMERICAS, THE
2091 Partridge Ln., Binghamton, NY 13903
Phone: 607-722-4939

Founded: 1989; Membership: 200
Scope: National

Description: The organization is concerned with all factors relevant to the world species assemblage of odonata (Insecta: Dragonflies). We study their systematics, biology, and taxonomy. The organization is also concerned with maintaining and improving the environmental conditions for Odonata through better water quality management, wetlands conservation, and aquatic habitat preservation.

Contact(s):
President: R.W. GARRISON, 1030 Fondale, Aqusa, CA 91702-0821
Secretary: S.W. DUNKLE, Biology Department, Collin Co. Community College, Plano, TX 75074
Treasurer: J.J. DAIGLE, 2166 Kimberly Ln., Tallahassee, FL 32301
Editor: T.W. DONNELLY, 2091 Partridge Lane, Binghamton, NY 13903

Publication(s): *ARGIA; Bulletin of American Odonatology*

Keyword(s): Aquatic Habitats, Environmental Preservation, Insects and Butterflies, Rivers, Wetlands

DUCKS UNLIMITED (Alberta, Canada)
#202, 10470 - 176 St., Edmonton, Alberta T5S 1L3 Canada
Phone: 403-489-2002; Fax: 403-489-1856
Scope: Statewide
Contact(s):
Alberta NAWMP Coordinator: BRETT CALVERLEY
Conserevation Programs Biologist: GARY STEWART
Conservation Programs Biologist: LES WETTER
Pacific Regional Director: JIM WOHL
Pacific Regional Director: GORDON EDWARDS
Publication(s): *Conservator*

DUCKS UNLIMITED (Manitoba, Canada)
Box 1160, Stonewall, Manitoba R0C 2Z0 Canada
Phone: 204-467-9028
Founded: 1938
Scope: Statewide
Description: Ducks Unlimited Canada's mission is to conserve wetlands and associated habitats for the benefit of North America's waterfowl, which in turn provide healthy environments for wildlife and people.
Contact(s):
President: GEORGE C. REIFEL, Reifel Cooke Group, 440-1055 West Hasings St., Vancouver, British Columbia V6E 2E9 Canada; Phone: 604-688-1055
Vice President: G. TOD WRIGHT, Suite 500 - 1 King St. W., Hamilton, Ontario L8P 1A4 Canada
Vice President: JAMES RICHARDSON, Richardson Oil and Gas Limited, 30th Fl., Richardson Bldg., One Lombard Pl., Winnipeg, Manitoba R3B 0Y1 Canada; Phone: 204-934-5860
Secretary: ROLAND E. RIVALIN, Tupper and Adams, 4th Fl., 200 Portage Ave., Winnipeg, Manitoba R3C 3X2 Canada; Phone: 204-942-0161
Secretary: ROLAND E. RIVALIN, Tupper and Adams, 4th Fl., 200 Portage Ave., Winnipeg, Manitoba R3C 3X2 Canada; Phone: 204-942-0161
Treasurer: H. LeBOURVEAU, 2921 - 10th St., SW, Calgary, Alberta T2T 3H4 Canada
Treasurer: H. LEBOURVEAU, 2921 - 10th St., SW, Calgary, Alberta T2T 3H4 Canada
Assistant Director of Institute for Wetlands and Waterfowl Research: DR. M. G. ANDERSON
Chairman of the Board: WILLIAM G. TURNBULL, Ste 320, 447-5th Ave., Calgary, Alberta T2P 2V1 Canada; Phone: 403-233-0333
Chairman of the Board: WILLIAM G. TURNBULL, Suite 320, 441-5th Ave. S.W., Calgary, Alberta T2P 2V1 Canada; Phone: 403-233-0333
Chief Biologist: DR. T. G. NERAASEN
Chief Chief Engineer: R. W. COLEY
Chief Engineer: R. W. COLEY
Chief Financial Officer: L. J. WARREN
Communications Manager: ROBERT KINDRACHUK
Communications Manager: GARY GOODWIN
Corporate Counsel: GARY GOODWIN
Executive Vice President: DON A. YOUNG
Executive Vice President: DON A. YOUNG
Institute for Wetlands and Waterfoul Research, Assistant Director: DR. BRIAN T. GRAY
Manager of Conservation: R. B. FOWLER
Manager of Finance and Administration: L. J. WARREN
Manager of Habitat Programs: R. B. FOWLER
Manager of Membership Services, Development, and Education: DR. RICK WISHART
Manager, Education Programs: DR. RICK WISHART
National Director of Fundraising, Marketing and Membership: RICHARD L.H. WALKER

DUCKS UNLIMITED (Nova Scotia, Canada)
9 Havelock St., Amherst, Nova Scotia B4H 3Z5 Canada
Phone: 902-667-8726; Fax: 902-667-0916
Scope: Statewide
Contact(s):
Provincial Biologist: KEITH McALONEY
Provincial Engineer: BRIAN ROYAL
Provincial Manager: ALLAN GLOVER

DUCKS UNLIMITED (Ontario, Canada)
566 Welham Rd., Barrie, Ontario L4N 8Z7 Canada
Phone: 705-721-4444; Fax: 705-721-4999; Email: du_barrier@ducks.ca
Scope: Statewide
Contact(s):
Director of Regional Operation: TED GADAWSKI
Manager Eastern Ontario Field Office: RON MAHER
Manager Western Ontario Field Office: BOB CLAY

DUCKS UNLIMITED (Quebec, Canada)
Suite 260, 710 Bouvier St., Quebec City, Quebec G2J 1C2 Canada
Phone: 418-623-1650
Founded: 1937; Membership: 140,000
Scope: Statewide
Description: Ducks Unlimited is an international, private, nonprofit conservation organization dedicated to the perpetuation and increase of North American's waterfowl resources through restoration, preservation, and creation of prime breeding habitat in Canada. Development of this habitat on a multiuse concept benefits wildlife and the general environment and provides water for agriculture, domestic, and recreational use.
Contact(s):
Director of Regional Operations: PATRICK PLANTE
Manager of Field Operations: BERNARD FILION
Publication(s): *Ducks Unlimited; Conservator; Conservationniste*

DUCKS UNLIMITED (Saskatchewan Operation, Canada)
P.O. Box 4465, 1606-4th Ave., Regina, Saskatchewan S4P 3W7 Canada
Phone: 306-569-0424; Fax: 306-565-3699
Founded: 1938
Scope: Statewide
Description: A private, nonprofit, conservation organization dedicated to preserving waterfowl by creating and restoring breeding habitat in Canada. This organization is funded by sportsmen of United States and Canada.
Contact(s):
Agricultural Program Specialist: L. R. MOATS
Director of Public Policy: D. A. CHEKAY
Manager of field Operations: TIM THIELE
Publication(s): *Newsletter*

DUCKS UNLIMITED, INC.
Headquarters, One Waterfowl Way, Memphis, TN 38120
Phone: 901-758-3825; Fax: 901-758-3850
Founded: 1937; Membership: 600,000
Scope: National
Description: The mission of Ducks Unlimited is to fulfill the annual life cycle needs of North American waterfowl by protecting, enhancing, restoring, and managing important wetlands and associated uplands. Only those activities which contribute directly toward that end shall be undertaken by Ducks Unlimited, Inc.
Contact(s):
President: JULIUS F. WALL, P.O. Box 226, Clinton, MD 64735; Phone: 660-885-2221
Secretary: MICHAEL J. BROOKS, One Branch Place 181-4, St. Louis, MO 63118; Phone: 314-577-7717
Executive Secretary: BILL R. WILLSEY, One Waterfowl Way, Memphis, TN 38120; Phone: 901-758-3825
1st Vice President and Treasurer: W. BRUCE LEWIS, P.O. Box 1344, Natchez, MS 39180; Phone: 601-446-6621

NON-GOVERNMENTAL ORGANIZATIONS

Chairman of the Board: GENE M. HENRY, P.O. Box 35, McFarland, WI 53558; Phone: 608-838-3188
Chief Biologist: DR. BRUCE BATT
Chief Financial Officer: RANDY L. GRAVES
Conatct for Minnesota: BILL ALLEN, R.R. #2 Box 148, Wabasha, MN 55981; Phone: 651-565-2369
Contact for Alabama: DOUGLAS N. LASHER, 209 Willow Bend, Wetumpka, AL 36093; Phone: 334-514-0561; Fax: 334-514-0562
Contact for Alaska: JAMES KING, P.O. Box 4073, 1870 N. Kentucky Derby Dr., Palmer, AK 99645; Phone: 907-745-3946; Fax: 907-745-3947
Contact for Arizona: MIKE SHIRE, 5938 E. Corrine Dr., Scottsdale, AZ 85254; Phone: 602-483-6186; Fax: 602-483-92551
Contact for Arkansas: STEVEN W. FRICK, 618 E. Parkway Dr., Russellville, AR 72801; Phone: 501-968-5801; Fax: 501-968-5514
Contact for California: PAUL WOODBURY, 3074 Gold Canal Dr., Rancho Cordova, CA 95670-6116; Phone: 916-852-2000; Fax: 916-852-2200
Contact for Colorado: DR. JOHN L. SCHMIDT, 9887B Grove St., Westminster, CO 80030; Phone: 303-465-3628; Fax: 303-465-3638
Contact for Connecticut: CRAIG FERRIS, 75 Glenn Rd., Suite 108, Sandy Hook, CT 06482; Phone: 203-426-2466; Fax: 203-426-2733
Contact for Delaware: JOSEPH F. ROWAN, 204 Friendship Dr., Centreville, MD 21617; Phone: 410-758-3145; Fax: 410-758-3998
Contact for Florida: DOUG WILLIAMS, 1862 Jefferson Rd., Tallahassee, FL 32311; Phone: 850-656-0053; Fax: 850-656-1313
Contact for Georgia: DAN DENTON, P.O. Box 870131, Mountain Park Branch, Stone Mountain, GA 30087; Phone: 770-985-5922; Fax: 770-985-4065
Contact for Hawii: BOB MAZGAJ, 4186 Brooks Rd., Valley Springs, CA 95252; Phone: 209-772-1966; Fax: 209-772-1883
Contact for Idaho: STEVE HALL, 6613 Wright Lane, Nampa, ID 83686; Phone: 208-463-9900; Fax: 208-463-9944
Contact for Illinios: GARY ERICKSON, 31764 North Harris Rd., Libertyville, IL 60048; Phone: 660-223-9426; Fax: 660-223-3437
Contact for Indiana: BRUCE MARHEINE, 2761 E. County Rd., 350 N., Sullivan, IN 47882; Phone: 812-397-2740; Fax: 812-397-5156
Contact for Iowa: ROCK BRIDGES, P.O. Box 223 (UPS-225 W. Main, Lower Level), Lake Mills, IA 50450; Phone: 515-397-5156; Fax: 515-592-3602
Contact for Kansas: RICHARD E. BURCH, P.O. Box 259, 116 Meadow Lane Ave., Buhler, KS 67522; Phone: 316-543-6806; Fax: 316-543-2327
Contact for Kentucky: BEN R. BURNLEY, 6887 Corydon Rd., Henderson, KY 42420; Phone: 502-826-9507; Fax: 502-826-5949
Contact for Louisiana: EARL D. NORWOOD JR., 1009 Frazier Rd., P.O. Box 578, Ruston, LA 71270; Phone: 318-265-6768; Fax: 318-255-2844
Contact for Maine: ERIC GOODENOUGH, HCR 72 Box 3800, Ossipee Hill Rd., E. Waterboro, ME 04030; Phone: 207-247-8448; Fax: 207-247-8333
Contact for Maryland: CHIP HEAPS, 136 Goucher Way, Churchville, MD 21028-1218; Phone: 410-399-4093; Fax: 410-734-6247
Contact for Massachusetts: PHILIP D. WARREN, Hill Rd., P.O. Box 488, Alstead, NH 03602; Phone: 603-835-2490; Fax: 603-835-6243
Contact for Michigan: FRED K. KNIGHT, 12473 Tuscola Rd., Clio, MI 48420; Phone: 810-686-5939; Fax: 810-686-9786
Contact for Mississippi: BILLY JOE CROSS, 193 Business Park, Suite L, Ridgeland, MS 39157-6026; Phone: 601-956-1936; Fax: 601-956-7814
Contact for Missouri: MITCHELL J. ROGERS, P.O. Box 385, 110 1/2 West Jefferson, Clinton, MO 64735; Phone: 660-885-7555; Fax: 660-885-8626
Contact for Montana: STEVE R. BAYLESS, 5225 Collins Dr., Helena, MT 59602; Phone: 406-458-5794; Fax: 406-458-1907
Contact for Nebraska: JOSEPH M. HYLAND, Rt. 9, 9909 South 56th St., Lincoln, NE 68506; Phone: 402-423-8188; Fax: 402-43-3753
Contact for Nevada: DR. JOHN LUDWIG, 1595 Watt St., Reno, NV 89509; Phone: 702-786-1021; Fax: 702-786-0472
Contact for New Hampshire: ERIC GOODENOUGH, HCR Box 72, Ossipee Hill Rd., E. Waterboro, ME 04030; Phone: 207-247-8448; Fax: 207-247-8333
Contact for New Jersey: JOSEPH DEMARTINO, 133 Fox Hollow Dr., Lanoka Harbor, NJ 08734; Phone: **Publication(s):** *Ducks Unlimited Magazine; Puddler Magazine;*
609-971-5845; Fax: 609-971-7365
Flightlines
Contact for New Mexico: MIKE SHIRE, 5938 E. Corrine Dr., Scottsdale, AZ 85254; Phone: 602-483-6168; Fax: 602-483-9251
Contact for New York: D. ALLEN STARLING, Allen's Point, R.D. #1 Box 182, Union Springs, NY 13160; Phone: 315-889-7210; Fax: 315-889-9941
Contact for North Carolina: DONALD J. MANLEY, 25 Scott Pl., Clinton, NC 28328; Phone: 910-592-3898; Fax: 910-590-3000
Contact for North Dakota: CONRAD N. HILLMAN, 3502 Franklin Ave., Bismarck, ND 58501-0761; Phone: 701-258-5599; Fax: 701-258-8364
Contact for Ohio: LARRY HARMON, 341 Deer Trail Rd., Thornville, OH 43076; Phone: 740-323-0703; Fax: 740-323-0793
Contact for Oklahoma: LARRY E. KRAMER, 1700 E. Walking Sky, Edmond, OK 73013; Phone: 405-330-3549; Fax: 405-330-3551
Contact for Oregon: BRENT LAWS, 20555 Dorchester East, Bend, OR 97702; Phone: 541-382-5662; Fax: 541-382-4425
Contact for Pennsylvania: PETER G. BROWN, 217 Pfulgh Rd., Butler, PA 16001; Phone: 724-865-2422; Fax: 724-865-2691
Contact for Rhode Island: CRAIG FERRIS, 3 Orange Pippin Rd., Sandy Hook, CT 06482; Phone: 203-426-2466; Fax: 203-426-2733
Contact for South Carolina: CURTIS WOOTEN, 391 Creole Pl., Mt Pleasant, SC 29464; Phone: 843-884-5972; Fax: 843-849-6821
Contact for South Dakota: DOUG JONES, 2018 Antelope, Pierre, SD 57501; Phone: 605-224-0563; Fax: 605-224-4356
Contact for Tennessee: JOHN C. KRUZAN, 20 Lock 8 Ln., Carthage, TN 37030; Phone: 615-774-3192; Fax: 615-774-3850
Contact for Texas: JIMMY DUNKS, 7806 Phoenix Pass, Austin, TX 78737; Phone: 512-288-3615; Fax: 512-288-8315
Contact for Utah: PHILLIP WAGNER, 1617 West Galbrath Ln., Kaysville, UT 84037; Phone: 801-546-4619; Fax: 801-359-9457
Contact for Vermont: PHILIP D. WARREN, Hill Rd., P.O. Box 488, Alstead, NH 03602; Phone: 603-835-2490; Fax: 603-835-6243
Contact for Virginia: CHIP HEAPS, 136 Goucher Way, Churchville, MD 21028-1218; Phone: 410-399-4093; Fax: 410-734-6247
Contact for Washington: FRANK R. LOCKARD, 4251 Green Cove, NW, Olympia, WA 98502; Phone: 360-866-0525; Fax: 360-866-5519
Contact for West Virginia: DONNIE L. STACEY, H.C. 37, Box 201, Frankfort, WV 24938; Phone: 304-497-0888; Fax: 304-497-4352
Contact for Wisconsin: BRUCE GRUTHOFF, W8840 E. Jason Dr., Beaver Dam, WI 53916; Phone: 920-887-8972; Fax: 920-887-8865
Contact for Wyoming: BARRY FLOYD, 760 West 54th St., Casper, WY 82601; Phone: 307-472-6980; Fax: 307-472-3130
Controller: ROBERT D. MIMS
Director of Communication and Corporations for Conservation: PETER C. NIEDBALA
Director of Conservation Policy: FRED ABRAHAM, 1301 Pennsylvania Ave, NW, Suite 402, Washington, D.C. 20004
Director of Database Marketing: BOB DAVIS
Director of Development Atlantic Region: DAVID H. TREVETT
Director of Development Central Region: MIKE BURTON

Director of Development Southern Region: JOHN BELZ
Director of Development Western Region: JIM GLEASON
Director of Field Operations Programs Support: DAN GARDNER Ph.D.
Director of Human Resources and Staff Development: DAVID T. RILEY
Director of Latin American Program: ROBERT G. STREEGER, 3204 Shoce Rd., Fort Collins, CO 80524-16885; Phone: 970-495-1973; Fax: 970-495-1973; Email: batneader@ducks.org
Director of Leadership Giving: JONATHON KRONSBERG
Director of Licensing: STEPHEN TONNING
Director of Marketing: MICHAEL CLEARY
Director of Meetings and Conferences: CLIFFORD J. SCHULTZ
Director of Membership Programs: KENNETH S. CHASE
Director of Operations Great Lakes/ Altlantic Regional Office: RICHARD B. PIERCE, 331 Metty Dr., Suite 4, Ann Arbor, MI 48103; Phone: 734-623-2000; Fax: 734-623-2035
Director of Operations, Great Plains Regional Office: JEFFREY NELSON, 3502 Franklin Ave., Bismarck, ND 58501; Phone: 701-956-1936; Fax: 701-258-8364
Director of Operations, Southern Regional Office: RONALD A. STROMSTAD, 3074 Gold Canal Dr., Rancho Cordova, CA 95670; Phone: 916-852-2000; Fax: 916-852-2200
Director of Operations, Western Regional Office: MARC PIERCE
Director of Operations, Western Regional Office: KENNETH BABCOCK, 193 Business Park Dr., #E, Jackson, MS 39231; Phone: 601-956-1936; Fax: 601-956-7814
Director of Publishing and Communications: LEE SALBER
Editor-in-Chief: TOM FULGHAM
Executive Vice President: MATTHEW B. CONNOLLY JR., One Waterfowl Way, Memphis, TN 38120; Phone: 901-758-3825
General Counsel: JAMES FLOOD
Group Manager of Conservation Programs: DR. W. ALAN WENTZ
Group Manager of Publishing and Communications: CHRIS DORSEY
National Director of Conservation: DR. JACK PAYNE
National Director of Development: DELBERT W. CASE
National Director of Field Operations: GARY GOODPASTER
North Atlantic Flyway Vice President: PAUL MAKAREVICH JR.
North Central Flyway Vice President: STEVE TONSO
North Pacific Flyway Vice President: HARLEY HANSON
Northeast Mississippi Flyway Vice President: DOUG BIECHELE
Northwest Mississippi Flyway Vice President: JACK NUGENT
Senior Group Manager of Field Operations and Administration: JAMES L. WARE
Senior Vice President (Advisory to the President) of Communications: JILL OLSEN
Senior Vice President (Advisory to the President) of Conservation: WICKHAM CORWIN
Senior Vice President (Advisory to the President) of Development: JAMES HUBERT
Senior Vice President (Advisory to the President) of Event Management: WILLIAM COLVIN
Senior Vice President (Advisory to the President) of Membership: BARRY E. WOOD
Senior Vice President (Advisory to the President) of Strategic Planning: JAMES F. DODD III
South Atlantic Flyway Vice President: RICHARD S. JOHNSON
South Central Flyway Vice President: MICHAEL SIMPSON
South Mississippi Flyway Vice President: DR. L. J. MAYEUX
South Pacific Flyway Vice President: STEPHEN G. DENKERS

DUCKS UNLIMITED, INC. (Central Flyway Office)
GPRO 3502 Frankling Ave., Bismarck, ND 58501
Phone: 701-258-5599
Scope: Regional
Contact(s):
Regional Operations Supervisor: JIM RINGLEMAN

DUCKS UNLIMITED, INC. (Low Country Initiative)
100 S. Main St., #L, Summerville, SC 29483
Phone: 803-832-8889; Fax: 803-832-8875
Scope: Regional
Contact(s):
Director: COY JOHNSON

DUCKS UNLIMITED, INC. (Meadowlands Office)
One DeKorte Park Plaza, Lyndhurst, NJ 07071
Phone: 201-460-1700
Scope: Regional
Contact(s):
Regional Biologist: ROBERT JORDAN

DUCKS UNLIMITED, INC. (North Atlantic Flyway and Ohio)
219 County Rd., Bedford, NH 03110
Phone: 603-626-7706
Scope: Regional
Contact(s):
Regional Biologist: RAY WHITTEMORE

DUCKS UNLIMITED, INC. (South Atlantic Flyway)
100 S. Main St., Suite L, Summerville, SC 29483
Phone: 803-832-8889
Scope: Regional
Contact(s):
Regional Biologist: KENNY WILLIAMS

DUCKS UNLIMITED, INC. (South Mississippi and South Central Flyways)
SRO 193 Business Park Dr., #E, Jackson, MS 39213
Phone: 601-956-1936
Scope: Regional
Contact(s):
Regional Operations Supervisor: DONALD W. THOMPSON

DUCKS UNLIMITED, INC. (Wetlands America Trust, Inc. Office)
One Waterfowl Way, Memphis, TN 38120
Phone: 901-758-3825
Scope: Regional
Description: A nonprofit trust organized to operate exclusively for charitable, educational, scientific and conservation purposes. The Trust seeks to protect the natural balance of our continent's wetland ecosystems, ensuring the future viability of waterfowl and other wetland wildlife.
Contact(s):
President: JAMES C. KENNEDY
Assistant Secretary: BILL R. WILLSEY
Chief Operating Officer: MATTHEW B. CONNOLLY JR.
Keyword(s): International Conservation, Water Resources, Waterfowl, Wetlands, Wildlife and Wildlife Habitat

E-P EDUCATION SERVICES, INC.
15 Brittany Ct., Cheshire, CT 06410
Phone: 203-271-2756; Fax: 203-271-2756
Founded: 1972
Scope: Statewide
Description: A nonprofit group formed to promote environmental and population education in Connecticut and committed to assisting educators in the task of providing quality environmental education for the citizens of our state.
Contact(s):
Vice President: MICHAEL SCHAEFER
Secretary: LINA ANN LAWALL
Treasurer: J. ROBERT BOUCHARD
President and Executive Director: LARRY SCHAEFER
Keyword(s): Environmental and Conservation Education, Land Use Planning, Pesticides, Planning Management, Wetlands

NON-GOVERNMENTAL ORGANIZATIONS

EAGLE NATURE FOUNDATION, LTD.
300 East Hickory, Apple River, IL 61001
Phone: 815-594-2306; Fax: 815-594-2305; Email: eaglenature.tni@june.com
Founded: 1995; Membership: 1,250+
Scope: International
Description: ENF is a nonprofit international organization, which develops and implements habitat preservation strategies, conducts a wide variety of nature education and awareness programs, and engages in and supports bald eagle research.
Contact(s):
Vice President: EUGENE L. SMALL; Phone: 773-434-8328
Secretary: SUSAN ERTMER; Phone: 815-845-2253
Treasurer: ROBERT TORSBERG; Phone: 815-652-4443
Director: JOSEPH LUKASCYK; Phone: 708-430-0779
Director: PAMELA BERNSTEIN; Phone: 815-777-1874
President and Executive Director: TERRENCE N. INGRAM
Publication(s): *Bald Eagle News; Nature News; The Bald Eagle - Our National Symbol*
Keyword(s): Endangered and Threatened Species, Environmental and Conservation Education, Preservation

EARTH DAY NEW YORK
205 E. 42nd St., #1314, New York, NY 10017
Phone: 212-922-0048; Fax: 212-922-1936; Email: plippe@aol.Com; WWW: www.emedia.net/earthday/
Founded: 1989
Scope: National
Description: Earth Day New York is a low-overhead, broadly educational nonprofir 501c(3) organization that promotes environmental awareness and solutions through a three-pronged program: 1) involving schools, teachers, and students through the Earth Day Education Program; 2) educating public and private policymakers through conferences; and 3) involving the general public in annual Earth Day events.
Contact(s):
Chairman: DOUGLAS DURST; Phone: 212-789-1132; Fax: 212-789-1993
President: FRED KENT; Phone: 212-620-5660; Fax: 212-620-3821
Secretary: JIM TRIPP; Phone: 212-505-2100; Fax: 212-505-2375
Treasurer: TIMON MALLOY; Phone: 203-535-5326; Fax: 203-353-5329
Executive Director and Vice President: PAMELA LIPPE; Phone: 212-922-0048; Fax: 212-922-1936
Publication(s): *Lessons Learned Four Times Square; Building the Sustainable Economy Conference I Proceedings; Earth Day Education Program 1991-1999*
Keyword(s): Environmental and Conservation Education, Green Building, Internships

EARTH FORCE
1908 Mount Vernon Ave., 2nd Flr., Alexandria, VA 22301
Phone: 703-299--9400; Fax: 703-299-9485; Email: earthforce@earthforce.org
Founded: 1993
Scope: National
Description: Earth Force is a national nonprofit environmental organization. Earth Force is dedicated to young people changing their communities and caring for our environment now, while developing life-long habits of active citizenship and environmental stewardship.
Contact(s):
President: THOMAS D. MARTIN
Secretary: F. JOHN HAGELE, 9th Flr., 1515 Market St., Philadelphia, PA 19102; Phone: 212-851-8640
Board of Directors Chair: DOUGLAS FOY; Phone: 617-350-0990; Fax: 617-350-4030
President and Director: TOM D. MARTIN; Phone: 703-519-6867; Fax: 703-299-9485
Vice President for Local Programs: DONNA POWER
Vice President for National Programs: ANNIE BRODY
Publication(s): *Free Campaign Materials for Kids and Educators*
Keyword(s): Environmental and Conservation Education, Youth Organizations

EARTH FOUNDATION
5151 Mitchelldale Suite B-11, Houston, TX 77092
Phone: 713-686-9453
Founded: 1990; Membership: 15,000 Schools
Scope: National
Description: The purpose of Earth Foundation is to empower educators and students to work towards a sustainable economy, just society, and healthy environment. Our focus is on education, fundraising for conservation, and cooperative programs with conservation groups and indigenous organizations working in the race to save the planet.
Contact(s):
Vice President: DONNA LAX-EDISON, 5151 Mitchelldale B11
President and Director: CYNTHIA EVERAGE, 5151 Mitchelldale B11, Houston, TX 77092
Publication(s): *Rainforest Rescue Campaign Teacher* **Keyword(s):** Biodiversity, Coral Reefs, Endangered and Threatened Species, Environmental and Conservation Education, Environmental Preservation, International Conservation, Land Purchase, Rainforests

EARTH ISLAND INSTITUTE
300 Broadway, Suite 28, San Francisco, CA 94133
Phone: 415-788-3666; Fax: 415-788-7324; Email: earthisland@earthisland.org; WWW: www.earthisland.org
Founded: 1982; Membership: 20,000
Scope: National
Description: Through education and activism, Earth Island Institute counteracts threats to the biological and cultural diversity that sustains and enriches the global environment. The Institute develops and supports projects that promote the conservation, preservation, and restoration of the Earth. The Institute was founded by David Brower, veteran environmental leader.
Contact(s):
Chair: DAVID R. BROWER
President: BOB WILKINSON
Secretary: MARIA MOYER-ANGUS
Treasurer: TIM RANDS
Executive Director: JOHN A. KNOX
Executive Director: DAVID PHILLIPS
Publication(s): *Earth Island Journal; Paper Locator; Ocean Alert*
Keyword(s): Endangered and Threatened Species, International Conservation, Marine Mammals, Sustainable Development, Urban Environment

EARTH SHARE
3400 International Dr., NW, Suite 2K, Washington, DC 20008
Phone: 1-800-875-3863/202-537-7100; Fax: 202-537-7101; WWW: www.earthshare.org
Founded: 1988
Scope: National
Description: Earth Share is a nonprofit, federated fund-raising organization that represents 44 nonprofit environmental and conservation organizations in workplace payroll deduction campaigns nationwide. Funds raised support these organizations' environmental and conservation programs and services. Earth Share also provides educational public service announcements about the environment.
Contact(s):
Chairman: JAY FELDMAN, 701 E St. SE, Washington, DC 20003; Phone: 202-543-5450; Fax: 202-543-4791
President: KALMAN STEIN
Secretary: CHUCK PAQUETTE, 8925 Leesburg Pike, Vienna, VA 22184; Phone: 703-790-4016
Keyword(s): Air Quality and Pollution, Environmental and Conservation Education, Environmental Preservation, Water Resources, Wildlife and Wildlife Habitat

EARTHJUSTICE LEGAL DEFENSE FUND (formerly Sierra Club Legal Defense Fund, Inc.)
Headquarters, 180 Montgomery St., Suite 1400, San Francisco, CA 94104-4209
Phone: 415-627-6700; Fax: 415-627-6740
Scope: National
Description: A nonprofit, tax-deductible public-interest law firm created to bring lawsuits on behalf of environmental and citizens' organizations to protect the environment. As such, provides staff lawyers to initiate legal action. Also engages in administrative proceedings before federal, state, and local agencies, and negotiates settlement agreements whenever possible.
Contact(s):
Executive Director: BUCK PARKER
Editor: TOM TURNER
Managing Attorney: BILL CURTISS
Vice President for Finance and Administration: BRUCE NEIGHBOR
Vice President of Development: TJISKA VAN WYK
Vice President of Human Resources: NANCI PATTERSON
Publication(s): *Annual Report; In Brief* (newsletter); *Ka Palila* (Hawaii newsletter)
Keyword(s): Air Quality and Pollution, Environmental Law, Forests and Forestry, Public Lands, Wildlife and Wildlife Habitat

Florida Office
111 S. Martin Luther King Jr. Blvd., P.O. Box 1329, Tallahassee, FL 32302
Phone: 904-681-0031
Scope: Regional
Contact(s):
Managing Attorney: DAVID G. GUEST

Hawaii Office
223 S. King, 4th Fl., Honolulu, HI 96813
Phone: 808-599-2436
Scope: Regional
Contact(s):
Managing Attorney: PAUL ACHITOFF

Louisiana Office
400 Magazine St., 4th Fl., New Orleans, LA 70130
Phone: 504-522-1394
Scope: Regional
Contact(s):
Associate Attorney: ESTHER BOYKIN
Managing Attorney: NATHALIE WALKER
Project Attorney: ERIC HUBER

Montana Office
222 E. Main St., Suite 300, Bozeman, MT 59715
Phone: 406-586-9699
Scope: Regional
Contact(s):
Managing Attorney: DOUGLAS L. HONNOLD

Rocky Mountain Office
1631 Glenarm Pl., Suite 300, Denver, CO 80202
Phone: 303-623-9466
Scope: Regional
Contact(s):
Managing Attorney: ROBERT WIYGUL
Staff Attorney: SUSAN DAGGETT

Seattle, Washington Office
705 Second Ave., Suite 203, Seattle, WA 98104
Phone: 206-343-7340
Scope: Regional
Contact(s):
Managing Attorney: PATTI GOLDMAN
Staff Attorney: TODD TRUE

Southeast Alaska Office
325 4th St., Juneau, AK 99801
Phone: 907-586-2751; Fax: 907-463-5891
Scope: Regional
Contact(s):
Managing Attorney: ERIC JORGENSEN
Staff Attorney: THOMAS S. WALDO

Washington, DC Office
1625 Massachusetts Ave., NW, Suite 702, Washington, DC 20036
Phone: 202-667-4500
Scope: Regional
Contact(s):
Managing Attorney: HOWARD FOX

EARTHLAW
Universitry of Denver, Forbes House, 1714 Poplar St., Denver, CO 80220
Phone: 303-871-6996; Fax: 303-871-6991; Email: earthlaw@du.edu; WWW: www.earthlaw.org
Scope: Regional
Description: Earthlaw protects and preserves our environment by providing free legal services to grassroots environmental groups and activists.
Contact(s):
Executive Director: MARK HUGHES

EARTHSCAN
120 Pentonville Rd., London, London N1 9JN United Kingdom
Phone: 0171-278-0433; Fax: 0171-278-1142; Email: earthinfo@earthscan.co.uk; WWW: www.earthscan.co.uk
Scope: National
Description: A publishing house for books addressing environment and development issues in both industrialized countries and the developing world, taking as a starting point the inescapable link between poverty and environmental degradation. All aspects of sustainable development are covered, including international relations, environmental law and institutions, global environmental change, population growth, and the management of resources and economics, as well as social and cultural questions such as the role of women.
Contact(s):
Editor: FRANCES MACDERMOTT
Editor: RUTH COLEMAN
Marketing Executive: CLAIRE BAGNALL
Publishing Director: JONATHAN SINCLAIR WILSON
Keyword(s): Environmental Planning, Population Growth, Sustainable Development, Urban Environment

EARTHSTEWARDS NETWORK
P.O. Box 10697, Bainbridge Island, WA 98110
Phone: 206-842-7986
Founded: 1980; Membership: 1,800
Scope: International
Description: International network for global conflict resolution. Utilizes rainforest reforestation and urban forestry projects to bring together peoples of cultures-in-conflict to work to heal the environment.
Contact(s):
Board President: DAVE BROWNING
Director of Compossionate Listening Project: LEAH GREEN
Director of Peace Trees Vietnam: JERILYN BREAUSSEAU
Office Manager: G. R. SHERRILL
Publication(s): *Earthstewards Handbook; Warriors of the Heart; Earthstewards Newsletter; Essence Book of Days - 1998; Essence Book of Meditations and Blessings*
Keyword(s): Communications, International Conservation, Urban Forestry, Youth Organizations

NON-GOVERNMENTAL ORGANIZATIONS

EARTHTRUST
25 Kaneohe Bay Dr., Kailua, HI 96734
Phone: 808-254-2866; Fax: 808-254-6409; Email: earthtrust@aloha.net; WWW: www.earthtrust.org
Founded: 1976
Scope: International
Description: Earthtrust is an international nonprofit wildlife conservation organization. It involves small groups of highly capable people, involved with innovative investigations and projects, in partnership with private industry, governments and other environmental groups. Earthtrust is aimed at resolving wildlife crisis situations. Earthtrust's focus in 1997-1998 is to expose the poaching of endangered species and the sale of endangered whale meat in Asian markets through the use of DNA analysis.
Contact(s):
President: DONALD WHITE
Keyword(s): Endangered and Threatened Species, Environmental Law, International Conservation, Marine Mammals, Wildlife and Wildlife Habitat

EARTHWATCH INSTITUTE
680 Mt. Auburn St., Box 9104, Watertown, MA 02471
Phone: 617-926-8200; Fax: 617-926-8532; Email: info@earthwatch.org; WWW: www.earthwatch.org
Founded: 1971; Membership: 23,000 US/35,000 internationally
Scope: International
Description: Earthwatch is a nonprofit organization which sponsors scientific field research worldwide. It recruits paying volunteers to help scholars of their field expeditions in 50 countries and 25 US states.
Contact(s):
President: ROGER BERGEN
Vice President: ANDREW MITCHELL
Chief Financial Officer: STELLA CHAN
Executive Director of Center for Field Research: DR. MARIE STUDER
Publication(s): *Earthwatch Magazine; Earthwatch Expedition Guide; Solutions*
Keyword(s): Biodiversity, Coral Reefs, Cultural Preservation, Endangered and Threatened Species, Environmental and Conservation Education, Flowers, Plants, and Trees, Geology, Grants, International Conservation, Internships, Research, Sustainable Development, Sustainable Ecosystems, Wildlife Management, Zoology

EAST CENTRAL ILLINOIS FUR TAKERS
R.R. 2, Paxton, IL 60957
Phone: 217-379-4067
Founded: 1974; Membership: 200
Scope: Statewide
Description: State chapter of Fur Takers of America. Helps monitor furbearing wildlife populations in the state and helps conserve this renewable resource.
Contact(s):
President: GREG ANDERSON
Vice President: JIM LIFT
Secretary-Treasurer: MIKE WILSON; Phone: 217-949-5221

EASTERN SHORE LAND CONSERVANCY
P.O. Box 169, Queenstown, MD 21658
Phone: 410-827-9756; Fax: 410-827-9039
Founded: 1990; Membership: 400
Scope: Statewide
Description: The Eastern Shore Land Conservancy works towards preserving farms, forests, and natural areas for future generations, and managing them for economic and community benefit.
Contact(s):
Executive Director: ROBERT J. ETGEN
Publication(s): *Conservancy Update; Preserving Land for Our Future; fact sheets*
Keyword(s): Land Preservation, Natural Areas, Nature Preservation, Open Space

ECOLOGICAL SOCIETY OF AMERICA, THE
2010 Massachusetts Ave., NW, Suite 400, Washington, DC 20036
Phone: 202-833-8773; Email: esahq@esa.org
Founded: 1915; Membership: 7,200
Scope: National
Description: The Ecological Society of America is the nation's premier professional society of ecologists. ESA promotes the responsible application of ecological principles to the solution of environmental problems through ESA reports, journals, and expert testimony to Congress. Each summer, ESA convenes a conference featuring the latest findings in ecological research.
Contact(s):
President: KAY GROSS
Executive Director: KATHERINE S. McCARTER
Associate Director for Public Affairs: NADINE LYMN
Publication(s): *Ecology; Ecological Applications; Ecological Monographs; Bulletin of the Ecological Society of America; Conservation Ecology; Issues in Ecology*
Keyword(s): Biodiversity, Biology, Ecology, Endangered and Threatened Species, Environment, Environmental and Conservation Education, Internships, Sustainable Ecosystems, Wildlife and Wildlife Habitat

ECOLOGY CENTER
2530 San Pablo Ave., Berkeley, CA 94702
Phone: 510-548-2220; Email: info@ecologycenter.org; WWW: www.ecologycenter.org
Founded: 1969
Scope: Statewide
Description: A nonprofit organization working to develop a more responsible society by identifying environmentally destructive practices and demonstrating sound alternatives. Programs include an environmental information clearinghouse, library, classes, book and ecoproducts store, sponsorship of three weekly farmers' markets, and weekly residential curbside recycling service in the city of Berkeley, CA. Primary service area: Greater San Francisco Bay region.
Contact(s):
Editor: LAIRD TOWNSEND
Publication(s): *Terrain*
Keyword(s): Ancient Forests, EcoAction, Endangered and Threatened Species, Environment, Environmental and Conservation Education, Environmental Justice, Gardening and Horticulture, Internships, Land Preservation, People of Color in the Environment, Pesticides, Public Lands, Renewable Resources, Wildlife and Wildlife Habitat, Women in the Environment

ECOTOURISM SOCIETY, THE
P.O. Box 755, North Bennington, VT 05257
Phone: 802-447-2121; Fax: 802-447-2122; Email: ecomail@ecotourism.org; WWW: www.ecotourism.org
Founded: 1990; Membership: 1,400
Scope: International
Description: The Ecotourism Society is an international nonprofit organization dedicated to finding the resources and building the expertise to make tourism a viable tool for conservation and sustainable development.
Contact(s):
Chairman: DR. RICHARD RYEL
President: MEGAN EPLER WOOD, P.O. Box 755, North Bennington, VT 05257; Phone: 802-447-2121; Fax: 802-447-2122; Email: ecomail@ecotourism.org
Publication(s): *Ecotourism: A Guide for Planners and Managers Volume I&II; Ecotourism Bibliography; Ecotourism Guidelines for Nature Tour Operators; Ecotourism Society Quarterly Newsletter; Ecolodge Sourcebook for Planners and Developers*
Keyword(s): Biodiversity, Developing Countries, Ecotourism, Environmental and Conservation Education, International Conservation, Outdoor Recreation, Sustainable Development, Tourism, Travel

EDUCATIONAL COMMUNICATIONS, INC.
P.O. Box 351419, Los Angeles, CA 90035
Phone: 310-559-9160; Fax: 310-559-9160; Email: ECNP@aol.com; WWW: home.earthlink.net/~dragonflight/ecoprojects.htm

Founded: 1958
Scope: National

Description: EC creates and promotes educational and scientific projects and programs for the public, focusing on environmental concerns. It publishes the Compendium Newsletter, a guide to ecological activism; founded The Ecology Center of Southern California in 1972, serving a 15-million-person area; since 1977 has sponsored the award-winning Environmental Directions, a weekly national and international radio series heard on 15 stations; and since 1984 has produced three-time Emmy-nominated ECONEWS, a weekly television series broadcast on over 100 cable and PBS outlets nationally. Educational Communications, Inc. is credited with over 375 award-winning programs including "Gem in the Heart of the City", "Wind! Energy for the '90's and Beyond" and "Population Crisis USA."

Contact(s):
Administrative Coordinator: LESLIE LEWIS
Associate Director: ANNA HARLOWE
Executive Producer and Director: NANCY PEARLMAN

Keyword(s): Communications, Environmental and Conservation Education, International Conservation, Population Growth, Wildlife and Wildlife Habitat

ELM RESEARCH INSTITUTE
867 Rt. 12, Unit 5, Westmoreland, NH 03467
Phone: 603-358-6198; Fax: 603-358-6305; WWW: www.forelms.org

Founded: 1967; Membership: 3,200
Scope: National

Description: A nonprofit organization which has funded over $1,000,000 in research for the treatment of Dutch elm disease and development of the disease-resistant American Liberty Elm, supplies equipment and information pertaining to elm care and treatment of Dutch elm disease, propagates the American Liberty Elm and distributes it under the auspices of the Johnny Elmseed Project with the assistance of local Boy Scouts and other nonprofit groups. Over 750 nurseries have been established since 1984. ERI provides a free ceremonial tree and commemorative plaque to the first 100 communities which agree to plant 10 more trees in 1999.

Contact(s):
Assistant Director: YVONNE SPALTHOFF
Executive Director: JOHN P. HANSEL

Publication(s): *Specialized Elm Care Information; ELM LEAVES; Data on Elm Injections*

Keyword(s): Endangered and Threatened Species, Flowers, Plants, and Trees, Historic Preservation, Urban Forestry

ELSA WILD ANIMAL APPEAL (Louisiana Chapter)
210 W. Railroad Ave., Lake Charles, LA 70601
Phone: 318-439-8879

Scope: Statewide

Description: Regional branch of ELSA WILD ANIMAL APPEAL; concerned with wildlife matters, educational programs, liaison with other wildlife and governmental groups for the betterment of natural environment and wildlife protection; establishes local volunteer corps to implement programs in conjunction with the Calcasieu Parish Animal Control and Protection Department; and participates in Wildlife Rehabilitation Programs with Heck Haven and Westlake Bird Sanctuary.

Contact(s):
Contact: LAURA LANZA

Keyword(s): Birds, Endangered and Threatened Species, Mammals, Urban Environment, Wildlife Rehabilitation

ENDANGERED SPECIES COALITION
1101 14th St., NW, Suite 1400, Washington, DC 20005
Phone: 202-682-9400

Founded: 1982; Membership: 450 environmental, scientific, and religious organizations
Scope: National

Description: The goal of the Coalition is to broaden and mobilize public support for protecting endangered species.

Contact(s):
Executive Director: BROCK EVANS

Publication(s): *Activist Tools; Newsletter*

Keyword(s): Biodiversity, Endangered and Threatened Species, Environmental Law

ENTOMOLOGICAL SOCIETY OF AMERICA
9301 Annapolis Rd., Lanham, MD 20706-3115
Phone: 301-731-4535

Founded: 1889
Scope: National

Description: To promote the scientific study of insects and related arthropods. Specialty sections include systematic behavior, toxicology, biogenetics, plant protection, medical and veterinary, regulatory and extension, and related scientific disciplines.

Contact(s):
President: DR. DOUGLAS DAHLMAN
Executive Director: HARRY BRADLEY
Past President: DR. MANYA STOETZEL
President Elect: DR. GEORGE KENNEDY

Publication(s): *Annals of the Entomological Society of America; Journal of Economic Entomology; Environmental Entomology; Medical Entomology; American Entomologist; ESA Newsletter*

Keyword(s): Agriculture, Biology, Biotechnology, Insects and Butterflies, Zoology

ENVIRONMENT COUNCIL OF RHODE ISLAND
P.O. Box 9061, Providence, RI 02940
Phone: Phone & Fax: 401-621-8048; Email: ecri@studentweb.providence.edu

Scope: Statewide

Description: A representative statewide organization, affiliated with the National Wildlife Federation, dedicated to the protection and enhancement of wildlife and its habitat through public education and government interaction.

Contact(s):
President: KRIS STUART
Affiliate Representative: PAUL BEAUDETTE
Alternate Representative: LAURA LANDEN
Editor: AIMEE TAVARES

Publication(s): *Audubon Society of Rhode Island Report; Checklist of RI Birds - 1900-1989; Fields Note of RI Birds*

Keyword(s): Birds, Environmental and Conservation Education, Natural History, Renewable Resources, Wildlife and Wildlife Habitat

ENVIRONMENTAL ACTION FUND (EAF)
P.O. Box 22421, Nashville, TN 37202
Phone: 615-385-4389

Founded: 1976
Scope: Statewide

Description: A nonprofit, nonpartisan union of citizen groups joined to preserve and protect Tennessee's natural resources and environmental health. EAF works for strong environmental legislative programs and policies.

Contact(s):
President: MARK MANNER, 2424 Golf Club Ln., Nashville, TN 37215
Secretary: SANDY BIVENS, 3504 General Bates Dr., Nashville, TN 37204
Treasurer: PAUL DAVIS, 5462 Vanderbilt Rd., Old Hickory, TN 37138

NON-GOVERNMENTAL ORGANIZATIONS

ENVIRONMENTAL ADVOCATES
353 Hamilton St., Albany, NY 12210
Phone: 518-462-5526; Fax: 518-427-0381; Email: info@envadvocates.org; WWW: www.enadvocates.org
Founded: 1969
Scope: Statewide
Description: A representative statewide organization, affiliated with the National Wildllife Federation, dedicated to the protection and enhancement of wildlife and its habitat through public education and government interaction.
Contact(s):
President: OAKES AMES
Affiliate Representative: CHARLES KRUZANSKY
Alternate Representative and Executive Director: VAL WASHINGTON
Editor: JEFF JONES
Publication(s): *Albany Report; Environmental Voter's Guide; Greensheets*

ENVIRONMENTAL AIR FORCE
22 Rittenhouse Rd., Broomll, PA 19008
Phone: 610-353-1535; Fax: 610-356-5814
Founded: 1989; Membership: 280
Scope: National
Description: A nonprofit membership organization dedicated to providing free aviation services to environmental and conservation groups worldwide. These services are provided through a network of member pilots and include aerial surveys and photography, flying essential observers, etc.
Contact(s):
Executive Director: ALAN M. BRECHER
Publication(s): *Despatches*
Keyword(s): Environmental and Conservation Education, Environmental Preservation, International Conservation, Land Preservation, Wildlife and Wildlife Habitat

ENVIRONMENTAL AND ENERGY STUDY INSTITUTE (EESI)
122 C St., NW, Suite 700, Washington, DC 20001
Phone: 202-628-1400; Fax: 202-628-1825
Founded: 1985
Scope: National
Description: The EESI is dedicated to promoting environmentally sustainable societies. EESI produces credible, timely information, and innovative public policy initiatives that lead to transitions to social and economic patterns that sustain people, the environment, and the natural resources upon which present and future generations depend.
Contact(s):
Chair: RICHARD L. OTTINGER
Executive Director: CAROL WERNER
Director and Senior Fellow of the Sustainable Communities Program: DON GRAY
Director of Energy and Climate Change Program: CAROL WERNER
Publication(s): *Environment and Energy Weekly; Environment and Energy Update; CMAQ Update*
Keyword(s): Energy, Greenhouse Effect/Global Warming, International Conservation, Transportation, Water Resources

ENVIRONMENTAL CAREER CENTER
100 Bridge St., Suite A1, Hampton, VA 23669
Phone: 757-727-7891; Fax: 757-727-7904; Email: ecc@visi.net
Founded: 1980
Scope: National
Description: Dedicated to helping people help the environment through internships, career counseling, diversity achievement program, career research, newsletters, and career seminars. Environmental Partnership Program provides paid apprenticeships in natural resources management and environmental protection. Partnerships with environmental employers and universities. Conducts career seminars for professional societies, universities, and agencies.
Contact(s):
Vice President: DR. JOHN E. DAMRON
Secretary: BARBARA ROUTTEN
Treasurer: KESHA A. OLIVER
President and Executive Director: JOHN ESSON
Keyword(s): Environmental and Conservation Education, Internships, People of Color in the Environment, Training

ENVIRONMENTAL CAREERS ORGANIZATION INC., THE
179 South St., 3rd Fl., Boston, MA 02111
Phone: 617-426-4375; WWW: www.eco.org
Founded: 1972
Scope: National
Description: ECO protects and enhances the environment through the development of professionals, the promotion of careers, and the inspiration of individual action. This is accomplished through placement, career advisement, career products and research, and consulting. ECO has five regional offices and an alumni network of over 6,000 individuals.
Contact(s):
President: JOHN R. COOK JR.
Treasurer: JUDITH M. STOCKDALE
Publication(s): *Complete Guide to Environmental Careers, The; Beyond the Green*
Keyword(s): Internships, People of Color in the Environment, Toxic Substances, Water Pollution

ENVIRONMENTAL CONCERN, INC.
210 W. Chew Ave., P.O. Box P, St. Michaels, MD 21663
Phone: 410-745-9620; Fax: 410-745-3517
Founded: 1972
Scope: National
Description: A nonprofit corporation founded for the purpose of researching, developing, and applying the technology and methodologies used in creating, restoring, and preserving wetlands; focus on consulting, wetland horticulture, professional and scholastic educational programs.
Contact(s):
President: EDGAR W. GARBISCH
Vice President: F. ALBERT MCCULLOUGH III
Vice President: JOANNA L. GARBISCH
Secretary and Treasurer: GLORIA SMITH
Publication(s): *Wetland Journal; Wow! The Wonders of Wetlands; Wetland Planting Guide for the Northeastern United States; Evaluation for Planned Wetlands: A Procedure for Assessing Wetland Functions and a Guide to Functional Design; "A Comprehensive Review of Wetlands Assessment Procedures: A Guide for Wetland Practitioners*
Keyword(s): Environmental and Conservation Education, Gardening and Horticulture, Renewable Resources, Research, Wetlands

ENVIRONMENTAL DEFENSE CENTER, INC.
906 Garden St., Santa Barbara, CA 93101
Phone: 805-963-1622; Fax: 805-962-3152
Founded: 1977
Scope: Statewide
Description: A nonprofit, public-interest environmental law firm providing legal services to citizens' groups and environmental organizations on environmental issues facing California's central coast region since 1977. The Center focuses on a wide range of issues, including oil development, toxic wastes, air and water pollution, species and habitat protection, open space preservation, land use, and coastal access.
Contact(s):
Chairman of the Board: KEN FALSTROM
Chief Counsel: MARC CHYTILO
Counsel: MARC McGINNES
Staff Attorney: JOHN BUSE
Staff Attorney: CAMERON BENSON
Staff Attorney: LINDA KROP

Keyword(s): Environmental Law, Land Use Planning, Water Resources, Wildlife and Wildlife Habitat

ENVIRONMENTAL DEFENSE FUND, INC.
Headquarters, 257 Park Ave., S., New York, NY 10010
Phone: 212-505-2100; Fax: 212-505-2375; WWW: www.edf.org
Founded: 1967; Membership: 300,000
Scope: National
Description: The Environmental Defense Fund (EDF), headquartered in New York and with five other offices nationwide, is a leading nonprofit, tax-exempt environmental advocacy organization active in a wide range of issues, including protection of the global and regional atmosphere, promotion of environmental health through reduced exposure to toxic chemicals, protecting and restoring biodiversity and critical rivers and wetlands, and restoring the health of our oceans.
Contact(s):
Executive Director: FRED KRUPP; Phone: 212-505-2100
Chairman of the Board of Trustees: JOHN H. WILSON
Deputy Director of Operations: ED BAILEY
Deputy Director of Programs: MARCIA ARONOFF
Editor: NORMA H. WATSON; Phone: 212-505-2100
General Counsel: JAMES T. TRIPP
International Counsel: ANNIE PETSONK
Legislative Director: STEVE COCHRAN
Strategic Communications Director: WILLIAM ROBERTS
Publication(s): *EDF Letter*
Keyword(s): Air Quality and Pollution, Aquatic Habitats, Biodiversity, Biotechnology, Chemical Pollution Control, Energy, Fisheries, International Conservation, Pollution Prevention, Transportation, Water Quality, Water Resources, Watersheds, Wetlands

Alliance for Environmental In Innovation
6 North Market Bldg., Faneuil Hall Marketplace, Boston, MA 02109
Phone: 617-723-2996; Fax: 617-723-7996
Scope: Regional
Description: The Alliance for Environmental Innovation is a joint project of EDF and The Pew Charitable Trusts.
Contact(s):
Director: JACKIE PRINCE ROBERTS

Capital Office
1875 Connecticut Ave., NW, Washington, DC 20009
Phone: 202-387-3500; Fax: 202-234-6049
Scope: Regional

North Carolina Office
2500 Blue Ridge Rd., Suite 330, Raleigh, NC 27607
Phone: 919-881-2601; Fax: 919-881-2607
Scope: Regional

Rocky Mountain Office
1405 Arapahoe, Boulder, CO 80302
Phone: 303-440-4901; Fax: 303-440-8052
Scope: Regional

Texas Office
44 East Ave., Austin, TX 78701
Phone: 512-478-5161; Fax: 512-478-8140
Scope: Regional

West Coast Office
5655 College Ave., Oakland, CA 94618
Phone: 510-658-8008; Fax: 510-658-0630
Scope: Regional

ENVIRONMENTAL EDUCATION ASSOCIATION OF ILLINOIS
(Iron Oaks Environmental Learning Center)
2453 Vollmer Rd., Olympia Fields, IL 60461
Phone: 708-481-2330
Founded: 1970; Membership: 600
Scope: Statewide
Description: Environmental Education Association of Illinois is the only organization in Illinois that makes environmental literacy its primary goal as it strives to instill a sense of community between the native ecosystems and people.
Contact(s):
President: JUDY MANN
Vice President: DEB CHAPMAN; Phone: 847-835-8239
Secretary: KIM PETZING; Phone: 217-384-4062
Treasurer: DAVE GURITZ; Phone: 847-428-2240
Membership: CURT CARTER, S.I.U.E. Mail Code 6888, Carbondale, IL 62901; Phone: 618-453-1121
Publication(s): *Illinois Environmental Education UPDATE*
Keyword(s): Aquatic Habitats, Environmental and Conservation Education, Flowers, Plants, and Trees, Solid Waste Management, Wildlife and Wildlife Habitat

ENVIRONMENTAL EDUCATION ASSOCIATION OF INDIANA
ATTN: President, Richardson Wildlife Sanctuary, 64 West Rd., Dune Acres, Chesterton, IN 46304
Founded: 1969
Scope: Statewide
Description: A statewide, nonprofit organization dedicated to the wise use and management of natural resources through environmental conservation education. Activities include an annual meeting, workshops, teaching materials, exhibits, and youth environmental summit.
Contact(s):
President: JOHN THIELE JR., Richardson Wildlife Sanctuary, 64 West Rd., Dune Acres, Chesterton, IN 46304; Phone: 219-787-8983
Treasurer: DOUG WALDMAN, 11832 Kress Rd., Roanoke, IN 46783; Phone: 317-672-3842
Editor: SAM CARMAN, 5822 E CR 1000N, Pittsboro, IN 46167; Phone: 317-232-4105
Immediate Past President: CATHY MEYER, 119 W 7th, Bloomington, IN 47404; Phone: 812-349-2800
Publication(s): *CREED Newsletter*
Keyword(s): Environmental and Conservation Education

NON-GOVERNMENTAL ORGANIZATIONS

ENVIRONMENTAL EDUCATION ASSOCIATION OF WASHINGTON
P.O. Box 4122, Bellingham, WA 98227
Phone: 206-365-3893; WWW: www.halcyon.com/eeaw/
Scope: Statewide
Description: EEAW is a dynamic, nonprofit organization comprised of teachers, agency people, business representatives, and community educators, dedicated to offering and promoting effective environmental education to all sectors of Washington.
Contact(s):
President: MICHELE HALFHILL

ENVIRONMENTAL EDUCATION COUNCIL OF OHIO
P.O. Box 2911, Akron, OH 44309-2911
Phone: 330-761-0855
Founded: 1967; Membership: 450
Scope: Statewide
Description: EECO is a statewide organization whose purpose is to promote environmental education which nurtures knowledge, attitudes, and behaviors that foster global stewardship. EECO brings together educators from many settings to provide opportunities to share ideas, materials, and techniques. Members include classroom teachers, naturalists, camp staff, teacher educators, youth leaders, and agency personnel.
Contact(s):
President: DEBORAH YANDALA, 2410 Thurmont Rd., Akron, OH 44313; Phone: 330-657-2796
Vice President: PAT BARRON, 611 Overbrook Dr., Columbus, OH 43214; Phone: 614-485-9800
Secretary: SABINA DAUDI, 2754 Clifton Rd., Upper Arlington, OH 43221; Phone: 614-481-8483
Treasurer: TIM TAYLOR; Phone: 740-366-3276
Executive Director: TERESA M. MOURAD; Phone: 330-761-0855
Publication(s): *EECO Newsletter; Ohio Sampler: Outdoor and Environmental Education*
Keyword(s): Environmental and Conservation Education, Stewardship, Youth Organizations

ENVIRONMENTAL EDUCATION PROJECT (John Inskeep Environmental Learning Center)
19600 S. Molalla Ave., Oregon City, OR 97045
Phone: 503-657-6958 ext2351; Email: elc@clackamas.cc.or.us
Founded: 1972
Scope: Statewide
Description: A source of teacher training and community education on environmental education topics, focusing on urban watershed issues. Located on a restored industrial site featuring buildings made from salvaged and recycled materials.
Contact(s):
Director: JOHN LeCAVALIER

ENVIRONMENTAL ENTERPRISES ASSISTANCE FUND, INC.
1901 N. Moore St. #1004, Arlington, VA 22209
Phone: 703-522-5928; Fax: 703-522-6450; Email: eeaf@igc.apc.org
Founded: 1990
Scope: National
Description: EEAF is a non-profit organization that operates as a venture capital fund; it provides long term risk capital and management asistance to environmentally beneficial businesses in developing countries, where such capital is otherwise unavailable.
Contact(s):
President: BROOKS BROWNE
Vice President: J. D. DOLINER
Senior Vice President: HELEN CHAIKOVSKY
Keyword(s): Agriculture, Biodiversity, Developing Countries, Energy, Energy Conservation, Fisheries, Pollution Prevention, Renewable Resources, Solar Energy, Sustainable Development, Water Pollution

ENVIRONMENTAL LAW ALLIANCE WORLDWIDE (E-LAW)
U.S. Office: 1877 Garden Ave., Eugene, OR 97403
Phone: 503-687-8454; Fax: 503-687-0535; Email: elawus@igc.apc.org; WWW: www.igc.apc.org/elaw/
Founded: 1989
Scope: International
Description: E-LAW is an international network of public-interest attorneys and scientists dedicated to using law to protect the environment. E-LAW's twenty offices, located around the world, exchange vital legal and scientific information via electronic and other media. Advocates in more than 50 countries call on E-LAW for information to support their environmental protection work.
Contact(s):
Chair: JOHN BONINE, School of Law, University of Oregon, Eugene, OR 97403; Phone: 503-346-3823
President: MICHAEL AXLINE, School of Law, University of Oregon, Eugene, OR 97403; Phone: 503-346-3823
Executive Director: BERN JOHNSON
Publication(s): *E-LAW Update*
Keyword(s): Environmental Law, International Conservation

ENVIRONMENTAL LAW INSTITUTE, THE
1616 P St., NW, Suite 200, Washington, DC 20036
Phone: 202-939-3800; Fax: 202-939-3868; WWW: www.eli.org
Founded: 1969
Scope: National
Description: The Environmental Law Institute advances environmental protection by improving law, management, and policy. ELI researches pressing problems, educates professionals and citizens about the nature of these issues, and convenes all sectors in forging effective solutions. ELI is an independent, internationally recognized research and education center on pollution abatement and resource conservation matters.
Contact(s):
President: J. WILLIAM FUTRELL
Chairman of the Board: TURNER SMITH JR.
Director of Communications: STEPHEN R. DUJACK
Head Librarian: LAWRENCE ROSS; Phone: 202-328-5150
Secretary and Treasurer: MICHAEL RICHARDSON
Publication(s): *ELR - Environmental Law Reporter, The; National Wetlands Newsletter; Environmental Forum*
Keyword(s): Biodiversity, Environmental and Conservation Education, Environmental Law, International Conservation, Sustainable Development, Wetlands

ENVIRONMENTAL LEAGUE OF MASSACHUSETTS (ELM)
Three Joy St., Boston, MA 02108
Phone: 617-742-2553; Fax: 617-742-9656; Email: elm@environmentalleague.org; WWW: www.environmentalleague.org
Founded: 1898
Scope: Statewide
Description: Advocates for responsible environmental policy on the state level and the effective implementation of state programs, e.g., land use, toxics use reduction, recycling, water resources protection, funding for environmental programs.
Contact(s):
Chairman: RICHARD H. JOHNSON
President: JAMES R. GOMES
Treasurer: JOHN A. CRONIN
Development Director: KIMBERLY A. MITCHELL
Environmental Collaborative Director: AMY LUCKEY
Legislative Director: NAMRITA KAPUR
Researcher/Advocate: NANCY GOODMAN
Publication(s): *ELM Bulletin; ELM Action Alerts*
Keyword(s): Air Quality and Pollution, Chemical Pollution Control, Environment, Environmental Law, Land Preservation, Land Use Planning, Open Space, Pesticides, Rivers, Sustainable Development, Toxic Substances, Water Pollution, Water Quality, Water Resources, Watersheds

ENVIRONMENTAL MEDIA ASSOCIATION
10780 Santa Monica Blvd., Suite 210, Los Angeles, CA 91770
Phone: 310-446-6244; Fax: 310-446-6255; Email: ema@ema1.org; WWW: www.ema-online.org
Founded: 1989
Scope: National
Description: EMA works to mobilize the entertainment community in a global effort to educate people about environmental problems, and inspire them to act on those problems now.
Contact(s):
President: WENDY M. JONES; Email: wendy@ema1.org
Vice President: JOYCE SHELBY; Email: joyce@ema1.org
Publication(s): *Green Light; Stories Kids Care About; Thinking Outside the Box*
Keyword(s): Environmental Communication

ENVIRONMENTAL PROTECTION ASSOCIATION OF GHANA
P.O. Box AS 32, Asawasi-Kumasi, Asawasi-Kumasi Ghana
Phone: 0233-051-29950; Fax: 233-51-22537
Founded: 1987; Membership: 220
Scope: International
Description: The Association was established with the major objective of promoting an environmentally clean society and ecologically sustainable development. Association activities have been concentrated on the following: tree planting, afforestation, education, awareness, seminars and workshops, health, women and development, income generation, and rural development.
Contact(s):
Director: F. A. JANTUAH
First Deputy Director: KWABENA ANTWI
Project Manager: JOHN KWADWO OWUSU
Second Deputy Director: F. A. OWUSU
Publication(s): *Annual Report*

ENVIRONMENTAL RESOURCE CENTER (ERC)
411 East Sixth St., P.O. Box 819, Ketchum, ID 83340
Phone: 208-726-4333; Fax: 208-726-1531; Email: erc@sunvalley.net
Founded: 1989; Membership: 800
Scope: National
Description: The ERC is a nonprofit organization that provides resources and educational programs to the public about local, regional, and global environmental issues.
Contact(s):
Acting Executive Director: DR. LEE BROWN
Publication(s): *Aquila*
Keyword(s): Ecology, Energy Conservation, Environmental and Conservation Education, Internships, Natural History

ENVIROSOUTH, INC.
P.O. Box 11468, Montgomery, AL 36111
Phone: 205-277-7050; Fax: 205-277-7080
Founded: 1975
Scope: National
Description: A private nonprofit organization specializing in recycling information and related services for the Southeast Recycling Market Council, and the annual Southeast Recycling Conference and Trade Show.
Contact(s):
President: MARTHA McINNIS; Phone: 205-277-7050
Publication(s): *EnviroSouth Magazine*
Keyword(s): Communications, Environmental and Conservation Education, Natural History, Renewable Resources, Solid Waste Management

EUROPARC FEDERATION
Kroellstrasse 5, Grafenau, Grafenau 94481 Germany
Phone: 01149-8552/96100; Fax: 01149-8552/961019
Founded: 1973; Membership: 295
Scope: International
Description: The EUROPARC Federation (formally known as the Federation of Nature and National Parks of Europe) is a pan-European, not-for-profit, non-governmental organisation, which promotes and supports the full range of protected areas in Europe. EUROPARC aims to facilitate the exchange of technical and scientific expertise, information and personnel between parks and reserves. It organizes training and exchange programmes, and provides professional advice on the establishment and development of protected areas.
Contact(s):
President: DR. HANS BIBELRIETHER
Director: EVA PONGRATZ
Publication(s): *European Bulletin: Nature and National Parks, Loving Them to Death--Sustainable Tourism in Europe's Nature and National Parks; EUROPARC 1L92, 1L93, 1994, 1995/ L9/ 1996, 1997: Proceedings of the Federation's Annual Conference and General Assembly.*
Keyword(s): Conservation of Protected Areas, International Conservation

EUROPEAN ASSOCIATION FOR AQUATIC MAMMALS
P.O. Box 58, 3910AB, Rhenen, Rhenen The Netherlands
Phone: 31-317-612294
Founded: 1973; Membership: 175
Scope: National
Description: To promote the free exchange of knowledge and to further scientific progress pertaining to the treatment, management, and conservation of aquatic mammals; to provide an organization for the above individuals, to improve practical husbandry; and to advance, by continued study, the basis for maintaining aquatic mammals in captivity.
Contact(s):
President: DR. JOHN R. BAKER
President Elect: GERALDINE LACAVE
Secretary and Treasurer: FRANS J. ENGELSMA
Publication(s): *Aquatic Mammals; Newletters*
Keyword(s): Endangered and Threatened Species, Environmental and Conservation Education, Marine Mammals, Water Pollution Management, Zoological Parks

EUROPEAN CETACEAN SOCIETY
c/o Deutsches Museum for Meereskunde und Fischerei, Katharinenberg 14, Stralsund 18439 Germany
Phone: 49-3831-265021; Fax: 49-3831-265060
Founded: 1987; Membership: 450
Scope: National
Description: The European Cetacean Society's main focus is to promote and coordinate scientific study and conservation of cetaceans and to gather and disseminate information to members and to the public.
Contact(s):
Chairman: CHRISTINA LOCKYER
Secretary: BEATRICE JANN
Treasurer: ROLAND LICK
Editor: PETER EVANS
Publication(s): *European Cetacean Society Newsletter; European Research on Cetaceans*
Keyword(s): Biodiversity, Endangered and Threatened Species, Environmental Preservation, Marine Mammals, Wildlife Management

EVERGLADES COORDINATING COUNCIL (ECC)
7901 W. 25 Ct., Hialeah, FL 33106
Phone: 305-248-9924
Founded: 1970; Membership: 14 affiliate organizations
Scope: Statewide
Description: ECC is an umbrella organization of south Florida sportspersons and conservation organizations united in a desire to protect wildlife habitat, assure sound wildlife management practices, and provide for properly regulated outdoor recreational activities.
Contact(s):
President: LEE CHAMBERLAIN, 4251 SW 77th Ave., Davie, FL 33328; Phone: 305-791-8711

NON-GOVERNMENTAL ORGANIZATIONS

Vice President: HAROLD L. JOHNSON, 3701 NW 66th Ave., Miami, FL 33166; Phone: 305-871-1860
Secretary: BARBARA JEAN POWELL, 22951 SW 190th Ave., Miami, FL 33170; Phone: 305-246-1381
Treasurer: DAVE CHARLAND, 3559 NW 52nd St., Ft. Lauderdale, FL 33309; Phone: 305-484-7777
Director: RALPH JOHNSON, 7901 W. 25th Ct., Hialeah, FL 33016; Phone: 305-825-4667
Publication(s): *Newsletter*
Keyword(s): Hunting, Outdoor Recreation, Wetlands, Wildlife and Wildlife Habitat, Wildlife Management

FAIRFAX AUDUBON SOCIETY
P.O. Box 128, Annandale, VA 22003-0128
Phone: 703-256-6895; Fax: 703-256-2060
Founded: 1980; Membership: 4,500
Scope: Statewide
Description: The Fairfax Audubon Society--a chapter of the National Audubon Society, is committed to the Audubon mission which is to conserve and restore natural ecosystems, focusing on birds and other wildlife, and their habitats.
Contact(s):
President: TISH TYSON, 8641 Mt. Vernon Hwy., Alexandria, VA 22309; Phone: 703-780-0925
Treasurer: DUNCAN LOVE, 9204 Holborn Ave., Anandale, VA 22003; Phone: 703-978-3262
Publication(s): *Potomac Flier*
Keyword(s): Biodiversity, Birds, Conservation of Protected Areas, Ecology, Environmental and Conservation Education, Environmental Planning, Environmental Preservation, Environmental Protection, Natural Areas, Nongame Wildlife, Raptors, Wildlife and Wildlife Habitat

FEDERAL CARTRIDGE COMPANY
900 Ehlen Dr., Anoka, MN 55303
Phone: 612-323-3827; Fax: 612-323-2506
Scope: National
Contact(s):
Conservation Manager: WILLIAM STEVENS
Keyword(s): Hunting, Wildlife Management

FEDERAL WILDLIFE OFFICER'S ASSOCIATION
P.O. Box 45614, Madison, WI 53744-5614
Phone: 603-433-0502; Fax: 603-433-0509; WWW: www.fwoq.org
Scope: National
Description: The Federal Wildlife Officer's Association is an organization dedicated to the protection of wildlife and plants, the enforcement of federal wildlife law, the fostering of cooperation and communication among federal wildlife officers, and the perpetuation, enhancement and defense of the wildlife officer profession.
Contact(s):
President: KEVIN O'BRIEN
Vice President: MIKE LUCCKINO; Phone: 602-835-8289; Fax: 602-890-1957
Secretary and Treasurer: ED SPOON; Phone: 608-221-1206 ext 15; Fax: 608-221-1357
Publication(s): *The Federal Wildlife Officer Newsletter (Quarterly)*
Keyword(s): Birds, Endangered and Threatened Species, Environmental and Conservation Education, Environmental Justice, Environmental Protection, Hunting, International Conservation, Mammals, Marine Mammals, Nongame Wildlife, Pesticides, Predators, Raptors, Toxic Substances

FEDERATION OF ALBERTA NATURALIST
Box 1472, Edmonton, Alberta T5J 2N5 Canada
Phone: 708-427-8124
Founded: 1970; Membership: 18 Clubs
Scope: Statewide
Description: To increase Albertans' knowledge of natural history; foster creation of new natural history groups; promote natural areas; and provide a forum for discussion and means of taking action on environmental problems of concern to naturalists.
Contact(s):
President: DEREK JOHNSON
Treasurer: PAT CLAYTON, Box 1472, Edmonton, AB T5X 5R8 Canada
Executive Director: GLEN SEMENCHUK
Editor: BRAIN PARKER
Publication(s): *Alberta Naturalist*
Keyword(s): Birds, Environmental and Conservation Education, Natural History, Nature Preservation, Public Lands

FEDERATION OF FLY FISHERS
P.O. Box 1595, 502 S. 19th, Suite #1, Bozeman, MT 59771
Phone: 406-585-7592; Fax: 406-585-7596; Email: 74504.2605@compuserve.com; WWW: www.fedflyfishers.org
Founded: 1965
Scope: National
Description: To promote international fly fishing as a most enjoyable and sportsmanlike method of fishing and to preserve all species of fish in all classes of waters through local stream and fisher restoration projects, conservation grants, audiovisual programs, public education, and international committees. The International Business and Membership Office is located in Bozeman, MT. The International Fly Fishing Center (IFFC) in Livingston, MT was developed by the FFF to promote the conservation and preservation of our aquatic resources.
Contact(s):
President: TOM JINDRA
Secretary: GARY GRANT
Treasurer: MARC FE-BORNSTEIN
Contact for Salt Water Committee: RON WINN; Phone: 407-777-3341
Contact for Steelhead Committee: HOWARD JOHNSON
Contact for Warm Water Committee: FRED STEVENSON; Phone: 205-881-2754
IFFC Director: BOB WILTSHIRE, 215 E. Lewis, Livingston, MT 59047; Phone: 406-222-9369
Planning Director: LAUREN BAGLEY
Vice President of Communications: RICHARD IZMIRIAN
Vice President of Conservation: VERNE LEHMBERG
Vice President of Education: DAVID BARRON
Vice President of Fund Raising: TRACIE MALER
Vice President of Membership: KYLE MOPPERT
Publication(s): *Flyfisher, The*
Keyword(s): Environmental and Conservation Education, Environmental Preservation, Fisheries, Sport Fishing

FEDERATION OF NEW YORK STATE BIRD CLUBS, INC.
P.O. Box 440, Lock Sheldrake, NY 12759
Founded: 1947; Membership: 42 clubs, 750 individuals
Scope: Statewide
Description: To further the study of birdlife in New York state and to disseminate knowlege thereof, to educate the public on the need for conserving natural resources and to encourage the establishment and maintenance of sanctuaries and protected areas.
Contact(s):
President: VALERIE M. FREER, 686 Cape Rd., Ellenville, NY 12428; Phone: 914-647-5496
Vice President: MARY ALICE KOENEKE, 362 Nine Mile Point Rd., Oswego, NY 13126; Phone: 315-342-3402
Treasurer: SUE ADAIR, 107 Fox Run Drive, Schenectady, NY 12303; Phone: 518-355-8008
Corresponding Secretary: WILLIAM B. REEVES, 107 Elberta Dr., E. Northport, NY 11731; Phone: 516-499-1688
Editor: PHYLLIS JONES, 9 Hallock Rd., Pond Eddy, NY 12770; Phone: 914-557-6591
Editor: DONALD A. WINDSOR, P.O. Box 604, Norwich, NY 13815; Phone: 607-336-4628
Recording Secretary: LINDA PARR, 22B Ellsworth Ave., Delmar, NY 12054
Publication(s): *Kingbird, The; New York Birders; Checklist of the Birds of New York State*
Keyword(s): Birds, Wildlife and Wildlife Habitat

FEDERATION OF ONTARIO NATURALISTS
355 Lesmill Rd., Don Mills, Ontario M3B 2W8 Canada
Phone: 416-444-8419; Fax: 416-444-9866; Email: info@ontarionature.org; WWW: www.ontarionature.org
Founded: 1931; Membership: 15,000
Scope: Statewide
Description: Committed to protecting and increasing awareness of Ontario's natural areas and wildlife, and exerts influence to protect our natural environment. Eighty-three federated clubs across Ontario.
Contact(s):
President: JANE TOPPING
Vice President: MARK DORFMAN
Executive Director: STEPHEN FULLER
Chief Administrative Officer: JEAN LABRECQUE
Director of Conservation and Environment: JOHN RILEY
Editor: NANCY CLARKE
Manager of Conservation and Stewardship: JUDY EISING
Secretary and Treasurer: ED HAZELL
Publication(s): *Seasons*

FEDERATION OF WESTERN OUTDOOR CLUBS
512 Boylston Ave. E., #106, Seattle, WA 98102
Phone: 206-322-3041
Founded: 1932; Membership: 385
Scope: National
Description: Established for mutual service and for the promotion of the proper use, enjoyment, and protection of America's scenic, wilderness, and outdoor recreation resources. Forty-five affiliated clubs in Alaska, British Columbia, and the western states.
Contact(s):
President: BROCK EVANS
Secretary: NANCY KROENING
Treasurer: MARTIN HUEBNER
Editor: HAZEL WOLF
Publication(s): *Outdoors West*
Keyword(s): Deserts, Environmental and Conservation Education, Forests and Forestry, Outdoor Recreation, Wildlife and Wildlife Habitat

FISH AND WILDLIFE INFORMATION EXCHANGE
203 W. Roanoke St., Blacksburg, VA 24061
Phone: 703-231-7348; Fax: 703-231-7019; Email: fwiexchg@vt.edu
Founded: 1984
Scope: National
Description: The FWIE is a clearinghouse and technical assistance center to state and federal fish and wildlife agencies in the area of fish and wildlife databases and computer applications. The FWIE is available to help agencies with biological and administrative information management for application to environmental assessment, planning, extension, research, and education. The FWIE is a unit within the Department of Fisheries and Wildlife Sciences, Virginia Tech.
Contact(s):
Project Leader: JEFFERSON L. WALDON
Keyword(s): Aquatic Habitats, Biodiversity, Birds, Ecology, Endangered and Threatened Species, Fisheries, Insects and Butterflies, Mammals, Nongame Wildlife, Reptiles and Amphibians, Sport Fishing, Terrestrial Habitats, Wildlife and Wildlife Habitat, Wildlife Management

FISH AND WILDLIFE REFERENCE SERVICE
5430 Grosvenor Ln., Bethesda, MD 20814
Phone: 800-582-3421; Fax: 301-564-4059; Email: fwrs@mail.fws.gov
Founded: 1965
Scope: National
Description: A computerized information retrieval system and clearinghouse, providing selected reports on fish and wildlife management. Operated under a contract with the U.S. Fish and Wildlife Service to provide access to reports produced by the Federal Aid in Fish and Wildlife Restoration Program, the Cooperative Fishery and Wildlife Research Units Program, the Endangered Species Grants Program, and the Anadromous sport Fish Conservation Program.
Contact(s):
Editor: GEOFFREY YEADON
Project Leader: PAUL WILSON
Publication(s): *Fish and Wildlife Reference Service*
Keyword(s): Endangered and Threatened Species, Fisheries, Nongame Wildlife, Wildlife and Wildlife Habitat, Wildlife Management

FISHAMERICA FOUNDATION
1033 N. Fairfax St., Suite 200, Alexandria, VA 22314
Phone: 703-548-6338
Scope: National
Description: FishAmerica Foundation is the conservation arm of the American Sportfishing Association. The Foundation is a nonprofit organization dedicated to enhancing the water quality and fish populations of North America.
Contact(s):
Managing Director: TOM MARSHALL
Keyword(s): Environmental and Conservation Education, Outdoor Recreation, Sport Fishing, Water Pollution, Water Resources

FLORIDA ASSOCIATION OF SOIL AND WATER CONSERVATION DISTRICTS
ATTN: President, 16806 NW 40th PL, Newberry, FL 32669
Scope: Statewide
Contact(s):
President: TIM FORD, 16806 NW 40th Pl., Newberry, FL 32669; Phone: 352-472-5462; Fax: 352-472-4473
Executive Director: FREEDY COCKRELL, 540 W. Mill St., Baldwin, FL 32234; Phone: 904-266-4784; Fax: 904-266-4038
1st Vice President: TODD UNDERHILL, 6408 Goldfinch St., Sarastota, FL 34241; Phone: 941-923-3782; Fax: 941-924-3422
2nd Vice President: LYNDA JACOBS, 1811 West Cr. 419, Chulota, FL 32766; Phone: 407-365-6031; Fax: 407-365-5067
Administrative Consultant: SANDY HOWE, 16808 NW 40th Place, Newberry, FL 32669; Phone: 352-472-5462; Fax: 352-472-4473
Administrative Consultant: SANDY HOWE, 16806 NW 40th Place, Newberry, FL 32669; Phone: 352-472-5462; Fax: 352-472-4473
Board Member: TOM FORD, Rt. 2 Box 1077, Bryceville, FL 32009; Phone: 904-879-1002
Secretary and Treasurer: VIRGINIA MCCALL, P.O. Box 276, Salem, FL 32356; Phone: 850-584-2721; Fax: 850-584-2619

FLORIDA AUDUBON SOCIETY
1331 Palmetto Ave., Suite 110, Winter Park, FL 32789
Founded: 1900; Membership: 35,000
Scope: Statewide
Description: A statewide organization formed to promote public interest, understanding, and protection of Florida wildlife, and of the environment and habitats that support it.
Contact(s):
President: CLAY HENDERSON
Secretary: WILLIAM MCQUILKIN
Treasurer: GARY FROHMAN
Chairman of the Board: CAPT. ED DAVIDSON, 10800 Overseas Highway, Marathon, FL 33050
Editor: SANDRA BOGAN
Ornithologist: DR. GIANFRANCO BASILI
Senior Vice President: CHARLES LEE
Vice President of Chapter Relations: LARRY THOMPSON
Vice President, Center for Birds of Prey: RESEE COLLINS
Publication(s): *Florida Naturalist, The*
Keyword(s): Birds, Conservation of Protected Areas, Coral Reefs, Endangered and Threatened Species, Environmental and Conservation Education, Forest Management, Lakes, Land Use

NON-GOVERNMENTAL ORGANIZATIONS

Planning, Population Growth, Public Lands, Raptors, Rivers, Sea Grass, Wildlife and Wildlife Habitat

FLORIDA B.A.S.S. CHAPTER FEDERATION
ATTN: President, P.O. Box 30, Welaka, FL 32193
Phone: 904-467-9499
Scope: Statewide
Description: An organization of Bassmaster chapters, affiliated with the Bass Anglers Sportsman Society, organized to fight pollution, assist state and national conservation agencies in their efforts, and teach young people of our good conservation practices. Dedicated to the realistic conservation of our water resources.
Contact(s):
President: MIKE WESTNEY, P.O. Box 30, Welaka, FL 32193; Phone: 904-467-9499
Conservation Director: CHARLIE YOUNGERS, 1783 Marsh Rd., Oviedo, FL 32765; Phone: 407-349-0846; Email: westney@gbso.net

FLORIDA CONSERVATION FOUNDATION, INC.
1251-B Miller Ave., Winter Park, FL 32789
Phone: 407-644-5377
Founded: 1968
Scope: Statewide
Description: A nonprofit, tax-exempt organization engaged in research and dissemination of environmental information of concern to Florida.
Contact(s):
Director: DOUG HEAD
Assistant to the Director: HEATHER MOORE
Editor: LINDA LORD, 1251-B Miller Ave., Winter Park, FL 32789
Publication(s): *ENFO Reports; Publications Guide to Florida Environmental Issues and Information; Solar Florida: A Sustainable Energy Future; Solar Heating for Swimming Pools; Build Your Own Solar Water Heater; Florida's Calamity Calendar; brochures; Florida's Water and Common Natural Areas*
Keyword(s): Energy, Environmental and Conservation Education, Solar Energy, Water Resources, Wildlife and Wildlife Habitat

FLORIDA DEFENDERS OF THE ENVIRONMENT, INC. (Home Office)
4424 NW 13 St., Suite C-8, Gainesville, FL 32609
Phone: 352-378-8465; Fax: 352-377-0869; Email: fde@bellsouth.net
Scope: Statewide
Description: FDE promotes conservation, restoration, and sustainable use of Florida's natural resources by providing the public and private sector with objective information and analysis developed through a statewide network of voluteer specialists. Guided by the motto "FDE gets the facts," the organization achieves realistic goals by targeting a limited number of complex environmental issues and providing expert scientific analysis, sustained tracking, advocacy, and litigation when necessary.
Contact(s):
President: RICHARD HAMANN ESQ; Phone: 352-392-2237; Fax: 352-392-1457
Vice President: DR. JOE SIRY
Secretary: BRAM D.E. CANTER ESQ
Treasurer: DR. SUSAN VINCE ESQ
Executive Director: ROBIN MITCHELL
Coordinator of Apalachicola River: STEVE LEITMAN
Coordinator of Ocklawaha River: DAVID J. WHITE
Coordinator of Suwannee River: SUSAN VINCE
Coordinator of Suwannee River: BOB SIMONS
Publication(s): *Monitor, The*
Keyword(s): Biodiversity, Land Use Planning, Rivers, Water Quality, Water Resources, Watersheds, Wildlife and Wildlife Habitat

FLORIDA EXOTIC PEST PLANT COUNCIL
P.O. Box 24680, West Palm Beach, FL 33416
Founded: 1984; Membership: 225
Scope: Statewide
Description: FLEPPC goals are directed toward building public awareness about the serious threat invasive plants pose to native ecosystems, secure funding, and support for control and management of exotic plants, and developing integrated management and control methods.
Contact(s):
Secretary: JACKIE SMITH; Phone: 561-791-4720
Treasurer: DAN THUYER; Phone: 561-687-6129; Fax: 561-687-6436
Chairperson: ANTONIO J. PERNAS; Phone: 941-695-4111; Fax: 941-695-5495; Email: tony-pernas@nps.gov
Past Chair: GREG JUBINSKY; Phone: 850-487-2600; Fax: 850-488-2216; Email: jubinsky-q@ngw.state.fl.us
Publication(s): *Wildland Weeds; Florida Exotic Pest Plant Council Newsletter*
Keyword(s): Biology, Conservation, Environmental Preservation, Natural Areas

FLORIDA FORESTRY ASSOCIATION
P.O. Box 1696, Tallahassee, FL 32302
Phone: 904-222-5646; Fax: 904-222-6179
Founded: 1923
Scope: Statewide
Description: Nonprofit, trade-supported organization of industries, businesses, and individuals who encourage the promotion, development, and protection of forestry in Florida.
Contact(s):
President: CLAY SMALLWOOD, P.O. Box 908, Port St. Joe, FL 32457
Editor: JEFF DORAN
Executive Vice President: JEFF DORAN
President-Elect: ROBERT LUNDBERG, P.O. Box 2565, Panama City, FL 32402-2565
Secretary and Treasurer: HARRY VAN LOOCK, Rt. 3 Box 260, Perry, FL 32347
Publication(s): *Pines and Needles; Florida Forests*

FLORIDA NATIVE PLANT SOCIETY
P.O. Box 6116, Spring Hill, FL 34606
Phone: 813-856-8202
Founded: 1980; Membership: 3,400
Scope: Statewide
Description: Promotes preservation, conservation, and restoration of native plants and native plant communities of Florida, and provides information through publications, conferences, workshops, and a statewide membership organized by local chapters.
Contact(s):
President: DAVID PAIS, 2306 NW 47th Terr., Gainesville, FL 32604; Phone: 904-372-3899
Vice President: KIM ZARILLO, 760 Cajeput Cir., Melbourne Village, FL 32904; Phone: 407-727-1713
Vice President: JANICE BRODA, 9335 Frangipani Dr., Vero Beach, FL 32963; Phone: 407-589-0319
Treasurer: CANDACE WELLER, 1515 Country Club Rd. N., St. Petersburg, FL 33710; Phone: 813-345-4619
Publication(s): *Palmetto, The; Florida's Incredible Wild Edibles; Planning and Planting Your Native Plant Yard; Butterfly Gardening with Florida's Native Plants*
Keyword(s): Biodiversity, Endangered and Threatened Species, Environmental and Conservation Education, Flowers, Plants, and Trees, Natural Areas

FLORIDA ORNITHOLOGICAL SOCIETY
c/o Richard L. West, 2808 Rabbit Hill Rd., Tallahassee, FL 32312
Phone: 904-386-6371; Fax: 904-531-9077
Founded: 1072; Membership: 500
Scope: Statewide
Description: To engage in pursuits that advance ornithology in Florida; to facilitate education about birds in the wild; to unite amateurs and professionals on the study of birds in the wild; and to publish a scientific journal and other publications, relevant to the member's common interests.
Contact(s):
President: BRUCE H. ANDERSON, 2917 Scarlet Rd., Winter Park, FL 32972; Phone: 407-671-3137
Vice President: THEODORE H. BELOW, 3697 North Rd., Naples, FL 33942; Phone: 941-643-2249
Secretary: DR. RICHARD L. WEST, 2808 Rabbit Hill Rd., Tallhassee, FL 32312; Phone: 904-386-6371
Treasurer: LINDA DOUGLAS, 3675 First Ave. NW, Naples, FL 33964; Phone: 813-455-8340
Editor: DR. WALTER K. TAYLOR
Librarian: FRED LOHRER, Florida Ornithological Society Collection Archbold Biological Station P.O. Box 2057, Lake Placid, FL 33852; Phone: 813-465-2571; Fax: 813-699-1927
Past President: FRED E. LOHRER
Publication(s): *Florida Field Naturalist; Florida Ornithological Society Newsletter*
Keyword(s): Birds, Endangered and Threatened Species, Environmental and Conservation Education, Natural History, Nongame Wildlife

FLORIDA PANTHER PROJECT, INC., THE
P.O. Box 19866, Sarasota, FL 34276
Phone: 941-379-2221
Founded: 1993
Scope: Statewide
Description: To assist in the sensible and responsible recovery of the Florida Panther in Florida, by raising funds to purchase environmentally sensitive panther habitat across Florida. Guest Speakers Available
Contact(s):
President: WILLIAM SAMUELS, P.O. Box 19866, Sarasota, FL 34276; Phone: 941-379-2221
Executive Director: BOB MILLS, Gifts and Fundraising 4269 Hearthstone Pl., Sarasota, FL 34238; Phone: 941-966-7765
Advisory Board: TIM MALLON, 3715 Felda St., Cocoa, FL 32926; Phone: 407-633-4799
Board of Directors: JUDY CONDA, 6551 Gulfgate Pl., Sarasota, FL 34321; Phone: 941-921-7300
Keyword(s): Endangered and Threatened Species, Environmental and Conservation Education, Land Purchase, Nongame Wildlife, Wildlife and Wildlife Habitat

FLORIDA PUBLIC INTEREST RESEARCH GROUP (Florida PIRG)
704 West Madison St., Tallahassee, FL 32304
Phone: 850-224-3321; Email: floridapirg@pirg.org; WWW: www.pirg.org/floridapirg
Founded: 1981; Membership: 35,000
Scope: Statewide
Description: Florida PIRG is a nonprofit organization committed to researching, educating, organizing, and advocating programs to protect Florida's environment. These programs include preventing offshore drilling, promoting recycling, and other vital issues.
Contact(s):
Executive Director: MARK FERRULO
Publication(s): *Citizen Agenda; Florida PIRG reports*
Keyword(s): Environmental Protection

FLORIDA SPORTSMEN'S CONSERVATION ASSOCIATION
P.O. Box 20051, West Palm Beach, FL 33416-0051
Phone: 561-478-5965
Founded: 1994; Membership: 288
Scope: Statewide
Description: The Florida Sportsmen's Conservation Association promotes conservation, preservation, and propagation of all forms of game wildlife species, nongame wildlife species, and marine life. The Association stimulates a greater interest in any and all legitimate outdoor recreational activities, assures sportsmen that they may continue to use areas for legitimate outdoor recreational activities, works towards the opening of all lands and waters for legitimate outdoor recreational activities, where feasible, and promote the enactment of fair game and fisheries laws and to assist in the enforcement of the laws.
Contact(s):
President: BISHOP WRIGHT, 15439-94th St. N., West Palm Beach, FL 33412; Phone: 561-795-1375
Secretary: KEVIN SMITH, 15856-93rd St. N., West Palm Beach, FL 33412; Phone: 561-795-4112
Treasurer: RICHARD ANDREA, 12334-77th Pl. N., West Palm Beach, FL 33412; Phone: 561-795-1136
1st Vice President: ROBERT STOSSEL JR., 14241-77th Pl. N., Loxahatchee, FL 33470; Phone: 561-753-7880
2nd Vice President: MARK DOMBROSKI, 1842 Lynton Cir., Wellington, FL 33414; Phone: 561-793-7200
Publication Director: BRUCE BRITT, 7407 Southern Blvd., West Palm Beach, FL 33413; Phone: 561-688-2553
Keyword(s): Environmental and Conservation Education, Land Use Planning, Outdoor Recreation, Public Lands, Wildlife and Wildlife Habitat

FLORIDA TRAIL ASSOCIATION, INC.
P.O. Box 13708, Gainesville, FL 32604-1708
Phone: 352-378-8823/800-343-1882
Founded: 1964; Membership: 5,500
Scope: Statewide
Description: This association was formed to instill in Floridians and in visitors to Florida an appreciation and a desire to conserve the natural beauty of Florida by all lawful means; to promote the creation of a hiking trail, to be called the Florida Trail, to run the length of the state; and to provide an opportunity for hiking and camping.
Contact(s):
President: RICHARD SCHULER
Secretary: MARY ANNE FREYER
Treasurer: DENNIS NYMARK
1st Vice Presiden for Administration: KENT WIMMER
2nd Vice President for Membership: SHIRLEY SORENSEN
3rd Vice President for Trails: FRED SCHILLER
4th Vice President for Public Relations: SYLVIA DUNNAM
Publication(s): *Footprint, The*
Keyword(s): Environmental and Conservation Education, Natural Areas, Outdoor Recreation, Pedestrian Environment

FLORIDA WILDLIFE FEDERATION
P.O. Box 6870, Tallahassee, FL 32314-6870
Phone: 850-942-7113; Fax: 850-942-4431; Email: wildfed@aol.com; WWW: www.ssnow.com/fwf/org.htm
Founded: 1935
Scope: Statewide
Description: A representative statewide organization, affiliated with the National Wildlife Federation, dedicated to the protection and enhancement of wildlife and its habitat through public education and government interaction.
Contact(s):
Chair: JENNY BROCK
President: MANLEY F. FULLER
Affiliate Representative: STEPHEN J. O'HARA
Editor: RICHARD FARREN
Publication(s): *Florida Fish and Wildlife News*

NON-GOVERNMENTAL ORGANIZATIONS

FOOD AND AGRICULTURE ORGANIZATION OF THE UNITED NATIONS
Viale delle Terme di Caracalla, Rome 00100 Italy
Phone: 57051; WWW: www.fao.org
Founded: 1945; Membership: 174
Scope: International
Description: To raise levels of nutrition and standards of living, to improve the production and distribution of agricultural products, and to better the conditions of rural populations. FAO has adopted an overriding strategy of integrated sustainable development. All operations are geared to meet basic human needs without compromising those of future generations.
Contact(s):
Contact for the Sustainable Development Department: H. CARSALAD
Deputy Director-General: H. W. HJORT
Director of Information Division: K. L. SVARRE
Director-General: JACQUES DIOUF
Inspector-General: P. G. WILSON
Publication(s): *State of Food and Agriculture; Unasylva*
Keyword(s): Agriculture, Fisheries, Forests and Forestry, Health and Nutrition, Rural Development

FOREST HISTORY SOCIETY, INC.
701 Vickers Ave., Durham, NC 27701
Phone: 919-682-9319
Founded: 1946; Membership: 1,500
Scope: National
Description: A nonprofit educational institution, the Forest History Society is dedicated to the advancement of historical understanding of man's interaction with the forest environment--forest industries, forestry, conservation, and other forms of use and appreciation. A membership organization, it sponsors programs in research, publication, archives-library, and professional service.
Contact(s):
Chairman: THOMAS R. DUNLAP
President: STEVE ANDERSON
Editor: HAL ROTHMAN
Librarian: CHERYL OAKES
Publication(s): *Forest History Today; Environmental History*
Keyword(s): Conservation of Protected Areas, Environmental Law, Forests and Forestry, Land Use Planning, Public Lands

FOREST LANDOWNERS ASSOCIATION, INC.
Suite 120, 4 Executive Park, E., P.O. Box 95385, Atlanta, GA 30347
Phone: 404-325-2954; Fax: 404-325-2955
Founded: 1941
Scope: National
Description: Nonprofit forestry organization of timberland owners large and small in 17 southern states seeking to give private timberland owners and related interests a greater voice in matters affecting their business.
Contact(s):
President: KIRK RODGERS
Editor: STACIE LEWIS
Executive Vice President: STEVE NEWTON
Regional Vice President: RON BOST, Crescent Resources, Inc., Box 1003, Charlotte, NC 28201-1003
Regional Vice President: ACE PARKER, Parker Forestry Services, Box 2171, Salisbury, MD 21802
Regional Vice President: ED M. JUSO, Southern Region Manager, Westvaco, Box 1950, Summerville, SC 29484
Regional Vice President: PEGGY CLARK, 1203 Pine St., Arkadelphia, AR 71923
Regional Vice President: WILLIAMS S. STUDY JR., 4601 Willard Ave., Chevy Chase, MD 20815
Publication(s): *Forest Magazine; Forest Farmer Manual*
Keyword(s): Environmental and Conservation Education, Forests and Forestry, Renewable Resources, Urban Forestry

FOREST LANDOWNERS OF CALIFORNIA
980 9th St., Suite 1600, Sacramento, CA 95814
Phone: 916-972-0273; Fax: 916-971-1504
Founded: 1974; Membership: 1,000
Scope: Statewide
Description: A statewide organization affiliated with the National Woodland Owners Association that provides educational programs, information services, and legislative representation to families who own forest land for long-term investment, recreational, and conservation reasons.
Contact(s):
President: LEN LINSTRAND, Altadena, CA
Secretary: RON ADAMS, Shingletown, CA
Treasurer: JIM CHAPIN, Placerville, CA
Executive Director: DANIEL M. WELDON
1st Vice President: FOREST TILLEY, Redding, CA
2nd Vice President: ALLEN EDWARDS, Lafayette, CA
Editor: DANIEL M. WELDON
Publication(s): *Forest Landowner*
Keyword(s): Forests and Forestry

FOREST OWNERS ASSOCIATION (GEORGIA)
3402 Manchester Dr., Waycross, GA 31501
Phone: 912-283-0871
Founded: 1974; Membership: 120
Scope: Statewide
Description: A statewide organization affiliated with the National Woodland Owners Association to perpetuate good forest practices on private woodlands in Georgia including soil and water conservation, wildlife management, reforestation, and utilization of forest products.
Contact(s):
President: BOB PATTON, Crossville
President: SPENCER DAVIS, Mershon
Vice President: ROBERT HARRISON, Crossville
Secretary/Treasurer: ARCHIE MCEUEN, Waycross

FOREST SERVICE EMPLOYEES FOR ENVIRONMENTAL ETHICS (FSEEE)
P.O. Box 11615, Eugene, OR 97440
Phone: 541-484-2692; Fax: 541-484-3004; Email: afseee@afseee.org; WWW: www.afseee.org
Founded: 1989; Membership: 12,000
Scope: National
Description: A national nonprofit organization of Forest Service employees, retirees, other resource professionals, and concerned citizens working to change from within the Forest Service's basic management philosophy to a land ethic that ensures ecologically and economically sustainable management.
Contact(s):
President: DAVE IVERSON
Executive Director: ANDY STAHL
Editor: MATT RASMUSSEN
Field Director: BOB DALE
Secretary and Treasurer: CYNTHIA REICHELT
Publication(s): *Inner Voice; AFSEEE Activist*
Keyword(s): Biodiversity, Environmental and Conservation Education, Forests and Forestry, Public Lands, Wildlife and Wildlife Habitat

FOREST TRUST
P.O. Box 519, Santa Fe, NM 87504-0519
Phone: 505-983-8992; Fax: 505-986-0798; Email: foresttrust@igc.apc.org
Founded: 1984
Scope: National
Description: A nonprofit organization dedicated to protecting the integrity of the forest ecosystem and improving the lives of people in rural communities. The Trust challenges conventional forest management philosophies and provides protection strategies to grassroots environmental organizations, rural communities, and public agencies. The Trust also provides land management services

to owners of private lands with significant conservation values and serves as the institutional home for the Forest Stewards Guild and the National Network of Forest Practitioners
Contact(s):
Director: HENRY H. CAREY
Accountant: RON DRYDEN
Community Forestry Program: RYAN S. TEMPLE
Development Coordinator: LAURA McCARTHY
Forest Stewards Guild: STEVEN A. HARRINGTON
Land Stewardship Natinal Network of Forest Practitioners: THOMAS BRENDLER
National Forest Program: SHIRL CROSMAN
Publication(s): *Forest Trust Quarterly Report; Practitioner; El Cuartonero; Distant Thunder*
Keyword(s): Environmental Preservation, Forests and Forestry, Land Use Planning, Rural Development, Sustainable Development

FOSSIL FUELS POLICY ACTION INSTITUTE/ALLIANCE FOR A PAVING MORATORIUM
P.O. Box 4347, Arcata, CA 95518-4347
Phone: 707-826-7775; Fax: 707-822-7007
Founded: 1988; Membership: 1,200
Scope: National
Description: As the founder of the Alliance for a Paving Moratorium, Fossil Fuels Action directs road-fighting and education to address loss of farmland, wilderness, and community. APM unites over 150 groups and businesses in a call for an end to new road construction while promoting alternative transportation and the car-free lifestyle. We oppose NAFTA superhighways, and promote local self-sufficiency (bioregionalism).
Contact(s):
Board of Directors Member: RICHARD REGISTER
Board of Directors Member: LONNIE MAXFIELD
Board of Directors Member: DEBBIE LUKAS
Board of Directors President: JAN LUNDBERG
Publication(s): *Auto-Free Times; Road Fighters Alert*
Keyword(s): Air Quality and Pollution, Energy, Environmental Planning, Environmental Preservation, Land Use Planning, NAFTA Superhighway, Population Growth, Road Construction, Sustainable Development, Transportation, Urban Environment, Watersheds, Wilderness

FOSSIL FUELS POLICY ACTION INSTITUTE/ALLIANCE FOR A PAVING MORATORIUM (South American Bureau Office)
P.O. Box 1394, Correo Central, Buenos Aires 1000 Argentina
Scope: National
Contact(s):
Contact: RAUL A. RUATOR

FOSSIL RIM WILDLIFE CENTER
P.O. Box 2189, Glen Rose, TX 76043
Phone: 254-897-2960
Founded: 1987
Scope: National
Description: A 3,000-acre wildlife preserve dedicated to the preservation of endangered and rare species with the ultimate goal of returning these species to the wild. Sixty animal species are represented, and Fossil Rim participates in nine Species Survival Plan programs. Programs include public education, research into the management and propagation of endangered species, training of conservation professionals, and support for the creation of similar efforts around the world. Public programs promote personal commitment and involvement in conservation. Conservation programs are funded through revenue producing conservation-based tourism activities
Contact(s):
Chairman of the Board: M. CHRISTINE JURZYKOWSKI
Chief Operating Officer: CRAIG BRESTRUD; Phone: 254-897-2960x202
Director of Communications: YOLA CARLOUGH; Phone: 254-897-2960x206
Vice President of Conservation: BRUCE A. WILLIAMS; Phone: 254-897-2960x304
Publication(s): *Fossil Rim News*
Keyword(s): Endangered and Threatened Species, Environmental and Conservation Education, International Conservation, Internships, Sustainable Ecosystems

FOUNDATION FOR NORTH AMERICAN BIG GAME
P.O. Box 2710, Woodbridge, VA 22193
Phone: 703-878-2119
Founded: 1992; Membership: 1,000
Scope: National
Description: A nonprofit membership organization with major objectives of protection and encouragement of sport hunting in North America; education of the general public to the values of sport hunting, both direct and indirect; and the conservation and welfare of the big-game species of the continent.
Contact(s):
President: DON J. KIRN; Phone: 816-761-4351; Fax: 816-761-8737
Vice President: WARREN K. PARKER; Phone: 816-229-8899; Fax: 816-229-5933
Secretary: DON R. MORGAN; Phone: 352-473-2662; Fax: 352-473-2166
Treasurer: E. WAYNE POCIUS; Phone: 215-536-9616; Fax: 215-536-5815
Executive Director: WILLIAM HAROLD NESBITT; Phone: 703-590-4449; Fax: 703-878-2119
Board Member: TAZ RIDLEY; Phone: 913-661-3532; Fax: 913-661-3510
Board Member: EDWARD N. NANNINI; Phone: 916-485-8111; Fax: 916-485-1709
Publication(s): *North American Big Game (quarterly magazine)*
Keyword(s): Environmental and Conservation Education, Hunting, Mammals, Wildlife and Wildlife Habitat, Wildlife Management

FOUNDATION FOR NORTH AMERICAN WILD SHEEP
720 Allen Ave., Cody, WY 82414
Founded: 1977; Membership: 5,000
Scope: National
Description: A nonprofit organization whose purposes are to: promote the management of and safeguard against the extinction of all species of wild sheep native to the continent of North America; promote the protection and intensive management of the remaining wild sheep populations and their habitat; and promote the re-establishment of wild sheep populations in suitable historic habitat in North America. The Foundation funds wild sheep research, wildlife studies, improves habitat, finances sheep transplants, and supports hunting and game management policies based on sound, proven principles.
Contact(s):
President: LeLAND SPEAKES JR., P.O. Box 1073, Cleveland, MS 38732; Phone: 601-843-2772; Fax: 601-843-3091
Secretary: DUNCAN GILCHRIST, P.O. Box 696, Corvallis, MT 59828; Phone: 406-961-4314
Treasurer: MIKE BAUMANN, 7436 W. 83rd Way, Arvada, CO 80003-1637; Phone: 303-940-6690; Fax: 303-940-6659
1st Vice President: TED SCHUTTE, 5554 180th St., Sibley, IA 51249; Phone: 712-754-3729; Fax: 712-754-3195
2nd Vice President: ROYCE WOOD, 4245 Production Court, N. Las Vegas, NV 89115; Phone: 702-643-3078; Fax: 702-643-7899
Publication(s): *Wild Sheep*
Keyword(s): Environmental and Conservation Education, Wildlife and Wildlife Habitat, Wildlife Disease, Wildlife Management, Wildlife Rehabilitation

NON-GOVERNMENTAL ORGANIZATIONS

FRANKFURT ZOOLOGICAL SOCIETY--HELP FOR THREATENED WILDLIFE
Alfred-Brehm-Platz 16, Frankfurt, Frankfurt D-60316 Germany
Phone: 069-94344644; Fax: 069-439348
Founded: 1858; Membership: 6,000
Scope: International
Description: A private organization that supports wildlife/nature conservation and environmental/conservation education with international, national, and regional projects.
Contact(s):
President: DR. RICHARD FAUST
Projects Officer and Executive Assistant to the President: INGRID KOBERSTEIN
Regional Representative for Eastern Africa: DR. MARKUS BORNER
Publication(s): *Mitteilungen an die Mitglieder*

FRESHWATER FOUNDATION
Spring Hill Center 725 County Rd. 6, Wayzata, MN 55391
Phone: 612-449-0092
Founded: 1968
Scope: National
Description: The FF is an international nonprofit organization established to support research and education. The Foundation encourages proper use and management to keep surface water and groundwater usable for human consumption, industry, and recreation. Through publications, conferences, media, and other information programs, the Foundation seeks to help people understand water issues and their environmental, political, social, and economic impact. Individual, professional, corporate, and organization memberships are available.
Contact(s):
Chairman: RICHARD GRAY
Director of Water Programs: ANN CONRAD
President and CEO: DONALD P. BROWN
Publication(s): *Facets of Freshwater Newsletter; Health and Environment Digest; U.S. Water News; Aquatic Nuisance Species Digest; National Water Quality News; various special reports; Minnesota weather guide calendars*
Keyword(s): Environmental and Conservation Education, Lakes, Water Pollution, Water Resources, Wetlands

FRIENDS OF ACADIA
P.O. Box 725, Bar Harbor, ME 04609
Phone: 207-288-3340; Fax: 207-288-8938; Email: stephanie@foa.acadia; WWW: www.foacadia.org
Founded: 1986; Membership: 2,500
Scope: Statewide
Description: Friends of Acadia is a nonprofit organization providing citizen support in partnership with the National Park Service to preserve and protect Acadia National Park and the communities that surround it.
Contact(s):
President: W. KENT OLSON
Board of Directors Chairman: H. LEE JUDD
Director of Association Conservation: MARLA MAJOR
Director of Conservation: STEPHANIE M. CLEMENT
Director of Operations: EILEEN ST.GERMAIN
Publication(s): *Friends of Acadia Journal*
Keyword(s): Conservation of Protected Areas, Outdoor Recreation, Public Lands

FRIENDS OF ANIMALS INC.
777 Post Rd. Suite 205, Darien, CT 06820
Phone: 203-656-1522; Fax: 203-656-0267; Email: foa@igc.apc.org; WWW: www.friendsofanimals.org
Founded: 1957; Membership: 200,000
Scope: National
Description: An international animal protection organization that works to protect animals from cruelty, abuse, and institutionalized exploitation. FOA's efforts protect and preserve animals and their habitats around the world.
Contact(s):
President and Editor: PRISCILLA FERAL
Secretary and Treasurer: SALLY LEINER-MALANGA
Publication(s): *Act'ionLine*
Keyword(s): Endangered and Threatened Species, Hunting, Marine Mammals, Trapping, Wildlife and Wildlife Habitat

FRIENDS OF DISCOVERY PARK
3801 W. Government Way, Seattle, WA Phone: 206-285-6862
Founded: 1974; Membership: 540
Scope: Statewide
Description: To create and protect an open space of quiet and tranquility where the works of man are minimized. A place which emphasizes its natural environment and to promote the development of Discovery Park according to a master plan responsive to these goals.
Contact(s):
President: ROBERT E. KILDALL
Vice President: GAYLE PODRABSKY
Secretary: ELIZABETH BERGGREN
Treasurer: ROSEALMA SMITH
Publication(s): *HCLT Newsletter*
Keyword(s): Environmental Planning, Landscape Architecture, Nongame Wildlife, Sustainable Ecosystems, Wetlands

FRIENDS OF THE BOUNDARY WATERS WILDERNESS
1313 5th St., SE, Suite 329, Minneapolis, MN 55414
Phone: 612-379-3835; Fax: 612-379-3842; Email: kevin@friends-bwca.org; WWW: www.friends-bwca.org
Founded: 1976; Membership: 4,000
Scope: Statewide
Description: Established to protect and preserve the wilderness character of northeastern Minnesota's million-acre Boundary Waters Canoe Area (BWCA) Wilderness and the surrounding areas in the international Quetico-Superior Ecosystem. Works on wilderness protection, acid rain, forestry issues, water quality, rivers protection, wilderness management, and wildlife species, such as the wolf.
Contact(s):
Secretary: CHEL ANDERSON
Treasurer: JEFF EVANS
Chairperson: JON NELSON
Executive Director and Editor: KEVIN PROESCHOLDT
Vice-Chairperson: BECKY ROM
Publication(s): *BWCA Wilderness News*
Keyword(s): Biodiversity, Endangered and Threatened Species, Forests and Forestry, Wilderness, Wildlands

FRIENDS OF THE EARTH
The Global Bldg., 1025 Vermont Ave., NW, Suite 300, Washington, DC 20005
Phone: 202-783-7400; Fax: 202-783-0444; Email: foe@foe.org; WWW: www.foe.org
Scope: National
Description: A global advocacy organization based in Washington, DC, with 61 international affiliates. Merged with Environmental Policy Institute and the Oceanic Society in 1990. Dedicated to protecting the planet from environmental disaster and preserving biological, cultural, and ethnic diversity. With strong ties to the grassroots in the U.S. and around the world, Friends of the Earth believes individuals and communities must have a voice in environmental policymaking that affects their lives. Fights ozone depletion, global warming, toxic chemical threats, nuclear hazards, groundwater contamination, environmentally unsound international lending policies, and irresponsible corporate practices. Produces the Earth Budget; works to change tax code to support environmentally sustainable policies. Budget is $2.7 million.
Contact(s):
President: BRENT BLACKWELDER
Publication(s): *Friends of the Earth Newsmagazine; Anatomy of a Deal, The Technical and Economic Feasability of Replacing Methyl Bromide, River of Red Ink; Green Scissors Annual Report*

Keyword(s): Air Quality and Pollution, Environmental Protection, Pesticides, Transportation, Water Quality

Northwest Regional Office (WA, OR, ID)
4512 University Way, NE, Seattle, WA 98105
Phone: 206-633-1661; Fax: 206-633-1935
Scope: National
Contact(s):
Contact: SHAWN CANTRELL

FRIENDS OF THE RIVER
128 J St. 2nd Fl., Sacramento, CA 95814
Phone: 916-442-3155; Fax: 916-442-3396; Email: ftr@igc.apc.org
Founded: 1973; Membership: 10,000
Scope: National
Description: A nonprofit membership organization dedicated to the preservation, protection, and restoration of rivers, streams, and watersheds through public education, citizen activist training and organizing, and expert advocacy to influence public policy.
Contact(s):
Executive Director: BETSY REIFSNIDER
Board of Directors Chair: JIM WHEATON
Editor and Advertising: CHARLIE CASEY
Publication(s): *Headwaters*
Keyword(s): Energy, Environmental and Conservation Education, Outdoor Recreation, Rivers, Water Resources

FRIENDS OF THE SAN JUANS
P.O. Box 1344, Friday Harbor, WA 98250
Phone: 206-378-2319; Fax: 360-378-2324; Email: friends@sanjuans.org; WWW: www.sanjuans.org
Founded: 1979; Membership: 700
Scope: National
Description: To protect to the fullest extent possible the scenic, aesthetic, ecological and sociological qualities, and resources of the San Juan Islands and the Northwest straits marine ecosystem. Promoting long-range planning and monitoring development.
Contact(s):
Executive Director: DOUGLAS SCOTT
Publication(s): *Friends of the San Juan Newsletter*
Keyword(s): Aquatic Habitats, Coasts, Forest Management, Islands, Land Use Planning, Marine Mammals, Oceanography, Sea Grass, Sustainable Development

FRIENDS OF THE SEA OTTER
2150 Garden Rd., B-4, Monterey, CA 93940
Phone: 408-373-2747; Fax: 408-373-2749; WWW: www.seaotter@seaotters.org
Founded: 1968; Membership: 4,000
Scope: Statewide
Description: A nonprofit organization dedicated to the protection and maintenance of a healthy population of southern sea otters, a threatened species, as well as sea otters throughout their north pacific range, and all sea otter habitat. Encourages research and public education to develop a sound conservation program.
Contact(s):
President: JOHN FISCHER
Vice President: RON STEVENS
Secretary: JEAN MANN MACDONALD
Administrative Assistant: JEAN HALLETT
Attorney: STUART SOMACH; Phone: 916-444-3900
Center Director: CATHY COLE
Executive Director for Education: ROSE DEAN
President Emerita: MARGARET OWINGS
Science Director: ELLEN FAUROT-DANIELS
Publication(s): *Otter Raft, The*
Keyword(s): Aquatic Habitats, Biodiversity, Biology, Coasts, Endangered and Threatened Species, Environment, Fisheries, Mammals, Water Pollution

FUND FOR ANIMALS INC., THE
200 W. 57th St., New York, NY 10019
Phone: 212-246-2096
Founded: 1967; Membership: 250,000
Scope: National
Description: National nonprofit animal-protection organization whose purpose is to preserve wildlife and promote humane treatment for all animals. Primarily serves as an advocacy group and information and education agency to help domestic and wild animals. The Fund operates six hands-on facilities.
Contact(s):
President: CLEVELAND AMORY
Chief of Legislative Services: CHRISTINE WOLF, 8121 Georgia Ave., Silver Spring, MD 20910
Field Officer: VIRGINIA HANDLEY, Fort Mason Center, Rm. 3262, San Francisco, CA 94123; Phone: 415-474-4020
Field Officer: CATHY SUE ANUNSEN, 5778 Commercial St. SE, Salem, OR 97308
Field Officer: DORIS DIXON, 2841 Colony Rd., Ann Arbor, MI 48104; Phone: 313-971-4632
Field Officer: LAURA SIMON, 21 Sperry Rd., Betany, CT 06524; Phone: 203-393-3669
Field Officer: SEAN HAWKINS, 401 Studenwood St., Houston, TX 77007
Field Officer: JULIE LEWIN, 16 Vera St., West Hartford, CT 06119
Field Officer: HEIDI PRESCOTT, 850 Sligo Ave., Silver Spring, MD 20910
Field Officer: ANDREA REED, P.O. Box 11294, Jackson, WY ; Phone: 307-859-8840
Field Officer: MARION STARK, P.O. Box 9029, Albany, NY 12209
Field Officer: KIMBERLY STURLA, 808 Alamo Dr., Suite 306, Vacaville, CA 95688
Field Officer: CHRIS BYRNE, Manager of Black Beauty Ranch, P.O. Box 367, Murchison, TX 75778
Field Officer: CHUCK TRAISI, Manager of Animal Trust Santuary, 18740 Highland Valley Rd., Ramona, CA 92065
Field Officer: CAROLINE GILBERT, Rt. 2 Box 559, Simponsville, SC 29681; Phone: 803-963-4389
Field Officer, Manager of Have a Heart Clinic: LIA ALBO, 335 W. 52nd St., New York, NY 10019
Legal Counsel: EDWARD J. WALSH JR., Vedder, Price, Kaufman, Kammholz, and Day, 805 3rd Ave., New York, NY 10022; Phone: 212-407-7740
National Director: HEIDI PRESCOTT, 8121 Georgia Ave., Silver Spring, MD 20910
Secretary and Treasurer: MARIAN PROBST
Keyword(s): Endangered and Threatened Species, Marine Mammals, Trapping, Wildlife and Wildlife Habitat, Wildlife Rehabilitation

FUNDACION NATURA - COLOMBIA
A. A. 55402, Santa Fe De Bogota, Santa Fe De Bogata Colombia
Phone: 571-3400569-3400137; Fax: 571-3400124; Email: snatura@xolnodo.apc.org
Founded: 1984
Scope: Regional
Description: Fundacion Natura is a Colombian nonprofit, non-governmental organization. It works with other national governmental and non-governmental organizations as well as international partners to attain the required knowledge to design viable conservation strategies which encompass biological, social, political, and economic variables.
Contact(s):
Executive Director: ELSA M. ANGEL
Publication(s): *Annual Report; Tropical Newsletter; Trua Wuandra*

NON-GOVERNMENTAL ORGANIZATIONS

FUTURE FISHERMAN FOUNDATION
1033 N. Fairfax St., Suite 200, Alexandria, VA 22314
Phone: 703-519-9691; Fax: 703-519-1872
Scope: National
Description: The educational arm of the American Sportfishing Association, the Foundation is a nonprofit organization dedicated to promoting participation and education in fishing as well as enhancement and protection of aquatic resources. Develops and coordinates the national program "Hooked On Fishing - Not on Drugs". The Foundation is a national leader in recreational fishing and aquatic resource education and offers student and instructor educational materials.
Contact(s):
President: MIKE HAYDEN
Director: DRISCOLL MCKEE
Keyword(s): Environmental and Conservation Education, Outdoor Recreation, Sport Fishing, Water Pollution, Water Resources

GALIANO CONSERVANCY ASSOCIATION
R.R. 1, Porlier Pass Rd., Galiano Island, British Columbia V0N 1P0 Canada
Phone: 250-539-2424; Fax: 250-539-2424; Email: galiano_conservancy@gulcislands.com
Founded: 1989; Membership: 300
Scope: Statewide
Description: The Galiano Conservancy Association is a community-based, regionally-oriented conservation organization and land trust. Its purposes are to preserve, protect, and enhance the quality of the human and natural environment of the area through public education; management, and ownership of conservatrion land; and research and restoration projects.
Contact(s):
Secretary: ROSE LONGINI; Phone: 250-539-3007; Fax: 250-539-2424
Co-Coordinator: JILLIAN RIDINGTON; Phone: 250-539-3095; Fax: 250-539-3096; Email: ridington@gulfislands.com
Coordinator: KEN MILLARD; Phone: 250-539-5878; Fax: 250-539-2424
Publication(s): *Archipelago; Newsletter; Bulletin*
Keyword(s): Aquatic Habitats, Biodiversity, Coasts, Conservation of Protected Areas, Environmental and Conservation Education, Environmental Planning, Fisheries, Forest Management, Islands, Land Preservation, Land Purchase, Land Use Planning, Natural Areas, Pesticides

GAME CONSERVANCY U.S.A. (formerly American Friends of the Game Conservancy)
P.O. Box 8328, Vero Beach, FL 71106
Phone: 561-234-8718; Fax: 561-234-6081
Founded: 1985; Membership: 525
Scope: National
Description: Game Conservancy USA's primary functions are to raise funds to support the research and educational activities of The Game Conservancy Trust in the U.K., to support antipoaching efforts in Tanzania, and to promote beneficial programs that pertain to the conservation of wildlife resources worldwide.
Contact(s):
President: F. WARRINGTON GILLET JR., 159 Via del Lago, Palm Beach, FL 33480; Phone: 407-655-6789; Fax: 407-832-1762
Secretary: WILLIAM E. MURRAY, 200 E. 61st ST. #4-G, New York, NY 10021; Phone: 212-832-23232; Fax: 212-319-5238
Executive Director: GEORGE F. MORRIS, 190 Camelia Ct. N., Vero Beach, FL 32963; Phone: 561-234-8718; Fax: 561-234-6081
Administrative Director: KIMBERLY A. MCMAHON, 365-20th Ave, Vero Beach, FL 32962; Phone: 516-234-8718; Fax: 561-234-6081
Librarian: JAMES LONG, The Game Conservancy Trust Fordingbridge, Hampshire, SP61EF United Kingdom; Phone: 011-44-1425-652381; Fax: 011-44-1425-655848
Publication(s): *American Friends of the Game Conservancy Newsletter*
Keyword(s): Scholarships and Grants, Wildlife and Wildlife Habitat, Wildlife Disease, Wildlife Management, Wildlife Rehabilitation

GAME CONSERVATION INTERNATIONAL (GAME COIN)
4600 Broad Ave., Ft. Worth, TX 76107
Phone: 817-738-5438
Founded: 1967; Membership: 1,500
Scope: International
Description: A nonprofit organization dedicated to responsible sustainable use of fish and wildlife and preserving the hunting and fishing heritage for future generations. Supports strong educational programs for classrooms and sponsors the state and province Outstanding Hunter Education awards from Mexico to Canada. Its National Junior Wildlife Artist competition encourages high school youngsters to compete for thousands of dollars in prizes under the theme: OUR WILDLIFE HERITAGE: PASS IT ON!. Created the 4-H Shooting Competition in Texas which now has been copied nationwide.
Contact(s):
Director: HARRY TENNISON; Phone: 210-271-0448
Keyword(s): Endangered and Threatened Species, International Conservation, Wildlife and Wildlife Habitat, Wildlife Management

GARDEN CLUB OF AMERICA, THE
14 East 60th St., New York, NY 10022
Phone: 212-753-8287
Founded: 1913
Scope: National
Description: A national nonprofit organization with member clubs from coast to coast and in Hawaii. Its purpose is to stimulate the knowledge and love of gardening, to share the advantages of association by means of educational meetings, conferences, correspondence and publications, and to restore, improve, and protect the quality of the environment through educational programs and action in the fields of conservation and civic improvement.
Contact(s):
President: MRS. ALAN M. WILLEMSEN
Conservation Chairman: MRS. WILLIAM P. BOGGESS II
Corresponding Secretary: MRS. GRAHAM A. MARX
Horticulture Chairman: MRS. ALEXANDER J. SCHLEUNING II
National Affairs and Legislation Committee: MRS. R. PAGE HENLEY JR.
Keyword(s): Endangered and Threatened Species, Environmental and Conservation Education, Flowers, Plants, and Trees, Gardening and Horticulture, Scholarships and Grants

GENERAL FEDERATION OF WOMEN'S CLUBS
1734 N St., NW, Washington, DC 20036
Phone: 202-347-3168; Fax: 202-835-0246; Email: gfwc@gfwc.org
Founded: 1890
Scope: National
Description: The General Foundation of Women's Clubs (GFWC) is an international organization of community-based volunteer women's clubs dedicates to community service since 1890. GFWC programs and projects encompass the major issues of our time including literacy, health, preservation of natural resources, abuse prevention, and solid waste management.
Contact(s):
President: MAXINE S. SCARBRO
Treasurer: ROSE M. DITTO
1st Vice President: JUDY LUTZ
2nd Vice President: ERNIE SHRINER
Beautification Program Chair: JOYCE SCHAEFER, Rd #4 Box 32, Seaford, DE 19973
Conservation Department Coordinator: TERRI WOGAN, 5401 E. Marilyn Rd., Scottsdale, AZ 85254
Director of Junior Clubs: BABS CONDON
Editor: NANCY HOFFMAN
President-Elect: SHELBY P. HAMLETT
Program Director: PAT NOLAN
Recording Secretary: JACQUELYN PIERCE

Resource Conservation Program Chair: BARBARA NUNNARI, 13200 Ridge Dr., Rockville, MD 20850
Water Quality Program Chair: NORMA CHESNEY, 1331 Jill Terrace, Homewood, IL 60430
Publication(s): *GFWC CLUBWOMAN*
Keyword(s): Energy, Environmental and Conservation Education, Environmental Preservation, Nature Preservation, Solid Waste Management

GEORGE MIKSCH SUTTON AVIAN RESEARCH CENTER INC.
P.O. Box 2007, Bartlesville, OK 74005
Phone: 918-336-7778; Fax: 918-336-7783; Email: gmsarc@aol.com
Founded: 1983
Scope: National
Description: Finding cooperative conservation solutions for birds and the natural world through science and education. The Sutton Research Center is a non-profit, tax-exempt organization conducting scientific studies, conservation projects, and educational programs regarding avian species worldwide. Topics of particular interest include raptor population surveys and studies, bald eagle population monitoring, avian captive breeding and reintroductions, ecological studies of grassland birds including songbirds and gamebirds, public education projects, and cooperative wildlife conservation efforts with landowners.
Contact(s):
Treasurer: HOWARD R. BURMAN
Executive Director: DR. STEVE K. SHERROD
Board Chairman: JOHN A. BROCK
Publication(s): *The Sutton Newsletter*
Keyword(s): Biodiversity, Birds, Conservation of Protected Areas, Endangered and Threatened Species, Environment, Environmental and Conservation Education, Environmental Preservation, Environmental Protection, International Conservation, Nature Preservation, Nongame Wildlife, Prairies, Predators, Raptors, Renewable Resources

GEORGE WRIGHT SOCIETY, THE
P.O. Box 65 210 Quincy St., Hancock, MI 49930
Phone: 906-487-9722; Fax: 906-487-9405; Email: gws@mail.portup.com
Founded: 1980; Membership: 600
Scope: National
Description: The George Wright Society is organized for the purposes of promoting the application of knowledge, fostering communication, improving resource management, and providing information to improve public understanding and appreciation of the basic purposes of natural and cultural parks and equivalent reserves.
Contact(s):
President: RICHARD W. SELLARS, National Park Service, P.O. Box 728, Santa Fe, NM 87504-0728; Phone: 505-988-6020
Executive Director: DAVID HARMON, Hancock Office
Publication(s): *George Wright Forum, The*
Keyword(s): Environmental Preservation, Environmental Protection, Historic Preservation

GEORGIA ASSOCIATION OF CONSERVATION DISTRICT SUPERVISORS
P.O. Box 8024, Athens, GA 30603
Phone: 706-542-3065
Scope: Statewide
Contact(s):
President: SAM T. RIGDON, P.O. Box 684, Buena Vista, GA 31803; Phone: 912-649-7547
Board Member: JOHN H. REDDING, P.O. Box 409, Monroe, GA 30655; Phone: 770-267-5283; Fax: 770-267-0014
President Elect, Alternate Board Member: RALPH HARRINGTON, 321 Glenhaven Dr., Milledgeville, GA 31061; Phone: 912-452-2609
Secretary and Treasurer: T. LARRY NIX, 3776 Anglin Dr., Gainesville, GA 30507; Phone: 770-534-7890

GEORGIA B.A.S.S. CHAPTER FEDERATION
ATTN: President, 11575 Northgate Trail, Roswell, GA 30075
Phone: 770-993-6597
Scope: Statewide
Description: An organization of Bassmaster chapters, affiliated with the Bass Anglers Sportsman Society, organized to fight pollution, assist state and national conservation agencies in their efforts, and teach young people of our country's good conservation practices. Dedicated to the realistic conservation of our water resources.
Contact(s):
President: LARRY S. LEWIS, 11575 Northgate Trail, Roswell, GA 30075; Phone: 770-993-6597
Conservation Director: SCOTT HENDRICKS, 5131 Maner Rd., Smyrna, GA 30080; Phone: 404-799-2159
Publication(s): *Georgia Federation Newsletter; Georgia Outdoor News*

GEORGIA CONSERVANCY, INC., THE
1776 Peachtree St., NW, Suite 400, S., Atlanta, GA 30309
Phone: 404-876-2900; Fax: 404-872-9229
Founded: 1967; Membership: 7,000
Scope: Statewide
Description: The Georgia Conservancy is a nonprofit organization of people dedicated to the responsible stewardship of Georgia's vital natural resources. We strive to balance the demands of social and economic progress with our commitment to protect the environment.
Contact(s):
Chairman: SUSAN M. BLEDSOE
Secretary: BETTY N. MORI
Treasurer: FLORIDA ELLIS
Assistant Treasurer: JAMES E. BOSTIC JR.
Chief Operating Officer and Senior Vice President: JAMES F. DURRETT III
Coastal Office: , 711 Sandtown Rd., Savannah, GA 31410; Phone: 912-897-6462; Fax: 912-897-6470
Publication Director: LISA P. PATRICK
Vice Chairman: MICHAEL RUMKE
Vice President for Education: ELLEN G. KEYS
Vice President for Environmental Policy: JOHN A. SIBLEY III
Vice President for Planning and Development: ROBERT D. SMULIAN
Publication(s): *Panorama: A Guide to the North Georgia Mountains; A guide to the Georgia Coast; Stream of Conscience: Natural Solutions for Clean Water; The Hiking Trails of North Georgia; Wetlands: Georgia's Vanishing Treasure*
Keyword(s): Air Quality and Pollution, Chemical Pollution Control, Conservation of Protected Areas, Ecology, Environment, Environmental Protection, Forest Management, Land Use Planning, Open Space, Pollution Prevention, Renewable Resources, Transportation, Urban Environment, Water Resources, Wetlands

GEORGIA ENVIRONMENTAL COUNCIL, INC.
P.O. Box 2388, Decatur, GA 30031-2388
Membership: 70+ organizations, 20+ subcribers
Scope: Statewide
Description: A statewide umbrella for organizations interested in environmental protection that seeks to facilitate the exchange of information among member organizations, to provide a forum for discussion of environmental issues of interest to the members, and to monitor state government legislative activities having to do with the environment.
Contact(s):
President: SUSAN VARLAMOFF; Phone: 770-978-0752
Secretary: TONY SCARDAC; Phone: 404-634-6511
Treasurer: TREY GIBBS; Phone: 404-633-2343
Past President: SUSAN WOOTTON; Phone: 770-953-8759
Publication(s): *GEC Monitor; Directory of Environmental Groups in Georgia; Legislative Monitor*
Keyword(s): Environmental and Conservation Education

NON-GOVERNMENTAL ORGANIZATIONS

GEORGIA ENVIRONMENTAL ORGANIZATION, INC (GEO)
3185 Center St., Smyrna, GA 30080-7039
Phone: 404-605-0000; Fax: 404-350-9997; Email: geoeco@compserve.com; WWW: www.sustainablesouth.org
Founded: 1991; Membership: 2,000
Scope: Statewide
Description: GEO is a non-profit, citizen-oriented organization established to preserve and protect Georgia's environment through education, collaboration, research, planning, legislation, and grassroots organizing. The mission of GEO is to create an ecologically sound, sustainable society by developing and implementing cooperative, long-range policies, plans and programs and by carrying out hands-on projects within local communities.
Contact(s):
Executive Director: DR. OLIN M. IVEY
President, Board of Directors: SUSANNA MACKENZIE EUSTON
Publication(s): *Georgians on Sustainbility; GEOdyssey; In My Backyard - A Citizens Guide to Watershed Planning and Protection; RIO-River Inventory for Organizing: Watershed Atlas-Directory; Case Studies for Watershed Protection*

GEORGIA FORESTRY ASSOCIATION, INC.
505 Pinnacle Ct., Norcross, GA 30071-3656
Phone: 770-416-7621; Fax: 770-840-8961; Email: gfagrowga@aol.com; WWW: www.gfagrow.com
Founded: 1907; Membership: 4,300
Scope: Statewide
Contact(s):
President: GIL MORGAN
Vice President: MARSHAL THOMAS
Treasurer: DALE GREENE
Executive Director and Editor: CHRIS BARNEY CASTLE
Publication(s): *Tops; GFA News; Legislative Bulletin*
Keyword(s): Communications, Forests and Forestry, Training, Transportation

GEORGIA TRAPPERS ASSOCIATION
P.O. Box 335, Doerun, GA 31744
Phone: 912-782-5417
Founded: 1979; Membership: 630
Scope: Statewide
Description: An organization of Georgia trappers and friends of trappers, affiliated with Georgia Wildlife Federation and National Trappers Association, organized to protect the rights of trappers to trap, to coordinate a trappers education program with the Georgia Department of Natural Resources and to conserve and protect the natural resources of Georgia.
Contact(s):
President: TOM ETHRIDGE, P.O. Box 335, Doerun, GA 31744
Vice President:
General Organizer: TOMMY KEY, Rt. 2, Newnan, GA 30623
NTA Director: RALPH GOODSON, P.O. Box 4398, Albany, GA 31706
Secretary and Treasurer: GRACE M. CONDER, P.O. Box 474, Brooklet, GA 30415

GEORGIA WILDLIFE FEDERATION
1930 Iris Dr., Conyers, GA 30094-5046
Phone: 770-929-3350; Fax: 770-929-3534; Email: gwf@gwf.org; WWW: www.gwf.org
Founded: 1936
Scope: Statewide
Description: A representative statewide organization, affiliated with the National Wildlife Federation, dedicated to the protection and enhancement of wildlife and its habitat through public education and government interaction.
Contact(s):
Chair: JOCELYN MOORE
Affiliate Representative: CHARLIE MILLER
Executive Vice President and COO: JAMES R. WILSON
President and CEO: JERRY McCOLLUM
Publication(s): *Southern Wildlife*

GIRL SCOUTS OF THE UNITED STATES OF AMERICA
420 5th Ave., New York, NY 10018-2798
Phone: 212-852-8000
Founded: 1912
Scope: National
Description: The national organization offers an informal education and recreation program designed to help each girl develop her own values and sense of worth as an individual. It provides opportunities for girls to experience, to discover, and to share planned activities that meet their interests. These activities encourage personal development through a wide variety of projects in social action, environmental action, wildlife values education, youth leadership, career exploration, and community service. Membership includes more than three million girls and adults.
Contact(s):
President: ELINOR FERNDON
Membership and Program Consultant: LAURAINE MERLINI
National Director of Membership and Program Cluster: SHARON WOODS HUSSEY
National Executive Director: MARSHA JOHNSON EVANS
Washington Representative: LaVERNE ALEXANDER, 1025 Connecticut Ave. NW, Suite 309, Washington, DC 20036-5405; Phone: 202-659-3780
Publication(s): *Outdoor Education in Girl Scouting; Earth Matters; Investigaciones divertidas y faciles de la naturaleza y ciencia; Fun and Easy Activities with Nature and Science; Fun and Easy Nature and Science Investigations*
Keyword(s): Environmental and Conservation Education, Outdoor Recreation, Urban Environment, Women in the Environment, Youth Organizations

GLOBAL CITIES PROJECT, THE
2962 Fillmore St., San Francisco, CA 94123
Phone: 415-775-0791; Fax: 415-775-4159; Email: epc@globalcities.org; WWW: http://www.globalcities.org
Founded: 1989
Scope: National
Description: The Global Cities Project provides local governments, businesses, and citizens with comprehensive, up-to-date information on local environmental policies and programs, promoting the development of environmentally and economically sound policy at the local level.
Contact(s):
President: WALTER McGUIRE
Chief Financial Officer: COLLEEN McCARTY, 2962 Fillmore St., San Francisco, CA 94123; Phone: 415-775-0791
Publication(s): *Building Sustainable Communities: A Guide for Local Government; Case Studies*
Keyword(s): Air Quality and Pollution, Energy, Energy Conservation, Environment, Land Use Planning, Open Space, Pollution Prevention, Solid Waste Management, Sustainable Development, Transportation, Urban Forestry, Water Quality

GLOBAL ENVIRONMENTAL MANAGEMENT INITIATIVE (GEMI)
818 Connecticut Ave., NW, 2nd Fl., Washington, DC 20006
Phone: 202-296-7449
Founded: 1990; Membership: 27
Scope: National
Description: The Global Environmental Management Initiative (GEMI), an industry-initiated coalition of domestic and multinational Fortune 500 companies, is dedicated to helping businesses achieve environmental, health, and safety excellence. Through the activities of its workgroups, it has generated and distributed concrete tools for industry use in a number of environmental management fields.
Contact(s):
Chairman: ROBERT SHERMAN
Executive Director: STEVEN B. HELLEM
Contact: MARY BETH PARKER
Publication(s): *Total Quality Environmental Management Primer; Corporate Quality and Environmental Management II: Measurements and Communications; Environmental Self-Assessment Program; Benchmarking Primer*

Keyword(s): Communications, Environmental and Conservation Education, International Conservation, Planning Management, Sustainable Development

GLOBAL INDUSTRIAL AND SOCIAL PROGRESS RESEARCH INSTITUTE (GISPRI)
3rd Floor, Skousenmitsui Bldg., 2-1-1 Toranomon, Minato-ku, Tokyo 105-0001 Japan
Phone: 81-3-5563-8800; Fax: 81-3-5563-8810; WWW: www.glocomnet.or.jp/gispri

Founded: 1988
Scope: International

Description: A nonprofi foundation established to conduct research and submit policy proposals in such areas as resource conservation, global environmental problems, and relationship between industry and economy.

Contact(s):
President: GAISHI HIRAIWA
Executive Director: KATSUO SEIKI
Secretary General: KIYOSHI KAWAMATSU
Publication(s): *GISPRI Newsletter (Japanese); GISPRI (English)*

GOPHER TORTOISE COUNCIL
Florida Museum of Natural History University of Florida, Gainesville, FL 32611
Phone: 904-392-1721

Founded: 1978; Membership: 500
Scope: National

Description: A nonprofit organization formed to assure the continued survival of viable populations of the gopher tortoise, Gopherus polyphemus, and its associated upland habitat in the southeastern United States.

Contact(s):
Secretary: CHRISTINE SMALL, 8300 West State Road 46, Sanford, FL 32771; Phone: 407-322-0268
Treasurer: CHRISTIAN NEWMAN, 3839 NW 67th Pl., Gainesville, FL 32653
Co-Chair: DEBORAH EPPERSON, MS Natural Heritage Program, CSTS-DPW-E Bldg. 6678, Camp Shelby, MS 39407-5500
Editor: PARKS SMALL, Florida Park Service, 1800 Wekiva Cir., Apopaka, FL 32712
Membership Secretary: LORA SMITH, c/o The GTC Florida Museum of Natural History, P.O. Box 117800, University of Florida, Gainesville, FL 32611-7800
Publication(s): *Tortoise Burrow, The Bulletin*
Keyword(s): Endangered and Threatened Species, Nongame Wildlife, Reptiles and Amphibians, Wildlife and Wildlife Habitat, Wildlife Management

GRAND CANYON TRUST
Headquarters, 2601 N Fort Valley Rd., Flagstaff, AZ 86001
Phone: 520-774-7488; Email: info@grandcanyontrust.org

Founded: 1986; Membership: 3,500
Scope: National

Description: The mission of the Grand Canyon is to protect and restore the canyon country of the Colorado Plateau---its spectacular landscapes, flowing rivers, clean air, diversity of plants and animals, and areas of beauty and solitude.

Contact(s):
President: GEOFFREY S. BARNARD; Phone: 520-774-7488
Communication Manager: TERI WALKER
Director of Conservation Field Programs: BRAD ACK
Director of Conservation Policy: TOM ROBINSON
Director of Development: KATRINA ROGERS
Membership Coordinator: DARCY ALLEN
Utah Conservation Director: BILL HEDDEN
Publication(s): *Colorado Plateau Advocate; Annual Report; Action Alerts*

GRAND CANYON TRUST (Utah Office)
Ancestor Square 2 West St. George Blvd., St. George, UT 84770
Phone: 801-673-8558
Scope: Regional

GRAND CANYON TRUST (Washington, DC Office)
900 17th St., NW, Suite 300, Washington, DC 20006
Phone: 202-429-2637; Fax: 202-429-2610
Scope: Regional
Contact(s):
Director: JULIE GALE
Keyword(s): Land Preservation, Land Use Planning, Public Lands, Sustainable Development, Water Resources

GRASSLAND HERITAGE FOUNDATION
P.O. Box 394, Shawnee Mission, KS 66201
Phone: 913-262-3506

Founded: 1976; Membership: 700
Scope: National

Description: A tax-exempt, nonprofit organization dedicated to prairie preservation and education. We encourage the preservation of all remaining prairies and work to increase public awareness of our prairie heritage.

Contact(s):
President: ANN SIMPSON
Publication(s): *GHF News*

GREAT BEAR FOUNDATION
P.O. Box No. 9383, Missoula, MT 59807
Phone: 406-728-9380; Fax: 406-728-2881

Founded: 1982; Membership: 2,500
Scope: National

Description: A membership-based organization dedicated to protecting all eight species of bears and their habitat. Programs range from supporting scientific research to educational outreach in schools.

Contact(s):
President: CHARLES JONKEL
Publication(s): *Bear News*
Keyword(s): Endangered and Threatened Species, Environmental and Conservation Education, International Conservation, Public Lands, Wildlife and Wildlife Habitat

GREAT LAKES SPORT FISHING COUNCIL
P.O. Box 297, Elmhurst, IL 60126
Phone: 630-941-1351; Fax: 630-941-1196; Email: hdqtrs@great-lakes.org; WWW: www.great-lakes.org

Founded: 1973; Membership: 325,000
Scope: National

Description: A nonprofit confederation of organizations and individuals throughout the Great Lakes states and provinces whose members are concerned with the present and future of sport fishing in the Great Lakes and adjoining waters. The Council, which acts as a clearinghouse for the exchange of information among members, also seeks to protect the Great Lakes against pollution and exploitation by commercial, individual, or other interests. over 100 U.S. and Canadian organizations with a combined membership of more than 325,000 families.

Contact(s):
President: DAN THOMAS
Vice President: ROBERT MITCHELL, 6466 Parkview, Troy, MI 48098; Phone: 810-558-6547; Fax: 810-575-9713
Secretary: MEL BOTH, 3538 S. Whitnall Ave., Milwaukee, WI 53207; Phone: 414-744-8711
Treasurer: TOM COUSTON, 12 W. Schaumburg Rd, Schaumburg, IL 60194; Phone: 847-519-1711
Editor: DAN THOMAS, P.O. Box 297, Elmhurst, IL 60126
Publication(s): *Great Lakes Basin Report*
Keyword(s): Aquatic Habitats, Environmental and Conservation Education, Fisheries, Sport Fishing, Wetlands

NON-GOVERNMENTAL ORGANIZATIONS

GREAT LAKES UNITED
Headquarters, Buffalo State College, Cassety Hall, 1300 Elmwood Ave., Buffalo, NY 14222
Phone: 716-886-0142; Fax: 716-886-0303
Scope: International
Description: An international coalition of environmental, conservation sports, labor, business, and native people organizations, and individuals throughout the eight Great Lakes states and two Canadian Provinces. GLU is dedicated to the protection, conservation, and restoration of the Great Lakes-St. Lawrence River Basin Ecosystem.
Contact(s):
President: JACK MANNO, Great Lakes Research Consortium, 24 Bray Hall, SUNY College of Environmental Science and Forestry, Syracuse, NY 13210; Phone: 315-470-6816; Fax: 315-470-6970; Email: jpmanno@mailbox.syr.edu
Vice President: JANE WILKINS, Sierra Club of Eastern Canada, 699 Bush St., Bel Fountain, Ontario L0N1B0 Canada; Phone: 519-927-5924; Fax: 519-927-9828
Secretary: TIM BROWN, Lake Michigan Federation, 1825 West Wabanasia, Chicago, IL 60622; Phone: 312-554-0900; Fax: 312-554-0193; Email: timbrown@igc.org
Canadian Treasurer: MANFRED KOECHLIN, Bay of Quinte RAP Team, 276 Dufferein Avenue, Belleville, Ontario K8N 3X7 Canada; Phone: 613-962-9492; Fax: 613-962-9492
Past President: JOHN JACKSON, Ontario Toxic Waste Research Coalition, 17 Major St., Kitchener, Ontario N2H4R1 Canada; Phone: 519-744-7503; Fax: 519-744-1546; Email: jjackson@web.net
Regional Director: MARC HUDON, Strategies Saint-Laurent, 343 rue Pere Fiset, Chicoutimi, Quebec G7H3E4 Canada; Phone: 418-698-4562; Fax: 418-543-8294
Regional Director: JAN CONLEY, Lake Superior Greens, 2406 Hughitt Ave., Superior, WI 54880; Phone: 218-726-1828; Fax: 715-392-5782; Email: jconley@cp.duluth.mn.us
Regional Director: KIRA MEDLIN-HENSCHEL, Mining Impact Coalition, 3805 Paunack Avenue, Madison, WI 53711; Phone: 608-231-9721; Fax: 608-236-9111; Email: Regional Director, Canada at Large: LYNDA LUKASIK, Bay Area Restoration Council, 148 Oakland Dr., Hamilton, ON L8E 1B6 Canada; Phone: 905-560-1177; Email: llukasik@worldwatch.com
Regional Director, Canadian At-Large: JULIAN HOLENSTEIN, Thunder Bay Field Naturalists, 427 Queen St., Thunder Bay, Ontario P7B2K3 Canada; Phone: 807-345-7784; Email: julian@tbaytel.net
Regional Director, Canadian At-Large: RICH WHATE, Toronto Environmental Alliance, 122 St. Patrick St. #209, Toronto, Ontario M5T 2X8 Canada; Phone: 416-596-0660; Fax: 416-596-0345; Email: tea@web.net
Regional Director, Canadian At-Large: JIM MAHON, Canadian Auto Workers Local 1520, 120 Tufton Place, London, Ontario N6C 4W9 Canada; Phone: 519-644-0960; Fax: 519-652-0586; Email: jim.mahon@odyssey.on.ca
Regional Director, Canadian At-Large: LILIANE COTNOIR, Front Commun Quebecois pour une Gestion Ecologique des Dechets, 2025 A Masson 001, Montreal, Quebec H2H2P7 Canada; Phone: 514-521-8989; Fax: 514-521-9041; Email: fcqged@enter-net.com
Regional Director, Canadian At-Large: DANIEL GREEN, Societe pour Vaincre la Pollution, C.P. 65 Place D'Armes, Montreal, Quebec H2Y 3E9 Canada; Phone: 514-844-5477; Fax: 514-844-1446
Regional Director, First Nation/Tribal: CLYNT KING, Six Nations Council, Box 5000, Ohsweken, ON N0A 1M0 Canada; Phone: 579-445-0853; Fax: 579-445-0155; Email: edp@execulink.com
Regional Director, Lake Erie Region: ELAINE MARSH, Rivers Unlimited, 4570 Akron Penninsula Rd., Penninsula, OH 44264; Phone: 216-657-2055; Fax: 216-657-2955; Email: ohgreenway@aol.com
Regional Director, Lake Huron Region: ZIGGY KLEINAU, Citizens for Renewable Energy, R.R. 4, Lion's Head, Ontario N0H 1W0 Canada; Phone: 519-795-7725; Fax: 519-795-7725
Regional Director, U.S. at Large: SUE MIHALYE, New York Sustainable Agriculture Working Group, 121 N. Fitzhugh St., Rochester, NY 14614; Phone: 716-232-1463; Fax: 716-232-1465; Email: mysauig@frontiernet.net
Regional Director, U.S. at Large: EMILY GREEN, Sierra Club Great Lakes Program, 214 N. Henry St #213., Madison, WI 53703; Phone: 608-257-4994; Fax: 608-257-3513; Email: sierra@expecpc.ocm
Regional Director, U.S. At-Large: MARTY VISNOSKY, Erie County Environmental Coalition, 900 State St., Erie, PA 16501; Phone: 814-456-4148; Fax: 814-453-2480; Email: martykanpa@juno.com
Regional Director, U.S. At-Large: DAN EMERTON, United Auto Workers Local #599, Environmental Committee, 812 Leith St., Flint, MI 48505; Phone: 810-238-1616ext.19; Fax: 810-238-3378
Regional Director, U.S. At-Large: MARK MULLER, Institute for Agriculture & Trade Policy, 2105 First Ave. S., Minneapolis, MN 55404; Phone: 612-870-0453; Fax: 612-870-4846; Email: mmuller@iatp.org
United States Treasurer: ED MICHAEL, Trout Unlimited, 223 Barberry Road, Highland Park, IL 60035; Phone: 847-831-4159; Fax: 847-831-1035; Email: 71750.1477@compuserve.com
Publication(s): *Great Lakes United, The; Pollution Prevention Bulletin; GLU Action Updates, occasional reports.*
Keyword(s): Biodiversity, Communications, Conservation of Protected Areas, Environmental Justice, Environmental Protection Fisheries, International Conservation, Pollution Prevention, Toxic Substances, Water Pollution, Water Quality, Water Resources, Watersheds, Wetlands

GREAT LAKES UNITED (Montreal Office)
460 St. Catherine W., #805, Montreal, Quebec H3B 1A7 Canada
Phone: 514-396-3333; Email: sgingras@igc.org
Scope: National

GREAT SMOKY MOUNTAINS INSTITUTE AT TREMONT
9275 Tremont Rd., Townsend, TN 37882
Phone: 423-448-6709; Fax: 423-448-9250; Email: gsmit@smokiesnha.org; WWW: www.nps.gov/grsm/tremont.htm
Founded: 1969
Scope: Statewide
Description: A residential environmental education center in the Great Smoky Mountains National Parks. Programs promote awareness, appreciation, and stewardship of national parks and are offered for children and adults.
Contact(s):
Chairman: TOM TAYLOR; Phone: 800-721-6064; Fax: 423-982-6583
Secretary: JOHN MINCEY; Phone: 803-635-3561; Fax: 803-635-3561
Treasurer: HARTWELL HERRING; Phone: 423-974-1755; Fax: 423-974-4631
Executive Director: TERRY MADDOX
Director: KEN VOORHIS; Phone: 423-448-6709; Fax: 423-448-9250; Email: ken@smokiesnha.org
Publication(s): *Connecting People and Nature; Trees of the Smokies; Hiking Guide to the Smokies*
Keyword(s): Environmental and Conservation Education, National Parks, Natural History

GREATER YELLOWSTONE COALITION
P.O. Box 1874 13 S. Willson, Bozeman, MT 59771
Phone: 406-586-1593; Fax: 406-586-0851; Email: gyc@greatyellowstone.org; WWW: www.greatyellowstone.org
Founded: 1983; **Membership:** 7,500
Scope: National
Description: A nonprofit, tax-exempt organization to preserve and protect the Greater Yellowstone Ecosystem and its unique quality of life by enhancing the ecosystem concept, raising the national public

consciousness about the Greater Yellowstone Ecosystem, and combining the political effectiveness of the coalition's 7,500 individual members and more than 120 national and regional member organizations.
Contact(s):
President: DWIGHT MINTON
Vice President: RUTH SHEA
Executive Director: MIKE CLARK
Editor: JON CATTON
Secretary and Treasurer: ROBERT KEITH
Publication(s): *Greater Yellowstone Report; Greater Yellowstone Today; Annual Report; EcoAction Alerts*
Keyword(s): Endangered and Threatened Species, Forests and Forestry, Private Land Development, Public Lands, Wildlife and Wildlife Habitat, Wildlife Management

GREEN (GLOBAL RIVERS ENVIRONMENTAL EDUCATION NETWORK)
206 S. Fifth Ave., Suite 150, Ann Arbor, MI 48104
Phone: 734-761-8142; Fax: 734-761-4951; Email: green@green.org
Founded: 1989
Scope: National
Description: The Global Rivers Environmental Education Network (GREEN) seeks to improve education through a global network that promotes watershed stewardship.
Contact(s):
Chairman: LORI WINGERTER, General Motors Corporation, Environmental and Energy Staff, 3044 W. Grand Blvd., GM Bldg. 12th Fl., Detroit, MI 48202-3220; Phone: 313-556-7652; Fax: 313-556-2644
Executive Director: DAVID BRUBAKER, 206 S. Fifth Ave., Suite 150, Ann Arbor, MI 48104; Phone: 734-761-8142; Fax: 734-761-4951
Honorary Director: WILLIAM STAPP, University of Michigan, 2050 Delaware Ave., Ann Arbor, MI 48104; Phone: 734-761-8142
Secretary and Treasurer: LINDA SEGEBRECHT, The Earth Works, 8300 NE Underground Dr., Pillar 108 H, Kansas City, MO 64141
Publication(s): *Cross-Cultural Partners Activities Manual; Heavy Metals Manual: Investigating Streams and Rivers; Air Pollution: Ozone Study and Action; Sourcebook for Watershed Education*
Keyword(s): Biology, Environment, Environmental and Conservation Education, Environmental Preservation, Environmental Protection, Inquiry Based Education, Pollution Prevention, Rivers, Water Pollution, Water Quality, Water Resources, Watersheds, Wetlands

GREEN MOUNTAIN AUDUBON SOCIETY
255 Sherman Hollow Rd., Huntington, VT 05462
Phone: 802-434-3068; Email: audubonmtn@aol.com
Founded: 1962; Membership: 2,000
Scope: Statewide
Description: Green Mountain Audubon Society is a chapter of the National Audubon Society. The Society operates nature center and wildlife sanctuary areas in Huntington, Shelburne, and Popasquash Island in Lake Champlain. The Nature Center offers environmental education programs for visitors and local schools year-around.
Contact(s):
Executive Director: WILLIAM G. HOWLAND

GREEN MOUNTAIN CLUB INC., THE
Rt. 100 R.R. 1 Box 650, Waterbury Center, VT 05677
Phone: 802-244-7037; Fax: 802-244-5867
Founded: 1910; Membership: 8,000
Scope: National
Description: A nonprofit organization organized to manage, maintain, and protect the Long Trail, a footpath completed in 1931 that follows the crest of the Green Mountains from Massachusetts to the Canadian border. The Club operates field programs and publishes guidebooks, maps, and educational materials in its efforts to maintain and protect the,440-mile Long Trail system. It is the advocate group for hiking in Vermont.
Contact(s):
President: ROLF ANDERSON, Rt. 242 Box 1010-G, Montgomery Center, VT 05471; Phone: 802-326-4789
Vice President: MARTY LAWTHERS, 4 Hillside Dr., Peru, NY 12927
Secretary: ANDREW NUQUIST, 29 Bailey Ave., Montpelier, VT 05602
Treasurer: PHIL BECKER, RR 2 Platinum Plain Rd., Barre, VT 05641
Executive Director: BEN ROSE
Editor: SYLVIA PLUMB
Publication(s): *Long Trail News, The Long Trail Guide; Day Hiker's Guide to Vermont; Long Trail End-to-Ender's Guide, Green Mountain Adventure, Vermont's Long Trail*
Keyword(s): Environmental and Conservation Education, Internships, Natural History, Outdoor Recreation

GREEN PARTY USA
P.O. Box 1134, Lawrence, NY 01842
Phone: 978-682-4353; Fax: 607-758-5417-callfirst; Email: gpusa@igc.apc.org; WWW: www.greens.org/
Founded: 1984
Scope: National
Contact(s):
Coordinator: JENNIFER GAUDET
Keyword(s): Air Quality and Pollution, Environmental Justice, Nuclear/Radiation, Sustainable Development, Water Quality

GREEN SEAL
1400 16th St., NW, Suite 300, Washington, DC 20036
Phone: 202-588-8400; Fax: 202-588-8465
Founded: 1989
Scope: National
Description: Green Seal helps organizations and individuals make environmentally responsible choices in their purchases. Green Seal reduces the adverse environmental impacts associated with the production, use, and disposal of consumer products through the award of an environmental "seal of approval." It develops environmental standards and tests products against those standards to identify for consumers those products that are environmentally responsible. The Environmental Partners Program also helps businesses develop green procurement plans through buying guides and monthly reports on green products.
Contact(s):
President: ARTHUR WEISSMAN
Chair of the Board: BRYAN THOMLISON; Phone: 609-737-8841
Publication(s): *Environmental Criteria and Standards; Catalog of Green Seal-Certified Products; Campus Green Buying Guide; Office Green Buying Guide; Monthly Choose Green Reports; Greening Your Property (A buying guide for hotels and motels)*
Keyword(s): Air Quality and Pollution, Energy, Environmental and Conservation Education, Renewable Resources, Sustainable Development

GREENHOUSE ACTION
2120 N. 140th St., Seattle, WA 98133
Phone: 206-361-0282
Founded: 1989; Membership: 500
Scope: National
Description: A nonprofit organization dedicated to reducing global warming and ozone depletion in the upper atmosphere through public education and citizen advocacy.
Contact(s):
President: GEORGE LOWE
Vice President: JOANNE LATHAN
Publication(s): *Warming Trends*
Keyword(s): Air Quality and Pollution, Energy, Greenhouse Effect/Global Warming, Population Growth, Renewable Resources

NON-GOVERNMENTAL ORGANIZATIONS

GREENPEACE, INC.
   1436 U St., NW, Washington, DC 20009
   Phone: 202-462-1177
Founded: 1971; Membership: 420,000
Scope: National
Description: A nonprofit organization dedicated to preserving the earth and the life it supports through nonviolent direct action, lobbying, public education, and research. Greenpeace seeks to protect biodiversity in all its forms; prevents pollution and abuse of the earth's ocean, land, air, and fresh water; end all nuclear threats; and promotes peace, global disarmament, and nonviolence.
Contact(s):
Executive Director: KRISTEN ENGBERG
Biodiversity and Ocean Ecology Campaign Coordinator: SUSAN SABELLA
Climate: KALEE KREIDER
Director of Communications: ADLAI AMOR
Director of Development: JULIE CRUDELE
Editor-in-Chief: DAVID BARRE
National Campaigns Director: LYNN THORP
Toxins and Energy: BILL WALSH
Publication(s): *Greenpeace Quarterly (magazine)*
Keyword(s): Energy, Fisheries, Greenhouse Effect/Global Warming, Nuclear/Radiation, Toxic Substances

GROUNDWATER FOUNDATION, THE
   P.O. Box 22558, Lincoln, NE 68542-2558
   Phone: 402-434-2740, 1-800-858-4844; Fax: 402-434-2742; Email: info@groundwater.org; WWW: www.groundwater.org
Founded: 1985; Membership: 4,000
Scope: National
Description: The Groundwater Foundation is a nonprofit education foundation dedicated to educating the public about conservation and management of groundwater. The Foundation is a clearinghouse for general groundwater information, sponsors the Nebraska Children Groundwater Festival, and coordinates the "Groundwater Guardian", a national community recognition program.
Contact(s):
President: SUSAN SEACREST
Groundwater Guardian Program Director: CINDY KREIFELS
Youth Programs Director: AMY KILLHAM
Publication(s): *Aquifer, The; The Groundwater Catalog*
Keyword(s): Environmental and Conservation Education, Pollution Prevention, Water Resources

GULF AND CARIBBEAN FISHERIES INSTITUTE
   c/o South Carolina Sea Grant Corsortium 287 Meeting St., Charleston, SC 29401
   Phone: 803-727-2078
Founded: 1948; Membership: 600
Scope: National
Description: Promotes fishery research by holding an annual meeting at which scientists, members of the fishing industry, and administrators can discuss status of various fisheries of the region; assists countries of the Caribbean in development and management of their fisheries; and makes information available on fisheries of the region and on research findings through the publication of the proceedings of the annual meeting.
Contact(s):
Executive Secretary: DR. MELVIN GOODWIN

GULF OF MEXICO FISHERY MANAGEMENT COUNCIL
   The Commons at Rivergate, Suite 1000; 3018 U.S. Highway 301 North, Tampa, FL 33619-2266
   Phone: 813-228-2815; Fax: 813-225-7015; Email: wayne.swingle@gulfcouncil.org
Founded: 1976; Membership: 21
Scope: National
Description: The Gulf Council is responsible for developing and monitoring fishery management plans to provide for the best use of the fishery resources in the federal waters of Gulf of Mexico.
Contact(s):
Executive Director: WAYNE E. SWINGLE
Keyword(s): Fisheries

H. JOHN HEINZ III CENTER FOR SCIENCE, ECONOMICS, AND THE ENVIRONMENT
   1001 Pennsylvania Ave., NW, Suite 735, South, Washington, DC 20004
   Phone: 202-737-6307; Fax: 202-737-6410; Email: info@heinzctr.org; WWW: www.heinzctr.org
Founded: 1995
Scope: National
Description: The H. John Heinz III Center is a nonprofit institution dedicated to improving the scientific and economic foundation of environmental policy. The Center's mission is to collaboratively identify emerging environmental issues, conduct related scientific research and economic analyses, and create and disseminate nonpartisan policy options for solving environmental problems.
Contact(s):
Board of Trustees Chair: JOHN SAWHILL
Senior Fellow and President: WILLIAM J. MERRELL
Senior Fellow and Vice President for Programs: MARY HOPE KATSOUROS
Senior Fellow and Vice President for Research: ROBERT FRIEDMAN
Keyword(s): Coasts, Environmental Protection, Fisheries, Research

HARDWOOD FOREST FOUNDATION
   P.O. Box 34518, Memphis, TN 38184-0518
   Phone: 901-377-1818; Fax: 901-382-6419
Founded: 1989; Membership: 400
Scope: National
Description: The Hardwood Forest Foundation is a public, nonprofit organization dedicated to supporting research and education about North American hardwood forests. The main programs focus on distributing factual information about forest management and forest-related issues in the form of video tapes, computer programs, and publications to elementary and high schools.
Contact(s):
President: NORMAN MURRAY
Executive Vice President: PAUL HOUGHLAND JR.
Keyword(s): Forest Management

HAWAII ASSOCIATION OF CONSERVATION DISTRICTS
   ATTN: President, P.O. Box 1170, Waiuku, HI 96793
Founded: 1939; Membership: 2,200
Scope: Statewide
Description: For better understanding, appreciation, and conservation of Hawaii's native wildlife resources, especially its unique and endangered bird species and their associated ecosystems.
Contact(s):
President: DAVID NORBRIGA, P.O. Box 1170, Waiuku, HI 96793; Phone: 808-935-0992; Fax: 808-935-0773
Executive Director: MIKE TULANG, 919 Ala Moana Blvd. Rm. 309, Honolulu, HI 96814; Phone: 808-586-4389; Fax: 808-586-4300
1st Vice President: DANIEL KANIHO, P.O. Box 2217, Kamuela, HI 96743; Phone: 808-885-1675; Fax: 808-885-1822
Alternate Board Member: SKIP COWELL, P.O. Box 783, Captain Cook, HI 96704; Phone: 808-328-9175; Fax: 808-328-8367

HAWAII AUDUBON SOCIETY
   850 Richards Street, #505, Honolulu, HI 96813-4709
   Phone: 808-528-1432; Fax: 808-537-5294; Email: hisocaude@pixi.com
Founded: 1939; Membership: 1,800
Scope: Statewide
Description: For better understanding, appreciation, and conservation of Hawaii's native wildlife resources, especially its unique and endangered bird species and their associated ecosystems.

NON-GOVERNMENTAL ORGANIZATIONS

Contact(s):
President: LINDA M.B. PAUL
Vice President: JOHN T. HARRISON
Recording Secretary: EDITH H. CHAVE
Publication(s): *Elepaio (Journal); Hawaii's Birds; Voice of Hawaii's Birds (cassette tapes); checklists; field card checklist*
Keyword(s): Aquatic Habitats, Biodiversity, Birds, Conservation of Protected Areas, Endangered and Threatened Species, Environmental and Conservation Education, Environmental Preservation, Islands, Natural Areas, Nongame Wildlife, Public Lands, Wildlife and Wildlife Habitat

HAWAII NATURE CENTER
2131 Makiki Heights Dr., Honolulu, HI 96822
Phone: 808-955-0100; Fax: 808-955-0116
Founded: 1981; Membership: 2,000
Scope: Statewide
Description: The Hawaii Nature Center's purpose is to foster awareness, appreciation, and understanding of Hawaii and encourage wise stewardship of the Islands in the future by providing hands-on environmental education field programs for school children, and community programs for families and the general public. Community programs include family nature adventures, interpretive hikes, and field adventures for scouts, senior citizens, and mentally and physically challenged groups. Focuses on full-day, environmental education field adventures for school children. Field sites on Oahu, HI and Maui, HI.
Contact(s):
Education Director: DIANA KING
Keyword(s): Aquatic Habitats, Biodiversity, Birds, Ecology, Endangered and Threatened Species, Environment, Environmental and Conservation Education, Insects and Butterflies, Interpretive Center, Natural History, Rainforests, Terrestrial Habitats, Wetlands

HAWAII SOCIETY OF AMERICAN FORESTERS
1151 Punchbowl St., Rm. 323, Honolulu, HI 96813
Founded: 1970
Scope: Statewide
Description: A nonprofit, tax-exempt organization working on environmental issues facing the state of Hawaii. Concerned with land use, native forests, water pollution, pesticides, coastal issues, and overdevelopment.
Contact(s):
Chairperson: NICK DUDLEY; Phone: 808-487-5561
Past Chair: LEONARD NEWELL; Phone: 808-522-8230
Secretary and Treasurer: TOM COLE; Phone: 808-522-8230
Keyword(s): Biodiversity, Endangered and Threatened Species, Forests and Forestry, Islands, Sustainable Development

HAWAIIAN BOTANICAL SOCIETY
c/o Botany Dept., University of Hawaii, 3190 Maile Way, Honolulu, HI 96822
Phone: 808-956-8072/ 683-0274
Founded: 1924; Membership: 200
Scope: Statewide
Description: Objectives of society are: to advance the science of botany in all of its applications; To encourage research in botany in all of its phases; to promote the botanical welfare of its members; and to develop the spirit of good fellowship and cooperation in botanical matters. The Society is particularly interested in the preservation of the Hawaiian flora.
Contact(s):
President: MINDY WILKINSON
Vice President: ALVIN YOSHINAGA
Secretary: LEILANI DURAND
Treasurer: RON FENSTEMACHER
Editor: CLIFFORD MORDEN
Publication(s): *Newsletter of the Hawaiian Botanical*

HAWK AND OWL TRUST, THE
c/o Zoological Society of London, Regent's Park, London, London NW1 4RY United Kingdom
Phone: 0181-450-0662; Fax: 0181-450-0662
Founded: 1969
Scope: National
Description: The Hawk and Owl Trust works for the conservation and appreciation of wild birds of prey and their habitats through projects which involve practical research, creative conservation, and imaginative education. Current projects include: Barn Owl Conservation Network; Operation Raptor Link; Farmland, Riverside and Forestry Link Scheme; Habitat Link. Its National Conservation and Education Centre is situated in Buckinghamshire
Contact(s):
Chairman: BARBARA HANDLEY
President: THE RIGHT HONORABLE THE EARL OF SHAFTESBURY
Director of Conservation and Research: COLIN SHAWYER
Press and Public Relations: BARBARA HALL
Vice Chairman: ROBIN REES-WEBBE
Publication(s): *The Raptor (journal/annual report); newsletters: Peregrine, Network Newslink, Adopt a Box*
Keyword(s): Birds, Environment, Environmental and Conservation Education, Raptors, Wildlife and Wildlife Habitat

HAWK MIGRATION ASSOCIATION OF NORTH AMERICA
Attn: Treasurer, R.R. 2 Box 301-A, New Ringgold, PA 17960
Founded: 1974; Membership: 1,000
Scope: National
Description: A nonprofit organization whose purpose is to advance the knowledge of bird-of-prey migration across the continent, to monitor raptor populations as an indicator of environmental health, to study further the behavior of raptors, and to contribute to greater public understanding of birds of prey.
Contact(s):
Chair: WILLIAM H. BARNARD, Norwich University, Biology Department, Northfield, VT 05663; Phone: 802-485-2342
Secretary: WILLIAM J. GALLAGHER, P.O. Box 822, Boonton, NJ 07005-0822; Phone: 973-335-0674
Treasurer: DOUGLAS WOOD, R.R. 2 Box 301-A, New Ringgold, PA 17960
Publication(s): *Hawk Migration Studies*
Keyword(s): Raptors

HAWK MOUNTAIN SANCTUARY ASSOCIATION
1700 Hawk Mountain Rd., Kempton, PA 19529
Phone: 610-756-6961; Fax: 610-756-4468; WWW: www.hawkmountain.org
Founded: 1934; Membership: 10,000
Scope: Regional
Description: The Association is a nonprofit organization devoted to the conservation of birds of prey and a greater understanding of the central Appalachian environment. A full-time staff assisted by interns and volunteers, carries out coordinated programs in education, research, monitoring, and sanctuary management. A visitor center is open year-round, and the 2,380-acre Sanctuary is maintained as a high-quality natural area with trails open to the public.
Contact(s):
Chairman: CLIFFORD L. JONES
Treasurer: JOHN B. BEINECKE
Executive Director: CYNTHIA R. LENHART
Publication(s): *Hawk Mountain News; Mountain and the Migration, The; Hawks Aloft*
Keyword(s): Birds, Mountain Ecosystems, Nongame Wildlife, Raptors

NON-GOVERNMENTAL ORGANIZATIONS

HAWKWATCH INTERNATIONAL INC.
P.O. Box 660, Salt Lake City, UT 84110-0660
Phone: 800-726-4295/801; Fax: 801-524-8520; Email: hawkwatch@charitiesusa.com; WWW: www.vpp.com/hawkwatch

Founded: 1986; Membership: 3,000
Scope: International

Description: HawkWatch International is a nonprofit research and educational institution dedicated to the study and conservation of raptors and to enhancing the public's knowledge of environmental issues affecting raptors and the ecosystems that support them.

Contact(s):
Chairman: DAVID NIMKIN, 3016 Kennedy, Salt Lake City, UT 84108; Phone: 801-582-1663
Secretary: ARDEAN WATTS, 660 S. University, Salt Lake City, UT 84120; Phone: 801-581-1931
Treasurer: SCOTT PICKETT, 36 S. State, Suite 1700, Salt Lake City, UT 84111
Executive Director: TIM FUNK, P.O. Box 660, Salt Lake City, UT 84110; Phone: 801-524-8511
Education Director: PAM HARDY, P.O. Box 660, Salt Lake City, UT 84110; Phone: 801-524-8511
Program Director: STEPHEN HOFFMAN, P.O. Box 660, Salt Lake City, UT 84110; Phone: 801-524-8511
Vice Chair: DAWN SEBESTA, 1399 Devonshire, Salt Lake City, UT 84108; Phone: 801-583-2223

Publication(s): *Raptorwatch; Hawkflash*

Keyword(s): Birds, Endangered and Threatened Species, Environmental and Conservation Education, Raptors, Wildlife and Wildlife Habitat

HEADLANDS INSTITUTE
Golden Gate National Recreation Area Bldg. 1033, Sausalito, CA 94965
Phone: 415-332-5771; Fax: 415-332-5784

Founded: 1979; Membership: 8,000
Scope: National

Description: To create sustained global environmental stewardship through educational adventures in nature's classroom.

Contact(s):
Chairman: DAVID JAY FLOOD
Executive Director: BRUCE A. TRUITT

Keyword(s): Environmental and Conservation Education, International Conservation, Natural History, Sustainable Development, Urban Environment

HENRY A. WALLACE INSTITUTE FOR ALTERNATIVE AGRICULTURE (HAWIAA)
9200 Edmonston Rd., Suite 117, Greenbelt, MD 20770-1551
Phone: 301-441-8777; Fax: 301-220-0164; Email: hawiaa@access.digex.net; WWW: www.hawiaa.org

Founded: 1983
Scope: National

Description: HAWIAA is a nonprofit, membership research and education organization established to encourage and facilitate adoption of resource-conserving, low-cost, environmentally sound, and economically viable farming systems.

Contact(s):
Executive Director: GARTH YOUNGBERG
Policy Studies Program Director: DAVID E. ERVIN

HERITAGE INTERPRETATION INTERNATIONAL
P.O. Box 7451, NECSC, Edmonton, Alberta T5E 6K1 Canada
Phone: 403-973-5931; Fax: 403-973-5931

Founded: 1985; Membership: 300
Scope: International

Description: Heritage Interpretation International works to provide an international network of interpreters; to foster professional recognition; to provide contacts between volunteers and projects; to convene a triennial congress; and to support national and regional organizations.

Contact(s):
President: CHRISTINE O'BRIEN, 96 Darghan St., Glebe 2037 NSW, Australia; Phone: 02-660-2165
Executive Board Chair: HELEN LOTTINSM, #97 St. Stephen's College, 8820 112 St., Edmunton, AB TG6 2P8 Canada; Fax: 403-427-0808
Past President: PER KRISTIAN SKULBERG, P.O. Box 100N, 1820 Spydeberg, Norway; Phone: 47-99-882395

Publication(s): *HII News; Membership Directory; Congress Proceedings*

HIGH DESERT MUSEUM, THE
59800 S. Highway 97, Bend, OR 97702-7963
Phone: 503-382-4754

Founded: 1974; Membership: 5,300
Scope: National

Description: Created to broaden the knowledge and understanding of the natural and cultural history and resources of the high desert country for the purpose of promoting thoughtful decision-making that will sustain the region's natural and cultural heritage. It is a "living," participation-oriented museum which focuses on the Intermountain West -- portions of eight Western states and the Canadian province of British Columbia. Opened to the public in 1982.

Contact(s):
Chairman of the Board of Trustees: MICHAEL HOLLERN
Director of Education: KATHLEEN RONNING
Editor and Communications Director: JACK COOPER
Native Heritage Curator: VIVIAN ADAMS
President (Acting): JERRY N. MOORE
Vice President of Development: WILLIAM A. REICHARDT
Western Heritage Curator: ROBERT BOYD

Publication(s): *High Desert Quarterly; Sagebrush Legacy*

Keyword(s): Cultural Preservation, Deserts, Environmental and Conservation Education, Natural History, Wildlife and Wildlife Habitat

HIMALAYAN WILDLIFE PROJECT
Centre One, House 1, Street 15, Islamabad F 7/2 Pakistan
Phone: 92-51-276113; Fax: 92-51-824484; Email: vzakaria@hbp.sdnpk.undp.org

Founded: 1993
Scope: International

Description: HWP is a nonprofit, nongovernmental organization dedicated to safeguarding the biodiversity of Pakistan's Northern areas. The efforts of HWP have included: involving local communities in the conservation process, coordinating protection and park management activities with the local administration and wildlife department.

Contact(s):
Contact: DR. ANIS UR RAHMAN

Keyword(s): Bears, Himalayan Range, National Parks

HOLDEN ARBORETUM, THE
9500 Sperry Rd., Kirtland, OH 44094
Phone: 440-256-1110; Fax: 440-256-1655; Email: holden@holdenarb.org

Founded: 1931; Membership: 7,200
Scope: National

Description: The Holden Arboretum's mission is to promote the knowledge and appreciation of plants for personal enjoyment, inspiration, and recreation, for scientific research; and educational and aesthetic purposes, and to develop documented collections, and study and conserve the natural environment, and to engage in horticultural research and education.

Contact(s):
Executive Director: DR. RICHARD H. MUNSON
Director of Education: PAUL C. SPECTOR
Director of Horticulture: PETER BRISTOL
Director of Research: ROBERT MARQUARD
Head Librarian: NADIA AUFDERHEIDE, Warren H. Corning Library, 9500 Sperry Rd., Kirtland, OH 44094; Phone: 440-256-1110 ext225; Fax: 440-256-5836

Publication(s): *Arboretum Leaves, The; Environmental Thinking and Learning (ETAL)*
Keyword(s): Botanical Gardens, Ecology, Environmental and Conservation Education, Flowers, Plants, and Trees, Gardening and Horticulture

HOLLY SOCIETY OF AMERICA, INC.
11318 W. Murdock, Wichita, KS 67212-6609
Founded: 1947; Membership: 600
Scope: National
Description: National nonprofit organization dedicated to bringing together persons interested in any phase of holly culture. Collects and disseminates information about holly; studies methods of conservatively cutting and marketing holly; promotes research and hybridization; publishes research papers; and popularizes the use of holly as a landscape material.
Contact(s):
President: BARBARA TAYLOR
Secretary: LINDA R. RICHARDSON
Treasurer: RUTH S. BRADLEY
Administrative Vice President: MICHAEL R. PONTTI
Editor: DR. SANDRA F. MCDONALD, 4302 Chesapeake Ave., Hampton, VA 23699-4638
Executive Vice President: DANIEL C. TURNER
Publication(s): *Holly Society Journal (including the proceedings); H.S.A. Books*

HOOD CANAL LAND TRUST
P.O. Box 861, Belfair, WA 98528
Scope: Statewide
Description: In 1986, the HCLT received its 501 c (3) status. Its primary aim is to preserve wetlands, wildlife habitat, and scenic outlooks along the Hood Canal. We currently hold title to 126 acres of estuary and upland fir forest. Under conservation easement we manage 222 acres.
Contact(s):
President: JOSEPH K. TESTU
Vice President: JEAN MOORE
Secretary: DIANA TIMM-DRYDEN
Treasurer: VIRGINIA M. TESTU
Keyword(s): Environmental Preservation, Hunting, Sport Fishing, Waterfowl, Wildlife and Wildlife Habitat

HOOSIER ENVIRONMENTAL COUNCIL
1002 E. Washington St., Suite 300, Indianapolis, IN 46202
Phone: 317-685-8800; Fax: 317-686-4794
Founded: 1983; Membership: 40,000 individual members & 65 group members
Scope: Statewide
Description: To encourage and promote more aggressive environmental regulation and enforcement in the state of Indiana. The Council objectives are as follows: Facilitation of communication between environmental groups and individuals; coordination of action on current environmental issues, educational programs and publications; and representation of the concerns of the membership before administrative officials and regulatory boards/agencies of the state and federal government.
Contact(s):
President: ERIC MAYER, 2020 First Indiana Plaza 135 N. Penn, Indianapolis, IN 46204; Phone: 317-634-7477
Secretary: CHARLOTTE ROBERTSON, 980 N. 400 East, Chesterton, IN 46304
Treasurer: ALICE SCHLOSS, 4525 N. Park Ave., Indianapolis, IN 46205
Executive Director: JEFFREY STANT, 1002 E. Washington St. Suite 300, Indianapolis, IN 46202; Phone: 317-685-8800
Editor: JEFF STANT, 1002 E. Washington St. Suite 300, Indianapolis, IN 46202; Phone: 317-685-8800
Publication(s): *Monitor; Boardwatch*
Keyword(s): Air Quality and Pollution, Biodiversity, Environmental and Conservation Education, Solid Waste Management, Water Quality

HUDSONIA LIMITED
Bard College Field Station, Annandale, NY 12504-0500
Phone: 914-758-7053/7023; Fax: 914-758-7033; Email: kiviat@bard.edu
Founded: 1981
Scope: National
Description: Hudsonia Limited is a nonprofit, nonadvocacy institute for research, education, and technical assistance in the environmental sciences. There are over 25 research associates and other technical personnel. Hudsonia conducts pure and applied research on natural and social-sciences aspects of the environment, produces educational publications, and offers natural history courses. Current activities include preparation of a Hudson River biodiversity manual, monitoring of constructed habitats for a threatened turtle, review of development sites, and research on fish, marsh insects, invasive plants, fresh-tidal wetlands, and rare species.
Contact(s):
Executive Director: ERIK KIVIAT
Staff Botanist: GRETCHEN STEVENS
Publication(s): *News From Hudsonia*
Keyword(s): Aquatic Habitats, Endangered and Threatened Species, Fisheries, Flowers, Plants, and Trees

HUMAN ECOLOGY ACTION LEAGUE INC. THE (HEAL)
P.O. Box 29629, Atlanta, GA 30359-0629
Phone: 404-248-1898; Fax: 404-248-0162; Email: HEALNatnl@aol.com; WWW: members.aol.com/HEALNatnl/index.html
Founded: 1977; Membership: 9,000
Scope: National
Description: A nonprofit volunteer organization of people affected by or concerned about environmental conditions that are hazardous to human health. It serves as an information clearinghouse on exposure-related illness; alerts the general public about the potential dangers of chemicals; and encourages healthy lifestyles that minimize potentially hazardous environmental exposures.
Contact(s):
President: MURIEL A. DANDO
Secretary: DR. KENNETH V. KING JR.
Treasurer: LYDIA C. JONES
Editor: DIANE C. THOMAS
Founding Advisor: THERON G. RANDOLPH
Publication(s): *Human Ecologist, The*
Keyword(s): Air Quality and Pollution, Health and Nutrition, Pesticides, Toxic Substances, Urban Environment

HUMANE SOCIETY OF THE UNITED STATES, THE
2100 L St., NW, Washington, DC 20037
Phone: 202-452-1100; Fax: 301-258-3077
Founded: 1954; Membership: 6,200,000
Scope: National
Description: A nonprofit organization dedicated to the protection of animals, both domestic and wild. Professional staff experienced in animal control, cruelty investigation, humane and environmental education, farm animals, federal and state legislative activities, wildlife and habitat protection, and laboratory animal welfare; offer resources to local organizations, government, media, and the general public.
Contact(s):
Secretary: DR. AMY FREEMAN LEE
CFO: G. THOMAS WAITE III
Chairman of the Board: O. J. RAMSEY
Director of The Center for Respect of Life and Environment: DR. RICHARD M. CLUGSTON
Executive Vice President: PATRICIA FORKAN
Library Assistant: SHARON GEIGER, The Joyce Mertz Gilmore Library, HSUS Offices, 700 Professional Dr., Gaithersburg, MD 20879; Phone: 202-452-1100
President of Earthvoice: PAUL G. IRWIN
President, CEO: PAUL G. IRWIN
President, Humane Society International: PAUL G. IRWIN

NON-GOVERNMENTAL ORGANIZATIONS

Senior Vice President of Wildlife: DR. JOHN W. GRANDY
Vice Chairman: DR. DAVID O. WIEBERS
Vice President and General Counsel: ROGER A. KINDLER
Publication(s): *HSUS News; Kind News; Shelter Sense; Kind Teacher;*
Keyword(s): Endangered and Threatened Species, Hunting, Marine Mammals, Trapping, Wildlife and Wildlife Habitat

HUMBOLT FIELD RESEARCH INSTITUTE
ATTN: Director, P.O. Box 9, Steuben, ME 04680
Phone: 207-546-2821; Fax: 207-546-3042
Founded: 1981
Scope: Statewide
Description: A nonprofit educational and research organization providing advanced and professional training programs in all aspects of natural history (terrestrial, freshwater and marine) and encouraging similar scholarly persuits. Program activities are based in coastal Maine, Central America, South American, and the Caribbean.
Contact(s):
Director: JOERG-HENNER LOTZE
Publication(s): *Norhteastern Naturalist*
Keyword(s): Biodiversity, Environmental and Conservation Education, Natural History, Wetlands

HUMMINGBIRD SOCIETY, THE
249 E. Main St., Suite 4, Newark, DE 19711
Phone: 302-369-3699; Fax: 302-369-1816; Email: info@hummingbird.org; WWW: www.hummingbird.org
Founded: 1996; Membership: 1,200
Scope: Regional
Description: The Hummingbird Society is a nonprofit corporation dedicated solely to hummingbirds, through disseminating information, education, support of scientific research, and protection of habitat.
Contact(s):
President: DR. H. ROSS HAWKINS
Vice President: GARY A. GRIFFITH; Phone: 410-398-4300; Email: brdnsum@pnet.net
Secretary: FRANCES HAMILTON OATES; Phone: 610-274-0551; Email: landenberg@aol.com
Treasurer: WILLIAM N. BARRY; Phone: 302-239-1797; Email: billb@wserve.com
Director: DR. ROBERT L. GELL; Phone: 410-287-1025; Email: rgell@ed.cecil.cc.md.us
Publication(s): *The Hummingbird Connection*
Keyword(s): Birds, Conservation, Endangered and Threatened Species, Environmental and Conservation Education, International Conservation, Research

HUNTSMAN MARINE SCIENCE CENTRE
Brandy Cove, St. Andrews, New Brunswick E0G 2X0 Canada
Phone: 506-529-1200; Fax: 506-529-1212; WWW: www.unb.ca\web\huntsman
Founded: 1969
Scope: National
Description: The HMSC is a nonprofit organization with a reputation for excellence in marine science research and education. It is supported by,universities, corporations, federal and provincial government agencies, and the public. Located on one of the most biologically active bodies of water in the world, it provides information, research, education, and training opportunities for students, investigators, and the public.
Contact(s):
Chair: JOHN M. ANDERSON, Atlantic Salmon Federation, St. Andrews, New Brunswick E0G 2X0 Canada; Phone: 506-529-1023
Director: JOHN H. ALLEN; Phone: 506-529-1200
Publication(s): *Huntsman Marine Science News; Seawords; Sea Trek Bulletin; Atlantic Reference Centre Species Identification Series*
Keyword(s): Air Quality and Pollution, Aquariums, Aquatic Habitats, Biodiversity, Biology, Birds, Ecology, Environment, Fisheries, Geology, Oceanography, Research, Sustainable Ecosystems, Training, Waterfowl

IDAHO ASSOCIATION OF SOIL CONSERVATION DISTRICTS
ATTN: President, Box 697, Lava Hot Springs, ID 83246
Scope: Statewide
Contact(s):
President, alternate board member: KEVIN KOESTER, Box 697, Lava Hot Springs, ID 83246; Phone: 208-776-5382; Fax: 208-776-5043
Vice President: ALICE WALLACE, 1005 N. 5th Avenue, Sandpoint, ID 83864; Phone: 208-263-0895; Fax: 208-265-8486
Secretary: KYLE HAWLEY, 1180 Lewis Rd., Moscow, ID 83843; Phone: 208-882-1290; Fax: 208-883-4239
Treasurer: ROGER STUTZMAN, Rt. 4, Buhl, ID 83316; Phone: 208-543-6824; Fax: 208-543-6824
Executive Director: KENT FOSTER, 802 W. Bannock Suite 1006 P.O. Box 2637, Boise, ID 83701; Phone: 208-338-5900; Fax: 208-338-9537
Board Member: ROD ROBISON, 2697 W 6300S, Rexburg, ID 83440; Phone: 208-356-7110; Fax: 208-356-7240

IDAHO B.A.S.S. CHAPTER FEDERATION
ATTN: President, 1010 Lilac, Meridian, ID 83642
Phone: 208-888-5060
Scope: Statewide
Description: An organization of Bassmaster chapters, affiliated with the Bass Anglers Sportsman Society, organized to fight pollution, assist state and national conservation agencies in their efforts, and teach the young people of our country good conservation practices. Dedicated to the realistic conservation of our water resources.
Contact(s):
President: STEVE WEEKES, 1010 Lilac, Meridian, ID 83642; Phone: 208-888-5060
Conservation Director: JIM DESARO, 8012 W. Arapaho Ct., Boise, ID 83703; Phone: 208-853-6840

IDAHO CONSERVATION LEAGUE
P.O. Box 884, Boise, ID 83701
Phone: 208-345-6933; Fax: 208-344-0344
Founded: 1973; Membership: 2,600
Scope: Statewide
Description: The Idaho Conservation League is Idaho's largest statewide conservation organization. Based on grassroots activism and a professional staff, ICL works to preserve and protect Idaho's wild country, water, and wildlife.
Contact(s):
President: MICHELE TAE, 2360 Table Rock Rd., Boise, ID 83703; Phone: 208-383-9616
Vice President: MARK SOLOMON, P.O. Box 8145, Moscow, ID 83843; Phone: 208-882-4087
Secretary: DOUG CHRISTENSEN, HC 64, Box 8288, Ketchum, ID 83340; Phone: 208-726-3668
Treasurer: GEORGE WALTER, 3023 Hilliary Dr., Boise, ID 83702; Phone: 208-336-4518
Associate Director: SUKI MOLINA
Central Idaho Associate: LINN KINCANNON
Conservation Director: JOHN McCARTHY
Executive Director (Acting): RICK JOHNSON
North Idaho Associate: LARRY McLAUD
State Affairs Director: MINDY HARM
Publication(s): *Idaho Conservation League News; Citizen's Guide to the Legislature*
Keyword(s): Biodiversity, Environmental Preservation, Public Lands, Water Pollution, Wilderness

IDAHO ENVIRONMENTAL COUNCIL
1568 Lola St., Idaho Falls, ID 83402
Scope: Statewide
Description: Founded to coordinate and stimulate the creative ideas, manpower, and financial resources of conservation-minded

individuals and organizations; and to provide an increased understanding of modern man's impact upon his environment. Action, the objective, is based on information and research.

Contact(s):
President: ALAN HAUSRATH; Phone: 208-336-4930
Editor: JERRY JAYNE; Phone: 208-523-6692
Vice President for Northern Idaho: DENNIS BAIRD; Phone: 208-882-8289
Vice President for Southeastern Idaho: RALPH MAUGHAN; Phone: 208-233-7091

Publication(s): *IEC Newsletter*

IDAHO FOREST OWNERS ASSOCIATION
P.O. Box 1257, Coeur d'Alene, ID 83816
Phone: 208-762-9303

Founded: 1983; Membership: 300
Scope: Statewide

Description: A statewide organization, affiliated with the National Woodland Owners Association, of forest landowners dedicated to the management, use, and protection of private forest resources in Idaho.

Contact(s):
President: BILL LUKENS, Sandpoint, ID ; Phone: 208-263-4440
Vice President: KIM DUFFY, Sandpoint, ID ; Phone: 208-265-4719
Secretary: KIRK DAVID, Athol, ID ; Phone: 208-769-1525
Treasurer: OZZIE OSBORN, Coeur d'Alene, ID ; Phone: 208-664-3889
Executive Director: AMY GILLETTE, Coeur d'Alene, ID ; Phone: 208-762-9303
Editor: LORI D. RASOR, 4033 SW Canyon Rd., Portland, OR 97221; Phone: 503-288-1367 ext104

Publication(s): *Northwest Woodlands*
Keyword(s): Forests and Forestry

IDAHO WILDLIFE FEDERATION
P.O. Box 6426, Boise, ID 83707
Phone: 208-342-7055; Fax: 208-342-7097; Email: IWFBOI@cyberhighway.net; WWW: www.buytheworld.com/norest/iwf/iwf/htm

Scope: Statewide

Description: A representative statewide organization, affiliated with the National Wildlife Federation, dedicated to the protection and enhancement of wildlife and its habitat through public education and government interaction.

Contact(s):
President: RUSS BIAGGNE
Executive Director: KENT LAVERTY
Affiliate Representative: JEFF BARNEY
Alternate Representative: RUSS BIAGGNE
Editor: BILL GOODNIGHT

Publication(s): *Idaho Wildlife News*

ILLINOIS ASSOCIATION OF CONSERVATION DISTRICTS
9313 Bull Valley Rd., Woodstock, IL 60098
Phone: 815-338-7664; Fax: 815-338-2773; Email: conserve@Delphi.com

Founded: 1973; Membership: 40
Scope: Statewide

Description: To promote the objectives and activities of the Conservation District of Illinois as set forth in the Illinois Conservation District Act and to cooperate with county, state, federal, and private agencies in resource management.

Contact(s):
President: KEN KONSIS; Phone: 217-442-1691
Vice President: PAUL HAGAN; Phone: 217-423-7708
Assistant Secretary and Treasurer: KEN FISKE; Phone: 815-338-7664
Secretary and Treasurer: JOHN KREMER; Phone: 815-547-7935

Keyword(s): Cultural Preservation, Endangered and Threatened Species, Environmental and Conservation Education, Land Preservation, Sustainable Ecosystems

ILLINOIS ASSOCIATION OF SOIL AND WATER CONSERVATION DISTRICTS
ATTN: President, Rt. 1 Box 186, Henry, IL 61537

Scope: Statewide

Contact(s):
President, Board Member: TERRY BOGNER, Rt. 1 Box 186, Henry, IL 61537; Phone: 309-364-3478; Fax: 309-364-3802
Secretary: JERRY SNODGRASS, 13501 N 1700th Ave., Geneseo, IL 61254; Phone: 309-944-2869; Fax: 309-937-2171
Treasurer: RICHARD BRECKENRIDGE, P.O. Box 170, Rt2 Box 317, Taylorville, IL 62568; Phone: 217-824-8002; Fax: 217-824-4834
Executive Director: STEVE STALCUP, 2520 Main St., Springfield, IL 62702-1262; Phone: 217-744-3414; Fax: 217-744-3420
Vice President, Alternate Board Member: DEBORAH CAVANAUGH-GRANT, Rt. 1 Box 680, Greenview, IL 62642; Phone: 217-968-5583; Fax: 217-968-5512

ILLINOIS AUDUBON SOCIETY
425 B N. Gilbert St., P.O. Box 2418, Danville, IL 61834
Phone: 217-446-5085; Fax: 217-446-6375

Founded: 1897
Scope: Statewide

Description: The Society is dedicated to the preservation and enjoyment of wildlife and their habitats.

Contact(s):
President: RITA RENWICK, 1508 W. Acres Rd., Joliet, IL 60435
Vice President: DAVID MILLER, 813 N. Center, McHenry, IL 60050
Executive Director: MARILYN F. CAMPBELL
Editor: MARILYN F. CAMPBELL
Editor: DEBBIE SCOTT NEWMAN

Publication(s): *Illinois Audubon; Cardinal News, The*
Keyword(s): Biodiversity, Birds, Endangered and Threatened Species, Land Preservation, Wildlife and Wildlife Habitat

ILLINOIS B.A.S.S. CHAPTER FEDERATION
ATTN: President, 1208 West Loucks, Peoria, IL 61604
Phone: 309-692-4036

Scope: Statewide

Description: An organization of Bassmaster chapters, affiliated with the Bass Anglers Sportsman Society, organized to fight pollution, assist state and national conservation agencies in their efforts, and to teach the young people of our country good conservation practices. Dedicated to the realistic conservation of our water resources.

Contact(s):
President: JEFF PETERSON, 1208 West Loucks, Peoria, IL 61604; Phone: 309-692-4036
Conservation Director: JOHN GROSS, 2425 Huntington Rd., Springfield, IL 62703; Phone: 217-529-8341(H)/217-529-5411(W)

Publication(s): *Illinois B.A.S.S. Federation Newsletter inserted in "Midwest Outdoors" magazine*

ILLINOIS ENVIRONMENTAL COUNCIL
319 W. Cook St., Springfield, IL 62704
Phone: 217-544-5954; Fax: 217-544-5958; Email: iec@eosinc.com

Founded: 1975; Membership: 70 groups plus individual members
Scope: Statewide

Description: Statewide coalition committed to lobbying for Illinois laws and policies that promote a healthful environment and conservation of resources. The Illinois Environmental Council Education Fund administers programs of education and outreach for the coalition.

Contact(s):
Board of Directors President: RON BURKE
Coordinator for Power Plant Clean-up Project: JOHN THOMPSON; Phone: 618-457-0137
Coordinator for Safer Pest Control Project: JILL VIEHWEG, 17 E. Monroe #212, Chicago, IL 60603; Phone: 312-641-5575

NON-GOVERNMENTAL ORGANIZATIONS

Director of Administration: ELLEN SCHMIDT
Executive Director and Legislative Liaison: LYNNE PADOVAN
Publication(s): *IEC Bulletin; Action Alerts; Environmental Voting Record and Affiliate Notes*
Keyword(s): Air Quality and Pollution, Pesticides, Solid Waste, Water Resources, Wildlife and Wildlife Habitat

ILLINOIS NATIVE PLANT SOCIETY
Forest Glen Preserve, 20301 E. 900 N. Rd., Westville, IL 61883
Phone: 217-662-2142; Email: kenkonsis@aol.com; WWW: www.vccd.org
Founded: 1982; Membership: 450
Scope: Statewide
Description: Dedicated to the preservation, conservation, and study of the native plants and vegetation of Illinois.
Contact(s):
Executive Board: KEN KONSIS
Publication(s): *Erigenia; Harbinger*
Keyword(s): Aquatic Habitats, Biodiversity, Botanical Gardens, Conservation of Protected Areas, Endangered and Threatened Species, Environmental Preservation, Environmental Protection, Flowers, Plants, and Trees, Natural Areas, Prairies, Wetlands

ILLINOIS NATURAL HERITAGE FOUNDATION
320 S. 3rd St., Rockford, IL 61104
Phone: 815-964-6666; Fax: 815-964-6666
Founded: 1982
Scope: Statewide
Description: A nonprofit organization to protect Illinois's native flora and fauna, and to encourage wise stewardship of the natural resources that affect them.
Contact(s):
President: GORDON EGGERS
Vice President: GARY McINTYRE
Secretary: RANDALL VINCENT
Treasurer: BRUCE ROSS-SHANNON
Executive Director: ED STIRLILNG
Director of Research and Management: MICHAEL JONES
Land Preservation Specialist: TODD CAGNONI
Manager of Resources: JILL KENNAY
Keyword(s): Biodiversity, Endangered and Threatened Species, Environmental Preservation

ILLINOIS PRAIRIE PATH
P.O. Box 1086, Wheaton, IL 60189
Phone: 708-752-0120
Founded: 1963; Membership: 2,000
Scope: Statewide
Description: To preserve natural areas and establish footpaths and other protected areas to be used for scientific, educational, and recreational purposes by the public. Promotes development of a 61-mile path for bicyclists, hikers, and joggers on former railroad right-of-way spanning DuPage County, extended Jan. 1972 into Kane County to Fox River, AND extended Dec. 1979 4 1/2 miles into Cook County. Incorporated: 1965. In 1971 designated part of National Trails System.
Contact(s):
President: DAVID TATE
Secretary: NANCY BECKER
Treasurer: PAUL MOORING
Editor: JEAN MOORING, 295 Abbotsford Ct., Glen Ellyn, IL 60137; Phone: 708-469-4289
Publication(s): *Newsletter; Illinois Prairie Path, The; Trail*
Keyword(s): Bicycle, Environmental and Conservation Education, Environmental Preservation, Outdoor Recreation, Public Lands, Trail, Wildlife and Wildlife Habitat

ILLINOIS WALNUT COUNCIL
Forest Glen Preserve, 20301 E. 900 N. Rd., Westville, IL 61883
Phone: 217-662-2142; Email: vccd@soltec.net; WWW: www.vccd.org
Membership: 130
Scope: Statewide
Description: To promote the growth and use of the black walnut (Juglans nigra, and the education of good forestry practices with concerns toward wildlife and soil erosion.
Contact(s):
President: BOB TRIMBLE, 804 Tyler Court, Monticello, IL 61856
Vice President: WAYNE WILDY, 7718 Wildy Rd., New Athens, IL 62264
Secretary: STEVE FELT, 522 Roberts Ln., Sherrard, IL 61281
Publication(s): *Walnut Council Bulletin; Juglans*
Keyword(s): Forest Management, Pesticides, Renewable Resources, Research, Soil Conservation, Sustainable Development, Watersheds, Wildlife and Wildlife Habitat

ILLINOIS WOODLAND OWNERS AND USERS ASSOCIATION
R.R. 1, Box 57, Mason, IL 62443
Phone: 618-245-6392
Membership: 300
Scope: Statewide
Description: A statewide organization affiliated with the National Woodland Owners Association. Dedicated to promoting good forestry practices and multiple use of woodlands.
Contact(s):
President: HILLIARD MORRIS, Mason, IL
Editor: TONY WAGNER, Kinmundy, IL ; Phone: 618-547-3477
Publication(s): *Illinois Woodlands*
Keyword(s): Forests and Forestry

INDIAN CREEK NATURE CENTER
6665 Otis Rd., SE, Cedar Rapids, IA 52403
Phone: 319-362-0664; Fax: 319-362-2876; Email: tbnature@aol.com
Founded: 1973; Membership: 600
Scope: Statewide
Description: The Indian Creek Nature Center is dedicated to fostering an appreciation of nature through environmental education and providing a natural facility for education and non-obtrusive recreation.
Contact(s):
President: MARK OGDEN; Phone: 319-366-7641
Executive Director: RICH PATTERSON
Chief Executive Officer: DENNIS REDMOND; Phone: 319-366-2163
Publication(s): *Currents*

INDIANA ASSOCIATION OF SOIL AND WATER CONSERVATION DISTRICTS, INC.
ATTN: President, 5377 E. 800 N., Syracuse, IN 46567-9548
Scope: Statewide
Contact(s):
President: GARRY TOM, 5377 E. 800 N., Syracuse, IN 46567-9548; Phone: 219-834-2416; Fax: 219-834-5636
Vice President: CAREY McKIBBEN, 2840 SR 9, LaGrange, IN 46761-9774; Phone: 219-463-2355
Secretary: LINDA YERKS, 20216 Notestine Rd., Woodburn, IN 46797-9791; Phone: 219-657-5318
Treasurer: SHERMAN BRYANT, 7343 N 650 E., N. Webster, IN 46555-9332; Phone: 219-834-2496
Executive Director: CHRISTA JONES, 225 SE St. Suite 740, Indianapolis, IN 46202; Phone: 317-692-7374; Fax: 317-692-7363; Email: iaswod@indy.net
Board Member: GENE SCHMIDT, 15722 S 400 W, Hanna, IN 46340; Phone: 219-797-5045

NON-GOVERNMENTAL ORGANIZATIONS

INDIANA AUDUBON SOCIETY, INC.
Mary Gray Bird Sanctuary, R.R. 6 Box 163, Connersville, IN 47331
Phone: 317-827-0908
Founded: 1898; Membership: 980
Scope: Statewide
Description: Works for the conservation of wildlife, especially birds.
Contact(s):
President: JANE MILLER, 4020 S. Rural, Independence, IN 46227-3865
Vice President: LARRY CARTER, 7496 N. Co. Rd. 2005, Ridgeville, IN 47380-9546
Secretary: SUSANNA BARRICLOW-ARVIN, 5992 W. Hilltop Dr., Frankfort, IN 46041
Treasurer: CLARE OSKAY, 551 Teton Trail, Indianapolis, IN 46217-3927
Editor: MARY GOUGH, 901 Maplewood Dr., New Castle, IN 47362; Phone: 317-529-5225
Editor: CHARLES E. KELLER, 2505 E. Maynard Dr., Indianapolis, IN 46226; Phone: 317-786-5822
Resident Agent and Manager of Sanctuary Management: DEANNA BARRICKLOW, 3499 S. Bird Sanctuary Rd., Connersville, IN 47331-8721; Phone: 317-825-9788
Keyword(s): Birds, Conservation of Protected Areas, Ecology, Environmental and Conservation Education, Flowers, Plants, and Trees, Insects and Butterflies, Waterfowl

INDIANA B.A.S.S. CHAPTER FEDERATION
ATTN: President, 7244 N. Homestead Rd., Morgantown, IN 46160
Phone: 812-988-8763
Scope: Statewide
Description: An organization of Bassmaster chapters, affiliated with the Bass Anglers Sportsman Society, organized to fight pollution, assist state and national conservation agencies in their efforts, and teach the young people of our country good conservation practices. Dedicated to the realistic conservation of our water resources.
Contact(s):
President: DAN PARDUE, 7244 N. Homestead Rd., Morgantown, IN 46160; Phone: 812-988-8763
Conservation Director: PAUL HOLLABAUGH, 1415 Cherokee Rd., Ft. Wayne, IN 46808; Phone: 219-422-2261

INDIANA FORESTRY AND WOODLAND OWNERS ASSOCIATION
5578 South 500 W., Atlanta, IN 46031-9363
Phone: 317-758-4735
Founded: 1977; Membership: 1,100
Scope: Statewide
Description: A statewide organization affiliated with the National Woodland Owners Association, providing leadership and programs to advance forestry in Indiana.
Contact(s):
President: EVERETTE BALLENTIN
Secretary: WILLIAM SIGMAN
Treasurer: WARREN BAIRD
1st Vice President: ROBERT KOENIG
2nd Vice President: THOMAS A. EWBANK
Editor: JAN MYERS; Phone: 317-583-2422
Forestry Educational Foundation: PETE HALSTEAD
Past President: WILLIAM BAITON
Publication(s): *Leaves and Limbs*
Keyword(s): Forests and Forestry

INDIANA NATIVE PLANT AND WILDFLOWER SOCIETY
6106 Kingsley Dr., Indianapolis, IN 46220
Phone: 317-253-3863; Email: rai38@aol.com; WWW: www.inpaws.org
Founded: 1993; Membership: 550
Scope: Statewide
Description: To promote the appreciation, preservation, conservation, utilization and scientific study of the flora native to Indiana; and to educate the public about the values, beauty, diversity, and environmental importance of indigenous vegetation.
Contact(s):
President: RUTH ANN INGRAHAM; Phone: 317-253-3863
Vice President: KEVIN TUNGESVICK; Phone: 317-354-2775
Treasurer: JEAN VIETOR; Phone: 317-823-1542
Corresponding Secretary: ROGER HEDGE; Phone: 317-232-4052
Recording Secretary: CAROLYN BRYSON; Phone: 317-873-4205
Publication(s): *Indiana Native Plant and Wildflower Society News*
Keyword(s): Biodiversity, Flowers, Plants, and Trees, Nature Preservation, Prairies, Sustainable Ecosystems

INDIANA STATE TRAPPERS ASSOCIATION, INC.
ATTN: President, 828 Elm St., Huntington, IN 46750
Founded: 1961; Membership: 265
Scope: Statewide
Description: A statewide organization dedicated to the conservation, restoration, and wise use of wildlife and other renewable natural resources. Provides public education concerning the role of trapping in the management of wildlife.
Contact(s):
President: KEN BROSMAN, 828 Elm St., Huntington, IN 46750; Phone: 812-939-3215
Vice President: JERRY MILLER, R.R. 1 21 N. 300 W., Bluffton, IN 46714
Director: NELSON TEETERS, R.R. 1 Box 140A, West Union, IN 60180
Director: JOHN DREIMAN, R.R. 1 Box 179, Monroe City, IN 47557
Director: ROBERT COATS, R.R. 1 Box 300, Portland, IN 47371
Secretary and Treasurer: KAREN MOSS, R.R. 1 Box 57, Clay City, IN 47841; Phone: 219-369-1573

INDIANA WILDLIFE FEDERATION
950 N. Rangeline Rd., Suite A, Carmel, IN 46032-1315
Phone: 317-571-1220/1-800-347-3445; Fax: 317-571-1223; Email: iwf@indy.net
Scope: Statewide
Description: A representative statewide organization, affiliated with the National Wildlife Federation, dedicated to the protection and enhancement of wildlife and its habitat through public education and government interaction.
Contact(s):
President: CHARLES O'NEILL
Affiliate Representative: DWIGHT SHELTON
Editor: MICKEY KOEHLER
Publication(s): *Hoosier Conservation*

INFORM, INC.
120 Wall St., 16th Flr., New York, NY 10005
Phone: 212-361-2400; Fax: 212-361-2412; Email: inform@informinc.org; WWW: www.informinc.org
Founded: 1973; Membership: 1,000
Scope: National
Description: A nonprofit tax-exempt environmental research and education organization that identifies and reports on practical solutions for problems in municipal solid waste, chemical hazards, air quality, and alternative vehicle fuels, with an emphasis on pollution prevention and waste reduction.
Contact(s):
President: JOANNA D. UNDERWOOD
Chairman of the Board: CHARLES A. MORAN
Director of Research: DR. NEVIN COHEN
Publication(s): *INFORM Reports* (Newsletter); *China at the Crossroads; Gearing up for Hydrogen; Building for the Future; Tracking Toxic Chemicals; Rethinking Resources*
Keyword(s): Air Quality and Pollution, Energy, Solid Waste Management, Toxic Substances, Transportation

NON-GOVERNMENTAL ORGANIZATIONS

INLAND BIRD BANDING ASSOCIATION
R.D. 2 Box 26, Wisner, NE 68791
Phone: 402-529-6679
Founded: 1922
Scope: National
Description: Promotes cooperation among its members and other organizations, with state, federal, or other officials or individuals engaged in bird banding or other scientific work with birds; informs the public of the purposes and results secured by banding.
Contact(s):
President: JOHN J. FLORA, 3636 Williams, Dearborn, MI 48124
Secretary: CAROL RUDY, W. 3866 Hwy. H, Chilton, WI 53084
Treasurer: C. HOLMES SMITH, 6305 Cumberland Rd. SW, Sherrodsville, OH 44675
Editor: WILLETTA LUESHEN, R. 2 Box 26, Wisner, NE 68791
Editor: DAN KRAMER, 3451 Co. Rd. 256, Victory, OH 43464
Membership Secretary: AL VALENTINE, 17403 Oakington Ct., Dallas, TX 75252
Publication(s): *North American Bird Bander; Inland Bird Banding Newsletter*

INSTITUTE AND SCHOOL FOR ENVIRONMENT AND NATURAL RESOURCES, Univeristy of Wyoming (IENR and SENR)
P.O. Box 3971, Laramie, WY 82071
Phone: 307-766-5080; Fax: 307-766-5099; Email: ienr@uwyo.edu; WWW: www.uwyo.edu/enr/ienr.htm
Founded: 1994; Membership: 43 Member Board of Directors
Scope: Statewide
Description: Current projects include workshops on ESA and NEPA, reports on Brucellosis in the Greater Yellowstone Area, and an open spaces inititatives in Grand Teton National Park
Contact(s):
Assistant Director: BRENDA KELLEY
Director: DR. HAROLD BERGMAN; Phone: 307-766-5677
Keyword(s): Endangered and Threatened Species, Open Spaces

INSTITUTE FOR CONSERVATION LEADERSHIP
6930 Carroll Ave. Suite 420, Takoma Park, MD 20912
Phone: 301-270-2900; Fax: 301-270-0610; Email: ici@ici.org
Scope: National
Description: The mission of the Institute is to train and empower volunteer leaders and to build volunteer institutions that protect and conserve the earth's environment. Services offered include training and technical assistance for nonprofit organizations and leaders in organizational development, fundraising, board development, volunteer recruitment, strategic planning, and related topics. Services also include meeting facilitation, coalition development, and network building.
Contact(s):
Executive Director: DIANNE RUSSELL
Administrative Assistant: ROSE WILLIAMS
Associate Director: BAIRD STRAUGHAN
Office Manager: CHIQUITA EDWARDS
Project Manager: PETER LANE
Keyword(s): Communications, Environment, Pollution Prevention, Training

INSTITUTE FOR EARTH EDUCATION, THE
Cedar Cove, Greenville, WV 24945
Phone: 304-832-6404; Fax: 304-832-6077; Email: iee1@aol.com
Founded: 1974; Membership: 2,000
Scope: National
Description: The Institute for Earth Education develops and disseminates focused educational programs to promote an understanding of, appreciation for, and harmony with the earth's natural systems and communities. The Institute conducts workshops, provides a seasonal journal, hosts an international conference, supports local and international branches, and publishes numerous books and program materials.
Contact(s):
Chair: STEVE VAN MATRE

Executive Staff Chair: BILL WEILER
International Internship Coordinator: FRAN BIRES
International Membership Services Coordinator: LAURIE FARBER
International Program Coordinator: BRUCE JOHNSON
International Training Coordinator: MIKE MAYER
Publication(s): *Talking Leaves Journal; Earth Education Sourcebook; Earth Education: A New Beginning; Earthkeepers; Earth Speaks, The; Sunship III*
Keyword(s): Ecology, Environmental and Conservation Education, Environmental Preservation, International Conservation, Internships

INSTITUTE OF ECOSYSTEM STUDIES
Mary Flagler Cary Arboretum, Box AB, Millbrook, NY 12545-0129
Phone: 914-677-5343; Fax: 914-677-5976; WWW: www.ecostudies.org
Scope: Statewide
Description: Devoted to the understanding of ecosystem structure and function. The program focus is on disturbance and recovery of northern temperate ecosystems. Education and research interests include wildlife management, biogeochemistry, landscape ecology, aquatic ecology, plant-animal interactions, microbial ecology, forest ecology, chemical ecology, and air and water quality.
Contact(s):
Director: DR. GENE E. LIKENS
Administrator: JOSEPH S. WARNER
Animal Ecologist: DR. RICHARD S. OSTFELD
Aquatic Ecologist: DR. STUART E.G. FINDLAY
Aquatic Ecologist: DR. MICHAEL L. PACE
Aquatic Microbiologist: DR. JONATHAN J. COLE
Biogeochemist: DR. NINA M. CARACO
Chemical Ecologist: DR. CLIVE G. JONES
Educational Research and Development Specialist: DR. KATHLEEN HOGAN; Phone: 914-677-5359
Forest Ecologist: DR. KATHLEEN C. WEATHERS
Forest Ecologist: DR. DAVID L. STRAYER
Head of Education: DR. ALAN R. BERKOWITZ; Phone: 914-677-5359
Librarian: ANNETTE R. FRANK
Microbial Ecologist: DR. PETER M. GROFFMAN
Plant Ecologist: DR. STEWARD T.A. PICKETT
Plant Ecologist: DR. GARY M. LOVETT
Plant Ecologist: DR. CHARLES D. CANHAM
Wildlife Biologist and Manager: RAYMOND J. WINCHCOMBE; Phone: 914-677-9818
Publication(s): *Newsletter; Occasional Publications*
Keyword(s): Acid Rain, Air Quality and Pollution, Environmental and Conservation Education

INTERFAITH COUNCIL FOR THE PROTECTION OF ANIMALS AND NATURE INC. (ICPAN)
3691 Tuxedo Rd. NW, Atlanta, GA 30305
Phone: 404-814-1371
Founded: 1980; Membership: 3,000
Scope: National
Description: Composed of people of all faiths, ICPAN works to promote conservation and environmental and humane education, mainly within the religious community. We try to make religious leaders, institutions, and the general public aware of our moral spiritual obligations, as emphasized in the Bible, to protect animals and the natural environment.
Contact(s):
Chairman: JOHN A. HOYT, 2100 L St. NW, Washington, DC 20037; Phone: 202-452-1100
President: LEWIS G. REGENSTEIN, 3691 Tuxedo Rd. NW, Atlanta, GA 30327; Phone: 404-814-1371
Director: PAUL G. IRWIN, 2100 L St. NW, Washington, DC 20037; Phone: 202-452-1100
Publication(s): *Replenish the Earth: The Teachings of the World's Religions on Protecting Animals and Nature; Replenish the Earth: A Booklet on The Bible's Message of Conservation and Kindness to Animals; Cleaning up America the Poisoned: How to Survive our Polluted Society*

Keyword(s): Endangered and Threatened Species, Environmental and Conservation Education, International Conservation, Sustainable Development, Wildlife and Wildlife Habitat

INTERNATIONAL ASSOCIATION FOR BEAR RESEARCH AND MANAGEMENT
c/o Bernie Peyton, 2841 Forest Ave., Berkley, CA 94705
Fax: 510-549-3116; Email: ucumari@aol.com

Founded: 1968
Scope: International
Description: A professional organization of biologists, animal or land managers, and private citizens with an interest or involvement in bear research and management. The Association encourages and reports research and management by various agencies or university research groups, sponsors the triannual International Conference on Bear Research and Management, publishes the proceedings of the conference, and sponsors or aids a world network of regional bear workshops, groups, and committees, and the IUCN Bear Group.
Contact(s):
President: BRUCE MCLELLAN, British Columbia Service Research Branch, RPO #3 Box 9158, Relestoke, Bristish Columbia V0E 3K0 Canada; Fax: 250-837-7626; Email: bruce.mclellan@gems9.gov.bc.ca
Vice President: KATE KENDALL, Glacier Science Center, Glacier National Park, West Glacier, MT 59936-0128; Fax: 406-888-7990; Email: katherine_kendall@usgs.gov
Secretary: BERNIE PEYTON
Treasurer: GORDON WARBURTON, North Carolina Wildlife Resource Commission, 4470 Hidden View Loop, Marion, NC 28752; Fax: 828-652-8170; Email: warburg@mail.wildlife.state.nc.us
Publication(s): *Ursus, formerly Bears: Their Biology and Management (Conference Proceedings); International Bear News (Quarterly Newsletter)*
Keyword(s): Bears, Biology, Endangered and Threatened Species, Land Use Planning, Public Lands, Wildlife Management

INTERNATIONAL ASSOCIATION FOR ENVIRONMENTAL HYDROLOGY (IAEH)
P.O. Box 35324, San Antonio, TX 78235
Phone: 210-344-5418; Fax: 210-344-9941; Email: hydroweb@mail.org; WWW: www.hydroweb.com

Founded: 1991; Membership: 500
Scope: International
Description: IAEH works to foster a global interchange of ideas, approaches, and technologies for environmental cleanup and protection of fresh water resources and pollution prevention; to place special focus on approaches to cleanup, prevention, and protection that are practical in less affluent countries; to further the development of environmentally sound solutions that are realistic from the economic standpoint; to seek solutions to cleanup, pollution prevention, and environmental protection; and to place pollution cleanup and prevention in the context of broader water resource and environmental issues.
Contact(s):
President: DR. ROGER W. PEEBLES, 308 Montfort Dr., San Antonio, TX 78216; Phone: 210-344-5418
Publication(s): *Journal of Environmental Hydrology; Environmental Hydrology Report Software: HYDROKIT, a two-CD-ROM set with over 60 popular groundwater and surface water modeling programs*
Keyword(s): Developing Countries, Environment, Environmental and Conservation Education, International Conservation, Pollution Prevention, Water Pollution, Water Resources

INTERNATIONAL ASSOCIATION OF FISH AND WILDLIFE AGENCIES
444 North Capitol St. NW Suite 544, Washington, DC 20001
Phone: 202-624-7890; Fax: 202-624-7891

Scope: International
Description: Association of states or territories of the United States, provinces of Canada, the Commonwealth of Puerto Rico, the United States Government, the Dominion Government of Canada, and governments of countries located in the western hemisphere, as well as individual associate members whose principal objective is conservation, protection, and management of wildlife and related natural resources.
Contact(s):
President: ROGER HOLMES, Director Division of Fish and Wildlife, Minnesota Dept. of Natural Resources, 500 Lafayette Rd., St. Paul, MN 55155
Annual Proceedings Editor: WM. HAROLD NESBITT
Counselor Emeritus: JACK H. BERRYMAN
Executive Committee Chariman: PATRICK GRAHAM, Director, Montana Department of Fish, Wildlife and Parks, 1420 E. 6th, Helena, MT 59620
Executive Committee Vice-Chairman: ROBERT MCDOWELL, Director, New Jersey Division of Fish, Game and Wildlife, CN 400, Trenton, NJ 08625-0400
Executive Vice-President: R. MAX PETERSON, Washington, DC
International Resource Director: DONALD E. MACLAUCHLAN
Legal Counsel: PAUL A. LENZINI, Washington, DC
Legislative Director: GARY J. TAYLOR
NAWMP Coordinator: LEN UGARENKO
Newsletter Editor: MARY JANE WILLIAMSON
Resource Director: ROBERT L. MILES
Secretary/Treasurer: C. THOMAS BENNETT, Commissioner, Kentucky Department of Fish, Wildlife and Resources, One Game Farm Rd., Frankfurt, KY 40601
Sportfish and Wildlife Restoration Outreach Project Manager: MARY JANE WILLIAMSON
Vice-President: DAVID WALLER, Director, Wildlife Resources Division, Georgia DNR, 2070 U.S. Highway 278, SE, Social Circle, GA 30025
Publication(s): *Newsletter; Annual Proceedings*

INTERNATIONAL ASSOCIATION OF NATURAL RESOURCE PILOTS
200 Patrick St. SW, Vienna, VA 22180-6703
Phone: 703-560-1271

Membership: 200
Scope: International
Description: Performs aviation and aircrew conservation-related responsibilities for federal and state game and fish divisions and departments of natural resources throughout the U.S. and for their counterparts in the Canadian provinces. Additional membership includes a variety of aviation-oriented corporations and advanced technological suppliers of equipment used in the performance of the aviation missions.
Contact(s):
President: MICHAEL DERENDINGER, Missouri Conservation Dept., 11077 Co. Rd. 391, Holts Summit, MO 65043; Phone: 314-751-2727; Email: mderendi@mail.state.mo.us
Vice President: DAVE YOUNKIN, Colorado Division of Wildlife, 1200 Gregory Dr., Plain City, OH 43143; Phone: 970-484-2836; Email: dave.younklin@state.co.us
Secretary: JIM BREEDY, US Fish&Wildlife Service, P.O. Box 1461, Cedar Crest, NM 87008; Phone: 505-248-6802; Email: jim_breedy@mail.fws.gov
Newsletter Editor: PETE HOBSTETTER, Ohio Department of Transportation, 2829 W. Granville Rd., Columbus, OH 43085; Phone: 614-793-5088; Email: MAG10@prodigy.net
Past President: JACK KEATON, Ohio Department of Transportation, 13618 Woods Opossum Road, Mt. Sterling, OH 43143; Phone: 614-793-5050; Email: skyking33@juno.com
Public Affairs Officer and Editor: FRANCIS SATTERLEE, 200 Patrick St. SW, Vienna, VA 22180-6703; Phone: 703-560-1271
Treasurer and Librarian: JOHN C. CLEM, Ohio Division of Wildlife (ret), 9740 Briarwood Drive, Plain City, OH 43064; Phone: 614-873-4163; Email: john_clem@compuserve.com
Publication(s): *Conservation Aviation*
Keyword(s): Agriculture, Biodiversity, Birds, Chemical Pollution Control, Conservation of Protected Areas, Endangered and Threatened Species, Environmental Law, Environmental Planning,

NON-GOVERNMENTAL ORGANIZATIONS

Fisheries, Forest Management, Hunting, Lakes, Land Use Planning, Natural Areas, Nongame Wildlife

INTERNATIONAL ASSOCIATION OF WILDLAND FIRE (formerly Fire Research Institute)
E. 8109 Bratt Rd., Fairfield, WA 99012
Phone: 509-523-4003; Fax: 509-523-5001; Email: greenlee@cet.com; WWW: www.wildfiremagazine.com
Founded: 1991; Membership: 1,500
Scope: International
Description: The International Association of Wildland Fire was organized to promote a fuller understanding of wildland fire. The Association is built on the belief that an understanding of this dynamic natural force is vital for natural resource management, firefighter safety, and harmonious interactions between people and their environment.
Contact(s):
President: MIKE DEGROSKY; Phone: 307-543-0949
Executive Director: JASON GREENLEE; Phone: 509-283-2397
Editor: MIKE WEBER; Phone: 403-435-7210
Publication(s): *International Directory of Wildland Fire; International Bibliography of Wildland Fire; International Journal of Wildland Fire; Wildfire Magazine; Current Titles in Wildland Fire*
Keyword(s): Ecology, Endangered and Threatened Species, Forests and Forestry, Terrestrial Habitats, Wildlands

INTERNATIONAL BICYCLE FUND
4887 Columbia Dr. S., Seattle, WA 98108-1919
Phone: 206-767-0848; Email: ibike@ibike.org; WWW: www.ibike.org
Founded: 1983
Scope: International
Description: The International Bicycle Fund's programs fall into the areas of transportation planning, sustainable economic development, safety education, and promoting international understanding. Within these programs we address issues of the environment, energy policy, public health, appropriate technology, land use patterns, sustainable systems, resource conservation, and employment generation. IBF coordinates and cooperates with organizations and individuals worldwide. IBF is a nonprofit organization.
Contact(s):
President: DAVID MOZER
Publication(s): *IBF News*
Keyword(s): Environmental and Conservation Education, Land Use Planning, Pedestrian Environment, Sustainable Development, Transportation

INTERNATIONAL CENTER FOR EARTH CONCERNS
2162 Baldwin Rd., Ojai, CA 93023
Phone: 805-649-3535; Fax: 805-649-1757
Founded: 1994
Scope: International
Description: The ICEC involves people with nature by fostering their appreciation of the natural world through environmental education and training.
Contact(s):
Chairman: JOHN TAFT
President: PAUL IRWIN
Secretary: RICK GOULD
Publication(s): *Earth Pulse*
Keyword(s): Botanical Gardens, Ecology, Environmental and Conservation Education, Environmental Protection

INTERNATIONAL CENTER FOR GIBBON STUDIES
P.O. Box 800249, Santa Clarita, CA 91380
Phone: 805-296-2737; Fax: 805-296-1237
Founded: 1977
Scope: International
Description: The International Center for Gibbon Studies ensures the preservation and propagation and a safe haven for all gibbon species living in the wild and in captivity; supports ongoing field conservation projects; and educates the public about the importance of this species and saving their natural habitat.
Contact(s):
Acting Director of Research: DR. BJORN MERKER, Institute for Biomusicology, Mid Sweden, Ostersund, S-83125 Sweden
Assistant Director of Research: DR. ELAINE BAKER, Department of Psychology, Marshall University, Huntington, WV 25755
Board of Directors President, Facility Director, and Chairman of the Board: ALAN MOOTNICK, P.O. Box 800249, Santa Clarita, CA 91380; Phone: 805-296-2737
Board of Directors Vice President: DR. GERI-ANN GALANTI, 2906 Ocean Ave., Venice, CA 90291; Phone: 310-827-0937
Director of Education and Conservation: DR. LORI SHEERAN, California State University at Fullerton, ; Phone: 714-773-2765
Keyword(s): Environmental and Conservation Education, Research, Training, Wildlife Management, Zoology

INTERNATIONAL CENTER FOR TROPICAL ECOLOGY
The University of Missouri at St. Louis, R224 Research Bldg., 8001 Natural Bridge Rd., St. Louis, MO 63121-4499
Phone: 314-516-5219; Fax: 314-516-6233; WWW: www.ecology.umsl.edu
Founded: 1990
Scope: International
Description: The ICTE is one of the premier institutes in the United States for the study of tropical biology and conservation. The Center's three primary missions include the training of graduate students in the vital areas of tropical ecology and conservation, the education of undergraduates about the importance of these areas, and involvement of the community in educational actvities with respect to issues related to conservation and biodiversity.
Contact(s):
Secretary: BERNADETTE DALTON; Phone: 314-516-6203; Fax: 314-516-6233; Email: bdalton@umsl.edu
Executive Director: DR. PATRICK OSBORNE; Phone: 314-516-5219; Fax: 314-516-6233; Email: posborne@jinx.umsl.edu
Director: DR. BETTE LOISELLE; Phone: 314-516-6224; Fax: 314-516-6233; Email: loiselle@jimx.umsl.edu

INTERNATIONAL CENTRE FOR CONSERVATION EDUCATION
Greenfield House, Guiting Power, Cheltenham GL54 5TZ
United Kingdom
Phone: 144-1242-674839; Fax: 144-1242-674839; Email: maikcec@aol.com
Founded: 1984
Scope: International
Description: ICCE works to promote a greater understanding of global environmental issues and sustainable development.
Contact(s):
Director: MARK N. BOULTON, Greenfield House Guiting Power, Cheltenham, GL545TZ United Kingdom; Phone: 144-1242-674839
Publication(s): *Environmental Audio-Visual Materials; Annual Review; Environmental Education Resources; Organise International Training Programmes in Environmental Education.*
Keyword(s): Biodiversity, Communications, Environmental and Conservation Education, International Conservation, Sustainable Development

INTERNATIONAL COUNCIL OF ENVIRONMENTAL LAW
D-53113, Bonn, Adenaueralle 214 Germany
Phone: 49-228-2692-240; Fax: 49228/2692-250
Founded: 1969
Scope: International
Description: A nonprofit, nongovernmental international organization with elected membership, structured in ten regions worldwide, for the purpose of exchange of information on international environmental law, policy, and administration and mutual assistance among members.
Contact(s):
Editor: TORSTEN WAESCH, Germany
Editor: MARLENE JAHNKE, Ireland
Executive Governor: W. E. BURHENNE, Germany

Publication(s): *Environmental Policy and Law; ICEL References to Environmental Policy and Law Literature; Directory of Members; International Environmental Soft Law*
Keyword(s): Environmental Law, International Conservation

INTERNATIONAL CRANE FOUNDATION
E-11376 Shady Ln. Rd. P.O. Box 447, Baraboo, WI 53913-0447
Phone: 608-356-9462
Founded: 1973; Membership: 7,000
Scope: International
Description: Preservation of cranes through research, conservation, captive propagation, restocking, field ecology, and public education.
Contact(s):
Deputy Director: JAMES HARRIS
Director: GEORGE ARCHIBALD
Assistant to the Director: SUSAN FINN
Conservation Coordinator: CLAIRE MIRANDE
Curator of Birds: SCOTT SWENGEL
Deputy Director of Finance and Administration: PETER MURRAY
Development: ROBERT HALLAM
Field Ecologist: JEB BARZEN
Librarian: BETSY DIDRICKSON, The Ron Sauey Memorial Library For Bird Conservation, E-11376 Shady Lane Rd., P.O. Box 447, Baraboo, WI 53913-0447; Phone: 608-356-9462
Site Manager: DAVID CHESKY
Publication(s): *ICF Bugle, The (Quarterly Magazine); Proceedings of the 7th N. American Crane Workshop, 1997; Reflections: The Story of Cranes*
Keyword(s): Birds, Endangered and Threatened Species, Environmental and Conservation Education, International Conservation, Wetlands

INTERNATIONAL ECOLOGY SOCIETY (IES)
1471 Barclay St., St. Paul, MN 55106-1405
Phone: 612-579-7008
Founded: 1975; Membership: 6,000
Scope: International
Description: One hundred percent volunteer-staffed, nonprofit international organization dedicated to the protection of the environment and the encouragement of better understanding of all life forms.
Contact(s):
Vice President: GEORGE E. JOHNSON
Central America Representative (Barranco Village, Toledo District, Belize): RICHARD J. EBENSTEINER
Contact (Dakota): MAGGIE WARREN, Hermosa, SD
North East Representative: BINA ROBINSON, Box 26, Swain, NY 14884-0026
President and Publisher: R. J. KRAMER
Publication(s): *Eco-Humane Letter; Sunrise (neighborhood news); Action Alerts*
Keyword(s): Endangered and Threatened Species, Marine Mammals, Trapping, Wildlife and Wildlife Habitat, Wildlife Management

INTERNATIONAL EROSION CONTROL ASSOCIATION (IECA)
P.O. Box 4904, Steamboat Springs, CO 80477
Phone: 970-879-3010; Fax: 970-879-8563
Founded: 1972; Membership: 1,900
Scope: International
Description: To provide opportunities for the worldwide exchange of information and economic methods of erosion control.
Contact(s):
Executive Director: BEN NORTHCUTT
Publication(s): *Proceedings of Annual Conference; Membership Directory; Products and Services Directory; bimonthyl magazine, quarterly newsletter, IECA Resource Catalog, IECA compilations*
Keyword(s): Engineering, Environmental and Conservation Education, International Conservation, Soil Conservation, Water Pollution

INTERNATIONAL FUND FOR ANIMAL WELFARE
411 Main St., Yarmouth Port, MA 02675
Phone: 508-362-4944; WWW: www.wfaw.org
Founded: 1969; Membership: 1.7 million
Scope: International
Description: An international nonprofit, tax-exempt organization in the U.S. dedicated to the protection of wild and domestic animals and their habitats. IFAW's goals are pursued through a strategic plan consisting of three distinct program areas: Commercial Expoitation and Trade of Wild Animals, Animals in Crisis and Distress, and Habitat for Animals.
Contact(s):
Chief Executive Officer: FRED O'REGAN
Founder: BRIAN D. DAVIES

Australian Office
P.O. BOX 322, Helensburg, New SouthWales 2058 Australia
Scope: International
Contact(s):
Contact: SALLY WILSON

Belgium Office
50 Rue du Taciturne, 1040 Brussels, Brussels Belgium
Scope: International
Contact(s):
Contact: STANLEY JOHNSON

French Office
BP 78 51170, Fismes, Fismes France
Scope: International
Contact(s):
Contact: CHANTAL DERTY

German Office
Postfach 55 04 67 D-22564, Hamburg, Hamburg Germany
Scope: International
Contact(s):
Contact: TOM MARTENS

Holland Office
Sterrenweg 3B, 2651 HZ Berkel en Rodenrijs, Holland United Kingdom
Scope: International
Contact(s):
Office Manager: JETTY TAK

Hong Kong Office
P.O. Box 82 Sai Kung PO, Kowloon, Kowloon China
Scope: International
Contact(s):
Contact: JILL ROBINSON

Italian Office
Via Bocca di Leone 36-Int 4, Rome 187 Italy
Scope: International
Contact(s):
Contact: WALTER CAPORALE

Philippines Office
14 East Maya, Phil-Am Homes, Quezon City 1100 Phillipines
Scope: International
Contact(s):
Contact: MEL ALIPIO

Russian Office
Apt. 84, Protochniy Pereulok 11, Moscow 21099 Russia
Scope: International
Contact(s):
Contact: MASHA VORONTSOVA

NON-GOVERNMENTAL ORGANIZATIONS

South African Office
P.O. Box 2587, Rivonia, Rivonia 2128 South Africa
Scope: International
Contact(s):
Contact: DAVID BARRITT

United Kingdom
Warren Court Park Rd., Crownborough, E.Sussex TN6 2QH United Kingdom
Scope: International
Contact(s):
Director: CINDY MILBURN

INTERNATIONAL GAME FISH ASSOCIATION
1301 E. Atlantic Blvd., Pompano Beach, FL 33060
Phone: 954-954-3474; Fax: 954-954-5868; Email: IGFAHQ@aol.com
Founded: 1939
Scope: International
Description: A nonprofit, tax-deductible organization which maintains and promotes ethical international angling regulations and compiles world game fish records for saltwater, freshwater, and fly fishing. Also represents and informs recreational fishermen regarding research, conservation, and legislative developments related to their sport. Encourages and supports game fish tagging programs and other scientific data collection efforts. There are over 250 international representatives and 1,000 affiliated fishing clubs.
Contact(s):
Chairman: GEORGE C. MATTHEWS
President: MICHAEL LEECH
Treasurer and Secretary: ROY E. NAFTZGER
Vice Chairman: JOHN W. ANDERSON II
Publication(s): *World Record Game Fishes; International Angler, The; Rule Book for Freshwater, Saltwater and Fly Fishing*
Keyword(s): Fisheries, Sport Fishing

INTERNATIONAL HUNTER EDUCATION ASSOCIATION
PO. Box 490, Wellington, CO 80549
Phone: 970-568-7954; Fax: 970-568-7955; Email: ihea@webaccess.net; WWW: ihea.com
Membership: 65,000
Scope: International
Description: To provide leadership and establish standards in the development of hunters to be safe, responsible, knowledgeable, and involved.
Contact(s):
President: CAPT. ED TYER
Vice President: TIM LAWHERN
Vice President: PHIL HAUGHIAN
Vice President: TONY BURTT
Secretary: MAC LANG
Treasurer: ALAN HIERONYMOUS
Executive Vice President: DR. DAVID M. KNOTTS
Instructor Board Member: RICHARD McQUILLAN
Instructor Board Member: ED AUGUSTINE
Instructor Board Member: JOHN PANIO JR.
President Elect: LES SMITH
Publication(s): *Hunter Education Journal; Hunter Education Student Guide*
Keyword(s): Environmental and Conservation Education, Hunting, Outdoor Recreation, Training, Wildlife Management

INTERNATIONAL INSTITUTE FOR ENERGY CONSERVATION
750 1st St., Suite 940 NE, Washington, DC 20002
Phone: 202-842-3388; Fax: 202-842-1565; Email: iiec@iiec.org
Founded: 1984
Scope: International
Description: A nonprofit organization established to accelerate the global adoption of energy-efficiency policies, technologies, and practices to enable econimically and ecologically sustainable development.
Contact(s):
Director: STEWART BOYLE
Director: STEVE HALL
Director: TERRY KRAFT OLIVER
Chairman of the Board: JOHN C. FOX
Executive Director and President: RUSSELL STURM
Publication(s): *E-Notes; Integrated Transport Management and Development, Opportunities for the U.S. Energy Efficiency Industry in Chile; Global Energy Efficiency Initiative Sustainable Energy Guide*
Keyword(s): Energy, Greenhouse Effect/Global Warming, International Conservation, Sustainable Development, Transportation

INTERNATIONAL MARINE MAMMAL PROJECT, THE
Earth Island Institute, 300 Broadway, Suite 28, San Francisco, CA 94133
Phone: 415-788-3666l/1-800-DOLPHIN; Fax: 415-788-7324; Email: marinemammal@earthisland.org
Founded: 1982; Membership: 35,000
Scope: International
Description: IMMP is a nonprofit research, education, and monitoring project of Earth Island Institute. IMMP is committed to ending dolphin mortality caused by the U.S. and international tuna industries, stopping the use of driftnets, and promoting sustainable fishing practices. In addition, IMMP aims to halt commercial whaling worldwide and ban live capture and display of marine mammals.
Contact(s):
Executive Director: DAVID PHILLIPS
Publication(s): *Earth Island Journal; Ocean Alert*
Keyword(s): Aquariums, Aquatic Habitats, Biodiversity, Endangered and Threatened Species, Environmental and Conservation Education, Environmental Law, Fisheries, International Conservation, Internships, Mammals, Marine Mammals, Nature Preservation, Wildlife and Wildlife Habitat

INTERNATIONAL MARITIME ORGANIZATION
4 Albert Embankment, London SE1 7SR United Kingdom
Phone: 0171-735-7611; Fax: 0717-857-3210; Email: info@imo.org; WWW: www.imo.org
Founded: 1959; Membership: 156
Scope: International
Description: To improve maritime safety and to prevent marine pollution from ships, through the adoption of international conventions, protocols, codes, and recommendations.
Contact(s):
Secretary-General: WILLIAM A. O'NEIL
Publication(s): *IMO News*
Keyword(s): Environmental Law, Greenhouse Effect/Global Warming, Sustainable Development, Transportation, Water Pollution Management

INTERNATIONAL OCEANOGRAPHIC FOUNDATION
University of Miami, Rosenstiel School of Marine & Atmosphere Science, 4600 Rickenbacker Causeway Virginia Key, Miami, FL 33149
Phone: 305-361-4061
Founded: 1953; Membership: 55,000
Scope: International
Description: Nonprofit foundation organized to encourage the extension of human knowledge by scientific study and exploration of the oceans in all their aspects and to acquaint and educate the general public concerning the vital role of the oceans to all life on this planet.
Contact(s):
President: EDWARD T. FOOTE II
Vice President: DAVID A. LIEBERMAN
Vice President: OTIS BROWN
Vice President: LUIS GLASER
Secretary: LOURDES LaPAZ, 400 SE 2nd Ave., 4th Fl., Miami, FL 33131; Phone: 305-375-8498; Fax: 305-375-9188
Treasurer: DIANE M. COOK

Keyword(s): Environmental and Conservation Education, Fisheries, Marine Mammals, Oceanography, Outdoor Recreation

INTERNATIONAL OSPREY FOUNDATION INC., THE
P.O. Box 250, Sanibel, FL 33957
Phone: 941-472-1862
Founded: 1981; Membership: 300
Scope: International
Description: A nonprofit organization dedicated to studying the problem of restoring osprey numbers to a stable population, making recommendations to enhance the continued survival of the osprey and initiating educational programs. Yearly grant of up to $1000.00 given for graduate work. Work relating to all raptors is acceptable, but osprey study is given priority.
Contact(s):
President: DAVID LOVELAND
Vice President: ANNE MITCHELL
Secretary and Treasurer: INGE GLISSMAN
Publication(s): *TIOF Newsletter - one International NL - one 'local' NL*
Keyword(s): Birds, International Wildlife, Nongame Wildlife, Raptors, Wildlife Management

INTERNATIONAL PLANT PROPAGATION SOCIETY, INC., THE
Washington Park Arboretum, 2300 Arboretum Dr., Seattle, WA 98112
Phone: 206-543-8602; Fax: 206-527-2796
Founded: 1950; Membership: 3,200
Scope: International
Description: The Society was founded to seek and share information on plant propagation. The Sociey has nine regional chapters, three in USA and Canada, Australia, New Zealand, Great Britain and Ireland, Scandinavian, Japan and Southern Africa.
Contact(s):
Executive Secretary and Treasurer: JOHN A. WOTT
Publication(s): *Annual Proceeding of all regional meetings and papers; regional newsletters of meetings for members*
Keyword(s): Flowers, Plants, and Trees, Plant Propagation, Urban Environment, Urban Forestry

INTERNATIONAL PRIMATE PROTECTION LEAGUE
P.O. Box 766, Summerville, SC 29484
Phone: 843-871-2280; Fax: 843-871-7988; Email: ippl@awod.com; WWW: www.ippl.org/
Founded: 1973; Membership: 16,000
Scope: International
Description: A nonprofit international organization devoted to the conservation and protection of nonhuman primates. There are branches in the United States, United Kingdom and field representatives in 32 countries.
Contact(s):
Secretary: MARJORIE DOGGETT, 1 Toh Heights, 507802 Singapore
Treasurer: DIANE WALTERS
Chairperson: DR. SHIRLEY McGREAL
Publication(s): *International Primate Protection League*
Keyword(s): Endangered and Threatened Species, Forests and Forestry, International Conservation, Mammals, Wildlife Rehabilitation

INTERNATIONAL PROFESSIONAL HUNTERS' ASSOCIATION
P.O. Box 17444, San Antonio, TX 78217
Phone: 210-824-7506
Founded: 1969; Membership: 500
Scope: International
Description: International organization of wildlife professionals dedicated to promoting the good management of wildlife worldwide; collaborates internationally with officers of Game Departments, National Parks and Reserves in conservation and management of fauna and flora; supports antipoaching programs and game surveys; members pledged to fair chase and sportsmanlike conduct in sport hunting and game photography.
Contact(s):
President: DONALD LINDSAY, P.O. Box 770, Cramerview, 2060 South Africa; Phone: 27-11-706-7724
Administrative Officer: CASSIE WALKER, P.O. Box 770, Cramerview, 2060 South Africa; Phone: 27-11-707-7725
Executive Officer: DI PIETERSE, P.O. Box 770, Cramerview, 2060 South Africa; Phone: 27-11-706-7725
Vice President of Eastern Sector: COENRAAD VERMAAK, P.O. Box 739, Dundee, 3000 South Africa; Phone: 27-34-25-729
Vice President of Eastern Sector: TERRY PIERSON, P.O. Box 4058, Christchurch, New Zealand; Phone: 64-33-55-8243
Vice President of Eastern Sector: ROBIN HURT, P.O. Box 24988, Nairobi, Kenya; Phone: 25-42-882-826
Vice President of Eastern Sector: TONY SANCHEZ-ARINO, Felix Pizcueta 6, Valencia, 46004 Spain; Phone: 6-35-1-0424
Vice President of Western Sector: RON YOUNG, 4028 Weber Rd., Corpus Christi, TX 78411; Phone: 512-833-1989
Vice President of Western Sector: BETH JONES-LEVITZ, Tower 1 Suite 1407 1000 Quayside Terr., Miami, FL 33138; Phone: 305-893-1162
Vice President of Western Sector: DOOLEY GILCHRIST, P.O. Box 6127, Jackson, MS 39288; Phone: 601-969-1777
Vice President of Western Sector: MIKE BRANHAM, P.O. Box 27, Hurricane, UT 84737; Phone: 801-635-2340
Keyword(s): Endangered and Threatened Species, Hunting, International Conservation, Wildlife and Wildlife Habitat, Wildlife Management

INTERNATIONAL RIVERS NETWORK
1847 Berkeley Way, Berkeley, CA 94703
Phone: 510-848-1155; Fax: 510-848-1008; Email: irn@irn.org
Founded: 1986; Membership: 1,600
Scope: International
Description: A nonprofit network dedicated to preserving the world's rivers and watersheds. Members include environmentalists, engineers, hydrologists, human rights activists, and academics who are committed to the study and defense of rivers and riverine communities. Since its inception, IRN has built a network of citizen organizations and technical experts in more than 80 countries who are working to protect freshwater resources, endangered ecosystems, and the rights of indigenous peoples worldwide.
Contact(s):
President: PHIL WILLIAMS
Director: OWEN LAMMERS
Africa Campaigns: LORI POTTINGER
Campaign Director: PATRICK McCULLY
Editor: JULIETTE MAJOT
Executive Assistant: RANI DERASARY
Library Coordinator: YVONNE CUELLAR
Office Operations: PETRA YEE
South America Campaigns: GLEN SWITKES
Publication(s): *World Rivers Review; Bank Check; special briefings; action alerts; working papers; IRN Reader*

INTERNATIONAL SNOW LEOPARD TRUST
4649 Sunnyside Ave., N., Suite 325, Seattle, WA 98103
Phone: 206-632-2421; Fax: 206-632-3967; Email: islt@serv.net
Founded: 1982; Membership: 950
Scope: International
Description: A nonprofit organization dedicated to the conservation of the endangered snow leopard and its mountain habitat through a balanced approach that considers the needs of the local people and the environment; and provides workshops, field training, equipment, publications, conservation education programs, and a centralized database for organizing and disseminating information.
Contact(s):
President: CHARLIE MORSE
Vice President: BONNIE ROBBINS
Treasurer: CAROLYN ANDERSON
Executive Director: JEFF DEMETRESCU; Phone: 206-632-2421
Chair and Founder: HELEN FREEMAN

NON-GOVERNMENTAL ORGANIZATIONS

Keyword(s): Biodiversity, Endangered and Threatened Species, Environmental and Conservation Education, International Conservation, Sustainable Ecosystems

INTERNATIONAL SOCIETY FOR ECOLOGICAL ECONOMICS
P.O. Box 1589, Solomons, MD 20688
Phone: 410-326-0794; Email: beckman@cbl.umces.edu
Founded: 1988; Membership: 1,600
Scope: International
Description: ISEE actively encourages the integration of the study and the management of ecology and economics in order to achieve an ecologically and economically sustainable world.
Contact(s):
President of Board of Directors: ROBERT COSTANZA
Publication(s): *Ecological Economics; Ecological Economics Bulletin, The*
Keyword(s): Biodiversity, Environmental Planning, Sustainable Development, Sustainable Ecosystems

INTERNATIONAL SOCIETY FOR ENDANGERED CATS (ISEC)
3070 Riverside Dr., Suite 160, Columbus, OH 43221
Phone: 614-487-8760; Fax: 614-487-8769
Founded: 1988; Membership: 600
Scope: International
Description: ISEC's purpose is to raise awareness of the plight of endangered wild cats, and thereby prevent their extinction. ISEC offers conservation education programs, collects and disseminates information about wild cats, and supports specific conservation projects around the world. Member IUCN
Contact(s):
President: BILL SIMPSON, 3070 Riverside Dr., Suite 160, Columbus, OH 43221
Executive Director: PATRICIA CURRIE, 196 W. Central, Delaware, OH 43015; Phone: 740-369-9794
Publication(s): *Cat Tales*
Keyword(s): Endangered and Threatened Species, Environmental and Conservation Education, International Conservation, Wild Cats, Wildlife and Wildlife Habitat

INTERNATIONAL SOCIETY FOR ENVIRONMENTAL ETHICS
Department of Philosophy, University of Windsor, Windsor, Ontario N9B 3P4 Canada
Phone: 519-253-4232
Founded: 1990; Membership: 650
Scope: International
Description: The International Society for Environmental Ethics' main purpose is to promote the critical analysis of ethical issues related to the natural environment, to further and support philosophical and scientific meetings and conferences nationally and internationally, and to provide material and media aids suitable for teaching environmental philosophy and environmental ethics.
Contact(s):
President: MARK SAGOFF, Director of Institute for Philosophy and Public Policy, University of Maryland, Baltimore, MD 20742 UnitedStates
Vice President: J. BAIRD CALLICOTT, Philosophy Department, University of Wisconsin at Stevens Point, Stevens Point, WI 54481 UnitedStates
Secretary: DR. LAURA WESTRA, University of Windsor, Windsor, Ontario N9B 3P4 Canada; Phone: 519-253-4232
Treasurer: EDWARD HETTINGER, College of Charleston, Charleston, SC 29424 UnitedStates
Publication(s): *International Society for Environmental Ethics Newsletter*

INTERNATIONAL SOCIETY FOR THE PRESERVATION OF THE TROPICAL RAINFOREST, THE
3931 Camino De La Cumbre, Sherman Oaks, CA 91423
Phone: 818-788-2002; Fax: 818-990-3333
Founded: 1984; Membership: 12,000
Scope: International
Description: The International Society for the Preservation of the Tropical Rainforest is dedicated to the global conservation of tropical forest resources through the promotion of park implementation, sustainable agriculture, and timber harvesting.
Contact(s):
Director: EDWARD ASNER, 3931 Camino De La Cumbre, Sherman Oaks, CA 91423; Phone: 818-788-2002
President and Director: ARNOLD NEWMAN, 3931 Camino De La Cumbre, Sherman Oaks, CA 91423; Phone: 818-788-2002
Vice President and Director: ROXANNE KREMER, 3931 Camino De La Cumbre, Sherman Oaks, CA 91423; Phone: 818-788-2002
Publication(s): *Tropical Rainforest: A World Survey of Our Most Valuable and Endangered Habitat (contains a blueprint for survival); Amazon Hotline*
Keyword(s): Biodiversity, Cultural Preservation, Endangered and Threatened Species, Environmental Preservation, Greenhouse Effect/Global Warming

INTERNATIONAL SOCIETY OF ARBORICULTURE
P.O. Box GG, Savoy, IL 61874
Phone: 217-355-9411; Fax: 217-355-9516
Founded: 1924; Membership: 10,500
Scope: International
Description: To promote and improve the care and preservation of shade and ornamental trees through research and education.
Contact(s):
President: AL CHERRY, Horsham, PA
Vice President: DR. GARY WATSON, Lisle, IL
Executive Director: BILL KRUIDENIER
Editor: DEREK VANNICE, P.O. Box GG, Savoy, IL 61874
Editor: DR. ROBERT MILLER, College of Natural Resources, University of Wisconsin/Stevens Point, Stevens Point, WI 54481
President-Elect: DR. DAN NEELY, Scott City, MO
Publication(s): *Journal of Arboriculture; Arborist News; Valuation of Landscape Trees, Shrubs, and Other Plants; Planting Tree and Shrubs; Publication listings to include "A Photographic Guide for Evaluation of Hazard Trees in Urban Areas"; " Arborist Certificate Guide"; VHS Video Tapes on Construction Damage to Trees on Wooded Lots*

INTERNATIONAL SOCIETY OF TROPICAL FORESTERS INC.
5400 Grosvenor Ln., Bethesda, MD 20814
Phone: 301-897-8720; Fax: 301-897-3690; Email: istfiust@igc.apc.org
Founded: 1950; Membership: 2,000
Scope: International
Description: A nonprofit organization founded with the objective of providing an information exchange for members involved in the management, protection, and wise use of tropical forests.
Contact(s):
President: WARREN T. DOOLITTLE, USA
Vice President: MARILYN W. HOSKINS, USA
Director of Africa: YEMI M. KATERERE, Zimbabwe
Director of Asia: CHUN K. LAI, Indonesia
Director of Latin America: RODOLFO SALAZAR, Costa Rica
Editor: FRANK H. WADSWORTH
Publication(s): *ISTF News; ISTF Noticis*
Keyword(s): Biodiversity, Forest Management, International Conservation, Renewable Resources, Sustainable Ecosystems, Urban Forestry

INTERNATIONAL SONORAN DESERT ALLIANCE
201 Esperanza Ave., P.O. Box 687, Ajo, AZ 85321
Phone: 520-387-6823; Fax: 520-387-5626
Founded: 1992; Membership: 673
Scope: International
Description: The purpose of the International Sonoran Desert Alliance is to promote environmentally sustainable and culturally sound economic development while protecting the natural and tri-cultural heritage of the western Sonoran Desert.
Contact(s):
President: JOSEPH JOAQUIN
Vice President: MANUEL GONZALEZ
Vice President: GRACIELA BARAJAS
Secretary: KENIA CASTANZDA
Treasurer: DIANA VEGA
Director: REYNALDO CANTU
Keyword(s): Cultural Preservation, Deserts, International Conservation, People of Color in the Environment, Sustainable Development

INTERNATIONAL UNION FOR CONSERVATION OF NATURE AND NATURAL RESOURCES (IUCN) THE WORLD CONSERVATION UNION
Headquarters, Rue Mauverney 28, CH-1196, Gland Switzerland
Phone: 022.9990001/4-419624/IUCN CH-22.999
Founded: 1948
Scope: International
Description: An independent body to promote scientifically-based action for the conservation of nature and to ensure that development is sustainable and provides a lasting improvement in the quality of life for people all over the world. Eight hundred eighty voting members in 138 countries; 73 states, 107 government agencies, and 623 non-governmental organizations. Also 35 non-voting affiliate members. Maintains a global network of more than 6,000 scientists and professionals organized into six commissions.
Contact(s):
President: YOLANDA N. KAKABADSE
Treasurer: CLAES DE DARDEL
Assistant Director of General Constituency Development: GEORGE GREENE
Chairman for Species Survival Commission (SSC) (Canada): DAVID BRACKETT
Chairman of Commission on Ecosystem Management (United Kingdom): EDWARD MALTBY
Chairman of Commission on Education and Communication (The Netherlands): DR. FRITZ HESSELINK
Chairman of Commission on Environmental Economic and Social Policy (United Kingdom): DR. TARIQ J. BUNURI
Chairman of Commission on Environmental Law (CEL) (US): PROF. NICHOLAS ROBINSON
Chairman of Commission on Protected Areas (WCPPA) (United Kingdom): PROF. ADRIAN PHILLIPS
Chairman of the Bureau (Eduador): SRA YOLANDA N. KAKABADSE
Director General (New Zealand): DAVID McDOWELL
Director of Biodiversity Policy Coordination Division: JEFFREY A. McNEELY
Director of Finance: MARIA GRAZIA IURI
Director of Global Programme (Switzerland): PATRICK DUGAN
Head of Environmental Law Centre (Bonn, FRG) (Belgium): FRANCOISE BURHENNE-GUILMIN
Publication(s): *World Conservation Bulletin; Red Data Books* (describing threatened species of mammals, amphibia and reptilia, invertebrates and plants); *United Nations List of National Parks and Protected Areas;* Books on conservation and development, land and freshwater animals, marine and coastal ecology and management, national parks and other protected areas, and regional conservation; *Environmental Policy and Law Papers; World Conservation Strategy: Living Resource Conservation for Sustainable Development; Caring for the Earth--A Strategy for Sustainable Living; A Pocket Guide to IUCN.*

Bangladesh Office
House #13, Road 3, Dhanmond, RIA 1205, Dhaka 1205 Bangladesh
Scope: International
Contact(s):
Head: ANWARUL ISLAM

Burkina Fasso Office
01 BP 3133, 515 Rue Agostino Neto, Ouagadougou 01, Ouagadougou 01 Burkina Fasso
Scope: International
Contact(s):
Country Representative: MICHEL KOUDA

Coordination Office of South and South East Asia
P.O. Box 4, 302 Outreach Bldg., AIT, Klong Luang, Pathumthani 12120 Thailand
Scope: International
Contact(s):
Head: DR. MOHAMMED ZAKIR HUSSAIN

Country Liaison Botswana Office
Private Bag 00300, Gaborone Botswana
Scope: International
Contact(s):
Country Representative: RUUD JANSEN

Mali Office
BP 1567, Bamako Mali
Scope: International
Contact(s):
Chef de Mission (Acting): ADAMA DAOU

Nepal Office
P.O. Box 3923, Lalitpur, Dhobighat, Kathmandu Nepal
Scope: International
Contact(s):
Country Representative: DR. AMBIKA ADHIKARI

Office for Southern Africa (ROSA)
P.O. Box 745, Harare Zimbabwe
Scope: International
Contact(s):
Regional Representative: YEMI KATERERE

Office of Sri Lanka
48 Vajira Ln., Colombo 5 Sri Lanka
Scope: International
Contact(s):
Country Representative: SHIRANEE YESARATNE

Outposted Centre Canada
380 St. Antoine St. W., Office 3200, Montreal, Quebec H2Y 3X7 Canada
Scope: International
Contact(s):
Head: MALCOLM MERCER

Outposted Centre European Programme
Marienhof, Bredaseweg 387, 5037 LD, Tilburg Netherlands
Scope: International
Contact(s):
European Programme Coordinator: ZBIGNIEW KARPOWICZ

Outposted Centre-Environmental Law Centre
Adenauerallee 214, Bonn 53113 Germany
Scope: International
Contact(s):
Head: DR. FRANCOISE BURHENNE-GUILMIN

NON-GOVERNMENTAL ORGANIZATIONS

Outposted Office
1400 16th St., NW, Washington, DC 20036
Scope: International
Contact(s):
Executive Director: SCOTT A. HAJOST

Pakistan Office
1 Bath Island Rd., Karachi 75530 Pakistan
Scope: International
Contact(s):
Country Representative: ABAN MARKER KABRAJI

Regional Coordination Office for West Africa
BP 10933, Niamey, Niger West Africa
Scope: International
Contact(s):
Country Representative and Regional Coordinator: M. M. MAMANE

Regional Office for Eastern Africa
P.O. Box 68200, Mukoma Rd., Langata, Nairobi Kenya
Scope: International
Contact(s):
Regional Representative: ELDAD TUKAHIRWA

Regional Office for Meso America
Apartado 0146-2150, Moravia, San Jose Costa Rica
Scope: International
Contact(s):
Regional Director: DR. ENRIQUE LAHMANN VANNICE

Regional Office for South America
Casilla Postal 17-17-626, Avenida Atahualpa 955 y Republica Edificio Digicom Piso 4, Quito Ecuador
Scope: International
Contact(s):
Regional Representative: JUANITA CASTANO

Regonal Office for Central Africa
B.P. 5506, c/o IUCN Project Office DHA, Yaounde, Cameroon Brazil
Scope: International
Contact(s):
Coordinator for Central Africa: ASSITOU NDINGA

Senegal Office
BP 3215 Ave. Bourguiba x rue 3, Castors, Dakar Senegal
Scope: International
Contact(s):
Chef de Mission: ABDOULAYE NDIAYE

U.S. Office, Washington, DC
1400 16th St., NW, Washington, DC 20036
Phone: 202-797-5454; Fax: 202-797-5461; Email: postmaster@iucnus.org; WWW: www.iucn.org
Scope: International

Uganda Office
P.O. Box 10950, Plot 39 Acacia Ave., Kampala Uganda
Scope: International
Contact(s):
Country Representative: ALEX MUHWEEZI

Zambia Office
Asco Bldg., Private Bag W, 356 Luanshya Rd., Plot No 5116, Lusaka Zambia
Scope: International
Contact(s):
Country Representative: SALLY LINDA MULALA

INTERNATIONAL WILD WATERFOWL ASSOCIATION
5614 River Styx Rd., Medina, OH 44256
Founded: 1958; Membership: 500
Scope: International
Description: Works toward protection, conservation, and reproduction of any species of wild waterfowl considered in danger of eventual extinction; encourages breeding of well known and rare species in captivity. Established Avicultural Hall of Fame. Sponsors annual conference and gives grants in field.
Contact(s):
President: WALTER B. STURGEON JR., 7 James Farm, Durham, NH 03824; Phone: 603-659-5442
Secretary: NANCY COLLINS, 5614 River Styx Rd., Medina, OH 44256; Phone: 216-725-8782
Treasurer: WILLIAM R. LOWE, 3010 Shady Ln., Billings, MT 59102; Phone: 406-245-6119
1st Vice President: EDWARD ASPER, Vice President of Sea World, 7007 Sea World Dr., Orlando, FL 32821; Phone: 407-351-3600
2nd Vice President: PAUL DYE, 10114 54th Pl. NE, Everett, WA 98205; Phone: 206-342-8346
Publication(s): *IWWA Newsletter*
Keyword(s): Endangered and Threatened Species, International Conservation, Scholarships and Grants, Waterfowl, Wildlife and Wildlife Habitat

INTERNATIONAL WILDERNESS LEADERSHIP (WILD) FOUNDATION
P.O. Box 1380, Ojai, CA 93024
Email: info@wild.org
Founded: 1974; Membership: 5,000
Scope: International
Description: The International Wilderness Leadership Foundation is dedicated to protect wilderness and wildlife, to provide environmental experience and training, and to promote the correct use of wildlands worldwide.
Contact(s):
Chairman: ROBERT BARON, 350 Indiana St., Golden, CO 80401
President: VANCE G. MARTIN; Phone: 805-640-0390
Treasurer: MICHAEL SWEATMAN VANNICE, P.O. Box 659, Stowe, VT 05672; Phone: 802-244-8981
Vice Presiden of Science and Education: DR. JOHN HENDEE, College of Forestry, University of Idaho, Moscow, ID 83843; Phone: 208-885-2267
Publication(s): *Leaf Newsletter, The; Wilderness Management; For the Conservation of Earth; Wilderness, the Way Ahead; Arctic Wilderness; International Journal of Wilderness*
Keyword(s): Environmental and Conservation Education, International Conservation, Wilderness

INTERNATIONAL WILDLIFE COALITION (IWC) AND THE WHALE ADOPTION PROJECT
70 E. Falmouth Highway, E. Falmouth, MA 02536
Phone: 508-548-8328; Fax: 508-548-8542; WWW: www.iwc.org
Founded: 1984; Membership: 275,000
Scope: International
Description: IWC is a nonprofit, tax-exempt organization dedicated to preserving wildlife and their habitats. As an internationally recognized non-governmental organization, IWC's achievements have been accomplished through grassroots advocacy, activism, research, and education efforts. IWC's Whale Adoption Project protects and researches marine mammals.
Contact(s):
President: DANIEL MORAST, 70 E. Falmouth Highway, E. Falmouth, MA 02536; Phone: 508-548-8328; Fax: 508-548-8542; Email: dmorast@iwc.org
Vice President: STEPHEN BEST, P.O. Box 988, Shelburne, Ontario L0N1S0 Canada; Phone: 519-925-3440; Fax: 519-925-2003; Email: sbest@iwc.org
Brazil Project Coordinator: JOSE TRUDA PALAZZO JR., P.O. Box 5087, Florianopolis, S.C. 88040-970 Brazil; Phone: 55-482-

340021; Fax: 55-482-341580; Email: BRAZILIAN_WILDLIFE@zaz.com.br

Canada Director: ANNE DONCASTER, P.O. Box 340, Carling, Ontario POB1J0 Canada; Phone: 705-765-6341; Fax: 705-765-6435; Email: adncstr@muskoka.com

Canada Project Director: DR. RONALD ORENSTEIN, 130 Adelaide St. West, Suite 1940, Toronto, Ontario M5H3P5 Canada; Phone: 905-820-7886; Fax: 905-569-0116; Email: ornstn@inforamp.net

Sri Lanka Representative: DR. HIRAN JAYEWARDENE, 218/1 Bauddhaloka Mawatha, Colombo 7, Sri Lanka; Phone: 94-1-580236; Fax: 94-1-580236

United Kingdom Director: CHARLES WARTENBERG, 141A, High St., Edenbridge, Kent TN85AX England; Phone: 44-1732-86695; Fax: 44-1732-866995

Vice President of Programs: DONNA HART, P.O. Box 138, Elsberry, MO 63343; Phone: 314-898-5600; Fax: 314-898-5411; Email: dlhart@inlink.com

Publication(s): *WhaleWatch; Wildlife Watch; Whales of the World Teacher's Kit; Wildlife and You and What You Can Do To Help*

Keyword(s): Endangered and Threatened Species, International Conservation, Mammals, Marine Mammals, Whales, Wildlife and Wildlife Habitat

INTERNATIONAL WILDLIFE REHABILITATION COUNCIL (IWRC)
4437 Central Pl., Suite B-4, Suisun, CA 94585-1633
Phone: 707-864-1761/Wildlife Care Referral Line 707-864-1762; Fax: 707-864-3106; Email: iwrc@inreach.com; WWW: www.iwrc-online.org

Founded: 1972; Membership: 1,700
Scope: International

Description: IWRC is a membership-supported organization dedicated to the care and rehabilitation of injured and orphaned wildlife and their eventual return into the wild. Committed to the training and education of wildlife rehabilitators, with a goal towards professionalism and expertise in the field.

Contact(s):
President: MARGE GIBSON
Vice President: SUSAN HECKLY
Secretary: THEISEN WATT
Treasurer: MARY BOTTI
Executive Director: MARY REYNOLDS

Publication(s): *Journal of Wildlife Rehabilitation; Basic Wildlife Rehabilitation; Minimum Standards and Accreditation; Current Protocol for Treatment of Oil Contaminated Birds; other publications and catalog available.*

Keyword(s): Biology, Natural History, Wildlife and Wildlife Habitat, Wildlife Disease, Wildlife Rehabilitation

INTERNATIONAL WOLF CENTER (Administrative Offices)
5930 Brooklyn Blvd., Minneapolis, MN 55429
Phone: 612-560-7374; Fax: 612-560-7368

Scope: International

INTERNATIONAL WOLF CENTER (Educational Services)
1396 Hwy. 169, Ely, MN 55731
Phone: 218-365-4695; Fax: 218-365-3318; Email: wolfinfo@wolf.org; WWW: www.wolf.org

Founded: 1985; Membership: 8,400
Scope: International

Description: The International Wolf Center supports the survival of the wolf around the world by teaching about its life, its associations with other species, and its dynamite relationship to humans.

Contact(s):
Chair: NANCY JO TUBBS
Secretary: ROLF PETERSON
Treasurer: PAUL ANDERSON
Executive Director: WALTER M. MEDWID
Information Resources Coordinator: LINDA AYLSWORTH
Vice Chair: DR. L. DAVID MECH

Publication(s): *International Wolf Magazine; Guidelines for Gray Wolf Management; various educational pamphlets*

Keyword(s): Endangered and Threatened Species, Environmental and Conservation Education, International Conservation, Mammals, Wildlife and Wildlife Habitat, Wildlife Management

INTERPRETATION CANADA
P.O. Box 2667, Station D, Ottawa, Ontario K1P 5W7 Canada

Founded: 1973; Membership: 625
Scope: National

Description: Interpretation Canada is dedicated to raising public awareness, understanding, and appreciation for Canada's natural and cultural heritage, provides training, networking, and advocacy for interpreters, and promotes the role of interpretation in fields such as conservation, education, recreation, and tourism.

Contact(s):
Chairperson: ANNA ROBERTSON, R.R.2, Lacombe, ABTOCISO Canada; Phone: 403-342-6889; Fax: 403-347-1666; Email: kwn@supernet.ab.ca

Member Services: JIM ROBERTSON, Kerrywood Nature Centre, 6300-45 Ave., Red Deer, Alberta T4N 3M4 403-346-2010 Canada; Phone: 403-347-2590; Email: kwnc@supernet.ab.ca

Publication(s): *Interpscan - national journal; regional newsletters from Northwest Territories, British Columbia, Alberta, Ontario, and Atlantic region; annual membership directory*

INTERTRIBAL BISON COOPERATIVE (ITBC)
124 East St. Joseph St., P.O. Box 8105, Rapid City, SD 57701
Phone: 605-394-9730; Fax: 605-394-7742; Email: itbc@enetis.net

Founded: 1991; Membership: 45 Tribes, Honorary & Associate
Scope: National

Description: The ITBC is dedicated to the restoration of buffalo to Indian lands in a manner which is compatible with the cultural practices and spiritual beliefs of the respective tribes.

Contact(s):
President: MIKE FOX, Gros Ventre & Assiniboine, R.R. 1 Box 66, Harlem, MT 59526; Phone: 406-353-2205

Vice President: CARL A. TSOSIE, Picuris Pueblo, P.O. Box 127, Penasco, NM 87553; Phone: 505-587-2519

Secretary: ARTHUR DENNY JR., Rt. 2 Box 163, Ncobrara, NE 68760; Phone: 402-857-2302

Treasurer: RICHARD ARCHULETA, Taos Pueblo, P.O. Box 3164, Taos, NM 87571; Phone: 505-758-3883

Executive Director: MARK HECKERT

Publication(s): *Buffalo Tracks*

Keyword(s): Cultural Preservation, Land Preservation, Prairies, Sustainable Development, Wildlife and Wildlife Habitat

IOWA ACADEMY OF SCIENCE
University of Northern Iowa, Cedar Falls, IA 50614-0508
Phone: 319-273-2021; Fax: 319-273-2807

Founded: 1875; Membership: 1,275
Scope: Statewide

Description: To further the work of scientists, facilitate cooperation among them, and increase public understanding and appreciation of the importance and promise of the methods of science in human progress. A conservation section meets each year as part of an annual convention submitting papers dealing with all conservation happenings.

Contact(s):
President: JIM CHRISTENSEN, Bioloby Dept., Drake University, Des Moines, IA 50311

Executive Director and Manager Editor: PAUL E. RIDER SR.

President-Elect: NEIL BERNSTEIN, Mt. Mercy College, 1330 Elmhurst Dr. NE, Cedar Rapids, IA 52402

Publication(s): *Journal of the Iowa Academy of Science; Iowa Science Teachers Newsletter; Iowa's Natural Heritage; IAS Bulletin*

NON-GOVERNMENTAL ORGANIZATIONS

IOWA ASSOCIATION OF NATURALISTS
R.R. 1 Box 53, Guthrie Center, IA 50115
Phone: 515-747-8383
Founded: 1978; Membership: 120
Scope: Statewide
Description: Organization of persons interested in promoting the development of skills and education within the art of interpreting the natural and cultural environment. Members representing county, state, federal, and private conservation education agencies, organizations, and facilities.
Contact(s):
President of the Board: TODD VON EHWEGAN, Cerro Gordo County Conservation Board 3501 Lime Creek Rd., Mason City, IA 50401
Secretary of the Board: SANDY FULCHER, Black Hawk County Conservation Board, 657 Reserve Dr., Cedar Falls, IA 50613; Phone: 319-277-2187
Treasurer of the Board: JOEL VAN ROEKEL, Warren County Conservation Board 1565 118th Ave., Indianola, IA 50125; Phone: 515-961-6169
Vice President of the Board: STEVE MARTIN, Butler County Conservatoin Board, Henry Woods State Park, 28727 Timber Rd., Clarkville, IA 50619; Phone: 319-278-1130
Workshop Coordinator: BRUCE VOIGHTS, Wright County Conservation Board, 1720 O'Brien Ave., Clarion, IA 50525; Phone: 515-532-3185
Keyword(s): Environmental and Conservation Education, Interpretation

IOWA ASSOCIATION OF SOIL AND WATER CONSERVATION DISTRICT COMMISSIONERS
ATTN: President, 1152 160th St., Gladbrook, IA 50131
Scope: Statewide
Contact(s):
President, Board Member: DAN BRUENE, 1152 160th St., Gladbrook, IA 50635; Phone: 515-473-2338; Fax: 515-473-2455
Vice President: WILLIAM BENNETT, 4331 Dove Rd., Elgin, IA 82141-9526; Phone: 319-426-5695; Fax: 319-426-5695
Secretary: BERNIE BOLTON, 38995 Honeysuckle Rd., Oakland, IA 52560-9686; Phone: 712-482-3386; Fax: 712-482-3561
Treasurer: ART RALSTON, 2629 200th St., Moville, IA 51039-8036; Phone: 712-873-3719
Executive Director: JILL KNAPP, P.O. Box 649, Johnston, IA 50131; Phone: 515-278-5362; Fax: 515-278-5362

IOWA AUDUBON COUNCIL
734 16th Ave. #6, Grinnell, IA 50112
Phone: 515-236-5403
Scope: Statewide
Description: A statewide council of representatives of the 11 National Audubon Society chapters in Iowa. The council's purpose is to promote the protection of natural resources through coordinating the efforts of Iowa Audubon chapters and by communicating to Iowans about environmental concerns.
Contact(s):
President: CHARLIE MANLY, 734 16th Ave. #6, Grinnell, IA 50112; Phone: 515-236-5403
Secretary: PHYLLIS BARBER, 4400 Ellis Rd. NW, Cedar Rapids, IA 52405; Phone: 319-396-5324
Treasurer: BILL HEIDENREICH, P.O. Box 296, Marquette, IA 52158; Phone: 319-873-3736
Keyword(s): Biodiversity, Birds, Environmental Preservation, Environmental Protection, Wildlife and Wildlife Habitat

IOWA B.A.S.S. CHAPTER FEDERATION
ATTN: President, 3282 Midway, Marion, IA 52302
Phone: 319-393-1481
Scope: Statewide
Description: An organization of Bassmaster chapters, affiliated with the Bass Anglers Sportsman Society, organized to fight pollution, assist state and national conservation agencies in their efforts, and teach the young people of our country good conservation practices. Dedicated to the realistic conservation of our water resources.
Contact(s):
President: TOM BOWLER, 3282 Midway, Marion, IA 52302; Phone: 319-393-1481
Conservation Director: NORMAN THEOBALD, 1207 Creston Ave., Des Moines, IA 50315; Phone: 515-244-8777

IOWA CONSERVATION EDUCATION COUNCIL, INC.
c/o Conservation Education Center, Rt. 1, Box 53, Guthrie Center, IA 50115
Phone: 515-747-8383
Founded: 1958; Membership: 800
Scope: Statewide
Description: To encourage and lead the development and practice of a widespread and effective conservation education program in Iowa.
Contact(s):
Bookkeeper: DOROTHY PIMLOTT, 205 I Ave., Nevada, IA 50319; Phone: 515-281-3146
Chairperson: STACEY SNYDER NEWBROUGH, P.O. Box 210, Tripoli, IA 50676
Editor: NANCY GESKE, 2400 Timberland, Ames, IA 50010; Phone: 515-292-2981
Editor: JOEL GESKE, 2400 Timberland, Ames, IA 50010; Phone: 515-292-2981
Vice Chairperson: MARILYN IRWIN, 2046 F Ave., Perry, IA 50220; Phone: 515-465-4755
Vice Chairperson: KATHY McKEE, 1002 Prairie, Gutherie Center, IA 50115; Phone: 515-747-3771
Vice Chairperson: CRAIG ZOELLNER, 500 College Dr., Mason City, IA 50401; Phone: 515-421-4319

IOWA ENVIRONMENTAL COUNCIL
7031 Douglas Ave., Des Moines, IA 50322
Phone: 515-237-5321; Fax: 515-237-5376; Email: iecmail@earthweshare.org; WWW: www.earthweshare.org
Founded: 1994; Membership: 57 organizations, 320 individuals
Scope: Statewide
Description: The Iowa Environmental Council is an alliance of diverse organizations and individuals working with all Iowans to protect our natural environment. We seek a sustainable future through shaping public policy, research and education, coalition-building, and advocacy.
Contact(s):
President: CHARLOTTE HUBBELL
Vice President: DARRELL HANSON
Secretary: COLLEEN SCHNEIDER
Treasurer: MARK ACKELSON
Executive Director: LINDA D. APPELGATE
Publication(s): *Iowa Environmental Council Journal; IEC Fax Bulletin*
Keyword(s): Agriculture, Biodiversity, Pesticides, Water Pollution, Water Quality

IOWA NATIVE PLANT SOCIETY
Botany Department, Iowa State University, Ames, IA 50011-1020
Phone: 515-294-9499; Fax: 515-294-1337
Founded: 1995; Membership: 175
Scope: Statewide
Description: Iowa Native Plant Society is an organization of amateurs and professionals who are interested in the scientific, educational, cultural aspects, preservation, and conservation of Iowa's native plants.
Contact(s):
President: ED FREESE
Vice President: FRED CRANE; Phone: 515-279-8440
Secretary and Treasurer: MARY BROWN; Phone: 319-338-3875
Publication(s): *Iowa Native Plant Society Newsletter*
Keyword(s): Biodiversity, Conservation, Endangered and Threatened Species, Environmental and Conservation Education,

Environmental Preservation, Flowers, Plants, and Trees, Prairies, Wetlands

IOWA NATURAL HERITAGE FOUNDATION
Insurance Exchange Bldg., Suite 444, 505 Fifth Ave., Des Moines, IA 50309
Phone: 515-288-1846; Fax: 515-288-0137
Founded: 1979; Membership: 5,000
Scope: Statewide
Description: An independent, statewide, nonprofit organization founded by business and community leaders to involve the private sector in protecting Iowa's natural resources. Program emphasis on land protection, landowner education, resource planning, wetland restoration, and rail-trail development in Iowa.
Contact(s):
Chairman: THEODORE HUTCHISON
President: MARK C. ACKELSON
Secretary: RICHARD E. RAMSAY
Treasurer: MICHAEL E. RILEY
Director of Communications: ANITA O'GARA
Director of Development: KARMIN WILSON
Director of Finance: LAURA McVAY
Director of Land Projects: BRUCE MOUNTAIN
Director of Land Stewardship: KYLE SWANSON
Director of Trails and Greenways: LISA HEIN
Vice Chairman: BARBARA MacGREGOR
Publication(s): *Iowa Natural Heritage; The Landowner's Options; Enjoy Iowa's Recreation Trails Guidebook*
Keyword(s): Biodiversity, Conservation of Protected Areas, Endangered and Threatened Species, Flowers, Plants, and Trees, Internships, Land Preservation, Natural Areas, Nature Preservation, Outdoor Recreation, Prairies, Rivers, Sustainable Development, Wetlands, Wildlands, Wildlife and Wildlife Habitat

IOWA PRAIRIE NETWORK
6736 Laural, Omaha, NE 68104
Phone: 402-571-6230; Fax: 402-571-6230; Email: pollockg@top.net; WWW: www.netins.net/showcase/bluestem/1pnapp.htm
Founded: 1990; Membership: 300
Scope: Statewide
Description: The Iowa Prairie Network is dedicated to protecting Iowa prairie heritage.
Contact(s):
President: GLENN POLLOCK
Vice President: CINDY HILDEBRAND
Treasurer: CAROLE KERN; Phone: 319-273-2813
Director: DAVID HANSEN; Phone: 515-357-3665
Publication(s): *IPN News; Native Prairie Management Guide; A Prairie Bioliography*
Keyword(s): Prairies

IOWA TRAILS COUNCIL
P.O. Box 131, Center Point, IA 52213
Phone: 319-849-1844
Founded: 1983; Membership: 1,200
Scope: Statewide
Description: A membership nonprofit organization primarily active in the Midwest, but with membership in over one-half the states and in several foreign countries. Primary purpose is to acquire and convert former railroad rights-of-way into recreational trails.
Contact(s):
Chairman: ELDON L. COLTON, 716 Oakland Rd. NE, Cedar Rapids, IA 52402
Secretary/Treasurer and Executive Director: TOM F. NEENAN, P.O. Box 131, Center Point, IA 52213-0131; Phone: 319-849-1844
Vice Chairman: DR. DAVID LYON, 116 10th Ave. S., Mt. Vernon, IA 52314; Phone: 319-895-8240
Publication(s): *Trails Advocate; Bicycle Trails of Iowa (128 Page color illustrated book of over 85 trails and points of interest throughout*

Keyword(s): Energy Conservation, Environmental Preservation, Land Preservation, Land Use Planning, Nature Preservation, Outdoor Recreation, Pollution Prevention, Transportation

IOWA TRAPPERS ASSOCIATION, INC.
c/o Anna Marie Scalf, 123 N. Madison Ave., Ottumwa, IA 52501
Phone: 515-682-3937
Founded: 1950; Membership: 2,000
Scope: Statewide
Description: A nonprofit organization that works to continue the wise use and harvest of Iowa's renewable resource of furbearing animals. Cooperates with all recognized conservation agencies, law enforcement agencies, and legislative committees, and provides input on the benefits and necessity of trapping.
Contact(s):
President: TOM WALTERS, 1723 20th St., Bettendorf, IA 52722-3829; Phone: 319-359-6949
Vice President: JAMES L. STAUFFER, 29602 202nd St., Clarksville, IA 50619-9801; Phone: 319-278-4004
Secretary: CHRIS GRILLOT, 2769 110th Ave., Wheatland, IA 52777; Phone: 319-374-1074
Treasurer: ANNA MARIE SCALF, 123 N. Madison Ave., Ottumwa, IA 52501; Phone: 515-682-3937
Editor: GORDY KRAHN, 700 E. State St., Iola, WI 54990; Phone: 715-445-2214
Publication(s): *Trapper and Predator Caller, The*
Keyword(s): Environmental and Conservation Education, Outdoor Recreation, Trapping, Wildlife and Wildlife Habitat, Wildlife Management

IOWA WILDLIFE FEDERATION
3125 Douglas, Suite 103, Des Moines, IA 50310
Phone: 515-279-0655
Scope: Statewide
Description: A representative statewide organization, affiliated with the National Wildlife Federation, dedicated to the protection and enhancement of wildlife and its habitat through public education and government interaction.
Contact(s):
President: JOE WILKINSON
Affiliate Representative: DOUG THOMPSON
Alternate Representative: CARLTON HARFORD
Editor: MIKE HODGES
Publication(s): *Iowa Wildlife*

IOWA WILDLIFE REHABILITATORS ASSOCIATION
1005 Harken Hill Dr., P.O. Box 217, Osceola, IA 50036
Phone: 515-342-2783
Founded: 1986; Membership: 50
Scope: Statewide
Description: A nonprofit organization established to disseminate information pertaining to wildlife rehabilitation and medicine to veterinarians, rehabilitators, naturalists, and others; to communicate and cooperate with state, federal, and private environmental/conservation organizations; and to encourage the public to become more aware of the need to care for the earth and its wild creatures. This is done largely through newsletters, educational material, state and regional conferences, and presentations.
Contact(s):
President: MARLENE EHRESMAN; Phone: 515-296-2995
Vice President: SUE BURGSTRUM; Phone: 319-242-6535
Secretary: WENDY VAN DeWALLE; Phone: 515-964-9592
Treasurer: BETH BROWN; Phone: 515-342-2783

IOWA WOMEN IN NATURAL RESOURCES
P.O. Box 20083, Des Moines, IA 50320-0083
Founded: 1988; Membership: 150
Scope: Statewide
Description: A nonprofit organiaztion dedicated to providing professional development to individuals interested in all natural

NON-GOVERNMENTAL ORGANIZATIONS

resource careers by promoting communication among professionals, encouraging girls and women to consider natural resource careers, conducting outdoor skills workshops, providing networking and support systems for women working in natural resources, and providing career enhancement training.
Contact(s):
President: PATRICIA PETERSEN-KEYS; Phone: 515-999-2557; Fax: 515-999-2709
Vice President: LISA HEMESATH; Phone: 515-432-2823; Fax: 515-432-2835
Secretary: MIKE BONSER; Phone: 319-266-2228
Treasurer: ANJEANETTE PERKINS; Phone: 515-432-2823; Fax: 515-432-2835
Publication(s): *IWINR News; IWINR Membership Directory*
Keyword(s): Environment, Training, Women in the Environment

IOWA WOODLAND OWNERS ASSOCIATION
2735 14th Ave., Marion, IA 52302-1848
Phone: 515-233-1161
Founded: 1987; Membership: 450
Scope: Statewide
Description: A statewide organization affiliated with the National Woodland Owners Association, organized to advance good forestry on the 1.5 million acres of timberland owned by 28,000 nonindustrial private landowners in Iowa.
Contact(s):
President: AL MANNING
Vice President: GREG TWEDT
Secretary and Editor: E. O. FRYE; Phone: 319-377-2540
Treasurer: JOANNE MENSINGER; Phone: 319-259-1160
Publication(s): *Timber Talk*
Keyword(s): Forests and Forestry

ISLAND CONSERVATION EFFORT
90 Edgewater Dr. #901, Coral Gables, FL 33133
Phone: 305-666-7848; Fax: 305-663-9941
Founded: 1988; Membership: 200
Scope: National
Description: Island Conservation Effort is dedicated to the preservation of island natural resources, fauna, and habitats on which their preservation depends. We promote conservation, education, and research to obtain necessary data to support conservation measures.
Contact(s):
President: MARTHA WALSH-McGEHEE, 90 Edgewater Dr. #901, Coral Gables, FL 33133; Phone: 305-666-5381
Vice President: PETER J. CARRE, 1700 K St. NW, Suite 1100, Washington, DC 20006; Phone: 202-828-5349
Secretary and Treasurer: DR. ROSEMARIE GNAM, 13 East Rosemont Ave., Alexandria, VA 22301; Phone: 703-739-9803
Keyword(s): Birds, Coral Reefs, Endangered and Threatened Species, Environmental and Conservation Education, Research

ISLAND INSTITUTE, THE
410 Main St., Rockland, ME 04841
Phone: 207-594-9209; Fax: 207-594-9314
Founded: 1983; Membership: 5,000
Scope: National
Description: Private, nonprofit conservation organization dedicated to sustaining islands and island communities through community services, publications, resource management, science, and marine research.
Contact(s):
Chairman: HORACE A. HILDRETH JR.; Phone: 207-774-5981
President: PHILIP W. CONKLING; Phone: 207-594-9209
Vice President: PETER RALSTON; Phone: 207-594-9209
Director of Science Stewardship: ANNETTE S. NAEGEL; Phone: 207-594-9209
Managing Editor: DAVID PLATT; Phone: 207-594-9209
Publication(s): *Island Journal; Inter-Island News; Working Waterfronts; Gulf of Maine Environmental Atlas*
Keyword(s): Cultural Preservation, Fisheries, Forests and Forestry, Islands, Sustainable Ecosystems

ISLAND RESOURCES FOUNDATION
Headquarters, 1718 P St., NW, Suite T-4, Washington, DC 20036
Phone: 202-265-9712; Fax: 202-232-0748; Email: irf@irf.org; WWW: www.irf.org
Founded: 1972
Scope: National
Description: An independent center for the study of island systems, dedicated to improved resources management, comprehensive development planning, the conservation of cultural, physical, and natural resources of islands.
Contact(s):
Chairman: DR. EDWARD L. TOWLE
Secretary: CHARLES W. CONSOLVO
Treasurer: JUDITH A. TOWLE
President and Executive Director: BRUCE G. POTTER
Vice Chairman: HENRY U. WHEATLEY
Keyword(s): Coasts, International Conservation, Islands, Land Use Planning, Water Resources

Eastern Caribbean Biodiversity Program Office
P.O. Box 2103, St. Johns, St. Johns Antigua, West Indies
Phone: 268-460-1740; Fax: 268-463-7740; Email: klinsay@irf.org
Scope: National

Washington, DC Office
Webster House Suite T-4 1718 P St. NW, Washington, DC 20036
Phone: 202-265-9712; Fax: 202-232-0748
Scope: National

ISSAQUAH ALPS TRAILS CLUB (I.A.T.C.)
P.O. Box 351, Issaquah, WA 98027
Phone: 206-328-0480
Founded: 1979; Membership: 3,500
Scope: Statewide
Description: A nonprofit membership organization established to preserve and promote trails and open space in the area east of Seattle along the I-90 highway corridor from Lake Washington to the Cascades, primarily in the area known as the "Issaquah Alps."
Contact(s):
President: KEN KONIGSMARK
Vice President: MARILYN MOON
Secretary: PAM WALLENSTEIN
Treasurer: BARBARA HALVERSON
Chairman of the Board: HARVEY MANNING
Publication(s): *Washington State We're In The; Targeting Tomorrow - Washington's Economy Adjusts to the 90's; Speaking of Ground Water; Washington State Public Port Districts*
Keyword(s): Air Quality and Pollution, Energy, Planning Management, Solid Waste, Wetlands

IZAAK WALTON LEAGUE OF AMERICA ENDOWMENT
P.O. Box 824, Iowa City, IA 52244
Phone: 319-351-7037
Founded: 1943
Scope: National
Description: Organized to help rebuild Outdoor America by the acquisition for governmental agencies of unique natural areas for the use of future generations. Members of the Izaak Walton League of America.
Contact(s):
President: WENDELL P. HALEY, 1840 NE 92nd Ave., Portland, OR 97220; Phone: 503-253-9749
Vice President: DR. LARRY C. SMITH, 1611 Alderman Dr., Greensboro, NC 27408; Phone: 336-834-0018
Secretary: CHARLES L. ELDRIDGE, 2008-7th St., Des Moines, IA 50322; Phone: 515-244-0932

NON-GOVERNMENTAL ORGANIZATIONS

Treasurer: WILLIAM D. WEBER, 6357 W. Encantado Ct., Rockford, MI 49341; Phone: 616-456-8691; Fax: 616-456-1915
Executive Secretary: ROBERT C. RUSSELL, P.O. Box 824, Iowa City, IA 52244; Phone: 319-351-7037
Honorary President: HOWARD S. WHITE, 302 S. McKinley St., Havana, IL 62644; Phone: 309-543-4391
Keyword(s): Acid Rain, Environmental and Conservation Education, Fisheries, Hunting, Outdoor Recreation

IZAAK WALTON LEAGUE OF AMERICA, INC., THE
707 Conservation Ln., Gaithersburg, MD 20878-2983
Phone: 301-548-0150; Conservation Info. Hotline 888-IKE-HILL; Fax: 301-548-0146; WWW: www.iwla.org
Membership: 50,000
Scope: National
Description: Promotes means and opportunities for educating the public to conserve, maintain, protect, and restore the soil, forest, water, air, and other natural resources of the U.S. and promotes the enjoyment and wholesome utilization of those resources.
Contact(s):
President: WILLIAM R. WEST
Vice President: DONALD FERRIS
Secretary: BIRTRUN KIDWELL JR.
Treasurer: CHARLES WILES
Executive Director: PAUL HANSEN
Chairman of the Executive Board: TIMOTHY W. REID
Conservation Director: JIM MOSHER
Director of Midwest Office: WILLIAM GRANT, 1619 Dayton Ave., Suite 202, St. Paul, MN 55104; Phone: 651-649-1446; Fax: 651-649-1494
Editor: ZACHARY HOSKINS
Media Director: DENNY JOHNSON
Publication(s): *Outdoor America; League Leader*
Keyword(s): Environmental Protection, Hunting, Outdoor Ethics, Public Lands, Sustainability, Water Quality, Wildlife Management

Alaska Division
2640 Kingsbridge Cir., Anchorage, AK 99504-3366
Scope: Statewide
Contact(s):
President: THOMAS CARTER; Phone: 907-333-0243

California Division
Reifel Cooke Group, 440-1055 W. Hastings St., Vancouver, British Columbia V6E 2E9 Canada
Phone: 604-688-1055
Founded: 1938
Scope: Statewide
Contact(s):
President: GEORGE C. REIFEL

Colorado Division
ATTN: President, 1314 Margo Ln., Colorado Spring, CO 80909-3064
Scope: Statewide
Contact(s):
President: NELSON BURTON, 1314 Margo Ln., Colorado Springs, CO 80909-3064; Phone: 719-473-0700
Secretary: AMY MILLER, 513 Strachan Dr., Fort Collins, CO 80525-2130; Phone: 970-223-5379

Florida Division
ATTN: President, P.O. Box 10382, Bradenton, FL 34282-0382
Scope: Statewide
Contact(s):
President: CARL R. KEELER, P.O. Box 10382, Bradenton, FL 34282-0382; Phone: 941-749-5656
Secretary: MIKE CHENOWITH, 31 Garden Cove Dr., Key Largo, FL 33037; Phone: 305-451-0993

Illinois Division
ATTN: President, 1005 S. Busey Ave., Urbana, IL 61801-4028
Scope: Statewide
Contact(s):
President: JOHN R. DICKLE, 1005 S. Busey Ave., Urbana, IL 61801-4028; Phone: 217-344-5108
Secretary: MARSHA JOHNSON, 1512 45th St., Moline, IL 61265-3544; Phone: 309-797-8255

Indiana Division
ATTN: President, 2173 Pennsylvania St., Portage, IN 46368-2444
Scope: Statewide
Contact(s):
President: CHARLES SIAR, 2173 Pennsylvania St., Portage, IN 46368-2444; Phone: 219-762-4876
Secretary: EDWARD R. BOHLE, JR., 206 Greenwood Ave., Michigan City, IN 46360; Phone: 219-925-5368
Editor: STEVE PARKS
Publication(s): *Hoosier Waltonian, The*

Iowa Division
3716 Ingersoll, Suite E, Des Moines, IA 50312
Phone: 800-956-4340
Scope: Statewide
Contact(s):
President: THOMAS RODD, 1201 Greenwood, Ankeny, IA 50021-1019; Phone: 515-964-8951

Maryland Division
Attn: Secretary, 14110 Clopper Rd., Boyds, MD 20841-9721
Phone: 301-972-1627
Scope: Statewide
Contact(s):
President: ROBERT HUDDLESTON, 301 Glenville Rd., Churchville, MD 21028; Phone: 410-734-7608
Secretary: THOMAS W. FISHER, 14110 Clopper Rd., Boyds, MD 20841-9721; Phone: 301-972-1627

Michigan Division
55 Kenton SE, Grand Rapids, MI 49548
Phone: 616-281-3026
Scope: Statewide
Contact(s):
President: DAN SPALINK, 55 Kenton SE, Grand Rapids, MI 49548; Phone: 616-281-3026
Secretary: ROBERT STEGMIER, 5285 Windmill Dr. NE, Rockford, MI 49341-9311; Phone: 616-866-4769

Minnesota Division
555 Park St., #140, St. Paul, MN 55103
Phone: 612-221-0215
Scope: Statewide
Contact(s):
President: GARY SCHVARTZ, 100 Shady Ave, Owatonna, MN 55060-3144; Phone: 507-451-6676
Secretary: CHERRY SCHWARTZ, 100 Shady Ave., Owatonna, MN 55060; Phone: 507-451-6676

Nebraska Division
ATTN: President, 4828 J St., Lincoln, NE 68510
Phone: 402-488-1640
Scope: Statewide
Contact(s):
President: DELMER MILLER, 4828 J St., Lincoln, NE 68510; Phone: 402-488-1640
Secretary: ART BRYANT, 5015 S 69th St., Lincoln, NE 68516-1566; Phone: 402-488-7781

NON-GOVERNMENTAL ORGANIZATIONS

New York Division
125 Euclid Dr., Fayetteville, NY 13066
Phone: 315-637-6735
Scope: Statewide
Contact(s):
President: LES MONOSTORY, 125 Euclid Dr., Fayetteville, NY 13066; Phone: 315-637-6735
Secretary: WARREN GILES, 118 Clinton St., Penn Yan, NY 14527-1701; Phone: 315-536-4249

Ohio Division
Attn: Executive Secretary, 900 Morman Rd., Hamilton, OH 45011-1817
Phone: 513-863-8018
Scope: Statewide
Contact(s):
President: DANIEL C. HAYES, 953 Greenwood Ave., Hamilton, OH 45011-1817; Phone: 513-863-8018
Executive Secretary: RAY ZEHLER, 900 Morman Rd., Hamilton, OH 45013; Phone: 513-868-3179

Oregon Divison
ATTN: President, 1539 SE 30th Ave., Portland, OR 97214-4928
Phone: 503-235-7634
Founded: 1930
Scope: Statewide
Description: To protect, perpetuate, and strive for renewal of Oregon's natural resources, including the air, soil, woods, waters, and wildlife; to promote means and opportunities for education of the public in respect to such resources and the enjoyment and utilization thereof.
Contact(s):
President: JEANNE NORTON, 1539 SE 30th Ave., Portland, OR 97214-4928; Phone: 503-235-7634
Secretary: CORAL TORLEY, 1820 NW Woodland Dr., Corvallis, OR 97330-1019; Phone: 541-752-0114

Pennsylvania Division
ATTN: President, 100 1st Ave., Red Lion, PA 17356-1610
Phone: 717-246-2748
Scope: Statewide
Contact(s):
President: PAUL L. WILSON, 100 1st Ave., Red Lion, PA 17356-1610; Phone: 717-246-2748
Secretary: RAY KOFFLER, 460 New Salem Rd., Uniontown, PA 15401-9023; Phone: 412-437-5356
Keyword(s): Land Preservation, Land Purchase, Land Use Planning, Natural Areas

South Dakota Division
Attn: President, 798 11th St., SW, Watertown, SD 57350-3060
Phone: 605-352-2598
Scope: Statewide
Contact(s):
President: CHARLES CLAYTON, 798 11th St., SW, Watertown, SD 57350-3060; Phone: 605-352-2598
Secretary: SIDNEY WAGNER, JR., 367 Lakeshore Dr., McCook, SD 57046-4002; Phone: 605-232-4511

Virginia Division
Attn: President, 5235 Richardson Dr., Fairfax, VA 22032-3930
Phone: 703-323-6563
Scope: Statewide
Contact(s):
President: BIRTRUN KIDWELL JR., 5235 Richardson Dr., Fairfax, VA 22032-3930; Phone: 703-232-6563
Secretary: JEANNE M. KLING, 6110 Occoquan Forst Drive, Manassas, VA 20112-3018
Publication(s): *PEC Newsreporter; Periodic books and special reports.*

Washington Division
ATTN: President, 400 95th Ave. NE, Bellevue, WA 98004-1359
Scope: Statewide
Contact(s):
President: RONNI McGLENN, 400 95th Ave. NE, Bellevue, WA 98004-1359; Phone: 206-455-1986
Secretary: GORDON PETERSON, 3806 N 24th, Tacoma, WA 98406-5313; Phone: 206-761-8758

West Virginia Division
ATTN: President, RR4, Box 334, Morgantown, WV 26505-9423
Phone: 304-599-9237
Scope: Statewide
Contact(s):
President: MARIE CYPHERT, RR4, Box 334, Morgantown, WV 26505-9423; Phone: 304-599-9237
Secretary: PAT LAROCCO, 101 Lavendar St., Oak Hill, WV 25901; Phone: 304-465-8107

Wisconsin Division
ATTN: President, 2631 Oakwood Ave., Green Bay, WI 54301-1811
Phone: 715-824-3175
Scope: Statewide
Contact(s):
President: JEANNE AGNEESSENS, 2631 Oakwood Ave., Green Bay, WI 54301-1811; Phone: 414-432-2273
Secretary: ROBERT ELLIKER, 5316 Forest Cir. N., Stevens Point, WI 54481-5605; Phone: 715-344-1803
Publication(s): *Wisconsin Rivers; Periodic Action Alerts and News Bulletins*
Keyword(s): Environmental and Conservation Education, Rivers, Water Quality, Water Resources, Watersheds

Wyoming Divisoin
ATTN: President, 1072 Empinado, Laramie, WY 82070
Phone: 307-742-2785
Scope: Statewide
Description: To encourage the protection and wise use of our lands, our forests, our scenic and recreational areas, our waters, minerals, wildlife, and other conservation and environmental values.
Contact(s):
President: RAYMOND G. JACQUOT, 1072 Empinado, Laramie, WY 82070; Phone: 307-742-2785
Publication(s): *Powder River Breaks*
Keyword(s): Agriculture, Energy, Environment, Solid Waste Management, Water Resources

J.N. (DING) DARLING FOUNDATION
785 Crandon Blvd #1206, Key Biscayne, FL 33149
Phone: 305-361-9788; Fax: 305-361-9789; Email: kipkoss@compuserve.com
Founded: 1962
Scope: National
Description: A nonprofit organization formed to continue the ideals and work of pioneer conservationist "Ding" Darling, with an emphasis on conservation education. The Foundation has no paid staff. With all services, including legal and accounting, provided by its trustees, the Foundation is able to funnel 100% of contributed funds into selected projects.
Contact(s):
President of Board of Trustees and Chairman of Executive Committee: CHRISTOPHER D. KOSS, 785 Crandon Blvd #1206, Key Biscayne, FL 33149; Phone: 305-361-9788; Fax: 305-361-9789
Keyword(s): Environmental and Conservation Education, Water Resources, Waterfowl, Wildlife and Wildlife Habitat

JACK H. BERRYMAN INSTITUTE FOR WILDLIFE DAMAGE MANAGEMENT
Department of Fisheries and Wildlife, Utah State University, Logan, UT 84322-5210
Phone: 435-797-2436
Scope: National
Description: The Jack H. Berryman Institute is a national non-profit organization which is centered at Utah State University. It engages in research, education, and extension activities aimed at resolving human and wildlife conflicts, enhancing the positive aspects of wildlife, and increasing human tolerance of wildlife problems.

JACK MINER MIGRATORY BIRD FOUNDATION, INC.
P.O. Box 39, Kingsville, Ontario N9Y 2E8 Canada
Phone: 519-733-4034; Email: info@jackminer.com; WWW: www.jackminer.com
Founded: 1904
Scope: Statewide
Description: A nonprofit, tax deductible, public foundation inc. in both the U.S. and Canada. This sanctuary and its founder, Jack Miner, have become internationally known as one of the earliest efforts in waterfowl conservation. Often referred to as "The Father of Conservation", Jack Miner pioneered the tagging of waterfowl in 1909.
Contact(s):
Vice President: EDNA MINER
Secretary: MARILYN HAGENIERS
President and Treasurer: KIRK W. MINER

JACKSON HOLE CONSERVATION ALLIANCE
P.O. Box 2728, Jackson, WY 83001
Phone: 307-733-9417; Fax: 307-733-9008; Email: jhca@wyoming.com; WWW: www.jacksonwy.com/jhalliance/
Founded: 1979; Membership: 1,555
Scope: Regional
Description: The Alliance is a nonprofit organization dedicated to responsible land stewardship in Jackson Hole, Wyoming, to ensure that human activities are in harmony with the area's irreplaceable natural resources.
Contact(s):
President: KARLA PENDEXTER; Phone: 307-739-1729
Vice President: DAVID HARDIE; Phone: 307-733-8018
Secretary: KIM SPRINGER; Phone: 307-733-1230
Treasurer: EDMUND A. DONNAN JR.; Phone: 307-733-3278
Executive Director: DR. FRANZ J. CAMENZIND
Program Director: PAMELA LICHTMAN
Publication(s): *Alliance News, The; Mosquito Abatement Program in teton County, Wyoming, The; Welcome to the Neighborhood*
Keyword(s): Biodiversity, Conservation, Endangered and Threatened Species, Environment, Fisheries, Forest Management, Land Use Planning, Open Space, Wilderness, Wildlife and Wildlife Habitat

JACKSON HOLE LAND TRUST
P.O. Box 2897, Jackson, WY 83001
Phone: 307-733-4707
Founded: 1980
Scope: Statewide
Description: A private, nonprofit land conservation organization which works to preserve open space and the scenic, ranching, and wildlife values of Jackson Hole by assisting landowners who wish to protect their land in perpetuity. Not a membership organization.
Contact(s):
President: ALLAN TESSLER
Vice President: JOHN BECKER
Secretary: JOHN KREMER
Treasurer: MIA JENSEN
Executive Director: LESLIE MATTSON
Publication(s): *Land Trust Newsletter*
Keyword(s): Agriculture, Land Preservation, Land Purchase, Open Space, Wildlife and Wildlife Habitat

JACKSON HOLE PRESERVE, INC.
30 Rockefeller Plaza, Rm. 5600, New York, NY 10112
Phone: 212-649-5819
Founded: 1940
Scope: National
Description: Nonprofit, charitable, and educational organization, established to conserve areas of outstanding primitive grandeur and natural beauty and to provide facilities for their use and enjoyment by the public.
Contact(s):
President: GEORGE R. LAMB
Secretary: ANTONIA M. GRUMBACH
Treasurer: CARMEN REYES
Chairman of the Board: LAURANCE S. ROCKEFELLER
Vice Chairman of the Board: CLAYTON W. FRYE JR.

JANE GOODALL INSTITUTE, THE
P.O. Box 14890, Silver Spring, MD 20911
Phone: 301-565-0086/1-800-592-JANE; Fax: 301-565-3188; Email: JGIinformation@janegoodall.org; WWW: www.janegoodall.org
Founded: 1977; Membership: 17,000
Scope: International
Description: The Jane Goodall Institute is an international organization dedicated to the conservation and understanding of wildlife, particularly chimpanzees, and to promoting environmental education, reforestation, and humanitarianism worldwide.
Contact(s):
Executive Director: STEWART HUDSON; Email: shudson@janegoodall.org
Director of Communications: JENNIFER LINDSEY; Email: jlindsey@janegoodall.org
Deputy Director of Roots and Shoots: MARCIA WHITNEY; Email: m.whitney@janegoodall.org
Deputy Director of Project Development: KELLY COLADARCI; Email: kcoladarci@janegoodall.org
Publication(s): *Annual JGI World Report; Semi-annual Roots and Shoots Network; ChimpanZOO Newsletter*
Keyword(s): Reforestation, Wildlife and Wildlife Habitat, Environmental and Humanitarian Education, Animal Welfare, Wildlife Research

JAPAN WILDLIFE RESEARCH CENTER (JWRC)
Yushima 2-29-3, Bunkyo-ku, Tokyo 113 Japan
Phone: 81-3-3813-8806; Fax: 81-3-3813-8958; Email: mkomoda@jwrc.or.jp
Founded: 1978
Scope: International
Description: JWRC has carried out research works and has accumulated data on nature of Japan and developed techniques for research and management of wildlife and its habitat. JWRC is also trying to contribute to the conservation of nature through fact finding and accumulation of basic data.
Contact(s):
President: YASUYUKI OSHIMA
Executive Director: KAZUHIRO YAMASE

KANSAS ACADEMY OF SCIENCE
ATTN: President, Division of Biological Sciences, Emporia State University, Emporia, KS 66901
Founded: 1868; Membership: 500
Scope: Statewide
Description: A nonprofit organization to increase, diffuse, and promote knowledge in various departments of science; interest young people in science and encourage them to consider science as their profession; aid the improvement of science teaching; and aid in development of the state's economic growth.
Contact(s):
President: KAREN DeBRES, Department of Geography Kansas State University, Manhattan, KS 66506; Phone: 913-532-6727

NON-GOVERNMENTAL ORGANIZATIONS

Secretary: PIETER BERENDSEN, Kansas Geological Survey University of Kansas, Lawrence, KS 66047; Phone: 913-864-4991
Editor: DAN MERRIAM, Kansas Geological Survey University of Kansas, Lawrence, KS 66047; Phone: 913-864-4991
President-Elect: DAVID K. SAUNDERS, Division of Biological Sciences Emporia State University, Emporia, KS 66901; Phone: 316-341-5610
Publication(s): *Transactions of the Kansas Academy of Science*
Keyword(s): Biology, Chemistry, Geography, Geology, Natural History

KANSAS ADVISORY COUNCIL FOR ENVIRONMENTAL EDUCATION
ATTN: President, 1005 Merchants Tower, Topeka, KS 66612
Founded: 1969
Scope: Statewide
Description: Organized to promote and support effective environmental education in order to enhance awareness, knowledge, and concern about the environment among the citizens of Kansas. The advisory council is made up of representatives of over 180 public and private organizations, institutions, business organizations, and individuals.
Contact(s):
President and Council Member: CLARK DUFFY, 1005 Merchants Tower, Topeka, KS 66612; Phone: 913-234-0589
Vice President: CAROL WILLIAMSON, 1209 Willow Dr., Olathe, KS 66061; Phone: 913-764-6036
Secretary: CONNIE ELDERS, 455 N. Main 11th Fl., Wichita, KS 67202; Phone: 316-264-8323
Treasurer: RUTH GENNRICH, Museum of Natural History University of Kansas, Lawrence, KS 66045-2454; Phone: 913-864-4173
Publication(s): *KACEE News*

KANSAS ASSOCIATION FOR CONSVERATION AND ENVIRONMENTAL EDUCATION
2610 Claflin Rd., Manhattan, KS 66502-2743
Phone: 785-532-3314; Fax: 785-532-3305; Email: jstrick@oz.oznet.ksu.edu
Founded: 1969; Membership: 110 organizations/106 individuals
Scope: Statewide
Description: Kansas Association for Conservation and Environmenal Education was organized to promote and support effective conservation and environmental education in Kansas. The Association is made up of over 200 public and private organizations and individulals.
Contact(s):
Assistant Director: LAURA DOWNEY; Phone: 785-532-3322
President: DEE TURNER; Phone: 785-296-1036; Fax: 785-296-6172; Email: dturner@scc.state.ks.us
Vice President: CINDY FORD; Phone: 316-235-4728; Fax: 316-235-4194; Email: cford@pittstate.edu
Treasurer: CLARK DUFFY; Phone: 785-296-3185; Fax: 785-296-0878
Executive Director: JOHN STRICKLER
Publication(s): *KACEE NEWS; Annual Report; Workshop Brochure*
Keyword(s): Environment, Environmental and Conservation Education

KANSAS ASSOCIATION OF CONSERVATION DISTRICTS
ATTN: President, Rt. 2 Box 36, Durham, KS 67438
Scope: Statewide
Contact(s):
President: DENNIS YOUK, Rt. 2 Box 36, Durham, KS 67438; Phone: 316-732-2765
Executive Director: RICHARD G. JONES, 522 Winn Rd., Salina, KS 67401-3668; Phone: 785-827-5847; Fax: 785-827-7784
Board Member: DON PAXSON, P.O. Box 487, Penokee, KS 67659; Phone: 785-421-2480; Fax: 785-421-5662
Secretary-Treasurer: SANDRA JONES, 5160 E Rd 17, Johnson, KS 67855; Phone: 316-492-6495; Fax: 316-492-2772

Vice President, Alternate Board Member: CARL JORDAN, Rt. 1 Box 110, Glen Elder, KS 67446; Phone: 785-545-3361; Fax: 785-545-3659

KANSAS AUDUBON COUNCIL
2328 Bailey Dr., Manhattan, KS 66044
Phone: 913-537-4143
Founded: 1974; Membership: 4,900
Scope: Statewide
Description: The Kansas Audubon Council is comprised of representatives from 10 chapters and members of the National Audubon Society throughout the state. The Council supports protection of our natural resources. It encourages members to become informed so that they can act at local and state levels to advocate adoption of sound environmental policy and legislation.
Contact(s):
Chairperson: CHRIS COKINOS

KANSAS B.A.S.S. CHAPTER FEDERATION
ATTN: President, 6711 Haskins, Shawnee, KS 66216
Phone: 913-631-7070
Scope: Statewide
Description: An organization of Bassmaster chapters, affiliated with the Bass Anglers Sportsman Society, organized to fight pollution, assist state and national conservation agencies in their efforts, and teach the young people of our country good conservation practices. Dedicated to the realistic conservation of our water resources.
Contact(s):
President: STEVE GRIGSBY, 6711 Haskins, Shawnee, KS 66216; Phone: 913-631-7070
Conservation Director: KIM HUEY, 9914 North Plum, Hutchinson, KS 67502; Phone: 316-662-1638

KANSAS HERPETOLOGICAL SOCIETY
University of Kansas Natural History Museum, Dyche Hall, Lawrence, KS 66045
Founded: 1974; Membership: 250
Scope: Statewide
Description: The Kansas Herpetological Society is a nonprofit organization designed to encourage education and dissemination of scientific information through the facilities of the Society; and to encourage conservation of wildlife in general and of amphibians and reptiles in Kansas in particular.
Contact(s):
Editor: ERIC RUNDQUIST, Animal Care Unit, B054 Malov, University of Kansas, Lawrence, KS 66045
Secretary and Treasurer: KAREN TOEPFER, 303 W. 39th St., Hays, KS 67601; Phone: 913-628-1437
Publication(s): *Kansas Herpetological Society Newsletter*
Keyword(s): Ecology, Environmental and Conservation Education, Natural History, Nongame Wildlife, Reptiles and Amphibians

KANSAS NATURAL RESOURCE COUNCIL
P.O. Box 2635, Topeka, KS 66601
Phone: 913-232-1555; Fax: 913-232-2232
Founded: 1981; Membership: 500
Scope: Statewide
Description: Environmental advocacy including public education, lobbying, and litigation.
Contact(s):
President: BILL WARD, 2145 Barker, Lawrence, KS 66046; Phone: 913-841-6118
Vice President: JOAN VIBERT, 1981 Indiana, Ottawa, KS 66067; Phone: 913-746-8885
Director: BILL CRAVEN, 935 S. Kansas Ave. Suite 200, Topeka, KS 66612
Publication(s): *KNRC Journal; Weekly Legislative Updates*
Keyword(s): Agriculture, Energy, Prairies, Rivers, Water Resources

NON-GOVERNMENTAL ORGANIZATIONS

KANSAS ORNITHOLOGICAL SOCIETY
ATTN: President, P.O. Box 395, Wilson, KS 67490
Founded: 1949; Membership: 430
Scope: Statewide
Description: Formed to promote the study of ornithology, to advance the members in ornithological science, to promote conservation, and the appreciation of birds by the general public.
Contact(s):
President: MIKE RADER, P.O. Box 395, Wilson, KS 67490; Phone: 913-658-2595
Vice President: ROY BECKEMEYER, 957 Perry, Wichita, KS 67203; Phone: 316-264-0049
Treasurer: GREGG FRIESEN, 515 E. 4th, Newton, KS 67114; Phone: 316-283-4721
Business Manager: DAWN SHARP, 1324 Prairie Ave., Lawrence, KS 66044; Phone: 913-842-8692
Editor: CHUCK OTTE, 613 Tamerisk, Junction City, KS 66441-3359; Phone: 913-238-8800
Editor: MAX C. THOMPSON, 1729 East 11th St., Winfield, KS 67156; Phone: 316-221-1856
Membership Secretary: MARGARET WEDGE, 1645 Louisiana, Lawrence, KS 66044; Phone: 913-842-5706
Recording and Corresponding Secretary: DWIGHT PLATT, 702 NE 24th St., Newton, KS 67114; Phone: 316-283-6708
Publication(s): *K.O.S. Bulletin; Horned Lark, The*
Keyword(s): Birds, Endangered and Threatened Species, Environmental and Conservation Education, Raptors, Wildlife and Wildlife Habitat

KANSAS WILDFLOWER SOCIETY
R.L. McGregor Herbarium, 2045 Constant Ave., Lawrence, KS 66047-3729
Phone: 785-864-3453; Fax: 785-864-5093
Founded: 1978; Membership: 300
Scope: Statewide
Description: The Society provides educational materials and sponsors activities to promote the conservation and cultivation of the native plants of Kansas.
Contact(s):
President: DWIGHT R. PLATT; Phone: 316-283-2500; Fax: 316-284-5286
Secretary: CYNTHIA FORD; Phone: 316-235-4726
Treasurer: SISTER PATRICIA M. STANLEY; Phone: 316-689-4070; Email: wichitacsj@feist.com
Agent: CRAIG C. FREEMAN
Publication(s): *KWS Newsletter*
Keyword(s): Conservation, Flowers, Plants, and Trees, Prairies

KANSAS WILDLIFE FEDERATION
4840 W. 15th St., Suite 1000, Lawrence, KS 66049-3876
Phone: 785-843-7786; Fax: 785-843-7555; Email: KWF@kswildlife.org; WWW: www.kswildlife.org
Scope: Statewide
Description: A representative statewide organization, affiliated with the National Wildlife Federation, dedicated to the protection and enhancement of wildlife and its habitat through public education and government interaction.
Contact(s):
President: STEVEN SORENSEN
Alternate Representative: STEVE MONTGOMERY
Editor: STEVE MILANO
Publication(s): *Kansas Sportsman*

KANSAS WILDSCAPE FOUNDATION
P.O. Box 4029, Lawrence, KS 66046
Phone: 785-843-9453; Fax: 785-843-6379; Email: kansaswild@aol.com
Founded: 1991; Membership: 650
Scope: Statewide
Description: The Kansas Wildscape Foundation is dedicated to conserving and perpetuating the land, wild species, and the rich beauty of Kansas for the use and enjoyment of all. Wildscape is a public/private partnership with the Kansas Department of Wildlife and Parks.
Contact(s):
President: WARREN GFELLER, 10370 Hollis Ln., Olathe, KS 66061; Phone: 913-768-9865
Vice President: GENE ARGO, Midwest Energy, Inc., 1330 Canterbury Rd., Hays, KS 67601; Phone: 785-625-1402
Vice President: WILLIAM A. ANDERSON JR., 4330 Shawnee Mission Parkway, Suite 135, Shawnee Mission, KS 66205; Phone: 913-262-2252
Vice President: ROBERT L. RING, P.O. Box 4067, Wichita, KS 67204; Phone: 316-838-9093
Secretary: JIM HUNTINGTON, 9200 Cody, Overland Park, KS 66214; Phone: 913-752-3440
Treasurer: MICHAEL G. VINEYARD, 14800 W. 83rd St., Lenexa, KS 66215; Phone: 913-888-1926
Keyword(s): Land Preservation, Wetlands, Wildlife and Wildlife Habitat, Youth Organizations

KEEP AMERICA BEAUTIFUL, INC.
1010 Washington Blvd., 7th Fl., Stamford, CT 06901
Phone: 203-323-8987
Founded: 1953
Scope: National
Description: A national nonprofit public education organization dedicated to litter prevention and improved waste handling practices in American communities. Keep America Beautiful trains and certifies communities into the Keep America Beautiful System, a behavior-based approach to improved waste handling.
Contact(s):
President: G. RAYMOND EMPSON
Chairman of the Board: MELINDA M. SWEET
Senior Vice President of Development and Environmental Programming: SUSANNE WOODS
Vice Chairman of the Board: JOHN F. BARD
Publication(s): *Network News*
Keyword(s): Communications, Environmental and Conservation Education, Environmental Preservation, Public Lands, Solid Waste Management

KEEP FLORIDA BEAUTIFUL, INC.
325 John Knox Rd., Suite M-240, Tallahassee, FL 32303
Phone: 904-385-1528; Fax: 904-385-4020
Founded: 1991
Scope: Statewide
Description: Our mission is to protect the environment and improve the quality of life in Florida by providing public education, using mass communications and grassroots activities, which will result in understanding and action by individuals, business, civic, environmental and governmental organizations to protect Florida's air, water, and natural resources.
Contact(s):
Executive Director: FRANK WALPER
Chairman, Board of Directors: M. CLAYTON HOLLIS JR.
Publication(s): *Keep Florida Beautiful Magazine;* **Keyword(s):** Aquatic Habitats, Communications, Environmental Preservation, Renewable Resources, Solid Waste Management

KENTUCKY ACADEMY OF SCIENCE
ATTN: President, Dept. of Biology, Cammpbellsville University, Campbelsville, KY 42718
Founded: 1914; Membership: 612
Scope: Statewide
Description: To encourage scientific research, promote the diffusion of scientific knowledge, and unify the scientific interests of Kentucky.
Contact(s):
President-Elect: GORDON K. WEDDLE, Dept. of Biology, Cammpbellsville University, Campbelsville, KY 42718
President: PATRICIA K. DOOLIN, Ashland Petroleum Co., Ashland, KY 41114

NON-GOVERNMENTAL ORGANIZATIONS

Vice President: BLAINE FERRELL, Dept. of Biology, Western Kentucky Univeristy, Bowling Green, KY 42101
Secretary: JOSEPH W. WILSON, Dept. of Chemistry, University of Kentucky, Lexington, KY 40506
Treasurer: WILLIAM E. HARTMAN, Western Kentucky University, Bowling Green, KY 42103
Editor: JOHN W. THIERET, Dept. of Biological Sciences, Northern Kentucky University, Highland Heights, KY 41099
Publication(s): *Journal of the Kentucky Academy of*

KENTUCKY ASSOCIATION FOR ENVIRONMENTAL EDUCATION (KAEE)
Blackacre Nature Preserve, 3200 Tucker Station Rd., Jeffersontown, KY 40299
Phone: 502-473-3437
Scope: Statewide
Description: Organized to promote and support formal and nonformal environmental education programs throughout the state. Promotes information sharing, research, and development of EE programs and activities. Annually sponsors a three-day conference.
Contact(s):
President: EVELYN MORGAN, U.S. Forest Service, 2375 KY 801 S., Morehead, KY 40351; Phone: 606-784-6428
Executive Director: KAREN P. REAGOR, P.O. Box 176055, Covington, KY 41017; Phone: 606-578-0312
Publication(s): *Newsletter; E.E. Resource Guide; Earth Day Handbook*
Keyword(s): Environmental and Conservation Education

KENTUCKY ASSOCIATION OF CONSERVATION DISTRICTS
ATTN: President, 1299 Lillies Ferry Rd., Winchester, KY 40391
Scope: Statewide
Contact(s):
President, Alternate Board Member: JOHN E. CHISM, 1299 Lillies Ferry Rd., Winchester, KY 40391; Phone: 606-744-8909; Fax: 502-564-9195
Vice President: PATRICK M. HENDERSON, Rt. 1 Box 146, Irvington, KY 40146; Phone: 502-547-6206; Fax: 502-564-9195
Board Member: JAMES LACY, Box 432, Campton, KY 41301; Phone: 606-662-4161; Fax: 502-564-9195
Secretary-Treasurer: KEVIN JEFFRIES, 1503 E. Hwy. 22, Crestwood, KY 40014; Phone: 502-222-9877; Fax: 502-222-0046

KENTUCKY AUDUBON COUNCIL
ATTN: President, 16509 Bradbe Rd., Fisherville, KY 40023
Founded: 1971
Scope: Statewide
Description: A statewide Audubon Council for the seven key chapters of the National Audubon Society. Works to promote, foster, and encourage the conservation and preservation of all wildlife, plants, soils, water, air, and other natural resources for the benefit of all people.
Contact(s):
President: JEFF FRANK, 16509 Bradbe Rd., Fisherville, KY 40023; Phone: 502-266-7181
Vice President: JOAN NOEL, 645 Foxfire Dr., Elizabethtown, KY 42701
Secretary: MAGGIE SELVIDGE, 904 North Dr., Hopkinsville, KY 42240; Phone: 502-886-8078
Treasurer: BERTHA M. TIMMEL, 3604 Graham Rd., Louisville, KY 40207; Phone: 502-893-5601

KENTUCKY B.A.S.S. CHAPTER FEDERATION
ATTN: President, 5036 Huntington Woods Rd., Frankfort, KY 40601
Phone: 502-223-8611
Scope: Statewide
Description: An organization of Bassmaster chapters, affiliated with the Bass Anglers Sportsman Society, organized to fight pollution, assist state and national conservation agencies in their efforts, and teach the young people of our country good conservation practices. Dedicated to the realistic conservation of our water resources.
Contact(s):
President: SCOTT KING, 5036 Huntington Woods Rd., Frankfort, KY 40601; Phone: 502-223-8611
Conservation Director: DAVE KIK, P.O. Box 724, Prospect, KY 40059; Phone: 502-228-1214

KENTUCKY RESOURCES COUNCIL
P.O. Box 1070, Frankfort, KY 40602
Phone: 502-875-2428; Fax: 502-875-2845; Email: fitzkrc@aol.com
Scope: Statewide
Description: The KRC is a nonprofit, membership-based statewide organization dedicated to the conservation and prudent use of Kentucky's natural resources. The Council is comprised of Kentuckians from all walks of life: Urban dwellers and rural residents, farmers, river recreationists, and conservationists. This broad-based membership shares a common concern with the impact of mineral extraction, natural resource development, and economic development on our homes, health, and quality of life.
Contact(s):
Director: TOM FITZGERALD
Keyword(s): Environmental Law, Environmental Protection, Toxic Substances, Water Pollution Management

KENTUCKY WOODLAND OWNERS ASSOCIATION
3395 Upper Tug Fork Rd., Alexandria, KY 41001
Phone: 606-635-7826
Founded: 1991; Membership: 350
Scope: Statewide
Description: A statewide nonprofit organization, affiliated with the National Woodland Owners Association, organized to promote good forest stewardship, circulate information on timber marketing, and encourage private property responsibility among woodland owners throughout the Commonwealth of Kentucky.
Contact(s):
President: DON GIRTON, Alexandria, KY
Secretary: PASCHAL PHILLIPS, Bardstown, KY
Treasurer: HERB LLOYD, Lexington, KY
Editor: DON GIRTON, Alexandria, KY
Publication(s): *Kentucky Timber*

KENTUCKY-TENNESSEE SOCIETY OF AMERICAN FORESTERS
100 Van Morgan Dr., Golden Pond, KY 42211
Scope: Statewide
Description: K-T SAF is the Kentucky-Tennessee section of the Society of American Foresters, and carries out the policies and programs of SAF within these two states. See the Society of American Foresters listing for more information.
Contact(s):
Chair: ERIC J. SCHMECKPEPER, 503 Meadow Ln., Murray, KY 42071; Phone: 502-753-9369
Chair-Elect: WAYNE K. CLATTERBUCK, Univ. of TN, Dept. of Forestry, Wildlife, and Fisheries, P.O. Box 1071, Knoxville, TN 37901; Phone: 423-974-7346
Editor: ROBERT SCHNELL; Phone: 615-494-7613
Secretary and Treasurer: PAT CLEARY, P.O. Box 189, Betsy Lane, KY 41605; Phone: 606-478-4495
Publication(s): *KT-SAF Newsletter*
Keyword(s): Environmental Planning, Renewable Resources, Urban Forestry

KEYSTONE CENTER, THE
Headquarters, 1628 Saints John Rd., Keystone, CO 80435
Phone: 970-513-5800; Fax: 970-262-0152; WWW: www.keystone.org
Founded: 1975
Scope: National
Description: A nonprofit center for environmental dispute resolution, mediation, and facilitation. Conducts national policy dialogues on environmental, energy, natural resources, health, and science/technology issues; assists in environmental decisionmaking and regulatory negotiations; provides environmental mediation

services; provides training and organizational development services in environmental conflict resolution.
Contact(s):
Chairman: WALLY QUANSTROM
President: KATHY PROSSER
Chief Financial Officer: JUDITH CAMP
Chief Operating Officer: CHARLES TAYLOR
Publication(s): *Consensus; Discovery*
Keyword(s): Biotechnology, Energy, Environmental and Conservation Education, Health and Nutrition, Natural Resource Conservation

KEYSTONE CENTER, THE (Washington, D.C. Office)
1030 15th St., NW, Suite 300, Washington, DC 20005
Phone: 202-783-0248; Fax: 202-783-0328
Scope: Statewide

KIDS FOR SAVING EARTH WORLDWIDE
P.O. Box 421118, Minneapolis, MN 55442
Phone: 612-559-1234; Fax: 612-559-6980; Email: kseww@aol.com
Founded: 1994
Scope: National
Description: KSEW's mission is to educate and empower children to help to protect the Earth's environment by providing free educational materials to kids, schools, and organizations through the KSE Network. Curriculum guides are also available.
Contact(s):
President and Director: TESSA HILL
Publication(s): *List available upon request.*
Keyword(s): Air Quality and Pollution, Aquatic Habitats, Conservation of Protected Areas, Endangered and Threatened Species, Energy Conservation, Environment, Environmental and Conservation Education, Environmental Preservation, Environmental Protection, Flowers, Plants, and Trees, International Conservation, Land Preservation, Nature Preservation, Pollution Prevention, Youth Organizations

KODIAK BROWN BEAR TRUST
11930 Circle Dr., Anchorage, AK 99516
Phone: 907-345-2939
Founded: 1981
Scope: National
Description: The Kodiak Brown Bear Trust is an Alaska-based nonprofit wildlife conservation trust which funds brown bear research and habitat protection in the Kodiak Archipelago. The Trust successfully partners with other funders to acquire private inholdings in the Kodiak National Wildlife Refuge, and fund essential brown bear research projects.
Contact(s):
Chairman: DAVE CLINE
Executive Director: TIM RICHARDSON, 4104 Denfeld Ave., Kensington, MD 20895; Phone: 301-946-8285

LADY BIRD JOHNSON WILDFLOWER CENTER (formerly the National Wildflower Research Center)
4801 La Crosse Ave., Austin, TX 78739
Phone: 512-292-4200
Founded: 1982; Membership: 19,000
Scope: National
Description: The Lady Bird Johnson Wildflower Center's (formerly the National Wildflower Research Center) purpose is to educate people about the environmental necessity, economic value, and natural beauty of native plants. The Wildflower Center, a nonprofit organization, serves North America by promoting the preservation and use of native plants through education programs, information dissemination, and by example.
Contact(s):
Editor: KAREN BASSETT
Education Director: JULIE BARRETT-HEFFINGTON
Executive Directory: ROBERT G. BREUTING Ph.D.
Founder: LADY BIRD JOHNSON
Founder: HELEN HAYES
Public Programs Manager and Senior Botanist: FLO OXLEY
Senior Horticulturist: DENISE DELANEY
Publication(s): *WILDFLOWER Newsletter*
Keyword(s): Endangered and Threatened Species, Environmental and Conservation Education, Flowers, Plants, and Trees, Landscape Architecture, Native Plants, Trees, Wildflowers

LAKE ERIE CLEAN-UP COMMITTEE, INC.
ATTN: President, 29789 Fort Rd., Rockwood, MI 48173
Founded: 1959
Scope: National
Description: The LECC's mission is to stop pollution of Lake Erie and of all freshwater lakes and streams; to inform the public of the need for greater pollution controls; to prevent the return to the methods of the past; and to encourage industry to do more research. Our Great Lakes are a fragile part of our ecosystem and we must continue to protect them. Membership includes representatives of Michigan and Ohio citizen groups.
Contact(s):
President: LEONARD MANNAUSA, 29789 Fort Rd., Rockwood, MI 48173; Phone: 313-379-3891
Secretary: RICHARD G. MICKA, 47 E. Elm, Monroe, MI 48162; Phone: 313-242-0909
Treasurer: JEROME C. FALWELL, 30251 Worth, Gibraltor, MI 48173
Keyword(s): Coasts, Remedial Action Plans, Water Pollution Management, Water Resources, Waterfowl, Wetlands

LAKE MICHIGAN FEDERATION
220 S. State St., Suite 2108, Chicago, IL 60604
Phone: 312-939-0838; Fax: 312-939-2708; Email: lmfool@aol.com
Founded: 1970
Scope: National
Description: A coalition of citizens and citizen organizations in Wisconsin, Illinois, Indiana, and Michigan dedicated to protecting Lake Michigan through community action and research. Supported by foundation and corporate grants, membership and contributions.
Contact(s):
Treasurer: ARTHUR MARTIN
Executive Director: CAMERON DAVIS
Board of Directors President: TIM BROWN
Publication(s): *Lake Michigan Monitor; A Citizen's Action Guide; A Citizen's Guide to Cleaning Up Contaminated Sediments (book); Wetlands and Water Quality: A Citizen's Guide.*
Keyword(s): EcoAction, Environment, Lakes, Pollution Prevention, Protecting Special Places, Water Pollution, Watersheds

LAKE SUPERIOR GREENS
P.O. Box 1144, Superior, WI 54880
Phone: 715-392-5782; Fax: 715-394-6856
Founded: 1991; Membership: 100
Scope: National
Description: Lake Superior Greens is a grassroots group joined to other Green groups in our dedication to a more sustainable lifestyle and a healthy planet. We are active locally as well as on a state, national, and international basis, recognizing that all issues are interrelated.
Contact(s):
Contact: MARTYE ALLEN, 10350 E. Kizlak Rd., Lake Nebagamon, WI 54849; Phone: 715-374-2203
Contact: JOHN SCHRAUFNAGEL, 1506 N. 19th, Superior, WI 54880; Phone: 715-394-6660
Contact: BOB BROWN, 422 Fisher Ogden, Superior, WI 54880; Phone: 715-394-6235
Steering Committee: JAN CONLEY, 2406 Hughitt, Superior, WI 54880; Phone: 715-392-5782
Publication(s): *monthly newsletter*
Keyword(s): Endangered and Threatened Species, Environmental and Conservation Education, Pesticides, Toxic Substances, Wildlands

NON-GOVERNMENTAL ORGANIZATIONS

LAND BETWEEN THE LAKES ASSOCIATION
Land Between The Lakes, 100 Van Morgan Dr., Golden Pond, KY 42211-9001
Phone: 502-924-2088
Founded: 1983; Membership: 3,000
Scope: National
Description: A private nonprofit membership organization supporting and promoting Tennessee Valley Authority's Land Between The Lakes, a 170,000-acre national demonstration in natural resource management, environmental education, and recreation.
Contact(s):
Chairman: AUSTIN CARROLL, General Manager, Hopkinsville Electric System, P.O. Box 544, Hopkinsville, KY 42240; Phone: 502-887-4210
President: CHARLES MATHENY
Director: GAYE LUBER
Keyword(s): Cultural Preservation, Environmental and Conservation Education, Lakes, Natural Areas, Prairies, Public Lands

LAND TRUST ALLIANCE, THE
1319 F St., NW, Suite 501, Washington, DC 20004
Phone: 202-638-4725; WWW: www.lta.org
Founded: 1982; Membership: 2,100
Scope: National
Description: Provides services and programs for local and regional land trusts to increase their skills and competence; fosters public policies that further land trusts' goals; and builds awareness among a broad constituency of the consequences of diminishing land resources and the role of land trusts in saving land.
Contact(s):
Chairman: JAMES J. ESPY
President: JEAN W. HOCKER
Vice President: ANDREW ZEPP
Secretary: CONSTANCE BEST
Treasurer: DAVID HARTWELL
Vice Chair: JOHN TURNER
Vice President of Administration: PHIL JONES
Vice President of Development: JOHN CHAPPELL
Publication(s): *Exchange; Conservation Easement Handbook; Appraising Easements; Federal Tax Law of Conservation Easements; Starting a Land Trust; National Directory of Conservation Land Trusts; Conservation Easement Stewardship Guide*
Keyword(s): Conservation Easements, Environmental and Conservation Education, Environmental Law, Environmental Preservation, Land Conservation, Land Protection, Land Purchase, Land Use Planning

LEAGUE OF CONSERVATION VOTERS
1707 L St., NW, Suite 750, Washington, DC 20036
Phone: 202-785-8683; Fax: 202-835-0491; Email: lcv@lcv.org; WWW: www.lcv.org
Founded: 1970; Membership: 25,000
Scope: National
Description: The LCV is the national, bipartisan political action arm of the environmental movement. LCV works to elect pro-environment candidates to Congress; publishes the National Environmental Scorecard, which rates members of Congress on key environmental votes; raises funds for campaigns through its Political Action Committee and Earthlist; and is governed by a Board of Directors made up of leaders from major national environmental organizations.
Contact(s):
Chair: MICHAEL HAYDEN
President: DEB CALLAHAN
Secretary: WADE GREENE
Treasurer: WINSOME McINTOSH
Executive Director: BETH SULLIVAN
Chief Financial Officer: ANNE SAER
Publication(s): *National Environmental Scorecard; Presidential Scorecard; LCV Insider Newsletter.*

LEAGUE OF KENTUCKY SPORTSMEN, INC.
P.O. Box 406, 4776 U.S. 27 S., Alexandria, KY 41075
Phone: Phone & Fax: 606-635-8896; Email: ksportsmen@fuse.net; WWW: www.loks.org
Scope: Statewide
Description: A representative statewide organization, affiliated with the National Wildlife Federation, dedicated to the protection and enhancement of wildlife and its habitat through public education and government interaction.
Contact(s):
President: BEN HALL
Executive Director: ROBERT SMITH
Affiliate Representative: LINDA SAUNDERS
Editor: HANK STRONG
Publication(s): *Kentucky Sportsman*

LEAGUE OF OHIO SPORTSMEN
3953 Indianola Ave., Columbus, OH 43214
Phone: 614-268-9924
Scope: Statewide
Description: A representative statewide organization, affiliated with the National Wildlife Federation, dedicated to the protection and enhancement of wildlife and its habitat through public education and government interaction.
Contact(s):
President: DON SEEDORF
Affiliate Representative: MARILYN M. LIEB
Alternate Representative: GEORGE LYNCH
Editor: BOB WALLACE
Publication(s): *Ohio Out-Of-Doors*

LEAGUE OF WOMEN VOTERS OF IOWA
200 10th St., 5th Fl., Des Moines, IA 50309
Phone: 515-883-1447; Fax: 515-243-5941
Founded: 1920; Membership: 750
Scope: Statewide
Description: A nonpartisan organization of local chapters and members-at-large, affiliated with the League of Women Voters of the U.S., whose purpose is to promote political responsibility through informed and active participation of citizens in government and to act on selected governmental issues. We promote and support management, preservation, and conservation of our natural resources. Activities: Public Forum, material distribution to communities and public officials, testimony.
Contact(s):
President: MARY DAILY LANGE; Phone: 515-277-4485
Vice President: MYRNA LOEHRLEIN; Phone: 319-365-3199
Environmental Coordinator: JUDIE HOFFMAN; Phone: 515-292-2660
Lead Staff: RUTH SPARKS MELONE; Phone: 515-883-1447
Publication(s): *Iowa Voter; Legislative Newsletter*
Keyword(s): Air Quality and Pollution, Chemical Pollution Control, Energy Conservation, Environmental Protection, Land Use Planning, Pollution Prevention, Soil Conservation, Solid Waste Management, Water Quality

LEAGUE OF WOMEN VOTERS OF THE U.S.
1730 M St. NW, Washington, DC 20036
Phone: 202-429-1965; Fax: 202-429-0854
Founded: 1920; Membership: 100,000
Scope: National
Description: Nonpartisan organization of 100,000 members located in all 50 states, the District of Columbia, Hong Kong, and the Virgin Islands, working to promote political responsibility through informed and active participation of citizens in government. Takes political action on water and air quality, solid and hazardous waste management, land use, and energy. The League of Women Voters Education Fund carries out educational projects, publishes materials, and arranges conferences on water and energy issues.

Contact(s):
President: CAROLYN JEFFERSON JENKINS
Executive Director: JANE GRUENEBAUM
Editor: MONICA SULLIVAN
Program Manager of Water Resources: ELANA COHEN
Program Manager, Energy Resources: SHARON LLOYD-O'CONNOR
Publication(s): *National Voter, The*
Keyword(s): Communications, Energy, Environmental and Conservation Education, Water Resources

LEAGUE OF WOMEN VOTERS OF WASHINGTON
1411 4th Ave., Bldg., #803, Seattle, WA Phone: 206-622-8961
Membership: 2,218
Scope: Statewide
Description: The League of Women Voters is a nonpartisan political organization that encourages the informed and active participation of citizens in government and influences public policy through education and advocacy. Any citizen over 18 may become a voting member.
Contact(s):
President: ELIZABETH PIERINI
Vice President: JUDY GOLBERG
Vice President: LUCY COPASS
Secretary: BETSY GREENE
Treasurer: MYRA HOWREY
Publication(s): *A State We're In, The; Washington; Targeting Tomorrow - Washington's Economy Adjusts to the 90's; Speaking of Ground Water; Washington State Public Port Districts; Public Assistance as Social Policy; Higher Education in Washington State; Gun Control in Washington; Direct Democracy: The Initiative/Referendum Process in Washington State.*
Keyword(s): Forests and Forestry, Outdoor Recreation, Public Lands, Rivers, Wildlife and Wildlife Habitat

LEAGUE TO SAVE LAKE TAHOE
955 Emerald Bay Rd., South Lake Tahoe, CA 96150
Phone: 530-541-5388; WWW: www.KeepTahoeBlue.com
Founded: 1957; Membership: 4,800
Scope: National
Description: A private, nonprofit corporation dedicated to preserving the environmental balance, scenic beauty, and recreational opportunities of the Lake Tahoe Basin.
Contact(s):
President: WILLIAM A. CALLENDER
Vice President: ADOLPHUS ANDREWS JR.
Vice President: CHARLES MCLEOD
Vice President: TOM MERTENS
Secretary: STEFFI MOOERS
Treasurer: WILLIAM R. MARKEN, 680 Milverton Rd., Los Altos, CA 94022
Executive Director: ROCHELLE NASON
Publication(s): *Keep Tahoe Blue*
Keyword(s): Environmental and Conservation Education, Environmental Preservation, Lakes, Land Use Planning, Water Pollution

LEGACY INTERNATIONAL
128 N. Fayette St., Alexandria, VA 22314
Phone: 703-549-3630; Fax: 703-549-0262
Founded: 1979
Scope: National
Description: Legacy International is a nonprofit, private voluntary organization serving public and private organizations facing the need to manage change. Legacy's expertise and experience bring about practical designs. Creative and innovative projects use interdisciplinary teams, extended networks, public and private partnerships, and citizen exchanges. Legacy has achieved international recognition for its accomplishments in environmentally sound development, conflict resolution, curriculum design, and leadership training.
Contact(s):
President: J. E. RASH, Rt. 4 Box 265, Bedford, VA 24523; Phone: 703-297-5982
Executive Director: DR. IRA KAUFMAN, 128 N. Fayette St., Alexandria, VA 22314; Phone: 703-549-3630
Publication(s): *Legacy World*
Keyword(s): Environmental and Conservation Education, Environmental Planning, Planning Management, Sustainable Development, Youth Organizations

LEGAL ENVIRONMENTAL ASSISTANCE FOUNDATION INC. (LEAF)
1114 Thomasville Rd., Suite E, Tallahassee, FL 32303-6290
Phone: 850-681-2591; Email: leaf@lewisweb.net; WWW: www.lewisweb.net/leaf
Founded: 1979
Scope: National
Description: LEAF is a charitable public-interest environmental law firm that protects human health from pollution. We provide legal and technical assistance to citizens and grassroots organizations in Florida, Georgia, and Alabama. LEAF is a membership organization and provides assistance and services free of charge.
Contact(s):
Chairman: LARRY THOMPSON
President: B. SUZI RUHL
Vice President: DAVID LUDDER
Vice President: CYNTHIA VALENCIC
Secretary: VICTOR JOHNSON
Treasurer: ROBERT WEBB
Publication(s): *LEAF BRIEFS; various educational documents. Citizens may write for a publications list.*
Keyword(s): Energy, Energy Conservation, Environmental Justice, Environmental Law, Environmental Protection, Pesticides, Pollution Prevention, Rivers, Solar Energy, Water Pollution

LIFE OF THE LAND
1111 Bishop St., Suite 503, Honolulu, HI 96813
Phone: 808-533-3454; Fax: 808-533-0993
Membership: 40
Scope: Statewide
Description: To advance the science, technology, education, and practice of professional forestry in America, and to use the knowledge and skills of the profession to benefit society.
Contact(s):
President: GUY NAKAMOTO
Vice President: ART MORI
Administrator: HENRY Q. CURTIS

LIGHTHAWK
Headquarters, 230 California St., Suite 207, San Francisco, CA 94111
Phone: 415-715-6400; Fax: 415-715-6401; Email: julied@lighthawk.org; WWW: www.sni.net/lighthawk
Founded: 1979
Scope: National
Description: An international non-profit organization that brings the power of flight to conservation by designing creative environmental campaigns and by partnering with earthbound environmentalists. Current programs include flights in Alaska, British Columbia, Washington, Oregon, the Rocky Mountain Region, Central America, and Florida.
Contact(s):
President: JOHN WYLDE
Secretary: PATRICIA SCHIFFERLE
Treasurer: TOM SARGENT
Executive Director: WILL PARISH
Publication(s): *Lighthawk Newsletter; Intercom*
Keyword(s): Ancient Forests, Aquatic Habitats, Biodiversity, Birds, Coasts, Conservation of Protected Areas, Endangered and Threatened Species, Environment, Environmental and Conservation Education, Environmental Planning, Environmental Preservation, Environmental Protection, Forest Management, Geography

NON-GOVERNMENTAL ORGANIZATIONS

Northwest Field Office
2915 E. Madison St., Suite 306, Seattle, WA 98112
Phone: 206-860-2832; Fax: 206-860-2836; Email: jenny1@lighthawk.org
Scope: Regional
Contact(s):
Director of Flight Operations: KEMP HIATT
Executive Director (Acting): LES WELSH

Rocky Mountain Field Office
303 Unit F AABC, Aspen, CO 81611
Phone: 970-925-6987; Fax: 970-925-2701
Scope: Regional
Contact(s):
Associate Executive Director: BRUCE GORDON

LONG LIVE THE KINGS
19435 184th Pl., NE, Woodinville, WA 98072
Phone: 206-788-6023
Founded: 1985
Scope: Regional
Description: To rebuild wild salmon populations in specific Northwest Rivers and to enhance their habitat. We are supported by foundations, corporations, individuals, Indian tribes, and fishing and environmental organizations. We are not a membership group.
Contact(s):
Executive Director: JOHN A. SAYRE
Chairman of the Board: JIM YOUNGREN
Publication(s): *Long Live the Kings Newsletter*
Keyword(s): Aquatic Habitats, Endangered and Threatened Species, Fisheries, Rivers, Water Resources

LOUISIANA ASSOCIATION OF CONSERVATION DISTRICTS
ATTN: President, 663 Holmes Rd., Keatchie, LA 71046
Scope: Statewide
Contact(s):
President: JERRY HOLMES, 663 Holmes Rd., Keatchie, LA 71046; Phone: 318-933-5375; Fax: 318-872-3178
Secretary/Treasurer and Board Member: CHARLES DUPUY, 313 N. Monroe St, Ste #4, Marksville, LA 71351; Phone: 318-253-7603; Fax: 318-253-8890
Vice President, Alternate Board Member: JOHN WOODWARD, 1251 Bayou LaCarpe Rd, Houma, LA 70363; Phone: 504-879-3528; Fax: 504-876-5267

LOUISIANA AUDUBON COUNCIL
355 Napoleon St., Baton Rouge, LA 70802-5964
Phone: 504-346-8761
Founded: 1989
Scope: Statewide
Description: To implement the Audubon cause in Louisiana on issues of statewide concern; coordinate activities among the Audubon chapters in Louisiana; and advocate on behalf of birds, wildlife, and their habitat.
Contact(s):
President: BILL ROBERTSON
Vice President: BARRY KOHL
Secretary: ANDREA MATTISON
Treasurer: DORIS FALKENHEINER
Keyword(s): Birds, Endangered and Threatened Species, Nongame Wildlife, Wetlands, Wildlife and Wildlife Habitat

LOUISIANA B.A.S.S. CHAPTER FEDERATION
ATTN: President, 107 Radeke St., Welsh, LA 70591
Phone: 318-734-3784
Scope: Statewide
Description: An organization of Bassmaster chapters, affiliated with the Bass Anglers Sportsman Society, organized to fight pollution, assist state and national conservation agencies in their efforts, and teach the young people of our country good conservation practices. Dedicated to the realistic conservation of our water resources.
Contact(s):
President: MIKE COOLEY, 107 Radeke St., Welsh, LA 70591; Phone: 318-734-3784
Conservation Director: WILL COURTNEY, 4548 Chelsea Dr., Baton Rouge, LA 70809; Phone: 504-923-1908

LOUISIANA FORESTRY ASSOCIATION
P.O. Drawer 5067, Alexandria, LA 71307
Phone: 318-443-2558
Founded: 1947; Membership: 2,300
Scope: Statewide
Description: Trade-supported association whose purpose is the conservation of the state's forest land and the promotion of the products and services derived therefrom.
Contact(s):
President: ED MYERS, 71270
Treasurer: BILL WIEGER, 71301
Executive Director: CHARLES A. VANDERSTEEN
1st Vice President: TOM RHODEA, 70634
2nd Vice President: JOHN MONK, 75941
3rd Vice President: DENNIS AUCOIN, 70722
Staff Forester: CLYDE M. TODD
Publication(s): *Forests and People*
Keyword(s): Forests and Forestry, Research, Scholarships and Grants, Training, Wildlife and Wildlife Habitat

LOUISIANA WILDLIFE FEDERATION, INC.
P.O. Box 65239, 337 S. Acadian Thruway, Baton Rouge, LA 70896-5239
Phone: Phone & Fax: 504-344-6707
Scope: Statewide
Description: A representative statewide organization, affiliated with the National Wildlife Federation, dedicated to the protection and enhancement of wildlife and its habitat through public education and government interaction.
Contact(s):
President: KATHY WASCOM
Affiliate Representative: EDGAR F. VEILLON
Executive Director and Editor: RANDY P. LANCTOT
Publication(s): *Louisiana Out-of-Doors*

LOWER MISSISSIPPI RIVER CONSERVATION COMMITTEE
2524 S. Frontage Rd. Suite C, Vicksburg, MS 39180-5269
Phone: 601-629-6602; Fax: 601-636-9541; Email: rf4r_lmrcc@fws.gov
Scope: Regional
Description: The Committee provides an organizational structure and forum for coordinating and facilitating cooperative activities involving the natural resources of the Lower Mississippi River. Also encourages sustainable use of Lower Mississippi River natural resources for long-term environmental, social, and economic benefits.
Contact(s):
Chairman: JERRY D. VINEYARD, Missouri Department of Natural Resources, P.O. Box 250, Rolla, MO 65402-0250; Phone: 573-368-2148
Coordinator: RON NASSAR, 2524 S. Frontage Rd., Ste. C, Vicksburg, MS 39180-5269; Phone: 601-629-6602
Publication(s): *LMRCC Newsletter, The*
Keyword(s): Fisheries, Land Use Planning, Rivers, Sustainable Ecosystems, Water Quality

MACBRIDE RAPTOR PROJECT
W.H., KCC, 6301 Kirkwood Blvd., SW, Cedar Rapids, IA 52406
Phone: 319-398-5495
Founded: 1985
Scope: Statewide
Description: The Macbride Raptor Project is devoted to the preservation of Iowa's birds of prey and their natural habitats through rehabilitation of sick or injured raptors, education of the public to the role of raptors in our environment, and research on various aspects of raptor biology.

Contact(s):
Director: JODEANE CANCILLA
Veterinarian: DR. STAN HOLST
Volunteer Coordinator: KATHY KELLY
Publication(s): *Raptor Review*

MAGIC
P.O. Box 5894, Stanford, CA 94309
Phone: 650-323-7333; Fax: 650-323-4232; Email: magic@ecomagic.org; WWW: www.ecomagic.org
Founded: 1979; Membership: 200
Scope: Statewide
Description: Magic's programs apply methods and principles of ecology to clarify values, improve health, increase cooperation, and steward the environment. Activities include lectures and seminars about the nature of value; life-planning workshops, swim, run, and hatha yoga instruction; mentoring, community organizing, habitat enhancement, water and land, resource planning; neighborhood design and publishing.
Contact(s):
President: ROBIN BAYER; Email: robin@ecomagic.org
Treasurer: DAVID SCHROM; Email: david@ecomagic.org
Publication(s): *Oak Regeneration on Stanford Lands; Liveable City; Human Ecology, A Science for Living Well*
Keyword(s): EcoAction, Ecology, Environmental and Conservation Education, Health and Nutrition, Sustainable Ecosystems, Urban Environment, Water Resources, Wildlife and Wildlife Habitat

MAINE ASSOCIATION OF CONSERVATION COMMISSIONS (MACC)
P.O. Box 702, Bath, ME 04330
Founded: 1969; Membership: 80 commissions
Scope: Statewide
Description: A membership organization whose objectives are twofold: to assist Maine municipalities in establishing conservation commissions; to assist the existing 200+ conservation commissions through technical assistance and educational programs.
Contact(s):
President: MIKE CLINE
Executive Director: BOB CUMMINGS
Publication(s): *Grass Roots*
Keyword(s): Environmental and Conservation Education, Environmental Planning, Environmental Protection, Solid Waste, Water Resources

MAINE ASSOCIATION OF CONSERVATION DISTRICTS
ATTN: President, 2467 Exeter Rd., Exeter, ME 04435-3107
Scope: Statewide
Contact(s):
President, Alternate Board Member: NEIL CRANE, 2467 Exeter Rd, Exeter, ME 04435-3107; Phone: 207-379-2641; Fax: 207-379-2644
Vice President: JOHN A. HEMOND, 46 N. Verreill Rd, Minot, ME 04258; Phone: 207-345-5322
Secretary: LARRY MacDONALD, Box 1187, Greenville, ME 04441; Phone: 207-695-2639
Treasurer: FRED HARDY, Rt. 1 Box 1501, Farmington, ME 04938; Phone: 207-778-4320
Executive Director: WILLIAM BELL, P.O. Box 228, Augusta, ME 04330; Phone: 207-622-4443; Fax: 207-623-3748; Email: newengag@mint.net
Board Member: RAYMOND HARRIS, Rt. 1 Box 8396, Washburn, ME 04786; Phone: 207-764-4320

MAINE AUDUBON SOCIETY
Gilsland Farm, 118 U.S. Rt. 1, P.O. Box 6009, Falmouth, ME 04105
Phone: 207-781-2330; Email: maineaudubon@maineaudubon.org; WWW: www.maineaudubon.org
Founded: 1843; Membership: 6,500
Scope: Statewide
Description: Dedicated to the protection, conservation, and enhancement of Maine's ecosystems through the promotion of individual understanding and actions. Programs focusing on forest conservation, endangered and threatened species protection, wildlife and wildlife habitats, grassroots activism, environmental education, and school curriculum enhancement. Nature day camp, field trip and world tour program, store, and 13 sanctuaries.
Contact(s):
Executive Director: THOMAS A. URQUHART
Editor: MARK CONDON
Publication(s): *Habitat: Journal of the Maine Audubon* **Keyword(s):** Coasts, Endangered and Threatened Species, Environmental and Conservation Education, Forests and Forestry, Natural History

MAINE B.A.S.S. CHAPTER FEDERATION
ATTN: President, R.R. 1 Box 332, Hollis Center, ME 04042
Phone: 207-929-8553
Scope: Statewide
Description: An organization of Bassmaster chapters, affiliated with the Bass Anglers Sportsman Society, organized to fight pollution, assist state and national conservation agencies in their efforts, and teach young people of our country good conservation practices. Dedicated to the realistic conservation of our water resources.
Contact(s):
President: ERIC LOW, R.R. 1 Box 332, Hollis Center, ME 04042; Phone: 207-929-8553
Conservation Director: NORM MOULTON, R.R. 1 Box 103D, Ellsworth, ME 04605; Phone: 207-667-6913; Email: bassme@midmaine.com
Publication(s): *Federation Guide*

MAINE COAST HERITAGE TRUST
169 Park Row, Brunswick, ME 04011
Phone: 207-729-7366; Fax: 207-729-6863
Founded: 1970
Scope: Statewide
Description: To protect land that is essential to the character of Maine, in particular its coastline and islands. Provides free advisory services on open-space protection to landowners, town officials, state and federal agencies, land trusts, and other private conservation organizations.
Contact(s):
Chairman: HAROLD E. WOODSUM JR.
President: JAMES J. ESPY JR.
Treasurer: JOHN M. ROBINSON
Editor: CHRIS HAMILTON
Publication(s): *Conservation Options, A Guide For Maine Landowners; Directory of Maine Land Conservation Trusts; Annual Report; Maine Heritage; Technical Bulletins*
Keyword(s): Coasts, Islands, Land Preservation, Natural Areas, Open Space

MAINE ENVIRONMENTAL EDUCATION ASSOCIATION, INC.
P.O. Box 9, Wiscasset, ME 04578
Phone: 207-882-7323
Founded: 1981; Membership: 225
Scope: Statewide
Description: A nonprofit organization dedicated to the promotion of environmental education in Maine by working for inclusion of K-12 EE in all schools, by providing methodological information and materials to teachers and parents, publishing a newsletter, and by coordinating the work of organizations involved in EE.

NON-GOVERNMENTAL ORGANIZATIONS

Contact(s):
President: LISA SILVERMAN-GENT, 1026 Sawyer Rd., Cape Elizabeth, ME 04107; Phone: 207-799-9339
Vice President: DAVID GALIN, 39 Howard St. #2, Portland, ME 04101; Phone: 207-775-5942
Secretary: BARBARA WELCH, DEP State House Station #7, Augusta, ME 04333; Phone: 207-287-7682
Treasurer: DON HUDSON, Chewonki Foundation, Wiscasset, ME 04578; Phone: 207-882-7323
Editor: LISA SILVERMAN-GENT
Publication(s): *Connections*
Keyword(s): Environmental and Conservation Education, Natural History

MANASOTA-88
5314 Bay State Rd., Palmetto, FL 34221
Scope: Statewide
Contact(s):
Chairman: GLORIA RAINS; Phone: 813-722-7413
Editor: GLORIA RAINS
Vice Chairman: MRS. LAURENCE QUY, Bradenton, FL 34209; Phone: 941-792-5509
Vice Chairman: REBECCA EGER, 324 W. Royal Flamingo Dr., Sarasota, FL 33578; Phone: 813-366-1765
Keyword(s): Biodiversity, Environmental Law, Nuclear/Radiation, Sustainable Ecosystems, Toxic Substances

MANITOBA NATURALISTS SOCIETY
401-63 Albert St., Winnipeg, Manitoba R3B 1G4 Canada
Phone: 204-943-9029
Founded: 1920; Membership: 1,500
Scope: Statewide
Description: Fosters an awareness and appreciation of the natural environment and an understanding of humanity's place therein; and sponsors lectures, workshops, field trips on natural history topics, and recreational outings that are environmentally friendly.
Contact(s):
President: WES TRETIAK; Phone: 204-261-1966
Secretary: FRANK PENNER; Phone: 204-667-1513
Executive Director: HERTA GUDAUSKAS; Phone: 204-943-9029
Editor: MARGARET KAPINGA; Phone: 204-269-1814
Publication(s): *Bulletin; Manitoba's Tall Grass Prairie: A Field Guide to an Endangered Space; The Birds of Southeastern Manitoba; Wings Along Winnipeg; The Wild Plants of Birds Hill Park*

MANITOBA WILDLIFE FEDERATION
70 Stevenson Rd., Winnipeg, Manitoba R3H 0W7 Canada
Phone: 204-633-5967; Fax: 204-632-5200
Founded: 1944; Membership: 14,000
Scope: Statewide
Description: Promotes conservation, safety, and good sportsmanship. Manages the Habitat Trust Fund which secures critical land to ensure habitat for wildlife. Protects the interests of anglers and hunters.
Contact(s):
President: LARRY THIESSEN
Vice President: RANDY WALKER
Vice President: SANDRA TAIT
Vice President: LIONEL NOBISS
Vice President: LLOYD LINTOTT
Vice President: LAWRIE HILTON
Vice President: JOHN HAWKINS
Vice President: DALE GARNHAM
Secretary: DARLENE GARNHAM
Treasurer: LAWRIE HILTON
Publication(s): *Wildlife Crusader/Outdoor Edge*

MANOMET OBSERVATORY
81 Stage Point Rd. P.O. Box 1770, Manomet, MA 02345
Phone: 508-224-6521; Fax: 508-224-9220; WWW: www.manomet.org
Founded: 1969; Membership: 3,000
Scope: National
Description: Manomet is a non-profit conservation research institute dedicated to promoting informed conservation policy and natural resource management through applied research. At study sites throughout the Americas, Manomet scientists and volunteers monitor migrant songbird and shorebird populations, identify critical wetlands habitats, design fisheries conservation and management strategies, and develop plans for sustainable management of temperate and tropical forest ecosystems. Manomet's environmental education program serves as the interpretive link between our research work and the information needs of the public. Manomet is membership supported.
Contact(s):
Chair: MRS JEPTHA H. WADE
Director of Programs: DR. KATHARINE C. PARSONS
President and Director: LINDA E. LEDDY
Keyword(s): Biodiversity, Birds, Coasts, Ecology, Endangered and Threatened Species, Environment, Fisheries, Forest Management, Internships, Land Use Planning, Natural Areas, Nongame Wildlife, Pesticides, Research

MARIN CONSERVATION LEAGUE
55 Mitchell Blvd., Suite 21, San Rafael, CA 94903
Phone: 415-472-6170
Founded: 1934; Membership: 4,000
Scope: Statewide
Description: The Marin Conservation League has worked to preserve and protect the natural assets of Marin County. The league works on all issues affecting the county environment, seeking partnerships with diverse groups to influence public policy and educate citizens and decisionmakers in understanding critical issues and options.
Contact(s):
President: KATHY LOWREY
Secretary: ROBERT BERNER
Treasurer: LAWRENCE SMITH
Executive Director: JERRY EDELBROCK
1st Vice President: DON NEUBACHER
2nd Vice President: JEAN STARKWEATHER
Education Coordinator: ANITA FRANZI
Publication(s): *MCL News*
Keyword(s): Agriculture, Environmental and Conservation Education, Environmental Preservation, Land Use Planning, Public Lands

MARINE CONSERVATION BIOLOGY INSTITUTE
Headquarters, 15806 NE 47th Ct., Redmond, WA 98052-5208
Phone: 425-883-8914; Fax: 425-883-3017; Email: caroline@mcbi.org; WWW: www.mcbi.org
Founded: 1996
Scope: National
Description: MCBI is a nonprofit, non-partisan, tax-exempt organization dedicated to advancing the multidisciplinary science of marine conservation biology. MCBI helps scientists to generate information that arms people with knowledge crucial for informed decision-making.
Contact(s):
President: DR. ELLIOTT A. NORSE
Program Director: AMY MATHEWS-AMOS, 205 Edgewood St., Arlington, VA 22201; Phone: 8703-276-1434; Fax: 703-276-1528; Email: amymcbi@mcbi.org
Keyword(s): Biodiversity, Marine Protected Areas, Seabed Disturbance

MARINE ENVIRONMENTAL RESEARCH INSTITUTE (MERI)
772 W. End Ave., New York, NY 10025
Phone: 212-864-6285; Fax: 212-864-1470; Email: meri@interport.net
Founded: 1990; Membership: 400
Scope: National
Description: MERI is a nonprofit organization dedicated to protecting the health and biodiversity of the marine environment. MERI's programs are international in scope and include direct field research, environmental and conservation education, training, and collaboration with the world's scientific community. MERI strives to address the problems of global marine pollution, endangered species and habitat degradation, and environmental emergencies affecting marine life.
Contact(s):
Chairman: DR. LEMUEL A. EVANS, 3536 Paintwater Pl., Las Vegas, NV 89129-7338
President: DR. SUSAN D. SHAW, P.O. Box 179, Brooklin, ME 04616
Vice President: SUZANNE B. HOPKINS, 15200 Old York Road, Monkton, MD 21111
Secretary: JOAN F. KOVEN, Astrolabe Inc., 4812 V St. NW, Washington, DC 20007
Resource Center Director: PATRICE FARREY, MERI Resource Center, Main St., P.O. Box 300, Brooklin, ME 04616; Phone: 207-359-8078; Fax: 207-359-8079; Email: meri@downeast.net
Publication(s): *MERI News; MERI Resource Center News; research publications*
Keyword(s): Biodiversity, Endangered and Threatened Species, Environmental and Conservation Education, Marine Mammals

MARINE MAMMAL CENTER, THE
Marin Headlands, Golden Gate National Recreation Area (GGNRA, Sausalito, CA 94965
Phone: 415-289-7325
Founded: 1975; Membership: 35,000
Scope: National
Description: The Marine Mammal Center is a nonprofit organization licensed to rescue and rehabilitate sick, injured, and orphaned marine mammals that strand along the northern and central California coast. Information derived from routine medical treatment is shared with scientists worldwide. Through education programs, the Center promotes public awareness of the ocean environment among over 100,000 visitors annually.
Contact(s):
Chair: JERRY GIBBONS, 130 Battery Street, Suite 330, San Francisco, CA 94111; Phone: 415-291-4999
Treasurer: SHELDON WOLFE, Steefel, Levitt, & Weiss, One Embarcadero Center, 30th Floor, San Francisco, CA 94111-3784; Phone: 415-788-0900
Executive Director: MARGARET BURKS
Publication(s): *Release, The; Annual Report; various scientific papers.*
Keyword(s): Environmental and Conservation Education, Marine Mammals, Wildlife Disease, Wildlife Rehabilitation

MARINE TECHNOLOGY SOCIETY
1828 L St., NW, Suite 906, Washington, DC 20036-5104
Phone: 202-775-5966
Founded: 1963; Membership: 2,500
Scope: International
Description: An ocean-oriented, multidisciplinary, international professional society, formed to encourage the development of the technology, education, operational expertise, and public awareness needed to advance man's capability to work effectively in all ocean areas and depths.
Contact(s):
President: NORMAN B. EDTABROOK
Executive Director: MARTIN J. FINERTY JR.
Managing Editor: I. CLAYTON LIGHTLY
Publication(s): *Marine Technology Society Journal; MTS Newsletter Currents; various proceedings*
Keyword(s): Engineering, Oceanography, Water Resources

MARYLAND ASSOCIATION OF CONSERVATION DISTRICTS
ATTN: President, 14919 Roxbury Rd., P.O. Box 189, Gleneig, MD 21737
Scope: Statewide
Contact(s):
President: MARTHA CLARK, 14919 Roxbury Rd. P.O. Box 189, Gleneig, MD 21737; Phone: 410-531-3456
Vice President: PARKER SMITH, 2426 Old New Windsor Pike, New Windsor, MD 21776; Phone: 410-751-8412
Secretary: ROBERT ZIEHM, 9025 Chevrolet Dr., Ste J, Ellicott City, MD 21042; Phone: 410-465-3180
Executive Director: LYNNE HOOT, 53 Slama Rd., Edgewater, MD 21037; Phone: 410-956-5771; Fax: 410-956-0161
Alternate Board Member: GEORGE LECHLIDER, 24110 Laytonsville Rd., Gaithersburg, MD 20882; Phone: 301-253-1501
Treasurer and Council Member: DONALD SPICKLER, 14854 Hicksville Rd., Clear Spring, MD 21722; Phone: 301-842-2534; Fax: 301-842-2534; Email: dspick@erols.com

MARYLAND B.A.S.S. CHAPTER FEDERATION
ATTN: President, 14500 Woodstar Ct., Leesbury, MD 20176
Phone: 301-898-3717
Scope: Statewide
Description: An organization of Bassmaster chapters, affiliated with the Bass Anglers Sportsman Society, organized to fight pollution, assist state and national conservation agencies in their efforts, and teach the young people of our country good conservation practices. Dedicated to the realistic conservation of our water resources.
Contact(s):
President: BRIAN LANCASTER, 14500 Woodstar Ct., Leesburg, VA 20176; Phone: 301-898-3717
Conservation Director: BILL SHEPARD, 1508 Dover Ct., Glen Burnie, MD 21722; Phone: 301-842-3200; Email: shepdeal@erols.com
Publication(s): *Maryland State Federation Update*

MARYLAND FORESTS ASSOCIATION
P.O. Box 599, Grantsville, MD 21536
Phone: 301-895-5369; Fax: 301-895-5369; Email: mfa@hereintown.net; WWW: mdforests.org
Membership: 525
Scope: Statewide
Description: A nonprofit 501c (3) citizens organization for people interested in trees, forests, related natural resources, and forestry. To promote the maintenance of a healthy and productive forestland base to enhance the economic, environmental, and social well-being of all who live in the state.
Contact(s):
President: CALVIN D. LUBBEN
Vice President: PETER A. ALEXANDER
Vice President: GEORGE GILMORE
Vice President: JOHN H. COLTON
Executive Director: KARIN E. MILLER
Secretary and Treasurer: DANIEL R. RIDER
Publication(s): *Crosscut, The; MFA Legislative Update*
Keyword(s): Environment, Environmental and Conservation Education, Forests and Forestry, Renewable Resources, Sustainable Ecosystems

MARYLAND NATIVE PLANT SOCIETY
P.O. Box 4877, Silver Spring, MD 20914
WWW: www.geocities.com.rainforest/vines/2996
Founded: 1990; Membership: 1,000
Scope: Statewide
Description: MNPS is a nonprofit organization that uses education, research, and community service to foster awareness and appreciation for Maryland's native flora and habitats, leading to their conservation.

NON-GOVERNMENTAL ORGANIZATIONS

Contact(s):
President: RODERICK HOYT SIMMONS; Phone: 703-256-7671
Vice President: LOUIS ARONICA; Phone: 202-722-1081
Secretary: SAMUEL JONES; Phone: 410-838-7950
Treasurer: CHARMANE TRUESDELL; Phone: 301-470-4462
Director: MARC IMLAY; Phone: 301-283-0808
Publication(s): *Native News*
Keyword(s): Biodiversity

MARYLAND ORNITHOLOGICAL SOCIETY, INC.
Cylburn Mansion, 4915 Greenspring Ave., Baltimore, MD 21209
Phone: 410-244-0032
Founded: 1945; Membership: 2,400
Scope: Statewide
Description: Nonprofit statewide organization of 16 chapters. Aims to promote the knowledge, protection, and conservation of wildlife and natural resources; to foster appreciation of the natural environment; to establish educational and scientific projects to inform and enrich the public; and to record, evaluate, and publish observations of birdlife in Maryland.
Contact(s):
President: ROBERT RINEER, 8326 Philadelphia Rd., Baltimore, MD 21237; Phone: 410-391-8499
Vice President: NORM SAUNDERS, 1261 Cavendish Rd., Colesville, MD 20905; Phone: 301-989-9035
Secretary: SYBIL WILLIAMS, 2000 Baltimore Rd. #A24, Rockville, MD 20851; Phone: 301-762-0560
Treasurer: JEFF METTER, 1301 N. Rolling Rd., Catonsville, MD 21228; Phone: 410-788-4877
Executive Secretary: WILL TRESS, 203 Gittings Ave., Baltimore, MD 21212; Phone: 410-433-1058; Email: wtress@ubmail.ubalt.edu
Editor: CHANDLER S. ROBBINS, Patuxent Wildlife Research Center, Laurel, MD 20811; Phone: 301-498-0281
Publication(s): *Maryland Birdlife; Maryland Yellowthroat,*
Keyword(s): Birds, Environmental and Conservation Education, Natural History, Wildlife and Wildlife Habitat

MASSACHUSETTS ASSOCIATION OF CONSERVATION COMMISSIONS (MACC)
10 Juniper Rd., Belmont, MA 02178
Phone: 617-489-3930
Founded: 1961; Membership: 3,200
Scope: Statewide
Description: Protects wetlands and open space through education and advocacy.
Contact(s):
President: GREGOR I. McGREGOR
Secretary: DONALD MacIVER
Executive Director: DR. SALLY A. ZIELINSKI
1st Vice President: GEORGE A. HALL
2nd Vice President: INGEBORG HEGEMAN
3rd Vice President: HELEN D. BETHELL
Publication(s): *Environmental Handbook for Massachusetts Conservation Commissioners, 1991 Edition; Newsletter of the Association for members of conservation commissions, government agencies, educational institutions, and environmental organizations*
Keyword(s): Environmental and Conservation Education, Environmental Preservation, Land Purchase, Public Lands, Wetlands

MASSACHUSETTS ASSOCIATION OF CONSERVATION DISTRICTS
ATTN: President, 25 Shore Rd., Bourne, MA 02532
Scope: Statewide
Contact(s):
President, Alternate Board Member: PEGGY FANTOZZI PACHECO, 25 Shore Rd., Bourne, MA 02532; Phone: 508-759-4363; Fax: 508-759-4363
Vice President: ED HIMLAN, P.O. Box 577, Leaminister, MA 01453; Phone: 978-534-0379; Fax: 978-534-1329
Secretary: ANNE MERRIAM, 157 State Rd E, Westminster, MA 01473; Phone: 978-874-2432
Treasurer: DONALD LAMBERT, 178 Moulton Hill Rd, Monson, MA 01057; Phone: 413-267-4837
Board Member: THOMAS QUINK, 67 Church St., Gilbertville, MA 01031-9864; Phone: 413-477-8870; Fax: 413-477-8870

MASSACHUSETTS AUDUBON SOCIETY, INC.
208 S. Great Rd., Lincoln, MA 01773
Phone: 617-259-9500; Fax: 617-259-8899
Founded: 1896; Membership: 55,000
Scope: Statewide
Description: A nonprofit organization committed to the protection of the environment for people and wildlife. One of the oldest conservation organizations in the world and the largest in New England. Owns and protects 24,000 acres with 19 staffed sanctuaries across Massachusetts. Programming priorities: Conservation, education, advocacy, and research.
Contact(s):
President: GERARD A. BERTRAND
Secretary: ALYNN D. HARVEY
Board of Directors Chairman: LEE SPELKE
Editor: JOHN HANSON MITCHELL
Publication(s): *Sanctuary*
Keyword(s): Biodiversity, Birds, Ecology, Environment, Environmental Protection, Land Preservation, Natural History

MASSACHUSETTS B.A.S.S. CHAPTER FEDERATION
ATTN: President 52 Elm St., Clinton, MA 01510
Phone: 978-365-6987
Scope: Statewide
Description: An organization of Bassmaster chapters, affiliated with the Bass Anglers Sportsman Society, organized to fight pollution, assist state and national conservation agencies in their efforts, and teach young people of our country good conservation practices. Dedicated to the realistic conservation of our water resources.
Contact(s):
President: JIM MARINO, 52 Elm St., Clinton, MA 01510; Phone: 978-365-6987
Conservation Director: DEAN PERCIVAL, 396 Green St., Northboro, MA 01532; Phone: 508-366-2030; Email: massbass@whiznet.com

MASSACHUSETTS ENVIRONMENTAL EDUCATION SOCIETY
Box 105, 290 Turnpike Rd., Westboro, MA 01581
Phone: 508-929-2751
Founded: 1977; Membership: 325
Scope: Statewide
Description: Massachusetts Environmental Education Society is a professional organization dedicated to the promotion of environmental education in Massachusetts. Members include teachers, naturalists, youth group leaders, education consultants, agencies, and organizations. Annual conference is held for professional development.
Contact(s):
President: CARY BUTTFIELD; Phone: 617-731-2992
Vice President: DAWN SATHER
Secretary: JENNIFER WIEST
Treasurer: ROBERT BARKMAN
Publication(s): *MEES Observer*
Keyword(s): Environment, Environmental and Conservation Education, Training

MASSACHUSETTS FORESTRY ASSOCIATION
P.O. Box 1096, Belchertown, MA 01007-1096
Phone: 413-323-7326
Founded: 1970; Membership: 1,100
Scope: Statewide
Description: A voluntary nonprofit association, affiliated with the National Woodland Owners Association; dedicated to conservation, stewardship, and advocacy of the forestland of Massachusetts. An educational organization offering information, workshops, conferences, publications, and professional assistance. Begun in

1970 as the Massachusetts Land League, changed to present name in 1986.
Contact(s):
President: MARY ELLEN LEES
Vice President: HUGH PUTNAM JR.
Executive Director: GREGORY COX
Editor: GREGORY COX
Secretary and Treasurer: TIM FOWLER
Publication(s): *Woodland Steward, The*
Keyword(s): Forests and Forestry

MASSACHUSETTS TRAPPER'S ASSOCIATION, INC.
155 Williams Rd., Concord, MA 01742
Phone: 508-369-5065
Founded: 1950
Scope: Statewide
Description: Objectives are to develop leadership for the advancement of the interests of the trapper and the fur industry, and to promote sound management for the conservation of furbearing animals.
Contact(s):
President: WILLIAM ANDRADE, 8 Williams St., Bedford, MA 01730; Phone: 617-275-1809
Secretary: IRENE HAYES, 155 Williams Rd., Concord, MA 01742; Phone: 508-369-5065
Treasurer: DEBRA BENEDETTO, P.O. Box 60, Wakefield, MA 01880; Phone: 617-246-2136
Public Relations: TOM HAYES, 155 Williams Rd., Concord, MA 01742; Phone: 508-369-5065
Vice President of East: DAN PROVOST, 16 Orchard St., Westford, MA 01886; Phone: 508-692-2097
Vice President of West: ROGER SARGENT, 28 Coburn Rd., Berlin, MA 61503; Phone: 508-838-2434
Publication(s): *Fur Ever*
Keyword(s): Mammals, Trapping, Wetlands, Wildlife and Wildlife Habitat, Wildlife Management

MAX McGRAW WILDLIFE FOUNDATION
P.O. Box 9, Dundee, IL 60118
Phone: 847-741-8000; Fax: 847-741-8157; Email: mcgrawwild@aol.com
Founded: 1962
Scope: National
Description: Conducts wildlife and fisheries research and management and conservation education projects; cooperates with other conservation agencies and institutions.
Contact(s):
President: FREDERICK G. ACKER
Vice President: RICHARD T. SCHROEDER
Vice President: SCOTT M. ELROD
Treasurer: TIMOTHY N. THOELECKE
Director of Research: JOHN D. THOMPSON
Secretary and Executive Director: STANLEY W. KOENIG
Publication(s): *Descriptive brochure; Wildlife Management Notes Series; Annual Research Report*
Keyword(s): Biodiversity, Biology, Birds, Conservation Tillage, Endangered and Threatened Species, Environmental and Conservation Education, Environmental Preservation, Fisheries, Hunting, Internships, Land Use Planning, Mammals, Natural Areas, Nature Preservation, Nongame Wildlife

MERCK FOREST AND FARMLAND CENTER, INC.
Rt. 315, Box 86, Rupert, VT 05768
Phone: 802-394-7836; Fax: 802-394-2519; Email: merck@vermontel.com; WWW: www.merckforest.com
Scope: Statewide
Description: Over 3,100 acres of field, farm, and forest open year-round to the public in the heart of the Taconic range in southwestern Vermont. Outdoor and environmental education experiences for individuals, families, and organized groups. Over 28 miles of trails, 65-acre organic demonstration farm, camping cabins and sites, and sustainable forestry.

Contact(s):
President: ALAN CALFEE
Director: RICHARD THOMPSON TUCKER

MICHIGAN ASSOCIATION OF CONSERVATION DISTRICTS
ATTN: President, 14302, OP Ave. E., Climax, MI 49034
Scope: Statewide
Contact(s):
President and Board Member: LARRY LEACH, 14302 OP Ave E, Climax, MI 49034; Phone: 616-746-4648; Fax: 616-746-4393
Vice President: JOE SLATER, 6780 Brunswick Rd, Holton, MI 49425; Phone: 616-821-2843
Executive Director: MARILYN SHY, 101 S. Main P.O. Box 539, Lake City, MI 49651; Phone: 616-839-3360; Fax: 616-839-3361; Email: mdistricts@aol.com
Administrative Assistant: CAROL BOGARD, 101 S. Main, P.O. Box 539, Lake City, MI 49651; Phone: 616-839-3360; Fax: 616-839-3361
Secretary and Treasurer, Alternate Board Member: RODNEY DRAGICEVICH, 29396 Heritage Lane, PawPaw, MI 49079; Phone: 616-375-3005

MICHIGAN AUDUBON SOCIETY
6011 W. St. Joseph, Suite 403, P.O. Box 80527, Lansing, MI 48908-0527
Phone: 517-886-9144; Fax: 517-886-9466
Founded: 1904; Membership: 8,500
Scope: Statewide
Description: The Michigan Audubon Society works to protect the Great Lakes ecosystem for people and wildlife. The society conducts scientific research, educates, and advocates for the protection of species and habitats through five major centers, three affiliate organizations, forty-six chapters, and sanctuaries totalling over 5,000 acres of land.
Contact(s):
President: NANCY TAR, 1381 West Blvd., Berkley, MI 48072
Secretary: DAVID YOUNG, 1223 Holyrood, Midland, MI 48640
Treasurer: CHARLES MACDONALD, 945 Tihart, Okemos, MI 48864; Phone: 517-339-0427
1st Vice President: LORETTA GOLD, 143 Lillie Ave., Battle Creek, MI 49015
2nd Vice President: GARY SIEGRIST, 11772 Trist Rd., Grass Lake, MI 49240
Business Manager: EILEEN SCAMEHORN
Editor-in-Chief: JULIE CRAVES
Editor-in-Chief: JOHN ELDER
Publication(s): *Jack-Pine Warbler; Michigan Birds & Natural History*
Keyword(s): Birds, EcoAction, Environmental and Conservation Education, Land Preservation

MICHIGAN B.A.S.S. CHAPTER FEDERATION
ATTN: 1010 S. West Ave., Jackson, MI 49203
Phone: 517-789-1008
Scope: Statewide
Description: An organization of Bassmaster chapters, affiliated with the Bass Anglers Sportsman Society, organized to fight pollution, assist state and national conservation agencies in their efforts, and teach the young people of our country good conservation practice. Dedicated to the realistic conservation of our water resources.
Contact(s):
President: JIM RICE, 1010 South West Ave., Jackson, MI 49203; Phone: 517-789-1008
Conservation Director: GLENN COOK, 1514 Tacoma, Flint, MI 48503; Phone: 810-232-2970

NON-GOVERNMENTAL ORGANIZATIONS

MICHIGAN ENVIRONMENTAL COUNCIL
115 W. Allegan, Suite 10B, Lansing, MI 48933
Phone: 517-487-9539; Fax: 917-487-9541; Email: mlenvcouncil@igc.apc.org
Founded: 1980
Scope: Statewide
Description: A statewide coalition of 37 citizen environmental and conservation organizations united to protect and enhance Michigan's human and natural environment and to ensure its sustainability. The Council acts through networking, advocacy, education, and research.
Contact(s):
Chairman: ELIZABETH HARRIS, E. Michigan Environmental Action Council 21220 W. 14 Mile Rd., Bloomfield Township, MI 48301-4000; Phone: 313-258-5188
Executive Director: CAROL K. MISSELDINE
Secretary (At-Large Board Member): JOEL HUNT
Vice Chair: ALISON HORTON
Vice Chair: ALICE AUSTIN; Phone: 517-663-2400
Publication(s): *Michigan Environmental Report; Land: Michigan's Promise, Michigan's Future; Groundwater at Risk: A Citizen's Guide*
Keyword(s): Communications, Energy, Land Use Planning, Pollution Prevention, Urban Environment

MICHIGAN FOREST ASSOCIATION
1558 Barrington St., Ann Arbor, MI 48103-5603
Phone: 734-913-9167
Founded: 1951; Membership: 1,100
Scope: Statewide
Description: A statewide organization affiliated with the National Woodland Owners Association, with concern for the full spectrum of forest activity, enterprise, development, and conservation in Michigan.
Contact(s):
President: JOHN F. VAN DYKE
Vice President: BYRON SAILOR
Treasurer: ALLAN KERTON
Executive Director: McCLAIN SMITH
Editor: DON INGLE, P.O. Box 78, Baldwin, MI 48103
Editor: McCLAIN SMITH
Publication(s): *MFA Leaves; Michigan Forests*
Keyword(s): Forests and Forestry

MICHIGAN LAND USE INSTITUTE
P.O. Box 228, Benzonia, MI 49016
Phone: 616-882-4723; Fax: 616-882-7350; Email: mlui@traverse.com; WWW: www.mlui.org
Founded: 1995; Membership: 1,100
Scope: Statewide
Description: Michigan Land Use Institute is a nonprofit environmental economic policy research organization focused on reforming land use policy and curbing sprawl.
Contact(s):
Treasurer: RICHARD HITCHINGHAM
Executive Director: KEITH SCHNEIDER
Managing Director: HANS VOSS
Publication(s): *Great Lakes Bulletin; Rivers at Risk; Benzie County Wetlands - A Resource Worth Protecting*
Keyword(s): Environment, Environmental and Conservation Education, Environmental Protection

MICHIGAN NATURAL AREAS COUNCIL
University of Michigan, Botanical Gardens, 1800 N. Dixboro Rd., Ann Arbor, MI 48105
Email: mnac@cyberspace.org; WWW: www.cyberspace.org/~mnacl
Founded: 1947; Membership: 150
Scope: Statewide
Description: The Michigan Natural Areas Council promotes the preservation of outstanding natural areas, prepares reports based on field investigations, and serves as an informed-citizens advisory on such matters.
Contact(s):
Chair: DR. SYLVIA M. TAYLOR, 10353J udd Rd., Willis, MI 48191; Phone: 313-461-9390; Email: smtaylot@umich.edu
Treasurer: CHRISTOPHER L. GRAHAM, 725 Peninsula Ct., Ann Arbor, MI 48105; Email: kfdh64@prodigy.com
Editor: ROBERT GRESE
Vice Chair: ROBERT GRESE, 1512 Carlton, Ann Arbor, MI 48103; Email: bgrese@umich.edu
Publication(s): *Michigan Natural Areas News and Views (natural areas, endangered species, and relevant conservation news*
Keyword(s): Endangered and Threatened Species, Flowers, Plants, and Trees, Islands, Nature Preservation, Prairies, Wilderness

MICHIGAN NATURE ASSOCIATION
7981 Beard Rd., Box 102, Avoca, MI 48006-0102
Phone: 313-324-2626
Founded: 1952; Membership: 1,400
Scope: Statewide
Description: Purpose is to acquire and maintain nature sanctuaries that contain examples of Michigan's original flora and fauna. Holds title to 149 properties totaling 7,702 acres in 52 counties of Michigan. MNA lands contain 206 of Michigan's endangered, threatened, and of special concern species. Available to public for nature education and appreciation.
Contact(s):
President: KAREN WEINGARDEN; Phone: 810-546-5429
Editor: BERTHA DAUBENDIEK, Box 102, Avoca, MI 48006
Executive Secretary and Treasurer: BERTHA DAUBENDIEK; Phone: 810-324-2626
Publication(s): *Members' Newsletter; MNA Nature Sanctuary Guidebook 7th edition, 1993; MNA--In Retrospect: A Celebration of 28 Years of Preserving Michigan's Wild and Rare Natural Lands 1960-1988; Walking Paths in Keweenaw; In Our Trust (1990-91, 30-minute Wildlife Video)*
Keyword(s): Birds, Endangered and Threatened Species, Flowers, Plants, and Trees, Insects and Butterflies, Land Preservation, Land Purchase, Mammals, Natural Areas, Natural History, Nature Preservation, Nongame Wildlife, Prairies, Reptiles and Amphibians, Wetlands, Wildlife and Wildlife Habitat

MICHIGAN UNITED CONSERVATION CLUBS, INC.
2101 Wood St., Lansing, MI 48912-3728
Phone: 517-371-1041; Fax: 517-371-1505; Email: mucc@mucc.org; WWW: www.mucc.org
Scope: Statewide
Description: A representative statewide organization, affiliated with the National Wildlife Federation, dedicated to the protection and enhancement of wildlife and its habitat through public education and government interaction.
Contact(s):
Executive Director: JIM GOODHEART
President: WILLIAM WHIPPEN
Alternate Representative: JAMES CAMPBELL
Editor: DENNIS KNICKERBOCKER
Representative: ARTHUR DITTMAR
Publication(s): *Michigan Out-of-Doors*

MICHIGAN WILDLIFE HABITAT FOUNDATION
6425 S. Pennsylvania, Suite 9, Lansing, MI 48911
Phone: 517-882-3110; Fax: 517-882-3687
Founded: 1982; Membership: 25,000
Scope: Statewide
Description: The Michigan Wildlife Habitat Foundation is a nonprofit membership organization, which restores and improves wildlife habitat through cost-effective projects. We want future generations to enjoy the same world of natural experiences we do today.
Contact(s):
Chairman: DR. MARK MERCER
President: MICHAEL DePOLO
Executive Director: DENNIS FIJALKOWSKI
Publication(s): *Wildlife Volunteer, The*

MID-ATLANTIC COUNCIL OF WATERSHED ASSOCIATIONS
12 Morris Rd., Ambler, PA 19002
Scope: National
Description: Promotes exchange of ideas on citizen watershed association activities and advises any group wishing to start a new watershed association.
Contact(s):
President: LORAH HOPKINS, 960 Old Mill Rd., Wyomissing, PA 19610; Phone: 215-372-3916
Secretary: ROBERT STRUBLE JR., Brandywine Valley Association, Inc. 1760 Unionville-Wawaset Rd., West Chester, PA 19382; Phone: 215-793-1090
Treasurer: DAVID FROCHLICH, Wissahickon Valley Watershed Associatoin, 12 Morris Rd., Ambler, PA 19002; Phone: 215-646-8866
Keyword(s): Environmental and Conservation Education, Land Use Planning, Rivers, Water Pollution, Water Resources

MID-ATLANTIC FISHERY MANAGEMENT COUNCIL
300 S. New St. Rm. 2115, Dover, DE 19901
Phone: 302-674-2331; Fax: 302-674-5399
Founded: 1976
Scope: National
Description: Mid-Atlantic Fishery Management Council is one of eight regional fishery management councils established to serve as planning units to carry out provisions of Magnuson Fishery Conservation and Management Act, charged with responsibility to prepare fishery management plans for implmentation by Secretary of Commerce.
Contact(s):
Chairman: DR. LEE G. ANDERSON, College of Marine Studies, University of Delaware, Newark, DE 19711; Phone: 302-831-2650
Executive Director: JOHN C. BRYSON, MAFMC, 300 S. New St., Rm. 2115, Dover, DE 19901; Phone: 302-674-2331
Vice Chairman: WILLIAM WELLS III, Wells Scallop Company, P.O. Box 600, Seaford, VA 23696; Phone: 804-898-8512
Publication(s): *Newsletter*
Keyword(s): Aquatic Habitats, Endangered and Threatened Species, Fisheries, Marine Mammals, Wetlands

MINERAL POLICY CENTER
1612 K St., NW, Suite 808, Washington, DC 20006
Phone: 202-887-1872; Fax: 202-887-1875
Founded: 1988; Membership: 2,500
Scope: National
Description: MPC is a national environmental membership organization. The Center is a research, education, and advocacy organization dedicated to cleaning up and preventing pollution from mining. The Center works for common sense environmental reform of mineral policy. The Center produces educational materials on mining impact, offers training for, and works closely with, citizens groups affected by mining damage.
Contact(s):
President: STEPHEN D'ESPOSITO
Board of Director: THOMAS A. TROYER
Board of Director: KARIN P. SHELDON
Board of Director: SHARON K. BENJAMIN
Board of Directors Chairman: J. MICHAEL MCCLOSKEY
Communication Director: SUSAN A BRACKETT
Vice President for Operations: VALERIE KEELS
Publication(s): *MPC News; Mining Conservation Directory; Canary Calls*
Keyword(s): Environmental Law, Public Lands, Solid Waste, Toxic Substances, Water Pollution

MINNESOTA ASSOCIATION OF SOIL AND WATER CONSERVATION DISTRICTS
ATTN: President, 775 Riverwood Dr., St. Paul, MN 55116
Scope: Statewide
Contact(s):
President and Board Member: VERN WILKER, 775 Riverwood Drive, Owatonna, MN 55060; Phone: 507-451-3655; Fax: 507-444-0172
Vice President: OWEN KNUTSON, 50066 County 43 Blvd., Pine Island, MN 55963; Phone: 507-356-8781; Fax: 507-732-7651; Email: knutsonoa@pioneer.com
Treasurer: RICHARD ZUPP, Rt. 4 Box 139, Pipestone, MN 56164; Phone: 507-825-3024
Executive Director: D'WAYNE DEZIEL, 790 Cleveland Ave. S. Suite 216, St. Paul, MN 55116; Phone: 612-690-9028; Fax: 612-690-9065; Email: dwaynez@pioneerplanet.infi.net

MINNESOTA B.A.S.S. CHAPTER FEDERATION
ATTN: President, 4822 Freemont Ave., North Minneapolis, MN 55430
Phone: 612-522-6567
Scope: Statewide
Description: An organization of Bassmaster chapters, affiliated with the Bass Anglers Sportsman Society, organized to fight pollution, assist state and national conservation agencies in their efforts, and teach the young people of our country good conservation practices. Dedicated to the realistic conservation of our water resources.
Contact(s):
President: DUANE CASE, 4822 Freemont Ave., North Minneapolis, MN 55430; Phone: 612-522-6567
Conservation Director: JOHN SCHNEIDER, 2865 Matilda St., Roseville, MN 55113; Phone: 612-481-8685

MINNESOTA CENTER FOR ENVIRONMENTAL ADVOCACY (MCEA)
26 E. Exchange St., Suite 206, St. Paul, MN 55101-2264
Phone: 651-223-5969
Founded: 1974; Membership: 800
Scope: Statewide
Description: The Minnesota Center for Environmental Advocacy is a nonprofit organization that uses law, science, and research to protect Minnesota's natural resources, wildlife, and the health of its people.
Contact(s):
Chair: ANGUS M. VAUGHAN
Secretary: STEVEN M. HOFFMAN
Treasurer: GAYLE PETERSON
Executive Director: PETER H. BACHMAN
Vice Chair: ROBERT G. DUNN
Publication(s): *Advocacy Update*
Keyword(s): Air Quality and Pollution, Feedlots and Pollution, Legal Advocacy, Pesticides, Toxic Reduction, Water Quality

MINNESOTA CONSERVATION FEDERATION
551 S. Snelling Ave., #B, St. Paul, MN 55116-1525
Phone: Phone & Fax: 612-690-3077; Email: mncf@mtn.org
Scope: Statewide
Description: A representative statewide organization, affiliated with the National Wildlife Federation, dedicated to the protection and enhancement of wildlife and its habitat through public education and government interaction.
Contact(s):
President: DAVE MORAN
Affiliate Representative: FRED PRINDLE
Editor: SHANNON LONG
Publication(s): *Minnesota Out-of-Doors*

Keyword(s): Aquatic Habitats, Renewable Resources, Terrestrial Habitats, Wetlands, Wildlife and Wildlife Habitat

NON-GOVERNMENTAL ORGANIZATIONS

MINNESOTA FORESTRY ASSOCIATION
P.O. Box 496, Grand Rapids, MN 55744
Phone: 218-326-3000
Membership: 1,200
Scope: Statewide
Description: A nonprofit organization, affiliated with the National Woodland Owners Association, dedicated to promoting the high potential advantages of intensive scientific management of forests, woodlots, and other renewable resources.
Contact(s):
President: DARRELL LAUBER; Phone: 218-326-5791
Vice President: JAMES LEMMERMAN, Duluth, MN ; Phone: 218-624-3847
Secretary: LANSIN R. HAMILTON; Phone: 218-534-3398
Treasurer: DAVID PARENT, Andover, MN ; Phone: 612-753-1619
Executive Director and Editor: TERRANCE WEBER
Publication(s): *Minnesota Better Forests*
Keyword(s): Forests and Forestry

MINNESOTA GROUND WATER ASSOCIATION
4779 126th St., N., White Bear Lake, MN 55110-5910
Founded: 1981; Membership: 500
Scope: Statewide
Description: MGWA's mission is to advocate the wise use and protection of gound water, and to provide education to the users of Minnesota's ground water.
Contact(s):
President: PAULA A. BERGER; Phone: 612-343-0510; Fax: 612-343-0506
Treasurer: PAUL BULGER; Phone: 651-296-7827
Advertising Manager: LEIGH HARROD; Phone: 651-4748678
Business Manager for Publications: DR. JEANETTE LEETE; Phone: 651-426-8795; Fax: 651-426-5449
Editor: TOM CLARK; Phone: 651-296-8580; Fax: 651-297-7709; Email: tom.p.clark@pca.state.mn.us
Past President: RAY WUOLO; Phone: 612-832-2696; Fax: 612-832-2601; Email: rwuolo@barr.com
Secretary and Membership: JAN FALTEISEK; Phone: 651-296-3877; Fax: 651-296-0445; Email: jan.falteisek@dnr.state.mn.us
Publication(s): *Minnesota Ground Water Association Newsletter; Minnesota Ground Water Association Directory*
Keyword(s): Environmental and Conservation Education, Environmental Planning, Environmental Preservation

MINNESOTA HERPETOLOGICAL SOCIETY (James Ford Bell Museum of Natural History)
10 Church St., SE, University of Minnesota, Minneapolis, MN 55455-0104
Phone: 612-624-7065
Founded: 1981; Membership: 350
Scope: Statewide
Description: A nonprofit organization chartered for the conservation and preservation of reptiles and amphibians, through the education of members and the public.
Publication(s): *MHS Newsletter*
Keyword(s): Endangered and Threatened Species, Environmental and Conservation Education, Nature Preservation, Nongame Wildlife, Reptiles and Amphibians

MINNESOTA NATIVE PLANT SOCIETY
220 Biological Sciences Center, 1445 Gortner Ave., University of Minnesota, St. Paul, MN 55108
Founded: 1982; Membership: 306
Scope: Statewide
Description: A nonprofit organization dedicated to education about native Minnesota flora and to its preservation and conservation.
Contact(s):
President: CHAR BEZANSON; Phone: 507-646-3605
Vice President: CHARLES UMBANHOWAR; Phone: 507-645-4386
Secretary: CHRIS DRASSAL; Phone: 612-444=9753
Treasurer: PAT RYAN; Phone: Editor: THOR KOMMEDAHL; Phone: 612-625-3164
Publication(s): *Minnesota Plant Press*
Keyword(s): Biodiversity, Endangered and Threatened Species, Environmental and Conservation Education, Environmental Preservation, Prairies

MINNESOTA ORNITHOLOGISTS' UNION
James Ford Bell Museum of Natural History, 10 Church St. SE, University of Minnesota, Minneapolis, MN 55455
Founded: 1937; Membership: 1,400
Scope: Statewide
Description: Statewide organization contributing to scientific knowledge through bird observations; stimulating public interest in birds; and working to preserve bird life and bird habitat.
Contact(s):
President: ANN KESSEN, 31145 Gensis Ave., Stacey, MN 55079
Treasurer: MARK CITSAY, 210 Mariner Way, Bayport, MN 55003
Editor: ANTHONY HERTZEL, 8461 Pleasant View Dr., Mounds View, MN 55112
Editor: JIM WILLIAMS, 5239 Cranberry Lane, Webster, WI 54893
Membership Secretary: ELIZABETH BELL, 5868 Pioneer Rd., St. Paul, MN 55071
Recording Secretary: AL BATT, Rt 1 Box 56A, Hartland, MN 56042
Publication(s): *Loon, The; Minnesota Birder*
Keyword(s): Biology, Birds, Geography, Nongame Wildlife, Waterfowl

MINNESOTA PARKS AND TRAILS COUNCIL
26 Exchange St. E, Suite 214, St. Paul, MN 55101-2264
Phone: 612-281-0508
Founded: 1954; Membership: 1,000
Scope: Statewide
Description: The mission of the Council is to further the establishment, development, and enhancement of parks and trails within the state of Minnesota, and to encourage their prudent use and protection.
Contact(s):
President: NADINE BLACKLOCK
Vice President: MARK STROBEL
Vice President: ELEANOR WINSTON
Secretary: MARC HUGUNIN
Treasurer: PETER SEED
Executive Director: DORIAN GRILLEY
Publication(s): *Newsletter*
Keyword(s): Environmental and Conservation Education, Environmental Preservation, Land Purchase, Outdoor Recreation, Public Lands

MINNESOTA WILDLIFE HERITAGE FOUNDATION, INC.
5701 Normandale Rd., Suite 325, Minneapolis, MN 55424
Phone: 612-925-1923
Scope: Statewide
Description: Formed to promote the idea of charitable giving for conservation purposes and to assist people in making charitable donations of property for wildlife habitat.
Contact(s):
President: JAMES MADY, 7338 Frontier Trail, Chanhassen, MN 55317
Secretary and Legal Counsel: LAURENCE F. KOLL, 633 Sunset Ln., Mendota Heights, MN 55118; Phone: 612-291-9155
Vice President and Director: HUGH C. PRICE, 4424 Dunham Dr., Edina, MN 55435; Phone: 612-925-2486

MINNESOTA WINGS SOCIETY, INC.
P.O. Box 11323, Minneapolis, MN 55411
Phone: 612-588-2966
Founded: 1978; Membership: 200
Scope: Statewide
Description: To present a program to high school students called "Sight and Save Wildlife Management." This program helps students and enables them to improve wildlife habitat around some of the species they see every day.

NON-GOVERNMENTAL ORGANIZATIONS

Contact(s):
President: THURMAN TUCKER, 1321 N. Irving Ave., Minneapolis, MN 55411; Phone: 612-588-2466
Vice President: DAVID DONNA, 4200 IDS Center, 80 S. 8th St., Minneapolis, MN 55402; Phone: 612-371-3211
Secretary: MARTIN HANSON, 1530 Quinlan Ave., So., St. Croix Beach, MN 55043; Phone: 612-436-8242
Treasurer: JIM McLELLAN, 10273 Yellow Cir. Dr., Minnetonka, MN 55343; Phone: 612-933-2263
Publication(s): *Wings (newsletter*
Keyword(s): Birds, Environmental and Conservation Education, Land Preservation, Wildlife and Wildlife Habitat, Wildlife Management

MISSISSIPPI ASSOCIATION OF CONSERVATION DISTRICTS, INC.
ATTN: President, P.O. Box 23005, Jackson, MS 38922
Scope: Statewide
Contact(s):
President and Board Member: DARYL BURNEY, P.O. Box 603, Coffeeville, MS 38922; Phone: 601-675-2786; Fax: 601-675-2786
1st Vice President: BENNY GOFF, 250044 Yellow Bluff Rd, Lucedale, MS 39452; Phone: 601-588-6362
2nd Vice President: MARC CURTIS, P.O. Box 958, Leland, MS 38756; Phone: 601-686-2321
Secretary and Treasurer: GALE MARTIN, P.O. Box 23005, Jackson, MS 39225-3005; Phone: 601-354-7645; Fax: 601-354-6628

MISSISSIPPI B.A.S.S. CHAPTER FEDERATION
ATTN: President, 404 Meadowlane, Aberdeen, MS 39730
Phone: 601-369-8290
Scope: Statewide
Description: An organization of Bassmaster chapters, affiliated with the Bass Anglers Sportsman Society, organized to fight pollution, assist state and national conservation agencies in their efforts, and teach the young people of our country good conservation practices. Dedicated to the realistic conservation of our water resources.
Contact(s):
President: JOHN HAMILTON, 404 Meadowlane, Aberdeen, MS 39730; Phone: 601-369-8290
Conservation Director: BILLY LING, 50012 Ling Lane, Amory, MS 38821; Phone: 601-256-5428

MISSISSIPPI INTERSTATE COOPERATIVE RESOURCE ASSOCIATION
P.O. Box 774, Bettendorf, IA 52722-0774
Phone: 309-793-5811
Founded: 1989; Membership: 180
Scope: National
Description: An interstate organization of 28 state departments of conservation and natural resources working in collaboration with federal agencies, Native American tribes, and other interests to improve the conservation, development, management, and utilization of interjurisdictional fishery resources in the Mississippi River basin through improved coordination and communication among the responsible management entities.
Contact(s):
Chairman: MARION CONOVER, Iowa Department of Natural Resources, E. Ninth and Grand Ave., Wallace Bldg., Des Moines, IA 50319-0034
Coordinator and Executive Secretary: JERRY L. RASMUSSEN, P.O. Box 774, Bettendorf, IA 52722-0774
Vice Chairman: BILL REEVES, Tennessee Wildlife Resources Agency, P.O. Box 40747, Ellington Agricultural Center, Nashville, TN 37204
Publication(s): *River Crossings; Other Periodic Reports*
Keyword(s): Endangered and Threatened Species, Fisheries, Rivers, Sport Fishing, Water Resources

MISSISSIPPI NATIVE PLANT SOCIETY
Mississippi Museum of Natural Science, 111 N. Jefferson St., Jackson, MS 39201
Founded: 1981; Membership: 300
Scope: Statewide
Description: The Mississippi Native Plant Society promotes the study and use of native and naturalized species of Mississippi, their use in landscaping, the appreciation of natural ecological communities of the state, and the conservation or preservation of these species, habitats and plant associations, using the principles of conservation biology and ecosystem management.
Contact(s):
President: RONALD WIELAND; Phone: 601-354-7303; Fax: 601-354-7227
Vice President: LIZ COX, 52 Cable Ridge Rd., Perkinston, MS 39573; Phone: 601-928-5837
Secretary and Treasurer: DEBORA MANN, 114 Auburn Dr., Clinton, MS 39056-6002; Phone: 601-974-1415
Publication(s): *Mississippi Native Plants*
Keyword(s): Environmental and Conservation Education, Flowers, Plants, and Trees, Landscape Architecture, Natural History

MISSISSIPPI RIVER BASIN ALLIANCE
2105 First Ave., South, Suite 301, Minneapolis, MN 55404
Phone: 612-870-3441; Fax: 612-870-4846; Email: mrbaoffice@mrba.org; WWW: www.mrba.org
Founded: 1992; Membership: 115
Scope: Regional
Description: To protect and restore the ecological, economic, cultural, historical, and recreational resources in the Basin, and to eliminate barriers of race, class, and economic status which divide us in the quest to achieve these purposes.
Contact(s):
President: DARRYL MALEK-WILEY, Sierra Club, 618 Adams St., New Orleans, LA 70118; Phone: 504-865-8708
Vice President: BILL REDDING S, Sierra Club, Midwest Office, 214 N. Henry St., Suite 203, Madison, WI 53703; Phone: 608-257-4994
Secretary: MICHELLE THELEN, C.U.B.E., 405 N. 8th St., Montevideo, MN 56265; Phone: 320-269-9326
Treasurer: MICHELE FROME, Soil and Water Conservation Society, 10802 Lockridge Dr., Silver Springs, MD 20901; Phone: 301-593-7814
Executive Director: TIMOTHY SULLIVAN, 2105 First Ave. South, Minneapolis, MN 55404; Phone: 612-870-3441
Publication(s): *Alliance Newsletter; Mississippi River Basin Directory*
Keyword(s): Greenways, Navigation, People of Color in the Environment, Rivers, Water Quality, Wetlands

MISSISSIPPI WILDLIFE FEDERATION
P.O. Box 1814, Jackson, MS 39215-1814
Phone: 601-353-6922; Fax: 601-352-3437; Email: mwf@netdoor.com
Scope: Statewide
Description: A representative statewide organization, affiliated with the National Wildlife Federation, dedicated to the protection and enhancement of wildlife and its habitat through public education and government interaction.
Contact(s):
President: LONNIE BAILEY
Executive Director: MARLA HUFFSTATLER
Affiliate Representative: BOB FAIRBANK
Alternate Representative: JIMMY BULLOCK
Editor: ALAN HUFFMAN
Publication(s): *Mississippi Wildlife Magazine*

NON-GOVERNMENTAL ORGANIZATIONS

MISSOURI ASSOCIATION OF SOIL AND WATER CONSERVATION DISTRICTS
ATTN: President, Rt. 2 Box 7, Tarkio, MO 64491
Scope: Statewide
Contact(s):
Vice President, Alternate Board Member: SAM BRUCE GRAVES SR., Rt. 2 Box 7, Tarkio, MO 64491; Phone: 660-736-4368
Treasurer: DAVID DIX, P.O. Box 756, Eminence, MO 65466; Phone: 573-226-3787
Executive Secretary: PEGGY LEMONS, 1209 Biscayne Dr., Jefferson City, MO 65109; Phone: 573-893-5188; Fax: 573-893-7328; Email: peggy@mojefferso.fsc.usda.gov
President and Board Member: STEVE HOPPER, Rt. 5 Box 132, Chillicothe, MO 64601; Phone: 660-639-2575

MISSOURI AUDUBON COUNCIL
619 Norris Dr., Jefferson City, MO 65109
Phone: 314-635-6018
Membership: 9,000
Scope: Statewide
Description: A statewide council composed of delegates from 14 National Audubon chapters and the Audubon Society of Missouri. Formed to coordinate efforts on various conservation and environmental issues in Missouri. Advised and assisted by the National Audubon Society.
Contact(s):
Chairperson: KAREN UHLENHUTH, 3714 E. Roanoke Dr., Kansas City, MO 64111; Phone: 816-561-1371
Keyword(s): Biodiversity, Birds, Endangered and Threatened Species, Environment, Water Quality

MISSOURI B.A.S.S. CHAPTER FEDERATION
ATTN: President, 29 Eagles Way Ln., Lakes St. Louis, MO 63367
Phone: 314-561-1139; WWW: www.geocities.com/yosemite/4194/
Scope: Statewide
Description: An organization of Bassmaster chapters, affiliated with the Bass Anglers Sportsman Society, organized to fight pollution, assist state and national conservation agencies in their efforts, and teach the young people of our country good conservation practices. Dedicated to the realistic conservation of our water resources.
Contact(s):
President: RON HAUSER, 29 Eagles Way Ln., Lake St. Louis, MO 63367; Phone: 314-561-1139; Email: hausers@inlink.com
Conservation Director: JIM NOAH, 916 SE 5th St. Terrace, Lee's Summit, MO 64063; Phone: 816-524-8360(H)/816-854-3175(W); Email: jimnoah@compuserve.com

MISSOURI NATIVE PLANT SOCIETY
P.O. Box 20073, St. Louis, MO 63144-0073
Phone: 618-614-5964; Email: larry.morrison@scott.af.mil; WWW: www.missouri.edu/~umo-herb/monps
Founded: 1979; Membership: 350
Scope: Statewide
Description: To promote the enjoyment, preservation, conservation, restoration, and study of the flora native to Missouri; to educate the public about the values of the beauty, diversity, and environmental importance of indigenous vegetation; and to publish related information.
Contact(s):
President: LARRY R. MORRISON; Phone: 618-624-5964
Vice President: SUE HOLLIS; Phone: 816-561-9419
Secretary: LYNDA RICHARDS; Phone: 573-364-8567
Treasurer: JACK H. HARRIS; Phone: 314-894-9021
Editor: PAT HARRIS; Phone: 314-894-9021
Editor: GEORGE YATSKIEVYCH; Phone: 314-577-9522
Publication(s): *Missouriensis; Petal Pusher*
Keyword(s): Biodiversity, Endangered and Threatened Species, Environment, Environmental Preservation, Environmental Protection, Flowers, Plants, and Trees, Forest Management, Gardening and Horticulture, Natural Areas, Natural History, Nature Preservation, Prairies, Public Lands, Wetlands, Wildlands

MISSOURI PRAIRIE FOUNDATION
P.O. Box 200, Columbia, MO 65205
Fax: 573-442-0260; Email: qfreeman@mail.com.missouri.edu
Founded: 1966
Scope: Statewide
Description: A nonprofit citizens' group organized to ensure the preservation of native prairie along with associated plant and animal life by acquisition, management protection, control, and perpetuation of the prairie; to carry on educational programs; and to provide scientific research relative to native prairie.
Contact(s):
President: GEORGE D. NICHOLS; Phone: 417-682-8768
Vice President: DR. ELIZABETH A. GARRETT; Phone: 573-446-3778
Secretary: RUSSELL RUNGE; Phone: 573-581-8754
Treasurer: JOHN R. CLINE; Phone: 314-581-6566
Advisor to the Board: D. M. CHRISTISEN
Editor: CAROL DAVIT, 728 East Capitol, #2W, Jefferson City, MO 65101; Phone: 573-635-7036
Publication(s): *Missouri Prairie Journal*
Keyword(s): Biodiversity, Conservation of Protected Areas, Endangered and Threatened Species, Environmental and Conservation Education, Land Preservation, Land Purchase, Prairies

MONITOR INTERNATIONAL
154 Quiet Waters Pl., Annapolis, MD 21403
Phone: 410-268-5155; Fax: 410-268-8788; Email: info@monitorinternational.org; WWW: www.monitorinternational.org
Founded: 1978
Scope: International
Description: Monitor International is a nonprofit corporation, conserves biological diversity and cultural heritage, and promotes environmentally sustainable development or marine and freshwater ecosystems throughout the world.
Contact(s):
President: DAVID READ BARKER
Vice President: LISA BORRE
Secretary: JOHN DOLAN
Treasurer: RICHARD TOBIN
Board of Trustees Chairman: MILTON M. KAUFMANN
Publication(s): *Sustainable Development; Success Stories; Lake Toba-Lake Champlain Exchange*
Keyword(s): Coasts, Developing Countries, Lakes, Sustainable Development

MONO LAKE COMMITTEE
P.O. Box 29, Lee Vining, CA 93541
Phone: 760-647-6595
Founded: 1978; Membership: 18,000
Scope: Statewide
Description: The Mono Lake Committee is a nonprofit citizens' group dedicated to protecting and restoring the Mono Basin ecosystem; educating the public about Mono Lake and the impacts on the environment of excessive water use; and promoting cooperative solutions that protect Mono Lake and meet real water needs without transferring environmental problems to other areas.
Contact(s):
Chair: ED MANNING
Chair: SALLY GAINES
Secretary: TOM SOTO
Executive Director: FRANCIS SPIVY-WEBER; Phone: 310-316-0041
Editor: GEOFFREY McQUILKIN
Publication(s): *Mono Lake Newsletter; Mono Lake Guidebook; Plants of the Mono Basin; Geology of the Mono Basin*
Keyword(s): Birds, Lakes, Sustainable Development, Water Resources, Wetlands

NON-GOVERNMENTAL ORGANIZATIONS

MONTANA ASSOCIATION OF CONSERVATION DISTRICTS
ATTN: President, P.O. Box 562, Polson, MT 59680
Phone: 406-443-5711
Scope: Statewide
Contact(s):
President, Board Member: DENNIS DeVRIES, P.O. Box 562, Polson, MT 59860; Phone: 406-883-6848; Fax: 406-883-2356; Email: sddvsb@digisys.net
Vice President: LUTHER WATERLAND, P.O. Box 21, Ekalaka, MT 59324; Phone: 406-775-6347
Treasurer: DALE MARXER, 654 Millegan Rd., Great Falls, MT 59405; Phone: 406-866-3259
Administrative Secretary: JAN McINERNEY, 501 N. Sanders, Suite 2, Helena, MT 59601; Phone: 406-443-5711; Fax: 406-443-0174
Alternate Board Member: MARIEANNE HANSER, 624 Ave. C, Billings, MT 59102; Phone: 406-259-9655
Executive Vice President: MIKE VOLESKY, 501 N. Sanders, Suite 2, Helena, MT 59601; Phone: 406-443-5711; Fax: 406-449-0174; Email: macd@mt.net

MONTANA AUDUBON
P.O. Box 595, Helena, MT 59624
Phone: 406-443-3949; Email: mtaudubon@desktop.org
Founded: 1976
Scope: Statewide
Description: The statewide organizationl of the nine National Audubon Society chapters in Montana. The Montana Audubon is involved in education, research, conservation, and public advocacy on issues affecting Montana's birds, wildlife, and other natural heritage. We enable Montana's 2,600 Audubon members to work together for the Audubon cause.
Contact(s):
President: HOWARD STRAUSE, 1917 W. Hill Pl., Great Falls, MT 59404; Phone: 406-727-7516
Vice President: DOROTHY POULSEN, 42 Olive, Helena, MT 59601; Phone: 406-449-7129
Secretary: CHUCK CARLSON, P.O. Box 227, Ft. Peck, MT 59223; Phone: 406-526-3245
Treasurer: BEA VOGEL, 46 S. Howie, Helena, MT 59601; Phone: 406-442-1514
Executive Director: JANET ELLIS
Keyword(s): Biodiversity, Birds, Land Use Planning, Wetlands

MONTANA B.A.S.S. CHAPTER FEDERATION
ATTN: Conservation Director, 583 Greer's Ferry, Libby, MT 59923
Phone: 406-752-8164
Scope: Statewide
Description: An organization of Bassmaster chapters, affiliated with the Bass Anglers Sportsman Society, organized to fight pollution, assist state and national conservation agencies in their efforts, and teach the young people of our country good conservation practice. Dedicated to the realistic conservation of our water resources.
Contact(s):
President: STEVE McGUIRE, 221 Garland St., Kalispell, MT 59901; Phone: 406-752-8164
Conservation Director: BOB KREPPS, 583 Greer's Ferry, Libby, MT 59923; Phone: 406-293-6211

MONTANA ENVIRONMENTAL INFORMATION CENTER
P.O. Box 1184, Helena, MT 59624
Phone: 406-443-2520; Fax: 406-443-2507; Email: meic@desktop.org
Founded: 1973; Membership: 4,000
Scope: Statewide
Description: Overall purpose is to protect and restore Montana's natural environment. Educates and mobilizes citizens on Montana environmental issues to press for wise decisions at local, state, and federal levels. Priority issues include: Water quality, solid waste, hardrock mining, hazardous waste, environmental policy, air quality, land use planning, toxic chemicals, and energy conservation.

Contact(s):
Executive Director: JIM JENSEN
Board of Directors President: COLLEEN MURPHY
Board of Directors Vice President: PAT CLANCEY
Publication(s): *Down to Earth; Capitol Monitor; Blackfoot Activist*
Keyword(s): Air Quality, Energy, Land Use Planning, Mining, Solid Waste Management, Toxic Substances, Water Quality

MONTANA FOREST OWNERS ASSOCIATION
17975 Ryan's Ln., Evaro, MT 59802
Phone: 406-726-3787; Fax: 406-549-2287
Scope: Statewide
Description: A statewide organization affiliated with the National Woodland Owners Association, dedicated to the careful use and active enjoyment of private forest lands in Montana. Goals are achieved through active forestry education programs, public communications, networking, and political advocacy.
Contact(s):
President: THORN LIECHTY
Vice President: DAVE HEIN
Vice President: TOM CASTLES
Secretary: LAURA GREGORY
Treasurer: JIM HAVILAND
Publication(s): *Big Sky NIPF-TY Notes*

MONTANA LAND RELIANCE
P.O. Box 355, Helena, MT 59624
Phone: 406-443-7027; Email: mlredesktop.org
Scope: Statewide
Description: A private nonprofit land trust protecting and conserving ecologically and agriculturally significant land in Montana, as well as sharing knowledge of voluntary, private-sector land conservation techniques. Pioneering ways to assure a legacy of responsibly managed private land.
Contact(s):
President: SUSAN HEYNEMAN, Bench Ranch, Fishtail, MT 59028
Vice President: DUDE TYLER, Two River Ranch, HC89, Box 4306, Big Timber, MT 59011
Director of Development: JOHN WILSON
Director of Financial: WILLIAM LONG
Director of Glacier/Flathead Office: AMY EATON, P.O. Box 460, Bigfork, MT 59911; Phone: 406-837-2178; Email: mlrnw@digisys.net
Director of Lands: ROCK RINGLING
Secretary and Treasurer: GEORGE OLSEN, Galusha, Higgens & Galusha, Box 1699, Helena, MT 59601
Publication(s): *Annual Report; Montana Spaces; Better Trout Habitat; Tax Implications of Donated Conservation Easements: An Introduction to Conservation Easements*
Keyword(s): Agriculture, Environment, Environmental Protection, Fisheries, Forest Management, Land Preservation, Natural Areas, Nature Preservation, Open Space, Rivers, Water Resources, Watersheds, Wetlands, Wildlife and Wildlife Habitat

MONTANA LAND RELIANCE (Eastern Office)
P.O. Box 171, Billings, MT 59103
Phone: 406-259-1328; Email: mlr@mcn.net
Scope: Statewide

MONTANA WILDERNESS ASSOCIATION
P.O. Box 635, Helena, MT 59624
Phone: 406-443-7350; Fax: 406-443-0750; Email: mwa@desktop.org
Founded: 1958; Membership: 2,900
Scope: Statewide
Description: A nonprofit membership organization dedicated to the preservation and proper management of Montana's wild lands, including designated and de facto wilderness areas, national parks, national forests, wildlife refuges, and BLM lands in Montana. The Montana Wilderness Association has six chapter affiliates and four field offices.

NON-GOVERNMENTAL ORGANIZATIONS

Contact(s):
President: DENNIS TIGHE; Phone: 406-761-5463
Vice President: KEN SINAY; Phone: 406-586-1155
Director: BOB DECKER
Education Director: SUSAN MILES BRYAN
Program Director: JOHN GATCHELL
Publication(s): *Wild Montana; Wilderness Walks Program*
Keyword(s): Biodiversity, Forests and Forestry, Public Lands, Sustainable Ecosystems, Wildlife and Wildlife Habitat

MONTANA WILDLIFE FEDERATION
P.O. Box 1175, Helena, MT 59624-1175
Phone: 406-449-7604; Fax: 406-449-8946; Email: mwf@desktop.org; WWW: www.montanawildlife.com
Scope: Statewide
Description: A representative statewide organization, affiliated with the National Wildlife Federation, dedicated to the protection and enhancement of wildlife and its habitat through public education and government interaction.
Contact(s):
President: STAN FRASIER
Executive Director and Editor: TONY JEWETT
Affiliate Representative: KATHY HADLEY
Publication(s): *Montana Wildlife*

MOTE MARINE LABORATORY
1600 Ken Thompson Parkway, Sarasota, FL 34236
Phone: 941-388-4441; Fax: 941-388-4312; Email: info@mote.org
Founded: 1955; Membership: 4,000
Scope: National
Description: MML is an independent, nonprofit research organization dedicated to excellence in marine and environmental sciences. Since its inception, the laboratory's primary missions have been the pursuit of excellence in scientific research and the dissemination of information to the scientific community as well to the general public. MML operates a public aquarium and a marine science education and long distance learning program.
Contact(s):
Chairman: ALFRED GOLDSTEIN, 1600 Ken Thompson Pkwy, Sarasota, FL 34236
President: WILLIAM R. MOTE, 1600 Ken Thompson Pkwy, Sarasota, FL 34236
Secretary: J. ROBERT LONG, 1486 Hillview Dr., Sarasota, FL 34239
Treasurer: ROBERT R. NELSON, 1600 Ken Thompson Pkwy, Sarasota, FL 34236
Executive Director: DR. KUMAR MAHADEVAN, 1600 Ken Thompson Pkwy., Sarasota, FL 34236
Head of Arthur Vining Davis Library: SUSAN STOVER
Vice Chairman: FREDERICK M. DERR, 1600 Ken Thonpson Pkwy, Sarasota, FL 34236
Publication(s): *Mote News; Views from Mote; Mote Marine Laboratory Collected Papers (list upon request)*
Keyword(s): Biology, Chemistry, Dolphins, Endangered and Threatened Species, Environmental and Conservation Education, Fisheries, Manatees, Sea Turtles

MOUNT GRACE LAND CONSERVATION TRUST
137 N. Main St., New Salem, MA 01355
Phone: 978-544-7170; Fax: 978-544-3877; Email: mtgrace@shaysnet.com
Founded: 1987; Membership: 500
Scope: Statewide
Description: Mount Grace Land Conservation Trust is dedicated to the protection of forests, agricultural land, and other open space in North Central Massachusetts.
Contact(s):
President: SHAUN BENNETT
Keyword(s): Agriculture, Conservation of Protected Areas, Forest Management, Nature Preservation, Open Space

MOUNT SHASTA AREA AUDUBON SOCIETY
P.O. Box 530, Mount Shasta, CA 96067
Phone: 916-842-2537
Founded: 1971; Membership: 124
Scope: Statewide
Description: Protects, enhances, and enjoys the natural environment of the Mount Shasta region, including its birds, wildlife, forests, mountains, meadows, and waters.
Contact(s):
President: BETTE KOERNER
Secretary: WILLO BALFREY, 2934 Nighthawk Ln., Weed, CA 96094; Phone: 916-938-2342
Editor: MIKE HAUPTMAN; Phone: 916-842-2537
Publication(s): *Endeavor*

MOUNTAIN LION FOUNDATION
P.O. Box 1896, Sacramento, CA 95812
Phone: 916-442-2666; Fax: 916-442-2871; Email: MLF@mountainlion.org
Founded: 1986; Membership: 30,000
Scope: Statewide
Description: The Mountain Lion Foundation is a nonprofit conservation and education organization dedicated to protecting wildlife and their habitat throughout California.
Contact(s):
President: KATHY FLETCHER
Vice President: JOSEPH HURWITZ
Secretary: SHARON CAVALLO
Treasurer: TOBY COOPER
Executive Director: LYNN SADLER; Phone: 916-442-2666
Director of Conservation Programs: TOM MARTENS
Director of Education: CAITLIN RIVERS
Legal Program Director: J. WILLIAM YEATES
Publication(s): *Mountain Lion Update; Cougar: The American Lion; Preserving Cougar Country; Crimes Against the Wild: Poaching in California*
Keyword(s): Biodiversity, Conservation of Protected Areas, Endangered and Threatened Species, Environmental Law, Hunting, Land Preservation, Mammals, Nongame Wildlife, Predators, Wildlife and Wildlife Habitat, Wildlife Management

MOUNTAINEERS, THE (Conservation Division)
300 3rd Ave., W., Seattle, WA 98119
Phone: 206-284-6310
Founded: 1906; Membership: 15,000
Scope: Statewide
Description: The Mountaineers is a volunteer club that provides the opportunity for outdoor recreation and training for its members and strives to protect the environment through community outreach, education, and political action.
Contact(s):
President: MARCIA HANSON
Secretary: PETE BENGTSON
Treasurer: CRAIG ROWLEY
Executive Director: SUE WECKERLY
Conservation Chair: FRAN TROJE
Librarian: CHRISTI BURCHARD, The Mountaineers Library, 300 Third Ave., W., Seattle, WA 98119; Phone: 206-284-6310; Fax: 206-284-4977
Presiden Elect: JERRY SCOTT
Public Policy Manager: BROOKE DRURY
Publication(s): *Voice of the Wild Olympics*
Keyword(s): Coasts, Public Lands, Rivers, Wilderness, Wildlife and Wildlife Habitat

MULE DEER FOUNDATION, THE
1005 Terminal Way, Suite 170, Reno, NV 89502
Phone: 702-322-2800; Fax: 702-322-3421
Founded: 1988; Membership: 5,500
Scope: National
Description: The Mule Deer Foundation is a wildlife conservation organization that focuses on mule deer and their subspecies for habitat improvement.
Contact(s):
Chairman: GARY WILLIAMS, 19151 Kantara Ct., West Linn, OR 07068; Phone: 503-526-1426
President: RICH FLETCHER, 1508 Catalina Ct., Livermore, CA 94550; Phone: 925-373-6601
Publication(s): *Mule Deer*
Keyword(s): Environmental and Conservation Education, Hunting, Outdoor Recreation, Wildlife and Wildlife Habitat, Wildlife Management

MUSKIES, INC.
2301 7th St. N., Fargo, ND 58102
Phone: 701-239-9540
Founded: 1966; Membership: 6,864
Scope: National
Description: A nonprofit organization dedicated to establishing hatcheries and introducing the Muskellunge into suitable waters, abating water pollution, promoting a high quality muskellunge sport fishery, supporting selected conservation practices, promoting muskellunge research, disseminating muskellunge information, maintaining records of habits, growth, and range, and promoting good fellowship and sportsmanship.
Contact(s):
President: JIM SMITH, 1299 S. Carson Way, Aurora, CO 80012; Phone: 303-745-0630
President: STEVE BUDNIK, 5751 Monticello Way, Madison, WI 53719; Phone: 608-271-2872
Secretary: MIKE BRANDT, R.R. #7, Hayward, WI 54843; Phone: 715-462-3563
Treasurer: DAN RILEY, 3031 14th Avenue S., Moorhead, MN 56560; Phone: 218-236-8160
1st Vice President: SMOKEY SWENSON, 4023 Girard Avenue, Minneapolis, MN 55412; Phone: 612-522-9744
2nd Vice President: PAUL FRAMSTEAD, 7079 S. Uinta Street, Englewood, CO 80112; Phone: 303-694-3287
Administrative Secretary: PAT JOHNSON, 2301 7th St. N., Fargo, ND 58102; Phone: 701-239-9540
Editor: KEITH OGDEN, Rt. 1 Box 185, Cavalier, ND 58220; Phone: 701-265-8023
Publication(s): *Muskie*
Keyword(s): Lakes, Outdoor Recreation, Sport Fishing, Water Resources, Wildlife Management

NATIONAL 4-H COUNCIL
7100 Connecticut Ave., Chevy Chase, MD 20815-4999
Phone: 301-961-2915
Founded: 1976
Scope: National
Description: Builds partnerships for community youth development that value and involve youth in solving issues critical to their lives, their families, and society. 4-H Environmental Stewardship helps youth turn concern for the environment into action and develop balanced approaches to community problem-solving, protecting the environment, managing resources, and taking appropriate action.
Contact(s):
President and CEO: RICHARD SAUER, 7100 Connecticut Ave., Chevy Chase, MD 20815-4999; Phone: 301-961-2830; Fax: 301-961-2894
Project Director, Environmental Stewardship and Workforce Preparation: KASHYAP CHOKSI, 7100 Connecticut Ave., Chevy Chase, MD 20815-4999; Phone: 301-961-2833; Fax: 301-961-2894; Email: choksi@fourhcouncil.edu
Vice President and COO: DON FLOYD, 7100 Connecticut Ave., Chevy Chase, MD 20815-4999; Phone: 301-961-2825; Fax: 301-961-2894
Publication(s): *Program Highlights; On Common Ground; Annual Report; various curricula*
Keyword(s): Energy, Environmental and Conservation Education, Pesticides, Renewable Resources, Wildlife and Wildlife Habitat, Youth Organizations

NATIONAL ARBOR DAY FOUNDATION
100 Arbor Ave., Nebraska City, NE 68410
Phone: 402-474-5655
Founded: 1971; Membership: 1,000,000
Scope: National
Description: A nonprofit, membership organization, sponsors Trees for America, Arbor Day, Tree City USA, Conservation Trees, and Rain Forest Rescue educational programs. The Foundation publishes "Grow Your Own Tree," "Trees are Terrific," and " Arbor Day National Poster Contest Activities Guide," instructional units for grade schools.
Contact(s):
Chair: TONY DORRELL
Conference Services Director: KATHY AUSTIN, 211 N 12th St., Lincoln, NE 68508
Corporate Marketing Representative: KEVIN SANDER, 211 N 12th St., Lincoln, NE 68508
Editor: JOHN ROSENOW
Honorary Trustee and Chairman: STEWART UDALL
Information Director: GARY BRIENZO
President of Board of Trustees: JOHN ROSENOW
Program Director: MARY YAGER, 211 N. 12th St., Lincoln, NE 68508
Vice Chair: PRESTON COLE, 211 N. 12th St., Lincoln, NE 68508
Publication(s): *Arbor Day; Tree City USA Bulletin; Conservation Trees booklet; Celebrate Arbor Day booklet; Library of Trees*
Keyword(s): Environmental and Conservation Education, Flowers, Plants, and Trees, Forests and Forestry, Soil Conservation, Urban Forestry

NATIONAL ASSOCIATION FOR INTERPRETATION
P.O. Box 2246, Fort Collins, CO 80522
Phone: 970-484-8283/1-888-900-8283
Founded: 1961
Scope: National
Description: A nonprofit professional organization serving 3,500 members, employed by agencies and organizations concerned with natural and cultural resources, conservation and management, and with the interpretation of the natural, and historical environment as a service to the public.
Contact(s):
President: CEM BASMAN, So. Illinois University, Dept. of Forestry, Carbondale, IL 62901-4411; Phone: 618-453-7476; Fax: 618-453-7475; Email: cbasman@aol.com
Executive Director: DR. TIM MERRIMAN, P.O. Box 2246, Fort Collins, CO 80522; Phone: 970-484-8283; Fax: 970-484-8179; Email: naiexec@aol.com
Editor: NANCY NICHOLS, Communication Director of NAI, P.O. Box 2246, Fort Collins, CO 80522; Phone: 970-484-8283; Email: naicom@aol.com
Publication(s): *Legacy; NAI News; Jobs in Interpretation; Journal of Interpretation Research*
Keyword(s): Communications, Environmental and Conservation Education, Historic Preservation, Internships, Natural History

NATIONAL ASSOCIATION OF BIOLOGY TEACHERS
11250 Roger Bacon Dr. #19, Reston, VA 20190-5202
Phone: 703-471-1134 or 800-406-0775; Email: nabter@aol.com
Founded: 1938; Membership: 7,500
Scope: National
Description: The only national association specifically organized to assist teachers in the improvement of biology/life science teaching.

NABT offers teachers an opportunity to develop professionally through its journal, annual convention, summer workshops, and other publication programs.
Contact(s):
President: VIVIANLEE WARD, Access Excellence-Genentech, Inc., Mail Stop 16B, 460 Point San Bruno Blvd., South San Francisco, CA 94080; Phone: 650-225-8750; Email: vlward@gene.com
Executive Director: DR. WAYNE W. CARLEY, NABT, 11250 Roger Bacon Drive, #19, Reston, VA 20190-5202; Phone: 703-471-1134 or 800-406-0775; Email: wcarley@aol.com
Editor: RANDY MOORE, College of Arts & Sciences, University of Louisville, Louisville, KY 40292; Phone: 502-852-6490; Email: r0moor01@homer.louisville.edu
Managing Editor: CHRISTINE CHANTRY, NABT, 11250 Roger Bacon Drive, #19, Reston, VA 20190-5202; Phone: 703-471-1134 or 800-406-0775; Email: nabter@aol.com
Past President: ALAN McCORMACK, 9280 Lake Murray Blvd., Unit A, San Diego, CA 92119; Phone: 619-594-4807; Email: amccorma@mail.sdsu.edu
President-Elect: RICHARD D. STOREY, Chair, Dept. of Biology, The Colorado College, Colorado Springs, CO 80903; Phone: 719-389-6406; Email: rstorey@cc.colorado.edu
Secretary and Treasurer: CATHERINE WILCOXSON, Department of Biological Sciences Northern Arizona University, P.O. Box 5640, Flagstaff, AZ 86011-5640; Phone: 520-523-7026; Email: catherine.wilcoxson@nau.edu
Publication(s): *American Biology Teacher, The; News and Views; The Monograph Series*
Keyword(s): Biology, Biotechnology, Environmental and Conservation Education, Zoology

NATIONAL ASSOCIATION OF CONSERVATION DISTRICTS
Headquarters, 509 Capitol Ct. NE, Washington, DC 20002
Phone: 202-547-6223; Fax: 202-547-6450; Email: info@nacdnet.org; WWW: www.nacdnet.org
Founded: 1946
Scope: National
Description: A nonprofit organization serving as the national instrument of its membership - 3,000 local districts and 54 state and territorial associations. Conservation districts, local subdivisions of state government, work to promote the conservation, wise use and orderly development of land, water, forests, wildlife, and related natural resources.
Contact(s):
President: RUDY RICE, 8310 State Rte 14, DuQoin, IL 62832-9741; Phone: 618-542-4102; Fax: 618-542-3966
1st Vice President: J. READ SMITH, 11751 Lancaster Rd., St. John, WA 99171-9723; Phone: 509-648-3922; Fax: 509-648-3293
2nd Vice President: GARY MAST, 6055 CR 203 Rte 4, Millersburg, OH 44654; Phone: 330-674-6278; Fax: 330-674-3690
Capacity Center Contact: RAY LEDGERWOD, NE 1615 Eastgate Blvd., Suite B, Pullman, WA 99163; Phone: 509-334-1823; Fax: 509-334-3453
Chief Executive Officer: ERNEST C. SHEA, 509 Capitol Court NE, Washington, DC 20002-4946; Phone: 202-547-6223; Fax: 202-547-6450
Director of Development/Membership: TERRY BOYKIE
Director of Leadership Services, North: DEBRA A. BOGAR, 9150 W. Jewell Ave Ste 111, Lakewood, CO 80232-6469; Phone: 303-988-1893; Fax: 303-988-1896
Director of Leadership Services, South: ROBERT TOOLE, P.O. Box 2334, Edmond, OK 73083-2334; Phone: 405-359-9011; Fax: 405-359-9047
Director of Meeting and Convention Services: BOB RASCHKE, 9150 W. Jewell Ave Ste 102, Lakewood, CO 80232-6469; Phone: 303-988-1810; Fax: 303-988-1896
Director of NACD Policy Center: BILL HORVATH, 1052 Main St. Ste 204, Stevens Point, WI 54481-2895; Phone: 715-341-1022; Fax: 715-341-1023
Director of National Wetlands Conservation Alliance: GENE WHITAKER
Director of Programs: GENE LAMB
Government Affairs/Communications Specialist: LAURA MCNICHOL
Secretary/Treasurer: DELBERT WINTERFELD, Box 97, Swan Valley, ID 83449; Phone: 208-483-3683; Fax: 208-483-3684
Publication(s): *Tuesday Letter; District Leader, The; America's Conservation Districts; Guide to Conservation Careers; Environmental Film Service Catalogue; Service Center Catalogue; other conservation-related informational and educational publications*
Keyword(s): Agriculture, Environmental and Conservation Education, Soil Conservation, Urban Environment, Water Pollution

NATIONAL ASSOCIATION OF CONSERVATION DISTRICTS (League City Office)
P.O. Box 855, League City, TX 77574
Phone: 281-332-3402, Order: 1-800-825-5547; Fax: 281-332-5259
Scope: National
Contact(s):
Catalog Sales Representative: TAMMY JONES
Office of Public Affairs Director: RONALD G. FRANCIS
Office of Public Affairs Director of Marketing: BRENDA McKEEHAN
Office of Public Affairs Editorial Specialist: LESLIE SANDERSON
Office of Public Affairs Education Specialist: BRENDA WEISER
Office of Public Affairs Publications Editor: LAURIE ADCOX
Service Center Director of Association and Administrative Services: S. JEFF WINTERS
Service Center Membership Services Specialist: KAY ADAMS
Service Center Production Manager: MAXINE MATHIS

NATIONAL ASSOCIATION OF ENVIRONMENTAL PROFESSIONALS, THE (National Office)
6524 Ramoth Dr., Jacksonville, DC 32226-9900
Phone: 904-251-9900; Fax: 904-251-9901; Email: naep@ilink.com; WWW: www.naep.org
Founded: 1975; Membership: 2,000
Scope: National
Description: NAEP is the professional association of the environmental professions, dedicated to the promotion of ethical practice, technical competency, and professional standards in the environmental field and recognition of the environmental profession since 1975.
Keyword(s): Air Quality and Pollution, Energy, Environmental Planning, Solid Waste Management, Water Resources

NATIONAL ASSOCIATION OF RECREATION RESOURCE PLANNERS
c/o Tim Bradle, Treasurer, Texas Parks & Wildlife Dept., 4200 Smith School Rd., Austin, SC 78744-3291
Phone: 512-912-7109; Fax: 512-707-2742
Scope: National
Description: A nonprofit organization involved in the exchange of recreation resource planning information among fedreal, state and regional agencies. Participates in national recreation concerns, promotes improvements in the state-of-the-art of recreation planning and professionalism among its members and acts as an advocate for conservation and recreation opportunities for the future.
Contact(s):
President: GORDON KIMBALL, Minnesota
Vice President: ROBERT SAMMON, New Hampshire
Treasurer: TIM BRADLE, Texas
Publication(s): *NARRP Newsletter*
Keyword(s): Land Use Planning, Open Space, Outdoor Recreation, Planning Management, Public Lands

NATIONAL ASSOCIATION OF SERVICE AND CONSERVATION CORPS (NASCC)
666 11th St., NW, Suite 1000, Washington, DC 20001
Phone: 202-737-6272; Fax: 202-737-6277; Email: nascc@nascc.org; WWW: www.nascc.org
Founded: 1985; Membership: 180
Scope: National
Description: NASCC unites and supports youth corps as a preminent strategy for achieving the nation's youth development, community service, and environmental restoration goals. NASCC serves as an advocate, central reference point, and source of assistance for the growing number of state and local youth corps around the country.
Contact(s):
President: KATHLEEN SELZ
Director for Member Services: LESLIE WILKOFF
Director for Training and Technical Assistance: HARRY BRUELL
Vice President for Government Relations: ANDREW MOORE
Publication(s): *Youth Corps Profiles; Youth Corps Resource Book; NASCC News; Corpsmember Wellness Guide; Urban Waterways Restoration Training Manual*
Keyword(s): Environmental and Conservation Education, People of Color in the Environment, Training, Urban Environment, Youth Organizations

NATIONAL ASSOCIATION OF STATE DEPARTMENTS OF AGRICULTURE
1156 15th St., NW, Suite 1020, Washington, DC 20005
Phone: 202-296-9680; Fax: 202-296-9686; Email: nasda@patriot.net; WWW: www.nasda-hq.org
Scope: National
Description: The National Association of State Departments of Agriculture (NASDA) is a nonprofit, nonpartisan association of public officials comprised of the executive heads of the fifty State Departments of Agriculture and those from territories of Puerto Rico, Guam, American Samoa, and the Virgin Islands. NASDA's mission is to support and promote the American agriculture industry, while protecting consumers and the environment, through the development, implementation, and communication of sound policy and programs.
Contact(s):
Chief Executive Officer: RICHARD W. KIRCHHOFF
Publication(s): *NASDA News (weekly); Ag In Perspective (quarterly)*
Keyword(s): Agriculture, Biotechnology, Conservation of Protected Areas, Conservation Tillage, Environmental Protection, Health and Nutrition, Pesticides, Precision Farming, Public Farming, Public Lands, Rural Development, Water Pollution, Water Quality, Water Resources, Wetlands

NATIONAL ASSOCIATION OF STATE FORESTERS
NASF Executive Director: BILL IMBERGAMO 444 N. Capitol St. NW Suite 540, Washington, DC 20001
Phone: 202-624-5415; Email: nasf@sso.org; WWW: www.sso.org/nasf.html
Scope: National
Description: Members are state foresters or equivalent officials whose agencies are the legally-constituted authorities for public forestry work within the states. In cooperation with federal agencies, private organizations, and individuals, NASF promotes sound forest management on public and private lands.
Contact(s):
President: MARVIN BROWN, Missouri Department of Conservation, 2901 W. Truman Blvd., P.O. Box 180, Jefferson City, MO 65102; Phone: 537-751-4115
Vice President: GARY HERGENRADER, Department of Forestry, Fish, and Wildlife, Rm. 101, Plant Industries Bldg., Lincoln, NE 68583-0814; Phone: 402-472-2944
Treasurer: STAN ADAMS, NC Div. Of Forest Resources, P.O. Box 29581, Raleigh, NC 27626-0581; Phone: 919-733-2162 x202
NASF Executive Director: BILL IMBERGAMO, 444 N. Capitol St., NW, Suite 540, Washington, DC 20001; Phone: 202-624-5415; Email: nasf@sso.org
Northeastern Area Regional Representative: WARREN ARCHEY, MA Dept. of Env. Mgmt., P.O. Box 1433, Pittsfield, MA 01202; Phone: 413-442-4963
Southern Group Regional Representative: HUGH RYAN, SC Forestry Commission, P.O. Box 21707, Columbia, SC 29221; Phone: 803-896-8800
Western Council Regional Representative: ARTHUR DU FAULT, US Div. Of Forestry, Fire, & State Lands, 1594 W. North Temple, Suite 3520, Salt Lake City, UT 84114-5703; Phone: 801-538-5555
Publication(s): *NASF Washington Update*
Keyword(s): Forests and Forestry, Public Lands, Soil Conservation, Urban Forestry, Water Resources

NATIONAL ASSOCIATION OF STATE OUTDOOR RECREATION LIAISON OFFICERS
ATTN: President, Administrator for Division of Customer Assistance and External Relations, Dept. of Natural Resources, P.O. Box 7921, Madison, WI 53707
Founded: 1967
Scope: National
Description: An organization of 56 gubernatorial-appointed state and territorial officials working with the National Park Service and the Department of the Interior to strengthen the nation's total outdoor recreation program. Represents state and local interests in administration of the Land and Water Conservation Fund Program, which provides money for acquisition and development of recreation land and facilities.
Contact(s):
President: CRAIG L. KARR, Administrator for Division of Customer Assistance and External Relations, Department of Natural Resources, P.O. Box 7921, Madison, WI 53707; Phone: 608-266-5896
Vice President: COURTLAND C. NELSON, Director of Division of Parks and Recreation, P.O. Box 146001, Salt Lake City, UT 84114-6001; Phone: 801-538-7362
Secretary: CHARLES A. SALKIN, Director of Division of Parks and Recreation, 89 Kings Hwy, Dover, DE 19901; Phone: 302-739-4401
Executive Director: NEY C. LANDRUM, 126 Mill Branch Rd., Tallahassee, FL 32312; Phone: 850-893-4959
Keyword(s): Land Purchase, Outdoor Recreation, Planning Management

NATIONAL ASSOCIATION OF STATE PARK DIRECTORS
Attn: Executive Director, 9894 E. Holden Pl., Tucson, AZ 85748
Founded: 1962; Membership: 50
Scope: National
Description: Works to unite the states on a common ground for the development of park systems to meet the intensive public demand for out-of-doors recreational opportunities; to promote the exchange of ideas regarding the development of state park systems; to encourage and develop professional leadership; and to expand and improve park policies and practices.
Contact(s):
President: FRAN P. MAINELLA, Director of Division of Recreation and Parks, Department of Environmental Protection, 3900 Commonwealth Blvd., Mail Station 500, Tallahassee, FL 32399-3000
Executive Director: GLEN ALEXANDER, 9894 E. Holden Pl., Tucson, AZ 85748
Secretary and Treasurer: YVONNE FERRELL, Director, Dept. of Parks & Rec., PO Box 83720-0065, Boise, ID 83720-00665
Vice-President: KENNETH E. TRAVOUS, Executive Director of Arizona State Parks, 1300 W. Washington, Phoenix, AZ 85007
Keyword(s): Environmental and Conservation Education, Land Purchase, Land Use Planning, Outdoor Recreation, Public Lands

NON-GOVERNMENTAL ORGANIZATIONS

NATIONAL ASSOCIATION OF UNIVERSITY FISHERIES AND WILDLIFE PROGRAMS
ATTN: President, Department of Animal Ecology, Iowa State University, Ames, IA 50011-3221
Founded: 1991
Scope: National
Description: Meets annually at the North American Wildlife and Natural Resources Conference. The purpose is to foster improved communications among members and between other agencies, organizations, and the general public in order to provide a unified voice for academic fisheries and wildlife programs.
Contact(s):
President: CHARLES G. SCALET, Department of Wildlife and Fisheries Sciences, South Dakota State University, Brookings, SD 57007-1696; Phone: 605-688-6121
President-Elect: BRUCE W. MENZEL, Department of Animal Ecology, Iowa State University, Ames, IA 50011-3221; Phone: 515-294-7419
Secretary and Treasurer: ERIK FRITZELL, Department of Fisheries and Wildlife, Oregon State University, Corvallis, OR 97331; Phone: 541-737-2910
Keyword(s): Environmental and Conservation Education, Fisheries, Wildlife and Wildlife Habitat

NATIONAL AUDUBON SOCIETY
700 Broadway, New York, NY 10003-9501
Phone: 212-979-3000
Founded: 1905; Membership: 550,000
Scope: National
Description: Solid Science, policy research, lobbying, citizen science and action, and education -- these are the tools used by the Audubon Society to protect the land and habitat that are critical to our health and the health of the planet. With the support of 550,000 members (in addition to the 500,000 elementary school students in the Audubon Adventures Program) and an extensive chapter network in the United States and Latin America, Audubon draws on the enthusiasm and power of the grassroots to save our threatened ecosystems.
Contact(s):
Chairman of the Board: DONAL C. O'BRIEN JR.; Fax: 212-353-0377
President and CEO: JOHN FLICKER
Senior Vice President of Education and Communications: VICTORIA A. SHAW
Senior Vice President of Field Operations and Sancturaies: GLENN E. OLSON
Senior Vice President of Operations: JAMES A. CUNNINGHAM
Senior Vice President of Public Policy: DANIEL BEARD
Senior Vice President of Science: FRANK GILL
Vice President of Campaigns: ERIN DRAPER
Vice President of Education: TALBERT SPENCE
Vice President of Membership: CELIA TENNENBAUM
Vice President of Public Policy: DANIEL BEARD
Vice President of Publishing: JAMES FISHMAN
Vice President/Controller: CAROLE J. MCNAMARA
Publication(s): *Audubon; Audubon Field Notes; Audubon Adventures*

Everglades Campaign Office
444 Brickell Ave., Suite 850, Miami, FL 33131
Phone: 305-371-6399; Fax: 305-371-6398
Scope: Regional
Contact(s):
Director: STUART STRAHL
Human Population and Resource Use Director: PATRICIA WAAK, 4150 Darley Ave., Suite 7, Boulder, CO 80303; Phone: 303-499-5155; Fax: 303-499-0286

Great Lakes, IL, IN, KY, MI, MN, OH, WI
692 N. High St. Suite 208, Columbus, OH 43215
Phone: 614-224-3303; Fax: 614-224-3305
Scope: Regional
Contact(s):
Vice President: STEPHEN SEDAM

Project Puffin
159 Sapsucker Woods Rd., Ithaca, NY 14850
Scope: Regional
Contact(s):
Director: STEPHEN KRESS

Scully Science Center
306 S. Bay Ave., Islip, NY 11751
Phone: 516-277-4289; Fax: 516-581-5268
Scope: Regional
Contact(s):
Director: DR. CARL SAFINA

Tavernier Science Center
115 Indian Mound Tr., Tavernier, FL 33070
Phone: 305-852-5092; Fax: 305-852-4889
Scope: Regional
Contact(s):
Coordinator: JEROME LORENZ

Washington, D.C. Office
1901 Pennsylvania Ave., NW, Suite 1100, Washington, DC 20006
Phone: 202-861-2242; Fax: 202-861-4290
Scope: Regional

NATIONAL AUDUBON SOCIETY, LIVING OCEANS PROGRAM
550 South Bay Ave., Islip, NY 11751
Phone: 516-859-3032; Fax: 516-581-5268; Email: mlee@audubon.org; WWW: www.audubon.org/campaign/10
Founded: 1993; Membership: 4,000
Scope: National
Description: Living Oceans is the marine conservation program of National Audubon Society. The program is dedicated to reversing the mismanagement of marine fisheries which has led to the depletion of marine wildlife, and to restore the health of our marine environment and coastal habitats.
Contact(s):
Assistant Director: MERCEDES LEE; Phone: 516-224-3669
Director: DR. CARL SAFINA
Staff Scientist: DR. MERRY CAMHI; Phone: 516-581-2927
Publication(s): *Living Oceans News; Audubon Guide to Seafood*
Keyword(s): Marine Conservation, Ocean Conservation

NATIONAL AVIARY IN PITTSBURGH
Allegheny Commons West, Pittsburg, PA 15212-5248
Phone: 412-323-7235; Fax: 412-321-4364; Email: ntlaviary@aol.org; WWW: www.aviary.org
Founded: 1952; Membership: 1,300
Scope: National
Description: The National Aviary's mission is to be the leader in avian conservation, education, and recreation, and to instill within the individuals we touch an environmental ethic which teaches our immense responsibility as stewards of the planet.
Contact(s):
Executive Director: DAYTON BAKER
Publication(s): *Bird Talk*
Keyword(s): Biodiversity, Birds, Botanical Gardens, Conservation, Endangered and Threatened Species, Environmental and Conservation Education, Flowers, Plants, and Trees, Raptors, Wildlife and Wildlife Habitat, Zoology

NON-GOVERNMENTAL ORGANIZATIONS

NATIONAL BIRD-FEEDING SOCIETY
P.O. Box 23, Northbrook, IL 60065-0023
Phone: 847-272-0135; Email: birdseye1@aol.com
Founded: 1989; Membership: 15,000
Scope: National
Description: The National Bird-Feeding Society works to make feeding of wild birds better for birds as well as for people. The Society also works to encourage suitable feeding and nesting habitats for backyard birds to thrive; sponsors education and research on backyard birds; and helps people learn more ways to attract and care for birds, to share bird-feeding experiences, observations, and to help the environment through the backyard.
Contact(s):
Executive Director: SUE WELLS
Chairman Emeritus: DONALD STOKES
Chairman of Board of **Publication(s):** *The Bird's-Eye reView*
Keyword(s): Birds, Conservation of Protected Areas, Environment, Flowers, Plants, and Trees, Research

NATIONAL BOATING FEDERATION
P.O. Box 4111, Annapolis, MD 21403
Phone: 410-280-1911
Founded: 1966; Membership: 2 million
Scope: National
Description: National, all-volunteer, non-profit boating organization consisting principally of regional or special interest boating organizations and yacht clubs. Activities included monitoring federal legislation and rule-making as they affect recreational boating. The NBF promotes the interests of those who use boats for cruising, water skiing, fishing, and other water sports.
Contact(s):
President: WILLIAM D. MITCHELSON, 9483 N. Fairway Cr., Milwaukee, WI 53217-1316
Immediate past president: LEWIS A. AHNER JR., 9125 Mayfield Ave., Oaklawn, IL 60453-1526; Phone: 708-424-6470; Fax: 708-868-1255
Public Relations and Editor: JILL BROGGI, P.O. Boxk 211, Salem, OR 97303-3903; Phone: 503-580-0769
Secretary and Treasurer: WILLIAM A. HEIDER, 1114 Apple Tree Lane, Erie, PA 16509-3917; Phone: 814-825-3011; Fax: 814-825-5284
Vice-President: ROBERT DAVID, 70 Garfield Lane, West Dennis, MA 02670-2321; Phone: 508-394-5670; Fax: 508-394-7236
Publication(s): *The LOOKOUT; Marine Sanitation Devices and Pollution From Small Recreational Boats; Boating Safety For Violators; assorted safety materials*
Keyword(s): Coasts, Lakes, Outdoor Recreation, Rivers, Water Pollution

NATIONAL COALITION AGAINST THE MISUSE OF PESTICIDES
701 E St. SE Suite 200, Washington, DC 20003
Phone: 202-543-5450; Email: ncamp@ncamping.org; WWW: www.ncamp.org
Founded: 1981
Scope: National
Description: Nonprofit membership organization committed to assisting individuals, organizations, and communities with useful information on pesticides and their alternatives. NCAMP's information clearinghouse provides material on a wide range of both agricultural and urban issues concerning farm protection of children, workers' safety, food safety, lawn care safety, groundwater problems, and alternatives to pesticides, as well as legislation.
Contact(s):
Executive Director: JAY FELDMAN
Editor: JAY FELDMAN
President Board of Directors: ALLEN SPALT
Publication(s): *Pesticides and You Newsletter (Quarterly); NCAMP's Technical Report (Monthly); Poison Poles: Their Toxic Trial and the Safer Alternatives; A Failure to Protect: The Unnecessary Use of Hazardous Pesticides at Federal Facilities; Safety at Home: A Guide to the Hazards of Lawn and Garden Pesticides and Safer Ways to Manage Pests; Unnecessary Risks: The Benefit Side of the Pesticides Risk-Benefit Equation*
Keyword(s): Agriculture, Environment, Insects and Butterflies, Pesticides, Toxicology

NATIONAL COALITION FOR MARINE CONSERVATION
3 W. Market St., Leesburg, VA 20176
Phone: 703-777-0037; Fax: 703-777-1107
Founded: 1973
Scope: National
Description: A nonprofit, privately-supported organization devoted exclusively to the conservation of ocean fish and the protection of their environment. Promotes public awareness of marine conservation issues and stimulates the formulation of responsible public policy.
Contact(s):
President: KEN HINMAN
Chairman of the Board: CHRISTOPHER M. WELD, One Post Office Square 24th Fl., Boston, MA 02109; Phone: 617-338-2909
Director of Communication and Development: CHRISTINE WILKINS
Editor: KEN HINMAN
Publication(s): *Marine Bulletin*
Keyword(s): Coasts, Environmental and Conservation Education, Fisheries, Sport Fishing, Wetlands

NATIONAL COUNCIL FOR GEOGRAPHIC EDUCATION
16A Leonard Hall Indiana University of Pennsylvania, Indiana, PA 15705
Phone: 412-357-6290
Founded: 1915; Membership: 4,000
Scope: National
Description: To promote and advance geographic and environmental education in the public schools and colleges of the U.S. and Canada.
Contact(s):
President: GAIL HOBBS
Secretary: SANDRA MATHER
Executive Director: RUTH I. SHIREY
Editor: JONATHAN LEIB, Department of Geography, Florida State University, Tallahassee, FL 32306-4016
Vice President of Curriculum and Instruction: ROBERT BEDNARZ
Vice President of Finance: CELESTE FRASER
Vice President of Publications and Products: GARY ELBOW
Vice President of Research and External Resources: JAMES PETERSON
Publication(s): *Journal of Geography; Water In the Global Environment;* list of other publications available upon request.

NATIONAL COUNCIL OF STATE GARDEN CLUBS, INC.
4401 Magnolia Ave., St. Louis, MO 63110
Phone: 314-776-7574
Founded: 1929; Membership: 285,255
Scope: National
Description: Coordinates and furthers the interests and activities of the State Federations of Garden Clubs, together with similar organizations in the U.S. and foreign countries; aids in the protection and conservation of natural resources; protects civic beauty and encourages the improvement of roadsides and parks; encourages and assists in establishing and maintaining botanical gardens and horticultural centers; and advances the arts of gardening and landscape design, and study of horticulture.
Contact(s):
President: MRS. C. MANNING SMITH, P.O. Box 450, Charles Town, WV 25414
Treasurer: MRS. THOMAS A. WIPPERMAN, 3206 Allison Way, Louisville, KY 40220
1st Vice President: MRS. JAMES DAWSON, 165 Olive St., Elmhurst, IL 60126
2nd Vice President: MRS. GRAEM YATES, 9516 Glenbrook Dr., Charlotte, NC 28215
Corresponding Secretary: MRS. C. VINCENT TOWNSEND, 123 Old Mill Rd., Martinsburg, WV 25401

Editor (Acting): SUSAN DAVIDSON, 102 S. Elm St., St. Louis, MO 63119
Environmental Education: M. SUE DAUGHERTY, 131 Old Ford Dr., Camp Hill, PA 17011
Office Manager: MRS. CHARLES MANTLER; Phone: 314-776-7574
Publication(s): *National Gardener, The*
Keyword(s): Gardening and Horticulture

NATIONAL EDUCATION ASSOCIATION
1201 16th St., NW, Washington, DC 20036
Phone: 202-833-4000
Founded: 1857; Membership: 2,000,000
Scope: National
Description: Works to elevate the character and advance the interests of the teaching profession and to promote the cause of education in the U.S.
Contact(s):
President: ROBERT F. CHASE
Vice President: REG WEAVER
Executive Director: DON CAMERON
Secretary and Treasurer: DENNIS VAN ROEKEL

NATIONAL ENVIRONMENTAL HEALTH ASSOCIATION
720 S. Colorado Blvd., S. Tower, Suite 970, Denver, CO 80246-1925
Phone: 303-756-9090; Fax: 303-691-9490; Email: staff@neha.org; WWW: www.neha.org
Founded: 1937; Membership: 5,000
Scope: National
Description: NEHA is a member nonprofit organization that offers a wide variety of educational credentialing and advancement opportunities for people involved or interested in environmental health issues. It is the largest society of environmental health practitioners in the nation today, numbering almost 5,000 members and growing.
Contact(s):
Executive Director: NELSON E. FABIAN
Publication(s): *Journal of Environmental Health; Self Paced Learning Modules; Environment News Digest;* various books, manuals, etc.
Keyword(s): Air Quality and Pollution, Environmental Health, Food Safety, Solid Waste, Toxic Substances, Water Pollution, Water Resources

NATIONAL FARMERS UNION
11900E. Cornell Ave., Aurora, CO 80014-3194
Phone: 303-337-5500
Founded: 1902
Scope: National
Description: Believes that the soil, water, forest and other natural resources of the nation should be used and conserved in a manner to pass these resources on undiminished to future generations and that publicly and privately owned land and resources should be administered in the interest of all the public.
Contact(s):
President: LELAND H. SWENSON
Vice President: CHARLES NASH
Editor: MARILYN WENTZ, 11900 E. Cornell Ave., Aurora, CO 80014-3194; Phone: 303-337-5500
Treasurer/Secretary: DAVID CARTER
Vice President of Legislative Services: LARRY MITCHELL, 400 Virginia Ave. SW, Suite 710, Washington, DC 20024; Phone: 202-554-1600
Publication(s): *National Farmers Union News*
Keyword(s): Agriculture, Environmental Law, Health and Nutrition, Renewable Resources, Soil Conservation

NATIONAL FFA ORGANIZATION
P.O. Box 15160, National FFA Center, Alexandria, VA 22309
Phone: 703-360-3600
Founded: 1928
Scope: National
Description: The FFA is a national organization of high school agriculture students in public secondary schools. Congress granted the organization a federal charter in 1950, making it an integral part of the high school agriculture program. Major aims are to provide activities that will stimulate students to higher achievement in the study of production agriculture, agriscience, agribusiness, and agrimarketing, and give them opportunities through student-planned programs for leadership and self-development.
Contact(s):
Executive Secretary: C. COLEMAN HARRIS; Phone: 703-360-3600
Advisor: DR. LARRY D. CASE; Phone: 703-360-3600
Publication(s): *FFA New Horizons Magazine, The; FFA Advisor Publication; Update Newsletter*
Keyword(s): Agriculture, Biotechnology, Gardening and Horticulture, Renewable Resources, Youth Organizations

NATIONAL FIELD ARCHERY ASSOCIATION
31407 Outer I-10, Redlands, CA 92373
Phone: 1-800-811-2331 909-794-2133
Membership: 20,000
Scope: National
Description: A nonprofit national membership headquarters for all archers.
Contact(s):
President: CHUCK CROWELL, 23 Wilderness Ln., Great Falls, MT 59401
Bowhunting Committee Chairman: TIM ATWOOD, 3175 Racine, Riverside, CA 92503
Editor: ARLYNE RHODE
Executive Secretary and Editor: MARIHELEN ROGERS
Publication(s): *Archery Magazine*
Keyword(s): Hunting, Scholarships and Grants, Sport Fishing, Youth Organizations

NATIONAL FISH AND WILDLIFE FOUNDATION
1120 Connecticut Ave., NW, Suite 900, Washington, DC 20036
Phone: 202-857-0166; Fax: 202-857-0162; Email: info@nfwf.org
Founded: 1984
Scope: National
Description: A national nonprofit grant-making and grant-seeking organization dedicated to the conservation of natural resources -- fish, wildlife, and plants. NFWF was established by Congress to leverage federally, appropriated funds by forging public and private partnerships which result in conservation activities that pinpoint and solve root causes of environmental problems.
Contact(s):
Deputy Director: ALEX ECHOLS
Executive Director: AMOS S. ENO
Chairman of the Board: MAGALEN O. BRYANT
Director of Conservation Education Initiative: TOM KELSCH
Director of Conservation Policy: NEAL SIGMON
Director of Conservation Programs: WHITNEY C. TILT
Director of Development and Marketing: JOHN FRITTS
Director of Finance and Administration: GINETTE RING
Director of Fisheries, Conservation and Management Initiative: JERRY CLARK
Director of Neotropical Migratory Bird Conservation Program: PETER W. STANGEL
Director of Wetlands and Private Lands: MOIRA MCDONALD
Director of Wildlife and Habitat Initiative: GARY KANIA
Keyword(s): Birds, Endangered and Threatened Species, Environmental and Conservation Education, Fisheries, Wildlife and Wildlife Habitat

NATIONAL FLYWAY COUNCIL
South Dakota Game Fish and Parks, 523 E. Capitol, Pierre, SD 57501
Scope: National
Contact(s):
Chairman: GEORGE VANDEL, South Dakota Game, Fish, and Parks Department, 523 E. Capitol, Pierre, SD 57501

Atlantic Flyway Office
Division of Fish and Wildlife Department of Environmental Conservation 50 Wolf Rd., Albany, NY 12233
Phone: 518-457-5690
Scope: Regional
Contact(s):
Chairman: KENNETH WICH

Central Flyway Office
Kansas Department of Wildlife and Parks Rt. 2 Box 54A, Pratt, KS 67124
Scope: Regional
Contact(s):
Chairman: JOE KRAMER

Mississippi Flyway Office
Section of Wildlife Natural Resources, 500 Lafayette Rd., St. Paul, MN 55155
Scope: Regional
Contact(s):
Chairman: ROGER HOLMES

NATIONAL FOREST FOUNDATION
1099 14th St., NW, Suite 5600W, Washington, DC 20005
Phone: 202-501-2473; Fax: 202-219-6585; Email: 1.girard@if.arctic.com
Founded: 1993
Scope: National
Description: The National Forest Foundation supports the U.S. Forest Service in its management, protection and use of the nation's forest lands by increasing awareness and appreciation to further the purposes of the National Forest System, including support for research and cooperative programs, and by raising private funds to better protect and nurture forest lands.
Contact(s):
Acting President: TERRY AUSTIN
Assistant Vice President for Conservation Programs: KENNETH GALLIK
Chief Financial Officer: BRENDA A. JONES
Events Coordinator: JULIA LAM
Vice President for Membership: CINDA JONES
Publication(s): *Forest Leader*
Keyword(s): Environmental and Conservation Education, Forests and Forestry, Outdoor Recreation, Public Lands, Wildlife and Wildlife Habitat

NATIONAL FORESTRY ASSOCIATION
374 Maple Ave., E., Suite 310, Vienna, VA 22180
Phone: 703-255-2300; Fax: 703-281-9200
Founded: 1981; Membership: 42,000
Scope: National
Description: A nationwide advocate of sustainable forestry on private and public lands. Programs include the National Forestry Network, Green Tag Forestry, the American Hardwood Management Advisory Board., and the National Historic Lookout Register.
Contact(s):
President: KEITH A. ARGOW; Email: nwoa@mindspring.com
Staff Forester: SUZANNE MANGINO
National Historic Lookout Register: NANCY GABRIEL
Hardwood Management Advisory Board: ARLYN PERKEY; Phone: 304-285-1523
Editor: ERIC A. JOHNSON; Phone: 315-369-3078
Publication(s): *Forestry Advantage, The*
Keyword(s): Conservation of Protected Areas, Forest Management, Forests and Forestry, Renewable Resources, Sustainable Resources, Green Certification

NATIONAL FOUNDATION TO PROTECT AMERICA'S EAGLES (Save The Eagle)
P.O. Box 120206, Nashville, TN 37212
Phone: 615-847-4171
Founded: 1985
Scope: National
Description: Dedicated to saving, restoring, and protecting America's endangered national symbol, the Bald Eagle, and preserving America's wildlife, waterways, forests, natural resources, ecosystems, and environment.
Contact(s):
Vice President: BOBBY J. HALLIBURTON, Nashville, TN
Secretary: STEVEN C. COMPTON, Brentwood, TN
Treasurer: JULIETTE INGRAM, Nashville, TN
President and CEO: AL LOUIS CECERE, P.O. Box 120206, Nashville, TN 37212
Publication(s): *American Eagle News*

NATIONAL GARDENING ASSOCIATION
180 Flynn Ave., Burlington, VT 5401
Phone: 802-863-1308; Fax: 802-863-5962
Founded: 1972; Membership: 200,000
Scope: National
Description: The mission of the National Gardening Association is to sustain the essential values of life and community, renewing the fundamental links between people, plants, and the earth. Through gardening, we promote environmental responsibility, advance multidisciplinary learning and scientific literacy, and create partnerships that restore and enhance communities.
Contact(s):
President: DAVID E. ELS
Administrative Coordinator of GrowLab: JIM FLINT
Assistant Treasurer and CFO: A. WILLIAM MILLER II
Associate Director of Education: EVE PRANIS
Board of Directors Vice Chair: JAMES SCHASSER
Director of Advertising: LARRY SOMMERS
Director of Circulation: BETSY BRADBURY
Director of Development: RETTA HUTTLINGER
Director of Education Programs: DOUGLAS HARRIS
Editor-in-Chief: MICHAEL MacCASKEY
Horticulturist: CHARLIE NARDOZZI
Managing Editor: DAN HICKEY
Market Research: BRUCE BUTTERFIELD
Senior Editor: JACK RUTTLE
Publication(s): *National Gardening Magazine; Guide to Kids Gardening; Community Garden Book, The; National Gardening Survey; Gardening; Gardening Video Series; GrowLab: A Complete Guide to Gardening in the Classroom; Ruth Page's Gardening Journal; GROWLAB: Activities for*
Keyword(s): Environmental and Conservation Education, Flowers, Plants, and Trees, Gardening and Horticulture, Youth Organizations

NATIONAL GEOGRAPHIC SOCIETY
1145 17th St., NW, Washington, DC 20036
Phone: 202-857-7000
Founded: 1888; Membership: 9,000,000
Scope: National
Description: For the increase and diffusion of geographic knowledge.
Contact(s):
Chairman of the Board: GILBERT M. GROSVENOR
Chief Financial Officer and Treasurer: H. GREGORY PLATTS
Editor of National Geographic: WILLIAM L. ALLEN
President and CEO: JOHN M. FAHEY JR.
Senior Vice President: DALE A. PETROSKEY
Senior Vice President: NINA HOFFMAN
Senior Vice President: SANDRA H. GILL
Senior Vice President: TERRENCE B. ADAMSON

NON-GOVERNMENTAL ORGANIZATIONS

Senior Vice President: ROBERT B. SIMS
Vice Chairman of the Board: REG MURPHY
Publication(s): *National Geographic; National Geographic World Magazine (for children); National Geographic Traveler; Books; Atlases; Maps; Globes; Filmstrips; Documentary Films; Classroom Materials*
Keyword(s): Environmental and Conservation Education, Geography, Natural History, Oceanography, Public Lands

NATIONAL GRANGE, THE
1616 H St. NW, Washington, DC 20006-4999
Phone: 202-628-3507
Founded: 1867; Membership: 300,000
Scope: National
Description: Rural family service organization with special interests in community service and agriculture.
Contact(s):
Secretary: SHIRLEY LAWSON, 120 Wilson Ave., Rumford, RI 02916; Phone: 401-434-1491
Executive Committee Chairman: JOHN MAPLE; Phone: 609-896-0935
Executive Committee Secretary: ROBERT CLARK; Phone: 360-683-4431
Legislative Director: TOM RUGG, Washington D.C. Office
Master: KERMIT W. RICHARDSON, Washington DC Office
Publication(s): *View From The Hill; Grange Today*
Keyword(s): Agriculture, Environmental Law, Land Use Planning, Soil Conservation, Transportation

NATIONAL GROUND WATER ASSOCIATION, THE
601 Dempsey Rd., Westerville, OH 43081
Phone: 1-800-551-7379/614-898-7791; Fax: 614-898-7786; WWW: www.ngwa.org
Founded: 1948
Scope: National
Description: The NGWA is the world's leading organization committed to the study of the occurrence, development, and protection of ground water. The Association annually sponsors educational programs dealing with a wide variety of water issues, including toxic substances, solid waste, and water pollution. Operates on-line data bases at Web Site.
Contact(s):
Executive Director: KEVIN McCRAY
Information: SANDY MASTERS, National Ground Water Information Center, 601 Dempsey Dr., Westerville, OH 43081
Publication(s): *Water Well Journal; Ground Water Monitoring and Remediation; Journal of Ground Water*
Keyword(s): Environmental and Conservation Education, Geology, Water Pollution, Water Resources

NATIONAL HUNTERS ASSOCIATION, INC.
P.O. Box 820, Knightdale, NC 27545
Phone: 919-365-7157
Founded: 1976
Scope: National
Description: The National Hunters Association, Inc. was incorporated under the laws of NC to protect your hunting rights in the U.S. and around the world. Dedicated to hunter safety, the preservation of the rights of the individual sportsman to pursue the sport of hunting and the preservation of an adequate supply of game for the sportsman to hunt -- now and in the future.
Contact(s):
President: D. V. SMITH
Vice President: JIM HUNTER
Secretary and Treasurer: FAYE M. SMITH
Publication(s): *NHA Newsletter*
Keyword(s): Environmental and Conservation Education, Hunting, Trapping, Youth Organizations

NATIONAL MILITARY FISH AND WILDLIFE ASSOCIATION
12428 Pinecrest Ln., Newburg, MD 20664
Founded: 1983; Membership: 700
Scope: National
Description: A nonprofit organization established to promote professional natural resources management on the over 25.5 million acres of United States Department of Defense lands worldwide. Membership is primarily comprised of professional Department of Defense natural resources personnel..
Contact(s):
President: MARJORIE McHENRY
Vice President: DAVE TAZIK; Phone: 601-634-2610
Director-At-Large: SCOTT SMITH; Phone: 919-736-6318
Director-At-Large: SHARON JONES; Phone: 760-830-7883
Eastern Regional Director: PAT WALSH; Phone: 941-452-4254
Eastern Regional Director: RICHARD McWHITE, AFDTC/EMN, Eglin AFB, FL 32542-5133; Phone: 904-882-4164
Eastern Regional Director: JAMES BEEMER, U.S. Military Academy, West Point, NY 10996-1592; Phone: 914-938-2314
Editor of Newsletter: RICHARD BUNN; Phone: 719-576-8074
Immediate Past President: RICK GRIFFITH
President-Elect: MARK HAGAN
Secretary and Treasurer: DON MEUSCHKE; Phone: 816-687-1227
Western Regional Director: TAMMY CONKLE; Phone: 619-537-6498
Western Regional Director: DON PITTS; Phone: 915-696-5049
Publication(s): *Fish and Wildlife News*
Keyword(s): Biodiversity, Fisheries, Land Use Planning, Public Lands, Wildlife and Wildlife Habitat

NATIONAL ORGANIZATION FOR RIVERS (NORS)
P.O. Box 6847, Colorado Springs, CO 80934
Phone: 719-579-8759
Founded: 1979; Membership: 10,000
Scope: National
Description: A nonprofit organization dedicated to education about whitewater river sports, including kayaking, rafting, and canoeing; to preserving rivers; and to protecting river access rights of the general public.
Contact(s):
President: GARY LACY
Vice President: BEN HARDING
Board Member: EARL PERRY
Board Member: FLETCHER ANDERSON
Editor: GREG MOORE
Membership Director: MARY McCURDY
Secretary, Treasurer, and Executive Director: ERIC LEAPER
Publication(s): *Currents*

NATIONAL PARK FOUNDATION
1101 17th St., NW, Suite 1102, Washington, DC 20036
Phone: 202-785-4500; Fax: 202-785-3539; WWW: NATIONALPARKS.ORG
Founded: 1967
Scope: National
Description: The National Park Foundation is the official nonprofit partner of the National Park Service. Created by Congress in 1967, the Foundation raises support from corporations, foundations, and individuals to preserve and enhance America's National Parks. Over the past five years, the National Park Foundation has raised more than $21 million in direct support for the National Parks.
Contact(s):
Chairman: BRUCE BABBITT
President: JAMES D. MADDY
Secretary: ROBERT G. STANTON
Treasurer: CLAUDIA SCHECHTER
Executive Vice President: JILL NICOLL
Vice Chairman: B. KENNETH WEST
Publication(s): *Complete Guide to America's National Parks, The; National Park Portfolio(periodical)*

Keyword(s): Cultural Preservation, Environmental and Conservation Education, Historic Preservation, National Parks, Nature Preservation, Outdoor Recreation, Public Lands

NATIONAL PARK TRUST
415 2nd St., NE, Suite 210, Washington, DC 20002
Phone: 202-548-0500; Fax: 202-548-0595; Email: Nptrust@aol.com; WWW: www.parktrust.org

Founded: 1983
Scope: National

Description: The private nonprofit land conservancy dedicated exclusively to protecting resources within and around national parklands and other natural and historic properties. The Trust is the only private citizen group recognized by Congress to own and manage, in cooperation with the National Park Service, a unit of the National Park System, The Tallgrass Prairie National Preserve, established in 1996. The Trust has aquired land in over 40 other parks units and finished 4 parks.

Contact(s):
President: PAUL C. PRITCHARD
Vice President: DAVINDER KHANNA
Secretary: WILLIAM BROWNELL
Treasurer: FRED MEYER
Chairman of the Board of Trustee: DALE CRANE
Development Director: SUSAN HAWLEY

Publication(s): *NPT News*, newsletter

Keyword(s): Historic Preservation, Land Purchase, Public Lands, Wildlife and Wildlife Habitat

NATIONAL PARKS AND CONSERVATION ASSOCIATION (NPCA)
Headquarters, 1776 Massachusetts Ave., NW, Washington, DC 20036
Phone: 202-223-6722; Fax: 202-659-0650; Email: natparks@aol.com; WWW: www.npca.org

Founded: 1919; Membership: 500,000
Scope: National

Description: A private nonprofit citizen organization, dedicated solely to preserving, protecting, and enhancing the U.S. National Park System. As a "watchdog" group, NPCA has been an advocate as well as a constructive critic of the National Park Service. NPCA has focused on the health of the entire system, from specific sites and programs to the processes of planning, management, and evaluation.

Contact(s):
Vice President: CAROL ATEN
Secretary: JENNIFER B. ROBERTSON
Director of Communications: JEROME UHER
Vice President of Development: JESSIE BRINKLEY
Vice President of Conservation Policy: WILLIAM J. CHANDLER
Vice President of Membership: TERRY L. VINES

Publication(s): *National Parks; ParkWatcher*

Keyword(s): Cultural Preservation, Land Preservation, National Parks, Public Lands

Alaska Regional Office
329 F St., Suite 208, Anchorage, AK 99501
Phone: 907-277-6722; Fax: 907-277-6723; Email: CHIPNPCA@aol.com
Scope: Regional
Contact(s):
Director: CHIP DENNERLEIN

Heartland Regional Office
P.O. Box 25354, Woodbury, MN 55125-5354
Phone: 612-735-8008; Email: LORINPCA@aol.com
Scope: Regional
Contact(s):
Director: LORI NELSON

Northeast Regional Office
P.O. Box 382372, Cambridge, MA 02238-0354
Phone: 617-354-8940; Email: EILEENNPCA@aol.com
Scope: Regional
Contact(s):
Director: EILEEN WOODFORD

Pacific Regional Office
P.O. Box 1289, Oakland, CA 94604
Phone: 510-839-9922; Fax: 510-839-9926; Email: BRIANNPCA@aol.com
Scope: Regional
Contact(s):
Director: BRIAN HUSE

Rocky Mountain Regional Office
100 Eagle Lake Dr., Fort Collins, CO 80524
Phone: 970-493-2545; Fax: 970-493-2527; Email: mpeterson@npca.org
Scope: Regional
Contact(s):
Director: MARK PETERSON

Southeast Regional Office
P.O. Box 930, Norris, TN 37828
Phone: 423-494-7008; Fax: 423-494-0426; Email: DONNPCA@aol.com
Scope: Regional
Contact(s):
Director: DON BARGER

Southwest Regional Office
823 Gold Ave., SW, Albuquerque, NM 87102
Phone: 505-247-1221; Fax: 505-247-1222; Email: DAVENPCA@aol.com
Scope: Regional
Contact(s):
Director: DAVID SIMON

NATIONAL RECREATION AND PARK ASSOCIATION
22377 Belmont Ridge Rd., Ashburn, VA 20148
Phone: 703-858-0784; Fax: 703-858-0794

Membership: 23,500
Scope: National

Description: A national nonprofit service, education, and research organization dedicated to the improvement of park and recreation leadership, programs, and facilities. The Association attempts to build public understanding that leisure programs and environments are indispensable to the well-being of a nation and its citizens.

Contact(s):
Secretary: ALICE CONKEY
Executive Director: R. DEAN TICE
Chairman of the Board: ERIC O'BRIEN
Chairman of the Executive Committee and President: CHRIS JARVI
Coordinator of Friends of Parks and Recreation: SUZANNE MATHIS
Director of Public Policy: BARRY TINDALL
Great Lakes Regional Director: WALTER JOHNSON, 650 W. Higgins, Hoffman Estates, IL 60195; Phone: 708-843-7529
Northeast Regional Director: KATHY SPANGLER, Recreation and Park Assoc., 22377 Belmont Ridge Road, Ashburn, VA 20148; Phone: 703-858-0784
Pacific Regional Director: PAMELA EARLE, 350 S. 333rd St., #103, Federal Way, WA 98003; Phone: 206-661-2265
Southeast Regional Director: W. TOM MARTIN, JR, 1285 Parker Rd., Conyers, GA 30207; Phone: 404-760-1668
Vice Chairman: RIP WILKENSON, Baton Rouge, LA
Western Regional Director: DICK HORTON, CO ; Phone: 719-632-7031

Publication(s): *Parks and Recreation Magazine; Journal of Leisure Research; Therapeutic Recreation Journal; Recreation and Parks Law Reporter; Park Practice Program; Dateline: NRPA*

NON-GOVERNMENTAL ORGANIZATIONS

NATIONAL RESEARCH COUNCIL
2101 Constitution Ave. NW, Washington, DC 20418
Phone: 202-334-2000
Founded: 1916
Scope: National
Description: An independent advisor to the federal government on scientific and technical questions of national importance. Jointly administered by the National Academies of Sciences and Engineering and the Institute of Medicine.
Contact(s):
Chairman: DR. BRUCE M. ALBERTS
Chief Operating Officer: SUZANNE H. WOOLSEY
Director of Office of News and Public Information: SUSAN TURNER-LOWE VINES
Publication(s): *Catalogue available upon request.*

NATIONAL RIFLE ASSOCIATION OF AMERICA
Headquarters, 11250 Waples Mill Rd., Fairfax, VA 22030
Phone: 703-267-1000; Fax: 703-267-3909
Founded: 1871; Membership: 2,800,000
Scope: National
Description: A nonprofit organization dedicated to protect and defend the Constitution of the United States, especially the right to possess and use firearms for recreation and personal protection; to promote public safety, law and order, and the national defense; and to train members of law enforcement agencies, the military, and private citizens of good repute in marksmanship and the safe handling and efficient use of small arms.
Contact(s):
President: CHARLTON HESTON
Secretary: EDWARD J. LAND JR.
Treasurer: WILSON H. PHILLIPS JR.
1st Vice President: KAYNE B. ROBINSON
2nd Vice President: SANDRA S. FROMAN
Assistant Manager of Hunter Services: JANICE E. TAYLOR; Phone: 703-267-1523
Credentials Program Coordinator for Training: KAREN DRUMMOND; Phone: 703-267-1481
Director of Conservation, Wildlife and Natural Resources Division: SUSAN LAMSON; Phone: 703-267-1541
Director of Education and Training Division: WILLIAM J. POOLE JR.; Phone: 703-267-1414
Executive Director of General Operations: CRAIG D. SANDLER
Executive Vice President: WAYNE R. LAPIERRE JR.
Instructor and Coach Trainer for Training: HOWARD H. MOODY; Phone: 703-267-1401
Manager for Training: CHARLES MITCHELL; Phone: 703-267-1431
Manager for Youth Programs: J. R. ROBBINS; Phone: 703-267-1596
Manager of Hunter Services: ROBERT L. DAVIS JR.; Phone: 703-267-1522
Program Assistant of Hunter Services: JOHN BAILEY; Phone: 703-267-1503
Program Coordinator of Hunter Services: BRITT J. FORD; Phone: 703-267-1516
Wildlife Management Specialist of Hunter Services (ECHO): BILLY R. TEMPLETON; Phone: 703-267-1501
Publication(s): *American Rifleman, American Hunter, American Guardian & Insights*
Keyword(s): Environmental and Conservation Education, Hunting, Outdoor Recreation, Wildlife and Wildlife Habitat, Youth Organizations

NATIONAL SCIENCE TEACHERS ASSOCIATION
1840 Wilson Blvd., Arlington, VA 22201
Phone: 703-243-7100; Fax: 703-243-7177; Email: maiser@nsta.org; WWW: www.nsta.org
Founded: 1944; Membership: 53,000
Scope: National
Description: NSTA is the world's largest organization committed to improving science education at all levels - preschool through college. NSTA's membership includes science teachers, science supervisors, administrators, scientists, business and industry representatives, and others involved in science education.
Contact(s):
President: FRED JOHNSON; Phone: 901-321-2527
Executive Director: GERALD F. WHEELER; Phone: 703-312-9254
Editor: JOAN McSHANE
President-Elect: STEVE RAKOW; Phone: 281-283-3593
Publication(s): *Science and Children; Science Scope; The Science Teacher; Journal of College Science Teaching; NSTA Reports!; Quantum; Dragonfly*
Keyword(s): Environmental and Conservation Education

NATIONAL SHOOTING SPORTS FOUNDATION, INC.
Flintlock Ridge Office Center, 11 Mile Hill Rd., Newtown, CT 06470-2359
Phone: 203-426-1320; Fax: 203-426-1087; Email: info@nssf.org
Founded: 1960
Scope: National
Description: Nonprofit educational, trade-supported association sponsors a wide variety of programs to create a better understanding of and a more active participation in the shooting sports and in practical conservation.
Contact(s):
Director of Conservation Partnerships: CHRIS CHAFFIN
Director of Facility Development: RICK PATTERSON
Director of Research and Information Services: LARRY FERENCE
National Coordinator of STEP OUTSIDE: JODI DiCAMILLO
President and CEO: ROBERT T. DELFAY
Vice President Marketing Administration: DOUGLAS PAINTER
Keyword(s): Environmental and Conservation Education, Hunting, Outdoor Recreation, Renewable Resources, Wildlife and Wildlife Habitat

NATIONAL SPELEOLOGICAL SOCIETY, INC.
2813 Cave Ave., Huntsville, AL 35810-4431
Email: nss@caves.org; WWW: www.caves.org
Founded: 1941; Membership: 12,000
Scope: National
Description: A nonprofit membership organization dedicated to the exploration, study, and conservation of America's caves and caverns, related features, and the ecology of caves.
Contact(s):
President: FRED L. WEFER, P.O. Box 47, McDowell, VA 24458-0047; Phone: 540-396-3543
Conservation Chairman: DAVID JAGNOW, 1300 Iris St., Apt. 103, Los Alamos, NM 87544-3140; Phone: 505-662-0553; Email: djagnow@roadrunner.com
International Secretary: JOHN LEE MOSES, 15807 River Roads Dr., Houston, TX 77079-5041; Phone: 281-597-1494
Publication(s): *NSS News; Journal of Cave and Karst Studies; publishers of speleological books*
Keyword(s): Biology, Endangered and Threatened Species, Environmental and Conservation Education, Geology

NATIONAL TRAPPERS ASSOCIATION, INC.
207 W. Jefferson St., P.O. Box 3667, Bloomington, IL 61702
Phone: 309-829-2422; Fax: 309-829-7615
Founded: 1959
Scope: National
Description: A national trappers organization dedicated to promoting sound conservation legislation; to conserving the nation's natural resources; to helping implement environmental education programs; and to promoting a continued annual furbearer harvest as a necessary wildlife management tool.
Contact(s):
President: CRAIG SPOORES, 18384 Weston Rd., Grand Rapids, OH 43522; Phone: 419-832-7903; Fax: 419-832-7903
Vice President: JOHN H. BECHTEL III, 164 Wheatland Dr., Gettysburg, PA 17325; Phone: 717-337-0734; Fax: 717-337-0734

Conservation Director: LAWRENCE KLINE, 1373 Ironwood St., Woodbridge, VA 22191; Phone: 703-494-8995; Fax: 703-494-8995

Director of Marketing and Public Relations: STEVE GREENE, 6901 Marlowe Rd. Apt. #514, Richmond, VA 23225; Phone: 804-560-4898; Fax: 804-560-0771

Director of National and International Affairs: SCOTT HARTMAN, Rt. 1 Box 43, New Martinsville, WV 26155; Phone: 304-455-4865; Fax: 304-455-5735; Email: trappers@ovnet.com

Editor and Advertising Manager: TOM KRAUSE, P.O. Box 513, Riverton, WY 82501; Phone: 307-856-3830; Fax: 307-857-2993

General Organizer: DAVID SOLLMAN, R.R. 1 Box391-1, Heltonville, IN 47436; Phone: 812-834-5334; Fax: 812-834-5334

Membership Secretary: KAREN LAVALLIER

Office Manager: CHRIS FORREST

Publication(s): *American Trapper*

Keyword(s): Renewable Resources, Sustainable Development, Trapping, Wildlife and Wildlife Habitat, Wildlife Management

NATIONAL TREE TRUST

1120 G St., NW, Suite 770, Washington, DC 20005
Phone: 202-628-8733; Fax: 202-628-8735

Founded: 1990
Scope: National

Description: The National Tree Trust serves as a catalyst for local volunteer and community service groups in growing, planting, and maintaining trees in rural communities, urban areas, and along the nation's highways. NTT mobilizes volunteer groups, promotes public awareness, provides educational and tree planting grants, and unites civic and corporate institutions in support of public land tree plantings.

Contact(s):
Executive Director: GEORGE L. CATES, Major General, USMC (Ret.) National Tree Trust, 1120 G St, NW, Ste. 770, Washington, DC 20005; Phone: 202-628-8733; Fax: 202-628-8735

Publication(s): *National Tree Trust News, The*

Keyword(s): Environment, Environmental and Conservation Education, Forests and Forestry, Public Lands, Urban Forestry

NATIONAL TRUST FOR HISTORIC PRESERVATION

Headquarters, 1785 Massachusetts Ave., NW, Washington, DC 20036
Phone: 202-588-6000

Founded: 1949; Membership: 250,000
Scope: National

Description: Private nonprofit membership organization chartered by Congress to encourage the public to participate in the preservation of America's historic and cultural heritage through advocacy, education, technical assistance, financial aid to nonprofit groups, and demonstration programs.

Contact(s):
President: RICHARD MOE

Publication(s): *Historic Preservation News; Historic Preservation Magazine; Preservation Law Reporter; Historic Preservation Forum*

Keyword(s): Environmental and Conservation Education, Historic Preservation, Land Use Planning, Renewable Resources, Urban Environment

Mid Atlantic
One Penn Center at Suburban Station, Suite 1520, 1617 John F. Kennedy Blvd., Philadelphia, PA 19144
Phone: 215-568-8162
Scope: Regional
Contact(s):
Director: PATRICIA WILSON

Midwest Office
53 W. Jackson Blvd., Suite 1135, Chicago, IL 60604
Phone: 312-939-5547
Scope: Regional
Contact(s):
Director: TIM TURNER

Mountains and Plains
511 16th St., Suite 700, Denver, CO 80202
Phone: 303-623-1504
Scope: Regional
Contact(s):
Director: BARBARA PAHL

Northeast Office
7 Faneuil Hall Marketplace, 5th Fl., Boston, MA 02109
Phone: 617-523-0885
Scope: Regional
Contact(s):
Director: WENDY NICHOLAS

Southern Office
456 King St., Charleston, SC 29403
Phone: 803-722-8552
Scope: Regional
Contact(s):
Director: SUSAN KIDD

Texas and New Mexico Offices
500 Main St., Suite 606, Fort Worth, TX 76102
Phone: 817-332-4398
Scope: Regional
Contact(s):
Director: ELIZABETH WILLIS

Western
One Sutter St., Suite 707, San Francisco, CA 94104
Phone: 419-956-0610
Scope: Regional
Contact(s):
Director: KATHRYN BURNS

NATIONAL WATER RESOURCES ASSOCIATION

3800 N. Fairfax Dr., Suite #4, Arlington, VA 22203
Phone: 703-524-1544; Fax: 703-524-1548; Email: nwra@erols.com; WWW: www.nwrs.org

Scope: National

Description: Promotes development, conservation and management of the water resources of 17 western state associations, including cities, counties, conservation districts, and individual members.

Contact(s):
President: DEWITT MOSS, 269-B S. 300E, Jerome, ID 83338
Executive Vice President: THOMAS F. DONNELLY

Publication(s): *National Waterline; Water Writes; Water Report*

Keyword(s): Agriculture, Endangered and Threatened Species, Nonpoint Source Pollution, Water Pollution, Water Resources, Wetlands

NATIONAL WATERSHED COALITION

9304 Lundy Ct., Burke, VA 22015
Phone: 703-455-6886; Fax: 703-455-6888; Email: jwpeterson@erols.com

Founded: 1989
Scope: National

Description: The NWC is a nonprofit coalition made up of national, regional, state, and local organizations, associations, and individuals, that advocate dealing with natural resources problems and issues using the watershed as the planning and implementation unit.

Contact(s):
Chair: B. BOWDEN

NON-GOVERNMENTAL ORGANIZATIONS

Secretary: D. SEBERT
Executive Director and Specialist: JOHN W. PETERSON
Vice Chair: B. HAMM
Publication(s): *Watershed News*

NATIONAL WATERWAYS CONFERENCE INC.
1130 17th St., NW, Washington, DC 20036
Phone: 202-296-4415
Founded: 1960; Membership: 500
Scope: National
Description: To promote a better understanding of the public value of water resource and water transportation programs and to show their importance to the total environment.
Contact(s):
Chairman: DENNIS L. KIRWIN, Executive Vice President of Midland Marine Corporation, 2550 N. Loop West, #115, Houston, TX 77092; Phone: 713-497-2100
Secretary: MICHAEL J. TOOHEY, Director of Federal Government Relations, Ashland, Inc., 601 Pennsylvania Ave., NW, #540-N, Washington, DC 20004; Phone: 202-223-8290
Treasurer: SCOTT ROBINSON, Port Director of Muskogee City-County Port Authority, 4901 Harodl Scoggins Dr., Muskogee, OK 74403; Phone: 918-682-7886
President and Editor: HARRY N. COOK
Vice Chairman: CRAIG E. PHILIP, President of Ingram Barge Company, P.O. Box 23049, Nashville, TN 37202; Phone: 615-298-8223
Publication(s): *Newsletter*
Keyword(s): Coasts, Energy, Rivers, Water Resources

NATIONAL WHISTLEBLOWER CENTER
National Whistleblower Legal Defense and Education Fund, P.O. Box 3768, Washington, DC 20007-2756
Phone: 202-667-7515
Founded: 1988
Scope: National
Description: The Fund is the only public insterest law firm dedicated to enforcing and enhancing the legal protections of employees who blow the whistle on significant violations of law, environmental protection, nuclear safety, and first amendment rights. The Fund provides legal advice, resources, and referrals for counsel to whistleblowers nationwide and conducts seminars and other outreach activities.
Contact(s):
Chairperson: STEPHEN M. KOHN, 3233 P. St. NW, Washington, DC 20007-2756; Phone: 202-342-6880
Publication(s): *Whistleblower News; Law Reporter*
Keyword(s): Environmental Ethics, Environmental Justice, Environmental Law, Training

NATIONAL WILD TURKEY FEDERATION, INC., THE
770 Augusta Rd., P.O. Box 530, Edgefield, SC 29824-0530
Phone: 803-637-3106; Fax: 803-637-0034
Founded: 1973; Membership: 180,000
Scope: National
Description: A nonprofit organization dedicated to the wise conservation and management of the American Wild Turkey and protecting the turkey hunting tradition. Comprised of 1,050 state and local affiliates. Supports annual research grants program.
Contact(s):
President: DR. JAMES G. DICKSON, P.O. Box 7600, SF#, Nacogdoches, TX 75962; Phone: 409-569-7981
Vice President: MICHAEL TULL, 1475 Holcomb Bridge Rd., Suite 113, Rosewell, GA 30076; Phone: 720-998-7830
Secretary: GLENN TEACHEY, 258 Harrison Bridge Rd., Simpsonville, SC 29861; Phone: 803-967-2917
Treasurer: EARL GROVES, New South Athletic Co., Inc; 301 E. Main St., Dallas, NC 28034; Phone: 704-922-1557
Chairman of the Board: LYNN BOYKIN, 1957 Point Legere, Mobile, AL 36605; Phone: 334-478-3152
Chief Financial Officer: JAMES SPARKS
Director of Communications: TAMMY LITZER
Director of Development: DONNA LEGGETT
Editor: JAY LANGSTON
Editor: RUSS LUMPKIN
Executive Vice President and CEO: ROB KECK; Phone: 409-569-7981
Vice President for Conservation Programs: JAMES EALR KENNAMER Ph.D.
Vice President of Operations: CARL BROWN
Publication(s): *Turkey Call Magazine; Caller, The*
Keyword(s): Forests and Forestry, Hunting, Public Lands, Scholarships and Grants, Wildlife Management

NATIONAL WILDLIFE FEDERATION
Headquarters, 8925 Leesburg Pike, Vienna, VA 22184-0001
Phone: 703-790-4000; Fax: 703-442-7332;
WWW: www.nwf.org
Founded: 1936; Membership: 4 million+
Scope: National
Description: A nonprofit organization whose mission is to educate, inspire, and assist individuals and organizations of diverse cultures to conserve wildlife and other natural resources and to protect the Earth's environment in order to achieve a peaceful, equitable, and sustainable future. **NOTE. Any correspondence for a member of the Board of Directors of the National Wildlife Federation should be directed to the National Wildlife Federation mailing address or fax number.**
Contact(s):
Chair of the Board: GERALD R. BARBER
Vice Chair of Central Region (IN): BECKY SCHEIBELHUT
Vice Chair of Eastern Region (VA): EDWARD CLARK JR.
Vice Chair of Western Region (NV): PAULA DEL GIUDICE
Director-At-Large: MAXINE S. THOMAS
Director-At-Large: VIRGINIA P. ALLERY
Director-At-Large: RICHARD J. BALDES
Director-At-Large: JUDITH ESPINOSA
Director-At-Large: TOM GONZALES
Director-At-Large: MARY C. HARRIS
Director-At-Large: STANLEY A. MOBERLY
Director-At-Large: JOHN S. RAINEY
Director-At-Large: JEROME C. RINGO
Regional Director of Region 1 (CT, MA, ME, NH, RI, VT): STEPHEN E. PETRON, Windham, NH
Regional Director of Region 10 (AZ, CO, NM, UT): BRYAN PRITCHETT, Littleton, CO
Regional Director of Region 11 (AK, OR, WA): ALLEN W. GUISINGER, Redmond, WA
Regional Director of Region 12 (CA, HI, NV): STEVEN L. MONTGOMERY, Waipahu, HI
Regional Director of Region 13 (ID, MT, WY): JO LYN REEVES, Laramie, WY
Regional Director of Region 2 (DC, DE, MD, NJ, NY, PA): CHARLES BROWN JR., Philadelphia, PA
Regional Director of Region 3 (NC, SC, VA, WV): HARMON SHADE, Isle of Palms, SC
Regional Director of Region 4 (AL, FL, GA, MS, VI): JAMES L. CARROLL, Jackson, MS
Regional Director of Region 5 (AR, KY, MO, TN): DARYL DURHAM, Eads, TN
Regional Director of Region 6 (IL, In, OH): DAN DEEB, Fort Wayne, IN
Regional Director of Region 7 (MI, MN, WI): JAMES BALDOCK, Waukesha, WI
Regional Director of Region 8 (LA, OK, TX): TOM MARTINE, Austin, TX
Regional Director of Region 9 (IA, KS, NE, ND, SD): SPENCER TOMB, Manhattan, KS
Headquarters Staff
President and Chief Executive Officer: MARK VAN PUTTEN
President and Chief Executive Officer of National Wildlife Productions: CHRISTOPHER PALMER
General Counsel: EILEEN MORGAN JOHNSON

Senior Vice President of Constituent Programs: NATALIE WAUGH
Chief Information Technology Officer: KENNETH HERMAN
Vice President and Coordinator for Conservation Programs: R. MONTGOMERY FISCHER
Vice President for Finance and Administration and Chief Executive Officer: LAWRENCE J. AMON
Vice President for Strategic Programs Initiative: BARBARA J. BRAMBLE
Vice President of Communications: PHILIP B. KAVITS
Vice President of Cause Related Marketing: JAIME MATYAS
Vice President of Educational Outreach (Acting): JAMES S. LYON
Vice President of Federal and International Affairs: STEVEN J. SHIMBERG
Vice President of Human Resources: ROBERT S. ERTTER
Vice President of Nature Education and Merchandise: JOHN H. GIESECKE
Vice President of Publications: ROBERT D. STROHM
Vice President of Southeastern Region: CAROLYN WALDON
Vice President of Western Region: J. SCOTT FEIERABEND
Past President: JAY D. HAIR
Past President: THOMAS L. KIMBALL
Editor of Conservation Directory: RUE E. GORDON
Editor of International Wildlife: JONATHAN FISHER
Editor of National Wildlife: MARK WEXLER
Editor of Ranger Rick: GERALD BISHOP
Editor of Your Big Backyard: DONNA JOHNSON
Publication(s): National Wildlife; International Wildlife; Ranger Rick; Conservation Directory;Your Big Backyard; EnviroAction; Campus Environmental Yearbook; Ecodemia; NatureScope; National Wildlife Week; Animal Tracks; EarthSavers
Keyword(s): Endangered and Threatened Species, International Conservation, Land Preservation, Sustainable Development, Water Quality, Wetlands

Office of Federal and International Affairs
1400 16th St., NW, Suite 501, Washington, DC 20036
Phone: 202-797-6800; Fax: 202-797-6646
Scope: National
Description: Efforts focus on the United States Congress, federal agencies, and non-governmental organizations (foreign and domestic). Domestic priority issues include endangered habitats, water quality, wetlands, public and private lands stewardship, and sustainable communities, including specific property rights issues (takings). International priority issues include population, trade and environment, climate change and wildlife habitats, and the environmental practices of international financial institutions.
Contact(s):
Vice President: STEVEN SHIMBERG

Alaska Project Office (AK, HI)
750 W. Second Ave., Suite 200, Anchorage, AK 99501
Phone: 907-258-4800; Fax: 907-258-4811
Scope: Regional
Description: The Alaska Project Office specializes in wetlands protection. The staff use litigation, education, and other tools to influence national wetlands policy and establish legal precedents while pursuing regional projects to protect Alaska's incomparable wetlands resources.
Contact(s):
Director: TONY TURRINI

Everglades Project Office
5051 Castello Dr., Suite 240, Naples, FL 34103
Phone: 941-643-4111; Fax: 941-643-5130
Scope: Regional
Description: The Everglades Project Office specializes in conserving and protecting the Big Cypress Watershed region of the Everglades. Advocating conservation-based land use planning, staff engages policy and decision-makers at the federal, state, and local level, and uses litigation and educational programs to influence management, legal, and legislative issues effecting the Everglades.
Contact(s):
Director: KRIS THOEMKE

Great Lakes Natural Resource Center (IL, IN, MI, OH, WI)
506 E. Liberty, Ann Arbor, MI 48104-2210
Phone: 313-769-3351; Fax: 313-769-1449; Email: nwfgrlks@igc.apc.org; WWW: www.nwf.org/greatlakes
Scope: Regional
Description: The Great Lakes Natural Resource Center is working to educate, inspire, and assist people who care to end the toxic pollution and habitat destruction that threaten the health of people, fish, and wildlife in the Great Lakes.
Contact(s):
Director: TIM EDER

Gulf States Natural Resource Center (AR, LA, MS, TX)
4505 Spicewood Springs, Suite 300, Austin, TX 78759
Phone: 512-346-3934; Fax: 512-346-3709
Scope: Regional
Description: The Gulf States Natural Resource Center is working to protect threatened rivers and important wetlands in the region and to restore polluted watersheds. The Center also promotes NWF's educational programs by working with schools and other organizations.
Contact(s):
Senior Director: SUSAN RIEFF

Northeast Natural Resource Center (CT, MA, ME, NH, NY, RI, VT)
58 State St., Montpelier, VT 05602
Phone: 802-229-0650; Fax: 802-229-4532
Scope: Regional
Description: The Northeastern Natural Resource Center is working for protection and sustainable use of northern forests through policy, advocacy, and education. The Center also concentrates its effort on protecting and restoring water quality in the northeast through research on the economic benefits of water quality and using a watershed-based approach to reduce polluted run-off. The Center focuses its education efforts on teachers, students, and citizens working to protect and restore key wildlife species such as wolves, peregrines, and amphibians in the northeast.
Contact(s):
Director: ERIC PALOLA

Northern Rockies Natural Resource Center (ID, MT, WY)
240 N. Higgins, Suite 2, Missoula, MT 59802
Phone: 406-721-6705; Fax: 406-721-6714
Scope: Regional
Description: The Northern Rockies Natural Resource Center focuses on safeguarding the ecosystems of our national norests and other public lands important to wildlife and people.
Contact(s):
Director: RICHARD DAY

Rocky Mountain Natural Resource Center (AZ, CO, NM, UT)
2260 Baseline Rd., Suite 100, Boulder, CO 80302
Phone: 303-786-8001; Fax: 303-786-8911
Scope: Regional
Description: The Rocky Mountain Natural Resource Center is dedicated to the conservation of wildlife and natural resources on public and private lands throughout the

NON-GOVERNMENTAL ORGANIZATIONS

Rocky Mountains. Center staff are working to restore biological diversity on millions of acres of native grasslands, to promote the restoration of water quality in western streams and rivers, and to promote the restoration of bison populations residing in Yellowstone National Park to lands throughout their historic range.
Contact(s):
Director: CATHY CARLSON

Southeastern Natural Resource Center (AL, FL, GA, NC, SC, TN, VI)
1330 West Peachtree St., Suite 475, Atlanta, GA 30309
Phone: 404-876-8733; Fax: 404-892-1744
Scope: Regional
Description: The Southeastern Natural Resource Center in Atlanta forges links between people and the environment, promoting sustainable practices to enhance the quality of life in our communities for people and wildlife. For example, NWF helps lead the Carver Hills Initiative to clean up and revitalize Atlanta's most polluted neighborhood, and is protecting wetlands like the Okefenokee Swamp.
Contact(s):
Director: ANDREW SCHOCK

Western Natural Resource Center (CA, NV, OR, WA)
2031 SE Belmont, Portland, OR 97214
Phone: 503-230-0421; Fax: 503-230-0677
Scope: Regional
Description: NWF's Western Natural Resource Center works to protect and restore wild salmon, wildlife such as bighorn sheep and the northern goshawk, and the rivers, forests, and grasslands on which these and other species depend. The Center also works with commuities and schools to create Backyard Wildlife Habitat sites to save water, eliminate chemicals, and support urban wildiife.
Contact(s):
Director: PETER FROST

NATIONAL WILDLIFE FEDERATION ENDOWMENT, INC.
8925 Leesburg Pike, Vienna, VA 22184-0001
Phone: 703-790-4000
Scope: National
Description: Established to support the conservation education and resource management programs of the National Wildlife Federation. Gifts and bequests are invested, and income is transferred to the National Wildlife Federation.
Contact(s):
Secretary: EILEEN MORGAN JOHNSON
Treasurer: LAWRENCE J. AMON
Assistant Secretary: NATALIE WAUGH
Board of Trustee: RAYMOND L. GOLDEN, New York, NY
Board of Trustee: MARY C. HARRIS, Arlington, VA
Board of Trustee: FRANCIS C. FARWELL, Madison, WI
Board of Trustee and Ex-Officio: GERALD R. BARBER, Ridgeland, MS
Board of Trustee Vice Chair: ALLEN W. GUISINGER, Redmond, WA
Chairman and Trustee: JOHN S. RAINEY, Columbia, SC

NATIONAL WILDLIFE PRODUCTIONS, INC.
8925 Leesburg Pike, Vienna, VA 22184
Phone: 703-790-4077
Scope: National
Description: National Wildlife Productions is the television, film, and multimedia arm of the National Wildlife Federation (NWF). The goal of NWP is to fulfill NWF's conservation mission by creating and producing television and mass-media projects, including children's television programs, documentaries, giant-screen films for IMAX theaters, feature films, TV movies, and interactive multimedia programs.
Contact(s):
President and Chief Executive Officer: CHRISTOPHER PALMER

Chairman: MARK VAN PUTTEN
Secretary: EILEEN MORGAN JOHNSON
Treasurer: LAWRENCE J. AMON

NATIONAL WILDLIFE REFUGE ASSOCIATION
1776 Massachusetts Ave., NW, Suite 200, Washington, DC 20036
Phone: 202-296-9729; Fax: 202-296-6030; Email: nwra@refugenet.org; WWW: www.refugenet.org
Founded: 1975
Scope: National
Description: The NWRA is the only national membership, nonprofit organization dedicated solely to protecting and preserving the National Wildlife Refuge System and to increasing public understanding and appreciation of it. Our mission is to preserve and enhance the integrity of the nation's largest network of lands and waters set aside primarily for the benefit of wildlife. Membership open to interested persons, organizations, institutions.
Contact(s):
President: DAVID TOBIN; Phone: 301-947-1921; Email: nwra_david@refugenet.org
Adiministration: SAM PAGE; Email: nwra_sam@refugenet.org
Associate Director: ANNE CRISS; Email: nwra_anne@refugenet.org
Director, Field Services: HEATH G. PACKARD; Email: nwra_heath@refugenet.org
Friends Initiative: BEVERLY HEINZE-LACEY, c/o Parker River NWR, 261 Northern Blvd., Newburport, MA 01950; Phone: 978-465-4178; Fax: 978-465-2807; Email: Regional Representative of Alaska: CALVIN LENSINK, 13641Jarvi Dr., Anchorage, AK 99515; Phone: 907-345-3096; Fax: 907-345-4693; Email: clensink@aol.com
Regional Representative of Great Lakes-Big Rivers: HAROLD W. BENSON, North 3042 State Road #13, Ogena, WI 54459; Phone: 715-767-5512; Fax: 715-767-5607
Regional Representative of Gulf Coast: RUSSELL W. CLAPPER, P.O. Box 1453, Anahuac, TX 77514; Phone: 409-252-3346; Fax: c/o State Farm 409-267-3802
Regional Representative of Mountain-Prairie: DALE HENRY, 7101 W Yale Ave. #405, Denver, CO 80227; Phone: 303-986-0583; Email: dbhenry@denver.net
Regional Representative of Pacific: ROBERT C. FIELDS, 1030 NW 176th Avenue, Beaverton, OR 97006; Phone: 503-645-3510; Email: bjfields@aol.com
Regional Representative of Southeast: PHILLIP S. MORGAN, 2032 Emadell Place, Loganville, GA 30052-5376; Phone: 770-972-6294; Fax: 770-978-6504
Regional Representative of Southwest: LAWRENCE S. SMITH, 1525 Cedar Ridge Dr. NE, Albuquerque, NM 87112; Phone: 505-293-0454; Fax: c/o Kinko's 505-293-3151; Email: cmfs00a@prodigy.com
Publication(s): *Blue Goose Flyer (Quarterly); Friends Flyer (Quarterly); Taking Flight - An Introduction to building refuge friends organizations, Annual Refuge Friends Group Directory, Annual National Wildlife Refugees Calandar*
Keyword(s): Conservation of Protected Areas, Environmental Preservation, Environmental Protection, Public Lands, Wildlife and Wildlife Habitat

NATIONAL WILDLIFE REHABILITATORS ASSOCIATION
14 N. 7th Ave., St. Cloud, MN 56303
Phone: 320-259-4086
Founded: 1982
Scope: National
Description: A nonprofit membership organization committed to promoting and improving the integrity and professionalism of wildlife rehabilitation and contributing to the preservation of natural ecosystems. The Organization disseminates information, provides training, and encourages networking through a quarterly journal, an annual membership directory, reviewed publications, annual symposia, and active committees for standards, wildlife medicine, education, awards, and grants.
Contact(s):
President: ELAINE M. THRUNE; Phone: 320-255-4911

Vice President: MICHAEL COX
Secretary: ERICA A. MILLER DVM
Treasurer: MARTHA POKRAS
Editor: DR. DANEIL R. LUDWIG, P.O. Box 2339, Glen Ellyn, IL 60138
Editor: BEA ORENDORFF, P.O. Box 245, Butler, KY 41006
Publication(s): *Wildlife Rehabilitation annual volumes; Principles of Wildlife Rehabilitation; Training Opportunities in Wildlife Rehabilitation; Minimum Standards for Wildlife Rehabilitation; NWRA Quarterly Journal*
Keyword(s): Birds, Environmental and Conservation Education, Mammals, Wildlife and Wildlife Habitat, Wildlife Rehabilitation

NATIONAL WOODLAND OWNERS ASSOCIATION
374 Maple Ave., E., Suite 210, Vienna, VA 22180
Phone: 703-255-2700
Founded: 1983; Membership: 41,000
Scope: National
Description: A nationwide association of woodland owners united to foster good stewardship of their nonindustrial private forest lands. Working together with cooperating and affiliated state woodland owners and forestry associations, the Association is a voice for private landowners on forestry, wildlife, and resource conservation issues. Sponsors the American Federation of Forest and Woodland Owner Associations with 31 state affiliates.
Contact(s):
President: MARK BURKE
Vice President: PAT PLITT, Frederick, MD
Secretary: EDWARD MURRINER
Treasurer: HOWARD KNOTTS
Editor (Interim): DAN KINCAID; Phone: 304-285-1524
Forestry Advisor: BOB WHIPKEY; Phone: 304-558-2788
Publication(s): *West Virginia Woods*
Keyword(s): Forests and Forestry

NATIONAL WOODLAND OWNERS ASSOCIATION (FORMERLY WISCONSIN WOODLAND OWNERS ASSOCIATION)
P.O. Box 285, Stevens Point, WI 54481-0285
Phone: 715-346-4798
Founded: 1979; Membership: 1,900
Scope: Statewide
Description: A statewide organization affiliated with the National Woodland Owners Association, established to advance the interests of woodland owners and the cause of forestry in Wisconsin.
Contact(s):
President: JACK D. EDSON, Strum, WI ; Phone: 715-878-4331
Vice President: JIM JOHNSON; Phone: 608-271-9718
Secretary: BEVERLY SCHENDEL, Bloomington, WI ; Phone: 612-881-7610
Treasurer: WALTER NAAB, Wautoma, WI ; Phone: 920-787-2174
Executive Director: NANCY C. BOZEK
Editor: JEANNE DOSCH, Madison, WI ; Phone: 608-231-5982
Publication(s): *Woodland Management*

NATIVE AMERICAN FISH AND WILDLIFE SOCIETY (NAFWS)
750 Burbank St., Broomfield, CO 80020
Phone: 303-466-1725; Fax: 303-466-5414
Founded: 1982; Membership: 1,500
Scope: National
Description: The Native American Fish and Wildlife Society is a nonprofit organization serving the needs of fish, wildlife, and natural resources on Tribal lands across the United States, including Alaska. The Society membership is comprised of approximately 1,500 professional and technical personnel associated with Native American natural resource programs. One hundred thirty seven federally-recognized tribes represent the Society, and many federal agencies rely on the Society's expertise and established network.
Contact(s):
President: ARTHUR BLAZER
Vice President: RANDY NOKA
Executive Director: KEN Q. POYNTER
Secretary and Treasurer: CAMERON MARTINEZ
Technical Director: PATRICK DURHAM
Publication(s): *From the Eagle's Nest*
Keyword(s): Cultural Preservation, Environmental Planning, Fisheries, Forests and Forestry, Wildlife Management

NATIVE AMERICANS FOR A CLEAN ENVIRONMENT (NACE)
P.O. BOX 1671, Tahlequah, OK 74465
Phone: 918-458-4322
Membership: 700
Scope: National
Description: NACE is an established Indian citizens environmental organization. The NACE held its first board meeting May 17, 1985. The purpose of NACE is to raise the consciousness of Indian people and the general public about environmental hazards, with an emphasis on the nuclear industry. NACE feels that we are caretakers of the earth and are responsible for her well-being.
Contact(s):
President: PAME KINGFISHER
Treasurer: NORMA FOURKILLER
Director: LANCE HUGHES
Publication(s): *NACE News*
Keyword(s): Nuclear/Radiation

NATIVE PLANT SOCIETY OF NORTHEASTERN OHIO
2651 Kerwick, University Heights, OH 44118
Phone: 216-371-4454
Founded: 1982; Membership: 100
Scope: Statewide
Description: The Native Plant Society of Northeastern Ohio protects and preserves native plants, trees, and shrubs.
Contact(s):
President: TOM SAMPLINER
Vice President: GEORGE WILDER; Phone: 216-932-3351
Secretary: BRIAN GILBERT; Phone: 216-486-8765
Treasurer: JOHN AUGUSTINE; Phone: 440-548-2414
Publication(s): *On the Fringe*
Keyword(s): Ancient Forests, Aquatic Habitats, Botanical Gardens, Conservation, Endangered and Threatened Species, Flowers, Plants, and Trees, Prairies, Wetlands

NATIVE PLANT SOCIETY OF OREGON
P.O. Box 902, Eugene, OR 97440
WWW: www.tekeport.com/nonprofit/npso
Founded: 1961; Membership: 919
Scope: Statewide
Description: The Native Plant Society of Oregon is a nonprofit statewide organization. The Society is dedicated to the enjoyment, conservation, and study of Oregon's native vegetation.
Contact(s):
President: MICHAEL FAHEY JR.; Phone: 360-694-2902
Vice President: MICHAEL McKEAG; Phone: 503-642-3965
Secretary: HEATHER LAUB; Phone: 541-386-2495
Treasurer: JEAN FRANCE; Phone: 503-639-0741
Publication(s): *Bulletin of the Native Plant Society of Oregon; Conservation and Management of Native Plants and Fungi; Proceedings from a Conference of the Native Plant of Oregon; KALMIOPSIS: Journal of the Native Plant Society of Oregon*
Keyword(s): Biodiversity, Conservation, Endangered and Threatened Species, Environmental Protection, Native Plants

NATIVE PLANT SOCIETY OF TEXAS
P.O. Box 891, Georgetown, TX 78627
Phone: 512-238-0695
Founded: 1980; Membership: 1,600
Scope: Statewide
Description: A nonprofit organization dedicated to the education and promotion of conservation, preservation, and utilization of the native plants and the plant habitats of Texas.
Contact(s):
President: MARY ANNE PICKENS; Phone: 409-732-5058
Coordinator: DANA TUCKER; Phone: 512-238-0695
Editor: BILL BISBEE; Phone: 713-966-3519

NON-GOVERNMENTAL ORGANIZATIONS

President-Elect: PETER LOOS; Phone: 281-362-1107
Vice President of Administration: MARK BARNETT; Phone: 817-666-3223
Vice President of Chapter Liaison: ERNEST TREMAYNE; Phone: 210-895-1106
Vice President of Finance: SUZANNE TUTTLE; Phone: 817-481-3301
Publication(s): Native Plant Society of Texas News

NATIVE PRAIRIES ASSOCIATION OF TEXAS
3503 Lafayette Ave., Austin, TX 78722
Phone: 512-476-1663; Fax: 512-476-1663; Email: buzzandlee@sprintmail.com
Membership: 200
Scope: National
Description: Native Prairies Association of Texas is dedicated to conservation and restoration of native prairies, through education, research, public awareness, agency cooperation, management, restoration, and acquisitions.
Contact(s):
President: JAMES ALDERSON; Phone: 258-742-9888; Fax: 254-298-1273
Vice President: GENE HEINEMANN; Phone: 512-337-0618
Secretary: LEE STONE
Treasurer: PAUL McCYNSKI; Phone: 254-896-5534
Publication(s): Prairie Dog, The
Keyword(s): Conservation Easements, Prairies, Restoration

NATURAL AREAS ASSOCIATION
P.O. Box 1504, Bend, OR 97709
Phone: 541-317-0199; Fax: 541-317-0140; Email: naa@natareas.org
Founded: 1980; Membership: 2,200
Scope: National
Description: A nonprofit organization of professional and active volunteers in natural area identification, preservation, protection, management, and research. Provides a medium of exchange and coordination to advance the understanding and appreciation of natural areas and natural diversity.
Contact(s):
President: HARRY R. TYLER JR., Maine State Planning Office, 184 State St., State House Station 38, Augusta, ME 04333; Phone: 207-287-1489; Fax: 207-287-7379; Email: hank.tyler@state.me.us
Vice President: NANCY MATHEWS, University of Wisconsin-Madison, Department of Wildlife Ecology, 215 Russell Labs, 1630 Linden Drive, Madison, WI 53706; Phone: 608-263-6697; Fax: 608-262-6099; Email: nemathew@facstaff.wisc.edu
Secretary: CARL BECKER, Natural Heritage Division, Illinois Dept. of Natural Resources, 524 Second St., Springfield, IL 62701-1787; Phone: 217-785-8774; Fax: 217-785-8277; Email: cbecker@dnrmail.state.il.us
Treasurer: GARY BURNETT, Rocky Mountain Elk Foundation, P.O. box 8249, Missoula, MT 59807-8249; Phone: 406-523-4516; Fax: 406-523-4550; Email: garyb@rmef.org
Executive Director: REID SCHULLER, P.O. Box 1504, Bend, OR 97709; Phone: 541-317-0199; Fax: 541-317-0140; Email: naa@natareas.org
Journal Editor: DON LEOPOLD, State University of New York, College of Environmental Science and Forestry, Syracuse, NY 13210; Phone: 315-470-6784; Fax: 315-470-6934; Email: dendro@mailbox.syr.edu
Publication(s): Natural Areas Journal, Natural Area News
Keyword(s): Biodiversity, Conservation of Protected Areas, Endangered and Threatened Species, Land Preservation, Natural Areas, Nature Preservation, Nongame Wildlife, Wildlands

NATURAL HISTORY SOCIETY OF MARYLAND, INC., THE
2643 N. Charles St., Baltimore, MD 21218-4590
Phone: 410-235-6116
Founded: 1929; Membership: 300
Scope: Statewide
Description: A nonprofit membership organization formed to promote the appreciation of natural history through education, research, and publication--thereby fostering stewardship of natural and cultural resources. The Society maintains a museum of Maryland objects and a library, and bestows the Edmund B. Fladung Award to recognize persons exemplifying the society's goals.
Contact(s):
President: DONNELL E. REDMAN
Vice President: JEFFREY A. WOLINSKI
Treasurer: RICHARD LEADER
Board of Trustees Chairman: CHARLES A. DAVIS
Editor: JOSEPH McSHARRY
Editor: ARNOLD NORDEN
Editor: HERBERT S. HARRIS JR.
Editor: DANIELL E. REDMAN
Librarian: C. HAVEN KOLB
Recording Secretary: WILLIAM F. SEIP
Publication(s): Bulletin of the Maryland Herpetological Society; The Maryland Naturalist; News and Views; Proceedings of the Natural History Society of Maryland
Keyword(s): Birds, Flowers, Plants, and Trees, Insects and Butterflies, Mammals, Natural History, Reptiles and Amphibians

NATURAL LAND INSTITUTE
320 S. 3rd St., Rockford, IL 61104
Phone: 815-964-6666; Fax: 815-964-6661; Email: nli@aol.com
Founded: 1958; Membership: 650
Scope: Statewide
Description: A nonprofit organization dedicated to preserving natural areas and natural diversity through a comprehensive program of land protection, stewardship, research, education, and advocacy.
Contact(s):
President: GORDON EGGERS
Vice President: GARY McINTYRE
Secretary: RANDY G. VINCENT
Treasurer: BRYCE ROSS-SHANNON
Executive Director: EDWIN W. STIRLING
Land Preservation Specialist: DAVID CLUTTER
Publication(s): Land and Nature; Boone and Winnebago Regional Greenways Plan
Keyword(s): Aquatic Habitats, Biodiversity, Birds, Conservation of Protected Areas, Ecology, Endangered and Threatened Species, Environmental Planning, Environmental Preservation, Environmental Protection, Land Preservation, Land Purchase, Land Use Planning, Natural Areas, Watersheds

NATURAL LANDS TRUST, INC.
Hildacy Farm, 1031 Palmers Mill Rd., Media, PA 19063
Phone: 610-353-5587; Fax: 610-353-0517
Founded: 1961; Membership: 1,100
Scope: Regional
Description: Natural Lands Trust is a regional land trust dedicated to working with people to conserve land in the Philadelphia metropolitan region and other nearby areas of environmental concern by acquiring and managing preserve properties, accepting conservation easements, and encouraging and supporting the conservation efforts of landowners, communities, government agencies, and other nonprofit organizations.
Contact(s):
President: PHILIP S. WALLIS
Board of Trustees Chairman: DOUGLAS C. WALKER
Vice President for Conservation Planning: RANDALL G. ARENDT
Vice President of Finance and Administration: JILL A. BEMIS
Vice President of Landowner Stewardship: PETER J. SMYRL
Publication(s): Nature Lands

NATURAL RESOURCES COUNCIL OF AMERICA
1025 Thomas Jefferson St. NW Suite 109, Washington, DC 20007-5291
Phone: 202-333-0411
Founded: 1946; Membership: 69
Scope: National
Description: An association of nonprofit environmental and conservation organizations dedicated to the protection, conservation, and responsible management of the nation's natural resources. The Council coordinates cooperative efforts between its members, government agencies, private citizens, and businesses. The Council also administers the Conservation Round Table Luncheon series, an annual Conservation Community Banquet and Awards program, and publishes a quarterly newsletter.
Contact(s):
Executive Director: ANDREA J. YANK, 1025 Thomas Jefferson St. NW, Suite 109, Washington, DC 20009-5201; Phone: 202-333-0411; Fax: 202-333-0412
Keyword(s): Fisheries, Forests and Forestry, Public Lands, Water Resources, Wildlife and Wildlife Habitat

NATURAL RESOURCES COUNCIL OF MAINE
3 Wade St., Augusta, ME 04330
Phone: 207-622-3101; Fax: 207-622-4343; Email: nrcm@nrcm.org
Scope: Statewide
Description: A representative statewide organization, affiliated with the National Wildlife Federation, dedicated to the protection and enhancement of wildlife and its habitat through public education and government interaction.
Contact(s):
President: BEN LUND
Executive Director and Affiliate Representative: EVERETT B. CARSON
Alternate Representative: TIM GLIDDEN
Editor: LESLIE E. HAHN
Publication(s): *Maine Environment*

NATURAL RESOURCES DEFENSE COUNCIL, INC.
Headquarters, 40 W. 20th St., New York, NY 10011
Phone: 212-727-2700; Email: nrdcinfo@nrdc.org; WWW: www.nrdc.org
Founded: 1970; Membership: 400,000
Scope: National
Description: Nonprofit membership organization dedicated to protecting America's endangered natural resources and to improving the quality of the human environment. Combines interdisciplinary legal and scientific approach in crafting innovative solutions, monitoring government agencies, bringing legal action, and disseminating citizen information. Areas of concentration: air and water pollution, global warming, nuclear safety, land use, urban environment, pollution prevention, ecosystem management, wilderness and wildlife protection, international environment, Alaska, energy efficiency, forestry, and ocean and fisheries protection.
Contact(s):
Executive Director: JOHN H. ADAMS; Phone: 212-727-2700
Chairman of the Board: FREDERICK A. SCHWARZ JR.; Phone: 212-727-2700
Editor: DANA FOLEY
Editor: KATHRIN LASSILA
Publication(s): *Amicus Journal, The; A complete list of NRDC's books and reports is available upon request.*

Los Angeles, California Office
6310 San Vicente Blvd., Suite 250, Los Angeles, CA 90048
Phone: 213-934-6900
Scope: National

San Francisco, California Office
71 Stevenson St., #1825, San Francisco, CA Phone: 415-777-0220
Scope: National

Washington, D.C. Office
1200 New York Ave., NW, Suite 400, Washington, DC 20005
Phone: 202-289-6868
Scope: National

NATURAL RESOURCES INFORMATION COUNCIL
Anne Hedrich Science & Technology Library, 3100 Old Main Hill, Logan, UT 84322-3100
Phone: 435-797-2165; Fax: 435-797-7475; Email: annhed@cc.usu.edu; WWW: www.usu.edu/~cnr/quinney/nrichome.html
Founded: 1991; Membership: 25
Scope: National
Description: Federal, state, provincial, academic, and special research librarians and information specialists from U.S. and Canada who facilitate the exchange of information on sustainable natural resources. Goals are to build a network of resource people to collect and disseminate information on sustainable natural resources and to provide continuing education.
Contact(s):
Membership: ANNE HEDRICH; Phone: 435-797-2165; Fax: 435-797-7475; Email: annhed@cc.usu.edu
Treasurer: BARBARA VOELTZ; Email: bvoeltz@ngpc.state.ne.us
Publication(s): *Fish and Game Natural Resource Library Survey, Annual Newsletter*
Keyword(s): Natural History, Natural Science, Sustainability, Sustainable Resources, Librarians/Information Professionals

NATURAL SCIENCE FOR YOUTH FOUNDATION
130 Azalea Dr., Roswell, GA 30075
Phone: 404-594-9367
Scope: National
Description: Provides counseling to community groups in the planning and development of environmental and natural science centers, museums, and native animal parks which are designed particularly to meet the needs and interests of children and young people. Conducts an annual conference as part of its widespread effort to promote professional excellence in environmental and natural science centers and museums.
Contact(s):
President: CHARLES S. COCHRANE
Secretary: GEORGINE PINDAR
Treasurer: JOHN L. HAMMAKER
Founder and President Emeritus: JOHN RIPLEY FORBES
Publications Director: OWEN D. WINTERS
Publication(s): *Directory of Natural Science Centers; Natural Science Center News; Opportunities Jobs Bulletin*
Keyword(s): Environmental and Conservation Education, Natural History, Outdoor Recreation, Wildlife Rehabilitation, Youth Organizations

NON-GOVERNMENTAL ORGANIZATIONS

NATURE CONSERVACNY, THE, NEW YORK EASTER CHAPTER
200 Broadway, 3rd Floor, Troy, NY 12180
Phone: 518-272-0195
Scope: Regional

NATURE CONSERVANCY OF CANADA, THE
110 Eglinton Ave., W., Suite 400, Toronto, Ontario M4R 1A2 Canada
Phone: 416-932-3202; Fax: 416-932-3208; Email: nature@natureconservancy.ca
Founded: 1963
Scope: National
Description: A national nonprofit organization dedicated to the acquisition and preservation of ecologically-significant natural land areas throughout Canada in cooperation with industry, governments, conservation groups, and individuals. Raises and contributes funds to support the conservation of natural areas.
Contact(s):
Chairman: ELVA KYLE
Executive Director: JOHN LAUNDS
Associate Director of Development: SHERI-LYNN ARMSTRONG
Publication(s): *Annual Report; Ark, The*

NATURE CONSERVANCY OF COLORADO, THE
1244 Pine St., Boulder, CO 80302
Phone: 303-444-2950; Fax: 303-444-2986
Founded: 1965; Membership: 22,000
Scope: Statewide
Description: To preserve the plants, animals, and natural communities that represent the diversity of life in Colorado by protecting the land and water they need to survive.
Contact(s):
Treasurer: GRAYDON HUBBARD
Board of Trustees Chair: THOMAS A. GOUGEON
Vice Chair: ROBERT COLLINS
Vice Chair: BONNIE MACDONALD
Vice Chair: JUDITH SELLERS
Publication(s): *Landmark Newsletter*
Keyword(s): Aquatic Habitats, Biodiversity, Biology, Birds, Conservation of Protected Areas, Ecology, Endangered and Threatened Species, Environment, Environmental Preservation, Environmental Protection, Fisheries, Flowers, Plants, and Trees, Insects and Butterflies, International Conservation, Internships

NATURE CONSERVANCY, THE
Headquarters, 4245 North Fairfax Dr., Arlington, VA 22208
Phone: 703-841-5300; Fax: 703-841-1283; WWW: www.tnc.org
Founded: 1951; Membership: 832,000
Scope: International
Description: International nonprofit membership organization committed to preserving biological diversity by protecting natural lands, and the life they harbor; cooperates with educational institutions, public and private conservation agencies. Works with states through "natural heritage programs" to identify ecologically significant natural areas. Manages a system of over 1,600 nature sanctuaries nationwide.
Contact(s):
President: JOHN C. SAWHILL
Chairman of the Board: SAM JOHNSON
Chief Conservation Officer: BILL WEEKS
Chief Operations Officer: DOUG HALL
Conservation Science: DEBORAH JENSEN
Development and Marketing: STEPHANIE MEEKS
General Counsel: MIKE DENNIS
Human Resources and Organizational Development: PRISCILLA VASQUEZ
Latin America: ALEXANDER WATSON
Membership Development: DONNA CHEREL
Membership Services: PAT SCHNEIDER
Stewardship: LIZ CHORNESKY
Vice President for Administration: RAY CULTER

Eastern Office
201 Devonshire St. 5th Fl., Boston, MA 02110
Phone: 617-542-1908
Scope: Regional
Contact(s):
Vice President: LAURA JOHNSON, 201 Devonshire St., 5th Fl., Boston, MA 02110; Phone: 617-542-1908
Editor-in-Chief: RON GEATZ
Executive Editor: MARK CHEATER
Hawaii Director: REX JOHNSON; Phone: 808-537-4508
Publication(s): *Nature Conservancy, Magazine; The* **Keyword(s):** Biodiversity, Endangered and Threatened Species, International Conservation, Land Purchase, Wildlife and Wildlife Habitat

Midwest Office
1313 5th St. SE314, Minneapolis, MN 55414
Phone: 612-331-0700
Scope: Regional
Contact(s):
Contact: JANE PROHASKA

New York Region Office
91 Broadway, Albany, NY 12204
Phone: 518-463-6133
Scope: Regional
Contact(s):
Contact: CAROL ASH

Pacific Office
1116 Smith St. Suite 201, Honolulu, HI 96817
Phone: 808-537-4508
Scope: Regional
Contact(s):
Director: KELVIN TAKETA

Southeast Office
P.O. Box 2267, Chapel Hill, NC 27515-2267
Phone: 919-967-5493
Scope: Regional
Contact(s):
Vice-President: MICHAEL ANDREWS

Western Region Office
2060 Broadway Suite 230, Boulder, CO 80302
Phone: 303-444-1060
Scope: Regional
Contact(s):
Director: DENNIS DONALD

NATURE CONSERVANCY, THE, ALABAMA CHAPTER
2821 C 2nd Ave., Birmingham, AL 35233
Phone: 205-251-1155
Scope: Regional

NATURE CONSERVANCY, THE, ALASKA CHAPTER
421 W. First Ave., #200, Anchorage, AK 99501
Phone: 907-276-3133
Scope: Regional

NATURE CONSERVANCY, THE, ARIZONA CHAPTER
300 E. University Blvd., #230, Tuscon, AZ 85705
Phone: 520-622-3861
Scope: Regional

NATURE CONSERVANCY, THE, ARKANSAS CHAPTER
601 N. University Ave., Little Rock, AR 72205
Phone: 501-663-6699
Scope: Regional

NATURE CONSERVANCY, THE, ASIA/PACIFIC PROGRAM
1116 Smith St., #201, Honolulu, HI 96817
Phone: 808-537-4508
Scope: International

NATURE CONSERVANCY, THE, CALIFORNIA CHAPTER
201 Mission St. 4th Fl., San Francisco, CA 94105
Phone: 415-777-0487
Scope: Regional
Contact(s):
Contact: STEVE McCORMICK

NATURE CONSERVANCY, THE, COLORADO CHAPTER
1244 Pine St., 4th Floor, Boulder, CO 80302
Phone: 303-444-2950
Scope: Regional

NATURE CONSERVANCY, THE, CONNECTICUT CHAPTER
55 High St., Middletown, CT 06457
Phone: 860-344-0716
Scope: Regional

NATURE CONSERVANCY, THE, DELAWARE CHAPTER
260 Chapman Rd., #210D, Newark, DE 19702
Phone: 302-369-4144
Scope: Regional

NATURE CONSERVANCY, THE, FLORIDA CHAPTER
222 S. Westmonte Dr. Suite 300, Altamonte Springs, FL 32714
Phone: 407-682-3664
Scope: Regional
Contact(s):
Contact: ROBERT BENDICK

NATURE CONSERVANCY, THE, HAWAII CHAPTER
1116 Smith St., #201, Honolulu, HI 96817
Phone: 808-537-4508
Scope: Regional

NATURE CONSERVANCY, THE, IDAHO CHAPTER
P.O. Box 165, Sun Valley, ID 83353
Phone: 208-726-3007
Scope: Regional

NATURE CONSERVANCY, THE, ILLINOIS CHAPTER
8 S. Michigan Ave., #900, Chicago, IL 60603
Phone: 312-346-8166
Scope: Regional

NATURE CONSERVANCY, THE, INDIANA CHAPTER
1330 W. 38th St., Indianapolis, IN 46208
Phone: 317-923-7547
Scope: Regional

NATURE CONSERVANCY, THE, IOWA CHAPTER
108 3rd St., Suite 300, Des Moines, IA 50309-4759
Phone: 515-244-5044
Founded: 1963; Membership: 7,000
Scope: Statewide
Description: The mission of The Nature Conservancy is to preserve plants, animals, and natural communities that represent the diversity of life on earth by protecting the lands and water they need to survive.
Contact(s):
Chairman: G. DAVID HURD; Phone: 515-247-5479
Secretary: DR. CHARISSE BUISING; Phone: 515-271-2756
Treasurer: BARBARA MENDENHALL; Phone: 712-332-2900
Director: GARY B. REINERS; Phone: 515-244-5044
Co-Vice Chairman: MARILYN MAGID; Phone: 319-365-6018
Co-Vice Chairman: FRED WEITZ; Phone: 515-245-7611
Publication(s): *Field Notes*
Keyword(s): Biodiversity, Endangered and Threatened Species, Environmental Preservation, Land Purchase, Sustainable Development

NON-GOVERNMENTAL ORGANIZATIONS

NATURE CONSERVANCY, THE, KANSAS CHAPTER
820 S.E. Quincy, #301, Topeka, KS 66612
Phone: 785-233-4400
Scope: Regional

NATURE CONSERVANCY, THE, KENTUCKY CHAPTER
642 W. Main St., Lexington, KY 40508
Phone: 606-259-9655
Scope: Regional

NATURE CONSERVANCY, THE, LATIN AMERICA AND CARRIBBEAN DIVISION
4245 N. Fairfax Dr., Suite 100, Arlington, VA 22203
Phone: 703-841-5300
Scope: International

NATURE CONSERVANCY, THE, LOUISIANA CHAPTER
P.O. Box 4125, Baton Rouge, LA 70821
Phone: 504-338-1040
Scope: Regional

NATURE CONSERVANCY, THE, MAINE CHAPTER
14 Maine St., #401, Brunswick, ME 04011
Phone: 207-729-5181
Scope: Regional

NATURE CONSERVANCY, THE, MARYLAND/D.C. CHAPTER
2 Wisconsin Circle, #300, Chevy Chase, MD 20815
Phone: 301-656-8673
Scope: Regional

NATURE CONSERVANCY, THE, MASSACHUSETTS CHAPTER
70 Milk St., #300, Boston, MA 02109
Phone: 617-423-2545
Scope: Regional

NATURE CONSERVANCY, THE, MICHIGAN CHAPTER
2840 E. Grand River, #5, East Lansing, MI 48823
Phone: 517-332-1741
Scope: Regional

NATURE CONSERVANCY, THE, MINNESOTA CHAPTER
1313 Fifth St., SE, #320, Minneapolis, MN 55414
Phone: 612-331-0750
Scope: Regional

NATURE CONSERVANCY, THE, MISSISSIPPI CHAPTER
6400 Lakeover Rd., Jackson, MS 39213
Phone: 601-713-3355
Scope: Regional

NATURE CONSERVANCY, THE, MISSOURI CHAPTER
2800 S. Brentwood Blvd., St. Louis, MO 63144
Phone: 314-968-1105
Scope: Regional

NATURE CONSERVANCY, THE, MONTANA CHAPTER
32 South Ewing, Helena, MT 59601
Phone: 406-443-0303
Scope: Regional

NATURE CONSERVANCY, THE, NEBRASKA CHAPTER
1722 St. Mary's Ave., #403, Omaha, NE 68102
Phone: 402-342-0282
Scope: Regional

NATURE CONSERVANCY, THE, NEVADA CHAPTER
1771 E. Flamingo, #111B, Las Vegas, NV 89119
Phone: 702-737-8744
Scope: Regional

NATURE CONSERVANCY, THE, NEW HAMPSHIRE CHAPTER
2 1/2 Beacon St., #6, Concord, NH 03301
Phone: 603-224-5853
Scope: Regional

NATURE CONSERVANCY, THE, NEW JERSEY CHAPTER
200 Pottersville Rd., Chester, NJ 07930
Phone: 908-879-7262
Scope: Regional

NATURE CONSERVANCY, THE, NEW MEXICO CHAPTER
212 E. Marcy, #200, Santa Fe, NM 87501
Phone: 505-988-3867
Scope: Regional

NATURE CONSERVANCY, THE, NEW YORK ADIRONDACK CHAPTER
P.O. Box 65, Route 73, Keene Valley, NY 12943
Phone: 518-576-2082
Scope: Regional

NATURE CONSERVANCY, THE, NEW YORK CENTRAL/WESTERN CHAPTER
315 Alexander St., 2nd Floor, Rochester, NY 14604
Phone: 716-546-8030
Scope: Regional

NATURE CONSERVANCY, THE, NEW YORK LONG ISLAND CHAPTER
250 Lawrence Hill Rd., Cold Spring Harbor, NY 11724
Phone: 516-367-3225
Scope: Regional

NATURE CONSERVANCY, THE, NEW YORK LOWER HUDSON CHAPTER
41 S. Moger Ave., Mt. Kisco, NY 10549
Phone: 914-244-3271
Scope: Regional

NATURE CONSERVANCY, THE, NEW YORK SOUTH FORK/SHELTER ISLAND CHAPTER
P.O. Box 5125, E. Hampton, NY 11937
Phone: 516-329-7689
Scope: Regional

NATURE CONSERVANCY, THE, NORTH CAROLINA CHAPTER
4011 Univeristy Dr., #201, Durham, NC 27707
Phone: 919-403-8558
Scope: Regional

NATURE CONSERVANCY, THE, NORTH DAKOTA CHAPTER
P.O. Box 1156, Bismarck, ND 58502-1156
Phone: 701-222-8464
Scope: Regional

NATURE CONSERVANCY, THE, OHO CHAPTER
6375 Riverside Dr., #50, Dublin, OH 43017
Phone: 614-717-2770
Scope: Regional

NATURE CONSERVANCY, THE, OKLAHOMA CHAPTER
23 West Fourth, #200, Tulsa, OK 74103
Phone: 918-585-1117
Scope: Regional

NATURE CONSERVANCY, THE, OREGON CHAPTER
821 SE 14th Ave., Portland, OR 97214
Phone: 503-230-1221
Scope: Regional

NATURE CONSERVANCY, THE, PENNSYLVANIA CHAPTER
1100 E. Hector St., #470, Conshohocken, PA 19428
Phone: 610-834-1323
Scope: Regional

NATURE CONSERVANCY, THE, RHODE ISLAND CHAPTER
45 S. Angell St., St. Providence, RI 02906

Phone: 401-331-7110
Scope: Regional

NATURE CONSERVANCY, THE, SOUTH CAROLINA CHAPTER
P.O. Box 5475, Columbia, SC 29250
Phone: 803-254-9049
Scope: Regional

NATURE CONSERVANCY, THE, SOUTH DAKOTA CHAPTER
1000 West Ave., N., #100, Sioux Falls, SD 57104
Phone: 605-331-0619
Scope: Regional

NATURE CONSERVANCY, THE, TENNESSEE CHAPTER
50 Vantage Way, #250, Nashville, TN 37228
Phone: 615-255-0303
Scope: Regional

NATURE CONSERVANCY, THE, TEXAS CHAPTER
P.O. Box 1440, San Antonio, TX 78295-1440
Phone: 210-224-8774
Scope: Regional

NATURE CONSERVANCY, THE, UTAH CHAPTER
559 E. South Temple, Salt Lake City, UT 84102
Phone: 801-531-0999
Scope: Regional

NATURE CONSERVANCY, THE, VERMONT CHAPTER
27 State. St., Montpelier, VT 05602
Phone: 802-229-4425
Scope: Regional

NATURE CONSERVANCY, THE, VIRGIN ISLANDS CHAPTER
148 Norre Gade, 2nd Flr., Charlotte Amue, VI 00802
Phone: 809-774-7633
Scope: Regional

NATURE CONSERVANCY, THE, VIRGINIA CHAPTER
1330 W. Peachtree St., #410, Atlanta, VA 30309
Phone: 404-873-6946
Scope: Regional
1233-A Cedars Court, Charlottesville, VA 22903
Phone: 804-295-6106
Scope: Regional

NATURE CONSERVANCY, THE, WASHINGTONG CHAPTER
217 Pine St., #1100, Seattle, WA 98101
Phone: 206-343-4344
Scope: Regional

NATURE CONSERVANCY, THE, WEST VIRGINIA CHAPTER
723 Kanawha Blvd. East, #500, Charleston, WV 25301
Phone: 304-345-4350
Scope: Regional

NATURE CONSERVANCY, THE, WISCONSIN CHAPTER
633 W. Main St., Madison, WI 53703
Phone: 608-251-8140
Scope: Regional

NATURE CONSERVANCY, THE, WYOMING CHAPTER
258 Main St., #200, Lander, WY 82520
Phone: 307-332-2971
Scope: Regional

NATURE CONSERVATION SOCIETY OF JAPAN, THE (NACS-J)
Nihon-Shizen-Hogo-Kyokai, Yamaji Saubauncho Bldg. 3F, 5-24 Sanbancho, Chiyoda Ku, Tokyo 102 Japan
Phone: 81-3-3265-0521; Fax: 81-3-3265-0527
Founded: 1951; Membership: 20,000
Scope: International
Description: A nonprofit, membership conservation organization devoted to promoting conservation, research, and education concerning the natural areas and wildlife in Japan, and also a recently launched international project to support biodiversity in developing countries.
Contact(s):
President: MAKOTO NUMATA
Director General: KIYOSHI OKUTOMI
Publication(s): *Nature Conservation (Japanese); Red List of Plant Species in Japan (Japanese); Red List of Plant Communities in Japan (Japanese)*

NATURE SASKATCHEWAN
206-1860 Lorne St., Regina, Saskatchewan S4P 2L7 Canada
Phone: 306-780-9273; Fax: 306-780-9263; Email: nature.sask@unibase.com; WWW: www.unibase.com/~naturesk
Founded: 1947; Membership: 2,000
Scope: Statewide
Description: Nature Saskatchewan is the largest non-profit nature organization in the province, committed to preserving our natural environment. We operate a nature bookshop, offer ecological tours, own nature sanctuaries, and support conservation and research activities and nature education.
Contact(s):
President: KATHLEEN DONAUER
Secretary: LEONA POLLOCK
Treasurer: DALE HJERTAAS
1st Vice President: DIANA BIZECKI ROBSON
2nd Vice President: BILL SARJEANT
Director of Administration: RUBY LaFAYETTE
Director of Conservation: GARTH NELSON
Director of Education: GREG FENTY
Honorary President: MARRY GILLILAND
Past President: BOB BERTHIAUME
Publication(s): *Blue Jay; Nature Views; special publication*
Keyword(s): Aquatic Habitats, Biodiversity, Birds, Conservation of Protected Areas, Ecology, Endangered and Threatened Species, Environment, Environmental Law, Flowers, Plants, and Trees, Insects and Butterflies, Land Preservation, Mammals, Natural Areas, Natural History

NEBRASKA ASSOCIATION OF NATURAL RESOURCE DISTRICTS
ATTN: President, 326 Road K, Richland, NE 68601
Scope: Statewide
Contact(s):
President, Alternate Board Member: CLINT JOHANNES, 326 Road K, Richland, NE 68601; Phone: 402-352-5640; Fax: 402-563-4272
Executive Director: DEAN EDSON, 601 S. 12th St., Suite 201, Lincoln, NE 68508; Phone: 402-471-7674; Fax: 402-471-7677
Board Member: MIKE MOSEL, R.R. 1, Ogallala, NE 69153; Phone: 308-352-4053; Fax: 308-352-4199
Secretary/Treasurer: DEAN RASMUSSEN, P.O. Box 1, N. Loup, NE 68859; Phone: 402-496-4284

NEBRASKA AUDUBON COUNCIL
11649, Burt St. #11, Omaha, NE 68154
Phone: 402-493-0373
Founded: 1985; Membership: 3,750
Scope: Statewide
Description: A statewide council of representatives of the eight National Audubon Society chapters in Nebraska. The Council's purpose is to coordinate efforts of the chapters on statewide environmental issues and advocate protection, preservation, and wise use of our soil, water, plants, and wildlife.
Contact(s):
President: ALICE RUMERY, 3911 Ave. E., Kearney, NE 68847; Phone: 308-237-3358
Treasurer: IONE WERTHMAN, 11649 Burt St., #11, Omaha, NE 68154; Phone: 402-493-0373

NON-GOVERNMENTAL ORGANIZATIONS

Legislative Coordinator: DAVID SANDS, The Apothecary, Suite 217, 140 N. 8th St., Lincoln, NE 68508; Phone: 402-475-1177

NEBRASKA B.A.S.S. CHAPTER FEDERATION
ATTN: President, 1518 Kozy Dr., Columbus, NE 68601
Phone: 402-563-2297
Scope: Statewide
Description: An organization of Bassmaster chapters, affiliated with the Bass Anglers Sportsman Society, organized to fight pollution, assist state and national conservation agencies in their efforts, and teach the young people of our country good conservation practices. Dedicated to the realistic conservation of our water resources.
Contact(s):
President: JOE CITTA, JR., 1518 Kozy Dr., Columbus, NE 68601; Phone: 402-563-2297
Conservation Director: BOB ALTWINE, 416 N. 5th St., Pierce, NE 68767; Phone: 402-329-4989

NEBRASKA CHAPTER OF THE AMERICAN FISHERIES SOCIETY
ATTN: President, Nebraska Chapter, 215 N. 17th St., Omaha, NE 68105
Founded: 1969; Membership: 60
Scope: Statewide
Description: The chapter is involved with issues pertaining to natural resources. Membership is composed of fishery science professionals and university students of fishery science. The Nebraska Chapter AFS is a state sub-unit chartered by the American Fisheries Society, a national organization. The Nebraska Chapter AFS supplies the parent society with annual activities by the chapter, provides information to legislative representatives on water issues, provides annual training sessions and technical seminars on fishery science studies for members, and provides awards for achievements in fisheries conservation.
Contact(s):
President: BECKY LATKA, Nebraska Chapter, 215 North 17 St., Omaha, NE 68105; Phone: 402-221-4602

NEBRASKA ORNITHOLOGISTS' UNION, INC. (University of Nebraska State Museum)
W436 Nebraska Hall, Lincoln, NE 68588-0514
Phone: 402-472-8366
Founded: 1899; Membership: 250
Scope: Statewide
Description: To promote the study of ornithology in Nebraska by both professionals and amateurs; to publish the results of independent studies; and to promote the passage and enforcement of judicious laws for bird protection.
Contact(s):
Vice President: LANNY RANDOLPH, 50374 24th Rd., Gibbon, NE 68840-9654; Phone: 308-468-5057
Secretary: ROBIN HARDING, 50374 24th Rd., Gibbon, NE 68840-9654; Phone: 308-468-5057
Treasurer: SUE AMIOTTE, 11 City Dam Rd., Chasron, NE 69337; Phone: 308-432-3783
Director: ALICE KENITZ, 190648 County Rd. 22, Gering, NE 69341; Phone: 308-436-2959
Director: MARK BROGIE, 508 Seeley, Box 316, Creighton, NE 68729; Phone: 402-358-5675
Director: TOM LABEDZ, 724 Glenarbor Cir., Lincoln, NE 68512; Phone: 402-423-1384
Librarian: MARY LOU PRITCHARD, 6325 O St. #515, Lincoln, NE 68510-2246
President and Newsletter Editor: BETTY ALLEN, 9628 Emmet St., Omaha, NE 68134
Publication(s): *Nebraska Bird Review, The*
Keyword(s): Birds

NEBRASKA WILDLIFE FEDERATION, INC.
P.O. Box 81437, Lincoln, NE 68501-1437
Phone: 402-476-9081; Fax: 402-994-2001
Founded: 1970
Scope: Statewide
Description: A representative statewide organization, affiliated with the National Wildlife Federation, dedicated to the protection and enhancement of wildlife and its habitat through public education and government interaction.
Contact(s):
President: DAVID KOUKOL
Affiliate Representative: GENE OGLESBY
Executive Director and Editor: DUANE HOVORKA
Publication(s): *Prairie Blade*

NEVADA ASSOCIATION OF CONSERVATION DISTRICTS
ATTN: President, 320 N. Crook Rd., Fallon, NV 89406
Scope: Statewide
Contact(s):
President, Alternate Board Member: FRANK SOARES, 320 N. Crook Rd., Fallon, NV 89406; Phone: 702-423-3955; Fax: 702-423-7594
Vice President: PATSY TOMERA, HC 65 Box 11, Carlin, NV 89822-9701; Phone: 702-754-2333
Executive Director: TERI KING, 111 Scheckler Rd., Fallon, NV 89406; Phone: 702-423-5124; Fax: 702-423-7594
Board Member: JOE SICKING, 1550 Cushman Rd., Fallon, NV 89406; Phone: 702-423-5216; Fax: 702-423-9574

NEVADA WILDLIFE FEDERATION
P.O. Box 71238, Reno, NV 89570
Phone: 702-645-5423; Fax: 702-885-0405; Email: dupree@pyramid.net; WWW: www.nvwf.org
Scope: Statewide
Description: A representative statewide organization, affiliated with the National Wildlife Federation, dedicated to the protection and enhancement of wildlife and its habitat through public education and government interaction.
Contact(s):
President: FRANK MAXWELL
Affiliate Representative: SUSAN SELBY
Alternate Representative: GALE DuPREE
Editor: ED JORGENSEN
Publication(s): *Western Sportsmen*

NEVIS HISTORICAL AND CONSERVATION SOCIETY
P.O. Box 563, Charlestown, Charlestown St. Kitts and Nevis
Phone: 869-469-5786; Fax: 869-469-0274
Founded: 1980; Membership: 500
Scope: National
Description: To foster the conservation of the natural, historic, and cultural aspects of Nevis and its surrounding waters by educational programs, publishing projects, and other awareness endeavors.
Contact(s):
President: LYRA RICHARDS; Phone: 869-469-2164,(W)869-469-5565/5796/1451
Vice President: CALVIN HOWELL; Phone: 869-469-1347
Secretary: EDRISE FELLOWS; Phone: 869-469-2147
Treasurer: JEFFIFER LOWREY
Publication(s): *Nevis Historical and Conservation Society Newsletter; FCO News; Nevis Environmentalist*
Keyword(s): Cultural Preservation, Environmental and Conservation Education, Historic Preservation, Nature Preservation, Sustainable Development

NEW BRUNSWICK WILDLIFE FEDERATION
Box 1066, Moncton, New Brunswick E1C 8P2 Canada
Phone: 506-859-1240
Founded: 1924
Scope: Statewide
Description: Promotes the wise use of renewable natural resources, with prime emphasis on education of the young. Affiliated with the Canadian Wildlife Federation.
Contact(s):
President and Executive Director: RICHARD DEBON

NEW ENGLAND ASSOCIATION OF ENVIRONMENTAL BIOLOGISTS (NEAEB)
60 Westview St., Lexington, MA 02173
Phone: 617-860-4300
Founded: 1976
Scope: Regional
Description: A professional society of environmental scientists, engineers and planners from industry and state and federal agencies in the northeast, working to coordinate and enhance environmental programs in each state. The organization advances technical information on environmental research, planning and management and evaluates the effectiveness of environmental regulations for protection of water quality.
Contact(s):
Executive Committee: ERNEST PIZZUTO
Information Officer: HOWARD DAVIS, EPA 60 Westview St., Lexington, MA 02173; Phone: 617-861-6700

NEW ENGLAND NATURAL RESOURCES CENTER
Box 44, Wayland, MA 01778
Phone: 508-358-2261
Founded: 1970; Membership: 15
Scope: National
Description: A nonprofit trust organized to provide a focal point for discussion and resolution of regional natural resource and environmental issues.
Contact(s):
Chairman: PERRY HAGENSTEIN, Box 44, Wayland, MA 01778
Vice Chairman: RUSSELL L. BRENNEMAN, Murtha, Cullina, Richter & Pinney, 101 Pearl St., Hartford, CT 06102
Keyword(s): Communications, Renewable Resources

NEW ENGLAND WILD FLOWER SOCIETY, INC.
180 Hemeway Rd., Framingham, MA 01701-2699
Phone: 508-877-7630; Fax: 508-877-3658; Email: newfs@newfs.org; WWW: www.newfs.org/newfs/
Founded: 1900; Membership: 5,000
Scope: National
Description: The New England Wild Flower Society is a nonprofit organization that promotes the conservation of temperate North American plants through conservation and research, education, horticulture, and habitat preservation.
Contact(s):
President: MOLLY BEARD
Vice President: GEORGE C. HARRINGTON
Secretary: DANA N. JOST
Treasurer: LALOR BURDICK
Executive Director: DAVID L. DeKING
Publication(s): *New England Wild Flower - Journal and Program Events; New England Wild Flower - Conservation Notes of New England Wild Flower Society; Curtis Trail Guide*
Keyword(s): Botanical Gardens, Conservation, Endangered and Threatened Species, Environmental and Conservation Education, Gardening and Horticulture, Natural History

NEW HAMPSHIRE ASSOCIATION OF CONSERVATION COMMISSIONS
54 Portsmouth St., Concord, NH 03301
Phone: 603-224-7867
Founded: 1970; Membership: 188 municipalities in NH/1,300 conservation commissioners
Scope: Statewide
Description: A nonprofit organization whose purpose is to foster conservation and wise use of NH's natural resources and to assist and facilitate communication and cooperation among the state's 200 conservation commissions.
Contact(s):
President: DIANE EADIE
Vice President: KATHERINE METZGER
Secretary: PATRICIA SCHLESINGER
Treasurer: RONALD KLEMARCZYK
Executive Director and Editor: MARJORY M. SWOPE
Publication(s): *NH Conservation News; Handbook for Municipal Conservation Commissions in New Hampshire; Legislative Updates*
Keyword(s): Environmental Law, Environmental Preservation, Land Use Planning, Water Resources, Wetlands

NEW HAMPSHIRE ASSOCIATION OF CONSERVATION DISTRICTS
ATTN: President, P.O. Box 404, Sunappe, NH 03782
Scope: Statewide
Contact(s):
President: ROBERT L. WARD, P.O. Box 404, Sunapee, NH 03782; Phone: 603-763-5425; Fax: 603-763-4194
1st Vice President: KITTY MILLER, 156 Concord Rd., Lee, NH 03824; Phone: 603-868-5217; Fax: 603-743-3667
2nd Vice President: HARRY E. KENNEDY III, Richardson Rd., Marlborough, NH 03455; Phone: 603-876-3838; Fax: 603-756-2978
Administrator: JOAN RICHARDSON, 44 Main St., P.O. Box 533, Conway, NH 03818-0533; Phone: 603-447-2771; Fax: 603-447-8945
Board Member: JOHN HODSDON, 85 Daniel Webster Hwy, Meredith, NH 03253; Phone: 603-279-6126; Fax: 603-528-8783
Secretary and Treasurer: STANELY GRIMES, 529 Buck St., Pembroke, NH 03275; Phone: 603-876-3838; Fax: 603-233-6030

NEW HAMPSHIRE B.A.S.S. CHAPTER FEDERATION
ATTN: President, 98 Chase Rd., Londonderry, NH 03053
Phone: 603-434-6759
Scope: Statewide
Description: An organization of Bassmaster chapters, affiliated with the Bass Anglers Sportsman Society, organized to fight pollution, assist state and national conservation agencies in their efforts, and teach the young people of our country good conservation practices. Dedicated to the realistic conservation of our water resources.
Contact(s):
President: DICK FRUCI, 98 Chase Rd., Londonderry, NH 03053; Phone: 603-434-6759

NEW HAMPSHIRE LAKES ASSOCIATION
7 South State St., Concord, NH 03301
Phone: 603-226-0299; Fax: 603-224-9442; Email: info@nhlakes.org; WWW: www.nhlakes.org
Founded: 1992; Membership: 2,100 individuals, 165 associations
Scope: Statewide
Description: The New Hampshire Lakes Association is a nonprofit education and advocacy organization dedicated to protecting and preserving New Hampshire's lakes for responsible, equitable enjoyment of everyone. The NHLA provides assistance to individuals and lake associations throughout New Hampshire.
Contact(s):
Executive Director: JACK CALHOUN; Email: jcalhoun@nhlakes.org

NON-GOVERNMENTAL ORGANIZATIONS

Special Projects Director: MICHELE L. TREMBLAY; Email: mtremblay@nhlakes.org
Publication(s): *Lakeside (quarterly magazine), Educational Brochures*
Keyword(s): Aquatic Habitats, Environment, Environmental and Conservation Education, Environmental Planning, Environmental Protection, Lakes, Land Use Planning, Open Space, Outdoor Recreation, Water Quality, Watersheds

NEW HAMPSHIRE TIMBERLAND OWNERS ASSOCIATION
54 Portsmouth St., Concord, NH 03301
Phone: 603-224-9699; Fax: 603-225-5898
Founded: 1911; Membership: 1,400
Scope: Statewide
Description: A statewide organization affiliated with the National Woodland Owners Association, dedicated to the promotion of wise forest management and the protection of forestry interests in New Hampshire.
Contact(s):
President: KEVIN EVANS
Secretary: SARAH SMITH
Treasurer: TED TICHY
Executive Director: ERIC W. KINGSLEY
Editor: PATRICK D. HACKLEY
President-Elect: JEFFREY PUTNAM
Publications: TIMBER CRIER
Keyword(s): Forests and Forestry

NEW HAMPSHIRE WILDLIFE FEDERATION
P.O. Box 239, 54 Portsmouth Rd., Concord, NH 03302
Phone: 603-224-5953; Fax: 603-228-0423; Email: nhwf@aol.com; WWW: www.nhwf.org
Scope: Statewide
Description: A representative statewide organization, affiliated with the National Wildlife Federation, dedicated to the protection and enhancement of wildlife and its habitat through public education and government interaction.
Contact(s):
President: MARIANNE CONRAD
Affiliate Representative: JOHN MONSON
Alternate Representative & Executive Director: KAREN COFFEY
Publication(s): *New Hampshire Wildlife*

NEW JERSEY AGRICULTURAL SOCIETY
CN 331, Trenton, NJ 08625
Phone: 609-394-7766
Founded: 1781; Membership: 1,100
Scope: Statewide
Description: The Society has continually worked to educate the public and promote agriculture in New Jersey. The Society is charitable, nonprofit, and conducts numerous educational programs about agriculture's vital role in the economy of New Jersey.
Contact(s):
President: RAYMOND L. BLEW JR.
Vice President: WILLIAM PETTIT; Phone: 609-292-3976
Assistant Secretary and Treasurer: EARL F. ERVEY
Editor: JONI ELLIOTT
Secretary and Treasurer: ARTHUR R. BROWN JR.
Publication(s): *Harbinger; Garden View*

NEW JERSEY ASSOCIATION OF CONSERVATION DISTRICTS
ATTN: 234 Chapel Heights Rd., Sewell, NJ 08080
Scope: Statewide
Contact(s):
President: JAY KANDLE, 234 Chapel Heights Rd., Sewell, NJ 08080; Phone: 609-589-7916
Secretary: EDWARD DIPOLVERE, 53 Cubberly Rd., Trenton, NJ 08690; Phone: 609-586-2684
Treasurer: ALLEN D. CARTER, P.O. Box 403, Tuckahoe, NJ 08250; Phone: 609-628-2466
1st Vice President: CLIFFORD R. LUNDIN, 8 Skytop Rd., Andover, NJ 07821; Phone: 973-398-2511

2nd Vice President: JOHN PERRY, 805 Brookside Dr., Toms River, NJ 08753; Phone: 732-349-2705
Past President: CATHERINE A. COSTA, 160 Indigo Dr., Mt. Laurel, NJ 08054; Phone: 609-727-4282

NEW JERSEY AUDUBON SOCIETY
P.O. Box 126, 9 Hardscrabble Rd., Bernardsville, NJ 07924
Phone: 908-204-8998
Founded: 1897; Membership: 16,000
Scope: Statewide
Description: Fosters environmental awareness and a conservation ethic among New Jersey citizens; protects New Jersey's birds, mammals, other animals, and plants, especially endangered and threatened species; and promotes preservation of New Jersey's valuable natural habitats.
Contact(s):
Board Chairperson: CHARLES F. WEST
Cape May Bird Observatory: , Northwood Center, 701 E. Lake Dr., P.O. Box 3, Cape May Point, NJ 08212; Phone: 609-884-2736
Director for Nature Center of Cape May: GRETCHEN FERRANTE, 1600 Delaware Ave., Cape May, NJ 08204; Phone: 609-898-8848
Director of Lorrimer Sanctuary: GORDON SCHULTZE, P.O. Box 125, 790 Ewing Ave., Franklin Lakes, NJ 07417; Phone: 201-891-2185
Director of Owl Haven Nature Center: PETE BACINSKI, 250 Route 522, P.O. Box 26, Tennent, NJ 07763; Phone: 732-780-7007
Director of Rancocas Nature Center: KARL ANDERSON, 794 Rancocas Rd., Mt. Holly, NJ 08060; Phone: 609-261-2495
Director of Weis Ecology Center: KARLA RISDON, 150 Snake Den Rd., Ringwood, NJ 07456; Phone: 973-835-2160
President and CEO: THOMAS J. GILMORE
Vice President for Conservation: RICHARD KANE
Vice President for Education: PATRICIA KANE, Sherman and Hoffman Sanctuaries, 111 Hardscrabble Rd., P.O. Box 693, Bernardsville, NJ 07924; Phone: 908-766-5787
Vice President of Natural History Information: PETER DUNNE, Cape May Bird Observatory, Center for Research and education, 600 Rt. 47 N., Cape May Court House, NJ 08210; Phone: 609-861-0700
Keyword(s): Environmental and Conservation Education, Land Preservation, Natural History

NEW JERSEY B.A.S.S. CHAPTER FEDERATION
ATTN: President, 77 Kenvil Ave., Succasunna, NJ 07876
Phone: 201-584-9387
Scope: Statewide
Description: An organization of Bassmaster chapters, affiliated with the Bass Anglers Sportsman Society, organized to fight pollution, assist state and national conservation agencies in their efforts, and teach the young people of our country good conservation practices. Dedicated to the realistic conservation of our water resources.
Contact(s):
President: TONY GOING, 77 Kenvil Ave., Succasunna, NJ 07876; Phone: 201-584-9387
Conservation Director: JOHN TURNEY, 13 Pumpkin Hill Rd., Warwick, NY 10990; Phone: 914-986-0669

NEW JERSEY CONSERVATION FOUNDATION
Bamboo Brook, 170 Longview Rd., Far Hills, NJ 07931
Phone: 908-234-1225; Fax: 908-234-1189; WWW: www.eclipse.net/~njcf
Founded: 1960; Membership: 6,400
Scope: Statewide
Description: A nonprofit membership organization concerned with environmental education issues related to land use and open-space acquisition and preservation through use of its revolving land fund. Formed from the Great Swamp Committee of the North American Wildlife Foundation.
Contact(s):
President: C. LAWRENCE KELLER
Secretary: PETER B. MOORE
Treasurer: LANGDON PALMER

Executive Director: DAVID F. MOORE
1st Vice President: HOPE E. ROBERTSON
2nd Vice President: CYNTHIA KELLOGG
Counsel: JAMES P. WYSE
Editor: PATRICIA J. BAXTER
Publication(s): *New Jersey Conservation; New Jersey Highlands, The: Treasures at Risk; Greenways to the Arthurkill; Charting a Course for the Delaware Bay Watershed*
Keyword(s): Agriculture, Biodiversity, Environmental and Conservation Education, Environmental Planning, Land Preservation, Land Purchase, Land Use Planning, Natural Areas, Nature Preservation, Open Space, Public Lands, Sustainable Development, Sustainable Ecosystems, Urban Environment, Watersheds

NEW JERSEY ENVIRONMENTAL LOBBY
204 W. State St., Trenton, NJ 08608
Phone: 609-396-3774; Fax: 609-396-4521
Founded: 1969; Membership: 1,000 individuals and 150 local and statewide environmental organizations
Scope: Statewide
Description: To advocate for legislation and regulation that is protective and preservative of both the natural and the built environment with a view, always, of protecting human health for all citizens and future generations. Conversely, we oppose those laws and regulations that are detrimental to the above.
Contact(s):
President: ANNE POOLE, 43 Four Mile Rd., Pemberton, NJ 08068; Phone: 609-894-4113
Vice President: KIM KAISER, 40 E. Valley Brook Rd., Long Valley, NJ 07853
Secretary: MARK HERZBERG, 24 Clinton Pl., Metuchen, NJ 08840; Phone: 908-494-4883
Treasurer: AL KENT, 39 Crystal Ave., West Orange, NJ 07052; Phone: 201-731-6546
Publication(s): *NJ Environmental Lobby News; periodic special reports*
Keyword(s): Air Quality and Pollution, Energy, Land Use Planning, Sustainable Development, Transportation

NEW JERSEY FORESTRY ASSOCIATION
1628 Prospect St., Trenton, NJ 08638
Phone: 609-771-8301
Founded: 1975; Membership: 900
Scope: Statewide
Description: A statewide organization affiliated with the National Woodland Owners Association. Formed to encourage the scientific management and perpetuation of woodlands in New Jersey.
Contact(s):
President: THOMAS F. BULLOCK, Haddonfield, NJ ; Phone: 609-696-5300
Vice President: GEORGE H. PIERSON, Pennington, NJ ; Phone: 609-737-0489
Executive Secretary: RON SHEAY, Trenton, NJ ; Phone: 609-771-8301
Editor: RICHARD WEST
Editor: RON SHEAY
Past President: RICHARD F. WEST, Jamesburg, NJ ; Phone: 908-521-6636
Publication(s): *New Jersey Woodlands*
Keyword(s): Forests and Forestry

NEW MEXICO ASSOCIATION OF CONSERVATION DISTRICTS
ATTN: President, P.O. Box 274, Hatch, NM 87194
Scope: Statewide
Contact(s):
President and Board Member: JOE PAUL LACK JR., P.O. Box 274, Hatch, NM 87194; Phone: 505-267-1016; Fax: 505-267-1234
Treasurer: THOMAS SHELLEY, P.O. Box 7, Hurley, NM 88043; Phone: 505-537-4111

Executive Director: DEBBIE HUGHES, 163 Trail Canyon Rd., Carlsbad, NM 88220; Phone: 505-981-2400; Fax: 505-981-2422
Vice President, Alternate Board Member: CAROL REED, P.O. Box 853, Rociada, MN 87742; Phone: 505-425-6564; Fax: 505-425-6564; Email: rc_reed@nmhu.campus.mci.net

NEW MEXICO BASS CHAPTER FEDERATION
Attn: Conservation Director, P.O. Box 717, Socorro, NM 87808
Phone: 505-744-4324
Scope: Statewide
Description: An organization of Bassmaster chapters, affiliated with the Bass Anglers Sportsman Society, organized to fight pollution, assist state and national conservation agencies in their efforts, and teach the young people of our nation good conservation practices. Dedicated to the realistic conservation of our water resources.
Contact(s):
President: BILL PATTERSON, P.O. Box 1487, Elephant Butte, NM 87935; Phone: 505-744-4324
Conservation Director: RON GILWORTH, P.O. Box 717, Socorro, NM 87801; Phone: 505-835-1200
Publication(s): *New Mexico B.A.S.S. Federation Newsletter "BigMouth"*

NEW MEXICO ENVIRONMENTAL LAW CENTER
1405 Luisa St. Suite 5, Santa Fe, NM 87505
Phone: 505-989-9022; Fax: 505-989-3769
Founded: 1987; Membership: 1,000
Scope: Statewide
Description: The New Mexico Environmental Law Center is a nonprofit, public interest law firm. The Law Center is the only New Mexico organization that provides free legal services for the preservation of the state's natural resources and protection of its citizens against environmental hazards. The Law Center represents grassroots organizations, individuals, and other environmental groups in site-specific efforts; participates in statewide and federal legislative advocacy; and provides public education.
Contact(s):
Executive Director: DOUGLAS MEIKLEJOHN
Board of Director: MIKE LILLEY
Board of Director: FRANK SANCHEZ
Board of Director: EDITH K. PIERPONT
Board of Director: ANTONIO LUJAN
Board of Director: DAVID HENDERSON
Board of Director: MARION DAVIDSON
Board of Director: RICHARD BARISH
Board of Director: LESLIE BARCLAY

NEW MEXICO WILDLIFE FEDERATION
3240-D Juan Tabo NE, Suite 204, Albuquerque, NM 87111
Phone: 505-299-5404
Scope: Statewide
Description: A representative statewide organization, affiliated with the National Wildlife Federation, dedicated to the protection and enhancement of wildlife and its habitat through public education and government interaction.
Contact(s):
President: CHUCK EASTON
Affiliate Representative: MARY REED
Alternate Representative: BILL REED
Publication(s): *New Mexico Outdoor Reporter*

NEW YORK ASSOCIATION OF CONSERVATION DISTRICTS, INC.
ATTN: President, P.O. Box 244, Panama, NY 14767
Scope: Statewide
Contact(s):
President, Board Member: DAVID STURGES, P.O. Box 244, Panama, NY 14767; Phone: 716-782-2697
Vice President: HARRY KELSEY, 6947 Macomber Rd., Oakfield, NY 14125; Phone: 716-948-5788

NON-GOVERNMENTAL ORGANIZATIONS

Secretary: CARL SEYMOUR, 242 Grange Hall Rd., Schuylerville, NY 12871; Phone: 518-695-9249
Treasurer: WILLIAM CHAMBERLAIN, Box 487, Henderson Harbor, NY 13651; Phone: 315-938-7106
Executive Vice President: ANITA CARTIN, 1 Winners Cir., Capital Plaza, Albany, NY 12235; Phone: 518-457-7229; Fax: 518-457-2716

NEW YORK B.A.S.S. CHAPTER FEDERATION
ATTN: President, 274 N. Goodman St., Rochester, NY 14607
Phone: 716-266-2083
Scope: Statewide
Description: An organization of Bassmaster chapters, affiliated with the Bass Anglers Sportsman Society, organized to fight pollution, assist state and national conservation agencies in their efforts, and teach the young people of our country good conservation practices. Dedicated to the realistic conservation of our water resources.
Contact(s):
President: SCOTT KELLER, 274 N. Goodman St., Rochester, NY 14607; Phone: 716-271-7000(W)/716-266-2083(H)
Conservation Director: SCOTT FRANCK, R.D. 2 Box 2073, Gilchrist Hill Rd., Hartford, NY 12838; Phone: 518-632-5829

NEW YORK FOREST OWNERS ASSOCIATION, INC.
P.O. Box 180, Fairport, NY 14450
Phone: 716-377-6060
Founded: 1962; Membership: 1,800
Scope: Statewide
Description: A statewide organization, affiliated with the National Woodland Owners Associaiton, organized to unite the 500,000 owners of 11 million acres of forest land in New York in encouraging the wise management of private woodland resources in New York State by promoting, protecting, representing, and serving the interests of woodland owners.
Contact(s):
President: JILL CORNELL, Johnsonville, NY ; Phone: 518-753-4336
Treasurer: DON WAGNER, Utica, NY ; Phone: 315-733-7391
Administrator: DEBORAH GILL, Fairport, NY ; Phone: 716-377-6060
Editor: RICHARD FOX; Phone: 315-497-1078
Publication(s): *Forest Owner*
Keyword(s): Forests and Forestry

NEW YORK PUBLIC INTEREST RESEARCH GROUP (NYPIRG
Main Office, 9 Murray St., 3rd Fl., New York, NY 10007
Phone: 212-349-6460; Fax: 212-349-7474
Founded: 1973; Membership: 80,000
Scope: Statewide
Description: The NYPIRG is a nonprofit, nonpartisan research group established and directed by New York state college students. Staff lawyers, researchers, and advocates work with students and other citizens developing citizenship skills and shaping public policy on environmental preservation, good government, and consumer issues.
Contact(s):
Executive Director: CHRIS MEYER
Chairperson: MICHAEL LIVERMORE
Publication(s): *NYPIRG Agenda; NYC CouncilWatch; Get the Lead Out*
Keyword(s): Environmental Justice, Pesticides, Solid Waste Management, Toxic Substances, Transportation

NEW YORK TURTLE AND TORTOISE SOCIETY
163 Amsterdam Ave., Suite 365, New York, NY 10023
Phone: 212-459-4803
Founded: 1970; Membership: 2,100
Scope: National
Description: The Society is dedicated to the conservation and preservation of habitat, and the promotion of proper husbandry and captive propagation of turtles. Education of members and the public is a key goal. Events held in the NYC area include a seminar, field trips, and show.
Contact(s):
President: SUZANNE DOHM
Vice President: ALLEN FOUST
Secretary: RITA DEVINE
Editor of Proceedings: JIM VAN ABBEMG
Membership: JOAN FRUMKIES
Treasurer of Wildlife Rehabilitation: LORI CRANER
Publication(s): *Plastron Papers; Journal of the New York Turtle and Tortoise Society; NYTTS; NewsNotes*
Keyword(s): Environmental and Conservation Education, Nongame Wildlife, Reptiles and Amphibians, Wildlife Rehabilitation, Zoology

NEW YORK-NEW JERSEY TRAIL CONFERENCE INC.
232 Madison Ave., New York, NY 10016
Phone: 212-685-9699
Founded: 1920; Membership: 10,000
Scope: Regional
Description: A nonprofit organization which coordinates the efforts of hiking and outdoor groups in New York and New Jersey to build and maintain over 1,300 miles of foot trails and whose purpose is to protect and conserve open space, wildlife, and places of natural beauty and interest.
Contact(s):
President: H. NEIL ZIMMERMAN
Vice President: GARY HAUGLAND
Secretary: DANIEL CHAZIN
Executive Director: JoANN DOLAN
Chairman of Trails Council: GARY HAUGLAND
Publication(s): *Trail Walker; New York Walk Book; New Jersey Walk BookGuide to the Appalachian Trail in New York and New Jersey; Guide To The Long Path; Catskill Trails Map Set; Hiking the Catskills; Iron Mine Trails; Delaware Water Gap National Recreation Area Hiking Guide; Health Hints for Hikers; Circuit Hikes; Harriman Trails Guide; Scenes and Walks in the Northern Shawongunks; several map sets.*
Keyword(s): Land Preservation, Natural Areas, Open Space, Outdoor Recreation

NEWFOUNDLAND LABRADOR WILDLIFE FEDERATION
ATTN: President, 67 Commonwealth Ave., Mount Pearl, Newfoundland A1N1W7 Canada
Phone: 709-364-8415
Membership: 900 - 24 Affiliated Clubs 5300 members
Scope: Statewide
Contact(s):
President: GORDON COOPER, 67 Commonwealth Ave., Mount Pearl, Newfoundland A1N 1W7 Canada; Phone: 709-368-6180
Secretary: FRANCES CLEARY, 14 Fairhaven Pl., St. John's, Newfoundland A1E 4S1 Canada; Phone: 709-335-2226
Keyword(s): Acid Rain, Air Quality and Pollution, Ancient Forests, Aquatic Habitats, Biodiversity, Birds, Ecology, Environmental Ethics, Forest Management, Lakes, Mammals, Nongame Wildlife, Solid Waste Management, Trapping, Wildlife and Wildlife Habitat

NIPPON ECOLOGY NETWORK
Ecology Center Bldg., 3 Fukuromachi, Shinjukku-ku, Tokyo 162 Japan
Phone: 81-3-5228-3344; Fax: 81-3-5228-6040; WWW: www.venture-web.or.jp/ecoland
Scope: International
Description: NEN is currently involved in many aspects of environment, agriculture, and food safety issues. Among NEN operations are: Radish boya, an organic and natural food home delivery system servicing over 55,000 homes; the Japan Ecology Center, an information center; Atopikko Chikyu no ko, a network of medical advisors and the allergy afflicted; and the Tree Free Club, an organization that promotes the use of alternatives to tree-based papers and manages the Tree Free Fund; the promotion and sales of water purification system and the Green Marketing Institute, an environmental marketing consultation and research firm.
Contact(s):
Chairman: MICHIAKI TOKUE
Publication(s): *Kurashi-no-ki (Environmental Lifestyle Magazine, Japanese); Japan Ecology Center News*

NORTH AMERICAN ASSOCIATION FOR ENVIRONMENTAL EDUCATION

Headquarters, 1255 23rd St., NW, Suite 400, Washington, DC 20037
Phone: 202-884-8912; Fax: 202-884-8701; Email: jthoreen@erinet.com; WWW: www.naaee.org

Founded: 1971
Scope: National
Description: NAAEE is dedicated to promoting environmental education and supporting the work of environmental educators in North America and around the world. NAAEE is made up of professionals who have thought seriously about how individuals become literate concerning environmental issues, and about how to prepare people to work together towards resolving environmental problems.
Contact(s):
President: JUDY BRAUS
Treasurer: SHERI SYKES SOYKA
Executive Director: EDWARD J. McCREA
Publication(s): *Environmental Communicator; Annual Conference Proceedings; NAAEE Directory of Environmental Educators*
Keyword(s): Communications, Environment, Environmental and Conservation Education, Environmental Literacy, International Conservation, Networking, Professional Development, Training, Urban Environment

NORTH AMERICAN ASSOCIATION FOR ENVIRONMENTAL EDUCATION (Membership and Publications Office)

P.O. Box 400, Troy, OH 45373
Phone: 513-676-2514

Scope: National

NORTH AMERICAN BENTHOLOGICAL SOCIETY

c/o The Allen Press Inc. 1041 New Hampshire St., Lawrence, KS 66044

Founded: 1953; *Membership:* 1,800
Scope: National
Description: The Society is an international scientific organization whose purpose is to promote better understanding of the biotic communities of lake and stream bottoms and their role in aquatic ecosystems. The Society provides media for disseminating results of scientific investigations and other information to aquatic biologists and to the scientific community at large.
Contact(s):
President: DR. COLBERT CUSHING; Phone: 509-376-9670
Secretary: DR. SUSAN DAVIES; Phone: 207-289-7778
Treasurer: DR. VIRGINIA R. TOLBERT; Phone: 615-574-7288
Editor: DR. DONALD W. WEBB, Illinois Natural History Survey, 607 E. Peabody St., Champaign, IL 61820
Editor: DR. STEVE CANTON, Chadwick and Associates Inc., 5575 S. Sycamore St., Suite 101, Littleton, CO 80120
Editor: DR. ROSEMARY J. MacKAY, Department of Zoology, University of Toronto, Ontario, M55IAl Canada
Publication(s): *Journal of the North American Benthological Society; Bulletin of the North American Benthological Society; Current and Selected Bibliography of Benthic Biology*

NORTH AMERICAN BLUEBIRD SOCIETY

PO Box 74, Darlington, WI 53530-0074
Phone: 608-329-6403; Fax: 608-329-7057; Email: nabluebird@aol.com; WWW: www.codeskill.edu./nabs/

Founded: 1978; *Membership:* 3,500
Scope: National
Description: A nonprofit conservation organization concerned with increasing the populations of the three species of North American bluebirds. On-going research, educational material development, including two slide programs, outreach initiatives through the NABS Speakers Bureau and a comprehensive website on bluebirding, address issues related to bluebirds and other native cavity-nesting bird species.
Contact(s):
President: RAY HARRIS, Box 2650, Pincher Creek, AB T0K 1W0 Canada
Vice President: DOUG LeVASSEUR, 20680 Township Rd. #120, Semecaville, OH 43780-9707
Treasurer: WILLIAM R. DAVIS, 1642 Humphrey Ave., Dayton, OH 45410-3309
Co-Executive Director: JOHN IVANKO, 7843 Count P, Browntown, WI 53522
Co-Executive Director: LISA KIVIRIST, 7843 County P, Browntown, WI 53522
Editor: JIM WILLIAMS, 5239 Cranberry Ln., Webster, WI 54893
Recording Secretary: ARLENE RIPLEY, 3513 Smithville Dr., Dunkirk, MD 20754
Vice President of Community Relations: CAROL McDANIEL, 4953 Highway 23, Darlington, WI 53530
Publication(s): *Bluebird Magazine (formerly Sialia)*

NORTH AMERICAN COALITION ON RELIGION AND ECOLOGY (NACRE)

5 Thomas Circle, NW, Washington, DC 20005
Founded: 1989; *Membership:* 6,300
Scope: National
Description: NACRE is an ecumenical and interfaith environmental organization designed to help the North American religious community enter into the environmental movement in the 1990s and to help environmental organizations and the wider society become aware and act upon these same ethical values.
Contact(s):
Chairman of the Board: BRUCE ANDERSON
President and CEO: DR. DONALD B. CONROY
Secretary and Treasurer: DR. CAROLYN M. GUTOWSKI
Publication(s): *ECO-Letter*
Keyword(s): Biodiversity, International Conservation, Renewable Resources, Urban Environment

NORTH AMERICAN CRANE WORKING GROUP

7030 Kilgor Road, Gibbon, NE 68840
Phone: 308-233-5576
Founded: 1988
Scope: National
Description: An organization of professional biologists, aviculturists, land managers, and other interested individuals dedicated to the conservation of cranes and their habitats in North America.
Contact(s):
President: SCOTT HEREFORD, Mississippi Crane Refuge, 7200 Crane Ln., Gauthier, MS 39553
Vice President: WENDY BROWN, 1208 Claire Ct. NW, Albuquerque, NM 87104
Secretary: STEPHEN A. NESBITT, 4005 S. Main St., Gainesville, FL 32601
Treasurer: GARY R. LINGLE, 7030 Kilger Rd., Gibbon, NE 68840; Phone: 308-233-5576
Editor: JANE NICOLICH, R.R. 2 Box 264A, Laurel, MD 20708
Publication(s): *Unison Call, The*
Keyword(s): Biodiversity, Birds, Endangered and Threatened Species, Wetlands, Wildlife and Wildlife Habitat

NORTH AMERICAN FALCONERS ASSOCIATION

ATTN: President, Rt. 1, Box 82A, Ellinwood, KS 67526-9801
Founded: 1962
Scope: National
Description: A nonprofit fraternal organization with the following purposes: improve and encourage competency in the practice of falconry; urge recognition of falconry as a legal field sport; and promote scientific study, conservation, and welfare of birds of prey with an appreciation of their value in nature.
Contact(s):
President: DR. J. TIMOTHY KIMMEL, Rt. 1, Box 82A, Ellinwood, KS 67526-9801
Treasurer: ALAN BESKE, HCR 76 Box 43, Hawk Springs, WY 82217-9716

NON-GOVERNMENTAL ORGANIZATIONS

Corresponding Secretary: ROBERT H. GLASS, 33 Tanager Ln., Robbinville, NJ 08691
Editor: SUE CECCHINI, 7220 Burgess Rd., Colorado Springs, CO 80908
Editor: DAN CECCHINI JR., 7220 Burgess Rd., Colorado Springs, CO 80908; Phone: 303-495-4506
Editor: WILLISTON SHOR, 318 Montford Ave., Mill Valley, CA 94941
Publication(s): *Hawk Chalk; Journal (annual)*
Keyword(s): Hunting, Raptors

NORTH AMERICAN FISHING CLUB
12301 Whitewater Dr., Suite 260, Minnetonka, MN 55343
Phone: 612-988-7401; Fax: 612-936-9755; Email: fishingclub@pclink.com
Founded: 1988; Membership: 500,000
Scope: International
Description: The North American Fishing Club is a membership organization dedicated to enhancing the fishing skills and enjoyment of anglers. The NAFC is the largest association of multi-species anglers in North America.
Contact(s):
President: STEVEN F. BURKE
Executive Director: STEVE PENNAZ
Publication(s): *North American Fisherman*
Keyword(s): Aquatic Habitats, Fisheries, Lakes, Sport Fishing

NORTH AMERICAN GAMEBIRD ASSOCIATION, INC.
1125 Brooks Ave., Raleigh, SC 27607
Phone: 919-782-6758; Fax: 919-515-5403; Email: gamebird@naga.org
Founded: 1932; Membership: 1,500
Scope: National
Description: To promote educational work and develop interest in game bird breeding and hunting preserves (nonprofit); to afford a means of cooperation with the federal and state governments in all matters of concern to the industry; and to encourage study of the sciences connected with the live production, preparation for markets, and marketing of game bird eggs and game birds.
Contact(s):
President: BILL MACFARLANE, 2821 South US Hwy 51, Janeville, WI 53546; Phone: 608-757-7881
Treasurer: MARY S. WALKER
Executive Director: DR. GARY S. DAVIS, 1214 Brooks Ave., Raleigh, NC 27607; Phone: 919-782-6758 or 919-515-5403
President-Elect: ROYD HATT, Box 134, Green River, UT 84525; Phone: 801-564-3224
Publication(s): *Wildlife Harvest Magazine; Membership Directory; Game Bird Propagation Book; List of Hunting Resort Members.*
Keyword(s): Birds, Hunting, Waterfowl, Wildlife and Wildlife Habitat, Wildlife Management

NORTH AMERICAN LOON FUND
6 Lily Pond Rd., Gilford, NH 03246
Phone: 603-528-4711
Founded: 1979
Scope: National
Description: A nonprofit organization established to sponsor loon conservation, public education, and scientific research projects across the U.S. and Canada. Sponsors annual grant program, and organizes annual research conference.
Contact(s):
Chairman: JORDAN S. PROUTY
Treasurer: SALLY STOCKWELL
Executive Director: LINDA OBARA
Clerk: GUY A. SWENSON
Publication(s): *Loon Call Newsletter; Annotated Bibliography of the Loons, Gaviidae; Educational poster and resource directory*
Keyword(s): Endangered and Threatened Species, Lakes, Nongame Wildlife, Scholarships and Grants, Wildlife and Wildlife Habitat

NORTH AMERICAN NATIVE FISHES ASSOCIATION
123 W. Mt. Airy Ave., Philadelphia, PA 19119
Founded: 1972; Membership: 450
Scope: National
Description: Membership includes ichthyologists, students, sportsmen, amateur naturalists, and aquarists who seek to promote the study, research, and conservation of North American native fishes. Goals are to promote the restoration and protection of habitat and to distribute information about native fishes.
Contact(s):
President: RAYMOND S. KATULA
Vice President: PHILIP NIXON
Treasurer: ROBERT E. SCHMIDT
Secretary and Editor: BRUCE GEBHARDT; Phone: 215-247-0384
Publication(s): *American Currents Magazine*
Keyword(s): Aquatic Habitats, Endangered and Threatened Species, Fisheries, Nongame Wildlife

NORTH AMERICAN WILDLIFE PARK FOUNDATION, INC.
Battle Ground, IN 47920
Phone: 765-567-2265; Email: wolfpark@dcwi.com; WWW: www.wolfpark.org
Founded: 1972; Membership: 1,500
Scope: National
Description: A nonprofit organization which operates a Wolf Park; provides continuous behavior research programs; offers lectures and a teaching program, as well as four Wolf Behavior seminars per year; monitors legislation on predators; and provides research opportunities for scientists and students.
Contact(s):
Assistant Treasurer and Assistant Secretary: ALBERT W. ZIMMERMANN, Suite 418, 3320 N. Meridian St., Indianapolis, IN 46204
President, Treasurer, and Editor: DR. ERICH KLINGHAMMER, Battle Ground, IN 47920
Publication(s): *Wolf Park News*

NORTH AMERICAN WOLF SOCIETY
850 37th St., Boulder, CO 80303
Founded: 1973
Scope: National
Description: Nonprofit, tax-exempt volunteer organization dedicated to the wise stewardship of the wolf and other wild canids found in North America. Produces educational materials appropriate to all age levels, as well as an annual summary of wolf recovery and management activities in North America.
Contact(s):
President:
Publication(s): *yearly summaries*
Keyword(s): Endangered and Threatened Species, Environmental and Conservation Education, Wildlife and Wildlife Habitat, Wildlife Management

NORTH ATLANTIC SALMON CONSERVATION ORGANIZATION
11 Rutland Square, Edinburgh, Edinburgh EH1 2AS United Kingdom
Phone: 131-228-2551; Fax: 131-228-4384; Email: hy@nusco.org.uk
Founded: 1984
Scope: National
Description: NASCO is an intergovernmental organization established to contribute to the conservation, restoration, enhancement, and rational management of salmon stocks in the North Atlantic Ocean through international cooperation. The member parties are: Canada, Denmark (in respect to the Faroe Islands and Greenland), the European Union, Iceland, Norway, the Russian Federation, and the USA.
Contact(s):
Secretary: DR. M.L. WINDSOR
Publication(s): *Biennial reports on the activities of the organization; Ten Year Review of the Activities of the North Atlantic Salmon*

NON-GOVERNMENTAL ORGANIZATIONS

Conservation Organization; annual reports of the meetings of the Council and Commissions; handbook of basic texts
Keyword(s): Acid Rain, Fisheries, Greenhouse Effect/Global Warming, International Conservation, North Atlantic Salmon

NORTH CAROLINA ASSOCIATION OF SOIL AND WATER CONSERVATION DISTRICTS
ATTN: President, 11416 Timber Ridge Rd., Charlotte, NC 28213
Scope: Statewide
Contact(s):
President: EDDIE STROUP, 11416 Timber Ridge Rd., Charlotte, NC 28213; Phone: 704-596-8394; Fax: 704-336-3486
Secretary: VASTINE MITCHELL, 505 W. 34th St., Lumberton, NC 28358; Phone: 910-738-5672; Fax: 910-739-8306
Treasurer: BRUCE WHITFIELD, 5968 Gordonton Rd., Hurdle Mills, NC 27541; Phone: 910-599-5672; Fax: 910-599-6516
1st Vice President: JEFF TURLINGTON, Rt. 1 Box 447, Coast, NC 27521; Phone: 910-897-6788
2nd Vice President: FRANKLIN WILLIAMS, 7530 S NC 41, Wallace, NC 28466; Phone: 910-285-7409
Alternate Board Member: JOHN FINCH, 5958 West NC 97, Spring Hope, NC 27882; Phone: 919-487-7230
Board Member: WADE CARRIGAN, 1245 Oak Ridge Rd., Mooresville, NC 28115; Phone: 704-663-1236

NORTH CAROLINA B.A.S.S. CHAPTER FEDERATION
Attn: Conservation Director, 415 Haywood St., Thomasville, NC 27360
Phone: 828-728-8550
Scope: Statewide
Description: An organization of Bassmaster chapters, affiliated with the Bass Anglers Sportsman Society, organized to fight pollution, assist state and national conservation agencies in their efforts and teach the young people of our country good conservation practices. Dedicated to the realistic conservation of our water resources.
Contact(s):
President: ED CANNON, 403 Red Wood Ct., Lenoir, NC 38645; Phone: 828-728-8550
Conservation Director: RICKY MURPHY, 415 Haywood St., Thomasville, NC 27360; Phone: 336-472-2398(W)/336-472-9139(H)

NORTH CAROLINA BEACH BUGGY ASSOCIATION, INC.
Box 940, Manteo, NC 27954
Phone: 252-473-4880
Membership: 4,414
Scope: Statewide
Description: NCBBA is an organization dedicated to preserving natural resources and coastal areas of North Carolina. Its purpose is to unite in an organization all persons interested in the natural beach resources of the Outer Banks of North Carolina and elsewhere, and establish a Code of Ethics of beach behavior to which each member must subscribe to uphold.
Contact(s):
President: JOHN P. NEWBOLD, 2400 Esplanade Dr., Virginia Beach, VA 23456; Phone: 252-480-2453
Vice President: W. JAMES KEENE, 23134 Homestead Lane, Franklin, VA 23851; Phone: 757-562-2554
Secretary: SHARON NEWBOLD, 2400 Esplanade Dr., Virginia Beach, VA 23456; Phone: 252-480-2453
Treasurer: BRENDA OUTLAW, P.O. Box 940, Manteo, NC 27954; Phone: 252-473-4880
Editor: JOHN NEWBOLD
Publication(s): *NCBBA News, The*
Keyword(s): Coasts, Endangered and Threatened Species, Fisheries, Outdoor Recreation, Sport Fishing

NORTH CAROLINA COASTAL FEDERATION, INC.
3609 Highway 24 (Ocean), Newport, NC 28570
Phone: 252-393-8185; Fax: 252-393-7508; Email: nccf@nccoast.org; WWW: www.nccoast.org
Founded: 1982; Membership: 5,000
Scope: Statewide
Description: The Coastal Federation focuses on the twenty coastal counties in North Carolina, with citizens working together for a healthy coast..
Contact(s):
President: MELVIN SHEPARD
Vice President: PRICEY TAYLOR
Secretary: MEG RAWLS
Treasurer: OLIVIA HOLDING
Chief Financial Officer: TODD MILLER
Publication(s): *Coastal Review; State of Coast Report; Sound Advice*
Keyword(s): Environmental and Conservation Education, Estuaries, Land Use Planning, Water Quality

NORTH CAROLINA FORESTRY ASSOCIATION
1600 Glenwood Ave., Suite I, Raleigh, NC 27608-2355
Phone: 919-834-3943 / 1-800-231-7723 NC only; Fax: 919-832-6188
Founded: 1911; Membership: 2,450
Scope: Statewide
Description: The North Carolina Forestry Association promotes and protects the long-term health and productivity of the forest ecosystem to enhance the environment and economy of North Carolina.
Contact(s):
President: DENNIS STONE, Canal Wood Corp., 308 East Fifth St., Lumberton, NC 28358
Executive Vice President: ROBERT W. SLOCUM JR., 1600 Glenwood Ave., Suite I, Raleigh, NC 27608-2355; Phone: 919-834-3943
President-Elect: ED KESSLER, Bunn Hardwoods, P.O. Box 188, Bunn, NC 27508
Publication(s): *TreeLine*
Keyword(s): Communications, Environmental and Conservation Education, Forests and Forestry, Renewable Resources

NORTH CAROLINA HERPETOLOGICAL SOCIETY
ATTN: President North Carolina Herpetological society, Department of Biology, UNC-6, Greensboro, NC 27412-5001
Founded: 1978
Scope: Statewide
Description: A nonprofit group formed to promote an interest in and to educate members and the general public concerning the ecological importance and conservation of reptiles and amphibians.
Contact(s):
President: ANN BERRY SOMERS, Department of Biology, UNC-6, Greensboro, NC 27412-5001; Phone: 910-334-5391
Vice President: MIKE LOOMIS, NC Zoological Park, 4401 Zoo Pkwy., Ashboro, NC 27203; Phone: 919-879-7630
Secretary: THAD HOWARD, 1422 Vanguard Pl., Durham, NC 27713-2032; Phone: 919-682-7947
Treasurer: DENNIS MOUNTAIN, 6612 Orchard Knoll, Apex, NC 27501; Phone: 919-387-1842
Advisor: ALVIN BRASWELL, NC State Museum of Natural Sciences, P.O. Box 27647, Raleigh, NC 27611; Phone: 919-733-7450
Editor: JEFF BEANE, North Carolina State Museum of Natural Sciences, P.O. Box 27647, Raleigh, NC 27611; Phone: 919-733-7450
Publication(s): *NC HERPS*
Keyword(s): Reptiles and Amphibians

NON-GOVERNMENTAL ORGANIZATIONS

NORTH CAROLINA RECREATION AND PARK SOCIETY, INC.
883 Washington St., Raleigh, NC 27605
Phone: 919-832-5868; Fax: 919-832-3323
Founded: 1944; Membership: 2,300
Scope: Statewide
Description: A nonprofit organization formed to promote the wise use of leisure and intelligent development of the state's recreation resources. An affiliate of The National Recreation and Park Association.
Contact(s):
President: HAROLD OWEN, Burlington Rec. & Parks, P.O. Box 1358, Burlington, NC 27216; Phone: 336-222-5030; Fax: 336-229-3106
Executive Director: MIKE WATERS, 883 Washington St., Raleigh, NC 27605
Editor: KARLA HENDERSON, UNC-Chapel Hill, LSRA Curriculum, Campus Box 3185, Evergreen House, Chapel Hill, NC 27599-3185; Phone: 919-962-1222; Fax: 919-962-1223
Publication(s): *North Carolina Recreation and Park Review; NCRPS News*
Keyword(s): Environmental Preservation, Open Space, Outdoor Recreation, Youth Organizations

NORTH CAROLINA WILDLIFE FEDERATION
Box 10626, Raleigh, NC 27605
Phone: 919-833-1923; Fax: 919-829-1192
Scope: Statewide
Description: A representative statewide organization, affiliated with the National Wildlife Federation, dedicated to the protection and enhancement of wildlife and its habitat through public education and government interaction.
Contact(s):
President: DALE MOSTELLER
Executive Director: DOCK KORNEGAY
Affiliate Representative: CHUCK RICE
Editor: EDDIE NICKENS
Publication(s): *Friend O'Wildlife*

NORTH CASCADES CONSERVATION COUNCIL
P.O. Box 95980, Seattle, WA 98145-2980
Phone: 206-282-1644; Fax: 206-684-1379; Email: steveB@premier.net
Founded: 1957; Membership: 500
Scope: Regional
Description: The Council seeks to protect and perserve the North Cascades' scenic, scientific, recreational, educational, wildlife, and wilderness values from the Columbia River to the US-Canadian border in the state of Washington.
Contact(s):
Chairman: PATRICK D. GOLDSWORTHY; Phone: 206-282-1644
President: MARC BARDSLEY; Phone: 206-684-1296; Fax: 206-684-1379; Email: marc.bardsley@metrokc.gov
Vice President: CHARLES EHLERT
Secretary: PHIL ZALESKY
Treasurer: THOMAS H. BRUCKER
Publication(s): *Wild Cascades, The*
Keyword(s): Ancient Forests, Biodiversity, Conservation of Protected Areas, Environmental Preservation, Environmental Protection, Fisheries, Forest Management, Lakes, Land Preservation, Land Use Planning, Mining, Natural Areas, Nature Preservation, Outdoor Recreation

NORTH DAKOTA ASSOCIATION OF SOIL CONSERVATION DISTRICTS
ATTN: President, 1736 16th St. NW, Minot, ND 58703-1116
Scope: Statewide
Contact(s):
President, Alternate Board Member: WES TOSSETT, 1736 16th St. NW, Minot, ND 58703-1116; Phone: 701-837-1162
Vice President: JACK LARSON, P.O. Box 218, Bisbee, ND 58317-0216; Phone: 701-656-3493
Board Member: TOM CHRISTENSEN, 7114 110th Ave. SE, Verona, ND 58490-9325; Phone: 701-432-5685; Fax: 701-432-5685; Email: ctomrun@yahoo.com
Executive Vice President: GARY PUPPE, P.O. Box 1601, 3310 University Dr., Bismarck, ND 58502-1601; Phone: 701-223-8518; Fax: 701-223-1291

NORTH DAKOTA NATURAL SCIENCE SOCIETY
Division of Biological Sciences, Box 4050, Emporia, KS 66801
Phone: 316-341-5623; WWW: www.imporia.edu/s/www/biosci/pn/pn.htm
Founded: 1967; Membership: 350
Scope: Statewide
Description: Dedicated to the observation, recording, study, and preservation of all aspects of the natural history of the Great Plains.
Contact(s):
President: DR. JANE AUSTIN, Northern Prairie Wildlife Research Center, Jamestown, ND 58401
Editor: DR. ELMER FINCK, Div. Of Biological Sciences, Box 4050, Emporia, KS 66801
Publication(s): *Prairie Naturalist, The*
Keyword(s): Fisheries, Great Plains, Natural History, Nongame Wildlife, Prairies, Wildlife and Wildlife Habitat

NORTH DAKOTA WILDLIFE FEDERATION, INC.
P.O. Box 7248, Bismarck, ND 58507-7248
Phone: 701-222-2557; Fax: 701-222-0334
Scope: Statewide
Description: A representative statewide organization, affiliated with the National Wildlife Federation, dedicated to the protection and enhancement of wildlife and its habitat through public education and government interaction.
Contact(s):
President: ART MIELKE
Affiliate Representative: JAMES LINNERTZ
Editor and Executive Administrator: MARY STEVENS
Publication(s): *Flickertales*

NORTHCOAST ENVIRONMENTAL CENTER
879 Ninth St., Arcata, CA 95521
Phone: 707-822-6918; Fax: 707-822-0827; Email: nec@igc.apc.org
Founded: 1971; Membership: 4,500
Scope: Statewide
Description: A tax-exempt educational organization dedicated to illuminating the relationships between humankind and the biosphere. Toward that end, the Center provides environmental information and referral services for northwestern California and operates a library open to the public.
Contact(s):
Director: TIM McKAY
Editor: SID DOMINITZ
Librarian: STAN LARSON
Office Manager: CONNIE STEWART
Publication(s): *Econews*
Keyword(s): Ancient Forests, Biodiversity, Endangered and Threatened Species, Environmental Protection, Forests and Forestry, Public Lands, Watersheds, Wilderness

NORTHEAST ASSOCIATION OF FISH AND WILDLIFE RESOURCE AGENCIES
ATTN: President, Director of Div. Of Fish & Wildlife, DNR and Environmental Control, 89 Kings Hwy., Dover, NJ 19901
Scope: Regional
Description: Consists of heads of fish and game agencies in 11 northeastern states, Canadian Maritime Provinces, Newfoundland, Ontario, and Quebec. Meets at least yearly to review progress, consider mutual problems, coordinate programs on a regional basis, and promote sound fish and game management programs.
Contact(s):
President: ANDREW MARCUS, Director of Division of Fish & Wildlife, DNR and Environmental Control, 89 Kings Hwy, Dover, DE 19901; Phone: 302-739-5295; Fax: 302-739-6157

Vice President: EDWARD PARKER, Chief of Connecticut Bureau of Natural Resources, 79 Elm Street, Hartford, CT 06106-5127; Phone: 860-424-3061; Fax: 860-424-4070

NORTHEAST CONSERVATION LAW ENFORCEMENT CHIEFS' ASSOCIATION (CLECA)
Attn: Secretary, RI Dept. of Environmental Management, 83 Park St., Providence, PA 02908
Phone: 401-277-2284
Scope: Regional
Contact(s):
President: RICHARD MURRAY, Director of Massachusetts Department of Fisheries, Wildlife, and Environmental Law Enforcement, 100 Cambridge St., Rm. 1901, Boston, MA 02202; Phone: 617-727-3905
Vice President: RONALD ALIE, Chief of New Hampshire Fish and Game Department, Law Enforcement Division, 2 Hazen Drive, Concord, NH 03301; Phone: 603-271-3422
Secretary and Treasurer: THOMAS GREENE

NORTHEAST SUSTAINABLE ENERGY ASSOCIATION
50 Miles St., Greenfield, MA 01301
Phone: 413-774-6051; Fax: 413-774-6053; Email: nesea@nesea.org; WWW: www.nesea.org
Founded: 1974; Membership: 1,200
Scope: Regional
Description: The Northeast Sustainable Energy Association (NESEA) aims to strengthen the economy and lessen our impact on the environment by bringing sustainable energy into everyday use. Through its programs and activities, NESEA offers an alternative vision of responsible energy use and works with policymakers, industry, educators, students, and the general public to make this vision a reality.
Contact(s):
Secretary: NANCY SCHALCH
Treasurer: PAUL ELDRENKAMP
Associate Director and Director of Administration: NANCY HAZARD; Email: nhazard@nesea.org
Board of Directors Chair: MICHAEL CORSO
Business Manager: RICHARD WITTY; Email: rwitty@nesea.org
Director of Education: KATE HARRIS; Email: kharris@nesea.org
Director of Energy Park: SANDY THOMAS; Email: sthomas@nesea.org
Executiuve Director of Administration: THOMAS THOMPSON; Email: tthompson@nesea.org
Manager of Building Program: DOUG MINOR; Email: dminor@nesea.org
Vice Chair: RICHARD F. MARK
Publication(s): *Northeast Sun; Getting Around Without Gasoline; Totally Tree-mendous Activities*
Keyword(s): Environmental and Conservation Education, Solar Energy, Sustainable Buildings, Sustainable Energy, Transportation

NORTHEAST WILDLIFE ADMINISTRATORS ASSOCIATION
c/o Wildlife Director, Vermont Dept. of Fish & Wildlife, 103 So. Main St., 10 South, Waterbury, PA 05671-0501
Phone: 802-241-3700; Fax: 802-241-3295; Email: ron@fwol.anr.state.vt.us
Founded: 1983
Scope: National
Description: Members include the wildlife management program administrators of the northeast U.S. state and eastern Canadian provincial fish and wildlife agencies. The goal of NEWAA is to coordinate and facilitate the work of regional technical wildlife management committees to promote sound wildlife management programs and to exchange ideas, methods, and approaches to administrative and operational problems in wildlife management.
Contact(s):
Chairman: RON REGAN, Wildlife Director, VT Dept. of Fish & Wildlife, 103 South Main St., 10 South, Waterbury, VT 05671-0501; Phone: 802-241-3700; Fax: 802-241-3295; Email: ron@fwol.anr.state.vt.us

Keyword(s): Endangered and Threatened Species, Hunting, Nongame Wildlife, Wildlife and Wildlife Habitat, Wildlife Management

NORTHERN ALASKA ENVIRONMENTAL CENTER
218 Driveway St., Fairbanks, AK 99701-2806
Phone: 907-452-5021; Fax: 907-452-3100; Email: naec@mosquitonet.com; WWW: http://www.mosquitonet.com/
Founded: 1971; Membership: 1,300
Scope: Statewide
Description: The Northern Alaska Environmental Center works to protect some of the wildest country left in North America -- the vast Interior and Arctic regions of Alaska -- through education, advocacy, grassroots organizing, and sheer perseverance. The Northern Center's priorities are to protect Alaska's Arctic from oil drilling; promote ecologically sound, sustainable management of Alaska's boreal forests; defend wild rivers from mining pollution and roads; and encourage better environmental understanding, particularly by our youth.
Contact(s):
President: PAM GROVES
Vice President: CLARICE DUKEMINIER
Secretary: LINDA DEFOLLIART
Treasurer: FRANZ MUETER
Executive Director: SYLVIA WARD
Boreal Forest Campaign Coordinator: AMY MARSH
Communication and Membership Director: BETH CALSSLE
Wilderness Campaign Coordinator: ROSS COEN
Publication(s): *Northern Line, The; Arctic Action; Boreal Briefs*
Keyword(s): Arctic, Environmental and Conservation Education, Forest Management, Natural Areas, Public Lands, Rivers, Sustainable Ecosystems, Taiga, Tundra, Water Quality, Wilderness, Wildlands

NORTHERN PLAINS RESOURCE COUNCIL
2401 Montana Ave., #200, Billings, MT 59101-2336
Phone: 406-248-1154
Founded: 1972; Membership: 3,000
Scope: National
Description: NPRC is a grassroots citizens' organization of farmers, ranchers, townspeople, and other conservationists. NPRC works on natural resource and agricultural issues to promote sustainable economic development, and to maintain Montana's unique rural quality of life. NPRC is dedicated to family agriculture and to stewardship of air, land, and water.
Contact(s):
Chair: JERRY SIKORSKI
Secretary: NELLIE ISRAEL
Treasurer: BARBARA VARNES
Research Coordinator: TED LANGE
Staff Director: TERESA ERICKSON
Vice Chair: DENA HOFF
Publication(s): *Plains Truth, The; Reclaiming the Wealth (A Citizens' Guide to Hard Rock Mining in Montana); Legislative Bulletin*
Keyword(s): Agriculture, Air Quality and Pollution, Energy, Mining, Solid Waste Management, Water Quality

NORTHWEST ATLANTIC FISHERIES ORGANIZATION (NAFO)
P.O. Box 638, Dartmouth, Nova Scotia B2Y 3Y9 Canada
Phone: 902-468-5590; Fax: 902-468-5538
Founded: 1979
Scope: National
Description: Works for the optimum utilization, rational management, and conservation of the fishery resources of the convention area in the Northwest Atlantic. Contracting Parties: Bulgaria, Canada, Cuba, Denmark for the Faroes and Greenland, Estonia, European Union, France (for St. Pierre and Miquelon), Iceland, Japan, Korea, Latvia, Lithuania, Norway, Poland, Romania, Russia and the USA.
Contact(s):
Executive Secretary: LEONARD I. CHEPEL

Assistant Executive Secretary: T. AMARATUNGA
Fisheries Commission Chairman: P. GULLESTAD, EU
Fisheries Commission Vice Chairman: D. SWANSON, Norway
General Council, Vice Chairman: R. DOMINGUEZ, Cuba
President of NAFO and Chairman of General Cousel: A. RODIN, Russia
Scientific Council Chairman: H. P. CORNUS, Canada
Scientific Council Vice Chairman: W. B. BRODIE, EU
Publication(s): *Annual Report; Journal of Northwest Atlantic Fishery Science; Statistical Bulletin; Scientific Council Studies; Sampling Yearbook; List of Fishing Vessels; Index of Meeting Documents*
Keyword(s): Biology, Fisheries, International Conservation, Oceanography

NORTHWEST ECOSYSTEM ALLIANCE
1421 Cornwall Ave., Suite 201, Bellingham, WA 98225
Phone: 360-671-9950; Fax: 360-671-8429; Email: nwea@ecosystem.org
Founded: 1989; Membership: 3,000
Scope: Regional
Description: The Northwest Ecosystem Alliance protects and restores wildlands in the Pacific Northwest and supports such efforts in British Columbia. The Alliance bridges science and advocacy, working with activists, policymakers, and the public to conserve our natural heritage.
Contact(s):
President: EMILY BARNETT
Secretary: JEFFREY JON BODE
Treasurer: TOM CAMPION
Executive Director: MITCH FRIEDMAN
Publication(s): *Northwest Conservation: News and Priorities; Wild Salmon and Trout Action Plan: Of Wolves and Washington; Cascadia Wild: Protecting an International Ecosystem; Conservation Biology and National Forest Management in the Inland Northwest: A Handbook for Activists*
Keyword(s): Ancient Forests, Biodiversity, Conservation of Protected Areas, Ecology, Endangered and Threatened Species, Environment, Forest Management, Internships, Nature Preservation, Predators, Raptors, Reptiles and Amphibians, Sustainable Ecosystems, Trapping, Wildlife and Wildlife Habitat

NORTHWEST ENVIRONMENT WATCH
1402 3rd Ave. #1127, Seattle, WA 98101
Phone: 206-447-1880; Fax: 206-447-2270; Email: new@northwestwatch.org; WWW: www.northwestwatch.org
Founded: 1993; Membership: 1,500
Scope: Regional
Description: NEW's mission is to foster sustainability in the Pacific Northwest. NEW provides citizens with intelligence reports on the latest findings from the natural and social sciences, and guides them in creating a sustainable economy.
Contact(s):
Executive Director: ALAN DURNING
Communications Director: PEG CHENG
Office Manager: RHEA CONNORS
Research Director: JOHN RYAN
Publication(s): *State of the Northwest; This Place on Earth; The Car and The City; Stuff, Misplaced Blame*
Keyword(s): Population Growth, Sustainable Development, Transportation

NORTHWEST INTERPRETIVE ASSOCIATION
909 1st Ave., Suite 630, Seattle, WA 98104
Phone: 206-220-4140
Founded: 1974
Scope: National
Description: The Association supports interpretation and education on public lands administered by the National Park Service, U.S. Forest Service, and other agencies in the Pacific Northwest. Proceeds from the sale of interpretive publications are donated to these agencies to educate visitors in the area's natural and cultural history.
Contact(s):
Executive Director: MARY QUACKENBUSH
Chairman of the Board: ERNEST KARLSTROM
Vice Chairman: JIM TORRENCE
Keyword(s): Cultural Preservation, Environmental and Conservation Education, Natural History, Outdoor Recreation, Wilderness

NORTHWEST RENEWABLE RESOURCES CENTER
1411 4th Ave. Suite 1510, Seattle, WA 98101-2216
Founded: 1984
Scope: National
Description: A nonprofit corporation founded by leaders of industry, Indian tribes, and environmental organizations to provide alternative dispute-resolution services on natural resources issues. The Center helps disputing parties identify opportunities for consensus and develop creative solutions to complex national resources problems.
Contact(s):
Board Member: JAMES C. WALDO
Co-Chairman: JAMES C. WALDO
Project Director: BETSY REYNOLDS
Publication(s): *Short Course on Tribal and County Intergovernmental Coordination; Working Effectively at the Local Level: Tribal and County Cooperation and Coordination; Videos: "Building Community Within A Watershed", "Voices of the Valley-A Skagit Valley Dialogue"*
Keyword(s): Forests and Forestry, Land Use Planning, Renewable Resources, Sustainable Development, Water Resources

NORTHWEST RESOURCE INFORMATION CENTER
2811 W. State St., P.O. Box 427, Eagle, ID 83616
Phone: 208-939-0714; Fax: 208-939-7263
Founded: 1976
Scope: National
Description: NRIC promotes through research, public education, technology transfer, and litigation the concept that ecological diversity and environmental quality are synonymous with long-term economic productivity and quality of life.
Contact(s):
Executive Director: ED CHANEY, 2811 W. State St., Eagle, ID 83616; Phone: 208-939-8731
Keyword(s): Environmental Protection, International Conservation, Sustainable Development, Sustainable Ecosystems, Watersheds

NOVA SCOTIA FORESTRY ASSOCIATION
P.O. Box 1113, Truro, Nova Scotia B2N 5G9 Canada
Phone: 902-893-4653; Fax: 902-893-1197
Founded: 1959
Scope: Statewide
Description: The Nova Scotia Forestry Association is a nonprofit, charitable organization dedicated to promoting the wise use and management of our forest resources through education programs for youth. Programs emphasize the importance of being good stewards of our natural resources.
Contact(s):
President: KEN MURRAY
Executive Director: JEFF VROOM
Project Coordinator: DALE LYON
Keyword(s): Environmental and Conservation Education, Pollution Prevention

NOVA SCOTIA WILDLIFE FEDERATION
P.O. Box 654, Halifax, Nova Scotia B3J 2T3 Canada
Phone: 902-423-6793; Email: tr.nswf@chebucto.ns.ca
Founded: 1930; Membership: 6,500
Scope: Statewide
Description: Affiliated with the Canadian Wildlife Federation and the National Coalition of Provincial and Territorial Wildlife Federations. Aims to unite all conservation organizations in Nova Scotia, fosters appreciation of wildlife and habitat, promotes fish and

game management, seeks enactment and enforcement of laws necessary for environmental controls as well as conservation of wildlife resources.
Contact(s):
President: RONNIE GILLIS
Executive Director: A. J. RODGERS

NW ENERGY COALITION
219 First Ave., So., Suite 100, Seattle, WA 98104
Phone: 206-621-0094; Fax: 206-621-0097; Email: nwec@nwenergy.org; WWW: www.nwenergy.org/nwec
Founded: 1981
Scope: National
Description: NWEC is a regionwide coalition of public interest groups and progressive utilities. The energy coalition works for a clean, affordable energy policy for the Pacific Northwest and British Columbia. The Coalition advocates for energy conservation and renewable resources, wild salmon, and low income/consumer protection.
Contact(s):
Chairman: JEFF SHIELDS
Director: SARA PATTON
Publication(s): *NW Energy Coalition Report; Energy Activist; Plugging People into Power;*
Keyword(s): Energy, Fisheries, Greenhouse Effect/Global Warming, Renewable Resources, Solar Energy

OCEAN VOICE INTERNATIONAL
P.O. Box 37026 3332 McCarthy Rd., Ottawa, Ontario K1V 0W0 Canada
Phone: 613-990-8819; Fax: 613-521-4205
Founded: 1987; Membership: 150
Scope: National
Description: To conserve the diversity of marine life, protect and restore marine ecosystems and ecological services, enhance the quality of life and equity of benefits for coastal peoples, and promote ecologically sustainable harvest of marine resources.
Contact(s):
President: DR. DON E. McALLISTER, P.O. Box 37026, 3332 McCarthy Rd., Ottawa, Ontario K1V 0W0 Canada; Phone: 613-264-8986
Secretary: KATJA RODRIGUEZ, 370 Metcalfe St., Apt. 712, Ottawa, Ontario K2P 159 Canada
Treasurer: PHYLLIS KOFMEL, 409 Huron Ave. S., Ottawa, Ontario K1Y 0X2 Canada; Phone: 613-729-1893
Publication(s): *Sea Wind; Save Our Coral Reefs; How Green is Your School?; Green School Biodiversity Booklet, The Status of the World Ocean and its Biodiversity; Global Freshwater Biodiversity; Striving for the Integrity of Freshwater Ecosystems*
Keyword(s): Aquatic Habitats, Biodiversity, Coral Reefs, Developing Countries, International Conservation

OHIO ACADEMY OF SCIENCE, THE
1500 W. 3rd Ave., Suite 223, Columbus, OH 43212-2817
Phone: 614-488-2228; Email: oas@iwaynet.net
Founded: 1891; Membership: 2,000
Scope: Statewide
Description: A nonprofit organization designed to stimulate interest in the sciences, to promote research, to improve instruction in the sciences, to disseminate scientific knowledge, and to recognize high achievement in attaining these objectives.
Contact(s):
President: SPENCER E. REAMES, Benjamin Logan HS, 6609 St. Rt. 47 E., Bellefontaine, OH 43311; Phone: 937-592-1666
Secretary: DR. RONALD L. STUCKEY, Ohio State University, Museum of Biolocial Diversity, 1315 Kinnear Ave., Columbus, OH 43212-1192; Phone: 614-292-6095
Treasurer: DR. MICHAEL HERSCHLER, Dept. of Life Sciences Otterbein College, Westerville, OH 43081; Phone: 614-823-1119

Editor: DR. THOMAS W. SCHMIDLIN, Kent State University Department of Geography, Kent, OH 44242; Phone: 330-672-4632
Executive Officer: LYNN EDWARD ELFNER
Publication(s): *Ohio Journal of Science, The; Ohio Academy of Science Newsletter*
Keyword(s): Biotechnology, Communications, Environmental and Conservation Education, Youth Organizations

OHIO ALLIANCE FOR THE ENVIRONMENT
1500 West Third Ave., Columbus, OH 43212
Phone: 614-487-9957; Fax: 614-487-9957; WWW: www.ohioalliance.org
Founded: 1977
Scope: Statewide
Description: A statewide nonprofit organization established to provide leadership in resolving environmental conflicts and to promote and support adult environmental education in Ohio. The Alliance is a nonadvocacy organization working to establish channels of communication among diverse groups with environmental concerns and to provide balanced environmental information through conferences, publications, roundtable discussions, and seminars.
Contact(s):
President: RANDY VAN DYNE, The National Center of Excellence for Environmental Management, The Univ. of Findlay, 1000 North Main St., Findlay, OH 45840-3695; Phone: 419-424-4572; Fax: 419-424-5303
Vice President: LOIS WHEALEY, Field Organizer, Lower Hocking Valley, Rural Action, 14 Oak St., Athens, OH 45701; Phone: 740-593-7490; Fax: 740-593-3228
Secretary: JEFF KNOOP, Director of Land Protection, Nature Conservancy, OH Field Office, 6375 Riverside Dr., Suite 50, Dublin, OH 43017; Phone: 614-717-2770; Fax: 614-717-2777
Treasurer: DR. JIM SWANEY, Dept. of Economics, Wright State Univ., Dayton, OH 45435; Phone: 937-775-2769; Fax: 937-775-3545
Executive Director: IRENE PROBASCO
Editor: JANE HAYNES, Natural Resources Specialist, League of Women Voters of Ohio Education Fund, 17 South High St.., Columbus, OH 43215; Phone: 614-469-1505
Past President: KARL GEBHARDT, Director of Office of Farm Land Preservation, OH Dept. of Agric., 8995 East Main St., Reynoldsburg, OH 43068; Phone: 614-466-2732
Publication(s): *Focus on the Issue; OAE Newsletter*

OHIO AUDUBON COUNCIL, INC.
121 Larchmont Rd., Springfield, OH 45503
Founded: 1969; Membership: 20,000
Scope: Statewide
Description: Associated with the National Audubon Society. Works to promote, foster, and encourage the conservation and preservation of all wildlife, plants, soil, water, air, and other natural resources for the benefit of all citizens. 20 chapters, two affiliates.
Contact(s):
President: JOYCE PELZ, Greater Akron AS, 560 Surfside Drive, Akron, OH 44319; Phone: 330-645-0953
Vice President: PETE PRECARIO, Columbus AS, 524 Blenheim Road, Columbus, OH 43214; Phone: 614-262-0050
Secretary: DOROTHY KOONTZ, Firelands AS, 740 Chestnut Lane, Huron, OH 44839; Phone: 216-433-2883
Treasurer: ALAN DOLAN, Canton AS, P.O. Box 935, Massillon, OH 44648; Phone: 330-832-2491
Past President: MIKE COOGAN, Dayton AS, 2477 W. Alex-Bell Rd., Dayton, OH 45459-1187; Phone: 513-643-1726
Keyword(s): Birds, Endangered and Threatened Species, Environmental and Conservation Education, Wetlands, Wildlife and Wildlife Habitat

NON-GOVERNMENTAL ORGANIZATIONS

OHIO B.A.S.S. CHAPTER FEDERATION
ATTN: President, 376 N. Dorset, Troy, OH 45373
Phone: 937-335-2078
Scope: Statewide
Description: An organization of Bassmaster chapters, affiliated with the Bass Anglers Sportsman Society, organized to fight pollution, assist state and national conservation agencies in their efforts, and teach the young people of our country good conservation practices. Dedicated to the realistic conservation of our water resources.
Contact(s):
President: DENNIS BECKER, 376 N. Dorset, Troy, OH 45373; Phone: 937-335-2078
Conservation Director: JIM DOSS, 43 Portsmouth Rd., Gallipolis, OH 45631; Phone: 614-446-9810

OHIO BIOLOGICAL SURVEY
1315 Kinnear Rd., Columbus, OH 43212-1192
Phone: 614-292-9645
Founded: 1912
Scope: Statewide
Description: An inter-institutional organization of 85 Ohio colleges, universities, museums, and other organizations. Produces and disseminates scientific and technical information concerning the flora and fauna of the Ohio environment, and larger areas of which Ohio is an integral part.
Contact(s):
Executive Director: DR. BRIAN J. ARMITAGE
Chairman of the Advisory Board: DR. TERRY D. KEISER, Ohio Northern University
Editor: VEDA M. CAFAZZO
Publication(s): *Bulletins; Miscellaneous Publications; Notes; Informative Publications*
Keyword(s): Biodiversity, Endangered and Threatened Species, Environmental and Conservation Education, Natural History, Nature Preservation

OHIO ENVIRONMENTAL COUNCIL, INC.
Suite 201, 1207 Grandview Ave., Columbus, OH 43212
Phone: 614-487-7506
Founded: 1969
Scope: Statewide
Description: The Ohio Environmental Council is a statewide umbrella organization providing resources for local environmental organizations across Ohio. The OEC promotes improved environmental quality in the state, advocacy, research, education and collaborative efforts.
Contact(s):
President: PAT HAMMEL, 217 E. Patterson, Columbus, OH 43202; Phone: 614-487-6954; Fax: 614-487-8506; Email: phammel@ocsea.org
Vice President: VIRGINIA AVENI, 1600 Clubside Rd., Lynhurst, OH 44124; Phone: 216-443-3716; Fax: 216-443-3737; Email: cpc@planning.co.cuyahoga.oh.us
Secretary: ANTHONY J. CELEBREZZE III, 253 H. E. Kossuth, Columbu, OH 43206; Phone: 614-644-7613; Fax: 614-446-4120(call first)
Treasurer: BRUCE CORNETT, Green Environmental Coalition, Box 266, Yellow Springs, OH 45387; Phone: 937-767-5000; Fax: 937-767-8587/9041; Email: bcornett@greenlink.org
Executive Director: VICKI LEE DEISNER
Publication(s): *Ohio Environmental Report Newsletter; Green Pages (listing of Ohio enviromental groups and resources; variety of other publications on critical environmental issues for Ohio*
Keyword(s): Air Quality and Pollution, Energy, Environmental and Conservation Education, Environmental Justice, Lakes, Pollution Prevention, Renewable Resources, Solid Waste Management, Sustainable Development, Sustainable Ecosystems, Toxic Substances, Water Pollution, Water Quality, Water Resources

OHIO FEDERATION OF SOIL AND WATER CONSERVATION DISTRICTS
ATTN: President, 660 Spruce St., Wauseon, OH 43567
Scope: Statewide
Contact(s):
President and Board Member: ROBERT CARROLL, 660 Spruce St., Wauseon, OH 43567; Phone: 419-337-5137; Fax: 419-337-4787
Secretary-Treasurer: DAVID LINKHART, 1782 Fawcett Rd., Xenia, OH 45385-9458; Phone: 937-376-5731
Vice President, Alternate Board Member: STEVE ROBINSON, 21199 SR 4, Marysville, OH 43040; Phone: 513-644-0452

OHIO FORESTRY ASSOCIATION, INC., THE
1335 Dublin Rd., Suite 203D, Columbus, OH 43215
Phone: 614-486-6767
Founded: 1903; Membership: 1,500
Scope: Statewide
Description: A statewide organization, affiliated with the National Woodland Owners Association, organized to promote the welfare of the people and private enterprise of Ohio by improving, through education, the wise management of Ohio's forest resource. Sponsors annual forestry camp for youths 14-19; assists schools' conservation activities and education; sponsors Paul Bunyan Show Exposition with Hocking Technical College; and coordinates American Tree Farm Program in Ohio.
Contact(s):
Chair: JOHN V. SCHMIDT
President: GARY KASTER, Coshocton, OH
1st Vice President: EUGENE WATTERS
2nd Vice President: ROBERT L. BOYLES
Editor: RONALD C. CORNELL
Secretary and Executive Director: RONALD C. CORNELL; Phone: 614-486-6767
Publication(s): *Ohio Woodlands*
Keyword(s): Forests and Forestry

OKLAHOMA ACADEMY OF SCIENCE
P.O. Box 701915, Tulsa, OK 74170-1915
Phone: 918-495-6944
Founded: 1909; Membership: 705 members, 60 libraries
Scope: Statewide
Description: To stimulate scientific research; to promote fraternal relationship among those engaged in scientific work in Oklahoma; to diffuse among the citizens of the state a knowledge of the various departments of science; and to investigate and make known the material, education, and other resources of the state.
Contact(s):
President: CONSTANCE E.S. TAYLOR, Department of Biology, Southeastern Oklahoma State University, Durant, OK 74701; Phone: 405-924-0121
Editor: FRANKLIN R. LEACH, Department of Biochemistry Oklahoma State University, Stillwater, OK 74078-0454; Phone: 405-744-6206
Executive Secretary and Treasurer: EDWARD N. NELSON, Department of Biology Oral Roberts University, Tulsa, OK 74171; Phone: 918-495-6944
President-Elect: RONALD J. TYRL, Department of Botany Oklahoma State University, Stillwater, OK 74078; Phone: 405-744-9558
Recording Secretary: CHARLES M. MATHER, Biology Department University of Sciences and Arts of Oklahoma, P.O. Box 82517, Chickasha, OK 73018; Phone: 405-224-3140
Publication(s): *Proceedings-Oklahoma Academy of Science; Annals-Oklahoma Academy of Science; Transactions-Oklahoma Junior Academy of Science; CAS Newsletter*
Keyword(s): Environmental and Conservation Education, Natural History, Research, Training, Wildlife and Wildlife Habitat

OKLAHOMA ASSOCIATION OF CONSERVATION DISTRICTS
ATTN: President, P.O. Box 107, Chelsea, OK 74016-0107
Scope: Statewide
Contact(s):
President: GEORGE FRALEY, P.O. Box 107, Chelsea, OK 74016-0107; Phone: 918-789-2511; Fax: 918-343-2807
Vice President: RICK JEANS, Rt 1 Box 184, Tonkawa, OK 74653; Phone: 405-628-2223
Vice President: MARK MOEHLE, 1601 Shadow Court, Edmond, OK 73013-2683; Phone: 405-340-8884; Fax: 405-842-8744
Secretary: CHRISTY KIMBLE, Oklahoma County CD, 1120 NW 63rd STE G101, Oklahoma City, OK 73116; Phone: 405-848-1933; Fax: 405-842-8744
Treasurer: WAYNE SMITH, 506 N. Pennsylvania, Mangum, OK 73554-3036; Phone: 405-782-3575; Fax: 405-782-3581
Board Member: BILLY WILSON, P.O. Box 208, Kinta, OK 74552-0208; Phone: 918-768-3542; Email: bwilson@cwis.net
Vice President, Alternate Board Member: CAROL GAUNT, Rt 5 Box 244, Weatherford, OK 73096-8815; Phone: 405-772-5107

OKLAHOMA AUDUBON COUNCIL
1728 S. Quaker, Tulsa, OK 74120
Phone: 918-592-1614
Founded: 1987; Membership: 4,000
Scope: Statewide
Description: A statewide council of representatives of the eight National Audubon Society chapters in Oklahoma. The council coordinates the efforts of the chapters on statewide environmental issues, and advocates protection, preservation, and wise use of soil, water, plants, and wildlife.
Contact(s):
President: SUE WOODWARD, 1728 S. Quaker, Tulsa, OK 74120; Phone: 918-592-1614
Treasurer: JOHN KENNINGTON, 11224 S. 83rd E. Ave., Bixby, OK 74008; Phone: 918-369-3923

OKLAHOMA B.A.S.S. CHAPTER FEDERATION
ATTN: President, 2300 E. Coleman Rd., Ponca City, OK 74604
Phone: 580-765-0165
Scope: Statewide
Description: An organization of Bassmaster chapters, affiliated with Bass Anglers Sportsman Society, organized to fight pollution, assist state and national conservation agencies in their efforts, and teach the young people of our country good conservation practices. Dedicated to the realistic conservation of our water resources.
Contact(s):
President: ROBERT CARTLIDGE, 2300 E. Coleman Rd., Ponca City, OK 74604; Phone: 580-765-0165
Conservation Director: DON LINDER, 2409 Cardinal, Ponca City, OK 74604; Phone: 405-762-3301
Publication(s): *Scissortail, The; Bulletin of the Oklahoma Ornithological Society, The; Oklahoma B.A.S.S. Federation Newsletter*

OKLAHOMA NATIVE PLANT SOCIETY
c/o Tulsa Garden Center, 2435 S. Peoria, Tulsa, OK 74114
Phone: 405-872-9652; Fax: 405-872-8361; Email: onps@aol.com
Founded: 1986; Membership: 375
Scope: Statewide
Description: Oklahoma Native Plant Society encourages the study, protection, propagation, appreciation, and use of Oklahoma's native plants.
Contact(s):
President: DR. SHEILA STRAWN; Phone: 405-733-0864
Vice President: TINA JULICH; Phone: 405-598-6742
Secretary: CLAIRE MILLER; Phone: 918-743-3149
Treasurer: JUDY JORDAN; Phone: 405-321-1611
Publication(s): *Gaillardia, The; Native Plant Selection Guide for Oklahoma Woody Plants*
Keyword(s): Aquatic Habitats, Biodiversity, Conservation, Ecology, Endangered and Threatened Species, Environmental Protection, Flowers, Plants, and Trees, Natural Areas, Prairies, Public Lands, Rivers, Rural Development, Terrestrial Habitats, Wetlands, Wilderness

OKLAHOMA ORNITHOLOGICAL SOCIETY
ATTN: Buiness Manager, 1701 W. Will Rogers, Claremore, OK 74017
Phone: 918-343-7706
Founded: 1950; Membership: 600
Scope: Statewide
Description: Affiliated with National Audubon Society and the Oklahoma Wildlife Federation. Dedicated to the observation, study, and conservation of birds in Oklahoma.
Contact(s):
President: JUNE KETCHUM, HCR 70, Box 156, Ardmore, OK 73401
Secretary: MICHAEL BAY, Dept. Biology, East Central state Univ., Ada, OK 74820
Treasurer: MARTY KAMP, 6422 s. Indianapolis Pl., Tulsa, OK 74136
Business Manager: KEITH W. MARTIN, Rogers Univ., 1701 W. Will Rogers, Claremore, OK 74017
Editor: JACK D. TYLER, Biology Dept., Cameron State University, Lawton, OK 73501
Editor: BONNIE GALL, Rt. 1, Box 515F, Bartlesville, OK 74006

OKLAHOMA WILDLIFE FEDERATION
P.O. Box 60126, Oklahoma City, OK 73118
Phone: 405-524-7009; Fax: 405-521-9270
Scope: Statewide
Description: A representative statewide organization, affiliated with the National Wildlife Federation, dedicated to the protection and enhancement of wildlife and its habitat through public education and government interaction.
Contact(s):
President: PAUL PURSER
Affiliate Representative: MICHAEL ENTZ
Alternate Representative: ROYCE MEEK
Editor: LANCE MEEK
Executive Officer: MARGARET RUFF
Publication(s): *Outdoor News*

OKLAHOMA WOODLAND OWNERS ASSOCIATION
2657 S. Trenton, Tulsa, OK 74114-2727
Phone: 918-569-4287
Membership: 754
Scope: Statewide
Description: A statewide organization affiliated with the National Woodland Owners Association to advance forest management skills of Oklahoma woodland owners. Other objectives are to promote education and networking, provide timber marketing, and to monitor and act upon legislation.
Contact(s):
Secretary: JOHN AHERN
Treasurer: AL REITER
1st Vice President: GEORGE PALMER
President and Editor: PATT NELSON
Publication(s): *Oklahoma Woodlands*

OLYMPIC PARK ASSOCIATES
13245,40th Ave., NE, Seattle, WA 98125-4617
Phone: 206-364-3933; WWW: www.halcyon.com/rdpayne/opa.html
Founded: 1948; Membership: 400
Scope: Statewide
Description: Dedicated to preservation of the integrity and wilderness of Olympic National Park and surrounding areas, as well as supporting wild land and wildlife habitat protection elsewhere in the nation. Currently working on restoration of the Elwha River ecosystem and elimination of exotic species from Olympic National Park.

NON-GOVERNMENTAL ORGANIZATIONS

Contact(s):
President: POLLY DYER, Seattle, WA ; Phone: 206-364-3933
Vice President: TIM McNULTY, Sequim, WA ; Phone: 360-681-2480
Secretary: PHILIP ZALESKY, Everett, WA ; Phone: 425-624-8901
Treasurer: JOHN W. ANDERSON; Phone: 206-523-5043
Editor: SALLY W. SOEST, Seattle, WA ; Phone: 206-860-2865
Publication(s): *Voice of the Wild Olympics*

OLYMPIC PARK INSTITUTE
111 Barnes Point Rd., Port Angeles, WA 98363
Phone: 360-928-3720; Fax: 360-928-3046; Email: opi@olympus.net; WWW: www.olympus.net/opi
Founded: 1987
Scope: National
Description: Mission is to inspire personal connection to the natural world and responsible actions to sustain it. OPI provides residential field science programs in Olympic National Park for adults, families, and K-12 classrooms. Programs introduce themes of ecology, sustainability, and stewardship.
Contact(s):
Chairman: KATHY NORTHROP, State Farm Insurance, P.O. Box 2147, Port Angeles, WA 98362; Phone: 360-457-6456
Executive Director: MAITLAND PEET, 111 Barnes Point Rd., Port Angeles, WA 98363; Phone: 360-938-3720
Keyword(s): Acid Rain, Ancient Forests, Biodiversity, Biology, Birds, Coasts, Conservation of Protected Areas, Cultural Preservation, Ecology, Endangered and Threatened Species, Energy, Environment, Environmental Preservation, Environmental Protection, Fisheries

OLYMPIC WILDLIFE RESCUE
1393 Mox-Chehaus Rd., McCleary, WA 98557
Phone: 360-495-3337
Scope: Statewide
Description: Olympic Wildlife Rescue is a nonprofit, tax-exempt organization dedicated to the care of injured, orphaned, and ill northwest wildlife. We operate a licensed wildlife rehabilitation center in McCleary, Washington (about 20 miles west of Olympia).
Contact(s):
President: GARY BANKERS
Vice President: SHAWN NEWMAN
Secretary: PAT PRINGLE
Treasurer: CAROL CHATWOOD
Director: CAROL CUSHING
Publication(s): *Ptarmigan Ptales*
Keyword(s): Environmental and Conservation Education, Outdoor Recreation, Renewable Resources, Wilderness, Wildlife and Wildlife Habitat

ONTARIO FEDERATION OF ANGLERS AND HUNTERS, INC., THE
4601 Guthrie Dr., Box 2800, Peterborough, Ontario K9J 8L5 Canada
Phone: 705-748-6324; Fax: 705-748-9577; Email: ofah@oncomdis
Founded: 1928; Membership: 74,000
Scope: Statewide
Description: Purpose is to conserve Ontario's natural resources and promote ethical angling and hunting practices.
Contact(s):
President: GERRY COURTEMANCHE
Treasurer: CHARLES ALEXANDER
Editor: MARK HOLMES
Executive Vice President: RICK MORGAN
Publication(s): *Call of the Loon; Hunter Education News; Canadian Fishing and Hunting Trade News; Angler and Hunter Hotline*

ONTARIO FORESTRY ASSOCIATION
200 Consumers Rd., Ste. 307, Willowdale, Ontario M2J 4R4 Canada
Phone: 416-493-4565; Fax: 416-493-4608; Email: forestry@oforest.on.ca; WWW: www.oforest.on.ca
Founded: 1949; Membership: 800+
Scope: Statewide
Description: Promotes sound land use and the full development, protection, and utilization of Ontario's forest resources for maximum public advantage. Programs include Envirothon, Community Woodland Steward Initiative, Smokey Bear, Honour Roll of Ontario Trees, Trees Ontario, Consultant Registry, National Forest Week, land use and forest management, Focus on Forests/Fires, advocacy, forestry publicity, and historical data.
Contact(s):
President: C. WALKER-GAYLE, Toronto, Ontario Canada
1st Vice President: ANNE KOVEN, Canada
2nd Vice President: ALEX RIGSBY, Canada
Editor: J. D. COATS
Executive Vice President: RICK MONZON, Canada
Publication(s): *Forest People; Ontario Forest Products Marketing Bulletin*

OPENLANDS PROJECT
220 S. State St., Suite 1880, Chicago, IL 60604
Phone: 312-427-4256; Fax: 312-427-6251; Email: openlands@aol.com; WWW: www.benefice.com
Scope: Statewide
Description: A private, nonprofit organization, Openlands Project was founded in 1963 to protect and enhance public open space in northeastern Illinois. Openlands preserves open space through land acquisition, greenways and watershed planning and restoration, urban greening initiatives, advocacy, and technical assistance.
Contact(s):
President: STEPHEN W. BAIRD
Secretary: J. BRADLEY DAVIS
Treasurer: THOMAS M. FLAVIN
Executive Director: GERALD W. ADELMANN
Vice President for Governmental Affairs: SAMUEL T. LAWTON JR.
Vice President for Programs: H. JAMES FOX
Vice President of Development: ANTHONY T. DEAN
Writer and Editor: GLENDA DANIEL
Publication(s): *Openlander; Annual Report*
Keyword(s): Environmental Preservation, Land Purchase, Land Use Planning, Urban Environment, Watersheds

OREGON ASSOCIATION OF CONSERVATION DISTRICTS
ATTN: President, 2524 Mitchell Butte Rd., Nyssa, OR 97913
Scope: Statewide
Contact(s):
President and Board Member: MIKE BARLOW, 2524 Mitchell Butte Rd., Nyssa, OR 97913; Phone: 541-372-2886; Fax: 541-889-4304
1st Vice President, Alternate Board Member: DON LUCAS, HC 60 Box 4000, Lakeview, OR 97630; Phone: 541-947-2482; Fax: 541-947-2070; Email: donald_lucas@yahoo.comdonald_lucas@yahoo.com
2nd Vice President: JOHN MCDONALD, 30730 SW Simpson Rd, Cornelius, OR 97113; Phone: 503-640-2841; Fax: 503-648-9606
Secretary/Treasurer: STAN CHRISTENSEN, 16350 Delashmutt Ln., McMinnville, OR 97128; Phone: 503-472-6307

OREGON B.A.S.S. CHAPTER FEDERATION
ATTN: President, P.O. Box 21139, Eugene, OR 97402
Phone: 541-484-9576
Scope: Statewide
Description: An organization of Bassmaster chapters, affiliated with Bass Anglers Sportsman Society, organized to fight pollution, assist state and national conservation agencies in their efforts, and teach the young people of our country good conservation practices. Dedicated to the realistic conservation of our water resources.

Contact(s):
President: HARRY RUTH, P.O. Box 21139, Eugene, OR 97402; Phone: 541-484-9576
Conservation Director: CHUCK LANG, 4775 Gardner Rd., SE, Salem, OR 97302; Phone: 503-588-1920; Email: ranger@transport.com
Publication(s): *EarthWatch Oregon*
Keyword(s): Air Quality and Pollution, Land Use Planning, Transportation, Water Quality, Water Resources

OREGON ENVIRONMENTAL COUNCIL
520 SW 6th, #940, Portland, OR 97204-1535
Phone: 503-222-1963; Fax: 506-222-1405; Email: oec@crcouncil.org
Founded: 1968; Membership: 40 organizations, 2,000 individuals
Scope: Statewide
Description: Oregon Environmental Council is a nonprofit organization whose mission is to restore and protect Oregon's clean water and air for future generations. OEC brings Oregonians together to create and promote socially just and economically sound environmental policies.
Contact(s):
President: ANN WHEELER-BARTOL
Vice President: ED MCNAMARA
Executive Director: JEFF ALLEN
Secretary and Treasurer: RANDY POZDENA
Publication(s): *EarthWatch Oregon*
Keyword(s): Air Quality and Pollution, Environmental Justice, Pesticides, Pollution Prevention, Rivers, Transportation, Water Pollution, Water Quality

OREGON NATURAL RESOURCES COUNCIL
5828 N. Greeley Avenue, Portland, OR 97217
Phone: 503-283-6343; Fax: 503-283-0756
Founded: 1972; Membership: 3,000 individuals
Scope: Statewide
Description: A nonprofit, state-wide organization to aggressively protect and restore Oregon's wildlands, wildlife, and waters as an enduring legacy, and dedicated to permanently protect public forest lands and protect and restore critical habitat for native species.
Contact(s):
President: JANE BECKWITH
President: JIM MIDDAUGH
Executive Director: MARC SMILEY; Email: ms@onrc.org
Advocacy Director: TIM LILLEBO, 16 NW Kansas, Bend, OR 97701; Phone: 541-382-2616; Fax: 503-385-3370; Email: tl@onrc.org
Associate Director: KEVIN GORMAN; Email: kg@onrc.org
Conservation Director: KEN RAIT; Email: kr@onrc.org
Klamath Basin Protection Advocate: WENDELL WOOD, 943 Lakeshore Drive, Klamath Falls, OR 97601-9107; Phone: 541-885-4886; Fax: 541-885-4887; Email: ww@onrc.org
Land Protection Advocate: DOUG HEIKEN, P.O. Box 11648, Eugene, OR 97440-3848; Phone: 541-344-0675; Fax: 541-343-0996; Email: onrcdoug@efn.org
Salmon Protection Advocate: DIANE VALANTINE; Email: dv@onrc.org
Water Protection Advocate: REGNA MERRITT; Email: rm@onrc.org
Publication(s): *Wild Oregon*
Keyword(s): Ancient Forests, Conservation of Protected Areas, Environmental Preservation, Environmental Protection, Natural Areas, Public Lands, Watersheds, Wilderness, Wildlands

OREGON SMALL WOODLANDS ASSOCIATION
P.O. Box 3079, Salem, OR 97302-0079
Phone: 503-588-1813
Founded: 1967; Membership: 3,500
Scope: Statewide
Description: A statewide organization affiliated with the National Woodland Owners Association, dedicated to the protection, management, use, and enhancement of Oregon's forest resources.
Contact(s):
President: ILENE WALDORF; Phone: 503-829-3181
Executive Director: DENNY MILES
1st Vice President: JOHN ROUNDS; Phone: 541-447-1342
2nd Vice President: GARY SPRINGER; Phone: 541-757-8665
2nd Vice President: WILLIAM ARSENAULT; Phone: 541-584-2272
2nd Vice President: LYNN BREESE; Phone: 541-447-6762
2nd Vice President: JOHN PIPPIN; Phone: 503-653-1678
Editor: LORI D. RASOR; Phone: 503-228-3624
Past President: JIM DENISON; Phone: 541-336-6639
Publication(s): *Northwest Woodlands, Update Newsletter*
Keyword(s): Environmental and Conservation Education, Forests and Forestry, Renewable Resources

OREGON SOCIETY OF AMERICAN FORESTERS
4033 SW Canyon Rd., Portland, OR 97221
Phone: 503-224-8046; Fax: 503-226-2515
Founded: 1900; Membership: 1,450
Scope: Statewide
Description: The mission of the society is to advance the science, education, technology, and practice of forestry; enhance its members' competency and professionalism; and use the knowledge and skills of the profession to benefit society.
Contact(s):
Chair: JULIE STANGELL, 41909 Deerhorn Rd., Springfield, OR 97478
Chair-Elect ('99): BLAIR MOODY, 564 Burgandy Circle, Medford, OR 97504
Manager and Editor: LORI RASOR, 4033 SW Canyon Rd., Portland, OR 97221; Phone: 503-224-8046

OREGON TROUT, INC.
117 SW Front Ave., Portland, OR 97204
Phone: 503-222-9091; Email: info@ortrout.org; WWW: www.ortrout.org
Scope: Statewide
Description: An Oregon-based organization focused on the protection and restoration of wild fish and their ecosystems throughout the Northwest.
Contact(s):
Executive Director: GEOFF PAMPUSH
Publication(s): *Heritage News*
Keyword(s): Fisheries, Hunting, Nongame Wildlife, Sport Fishing, Wildlife and Wildlife Habitat

OREGON WILDLIFE HERITAGE FOUNDATION
P.O. Box 30406, Portland, OR 97294-3406
Phone: 503-255-6059; Fax: 503-255-6467
Founded: 1981
Scope: Statewide
Description: The Oregon Wildlife Heritage Foundation is a nonprofit, tax-exempt foundation incorporated under the laws of the state of Oregon. It has a 501(c(3 determination under the I.R.S. code. It receives grants and contributions to be used to fund selected projects beneficial to the fish and wildlife resources of Oregon and the people who enjoy them.
Contact(s):
President: KIM MacCOLL JR.
Vice President: JIM MEIER
Secretary: MARCIA HARTMAN
Treasurer: DON BARTH
Executive Director: ROD BROBRCK
Director Emeiritus: ALLEN L. KELLY
Editor: ALLAN L. KELLY

ORGANIZATION OF WILDLIFE PLANNERS
1900 Kanawha Blvd., East Charleston, WV 25305
Phone: 304-558-2771
Founded: 1978
Scope: National
Description: A nonprofit, tax-exempt organization comprised of professional state and federal fish and wildlife resource planners,

NON-GOVERNMENTAL ORGANIZATIONS

natural resources educators, professional conservationists, and associated interests dedicated to improving, through education and training, the quality of state-level resources management and planning. The focus of the organization is on developing the necessary tools and skills to conduct effective planned management systems.
Contact(s):
President: DAN ZEKOR, Missouri Department of Conservation, P.O. Box 180, Jefferson City, MO 65102
Treasurer: ARTHUR M. JOHNSEN, New York Department of Environmental Conservation, Rt. 10, Stamford, NY 12167
1st Past President: TOMMY SHROPSHIRE, Mississippi Department of Wildlife, Fisheries, and Parks, P.O. Box 451, Jackson, MS 39205
2nd Past President: THOMAS WASSON, Ohio Division of Wildlife, 1840 Belcher Dr., Columbus, OH 43224-1329
Editor: SHERRY CROUCH, Arizona Game & Fish Department, 2221 West Greenway, Phoenix, AZ 85023
President-Elect: LARRY D. CARTEE, South Carolina Department of Natural Resources, P.O. Box 167, Columbia, SC 29202
Publication(s): *Tomorrow's Management, Newsletter*
Keyword(s): Planning Management

ORNITHOLOGICAL COUNCIL
1725 K St., NW, Suite 212, Washington, DC 20006-1401
Phone: 202-530-5810; Fax: 202-628-4311; Email: oc@cnie.org; WWW: www.nmnh.si.edu/BIRDNET
Founded: 1992; Membership: 9 scientific societies/7,000 ornithologists
Scope: National
Description: The Council provides impartial scientific information about birds for sound decisions, policies, or management actions; links the scientific community with public and private decision-makers; informs ornithologists of actions that affect birds or the study of birds; and speaks for scientific ornithology when the study of birds might be affected.
Contact(s):
Chair: DR. DAVID E. BLOCKSTEIN
Executive Director: ELLEN PAUL, 3713 Chevy Chase Lake Drive, Apt 3, Chevy Chase, MD 20815; Phone: 301-986-8568; Fax: 301-986-5205; Email: epaul@dclink.com
Publication(s): *Ornithological Newsletter; Use of Wild Birds in Research; Bird Issue Briefs*
Keyword(s): Biology, Birds, Environmental and Conservation Education, Raptors, Waterfowl

OUTDOOR CIRCLE, THE
1314 S. King, #306, Honolulu, HI 96814
Phone: 808-593-0300; Fax: 808-593-0525; Email: outdoorcircle.org
Founded: 1912
Scope: Statewide
Description: A nonprofit organization whose purpose is to work for and develop a more beautiful state, freeing it from disfigurement, conserving and developing its natural beauty, and cooperating in educational and other efforts towards preservation of open spaces, parklands, recycling, and antilitter.
Contact(s):
President: CAROL HENDRICKS
Treasurer: MARY FLEMING
1st Vice President: PAULA RESS
Chief Executive Officer: MARY STEINER
Publication(s): *Keep Hawaii Green; Pua Nani: Hawaii is a Garden; Majesty: Exceptional Trees of Hawaii; Majesty II; Exceptional Trees of Hawaii, The*
Keyword(s): Land Preservation, Natural Areas, Open Space, Public Lands, Urban Forestry

OUTDOOR RECREATION COUNCIL OF BRITISH COLUMBIA
334 - 1367 W. Broadway, Vancouver, British Columbia V6H 4A9 Canada
Phone: 604-737-3058; Email: orcbc@istar.ca; WWW: home.istar.ca/~orcbc/
Founded: 1976
Scope: Statewide
Description: The ORC of BC is a nonprofit society formed to serve as a mechanism independent from government, through which the interests and activities of groups organized on a provincial basis concerned with outdoor recreation, education, and conservation can be coordinated and represented to government, industry, and the public.
Contact(s):
Chair: DOUG LEAVERS
Executive Director: NORMA WILSON
Director: DON GRIFFITHS
Director: BEVERLY FELSKE
Director: JOHN CAMPBELL
Director: WAYNE BOURQUE
Secretary and Treasurer: GEORGEEN GOTT-JANZEN
Publication(s): *Outdoor Report*
Keyword(s): Conservation of Protected Areas, Land Use Planning, Outdoor Recreation, Research, Rivers, Wilderness

OUTDOOR WRITERS ASSOCIATION OF AMERICA INC.
2155 E. College Avenue, State College, PA 16801-7204
Phone: 814-234-1011
Founded: 1927; Membership: 2,000
Scope: National
Description: We strive to improve ourselves in the art and media of our craft and to increase our knowledge and understanding in supporting the conservation of our natural resources. To this end we pledge ourselves to maintain the highest ethical standards in the exercise of our craft.
Contact(s):
President: TOM WHARTON, 1024 Ramona Ave., Salt Lake City, UT 84105; Phone: 801-237-2039
Executive Director: STEVE WAGNER, 2155 E. College Ave., State College, PA 16801; Phone: 814-234-1011
1st Vice President: JIM CASADA, 1250 Yorkdale Dr., Rock Hill, SC 29730
2nd Vice President: CLIFF SHELBY, HCR 64, Box 522, Flippin, AR 72634; Phone: 870-453-8337
3rd Vice President: BILL MONROE, 14292 S. Forsythe Rd., Oregon City, OR 97045; Phone: 888-222-8231
Chairman of the Board: BETTY LOU FEGELY, 3699 Beech Drive, Walnutport, PA 18088; Phone: 610-760-9470
Editor: CAROL KERSAVAGE
Secretary and Treasurer: JOHN P. MCCOY JR., One Bluegrass Ln., Barboursville, WV 25504; Phone: 304-736-3585
Publication(s): *Outdoors Unlimited*
Keyword(s): Communications, Environmental and Conservation Education, Outdoor Recreation, Wildlife and Wildlife Habitat

OZARK SOCIETY, THE
P.O. Box 2914, Little Rock, AR 72203
Founded: 1962; Membership: 1,000
Scope: Statewide
Description: To promote the knowledge and enjoyment of the scenic and scientific resources (particularly free-flowing streams, wilderness areas, and unique natural areas of the Ozark-Ouachita mountain region, and to help protect those resources for present and future generations.
Contact(s):
President: STEWART NOLAND
Publication(s): *Pack and Paddle, The*

OZARKS RESOURCE CENTER
PO Box 1198, Ava, MO 65608
Phone: 417-683-6245; Email: jlorrain@goin.missouri.org
Founded: 1978; Membership: 1,750
Scope: National
Description: The Center provides research, education, technical assistance, and dissemination of information on renewable resources-based technolog, sustainable agriculture, environmentally responsible practices, sustainable community economic development, and self-reliance for the family, farm, community, Ozarks, and other bio-regions.
Contact(s):
President: DONNA JONES, RR 1 Box 68A-1, Dora, MO 65637; Phone: 417-261-2518
Vice President: CORLISS SCHAFFER, HCR 64 Box 221, West Plains, MO 65775; Phone: 417-257-0670
Secretary: KATHI TRANTHAM, 7969 Covnty Rd. 3010, West Plains, MO 65775; Phone: 417-256-6518
Treasurer: DENISE VAUGHN, Rt 3 Box 200, Mtn. View, MO 65548; Phone: 417-256-6518
Executive Director: JANICE LORRAIN, Rt. 1 Box 393, Ava, MO 65608; Phone: 417-683-5049
Publication(s): *Broadcaster, The (newsletter); Talking Oak Leaves (newsletter)*
Keyword(s): Cultural Preservation, Environmental and Conservation Education, Environmental Preservation, Rural Development, Sustainable Development

OZONE ACTION
1636 Connecticut Ave. NW; 3rd Floor, Washington, DC 20009
Phone: 202-265-6738; Fax: 202-986-6041; Email: ozone_action@ozone.org
Founded: 1992
Scope: National
Description: Ozone Action educates the public about threats from ozone depletion and human-induced climate change. Ozone Action investigates and publicizes attempts to weaken our global environmental protections and exposes attempts by industry to distort public debate.
Contact(s):
President: JOHN PASSACANTANDO
Board Chair: MIKE CLARK
Publication(s): *Ozone Action News; Ties That Blind; Black Market CFC Reports; Climate Change Current Effects Summaries*
Keyword(s): Greenhouse Effect/Global Warming, Ozone Depletion

PACIFIC BASIN ASSOCIATION OF SOIL AND WATER CONSERVATION DISTRICTS
c/o Secretary-Treasurer, 494 Rte 8, Ste 101, Barrigada, Guam 96913
Scope: Statewide
Contact(s):
President and Board Member: ESTANISLAO HOCOG, P.O. Box 12, Tinian MP, GU 96952; Phone: 670-433-0690; Fax: 670-433-3152
Secretary-Treasurer: PATRICK CALVO, P.O. Box 2795, Saipan, MP 96950; Phone: 670-234-6120; Fax: 670-235-6122
Vice President, Alternate Board Member: RAYMOND SAN AGUSTIN, 494 Rte 8, Ste 101, Barrigada, GU 96913; Phone: 671-735-2111; Fax: 671-735-2110

PACIFIC FISHERY MANAGEMENT COUNCIL
2130 SW 5th Ave., Suite 224, Portland, OR 97201
Phone: 503-326-6352; Fax: 503-326-6831
Scope: National
Description: Nonprofit organization established by the Magnuson Fishery Conservation and Management Act of 1976. Develops management plans for fisheries off the coasts of Washington, Oregon, and California. Fourteen voting and five nonvoting members, of which nine are appointed by the Secretary of Commerce. Members include state and federal fishery agency managers, knowledgable citizens, and a tribal representative.
Contact(s):
Executive Director: LAWRENCE D. SIX
Administrative Officer: JOHN RHOTON
Economic Analysis Coordinator: JAMES L. SEGER
Fishery Management Coordinator, Marine: JAMES W. GLOCK
Fishery Management Coordinator, Salmon: JOHN COON
Keyword(s): Aquatic Habitats, Fisheries, Renewable Resources, Sport Fishing

PACIFIC NORTHWEST TRAIL ASSOCIATION
13595 Avon Allen Road, Mount Vernon, WA 98273
Phone: 306-424-0407
Founded: 1977; Membership: 300
Scope: National
Description: The PNTA was formed to promote the development of a continuous foot and horse trail from the Continental Divide at Glacier National Park to the Pacific Ocean at Olympic National Park. The PNTA encourages land use and conservation education through exposure to the historic and natural diversity of the Pacific Northwest.
Contact(s):
Chair: Duane Melcher; Phone: 306-424-0407
Publication(s): *Nor'wester; Pacific Northwest Trail, The, a guidebook to the 1,100 mile PNT (available on diskette); Blanchard Hill and Chuckanut Mountain Map*
Keyword(s): Environmental and Conservation Education, Internships, Outdoor Recreation, Pedestrian Environment, Public Lands

PACIFIC RIVERS COUNCIL
P.O. Box 10798, Eugene, OR 97440
Phone: 541-345-0119; Fax: 541-345-0710
Founded: 1987; Membership: 1,200
Scope: National
Description: The purpose of the Pacific Rivers Council is to develop scientific tools and legislative policies; to restore the ecological integrity and sustainable human use of America's river systems.
Contact(s):
Executive Director: TRYG SLETTELAND
Conservation Director: DAVID BAYLES
Publication(s): *Entering the Watershed; Freeflow; Various Briefing books and reports*
Keyword(s): Biodiversity, Fisheries, Public Lands, Rivers, Sustainable Agriculture

PACIFIC SEABIRD GROUP
Box 179, 4505 University Way, NE, Seattle, WA 98105
Founded: 1972; Membership: 415
Scope: International
Description: An international organization to promote the knowledge, study and conservation of Pacific seabirds.
Contact(s):
Chair: ALAN BURGER, Dept. of Biology, Univ. of Victoria, Victoria, CANADA V8W 3N5; Phone: 250-721-7127; Fax: 250-721-7120
Secretary: KATHY KULETZ, USFWS, 1011 East Tudor Rd., Anchorage, AK 99503; Phone: 907-786-3453; Fax: 907-786-3641
Treasurer: JAN HODDER, Oregon Institute of Marine Bio., Univ. of Oregon, Charleston, OR 97420; Phone: 541-888-2581/ext. 215; Fax: 541-888-3240
Chair-Elect: ED MURPHY, Institute of Arctic Biology, Univ. of Alaska Fairbanks, Fairbanks, AK 99712-0180; Phone: 907-474-7154; Fax: 907-474-6967
Editor: STEVEN M. SPEICH, 4720 N. Oeste Pl., Tucson, AZ 85749; Phone: 520-760-2110; Fax: 520-760-0228
Publication(s): *Pacific Seabird Group Bulletin*
Keyword(s): Birds, Endangered and Threatened Species, Environmental and Conservation Education, Wildlife and Wildlife Habitat, Zoology

NON-GOVERNMENTAL ORGANIZATIONS

PACIFIC WHALE FOUNDATION
101 N. Kihei Rd., Kihei, HI 96753
Phone: 808-879-8860; Fax: 808-879-2615
Founded: 1980
Scope: National
Description: A nonprofit tax-exempt 501(c)(3) organization dedicated to saving whales, dolphins and their ocean habitats through marine research, public education, and marine conservation. Pacific Whale Foundation actively studies whales, dolphins and coral reef communities throughout the Pacific to ensure their survival and recovery. More than 700,000 people have been educated about marine conservation through Pacific Whale Foundation's award-winning Ocean Outreach Program. The program includes Research Internships, school programs, an Adopt-a-Whale program, and an Adopt-a-Dolphin program.
Contact(s):
President: GREGORY D. KAUFMAN
Vice President: DR. PAUL H. FORESTELL
Editor: ANNE RILLERO
Secretary and Treasurer: DIXIE BONGOLAN
Publication(s): *Fin and Fluke; Soundings*
Keyword(s): Aquatic Habitats, Dolphins, Endangered and Threatened Species, Environmental and Conservation Education, Internships, Marine Mammals, Whales

PANOS INSTITUTE, THE
1701 K St., NW, 11 Fl., Washington, DC 20036
Phone: 202-223-7940; Fax: 202-223-7947
Founded: 1986
Scope: International
Description: The Panos Institute consists of three autonomous nonprofit, nongovernmental organizations located in London, Paris, and Washington, DC, working to raise public understanding of sustainable development issues. The Washington, DC institute focuses its work on Latin America, the Caribbean, and the United States.
Contact(s):
Secretary: DIANE McGLYNN
Treasurer: JACOB SCHERR
Board of Directors Chair: WILLIAM D. CARMICHAEL
Vice President and Executive Director: MELANIE BETH OLIVIERO
Publication(s): *We Speak For Ourselves; SIDAmerica; Eco-Reports; From Information to Education*
Keyword(s): Communications, Environmental and Conservation Education, Internships, Population Growth, Sustainable Development

PARTNERS IN PARKS
4916 Butterworth Pl. NW, Washington, DC 20016
Phone: 202-364-7244; Fax: 202-364-7246; Email: partpark@cqi.com
Founded: 1988
Scope: National
Description: A nonprofit organization that encourages, promotes, and establishes professional level partnerships between national park and other public land managers and those who would contribute their time and skills to studying, protecting, and interpreting natural and cultural features.
Contact(s):
Chair and President: SARAH G. BISHOP
Secretary and Treasurer: DAVID A. KIKEL
Keyword(s): Conservation of Protected Areas, Cultural Preservation, Natural Areas, Nature Preservation, Public Lands, Research

PENNSYLVANIA ASSOCIATION OF CONSERVATION DISTRICT DIRECTORS, INC.
ATTN: President, 534 Kennedy Rd., Airville, PA 17032
Scope: Statewide
Contact(s):
President, Alternate Board Member: PATRICIA SUECK, 534 Kennedy Rd., Airville, PA 17032; Phone: 717-862-3486; Fax: 717-862-3486
Secretary: RONALD ROHALL, P.O. Box 27, Rector, PA 15677; Phone: 412-238-4973
Treasurer: CLOYD E. BRENNEMAN, 103 Courthouse, Mercer, PA 16137; Phone: 412-662-3800
Executive Director: SUSAN FOX, 225 Pine St., Harrisburg, PA 17101; Phone: 717-236-1006; Fax: 717-236-6410
1st Vice President: FRANKLIN LONG JR, Rd. 1 Box 441, Tyrone, PA 16886; Phone: 814-648-4838
2nd Vice President: MURRAY LAITE, 512 Electric Ave, Lewistown, PA 17044; Phone: 717-248-6733
Board Member: ROBERT WAGNER, 373 Scott Rd., Quarryville, PA 17566; Phone: 717-529-2831; Fax: 717-529-2155

PENNSYLVANIA AUDUBON SOCIETY
1104 Fernwood Ave., #300, Camp Hill, PA 17011
Phone: 717-763-4985; Fax: 717-763-4981; Email: kmeinhart@audubon.org
Founded: 1987; Membership: 27,000
Scope: Statewide
Description: The Pennsylvania Audubon Society promotes and encourages the conservation and protection of our natural resources through public education, communication with public officials, and sponsorship of programs to help children and adults become aware of their relationship to the environment.
Contact(s):
President: CARMEN SANTASANIA, 1410 Charles St., State College, PA 16801; Phone: 814-359-5760
Secretary: MARIAN CROSSMAN, 6 Tussey Circle, Pittsburgh, PA 15237; Phone: 412-366-3339
Treasurer: LEIGH ALTADONNA, 161 Greenwood Ave., Wyncote, PA 15834; Phone: 215-886-0656
Executive Director: CINDY ADAMS DUNN, 1104 Fernwood Ave., Suite 300, Camp Hill, PA 17011; Phone: 717-763-4985
Publication(s): *Quarterly Newsletter; Population&Habitat Newsletter; Pennsylvania Sonbirds - a K-12 Teacher's Guide; Important Bird Areas of Pennsylvania Report; Audubon Protecting Animals Through Habitat; Project Mayfly; Wetlands Action Guide*
Keyword(s): Birds, Environmental and Conservation Education, Natural History, Outdoor Recreation, Wetlands, Wildlife and Wildlife Habitat

PENNSYLVANIA B.A.S.S. CHAPTER FEDERATION, INC.
ATTN: President, 769 N. Cottage Rd., Mercer, PA 16137
Phone: 412-475-2422
Scope: Statewide
Description: An organization of Bassmaster chapters, affiliated with the Bass Anglers Sportsman Society, organized to fight pollution, assist state and national conservation agencies in their efforts, and teach the young people of our country good conservation practices. Dedicated to the realistic conservation of our water resources.
Contact(s):
President: MIKE DUNKERLEY, 769 N. Cottage Rd., Mercer, PA 16137; Phone: 412-475-2422
Conservation Director: JOE CERSKI, 135 Pine Run Rd., Wilkes-Barre, PA 18702; Phone: 717-829-2158

PENNSYLVANIA CITIZENS ADVISORY COUNCIL TO DEPARTMENT OF ENVIRONMENTAL PROTECTION
13th Fl., RCSOB P.O. Box 8459, Harrisburg, PA 17105-8459
Phone: 717-787-4527
Scope: Statewide
Description: Created by Act 275 of the PA General Assembly, 1971.

Contact(s):
Executive Director: SUSAN M. WILSON
Administrative Assistant: STEPHANIE MIOFF
Chairperson: JOLENE CHINCHILLI
Vice Chairperson: DAVID STRONG
Keyword(s): Air Resources, Public Participation, Waste Resources, Water Resources

PENNSYLVANIA ENVIRONMENTAL COUNCIL, INC. (PEC)
1211 Chestnut St., Suite 900, Philadelphia, PA 19107
Phone: 215-563-0250/1-800-322-9214 in PA
Founded: 1969; Membership: 3,500
Scope: Statewide
Description: Private nonprofit statewide membership organization devoted to the protection and improvement of Pennsylvania's environment through education, advocacy, and consensus-building. PEC brings together nonprofits, government agencies, businesses, and citizens to develop environmental policy, take action on environmental issues, and work for effective environmental legislation, regulation, and enforcement.
Contact(s):
Chair: JOSEPH M. MANKO
President: JOANNE R. DENWORTH
Regional Director of Northeastern PA Office: RUSSELL JOHNSON
Regional Director of Planning: ANNA BRIENICH
Regional Director of Southeastern Office: PATRICK STARR
Regional Director of Western PA Office: DAVITT WOODWELL
Publication(s): *Environmental Forum Newsletter; PA Legislative Updates; Guiding Growth; Building Better Communities and Preserving our Countryside; Environmental Advisory Council Handbook; Transit-Oriented Development Handbook; Urban Vacant Land Handbook*

PENNSYLVANIA FEDERATION OF SPORTSMEN'S CLUBS
2426 N. Second St., Harrisburg, PA 17110
Phone: 717-232-3480; Fax: 717-231-3524; Email: pawild@paonline.com
Scope: Statewide
Description: A representative statewide organization, affiliated with the National Wildlife Federation, dedicated to the protection and enhancement of wildlife and its habitat through public education and government interaction.
Contact(s):
President: RAY MARTIN
Executive Director: JOSEPH NEVILLE
Affiliate Representative: MARK HENRY
Alternate Representative: ED ZYGMUT
Editor: DAVE WOLF
Keyword(s): Aquatic Habitats, Fisheries, Renewable Resources, Water Pollution Management, Wetlands

PENNSYLVANIA FORESTRY ASSOCIATION, THE
56 E. Main St., Mechanicsburg, PA 17055
Phone: 717-766-5371
Founded: 1886; Membership: 1,700
Scope: Statewide
Description: An independent nonprofit conservation organization, affiliated with the National Woodland Owners Association dedicated to environmental improvement and wise use of natural resources in Pennsylvania. Membership includes a cross section of all groups and individuals interested in true conservation.
Contact(s):
President: LINDA FITTERER; Phone: 717-534-2955
Vice President: SCOTT KURTZMAN; Phone: 717-225-4711
Secretary: WILLIAM S. CORLETT; Phone: 717-737-7118
Treasurer: JOHN BEVERLY; Phone: 717-787-2039
Editor: JAN ZINN
Past President: JOHN R. PETERS; Phone: 215-975-4075
Publication(s): *Pennsylvania Recreation and Parks*
Keyword(s): Environmental and Conservation Education, Health and Nutrition, Outdoor Recreation, Public Lands, Youth Organizations

PENNSYLVANIA RECREATION AND PARK SOCIETY, INC.
1315 W. College Ave., Suite 200, State College, PA 16801-2776
Phone: 814-234-4272; Fax: 814-234-5276
Founded: 1935; Membership: 1,700
Scope: Statewide
Description: To promote quality recreation and park opportunities for all the citizens of the Commonwealth of Pennsylvania by actively involving professionals and citizens in recreation, park, and conservation programs, by fostering and maintaining high standards of professional qualifications and ethics, and by providing quality educational opportunities.
Contact(s):
President: KAREN L. HESSER, Chester Co. Parks and Recreation, Gov't Services Ctr, Ste 160, 60 Westtown Rd., West Chester, PA 19382; Phone: 610-344-6415
Secretary: DOUGLAS J. WENDELL, Abington Twp. Parks and Recreation, 515 Meetinghouse Rd., Jenkintown, PA 19046; Phone: 215-576-5213
Treasurer: R. BRUCE McFATE, Calendonia State Park, 40 Rocky Mount Rd., Fayetteville, PA 17222; Phone: 717-352-2161
Executive Director: ROBERT D. GRIFFITH, Pennsylvania Recreation and Park Society, Inc., 1315 W. College Ave., Suite 200, State College, PA 16801-2776
Editor: VANYLA S. TIERNEY
President-Elect: CARNEN S. WILLIAMS, West Shore Recreation and Leisure Serv., PO Box 442, New Cumberland, PA 17070-0442; Phone: 717-938-8525
Publication(s): *Pennsylvania Recreation and Parks*
Keyword(s): Environmental and Conservation Education, Flowers, Plants, and Trees, Pesticides, Solid Waste, Water Pollution

PENNSYLVANIA RESOURCES COUNCIL, INC., (formerly PA Roadside Council)
3606 Providence Rd., Newtown Square, PA 19073
Phone: 610-353-1555; Fax: 610-353-6257; WWW: www.prc.org
Founded: 1939
Scope: Statewide
Description: The Pennsylvania Resources Council (PRC) is recognized nationally for its expertise in recycling, waste reduction, and litter control. PRC produces educational materials, as well as seminars and conferences for citizens, municipalities, civic groups and corporations. PRC also sponsors the nation's only environmental shopping hotline (1-800-Go-To-PRC). Open to the public, PRC's environmental living center has exhibits and workshops to show the impact of lifestyle choices on the environment.
Contact(s):
President: JOAN BATORY; Phone: 610-344-6257
Vice President: HOWARD WEIN; Phone: 412-392-2128
Vice President: TIM WILLIAMS; Phone: 717-234-4067
Vice President: RICHARD BAPST; Phone: 215-984-7113
Publication(s): *PEEC Seasons; All About Recycling; Environmental Living Up Date; PRC Newsletter*
Keyword(s): Beautification, Environmental and Conservation Education, Environmental Living, Healthy Home, Litter, Natural History, Nature Study, Outdoor Recreation, Pollution Prevention, Recycling, Waste Management, Wildlife and Wildlife Habitat

PEOPLE'S FORUM 2001, JAPAN
Maruko Bld. 3F, 1-20-6 Higashiueno, Taitou-ku, Tokyo 110-0015 Japan
Phone: 81-3-3834-2436; Fax: 81-3-3834-2406; Email: pf2001jp@jca.ax.apc.org
Scope: International
Description: People's Forum 2001, Japan is an NGO network of national environmental NGO's, CBO's, and individuals being active to bring about sustainable society. The Forum's task is to serve as a clearing house as well as to provide a framework of activities for the members. The Forum's activities include research, education, publication, and policy dialogues with different sectors to alter

current economic and political systems to be ecologically and socially sustainable.
Contact(s):
Director: TOMOKO SAKUMA

PEREGRINE FUND, THE
5666 W. Flying Hawk Ln., Boise, ID 83709
Phone: 208-362-3716; Fax: 208-362-2376; Email: tpf@peregrinefund.org; WWW: www.peregrinefund.org
Founded: 1970
Scope: National
Description: The Peregrine Fund works nationally and internationally to conserve biological diversity and enhance environmental health by working with birds through management and conservation of species and their habitat, and through education and scientific investigation. Although best known nationally for species restoration, they have assisted on conservation projects in over 40 countries.
Contact(s):
Vice President: JEFFREY R. CILEK
Vice President: J. PETER JENNY
Secretary: RONALD C. YANKE
Treasurer: PAXSON H. OFFIELD
Chairman of Board: HENRY M. PAULSON, JR
Editor: WILLIAM BURNHAM
Founding Chairman of Board: DR. TOM J. CADE
Librarian: LLOYD F. KIFF
President and CEO: DR. WILLIAM A. BURNHAM
Vice Chairman of the Board: D. JAMES NELSON
Publication(s): *The Peregrine Fund Newsletter; Annual Report; Operation Report; progress reports*
Keyword(s): Birds, Endangered and Threatened Species, International Conservation, Raptors, Wildlife Management

PHEASANTS FOREVER INC.
P.O. Box 75473, St. Paul, MN 55175
Phone: 612-773-2000
Founded: 1982; Membership: 76000 and 500 chapters
Scope: National
Description: Pheasants Forever, Inc. is a nonprofit conservation organization formed in response to the continued decline of ring-necked pheasants. The mission of Pheasants Forever is to protect and to enhance pheasant and other upland wildlife populations through habitat improvement, public awareness and education programs, and land management policy refinement. Pheasants Forever accomplishes its goals primarily through a nationwide network of chapters that raises money at annual banquets and uses 100% of the net funds for local habitat projects.
Contact(s):
Chairman: GEORGE A. WILSON
Secretary: ROBERT P. LARSON
Treasurer: RICHARD O. HANOUSEK
Chief Executive Officer: JEFFREY S. FINDEN
Chief Executive Officer: JEFFERY S. FINDEN
Director of Development and Public Affairs: JOSEPH J. DUGGAN
Director of Education: RUSSELL W. SEWELL
Director of Governmental Affairs: DAVID E. NOMSEN, 2101 Ridgewood Dr., Alexandria, MN 56308; Phone: 612-763-6103
Editor: MARK HERWIG
Regional Field Representative: MATTHEW B. O'CONNOR, 2880 Thunder Rd., Hopkinton, IA 52237; Phone: 319-926-2357
Regional Represenative: RICHARD E. YOUNG, 6200 Knollwood, Oregon, WI 53575; Phone: 608-835-8914
Regional Representative: THOMAS R. KIRSCHENMANN, 420 Dawn Ave., Danville, IL 61832; Phone: 217-446-2958
Regional Representative: KEITH BRUS, 5995 W. Little Portage Rd., Pt. Clinton, OH 43452; Phone: 419-732-7149
Regional Representative: KENNETH E. SOLOMON, 557 Utah Ave. SE, Huron, SD 57350; Phone: 605-352-5268
Regional Representative: DAVID R. LOCKWOOD, 5525 Randolph Dr., Boise, ID 83705; Phone: 208-378-4371
Regional Representative: PETER S. BERTHELSEN, 101 Alexander Ave., Elba, NE 68835; Phone: 308-754-5339
Regional Representative: DAVID E. NOMSEN, 2101 Ridgewood Dr., Alexandria, MN 56308; Phone: 612-763-6103
Regional Representative: BARTH V. CROUCH, 1625 E. Beloit Ave., Salina, KS 67401; Phone: 913-823-9427
Regional Reptresentative: JAMES R. GOODHEART, 8401 Stoney Creek Ct., Davison, MI 48423; Phone: 810-658-2209
Senior Regional Wildlife Biologist: JAMES B. WOOLEY JR., 1205 Ilion Ave., Chariton, IA 50049; Phone: 515-774-2238
Senior Vice President and Chief Financial Officer: HOWARD K. VINCENT
Publication(s): *Pheasants Forever*
Keyword(s): Agriculture, Birds, Environmental and Conservation Education, Hunting, Wildlife and Wildlife Habitat

PHYSICIANS FOR SOCIAL RESPONSIBILITY
1101 14th St. NW 7th Floor, Washington, DC 20005
Phone: 202-898-0150
Founded: 1961; Membership: 20,000
Scope: National
Description: Promotes arms reduction, international cooperation to protect the environment, and education and programs aimed at reducing violence.
Contact(s):
President: DR. DAVE HALL
Executive Director: DR. ROBERT K. MUSIL
Publication(s): *Monitor; PSR Reports.*
Keyword(s): Energy, Environmental and Conservation Education, Nuclear/Radiation, Pesticides, Toxic Substances

PIEDMONT ENVIRONMENTAL COUNCIL
P.O. Box 460, Warrenton, VA 20188
Phone: 540-347-2334; Fax: 540-349-9003
Founded: 1972
Scope: Statewide
Description: A nonprofit organization formed to conserve natural resources and the pastoral landscape of a nine-county region of the Northern Virginia Piedmont. Public education and services to public officials and citizens, covering: land use; farmland retention; open space conservation; historic preservation; rural transportation policy; and rural planning legislation. Active statewide and federally on rural conservation issues.
Contact(s):
Chairman: EVE D. FOUT
President: CHRISTOPHER G. MILLER
Vice Chairman: JOHN BIRDSALL
Publication(s): *Potomac Appalachian; various topographical maps and hiking guidebooks*
Keyword(s): Environmental Preservation, Land Purchase, Outdoor Recreation, Pedestrian Environment, Public Lands

PINCHOT INSTITUTE FOR CONSERVATION
1616 P St. NW Suite 100, Washington, DC 20036
Phone: 202-797-6580; Fax: 202-797-6583; Email: alsample@pinchot.org
Founded: 1963
Scope: National
Description: The Pinchot Institute for Conservation is an independent nonprofit organization established to advance forest conservation thought, policy, and action. Serves as a bridge between the scientific and policymaking communities, providing timely, objective policy research, facilitation, leadership, training, and environmental education on issues relating to the protection and sustainable management of forests.
Contact(s):
Chair: JACKSON F. ENO
President: V. ALARIC SAMPLE
Secretary: MARY COULOMBE
Treasurer: JOHN FRY
Director of Grey Towers National Historic Landmark: EDGAR B. BRANNON, P.O. Box 188, Milford, PA 18337; Phone: 717-296-9630; Fax: 717-296-9675
Vice Chair: DENNIS LeMASTER

Publication(s): *The Pinchot Letter; Grey Towers Press books; numerous policy studies*

Keyword(s): Forests and Forestry, Planning Management, Public Lands, Research, Sustainable Ecosystems

PLANNED PARENTHOOD FEDERATION OF AMERICA INC.
810 Seventh Ave., New York, NY 10019
Phone: 212-541-7800; WWW: www.plannedparenthood.org

Founded: *1916*
Scope: *National*

Description: Planned Parenthood Federation of America (PPFA) is a federation of 136 not-for-profit affiliates operating nearly 900 medically-supervised health centers nationwide. Planned Parenthood centers provide a wide range of services--including family planning counseling, contraception, prenatal care, adoption referrals, abortion services, cancer screening, testing and treatment for HIV/AIDS, and other sexually transmitted infections, and sexuality education--to nearly five million men and women each year. For the Planned Parenthood center nearest you, call 1-800-230-PLAN. Contact: PPFA, 810 Seventh Ave., New York, NY ,10019, 212-541-7800, www.plannedparenthood.org.

Contact(s):
President: GLORIA FELDT
Secretary: JOHN ROMO
Treasurer: BARBARA SINGHAUS
1st Vice Chairperson: ELLEN OFFNER
2nd Vice Chairperson: MARK MUNGER
Chairperson: SHARON W. ALLISON
Chief Operating Officer: R. JAMES LeFEVRE
Librarian: TRACEY FRIESENG, Katherine Dexter McCormick Library, 810 Seventh Ave., New York, NY 10019; Phone: 212-261-4637

Keyword(s): Family Planning, Health and Nutrition, Population Growth, Reproductive Rights

PLANNING AND CONSERVATION LEAGUE
926 J St., Suite 612, Sacramento, CA 95814
Phone: 916-444-8726; Fax: 916-448-1789; Email: pclmail@pcl.org; WWW: www.pcl.org/pcl

Founded: *1965;* **Membership:** *10,000*
Scope: *Statewide*

Description: A representative statewide organization, affiliated with the National Wildlife Federation, dedicated to the protection and enhancement of wildlife and its habitat through public education and government interaction.

Contact(s):
Affiliate Representative: DAN FROST
Executive Director: DR. GERALD H. MERAL

POCONO ENVIRONMENTAL EDUCATION CENTER
R.R. 2 Box 1010, Dingmans Ferry, PA 18328
Phone: 717-828-2319; Fax: 717-828-9695; Email: peec@ptd.net; WWW: www.peec.org

Founded: *1986*
Scope: *Statewide*

Description: The Pocono Environmental Education Center (PEEC) advances environmental awareness, knowledge, and skills through education, in order that those who inhabit and will inherit the planet may better understand the complexities of natural and human-designed environments.

Contact(s):
Assistant Director: THOMAS SHIMALLA
President: JOHN PADALINO; Email: jack.peec@oal.com
Director: FLORENCE MAURO
Associate Director: PAUL F. BRANDWEIN

POLLUTION PROBE FOUNDATION
12 Madison Ave., Toronto, Ontario M5R 2S1 Canada
Phone: 416-926-1907; Fax: 416-926-1601; Email: pprobe@pollutionprobe.org; WWW: www.pollutionprobe.org

Founded: *1969;* **Membership:** *10,000*
Scope: *National*

Description: Pollution Probe is a Canadian nonprofit organization that exists to define environmental problems through research; to promote understanding through education; and to press for practical solutions through advocacy.

Contact(s):
Executive Director: KEN OGILVIE; Phone: 416-926-1907 ext231
Chairman of Pollution Probe Foundation: EDWARD BABIN

Publication(s): *Canadian Green Consumer Guide, The; Canadian Junior Green Guide, The; Kitchen Handbook, An Environmental Guide; Profit from Pollution Prevention: A Guide to Waste Reduction and Recycling in Canada*

POPE AND YOUNG CLUB
15 E. 2nd St. P.O. Box 548, Chatfield, MN 55923
Phone: 507-867-4144; Fax: 507-867-4144; Email: pyclub@isl.net

Founded: *1961;* **Membership:** *3,500*
Scope: *National*

Description: A North American bowhunting and wildlife conservation organization dedicated to the promotion and protection of our bowhunting heritage and North America's wildlife.

Contact(s):
President: G. FRED ASBELL
Treasurer: DONALD ACE MORGAN
Executive Secretary: GLENN E. HISEY
First Vice President: M. R. JAMES

POPULATION ACTION INTERNATIONAL
Suite 550 1120 19th St. NW, Washington, DC 20036
Phone: 202-659-1833

Founded: *1965*
Scope: *National*

Description: Develops worldwide support for international population and family planning programs through public education, policy analysis, and liaison with international leaders and organizations.

Contact(s):
President: HUGO HOOGENBOOM
Vice President: VICTORIA MARKELL
Secretary: PHYLLIS T. PIOTROW
Treasurer: WILLIAM C. EDWARDS
Director of Population and Environment Program: ROBERT ENGELMAN
Director of Publications: JUDITH HINDS
Founder: WILLIAM H. DRAPER JR.
Information Services Manager and Senior Librarian: ANNE MARIE B. AMANTIA
National Chair: ROBIN CHANDLER DUKE
National Co-Chair: VICKI SANT
National Co-Chair: ROBERT B. WALLACE
National Co-Chair: JOSEPH D. TYDINGS

Publication(s): *Population briefing sheets; country status reports; legislative and policy updates; annual report of activities; studies of population-environment linkages*

Keyword(s): Environment, Health and Nutrition, Population Growth, Renewable Resources, Sustainable Development

POPULATION COMMUNICATIONS INTERNATIONAL
777 United Nations Plaza 7C, New York, NY 10017
Phone: 212-687-3366; Fax: 212-661-4188; Email: pci@together.org

Founded: *1985;* **Membership:** *10,000*
Scope: *National*

Description: PCI works through mass media and nongovernmental organizations to promote elevation of women's status, use of family planning, and small family norms. PCI's social-content soap operas

NON-GOVERNMENTAL ORGANIZATIONS

in developing countries are locally researched and produced and weave social themes into long-term script development for radio and television dramas. In the United States PCI also works with broadcasters and NGOs. Currently PCI is collaborating with NWF to develop an environmental/human sexuality soap opera for U.S. audiences.
Contact(s):
President: DAVID O. POINDEXTER, 777 United Nations Plaza, New York, NY 10017; Phone: 212-687-3366
Publication(s): *International Dateline; Beyond Cairo; Teletipo Poblacion; Member News*
Keyword(s): Communications, Population Growth

POPULATION INSTITUTE, THE
107 Second St. NE, Washington, DC 20002
Phone: 202-544-3300; Fax: 202-544-0068; Email: web@populationinstitute.org
Founded: 1969
Scope: National
Description: To enlist and motivate key leadership groups to participate in the effort to bring population growth into balance with resources by means consistent with human dignity and freedom. Works in communications and with mass membership organizations, educational leaders, and policy leaders.
Contact(s):
President: WERNER FORNOS; Phone: 202-544-3300
Secretary: STEPHEN KEESE
Treasurer: JOYCE W. CRAMER
Chairperson of the Board: BETTYE WARD
Vice Chairperson: SARAH G. EPSTEIN
Publication(s): *POPLINE - World Population News Service; Annual Report; Towards The 21st Century (Monograph Series)*
Keyword(s): Air Quality and Pollution, Developing Countries, Environment, Internships, Population Growth, Water Resources

POPULATION REFERENCE BUREAU INC.
1875 Connecticut Ave. NW #520, Washington, DC 20009
Phone: 202-483-1100
Founded: 1929; Membership: 4,000
Scope: National
Description: PRB is a private, nonprofit educational organization which gathers, interprets, and disseminates information on population dynamics and their public-policy implications, globally and in the United States. Program areas include: international population communications, domestic (U.S.) policy studies, library and information services, educational programs, and an extensive publications program.
Contact(s):
President: PETER DONALDSON
Treasurer: BERT T. EDWARDS
Chair of the Board: MONTAGUE YUDELMAN
Director of International Programs: ALENE GELBARD
Librarian: ZUALI MALSAWMA
Publications Director: ELLEN CARNEVALE
Senior Denographer: CARL HAUB
Publication(s): *Population Bulletin; Population Today; World and U.S. Population Data Sheets, teaching kits on population topics; list available on request.*
Keyword(s): Communications, Environmental and Conservation Education, Geography, Population Growth, Sustainable Development

POPULATION-ENVIRONMENT BALANCE INC.
2000 P St. NW Suite 210, Washington, DC 20036-5915
Phone: 202-955-5700; Fax: 202-955-6161; Email: uspop@balance.org; WWW: www.balance.org
Founded: 1973; Membership: 10,000
Scope: National
Description: Population-Environment Balance is a grassroots membership organization dedicated to public education regarding the adverse effects of population growth on the environment. "BALANCE" advocates measures that would encourage population stabilization in the U.S.; encourages a responsible immigration policy for the U.S.; and promotes increased funding for contraceptive research and availability. Activities include public education, advocacy, media campaigns, and publications.
Contact(s):
Executive Director: MARIA SEPULVEDA
Chairman of the Board: DR. VIRGINIA ABERNETHY
Publication(s): *Balance Activist; BALANCE data; Action Alerts*
Keyword(s): Air Quality and Pollution, Environment, Population Growth

POTOMAC APPALACHIAN TRAIL CLUB
118 Park St., SE, Vienna, VA 22180
Phone: 703-242-0693; Fax: 703-242-0968; WWW: patc.simplenet.com
Founded: 1927; Membership: 6,100
Scope: Statewide
Description: Maintains 240 miles of the Appalachian Trail from Rock Fish Gap in Virginia to Pine Grove Furnace State Park in Pennsylvania. Also maintains an additional 750 miles of trails. Activities include publication of maps and guidebooks, mountaineering, ski-touring, construction and maintenance of trails, shelters, and cabins, and many conservation activities.
Contact(s):
President: SANDRA MARRA
Treasurer: RICHARD NEWCOMER
Director of Administration: WILSON RILEY
Editor: BIANCA MENEDEZ
General Secretary: WARREN SHARP
Supervisor of Trails: PETER GATJE
Keyword(s): Environmental and Conservation Education

POWDER RIVER BASIN RESOURCE COUNCIL
P.O. Box 1178, Douglas, WY 82633
Phone: 307-358-5002; Fax: 307-358-6771
Founded: 1973; Membership: 600
Scope: Statewide
Description: Nonprofit grassroots organization whose major purpose is to help Wyoming people work to prevent and alleviate environmental and rural problems. Major issues include: Coal mining, water development, toxics, wastes, energy conservation, agriculture, and accountable government.
Contact(s):
Chair: MARY WEBER
Treasurer: STACY PAGE
Vice Chairman: BOB STRAYER

PRAIRIE CLUB, THE
203 N. Wabash Suite 1620, Chicago, IL 60601
Phone: 312-899-1539; Fax: 312-899-1541
Founded: 1911; Membership: 900
Scope: National
Description: Organized for the promotion of outdoor recreation in the form of walks, outings, camping, and canoeing; the establishment and maintenance of permanent and temporary camps; and the encouragement of the love of nature.
Contact(s):
President: ROGER FAVORITE
Secretary: ELIZABETH DURKIN
Treasurer: HENRY GRAEF
1st Vice President: HERB CARLSON
2nd Vice President: LAYTON OLSON
Chairman of Conservation Committee: KAY LINCICOME
Editor: SUSAN MESSER
Publication(s): *The Bulletin*
Keyword(s): Biodiversity, Environmental Preservation, Land Purchase, Outdoor Recreation, Wildlife and Wildlife Habitat

PRAIRIE GROUSE TECHNICAL COUNCIL
Wildlife and Fisheries Sciences Department Texas A&M University, College Station, TX 77843
Phone: 409-845-5777; Fax: 409-845-3786

Membership: 200
Scope: National
Description: Comprises federal, state, and private agency biologists or administrators concerned with the status, research, and management of the prairie-chicken and sharp-tailed grouse in North America.
Contact(s):
Executive Committee: KENNETH GIESEN, 317 W. Prospect, Ft.Collins, CO 80526
Publication(s): *Newsletter and Proceedings*
Keyword(s): Birds, Endangered and Threatened Species, Prairies, Wildlife and Wildlife Habitat, Wildlife Management

PREDATOR PROJECT
P.O. Box 6733, Bozeman, MT 59771
Phone: 406-587-3389; Fax: 406-587-3178; Email: predproj@avicom.net; WWW: www.wildrockies.org/predproj

Founded: 1991; Membership: 1000
Scope: National
Description: Since its inception in 1991, Predator Project has worked to conserve and restore ecosystem integrity by protecting predators and their habitats--saving a place for America's predators. We advocate on behalf of over twelve species that otherwise receive inadequate attention: primarily the grizzly bear, wolf, lynx, wolverine, fisher, marten, black-footed ferret, swift fox, burrowing owl, coyote, mountain lion, and black bear. Of these, nine are imperiled. We also work on behalf of important prey species, such as prairie dogs, because these animals provide predators with essential food and/or habitat.
Contact(s):
President: STEVE FORREST
Vice President: SHARON NEGRI
Executive Director: TOM SKEELE
Secretary/Treasurer: JIM STOLTZ
Publication(s): *The Home Range (quarterly newsletter; membership of $20 or more); Conservation of Prairie Dog Ecosystems: Learning From the Past to Insure the Prairie Dog's Future (a 32-page report; $7); The Wild Bunch (free 12-page booklet on the lynx, wolverine, fisher, and marten;Ten Myths that Perpetuate Environmental Destruction and Government Waste (a 12 page booklet, $1); Motorizing Montana's National Forest Trails (a 13 page report $3)*
Keyword(s): Biodiversity, Endangered and Threatened Species, Environmental Protection, Mammals, Nongame Wildlife, Prairies, Predators, Public Lands, Wildlife and Wildlife Habitat, Wildlife Management

PROFESSIONAL BOWHUNTERS SOCIETY
P.O. Box 246, Terrell, NC 28682
Phone: 704-664-2534; Fax: 704-664-2534

Founded: 1963; Membership: 3,000
Scope: National
Description: Created as an organization of dedicated bowhunters interested in promoting a high level of ethics in the taking of wild game with bow and arrow. To provide training for others in safety, shooting skill, and hunting techniques. To practice and promote the wise use of our natural resources and conservation of wildlife.
Contact(s):
President: JIM CHINN, P.O. Box 1315, Hamilton, MT 59840; Phone: 406-363-3816
Vice President: JERRY BRUMM, 8525 Thornapple Lake Rd., Nashville, MI 49073; Phone: 517-852-9340
Council At-Large: TIM REED, P.O. Box 60, Valley Grove, WV 26060; Phone: 304-547-9077
Councilman: DENNIS ALLMAN, 2600 Hill Dr., Morganton, NC 28655; Phone: 704-433-9494
Editor: JACK SMITH
PBS Office: BRENDA KISNER; Phone: 704-664-2534; Fax: 704-664-7471
Secretary and Treasurer: JACK SMITH, P.O. Box 246, Terrell, NC 28682; Phone: 704-664-2534; Fax: 704-664-7471
Senior Councilman: DOUG KERR, R.R. 1, Box 312D, Stoney Lake Rd., Glenfield, NY 13343; Phone: 315-376-8660
Publication(s): *Professional Bowhunter Magazine, The*

PROVINCE OF QUEBEC SOCIETY FOR THE PROTECTION OF BIRDS, INC.
P.O. Box 43, Station B, Montreal, Quebec H3B 3J5 Canada
Phone: 514-637-2141

Founded: 1917; Membership: 708
Scope: Statewide
Contact(s):
President: DAVID MULHOLLAND, 60 Angell, Beaconsfield, Quebec H9W 4V5 Canada; Phone: 514-630-3968
Vice President: BARBARA MacDUFF, 101 Birch Hill, Hudson, Quebec J0P 1J0 Canada; Phone: 514-458-4751
Vice President: BESS MUHLSTOCK, 4807 Jeanne Mance, Montreal, Quebec H2V 4J6 Canada; Phone: 514-274-3810
Editor: SHEILA ARTHUR, 3804 Royal Ave., Montreal, Quebec H4E 1P1 Canada; Phone: 514-487-4047
Hon. Secretary: KYRA EMO, 140 Irvine Ave., Westmount, Quebec H3Z 2K2 Canada; Phone: 514-939-9666
Hon. Treasurer: KENNETH THORPE, 5615 Eldridge, Cote St-Luc, Quebec H4W 2C9 Canada; Phone: 514-483-5031
Publication(s): *Tchebec (Annual Review); Field Check List of Birds in the Montreal Area; Birdfinding in the Montreal Area; Monthly Newsletter*

PTARMIGANS, THE
P.O. Box 1821, Vancouver, WA 98668
Phone: 206-687-2436/206; Fax: 695-5385

Founded: 1960; Membership: 125
Scope: Statewide
Description: The Ptarmigans were established for the purpose of conducting mountaineering activities in the northwest and in promoting the preservation of the northwest forests, wilderness lands, and mountain scenery. The only membership requirement is a love of the outdoors. Offer a variety of outdoor activities led in an ecologically-minded manner. Help maintain several local trail systems and conduct an annual Basic Climbing School. Visit and observe changes proposed in our northwest forests and mountains. The conservation committee studies issues that affect our outdoor recreation area.
Contact(s):
President: JIM PEDERSEN
1st Vice President: MIKE DIANICH
2nd Vice President: RICHARD CHENOWETH
Secretary: JIM EPLIN
Treasurer: FREDA SHERBURNE
Publication(s): *Preserve Farmlands; A Place in the Islands; Landowner's Guide; Mom's Marsh and Other Fine Places (video)*
Keyword(s): Birds, Environmental and Conservation Education, Environmental Preservation, Islands, Wildlife and Wildlife Habitat

PUBLIC EMPLOYEES FOR ENVIRONMENTAL RESPONSIBILITY (PEER)
2001 S St., NW, Suite 570, Washington, DC 20009
Phone: 202-265-7337; Fax: 202-265-4192; Email: info@peer.org

Founded: 1993
Scope: National
Description: PEER is an association of resource managers, scientists, biologists, law enforcement officials, and other government professionals dedicated to the responsible management of the nation's environment. PEER advocates the sustainable management of public resources and promotes environmental ethics and professional integrity within their agency.
Contact(s):
Vice President: HOWARD WILSHIRE

NON-GOVERNMENTAL ORGANIZATIONS

Executive Director: JEFFREY RUCH
Administrative Director: HEIDI M. POOR
Board Chair: JEFF DeBONIS
Board President: JEFF RUCH
Development Director: MELISSA HIPPLER
Director of Membership: SHIRLEY HARRIS
General Counsel: TODD ROBINS
Membership Coordinator: PETULA CAESAR
National Field Director: ROB PERKS
Publication(s): *PEEReview; various issue papers*
Keyword(s): Environmental Ethics, Environmental Protection, Forests and Forestry, Public Lands, Water Resources

PUBLIC EMPLOYEES FOR ENVIRONMENTAL RESPONSIBILITY (PEER) (West Coast Office)
P.O. Box 30, Hood River, OR 97031
Phone: 541-387-4781; Fax: 541-387-4783
Scope: National

PUBLIC LANDS FOUNDATION
P.O. Box 7226 Arlington, McLean, VA 22207
Phone: 703-790-1988
Founded: 1987
Scope: National
Description: A national, nonprofit, independent advocate to keep the public lands public and for the proper use and protection of the public lands administered by the Bureau of Land Management; implementation of the Federal Land Policy and Management Act (FLPMA); and for professional land management by professional employees.
Contact(s):
President: GEORGE D. LEA; Phone: 703-790-1988
Editor: GEORGE D. LEA
President-Elect: VINCE HECKER; Phone: 301-881-0964
Secretary and Treasurer: VINCE RILEY; Phone: 703-536-7939
Publication(s): *Public Lands Monitor, The*
Keyword(s): Environmental and Conservation Education, Land Use Planning, Public Lands, Renewable Resources, Soil Conservation

PUERTO RICO ASSOCIATION OF SOIL AND WATER CONSERVATION DISTRICTS
ATTN: President, P.O. Box 91, Orocovis, PR 00720
Scope: Statewide
Contact(s):
President: PEDRO J. FUENTES, P.O. Box 91, Orocovis, PR 00720; Phone: 787-867-4707
Secretary: HILDA BONILLA, HC 1 Box 8162, Manati, PR 00773; Phone: 787-860-0045
Treasurer: VOLTAIRE LOPEZ, P.O. Box 288, Orcovis, PR 00720; Phone: 787-854-0143
Administrative Secretary: MIGDALIA RODRIGUEZ, P.O. Box 1225, Casguas, PR 00726; Phone: 787-258-0490; Fax: 787-258-0490
Vice President, Board Member: CARLOS MANTRAS, 1722 Pastemark St., Urb Purple Tree, PR 00926; Phone: 787-761-6247
Publication(s): *Verde Luz Newsletter; Puerto Rico Environmental Laws; Puerto Rico Conservation Directory; Puerto Rican Parrot Teacher's Kit, Pablo y Marisol van a la Playa*
Keyword(s): Biodiversity, Coasts, Endangered and Threatened Species, Environmental and Conservation Education, Land Purchase, Wetlands

PUERTO RICO CONSERVATION FOUNDATION, THE (PRCF
G-11 O'Neill, Apt. 1, San Juan, PR 00918-2301
Phone: 787-763-9875; Fax: 787-763-9895; Email: 104203.430@compuserve.com
Founded: 1987
Scope: Statewide
Description: The PRCF is a private nonprofit tax-exempt 501(c)3 organization. The organization began and continues its work with the support of the MacArthur Foundation, The Nature Conservancy, U.S. Fish and Wildlife Service, U.S. Forest Service, and private corporations. The main purpose of PRCF is the conservation of Puerto Rico's biological biodiversity, not only endangered species, but other lesser known species as well, their habitats and those natural areas required for their survival.
Contact(s):
President: JUAN L. RICART
Secretary: JOSE A. DUENO
Director: ANDRES GARCIA
Director: HELEN NUNCI
Director: MIGUEL ITURREGUI
Executive Director (Acting): ESTHER ROJAS
Vice President and Treasurer: ROBERTO E. BIAGGI
Publication(s): *Verde Luz Newsletter; Puerto Rico Environmental Laws; Puerto Rico NGOs Directory; Puerto Rican Parrot Teacher's Kit; Pablo y Marisol van Playa; Sea Turtle Kit and various brochures*
Keyword(s): Conservation, Endangered and Threatened Species, Environmental and Conservation Education, Research

PUGET SOUNDKEEPER ALLIANCE
1415 W. Dravus, Seattle, WA 98119
Phone: 206-286-1309; Fax: 206-286-1082; Email: pskeeper@halcyon.com; WWW: www.halcyon.com/pskeeper
Founded: 1984; Membership: 400
Scope: National
Description: A nonprofit organization whose mission is to serve as stewards for the protection and enhancement of Puget Sound through education, advocacy, monitoring, and celebration.
Contact(s):
President: TOM DILLER, Seattle, WA
Executive Director: ROBERTA M. GUNN, Seattle, WA ; Phone: 206-286-1309
SoundKeeper: B. J. CUMMINGS, Seattle, WA ; Phone: 206-286-1309/1-800-42-PUGET
Treasurer and Secretary: BRAD MCMULLEN
Publication(s): *Sounder*
Keyword(s): Coasts, Environmental and Conservation Education, Environmental Law, Water Pollution, Water Quality

PURPLE MARTIN CONSERVATION ASSOCIATION
Edinboro University of Pennsylvania, Edinboro, PA 16444
Phone: 814-734-4420; Fax: 814-734-5803; Email: PMCA@edinboro.edu; WWW: www.purplemartin.org
Founded: 1987; Membership: 6,500
Scope: International
Description: An international tax-exempt, nonprofit organization dedicated to the conservation of the Purple Martin (Progne subis) species of bird through scientific research, state-of-the-art wildlife management techniques, and public education. The PMCA's scientific staff conducts research on all aspects of martin biology throughout the bird's North, South, and Middle American breeding, wintering, and migratory ranges. The organization functions as a centralized data-gathering and information source on the species, serving both the scientist and the martin enthusiast. Its major mission is educating martin enthusiasts in the proper techniques for managing this human-dependent species.
Contact(s):
Director and Editor: JAMES R. HILL II
Publication(s): *Purple Martin Update*
Keyword(s): Birds, Endangered and Threatened Species, Environmental and Conservation Education, Nongame Wildlife, Wildlife Management

QUAIL UNLIMITED, INC.
31 Quail Run, P.O. Box 610, Edgefield, SC 29824-0610
Phone: 803-637-5731; Fax: 803-637-0037; Email: quail@jetbn.net
Founded: 1981; Membership: 50,000
Scope: National
Description: A national nonprofit conservation organization dedicated to improving quail and upland game bird populations through habitat management and research. Organized to re-establish and manage suitable upland game habitat, both public and

private lands across the country, and to educate the public to the needs for wildlife habitat management.
Contact(s):
President: STEVE McGHEE, 100 Patterson Circle, Oliver Springs, TN 37840; Phone: 423-574-3685
Administrative Vice President: JERRY W. ALLEN, 1884 Highway 23 West, Edgefield, SC 29824; Phone: 803-637-5877
Director of Chapter Development: TOMMY DEAN, 815 Shawnee Dr., N. Arlington, SC 29841; Phone: 803-637-5731
Editor: D. KOGON
Executive Vice President: JOSEPH R. EVANS, 3012 Sussex Rd., Augusta, GA 30909; Phone: 706-738-0692
National Habitat Coordinator: ROGER WELLS, 868 Road 290, Americus, KS ; Phone: 316-443-5834
Publication(s): *Quail Unlimited Magazine*
Keyword(s): Wildlife and Wildlife Habitat

QUEBEC WILDLIFE FEDERATION
6780 1st Ave. Bureau 109, Charlesbourg, Quebec G1H 2W8 Canada
Phone: 418-626-6858; Fax: 418-622-6168; Email: fede@fgf.gc.ca
Founded: 1945; Membership: 175,000
Scope: Statewide
Contact(s):
Executive Director: GERALD LAVOIE
President: CLAUDE GAUTHIER
1st Vice President: ALAIN GAGNON
2nd Vice President: YVON LaPRADE
Secretary: ALAIN BISSON
Treasurer: YVON LAFLAMME
Biologist: JEAN-PIERRE TREMBLAY
Communication Coordinator: MANON GAGNON
Forest Engineer: PATRICK FILIATRAULT
Keyword(s): Hunting, Outdoor Recreation, Public Lands, Renewable Resources, Sport Fishing, Sustainable Development, Training, Waterfowl, Wildlife and Wildlife Habitat, Wildlife Management

RACHEL CARSON COUNCIL INC. (formerly Rachel Carson Trust for the Living Environment Inc.)
8940 Jones Mill Rd., Chevy Chase, MD 20815
Phone: 301-652-1877; Fax: 301-951-7179; Email: rccouncil@aol.com; WWW: members.aol.com/rccouncil/ourpage
Founded: 1965
Scope: National
Description: An international clearinghouse for information on toxic substances, particularly pesticides for both scientists and laymen, distributed by means of publications, conferences, and response to specific questions. Rachel Carson Council is devoted to fostering a sense of wonder and respect toward nature and helping society realize Rachel Carson's vision of a healthy and diverse environment.
Contact(s):
President: DAVID B. McGRATH
Vice President: MARTHA H. TALBOT
Treasurer: FREEBORN G. JEWETT JR.
Executive Director and Secretary: DR. DIANA M. POST
Liaison to the Board: DR. AARON BLAIR
Publication(s): *Basic Guide to Pesticides; Rachel Carson Council News;* books, pamphlets and sheets on specific alternative pest control methods and on pesticides effects; list of current publications available on request.
Keyword(s): Agriculture, Environmental and Conservation Education, Pesticides, Toxic Substances, Water Pollution

RAILS-TO-TRAILS CONSERVANCY
1100 17th S., NW, 10th Floor, Washington, DC 20036
Phone: 202-331-9696; Fax: 202-331-9680
Founded: 1986; Membership: 80,000
Scope: National
Description: The mission of the Rails-to-Trails Conservancy is to enhance America's communities and countrysides by converting thousands of miles of abandoned rail corridors, and connecting open space into a nationwide network of public trails.
Contact(s):
President: DAVID BURWELL
Board of Directors Chair: MARK ACKELSON
Board of Directors Treasurer: RICHARD W. ANGLE JR.
Executive Vice President: MARK WOLF-ARMSTRONG
Publication(s): *Trailblazer; Seven-Hundred Great Rail-Trails: A Directory of Multi-Use Paths Created from Abandoned Railroads; Secrets of Successful Rail-Trails: An Acquisition and Organizing Manual for Converting Rails into Trails; Enhancing America's Communities: A Nationwide Survey of The Transportation Enhancements Provisions of ISTEALibrary: (202-331-9696)*
Keyword(s): Environment, Internships, Land Preservation, Outdoor Recreation, Research

RAINBOW PUSH COALITION
1002 Wisconsin Ave., NW, Washington, DC 20007
Phone: 202-333-5270
Founded: 1984
Scope: National
Description: RPC is a national progressive membership organization committed to public education, empowerment, economic and social justice, and gender and racial equality. The Rainbow Push Coalition has state chapters and a national membership base. The Rainbow Push Coalition addresses such issues as education, voter registration, economic justice, civil rights, environment, labor, and working people's rights.
Contact(s):
Co-chairman of the Board: WILLIE T. BARROW
Co-chairman of the Board: DENNIS RIVERA
President and Founder: REV. JESSE L. JACKSON
Publication(s): *Rainbow Newsletter; Labor Newsletter;* various issue papers, speeches, and briefings; *Rainbow Push Magazine or The Rainbow JaxFax*
Keyword(s): Environmental and Conservation Education, Sustainable Development, Toxic Substances, Urban Environment

RAINFOREST ACTION NETWORK
221 Pine St., Suite 500, San Francisco, CA 94104
Phone: 415-398-4404; Fax: 415-398-2732; Email: rainforest@ran.org; WWW: www.ran.org
Founded: 1985; Membership: 30,000
Scope: National
Description: RAN works nationally and internationally on major campaigns to protect rainforests and defend the rights of indigenous people, using non-violent direct action such as: letter-writing campaigns, boycotts, and demonstrations against corporations and lending agencies contributing to rainforest destruction. RAN also produces educational materials, a teachers' packet, and fact sheets for community organizers.
Contact(s):
President: RANDALL MEYERS
Executive Director: KELLY AUIRKE
Board Chair: MICHAEL KLEIN
Board Secretary: DAVID WEIR
Board Treasurer: SCOTT PRICE
Communications Director: MARK WESTLUND
Information Director: LAURA FAUTH
Publication(s): *World Rainforest Report; Action Alert; RAG-RAG Rainforest Action Group Newsletter; World Rainforest Week Organizers' Manual*
Keyword(s): Biodiversity, Environmental and Conservation Education, Forests and Forestry, International Conservation

NON-GOVERNMENTAL ORGANIZATIONS

RAINFOREST ALLIANCE
65 Bleecker St., New York, NY 10012
Phone: 212-677-1900; Fax: 212-677-2187; Email: canopy@ra.org
Founded: 1986; Membership: 20,000
Scope: International
Description: The Rainforest Alliance is an international nonprofit organization dedicated to the conservation of tropical forests for the benefit of the global community. Its primary mission is to develop and promote economically viable and socially desirable alternatives to the destruction of tropical forests.
Contact(s):
President: DANIEL R. KATZ
Secretary: MARGIE AMBROSINO
Vice President and Treasurer: KARIN KREIDER
Publication(s): *CANOPY, The; Floods of Fortune; Tales from the Jungle; So Fruitful a Fish; Tales from the Jungle; Catfish Connection, The*
Keyword(s): Biodiversity, Forests and Forestry, Grants, International Conservation, Sustainable Development

RAINFOREST RELIEF
P.O. Box 150566, Brooklyn, NY 11215
Phone: 718-398-3760; Fax: 718-398-3760; Email: relief@igc.org; WWW: host.environlink.org/relief
Founded: 1989; Membership: 250
Scope: National
Description: Rainforest Relief, a nonprofit 501(c)3, works to end the loss of tropical and temperate rain forests through education and actions that increase awareness of the causes and consequences of rain forest destruction. Rainforest Relief focuses on the impact on rain forests of materials consumption, such as tropical wood and paper by the industrial world.
Contact(s):
Vice President: JEFFREY LOCKWOOD
Treasurer: ROSANE BARLUFFE
Montpelier Vermont Chpater, President: JANE GEARING, P.O. Box 454, Montpelier, VT 05601; Phone: 802-479-6121
Portland Oregon Chapter, President: JEFFREY LOCKWOOD, P.O. Box 14232, Portland, OR 97293; Phone: 503-236-3031; Email: rainrelief@hotmail.com
President and Director: TIM KEATING
Publication(s): *Roots; Raindrops; Rainforest Relief Reports*
Keyword(s): Biodiversity, Cultural Preservation, Environmental and Conservation Education, Forests and Forestry, International Conservation, Overconsumption

RAINFOREST TRUST INC., THE
6001 S.W. 63rd Avenue, Miame, FL 33143
Phone: 305-665-0691; Fax: 305-665-0691; Email: rforest@rainforesttrust.com; WWW: www.rainforesttrust.com
Scope: National
Description: The Trust has established a jaguar sanctuary and rainforest preserve in Belize. It also promotes eco-tourism and alternative rainforest sustainable agriculture as economically viable alternatives to deforestation, particularly in Jamaica; and promotes programmes to educate public school children and farmers about conservation of eco-systems, organic agriculture, and wildlife. The trust has established a second wildlife sanctuary and rainforest preserve in Jamaica.
Contact(s):
Chairman: T. EVELYN HAWKINS; Phone: 305-666-2158
President: BRETT EVELYN ASHMEADE-HAWKINS
Director: CURTIS RUSSELL PULFORD-EARLE
Director: ENRIQUE JOSE AGUILERA-CALZADILLA
Director: HON. MRS. LEMERCIER DUQUESNAY
Director: PRINCE EGON VON FURSTENBERG
Secretary and Treasurer: MARK EVELYN ASHMEADE-HAWKINS
Keyword(s): Agriculture, Ancient Forests, Conservation of Protected Areas, Endangered and Threatened Species, Environmental and Conservation Education, Environmental Protection, Historic Preservation, Sustainable Ecosystems, Wildlife and Wildlife Habitat

RAPTOR CENTER, THE
University of Minnesota 1920 Fitch Ave., St. Paul, MN 55108
Phone: 612-624-8740; Email: raptor@umn.edu; WWW: www.raptor.cvm.umn.edu
Founded: 1974; Membership: 4,500
Scope: National
Description: To preserve biological diversity among raptors and other avian species through medical treatment, scientific investigation, education, and management of wild populations.
Contact(s):
Director: PATRICK T. REDIG
Associate Director: RON OSTERBAUER
Board Chair: DEBBIE REYNOLDS
Publication(s): *Raptor Release, The; Medical Management of Birds of Prey; Care and Management of Captive Raptors*
Keyword(s): Birds, Endangered and Threatened Species, Environmental and Conservation Education, Raptors, Wildlife Rehabilitation

RAPTOR EDUCATION FOUNDATION INC.
21901 E. Hampden Ave., Aurora, CO 80013
Phone: 303-680-8500; Fax: 303-680-8502
Founded: 1980
Scope: National
Description: A nonprofit, charitable educational organization utilizing nonreleasable raptors to promote environmental literacy. Lecturers travel nationwide.
Contact(s):
Vice President: WILLIAM F. GREVE JR.
Vice President: ROBERT P. KOEHLER
President and Editor: PETER RESHETNIAK
Secretary and Editor: SHERRIE YORK
Publication(s): *Talon; Talon Supplement; Eagles, Hawks, Falcons, and Owls of America (a coloring album); Castings (volunteer newsletter)*
Keyword(s): Environmental and Conservation Education, Environmental Preservation, Environmental Protection, Raptors

RAPTOR RESEARCH FOUNDATION, INC.
ATTN: President, Raptor Research and Technical Assistance Center, 3948 Development St., Boise, ID 83706
Founded: 1966
Scope: National
Description: A nonprofit corporation formed to stimulate and coordinate the dissemination of information on the biology and management of birds of prey and their habitats. Areas of particular interest include: raptor banding, behavior, captive breeding, conservation, ecology, research techniques, management, migration, population monitoring, pathology, and rehabilitation.
Contact(s):
President: MICHAEL N. KOCHERT, Raptor Research and Technical Assistance Center, 3948 Development St., Boise, ID 83706
Vice President: KEITH L. BILDSTEIN, Hawk Mountain Sanctuary, Route 2, Box 191, Kempton, PA 19529; Phone: 910-756-6961
Secretary: PATRICIA HALL, 436 David Dr. E, Flagstaff, AZ 86001; Phone: 520-774-0041
Editor-in-Chief: DR. MARC J. BECHARD, Department of Biology, Boise State University, Boise, ID 83725
Treasurer and Membership Information: JIM FITZPATRICK, Carpenter, St. Croix Valley Nature Center, 12805 St. Croix Tr., Hastings, MN 55033; Phone: 612-437-4359
Publication(s): *Journal of Raptor Research; Wingspan; Kettle; (RRF Membership Directory and Handbook - published even-numbered years)*
Keyword(s): Endangered and Threatened Species, Environmental and Conservation Education, Nongame Wildlife, Raptors, Wildlife and Wildlife Habitat

RARE CENTER FOR TROPICAL CONSERVATION
1616 Walnut St. Suite 1010, Philadelphia, PA 19103
Phone: 215-735-3510; Fax: 215-735-3515; Email:
rare@rarecenter.org
Founded: 1973; Membership: 2,400
Scope: National
Description: RARE Center is a small organization doing innovative work to preserve threatened habitats and ecosystems in Latin America, the Caribbean, and the Pacific. Our programs focus on education and training, habitat protection, and research.
Contact(s):
Chairman: ROGER F. PASQUIER
President: PETER T. HAZLEWOOD
Secretary: EMILIE M. PRYOR
Treasurer: DAVID AYER
Director, Conservation Education: PAUL J. BUTLER
Director, Ecotourism and Community Development Program: BRETT JENKS
Vice Chairman: JOHN E. EARHART
Keyword(s): Environmental and Conservation Education, Environmental Preservation

REEF RELIEF
P.O. Box 430, Key West, FL 33041
Phone: 305-294-3100; Fax: 305-293-9515; WWW: www.reefrelief.org
Founded: 1989
Scope: National
Description: Reef Relief is a nonprofit membership organization dedicated to preserve and protect Living Coral Reef Ecosystems through local, regional, and global efforts.
Contact(s):
President: DR. BRIAN LaPOINTE
President: VICTORIA IMPALLOMENI
Secretary: ROBIN ORLANDI
Educational Coordinator: JOEL BIDDLE
Founder and Director of Marine Projects: CRAIG QUIROLO
Past President and First Vice President: CAPT. VICTORIA IMPALLOMENI
Project Coordinator: MICHAEL BLADES
Second Vice President: MARCI L. ROSE
Treasurer and Project Director: DEEVON QUIROLO
Publication(s): *Reef Line; Florida's Coral Reef Ecosystem;* booklets; flyers Library and Public Educational Facility: Reef Relief Environmental Center and Store, 201 William St., Key West, FL 33040
Keyword(s): Biodiversity, Coral Reefs, Environmental and Conservation Education, Sustainable Ecosystems, Water Pollution Management

RENEW AMERICA
1200 18TH St., NW, Suite 1100, Washington, DC 20036
Phone: 202-721-1545; Fax: 202-467-5780; Email:
renewamerica@counterpart.org
Founded: 1978; Membership: 2,000
Scope: National
Description: Renew America is the nation's only organization specializing in broad-based environmental program identification, verification, and promotion of positive models for change. We advance solutions to environmental problems by encouraging the replication of successful community-based initiatives. By seeking out, promoting, and awarding exemplary programs among all sectors, we offer innovative, constructive models to inspire communities and businesses to meet environmental challenges.
Contact(s):
Executive Director: ANNA SLAFER
Publication(s): *Environmental Success Index*
Keyword(s): Environmental and Conservation Education

RENEWABLE NATURAL RESOURCES FOUNDATION
5430 Grosvenor Ln., Bethesda, MD 20814
Phone: 301-493-9101; Fax: 301-493-6148; Email:
RNRF@aol.com; WWW: members.aol.com/RNRF
Founded: 1972
Scope: National
Description: A public, nonprofit, operating foundation. Conducts conferences and symposia on renewable natural resource subjects and public policy alternatives. Developer of the Renewable Natural Resources Center, an office-park complex for natural resource organizations.
Contact(s):
Executive Director: ROBERT D. DAY
Chairman of Board of Directors: RICHARD L. DUESTERHAUS, (SWCS)
Director of Administration and Finance: CHANDRU KRISHNA
Director of Programs: KRISTEN L. KRAPF
Vice Chairman of the Board: DAVID W. MOODY, (AWRA)
Publication(s): *Renewable Resources Journal*
Keyword(s): Environmental and Conservation Education, International Conservation, Land Use Planning, Renewable Resources, Urban Environment

RESOURCE RENEWAL INSTITUTE, THE
Fort Mason Center Building A, San Francisco, CA 94123
Phone: 415-928-3774; Fax: 415-928-6529; Email: info@rri.org
Founded: 1983
Scope: National
Description: The RRI is a national, nonprofit organization advocating state and national comprehensive, integrated environmental strategies (known as Green Plans), modeled on those of the Netherlands and New Zealand. RRI has set up a Global Green Plan Center to act as a clearinghouse for information on Green Plans. For more information, use RRI's e-mail address.
Contact(s):
President: HUEY D. JOHNSON
Vice President: PEGGY LAUER
Publication(s): *Saving Cities, Saving Money; The International Green Planner; Green Plans: Greenprint for Sustainability*
Keyword(s): Environmental and Conservation Education, Environmental Planning, Renewable Resources, Sustainable Development, Sustainable Ecosystems

RESOURCE-USE EDUCATION COUNCIL
ATTN: Chairman Resource-Use Education Council, Dept. of Environmental Quality, P.O. Box 10009, Richmond, VA 23240-0009
Founded: 1952
Scope: Statewide
Description: A volunteer, nonprofit organization, composed of members of the state and federal government, colleges, and private industry, working to promote the broad principle of environmental education. The Council offers conservation education workshops for educators across Virginia. Scholarships for teachers are available.
Contact(s):
Chairman: ANN REGN, Department of Environmental Quality, P.O. Box 10009, Richmond, VA 23240-0009; Phone: 804-762-4442
Secretary: SUSAN GILLEY, Department of Game and Inland Fisheries, Box 11104, Richmond, VA 23230; Phone: 804-367-1000
Treasurer: DIANA DUTTEN, P.O. Box 339, Calverton, VA 22016; Phone: 703-361-1710
Publication(s): *Coldwater Conservationist, The*

RESOURCES FOR THE FUTURE
1616 P St., NW, Washington, DC 20036
Phone: 202-328-5000; Fax: 202-939-3460
Founded: 1952
Scope: National
Description: An independent nonprofit organization that works to advance research and education in the development, conservation, and use of environmental and natural resources. Staff is comprised

NON-GOVERNMENTAL ORGANIZATIONS

primarily of economists and policy analysts who research a variety of environmental and natural resource issues.
Contact(s):
President: PAUL R. PORTNEY; Phone: 202-328-5000
Board of Directors Chairman: DARIUS W. GASKINS JR.
Center for Risk Management Director: J. CLARENCE DAVIES III; Phone: 202-328-5093
Director of Development: EVITA SHERMAN-DIXON
Energy and Natural Resources Division Director: MICHAEL TOMAN; Phone: 202-328-5091
Librarian: CHRISTOPHER CLOTWORTHY; Phone: 202-328-5089
Manager of Public Affairs: MICHAEL TEBO; Phone: 202-328-5019
Quality of the Environment Division Director: ALAN KRUPNICK; Phone: 202-328-5059
Vice President of Finance and Administration: EDWARD F. HAND; Phone: 202-328-5029
Publication(s): *Resources*
Keyword(s): Air Quality and Pollution, Biodiversity, Developing Countries, Endangered and Threatened Species, Energy, Energy Conservation, Environment, Environmental Protection, Forest Management, Land Use Planning, Mining, Renewable Resources, Sustainable Development, Transportation

RESPONSIVE MANAGEMENT
P.O. Box 389, Harrisonburg, VA 22801
Phone: 540-432-1888; Fax: 540-432-1892; Email: mdduda@rica.net
Founded: 1986
Scope: National
Description: Developed to help fish and wildlife organizations understand and work with their constituents. Responsive Management conducts focus group research, telephone and mail surveys, public opinion and attitude research, literature reviews, demographic analysis, and workshops in public opinion polling, marketing change, communications, dispute resolution, and human dimensions of natural resource management.
Contact(s):
Executive Director: MARK DAMIAN DUDA, P.O. Box 389, Harrisonburg, VA 22801-0389; Phone: 540-432-1888
Board of Directors: PAT GRAHAM, Chairman of the Board of Montana Department of Fish, Wildlife, and Parks, 1420 E. 6th, Helena, MT 59620; Phone: 406-444-2535
Research Statistician: KIRA YOUNG, P.O. Box 389, Harrisonburg, VA 22801-0389; Phone: 540-432-1888
Publication(s): *Responsive Management Report*
Keyword(s): Communications, Research, Training

RETURNED PEACE CORPS VOLUNTEER FOR ENVIRONMENT AND DEVELOPMENT (RPCV-ED)
P.O. Box 256, Orange City, IA 51041
Phone: 712-737-2700
Founded: 1991; Membership: 450
Scope: National
Description: The RPCVs-ED was formed to serve as a focal point for action on environment and development issues by Peace Corps alumni and friends.
Contact(s):
Co-chair: MARY STEINMAUS, 216 Sycamore St., Suite. 500, Muscatine, IA 52761; Phone: 319-264-1500
Co-chair: KATY HANSEN
Editor: SUSAN SINGH, 1762 E. 60th St., Tulsa, OK 74105; Phone: 918-749-7004
Keyword(s): Developing Countries, Environment, Sustainable Development

RHODE ISLAND B.A.S.S. CHAPTER FEDERATION
ATTN: President, 64 Oakton St., Woonsockey, RI 02895
Phone: 401-766-7082
Scope: Statewide
Description: An organization of Bassmaster chapters, affiliated with the Bass Anglers Sportsman Society, organized to fight pollution, assist state and national conservation agencies in their efforts, and teach the young people of our country good conservation practices. Dedicated to the realistic conservation of our water resources.
Contact(s):
President: LUCIEN BIBEAULT, 64 Oakton St., Woonsocket, RI 02895; Phone: 401-766-7082
Conservation Director: BILL WEIKERT, 156 Ridgewood Rd., Middletown, RI 02842; Phone: 401-846-0512
Publication(s): *Forest Conservationist, The*
Keyword(s): Forests and Forestry

RHODE ISLAND FOREST CONSERVATORS ASSOCIATION
P.O. Box 40328, Providence, RI 02908
Phone: 401-273-8037
Founded: 1989; Membership: 250
Scope: Statewide
Description: A statewide organization affiliated with the National Woodland Owners Association organized to promote stewardship of Rhode Island's wooded lands and watersheds and protect their heritage for future generations.
Contact(s):
President: MARC J. TREMBLAY, Cranston, RI
Vice President: ALEX MERRIMIAN, Smithfield, RI
Secretary: MILTON SCHUMACHER
Treasurer: HANS BERGEY, Providence, RI
Editor: MARC J. TREMBLAY, Smithfield, RI ; Phone: 401-273-8037

RHODE ISLAND STATE ASSOCIATION OF CONSERVATION DISTRICTS
ATTN: President, 35 Abbott Run Valley Rd., Cumberland, RI 02864
Scope: Statewide
Contact(s):
President: JESSE A. CARPENTER, 35 Abbott Run Valley Rd., Cumberland, RI 02864; Phone: 401-762-7346; Email: Fahma1@aol.com
Vice President: EMERSON WILDES, Whimshaw Farm, Shaw Rd., Little Compton, RI 02837; Phone: 401-635-2935
Secretary: ROBERT SWANSON, 39 Shannock Hill Rd., Carolina, RI 02812; Phone: 401-364-4069
Treasurer: WILLIAM COLBURN, 5 Pierce Rd., Foster, RI 02825; Phone: 401-397-5989
Board Member: G. W. HUMPHREY, P.O. Box 484, Little Compton, RI 02837; Phone: 401-635-2998; Fax: 401-635-2998
Publication(s): *Bi-Annual Newsletter; Cultivation Notes 1-16; Wild Plants! (some basic information; other resources and fact sheets)*
Keyword(s): Endangered and Threatened Species, Environmental and Conservation Education, Flowers, Plants, and Trees, Nature Preservation, Terrestrial Habitats

RHODE ISLAND WILD PLANT SOCIETY
12 Sanderson Rd., Smithfield, RI 02917-2606
Phone: 401-949-0195
Founded: 1987; Membership: 500
Scope: Statewide
Description: The Rhode Island Wild Plant Society is a nonprofit conservation organization dedicated to the preservation and protection of Rhode Island's native plants and their habitats.
Contact(s):
President: RICHARD HULL, 8 Bramblewood Ln., Wakefield, RI 02879
President: MABEL S. HEMPSTEAD, 1474 Ten Rod Rd., N. Kingston, RI 02852
Secretary:
Treasurer: MARY LOU UPHAM, 550 Shermantown Rd., Saunderstown, RI 02874
Publication(s): *Bay Bulletin, The,; special reports on land use issues, wastewater treatment plan performance, and water quality*
Keyword(s): Environmental and Conservation Education, Environmental Preservation, Land Use Planning, Sustainable Development, Water Pollution

RINCON INSTITUTE, THE
7650 E. Broadway Blvd. Suite 203, Tucson, AZ 85710
Phone: 520-290-0828; Fax: 520-290-0969; Email: rincon@sonoran.org
Founded: 1990
Scope: Statewide
Description: The Rincon Institute protects the ecological integrity of Saguaro National Park by ensuring that development adjacent to the park adheres to the highest ecological and social standards. This goal is accomplished primarily through ecological research, environmental education, and the development of cooperative approaches to resolving land use conflicts.
Contact(s):
Executive Director: LUTHER PROPST
Chairman of the Board: PETER BACKUS
Director of Research: MARK BRIGGS
Outreach Director: JAN GINGOLD
Program Assistant: MARY VINT
Keyword(s): Environmental and Conservation Education, Sustainable Development, Sustainable Ecosystems, Terrestrial Habitats

RIVER ALLIANCE OF WISCONSIN
122 State St., Suite 202, Madison, WI 53703
Phone: 608-257-2424; Fax: 608-251-1655; Email: wisrivers@igc.apc.org; WWW: www.igc.org/wisrivers
Founded: 1993; Membership: 700
Scope: Statewide
Description: The River Alliance is a nonprofit, nonpartisan citizen advocacy organization for rivers. Our mission is to lead the growing statewide effort to protect, enhance and restore Wisconsin's rivers and watersheds for their ecological, recreational, aesthetic, and cultural values. Recent program work includes education and information about the impacts of dams on river system health, minimizing ecosystem damage through federal relicensing of hydro dams, and advocacy for selective removal of uneconomical dams for purpose of river restoration.
Contact(s):
Executive Director: SARA E. JOHNSON
Publication(s): *Wisconsin Rivers (Quarterly); Periodic Action Alerts; News Bulletins and fact Sheets*
Keyword(s): Aquatic Habitats, Dams, Fisheries, Rivers, Watersheds

RIVER FEDERATION
1428 Fenwick Ln., Silver Spring, MD 20910
Phone: 301-589-9454; Fax: 301-589-6121; Email: riverfed1@aol.com
Founded: 1981; Membership: 100
Scope: National
Description: River Federation's mission is to work in partnership to conserve and revitalize the nation's rivers. It is a forum for and publishes information on river conservation and revitalization management for river professionals and leaders. It ensures that states are represented in the formulation of national river conservation and revitalization policy. It provides technical communications, planning, and management services to river conservation programs.
Contact(s):
President: DOUGLAS CARTER, Michigan Department of Natural Resources, ; Phone: 517-373-1172; Fax: 517-373-9965
Vice President: EDWARD D. FITE III, Oklahoma Scenic Rivers Commission, ; Phone: 918-456-3281; Fax: 918-456-3281
Executive Director: ROBERT C. HOFFMAN; Phone: 301-589-9454; Fax: 301-589-6121; Email: riverfed1@aol.com
Secretary and Treasurer: MOLLY MacGREGOR, Mississippi Headwaters Board, ; Phone: 218-547-3300; Fax: 218-547-2440
Publication(s): *Institutional Frameworks for Watershed Management Programs (1994); Profiles in River Management; River Federation Newsletter; River Conservation Directory (1990)*
Keyword(s): Land Use Planning, Outdoor Recreation, Planning Management, Rivers, Water Resources

RIVER NETWORK
Headquarters, P.O. Box 8787, 520 SW 6th Ave., Suite 1130, Portland, OR 97204
Phone: 503-241-3506, 1-800-423-6747; Fax: 503-241-9256; Email: rivernet@igc.org; WWW: www.rivernetwork.org
Founded: 1988
Scope: National
Description: A national nonprofit organization whose mission is to help people organize to protect and restore rivers and watersheds. River Network supports river advocates at the grassroots, state and regional levels; helps them build effective organizations; and links them together in a national movement to protect and restore America's rivers and watersheds. River Network also works with river conservationists to acquire and conserve riverlands and riparian areas critical for wildlife, fisheries, drinking water, flood plain management, and recreation.
Contact(s):
President: KEN MARGOLIS
Administrative Director: LINDY WALSH
Chairman of Board of Directors: JIM COMPTON, Saratoga, CA
Communications Director: THALIA A. ZEPATOS
Director of Development: BRIGETTE SARABI
Director of Watershed Programs: DON ELDER
Northwest (RLC): SUE DOROFF
Riverlands Conservancy Director: PHIL WALLIN
Watershed Program Associate: ALISON COOK
Watershed Program Associates: KATHY LUSCHER
Watershed Program Manager: GEORGE CONSTANTZ
Watershed Program Manager: PAT MUNOZ
Watershed Program Manager: LIZ RAISBECK
Publication(s): *The Watershed Innovators Workshop: Proceedings and The Swift River Principles; How to save a River; River Voices; 1998-1999 River and Watershed Conservation Directory; River Fundraising Alert; Starting Up: A Handbook for New River and Watershed Organizations; Directory of Funding Sources for Grassroots River and Watershed Groups.*
Keyword(s): Land Purchase, Rivers, Watersheds

Eastern Office
4000 Albemarle St., NW, #303, Washington, DC 20016
Phone: 202-364-2550; Fax: 202-364-2520; Email: rivernet2@aol.com
Scope: National
Contact(s):
Contact: ALISON COOK

Northern Rockes Office: Riverlands Conservancy Field Office
44 North Last Chance Gulch, #4, Helena, MT 59601
Phone: 406-442-4777; Fax: 406-442-8883
Scope: National
Contact(s):
Contact: HUGH ZACKHEIM
Keyword(s): Air Quality and Pollution, Ancient Forests, Aquatic Habitats, Chemical Pollution Control, Cultural Preservation, EcoAction, Environment, Environmental and Conservation Education, Environmental Justice, Environmental Protection, Sustainable Development, Wetlands, Wilderness

RIVER OTTER ALLIANCE, THE
6733 S. Locust Ct., Englewood, CO 80112
Phone: 303-773-2749; Fax: 303-722-7703
Founded: 1990; Membership: 150
Scope: National
Description: The River Otter Alliance promotes the survival of the North American River Otter through education, research, and habitat protection. We support current research and reintroduction programs, monitor abundance and distribution in the United States, and educate through our newsletter on the need to restore and sustain river otter populations.
Contact(s):
President: JUDITH BERG, 4421 S. Parkview Dr., Salt Lake City, UT 84124

NON-GOVERNMENTAL ORGANIZATIONS

Vice President: DAVID BERG
Secretary: TRACY JOHNSTON, 2715 S. Pierce St., Denver, CO 80227-3531
Treasurer: JOHN MULVIHILL, 6733 S. Locust Ct., Englewood, CO 80112-1007
Publication(s): *River Otter Journal, The*
Keyword(s): Endangered and Threatened Species, Rivers, Trapping, Water Quality, Wildlife Rehabilitation

RIVERS COUNCIL OF WASHINGTON (formerly Northwest Rivers Council)
1731 Westlake Ave. N. Suite 202, Seattle, WA 98109
Phone: 206-283-4988; Fax: 206-283-4824; Email: riverswa@brigadoon.com
Founded: 1984; **Membership:** 1,000
Scope: National
Description: The mission of the Rivers Council of Washington is to lead an expanding grassroots effort to preserve, enhance, and restore rivers and their watersheds in Washington state for their natural, recreational, and cultural values, and support compatible efforts of other organizations in the Pacific Northwest.
Contact(s):
President: DAN CLARKSON
Vice President: JOHN MACLEAN
Secretary: BARBARA GEYER BROCK
Treasurer: JULIE STEPHENSON
Executive Director: JOY HUBER
Chair of Trustees: DOUG NORTH
Publication(s): *Washington Rivers*
Keyword(s): Environmental and Conservation Education, Outdoor Recreation, Rivers, Sustainable Ecosystems, Water Resources

ROCKY MOUNTAIN BIGHORN SOCIETY
P.O. Box 8320, Denver, CO 80201
Founded: 1975; **Membership:** 1,000
Scope: Statewide
Description: The purpose of the Society is to support the sound management of the Rocky Mountain bighorn sheep and its habitat and to promote the advancement and knowledge of the bighorn.
Contact(s):
President: J. MICHAEL BAUMANN, 6126 W. 64th Ave., Arvada, CO 80003; Phone: 303-421-4807
Vice President: PETER KUMMERFELDT, 6612 Frederick Dr., Colorado Springs, CO 80918; Phone: 719-593-5852
Secretary: TERRY SANDMEIER, P.O. Box 771, Conifer, CO 80433; Phone: 303-838-6311
Treasurer: FRED RATLIFF, 6920 W. 5th Ave., Lakewood, CO 80206; Phone: 303-572-3125
Area Representative of Northcentral: GREG JUNGMAN, P.O. Box 1827, Dillon, CO 80435; Phone: 303-468-5995
Area Representative of Northwest: DARYL ISER, 537 28 3/4 Rd., Grand Junction, CO 81501; Phone: 303-242-5478
Area Representative of Southeast: JAMES GARRISON, 4555 S. 103rd Rd., Alamosa, CO 81101; Phone: 719-589-6144
Area Representative of Southwest: GEORGE VAN DEN BERG, P.O. Box 157, Durango, CO 81301
Publication(s): *Bighorn, The*; *Guide to Sheep Hunting in Colorado*
Keyword(s): Hunting, Trapping, Wildlife and Wildlife Habitat, Wildlife Management, Wildlife Rehabilitation

ROCKY MOUNTAIN ELK FOUNDATION
P.O. Box 8249, Missoula, MT 59807-8249
Phone: 406-523-4500; Fax: 406-523-4550
Founded: 1984; **Membership:** 110,000
Scope: National
Description: The Foundation's mission is to ensure the future of elk, other wildlife, and their habitat. Projects funded by RMEF include: land protection, habitat enhancement, management, research, conservation education, and hunting heritage.
Contact(s):
Chairman, Board of Directors: ROBERT KOONS
President & CEO: GARY J. WOLFE Ph.D.
President Emeritus: ROBERT W. MUNSON
Senior Vice President, Finance & Administration/CFO: LARRY PUGH
Vice Chairman: PAT GILLIGAN
Vice Chairman, Board of Directors: PAT GILLIGAN
Vice President of Communication/Public Relations: LANCE SCHELVAN
Vice President of Conservation Programs: ALAN CHRISTENSEN
Vice President of Field Operations/Membership: BILL GEER
Vice President, Communications/Public Relations: LANCE SCHELVAN
Vice President, Conservation Programs: ALAN CHRISTENSEN
Vice President, Development & Marketing: DAVID WESLEY
Vice President, Field Operations: WILLIAM H. GEER
Vice President, Legal Affairs/General Counsel: GRANT PARKER
Publication(s): *BUGLE: Journal of Elk and the Hunt*; *Wild Outdoor World (W.O.W.: Kids Conservation Magazine)*
Keyword(s): Environmental and Conservation Education, Hunting, Land Purchase, Open Space, Wildlife and Wildlife Habitat

Intermountain Region Office
211 E George Drive, Pueblo West, MT 81007
Scope: Regional
Contact(s):
Regional Director: MARTY HOLMES; Phone: 505-445-8788
Contact for CO: TOM BROWN; Phone: 303-279-7974
Contact for NM: RICHARD BROWN; Phone: 505-866-0129
Contact for UT: BILL CHRISTENSEN; Phone: 801-254-1922
Contact for WY: DAMIEN MILLER; Phone: 307-332-6084

North-Central Region Office
R.R. #1, Box 85D, Custer, MT 57730
Scope: Regional
Contact(s):
Regional Director: MIKE MUELLER; Phone: 605-673-2396
Contact for MN and IA: RALPH CINFIO; Phone: 320-203-0932
Contact for ND: MIKE MUELLER; Phone: 605-673-2396
Contact for SD: TIM CHRISTIAN; Phone: 605-644-2396
Contact for WI: BILL HUNYADI; Phone: 715-769-3559

Northeast Region Office
198 Bennett Rd., Julian, MT 16844
Scope: Regional
Contact(s):
Regional Director: DAVE MESSICS; Phone: 814-353-1667
Contact for DC, DE, MD, NJ, PA: LANCE SCHUL; Phone: 814-355-5589
Contact for ME, NH, VT, NY, CT, MA, RI: DAVE RAGANTESI; Phone: 717-756-3867
Contact for MI and OH: WAYNE BIVANS; Phone: 616-874-9222

Northwest Region Office
9908 Wilbath Ln., Nampa, MT 93686
Scope: Regional
Contact(s):
Regional Director: ART TALSMA; Phone: 208-466-0204
Contact for AK, and Western WA: LLORAN JOHNSON; Phone: 253-539-7651
Contact for Eastern WA: RANCE BLOCK; Phone: 509-226-0388
Contact for MT: KIRK MURPHY; Phone: 406-883-1147
Contact for OR: TOM LYTLE; Phone: 503-362-3062
Contact for Southern ID: ART TALSMA; Phone: 208-466-0204
Contact for Southwest MT and Eastern ID: DAVE TORELL; Phone: 208-528-8914

Pacific Southwest Region Office
P.O. Box 25902, Munds Park, MT 86701
Scope: Regional
Contact(s):
Contact for AZ: BRUCE SITKO; Phone: 520-368-4105
Contact for Northern CA: MIKE FORD; Phone: 530-842-2021
Contact for NV: TONY KAVALOK; Phone: 702-971-9000
Contact for Southern CA: BILL HARRIS; Phone: 619-486-5601

Regional Director: DAKOTA LIVESAY; Phone: 520-286-1833

South-Central Region Office
1480 8th NE, 1086th St., Holt, MT 64048
Scope: Regional
Contact(s):
Regional Director: TERRY CLOUTIER; Phone: 816-320-2618
Contact for IN and IL: DON BLAKELY; Phone: 618-893-4142
Contact for KS and NE: MARK JOHNSON; Phone: 316-672-2201
Contact for MO: DOUG SONNTAG; Phone: 417-581-8062
Contact for OK and TX: RANDY PORTERFIELD; Phone: 903-677-5740
Contact for West TX: RICHARD BROWN; Phone: 505-866-0129

Southeast Region Office
1323 Robert E. Lee Ln., Brentwood, MT 37021
Scope: Regional
Contact(s):
Regional Director: RON WHITE; Phone: 615-370-0370
Contact for AL, AR, LA, MS: HOLLY FRENCH; Phone: 601-978-3588
Contact for GA, FL, NC, SC, VA, WV: JOHN MECHLER; Phone: 502-767-0095
Contact for KY: RON WHITE; Phone: 615-370-0370

ROGER TORY PETERSON INSTITUTE
311 Curtis St., Jamestown, NY 14701
Phone: 716-665-2473; Fax: 716-665-3794; Email: webmaster@rtpi.org; WWW: www.rtpi.org
Founded: 1984; Membership: 3,000
Scope: Statewide
Description: The mission of the Roger Tory Peterson Institute is to create a passion for and knowledge of the natural world in the hearts and minds of children by guiding and inspiring the study of nature in our schools and communities.
Contact(s):
President: JIM BERRY; Phone: 716-665-2473; Fax: 716-665-3794; Email: jim@rtpi.org
Director of Development: MIKE LYONS; Phone: 716-665-2473; Fax: 716-665-3794; Email: mike@rtpi.org
Director of Education: MARK BALDWIN; Phone: 716-665-2473; Fax: 716-665-3794; Email: mark@rtpi.org
Keyword(s): Environment, Environmental and Conservation Education, Natural History, Nature Study, Urban and Rural Development

RUFFED GROUSE SOCIETY, THE
451 McCormick Rd., Coraopolis, PA 15108
Phone: 412-262-4044; Email: rgshg@aol.com; WWW: www.ruffedgrousesociety.org
Founded: 1961; Membership: 23,000
Scope: National
Description: Nonprofit conservation organization dedicated to improving the environment for ruffed grouse, woodcock, and other forest wildlife through maintenance, improvement, and expansion of their habitat. Assists private, industrial, county, state, and federal landholders in forest wildlife habitat improvement programs.
Contact(s):
President: JOE R. IRWIN
Vice President: EDWIN H. GOTT JR.
Secretary: GAYLEN J. BYKER
Treasurer: STEPHEN F. QUILL
Executive Director: DR. SAMUEL R. PURSGLOVE
Associate Executive Director of Development: RONALD P. BURKERT
Associate Executive Director of Operations: BRENDA K. OSBORN
Chief Biologist (All Areas): DAN DESSECKER; Phone: 715-234-8302
Editor and Director of Information and Education: PAUL E. CARSON
Executive Vice President: S. PROSSER MELLON
Regional Biologist (MI, OH): MARK E. BANKER; Phone: 616-829-4797
Regional Director (MD, OH, PA, Washington, DC, VA, Southeastern States): BILL KLEIN; Phone: 724-938-3705
Regional Director (MI): DAVID B. MADEMA; Phone: 616-245-1161
Regional Director (MN): DONALD A. BASSETT; Phone: 218-894-1321
Regional Director (NJ, NY, New England): DON NICKERSON; Phone: 607-638-5456
Regional Director (WI): PAUL V. CLARTEN; Phone: 715-389-1606
Regional Supervisor of Eastern States: BILL GOUDY; Phone: 717-745-7313
Regional Supervisor of Western States: LOU GEORGE; Phone: 608-788-1786
RGS-Canada Executive Director (All Canada): JIM ABBOY; Phone: 519-842-6027
Publication(s): *RGS*
Keyword(s): Birds, Environmental and Conservation Education, Forests and Forestry, Wildlife and Wildlife Habitat, Wildlife Management

SAFARI CLUB INTERNATIONAL
Headquarters, 4800 W. Gates Pass Rd., Tucson, AZ 85745
Phone: 520-620-1220; Fax: 520-622-1205
Scope: National
Description: Nonprofit organization formed to promote good fellowship and communication among sportsmen conservationists. To promote conservation of the wildlife of the world as a valuable renewable resource in which hunting is one management tool among many; to stimulate conservation education programs and teacher training workshops emphasizing the wise use and management of renewable natural resources. Sponsors wildlife management research, Sportsmen Against Hunger, field projects, and emergency game animal relief programs; operates two educational facilities: the International Wildlife Museum and headquarters in Tucson, AZ, and the American Wilderness Leadership School near Jackson, WY. Maintains offices in Washington, DC and South Africa.
Contact(s):
President: ALFRED S. DONAU
Secretary: TAZ RIDLEY
Treasurer: MIKE ROGERS SR.
Administrative Director: RUDY ROSEN
Director of Governmental and Conservation Affairs: RICHARD PARSONS
Education Director: DONALD BROWN
President-Elect: LARRY KATZ
Publications Director: BILL QUIMBY
Sportsmen Against Hunger Coordinator: RAY STROUP
Washington Counsel: RICHARD PARSONS
Publication(s): *Safari Magazine; Worldwide Hunting Annual; Record Book of Trophy Animals; Sheep Special, The; Deer Special, The; Safari Times; African Special, The; North of the 48*
Keyword(s): Endangered and Threatened Species, Environmental and Conservation Education, Hunting, Wildlife and Wildlife Habitat

Michigan Office
4285 Van Buren, Hudsonville, MI 49426
Founded: 1973; Membership: 200
Scope: Statewide
Description: Goals are to educate the public, especially children, in the realm of conservation as it relates to the hunter. Especially concerned with environmental respect and the preservation of any endangered species.
Contact(s):
President: TERRY BLAUWKAMP; Phone: 616-669-1610
Education: BETTY DYKSTRA; Phone: 616-676-9704
President-Elect: LEN VINING; Phone: 616-698-7440
Program: LANCE NORRIS; Phone: 616-798-3410
Secretary and Treasurer: DENNY ANASTOR; Phone: 616-942-8877

NON-GOVERNMENTAL ORGANIZATIONS

South Africa Office
P.O. Box 10362, Hennopsmeer, Hennopsmeer 46 South Africa
Phone: 27-12/663-8073; Fax: 27-12/663-8075
Scope: National

Washington, DC Office
445-B Carlisle Dr., Herndon, VA 20170
Phone: 703-709-2293; Fax: 703-709-2296
Scope: National

SAFE ENERGY COMMUNICATION COUNCIL
1717 Massachusetts Ave., NW, Suite 805, Washington, DC 20036
Phone: 202-483-8491; Fax: 202-234-9194
Founded: 1980
Scope: National
Description: A coalition of 10 national environmental, safe energy, and public interest media groups. SECC produces broadcast and print ads, studies, commentaries, and graphic editorial services to promote sustainable energy policies and respond to nuclear industry and utility campaigns and helps groups develop media skills.
Contact(s):
President: ANDREW SCHWARTZMAN
Executive Director: SCOTT DENMAN
Administrative Director: SARAH SWEETMAN
Communications Director: LINDA PENTZ
Publication(s): *MYTHBusters Series, Viewpoint; Enfacts; Polls and various Energy Reports*
Keyword(s): Energy, Energy Conservation, Environment, Nuclear Energy, Renewable Resources, Training

SAN JUAN PRESERVATION TRUST, THE
Box 327, Lopez Island, WA 98261
Phone: 360-468-3202; Fax: 360-468-3509; Email: sjptrust@rockisland.com; WWW: www.rockisland.com/sjptrust/
Founded: 1979; Membership: 1,200
Scope: Statewide
Description: The trust is supported by voluntary contributions from members who support the preservation of wildlife, scenery, and natural heritage of the San Juan Islands of Washington state.
Contact(s):
President: JUDY GILSON MOOD
Vice President: DALE HAZEN
Secretary: BOB DITTMER
Treasurer: MORRIS DALTON
Publication(s): *Preserve Farmlands; A Place in the Islands; Landowner's Guide; Mom's Marsh and Other Fine Places (video)*

SANIBEL-CAPTIVA CONSERVATION FOUNDATION, INC.
P.O. Box 839, 3333 Sanibel-Captiva Rd., Sanibel, FL 33957
Phone: 941-472-1932; Fax: 941-472-6421; Email: sccfc@scccf.org; WWW: www.sccf.org
Founded: 1967
Scope: Statewide
Description: The Sanibel-Captiva Conservation Foundation is a not-for-profit organization dedicated to the preservation of natural resources and wildlife habitat on and around Sanibel and Captiva Islands. Community programs include: Land acquisition, habitat management, landscaping for wildlife, research, education, wildlife assistance, and sea turtle conservation program. The Foundation utilizes the time and talent of over 200 dedicated volunteers.
Contact(s):
Executive Director: ERICK LINDBLAD
Business Manager: DIANNE ALTIERI
Education Director: KRISTIE ANDERS
Native Plant Nursery Manager: KATHY BOONE
Publication(s): *Conservation Update; Walk in the Wetlands; Growing Native*
Keyword(s): Environmental and Conservation Education, Islands, Land Purchase, Wetlands, Wildlife and Wildlife Habitat

SASKATCHEWAN WILDLIFE FEDERATION
444 River St. W., Moose Jaw, Saskatchewan S6H 6J6 Canada
Phone: 306-692-8812; Fax: 306-692-4370
Founded: 1929
Scope: Statewide
Description: Affiliated with the Canadian Wildlife Federation. A nonprofit, citizens' conservation group established for the protection and enhancement of fish and wildlife habitat. One hundred and thirty-seven local branches representing 32,000 members. Includes the Habitat Trust Fund holding title to 15,000 purchased and donated acres, and the Wildlife Tomorrow Program with 400,000 acres under free easement.
Contact(s):
President: JOYCE LORENZ, Box 545, Raymore, Saskatchewan S0A 3J0 Canada; Phone: 306-746--4313; Fax: 306-746-5810
Executive Director: ROBERT NOWASAD, 444 River St. W., Moose Jaw, Saskatchewan S6H 6J6 Canada; Phone: 306-692-7772
Land Coordinator: JAMES KROSHUS, 444 River St. W., Moose Jaw, Saskatchewan S6H 6J6 Canada; Phone: 306-693-9022
Officer Manager: SANDRA DEWALD, 444 River St. W., Moose Jaw, Saskatchewan S6H 6J6 Canada; Phone: 306-692-8812
Wildlife Tomorrow Coordinator: CLINT SANBORN, 444 River St. West, Moose Jaw, Saskatchewan S6H 6J6 Canada; Phone: 306-692-3374
Publication(s): *Outdoor Edge*

SAVE AMERICA'S FORESTS
4 Library Ct., SE, Washington, DC 20003
Phone: 202-544-9219
Founded: 1990; Membership: 6,000
Scope: National
Description: A nationwide coalition of grassroots regional and national environmental groups, public interest groups, responsible businesses, and individuals working together to pass strong forest protection legislation in the U.S. Congress.
Contact(s):
Director: CARL ROSS
Co-Director: MARK WINSTEIN
Publication(s): *Save America's Forests Magazine*
Keyword(s): Biodiversity, Forests and Forestry, National Forests, Public Lands, Sustainable Development, Sustainable Ecosystems

SAVE SAN FRANCISCO BAY ASSOCIATION
1736 Franklin St., 4th Fl., Oakland, CA 94612
Phone: 510-452-9261; Fax: 510-452-9266; Email: savesfbay@igc.apc.org; WWW: http://www.savesfbay.org
Founded: 1961; Membership: 20,000
Scope: Statewide
Description: Nonprofit, tax-exempt organization dedicated to the protection and enhancement of San Francisco Bay's many natural and public values. Current priorities include: protecting wetlands, improving water quality, providing shoreline parks and trails, preventing unnecessary bay fill, and preventing additional fresh water diversion from the estuary. Established by Mrs. Clark Kerr, Mrs. Charles A. Gulick, and Mrs. Donald H. McLaughlin.
Contact(s):
President: DONALD R. WEDEN
Vice President: JAKE WARNER
Vice President: POLLY SMITH
Vice President: NANCY WAKEMAN
Executive Director: BARRY M. NELSON
Editor: PATTY O'BISO
Publication(s): *Watershed; information fact sheets*
Keyword(s): Environmental and Conservation Education, Water Pollution, Water Resources, Wetlands, Wildlife and Wildlife Habitat

SAVE THE BAY, INC.
434 Smith St., Providence, RI 02908-3770
Phone: 401-272-3540; Fax: 401-273-7153; WWW: www.savethebay.org
Founded: 1970; Membership: 20,000
Scope: Statewide
Description: Save The Bay is dedicated to restoring and protecting Narragansett Bay--a designated estuary of national significance. As a nonprofit, member-supported environmental organization, Save The Bay works to ensure that the environmental quality of Narragansett Bay and its watershed is restored and protected from the harmful effects of human activity.
Contact(s):
President: KATE KILGUSS
Executive Director: H. CURTIS SPALDING
Editor: MARISA J. POLI
Publication(s): *Bay Bulletin*

SAVE THE DUNES COUNCIL
444 Barker Rd., Michigan City, IN 46360
Phone: 219-879-3937; Fax: 219-872-4875; Email: std@savedunes.org; WWW: www.savedunes.org
Founded: 1952; Membership: 2,000
Scope: National
Description: Dedicated to the preservation of the Indiana Dunes National Lakeshore for public use and enjoyment. Concerned with protecting the ecological values of the dunes region, preserving Lake Michigan, and combating air, water, and hazardous waste pollution. Established by Dorothy Buell.
Contact(s):
Assistant Director: CHARLOTTE J. READ
President: THOMAS SERYNEK, 1000 N. Warrick, Gary, IN 46403; Phone: 219-938-5410
Treasurer: MARK MIHALO, 8 Diana Road, Ogden Dunes, Portage, IN 46368; Phone: 219-763-4871
Executive Director: THOMAS R. ANDERSON
1st Vice President: DOROTHY POTUCEK, 1608 Parkview Ave., Whiting, IN 46394
Editor: CHARLOTTE J. READ
Publication(s): *Challenging the Agency; Newsletter*
Keyword(s): Air Quality and Pollution, Land Preservation, Outdoor Recreation, Public Lands, Water Pollution

Save the Dunes Conservation Fund
444 Barker Rd., Michigan City, IN 46360
Scope: National
Description: Educational and non-lobbying 501©(3) fund to support the goals of the Save the Dunes Council.
Contact(s):
Executive Director: THOMAS R. ANDERSON
Fund Director: SANDRA WILMORE
Keyword(s): Environmental and Conservation Education, Research, Streams, Watersheds

SAVE THE HARBOR/SAVE THE BAY
59 Temple Pl., Suite 304, Boston, MA 02111
Phone: 617-451-2860; Fax: 617-451-0496
Founded: 1986; Membership: 2,000
Scope: Statewide
Description: Save the Harbor/Save the Bay is a nonprofit organization whose mission is to foster a positive vision of Boston Harbor and Massachusetts Bay, and to build a broad-based constituency to promote the restoration and protection of these valuable resources. Services include narrated boat tours of Boston Harbor, discussions of harbor pollution, cleanup projects, history, celebratory events, summer youth program, and a Baywatch Program.
Contact(s):
Chairperson: BETH NICHOLSON
Director of Operations: JODEEN WETHERELL
Director of Policy: CATE DOHERTY

Keyword(s): Environment, Water Pollution, Water Quality, Water Resources, Watersheds

SAVE THE MANATEE CLUB
500 N. Maitland Ave., Maitland, FL 32751
Phone: 407-539-0990; Fax: 407-539-0871; Email: education@savethemanatee.org; WWW: www.savethemanatee.org
Founded: 1981; Membership: 40,000
Scope: National
Description: A national nonprofit organization founded by Governor Bob Graham and singer and songwriter Jimmy Buffett. Objectives are public awareness and education; funding research, rescue, rehabilitation and advocacy and appropriate legal action for the endangered West Indian manatee and its habitat. Funded primarily by the club's Adopt-A-Manatee program.
Contact(s):
Executive Director: JUDITH VALLEE
Co-Chairman: E. F. STALLINGS, P.O. Box 8776, Naples, FL 34101
Co-Chairman: JIMMY BUFFETT, c/o Margaritaville Store, 424A Fleming St., Key West, FL 33040; Phone: 305-296-9089
Keyword(s): Endangered and Threatened Species, Environmental and Conservation Education, Marine Mammals, Wildlife and Wildlife Habitat

SAVE THE SOUND, INC.
185 Magee Ave., Stamford, CT 06902
Phone: 203-327-9786; Fax: 203-967-2677; Email: savethesound@snet.net; WWW: www.savethesound.org
Founded: 1972; Membership: 4,000
Scope: Statewide
Description: Save the Sound, Inc. is devoted to protecting, restoring, and appreciating Long Island Sound and its watershed. With a staff of nine full-time employees and additional seasonal employees, STS operates year-round programs in education, research, and advocacy, including Sea Camp, Soundshore Ecology, water quality monitoring, habitat restoration beach cleanups, and an extensive library.
Contact(s):
Chairman: SHEILA O'NEILL
President: JOHN ATKIN
Secretary: LARRY McGAUGHEY
Treasurer: WILLIAM JESSUP
Chairman Emeritus: ARTHUR GLOWKA
Vice Chairman: LARRY BINGAMAN
Publication(s): *Save the Sound News (Quarterly Newsletter); Water Quality Monitoring: A Guide for Concerned Citizens; Harbor Watch Report (1986-1992); The Sound Connection Curriculum Guide*
Keyword(s): Coasts, Environmental and Conservation Education, Environmental Preservation, Water Pollution, Wetlands

SAVE THE SOUND, INC. (GARVIES POINT MUSEUM)
50 Barry Dr., Glen Cove, NY 11542
Phone: 516-759-2165
Scope: Statewide

SAVE WETLANDS AND BAYS
R.D. 6, Box 98, Millsboro, DE 19966
Phone: 302-945-1317
Founded: 1989; Membership: 230
Scope: Statewide
Description: To protect Delaware's inland bays and fringing marshes from perceived threats.
Contact(s):
Contact: TIL PURNELL

NON-GOVERNMENTAL ORGANIZATIONS

SAVE-THE-REDWOODS LEAGUE
114 Sansome St. Rm. 605, San Francisco, CA 94104
Phone: 415-362-2352
Founded: 1918
Scope: National
Description: Established to rescue from destruction representative areas of our primeval forests; to cooperate with the California Department of Parks and Recreation, the National Park Service, and other agencies in establishing redwood parks and other parks and reservations; to purchase redwood groves by private subscription; to support reforestation and conservation of our forest areas.
Contact(s):
President: RICHARD C. OTTER
Vice President: R.A.L. MENZIES
Treasurer: FRANK W. WESTWORTH, P.O. Box 44614, San Francisco, CA 94144-0001
Assistant Secretary: C. MACK SHAVER
Chairman of the Board: BRUCE S. HOWARD
General Counsel: KATE ANDERTON
Secretary and Executive Director: MARY A. ANGLE-FRANZINE
Publication(s): *California Redwood Parks and Preserves; Trees, Shrubs and Flowers of the Redwood Region; Redwoods of the Past; Story Told by a Fallen Redwood*
Keyword(s): Forests and Forestry, Land Purchase, Public Lands

SCENIC AMERICA
Headquarters, 801 Pennsylvania Ave., SE, Suite 300, Washington, DC 20003
Phone: 202-543-6200; Fax: 202-543-9130; Email: scenic@scenic.org; WWW: www.scenic.org
Founded: 1978
Scope: National
Description: National membership organization dedicated to preserving and enhancing the scenic character of America's communities and countryside. Provides information and technical assistance on billboard and sign control, scenic byways, tree preservation, highway design, cellular tower siting, and other scenic conservation issues.
Contact(s):
Chair: MADELEINE APPEL; Phone: 202-833-4300
President: MEG MAGUIRE
Vice President for Policy and Communications: FRANK VESPE
Vice President for Program Development: RAY FOOTE
Publication(s): *Viewpoints; The Grassroots Advocate;* series of technical bulletins
Keyword(s): Environmental and Conservation Education, Land Preservation, Land Use Planning, Landscape Architecture, Urban Environment

Scenic Kentucky
c/o Hilliard Lyons, P.O. Box 32760, Louisville, KY 40232
Phone: 502-588-8839; Fax: 502-588-8612
Scope: Statewide
Description: The only statewide organization devoted to protecting Kentucky's scenic resources and visual environment. Scenic Kentucky has the following three major objectives: 1) clean up billboard blight, 2) improve community appearance, and 3) protect scenic roads.
Contact(s):
Executive Director: B. LOEB

Scenic Michigan
P.O. Box 30235, Lansing, MI 48909
Phone: 517-371-1041; Fax: 517-371-1505; Email: mtanton@freeway.net
Scope: Statewide
Description: Scenic Michigan started under the aegis of Michigan United Conservation Clubs, the largest nonprofit conservation organization in the United States, as a billboard control task in 1989. The mission of Scenic Michigan is to protect and enhance the appearance and scenic character of Michigan's communities and countryside.
Contact(s):
Executive

Scenic Missouri
5650A South Sinclair, Columbia, MO 65203
Phone: 573-446-3129; Fax: 573-443-3748; Email: scenicmo@tranquility.net
Founded: 1993
Scope: Statewide
Description: Scenic Missouri was founded because of a growing concern about the loss of Missouri's scenic heritage. Its mission is to preserve and enhance the distinctive appearance and scenic character of Missouri's communities and countryside.
Contact(s):
Executive Director: KARL KRUSE

Scenic North Carolina
P.O. Box 628, Raleigh, NC 27602
Phone: 919-832-3687; Fax: 919-832-3299; Email: scenic.nc@worldnct.att.net
Scope: Statewide
Description: Our sense of identity as North Carolinians is tied to special places and buildings and views. Each type of landscape has its own kind of beauty, character and uniqueness. Scenic North Carolina is a statewide organization dedicated to preserving and enhancing scenic resources and community appearance in North Carolina.
Contact(s):
Executive Director: DALE McKEEL

Scenic Ohio
85 East Gay St., Suite 702, Columbus, OH 43215
Phone: 614-228-3274; Fax: 614-228-7210; Email: mjvance@iwaynet.nct
Scope: Statewide
Description: Scenic Ohio, formerly the Ohio Roadside Council, was founded in the fall of 1966. Scenic Ohio's mission is to protect and enhance the visual quality and scenic character of Ohio's commuities and countryside.
Contact(s):
Executive Director: MARIAN VANCE

Scenic Texas
1200 Post Oak Blvd., Suite 324, Houston, TX 77056
Phone: 713-629-0481; Fax: 713-629-0485; Email: scenicvu@ncosoft.com
Scope: Statewide
Description: The mission of Scenic Texas is to preserve and enhance the scenic character of the visual environment. Scenic Texas has chapters in Houston, Austin, San Antonio, Fort Worth, and Galveston.

SCENIC HUDSON, INC.
9 Vassar St., Poughkeepsie, NY 12601
Phone: 914-473-4440; Fax: 914-473-2648; Email: scenichu@mhv.net
Founded: 1963
Scope: Statewide
Description: A nonprofit conservation and environmental organization dedicated to the preservation and improvement of natural, recreational, historic, and scenic resources of the Hudson River Valley. Speakers' Bureau available to the public.
Contact(s):
Chairman: DAVID N. REDDEN; Phone: 914-473-4440
Secretary: ELIZABETH B. PUGH
Treasurer: MARJORIE L. HART
Executive Director: KLARA B. SAUER
Editor: KLARA SAUER
Editor: BARBARA MURPHY
Vice Chairman: FREDERICK OSBORN III
Publication(s): *Scenic Hudson News; Signs of the Times (Creative Ideas for Signage; Dealing with Airport Growth; Cooling Tower Report; Understanding Traffic and its Impacts; Dredging Report*

Keyword(s): Air Quality and Pollution, Environmental Preservation, Land Preservation, Rivers, Transportation

SCIENTISTS CENTER FOR ANIMAL WELFARE
7833 Walker Dr. Suite 340, Greenbelt, MD 20770
Phone: 301-345-3500; Fax: 301-345-3503; Email: SCAW@erols.com; WWW: www.erols.com/scaw/
Scope: National
Description: A nonprofit educational organization that promotes the belief that high standards of animal welfare complement the quality of scientific results. SCAW publishes educational material about current issues of animal use in research, testing, and teaching.
Contact(s):
Executive Director: LEE KRULISCH
Keyword(s): Agriculture, Aquariums, Biology, Biotechnology, Birds, Endangered and Threatened Species, Environmental Ethics, Fisheries, Health and Nutrition, Mammals, Marine Mammals, Nongame Wildlife, Public Health Protection, Reptiles and Amphibians, Research

SEA SHEPHERD CONSERVATION SOCIETY
P.O. Box 628, Venice, CA 90294
Phone: 310-301-7325; Fax: 310-574-3161
Founded: 1977; Membership: 28,600
Scope: National
Description: An international direct action marine mammal conservation organization involved in stopping marine mammal slaughters. Special projects include: campaigns against drift net fishing, whaling, the faeroese pilot whale slaughter, and sealing. The Society owns and operates three ships, the Sea Shepard III, the submarine Mirage, and the Edward Abbey.
Contact(s):
Editor: PAUL WATSON
Founder: CAPT. PAUL WATSON
Publication(s): *Sea Shepherd Log*
Keyword(s): Endangered and Threatened Species, Environmental and Conservation Education, Fisheries, International Conservation, Marine Mammals

Australia Office
P.O. Box 334, Clifton Hill, Clifton Hill VIC 3068 Australia
Scope: National

Canada Office
P.O. Box 48446, Vancouver, British Columbia V7X 1A2 Canada
Scope: National

Great Britain Office
35 Vicarage Grove, London, London SE5 7LY United Kingdom
Scope: National

Netherlands Office
P.O. Box 97702, 2509 GC The Hague, The Hague Netherlands
Scope: National

USA Office
3107A Washington Blvd., Marina del Rey, CA 90292
Phone: 310-301-7325; Fax: 310-574-3161
Scope: National

SEACOAST ANTI-POLLUTION LEAGUE
P.O. Box 1136, Portsmouth, NH 03802
Phone: 603-431-5089
Founded: 1969; Membership: 600
Scope: Statewide
Description: To promote the wise use of natural resources of the seacoast region, and to alert and educate the community and relevant government agencies of threats to the environment. SAPL works to prevent ecological, economic, and public health damage from the Seabrook nuclear reactor, and monitors the clean-up effort at the Portsmouth Naval Shipyard.

Contact(s):
President: DAVIE HILLS
Vice President: MARY METCALF
Secretary: JOHANNA LYONS
Treasurer: JIM HORRIGAN
Staff Director: STEVE HABERWAVY
Tag Coordinator: PETER VANDERMARK

SEAPLANE PILOTS ASSOCIATION
421 Aviation Way, Frederick, MD 21701
Phone: 301-695-2083
Founded: 1972; Membership: 6,500
Scope: National
Description: A unit formed to provide seaplane services to agencies and environmental groups involved in forest fire detection, search and rescue, wildlife surveys, pollution patrols, and other related environmental and ecological projects.
Contact(s):
President: . J. J. FREY
Vice President: WALTER WINDUS
Secretary: MICHAEL VOLK
Executive Director: ROBERT A. RICHARDSON
Publication(s): *Water Flying; Water Flying Annual; Water Landing Directory*
Keyword(s): Coasts, Lakes, Outdoor Recreation, Rivers, Water Resources

SIERRA CLUB
Headquaters, 85 2nd St., 2nd Fl., San Francisco, CA 94105-3459
Phone: 415-977-5500
Founded: 1892; Membership: 550,000
Scope: National
Description: To explore, enjoy, and protect the wild places of the earth; to practice and promote the responsible use of the earth's ecosystems and resources; to educate and enlist humanity to protect and restore the quality of the natural and human environment; and to use all lawful means to carry out these objectives. With 65 chapters and 396 groups in North America, the Club's nonprofit program work includes legislation, litigation, public information, publishing, wilderness outings, and conferences. Founded by John Muir.
Contact(s):
Chairman: MICHAEL McCLOSKEY
President: J. ROBERT COX
Vice President: KATHY FLETCHER
Secretary: CAROLYN CARR
Treasurer: TONY RUCKEL
Executive Director: CARL POPE
Associate Executive Director of Conservation and Communications: BRUCE HAMILTON
Associate Publisher of Sierra: KATHLEEN SACKS
Communication Director: JEAN FREEDBERG
Director of Conservation Field Services: BOB BINGMAN
Editor-in-Chief of Sierra: JOAN HAMILTON
Fifth Officer: DAVE FOREMAN
Publisher of Books: PETER BEREN
Senior Advisor to the Executive Director: GENE COAN
Publication(s): *Sierra; Planet, The; chapter and group newsletters*
Keyword(s): Air Quality and Pollution, Energy, International Conservation, Public Lands, Toxic Substances

Alaska Office
241 E. 5th Ave., #205, Anchorage, AK 99501
Phone: 907-276-4048; Fax: 907-258-6807
Scope: Regional
Contact(s):
Associate Representative: PAM BRODIE, 241 E. 5th Ave. #205, Anchorage, AK 99501; Phone: 907-276-4048; Fax: 907-258-6807
Senior Alaska Specialist: JACK HESSION

NON-GOVERNMENTAL ORGANIZATIONS

Canada Office
#1 Nicholas St., Suite 412, Ottawa, Ontario K1N 7B7 Canada
Phone: 613-241-4611; Fax: 613-241-2292
Scope: Regional

Midwest Office
214 N. Henry St., #203, Madison, WI 53703
Phone: 608-257-4994; Fax: 608-257-3513
Scope: Regional
Contact(s):
Associate Representative: BILL REDDING
Regional Representative: BRETT HULSEY
Staff Director: CARL ZICHELLA

Northeast Office
85 Washington St., Saratoga Springs, NY 12866
Phone: 518-587-9166; Fax: 518-583-9062
Scope: Regional
Contact(s):
Associate Representative: MARION TRIESTE
Associate Representative: MARK BETTINGER
Staff Director: CHRIS BALLANTYNE

Northern Plains
23 N. Scott St., #27, Sheridan, WY 82801
Phone: 307-672-0425; Fax: 307-674-6187
Scope: Regional
Contact(s):
Associate Representative: KIRK KOEPSEL
Senior Regional Staff Director: LARRY MEHLHAFF

Northwest Office
1516 Melrose Ave., Seattle, WA 98122
Phone: 206-621-1696; Fax: 206-621-9110
Scope: Regional
Contact(s):
Associate Representative: JIM YOUNG
Associate Representative: JULIA REITAN
Staff Director: BILL ARTHUR

Southeast Office
1330 21st Way South, #100B, Birmingham, AL 35205
Phone: 205-933-9111; Fax: 205-939-1020
Scope: Regional
Contact(s):
Grassroots Organizer: JOHN McCOWN
Senior Regional Staff Director: JIM PRICE

Southern California/Nevada Branch
3345 Wilshire Blvd., Suite #508, Los Angeles, CA 90010
Phone: 213-387-6528; Fax: 213-387-9862
Scope: Regional
Contact(s):
Associate Representative: BRENT SCOTT

Southwest Office
516 E. Portland St., Phoenix, AZ 85004-1843
Phone: 602-254-9330
Scope: Regional
Contact(s):
Staff Director: ROB SMITH

Texas Office
7502 Greenville Ave., #670, Dallas, TX 75231
Phone: 214-369-8181; Fax: 214-369-8183
Scope: Regional
Contact(s):
Regional Representative: LARRY FREILICH

Washington, DC Office
408 C St., NE, Washington, DC 20002
Phone: 202-547-1141; Fax: 202-547-6009
Scope: Regional
Contact(s):
Legislative Director: DEBBIE SEASE

SIERRA CLUB FOUNDATION, THE
220 Sansome St., Suite 1100, San Francisco, CA 94104
Phone: 415-291-1800
Founded: 1960
Scope: National
Description: A nonprofit, tax-deductible, public foundation established to finance the educational, literary, and scientific projects of citizen-based groups working on national and international environmental problems. Manages assets in excess of $25 million and over 600 regional or special interest funds principally for charitable conservation purposes. Also manages charitable remainder unitrusts and a pooled income fund with assets over $8.2 million.
Contact(s):
President: ROBERT B. FLINT JR.
Vice President: MARLENE FLUHARTY
Secretary: ROGER W. HERSHEY
Treasurer: RICHARD CELLARIUS JR.
Executive Director: JOHN DECOOK
Controller: IQBAL PARUPIA
Director of Finance and Administration: MONA CANNON
Fifth Officer: MICHAEL LOEB
Grants Manager: ANDREA MANION
Keyword(s): Environmental and Conservation Education, Environmental Law, Land Use Planning, Public Lands, Urban Environment

SINAPU
Box 3243, Boulder, CO 80307
Phone: 303-447-8655; Fax: 303-447-8612; Email: sinapu@sinapu.org; WWW: http://www.sinapu.org/
Founded: 1991; Membership: 1,400
Scope: Statewide
Description: Sinapu was named after the Ute word for wolves. Sinapu is dedicated to the recovery of the gray wolf in the Southern Rocky Montains, and to restoration of the wild habitat in which all species flourish.
Contact(s):
Program Director: ROB EDWARD
Publication(s): *Southern Rockies Wolf Tracks*
Keyword(s): Ancient Forests, Biodiversity, EcoAction, Ecology, Endangered and Threatened Species, Forest Management, Predators, Public Lands, Wildlands, Wildlife and Wildlife Habitat, Wildlife Management

SMALL WOODLAND OWNERS ASSOCIATION OF MAINE, INC.
153 Hostpital St., P.O. Box 926, Augusta, ME 04332
Phone: 207-626-0005
Founded: 1975; Membership: 1,500
Scope: Statewide
Description: A statewide nonprofit organization, affiliated with the National Woodland Owners Association, which pursues better understandings, skills, and directions in small woodland ownership/management under integrated use objectives.
Contact(s):
President: EVERETT TOWLE; Phone: 207-929-6481
Vice President: ANCYL THURSTON; Phone: 207-623-9147
Secretary: CARL VAN HUSEN; Phone: 207-696-3665
Treasurer: RICHARD PIERCE; Phone: 207-562-7042
Editor and Executive Director: JEFFREY ROMANO
Publication(s): *SWOAM NEWS*
Keyword(s): Forests and Forestry

SMITHSONIAN INSTITUTION
1000 Jefferson Dr. SW, Washington, DC 20560
Phone: 202-357-2700, Voic TTY 202-357-1729
Founded: 1846
Scope: National
Description: An education, museum, and research complex as well as an independent trust instrumentality of the United States, established for the increase and diffusion of knowledge. Mission accomplished by: field investigations; national collections development in arts, history, and science, and their preservation for study, reference, and exhibition; scientific research and publications; programs of national and international cooperative research, conservation, education, and training; answering inquiries from the general public and educational and scientific organizations; long-term loan of selected objects; and sharing of research and educational material on the World Wide Web.
Contact(s):
Secretary: IRA MICHAEL HEYMAN
Provost: J. DENNIS O'CONNOR
Under Secretary: CONSTANCE BERRY NEWMAN; Phone: 202-357-3258
Keyword(s): Ancient Forests, Aquatic Habitats, Biodiversity, Birds, Coral Reefs, Cultural Preservation, Culture, Endangered and Threatened Species, Gardening and Horticulture, Historic Preservation, Insects and Butterflies, Mammals, Marine Mammals, Natural History, Reptiles and Amphibians

National Museum of Natural History
10th St. and Constitution Ave., NW, Washington, DC 20560
Phone: 202-357-2700; Fax: TTY357-1729
Scope: National
Description: A center for the study of humans, plants, animals, fossil organisms, terrestrial and extraterrestrial rocks, and minerals as well as other fields of scientific investigation.
Contact(s):
Director: ROBERT FRI
Chief Scientist of Environmental Research Center: DAVID L. CORRELL, Smithsonian Environmental Research Center, P.O. Box 28, Edgewater, MD 21037; Phone: 301-261-4190

National Zoological Park
3000 Block of Connecticut Ave. NW, Washington, DC 20008
Phone: 202-673-4717/Press:673-4840
Scope: National
Description: Research concentrates on a better understanding of animal behavior and health, particularly endangered species. Through the operation of the zoo's Conservation and Research Center in Front Royal, VA, the NZP is developing a program of animal propagation which will aid in the survival of threatened and endangered species. Undertakes a number of programs overseas to develop new methodology and increase knowledge of species in the wild. The Migratory Bird Center is located at the zoo.
Contact(s):
Director: MICHAEL ROBINSON

Office of Fellowships and Grants
Smithsonian Institution L'Enfant Plaza SW Rm. 7300, Washington, DC 20560
Phone: 202-287-3271
Scope: National
Description: Oversees all Smithsonian fellowships and supports a wide range of research activities. It also provides program and administrative assistance for cooperative teaching arrangements between the Institution and local universities in American history, museum studies, and other areas.
Contact(s):
Director: ROBERTA RUBINOFF

Office of International Relations
Smithsonian Institution 1100 Jefferson Dr. SW Rm. 3123, Washington, DC 20560
Phone: 202-357-4795
Scope: National
Description: The Foreign Currency Program supports the research activities of American institutions of higher learning through grants in U.S.-owned local currencies.
Contact(s):
Director: FRANCINE BERKOWITZ

Smithsonian Marine Station at Link Port
5612 Old Dixie Highway, Fort Pierce, FL 34946
Phone: 561-465-6632
Scope: National
Description: Marine studies aim at understanding the ecological function of inland waterways and their relationship to land use policy.
Contact(s):
Director: MARY E. RICE

Smithsonian Press/Smithsonian Productions
470 L'Enfant Plaza Suite 7100, Washington, DC 20560
Phone: 202-287-3738
Scope: National
Description: Information on history, art, and science research is presented in non-technical style in Smithsonian Institution Research Reports issued four times a year by the Office of Public Affairs (202-357-2627). Smithsonian, the official magazine of the Institution, presents general interest feature articles each month in every subject area of the Smithsonian museums: art, culture, history, science, and technology.
Contact(s):
Director: DANIEL GOODWIN
Director of Communications: DAVID UMANSKY, Arts and Industries Bldg., 900 Jefferson Dr. SW, Rm. 4210, Washington, DC 20560; Phone: 202-357-2627
Editor: DON MOSER, Smithsonian Magazine Arts and Industries, Bldg. 900 Jefferson Dr. SW, RM. 1310C, Washington, DC 20560
Publication(s): *Research in various fields is reported in a continuing series of publications by the Smithsonian Institution Press under the following general headings: Smithsonian contributions to Anthropology, to Astrophysics, Botany, Earth Sciences, Marine Sciences, Paleobiology, Zoology, Air and Space, History and Technology, Folklife and Culture.*

Smithsonian Tropical Research Institute
APO AA, FL 34002-0948
Scope: National
Description: A center for advanced studies in tropical biology. Ecology and evolution of tropical organisms are the primary research interests of the staff. The reserve and laboratories on Barro Colorado Island, as well as marine facilities on both coasts, are available to visiting scientists and students.
Contact(s):
Director: IRA RUBINOFF

SOCIETY FOR ANIMAL PROTECTIVE LEGISLATION
P.O. Box 3719 Georgetown Station, Washington, DC 20007
Phone: 202-337-2334
Founded: 1955
Scope: National
Description: Nonprofit organization which keeps its 7,000 correspondents apprised of current developments in legislation for the protection of animals. Has been instrumental in obtaining enactment of 14 federal laws.
Contact(s):
President: MADELEINE BEMELMANS
Vice President: JOHN F. KULLBERG
Secretary: CHRISTINE STEVENS; Phone: 202-337-2334
Treasurer: ROGER L. STEVENS

NON-GOVERNMENTAL ORGANIZATIONS

Executive Secretary: JOHN GLEIBER; Phone: 202-337-2334
Keyword(s): Endangered and Threatened Species, Mammals, Marine Mammals, Trapping, Wildlife and Wildlife Habitat

SOCIETY FOR CONSERVATION BIOLOGY
Univ. of Washington, Box 351800, Seattle, WA 98195-1800
Phone: 206-616-4054
Founded: 1985; Membership: 5,700
Scope: National
Description: A professional society dedicated to providing the scientific information and expertise required to protect the world's biological diversity. Incorporated as a tax-exempt scientific organization, the Society has a board composed of scholars, government personnel, and members of both national and international scientific and conservation organizations.
Contact(s):
President: P. DEE BOERSMA; Phone: 206-616-2185
Secretary: SANDY ANDELMAN
Treasurer: STEPHEN R. HUMPHREY; Phone: 352-392-9230
Editor: GARY MEFFE; Phone: 352-846-0557
Publication(s): *Conservation Biology*
Keyword(s): Biodiversity, Endangered and Threatened Species, Environmental and Conservation Education, International Conservation, Sustainable Development

SOCIETY FOR ECOLOGICAL RESTORATION
1207 Seminole Highway Suite B, Madison, WI 53711
Phone: 608-262-9547; Fax: 608-265-8557
Founded: 1987; Membership: 2,200
Scope: National
Description: Created to promote the development of ecological restoration both as a discipline and as a model for a healthy relationship with nature, and to raise awareness of the value and limitations of restoration as a conservation strategy.
Contact(s):
Chair: NIK LOPOUKHINE; Phone: 819-944-2639
Secretary: ERIC HIGGS; Phone: 403-492-5469
Treasurer: DR. WILLIAM HALVORSON; Phone: 520-670-6885
Executive Director: DONALD A. FALK; Phone: 520-626-7201
Editor: WILLIAM R. JORDAN, III
Vice Chair: GEORGE GANN; Phone: 305-245-6547
Publication(s): *Restoration and Management Notes; SER News; Restoration Ecology; Ecological Restoration: The New Management Challenge; Proceedings of the First SER Conference, 1989; Proceedings from the Seventh SER Conference, 1995*
Keyword(s): Conservation of Protected Areas, Ecology, Environmental and Conservation Education, Renewable Resources, Wildlife Management

SOCIETY FOR MARINE MAMMALOGY, THE
ATTN: Secretary, Department of Biology, EMS Building, University of California-Santa Cruz, Santa Cruz, CA 95064
Founded: 1981; Membership: 1,000
Scope: National
Description: To promote the educational, scientific, and managerial advancement of marine mammal science; gather and disseminate scientific, technical, and management information, through publications and meetings to members of the society, the public, and public and private institutions; and promote the wise conservation and management of marine mammal resources.
Contact(s):
President: IAN STIRLING, Canadian Wildlife Service, 5330 122 Street, Edmonton, Alberta T6H 3S5 Canada; Phone: 403-435-7349; Fax: 403-435-7359; Email: stirling@ec.gc.ca
Secretary: TERRI E. M. WILLIAMS, Department of Biology, EMS Building, University of California-Santa Cruz, Santa Cruz, CA 95064; Phone: 408-459-5123; Fax: 408-459-4882; Email: williams@biology.ucsc.edu
Treasurer: JAMES T. HARVEY, Moss Landing Marine Laboratory, P.O. Box 450, Moss Landing, CA 95039; Phone: 408-755-8699; Fax: 408-753-2826; Email: harvey@mlml.calstate.edu
Chairman of Awards/Scholarship Committee: CAROL PRICE FAIRFIELD, Office of Protected Resources, National Marine Fisheries Service, 1335 East-West Highway, Silver Spring, MD 21403; Phone: 301-713-2289; Fax: 301-713-0376; Email: cfairfield@rdc.noaa.gov
Chairman of Board of Editors: WILLIAM F. PERRIN, Southwest Fisheries Science Center, P.O. Box 271, La Jolla, CA 92038; Phone: 619-546-7096; Fax: 619-546-7003; Email: wperrin@its.ucsd.edu
Chairman of Committee of Scientific Advisors: STEVEN L. SWARTZ, National Marine Fisheries Service, 1335 East-West Highway, Silver Spring, MD 20910; Phone: 301-713-2239; Email: sswartz@shark.ssp.nmfs.gov
Chairman of Education Committee: DANIEL K. ODELL, Sea World, Inc., 7007 Sea World Drive, Orlando, CA 32821-8097; Phone: 407-363-2662; Fax: 407-345-5397; Email: odell@pegasus.cc.ucf.edu
Chairman of Nominations/Elections: JOHN E. REYNOLDS III, Marine Science and Biology Department, Eckerd College, 4200 54th Avenue S., St. Petersburg, FL 33711; Phone: 813-864-8431; Fax: 813-864-8388; Email: reynolje@eckerd.edu
Member-at-Large: PETER B. BEST, Whale Unit, c/o South African Museum, P.O. Box 61, Cape Town, 8000 South Africa; Phone: 27-21-243330; Fax: 27-21-246726; Email: pbest@nv1.samuseum.ac.za
Member-at-Large: ALEX AGUILAR, Department of Animal Biology, University of Barcelona, Barcelona, 08071 Spain; Phone: 3-402-1453; Fax: 3-411-0887; Email: alexa@porthos.bio.ub.es
Newsletter Editor: RANDALL S. WELLS, Chicago Zoological Society, c/o Mote Marine Laboratory, 1600 Thompson Parkway, Sarasota, FL 34236; Phone: 941-388-4441; Fax: 941-388-4223; Email: mmlrwells@aol.com
President-Elect: DOUGLAS P. DeMASTER, National Marine Fisheries Service, 7600 Sand Point Way NE, Seattle, WA 98115; Phone: 206-526-4021; Fax: 206-526-6615; Email: demaster@afsc.noaa.gov
Student Member-at-Large: LEAH GERBER, Washington Cooperative Fish and Wildlife Research Unit, School of Fisheries, Box 357980, University of Washington, Seattle, WA 98195; Phone: 206-526-6331; Fax: 206-685-7471; Email: leah@fish.washington.edu
Publication(s): *Marine Mammal Science*
Keyword(s): Endangered and Threatened Species, International Conservation, Marine Mammals, Natural History, Wildlife Management

SOCIETY FOR RANGE MANAGEMENT
1839 York St., Denver, CO 80206
Phone: 303-355-7070
Founded: 1948; Membership: 4,000
Scope: National
Description: Professional society which promotes understanding of rangeland ecosystems and their management and use for tangible products and intangible values; reports new findings and techniques in range science; promotes public appreciation of rangelands and benefits derived from them; promotes professional development of members.
Contact(s):
President: KENDALL JOHNSON, University of Idaho, Rangeland Resources, Moscow, ID 83844
Director: RONALD E. SOSEBEE, 6902 Geneva, Lubbock, TX 79413
Director: RODNEY K. HEITSCHMIDT, Route 1 Box 2021, Miles City, MT 59301
Director: CAROLYN HHULL-SEIG, 501 E. St. Joseph, Rapid City, SD 57701
Director: PAT SHAVER, 2510 Meadow Ln., Woodburn, OR 97071
Director: ANGELA WILLIAMS, Route 1 Box 108, Paoli, OK 73074
Director: BOB BUDD, Red Canyon Ranch, 350 Red Canyon Rd., Lander, WY 82520
1st Vice President: JOHN McLAIN, 340 N. Minnesota St., Carson City, NV 89703-4152

Executive Vice President: J. C. WHITTEKIEND, 1839 York St., Denver, CO 80206; Phone: 303-355-7070; Email: srmden@ix.netcom.com
Past President: LAMAR SMITH, 4963 N Cascabel Rd., Benson, AZ 85602
Technical Editor: GARY FRASIER, 7820 Stag Hollow Rd., Loveland, CO 80538
Publication(s): *Journal of Range Management; Rangelands*
Keyword(s): Agriculture, Ecology, Environment, Land Use Planning, Prairies, Public Lands, Renewable Resources, Sustainable Resources, Water Quality, Water Resources, Watersheds, Wetlands

SOCIETY FOR THE PRESERVATION OF BIRDS OF PREY
P.O. Box 66070 Mar Vista Station, Los Angeles, CA 90066-0070
Phone: 310-840-2322
Founded: 1966
Scope: National
Description: A private charity, non-membership, national association which advocates the strictest possible protection for birds of prey; educates the public about the role of raptors in the ecosystem; opposes harvesting for falconry and the sale of birds of prey for profit; endorses captive raptor breeding as a conservation technique; and supports the largest collection of literature on birds of prey for use by the public. The Society is the only and oldest raptor organization which places emphasis on protection of birds of prey in the wild and whose officers, trustees and spokesperson receive no salary, compensation, or reimbursement for their volunteer service to the Society.
Contact(s):
Vice President: CHUCK ARAMAKI
Vice President: MRS. KARLA SATOU
Treasurer: DR. HAROLD WILKINSON
Director At-Large: DR. LESLIE GIERSON
President and Editor: J. RICHARD HILTON; Phone: 310-636-0072
Publication(s): *Raptor Report, The; Leaflet Series*
Keyword(s): Endangered and Threatened Species, Falconry, Predators, Raptors

SOCIETY FOR THE PROTECTION OF NEW HAMPSHIRE FORESTS
54 Portsmouth St., Concord, NH 03301-5400
Phone: 603-224-9945; Fax: 603-228-0423
Founded: 1901; Membership: 10,000
Scope: Statewide
Description: A voluntary nonprofit organization promoting balanced conservation of New Hampshire's renewable natural resources through land protection, education, advocacy, and forestry.
Contact(s):
Secretary: PETER POWELL
Chairman of the Board: BEN GAYMAN
Editor and Senior Director of Communications and Development: RICHARD OBER
President and Senior Director of Conservation Programs: PAUL A. DOSCHER
Vice President of Finance and Development: ELLEN POPE
Publication(s): *Forest Notes*
Keyword(s): Environmental and Conservation Education, Forests and Forestry, Land Purchase, Wildlife and Wildlife Habitat, Wildlife Management

SOCIETY OF AMERICAN FORESTERS
5400 Grosvenor Ln., Bethesda, MD 20814
Phone: 301-897-8720; Fax: 301-897-3690; Email: safweb@safnet.org
Founded: 1900; Membership: 18,000
Scope: National
Description: The national organization representing all segments of the forestry profession and the accreditation authority for professional forestry education in the U.S. Objectives are to advance the science, technology, education, and practice of professional forestry and to use the knowledge and skills of the profession to benefit society.
Contact(s):
President: KARL F. WENGER
Vice President: JAMES E. COUFAL
Director of Communications and Marketing Services: LORI GARDNER
Director of Conventions and Meetings: DIANE M. PERL
Director of Finance and Administration: CHARLES N. JACKSON
Director of Resource Policy: LAWRENCE W. HILL
Director of Science and Education: P. GREGORY SMITH
Editorial Director and Director of Publications: REBECCA N. STAEBLER
Executive Vice President: WILLIAM H. BANZHAF
Past President: ROBERT W. BOSWORTH
Past President: HARRY V. WIANT JR.
Publication(s): *Journal of Forestry; Forest Science; Southern Journal of Applied Forestry; Northern Journal of Applied Forestry; Western Journal of Applied Forestry; Forestry Source, The*
Keyword(s): Environmental and Conservation Education, Environmental Law, Forests and Forestry, Public Lands, Renewable Resources

SOCIETY OF TYMPANUCHUS CUPIDO PINNATUS LTD.
Stone Ridge II, Ste. 280; N 14 W23777 Stone Ridge Dr., Waukeha, WI 53188-1188
Phone: 414-523-3600; Fax: 414-523-3601; Email: mihal@execpc.com
Founded: 1961; Membership: 700
Scope: National
Description: Nonprofit organization dedicated to the preservation of the prairie chicken for all future generations in Wisconsin and all threatened and endangered species native to the state of Wisconsin.
Contact(s):
President: RUSSELL C. SCHALLERT
Vice President: LAWRENCE N. DeLEERS, JR., 4665 Highway Y, Saukville, WI 53080
Vice President: GREGORY SEPTON, Milwaukee Public Museum; 800 W. Wells Street, Milwaukee, WI 53233
Vice President: WILLIAM H. EMORY, Klug and Smith Company, 4425 W. Mitchell, Milwaukee, WI 53214
Secretary: KURT W. REMUS, JR., 3860 N. Port Washington Rd., Milwaukee, WI 53217
Treasurer: GLENN N. GOERGEN, Deloitte and Touche, 250 E. Wisconsin Ave., Milwaukee, WI 53202
Publication(s): *Boom*
Keyword(s): Endangered and Threatened Species, Prairies, Wildlife and Wildlife Habitat, Wildlife Management

SOCIETY OF WETLAND SCIENTISTS
P.O. Box 1897, Lawrence, KS 66044-8897
Phone: 913-843-1221; Fax: 913-843-1274; WWW: www.sws.org
Founded: 1979; Membership: 4,200
Scope: International
Description: International nonprofit education and charitable society of persons interested in wetland science, technology, and related fields. Encourages educational, scientific, and technological development and advancement in all fields of wetland science. Encourages protection, restoration, and stewardship of wetlands. Student memberships and scholarships.
Contact(s):
President: DUNCAN PATTEN, Arizona State University, Center for Environmental Studies, ; Phone: 602-965-2975
Vice President: DONALD CAHOON, National Wetlands Resource Center, 700 Cajundome Blvd., Lafayette, LA 70506; Phone: 318-266-8634
Secretary: JANET KEOUGH, Northern Prairie Science Center, 8711 37th St. SE, Jamestown, ND 58401-7317; Phone: 701-252-5363

NON-GOVERNMENTAL ORGANIZATIONS

Treasurer: BARBARA KLEISS, 197 Skyline, Clinton, MS 39056-5844; Phone: 601-965-4600ext.5682
Past President: WILLIAM MITSCH, OSU School of Natural Resources, Columbus, OH 43210; Phone: 614-292-9774
Publication(s): *Wetlands; SWS Bulletin*
Keyword(s): Aquatic Habitats, Environmental and Conservation Education, Sustainable Ecosystems, Water Resources, Wetlands

SOIL AND WATER CONSERVATION SOCIETY (formerly Soil Conservation Society of America)
7515 NE Ankeny Rd., Ankeny, IA 50021-9764
Phone: 515-289-2331; Fax: 515-289-1227
Founded: 1945; Membership: 12,000
Scope: National
Description: The Soil and Water Conservation Society is a multidisciplinary membership organization advocating protection, enhancement, and wise use of soil, water, and related natural resources. SWCS programs emphasize the interdependence of natural resources through education, publications, and a network of local chapters throughout the U.S. and Canada. SWCS also manages the World Association of Soil and Water Conservation.
Contact(s):
President: ANIKO SZOJKA-PARNELL, Alberta Environmental Protection, 9820 103rd St., Edmonton, ART5K2J6 Canada; Phone: 403-427-0047; Fax: 403-422-5136
Vice President: DENNIS PATE, 9644 Quail Ridge, Urbandale, IA 50322; Phone: 515-284-4393; Fax: 515-284-4394
Secretary: DANA CHAPMAN, Watershed Agricultural Council, RR #1, Box 74, NYS Route 10, Walton, NY 13856; Phone: 607-865-7790; Fax: 607-865-4932
Treasurer: SARAH FAST, Missouri Department of Natural Resources, P.O. Box 176, Jefferson City, MO 65102; Phone: 573-751-4932; Fax: 573-526-3508
Executive Vice President: DOUGLAS M. KLEINE, CAE SWCS 7515 NE Ankeny Rd., Ankeny, IA 50021-9764; Phone: 515-289-2331; Fax: 515-289-1227; Email: dougk@swcs.org
Marketing: KAREN HOWE
Ottawa, Canada Representative: JAMES R. BRUCE
Program Development: CHARLES PERSINGER
Publications: SUE BALLANTINE
Washington, DC Representative: NORMAN A. BERG
Publication(s): *Journal of Soil and Water Conservation; Conservation Voices: Listening to the Land.*
Keyword(s): Agriculture, Conservation Tillage, Environmental and Conservation Education, Environmental Protection, International Conservation, Renewable Resources, Research, Soil Conservation, Sustainable Development, Sustainable Ecosystems, Training, Water Quality, Watersheds, Wetlands, Wildlife and Wildlife Habitat

SONORAN INSTITUTE
7650 E. Broadway Blvd., Suite 203, Tucson, AZ 85710
Phone: 520-290-0828; Fax: 520-290-0969; Email: sonoran@sonoran.org; WWW: www.sonoran.org
Founded: 1990
Scope: National
Description: The mission of the Sonoran Institute is to promote community-based conservation strategies that preserve the ecological integrity of protected lands and at the same time meet the economic aspirations of adjoining landowners and communities. Underlying this mission is the conviction that locally-driven and inclusive approaches produce the best results.
Contact(s):
Executive Director: LUTHER PROPST
Administrative Assistant: KARIN LAWRENCE
Associate Director: JOHN SHEPARD
Associate Director of Boarderlands Programs: JOANQUIN MURRIETA
Board Chairman: FRANK GREGG
Community Outreach Coordinator: MARY VINT
Director of Boarderlands Programs: STEVE CORNELIUS
Director of Communications: LARA SCHMIT
Director of Northwest Office: DR. RAY RASKER, 105 W. Main St., Suite D, Bozeman, MT 59715; Phone: 406-587-7331; Fax: 406-587-2027
Director of Research: MARK BRIGGS
Officer Manager: ANA CRISTINA WILSON
Program Associate of Northwest Office: BARB CESTERO
Program Associate of Northwest Office: BEN ALEXANDER
Keyword(s): Land Use Planning, Public Lands, Riparian Restoration, Stewardship, Sustainable Development

SOUND EXPERIENCE
2730 Washington St. #D, Port Townsend, WA 98368
Phone: 360-379-0438
Founded: 1988
Scope: National
Description: Sound Experience involves participants in exploration of Puget Sound from the decks of a traditional sailing ship (the 101' Schooner Adventuress). Our mission is protecting Puget Sound through education.
Contact(s):
President: JAN GRAY
Vice President: JAN VULK
Secretary: DEDE CHINLUND
Treasurer: MARY ANDERSON
Executive Director: JENELL DeMATTEO
Keyword(s): Environmental and Conservation Education, Historic Preservation, Outdoor Recreation, Youth Organizations

SOUTH ATLANTIC FISHERY MANAGEMENT COUNCIL
One Southpark Cir. Suite 306, Charleston, SC 29407-4699
Phone: 803-571-4366; Email: safmc@noaa.gov
Founded: 1976
Scope: National
Description: Responsible for the conservation and management of fish stocks within the,200-mile limit (federal waters) of the Atlantic off the coasts of North Carolina, South Carolina, Georgia, and Florida.
Contact(s):
Chairman: BENJAMIN C. HARTIG
Executive Director: ROBERT K. MAHOOD
Publication(s): *South Atlantic Update; Fishery Management Plans*
Keyword(s): Fisheries

SOUTH CAROLINA ASSOCIATION OF CONSERVATION DISTRICTS
ATTN: President, P.O. Box 612, Camden, SC 29020
Scope: Statewide
Contact(s):
President, Alternate Board Member: JAMES McLEOD, P.O. Box 612, Camden, SC 29020; Phone: 803-432-3516; Fax: 803-425-6749
Vice President: LARRY E. NATES, 112 Luther Dr., Gaston, SC 29053; Phone: 803-755-0319
Secretary: DOROTHY LEE, 202 Indian Trail Rd., Seneca, SC 29672; Phone: 864-888-2925
Treasurer: VENNING MORRISON, 917 State St., West Columbia, SC 29169; Phone: 803-796-9204
Board Member: WALTER B. COUSINS, P.O. Box 622, Newberry, SC 29108; Phone: 803-276-1522; Fax: 803-276-4157

SOUTH CAROLINA B.A.S.S. CHAPTER FEDERATION
ATTN: President, 1469 Schurlknight Rd., St. Stephen, SC 29479
Phone: 803-567-4680
Scope: Statewide
Description: An organization of Bassmaster chapters, affiliated with the Bass Anglers Sportsman Society, organized to fight pollution, assist state and national conservation agencies in their efforts, and teach the young people of our country good conservation practices. Dedicated to the realistic conservation of our water resources.
Contact(s):
President: TONY BENNETT, 1469 Schurlknight Rd., St.Stephen, SC 29479; Phone: 803-567-4680

Conservation Director: TOM HUEBLE, 446 Baker Rd., Whitmire, SC 29178; Phone: 803-694-3602
Publication(s): *South Carolina Forestry Journal; South Carolina B.A.S.S. Federation, Inc. Newsletter*
Keyword(s): Forests and Forestry, Land Use Planning, Transportation, Wetlands, Wildlife and Wildlife Habitat

SOUTH CAROLINA FORESTRY ASSOCIATION
4901 Broad River Rd., P.O. Box 21303, Columbia, SC 29221
Phone: 803-798-4170
Founded: 1968
Scope: Statewide
Description: A nonprofit educational organization with a membership of timberland owners, wood dealers, wood-using industries, equipment suppliers, and individuals interested in forest conservation and wise use of natural resources.
Contact(s):
President: ROBERT R. SCOTT
Chairman of the Board: W. VIRGIL WALL JR.

SOUTH CAROLINA WILDLIFE FEDERATION
2711 Middleburg Dr., Suite 104, Columbia, SC 29204
Phone: 803-256-0670; Fax: 803-256-0690; Email: mail@scwf.org; WWW: www.scwf.org
Scope: Statewide
Description: A representative statewide organization, affiliated with the National Wildlife Federation, dedicated to the protection and enhancement of wildlife and its habitat through public education and government interaction.
Contact(s):
President: DENTON LINDSAY
Affiliate Representative: CHRISTINE THOMPSON
Alternate Representative: JOHN HELMS
Executive Director & Editor: ANGELA VINEY
Publication(s): *South Carolina Out-of-Doors*
Keyword(s): Aquatic Habitats, Fisheries, Renewable Resources, Water Pollution Management, Wetlands

SOUTH DAKOTA ASSOCIATION OF CONSERVATION DISTRICTS
ATTN: President, 15074 372nd Ave., Chelsea, SD 57465
Scope: Statewide
Contact(s):
President, Alternate Board Member: HENRY ELSING, 15074 372nd Ave., Chelsea, SD 57465; Phone: 605-887-3337; Fax: 605-887-3337
Vice President: GERALD THADEN, 14321 465th Ave., Marvin, SD 57251-9720; Phone: 605-938-4579
Secretary/Treasurer: JOHN D. MAJERES, RR2 Box 122, Dell Rapids, SD 57022-0208; Phone: 605-428-3090; Fax: 605-988-5773
Executive Secretary: ANGELA EHLERS, 116 N. Euclid, P.O. Box 275, Pierre, SD 57501-0275; Phone: 605-224-0361; Fax: 605-773-4531
Board Member: GENE S. WILLIAMS, P.O. Box 2, Interior, SD 57750-0002; Phone: 605-433-5469; Fax: 605-433-5470; Email: gwilliams@sioux.sodak.net

SOUTH DAKOTA B.A.S.S. CHAPTER FEDERATION
ATTN: President, P.O. Box 266, Winner, SD 57580
Phone: 605-842-0746
Scope: Statewide
Description: An organization of Bassmaster chapters, affiliated with the Bass Anglers Sportsman Society, organized to fight pollution, assist state and national conservation agencies in their efforts, and teach young people of our country good conservation practices. Dedicated to the realistic conservation of our water resources.
Contact(s):
President: CHUCK DOOM, P.O. Box 266, Winner, SD 57580; Phone: 605-842-0746
Conservation Director: PHILLIP RISNES, 26643 461st. Ave., Hartford, SD 57033; Phone: 605-332-4755
Publication(s): *South Dakota Bird Notes; Birds of South Dakota, 1991; The South Dakota Breeding Bird Atlas, 1995; B.A.S.S. Federation Newsletter "Dakota Bassin"*
Keyword(s): Birds, Endangered and Threatened Species, Natural History, Raptors, Waterfowl

SOUTH DAKOTA ORNITHOLOGISTS' UNION
P.O. Box 277, Ipswich, SD 57451
Founded: 1949; Membership: 350
Scope: Statewide
Description: To encourage the study of birds in South Dakota and to promote the study of ornithology by more closely uniting the students of this branch of natural science.
Contact(s):
President: DAVID SWANSON, Biology Department University of South Dakota, Vermillion, SD 57069; Phone: 605-624-0203
Vice President: JEFFREY PALMER, 821 NW Fifth St., Madison, SD 57041; Phone: 605-256-9745
Secretary: J. DAVID WILLIAMS; Phone: 605-426-6974
Treasurer: NELDA HOLDEN, 1620 Elmwood Dr., Brookings, SD 57006; Phone: 605-692-8278
Editor: DAN TALLMAN, Box 740, Northern State University, Aberdeen, SD 57401; Phone: 605-226-2255
Publication(s): *South Dakota Bird Notes; Birds of South Dakota (1991); South Dakota Breeding Bird Atlas, The (1995)*
Keyword(s): Agriculture, Air Quality and Pollution, Energy, Solid Waste Management, Water Resources

SOUTH DAKOTA RESOURCES COALITION
P.O. Box 66, Brookings, SD 57006
Founded: 1972
Scope: Statewide
Description: Seeks to promote the survival and integrity of water, energy, land, wildlife, and air resources, along with justice in their allocation.
Contact(s):
Chair: DAVID NELSON; Phone: 605-693-4893
Secretary: LAWRENCE NOVOTNY; Phone: 605-688-6172
Treasurer: ROBERT ROBY, 4512 Belmont St., Sioux Falls, SD 57102; Phone: 605-371-0743
Editor: BRUCE PENGRA; Phone: 605-692-8579
Vice Chair: KAYE HUNT, P.O. Box 309, Garretson, SD 57030; Phone: 605-594-3558
Publication(s): *ECO-Forum*

SOUTH DAKOTA WILDLIFE FEDERATION
P.O. Box 7075, Pierre, SD 57501
Phone: Phone & Fax: 605-224-7524; Email: sdwf@cam-walnet.com; WWW: www.sdwf.org
Scope: Statewide
Description: A representative statewide organization, affiliated with the National Wildlife Federation, dedicated to the protection and enhancement of wildlife and its habitat through public education and government interaction.
Contact(s):
President: MIKE LARSEN
Affiliate Representative: CHUCK CLAYTON
Alternate Representative: GINGER SCALET
Executive Director and Editor: CHRIS HESLA
Publication(s): *South Dakota Out-of-Doors*
Keyword(s): Aquatic Habitats, Fisheries, Renewable Resources, Water Pollution Management, Wetlands

SOUTHEAST ALASKA CONSERVATION COUNCIL (SEACC)
419 6th St., #328, Juneau, AK 99801
Phone: 907-586-6942; Fax: 907-463-3312; Email: info@seacc.org
Founded: 1969; Membership: 1,200
Scope: Statewide
Description: SEACC is a coalition of sixteen local conservation groups, dedicated to preserving the integrity of Southeast Alaska's magnificent natural environment. Protection of the region's pristine

NON-GOVERNMENTAL ORGANIZATIONS

coastal rainforests, abundant fish and wildlife, and outstanding scenery. Provides for a sustainable approach to economic stability, subsistence use areas, recreational opportunities, and a unique way of life.
Contact(s):
President: KATYA KIRSCH, Box 521, Haines, AK 99827
Vice President: BRUCE BAKER, P.O. Box 211384, Auke Bay, AK 99821
Secretary: JULIE PENN, P.O. Box 22474, Juneau, AK 99802
Treasurer: DANA OWEN, 949 Goldbelt, Juneau, AK 99801
Executive Director: BART KOEHLER
Administrative Assistant: SERENA DOWN
Administrative Coordinator: MICHELLE KAELKE
Conservation Director and Staff Attorney: BUCK LINDEKUGEL
Grassroots Organizer: TIM BRISTOL
Grassroots Organizer: MARC WHEELER
Publication(s): *RAVENCALL; Action Alerts*
Keyword(s): Conservation of Protected Areas, Environment, Fisheries, Forest Management, Internships, Land Use Planning, Outdoor Recreation, Public Lands, Rivers, Sustainable Development, Water Pollution, Water Quality, Watersheds

SOUTHEASTERN ASSOCIATION OF FISH AND WILDLIFE AGENCIES
ATTN: President, Commissoiner of Kentucky Department of Fish and Wildlfie Resources, #1 Game Farm Rd., Frankfort, KY 40601
Scope: Regional
Description: To protect the best interests of the southeastern states by maintaining their right of jurisdiction over their wildlife resources on public and private lands, by supporting or opposing state and federal wildlife legislation, and by making recommendations on federal programs involving aid. Conducts annual conference for the exchange of ideas and research and land management information concerning wildlife and native and fresh water fisheries.
Contact(s):
President: C. TOM BENNETT, Commissioner of Kentucky Department of Fish and Wildlife Resources, #1 Game Farm Rd., Frankfort, KY 40601; Phone: 502-564-3400
Vice President: GREG DUFFY, Director, Oklahoma Dept. of Conservation; 1801 North Lincoln, Oklahoma City, OK 73105; Phone: 405-521-4660
Executive Secretary: ROBERT M. BRANTLY, 7221 Covey Trace, Tallahassee, FL 32308; Phone: 850-893-1204
Secretary-Treasurer: BILL WOODFIN, Director, Virginia Dept. of Game and Inland Fisheries, 4010 W. Broad St., Richmond, VA 23230; Phone: 804-367-1000
Keyword(s): Biology, Fisheries, Forest Management, Wildlife and Wildlife Habitat, Wildlife Management

SOUTHEASTERN COOPERATIVE WILDLIFE DISEASE STUDY
College of Veterinary Medicine University of Georgia, Athens, GA 30602
Phone: 706-542-1741; Fax: 706-542-5865
Founded: 1957
Scope: National
Description: The first regional diagnostic and research service in the U.S. for the specific purpose of investigating wildlife diseases. This joint-state organization currently is sponsored by the Southeastern Association of Fish and Wildlife Agencies; Veterinary Services of APHIS, USDA; and the Biological Resources Division of USDI. Participating states: AL, AR, FL, GA, KY, LA, MD, MO, MS, NC, PR, SC, TN, VA, WV.
Contact(s):
Director: VICTOR F. NETTLES
Publication(s): *SCWDS BRIEFS Newsletter*
Keyword(s): Agriculture, Environmental and Conservation Education, Health and Nutrition, Wildlife Disease, Wildlife Management

SOUTHEASTERN FISHES COUNCIL
c/o U.S.D.A. Forest Service; Southern Research Station; 1000 Front St., Oxford, FL 38655-4915
Scope: National
Description: Objectives are to provide for the pursuit and transmittal of information on the status and protection of southeastern fishes and their habitats, and to promote the perpetuation of rich natural assemblages of fishes and their habitats, as well as the localized unique forms and their habitats.
Contact(s):
Chair: DR. MELVIN L. WARREN, JR., USDA Forest Service; Southern Research Station; 1000 Front Street, Oxford, MS 38655-4915
Secretary: GERRY DINKINS, 3D International Environmental Group, 7039 Maynardville Highway, Knoxville, TN 37830-7976
Treasurer: DR. MARY C. FREEMAN, U.S. Geological Survey, Biological Resources Division, Institute of Ecology, University of Georgia, Athens, GA 30602
Editor: DR. MICHAEL M. STEVENSON, Department of Biological Sciences, University of New Orleans, New Orleans, LA 70148; Phone: 504-286-7057
Past Chair: DR. STEPHEN J. WALSH
Publication(s): *Proceedings of the Southeastern Fishes Council*
Keyword(s): Aquatic Habitats, Biodiversity, Conservation of Protected Areas, Endangered and Threatened Species, Fisheries, Natural History, Rivers, Watersheds

SOUTHERN AFRICAN INSTITUTE OF FORESTRY
Postnet Suite 329, P/Bag X4, Menlo Park, Pretoria 0102 South Africa
Phone: 2712-3481745
Founded: 1967; Membership: 550
Scope: International
Description: Represents professional forestry science at all levels in silviculture, forestry conservation, and timber processing, and disseminates information about forestry inside and outside of the profession.
Contact(s):
President: W. S. OLIVIER
Vice President: P. L. KIME
Secretary: C. VILJOEN
Publicity Officer: DR. D. W. VAN DER ZEL, P.O. Box 1673, Pretoria, 0001 South Africa; Phone: 271-254-59269
Publication(s): *Southern African Forestry Journal; South African Forestry Handbook*

SOUTHERN ENVIRONMENTAL LAW CENTER
201 W. Main St. Suite 14, Charlottesville, VA 22902-5065
Phone: 804-977-4090; Fax: 804-977-1483; Email: selcva@selcva.org
Founded: 1985; Membership: 2,000
Scope: National
Description: A regional nonprofit public interest advocacy organization committed to protecting the natural resources of the southeast through direct advocacy in court and before regulatory agencies; through assistance to state and local environmental groups in the region; and through providing regional leadership on key southeastern environmental issues.
Contact(s):
Vice President: TERENCE Y. SIEG
Secretary: MARY RICE
Treasurer: FREDERICK S. MIDDLETON III
Executive Director: FREDERICK S. MIDDLETON III; Phone: 804-977-4090
Board Officers and Chairman of the Board of Trustees: DEADERICK C. MONTAGUE
Communications Coordinator: CATHRYN McCUE; Phone: 804-977-4090
Director of Carolinas Office: LARK HAYES; Phone: 919-967-1450
Publication(s): *Energy 2000: A Blueprint for an Energy Efficient Virginia; Energy Choices: A Primer on Electric Utility Industry Restructuring; Citizen's Guides to Protecting Wetlands in South*

Carolina, Alabama, and Georgia; *Visual Pollution and Sign Control; A Legal Handbook on Billboard Control; Southern Resources* (newsletter); *Southeast Energy New* (newsletter).
Keyword(s): Acid Rain, Air Quality and Pollution, Coasts, Energy, Energy Conservation, Environmental Law, Forests and Forestry, Land Preservation, Natural Areas, Open Space, Planning Management, Public Lands, Transportation, Water Pollution Management, Wetlands

SOUTHERN ENVIRONMENTAL LAW CENTER (North Carolina Office)
137 E. Franklin St. Suite 404, Chapel Hill, NC 27514-3628
Phone: 919-967-1450; Fax: 919-929-9421; Email: selcnc@selcnc.org
Scope: National

SOUTHERN NEW ENGLAND FOREST CONSORTIUM, INC.
P.O. Box 760, Chepachet, RI 02816
Phone: 401-568-1610; Fax: 401-568-7874
Founded: 1985
Scope: Regional
Description: The SNEFCI promotes wise conservation practices in Southern New England. Our goals are to reduce forest fragmentation, promote stewardship of forest resources, and enhance urban and community forst resources.
Contact(s):
President: THOMAS DuPREE; Phone: 401-277-1414; Fax: 401-647-3590
Vice President: DONALD SMITH; Phone: 860-424-3630; Fax: 860-424-4070
Secretary: GAIL MICHAELS; Phone: 603-868-7694; Fax: 603-868-7604
Treasurer: HANS BERGEY; Phone: 401-821-8746; Fax: 401-821-8746
Executive Director: CHRISTOPHER MODISETTE; Phone: 401-568-1610; Fax: 401-568-7874
Publication(s): *Your Family Land: Legacy or Memory; Your Family Lands: Legacy or Memory: Commonly Asked Questions; Cost of Community Services in Southern New England; Foresters and The Care of Your Land*
Keyword(s): Forest Management, Planning Management, Urban Forestry

SOUTHERN UTAH WILDERNESS ALLIANCE (Moab Office)
P.O.Box 968, Moab, UT 84532-0968
Phone: 801-259-5440
Scope: Statewide

SOUTHERN UTAH WILDERNESS ALLIANCE (St. George Office)
P.O. Box 1726, Cedar City, UT 84721
Scope: Statewide

SOUTHERN UTAH WILDERNESS ALLIANCE (SUWA)
Headquarters, 1471 S. 1100 E., Salt Lake City, UT 84105-2423
Phone: 801-486-3161
Founded: 1983; Membership: 25,000
Scope: Statewide
Description: SUWA advocates wilderness preservation for qualifying federal public lands in Utah's incomparable canyon country. Through the allied efforts of SUWA's staff, Utah activists, and concerned citizens across the United States, SUWA seeks to give its members and the general public a voice in deciding the fate of America's redrock wilderness.
Contact(s):
Chairman: HANSJORG WYSS
Secretary: JAMES MARTIN
Treasurer: MARK RISTOW
Executive Director: MIKE MATZ
Vice Chairman: TED WILSON
Publication(s): *Quarterly newsletter; bulletins*

SOUTHERN UTAH WILDERNESS ALLIANCE (Washington, DC Office)
215 Pennsylvania Ave., SE, Washington, DC 20002
Phone: 202-546-2215
Scope: Statewide

SOUTHFACE ENERGY INSTITUTE
241 Pine St., Atlanta, GA 30308
Phone: 404-872-3549; Fax: 404-872-5009; Email: info@southface.org; WWW: www.southface.org
Founded: 1978; Membership: 350
Scope: Regional
Description: The Southface is a nonprofit organization that promotes the use of sustainable energy and environmental technologies and policies in the building sciences through education, research, and technical assistance.
Contact(s):
President: TILLMAN DOUGLAS; Email: tillman@inweb.net
Executive Director: DENNIS CREECH; Email: dcreech@southface.org
Publication(s): *The Southface Journal of Energy and Building Technology; A Builder's Guide to Energy Efficient Homes in Georgia; Home Energy Projects*
Keyword(s): Energy Conservation, Environment, Internships, Sustainable Development

SOUTHWEST CENTER FOR BIOLOGICAL DIVERSITY
P.O. Box 710, Tuscon, AZ 85702-0710
Phone: 520-623-5252; Fax: 520-623-9797; Email: swcbd@sw-center.org; WWW: www.sw-center.org
Founded: 1989; Membership: 4,200
Scope: Regional
Description: The Southwest Center for Biological Diversity uses a combination of scientific research, public education, and strategic litigation to defend the Southwest's forests, rivers, and deserts.
Contact(s):
Conservation Chair: DR. ROBIN SILVER; Phone: 602-246-4170; Fax: 602-249-2576; Email: rsilver@sw-center.org
President and Executive Director: KIERAN SUCKLING; Email: ksuckling@sw-center.org
Publication(s): *Wild Southwest, The; Action Alerts of the SW Center For Biologival Diversity*
Keyword(s): Biodiversity, Deserts, Endangered and Threatened Species, Forest Management, Mining, Public Lands, Watersheds

SOUTHWEST RESEARCH AND INFORMATION CENTER
P.O. Box 4524, Albuquerque, NM 87106
Phone: 505-346-1455; Fax: 505-346-1459; Email: sric@igc.org; WWW: www.sric.org
Founded: 1971
Scope: National
Description: SRIC is a nonprofit organization founded to provide timely, accurate information to the public on a broad range of issues related to the environment, human, and natural resources. SRIC's twin objectives are to promote citizen participation and environmental justice, and to protect natural resources.
Contact(s):
President: MARY ANN TSOSIE
Vice President: ANNE ALBRINK
Secretary: LALORA CHARLES
Treasurer: WILFRED RAEL
Administrator: DON HANCOCK
Publication(s): *Workbook, The*
Keyword(s): Environmental Justice, Mining, Water Pollution

SPORTSMAN'S ALLIANCE OF MAINE
R.R. 1, Box 1174, Church Hill Rd., Augusta, ME 04330-9749
Phone: 207-622-5503
Founded: 1975; Membership: 13,202
Scope: Statewide
Description: SAM is a statewide nonprofit organization of sportsmen and women dedicated to hunting, fishing, trapping,

NON-GOVERNMENTAL ORGANIZATIONS

protection of wildlife habitat, and conservation. Lobbies and works with state agencies on behalf of Maine sportsmen.
Contact(s):
President: EDYE CRONK
Treasurer: RICHARD PARADIS
1st Vice President: JAMES HILLY
2nd Vice President: ROBERT CRAM
Executive Director and Editor: GEORGE A. SMITH
Secretary and Clerk: HERBERT MORSE
Publication(s): SAM NEWS

SPORTSMAN'S NETWORK, INC., THE
111 South Main St., P.O. Box 257, Dry Ridge, KY 41035
Phone: 606-824-6526; Fax: 606-824-0556
Founded: 1991; **Membership:** 1.5
Scope: Statewide
Description: The Sportsman's Network is a statewide nonprofit conservation organization dedicated to educating the public and raising awareness of the need for wildlife conservation, through controlled hunting, fishing, and other related programs. Also promotes "A Moment in Conservation" radio program.
Contact(s):
Vice President: GARY PFERRMAN
Secretary: PAUL COOKENDORFER
Treasurer: WILLIAM A. KREBS
State Chairman: PETER O. SAMPLES
Keyword(s): Hunting, Land Preservation, Nature Preservation, Rehabilitation, Rivers, Sport Fishing, Training, Trapping, Wetlands, Wildlands, Wildlife and Wildlife Habitat, Wildlife Management

ST. REGIS MOHAWK TRIBE
Environment Division Community Bldg., Hogansburg, NY 13655
Phone: 518-358-5937; Fax: 518-358-6252
Scope: National
Description: To monitor, maintain, and protect the environment of the St. Regis Mohawk Tribe for the prevention of disease and injury to body, mind, and spirit. Participation in hazardous waste remediation, Superfund site cleanups, reservation environmental protection, and air and water quality.
Contact(s):
Akwesasne Library/Cultural Center Librarian: CAROL WHITE
Assistant Director of Environment Division: LES BENEDICT
Director of Environment Division: KEN JOCK
Publication(s): Iroquois Environmental Newsletter
Keyword(s): Environmental Protection

STANFORD ENVIRONMENTAL LAW SOCIETY
Stanford Law School, Stanford, CA 94305
Phone: 415-723-4421
Founded: 1969
Scope: Statewide
Description: The Stanford Environmental Law Society is the oldest student organization of its kind in the United States. Its primary function is sponsorship of original research in developing areas of environmental law. The Society relies on contributions, grants, and proceeds from the sale of publications.
Contact(s):
Board Officer: CRAIG GARBY
Board Officer: DAVID ADELMAN
Board Officer: ERIC FROTHINGHAM
Board Officer: AMY SPENCE
Publication(s): Stanford Environmental Law Journal; Endangered Species Act, The: A Guide to its Protections and Implementation; Hazardous Waste Disposal Sites; Who Runs the Rivers?

STATE AND TERRITORIAL AIR POLLUTION PROGRAM ADMINISTRATORS AND THE ASSOCIATION OF LOCAL AIR POLLUTION CONTROL OFFICIALS (STAPPA and ALAPCO
444 N. Capitol St. NW Suite 307, Washington, DC 20001
Phone: 202-624-7864
Founded: 1980; **Membership:** STAPPA 55/ALAPCO 210
Scope: National
Description: The national associations of air pollution control agencies in the states, territories, and major metropolitan areas. The associations' members have primary responsibility for ensuring healthy air quality and represent the technical expertise behind the implementation of our nation's air pollution control laws and regulations.
Contact(s):
Executive Director: S. WILLIAM BECKER
Publication(s): Meeting the 15% Rate of Progress Requirement Under The Clean Air Act: A Menu of Options (1993); <S> Controlling Nitrogen Oxides Under The Clean Air Act: A Menu of Options (1994); Controlling Particulate Matter Under The Clean Air Act: A Menu of Options (1
Keyword(s): Acid Rain, Air Quality and Pollution, Environment, Greenhouse Effect/Global Warming, Pollution Prevention

STATEWIDE PROGRAM OF ACTION TO CONSERVE OUR ENVIRONMENT (SPACE
N.H.'s Current Use Coalition, 54 Portsmouth St., Concord, NH 03301
Phone: 603-224-3306
Founded: 1966
Scope: Statewide
Description: A private, not-for-profit advocacy coalition of groups dedcated to conserving open space land. S.P.A.C.E.'s work includes advocacy, education, supporting research and working with the state, towns, and individuals on the administration and monitoring of the current use program.
Contact(s):
Chairman: DENNIS D. McKENNEY, 569 N. Bennington Rd., Bennington, NH 03442-4505
Treasurer: KENNETH MARSHALL, 169 N. Main St., Boscawen, NH 03303
Clerk: JOHN BARTO ESQ, Christian Mutual Bldg., 6 Loudon Rd., Concord, NH 03301
Publication(s): SPACE Newsletter
Keyword(s): Land Preservation

STEAMBOATERS, THE
P.O. Box 176, Idleyld Park, OR 97447
Phone: 503-496-3003
Founded: 1966; **Membership:** 400
Scope: National
Description: Formed to preserve, promote, and restore the natural production of wild fish populations, the habitat which sustains them, and the unique aesthetic values of the North Umpqua River for present and future generations.
Contact(s):
President: JIM WATSON; Phone: 541-496-3512; Email: samnjim@rosenet.net
Vice President: LEN JANSSEN; Phone: 541-440-9375
Secretary: CHARLIE SPOONER
Treasurer: PAUL MOORE
Keyword(s): Biodiversity, Endangered and Threatened Species, Environmental and Conservation Education, Environmental Law, Planning Management

STOP

130-651 Notre Dame West, Montreal, Quebec H3C 1H9
Canada
Phone: 514-393-9559; Fax: 514-393-9588
Founded: 1970; Membership: 200
Scope: Statewide
Description: Devoted to preserving and improving the quality of the physical and human environment, and to promoting rational utilization of natural resources.
Contact(s):
President: GEORGES HEBERT
Research Director: BRUCE WALKER
Publication(s): *Stop Press*
Keyword(s): Acid Rain, Air Quality and Pollution, Chemical Pollution Control, Environmental and Conservation Education, Solid Waste Management, Toxic Substances, Transportation, Urban Environment, Water Pollution

STRIPERS UNLIMITED INC.

P.O. Box 3045, S. Attleboro, MA 02703
Phone: 508-761-7983; Fax: 508-761-7973
Founded: 1965
Scope: National
Description: Nonprofit organization formed to promote, conserve, and protect striped bass and to protect and restore its environment. Promotes and encourages research on striped bass in order to preserve it as a natural resource and to increase its areas of reproduction. Members in 21 states and two Canadian provinces.
Contact(s):
President: NORMAN WHIFFEN, 24 Ellsworth Terr., Lynn, MA 01904
Treasurer: ROBERT B. POND, P.O. Box 3045, S. Attleboro, MA 02703; Phone: 508-761-7983
Executive Director: ROBERT B. POND
Executive Secretary: AVIS E. BOYD, P.O. Box 3166, S. Attleboro, MA 02703; Phone: 508-761-4627
Editor: AVIS E. BOYD
Publication(s): *Newsletter in North East Woods & Waters, monthly*
Keyword(s): Environmental and Conservation Education, Fisheries, Sport Fishing, Toxic Substances, Water Pollution

STUDENT CONSERVATION ASSOCIATION, INC.

National Headquarters, Box 550, Charlestown, NH 03603
Phone: 603-543-1700; Fax: 603-543-1828; Email: earthwork@sca-inc.org; WWW: www.sca-inc.org
Founded: 1957; Membership: 24,000
Scope: National
Description: SCA was founded by Elizabeth Titus Putnam in 1957 and continues to be guided by two premises: high school and college-age men and women volunteers can accomplish a variety of conservation tasks vital to the protection of America's natural resources, and the experience gained by these volunteers can significantly impact their education, personal development, and career goals.
Contact(s):
President: DALE PENNY
Chair of the Board: JOHN R. TWISS JR.
Chief Financial Officer: MARK BODIN
Editor: LISA YOUNGER
Executive Vice President: VALERIE J. SHAND
Founding President: ELIZABETH C. TITUS
SCA California Office: , 655 13th St., Suite 304, Oakland, CA 94612; Phone: 510-832-1966
SCA Capital Office: , 1800 N. Kent St., Suite 1260, Arlington, VA 22209; Phone: 703-524-2441
SCA Inter-Mountain Office: , 1370 Pennsylvania Ave., Suite 330, Denver, CO 80302; Phone: 303-831-7172
SCA Newark Office: , P.O. Box 32369, 24 Commerce St., Suite 1430, Newark, NJ 07102; Phone: 973-733-4450
SCA Northwest Office: , 605 13th Ave., Seattle, WA 98122; Phone: 206-324-4760
Vice President of Development: ROBERT D. HOLLEY
Vice President of Programs: SCOTT C. WEAVER
Publication(s): *Earth Work*
Keyword(s): Careers, Cultural Preservation, Environment, Environmental and Conservation Education, Internships, People of Color in the Environment, Public Lands, Renewable Resources, Youth Organizations

STUDENT ENVIRONMENTAL ACTION COALITION (SEAC)

P.O. Box 31909, Philadelphia, PA 19104
Phone: 215-222-4711; Fax: 215-222-2896; Email: seac@seac.org; WWW: www.seac.org
Founded: 1988; Membership: 2,000
Scope: National
Description: SEAC is a national student-run and student-led network of progressive organizations and individuals whose aim is to uproot environmental injustices through action and education. We define the environment to include the physical, economical, political, and cultural conditions in which we live. By challenging the power structure which threatens these environmental conditions, SEAC works to create progressive social change on both the local and global levels.
Publication(s): *Threshold*
Keyword(s): Environmental Justice, Social Justice, Solid Waste Management, Wilderness, Youth Organizations

STUDENT PUGWASH USA

815 15th St. NW Suite 814, Washington, DC 20005
Phone: 202-393-6555; Fax: 202-393-6550; Email: spusa@spusa.org
Scope: National
Description: The mission of Student Pugwash USA is to promote the socially-responsible application of science and technology in the 21st century. As a student organization, Student Pugwash USA encourages young people to examine the ethical, social, and global implications of science and technology, and to make these concerns a guiding focus of their academic and professional endeavors.
Contact(s):
Executive Director: SANDRA IONNO
Executive Committee Chairman: CONSTANCE PECHURA
Publication(s): *Jobs You Can Live With: Working at the Crossroads of Science, Technology, and Society; Tough Questions; Pugwatch; mindfull: a brainsnack for future leaders with ethical appetites; Global Issues Guidebook*
Keyword(s): Biotechnology, Communications, Energy, Environmental and Conservation Education, Nuclear/Radiation

SUNCOAST SEABIRD SANCTUARY INC.

18328 Gulf Blvd., Indian Shores, FL 33785
Phone: 727-391-6211; Fax: 727-399-2923
Founded: 1972; Membership: 30,000
Scope: National
Description: A private, nonprofit, membership organization dedicated to the rescue, repair, recuperation, and release of healed sick and injured wild birds. The Sanctuary treats and releases over 9,000 birds each year. It provides a safe home for over 600 permanently injured avian species. The Sanctuary is open for visitation every day from 9:00 a.m. till dusk. Guided tours available - free admission.
Contact(s):
Secretary: KEITH RINGELSPAUGH, 3347 49th St. N., St. Petersburg, FL 33710; Phone: 727-525-1958
Treasurer: HELEN B. HEATH, 18383 Sunset Blvd., Redington Shores, FL 33708; Phone: 727-393-0933
Founder and Director: RALPH T. HEATH JR., 18323 Sunset Blvd., Redington Shores, FL 33708; Phone: 727-391-6211
Publication(s): *Suncoast Seabird Sanctuary Newsletter; S.S.S. Brochure (Blue); If You Find A Baby Bird Book*
Keyword(s): Birds, Endangered and Threatened Species, Environmental and Conservation Education, Waterfowl, Wildlife Rehabilitation

NON-GOVERNMENTAL ORGANIZATIONS

TAHOE REGIONAL PLANNING AGENCY
308 Dorla Ct. P.O. Box 1038, Zephyr Cove, NV 89448-1038
Phone: 702-588-4547
Founded: 1969
Scope: National
Description: To establish and implement land use and environmental plans and regulations in the Lake Tahoe Region. Established by Public Law No. 91-148, December 1969, amended by Public Law No. 96-551, December 1980.
Contact(s):
Executive Director: JIM BAETGE
Legal Counsel: JOHN MARSHALL
Legal Counsel: SUSAN SCHOLLEY
Keyword(s): Air Quality and Pollution, Lakes, Land Use Planning, Water Pollution, Wetlands

TALL TIMBERS RESEARCH INC.
Rt. 1 Box 678, Tallahassee, FL 32312-9712
Phone: 904-893-4153
Founded: 1958; Membership: 2,100
Scope: National
Description: A nonprofit, tax-exempt scientific and educational organization with a focus on land management, conservation, ecological research, and fire ecology. Information is exchanged in print and on the Internet. Tall Timbers provides publications, seminars, conferences and training programs for land owners and managers, scholars, research scientists, students and concerned citizens.
Contact(s):
Chairman: WALTER C. SEDGWICK
Secretary: LOUISE HUMPHREY
Treasurer: GEORGE R. LANGFORD
Executive Director: LANE GREEN
Development Director: SHARON A. LIGGETT
Librarian: ANN BRUCE, Tall Timbers Library, ; Fax: 904-668-7781
Research Director: DR. LEONARD A. BRENNAN
Vice Chairperson: KATE IRELAND
Publication(s): *Newsletters, annual reports, proceedings, technical reports, and informational bulletins.Services: Literature and data searches, publications and periodicals.*
Keyword(s): Endangered and Threatened Species, Environmental and Conservation Education, Flowers, Plants, and Trees, Wildlife and Wildlife Habitat, Wildlife Management

TALLAHASSEE MUSEUM OF HISTORY AND NATURAL SCIENCE
3945 Museum Dr., Tallahassee, FL 32310
Phone: 850-575-8684; Fax: 850-574-8243; WWW: www.tallahasseemuseum.org
Founded: 1957; Membership: 5,000
Scope: Statewide
Description: To educate residents and visitors of Tallahassee and the Big Bend area about the region's natural and cultural history, from the beginning of the 19th-century until the present. For this purpose, the museum collects, preserves, and exhibits artifacts and historic buildings, maintains native animals in natural habitats, and operates a 19th century farmstead.
Contact(s):
Curator of Animals: MIKE JONES
Curator of Collections and Exhibits: LINDA DEATON
Director of Education: JENNIFER GOLDEN
Director of Institutional Advancement: JANET BORNEMAN
Executive Director/CEO: RUSSELL DAWS
Publication(s): *The Newsletter of The Tallahassee Museum of History and Natural Science*
Keyword(s): Biodiversity, Culture, Ecology, Endangered and Threatened Species, Environment, Environmental and Conservation Education, Historic Preservation, Mammals, Natural Areas, Natural History, Nongame Wildlife, Zoological Parks, Zoology

TEENS FOR RECREATION AND ENVIRONMENTAL CONSERVATION (TREC)
Seattle Department of Parks and Recreation, 100 Dexter Ave., N., Seattle, WA 98109-5199
Phone: 206-684-7097; Fax: 206-684-7025; Email: robert.warner@Cl.Seattle.WA.US; WWW: www.wawebsites.com/trec
Founded: 1992; Membership: 80 active teen/500-600 teens throughout the community
Scope: Statewide
Description: TREC is an outdoor expedition-level program designed to expose multi-ethnic teens to environmental education, urban conservation, and stewardship, while creating an environment for community leadership and empowerment.
Contact(s):
Contact: ROBERT WARNER

TENNESSEE ASSOCIATION OF CONSERVATION DISTRICTS
ATTN: President, 2205 Armour Dr. Rt2, Box 372, Somerville, TN 38068
Scope: Statewide
Contact(s):
President: HARRIS A. ARMOUR III, 2205 Armour Dr. Rt. 2, Box 372, Somerville, TN 38068; Phone: 901-465-9684
Vice President: ROY GILLS, 419 Nofattie Rd., Limestone, TN 37615; Phone: 423-257-2305
Executive Director: MISSY L. KILGORE, 144 Southeast Parkway #210, Franklin, TN 37064; Phone: 615-595-9979; Fax: 615-595-9982
Board Member: JOHN CHARLES WILSON, 560 Orr Rd., Arlington, TN 38002; Phone: 901-867-8289
Secretary-Treasurer: BARRY LAKE, P.O. Box 107, Hickory Valley, TN 38042; Phone: 901-764-2909

TENNESSEE B.A.S.S. CHAPTER FEDERATION
ATTN: President, P.O. Box 246, Waverly, TN 37185
Phone: 931-296-4428
Scope: Statewide
Description: An organization of Bassmaster chapters, affiliated with the Bass Anglers Sportsman Society, organized to fight pollution, assist state and national conservation agencies in their efforts, and teach the young people of our country good conservation practices. Dedicated to the realistic conservation of our water resources.
Contact(s):
President: CHARLES MITCHELL, P.O. Box 246, Waverly, TN 37185; Phone: 931-296-4428; Email: cjmitchell@waverly.net
Conservation Director: ERIC NEWBERRY, 2853 Crooked Oak Dr., Lenore City, TN 37771; Phone: 423-986-6864
Publication(s): *Chapter Newsletter*
Keyword(s): Aquatic Habitats, Fisheries

TENNESSEE CITIZENS FOR WILDERNESS PLANNING
130 Tabor Rd., Oak Ridge, TN 37830
Phone: 615-482-2153
Founded: 1966; Membership: 400
Scope: Statewide
Description: Dedicated to achieving and perpetuating protection of natural lands and waters by means of public ownership, legislation, or cooperation with the private sector. Our first focus is the Cumberland and Appalachian regions of East Tennessee, but efforts may extend to the rest of the state and the nation.
Contact(s):
President: JIMMY GROTON, 87 Outer Dr., Oak Ridge, TN 37830; Phone: 423-482-5799
Vice President: ERIC HIRST, 106 Capital Cir., Oak Ridge, TN 37830; Phone: 423-483-1289
Secretary: TOM THORNBURGH, 94 Tempura Dr., Oak Ridge, TN 37830; Phone: 423-483-8761
Treasurer: CHARLES KLABUNDE, 219 E. Vanderbilt Dr., Oak Ridge, TN 37830; Phone: 423-483-8055
Executive Director: MARCY REED, 657 W. Outer Dr., Oak Ridge, TN 37830; Phone: 423-481-0623

Editor: LIANE B. RUSSELL, 130 Tabor Rd., Oak Ridge, TN 37830; Phone: 423-482-2153
Publication(s): *TCWP Newsletter*
Keyword(s): Biodiversity, Forest Management, Natural Areas, Nongame Wildlife, Public Lands, Rivers, Water Resources, Watersheds, Wilderness

TENNESSEE CONSERVATION LEAGUE
300 Orlando Ave., Nashville, TN 37209-3257
Phone: 615-353-1133; Fax: 615-353-0083; Email: conserve.tcl@nashville.com
Scope: *Statewide*
Description: A representative statewide organization, affiliated with the National Wildlife Federation, dedicated to the protection and enhancement of wildlife and its habitat through public education and government interaction.
Contact(s):
President: DICK URBAN
Executive Director: ANN P. MURRAY
Alternate Representative: MIKE PEARIGEN
Editor: SUE GARNER
Publication(s): *Tennessee Out-of-Doors*
Keyword(s): Aquatic Habitats, Fisheries, Renewable Resources, Water Pollution Management, Wetlands

TENNESSEE ENVIRONMENTAL COUNCIL
1700 Hayes St., Suite 101, Nashville, TN 37203
Phone: 615-321-5075; Fax: 615-321-5082; Email: tec@nol.com
Founded: *1970; Membership: 44 organizations, 2,200 individuals*
Scope: *Statewide*
Description: A nonprofit coalition working to protect and improve Tennessee's public health, quality of life,, and natural heritage. TEC is a 28-year old organiaztion, focused on carrying out the state's environmental policies and regulations on behalf of Tennessee citizens.
Contact(s):
President: PATRICK WILLARD; Phone: 615-297-7243
Secretary: SANDI KURTZ; Phone: 423-892-4403
Treasurer: DR. WILLIAM R. MILLER III; Phone: 931-486-9504
Executive Director: ALAN JONES
Publication(s): *ProTECt*
Keyword(s): Air Quality and Pollution, Chemical Pollution Control, Environment, Environmental Justice, Environmental Protection, Forest Management, Planning Management, Public Health Protection, Solid Waste Management, Sustainable Development, Toxic Substances, Water Pollution

TENNESSEE FORESTRY ASSOCIATION
P.O. Box 290693, Nashville, TN 37229
Phone: 615-883-3832
Founded: *1951*
Scope: *Statewide*
Description: A nonprofit conservation group of about 1300 woodland owners, public and private foresters, educators, and wood using companies, as well as individual citizens and allied businesses, encouraging the development and wise use of Tennessee's forest resources.
Contact(s):
President: WALLACE JOHNSTON
Vice President: STEVE MAVNEY
Vice President: WAYNE TURNER
Vice President: BUSTER JOHNSON
1st Vice President: JOE SAVERY

TENNESSEE WOODLAND OWNERS ASSOCIATION
P.O. Box 1400, Crossville, TN 38557
Phone: 615-484-5535
Founded: *1976; Membership: 80*
Scope: *Statewide*
Description: A statewide organization affiliated with the National Woodland Owners Association to focus on the special needs and concerns of non-industrial private forest owners throughout Tennessee and to promote responsible resource sttewardhip.

TERRENE INSTITUTE, THE
4 Herbert St., Alexandria, VA 22305
Phone: 703-548-5473; Fax: 703-548-6299; Email: terrinst@aol.com; WWW: www.terrence.org
Founded: *1990*
Scope: *National*
Description: The Terrene Institute is a nonprofit organization that works with corporate, environmental, and government partners to promote innovative and economical solutions for improving environmental quality. Terrene is an environmental education organization that develops conferences, issues forums, and publications that serve both corporate and nonprofit audiences. Terrene's principal work is in wetlands, including the coordination of American Wetlands Month activities, and nonpoint source water quality. A catlaog of Terrene publications is available.
Contact(s):
President: DR. WILLIAM FUNK, 330 Kimball SW, Pullman, WA 99163; Phone: 509-335-5531
Executive Director: CHRISTOPHER A. NOVAK, 4 Herbert St., Alexandria, VA 22305; Phone: 703-548-5473; Email: c-novak@erols.com
Publication(s): *Terrene publishes the newsletter "Runoff Report".Ask for catalog of books, posters, and other products.*
Keyword(s): Water Resources, Watersheds, Wetlands

TEXAS ASSOCIATION OF SOIL AND WATER CONSERVATION DISTRICTS
ATTN: President, Rt. 1 Box 3238, New Waverly, TX 77358
Scope: *Statewide*
Contact(s):
President: WAYNE REGISTER, Rt 1 Box 3283, New Waverly, TX 77358; Phone: 713-237-9793; Fax: 713-237-1209
Secretary: BEATRICE E. WHITE, P.O. Box 658, Temple, TX 76503; Phone: 254-778-8741; Fax: 254-773-3311
Secretary-Treasurer: DAYTON ELAM, Rt. # Box 66AA, Seminole, TX 79360; Phone: 915-758-3504
Vice President, Board Member: JOHN EARL SMITH, Rt 1 Box 57, Quemado, TX 78877; Phone: 830-757-1233
Publication(s): *Big Bend Paisano, The; official park newspaper; Big Bend seminars and sales catalog available on request.*

TEXAS B.A.S.S. CHAPTER FEDERATION
ATTN: President, 10301 NW Freeway 302, Houston, TX 77092
Phone: 281-807-1625
Scope: *Statewide*
Description: An organization of Bassmaster chapters, affiliated with the Bass Anglers Sportsman Society, organized to fight pollution, assist state and national conservation agencies in their efforts, and teach the young people of our country good conservation practices. Dedicated to the realistic conservation of our water resources.
Contact(s):
President: RANDY KINDLER, 10301 NW Freeway 302, Houston, TX 77092; Phone: 281-807-1625
Conservation Director: ALAN ALLEN, 807 Brazos Suite 311, Austin, TX 78701; Phone: 512-472-2267
Publication(s): *Conservation Progress; Forest Reform Network Newsletter*
Keyword(s): Environmental and Conservation Education, Forests and Forestry, Rivers, Water Resources, Wilderness

NON-GOVERNMENTAL ORGANIZATIONS

TEXAS COMMITTEE ON NATURAL RESOURCES
601 Westlake Dr., Austin, TX 78746
Phone: 512-327-4119; Fax: 512-328-3399; Email: tconr@eden.com; WWW: www.eden.com/tconr
Founded: 1968
Scope: Statewide
Description: A representative statewide organization, affiliated with the National Wildlife Federation, dedicated to the protection and enhancement of wildlife and its habitat through public education and government interaction.
Contact(s):
Chairman: DAVID GRAY
Executive Director: JANICE BEZANSON
Affiliate Representative: DR. EARL MATTHEW

TEXAS FORESTRY ASSOCIATION
P.O. 1488, Lufkin, TX 75902-1488
Phone: 409-632-TREE
Founded: 1914
Scope: Statewide
Description: Private nonprofit statewide organization promoting the conservation, fullest economic development, and utilization of forest and related resources.
Contact(s):
President: TOMMY BURCH, B&W Contractors, Brookeland, TX
Executive Vice President: RONALD H. HUFFORD
Publication(s): *TOES News & Notes*
Keyword(s): Biodiversity, Endangered and Threatened Species, Environmental and Conservation Education, Reforestation, Scholarships and Grants, Sustainability

TEXAS ORGANIZATION FOR ENDANGERED SPECIES
P.O. Box 12773, Austin, TX 78711-2773
Founded: 1972; Membership: 275
Scope: Statewide
Description: A nonprofit statewide organization dedicated to the conservation of endangered, threatened, or rare species and biotic communities of Texas.
Contact(s):
President: GARY VALENTINE; Phone: 254-297-1291
Secretary: DEBORAH HOLLE; Phone: 512-482-5700
Treasurer: C. LEE SHERROD; Phone: 512-328-2430
Chair of Conservation Committee: JASON SINGHURST; Phone: 512-912-7011
Chair of Education Committee: LINDA CAMPBELL; Phone: 512-912-7044
Chair of Natural Resources: PEGGY HOMER; Phone: 512-912-7047
Editor: DAVID LEMKE; Phone: 512-245-2178
Past-President: LEE ANN LINAM; Phone: 512-847-9480
Publication(s): *TOES News & Notes*
Keyword(s): Hunting, Outdoor Recreation, Sustainable Development, Wildlife and Wildlife Habitat, Wildlife Management

TEXAS WILDLIFE ASSOCIATION
1635 NE Loop 410, Suite 108, San Antonio, TX 78209
Phone: 512-826-2904
Founded: 1985; Membership: 5,000
Scope: Statewide
Description: Texas Wildlife Association is a nonprofit corporation, formed to protect and promote the rights of Texas' wildlife managers, land owners, sportsmen, and the state's wildlife resources--especially on private lands.
Contact(s):
President: PAUL E. McSWEEN III; Phone: 210-731-4626
Vice President: JAMES L. HAYNE; Phone: 210-226-2161
Secretary: JOSEPH B.C. FITZSIMONS; Phone: 210-736-2220
Treasurer: JIMMIE V. THURMOND III; Phone: 210-923-4317
Executive Vice President: DAVID K. LANGFORD; Phone: 210-821-3377
Publication(s): *Texas Wildlife*

THE CROSBY ABORETUM, Mississippi State University
P.O. Box 1639, Picayune, MS 39466
Phone: 601-799-2311; Fax: 601-799-2372; Email: crosbyar@datastar.net; WWW: www.crosbyarboretum.org
Founded: 1980; Membership: 700
Scope: Statewide
Description: The main activity of the Arboretum is to preserve, protect and display plants native to the pearl river drainage basin. Additionally, we provide environmental and horticultural research oppurtunities and offer educational, scientific, and recreational programs.
Contact(s):
President: DOUGLAS K. WILDS; Phone: 504-641-9731
Vice President: FAY BRIGHT; Phone: 504-542-9477; Fax: 504-345-1696
Secretary: BERTHA PAGE; Phone: 601-798-3116; Fax: 601-798-5650
Treasurer: STEWART GAMILL III; Phone: 601-264-5246; Fax: 601-271-2064
Executive Director: LARRY G. PARONE; Phone: 601-799-2311; Fax: 601-799-2372
Publication(s): *Native Trees for Urban Landscapes*
Keyword(s): Biodiversity, Conservation, Ecology, Environmental and Conservation Education

THE GLACIER INSTITUTE
P.O. Box 7475, Kalispell, MT 59904
Phone: 406-755-1211; Fax: 406-755-7154; Email: glacinst@digisys.net; WWW: www.digisys.net/glacinst
Founded: 1983
Scope: Statewide
Description: The Glacier Institute serves students of all ages as an educational leader in the Crown of the Continent Ecosystem, emphasizing hands-on, field-based experiences promoting a balanced understanding of the science of ecology and human interaction with the environment.
Contact(s):
President: JODIE JOHNSON
Vice President: DOUG MOREHOUSE
Secretary: SCOTT C. WURSTER
General Manager: KRISTIN RIPPETO BRUNINGA
Program Director: CHRIS BARTH
Program Director: R. J. DEVITT
Keyword(s): Aquatic Habitats, Conservation, Ecology, Geology, Internships, Natural History, Sustainable Ecosystems, Wildlife and Wildlife Habitat

THORNE ECOLOGICAL INSTITUTE
5398 Manhattan Cir., Suite 120, Boulder, CO 80303-4239
Phone: 303-499-3647; Fax: 303-499-8340
Founded: 1954
Scope: National
Description: A nonprofit educational institute creating inovative outdoor learning experiences and other educational opportunities that teach stewardship of the earth to children and adults. The Institute offers a variety of environmental education classes to children from the Boulder, Denver area with science-based activities and exciting hands-on lessons.
Contact(s):
Executive Director: PERI CHICKERING
Chairman of the Board: SHAWN MULLIGAN
Founder and President: DR. OAKLEIGH THORNE II
Keyword(s): Camp, Ecology, Environmental and Conservation Education, Fieldwork, Internships, Natural Science, Watersheds, Wetlands, Wildlife and Wildlife Habitat

THREE CIRCLES CENTER FOR MULTICULTURAL ENVIRONMENTAL EDUCATION

P.O. Box 1946, Sausalito, CA 94965
Phone: 415-331-4540; Email: circlecenter@igc.apc.org

Founded: 1990
Scope: National

Description: Three Circles Center introduces, encourages, and cultivates multicultural perspectives and values in environmental and outdoor education, recreation, and interpretation.

Contact(s):
Executive Director: RUNNING-GRASS, P.O. Box 1946, Sausalito, CA 94965; Phone: 415-331-4540

Publication(s): *Journal of Multicultural Environmental Education; Perspectives; Monographs; Research Papers*

Keyword(s): Culture, Environment, Environmental and Conservation Education, Justice, Training

THRESHOLD INC.

International Center for Environmental Renewal Drawer CU, Bisbee, AZ 85603
Phone: 602-432-7353

Founded: 1972
Scope: National

Description: An independent, nongovernmental, nonprofit, and international center seeking to improve mankind's understanding of and relationship to the environment at five levels: Individual and home, neighborhood, city, bioregion, national, and international. Projects involve environmental research, case studies, planning, education, communication, conferencing, and demonstration activities. A major focus is on the development of ecologically sound alternatives for practical application in human society. Tropical forests protection, acid rain reduction, solar energy, international park planning, wilderness solo retreats, community sacred parks, pollution control, bioregional education, and river basin studies are other major activities.

Contact(s):
Chairman: JOHN P. MILTON; Phone: 602-432-5814
Director of San Francisco Office: JOHN DIAMANTE; Phone: 415-986-0999
Director of Washington, DC Office: CRAIG PERKINS; Phone: 1-800-356-0195
Secretary/Treasurer and Administrative Officer of Arizona Office: LISA SANTA-CRUZ; Phone: 602-432-7353
Vice Chairman: GEORGE A. BINNEY; Phone: 602-398-9163

Keyword(s): Environmental and Conservation Education, International Conservation, Internships, Land Use Planning, Wildlife and Wildlife Habitat

TOGETHER FOUNDATION, THE

130 S. Willard St., Burlington, VT 05401
Phone: 802-862-2030

Founded: 1989; Membership: 1,000
Scope: National

Description: To facilitate positive global change by establishing communications and information systems that inventory and integrate the resources and needs of people, projects, and organizations working on environment, sustainable development, and human rights.

Contact(s):
President: ELLA CISNEROS
Vice President: JAMES MacINTYRE
Secretary: ROBIN RUGG

Publication(s): *The Together Foundation Newsletter*

Keyword(s): Communications, Environmental and Conservation Education, Environmental Planning, Sustainable Development

TRAFFIC USA

c/o World Wildlife Fund, 1250 24th St., NW, Washington, DC 20037
Phone: 202-293-4800; Fax: 202-775-8287

Scope: National

Description: Trade Records Analysis of Flora and Fauna in Commerce is a scientific, information-gathering program that monitors the trade in wild animals and plants and the products made from them. It is a program of World Wildlife Fund and is a part of an international network of TRAFFIC offices.

Contact(s):
Director: GINA DEFERRARI
Director of Program Assistant: HOLLY REED
Program Officer: CHRIS ROBBINS

Publication(s): *TRAFFIC USA; Special Reports*

Keyword(s): Birds, Endangered and Threatened Species, Mammals, Wildlife Management

TREAD LIGHTLY! INC.

298 24th St. Suite 325, Ogden, UT 84401
Phone: 801-627-0077

Founded: 1990
Scope: National

Description: Tread Lightly!, Inc. is a nonprofit organization dedicated to protecting public and private lands through education. Emphasis is placed on responsible use of off-highway vehicles, other forms of backcountry travel, and on low-impact principles applicable to all recreational activities.

Contact(s):
Chairman: ROBERT E. CLEVER, 1919 Torrance Blvd., Torrance, CA 90501-2746; Phone: 310-783-3795
Executive Director: LORI McNEELY, 298 24th St., Suite 325C, Ogden, UT 84401; Phone: 801-627-0077
Secretary and Treasurer: VON KREITZ, 13270 SE Pheasant Court, Milwaukee, OR 97222; Phone: 503-786-4428
Vice Chairman: SUSAN HALBERT, 7100 Connecticut Ave., Chevy Chase, MD 20815-4999; Phone: 301-961-2913

Publication(s): *Tread Lightly! Trails Quarterly Newsletter; Guide to Responsible 4 Wheeling; Guide to Responsible Mountain Biking; Guide to Responsible Dirt Biking*

Keyword(s): Environmental and Conservation Education, Environmental Preservation, International Conservation, Outdoor Recreation, Public Lands

TREE PEOPLE

12601 Mulholland Dr., Beverly Hills, CA 90210
Phone: 818-753-4600

Founded: 1973; Membership: 20,000
Scope: Statewide

Description: Andy Lipkis and his teenage friends became known as the "TreePeople" when they began planting trees to restore a dying forest. Through innovative education and training programs, TreePeople has involved thousands of students and volunteers in neighborhood renewal and community service throughout southern California. Today, TreePeople is at the forefront of the urban forestry movement, offering sustainable solutions for the urban ecosystem.

Contact(s):
President: ANDY LIPKIS
Vice President and Editor: KATIE LIPKIS

Publication(s): *Seedling News; A Planters' Guide to The Urban Forest; TreePeople Membership Newsletter; Simple Act of Planting a Tree, The*

Keyword(s): Environmental and Conservation Education, Forests and Forestry, Urban Environment, Urban Forestry, Youth Organizations

NON-GOVERNMENTAL ORGANIZATIONS

TREES FOR THE FUTURE, INC.
P.O. Box 1786, Silver Spring, MD 20915
Phone: 301-929-0238; Fax: 301-929-0439; Email: treesftf@aol.com; WWW: www.treesftf.org
Founded: 1989; Membership: 6,600
Scope: National
Description: Trees for the Future offers multi-purpose tree seeds, training materials, and technical assistance for requesting communities throughout the developing regions of the world. In addition, Trees for the Future creates awareness of the potential threat of Global Climatic Change and the simple cost-effective solutions of tree-planting to counter the "Global Warming" effect.
Contact(s):
Chairman: DR. JOHN R. MOORE
President: DAVE DEPPNER
Secretary: PATRICIA AIKEN
Treasurer: OSCAR V. GRUSPE
Administrator: DAVID MITZEL
Africa Program Coordinator: PHUONG MAI
Latin America/Caribbean Coordinator: ERIC SPILDE
Vice Chairman: CELSO MATAAC
Women's and Children's Programs: REMEDIOS G. DEPPNER
Publication(s): *Johnny Ipil-Seed News; Technical Papers*
Keyword(s): Agriculture, Air Quality and Pollution, Chemical Pollution Control, Developing Countries, Energy Conservation, Environment, Environmental Planning, Environmental Preservation, Flowers, Plants, and Trees, Greenhouse Effect/Global Warming, International Conservation, Renewable Resources, Rural Development

TREES FOR TOMORROW, INC., NATURAL RESOURCES EDUCATION CENTER
P.O. Box 609, Eagle River, WI 54521
Phone: 715-479-6456/1-800-838-9472; Fax: 715-479-2318
Founded: 1944
Scope: Statewide
Description: Original purpose to help reforest northern Wisconsin and provide land management assistance; currently an education center which conducts multi-day workshops on the sensible management and use of natural resources. Also sells tree seedlings.
Contact(s):
President: DONALD HOLLATZ, Madison Gas and Electric Co. P.O. Box 1231, Madison, WI 53701
Secretary: BILL ZABOR, Procter & Gamble Paper Products, P.O. Box 8020, Green Bay, WI 54308-8020
Treasurer: FRED SOUBA JR., Consolidated Paper, P.O. Box 8050, Wisconsin Rapids, WI 54495-8050
Director: JIM HOLPERIN
President-elect: JON SMITH, Pacific Corp., P.O. Box 190, Tomahawk, WI 54487-0190

TRI-STATE BIRD RESCUE AND RESEARCH, INC.
110 Possum Hollow Rd., Newark, DE 19711
Phone: 302-737-9543; Fax: 302-737-9562
Founded: 1976; Membership: 2,000
Scope: Regional
Description: To study and promote healthy populations of native wildlife by rehabilitation of oiled birds; rehabilitation of injured, diseased, and orphaned birds for release back into the wild; conducting training and education programs for colleagues, peers, and the general public; and conducting medical and biological research consistent with goals of providing for the general well-being of native wildlife.
Contact(s):
President: DR. DAVID D. MOOBERRY, 106 Spottswood Ln., Kennett Square, PA 19348; Phone: 215-444-5495
Vice President: JOHN FRINK, 400 Milton Dr., Wilmington, DE 19802
Secretary: BARBARA DRUDING, 110 Possum Hollow Rd., Newark, DE 19711
Treasurer: MARY ROBINSON, 412 Ribblett Ln., Wilmington, DE 19808; Phone: 302-998-3288
Executive Director: DR. VIRGINIA PIERCE, 110 Possum Hollow Rd., Newark, DE 19711
Contact for Human Resources: JULIE BARTLEY
Publication(s): *Effects of Oil on Wildlife, The; Medical Notes for Rehabilitators; Oiled Bird Rehabilitation; Wildlife and Oil Spills Bulletin; Wildlife and Oil Spills: Rehabilitation, Research, and Contingency Planning*
Keyword(s): Birds, Endangered and Threatened Species, Environmental and Conservation Education, Wildlife Disease, Wildlife Rehabilitation

TROUT UNLIMITED
National Headquarters, 1500 Wilson Blvd., Suite 310, Arlington, VA 22209-2404
Phone: 703-522-0200; Fax: 703-284-9400; Email: trout@tu.org; WWW: http://tu.org
Founded: 1959; Membership: 100,000
Scope: National
Description: A nonprofit, tax-deductible international coldwater fisheries organization dedicated to the conservation, protection, and restoration of coldwater fisheries and their watersheds. Affiliates in Canada, New Zealand, and Australia.
Contact(s):
Chairman of National Resource Board: STEPHEN BORN, 424 Washburn Pl., Madison, WI 53403; Phone: 608-257-6625
Chairman of the Board: GEORGE WIEGERS
Chief Operating and Financial Officer: KENNETH MENDEZ
Conservation Counsel: MONA JANOPAUL
Controller: BRUCE APSLEY
Coordinator of TU and FS: DON DUFF
Director of Development: WHIT FOSBURGH
Director of Government Affairs: STEVEN N. MOYER
Director of Resources: JOSEPH McGURRIN
Editor: CHRISTINE ARENA
Editor: PETER RAFLE
Manager of Membership Services: WENDY G. REED
New Zealand Office President: PHIL GATES, U.S. Trade Commission, U.S. Consulate, Private Bag 92022, Auckland, NewZealand
President and Chief Executive Officer: CHARLES F. GAUVIN
Regional Director of Southern Rockies: DAVID NICKUM, 1900 13th St., Ste 101, Boulder, CO 80302; Phone: 303-440-2937; Fax: 303-440-7933
Regional Vice President of Great Lakes: ELLIOTT OLSON, 1500 Xanthus Ln., N., Plymouth, WI 55447-2563; Phone: 612-835-4505; Email: dakotaww@goldengate.net
Regional Vice President of Mid-Atlantic: LOU SCHMIDT, Rt. 1 Box 109-A, Bristol, WV 26332-9801; Phone: 304-367-2724; Fax: 304-367-2727
Regional Vice President of Midwest: RAY SMITH, 70 N. College Ave., #11, Fayetteville, AR 72701; Phone: 501-521-7011; Fax: 501-443-4333; Email: franksmith@worldnet.att.net
Regional Vice President of New England: DAVID BOWIE, 540 Duck Pond Rd., Westbrook, ME 04092-2510; Phone: 207-854-9978; Email: usunmz6m@ibmmail.com
Regional Vice President of Northeast: THOMAS LOPEZZO, 47 Flintlock Dr., Long Valley, NJ 07835-0320; Phone: 701-765-5673; Email: 72077,1327@compuserve.com
Regional Vice President of Northern Rockies: KIRK EVENSON, P.O. Box 1525, Great Falls, MT 59403-1525; Phone: 406-454-1384; Fax: 406-761-2610; Email: evenson@mch.net
Regional Vice President of Pacific Northwest: RONALD HOLTCAMP, 525 Eskridge Way, Olympia, WA 98501-3451; Phone: 360-902-1709; Email: ahh525@aol.com
Regional Vice President of Southeast: RAY MORTENSEN, 22 Beacon Ridge Cir., Salem, SC 29676-0544; Phone: 864-944-6136; Fax: 864-944-6136; Email: sertuvp@aol.com
Regional Vice President of Southern Rockies: JAY ENGEL, 225 County Rd. #516, Ignacio, CO 81137-9728; Phone: 790-563-9599; Email: engelbj@compuserve.com
Regional Vice President of Southwest: STAN GRIFFIN, California Council of Trout Unlimited 5200 Huntington Ave., Suite 300,

Richmond, CA 94804-5416; Phone: 510-528-5390; Email: tucalif@ziplink.net

TU and BLM Bring Back The Natives Program Coordinator: DAVID NOLTE, 6322 NW Atkinson Ave., Redmond, OR 97756; Phone: 541-548-FISH; Fax: 541-548-3473; Email: dnotte@bend-or.com

Wyoming TU Office Administrator: KATHY BUCHNER, P.O. Box 4069, Jackson, WY 83001; Phone: 307-733-6991; Fax: 307-733-9678; Email: kbuchner@wyoming.com

Publication(s): *TROUT magazine; Lines To Leaders; Emerger, The*
Keyword(s): Acid Rain, Aquatic Habitats, Endangered and Threatened Species, Environmental and Conservation Education, Rivers

TROUT UNLIMITED, ALASKA COUNCIL
P.O. Box 3324, Homer, AK 99603-3324
Email: tujackak@alaska.net
Scope: Statewide
Description: A statewide council with ten active chapters dedicated to the protection and enhancement of the cold water fishery resource.
Contact(s):
Chairman: JACK WILLIS, P.O. Box 3324, Homer, AK 99603-3324; Phone: (H)907-235-3860

TROUT UNLIMITED, ARIZONA COUNCIL
Arizona Council TU; 77 E. Columbus Ave #200, Phoenix, AZ 85012
Phone: 602-264-5840
Scope: Statewide
Description: A statewide council with four active chapters working for the protection and enhancement of coldwater fishery resources.
Contact(s):
Chairman: CARM MOEHLE, Arizona Council TU, 77 E. Columbus Ave. #200, Phoenix, AZ 85012; Phone: 602-264-5840

TROUT UNLIMITED, ARKANSAS COUNCIL
784 Texas Way, Fayetteville, AR 72701-4449
Phone: 501-521-0837
Scope: Statewide
Description: A statewide council with 3 active chapters working for the protection and enhancement of coldwater fishery resources.
Contact(s):
Chairman: JOHN HEHR, 784 Texas Way, Fayetteville, AR 72701-4449; Phone: 501-521-0837

TROUT UNLIMITED, CALIFORNIA COUNCIL
State Office, 828 San Pablo Ave., Ste 244, Albany, CA 94706
Phone: 510-528-7880
Scope: Statewide
Description: A statewide council with ten active chapters working for the protection and enhancement of coldwater fishery resources.
Contact(s):
Chairman: CHARLES SCHULTZ, 1024 C Los Gamos, San Rafael, CA 94903-2517; Phone: 415-472-5837
Office Director: STAN GRIFFIN, 828 San Pablo Ave., Ste 244, Albany, CA 94706; Phone: 510-528-4772; Fax: 510-528-7880

TROUT UNLIMITED, COLORADO COUNCIL
1900 13th Ste 101, Boulder, CO 80302
Phone: 303-837-9383
Scope: Statewide
Description: A statewide council with 28 active chapters working for the protection and enhancement of coldwater fishery resources.
Contact(s):
Chair: DAVID TAYLOR, 1487 Cross Creek Court, Lafayette, CO 80026-8000; Phone: (H)303-673-9815 (W)800-525-3786; Fax: 303-277-6246; Email: dave.taylor@coors.com

TROUT UNLIMITED, CONNECTICUT COUNCIL
186 Sandy Hollow Rd, Gales Ferry, CT 06335-1709
Phone: 860-464-8246
Scope: Statewide
Description: A statewide council with nine active chapters working for the protection and enhancement of coldwater fishery resources.
Contact(s):
Chairman: CURTIS NELSON, 186 Sandy Hollow Rd, Gales Ferry, CT 06335-1709; Phone: 860-464-8246

TROUT UNLIMITED, DELAWARE STATE COUNCIL
ATTN: President, 118 St. Regis Dr., Newark, DE 19711-3823
Scope: Statewide
Description: A statewide chapter dedicated to the protection and enhancement of coldwater fishery resource.
Contact(s):
President: JOHN MCMINN, 118 St. Regis Dr., Newark, DE 19711-3823; Phone: (H)302-368-2903 (W)302-695-2237; Email: ritamcm@bellatlantic.net

TROUT UNLIMITED, GEORGIA COUNCIL
ATTN: Chairman, 3836 Foxwood Rd., Duluth, GA 30136-2985
Scope: Statewide
Description: A statewide council with 14 active chapters working for the protection and enhancement of coldwater fishery resources.
Contact(s):
Chairman: ROBERT BECK, 3836 Foxwood Rd., Duluth, GA 30136-2985; Phone: (H)770-447-9772 (W)404-506-7232; Fax: 404-506-1019; Email: RJBECK@southernco.com
Secretary: GENE BARRINGTON, 910 Wood Valley Ct., Cumming, GA 30130
Treasurer: JOE BISHOP, 1640 Powers Ferry Rd., Bldg. 22, Marietta, GA 30067; Phone: 404-933-1919
Environmental Affairs: BILL FOWLER, 3188 Argonne Dr., NE, Atlanta, GA 30305; Phone: 404-231-0898
Membership Director: BOB FOSTER, 5074 Odins Way, Marietta, GA 30067; Phone: 404-992-8789
Resource Director: GARLAND STEWART, 4453 Abingdon Dr., Stone Mountain, GA 30083; Phone: 404-294-0471
Vice Chairman: KEN LOUKO, 2490 Sharondale Dr., NE., Atlanta, GA 30305

TROUT UNLIMITED, GUADELOUPE RIVER COUNCIL
c/o president, 3601 Lovage Dr., Austin, TX 78727-3085
Phone: 512-451-7696; Email: billtrim@jumpnet.com
Scope: Statewide
Description: Dedicated to the protection and enhancement of the coldwater fishery resource.
Contact(s):
President: BILLY TRIMBLE, 3601 Lovage Dr., Austin, TX 78727-3058; Phone: 512-451-7696; Email: billtrim@junpnet.com
Publication(s): *Texas Wetlands*
Keyword(s): Hunting, Outdoor Recreation, Waterfowl, Wetlands, Wildlife and Wildlife Habitat

TROUT UNLIMITED, IDAHO COUNCIL
Attn: Chairman, P.O. Box AX, McCall, ID 83638-2551
Scope: Statewide
Description: A statewide council with eight active chapters dedicated to the protection and enhancement of the coldwater fishery resource.
Contact(s):
Chairman: Shawn Miller; Phone: (H)208-634-2775 (W)208-634-5433; Fax: 208-634-3009

TROUT UNLIMITED, ILLINOIS COUNCIL
ATTN: Chairman, 2580 Forest View Ave., River Grove, IL 60171-1602
Email: jhammon@aol.com or jdhammon@attmail.com
Scope: Statewide
Description: A statewide council with four active chapters working for the protection and enhancement of coldwater fishery resources.

NON-GOVERNMENTAL ORGANIZATIONS

Contact(s):
Chairman: JOSEPH HAMMON, 2580 Forest View Ave., River Grove, IL 60171-1602; Phone: (H)708-453-8102 (W)312-751-4730

TROUT UNLIMITED, KENTUCKY COUNCIL
ATTN: Chairman, 75 Valley Rd., Louisville, KY 40204-1516
Scope: Statewide
Description: A statewide council with three active chapters working for the protection and enhancement of coldwater fishery resources.
Contact(s):
Chairman: STEPHEN WOODRING, 75 Valley Rd., Louisville, KY 40204-1516; Phone: (H)502-458-8113 (W)502-562-0115

TROUT UNLIMITED, MAINE COUNCIL
ATTN: President, 80 River Rd., Whitefield, ME 04353-9730
Scope: Statewide
Description: A statewide council with six active chapters working for the protection and enhancement of coldwater fishery resources.
Contact(s):
Chairman: SEAN McCORMICK, 80 E. River Rd., Whitefield, ME 04353-9730; Phone: 207-549-3355; Fax: 207-549-9906; Email: seanmc@gwi.net

TROUT UNLIMITED, MARYLAND COUNCIL (Mid-Atlantic)
ATTN: President, 6586 Guilford Rd., Clarksville, MD 21029
Scope: Statewide
Description: A statewide council with seven active chapters working for the protection and enhancement of coldwater fishery resources.
Contact(s):
Chairman: BRUCE EBERLE, 6586 Guilford Rd., Clarksville, MD 21029; Phone: (H)301-854-3142 (W)202-366-2060; Fax: 202-366-3409

TROUT UNLIMITED, MASSACHUSETTS/RHODE ISLAND COUNCIL
ATTN: Chairman, 11 Obeline Dr., N. Smithfield, MA 02896-6927
Scope: Statewide
Description: A statewide council with 12 active chapters working for the protection and enhancement of coldwater fishery resources.
Contact(s):
Chairman: FRED RUGO, 11 Obeline Dr., N. Smithfield, RI 02896-6927; Phone: (H)401-766-6404 (W)860-441-4589

TROUT UNLIMITED, MICHIGAN COUNCIL
ATTN: President, 106 Pheasant Run Drive, Troy, MI 48098-1796
Scope: Statewide
Description: A statewide council with 21 active chapters working for the protection and enhancement of coldwater fishery resources.
Contact(s):
Chairman: JOHN SABININA, 106 Pheasant Run Drive, Troy, MI 48098-1796; Phone: (H) 248-828-0688 (W) 248-753-1168; Fax: 248-573-1823; Email: jjsabina@tir.com

TROUT UNLIMITED, MINNESOTA COUNCIL
1500 Xanthus Ln., Plymouth, MN 55447
Phone: 612-470-0078
Scope: Statewide
Description: A statewide council with nine active chapters working for the protection and enhancement of coldwater fishery resources.
Contact(s):
Chairman: ELLIOTT OLSON, 1500 Xanthus Ln., Plymouth, MN 55447; Phone: (H)612-470-0078 (W) 612-835-4505; Email: dakotaww@goldengate.net

TROUT UNLIMITED, MISSOURI COUNCIL
2010 Daisy Ln., Jefferson, MO 65109-1810
Phone: (W)573-634-3096 (H)573-751-1039; Fax: 573-634-3096
Scope: Statewide
Description: A statewide council with four active chapters working for the protection and enhancement of coldwater fishery resources.
Contact(s):
Chairman: JOHN WENZLICK, 2010 Daisy Ln, Jefferson, MO 65109-1810; Phone: (H) 573-634-3096 (W)573-751-1039; Fax: 573-634-3096; Email: jdwenzlick@juno.com

TROUT UNLIMITED, MONTANA COUNCIL
Attn: Chairman, P.O. Box 1638, Polson, MT 59860
Phone: 406-887-2495
Scope: Statewide
Description: A statewide council with 12 chapters working for the protection and enhancement of coldwater fishery resources.
Contact(s):
Chairman: RIC SMITH, P.O. Box 1638, Polson, MT 59860; Phone: 406-887-2495
Resource Director: L. FRANK COOPER, 1804 Beltview Dr., Helena, MT 59601-5801; Phone: 406-443-6441; Fax: 406-442-6748; Email: FrankCoop@aol.com

TROUT UNLIMITED, NATIONAL CAPITAL COUNCIL
ATTN: President, 4914 Earlston Dr., Bethesda, DC 20816-1732
Scope: Statewide
Description: Dedicated to the protection and enhancement of coldwater fishing resources.
Contact(s):
President: FRED PARMENTER, 4914 Earlston Dr., Bethesda, MD 20816-1732; Phone: (H) 301-320-0760 (W)202-307-0620; Fax: 202-307-6283

TROUT UNLIMITED, NEVADA COUNCIL
P.O. Box 5882, Elko, NV 889802-5882
Phone: 702-853-9676; Email: crkwrks@sierra.net
Scope: Statewide
Description: A statewide council with three active chapters, dedicated to the protection and enhancement of coldwater fishing resources.
Contact(s):
Contact: MATT HOLFORD, P.O. Box 5882, Elko, NV 89802-5882; Phone: (H) 702-753-4306 (W)702-753-9676; Fax: 702-753-4306; Email: crlwrks@elko.net

TROUT UNLIMITED, NEW HAMPSHIRE COUNCIL
9 Sirod Rd., Windham, NH 03087-1401
Phone: 603-432-3254
Scope: Statewide
Description: A statewide council with six active chapters working for the protection and enhancement of coldwater fishery resources.
Contact(s):
Chairman: JAMES NORTON, 9 Sirod Rd., Windham, NH 03087-1401; Phone: 603-432-3254

TROUT UNLIMITED, NEW JERSEY COUNCIL
17 Braemar Court, Andover, NJ 07821-3510
Phone: 800-524-2784; Fax: 201-691-0441
Scope: Statewide
Description: A statewide council with eight active chapters for the protection and enhancement of coldwater fishery resource.
Contact(s):
Chairman: FREDERICK EGE, 17 Braemar Court, Andover, NJ 07821-3510; Phone: 800-524-2784; Fax: 201-691-0441

TROUT UNLIMITED, NEW YORK COUNCIL
ATTN: Chairman, 2711 Girdle Rd., Elma, NY 14059
Scope: Statewide
Description: A statewide council with 37 active chapters working for the protection and enhancement of coldwater fishery resources.

Contact(s):
Chairman: PAUL MACIEJEWSKI, 2711 Girdle Rd., Elma, NY 14059; Phone: 716-655-1331 (Home); Email: dryfly@bafnet.net
Editor: KEN GAHERTY, 10 Bellewood Ave., Centereach, NY 11720
Publication(s): *Long Casts*

TROUT UNLIMITED, NORTH CAROLINA COUNCIL
135 Tacoma Cir., Asheville, NC 28801-1625
Phone: 704-684-5178; Fax: 704-687-1689
Scope: Statewide
Description: A statewide council with 18 active chapters working for the protection and enhancement of coldwater fishery resource.
Contact(s):
Chairman: KIRK OTEY, 1308 Lexington Ave., Charlotte, NC 28203; Phone: (H)704-332-8232 (W)800-432-6268; Fax: 704-375-6425

TROUT UNLIMITED, NORTH FLORIDA COUNCIL
ATTN: Chairman, 4006 S. Florida Ave., Lakeland, FL 33813
Scope: Statewide
Description: A statewide council with two chapters working for the protection of coldwater fishery resources.
Contact(s):
Chairman: ROBERT JACKSON, 4006 S. Florida Ave., Lakeland, FL 33813; Phone: (H) 941-680-1143 (W) 941-646-1476

TROUT UNLIMITED, OHIO COUNCIL
1487 New Way Drive, Beaver Creek, OH 45434-6925
Phone: 800-227-9597; Email: mark*blauvelt@lexis-nexis.com
Scope: Statewide
Description: Dedicated to the protection and enhancement of the coldwater fishery resource.
Contact(s):
President: MARK BLAUVELT, 1487 New Way Drive, Beaver Creek, OH 45434-6925; Phone: 800-227-9597

TROUT UNLIMITED, OKLAHOMA COUNCIL
9528 E. 55th St. Ste A, Tulsa, OK 74145
Phone: (H)918-455-5573 (W)918-622-6633
Scope: Statewide
Description: A statewide council with three active chapters dedicated to the protection and enhancement of coldwater fishing resources.
Contact(s):
President: DALE DEUVALL, Advanced Filing Systems Inc., 9528 E. 55th St. Ste A, Tulsa, OK 74145; Phone: (H)918-455-5573 (W)918-622-6633
Keyword(s): Aquatic Habitats, Fisheries, Renewable Resources, Water Pollution Management, Wetlands

TROUT UNLIMITED, OREGON COUNCIL
22875,NW Chestnut St., Hillsboro, OR 97124-6545
Phone: 541-640-2123; Fax: 503-844-9929; Email: lindawolf@aol.com
Scope: Statewide
Description: A statewide council with seven active chapters working for the protection and enhancement of the coldwater fishery resource.
Contact(s):
Chairman: THOMAS WOLF, 22875 NW Chestnut St., Hillsboro, OR 97124-6545; Phone: (H)503-640-2123 (W)503-844-4519; Email: tmilowolf@aol.com

TROUT UNLIMITED, PENNSYLVANIA COUNCIL
ATTN: Chairman, RD 1 Box 371C, East Bradley, PA 16208-9740
Scope: Statewide
Description: A statewide council with 56 active chapters working for the protection and enhancement of the coldwater fishery resource.
Contact(s):
Chairman: DAVID CURAN, RD 1 Box 371C, East Bradley, PA 16028-9740; Phone: 724-526-5487; Email: dcurran@alltel.net

Publication(s): *TCWA Report*
Keyword(s): Environmental and Conservation Education, Land Use Planning, Water Quality, Watersheds, Wildlife Rehabilitation

TROUT UNLIMITED, RHODE ISLAND COUNCIL (Narragansett)
ATTN: President, 553 Kenyon Ave., Pawtucket, RI 02861-1254
Scope: Statewide
Description: A statewide chapter, dedicated to the protection and enhancement of coldwater fishery resources.
Contact(s):
President: PATRICK KAPSNER, 553 Kenyon Ave., Pawtucket, RI 02861-1254; Phone: (H)401-724-2932 (W)401-724-2932; Email: patkapsner@prodigy.net
Publication(s): *South Carolina Out-Of-Doors*

TROUT UNLIMITED, RIVERSIDE COUNCIL
Rt. 1 Box 419, Jasper, AL 35501
Phone: 205-287-0050
Scope: Statewide
Contact(s):
President: JOHN EISENBARTH

TROUT UNLIMITED, SHADES VALLEY COUNCIL
508 Sharpsburg Cir., Birmingham, AL 35213
Phone: 205-956-9590
Scope: Statewide
Contact(s):
President: JAMES D. HILLHOUSE, 508 Sharpsburg Cir., Birmingham, AL 35213; Phone: 205-956-9590

TROUT UNLIMITED, SOUTH CAROLINA COUNCIL
ATTN: Chairman, 204 Bent Oak Way, Spartanburg, SC 20301
Email: jcarter@globalvision.com
Scope: Statewide
Description: A statewide council with four active chapters working for the protection and enhancement of coldwater fishery resources.
Contact(s):
Chairman: JIM CARTER, 204 Bent Oak Way, Spartanburg, SC 20301; Email: jcarter @globalvision.com

TROUT UNLIMITED, SOUTH FLORIDA CHAPTER
7439 NW 34th St., Lauderdale, FL 33319
Scope: Statewide
Description: The Trout Unlimited South Florida Chapter is dedicated to the protection and enhancement of coldwater fishing resources.
Contact(s):
Contact: SCOTT FOULKE; Phone: 954-742-7876

TROUT UNLIMITED, TENNESSEE COUNCIL
ATTN: Chairman, 2611 Oakland Ave., Nashville, TN 37212
Scope: Statewide
Description: A statewide council with 10 active chapters working for the protection and enhancement of the coldwater fishery resource.
Contact(s):
Chairman: JIM MAURIES, 2611 Oakland Ave, Nashville, TN 37212; Phone: (H)615-298-3840 (W)615-321-4069

TROUT UNLIMITED, UTAH COUNCIL
1471 E. Canyon Dr., South Weber, UT
Phone: (H)801-479-8846 (W)801-538-7353; Fax: 801-538-7278
Scope: Statewide
Description: Dedicated to the protection and enhancement of the coldwater fishery resource.
Contact(s):
Chairman: WES JOHNSON, 1471 E. Canyon Dr., South Weber, UT 84405-9629; Phone: (H)801-479-846 (W)801-538-7353; Fax: 801-538-7278; Email: rwj@utw.com

NON-GOVERNMENTAL ORGANIZATIONS

TROUT UNLIMITED, VERMONT COUNCIL
ATTN: President, P.O. Box 497, Derby, VT 05289-0497
Scope: Statewide
Description: A statewide council with six chapters working for the protection and enhancement of the coldwater fishery resource.
Contact(s):
Chairman: FRANCIS SMITH, P.O. Box 497, Derby, VT 05289-0497; Phone: (H)802-766-8013 (W)802-334-1674; Fax: 802-334-2991

TROUT UNLIMITED, VIRGINIA COUNCIL
ATTN: Chairman, 4615 Norris Court, Chantilly, VA 20151-1407
Email: EmailTrouto@aol.com
Scope: Statewide
Description: A statewide organization with 16 active chapters working for the protection and enhancement of the coldwater fishery resource.
Contact(s):
Chairman: WILLIAM HOBSON, 4615 Norris Court, Chantilly, VA 20151-1407; Phone: (H)703-378-0356 (W)703-850-8484; Email: willhobson@aol.com
Editor: CHARLES E. HUDSON, 211 Shady Oak Ln., Forest, VA 24551-1113; Phone: 804-525-6004

TROUT UNLIMITED, WASHINGTON COUNCIL
2401 Briston Court, SW Olympia, WA 98502
Phone: 360-754-2131
Scope: Statewide
Description: A statewide council with 31 active chapters working for the protection and enhancement of coldwater fishery resources.
Contact(s):
Chairman: ROBERT JOHNSON, 14727 SE 145th Pl., Renton, WA 98059-7336; Phone: 425-865-7404; Fax: 360-754-4240; Email: kbob@halycon.com
Editor: BILL LINDSTROM, 2401 Bristol Ct., SW, Suite 18, Olympia, WA 98502
Publication(s): *Trout and Salmon Leader*

TROUT UNLIMITED, WEST VIRGINIA COUNCIL
ATTN: Chairman, 180 Oriole Rd., Frasers Bottom, WV 25082
Scope: Statewide
Description: A statewide council with 8 active chapters working for the protection and enhancement of coldwater fishery resources.
Contact(s):
Chairman: ED CRUM, 180 Oriole Rd., Frasers Bottom, WV 25082; Phone: 304-937-2214

TROUT UNLIMITED, WISCONSIN COUNCIL
P.O. Box 228, Eau Claire, WI 54702-0228
Phone: (H)715-833-7028 (W)715-831-9568; Fax: 715-831-9568; Email: jwelter@discover-net.net
Scope: Statewide
Description: A statewide council with 21 active chapters working for the protection and enhancement of coldwater fishery resources.
Contact(s):
Chairman: JOHN WELTER, P.O. Box 228, Eau Claire, WI 54702-0228; Phone: (H)715-833-7028 (W)715-831-9565; Fax: 715-831-9568; Email: jwelter@discover-net.net
Editor: MITCH BENT, 1282 Monterey Trail, De Pere, WI 54115; Phone: 414-336-4983
Publication(s): *Wisconsin Trout*

TROUT UNLIMITED, WYOMING COUNCIL
ATTN: President, P.O. Box 1022, Jackson, WY 83001
Email: Email103062.442@compuserve.com
Scope: Statewide
Description: A statewide council with 16 active chapters dedicated to the protection and enhancement of the coldwater fishery resource.
Contact(s):
Chairman: JAY BUCHNER, P.O. Box 1022, Jackson, WY 83001; Phone: 307-733-1530; Email: 103062.442@compuserve.com

Executive Director: JOHN ZELAZNY, T.U. Wyoming, P.O. Box 4069, Jackson, WY 83001; Phone: 307-733-1486

TRUMPETER SWAN SOCIETY, THE
3800 County Rd. 24, Maple Plain, MN 55359
Phone: 612-476-4663; Fax: 612-476-1514; Email: hpwlttss@aol.com
Founded: 1968; Membership: 500
Scope: National
Description: International scientific and educational organization dedicated to assuring the vitality and welfare of wild Trumpeter Swan populations in North America, and to restoring the species to its original range. The Society promotes research into Trumpeter ecology and management, and provides a framework for exchange of knowledge about the species.
Contact(s):
President: RUTH E. SHEA, 3346 E. 200 N., Rigby, ID 83442
Vice President: BRUCE CONANT, USFWS, 3000 Vintage Blvd, Suite 240, Juneau, AK 99801-7100
Editor: DONNA C. COMPTON
Editor: JANE NOLL WEST
Editor: MADELEINE LINCK
Publication(s): *North American Swans, Bulletin of the Trumpeter Swan Society; Trumpetings; Proceedings and Papers of the 14th Trumpeter Swan Society Conference; Proceedings and Papers of the 15th Trumpeter Swan Society Conference.*
Keyword(s): Birds, Nongame Wildlife, Waterfowl, Wetlands, Wildlife and Wildlife Habitat

TRUST FOR PUBLIC LAND, THE
National Office, 116 New Montgomery St. 4th Fl., San Francisco, CA 94105
Phone: 415-495-4014/1-800-714-LAND; Fax: 415-495-4103; Email: mailbox@tpl.org
Founded: 1972
Scope: National
Description: The Trust for Public Land (TPL) is a private, nonprofit land conservation organization that works nationwide to conserve land for people. Founded in 1972, the TPL specializes in conservation real estate. The TPL applies its expertise in negotiation, public finance, and law to protect land for public use. Working with private landowners, communities, and government agencies, TPL has helped protect more than 1,400 special places nationwide for people to enjoy as parks, playgrounds, community gardens, recreation areas, historic landmarks and wilderness areas.
Contact(s):
President: MARTIN J. ROSEN
Vice President: ERNEST COOK, 33 Union St., 4th Fl., Boston, MA 02108; Phone: 617-367-6200
Vice President: LISA CASHDAN, P.O. Box 1257, The Aldrich House, 16 Beaver Meadow Rd., Norwich, VT 05055; Phone: 802-649-3611
Atlanta Field Office Director: RAND WENTWORTH, 1447 Peachtree St., NE, Suite 601, Atlanta, GA 30309; Phone: 404-873-7306
Director of Federal Affairs: ALAN FRONT
Director of Oregon Field Office: BOWEN BLAIR, 1211 SW Sixth Ave., Portland, OR 97204; Phone: 503-228-6620
Director of Public Affairs: SUSAN IVES
Editor: SUSAN IVES
Executive Vice President: RALPH W. BENSON
General Counsel: NELSON LEE
Mid-Atlantic Regional Manager: ROSE HARVEY, 666 Broadway, New York, NY 10012; Phone: 212-677-7171
New England Regional Manager: PETER FORBES, 33 Union St., 4th Fl., Boston, MA 02108; Phone: 617-367-6200
Northwest Regional Manager: CRAIG LEE, Smith Tower, Suite 1510, 506 2nd Ave., Seattle, WA 98104; Phone: 206-587-2447
Senior Vice President and CFO: ROBERT W. McINTYRE
Southwest Regional Manager: TED HARRISON, 418 Montezuma, Santa Fe, NM 87501; Phone: 505-988-5922
Vice President and Senior Project Manager: KATHY BLAHA, 666 Pennsylvania Ave. SE, Washington, DC 20003; Phone: 202-543-7552

Vice President and Southeast Regional Manager: W. DALE ALLEN, 306 N. Monroe St., Tallahassee, FL 32301-7635; Phone: 904-222-7911
Vice President of External Affairs: JENNIE GERARD
Vice President of Land Transactions: STEPHEN E. THOMPSON, 418 Montezuma, Santa Fe, NM 87501; Phone: 505-988-5922
Western Regional Manager: WILL ROGERS, 116 New Montgomery, 3rd Fl., San Francisco, CA 94105; Phone: 415-495-5660

Publication(s): *Land and People; GreenSense; Regional newsletters*
Keyword(s): Land Purchase, Open Space, Outdoor Recreation, Watersheds, Wilderness

TRUST FOR WILDLIFE, INC.
Ehrich Rd., RR1, Box 366, Shaftsbury, VT 05262
Phone: 802-447-0746
Founded: 1983
Scope: National
Description: Dedicated to wildlife conservation and education with a focus on wildlife habitats, international partnerships with a focus on Russia, and wildlife rehabilitation with an emphasis on public education.
Contact(s):
President: MARSHAL T. CASE, Ehrich Rd., R.R. 1 Box 366, Shaftsbury, VT 05262; Phone: 802-447-0746
Secretary: GREGORY SHARP, 225 Reeds Gap Rd., East Northford, CT 6472; Phone: 203-240-6046
Director: LES LINE, P.O. Box 323, Amenia, NY 12501; Phone: 914-373-9135
Keyword(s): Biodiversity, Communications, Environmental and Conservation Education, International Conservation, Land Preservation, Natural History, Nature Preservation, Wildlife and Wildlife Habitat, Wildlife Rehabilitation, Youth Organizations

TRUSTEES FOR ALASKA
725 Christensen Dr., Suite 4, Anchorage, AK 99501-2101
Phone: 907-276-4244; Fax: 907-276-7110; Email: ecolaw@trustees.org; WWW: www.trustees.org
Founded: 1974; Membership: 1,200
Scope: Statewide
Description: Nonprofit, public-interest, environmental law firm working to ensure that Alaska's unique environmental values are not lost to future generations through irresponsible development or irrational public management. Primarily concerned with protection of Alaska's environment and the wise management of Alaska's resources.
Contact(s):
Chair: KEN ROBERTSON
Secretary: CHRIS ROSE
Treasurer: DAN DICKENSON
Executive Director: ANN L. ROTHE
Litigation Director: PETER VAN TUYN
Staff Attorney: VALERIE BROWN
Staff Attorney: ROBERT RANDALL
Staff Attorney: MICHAEL FRANK
Vice Chair: MARY McBURNEY
Keyword(s): Environmental Law

TRUSTEES OF RESERVATIONS, THE
572 Essex St., Beverly, MA 01915-1530
Phone: 978-921-1944; Fax: 978-921-1948; Email: TTofR@aol.com
Founded: 1891; Membership: 18,000
Scope: Statewide
Description: The Trustees of Reservations is the nation's oldest regional land trust, dedicated to preserving, for public use and enjoyment properties of exceptional scenic, historic, and ecological value throughout Massachusetts.
Contact(s):
Chairman: ELLIOT SURKIN
President: ALBERT CREIGHTON JR.
Secretary: HERBERT VAUGHAN
Treasurer: JOHN PARKER
Executive Director: FREDERIC WINTHROP
Director of Communications and Marketing: MICHAEL TRIFF
Director of Development: ANN POWELL
Director of Finance and Administration: JOHN COLEMAN
Director of Land Conservation: WESLEY WARD
Director of Planned Giving: ELOISE HODGES
Director of Property Management: RICHARD HOWE
Publication(s): *Annual Report; Land Conservation Methods: A Guide For Massachusetts Landowners; Land In Trust: Conservation Options For Private Landowners; Newsletter; Reservations Guidebook*
Keyword(s): Gardening and Horticulture, Historic Preservation, Land Preservation, Nature Preservation, Open Space

TUG HILL TOMORROW, INC.
P.O. Box 6063, Watertown, NY 13601
Phone: 315-785-2382; Email: THTomorrow@imcnet.net
Founded: 1990; Membership: 100
Scope: National
Description: Tug Hill Tomorrow is a private nonprofit corporation that works to help retain the forests, farms, recreational, and wild lands of the Tug Hill region through education, research, and voluntary land protection.
Contact(s):
Chair: STACEY SMITH, 8978 Church St., Remsen, NY 13438; Phone: 315-896-2814
Secretary: THOMAS J. YOUSEY III, R.D. 1 Box 309, Glenfield, NY 13343; Phone: 315-376-7633
Treasurer: DOUGLAS MURRAY, 31151 NYS Rt. 12, Watertown, NY 13601; Phone: 315-788-4969
Vice Chair: PAUL MILLER, 3825 Miller Rd., Blossvale, NY 13308-9781; Phone: 315-363-2629
Publication(s): *Greenings; Tug Hill Recreation Guide: A Guide to Cross-Country Skiing, Hiking, Biking, and Fishing; Tug Hill Working Lands; Tug Hill Resource Guide to Educational Programs; Tug Hill National History Field Guide*
Keyword(s): Environmental and Conservation Education, Forests and Forestry, Land Preservation, Natural Areas, Open Space

TURTLE CREEK WATERSHED ASSOCIATION, INC.
600 Braddock Ave., Suite G, Turtle Creek, PA 15145
Phone: 412-829-5042; Fax: 412-829-5042; Email: Gdomestic@turtlecreekwatershed.org; WWW: www.turtlecreekwatershed.org
Founded: 1969; Membership: 250
Scope: Statewide
Description: The objective of the Turtle Creek Watershed Association, Inc. is to preserve and protect natural resources; educate the community about important environmental issues; monitor and improve water quality; and work with responsible agencies to encourage wise land use planning in the Turtle Creek Watershed.
Contact(s):
President: ROBERT A. MAZIK SR.
Vice President: HENRY HOFFMAN
Secretary: EDWARD FISCHER
Treasurer: A.B. CARL
Executive Director: G. DOMENIC SPINO
Director Emeritus: JAMES TEMPERO
Publication(s): *Conserve; Business Associate; TCWA* **Keyword(s):** Endangered and Threatened Species, Environmental and Conservation Education, Environmental Protection, Land Purchase, Rivers, Water Quality, Wildlife and Wildlife Habitat

NON-GOVERNMENTAL ORGANIZATIONS

U.S. PUBLIC INTEREST RESEARCH GROUP
218 D St., SE, Washington, DC 20003
Phone: 202-546-9707; Fax: 202-546-2461; Email: usping@pirg.org; WWW: www.pirg.org1
Founded: 1983
Scope: National
Description: U.S. PIRG is the national lobbying office for state PIRGs around the country, representing more than one million members. We conduct independent research and lobby for national environmental and consumer protections.
Contact(s):
Director: GENE KARPINSKI
Publication(s): *Citizen Agenda; A publication list available upon request.*
Keyword(s): Air Quality and Pollution, Chemical Pollution Control, Conservation of Protected Areas, Endangered and Threatened Species, Energy, Energy Conservation, Environment, Environmental Protection, Pollution Prevention, Solid Waste Management, Water Pollution, Wetlands

UNION OF CONCERNED SCIENTISTS
Two Brattle Square, Cambridge, MA 2238
Phone: 617-547-5552; WWW: www.uscusa.org
Founded: 1969; Membership: 70,000
Scope: National
Description: The Union of Concerned Scientists is a national non-profit working for a cleaner environment and a safer world. UCS is working to encourage preservation of life-sustaining resources, promote energy technologies that are renewable, safe, and cost-effective, promote advanced transportation technologies, encourage sustainable agriculture, and curtail weapons proliferation.
Contact(s):
Chairman: HENRY KENDALL
Executive Director: HOWARD RIS JR.
Publication(s): *Newsletter: NUCLEUS; The Gene Exchange; Energy Innovations, Keeping the Earth (video)*
Keyword(s): Agriculture, Biodiversity, Biotechnology, Energy, Environment, Environmental and Conservation Education, Greenhouse Effect/Global Warming, Nuclear Energy, Renewable Resources, Solar Energy, Sustainable Development, Transportation

UNITED NATIONS ENVIRONMENT PROGRAMME
P.O. Box 30552, Nairobi Kenya
Phone: 254--2-623089; Fax: 254-2-623692; Email: anila.shah@unep.org; WWW: www.unep.org
Founded: 1972
Scope: International
Description: The United Nations Environment Programme (UNEP) was established by the U.N. General Assembly to be the environmental conscience of the U.N. system. It assesses the state of the world's environment; environmental management capacity of developing countries; and raises environmental considerations for the social and economic policies and programmes of UN agencies. UNEP provides a unique forum to bring countries to the table for negotiations, to build consensus and forge international agreements. In doing so, it makes a particular effort to nurture partnerships with business and industry, the scientific and academic community, non-governmental organizations, community groups, youth, women and sports organizations.
Contact(s):
Deputy Executive Director: SHAFQAT KAKAKHEL
Under Secretary General of the United Nations and Executive Director: KLAUS TOEPFER
Publication(s): *Our Planet Magazine; The Environment in Print; Global Environment Outlook, For Life on Earth (CD-ROM)*
Keyword(s): Air Quality and Pollution, Biodiversity, Biotechnology, Chemical Pollution Control, Coasts, Ecology, Endangered and Threatened Species, Environment, Environmental Ethics, Environmental Law, Environmental Planning, Environmental Protection, International Conservation, Urban Environment, Water Resources

UNITED NATIONS ENVIRONMENT PROGRAMME (Latin America and Carribean Region)
UNEP-ROLAC (United Nations Environment Programme Apdo.), Postal 10.793, Mexico, D.F. 11000 Mexico
Phone: 52-5202-4841/6394; Fax: 52-5-202-0950; Email: rolac@rolac.unep.mx
Scope: International

UNITED NATIONS ENVIRONMENT PROGRAMME (North America Regional Office)
United Nations, Rm. DC2-0803, New York, NY 10017
Phone: 212-963-8210; Fax: 212-963-7341; Email: uneprona@un.org
Scope: International
Contact(s):
Director: DR. JOANNE FOX-PRZEWORSKI
Information Officer: JAMES SNIFFEN

UNITED STATES CHAMBER OF COMMERCE
1615 H St. NW, Washington, DC 20062
Founded: 1912
Scope: National
Description: Created to provide business representation on major national issues. Membership includes 3,000 chambers of commerce, 1,200 trade and professional associations, and 215,000 business firms.
Contact(s):
Manager of Energy and Natural Resources Policy: STUART HARDY; Phone: 202-463-5533
Manager of Environmental Policy: MARY BERNHARD; Phone: 202-463-5533
Manager of Food & Agriculture Policy: STUART HARDY; Phone: 202-463-5533
Manager of Resources Policy Department: DR. HARVEY ALTER; Phone: 202-463-5531
Manager of Small Business Policy: DAVID VOIGHT; Phone: 202-463-5533
President and CEO: THOMAS N. DONOHUE

UNITED STATES COMMITTEE FOR THE UNITED NATIONS ENVIRONMENT PROGRAMME THE (U.S. and UNEP)
2013 Q St., NW, Washington, DC 20009
Phone: 202-234-3600
Scope: National
Description: A nonprofit support group for the U.N. Environment Programme, U.S. and UNEP generates public awareness of global environmental issues, including ozone layer depletion, the greenhouse effect, and the transport of hazardous chemicals, and UNEP's response to these issues. The organization links UNEP to environmental groups across the U.S.
Contact(s):
President: RICHARD A. HELLMAN
Vice President: MICHAEL D. GRANOFF
Editor: ANN R. ULRICH
Publication(s): *US and UNEP NEWS*
Keyword(s): Agriculture, Endangered and Threatened Species, Environmental and Conservation Education, Greenhouse Effect/Global Warming, International Conservation

UNITED STATES TOURIST COUNCIL
Drawer 1875, Washington, DC 20013-1875
Scope: National
Description: A nonprofit association of conservation-concerned individuals, industries, and institutions who travel or cater to the traveler. Emphasis is on historic and scenic preservation, wilderness and roadside development, ecology through sound planning and education, and support of scientific studies of natural wilderness.
Contact(s):
Chairman of Board of Trustees and Executive Director: DR. STANFORD WEST
Keyword(s): Aquatic Habitats, Forests and Forestry, Historic Preservation, International Conservation, Wetlands

UPPER MISSISSIPPI RIVER CONSERVATION COMMITTEE
4469 - 48th Ave. Ct., Rock Island, IL 61201
Phone: 309-793-5800
Founded: 1943
Scope: Regional
Description: Promotes preservation, development, and wise use of the natural and recreational resources of the Upper Mississippi River and formulates policies, plans, and programs for conducting cooperative studies. Members: state conservation departments of Illinois, Iowa, Minnesota, Missouri, and Wisconsin.
Contact(s):
Chairperson: BILL BERTRAND, Illinois Department of Resources, Box 149, Aledo, IL 61231; Phone: 309-582-5611
Coordinator: JON DUYVEJONCK, 4469 48th Avenue Ct., Rock Island, IL 61201; Phone: 309-793-5800
Secretary and Treasurer: DAN SALLEE, Illinois Department of Conservation, Box 149, Aledo, IL 61231; Phone: 309-582-5611
Publication(s): *Annual Proceedings; Newsletter; and miscellaneous technical reports*
Keyword(s): Aquatic Habitats, Biology, Fisheries, Rivers, Sustainable Development, Water Quality, Water Resources

URBAN HABITAT PROGRAM
P.O. Box 29908, Presidio Station, San Francisco, CA 94129
Phone: 415-561-3333; Fax: 415-561-3334
Founded: 1989
Scope: National
Description: The Urban Habitat Program is a project of Tides Center. Its mission is to build multi-cultural urban environmental leadership for socially-just and sustainable communities in the San Francisco Bay area. Our project areas include transportation, regional land use and social justice, land recycling and brown fields, leadership institute for sustainability and justice, and the goal of ecological literacy, all from an ecological and social justice perspective.
Contact(s):
Director: CARL ANTHONY
Publication(s): *Race, Poverty & the Environment*
Keyword(s): Brown Fields, Cultural Preservation, Environmental Justice, Land Use Planning, People of Color in the Environment, Transportation, Urban Environment

UTAH ASSOCIATION OF SOIL CONSERVATION DISTRICTS
ATTN: President, 16116 N. Main, Centerville, UT 84014
Scope: Statewide
Contact(s):
President, Board Member: WILLIAM RIGBY, 1616 N. Main, Centerville, UT 84014; Phone: 801-292-0245; Fax: 801-296-8586
Vice President, Alternate Board Member: RANDY GREENHALGH, 403 E. Center, Nephi, UT 84648; Phone: 801-623-0845; Email: rgreen@ext.usu.edu
Executive Vice President: GORDON YOUNKER, 1860 N 100 E, North Logan, UT 84341-2215; Phone: 801-753-6029; Fax: 801-755-2117; Email: gyounker@ext.usu.edu
Secretary and Treasurer: BEN A. THURGOOD, 1649 West 700 South, Syracuse, UT 84075; Phone: 801-825-1772

UTAH B.A.S.S. CHAPTER FEDERATION
ATTN: President, 3460 S. Scott Cir., SLC, UT 84115
Phone: 801-487-8711
Scope: Statewide
Description: An organization of Bassmaster chapters, affiliated with the Bass Anglers Sportsman Society, organized to fight pollution, assist state and national conservation agencies in their efforts, and teach young people of our country good conservation practices. Dedicated to the realistic conservation of our water resources.
Contact(s):
President: GEORGE SOMMER, 3460 South Scott Cir., SLC, UT 84115; Phone: 801-487-8711
Conservation Director: WALTER MALDONADO, P.O. Box 482, Green River, UT 84525-0482; Phone: 435-564-8147

Publication(s): *Nature News Notes*
Keyword(s): Environmental and Conservation Education, Natural Areas, Nature Preservation, Nongame Wildlife, Wildlife and Wildlife Habitat

UTAH NATURE STUDY SOCIETY
ATTN: President Utah Nature Study Society, 2853 S. 23rd East, Salt Lake City, UT 84109
Founded: 1954
Scope: Statewide
Description: Promotes conservation and nature education through workshops and field trips for members; publicizes conservation problems and issues through meetings and its newsletter. Member of Utah Associated Garden Clubs.
Contact(s):
President: DOROTHY K. PLATT, 2853 S. 23rd East, Salt Lake City, UT 84109
Secretary: MARIA DICKERSON, 323 S. 2nd W., Tooele, UT 84074
Executive Secretary: JEAN WHITE, 377 E. 5300 S., Murray, UT 84107-6019
Editor: CATHERINE QUINN, 1383 S. 300 East, Salt Lake City, UT 84115
Publication(s): *UWA Review*
Keyword(s): Biodiversity, Environmental and Conservation Education, Public Lands, Wilderness, Wildlife Management

UTAH WILDERNESS COALITION
P.O. Box 520974, Salt Lake City, UT 84152-0974
Phone: 801-486-2872; Fax: 801-485-5572
Founded: 1985
Scope: Statewide
Description: Promote and coordinate the preservation of U.S. BLM and Forest Service wildlands in southern and western Utah. The goal includes protection of the remaining wilderness quality public lands under the National Wilderness Preservation System.
Contact(s):
Board Member: WAYNE HOSKISSON, The Sierra Club, 2273 South Highland Drive, Salt Lake City, UT 84106; Phone: 801-467-9294
Board Member: PAM EATON, The Wilderness Society, 7475 Dankin Street, #410, Denver, CO 80221; Phone: 303-650-5818
Board Member: MIKE MATZ, Southern Utah Wilderness Alliance, 1471 S. 1100 E., Salt Lake City, UT 84105; Phone: 801-486-3161
Board Member: JOHN VERANTH, Wasatch Mountain Club, 1390 South 1100 East STE 103, Salt Lake City, UT 84105; Phone: 801-463-9842
Co-Chairperson: BOB BINGAMAN, National Field Director of the Sierra Club, 408 C Street NE, Washington, DC 20002; Phone: 202-547-1141
Co-Chairperson: LARRY YOUNG, 1390 South 1100 East, Salt Lake City, UT 84105; Phone: 801-486-2872
Publication(s): *Wilderness at the Edge*
Keyword(s): Outdoor Recreation, Public Lands, Wilderness

UTAH WILDLIFE FEDERATION
P.O. Box 526367, Salt Lake City, UT 84152-6367
Phone: 801-487-1946; Fax: 801-846-0611
Scope: Statewide
Description: A representative statewide organization, affiliated with the National Wildlife Federation, dedicated to the protection and enhancement of wildlife and its habitat through public education and government interaction.
Contact(s):
President: GERALD GORDON
Editor: RAY SCHELBLE
Publication(s): *Utah Wildlife News*
Keyword(s): Aquatic Habitats, Fisheries, Renewable Resources, Water Pollution Management, Wetlands

NON-GOVERNMENTAL ORGANIZATIONS

UTAH WOODLAND OWNERS COUNCIL
2829 Sleep Hollow Dr., Salt Lake City, UT 84117
Phone: 801-277-1615
Founded: 1997; Membership: 75
Scope: Statewide
Description: A statewide organization affiliated with the National Woodland Owners Association and associated with Utah Farms Bureau, that is working for good forest management practices on the private forest and ranch land in Utah.
Contact(s):
Chairman: RICHARD OLDROYD

VERMONT ASSOCIATION OF CONSERVATION DISTRICTS
ATTN: President, 504 Thompson Hill Rd., Waybridge, VT 05753
Scope: Statewide
Contact(s):
President and Baord Member: CLAIRE AYER, 504 Thompson Hill Rd., Waybridge, VT 05753; Phone: 802-545-2142; Fax: 802-545-2142; Email: ayer@together.net
Vice President: STEVE DARROW, Westhill Rd., P.O. Box 880-N, Putney, VT 05346; Phone: 802-254-7454; Fax: 802-254-3307
Secretary: NOAH HUDSON, Rt. 4 Box 2025, Montpelier, VT 05602; Phone: 802-223-3593; Fax: 802-828-4493
Treasurer: DAVID STEVENS, Terrace Rd., Rt. 1 Box 13, Wells River, VT 05081; Phone: 802-757-2318; Fax: 802-296-3654

VERMONT AUDUBON COUNCIL
65 Millet St., Richmond, VT 05477
Phone: 802-434-4300
Scope: Statewide
Description: A statewide council consisting of eight chapters of the National Audubon Society formed to protect and enhance all elements of the precious and irreplaceable natural environment.
Contact(s):
President: WARREN KING, P.O. Box 77, Ripton, VT 05766; Phone: 802-388-4082
Vice President: KATHY ARCHER, P.O. Box 77, Ripton, VT 06766; Phone: 802-388-4082
Treasurer: SUZANNA LIEPMANN, P.O. Box 112, South Strafford, VT 05070; Phone: 802-765-4118
Keyword(s): Environmental and Conservation Education, Forests and Forestry, Nongame Wildlife, Planning Management, Wetlands

VERMONT B.A.S.S. CHAPTER FEDERATION
ATTN: President, 19 Pinewood Rd., Montpelier, VT 05602
Phone: 802-223-7793
Scope: Statewide
Description: An organization of Bassmaster chapters, affiliated with the Bass Anglers Sportman Society, organized to fight pollution, assist state and national conservation agencies in their efforts, and teach the young people of our country good conservation practices. Dedicated to the realistic conservation of our water resources.
Contact(s):
President: NORM WHITE, 19 Pinewood Rd., Montpelier, VT 05602; Phone: 802-223-7793
Conservation Director: JIM EDELMAN, 15 John Rowley Rd., Milton, VT 05468; Phone: 802-893-6571
Publication(s): *Vermont Institute of Natural Science; Records of Vermont Birds; Hands on Nature; Atlas of Breeding Birds of Vermont; Waste Away, Annual Report*
Keyword(s): Birds, Endangered and Threatened Species, Environmental and Conservation Education, Natural History, Raptors

VERMONT INSTITUTE OF NATURAL SCIENCE
R.R. 2 Box 532, Woodstock, VT 05091
Phone: 802-457-2779; Fax: 802-457-1053
Founded: 1972; Membership: 5,000
Scope: Statewide
Description: The mission of VINS is to protect Vermont's natural heritage through environmental education and research. VINS Raptor Center, Living Museum of birds of prey, on VINS nature preserve.
Contact(s):
President: DEBORAH GRANQUIST
Vice President: JENEPHER LINGLEBACH
Secretary: DEBORAH SCHOCH
Treasurer: JUDY PETERSON
Executive Director: TIM TRAVER
Education Director: JENNIFER GUARINO
Research Director: CHRISTOPHER RIMMER
Publication(s): *Vermont Institute of Natural Science; Records of Vermont; Hands on Nature; atlas of Breeding Birds of Vermont; Waste Away, Annual Report*
Keyword(s): Agriculture, Environmental and Conservation Education, Forests and Forestry, Land Preservation

VERMONT LAND TRUST
8 Bailey Ave., Montpelier, VT 05602
Phone: 802-223-5234; Fax: 802-223-4223; WWW: http://www.vlt.org
Founded: 1977; Membership: 4,000
Scope: Statewide
Description: Conserving the productive, recreational, and scenic lands that help give Vermont and its communities their distinctive rural character.
Contact(s):
President: DARBY BRADLEY, 8 Bailey Ave., Montpelier, VT 05602; Phone: 802-223-5234
Vice President for Land Conservation: GIL LIVINGSTON, 8 Bailey Ave., Montpelier, VT 05602; Phone: 802-223-5234
Vice President of Operations: BARBARA WAGNER, 8 Bailey Ave., Montpelier, VT 05602; Phone: 802-223-5234
Publication(s): *Quarterly newsletters, Annual Report*
Keyword(s): Environmental and Conservation Education

VERMONT NATURAL RESOURCES COUNCIL
9 Bailey Ave., Montpelier, VT 05602
Phone: 802-223-2328; Fax: 802-223-0287; Email: vnrc@together.net
Scope: Statewide
Description: A representative statewide organization, affiliated with the National Wildlife Federation, dedicated to the protection and enhancement of wildlife and its habitat through public education and government interaction.
Contact(s):
Chair: MARY ASHCROFT
Executive Director: ELIZABETH COURTNEY
Affiliate Representative: LEONARD WILSON
Editor: SUE HIGBY
Publication(s): *Vermont Environmental Report*
Keyword(s): Agriculture, Environmental and Conservation Education, Forests and Forestry, Outdoor Recreation, Wildlife Management

VERMONT STATE-WIDE ENVIRONMENTAL EDUCATION PROGRAMS (SWEEP)
c/o Vermont Natural Resources Council, 9 Bailey Ave., Montpelier, VT 05602
Founded: 1973
Scope: Statewide
Description: SWEEP is a coalition of individuals and organizations promoting environmental education in Vermont. SWEEP's purpose is to foster environmental appreciation and understanding in order to enable Vermonters to make responsible decisions affecting the environment.
Contact(s):
Chair: MARIE LEVESQUE CADUTO, 198 Kerwin Hill Rd., Norwich, VT 05055; Phone: 802-649-8116
Chair: SUSAN CLARK, R.D. 2 Box 3230, Worcester, VT 05682; Phone: 802-223-5824
Secretary: EVELEEN CECCHINI, OFES, 102 Harbor Rd., Shelburne, VT 05482; Phone: 802-985-8738

Treasurer: BARRY KING, Keewaydin Environmental Education Center, Salisbury, VT 05769; Phone: 802-352-9011
Publication(s): *VTOA Newsletter*
Keyword(s): Forests and Forestry

VERMONT WOODLANDS ASSOCIATION
9 Bailey Ave., Montpelier, VT 05602
Phone: 802-584-3333
Scope: Statewide
Description: A statewide organization, affiliated with the National Woodland Owners Association, organized to promote sound forest management throughout Vermont.
Contact(s):
President: ROBERT DARROW M.D., Rutland, VT ; Phone: 802-773-7144
Vice President: JOHN HEMENWAY, Stafford, VT ; Phone: 802-765-4324
Executive Director: HARRY CHANDLER
Editor: STEPHEN LONG
Editor: VIRGINIA BARLOW
Publication(s): *VTOA Newsletter, Vermont Woodlands Magazine*

VIRGIN ISLANDS CONSERVATION DISTRICT
ATTN: President, P.O. Box 1576, Fredericksted, VI 00841
Scope: Statewide
Contact(s):
President and Board Member: HANS LAWAETZ, P.O. Box 1576, Fredericksted, VI 00841; Phone: 340-788-2229; Fax: 340-778-0270
Vice President: JOSEPH SAMUEL, P.O. Box 241, Fredericksted, St. Croix, VI 00841; Phone: 340-772-3168
Alternate Board Member: CEDRICK LEWIS, P.O. Box 303142, St. Thomas, VI 00803; Phone: 340-775-7393
Secretary and Treasurer: ENRICO GASPERI, P.O. Box 895, Christiansted, VI 00824; Phone: 340-773-2386
Publication(s): *Federation Record, The*

VIRGIN ISLANDS CONSERVATION SOCIETY, INC.
Arawak Bldg., #3, Gallows Bay, Christiansted, VI 00820
Phone: 340-773-1989; Fax: 340-773-7545; Email: sea@viaccess.net; WWW: www.ecani.com/environassoc
Founded: 1968
Scope: Statewide
Description: A representative statewide organization, affiliated with the National Wildlife Federation, dedicated to the protection and enhancement of wildlife and its habitat through public education and government interaction.
Contact(s):
President: ANDY SIMPSON
Executive Director: ROBIN FREEMAN, St Croix Environmental Association, Arawak Bldg., #3, Gallows Bay, St. Croix, VI 00820
Affiliate Representative: NICOLE BALLENTINI, c/o East, P.O. Box 12379, St. Thomas, VI 00801
Alternate Representative: DEVORATH ELCOCK
Editor: EMY THOMAS, SEA, 9003 Salt River, Christiansted, VI 00820
Executive Director and Editor: GRETHELYN PIPER, East, P.O. Box 12379, St. Thomas, VI 00801
Keyword(s): Agriculture, Coral Reefs, Environmental and Conservation Education, Pollution Prevention, Soil Conservation

VIRGINIA ASSOCIATION OF CONSERVATION DISTRICTS
ATTN: President, P.O. Box 127, North, VA 23128
Scope: Statewide
Contact(s):
President, Alternate Board Member: MARILYN W. LAYER, P.O. Box 127, North, VA 23128; Phone: 804-725-4622; Fax: 804-725-4622; Email: layer@inna.net
Secretary/Treasurer: ANDREW H. GRANT II, 12615 Norwood Rd., Wingina, VA 24599; Phone: 804-263-8680; Fax: 804-975-0224
Executive Secretary: ANGELA CHAPLIN, 7293 Hanover Green Dr. Ste B101, Mechanicsville, VA 23111; Phone: 804-559-0324; Fax: 804-559-0325
1st Vice President: JOHN R. DIXON, 1228 Rendezous Ln., Bedford, VA 24523; Phone: 304-392-6058; Fax: 304-392-6058
2nd Vice President: DAPHNE W. JAMISON, 290 River Creek Rd., Wirtz, VA 24184; Phone: 540-721-2361; Fax: 540-483-0006; Email: Rjam229@aol.com
Board Member: HUDSON REESE, 8125 James D. Hagwood Hwy, Scottsbrg, VA 24589; Phone: 703-787-2637

VIRGINIA B.A.S.S. CHAPTER FEDERATION
ATTN: President, 11210 Brewer Rd., Richmond, VA 23233
Phone: 804-360-8922; WWW: www.mscc.vt.edu/orgs.vabass
Scope: Statewide
Description: An organization of Bassmaster chapters, affiliated with the Bass Anglers Sportsman Society, organized to fight pollution, assist state and national conservation agencies in their efforts, and teach the young people of our country good conservation practices. Dedicated to the realistic conservation of our water resources.
Contact(s):
President and Conservation Director: ED RHODES, 11210 Brewer Rd., Richmond, VA 23233; Phone: 804-360-8922; Email: edrhodz@worldnet.att.net
Publication(s): *VCN News; Environmental Voting Summary; Virginia B.A.S.S. Federation Newsletter "Tightlines"*
Keyword(s): Air Quality and Pollution, Land Use Planning, Water Quality

VIRGINIA CONSERVATION NETWORK
1001 E. Broad St., Suite 410, Richmond, VA 23219
Phone: 804-644-0283; Fax: 804-644-0286
Founded: 1969; Membership: 111 organizatons organizations
Scope: Statewide
Description: The Conservation Council of Virginia merged with the Virginia Environmental Network in 1994 to form the Virginia Conservation Network. The Network's member organizations are devoted to advancing a common, environmentally-sound vision for Virginia.
Contact(s):
President: CHRIS MILLER, P.O. Box 460, Warrenton, VA 22186; Phone: 540-347-2334
Vice President: JACK WHITNEY, 318 Kemp Lane, Chesapeake, VA 23325; Phone: 757-473-2000
Secretary: LAWRENCE JAHN, 2435 Rivera Drive, Vienna, VA 22181; Phone: 703-281-9768
Treasurer: PATTI JACKSON, P.O. Box 110, Richmond, VA 23218; Phone: 804-730-2898
Office Manager: SUSAN WERMUS
Publication(s): *Virginia Forests Magazine; Forestry News*
Keyword(s): Environmental Legislation

VIRGINIA FORESTRY ASSOCIATION
8810B Patterson Ave., Richmond, VA 23229
Phone: 804-741-0836; Fax: 804-741-0838; Email: vafa@erols.com
Founded: 1943; Membership: 1,600
Scope: Statewide
Description: An association of landowners and forest industry that promotes stewardship and wise use of forest resources for the economic and environmental benefits of all Virginians.
Contact(s):
President: CROCKETT MORRIS, Waverly, VA
Vice President: DENICE TAPPERO, Hopewell, VA
Treasurer: JOHN CARROLL
Editor: PAUL HOWE
Executive Vice President: PAUL R. HOWE
Past President: RICHARD L. MALM, Franklin, VA
Publication(s): *Bulletin; chapter newsletters; wildflower conservation guidelines; checklists; nursery source list; fact sheets; brochure; invasive alien plant list*

NON-GOVERNMENTAL ORGANIZATIONS

Keyword(s): Endangered and Threatened Species, Environmental and Conservation Education, Flowers, Plants, and Trees, Gardening and Horticulture, Natural Areas

VIRGINIA NATIVE PLANT SOCIETY
P.O. Box 844, Annandale, VA 22003
Phone: 703-368-9803; Email: mfminor@inna.net; WWW: www.hort.vt.edu/vnps
Founded: 1982; Membership: 1,750
Scope: Statewide
Description: The VNPS and nine chapters throughout Virginia seek further appreciation and conservation of Virginia's wild plants and habitats. Programs emphasize public education, protection of endangered species, habitat preservation, control of invasive alien plants, and encouragement of appropriate landscape use of native plants. Includes both amateurs and professionals. Membership brochures available.
Contact(s):
President: MARIE F. MINOR; Phone: 804-443-5950
Treasurer: JOHN FRY; Phone: 540-364-3046
1st Vice President: RICHARD KELLY; Phone: 540-384-7429
2nd Vice President: BEN FITZGERALD
Corresponding Secretary: ELAINE SMITH; Phone: 540-432-6833; Fax: 540-568-3332
Director of Blue Ridge Chapter: BOB EUBANK; Phone: 804-239-9756
Director of Botany: DR. STANWYN SHETLER; Phone: 703-430-6523
Director of Conservation: NICKY STAUNTON; Phone: 703-368-9803
Director of Education: EFFIE FOX; Phone: 540-347-2788
Director of Horticulture: NANCY ARRINGTON; Phone: 703-368-9711
Director of Jefferson Chapter: PAT WILLIS; Phone: 540-967-1776
Director of John Clayton Chapter: GORDON CHAPPELL; Phone: 757-220-0914
Director of Membership: CHARLES SMITH; Phone: 703-361-5125
Director of Piedmont Chapter: JOHN FRY; Phone: 540-364-3046
Director of Pocahontas Chapter: RICHARD MOSS; Phone: 804-748-2940
Director of Potomac Chapter: NORMA VERMILLION; Phone: 703-451-0572
Director of Prince William Chapter: HELEN WALTER; Phone: 703-330-9614
Director of Publicity: NANCY HUGO; Phone: 804-798-6364
Director of Registry: BOLEYN DALE; Phone: 804-725-5451
Director of Shenandoah Chapter: BONNIE HOHN; Phone: 540-885-2393
Director of South Hampton Roads Chapter: HOLLY CRUSER; Phone: 757-481-2285
Recording Secretary: JUNE GRIFFIN; Phone: 804-296-3219
Publication(s): *BULLETIN; Virginia Wildflower of the Year; Nursery Sources fo Native Plants*
Keyword(s): Botany, Conservation of Protected Areas, Endangered and Threatened Species, Environment, Flowers, Plants, and Trees, Forest Management, Habitat Conservation, Landscape Architecture, Natural Areas, Prairies, Public Lands, Urban Forestry, Watersheds, Wetlands

VIRGINIA SOCIETY OF ORNITHOLOGY
7451 Little River Turnpike, #202, Annandale, VA 22003
Phone: 703-305-7381
Founded: 1929; Membership: 1,000
Scope: Statewide
Description: Dedicated to all aspects of the birds of Virginia, including conservation, field research, education of any interested person or group, and dissemination of all types of information. The VSO coordinates with state agencies and with other private organizations in this mission.
Contact(s):
President: THELMA DALMAS, 1230 Viewmont Dr., Evington, VA 24550; Phone: 804-821-1136
Vice President: LARRY LYNCH, 9430 Tuxford Rd., Richmond, VA 23236; Phone: 804-272-8582
Secretary: LISA HAMILTON, 321 York Ave, Staunton, VA 24401; Phone: 540-885-4808
Treasurer: BARBARA SUE THRASHER, 120 Woodbine Dr., Lynchburg, VA 24502; Phone: 804-239-5850
Publication(s): *Raven, The; VSO Newsletter*

VIRGINIA WILDLIFE FEDERATION
1001 E. Broad St., LL-5, Richmond, VA 23219-1928
Phone: 804-648-3136; Fax: 804-648-8010
Scope: Statewide
Description: A representative statewide organization, affiliated with the National Wildlife Federation, dedicated to the protection and enhancement of wildlife and its habitat through public education and government interaction.
Contact(s):
President: DON HINCHEY
Affiliate Representative: KEMPER E. EAGLE
Editor: THOMAS W. EVANS
Publication(s): *Federation Record, The*
Keyword(s): Aquatic Habitats, Fisheries, Renewable Resources, Water Pollution Management, Wetlands

WASHINGTON ASSOCIATION OF CONSERVATION DISTRICTS
ATTN: President, 1301 Crumbaker Rd., Colfax, WA 99111
Scope: Statewide
Contact(s):
President, Alternate Board Member: LARRY COCHRAN, 1301 Crumbaker Rd., Colfax, WA 99111; Phone: 509-397-3302; Fax: 590-397-3302
Vice President: COLIN BENNETT, 185 Beebe Rd., Goldendale, WA 98620; Phone: 509-773-5065; Fax: 509-773-5600; Email: cbennett@gorge.net
Executive Director: DON STUART, P.O. Box 60055, Shoreline, WA 98160; Phone: 206-546-7690; Fax: 206-546-7740
Board Member: BOB HABERMAN, 771 Hungry Junction Rd., Ellensburg, WA 98926; Phone: 509-925-1713; Fax: 509-925-7730; Email: bobhaber@eburg.net
Secretary and Treasurer: MONTE MARTI, 11605 33rd Ct, NE, Lake Stevens, WA 98258; Phone: 425-261-6678; Fax: 425-258-4839

WASHINGTON B.A.S.S. CHAPTER FEDERATION
ATTN: President, 16569 162nd Pl. SE, Renton, WA 98058
Phone: 425-271-6569; WWW: www.accessone.com/~kreigbaum
Scope: Statewide
Description: An organization of Bassmaster chapters, affiliated with the Bass Anglers Sportsman Society, organized to fight pollution, assist state and national conservation agencies in their efforts, and teach the young people of our country good conservation practices. Dedicated to the realistic conservation of our water resources.
Contact(s):
President: JIM OWENS, 16569 162nd Pl. SE, Renton, WA 98058; Phone: 425-271-6569
Conservation Director: DAN PFEIFFER, 4243 E. 29th Ave., Spokane, WA 99223; Phone: 509-482-4416
Keyword(s): Energy, Environmental and Conservation Education, Environmental Preservation, Renewable Resources, Solid Waste

WASHINGTON ENVIRONMENTAL COUNCIL
615 2nd Avenue, #380, Seattle, WA 98104
Phone: 206-622-8103; Fax: 206-622-8113; Email: greenwec@aol.com
Founded: 1967; Membership: 2,500
Scope: Statewide
Description: A statewide nonprofit organization of 2,500 individual volunteers and 85 affiliated organizations working to protect, preserve, and restore the environment of Washington state and the Pacific Northwest.
Contact(s):
President: DAVE MANN
Vice President: AARON OSTROM

Secretary: LAURI AUNAN
Treasurer: JOHN ANDERSON
Executive Director: JOAN CROOKS
Editor: TOM GEIGER
Vice President, Legislative Affairs: LOREN DUNN
Vice President, Organizational Liasion: LEEANNE TRYON
Publication(s): *WEC Voices; Forest Resources News*
Keyword(s): Forests and Forestry

WASHINGTON FARM FORESTRY ASSOCIATION
P.O. Box 7663, Olympia, WA 98507
Phone: 360-459-0984
Founded: 1944; Membership: 1,250
Scope: Statewide
Description: A statewide organization affiliated with the National Woodland Owners Association, founded to help small woodland owners acquire information on better management of small timber tracts.
Contact(s):
President: CHANDLER NOERENBERG, Castle Rock, WA
Vice President: SHERRY FOX, Ethel, WA
Secretary: BILL AND ERIN WOODS, Redmond, WA
Treasurer: BOB FALKNER, Raymond, WA
Executive Director: NELS HANSON; Phone: 360-943-3875
Editor: NELS HANSON; Phone: 360-943-3875
Editor: LORI D. RASOR, 4033 SW Canyon Rd., Portland, OR 97221; Phone: 503-226-2515
Past President: MAURICE WILLIAMSON
Publication(s): *Northwest Woodlands; Landowner News*
Keyword(s): Environmental and Conservation Education, Environmental Law, Natural History, Scholarships and Grants, Wildlife and Wildlife Habitat

WASHINGTON FOUNDATION FOR THE ENVIRONMENT
P.O. Box 2123, Seattle, WA 98111
Founded: 1979
Scope: Statewide
Description: Dedicated to preserving and enhancing the environmental heritage of Washington state by supporting educational and innovative projects in both the public and private sectors.
Contact(s):
President: PATRICIA SERIE, 1147 21st Avenu., E, Seattle, WA 98112; Phone: 206-324-9319
Vice President: WICK DUFFORD, 620 16th NE, Bellevue, WA 98008; Phone: 206-747-8215
Secretary: KATHY FLETCHER, 1916 7th Avenue, W, Seattle, WA 98119; Phone: 206-382-7007
Treasurer: BILL JOLLY, 4007 Green Cove, NW, Olympia, WA 98502; Phone: 206-866-9204
Publication(s): *Public trust Doctrine, The; Conference Proceedings; Washington Natural Hertage Eduation*
Keyword(s): Environmental and Conservation Education, Environmental Preservation, Environmental Protection

WASHINGTON NATIVE PLANT SOCIETY
P.O. Box 28690, Seattle, WA 98118-8690
Phone: 206-760-8022
Founded: 1976; Membership: 1,500
Scope: Statewide
Description: To promote the appreciation and conservation of Washington's native plants and their habitats through study, education, and advocacy.
Contact(s):
President: SARAH GAGE, 836 NE 58th St., Seattle, WA 98105; Phone: 206-522-2242
Vice President: LAURA POTASH, 2112 N. 44th St., Seattle, WA 98103; Phone: 206-547-3199
Secretary: JOAN FRAZEE, P.O. Box 2435, Poulsboro, WA 98370; Phone: 360-598-1993
Treasurer: PEGGY BUTLER, 7710 Brown Rd., SW, Olympia, WA 98502; Phone: 360-943-8711

Publication(s): *Publicationss: Syllabus*
Keyword(s): Outdoor Recreation, Public Lands, Urban Forestry, Wetlands, Youth Organizations

WASHINGTON RECREATION AND PARK ASSOCIATION
350 S. 333rd St., Suite 103, Federal Way, WA 98003
Phone: 253-874-1283; Fax: 253-661-3929
Founded: 1947; Membership: 1,200
Scope: Statewide
Description: Dedicated to enhanching and promoting parks, recreation, and leisure pursuits in Washington state, and plays a vital role in promoting public support for parks and recreation.
Contact(s):
President: JUDY QUINLIVAN, 808 W. Spokane Falls Blvd., Spokane, WA 99201
Secretary: LORI CUMMINGS, 802 Mukilteo Blvd, Everett, WA 98203
President-elect: JOHN COUCH, P.O. Box 97010, Redmond, WA 98073
Publication(s): *Syllabus*

WASHINGTON SOCIETY OF AMERICAN FORESTERS
4033 SW Canyon Rd., Portland, OR 97221
Phone: 503-224-8046
Founded: 1900; Membership: 925 (WA)
Scope: Statewide
Description: Represents the forestry profession in advancing the science, technology, education, and practice of forestry for the benefit of forests, forest managers, and the public.
Contact(s):
Chair: JOCKO BURKS, 3302 Sounview Dr. West, University Place, WA 98466
Chair-Elect ('99): ART SCHICK, 2585 NE Ortis Rd., Poulsbo, WA 98370
Manager/Editor: LORI RASOR, 4033 SW Canyon Rd., Portland, OR 97221

WASHINGTON TOXICS COALITION
4649 Sunnyside Ave., N., Suite 540 East, Seattle, WA 98103
Phone: 206-632-1545; Email: info@watoxics.org; WWW: www.accessone.com/~watoxics/
Founded: 1981; Membership: 1,500
Scope: Statewide
Description: Works to reduce society's reliance on toxic chemicals through research, education, advocacy, organizing, and litigation.
Contact(s):
President: DAVID STITZHAL
Secretary: JENNIFER DOLD
Treasurer: DON BOLLINGER
Publication(s): *Alternatives; Buy Smart, Grow Smart, Grow Safe: A Consumer Guide to Lawn and Garden Products; Trumbling Bubbles: The Case for Replacing Alkylphenol Ethozylate Surfacants; No Place For Poisons: Reducing Pesticides in School; Home Safe Home (fact sheets); Smokescreen: Myth & Incinerator Need; Fact sheets on industry source reduction; Poisons in the Web of Life: The Case for Toxics Reform*
Keyword(s): Cultural Preservation, Environmental and Conservation Education, Outdoor Recreation, Public Lands, Transportation

WASHINGTON TRAILS ASSOCIATION
1305 4th Ave., #512, Seattle, WA 98101-2401
Phone: 206-625-1367
Founded: 1973; Membership: 4,100
Scope: Statewide
Description: Washington Trails Association works to protect and enhance Washington's diverse trail system through education and information programs, direct involvement in trail planning and maintenance and management activities, and by encouraging cooperation in finding solutions to trail problems statewide.
Contact(s):
President: PETER SANBORN

NON-GOVERNMENTAL ORGANIZATIONS

Director of Operations: GREG BALL
Keyword(s): Environmental and Conservation Education, Natural Areas, Open Space, Outdoor Recreation, Wildlife and Wildlife Habitat, Wildlife Management

WASHINGTON WILDERNESS COALITION
4649 Sunnyside Ave., N.#242, Seattle, WA 98103
Phone: 206-633-1992; Fax: 206-633-1996; Email: wawild@aol.com
Founded: 1979; Membership: 10,000
Scope: Statewide
Description: WWC is a statewide organization of individuals and groups dedicated to preserving wilderness and biodiversity for the benefit of future generations. WWC works to protect and restore wildlands and waters in Washington State through outreach, public education, organizing, and support of grassroots conservation groups.
Contact(s):
President: MARTIN LOESCH
Vice President: DONA WUTHNOW
Secretary: JOHN OSBORN
Treasurer: MICHELLE KINSCH
Executive Director: JOHN LEARY
Canvass Director: PHIL COCHRAN
Field Director: JON OWEN
Membership & Development Coordinator: JULIE HOFFMAN
Policy Director: TREVOR FITZGIBBON
Publication(s): *Washington Wildfire*

WASHINGTON WILDLIFE AND RECREATION COALITION
4001 SW Cloverdale, Seattle, WA 98136-2363
Phone: 206-938-4513; Fax: 206-932-5651
Founded: 1989
Scope: Statewide
Description: The Washington Wildlife and Recreation Coalition was formed in 1989 to promote the acquisition of land for wildlife and outdoor recreation through public education, support of appropriate legislation, and research into outdoor recreation and conservation needs in Washington state. Our long-range goal is to secure state funding for a $450 million, 8-10 year program to acquire and develop parks, trails, water access, wildlife habitat, and natural areas. To date, the state legislature has allocated over $270 million towards that goal.
Contact(s):
Assistant Director: KRISTEN QUIGLEY
President: KENT HULL
Vice President: JOANNE ROBERTS
Vice President: JOHN McGLENN
Secretary: KAREN MUNRO
Treasurer: PETER SCHOLES
Executive Director: JANET WAINWRIGHT
Program Coordinator: LINDSEY AMTMANN
Publication(s): *Land News*
Keyword(s): Land Preservation, Land Purchase, Nature Preservation, Public Lands, Wildlife and Wildlife Habitat

WASHINGTON WILDLIFE FEDERATION
P.O. Box 1966, Olympia, WA 98507-1966
Phone: 360-705-1903; WWW: www.washingtonwildlife.org
Scope: Statewide
Description: A representative statewide organization, affiliated with the National Wildlife Federation, dedicated to the protection and enhancement of wildlife and its habitat through public education and government interaction.
Contact(s):
President: KEN HILTON
Affiliate Representative: THEA LEVKOVITZ
Keyword(s): Environmental and Conservation Education, Environmental Preservation, Land Purchase, Water Pollution Management, Wetlands

WASHINGTON WILDLIFE HERITAGE FOUNDATION (including Heritage Land Trust
32610 Pacific Highway South, Federal Way, WA 98003
Scope: Statewide
Description: The Foundation is dedicated to fish and wildlife/water and land conservation through resource management, and enhancing habitat and public education, with the involvement, support, and cooperation of both the public and private sector.
Contact(s):
Chairman: BRUCE STUWE, 4727 Crisman Ct., SE, Olympia, WA 98501; Phone: 360-491-9195
Secretary: ROBERT GRIBBLE, 26442 164th SE, Kent, WA 98042; Phone: 253-631-9244
Publication(s): *Land News*
Keyword(s): Land Management, Outdoor Recreation, Wildlife and Wildlife Habitat

WATER ENVIRONMENT FEDERATION
601 Wythe St., Alexandria, VA 22314-1994
Phone: 703-684-2400
Founded: 1928; Membership: 41,000
Scope: National
Description: A nonprofit technical and educational organization. Its mission is to preserve and enhance the global water environment. Federation members are water quality specialists from around the world, including environmental, civil and chemical engineers, biologists, government officials, treatment plant managers and operators, laboratory technicians, college professors, students, and equipment manufacturers and distributors.
Contact(s):
President: RHONDA HARRIS
Vice President: JOE C. STOWE
Treasurer: PRAD KHARE
Executive Director: DR. QUINCALEE BROWN
President-Elect: ALBERT GOODMAN
Publication(s): *Water Environment Research; Water Environment and Technology; WEF Highlights; Operations Forum; Water Environment Regulation Watch*
Keyword(s): Asia Water Environment, Engineering, Environmental and Conservation Education, Toxic Substances, Water Pollution Management, Water Resources

WATER RESOURCES ASSOCIATION OF THE DELAWARE RIVER BASIN
P.O. Box 867, Valley Forge, PA 19482-0867
Phone: 610-917-0090; Fax: 610-917-0091; Email: wradrb@aol.com
Founded: 1959
Scope: National
Description: Nonprofit federation of businesses, industries, academia, government, environmental, and citizen organizations which serves to advise of and advocate the need for adequate water supplies through the orderly conservation, development, and equitable use and reuse of the water and related land resources of the Delaware River Basin.
Contact(s):
Chair: JEREMIAH J. CARDAMONE ESQ
Executive Director: WILLIAM H. PALMER
Keyword(s): Environmental and Conservation Education, Rivers, Water Pollution, Water Resources, Wetlands

WELDER WILDLIFE FOUNDATION
P.O. Box 1400, Sinton, TX 78387
Phone: 512-364-2643; Fax: 512-364-2650; Email: welderwf@aol.com
Founded: 1954
Scope: National
Description: Established by the will of the late Rob Welder, the Foundation is dedicated to the cause of conservation through research and education in wildlife ecology and management and closely related fields. Operates through a small staff, with research fellowships to graduate students only.

Contact(s):
Director: D. LYNN DRAWE
Assistant Director/Conservatin Educator: SELMA N. GLASSCOCK
Assistant Director/Wildlife Biologist: TERRY L. BLANKENSHIP
Keyword(s): Birds, Mammals, Scholarships and Grants, Wildlife and Wildlife Habitat, Wildlife Management

WEST MICHIGAN ENVIRONMENTAL ACTION COUNCIL
1432 Wealthy, SE, Grand Rapids, MI 49506
Phone: 616-451-3051; Fax: 616-451-3054
Founded: 1968; Membership: 700 individuals, 30 organizations
Scope: Statewide
Description: Provide leadership in environmental protection and preservation in west Michigan and throughout Michigan on issues such as water quality, land use planning, and urban environment. Through the involvement of concerned volunteers, WMEAC has helped landmark environmental legislation and assured application of existing laws.
Contact(s):
President: THOM PETERSON
Executive Director: TOM LEONARD
Publication(s): *Action Issue*
Keyword(s): Air Quality and Pollution, Conservation, Environmental and Conservation Education, Land Use Planning, Waste Management, Water Resources

WEST VIRGINIA ASSOCIATION OF CONSERVATION DISTRICT SUPERVISORS ASSOCIATION, INC.
ATTN: President, Rt. 1 Box 543A, Berkeley Springs, WV 25411
Scope: Statewide
Contact(s):
President and Board Member: LARRY C. SMITH, Rt. 1 Box 543A, Berkeley Springs, WV 25411; Phone: 304-258-2534
Secretary: CARROLL CUMBERLEDGE, Box 11, Hundred, WV 26575; Phone: 304-775-7611
Treasurer: CLINTON LUCAS, Rt. 1 Box 303-E, West Hamlin, WV 25571; Phone: 304-778-7234
Vice President, Alternate Board Membe: ROBERT BAIRD, P.O. Box 711, Gallipolis Ferry, WV 25515; Phone: 304-675-6873

WEST VIRGINIA B.A.S.S. CHAPTER FEDERATION
ATTN: President, 12 N. Kanawha St., Buckhannon, WV 26201
Phone: 304-472-3600
Scope: Statewide
Description: An organization of Bassmaster chapters, affiliated with the Bass Anglers Sportsman Society, organized to fight pollution, assist state and national conservation agencies in their efforts, and teach the young people of our country good conservation practices. Dedicated to the realistic conservation of our water resources.
Contact(s):
President: JOHN BURDETTE, 12 N. Kanawha St., Buckhannon, WV 26201; Phone: 304-472-3600
Conservation Director: JIM SUMMERS, Rt. 1 Box 205, Worthington, WV 26591; Phone: 304-287-7700
Publication(s): *Highlands Voice, The; Monongahela National Forest Hiking Guide, The*
Keyword(s): Forests and Forestry, Public Lands, Rivers, Water Pollution Management, Wilderness

WEST VIRGINIA HIGHLANDS CONSERVANCY
P.O. Box 306, Charleston, WV 25321
Founded: 1967
Scope: Statewide
Description: An organization devoted to the conservation and wise management of West Virginia's natural and historic resources. Active in wilderness preservation, river conservation, public lands management, mining, air and water quality, water resources management, and a wide variety of other environmental and conservation issues.
Contact(s):
President: JOHN McFERRIN, 114 Beckley Ave., Beckley, WV 25801; Phone: 304-252-8733
Secretary: JACQUELINE HALLINAN, 1120 Swan Rd., Charleston, WV 25314; Phone: 304-345-3718
Treasurer: TOM MICHAEL, Rt. 2, Box 217, Lost Creek, WV 26385; Phone: 304-623-3447
Editor: BILL REED, 350 Bucks Branch, Beckley, WV 25801; Phone: 304-934-5828
Membership Secretary: DAVE SAVILLE, P.O. Box 569, Morgantown, WV 26507; Phone: 304-594-2276
Past President: CINDY RANK, HC 78, Box 227, Rock Cave, WV 26234; Phone: 304-924-5802
Senior Vice President: FRANK YOUNG, Rt. 1, Box 108, Ripley, WV 25271; Phone: 304-372-9329
Vice President of State Affairs: NORM STEENSTRA, 1001 Valley Rd., Charleston, WV 25302; Phone: 304-346-5891

WEST VIRGINIA WILDLIFE FEDERATION, INC.
P.O. Box 275, Paden City, WV 26159
Phone: 304-782-3685; Email: pleinbach@aol.com
Scope: Statewide
Description: A representative statewide organization, affiliated with the National Wildlife Federation, dedicated to the protection and enhancement of wildlife and its habitat through public education and government interaction.
Contact(s):
President: ART MULLINS
Affiliate Representative: PAUL JOHANSEN
Editor: PHIL LEINBACH

WESTERN ASSOCIATION OF FISH AND WILDLIFE AGENCIES
Game and Fish Department, 5400 Bishop Blvd., Cheyenne, WY 82006
Scope: Regional
Description: A regional organization including 18 fish and wildlife agencies of 15 states and three Canadian provinces. Meets annually to consider mutual problems and provide a forum for the exchange of information at both administrative and technical levels.
Contact(s):
President: JOHN BAUGHMAN; Phone: 307-777-4600
1st Vice President: JOHN MUMMA; Phone: 303-291-7208
2rd Vice President: JIM GREER; Phone: 503-872-5272
Secretary and Treasurer: LARRY KRUCKENBERG, Game and Fish Department, 5400 Bishop Blvd., Cheyenne, WY 82006; Phone: 307-7774569

WESTERN ENVIRONMENTAL LAW CENTER
1216 Lincoln St., Eugene, OR 97401
Phone: 541-485-2471; Fax: 541-485-2457; Email: westernlaw@igc.org; WWW: www.welc.org
Founded: 1993; Membership: 900
Scope: Statewide
Description: WELC specializes in environmental law enforcement, working with grassroots citizen groups and native American tribes to implement our nation's environmental laws. WELC has offices in Eugene, Oregon and Taos, New Mexico.
Contact(s):
President: LORI MADDOX
Vice President: CORRIE YACKULIC
Executive Director: MICHAEL AXLINE
Director of Taos Office: GROVE BURNETT; Phone: 505-751-0351; Fax: 505-751-1775; Email: taoslaw@laplaza.org
Secretary and Treasurer: MARY WOOD
Publication(s): *Defending the West; Biennial Report*
Keyword(s): Air Quality and Pollution, Cultural Preservation, Environmental Law, Mining, Pesticides, Toxic Substances, Water Quality, Wildlife and Wildlife Habitat

NON-GOVERNMENTAL ORGANIZATIONS

WESTERN FORESTRY AND CONSERVATION ASSOCIATION
4033 SW Canyon Rd., Portland, OR 97221
Phone: 503-226-4562; Fax: 503-226-2515; Email: richard@westernforestry.org
Founded: 1909
Scope: National
Description: The mission of the WFCA is to promote forest stewardship in western North America. The Association's objectives are to promote the science and practice of forestry, promote the dissemination of forestry research and technical information, and foster cooperation between federal, state, provincial, and private forest agencies.
Contact(s):
President: BOB ANDERSON
Treasurer: BLAIR HOLMAN
Executive Director: RICHARD ZABEL
Past President: WADE BOYD
Keyword(s): Forest Management

WESTERN HEMISPHERE SHOREBIRD RESERVE NETWORK (WHSRN)
c/o Manomet Center for Conservation Services, 81 Stage Point Rd., P.O. Box 1770, Manomet, MA 02345
Phone: 508-224-6521; Fax: 508-224-9220; Email: jmcorven@manomet.org; WWW: www.manomet.org/WHSRN.htm
Founded: 1985; Membership: 120 organizations
Scope: National
Description: As a partnership of Manomet and Wetlands International: the Americas, WHSRN is a voluntary nonregulatory network of 35 critical wetland sites in seven countries which have joined together to study, manage, and promote the sustainable conservation of shorebirds and their habitats for the benefit of the ecosystems and people. WHSRN's strategy promotes a multiple species ecosystem approach to protection of over nine million acres of habitats that are critical staging, nesting, and nonbreeding sites of migratory shorebirds, throughout North and South America.
Contact(s):
Director: JIM CORVEN
Publication(s): *WHSRNews; Important Shorebird Staging Sites Meeting WHSRN Criteria in the U.S.; Transcripts from the WHSRN Workshop; Save Our Migratory Shorebirds (curriculum guide and game), Shorebird Atlas*
Keyword(s): Birds, International Conservation, Sustainable Ecosystems, Wetlands, Wildlife Management

WESTERN PACIFIC REGIONAL FISHERY MANAGEMENT COUNCIL
1164 Bishop St. Suite 1400, Honolulu, HI 96813
Phone: 808-522-8220; Fax: 808-522-8226
Founded: 1977; Membership: 16
Scope: National
Description: The Council is the policy-making organization for the management of fisheries in and around the EEZs of American Samoa, Guam, Hawaii, and the Northern Mariana Islands, and U.S. possessions in the Pacific Ocean. Council members and members of its advisory bodies: Scientific and Statistical Committee, Plan Teams, and Advisory Panels represent the fishing community, government agencies, and national international fisheries management organizations throughout the region.
Contact(s):
Chairman: JIM D. COOK
Executive Director: KITTY M. SIMONDS
Publication(s): *Pacific Islands Fishery News*
Keyword(s): Commercial Sport Fishing, Fish Wildlife Management, Fisheries, Highly Migratory Species, Islands, Management Plans

WESTERN PENNSYLVANIA CONSERVANCY
209 4th Ave., Pittsburgh, PA 15222
Phone: 412-288-2777
Founded: 1932; Membership: 18,000
Scope: Statewide
Description: The Western Pennsylvania Conservancy, working together to save the places we care about, protects natural lands, promotes healthy and attractive communities, and preserves Faiingwater.
Contact(s):
Chairman: JARVIS B. CECIL
Secretary: GEORGE F. KESEL
Treasurer: ALEXANDER C. SPEYER III
Director of Administration and CFO: MICHAEL E. AUGUSTINE
Editor and Senior Director of Public Affairs: JULIE LALO
Executive Vice President and COO: CYNTHIA CARROW
President and CEO: LARRY J. SCHWEIGER
Senior Director of Community Conservation: JEFF GERSON
Senior Director of Constituent Programs: SUSAN NESZPAUL
Vice Chairman: E. MICHAEL BOYLE
Vice President and Director of Fallingwater: LYNDA WAGGONER
Vice President of Resource Conservation: PAUL G. WIEGMAN
Publication(s): *Conserve; Annual Calendar*
Keyword(s): Conservation of Protected Areas, Endangered and Threatened Species, Gardening and Horticulture, Land Preservation, Sustainable Ecosystems, Urban Environment

WESTERN REGIONAL ENVIRONMENTAL EDUCATION COUNCIL
c/o Josetta Hawthorne Executive Director 4014 Chatham Ln., Houston, TX 77027
Phone: 713-520-1936
Scope: National
Description: Membership includes department of education and resource management personnel from 13 western states. Works to advance national, state, and regional level formal and nonformal environmental education programs in cooperation with public and private agencies. Conducts materials development and in-service training activities, and provides consultant services to various organizations developing environmental education materials and programs. Produced Project WILD and Project Learning Tree, interdisciplinary, supplemental environmental education programs for use in grades K-12. Co-sponsors National Project WET (Water Education for Teachers).
Contact(s):
President: DAVE SANGER, Nevada Department of Wildlife, ;
  Phone: 702-688-1555
Executive Director: JOSETTA HAWTHORNE; Phone: 713-520-1936
Past President: JOHN GAHL; Phone: 208-334-2633
Project Learning Tree Director: KATHY McGLAUFLIN, 1250
  Connecticut Ave. NW, Suite 320, Washington, DC 20036;
  Phone: 202-463-2455
Project WET Director: DENNIS NELSON, Montana State University,
  Culbertson Hall, Bozeman, MT 59717; Phone: 406-994-5392
Project WILD Director: BETTY OLIVOLO, 5430 Grosvenor Ln.,
  Bethesda, MD 20814; Phone: 301-493-5447
Keyword(s): Environmental and Conservation Education

WETLAND HABITAT ALLIANCE OF TEXAS
118 E. Hospital, Suite 208, Nacogdoches, TX 75961
Phone: 409-569-9428; Fax: 409-569-6349; Email: whatduck@lcc.net
Founded: 1984; Membership: 7,000
Scope: Statewide
Description: A nonprofit organization of conservationists, dedicated to preserving, reclaiming, and enhancing Texas wetland habitat, that promotes the wise use of our natural resources and the progress of our society. Constructs habitat improvement projects on public and private lands, promotes educational programs, performs priority wetland research, and supports legislative conservation efforts.
Contact(s):
Chairman: BRUCE KLINGMAN

Vice President: RICHARD TINSLEY
Treasurer: NEAL JENKINS
Executive Director: JOHN E. FRASIER
Publication(s): *Texas Wetlands*

WHALE AND DOLPHIN CONSERVATION SOCIETY
Alexander House, James Street, West, Bath, Somerset BA1 2BT United Kingdom
Phone: 01225-334511; Fax: 01225-480097; Email: campaign@wdcs.org; WWW: www.wdcs.org
Founded: 1987; Membership: 75,000
Scope: International
Description: The WDCS is dedicated to the conservation, walfare, and appreciation of all species of whale, dolphins, and porpoises.
Contact(s):
Director of Campaigns: CHRIS STROUD
Director of Conservation: ALSON M. SMITH
Director of Fundraising: CHRIS VICK
Manager of Accounts: S. DAVIS-HAMILTON
Publication(s): *Sonar Magazine; Echo; Orcalog*
Keyword(s): Endangered and Threatened Species, Environmental Protection, Fisheries, Hunting, International Conservation, Marine Mammals, Water Pollution, Wildlife and Wildlife Habitat

WHITE CLAY WATERSHED ASSOCIATION
760 Chambers Rock Rd., Landenberg, PA 19350
Phone: 215-255-4314
Founded: 1965
Scope: Regional
Description: The White Clay Watershed Association is a nonprofit organization devoted to protection and improvement of the environmental quality of the White Clay Creek and valley. The Association works to improve water quality in local streams, conserve open space, woodlands, wetlands and geological features; aid in the preservation of cultural, historical and archaeological sites; increase outdoor recreation oppotunities; and conduct educational programs relating to the environment.
Contact(s):
President: JOHN A. MURRAY
Vice President: ROBERT M. STARK
Secretary: CAROL CATANESE
Treasurer: DONNA BUSH
Keyword(s): Cultural Preservation, Environmental Protection, Nature Preservation, Water Quality, Watersheds

WHITETAILS UNLIMITED INC.
P.O. Box 720 Rhode Island St., Sturgeon Bay, WI 54235
Phone: 414-743-6777
Founded: 1982; Membership: 40,000
Scope: National
Description: Whitetails Unlimited is a national, nonprofit conservation organization. Its purpose is to raise funds in support of education, habitat enhancement, and the preservation of the hunting tradition for the direct benefit of the white-tailed deer and other wildlife species.
Contact(s):
President: JEFFREY B. SCHINKTEN
Executive Director: PETER J. GERL
Chapter Services: KIM MCKINNEY
Field Editor: PETER R. SCHOONMAKER
Field Editor: KEVIN NAZE
Membership Services: CHERYL UECKER
Merchandise: ARLENE PETERSON
National Advisory Board: DANIEL O. TRAINER
National Executive Board: PETER J. GERL
Office Manager: JANET GERL
Production Manager: PETER J. GERL
Production/Design: DENISE DUBICK
Vice President of Finance: WILLIAM E. GERL JR.
Vice President of Marketing: DAVID J. HAWKEY
Publication(s): *Whitetails Unlimited Magazine; WTU Chapter Connections*
Keyword(s): Environmental and Conservation Education, Hunting, Wildlife and Wildlife Habitat, Wildlife Management

WHOOPING CRANE CONSERVATION ASSOCIATION INC.
1393 Henderson Highway, Breaux Bridge, LA Phone: 318-228-7563
Founded: 1961; Membership: 700
Scope: National
Description: A scientific and educational organization, international in scope, working to prevent the extinction of the whooping crane and save wetland habitats.
Contact(s):
Editor: JEROME J. PRATT, 3000 Meadowlark Dr., Sierra Vista, AZ 85635
Secretary and Treasurer: MARY L. COURVILLE
Publication(s): *Grus Americana*
Keyword(s): Endangered and Threatened Species

WILD CANINE SURVIVAL AND RESEARCH CENTER AND WOLF SANCTUARY
P.O. Box 760, Eureka, MO 63025
Phone: 314-938-5900; Fax: 314-938-6490; Email: wolf@spawn.il.net; WWW: www.wolfsanctuary.org
Founded: 1971; Membership: 2,000
Scope: National
Description: A nonprofit, conservation organization dedicated to the preservation of the wolf and its place in the natural ecosystem through education, research, and captive breeding.
Contact(s):
President: FRANK OLIVE
Secretary: NINA WARE
Treasurer: KATHRYN STREET
Executive Director: DR. SUE LINDSEY
Co-Vice President: SHEILA COLES
Co-Vice President: DICK COLES
Publication(s): *Wolf Sanctuary Review; Wolf Pack Press*
Keyword(s): Endangered and Threatened Species, Environmental and Conservation Education, Predators, Reintroduction, Research

WILD EARTH
P.O. Box 455, Richmond, VT 05477
Phone: 802-434-4077
Founded: 1991; Membership: 4,000
Scope: National
Description: Wild Earth, formerly Cenozoic Society, combines conservation biology and wildlands activism and is the sister organization of the Wildllands Project. It is a voice for the new conservation movement and The Wildlands Project.
Contact(s):
Executive Director: MONIQUE MILLER
Board Member and Executive Editor: DAVE FOREMAN
Editor: TOM BUTLER, University of Vermont Bailey Howe Library, University of Vermont, Burlington, VT 05405
Publication(s): *Wild Earth*
Keyword(s): Biodiversity, Environment, Population Growth, Wilderness, Wildlands

WILD HORSE ORGANIZED ASSISTANCE, INC. (WHOA)
P.O. Box 555, Reno, NV 89504
Phone: 702-323-5908
Founded: 1971; Membership: 12,000
Scope: National
Description: Directs efforts toward the welfare of wild horses and burros; implementation of federal efforts in carrying out terms of the management, protection, and control program for their welfare; student projects pertaining to all phases of our heritage.
Contact(s):
Secretary: BERT LAPPIN; Phone: 702-851-4817
Treasurer: LESLIE JOHNSON; Phone: 702-851-4817
Executive Director and Chairman of the Board: DAWN Y. LAPPIN; Phone: 702-851-4817
Vice Chairman: RUSSELL JOHNSON; Phone: 702-786-7600

NON-GOVERNMENTAL ORGANIZATIONS

WILD ONES - NATURAL LANDSCAPERS, LTD
Headquarters, P.O. Box 23576, Milwaukee, WI 53223-0576
Phone: 500-367-9453; Fax: 920-730-8654; Email: woresource@aol.com; WWW: www.for-wild.org
Founded: 1977; Membership: 2,300
Scope: National
Description: Wild Ones is a nonprofit organization seeking to educate and inform members and public at the plants-root level and to promote biodiversity and environmental sound practices, thru natural landscaping using native species in developing plant communities.
Contact(s):
President: BRET RAPPAPORT
Vice President: MANDY PLOCH
Secretary: PATRICIA BRUST
Treasurer: DOROTHY BOYER
Administrative Director: DONNA VAN BUECKEN
Publication(s): *Wild Ones Handbook; Wild Ones Journal*
Keyword(s): Ancient Forests, Aquatic Habitats, Birds, Conservation, Endangered and Threatened Species, Environmental Ethics, Environmental Preservation, Flowers, Plants, and Trees, Gardening and Horticulture, Grants, Insects and Butterflies, Land Preservation, Natural Areas, Nature Preservation, Nongame Wildlife

WILDERNESS EDUCATION ASSOCIATION
W.E.A. Department of Natural Resource Recreation and Tourism Colorado State University, Fort Collins, CO 80523
Phone: 970-223-6252; Email: wea@lamar.colostate.edu; WWW: www.prarienet.org/
Founded: 1977; Membership: 2,500
Scope: National
Description: WEA is a nonprofit membership organization. It promotes national wilderness education and preservation programs by providing for-credit, expedition-based wilderness leadership training programs, developing and publishing state-of-the-art wilderness education publications and training manuals, promoting scholarly research programs, establishing and maintaining national outdoor leadership certification standards, providing support to wildland management agencies to promote wilderness education, and help foster a preservationist land ethic.
Contact(s):
President: DR. DAVID COCKRELL, Department of Human Performance and Leisure Studies, University of Southern Colorado, 2200 Bonforte Blvd., Pueblo, CO 81001-4901; Phone: 719-549-2775; Fax: 719-549-2732
Vice President: DR. MITCHELL SAKOFS, Outward Bound USA, Rt. 9, R. D. 2, Box 280, Garrison, NY 10524-9757; Phone: 914-424-4000
Secretary: JEFF OLSON, Confidence Learning Center, 6260 Mary Fawcett Memorial Dr., Brainerd, MN 56401; Phone: 218-828-2344
Treasurer: DR. WILLIAM W. FORGEY, One Tower Plaza, 109 E. 89th Ave., Merrillville, IN 46410; Phone: 219-769-6055; Fax: 219-769-6035
Executive Director: DARLA S. DERUITER, WEA Department of Natural Resource Recreation and Tourism, Colorado State University, Fort Collins, CO 80523; Phone: 970-223-6252; Fax: 970-223-6252
Publisher: W. W. NORTON
Publication(s): *WEA Legend; Trustees and Affiliates Briefing System (TABS); The Backcountry Classroom; WEA Affiliate Handbook; New Wilderness Handbook; Wilderness Educator*
Keyword(s): Environmental and Conservation Education, Environmental Preservation, Internships, Outdoor Recreation, Wilderness

WILDERNESS LAND TRUST, THE (Colorado Office)
642 Surrey Rd., Carbondale, CO 81623
Phone: 970-963-9688; Fax: 970-963-9670; Email: jon@wildernessland.org; WWW: www.widlernessland.org
Founded: 1992; Membership: 400
Scope: National
Description: To facilitate public acquisition of private lands (inholdings) within units of the National Wilderness Preservation System to fulfill the promise of Congress made in The Wilderness Act of 1964 that all generations of Americans will enjoy an enduring resource of wilderness.
Contact(s):
Chairman: JOHN FIELDER, P.O. Box 1261, Englewood, CO 80150; Phone: 303-935-0900
President: JON K. MULFORD
Secretary and Treasurer: ANDY WIESSNER, 811 Potato Patch Dr., Vail, CO 81657; Phone: 303-393-7561
Publication(s): *Wilderness Heritage Newsletter*
Keyword(s): Conservation of Protected Areas, Environmental Protection, Land Preservation, Land Purchase, Wilderness

WILDERNESS LAND TRUST, THE (Oregon Office)
4060 Post Canyon Dr., Hood River, OR 97031
Phone: 541-386-9546; WWW: www.wildernessland.org
Scope: National

WILDERNESS SOCIETY, THE
900 17th St., NW, Washington, DC 20006-2596
Phone: 202-833-2300
Founded: 1935; Membership: 300,000
Scope: National
Description: A nonprofit membership organization devoted to preserving wilderness and wildlife, protecting America's prime forests, parks, rivers, and shorelands, and fostering an American land ethic. The Society welcomes membership inquiries, contributions, and bequests.
Contact(s):
Chair: BERT FINGERHUT
President: WILLIAM H. MEADOWS III
Counselor: GAYLORD NELSON
Director of LWEF: SUE GUNN
Director of National Forest Issues: MICHAEL FRANCIS
Director of National Parks and Alaska Issues: BILL REFFALT
Director of National Wildlife Refuges and Endangered Species Issues: JIM WALTMAN
Finance and Administration: STEVE KALLAN
Program Director of BLM Issues: FRAN HUNT
Regional and State Director: CRAIG GEHRKE, 413 W. Idaho St., Suite 102, Boise, ID 83702; Phone: 208-343-8153
Regional Director: ALLEN SMITH, 430 W. 7th Ave., #210, Anchorage, AK 99501; Phone: 907-272-9453
Regional Director: ROBERT EKEY, 105 W. Main St., Suite E, Bozeman, MT 59715; Phone: 406-586-1600
Regional Director: JAY WATSON, Presidio Bldg. 1016, P.O. Box 29241, San Francisco, CA 94129; Phone: 415-561-6641
Regional Director: PAMELA EATON, 7475 Dakin St., Suite 410, Denver, CO 80221; Phone: 303-650-5818
Regional Director: STEVE WHITNEY, 1424 Fourth Ave., Suite 816, Seattle, WA 98101; Phone: 206-624-6430
Regional Director: ROBERT PERSCHEL, 45 Bromfield St., Suite 1101, Boston, MA 02108; Phone: 617-350-8866
Vice President of Communications: SUE LOMENZO
Vice President of Ecology and Economics Research: THOMAS BANCROFT
Vice President of Public Policy: RINDY O'BRIEN
Vice President of Regional Conservation: DARRELL KNUFFKE
Vice President of Resource Development: SANDRA ADAMS
Publication(s): *Wilderness Year, The; Annual: Wilderness America; Newsletter*
Keyword(s): Biodiversity, Forests and Forestry, Public Lands, Sustainable Ecosystems, Wilderness

WILDERNESS WATCH
P.O. Box 9175, Missoula, MT 59807
Phone: 406-542-2048; Fax: 406-542-7714; Email: wild@wildernesswatch.org; WWW: www.wildernesswatch.org
Scope: National
Description: Wilderness Watch is a national, nonprofit, citizen organization dedicated solely to the protection and proper administration of lands within the National Wilderness Preservation System and Wild and Scenic Rivers System. We achieve our goals through the efforts of citizen activists, local chapters, wilderness "adopters", and by working with other local organizations concerned about wilderness and wild river issues.
Contact(s):
Executive Director: GEORGE NICKAS
Publication(s): *Wilderness Watcher*

WILDFOWL TRUST OF NORTH AMERICA INC., THE
P.O. Box 519, Discovery Lane, Grasonville, MD 21638
Phone: 410-827-6694
Founded: 1979; Membership: 500
Scope: National
Description: A nonprofit, tax-exempt organization dedicated to the preservation of wildlife and wetlands through education, conservation, and research. The Trust operates The Horsehead Wetlands Center on its, 500-acre wetland refuge on the Chesapeake Bay's Eastern Shore. The Center provides environmental education programs, a collection of resident waterfowl and raptors in natural habitat settings, a Visitor's Center, trails, and observation blinds and towers. Canoes are available to members.
Contact(s):
President: DR. TORREY C. BROWN
Vice President: WILLIAM STOTT
Executive Director: DR. EDWARD L. DELANEY
Publication(s): *Newsletter*
Keyword(s): Biodiversity, Environmental and Conservation Education, Research, Wetlands, Wildlife and Wildlife Habitat

WILDLANDS CONSERVANCY
3701 Orchid Pl., Emmaus, PA 18049-1637
Phone: 610-965-4397; Email: wildlands@aol.com
Founded: 1973
Scope: Statewide
Description: A nonprofit, member-supported organization serving eastern Pennsylvania. Involved in land and river preservation and environmental education. Preserved over 20,000 acres of open space, much of it in cooperation with the Pennsylvania Game Commission. Operates nature preserves and sanctuaries with concomitant education programs for students and families; develops and implements plans for rivers conservation and other types of preservation projects; created a curriculum (kindergarten through college, that teaches responsible watershed stewardship; operates a conservation-easement program; operates a Trash-Pick-Up Group; operates the Friends of the Parks, an advocacy group for Lehigh County parks; and provides technical assistance to governmental bodies, supports citizen environmental advocacy groups, and accomplishes topical research.
Contact(s):
President: PAUL C. WESSEL; Phone: 610-965-4397
Executive Director: THOMAS J. KERR; Phone: 610-965-4397

WILDLANDS PROJECT, THE
1955 W Grant Dr., #148, Tucson, AZ 85745-1147
Phone: 520-884-0875; Fax: 520-884-0962; Email: wildland@earthlink.net; WWW: www.twp.org
Founded: 1992
Scope: Regional
Description: The mission of The Wildlands Project is to protect and restore the ecological integrity and native biodiversity of North America, through the establishment of a connected system of conservation reserves. TWP coordinates the efforts of regional organizations and individuals in the development of reserve design proposals for a continental vision.
Contact(s):
Chairman: DAVE FOREMAN
President: MICHAEL SOULE; Email: soule@co.tds.net
Executive Director: STEVE GATEWOOD
Secretary and Treasurer: DAVID JOHNS
Publication(s): *Wildlands Project, The: Plotting A North American Wilderness Recovery Strategy; Wildlands Project, The: First Thousands Days of the Next Thousand Years; Wild Earth*
Keyword(s): Biodiversity, Conservation of Protected Areas, International Conservation, Wilderness, Wildlands

WILDLIFE ACTION, INC.
P.O. Box 866, Mullins, SC 29574
Phone: 803-464-8473/1-800-753-2264; Fax: 803-464-1914
Founded: 1977; Membership: 14,000
Scope: National
Description: Wildlife Action is a private nonprofit 501(c)3 tax-exempt organization dedicated to the appreciation and enjoyment of our wildlife heritage and to educating the public in the value of protection, restoration, enhancement, and wise use of our natural resources.
Contact(s):
Vice President: TOMMY SIMPSON
Secretary: SANDRA O. BANE
Treasurer: RUSTY RICHARDSON
President and CEO: M. GAULT BEESON JR.
Publication(s): *Wildlife Pride; Wild Things - Our Resource Education Center*
Keyword(s): Environmental and Conservation Education, Environmental Ethics, Environmental Preservation, Outdoor Recreation, Youth Organizations

WILDLIFE CENTER OF VIRGINIA, THE
P.O. Box 1557, Waynesboro, VA 22980-1414
Phone: 540-942-9453; Fax: 540-943-9453
Founded: 1982
Scope: National
Description: A nonprofit organization that operates the nation's largest professionally-staffed veterinary teaching and research hospital for native wildlife. The Center treats 3,000 wild animals annually, from more than 200 species. Study and documentation of environmental factors that cause injuries, especially pesticide poisoning, are used to monitor environmental and wildlife health trends and support public policy positions. The insight gained is disseminated through a nationally-recognized environmental and public education program. The Center also trains students and professionals from the fields of veterinary medicine, wildlife management, and wildlife rehabilitation.
Contact(s):
President: EDWARD E. CLARK JR.
Vice President: SERENA BENSON
Chairman of the Board: ERWIN BOHMFALK
Director of Environmental Education: LISA M. BRISKEY
Director of Veterinary Services: EDWARD J. GENTZ
Publication(s): *Handbook of Wildlife Medicine; The Wildlife Center Teacher's Packet; Annual and Mid-year reports, reprints of articles and papers on various topics.*
Keyword(s): Birds, Endangered and Threatened Species, Environmental and Conservation Education, Mammals, Nongame Wildlife, Raptors, Wildlife and Wildlife Habitat, Wildlife Disease, Wildlife Rehabilitation

WILDLIFE CONSERVATION SOCIETY
185th St. and Southern Blvd., Bronx, NY 10460-1099
Phone: 718-220-5100; WWW: www.wcs.org
Founded: 1895; Membership: 100,000
Scope: National
Description: A nonprofit, membership organization which operates an international wildlife and wildlands conservation program (300 projects, 53 countries) with a full-time staff of wildlife biologists

conducting field research and training programs around the world. The Society believes that successful conservation requires in-depth understanding through species and ecosystem research analyzed within the human context. Headquartered in New York City, the Society also operates the Bronx Zoo; The New York Aquarium, Central Park Wildlife Center and Tisch Childhood Zoo, Queens Wildlife Center, Prospect Park Wildlife Center, and St. Catherines Island Wildlife Survival Center.
Contact(s):
Chairman: DAVID T. SCHIFF
Director for Africa: AMY VEDDER
Director for Asia: JOSHUA GINSBERG
Director for Latin America: ANDREW TABER
Director for North America: WILLIAM WEBER
Director for Science: GEORGE SCHALLER
Director of Design: JOHN GWYNNE
Director of Wildlife Health Center: ROBERT COOK
Editor-in-Chief: JOAN DOWNS
General Curator of the Wildlife Conservation Park: JAMES DOHERTY
Librarian: STEVE JOHNSON
President and General Director: WILLIAM CONWAY
Regional Coordinator for Mesoamerica: ARCHIE CARR III
Vice President of Administrative Services: JOHN MCKEW
Vice President of Aquarium Science: LOUIS GARIBALDI
Vice President of Conservation Centers: RICHARD LATTIS
Vice President of Education: ANNETTE BEROVITS
Vice President of Financial Services: JOHN HOARE
Vice President of International Conservation: JOHN ROBINSON
Vice President of Public Affairs and Development: JENNIFER HERRING
Publication(s): *Wildlife Conservation; Annual Report*
Keyword(s): Endangered and Threatened Species, International Conservation, Wildlife and Wildlife Habitat, Wildlife Management, Zoological Parks

WILDLIFE DAMAGE REVIEW (WDR)
P.O. Box 85218, Tucson, AZ 85754
Phone: 520-884-0883; Fax: 520-884-0962; Email: wdr@azstarnet.com
Founded: 1991; Membership: 3,500
Scope: Statewide
Description: Wildlife Damage Review's mission is to bring much needed public attention to the USDA's Animal Damage Control (ADC) program. This taxpayer supported program traps, snares, poisons, and aerial guns 1-2 million of America's wildlife yearly for private interests. WDR's ultimate goal is to place wildlife management into the hands of those agencies whose vested interest is protection of biodiversity and banish management guided by predator prejudice.
Contact(s):
Executive Director: NANCY ZIERENBERG
Publication(s): *Special Edition Update; Waste, Fraud, Abuse in the U.S. Animal Damage Control Program; Wildlife Damage Review; Audit of the USDA Animal Damage Control Program*
Keyword(s): Agriculture, Biodiversity, Birds, Chemical Pollution Control, Endangered and Threatened Species, Environmental and Conservation Education, Mammals, Pesticides, Predators, Toxic Substances, Trapping, Wildlife Management

WILDLIFE DISEASE ASSOCIATION
P.O. Box 1897, Lawrence, KS 66044-8897
Founded: 1951; Membership: 1,500
Scope: National
Description: An international nonprofit organization of scientists interested in advancing knowledge of the effects of infectious, parasitic, toxic, genetic, and physiologic diseases and environmental factors upon the health and survival of free-living and captive wild animals, and upon their relationships to man.
Contact(s):
President: DR. DAVID JESSUP
Secretary: DR. KATHY CONVERSE
Treasurer: DR. BILL ADRIAN
Business Manager: DICK DALE
Editor: DR. R. BOTZLER, Department of Wildlife, Humboldt State University, Arcata, CA 95521
Publication(s): *Journal of Wildlife Diseases; Newsletter*
Keyword(s): Biology, Health and Nutrition, Wildlife Disease

WILDLIFE EDUCATION PROGRAM AND DESIGN
44781 Bittner Point Rd., Bovey, MN 55709
Phone: 218-245-3049; Email: karlyn@uslink.net
Scope: National
Description: A nonprofit, education organization with several slide lectures, Wolf Display, educational programs, and teacher's workshops with "Wolves and Humans" curriculum, and a Wolf Learning Stations Box of environmental education materials dedicated to understanding the predatory animal; to inform people of predators vital role within the balance of nature; stress importance of preservation of total ecosystem; to promote realistic solutions for man and nature to coexist. Nationwide program available; special emphasis on predators, wolves, historical relationship between man and wolves, and global perspective on the wolf of Minnesota. Contract to design environmental education materials, such as the newly-created Wetland Learning Stations and Wolf Track Pack. No employment positions.
Contact(s):
Director: KARLYN ATKINSON BERG
Keyword(s): Endangered and Threatened Species, Environmental and Conservation Education, Mammals, Natural History, Wildlife and Wildlife Habitat

WILDLIFE FEDERATION OF ALASKA
750 W. Second Ave., Suite 200-B, Anchorage, AK 99501
Phone: 907-274-3388; Fax: 907-258-4811; Email: wfa@micronet.net; WWW: www.micronet/users/~wfa/
Founded: 1984
Scope: Statewide
Description: A representative statewide organization, affiliated with the National Wildlife Federation, dedicated to the protection and enhancement of wildlife ands its habitat through public education and government interaction.
Contact(s):
President: ROSA MEEHAN
Affiliate Representative: NANCY WAINWRIGHT
Editor: BUCKY DENNERLEIN
Publication(s): *Tracks*

WILDLIFE FOREVER
12301Whitewater Dr., Suite 210, Minnetonka, MN 55343
Phone: 612-936-0605; Fax: 612-936-0915; Email: wildlife.forever@pclink.com; WWW: www.wildlifeforever.org
Founded: 1987; Membership: 65,000
Scope: National
Description: A charitable, nonprofit organization dedicated to preserving America's wildlife heritage through preservation, conservation and management of habitats, plant life, and wildlife. Projects include acquisition, grassroots activities, management, research, education, and ethics for wildlife conservation.
Contact(s):
President: STEVEN F. BURKE
Executive Director: DOUGLAS H. GRANN
Director of Development: ROSS SUBLETT
Director of Marketing: PETE WUEBKER
Publication(s): *Cry of the Wild; Wildlife Forever; The First Decade*
Keyword(s): Aquatic Habitats, Environment, Fisheries, Flowers, Plants, and Trees, Hunting, Land Purchase, Mammals, Nongame Wildlife, Outdoor Recreation, Public Lands, Raptors, Sport Fishing, Waterfowl, Women in the Environment

WILDLIFE FOUNDATION OF FLORIDA, INC.
620 S. Meridian St., Tallahassee, FL 32399-1600
Phone: 850-487-3794; Fax: 850-488-6988
Founded: 1994
Scope: Statewide
Description: The mission of the Wildlife Foundation of Florida, Inc. is to provide assistance, funding, and promotional support for the Florida Game and Fresh Water Fish Commission, and in so doing, contribute to the health and well-being of Florida's fish and wildlife resources and their habitats.
Contact(s):
Board of Director: ALLAN L. EGBERT
Board of Director: ROBERT M. BRANTLY
Board of Director: WILLIAM M. BLAKE
Board of Director: GEORGE G. MATTHEWS
Board of Director: LINDA M. BREMER
Board of Director: WILLIAM G. BOSTICK JR.
Board of Director: C. TOM RAINEY
Board of Director: KATE IRELAND
Keyword(s): Fisheries, Hunting, Sport Fishing, Wildlife and Wildlife Habitat, Wildlife Management

WILDLIFE HABITAT CANADA
7 Hinton Ave.North, Ste. 200, Ottawa, Ontario K1Y 4P1 Canada
Phone: 613-722-2090; Fax: 613-722-3318; Email: receptio@wtc.org
Founded: 1984
Scope: National
Description: Wildlife Habitat Canada is a national non-profit organization dedicated to working with private citizens, governments, non-government organizations, and industry to conserve the great variety of wildlife habitats across Canada. The organization develops and implements its own conservation initiatives, such as the Forest Biodiversity Program, but also provides grants for conservation, research, and communication and education projects and has a graduate scholarship program.
Contact(s):
Executive Director: DAVID J. NEAVE
Program Manager: JAMES FORTUNE
Science Advisor: DR. CAROLINE CAZA
Publication(s): *Annual Reports (a list of free publications is contained therein; publications are available upon request.*
Keyword(s): Agriculture, Biodiversity, Fisheries, Forest Management, Scholarships and Grants, Wetlands, Wildlife and Wildlife Habitat

WILDLIFE HABITAT COUNCIL
1010 Wayne Ave. Suite 920, Silver Spring, MD 20910
Phone: 301-588-8994; Fax: 301-588-4629; Email: whc@wildlifehc.org; WWW: www.wildlifehc.org
Founded: 1987; Membership: 130
Scope: National
Description: A joint effort between the conservation and corporate communities, WHC is an international, nonprofit organization formed to assist corporations in enhancing their lands for the benefit of wildlife. WHC's program includes technical assistance in establishing and maintaining responsible corporate wildlife management practices, environmental mediation, habitat certification, information sharing, employee involvement, and community outreach.
Contact(s):
President: WILLIAM W. HOWARD
Vice President: ROBERT J. JOHNSON
Board of Directors Chairman: DR. CHARLES G. CARSON III
Board of Directors Secretary and Treasurer: HUGH J. DILLINGHAM III
Board of Directors Vice Chair: ROBERT W. MUNSON
Controller: LAURIE CORAN
Publication(s): *Habitat Quarterly;Wildlife Habitat; Registry of certified and internationally accredited corporate wildlife habitat programs*
Keyword(s): Biodiversity, Environmental and Conservation Education, Sustainable Development, Wildlife and Wildlife Habitat, Wildlife Management

WILDLIFE INFORMATION CENTER, INC.
P.O. Box 198, Slatington, PA 18080
Phone: 610-760-8889
Founded: 1986
Scope: National
Description: A nonprofit, tax-exempt organization whose purpose is to secure and disseminate wildlife conservation, education, recreation, and scientific research information. Programs include: Sponsoring and conducting The Kittatinny Raptor Corridor Project and long-term hawk migration field studies at Bake Oven Knob, PA.; in-service teacher training courses and public education; research and preparation of conservation-education papers and reports; maintaining wildlife libraries, photographs, computer databases; sponsoring conferences and workshops; and advocating wildlife observation, photography, sound recording, drawing and painting, and wilidlife tourism. The Center currently is raising funds for the purchase of land for its own wildlife refuge and headquarters.
Contact(s):
President: DAN R. KUNKLE
Secretary: KATHIE ROMANO
Treasurer: MARGARET LIBONATI M.D.
Editor: DAN R. KUNKLE
Publication(s): *Wildlife Conservation Reports; Wildlife Activist; American Hawkwatcher*
Keyword(s): Biodiversity, Birds, Environmental and Conservation Education, Raptors, Wildlife and Wildlife Habitat

WILDLIFE LEGISLATIVE FUND OF AMERICA, THE, AND WILDLIFE CONSERVATION FUND OF AMERICA, THE
801 Kingsmill Parkway, Columbus, OH 43229-1137
Phone: 614-888-4868
Founded: 1978; Membership: 2
Scope: National
Description: Companion nonprofit organizations established to protect America's hunting, trapping, and fishing heritage, and the scientific wildlife management practices which support it. The WLFA is the legislative arm. The WCFA is the legal defense, public education, and research arm.
Contact(s):
Vice President: RICK STORY
Treasurer: MRS. GILBERT W. HUMPHREY
Chairman of the Board: JAMES H. GLASS
Director of Federal Affairs: WILLIAM F. BRAGG
Director of National and International Affairs and Washington, D.C. Counsel: WILLIAM P. HORN
Director of State Services: ROBERT T. SEXTON
General Counsel: THOMAS L. SHERMAN
Vice Chairman: DR. VINCENT W. SHIEL
Publication(s): *Update*
Keyword(s): Hunting, Sport Fishing, Trapping, Wildlife and Wildlife Habitat, Wildlife Management

Washington, D.C.National Affairs Office
Washington, DC
Phone: 202-862-8364; Fax: 202-659-1027
Scope: National

WILDLIFE MANAGEMENT INSTITUTE
Suite 801, 1101 14th St., NW, Washington, DC 20005
Phone: 202-371-1808; Fax: 202-408-5059; Email: wmihq@aol.com; WWW: www.wildlifemgt.org/wmi
Scope: National
Description: International nonprofit scientific and educational private membership organization, supported by industries, groups, and individuals, promoting improved professional management of natural resources for the benefit of those resources and North American, including its people.

NON-GOVERNMENTAL ORGANIZATIONS

Contact(s):
President: ROLLIN D. SPARROWE
Vice President: LONNIE L. WILLIAMSON
Conservation Policy Specialist: RONALD R. HELINSKI
Field Representative: LEN CARPENTER, 4015 Cheney Dr., Fort Collins, CO 80526; Phone: 970-223-1099; Fax: 970-204-9198; Email: carpent1@interserv.com
Field Representative: SCOT J. WILLIAMSON, R.R. 1, Box 587, Spur Rd., North Stratford, NH 03590; Phone: 603-636-9846; Fax: 603-636-9853; Email: wmisw@together.net
Field Representative: E. CHARLES MESLOW, 8035 NW Oxbow Dr., Corvallis, OR 97330; Phone: 541-752-7205; Fax: 541-753-8772; Email: wmicm@aol.com
Field Representative: TERRY Z. RILEY, 13377 382nd Ave., Aberdeen, SD 57401; Phone: 605-229-2067; Fax: 605-229-2187; Email: wmitr@hdc.net
Field Representative: CHESTER A. McCONNELL, 110 Wildwoods Ln., Lawrenceburg, TN 38464; Phone: 615-762-7718; Fax: 615-766-1087; Email: wmicmc@usit.net
Finance Manager: CAROL J. PEDDICORD
Partners Program Director: PATRICIA PEACOCK
Secretary and Publications Director: RICHARD E. McCABE
Senior Scientist: JAMES R. WOEHR
Wildlife Program Coordinator: ROBERT L. BYRNE
Publication(s): *Outdoor News Bulletin; Transactions North American Wildlife and Natural Resources Conference; books and booklets*
Keyword(s): Wildlife Management

WILDLIFE PRESERVATION TRUST INTERNATIONAL, INC.
1520 Locust St., Suite 704, Philadelphia, PA 19102
Phone: 215-731-9770; Fax: 215-731-9766; Email: homeoffice@wpti.org
Founded: 1971; Membership: 7,000
Scope: National
Description: Supports the preservation of endangered species through hands-on field work, research, education, and training. Awards grants internationally in these areas. Affiliated with the Jersey Wildlife Preservation Trust, Jersey, Channel Islands.
Contact(s):
President: THOMAS J. P. McHENRY
Vice President: VIRGINIA C. MARS
Vice President: MRS. GEORGE MOSS
Secretary: JON M. JENSEN
Treasurer: JOHN C. TUTEN JR.
Executive Director: MARY C. PEARL
Founder: GERALD M. DURRELL
Honorary Chairman: THOMAS E. LOVEJOY
Publication(s): *On the Edge; Dodo, The; Dodo Dispatch; Wild Times, The; Annual Report*
Keyword(s): Endangered and Threatened Species, Environmental and Conservation Education, International Conservation, Scholarships and Grants, Wildlife and Wildlife Habitat

WILDLIFE SOCIETY, ALABAMA CHAPTER
ATTN: President, P.O. Box 311, Auburn, AL 36830
Scope: Statewide
Contact(s):
President: TOM U. COUNTS, P.O. Box 311, Auburn, AL 36830; Phone: 334-887-4510
Secretary and Treasurer: MICHAEL KEITH HUDSON, 309 Knights Bridge Rd., Florence, AL 35631; Phone: 205-760-8233

WILDLIFE SOCIETY, ALASKA CHAPTER
ATTN: President, P.O. Box 72962, Fairbanks, AK 99707
Scope: Statewide
Contact(s):
President: ROGER A. POST, P.O. Box 72962, Fairbanks, AK 99707; Phone: 907-459-7287
President-Elect: GINO DEL FRATE, P.O. Box 1413, Homer, AK 99801; Phone: 907-235-8191
Secretary and Treasurer: ANNE MORKILL, P.O. Box 83381, Fairbanks, AK 99708; Phone: 907-474-2340

WILDLIFE SOCIETY, ALBERTA CHAPTER
ATTN: President, 110 Seabolt Dr., Hinton, Alberta T7V1K2 Canada
Scope: Statewide
Contact(s):
President: BETH MCCALLUM, 110 Seabolt Dr., Hinton, AB T7V 1K2 Canada; Phone: 406-865-3390
President-Elect: MIKE TORRANCE, Rural Route 4, Sherwood Park, AB T8A 3K4 Canada; Phone: 403-467-4396
Secretary and Treasurer: JOHN JORGENSON, Natural Resources Services, 800 Railway Ave., Suite 201, Canmore, AB T1W 1P1 Canada; Phone: 403-678-2373

WILDLIFE SOCIETY, ARIZONA CHAPTER
ATTN: President, U.S. Fish & Wildlife Service, 5075 N. Hwy 89, Flagstaff, AZ 86004
Scope: Statewide
Contact(s):
President: BILL AUSTIN, U.S. Fish & Wildlife Service, 5075 N. Highway 89, Flagstaff, AZ 86004; Phone: 520-527-3042
Treasurer: MARY ANN BENOIT, HC 31, Box 68, Happy Jack, AZ 86024; Phone: 520-354-2580
Corresponding Secretary: BILL BURGER, AZ Game & Fish Dept., 7220 E. University Drive, Mesa, AZ 85296; Phone: 602-981-9400
President-elect: REED SANDERSON, 130 W. Calle Melendroz, Green Valley, AZ 85614; Phone: 510-648-6556
Recording Secretary: GENICE FROEHLICH, P.O. Box 709, Stafford, AZ 85548; Phone: 520-428-4150

WILDLIFE SOCIETY, ARKANSAS CHAPTER
ATTN: President, 172 Heritage Dr., Hot Springs, AR 71901-9300
Scope: Statewide
Contact(s):
President: JERRY DAVIS, 172 Heritage Dr., Hot Springs, AR 71901-9300; Phone: 501-321-5201
Secretary and Treasurer: LINDA KNIGHTON, 1685 CR 35N, Columbus, AR 71831; Phone: 870-983-2790

WILDLIFE SOCIETY, CALIFORNIA CENTRAL COAST CHAPTER
ATTN: President, USDA Forest Service 6144 Calle Real, Goleta, CA 93117
Scope: Statewide
Contact(s):
President: PATRICK J. WHITE, Headquarters, Camp Roberts, CA 93415-5000; Phone: 805-238-8265
Secretary: JUSTIN VREELAND, University of California Extension, 2156 Sierra Way, Suite C, San Luis Obispo, CA 93401; Phone: 805-781-5940
Treasurer: MICHAEL T. HANSON, 1203 Madonna Road, San Luis Obispo, CA 93405; Phone: 805-541-0272
President-Elect: MAETON FREEL, USDA Forest Service 6144 Calle Real, Goleta, CA 93117; Phone: 805-681-2764
Vice-President: KEVIN COOPER, USDA Forest Service, 1616 Carlotti Drive, Santa Maria, CA 93117; Phone: 805-681-2764

WILDLIFE SOCIETY, CALIFORNIA NORTH COAST CHAPTER
ATTN: President, Simpson Timber Co., P.O. Box 68, Korbel, CA 95550
Scope: Statewide
Contact(s):
President: LOWELL DILLER, Simpson Timber Co., P.O. Box 68, Korbel, CA 95550; Phone: 707-668-4428
Secretary: CHESTER OGAN, 811 'O' Street, Eureka, CA 95501; Phone: 707-825-2952
Treasurer: SANDRA VON ARB, P.O. Box 4553, Arcata, CA 95518; Phone: 707-445-7805
President-Elect: CYNTHIA ZABEL, U.S. Fish & Wildlife Service, PSW, Redwood Science Lab, 1700 Bayview Dr., Arcata, CA 95521; Phone: 707-825-2958

NON-GOVERNMENTAL ORGANIZATIONS

WILDLIFE SOCIETY, COLORADO CHAPTER
ATTN: President, Colorado Division of Wildlife, 317 W. Prospect St., Fort Collins, CO 80526
Scope: Statewide
Contact(s):
President: KIRK NAVO, 0772 S. Rd. 1E, Monte Vista, CO 8114; Phone: 719-852-4783
Secretary: ROBIN SELL, 810 Taylor Street, Craig, CO 81625; Phone: 970-824-4441
Treasurer: DOUGLAS HALFORD, 2597 B 3/4 Road, Grand Junction, CO 81503-1789
President-Elect: TOM POLAR, Colorado Division of Wildlife, 317 W. Prospect St., Fort Collins, CO 80526

WILDLIFE SOCIETY, FLORIDA CHAPTER
ATTN: President, Apalachicola National Forest, P.O. Box 579, Bristol, FL 32321
Scope: Statewide
Contact(s):
President: JULIE HOVIS, 1239 SW 10th Street, Ocala, FL 34474; Phone: 352-732-1225
Vice President: PETE DAVID, 23500 SW Kanner Hwy, Canal Point, FL 33438; Phone: 561-924-5310
President-elect: SUSAN FITZGERALD, Apalachicola National Forest, P.O. Box 579, Bristol, FL 32321; Phone: 850-643-2282
Secretary and Treasurer: CAROLYN SEKERAK, P.O. Box 275, Trilby, FL 33593; Phone: 352-669-3153

WILDLIFE SOCIETY, GEORGIA CHAPTER
ATTN: President, School of Forest Resources, University of Georgia, Athens, GA 30602
Scope: Statewide
Contact(s):
President: DOUG HALL, USDA-ADC, School of Forest Resources, University of Georgia, Athens, GA 30602; Phone: 706-546-2020
President-elect: SARAH SCHWEITZER, School of Forest Resources, University of Georgia, Athens, GA 30602; Phone: 706-542-1150
Secretary and Treasurer: JIM WENTWORTH, USDA Forest Service, P.O. Box 9, Blairville, GA 30514; Phone: 709-745-6928

WILDLIFE SOCIETY, HAWAII CHAPTER
P.O. Box 4632, Honolulu, HI 96813
Scope: Statewide
Contact(s):
President: CATHLEEN HODGES, P.O. Box 6, Makawao, HI 96768-0006; Phone: 808-572-4491
Secretary: JOY TAMAYOSE, c/o Haleakala National Park, P.O. Box 369, Makawao, HI 96768; Phone: 808-572-4492
Treasurer: VIKKI GRIEVE, 443 Crater Rd., Kula, HI 96790; Phone: 808-572-4499

WILDLIFE SOCIETY, IDAHO CHAPTER
ATTN: President, College of Forestry, Wildlife & Range Sciences, University of Idaho, Moscow, ID 83843-1136
Scope: Statewide
Contact(s):
President: KERRY PAUL REESE, College of Forestry, Wildlife & Range Sciences, University of Idaho, Moscow, ID 83843-1136; Phone: 208-885-6435
Secretary: CHARLES PETERSON, Box 8007, Idaho State University, Pocatello, ID 83209; Phone: 208-465-8465
Treasurer: TONY APA, ID Dept. of Fish & Game, 686 E. Main, Jerome, ID 83338; Phone: 208-324-4359

WILDLIFE SOCIETY, ILLINOIS CHAPTER
ATTN: President, Max McGraw Wildlife Foundation, P.O. Box 9, Dundee, IL 60118
Scope: Statewide
Contact(s):
President: THOMAS NELSON, Zoology Dept., Eastern Illinois Univ., Charleston, IL 61920; Phone: 217-581-2500
President-elect: JOHN D. THOMPSON, Max McGraw Wildlife Foundation, P.O. Box 9, Dundee, IL 60118; Phone: 847-741-8000
Secretary-Treasurer: TERRY L. MOYER, Richardson Wildlife Foundation, 2316 Shaw Road, West Brooklyn, IL 61378; Phone: 815-628-3300

WILDLIFE SOCIETY, INDIANA CHAPTER
ATTN: President, Div. Of State Parks and Reservoirs, 402 W. Washington, Rm. W298, Indianapolis, IN 46204
Scope: Statewide
Contact(s):
President: HARMON WEEKS JR., Dept. of Forestry & Natural Resources, Purdue University, Lafayette, IN 47907; Phone: 765-494-3567
President-elect: JIM GERBRACHT, Div. Of State Parks and Reservoirs, 402 W. Washington, Room W298, Indianapolis, IN 46204; Phone: 312-232-4124
Secretary and Treasurer: BRIAN FRAWLEY, IN Division of Fish & Wildlife, 3900 Soldiers Home Road, West Lafayette, IN 47906; Phone: 765-463-0032

WILDLIFE SOCIETY, IOWA CHAPTER
ATTN: President, 106 W. Wilcoxway, Jefferson, IA 50129
Scope: Statewide
Contact(s):
President: JAMES PEASE, 124 Science II, Iowa State University, Ames, IA 50011; Phone: 515-294-7429
President-Elect: DONALD SIEVERS, 106 W. Wilcoxway, Jefferson, IA 50129; Phone: 515-386-3073
Secretary and Treasurer: CHUCK STEFFEN, 700 Farm Credit Drive, Ottumwa, IA 52501; Phone: 515-682-3552

WILDLIFE SOCIETY, KANSAS CHAPTER
ATTN: President, Emporia State University, Biology Dept. Box 4050, Emporia, KS 66854
Scope: Statewide
Contact(s):
President: MIKE McFADDEN, Kansas Dept. Wildlife and Parks, 1110 North 900 Road, Lawrence, KS 66047-9474; Phone: 913-273-6740
President-Elect: ELMER FINCK, Emporia State University, Biology Dept., Box 4050, Emporia, KS 66854; Phone: 316-341-5623
Secretary-Treasurer: CHARLES LEE, Kansas State University, Room 127, Call Hall, Manhattan, KS 66506-1600; Phone: 913-539-2210

WILDLIFE SOCIETY, KENTUCKY CHAPTER
ATTN: President, KY Dept. Fish & Wildlife, #1 Game Farm Rd., Frankfort, KY 40601
Scope: Statewide
Contact(s):
President: ROBERT M. MORTON, 9956 Hwy 268, Corydon, KY 42406; Phone: 502-827-2673
President-elect: ROY GRIMES, KY Dept. Fish & Wildlife, #1 Game Farm Rd, Frankfort, KY 40601; Phone: 502-564-4858
Secretary and Treasurer: WILLIAM BALDA, KY Dept. Fish & Wildlife, #1 Game Farm Road, Frankfort, KY 40601; Phone: 502-564-4858

NON-GOVERNMENTAL ORGANIZATIONS

WILDLIFE SOCIETY, LOUISIANA CHAPTER
ATTN: President, 2415 Darnall Rd., New Ibeia, LA 70560
Scope: Statewide
Contact(s):
President: THOMAS HESS JR., 5492 Grand Chenier Hwy, Grand Chenier, LA 70643; Phone: 318-538-2165
President-Elect: EDMOND MOUTON LDWF, 2415 Darnall Road, New Iberia, LA 70560; Phone: 318-373-0032
Secretary and Treasurer: CECILIA WALTHER, 4110 Janet Avenue, #6, Baton Rouge, LA 70800; Phone: 504-761-0963

WILDLIFE SOCIETY, MAINE CHAPTER
Attn: Secretary, ME Dept. Inland Fish & Wildlife, P.O. Box 416, Ashland, ME 04732
Scope: Statewide
Contact(s):
President: MARK McCOLLOUGH, ME Inland Fisheries & Wildlife, 650 State Road, Bangor, ME 04401; Phone: 207-941-4475
President-elect: MITSCHKA J. HARTLEY, Dept. Wildlife Ecology, 5755 Nutting Hall, Unvieristy of Maine, Orono, ME 04467; Phone: 207-581-2939
Secretary-Treasurer: RICHARD T. HOPPE, ME Dept. of Inland Fish & Wildlife, P.O. Box 416, Ashland, ME 04732; Phone: 207-435-3231

WILDLIFE SOCIETY, MANITOBA CHAPTER
ATTN: President (Rhian Christie), Dillion Consulting Ltd., 6 Donald St. S., Winnipeg, Manitoba R3L0K6 Canada
Scope: Statewide
Contact(s):
President: BOB EMERY, Ducks Unlimited Canada, P.O. box 1160, Stonewall, Manitoba R0C2Z0 Canada; Phone: 204-467-3238
President-Elect: RHIAN CHRISTIE, Dillion Consulting Ltd., 6 Donald St. S., Winnipeg, Manitoba R3L 0K6 Canada; Phone: 204-453-2301
Secretary and Treasurer: TANYS UHMANN, 1017 Kilkenny Dr., Winnipeg, Manitoba R2T 2N2 Canada; Phone: 204-474-8373

WILDLIFE SOCIETY, MARYLAND-DELAWARE CHAPTER
ATTN: President, Oakland Mills Rd., Columbia, MD 21046
Scope: Statewide
Contact(s):
President: CAROL BERNSTEIN, 1053 Hampton Drive, Crownsville, MD 21032-1315; Phone: 410-962-2942
Secretary: ELAINE JOHNSON, Blackwater Refuge, 2145 Key Wallace Dr., Cambridge, MD 21613; Phone: 410-228-2692
Treasurer: DONALD H. ROHRBACK, 11107 Fort Frederick Rd., Big Pool, MD 21711; Phone: 301-478-2525
President-elect: PHILIP E. NORMAN, Oakland Mills Rd., Columbia, MD 21046; Phone: 410-213-4727

WILDLIFE SOCIETY, MICHIGAN CHAPTER
ATTN: President, 314 Silsby Dr., Roscommon, MI 48653
Scope: Statewide
Contact(s):
President: DEAN E. BEYER JR., 766 Lakewood Lane, Marquette, MI 49853; Phone: 906-227-1627
President-elect: BRIAN G. MASTENBROOK, 314 Silsby Drive, Roscommon, MI 48653
Secretary and Treasurer: HENRY CAMPA III, Dept. Fisheries & Wildlife, Michigan State University, East Lansing, MI 48824; Phone: 517-353-2979

WILDLIFE SOCIETY, MINNESOTA CHAPTER
ATTN: President, 683 Country Rd., Bovey, MN 55709
Scope: Statewide
Contact(s):
President: JOHN J. MOOTY, 401 Birch Hill Dr., Grand Rapids, MN 55744; Phone: 218-326-6231
President-elect: JANET BOE, 683 Country Rd. 10, Bovey, MN 55709; Phone: 218-326-6231
Secretary and Treasurer: GRETCHEN MEHMEL, P.O. Box 100, Roosevelt, MN 56673; Phone: 218-783-6861

WILDLIFE SOCIETY, MISSISSIPPI CHAPTER
ATTN: President, P.O. Box 451, Jackson, MS 39205
Scope: Statewide
Contact(s):
President: JACKIE HENNE-KERR, Crown Vantage, 5925 N. Washington Street, Vicksburg, MS 39159; Phone: 601-638-9275
President-elect: RANDY SPENCER, P.O. Box 451, Jackson, MS 39205; Phone: 601-364-2229
Secretary and Treasurer: DARREN A. MILLER, P.O. Box 2288, Columbus, MS 39704; Phone: 601-245-5249

WILDLIFE SOCIETY, MISSOURI CHAPTER
Missouri Department of Conservation, 1110 S. College Ave., Columbia, MO 65201
Phone: 314-882-9880
Scope: Statewide
Contact(s):
President: JOHN L. BOYLES, 2500 S. Halliburton, Kirksville, MO 63501; Phone: 660-785-2420
Secretary: LAUREL L. DOHM, 8616 E. 63rd St., Kansas City, MO 64133; Phone: 816-336-2280
Treasurer: MARY RATNASWAMY, 112 Stephens Hall, University of Missouri, Columbia, MO 65211; Phone: 816-882-9424
President-Elect: R. MARK JACKSON, 21999 Hwy B, Maitland, MO 64466; Phone: 660-446-3371

WILDLIFE SOCIETY, MONTANA CHAPTER
ATTN: President, MT Fish, Wildlife & Parks, 490 N. Meriden, Kalispell, MT 59901
Scope: Statewide
Contact(s):
President: DALE BECKER, 107 Mark Jensen Lane, Polson, MT 59860; Phone: 406-675-2700
President-elect: JOHN VORE, MT Fish, Wildlife & Parks, 490 N. Meriden, Kalispell, MT 59901; Phone: 406-752-5501
Secretary and Treasurer: FRANK PICKETT, 40 E. Boadway, Butte, MT 59701; Phone: 406-497-3000

WILDLIFE SOCIETY, NATIONAL CAPITAL CHAPTER
ATTN: President, ECS Division, NRCS, P.O. Box 2890, Washington, DC 20013
Scope: Statewide
Contact(s):
President: ERIC W. SCHENCK, Ducks Unlimited, Inc., 1709 New York Avenue, NW, Suite 202, Washington, DC 20006; Phone: 202-347-1530
President-elect: MIKE ANDERSON, ECS Division, NRCS, P.O. Box 2890, Washington, DC 20013; Phone: 202-689-0856
Secretary and Treasurer: KRISTEN LaVINE, The Rockland Group, 1801 K Street, NW Suite 203L, Washington, DC 20006; Phone: 202-822-8540

WILDLIFE SOCIETY, NEBRASKA CHAPTER
ATTN: President, 202 Natural Resources Hall, University of Nebraska, Lincoln, NE 68583-0819
Scope: Statewide
Contact(s):
President-elect: KURT VER CAUTEREN, 202 Natural Resources Hall, University of Nebraska, Lincoln, NE 68583-0819; Phone: 402-472-6822
President: MARK LINDVALL, 526 Elenora Drive, Valentine, NE 69201; Phone: 402-376-3789
Secretary: JUSTIN KING, 375 South 7th Avenue, Columbus, NE 68601; Phone: 402-563-5088
Treasurer: JENNIFER DELISLE, NE Game & Parks Commission, P.O. Box 30370, Lincoln, NE 68503; Phone: 402-471-5412

WILDLIFE SOCIETY, NEVADA CHAPTER
ATTN: President, 4321 Jody Ave., Las Vegas, NV 89120
Scope: Statewide
Contact(s):
President: JAMES RAMAKKA, 3055 Holly Lane, Carson City, NV 89704; Phone: 702-885-6174

NON-GOVERNMENTAL ORGANIZATIONS

President-Elect: ROBERT TURNER, 4321 Jody Ave., Las Vegas, NV 89120; Phone: 702-263-7600
Secretary and Treasurer: ALAN JENNE, 79 Kendall St., Winnemucca, NV 89445; Phone: 702-623-6505

WILDLIFE SOCIETY, NEW ENGLAND CHAPTER
Headquarters, 79 Elm St., Hartford, CT 06101
Phone: 860-424-3499
Scope: National
Contact(s):
President: DALE MAY, P.O. Box 165, Hampton, CT 06247; Phone: 860-642-3011
President-Elect: PAUL REGO, Sessions Woods, WMA, P.O. Box 1550, Burlington, CT 06013; Phone: 860-675-8130
Secretary and Treasurer: DAVID FULLER, 45 Nichewaug Road, Petersham, MA 01366; Phone: 508-835-3607

WILDLIFE SOCIETY, NEW JERSEY CHAPTER
ATTN: President, P.O. Box 34, Oceanville, NJ 08231-0034
Scope: Statewide
Contact(s):
President: TRACY CASSELMAN, P.O. Box 34, Oceanville, NJ 08231-0034; Phone: 609-652-1665
Secretary: ANNETTE BAKER, 33-31 Bloomingdale Drive, Somerville, NJ 08876; Phone: 609-259-7954
Treasurer: JAMES SCIASCA, NJ Division of Fish, Game & Wildlife, 26 Route 173 W., Hampton, NJ 08827; Phone: 908-735-8975

WILDLIFE SOCIETY, NEW MEXICO CHAPTER
ATTN: President, 331 Camino de la Tietta, Corrales, NM 87048-8554
Scope: Statewide
Contact(s):
President: DALE A. JONES, 1191 John Road, Belen, NM 87002; Phone: 505-864-7223
President-elect: GAIL TUNBERG, 331 Camino de la Tietta, Corrales, NM 87048-8554; Phone: 505-842-3151
Secretary and Treasurer: DAN SUTCLIFFE, 1898 Quemado, Santa Fe, NM 87505; Phone: 505-473-1436

WILDLIFE SOCIETY, NEW YORK CHAPTER
Wildlife Resources Center, Delmar, NY 12054
Scope: Statewide
Contact(s):
President: MICHAEL J. MATTHEWS, 281 Swift Road, Voorheesville, NY 12186-5031; Phone: 518-429-1662
Secretary: RICHARD B. CHIPMAN, USDA/APHIS/WS, 1930 Route 9, Castleton, NY 12033-9653; Phone: 518-477-4837
Treasurer: JAMES G. DALEY, Clermont St., Albany, NY 12203; Phone: 518-783-5733
Vice-President: CHUCK R. DENTE, 14 Marvin Ave., Demar, NY 12054; Phone: 518-429-1662

WILDLIFE SOCIETY, NORTH CAROLINA CHAPTER
ATTN: President, 4470 Hidden View Loop, Marion, NC 28752
Scope: Statewide
Contact(s):
President-Elect: GORDON S. WARBURTON, 4470 Hidden View Loop, Marion, NC 28752; Phone: 704-724-9162
President: CARL BETSILL, 512 N. Salisbury St., Raleigh, NC 27604-1188; Phone: 919-783-7291
Secretary: JON HEITSERBERG, 6213-E Angus Dr., Raleigh, NC 27613; Phone: 919-856-4124
Treasurer: CHRIS MCGRATH, 315 Morgan Branch Rd., Leicester, NC 28748; Phone: 828-683-0671

WILDLIFE SOCIETY, NORTH DAKOTA CHAPTER
ATTN: President, 5901 Ponderosa Ave., Bismarck, ND 58501
Scope: Statewide
Contact(s):
President: SCOTT PETERSON, 1851 23rd Ave. N.E., Harvey, ND 58341-9112; Phone: 701-324-2211

President-Elect: WILLIAM B. BICKNELL, 4435 Riverbend, Bismarck, ND 58504; Phone: 701-250-4414
Secretary and Treasurer: DAVE HIRSCH, 5901 Ponderosa Avenue, Bismarck, ND 58501; Phone: 701-250-4473

WILDLIFE SOCIETY, OHIO CHAPTER
ATTN: President, 9660 Street, Route 356, New Marshfield, OH 45766
Scope: Statewide
Contact(s):
President: DAVE SWANSON, 9660 Street, Route 356, New Marshfield, OH 45766; Phone: 740-654-2745
Secretary: FRED DIERKES, 19098 CH 115, Harpster, OH 43323; Phone: 740-496-2254
Treasurer: TIM PLAGEMAN, 952 Lima Ave., Box A, Findlay, OH 45840; Phone: 419-424-5000

WILDLIFE SOCIETY, OKLAHOMA CHAPTERWILDLIFE SOCIETY, OKLAHOMA CHAPTER
ATTN: President, 011 AG Hall, Oklahoma State University, Stillwater, OK 74078-3051
Scope: Statewide
Contact(s):
President-Elect: CHAMPE B GREEN, 011 AG Hall, Oklahoma State Univeristy, Stillwater, OK 74078-3051; Phone: 405-744-5445
President: DAVID M. LESLIE JR., 404 LSW, Oklahoma State University, Stillwater, OK 74078-3051; Phone: 405-744-6342
Secretary: NOREEN WALSH, USFWS, 222 S. Houston, Suite A, Tulsa, OK 74127; Phone: 918-581-7458
Treasurer: JERRY BRABANDER, U.S. Fish & Wildlife Service, Tulsa Ecological Services Office, 222 S. Houston, Tulsa, OK 74127

WILDLIFE SOCIETY, OREGON CHAPTER
ATTN: President, BLM-Bio Resources, P.O. Box 2965, Portland, OR 97208
Scope: Statewide
Contact(s):
President: BARBARA HILL, BLM-Bio Resources, P.O. Box 2965, Portland, OR 97208; Phone: 503-952-6052
Vice President: LAURA TODD, USFWS, 2600 SE 98th, #100, Portland, OR 97266; Phone: 503-231-6179
Secretary and Treasurer: ED ARNETT, Weyerhauser Company, P.O. Box 275, Springfield, OR 97477; Phone: 541-741-5536
Vice President-Elect: SARAH MADSEN, P.O. Box 234, Philomath, OR 97370; Phone: 541-929-5608
Publication(s): *On Target*

WILDLIFE SOCIETY, PENNSYLVANIA CHAPTER
ATTN: President, Rural Delivery #2, Box 140, Corry, PA 16407
Scope: Statewide
Contact(s):
President: KRISTI SULLIVAN, 415 E. McCormick Ave., State College, PA 16801; Phone: 814-863-2865
President-Elect: SHAYNE HOACHLANDER, Rural Delivery #2, Box 140, Corry, PA 16407; Phone: 814-664-8867
Secretary: TIM SULLIVAN, 415 E. McCormick Ave., State College, PA 16801
Treasurer: TOM HARDISKY, Rural Route 1, Box 84-D, Loganton, PA 17747; Phone: 717-725-2287
Keyword(s): Environmental and Conservation Education, Solid Waste, Sustainable Development, Toxic Substances, Water Resources

WILDLIFE SOCIETY, SACRAMENTO-SHASTA CHAPTER
ATTN: President, Dept. of Water Resources, 3251 S. Street, Sacramento, CA 95816
Scope: Statewide
Contact(s):
President: MICHAEL BRADBURY, Dept. of Water Resources, 3251 S. Street, Sacramento, CA 95816; Phone: 916-227-7527

NON-GOVERNMENTAL ORGANIZATIONS

Vice President: ROBERT L. CAREY, W.M. Beaty and Associates, Inc., P.O. Box 990898, Redding, CA 96099-0898; Phone: 916-227-2657

Secretary and Treasurer: LINNEA HALL, Dept. of Biological Sciences, California State Univeristy, Sacremento, 6000 J St., Sacramento, CA 95819-6077; Phone: 916-278-6573

WILDLIFE SOCIETY, SAN FRANCISCO BAY AREA CHAPTER
ATTN: President, 210 Maclavey Drive, Martinez, CA 94553
Scope: Statewide
Contact(s):
President: STEVEN BOBZIEN, c/o East Bay Regional Park District, 2960 Peralta Oaks Court, P.O. Box 5318, Oakland, CA 94605-0381
President-Elect: JOHN M. BAAS, 210 Maclavey Drive, Martinez, CA 94553; Phone: 510-335-9778
Secretary and Treasurer: TRISH TATARIAN, 1010 Lakeview St., Suite 3A, Petaluma, CA 94952; Phone: 707-763-6492

WILDLIFE SOCIETY, SAN JOAQUIN VALLEY CHAPTER
ATTN: President, Dept. Water Resources, 3374 Shields Ave., Fresno, CA 93726
Scope: Statewide
Contact(s):
President: KAREN J. BROWN, Dept. Water Resources, 3374 E. Shields Ave., Fresno, CA 93726; Phone: 209-445-5386
Secretary: GERRIT BUMA, 153 E. Spruce, LeMoore, CA 93245; Phone: 209-998-4103
Treasurer: LARRY SASLAW, BLM, 3801 Pegasus, Bakersfield, CA 93308; Phone: 805-391-6068
President-Elect: BRIAN CYPHER, P.O. Box 9622, Bakersfield, CA 93309-9622; Phone: 805-398-2201

WILDLIFE SOCIETY, SOUTH CAROLINA CHAPTER
ATTN: President, P.O. Box 167, Columbia, SC 29202
Scope: Statewide
Contact(s):
President: BEN MILLER, 1904 N. Mulberry Drive, Moncks Corner, SC 29461; Phone: 803-899-5780
President-Elect: JUDY BARNES, P.O. Box 167, Columbia, SC 29202; Phone: 803-734-3609
Secretary and Treasurer: PAUL JOHNS, 2441 Williston Road, Aiken, SC 29802; Phone: 803-725-5337
Publication(s): *South Dakota Out-of-Doors*

WILDLIFE SOCIETY, SOUTH DAKOTA CHAPTER
ATTN: President, SD Game, Fish, and Parks, 4500 S. Oxbow Ave., Sioux Falls, SD 57106-4114
Scope: Statewide
Contact(s):
President: THOMAS R. TORNOW, Madison Wetland Management District, P.O. Box 48, Madison, SD 57042; Phone: 605-256-2974
President-Elect: RON SCHAUER, SD Game, Fish & Parks, 4500 S. Oxbow Ave., Sioux Falls, SD 57106-4114; Phone: 605-362-2700
Secretary and Treasurer: PAUL F. COUGHLIN, SD Game, Fish & Parks, Box 218, Desmet, SD 57231; Phone: 605-854-9105
Publication(s): *Tennessee Out of Doors*

WILDLIFE SOCIETY, SOUTHERN CALIFORNIA CHAPTER
ATTN: President, 15644 Kingman Rd., Poway, CA 92064
Scope: Statewide
Contact(s):
President: JEFFREY L. LINCER, 15644 Kingman Rd., Poway, CA 92064; Phone: 609-486-9995
Treasurer: JOHN STEPHENSON, 199 Via Del Cerrito, Encinitas, CA 92024; Phone: 619-674-2951

WILDLIFE SOCIETY, TENNESSEE CHAPTER
ATTN: President Tennessee Chapter, Dept. of Forestry, Wildlfie & Fish, University of Tennessee, P.O. Box 1071, Knoxville, TN 37901
Scope: Statewide
Contact(s):
President: ROBERT WYATT, 1219 Sweet Williams Lane, New Market, TN 37820; Phone: 423-471-0146
President-Elect: DAVID BUEHLER, Dept. Forestry, Wildlife & Fish, University of Tennessee, P.O. Box 1071, Knoxville, TN 37901; Phone: 615-781-6610
Secretary and Treasurer: DAVID WHITEHEAD, 172 Steele Road, Vonore, TN 37885; Phone: 423-884-6767

WILDLIFE SOCIETY, TEXAS CHAPTER
ATTN: President, 4200 Smith School Rd., Austin, TX 78744
Scope: Statewide
Contact(s):
President: LINDA CAMPBELL, TPWD, 3000 1H 35 S., Suite 100, Austin, TX 78704; Phone: 512-912-7044
President-Elect: PENNY BARTNICKI, 4200 Smith School Rd., Austin, TX 78744; Phone: 512-389-4767
Secretary and Treasurer: SCOTT HENKE, CKWRI, Texas A&M Univeristy Kinsville, Kingsville, TX 78363; Phone: 512-593-3689
Vice President-elect: CLARKE E. ADAMS, Texas A&M University, Dept. of Wildlife & Fisheries Sciences, College Station, TX 78743-2258; Phone: 409-845-8824
Publication(s): *Utah Wildlife News*

WILDLIFE SOCIETY, THE
5410 Grosvenor Ln., Bethesda, MD 20814
Phone: 301-897-9770
Founded: 1937; Membership: 9,500
Scope: National
Description: International scientific and educational organization of professionals and students engaged in wildlife research, management, education, and administration. Dedicated to sound stewardship of wildlife resources and the environments upon which wildlife and humans depend; undertakes an active role in preventing human-induced environmental degradation; increases awareness and appreciation of wildlife values; and seeks the highest standards in all activities of the wildlife profession.
Contact(s):
President: JAMES E. MILLER, USDA-CSREES.NRE, AG Box 2210, Room 829, Aerospace Center, Washington, DC 20250-2210; Phone: 202-401-6602
Executive Director: HARRY E. HODGDON
Past-President: ROBERT G. ANTHONY, OR Coop. Wildlife Research Unit, Dept. of Fish and Wildlife, Oregon State University, Corvallis, OR 97331; Phone: 541-737-1954
President-elect: NOVA SILVY, 210 Nagle Hall, Dept. of Wildlife and Fisheries Sciences, Texas A&M University, College Station, TX 77843; Phone: 409-845-5777
Program Directoy: SANDRA STAPLES-BORTNER, 18214 NE 125th Way, Brush Prairie, WA 98606; Phone: 360-253-4611
Serial Publicaitons: Central Mountains & Plains Section: ROBERT D. WOOD, 502 S. Commodore, Pratt, KS 67124; Phone: 316-672-2562
Serial Publicaitons: North Central Section: W. DANIEL SVEDARSKY, Northwest Experimental Station, University of Minnesota, ARC Building, Crookston, MN 56716; Phone: 218-281-8129
Serial Publications: Northeast Section: DANIEL J. DECKER, Dept. of Natural Resources, Fernow Hall, Cornell University, Ithaca, NY 14853; Phone: 573-882-9880
Serial Publications: Northwest Section: W. DANIEL EDGE, Dept. of Fisheries & Wildlife, Oregon State University, 104 Nash Hall, Corvallis, OR 97331-3803; Phone: 506-737-4531
Serial Publications: Southeastern Section: ROBERT J. WARREN, Warnell School of Forest Resources, University of Georgia, Athens, GA 30602-2152; Phone: 706-542-6474

Serial Publications: Southwest Section: ROBERT D. BROWN, Dept. of Wildlife & Fisheries Sciences, 210 Nagle Hall, Texas A&M Univeristy, College Station, TX 77843-2258; Phone: 409-845-1261
Serial Publications: Western Section: BRADLEY E. VALENTINE, California Dept. of Forestry, P.O. Box 670, Santa Rosa, CA 95401; Phone: 707-576-2937
Vice-President: LEN H. CARPENTER, Wildllife Management Institute, 4015 Cheney Dr., Fort Collins, CO 80526; Phone: 970-223-1099
Wildlife Policy Directoy: THOMAS M. FRANKLIN
Publication(s): Serial *Journal of Wildlife Management, The; Wildlife Monographs; Wildlife Society Bulletin; Wildlifer, The*
Keyword(s): Nongame Wildlife, Renewable Resources, Wildlife and Wildlife Habitat, Wildlife Management

WILDLIFE SOCIETY, UTAH CHAPTER
ATTN: President Utah Chapter, Bureau of Land Management, 318 N. 100 E., Kanab, UT 84741
Scope: Statewide
Contact(s):
President: DEAN L. MITCHELL, UT Divison of Wildlife Resources, 1594 W. North Temple, Suite 2110, Box 146301, Salt Lake City, UT 84114-6301; Phone: 801-538-4786
President-Elect: HARRY A. BARBER, Bureau of Land Management, 318 N. 100 E., Kanab, UT 84741; Phone: 435-644-2672
Secretary: LESLIE ROCK, UT Div. Wildlife Resources, 515 E. 5330 Street, Ogden, UT 84405; Phone: 801-476-2740
Treasurer: CECILE LeBLANC, 295 N. 6th St., Tooele, UT 84074; Phone: 435-882-2070
Publication(s): *Vermont Environmental Report*

WILDLIFE SOCIETY, VIRGINIA CHAPTER
ATTN: President Virginia Chapter, USDA Forest Service, 110 Southpark Dr., Blacksburg, VA 24060
Scope: Statewide
Contact(s):
President: MICHAEL T. MENGAK, Ferrmun College, Box 2283, Ferrmun, VA 24088; Phone: 540-365-4373
President-elect: JESSE L. OVERCASH, USDA Forest Service, 110 Southpark Dr., Blacksburg, VA 24060; Phone: 540-522-4641
Secretary: JESSICA W. DEWEY, Reagan National Airport, Terminal A, Room 1171, c/o Operations, Washington, DC 20007; Phone: 703-572-6836
Treasurer: MICHAEL L. FIES, P.O. Box 996, Verona, VA 24482; Phone: 540-248-9390
Vice President-elect: BRUCE A. LEMMERT, 21 S. Church St., Lovettsville, VA 20180; Phone: 540-822-4219

WILDLIFE SOCIETY, WASHINGTON CHAPTER
ATTN: President Washington Chapter, DNR Forest Stewardship, 1111 Washington St., SE, P.O. Box43155, Olympia, WA 98504-3155
Founded: 1966; Membership: 200
Scope: Statewide
Description: The Washington Chapter of The Wildlife Society is a state organization of professional wildlife biologists providing support and training for its members, a forum for presenting wildlife research results and management ideas, and a professional voice in state conservation issues.
Contact(s):
President: JIM BOTTORFF, DNR Forest Stewardship, 1111 Washington Street, SE, P.O. Box 43155, Olympia, WA 98504-3155; Phone: 360-902-2599
Secretary: ANN SPRAGUE, Methow Valley Ranger District, P.O. Box 188, Twisp, WA 98856; Phone: 509-997-2131
Treasurer: CATHERINE RALEY, Forest Sciences Lab, 3625 93rd Ave., S.W., Olympia, WA 98512; Phone: 360-753-7686
Publication(s): *Wildlife Notes*

WILDLIFE SOCIETY, WEST VIRGINIA CHAPTER
ATTN: President W. Virginia Chapter, WV Div. Natural Resources, P.O. Box 67, Elkins, WV 26241
Scope: Statewide
Contact(s):
President: SHAWN HEAD, WV Div. Natural Resources, P.O. Box 67, Elkins, WV 26241; Phone: 304-637-0245
Vice President: TIM FERGUSON, 1304 Goose Run Road, Fairmont, WV 26554; Phone: 304-557-2720
Secretary and Treasurer: ROBERT SILVESTER, 2006 Robert C. Byrd Drive, Beckly, WV 25801-8320; Phone: 304-557-6947
Publication(s): *Wisconservation*

WILDLIFE SOCIETY, WISCONSIN CHAPTER
ATTN: President Wisconisn Chapter, Wisconsin DNR, 3911 Fish Hatchery Rd., Fitchburh, WI 53711
Scope: Statewide
Contact(s):
President: MARK S. BOYCE, College of Natural Resources, University fo Wisconsin, Stevens Point, WI 54481-3897; Phone: 715-346-3873
President-Elect: MIKE FOY, Wisonsin DNR, 3911 Fish Hatchery Road, Fitchburg, WI 53711; Phone: 608-273-6275
Secretary and Treasurer: JAMES R. KEIR, DNR Ranger Station, Friendship, WI 53934; Phone: 608-339-4819
Publication(s): *Wisconsin Association for Environmental Education Bulletin;*

WILDLIFE SOCIETY, WYOMING CHAPTER
ATTN: President, 260 Buena Vista, Lander, WY 82520
Scope: Statewide
Contact(s):
President: DAVE MOODY, WY Game & Fish Dept., 260 Buena Vista Blvd., Lnader, WY 82070; Phone: 307-332-2689
President-Elect: ANDREA CERVOSKI, 260 Buena Vista, Lander, WY 82520; Phone: 307-332-2589
Secretary: BRAD PHILLIPS, 1627 South Summit, Newcastle, WY 82701; Phone: 307-746-2383
Treasurer: TIMOTHY P. THOMAS, WY Game & Fish Dept., P.O. Box 6249, Sheridan, WY 82801; Phone: 307-672-7418

WILDLIFE WAYSTATION
14831 Little Tujunga Canyon Rd., Angeles National Forest, CA 91342-5999
Phone: 818-899-5201
Founded: 1969; Membership: 21,000
Scope: National
Description: A southern California nonprofit refuge providing medical care, refuge, rehabilitation, and placement services for over 4,000 wild and exotic animals annually. Public tours and educational programs available.
Contact(s):
Founder and President: MARTINE COLETTE
Publication(s): *Wildlife Waystation (newsletter); Wild Proofing the Human Habitat (brochure)*
Keyword(s): Endangered and Threatened Species, Environmental and Conservation Education, Mammals, Raptors, Wildlife Rehabilitation

WILSON ORNITHOLOGICAL SOCIETY
ATTN: President, Wilson Ornithological Society, Dept. Of Zoology, Ohio Wesleyan University, Delaware, OH 43015
Founded: 1888; Membership: 3,170
Scope: National
Description: To advance the science of ornithology and to secure cooperation in measures tending to this end.
Contact(s):
President: EDWARD H. BURTT JR., Department of Zoology, Ohio Wesleyan University, Delaware, OH 43015; Phone: 740-368-3886; Fax: 740-368-3011; Email: EHBURTT@CC.OWU.EDU
Secretary: JOHN A. SMALLWOOD, Department of Biology, Montclair State University, Upper Montclair, NJ 07043; Phone:

NON-GOVERNMENTAL ORGANIZATIONS

973-655-5345; Fax: 973-655-7047; Email: SMALLWOOD@SATURN.MONTCLAIR.EDU
Treasurer: DORIS J. WATT, Department of Biology, Saint Mary's College, Notre Dame, IN 46556-5001; Phone: 219-284-4668; Fax: 219-284-4716; Email: DWATT@JADE.SAINTMARYS.EDU
Editor: ROBERT C. BEASON, Department of Biology, State University of New York, 1 College Circle, Geneseo, NY 14454; Phone: 716-245-5310; Fax: 716-245-5007; Email: wilsonbull@uno.cc.geneseo.edu
First Vice President: JOHN C. KRICHER, Department of Biology, Wheaton College, Norton, MA 02766; Phone: 508-285-8200; Email: jkricher@wheatonma.edu
Second Vice President: WILLIAM E. DAVIS, College of General Studies, 871 Commonwealth Avenue, Boston University, Boston, MA 02215; Phone: 617-353-2886; Fax: 617-353-5868; Email: wedavis@bu.edu

Publication(s): Wilson Bulletin, The
Keyword(s): Biodiversity, Biology, Birds, Ecology, Environment, Grants, International Conservation, Natural History, Research, Wildlife and Wildlife Habitat, Zoology

WINCHESTER NILO FARMS
Olin Corporation, E. Alton, IL 62024
Phone: 618-258-3133
Scope: National
Contact(s):
Manager: ROGER JONES; Phone: 618-466-0613

WINDSTAR FOUNDATION, THE
2317 Snowmass Creek Rd., Snowmass, CO 81654
Phone: 303-927-4777; Fax: 303-927-4779
Founded: 1976
Scope: National
Description: A nonprofit membership organization co-founded by John Denver and Tom Crum. Windstar works to inspire individuals to make responsible choices and take direct action to achieve a peaceful and environmentally sustainable future. Programs include: educational programs, and Choices For the Future symposium.
Contact(s):
Chairman of Board of Trustees: DR. JAY D. HAIR
Managing Director (Acting): TERI L. PAUL, The Windstar Foundation, 2317 Snowmass Creek Rd., Snowmass, CO 81654; Phone: 303-927-4777
Secretary and Treasurer: JOEL T. THOMAS
Keyword(s): Air Quality and Pollution, Environmental and Conservation Education, Gardening and Horticulture, Greenhouse Effect/Global Warming, Renewable Resources

WISCONSIN ASSOCIATION FOR ENVIRONMENTAL EDUCATION, INC.
Nelson Hall, UWSP, Steven's Point, WI 54481
Phone: 715-346-2796
Founded: 1974; Membership: 450
Scope: Statewide
Description: Promotes environmental education in schools and other institutions and organizations in Wisconsin.
Contact(s):
Administrative Assistant: GINNY CARLTON, WAEE, Nelson Hall, UWSP, Steven Point, WI 54481
Chairperson: STERLING STRATHE, College of Natural Resources, UWSP, Stevens Point, WI 54481
Vice Chairperson: NANCY PIRAINO
Publication(s): Lake Connection, The
Keyword(s): Environmental and Conservation Education, Environmental Law, Lakes, Water Pollution Management, Water Resources

WISCONSIN ASSOCIATION OF LAKES (WAL)
P.O. Box 126, Stevens Point, WI 54481-0126
Phone: 715-346-3424; Fax: 715-346-3436; Email: wal@coredcs.com
Founded: 1980; Membership: 275
Scope: Statewide
Description: WAL is a coalition of approximately 250 lake management organizations, as well as hundreds of individual members. The organization is dedicated to the protection of lake ecosystems in Wisconsin. WAL works closely with the Wisconsin Department of Natural Resources and University Extension in the Wisconsin Lakes Partnership.
Contact(s):
President: YVONNE FEAVEL; Phone: 715-258-8034
Secretary: JUDY JOOSS; Phone: 414-877-9301; Email: jjooss@techheadnet.com
Treasurer: JOHN SEIBEL; Phone: 715-479-4714; Email: jpsmis@nnex.net
Publication(s): Lake Connection, The
Keyword(s): Aquatic Habitats, Environmental Preservation, Environmental Protection, Lakes, Land Use Planning, Pollution Prevention, Sustainable Ecosystems, Watersheds, Wetlands

WISCONSIN B.A.S.S. CHAPTER FEDERATION
c/o President, 6503 Lani Ln., McFarland, WI 53558
Phone: 608-838-3040
Scope: Statewide
Description: An organization of Bassmaster chapters, affiliated with the Bass Anglers Sportsman Society, organized to fight pollution, assist state and national conservation agencies in their efforts, and teach young people good conservation practices. Dedicated to the realistic conservation of our water resources.
Contact(s):
President: CHUCK ROLFSMEYER, 6503 Lani Ln., McFarland, WI 53558; Phone: 608-262-2409(W)/608-838-3040(H)
Conservation Director: DON HILDEBRANDT, 2310 N. 6th St., Wausau, WI 54403; Phone: 715-842-3397; Email: hilde1com@aol.com
Publication(s): Wisconsin Bass News

WISCONSIN LAND AND WATER CONSERVATION ASSOCIATION
ATTN: President, N2538 Cty Rd., J, Kaulauha, WI 54130
Phone: 608-833-1833; Fax: 608-833-7179; Email: wlwca@execpc.com; WWW: www.execpc.com/~wlwca
Scope: Statewide
Description: Wisconsin Land and Water Conservation Association is a 501(c) (3) non-profit organization representing Wisconsin's 72 county land conservation committees and departments, assisting them with the protection, enhancement and sustainable use of Wisconsin's natural resources, and representing them through education and government interaction.
Contact(s):
President: MARVIN FOX, N2538 Cty Road, J, Kaulauha, WI 54130; Phone: 414-766-3242
Vice President: JOSEPH WISNIEWSKI, 4080 Deerskin Rd., Phelps, WI 54554; Phone: 715-545-2787
Executive Director: ADAM PAYNE, One Point Place, Ste 202, Madison, WI 53719-2809; Phone: 608-833-1833; Fax: 608-833-7179; Email: apayne@execpc.com
Board Member: JOHN KOHL, 1412 Highway 175, Hubertus, WI 53033; Phone: 414-628-1219; Fax: 414-628-0570
Publication(s): Thursday Note; Conservation Catalyst
Keyword(s): Acid Rain, Air Quality, Biodiversity, Biotechnology, Birds, Chemical Pollution Control, Coasts, Communications, Conservation of Protected Areas, Conservation Tillage, EcoAction, Ecology, Endangered and Threatened Species, Energy, Public Lands

NON-GOVERNMENTAL ORGANIZATIONS

WISCONSIN PARK AND RECREATION ASSOCIATION
7000 Greenway, Suite 201, Greendale, WI 53129
Phone: 414-423-1210; Fax: 414-423-1296; Email: wpra@execpc.com
Membership: 1,200
Scope: Statewide
Description: A nonprofit organization, affiliated with the National Recreation and Park Association, working with other groups and organizations to achieve the best in park services and recreational opportunities.
Contact(s):
President: PAUL LEUTHOLD, 3805 S. Casper Dr., New Berlin, WI 53151; Phone: 414-797-2443
Editor: STEVE THOMPSON, 7000 Greenway, Suite 201, Greendale, WI 53129; Phone: 414-423-1210
Publication(s): *Badger Birder; Passenger Pigeon*
Keyword(s): Birds, Environment, Environmental and Conservation Education, Environmental Preservation, Environmental Protection

WISCONSIN SOCIETY FOR ORNITHOLOGY, INC., THE
5188 Bittersweet Ln., Oshkosh, WI 54901
Phone: 414-233-1973
Founded: 1939; Membership: 1,200
Scope: Statewide
Description: To stimulate interest in and promote the study of birds in Wisconsin for a better understanding of their biology and basis for their preservation.
Contact(s):
President: JAMES S. ANDERSON, Mosquito Hill Nature Center, N3880 Rogers Rd., New London, WI 54961; Phone: 414-779-6433
Vice President: SUMNER MATTESON, WDNR, Bureau of Endangered Resources, Box 7921, Madison, WI 53707; Phone: 608-266-1571
Secretary: JANE DENNIS, 138 S. Franklin Ave., Madison, WI 53705-5248; Phone: 608-231-1741
Treasurer: ALEX F. KAILING, W330 N8275 W. Shore Dr., Hartland, WI 53029; Phone: 414-966-1072
Editor: R. TOD HIGHSMITH, 702 Schiller Ct., Madison, WI 53704; Phone: 608-242-1168
Editor: JENNIFER NIELAND, 1066 Harwood Ave., #2, Green Bay, WI 54313; Phone: 414-434-1229
Publicity Chair: BETTIE R. HARRIMAN, 5188 Bittersweet Ln., Oshkosh, WI 54901; Phone: 414-233-1973
Publication(s): *Badger Birder; Passenger Pigeon*
Keyword(s): Birds, Environmental and Conservation Education, Environmental Law, Waterfowl, Wetlands, Wildlife and Wildlife Habitat

WISCONSIN WATERFOWL ASSOCIATION, INC.
131 W. Broadway, P.O. Box 792, Waukesha, WI 53187-0792
Phone: 414-524-8460
Founded: 1983; Membership: 7,800
Scope: Statewide
Description: A statewide nonprofit environmental/educational organization that establishes, promotes, assists, and contributes to conservation, restoration, and management of Wisconsin wetlands to perpetuate waterfowl and wildlife. Represents waterfowl enthusiasts via a unified statewide voice on Wisconsin migratory bird hunting regulations and conservation legislation benefiting the protection of wetlands. Educational programs and waterfowl hunting seminars.
Contact(s):
President: JOEL WATSON, W359 N7660 Brown St., Oconomowoc, WI 53066; Phone: 414-474-7635
Vice President: ELDON McLAURY, 5715 Richardson Cir., Madison, WI 53711; Phone: 608-274-9081
Secretary: TIM HENZEL, 18403 W. Beloit Rd., New Berlin, WI 53146; Phone: 414-679-8791
Treasurer: ROGER BORD, W2667 Kittie Ct., East Troy, WI 53120; Phone: 414-642-5655
Administrator: CHRISTINE BELL
Operations Manager: JEFF BORD
Project Director: JEFF NANIA
Publication(s): *Wisconsin Waterfowl*
Keyword(s): Forests and Forestry

WISCONSIN WILDLIFE FEDERATION
242 Keoller Ave., Oshkosh, WI 54901
Phone: 414-235-9136; Fax: 414-235-6030; Email: wwf@POP.prodigy.net
Scope: Statewide
Description: A representative statewide organization, affiliated with the National Wildlife Federation, dedicated to the protection and enhancement of wildlife and its habitat through public education and government interaction.
Contact(s):
President: BILL BUCKLEY
Affiliate Representative: RUSSELL HITZ
Alternate Representative: MARTHA KILLISHEK
Editor: DANIEL GRIES
Publication(s): *Wisconservation*
Keyword(s): Aquatic Habitats, Fisheries, Renewable Resources, Water Pollution Management, Wetlands

WOLF EDUCATION AND RESEARCH CENTER
P.O. Box 917, Boise, ID 83701
Phone: 208-343-2248; Fax: 208-343-1601; Email: wolfcenter@rmci.net; WWW: www.wolfcenter.org
Founded: 1992; Membership: 14,000 plus 80,000 sponsors
Scope: National
Description: The Wolf Education and Research Center is dedicated to providing public information, education, and research concerning endangered species, with an emphasis on the gray wolf, its habitat and ecosystem in the Northern Rocky Mountain region. Our efforts seek to improve public awareness of endangered and threatened species in the area and to develop, in concert with regional cultures and residents, ways to coexist with these species. It is our goal to be an inclusive organization that offers factual and balanced information.
Contact(s):
President: DIANNA HEWETT; Phone: 208-788-3868; Fax: 208-788-1501
Vice President: ROY FARRAR; Phone: 208-336-6562; Fax: 208-384-0540
Secretary: SALLY FARRAR; Phone: 208-336-6562; Fax: 208-384-0540
Executive Director: KATHY MAECHTLE; Phone: 208-343-2248; Fax: 208-343-1601
Publication(s): *Sawtooth Pack Sponsorship Newsletter; Wild Wolves Sponsorship Newsletter; Wolf Education and Research Center Membership Newsletter*
Keyword(s): Biodiversity, Cultural Preservation, Endangered and Threatened Species, Environmental and Conservation Education, Nature Preservation, Nongame Wildlife, Outdoor Recreation, Predators, Research, Training

WOLF FUND, THE
P.O. Box 471, Moose, WY 83012
Phone: 307-733-0740; Fax: 307-733-0962
Founded: 1986
Scope: National
Description: A project of the Center for the Humanities and the Environment. The sole mission of The Wolf Fund is to facilitate the recovery of the gray wolf to Yellowstone National Park. The Wolf Fund maintains an active mailing list. Received 501 (c) (3 status in March of 1990.
Contact(s):
Executive Director: RENEE ASKINS
Publication(s): *Wolf Fund Newsletter, The; Wolf Fund Children's brochure: Wolves, People, and Yellowstone*
Keyword(s): Endangered and Threatened Species, Environmental and Conservation Education, Wildlife and Wildlife Habitat, Wildlife Management, Wildlife Rehabilitation

NON-GOVERNMENTAL ORGANIZATIONS

WOLF HAVEN INTERNATIONAL
3111 Offut Lake Rd., Tenino, WA 98589
Phone: 360-264-4695
Scope: National
Description: The organization's mission is "Working for Wolf Conservation". With the intent on making a difference, all of Wolf Haven's activities have been undergoing changes that seek to strenghten our involvement in research and education.
Contact(s):
President: RICK SCHAEFER
Vice President: ELLEN FORD
Secretary: NANCY JUDGE
Treasurer: GARY BANKERS, 7447 Boston Harbor Rd. NE, Olympia, WA 98506
Executive Director: MAUREEN L. GREELEY
Publication(s): *Wolf Tracks*
Keyword(s): Endangered and Threatened Species

WOMEN'S ENVIRONMENT AND DEVELOPMENT ORGANIZATION (WEDO)
355 Lexington Avenue, 3rd Floor, New York, NY 10017
Phone: 212-973-0325; Fax: 212-973-0335; Email: wedo@igc.apc.org; WWW: http://www.wedo.org
Founded: 1990
Scope: National
Description: On January 27, 1995, Women USA Fund, Inc. changed its name to WEDO. The organization is an international advocacy network actively working to transform society to achieve social, political, economic, and environmental justice for all through the empowerment of women, in all their diversity, and through their equal participation with men in decision-making from grassroots to global arenas.
Contact(s):
President: BELLA ABZUG
Vice President: CHIEF BISI OGUNLEYE
Vice President: JOCELYN DOW
Vice President: THAIS CORRAL
Secretary: MIM KELBER
Treasurer: BROWNIE LEDBETTER
Publication(s): *News and Views (contact WEDO for a comprehensive list)*
Keyword(s): Biotechnology, Environmental and Conservation Education, International Conservation, Population Growth, Renewable Resources

WOMEN'S SHOOTING SPORTS FOUNDATION
4620 Edison Ave., Suite C, Colorado Springs, CO 80915
Phone: 1-800-820-9773
Founded: 1993; Membership: 3,500
Scope: National
Description: The Women's Shooting Sports Foundation is a national, nonprofit membership organization offering an ongoing series of programs to expand shooting opportunities for women.
Contact(s):
Executive Director: SHARI LeGATE
Publication(s): *Open Sights; Women's Resource List, The*
Keyword(s): Hunting, Training, Waterfowl, Women in the Environment

WOODLAND OWNERS ASSOCIATION OF WEST VIRGINIA
P.O. Box 13695, Sissonville, WV 25360
Phone: 304-594-3648
Founded: 1991; Membership: 425
Scope: Statewide
Description: A statewide organization affiliated with the National Woodland Owners Association that promotes good forestry and sustainable management by non-industrial private owners in West Virginia.
Contact(s):
President: MARK A. BURKE, Sissonville, WV ; Phone: 304-594-3648
Secretary: EDWARD MURRINER, Charleston, WV

WORLD ASSOCIATION OF GIRL GUIDES AND GIRL SCOUTS (WAGGGS)
World Bureau Olave Centre 12c Lyndhurst Rd., Hampstead, London, London NW35PQ United Kingdom
Founded: 1928; Membership: 135
Scope: National
Description: WAGGGS is a voluntary worldwide movement open to all girls and young women. Based on spiritual values and dedicated to the education of girls and young women, WAGGGS provides them with opportunities of self-training in the development of character, responsible citizenship, and service in their own and world communities. WAGGGS works for peace by promoting increased understanding between individuals through community, environmental, and international projects.
Contact(s):
Treasurer: SUSAN PATTEN
Director: JAN HOLT
World Board Chairman: HEATHER BRANDON
World Board Vice Chairman: TERESITA CHOA
Publication(s): *Peace Modules; World Issues Series Booklets-Food and Nutrition, AIDS, and Street Children; Our World News*
Keyword(s): Health and Nutrition, Sustainable Development, Training, Women in the Environment, Youth Organizations

WORLD BIRD SANCTUARY (formerly Raptor Rehabilitation and Propagation Project Inc. The)
Box 270270, St. Louis, MO 63127
Phone: 314-938-6193; Fax: 314-938-9464
Founded: 1977; Membership: 1,500
Scope: National
Description: The WBS was established by Walter C. Crawford, Jr. near St. Louis, Missouri. It is a nonprofit, tax-exempt organization whose mission is to preserve the earth's biological diversity and to secure the future of threatened bird species in their natural environments. We work to fullfill that mission through education, propagation, and rehabilitation. We also have a hands-on internship program.
Contact(s):
President: DR. LEON P. ULLENSVANG
Vice President: SUSAN SEDGWICK-POLING
Secretary: ROBERT J. BRACE
Treasurer: DENNIS V. BREITE
Executive Director: WALTER C. CRAWFORD JR.; Phone: 314-938-6193
Editor: MARION V. ERNST
Publication(s): *Mews News; Methods of Feather Replacement in Birds of Prey; Techniques for Artificial Incubation and Hand-rearing of Raptors; Stress in Captive Birds of Prey*
Keyword(s): Biodiversity, Birds, Endangered and Threatened Species, Environment, Raptors

WORLD CONSERVATION MONITORING CENTRE
219 Huntingdon Rd., Cambridge, Cambridge CB3 0DL United Kingdom
Phone: 0123277314; Fax: 01223277136; Email: info@wcmc.org.uk; WWW: www.wcmc.org.uk
Scope: National
Description: The WCMC supports conservation and sustainable development through the provision of information services on issues relating to nature conservation, and through supporting others in the development of their own information management activities. WCMC works in a collaborative manner with a wide range of organizations, and is jointly managed by three of the foremost global agencies concerned with the environment and nature conservation, IUCN, WWF, and UNEP.
Contact(s):
Director: DR. MARK COLLINS
Head of Information Services: JEREMY HARRISON
Information Officer: JO TAYLOR
Publication(s): *Global Biodiversity: Status of the Earth's living resources; IUCN Red List of Threatened Animals (1996); IUCN Red*

List of Threatened Plants (1997); Conservation Atlas of Tropical Rainforests
Keyword(s): Ancient Forests, Aquatic Habitats, Biodiversity, Birds, Botanical Gardens, Coasts, Conservation of Protected Areas, Coral Reefs, Deserts, Developing Countries, Ecology, Endangered and Threatened Species, Environmental and Conservation Education, International Conservation, Wildlife and Wildlife Habitat

WORLD FORESTRY CENTER
4033 SW Canyon Rd., Portland, OR 97221
Phone: 503-228-1367; Fax: 503-228-4608
Founded: 1966
Scope: National
Description: The World Forestry Center is a nonprofit organization promoting a greater appreciation and understanding of the world's forests and related natural resources. The Center operates a forestry museum adjacent to the Hoyt Arboretum, conference facilities, an international institute, and an 80-acre demonstration forest and outdoor education site. Public tours and classes, school programs, exhibits and special events, conferences, curriculum materials, and publications are available.
Contact(s):
President: JOHN BLACKWELL
Education Director: RICK ZENN
Publication(s): *Forest Education Program Guide; Branching out Newsletter*
Keyword(s): Environmental and Conservation Education, Forests and Forestry, International Conservation, Natural History, Renewable Resources

WORLD NATURE ASSOCIATION INC.
P.O. Box 673, Silver Spring, MD 20918
Phone: 301-593-5924; Fax: 301-593-2522; Email: dm88@umail.umd.edu
Founded: 1969; Membership: 250
Scope: National
Description: The Association supports educational and conservation projects in other parts of the world. We seek out small projects that are not able to be funded by other means and are often the work of a few individuals. We also sponsor a scholarship for young Maryland educators.
Contact(s):
President: DONALD MESSERSMITH, 10418 Brookmoor Dr., Silver Spring, MD 20901; Phone: 301-593-5924
Vice President: MICHAEL KREGER, 7511 Brooklyn Bridge Rd., Laurel, MD 20707
Secretary: PATRICIA TONKIN, 602 Winhall Way, Silver Spring, MD 20904
Treasurer: DR. PHILLIPS FOSTER, 7526 Sweetbriar Dr., College Park, MD 20740
Crowder Memorial Library Librarian: DONALD MESSERSMITH, P.O. Box 673, Silver Spring, MD 20918
Publication(s): *World Nature News*
Keyword(s): Biodiversity, Birds, Conservation of Protected Areas, Endangered and Threatened Species, Environmental and Conservation Education, Grants, Nature Preservation, Research

WORLD PAL (WORLD POPULATION ALLOCATION LIMITED INC.)
P.O. Box 2568, Peekskill, NY 10566
Phone: 914-424-4805; Fax: 914-424-4805; Email: anderson@worldpal.org
Scope: National
Description: World Pal is concerned with increasing the awareness that young people have for their environment. World Pal conducts educational awareness programs on the decks of a newly-built, four-masted barquetine. The programs are offered in many ports throughout Latin America, from the Rio Grande to Patagonia. While on board, passagers are encouraged to participate in the educational program.
Contact(s):
Executive Director: CAPT. D. C. ANDERSON

Keyword(s): Ecosystems, Environment, Environmental Protection, Population Growth, Sustainable Development

WORLD PARKS ENDOWMENT INC.
99 Park Ave., New York, NY 10016
Founded: 1988
Scope: National
Description: World Parks Endowment, Inc. is a unique organization which acquires land in the rain forest and other critical sites for biological diversity. It also provides funds for park management of tropical rain forests and other ecosystems of great conservation importance around the world, and has developed projects in over eight countries.
Contact(s):
Chairman and President: DANIEL KATZ, 319 Garfield Pl. 3A, Brooklyn, NY 11215; Phone: 212-677-1900
Secretary and Executive Director: BYRON SWIFT, 1400 16th St. NW, Washington, DC 20036; Phone: 202-939-3808
Vice President and Treasurer: ROGER PASQUIER, 257 Park Ave. S., New York, NY 10010; Phone: 212-505-2100
Publication(s): *Annual Report*
Keyword(s): Land Preservation, Land Purchase

WORLD PHEASANT ASSOCIATION
P.O. Box 5 Lower Basildon, Reading, Berks RG8 9PF United Kingdom
Phone: 01189-845140; Fax: 01189-843369; Email: wpa@gr.apc.org
Founded: 1975
Scope: National
Description: Aims are to develop, promote, and support conservation of all species of the order galliformes with initial emphasis on the family phasianidae.
Contact(s):
Chairman: RICHARD P. HOWARD
President: KEITH HOWMAN
Administrator: NICOLA CHALMERS-WATSON
Editor: DEREK BINGHAM, c/o World Pheasant Association, P.O. Box 5, Lower Basildon, Reading, Berks RG8 9PF United Kingdom
Publication(s): *Annual Review; Newsletters*

WORLD PHEASANT ASSOCIATION OF U.S.A. INC.
15545Regaldo St., Hasienda Heights, CA 91745
Phone: 602-455-5522
Founded: 1982
Scope: National
Description: A nonprofit, tax-exempt membership organization devoted to support of research, education, propagation, and conservation of galliform birds throughout the world. Participates in the development of a World Conservation Strategy for the galliformes and serves in collaboration with other national chapters such as the ICBP and IUCN Specialist Group on galliform birds.
Contact(s):
President: DON TUCKER
Vice President: DAVID J. CALVIN
Chairman of Executive Committee: MICHAEL BARRETT
Editor: IAIN GRAHAME
General Counsel: JAMES D. GUNDERSON
Honorary President: DIDY GRAHAME
Secretary and Treasurer: EDWARD C. SCHMITT
Publication(s): *WPA Newsletter; Annual Journal; Annual Report*

WORLD RESOURCES INSTITUTE
1709 New York Ave., NW, Washington, DC 20006
Phone: 202-638-6300; Fax: 202-638-0036; Email: nkete@wri.org
Founded: 1982
Scope: National
Description: A policy research center created with funding from the John D. and Catherine T. MacArthur Foundation and others, to help governments, international organizations, the private sector, and

NON-GOVERNMENTAL ORGANIZATIONS

others address vital issues of environmental integrity, natural resource management, economic growth, and international security.
Contact(s):
President: JONATHAN LASH
Corporate Secretary and Treasurer: MARJORIE BEANE
Senior Vice President: ALAN BREWSTER
Publication(s): *Policy Studies Series; Research Report Series; World Resources Report*
Keyword(s): Air Quality and Pollution, Forests and Forestry, Greenhouse Effect/Global Warming, Renewable Resources, Sustainable Development

WORLD SOCIETY FOR THE PROTECTION OF ANIMALS (WSPA)
29 Perkins St. P. O. Box 190, Boston, MA 02130
Phone: 617-522-7000; Fax: 617-522-7077
Founded: 1981
Scope: National
Description: The World Society for the Protection of Animals (WSPA) aims to promote the protection of animals, to prevent cruelty to animals, and to relieve animal suffering in every part of the world. For decades, our tools have been hands-on field work, along with humane education and legislative action as we strive for the humans treatment and safety of animals. WSPA has over 350 members societies in 75 nations that provide support for our many animal protection initiatives.
Contact(s):
President: PAUL G. IRWIN
Vice President: PETER DAVIES
Vice President: HANS PETER HAERING
Secretary: MURDAUGH MADDEN
Treasurer: ROBERT CUMMINGS
Chief Executive: ANDREW DICKSON
International Projects Director: JOHN WALSH
Publication(s): *Animals International; WSPA World; WSPA Campaign News; Annual Report, By-Laws, Policy Statement*
Keyword(s): Endangered and Threatened Species, Mammals, Marine Mammals, Nongame Wildlife, Wildlife Rehabilitation

WORLD WILDLIFE FUND
1250 24th St., NW, Washington, DC 20037
Phone: 202-293-4800; Fax: 202-293-9211
Founded: 1961; **Membership:** 1.2 million
Scope: National
Description: WWF is the largest private U.S. organization working worldwide to protect wildlife and wildlands--especially in the tropical forests of Latin America, Asia, and Africa. WWF has helped create and protect more than 450 national parks and nature reserves; supports scientific investigations; monitors international trade in wildlife; promotes ecologically- sound development; assists local groups to take the lead in needed conservation projects; and seeks to influence public opinion and the policies of governments and private institutions to promote conservation of the earth's living resources.
Contact(s):
President: KATHRYN S. FULLER
Secretary: ADRIENNE MARS
Treasurer: HUNTER LEWIS
Africa and Madagascar Vice President: HENRI NSANJAMA
Asia and Pacific Vice President: BRUCE W. BUNTING
Chairman of Board: ROGER W. SANT
Chairman of Executive Committee: EDWARD P. BASS
General Counsel: PATRICIA EWING
Latin America and Caribbean Vice President: TWIG JOHNSON
Managing Vice President for Operations: DEBORAH S. HECHINGER
Public Affairs Vice President: MARK J. ROVNER
Senior Vice President: JAMES P. LEAPE
U.S. Land and Wildlife Vice President: WILLIAM M. EICHBAUM
Vice President of Research and Development: DIANE W. WOOD
Publication(s): *FOCUS*
Keyword(s): Endangered and Threatened Species, International Conservation, Urban Environment, Wildlife and Wildlife Habitat

WORLD WOMEN IN THE DEFENSE OF THE ENVIRONMENT
1200 18th St., NW, Suite 1100, Washington, DC 20036
Phone: 202- 721-1541; Fax: 202-296-9679
Founded: 1981
Scope: International
Description: An international membership organization established to strengthen the role of women in developing and implementing sound policies for managing the environment and natural resources. WORLDWIDE's goals are: (1 to educate the public and policymakers about the vital linkages between women, natural resources, and sustainable development; and (2 to promote the inclusion of women and their environmental perceptions in the design and implementation of development policies and programs.
Contact(s):
Executive Director: ANNABELL HERTZ
Publication(s): *WorldWIDE News (International Newsletter); WorldWIDE Directory of Women in Environment; Proceedings from 1991 Global Assembly of Women and the Environment*
Keyword(s): Environmental and Conservation Education, International Conservation, Public Health Protection, Women in the Environment

WORLDWATCH INSTITUTE
1776 Massachusetts Ave. NW, Washington, DC 20036-1904
Phone: 202-452-1999 Publications 800-555-2028; Email: worldwatch@worldwatch.org; WWW: www.worldwatch.org
Founded: 1974
Scope: National
Description: A nonprofit research organization designed to inform policymakers and the public about emerging global problems and trends and the complex links between the world economy and its environmental support systems. Recent studies have covered global warming, world water shortages, soil erosion, and the decline in food production compared to population growth, renewable energy, deforestation, transportation, oceans, fisheries, carrying capacity, environmental refugees, etc.
Contact(s):
President: LESTER R. BROWN
Vice President: CHRISTOPHER FLAVIN
Assistant to the Vice President: REAH JANISE KAUFFMAN
Librarian: LORI BALDWIN
Vice President of Communications: DICK BELL
Vice President of Operations: JAMES GILLEPSIE
WorldWatch Magazine Editor: ED AYRES
Publication(s): *Worldwatch papers; State of the World; World Watch magazine; Vital Signs; Environmental Alert book series; Database Diskette*
Keyword(s): Agriculture, Energy, Population Growth, Renewable Resources, Water Resources

WWF JAPAN (WORLD WIDE FUND FOR NATURE JAPAN)
Nihonseimei Akabanebashi Bldg., 3-1-14 Shiba, Minato-Ku, Tokyo 1050-0014 Japan
Phone: 03-3769-1711; Fax: 03-3769-1717
Founded: 1971; **Membership:** 40,000
Scope: International
Description: WWF Japan is a national organization of WWF - World Wide Fund for Nature - which is one of the world's largest private international conservation organizations.
Contact(s):
Chairperson: HISAKO HATAKEYAMA
Chief Executive Director: MAKOTO HOSHINO
Honorary President: PRINCE AKISHINO
Vice Chairman: TOMIO YOSHIDA
Vice Chairman: MITSUGU KAWAMURA
Publication(s): *WWF News (Japanese); Panda News (Japanese); TRAFFIC Newsletter (Japanese); Environment Education Newsletter (Japanese)*

WYOMING ASSOCIATION OF CONSERVATION DISTRICTS
ATTN: President, Box 271, Meeteetse, WY 82422
Scope: Statewide
Contact(s):
President: TRACY RENNER, Box 271, Meeteetse, WY 82422; Phone: 307-868-2235; Fax: 307-868-2470
Vice President: DENNIS THALER, Rt. 77, Box 167, LaGrange, WY 82221; Phone: 307-834-2279; Fax: 307-834-2279
Executive Director: BOBBI FRANK, 2304 E. 13th St., Cheyenne, WY 82001; Phone: 307-632-5716; Fax: 307-638-4099; Email: wacod@trib.com
Alternate Board Member: KEITH SCHOENE, 5307 I-80 Service Rd., Burns, WY 82053; Phone: 307-547-3320; Fax: 307-772-2120
Board Member: DARRELL WALKER, P.O. Box 121, Daniel, WY 83115; Phone: 307-859-8264; Fax: 307-367-2272

WYOMING B.A.S.S. CHAPTER FEDERATION
c/o president, 1819 Hollipark Dr., Idaho Falls, WY 83401
Phone: 208-525-2028
Scope: Statewide
Description: An organization of Bassmaster chapters, affiliated with the Bass Anglers Sportsman Society, organized to fight pollution, assist state and national conservation agencies in their efforts, and teach the young people of our country good conservation practices. Dedicated to the realistic conservation of our water resources.
Contact(s):
President: CHUCK WIEGAND, 1819 Hollipark Dr., Idaho Falls, ID 83401; Phone: 208-525-2028
Conservation Director: DAVID CHANNEL, 317 Winterhawk Dr., Rock Springs, WY 82901; Phone: 307-382-4742

WYOMING NATIVE PLANT SOCIETY
1604 Grand Ave., Laramie, WY 82070
Phone: 307-745-5026; Email: clyde@uwyo.edu
Founded: 1981; Membership: 200
Scope: Statewide
Description: The Wyoming Native Plant Society promotes the use and appreciation of the state's native flora through education and supporting research.
Contact(s):
President: CHARMAINE REFSDAL DELMATIER
Vice President: JIM OZENBERGER
Secretary and Treasurer: WALTER FERTIG; Phone: 307-745-3509
Publication(s): *Castilleja; Landscaping with Wildflowers and Native Plants*
Keyword(s): Endangered and Threatened Species, Flowers, Plants, and Trees, Gardening and Horticulture, Natural Areas, Natural History, Wildlands

WYOMING OUTDOOR COUNCIL
262 Lincoln St., Lander, WY 82520
Phone: 307-332-7031; Fax: 307-332-6899; Email: woc@rmisp.com; WWW: www.wocnet.org
Founded: 1967
Scope: Statewide
Description: A statewide membership organization dedicated to the conservation of Wyoming's natural resources. Promotes sound environmental policy and education of the public for wise decisionmaking. Serves as an active citizen lobby for environmental policies, conducts research, and monitors state and federal agencies.
Contact(s):
President: CHIP RAWLINS, P.O. Box 1262, Pinedale, WY 82941
Treasurer: MICHELE BARLOW, 718 S. 5th, Laramie, WY 82070
Executive Directory: DAN HEILIG
President-elect: LIZ HOWELL, P.O. Box 345, Story, WY 82824
Publication(s): *State Legislative Analysis; Frontline Report* (newsletter); various reports and alerts
Keyword(s): Environmental and Conservation Education, Public Lands, Solid Waste, Toxic Substances, Wildlife and Wildlife Habitat

WYOMING WILDLIFE FEDERATION
P.O. Box 106, Cheyenne, WY 82003
Phone: 307-637-5433; Fax: 307-637-6629; Email: admin@wyomingwildlife.org; WWW: www.wyomingwildlife.org
Scope: Statewide
Description: A representative statewide organization, affiliated with the National Wildlife Federation, dedicated to the protection and enhancement of wildlife and its habitat through public education and government interaction.
Contact(s):
President: HAROLD SCHULTZ
Affiliate Representative: CRAIG THOMPSON
Editor: KRISTIN SPAN

XERCES SOCIETY, THE
4828 SE Hawthorne Blvd., Portland, OR 97215
Phone: 503-232-6639; Fax: 503-233-6794; Email: xerces@teleport.com
Founded: 1971; Membership: 7,700
Scope: National
Description: An international nonprofit organization dedicated to invertebrates and the preservation of critical biosystems worldwide. The Society is committed to protecting invertebrates as major components of biological diversity. Emphasis: aquatic invertebrate monitoring to assist in conservation of Pacific Northwest watersheds, butterfly farming in NE Costa Rica, enhancing wild pollinator populations in out-of-play areas of selected Columbia Plateau golf courses, and education through publications.
Contact(s):
President: THOMAS EISNER, Cornell University, Neurobiology and Behavior, W347 Mudd Hall, Ithaca, NY 14853-2702; Phone: 607-255-4464
Vice President: PAUL OPLER, Midcontinent Ecological Science Center, 4512 McMurry Avenue, Ft. Collins, CO 80525; Phone: 970-226-9409
Secretary: ED GROSSWILER, Robertson, Grosswiler, Crown Plaza, Suite 1005, 1500 SW 1st, Portland, OR 97201; Phone: 503-228-3282
Treasurer: KATHERINE JANEWAY, 1932 First Avenue, Suite 510, Seattle, WA 98101; Phone: 206-583-8304
Executive Director: MELODY ALLEN, 4828 SE Hawthorne Blvd., Portland, OR 97215; Phone: 503-232-6639
Editor: MARY TROYCHAK, 4828 SE Hawthorne Blvd., Portland, OR 97215
Publication(s): *Wings: Essays on Invertebrate Conservation* (membership magazine); *Butterfly Gardening: Creating Summer Magic in Your Garden; Common Names of North American Butterflies, The*
Keyword(s): Biodiversity, Endangered and Threatened Species, Insects and Butterflies

YELLOWSTONE GRIZZLY FOUNDATION (YGF)
104 Hillside Ct., Boulder, CO 80302-9452
Phone: 303-939-8126
Founded: 1986; Membership: 500
Scope: National
Description: The YGF is a nonprofit organization dedicated to the conservation of the threatened grizzly bear and habitat preservation in the Greater Yellowstone Ecosystem. It conducts independent research and draws from that to produce educational materials and programs for both professional and general public audiences.
Contact(s):
President: MARILYN FRENCH, 6675 Upper Cascade Dr., Jackson, WY 83001; Phone: 307-733-8630
Vice President: KAREN SHIRLEY, P.O. Box 3468, Jackson, WY 83001; Phone: 307-733-5311
Secretary: DR. TIMOTHY FLOYD, P.O. Box 3229, Hailey, ID 83333; Phone: 208-726-3968
Treasurer: STEVEN P. FRENCH
Publication(s): *Yellowtone Grizzly Journal*

Keyword(s): Endangered and Threatened Species, Environmental and Conservation Education, Mammals, Wildlife and Wildlife Habitat, Wildlife Management

YMCA EARTH SERVICE CORPS
909 4th Ave., Seattle, WA 98104
Phone: 206-382-5013
Founded: 1989
Scope: National
Description: YMCA Earth Service Corps empowers young people to be effective, responsible global citizens by providing opportunities for environmental education and action, leadership development, and international and cross-cultural exchange. Students, working with teachers and the YMCA staff, initiate environmental community service projects, such as tree plantings, water quality monitoring, recycling, and working with younger students.
Contact(s):
National Program Director: KRISTIN JOHNSTAD, 909 4th Ave., Seattle, WA 98104; Phone: 206-382-5013 ext.5087
Operations and Communications and Development Coordinator: KATHLEEN WONG, 909 4th Ave., Seattle, WA 98104; Phone: 206-382-5013 ext.5115
Training Director: CHARLIE MURPHY; Phone: 206-382-5013 ext.5079
Publication(s): *Only Green World*
Keyword(s): Environmental and Conservation Education, Environmental Preservation, Urban Environment, Urban Forestry, Youth Organizations

YOSEMITE RESTORATION TRUST
1212 Broadway, Suite 814, Oakland, CA 94612
Phone: 510-763-1403; Fax: 510-208-4435
Founded: 1990
Scope: National
Description: To ensure protection of the natural, scenic, and historic resources of Yosemite National Park and its ecosystems, and to ensure that visitors have the highest quality experience of the park's natural environment.
Contact(s):
President: JANET S. COBB
Vice President: WALTER F. KIESER
Vice President: HAL C. BROWDER
Secretary: JULIE MCDONALD
Treasurer: THOMAS W. GWYN
Publication(s): *Yosemite Viewpoints (Newsletter); special reports on regional transportation, day-use reservations, and housing.*
Keyword(s): Nature Preservation, Outdoor Recreation, Rural Development, Transportation, Wilderness

YOUNG ENTOMOLOGISTS' SOCIETY INC.
1915 Peggy Pl., Lansing, MI 48910-2553
Phone: 517-887-0499; Email: YESbugs@aol.com; WWW: YESbugs/bugclub.html
Founded: 1965; Membership: 750
Scope: National
Description: An international nonprofit organization educates and serves youth and amateur entomologists via publications and programs; assists in information, talent, scientific literature, and insect specimen exchanges (informational networks); distributes and develops resource materials; and promotes awareness of arthropod importance and the contributions youth and amateur entomologists make to the science of entomology. Founded as Teen International Entomology Group.
Contact(s):
Executive Director: DIANNA K. DUNN; Phone: 517-887-0499
Director of Education: GARY A. DUNN; Phone: 517-887-0499
Publication(s): *Caring for Insect Livestock; Insect World; Flea Market; Insect Study Sourcebook, The; Project B.U.G.S.; Insect Indentification Guide*
Keyword(s): Environmental and Conservation Education, Insects and Butterflies, Outdoor Recreation, Youth Organizations, Zoology

YUKON FISH AND GAME ASSOCIATION
P.O. Box 4434, Whitehorse, Yukon Territory Y1A 3T5 Canada
Phone: 403-667-2843
Scope: Statewide
Description: Affiliated with the Canadian Wildlife Federation.

ZERO (REGIONAL ENVIRONMENTAL ORGANIZATION)
158 Fife Ave., Greenwood Park, P.O. Box 5338, Harare Zimbabwe
Phone: 263-4-791333; Fax: 263-4-732858; Email: zero@harare.iafrica.com
Founded: 1987
Scope: International
Description: ZERO, a regional environmental organization, is an independent professional, not-for-profit institution dedicated to the development of the rural peoples of southern Africa, especially through the promotion of sustainable management of land resources. ZERO pursues this goal through applied research, policy analysis and influencing national, regional, and international environmental policy making.
Contact(s):
Director: DR. JOSEPH Z. MATOWANYIKA
Chairperson to the Board: DR. YEMI KATERERE
Librarian and Information Officer: J. K. MUTSIGWA
Secretary to the Board: PROF. SAM MOYO
Publication(s): *Books, Working Paper Series, Special Paper Series, and Rural Industries Training Manuals.*

ZERO POPULATION GROWTH INC.
1400 16th St. NW Suite 320, Washington, DC 20036
Phone: 202-332-2200; Fax: 202-332-2302; Email: info@zpg.org; WWW: www.zpg.org
Founded: 1968; Membership: 56,000
Scope: National
Description: ZPG is a national nonprofit membership organization that works to educate and motivate Americans to help meet the global population challenge. ZPG mobilizes grassroots support for the adoption of policies and programs necessary to stabilize global population growth.
Contact(s):
President: DR. JUDITH E. JACOBSEN
Executive Director: PETER H. KOSTMAYER
Director of Communications: TIM CLINE
Director of Communications: JOHN SEAGER
Director of Government Relations: BRIAN DIXON
Director of Membership and Development: SUE WOODWARD
Director of Policy, Field and Communications: JOHN SEAGER
Director of Population Education: PAMELA WASSERMAN
Field Director: JAY KELLER
Honorary President: DR. PAUL R. EHRLICH
Political Representative: BRIAN DIXON
Publication(s): *ZPG Reporter; Teachers' PET Term Paper; Action Alerts, Factsheets, Backgrounders, Media Targets, reports, and promotional brochures*
Keyword(s): Environmental and Conservation Education, Population Growth, Public Health Protection, Renewable Resources, Sustainable Development

EDUCATIONAL INSTITUTIONS

ALABAMA

AUBURN UNIVERSITY, College of Agriculture
Swingle Hall, Auburn, AL 36849
Contact(s):
Allied Aquacultures, (B.S., M.S., M.Aq., Ph.D.), Dean Of Libraries: DR. STELLA BENTLEY
Department of Fisheries, (B.S., M.S., Ph.D.), Department Head: DR. JOHN W. JENSEN; Phone: 344-844-4786

AUBURN UNIVERSITY, College of Sciences and Mathematics
Auburn, AL 36849
Contact(s):
Department of Zoology, Department Head: DR. MICHAEL C. WOOTEN, 331 Furnchess Hall, Auburn, AL 36849; Phone: 334-844-4850
Marine Biology, (B.S.):
Wildlife Science, (B.S., M.S., Ph.D.):
Zoology, (B.S., M.S., Ph.D.):

AUBURN UNIVERSITY, Ralph Brown Draughon Library
Auburn, AL 36849
Phone: 334-844-1714
Contact(s):
Project Director: DR. JOHN A. PLUMB

AUBURN UNIVERSITY, School of Forestry
108 M. White Smith Hall, Auburn, AL 36849-5418
Phone: 334-844-1007
Degrees: (B.S., M.F., M.S., Ph.D.)
Contact(s):
Dean: DR. RICHARD W. BRIKER

AUBURN UNIVERSITY, Southeastern Cooperative Fish Disease Project
Department of Fisheries and Allied Aquacultures, Auburn, AL 36849
Phone: 334-844-4786; Fax: 334-844-9208
Founded: 1964
Description: The project was founded in 1964 to provide a fish-kill diagnostic service, training in fish diseases, and research on fish diseases to the cooperating member states.
Contact(s):
Associate Project Director: DR. JOHN M. GRIZZLE

ALASKA

UNIVERSITY OF ALASKA AT FAIRBANKS
Fairbanks, AK 99775
Contact(s):
Alaska Cooperative Fish and Wildlife Research Unit, Leader: DR. JAMES B. REYNOLDS; Phone: 907-474-7661
Department of Biology and Wildlife, Head: DR. GERALD F. SHIELDS; Phone: 907-474-5493
Institute of Arctic Biology, Interim Director: DR. JAMES S. SEDINGER; Phone: 907-474-7640

UNIVERSITY OF ALASKA AT FAIRBANKS, College of Science/Engineering and Mathematics
Fairbanks, AK 99775
Phone: 907-474-7608
Contact(s):
Interim Dean: DR. EDWARD C. MURPHY

UNIVERSITY OF ALASKA AT FAIRBANKS, School of Fisheries and Ocean Sciences
Fairbanks, AK 99775
Phone: 907-474-7824
Contact(s):
Dean: DR. VERA ALEXANDER

ALBERTA

UNIVERSITY OF ALBERTA, Faculty of Agriculture, Forestry, and Home Economics
2-14 Agriculture Forestry Centre, Edmonton, Alberta T6G 2P5 Canada
Phone: 403-492-4933/1-800-804-6417 (Western Canada); Email: dean.agforhe@ualberta.ca; WWW: www.afhe.ualberta.ca/
Description: Undergraduate Degree Programs: B.Sc. in Agricultural and Food Business Management, Agriculture, Environmental and Conservation Sciences, Forest Business Management, Forestry, Human Ecology, Nutrition, and Food Sciences. Graduate Degree Programs: M.Sc., M. Ag., M.Eng., Ph.D. in Agricultural Food and Nutritional Science; M.A. and MSc. in Human Ecology; M.Sc., M. Ag., M.F., Ph. D., MBA/MF in Renewable Resources; MSc., MAg., Ph.D., MBA/MAg in Rural Economy.
Contact(s):
Agricultural, Food, and Nutritional Science, Chair: DR. JOHN J. KENNELLY; Phone: 403-492-3239
Human Ecology, Acting Chair: DR. NANCY KERR; Phone: 403-492-3824
Renewable Resources, Chair: DR. JIM A. BECK; Phone: 403-492-4413
Rural Economy, Acting Chair: DR. MEL I. LEROHL; Phone: 403-492-4225

ARIZONA

ARIZONA STATE UNIVERSITY, Center for Environmental Studies
Box 873211, Arizona State University, Tempe, AZ 85287-1501
Phone: 602-965-2975; Fax: 602-965-8087; WWW: www.asu.edu/ces or caplter.asu.edu
Description: The Center is involved in the Central Arizona-Phoenix Long Term Ecological Research (CAPLTER) project at Arizona State University, funded by the National Science Foundation and is one of the first urban sites in the LTER network. CAPLTER provides a unique addition to CAPLTER research by focusing upon an arid-land ecosystem profoundly influenced, even defined by the presence and activities of humans. Investigations of land-use and ecological consequences in an urban environmental also involves community partners and K-12 schools. Our aim is to understand the changing urban fabric of our arid urban ecosystems and to offer applications to arid cities across the globe.
Contact(s):
Co-Project Director: CHARLES L. REDMOND
Co-Project Director: NANCY GRIMM
Director: CHARLES REDMOND

NORTHERN ARIZONA UNIVERSITY
Flagstaff, AZ 86011-5016
Contact(s):
College of Ecosystem Science and Management, Dean: DAVID R. PATTON; Phone: 520-523-6629
Department of Geography and Public Planning, (Geography, B.S., Applied Geography, B.S., Public Planning, B.S., Rural Geography, M.S.), Chair: ROBERT O. CLARK, Box 15016, Flagstaff, AZ 86011-5016; Phone: 520-523-2650/1321

EDUCATIONAL INSTITUTIONS - ARKANSAS/ARKANSAS

Forest Science, (B.S., M.S., M.Agr., Ph.D.), Interim Head: DR. ROBERT G. MERRIFIELD; Phone: 409-845-5000
Institute for Renewable Natural Resources, (B.S., M.Agr.), Director: DR. BOB BROWN; Phone: 409-845-5777
Rangeland Ecology and Management, (B.S., M.S., M.Agr., Ph.D.), Head: DR. BOB WHITSON; Phone: 409-845-5579
Recreation, Parks, and Tourism Sciences, (B.S., M.S., M.Agr., Ph.D.), Head: DR. PETER A. WITT; Phone: 409-845-7324
Wildlife and Fisheries Sciences, (B.S., M.S., M.Agr., Ph.D.), Head: DR. BOB BROWN; Phone: 409-845-5777

NORTHERN ARIZONA UNIVERSITY, School of Forestry
Box 15018, Flagstaff, AZ 86011-5018
Phone: 520-523-3031

Description: Norhtern Arizona University is in an ideal location for the study of both forestry and recreation. Near Flagstaff are the largest ponderosa pine forest in America, five life zones within fifty miles, recreartion and aesthetic areas, and extensive wildlife, grazing, and watershed areas.

Contact(s):
Chair: DONALD G. ARGANBRIGHT
Forestry, (B.S., M.S., Ph.D.):
Park and Recreation Management, (B.S. and certification in Natural Resource Law Enforcement):

PRESCOTT COLLEGE, Environmental Studies Program
220 Grove Ave., Prescott, AZ 86301
Phone: 520-778-2090; Fax: 520-776-5137

Description: The Environmental Studies Program is one of four programs within Prescott College. The program emphasizes experiential and interdisciplinary learning, and focuses on the interrelationships between the human and nonhuman worlds and the reciprocal influences each has on the other.

Contact(s):
Program Coordinator: DR. PAUL SNEED

UNIVERSITY OF ARIZONA, Department of Hydrology and Water Resources
122 Harshbarger Bldg. #11, Tucson, AZ 85721
Phone: 520-621-5082; Fax: 520-621-1422; Email: programs@hwr.arizona.edu; WWW: www.arizona.edu

Description: The mission of the department is to provide education, research, and service in the fields of hydrology and water resources at the B.S., M.S., and Ph.D. levels and to engage in basic and applied research. The department offers comprehensive programs in all areas of surface and subsurface hydrology, water quality, and water resources systems (management, administration, engineering).

Contact(s):
Academic Advising Coordinator: TERRIE H. THOMPSON; Phone: 520-621-3131
Dean of Libraries: CARLA J. STOFFLE; Phone: 520-621-2101
Department Head: VIC R. BAKER; Phone: 520-621-7120
Main Library: ; Phone: 520-621-6441; Fax: 520-621-9722
Undergraduate Coordinator: DONALD R. DAVIS; Phone: 520-621-3801

UNIVERSITY OF ARIZONA, School of Renewable Resources
325 Biological Sciences East, P.O. Box 210043, Tucson, AZ 85721-0043
WWW: www.srnr.arizona.edu/

Description: The School of Renewable Natural Resources provides instruction, research, and extension in a range of disciplines. The specific academic programs of landscape resources, rangeland and forest resources, watershed resources, and wildlife and fisheries resources provide undergraduate and graduate education. Physical and biological sciences are integrated with socioeconomic and political factors necessary for the conservation, protection, and management of renewable natural resources.

Contact(s):
Associate Director: DR. C.P. PATRICK REID; Phone: 520-621-7257; Fax: 520-621-8801
Cooperative Fish and Wildlife Research Unit (U.S. Department of Interior), Leader: DR. O. EUGENE MAUGHAN; Phone: 520-621-1959
Cooperative National Park Resources Studies Unit (U.S. Department of Interior), Leader: DR. WILLIAM HALVORSON; Phone: 520-621-1174
Cooperative Social Sciences Institute (USDA Natural Resources Conservation Service), (M.L.A.), Contact: MICHAEL JOHNSON; Phone: 520-626-4685
Director: DR. MALCOM J. ZWOLINSKI; Phone: 520-621-1432
Forest Service Cooperative Research Unit (USDA, Rocky Mountain Research Station), Leader: DR. CARL EDMINSTER; Phone: 520-621-2543/970-498-1264
Rangeland and Forest Resources, (B.S., M.S., Ph.D.): DR. GEORGE RUYLE; Phone: 520-621-1384
Renewable Natural Resources Studies, (M.S., Ph.D.): DR. MITCHEL MCCLAREN; Phone: 520-621-1673
Watershed Resources Science and Management, (B.S., M.S., Ph.D.): DR. RICHARD HAWKINS; Phone: 520-621-7273
Wildlife and Fisheries Resources, (B.S., M.S., Ph.D.): DR. WILLIAM W. SHAW; Phone: 520-621-7265

ARKANSAS

ARKANSAS STATE UNIVERSITY
State University, AR 72467
Phone: 870-972-3082; Fax: 870-972-3638; Email: jbednarz@navajo.astate.edu

Contact(s):
Biology Degrees, (B.S., B.S.E., M.S.):
Botany Degrees, (B.S.):
Department of Biological Sciences, Chair: DR. ROGER BUCHANAN
Environmental Biology, (B.S.):
Wildlife Ecology and Management, (B.S.):
Zoology, (B.S.):

ARKANSAS TECH UNIVERSITY
Russellville, AR 72801
Phone: 501-964-0852; Fax: 501-964-0837; Email: fwjs@atuvm.atu.edu

Contact(s):
Fisheries and Wildlife Biology, (B.S.), Director: DR. JOSEPH STOECKEL
Park Administration, (B.S.), Director: DR. THERESA HERRICK
Recreation Administration, (B.S.), Director: DR. THERESA HERRICK

UNIVERSITY OF ARKANSAS AT LITTLE ROCK, Department of Biology/Environmental Health Sciences Program
Rm. NS406C, 2801 S. University Ave., Little Rock, AR 72204
Phone: 501-569-3501

Description: The program curriculum consists of a common core and a choice from four areas of concentrated study: Environmental quality management; occupational safety and health; environmental planning; and environmental/public health sciences. Internships are available.

UNIVERSITY OF ARKANSAS AT MONTICELLO, School of Forest Resources/Arkansas Forest Resources Center
Monticello, AR 71656
Phone: 870-460-1052

Degrees: B.S. in Forestry, B.S. in Wildlife Management, M.S. in Forest Resources

Contact(s):
Dean: DR. BOB BLACKMON

BRITISH COLUMBIA

UNIVERSITY OF BRITISH COLUMBIA
British Columbia
Contact(s):
Agricultral Sciences, Dean: PROF. MOURA QUAYLE, 248-2357 Main Mall University Campus, Vancouver, British Columbia V6T 1Z4 Canada
Animal Sciences Department, Contact: DR. M. SHACKLETON, 248-2357 Main Mall University Campus, Vancouver, British Columbia V6T 1Z4 Canada
Civil Engineering Department, Head: DR. M. ISAACSON, 2324 Main Mall, Vancouver, British Columbia V6T 1Z4 Canada
Forestry, Dean: DR. C. S. BINKLEY, #207-2357 Main Mall, Vancouver, British Columbia V6T 1Z4 Canada
Geography Department, Head: DR. G. WYNN, 1984 West Mall, Vancouver, British Columbia V6T 1Z5 Canada
Institute for Resources and Environment, Director: DR. L. M. LAVKULICH, Rm 436E, 2206 E. Mall, Vancouver, British Columbia V6T 1Z3 Canada
Oceanography Department, Head: DR. A. LEWIS, 6270 University Blvd., Vancouver, British Columbia V6T 1Z2 Canada
Westwater Research Centre, Director: DR. M. HEALEY, 1933 W. Mall Annex, Rm 200, Vancouver, British Columbia V6T 1Z2 Canada
Zoology Department, Head: DR. J. BURGER, 6270 University Blvd., Vancouver, British Columbia V6T 1Z4 Canada

UNIVERSITY OF NORTHERN BRITISH COLUMBIA
3333 University Way, Prince George, British Columbia V2N 4Z9 Canada
Phone: 250-960-5830; Fax: 250-960-5537; WWW: quarles.unbc.edu/nres/nres/htm
Founded: 1990
Description: The faculty of Natural Resources and Environmental Studies educates managers and scientists to effectively meet the demands for services and products from natural resources while maintaining a quality environment.
Contact(s):
Dean: LEE KEENER

CALIFORNIA

CALIFORNIA POLYTECHNIC STATE UNIVERSITY
San Luis Obispo, CA 93407
Phone: 805-756-1111
Contact(s):
Architecture, (B.A., M.S.), Director: GILBERT COOKE
City and Regional Planning, (MCRP, B.S.), Department Head: DR. WILLIAM SIEMBIEDA
Landscape Architecture, Contact: WALTER D. BREMIER

CALIFORNIA STATE UNIVERSITY AT CHICO
Chico, CA 95929-0560
Phone: 530-898-6408; Fax: 530-898-6557; Email: dsimcox@oqvax.csuchica.edu
Description: Areas of study include environmental education and interpretation, recreation and natural resource management, parks maintenance and operations, and planning and design.
Contact(s):
Parks and Natural Resources Management Option, Coordinator: DR. JON HOOPER
Recreation and Parks Management, (B.S., M.A.), Chairman: DAVID E. SIMCOX

CALIFORNIA STATE UNIVERSITY AT FULLERTON, Environmental Studies Master of Science Degree
Fullerton, CA 92834
Phone: 714-278-2011
Founded: 1970
Description: Interdisciplinary graduate program leading to master's degree in environmental sciences, environmental policy and planning, or environmental education and communication.
Contact(s):
Program Coordinator: STEWART LONG

CALIFORNIA STATE UNIVERSITY AT SACRAMENTO
Sacramento, CA 95819
Phone: 916-278-6011
Contact(s):
Biological Conservation, (B.S., M.S.): DR. C. DAVID VANICEK
Environmental Studies, (B.A.): DR. ANGUS WRIGHT
Recreation and Leisure Studies with options in recreationa and park administration recreation, (B.S., M.S.): STEPHEN WALKER

HUMBOLDT STATE UNIVERSITY, College of Natural Resources and Sciences
Arcata, CA 95521
Phone: 707-826-3256
Contact(s):
Biological Sciences, (B.S., M.S.), Chairman: DR. TIMOTHY LAWLOR; Phone: 707-826-3246
Cooperative Fishery Research Unit, Leader: DR. WALTER DUFFY; Phone: 707-826-3268
Dean: STEVEN A. CARISON
Experiment Station, Pacific Southwest Forest and Range Station, Project Leader: DR. ROBERT R. ZIEMER; Phone: 707-825-2936
Fisheries, (B.S., M.S.), Chairman: DR. TIM MULLIGAN; Phone: 707-825-5645
Forestry, (B.S., M.S.), Charman: DR. GERALD ALLEN; Phone: 707-826-4243
Indian Natural Resources, Sciences, and Engineering Program, Director: RUSSEL BOHAM; Phone: 707-826-4994
Library, Librarian: DR. SHARMAN KENYON; Phone: 707-826-3441
Natural Resources Planning and Interpretation, (B.S., M.S.), Chairman: DR. KEN FULGHAM; Phone: 707-826-4147
Oceanography, (B.S.), Chairman: DR. MARIE DEANGELIS; Phone: 707-826-4147
Rangeland Resources and Wildland Soils, (B.S.), Chairman: DR. KEN FULGHAM; Phone: 707-826-4147
Watershed Management, (M.S.), Chairman: DR. GERALD ALLEN; Phone: 707-826-4243
Wildlife, (B.S., M.S.), Chairman: DR. MARK COLWELL; Phone: 707-826-3723

SAN FRANCISCO STATE UNIVERSITY, Wildlands Studies Program
3 Mosswood Cir., Cazadero, CA 95421
Phone: 707-632-5665; Email: wildlnds@sonic.net; WWW: wildlandsstudies.com/ws
Founded: 1979
Description: Wildlands Studies offers a year-round series of field study programs in North American and international wilderness locations. Participants join backcountry research teams in a search for answers to important environmental problems concerning wildlife populations and/or wildlands habitats. Participants can earn 3-14 units of university credit.
Contact(s):
Director: CRANDALL BAY; Phone: 707-632-5665

EDUCATIONAL INSTITUTIONS - CALIFORNIA/CALIFORNIA

SAN JOSE STATE UNIVERSITY, Department of Environmental Studies
San Jose, CA 95192-0115
Phone: 408-924-5450; Fax: 408-924-5477; Email: envstdy@email.sjsu.edu; WWW: www.sjsu.edu/depts/EnvStudies/
Founded: 1970
Description: The department offers a B.S. in Environmental Studies, a B.A. in Environmental Studies, a B.A in Environmental Studies preparation for teaching, a M.S. in Environmental Studies, a minor in Environmental Studies, and a minor in energy and the environment. Special interests of the faculty include habitat restoration, environmental empact assessment, energy, water, and forest resource management, human ecology, international development, coastal resource management, solid waste management, and environmental education for teachers. Credit is given for beyond-the-classroom experiences for appropriate Peace Corps Service, Internships programs, Center for Development of Recycling (CDR), and Environmental Resource Center (ERC)
Contact(s):
Department Chairperson: DR. LESTER ROWNTREE

SONOMA STATE UNIVERSITY, Department of Environemental Studies and Planning
1801 E. Cotati Ave., Rohnert Park, CA 94928
Phone: 707-664-2306; Fax: 707-664-2505; WWW: www.sonoma.edu/ensp/
Description: Interdisciplinary academic program with B.S. and B.A. degrees. Study tracks in environmental education, energy management and design, city and regional planning, water quality, hazardous materials management, and environmental conservation and restoration

SONOMA STATE UNIVERSITY, Earth Lab
1801 E. Cotati Ave., Rohnert Park, CA 94928
Phone: 707-664-2430; Fax: 707-664-2505
Description: The Earthlab is an on-campus demonstration, education, and research center which serves the campus and surrounding communities through programs in environmental education, professional training, teacher workshops, demonstration projects, and scientific research.
Contact(s):
Director: DR. JEAN A. FALBO

STANFORD UNIVERSITY, Center for Conservation Biology, Department of Biological Sciences
Stanford, CA 94305-5020
Phone: 650-723-5924
Founded: 1984
Description: To develop the science of conservation biology, including its application to solutions for critical conservation problems. The Center conducts scientific and policy research that is building a sound basis for the conservation, management, and restoration of biotic diversity around the world. The overall goal is to develop ways and means for protecting Earth's life support systems and thus enhancing future human well-being.
Contact(s):
President: PROF. PAUL R. EHRLICH

STANFORD UNIVERSITY, Morrison Institute for Population and Resource Studies
Gilbert Bldg., Stanford, CA 94305-5020
Phone: 415-723-7518; Fax: 415-725-8244; Email: morrison@forsythe.stanford.edu
Founded: 1986
Description: To support research and education in the interconnected global issues of population growth, its effects on the environment, the pressure on natural resources, and the capacity of many nations to achieve sustainable socioeconomic development. Issues are approached through interdisciplinary perspectives of population biology, economics, and social and medical sciences.
Contact(s):
Director: DR. MARCUS W. FELDMAN

UNIVERSITY OF CALIFORNIA AT BERKELEY
Berkeley, CA 94720-3114
Phone: 510-642-0376
Contact(s):
Cooperative Extension, Forestry Integrated Hardwood Range Management Program, Director: DR. RICHARD B. STANIFORD
Forestry and Resource Management, (B.S., M.S., Ph.D.), Division Head: JAMES W. BARTOLOME

UNIVERSITY OF CALIFORNIA AT DAVIS, Herbarium
University of California at Davis, Davis, CA 95616
Phone: 916-752-1091; Fax: 916-752-5410; Email: eadean@ucdavis.edu.)
Founded: 1923
Description: The UC Davis Herbarium is the center for research in plant systematics at the University of California, Davis. The Herbarium, of worldwide scope, includes 200,000 specimens. Holdings from California include documentation for many rare and endangered species.
Contact(s):
Director and Curator: ELLEN A. DEAN

UNIVERSITY OF CALIFORNIA AT LOS ANGELES
Los Angeles, CA 90095
Phone: 310-825-4321
Contact(s):
Biogeography and Conservation, (M.A., Ph.D.), Contact: DR. HARTMUT S. WALTER
Ecology, Behavior, and Evolution, (B.S., M.A, Ph.D.): DR. MARTIN L. CODY
Environmental Science and Engineering, (D.Env.), Contact: DR. ARTHUR M. WINER
Environmentla Systems Engineering, (B.S., M.S., Ph.D.), Contact: DR. MICHAEL K. STENSTROM
Geography/Environmental Studies, (B.A), Contact: DR. HARTMUT S. WALTER

UNIVERSITY OF CALIFORNIA AT RIVERSIDE, Environmental Science Program
River, CA 92521
Phone: 714-787-4551
Founded: 1971
Description: The Environmental Sciences Program offers four curriculum tracks: Natural Science, Social Science, Environmental Toxicology, and Soil Science. Opportunities are available for students to conduct research and to engage in environmental internships.
Degrees: (B.S., B.A.)
Contact(s):
Advisor: PETER H. DIAGE; Phone: 909-787-3850; Fax: 909-787-3993; Email: phdiage@ucrac1.ucr.edu
Chairman: DR. LANNY J. LUND; Phone: 909-787-5116

UNIVERSITY OF CALIFORNIA AT SANTA BARBARA, Environmental Studies
Santa Barbara, CA 93106
Phone: 805-893-2968; Email: envst_info@envst.ucsb.edu; WWW: ucsbuxa.ucsb.edu/es
Description: The Environmental Studies Program at UCSB remains one of the strongest in terms of student demand and national reputation. The Environmental Studies curriculum is designed to provide students with the scholarly background and intellectual skills necessary to understand complex environmental problems and formulate decsions that are environmentally sound. While the E.S. Program offers both a B.S. and B.A. degree. Both majors recognize and stress the importance of understanding the interrelationships between the hamanities, social sciences, and natural science disciplines within the environment.
Contact(s):
Program Chair: JO-ANN SHELTON

EDUCATIONAL INSTITUTIONS - COLORADO/CONNECTICUT

UNIVERSITY OF CALIFORNIA AT SANTA CRUZ
Santa Cruz, CA 95064
Phone: 331-459-2634
Contact(s):
Environmental Studies, (B.A., Ph.D.), Chairperson: PROF. DAVID GOODMAN

UNIVERSITY OF CALIFORNIA, Scripps Institution of Oceanography
CA
Founded: 1903
Description: A part of the University of California, San Diego, the Scripps Institution of Oceanography is one of the oldest, largest, and most important centers for marine science research and graduate training in the world. The Birch Aquarium serves as the public education center for the institution.
Contact(s):
Interim Director: DR. WOLFGANG BERGER

UNIVERSITY OF SOUTHERN CALIFORNIA
Los Angeles, CA 90089-0231
Phone: 213-743-7517
Contact(s):
Environmental Engineering Program, (M.S., Ph.D.), Director: MIHRAN S. AGBABIAN
Environmental Social Sciences Program, Dean of the Division: DR. DONALD LEWIS

COLORADO

COLORADO MOUNTAIN COLLEGE
Leadville, CO 80461
Phone: 719-486-2015; Fax: 719-486-3212
Description: Colorado Mountain College is a public two-year community college. The College is fully accredited by the North Central Accrediting Association.
Contact(s):
Contact: PETER G. MOLLER

COLORADO MOUNTAIN COLLEGE, Timberline Campus
Leadville, CO 80461
Phone: 719-486-2015; Fax: 719-486-3212
Founded: 1967
Description: The Timberline Campus offers a number of programs focusing on the environment and outdoor recreation.
Contact(s):
President: DR. CYNTHIA HEELAN

COLORADO STATE UNIVERSITY, College of Natural Resources
Fort Collins, CO 80523
Contact(s):
Cooperative Fish and Wildlife Research Unit, Leader: DR. DAVID ANDERSON; Phone: 970-491-1414
Dean: DR. A. ALLEN DYER; Phone: 970-491-4997
Earth Resources, (B.S., M.S., Ph.D.), Head: DR. JUDITH HANNAH; Phone: 970-491-5662
Fishery and Wildlife Biology, (B.S., M.S., Ph.D.), Interim Dept. Head: DR. STEPHEN FLICKINGER; Phone: 970-491-5020
Forest Sciences, (B.S., M.S., M.F., Ph.D.), Head: DR. SUSAN STAFFORD; Phone: 970-491-6911
Natural Resources Ecology Laboratory, Contact: DR. DIANA WALL; Phone: 970-491-1982
Natural Resources Recreation and Tourism, (B.S., M.S., Ph.D.), Head: DR. MICHAEL MANFREDO; Phone: 970-491-6521
Rangeland Ecosystem Science, (B.S., M.S., Ph.D.), Head: DR. DENNIS CHILD; Phone: 970-491-4994

COLORADO STATE UNIVERSITY, Doctoral Program in Environmental Politics and Policy Department of Political Science
Department of Political Science, Colorado State University, Fort Collins, CO 80523
Phone: 970-491-5156; Fax: 970-491-2490
Founded: 1975
Description: All Ph.D. students in the program choose Environmental Politics and Policy as one of three subfields in political science offered in preparation for their degree. The program prepares doctoral students for university positions and a wide variety of private and public sector careers related to environmental politics and policy.
Contact(s):
Chair: DR. WAYNE PEAK
Graduate Coordinator: DR. ALAN LAMBORN

COLORADO STATE UNIVERSITY, William E. Morgan Library
Fort Collins, CO 80523
Phone: 970-491-1101
Contact(s):
Director: CAMILA ALIRE; Phone: 970-491-1833; Fax: 970-491-1195

UNIVERSITY OF COLORADO AT BOULDER, Environmental Center
Campus Box 207, Boulder, CO 80309
Phone: 303-492-8308; Fax: 303-492-1897; Email: ecology@stripe.colorado.edu)
Founded: 1970
Description: The Environmental Center is a student-funded campus organization which educates students and the community on environmental issues through conferences, programs, direct actions, resource files, and a library. We house the largest campus recycling program in the country as well as various activist groups: Animal Rights, Ecological Living, Congressional Action Committee, Wilderness Study, Rainforest Action Group, Earth Education, and the Student Environmental Action Coalition.
Contact(s):
Director: WILL TOOR; Phone: 303-492-8308

UNIVERSITY OF COLORADO, Natural Resources Law Center University of Colorado School of Law
Campus Box 401, Boulder, CO 80309-0401
Phone: 303-492-1286; Fax: 303-492-1297
Description: Conducts research on environmental and natural resources law and policy, including water, public lands, minerals, Indian law, etc. Sponsors conferences and workshops and hosts visiting scholars. Publishes books, research papers, and Resource Law Notes newsletter.
Contact(s):
Director: BETSY RIEKE

CONNECTICUT

CONNECTICUT COLLEGE
270 Mohegan Ave., New London, CT 06320
Phone: 860-439-2140; Fax: 860-439-2519
Description: Environmental Studies has a long and successful history at Connecticut College beginning in 1931 with the establishment of the Connecticut College Arboretum. Since then, a common theme in the program has been to understand the structure and functioning of both natural and managed ecosystems.
Contact(s):
Botany Department, Chair: SCOTT R. WARREN
Center for Conservation Biology and Environmental Studies, Director: GLENN D. DREYER
Environmental Studies Program, (B.A.), Director: DR. PETER A. SIVER
Zoology Department, Chair: ROBERT A. ASKINS

EDUCATIONAL INSTITUTIONS - DELAWARE/FLORIDA

SOUTHERN CONNECTICUT STATE UNIVERSITY, Center for the Environment
501 Crescent St. Jennings Hall Rm. 309, New Haven, CT 06515
Phone: 203-392-6600; Email: hageman@scsu.ctstateu.edu)
Description: The Center for the Environment is an academic center granting graduate and undergraduate degrees in environmental areas, conducting research, and developing epistemological models.

UNIVERSITY OF CONNECTICUT
Box U-87, 1376 Storrs Road, WBY, Room 308, Storrs, CT 06269-4087
Phone: 203-486-2840
Description: Department of Natural Resources Management and Engineering offers B.S. and M.S. in natural resources with emphasis in forestry, fisheries, wildlife, biometeorology, watershed hydrology, remote sensing, soil and water conservation, and natural resources engineering.
Contact(s):
Department of Natural Resources Management and Engineering, (B.S., M.S.), Head: DR. DAVID B. SCHROEDER

UNIVERSITY OF NEW HAVEN
300 Orange Ave., West Haven, CT 06516
Phone: 203-932-7101; Fax: 203-933-2036
Contact(s):
Department of Biology and Environmental Science, (B.S., M.S.), Chairman: CHARLES VIGUE

YALE UNIVERSITY, Graves Memorial Library
205 Prospect St., New Haven, CT 06511
Phone: 203-432-5100; Fax: 203-432-5942
Contact(s):
Acting Librarian: PAUL DRAGHI

YALE UNIVERSITY, School of Forestry and Environmental Studies
205 Prospect St., New Haven, CT 06511
Phone: 203-432-5100; Fax: 203-432-5942
Description: The mission of the school is to provide leadership in the science and management of natural resource and environmental systems. The school trains managers for governmental, non-governmental, and corporate institutions, and educates teachers and researchers
Degrees: D.F. & E.S., M.F., M.F.S, M.E.S, Ph.D.

DELAWARE

UNIVERSITY OF DELAWARE, College of Agriculture and Natural Resources
Newark, DE 19717
Phone: 302-831-2501
Contact(s):
Department of Entomology and Applied Ecology, (B.S. entomology with wildlife conservation concentration, M.S.), Chairperson: DR. JUDITH A. HOUGH-GOLDSTEIN; Phone: 302-831-2526; Fax: 302-831-3651; Email: jhough@udel.edu

DISTRICT OF COLUMBIA

GEORGE WASHINGTON UNIVERSITY
Washington, DC 20052
Phone: 202-994-1000
Contact(s):
Environmental and Resource Policy, (M.A., Ph.D.), Chairman: HENRY MERCHANT; Phone: 202-994-7118
Environmental Engineering, (M.S., D.Sc.), Acting Chair: THEODORE TORIDIS; Phone: 202-994-5450
Environmental Law Program, (J.D., L.L.M.), Co-Director and Associate Professor of Environmental Law: LAURENT R. HOURCLE; Phone: 202-994-4823
Environmental Management, (MEA), Associate Professor of Engineering Administration: BARRY SILVERMAN; Phone: 202-994-5079
Environmental Science, (M.S.), Chairman: HENRY MERCHANT; Phone: 202-994-7123
Environmental Studies, (B.A., B.S.), Director: HENRY MERCHANT; Phone: 202-994-7118

GEORGE WASHINGTON UNIVERSITY, Law School
720 20th St., NW, Washington, DC 20052
Phone: 202-994-4500
Founded: 1865
Description: Nation's largest graduate and undergraduate environmental law program. Twenty-two environmental courses for J.D. and LL.M. students in addition to land use and other related topics. Emphasizes a practical approach.

GEORGETOWN UNIVERSITY, Law Center
600 New Jersey Ave., NW, Washington, DC 20001
Contact(s):
Dean: JUDITH AREEN

HOWARD UNIVERSITY, Department of Environmental Sciences
P.O. Box 2232, Washington, DC 20013
Phone: 202-234-2490
Founded: 1974
Description: Strongly interdisciplinary, with a dual curriculum in environmental health sciences and environmental policy management. The department provides training at both the undergraduate and graduate levels. The focus of the department prevention through human intervention in promoting a quality environment.

UNIVERSITY OF DC (VAN NESS CAMPUS)
Washington, DC 20008
Phone: 202-282-7370
Contact(s):
Department of Environmental Science, (A.A.S., B.S.), Chairperson: A. JOSE JONES

FLORIDA

FLORIDA ATLANTIC UNIVERSITY, Pine Jog Environmental Education Center
6301 Summit Blvd., West Palm Beach, FL 33415
Phone: 561-686-6600; Fax: 561-687-4968
Founded: 1960
Description: Pine Jog is an environmental education center within the College of Education of Florida Atlantic University. The purpose of the Center is to provide environmental education programs which foster an awareness and appreciation of the natural world, promote an understanding of ecological concepts, and instill a sense of stewardship towards the earth and all of its inhabitants.
Contact(s):
Chair: BONNIE WEAVER, 103 Elwa Pl., West Palm Beach, FL 33405-4107; Phone: 561-588-7523
Chair-elect: DONALD MATHIS, Sartory, Mathis, & Beedle, 5840 Corporate Way, West Palm Beach, FL 33407; Phone: 561-683-7500
Executive Director: PATRICIA WELCH; Phone: 561-686-6600
Secretary: JEFF KOONS, Commissioner, Citry of West Palm Beach, P.O. Box 3366, West Palm Beach, FL 33402; Phone: 561-659-8099

EDUCATIONAL INSTITUTIONS - GEORGIA/IDAHO

FLORIDA STATE UNIVERSITY
Tallahassee, FL 32306
Phone: 904-644-2525
Contact(s):
Anthropology, (B.S., M.S., Ph.D.), Chairman: DR. BRUCE T. GRINDAL
Biological Science, (B.S., M.S., Ph.D.), Chairman: DR. LAWRENCE G. ABELE
Center for Aquatic Research and Resource Management, Director: DR. ROBERT J. LIVINGSTON
Center for Biomedical and Toxicologica Research, Executive Director: DR. E. A. FERNALD
Center for Polar Desert Research, Director: DR. IRMIE FRIEDMAN
Geography, (B.S., M.S., Ph.D.), Chairman: DR. PATRICK O'SULLIVAN
Geology, (B.S., M.S., Ph.D.), Chairman: DR. J F. TULL
Meteorology, (B.S., M.S., Ph.D.), Chairman: DR. DAVID W. STUART
Oceanography, (M.S., Ph.D.), Chairman: DR. WILTON STURGES

UNIVERSITY OF MIAMI, Rosenstiel School of Marine and Atmospheric Science
4600 Rickenbacker Causeway, Miami, FL 33149
Phone: 305-361-4000; Fax: 305-361-4711
Contact(s):
Applied Marine Physics, (M.S., Ph.D.), Dean: DR. OTIS B. BROWN

UNIVERSITY OF FLORIDA, School of Forest Resources and Conservation
118 Newins Ziegler Hall P.O. Box 110410, Gainesville, FL 32611-0410
Phone: 352-846-0851; Fax: 352-392-1701; Email: sfrc@gnv.ifas.ufl.edu
Founded: 1937
Description: The school seeks to advance understanding of forests: interactions of their components and environment, their relationships with other ecosystems, and appropriate management practices and conservation strategies. Communicating this knowledge to students, public and other professionals is central to this mission; working together with other disciplines is essential to meeting its challenges. Degrees: B.S., M.S., Ph.D.
Contact(s):
Director: DR. WAYNE H. SMITH
Graduate Programs Coordinator: DR. HENRY L. GHOLZ
Undergraduate Programs Coordinator: DR. GEORGE M. BLAKESLEE

UNIVERSITY OF FLORIDA, Solar Energy and Energy Conversion Laboratories
237 MEB, Gainesville, FL 32611-2050
Phone: 352-392-0812; Fax: 352-392-1071; Email: solar@cimar.me.ufl.edu
Contact(s):
Director: DR. D. YOGI GOSWAMI

UNIVERSITY OF WEST FLORIDA
Pensacola, FL 32514
Phone: 850-474-2745
Contact(s):
Department of Biology, (B.S., M.S.), Chair and Professor: DR. JOHN P. RIEHM
Program in Coastal Zone Studies, (M.S.):

GEORGIA

EMORY UNIVERSITY
Contact(s):
Biology (terrestrial ecology/systems ecology), (M.S., Ph.D.):

GEORGIA INSTITUTE OF TECHNOLOGY
Atlanta, GA 30332
Phone: 404-894-3776
Contact(s):
Environmental Resources Center, Director: DR. BERND KAHN

UNIVERSITY OF GEORGIA
Athens, GA 30602
Contact(s):
Cooperative Fish and Wildlife Research Unit Graduate Program: DR. ROBERT O. TESKEY; Phone: 706-542-5055; Fax: 706-542-8356
Daniel B. Warnell School of Forest Resources: ; Phone: 706-542-2686
Undergraduate Program: SANDRA CHAPMAN; Phone: 706-542-8356; Fax: 706-542-8356

UNIVERSITY OF GEORGIA, Marine Institute
Sapelo Island, GA 31327
Phone: 912-485-2221
Founded: 1953
Description: Concerned with research into the system-ecology, biology, chemistry, and geology of the salt marshes, barrier islands, and nearshore zone of the Georgia coast.
Contact(s):
Director: JAMES J. ALBERTS

HAWAII

UNIVERSITY OF HAWAII, Cooperative Fishery Research Unit
2538 The Mall, Honolulu, HI 96822
Phone: 808-956-8350, 808-956-4708
Contact(s):
Leader: DR. JAMES D. PARRISH

IDAHO

IDAHO STATE UNIVERSITY, Department of Biological Sciences
Box 8007, Pocatello, ID 83209
Phone: 208-236-3765; Fax: 208-236-4570; E-mail; Email: seehrodn@isu.edu)
Description: The Department of Biological Sciences at Idaho State University has high quality degree programs in ecology. Strong basic coursework and original investigations are emphasized at the undergraduate and graduate levels. Habitats available for study range from cold sagebrush deserts to heavily forested areas and includes streams and riparian areas in the Snake River Canyon to its headwaters in Yellowstone National Park.
Contact(s):
Ecology, (B.S., M.S., Ph.D.), Chairman: ROD R. SEELEY

UNIVERSITY OF IDAHO, Bowers Laboratory
Moscow, ID 83844-1114
Phone: 208-885-6754; Fax: 208-885-5878; Email: dixie@uidaho.edu
Contact(s):
Contact and Editor: DIXIE L. EHRENREICH

UNIVERSITY OF IDAHO, College of Forestry/Wildlife and Range Sciences
Moscow, ID 83843
Phone: 208-885-6441; Fax: 208-885-6226
Contact(s):
Cooperative Fish and Wildlife Research Unit, Leader: DR. J. MICHAEL SCOTT; Phone: 208-855-6336
Cooperative Park Studies Unit, Leader: DR. GARY MACHLIS; Phone: 208-855-7054
Dean: DR. CHARLES R. HATCH; Phone: 208-885-6442
Forest Products, (B.S., M.S., Ph.D.), Contact: DR. LEONARD R. JOHNSON; Phone: 208-855-6126

EDUCATIONAL INSTITUTIONS - ILLINOIS/INDIANA

Forest Resources, (B.S., M.S., Ph.D.), Contact: DR. JO ELLEN FORCE; Phone: 208-885-7311
Policy Analysis Group, Contact: DR. JAY O'LAUGLIN; Phone: 208-885-5776
Range Resources, (B.S., M.S., Ph.D.), Contact: DR. KENDALL JOHNSON; Phone: 208-885-6536
Resource Recreation and Tourism, (B.S., M.S., Ph.D.), Contact: DR. JOHN D. HUNT; Phone: 208-885-7911
Wilderness Research Center, Director: DR. JOHN C. HENDEE; Phone: 208-885-2267

ILLINOIS

BRADLEY UNIVERSITY
Peoria, IL 61625
Phone: 309-677-3020
Contact(s):
Biology, (B.S., B.A., M.S.), Chairman: JOHN A. DEPINTO
Environmental Science, (B.S.), Chairman of Coordinating Committee: K. MCCONNAUGHAY

EASTERN ILLINOIS UNIVERSITY
Charleston, IL 61920
Phone: 217-581-3763
Description: Eastern Illinois University offers undergraduate degrees in botany, environmental biology, zoology, and the biological sciences. Emphasis is placed upon a fundamental understanding of biology and environmental concerns.
Contact(s):
Biological Sciences, (M.S.), Contact: ANDREW METHVEN; Phone: 217-581-6241
Botany, (B.S.), Chair: JANICE COONS; Phone: 214-581-6243
Environmental Biology, (B.S.), Chairperson: CHARLES L. PEDERSON; Phone: 217-581-6239; Fax: 217-581-2772; Email: cfclpi@eiu.edu
Zoology (B.S.), Chair: KIPP C. KRUSE; Phone: 217-581-3011; Email: cfkck@eiu.edu

ILLINOIS STATE UNIVERSITY, Environmental Health Program
Department of Health Sciences
Campus Box 5220, Normal, IL 61790-5220
Phone: 309-438-8329; Fax: 309-438-2450
Founded: 1974
Description: Undergraduate education for B.S. in environmental health. Seven faculty persons and 165 enrolled students. Four-year curriculum accredited by National Environmental Health Science and Protection Accreditation Council.
Degrees: B.S.
Contact(s):
Program Director: STEPHEN D. ARNOLD

NORTHEASTERN UNIVERSITY
Contact(s):
Center for Vertebrate Studies/Vertebrate Ecology and Systematics, (B.S., M.S., Ph.D.), Director: DR. GWILYM S. JONES; Phone: 617-373-2851
Department of Biology: ; Phone: 617-373-2260; Fax: 617-373-3724
Marine Science Center/Marine Biology, (B.S., M.S., Ph.D.), Director: DR. JOSEPH AYERS; Phone: 617-581-7370
Salt Marsh Ecology, (B.S., M.S., Ph.D.), Contact: DR. ERNEST RUBER; Phone: 617-373-2260

SOUTHERN ILLINOIS UNIVERSITY
Carbondale, IL 62901
Phone: 618-453-2121
Contact(s):
Cooperative Fisheries Research Lab, (M.S., Ph.D.), Director: DR. ROY C HEIDINGER; Phone: 618-536-7761
Cooperative Wildlife Research Lab, (M.S., Ph.D.), Director: DR. ALAN WOOLF; Phone: 618-536-7766
Forestry, (B.S., M.S.), Chair: DR. JOHN E. PHELPS; Phone: 618-453-3341
Plant and Soil Science, (B.S., M.S.), Chair: DR. DONALD J. STUCKY; Phone: 618-453-2496

UNIVERSITY OF ILLINOIS AT URBANA-CHAMPAIGN
Urbana, IL 61801
Phone: 217-333-1000
Contact(s):
Center for Wildlife Ecology, Nature History Survey, Director: PATRICK W. BROWN
Civil Engineering, (B.S., M.S., Ph.D.), Head: DAVID E. DANIEL
Ecology, Ethology, and Evolution, (B.A., Ph.D.), Acting Head: GEORGE O. BATZLI
Geography, (B.S., M.S, Ph.D.), Head: COLIN E. THORN
Landscape Architecture, (B.L.A., M.L.A.), Head: VINCENT J. BELLAFIORE
Natural Resources and Environmental Sciences, (B.S., M.S., Ph.D.), Head: GARY L. ROLFE
Urban and Regional Planning, (B.A., M.U.P., Ph.D.), Head: LEWIS D. HOPKINS

WESTERN ILLINOIS UNIVERSITY
Macomb, IL 61455
Phone: 309-298-1546
Contact(s):
Fisheries, (B.S., M.S.): DR. LARRY A JAHN
Wildlife, (B.S., M.S.): DR. THOMAS C. DUNSTAN

INDIANA

BALL STATE UNIVERSITY
Muncie, IN 47306
Phone: 765-285-5780; Fax: 765-285-2606; Email: nrem@bsu.edu; WWW: www.bsu.edu/nrem
Contact(s):
Departmental Minor in Environmental Management, Advisor: DR. JOHN R. PICHTEL
Departmental Minor in Natural Resources, Advisor: DR. CHARLES O. MORTENSEN
Environmental Interpretation and Outdoor Recreation Management Option, Advisor: DR. CHARLES O. MORTENSEN
Environmental Protection Option, Advisor: DR. THAD GODISH, DR. JOHN PICHTELL, DR. FRED SIEWERT
Interdepartmental Minors in Energy Resources and Environmental Policy, Advisor: DR. JAMES EFLIN
Land Management Option, Advisor: DR. HUGH J. BROWN
Natural Resources and Environmental Managament, (B.S., B.A., M.A., M.S.), Chair: DR. CHARLES O. MORTENSEN
Natural Resources Studies Option, Advisor: DR. TIMOTHY F. LYON, DR. PAUL CHANDLER
Occupational and Industrial Hygiene Option, Advisor: DR. THAD GODISH
Teaching Minor in Environmental Studies, Advisor: DR. TIMOTHY F. LYON

INDIANA STATE UNIVERSITY
Terre Haute, IN 47809
Phone: 317-237-2261
Contact(s):
Conservation, Contact: DR. JOHN E. OLIVER
Ecology and Wildlife, (B.S., M.S., Ph.D), Contact: DR. MARION T. JACKSON

INDIANA UNIVERSITY, School of Public and Environmental Affairs
Bloomington, IN 47405
Phone: 812-855-2457; Fax: 812-855-7802; Email: speainfo@indiana.edu; WWW: www.indiana.edu/~speaweb
Founded: 1972
Description: The School of Public Environmental Affairs brings an interdisciplinary approach to the study of the environmental

sciences. The focus of the academic programs is to teach techniques that will help graduates preserve and protect the quality of natural resources, identify environmental hazards, and significantly contribute to solutions to enhance quality of life in the world's communities.
Contact(s):
Associate Dean: BARRY M. RUBIN
Dean: A. JAMES BARNES
Director of Graduate Programs: C. KURT ZORN
Director of Ph.D. Programs in Public Policy and Public Affairs: LARRY SCHROEDER
Director of Undergraduate Programs: E. PHILIP MORGAN

MANCHESTER COLLEGE, Koinonia Environmental and Retreat Center
Box 36, North Manchester, IN 46962
Phone: 219-982-5010; Fax: 219-982-5043; Email: bjehrhardt@manchester.edu.)
Founded: 1974
Description: The 100-acre facility is used extensively to provide hands-on environmental science education for area students in grades, K,-12. A two-story building houses the nature center with many educational displays. The retreat facility will accommodate 32 persons.
Contact(s):
Director: BARBARA J. EHRHARDT

PURDUE UNIVERSITY
1159 Forestry Bldg., West Lafayette, IN Contact(s):
Department of Forestry and Natural Resources, Head: DR. DENNIS C. LEMASTER; Phone: 765-494-3590; Fax: 765-496-2422
Fisheries and Aquatic Sciences, (B.S., M.S., Ph.D.):
Forestry, (B.S.F., M.S., Ph.D.):
Graduate Program, Director of Graduate Studies: DR. ANNE SPACIE; Phone: 765-494-3621; Fax: 765-496-2422
Natural Resources, (B.S., M.S, Ph.D.):
Undergraduate Programs, Director of Student Services: DR. W. L. MILLS JR.; Phone: 765-494-3575; Fax: 765-496-2422
Wildlife, (B.S., M.S., Ph.D.):
Wood Products Manufacturing Technology, (B.S., M.S., Ph.D.):

IOWA

IOWA STATE UNIVERSITY
Ames, IA 50011
Contact(s):
Cooperative Fish and Wildlife Research Unit, Leader: ERWIN KLAAS; Phone: 515-294-3056
Fisheries, Wildlife Biology, and Animal Ecology, (B.S., M.S., Ph.D.), Chairman: DR. BRUCE W. MENZEL; Phone: 515-294-6148
Forestry, (B.S., M.S., Ph.D.), Chairman: DR. J. MICHAEL KELLY; Phone: 515-294-1166
Landscape Architecture, (B.L.A., M.L.A.), Chairman: DR. J. TIMOTHY KELLER; Phone: 515-294-5676

UNIVERSITY OF IOWA
Iowa City, IA 52242
Phone: 319-353-2121
Contact(s):
Environmental Engineering Program and Science, Department of Civil and Environmetal Engineering, (M.S., Ph.D.):
Environmental Program Director: DR. KEITH R. LONG
Environmental Sciences, (B.S.), Chairman: STEPHEN HENDRIX; Phone: 319-335-3680
Preventive Medicine and Environmental Health, (M.S., Ph.D.):

KANSAS

EMPORIA STATE UNIVERSITY
Emporia, KS 66801
Phone: 316-341-5311
Contact(s):
Division of Biological Sciences, Ecology and Wildlife Biology, (B.S., M.S.), Contact: DR. DIANA BARSHAW

KANSAS STATE UNIVERSITY
Manhatten, KS 66506
Phone: 785-532-6011
Contact(s):
Fisheries, (B.S., M.S., Ph.D.), Contact: DR. HAROLD E. KLAASSEN; Phone: 785-532-6654
Konza Prairie Research Natural Area, Contact: DR. DAVID C. HARTNETT; Phone: 785-532-5925
Landscape Architecture, (B.L.A.), Contact: DAN DONELIN; Phone: 785-532-5961
Pre-Forestry and Park Resource Management (B.S.), Contact: DR. TED T. CABLE; Phone: 785-532-7232
Range Mangement, (B.S., M.S., Ph.D.), Contact: DR. CLENTON OWENSBY; Phone: 785-532-7232
Regional and Community Planning, Contact: DR. C. A. KEITHLEY; Phone: 785-532-5958
Soil and Water Conservation, (B.S.), Contact: DR. MICHEL D. RANSOM; Phone: 785-532-7203
Wildlife (B.S., M.S., Ph.D.), Contact: DR. ROBERT J. ROBEL; Phone: 785-532-6644

KANSAS STATE UNIVERSITY, Cooperative Fish and Wildlife Research Unit
Leasure Hall, Manhattan, KS 66506-3501
Phone: 785-532-6070
Description: Provides graduate training and research in fisheries and wildlife biology, research, management, ecology, population dynamics, genetics, and related areas. Supported cooperatively by Kansas State University, The Kansas Department of Wildlife and Parks, the National Biological Service and the Wildlife Management Institute.
Contact(s):
Assistant Leader of Fisheries: DR. CHRISTOPHER S. GUY
Assistant Leader of Wildlife: DR. JACK F. CULLY JR.
Leader: DR. PHILIP S. GIPSON

UNIVERSITY OF KANSAS
Lawrence, KS 66045
Phone: 785-864-2700; Email: env-stud@ukans.edu; WWW: www.cc.ukans.edu/~kuesp
Contact(s):
Environmental Studies Program with options in ecology and field biology, environental policy, environmental impact analysis, environmental health, geology and meterology, water resources, and environmental land-use analysis, (B.A., B.G.S., B.S.), Director: STANFORD LOEB; Phone: 785-842-2059
Experimental and Applied Ecology, with emphsis in aquatic ecology and population biology of small mammals and plants, (M.A., Ph.D.), Director: W. JOHN O'BRIEN; Phone: 785-864-4375
Kansas Applied Remote Sensing Program with emphasis in natural resources management, Director: ED MARTINKO; Phone: 785-864-7770
Systematics and Ecology, with specialty in animal behavior, aquatic ecology, community and ecosystem ecology, biodiversity, population and ecological biology/genetics, systematics, tropicalbiology, and paleontology/paleoncology, (B.S., M.A., Ph.D.), Chair: THOMAS N. TAYLOR; Phone: 785-864-3625

KENTUCKY

EASTERN KENTUCKY UNIVERSITY
Richmond, KY 40475-3124
Contact(s):
Applied Ecology, (M.S.), Contact: DR. ROSS CLARK; Phone: 606-622-1531
Envirnomental Resources, (B.S.), Contact: DR. M. PETE THOMPSON; Phone: 606-622-1540
Lillie Woods Research Natural Area: DR. JON MAKI; Phone: 606-622-1476
Wildlife Management, (B.S.), Contact: DR. M. PETE THOMPSON; Phone: 606-622-1540

GEORGETOWN COLLEGE
400 E. College St., Georgetown, KY 40324
Phone: 502-863-8088
Contact(s):
Environmental Science Program, (B.S.), Coordinator: DR. RICK KOPP

MOREHEAD STATE UNIVERSITY
Morehead, KY 40351
Phone: 606-783-2944
Contact(s):
Biology, a major in biology (organismal, genetics, microbiology, cell biology, physiology, ecology) is offered (39 semester hours); A minor is also available, (B.S., M.S.): DR. JOE E. WINSTEAD; Phone: 606-783-2944; Email: j.winstead@morehead-st.edu
Environmental Science, an area of concentration in environmental science (biology, ecology, environment, environmental planning, wildlife management) is offered (61-62 semester hours) A minor is also available, (B.S.): DR. JOE E. WINSTEAD; Phone: 606-783-2944; Email: j.winstead@morehead-st.edu

MURRAY STATE UNIVERSITY
P.O. Box 9, Murray, KY 42071-0009
Phone: 502-762-3011; WWW: www.murraystate.edu
Contact(s):
Center for Resevoir Research, Contact: DR. DAVID WHITE; Phone: 502-474-2272; Email: David,White@murraystate.edu
Department of Biolgical Sciences, Chairman: DR. TOM J. TIMMONS; Email: Tom,Timmons@murraystate.edu
Fisheries, (B.S., M.S.), Contact: DR. TOM J. TIMMONS; Phone: 502-762-6185; Email: Tom,Timmons@murraystate.edu
Wildlife, (B.S., M.S.), Contact: DR. STEPHEN B. WHITE; Phone: 502-762-6298; Email: Steve,White@murraystate.edu

UNIVERSITY OF KENTUCKY
Lexington, KY 40546
Phone: 606-257-7596
Contact(s):
Forestry, (B.S., M.S., M.S.F.), Chairman: DR. DONALD H. GRAVES
Natural Resource Conservation and Management, (B.S.):

UNIVERSITY OF LOUISVILLE
Lexington, KY 40546
Phone: 606-257-7596
Description: The Water Resources Laboratory was established in the early 1960s to conduct research on freshwater systems in Kentucky and surrounding states. Community and population studies of rivers and smaller streams constitute the primary focus of the laboratory;
Contact(s):
Water Resources Laboratory (Fisheries), (M.S., Ph.D.), Professor: DR. WILLIAM D. PEARSON

LOUISIANA

LOUISIANA STATE UNIVERSITY, School of Forestry
Baton Rouge, LA 70803
Phone: 225-388-4131
Contact(s):
Cooperative Fish and Wildlife Research Unit, Leader: DR. CHARLES F. BRYAN
Fisheries, (B.S., M.S., Ph.D.):
Wildlife and Fisheries Sciences, (Ph.D.):
Wildlife, (M.S., Ph.D.):

LOUISIANA TECH UNIVERSITY, School of Forestry
Ruston, LA 71272
Phone: 318-257-4985
Description: The School of Forestry offers a Bachelor of Science degree in Forestry in a program that is fully accredited by the Society of American Foresters. Areas of concentration for studies in this program include Forest Management, Business, Natural Resources Management, and Wildlife Management.
Degrees: (B.S.)
Contact(s):
Director: G. H. WEAVER

MCNEESE STATE UNIVERSITY
Lake Charles, LA 70609
Contact(s):
Department of Agriculture, Head: DR. HAROLD J. AYMOND; Phone: 318-475-5690

NORTHWESTERN STATE UNIVERSITY OF LOUISIANA
Natchitoches, LA 71497
Phone: 318-357-5375/5323; Fax: 318-357-4518
Description: To educate students in principles and science of wildlife management; to prepare students for management of natural resources at the professional entry levels; and to provide an emphasis on biodiversity and ecosystems; to orient students toward interpersonal communication
Contact(s):
Biology Sciences, Head: DR. DICK STALLING
Biology/Wildlife Management, (B.S.), Advisor: DR. ARTHUR S. ALLEN; Email: allena@alpha.nsula.edu
Watson Memorial Library, Librarian: DR. ADA JARRED; Phone: 318-357-4403

TULANE UNIVERSITY
New Orleans, LA 70118
Phone: 504-865-5191; Fax: 504-862-8706; Email: miltonf@mailhost.tcs.tulane.edu
Contact(s):
Environmental Biology (ecology and systematics), (B.S., M.S., Ph.D.), Chairman: DR. MILTON FINGERMAN

TULANE UNIVERSITY, Environmental Law Program
6801 Freret St., New Orleans, LA 70118
Phone: 504-865-5946; Fax: 504-862-8855; Email: Ohouck@law.tulane.edu; WWW: www.law.tulane.edu/studorg/els/elsnews.htm
Founded: 1981
Description: Environmental law education, research, and advocacy through faculty, staff, JD and graduate student body.
Contact(s):
Director: PROF OLIVER A. HOUCK

TULANE UNIVERSITY. Environmental Law Clinic
6329 Freret St., New Orleans, LA 70118-5670
Phone: 504-865-5789; Fax: 504-862-8721
Founded: 1989
Description: Provides free legal assistance through its student attorneys to community organizations and indigent persons seeking to protect public health and the environment.
Contact(s):
Director: ROBERT R. KUEHN

MAINE

COLLEGE OF THE ATLANTIC
105 Eden St., Bar Harbor, ME 04609
Phone: 207-288-5015
Description: The College of the Atlantic is a fully accredited four-year residential college. Students are attracted to its excellent programs in marine biology, environmental studies and ecology, environmental design, public policy, education, and selected humanities. Over 250 students. Awards a B.A. and M. pH. In human ecology. Summer programs in field studies for teachers.
Contact(s):
President: STEVEN KATONA

UNITY COLLEGE
Unity, ME 04988
Phone: 207-948-3131
Founded: 1966
Description: Unity College is a small, liberal arts college in rural Maine with degree programs specializing in natural resource management and wilderness-based recreation.
Contact(s):
Aquaculture, Contact: A. JIM CHACKO
Arboriculture, Contact: DOUG FOX
Botany and Ecology, Contact: ED BEALS
Conservation Law Enforcement, Contact: LARRY FARNSWORTH
Environmental Science, (A.A.S., B.S.), Contact: DAVE POTTER
Fisheries, Contact: GRANT ESTELL
Park Management, Contact: CRAIG RIORDAN
Wildlife, Contact: JIM NELSON

UNIVERSITY OF MAINE AT FORT KENT
25 Pleasant St., Fort Kent, ME 04743
Phone: 207-834-7617; Fax: 207-834-7503
Description: Located in the heart of Maine's Acadian forest region. Our Bachelor of Science in Environmental Studies degree program provides a solid experiential and academic background to students preparing for careers in education, industry, and public service.
Contact(s):
Environmental Studies, Director: DR. STEVEN SELVA; Email: selva@main.maine.edu
President: CHARLES LYONS

UNIVERSITY OF MAINE AT ORONO, College of Natural Sciences Forestry and Agriculture
Orono, ME 04469
Phone: 207-581-1110
Contact(s):
Cooperative Fish and Wildlife Research Unit, Leader: DR. WILLIAM B. KROHN; Phone: 207-581-2870
Dean: DR. BRUCE WIERSMA; Phone: 207-581-3202
Department of Bio-systems Science and Engineering, (B.S., M.E., M.P.S., Ph.D.), Chairman: DR. CHARLES R. WALLACE; Phone: 207-581-2770
Department of Biochemistry, Microbiology and Molecular Biology, (B.A., B.S., M.S., M.P.S., Ph.D.), Chairman: DR. JOHN SINGER; Phone: 207-581-2810
Department of Biological Sciences, (B.A., B.S., M.S., Ph.D.), Chairman: DR. J. MALCOLM SHICK; Phone: 207-581-2551
Department of Food Science and Human Nutrition, Food and Nutrition Sciences, (B.S., M.S., Ph.D.), Chair: DR. RODNEY BUSHWAY; Phone: 207-581-1621
Department of Forest Ecosystem Science, Chairman: DR. WILLIAM LIVINGSTON; Phone: 207-581-2884
Department of Forest Management, (B.S., M.F., M.S., Ph.D.), Chairman: DR. DAVID B. FIELD; Phone: 207-581-2856
Department of Geological Sciences, (B.A., B.S., M.S., Ph.D.), Chair: DR. STEPHEN NORTON; Phone: 207-581-2156
Department of Plant, Soil, and Environmental Science, (B.S., M.S., Ph.D.), Chairman: DR. IVAN FERNANDEZ; Phone: 207-581-2932
Department of Resource Economics and Policy, (B.S., M.S.), Chairman: DR. GEORGE CRINER; Phone: 207-581-3150
Department of Wildlife Ecology, (B.S., M.S., M.W.C., Ph.D.): DR. JAMES R. GILBERT; Phone: 207-581-2866
Natural Resources Program, (B.S.), Coordinator: SUE ERICH; Phone: 207-581-2997

UNIVERSITY OF MAINE AT ORONO, School of Marine Sciences
Orono, ME 04469
Degrees: (B.S., M.S., Ph.D.)
Contact(s):
Chair: BRUCE SIDELL; Phone: 207-581-4381207-581-4381

MANITOBA

UNIVERSITY OF MANITOBA, Natural Resources Institute
Winnipeg, Manitoba R3T 2N2 Canada
Contact(s):
Associate Director and Professor: DR. RICHARD BAYDACK
Director and Professor: DR. SLOBODAN SOMONOVIC

MARYLAND

JOHNS HOPKINS UNIVERSITY THE
Baltimore, MD 21218
Phone: 410-516-7092
Contact(s):
Ecology, (M.A., Ph.D.), Contact: GRACE S. BRUSH
Environmental Chemistry, (M.A., M.S., Ph.D.), Contact: ALAN T. STONE
Environmental Engineering, (M.S.E., Ph.D.), Contact: EDWARD J. BOVWER
Natural Resources, (M.A., M.S., Ph.D.), Contact: M. GORDON WOLMAN

UNIVERSITY OF MARYLAND AT BALTIMORE COUNTY, Department of Biological Sciences
Baltimore, MD 21250
Phone: 410-455-2261; Fax: 410-455-3875; Email: lindahl@umbc.edu
Degrees: B.S., B.A., M.S., Ph.D
Contact(s):
Professor and Chair: DR. LASSE LINDAHL; Phone: 410-455-2261; Fax: 410-455-3875; Email: lindahl@umbc.edu

UNIVERSITY OF MARYLAND AT CAMBRIDGE, Appalachian Laboratory
301 Braddock Rd., Frostburg, MD 21532
Phone: 301-689-3115
Contact(s):
Director and Professor: DR. LOUIS F. PITELKA

UNIVERSITY OF MARYLAND AT CAMBRIDGE, Chesapeake Biological Laboratory
P.O. Box 38, Solomons, MD 20688
Phone: 410-326-4281
Contact(s):
Director and Professor: DR. KENNETH R. TENORE

UNIVERSITY OF MARYLAND AT CAMBRIDGE, Horn Point Laboratory
P.O. Box 775, Cambridge, MD 21613
Phone: 410-228-8200
Contact(s):
Director and Professor: DR. THOMAS C. MALONE

EDUCATIONAL INSTITUTIONS - MASSACHUSETTS/MASSACHUSETTS

UNIVERSITY OF MARYLAND AT COLLEGE PARK
College Park, MD 20742
Phone: 301-405-1000
Contact(s):
Agricultural and Resource Economics, (B.S., M.S., Ph.D.), Chairman: DR. R. E. JUST
Agricultural Engineering, (B.S., M.S., Ph.D), Acting Chairman: DR. FRED WHEATON
Agronomy, (B.S., M.S., Ph.D.), Acting Chairman: DR. R. A. WEISMILLER
Animal Sciences Graduate Program, (M.S., Ph.D.), Chairman: DR. D. S. WESTHOFF
Civil Engineering, (B.S., M.S., Ph.D.), Chairman: DR. D. S. WESTHOFF
Entomology, (B.S., M.S. Ph.D.), Chairman: M. J. RAUPP
Environmental Education (M.S.), Coordinator: DR. P. KANGAS
Geography, (B.S., M.S., Ph.D.), Chairman: DR. R. J. TOWNSHEND
Natural Resources Management (B.S), Coordinator: DR. P KANGAS
Recreation, (B.A., M.A., Ed.D., Ph.D.), Coordinator: DR. S. ISO-AHOLA

UNIVERSITY OF MARYLAND AT COLLEGE PARK, Department of Government and Politics and Renewalble Energy (REPP)
1612 K St., NW, Suite 410, Washington, MD 20006
Phone: 202-293-2833; Fax: 202-293-5857
Description: REPP identifies and explores key policy issues concerning the accelerated adoption of renewable energy technologies. REPP undertakes in-house research projects; provides small grants for external research; collaborates with professional associations, academics, national laboratories, and others; and suggests strategic paths for long-range planning by the renewable energy community.
Contact(s):
Chairman of the Board of Directors: CARL WEINBERG
Executive Director: ROBY ROBERTS
Research Director: ADAM SERCHUK

UNIVERSITY OF MARYLAND AT EASTERN SHORE
Princess Anne, MD 21853
Phone: 301-651-2200
Contact(s):
Coastal Ecology Research Center, Contact: DR. CHARLES HOCUTT
Environmental Scientist, Contact: GIAN GUPTA
Marine, Estuarine, and Environmental Sciences, Contact: DR. STEVE REBACH
Natural Sciences, (B.S., M.S., Ph.D.), Chairman: DR. ROBERT M. OKOH
Undergraduate Marine Science Program, Contact: DR. GIAN GUPTA

UNIVERSITY OF MARYLAND AT FROSTBURG STATE UNIVERSITY
Consortium, Frostburg, MD 21532
Contact(s):
Appalachian Environmental Laboratory: DR. LOUIS F. PITELKA, Frostburg State University Campus, Frostburg, MD ; Phone: 301-689-3115
Department of Applied Ecology and Conservation Biology (B.S., M.S., Ph.D.):
Department of Biology (B.S., Ph.D.), Chairman: DR. DAVID MORTON; Phone: 301-687-4255
Department of Wildlife and Fishereis (B.A, M.A., Ph.D.):
Wildlife and Fisheries (M.S., Ph.D.):

UNIVERSITY OF MARYLAND, Center for Environmental Science
P.O. Box 775, Cambridge, MD 21613
Phone: 410-228-9250; Fax: 410 228-3843
Founded: 1925
Description: UMCES is an institution of the University System of Maryland, with a special mission in multidisciplinary environmental research on Chesapeake Bay, the mid-Atlantic region, and coastal systems around the world.
Contact(s):
President and Professor: DR. DONALD F. BOESCH

MASSACHUSETTS

CLARK UNIVERSITY, International Development Program
950 Main St., Worcester, MA 1610
Phone: 508-793-7201; Fax: 508-793-8820
Founded: 1972
Description: The International Development Program uses a multidisciplinary approach in research and teaching to analyze issues of underdevelopment in Asia, Africa, and Latin America. It draws on faculty from the fields of geography (including GIS), environmental studies, management, anthropology, economics, politics, and history, and serves both U.S. and international students. (B.A. and M.A. degree offered)
Contact(s):
Director Center for Community-Based Development: DR. RICHARD FORD
Director of International Development Program: DR. BARBARA P. THOMAS-SLAYTER

NORTHEASTERN UNIVERSITY, School For Field Studies, The
16 Broadway, Beverly, MA 01915-4499
Phone: 1-800-989-4435; Fax: 978-927-5127; Email: sfshome@igc.apc.org.; WWW: www.fieldstudies.org
Founded: 1980
Description: The mission of The School for Field Studies is to provide highly motivated young people from the U.S. and abroad with an excellent practical education in environmental studies, in order that tomorrow's leaders may become more environmentally literate/aware as well as make immediate and future contributions toward the sustainable management of natural resources.
Contact(s):
President: TERRY L. ANDREAS

TUFTS UNIVERSITY
Medford, MA 02155
Phone: 617-627-3211
Contact(s):
Department of Civil Engineering, Chair: STEPHEN LEVINE
Department of Environmental Leadership, Contact: LINFIELD C. BROWN
Environmental Engineering, Contact: LINFIELD C. BROWN
Environmetnal Geotechnology, Contact: CHRISTOPHER SWAN
Hazardous Material Management, Contact: JOHN DURANT
Water Resources, Contact: RICHARD M. VOGEL

UNIVERSITY OF MASSACHUSETTS
Amherst, MA 01003-4210
Phone: 413-545-2665
Contact(s):
Department of Forestry and Wildlife Management, Head: DR. WILLIAM C. MCCOMB
Environmental Sciences, Program Director: DR. GUY R. LANZA; Phone: 413-545-3747
U.S. Forest Service Cooperative Wildlife Research Unit, Leader: DR. RICHARD M. DEGRAAF
U.S. Geological Survey, Massachusetts Cooperative Fish and Wildlife Research Unit, Assistant Leader: DR. REBECCA FIELD; Phone: 413-545-4888
U.S. National Oceanic and Atmospheric Administration Cooperative Education and Researh Program, Director: DR. JOHN G. BOREMAN; Phone: 413-545-2842

UNIVERSITY OF MASSACHUSETTS, Urban Harbors Institute
100 Morrissey Blvd., Boston, MA 02125-3393
Phone: 617-287-5570; Fax: 617-287-5575; Email: urbharbors@umbsky.cc.edu
Founded: 1989
Description: The Urban Harbors Institute was founded as a center for the study of harbor issues. It Conducts multidisciplinary research on the policy and management issues affecting the coastal area, with emphasis on the urban waterfront. It also promotes linkages between scientists, government, academic, and business communitites to improve decision-making. The institute publishes research, sponsors seminars, conferences, and public forums to disseminate and exchange information.
Contact(s):
Director: RICHARD F. DELANEY

WILLIAMS COLLEGE, Center for Environmental Studies Program
Box 632, Williamstown, MA 01267
Phone: 413-597-2346
Founded: 1967
Description: The Center for Environmental Studies offers an integrated undergraduate program of studies to liberal arts students in combination with their major discipline. The Center also administers the 2,400 acre Hopkins Forest, a research and educational facility, as well as the Environmental Science Laboratory and the Matt Cole Memorial Library.
Contact(s):
Director: KAI N. LEE

MICHIGAN

CENTRAL MICHIGAN UNIVERSITY
Mt. Pleasant, MI 48859
Contact(s):
Fisheries, (B.S.,M.S), Contact: DR. HERBERT L. LENON; Phone: 517-774-3531
Wildlife, (B.S., M.S.), Contact: DR. JOHN N. KRULL; Phone: 517-774-3412

EASTERN MICHIGAN UNIVERSITY
Ypsilanti, MI 48197
Phone: 313-487-1849
Contact(s):
Biology, (B.S., M.S.), Head: DR. DOUGLAS Y. SHAPIRO; Phone: 313-487-4242
Conservation Resource Use, Contact: DR. CATHERINE BACH; Phone: 313-487-0212
Ecosystems Biology Concentration, Advisor: DR. ROBERT K. NEELY; Phone: 313-487-0332
Geography and Geology, (B.S., M.S.), Head: ANDREW A. NAZZARO; Phone: 313-487-0218
Kresge Environmental Education Center, Resident Manager: BEN CZINSKI; Phone: 313-487-2350

FERRIS STATE UNIVERSITY, College of Allied Health Sciences
200 Ferris Dr., Big Rapids, MI 49307-2740
Phone: 616-592-2314; Fax: 616-592-3788; Email: janice_m_webster@ferris.edu
Founded: 1964
Description: Educational institution offering bachelor of science degree in industrial and environmental health management, with options in general environmental health, hazardous materials management, industrial hygiene, and industrial safety.
Contact(s):
Environmental and Clinical Sciences Departmen, Head: DR. JANICE WEBSTER; Phone: 616-592-2314; Email: janice_m_webster@ferris.edu

LAKE SUPERIOR STATE UNIVERSITY, College of Natural and Health Sciences
Description: Degrees offered in biological science, conservation law enforcement, environmental chemistry, environmental science, fisheries/wildlife management, geology, and natural resources technology (A.D.).
Degrees: A.D., B.A., B.S.
Contact(s):
Dean: DONALD A. MCCRIMMON

MICHIGAN STATE UNIVERSITY
323 Natural Resources Bldg. MSU, East Lansing, MI 48824-1222
Phone: 517-355-3421; Fax: 517-353-8994; Email: fridgenc@pilot.msu.edu
Contact(s):
Department of Resources Development, (B.S., M.S., Ph.D.), Chairperson: DR. CYNTHIA FRIDGEN
Fisheries and Wildlife, (B.S., M.S., Ph.D.), Chairperson: WILLIAM TAYLOR
Forestry, (B.S., M.S., Ph.D.), Chairperson: DR. DANIEL E. KEATHLEY
Park and Recreation Resources, (B.S., M.S., Ph.D.), Chairperson: JOSEPH D. FRIDGEN

MICHIGAN TECHNOLOGICAL UNIVERSITY, School of Forestry and Wood Products
1400 Townsend Dr., Houghton, MI 49931
Phone: 906-487-2454; Fax: 906-487-2915; Email: wefrayer@mtu.edu)
Description: Undergraduate concentrations and graduate programs in forest management science, forest biology and ecology, wildlife biology and ecology, and wood science and technology.
Contact(s):
Forestry, (B.S., M.S., Ph.D.), Dean: W E. FRAYER

NORTHERN MICHIGAN UNIVERSITY
Marquette, MI 49855
Phone: 906-227-1000
Contact(s):
Department of Biology, (B.A., B.S., M.S.), Head: DR. THOMAS FROILAND; Phone: 906-227-2310
Department of Geography, Earth Science, Conservation, and Planning, (B.A., B.S.), Head: PROF. J. PAT FARRELL; Phone: 906-227-2500

UNIVERSITY OF MICHIGAN, School of Natural Resources and Environment
Ann Arbor, MI 48109-1115
Phone: 313-764-2550
Contact(s):
Dean: DANIEL A. MAZMANIAN
Landscape Architecture, (M.L.A., B.S., M.S), Concentration Chair: DONNA ERICKSON
Resource Ecology and Management, (B.S., M.S., Ph.D.), Concentration Chair: JAMES S. DIANA
Resource Policy and Behavior, (B.S., M.S., Ph.D.), Concetration Chair: PAUL MOHAI

WAYNE STATE UNIVERSITY, Department of Biological Sciences
Description: Courses offered in such subjects as limnology, ornithology, mammalogy, biogeography, natural history of vertebrates, animal behavior, population genetics, population ecology, microbial ecology, aquatic botany, ecology, advanced ecology, and evolutionary ecology.
Degrees: B.A., B.S., M.S., Ph.D.
Contact(s):
Chairman: JACK LILIEN

EDUCATIONAL INSTITUTIONS - MINNESOTA/MISSOURI

WESTERN MICHIGAN UNIVERSITY, Environmental Studies Program
Kalamazoo, MI 49008
Phone: 616-387-2716
Description: This undergraduate interdisciplinary program provides intellectual and practical experience that provokes thought about the complex interrelationships between humans, the social and technological systems they develop, and the natural environment. The program encourages students to develop an appreciation for the many elements of planetary health and to devise creative solutions to environmental problems.
Contact(s):
Program Coordinator: MOLLY COLE

MINNESOTA

BEMIDJI STATE UNIVERSITY, Center for Environmetnal Studies
Bemidji, MN 56601
Phone: 218-755-2000
Founded: 1968
Description: The Center for Environmental Studies is a research and teaching unit directed towards understanding our physical, biological, and social environment, and preventing its deterioration. The center conducts laboratory and field studies, both internally and externally funded, and offers baccalaureate and master's degree programs.
Degrees: B.S., M.S.
Contact(s):
Director: STEVEN A. SPIGARELLI; Phone: 218-755-2910; Fax: 218-755-4107; Email: saspigarelli@vax1.bemidji.msus.edu

HAMLINE UNIVERSITY'S CENTER FOR GLOBAL ENVIRONMENTAL EDUCATION
1536 Hewitt Ave., St. Paul, MN 55104-1284
Phone: 651-523-2480; Fax: 651-523-2987; Email: tfredin@gw.hamline.edu; WWW: cgee.hamline.edu
Founded: 1990
Description: CGEE was founded to nurture greater understanding of the interconnectedness of local and global environments among educators, students, scientists, and citizens.
Contact(s):
Director: TRACY FREDIN; Phone: 651-523-3105; Fax: 651-523-2987; Email: tfredin@gw.hamline.edu

UNIVERSITY OF MINNESOTA AT CROOKSTON
Crookston, MN 56716
Phone: 218-281-8129
Description: Offers a broadly-oriented natural resource major which prepares students for entry-level resource management positions. Practical and field instruction in integrated land management is emphasized leading, to a B.S. degree in Natural Resource Management, Park Management, Soil and Water Technology, or Conservation Law Enforcement.
Contact(s):
Head: DANIEL SVEDARSKY

UNIVERSITY OF MINNESOTA AT ST. PAUL, College of Natural Resources
St. Paul, MN 55108
Phone: 612-624-1234
Description: The mission of the College of Natural Resources is to foster a quality environment by contributing to the management, protection, and sustainable use of our natural resources through teaching, research, and outreach.
Contact(s):
Cooperative Park Studies Unit, (B.S., M.S., D.F.), Senior Research Associate: DR. DAVIE W. LIME; Phone: 612-624-2250
Dean of College of Natural Resources, (B.S., M.S., Ph.D.): DR. ALFRED D. SULLIVAN
Department of Ecology, Evolution, and Behavior, Head: DR. PARTICE A. MORROW, 1987 Upper Buford Cir., St. Paul, MN 55108; Phone: 612-625-5700
Department of Fisheries and Wildlife, (B.S., M.S., Ph.D.): DR. IRA R. ADELMAN; Phone: 612-624-3600
Department of Forest Resources, (B.S., M.S., Ph.D.), Head: DR. ALAN EK; Phone: 612-624-3400
Department of Wood and Paper Science, (B.S., M.S., Ph.D.), Head: DR. JOSEPH G. MASSEY; Phone: 612-624-5200
Forestry Library, B-50 Natural Resources Administration Bldg., Librarian: JEAN ALBRECHT, 2003 Upper Buford Cir., St. Paul, MN 55108; Phone: 612-624-3222
Graduate Studies/Conservation Biology Program, Director: DR. DAVID SMITH and FRANCESCA CUTHBERT
Graduate Studies/Ecology Graduate Program, Director: DR. ROBERT STERNER
Minnesota Cooperative Fish and Wildlife Research Unit, (B.S., M.S., Ph.D.), Leader: DR. DAVID E. ANDERSON; Phone: 612-624-3421
Outreach and Extension, (B.S., M.S., Ph.D.), Associate Dean: DR. STEVEN B. DALEYLAURSEN; Phone: 612-624-9298
Student Services Office, (B.S., M.S.), Director: BILL K. GANZLIN; Phone: 612-624-6768
Water Resources Center, (B.S., M.S., Ph.D.), Direcoty: DR. PATRICK BREZONIK; Phone: 612-624-9282

MISSISSIPPI

MISSISSIPPI STATE UNIVERSITY
Box 9680, Mississippi State, MS 39762-9680
Phone: 601-325-2952
Contact(s):
Associate Dean: DR. BOB L. KARR
Forest Products, (B.S., M.S.), Interim Head: DR. PHILIP H. STEELE; Phone: 601-325-2119
Forest Resources, (Ph.D), Dean: DR. JOHN E. GUNTER
Forestry, (B.S., M.S.), Head: DR. DOUGLAS P. RICHARDS; Phone: 601-325-2949
Wildlife and Fisheries, (B.S., M.S.), Head: DR. H. RANDALL ROBINETTE; Phone: 601-325-3830

UNIVERSITY OF SOUTHERN MISSISSIPPI
Hattiesburg, MS 39401
Phone: 601-266-7011
Contact(s):
Aquatic Biology, (M.S., Ph.D.), Contact: DR. GORDON GODSHALK
Aquatic Ecology, Contact: DR. JEAN W. WOOTEN
Fisheries Biology, (M.S., Ph.D.), Contact: DR. STEPHEN T. ROSS
Marine Biology, (M.S., Ph.D.), Contact: DR. R. S. PREZANT
Recreation Planning and Resources Management, (B.S., M.S.), Contact: DR. L. CHARLES BURCHELL
Resource Mangement and Environmental Planning, (B.S., M.S., Ph.D.), Contact: DR. ROBERT W. WALES
Zoology, (M.S., Ph.D.), Contact: DR. J. W. CLIBURN

MISSOURI

UNIVERSITY OF MISSOURI, The School of Natural Resources
103 Anheuser-Busch Natural Resource Bldg., Columbia, MO 65211-7220
Phone: 573-882-6445
Contact(s):
Cooperative Fish and Wildlife Research Unit, Leader: DR. CHARLES RABENI, 302 Annheuser-Busch Natural Resource Bldg., ; Phone: 573-882-3524
Director, (B.S., M.S., Ph.D.): DR. ALBERT R. VOGT
Fisheries and Wildlife Program, (B.S., M.S., Ph.D.), Program Leader: DR. JACK JONES, 302 Annheuser-Busch Natural Resource Bldg., ; Phone: 573-882-3436

Forestry Program, (B.S., M.S., Ph.D.), Program Leader: DR. CARL SETTERGREN, 302 Annheuser-Busch Natrual Resource Bldg., ; Phone: 573-882-2627

Parks, Recreation and Tourism Department, (B.S., M.S.), Chair and Graduate Director: DR. C. RANDALL VESSELL, 105 Annheuser-Busch Natural Resource Bldg., ; Phone: 573-882-7088

Soil and Atmospheric Sciences Department, (B.S., M.S., Ph.D.), Chair: DR. R. DAVID HAMMER, 302 Annheuser-Busch Natural Resource Bldg., ; Phone: 573-882-6591

WASHINGTON UNIVERSITY
St. Louis, MO 63130
Phone: 314-935-6868

Description: The laboratory is active in applying modern genetic techniques to problems in conservation biology such as conservation forensics (e.g., DNA fingerprinting of elephant tusks), systematics (identifying taxa that are significant evolutionary units), inter- and intraspefic hybridizataion, and genetic management of captive, translocated, and natural populations.

Contact(s):
Department of Biology, Head: DR. ALAN R. TEMPLETON; Phone: 314-935-6868

MONTANA

MONTANA STATE UNIVERSITY
Bozeman, MT 59717

Contact(s):
Cooperative Fishery Research Unit, Leader: DR. ROBERT G. WHITE
Department of Biology: , P.O. Box 173460, Bozeman, MT 59717; Phone: 406-994-4549; Fax: 406-994-7479; Email: tbi70001@montana.edu
Fish and Wildlife Management Program, (B.S., M.S., Ph.D), Director: DR. LYNN R. IRBY
Fisheries: DR. THOMAS McMAHON

UNIVERSITY OF MONTANA, School of Forestry
Missoula, MT 59812
Phone: 406-243-5521; Fax: 406-243-4845

Contact(s):
Bolle Center for People and Forests: DR. JAMES BURCHFIELD; Phone: 406-243-6650
Boone and Crocket Wildlife Conservation Program: DR. JACK WARD THOMAS; Phone: 406-243-5566
Forestry (B.S., M.S., M.E.M., Ph.D):
Inland Northwest Growth and Yield Cooperative: DR. KELSEY MILNER; Phone: 406-243-6653
Institute for Tourism and Recreation Research: DR. NORMA NICKERSON; Phone: 406-243-5686
Mission Oriented Research Program: DR. ROBERT PFISTER; Phone: 406-243-6582
Montana Forest and Conservation Experiment Station, Director: DR. PERRY J. BROWN; Phone: 406-243-5522
Numerical Terradynamic Simulation Group: DR. STEVEN RUNNING; Phone: 406-243-6311
Quantitative Services Group: DR. HANS R. ZUURING; Phone: 406-243-6465
Range Management (B.S., M.S.):
Recreation Management (B.S., M.S.):
Resource Conservation (B.S., M.S.):
Riparian/Wetland Research Program: DR. PAUL HANSEN; Phone: 406-243-2050
School of Forestry Dean: DR. PERRY J. BROWN
Wilderness Institute: DR. WAYNE FERMUND; Phone: 406-243-5184
Wildlife Biology (B.S., M.S., Ph.D.), Dean: DR. PERRY J. BROWN
Wildlife Biology Program, Director: DR. DANIEL H. PLETSCHER; Phone: 406-243-5272

UNIVERSITY OF MONTANA, School of Law
Missoula, MT 59812
Contact(s):
Dean: E. EDWIN ECH

NEBRASKA

UNIVERSITY OF NEBRASKA, Institute of Agriculture and Natural Resources
Lincoln, NE 68583
Phone: 403-472-7211

Contact(s):
Fisheries Management, (B.S., M.S., Ph.D.): EDWARD PETERS, 203 Natural Resources Hall, Lincoln, NE 68583; Phone: 402-472-6824
Forestry: JAMES BRANDLE, 002 Plant Industry, Lincoln, NE 68583; Phone: 402-472-6626
Range Science, (B.S., M.S., Ph.D.): JAMES STUBBENDIECK, 349 Keirn Hall, Lincoln, NE 68583; Phone: 402-472-1519
Wildlife Management, (B.S., M.S., Ph.D.): RONALD M CASE, 204 Natural Resources Hall, Lincoln, NE 68583; Phone: 402-472-6825

NEVADA

UNIVERSITY OF NEVADA AT LAS VEGAS
Las Vegas, NV 89154-4029

Contact(s):
Conservation Biology, (B.S., M.S., Ph.D): DR. JOEL BERGER
Department of Environmental and Resource Sciences, Chairman: DR. GERALD F. GIFFORD
Environmental Science, (B.S., M.S.), Contact: DR. GLENN MILLER
Interdisciplinary Hydrology, (B.S., M.S., Ph.D.): DR. JOHN C. GUITJENS
Natural Resource Management, (B.S., M.S.): DR. DALE JOHNSON

UNIVERSITY OF NEVADA AT LAS VEGAS, Water Resources Program
4505 Maryland Pkwy., Las Vegas, NV 89154-4029
Phone: 702-895-4006

Description: The Water Resources Management Graduate Program at the University of Nevada is an interdisciplinary environmental program. The curriculum includes studies in water quality and quantity; surface water and groundwater; and water law, regulation, and management. Offers environmental programs at graduate level.

Contact(s):
Director: DR. DAVID KREAMER, University of Nevada at Las Vegas, 1000 Valley Rd., Reno, NV 89512; Phone: 702-784-4000; Fax: 702-784-4583

UNIVERSITY OF NEVADA AT RENO
1000 Valley Rd., Reno, NV 89512
Phone: 702-784-4000; Fax: 702-784-4583

Contact(s):
Conservation Biology, (B.S., M.S., Ph.D.): DR. JOEL BERGER
Department of Environmental and Resource Sciences, Chairman: DR. GERALD F. GIFFORD
Environmental Science, (B.S., M.S.): DR. GLENN MILLER
Interdisciplinary Hydrology, (B.S., M.S., Ph.D.): DR. JOHN C. GUITJENS
Natural Resource Management, (B.S., M.S.): DR. DALE JOHNSON

EDUCATIONAL INSTITUTIONS - NEW BRUNSWICK/NEW JERSEY

NEW BRUNSWICK

UNIVERSITY OF NEW BRUNSWICK
Fredericton, New Brunswick E3B 6C2 Canada
Contact(s):
Atlantic Cooperative Wildlife Ecology Research Network: ; Phone: 506-453-4501; Fax: 506-453-3538
Biology, (B.Sc., M.Sc., Ph.D), Chairperson: TIM DILWORTH; Phone: 506-453-4583
Cooperative Wildlife Research Unit: G. J. FORBES; Phone: 506-453-4583
Forestry and Environmental Management and Department of Biology, (B.Sc.F., M.Sc.F., Ph.D.), Acting Dean: E. W. ROBAK, P.O. Box 44555, Fredericton, New Brunswick E3J 6C2 Canada; Phone: 506-453-4501; Fax: 506-453-3538
Science Library, Contact: A W. DIAMOND, P.O. Box 7500, Fredericton, New Brunswick E3J 5H5 Canada; Phone: 506-453-4601

NEW HAMPSHIRE

ANTIOCH NEW ENGLAND GRADUATE SCHOOL
40 Avon St., Keene, NH 03431
Phone: 603-357-6265; Fax: 603-357-0718; Email: admissions@antiochne.edu; WWW: www.antiochne.edu
Description: Antioch New England Graduate School offers professional training for effective, reflective, environmental leadership. The M.S. Degree in Environmental Studies is a field-oriented program that stresses professional preparation in environmental biology, teaching, communication, administration, policy, and environmental education. Biology and general science teacher certifications are available. The M.S. degree in Resource Management and Administration integrates environmental science, natural resources policy, and administration. The Ph.D Program in Environmental Studies offers an interdisciplinary approach to research in Environmental Education and Environmental Policy.
Contact(s):
Environmental Studies, (M.S.): DR. THOMAS WESSELS
Environmental Studies, (Ph.D.): DR. MITCHELL THOMASHOW
Resource Management, (M.S.): DR. THOMAS WESSELS

DARTMOUTH COLLEGE, Environmental Studies Program
6182 Steele Hall, Rm. 306, Hanover, NH 03755-3577
Phone: 603-646-2838
Founded: 1970
Description: Interdisciplinary academic program providing students with the opportunity to assess the seriousness and complexity of environmental problems and to understand how to search for solutions. Faculty research interests include biological conservation, ecosystem ecology, air pollution, economics, and international environmental governance.
Contact(s):
Chairman: ROSS A. VIRGINIA

KEENE STATE COLLEGE OF THE UNIVERSITY SYSTEM OF NEW HAMPSHIRE
229 Main St., Keene, NH 03431-1504
Phone: 603-352-1909
Founded: 1909
Description: A multipurpose, predominantly undergraduate college with a central focus in the liberal arts and sciences. Total numbers of students (graduate and undergraduate): 4,900.
Contact(s):
President: STANLEY J. YAROSEWICK

UNIVERSITY OF NEW HAMPSHIRE
Durham, NH 03824
Phone: 603-862-1020
Contact(s):
Department of Natural Resources, James Hall, Chair: DR. THEODORE E. HOWARD
Environmental Conservation, (B.S., M.S.), Program Coordinator: DR. ROBERT T. ECKERT
Forestry, (B.S., M.S.) Program Coordinator: DR. RICHARD WEYRICK
Natural Resources, (Ph.D.), Program Coordinator: DR. JOHN ABER
Soil Science, (B.S., M.S.), Program Coordinator: DR. ROBERT HARTER
Water Resources Management, (B.S., M.S.), Program Coordinator: DR. WILLIAM MCDOWELL
Wildlife Ecology, (B.S., M.S.), Program Coordinator: DR. PETER PEKINS

NEW JERSEY

MONTCLAIR STATE COLLEGE
Upper Montclair, NJ 07043
Phone: 201-893-5258
Contact(s):
Director: DR. DAVID K. ROBERTSON
Environmental Studies, (M.A.), Student Advisor: DR. W. AUGUSTUS RENSCH

ROWAN UNIVERSITY
Glassboro, NJ 08028
Phone: 609-256-4500/ext.3587
Contact(s):
Conservation and Environmental Education, (M.A.), Advisor: GARY PATTERSON

ROWAN UNIVERSITY, Pinelands Institute for Natural and Environmental Studies
120-13 Whitesbog Rd., Browns Mills, NJ 08015
Phone: 609-893-1765
Contact(s):
Director: GARY PATTERSON

RUTGERS UNIVERSITY, Cook College
P.O. Box 231, New Brunswick, NJ 08903
Phone: 201-932-9336
Contact(s):
Agriculture/Environmental Sciences/ Conservation/Wildlife Science, (B.S., M.S., Ph.D), Director of Resident Instruction: DR. IAN MAW
Forestry, (B.S., M.S., Ph.D.), Associate Professor: DR. JOHN KUSER
Landscape Architecture, (B.S.), Chairman: PROF. STEVEN STROM
Wildlife, (B.S., M.S., Ph.D), Coordinator: DR. JAMES E. APPELGATE

STOCKTON STATE COLLEGE
Jim Leeds Rd., Pomona, NJ 08240
Phone: 609-652-4546; Fax: 609-748-5515; Email: iaprod573f@vax003.stockton.edu)
Founded: 1969
Contact(s):
Division of Natural Sciences and Mathematics Energy Certificate, Program Coordinator: DR. LYNN STILES
Division of Natural Sciences and Mathematics-Biology, (B.A.), Program Coordinator: DR. RICHARD COLBY; Phone: 609-652-4355
Division of Natural Sciences and Mathematics-Chemistry, (B.A., B.S.), Program Coordinator: DR. ROGERS BARLAT
Division of Natural Sciences and Mathematics-Environmental Studies and Geology, (B.A., B.S.), Program Coordinator: DR. MICHAEL D. GELLER; Phone: 609-652-4578
Division of Natural Sciences and Mathematics-Marine Science, (B.A., B.S.), Program Coordinator: DR. MATHEW LANDAU; Phone: 609-652-4578
Division of Professional Studies, Coordinator of Public Health: BRUCE DELUSSA
Office of Continuing Education, Director: BARBARA KENNEDY; Phone: 609-652-4227

President: VERA KING FARRIS

NEW MEXICO

NEW MEXICO STATE UNIVERSITY
Contact(s):
Department of Animal and Range Science, (B.S., M.S., Ph.D.), Department Head: DR. BOBBY J. RANKIN; Phone: 505-646-2514
Department of Fishery and Wildlife Sciences, (B.S., M.S.) Acting Head: DR. RICHARD A. COLE, Box 300003 Dept. 4901, Las Cruces, NM 88003-0003; Phone: 505-646-1544; Fax: 505-646-1281; Email: cdavis@nmsu.edu

NEW YORK

ALFRED UNIVERSITY, Division of Environmental Studies
Saxon Dr., Alfred, NY 14802-1205
Phone: 607-871-2634; Fax: 607-871-2697; Email: ens@bigvax.alfred.edu
Founded: 1971
Description: The program offers an undergraduate degree in multidisciplinary environmental studies in a liberal arts setting. Students can focus on either natural or social sciences, and many take a second major in biology, geology, political science, economics, etc. The project-oriented program is supervised by fifteen faculty members from different disciplines.
Contact(s):
Chair: DR. MICHELE M. HLUCHY

BARD COLLEGE, Graduate School in Environmental Studies
Annandale-on-Hudson, NY 12504-5000
Description: The school offers an interdisciplinary graduate program that combines training in the natural and social sciences. Students receive an M.S. in environmental studies after two summers of intensive coursework and a third season completing a research thesis. Recent thesis projects have included multinational corporations and environmental responsibility; habitat utilization of a local endagered species; population growth rates of marine fishes; and sociological analysis of a small rural town.
Contact(s):
Director: DR. JANE L. WOLFSON; Phone: 914-758-7483

CITY UNIVERSITY OF NEW YORK, College of Staten Island
2800 Victory Blvd., Staten Island, NY 10314
Phone: 718-982-3921; Fax: 718-982-3923
Description: An interdisciplinary program is provided, including ecology, geology, chemistry, environmental engineering, and computer modeling. The objective of the masters program is to expose the students to the scientific principles underlying environmental problems. Research is carried out on wetlands, park planning, air pollution, waste disposal, environmental epidemiology, and risk analysis.
Contact(s):
Environmental Science Masters Program, Center for Environmental Science 6S-308, Center of Applied Sciences, Center and Lecturere in Mathmatics, Director: DR. JOHN R. OPPENHEIMER

CITY UNIVERSITY OF NEW YORK, Hunter College
695 Park Ave., New York, NY 10021
Phone: 212-772-4146; Fax: 212-772-4142
Contact(s):
Department of Geography, affiliated with City University of New York Ph.D program in Earth and Environmental Science, Chairman: PROF. CHARLES A. HEATWOLE
Wexler Library Chief Librarian: LOUISE SHERBY, 695 Park Ave., New York, NY 10021; Phone: 212-772-4146; Fax: 212-772-4142

CORNELL UNIVERSITY
Ithaca, NY 14853
Phone: 607-255-2810; Fax: 607-255-0349
Contact(s):
Adirondack Fishery Research Program, Arnot Teaching and Research Forest: DR. CHARLES R. SMITH; Phone: 607-255-3219
Cooperative Fish and Wildlife Research Unit: DR. MILO E. RICHMOND; Phone: 607-255-2839
Cornell Biological Field Station: DR. EDWARD L. MILLS; Phone: 315-633-9243
Department of Natural Resources: DR. JAMES P. LASSOIE
Environmental Ethics: DR. RICHARD A. BAER; Phone: 607-255-7797
Fisheries and Aquatic Sciences: DR. CHARLES C. KRUEGER; Phone: 315-633-9243
Forest Science: DR. TIMOTHY J. FAHEY; Phone: 607-255-5470
Graduate Field Faculty: DR. MARIANNE E. KRASNY; Phone: 607-255-2823
Human Dimensions Research Unit: TOMMY L. BROWN; Phone: 607-255-7695
Natural Resources Extension: DR. DAVID W. GROSS; Phone: 607-255-2825
Resource Policy and Management: DR. BARBARA KNUTH; Phone: 607-255-2827
Uihlein Sugar Maple Research and Extension Field Station: LEWIS J. STAATS; Phone: 518-523-9337
Undergraduate Program, Coordinator: DR. RICHARD J. MCNEIL; Phone: 607-255-7703
Wildlife Science: DR. AARON N. MOEN; Phone: 607-255-3182

CORNELL UNIVERSITY, Resource Center
7 Business and Technology Park, Ithaca, NY 14850
Phone: 607-255-2080
Description: To extend the research-based knowledge from the university to others who can use this information. Educational materials are available in print and nonprint formats.
Contact(s):
Audiovisual Librarian: RICHARD GRAY

POLYTECHNIC UNIVERSITY, Civil and Environmental Engineering Department
333 Jay St., Brooklyn, NY 11201
Phone: 718-260-3220
Description: The Department is engaged in teaching and research in several areas of environmental science and engineering. Masters degrees with environmental focus are offered in civil engineering, environmental engineering, and environmental health science. The Ph.D. is also offered.
Contact(s):
President: DAVID CHANG

POLYTECHNIC UNIVERSITY, Rensselaer Polytechnic Institute
Environmental Management and Policy, Troy, NY 12180-3590
Phone: 518-274-6562
Description: Rensselaer's EMP program educates students at the masters of science level to undertake a professional role in companies, governmental agencies, and other organizations dealing with environmental and energy matters from a base of technical and managerial knowledge and understanding.
Contact(s):
Director: DR. BRUCE W. PIASECKI

ST. LAWRENCE UNIVERSITY
Canton, NY 13617
Phone: 315-379-5011
Founded: 1856
Description: St. Lawrence University is a liberal arts and sciences institution. The institution offers one of the oldest environmental studies programs in the nation. The university is committed to environmentally responsible management practices and comprehensive outdoor education programs.

EDUCATIONAL INSTITUTIONS - NORTH CAROLINA/NORTH CAROLINA

Contact(s):
President: DANIEL F. SULLIVAN; Phone: 315-229-5895
Vice President: THOMAS COBURN; Phone: 315-229-5993

STATE UNIVERSITY OF NEW YORK AT CORTLAND
Cortland, NY 13045
Phone: 607-753-2011
Contact(s):
Center for Environmental and Outdooor Education, Director: DR. THOMAS PASQUARELLO; Phone: 607-753-5772
Environmental Sciences (Concentration for majors in Biology, Geology, Chemistry and Physics), Coordnator: DR. JOHN L. FAUTH; Phone: 607-753-2816
Recreation and Environmental Interpretation, Chair: DR. ANDERSON B. YOUNG; Phone: 607-753-4941

STATE UNIVERSITY OF NEW YORK, College of Environmental Science and Forestry
One Forestry Dr., Syracuse, NY 13210-2778
Phone: 315-470-6500; Fax: 315-470-6977
Founded: 1911
Description: Research has been a hallmark of ESF since its inception. Recent wildlife studies have aimed toward reintroducing lynx and moose to the Adirondack Park; application of molecular biology techniques to identify migrant bird populations; restoration of muskellunge and sturgeon in the St. Lawrence River system; analysis of Flamingo population dynamics in Mexico; tailoring black cherry clones for fast growth and straight limbs; researching willow plantations as a source of biomass energy; cooperating with NASA to analyze polarized-light photographs of Earth; and detailing the effects of acid precipitation on forest ecosystems.
Contact(s):
Academic Affairs Provost and Vice President: WILLIAM P. TULLY; Phone: 315-470-6510
Adirondack Ecological Center, Director: WILLIAM F. PORTER; Phone: 315-470-6798
Administration, Vice President: CONNIE WEBB; Phone: 315-470-6622
Cellulose Research Institute, Acting Director: ANATOLE SARKO; Phone: 315-470-6855
Cooperative Park Studies Unit, Director: H. BRIAN UNDERWOOD; Phone: 315-470-6820
Cranberry Lake Regional Campus: ; Phone: 315-470-3444
Empire State Paper Research Institute, Director: HANNU MAKKONEN; Phone: 315-470-6900
Environmental Institute, Randof G. Park, Director: RICHARD C. SMARDON; Phone: 315-470-6636
F.Franklin Moon Library, Director: ELIZABETH A. ELKINS; Phone: 315-470-6716
Faculty of Chemistry, (B.S., M.S., Ph.D.), Chair: JOHN HASSETT; Phone: 315-470-6855
Faculty of Construction Management and Wood Products Engineering, (B.S., M.S., Ph.D.), Chair: GEORGE H. KYANKA; Phone: 315-470-6880
Faculty of Environmental and Forest Biology, (B.S., M.S., Ph.D.), Chair: NEIL H. RINGLER; Phone: 315-470-6743
Faculty of Environmental Resources and Forest Engineering, (B.S., M.S., Ph.D.), Chair: ROBERT H. BROCK JR.; Phone: 315-470-6633
Faculty of Environmental Studies, (B.S., M.S., Ph.D.), Chair: RICHARD C. SMARDON; Phone: 315-470-6636
Faculty of Forestry, (B.S., M.S., Ph.D.), Chair: WILLIAM R. BENTLEY; Phone: 315-470-6536
Faculty of Landscape Architecture, (B.L.A., M.L.A.), Chair: RICHARD HAWKS; Phone: 315-470-6544
Faculty of Paper Science and Engineering, (B.S., M.S., Ph.D.), Chair: LELAND SCHROEDER; Phone: 315-470-6502
Forest Technician Program, (A.A.S.), Director: CHRISTOPHER WESTBROOK; Phone: 315-470-2566
Great Lakes Research Consortium, Co-Director: RICHARD C. SMARDON; Phone: 315-470-6816
N.C. Brown Laboratory for Ultrastructure Studies, Director: ROBERT B. HANNA; Phone: 315-470-6880
Newcomb Regional Campus: ; Phone: 518-582-4551
Office of Nonresident Programs, Dean: ROBERT C. KOEPPER; Phone: 315-470-6891
Polymer Research Institute, Director: ISRAEL CABASSO; Phone: 315-470-4767
President: ROSS S. WHALEY; Phone: 315-470-6681
Roosevelt Wildlife Station, Director: NEIL H. RINGLER; Phone: 315-470-6770
Tully Regional Campus: ; Phone: 315-696-5541
U.S. Forest Service Unit, Deputy Project Leader: WAYNE ZIPPERER; Phone: 315-448-3201
Wanakena Regional Campus, (A.A.S.), Director: CHRISTOPHER WESTBROOK; Phone: 315-848-2566

NORTH CAROLINA

APPALACHIAN STATE UNIVERSITY
Boone, NC 28608
Phone: 704-262-2179
Contact(s):
Commercial Recreatin: DR. LYNN MASTERSON; Phone: 704-262-6337
Department of Biology, Chairperson: DR. DOUG MEIKLE; Phone: 704-262-2674
Department of Health, Leisure and Exercise Science, Director: DR. WAYNE WILLIAMS; Phone: 704-262-6335
Environmental Education Program, Naturalist: DR. RICHARD HENSON; Phone: 704-262-2677
Outdoor Recreation: DR. DEL BACHERT; Phone: 704-262-2540
Recreation and Park Management: DR. PAUL GASKILL; Phone: 704-262-6336
Travel and Tourism: DR. BILL NORMAN; Phone: 704-262-6338

DUKE UNIVERSITY, Center for Tropical Conservation
P.O. Box 90381, Durham, NC 27708-0381
Phone: 919-490-9081; Fax: 919-493-3695
Founded: 1988
Description: The goal of the Center is to contribute to the alleviation of the world environmental crisis, particularly as it affects the developing countries of the tropics. The CTC works toward this goal through interdisciplinary research into issues of environmental policy relevance, training in environmental management, and dissemination of information.
Contact(s):
Co-Director: DR. JOHN W. TERBORGH

DUKE UNIVERSITY, Nicholas School of the Environment
Durham, NC 27708
Phone: 919-613-8000
Degrees: M.F., M.E.M., Ph.D.
Contact(s):
Coastal Environmental Management: DR. MICHAEL K. ORBACH
Dean: DR. NORMAN L. CHRISTENSEN
Division of Earth Sciences, Chair: DR. JEFFREY A. KARSON
Duke University Marine Laboratory, Director: DR. JOSEPH S. RAMUS
Environmental Toxicology: DR. RICHARD T. DIGIULO
Forest Resource Management: DR. DANIEL D. RICHTER
Resource Ecology: DR. DANIEL D. RICHTER
Resource Economics and Policy: DR. RANDAL A. KRAMER
Water Resouces: DR. KENNETH H. RECKHOW

NORTH CAROLINA STATE UNIVERSITY
Box 7103, Raleigh, NC 27695-7103
Contact(s):
Department of Biological and Agricultural Engineering, (B.S., M.S., M.B.A.E., Ph.D.), Head: DR. DAVID B. BEASLEY; Phone: 919-515-2694
Department of Botany, (B.S., M.S., M.L.S., Ph.D.), Interim Head: DR. UDO BLUM; Phone: 919-515-2727
Department of Forestry, (B.S., M.S., M.F.S., M.N.R.A., Ph.D.), Head: DR. FREDERICK W. CUBBAGE; Phone: 919-515-7789

EDUCATIONAL INSTITUTIONS - NORTH DAKOTA/NOVA SCOTIA

Department of Landscape Architecture, (B.L.A., E.D.L., M.LAR.), Head: ARTHUR R. RICE; Phone: 919-515-2204
Department of Marine, Earth, and Atmospheric Sciences, (B.S., M.S., Ph.D.), Head: DR. LEONARD J. PIETRAFESA; Phone: 919-515-3717
Department of Parks, Recreation, and Tourism Management, (B.S., M.S., M.R.R.), Head: DR. PHILLIP S. REA; Phone: 919-515-3675
Department of Soil Science, (B.S., M.S., M.N.R.A., Ph.D.), Head: DR. EUGENE J. KAMPRATH; Phone: 919-515-2655
Department of Toxicology, (M.S., M.T., Ph.D.), Head: DR. ERNEST HODGSON; Phone: 919-515-2274
Department of Zoology, (B.S., M.S., M.L.S., M.W.B., Ph.D.), Head: DR. HAROLD F. HEATWOLE; Phone: 919-515-2741
Program in Ecology, (M.S.); Program in Environmental Sciences, (B.S.), Coordinator: DR. JAMES D. GREGORY; Phone: 919-515-1963
Program in Fisheries and Wildlife Sciences, (B.S.), Coordinator: DR. RICHARD L. NOBLE; Phone: 919-515-7586
Program in Natural Resources, (B.S.), Coordinator: DR. JAMES D. GREGORY; Phone: 919-515-7567
Program in Wildlife Biology, (M.S., M.W.B.), Coordinator: DR. RICHARD L. NOBLE; Phone: 919-515-7586

NORTH CAROLINA STATE UNIVERSITY, Center for World Environment and Sustainable Development
Campus Box 7621, Raleigh, NC 27695-7621
Phone: 919-515-5300
Founded: 1989
Description: The Center is a research and teaching consortium involving nearly 400 faculty members of Duke University, North Carolina State University, and the University of North Carolina at Chapel Hill, who work on international environmental issues. Areas of interest include; tropical conservation and development; environment in central Asia and Eastern Europe; and global climate change.
Contact(s):
Chair: DR. ROBERT G. HEALY; Phone: 919-684-6090

UNIVERSITY OF NORTH CAROLINA AT ASHEVILLE, Environmental Science Program
One University Heights, Asheville, NC 28804-3299
Phone: 704-251-6441; Fax: 704-251-6041; Email: drobbins@unca.edu
Description: The undergraduate environmental education offers four degrees options in ecology, pollution control, earth science, and natural resource management. The program started in 1983 and presently has about 200 majors. Required internship program, numerous research opportunities in an environmentally diverse region in areas such as ecology, wetlands restoration, lead and pesticides contamination, and waste analysis.
Contact(s):
Contact: DR. RICHARD P. MAAS, Robinson Hall, Univ. of NC at Asheville, Asheville, NC 28804

UNIVERSITY OF NORTH CAROLINA AT CHAPEL HILL
Chapel Hill, NC 27599-7400
Phone: 919-966-1171
Contact(s):
Air, Radiation, and Industrial Hygiene: DR. RICHARD KAMENS; Phone: 919-966-5452
Aquatic and Atmospheric Sciences: DR. RUSSELL F. CHRISTMAN; Phone: 919-966-1683
Ecology, (M.S., Ph.D.), Chairman: DR. SETH R. REICE; Phone: 919-962-1375
Environmental Health Sciences: DR. LOUISE M. BALL; Phone: 919-966-7306
Environmental Management and Policy: DR. AL TURNER JR.; Phone: 919-966-3850
Environmental Sciences and Engineering, Chairman: DR. WILLIAM H. GLAZE; Phone: 919-966-1024
Institute for Environmental Studies, Director: DR. FREDERIC PFAENDER; Phone: 919-966-3842
Marine Sciences, Chairman: CHRISTOPHER MARTENS; Phone: 919-962-0152
Water Resources Engineering: DR. PHILIP C. SINGER; Phone: 919-962-3865

UNIVERSITY OF NORTH CAROLINA AT CHAPEL HILL, School of Public Health/Environmental Resource Program
CB# 7400 Rosenau Hall, Chapel Hill, NC 27514
Phone: 919-966-7754; Fax: 919-966-5692
Founded: 1985
Description: The ERP was established to link the resources of the University with the citizens of North Carolina. Since its inception, the ERP has provided information, technical assistance, and training to citizen groups, local governments, and school teachers, and has facilitated collaborative decisionmaking about environmental issues. The ERP has three main program areas: community environmental education, teacher training, and collaborative decisionmaking.
Contact(s):
Associate Director: DR. MELVA OKUN
Director: DR. FRANCES LYNN
Outreach Coordinator: MARGARET NEWBOLD
Research Coordinator: GINA SANGUINETTI

NORTH DAKOTA

NORTH DAKOTA STATE UNIVERSITY
Stevens Hall, Fargo, ND 58105
Phone: 701-231-7087; Fax: 701-231-7149; Email: bleier@plains.nodak.edu; WWW: www.ndsu.nodak.edu/zoology/
Contact(s):
Wildlife and Fisheries Biology Option in Zoology, (B.A., B.S., M.S., Ph.D.), Advisor: DR. W. J. BLEIER

UNIVERSITY OF NORTH DAKOTA
Grand Forks, ND 58202-9019
Phone: 701-777-2621
Contact(s):
Fishery Research Unit, (B.S., M.S., Ph.D.), Leader: DR. STEVEN KELSCH
Wildlife, (B.S., M.S., Ph.D.), Coordinator: DR. RICHARD D. CRAWFORD

NOVA SCOTIA

ACADIA UNIVERSITY
Wolfville, Nova Scotia B0P 1X0 Canada
Phone: 902-542-2201
Founded: 1838
Description: Primarily an undergraduate university, emphasizing a liberal education in a balanced blend of arts, science, and professional studies. Masters degrees are offered in biology, chemistry, computer science, economics, education, english, geology, political sciecne, physiology, and sociology.
Contact(s):
Environmental Chemistry, (B.Sc., Hon., M.Sc.): DAVID A. STILES
Environmental Geology, (B.Sc., Hon., M.Sc.): BARRY CAMERON
Recreation Management, (B.A., B.Sc.): JUDE HIRSCH
Wildlife, Fisheries, Aquatic Biology, Marine Ecology, Mammalogy, Animal Behavior, Ornithology, (B.Sc., Hon.; M.Sc.): SOREN BONDRUP-NIELS

EDUCATIONAL INSTITUTIONS - OHIO/ONTARIO

DALHOUSIE UNIVERSITY, School for Resource and Environmental Studies (SRES)
1312 Robie St., Halifax, Nova Scotia B3H 3E2 Canada
Phone: 902-494-3632; Fax: 902-494-3728; Email: sres@is.dal.ca
Founded: 1975
Description: Graduate school within the Faculty of Management of Dalhousie University, offering a master of environmental studies (M.E.S.) degree, through two year programme (thesis required). Emphasis of programme is on policy and management aspects.
Contact(s):
Director: PETER M. DUIKER
Librarian: JUDITH G. READE; Phone: 902-494-1359; Fax: 902-494-3728; Email: reade@is.dal.ca

OHIO

ANTIOCH COLLEGE
Yellow Springs, OH 45387
Phone: 937-767-7331; Fax: 937-767-6323
Contact(s):
Biology: JILL YAGER; Email: jyager@antioch-college.edu
Chemistry: KABUIKA BUTAMINA; Email: kbutamina@antioch-college.edu
Geology: TOM ARSMAN; Email: tayrsman@antioch-college.edu
Physics and Solar Energy/Alternative Technology: CHARLES TAYLOR; Email: ctaylor@antioch-college.edu

BOWLING GREEN STATE UNIVERSITY
Center for Environmental Programs, Bowling Green, OH 43403
Phone: 419-372-8207; Email: rthibau@bgnet.bgsu.edu)
Description: Offer undergraduate environmental degree programs in Arts and Sciences, Environmental Policy, and Analysis/Environmental Science)/Health and Human Services.
Contact(s):
Director: ROGER E. THIBAULT
Environmental Resource Library, Librarian: ELEANOR CONNOR

HOCKING COLLEGE, School of Natural Resources and Ecological Sciences
3301 Hocking Parkway, Nelsonville, OH 45764
Phone: 740-753-3591; Fax: 740-753-2021; WWW: www.hockng.edu
Founded: 1969
Description: The mission of our Hocking College School of Natural Resources and Ecological Sciences is to prepare individuals for careers as technicians in the natural resources profession. Emphasis is placed on basic theory, developing a sustained postive work ethic, and the practical application of the development of the competencies required for entry-level positions in recreation and wildlife, forestry,timber harvesting/tree care, and a wide variety of land managemetn technology fields.
Contact(s):
Dean: RUSSELL K. TIPPETT; Phone: 740-753-3591 ext 2317; Email: tippet_r@hocking.edu
Fisheries, Biologist: LLOYD D. WRIGHT
Wildlife, Biologist: ALBERT LECOUNT

MIAMI UNIVERSITY
Boyd Hall, Oxford, OH 45056
Phone: 513-529-5811; Fax: 513-529-5814
Contact(s):
Architecture, (A.B., M.A.), Chairman: ROBERT A. BENSON
Botany, (A.B., B.S., M.A., Ph.D.), Chairman: DAVID A. FRANCKO
Chemistry, (A.B., B.S., M.S., Ph.D.), Chairman: MICHAEL NOVAK
Geography, (A.B., M.A.) Chairman: JOHN C. KLINK
Institute of Environmental Sciences, (M.En.), Director: GENE E. WILLEKE; Email: willekge@muohio.edu
Zoology, (A.B., B.S., M.A., M.S., Ph.D.), Chairman: DOUGLAS B. MEIKLE

OBERLIN COLLEGE, Environmental Studies Program
Rice Hall, OH
Phone: 216-775-8747; Fax: 216-775-8124; WWW: www.oberlin.edu/~envs/
Description: An interdisciplinary program which includes 30+ courses across ten departments. Students are required to do significant academic work that spans the sciences, social sciences, and the humanities. The program offers significant off-campus opportunities for students through a Watershed Education Program, a local initiative in sustainable agriculture, and work with the city on energy and development issues.
Contact(s):
Director: DAVID ORR

OHIO STATE UNIVERSITY, School of Natural Resources
2021 Coffey Rd., Columbus, OH 43210
Phone: 614-292-2265
Contact(s):
Cooperative Wildlife and Fishery Research Unit, (B.S., M.S., Ph.D.), Leader: DR. DEANA STOUDER
Cooperative Wildlife and Fishery Research, Assistant Leader: MARTIN STAPANIAN
Department of Landscape Architecture, (B.L.A., M.L.A.):
Department of Zoology, College of Biological Fisheries Biology, (B.S., M.S., Ph.D.): DR. PETER PAPPAS
Interim Director, (B.S., M.S., Ph.D.): DR. GARY W. MULLINS

SHAWNEE STATE UNIVERSITY
940 Second St., Portsmouth, OH 45662
Phone: 614-354-3205; Fax: 614-355-2416
Contact(s):
Natural Science, (B.S.), Environmental Certificate Advisor: JEFFREY BAUER; Phone: 614-355-2239; Fax: 614-355-2546

UNIVERSITY OF AKRON, Center for Environmental Studies
Akron, OH 44325-4102
Phone: 330-972-7991; Email: AFOOS@uakron.edu; WWW: www.uakron.edu/envstudies/
Contact(s):
Director: DR. ANNABELLE FOOS

OKLAHOMA

OKLAHOMA STATE UNIVERSITY
Stillwater, OK 74078
Phone: 405-744-5000
Contact(s):
Cooperative Fish and Wildlife Research Unit, Leader: DR. DAVID M. LESLIE JR., 404 Life Sciences West, ; Phone: 405-744-6243
Department of Botany, (B.S., M.S., Ph.D.), Head: DR. JAMES D. OWNBY; Phone: 405-744-5559
Department of Forestry, (B.S., M.S.), Head: DR. EDWIN L. MILLER; Phone: 405-744-5437
Department of Wildlife/Fisheries/Ecology/Zoology, (B.S., M.S., Ph.D.), Head: DR. JAMES H. SHAW; Phone: 405-744-5555
Environmental Science, (M.S., Ph.D), Program Coordinator: DR. EDWARD T. KNOBBE; Phone: 405-744-9229
Range Management, (B.S., M.S., Ph.D.), Program Coordinator: DR. DAVID M. ENGLE, 477 Ag Hall, Stillwater, OK 74078; Phone: 405-744-6410

ONTARIO

LAKEHEAD UNIVERSITY
Thunder Bay, Ontario P7B 5E1 Canada
Contact(s):
Forestry/Diploma in Integrated Forest Resources Management, Dean: DR. D. EULER; Phone: 807-343-8623
Wildlife, Emeritus: DR. HAROLD G. CUMMING; Phone: 807-343-8280

UNIVERSITY OF GUELPH
Guelph, Ontario N1G 2W1 Canada
Phone: 519-824-4120
Contact(s):
Fisheries Biology: DR. G. VON DERKROAK
Fisheris Science:
Marine Biology: DR. J. BALLANTYNE
Wildlife Diseases: DR. R. C. ANDERSON
Wildlife Ecology: DR. R. J. BROOKS
Wildlife Ethology: DR. D. NOAKE
Wildlife Management: DR. V. G. THOMAS

UNIVERSITY OF TORONTO
Toronto, Ontario M5S 3B3 Canada
Phone: 416-978-6152; Email: gradprog@forestry.utoronto.ca;
WWW: www.forestry.utoronto.ca
Contact(s):
Faculty of Forestry, (B.A., M.F.C., M.Sc.F., Ph.D.), Dean: DR. RORKE B. BRYAN

YORK UNIVERSITY, Environmental Studies
355 Lumbers Bldg. 4700 Keele St., Toronto, Ontario M3J 1P3 Canada
Phone: 416-736-5252; Fax: 416-736-5679; Email: fesinfo@yorku.ca; WWW: www.yorku.ca/faculty/fes
Founded: 1968
Description: The faculty of Environmental Studies offers interdisciplinary, flexible, individualized programs at both the undergraduate and graduate levels. FES is committed to a broad definition of environment, offering the opportunity to study natural, built, organizational, and social environments.
Contact(s):
Dean: PETER VICTOR

OREGON

OREGON STATE UNIVERSITY
Corvallis, OR 97331
Phone: 503-737-0123
Contact(s):
Center for Analysis of Environmental Change, Director of Environment: DR. MICHAEL H. UNSWORTH
Consortium on Social Values of Natural Resources, Coordinator of Outdoor Recreation: DR. GEORGE H. STANKEY
Cooperative Fishery Research Unit, Leader of Fishery: DR. CARL B. SCHRECK
Cooperative Park Studies Unit, Leader of Outdoor Recreation: DR. EDWARD E. STARKEY
Cooperative Wildlife Research Unit, Leader of Wildlife: DR. ROBERT G. ANTHONY
Fisheries and Wildlife, (B.S., M.S., Ph.D.), Head of Wildlife: DR. ERIK K. FRITZELL
Forest and Rangeland Ecosystem Science Center, Director of Forestry: DR. MICHAEL W. COLLOPY
Forestry and Forest Recreation, (B.S., M.S., Ph.D.), Dean: DR. GEORGE W. BROWN
Rangeland Resources, (B.S., M.S., Ph.D), Head of Range: DR. WILLIAM KRUEGER
Sustainable Forestry Program, Leader of Forestry: DR. STEVEN R. RADOSEVICH

OREGON STATE UNIVERSITY, Lewis and Clark College
Portland, OR 97219
Description: Strong environmental law training program (Environmental Law Certificate at J.D. level and specialized LL.M. in Environmental and Natural Resources Law); publish journal of Environmental Law; research program in Natural Resources Law Institute (newsletter: NRLI News); conferences and workshops through continuing education program; internships in natural resources; and environmental clinical opportunities.

OREGON STATE UNIVERSITY, Northwestern School of Law
10015 SW Terwilliger Blvd., Portland, OR 97219
Contact(s):
Dean: JAMES HUFFMAN; Phone: 503-768-6602
Environmental and Natural Resources Law Program, Director: JANICE WEIS; Phone: 503-768-6649; Fax: 503-768-6671; Email: jweis@clark.edu

PORTLAND STATE UNIVERSITY, Environmental Sciences and Resources
P.O. Box 751, Portland, OR 97207-0751
Phone: 503-725-4980; Fax: 503-725-3888; Email: envir@pdx.edu
Description: The focus of the program is research on the problems of the environment and resources. The program offers Ph.D. degrees in cooperation with the participating departments of biology, chemistry, civil engineering, economics, geography, geology, and physics. Master programs include MS, MEM (Master of Environmental Management), and MST (Master of Science in Teaching). Bachelor's programs (B.A., B.S.) include tracks in environmental science and environmental policy and management.
Contact(s):
Director: JAMES R. PRATT

SOUTHERN OREGON STATE COLLEGE, Treasure Valley Community College
650 College Blvd., Ontario, OR 97914
Phone: 503-889-6493
Description: Offers natural resource education, both lower division transfer and professional/technical. Forestry, range management surveying, wildland fire management, and wildlife management.
Contact(s):
Department of Natural Resources, Chairman: KEN KNOTHE

SOUTHERN OREGON UNIVERSITY, Environmental Education Program
Biology Department, Ashland, OR 97520
Phone: 541-552-6797; Email: janes@sou.edu,jessup@sou.edu
Founded: 1990
Description: This graduate program grants a Master of Science degree, and provides hands-on learning experiences in conservation biology, interpretive practices, field interpretation, and field studies in southwestern Oregon and elsewhere in the state for students committed to careers in environmental education. Studies are also required in biology and related disciplines of choice to complete the program.
Contact(s):
Contact: DR. STEWART JANES

UNIVERSITY OF OREGON, School of Law
Eugene, OR 97403
Phone: 503-686-3823
Contact(s):
Dean: MAURICE J. HOLLAND
Western Natural Resource Law Clinic, Director: MICHAEL D. AXLINE

PENNSYLVANIA

CALIFORNIA UNIVERSITY OF PENNSYLVANIA
250 University Ave., California, PA 15419-1394
Phone: 724-938-4200; Fax: 724-938-5743
Contact(s):
Biology, (B.S., M.S.Option), Chair: DR. DAVID BOEHM; Phone: 724-938-4200
Environmental Conservation (Option): DR. THOMAS MOON; Phone: 724-938-4200
Environmetnal Pollution Control (Option): DR. WILLIAM KIMMEL; Phone: 724-938-4213
Environmetnal Science (Option): DR. ALLAN MILLER; Phone: 724-938-4200

EDUCATIONAL INSTITUTIONS - QUEBEC/QUEBEC

Wildlife Biology (Option): DR. WILLIAM GUILIANO; Phone: 724-938-4215

CALIFORNIA UNIVERSITY OF PENNSYLVANIA, Environmental Studies
Description: The emphasis of this program is in applied aspects of environmental problems and human interactions with the environment. The program is biology and science based with options in conservation, science, pollution control, and wildlife biology. Master of Sc
Degrees: B.S.
Contact(s):
Program Director: DR. ALLAN MILLER; Phone: 724-938-4462

DREXEL UNIVERSITY, School of Environmental Science, Engineering, and Policy
32nd and Chestnut St., Philadelphia, PA 19104
Phone: 215-895-2266
Description: Environmental Engineering and Science undergraduate and graduate study is offered by the School of Environmental Science, Engineering, and Policy at Drexel University. Over 25 faculty participate in SESEP programs. Degrees available with specializations in air pollution, environmental assessment, environmental biotechnology, environmental chemistry, environmental health, hazardous and solid waste, subsurface contaminant hydrology, water and wastewater treatment, and wataer resources. Programs are offered on a full or part-time basis.
Degrees: (B.S., M.S., Ph.D.)
Contact(s):
Associate Director: CLAIRE WELTY; Phone: 215-895-2281; Email: weltyc@dunxl.ocs.drexel.edu
Director: MICHAEL A. GEALT; Phone: 215-895-2265; Email: gealt@dunxl.ocs.drexel.edu

PENNSYLVANIA STATE UNIVERSITY, School of Forest Resources
113 Ferguson Bldg., University Park, PA 16802
Phone: 814-863-7093
Contact(s):
Director: DR. LARRY A. NIELSEN; Phone: 814-863-7093
Ecology, (M.S., M.E.P.C., M.Eng), Chair: DR. HERSCHEL ELLIOT, 208 Ag Sciences and Industries Bldg., ; Phone: 814-865-6942
Environmental Resource Management, (B.S.), Coordinator: DR. LAMARTING HOOD, 208 Ag Sciences and Industries Bldg., ; Phone: 814-865-6942
Fisheries and Wildlife Cooperative Research Unit, Leader: DR. ROBERT F. CARLINE, 112A Merkle Bldg., ; Phone: 814-865-4511
Forest Resources, (B.S., M.S., Ph.D.), Professor: DR. KIM C. STEINER, 213 Ferguson Bldg., ; Phone: 814-865-9351
Wildlife and Fisheries, (B.S., M.S., Ph.D.), Contact: DR. JAY R. STAUFFER JR., 2C Ferguson Bldg., ; Phone: 814-865-0645
Wood Products, (B.S., M.S., Ph.D.), Professor: DR. PETER LABOSKY, 309 Forest Resources Laboratory, ; Phone: 814-865-7423

SLIPPERY ROCK UNIVERSITY
Slippery Rock, PA 16057
Phone: 724-738-0512
Contact(s):
Environmental Education, (B.S., M.Ed.), Coordinator: DR. DAN DZIUBEK; Phone: 724-738-2958
Environmental Science, (B.S.), Program Coordinator: DR. MICHAEL STAPLETON; Phone: 724-738-2495
Environmental Studies, (B.S.), Coordinator: DR. BEVERLY BUCHERT; Phone: 724-738-2389
Institute for the Environment Executive, Committee Chair: DR. DAN DZIUBEK; Phone: 724-738-2958
Park and Resource Management, (B.S., M.S.), Chairman: BRUCE BOLIVER; Phone: 724-738-2068
Pennsylvania Center for Environmental Education, Director: DR. PAULETTE JOHNSON; Phone: 724-738-4555

Sustainable Systems, (M.S.), Coordinator: DR. KAREN KAINER; Phone: 724-738-2622

UNIVERSITY OF PENNSYLVANIA
Philadelphia, PA 19104-6311
Phone: 215-898-6591; Fax: 215-573-3770; Email: jdhunt@pobox.upenn.edu; WWW: www.upenn.edu/gsfa/larp
Contact(s):
Departmen of Landscape Architecture and Regional Planning, (M.L.A., M.R.P.), Chairman: JOHN DIXON HUNT

UNIVERSITY OF PITTSBURGH
Pittsburgh, PA 15260
Phone: 412-624-4141
Contact(s):
Department of Biological Sciences, Chairman: DR. DAVID BURGESS; Phone: 412-624-4350; Fax: 412-624-4759
Ecology and Pymatuning Laboratory of Ecology, (M.S., Ph.D.), Director: STEPHEN J. TONSOR, 13142 Hartstown Rd., Linesville, PA 16424; Phone: 814-683-5813; Fax: 814-683-2302; Email: pymatuning@gremian.org
Environmental Health, (M.P.H., M.S., D.Sci.), Dean: DR. DONALD R. MATTISON; Phone: 412-624-3001

WIDENER UNIVERSITY, Department of Civil Engineering
One University Pl., Chester, PA 19013-5792
Phone: 610-499-4042; Fax: 610-499-4059
Description: The Department of Civil Engineering at Widener University offers undergraduate and graduate degrees which include courses in water resources, solid waste management, and environmental engineering. Continuing education seminars are taught in solid waste management and recycling. Research and development performed in solid waste and recycling.
Contact(s):
Chair: DR. CHARLES L. BARTHOLOMEW
Waste Management Programs, Coordinator: DR. RONALD L. MERSKY
Wolfgram Memorial Library: THERESEA TABORSKY, One University Pl., Chester, PA 19013-5792; Phone: 610-499-4087

WILKES UNIVERSITY, Geo-Environmental Sciences/Engineering Dept.
Wilkes Barre, PA 18766
Description: The department offers two degree programs. The Environmental Engineering cirriculum highlights a balance among the basic areas of water and waste-water engineering, water quality measurement, air pollution measurement and control technology, as well as the more recent demands in the areas of hazardous and solid waste management. The Earth and Environmental Science cirriculum requires a concentration of departmental electives that can be used to create an area of specialization such as geology or environmental science.
Contact(s):
Chairman: DALE A. BRUNS; Phone: 717-408-4610; Fax: 717-408-1003

QUEBEC

UNIVERSITE LAVAL
Quebec G1K 7P4 Canada
Contact(s):
Argiculture, (M.S., Ph.D.), Contact: ANDRE GOSSELIN; Phone: 418-656-7234; Fax: 416-656-7856
Forestry, Wood, and Forest Sciences Department, (B.S., M.S., Ph.D.), Contact: MICHEL DESSUREAULT; Phone: 418-656-7128; Fax: 418-656-3177

RHODE ISLAND

BROWN UNIVERSITY, Center for Environmental Studies
Box 1943, Providence, RI 02912
Phone: 401-863-3449; Fax: 401-863-3503; WWW: www.brown.edu/departments/environmental_studies
Founded: 1978
Description: The Center for Environmental Studies offers three interdisciplinary degrees (A.B., Sc.B., and M.A.) in environmental problem-solving; coordinates and facilitates environmental efforts within the university community; and collaborates with both state government agencies and community-based groups on projects to improve environmental quality for all Rhode Island residents. All programs aim to integrate teaching, scholarship, and service.
Contact(s):
Administrator Manager: PATTI CATON
Director: HAROLD R. WARD

BROWN UNIVERSITY, Rhode Island School of Design
Providence, RI 02903
Phone: 401-331-3511
Contact(s):
Landscape Architecture, (B.L.A., M.L.A.), Head: COLGATE SEARLE

ROGER WILLIAMS UNIVERSITY, College of Arts and Sciences
Bristol, RI 02903
Contact(s):
Dean: RON AMBROSETTI
Director: Center for Economic and Environmental Development: MARK GOULD

ROGER WILLIAMS UNIVERSITY, Division of Science and Mathematics
Bristol, RI 02809
Phone: 401-254-3087; Fax: 401-254-3480; E-mail; Email: mgould@acc.rwu.edu
Founded: 1969
Description: Provides undergraduate training in the sciences. Specializes in marine biology and biotechnology.
Contact(s):
President: ANTHONY SANTORO

UNIVERSITY OF RHODE ISLAND, Department of Natural Resources Science
Kingston, RI 02881
Phone: 401-792-2495; Fax: 401-874-4561; E-mail; Email: NATRES@uriacc.uri.edu)
Description: The teaching mission of the Department of Natural Resources Science is to help students acquire the technical knowledge and practical skills needed to understand and wisely manage natural and disturbed ecosystems and their basic components: soil, water, air and biota. The research mission of the department is to use hypthesis-based methods of scientific inquiry toward development of applicable solutions to environmental problems.
Contact(s):
Wildlife Biology and Mangement/Environmental Management/Soil and Water Resources, (B.S., M.S.), Chairman: DR. PETER V. AUGUST

SASKATCHEWAN

UNIVERSITY OF REGINA
Regina, Saskatchewan S4S 0A2 Canada
Phone: 306-585-4145
Contact(s):
Department of Biology/Wildlife/Animal Behavior/Plant Ecology, (B.Sc., B.Ssc. Hon., M.Sc., Ph.D.), Contact: DR. WILLIAM CHAPCO

UNIVERSITY OF SASKATCHEWAN
Saskatoon, Saskatchewan S7N 0W0 Canada
Phone: 306-966-4944
Contact(s):
Department of Crop Science and Plant Ecology, Chairman: DR. M. D. DEVINE

SOUTH CAROLINA

CLEMSON UNIVERSITY
Contact(s):
Clemson Institute of Environmenal Toxicology, (M.S., Ph.D.), Chair: DR. JOHN RODGERS, 509 Westinghouse Drive, Pendleton, SC 29670; Phone: 864-646-2239
Environmental Engineering and Science, (M.Engr., M.S., Ph.D.), Chair: DR. ALAN W. ELZERMAN, 156 Linvil G. Rich Environmental Research Laboratory, Clemson, SC 29634; Phone: 864-656-5568
Forest Resources, (M.F.R., M.S., Ph.D.), Interim Chair: DR. ALLEN DUNN, 261 Lehotsky Hall, Clemson, SC 29634; Phone: 964-656-3302
Park, Recreation & Tourism Management, (M.P.R.T.M, M.S., Ph.D.), Chair: DR. ANN JAMES, 263 Lehofsky Hall, Clemson, SC 29634; Phone: 864-656-3400

CLEMSON UNIVERSITY, Aquaculture, Fisheries,and Wildlife
G08 Lehotsky Hall, Clemson, SC 29634
Phone: 803-656-3117
Description: The curriculum leading to a B.S. degree provides a solid foundation in basic and applied science, social science, and communication skills. Emphasis areas permit students to broaden their technical knowledge in their chosen career path. Those interested in pursuing a graduate degree program in aquaculture, fisheries, or wildlife management shoud have sound undergraduate training in the biological or related sciences. Programs of study are designed to emphasize relationships between wild animals and their changing environments, or production of aquatic organisms. The graduate program in wildlife biology is accredited by the Southeastern Section of the Wildlife Society.
Degrees: (B.S., M.S., Ph.D.)
Contact(s):
Chair: DR. JOHN R. SWEENEY

UNIVERSITY OF SOUTH CAROLINA, Baruch Marine Field Laboratory
P.O. Box 1630, Georgetown, SC 29442
Phone: 843-546-3623
Contact(s):
Resident Director: DR. DENNIS M. ALLEN; Phone: 843-546-3623; Email: dallen@belle.baruch.sc.edu

UNIVERSITY OF SOUTH CAROLINA, The Marine Science Program
Columbia, SC 29208
Description: The Marine Science Program, in the College of Science and Mathematics at the University of South Carolina, is an interdisciplinary educational program offering curricula which lead to the bachelor of science, master of science, and doctor pf philosophy degrees.
Contact(s):
Belle W. Baruch Institute for Marine Biology and Coastal Research, Director: DR. MADYLYN FLETCHER; Phone: 803-777-5288; Email: fletcher@brol.sc.edu
Marine Science Program, (B.S., M.S., Ph.D.), Director: DR. MADYLYN FLETCHER; Phone: 803-777-5288

EDUCATIONAL INSTITUTIONS - SOUTH DAKOTA/TEXAS

SOUTH DAKOTA

SOUTH DAKOTA STATE UNIVERSITY, Department of Wildlife Fisheries Sciences
P.O. Box 2140B, Brookings, SD 57007-1696
Phone: 605-688-6121; Fax: 605-688-4515; Email: longielj@mg.sdstate.edu
Description: Fish and wildlife research, education, and services with emphasis on prairie pothole ecology, fisheries management, wildlife management, and fisheries and wildlife ecology.
Contact(s):
Cooperative Fish and Wildlife Research Unit, Leader: DR. CHARLES R. BERRY
Head: DR. CHARLES G. SCALET
Wildlife and Fisheries Sciences, (B.S., M.S., Ph.D.):

TENNESSEE

MIDDLE TENNESSEE STATE UNIVERSITY, Biology Department
Box 60, Murfreesboro, TN 37132
Phone: 615-898-5615/5449
Contact(s):
DR. CINDI SMITH-WALTERS
DR. PADGETT KELLY

MIDDLE TENNESSEE STATE UNIVERSITY, Center for Environmental/Energy Education
Description: The MTSU Center for Environmental and Energy Education (CEEE) provides a wide range of workshops and activities in the MTSU service area. The Center maintains a video and material library that is free to area educators.

TENNESSEE TECHNOLOGICAL UNIVERSITY
Cookeville, TN 38505
Phone: 615-372-3134
Contact(s):
Cooperative Fishery Research Unit, Acting Leader: DR. JAMES B. LAYZER
Wildlife and Fisheries Science, (B.S., M.S.), Chairman: DR. M. J. HARVEY

UNIVERSITY OF TENNESSEE AT KNOXVILLE
Knoxville, TN 37901
Phone: 423-974-7126; Fax: 423-974-4714
Description: Offer B.S. degree in forestry, forest management concentration, wildland recreation concentration, M.S.in forestry, Thesis and Non-Thesis Option, and B.S. and M.S. degrees in wildlife and fisheries science.
Contact(s):
Professor and Department Head: DR. GEORGE M. HOPPER

UNIVERSITY OF TENNESSEE AT MARTIN, School of Agriculture and Human Environment
Martin, TN 38238
Phone: 901-587-7250
Description: Provides a B.S. degree in natural resources management with concentrations in wildlife biology, environmental management, soil and water conservation, and park and recreation administration.
Contact(s):
Dean: DR. JIM BYFORD

UNIVERSITY OF THE SOUTH
Sewanee, TN 37901
Phone: 615-598-1479
Contact(s):
Natural Resources/Department of ForestryGeology, (B.S.), Chairman: PROF STEPHEN SHAVER

VANDERBILT UNIVERSITY
Box 1831-Station B, Nashville, TN 37235
Phone: 615-322-2697; WWW: www.vuse.@vanderbilt.edu/ceeinfo/cee.htm
Contact(s):
Environmetnal Engineering, (B.E., B.S., M.E., M.S., Ph.D.), Chairman: EDWARD L. THACKSTON

TEXAS

RICE UNIVERSITY
Houston, TX 77251
Phone: 713-527-8101
Contact(s):
Ecology and Evolutionary Biology, (B.S., M.A., Ph.D.): PAULA A. HARCOMBE
Energy and Environmental Systems Institute, (B.A., M.E.S., M.E.E., M.S., Ph.D.), Directory: C. H. WARD

RICE UNIVERSITY, School of Architecture
Houston, TX 77251
Contact(s):
Biochemistry and Cell Biology, Chair: KATHLEEN S. MATTHEWS
Dean: LARS LERUD

STEPHEN F. AUSTIN STATE UNIVERSITY, Arthur Temple College of Forestry
Nacogdoches, TX 75962-6109
Phone: 409-468-3301; Fax: 409-468-2489
Contact(s):
Biometrics, (Ph.D.): DR. DAVID LENHART
Dean: DR. R. SCOTT BEASLEY
Fire Ecology and Silviculture, (Ph.D.): DR. BRIAN OSWALD
Forest Eco-Physiology, (Ph.D.): DR. HANS M. WILLIAMS
Forest Economics, (Ph.D.): DR. GARY D. KRONRAD
Forest Entomology, (Ph.D.): DR. DAVID KULHAVY
Forest Hydrology, (Ph.D.): DR. MINGTEH CHANG
Forest Prodcuts, (D.F.): DR. EDWARD DOUGAL
Forest Recreation Management, (Ph.D.): DR. MICHAEL LEGG
Forest Wildlife Management, (Ph.D.): DR. JAMES C. KROLL
GIS/Remote Sensing, Contact: DR. ABU BADRUDDIN
Interpretation/Conflict Resolution, (Ph.D.): DR. PAUL H. RISK
Remote Sensins/Mensuration, Contact: DR. DANIEL UNGER
Siviculture/Forest Ecology, (Ph.D.): DR. MICHAEL FOUNTAIN
Soil Science, (Ph.D.): DR. KENNETH FARRISH
Wildlife Management, (Ph.D.): DR. R. MONTAGUE WHITING
Wood Science, (D.F.): DR. MALCOLM MACPEACK

TEXAS A&M UNIVERSITY AT COLLEGE STATION
College Station, TX 77843
Contact(s):
Forest Science, (B.S., M.S., M.Agr., Ph.D.), Interim Head: DR. ROBERT G. MERRIFIELD; Phone: 409-845-5000
Institute for Renewable Natural Resources, (B.S., M.Agr.), Director: DR. BOB BROWN; Phone: 409-845-5777
Rangeland Ecology and Management, (B.S., M.S., M.Agr., Ph.D.), Head: DR. BOB WHITSON; Phone: 409-845-5579
Recreation Parks, and Tourism Sciences, (B.S., M.S., M.Agr., Ph.D.), Head: DR. PETER A. WITT; Phone: 409-845-7324
Wildlife and Fisheries Sciences, (B.S., M.S., M.Agr., Ph.D.), Head: DR. BOB BROWN; Phone: 409-845-5777

TEXAS A&M UNIVERSITY AT COMMERCE
Phone: 903-886-5350
Founded: 1889
Description: Educational institution offering B.S. and M.S. degrees in agricultural fields, including pre-wildlife management programs.
Contact(s):
Department of Agricultural Sciences, (B.S., M.S.), Head: DR. DON CAWTHON

TEXAS A&M UNIVERSITY AT KINGSVILLE, Caesar Kleberg Wildlife Research Institute
Campus Box 218, Kingsville, TX 78363
Phone: 512-595-3922; Fax: 512-593-3924
Founded: 1981
Description: A nonprofit institute that emphasizes research on wildlife and range management in Texas. Some work also done in Mexico and Canada. Research specialties include deer, quail, waterfowl, endangered cats, and nongame wildlife.
Contact(s):
Director: DR. FRED C. BRYANT; Phone: 512-593-4025

TEXAS CHRISTIAN UNIVERSITY
P.O. Box 30798, Fort Worth, TX 76129
Phone: 817-921-7271; Fax: 817-921-7789; Email: L.Newland@tcu.edu
Contact(s):
Environmental Sciences, (B.S., M.S.), Director: DR. LEO NEWLAND

TEXAS TECH UNIVERSITY
Lubbock, TX 79409-2125
Phone: 806-742-2841; Fax: 806-742-2280; Email: c7wez@ttacs.ttu.edu; WWW: www.ttu.edu~rwfmhp
Contact(s):
Environmental Conservation of Natural Resources, (B.S.):
Range Management, (B.S.):
Range Science, (M.S., Ph.D.):
Wildlife and Fisheries Management, (B.S.):
Wildlife Science and Fisheries Science, (M.S., Ph.D.), Chairman: DR. PHILLIP J. ZWANK

UNIVERSITY OF HOUSTON, Cullen College of Engineering
Houston, TX 77204-4791
Contact(s):
Environmental Engineering Program, Program Director: DR. THEODORE G. CLEVELAND; Phone: 713-743-4250

UNIVERSITY OF NORTH TEXAS, Institute of Applied Sciences
NT Box 13078, Denton, TX 76203
Phone: 817-565-2694; Fax: 817-565-4297
Founded: 1976
Description: An interdisciplinary unit whose primary research activities are oriented towards land and water resources. Research includes aquatic toxicology, surface and groundwater quality, archaelogy, remote sensing, geographic information systems, and environmental modeling. Over 100 scientists, support staff, graduate and undergraduate students are involved in these activities.
Contact(s):
Aquatic Toxicology and Reservoir Limnology, Director: DR. WILLIAM T. WALLER; Phone: 817-565-2694
Center for Environmental Archaeology, Director: DR. REID FERRING; Phone: 817-565-2694
Center for Environmental Ecoonmics, Director: DR. MIKE NIESWIADOMY; Phone: 817-565-2573
Center for Remote Sensing, Director: DR. SAMUEL F. ATKINSON; Phone: 817-565-2694
Center for Spatial Analysis, Director: DR. ANDY SCHOOLMASTER; Phone: 817-565-2901
Director: DR. KENNETH L DICKSON
Environmental Chemistry Laboratory, Director: DR. FARIDA SALEH; Phone: 817-565-2694
Environmental Modeling Laboratory, Director: DR. MIGUEL ACEVEDO; Phone: 817-565-2091
Environmental Visualization Laboratory, Director: BRUCE HUNTER; Phone: 817-565-2694
Faculty for Environmental Ethics, Coordinator: DR. MAX OELSHLAEGER; Phone: 817-565-2266
Faculty for Environmental Philosophy, Executive Director: JAN DICKSON; Phone: 817-565-2727
Graduate Program in Environmental Ethics, (M.A.), Coordinator: DR. EUGENE C. HARGROVE; Phone: 817-565-2266
Graduate Program in Environmental Science, (M.S., Ph.D.), Coordinator: DR. SAMUEL F. ATKINSON; Phone: 817-565-2694
Interdisciplinary Graduate Studies, Dean: DR. SANDRA TERRELL
Water Research Field Station, Director: DR. JAMES H. KENNEDY; Phone: 817-565-2694
Wetlands Research, Director: DR. ROBERT DOYLE; Phone: 817-565-2694

UTAH

UTAH STATE UNIVERSITY, Berryman Institute for Wildlife Damage Management
Logan, UT 84321
Phone: 435-797-2436
Founded: 1990
Description: The Jack H. Berryman Institute is a national non-profit organization which is centered at Utah State University. It engages in research, education, and extension activities aimed at resolving human and wildlife conflicts, enhancing the positive aspects of wildlife, and increasing human tolerance of wildlife problems.
Contact(s):
Director: DR. MICHAEL CONOVER

UTAH STATE UNIVERSITY, College of Natural Resources
Logan, UT 84322
Phone: 801-797-2445
Contact(s):
Associate Dean: DR. FREDERICH H. WAGNER
Dean: DR. JOHN KADLEC
Division of Environmental Engineering, (M.S., Ph.D.), Head: DR. RONALD CHARLES SIMS
Fisheries and Wildlife, (B.S., M.S., Ph.D.), Head: DR. CHRIS LUECKE
Fisheries, Assistant Leader: DR. DAVID A. BEAUCHAMMP
Forest Resources, (B.S., M.S., Ph.D.), Head: DR. TERRY SHARIK
Geography and Earth Resources (B.S.), Head: DR. ALLAN FALCONER
Landscape Architecture, (B.L.A., M.L.A., B.S., M.S.), Head: RICHARD E. TOTH
Range Science, (B.S., M.S., Ph.D.), Head: DR. JOHN C. MALECHEK
S.J. and Jessie E. Quinney Natural Resources Research Library: CARLA HEISTER; Phone: 801-750-2464
Utah Cooperative Fishery and Wildlife Research Unit, Leader: DR. JOHN A. BISSONETTE
Watershed Science Unit, (B.S., M.S., Ph.D.), Director: DR. JAMES P. DOBROWOLSKI
Wildlife, Assistant Leader: DR. THOMAS C. EDWARDS JR.

UTAH STATE UNIVERSITY, Johnson State College
Logan, UT 84322
Contact(s):
Babcock Nature Preserve, Director: DR. JOHN WRAZEN
Biology, (B.S.): DR. CYRUS MCQUEEN
Department of Environmental and Health Sciences: ; Phone: 802-635-2356
Ecology: DR. JOHN WRAZEN
Environmental Chemistry and Environmental Education: DR. PAUL ABAJIAN
Environmental Science and Natural Resources, (B.S.): DR. MARGARET OTTUM
Life Science Teacher Certification: DR. CYRUS MCQUEEN

EDUCATIONAL INSTITUTIONS - VERMONT/VIRGINIA

VERMONT

STERLING COLLEGE
P.O. Box 72, Craftsbury Common, VT 05827-0072
Phone: 802-586-7711; Fax: 802-586-2596; Email: sterling@sterlingcollege.craftsbury.vt.us
Founded: 1958
Description: Sterling College offers one-and two-year college programs to provide a liberal education using environmental and natural resource studies in tandem with outdoor challenge activities, all within the context of an environmentally sustainable working model.
Contact(s):
Dean: EDWARD HOUSTON
Director of Admissions: JOHN ZABER
Director of Student Affairs: JIM ESDEN
Librarian: LISA SAMMET
President: JOHN E. WILLIAMSON

UNIVERSITY OF VERMONT, School of Natural Resources
Burlington, VT 05405
Phone: 802-656-4280
Contact(s):
Cooperative Fish and Wildlife Research Unit, Acting Leader: DR. DONALD L. PARRISH
Dean: DR. DONALD H. DEHAYES
Forestry, (B.S., M.S.): DR. CARLTON M. NEWTON
Natural Resources Planning, (M.S.): DR. CARLTON M. NEWTON
Natural Resources, (B.S., Ph.D.): DR. DONALD H. DEHAYES
Recreation Management, (B.S.): DR. ALPHONSE H. GILBERT
Resource Economics, (B.S.): DR. ALPHONSE H. GILBERT
The Environmental Sciences Program, (B.S.): DR. ALAN MCINTOSH
The Environmental Studies Program, (B.S., B.A.), Interim Director: DR. IAN A. WORLEY
Water Resources and Lake Studies Center, (M.S.), Director: DR. ALAN W. MCINTOSH
Wildlife and Fisheries Biology Program, (B.S., M.S.): DR. DAVID H. HIRTH

VERMONT LAW SCHOOL, Environmental Law Center
South Royalton, VT 05068
Phone: 802-763-8303
Description: The Environmental Law Center offers an accredited, interdisciplinary academic program leading to the degree of Master of Studies in Environmental Law (M.S.L.). The 30-credit, 12-month program is open to scientists, planners, administrators, lawyers, recent college graduates, and, on a joint-degree basis, to law students. The center also offers a summer session of environmental law and policy courses, open to nondegree and MSEL students.
Degrees: M.S.E.L., J.D.
Contact(s):
Dean: KINVIN L. WROTH
Director: PATRICK PARENTEAU

VIRGIN ISLANDS

UNIVERSITY OF THE VIRGIN ISLANDS
St. Thomas, VI 00802
Phone: 809-776-9200
Contact(s):
Division of Science and Mathematics, Chair: DR. LYNN ROSENTHAL; Phone: 340-693-1211; Fax: 340-693-1245
Eastern Caribbean Center, Director: DR. HENRY H. SMITH; Phone: 809-693-1021; Fax: 340-693-1025
MacLean Marine Science Center, Acting Director: DR. JAMES F. BATTEY; Phone: 340-693-1381; Fax: 340-693-1385
Maring Biology Major, St Thomas Campus, (B.S., B.S.), Vice President for Academic Affairs: DR. DENNIS F. PAUL; Phone: 340-693-1201; Fax: 340-693-1205

VIRGINIA

COLLEGE OF WILLIAM AND MARY, Virginia Institute of Marine Science/School of Marine Science
Gloucester Point, VA 23062
Phone: 804-642-7000
Founded: 1940
Description: A state institution founded for providing research, advisory services, and education for the public and for state and federal agencies responsible for managing marine resources.
Contact(s):
Associate Director of Development: PAGE HAYHURST; Phone: 804-684-7107
Biological Sciences, Chair: H. W. DUCKLOW; Phone: 804-684-7180
Dean and Director: L. DONELSON WRIGHT; Phone: 804-684-7103
Dean of Graduate Studies: JOHN D. MILLIMAN; Phone: 804-684-7105
Director of Library: CHARLES McFADDEN; Phone: 804-684-7114
Director of Planning and Budget: CAROLYN RIDGEWAY COOK; Phone: 804-684-7003
Director of Research and Advisory Services: E. M. BURRESON; Phone: 804-684-7108
Environmental Sciences, Chair: M. H. ROBERTS; Phone: 804-684-7260
Fisheries Sciences, Chair: J. E. GRAVES; Phone: 804-684-7352
Head of Marine Advisory Services: WILLIAM D. DUPAUL; Phone: 804-684-7164
Physical Sciences, Chair: S. A. KUEHL; Phone: 804-684-7118
Resource Management & Policy, Chair: C. H. HERSHNER JR.; Phone: 804-684-7387

FERRUM COLLEGE
Ferrum, VA 24088
Phone: 540-365-2121
Contact(s):
Agriculture, (B.S.): DR. WILLIAM MOORE; Phone: 540-365-4363
Biology, (B.S.): DR. BOB R. POHLAD; Phone: 540-365-4367
Chemistry, (B.S.):
Environmental Studies, (B.S.): DR. JOSEPH D. STOGNER; Phone: 540-365-4369
Forestry and Wildlife: DR. MICHAEL MENGAK; Phone: 540-365-4373; Email: mmengak@ferrum.edu
Leisure Services, (B.S., B.A.): DR. DEMPSLY HENSLEY; Phone: 540-365-4494
Medical Technology, (B.S.): RONALD STEPHENS
Recreation: DR. DEMPSLY HENSLEY
Stanley Library: DR. C. I. DILLION III; Phone: 540-365-2121

VIRGINIA POLYTECHNIC INSTITUTE AND STATE UNIVERSITY, College of Forestry & Wildlife Resources
Attn: Peggy Quarterman, 324 Cheatham Hall, Blacksburg, VA 24061-0324
Phone: 540-231-5481; Fax: 540-231-7664; Email: pquarter@vt.edu
Contact(s):
Center for Environmental and Hazardous Materials Studies, Director: DR. JOHN CAIRNS JR.; Phone: 540-231-7075
Cooperative Fish and Wildlife Unit, Leader: RICHARD J. NEVES; Phone: 540-231-5927; Email: mussel@vt.edu
Dean: DR. GREGORY N. BROWN; Email: browngn@vt.edu
Department of Fisheries and Wildlife Sciences, (B.S., M.S., Ph.D.), Head: DR. BRIAN R. MURPHY; Phone: 540-231-5573; Email: murphybr@vt.edu
Department of Forestry, (B.S., M.S., Ph.D.), Head: DR. HAROLD E. BURKHART; Phone: 540-231-5483; Email: burkhart@vt.edu
Department of Wood Science and Forest Products, (B.S., M.S., Ph.D.), Head: DR. GEZA IFJU; Phone: 540-231-8853; Email: ifju@vt.edu
U.S. Forest Service Coldwater and Trout Research Unit, Leader: DR. C. ANDREW DOLLOFF; Phone: 540-231-4864; Email: adoll@vt.edu

EDUCATIONAL INSTITUTIONS - WASHINGTON/WISCONSIN

WASHINGTON

HUXLEY COLLEGE OF ENVIRONMENTAL STUDIES, Division of Western Washington University
Bellingham, WA 98225
Phone: 360-650-3521
Description: Principally a two-year, upper division and M.S. program; B.A., B.S. in environmental studies; M.S. in environmental science. Also cooperative programs, M.S. in marine and estuarine science and M.A. in political science and environmental studies.
Contact(s):
Dean: Undergraduate majors in environmental policy and assessment, environmental education, environmental science, environmental studies, graduate tracks in environmental toxicology, applied ecology, and environmental chemistry: DR. BRADLEY F. SMITH
Director: Associated Research Institutes, Institute of Environmental Toxicology and Chemistry: DR. WAYNE LANDIS
Director: Institute for Watershed Studies: DR. ROBIN MATHEWS

MARINE SCIENCE CENTER
18743 Front St., NE, P.O. Box 2079, Poulsbo, WA 98370
Phone: 206-779-5549; Fax: 206-779-8960
Founded: 1968
Description: The Marine Science Center works to meet the science education needs of public citizens and of students and teachers nationally, regionally, and locally. Hands-on environmental education is at the heart of its mission and is reflected in direct instruction from its facility on Washington's State's Liberty Bay, part of the Puget Sound.
Contact(s):
Society President: MIKE SCOTT

WASHINGTON STATE UNIVERSITY
Pullman, WA 99164
Description: WSU has tripartite goals of providing higher education, research, and outreach/service programs relevant to the needs of Washington's citizens. The Department of Natural Resource Sciences (NRS) and Program in Environmental Science and Regional Planning (ESRP) are the chief academic units at WSU devoted to understanding, conserving, and managing natural resources, the environments they create, and the values such resources and environments provide to society. Landscape Architecture (L.A.) offers related programs focused on planning and designing land resources in an environmentally sound manner.
Contact(s):
Environmental Science and Regional Planning, (B.S., M.S., M.R.P., Ph.D.), Chair: WILLIAM BUDD; Phone: 509-335-8536
Horticulture and Landscape Architecture, (B.S., B.L.A.), Chair: CHARLES R. JOHNSON; Phone: 509-335-9502; Fax: 509-335-8690
Natural Resource Sciences, (B.S., M.S., Ph.D.), Chair: EDWARD J. DEPUIT; Phone: 509-335-6166; Fax: 509-335-7862

WEST VIRGINIA

SHEPHERD COLLEGE
Shepherdstown, WV 25443
Contact(s):
Park Administration, (B.S), Head: DR. CHARLES A. HULSE; Phone: 304-876-2511

WEST VIRGINIA UNIVERSITY
P.O. Box 6125, Morgantown, WV 26506
Phone: 304-293-2941
Contact(s):
Appalachian Hardwood Center, Director: DR. CURT HASSLER; Phone: 304-293-2941 ext 2451
Division of Forestry, (B.S., M.S., Ph.D.), Interim Director: DR. JAMES ARMSTRONG
Recreation and Parks Management, (B.S.R., M.S., Ph.D.), Program Coordinator: DR. GENE BAMMEL; Phone: 304-293-2941 ext 2415
Wildlife and Fisheries Management, (B.S., M.S., Ph.D.), Program Coordinator: DR. DAVE SAMUEL; Phone: 304-293-4797 ext 2496
Wood Industries, (B.S.F., M.S., Ph.D.), Program Coordinator: DR. JAMES ARMSTRONG; Phone: 304-293-2941 ext 2486

WISCONSIN

NORTHLAND COLLEGE, Sigurd Olson Environmental Institute
Ashland, WI 54806
Phone: 715-682-1223; Fax: 715-682-1218; Email: channa@wheeler.northland.edu
Founded: 1972
Description: The Sigurd Olson Environmental Institute was founded at Northland College in 1972 to increase public understanding of the complex relationships between natural and cultural environments in the Lake Superior region and to assist in developing workable solutions to regional environmental problems. The institute seeks to carry out Sigurd Olson's vision by fostering environmental citizenship and educating citizens for a sustainable future.
Contact(s):
Advisory Board Chair: EILEEN LONG
Communications Specialist: LAURENCE WILAND
Environmental Education Specialist: CLAYTON RUSSELL
Executive Director: KENNETH M. BRO
Lake Superior Program Coordinator: JANE SILBERSTEIN
LoonWatch Coordinator: TED GOSTOMSKI
Officer Manager: CAROLYN HANNA
Timber Wolf Alliance Coordinator: PAM TROXELL

ST. NORBERT COLLEGE, International Center
100 Grant St., De Pere, WI 54115-2099
Phone: 414-403-3100; Fax: 414-403-4083
Founded: 1990
Description: The Center conducts an Annual Global Ecology Series on themes such as the Great Lakes as an endangered Resource of north america, africa and women, population, and international policy-making. Instructional resources and in-service programs are provided for K-1
Contact(s):
President: DR. THOMAS A. MANION

UNIVERSITY OF WISCONSIN AT EAU CLAIRE
Eau Claire, WI 54701
Phone: 715-836-4166
Contact(s):
Biology, (B.S., M.S.), Chairman: DR. MICHAEL WEIL
Environmental Science; minor:
Geography, (B.S.), Chairman: DR. BRADY FOUST

UNIVERSITY OF WISCONSIN AT GREEN BAY, College of Environmental Science
2420 Nicolet Dr., Green Bay, WI 54311-7001
Phone: 920-465-2370
Description: Interdisciplinary curriculum with emphasis on the environment.
Contact(s):
Cofrin Arboretum, Director: DR. PAUL SAGER
Cofrin Library, Director: KATHY L PLETCHEN; Phone: 920-465-2383
College of Human Biology, (B.S., B.A.), Chair: DR. CHARLES IHRKE; Phone: 920-465-2681; Fax: 920-465-2376
Environmental Science and Policy, (M.S.) Coordinator: DR. CHARLES RHYNER; Phone: 920-465-2281
Environmental Science, (B.S.), Chair: DR. H. J. HARRIS; Phone: 920-465-2369; Fax: 920-465-2376
Public and Environmental Administration, (B.S., B.A.), Chair: DR. MICHAEL KRAFT; Phone: 920-465-2355; Fax: 920-465-2791

EDUCATIONAL INSTITUTIONS - WYOMING/WYOMING

Richter Natural History Museum, Curator: DR. ROBERT HOWE; Phone: 920-465-2272
UW-Green Bay Herbarium, Curator: DR. MICHAEL D. MORGAN; Phone: 920-465-2243

UNIVERSITY OF WISCONSIN AT LA CROSSE
4028-4032 Cowley Hall, La Crosse, WI 54601
Phone: 608-785-8238; Fax: 608-785-6959
Contact(s):
Biology and Microbiology including Aquatic Science Concentration, (B.S., M.S.), Chairman: DR. THOMAS CLAFLIN
Geography and Earth Science, (B.S.), Chairman: DR. GEORGE HUPPERT, 2004 Cowley Hall, ; Phone: 608-785-8333; Fax: 608-785-8332; Email: huppert@mail.uwlax.edu
River Studies Center, Director: MARK B. SANDHEINRICH

UNIVERSITY OF WISCONSIN AT MADISON, College of Agricultural and Life Sciences
1450 Linden Dr., Rm. 140, Madison, WI 53706
Phone: 608-262-4930
Contact(s):
Interim Dean: NEAL A. JORGENSEN

UNIVERSITY OF WISCONSIN AT MADISON, Institute for Environmental Studies (IES)
550 N. Park St., Science Hall, Madison, WI 53706
Phone: 608-265-5296
Description: The IES is an intercollege unit of the University of Wisconsin-Madison to promote, develop, and administer interdisciplinary environmental instruction, research, and public service programs. The Institute offers four graduate-level degrees, two optional graduate curricula, and an undergraduate certificate program.
Contact(s):
Director: DR. THOMAS M. YUILL

UNIVERSITY OF WISCONSIN AT MADISON, School of Natural Resources
1450 Linden Dr., Rm. 146, Madison, WI 53706
Phone: 608-262-6968
Description: The School of Natural Resources is within the college of Agricultural and Life Sciences. The school offers 13 undergraduate options in natural resources. Graduate instruction is available in many specialized and interdisciplinary areas.
Contact(s):
Director: KEVIN McSWEENEY

UNIVERSITY OF WISCONSIN AT STEVENS POINT
Stevens Point, WI 54481
Phone: 715-346-4617
Contact(s):
Cooperative Fishery Unit, (M.S.), Leader: DR. DANIEL W. COBLE
Environmental Education, (B.S., M.S.): DR. RANDY CHAMPEAU
Forestry, (B.S., M.S.): DR. ROBERT MILLER
Resources Management, (B.S., M.S.): DR. CHRISTING THOMAS
Soil Science, (B.S., M.S.): DR. RONALD HENSLER
Water Science, (B.S., M.S.): DR. STAN SZCZYTKO
Wildlife Degrees, (B.S., M.S.): DR. ERIC ANDERSON

UNIVERSITY OF WISCONSIN AT STEVENS POINT, College of Natural Resources
Description: Located in Central Wisconsin, the College of Natural Resources began in 1946 with the nation's first conservation education major. The College now has over 60 faculty and staff, 1,750 undergraduates and 80 graduate students. The college offers 16 majors and 13 minors.
Contact(s):
Associate Dean: DR. RICHARD WILKE
Dean: DR. ALAN HANEY

WYOMING

UNIVERSITY OF WYOMING
Laramie, WY 82071
Contact(s):
Department of Zoology and Physiology, (B.S., M.S., Ph.D.), Head: DR. NANCY STANTON, P.O. Box 3166, Laramie, WY 82071; Phone: 307-766-4207; Fax: 307-766-5625
National Park Service Research Center, Director: DR. HENRY J. HARLOW, P.O. Box 3166, Laramie, WY 82071; Phone: 307-766-4227
Wyoming Cooperative Fish and Wildlife Research Unit, (B.S., M.S., Ph.D.), Leader: DR. STEVEN H. ANDERSON, P.O. Box 3166, Laramie, WY 82071; Phone: 307-766-5415; Fax: 907-766-5400

CONSERVATION INFORMATION RESOURCES

FISH AND WILDLIFE COMMISSIONERS AND DIRECTORS OF THE UNITED STATES AND CANADA

UNITED STATES

Alabama Division of Game and Fish, 64 N. Union St., Montgomery, AL 36130 (334, 242-3465)
Director: CHARLES D. KELLEY

Alaska Department of Fish and Game, P.O. Box 25526, Juneau, AK 99802-5526 (907, 465-4100)
Commissioner: FRANK RUE

Arizona Game and Fish Department, 2221 W. Greenway Rd., Phoenix, AZ 85023 (602, 942-3000)
Director: DUANE SHROUFE

Arkansas Game and Fish Commission, #2 Natural Resources Dr., Little Rock, AR 72205 (501, 223-6305)
Director: STEVE N. WILSON

California Department of Fish and Game, P.O. Box 944209, Sacramento, CA 94244-2090 (916, 653-7664)
Director: JACQUELINE SCHAFER

Colorado Division of Wildlife, 6060 Broadway, Denver, CO 80216 (303, 291-7208)
Director: JOHN MUMMA

Connecticut Department of Environmental Protection, State Office Bldg., 79 Elm St., Hartford, CT 06106-5127 (860-424-3011)
Deputy Commissioner: THOMAS J. DUDCHIK; Director, Fisheries Division: ERNEST BECKWITH; Director, Wildlife Division: DALE MAY

Delaware Division of Fish and Wildlife, 89 Kings Highway, Dover, DE 19903 (302, 739-5295)
Director: ANDREW T. MANUS

District of Columbia Department of Conservation and Regulatory Affairs, Fisheries Management Program, 2100 Martin L. King Ave., SE, Suite 203, Washington, DC 20020 (202, 645-6064)
Director: IRA PALMER

Florida Game and Fresh Water Fish Commission, Farris Bryant Bldg., 620 S. Meridian, Tallahassee 32399-1600 (904, 488-2975)
Executive Director: ALLAN L. EGBERT

Georgia State Game and Fish Division, 2070 U.S. Highway 278, SE, Social Circle, GA 30025 (706, 57-3020)
Director: DAVID J. WALLER

Guam Department of Agriculture, Agana, Guam 96910 (671, 734-3941)
Director: ANTONIO S. QUITUGUA; Chief: ROBERT ANDERSON, Division of Aquatic and Wildlife Resources

Hawaii Department of Land and Natural Resources, P. O. Box 621, Honolulu, HI 96809 (808, 587-0400)
Chairman: MICHAEL WILSON

Idaho Fish and Game Department, 600 S. Walnut, Box 25, Boise 83707 (208, 334-5159)
Director: DEAN HILDEBRAND

Illinois Department of Natural Resources, Lincoln Tower Plaza, 524 S. Second St., Springfield, IL 62701-1787 (217, 785-0075)
Director: G. BRENT MANNING

Indiana Division of Fish and Wildlife, 402 W. Washington St., Rm. W-273, Indianapolis, IN 46204-2212 (317, 232-4080)
Director: GARY DOXTATER

Iowa Department of Natural Resources, Wallace State Office Bldg., East Ninth and Grand Ave., Des Moines, IA 50319-0034 (515, 281-5145)
Director: LARRY WILSON

Kansas Department of Wildlife and Parks, 900 Jackson St., Ste. 502, Topeka, KS 66612-1220 (913, 296-2281)
Secretary: STEVE WILLIAMS
Operations Office, Assistant Secretary: ROB MANES, Rt. 2, Box 54A, Pratt, KS 67124-9599 (316, 672-5911)

Kentucky Department of Fish and Wildlife Resources, #1 Game Farm Rd., Frankfort 40601 (502, 564-3400)
Commissioner: C. THOMAS BENNETT

Louisiana Department Wildlife and Fisheries, P.O. Box 98000, Baton Rouge, LA 70898-9000 (504, 765-2623)
Secretary: JAMES JENKINS

Maine Department of Inland Fisheries and Wildlife, 284 State St., Station #41, Augusta, ME 04333 (207, 287-5202)
Commissioner: LEE PERRY

Maryland Department of Natural Resources, Tawes State Office Bldg., Annapolis, MD 21401 (410, 260-5551)
Assistant Secretary for Resource Management: SARAH J. RAYLOY-ROGERS (410, 260-3548)
Tidewater Administration, Administrator: PAUL MASSICOT (410, 260-2926)
Director of Fisheries Service: ROBERT A. BACHMAN, Deputy Director (410, 260-8281)
Director of Wildlife Division: MIKE SLATTERY (410, 260-8540)

Massachusetts Department of Fisheries, Wildlife and Environmental Law Enforcement, Division of Fisheries and Wildlife, 100 Cambridge St., Boston, MA 02202 (617, 727-3155)
Directors: WAYNE MacCALLUM; PHILIP G. COATES, MA Division of Marine Fisheries (617, 727-3193)

Michigan Department of Natural Resources, Director: K.L. COOL, Stevens T. Mason Bldg., Box 30028, Lansing, MI 48909 (517, 373-2329)

Minnesota Department of Natural Resources, 500 Lafayette Rd., St. Paul, MN 55155-4020 (612, 296-2549)
Commissioner: RODNEY W. SANDO
Chief of Wildlife: TIM BREMICKER (612, 296-2549 ext. 3344)
Division of Fish and Wildlife: ROGER HOLMES (612, 297-1308)

Mississippi Department of Wildlife, Fisheries and Parks, P.O. Box 451, Jackson, MS 39205 (601, 364-2000)
Director: SAM POLLES

Missouri Department of Conservation, 2901 W. Truman Blvd., P.O. Box 180, Jefferson City, MO 65102-0180 (573, 751-4115)
Director: JERRY M. CONLEY

STATE AGENCY COORDINATORS FOR ENVIRONMENTAL EDUCATION

Montana Department of Fish, Wildlife, and Parks, 1420 E. Sixth Ave., Helena, MT 59620 (406, 444-3186)
Director: PAT GRAHAM

Nebraska Game and Parks Commission, P.O. Box 30370, 2200 N. 33rd, Lincoln, NE 68503 (402, 471-5539)
Director: REX AMACK

Division of Wildlife, Nevada Department of Conservation and Natural Resources, 1100 Valley Rd., Reno, NV 89512 (702, 688-1599)
Administrator: WILLIAM A. MOLINI

New Hampshire Fish and Game Department, 2 Hazen Dr., Concord, NH 03301 (603, 271-3422)
Executive Director: WAYNE VETTER

New Jersey Division of Fish, Game, and Wildlife, CN 400, Trenton, NJ 08625-0400 (609, 292-9410)
Director: ROBERT McDOWELL

New Mexico Natural Resources Department, Villagra Bldg., Santa Fe, NM 87503 (505, 827-7911)
Director: JERRY MARACCHINI (505, 827-7899)

New York Department of Environmental Conservation, 50 Wolf Rd., Albany, NY 12233
Division of Fish, Wildlife, and Marine Resources: GERRY BARNHART (518, 457-5690)

North Carolina Wildlife Resources Commission, Archdale Bldg., 512 N. Salisbury St., Raleigh, NC 27604-1188 (919, 733-3391)
Executive Director: CHARLES FULLWOOD

North Dakota State Game and Fish Department, 100 North Bismarck Expressway, Bismarck, ND 58501 (701, 221-6300)
Commissioner: DEAN HILDEBRAND

Ohio Division of Wildlife, 1840 Belcher Dr., Columbus, OH 43224-1329 (614, 265-6300)
Chief: MICHAEL J. BUDZIK

Oklahoma Department of Wildlife Conservation, 1801 N. Lincoln, P.O. Box 53465, Oklahoma City, OK 73152 (405, 521-3851)
Director: GREG DUFFY

Oregon Department Fish and Wildlife, Box 59, Portland, OR 97207 (503, 872-5410 ext. 401)
Director: JIM GREER

Pennsylvania Fish and Boat Commission, P.O. Box 67000, Harrisburg, PA 17106-7000 (717, 657-4515)
Executive Director: PETE COLANGELO

Pennsylvania Game Commission, 2001 Elmerton Ave., Harrisburg, PA 17110-9797 (717, 787-3633)
Executive Director: DONALD MADL

Puerto Rico Department of Natural Resources, P.O. Box 5887, Puerto DeTierra Station, San Juan, PR 00906 (787, 723-3090)
Secretary: PEDRO A. GELABERT

Rhode Island Department of Environmental Management, Division of Fish and Wildlife, Stedman Government Center, 4808 Tower Hill Rd., Wakefield, RI 02879 (401, 222-3075)
Chief: JOHN STOLGITIS

South Carolina Department of Natural Resources, Rembert C. Dennis Bldg., Box 167, Columbia, SC 29202 (803, 734-4007)
Executive Director: DR. PAUL A. SANDIFER

South Dakota Department of Game, Fish and Parks, Sigurd Anderson Bldg., 523 E. Capitol, Pierre, SD 57501-3182 (605, 773-3387)
Secretary: JOHN COOPER

Tennessee Wildlife Resources Agency, Box 40747, Ellington Agricultural Center, Nashville, TN 37204 (615, 781-6552)
Executive Director: GARY T. MYERS

Texas Parks and Wildlife Department, 4200 Smith School Rd., Austin, TX 78744 (512, 389-4802)
Executive Director: ANDREW SANSOM

Utah State Division of Wildlife Resources, 1596 WN Temple, Salt Lake City, UT 84116-3154 (801, 538-4702)
Director: JOHN KIMBALL

Vermont Fish and Game Department, 103 S. Main St., 10 South, Waterbury, VT 05671-0501 (802, 241-3730)
Commissioner: ALLEN ELSER

Virginia Department of Game and Inland Fisheries, 4010 W. Broad St., Box 11104, Richmond, VA 23230-1104 (804, 367-9231)
Executive Director: WILLIAM L. WOODFIN, JR.

Washington Department of Fish and Wildlife, 600 Capitol Way North, Olympia, WA 98501-1091 (360, 902-2225)
Director (Acting): LARRY PECK

West Virginia Division of Natural Resources, Wildlife Resources Section, 1900 Kanawha Blvd., E., Charleston, WV 25305 (304, 558-2771)
Chief: BERNARD DOWLER

Wisconsin Department of Natural Resources, Box 7921, Madison, WI 53707 (608, 266-2121)
Secretary: GEORGE E. MEYER

Wyoming Game and Fish Department, 5400 Bishop Blvd., Cheyenne, WY 82006 (307, 777-4601)
Director: JOHN BAUGHMAN

CANADA

Alberta Department of Forestry Lands and Wildlife, Petroleum Plaza, 9945-108 St., Edmonton, Canada T5K 2G6
Minister: TY LUND
Deputy Minister: PETER MELNYCHUK, Director of Wildlife, Fish and Wildlife Division, Department of Energy and Natural Resources, Petroleum Plaza, South Tower, 9945-108 St., Edmonton, Canada T5K 2G9 (403, 427-6733)
Assistant Deputy Minister: JIM R. NICHOLS (403, 427-6749)

British Columbia Ministry of the Environment, Parliament Bldg., Victoria, Canada V8V 1X5
Minister: BRUCE STRACHAN
Deputy Minister: THOMAS GUNTON (250, 387-5429)
Assistant Deputy Minister, Environmental Management Division: J. RIORDAN (250, 387-9877)
Director of Wildlife Branch: NANCY BIRCHER (250, 387-9731)
Director of Fisheries Branch: HARVEY ANDRUSAK (250, 387-9791)

Manitoba Department of Natural Resources, Natural Resources Division, Rm. 302, Legislative Bldg., Winnipeg, Canada R3C 0V8
Minister: ALBERT DRIEDGER, 314 Legislature Bldg., Winnipeg, Canada RC3 0V8

Conservation Information Resources

Deputy Minister: DAVID TOMASSON, P.O. Box 22, 1495 St. James St., Winnipeg, Canada R3H 0W9 (204, 945-3785)
Director of Wildlife Branch: BRIAN GILLESPIE (204, 945-7761)

New Brunswick Department of Natural Resources and Energy, Fish and Wildlife Branch, Centennial Bldg., P.O. Box 6000, Fredericton, Canada E3B 5H1
Minister: ALAN R. GRAHAM (506, 453-2510)
Deputy Minister: MAVIS HURLEY (506, 453-2501)
Director: ARNOLD BOER (506, 453-2433)

Newfoundland Department of Natural Resources, Wildlife Division
Minister: REX GIBBONS (709, 729-0659)
Deputy Minister: HAL STANLEY (709, 729-3555)

Newfoundland Department of Fisheries, P.O. Box 4750, St. John's, Canada A1C 5T7
Director: D.G. PIKE (709, 737-2817)

Nova Scotia Department of Natural Resources Wildlife Division
136 Exhibition St., Kentville, Nova Scotia, Canada B4N 4E5
Minister: DONALD DOWNE (902, 424-4037)
Deputy Minister: WILLIAM D. HOGG (902, 424-4121)
Director: BARRY SABEAN (902, 679-6091)

Ontario Ministry of Natural Resources
Policy Division, 99 Wellesley St., Rm. 2327, Whitney Block, Queen's Park, Toronto, Canada M7A 1W3
Minister: CHRIS HODGSON (416, 314-2301)
Deputy Minister: RON VRANCART (416, 314-2150)
Wildlife Director: PHIL SMITH (705-755-1909)

Prince Edward Island Department of the Environment
11 Kent St., P.O. Box 2000, Charlottetown, Canada C1A 7N8
Minister: HON. BARRY HICKEN (902, 368-6410)
Deputy Minister: DIANE F. GRIFFIN (902, 368-5340)

Quebec Ministere Du Loisir, De La Chasse Et De La Peche, 150 est boul, St.-Cyrille, Quebec City, Quebec, Canada G1R 4Y1
Minister: GASTON BLACKBURN
Sous-Minister: ANDRE MAGNY (418, 643-2207)
Director of Wildlife, Fisheries and Habitat: RENE` LESAGE (418, 644-2823)

Saskatchewan Natural Resources, Legislative Bldg., 3211 Albert St., Regina, Canada S4S 5W6
Minister: HON. BERNHARD H. WIENS (306, 787-0605)
Deputy Minister: MICHAEL SHAW (306, 787-2930)
Director, Fisheries Branch: MERV SWANSON (306, 787-2884)
Director, Wildlife Branch: DENNIS SHERRATT (306, 787-2309)

Northwest Territory Department of Renewable Resources
Box 21, Scotia Center, 5th Fl., 5102 50th Ave., #600, Yellowknife, Canada X1A 2L9
Minister: SILAS ARNGNA'NAAQ (403, 669-2344; Fax: 403, 873-0169
Deputy Minister: JOSEPH L. HANDLEY (403, 920-7420; Fax: 403-873-0114)
Director of Wildlife Management Division: DOUG STEWART (867, 873-7411; Fax: 867, 873-0293)

Yukon Department Renewable Resources
Wildlife Branch, P.O. Box 2703, Whitehorse, Yukon Territory, Canada Y1A 2C6
Minister: HON. BILL BREWSTER
Deputy Minister: MIRIAM McTIERNAN (867, 667-5460)
Director of Fish and Wildlife: ARTHUR HOOLE (867, 667-5715)
Chief of Habitat Management: MANFRED HOEFS (867, 667-5761)

STATE AGENCY COORDINATORS FOR ENVIRONMENTAL EDUCATION

ALABAMA: ROBERT S. DAVIS, Science Curriculum Development Specialist. Alabama Department of Education, Gordon Persons Bldg., 50 N Ripley St., Montgomery, AL 36104-3833

ALASKA: SUE ETHELBAH, Program Manager, Vocational Education, Alaska Department of Education, 801 W. 10th St., Ste. 200, Juneau, AK 99811 (907, 465-8729; Fax: 907, 465-3240; E-mail: sethelba@educ.state.ak.us.)

ARKANSAS: BILL FULTON, Science and Environmental Education Specialist, Arkansas Department of Education, #4 State Capitol Mall, Little Rock, AR 72201-1071 (501, 682-4471)
This office coordinates environmental education efforts with Arkansas public schools, and works with the Arkansas Department of Pollution Control and Ecology, Arkansas Game & Fish Commission, and Arkansas Forestry Commission. These Agencies provide all the environmental education training for the State.

CALIFORNIA: BILL ANDREWS, Office of Environmental Education, Policy and Program Coordination Unit A Consultant, Environmental/Conservation Education, 721 Capitol Mall, P.O. Box 944272, Sacramento, CA 94244-2720 (916, 657-5374)

COLORADO: DON HOLLUMS, Consultant, Conservation and Environmental Education Services, Colorado Department of Education, State Office Bldg., 201 E. Colfax, Denver, CO 80203 (303, 866-6787; Fax: 303-866-6836)

CONNECTICUT: STEVE WEINBERG, Science Consultant, Connecticut Department of Education, 165 Capitol Ave., Hartford, CT 06106 (203, 566-6018)

DELAWARE: LAURIE DRAPER, Chief of Environmental Education and Interpretation, Division of Parks and Recreation, 89 Kings Highway, P.O. Box 1401, Dover, DE 19903

FLORIDA: Vacant, Director of Special Programs and Projects, Florida Department of Education, Florida Education Center, Tallahassee, FL 32399 (904, 488-1701)

GEORGIA: BOB MOORE, Science Coordinator of K-12, Georgia Department of Education, 1766 Twin Towers East, Atlanta, GA 30334-5040 (404, 656-0913; Fax: 404, 657-7096; E-mail: b_moore@doe.k12.ga.us)

HAWAII: JOHN W. HAWKINS, Education Specialist-Environmental Education, Hawaii Department of Education, 189 Lunalilo Home Rd., 2nd Fl., Honolulu, HI 96825 (808, 395-9252)

IDAHO: RICHARD KAY, Consultant Science and Environmental Education, Idaho Department of Education, 650 W. State St., Boise, ID 83720 (208, 334-2281; Fax: 208, 334-2228)

ILLINOIS: GWEN POLLOCK, Educational Consultant, Illinois State Board of Education, N-242, 100 N. First St., Springfield, IL 62777 (217, 782-2826)

INDIANA: KEVIN BEARDMORE, Science Coordinator, Office of Program Development, Indiana Department of Education, Rm. 229, State House, Indianapolis, IN 46204 (317, 232-9153)

IOWA: DUANE TOOMSEN, Environmental Education Consultant, Curriculum Division, Iowa Department of Education, Grimes Office Bldg., Des Moines, IA 50319 (515, 281-3146)

PERIODICALS AND DIRECTORIES

KANSAS: GREG SCHELL, Science Consultant, Kansas Department of Education, 120 SE 10th, Topeka, KS 66612 (913, 296-8108)

LOUISIANA: PAUL A. LONG, Program Manager, Science and Environmental Education, Louisiana Department of Education, P.O. Box 94064, Baton Rouge, LA 70804-9064 (504, 342-1136 Fax: 504-342-9891; E-mail: plong@mail.doe.state.la.us.)

MARYLAND: DIANE HOUSEHOLDER, Science Specialist, Department of Education, 200 W. Baltimore St., Baltimore, MD 21201 (410, 767-0323); GARY HEATH, Environmental Education Specialist, Department of Education, 200 W. Baltimore St., Baltimore, MD 21201 (410, 767-0324)

MICHIGAN: MOZELL P. LANG, Science Specialist, Michigan Department of Education, P.O. Box 30008, Lansing, MI 48909 (517, 373-4223)

MINNESOTA: Vacant, Formal Environmental Education Coordinator, Environmental Education Advisory Board, Minnesota Department of Education, Capitol Square Bldg., 550 Cedar St., St. Paul, MN 55101 (612, 297-2228/282-5788 or 282-6474; Fax: 612, 297-3348 or 297-8687)

MISSISSIPPI: BRIAN S. KNIPPERS, Science Specialist, Mississippi Department of Education, P.O. Box 771, Jackson, MS 39205 (601, 359-3778; E-mail: bknippers@mdek12.state.ms.us)

MISSOURI: C.J. VARNON, Science Consultant Missouri Department of Elementary and Secondary Education, P.O. Box 480, Jefferson, MO 65102 (314, 751-4445)

MONTANA: SPENCER SARTORIUS, Specialist, Outdoor-Health-PE Education, Office of Public Instruction, Capitol Bldg., Helena, MT 59620 (406, 444-4434); LINDA PETERSON, Environmental Education, Social Studies, Education, Montana Office of Public Instruction, State Capitol Bldg., Helena, MT 59620 (406, 444-4439)

NEBRASKA: JIM WOODLAND, Director, Science Education, Nebraska Department of Education, P.O. Box 94987, Lincoln, NE 68509 (402, 471-4329; Fax: 402, 471-0117)

NEW HAMPSHIRE: EDWARD J. HENDRY, Consultant, Science Education, New Hampshire Department of Education, 101 Pleasant St., Concord, NH 03301 (603, 271-2632)

NEW JERSEY: DR. BRUCE MARGANOFF, Science Coordinator, New Jersey Department of Education, 100 Riverview Plaza, Trenton, NJ 08625-0500 (609, 984-7453; Fax: 609, 292-7276)

NEW YORK: BARRY W. JAMASON, Coordinator, Environmental Education, New York State Department of Education, Rm. 212EB, Albany, NY 12234 (518, 474-5890)

NORTH CAROLINA: CLINTON L. BROWN, Science Coordinator, North Carolina Department of Public Instruction, Raleigh, NC 27601-2825 (919, 715-1853)

NORTH DAKOTA: CURT ERIKSMOEN, Social Studies Coordinator, North Dakota Department of Public Instruction, Division of Independent Study, Box 5036, Fargo, ND 58105-5036 701-231-6062

OKLAHOMA: KATHY THOMAS CHRIST, Science Specialist, Oklahoma Department of Education, Oliver Hodge Bldg., 2500 N. Lincoln, Oklahoma City, OK 73105 (405, 522-3524; Fax: 405, 521-6205; kathy_christ@mail.sde.state.ok.us)

OREGON: Specialist, Science/Energy/Environment Education, Oregon Department of Education, 700 Pringle Parkway, SE, Salem, OR 97310-0290 (503, 373-3602; Fax: 503, 373-7968)

PENNSYLVANIA: DR. PATRICIA VATHIS, Director, Office of Environmental Education, Pennsylvania Department of Education, 333 Market St., 8th Floor, Harrisburg, PA 17126-0333 (717, 783-6994)

RHODE ISLAND: DR. DENNIS W.CHEEK, Coordinator of Mathematics, Science, Technology, and the Social Studies, Rhode Island Department of Elementary and Secondary Education, 255 Westminster St., Providence, RI 02903-3400, (401, 277-4600, ext. 2150; Fax: 401, 277-6033, E-mail: ststoday@aol.com)

SOUTH CAROLINA: LINDA D. SINCLAIR, Science and Environmental Education Associate, South Carolina Department of Education, 507 Rutledge Bldg., 1429 Senate St., Columbia, SC 29201 (803, 734-0887; Fax: 803, 734-4605; E-mail: lsinclai@sde.state.sc..us)

SOUTH DAKOTA: Science Director, South Dakota Department of Elementary and Secondary Education, Kneip Bldg., Pierre, SD 57501 (605, 741-2851)

TENNESSEE: KAREN HANNA JENKINS, Director, Office of Conservation Education, 8th Fl., Gateway Plaza, 710 James Robertson Parkway, Nashville, TN 37243-0379 (615, 532-6249; Fax: 615, 532-8536)

TEXAS: IRENE PICKHARDT, Environmental Education Coordinator, Texas Education Agency, 1701 W. Congress Ave., Austin, TX 78701 (512, 463-9566)

UTAH: BRETT D. MOULDING, Science Education Specialist, Utah State Office of Education, 250 East 500 S., Salt Lake City, UT 84111 (801, 538-7791; E-mail: brett.moulding@usoe.k12.ut.us)

VIRGINIA: JAMES C. FIREBAUGH, JR., Science Specialist, Virginia Department of Education, P.O. Box 2120, Richmond, VA 23218-2120 (804, 225-2651; Fax: 804, 786-1703; E-mail: jfirebau@pen.k12.va.us)

WASHINGTON: TONY ANGELL, Environmental Education Program Supervisor, Washington State Office of Environmental Education, Office of Superintendent of Public Instruction, 2800 NE 200th St., Seattle, WA 98155-1418 (206, 365-3893; Fax: 206, 367-4540)

WEST VIRGINIA: PHYLLIS BARNHART, State Science Director, West Virginia Department of Education, Bldg. 6, Rm. 330, 1900 Kanawha Blvd., East, Charleston, WV 25305-0330 (304, 558-7805; Fax: 304, 558-0459; E-mail: pbarnhar@access.K12.wv.us)

WYOMING: DR. WILLIAM M. FUTRELL, Coordinator, Science/Mathematics/Environmental Education, Wyoming Department of Education, 246 Hathaway Bldg., Cheyenne, WY 82002 (307, 777-6247; Fax: 307, 777-6247)

PERIODICALS AND DIRECTORIES

Air and Water Pollution Report's Environment Week
951 Pershing Dr., Silver Spring, MD 20910
(301, 587-6300); Weekly One-year subscription
$617.00 per year (50 issues)

Animals' Agenda
P.O. Box 25881, Baltimore, MD 21224

Conservation Information Resources

(410, 675-4566; Fax: 410, 675-0066; E-mail: office@animalsagenda.org; www.animalsagenda.org
One-year subscription; $24.00 U.S.; $30.00 Canada/Mexico $37.00 other foreign

BioCycle Journal of Composting & Recycling
The J G Press, Inc., 419 State Ave.
Emmaus, PA 18049 (610, 967-4135)

Boating Business
703 Evans Ave., Suite 202, Toronto
Ontario, Canada M9C 5E9 (416, 695-0311)

Boston College Environmental Affairs Law Review
(formerly Environmental Affairs)
Boston College Law School, 885 Centre St.
Newton Centre, MA 02159; Quarterly; $23.00 per year

Caretaker Gazette, The
P.O. Box 5887, Carefree, AZ 85377-5887
(Phone/Fax: 602, 488-1970; E-mail: caretaker@uswest.net; WWW: www.angelfire.com/wa/caretaker; Bimonthly

Clean Water Report
CJE Associates, 237 Gretna Green Ct.
Alexandria, VA 22304-5602
(703, 823-0662; Fax: 703, 823-5923)
Biweekly; $295.00 per year

Congressional Green Sheets, Inc., 406 E St., SE, Washington, D.C. 20003 (202, 546-2220; Fax: 202, 546-7490; E-mail: wb@greensheets.com; www.greensheets.com)

Clearing Magazine
John Inskeep Environmental Learning Center
19600 S. Molalla Ave., Oregon City, OR 97045
(503, 657-6958/ext. 2638; clearing@teleport.com
Bimonthly

Container Recycling Report
P.O. Box 10540, Portland, OR 97296-0540
(503, 227-1319; Fax: 503, 227-6135)
$49.00 per year (12 issues)

Ecology Law Quarterly
University of California, Boalt Hall School of Law, Berkeley, CA 94720; (510, 642-0457; Fax: 510, 643-9042; E-mail: elq@violet.berkeley.edu); Quarterly (Personal subscriptions)
$30.00 per volume/year individuals (U.S.)
$22.00 per volume/year students (U.S.)
$50.00 per volume/year institution (U.S.)
$6.00 per volume/year foreign postage (surface)
$32.00 per volume/year foreign postage (airmail)

Ecology USA
CJE Associates, 237 Gretna Green Ct.
Alexandria, VA 22304-5602
(703, 823-0662; Fax: 703,823-5923)
Biweekly; $135.00 per year

Endangered Species Bulletin
Division of Endangered Species,
U.S. Fish and Wildlife Service, Washington, DC 20240

Endangered Species & Wetlands Report
6717 Poplar Ave., Takoma Park, MD 20912
(301, 891-3791; Fax: 301, 891-3507)
E-mail: poplar@crosslink.net; WWW: www. eswr.com
Monthly; $245.00 a year; discount for new subscribers, qualified nonprofit groups, and students

Endangered Species UPDATE
School of Natural Resources and Environment
The University of Michigan, Ann Arbor, MI 48109-1115
(734, 763-3243; Fax: 734, 936-2195; E-mail: (esupdate@umich.edu); Annually (6 issues bimonthly)
$28.00 per year (U.S.); $23.00 for students

and senior citizens; $5.00 additional for foreign

Energy Today
Trends Publishing, Inc.
National Press Bldg., Washington, DC 20045
Monthly; $795.00 per year
(202, 393-0031; Fax: 202, 393-1732)

Environment Abstracts
Congressional Information Services, Inc.
4520 East-West Hwy., Bethesda, MD 20814-3389
Monthly print subscription: $1,245.00
Quarterly CD-Rom subscription: $1,500.00
(800-638-8380 or 301, 654-1550; Fax: 301, 654-4033)

Environment Reporter
Bureau of National Affairs, Inc.
1231 25th St., NW; Washington, DC 20037

Evironmental Abstracts Annual
Bowker A&I Publishing, 121 Chanlon Rd.
New Providence, NJ 07974
Annually; $495.00 per year

Environmental Building News
28 Birge St., Brattleboro, VT 05301
(802, 257-7300; Fax: 802, 257-7304; Orders: 800-861-0954
E-mail: ebn@ebuild.com; WWW: www.ebuild.com)
$67.00 per year; $127.00 per year for companies with 25 or more employees; $30.00 additional for addresses outside North America
10 issues per year plus annual supplement
E Build Library CD-ROM of all back issues, updated annually, first copy: subscribers $95.00, non-subscribers $149.00

National Environmental Employment Report
Environmental Careers World
100 Bridge St., Bldg. A, Hampton, VA 23669
(757, 727-7895; Fax: 757, 727-7904)
E-mail: ecwo@environmental-jobs.com
WWW: www. environmental-jobs.com
Monthly; $15.00 -three issues
$35.00 - six issues; $59.00 - 12 issues (individuals)
$89.00 - 12 issues (organizations & universities)
$159.00 - 24 issues

Environmental Law
Northwestern School of Law; Lewis and Clark College
10015 SW Terwilliger Blvd., Portland, OR 97219
(503, 768-6700; Fax: 503, 768-6671); Quarterly

Environmental Law Reporter, The (ELR)
Environmental Law Institute, 1616 P St., NW
Suite 200, Washington, DC 20036; Monthly

E/The Environmental Magazine
P.O. Box 5098, Westport, CT 06881
(203, 854-5559; Fax: 203, 866-0602)
E-mail: emagazine@prodigy.net
WWW: www.emagazine.com
$20.00 per year (six issues)
Subscription Department: P.O. Box 2047
Marion, OH 43306

Environmental Remediation Technology
Business Publishers, Inc., 951 Pershing Dr.
Silver Spring, MD 20910; (301, 587-6300)
Biweekly; One-year subscription
$459.00 per year (26 issues)

Environmental Science and Technology
American Chemical Society, 1155 16th St., NW
Washington, DC 20036
(202, 872-4582; Fax: 202, 872-4403)
E-mail: est@acs.org); Monthly
ACS members: $27.00; Individuals: $61.00
Non-members: $49.00; Individuals: $125.00

PERIODICALS AND DIRECTORIES

Institutions: $889.00; Students: $45.75

Game Manager, The
P.O. Box 1330, West Point, CA 95255
(209, 293-7087; Fax: 209, 293-7105)
Quarterly; $20.00 per year

Global Environmental Change Report
37 Broadway, Arlington, MA 02174
(617, 648-8700); Twice a month (24 issues)
$457.00 (U.S. and Canada); $557.00 (Foreign)

Groundwater Newsletter, The
Water Information Center, Inc., 2525 Arapahoe Ave., Suite E4-910,
Boulder, CO 80302 (303, 546-6900; Fax: 303, 546-9113)
Twice Monthly
1995-$347.00; 1996-$347.00 (Domestic and Canada)
1995-$377.00; 1996-$377.00 (Overseas-Airmail)
Two year subscriptions
1995-$567.00; 1996-$567.00 (domestic)
1995-$597.00; 1996-$597 (overseas)

Harvard Environmental Law Review
Harvard Law School, Cambridge, MA 02138
(617,495-3110, Fax: 617, 496-2148
E-mail: hlselr@hulaw1.harvard.edu)
Semi-annually (winter and summer)
$28.00 per year (U.S.)
$34.00 per year (foreign surface mail)
$46.00 per year (foreign air mail)

High Country News
Box 1090, Paonia, CO 81428
(970, 527-4898; Fax: 970, 527-4897); Biweekly
Subscriptions: 1-800-905-1155
$28.00 per year (Individual, school/public library)
$38.00 per year (business inst.)

Industry and Environment Review
United Nations Environment Programme Industry
and Environment (UNEP/IE)
Tour Mirabeau, 39-43 Quai Andre Citroen,
75739 Paris cedex 15, France
Telephone (331, 44 37 14 50)
Telefax (331, 44 37 14 74)
Sales price: 45.00 US$ surface mail/60.00 U.S.$ airmail

International Cleaner Production Information Clearinghouse
United Nations Environment Programme Industry
and Environment (UNEP/IE)
Tour Mirabeau, 39-43 Quai Andre Citroen
75739 Paris cedex 15, France
Phone: (33-1) 44 37 14 50
Telefax: (33-1 44 37 14 74); Sales price: $40.00 U.S.$

Land Letter (The Newsletter for Natural Resource Professionals)
EESI Publishing, 122 C St., NW, Suite 700
Washington, DC 20001
34 issues/year; $195.00 introductory rate

Land Use Law Report
Business Publishers, Inc., 951 Pershing Dr.
Silver Spring, MD 20910
Biweekly; $367.00 per year (Includes first class postage)

Landscape Journal
The University of Wisconsin Press
2537 Daniels St., Madison, WI 53718 (608, 224-3880)
Semi-annually; $33.00 (individual); $84.00 (institution)

Law and The Land, The
Robinson and Cole, LLP 280 Trumbull St.
Hartford, CT 06103-3597 (860, 275-8200)
Quarterly

Mother Earth News
49 East 21st St., 11th Fl., New York, NY 10010
Bimonthly (212, 260-7210)

National Boycott News
Institute for Consumer Responsibility (ICR)
3618 Wallingford Ave. N., Seattle, WA 98103
(206, 523-0421; 206, 523-0421)

National Wetlands Newsletter
Environmental Law Institute
1616 P St., NW, Suite 200, Washington, DC 20036
Bimonthly; $40.00 per year (800, 433-5120)

National Woodlands Magazine
National Woodland Owners Association
374 Maple Ave., E., Suite 210
Vienna, VA 22180; Quarterly

Natural Resources Journal
University of New Mexico School of Law
1117 Stanford, NE, Albuquerque, NM 87131
Quarterly; $35.00 per year (U.S.)
$40.00 per year (foreign)

Nuclear Waste News
Business Publishers, Inc.
951 Pershing Dr., Silver Spring, MD 20910
Weekly; (301, 587-6300)
One-year subscription
$774.00 per year (50 issues)

Organic Gardening Magazine
Rodale Press, Inc., 33 E. Minor St.
Emmaus, PA 18098
(610, 967-5171; Fax: 610, 967-7846)
$19.96 (6 issues per year)
(U.S. and U.S. possessions)

Outdoor Canada
703 Evans Ave., Ste. 202
Toronto, Ontario, M9C 5E9, Canada
(416, 695-0311; Fax: 416, 695-0381)

Plastics Recycling Update
P.O. Box 10540, Portland, OR 97296-0540
(503, 227-1319; Fax: 503, 227-6135)
$49.00 per year (twelve issues)

Pollution Abstracts
Cambridge Scientific Abstracts
7200 Wisconsin Ave., Bethesda, MD 20814
301-961-6700; Fax: 301-961-6720; E-mail: market@csa.com

Preserving Family Lands: Essential Tax Strategies for the Landowner; Preserving Family Lands: More Planning Strategies for the Future
Landowner Planning Center, P.O. Box 2242
Boston, MA 02101-4508 (617, 357-1644)

Refuge Reporter
AVOCET TWO, Publisher
Avocet Crossing, Millwood, VA 22646-0156
(540, 837-2152; E-mail: refrep@mnsinc.com)
Quarterly: $12.00/year, $22.00/2 yrs.

Tundra Talk Newsletter
Connecticut Caribou Clan, P.O. Box 9344
Bolton, CT 06043-9344; (860, 643-2948; captundra@aol.com)

Virginia Environmental Law Journal
University of Virginia School of Law
Charlottesville, VA 22903-1789
(804, 924-3683; Fax: 804, 924-7536; E-mail: acd5t@virginia.edu)

Water Newsletter and International Water Report
Water Information Center, Inc.
2525 Arapahoe Ave., Ste. E4-910, Boulder, CO 80302
(303, 391-8799; Fax: 303, 294-1239)
Monthly; $127.00 (Domestic & Canada
15% discount - $107.95); $157.00 (overseas-Airmail)
Individual issues - $10.58/copy - domestic; $13.08/copy - overseas
2nd copy (in same envelope) - $50/year; 3rd & 4th copies - $40/year; Two-year subscriptions - $216.00 (domestic); $246.00 (overseas)

Wild Earth
P.O. Box 455, Richmond, VT 05477
(Phone/Fax: 802, 434-4077) Quarterly

Wildlife Law News Quarterly
Center for Wildlife Law
School of Law, Institute of Public Law
1117 Stanford, NE, Albuquerque, NM 87131
(505, 277-5006; Fax: 505, 277-7064)
Quarterly; $60 (One-year subscription)
$48 - Student Price

Woodland Report (Forestry Newsletter)
374 Maple Ave., E., Suite 210
Vienna, VA 22180
Eight Issues a Year

World Environment Report
Business Publishers, Inc.
951 Pershing Dr., Silver Spring, MD 20910
Biweekly; (301, 587-6300)
One-year subscription
$494.00 per year (26 issues)

CALIFORNIA ENVIRONMENTAL DIRECTORY: A GUIDE TO ORGANIZATIONS AND RESOURCES
Order from California Institute of Public Affairs, P.O. Box 189040 Sacramento, CA 95818 (916, 442-2472; Fax: 916, 442-2478) This is the only systematic guide available to state and federal government agencies, university programs, major associations, and selected local and regional agencies in California (nearly 1,000 listings in all) that are concerned with protecting the environment and managing natural resources. Regular price $40.00. Special price for public, academic, and governmental libraries and for nonprofit public-interest associations ordering on letterhead: $25.00. Fifth edition - 1992.

CONGRESS AT YOUR FINGERTIPS - CONGRESSIONAL DIRECTORIES
(Published by Capitol Advantage), P.O. Box 1223, McLean, VA 22101 (703, 734-3266 or 800-659-8708 (outside Washington, DC area); Fax: 703, 847-0573)
The perfect resource for communicating with Congress easily and effectively. Includes: Photos; room, phone, fax numbers, and E-mail addresses; key staff members; leadership and officers; committee and subcommittee listings; information on the White House, selected federal agencies, the Supreme Court, and state governors; tips on writing and visiting congressional offices; detailed, fold-out map (8"x10") of Capitol Hill and office building layout; and congressional schedule. Pocket size (4"x 9") guide to Congress. Published annually. Single copy, spiral bound, Standard Version: $11.95 includes shipping. Personalized copies available. Other media available. Free catalog.

CONGRESSIONAL STAFF DIRECTORY, 1998
815 Slaters Ln., Alexandria, VA 22314 (703, 739-0900/1-800-252-1722; Fax: 703, 739-0234)
Published by CA Staff Directories, Inc., three times per year, spring, summer, and fall. Contains information concerning Congress, including Member contact and information, phone, fax, e-mail web, their photographs, biographies, election results, office staffs in Washington and in district offices, assignment of Members and staff to committees and subcommittees, 14,000 cities and counties and their congressional districts, 3,200 staff biographies, key-word subject index, and 19,000-name index of individuals with phone numbers. Subscription: $227.00 - three edition; individual - $89.00. Also available on Diskette and CD-ROM.

DIRECTORY OF NATURAL ENVIRONMENTAL SCIENCE CENTERS
Natural Science for Youth Foundation, 130 Azalea Dr., Roswell, GA 30075.
The directory lists over 1,100 centers located throughout the United States, Canada, and the Virgin Islands. Each center is listed together with its address, telephone number, business hours, and admission fees. The buildings, acreage, and any special features are also included. Single copy: $55.00 plus $3.50 for postage and handling.

DIRECTORY OF ENVIRONMENTAL GROUPS IN NEW ENGLAND
Environmental Protection Agency, Region I, REN, John F. Kennedy Federal Bldg., Boston, MA 02203; JOHN DEVILLARS, Regional Administrator

ENVIRONMENTAL GRANTMAKING FOUNDATIONS DIRECTORY
Resources for Global Sustainability (RGS), P.O. Box 3665, Cary, NC 27519 (800-724-1857; Fax: 919, 319-9237); Email: rgs@environmentalgrants.com; www.environmentalgrants.com
The Directory is the seventh edition of the best-selling annual guide to 800 independent, community, and corporate foundations that give environmental grants. The Foundation profiles include: contact information, history and philosophy, financial data, funding analysis, sample grants, application process, and emphases and restrictions. Multiple indexes allow easy cross-referencing. ISBN: 0-9631943-6-4. Cost: $100.00 (print 1,000 pages) and $110.00 (CD-ROM). Online directory to be available in 1999.

FEDERAL STAFF DIRECTORY, 815 Slaters Ln., Alexandria, VA 22314 (703, 739-0900; Fax: 703, 739-0234)
Published by CA Staff Directories, Inc., three times per year, spring, summer, and fall. Lists 38,000 Executive Branch officials by name, title, address, phone and fax numbers, e-mail, and web. Includes the White House, all departments, independent and quasi agencies, regulatory bodies, advisory organizations, regional offices outside the Washington area, and legal authority as well as responsibilities. Also includes biographies of 2,600 key officials, a key-word subject index, and an index of individuals. Single copy: $89.00 each. Subscription: $227.00, three editions. Also available on CD-ROM and mailing lists.

JUDICIAL STAFF DIRECTORY, 1998, 815 Slaters Ln., Alexandria, VA 22314
(703, 739-0900; Fax: 703, 739-0234)
Published by CA Staff Directories, Inc. Contains listings of all federal courts, judges, and staffs. Also includes magistrates, court clerks and deputies, probation officers, and U.S. Attorneys and U.S. Marshals and their staffs. Includes the Supreme Court, national courts, federal circuit, district, and bankruptcy courts, committees of the Judicial Conference, the Department of Justice, 14,000 cities and counties and their circuit and district courts, maps of judicial districts, indexes of judges alphabetically, by appointing presidents and by year of appointment, tables of judicial nominations and vacancies, court workload and case statistics, 1,900 biographies of judges and key staff, and an index of individuals. Single copy: $89.00 each. Also available on CD-ROM and mailing lists.

THE NEW ENGLAND ENVIRONMENTAL DIRECTORY (NEED)
8850 O'Brien Creek Rd., Missoula, MT 59801 (406, 543-3359)

SOURCES OF AUDIO-VISUAL MATERIALS

The New England Environmental Directory is designed to facilitate access to public agencies, environmental activists, and educators, to increase collaboration among organizations and agencies, and to encourage effective use of environmental education resources. The directory is updated and reprinted biannually. Cost: $15.00.

WHO'S WHO IN SERVICE TO THE EARTH DIRECTORY; WHO'S WHO AT THE EARTH SUMMIT DIRECTORY
Published by Vision Link Education Foundation, 181 Biodome, Waynesville, NC 28786
The Who's Who in Service to the Earth lists 8,000 cross-indexed entries for people, projects, and organizations. Edited by Hans T. Keller. Cost: $30.00. The Who's Who at the Earth Summit (Rio De Janeiro) lists 30,000 cross-indexed entries of all governmental and nongovernmental organizations. Cost: $30.00. Edited by Hans T. Keller

WORLD DIRECTORY OF ENVIRONMENTAL ORGANIZATIONS
California Institute of Public Affairs, P.O. Box 189040 Sacramento, CA 95818.
(916, 442-2472; Fax: 916, 442-2478; WWW: www.igc.org/cipa)
Published in cooperation with the Sierra Club and IUCN-The World Conservation Union. Fifth edition - 1996. Single copy: $50.00 plus $2.00 handling.
The only comprehensive guide to organizations in all parts of the world that are concerned with problems of the environment and natural resources. Describes more than 3,200 organizations in over 200 countries, and includes detailed profiles of environmental activities of international organizations, and listings of key national governmental and nongovernmental organizations.

SOURCES OF AUDIO-VISUAL MATERIALS

American Society of Mammalogists, Mammal Slide Library, 1907 Monument Canyon Dr., Grand Junction, CO 81503; Catalogues available.

Audiovisuals for the Environment, International Centre for Conservation Education (ICCE), Greenfield House, Guiting Power, Cheltenham, Glos. GL54 5TZ, United Kingdom (0451-850777; Fax: 0451-850705) Catalogue of Environmental Audiovisuals available on request.

Berlet Films, 1646 West Kimmel Rd., Jackson, MI 49201 (517, 784-6969; Fax: 517-796-2646) Sales, rental. Free catalogue available.

Brauer Productions, 530 S. Union St., Traverse City, MI 49684 (616, 941-0850) Full service film and video production company serving Traverse City and clients throughout Michigan and the N.W. since 1978.

Bullfrog Films, Oley, PA 19547 (800, 543-3764) Films and videos rented and sold worldwide to educational institutions. Programs come with study guide with suggested activities, research topics, debate subjects, and bibliographies. Free catalogue available.

Critical Index of Films on Man and His Environment, by Conservation Education Association, The Interstate, 19-27 N. Jackson St., Danville, IL 61832

Environment Film Review, Films and Research for an Endangered Environment, Ltd., Rt. 1, Box 454, Prarie Du Chien, WI 53821 (608, 326-4783); Film presentation available on request.

Environmental Film Service, National Association of Conservation Districts, 408 E. Main, P.O. Box 855, League City, TX 77573 281-332-3402 Catalogue available.

Environmental Media, P.O. Box 1016, Chapel Hill, NC 27514 (919, 933-3003; Fax: 919, 942-8785; E-mail: enveduc@aol.com;; www.envmedia.com
Founded: 1989.
Environmental Media designs, produces, and distributes media to support environmental education. Programs are curriculum-based and most are accompanied by teaching guides. Free catalogue available listing videocassettes, books, games, and other educational material.

Georgia Department of Natural Resources, Film and Video Unit, 205 Butler St., SE, Suite 1354, Atlanta, GA 30334 (404--657-9851; Fax: 404-651-5871) Free loan and sales. Free film catalogue available upon request.

Green Mountain Post Films, P.O. Box 229, Turners Falls, MA 01376 (413, 863-4754; Fax: 413, 863-8248)
A film/video production and distribution company founded in 1975 that specializes in media concerning environmental issues.

International Film Bureau, Inc., 332 S. Michigan Ave., Chicago, IL 60604 (312-427-4545; Fax: 312-427-4550) Sales, rentals; Free catalogue.

Jerry Mossier Productions/Underwater Images, P.O. Box 1415, Hayden, Idaho, 83835 (208-683-8112)
Contracts for producing fisheries, wildlife and natural history videos.

Montana Fish, Wildlife, and Parks Film Center, 1420 E. 6th Ave., P.O. Box 200701, Helena, MT 59620-0701 (406-444-2426; Fax: 406-444-4952). Brochure is available upon request.

Neal and Reed Communications, Inc., 169 Belle Forest Cr., Nashville, TN 37221 (615-662-1946; Fax: 615-662-1995)
Produce outreach videos supporting sustainable ecosystems and development, conservation of natural resources, wildlife, and cultural integrity. Specialists in translating complex issues into compelling, motivating communications.

South Carolina Wildlife and Marine Resources Department, Film Department, P.O. Box 167, Columbia, SC 29202; Catalogue available.

Tennessee Department of Conservation, Division of Information and Education, 2611 West End Ave., Nashville, TN 37203; Film catalogue and list of publications available upon request to Tennessee residents and organizations only.

U.S. Department of Agriculture Films, Available from film libraries of the 50 state land grant universities (see also U.S. Forest Service below). Catalogues available from university film libraries.

U.S. Department of the Interior Films, Catalogue available by writing Office of Public Affairs, U.S. Department of the Interior, 18th & C St. NW, Washington, DC 20240; Free.

U.S. Forest Service Films, Available through regional offices or private contractors. Free catalogues. Addresses: Alaska Region, Federal Office Bldg., P.O. Box 1628, Juneau, AK 99802; California Region, 630 Sansome St., San Francisco, CA 94111; Eastern Region, 633 W. Wisconsin Ave., Milwaukee, WI 53203; Intermountain Region, 324 25th St., Ogden, UT 84401; Northern Region, Federal Bldg., Missoula, MT 59801; Pacific Northwest Region, 319 SW Pine St., P.O. Box 3623, Portland, OR 97208; Rocky Mountain Region, Cromars, 1200 Stout St., Denver, CO 80204; Southern Region, 1720 Peachtree Rd., NW, Atlanta, GA

30309; Southwestern Region, Federal Bldg., 517 Gold Ave., SW, Albuquerque, NM 87102

30309; Southwestern Region, Federal Bldg., 517 Gold Ave., SW, Albuquerque, NM 87102

Video-Active Productions, 200 Boyden Rd., Canton, NY 13617 (315, 386-8797)
Founded: 1985
Part of the movement for environmental justice seeking to give a voice to victims, empower potential victims, promote a public dialogue, enhance informed decision making, stimulate local democracy, expose corruption, validate common sense, endorse sustainable development, and move to the front end of the problem.

Video Project, The, 5332 College Ave., Ste. 510, Berkeley, CA 94618 (415, 655-9050; Fax: 415, 655-9115)
Affordable films and videos on environmental and related issues. The project now offers over 150 programs for sale or rental. Free catalogues available.

Walkabout Productions, Inc., 632 Harberts Court, Annapolis, MD 21401 (410, 573-1228; Metro D.C.: 301, 970-2525)
Founded: 1975
Walkabout Productions, Inc., is an EMMY award winning production team that focuses on environment, wildlife, and science documentaries. Filmography is available.

Washington Department of Natural Resources, Public Information Office, Public Lands Bldg., Olympia, WA 98504; Catalogue available.

Media Designs Associates, Inc., 1898 S. Flatiron Ct., P.O. Box 3189, Boulder, CO 80307-3532 (303, 443-2800/1-800-228-8854; Fax: 303-443-2882; E-mail: mediades@indra.com; www.indra.com/mediades)
Founded: 1973
Produce and distribute film/video, including laser videodisc and CD-ROM formats. West Wind specializes in natural history and environmental subjects. Free catalogue available.

Wyoming Game and Fish Department, Film Librarian, 5400 Bishop Blvd.,Cheyenne, WY 82002 (307-777-4629; Fax: 307-777-4610.) Catalogue available.

NATURAL HERITAGE PROGRAMS AND CONSERVATION DATA CENTERS IN THE UNITED STATES, CANADA, AND LATIN AMERICA

Natural heritage programs and conservation data centers are computerized biodiversity surveys that focus on the distribution, status, and condition of species and ecosystems. Most individual heritage programs are administered by state natural resource agencies and operate in collaboration with The Nature Conservancy.

NATURAL HERITAGE NETWORK SUPPORT

The Nature Conservancy
Conservation Science Division
1815 N. Lynn St.
Arlington, VA 22209
(703, 841-5300; Fax: 703, 841-8796)
Director Heritage Operations: MARK SHAFFER

Association for Biodiversity Information
10401 Chesterwood Dr., Spotsylvania, VA 22553
(540-786-6360; Fax: 540-786-1026) , omarinc@msn.com
Executive Director: RICHARD WARNER

UNITED STATES NATURAL HERITAGE PROGRAMS

Alabama Natural Heritage Program
Huntington College
Massey Hall
1500 East Fairview Ave.
Montgomery, AL 36106-2148
(334, 834-4519; Fax: 334, 834-5439; E-mail: alnhp@wsnet.com)
Acting Coordinator: JAREL L. HILTON, ext. 3078

Alaska Natural Heritage Program
University of Alaska Anchorage
707 A St., Anchorage, AK 99501
(907, 257-2702; Fax: 907, 258-9139; E-mail: afdcd1@orion.alaska.edu)
Program Director: DAVID DUFFY (907, 257-2707)

Arizona Heritage Data Management System
Arizona Game & Fish Department
WM-H, 2221 W. Greenway Rd., Phoenix, AZ 85023
(602, 789-3612; Fax: 602, 789-3928;
E-mail: hdms@gf.state.as.us; hdms1@gf.state.as.us)
Coordinator, Data Mgmt. System: BARRY SPICER

Arkansas Natural Heritage Commission
Suite 1500, Tower Bldg.
323 Center St.
Little Rock, AR 72201
(501, 324-9150; Fax: 501, 324-9618)
Chief of Research: TOM FOTI (501, 324-9761; E-mail: tom@dah.state.ar.us)

California Natural Heritage Division
Department of Fish & Game
1220 S St., Sacramento, CA 95814
(916, 322-2493; Fax: 916, 324-0475)
Chief: SUSAN A. COCHRANE (916, 324-8348; Internet: scochran@gishost.dfg.ca.gov)

Colorado Natural Heritage Program
College of Natural Resources
Colorado State University
204 General Services Bldg.
Fort Collins, CO 80523
(970, 491-1309; Fax: 970, 491-0279)
Director/Chief Scientist: CHRIS PAGUE
(970, 491-1150; Internet: cpague@lamar.colostate.edu)

Connecticut Natural Diversity Database
Natural Resources Center
Department of Environmental Protection
79 Elm St., Store Level
Hartford, CT 06106-5127
(860, 424-3540; Fax: 860, 424-4058)
Coordinator: NANCY MURRAY (860, 424-3589; E-mail: nancy.murray@po.state.ct.us)

Delaware Natural Heritage Program
Division of Fish & Wildlife
Department of Natural Resources & Environmental Control
4876 Hay Point Landing Rd.
Smyrna, DE 19977
(302, 653-2880; Fax: 302, 653-3431)
Coordinator: LYNN BROADDUS
(Internet: lbroaddus@state.de.us)

District of Columbia Natural Heritage Program
National Park Service, 13025 Riley's Lock Rd.
Poolesville, MD 20837
(301, 427-1302; Fax: 301, 427-1355)
Coordinator: OLIN ALLEN

NATURAL HERITAGE PROGRAMS

Florida Natural Areas Inventory
1018 Thomasville Rd., Suite 200-c
Tallahassee, FL 32303
(904, 224-8207; Fax: 904, 681-9364)
Director: GARY KNIGHT

Georgia Natural Heritage Program
Wildlife Resources Division
Georgia Department of Natural Resources
2117 U.S. Hwy. 278 SE
Social Cir., GA 30279
(706, 557-3032; Fax: 706, 557-3040; Internet:
natural_heritage@mail.dnr.state.ga.us)
Program Manager: JOHN BOZEMAN

Hawaii Natural Heritage Program
The Nature Conservancy of Hawaii
1116 Smith St., Suite 201
Honolulu, HI 96817
(808, 537-4508; Fax: 808, 545-2019)
Director: DANIEL ORODENKER

Idaho Conservation Data Center
Department of Fish & Game
600 South Walnut St. Box 25
Boise, ID 83707
(208, 334-3402; Fax: 208, 334-2114)
Coordinator/Ecologist: BOB MOSELEY (Internet:
bmoseley@idfg.state.id.us)

Illinois Natural Heritage Division
Department of Resources
524 South 2nd St.
Springfield, IL 62701
(217, 785-8774; Fax: 217, 785-8277)
Division Chief: CARL BECKER

Indiana Natural Heritage Data Center
Division of Nature Preserves
Department of Natural Resources
402 West Washington St., Rm. W267
Indianapolis, IN 46204
(317, 232-4052; Fax: 317, 233-0133)
Coordinator: CLOYCE HEDGE

Iowa Natural Areas Inventory
Bureau of Preserves & Ecological Services
Department of Natural Resources
Wallace State Office Bldg.
Des Moines, IA 50319
(515, 281-8524; Fax: 515, 281-6794)
Coordinator: DARYL HOWELL (515, 281-8524)

Kansas Natural Heritage Inventory
Kansas Biological Survey
University of Kansas
2041 Constant Ave.
Lawrence, KS 66047-2906
(913, 864-3453; Fax: 913, 864-5093)
Coordinator/Botonist: CRAIG FREEMAN
(913, 864-3453; Internet: c-freeman@ukans.edu)

Kentucky Natural Heritage Program
Kentucky State Nature Preserves Commission
801 Schenkel Ln., Frankfort, KY 40601
(502, 573-2886; Fax: 502, 573-2355)
Director: ROBERT McCANE, JR.
(Internet: bmccance.ksnpc@mail.state.ky.us)

Louisiana Natural Heritage Program
Department of Wildlife & Fisheries
P.O. Box 98000, Baton Rouge, LA 70898-9000
(504, 765-2821; Fax: 504, 765-2607)
Coordinator: GARY LESTER (504, 765-2823)

Maine Natural Areas Program
Department of Conservation
(FedEx/UPS: 159 Hospital St.
93 State House Station
Augusta, ME 04333-0093
(207, 287-8044; Fax: 207, 287-8040;
E-mail: mnap@state.me.us; Internet:
http://www.state.me.us/doc/mnap.home.htm)
Coordinator: MOLLY DOCHERTY (207, 287-8045)

Maryland Heritage and Biodiversity Conservation Programs
Department of Natural Resources
Tawes State Office Bldg., E-1
Annapolis, MD 21401
(410, 974-3195; Fax: 410, 974-5590)
Associate Director: MIKE SLATTERY

Massachusetts Natural Heritage & Endangered Species Program
Division of Fisheries & Wildlife
Route 135, Westborough, MA 01581
(508, 792-7270/ext. 200; Fax: 508, 792-7275)
Coordinator: HENRY WOOLSEY (508, 792-7270 ext. 162;
E-mail: hwoolsey@state.ma.us)

Michigan Natural Features Inventory
(FedEx/ UPS: 530 W. Allegan, 48933)
Mason Bldg., 5th Fl., Box 30444
Lansing, MI 48909-7944
(517, 373-1552; Fax: 517, 373-6705)
Director: LENI WILSMANN (517, 373-7565;
Internet: wilsman1@wildlife.dnr.state.mi.us)

Minnesota Natural Heritage & Nongame Research
Department of Natural Resources
500 Lafayette Rd., Box 7, St. Paul, MN 55155
(612, 297-4964; Fax: 612, 297-4961)
Coordinator: BONITA ELIASON (612, 297-2276;
Internet: bonita.eliason@dnr.state.mn.us)

Mississippi Natural Heritage Program
Museum of Natural Science
111 North Jefferson St.
Jackson, MS 39201-2897
(601, 354-7303; Fax: 601, 354-7227)
Coordinator/Botanist: KEN GORDON

Missouri Natural Heritage Database
Missouri Department of Conservation
P.O. Box 180, (FedEx: 2901 West Truman Blvd)
Jefferson City, MO 65102
(314, 751-4115; Fax: 314, 526-5582)
Database Coordinator: DOROTHY BUTLER

Montana Natural Heritage Program
State Library Bldg.
1515 E. 6th Ave., Helena, MT 59620
(406, 444-3009; Fax: 406, 444-0581; mtnhp@nris.mt.gov;
nris.msl.mt.gov/mtnhp/nhp-dir.html)
Director/Zoologist: DAVID GENTER (406, 444-3019)
E-mail: dgenter@nris.msl.mt.gov

Nebraska Natural Heritage Program
Game and Parks Commission
2200 North 33rd St., P.O. Box 30370
Lincoln, NE 68503
(402, 471-5421; Fax: 402, 471-5528)
Coordinator/Biologist: RICK SCHNEIDER

Nevada Natural Heritage Program
Department of Conservation & Natural Resources
1550 E. College Parkway, Suite 145
Carson City, NV 89710
(702, 687-4245; Fax: 702, 885-0868)
Program Manager/Zoologist: GLENN CLEMMER

Conservation Information Resources

New Hampshire Natural Heritage Inventory
Department of Resources & Economic Development
172 Pembroke St., P.O. Box 1856
Concord, NH 03302
(603, 271-3623; Fax: 603, 271-2629)
Coordinator: DAVID VANLUVEN

New Jersey Natural Heritage Program
Office of Natural Lands Management
22 S. Clinton Ave. CN404
Trenton, NJ 08625-0404
(609, 984-1339; Fax: 609, 984-1427)
Coordinator/Ecologist: TOM BREDEN (609, 984-0097)

New Mexico Natural Heritage Program
University of New Mexico
851 University Blvd., SE, Suite 101
Albuquerque, NM 87131-1091
(505, 272-3545; Fax: 505, 272-3544)
Director/Research Zoologist: PAT MEHLHOP
(505, 277-5600; E-mail: pmehlhop@unm.edu)

New York Natural Heritage Program
Department of Environmental Conservation
700 Troy-Schenectady Rd.
Latham, NY 12110-2400
(518, 783-3932; Fax: 518, 783-3916)
Coordinator/Zoologist: KATHRYN SCHNEIDER
(518, 783-3937; Internet: kschneider@tnc.org)

North Carolina Heritage Program
NC Department of Environment, Health & Natural Resources
Division of Parks & Recreation
P.O. Box 27687, Raleigh, NC 27611
(919, 733-7701; Fax: 919, 715-3085)
Coordinator: LINDA PEARSALL

North Dakota Natural Heritage Inventory
North Dakota Parks & Recreation Department
1835 Bismarck Expressway
Bismarck, ND 58504
(701, 328-5357; Fax: 701, 328-5363)
Coordinator/Zoologist: KATHY ARMSTRONG

Ohio Natural Heritage Data Base
Division of Natural Areas & Preserves
Department of Natural Resources
1889 Fountain Square, Bldg. F-1
Columbus, OH 43224
(614, 265-6453; Fax: 614, 267-3096)
Division Chief: GUY DENNY

Oklahoma Natural Heritage Inventory
Oklahoma Biological Survey
111 East Chesapeake St., University of Oklahoma
Norman, OK 73019-0575
(405, 325-1985; Fax: 405, 325-7702;
obssun02.uoknor.edu/biosurvey/onhi/home.html)
Coordinator/Aquatic Zoologist: CARYN VAUGHN

Oregon Natural Heritage Program
Oregon Field Office
The Nature Conservancy
821 SE 14th Ave., Portland, OR 97214
(503, 731-3070, 230-1221; Fax: 503, 230-9639)
Coordinator/Ecologist: JIMMY KAGAN
(E-mail: jkagan@tnc.org)

Pennsylvania Natural Diversity Inventory PNDI-East
The Nature Conservancy
34 Airport Dr., Middletown, PA 17057
(717, 948-3962; Fax: 717, 948-3957)
Coordinator: ANTHONY DAVIS

Western Pennsylvania Conservancy
PNDI-West, 316 Fourth Ave.
Pittsburgh, PA 15222
(412, 288-2777; Fax: 412, 281-1792)
Coordinator/Botanist: PAUL WIEGMAN
(412, 288-2777)

PNDI-Central
Bureau of Forestry
P.O. Box 8552
Harrisburg, PA 17105-8552
(717, 783-0388; Fax: 717, 783-5109)
State Coordinator/Botanist: KATHY McKENNA
(717, 783-0388)

Rhode Island Natural Heritage Program
Department of Environmental Management
Division of Planning & Development
235 Promenade St., 3rd Floor
Providence, RI 02908
(401, 277-2776 x4308; Fax: 401, 277-2069)
Coordinator/Botanist: RICK ENSER

South Carolina Heritage Trust
SC Wildlife & Marine Resources Department
P.O. Box 167, Columbia, SC 29202
(803, 734-3893; Fax: 803, 734-6310 (call first))
Coordinator: STEVE BENNETT

South Dakota Natural Heritage Data Base
SD Department of Game, Fish & Parks
Wildlife Division, 523 E. Capitol Ave., Pierre, SD 57501-3182
(605, 773-4227; Fax: 605, 773-6245)
Botanist/Ecologist: DAVE ODE (605, 773-4227;
E-mail: daveo@gfp.state.sd.us)

Tennessee Division of Natural Heritage
Tennessee Department of Environment & Conservation
401 Church St., Life and Casualty Tower, 8th Fl.
Nashville, TN 37243-0447
(615, 532-0431; Fax: 615, 532-0046)
Heritage Coordinator: SMOOT MAJOR

Texas CDC
P.O. Box 1440, San Antonio, TX 78295-1440
210-224-8774; Fax: 210-228-9805
Coordinator: TERRY COOK

Utah Natural Heritage Program
Division of Wildlife Resources
1596 West North Temple
Salt Lake City, UT 84116
(801, 538-4761; Fax: 801, 538-4709)
Coordinator: DOUG STONE (801, 538-4761;
E-mail: nrdwr.dstone@email.state.ut.us)

Vermont Nongame & Natural Heritage Program
Vermont Fish & Wildlife Department
103 S. Main St., 10 S.
Waterbury, VT 05671-0501
(802, 241-3700; Fax: 802, 241-3295)
Program Coordinator: STEVE PARREN (802, 241-3717;
E-mail: sparren@fwd.anr.state.vt.us)

Virginia Division of Natural Heritage
Department of Conservation & Recreation
214 Governor St., 3rd Floor
Richmond, VA 23219
(804, 786-7951; Fax: 804, 371-2674)
www.state.va.us/~dcr/vaher.html
Division Director: TOM SMITH (804, 786-4554;
E-mail: tsmith.dcr@state.va.us)

Washington Natural Heritage Program
Department of Natural Resources
(FedEx: 1111 Washington St. SE)
P.O. Box 47016, Olympia, WA 98504-7016
(360, 902-1340; Fax: 360, 902-1783)

NATURAL HERITAGE PROGRAMS

Program Manager: MARK SHEEHAN (360, 902-1664;
E-mail: mamm490@wadnr.gov)

West Virginia Natural Heritage Program
Department of Natural Resources Operations Center
Ward Rd., P.O. Box 67, Elkins, WV 26241
(304, 637-0245; Fax: 304, 637-0250)
Coordinator: BRIAN McDONALD
(E-mail: bmcdonald@mail.dnr.state.wv.us)

Wisconsin Natural Heritage Program
Endangered Resources/4
Department of Natural Resources
101 S. Webster St., Box 7921
Madison, WI 53707
(608, 266-7012; Fax: 608, 266-2925)
Coordinator: BETTY LES
(608, 266-3369; E:mail: lesb@dnr.state.wis.us)

Wyoming Natural Diversity Database
1604 Grand Ave., Suite 2
Laramie, WY 82070
(307, 745-5026; Fax: 307, 745-5026 (call first);
Internet: wyndd@lariat.org)
Director: RICH LINDSEY

REGIONAL HERITAGE DATA CENTERS

Navajo Naural Heritage Program
Navajo Fish & Wildlife Department
P.O. Box 1480, Window Rock, AZ 86515-1480
(520, 871-6472; Fax: 520, 871-7069)
Coordinator: JACK MEYER (520, 871-7059
Internet: jmeyer@tnc.org

TVA Regional Natural Heritage
Resource Group Land Management
Norris, TN 37828 (423, 632-1593; Fax: 423, 632-1795)
Coordinator: WILLIAM H. REDMOND (423, 632-1593)
Internet: wredmond@mhs-tva.attmail.com

NATIONAL PARK DATA CENTERS

South Regional Office, National Park Service
Atlanta Federal Center, 1924 Bldg.
100 Alabama St., SW, Atlanta, GA 30303
404-562-3113; Fax: 404-562-3201
Natural Resource Data Manager: KELLEY WATSON

Great Smoky Mountains National Park
c/o Janet Rock, Keith Langdon
1314 Cherokee Orchard Rd.
Twin Creeks Natural Resources Center
Gatlinburg, TN 37738
(423, 436-1264; Fax: 423, 436-5598)
Coordinator and Supervisory Biologist: KEITH LANGDON

Gulf Islands National Seashore
1801 Gulf Breeze Parkway
Gulf Breeze, FL 32561
904, 934-2605

Mammoth Cave National Park
Division of Science & Resource Management
Mammoth Cave National Park
Mammoth Cave, KY 42259
(502, 758-2238)
Chief, Science & Research Mgmt: JEFF BRADYBAUGH

National Capital Region Conservation Data Center
13025 Riley's Lock Rd., Poolesville, MD 20837
(301, 427-1302; Fax: 301, 427-1355)
Coordinator and Zoologist: OLIN ALLEN; olin_allen@npa.gov

CANADA-ROVINCIAL PROGRAMS

Alberta Natural Heritage Inventory Center
Alberta Department of Environmental Protection
10405 Jasper Ave.
Edmonton, Alberta T5J 3N4
Canada (403, 427-5209; Fax: 403, 427-5980)
Joint Coordinator: PETER LEE
Internet: plee@env.gov.ab.ca

British Columbia Conservation Data Centre
Wildlife Branch, Ministry of Environment
780 Blanshard St., Victoria, BC V8V 1X5
Canada (604, 356-0928; Fax: 604, 387-2733)
Coordinator: ANDREW HARCOMBE (604, 387-9798)
Internet: aharcomb@fwhdept.env.gov.bc.ca

Manitoba Conservation Data Centre
Department of Natural Resources
Wildlife Branch, Box 24, 200 Saulteaux Crescent
Winnipeg, Manitoba R3J 3W3
Canada (204, 945-7743; Fax: 204, 945-1365)
Internet: mbcdc@lic.gov.mb.ca
Manager: CAROL SCOTT (204, 945-2911)

Le Centre de Données sur, le Patrimoine Naturel du Québec
Ministère de l'Environnement
Direction de la conservation et du patrimoine écologique
2360 Ch. Ste-Foy, 1er étage, Sainte-Foy, Québec G1V 4H2
Canada (418, 644-3358; Fax: 418, 646-6169)
Coordinator: GILDO LAVOIE

Natural Heritage Information Centre
P.O. Box 7000, 300 Walter St., 2nd Floor, North Tower
Peterborough, Ontario K9J 8M5
Canada (705, 745-6767; Fax: 705, 755-2168)
Coordinator: ROB PARRY (705, 755-2158)
Internet: parryro@epo.gov.on.ca

Saskatchewan Conservation Data Centre
SK Environment & Resource Management
3211 Albert St., Regina, SK S4S 5W6
Canada (306, 787-7196; Fax: 306, 787-7085)
Coordinator: MARLON KILLABY
Internet: mkillaby@unibase.unibase.com
Internet: jkeith@unibase.unibase.com

LATIN AMERICA/CARIBBEAN PROGRAMS

Centro de Datos para la Conservación de Bolivia Calle Juan
Jose Perez, No. 268 1er piso , Casilla 11250
La Paz, BOLIVIA (39-0565/USA: 011-59-12; Fax: 37-5371)
Internet: CDC@tropico.rds.org.bo)
Executive Director: EDUARDO FORNO

Centro de Datos para la Conservación de Colombia
Corporación Autónoma Regional del Valle del Cauca (CVC)
Carrera 56 No.11-36; Apartado Aéreo 2366
Cali, COLOMBIA (Tel: 30-6643; USA: 011-57-23; Fax: 39-3393)
Coordinator: EDUARDO VELASCO ABAD

Corporación Centro de Datos para la Conservación
Apartado 17-21-1332, Quito, ECUADOR
(Tel: 257-68; USA: 011-593-2; Fax: 24-5189)
Internet: cdc@vio.satnet.net
Executive Director: CARMEN JOSSE

Centro de Datos para la Conservación de Guatemala
Centro de Estudios Conservacionistas (CECON)
Universidad de San Carlos

Avenida de la Reforma 0-63, Zona 10
Ciudad de Guatemala, GUATEMALA 01010
(Tel: 34-7662, 34-6064 y 31-0904; USA: 011-502; Fax: 34-7664)
Internet: cecon@uvalle.edu.gt
Coordinator: OLGA ISABEL VALDEZ RODAS

Conservation Data Center - Jamaica
Department of Botany
University of the West Indies, Mona
Kingston 7, Jamaica
(Tel: 809 977-0743; Fax: 809 977-0743)
Data Manager: NELLA STEWART
Internet: nstewart@uwimona.edu.jm

Centro de Datos para la Conservación de la Naturaleza en Sonora
Centro Ecológico de Sonora
Carretera a Guaymas Km. 2.5
Apartado postal 1497
Hermosillo, Sonora, MEXICO 83240
(Tel: 50-1137 y 50-1225; USA: 011-52-62; Fax: 50-1034)
Coordinator: JOSE R. CAMPOY FAVELA

Netherlands Antilles Natural Heritage Program
Carmabi Foundation, P.O. Box 2090
Curaçao, NETHERLANDS ANTILLES
(Tel: 62-4242; USA: 011-599-9; Fax: 62-7680)
Coordinator: JOHN de FREITAS

Centro de Datos para la Conservación de Panamá
Asociación Nacional para la Conservación de
la Naturaleza (ANCON)
Apartado Postal 1387, Zona 1
Panamá, REPUBLICA DE PANAMA
(Tel: 2-64-8100; USA: 011-507; Fax: 2-64-2445)
Director: IVAN A. VALDESPINO

Centro de Datos para la Conservación de Paraguay
Sub-Secretaría de Recursos Naturales y Ganadería
25 de Mayo 640 - 12 B, Casilla 3303, Asunción, PARAGUAY
(Tel: 49-4914; USA: 011-595-21; Fax: 49-5568)
Coordinator: NELIDA RIVAROLA

Centro de Datos para la Conservación de Perú
Universidad Nacional Agraria La Molina
Facultad de Ciencias Forestales
Apartado 456, Lima 100, PERU
(Tel: 437-1143; USA: 011-511; Fax: 437-1143)
Internet: cdc@redinf.edu.pe
Director: PEDRO G. VASQUEZ

División de Patrimonio Natural Area de Planificación de Recusos Integral
Departamento de Recursos Naturales y Ambientales
P.O. Box 5887, Puerta de Tierra, PUERTO RICO 00906
(Tel: 809-722-1726; Fax: 809-725-9526)
Division Director: MYRIAM GONZALEZ TORRES

Instituto Nacional de Parques
Ministerio del Ambiente y Recursos Naturales Renovables
Apartado Postal 76471, Caracas 1070-A, VENEZUELA
(Tel: 285-4106, 285-4360, 285-4859; USA: 011-58-2; Fax: 285-3070) Biologist: LYA CARDENAS

ENVIRONMENTAL DATABASES AND SERVICES

This is a list of databases and services that can provide electronic access to environmental information. Entries in this section are arranged alphabetically by database name and include producer name, address, telephone number, and a description of the database.

ABSEARCH
Type: Abstracts and bibliographies
Subject: Fisheries, Ecology, Birds, Mammals, Waterfowl, Wetlands, Wildlife, Zoology, Fire Ecology, Herpetology, Conservation Biology.
Language: English, Conservation Biology offered in Spanish
Available Service through: ABSEARCH, Inc.
Producer: ABSEARCH, Inc., 121 Sweet Ave., Moscow, ID 83843
(Phone: 1-800-867-1877; Fax: 208-885-3803) E-mail: absearch@aol.com
Contact: NAOMI D. FERGUSON, Officer Manager
ABSEARCH databases include abstracts and citations from professional research journals. The databases allow keyword search strings and easy printing of bibliographies. Over a dozen natural resource topics are covered.

AGRICOLA
Type: Bibliographic
Subject: Natural Resources, Animal Welfare, Pollution, Pesticides, Land and Water Management.
Language: English and over 70 other languages.
Available Service Through: DIALOG, OCLC
Producer: National Agricultural Library, Information Systems Division, 10301 Baltimore Blvd., Beltsville, MD 20705
Phone: (301, 504-6813)
Contact: DAVID GOLDBERG
AGRICOLA is a database of bibliographic citations covering all aspects of agricultural and food sciences, including natural resources, animal welfare, pollution, pesticides, and land and water management. The database has over three million records, which are updated monthly at a rate of 9,000-10,000 per month.

Air and Water Pollution Report
Type: Full Text
Subject: Environmental Law, Air Quality and Pollution, Water Pollution Management, toxic substances.
Language: English
Available Service Through: Newsnet and Predicasts
Producer: Business Publishers, Inc., 951 Pershing Dr., Silver Spring, MD 20910-4464
Phone: (301, 587-6300; Fax: 301, 587-1081)
Contact: DAVID GOELLER
Covers policy regulation and legislation on the Clean Air and Water Acts, global warming research, acid rain, air toxics, indoor air pollutants, and much more, for the regulator and the regulated community.

AQUALINE
Type: Abstracts
Subject: Water Cycle
Language: English
Available Service Through: QUESTEL-ORBIT
Producer: WRc plc, Frankland Rd., Blagrove, Swindon, Wilts SN5 8YF, Great Britain
Phone: (01)793 511 711; Fax: (01) 793, 511 712; E-mail: aqualine@wrcplc.co.uk
Contact: KAREN HUTCHESON
Aqualine covers the world's literature on the complete hydrological cycle from source to sea, up to and including the continental shelf.

Aquatic Toxicity Information Retrieval (AQUIRE)
Type: Data extract from scientific papers
Subject: Toxicity of chemical substances to aquatic species.
Language: English
Available Service Through: Chemical Information System (CIS)
Producer: EPA, 810 Gleneagles Ct., #300, Towson, MD 21286
Phone: (410, 321-8440; 800- CIS-USER)
Contact: CIS User Support Group
AQUIRE includes more than 129,000 records detailing the effects of chemical substances on aquatic species, including chronic and acute toxicity data.

Arctic and Antarctic Regions (Cold Regions)
Type: Bibliographic

ENVIRONMENTAL DATABASES AND SERVICES

Subject: Arctic, Antarctic, Polar Regions, and Cold Regions.
Language: English
Available Service Through: CD-ROM and Internet
Producer: National Information Services Corporation, Suite 6, Wyman Towers, 3100 St. Paul St., Baltimore, MD 21218.
Phone: (410, 243-0797; Fax: 410, 243-0982)
Contact: Sales@NISC.com
Over 710,000 citations and abstracts from nine major polar files.

Australian Earth Sciences Information System
Type: Bibliographic
Subject: Environmental protection, pollution, rehabilitation
Language: English
Producer: Australian Mineral Foundation, 63 Conyngham St., Glenside, S.A., Australia 5065
(Phone: Aust: 08 83790444; International: 61 8 83790444; E-mail: amf@amf.com.au; www.amf.com.au/amf)
Contact: KEVIN BOND
AESIS covers Australian-generated published and unpublished documented material over the full range of the geo sciences. AESIS also covers material published on continental Australia by non-Australian sources. AESIS is the world's largest database on Australian geoscience, minerals and petroleum information. Also available on CD-ROM and via Dialog Corporation as file 105.

BAKER
Type: Data extracted from scientific papers
Subject: Chemical-physical properties, fire and health hazards, spill and disposal information, storage and handling information, and protective equipment information.
Language: English
Available Service Through: Chemical Information System (CIS)
Producer: J.T. Baker Chemical Company, 810 Gleneagles Ct., Suite 300, Towson, MD 21286
Phone: (410, 321-8440; 800-CIS-USER)
Contact: CIS User Support Group
BAKER is a collection of Material Safety Data Sheets (MSDS) for over 1,950 chemical substances. Each record of information represents one chemical. These MSDS's were prepared in accordance with guidelines issued by the U.S. Occupational Safety and Health Administration.

BIOSIS Previews®
Type: Bibliographic
Subject: Botany, Ecology, Environmental Biology, Evolution, Forestry, Horticulture, Plant Physiology, Soil Microbiology, Temperature.
Language: English
Available Service Through: OVID Online, Dialog, DIMDI, Data Star, Science and Technology Information Center, Royal Institute of Technology Library Information and Documentation Center, Royal Society of Chemistry, NERAC, Inc., OCLC Online Computer Library Center, Inc.
Producer: BIOSIS, 2100 Arch St., Philadelphia, PA 19103-1399
Phone: (1-800, 523-4806; 215, 587-4800; Fax: 215, 587-2016; E-mail: info@mail.biosis.org)
Contact: ALAN CLARKE
BIOSIS Previews is the on-line version of the citations found in the printed publications Biological Abstracts and Biological Abstracts/RRM (Reports, Reviews, and Meetings). This database contains bibliographic information and abstracts derived from original life science source publications, with indexing added by the BIOSIS editorial staff.

Business and the Environment
Type: Full Text Newsletter
Subject: Monthly International coverage of "green" corporate environmental initiatives, environmental regulations, and related topics.
Language: English
Available Service Through: hardcopy subscription; access via Website
Producer: Cutter Info. Corp., 37 Broadway, Suite 1, Arlington, MA 02174 USA
Phone: (1-800-964-5125; 617, 641-5125)
Contact: DENNIS CROWLEY
Subscription includes quarterly Meeting Planner listing of environment-related meetings and conferences worldwide, and the ISO 14000 Update, a monthly briefing on the ISO 14000 environmental management systems standards.

CERCLA Information System (CERCLIS)
Type: Full Text
Subject: SUPERFUND Sites.
Language: English
Available Service Through: Chemical Information System (CIS)
Producer: EPA, 810 Gleneagles Ct., Suite 300, Towson, MD 21286
Phone: (410, 321-8440; 800-CIS-USER)
Contact: CIS User Support Group
CERCLIS contains complete public disclosure records from EPA for more than 42,000 US sites, either proposed or chosen for cleanup under Superfund. It is searchable by name, locale (e.g., city, zip), and a variety of other methods. No Further Remedial Action Planned (NFRAP) sites and Potentially Responsible Parties (PRP) are included in the database.

Chemical Carcinogenesis Research Information System (CCRIS)
Type: Data extracted from scientific papers
Subject: Carcinogenicity, mutagenicity, cocarcinogenicity, and tumor promotion.
Language: English
Available Service Through: Chemical Information System (CIS)
Producer: NCI, 810 Gleneagles Ct., Suite 300, Towson, MD 21286
Phone: (410, 321-8440; 800-CIS-USER)
Contact: CIS User Support Group
CCRIS, originating from the National Cancer Institute of the National Institutes of Health. CCRIS contains individual assay results and test conditions for over 1,450 chemicals.

Chemical Evaluation Search and Retrieval System (CESARS)
Type: Text and Tabular
Subject: Toxicity of chemicals of concern to the environment.
Language: English
Available Service Through: CIS, CCINFOLINE (online), CCINFODISK (CD version)
Producer: Michigan Department of Environmental Quality, Surface Water Quality Division, P.O. Box 30273, Lansing, MI 48909 and Ontario Ministry of the Environment and Energy, Hazardous Contaminants Coordination Branch, 2 St. Clair Ave., West, 12th Fl., Toronto, Ontario, Canada M4V 1L5
Phone: (517, 335-3312; 335-3308)
Contact: GARY HURLBURT or DENNIS BUSH
Chemicals are evaluated for their toxicity by reviewing the primary literature sources.

Chemical Hazards Information System (ChemHazIS)
Type: Data extracted from scientific papers.
Subject: Toxicity, Health, Carcinogenicity, Chemical-Physical Properties, Transportation, Regulations, and uses.
Language: English
Available Service Through: Chemical Information System (CIS)
Producer: NTP, 810 Gleneagles Ct., Suite 300, Towson, MD 21286
Phone: (410, 321-8440; 800-CIS-USER)
Contact: CIS User Support Group
ChemHazIS contains over 2,280 chemical compiled by the National Toxicology Program (NTP). Each record closely resembles a Material Safety Data Sheet (MSDS) format.

Chemical Hazards Response Information System (CHRIS)
Type: Data extracted from scientific paper
Subject: Handling of hazardous materials.
Language: English

ENVIRONMENTAL DATABASES AND SERVICES

Available Service Through: Chemical Information System (CIS)
Producer: U.S. Coast Guard, 810 Gleneagles Ct., Suite 300, Towson, MD 21286
Phone: (410, 321-8440; 800-CIS-USER)
Contact: CIS User Support Group
CHRIS is the Coast Guard's principal database for providing information on safe handling of hazardous substances.

Computer-aided Environmental Legislative Data System (CELDS)
Type: Abstracts
Subject: Environmental Regulations.
Language: English
Available Service Through: N/A
Producer: Environmental Technical Information System, 611 E Lorado Taft Dr., #111 Champaign, IL 61820-6921
Phone: (217, 333-1369; Fax: 217, 244-1717)
Contact: ELIZABETH DENNISON
CELDS is an information bank of abstracted federal and state environmental regulations and standards. Intended for use by the layperson, abstracts classified within several environmental sector categories provide quick access to current regulations that relate to the environment.

ECOLINE
Type: Full text, key words
Subject: Acid Rain, Global Warming, Soil Erosion, Environmental Programs.
Language: English
Available Service Through: Together Foundation, 130 S. Willard St., Burlington, VT 05401
Producer: Together Foundation and the University of Vermont Environmental Program
Phone: (802, 682-2030; Fax: 802, 862-1890)
Contact: HANS KELLER

Ecology Abstracts
Type: Bibliographic
Subject: Ecology
Language: English
Available Service Through: Dialog
Producer: Cambridge Scientific Abstracts, 7200 Wisconsin Ave., Suite 601, Bethesda, MD 20814
Phone: (301, 961-6700)
Contact: ROBERT HILTON
A monthly printed abstracts journal available online through dialog, BIOSIS: Life Science Network, and BRS (as part of CSAL); CD ROM also; online updated monthly.

ECONET
Type: Various types
Subject: Energy, Environmental Education, Toxic Substances, Sustainable Development, Global Warming, Environmental Justice.
Language: English
Available Service Through: Institute for Global Communications, P.O. Box 29904, San Francisco, CA 94129-0904
Producer: Institute for Global Communications
Phone: (415, 561-6100; Fax: 415, 561-6101; E-mail: econet@igc.apc.org; Internet: www.igc.org)
Contact: MICHAEL STEIN, Outreach Director
Through the development of communication and information sharing systems, EcoNet seeks to increase collaboration and cooperation between organizations seeking environmental sustainability.

Emergency Release Notification System (ERNS)
Type: Data extracted from reference
Subject: Notifications of oil and hazardous substances releases and spills
Language: English
Available Service Through: Chemical Information System (CIS)
Producer: EPA, 810 Gleneagles Ct., Suite 300, Towson, MD 21286
Phone: (410, 321-8440; 800-CIS-USER)
Contact: CIS User Support Group
ERNS contains over 231,312 release and spill notifications of oil and/or hazardous substances. It can be used to examine the following categories: Transportation accident, equipment failure, operator error, natural phenomenon, dumping, and unknown.

Energy Design Update
Type: Full Text
Subject: Energy-efficient residential design and construction.
Language: English
Available Service Through: Newsnet
Producer: Cutter Info. Corp., 37 Broadway, Arlington, MA 02174
Phone: (1-800-964-5118)
Contact: KAREN KURR
Level-headed news and analysis of developments in energy-efficient home construction. Practical, hands-on information on the latest building techniques and products.

Energy, Economics, and Climate Change
Type: Full Text
Subject: Economic implications of climate change policies.
Language: English
Available Service Through: Newsnet, Predicasts
Producer: Cutter Information Corp., 37 Broadway, Arlington, MA 02174
Phone: (1-800-964-5118)
Contact: KAREN KURR
Analyses of latest economic studies and reports pertaining to climate change, legislative updates, and utility regulation.

ENVIROFATE
Type: Data extracted from scientific papers
Subject: Environmental fate of chemicals.
Language: English
Available Service Through: Chemical Information System (CIS)
Producer: EPA, 810 Gleneagles Ct., Suite 300, Towson, MD 21286
Phone: (410, 321-8440; 800- CIS-USER)
Contact: CIS User Support Group
ENVIROFATE deals with the environmental fate or behavior of chemicals released into the environment. It covers a variety of types of data. It includes more than 15,000 records on some 1,300 substances.

Enviroline
Subject: Acid Rain, Environment, Land Use Planning, Population Growth, and Transportation
Available Service Through: Dialog
Producer: Congressional Information Service, Inc., 4520 East-West Hwy., Bethesda, MD 20814-3389
Phone: (800-638-8380 or 301, 654-1550; Fax: 301, 654-4033)
Contact: DIANE KEELY, Director of Communications (Acting)
Publishes indexes, electronic databases, and microform collections that provide access to information published by government, private, and international sources.

Environment Abstracts
Type: Abstracting and Indexing
Subjects: Environment, Air, Water, Noise Pollution, Environmental Law, Wildlife Management, Solid and Toxic Wastes.
Language: English
Available Service Through: Dialog, ORBIT, Infoline, ESA-IRS, DIMDI, Data Star, FIZ-TECHNIK, Lexis-Nexis
Producer: Congressional Information Service, Inc., 4520 East-West Hwy., Suite 800, Bethesda, MD 20814-3389
Phone: (301, 654-1550)
Contact: LARRY SHERIDAN, Managing Editor
Abstracts and indexes information from scientific, technical, and business journals; conference and symposium proceedings; newsletters; and academic, corporate, and government reports. Formats in which service is available: Print monthly, quarterly, and annual indexes; CD-ROM; microfiche; magnetic tape.

Environmental Bibliography
Type: Bibliographic, Keywords

Subject: Ecology, Energy, Land Resources, Water Resources, Health.
Language: English
Available Service Through: Dialog-file 68, Compuserve (I-Quest), CSA-Environmental Routenet, CD-ROM (NISC)
Producer: International Academy, 5385 Hollister Ave., # 210, Santa Barbara, CA 93111
Phone: (805, 683-4927; Fax: 805,683-4637; www.iasb.org)
Contact: ELAINE MESSIER
Covers more than 400 scientific and popular journals in social, political and philosophical issues, air, energy, land and water resources, nutrition, and health. Authors abstracts, 1997 forward.

Environmental Information Connection
Type: N/A
Subject: N/A
Language: English
Available Service Through: N/A
Producer: Environmental Technical Information System, 1003 W. Nevada St., Urbana, IL 61801
Phone: (217, 333-1369; Fax: 217, 244-1717)
Contact: ELIZABETH DENNISON
The Environmental Information Connection provides literature searches, prepares bibliographies, obtains information about environmental databases and software, investigates information sources, and locates specialists or information centers.

Environmental Periodicals Bibliography
Type: Bibliographic
Subject: Air, Land, Water, Energy, Human Ecology, Nutrition, Health, Environment, Toxicity, Pollution, Waste Management.
Language: English
Available Service Through: CD-ROM
Producer: National Information Services Corporation, Suite 6, Wyman Towers, 3100 St. Paul St., Baltimore, MD 21218
Phone: (410, 243-0797; Fax: 410, 243-0982)
Contact: Sales@NISC.com
More than 578,000 citations from the Environmental Studies Institute of the International Academy make EPB the world's largest collection on environmental issues and research. Widely respected for the breadth and quality of its indexing, EPB is your reference to thousands of scientific, technical, and popular periodicals from around the world.

Environmental Resources Technology (ERTH)
Type: Bibliographic with abstracts
Subject: Petroleum exploration and production.
Language: English
Available Service Through: ORBIT-QUESTEL
Producer: Petroleum Abstracts/The University of Tulsa, 600 S. College, 101 Harwell, Tulsa, OK 74104-3189
Phone: (918, 631-2295; 1-800, 247-8678)
Contact: DAVID BROWN, Manager of Marketing
Available in print as E&P Health, Safety and Environment ($185.00/yr).
ERTH is a guide to information on ecology and pollution related to petroleum exploration, production and transportation, plus environmental, health, and safety topics. Over 36,000 entries. Updated monthly. 1965-present.

Facilities Index Data System (FINDS)
Type: Reference
Subject: EPA-regulated facilities and sites.
Language: English
Available Service Through: Chemical Information System (CIS)
Producer: EPA, 810 Gleneagles Ct., Suite 300, Towson, MD 21286
Phone: (410, 321-8440; 800-CIS-USER)
Contact: CIS User Support Group
FINDS contains several hundred thousand records pertaining to sites and facilities regulated by EPA. Also contains references to other databases (e.g., RCRIS, CERCLIS) containing information on these sites and facilities.

Fish and Fisheries Worldwide
Type: Abstracts and Bibliographic
Subjects: Aquaculture, Fish, Fisheries, Marine, Ocean, Water.
Language: English
Available Service Through: CD-ROM and Internet
Producer: National Information Services Corporation, Suite 6, Wyman Towers, 3100 St. Paul St., Baltimore, MD 21218
Phone: (410, 243-0797; Fax: 410, 243-0982)
Contact: Sales@NISC.com
Several leading files cover the world's literature on fisheries and fish-related topics. Over 180,000 citations are drawn from *Fisheries Review*, compiled by the U.S. National Biological Service, the Fish and Wildlife Reference Service file. Quarterly updates, $895.00 year subscription.

Fish and Wildlife Reference Service Database
Type: Bibliographic
Subjects: Fisheries, Wildlife, Habitat.
Language: English
Available Service Through: U.S. Fish and Wildlife Website (http://www.fws.gov)
Producer: Fish and Wildlife Reference Service, 5430 Grosvenor Ln., #110, Bethesda, MD 20814
Phone: (301, 492-6403; 1-800, 582-3421)
Contact: PAUL WILSON
Primarily state fish and wildlife agency research reports; some USFWS publications; and Coop Unit Theses and dissertations; some USNBS publications.

Florida Natural Areas Inventory
1018 Thomasville Rd., Suite 200-C, Tallahassee, FL 32303
Subject: Biodiversity, Endangered and Threatened Species, Natural Areas, Nature Preservation, and Wildlife/Wildlife Habitat
Contact: GARY KNIGHT, Director (850-224-8207)
Florida Natural Areas Inventory provides a continuous process for identifying important natural areas and making data available to decision-makers involved in land planning, research, acquisition, and resource management. Information on the status and distribution of natural communities, rare and endangered species of plants and animals, and other natural features is collected, processed, and analyzed through an integrated data management system.

Global Environmental Change Report
Type: Full Text
Subjects: Climate Change, Stratospheric Ozone Depletion, Deforestation, Acid Rain.
Language: English
Available Service Through: Newsnet, Predicasts
Producer: Cutter Info. Corp., 37 Broadway, Arlington, MA 02174
Phone: (1-800-964-5118)
Contact: KAREN KURR
Policy trends, industry actions, and scientific findings worldwide on global climate change, noted for its balanced, insightful approach to controversial topics.

GreenDisk Paperless Environmental Journal
Type: Full text, bibliographic, keywords
Subject: Environment
Language: English
Available service through: Disk by mail, EcoNet, and Internet FTP.
Producer: The GreenDisk, P.O. Box 32224, Washington, D.C. 20007. E-mail: greendisk@igc.apc.org
Phone: (1-888-GRN-DISK)
Contact: WILLIAM C. SUGG, Editor
Published six times per year in IBM or Macintosh format. Keyword searchable. Covers a wide range of environmental issues. Forum for the publication of research reports, press releases, action alerts, and news summaries from the world's environmental groups and governmental agencies. Audience: Environmental educators, professionals, journalists, activists. Browse a sample issue at www.igc.org/greendisk.

ENVIRONMENTAL DATABASES AND SERVICES

GreenNet
259 Dorchester Manor Blvd., North Charleston, SC 29420-8108 (Voice: 803, 552-2145; Fax: 803, 760-2109; BBS: 803, 552-4389; E-mail: greennet@f50.n372.z1fidonet.org or greennet@earthart.com)
Founded: 1991; Members: 3,300.
Subject: Biodiversity, Environmental/Conservation Education, International Conservation, Waterfowl, and Wildlife/Wildlife Habitat
Language: English
Available service through: Online Earth Art BBS in Green BBS Door
GreenNet is a free international environmental BBS network, created to further understanding of important ecological issues now facing the global community. We're best known for compiling The International GREEN BBS List, distributed worldwide over the internet serving as International Hub for the Sierra Club BBS Network. Hosted from Earth Art BBS (1:372/50).
President and Network Director: ROBERT B. CHAPMAN
Primary Contact Method: Earth Art BBS (803, 552-4389; Fax:803, 760-2109; Voice: 803, 552-2145)

Greenwire
3129 Mt. Vernon Ave., Alexandria, VA 22305
(703, 518-8724; Fax: 703, 518-8702; E-mail: greenwire@njdc.com.)
Founded: 1991.
Greenwire is the nation's leading online environmental news service. Editors distill news and commentary from 200+ news sources and publish original interviews, news analyses, and other current information. A companion online database provides instant access to more than 30,000 stories published in *Greenwire*.
Publisher: DALE CURTIS

Ground Water Monitor
Type: Full Text
Subjects: Ground Water Contamination and Remediation, Waste Management.
Language: English
Available Service Through: Newsnet and Predicasts
Producer: Business Publishers, Inc., 951 Pershing Dr., Silver Spring, MD 20910-4464
Phone: (301, 587-6300; Fax: 301, 587-1081)
Complete coverage of state and federal ground water policy and regulation in making new technologies for remediation of contaminants in ground water.

Ground Water Network
Type: Bibliographic database with 78,000 ground water abstracts.
Subject: Environmental Protection, Geology, Water Pollution Management, Water Resources, Water Quality, Rivers, Environmental Law.
Language: English
Producer: National Ground Water Information Center, 601 Dempsey Rd., Westerville, OH 43081
Phone: (800-551-7379/614,898-7791; Fax: 614, 898-7786)
Contact: SANDY MASTERS
The NGWIC is a fee-based information service which conducts literature searches and document delivery for NGWA members and the general public. It also maintains six databases related to ground water, water treatability, NGWA Certified Ground Water Contractors, and U.S. Census on housing and water source information.

Hazardous Waste News
Type: Full Text
Subject: Environmental Law, Hazardous Waste Management.
Language: English
Available Service Through: Newsnet and Predicasts
Producer: Business Publishers, Inc., 951 Pershing Dr., Silver Spring, MD 20910-4464
Phone: (301, 587-6300; Fax: 301, 587-1081)
Contact: LOUISE HARRIS, Editor
Covers U.S. news, legislation, and regulatory issues. RCRA, generation and source reduction, testing and classification, collection, storage and treatment, and disposal options.

H.E.R.M.A.N. (Hierarchial Environmental Retrieval for Management and Networking)
Type: Bibliographic Subject: Ocean, shore, marsh, waterfowl, upland game and raptor birds; bats, game and fur species, carnivores, big game, marine mammals.
Language: All languages (titles in English)
Available Service Through: Wildlife Information Service
Producer: Wildlife Information Service, 9956 N. Highway 185, Las Cruces, NM 88005-6021
Phone: (505, 527-2547; wildlife@greatwhite.com)
Contact: JULIE L. MOORE
Contains references and descriptions from 1934 to date. Available on diskettes (ASCII - IBM). Secondary sources taken from Biological Abstracts, Zoological Record, Wildlife Review, NTIS, Dissertation Abstracts, etc.

Indoor Air Quality Update
Type: Full Text
Subject: Prevention and control of indoor air pollution.
Language: English
Available Service Through: Newsnet
Producer: Cutter Info. Corp., 37 Broadway, Arlington, MA 02174
Phone: (1-800-964-5118)
Contact: KAREN KURR
Advice on controlling potential pollutant sources, suggestions on building and HVAC design, operation, and maintenance, detailed case studies, legislative updates, and related issues.

Information System for Hazardous Organics in Water (ISHOW)
Type: Data extracted from scientific papers.
Subject: Environmental fate or behavior of organic chemicals.
Language: English
Available Service Through: Chemical Information System (CIS)
Producer: EPA, 810 Gleneagles Ct., Suite 300, Towson, MD 21286
Phone: (410, 321-8440; 800-CIS-USER)
Contact: CIS User Support Group
ISHOW contains six types of data (melting point, boiling point, partition coefficient, acid dissociation constant, water solubility, vapor pressure) for more than 5,400 chemical substances.

Inter Press Service (IPS)/Global Information Network
Type: Full Text
Subject: International - special focus on developing countries.
Language: English and Spanish
Available Service Through: Dialog, Nexis, Electric Library, NewsBank, Compuserve Newsgrid, Dow Jones Interactive, BBS with IPS Environment Library, Modem: BBS (212, 463-9393) Homework Helper Infonautics
Producer: 275 Seventh Ave., #1206, New York, NY 10001
Phone: (212, 627-0123; Fax: 212, 627-6137; E-mail: ipsgin@igc.apc.org)
Contacts: K.C SEOL, MONICA CARRERA
Global Information Network is the distributor of Inter Press Service and other news wires from developing countries with special features on the environment.

Solar and Renewable Energy Outlook
Type: Full Text
Subject: Solar Energy, Renewable Resources.
Language: English
Available Service Through: Newsnet and Predicasts
Producer: Business Publishers, Inc., 951 Pershing Dr., Silver Spring, MD 20910-4464
Phone: (301, 587-6300; Fax: 301, 587-1081)
Contact: TODD LEEUWENBURGH
The only newsletter in the world that is dedicated exclusively to developments that affect the domestic and international market for a broad range of renewable energy technologies.

IRIS (Integrated Risk Information System)
Type: Data extract from scientific papers
Subject: Risk assessment of hazardous chemicals.
Language: English

ENVIRONMENTAL DATABASES AND SERVICES

Available Service Through: Chemical Information System (CIS)
Producer: EPA, 810 Gleneagles Ct., Suite 300, Towson, MD 21286
Phone: (410, 321-8440; 800-CIS-USER)
Contact: CIS User Support Group
IRIS is the EPA's principal database for assessing potential risk of exposure to hazardous chemical substances. It covers toxicity and carcinogenicity for over 660. Some chemical-physical data and regulatory information are also covered.

Land Use Law Report
Type: Full Text
Subject: Environment, Land Use Planning, Land Preservation.
Language: English
Available Service Through: Newsnet and Predicasts
Producer: Business Publishers, Inc., 951 Pershing Dr., Silver Spring, MD 20910-4464
Phone: (301, 587-6300; Fax: 301, 587-1081)
Contact: JIM LAWLOR
Covers U.S. news on legislation, regulatory issues, legal decisions, budget proposals, and more, affecting land use.

MALLIN
Type: Data extracted from scientific papers
Subject: Chemical-physical properties, fire and health hazards, spill and disposal information, storage and handling information, and protective equipment information
Language: English
Available Service Through: Chemical Information System (CIS)
Producer: Mallinckrodt, Inc., 810 Gleneagles Ct., Suite 300, Towson, MD 21286
Phone: (410, 321-8440; 800-CIS-USER)
Contact: CIS User Support Group
MALLIN is a collection of Material Safety Data Sheets (MSDS) for over 1,642 chemical substances. Each record of information represents one chemical. These MSDS's were prepared in accordance with guidelines issued by the U.S. Occupational Safety and Health Administration.

Master Species File, The
Type: Species Accounts (codes, keywords, text, and references)
Subject: Species taxonomy, status, distribution, ecology, management practices, and references.
Language: English
Available Service Through: WWW
Producer: Fish and Wildlife Information Exchange, Department of Fisheries and Wildlife, Virginia Polytechnic Institute and State University 203 W. Roanoke St., Blacksburg, VA 24060
E-mail: fwiexchg@vt-edu
Phone: (540, 231-7348; Fax: 540, 231-7019)
Contact: JEFF WALDON
The Master Species File is an archive of species accounts compiled by state and federal fish and wildlife agencies in North America. The Master Species file is available on the World Wide Web at fwie.fw.vt.edu/

Oil and Hazardous Materials Technical Assistance Data System (OHM/TADS)
Type: Data extracted from scientific papers
Subject: Handling of hazardous materials.
Language: English
Available Service Through: Chemical Information System (CIS)
Producer: EPA, 810 Gleneagles Ct., Suite 300, Towson, MD 21286
Phone: (410, 321-8440; 800- CIS-USER)
Contact: CIS User Support Group
OHM/TADS is the EPA's principal database for providing information on safe handling of hazardous substances.

Oil Spill Intelligence Report
Type: Full Text
Subject: Oil spills, prevention, cleanup, and control.
Language: English
Producer: Cutter Info. Corp., 37 Broadway, Arlington, MA 02174
Phone: (1-800-964-5125)
Contact: DENNIS CROWLEY
Detailed information on oil spills worldwide and related developments. Customized reports also available.

Oil Spill Intelligence Report International Spill Database
Type: N/A
Subject: Worldwide oil spills involving 10,000+ gallons.
Language: English
Available Service Through: N/A
Producer: Oil Spill Intelligence Report, Cutter Information, 37 Broadway, Arlington, MA 02174
Phone: (617, 641-5107; Fax: 617, 648-8707; E-mail: jwelch@cutter.com)
Contact: JEFF WELCH or DAGMAR ETKIN
Lists date, amount, type of oil, causes, damages, and more on over 2,500 oil spills that have occurred worldwide. Updated weekly.

Oil Spill U.S. Law Report
Type: Full Text
Subject: Legislation, litigation, regulations, and enforcement actions in the U.S. pertaining to oil spills.
Language: English
Available Service Through: Newsnet, Predicasts
Producer: Cutter Information Corp., 37 Broadway, Arlington, MA 02174
Phone: (1-800-964-5125)
Contact: DENNIS CROWLEY
U.S. federal and state oil spill legislation and regulations, litigation, and administrative actions, including news and interpretation of the ongoing implementation of the Oil Pollution Act of 1990 (OPA 1990).

Plant Toxicity Data (PHYTOTOX)
Type: Data extracted from scientific papers
Subject: Plant toxicity of organic chemicals
Language: English
Available Service Through: Chemical Information System (CIS)
Producer: University of Oklahoma, Department of Botany and Microbiology, 810 Gleneagles Ct., Suite 300, Towson, MD 21286
Phone: (410, 321-8440; 800-CIS-USER)
Contact: CIS User Support Group
PHYTOTOX contains over 70,000 records relating the biological effects of organic chemicals on terrestrial plants. The records of data include information about the effects observed in the experiment and bibliographic references to the source documents.

Registry of Toxic Effects of Chemical Substances (RTECS)
Type: Data extracted from scientific papers
Subject: Toxicity, irritation, mutagenicity, tumorigenicity, teratogenicity, carcinogenicity.
Language: English
Available Service Through: Chemical Information System (CIS)
Producer: NIOSH, 810 Gleneagles Ct., Suite 300, Towson, MD 21286
Phone: (410, 321-8440; 800-CIS-USER)
Contact: CIS User Support Group
RTECS contains data of more then 135,000 chemical substances.

SIRS Researcher
Type: Full Text
Subject: Earth science, physical science, life science, medical science, applied science, social issues, and global issues.
Language: English
Available Service Through: CD-ROM, Tape or online via www
Producer: SIRS Mandarin, Inc., P.O. Box 2348, Boca Raton, FL 33427-2348
Phone: (1-800, 232-SIRS; 561, 994-0079)
Contact: LINDA MIGNONE, Marketing Manager
SIRS Researcher is a general reference database containing thousands of full-text articles exploring social, scientific, historic, economic, political and global issues. Articles and graphics are selected from around 1,500 sources. Three search methods are provided: Subject Index, Title Browse, and Keyword. Print or save articles as full or partial text.

Solid Waste Report
Type: Full Text
Subject: Environment Waste
Language: English
Available Service Through: Newsnet and Predicasts
Producer: Business Publishers, Inc., 951 Pershing Dr., Silver Spring, MD 20910-4464
Phone: (301, 587-6300; Fax: 301, 587-1081)
Contact: DAVID R. JONES
SWR covers general collection, transportation, resource recovery, recycling and ultimate disposal of municipal, commercial, agricultural, and non-hazardous industrial refuse.

Toxic Release Inventory (TRI)
Type: Full Text
Subject: Toxic Chemicals
Language: English
Available Service Through: NLM's TOXNET
Producer: Office of Pollution Prevention and Toxics-EPA, 401 M St., NW, Washington, DC 20460
Phone: (202, 260-8387)
Contact: RUBY N. BOYA
Mandated by the Emergency Planning and Community Right-to-Know Act. TRI contains amounts for over 300 toxic chemicals that facilities release directly to air, water, or land or that are transported off-site.

Toxic Substances Control Act Test Submissions (TSCATS)
Type: Bibliographic
Subject: Toxicity, health, safety, environmental fate.
Language: English
Available Service Through: Chemical Information System (CIS)
Producer: EPA, 810 Gleneagles Ct., Suite 300, Towson, MD 21286
Phone: (410, 321-8440; 800-CIS-USER)
Contact: CIS User Support Group
TSCATS contains over 56,000 references to unpublished health, safety, toxicity, and environmental fate studies submitted to the EPA. Copies of referenced studies can be ordered through the system.

TOXLINE
Type: Bibliographic
Subject: Toxicology, pharmacology, physiology, biochemistry.
Language: English
Available Service Through: Dialog, DIMDI, Ovid Online, STN (Scientific and Technical Network) Silver Platter, and Ovid Technologies.
Producer: BIOSIS, 2100 Arch St., Philadelphia, PA 19103-1399
Phone: (1-800, 523-4806; 215, 587-4847; Fax: 215, 587-2016; E-mail: info@mail.biosis.org)
Contact: ALAN CLARKE
BIOSIS is one of five contributors to TOXLINE, an online file containing references to the effects of drugs and other chemicals. It includes information on toxicology, drug testing, drug interactions, and evaluations. The database is a collection of 15 subfiles derived from various secondary literature sources and special collections of material.

U.S. EPA Civil Enforcement Docket (DOCKET)
Type: Data extracted from documents
Subject: Civil judicial cases filed by the Department of Justice on behalf of the EPA.
Language: English
Available Service Through: Chemical Information System (CIS)
Producer: EPA, 810 Gleneagles Ct., Suite 300, Towson, MD 21286
Phone: (410, 321-8440; 800-CIS-USER)
Contact: CIS User Support Group
DOCKET contains over 4,200 records of civil lawsuits. The database was compiled by the EPA and is updated quarterly.

Waste Management Information Database
Type: Full Text and Bibliographic
Subject: Solid, liquid, hazardous, and nuclear wastes management; water quality, toxic substances, land reclamation, air pollution, and resources recovery.
Language: English
Available Service Through: ITTD Network
Producer: International Research and Evaluation, 21098 IRE Control Center, Eagan, MN 55121
Phone: (612, 888-9635; Fax: 612-888-9124)
Contact: DR. R. DANFORD
The WM/RR-ID is your one source ready-access to an entire environmental library for the practical application of knowledge, methods, and means. Company provides and manages Energy, Environment and Infrastructure Resource Center, 10740-BW Lyndale Avenue South, Bloomington, MN 55121. (612, 472-9222)

Water Resources Abstracts
Type: Abstracts and bibliographic
Subject: Water resources, ocean, groundwater, fish, and marine mammals.
Language: English
Available Service Through: CD-ROM
Producer: National Information Services Corporation, Suite 6, Wyman Towers, 3100 St. Paul St., Baltimore, MD 21218
Phone: (410, 243-0797; Fax: 410, 243-0982)
Contact: Sales@NISC.com
The exclusive two-disc set provides automated searching with the WRSIC Thesaurus. WRA is the best source for issues pertaining to groundwater, water quality, and water planning, law and rights. Over 50,000 citations and abstracts. Quarterly updates, $1,195.00 year subscription.

Water Resources Worldwide
Type: Abstracts and bibliographic
Subject: Water resources, pollution, waste management, recycling.
Language: French and English
Available Service Through: CD-ROM and Internet (BiblioLine)
Producer: National Information Services Corporation, Suite 6, Wyman Towers, 3100 St. Paul St., Baltimore, MD 21218
Phone: (410, 243-0797; Fax: 410, 243-0982)
Contact: Sales@NISC.com
Global, regional, national, and local coverage is provided by WATERLIT from the South African Water Information Center, AQUAREF from the Inland Waters Directorate of Environment Canada, and DELFT HYDRO from the Delft Hydraulics Laboratory of the Netherlands. This exclusive entomology provides roughly 390,000 citations and abstracts and features the WATERLIT thesaurus. Semi-annual updates, $895.00 per year subscription.

Wildlife Worldwide
Type: Abstracts and Bibliographic
Subject: Wildlife, endangered species, environment, and natural resources.
Language: English
Available Service Through: CD-ROM and Internet
Producer: National Information Services Corporation, Suite 6, Wyman Towers, 3100 St. Paul St., Baltimore, MD 21218
Phone: (410, 243-0797; Fax: 410, 243-0982)
Contact: Sales@NISC.com
The world's most extensive collection of wildlife databases on CD-ROM. Nearly 500,000 records are drawn from Wildlife Review and the Waterfowl and Wetlands Database, compiled by the U.S. National Biological Service; the WIS database from the Wildlife Information Service; BIODOC from the National University of Costa Rico; the Fish and Wildlife Reference Service file; and a book reviews database. Quarterly updates, $895.00 year subscription.

Marine Oceanographic and Freshwater Resources
Type: Bibliographic
Subject: Marine, Oceanographic and Freshwater Resources
Language: English
Producer: National Information Services Corporation, Suite, 6, Wyman Towers, 3100 St. Paul St., Baltimore, MD 21218

ENVIRONMENTAL DATABASES AND SERVICES

Phone: 410, 243-0797; Fax: 410, 243-0982)
Contact: Sales@NISC.com
The MOFR is an exclusive combination of the world's premier bibliographic database on marine, oceanographic, and related freshwater resources. Providing comprehensive coverage of over 885,000 records on international marine and oceanic information, as well as substantial coverage of estuarine, brackishwater, and freshwater environments.

Pollution Abstracts
Subject: Air, Marine, and Freshwater Pollution
Language: English
Producer: National Information Services Corporation, Suite, 6, Wyman Towers, 3100 St. Paul St., Baltimore, MD 21218
Phone: (410, 243-0797; Fax: 410, 243-0982)
Contact: Sales@NISC.com
Provides information on scientific research and government policies in a single resource; coverage of journal literature, conference proceedings, hard-to-find documents; and fast access to the environmental information necessary to resolve day-to-day problems.

Entomology Abstracts
Language: English
Producer: National Information Services Corporation, Suite, 6, Wyman Towers, 3100 St. Paul St., Baltimore, MD 21218
Phone: (410, 243-0797; Fax: 410, 243-0982)
Contact: Sales@NISC.com
Entomology Abstracts 1978-present provides important information on geographic distribution, nomenclature, new species, and more. 10,200 abstracts are added per year. Price: US$1,445.00, annual subscription.

Ecology Abstracts
Language: English
Producer: National Information Services Corporation, Suite, 6, Wyman Towers, 3100 St. Paul St., Baltimore, MD 21218
Phone: (410, 243-0797; Fax: 410, 243-0982)
Contact: Sales@NISC.com
This database from Cambridge Scientific Abstracts, focuses on how organisms of all kinds—microbes, plants, and animals—interact with their environments and with other organisms.

Biotechnology Abstracts
Language: English
Producer: National Information Services Corporation, Suite, 6, Wyman Towers, 3100 St. Paul St., Baltimore, MD 21218
Phone: (410, 243-0797; Fax: 410, 243-0982)
Contact: Sales@NISC.com
A recently published database from Cambridge Scientific Abstracts, gathers the world literature in which molecular biology and genetics are applied to these areas. Coverage includes agricultural products involving both plants and animals. Price: US$695.00, annual subscription.

World Environment Report
Type: Full Text
Subject: Environmental laws, regulations and environmental business worldwide.
Language: English
Available Service Through: Newsnet and Predicasts
Producer: Business Publishers, Inc., 951 Pershing Dr., Silver Spring, MD 20910-4464
Phone: (301, 587-6300; Fax: 301, 587-1081)
Contact: DAVID BOTTORFF
Providing news, information, and analysis on international environmental laws and regulations for companies operating abroad.

World Environmental Directory
Type: Full Text
Subject: Environmental Resources
Language: English
Available Service Through: Newsnet and Predicasts
Producer: Business Publishers, Inc., 951 Pershing Dr., Silver Spring, MD 20910-4464
Phone: (301, 587-6300; Fax: 301, 587-1081)
Contact: LARRY FISHBEIN
Helps you reach professional colleagues. Aids in your search for qualified consultants doing research and analysis. Puts you in touch with corporate officials, colleges, universities, and much more. The perfect tool for environmental resource information in USA and Canada. Contains source names and addresses to manufacturers, consultants, federal government, professional organizations, educational institutions, and more.

FEDERALLY PROTECTED AREAS

NATIONAL FORESTS IN THE UNTED STATES

ALABAMA: Conecuh, Talladega, and Tuskegee National Forests: JOHN YANCY, Supervisor, national forests in Alabama, 2946 Chestnutt St., Montgomery, AL 36107 (334, 832-4470)

ALASKA: Chugach National Forest: BRUCE VAN ZEE, Supervisor, 3301 C St., Ste. 300, Anchorage, AK 99503-3998 (907, 271-2500)
Tongass-Chatham Area National Forest: GARY MORRISON, Supervisor, 204 Siginaka Way, Sitka, AK 99835 (907, 747-6671)
Tongass-Ketchikan Area National Forest: DAVE RITTENHOUSE, Supervisor, Federal Bldg., Ketchikan, AK 99901 (907, 225-3101)
Tongass-Stikine Area National Forest: ABIGAIL KIMBELL, Supervisor, Box 309, Petersburg, AK 99833 (907, 772-3841)

ARIZONA: Apache-Sitgreaves National Forest: JOHN C. BEDELL, Supervisor, Federal Bldg., Box 640, Springerville, AZ 85938 (520, 333-4301)
Coconino National Forest: FRED TREVEY, Supervisor, 2323 E. Greenlaw Ln., Flagstaff, AZ 86004 (520, 527-3600)
Coronado National Forest: JAMES R. ABBOTT, Supervisor, 300 W. Congress, Tucson, AZ 85701 (520, 670-4552)
Kaibab National Forest: WILLIAM LANNAN, Supervisor, 800 South 6th St., Williams, AZ 86046 (520, 635-2681)
Prescott National Forest: COY JEMMETT, Supervisor, 344 S. Cortez, Prescott, AZ 86303 (520, 771-4700)
Tonto National Forest: CHARLES R. BAZAN, Supervisor, 2324 E. McDowell Rd., P.O. Box 5348, Phoenix, AZ 85006 (602, 225-5200)

ARKANSAS: Ouachita National Forest: MIKE CURRAN, Supervisor, Box 1270, Federal Bldg., Hot Springs National Park, AR 71902 (501, 321-5202)
Ozark and St. Francis National Forests: CHARLIE RICHMOND, Supervisor, 605 West Main, Box 1008, Russellville, AR 72801 (501, 968-2354)

CALIFORNIA: Angeles National Forest: MIKE ROGERS, Supervisor, 701 N. Santa Anita Ave., Arcadia, CA 91006 (818, 574-1613)
Cleveland National Forest: ANNE S. FEGE, Supervisor, 10845 Rancho Bernardo Rd., Ste. 200, San Diego, CA 92127-2107 (619, 673-6180)
Eldorado National Forest: JOHN PHIPPS, Supervisor, 100 Forni Rd., Placerville, CA 95667 (530, 622-5062)
Inyo National Forest: DENNIS W. MARTIN, 873 N. Main St., Bishop, CA 93514 (530, 873-2400)
Klamath National Forest: BARBARA HOLDER, Supervisor, 1312 Fairlane Rd., Yreka, CA 96097 (530, 842-6131)
Lassen National Forest: LEONARD ATENCIO, Supervisor, 55 S. Sacramento St., Susanville, CA 96130 (530, 257-2151)
Los Padres National Forest: DAVID W. DAHL, Supervisor, 6144 Calle Real, Goleta, CA 93117 (805, 683-6711)
Mendocino National Forest: DANIEL C. CHISHOLM, 420 E. Laurel St., Willows, CA 95988 (530, 934-3316)
Modoc National Forest: DIANE K. HENDERSON, Supervisor, 800 W. 12th St., Alturas, CA 96101 (530, 233-5811)
Plumas National Forest: WAYNE THORNTON, Supervisor, 159 Lawrence St., Box 11500, Quincy, CA 95971-6025 (530, 283-2050)
San Bernardino National Forest: GENE ZIMMERMAN, Supervisor, 1824 S. Commercenter Cir., San Bernardino, CA 92408-3430 (909, 383-5588)
Sequoia National Forest: SANDRA KEY, Supervisor, 900 W. Grand Ave., Porterville, CA 93257 (209, 784-1500)
Shasta-Trinity National Forest: STEPHEN A. FITCH, Supervisor, 2400 Washington Ave., Redding, CA 96001 (530, 246-5222)
Sierra National Forest: JAMES L. BOYNTON, Supervisor, 1600 Tollhouse Rd., Clovis, CA 93611 (209, 297-0706)
Six Rivers National Forest: MARTHA KETELLE, Supervisor, 1330 Bayshore Way, Eureka, CA 95501-3834 (707, 442-1721)
Stanislaus National Forest: JANET WOLD, Supervisor, 19777 Greenley Rd., Sonora, CA 95370 (209, 532-3671)
Tahoe National Forest: JOHN SKINNER, Supervisor, 631 Coyote St., P.O. Box 6003, Nevada City, CA 95959-6003 (530, 265-4531)

COLORADO: Arapaho and Roosevelt National Forests: M.M. UNDERWOOD, JR., Supervisor, 240 W. Prospect St., Fort Collins, CO 80526 (970, 498-1100)
Grand Mesa, Uncompahgre, and Gunnison National Forests: ROBERT L. STORCH, Supervisor, 2250 Highway 50, Delta, CO 81416 (970, 874-7691)
Pike and San Isabel National Forests: JACK A. WEISSLING, Supervisor, 1920 Valley Dr., Pueblo, CO 81008 (719, 545-8737)
Rio Grande National Forest: JAMES B. WEBB, Supervisor, 1803 West Highway 160, Monte Vista, CO 81144 (719, 852-5941)
Routt National Forest: JERRY E. SCHMIDT, Supervisor, 29587 W. US40, Ste. 20, Steamboat Springs, CO 80487-9550 (970, 879-1722)
San Juan National Forest: JAMES B. WEBB, Supervisor, Federal Bldg., 701 Camino Del Rio, Rm. 301, Durango, CO 81301 (970, 247-4874)
White River National Forest: VETO J. LASALLE, Supervisor, Old Federal Bldg., Box 948, Glenwood Springs, CO 81602 (970, 945-2521)

FLORIDA: Apalachicola, Ocala, and Osceola National Forests: Supervisor, National Forests in Florida, Woodcrest Office Park, 325 John Knox Rd., Ste. F-100, Tallahassee, FL 32303 (850, 942-9300)

GEORGIA: Chattahoochee and Oconee National Forests: GEORGE G. MARTIN, Supervisor, 508 Oak St., NW, Gainesville, GA 30501 (770, 536-0541)

IDAHO: Boise National Forest: STEPHEN P. MEALEY, Supervisor, 1750 Front St., Boise, ID 83702 (208, 364-4100)
Caribou National Forest: PAUL R. NORDWALL, 250 S. 4th Ave., Ste. 282, Federal Bldg., Pocatello, ID 83201 (208, 236-7500)
Challis National Forest: CHARLES C. WILDES, Supervisor, HC 63 Box 1671, F.S. Bldg., Challis, ID 83226 (208, 879-2285)
Clearwater National Forest: JAMES L. CASWELL, Supervisor, 12730 Highway 12, Orofino, ID 83544 (208, 476-4541)
Idaho Panhandle National Forests: DAVID J. WRIGHT, Supervisor, 1201 Ironwood Dr., Coeur d'Alene, ID 83814 (208, 765-7223)
Nez-Perce National Forest: MIKE KING, Supervisor, Rt. 2, Box 475, Grangeville, ID 83530 (208, 983-1950)
Payette National Forest: DAVID F. ALEXANDER, Supervisor, Forest Service Bldg., Box 1026, McCall, ID 83638 (208, 634-0700)
Salmon National Forest: JOHN E. BURNS, Supervisor, Forest Service, P.O. Box 729, Salmon, ID 83467-0729 (208, 756-2215)

FEDERALLY PROTECTED AREAS

Sawtooth National Forest: JACK E. BILLS, Supervisor, 2647 Kimberly Rd., East, Twin Falls, ID 83301-7976 (208, 737-3200) Targhee National Forest: JAMES L. COSWELL, 420 N. Bridge St., P.O. Box 208, St. Anthony, ID 83445 (208, 624-3151)

ILLINOIS: Shawnee National Forest: (Acting) LOUISE ODEGAARD, Supervisor, 901 S. Commercial St., Harrisburg, IL 62946 (618, 253-1000)

INDIANA: Wayne National Forest: KENNETH G. DAY, Supervisor, 811 Constitution Ave., Bedford, IN 47421 (812, 275-5987)

KENTUCKY: Daniel Boone National Forest: BRADLEY E. POWELL, Supervisor, 100 Vaught Rd., Winchester, KY 40391 (606, 745-3100)

LOUISIANA: Kisatchie National Forest: DANNY W. BRITT, Supervisor, P.O. Box 5500, 2500 Shreveport Hwy., Pineville, LA 71361-5500 (318, 473-7160)

MAINE: White Mountain National Forest: (see New Hampshire)

MICHIGAN: Hiawatha National Forest: WILLIAM F. SPINNER, Supervisor, 2727 N. Lincoln Rd., Escanaba, MI 49829 (906, 786-4062)
Huron-Manistee National Forest: STEVE KELLEY, Supervisor, 421 S. Mitchell St., Cadillac, MI 49601 (616, 775-2421)
Ottawa National Forest: DAVID H. MORTON, Supervisor, 2100 E. Cloverland Dr., Ironwood, MI 49938 (906, 932-1330)

MINNESOTA: Chippewa National Forest: STEVE EUBANKS, Supervisor, Cass Lake, MN 56633 (218, 335-8600)
Superior National Forest: KATHLEEN McALLISTER, Supervisor, Box 338, Duluth, MN 55802 (218, 720-5324)

MISSISSIPPI: Bienville, Delta, Desoto, Holly Springs, Homochitto, and Tombigbee National Forests: KENNETH R. JOHNSON, Supervisor, National Forests in Mississippi, 100 W Capital St., Ste. 1141, Jackson, MS 39269 (601, 965-4391)

MISSOURI: Mark Twain National Forest: B. ERIC MORSE, Supervisor, 401 Fairgrounds Rd., Rolla, MO 65401 (314, 364-4621)

MONTANA: Beaverhead National Forest: 420 Barrett St., Dillon, MT 59725-3572 (406, 683-3900)
Bitterroot National Forest: STEPHEN K. KELLY, Supervisor, 1801 N. 1st St., Hamilton, MT 59840 (406, 363-7121)
Custer National Forest: Supervisor, Box 2556, Billings, MT 59103 (406, 657-6361)
Deerlodge National Forest: VAN ELSBERND, Supervisor, Federal Bldg., Box 400, Butte, MT 59703 (406, 496-3400)
Flathead National Forest: JOEL HOLTROP, Supervisor, 1935 3rd Ave., E., Kalispell, MT 59901 (406, 755-5401)
Gallatin National Forest: DAVE GARBER, Supervisor, 10 E. Babcock Ave., Federal Bldg., Box 130, Bozeman, MT 59771 (406, 587-6701)
Helena National Forest: TOM CLIFFORD Supervisor, Federal Bldg., 2880 Skyway Dr., Helena, MT 59601 (406, 449-5201)
Kootenai National Forest: ROBERT L. SCHRENK, Supervisor, 506 Highway 2W, Libby, MT 59923 (406, 293-6211)
Lewis and Clark National Forest: J. DALE GORMAN, Supervisor, Box 869, 1101 15th St., N., Great Falls, MT 59403 (406, 791-7700)

Lolo National Forest: ORVILLE L. DANIELS, Supervisor, Bldg. 24, Ft. Missoula, Missoula, MT 59801 (406, 329-3750)

NEBRASKA: Nebraska National Forest: MARY H. PETERSON, Supervisor, 125 N. Main St., Chadron, NE 69337 (308, 432-0300)

NEVADA: Humboldt National Forest: JOHN INMAN, Supervisor, 976 Mountain City Hwy., Elko, NV 89801 (702, 738-5171)
Toiyabe National Forest: R.M. (Jim) NELSON, Supervisor, 1200 Franklin Way, Sparks, NV 89431, (702, 355-5300/702, 331-6444)

NEW HAMPSHIRE: White Mountain National Forest: RICK CABLES, Supervisor, Federal Bldg., 719 Main St., Box 638, Laconia, NH 03247 (603, 528-8721)

NEW MEXICO: Carson National Forest: LEONARD L. LUCERO, Supervisor, Fed. Bldg., 208 Cruz Alta Rd., Box 558, Taos, NM 87571 (505, 758-6200)
Cibola National Forest: JEANINE A. DERBY, Supervisor, 2113 Osuna Rd. NE, Ste. A, Albuquerque, NM 87111-1001 (505, 761-4650)
Gila National Forest: Supervisor, 3005 E. Camino del Bosque, Silver City, NM 88061 (505, 388-8201)
Lincoln National Forest: LEE POAGUE, Supervisor, Federal Bldg., 1101 New York Ave., Alamogordo, NM 88310-6992 (505, 434-7200)
Santa Fe National Forest: AL DEFLER, Supervisor, 1220 St. Francis Dr., Santa Fe, NM 87504 (505, 988-6940)

NORTH CAROLINA: Croatan, Nantahala, Pisgah, and Uwharrie National Forests: RANDLE G. PHILLIPS, Supervisor, National Forests in North Carolina, Post & Otis Sts., Box 2750, Asheville, NC 28802 (704, 257-4200)

OREGON: Deschutes National Forest: SALLY COLLINS, Supervisor, 1645 Highway 20 East, Bend, OR 97701 (541, 388-2715
Fremont National Forest: CHUCK GRAHAM, Supervisor, 524 North G St., Lakeview, OR 97630 (541, 947-2151)
Malheur National Forest: MARK BOCHE, Supervisor, 139 NE Dayton St., John Day, OR 97845 (541, 575-1731)
Mt. Hood National Forest: MIKE EDRINGTON, Supervisor, 2955 Division St., Gresham, OR 97030 (503, 666-1700)
Ochoco National Forest: TOM SCHMIDT, Supervisor, Box 490, Prineville, OR 97754 (541, 447-6247)
Rogue River National Forest: JAMES T. GLADEN, Supervisor, Federal Bldg., 333 W. 8th St., Box 520, Medford, OR 97501 (541, 776-3600)
Siskiyou National Forest: MICHAEL LUNN, Supervisor, Box 440, Grants Pass, OR 97526 (541, 471-6500)
Siuslaw National Forest: Supervisor, Box 1148, Corvallis, OR 97339 (541, 750-7000)
Umatilla National Forest: JOHN P. KLINE, Supervisor, 2517 SW Hailey Ave., Pendleton, OR 97801 (541, 278-3721)
Umpqua National Forest: DON OSTBY, Supervisor, Box 1008, Roseburg, OR 97470 (541, 672-6601)
Wallowa Whitman National Forests: ROBERT RICHMOND, Supervisor, Box 907, Baker City, OR 97814 (541, 523-6391)
Willamette National Forest: DARREL L. KENOPS, Supervisor, Box 10607, Eugene, OR 97440 (541, 465-6521)
Winema National Forest: BOB CASTANEDA, Supervisor, 2819 Dahlia, Klamath Falls, OR 97601 (541, 883-6714)

PENNSYLVANIA: Allegheny National Forest: JOHN E. PALMER, Supervisor, 222 Liberty St., Box 847, Warren, PA 16365 (814, 723-5150)

PUERTO RICO: Caribbean National Forest: PABLO CRUZ, Supervisor, Call Box 25000, Rio Piedras, PR 00928-2500 (809, 766-5335)

SOUTH CAROLINA: Francis Marion and Sumter National Forests: JEROME THOMAS, Supervisor, 4923 Broad River Rd., Columbia, SC 29212 (803, 561-4000)

SOUTH DAKOTA: Black Hills National Forest: JOHN C. TWISS, Supervisor, R.R. 2, Box 200, Custer, SD 57730-9504 (605, 673-2251)

TENNESSEE: Cherokee National Forest: ANNE ZIMMERMAN, Supervisor, 2800 N. Ocoee St., NE, Box 2010, Cleveland, TN 37320 (423, 476-9700)

TEXAS: Angelina, Davy Crockett, Sabine, and Sam Houston National Forests: RONNIE RAUM, Supervisor, National Forests in Texas, Homer Garrison Federal Bldg., 701 N. 1st St., Lufkin, TX 75901 (409, 639-8620)

UTAH: Ashley National Forest: BERT KULESZA, Supervisor, 355 N. Vernal Ave., Vernal, UT 84078 (801, 789-1181)
Dixie National Forest: HUGH C. THOMPSON, Supervisor, 82 N. 100 E. St., P.O. Box 580, Cedar City, UT 84721 (435, 865-3701)
Fishlake National Forest: ROBERT D. MROWAK, Supervisor, 115 East 900 North, Richfield, UT 84701 (435, 896-1001)
Manti-LaSal National Forest: J. KAISER, Supervisor, 599 West Price River Dr., Price, UT 84501 (435, 637-2817)
Uinta National Forest: PETE KARP, Supervisor, 88 West 100 North, Provo, UT 84601 (435, 636-3501)
Wasatch-Cache National Forest: BERNIE WANGART, Supervisor, 8236 Federal Bldg., 125 S. State St., Salt Lake City, UT 84138 (801, 524-5030)

VERMONT: Green Mountain National Forest: TERRY W. HOFFMAN, Supervisor, Federal Bldg., 231 N. Main, Rutland, VT 05701-0519 (802, 747-6700)

VIRGINIA: George Washington National Forest: GEORGE W. KELLY, Supervisor, P.O. Box 233, Harrison Plaza, Harrisonburg, VA 22801 (540-265-5100)
Jefferson National Forest: JOY BERG, Supervisor, 5162 Valleypointe Parkway, Roanoke, VA 24019 (540-265-5100)

WASHINGTON: Colville National Forest: ROBERT L. VAUGHT, Supervisor, 716 S. Main, Colville, WA 99114 (509, 662-4335)
Gifford Pinchot National Forest: TED STUBBLEFIELD, Supervisor, 6926 E. 4th Plain Blvd., Vancouver, WA 98668-8944 (360-891-5000)
Mt. Baker-Snoqualmie National Forest: Supervisor, 21905 64th Ave. West, Mountlake Terrace, Seattle, WA 98043 (425-775-4702)
Okanogan National Forest: SAMUEL GEHR, Supervisor, 1240 S. Second, Okanogan, WA 98840 (509, 826-3275)
Olympic National Forest: RONARO R. HUMPHREY, Supervisor, 1835 Blacklake Blvd., SW, Olympia, WA 98512 (360, 956-2300)
Wenatchee National Forest: SONNY O'NEAL, Supervisor, Box 811, Wenatchee, WA 98807 (509, 662-4335)

WEST VIRGINIA: Monongahela National Forest: JIM PAGE, Supervisor, USDA Bldg., 200 Sycamore St., Elkins, WV 26241-3962 (304, 636-1800)

WISCONSIN: Chequamegon National Forest: JACK G. TROYER, Supervisor, 1170 4th Ave., S., Park Falls, WI 54552 (715, 762-2461)
Nicolet National Forest: JACK G. TROYER, Supervisor, Federal Bldg., 68 S. Stevens, Rhinelander, WI 54501 (715, 362-1300)

WYOMING: Bridger-Teton National Forest: BRIAN STOUT, Supervisor, Forest Service Bldg., 340 N. Cache, Box 1888, Jackson, WY 83001 (307, 739-5500)
Bighorn National Forest: ABIGAIL KIMBELL, Supervisor, 1969 S. Sheridan Ave., Sheridan, WY 82801 (307, 674-2600)
Medicine Bow National Forest: JERRY SCHMIDT, 2468 Jackson St., Laramie, WY 82070-6535 (307, 745-8971)
Shoshone National Forest: REBECCA AUS, Supervisor, 808 Meadow Ln., Cody, WY 82414 (307, 527-6241)

NATIONAL MARINE SANCTUARIES AND

Channel Islands National Marine Sanctuary, 113 Harbor Way, Santa Barbara, CA 93109 (805, 966-7107; Fax: 805, 568-1582)
Manager: ED CASSANO

Cordell Bank National Marine Sanctuary, Ft. Mason, Bldg. #201, San Francisco, CA 94123 (415, 561-6622; Fax: 415, 561-6616)
Manager: EDWARD UEBER

Fagatele Bay National Marine Sanctuary, P.O. Box 4318, Pago Pago, American Samoa 96799 9-011 (684) 633-5155; Fax: 9-011 (684) 633-4195
Coordinator: NANCY DASCHBACH

Flower Garden Banks National Marine Sanctuary: Manager (Acting), SHELLY DuPUY, 216 W. 26th St., Suire 104, BryaN, tx 77803 (409, 779-27805; Fax: 409, 779-2334)

Gray's Reef National Marine Sanctuary, 10 Ocean Science Cir., Savannah, GA 31411 (912, 598-2345; Fax: 912, 598-2367)
Manager: REED BOHNE

Gulf of the Farallones National Marine Sanctuary, Fort Mason Bldg. #201, San Francisco, CA 94123 (415, 561-6622; Fax: 415, 561-6616)
Manager: EDWARD UEBER

Florida Keys National Marine Sanctuary, P.O. Box 500368, 5550 Overseas Highway, Marathon, FL 33050 (305, 743-2437; Fax: 305, 743-2357)
Sanctuary Superintendent: BILLY CAUSEY

Monitor National Marine Sanctuary, c/o The Mariners' Museum, 100 Museum Dr., Newport News, VA 23606 (757, 599-3122; Fax: 757, 591-7353)
Manager: JOHN BROADWATER

Monterey Bay National Marine Sanctuary: WILLIAM J. DOUROS,

FEDERALLY PROTECTED AREAS

299 Foam St., Suite D, Monterey, CA 93940 (831, 647-4201; Fax: 831, 647-4250)

Hawaiian Islands Humpback Whale National Marine Sanctuary, 726 South, Kihei, HI 96753 (808, 879-2818; Fax: 808, 874-3814)
Manager: ALLEN TOM

Olympic Coast National Marine Sanctuary, 138 W. First St., Port Angeles, WA 98362-2600 (360, 457-6622; Fax: 360, 457-8496)
Manager (Acting), GEORGE GALASSO

Stellwagen Bank National Marine Sanctuary, 14 Union St., Plymouth, MA 02360 (508, 747-1691, Fax: 508, 747-1949)
Manager: BRAD BARR

ACE Basin NERR, South Carolina Department of Natural Resources, P.O. Box 12559, Charleston, SC 29412 (843, 762-5062; Fax: 843, 762-5001)
Manager: MICHAEL McKENZIE

Delaware NERR, Delaware Department of Natural Resources and Environmental Control: BETSY ARCHER, 89 Kings Highway, Dover, DE 19901 (302, 739-3451; Fax: 302, 739-2048)

Great Bay NERR, Department of Fish and Game, 225 Main St., Durham, NH 03824 (603, 868-1095; Fax: 603, 271-1438)
Manager: PETER WELLENBERGER

Hudson River NERR, c/o Bard College Field Station, Annadale-on-Hudson, NY 12504 (914, 758-7010; Fax: 914, 758-7033)
Manager: ELIZABETH BLAIR

Narragansett Bay NERR, Department of Environmental Management, 55 South Reserve Dr.,Prudence Island, RI 02872 (401, 683-6780; Fax: 401, 277-6802)
Manager: AL BECK

North Carolina NERR, Center for Marine Science Research, University of North Carolina at Willmington, 7205 Wrightsville Ave., Wilmington, NC 28403 (919, 256-3721; Fax: 919, 256-8856)
Manager: JOHN TAGGART

North Inlet - Winyah Bay NERR, Baruch Marine Field Lab, P.O. Box 1630, Georgetown, SC 29440 (803, 546-3623; Fax: 803, 546-1632)
Manager, DENNIS ALLEN

Chesapeake Bay NERR in Maryland, Department of Natural Resources, Tawes State Office Bldg., B-3, 580 Taylor Ave., Annapolis, MD 21401 (410, 260-8740; Fax: 410, 260—8736)
Manager: KATHY ELLETT

Chesapeake Bay NERR in Virginia, Virginia Institute of Marine Science, Gloucester Point, VA 23062 (804, 684-7135; Fax: 804, 684-7120)
Manager: MAURICE LYNCH

Old Woman Creek NERR, 2514 Cleveland Rd., East, Huron, OH 44839 (419, 433-4601; Fax: 419, 433-2851)
Manager: EUGENE WRIGHT

Sapelo Island NERR, Georgia Department of Natural Resources, P.O. Box 15, Sapelo Island, GA 31327 (912, 485-2251; Fax: 912, 262-3143)
Manager: BUDDY SULLIVAN

Waquoit Bay NERR, Department of Environmental Management, P.O. Box 3092, Waquoit, MA 02536 (508, 457-0495; Fax: 617, 727-5537)
Manager: CHRISTINE GAULT

Wells NERR: Manager, KENT KIRKPATRICK, 342 Landholm Farm Rd., Wells, ME 04090 (207, 646-1555; Fax: 207, 646-2930)
Manager: JIM LIST

Apalachicola NERR, Department of Environmental Protection, 350 Carroll St., Eastpoint, FL 32328 (850, 670-4783; Fax: 850, 670-4324)
Manager, WOODWARD MILEY

Jobos Bay NERR, Department of Natural Resources, Call Box B, Aguirre, PR 00704 (787, 853-4617; Fax: 787, 853-4618)
Manager, CARMEN GONZALEZ

Rookery Bay NERR, Department of Environmental Protection, 300 Tower Rd., Naples, FL 34113 (941, 417-6310; Fax: 941, 417-6315)
Manager, GARY LYTTON

Weeks Bay NERR, 11300 U.S. Highway 98, Fairhope, AL 36532 (334, 928-9792; Fax: 334, 928-1792)
Manager, L.G. ADAMS

Elkhorn Slough NERR, 1700 Elkhorn Slough, Watsonville, CA 95076 (408, 728-2822; Fax: 408, 728-1056)
Manager: STEVE KIMPLE
Manager, BECKY CHRISTENSEN

Padilla Bay NERR, 1043 Bayview-Edison Rd., Mt. Vernon, WA 98273 (360, 428-1558; Fax: 360, 428-1491)
Manager: TERRY STEVENS

South Slough NERR, P.O. Box 5417, Charleston, OR 97420 (541, 888-5558; Fax: 541, 888-5559)
Manager: MIKE GRAYBILL

Tijuana River NERR, 301 Caspian Way, Imperial Beach, CA 91932 (619, 575-3613; Fax: 619, 575-6913)
Manager: JOANNE KERBAVAZ
Manager: PHIL JENKINS

NATIONAL PARKS IN THE UNITED STATES

ALASKA: Denali National Park: Supertendent, STEPHEN P. MARTIN, P.O. Box 9, McKinley Park, AK 99755 (907, 683-2294)
Gates of the Arctic National Park: DAVID MILLS, Supt., P.O. Box 74680, Fairbanks, AK 99707 (907, 456-0281)
Glacier Bay National Park: JAMES BRADY, Supt., Gustavus, AK 99826 (907, 697-2230)
Katmai National Park: BILL PIERCE, P.O. Box 7, King Salmon, AK 99613 (907, 246-3305)
Kenai Fjords National Park: ANNE CASTELLINA, Supt., P.O. Box 1727, Seward, AK 99664 (907, 224-3175)
Kobuk Valley National Park: DAVID SPIRTES, Supt., P.O. Box 1029,

Kotzebue, AK 99752 (907, 442-3890)
Lake Clark National Park: BILL PIERCE, Supt., 4230 University Dr., Ste. 311, Anchorage, AK 99508 (907, 271-3751)
Wrangell-St. Elias National Park: JON JARVIS, Supt., P.O. Box 29, Glennallen, AK 99588 (909, 822-5235)

AMERICAN SAMOA: National Park of American Samoa: CHRISTOPHER STEIN, Supt., Pago Pago, American Samoa 96799 (684, 633-7082)

ARIZONA: Grand Canyon National Park: ROBERT ARNBERGER, Supt., P.O. Box 129, Grand Canyon, AZ 86023 (602, 638-7701)
Petrified Forest National Park: MICHELLE HELLICKSON, Supt., P.O. Box 217, Petrified Forest National Park, AZ 86028 (602, 524-6228)

ARKANSAS: Hot Springs National Park: ROGER GIDDINGS, Supt., P.O. Box 1860, Hot Springs, AR 71902 (501, 624-3383)

CALIFORNIA: Lassen Volcanic National Park: MARILYN PARRIS, Supt., P.O. Box 100, Mineral, CA 96063 (916, 595-4444)
Redwood National Park: ANDREW RINGGOLD, Supt., 1111 Second St., Crescent City, CA 95531 (707, 464-6101)
Sequoia and Kings Canyon National Parks: MICHAEL TOLLEFSON, Supt., Three Rivers, CA 93271 (209, 565-3341)
Yosemite National Park: STANLEY ALBRIGHT, Supt., P.O. Box 577, Yosemite National Park, CA 95389 (209, 372-0200)
Channel Islands National Park: TIM SETNIKA, Supt., 1901 Spinnaker Dr., Ventura, CA 93001 (805, 658-5700)

COLORADO: Mesa Verde National Park: LARRY WIESE, Supt., Mesa Verde National Park, CO 81330 (303, 529-4465)
Rocky Mountain National Park: RANDY JONES, Supt., Estes Park, CO 80517 (303, 586-2371)

FLORIDA: Biscayne National Park: DICK FROST, Supt., P.O. Box 1369, Homestead, FL 33090 (305, 247-2044)
Everglades National Park: RICHARD RING, Supt., P.O. Box 279, Homestead, FL 33030 (305, 242-7700)

HAWAII: Haleakala National Park: DONALD W. REESER, Supt., P.O. Box 369, Makawao, Maui, HI 96768 (808, 572-9306)
Hawaii Volcanoes National Park: JIM MARTIN, Supt., Hawaii Volcanoes National Park, HI 96718 (808, 967-7311)

KENTUCKY: Mammoth Cave National Park: RONALD SWITZER, Supt., Mammoth Cave, KY 42259 (502, 758-2328)

MAINE: Acadia National Park: PAUL HAERTEL, Supt., P.O. Box 177, Bar Harbor, ME 04609 (207, 288-3338)

MICHIGAN: Isle Royale Natl. Park: DOUGLAS A. BARNARD, Supt., 800 E. Lakeshore Dr., Houghton, MI 49931 (906, 482-0984)

MINNESOTA: Voyageurs National Park: TIM COCHRANE, Supt., 3131 Highway 53, International Falls, MN 56649 (218, 283-9821)

MONTANA: Glacier National Park: DAVID MIHALIC, Supt., West Glacier, MT 59936 (406, 888-5441)

NEVADA: Great Basin National Park: REBECCA MILLS, Supt., Baker, NV 89311 (702, 234-7331)

NEW MEXICO: Carlsbad Caverns National Park: FRANK J. DECKERT, Supt., 3225 National Parks Hwy., Carlsbad, NM 88220 (505, 785-2232)

NORTH DAKOTA: Theodore Roosevelt National Park: NOEL POE, Supt., Medora, ND 58645 (701, 623-4466)

OREGON: Crater Lake National Park: ALBERT HENDRICKS, Supt., P.O. Box 7, Crater Lake, OR 97604 (503, 594-2211)

SOUTH DAKOTA: Wind Cave National Park: JIM TAYLOR, Supt., Hot Springs, SD 57747 (605, 745-4600)
Badlands National Park: WILLIAM SUPERNAUGH, Supt., P.O. Box 6, Interior, SD 57750 (605, 433-5361)

TENNESSEE: Great Smoky Mountains National Park: KAREN WADE, Supt., Gatlinburg, TN 37738 (615, 436-1200)

TEXAS: Big Bend National Park: JOSE CISNEROS, Supt., Big Bend National Park, TX 79834 (915, 477-2251)
Guadalupe Mountains National Park: LARRY HENDERSON, Supt., HC 60, Box 400, Salt Flat, TX 79847-9400 (915, 828-3351)

UTAH: Arches National Park: WALT DABNEY, Supt., Arches National Park, P.O. Box 907, Moab, UT 84532 (801, 259-8161)
Bryce Canyon National Park: FRED J. FAGERGREN, Supt., Bryce Canyon, UT 84717 (801, 834-5322)
Canyonlands National Park: WALTER DABNEY, Supt., 125 W. 200 South, Moab, UT 84532 (801, 259-3911)
Capitol Reef National Park: CHARLES LUNDY, Supt., HC70, Box 15, Torrey, UT 84775 (801, 425-3791)
Zion National Park: DON FALVEY, Supt., Springdale, UT 84767 (801, 772-3256)

VIRGIN ISLANDS: Virgin Islands National Park: RUSSELL BARRY, #10 Estate Nazareth, St. Thomas, VI 00802 (809, 775-6238)

VIRGINIA: Shenandoah National Park: DOUG MORRIS, Supt., Rt. 4, Box 348, Luray, VA 22835 (703, 999-2243)

WASHINGTON: Mount Rainier National Park: WILLIAM BRIGGLE, Supt., Tahoma Woods, Star Route, Ashford, WA 98304 (206, 569-2211)
North Cascades National Park: BILL PALECK, Supt., 2105 Highway 20, Sedro Woolley, WA 98284 (206, 856-5700)
Olympic National Park: DAVID MORRIS, Supt., 600 E. Park Ave., Port Angeles, WA 98362 (206, 452-4501)

WYOMING: Grand Teton National Park: JACK NECKELS, Supt., P.O. Drawer 170, Moose, WY 83012 (307, 739-3610)
Yellowstone National Park: MICHAEL FINLEY, Supt., P.O. Box 168, Yellowstone National Park, WY 82190 (307, 344-7381

NATIONAL SEASHORES IN THE UNITED STATES

CALIFORNIA: Point Reyes National Seashore: DON NEUBACHER, Supt., Point Reyes, CA 94956 (415, 663-8522)

FLORIDA: Canaveral National Seashore: WENDELL SIMPSON, Supt., 308 Julia St., Titusville, FL 32796-3521 (407, 267-1110)
Gulf Islands National Seashore: JERRY A. EUBANKS, Supt., 1801 Gulf Breeze Parkway, Gulf Breeze, FL 32561 (904, 934-2604)

FEDERALLY PROTECTED AREAS

GEORGIA: Cumberland Island National Seashore: DENIS DAVIS, Supt., P.O. Box 806, Saint Marys, GA 31558 (912, 882-4337)

MARYLAND: Assateague Island National Seashore: MARC A. KOENINGS, Supt., Rt. 611, 7206 National Seashore Ln., Berlin, MD 21811 (410, 641-1441)

MASSACHUSETTS: Cape Cod National Seashore: MARIA BURKS, Supt., South Wellfleet, MA 02663 (508, 349-3785)

MISSISSIPPI: Gulf Islands National Seashore: (see Florida)

NEW YORK: Fire Island National Seashore: DILLAN CONSTANTINE, Supt., 120 Laurel St., Patchogue, NY 11772 (516, 289-4810)

NORTH CAROLINA: Cape Lookout National Seashore: WILLIAM A. HARRIS, Supt., 131 Charles St., Harkers Island, NC 28531 (919, 728-2250)

Cape Hatteras National Seashore: ROBERT REYNOLDS, Supt., Rt. 1, Box 675, Manteo, NC 27954 (919, 473-2111)

TEXAS: Padre Island National Seashore: PATRICK McCRARY, Supt., 9405 S. Padre Island Dr., Corpus Christi, TX 78418 (512, 937-2621)

NATIONAL GRASSLANDS

Region I: Custer National Forest, Box 2556, Billings, MT 59103 (406, 248-9885)

Cedar River National Grassland, 1005 5th Ave., W., P.O. Box 390, Lemmon, SD 57638 (605, 374-3592)

Grand River National Grassland, 1005 5th Ave., W., P.O. Box 390, Lemmon, SD 57638 (605, 374-3592)

Little Missouri National Grassland, Medora Ranger District, Rt. 6, Box 131B, Dickinson, ND 58601 (701, 225-5151)

Little Missouri National Grassland, McKenzie Ranger District, BC02 Box 8, Watford City, ND 58854 (701, 842-2393)

Sheyenne National Grassland, Box 946, Lisbon, ND 58054 (701, 683-4342)

Region II: Arapaho and Roosevelt National Forests, 240 W. Prospect, Fort Collins, CO 80526 (970, 498-1100)

Pawnee National Grassland, 2017 9th St., Greeley, CO 80631 (970, 353-5004)

Medicine Bow National Forest, 605 Skyline Dr., Laramie, WY 82070 (307, 745-2300)

Thunder Basin National Grassland, 809 S. 9th, Douglas, WY 82633 (307, 358-4690)

Nebraska National Forest, 125 N. Main St., Chadron, NE 69337 (308, 432-0300)

Buffalo Gap National Grassland, Fall River Ranger District, 209 N. River, Hot Springs, SD 57747 (605, 745-4107)

Buffalo Gap National Grassland, Wall Raner District, 608 Main St., P.O. Box 425, Wall, SD 57790 (605, 279-2125)

Fort Pierre National Grassland, 124 South Euclid Ave., P.O. Box 417, Pierre, SD 57501 (605, 224-5517)

Oglala National Grassland, HC 75, Box 13A9, Chadron, NE 69337 (308, 432-4475)

Pike and San Isabel National Forest, 1920 Valley Dr., Pueblo, CO 81008 (719, 545-8737)

Cimarron National Grassland, 737 Villymaca St., P.O. Box J, Goodwin Bldg., Elkhart, KS 67950 (316, 697-4621)

Comanche National Grassland, 27162 Hwy. 287, P.O. Box 127, Springfield, CO 81073 (719, 384-2181)

Region III: Cibola National Forest, 2113 Osuna Rd., NE, Albuquerque, NM 87113-1001, (505, 346-2650)

Black Kettle National Grassland, Rt. 1, Box 55B, Cheyenne, OK 73628 (405, 497-2143)

Kiowa National Grassland, 16 N. 2nd St., Clayton, NM 88415 (505, 374-9652)

McClelland Creek National Grassland, Rt. 1, Box 55B, Cheyenne, OK 73628 (405, 497-2143)

Rita Blanca National Grassland, P.O. Box 38, Texline, TX 79087 (806, 362-4254)

Region IV: Caribou National Forest, 250 S. 4th Ave., Ste. 282, Federal Bldg., Pocatello, ID 83201 (208, 236-7500)

Curlew National Grassland, P.O. Box 142, Malad, ID 83252 (208, 766-4743)

Region V: Klamath National Forest, 1312 Fairlane Dr., Yreka, CA 96097 (530, 842-6131)

Butte Valley National Grassland, c/o Klamath National Forest, 1312 Fairlane Dr., Yreka, CA 96097 (530, 842-6131)

Region VI: Ochoco National Forest, Box 490, Prineville, OR 97754 (541, 447-6247)

Crooked River National Grassland, 2321 E. 3rd St., Prineville, OR 97754 (541, 475-9272)

Region VII: Caddo National Grassland, FM Rd. 730 South, P.O. Box 507, Decatur, TX 76234 (817, 627-5475)

Lyndon B. Johnson National Grassland, FM Rd. 730 South, P.O. Box 507, Decatur, TX 76234 (817, 627-5475)

BUREAU OF LAND MANAGEMENT DISTRICTS IN THE UNITED STATES

ALASKA: Anchorage District: Manager, NICHOLAS DOUGLAS (907, 267-1246)

Glennallen District: Team Leader CATHIE JENSEN (907, 822-3217)

Northern District: Manager, DEE RITCHIE

ARIZONA:

Arizona Strip Field Office: Manager, ROGER TAYLOR, 345 East River Dr., St. George, UT 84790 801-688-3301

Phoenix Field Office: Manager, GORDON CHENAIE, 2015 W. Deer Valley Rd., Phoenix, AZ 85027 (602-580-5600

Safford Field Office: Manager, BILL CIVISH, 711 South 14th Ave., Safford, AZ 85546 520-348-4201

Yuma Field Office: Manager, JUDY REED, 2555 East Gila Ridge Rd., Yuma, AZ 85365 520-317-3200

Lake Havasu Field Office: Manager, JOE LIEBHAUSER, 2610 Sweetwater Ave., Lake Havasu City, AZ 86406 (520, 505-1234)

Kingman Field Office: Manager, KEN DREW, 2475 Beverly Ave., Kingman, AZ 86401 (520, 757-3201

Tuscon Field Office: Manager, JESSE JUEN, 12661 East Broadway, Tucson, AZ 85748 (520, 722-4201

CALIFORNIA:

Bakersfield District: Manager, RON FELLOWS, 3801 Pegasus Ave., Bakersfield, CA 93308 (805, 391-6000)

California Desert District:Manager, HENRI BISSON, 6221 Box Springs Blvd., Riverside, CA 92507 (909, 697-5204)

Alturas Northern California Resource Area: Manager, RICH BURNS, Mgr., 708 W. 12th St., Alturas, CA 96101 (916, 233-4666)

Arcata Northern California Resource Area: Manager, LYNDA ROUSH, 1695 Heindon Rd., Arcata, CA 95521 (707, 825-2300)

Clear Lake Northern California Resource Area: Manager, RENEE SNYDER, 2550 N. State St., Ukiah, CA 95482 (707, 468-4000)

Eagle Lake Northern California Resource Area: Manager, LINDA HANSEN, 2950 Riverside Dr.,Susanville, CA 96130 (916, 257-0456)

Redding Northern California Resource Area: Manager, CHUCK SCHULTZ, 355 Hemsted Dr., Redding, CA 96002 (916, 224-2100)

Surprise Northern California Resource Area: Manager, SUSIE STOKE, 602 Cressler St., Cedarville, CA 96104 (916, 279-6101)

COLORADO:
Canon City District: Manager, DONNIE R. SPARKS, 3170 E. Main St., Canon City, CO 81212, (719,269-8500)

Craig District: Manager, MARK MORSE, 455 Emerson St., Craig, CO 81625, (970-824-8261)

Grand Junction District: Manager, MARK MORSE, 2815 H Rd., Grand Junction, CO 81506, (970-244-3000)

Montrose District: Manager, MARK STILES, 2465 S. Townsend, Montrose, CO 81401, (970-240-5300)

EASTERN STATES (All states bordering and east of the Mississippi River)
Jackson District: Manager, BRUCE DAWSON, Mgr., 411 Briarwood Dr., Suite 404, Jackson, MS 39206, (601, 977-5400)

Milwaukee District: Manager, JIM DRYDEN, 310 W. Wisconsin Ave., Suite 450, Milwaukee, WI 53203 (414, 297-4400; Fax: 414, 297-4409)

IDAHO: Lower Snake River District: Manager, JERRY KIDD, 3948 Development Ave., Boise, ID 83705 (208, 384-3300)

Idaho Falls District: Manager, HOWARD HEDRICK,1405 Holly Park Dr.,Idaho Falls, ID 83401 (208, 524-7500)

Coeur D'alene Field Office: Manager, FRITZ RENNEBAUM, 1808 North Third St., Coeur D'alene, ID 83814 (208-524-7500)

Upper Snake River-Burley Field Office: Manager, TOM DYER, 15 East 200 South, Burley, ID 83318, (208-677-6641)

MONTANA (Also North Dakota and South Dakota)
Butte District: Manager, JAMES OWINGS, 106 N. Parkmont, Butte, MT 59702-3388 (406, 494-5059)

Dakota District: Manager, DOUGLAS BURGER, 2933 Third Ave., W.est Dickinson, ND 58601-2617 (701, 225-9148)

Lewistown District:Manager, DAVE MARI, AirPort Rd., P.O. Box 1160, Lewistown, MT 59457-1160 (406, 538-7461)

Miles City District: Manager, RIM MURPHY, 111 Garryowen Rd., Miles City, MT 59301 (406, 232-4333)

NEVADA:
Battle Mountain Field Office: Manager, GERALD SMITH, 50 Bastian Rd., Battle Mountain, NV 89820 (702, 635-4000; Fax: 702, 635-4034)

Carson City Field Office: Manager, JOHN O. SINGLAUB, 1535 Hot Springs Rd., Carson City, NV 89706-0638 (702, 885-6000; Fax: 702, 885-6147)

Elko Field Office: Manager, HELEN M. HANKINS, 3900 East Idaho St., Elko, NV 89801 (702, 753-0200; Fax: 702, 753-0255)

Ely Field Office: Manager, GENE A. KOLKMAN, 702 North Industrial Way, Ely, NV 89301 (702, 289-1800; Fax: 702, 702, 289-1810)

Las Vegas District: Manager, MIKE F. DWYER, 4765 West Vegas Dr., Las Vegas, NV 89108 (702, 647-5000; Fax: 702, 647-5023)

Winnemucca District: Manager, RONALD B. WENKER, 5100 East Winnemucca Blvd., Winnemucca, NV 89445 (702, 623-1500; Fax: 702, 623-1503)

NEW MEXICO (Also Kansas, Oklahoma, and Texas)
Albuquerque District: Manager, MIKE FORD, 435 Montano Rd., NE, Albuquerque, NM 87107 (505, 761-8700; Fax: 505, 761-8911)

Farmington District: Manager, MIKE POOL, 1235 La Plata Hwy., Farmington, NM 87401 (505, 599-8900; Fax: 505, 599-8998)

Las Cruces District: Manager, LINDA RUNDELL, 1800 Marquess, Las Cruces, NM 87005-3371 (505, 525-4300; Fax: 505, 525-4412)

Roswell District: Manager, ED ROBERSON, 2909 W. Second St., Roswell, NM 88201-2019 (505, 627-0272; Fax: 505, 627-0276)

Tulsa District: Manager, JAMES F. SIMS,7906 East 33 St.,Tulsa, OK 74145-1352 (918, 621-4100; Fax: 918, 621-4130)

OREGON (Also Washington)
Burns District: Manager, MICHAEL GREEN, HC 74-12533 Hwy. 20 West, Hines, OR 97738 (541-574-4400)

Coos Bay District: Manager, Vacant, 1300 Airport Lane Rd., North Bend, OR 97459 (541-756-0100)

Eugene District: Manager, DENNIS WILLIAMSON, 2890 Chad Dr.,Eugene, OR 97408 (541- 683-6600)

Lakeview District: Manager, STEVEN A. ELLIS, 1000 South Ninth St., P.O. Box 151, Lakeview, OR 97630-0555, (503, 947-2177)

Medford District: Manager, DAVID A. JONES, 3040 Biddle Rd., Medford, OR 97504, (541-770-2411)

Prineville District: Manager, JAMES L. HANCOCK, P.O. Box 550, Prineville, OR 97754, (541-447-4115)

Roseburg District: Manager, CARY OSTRHAUS, 777 NW Garden Valley Blvd., Roseburg, OR 97470, (541-440-4930)

Salem District: Manager, VAN W. MANNING, 1717 Fabry Rd., SE, Salem, OR 97306, (541-375-5646)

Spokane District: Manager, JOSEPH BUESING, 1103 N. Fancher, Spokane, WA 99212, (509, 536-1200)

Vale District: Manager, EDWIN J. SINGLETON,100 Oregon St. Vale, OR 97918, (541-473-3144)

UTAH: Cedar City District: Manager, ART TAIT, 176 East D.L. Sargent Dr., Cedar City, UT 84720 (801, 865-3053; Fax: 801, 865-3058)

Moab District: Manager, KATE KITCHELL, 82 E. Dogwood, Moab, UT 84532, (801-259-6111)

Richfield District: Manager, JERRY W. GOODMAN, 150 E. 900 N., Richfield, UT 84701 (801, 896-8221)

Salt Lake District: Manager, GLENN CARPENTER, 2370 S. 2300 W., Salt Lake City, UT 84119 (801, 977-4300; Fax: 801, 997-4397)

Vernal District: Manager,DAVID HOWELL,170 S. 500 E., Vernal, UT 84078 (801, 781-4400; Fax: 801, 781-4410)

WYOMING (Also Nebraska)
Burns District: Manager, MIKE GREEN, HC 74-12533 Hwy 20 West, Hines, OR 97738 (541, 573-4400; Fax: 541, 573-4411)

Coos Bay District: Manager, LILLIE HIKIDA, 1300 Airport Ln., North Bend, OR 97459 (541, 756-0100; Fax: 541, 756-9303)

Eugene District: Manager, DENNIS WILLIAMSON,2890 Chad Dr., Eugene, OR 97440 (541, 683-6600)

Lakeview District: Manager, STEVE A. ELLIS, 1000 S. 9th St.,Lakeview, OR 97630-0555 (541-947-2177)

Medford District: Manager, DAVID A.JONES, 3040 Biddle Rd., Medford, OR 97504 (541, 770-2411; Fax: 541, 770-2400)

FEDERALLY PROTECTED AREAS

Prineville District: Manager, JIM HANCOCK, 3050 NE Third St., P.O. Box 550, Prineville, OR 97754 (541-447-4115)

Roseburg District: Manager, CARY OSTERHAUS, 777 N.W. Garden Valley Blvd., Roseburg, OR 97470 (541, 440-4930)

Salem District: Manager, VAN MANNING, 1717 Fabry Rd. S.E., Salem, OR 97306 (503, 375-5643; Fax: 503, 375-5622)

Spokane District: Manager, JOE BUESING, 1103 N. Fancher, Spokane, WA 99212 (509, 536-1200; Fax: 509, 536-1275)

Vale District: Manager, EDWIN J. SINGLETON, 100 Oregon St., Vale, OR 97918 (541, 473-3144; Fax: 541, 473-6213)

NATIONAL WILDLIFE REFUGES IN THE UNITED STATES

National Wildlife Refuges are administered by the United States Fish and Wildlife Service. Refuges are listed here by state. The abbreviation WMD refers to Wetlands Management District and WMA refers to Wildlife Management Area

ALABAMA: Bon Secour: Vacant, 12295 State Highway 180, Gulf Shores 36542 (334, 540-7720)

Choctaw: DOUGLAS J. BAUMGARTNER, Box 808, Jackson 36545 (334, 246-3583)

Eufaula: FRANK C. DUKES, 509 Old Highway 165, Eufaula 36027 (334, 687-4065)

Wheeler: (Blowing Wind Cave; Fern Cave; Watercress Darter): HARRY T. STONE, Rt. 4, Box 250, Decatur 35603 (205, 353-7243)

Grand Bay: (see Mississippi)

ALASKA: Alaska Maritime (Alaska Peninsula Unit; Bering Sea Unit; Chukchi Sea Unit; Gulf of Alaska Unit): JOHN L. MARTIN, 2355 Kachemak Bay Dr., Ste. 101, Homer 99603-8021 (907, 235-6546); Aleutian Islands Unit: DANIEL BOONE, PSC 486, Box 5251, FBO AP, AK 96506-5251 (907, 592-2406)

Alaska Peninsula (Becharof): RONALD HOOD, P.O. Box 277, King Salmon 99613 (907, 246-3339)

Arctic: JIM KURTH, 101-12th Ave., Box 20, Fairbanks 99701 (907, 456-0250)

Innoko: ED MERRITT, Box 69, McGrath 99627 (907, 524-3251)

Izembek: GREG SIEKANIEC, Box 127, Cold Bay 99571 (907, 532-2445)

Kanuti: TOM EARLY, 101-12th Ave., Box 11, Fairbanks 99701 (907, 456-0329)

Kenai: ROBIN WEST, P.O. Box 2139, Ski Hill Rd., Soldotna 99669-2139 (907, 262-7021)

Kodiak: JAY BELLINGER, 1390 Buskin River Rd., Kodiak 99615 (907, 487-2600)

Koyukuk/Nowitna: TOM ELEY, P.O. Box 287, Galena 99741 (907, 656-1231)

Selawik: LESLIE KERR, P.O. Box 270, Kotzebue 99752 (907, 442-3799)

Tetlin: RICHARD VOSS, P.O. Box 779, Tok 99780 (907, 883-5312)

Togiak: AARON ARCHIBEQUE, P.O. Box 270, Dillingham 99576 (907, 842-1063)

Yukon Delta: MICHAEL REARDON, P.O. Box 346, Bethel 99559 (907, 543-3151)

Yukon Flats: TED HEUER, 101-12th Ave., Box 14, Fairbanks 99701 (907, 456-0440)

ARIZONA: Buenos Aires: WAYNE A. SHIFFLETT, P.O. Box 109, Sasabe 85633 (520, 823-4251)

San Bernardino (Leslie Canyon): KEVIN S. COBBLE, P.O. Box 3509, Douglas 85607 (520, 364-2104)

Cabeza Prieta: ROBERT W. SCHUMACHER, 1611 N. Second Ave., Ajo 85321 (520, 387-6483)

Kofa: MILTON K. HADERLIE, P.O. Box 6290, Yuma 85366-6290 (602, 783-7861)

Imperial: Vacant, P.O. Box 72217, Yuma, AZ 85365 (520, 783-3371)

Lower Colorado River Complex: WES MARTIN, P.O. Box D, Yuma 85364 (520, 343-8112); Bill Williams: NANCY M. GILBERTSON, 60911 Highway 95, Parker, AZ 85344 (520, 667-4144); Cibola: RICHARD A. GILBERT, P.O. Box AP, 54D,Blythe, CA 92226 (602, 857-3253); Havasu: JAMES R. GOOD, P.O. Box 3009, Needles, CA 92363 (619, 326-3853)

ARKANSAS: Felsenthal (Pond Creek, Overflow): JIM C. JOHNSON, P.O. Box 1157, Crossett, AR 71635 (870, 364-3167)

Holla Bend (Logan Cave): BRUCE BLIHOVDE, Rt. 1, Box 59, Dardanelle 72834-9704 (501, 229-4300)

Cache River: DENNIS WIDNER, Rt. 2, Box 126-T, Augusta 72006 (501, 347-2614)

Bald Knob: BILL ALEXANDER

CALIFORNIA: Hopper Mountain Complex (Hopper Mountain, Battle Creek) MARC WEITZEL, P.O. Box 5839, Ventura 93005 (805, 644-5185)

Humboldt Bay: KIM FORRES, 1020 Ranch Rd., Loleta 95551 (707, 733-5406)

Kern (Blue Ridge; Pixley):DAVID A. HARDT, P.O. Box 670, Delano 93216-0219 (805, 725-2767)

Klamath Basin Refuges (Bear Valley, OR; Clear Lake, OR; Lower Klamath, OR & CA; Tule Lake; Upper Klamath, OR; Klamath Forest, OR): THOMAS STEWART, Rt. 1, Box 74, Tulelake 96134 (530, 667-2231)

Modoc: DAVID JOHNSON, P.O. Box 1610, Alturas 96101 (530, 233-3572)

Sacramento (Butte Sink WMA; Colusa; Delevan, North Central Valley; Sacramento River; Sutter; Willow Creek-Lurline WMA): GARY W. KRAMER, 752 County Rd., 99W, Willows 95988 (916, 934-2801)

Salton Sea (Coachella Valley): E. CLARK BLOOM, 906 W. Sinclair, Calipatria 92233 (760, 348-5278)

San Francisco Bay (Antioch Dunes; Don Edwards San Francisco Bay; Ellicott Slough; Farallon; Humbolt Bay; Marin Islands; Salinas River; San Pablo Bay): MARGARET T. KOLAR, P.O. Box 524, Newark 94560 (510, 792-0222); San Luis (Grasslands WMA; Kesterson; Merced; San Joaquin River): GARY R. ZAHM, P.O. Box 2176, Los Banos, CA 93635-2176 (209, 826-3508)

San Diego Complex (Tijuana Slough; Sweetwater Marsh; Seal Beach): DEAN RUNDLE, 2736 Loker Ave., West, Ste. A, Carlsbad, CA 92008 (619, 930-0168)

Stone Lakes: TOM HARVEY 2233 Watt Ave., Suite 375, Sacramento 95825-0509 (916, 979-2085)

COLORADO: Alamosa NWR (Monte Vista NWR): MICHAEL D. BLENDEN, 9383 El Rancho Ln., Alamosa, CO 81101-9003 (719, 589-4021)

Arapaho NWR (Hutton Lake, Bamforth, Mortenson Lake, and Pathfinder NWR): EUGENE C. PATTEN, P.O. Box 457, Walden, CO 80480 (970, 723-8202)

Browns Park: 1318 Highway 318, Maybell 81640 (970, 365-3613)

Rocky Mountain Arsenal Wildlife Area: RAY RAUCH, Bldg. 613, Commerce City, CO 80022-1748 (303, 289-0232); Two Ponds: DAVID JAMIEL

CONNECTICUT: BILL KOLODNICKI, P.O. Box 1030, Westbrook, CT 06498 (860, 399-2513)

DELAWARE: Bombay Hook (Prime Hook NWR): PAUL D. DALY, 2591 Whitehall Neck Rd., Smyrna, DE 19977 (302, 653-9345)
Prime Hook: GEORGE F. O'SHEA, R.D. Rt. 3, Box 195, Milton 19968 (302, 684-8419)

FLORIDA: Arthur R. Marshall Loxahatchee NWR (Hobe Sound NWR): BURKETT S. NEELY, JR., 10216 Lee Rd., Boynton Beach, FL 33437-4796 (561, 732-3684)
Chassahowitzka NWR (Crystal River NWR, Egmont Key NWR, Passage Key NWR, and Pinellas NWR): ELIZABETH SOUHEAVER, 1502 S.E. Kings Bay Dr., Crystal River, FL 34429 (352, 563-2088)
Florida Panther NWR; Ten Thousand Island: JIM KRAKOWSKI, 3860 Tollgate Blvd., Ste. 300, Naples, FL 34114 (941, 353-8442)
Hobe Sound NWR: RYAN M. NOEL, P.O. Box 645, Hobe Sound, FL 33475-0645 (561, 546-6141)
J.N. Ding Darling NWR (Caloosahatchee, Island Bay, Matlacha Pass and Pine Island NWRs): LOUIS S. HINDS, III, 1 Wildlife Dr., Sanibel, FL 33957 (941, 472-1100)
Lake Woodruff NWR: HENRY SANSING, P.O. Box 488, DeLeon Springs, FL 32130-0488 (904, 985-4673)
Lower Suwannee NWR (Cedar Keys NWR): KENNETH L. LITZENBERGER, 16450 NW 31st Place, Chiefland, FL 32626 (352, 493-0238)
Merritt Island NWR (Pelican Island NWR, Archie Carr NWR, Lake Wales Ridge NWR, and St. Johns NWR): ALBERT R. HIGHT, P.O. Box 6504, Titusville, FL 32782 (407, 859-2089)
National Key Deer Refuge (Key West, Great White Heron, and Crocodile Lake NWRs): STEVE KLETT, P.O. Box 43510, Big Pine Key, FL 33043-0510 (305, 872-2239)
St. Marks NWR: JAMES BURNETT, P.O. Box 68, St. Marks, FL 32355 (850, 925-6121)
St. Vincent NWR: DONALD J. KOSIN, P.O. Box 447, Apalachicola, FL 32329-0447 (850, 653-8808)

GEORGIA:Okefenokee NWR (Banks Lake NWR): MALLORY REEVES, Route 2, Box 3330, Folkston, GA 31537 (912, 496-7366)
Piedmont NWR (Bond Swamp NWR): RONNIE L. SHELL, Route 1 Box 670, Round Oak, GA 31038 (912, 986-5441)
Savannah Coastal Refuges (Savannah NWR), GENE SINGLETON; (Blackbeard Island), MICHAEL JOHNSON; Harris Neck, (Wassaw Island, Pinckney Island), REBECCA SCHAPANSKY (912-652-4415); (Tybee Island, and Wolf Island NWR): SAM O. DRAKE, JR., 1000 Business Center Dr., Ste. 10, Savannah, GA 31405 (912, 652-4415)

HAWAII: Hawaiian and Pacific Islands NWR Complex: JERRY F. LEINECKE, P.O. Box 50150167, Honolulu 96850 (808, 541-1201)
Guam: Vacant, P.O. Box 8134, MOU-3, Dededo, Guam 96912 (671-355-5096)
Hakalau Forest NWR: RICHARD C. WASS, 32 K Kincole St., Suite 101, Hilo, HI 96720 (808-933-6915
James Campbell NWR Pearl Harbor NWR): DONNA T. STOVALL, 66-590 Kamehameha Highway, Rm. 2C, Haleiwa, HI 96712 (808, 637-6330)
Johnston Island NWR: ROSA ROGER DI ROSA, Box 396, APO, AP 96558 (808, 621-3044)
Kealia Pond NWR (Kakahaia): KATHERINE C.E. SMITH, P.O. Box 1042, Kihei, HI 96753-1042 (808, 875-1582)
Kilauea Point NWR (Hanalei NWR and Huleia NWR): THOMAS R. ALEXANDER, P.O. Box 1125, Kilauea, Kauai, HI 96754-0087 (808, 828-1413)
Midway Atoll NWR: ROB SHALLENBERGER, P.O. Box 660099,
Midway Station, Annex Station 4, Lihue, HI 96766-0099 (808, 599-5888)
Pacific/Remote Islands Complex (Hawaiian Islands, Baker Island, Howland Island, Jarvis Island, Rose Atoll NWRs): P.O. Box 50167, Honolulu, HI 96850 (808, 541-1201)

IDAHO: Deer Flat, KEVIN RYAN, 13751 Upper Embankment Rd., Nampa 83686 (208, 467-9278)
Kootenai: DAN PENNINGTON, HCR 60, Box 283, Bonners Ferry 83805 (208, 267-3888)
Southeast Idaho Complex: MILTON K. HADERLIE, 1246 Yellowstone Ave., A-4, Pocatello 83201-4372 (208, 237-6616); Bear Lake: RICHARD SJOSTROM, Box 9, Montpelier 83253 (208, 847-1757); Camas: GERALD DEUTSCHER, 2150 E. 2350 N., Hamer 83425 (208, 662-5423); Grays Lake: MIKE FISHER, 74 Grays Lake Rd., Wayan 83285 (208, 574-2755); Minidoka: MIKE JOHNSON, 961 East Minidoka Dam, Rupert 83350 (208, 436-3589); Oxford Slough WPA: TERRY GLADWIN, 1246 Yellowstone Ave., Ste. A-4, Pocatello, ID 83201-4372 (208, 237-6616)

ILLINOIS: Illinois River National Wildlife and Fish Refuge (Chautauqua, Emiquon, Meredosia): ROSS ADAMS, 19031 E. County Rd. 2105N, Havana, IL 62644 (309, 535-2290)
Crab Orchard: DANIEL DOSHIER, 8588 Route 148, Marion, IL 62959 (618, 997-3344)
Cypress Creek: MARGUERITE HILLS, Rt. 1, Box 53D, Ullin 62992 (618, 634-2231)
Mark Twain/Brussels District: K.L. DREWS, HRC, Box 107, Brussels 62013-9711 (618, 883-2524)
Mark Twain/Wapello District: SUE JULISON, 10728 County Rd. X-61, Wapello, IA 52653-9477 (319, 523-6982)
Mark Twin NWR/Annada District: DAVID M. ELLIS, P.O. Box 88, Annada, MO 63330 (314-847-2333)

INDIANA: Muscatatuck: LELAND E. HERZBERGER, 12985 E. U.S. Highway 50, Seymour, IN 47274 (812, 522-4352)
Patoka River National Wetlands Project: WILLIAM McCOY, 510 1/2 West Morton St., P.O. Box 217, Oakland City, IN 47660 (812, 749-3199)

IOWA: De Soto (Boyer Chute NWR): GEORGE E. GAGE, 1434 316th Ln., Missouri Valley 51555 (712, 642-4121)
Union Slough: BARRETT CHRISTENSON, 1710 360th St., Titonka 50480 (515, 928-2523)
Walnut Creek: RICHARD BIRGER, P.O. Box 399, Prairie City 50228 (515, 994-2415)

KANSAS: Flint Hills (Marais des Cygnes NWR): JERRE L. GAMBLE, P.O. Box 128, 530 W. Maple, Hartford 66854 (316, 392-5553)
Kirwin: WILLIAM H. SCHAFF, R.R. 1, Box 103, Kirwin 67644 (913, 543-6673)
Quivira: DAVID HILLEY, R.R. 3 Box 48A, Stafford 67530 (316, 486-2393)

KENTUCKY: Reelfoot (see Tennessee)

LOUISIANA: Bayou Cocodrie: JEROME FORD, P.O. Box 1772,

FEDERALLY PROTECTED AREAS

Ferriday, LA 71334 (318, 336-7119)
Cameron Prairie: PAUL YAKUPZACK, 1428 Highway, Bell City, LA 70630 (318, 598-2216)
Catahoula: ERIC SIPCO, P.O. Drawer Z, Rhinehart, LA 71363-0201 (318, 992-5261)
North Louisiana Wildlife Refuge Complex (D'Arbonne,(Upper Ouachita): LEE R. FULTON, Rt. 2, Box 401-A, Farmerville, LA 71241 (318, 726-4222)
Lacassine: VICKI C. GRAFE, 209 Nature Rd., Lake Arthur, LA 70549 (318, 774-5923)
Lake Ophelia (Grand Cote): ERIC SMITH, 401 Island Rd., Marksville, LA 71351 (318, 253-4238)
Louisiana WMD (Handy Brake): KELBY OUCHLEY, Rt. 2, Box 401-A, Farmerville, LA 71241 (318, 726-4400)
Sabine: WILL NIDECKER, III, Holly Beach Highway, 3000 Main St., Hackberry, LA 70645 (318, 762-3816)
SE Louisiana Refuges (Bayou Sauvage, Big Branch Marsh, Bogue Chitto, Breton, Delta, Atchafalaya, Shell Keys): HOWARD E. POITEVINT, 1010 Gause Blvd., Bldg. 936, Slidell, LA 70458 (504, 646-7555)
Tensas River: GEORGE CHANDLER, JR. Rt. 2, Box 295, Tallulah 71282 (318, 574-2664)

MAINE: Moosehorn: MARK SWEENEY, R.R.1, Box 202, Suite 1, Baring, ME 04694 (207, 454-7161)
Petit Manan (Cross Island, Franklin Island, Seal Island, Pond Island, MA): STAN A. SKUTEK, P.O. Box 279, Milbridge 04658 (207, 546-2124)
Rachel Carson: WARD FEURT, Box 751, Wells, ME 04090 (207, 646-9226)
Sunkhaze Meadows (Carlton Pond): RAY VARNEY, 1033 S. Main St., Old Town 04468 (207, 827-6138)

MARYLAND: Blackwater (Martin; Susquehanna): GLENN A. CAROWAN, JR., 2145 Key Wallace Dr., Cambridge 21613 (410, 228-2692)
Eastern Neck: MARTIN KAEHNY, 1730 Eastern Neck Rd., Rock Hall 21661 (410, 639-7056)
Patuxent Research Refuge: SUSAN McMAHON, 12100 Beech Forest Rd., Ste. 4036, Laurel 20708-4036 (301, 497-5582)

MASSACHUSETTS: Great Meadows (John Hay, NH, Massasoit, Nantucket, Norman's Land Island, Oxbow, Wapack, NH): Vacant, Weir Hill Rd., Sudbury 01776 (508, 443-4661)
Monomoy: SHARON WARE, Wikis Way, Morris Island, Chatham 02633 (508, 945-0594)
Parker River (Thacher Island): JOHN L. FILLIO, Northern Blvd., Plum Island, Newburyport, MA 01950 (508, 465-5753)
Silvio O. Conte National Wildlife and Fish Refuge: LARRY BANDOLIN, 38 Ave. A, Turners Falls 01376 (413, 863-0209)

MICHIGAN: East Lansing WMD: JIM HUDGINS, 2651 Coolidge Rd., East Lansing, MI 48823 (517, 351-4230)
Seney (Harbor Island; Huron; Kirtland's Warbler WMA): MICHAEL TANSY, HCR #2, Box 1, Seney, MI 49883 (906, 586-9851)
Shiawassee (Michigan Islands; Wyandotte): DOUGLAS SPENCER, 6975 Mower Rd., Saginaw 48601 (517, 777-5930)

MINNESOTA: Agassiz NWR: MARGARET ANDERSON, R.R. 1, Box 74, Middle River 56737 (218, 449-4115)
Big Stone NWR: RICH PAPASSO R.R. Box 25, Odessa, MN 56276 (320-273-2191
Crane Meadows NWR: Route 6, Box 171A, Little Falls, MN 56345 (612, 632-1575)
Detroit Lakes WMD: RICK JULIAN, Rt. 3, Box 47D, Tower Rd., Detroit Lakes, MN 56501 (218, 847-4431); Fergus Falls WMD: KEVIN J. BRENNAN, Route 1, Box 76, Fergus Falls, MN 56537 (218, 739-2291); Hamden Slough NWR: MICHAEL T. MURPHY, Rt.1, Box 32, Audubon, MN 56511 (218, 439-6319); Litchfield WMD: THOMAS G. BELL, 971 East Frontage Rd., Litchfield, MN 55355 (320), 693-2849); Morris WMD: ALFRED L. RADTKE, Route 1, Box 877, Morris, MN 56267 (612, 589-1001)
Minnesota Valley NWR: RICHARD D. SCHULTZ, 3815 East 80th St., Bloomington, MN 55425-1600 (612, 854-5900)
Rice Lake NWR (Mille Lacs): RALPH O. LLOYD, Route 2, Box 67, McGregor, MN 55760 (218, 768-2402)
Sherburne NWR: CHARLES W. BLAIR, 17076 293rd Ave., Zimmerman, MN 55398 (612m 389-3323)
Tamarac NWR: JAY M. JOHNSON, HC 10, Box 145, Rochert, MN 56578 (218, 847-2641)
Upper Mississippi River W&FR/Winona District: ROBERT L. DRIESLEIN, 51 E. 4th St., Rm. 203, Winona, MN 55987 (507, 454-7351)
Upper Mississippi River Wildlife and Fish Refuge: JAMES R. FISHER, 51 E. 4th St., Rm. 101, Winona, MN 55987 (507-452-54232)
Upper Mississippi River National Wildlife and Fish Refuge: (see Minnesota); La Crosse District: JAMES M. NISSEN, Box 415, La Crosse 54601-0415 (608, 784-3910)
Upper Mississippi River National Wildlife and Fish Refuge/McGregor District: DOUGLAS MULLEN, P.O. Box 460, McGregor 52157 (319, 873-3423)
Upper Mississippi River National Wildlife and Fish Refuge: EDWARD BRITTON, P.O. Box 336, Savanna, MN 61074 (815-273-3153)

MISSISSIPPI: Mississippi Sandhill Crane (Grand Bay): JOE HARDY, 7200 Crane Ln., Gautier 39553 (601, 497-6322)
Noxubee: JIMMY L. TISDALE, Rt. 1, Box 142, Brooksville 39739 (601, 323-5548)
Mississippi WMD (Dahomey; Tallahatchie): STEVE GARD, P.O. Box 1070, 16736 Hwy 8 West, Grenada 38902 (601, 226-8286)
St. Catherine Creek: TOM PRUSA, P.O. Box 117, Sibley, MS 39165 (601, 442-6696)
Yazoo: (Hillside; Mathews Brake; Morgan Brake): TIMOTHY M. WILKINS, Route 1, Box 286, 728 Yazoo Refuge Rd.,Hollandale, MS 38748 (601, 839-2638); Panther Swamp: W.F. STEVENS, 13695 River Rd., Yazoo City, MS 39194 (601, 746-5060); Hillside: DAVID VIKER, 4349 Christmas Pl., Lexington, MS 39095 (601, 235-4989); TIM WILKINS, Rt. 1, Box 286, Hollandale 38748 (601, 839-2638)

MISSOURI: Big Muddy National Wildlife & Fish Refuge: J.C. BRYANT, Midwest Science Center, 4200 New Haven Rd., Columbia 65201-9634 (573, 876-1826)
Mark Twain/Annada District (Clarence Cannon): DAVID ELLIS, P.O. Box 88, Annada, MO 63330 (314, 847-2333)
Mingo (Pilot Knob, Ozark Cavefish): GERALD L. CLAWSON, R.R. 1, Box 103, Puxico, MO 63960 (314, 222-3589)
Squaw Creek: RONALD BELL, P.O. Box 158, Mound City 64470 (816, 442-3187)
Swan Lake: JOHN GUTHRIE, Rt. 1, Box 29A, Sumner 64681 (816, 856-3323)

MONTANA: Benton Lake: JIM McCOLLUM, 922 Bootlegger Trail, Great Falls 59404 (406, 727-7400)
Bowdoin (Black Coulee; Creedman Coulee; Hewitt Lake; Lake Thibadeau): HC 65 Box 5700, Malta 59538 (406, 654-2863)
Charles M. Russell (Hailstone; Halfbreed Lake; Lake Mason; UL Bend; War Horse): MIKE HEDRICK, P.O. Box 110, Lewistown

59457 (406, 538-8706)

Lee Metcalf: PAT GONZALES, P.O. Box 257, Stevensville 59870 (406, 777-5552)

Medicine Lake (Lamesteer): TED GUTZKE, 223 N. Shore Rd., Medicine Lake. MT 59247-9600 (406, 789-2305)

National Bison Range (Nine-Pipe; Pablo; Swan River): DAVID S. WISEMAN, 132 Bison Range Rd., Moiese, MT 59824 (406, 644-2211)

Red Rock Lakes: DANIEL GOMEZ, Monida Star Rt., Box 15, Lima 59739 (406, 276-3536)

NEBRASKA: Crescent Lake/North Platte NWR Complex: STEVE KNODA, P.O. Box 1346, Scottsbluff, NE 69363-1346 (308, 635-7851); Crescent Lake: Vacant, HC 68 Box 21, Ellsworth 69340 (308, 762-4893)

Fort Niobrara/Valentine: ROYCE HUBER, HC 14, Box 67, Valentine 69201 (402, 376-3789)

Rainwater Basin WMD: GENE MACK, P.O. Box 1686, Kearney 68848 (308, 236-5015)

NEVADA: Desert Refuge Complex (Desert Moapa Valley): KEN VOGET, 1500 N. Decatur Blvd., Las Vegas 89108 (702, 646-3401); Ash Meadows: ERIC HOPSON, P.O. Box 115, Amargosa Valley, NV 89020 (702, 372-5435); Pahranagat: Vacant, Box 510, Alamo 89001 (702, 725-3417)

Ruby Lake: KIM D. HANSON, HC 60, Box 860, Ruby Valley 89833 (702, 779-2237)

Stillwater (Anaho Island; Fallon): DAN WALSWORTH, P.O. Box 1236, Fallon 89407-1236 (702, 423-5128)

NEW HAMPSHIRE: Great Bay: SHARON D. VAUGHN, 601 Spaulding Tpke., Ste. 17, Portsmouth 03801 (603, 431-7511)

Lake Umbagog: PAUL CASEY, Box 280, Errol 03579 (603, 482-3415)

NEW JERSEY: Cape May: BRUCE LUEBKE, 24 Kimbles Beach Rd., Cape May Courthouse 08210-4207 (609, 463-0994)

Edwin B. Forsythe: Brigantine Division: STEPHEN ATZERT, Manager; TRACY CASSELMAN Great Creek Rd., Box 72, Oceanville, NJ 08231 (609, 652-1665); Barnegat Division: ALLISON BANKS, 70 Collinstown Rd., P.O. Box 544, Barnegat, NJ 08005 (609, 698-1378)

Great Swamp: WILLIAM KOCH, R.D. 1, Box 152, Basking Ridge 07920 (201, 425-1222)

Supawna Meadows: WALTER E. FORD, RD 3, Box 540, Salem, NJ 08079 (609, 935-1487)

Wallkill River: LIBBY HERLAND, P.O. Box 383, Sussex 07461 (201, 702-7266)

NEW MEXICO: Bitter Lake: WILLIAM R. RADKE, P.O. Box 7, Roswell 88202-0007 (505, 622-6755)

Bosque del Apache: PHILLIP W. NORTON, P.O. Box 1246, Socorro 87801 (505, 835-1828); Sevilleta: THEODORE M. STANS, P.O. Box 1248, Socorro 87801 (505, 864-4021)

Las Vegas: JOE B. RODRIGUEZ, JR., Rt. 1, Box 399, Las Vegas 87701 (505, 425-3581)

Maxwell: JERRY D. FRENCH, P.O. Box 276, Maxwell 87728 (505, 375-2331)

San Andres: GARY MONTOYA, P.O. Box 756, Las Cruces 88004 (505, 382-5047)

NEW YORK: Iroquois: Vacant, P.O. Box 517, 1101 Casey Rd., Alabama 14003 (716, 948-9154)

Long Island NWR Complex (Wertheim NWR, Target Rock NWR, Oyster Bay NWR, Seatuck NWR, Elizabeth A. Morton NWR, Amagansett NWR, Conscience Point NWR): PATRICIA MARTINKOVIC, P.O. Box 21, Shirley, NY 11967 (516, 286-0485)

Montezuma: THOMAS JASIKOFF, 3395 Rt. 5/20 East, Seneca Falls 13148 (315, 568-5987)

St. Lawrence WMD: Vacant, Boland Rd., St. Lawrence County, Richville, NY 13681 (315-393-9002)

NORTH CAROLINA: Alligator River (Pea Island): MICHAEL R. BRYANT, P.O. Box 1969, Manteo, NC 27954 (919, 473-1131)

Mackay Island (Currituck): JOHN D. WALLACE, P.O. Box 39, Knotts Island 27950 (919, 429-3100)

Mattamuskeet (Cedar Island; Swanquarter): DON TEMPLE, Rt. 1, Box N-2, Swanquarter 27885 (919, 926-4021)

Pee Dee: MIKE IELMINI, Rt. 1, Box 92, Wadesboro 28170 (704, 694-4424)

Pocosin Lakes: ELTON SAVERY, 3255 Shore Dr., Creswell 27928 (919, 797-4431)

Roanoke River: JERRY HOLLOMAN, P.O. Box 430, Windsor 27983 (919, 794-5326)

NORTH DAKOTA: Arrowwood Complex: MARK VANIMAN, 7745 11th St., SE, Pingree 58476-8308 (701, 285-3341); Valley City WMD: HARRIS HOISTAD, 11515 River Rd., Valley City, ND 58072-9619 (701, 845-3466)

Audubon NWR (Audubon WMD, Camp Lake NWR, Hiddenwood NWR, Lake Ilo NWR, Lake Nettie NWR, Lake Otis NWR, Lost Lake NWR, McLean NWR, Pretty Rock NWR, Lake Ilo NWR), DON J. BOZOVSKY, P.O. Box 127, Dunn Center, ND 58626 (701, 548-8110), Sheyenne Lake NWR, Stewart Lake NWR, and White Lake NWR): DAVE G. POTTER, RR1, P.O. Box 16, Colehabor, ND 58531 (701, 442-5474)

Chase Lake NWR: MICK ERICKSON, 5924 19TH St. SE, Woodworth, ND 58496 (701, 752-4218)

Crosby WMD (Lake Zahl NWR): TIM KESSLER, P.O. Box 148, Crosby, ND 58730-0148 (701, 965-6488)

Des Lacs NWR (Des Lacs NWR, Lostwood NWR, Shell Lake NWR, Lake Zahl NWR, Crosby WMD, Lostwood WMD):P.O. Box 578, Kenmare, ND 58746-0578 (701, 385-4046)

Devils Lake WMD (Brumba NWR, Kellys Slough NWR, Lake Alice NWR, Lake Ardoch NWR, Lambs Lake NWR, Little Goose NWR, Pleasant Lake NWR, Rock Lake NWR, Rose Lake NWR, Silver Lake NWR, Snyder Lake NWR, Stump Lake NWR, Sullys Hill NGP, Wood Lake NWR): ROGER HOLLEVOET, P.O. Box 908, Devils Lake, ND 58301 (701, 662-8611)

J.Clark Salyer NWR (J. Clark Salyer WMD, Buffalo Lake NWR, Cottonwood NWR, Lords Lake NWR, Rabb Lake NWR, School Section Lake NWR, Willow Lake NWR, and Wintering River NWR): ROBERT L. HOWARD, P.O. Box 66, Upham, ND 58789 (701, 768-2548)

Kulm WMD (Bone Hill Creek NWR, Dakota Lake NWR, Lake Patricia, and Maple River NWR): ROBERT J. VANDEN BERGE, P.O. Box E, Kulm, ND 58456-0170 (701, 647-2866)

Long Lake NWR (Long Lake NWR, Long Lake WMD, Florence Lake NWR, Slade NWR, Appert Lake NWR, Canfield Lake NWR, Hutchinson Lake NWR, Lake George NWR, Springwater NWR, and Sunburst Lake NWR); PAUL C. VAN NINGEN, 1200 353rd St. SE, Moffit, ND 58560-9740 (701, 387-4397)

Tewaukon NWR (Lake Elsie NWR, Storm Lake NWR, Wild Rice Lake NWR, and Tewaukon WMD: SANDRA SIEKANIEC, 9754 143 1/2 Ave. SE, Cayuga, ND 58013 (701, 724-3598)

Upper Souris NWR: DEAN F. KNAUER, RR 1, Box 163, Foxholm, ND 58718-9523 (701, 468-5467)

FEDERALLY PROTECTED AREAS

OHIO: Ottawa (Cedar Point; West Sister Island): LARRY MARTIN, 14000 W. State, Rt. 2, Oak Harbor 43449 (419, 898-0014)

OKLAHOMA: Deep Fork: JON M. BROCK, P.O. Box 816, Okmulgee, OK 74447 (918, 756-0815)

Little River (Little Sandy): BERLIN A. HECK, P.O. Box 340, Broken Bow 74728 (405, 584-6211)

Salt Plains: RODNEY F. KREY, Rt. 1, Box 76, Jet 73749 (405, 626-4794)

Sequoyah (Ozark Plateau NWR): STEPHEN L. BERENDZEN, Rt. 1, Box 18A, Vian 74962 (918, 773-5251)

Tishomingo: JOHNNY BEALL, Rt. 1, Box 151, Tishomingo 73460 (405, 371-2402)

Washita (Optima): RALPH L. BRYANT, Rt. 1, Box 68, Butler 73625 (405, 664-2205)

Wichita Mountains Wildlife Refuge: SAM WALDSTEIN, RR 1, Box 448, Indiahoma 73552 (405, 429-3221)

OREGON: Sheldon/Hart Mouintain Complex: Manager, MICHAEL L. NUNN, P.O. Box 111, Lakeview, OR 97630 (541-947-3315);

Hart Mountain National Antelope Refuge: DANIEL M. ALONSO, P.O. Box 21, Plush, OR 97637-0021 (541, 947-3315)

Klamath Forest NWR: HUGH NULL, HC 63, Box 303, Chiloquin, OR 97624-9616 (541, 783-3380)

Malheur NWR: FORREST W. CAMERON, HC 72, Box 245, Princeton, OR 97721-9505 (541, 493-2612)

Mid-Columbia River Complex (Umatilla, Cold Springs, McKay Creek, McNary, and Toppenish NWR): GARY A. HAGEDORN, P.O. Box 700, Umatilla, OR 97882-0700 (541, 922-3232)

Oregon Coastal Refuges (Bandon Marsh, Cape Meares, Nestucca Bay, Oregon Islands, Siletz Bay, and Three Arch Rocks NWR): ROY LOWE, 2127 SE OSU Dr., Newport, OR 97365-5258 (541, 867-4550)

Sheldon NWR: STEVEN E. CLAY, P.O. Box 111, Lakeview, OR 97630-0107 (541, 947-3315)

Sheldon/Hart Mountain Complex (Sheldon NWR and Hart Mountain National Antelope Refuge): MICHAEL L. NUNN, P.O. Box 111, Lakeview, OR 97630-0107 (503, 947-3315)

Tualatin River NWR: RALPH D. WEBBER, 16340 SW Beef Bend Rd., Sherwood, OR 97140-8306 (503, 590-5811)

Western Oregon Complex (Ankeny, Naskett Slough, Tualatin River, and William L. Finley NWRs, Bandon Marsh, Cape Meares, Nestucca Bay, Oregon Islands, Siletz Bay, and Three Rocks NWRs; JAMES E. HOUK, 26208 Finley Refuge Rd., Corvallis, OR 97333-9533 (541, 757-7236); Baskett Slough NWR: RICHARD J. GUADAGNO, 10995 Hwy. 22, Dallas, OR 97338-9343 (503, 623-2749); Ankeny NWR: 2301 Wintel Rd., Jefferson, OR 97352-9758 (503, 588-2701)

PENNSYLVANIA: Erie: THOMAS MOUNTAIN, R.D. 1, Wood Duck Ln., Guys Mills 16327 (814, 789-3585)

John Heinz NWR at Tinicum (Supawna Meadows NWR and Kilcohook Coordination Area): RICHARD F. NUGENT, Ste. 104, Scott Plaza 2, Philadelphia 19113 (2610 521-0662); WALTER E. FORD, 229 Lighthouse Rd., Salem, NJ 08079 (609-935-1487)

PUERTO RICO: Caribbean Islands Refuges (Cabo Rojo, JOSEPH J. SCHWAGERL; Desecheo, Laguna Cartagena; Sandy Point, Virgin Islands): VAL K. URBAN, P.O. Box 510, Boqueron, PR 00622 (809, 851-7258); (Culebra): TERESA TALLEVAST, P.O. Box 190, Culebra 00775 (787, 742-0115)

Sandy Point NWR: Vacant, Federal Bldg., 3013 Estate Golden Rock, Ste. 167, Christiansted, VI 00820-4355 (809, 773-4554)

RHODE ISLAND: Ninigret NWR (Block Island; Pettaquamscutt Cove NWR; Sachuest Point; Trustom Pond and Stewart B. McKinney NWR): CHARLES HEBERT, P.O. Box 307, Charlestown 02813 (401, 364-9124)

SOUTH CAROLINA: ACE Basin: JAMES BROWNING, P.O. Box 848, Hollywood 29449 (803, 889-3084)

Cape Romain (Santee NWR): Rt. 2 Box 370, Summerton, SC 29148 (803-478-2217); GEORGE R. GARRIS, 5801 Highway 17 N., Awendaw 29429 (803, 928-3368)

Carolina Sandhills: R. SCOTT LANIER, Rt. 2, Box 100, McBee 29101 (803, 335-8401)

SOUTH DAKOTA: Huron WMD: MARK HEISINGER, 200-4th St., SW, Rm. 317, Federal Bldg., Huron, SD 57350-2470 (605, 352-5894)

Lacreek (Bear Butte, LaCreek): ROLF H. KRAFT, HC 5, Box 14, Martin 57551 (605, 685-6508)

Lake Andes (Karl E. Mundt): SYLVIA PELIZZA, 38672 291st St., Lake Andes 57356 (605, 487-7603)

Madison WMD: DAVID L. GILBERT, P.O. Box 48, Madison 57042 (605, 256-2974)

Sand Lake (Pocasse): JOHN W. KOERNER, R.R. 1, Box 25, Columbia 57433 (605, 885-6320)

Waubay: DOUGLAS A. LESCHISIN, R.R. 1, Box 39, Wauba 57273 (605, 947-4521); Waubay WMD: CONNIE L. MUELLER

TENNESSEE: Cross Creeks NWR: JIM W. WIGGINTON, 643 Wildlife Rd., Dover, TN 37058 (931, 232-7477)

Hatchie NWR: MARVIN L. NICHOLS, 4172 Highway 76 South, Brownsville, TN 38012-8332 (901, 772-0501)

Reelfoot NWR, MARK WILLIAMS, 4343 Highway 157, Union City, TN 38261 (901-538-2481); (Lake Isom NWR, Chickasaw NWR, RANDY COOK; (Lower Hatchie NWR) EDWARD RODRIGUEZ, Federal Bldg., Rm. 129, 309 N. Church St., Dyersburg, TN 38024 (901, 287-0650); (Chickasaw NWR), BRYAN SCHULTZ, 1505 Sand Bluff Rd., Ripley, TN 38063 (901-635-7621)

Tennessee NWR: JOHN T. TAYLOR, P.O. Box 849, Paris, TN 38242 (901, 642-2091)

TEXAS: Anahuac (Moody, McFaddin, Texas Point); ANDY LORANGER, P.O. Box 278, Anahuac 77514 (409, 267-3337)

Aransas: J. BRENT GIEZENTANNER, P.O. Box 100, Austwell 77950 (512, 286-3559)

Attwater Prairie Chicken: TERRY A. ROSSIGNOL, JR., P.O. Box 519, Eagle Lake 77434-0519 (409, 234-3021)

Balcones Canyonlands: DEBORAH G. HOLLE, 10711 Burnet Rd., Ste. 201, Austin, TX 78758 (512, 339-9432)

Brazoria (San Bernard and Big Boggy): RONALD G. BISBEE, 1212 N. Velasco, Ste. 200, Angleton 77515-1088 (409, 849-7771); Big Boggy NWR: ALLEN C. JONES (409-064-3639)

Buffalo Lake: LYNN NYMEYER, P.O. Box 179, Umbarger 79091 (806, 499-3382)

Hagerman: JAMES M. WILLIAMS, Rt. 3, Box 123, Sherman 75091-9564 (903, 786-2826)

Laguna Atascosa: P.O. Box 450, Rio Hondo 78583 (210, 748-3607)

Muleshoe (Grulla, NM): DONALD R. CLAPP, P.O. Box 549, Muleshoe, TX 79347 (806, 946-3341)

Santa Ana/Lower Rio Grande Valley Complex: LARRY R. DITTO, Rt. 2 Box 202A, Almo, TX 78516 (210-787-3079); Lower Rio Grande Valley: MICHAEL R. BRYAN, Rt. 2, Box 202A, Rm. 225, Alamo 78516 (210, 787-3079); Santa Ana: Vacant

Trinity River NWR: STUART J. MARCUS, P.O. Box 10015, Liberty,

TX 77575 (409-336-9786)

UTAH: Bear River Migratory Bird Refuge: ALAN K. TROUT, 58 S. 950 West, Brigham City 84302 (801, 723-5887)
Fish Springs: JAY BANTA, P.O. Box 568, Dugway 84022 (801, 831-5353)
Ouray: STEVE BROCK, 266 West 100 North, Ste. #2, Vernal, UT 84078 (801, 789-0351)

VERMONT: Missisquoi: ROBERT A. ZELLEY, P.O. Box 163, Swanton 05488 (802, 868-4781)

VIRGINIA: Back Bay (Plum Tree Island): JOHN STASKO, 4005 Sandpiper Rd., Virginia Beach 23456 (757, 721-2412)
Chincoteague (Wallops Island): JOHN D. SCHROER, P.O. Box 62, Chincoteague 23336 (757, 336-6122)
Eastern Shore of VA (Fisherman Island): SUSAN RICE, RFD 1 Box 12B, Cape Charles 23310 (757, 331-2760)
Great Dismal Swamp (Nansemond): LLOYD CULP, JR., P.O. Box 349, Suffolk 23434 (757, 986-3705)
Mason Neck (Featherstone; Marumsco): GREG WEILER, 14344 Jefferson Davis Hwy., Woodbridge 22191 (703, 690-1297)
Rappahannock River Valley NWR (James River, Presquile): BARRY BRADY, P.O. Box 189, Prince George 23875 (804, 733-8042)

WASHINGTON: Columbia (Saddle Mountain): DAVID E. GOEKE, 735 E. Main St., P.O. Drawer F, Othello 99344 (509, 488-2668)
Little Pend Oreille NWR: LISA LANGELIER, 1310 Bear Creek Rd., Colville, WA 99114-9713 (509, 684-8384)
Nisqually NWR (Copalis, Dungeness), ROBERT H. EDENS, JR., 83 S. Barr Rd., Port Angeles, WA 98362 (360-457-8451); (Flattery Rocks, Grays Harbor, Protection Island, Quillayute Needles, and San Juan Islands NWRs): WILLARD B. HESSELBART, 100 Brown Farm Rd., Olympia, WA 98516-2302 (360, 753-9467)
Ridgefield NWR (Conboy Lake, Franz Lake, Pierce), JEFF W. HOLM, 36062 SR 14, Stevenson, WA 98648 (509-427-5208); and (Steigerwald Lake NWRs): THOMAS J. MELANSON, P.O. Box 457, Ridgefield, WA 98642-0457 (360, 887-4106); (Conboy Lake NWR): HAROLD E. COLE, Box 5, Glenwood, WA 98619-0005 (509, 364-3410)
Turnbull NWR: NANCY J. CURRY, 26010 South Smith Rd., Cheney, WA 99004-9326 (509, 235-4723)
Willapa NWR (Lewis and Clark NWR and Julia Butler Hansen Refuge for the Columbian White-tailed Deer): Vacant, HC 01, Box 910, Ilwaco, WA 98624-9707 (360, 484-3482); Julia Butler Hansen Refuge for the Columbian White-tailed Deer: ANNE M. SITTAUER, P.O. Box 566, Cathlamet, WA 98612-0566 (509, 795-3915)

WEST VIRGINIA: Ohio River Islands: JERRY L. WILSON, P.O. Box 1811, Parkersburg 26102-1811 (304, 422-0752)
Canaan Valley: GAIL BAKER, P.O. Box 1278, Rt. 250 S. Elkins 26241 (304, 637-7312)

WISCONSIN: Horicon Complex (Fox River; Gravel Island; Green Bay; Leopold WMD), STEVE LENZ; PATTI MEYERS, W 4279 Headquarters Rd., Mayville 53050 (414, 387-2658)
Necedah: LARRY A. WARGOWSKY, W. 7996 20th St., W., Necedah 54646-7531 (608, 565-2551)
St. Croix WMD: STEVE DELEHANTY, 1764 95th St.,, New Richmond, WI 54017 (715, 246-7784)
Trempealeau: RICHARD FRIETSCHE, Rt. 1, Box 1602, Trempealeau 54661-9781 (608, 539-2311)

WYOMING: National Elk Refuge: BARRY REISWIG, 675 E. Broadway, P.O. Box C, Jackson, WY 83001 (307, 733-9212)
Seedskadee (Cookeville Meadows): ANNE MARIE LAROSA, P O. Box 700, Green River, WY 82935 (307, 875-2187)

Regional Directors
Region 1: MICHAEL SPEAR, 911 NE 11th Ave., Eastside Federal Complex, Portland, OR 97232-4181 (503, 231-6118)
Region 2: NANCY KAUFMAN, P.O. Box 1306, Albuquerque, NM 87103 (505, 766-2321)
Region 3: WILLIAM F. HARTWIG, 1 Federal Dr., Federal Bldg., Fort Snelling, MN 55111-4056 (612, 725-3563)
Region 4: SAM HAMILTON, 1875 Century Blvd., NE, Rm. 324, Atlanta, GA 30345 (404, 679-4000)
Region 5: RONALD LAMBERTSON, 300 Westgate Center Dr., Hadley, MA 01035-9589 (413, 253-8200)
Region 6: RALPH MORGENWECK, Box 25486, Denver Federal Center, Denver, CO 80228 (303, 236-7920)
Region 7: DAVID B. ALLEN, 1011 East Tudor Rd., Anchorage, AK 99503 (907, 786-3542)

ORGANIZATION NAME INDEX

1000 FRIENDS OF FLORIDA 133
A. E. HOWELL WILDLIFE CONSERVATION CENTER 133
A.B. ENVIRONMENTAL EDUCATION CENTER 133
ABUNDANT LIFE SEED FOUNDATION 133
ACADIA UNIVERSITY 384
ACRES LAND TRUST 133
ACTION FOR NATURE, INC. 133
ADIRONDACK COUNCIL, THE 133
ADIRONDACK MOUNTAIN CLUB, INC., THE 134
ADIRONDACK NATURE CONSERVANCY/ADIRONDACK LAND TRUST, INC. 134
ADIRONDACK PARK AGENCY 90
ADKINS ARBORETUM 134
ADOPT-A-STREAM FOUNDATION, THE 134
ADVISORY COUNCIL ON HISTORIC PRESERVATION 34
AFRICAN WILDLIFE FOUNDATION 134
AFRICAN WILDLIFE NEWS SERVICE 135
AGENCY OF NATURAL RESOURCES 114
Department of Environmental Conservation 114
Department of Fish and Wildlife 114
Department of Forests, Parks, and Recreation 114
Environmental Board 115
Vermont Geological Survey 115
AGRICULTURAL EXTENSION SERVICE 110
AIR AND WASTE MANAGEMENT ASSOCIATION 135
ALABAMA ASSOCIATION OF SOIL AND WATER CONSERVATION DISTRICTS 135
ALABAMA B.A.S.S. CHAPTER FEDERATION 135
ALABAMA COOPERATIVE EXTENSION SYSTEM 39
ALABAMA COOPERATIVE FISH AND WILDLIFE RESEARCH UNIT (USDI) .. 39
ALABAMA DEPARTMENT OF AGRICULTURE AND INDUSTRIES 39
ALABAMA DEPARTMENT OF CONSERVATION AND NATURAL RESOURCES 39
ALABAMA DEPARTMENT OF ECONOMIC AND COMMUNITY AFFAIRS, COASTAL PROGRAMS (ADECA) 39
ALABAMA DEPARTMENT OF ENVIRONMENTAL MANAGEMENT 39
ALABAMA ENVIRONMENTAL COUNCIL 135
ALABAMA FORESTRY COMMISSION 39
ALABAMA NATURAL HERITAGE PROGRAM 135
ALABAMA SEA GRANT PROGRAM 40
ALABAMA SOIL AND WATER CONSERVATION COMMITTEE 40
ALABAMA WATERFOWL ASSOCIATION, INC. (AWA) 135
ALABAMA WILDLIFE FEDERATION 136
ALASKA ASSOCIATION OF SOIL AND WATER CONSERVATION DISTRICTS 136
ALASKA AUDUBON SOCIETY 136
ALASKA CENTER FOR THE ENVIRONMENT 136
ALASKA CONSERVATION ALLIANCE 136
ALASKA CONSERVATION FOUNDATION 136
ALASKA CONSERVATION VOICE 137
ALASKA COOPERATIVE FISH AND WILDLIFE RESEARCH UNIT 40
ALASKA DEPARTMENT OF ENVIRONMENTAL CONSERVATION 40
ALASKA DEPARTMENT OF FISH AND GAME 40
ALASKA DEPARTMENT OF NATURAL RESOURCES 41
ALASKA HEALTH PROJECT 41
ALASKA NATURAL RESOURCE AND OUTDOOR EDUCATION ASSOCIATION 137
ALASKA RAINFOREST CAMPAIGN 137
ALASKA SEA GRANT COLLEGE PROGRAM 41
ALASKA STATE EXTENSION SERVICES 41
ALASKA WILDLIFE ALLIANCE, THE 137
ALBERTA DEPARTMENT OF ENVIRONMENTAL PROTECTION 127
Communications Division 127
Corporate Management Service 127
Environmental Service 127
Land and Forest Service 127
Natural Resources Service 127
ALBERTA FISH AND GAME ASSOCIATION, THE 137
ALBERTA TRAPPERS ASSOCIATION 137
ALBERTA WILDERNESS ASSOCIATION 137
ALFRED UNIVERSITY, Division of Environmental Studies 382
ALLIANCE FOR THE CHESAPEAKE BAY 138
Balitmore Office 138
CRIS Office 138
Harrisburg Office 138
AMERICA THE BEAUTIFUL FUND 138
AMERICAN ALLIANCE FOR HEALTH PHYSICAL EDUCATION AND RECREATION AND DANCE 138
AMERICAN ASSOCIATION FOR LEISURE AND RECREATION (AALR) 139
AMERICAN ASSOCIATION FOR THE ADVANCEMENT OF SCIENCE 139
AMERICAN ASSOCIATION OF BOTANICAL GARDENS AND ARBORETA, INC. 139
AMERICAN ASSOCIATION OF FIELD BOTANISTS 139
AMERICAN ASSOCIATION OF ZOO KEEPERS, INC. 139
AMERICAN BASS ASSOCIATION OF CONNECTICUT, THE 140
AMERICAN BASS ASSOCIATION OF KENTUCKY, THE 140
AMERICAN BASS ASSOCIATION OF MAINE, THE 140
AMERICAN BASS ASSOCIATION OF MARYLAND, THE 140
AMERICAN BASS ASSOCIATION OF MASSACHUSETTS, THE 140
AMERICAN BASS ASSOCIATION OF NEW HAMPSHIRE, THE 140
AMERICAN BASS ASSOCIATION OF NEW JERSEY, THE 140
AMERICAN BASS ASSOCIATION OF WEST VIRGINIA, THE 140
AMERICAN BASS ASSOCIATION, INC. 140
AMERICAN BIRD CONSERVANCY 140
AMERICAN BIRDING ASSOCIATION 141
AMERICAN CAMPING ASSOCIATION, INC. 141
AMERICAN CANAL SOCIETY, INC. 141
AMERICAN CAVE CONSERVATION ASSOCIATION 141
AMERICAN CETACEAN SOCIETY 141
AMERICAN CHESTNUT FOUNDATION, THE 141
AMERICAN CONSERVATION ASSOCIATION, INC. 141
AMERICAN CONSERVATION ASSOCIATION, INC. (New York Office) 142
AMERICAN COUNCIL FOR AN ENERGY-EFFICIENT ECONOMY 142
AMERICAN FARMLAND TRUST 142
AMERICAN FEDERATION OF MINERALOGICAL SOCIETIES 142
AMERICAN FISHERIES SOCIETY 142
Bioengineering Section 142
Canadian Aquatic Resources Section 143
Computer User Section 143
Early Life History 143
Education Section 143
Equal Opportunities Section 143
Estuaries Section 143
Fish Culture Section 143
Fish Health Section 143
Fisheries Administrators Section 143
Fisheries History Section 143
Fisheries Law Section 143
Fisheries Management Section 143
Genetics Section 143
International Fisheries Section 143
Introduced Fish Section 143
Marine Fisheries Section 143
Native People Fisheries Section 143
North Central Division 143
Northeastern Division 144
Physiology Section 144
Socioeconomics Section 144
Southern Division 144
Southern Ontario Chapter 144
Water Quality Section 144
Western Division 144
AMERICAN FISHERIES SOCIETY, ALABAMA CHAPTER 144
AMERICAN FISHERIES SOCIETY, ALASKA CHAPTER 144
AMERICAN FISHERIES SOCIETY, ARIZONA-NEW MEXICO CHAPTER 144
AMERICAN FISHERIES SOCIETY, ARKANSAS CHAPTER 144
AMERICAN FISHERIES SOCIETY, ATLANTIC INTERNATIONAL CHAPTER 144
AMERICAN FISHERIES SOCIETY, AUBURN UNIVERSITY STUDENT CHAPTER 145
AMERICAN FISHERIES SOCIETY, BONNEVILLE CHAPTER 145
AMERICAN FISHERIES SOCIETY, CALIFORNIA-NEVADA CHAPTER 145
AMERICAN FISHERIES SOCIETY, COLLEGE OF ENVIRONMENTAL SCIENCE AND FORESTRY CHAPTER 145
AMERICAN FISHERIES SOCIETY, COLORADO and WYOMING CHAPTER 145
AMERICAN FISHERIES SOCIETY, DAKOTA CHAPTER 145
AMERICAN FISHERIES SOCIETY, FLORIDA CHAPTER 145
AMERICAN FISHERIES SOCIETY, GEORGIA CHAPTER 145
AMERICAN FISHERIES SOCIETY, GREATER PORTLAND, OR CHAPTER. 145
AMERICAN FISHERIES SOCIETY, HAWAII CHAPTER 146
AMERICAN FISHERIES SOCIETY, HUMBOLDT CHAPTER 146
AMERICAN FISHERIES SOCIETY, IDAHO CHAPTER 146
AMERICAN FISHERIES SOCIETY, ILLINOIS CHAPTER 146
AMERICAN FISHERIES SOCIETY, INDIANA CHAPTER 146
AMERICAN FISHERIES SOCIETY, IOWA CHAPTER 146
AMERICAN FISHERIES SOCIETY, KANSAS CHAPTER 146
AMERICAN FISHERIES SOCIETY, KENTUCKY CHAPTER 146
AMERICAN FISHERIES SOCIETY, LOUISIANA CHAPTER 146
AMERICAN FISHERIES SOCIETY, MICHIGAN CHAPTER 147
AMERICAN FISHERIES SOCIETY, MID-ATLANTIC CHAPTER 147
AMERICAN FISHERIES SOCIETY, MID-CANADA CHAPTER 147
AMERICAN FISHERIES SOCIETY, MINNESOTA CHAPTER 147
AMERICAN FISHERIES SOCIETY, MISSISSIPPI CHAPTER 147
AMERICAN FISHERIES SOCIETY, MISSOURI CHAPTER 147
AMERICAN FISHERIES SOCIETY, MONTANA CHAPTER 147
AMERICAN FISHERIES SOCIETY, NEW MEXICO STATE UNIVERSITY STUDENT CHAPTER 147
AMERICAN FISHERIES SOCIETY, NEW YORK CHAPTER 147
AMERICAN FISHERIES SOCIETY, NORTH CAROLINA CHAPTER 148
AMERICAN FISHERIES SOCIETY, NORTH PACIFIC INTERNATIONAL CHAPTER 148
AMERICAN FISHERIES SOCIETY, NORTHWESTERN ONTARIO CHAPTER 148
AMERICAN FISHERIES SOCIETY, OHIO CHAPTER 148
AMERICAN FISHERIES SOCIETY, OKLAHOMA CHAPTER 148

428 ORGANIZATION NAME INDEX

AMERICAN FISHERIES SOCIETY, OREGON CHAPTER 148
AMERICAN FISHERIES SOCIETY, PENNSYLVANIA CHAPTER 148
AMERICAN FISHERIES SOCIETY, POTOMAC CHAPTER 148
AMERICAN FISHERIES SOCIETY, SOUTH CAROLINA CHAPTER 148
AMERICAN FISHERIES SOCIETY, SOUTHERN NEW ENGLAND CHAPTER 149
AMERICAN FISHERIES SOCIETY, TENNESSEE CHAPTER 149
AMERICAN FISHERIES SOCIETY, TEXAS A&M CHAPTER 149
AMERICAN FISHERIES SOCIETY, TEXAS CHAPTER 149
AMERICAN FISHERIES SOCIETY, TIDEWATER CHAPTER 149
AMERICAN FISHERIES SOCIETY, VIRGINIA CHAPTER 149
AMERICAN FISHERIES SOCIETY, VIRGINIA TECH CHAPTER 149
AMERICAN FISHERIES SOCIETY, WEST VIRGINIA CHAPTER 149
AMERICAN FISHERIES SOCIETY, WISCONSIN CHAPTER 149
AMERICAN FOREST FOUNDATION 150
AMERICAN FORESTS (formerly American Forestry Association) 150
AMERICAN GEOGRAPHICAL SOCIETY 150
AMERICAN GEOLOGICAL INSTITUTE 150
AMERICAN GROUND WATER TRUST 150
AMERICAN HIKING SOCIETY 150
AMERICAN HORSE PROTECTION ASSOCIATION 151
AMERICAN HUMANE ASSOCIATION 151
AMERICAN INSTITUTE OF BIOLOGICAL SCIENCES 151
AMERICAN INSTITUTE OF FISHERY RESEARCH BIOLOGISTS 151
AMERICAN LAND CONSERVANCY 151
AMERICAN LANDS (formerly Western Ancient Forest Campaign) 151
AMERICAN LEAGUE OF ANGLERS AND BOATERS 152
AMERICAN LITTORAL SOCIETY 152
AMERICAN LITTORAL SOCIETY (Coral Reef Conservation Center Office) ... 152
AMERICAN LITTORAL SOCIETY (Delaware Riverkeeper Crossin) 152
AMERICAN LITTORAL SOCIETY (New York Office) 152
AMERICAN LIVESTOCK BREEDS CONSERVANCY 152
AMERICAN LUNG ASSOCIATION 152
AMERICAN LUNG ASSOCIATION OF LOUISIANA, INC. 152
AMERICAN MUSEUM OF NATURAL HISTORY 153
AMERICAN NATURE STUDY SOCIETY 153
AMERICAN OCEANS CAMPAIGN 153
AMERICAN OCEANS CAMPAIGN (Washington DC Office) 153
AMERICAN ORNITHOLOGISTS' UNION 153
AMERICAN PIE (PUBLIC INFORMATION ON THE ENVIRONMENT) 153
AMERICAN PLANNING ASSOCIATION 154
AMERICAN RECREATION COALITION 154
AMERICAN RESOURCES GROUP 154
AMERICAN RIVERS (formerly American Rivers Conservation Council) 154
AMERICAN SAMOA DEPARTMENT OF AGRICULTURE 41
AMERICAN SOCIETY FOR ENVIRONMENTAL HISTORY 154
AMERICAN SOCIETY OF ICHTHYOLOGISTS AND HERPETOLOGISTS 155
AMERICAN SOCIETY OF LANDSCAPE ARCHITECTS 155
AMERICAN SOCIETY OF LIMNOLOGY AND OCEANOGRAPHY 155
AMERICAN SOCIETY OF MAMMALOGISTS 155
AMERICAN SOCIETY OF ZOOLOGISTS 156
AMERICAN SPORTFISHING ASSOCIATION 156
AMERICAN WATER RESOURCES ASSOCIATION 156
AMERICAN WATER WORKS ASSOCIATION (AWWA) 156
AMERICAN WILDLANDS 156
AMERICAN WILDLIFE RESEARCH FOUNDATION, INC. 156
AMERICAN ZOO AND AQUARIUM ASSOCIATION (AZA) 157
AMERICANS FOR THE ENVIRONMENT 157
ANACOSTIA WATERSHED SOCIETY 157
ANCIENT FOREST INTERNATIONAL 157
ANGLERS FOR CLEAN WATER 157
ANIMAL PROTECTION INSTITUTE 157
ANIMAL WELFARE INSTITUTE 158
ANTARCTICA PROJECT 158
ANTIOCH COLLEGE 385
ANTIOCH NEW ENGLAND GRADUATE SCHOOL 381
APPALACHIAN REGIONAL COMMISSION 7
APPALACHIAN MOUNTAIN CLUB 158
APPALACHIAN STATE UNIVERSITY 383
APPALACHIAN TRAIL CONFERENCE 158
ARCHAEOLOGICAL CONSERVANCY 158
ARCHBOLD BIOLOGICAL STATION 159
ARCHERY MANUFACTURERS AND MERCHANTS ORGANIZATION (AMO) 159
ARCTIC INSTITUTE OF NORTH AMERICA 159
ARIZONA ASSOCIATION OF CONSERVATION DISTRICTS 159
ARIZONA B.A.S.S. CHAPTER FEDERATION 159
ARIZONA COOPERATIVE FISH AND WILDLIFE RESEARCH UNIT (USDI) ... 41
ARIZONA DEPARTMENT OF AGRICULTURE 41
  Animal Services Division 42
  Environmental Services Division 42
  Integrated Pest Management (IPM) 42
  Plant Services Division 42
ARIZONA DEPARTMENT OF ENVIRONMENTAL QUALITY 42
ARIZONA GAME AND FISH DEPARTMENT 42
ARIZONA GEOLOGICAL SURVEY 42
ARIZONA LAND DEPARTMENT 42
ARIZONA STATE EXTENSION SERVICES 43
ARIZONA STATE PARKS BOARD 43
ARIZONA STATE UNIVERSITY, Center for Environmental Studies 366
ARIZONA WILDLIFE FEDERATION 159
ARKANSAS ASSOCIATION OF CONSERVATION DISTRICTS 159
ARKANSAS B.A.S.S. CHAPTER FEDERATION 159
ARKANSAS COOPERATIVE RESEARCH UNIT 43
ARKANSAS DEPARTMENT OF PARKS AND TOURISM 43
ARKANSAS ENVIRONMENTAL EDUCATION ASSOCIATION 160
ARKANSAS GAME AND FISH COMMISSION 43
ARKANSAS STATE EXTENSION SERVICES 44
ARKANSAS STATE UNIVERSITY 367
ARKANSAS TECH UNIVERSITY 367
ARKANSAS WILDLIFE FEDERATION 160
ARLINGTON OUTDOOR EDUCATION ASSOCIATION, INC. 160
ASSOCIATION FOR CONSERVATION INFORMATION, INC. 160
ASSOCIATION FOR FISH AND WILDLIFE ENFORCEMENT TRAINING 160
ASSOCIATION FOR THE PROTECTION OF THE ADIRONDACKS, THE 160
ASSOCIATION OF AMERICAN GEOGRAPHERS 161
ASSOCIATION OF AVIAN VETERINARIANS 161
ASSOCIATION OF CONSERVATION ENGINEERS 161
ASSOCIATION OF CONSULTING FORESTERS OF AMERICA 161
ASSOCIATION OF FIELD ORNITHOLOGISTS 161
ASSOCIATION OF GREAT LAKES OUTDOOR WRITERS 162
ASSOCIATION OF MIDWEST FISH AND GAME LAW ENFORCEMENT OFFICERS 162
ASSOCIATION OF NEW JERSEY ENVIRONMENTAL COMMISSIONS 162
ASSOCIATION OF STATE AND TERRITORIAL HEALTH OFFICIALS 162
ATLANTIC CENTER FOR THE ENVIRONMENT 162, 163
ATLANTIC CENTER FOR THE ENVIRONMENT (New England Office) 162
ATLANTIC CENTER FOR THE ENVIRONMENT (QLF Canada Office) 163
ATLANTIC SALMON FEDERATION 163
ATLANTIC STATES LEGAL FOUNDATION 163
ATLANTIC STATES MARINE FISHERIES COMMISSION 7
AUBURN UNIVERSITY, College of Agriculture 366
AUBURN UNIVERSITY, College of Sciences and Mathematics 366
AUBURN UNIVERSITY, Ralph Brown Draughon Library 366
AUBURN UNIVERSITY, School of Forestry 366
AUBURN UNIVERSITY, Southeastern Cooperative Fish Disease Project 366
AUDUBON COUNCIL OF CONNECTICUT 163
AUDUBON COUNCIL OF ILLINOIS 163
AUDUBON INTERNATIONAL 163
AUDUBON NATURALIST SOCIETY OF THE CENTRAL ATLANTIC STATES 164
AUDUBON SOCIETY OF MISSOURI 164
AUDUBON SOCIETY OF NEW HAMPSHIRE 164
AUDUBON SOCIETY OF PORTLAND 164
AUDUBON SOCIETY OF RHODE ISLAND 164
AUDUBON SOCIETY OF WESTERN PENNSYLVANIA 165
AVSC INTERNATIONAL 165
BALL STATE UNIVERSITY 373
BARD COLLEGE, Graduate School in Environmental Studies 382
BARRIER ISLAND TRUST, INC. 165
BASS ANGLERS SPORTSMAN SOCIETY (B.A.S.S, INC.) 165
BASS RESEARCH FOUNDATION 165
BAT CONSERVATION INTERNATIONAL 165
BEMIDJI STATE UNIVERSITY, Center for Environmetnal Studies 379
BERKSHIRE-LITCHFIELD ENVIRONMENTAL COUNCIL, INC. 165
BIG BEND NATURAL HISTORY ASSOCIATION 166
BILLFISH FOUNDATION 166
BIODIVERSITY LEGAL FOUNDATION 166
BIO-INTEGRAL RESOURCE CENTER 166
BIOMASS USERS NETWORK 166
BIRDLIFE INTERNATIONAL 166
BLACK BASS FOUNDATION 166
BLUEBIRDS ACROSS VERMONT PROJECT 167
BOARD OF MINERALS AND ENVIRONMENT 109
BOONE AND CROCKETT CLUB 167
BOONE AND CROCKETT FOUNDATION 167
BORDER ECOLOGY PROJECT (BEP) 167
BOTANICAL CLUB OF WISCONSIN 167
BOTANICAL SOCIETY OF WESTERN PENNSYLVANIA 167
BOUNTY INFORMATION SERVICE 167
BOWLING GREEN STATE UNIVERSITY 385
BOY SCOUTS OF AMERICA 168
BRADLEY UNIVERSITY 373
BRANDYWINE CONSERVANCY, INC. 168
BRITISH COLUMBIA FIELD ORNITHOLOGISTS 168
BRITISH COLUMBIA WATERFOWL SOCIETY, THE 168
BROOKS BIRD CLUB INC., THE 168
BROTHERHOOD OF THE JUNGLE COCK, INC., THE 168
BROWN UNIVERSITY, Center for Environmental Studies 388
BROWN UNIVERSITY, Rhode Island School of Design 388
BUREAU OF ECONOMIC GEOLOGY 111
BUREAU OF MINES AND GEOLOGY 82
CA DEPARTMENT OF EDUCATION, OFFICE OF ENVIRONMENTAL EDUCATION 45
CADDO LAKE INSTITUTE, INC. 169
CALIFORNIA ACADEMY OF SCIENCES 45
  California Academy of Sciences Library 45

Organization Name Index

ORGANIZATION NAME INDEX 429

CALIFORNIA ASSOCIATION OF RESOURCE CONSERVATION DISTRICTS 169
CALIFORNIA B.A.S.S. CHAPTER FEDERATION 169
CALIFORNIA COOPERATIVE FISHERY RESEARCH UNIT (USGS) 45
CALIFORNIA ENVIRONMENTAL PROTECTION AGENCY 45
California Air Resources Board 46
Department of Pesticide Regulation 46
Department of Toxic Substances Control 46
Integrated Waste Management Board, IWMB 46
Office of Environmental Health Hazard Assessment 46
Water Resources Control Board 46
CALIFORNIA NATIVE PLANT SOCIETY (CNDS) 169
CALIFORNIA NATIVE PLANT SOCIETY, THE 169
CALIFORNIA POLYTECHNIC STATE UNIVERSITY 368
CALIFORNIA SEA GRANT COLLEGE SYSTEM 46
CALIFORNIA STATE EXTENSION SERVICES 47
CALIFORNIA STATE UNIVERSITY AT CHICO 368
CALIFORNIA STATE UNIVERSITY AT FULLERTON, Environmental Studies Master of Science Degree 368
CALIFORNIA STATE UNIVERSITY AT SACRAMENTO 368
CALIFORNIA TRAPPERS ASSOCIATION 170
CALIFORNIA TROUT, INC. 170
CALIFORNIA UNIVERSITY OF PENNSYLVANIA 386
CALIFORNIA UNIVERSITY OF PENNSYLVANIA, Environmental Studies 387
CALIFORNIA WATERFOWL ASSOCIATION 170
CALIFORNIA WILDLIFE DEFENDERS 170
CALIFORNIA WILDLIFE FEDERATION 170
CALIFORNIANS FOR POPULATION STABILIZATION (CAPS) 170
CAMP FIRE BOYS AND GIRLS 170
CAMP FIRE CLUB OF AMERICA, THE 171
CAMP FIRE CONSERVATION FUND 171
CAMPAIGN FOR A PROSPEROUS GEORGIA 171
CANADA-UNITED STATES ENVIRONMENTAL COUNCIL (United States Office) 171
CANADIAN ARCTIC RESOURCES COMMITTEE, INC. 171
CANADIAN COOPERATIVE WILDLIFE HEALTH CENTRE 171
CANADIAN ENVIRONMENTAL LAW ASSOCIATION 172
CANADIAN FEDERATION OF HUMANE SOCIETIES 172
CANADIAN FORESTRY ASSOCIATION 172
CANADIAN INSTITUTE FOR ENVIRONMENTAL LAW AND POLICY (CIELAP) 172
CANADIAN INSTITUTE OF FORESTRY/INSTITUT FORESTIER DU CANADA 172
CANADIAN NATIONAL SPORTSMEN'S SHOWS 172
CANADIAN NATURE FEDERATION 172
CANADIAN PARKS AND WILDERNESS SOCIETY 173
CANADIAN SOCIETY OF ENVIRONMENTAL BIOLOGISTS 173
CANADIAN WILDLIFE FEDERATION 173
CANVASBACK SOCIETY 173
CARIBBEAN CONSERVATION CORPORATION 173
CARIBBEAN CONSERVATION CORPORATION (Costa Rica Office) 173
CARIBBEAN NATURAL RESOURCES INSTITUTE 173
CAROLINA BIRD CLUB, INC. 173
CARRYING CAPACITY NETWORK 174
CASCADIA RESEARCH 174
CATSKILL CENTER FOR CONSERVATION AND DEVELOPMENT, INC., THE 174
CATSKILL FOREST ASSOCIATION 174
CAVE RESEARCH FOUNDATION 174
CENTER FOR ENVIRONMENT 174
CENTER FOR ENVIRONMENTAL EDUCATION 174
CENTER FOR ENVIRONMENTAL INFORMATION 175
CENTER FOR ENVIRONMENTAL PHILOSOPHY 175
CENTER FOR ENVIRONMENTAL STUDY 175
CENTER FOR HEALTH, ENVIRONMENT, AND JUSTICE 175
CENTER FOR INTERNATIONAL ENVIRONMENTAL LAW (CIEL) 175
CENTER FOR MARINE CONSERVATION 176
CENTER FOR PLANT CONSERVATION 176
CENTER FOR RESOURCE ECONOMICS 176
CENTER FOR RESOURCEFUL BUILDING TECHNOLOGY 176
CENTER FOR SCIENCE IN THE PUBLIC INTEREST 176
CENTER FOR SCIENCE INFORMATION 176
CENTER FOR THE STUDY OF TROPICAL BIRDS, INC. (Administative Office) 177
CENTER FOR THE STUDY OF TROPICAL BIRDS, INC. (Field Office) 177
CENTER FOR WATERSHED PROTECTION 177
CENTER FOR WILDLIFE LAW 177
CENTRAL MICHIGAN UNIVERSITY 378
CENTRAL OHIO ANGLERS AND HUNTERS CLUB 177
CENTRAL STATES EDUCATION CENTER 177
CENTRO de INFORMACION, INVESTIGACION y EDUCACION SOCIAL (CIIES) 177
CETACEAN SOCIETY INTERNATIONAL 177
CHARLES A. AND ANNE MORROW LINDBERGH FOUNDATION, THE 178
CHELONIA INSTITUTE 178
CHESAPEAKE BAY FOUNDATION, INC. 178
CHESAPEAKE BAY FOUNDATION, INC. (Maryland Office) 178
CHESAPEAKE BAY FOUNDATION, INC. (Pennsylvania Office) 178
CHESAPEAKE BAY FOUNDATION, INC. (Virginia Office) 178
CHESAPEAKE FARMS 179
CHESAPEAKE WILDLIFE HERITAGE (CWH) 179
CHICAGO HERPETOLOGICAL SOCIETY 179
CHIHUAHUAN DESERT RESEARCH INSTITUTE 179
CHINA REGION LAKES ALLIANCE 179
CHRISTINA CONSERVANCY, INC. 179
CIRCUMPOLAR CONSERVATION UNION 179
CITIZENS ALLIANCE FOR SAVING THE ATMOSPHERE AND THE EARTH (CASA) 179
CITIZENS NATURAL RESOURCES ASSOCIATION OF WISCONSIN, INC. 180
CITY UNIVERSITY OF NEW YORK, College of Staten Island 382
CITY UNIVERSITY OF NEW YORK, Hunter College 382
CLARK UNIVERSITY, International Development Program 377
CLEAN OCEAN ACTION 180
CLEAN WATER ACTION 180
CLEAN WATER FUND 180
CLEAN WATER NETWORK, THE 180
CLEMSON UNIVERSITY 388
CLEMSON UNIVERSITY, Aquaculture, Fisheries,and Wildlife 388
CLEVELAND MUSEUM OF NATURAL HISTORY, THE 180
CLIMATE INSTITUTE 180
COALITION FOR CLEAN AIR 181
COALITION FOR EDUCATION IN THE OUTDOORS 181
COALITION FOR NATURAL STREAM VALLEYS, INC. 181
COAST ALLIANCE 181
COASTAL CONSERVATION ASSOCIATION 181
COASTAL SOCIETY, THE 182
COLLEGE OF THE ATLANTIC 376
COLLEGE OF WILLIAM AND MARY, Virginia Institute of Marine Science/School of Marine Science 391
COLORADO ASSOCIATION OF SOIL CONSERVATION DISTRICTS 182
COLORADO B.A.S.S. CHAPTER FEDERATION 182
COLORADO COOPERATIVE FISH AND WILDLIFE RESEARCH UNIT (USDI) 50
COLORADO DEPARTMENT OF AGRICULTURE 50
COLORADO DEPARTMENT OF EDUCATION 50
COLORADO DEPARTMENT OF NATURAL RESOURCES 50
Colorado Geologic Survey 50
Division of Minerals and Geology 50
Division of Parks and Outdoor Recreation 50
Division of Water Resources 51
Division of Wildlife 51
Oil and Gas Conservation Commission 51
Soil Conservation Board 51
State Board of Land 51
Water Conservation Board 51
COLORADO DEPARTMENT OF PUBLIC HEALTH AND ENVIRONMENT 51
COLORADO ENVIRONMENTAL COALITION 182
COLORADO FORESTRY ASSOCIATION 182
COLORADO MOUNTAIN COLLEGE 370
COLORADO MOUNTAIN COLLEGE, Timberline Campus 370
COLORADO NATURAL HERITAGE PROGRAM 182
COLORADO STATE COOPERATIVE EXTENSION 51
COLORADO STATE FOREST SERVICE 51
COLORADO STATE UNIVERSITY, College of Natural Resources 370
COLORADO STATE UNIVERSITY, Doctoral Program in Environmental Politics and Policy Department of Political Science 370
COLORADO STATE UNIVERSITY, William E. Morgan Library 370
COLORADO TRAPPERS ASSOCIATION 183
COLORADO WATER CONGRESS 183
COLORADO WILDLIFE FEDERATION 183
COLORADO WILDLIFE HERITAGE FOUNDATION 183
COLUMBIA BASIN FISH AND WILDLIFE AUTHORITY 183
COLUMBIA RIVER GORGE COMMISSION 119
COLUMBIA RIVER INTER-TRIBAL FISH COMMISSION 7
COMITE DESPERTAR CIDRENO 105
COMMITTEE FOR NATIONAL ARBOR DAY 183
COMMITTEE FOR THE NATIONAL INSTITUTE FOR THE ENVIRONMENT (CNIE) 183
COMMITTEE ON AGRICULTURAL SUSTAINABILITY FOR DEVELOPING COUNTRIES 184
COMMUNITIES FOR A BETTER ENVIRONMENT 184
COMMUNITY CONSERVATION CONSULTANTS/HOWLERS FOREVER, INC. 184
COMMUNITY ENVIRONMENTAL COUNCIL 184
COMMUNITY RIGHTS COUNSEL 184
CONCERN, INC. 184
CONFEDERATED SALISH AND KOOTENAI TRIBES 185
CONFERENCE OF NATIONAL PARK COOPERATING ASSOCIATIONS 185
CONNECTICUT ASSOCIATION OF SOIL AND WATER CONSERVATION DISTRICTS, INC. 185
CONNECTICUT AUDUBON SOCIETY, INC. 185
CONNECTICUT B.A.S.S. CHAPTER FEDERATION 185
CONNECTICUT BOTANICAL SOCIETY 185
CONNECTICUT COLLEGE 370
CONNECTICUT DEPARTMENT OF AGRICULTURE 51
CONNECTICUT FOREST AND PARK ASSOCIATION 186
CONNECTICUT FUND FOR THE ENVIRONMENT 186
CONNECTICUT PUBLIC INTEREST RESEARCH GROUP (ConnPIRG) 186
CONNECTICUT RIVER WATERSHED COUNCIL INC. 186
CONNECTICUT WATERFOWL ASSOCIATION, INC. 186
CONSERVANCY OF SOUTHWEST FLORIDA, THE 186

Organization Name Index

ORGANIZATION NAME INDEX

Entry	Page
CONSERVATION AND RESEARCH FOUNDATION, INC., THE	186
CONSERVATION COUNCIL FOR HAWAII	187
CONSERVATION COUNCIL OF NORTH CAROLINA	187
CONSERVATION COUNCIL OF WESTERN AUSTRALIA, INC.	36
CONSERVATION DISTRICTS FOUNDATION INC.	187
CONSERVATION FEDERATION OF MARYLAND/For A Rural Maryland (F.A.R.M.)	187
CONSERVATION FEDERATION OF MISSOURI	187
CONSERVATION FUND, THE	187
CONSERVATION INTERNATIONAL	188
CONSERVATION LAW FOUNDATION, INC. (CLF)	188
CONSERVATION LAW FOUNDATION, INC. (CLF) (Maine Office)	188
CONSERVATION LAW FOUNDATION, INC. (CLF) (Vermont Office)	188
CONSERVATION TECHNOLOGY INFORMATION CENTER	188
CONSERVATION TREATY SUPPORT FUND	188
CONSERVATION TRUST OF PUERTO RICO	189
COOK INLET KEEPER	189
COOPER ORNITHOLOGICAL SOCIETY	189
COOPERATIVE EXTENSION SERVICE (NORTH CAROLINA)	94
COOPERATIVE EXTENSION SERVICE (VIRGIN ISLANDS)	115
COOPERATIVE EXTENSION SYSTEM (MASSACHUSETTS)	74
CORAL REEF ALLIANCE, THE (CORAL)	189
CORNELL LAB OF ORNITHOLOGY	189
CORNELL UNIVERSITY	382
CORNELL UNIVERSITY, Resource Center	382
COUNCIL FOR ENVIRONMENTAL EDUCATION	189
COUNCIL FOR PLANNING AND CONSERVATION	190
COUNCIL ON ENVIRONMENTAL QUALITY	10, 52
COUNCIL ON ENVIRONMENTAL QUALITY (CONNECTICUT)	52
COUNCIL ON RESOURCES AND DEVELOPMENT	85
COUSTEAU SOCIETY, INC., THE	190
COUSTEAU SOCIETY, INC., THE (France Office)	190
COUSTEAU SOCIETY, INC., THE (New York Office)	190
CRAIGHEAD ENVIRONMENTAL RESEARCH INSTITUTE	190
CRAIGHEAD WILDLIFE-WILDLANDS INSTITUTE	190
CRESTON VALLEY WILDLIFE MANAGEMENT AUTHORITY	190
DALHOUSIE UNIVERSITY, School for Resource and Environmental Studies (SRES)	385
DARTMOUTH COLLEGE, Environmental Studies Program	381
DAWES ARBORETUM, THE	191
DEEP-PORTAGE CONSERVATION RESERVE	191
DEFENDERS OF WILDLIFE	191
DELAWARE ASSOCIATION OF CONSERVATION DISTRICTS	191
DELAWARE AUDUBON SOCIETY	191
DELAWARE B.A.S.S. CHAPTER FEDERATION	191
DELAWARE DEPARTMENT OF AGRICULTURE	52
DELAWARE DEPARTMENT OF NATURAL RESOURCES AND ENVIRONMENTAL CONTROL	52
Division of Air and Waste Management	52
Division of Fish and Wildlife	53
Division of Parks and Recreation	53
Division of Water Resources	53
Division of Soil and Water Conservation	53
DELAWARE FORESTRY ASSOCIATION	192
DELAWARE GEOLOGICAL SURVEY	53
DELAWARE GREENWAYS, INC.	192
DELAWARE MUSEUM OF NATURAL HISTORY	192
DELAWARE NATURE SOCIETY	192
DELAWARE RIVER BASIN COMMISSION	7
DELAWARE SEA GRANT PROGRAM	53
DELAWARE SOLID WASTE AUTHORITY	53
DELAWARE STATE EXTENSION SERVICE	53
DELAWARE WILD LANDS, INC.	192
DELMARVA ORNITHOLOGICAL SOCIETY	192
DELTA WATERFOWL FOUNDATION	192
DELTA WILDLIFE FOUNDATION	192
DEPARTMENT FOR ENVIRONMENT, HERITAGE AND ABORIGINAL AFFAIRS	36
DEPARTMENT OF CANADIAN HERITAGE	36
DEPARTMENT OF COMMERCE	12
ECONOMIC DEVELOPMENT ADMINISTRATION	12
NATIONAL OCEANIC AND ATMOSPHERIC ADMINISTRATION	12
DEPARTMENT OF DEFENSE	13
DEPARTMENT OF ECOLOGY	119
Central Regional Office	119
Eastern Regional Office	119
Northwest Regional Office	119
Southwest Regional Office	119
DEPARTMENT OF EDUCATION	13
DEPARTMENT OF ENERGY	13
CARBON DIOXIDE INFORMATION ANALYSIS CENTER	14
FEDERAL ENERGY REGULATORY COMMISSION	14
DEPARTMENT OF ENVIRONMENT AND CONSERVATION (TENNESSEE)	109
DEPARTMENT OF ENVIRONMENT AND NATURAL RESOURCES (SOUTH DAKOTA)	109
DEPARTMENT OF ENVIRONMENT AND WILDLIFE (QUEBEC)	131
DEPARTMENT OF ENVIRONMENTAL CONSERVATION (NEW YORK)	90
Divisin of Environmental Permits	91
Division of Air Resources	91
Division of Environmental Enforcement	91
Division of Environmental Remediation	91
Division of Fish, Wildlife and Marine Resources	91
Division of Forest Protection & Fire Management	91
Division of in Mineral Resources	91
Division of Information Services	91
Division of Lands and Forests	91
Division of Law Enforcement	91
Division of Legal Affairs	91
Division of Management and Budget	91
Division of Operations	91
Division of Public Affairs and Education	91
Division of Solid & Hazardous Materials	91
Division of Transportation Services	91
Division of Water	91
Press Office	91
Regional Directors	91
DEPARTMENT OF ENVIRONMENTAL MANAGEMENT (RHODE ISLAND)	106
DEPARTMENT OF ENVIRONMENTAL PROTECTION (CONNECTICUT)	52
DEPARTMENT OF ENVIRONMENTAL PROTECTION (MAINE0	71
DEPARTMENT OF ENVIRONMENTAL PROTECTION (NEW JERSEY)	86
Division of Fish, Game, and Wildlife	87
Division of Parks and Forestry	87
Division of Publicly Funded Site Remediation	87
Division of Solid and Hazardous Waste	87
Geological Survey	87
Green Acres and Recreation Program	87
DEPARTMENT OF ENVIRONMENTAL PROTECTION (PENNSYLVANIA)	102
Citizens Advisory Council to DEP	103
DEPARTMENT OF ENVIRONMENTAL QUALITY (ARKANSAS)	44
DEPARTMENT OF ENVIRONMENTAL QUALITY (MISSISSIPPI)	79
Office of Land and Water Resources	79
DEPARTMENT OF ENVIRONMENTAL QUALITY (NEBRASKA)	83
DEPARTMENT OF ENVIRONMENTAL RESOURCES (PRINCE EDWARD ISLAND)	131
DEPARTMENT OF FISH AND WILDLIFE (OREGON)	100
DEPARTMENT OF FISH AND WILDLIFE (WASHINGTON)	119
DEPARTMENT OF FISHERIES AND AQUACULTURE	129
DEPARTMENT OF FISHERIES AND OCEANS	36
DEPARTMENT OF FOOD AND AGRICULTURE (CALIFORNIA)	47
DEPARTMENT OF FORESTRY	116
DEPARTMENT OF GAME AND INLAND FISHERIES	116
Region I	116
Region II	116
Region III	116
Region IV	116
Region V	116
DEPARTMENT OF GEOLOGY AND MINERAL INDUSTRIES	100
DEPARTMENT OF HEALTH AND HUMAN SERVICES	14
FOOD AND DRUG ADMINISTRATION	14
DEPARTMENT OF HEALTH, Environmental Health Administration, (District of Columbia)	53
DEPARTMENT OF HOUSING AND URBAN DEVELOPMENT	15
DEPARTMENT OF INDUSTRY, TRADE AND TOURISM	128
DEPARTMENT OF INLAND FISHERIES AND WILDLIFE	71
DEPARTMENT OF INTERIOR, U.S.G.S/B.R.D, SOUTH CAROLINA COOPERATIVE FISH AND WILDLIFE RESEARCH UNIT	107
DEPARTMENT OF JUSTICE	15
DEPARTMENT OF LABOR	15
JOB CORPS	15
MINE SAFETY AND HEALTH ADMINISTRATION	15
DEPARTMENT OF LAND AND NATURAL RESOURCES	
Division of Boating and Ocean Recreation (DOBOR	59
Division of Water Resource Management,	59
DEPARTMENT OF LAND AND NATURAL RESOURCES (HAWAII)	60
Division of Aquatic Resources	60
Division of Conservation and Resources Enforcement	60
Division of Forestry and Wildlife	60
Division of Historic Preservation	60
Division of State Parks	60
Land Division	60
DEPARTMENT OF LANDS (IDAHO)	61
DEPARTMENT OF MARINE RESOURCES	71
DEPARTMENT OF MINES, MINERALS AND ENERGY	116
Division of Energy	117
Division of Gas and Oil	117
Division of Mined Land Reclamation	117
Division of Mineral Mining	117
Division of Mineral Resources	117
Division of Mines	117
DEPARTMENT OF NATURAL RESOURCES	130
DEPARTMENT OF PARKS AND RECREATION (GUAM)	58
DEPARTMENT OF PARKS, RECREATION, AND TOURISM	107
DEPARTMENT OF PLANNING AND NATURAL RESOURCES	115
Division of Fish and Wildlife	116
DEPARTMENT OF PUBLIC SAFETY	41
Division of Fish and Wildlife Protection	41
DEPARTMENT OF PUBLIC WORKS	53
DEPARTMENT OF RENEWABLE RESOURCES	132

ORGANIZATION NAME INDEX 431

DEPARTMENT OF RESOURCES AND ECONOMIC DEVELOPMENT 85
DEPARTMENT OF RESOURCES, WILDLIFE AND ECONOMIC DEVELOPMENT, GOVERNMENT OF THE NORTHWEST TERRITORIES 129
DEPARTMENT OF STATE 16
BUREAU OF OCEANS AND INTERNATIONAL ENVIRONMENTAL AND SCIENTIFIC AFFAIRS 16
UNITED STATES MAN AND THE BIOSPHERE PROGRAM (U.S. MAB) 16
DEPARTMENT OF THE AIR FORCE 16
MAJOR AIR COMMANDS 16
MAJOR U.S. INSTALLATIONS 17
DEPARTMENT OF THE ARMY 19, 23
ARMY TRAINING AND DOCTRINE COMMAND 19
HEADQUARTERS, U.S. ARMY TRAINING AND DOCTRINE COMMAND 19
HQ ARMY MATERIAL COMMAND, INSTALLATIONS AND SERVICES ACTIVITY 20
U.S. ARMY CONSTRUCTION ENGINEERING RESEARCH LABORATORIES CERL 21
U.S. ARMY CORPS OF ENGINEERS 21
U.S. ARMY FORCES COMMAND 23
U.S. MILITARY ACADEMY 23
DEPARTMENT OF THE ARMY CONSERVATION DIVISION
ASSISTANT CHIEF OF STAFF FOR INSTALLATION MANAGEMENT 23
DEPARTMENT OF THE ENVIRONMENT 72
DEPARTMENT OF THE INTERIOR 23
BUREAU OF INDIAN AFFAIRS 24
BUREAU OF LAND MANAGEMENT 24
BUREAU OF RECLAMATION 24
NATIONAL PARK SERVICE 25
OFFICE OF SURFACE MINING RECLAMATION AND ENFORCEMENT 25
U.S. GEOLOGICAL SURVEY 25
U.S. GEOLOGICAL SURVEY BIOLOGICAL RESOURCES DIVISION 26
UNITED STATES FISH AND WILDLIFE SERVICE 26
DEPARTMENT OF THE NAVY 27
U.S. MARINE CORPS 27
DEPARTMENT OF TRANSPORTATION 27
FEDERAL AVIATION ADMINISTRATION 27
FEDERAL HIGHWAY ADMINISTRATION 27
FEDERAL RAILROAD ADMINISTRATION 28
FEDERAL TRANSIT ADMINISTRATION 28
NATIONAL HIGHWAY TRAFFIC SAFETY ADMINISTRATION 28
SAINT LAWRENCE SEAWAY DEVELOPMENT CORPORATION 28
U.S. COAST GUARD 28
DEPARTMENT OF TRANSPORTATION (OREGON) 100
DEPARTMENT OF TRANSPORTATION (RHODE ISLAND) 106
DEPARTMENT OF WATER RESOURCES (IDAHO) 61
DEPARTMENT OF WATER RESOURCES (NEBRASKA) 83
DEPARTMENT OF WILDLIFE CONSERVATION 98
DESERT FISHES COUNCIL 193
DESERT TORTOISE COUNCIL 193
DESERT TORTOISE PRESERVE COMMITTEE, INC. 193
DISTRICT OF COLUMBIA SOIL AND WATER CONSERVATION DISTRICT. 193
DISTRICT OF COLUMBIA STATE EXTENSION SERVICES 54
DIVISION OF AGRICULTURE 84
DIVISION OF FORESTRY AND SOIL RESOURCES (GUAM) 58
DIVISION OF NATURAL RESOURCES 122
DOGTOOTH GROUP 193
DRAGONFLY SOCIETY OF THE AMERICAS, THE 193
DREXEL UNIVERSITY, School of Environmental Science, Engineering, and Policy 387
DUCKS UNLIMITED (Alberta, Canada) 194
DUCKS UNLIMITED (Manitoba, Canada) 194
DUCKS UNLIMITED (Nova Scotia, Canada) 194
DUCKS UNLIMITED (Ontario, Canada) 194
DUCKS UNLIMITED (Quebec, Canada) 194
DUCKS UNLIMITED (Saskatchewan Operation, Canada) 194
DUCKS UNLIMITED, INC. 194, 196
DUCKS UNLIMITED, INC. (Central Flyway Office) 196
DUCKS UNLIMITED, INC. (Low Country Initiative) 196
DUCKS UNLIMITED, INC. (Meadowlands Office) 196
DUCKS UNLIMITED, INC. (North Atlantic Flyway and Ohio) 196
DUCKS UNLIMITED, INC. (South Atlantic Flyway) 196
DUCKS UNLIMITED, INC. (South Mississippi and South Central Flyways) 196
DUCKS UNLIMITED, INC. (Wetlands America Trust, Inc. Office) 196
DUKE UNIVERSITY, Center for Tropical Conservation 383
DUKE UNIVERSITY, Nicholas School of the Environment 383
EAGLE NATURE FOUNDATION, LTD. 197
EARTH DAY NEW YORK 197
EARTH FORCE 197
EARTH FOUNDATION 197
EARTH ISLAND INSTITUTE 197
EARTH SHARE 197
EARTHJUSTICE LEGAL DEFENSE FUND (formerly Sierra Club Legal Defense Fund, Inc.) 198
Florida Office 198
Hawaii Office 198
Louisiana Office 198
Montana Office 198
Rocky Mountain Office 198
Seattle, Washington Office 198
Southeast Alaska Office 198
Washington, DC Office 198
EARTHLAW 198
EARTHSCAN 198
EARTHSTEWARDS NETWORK 198
EARTHTRUST 199
EARTHWATCH INSTITUTE 199
EAST CENTRAL ILLINOIS FUR TAKERS 199
EASTERN ILLINOIS UNIVERSITY 373
EASTERN KENTUCKY UNIVERSITY 375
EASTERN MICHIGAN UNIVERSITY 378
EASTERN SHORE LAND CONSERVANCY 199
ECOLOGICAL SOCIETY OF AMERICA, THE 199
ECOLOGY CENTER 199
ECOTOURISM SOCIETY, THE 199
EDUCATIONAL COMMUNICATIONS, INC. 200
ELM RESEARCH INSTITUTE 200
ELSA WILD ANIMAL APPEAL (Louisiana Chapter) 200
EMORY UNIVERSITY 372
EMPORIA STATE UNIVERSITY 374
ENDANGERED SPECIES COALITION 200
ENERGY, MINERALS, AND NATURAL RESOURCES DEPARTMENT 88
Administrative Services Division 108
Energy Conservation and Management Division 88
Forestry and Resources Conservation Division 88
Mining and Minerals Division 88
Oil Conservation Division 88
State Parks and Recreation Division 88
ENTOMOLOGICAL SOCIETY OF AMERICA 200
ENVIRONMENT COUNCIL OF RHODE ISLAND 200
ENVIRONMENTAL ACTION FUND (EAF) 200
ENVIRONMENTAL ADVOCATES 201
ENVIRONMENTAL AIR FORCE 201
ENVIRONMENTAL AND ENERGY STUDY INSTITUTE (EESI) 201
ENVIRONMENTAL CAREER CENTER 201
ENVIRONMENTAL CAREERS ORGANIZATION INC., THE 201
ENVIRONMENTAL CENTER 60
ENVIRONMENTAL CONCERN, INC. 201
ENVIRONMENTAL CONSERVATION SERVICE 36
ENVIRONMENTAL DEFENSE CENTER, INC. 201
ENVIRONMENTAL DEFENSE FUND, INC. 202
Alliance for Environmental In Innovation 202
Capital Office 202
North Carolina Office 202
Rocky Mountain Office 202
Texas Office 202
West Coast Office 202
ENVIRONMENTAL EDUCATION ASSOCIATION OF ILLINOIS (Iron Oaks Environmental Learning Center) 202
ENVIRONMENTAL EDUCATION ASSOCIATION OF INDIANA 202
ENVIRONMENTAL EDUCATION ASSOCIATION OF WASHINGTON 203
ENVIRONMENTAL EDUCATION COUNCIL OF OHIO 203
ENVIRONMENTAL EDUCATION PROJECT (John Inskeep Environmental Learning Center) 203
ENVIRONMENTAL ENTERPRISES ASSISTANCE FUND, INC. 203
ENVIRONMENTAL LAW ALLIANCE WORLDWIDE (E-LAW) 203
ENVIRONMENTAL LAW INSTITUTE, THE 203
ENVIRONMENTAL LEAGUE OF MASSACHUSETTS (ELM) 203
ENVIRONMENTAL MEDIA ASSOCIATION 204
ENVIRONMENTAL PROTECTION AGENCY 10
ENVIRONMENTAL PROTECTION ASSOCIATION OF GHANA 204
ENVIRONMENTAL PROTECTION BUREAU 91
ENVIRONMENTAL PROTECTION SERVICE 37
ENVIRONMENTAL QUALITY COUNCIL 82
ENVIRONMENTAL QUALITY DEPARTMENT 125
ENVIRONMENTAL RESOURCE CENTER (ERC) 204
ENVIRONMENTAL REVIEW APPEALS COMMISSION 96
ENVIROSOUTH, INC. 204
E-P EDUCATION SERVICES, INC. 196
EUROPARC FEDERATION 204
EUROPEAN ASSOCIATION FOR AQUATIC MAMMALS 204
EUROPEAN CETACEAN SOCIETY 204
EVERGLADES COORDINATING COUNCIL (ECC) 204
EXECUTIVE OFFICE OF ENVIRONMENTAL AFFAIRS
Division of Fisheries and Wildlife 74
EXECUTIVE OFFICE OF ENVIRONMENTAL AFFAIRS (MASSACHUSETTS) 74
Animal Health 75
Bureau of Land Use 75
Bureau of Markets 75
Bureau of Pesticides 75
Department of Environmental Management 75
Department of Environmental Protection 75
Department of Fisheries, Wildlife, and Environmental Law Enforcement 75
Department of Food and Agriculture 75
Division of Agricultural Development 75
Division of Regulatory Services 75
Division of Wetlands and Waterways, ... 75
Metropolitan District Commission, ... 75
State Commission for Conservation of Soil, Water and Related Resources .. 75
Watershed Division 75
FAIRFAX AUDUBON SOCIETY 205

Organization Name Index

432 ORGANIZATION NAME INDEX

FEDERAL CARTRIDGE COMPANY ... 205
FEDERAL WILDLIFE OFFICER'S ASSOCIATION ... 205
FEDERATION OF ALBERTA NATURALIST ... 205
FEDERATION OF FLY FISHERS ... 205
FEDERATION OF NEW YORK STATE BIRD CLUBS, INC. ... 205
FEDERATION OF ONTARIO NATURALISTS ... 206
FEDERATION OF WESTERN OUTDOOR CLUBS ... 206
FERRIS STATE UNIVERSITY, College of Allied Health Sciences ... 378
FERRUM COLLEGE ... 391
FISH AND BOAT COMMISSION ... 103
Region 1 Northwest ... 103
Region 2 Southwest ... 103
Region 3 Northeast ... 103
Region IV Southeast ... 103
Region V North Central ... 103
Region VI South Central ... 103
FISH AND WILDLIFE DIVISION/DEPARTMENT OF STATE POLICE ... 100
FISH AND WILDLIFE INFORMATION EXCHANGE ... 206
FISH AND WILDLIFE REFERENCE SERVICE ... 206
FISHAMERICA FOUNDATION ... 206
FLORIDA ASSOCIATION OF SOIL AND WATER CONSERVATION DISTRICTS ... 206
FLORIDA ATLANTIC UNIVERSITY, Pine Jog Environmental Education Center ... 371
FLORIDA AUDUBON SOCIETY ... 206
FLORIDA B.A.S.S. CHAPTER FEDERATION ... 207
FLORIDA CONSERVATION FOUNDATION, INC. ... 207
FLORIDA COOPERATIVE FISH AND WILDLIFE RESEARCH UNIT (USDI) ... 54
FLORIDA DEFENDERS OF THE ENVIRONMENT, INC. (Home Office) ... 207
FLORIDA DEPARTMENT OF AGRICULTURE AND CONSUMER SERVICES 54
Division of Forestry ... 54
Office of Agricultural Water Policy ... 54
Soil and Water Conservation Board ... 54
FLORIDA DEPARTMENT OF ENVIRONMENTAL PROTECTION ... 54
Air Resources Management Division ... 54
Beaches and Shores Division ... 54
Ecosytem Management Division ... 54
Environmental Resource Permitting Division ... 55
Law Enforcement Division ... 55
Legislative and Cabinet Affairs Division ... 55
Marine Resource Division ... 55
Recreation and Parks division ... 55
State Lands Division ... 55
Waste Management Division ... 55
Water Facilities Division ... 55
FLORIDA EXOTIC PEST PLANT COUNCIL ... 207
FLORIDA FORESTRY ASSOCIATION ... 207
FLORIDA GAME AND FRESH WATER FISH COMMISSION ... 55
FLORIDA NATIVE PLANT SOCIETY ... 207
FLORIDA ORNITHOLOGICAL SOCIETY ... 208
FLORIDA PANTHER PROJECT, INC., THE ... 208
FLORIDA PUBLIC INTEREST RESEARCH GROUP (Florida PIRG) ... 208
FLORIDA SEA GRANT COLLEGE ... 55
FLORIDA SPORTSMEN'S CONSERVATION ASSOCIATION ... 208
FLORIDA STATE COOPERATIVE EXTENSION SERVICE ... 56
FLORIDA STATE DEPARTMENT OF HEALTH ... 56
FLORIDA STATE UNIVERSITY ... 372
FLORIDA TRAIL ASSOCIATION, INC. ... 208
FLORIDA WILDLIFE FEDERATION ... 208
FOOD AND AGRICULTURE ORGANIZATION OF THE UNITED NATIONS .. 209
FOREST HISTORY SOCIETY, INC. ... 209
FOREST LANDOWNERS ASSOCIATION, INC. ... 209
FOREST LANDOWNERS OF CALIFORNIA ... 209
FOREST OWNERS ASSOCIATION (GEORGIA) ... 209
FOREST SERVICE (Texas) ... 111
FOREST SERVICE EMPLOYEES FOR ENVIRONMENTAL ETHICS (FSEEE) ... 209
FOREST TRUST ... 209
FORESTRY COMMISSION (ARKANSAS) ... 44
FORESTRY COMMISSION (MISSISSIPPI) ... 79
FORESTRY COMMISSION (SOUTH CAROLINA) ... 107
FOSSIL FUELS POLICY ACTION INSTITUTE/ALLIANCE FOR A PAVING MORATORIUM ... 210
FOSSIL FUELS POLICY ACTION INSTITUTE/ALLIANCE FOR A PAVING MORATORIUM (South American Bureau Office) ... 210
FOSSIL RIM WILDLIFE CENTER ... 210
FOUNDATION FOR NORTH AMERICAN BIG GAME ... 210
FOUNDATION FOR NORTH AMERICAN WILD SHEEP ... 210
FRANKFURT ZOOLOGICAL SOCIETY--HELP FOR THREATENED WILDLIFE ... 211
FRESHWATER FOUNDATION ... 211
FRIENDS OF ACADIA ... 211
FRIENDS OF ANIMALS INC. ... 211
FRIENDS OF DISCOVERY PARK ... 211
FRIENDS OF THE BOUNDARY WATERS WILDERNESS ... 211
FRIENDS OF THE EARTH ... 211
Northwest Regional Office (WA, OR, ID) ... 212
FRIENDS OF THE RIVER ... 212
FRIENDS OF THE SAN JUANS ... 212
FRIENDS OF THE SEA OTTER ... 212
FUND FOR ANIMALS INC., THE ... 212
FUNDACION NATURA - COLOMBIA ... 212
FUTURE FISHERMAN FOUNDATION ... 213
GALIANO CONSERVANCY ASSOCIATION ... 213
GAME AND FISH DEPARTMENT ... 125
GAME AND PARKS COMMISSION ... 83
Game and Parks Commission ... 83
GAME AND PARKS COMMISSION-NEBRASKA
AK-Sar-Ben Aquarium ... 84
GAME COMMISSION ... 103
GAME CONSERVANCY U.S.A. (formerly American Friends of the Game Conservancy) ... 213
GAME CONSERVATION INTERNATIONAL (GAME COIN) ... 213
GARDEN CLUB OF AMERICA, THE ... 213
GENERAL FEDERATION OF WOMEN'S CLUBS ... 213
GENERAL SERVICES ADMINISTRATION ... 34
GEORGE MIKSCH SUTTON AVIAN RESEARCH CENTER INC. ... 214
GEORGE WASHINGTON UNIVERSITY ... 371
GEORGE WASHINGTON UNIVERSITY, Law School ... 371
GEORGE WRIGHT SOCIETY, THE ... 214
GEORGETOWN UNIVERSITY, Law Center ... 371
GEORGETOWN COLLEGE ... 375
GEORGIA ASSOCIATION OF CONSERVATION DISTRICT SUPERVISORS 214
GEORGIA B.A.S.S. CHAPTER FEDERATION ... 214
GEORGIA CONSERVANCY, INC., THE ... 214
GEORGIA COOPERATIVE FISH AND WILDLIFE RESEARCH UNIT (USDI) ... 57
GEORGIA DEPARTMENT OF AGRICULTURE ... 57
Consumers Services Library ... 57
GEORGIA DEPARTMENT OF EDUCATION ... 57
GEORGIA DEPARTMENT OF NATURAL RESOURCES ... 57
Coastal Resources Division ... 57
Environmental Protection Division ... 57
Historic Preservation Division ... 57
Parks, Recreation and Historic Sites Division ... 57
Pollution Prevention Assistance Division ... 57
Program Support Division ... 57
Wildlife Resources Division ... 57
GEORGIA ENVIRONMENTAL COUNCIL, INC. ... 214
GEORGIA ENVIRONMENTAL ORGANIZATION, INC (GEO) ... 215
GEORGIA FORESTRY ASSOCIATION, INC. ... 215
GEORGIA FORESTRY COMMISSION ... 57
GEORGIA INSTITUTE OF TECHNOLOGY ... 372
GEORGIA SEA GRANT COLLEGE PROGRAM ... 58
GEORGIA STATE EXTENSION SERVICES ... 58
GEORGIA TRAPPERS ASSOCIATION ... 215
GEORGIA WILDLIFE FEDERATION ... 215
GIRL SCOUTS OF THE UNITED STATES OF AMERICA ... 215
GLOBAL CITIES PROJECT, THE ... 215
GLOBAL ENVIRONMENTAL MANAGEMENT INITIATIVE (GEMI) ... 215
GLOBAL INDUSTRIAL AND SOCIAL PROGRESS RESEARCH INSTITUTE (GISPRI) ... 216
GOPHER TORTOISE COUNCIL ... 216
GOVERNOR OF ALABAMA, DONALD SIEGELMAN ... 39
GOVERNOR OF ALASKA, TONY KNOWLES ... 40
GOVERNOR OF AMERICAN SAMOA, TAUESE P.F. SUNIA ... 41
GOVERNOR OF ARIZONA, JANE DEE HULL ... 41
GOVERNOR OF ARKANSAS, MIKE HUCKABEE ... 43
GOVERNOR OF CALIFORNIA, GRAY DAVIS ... 45
GOVERNOR OF COLORADO, BILL OWENS ... 50
GOVERNOR OF CONNECTICUT, JOHN G. ROWLAND ... 51
GOVERNOR OF DELAWARE, THOMAS R. CARPER ... 52
GOVERNOR OF FLORIDA, JEB BUSH ... 54
GOVERNOR OF GEORGIA, ROY BARNES ... 57
GOVERNOR OF GUAM, CARL T.C. GUTIERREZ ... 58
GOVERNOR OF HAWAII, BENJAMIN CAYETANO ... 59
GOVERNOR OF IDAHO, DIRK KEMPTHORNE ... 61
GOVERNOR OF ILLINOIS, GEORGE RYAN ... 62
GOVERNOR OF INDIANA, FRANK O'BANNON ... 63
GOVERNOR OF IOWA, TOM VILSACK ... 65
GOVERNOR OF KANSAS, BILL GRAVES ... 66
GOVERNOR OF KENTUCKY, PAUL E. PATTON ... 68
GOVERNOR OF LOUISIANA, M. J. FOSTER, JR. ... 69
GOVERNOR OF MAINE, ANGUS S. KING, JR. ... 71
GOVERNOR OF MARYLAND, PARRIS N. GLENDENING ... 72
GOVERNOR OF MASSACHUSETTS, ARGEO PAUL CELLUCCI ... 74
GOVERNOR OF MICHIGAN, JOHN ENGLER ... 76
GOVERNOR OF MINNESOTA, JESSE VENTURA ... 77
GOVERNOR OF MISSISSIPPI, KIRK FORDICE ... 79
GOVERNOR OF MISSOURI, MEL CARNAHAN ... 81
GOVERNOR OF MONTANA, MARC RACICOT ... 82
GOVERNOR OF NEBRASKA, MIKE JOHANNS ... 83
GOVERNOR OF NEVADA, KENNY GUINN ... 84
GOVERNOR OF NEW HAMPSHIRE, JEANNE SHAHEEN ... 85
GOVERNOR OF NEW JERSEY, CHRISTINE T. WHITMAN ... 86
GOVERNOR OF NEW MEXICO, GARY JOHNSON ... 88
GOVERNOR OF NEW YORK, GEORGE E. PATAKI ... 90
GOVERNOR OF NORTH CAROLINA, JAMES B. HUNT, JR. ... 94
GOVERNOR OF NORTH DAKOTA, EDWARD T. SCHAFFER ... 95

Organization Name Index

ORGANIZATION NAME INDEX 433

GOVERNOR OF OHIO, ROBERT TAFT 96
GOVERNOR OF OKLAHOMA, FRANK KEATING 98
GOVERNOR OF OREGON, JOHN A. KITZHABER 100
GOVERNOR OF PENNSYLVANIA, TOM RIDGE 102
GOVERNOR OF PUERTO RICO, PEDRO J. ROSSELLO 105
GOVERNOR OF RHODE ISLAND, LINCOLN ALMOND 106
GOVERNOR OF SOUTH CAROLINA, JIM HODGES 107
GOVERNOR OF SOUTH DAKOTA, WILLIAM J. JANKLOW 109
GOVERNOR OF TENNESSEE, DON SUNDQUIST 109
GOVERNOR OF TEXAS, GEORGE W. BUSH 110
GOVERNOR OF THE VIRGIN ISLANDS, ROY L. SCHNEIDER 115
GOVERNOR OF UTAH, MIKE LEAVITT 113
GOVERNOR OF VERMONT, HOWARD DEAN 114
GOVERNOR OF VIRGINIA, JAMES S. GILMORE II 116
GOVERNOR OF WASHINGTON, GARY LOCKE 119
GOVERNOR OF WEST VIRGINIA, CECIL UNDERWOOD 122
GOVERNOR OF WISCONSIN, TOMMY G. THOMPSON 123
GOVERNOR OF WYOMING, JIM GERINGER 125
GRAND CANYON TRUST 216
GRAND CANYON TRUST (Utah Office) 216
GRAND CANYON TRUST (Washington, DC Office) 216
GRASSLAND HERITAGE FOUNDATION 216
GREAT BEAR FOUNDATION 216
GREAT LAKES FISHERY COMMISSION 7
GREAT LAKES INDIAN FISH AND WILDLIFE COMMISSION 7
GREAT LAKES SPORT FISHING COUNCIL 216
GREAT LAKES UNITED 217
GREAT LAKES UNITED (Montreal Office) 217
GREAT SMOKY MOUNTAINS INSTITUTE AT TREMONT 217
GREATER YELLOWSTONE COALITION 217
GREEN (GLOBAL RIVERS ENVIRONMENTAL EDUCATION NETWORK) 218
GREEN MOUNTAIN AUDUBON SOCIETY 218
GREEN MOUNTAIN CLUB INC., THE 218
GREEN PARTY USA 218
GREEN SEAL 218
GREENHOUSE ACTION 218
GREENPEACE, INC. 219
GROUNDWATER FOUNDATION, THE 219
GUADALUPE-BLANCO RIVER AUTHORITY 111
GUAM COASTAL MANAGEMENT PROGRAM 58
GUAM DEPARTMENT OF AGRICULTURE 58
Division of Aquatic and Wildlife Resources 58
GUAM ENVIRONMENTAL PROTECTION AGENCY 59
GUAM EXTENSION SERVICE 59
GUAM SEA GRANT PROGRAM 59
GULF AND CARIBBEAN FISHERIES INSTITUTE 219
GULF COAST RESEARCH LABORATORY 79
GULF OF MEXICO FISHERY MANAGEMENT COUNCIL 219
GULF STATES MARINE FISHERIES COMMISSION 7
H. JOHN HEINZ III CENTER FOR SCIENCE, ECONOMICS, AND THE ENVIRONMENT 219
HAMLINE UNIVERSITY'S CENTER FOR GLOBAL ENVIRONMENTAL EDUCATION 379
HARDWOOD FOREST FOUNDATION 219
HAWAII ASSOCIATION OF CONSERVATION DISTRICTS 219
HAWAII AUDUBON SOCIETY 219
HAWAII COOPERATIVE FISHERY RESEARCH UNIT (USDI) 60
HAWAII DEPARTMENT OF AGRICULTURE 60
HAWAII DEPARTMENT OF HEALTH 60
HAWAII NATURE CENTER 220
HAWAII SOCIETY OF AMERICAN FORESTERS 220
HAWAIIAN BOTANICAL SOCIETY 220
HAWK AND OWL TRUST, THE 220
HAWK MIGRATION ASSOCIATION OF NORTH AMERICA 220
HAWK MOUNTAIN SANCTUARY ASSOCIATION 220
HAWKWATCH INTERNATIONAL INC. 221
HEADLANDS INSTITUTE 221
HELSINKI COMMISSION/ BALTIC MARINE ENVIRONMENT PROTECTION COMMISSION 7
HENRY A. WALLACE INSTITUTE FOR ALTERNATIVE AGRICULTURE (HAWIAA) 221
HERITAGE INTERPRETATION INTERNATIONAL 221
HIGH DESERT MUSEUM, THE 221
HIMALAYAN WILDLIFE PROJECT 221
HOCKING COLLEGE, School of Natural Resources and Ecological Sciences 385
HOLDEN ARBORETUM, THE 221
HOLLY SOCIETY OF AMERICA, INC. 222
HOOD CANAL LAND TRUST 222
HOOSIER ENVIRONMENTAL COUNCIL 222
HOUSE COMMITTEE ON RESOURCES 4
HOUSE COMMITTEE ON AGRICULTURE 4
HOUSE COMMITTEE ON APPROPRIATIONS 5
HOUSE COMMITTEE ON COMMERCE 5
HOUSE COMMITTEE ON EDUCATION AND THE WORKFORCE 5
HOUSE COMMITTEE ON INTERNATIONAL RELATIONS 5
HOUSE COMMITTEE ON RULES 5
HOUSE COMMITTEE ON TRANSPORTATION AND INFRASTRUCTURE 5
HOWARD UNIVERSITY, Department of Environmental Sciences 371
HUDSONIA LIMITED 222
HUMAN ECOLOGY ACTION LEAGUE INC. THE (HEAL) 222
HUMANE SOCIETY OF THE UNITED STATES, THE 222
HUMBOLDT STATE UNIVERSITY, College of Natural Resources and Sciences 368
HUMBOLT FIELD RESEARCH INSTITUTE 223
HUMMINGBIRD SOCIETY, THE 223
HUNTSMAN MARINE SCIENCE CENTRE 223
HUXLEY COLLEGE OF ENVIRONMENTAL STUDIES, Division of Western Washington University 392
IDAHO ASSOCIATION OF SOIL CONSERVATION DISTRICTS 223
IDAHO B.A.S.S. CHAPTER FEDERATION 223
IDAHO CONSERVATION LEAGUE 223
IDAHO COOPERATIVE EXTENSION 61
IDAHO COOPERATIVE FISH AND WILDLIFE RESEARCH UNIT (USDI) 61
IDAHO DEPARTMENT OF PARKS AND RECREATION 61
IDAHO ENVIRONMENTAL COUNCIL 223
IDAHO FISH AND GAME DEPARTMENT 61
IDAHO FISH AND WILDLIFE FOUNDATION 62
IDAHO FOREST OWNERS ASSOCIATION 224
IDAHO GEOLOGICAL SURVEY 62
IDAHO STATE DEPARTMENT OF AGRICULTURE 62
IDAHO STATE UNIVERSITY, Department of Biological Sciences 372
IDAHO WILDLIFE FEDERATION 224
ILLINOIS ASSOCIATION OF CONSERVATION DISTRICTS 224
ILLINOIS ASSOCIATION OF SOIL AND WATER CONSERVATION DISTRICTS 224
ILLINOIS AUDUBON SOCIETY 224
ILLINOIS B.A.S.S. CHAPTER FEDERATION 224
ILLINOIS DEPARTMENT OF AGRICULTURE 62
Soil and Water Conservation Districts Advisory Board 63
ILLINOIS DEPARTMENT OF NATURAL RESOURCES 63
ILLINOIS DEPARTMENT OF TRANSPORTATION 63
ILLINOIS ENVIRONMENTAL COUNCIL 224
ILLINOIS ENVIRONMENTAL PROTECTION AGENCY 63
ILLINOIS NATIVE PLANT SOCIETY 225
ILLINOIS NATURAL HERITAGE FOUNDATION 225
ILLINOIS PRAIRIE PATH 225
ILLINOIS STATE UNIVERSITY, Environmental Health Program Department of Health Sciences 373
ILLINOIS WALNUT COUNCIL 225
ILLINOIS WOODLAND OWNERS AND USERS ASSOCIATION 225
INDIAN CREEK NATURE CENTER 225
INDIANA ASSOCIATION OF SOIL AND WATER CONSERVATION DISTRICTS, INC. 225
INDIANA AUDUBON SOCIETY, INC. 226
INDIANA B.A.S.S. CHAPTER FEDERATION 226
INDIANA DEPARTMENT OF ENVIRONMENTAL MANAGEMENT 63
INDIANA DEPARTMENT OF NATURAL RESOURCES 64
Division of Soil Conservation 64
INDIANA FORESTRY AND WOODLAND OWNERS ASSOCIATION 226
INDIANA NATIVE PLANT AND WILDFLOWER SOCIETY 226
INDIANA STATE DEPARTMENT OF HEALTH 64
INDIANA STATE GEOLOGICAL SURVEY 65
INDIANA STATE TRAPPERS ASSOCIATION, INC. 226
INDIANA STATE UNIVERSITY 373
INDIANA UNIVERSITY, School of Public and Environmental Affairs 373
INDIANA WILDLIFE FEDERATION 226
INDUSTRIAL SITING DIVISION/DEPARTMENT OF ENVIRONMENTAL QUALITY 126
INFORM, INC. 226
INLAND BIRD BANDING ASSOCIATION 227
INSTITUTE AND SCHOOL FOR ENVIRONMENT AND NATURAL RESOURCES, Univeristy of Wyoming (IENR and SENR) 227
INSTITUTE FOR CONSERVATION LEADERSHIP 227
INSTITUTE FOR EARTH EDUCATION, THE 227
INSTITUTE FOR ECOLOGICAL STUDIES 95
INSTITUTE OF ECOSYSTEM STUDIES 227
INSTITUTE OF MARINE BIOLOGY 60
INSTITUTE OF TROPICAL AGRICULTURE AND HUMAN RESOURCES 61
INSTITUTO NACIONAL DE BIODIVERSIDAD (INBIO) 37
INTERAGENCY COMMITTEE FOR OUTDOOR RECREATION (IAC) 120
INTER-AMERICAN TROPICAL TUNA COMMISSION 8
INTERFAITH COUNCIL FOR THE PROTECTION OF ANIMALS AND NATURE INC. (ICPAN) 227
INTERNATIONAL ASSOCIATION FOR BEAR RESEARCH AND MANAGEMENT 228
INTERNATIONAL ASSOCIATION FOR ENVIRONMENTAL HYDROLOGY (IAEH) 228
INTERNATIONAL ASSOCIATION OF FISH AND WILDLIFE AGENCIES 228
INTERNATIONAL ASSOCIATION OF NATURAL RESOURCE PILOTS 228
INTERNATIONAL ASSOCIATION OF WILDLAND FIRE (formerly Fire Research Institute) 229
INTERNATIONAL BICYCLE FUND 229
INTERNATIONAL CENTER FOR EARTH CONCERNS 229
INTERNATIONAL CENTER FOR GIBBON STUDIES 229
INTERNATIONAL CENTER FOR TROPICAL ECOLOGY 229
INTERNATIONAL CENTRE FOR CONSERVATION EDUCATION 229
INTERNATIONAL COUNCIL OF ENVIRONMENTAL LAW 229
INTERNATIONAL CRANE FOUNDATION 230
INTERNATIONAL ECOLOGY SOCIETY (IES) 230
INTERNATIONAL EROSION CONTROL ASSOCIATION (IECA) 230

Organization Name Index

INTERNATIONAL FUND FOR ANIMAL WELFARE	230
Austraian Office	230
Belgium Office	230
French Office	230
German Office	230
Holland Office	230
Hong Kong Office	230
Italian Office	230
Philippines Office	230
Russian Office	230
South African Office	231
United Kingdom	231
INTERNATIONAL GAME FISH ASSOCIATION	231
INTERNATIONAL HUNTER EDUCATION ASSOCIATION	231
INTERNATIONAL INSTITUTE FOR ENERGY CONSERVATION	231
INTERNATIONAL JOINT COMMISSION (Canada Office)	8
INTERNATIONAL JOINT COMMISSION (Great Lakes Regional Office)	8
INTERNATIONAL JOINT COMMISSION (Headquarters)	8
INTERNATIONAL MARINE MAMMAL PROJECT, THE	231
INTERNATIONAL MARITIME ORGANIZATION	231
INTERNATIONAL OCEANOGRAPHIC FOUNDATION	231
INTERNATIONAL OSPREY FOUNDATION INC., THE	232
INTERNATIONAL PACIFIC HALIBUT COMMISSION	8
INTERNATIONAL PLANT PROPAGATION SOCIETY, INC., THE	232
INTERNATIONAL PRIMATE PROTECTION LEAGUE	232
INTERNATIONAL PROFESSIONAL HUNTERS' ASSOCIATION	232
INTERNATIONAL RIVERS NETWORK	232
INTERNATIONAL SNOW LEOPARD TRUST	232
INTERNATIONAL SOCIETY FOR ECOLOGICAL ECONOMICS	233
INTERNATIONAL SOCIETY FOR ENDANGERED CATS (ISEC)	233
INTERNATIONAL SOCIETY FOR ENVIRONMENTAL ETHICS	233
INTERNATIONAL SOCIETY FOR THE PRESERVATION OF THE TROPICAL RAINFOREST, THE	233
INTERNATIONAL SOCIETY OF ARBORICULTURE	233
INTERNATIONAL SOCIETY OF TROPICAL FORESTERS INC.	233
INTERNATIONAL SONORAN DESERT ALLIANCE	234
INTERNATIONAL UNION FOR CONSERVATION OF NATURE AND NATURAL RESOURCES (IUCN) THE WORLD CONSERVATION UNION	234
Bangladesh Office	234
Burkina Fasso Office	234
Coordination Office of South and South East Asia	234
Country Liaison Botswana Office	234
Mali Office	234
Nepal Office	234
Office for Southern Africa (ROSA)	234
Office of Sri Lanka	234
Outposted Centre Canada	234
Outposted Centre European Programme	234
Outposted Centre-Environmental Law Centre	234
Outposted Office	235
Pakistan Office	235
Regional Coordination Office for West Africa	235
Regional Office for Eastern Africa	235
Regional Office for Meso America	235
Regional Office for South America	235
Regional Office for Central Africa	235
Senegal Office	235
U.S. Office, Washington, DC	235
Uganda Office	235
Zambia Office	235
INTERNATIONAL WHALING COMMISSION	8
INTERNATIONAL WILD WATERFOWL ASSOCIATION	235
INTERNATIONAL WILDERNESS LEADERSHIP (WILD) FOUNDATION	235
INTERNATIONAL WILDLIFE COALITION (IWC) AND THE WHALE ADOPTION PROJECT	235
INTERNATIONAL WILDLIFE REHABILITATION COUNCIL (IWRC)	236
INTERNATIONAL WOLF CENTER (Administrative Offices)	236
INTERNATIONAL WOLF CENTER (Educational Services)	236
INTERPRETATION CANADA	236
INTERSTATE COMMISSION ON THE POTOMAC RIVER BASIN	8
INTERTRIBAL BISON COOPERATIVE (ITBC)	236
IOWA ACADEMY OF SCIENCE	236
IOWA ASSOCIATION OF COUNTY CONSERVATION BOARDS	65
IOWA ASSOCIATION OF NATURALISTS	237
IOWA ASSOCIATION OF SOIL AND WATER CONSERVATION DISTRICT COMMISSIONERS	237
IOWA AUDUBON COUNCIL	237
IOWA B.A.S.S. CHAPTER FEDERATION	237
IOWA CONSERVATION EDUCATION COUNCIL, INC.	237
IOWA COOPERATIVE FISH AND WILDLIFE RESEARCH UNIT	65
IOWA DEPARTMENT OF AGRICULTURE AND LAND STEWARDSHIP	
Bureau of Field Services	65
Bureau of Financial Incentive Program	65
Bureau of Mines and Minerals	65
Bureau of Water Resources	65
Division of Soil Conservation	65
IOWA DEPARTMENT OF NATURAL RESOURCES	65
Administrative Services Division	65
Cooperative North American Shotgunning Education Program	66
Energy and Geological Resources Division	66
Environmental Protection Division	66
Fish and Wildlife Division	66
Forests and Forestry Division	66
Parks	66
Waste Management Division	66
IOWA ENVIRONMENTAL COUNCIL	237
IOWA NATIVE PLANT SOCIETY	237
IOWA NATURAL HERITAGE FOUNDATION	238
IOWA PRAIRIE NETWORK	238
IOWA STATE EXTENSION SERVICES	66
IOWA STATE UNIVERSITY	374
IOWA TRAILS COUNCIL	238
IOWA TRAPPERS ASSOCIATION, INC.	238
IOWA WILDLIFE FEDERATION	238
IOWA WILDLIFE REHABILITATORS ASSOCIATION	238
IOWA WOMEN IN NATURAL RESOURCES	238
IOWA WOODLAND OWNERS ASSOCIATION	239
ISLAND CONSERVATION EFFORT	239
ISLAND INSTITUTE, THE	239
ISLAND RESOURCES FOUNDATION	239
Eastern Caribbean Biodiversity Program Office	239
Washington, DC Office	239
ISSAQUAH ALPS TRAILS CLUB (I.A.T.C.)	239
IZAAK WALTON LEAGUE OF AMERICA ENDOWMENT	239
IZAAK WALTON LEAGUE OF AMERICA, INC., THE	240
Alaska Division	240
California Division	240
Colorado Division	240
Florida Division	240
Illinois Division	240
Indiana Division	240
Iowa Division	240
Maryland Division	240
Michigan Division	240
Minnesota Division	240
Nebraska Division	240
New York Division	241
Ohio Division	241
Oregon Divison	241
Pennsylvania Division	241
South Dakota Division	241
Virginia Division	241
Washington Division	241
West Virginia Division	241
Wisconsin Division	241
Wyoming Divisoin	241
J.N. (DING) DARLING FOUNDATION	241
JACK H. BERRYMAN INSTITUTE FOR WILDLIFE DAMAGE MANAGEMENT	242
JACK MINER MIGRATORY BIRD FOUNDATION, INC.	242
JACKSON HOLE CONSERVATION ALLIANCE	242
JACKSON HOLE LAND TRUST	242
JACKSON HOLE PRESERVE, INC.	242
JANE GOODALL INSTITUTE, THE	242
JAPAN WILDLIFE RESEARCH CENTER (JWRC)	242
JOHNS HOPKINS UNIVERSITY THE	376
KANSAS ACADEMY OF SCIENCE	242
KANSAS ADVISORY COUNCIL FOR ENVIRONMENTAL EDUCATION	243
KANSAS ASSOCIATION FOR CONSVERATION AND ENVIRONMENTAL EDUCATION	243
KANSAS ASSOCIATION OF CONSERVATION DISTRICTS	243
KANSAS AUDUBON COUNCIL	243
KANSAS B.A.S.S. CHAPTER FEDERATION	243
KANSAS BIOLOGICAL SURVEY	66
KANSAS COOPERATIVE FISH AND WILDLIFE RESEARCH UNIT	66
KANSAS DEPARTMENT OF AGRICULTURE	66
KANSAS DEPARTMENT OF WILDLIFE AND PARKS	67
Operations Office	67
Region 1	67
Region 2	67
Region 3	67
Region 4	67
KANSAS DEPARTMENT OF WILDLIFE AND PARKS, Region 5	67
KANSAS FOREST SERVICE	67
KANSAS GEOLOGICAL SURVEY	67
KANSAS HERPETOLOGICAL SOCIETY	243
KANSAS NATURAL RESOURCE COUNCIL	243
KANSAS ORNITHOLOGICAL SOCIETY	244
KANSAS STATE CONSERVATION COMMISSION	67
KANSAS STATE DEPARTMENT OF HEALTH AND ENVIRONMENT	67
KANSAS STATE EXTENSION SERVICES	68
KANSAS STATE UNIVERSITY	374
KANSAS STATE UNIVERSITY, Cooperative Fish and Wildlife Research Unit	374
KANSAS WATER OFFICE	68
KANSAS WILDFLOWER SOCIETY	244
KANSAS WILDLIFE FEDERATION	244
KANSAS WILDSCAPE FOUNDATION	244

ORGANIZATION NAME INDEX 435

KEENE STATE COLLEGE OF THE UNIVERSITY SYSTEM OF NEW HAMPSHIRE 381
KEEP AMERICA BEAUTIFUL, INC. 244
KEEP FLORIDA BEAUTIFUL, INC. 244
KENTUCKY ACADEMY OF SCIENCE 244
KENTUCKY ASSOCIATION FOR ENVIRONMENTAL EDUCATION (KAEE) . 245
KENTUCKY ASSOCIATION OF CONSERVATION DISTRICTS 245
KENTUCKY AUDUBON COUNCIL 245
KENTUCKY B.A.S.S. CHAPTER FEDERATION 245
KENTUCKY DEPARTMENT OF AGRICULTURE 68
KENTUCKY DEPARTMENT OF FISH AND WILDLIFE RESOURCES 68
KENTUCKY DEPARTMENT OF PARKS 68
KENTUCKY GEOLOGICAL SURVEY 68
KENTUCKY RESOURCES COUNCIL 245
KENTUCKY SOIL AND WATER CONSERVATION COMMISSION 69
KENTUCKY STATE EXTENSION SERVICES 69
KENTUCKY STATE NATURE PRESERVES COMMISSION 69
KENTUCKY WOODLAND OWNERS ASSOCIATION 245
KENTUCKY-TENNESSEE SOCIETY OF AMERICAN FORESTERS 245
KEYSTONE CENTER, THE 245
KEYSTONE CENTER, THE (Washington, D.C. Office) 246
KIDS FOR SAVING EARTH WORLDWIDE 246
KODIAK BROWN BEAR TRUST 246
LADY BIRD JOHNSON WILDFLOWER CENTER (formerly the National Wildflower Research Center) 246
LAKE ERIE CLEAN-UP COMMITTEE, INC. 246
LAKE MICHIGAN FEDERATION 246
LAKE SUPERIOR GREENS 246
LAKE SUPERIOR STATE UNIVERSITY, College of Natural and Health Sciences 378
LAKEHEAD UNIVERSITY 385
LAND BETWEEN THE LAKES ASSOCIATION 247
LAND TRUST ALLIANCE, THE 247
LEAGUE OF CONSERVATION VOTERS 247
LEAGUE OF KENTUCKY SPORTSMEN, INC. 247
LEAGUE OF OHIO SPORTSMEN 247
LEAGUE OF WOMEN VOTERS OF IOWA 247
LEAGUE OF WOMEN VOTERS OF THE U.S. 247
LEAGUE OF WOMEN VOTERS OF WASHINGTON 248
LEAGUE TO SAVE LAKE TAHOE 248
LEE COUNTY PARKS AND RECREATION SERVICES 56
LEGACY INTERNATIONAL 248
LEGAL ENVIRONMENTAL ASSISTANCE FOUNDATION INC. (LEAF) 248
LIFE OF THE LAND 248
LIGHTHAWK 248
  Northwest Field Office 249
  Rocky Mountain Field Office 249
LONG LIVE THE KINGS 249
LOUISIANA ASSOCIATION OF CONSERVATION DISTRICTS 249
LOUISIANA AUDUBON COUNCIL 249
LOUISIANA B.A.S.S. CHAPTER FEDERATION 249
LOUISIANA COOPERATIVE FISH AND WILDLIFE RESEARCH UNIT (USDI) 69
LOUISIANA DEPARTMENT OF AGRICULTURE
  Office of Forestry 69
  Office of Soil and Water Conservation, State Soil and Water Conservation Committee 70
LOUISIANA DEPARTMENT OF AGRICULTURE AND FORESTRY 70
LOUISIANA DEPARTMENT OF WILDLIFE AND FISHERIES 70
LOUISIANA FORESTRY ASSOCIATION 249
LOUISIANA GEOLOGICAL SURVEY 70
LOUISIANA SEA GRANT COLLEGE PROGRAM 70
LOUISIANA STATE EXTENSION SERVICES 70
LOUISIANA STATE UNIVERSITY, School of Forestry 375
LOUISIANA TECH UNIVERSITY, School of Forestry 375
LOUISIANA WILDLIFE FEDERATION, INC. 249
LOWER MISSISSIPPI RIVER CONSERVATION COMMITTEE 249
MACBRIDE RAPTOR PROJECT 249
MAGIC 250
MAINE ASSOCIATION OF CONSERVATION COMMISSIONS (MACC) 250
MAINE ASSOCIATION OF CONSERVATION DISTRICTS 250
MAINE ATLANTIC SALMON AUTHORITY (formerly Maine Atlantic Sea Run Salmon Commission) 71
MAINE AUDUBON SOCIETY 250
MAINE B.A.S.S. CHAPTER FEDERATION 250
MAINE COAST HERITAGE TRUST 250
MAINE COOPERATIVE FISH AND WILDLIFE RESEARCH UNIT (USDI) 72
MAINE DEPARTMENT OF AGRICULTURE, FOOD, AND RURAL RESOURCES 72
MAINE DEPARTMENT OF CONSERVATION 72
  Land Use Regulatin Commission 72
  Maine Forest Service 72
  Natural Resource Information & Mapping 72
MAINE DEPARTMENT OF CONSERVATION Bureau of Parks and Lands) 72
MAINE ENVIRONMENTAL EDUCATION ASSOCIATION, INC. 250
MAINE SEA GRANT PROGRAM 72
MANASOTA-88 251
MANCHESTER COLLEGE, Koinonia Environmental and Retreat Center 374
MANITOBA DEPARTMENT OF NATURAL RESOURCES 128
  Central Region 128
  Eastern Region 128
  Northeastern Region 128
  Northwestern Region 128
  Western Region 128
MANITOBA NATURALISTS SOCIETY 251
MANITOBA WILDLIFE FEDERATION 251
MANOMET OBSERVATORY 251
MARIN CONSERVATION LEAGUE 251
MARINE CONSERVATION BIOLOGY INSTITUTE 251
MARINE ENVIRONMENTAL RESEARCH INSTITUTE (MERI) 252
MARINE LABORATORY (FLORIDA) 56
MARINE MAMMAL CENTER, THE 252
MARINE MAMMAL COMMISSION 8
MARINE RESOURCES COMMISSION (VIRGINIA) 117
MARINE SCIENCE CENTER 392
MARINE SCIENCES RESEARCH CENTER (NEW YORK) 92
MARINE TECHNOLOGY SOCIETY 252
MARYLAND ASSOCIATION OF CONSERVATION DISTRICTS 252
MARYLAND B.A.S.S. CHAPTER FEDERATION 252
MARYLAND DEPARTMENT OF AGRICULTURE 73
  Agricultural Commission 73
  State Soil Conservation Committee 73
MARYLAND DEPARTMENT OF NATURAL RESOURCES 73
  Chesapeake Bay and Watershed Programs 73
  Management Services 73
  Public Lands Division 73
  Resource Management Services 74
MARYLAND FORESTS ASSOCIATION 252
MARYLAND NATIVE PLANT SOCIETY 252
MARYLAND ORNITHOLOGICAL SOCIETY, INC. 253
MARYLAND SEA GRANT COLLEGE 74
MARYLAND STATE EXTENSION SERVICES 74
MARYLAND-NATIONAL CAPITAL PARK AND PLANNING COMMISSION 74
MASSACHUSETTS ASSOCIATION OF CONSERVATION COMMISSIONS (MACC) 253
MASSACHUSETTS ASSOCIATION OF CONSERVATION DISTRICTS 253
MASSACHUSETTS AUDUBON SOCIETY, INC. 253
MASSACHUSETTS B.A.S.S. CHAPTER FEDERATION 253
MASSACHUSETTS COOPERATIVE FISH AND WILDLIFE RESEARCH UNIT (USDI) 75
MASSACHUSETTS ENVIRONMENTAL EDUCATION SOCIETY 253
MASSACHUSETTS FORESTRY ASSOCIATION 253
MASSACHUSETTS HIGHWAY DEPARTMENT 75
MASSACHUSETTS TRAPPER'S ASSOCIATION, INC. 254
MAX McGRAW WILDLIFE FOUNDATION 254
MCNEESE STATE UNIVERSITY 375
MERCK FOREST AND FARMLAND CENTER, INC. 254
MIAMI UNIVERSITY 385
MICHIGAN ASSOCIATION OF CONSERVATION DISTRICTS 254
MICHIGAN AUDUBON SOCIETY 254
MICHIGAN B.A.S.S. CHAPTER FEDERATION 254
MICHIGAN DEPARTMENT OF AGRICULTURE 76
MICHIGAN DEPARTMENT OF ENVIRONMENTAL QUALITY 76
MICHIGAN DEPARTMENT OF NATURAL RESOURCES 76
MICHIGAN DEPARTMENT OF PUBLIC HEALTH 77
MICHIGAN ENVIRONMENTAL COUNCIL 255
MICHIGAN FOREST ASSOCIATION 255
MICHIGAN LAND USE INSTITUTE 255
MICHIGAN NATURAL AREAS COUNCIL 255
MICHIGAN NATURE ASSOCIATION 255
MICHIGAN SEA GRANT COLLEGE PROGRAM 77
MICHIGAN STATE UNIVERSITY 378
MICHIGAN STATE UNIVERSITY EXTENSION 77
MICHIGAN TECHNOLOGICAL UNIVERSITY, School of Forestry and Wood Products 378
MICHIGAN UNITED CONSERVATION CLUBS, INC. 255
MICHIGAN WILDLIFE HABITAT FOUNDATION 255
MID-ATLANTIC COUNCIL OF WATERSHED ASSOCIATIONS 256
MID-ATLANTIC FISHERY MANAGEMENT COUNCIL 256
MIDDLE TENNESSEE STATE UNIVERSITY, Biology Department 389
MIDDLE TENNESSEE STATE UNIVERSITY, Center for Environmental/Energy Education 389
MIGRATORY BIRD CONSERVATION COMMISSION 8
MINERAL POLICY CENTER 256
MINISTRY OF ENVIRONMENT, LANDS, AND PARKS 127
MINISTRY OF FISHERIES 127
MINISTRY OF NATURAL RESOURCES
  Algonquin Forestry Authority 130
  Corporate Services Division 130
  Field Services Division 130
  Fish and Wildlife Branch 130
  Natural Resource Management Division 130
  Northeast Region 131
  Northwest Region 131
  Ontario131
  Science and Information Resources Division 131
  South Central Region 131
MINISTRY OF SMALL BUSINESS TOURISM AND CULTURE 127
MINISTRY OF THE ENVIRONMENT OF THE CZECH REPUBLIC 37
MINNESOTA ASSOCIATION OF SOIL AND WATER CONSERVATION DISTRICTS 256

Organization Name Index

436 ORGANIZATION NAME INDEX

MINNESOTA B.A.S.S. CHAPTER FEDERATION ... 256
MINNESOTA BOARD OF WATER AND SOIL RESOURCES ... 77
MINNESOTA CENTER FOR ENVIRONMENTAL ADVOCACY (MCEA) ... 256
MINNESOTA CONSERVATION FEDERATION ... 256
MINNESOTA COOPERATIVE FISH AND WILDLIFE RESEARCH UNIT ... 77
MINNESOTA DEPARTMENT OF AGRICULTURE ... 77
MINNESOTA DEPARTMENT OF NATURAL RESOURCES ... 78
MINNESOTA ENVIRONMENTAL QUALITY BOARD ... 78
MINNESOTA FORESTRY ASSOCIATION ... 257
MINNESOTA GEOLOGICAL SURVEY ... 78
MINNESOTA GROUND WATER ASSOCIATION ... 257
MINNESOTA HERPETOLOGICAL SOCIETY (James Ford Bell Museum of Natural History) ... 257
MINNESOTA NATIVE PLANT SOCIETY ... 257
MINNESOTA ORNITHOLOGISTS' UNION ... 257
MINNESOTA PARKS AND TRAILS COUNCIL ... 257
MINNESOTA POLLUTION CONTROL AGENCY ... 78
Brainerd, MN ... 78
Detroit Lakes, MN ... 79
Duluth, MN ... 79
Marshall, MN ... 79
Rochester, MN ... 79
MINNESOTA SEA GRANT COLLEGE PROGRAM ... 79
MINNESOTA STATE EXTENSION SERVICES ... 79
MINNESOTA WILDLIFE HERITAGE FOUNDATION, INC. ... 257
MINNESOTA WINGS SOCIETY, INC. ... 257
MINNESOTA-WISCONSIN BOUNDARY AREA COMMISSION ... 9
MISSISSIPPI ASSOCIATION OF CONSERVATION DISTRICTS, INC. ... 258
MISSISSIPPI B.A.S.S. CHAPTER FEDERATION ... 258
MISSISSIPPI COOPERATIVE FISH AND WILDLIFE RESEARCH UNIT (USDI) ... 79
MISSISSIPPI DEPARTMENT OF AGRICULTURE AND COMMERCE ... 80
MISSISSIPPI DEPARTMENT OF WILDLIFE, FISHERIES, AND PARKS ... 80
MISSISSIPPI INTERSTATE COOPERATIVE RESOURCE ASSOCIATION ... 258
MISSISSIPPI NATIVE PLANT SOCIETY ... 258
MISSISSIPPI RIVER BASIN ALLIANCE ... 258
MISSISSIPPI SEA GRANT PROGRAM ... 80
MISSISSIPPI SOIL AND WATER CONSERVATION COMMISSION ... 80
MISSISSIPPI STATE DEPARTMENT OF HEALTH ... 80
MISSISSIPPI STATE EXTENSION SERVICES ... 80
MISSISSIPPI STATE UNIVERSITY ... 379
MISSISSIPPI WILDLIFE FEDERATION ... 258
MISSOURI ASSOCIATION OF SOIL AND WATER CONSERVATION DISTRICTS ... 259
MISSOURI AUDUBON COUNCIL ... 259
MISSOURI B.A.S.S. CHAPTER FEDERATION ... 259
MISSOURI COOPERATIVE FISH AND WILDLIFE RESEARCH UNIT (USDI) .. 81
MISSOURI DEPARTMENT OF AGRICULTURE ... 81
MISSOURI DEPARTMENT OF CONSERVATION ... 81
Fisheries Division ... 81
Forestry Division ... 81
Protection Division ... 81
Wildlife Division ... 81
MISSOURI DEPARTMENT OF NATURAL RESOURCES ... 81
MISSOURI NATIVE PLANT SOCIETY ... 259
MISSOURI PRAIRIE FOUNDATION ... 259
MISSOURI STATE EXTENSION SERVICES ... 82
MONITOR INTERNATIONAL ... 259
MONO LAKE COMMITTEE ... 259
MONTANA ASSOCIATION OF CONSERVATION DISTRICTS ... 260
MONTANA AUDUBON ... 260
MONTANA B.A.S.S. CHAPTER FEDERATION ... 260
MONTANA COOPERATIVE FISHERY RESEARCH UNIT (USDI) ... 82
MONTANA COOPERATIVE WILDLIFE RESEARCH UNIT (USGS/BRD) ... 82
MONTANA DEPARTMENT OF AGRICULTURE ... 82
MONTANA DEPARTMENT OF FISH, WILDLIFE, AND PARKS ... 82
MONTANA DEPARTMENT OF NATURAL RESOURCES AND CONSERVATION ... 82
MONTANA ENVIRONMENTAL INFORMATION CENTER ... 260
MONTANA FOREST OWNERS ASSOCIATION ... 260
MONTANA LAND RELIANCE ... 260
MONTANA LAND RELIANCE (Eastern Office) ... 260
MONTANA NATURAL HERITAGE PROGRAM ... 83
MONTANA STATE EXTENSION SERVICES ... 83
MONTANA STATE UNIVERSITY ... 380
MONTANA WILDERNESS ASSOCIATION ... 260
MONTANA WILDLIFE FEDERATION ... 261
MONTCLAIR STATE COLLEGE ... 381
MOREHEAD STATE UNIVERSITY ... 375
MOTE MARINE LABORATORY ... 261
MOUNT GRACE LAND CONSERVATION TRUST ... 261
MOUNT SHASTA AREA AUDUBON SOCIETY ... 261
MOUNTAIN LION FOUNDATION ... 261
MOUNTAINEERS, THE (Conservation Division) ... 261
MULE DEER FOUNDATION, THE ... 262
MURRAY STATE UNIVERSITY ... 375
MUSKIES, INC. ... 262
NATIONAL 4-H COUNCIL ... 262
NATIONAL ARBOR DAY FOUNDATION ... 262
NATIONAL ASSOCIATION FOR INTERPRETATION ... 262
NATIONAL ASSOCIATION OF BIOLOGY TEACHERS ... 262
NATIONAL ASSOCIATION OF CONSERVATION DISTRICTS ... 263
NATIONAL ASSOCIATION OF CONSERVATION DISTRICTS (League City Office) ... 263
NATIONAL ASSOCIATION OF ENVIRONMENTAL PROFESSIONALS, THE (National Office) ... 263
NATIONAL ASSOCIATION OF RECREATION RESOURCE PLANNERS ... 263
NATIONAL ASSOCIATION OF SERVICE AND CONSERVATION CORPS (NASCC) ... 264
NATIONAL ASSOCIATION OF STATE DEPARTMENTS OF AGRICULTURE 264
NATIONAL ASSOCIATION OF STATE FORESTERS ... 264
NATIONAL ASSOCIATION OF STATE OUTDOOR RECREATION LIAISON OFFICERS ... 264
NATIONAL ASSOCIATION OF STATE PARK DIRECTORS ... 264
NATIONAL ASSOCIATION OF UNIVERSITY FISHERIES AND WILDLIFE PROGRAMS ... 265
NATIONAL AUDUBON SOCIETY ... 265
Everglades Campaign Office ... 265
Great Lakes, IL, IN, KY, MI, MN, OH, WI ... 265
Project Puffin ... 265
Scully Science Center ... 265
Tavernier Science Center ... 265
Washington, D.C. Office ... 265
NATIONAL AUDUBON SOCIETY, LIVING OCEANS PROGRAM ... 265
NATIONAL AVIARY IN PITTSBURGH ... 265
NATIONAL BIRD-FEEDING SOCIETY ... 266
NATIONAL BOATING FEDERATION ... 266
NATIONAL COALITION AGAINST THE MISUSE OF PESTICIDES ... 266
NATIONAL COALITION FOR MARINE CONSERVATION ... 266
NATIONAL COUNCIL FOR GEOGRAPHIC EDUCATION ... 266
NATIONAL COUNCIL OF STATE GARDEN CLUBS, INC. ... 266
NATIONAL EDUCATION ASSOCIATION ... 267
NATIONAL ENVIRONMENTAL HEALTH ASSOCIATION ... 267
NATIONAL FARMERS UNION ... 267
NATIONAL FFA ORGANIZATION ... 267
NATIONAL FIELD ARCHERY ASSOCIATION ... 267
NATIONAL FISH AND WILDLIFE FOUNDATION ... 267
NATIONAL FLYWAY COUNCIL ... 268
Atlantic Flyway Office ... 268
Central Flyway Office ... 268
Mississippi Flyway Office ... 268
NATIONAL FOREST FOUNDATION ... 268
NATIONAL FORESTRY ASSOCIATION ... 268
NATIONAL FOUNDATION TO PROTECT AMERICA'S EAGLES (Save The Eagle) ... 268
NATIONAL GARDENING ASSOCIATION ... 268
NATIONAL GEOGRAPHIC SOCIETY ... 268
NATIONAL GRANGE, THE ... 269
NATIONAL GROUND WATER ASSOCIATION, THE ... 269
NATIONAL HUNTERS ASSOCIATION, INC. ... 269
NATIONAL MILITARY FISH AND WILDLIFE ASSOCIATION ... 269
NATIONAL ORGANIZATION FOR RIVERS (NORS) ... 269
NATIONAL PARK FOUNDATION ... 269
NATIONAL PARK TRUST ... 270
NATIONAL PARKS AND CONSERVATION ASSOCIATION (NPCA) ... 270
Alaska Regional Office ... 270
Heartland Regional Office ... 270
Northeast Regional Office ... 270
Pacific Regional Office ... 270
Rocky Mountain Regional Office ... 270
Southeast Regional Office ... 270
Southwest Regional Office ... 270
NATIONAL RECREATION AND PARK ASSOCIATION ... 270
NATIONAL RESEARCH COUNCIL ... 271
NATIONAL RIFLE ASSOCIATION OF AMERICA ... 271
NATIONAL SCIENCE FOUNDATION ... 34
NATIONAL SCIENCE TEACHERS ASSOCIATION ... 271
NATIONAL SHOOTING SPORTS FOUNDATION, INC. ... 271
NATIONAL SPELEOLOGICAL SOCIETY, INC. ... 271
NATIONAL TRANSPORTATION SAFETY BOARD ... 34
NATIONAL TRAPPERS ASSOCIATION, INC. ... 271
NATIONAL TREE TRUST ... 272
NATIONAL TRUST FOR HISTORIC PRESERVATION ... 272
Mid Atlantic ... 272
Midwest Office ... 272
Mountains and Plains ... 272
Northeast Office ... 272
Southern Office ... 272
Texas and New Mexico Offices ... 272
Western ... 272
NATIONAL WATER RESOURCES ASSOCIATION ... 272
NATIONAL WATERSHED COALITION ... 272
NATIONAL WATERWAYS CONFERENCE INC. ... 273
NATIONAL WHISTLEBLOWER CENTER ... 273
NATIONAL WILD TURKEY FEDERATION, INC., THE ... 273
NATIONAL WILDLIFE FEDERATION ... 273
Alaska Project Office (AK, HI) ... 274
Everglades Project Office ... 274

Organization Name Index

ORGANIZATION NAME INDEX 437

Great Lakes Natural Resource Center (IL, IN, MI, OH, WI) ... 274
Gulf States Natural Resource Center (AR, LA, MS, TX) ... 274
Northeast Natural Resource Center (CT, MA, ME, NH, NY, RI, VT) ... 274
Northern Rockies Natural Resource Center (ID, MT, WY) ... 274
Office of Federal and International Affairs ... 274
Rocky Mountain Natural Resource Center (AZ, CO, NM, UT) ... 274
Southeastern Natural Resource Center (AL, FL, GA, NC, SC, TN, VI) ... 275
Western Natural Resource Center (CA, NV, OR, WA) ... 275
NATIONAL WILDLIFE FEDERATION ENDOWMENT, INC. ... 275
NATIONAL WILDLIFE PRODUCTIONS, INC. ... 275
NATIONAL WILDLIFE REFUGE ASSOCIATION ... 275
NATIONAL WILDLIFE REHABILITATORS ASSOCIATION ... 275
NATIONAL WOODLAND OWNERS ASSOCIATION ... 276
NATIONAL WOODLAND OWNERS ASSOCIATION (FORMERLY WISCONSIN WOODLAND OWNERS ASSOCIATION) ... 276
NATIVE AMERICAN FISH AND WILDLIFE SOCIETY (NAFWS) ... 276
NATIVE AMERICANS FOR A CLEAN ENVIRONMENT (NACE) ... 276
NATIVE PLANT SOCIETY OF NORTHEASTERN OHIO ... 276
NATIVE PLANT SOCIETY OF OREGON ... 276
NATIVE PLANT SOCIETY OF TEXAS ... 276
NATIVE PRAIRIES ASSOCIATION OF TEXAS ... 277
NATURAL AND SCENIC RIVERS COMMISSION (ARKANSAS) ... 45
NATURAL AREAS ASSOCIATION ... 277
NATURAL HERITAGE COMMISSION (ARKANSAS) ... 45
NATURAL HISTORY SOCIETY OF MARYLAND, INC., THE ... 277
NATURAL LAND INSTITUTE ... 277
NATURAL LANDS TRUST, INC. ... 277
NATURAL RESOURCES AND ENVIRONMENTAL PROTECTION CABINET .. 69
Department for Environmental Protection ... 69
Department for Natural Resources ... 69
Department for Surface Mining Reclamation and Enforcement ... 69
Environmental Quality Commission ... 69
Nature Preserves Commission ... 63, 69
NATURAL RESOURCES CANADA, CANADIAN FOREST SERVICE ... 37
NATURAL RESOURCES COUNCIL OF AMERICA ... 278
NATURAL RESOURCES COUNCIL OF MAINE ... 278
NATURAL RESOURCES DEFENSE COUNCIL, INC. ... 278
Los Angeles, California Office ... 278
San Francisco, California Office ... 278
Washington, D.C. Office ... 265, 278
NATURAL RESOURCES INFORMATION COUNCIL ... 278
NATURAL SCIENCE FOR YOUTH FOUNDATION ... 278
NATURE CONSERVACNY, THE, NEW YORK EASTER CHAPTER ... 279
NATURE CONSERVANCY OF CANADA, THE ... 279
NATURE CONSERVANCY OF COLORADO, THE ... 279
NATURE CONSERVANCY, THE ... 279
Eastern Office ... 279
Midwest Office ... 279
New York Region Office ... 279
Pacific Office ... 279
Southeast Office ... 279
Western Region Office ... 279
NATURE CONSERVANCY, THE, ALABAMA CHAPTER ... 280
NATURE CONSERVANCY, THE, ALASKA CHAPTER ... 280
NATURE CONSERVANCY, THE, ARIZONA CHAPTER ... 280
NATURE CONSERVANCY, THE, ARKANSAS CHAPTER ... 280
NATURE CONSERVANCY, THE, ASIA/PACIFIC PROGRAM ... 280
NATURE CONSERVANCY, THE, CALIFORNIA CHAPTER ... 280
NATURE CONSERVANCY, THE, COLORADO CHAPTER ... 280
NATURE CONSERVANCY, THE, CONNECTICUT CHAPTER ... 280
NATURE CONSERVANCY, THE, DELAWARE CHAPTER ... 280
NATURE CONSERVANCY, THE, FLORIDA CHAPTER ... 280
NATURE CONSERVANCY, THE, HAWAII CHAPTER ... 280
NATURE CONSERVANCY, THE, IDAHO CHAPTER ... 280
NATURE CONSERVANCY, THE, ILLINOIS CHAPTER ... 280
NATURE CONSERVANCY, THE, INDIANA CHAPTER ... 280
NATURE CONSERVANCY, THE, IOWA CHAPTER ... 280
NATURE CONSERVANCY, THE, KANSAS CHAPTER ... 281
NATURE CONSERVANCY, THE, KENTUCKY CHAPTER ... 281
NATURE CONSERVANCY, THE, LATIN AMERICA AND CARRIBBEAN DIVISION ... 281
NATURE CONSERVANCY, THE, LOUISIANA CHAPTER ... 281
NATURE CONSERVANCY, THE, MAINE CHAPTER ... 281
NATURE CONSERVANCY, THE, MARYLAND/D.C. CHAPTER ... 281
NATURE CONSERVANCY, THE, MASSACHUSETTS CHAPTER ... 281
NATURE CONSERVANCY, THE, MICHIGAN CHAPTER ... 281
NATURE CONSERVANCY, THE, MINNESOTA CHAPTER ... 281
NATURE CONSERVANCY, THE, MISSISSIPPI CHAPTER ... 281
NATURE CONSERVANCY, THE, MISSOURI CHAPTER ... 281
NATURE CONSERVANCY, THE, MONTANA CHAPTER ... 281
NATURE CONSERVANCY, THE, NEBRASKA CHAPTER ... 281
NATURE CONSERVANCY, THE, NEVADA CHAPTER ... 281
NATURE CONSERVANCY, THE, NEW HAMPSHIRE CHAPTER ... 281
NATURE CONSERVANCY, THE, NEW JERSEY CHAPTER ... 281
NATURE CONSERVANCY, THE, NEW MEXICO CHAPTER ... 281
NATURE CONSERVANCY, THE, NEW YORK ADIRONDACK CHAPTER ... 281
NATURE CONSERVANCY, THE, NEW YORK CENTRAL/WESTERN CHAPTER ... 281
NATURE CONSERVANCY, THE, NEW YORK LONG ISLAND CHAPTER ... 281
NATURE CONSERVANCY, THE, NEW YORK LOWER HUDSON CHAPTER281
NATURE CONSERVANCY, THE, NEW YORK SOUTH FORK/SHELTER ISLAND CHAPTER ... 281
NATURE CONSERVANCY, THE, NORTH CAROLINA CHAPTER ... 281
NATURE CONSERVANCY, THE, NORTH DAKOTA CHAPTER ... 281
NATURE CONSERVANCY, THE, OHO CHAPTER ... 281
NATURE CONSERVANCY, THE, OKLAHOMA CHAPTER ... 281
NATURE CONSERVANCY, THE, OREGON CHAPTER ... 281
NATURE CONSERVANCY, THE, PENNSYLVANIA CHAPTER ... 281
NATURE CONSERVANCY, THE, RHODE ISLAND CHAPTER ... 281
NATURE CONSERVANCY, THE, SOUTH CAROLINA CHAPTER ... 282
NATURE CONSERVANCY, THE, SOUTH DAKOTA CHAPTER ... 282
NATURE CONSERVANCY, THE, TENNESSEE CHAPTER ... 282
NATURE CONSERVANCY, THE, TEXAS CHAPTER ... 282
NATURE CONSERVANCY, THE, UTAH CHAPTER ... 282
NATURE CONSERVANCY, THE, VERMONT CHAPTER ... 282
NATURE CONSERVANCY, THE, VIRGIN ISLANDS CHAPTER ... 282
NATURE CONSERVANCY, THE, VIRGINIA CHAPTER ... 282
NATURE CONSERVANCY, THE, WASHINGTONG CHAPTER ... 282
NATURE CONSERVANCY, THE, WEST VIRGINIA CHAPTER ... 282
NATURE CONSERVANCY, THE, WISCONSIN CHAPTER ... 282
NATURE CONSERVANCY, THE, WYOMING CHAPTER ... 282
NATURE CONSERVATION SOCIETY OF JAPAN, THE (NACS-J) ... 282
NATURE PRESERVES COMMISSION ... 63
NATURE SASKATCHEWAN ... 282
NEBRASKA ASSOCIATION OF NATURAL RESOURCE DISTRICTS ... 282
NEBRASKA AUDUBON COUNCIL ... 282
NEBRASKA B.A.S.S. CHAPTER FEDERATION ... 283
NEBRASKA CHAPTER OF THE AMERICAN FISHERIES SOCIETY ... 283
NEBRASKA DEPARTMENT OF AGRICULTURE ... 84
NEBRASKA GEOLOGICAL SURVEY ... 84
NEBRASKA NATURAL RESOURCES COMMISSION ... 84
NEBRASKA ORNITHOLOGISTS' UNION, INC. (University of Nebraska State Museum) ... 283
NEBRASKA STATE EXTENSION SERVICES ... 84
NEBRASKA WILDLIFE FEDERATION, INC. ... 283
NEVADA ASSOCIATION OF CONSERVATION DISTRICTS ... 283
NEVADA BUREAU OF MINES AND GEOLOGY ... 84
NEVADA DEPARTMENT OF CONSERVATION AND NATURAL RESOURCES ... 84
State Conservation Commission ... 85
NEVADA DIVISION OF WILDLIFE ... 85
NEVADA NATURAL HERITAGE PROGRAM ... 85
NEVADA WILDLIFE FEDERATION ... 283
NEVEDA COOPERATIVE EXTENSION ... 85
NEVIS HISTORICAL AND CONSERVATION SOCIETY ... 283
NEW BRUNSWICK DEPARTMENT OF NATURAL RESOURCES AND ENERGY ... 128
NEW BRUNSWICK WILDLIFE FEDERATION ... 284
NEW ENGLAND ASSOCIATION OF ENVIRONMENTAL BIOLOGISTS (NEAEB) ... 284
NEW ENGLAND INTERSTATE WATER POLLUTION CONTROL COMMISSION ... 9
NEW ENGLAND NATURAL RESOURCES CENTER ... 284
NEW ENGLAND WILD FLOWER SOCIETY, INC. ... 284
NEW HAMPSHIRE ASSOCIATION OF CONSERVATION COMMISSIONS ... 284
NEW HAMPSHIRE ASSOCIATION OF CONSERVATION DISTRICTS ... 284
NEW HAMPSHIRE B.A.S.S. CHAPTER FEDERATION ... 284
NEW HAMPSHIRE DEPARTMENT OF AGRICULTURE, MARKETS, AND FOOD ... 85
State Conservation Committee ... 85
NEW HAMPSHIRE DEPARTMENT OF ENVIRONMENTAL SERVICES ... 86
NEW HAMPSHIRE FISH AND GAME DEPARTMENT ... 86
NEW HAMPSHIRE LAKES ASSOCIATION ... 284
NEW HAMPSHIRE NATURAL HERITAGE INVENTORY ... 86
NEW HAMPSHIRE SEA GRANT PROGRAM ... 86
NEW HAMPSHIRE TIMBERLAND OWNERS ASSOCIATION ... 285
NEW HAMPSHIRE WILDLIFE FEDERATION ... 285
NEW JERSEY AGRICULTURAL SOCIETY ... 285
NEW JERSEY ASSOCIATION OF CONSERVATION DISTRICTS ... 285
NEW JERSEY AUDUBON SOCIETY ... 285
NEW JERSEY B.A.S.S. CHAPTER FEDERATION ... 285
NEW JERSEY CONSERVATION FOUNDATION ... 285
NEW JERSEY DEPARTMENT OF AGRICULTURE ... 87
State Soil and Conservation Committee ... 87
NEW JERSEY ENVIRONMENTAL LOBBY ... 286
NEW JERSEY FORESTRY ASSOCIATION ... 286
NEW JERSEY PINELANDS COMMISSION ... 88
NEW JERSEY SEA GRANT PROGRAM ... 88
NEW JERSEY STATE EXTENSION SERVICES ... 88
NEW MEXICO ASSOCIATION OF CONSERVATION DISTRICTS ... 286
NEW MEXICO BASS CHAPTER FEDERATION ... 286
NEW MEXICO BUREAU OF MINES AND MINERAL RESOURCES ... 89
Geological Information Center Library ... 89
NEW MEXICO COOPERATIVE FISH AND WILDLIFE RESEARCH UNIT ... 89
NEW MEXICO DEPARTMENT OF AGRICULTURE ... 89
NEW MEXICO DEPARTMENT OF GAME AND FISH ... 89
Albuquerque NM Office ... 89
Las Cruces NM Office ... 89
Raton NM Office ... 89
Roswell NM Office ... 89

Organization Name Index

438 ORGANIZATION NAME INDEX

NEW MEXICO DEPARTMENT OF NATURAL RESOURCES
Corporate Service Unit ... 130
Land Services Division ... 130
Regional Services ... 130
Renewable Resources ... 130
NEW MEXICO ENVIRONMENT DEPARTMENT ... 89
NEW MEXICO ENVIRONMENTAL LAW CENTER ... 286
NEW MEXICO SOIL AND WATER CONSERVATION COMMISSION ... 90
NEW MEXICO STATE EXTENSION SERVICES ... 90
NEW MEXICO STATE UNIVERSITY ... 382
NEW MEXICO WILDLIFE FEDERATION ... 286
NEW YORK ASSOCIATION OF CONSERVATION DISTRICTS, INC. ... 286
NEW YORK B.A.S.S. CHAPTER FEDERATION ... 287
NEW YORK COOPERATIVE FISH AND WILDLIFE RESEARCH UNIT ... 92
NEW YORK DEPARTMENT OF AGRICULTURE AND MARKETS ... 92
State Soil and Water Conservation Committee ... 92
NEW YORK DEPARTMENT OF HEALTH ... 92
NEW YORK FOREST OWNERS ASSOCIATION, INC. ... 287
NEW YORK GEOLOGICAL SURVEY AND STATE MUSEUM ... 92
NEW YORK PUBLIC INTEREST RESEARCH GROUP (NYPIRG ... 287
NEW YORK SEA GRANT ... 92
NEW YORK STATE COOPERATIVE EXTENSION ... 93
NEW YORK STATE OFFICE OF PARKS, RECREATION AND HISTORIC PRESERVATION ... 93
NEW YORK TURTLE AND TORTOISE SOCIETY ... 287
NEW YORK-NEW JERSEY TRAIL CONFERENCE INC ... 287
NEWFOUNDLAND DEPARTMENT OF FOREST RESOURCES AND AGRIFOODS ... 128
Ecosystem Health Division ... 128
Inland Fish and Wildlife Division ... 129
Legislation and Compliance Division ... 129
Regional Offices ... 129
NEWFOUNDLAND LABRADOR WILDLIFE FEDERATION ... 287
NIAGARA ESCARPMENT COMMISSION ... 131
NIPPON ECOLOGY NETWORK ... 287
NORTH CAROLINA DEPARTMENT OF ENVIRONMENT AND NATURAL RESOURCES ... 94
NORTH AMERICAN ASSOCIATION FOR ENVIRONMENTAL EDUCATION ... 288
NORTH AMERICAN ASSOCIATION FOR ENVIRONMENTAL EDUCATION (Membership and Publications Office) ... 288
NORTH AMERICAN BENTHOLOGICAL SOCIETY ... 288
NORTH AMERICAN BLUEBIRD SOCIETY ... 288
NORTH AMERICAN COALITION ON RELIGION AND ECOLOGY (NACRE) ... 288
NORTH AMERICAN CRANE WORKING GROUP ... 288
NORTH AMERICAN FALCONERS ASSOCIATION ... 288
NORTH AMERICAN FISHING CLUB ... 289
NORTH AMERICAN GAMEBIRD ASSOCIATION, INC ... 289
NORTH AMERICAN LOON FUND ... 289
NORTH AMERICAN NATIVE FISHES ASSOCIATION ... 289
NORTH AMERICAN WETLANDS CONSERVATION COUNCIL ... 9
NORTH AMERICAN WILDLIFE PARK FOUNDATION, INC. ... 289
NORTH AMERICAN WOLF SOCIETY ... 289
NORTH ATLANTIC SALMON CONSERVATION ORGANIZATION ... 289
NORTH CAROLINA ASSOCIATION OF SOIL AND WATER CONSERVATION DISTRICTS ... 290
NORTH CAROLINA B.A.S.S. CHAPTER FEDERATION ... 290
NORTH CAROLINA BEACH BUGGY ASSOCIATION, INC. ... 290
NORTH CAROLINA COASTAL FEDERATION, INC. ... 290
NORTH CAROLINA COOPERATIVE FISH AND WILDLIFE RESEARCH UNIT (USDI) ... 94
NORTH CAROLINA DEPARTMENT OF AGRICULTURE ... 94
NORTH CAROLINA DEPARTMENT OF ENVIRONMENT AND NATURAL RESOURCES
State Soil and Water Conservation Commission ... 95
NORTH CAROLINA FORESTRY ASSOCIATION ... 290
NORTH CAROLINA HERPETOLOGICAL SOCIETY ... 290
NORTH CAROLINA RECREATION AND PARK SOCIETY, INC. ... 291
NORTH CAROLINA SEA GRANT PROGRAM ... 95
NORTH CAROLINA STATE UNIVERSITY ... 383
NORTH CAROLINA STATE UNIVERSITY, Center for World Environment and Sustainable Development ... 384
NORTH CAROLINA WILDLIFE FEDERATION ... 291
NORTH CASCADES CONSERVATION COUNCIL ... 291
NORTH DAKOTA ASSOCIATION OF SOIL CONSERVATION DISTRICTS ... 291
NORTH DAKOTA DEPARTMENT OF AGRICULTURE ... 95
NORTH DAKOTA DEPARTMENT OF HEALTH ... 95
NORTH DAKOTA GAME AND FISH DEPARTMENT ... 95
NORTH DAKOTA GEOLOGICAL SURVEY ... 96
NORTH DAKOTA NATURAL SCIENCE SOCIETY ... 291
NORTH DAKOTA STATE EXTENSION SERVICE ... 96
NORTH DAKOTA STATE FOREST SERVICE ... 96
NORTH DAKOTA STATE SOIL CONSERVATION COMMITTEE ... 96
NORTH DAKOTA STATE UNIVERSITY ... 384
NORTH DAKOTA WATER COMMISSION ... 96
NORTH DAKOTA WILDLIFE FEDERATION, INC. ... 291
NORTH PACIFIC ANADROMOUS FISH COMMISSION ... 9
NORTHCOAST ENVIRONMENTAL CENTER ... 291
NORTHEAST ASSOCIATION OF FISH AND WILDLIFE RESOURCE AGENCIES ... 291
NORTHEAST ATLANTIC FISHERIES COMMISSION ... 9
NORTHEAST CONSERVATION LAW ENFORCEMENT CHIEFS' ASSOCIATION (CLECA) ... 292
NORTHEAST SUSTAINABLE ENERGY ASSOCIATION ... 292
NORTHEAST WILDLIFE ADMINISTRATORS ASSOCIATION ... 292
NORTHEASTERN FOREST FIRE PROTECTION COMMISSION ... 9
NORTHEASTERN UNIVERSITY ... 377
NORTHEASTERN UNIVERSITY, School For Field Studies, The ... 377
NORTHERN ALASKA ENVIRONMENTAL CENTER ... 292
NORTHERN ARIZONA UNIVERSITY ... 366
NORTHERN ARIZONA UNIVERSITY, School of Forestry ... 367
NORTHERN MICHIGAN UNIVERSITY ... 378
NORTHERN PLAINS RESOURCE COUNCIL ... 292
NORTHERN VIRGINIA REGIONAL PARK AUTHORITY ... 117
NORTHLAND COLLEGE, Sigurd Olson Environmental Institute ... 392
NORTHWEST ATLANTIC FISHERIES ORGANIZATION (NAFO) ... 292
NORTHWEST ECOSYSTEM ALLIANCE ... 293
NORTHWEST ENVIRONMENT WATCH ... 293
NORTHWEST INTERPRETIVE ASSOCIATION ... 293
NORTHWEST RENEWABLE RESOURCES CENTER ... 293
NORTHWEST RESOURCE INFORMATION CENTER ... 293
NORTHWESTERN STATE UNIVERSITY OF LOUISIANA ... 375
NOVA SCOTIA FORESTRY ASSOCIATION ... 293
NOVA SCOTIA WILDLIFE FEDERATION ... 293
NUCLEAR REGULATORY COMMISSION ... 34
NW ENERGY COALITION ... 294
OBERLIN COLLEGE, Environmental Studies Program ... 385
OCEAN VOICE INTERNATIONAL ... 294
OFFICE OF ENERGY EFFICIENCY AND ENVIRONMENT ... 93
OFFICE OF STATE PARKS, DEPARTMENT OF CULTURE, RECREATION, AND TOURISM ... 71
OHIO ACADEMY OF SCIENCE, THE ... 294
OHIO ALLIANCE FOR THE ENVIRONMENT ... 294
OHIO AUDUBON COUNCIL, INC. ... 294
OHIO B.A.S.S. CHAPTER FEDERATION ... 295
OHIO BIOLOGICAL SURVEY ... 295
OHIO COOPERATIVE FISH AND WILDLIFE RESEARCH UNIT (USDI) ... 96
OHIO DEPARTMENT OF AGRICULTURE ... 96
OHIO DEPARTMENT OF NATURAL RESOURCES ... 97
OHIO ENVIRONMENTAL COUNCIL, INC. ... 295
OHIO ENVIRONMENTAL PROTECTION AGENCY ... 97
OHIO FEDERATION OF SOIL AND WATER CONSERVATION DISTRICTS ... 295
OHIO FORESTRY ASSOCIATION, INC., THE ... 295
OHIO RIVER VALLEY WATER SANITATION COMMISSION ... 9
OHIO SEA GRANT COLLEGE PROGRAM, F.T. STONE LABORATORY, AND GREAT LAKES AQUATIC ECOSYSTEM RESEARCH CONSORTIUM (GLAERC) ... 97
OHIO STATE EXTENSION SERVICES ... 97
OHIO STATE UNIVERSITY, School of Natural Resources ... 385
OKLAHOMA ACADEMY OF SCIENCE ... 295
OKLAHOMA ASSOCIATION OF CONSERVATION DISTRICTS ... 296
OKLAHOMA AUDUBON COUNCIL ... 296
OKLAHOMA B.A.S.S. CHAPTER FEDERATION ... 296
OKLAHOMA BIOLOGICAL SURVEY ... 98
OKLAHOMA COOPERATIVE FISH AND WILDLIFE RESEARCH UNIT (USDI) 98
OKLAHOMA DEPARTMENT OF ENVIRONMENTAL QUALITY ... 98
OKLAHOMA GEOLOGICAL SURVEY ... 98
OKLAHOMA NATIVE PLANT SOCIETY ... 296
OKLAHOMA ORNITHOLOGICAL SOCIETY ... 296
OKLAHOMA STATE BOARD OF AGRICULTURE ... 98
OKLAHOMA STATE CONSERVATION COMMISSION ... 99
OKLAHOMA STATE EXTENSION SERVICES ... 99
OKLAHOMA STATE UNIVERSITY ... 385
OKLAHOMA TOURISM AND RECREATION DEPARTMENT ... 99
OKLAHOMA WATER RESOURCES BOARD ... 99
OKLAHOMA WILDLIFE FEDERATION ... 296
OKLAHOMA WOODLAND OWNERS ASSOCIATION ... 296
OLYMPIC PARK ASSOCIATES ... 296
OLYMPIC PARK INSTITUTE ... 297
OLYMPIC WILDLIFE RESCUE ... 297
ONTARIO FEDERATION OF ANGLERS AND HUNTERS, INC., THE ... 297
ONTARIO FORESTRY ASSOCIATION ... 297
OPENLANDS PROJECT ... 297
OREGON ASSOCIATION OF CONSERVATION DISTRICTS ... 297
OREGON B.A.S.S. CHAPTER FEDERATION ... 297
OREGON COOPERATIVE FISH AND WILDLIFE RESEARCH UNIT (USDI) 100
OREGON COOPERATIVE FISH AND WILDLIFE RESEARCH UNIT (USDI) . 100
OREGON DEPARTMENT OF AGRICULTURE ... 100
OREGON DEPARTMENT OF ENVIRONMENTAL QUALITY (DEQ) ... 101
OREGON DEPARTMENT OF FORESTRY ... 101
OREGON ENVIRONMENTAL COUNCIL ... 298
OREGON NATURAL RESOURCES COUNCIL ... 298
OREGON PARKS AND RECREATION DEPARTMENT ... 101
OREGON SEA GRANT PROGRAM ... 101
OREGON SMALL WOODLANDS ASSOCIATION ... 298
OREGON SOCIETY OF AMERICAN FORESTERS ... 298
OREGON STATE EXTENSION SERVICES ... 101
OREGON STATE UNIVERSITY ... 386
OREGON STATE UNIVERSITY, Lewis and Clark College ... 386

Organization Name Index

ORGANIZATION NAME INDEX 439

OREGON STATE UNIVERSITY, Northwestern School of Law 386
OREGON TROUT, INC. 298
OREGON WILDLIFE HERITAGE FOUNDATION 298
ORGANIZATION OF WILDLIFE PLANNERS 298
ORNITHOLOGICAL COUNCIL 299
OUTDOOR CIRCLE, THE 299
OUTDOOR RECREATION COUNCIL OF BRITISH COLUMBIA 299
OUTDOOR WRITERS ASSOCIATION OF AMERICA INC. 299
OZARK SOCIETY, THE 299
OZARKS RESOURCE CENTER 300
OZONE ACTION 300
PACIFIC BASIN ASSOCIATION OF SOIL AND WATER CONSERVATION DISTRICTS 300
PACIFIC FISHERY MANAGEMENT COUNCIL 300
PACIFIC NORTHWEST TRAIL ASSOCIATION 300
PACIFIC RIVERS COUNCIL 300
PACIFIC SALMON COMMISSION 9
PACIFIC SEABIRD GROUP 300
PACIFIC STATES MARINE FISHERIES COMMISSION 10
PACIFIC WHALE FOUNDATION 301
PANOS INSTITUTE, THE 301
PARKS AND RECREATION DEPARTMENT (NORTH DAKOTA) 96
PARTNERS IN PARKS 301
PEACE CORPS OF THE UNITED STATES 35
PENNSYLVANIA ASSOCIATION OF CONSERVATION DISTRICT DIRECTORS, INC. 301
PENNSYLVANIA AUDUBON SOCIETY 301
PENNSYLVANIA B.A.S.S. CHAPTER FEDERATION, INC. 301
PENNSYLVANIA CITIZENS ADVISORY COUNCIL TO DEPARTMENT OF ENVIRONMENTAL PROTECTION 301
PENNSYLVANIA COOPERATIVE FISH AND WILDLIFE RESEARCH UNIT .. 104
PENNSYLVANIA DEPARTMENT OF AGRICULTURE 104
Region I 104
Region II 104
Region III 104
Region IV 104
Region V 104
Region VI 105
Region VII 105
State Conservation Commission 105
PENNSYLVANIA DEPARTMENT OF CONSERVATION AND NATURAL RESOURCES 105
PENNSYLVANIA ENVIRONMENTAL COUNCIL, INC. (PEC) 302
PENNSYLVANIA FEDERATION OF SPORTSMEN'S CLUBS 302
PENNSYLVANIA FOREST STEWARDSHIP PROGRAM 105
PENNSYLVANIA FORESTRY ASSOCIATION, THE 302
PENNSYLVANIA RECREATION AND PARK SOCIETY, INC. 302
PENNSYLVANIA RESOURCES COUNCIL, INC., (formerly PA Roadside Council) 302
PENNSYLVANIA STATE EXTENSION SERVICES 105
PENNSYLVANIA STATE UNIVERSITY, School of Forest Resources 387
PEREGRINE FUND, THE 303
PHEASANTS FOREVER INC. 303
PHYSICIANS FOR SOCIAL RESPONSIBILITY 303
PIEDMONT ENVIRONMENTAL COUNCIL 303
PINCHOT INSTITUTE FOR CONSERVATION 303
PINE BLUFF COOPERATIVE FISHERY RESEARCH PROJECT 45
PLANNED PARENTHOOD FEDERATION OF AMERICA INC. 304
PLANNING AND CONSERVATION LEAGUE 304
POCONO ENVIRONMENTAL EDUCATION CENTER 304
POLLUTION PROBE FOUNDATION 304
POLYTECHNIC UNIVERSITY, Civil and Environmental Engineering Department 382
POLYTECHNIC UNIVERSITY, Rensselaer Polytechnic Institute 382
POPE AND YOUNG CLUB 304
POPULATION ACTION INTERNATIONAL 304
POPULATION COMMUNICATIONS INTERNATIONAL 304
POPULATION INSTITUTE, THE 305
POPULATION REFERENCE BUREAU INC. 305
POPULATION-ENVIRONMENT BALANCE INC. 305
PORTLAND STATE UNIVERSITY, Environmental Sciences and Resources .. 386
POTOMAC APPALACHIAN TRAIL CLUB 305
POWDER RIVER BASIN RESOURCE COUNCIL 305
PRAIRIE CLUB, THE 305
PRAIRIE GROUSE TECHNICAL COUNCIL 306
PREDATOR PROJECT 306
PRESCOTT COLLEGE, Environmental Studies Program 367
PROFESSIONAL BOWHUNTERS SOCIETY 306
PROVINCE OF QUEBEC SOCIETY FOR THE PROTECTION OF BIRDS, INC. 306
PTARMIGANS, THE 306
PUBLIC EMPLOYEES FOR ENVIRONMENTAL RESPONSIBILITY (PEER) .. 306
PUBLIC EMPLOYEES FOR ENVIRONMENTAL RESPONSIBILITY (PEER) (West Coast Office) 307
PUBLIC LANDS FOUNDATION 307
PUERTO RICO ASSOCIATION OF SOIL AND WATER CONSERVATION DISTRICTS 307
PUERTO RICO CONSERVATION FOUNDATION, THE (PRCF 307
PUERTO RICO DEPARTMENT OF AGRICULTURE 105
PUERTO RICO DEPARTMENT OF NATURAL AND ENVIRONMENTAL RESOURCES 105
PUERTO RICO SEA GRANT PROGRAM 105
PUERTO RICO STATE EXTENSION SERVICES 106
PUGET SOUNDKEEPER ALLIANCE 307
PURDUE UNIVERSITY 374
PURDUE UNIVERSITY EXTENSION SERVICES 65
PURPLE MARTIN CONSERVATION ASSOCIATION 307
QUAIL UNLIMITED, INC. 307
QUEBEC WILDLIFE FEDERATION 308
RACHEL CARSON COUNCIL INC. (formerly Rachel Carson Trust for the Living Environment Inc.) 308
RAILS-TO-TRAILS CONSERVANCY 308
RAINBOW PUSH COALITION 308
RAINFOREST ACTION NETWORK 308
RAINFOREST ALLIANCE 309
RAINFOREST RELIEF 309
RAINFOREST TRUST INC., THE 309
RAPTOR CENTER, THE 309
RAPTOR EDUCATION FOUNDATION INC. 309
RAPTOR RESEARCH FOUNDATION, INC. 309
RARE CENTER FOR TROPICAL CONSERVATION 310
REEF RELIEF 310
RENEW AMERICA 310
RENEWABLE NATURAL RESOURCES FOUNDATION 310
RESOURCE RENEWAL INSTITUTE, THE 310
RESOURCES AGENCY, THE 47
California Coastal Commission 47
California Coastal Conservancy 47
California Conservation Corps 48
California Energy Commission 48
California Water Commission 48
Colorado River Board of California 48
Department of Boating and Waterways 48
Department of Conservation 48
Department of Fish and Game 48
Department of Forestry and Fire Protection 49
Department of Parks and Recreation 49
Department of Water Resources 49
Fish and Game Commission 49
Native American Heritage Commission 49
San Francisco Bay Conservation and Development Commission 49
State Reclamation Board 49
Wildlife Conservation Board 50
RESOURCES FOR THE FUTURE 310
RESOURCE-USE EDUCATION COUNCIL 310
RESPONSIVE MANAGEMENT 311
RETURNED PEACE CORPS VOLUNTEER FOR ENVIRONMENT AND DEVELOPMENT (RPCV-ED) 311
RHODE ISLAND B.A.S.S. CHAPTER FEDERATION 311
RHODE ISLAND COOPERATIVE EXTENSION 106
RHODE ISLAND FOREST CONSERVATORS ASSOCIATION 311
RHODE ISLAND STATE ASSOCIATION OF CONSERVATION DISTRICTS . 311
RHODE ISLAND STATE CONSERVATION COMMITTEE 107
RHODE ISLAND WILD PLANT SOCIETY 311
RICE UNIVERSITY 389
RICE UNIVERSITY, School of Architecture 389
RINCON INSTITUTE, THE 312
RIVER ALLIANCE OF WISCONSIN 312
RIVER FEDERATION 312
RIVER NETWORK 312
Eastern Office 312
Northern Rockes Office
Riverlands Conservancy Field Office 312
RIVER OTTER ALLIANCE, THE 312
RIVERS COUNCIL OF WASHINGTON (formerly Northwest Rivers Council) .. 313
ROCKY MOUNTAIN BIGHORN SOCIETY 313
ROCKY MOUNTAIN ELK FOUNDATION 313
Intermountain Region Office 313
North-Central Region Office 313
Northeast Region Office 313
Northwest Region Office 313
Pacific Southwest Region Office 313
South-Central Region Office 314
Southeast Region Office 314
ROGER TORY PETERSON INSTITUTE 314
ROGER WILLIAMS UNIVERSITY, College of Arts and Sciences 388
ROGER WILLIAMS UNIVERSITY, Division of Science and Mathematics 388
ROWAN UNIVERSITY 381
ROWAN UNIVERSITY, Pinelands Institute for Natural and Environmental Studies 381
RUFFED GROUSE SOCIETY, THE 314
RUTGERS UNIVERSITY, Cook College 381
SAFARI CLUB INTERNATIONAL 314
Michigan Office 314
South Africa Office 315
Washington, DC Office 315
SAFE ENERGY COMMUNICATION COUNCIL 315
SAN FRANCISCO STATE UNIVERSITY, Wildlands Studies Program 368
SAN JOSE STATE UNIVERSITY, Department of Environmental Studies 369

Organization Name Index

440 ORGANIZATION NAME INDEX

SAN JUAN PRESERVATION TRUST, THE 315
SANIBEL-CAPTIVA CONSERVATION FOUNDATION, INC. 315
SASKATCHEWAN ENVIRONMENT AND RESOURCE MANAGEMENT 132
Corporate Services 132
East Boreal 132
Enforcement and Compliance Branch 132
Fire Management and Forest Protection Branch 132
Grassland 132
Operations 132
Parkland 132
Policy and Assessment 132
Programs 132
Shield 132
West Boreal 132
SASKATCHEWAN WILDLIFE FEDERATION 315
SAVANNAH RIVER ECOLOGY LABORATORY 107
SAVE AMERICA'S FORESTS 315
SAVE SAN FRANCISCO BAY ASSOCIATION 315
SAVE THE BAY, INC. 316
SAVE THE DUNES COUNCIL 316
Save the Dunes Conservation Fund 316
SAVE THE HARBOR/SAVE THE BAY 316
SAVE THE MANATEE CLUB 316
SAVE THE SOUND, INC. 316
SAVE THE SOUND, INC. (GARVIES POINT MUSEUM) 316
SAVE WETLANDS AND BAYS 316
SAVE-THE-REDWOODS LEAGUE 317
SCENIC AMERICA 317
Scenic Kentucky 317
Scenic Michigan 317
Scenic Missouri 317
Scenic North Carolina 317
Scenic Ohio 317
Scenic Texas 317
SCENIC HUDSON, INC. 317
SCIENTISTS CENTER FOR ANIMAL WELFARE 318
SEA SHEPHERD CONSERVATION SOCIETY 318
Australia Office 318
Canada Office 319
Great Britain Office 318
Netherlands Office 318
USA Office 318
SEACOAST ANTI-POLLUTION LEAGUE 318
SEAPLANE PILOTS ASSOCIATION 318
SENATE COMMITTEE ON AGRICULTURE, NUTRITION, AND FORESTRY 5
SENATE COMMITTEE ON APPROPRIATIONS 6
SENATE COMMITTEE ON COMMERCE SCIENCE AND TRANSPORTATION 6
SENATE COMMITTEE ON ENERGY AND NATURAL RESOURCES 6
SENATE COMMITTEE ON ENVIRONMENT AND PUBLIC WORKS 6
SENATE COMMITTEE ON FOREIGN RELATIONS 6
SENATE COMMITTEE ON LABOR AND HUMAN RESOURCES 6
SHAWNEE STATE UNIVERSITY 385
SHEPHERD COLLEGE 392
SIERRA CLUB 318
Alaska Office 318
Canada Office 318
Midwest Office 319
Northeast Office 319
Northern Plains 319
Northwest Office 319
Southeast Office 319
Southern California/Nevada Branch 319
Southwest Office 319
Texas Office 319
Washington, DC Office 332
SIERRA CLUB FOUNDATION, THE 319
SINAPU 319
SLIPPERY ROCK UNIVERSITY 387
SMALL WOODLAND OWNERS ASSOCIATION OF MAINE, INC. 319
SMITHSONIAN INSTITUTION 320
National Museum of Natural History 320
National Zoological Park 320
Office of Fellowships and Grants 320
Office of International Relations 320
Smithsonian Marine Station at Link Port 320
Smithsonian Press/Smithsonian Productions 320
Smithsonian Tropical Research Institute 320
SOCIETY FOR ANIMAL PROTECTIVE LEGISLATION 320
SOCIETY FOR CONSERVATION BIOLOGY 321
SOCIETY FOR ECOLOGICAL RESTORATION 321
SOCIETY FOR MARINE MAMMALOGY, THE 321
SOCIETY FOR RANGE MANAGEMENT 321
SOCIETY FOR THE PRESERVATION OF BIRDS OF PREY 322
SOCIETY FOR THE PROTECTION OF NEW HAMPSHIRE FORESTS 322
SOCIETY OF AMERICAN FORESTERS 322
SOCIETY OF TYMPANUCHUS CUPIDO PINNATUS LTD 322
SOCIETY OF WETLAND SCIENTISTS 322
SOIL AND WATER CONSERVATION SOCIETY (formerly Soil Conservation Society of America) 323
SOIL CONSERVATION COMMITTEE OF PUERTO RICO 106
SONOMA STATE UNIVERSITY, Department of Environemental Studies and Planning 369
SONOMA STATE UNIVERSITY, Earth Lab 369
SONORAN INSTITUTE 323
SOUND EXPERIENCE 323
SOUTH ATLANTIC FISHERY MANAGEMENT COUNCIL 323
SOUTH CAROLINA ASSOCIATION OF CONSERVATION DISTRICTS 323
SOUTH CAROLINA B.A.S.S. CHAPTER FEDERATION 323
SOUTH CAROLINA DEPARTMENT OF AGRICULTURE 107
SOUTH CAROLINA DEPARTMENT OF HEALTH AND ENVIRONMENTAL CONTROL 108
Office of Ocean and Coastal Resource Management (OCRM) 108
SOUTH CAROLINA DEPARTMENT OF NATURAL RESOURCES 108
SOUTH CAROLINA ENERGY OFFICE 108
SOUTH CAROLINA FORESTRY ASSOCIATION 324
SOUTH CAROLINA SEA GRANT CONSORTIUM 108
SOUTH CAROLINA STATE EXTENSION SERVICES 108
SOUTH CAROLINA WILDLIFE FEDERATION 324
SOUTH DAKOTA ASSOCIATION OF CONSERVATION DISTRICTS 324
SOUTH DAKOTA B.A.S.S. CHAPTER FEDERATION 324
SOUTH DAKOTA COOPERATIVE FISH AND WILDLIFE RESEARCH UNIT (USDI) 109
SOUTH DAKOTA DEPARTMENT OF AGRICULTURE 109
Division of Resource Conservation and Forestry 109
State Conservation Commission 109
SOUTH DAKOTA GAME, FISH, AND PARKS DEPARTMENT 109
SOUTH DAKOTA ORNITHOLOGISTS' UNION 324
SOUTH DAKOTA RESOURCES COALITION 324
SOUTH DAKOTA STATE EXTENSION SERVICES 109
SOUTH DAKOTA STATE UNIVERSITY, Department of Wildlife Fisheries Sciences 389
SOUTH DAKOTA WILDLIFE FEDERATION 324
SOUTH FLORIDA WATER MANAGEMENT DISTRICT 56
SOUTHEAST ALASKA CONSERVATION COUNCIL (SEACC) 324
SOUTHEASTERN ASSOCIATION OF FISH AND WILDLIFE AGENCIES 325
SOUTHEASTERN COOPERATIVE WILDLIFE DISEASE STUDY 325
SOUTHEASTERN FISHES COUNCIL 325
SOUTHERN AFRICAN INSTITUTE OF FORESTRY 325
SOUTHERN CONNECTICUT STATE UNIVERSITY, Center for the Environment 371
SOUTHERN ENVIRONMENTAL LAW CENTER 325
SOUTHERN ENVIRONMENTAL LAW CENTER (North Carolina Office) 326
SOUTHERN ILLINOIS UNIVERSITY 373
SOUTHERN NEW ENGLAND FOREST CONSORTIUM, INC. 326
SOUTHERN OREGON STATE COLLEGE, Treasure Valley Community College 386
SOUTHERN OREGON UNIVERSITY, Environmental Education Program 386
SOUTHERN UTAH WILDERNESS ALLIANCE (Moab Office) 326
SOUTHERN UTAH WILDERNESS ALLIANCE (St. George Office) 326
SOUTHERN UTAH WILDERNESS ALLIANCE (SUWA) 326
SOUTHERN UTAH WILDERNESS ALLIANCE (Washington, DC Office) 326
SOUTHFACE ENERGY INSTITUTE 326
SOUTHWEST CENTER FOR BIOLOGICAL DIVERSITY 326
SOUTHWEST FLORIDA WATER MANAGEMENT DISTRICT (SWFWMD) 56
SOUTHWEST RESEARCH AND INFORMATION CENTER 326
ST. CROIX INTERNATIONAL WATERWAY COMMISSION 10
ST. CROIX INTERNATIONAL WATERWAY COMMISSION (Canadian Office) 10
ST. LAWRENCE UNIVERSITY 382
ST. NORBERT COLLEGE, International Center 392
ST. REGIS MOHAWK TRIBE 327
STANFORD ENVIRONMENTAL LAW SOCIETY 327
STANFORD UNIVERSITY, Center for Conservation Biology, Department of Biological Sciences 369
STANFORD UNIVERSITY, Morrison Institute for Population and Resource Studies 369
STATE ENGINEER OFFICE/INTERSTATE STREAM COMMISSION 90
STATE FISH AND WILDLIFE MANAGEMENT BOARD (NEW YORK) 93
Region 3 93
Region 4 93
Region 5 93
Region 6 93
Region 7 94
Region 8 94
Region 9 94
STATE FORESTRY DIVISION (WYOMING) 126
STATE LANDS COMMISSION (CALIFORNIA) 50
STATE MARINE BOARD (OREGON) 102
STATE OF IDAHO, DIVISION OF ENVIRONMENTAL QUALITY 62
STATE OFFICE OF CONSERVATION (LOUISIANA) 71
STATE PARKS AND RECREATION COMMISSION (WASHINGTON) 120
Eastern Region 120
Northwest Region 120
Puget Sound Region 120
Southwest Region 121
STATE PLANT BOARD (ARKANSAS) 45
STATE SOIL AND WATER CONSERVATION COMMISSION (GEORGIA) 58
STATE SOIL CONSERVATION COMMISSION (IDAHO) 62
STATE UNIVERSITY OF NEW YORK AT CORTLAND 383

Organization Name Index

ORGANIZATION NAME INDEX 441

STATE UNIVERSITY OF NEW YORK, College of Environmental Science and Forestry ... 383
STATE WATER RESOURCES BOARD (RHODE ISLAND) ... 107
STATEWIDE PROGRAM OF ACTION TO CONSERVE OUR ENVIRONMENT (SPACE ... 327
STEAMBOATERS, THE ... 327
STEPHEN F. AUSTIN STATE UNIVERSITY, Arthur Temple College of Forestry ... 389
STERLING COLLEGE ... 391
STOCKTON STATE COLLEGE ... 381
STOP ... 328
STRIPERS UNLIMITED INC. ... 328
STUDENT CONSERVATION ASSOCIATION, INC. ... 328
STUDENT ENVIRONMENTAL ACTION COALITION (SEAC) ... 328
STUDENT PUGWASH USA ... 328
SUNCOAST SEABIRD SANCTUARY INC. ... 328
SUSQUEHANNA RIVER BASIN COMMISSION ... 10
TAHOE REGIONAL PLANNING AGENCY ... 329
TALL TIMBERS RESEARCH INC. ... 329
TALLAHASSEE MUSEUM OF HISTORY AND NATURAL SCIENCE ... 329
TEENS FOR RECREATION AND ENVIRONMENTAL CONSERVATION (TREC) ... 329
TENNESSEE ASSOCIATION OF CONSERVATION DISTRICTS ... 329
TENNESSEE B.A.S.S. CHAPTER FEDERATION ... 329
TENNESSEE CITIZENS FOR WILDERNESS PLANNING ... 329
TENNESSEE CONSERVATION LEAGUE ... 330
TENNESSEE COOPERATIVE FISHERY RESEARCH UNIT (USDI) ... 110
TENNESSEE DEPARTMENT OF AGRICULTURE ... 110
State Soil Conservation Committee ... 110
TENNESSEE ENVIRONMENTAL COUNCIL ... 330
TENNESSEE FORESTRY ASSOCIATION ... 330
TENNESSEE STATE EXTENSION SERVICES ... 110
TENNESSEE TECHNOLOGICAL UNIVERSITY ... 389
TENNESSEE VALLEY AUTHORITY ... 36
TENNESSEE WOODLAND OWNERS ASSOCIATION ... 330
TERRENE INSTITUTE, THE ... 330
TEXAS A&M UNIVERSITY AT COLLEGE STATION ... 389
TEXAS A&M UNIVERSITY AT COMMERCE ... 389
TEXAS A&M UNIVERSITY AT KINGSVILLE, Caesar Kleberg Wildlife Research Institute ... 390
TEXAS ASSOCIATION OF SOIL AND WATER CONSERVATION DISTRICTS ... 330
TEXAS B.A.S.S. CHAPTER FEDERATION ... 330
TEXAS CHRISTIAN UNIVERSITY ... 390
TEXAS COMMITTEE ON NATURAL RESOURCES ... 331
TEXAS COOPERATIVE FISH AND WILDLIFE RESEARCH UNIT ... 111
TEXAS DEPARTMENT OF AGRICULTURE ... 111
TEXAS DEPARTMENT OF HEALTH ... 111
TEXAS FORESTRY ASSOCIATION ... 331
TEXAS GENERAL LAND OFFICE ... 112
TEXAS ORGANIZATION FOR ENDANGERED SPECIES ... 331
TEXAS PARKS AND WILDLIFE DEPARTMENT ... 112
TEXAS SEA GRANT PROGRAM ... 112
TEXAS STATE SOIL AND WATER CONSERVATION BOARD ... 112
TEXAS TECH UNIVERSITY ... 390
TEXAS WATER DEVELOPMENT BOARD ... 112
TEXAS WILDLIFE ASSOCIATION ... 331
THE CROSBY ABORETUM, Mississippi State University ... 331
THE GLACIER INSTITUTE ... 331
THORNE ECOLOGICAL INSTITUTE ... 331
THREE CIRCLES CENTER FOR MULTICULTURAL ENVIRONMENTAL EDUCATION ... 332
THRESHOLD INC. ... 332
TOGETHER FOUNDATION, THE ... 332
TRAFFIC USA ... 332
TREAD LIGHTLY! INC. ... 332
TREE PEOPLE ... 332
TREES FOR THE FUTURE, INC. ... 333
TREES FOR TOMORROW, INC., NATURAL RESOURCES EDUCATION CENTER ... 333
TRI-STATE BIRD RESCUE AND RESEARCH, INC. ... 333
TROUT UNLIMITED ... 333
TROUT UNLIMITED, ALASKA COUNCIL ... 334
TROUT UNLIMITED, ARIZONA COUNCIL ... 334
TROUT UNLIMITED, ARKANSAS COUNCIL ... 334
TROUT UNLIMITED, CALIFORNIA COUNCIL ... 334
TROUT UNLIMITED, COLORADO COUNCIL ... 334
TROUT UNLIMITED, CONNECTICUT COUNCIL ... 334
TROUT UNLIMITED, DELAWARE STATE COUNCIL ... 334
TROUT UNLIMITED, GEORGIA COUNCIL ... 334
TROUT UNLIMITED, GUADELOUPE RIVER COUNCIL ... 334
TROUT UNLIMITED, IDAHO COUNCIL ... 334
TROUT UNLIMITED, ILLINOIS COUNCIL ... 334
TROUT UNLIMITED, KENTUCKY COUNCIL ... 335
TROUT UNLIMITED, MAINE COUNCIL ... 335
TROUT UNLIMITED, MARYLAND COUNCIL (Mid-Atlantic) ... 335
TROUT UNLIMITED, MASSACHUSETTS/RHODE ISLAND COUNCIL ... 335
TROUT UNLIMITED, MICHIGAN COUNCIL ... 335
TROUT UNLIMITED, MINNESOTA COUNCIL ... 335
TROUT UNLIMITED, MISSOURI COUNCIL ... 335
TROUT UNLIMITED, MONTANA COUNCIL ... 335
TROUT UNLIMITED, NATIONAL CAPITAL COUNCIL ... 335
TROUT UNLIMITED, NEVADA COUNCIL ... 335
TROUT UNLIMITED, NEW HAMPSHIRE COUNCIL ... 335
TROUT UNLIMITED, NEW JERSEY COUNCIL ... 335
TROUT UNLIMITED, NEW YORK COUNCIL ... 335
TROUT UNLIMITED, NORTH CAROLINA COUNCIL ... 336
TROUT UNLIMITED, NORTH FLORIDA COUNCIL ... 336
TROUT UNLIMITED, OHIO COUNCIL ... 336
TROUT UNLIMITED, OKLAHOMA COUNCIL ... 336
TROUT UNLIMITED, OREGON COUNCIL ... 336
TROUT UNLIMITED, PENNSYLVANIA COUNCIL ... 336
TROUT UNLIMITED, RHODE ISLAND COUNCIL (Narragansett) ... 336
TROUT UNLIMITED, RIVERSIDE COUNCIL ... 336
TROUT UNLIMITED, SHADES VALLEY COUNCIL ... 336
TROUT UNLIMITED, SOUTH CAROLINA COUNCIL ... 336
TROUT UNLIMITED, SOUTH FLORIDA CHAPTER ... 336
TROUT UNLIMITED, TENNESSEE COUNCIL ... 336
TROUT UNLIMITED, UTAH COUNCIL ... 336
TROUT UNLIMITED, VERMONT COUNCIL ... 337
TROUT UNLIMITED, VIRGINIA COUNCIL ... 337
TROUT UNLIMITED, WASHINGTON COUNCIL ... 337
TROUT UNLIMITED, WEST VIRGINIA COUNCIL ... 337
TROUT UNLIMITED, WISCONSIN COUNCIL ... 337
TROUT UNLIMITED, WYOMING COUNCIL ... 337
TRUMPETER SWAN SOCIETY, THE ... 337
TRUST FOR PUBLIC LAND, THE ... 337
TRUST FOR WILDLIFE, INC. ... 338
TRUSTEES FOR ALASKA ... 338
TRUSTEES OF RESERVATIONS, THE ... 338
TUFTS UNIVERSITY ... 377
TUG HILL COMMISSION ... 94
TUG HILL TOMORROW, INC. ... 338
TULANE UNIVERSITY ... 375
TULANE UNIVERSITY, Environmental Law Program ... 375
TULANE UNIVERSITY. Environmental Law Clinic ... 375
TURTLE CREEK WATERSHED ASSOCIATION, INC. ... 338
U.S. DEPARTMENT OF AGRICULTURE ... 28
ANIMAL AND PLANT HEALTH INSPECTION SERVICE ... 29
ECONOMIC RESEARCH SERVICE ... 30
FARM SERVICE AGENCY (FSA), FORMERLY AGRICULTURAL STABILIZATION AND CONSERVATION SERVICE ... 30
NATURAL RESOURCES CONSERVATION SERVICE (formerly Soil Conservation Service) ... 30
RESEARCH EDUCATION AND ECONOMICS ... 32
UNITED STATES FOREST SERVICE ... 32
U.S. PUBLIC INTEREST RESEARCH GROUP ... 339
U.S. TREASURY DEPARTMENT ... 33
U.S CUSTOMS SERVICE ... 33
U.S. CUSTOMS SERVICE ... 33
UNION OF CONCERNED SCIENTISTS ... 339
UNITED NATIONS ENVIRONMENT PROGRAMME ... 339
UNITED NATIONS ENVIRONMENT PROGRAMME (Latin America and Carribean Region) ... 339
UNITED NATIONS ENVIRONMENT PROGRAMME (North America Regional Office) ... 339
UNITED NATIONS RESEARCH INSTITUTE FOR SOCIAL DEVELOPMENT (UNRISD) ... 38
UNITED STATES CHAMBER OF COMMERCE ... 339
UNITED STATES COMMITTEE FOR THE UNITED NATIONS ENVIRONMENT PROGRAMME THE (U.S. and UNEP) ... 339
UNITED STATES TOURIST COUNCIL ... 339
UNITY COLLEGE ... 376
UNIVERSITE LAVAL ... 387
UNIVERSITY OF MIAMI, Rosenstiel School of Marine and Atmospheric Science ... 372
UNIVERSITY OF AKRON, Center for Environmental Studies ... 385
UNIVERSITY OF ALASKA AT FAIRBANKS ... 366
UNIVERSITY OF ALASKA AT FAIRBANKS, College of Science/Engineering and Mathematics ... 366
UNIVERSITY OF ALASKA AT FAIRBANKS, School of Fisheries and Ocean Sciences ... 366
UNIVERSITY OF ALBERTA, Faculty of Agriculture, Forestry, and Home Economics ... 366
UNIVERSITY OF ARIZONA, Department of Hydrology and Water Resources 367
UNIVERSITY OF ARIZONA, School of Renewable Resources ... 367
UNIVERSITY OF ARKANSAS AT LITTLE ROCK, Department of Biology/Environmental Health Sciences Program ... 367
UNIVERSITY OF ARKANSAS AT MONTICELLO, School of Forest Resources/Arkansas Forest Resources Center ... 367
UNIVERSITY OF BRITISH COLUMBIA ... 368
UNIVERSITY OF CALIFORNIA AT BERKELEY ... 369
UNIVERSITY OF CALIFORNIA AT DAVIS, Herbarium ... 369
UNIVERSITY OF CALIFORNIA AT LOS ANGELES ... 369
UNIVERSITY OF CALIFORNIA AT RIVERSIDE, Environmental Science Program ... 369
UNIVERSITY OF CALIFORNIA AT SANTA BARBARA, Environmental Studies ... 369
UNIVERSITY OF CALIFORNIA AT SANTA CRUZ ... 370
UNIVERSITY OF CALIFORNIA, Scripps Institution of Oceanography ... 370

Organization Name Index

442 ORGANIZATION NAME INDEX

UNIVERSITY OF COLORADO AT BOULDER, Environmental Center 370
UNIVERSITY OF COLORADO, Natural Resources Law Center University of Colorado School of Law 370
UNIVERSITY OF CONNECTICUT 371
UNIVERSITY OF CONNECTICUT COOPERATIVE EXTENSION 52
UNIVERSITY OF DC (VAN NESS CAMPUS) 371
UNIVERSITY OF DELAWARE, College of Agriculture and Natural Resources 371
UNIVERSITY OF FLORIDA, School of Forest Resources and Conservation .. 372
UNIVERSITY OF FLORIDA, Solar Energy and Energy Conversion Laboratories 372
UNIVERSITY OF GEORGIA 372
UNIVERSITY OF GEORGIA, Marine Institute 372
UNIVERSITY OF GUELPH 386
UNIVERSITY OF HAWAII, Cooperative Fishery Research Unit 372
UNIVERSITY OF HOUSTON, Cullen College of Engineering 390
UNIVERSITY OF IDAHO, Bowers Laboratory 372
UNIVERSITY OF IDAHO, College of Forestry/Wildlife and Range Sciences ... 372
UNIVERSITY OF ILLINOIS AT URBANA-CHAMPAIGN 373
UNIVERSITY OF IOWA 374
UNIVERSITY OF KANSAS 374
UNIVERSITY OF KENTUCKY 375
UNIVERSITY OF LOUISVILLE 375
UNIVERSITY OF MAINE AT FORT KENT 376
UNIVERSITY OF MAINE AT ORONO, College of Natural Sciences Forestry and Agriculture 376
UNIVERSITY OF MAINE AT ORONO, School of Marine Sciences 376
UNIVERSITY OF MAINE COOPERATIVE EXTENSION 72
UNIVERSITY OF MANITOBA, Natural Resources Institute 376
UNIVERSITY OF MARYLAND AT BALTIMORE COUNTY, Department of Biological Sciences 376
UNIVERSITY OF MARYLAND AT CAMBRIDGE, Appalachian Laboratory 376
UNIVERSITY OF MARYLAND AT CAMBRIDGE, Chesapeake Biological Laboratory 376
UNIVERSITY OF MARYLAND AT CAMBRIDGE, Horn Point Laboratory 376
UNIVERSITY OF MARYLAND AT COLLEGE PARK 377
UNIVERSITY OF MARYLAND AT COLLEGE PARK, Department of Government and Politics and Renewalble Energy (REPP) 377
UNIVERSITY OF MARYLAND AT EASTERN SHORE 377
UNIVERSITY OF MARYLAND AT FROSTBURG STATE UNIVERSITY 377
UNIVERSITY OF MARYLAND, Center for Environmental Science 377
UNIVERSITY OF MASSACHUSETTS 377
UNIVERSITY OF MASSACHUSETTS, Urban Harbors Institute 378
UNIVERSITY OF MICHIGAN, School of Natural Resources and Environment 378
UNIVERSITY OF MINNESOTA AT CROOKSTON 379
UNIVERSITY OF MINNESOTA AT ST. PAUL, College of Natural Resources. 379
UNIVERSITY OF MISSOURI, The School of Natural Resources 379
UNIVERSITY OF MONTANA, School of Forestry 380
UNIVERSITY OF MONTANA, School of Law 380
UNIVERSITY OF NEBRASKA, Institute of Agriculture and Natural Resources 380
UNIVERSITY OF NEVADA AT LAS VEGAS 380
UNIVERSITY OF NEVADA AT LAS VEGAS, Water Resources Program 380
UNIVERSITY OF NEVADA AT RENO 380
UNIVERSITY OF NEW BRUNSWICK 381
UNIVERSITY OF NEW HAMPSHIRE 381
UNIVERSITY OF NEW HAMPSHIRE COOPERATIVE EXTENSION 86
UNIVERSITY OF NEW HAVEN 371
UNIVERSITY OF NORTH CAROLINA AT ASHEVILLE, Environmental Science Program 384
UNIVERSITY OF NORTH CAROLINA AT CHAPEL HILL 384
UNIVERSITY OF NORTH CAROLINA AT CHAPEL HILL, School of Public Health/Environmental Resource Program 384
UNIVERSITY OF NORTH DAKOTA 384
UNIVERSITY OF NORTH TEXAS, Institute of Applied Sciences 390
UNIVERSITY OF NORTHERN BRITISH COLUMBIA 368
UNIVERSITY OF OREGON, School of Law 386
UNIVERSITY OF PENNSYLVANIA 387
UNIVERSITY OF PITTSBURGH 387
UNIVERSITY OF REGINA 388
UNIVERSITY OF RHODE ISLAND, Department of Natural Resources Science 388
UNIVERSITY OF SASKATCHEWAN 388
UNIVERSITY OF SOUTH CAROLINA, Baruch Marine Field Laboratory 388
UNIVERSITY OF SOUTH CAROLINA, The Marine Science Program 388
UNIVERSITY OF SOUTHERN CALIFORNIA 370
UNIVERSITY OF SOUTHERN MISSISSIPPI 379
UNIVERSITY OF TENNESSEE AT KNOXVILLE 389
UNIVERSITY OF TENNESSEE AT MARTIN, School of Agriculture and Human Environment 389
UNIVERSITY OF THE SOUTH 389
UNIVERSITY OF THE VIRGIN ISLANDS 391
UNIVERSITY OF TORONTO 386
UNIVERSITY OF VERMONT EXTENSION 115
  Publications Office 115
UNIVERSITY OF VERMONT, School of Natural Resources 391
UNIVERSITY OF WEST FLORIDA 372
UNIVERSITY OF WISCONSIN AT EAU CLAIRE 392
UNIVERSITY OF WISCONSIN AT GREEN BAY, College of Environmental Science 392
UNIVERSITY OF WISCONSIN AT LA CROSSE 393
UNIVERSITY OF WISCONSIN AT MADISON, College of Agricultural and Life Sciences 393
UNIVERSITY OF WISCONSIN AT MADISON, Institute for Environmental Studies (IES) 393
UNIVERSITY OF WISCONSIN AT MADISON, School of Natural Resources.. 393
UNIVERSITY OF WISCONSIN AT STEVENS POINT 393
UNIVERSITY OF WISCONSIN AT STEVENS POINT, College of Natural Resources 393
UNIVERSITY OF WYOMING 393
UPPER COLORADO RIVER COMMISSION 10
UPPER MISSISSIPPI RIVER CONSERVATION COMMITTEE 340
URBAN HABITAT PROGRAM 340
UTAH ASSOCIATION OF SOIL CONSERVATION DISTRICTS 340
UTAH B.A.S.S. CHAPTER FEDERATION 340
UTAH COOPERATIVE FISH AND WILDLIFE RESEARCH UNIT (USDI-USGS-BRD-CRU) 113
UTAH DEPARTMENT OF AGRICULTURE 113
UTAH DEPARTMENT OF HEALTH 113
UTAH NATURE STUDY SOCIETY 340
UTAH STATE DEPARTMENT OF NATURAL RESOURCES 113
  Division of Forestry, Fire and State Lands 113
  Division of Oil, Gas and Mining 113
  Division of Parks and Recreation 113
  Division of Water Rights 113
  Division of Wildlife Resources 113
  Office of Energy and Resource Planning 113
  Regional Supervisors 113
  State Soil Conservation Committee 114
UTAH STATE DEPARTMENT OF NATURAL RESOURCES, Division of Water Resources 114
UTAH STATE EXTENSION SERVICES 114
UTAH STATE SOIL CONSERVATION COMMISSION 114
UTAH STATE UNIVERSITY, Berryman Institute for Wildlife Damage Management 390
UTAH STATE UNIVERSITY, College of Natural Resources 390
UTAH STATE UNIVERSITY, Johnson State College 390
UTAH WILDERNESS COALITION 340
UTAH WILDLIFE FEDERATION 340
UTAH WOODLAND OWNERS COUNCIL 341
VANDERBILT UNIVERSITY 389
VERMONT ASSOCIATION OF CONSERVATION DISTRICTS 341
VERMONT AUDUBON COUNCIL 341
VERMONT B.A.S.S. CHAPTER FEDERATION 341
VERMONT DEPARTMENT OF AGRICULTURE, FOOD, AND MARKETS 115
  Natural Resources Conservation Council 115
  State Conservation Commission 115
VERMONT DEPARTMENT OF HEALTH 115
VERMONT INSTITUTE OF NATURAL SCIENCE 341
VERMONT LAND TRUST 341
VERMONT LAW SCHOOL, Environmental Law Center 391
VERMONT NATURAL RESOURCES COUNCIL 341
VERMONT STATE-WIDE ENVIRONMENTAL EDUCATION PROGRAMS (SWEEP) 341
VERMONT WOODLANDS ASSOCIATION 342
VIRGIN ISLANDS CONSERVATION DISTRICT 342
VIRGIN ISLANDS CONSERVATION SOCIETY, INC. 342
VIRGIN ISLANDS SOIL AND WATER CONSERVATION DIVISION 116
VIRGINIA ASSOCIATION OF CONSERVATION DISTRICTS 342
VIRGINIA B.A.S.S. CHAPTER FEDERATION 342
VIRGINIA CONSERVATION NETWORK 342
VIRGINIA COOPERATIVE FISH AND WILDLIFE RESEARCH UNIT (USDI).. 117
VIRGINIA DEPARTMENT OF AGRICULTURE AND CONSUMER SERVICES 117
VIRGINIA DEPARTMENT OF CONSERVATION AND RECREATION 117
  Board of Conservation and Recreation 117
  Breaks Interstate Park Commission 117
  Chippokes Plantation Farm Foundation 117
  Conservation and Development of Public Beaches Board 117
  Division of Administration 118
  Division of Dam Safety 118
  Division of Natural Heritage 118
  Division of Planning and Recreation Resources 118
  Division of Soil and Water Conservation 118
  Division of State Parks 118
  Virginia Cave Board 118
  Virginia Soil and Water Conservation Board 118
VIRGINIA DEPARTMENT OF ENVIRONMENTAL QUALITY 118
VIRGINIA DEPARTMENT OF HEALTH 118
VIRGINIA FORESTRY ASSOCIATION 342
VIRGINIA MUSEUM OF NATURAL HISTORY 118
VIRGINIA NATIVE PLANT SOCIETY 343
VIRGINIA OUTDOORS FOUNDATION 118
VIRGINIA POLYTECHNIC INSTITUTE AND STATE UNIVERSITY, College of Forestry & Wildlife Resources 391
VIRGINIA SEA GRANT PROGRAM 119
VIRGINIA SOCIETY OF ORNITHOLOGY 343
VIRGINIA STATE EXTENSION SERVICES 119
VIRGINIA WILDLIFE FEDERATION 343
WASHINGTON ASSOCIATION OF CONSERVATION DISTRICTS 343

Organization Name Index

ORGANIZATION NAME INDEX 443

WASHINGTON B.A.S.S. CHAPTER FEDERATION ... 343
WASHINGTON COOPERATIVE FISH AND WILDLIFE RESEARCH UNIT (USDI) ... 120
WASHINGTON DEPARTMENT OF AGRICULTURE ... 120
WASHINGTON DEPARTMENT OF NATURAL RESOURCES ... 120
Central Region ... 121
Northeast Region ... 121
Northwest Region ... 121
Olympic Region ... 121
South Puget Sound Region ... 121
Southeast Region ... 121
Southwest Region ... 121
WASHINGTON ENVIRONMENTAL COUNCIL ... 343
WASHINGTON FARM FORESTRY ASSOCIATION ... 344
WASHINGTON FOUNDATION FOR THE ENVIRONMENT ... 344
WASHINGTON NATIVE PLANT SOCIETY ... 344
WASHINGTON NATURAL HERITAGE PROGRAM ... 121
WASHINGTON RECREATION AND PARK ASSOCIATION ... 344
WASHINGTON SEA GRANT PROGRAM ... 121
WASHINGTON SOCIETY OF AMERICAN FORESTERS ... 344
WASHINGTON STATE CONSERVATION COMMISSION ... 121
WASHINGTON STATE EXTENSION SERVICES ... 121
WASHINGTON STATE OFFICE OF ENVIRONMENTAL EDUCATION ... 122
WASHINGTON STATE UNIVERSITY ... 392
WASHINGTON TOXICS COALITION ... 344
WASHINGTON TRAILS ASSOCIATION ... 344
WASHINGTON UNIVERSITY ... 380
WASHINGTON WILDERNESS COALITION ... 345
WASHINGTON WILDLIFE AND RECREATION COALITION ... 345
WASHINGTON WILDLIFE FEDERATION ... 345
WASHINGTON WILDLIFE HERITAGE FOUNDATION (including Heritage Land Trust ... 345
WATER ENVIRONMENT FEDERATION ... 345
WATER RESOURCES ASSOCIATION OF THE DELAWARE RIVER BASIN. 345
WATER RESOURCES DEPARTMENT ... 102
Water Resources Commission ... 102
WATER RESOURCES RESEARCH CENTER ... 61
WAYNE STATE UNIVERSITY, Department of Biological Sciences ... 378
WELDER WILDLIFE FOUNDATION ... 345
WEST MICHIGAN ENVIRONMENTAL ACTION COUNCIL ... 346
WEST VIRGINIA ASSOCIATION OF CONSERVATION DISTRICT SUPERVISORS ASSOCIATION, INC. ... 346
WEST VIRGINIA B.A.S.S. CHAPTER FEDERATION ... 346
WEST VIRGINIA BUREAU OF ENVIRONMENT ... 122
WEST VIRGINIA COOPERATIVE FISH AND WILDLIFE RESEARCH UNIT .. 122
WEST VIRGINIA DEPARTMENT OF AGRICULTURE ... 122
West Virginia State Soil Conservation Committee ... 122
WEST VIRGINIA GEOLOGICAL AND ECONOMIC SURVEY ... 123
WEST VIRGINIA HIGHLANDS CONSERVANCY ... 346
WEST VIRGINIA STATE EXTENSION SERVICES ... 123
WEST VIRGINIA UNIVERSITY ... 392
WEST VIRGINIA WILDLIFE FEDERATION, INC. ... 346
WESTERN ASSOCIATION OF FISH AND WILDLIFE AGENCIES ... 346
WESTERN ENVIRONMENTAL LAW CENTER ... 346
WESTERN FORESTRY AND CONSERVATION ASSOCIATION ... 347
WESTERN HEMISPHERE SHOREBIRD RESERVE NETWORK (WHSRN) .. 347
WESTERN ILLINOIS UNIVERSITY ... 373
WESTERN MICHIGAN UNIVERSITY, Environmental Studies Program ... 379
WESTERN PACIFIC REGIONAL FISHERY MANAGEMENT COUNCIL ... 347
WESTERN PENNSYLVANIA CONSERVANCY ... 347
WESTERN REGIONAL ENVIRONMENTAL EDUCATION COUNCIL ... 347
WETLAND HABITAT ALLIANCE OF TEXAS ... 347
WHALE AND DOLPHIN CONSERVATION SOCIETY ... 348
WHITE CLAY WATERSHED ASSOCIATION ... 348
WHITETAILS UNLIMITED INC. ... 348
WHOOPING CRANE CONSERVATION ASSOCIATION INC. ... 348
WIDENER UNIVERSITY, Department of Civil Engineering ... 387
WILD CANINE SURVIVAL AND RESEARCH CENTER AND WOLF SANCTUARY ... 348
WILD EARTH ... 348
WILD HORSE ORGANIZED ASSISTANCE, INC. (WHOA) ... 348
WILD ONES - NATURAL LANDSCAPERS, LTD ... 349
WILDERNESS EDUCATION ASSOCIATION ... 349
WILDERNESS LAND TRUST, THE (Colorado Office) ... 349
WILDERNESS LAND TRUST, THE (Oregon Office) ... 349
WILDERNESS SOCIETY, THE ... 349
WILDERNESS WATCH ... 350
WILDFOWL TRUST OF NORTH AMERICA INC., THE ... 350
WILDLANDS CONSERVANCY ... 350
WILDLANDS PROJECT, THE ... 350
WILDLIFE ACTION, INC. ... 350
WILDLIFE CENTER OF VIRGINIA, THE ... 350
WILDLIFE CONSERVATION SOCIETY ... 350
WILDLIFE DAMAGE REVIEW (WDR) ... 351
WILDLIFE DISEASE ASSOCIATION ... 351
WILDLIFE EDUCATION PROGRAM AND DESIGN ... 351
WILDLIFE FEDERATION OF ALASKA ... 351
WILDLIFE FOREVER ... 351
WILDLIFE FOUNDATION OF FLORIDA, INC. ... 352
WILDLIFE HABITAT CANADA ... 352
WILDLIFE HABITAT COUNCIL ... 352
WILDLIFE INFORMATION CENTER, INC. ... 352
WILDLIFE LEGISLATIVE FUND OF AMERICA, THE, AND WILDLIFE CONSERVATION FUND OF AMERICA, THE ... 352
Washington, D.C.National Affairs Office ... 352
WILDLIFE MANAGEMENT INSTITUTE ... 352
WILDLIFE PRESERVATION TRUST INTERNATIONAL, INC. ... 353
WILDLIFE RESOURCES AGENCY ... 110
WILDLIFE RESOURCES COMMISSION ... 95
WILDLIFE SOCIETY, OKLAHOMA CHAPTER ... 356
WILDLIFE SOCIETY, ALABAMA CHAPTER ... 353
WILDLIFE SOCIETY, ALASKA CHAPTER ... 353
WILDLIFE SOCIETY, ALBERTA CHAPTER ... 353
WILDLIFE SOCIETY, ARIZONA CHAPTER ... 353
WILDLIFE SOCIETY, ARKANSAS CHAPTER ... 353
WILDLIFE SOCIETY, CALIFORNIA CENTRAL COAST CHAPTER ... 353
WILDLIFE SOCIETY, CALIFORNIA NORTH COAST CHAPTER ... 353
WILDLIFE SOCIETY, COLORADO CHAPTER ... 354
WILDLIFE SOCIETY, FLORIDA CHAPTER ... 354
WILDLIFE SOCIETY, GEORGIA CHAPTER ... 354
WILDLIFE SOCIETY, HAWAII CHAPTER ... 354
WILDLIFE SOCIETY, IDAHO CHAPTER ... 354
WILDLIFE SOCIETY, ILLINOIS CHAPTER ... 354
WILDLIFE SOCIETY, INDIANA CHAPTER ... 354
WILDLIFE SOCIETY, IOWA CHAPTER ... 354
WILDLIFE SOCIETY, KANSAS CHAPTER ... 354
WILDLIFE SOCIETY, KENTUCKY CHAPTER ... 354
WILDLIFE SOCIETY, LOUISIANA CHAPTER ... 355
WILDLIFE SOCIETY, MAINE CHAPTER ... 355
WILDLIFE SOCIETY, MANITOBA CHAPTER ... 355
WILDLIFE SOCIETY, MARYLAND-DELAWARE CHAPTER ... 355
WILDLIFE SOCIETY, MICHIGAN CHAPTER ... 355
WILDLIFE SOCIETY, MINNESOTA CHAPTER ... 355
WILDLIFE SOCIETY, MISSISSIPPI CHAPTER ... 355
WILDLIFE SOCIETY, MISSOURI CHAPTER ... 355
WILDLIFE SOCIETY, MONTANA CHAPTER ... 355
WILDLIFE SOCIETY, NATIONAL CAPITAL CHAPTER ... 355
WILDLIFE SOCIETY, NEBRASKA CHAPTER ... 355
WILDLIFE SOCIETY, NEVADA CHAPTER ... 355
WILDLIFE SOCIETY, NEW ENGLAND CHAPTER ... 356
WILDLIFE SOCIETY, NEW JERSEY CHAPTER ... 356
WILDLIFE SOCIETY, NEW MEXICO CHAPTER ... 356
WILDLIFE SOCIETY, NEW YORK CHAPTER ... 356
WILDLIFE SOCIETY, NORTH CAROLINA CHAPTER ... 356
WILDLIFE SOCIETY, NORTH DAKOTA CHAPTER ... 356
WILDLIFE SOCIETY, OHIO CHAPTER ... 356
WILDLIFE SOCIETY, OKLAHOMA CHAPTER ... 356
WILDLIFE SOCIETY, OREGON CHAPTER ... 356
WILDLIFE SOCIETY, PENNSYLVANIA CHAPTER ... 356
WILDLIFE SOCIETY, SACRAMENTO-SHASTA CHAPTER ... 356
WILDLIFE SOCIETY, SAN FRANCISCO BAY AREA CHAPTER ... 357
WILDLIFE SOCIETY, SAN JOAQUIN VALLEY CHAPTER ... 357
WILDLIFE SOCIETY, SOUTH CAROLINA CHAPTER ... 357
WILDLIFE SOCIETY, SOUTH DAKOTA CHAPTER ... 357
WILDLIFE SOCIETY, SOUTHERN CALIFORNIA CHAPTER ... 357
WILDLIFE SOCIETY, TENNESSEE CHAPTER ... 357
WILDLIFE SOCIETY, TEXAS CHAPTER ... 357
WILDLIFE SOCIETY, THE ... 357
WILDLIFE SOCIETY, UTAH CHAPTER ... 358
WILDLIFE SOCIETY, VIRGINIA CHAPTER ... 358
WILDLIFE SOCIETY, WASHINGTON CHAPTER ... 358
WILDLIFE SOCIETY, WEST VIRGINIA CHAPTER ... 358
WILDLIFE SOCIETY, WISCONSIN CHAPTER ... 358
WILDLIFE SOCIETY, WYOMING CHAPTER ... 358
WILDLIFE WAYSTATION ... 358
WILKES UNIVERSITY, Geo-Environmental Sciences/Engineering Dept. ... 387
WILLIAMS COLLEGE, Center for Environmental Studies Program ... 378
WILSON ORNITHOLOGICAL SOCIETY ... 358
WINCHESTER NILO FARMS ... 359
WINDSTAR FOUNDATION, THE ... 359
WISCONSIN ASSOCIATION FOR ENVIRONMENTAL EDUCATION, INC. ... 359
WISCONSIN ASSOCIATION OF LAKES (WAL) ... 359
WISCONSIN B.A.S.S. CHAPTER FEDERATION ... 359
WISCONSIN CONSERVATION CORPS ... 123
WISCONSIN COOPERATIVE FISHERY RESEARCH UNIT (USDI) ... 123
WISCONSIN COOPERATIVE WILDLIFE RESEARCH UNIT (USDI) ... 123
WISCONSIN DEPARTMENT OF AGRICULTURE ... 123
WISCONSIN DEPARTMENT OF AGRICULTURE (Land and Water Resources Bureau) ... 123
WISCONSIN DEPARTMENT OF NATURAL RESOURCES ... 124
WISCONSIN DEPARTMENT OF PUBLIC INSTRUCTION ... 124
WISCONSIN ENVIRONMENTAL EDUCATION BOARD (WEEB) ... 124
WISCONSIN GEOLOGICAL AND NATURAL HISTORY SURVEY ... 125
WISCONSIN LAND AND WATER CONSERVATION ASSOCIATION ... 359
WISCONSIN PARK AND RECREATION ASSOCIATION ... 360
WISCONSIN SEA GRANT INSTITUTE ... 125
WISCONSIN SOCIETY FOR ORNITHOLOGY, INC., THE ... 360
WISCONSIN STATE EXTENSION SERVICES ... 125
WISCONSIN WATERFOWL ASSOCIATION, INC. ... 360
WISCONSIN WILDLIFE FEDERATION ... 360

Organization Name Index

WOLF EDUCATION AND RESEARCH CENTER 360
WOLF FUND, THE 360
WOLF HAVEN INTERNATIONAL 361
WOODLAND OWNERS ASSOCIATION OF WEST VIRGINIA 361
WOODS HOLE OCEANOGRAPHIC INSITITUTION (WHOI) SEA GRANT PROGRAM 76
WORLD ASSOCIATION OF GIRL GUIDES AND GIRL SCOUTS (WAGGGS) 361
WORLD BIRD SANCTUARY (formerly Raptor Rehabilitation and Propagation Project Inc. The) 361
WORLD CONSERVATION MONITORING CENTRE 361
WORLD FORESTRY CENTER 362
WORLD NATURE ASSOCIATION INC. 362
WORLD PAL (WORLD POPULATION ALLOCATION LIMITED INC.) 362
WORLD PARKS ENDOWMENT INC. 362
WORLD PHEASANT ASSOCIATION 362
WORLD PHEASANT ASSOCIATION OF U.S.A. INC. 362
WORLD RESOURCES INSTITUTE 362
WORLD SOCIETY FOR THE PROTECTION OF ANIMALS (WSPA) 363
WORLD WILDLIFE FUND 363
WORLD WOMEN IN THE DEFENSE OF THE ENVIRONMENT 363
WORLDWATCH INSTITUTE 363
WWF JAPAN (WORLD WIDE FUND FOR NATURE JAPAN) 363
WYOMING ASSOCIATION OF CONSERVATION DISTRICTS 364
WYOMING B.A.S.S. CHAPTER FEDERATION 364
WYOMING COOPERATIVE FISH AND WILDLIFE RESEARCH UNIT (USDI) 126
WYOMING DEPARTMENT OF AGRICULTURE 126
WYOMING DEPARTMENT OF COMMERCE
   Division of State Parks and Historic Sites 126
WYOMING NATIVE PLANT SOCIETY 364
WYOMING OUTDOOR COUNCIL 364
WYOMING STATE BOARD OF LAND COMMISSIONERS 126
WYOMING STATE EXTENSION SERVICES 126
WYOMING STATE GEOLOGICAL SURVEY 126
WYOMING WILDLIFE FEDERATION 364
XERCES SOCIETY, THE 364
YALE UNIVERSITY, Graves Memorial Library 371
YALE UNIVERSITY, School of Forestry and Environmental Studies 371
YELLOWSTONE GRIZZLY FOUNDATION (YGF) 364
YMCA EARTH SERVICE CORPS 365
YORK UNIVERSITY, Environmental Studies 386
YOSEMITE RESTORATION TRUST 365
YOUNG ENTOMOLOGISTS' SOCIETY INC. 365
YUKON FISH AND GAME ASSOCIATION 365
ZERO (REGIONAL ENVIRONMENTAL ORGANIZATION) 365
ZERO POPULATION GROWTH INC. 365

KEYWORD INDEX

Abandoned Mine Land Reclamation

OKLAHOMA STATE CONSERVATION COMMISSION 99

Acid Rain

ADIRONDACK COUNCIL, THE.. 133
CENTER FOR ENVIRONMENTAL INFORMATION 175
INSTITUTE OF ECOSYSTEM STUDIES 227
IZAAK WALTON LEAGUE OF AMERICA ENDOWMENT 239
NEWFOUNDLAND LABRADOR WILDLIFE FEDERATION 287
NORTH ATLANTIC SALMON CONSERVATION ORGANIZATION 289
OFFICE OF ENERGY EFFICIENCY AND ENVIRONMENT......................... 93
OLYMPIC PARK INSTITUTE 297
SOUTHERN ENVIRONMENTAL LAW CENTER 325, 326
STOP 328
TROUT UNLIMITED 333, 334, 335, 336, 337
UNIVERSITY OF VERMONT EXTENSION... 115
WISCONSIN LAND AND WATER CONSERVATION ASSOCIATION 359

Afforestation

DIVISION OF FORESTRY AND SOIL RESOURCES (GUAM)...................... 58

Agriculture

ABUNDANT LIFE SEED FOUNDATION 133
ADIRONDACK NATURE CONSERVANCY/ADIRONDACK LAND TRUST, INC. 134
AGRICULTURAL EXTENSION SERVICE.. 110
ALABAMA COOPERATIVE EXTENSION SYSTEM 39
ALASKA DEPARTMENT OF NATURAL RESOURCES 41
AMERICA THE BEAUTIFUL FUND.. 138
AMERICAN FARMLAND TRUST 142
AMERICAN LIVESTOCK BREEDS CONSERVANCY 152
ARIZONA DEPARTMENT OF AGRICULTURE 41
ARKANSAS STATE EXTENSION SERVICES.. 44
ASSOCIATION OF AMERICAN GEOGRAPHERS 161
BERKSHIRE-LITCHFIELD ENVIRONMENTAL COUNCIL, INC................... 165
BIO-INTEGRAL RESOURCE CENTER 166
CANADIAN FEDERATION OF HUMANE SOCIETIES 172
CARRYING CAPACITY NETWORK... 174
CENTER FOR SCIENCE IN THE PUBLIC INTEREST 176
CENTER FOR SCIENCE INFORMATION 176
CHARLES A. AND ANNE MORROW LINDBERGH FOUNDATION, THE..... 178
COLORADO DEPARTMENT OF AGRICULTURE...................................... 50
COLORADO STATE COOPERATIVE EXTENSION 51
COLORADO TRAPPERS ASSOCIATION 183
COMMITTEE ON AGRICULTURAL SUSTAINABILITY FOR DEVELOPING COUNTRIES 184
CONSERVATION FEDERATION OF MARYLAND/For A Rural Maryland (F.A.R.M.) 187
COOPERATIVE EXTENSION SERVICE (NORTH CAROLINA)................... 94
DELAWARE ASSOCIATION OF CONSERVATION DISTRICTS 191
DELAWARE DEPARTMENT OF AGRICULTURE 52
DELAWARE STATE EXTENSION SERVICE 53
DELTA WILDLIFE FOUNDATION 192
ENTOMOLOGICAL SOCIETY OF AMERICA 200
ENVIRONMENTAL ENTERPRISES ASSISTANCE FUND, INC. 203
FOOD AND AGRICULTURE ORGANIZATION OF THE UNITED NATIONS 209
GEORGIA DEPARTMENT OF AGRICULTURE 57
GOVERNOR OF SOUTH CAROLINA, JIM HODGES 107
IDAHO STATE DEPARTMENT OF AGRICULTURE 62
ILLINOIS DEPARTMENT OF AGRICULTURE 62
INDIANA DEPARTMENT OF NATURAL RESOURCES 64
INSTITUTE OF TROPICAL AGRICULTURE AND HUMAN RESOURCES... 61
INTERNATIONAL ASSOCIATION OF NATURAL RESOURCE PILOTS 228
IOWA ENVIRONMENTAL COUNCIL 237
IZAAK WALTON LEAGUE OF AMERICA, INC., THE 240
JACKSON HOLE LAND TRUST.. 242
KANSAS DEPARTMENT OF AGRICULTURE 66
KANSAS DEPARTMENT OF WILDLIFE AND PARKS 67
KANSAS NATURAL RESOURCE COUNCIL 243
KENTUCKY DEPARTMENT OF AGRICULTURE...................................... 68
MARIN CONSERVATION LEAGUE 251
MARYLAND DEPARTMENT OF AGRICULTURE 73
MICHIGAN DEPARTMENT OF AGRICULTURE 76
MICHIGAN STATE UNIVERSITY EXTENSION.. 77
MINNESOTA DEPARTMENT OF AGRICULTURE 77
MONTANA DEPARTMENT OF AGRICULTURE 82
MONTANA DEPARTMENT OF NATURAL RESOURCES AND CONSERVATION 82
MONTANA LAND RELIANCE 260
MOUNT GRACE LAND CONSERVATION TRUST 261
NATIONAL ASSOCIATION OF CONSERVATION DISTRICTS 263
NATIONAL ASSOCIATION OF STATE DEPARTMENTS OF AGRICULTURE 264
NATIONAL COALITION AGAINST THE MISUSE OF PESTICIDES 266
NATIONAL FARMERS UNION 267
NATIONAL FFA ORGANIZATION... 267
NATIONAL GRANGE, THE 269
NATIONAL WATER RESOURCES ASSOCIATION 272
NEBRASKA STATE EXTENSION SERVICES.. 84
NEW HAMPSHIRE DEPARTMENT OF AGRICULTURE, MARKETS, AND FOOD 85
NEW JERSEY CONSERVATION FOUNDATION 285
NEW JERSEY DEPARTMENT OF AGRICULTURE 87
NEW JERSEY STATE EXTENSION SERVICES 88
NEW YORK DEPARTMENT OF AGRICULTURE AND MARKETS.............. 92
NEW YORK STATE COOPERATIVE EXTENSION 93
NORTH CAROLINA DEPARTMENT OF AGRICULTURE 94
NORTH DAKOTA STATE SOIL CONSERVATION COMMITTEE 96
NORTHERN PLAINS RESOURCE COUNCIL 292
OKLAHOMA STATE BOARD OF AGRICULTURE 98
PENNSYLVANIA DEPARTMENT OF AGRICULTURE............................. 104
PHEASANTS FOREVER INC... 303
PUERTO RICO STATE EXTENSION SERVICES 106
RACHEL CARSON COUNCIL INC. (formerly Rachel Carson Trust for the Living Environment Inc.) 308
RAINFOREST TRUST INC., THE 309
RHODE ISLAND COOPERATIVE EXTENSION 106
SCIENTISTS CENTER FOR ANIMAL WELFARE 318
SOCIETY FOR RANGE MANAGEMENT 321
SOIL AND WATER CONSERVATION SOCIETY (formerly Soil Conservation Society of America) 323
SOUTH CAROLINA DEPARTMENT OF AGRICULTURE 107
SOUTH DAKOTA ORNITHOLOGISTS' UNION 324
SOUTH DAKOTA STATE EXTENSION SERVICES 109
SOUTHEASTERN COOPERATIVE WILDLIFE DISEASE STUDY 325
STATE SOIL AND WATER CONSERVATION COMMISSION (GEORGIA).. 58
STATE SOIL CONSERVATION COMMISSION (IDAHO)........................... 62
TENNESSEE DEPARTMENT OF AGRICULTURE 110
TEXAS COOPERATIVE FISH AND WILDLIFE RESEARCH UNIT 111
TEXAS SEA GRANT PROGRAM.. 112
TEXAS STATE SOIL AND WATER CONSERVATION BOARD 112
TREES FOR THE FUTURE, INC. 333
UNION OF CONCERNED SCIENTISTS 339
UNITED STATES COMMITTEE FOR THE UNITED NATIONS ENVIRONMENT PROGRAMME THE (U.S. and UNEP) 339
UTAH STATE SOIL CONSERVATION COMMISSION.............................. 114
VERMONT DEPARTMENT OF AGRICULTURE, FOOD, AND MARKETS. 115
VERMONT INSTITUTE OF NATURAL SCIENCE 341
VERMONT NATURAL RESOURCES COUNCIL 341
VIRGIN ISLANDS CONSERVATION SOCIETY, INC. 342
VIRGINIA DEPARTMENT OF AGRICULTURE AND CONSUMER SERVICES 117
WASHINGTON DEPARTMENT OF AGRICULTURE 120
WASHINGTON STATE CONSERVATION COMMISSION 121
WASHINGTON STATE EXTENSION SERVICES 121
WEST VIRGINIA DEPARTMENT OF AGRICULTURE 122
WEST VIRGINIA STATE EXTENSION SERVICES 123
WILDLIFE DAMAGE REVIEW (WDR).. 351
WILDLIFE HABITAT CANADA 352
WISCONSIN DEPARTMENT OF AGRICULTURE 123
WORLDWATCH INSTITUTE.. 363
WYOMING STATE EXTENSION SERVICES 126

Air Quality

MASSACHUSETTS HIGHWAY DEPARTMENT 75
MONTANA ENVIRONMENTAL INFORMATION CENTER........................ 260
WISCONSIN LAND AND WATER CONSERVATION ASSOCIATION 359

Air Quality and Pollution

AGENCY OF NATURAL RESOURCES 114
AIR AND WASTE MANAGEMENT ASSOCIATION 135
ALABAMA DEPARTMENT OF ENVIRONMENTAL MANAGEMENT 39
ALASKA CONSERVATION ALLIANCE... 136
ALASKA CONSERVATION VOICE 137
ALASKA DEPARTMENT OF ENVIRONMENTAL CONSERVATION 40
AMERICAN CONSERVATION ASSOCIATION, INC. 141, 142
AMERICAN LUNG ASSOCIATION 152
APPALACHIAN MOUNTAIN CLUB 158
ARIZONA DEPARTMENT OF ENVIRONMENTAL QUALITY....................... 42

446 KEYWORD INDEX - Air Resources/Aquatic Habitats

Keyword Index

AUDUBON SOCIETY OF RHODE ISLAND 164
BORDER ECOLOGY PROJECT (BEP) 167
CA DEPARTMENT OF EDUCATION, OFFICE OF ENVIRONMENTAL EDUCATION 45
CALIFORNIA ENVIRONMENTAL PROTECTION AGENCY 45
CAMP FIRE BOYS AND GIRLS 170
CAMPAIGN FOR A PROSPEROUS GEORGIA 171
CANADA-UNITED STATES ENVIRONMENTAL COUNCIL (United States Office) 171
CENTER FOR ENVIRONMENTAL STUDY 175
CHESAPEAKE BAY FOUNDATION, INC. (Pennsylvania Office) 178
COALITION FOR CLEAN AIR 181
COMITE DESPERTAR CIDRENO 105
COMMUNITIES FOR A BETTER ENVIRONMENT 184
CONNECTICUT FUND FOR THE ENVIRONMENT 186
CONNECTICUT PUBLIC INTEREST RESEARCH GROUP (ConnPIRG) ... 186
CONSERVATION AND RESEARCH FOUNDATION, INC., THE 186
CONSERVATION COUNCIL OF NORTH CAROLINA 187
CONSERVATION LAW FOUNDATION, INC. (CLF) 188
DELAWARE DEPARTMENT OF NATURAL RESOURCES AND ENVIRONMENTAL CONTROL 52
DELAWARE NATURE SOCIETY 192
DEPARTMENT OF ENVIRONMENT AND NATURAL RESOURCES (SOUTH DAKOTA) 109
DEPARTMENT OF ENVIRONMENTAL PROTECTION (MAINEO 71
DEPARTMENT OF ENVIRONMENTAL QUALITY (ARKANSAS) 44
DEPARTMENT OF THE ENVIRONMENT 72
EARTH SHARE 197
EARTHJUSTICE LEGAL DEFENSE FUND (formerly Sierra Club Legal Defense Fund, Inc.) 198
ENVIRONMENTAL DEFENSE FUND, INC. 202
ENVIRONMENTAL LEAGUE OF MASSACHUSETTS (ELM) 203
ENVIRONMENTAL QUALITY COUNCIL 82
FOSSIL FUELS POLICY ACTION INSTITUTE/ALLIANCE FOR A PAVING MORATORIUM 210
FRIENDS OF THE EARTH 211
GEORGIA CONSERVANCY, INC., THE 214
GLOBAL CITIES PROJECT, THE 215
GREEN PARTY USA 218
GREEN SEAL 218
GREENHOUSE ACTION 218
HOOSIER ENVIRONMENTAL COUNCIL 222
HUMAN ECOLOGY ACTION LEAGUE INC. THE (HEAL) 222
HUNTSMAN MARINE SCIENCE CENTRE 223
ILLINOIS ENVIRONMENTAL COUNCIL 224
ILLINOIS ENVIRONMENTAL PROTECTION AGENCY 63
INFORM, INC. 226
INSTITUTE OF ECOSYSTEM STUDIES 227
IOWA DEPARTMENT OF NATURAL RESOURCES 65
ISSAQUAH ALPS TRAILS CLUB (I.A.T.C.) 239
KANSAS STATE DEPARTMENT OF HEALTH AND ENVIRONMENT 67
KIDS FOR SAVING EARTH WORLDWIDE 246
LEAGUE OF WOMEN VOTERS OF IOWA 247
MICHIGAN DEPARTMENT OF ENVIRONMENTAL QUALITY 76
MINNESOTA CENTER FOR ENVIRONMENTAL ADVOCACY (MCEA) 256
NATIONAL ASSOCIATION OF ENVIRONMENTAL PROFESSIONALS, THE (National Office) 263
NATIONAL ENVIRONMENTAL HEALTH ASSOCIATION 267
NEW HAMPSHIRE DEPARTMENT OF ENVIRONMENTAL SERVICES 86
NEW JERSEY ENVIRONMENTAL LOBBY 286
NEWFOUNDLAND LABRADOR WILDLIFE FEDERATION 287
NORTH DAKOTA DEPARTMENT OF HEALTH 95
NORTHERN PLAINS RESOURCE COUNCIL 292
OHIO ENVIRONMENTAL COUNCIL, INC. 295
OHIO ENVIRONMENTAL PROTECTION AGENCY 97
OKLAHOMA DEPARTMENT OF ENVIRONMENTAL QUALITY 98
OREGON B.A.S.S. CHAPTER FEDERATION 297
OREGON DEPARTMENT OF ENVIRONMENTAL QUALITY (DEQ) 101
OREGON ENVIRONMENTAL COUNCIL 298
POPULATION INSTITUTE, THE 305
POPULATION-ENVIRONMENT BALANCE INC. 305
RESOURCES FOR THE FUTURE 310
RIVER NETWORK 312
SAVE THE DUNES COUNCIL 316
SCENIC HUDSON, INC. 317
SIERRA CLUB 318, 319
SOUTH CAROLINA DEPARTMENT OF HEALTH AND ENVIRONMENTAL CONTROL 108
SOUTH DAKOTA ORNITHOLOGISTS' UNION 324
SOUTHERN ENVIRONMENTAL LAW CENTER 325, 326
STATE OF IDAHO, DIVISION OF ENVIRONMENTAL QUALITY 62
STOP 328
TAHOE REGIONAL PLANNING AGENCY 329
TENNESSEE ENVIRONMENTAL COUNCIL 330
TREES FOR THE FUTURE, INC. 333
U.S. PUBLIC INTEREST RESEARCH GROUP 339
UNITED NATIONS ENVIRONMENT PROGRAMME 339
VERMONT DEPARTMENT OF HEALTH 115
VIRGINIA B.A.S.S. CHAPTER FEDERATION 342
VIRGINIA DEPARTMENT OF ENVIRONMENTAL QUALITY 118
WEST MICHIGAN ENVIRONMENTAL ACTION COUNCIL 346
WESTERN ENVIRONMENTAL LAW CENTER 346
WINDSTAR FOUNDATION, THE 359
WISCONSIN DEPARTMENT OF NATURAL RESOURCES 124
WORLD RESOURCES INSTITUTE 362

Air Resources

PENNSYLVANIA CITIZENS ADVISORY COUNCIL TO DEPARTMENT OF ENVIRONMENTAL PROTECTION 301

Alternative Agriculture

CATSKILL CENTER FOR CONSERVATION AND DEVELOPMENT, INC., THE 174

Ancient Forests

ALASKA CONSERVATION ALLIANCE 136
ALASKA CONSERVATION VOICE 137
AUDUBON SOCIETY OF PORTLAND 164
ECOLOGY CENTER 199
LIGHTHAWK 248
NATIVE PLANT SOCIETY OF NORTHEASTERN OHIO 276
NEWFOUNDLAND LABRADOR WILDLIFE FEDERATION 287
NORTH CASCADES CONSERVATION COUNCIL 291
NORTHCOAST ENVIRONMENTAL CENTER 291
NORTHWEST ECOSYSTEM ALLIANCE 293
OLYMPIC PARK INSTITUTE 297
OREGON NATURAL RESOURCES COUNCIL 298
RAINFOREST TRUST INC., THE 309
RIVER NETWORK 312
SINAPU 319
SMITHSONIAN INSTITUTION 320
WILD ONES - NATURAL LANDSCAPERS, LTD 349
WORLD CONSERVATION MONITORING CENTRE 361

Animal Welfare

JANE GOODALL INSTITUTE, THE 242

Aquaculture

NORTH CAROLINA SEA GRANT PROGRAM 95
WOODS HOLE OCEANOGRAPHIC INSITITUTION (WHOI) SEA GRANT PROGRAM 76

Aquariums

AMERICAN ZOO AND AQUARIUM ASSOCIATION (AZA) 157
HUNTSMAN MARINE SCIENCE CENTRE 223
INTERNATIONAL MARINE MAMMAL PROJECT, THE 231
SCIENTISTS CENTER FOR ANIMAL WELFARE 318

Aquatic Habitats

A.B. ENVIRONMENTAL EDUCATION CENTER 133
ADOPT-A-STREAM FOUNDATION, THE 134
ALASKA CONSERVATION ALLIANCE 136
ALASKA CONSERVATION VOICE 137
ALASKA COOPERATIVE FISH AND WILDLIFE RESEARCH UNIT 40
AMERICAN CETACEAN SOCIETY 141
AMERICAN FISHERIES SOCIETY 142, 144, 145, 146, 147, 148, 149, 283
AMERICAN FISHERIES SOCIETY, ALABAMA CHAPTER 144
AMERICAN FISHERIES SOCIETY, ALASKA CHAPTER 144
AMERICAN FISHERIES SOCIETY, ARIZONA-NEW MEXICO CHAPTER. 144
AMERICAN FISHERIES SOCIETY, ARKANSAS CHAPTER 144
AMERICAN FISHERIES SOCIETY, AUBURN UNIVERSITY STUDENT CHAPTER 145
AMERICAN FISHERIES SOCIETY, CALIFORNIA-NEVADA CHAPTER 145
AMERICAN FISHERIES SOCIETY, COLLEGE OF ENVIRONMENTAL SCIENCE AND FORESTRY CHAPTER 145
AMERICAN FISHERIES SOCIETY, COLORADO and WYOMING CHAPTER 145
AMERICAN FISHERIES SOCIETY, FLORIDA CHAPTER 145
AMERICAN FISHERIES SOCIETY, GEORGIA CHAPTER 145
AMERICAN FISHERIES SOCIETY, HAWAII CHAPTER 146
AMERICAN FISHERIES SOCIETY, HUMBOLDT CHAPTER 146
AMERICAN FISHERIES SOCIETY, IDAHO CHAPTER 146

KEYWORD INDEX - Aquatic Species/Bears 447

AMERICAN FISHERIES SOCIETY, ILLINOIS CHAPTER 146
AMERICAN FISHERIES SOCIETY, INDIANA CHAPTER 146
AMERICAN FISHERIES SOCIETY, IOWA CHAPTER 146
AMERICAN FISHERIES SOCIETY, KANSAS CHAPTER 146
AMERICAN FISHERIES SOCIETY, KENTUCKY CHAPTER 146
AMERICAN FISHERIES SOCIETY, LOUISIANA CHAPTER 146
AMERICAN FISHERIES SOCIETY, MICHIGAN CHAPTER 147
AMERICAN FISHERIES SOCIETY, MID-ATLANTIC CHAPTER 147
AMERICAN FISHERIES SOCIETY, MINNESOTA CHAPTER 147
AMERICAN FISHERIES SOCIETY, MISSISSIPPI CHAPTER 147
AMERICAN FISHERIES SOCIETY, MISSOURI CHAPTER 147
AMERICAN FISHERIES SOCIETY, NEW YORK CHAPTER 147
AMERICAN FISHERIES SOCIETY, NORTH CAROLINA CHAPTER 148
AMERICAN FISHERIES SOCIETY, OHIO CHAPTER 148
AMERICAN FISHERIES SOCIETY, OKLAHOMA CHAPTER 148
AMERICAN FISHERIES SOCIETY, OREGON CHAPTER 148
AMERICAN FISHERIES SOCIETY, POTOMAC CHAPTER 148
AMERICAN FISHERIES SOCIETY, SOUTHERN NEW ENGLAND CHAPTER 149
AMERICAN FISHERIES SOCIETY, TEXAS A&M CHAPTER 149
AMERICAN FISHERIES SOCIETY, TIDEWATER CHAPTER 149
AMERICAN INSTITUTE OF FISHERY RESEARCH BIOLOGISTS 151
AMERICAN LANDS (formerly Western Ancient Forest Campaign) 151
AMERICAN LITTORAL SOCIETY 152
AMERICAN OCEANS CAMPAIGN 153
AMERICAN SOCIETY OF ICHTHYOLOGISTS AND HERPETOLOGISTS. 155
ANGLERS FOR CLEAN WATER 157
ARLINGTON OUTDOOR EDUCATION ASSOCIATION, INC. 160
CARIBBEAN CONSERVATION CORPORATION (Costa Rica Office) 173
CHESAPEAKE BAY FOUNDATION, INC. (Maryland Office) 178
COAST ALLIANCE 181
COASTAL CONSERVATION ASSOCIATION 181
DEPARTMENT OF FISH AND WILDLIFE (WASHINGTON) 119
DEPARTMENT OF MARINE RESOURCES 71
DEPARTMENT OF PLANNING AND NATURAL RESOURCES 115
DEPARTMENT OF WILDLIFE CONSERVATION 98
DESERT FISHES COUNCIL 193
DIVISION OF NATURAL RESOURCES 122
DRAGONFLY SOCIETY OF THE AMERICAS, THE 193
ENVIRONMENTAL DEFENSE FUND, INC. 202
ENVIRONMENTAL EDUCATION ASSOCIATION OF ILLINOIS (Iron Oaks Environmental Learning Center) 202
FISH AND BOAT COMMISSION 103
FISH AND WILDLIFE INFORMATION EXCHANGE 206
FLORIDA COOPERATIVE FISH AND WILDLIFE RESEARCH UNIT (USDI) 54
FLORIDA GAME AND FRESH WATER FISH COMMISSION 55
FRIENDS OF THE SAN JUANS 212
FRIENDS OF THE SEA OTTER 212
GALIANO CONSERVANCY ASSOCIATION 213
GEORGIA COOPERATIVE FISH AND WILDLIFE RESEARCH UNIT (USDI) 57
GREAT LAKES SPORT FISHING COUNCIL 216
HAWAII AUDUBON SOCIETY 219
HAWAII COOPERATIVE FISHERY RESEARCH UNIT (USDI) 60
HAWAII NATURE CENTER 220
HUDSONIA LIMITED 222
HUNTSMAN MARINE SCIENCE CENTRE 223
ILLINOIS NATIVE PLANT SOCIETY 225
INTERNATIONAL MARINE MAMMAL PROJECT, THE 231
IOWA DEPARTMENT OF NATURAL RESOURCES 65
KANSAS BIOLOGICAL SURVEY 66
KANSAS DEPARTMENT OF WILDLIFE AND PARKS 67
KEEP FLORIDA BEAUTIFUL, INC. 244
KIDS FOR SAVING EARTH WORLDWIDE 246
LIGHTHAWK 248
LONG LIVE THE KINGS 249
MAINE COOPERATIVE FISH AND WILDLIFE RESEARCH UNIT (USDI) 72
MAINE SEA GRANT PROGRAM 72
MARINE LABORATORY (FLORIDA) 56
MARYLAND SEA GRANT COLLEGE 74
MICHIGAN WILDLIFE HABITAT FOUNDATION 255
MID-ATLANTIC FISHERY MANAGEMENT COUNCIL 256
MINNESOTA COOPERATIVE FISH AND WILDLIFE RESEARCH UNIT 77
MINNESOTA SEA GRANT COLLEGE PROGRAM 79
MONTANA COOPERATIVE FISHERY RESEARCH UNIT (USDI) 82
NATIVE PLANT SOCIETY OF NORTHEASTERN OHIO 276
NATURAL LAND INSTITUTE 277
NATURE CONSERVANCY OF COLORADO, THE 279
NATURE SASKATCHEWAN 282
NEW HAMPSHIRE LAKES ASSOCIATION 284
NEW HAMPSHIRE SEA GRANT PROGRAM 86
NEW MEXICO COOPERATIVE FISH AND WILDLIFE RESEARCH UNIT ... 89
NEWFOUNDLAND LABRADOR WILDLIFE FEDERATION 287
NORTH AMERICAN FISHING CLUB 289
NORTH AMERICAN NATIVE FISHES ASSOCIATION 289
NORTH CAROLINA SEA GRANT PROGRAM 95
OCEAN VOICE INTERNATIONAL 294
OHIO COOPERATIVE FISH AND WILDLIFE RESEARCH UNIT (USDI) 96
OHIO SEA GRANT COLLEGE PROGRAM, F.T. STONE LABORATORY, AND GREAT LAKES AQUATIC ECOSYSTEM RESEARCH CONSORTIUM (GLAERC) 97
OKLAHOMA NATIVE PLANT SOCIETY 296
OREGON COOPERATIVE FISH AND WILDLIFE RESEARCH UNIT (USDI) 100
PACIFIC FISHERY MANAGEMENT COUNCIL 300
PACIFIC WHALE FOUNDATION 301
PENNSYLVANIA FEDERATION OF SPORTSMEN'S CLUBS 302
PUERTO RICO SEA GRANT PROGRAM 105
RIVER ALLIANCE OF WISCONSIN 312
RIVER NETWORK 312
SMITHSONIAN INSTITUTION 320
SOCIETY OF WETLAND SCIENTISTS 322
SOUTH CAROLINA WILDLIFE FEDERATION 324
SOUTH DAKOTA GAME, FISH, AND PARKS DEPARTMENT 109
SOUTH DAKOTA WILDLIFE FEDERATION 324
SOUTHEASTERN FISHES COUNCIL 325
TENNESSEE B.A.S.S. CHAPTER FEDERATION 329
TENNESSEE CONSERVATION LEAGUE 330
TEXAS SEA GRANT PROGRAM 112
TEXAS WATER DEVELOPMENT BOARD 112
THE GLACIER INSTITUTE 331
TROUT UNLIMITED 333, 334, 335, 336, 337
TROUT UNLIMITED, OKLAHOMA COUNCIL 336
UNITED STATES TOURIST COUNCIL 339
UPPER MISSISSIPPI RIVER CONSERVATION COMMITTEE 340
UTAH COOPERATIVE FISH AND WILDLIFE RESEARCH UNIT (USDI-USGS-BRD-CRU) 113
UTAH WILDLIFE FEDERATION 340
VIRGINIA COOPERATIVE FISH AND WILDLIFE RESEARCH UNIT (USDI) 117
VIRGINIA SEA GRANT PROGRAM 119
VIRGINIA WILDLIFE FEDERATION 343, 346
WASHINGTON COOPERATIVE FISH AND WILDLIFE RESEARCH UNIT (USDI) 120
WATER RESOURCES RESEARCH CENTER 61
WEST VIRGINIA COOPERATIVE FISH AND WILDLIFE RESEARCH UNIT 122
WILD ONES - NATURAL LANDSCAPERS, LTD 349
WILDLIFE FOREVER 351
WISCONSIN ASSOCIATION OF LAKES (WAL) 359
WISCONSIN COOPERATIVE FISHERY RESEARCH UNIT (USDI) 123
WISCONSIN SEA GRANT INSTITUTE 125
WISCONSIN WILDLIFE FEDERATION 360
WORLD CONSERVATION MONITORING CENTRE 361

Aquatic Species

NORTH CAROLINA SEA GRANT PROGRAM 95
OHIO SEA GRANT COLLEGE PROGRAM, F.T. STONE LABORATORY, AND GREAT LAKES AQUATIC ECOSYSTEM RESEARCH CONSORTIUM (GLAERC) 97

Arctic

CIRCUMPOLAR CONSERVATION UNION 179
NORTHERN ALASKA ENVIRONMENTAL CENTER 292

Arid Lands

NEW MEXICO COOPERATIVE FISH AND WILDLIFE RESEARCH UNIT ... 89

Asia Water Environment

WATER ENVIRONMENT FEDERATION 345

Atlantic Salmon

ATLANTIC SALMON FEDERATION 163
MAINE ATLANTIC SALMON AUTHORITY (formerly Maine Atlantic Sea Run Salmon Commission) 71

Beaches

AMERICAN OCEANS CAMPAIGN 153

Bears

HIMALAYAN WILDLIFE PROJECT 221

Keyword Index

INTERNATIONAL ASSOCIATION FOR BEAR RESEARCH AND MANAGEMENT 228

Beautification

PENNSYLVANIA RESOURCES COUNCIL, INC., (formerly PA Roadside Council) 302

Bicycle

ILLINOIS PRAIRIE PATH 225

Billfish

BILLFISH FOUNDATION 166

Biodiversity

ACRES LAND TRUST 133
ADKINS ARBORETUM 134
ALABAMA COOPERATIVE FISH AND WILDLIFE RESEARCH UNIT (USDI) 39
ALABAMA NATURAL HERITAGE PROGRAM 135
ALASKA AUDUBON SOCIETY 136
AMERICA THE BEAUTIFUL FUND 138
AMERICAN ASSOCIATION FOR THE ADVANCEMENT OF SCIENCE 139
AMERICAN ASSOCIATION OF FIELD BOTANISTS 139
AMERICAN BIRDING ASSOCIATION 141
AMERICAN CHESTNUT FOUNDATION, THE 141
AMERICAN FISHERIES SOCIETY, GREATER PORTLAND, OR CHAPTER 145
AMERICAN LIVESTOCK BREEDS CONSERVANCY 152
AMERICAN MUSEUM OF NATURAL HISTORY 153
AMERICAN WILDLANDS 156
ANCIENT FOREST INTERNATIONAL 157
ANTARCTICA PROJECT 158
ASSOCIATION FOR THE PROTECTION OF THE ADIRONDACKS, THE. 160
AUDUBON COUNCIL OF ILLINOIS 163
AUDUBON INTERNATIONAL 163
BAT CONSERVATION INTERNATIONAL 165
BERKSHIRE-LITCHFIELD ENVIRONMENTAL COUNCIL, INC. 165
BIODIVERSITY LEGAL FOUNDATION 166
CALIFORNIA NATIVE PLANT SOCIETY, THE 169
CALIFORNIA WILDLIFE FEDERATION 170
CATSKILL FOREST ASSOCIATION 174
CENTER FOR INTERNATIONAL ENVIRONMENTAL LAW (CIEL) 175
CENTER FOR MARINE CONSERVATION 176
CENTER FOR PLANT CONSERVATION 176
CENTER FOR RESOURCE ECONOMICS 176
CENTER FOR SCIENCE INFORMATION 176
CENTRO de INFORMACION, INVESTIGACION y EDUCACION SOCIAL (CIIES) 177
COLORADO NATURAL HERITAGE PROGRAM 182
CONSERVATION INTERNATIONAL 188
CONSERVATION TREATY SUPPORT FUND 188
CORNELL LAB OF ORNITHOLOGY 189
CRAIGHEAD WILDLIFE-WILDLANDS INSTITUTE 190
DEFENDERS OF WILDLIFE 191
EARTH FOUNDATION 197
EARTHWATCH INSTITUTE 199
ECOLOGICAL SOCIETY OF AMERICA, THE 199
ECOTOURISM SOCIETY, THE 199
ENDANGERED SPECIES COALITION 200
ENVIRONMENTAL DEFENSE FUND, INC. 202
ENVIRONMENTAL ENTERPRISES ASSISTANCE FUND, INC. 203
ENVIRONMENTAL LAW INSTITUTE, THE 203
EUROPEAN CETACEAN SOCIETY 204
FAIRFAX AUDUBON SOCIETY 205
FISH AND WILDLIFE INFORMATION EXCHANGE 206
FLORIDA COOPERATIVE FISH AND WILDLIFE RESEARCH UNIT (USDI) 54
FLORIDA DEFENDERS OF THE ENVIRONMENT, INC. (Home Office) 207
FLORIDA NATIVE PLANT SOCIETY 207
FOREST SERVICE EMPLOYEES FOR ENVIRONMENTAL ETHICS (FSEEE) 209
FRIENDS OF THE BOUNDARY WATERS WILDERNESS 211
FRIENDS OF THE SEA OTTER 212
GALIANO CONSERVANCY ASSOCIATION 213
GEORGE MIKSCH SUTTON AVIAN RESEARCH CENTER INC. 214
GREAT LAKES UNITED 217
HAWAII AUDUBON SOCIETY 219
HAWAII NATURE CENTER 220
HAWAII SOCIETY OF AMERICAN FORESTERS 220
HOOSIER ENVIRONMENTAL COUNCIL 222
HUMBOLT FIELD RESEARCH INSTITUTE 223
HUNTSMAN MARINE SCIENCE CENTRE 223
IDAHO CONSERVATION LEAGUE 223
IDAHO COOPERATIVE FISH AND WILDLIFE RESEARCH UNIT (USDI) 61
ILLINOIS AUDUBON SOCIETY 224
ILLINOIS DEPARTMENT OF NATURAL RESOURCES 63
ILLINOIS NATIVE PLANT SOCIETY 225
ILLINOIS NATURAL HERITAGE FOUNDATION 225
INDIANA NATIVE PLANT AND WILDFLOWER SOCIETY 226
INSTITUTE FOR ECOLOGICAL STUDIES 95
INTERNATIONAL ASSOCIATION OF NATURAL RESOURCE PILOTS 228
INTERNATIONAL CENTRE FOR CONSERVATION EDUCATION 229
INTERNATIONAL MARINE MAMMAL PROJECT, THE 231
INTERNATIONAL SNOW LEOPARD TRUST 232
INTERNATIONAL SOCIETY FOR ECOLOGICAL ECONOMICS 233
INTERNATIONAL SOCIETY FOR THE PRESERVATION OF THE TROPICAL RAINFOREST, THE 233
INTERNATIONAL SOCIETY OF TROPICAL FORESTERS INC. 233
IOWA AUDUBON COUNCIL 237
IOWA COOPERATIVE FISH AND WILDLIFE RESEARCH UNIT 65
IOWA ENVIRONMENTAL COUNCIL 237
IOWA NATIVE PLANT SOCIETY 237
IOWA NATURAL HERITAGE FOUNDATION 238
JACKSON HOLE CONSERVATION ALLIANCE 242
KANSAS BIOLOGICAL SURVEY 66
KANSAS DEPARTMENT OF WILDLIFE AND PARKS 67
KENTUCKY DEPARTMENT OF FISH AND WILDLIFE RESOURCES 68
LEE COUNTY PARKS AND RECREATION SERVICES 56
LIGHTHAWK 248
MAINE COOPERATIVE FISH AND WILDLIFE RESEARCH UNIT (USDI) 72
MANASOTA-88 251
MANOMET OBSERVATORY 251
MARINE CONSERVATION BIOLOGY INSTITUTE 251
MARINE ENVIRONMENTAL RESEARCH INSTITUTE (MERI) 252
MARYLAND NATIVE PLANT SOCIETY 252
MASSACHUSETTS AUDUBON SOCIETY, INC. 253
MASSACHUSETTS COOPERATIVE FISH AND WILDLIFE RESEARCH UNIT (USDI) 75
MAX McGRAW WILDLIFE FOUNDATION 254
MICHIGAN DEPARTMENT OF AGRICULTURE 76
MINNESOTA DEPARTMENT OF AGRICULTURE 77
MINNESOTA NATIVE PLANT SOCIETY 257
MISSOURI AUDUBON COUNCIL 259
MISSOURI NATIVE PLANT SOCIETY 259
MISSOURI PRAIRIE FOUNDATION 259
MONTANA AUDUBON 260
MONTANA WILDERNESS ASSOCIATION 260
MOUNTAIN LION FOUNDATION 261
NATIONAL AVIARY IN PITTSBURGH 265
NATIONAL MILITARY FISH AND WILDLIFE ASSOCIATION 269
NATIVE PLANT SOCIETY OF OREGON 276
NATURAL AREAS ASSOCIATION 277
NATURAL HERITAGE COMMISSION (ARKANSAS) 45
NATURAL LAND INSTITUTE 277
NATURE CONSERVANCY OF COLORADO, THE 279
NATURE CONSERVANCY, THE 279, 280, 281, 282
NATURE CONSERVANCY, THE, IOWA CHAPTER 280
NATURE SASKATCHEWAN 282
NEVADA NATURAL HERITAGE PROGRAM 85
NEW HAMPSHIRE NATURAL HERITAGE INVENTORY 86
NEW JERSEY CONSERVATION FOUNDATION 285
NEWFOUNDLAND LABRADOR WILDLIFE FEDERATION 287
NORTH AMERICAN COALITION ON RELIGION AND ECOLOGY (NACRE) 288
NORTH AMERICAN CRANE WORKING GROUP 288
NORTH CASCADES CONSERVATION COUNCIL 291
NORTHCOAST ENVIRONMENTAL CENTER 291
NORTHWEST ECOSYSTEM ALLIANCE 293
OCEAN VOICE INTERNATIONAL 294
OHIO BIOLOGICAL SURVEY 295
OHIO COOPERATIVE FISH AND WILDLIFE RESEARCH UNIT (USDI) 96
OKLAHOMA BIOLOGICAL SURVEY 98
OKLAHOMA NATIVE PLANT SOCIETY 296
OLYMPIC PARK INSTITUTE 297
OREGON COOPERATIVE FISH AND WILDLIFE RESEARCH UNIT (USDI) 100
PACIFIC RIVERS COUNCIL 300
PARKS AND RECREATION DEPARTMENT (NORTH DAKOTA) 96
PENNSYLVANIA DEPARTMENT OF CONSERVATION AND NATURAL RESOURCES 105
PENNSYLVANIA FOREST STEWARDSHIP PROGRAM 105
PRAIRIE CLUB, THE 305
PREDATOR PROJECT 306
PUERTO RICO ASSOCIATION OF SOIL AND WATER CONSERVATION DISTRICTS 307
PUERTO RICO DEPARTMENT OF NATURAL AND ENVIRONMENTAL RESOURCES 105
PUERTO RICO SEA GRANT PROGRAM 105
RAINFOREST ACTION NETWORK 308
RAINFOREST ALLIANCE 309

KEYWORD INDEX - Biology/Birds

RAINFOREST RELIEF	309
REEF RELIEF	310
RESOURCES FOR THE FUTURE	310
SAVANNAH RIVER ECOLOGY LABORATORY	107
SAVE AMERICA'S FORESTS	315
SINAPU	319
SMITHSONIAN INSTITUTION	320
SOCIETY FOR CONSERVATION BIOLOGY	321
SOUTHEASTERN FISHES COUNCIL	325
SOUTHWEST CENTER FOR BIOLOGICAL DIVERSITY	326
STEAMBOATERS, THE	327
TALLAHASSEE MUSEUM OF HISTORY AND NATURAL SCIENCE	329
TENNESSEE CITIZENS FOR WILDERNESS PLANNING	329
TEXAS COOPERATIVE FISH AND WILDLIFE RESEARCH UNIT	111
TEXAS FORESTRY ASSOCIATION	331
THE CROSBY ABORETUM, Mississippi State University	331
TRUST FOR WILDLIFE, INC.	338
UNION OF CONCERNED SCIENTISTS	339
UNITED NATIONS ENVIRONMENT PROGRAMME	339
UTAH COOPERATIVE FISH AND WILDLIFE RESEARCH UNIT (USDI-USGS-BRD-CRU)	113
UTAH NATURE STUDY SOCIETY	340
VIRGINIA MUSEUM OF NATURAL HISTORY	118
WASHINGTON COOPERATIVE FISH AND WILDLIFE RESEARCH UNIT (USDI)	120
WASHINGTON NATURAL HERITAGE PROGRAM	121
WILD EARTH	348
WILDERNESS SOCIETY, THE	349
WILDFOWL TRUST OF NORTH AMERICA INC., THE	350
WILDLANDS PROJECT, THE	350
WILDLIFE DAMAGE REVIEW (WDR)	351
WILDLIFE HABITAT CANADA	352
WILDLIFE HABITAT COUNCIL	352
WILDLIFE INFORMATION CENTER, INC.	352
WILSON ORNITHOLOGICAL SOCIETY	358
WISCONSIN LAND AND WATER CONSERVATION ASSOCIATION	359
WOLF EDUCATION AND RESEARCH CENTER	360
WOODS HOLE OCEANOGRAPHIC INSITITUTION (WHOI) SEA GRANT PROGRAM	76
WORLD BIRD SANCTUARY (formerly Raptor Rehabilitation and Propagation Project Inc. The)	361
WORLD CONSERVATION MONITORING CENTRE	361
WORLD NATURE ASSOCIATION INC.	362
XERCES SOCIETY, THE	364

Biology

ALASKA AUDUBON SOCIETY	136
AMERICAN ASSOCIATION FOR THE ADVANCEMENT OF SCIENCE	139
AMERICAN INSTITUTE OF BIOLOGICAL SCIENCES	151
AMERICAN SOCIETY OF ICHTHYOLOGISTS AND HERPETOLOGISTS	155
AMERICAN SOCIETY OF ZOOLOGISTS	156
ASSOCIATION OF FIELD ORNITHOLOGISTS	161
BAT CONSERVATION INTERNATIONAL	165
CALIFORNIA TRAPPERS ASSOCIATION	170
CENTER FOR MARINE CONSERVATION	176
CHICAGO HERPETOLOGICAL SOCIETY	179
CHIHUAHUAN DESERT RESEARCH INSTITUTE	179
DESERT TORTOISE COUNCIL	193
ECOLOGICAL SOCIETY OF AMERICA, THE	199
ENTOMOLOGICAL SOCIETY OF AMERICA	200
FLORIDA EXOTIC PEST PLANT COUNCIL	207
FRIENDS OF THE SEA OTTER	212
GREEN (GLOBAL RIVERS ENVIRONMENTAL EDUCATION NETWORK)	218
HUNTSMAN MARINE SCIENCE CENTRE	223
ILLINOIS DEPARTMENT OF NATURAL RESOURCES	63
INTERNATIONAL ASSOCIATION FOR BEAR RESEARCH AND MANAGEMENT	228
INTERNATIONAL WILDLIFE REHABILITATION COUNCIL (IWRC)	236
KANSAS ACADEMY OF SCIENCE	242
KANSAS DEPARTMENT OF WILDLIFE AND PARKS	67
MAINE ATLANTIC SALMON AUTHORITY (formerly Maine Atlantic Sea Run Salmon Commission)	71
MARINE LABORATORY (FLORIDA)	56
MAX McGRAW WILDLIFE FOUNDATION	254
MINNESOTA ORNITHOLOGISTS' UNION	257
MOTE MARINE LABORATORY	261
NATIONAL ASSOCIATION OF BIOLOGY TEACHERS	262
NATIONAL SPELEOLOGICAL SOCIETY, INC.	271
NATURE CONSERVANCY OF COLORADO, THE	279
NEW HAMPSHIRE FISH AND GAME DEPARTMENT	86
NEW HAMPSHIRE NATURAL HERITAGE INVENTORY	86
NORTHWEST ATLANTIC FISHERIES ORGANIZATION (NAFO)	292
OKLAHOMA BIOLOGICAL SURVEY	98
OLYMPIC PARK INSTITUTE	297
ORNITHOLOGICAL COUNCIL	299
SCIENTISTS CENTER FOR ANIMAL WELFARE	318
SOUTHEASTERN ASSOCIATION OF FISH AND WILDLIFE AGENCIES	325
TEXAS SEA GRANT PROGRAM	112
UPPER MISSISSIPPI RIVER CONSERVATION COMMITTEE	340
WILDLIFE DISEASE ASSOCIATION	351
WILSON ORNITHOLOGICAL SOCIETY	358

Biotechnology

CALIFORNIA SEA GRANT COLLEGE SYSTEM	46
COLORADO STATE COOPERATIVE EXTENSION	51
ENTOMOLOGICAL SOCIETY OF AMERICA	200
ENVIRONMENTAL DEFENSE FUND, INC.	202
IDAHO STATE DEPARTMENT OF AGRICULTURE	62
INSTITUTE OF TROPICAL AGRICULTURE AND HUMAN RESOURCES	61
KEYSTONE CENTER, THE	245, 246
MARYLAND SEA GRANT COLLEGE	74
MINNESOTA SEA GRANT COLLEGE PROGRAM	79
NATIONAL ASSOCIATION OF BIOLOGY TEACHERS	262
NATIONAL ASSOCIATION OF STATE DEPARTMENTS OF AGRICULTURE	264
NATIONAL FFA ORGANIZATION	267
NEW YORK DEPARTMENT OF AGRICULTURE AND MARKETS	92
OHIO ACADEMY OF SCIENCE, THE	294
OREGON SEA GRANT PROGRAM	101
SCIENTISTS CENTER FOR ANIMAL WELFARE	318
STUDENT PUGWASH USA	328
TEXAS COOPERATIVE FISH AND WILDLIFE RESEARCH UNIT	111
UNION OF CONCERNED SCIENTISTS	339
UNITED NATIONS ENVIRONMENT PROGRAMME	339
UTAH DEPARTMENT OF HEALTH	113
WASHINGTON SEA GRANT PROGRAM	121
WISCONSIN LAND AND WATER CONSERVATION ASSOCIATION	359
WISCONSIN SEA GRANT INSTITUTE	125

Birds

ALASKA AUDUBON SOCIETY	136
AMERICA THE BEAUTIFUL FUND	138
AMERICAN BIRD CONSERVANCY	140
AMERICAN BIRDING ASSOCIATION	141
AMERICAN FISHERIES SOCIETY, GREATER PORTLAND, OR CHAPTER	145
AMERICAN FISHERIES SOCIETY, PENNSYLVANIA CHAPTER	148
AMERICAN ORNITHOLOGISTS' UNION	153
ASSOCIATION OF AVIAN VETERINARIANS	161
ASSOCIATION OF FIELD ORNITHOLOGISTS	161
AUDUBON COUNCIL OF CONNECTICUT	163
AUDUBON COUNCIL OF ILLINOIS	163
AUDUBON INTERNATIONAL	163
AUDUBON NATURALIST SOCIETY OF THE CENTRAL ATLANTIC STATES	164
AUDUBON SOCIETY OF MISSOURI	164
AUDUBON SOCIETY OF PORTLAND	164
AUDUBON SOCIETY OF RHODE ISLAND	164
AUDUBON SOCIETY OF WESTERN PENNSYLVANIA	165
BIRDLIFE INTERNATIONAL	166
BRITISH COLUMBIA FIELD ORNITHOLOGISTS	168
BROOKS BIRD CLUB INC., THE	168
CANADIAN COOPERATIVE WILDLIFE HEALTH CENTRE	171
CASCADIA RESEARCH	174
CENTER FOR THE STUDY OF TROPICAL BIRDS, INC. (Administrative Office)	177
CHESAPEAKE BAY FOUNDATION, INC. (Virginia Office)	178
COLORADO COOPERATIVE FISH AND WILDLIFE RESEARCH UNIT (USDI)	50
CORNELL LAB OF ORNITHOLOGY	189
DELAWARE MUSEUM OF NATURAL HISTORY	192
DEPARTMENT OF INTERIOR, U.S.G.S/B.R.D, SOUTH CAROLINA COOPERATIVE FISH AND WILDLIFE RESEARCH UNIT	107
DEPARTMENT OF PLANNING AND NATURAL RESOURCES	115
ELSA WILD ANIMAL APPEAL (Louisiana Chapter)	200
ENVIRONMENT COUNCIL OF RHODE ISLAND	200
FAIRFAX AUDUBON SOCIETY	205
FEDERAL WILDLIFE OFFICER'S ASSOCIATION	205
FEDERATION OF ALBERTA NATURALIST	205
FEDERATION OF NEW YORK STATE BIRD CLUBS, INC.	205
FISH AND WILDLIFE INFORMATION EXCHANGE	206
FLORIDA AUDUBON SOCIETY	206
FLORIDA GAME AND FRESH WATER FISH COMMISSION	55
FLORIDA ORNITHOLOGICAL SOCIETY	208
GEORGE MIKSCH SUTTON AVIAN RESEARCH CENTER INC.	214
HAWAII AUDUBON SOCIETY	219
HAWAII NATURE CENTER	220
HAWK AND OWL TRUST, THE	220
HAWK MOUNTAIN SANCTUARY ASSOCIATION	220
HAWKWATCH INTERNATIONAL INC.	221
HUMMINGBIRD SOCIETY, THE	223
HUNTSMAN MARINE SCIENCE CENTRE	223

IDAHO COOPERATIVE FISH AND WILDLIFE RESEARCH UNIT (USDI).... 61
ILLINOIS AUDUBON SOCIETY 224
INDIANA AUDUBON SOCIETY, INC. 226
INTERNATIONAL ASSOCIATION OF NATURAL RESOURCE PILOTS 228
INTERNATIONAL CRANE FOUNDATION 230
INTERNATIONAL OSPREY FOUNDATION INC., THE 232
IOWA AUDUBON COUNCIL 237
IOWA DEPARTMENT OF NATURAL RESOURCES 65
ISLAND CONSERVATION EFFORT 239
KANSAS DEPARTMENT OF WILDLIFE AND PARKS 67
KANSAS ORNITHOLOGICAL SOCIETY 244
LEE COUNTY PARKS AND RECREATION SERVICES 56
LIGHTHAWK 248
LOUISIANA AUDUBON COUNCIL 249
MANOMET OBSERVATORY 251
MARYLAND ORNITHOLOGICAL SOCIETY, INC. 253
MASSACHUSETTS AUDUBON SOCIETY, INC. 253
MAX McGRAW WILDLIFE FOUNDATION 254
MICHIGAN AUDUBON SOCIETY 254
MICHIGAN NATURE ASSOCIATION 255
MINNESOTA ORNITHOLOGISTS' UNION 257
MINNESOTA WINGS SOCIETY, INC. 257
MISSOURI AUDUBON COUNCIL 259
MONO LAKE COMMITTEE 259
MONTANA AUDUBON 260
MONTANA COOPERATIVE WILDLIFE RESEARCH UNIT (USGS/BRD)..... 82
NATIONAL AVIARY IN PITTSBURGH 265
NATIONAL BIRD-FEEDING SOCIETY 266
NATIONAL FISH AND WILDLIFE FOUNDATION 267
NATIONAL WILDLIFE REHABILITATORS ASSOCIATION 275
NATURAL HISTORY SOCIETY OF MARYLAND, INC., THE 277
NATURAL LAND INSTITUTE 277
NATURE CONSERVANCY OF COLORADO, THE 279
NATURE SASKATCHEWAN 282
NEBRASKA ORNITHOLOGISTS' UNION, INC. (University of Nebraska State
  Museum)... 283
NEWFOUNDLAND LABRADOR WILDLIFE FEDERATION 287
NORTH AMERICAN CRANE WORKING GROUP 288
NORTH AMERICAN GAMEBIRD ASSOCIATION, INC. 289
OHIO AUDUBON COUNCIL, INC. 294
OHIO COOPERATIVE FISH AND WILDLIFE RESEARCH UNIT (USDI)...... 96
OLYMPIC PARK INSTITUTE 297
ORNITHOLOGICAL COUNCIL 299
PACIFIC SEABIRD GROUP 300
PENNSYLVANIA AUDUBON SOCIETY 301
PEREGRINE FUND, THE 303
PHEASANTS FOREVER INC. 303
PRAIRIE GROUSE TECHNICAL COUNCIL 306
PTARMIGANS, THE 306
PURPLE MARTIN CONSERVATION ASSOCIATION 307
RAPTOR CENTER, THE 309
RUFFED GROUSE SOCIETY, THE 314
SCIENTISTS CENTER FOR ANIMAL WELFARE 318
SMITHSONIAN INSTITUTION 320
SOUTH DAKOTA B.A.S.S. CHAPTER FEDERATION 324
SUNCOAST SEABIRD SANCTUARY INC. 328
TRAFFIC USA 332
TRI-STATE BIRD RESCUE AND RESEARCH, INC. 333
TRUMPETER SWAN SOCIETY, THE 337
UTAH COOPERATIVE FISH AND WILDLIFE RESEARCH UNIT (USDI-
  USGS-BRD-CRU) 113
VERMONT B.A.S.S. CHAPTER FEDERATION 341
WELDER WILDLIFE FOUNDATION 345
WESTERN HEMISPHERE SHOREBIRD RESERVE NETWORK (WHSRN)
  347
WILD ONES - NATURAL LANDSCAPERS, LTD 349
WILDLIFE CENTER OF VIRGINIA, THE 350
WILDLIFE DAMAGE REVIEW (WDR) 351
WILDLIFE INFORMATION CENTER, INC. 352
WILSON ORNITHOLOGICAL SOCIETY 358
WISCONSIN LAND AND WATER CONSERVATION ASSOCIATION 359
WISCONSIN PARK AND RECREATION ASSOCIATION 360
WISCONSIN SOCIETY FOR ORNITHOLOGY, INC., THE 360
WORLD BIRD SANCTUARY (formerly Raptor Rehabilitation and Propagation
  Project Inc. The) 361
WORLD CONSERVATION MONITORING CENTRE 361
WORLD NATURE ASSOCIATION INC. 362

Botanical Gardens

AMERICA THE BEAUTIFUL FUND 138
AMERICAN ASSOCIATION OF BOTANICAL GARDENS AND ARBORETA,
  INC. 139
ARIZONA STATE PARKS BOARD 43
CENTER FOR PLANT CONSERVATION 176
HOLDEN ARBORETUM, THE 221
ILLINOIS NATIVE PLANT SOCIETY 225
INTERNATIONAL CENTER FOR EARTH CONCERNS 229

NATIONAL AVIARY IN PITTSBURGH 265
NATIVE PLANT SOCIETY OF NORTHEASTERN OHIO 276
NEW ENGLAND WILD FLOWER SOCIETY, INC. 284
NORTHERN VIRGINIA REGIONAL PARK AUTHORITY 117
WORLD CONSERVATION MONITORING CENTRE 361

Botany

OKLAHOMA BIOLOGICAL SURVEY 98
VIRGINIA NATIVE PLANT SOCIETY 343
WASHINGTON NATURAL HERITAGE PROGRAM 121

Brown Fields

URBAN HABITAT PROGRAM 340

Camp

THORNE ECOLOGICAL INSTITUTE 331

Careers

STUDENT CONSERVATION ASSOCIATION, INC. 328

Cave

AMERICAN CAVE CONSERVATION ASSOCIATION 141

Chemical Pollution Control

ALASKA CONSERVATION ALLIANCE 136
ALASKA CONSERVATION VOICE 137
ATLANTIC STATES LEGAL FOUNDATION 163
DEPARTMENT OF ENVIRONMENT AND NATURAL RESOURCES (SOUTH
  DAKOTA) 109
ENVIRONMENTAL DEFENSE FUND, INC. 202
ENVIRONMENTAL LEAGUE OF MASSACHUSETTS (ELM) 203
GEORGIA CONSERVANCY, INC., THE 214
IDAHO STATE DEPARTMENT OF AGRICULTURE 62
INSTITUTE OF TROPICAL AGRICULTURE AND HUMAN RESOURCES... 61
INTERNATIONAL ASSOCIATION OF NATURAL RESOURCE PILOTS 228
IOWA DEPARTMENT OF NATURAL RESOURCES 65
LEAGUE OF WOMEN VOTERS OF IOWA 247
MICHIGAN DEPARTMENT OF ENVIRONMENTAL QUALITY 76
RIVER NETWORK 312
STOP 328
TENNESSEE ENVIRONMENTAL COUNCIL 330
TREES FOR THE FUTURE, INC. 333
U.S. PUBLIC INTEREST RESEARCH GROUP 339
UNITED NATIONS ENVIRONMENT PROGRAMME 339
WILDLIFE DAMAGE REVIEW (WDR) 351
WISCONSIN LAND AND WATER CONSERVATION ASSOCIATION 359

Chemistry

KANSAS ACADEMY OF SCIENCE 242
MOTE MARINE LABORATORY 261
NEW MEXICO BUREAU OF MINES AND MINERAL RESOURCES 89
SAVANNAH RIVER ECOLOGY LABORATORY 107
SOUTH CAROLINA DEPARTMENT OF AGRICULTURE 107

Coastal Construction and Erosion

NORTH CAROLINA SEA GRANT PROGRAM 95

Coasts

ALABAMA DEPARTMENT OF ECONOMIC AND COMMUNITY AFFAIRS,
  COASTAL PROGRAMS (ADECA) 39
ALABAMA DEPARTMENT OF ENVIRONMENTAL MANAGEMENT 39
ALASKA SEA GRANT COLLEGE PROGRAM 41
AMERICAN CONSERVATION ASSOCIATION, INC. 141, 142
AMERICAN LAND CONSERVANCY 151
AMERICAN LITTORAL SOCIETY 152
AMERICAN OCEANS CAMPAIGN 153
AUDUBON SOCIETY OF RHODE ISLAND 164
CALIFORNIA SEA GRANT COLLEGE SYSTEM 46
CLEAN OCEAN ACTION 180

KEYWORD INDEX - Commercial Sport Fishing/Conservation of Protected Areas

CLIMATE INSTITUTE	180
COAST ALLIANCE	181
COASTAL CONSERVATION ASSOCIATION	181
COASTAL SOCIETY, THE	182
CONSERVATION COUNCIL OF NORTH CAROLINA	187
CORAL REEF ALLIANCE, THE (CORAL)	189
FLORIDA SEA GRANT COLLEGE	55
FRIENDS OF THE SAN JUANS	212
FRIENDS OF THE SEA OTTER	212
GALIANO CONSERVANCY ASSOCIATION	213
GEORGIA SEA GRANT COLLEGE PROGRAM	58
GUAM COASTAL MANAGEMENT PROGRAM	58
H. JOHN HEINZ III CENTER FOR SCIENCE, ECONOMICS, AND THE ENVIRONMENT	219
ISLAND RESOURCES FOUNDATION	239
LAKE ERIE CLEAN-UP COMMITTEE, INC.	246
LIGHTHAWK	248
LOUISIANA GEOLOGICAL SURVEY	70
LOUISIANA SEA GRANT COLLEGE PROGRAM	70
MAINE AUDUBON SOCIETY	250
MAINE COAST HERITAGE TRUST	250
MAINE SEA GRANT PROGRAM	72
MANOMET OBSERVATORY	251
MARINE LABORATORY (FLORIDA)	56
MARINE SCIENCES RESEARCH CENTER (NEW YORK)	92
MICHIGAN DEPARTMENT OF ENVIRONMENTAL QUALITY	76
MONITOR INTERNATIONAL	259
MOUNTAINEERS, THE (Conservation Division)	261
NATIONAL BOATING FEDERATION	266
NATIONAL COALITION FOR MARINE CONSERVATION	266
NATIONAL WATERWAYS CONFERENCE INC.	273
NEW HAMPSHIRE SEA GRANT PROGRAM	86
NEW YORK GEOLOGICAL SURVEY AND STATE MUSEUM	92
NEW YORK SEA GRANT	92
NORTH CAROLINA BEACH BUGGY ASSOCIATION, INC.	290
NORTH CAROLINA SEA GRANT PROGRAM	95
OLYMPIC PARK INSTITUTE	297
OREGON SEA GRANT PROGRAM	101
PUERTO RICO ASSOCIATION OF SOIL AND WATER CONSERVATION DISTRICTS	307
PUERTO RICO SEA GRANT PROGRAM	105
PUGET SOUNDKEEPER ALLIANCE	307
RESOURCES AGENCY, THE	47
SAVE THE SOUND, INC.	316
SEAPLANE PILOTS ASSOCIATION	318
SOUTH CAROLINA DEPARTMENT OF HEALTH AND ENVIRONMENTAL CONTROL	108
SOUTHERN ENVIRONMENTAL LAW CENTER	325, 326
TEXAS GENERAL LAND OFFICE	112
TEXAS SEA GRANT PROGRAM	112
UNITED NATIONS ENVIRONMENT PROGRAMME	339
VIRGINIA SEA GRANT PROGRAM	119
WISCONSIN LAND AND WATER CONSERVATION ASSOCIATION	359
WOODS HOLE OCEANOGRAPHIC INSITITUTION (WHOI) SEA GRANT PROGRAM	76
WORLD CONSERVATION MONITORING CENTRE	361

Commercial Sport Fishing

WESTERN PACIFIC REGIONAL FISHERY MANAGEMENT COUNCIL	347

Communications

AGENCY OF NATURAL RESOURCES	114
ALASKA HEALTH PROJECT	41
AMERICAN ASSOCIATION FOR THE ADVANCEMENT OF SCIENCE	139
AMERICAN FOREST FOUNDATION	150
AMERICAN PIE (PUBLIC INFORMATION ON THE ENVIRONMENT)	153
ANGLERS FOR CLEAN WATER	157
ASSOCIATION OF STATE AND TERRITORIAL HEALTH OFFICIALS	162
CENTER FOR ENVIRONMENTAL INFORMATION	175
CENTER FOR ENVIRONMENTAL STUDY	175
CENTER FOR SCIENCE INFORMATION	176
COMMITTEE FOR THE NATIONAL INSTITUTE FOR THE ENVIRONMENT (CNIE)	183
DELTA WATERFOWL FOUNDATION	192
DELTA WILDLIFE FOUNDATION	192
EARTHSTEWARDS NETWORK	198
EDUCATIONAL COMMUNICATIONS, INC.	200
ENVIROSOUTH, INC.	204
GEORGIA FORESTRY ASSOCIATION, INC.	215
GLOBAL ENVIRONMENTAL MANAGEMENT INITIATIVE (GEMI)	215
GREAT LAKES UNITED	217
INSTITUTE FOR CONSERVATION LEADERSHIP	227
INTERNATIONAL CENTRE FOR CONSERVATION EDUCATION	229
KANSAS DEPARTMENT OF WILDLIFE AND PARKS	67
KEEP AMERICA BEAUTIFUL, INC.	244
KEEP FLORIDA BEAUTIFUL, INC.	244
LEAGUE OF WOMEN VOTERS OF THE U.S.	247
MICHIGAN ENVIRONMENTAL COUNCIL	255
MINNESOTA SEA GRANT COLLEGE PROGRAM	79
NATIONAL ASSOCIATION FOR INTERPRETATION	262
NEW ENGLAND NATURAL RESOURCES CENTER	284
NORTH AMERICAN ASSOCIATION FOR ENVIRONMENTAL EDUCATION	288
NORTH CAROLINA FORESTRY ASSOCIATION	290
OHIO ACADEMY OF SCIENCE, THE	294
OREGON SEA GRANT PROGRAM	101
OUTDOOR WRITERS ASSOCIATION OF AMERICA INC.	299
PANOS INSTITUTE, THE	301
POPULATION COMMUNICATIONS INTERNATIONAL	304
POPULATION REFERENCE BUREAU INC.	305
RESPONSIVE MANAGEMENT	311
STUDENT PUGWASH USA	328
TEXAS SEA GRANT PROGRAM	112
TOGETHER FOUNDATION, THE	332
TRUST FOR WILDLIFE, INC.	338
WISCONSIN LAND AND WATER CONSERVATION ASSOCIATION	359

Conservation

ALABAMA DEPARTMENT OF ECONOMIC AND COMMUNITY AFFAIRS, COASTAL PROGRAMS (ADECA)	39
ALABAMA NATURAL HERITAGE PROGRAM	135
AMERICAN RIVERS (formerly American Rivers Conservation Council)	154
AUDUBON SOCIETY OF PORTLAND	164
BOTANICAL SOCIETY OF WESTERN PENNSYLVANIA	167
CALIFORNIA NATIVE PLANT SOCIETY (CNDS)	169
COMMUNITY CONSERVATION CONSULTANTS/HOWLERS FOREVER, INC.	184
CONNECTICUT BOTANICAL SOCIETY	185
FLORIDA EXOTIC PEST PLANT COUNCIL	207
HUMMINGBIRD SOCIETY, THE	223
IOWA NATIVE PLANT SOCIETY	237
JACKSON HOLE CONSERVATION ALLIANCE	242
KANSAS WILDFLOWER SOCIETY	244
NATIONAL AVIARY IN PITTSBURGH	265
NATIVE PLANT SOCIETY OF NORTHEASTERN OHIO	276
NATIVE PLANT SOCIETY OF OREGON	276
NEVADA NATURAL HERITAGE PROGRAM	85
NEW ENGLAND WILD FLOWER SOCIETY, INC.	284
OKLAHOMA NATIVE PLANT SOCIETY	296
PUERTO RICO CONSERVATION FOUNDATION, THE (PRCF)	307
THE CROSBY ABORETUM, Mississippi State University	331
THE GLACIER INSTITUTE	331
WEST MICHIGAN ENVIRONMENTAL ACTION COUNCIL	346
WILD ONES - NATURAL LANDSCAPERS, LTD	349

Conservation Biology

ASSOCIATION OF FIELD ORNITHOLOGISTS	161

Conservation Easements

LAND TRUST ALLIANCE, THE	247
NATIVE PRAIRIES ASSOCIATION OF TEXAS	277

Conservation of Protected Areas

ADIRONDACK MOUNTAIN CLUB, INC., THE	134
ADKINS ARBORETUM	134
AFRICAN WILDLIFE FOUNDATION	134
AFRICAN WILDLIFE NEWS SERVICE	135
ALABAMA NATURAL HERITAGE PROGRAM	135
ALASKA AUDUBON SOCIETY	136
ALBERTA WILDERNESS ASSOCIATION	137
AMERICA THE BEAUTIFUL FUND	138
AMERICAN ASSOCIATION OF FIELD BOTANISTS	139
AMERICAN ASSOCIATION OF ZOO KEEPERS, INC.	139
AMERICAN BIRD CONSERVANCY	140
ANTARCTICA PROJECT	158
AUDUBON SOCIETY OF RHODE ISLAND	164
BIRDLIFE INTERNATIONAL	166
CENTER FOR MARINE CONSERVATION	176
CONSERVATION FEDERATION OF MARYLAND/For A Rural Maryland (F.A.R.M.)	187
CORAL REEF ALLIANCE, THE (CORAL)	189
DESERT FISHES COUNCIL	193
DESERT TORTOISE COUNCIL	193
EUROPARC FEDERATION	204
FAIRFAX AUDUBON SOCIETY	205
FLORIDA AUDUBON SOCIETY	206

FOREST HISTORY SOCIETY, INC.	209
FRIENDS OF ACADIA	211
GALIANO CONSERVANCY ASSOCIATION	213
GEORGE MIKSCH SUTTON AVIAN RESEARCH CENTER INC.	214
GEORGIA CONSERVANCY, INC., THE	214
GREAT LAKES UNITED	217
HAWAII AUDUBON SOCIETY	219
ILLINOIS DEPARTMENT OF NATURAL RESOURCES	63
ILLINOIS NATIVE PLANT SOCIETY	225
INDIANA AUDUBON SOCIETY, INC.	226
INTERNATIONAL ASSOCIATION OF NATURAL RESOURCE PILOTS	228
IOWA DEPARTMENT OF NATURAL RESOURCES	65
IOWA NATURAL HERITAGE FOUNDATION	238
KANSAS DEPARTMENT OF WILDLIFE AND PARKS	67
KIDS FOR SAVING EARTH WORLDWIDE	246
LEE COUNTY PARKS AND RECREATION SERVICES	56
LIGHTHAWK	248
MISSOURI PRAIRIE FOUNDATION	259
MOUNT GRACE LAND CONSERVATION TRUST	261
MOUNTAIN LION FOUNDATION	261
NATIONAL ASSOCIATION OF STATE DEPARTMENTS OF AGRICULTURE	264
NATIONAL BIRD-FEEDING SOCIETY	266
NATIONAL FORESTRY ASSOCIATION	268
NATIONAL WILDLIFE REFUGE ASSOCIATION	275
NATURAL AREAS ASSOCIATION	277
NATURAL LAND INSTITUTE	277
NATURE CONSERVANCY OF COLORADO, THE	279
NATURE SASKATCHEWAN	282
NEVADA NATURAL HERITAGE PROGRAM	85
NORTH CASCADES CONSERVATION COUNCIL	291
NORTHWEST ECOSYSTEM ALLIANCE	293
OHIO COOPERATIVE FISH AND WILDLIFE RESEARCH UNIT (USDI)	96
OKLAHOMA BIOLOGICAL SURVEY	98
OLYMPIC PARK INSTITUTE	297
OREGON NATURAL RESOURCES COUNCIL	298
OUTDOOR RECREATION COUNCIL OF BRITISH COLUMBIA	299
PARTNERS IN PARKS	301
PENNSYLVANIA DEPARTMENT OF CONSERVATION AND NATURAL RESOURCES	105
RAINFOREST TRUST INC., THE	309
SOCIETY FOR ECOLOGICAL RESTORATION	321
SOUTHEAST ALASKA CONSERVATION COUNCIL (SEACC)	324
SOUTHEASTERN FISHES COUNCIL	325
TEXAS SEA GRANT PROGRAM	112
U.S. PUBLIC INTEREST RESEARCH GROUP	339
VIRGINIA NATIVE PLANT SOCIETY	343
VIRGINIA OUTDOORS FOUNDATION	118
WESTERN PENNSYLVANIA CONSERVANCY	347
WILDERNESS LAND TRUST, THE (Colorado Office)	349
WILDLANDS PROJECT, THE	350
WISCONSIN LAND AND WATER CONSERVATION ASSOCIATION	359
WORLD CONSERVATION MONITORING CENTRE	361
WORLD NATURE ASSOCIATION INC.	362

Conservation Plannning

NEW MEXICO COOPERATIVE FISH AND WILDLIFE RESEARCH UNIT	89

Conservation Tillage

AMERICA THE BEAUTIFUL FUND	138
CONSERVATION TECHNOLOGY INFORMATION CENTER	188
DELAWARE STATE EXTENSION SERVICE	53
INSTITUTE OF TROPICAL AGRICULTURE AND HUMAN RESOURCES	61
KANSAS DEPARTMENT OF WILDLIFE AND PARKS	67
MAX McGRAW WILDLIFE FOUNDATION	254
MINNESOTA BOARD OF WATER AND SOIL RESOURCES	77
NATIONAL ASSOCIATION OF STATE DEPARTMENTS OF AGRICULTURE	264
SOIL AND WATER CONSERVATION SOCIETY (formerly Soil Conservation Society of America)	323
WISCONSIN LAND AND WATER CONSERVATION ASSOCIATION	359

Consumer Protection

GEORGIA DEPARTMENT OF AGRICULTURE	57

Consumer Services

GEORGIA DEPARTMENT OF AGRICULTURE	57

Contaminated Sediments

CLEAN OCEAN ACTION	180
COAST ALLIANCE	181

Coral Reefs

AMERICAN LITTORAL SOCIETY	152
CARIBBEAN NATURAL RESOURCES INSTITUTE	173
CENTER FOR MARINE CONSERVATION	176
CORAL REEF ALLIANCE, THE (CORAL)	189
EARTH FOUNDATION	197
EARTHWATCH INSTITUTE	199
FLORIDA AUDUBON SOCIETY	206
GUAM COASTAL MANAGEMENT PROGRAM	58
ISLAND CONSERVATION EFFORT	239
OCEAN VOICE INTERNATIONAL	294
PUERTO RICO SEA GRANT PROGRAM	105
REEF RELIEF	310
SMITHSONIAN INSTITUTION	320
TEXAS SEA GRANT PROGRAM	112
VIRGIN ISLANDS CONSERVATION SOCIETY, INC.	342
WORLD CONSERVATION MONITORING CENTRE	361

Cultural Preservation

ALASKA CONSERVATION ALLIANCE	136
ALASKA CONSERVATION VOICE	137
AMERICA THE BEAUTIFUL FUND	138
ARCHAEOLOGICAL CONSERVANCY	158
ARIZONA STATE PARKS BOARD	43
ARKANSAS DEPARTMENT OF PARKS AND TOURISM	43
CONFEDERATED SALISH AND KOOTENAI TRIBES	185
DELAWARE GREENWAYS, INC.	192
EARTHWATCH INSTITUTE	199
HIGH DESERT MUSEUM, THE	221
IDAHO DEPARTMENT OF PARKS AND RECREATION	61
ILLINOIS ASSOCIATION OF CONSERVATION DISTRICTS	224
INTERNATIONAL SOCIETY FOR THE PRESERVATION OF THE TROPICAL RAINFOREST, THE	233
INTERNATIONAL SONORAN DESERT ALLIANCE	234
INTERTRIBAL BISON COOPERATIVE (ITBC)	236
ISLAND INSTITUTE, THE	239
LAND BETWEEN THE LAKES ASSOCIATION	247
MASSACHUSETTS HIGHWAY DEPARTMENT	75
NATIONAL PARK FOUNDATION	269
NATIONAL PARKS AND CONSERVATION ASSOCIATION (NPCA)	270
NATIVE AMERICAN FISH AND WILDLIFE SOCIETY (NAFWS)	276
NEVIS HISTORICAL AND CONSERVATION SOCIETY	283
NEW YORK STATE OFFICE OF PARKS, RECREATION AND HISTORIC PRESERVATION	93
NORTHWEST INTERPRETIVE ASSOCIATION	293
OFFICE OF STATE PARKS, DEPARTMENT OF CULTURE, RECREATION, AND TOURISM	71
OLYMPIC PARK INSTITUTE	297
OZARKS RESOURCE CENTER	300
PARTNERS IN PARKS	301
RAINFOREST RELIEF	309
RIVER NETWORK	312
SMITHSONIAN INSTITUTION	320
STATE PARKS AND RECREATION COMMISSION (WASHINGTON)	120
STUDENT CONSERVATION ASSOCIATION, INC.	328
URBAN HABITAT PROGRAM	340
WASHINGTON TOXICS COALITION	344
WESTERN ENVIRONMENTAL LAW CENTER	346
WHITE CLAY WATERSHED ASSOCIATION	348
WOLF EDUCATION AND RESEARCH CENTER	360

Culture

AMERICA THE BEAUTIFUL FUND	138
CATSKILL CENTER FOR CONSERVATION AND DEVELOPMENT, INC., THE	174
SMITHSONIAN INSTITUTION	320
TALLAHASSEE MUSEUM OF HISTORY AND NATURAL SCIENCE	329
THREE CIRCLES CENTER FOR MULTICULTURAL ENVIRONMENTAL EDUCATION	332

Dams

RIVER ALLIANCE OF WISCONSIN	312

Deserts

AMERICAN FISHERIES SOCIETY, BONNEVILLE CHAPTER	145

KEYWORD INDEX - Developing Countries/Endangered and Threatened Species

AMERICAN LAND CONSERVANCY 151
CHIHUAHUAN DESERT RESEARCH INSTITUTE 179
DESERT FISHES COUNCIL 193
DESERT TORTOISE COUNCIL 193
FEDERATION OF WESTERN OUTDOOR CLUBS 206
HIGH DESERT MUSEUM, THE 221
INTERNATIONAL SONORAN DESERT ALLIANCE 234
SOUTHWEST CENTER FOR BIOLOGICAL DIVERSITY 326
WORLD CONSERVATION MONITORING CENTRE 361

Developing Countries

ATLANTIC STATES LEGAL FOUNDATION 163
COMMITTEE ON AGRICULTURAL SUSTAINABILITY FOR DEVELOPING
 COUNTRIES 184
ECOTOURISM SOCIETY, THE 199
ENVIRONMENTAL ENTERPRISES ASSISTANCE FUND, INC. ... 203
INTERNATIONAL ASSOCIATION FOR ENVIRONMENTAL HYDROLOGY
 (IAEH) 228
MONITOR INTERNATIONAL 259
OCEAN VOICE INTERNATIONAL 294
POPULATION INSTITUTE, THE 305
RESOURCES FOR THE FUTURE 310
RETURNED PEACE CORPS VOLUNTEER FOR ENVIRONMENT AND
 DEVELOPMENT (RPCV-ED) 311
TREES FOR THE FUTURE, INC. 333
WORLD CONSERVATION MONITORING CENTRE 361

Development

COAST ALLIANCE 181

Diseases

STATE FORESTRY DIVISION (WYOMING) 126

Dolphins

MOTE MARINE LABORATORY 261
PACIFIC WHALE FOUNDATION 301

Drinking Water Protection

MICHIGAN DEPARTMENT OF ENVIRONMENTAL QUALITY 76

EcoAction

ALASKA CONSERVATION ALLIANCE 136
ALASKA CONSERVATION VOICE 137
AMERICAN PIE (PUBLIC INFORMATION ON THE ENVIRONMENT) 153
ECOLOGY CENTER 199
LAKE MICHIGAN FEDERATION 246
LEE COUNTY PARKS AND RECREATION SERVICES 56
MAGIC 250
MICHIGAN AUDUBON SOCIETY 254
PUERTO RICO SEA GRANT PROGRAM 105
RIVER NETWORK 312
SINAPU 319
WISCONSIN LAND AND WATER CONSERVATION ASSOCIATION 359

Ecology

ADKINS ARBORETUM 134
ALASKA COOPERATIVE FISH AND WILDLIFE RESEARCH UNIT 40
AMERICA THE BEAUTIFUL FUND 138
AMERICAN ASSOCIATION OF FIELD BOTANISTS 139
ARCHBOLD BIOLOGICAL STATION 159
ARKANSAS COOPERATIVE RESEARCH UNIT 43
BAT CONSERVATION INTERNATIONAL 165
CADDO LAKE INSTITUTE, INC. 169
CENTER FOR ENVIRONMENTAL STUDY 175
CENTER FOR MARINE CONSERVATION 176
COLORADO NATURAL HERITAGE PROGRAM 182
CRAIGHEAD WILDLIFE-WILDLANDS INSTITUTE 190
DEPARTMENT OF ENVIRONMENTAL QUALITY (ARKANSAS) 44
DEPARTMENT OF MARINE RESOURCES 71
ECOLOGICAL SOCIETY OF AMERICA, THE 199
ENVIRONMENTAL RESOURCE CENTER (ERC) 204
FAIRFAX AUDUBON SOCIETY 205
FISH AND WILDLIFE INFORMATION EXCHANGE 206
GEORGIA CONSERVANCY, INC., THE 214

HAWAII NATURE CENTER 220
HOLDEN ARBORETUM, THE 221
HUNTSMAN MARINE SCIENCE CENTRE 223
INDIANA AUDUBON SOCIETY, INC. 226
INSTITUTE FOR EARTH EDUCATION, THE 227
INTERNATIONAL ASSOCIATION OF WILDLAND FIRE (formerly Fire
 Research Institute) 229
INTERNATIONAL CENTER FOR EARTH CONCERNS 229
KANSAS DEPARTMENT OF WILDLIFE AND PARKS 67
KANSAS HERPETOLOGICAL SOCIETY 243
MAGIC 250
MANOMET OBSERVATORY 251
MASSACHUSETTS AUDUBON SOCIETY, INC. 253
NATURAL LAND INSTITUTE 277
NATURE CONSERVANCY OF COLORADO, THE 279
NATURE SASKATCHEWAN 282
NEW HAMPSHIRE NATURAL HERITAGE INVENTORY 86
NEWFOUNDLAND LABRADOR WILDLIFE FEDERATION 287
NORTHWEST ECOSYSTEM ALLIANCE 293
OHIO COOPERATIVE FISH AND WILDLIFE RESEARCH UNIT (USDI) 96
OKLAHOMA BIOLOGICAL SURVEY 98
OKLAHOMA NATIVE PLANT SOCIETY 296
OLYMPIC PARK INSTITUTE 297
SINAPU 319
SOCIETY FOR ECOLOGICAL RESTORATION 321
SOCIETY FOR RANGE MANAGEMENT 321
TALLAHASSEE MUSEUM OF HISTORY AND NATURAL SCIENCE 329
TEXAS SEA GRANT PROGRAM 112
THE CROSBY ABORETUM, Mississippi State University 331
THE GLACIER INSTITUTE 331
THORNE ECOLOGICAL INSTITUTE 331
UNITED NATIONS ENVIRONMENT PROGRAMME 339
UTAH COOPERATIVE FISH AND WILDLIFE RESEARCH UNIT (USDI-
 USGS-BRD-CRU) 113
WILSON ORNITHOLOGICAL SOCIETY 358
WISCONSIN LAND AND WATER CONSERVATION ASSOCIATION 359
WORLD CONSERVATION MONITORING CENTRE 361

Ecosystems

WORLD PAL (WORLD POPULATION ALLOCATION LIMITED INC.) 362

Ecotourism

ECOTOURISM SOCIETY, THE 199

Endangered and Threatened Species

ABUNDANT LIFE SEED FOUNDATION 133
ACRES LAND TRUST 133
ADKINS ARBORETUM 134
AFRICAN WILDLIFE FOUNDATION 134
AFRICAN WILDLIFE NEWS SERVICE 135
ALABAMA COOPERATIVE FISH AND WILDLIFE RESEARCH UNIT (USDI)
 39
ALABAMA ENVIRONMENTAL COUNCIL 135
ALABAMA NATURAL HERITAGE PROGRAM 135
ALASKA AUDUBON SOCIETY 136
ALBERTA WILDERNESS ASSOCIATION 137
AMERICAN ASSOCIATION OF FIELD BOTANISTS 139
AMERICAN ASSOCIATION OF ZOO KEEPERS, INC. 139
AMERICAN BIRD CONSERVANCY 140
AMERICAN CAVE CONSERVATION ASSOCIATION 141
AMERICAN CETACEAN SOCIETY 141
AMERICAN CHESTNUT FOUNDATION, THE 141
AMERICAN FISHERIES SOCIETY, BONNEVILLE CHAPTER 145
AMERICAN FISHERIES SOCIETY, WISCONSIN CHAPTER 149
AMERICAN LIVESTOCK BREEDS CONSERVANCY 152
AMERICAN MUSEUM OF NATURAL HISTORY 153
AMERICAN SOCIETY OF ICHTHYOLOGISTS AND HERPETOLOGISTS. 155
AMERICAN SOCIETY OF MAMMALOGISTS 155
AMERICAN ZOO AND AQUARIUM ASSOCIATION (AZA) 157
ANCIENT FOREST INTERNATIONAL 157
ANIMAL PROTECTION INSTITUTE 157
ANIMAL WELFARE INSTITUTE 158
APPALACHIAN TRAIL CONFERENCE 158
ARCHBOLD BIOLOGICAL STATION 159
ARKANSAS COOPERATIVE RESEARCH UNIT 43
ASSOCIATION OF AVIAN VETERINARIANS 161
ATLANTIC SALMON FEDERATION 163
AUDUBON SOCIETY OF PORTLAND 164
AUDUBON SOCIETY OF RHODE ISLAND 164
BAT CONSERVATION INTERNATIONAL 165
BILLFISH FOUNDATION 166
BIODIVERSITY LEGAL FOUNDATION 166
BIRDLIFE INTERNATIONAL 166

KEYWORD INDEX - Endangered and Threatened Species/Endangered and Threatened Species

BROTHERHOOD OF THE JUNGLE COCK, INC., THE 168
CA DEPARTMENT OF EDUCATION, OFFICE OF ENVIRONMENTAL EDUCATION 45
CALIFORNIA NATIVE PLANT SOCIETY (CNDS) 169
CALIFORNIA NATIVE PLANT SOCIETY, THE 169
CALIFORNIA TRAPPERS ASSOCIATION 170
CALIFORNIA WILDLIFE FEDERATION 170
CAMP FIRE BOYS AND GIRLS 170
CAMP FIRE CONSERVATION FUND 171
CANADA-UNITED STATES ENVIRONMENTAL COUNCIL (United States Office) 171
CANADIAN FEDERATION OF HUMANE SOCIETIES 172
CASCADIA RESEARCH 174
CENTER FOR MARINE CONSERVATION 176
CENTER FOR PLANT CONSERVATION 176
CENTER FOR THE STUDY OF TROPICAL BIRDS, INC. (Administative Office) 177
CETACEAN SOCIETY INTERNATIONAL 177
CHIHUAHUAN DESERT RESEARCH INSTITUTE 179
COLORADO COOPERATIVE FISH AND WILDLIFE RESEARCH UNIT (USDI) 50
COLORADO WILDLIFE HERITAGE FOUNDATION 183
COMITE DESPERTAR CIDRENO 105
COMMUNITY RIGHTS COUNSEL 184
CONNECTICUT BOTANICAL SOCIETY 185
CONNECTICUT PUBLIC INTEREST RESEARCH GROUP (ConnPIRG) ... 186
CONSERVATION INTERNATIONAL 188
CRAIGHEAD WILDLIFE-WILDLANDS INSTITUTE 190
DEFENDERS OF WILDLIFE 191
DELAWARE NATURE SOCIETY 192
DEPARTMENT OF FISH AND WILDLIFE (WASHINGTON) 119
DEPARTMENT OF INLAND FISHERIES AND WILDLIFE 71
DEPARTMENT OF INTERIOR, U.S.G.S/B.R.D, SOUTH CAROLINA COOPERATIVE FISH AND WILDLIFE RESEARCH UNIT 107
DEPARTMENT OF PLANNING AND NATURAL RESOURCES 115
DEPARTMENT OF WILDLIFE CONSERVATION 98
DESERT FISHES COUNCIL 193
DESERT TORTOISE COUNCIL 193
DESERT TORTOISE PRESERVE COMMITTEE, INC. 193
EAGLE NATURE FOUNDATION, LTD. 197
EARTH FOUNDATION 197
EARTH ISLAND INSTITUTE 197
EARTHTRUST 199
EARTHWATCH INSTITUTE 199
ECOLOGICAL SOCIETY OF AMERICA, THE 199
ECOLOGY CENTER 199
ELM RESEARCH INSTITUTE 200
ELSA WILD ANIMAL APPEAL (Louisiana Chapter) 200
ENDANGERED SPECIES COALITION 200
EUROPEAN ASSOCIATION FOR AQUATIC MAMMALS 204
EUROPEAN CETACEAN SOCIETY 204
FEDERAL WILDLIFE OFFICER'S ASSOCIATION 205
FISH AND WILDLIFE DIVISION/DEPARTMENT OF STATE POLICE 100
FISH AND WILDLIFE INFORMATION EXCHANGE 206
FISH AND WILDLIFE REFERENCE SERVICE 206
FLORIDA AUDUBON SOCIETY 206
FLORIDA COOPERATIVE FISH AND WILDLIFE RESEARCH UNIT (USDI) 54
FLORIDA GAME AND FRESH WATER FISH COMMISSION 55
FLORIDA NATIVE PLANT SOCIETY 207
FLORIDA ORNITHOLOGICAL SOCIETY 208
FLORIDA PANTHER PROJECT, INC., THE 208
FOSSIL RIM WILDLIFE CENTER 210
FRIENDS OF ANIMALS INC. 211
FRIENDS OF THE BOUNDARY WATERS WILDERNESS 211
FRIENDS OF THE SEA OTTER 212
FUND FOR ANIMALS INC., THE 212
GAME CONSERVATION INTERNATIONAL (GAME COIN) 213
GARDEN CLUB OF AMERICA, THE 213
GEORGE MIKSCH SUTTON AVIAN RESEARCH CENTER INC. 214
GOPHER TORTOISE COUNCIL 216
GREAT BEAR FOUNDATION 216
GREATER YELLOWSTONE COALITION 217
HAWAII AUDUBON SOCIETY 219
HAWAII NATURE CENTER 220
HAWAII SOCIETY OF AMERICAN FORESTERS 220
HAWKWATCH INTERNATIONAL INC. 221
HUDSONIA LIMITED 222
HUMANE SOCIETY OF THE UNITED STATES, THE 222
HUMMINGBIRD SOCIETY, THE 223
IDAHO COOPERATIVE FISH AND WILDLIFE RESEARCH UNIT (USDI) ... 61
IDAHO STATE DEPARTMENT OF AGRICULTURE 62
ILLINOIS ASSOCIATION OF CONSERVATION DISTRICTS 224
ILLINOIS AUDUBON SOCIETY 224
ILLINOIS DEPARTMENT OF NATURAL RESOURCES 63
ILLINOIS NATIVE PLANT SOCIETY 225
ILLINOIS NATURAL HERITAGE FOUNDATION 225
INSTITUTE AND SCHOOL FOR ENVIRONMENT AND NATURAL RESOURCES, Univeristy of Wyoming (IENR and SENR) 227
INSTITUTE FOR ECOLOGICAL STUDIES 95
INTERFAITH COUNCIL FOR THE PROTECTION OF ANIMALS AND NATURE INC. (ICPAN) 227
INTERNATIONAL ASSOCIATION FOR BEAR RESEARCH AND MANAGEMENT 228
INTERNATIONAL ASSOCIATION OF NATURAL RESOURCE PILOTS 228
INTERNATIONAL ASSOCIATION OF WILDLAND FIRE (formerly Fire Research Institute) 229
INTERNATIONAL CRANE FOUNDATION 230
INTERNATIONAL ECOLOGY SOCIETY (IES) 230
INTERNATIONAL MARINE MAMMAL PROJECT, THE 231
INTERNATIONAL PRIMATE PROTECTION LEAGUE 232
INTERNATIONAL PROFESSIONAL HUNTERS' ASSOCIATION 232
INTERNATIONAL SNOW LEOPARD TRUST 232
INTERNATIONAL SOCIETY FOR ENDANGERED CATS (ISEC) 233
INTERNATIONAL SOCIETY FOR THE PRESERVATION OF THE TROPICAL RAINFOREST, THE 233
INTERNATIONAL WILD WATERFOWL ASSOCIATION 235
INTERNATIONAL WILDLIFE COALITION (IWC) AND THE WHALE ADOPTION PROJECT 235
INTERNATIONAL WOLF CENTER (Educational Services) 236
IOWA DEPARTMENT OF NATURAL RESOURCES 65
IOWA NATIVE PLANT SOCIETY 237
IOWA NATURAL HERITAGE FOUNDATION 238
ISLAND CONSERVATION EFFORT 239
JACKSON HOLE CONSERVATION ALLIANCE 242
KANSAS BIOLOGICAL SURVEY 66
KANSAS DEPARTMENT OF WILDLIFE AND PARKS 67
KANSAS ORNITHOLOGICAL SOCIETY 244
KIDS FOR SAVING EARTH WORLDWIDE 246
LADY BIRD JOHNSON WILDFLOWER CENTER (formerly the National Wildflower Research Center) 246
LAKE SUPERIOR GREENS 246
LEE COUNTY PARKS AND RECREATION SERVICES 56
LIGHTHAWK 248
LONG LIVE THE KINGS 249
LOUISIANA AUDUBON COUNCIL 249
MAINE ATLANTIC SALMON AUTHORITY (formerly Maine Atlantic Sea Run Salmon Commission) 71
MAINE AUDUBON SOCIETY 250
MANOMET OBSERVATORY 251
MARINE ENVIRONMENTAL RESEARCH INSTITUTE (MERI) 252
MAX McGRAW WILDLIFE FOUNDATION 254
MICHIGAN NATURAL AREAS COUNCIL 255
MICHIGAN NATURE ASSOCIATION 255
MID-ATLANTIC FISHERY MANAGEMENT COUNCIL 256
MINNESOTA HERPETOLOGICAL SOCIETY (James Ford Bell Museum of Natural History) 257
MINNESOTA NATIVE PLANT SOCIETY 257
MISSISSIPPI COOPERATIVE FISH AND WILDLIFE RESEARCH UNIT (USDI) 79
MISSISSIPPI DEPARTMENT OF WILDLIFE, FISHERIES, AND PARKS ... 80
MISSISSIPPI INTERSTATE COOPERATIVE RESOURCE ASSOCIATION 258
MISSOURI AUDUBON COUNCIL 259
MISSOURI NATIVE PLANT SOCIETY 259
MISSOURI PRAIRIE FOUNDATION 259
MONTANA COOPERATIVE FISHERY RESEARCH UNIT (USDI) 82
MONTANA DEPARTMENT OF AGRICULTURE 82
MOTE MARINE LABORATORY 261
MOUNTAIN LION FOUNDATION 261
NATIONAL AVIARY IN PITTSBURGH 265
NATIONAL FISH AND WILDLIFE FOUNDATION 267
NATIONAL SPELEOLOGICAL SOCIETY, INC. 271
NATIONAL WATER RESOURCES ASSOCIATION 272
NATIONAL WILDLIFE FEDERATION 273, 275
NATIVE PLANT SOCIETY OF NORTHEASTERN OHIO 276
NATIVE PLANT SOCIETY OF OREGON 276
NATURAL AREAS ASSOCIATION 277
NATURAL HERITAGE COMMISSION (ARKANSAS) 45
NATURAL LAND INSTITUTE 277
NATURE CONSERVANCY OF COLORADO, THE 279
NATURE CONSERVANCY, THE 279, 280, 281, 282
NATURE CONSERVANCY, THE, IOWA CHAPTER 280
NATURE SASKATCHEWAN 282
NEVADA NATURAL HERITAGE PROGRAM 85
NEW ENGLAND WILD FLOWER SOCIETY, INC. 284
NEW HAMPSHIRE FISH AND GAME DEPARTMENT 86
NEW HAMPSHIRE NATURAL HERITAGE INVENTORY 86
NEW MEXICO COOPERATIVE FISH AND WILDLIFE RESEARCH UNIT ... 89
NORTH AMERICAN CRANE WORKING GROUP 288
NORTH AMERICAN LOON FUND 289
NORTH AMERICAN NATIVE FISHES ASSOCIATION 289
NORTH AMERICAN WOLF SOCIETY 289
NORTH CAROLINA BEACH BUGGY ASSOCIATION, INC. 290
NORTHCOAST ENVIRONMENTAL CENTER 291
NORTHEAST WILDLIFE ADMINISTRATORS ASSOCIATION 292
NORTHWEST ECOSYSTEM ALLIANCE 293
OHIO AUDUBON COUNCIL, INC. 294
OHIO BIOLOGICAL SURVEY 295
OHIO COOPERATIVE FISH AND WILDLIFE RESEARCH UNIT (USDI) 96

KEYWORD INDEX - Endangered Resources/Energy Conservation

OKLAHOMA BIOLOGICAL SURVEY 98
OKLAHOMA COOPERATIVE FISH AND WILDLIFE RESEARCH UNIT (USDI) 98
OKLAHOMA NATIVE PLANT SOCIETY 296
OKLAHOMA STATE EXTENSION SERVICES 99
OLYMPIC PARK INSTITUTE 297
OREGON COOPERATIVE FISH AND WILDLIFE RESEARCH UNIT (USDI) 100
OREGON DEPARTMENT OF FORESTRY 101
PACiFIC SEABIRD GROUP 300
PACIFIC WHALE FOUNDATION 301
PEREGRINE FUND, THE 303
PINE BLUFF COOPERATIVE FISHERY RESEARCH PROJECT 45
PRAIRIE GROUSE TECHNICAL COUNCIL 306
PREDATOR PROJECT 306
PUERTO RICO ASSOCIATION OF SOIL AND WATER CONSERVATION DISTRICTS 307
PUERTO RICO CONSERVATION FOUNDATION, THE (PRCF 307
PUERTO RICO SEA GRANT PROGRAM 105
PURPLE MARTIN CONSERVATION ASSOCIATION 307
RAINFOREST TRUST INC., THE 309
RAPTOR CENTER, THE 309
RAPTOR RESEARCH FOUNDATION, INC. 309
RESOURCES FOR THE FUTURE 310
RHODE ISLAND STATE ASSOCIATION OF CONSERVATION DISTRICTS 311
RIVER OTTER ALLIANCE, THE 312
SAFARI CLUB INTERNATIONAL 314
SAVE THE MANATEE CLUB 316
SCIENTISTS CENTER FOR ANIMAL WELFARE 318
SEA SHEPHERD CONSERVATION SOCIETY 318
SINAPU 319
SMITHSONIAN INSTITUTION 320
SOCIETY FOR ANIMAL PROTECTIVE LEGISLATION 320
SOCIETY FOR CONSERVATION BIOLOGY 321
SOCIETY FOR MARINE MAMMALOGY, THE 321
SOCIETY FOR THE PRESERVATION OF BIRDS OF PREY 322
SOCIETY OF TYMPANUCHUS CUPIDO PINNATUS LTD. 322
SOUTH CAROLINA DEPARTMENT OF NATURAL RESOURCES ... 108
SOUTH DAKOTA B.A.S.S. CHAPTER FEDERATION 324
SOUTH DAKOTA COOPERATIVE FISH AND WILDLIFE RESEARCH UNIT (USDI) 109
SOUTHEASTERN FISHES COUNCIL 325
SOUTHWEST CENTER FOR BIOLOGICAL DIVERSITY 326
STEAMBOATERS, THE 327
SUNCOAST SEABIRD SANCTUARY INC. 328
TALL TIMBERS RESEARCH INC. 329
TALLAHASSEE MUSEUM OF HISTORY AND NATURAL SCIENCE ... 329
TEXAS FORESTRY ASSOCIATION 331
TEXAS SEA GRANT PROGRAM 112
TRAFFIC USA 332
TRI-STATE BIRD RESCUE AND RESEARCH, INC. 333
TROUT UNLIMITED 333, 334, 335, 336, 337
TURTLE CREEK WATERSHED ASSOCIATION, INC. 338
U.S. PUBLIC INTEREST RESEARCH GROUP 339
UNITED NATIONS ENVIRONMENT PROGRAMME 339
UNITED STATES COMMITTEE FOR THE UNITED NATIONS ENVIRONMENT PROGRAMME THE (U.S. and UNEP) 339
UTAH COOPERATIVE FISH AND WILDLIFE RESEARCH UNIT (USDI-USGS-BRD-CRU) 113
VERMONT B.A.S.S. CHAPTER FEDERATION 341
VIRGINIA COOPERATIVE FISH AND WILDLIFE RESEARCH UNIT (USDI) 117
VIRGINIA DEPARTMENT OF AGRICULTURE AND CONSUMER SERVICES 117
VIRGINIA FORESTRY ASSOCIATION 342
VIRGINIA MUSEUM OF NATURAL HISTORY 118
VIRGINIA NATIVE PLANT SOCIETY 343
WESTERN PENNSYLVANIA CONSERVANCY 347
WHALE AND DOLPHIN CONSERVATION SOCIETY 348
WHOOPING CRANE CONSERVATION ASSOCIATION INC. 348
WILD CANINE SURVIVAL AND RESEARCH CENTER AND WOLF SANCTUARY 348
WILD ONES - NATURAL LANDSCAPERS, LTD 349
WILDLIFE CENTER OF VIRGINIA, THE 350
WILDLIFE CONSERVATION SOCIETY 350
WILDLIFE DAMAGE REVIEW (WDR) 351
WILDLIFE EDUCATION PROGRAM AND DESIGN 351
WILDLIFE PRESERVATION TRUST INTERNATIONAL, INC. 353
WILDLIFE RESOURCES AGENCY 110
WILDLIFE WAYSTATION 358
WISCONSIN LAND AND WATER CONSERVATION ASSOCIATION ... 359
WOLF EDUCATION AND RESEARCH CENTER 360
WOLF FUND, THE 360
WOLF HAVEN INTERNATIONAL 361
WORLD BIRD SANCTUARY (formerly Raptor Rehabilitation and Propagation Project Inc. The) 361
WORLD CONSERVATION MONITORING CENTRE 361
WORLD NATURE ASSOCIATION INC. 362
WORLD SOCIETY FOR THE PROTECTION OF ANIMALS (WSPA) ... 363
WORLD WILDLIFE FUND 363
WYOMING COOPERATIVE FISH AND WILDLIFE RESEARCH UNIT (USDI) 126
WYOMING NATIVE PLANT SOCIETY 364
XERCES SOCIETY, THE 364
YELLOWSTONE GRIZZLY FOUNDATION (YGF) 364

Endangered Resources

WISCONSIN DEPARTMENT OF NATURAL RESOURCES 124

Energy

AMERICAN COUNCIL FOR AN ENERGY-EFFICIENT ECONOMY ... 142
ARIZONA GEOLOGICAL SURVEY 42
BIOMASS USERS NETWORK 166
BUREAU OF ECONOMIC GEOLOGY 111
BUREAU OF MINES AND GEOLOGY 82
CAMPAIGN FOR A PROSPEROUS GEORGIA 171
CENTER FOR ENVIRONMENTAL INFORMATION 175
CENTER FOR RESOURCE ECONOMICS 176
CHESAPEAKE BAY FOUNDATION, INC. (Pennsylvania Office) ... 178
CLIMATE INSTITUTE 180
CONNECTICUT FUND FOR THE ENVIRONMENT 186
CONSERVATION LAW FOUNDATION, INC. (CLF) 188
ENERGY, MINERALS, AND NATURAL RESOURCES DEPARTMENT ... 88
ENVIRONMENTAL AND ENERGY STUDY INSTITUTE (EESI) 201
ENVIRONMENTAL DEFENSE FUND, INC. 202
ENVIRONMENTAL ENTERPRISES ASSISTANCE FUND, INC. ... 203
FLORIDA CONSERVATION FOUNDATION, INC. 207
FOSSIL FUELS POLICY ACTION INSTITUTE/ALLIANCE FOR A PAVING MORATORIUM 210
FRIENDS OF THE RIVER 212
GENERAL FEDERATION OF WOMEN'S CLUBS 213
GLOBAL CITIES PROJECT, THE 215
GREEN SEAL 218
GREENHOUSE ACTION 218
GREENPEACE, INC. 219
INFORM, INC. 226
INTERNATIONAL INSTITUTE FOR ENERGY CONSERVATION ... 231
IOWA DEPARTMENT OF NATURAL RESOURCES 65
ISSAQUAH ALPS TRAILS CLUB (I.A.T.C.) 239
IZAAK WALTON LEAGUE OF AMERICA, INC., THE 240
KANSAS GEOLOGICAL SURVEY 67
KANSAS NATURAL RESOURCE COUNCIL 243
KEYSTONE CENTER, THE 245, 246
LEAGUE OF WOMEN VOTERS OF THE U.S. 247
LEGAL ENVIRONMENTAL ASSISTANCE FOUNDATION INC. (LEAF) ... 248
LOUISIANA GEOLOGICAL SURVEY 70
MICHIGAN ENVIRONMENTAL COUNCIL 255
MINNESOTA ENVIRONMENTAL QUALITY BOARD 78
MISSOURI DEPARTMENT OF NATURAL RESOURCES 81
MONTANA ENVIRONMENTAL INFORMATION CENTER 260
NATIONAL 4-H COUNCIL 262
NATIONAL ASSOCIATION OF ENVIRONMENTAL PROFESSIONALS, THE (National Office) 263
NATIONAL WATERWAYS CONFERENCE INC. 273
NEW JERSEY ENVIRONMENTAL LOBBY 286
NEW MEXICO BUREAU OF MINES AND MINERAL RESOURCES ... 89
NEW YORK GEOLOGICAL SURVEY AND STATE MUSEUM 92
NORTH DAKOTA GEOLOGICAL SURVEY 96
NORTHERN PLAINS RESOURCE COUNCIL 292
NW ENERGY COALITION 294
OFFICE OF ENERGY EFFICIENCY AND ENVIRONMENT 93
OHIO ENVIRONMENTAL COUNCIL, INC. 295
OKLAHOMA GEOLOGICAL SURVEY 98
OLYMPIC PARK INSTITUTE 297
PHYSICIANS FOR SOCIAL RESPONSIBILITY 303
RESOURCES FOR THE FUTURE 310
SAFE ENERGY COMMUNICATION COUNCIL 315
SIERRA CLUB 318, 319
SOUTH CAROLINA ENERGY OFFICE 108
SOUTH DAKOTA ORNITHOLOGISTS' UNION 324
SOUTHERN ENVIRONMENTAL LAW CENTER 325, 326
STATE OFFICE OF CONSERVATION (LOUISIANA) 71
STUDENT PUGWASH USA 328
U.S. PUBLIC INTEREST RESEARCH GROUP 339
UNION OF CONCERNED SCIENTISTS 339
WASHINGTON B.A.S.S. CHAPTER FEDERATION 343
WISCONSIN LAND AND WATER CONSERVATION ASSOCIATION ... 359
WORLDWATCH INSTITUTE 363
WYOMING STATE GEOLOGICAL SURVEY 126

Energy Conservation

DELAWARE STATE EXTENSION SERVICE 53

ENVIRONMENTAL ENTERPRISES ASSISTANCE FUND, INC. 203
ENVIRONMENTAL RESOURCE CENTER (ERC) 204
GLOBAL CITIES PROJECT, THE 215
IOWA TRAILS COUNCIL 238
KIDS FOR SAVING EARTH WORLDWIDE 246
LEAGUE OF WOMEN VOTERS OF IOWA 247
LEE COUNTY PARKS AND RECREATION SERVICES 56
LEGAL ENVIRONMENTAL ASSISTANCE FOUNDATION INC. (LEAF) 248
RESOURCES FOR THE FUTURE 310
SAFE ENERGY COMMUNICATION COUNCIL 315
SOUTHERN ENVIRONMENTAL LAW CENTER 325, 326
SOUTHFACE ENERGY INSTITUTE 326
TREES FOR THE FUTURE, INC. 333
U.S. PUBLIC INTEREST RESEARCH GROUP 339

Engineering

AIR AND WASTE MANAGEMENT ASSOCIATION 135
ALASKA HEALTH PROJECT 41
ARIZONA GEOLOGICAL SURVEY 42
ASSOCIATION OF CONSERVATION ENGINEERS 161
DELAWARE STATE EXTENSION SERVICE 53
DEPARTMENT OF TRANSPORTATION 27, 100, 106
DEPARTMENT OF TRANSPORTATION (OREGON) 100
DEPARTMENT OF TRANSPORTATION (RHODE ISLAND) 106
DEPARTMENT OF WATER RESOURCES (NEBRASKA) 83
INSTITUTE OF TROPICAL AGRICULTURE AND HUMAN RESOURCES ... 61
INTERNATIONAL EROSION CONTROL ASSOCIATION (IECA) 230
MARINE TECHNOLOGY SOCIETY 252
STATE OFFICE OF CONSERVATION (LOUISIANA) 71
WATER ENVIRONMENT FEDERATION 345

Environment

ADIRONDACK MOUNTAIN CLUB, INC., THE 134
ALASKA CONSERVATION ALLIANCE 136
ALASKA CONSERVATION VOICE 137
ALLIANCE FOR THE CHESAPEAKE BAY 138
AMERICANS FOR THE ENVIRONMENT 157
MANOMET OBSERVATORY 251
MARYLAND FORESTS ASSOCIATION 252
MASSACHUSETTS AUDUBON SOCIETY, INC. 253
MICHIGAN LAND USE INSTITUTE 255
MINNESOTA SEA GRANT COLLEGE PROGRAM 79
MISSOURI AUDUBON COUNCIL 259
MISSOURI NATIVE PLANT SOCIETY 259
MONTANA LAND RELIANCE 260
NATIONAL BIRD-FEEDING SOCIETY 266
NATIONAL COALITION AGAINST THE MISUSE OF PESTICIDES 266
NATIONAL TREE TRUST 272
NATURE CONSERVANCY OF COLORADO, THE 279
NATURE SASKATCHEWAN 282
NEW HAMPSHIRE LAKES ASSOCIATION 284
NORTH AMERICAN ASSOCIATION FOR ENVIRONMENTAL EDUCATION 288
NORTHWEST ECOSYSTEM ALLIANCE 293
OHIO COOPERATIVE FISH AND WILDLIFE RESEARCH UNIT (USDI) 96
OKLAHOMA GEOLOGICAL SURVEY 98
OLYMPIC PARK INSTITUTE 297
POPULATION ACTION INTERNATIONAL 304
POPULATION INSTITUTE, THE 305
POPULATION-ENVIRONMENT BALANCE INC. 305
RAILS-TO-TRAILS CONSERVANCY 308
RESOURCES FOR THE FUTURE 310
RETURNED PEACE CORPS VOLUNTEER FOR ENVIRONMENT AND DEVELOPMENT (RPCV-ED) 311
RIVER NETWORK 312
ROGER TORY PETERSON INSTITUTE 314
SAFE ENERGY COMMUNICATION COUNCIL 315
SAVE THE HARBOR/SAVE THE BAY 316
SOCIETY FOR RANGE MANAGEMENT 321
SOUTHEAST ALASKA CONSERVATION COUNCIL (SEACC) 324
SOUTHFACE ENERGY INSTITUTE 326
STUDENT CONSERVATION ASSOCIATION, INC. 328
TALLAHASSEE MUSEUM OF HISTORY AND NATURAL SCIENCE 329
TENNESSEE ENVIRONMENTAL COUNCIL 330
TEXAS COOPERATIVE FISH AND WILDLIFE RESEARCH UNIT 111
TEXAS SEA GRANT PROGRAM 112
THREE CIRCLES CENTER FOR MULTICULTURAL ENVIRONMENTAL EDUCATION 332
TREES FOR THE FUTURE, INC. 333
U.S. PUBLIC INTEREST RESEARCH GROUP 339
UNION OF CONCERNED SCIENTISTS 339
UNITED NATIONS ENVIRONMENT PROGRAMME 339
VIRGINIA DEPARTMENT OF ENVIRONMENTAL QUALITY 118
VIRGINIA NATIVE PLANT SOCIETY 343
WILD EARTH 348
ASSOCIATION OF STATE AND TERRITORIAL HEALTH OFFICIALS 162
AUDUBON COUNCIL OF CONNECTICUT 163
AUDUBON SOCIETY OF RHODE ISLAND 164
BAT CONSERVATION INTERNATIONAL 165
CALIFORNIA ACADEMY OF SCIENCES 45, 169
CARRYING CAPACITY NETWORK 174
CENTER FOR PLANT CONSERVATION 176
COMITE DESPERTAR CIDRENO 105
COUNCIL ON ENVIRONMENTAL QUALITY (CONNECTICUT) 52
DEFENDERS OF WILDLIFE 191
DEPARTMENT OF ENVIRONMENT AND NATURAL RESOURCES (SOUTH DAKOTA) 109
DEPARTMENT OF TRANSPORTATION (OREGON) 100
DESERT TORTOISE COUNCIL 193
ECOLOGICAL SOCIETY OF AMERICA, THE 199
ECOLOGY CENTER 199
ENVIRONMENTAL LEAGUE OF MASSACHUSETTS (ELM) 203
FLORIDA GAME AND FRESH WATER FISH COMMISSION 55
FRIENDS OF THE SEA OTTER 212
GEORGE MIKSCH SUTTON AVIAN RESEARCH CENTER INC. 214
GEORGIA CONSERVANCY, INC., THE 214
GLOBAL CITIES PROJECT, THE 215
GREEN (GLOBAL RIVERS ENVIRONMENTAL EDUCATION NETWORK) 218
HAWAII NATURE CENTER 220
HAWK AND OWL TRUST, THE 220
HUNTSMAN MARINE SCIENCE CENTRE 223
INSTITUTE FOR CONSERVATION LEADERSHIP 227
INSTITUTE OF TROPICAL AGRICULTURE AND HUMAN RESOURCES ... 61
INTERNATIONAL ASSOCIATION FOR ENVIRONMENTAL HYDROLOGY (IAEH) 228
IOWA DEPARTMENT OF NATURAL RESOURCES 65
IOWA WOMEN IN NATURAL RESOURCES 238
IZAAK WALTON LEAGUE OF AMERICA, INC., THE 240
JACKSON HOLE CONSERVATION ALLIANCE 242
KANSAS ASSOCIATION FOR CONSVERATION AND ENVIRONMENTAL EDUCATION 243
KANSAS DEPARTMENT OF WILDLIFE AND PARKS 67
KANSAS STATE DEPARTMENT OF HEALTH AND ENVIRONMENT 67
KIDS FOR SAVING EARTH WORLDWIDE 246
LAKE MICHIGAN FEDERATION 246
LIGHTHAWK 2
WILDLIFE FOREVER 351
WILSON ORNITHOLOGICAL SOCIETY 358
WISCONSIN DEPARTMENT OF AGRICULTURE (Land and Water Resources Bureau) 123
WISCONSIN PARK AND RECREATION ASSOCIATION 360
WORLD BIRD SANCTUARY (formerly Raptor Rehabilitation and Propagation Project Inc. The) 361
WORLD PAL (WORLD POPULATION ALLOCATION LIMITED INC.) 362
WYOMING STATE BOARD OF LAND COMMISSIONERS 126

Environmental and Conservation Education

1000 FRIENDS OF FLORIDA 133
A. E. HOWELL WILDLIFE CONSERVATION CENTER 133
ACRES LAND TRUST 133
ADIRONDACK MOUNTAIN CLUB, INC., THE 134
ADIRONDACK PARK AGENCY 90
ADKINS ARBORETUM 134
ADOPT-A-STREAM FOUNDATION, THE 134
AGRICULTURAL EXTENSION SERVICE 110
ALABAMA ENVIRONMENTAL COUNCIL 135
ALABAMA FORESTRY COMMISSION 39
ALASKA AUDUBON SOCIETY 136
ALASKA CONSERVATION ALLIANCE 136
ALASKA CONSERVATION VOICE 137
ALASKA HEALTH PROJECT 41
ALASKA NATURAL RESOURCE AND OUTDOOR EDUCATION ASSOCIATION 137
ALASKA SEA GRANT COLLEGE PROGRAM 41
ALLIANCE FOR THE CHESAPEAKE BAY 138
AMERICA THE BEAUTIFUL FUND 138
AMERICAN BASS ASSOCIATION OF WEST VIRGINIA, THE 140
AMERICAN BIRDING ASSOCIATION 141
AMERICAN CAMPING ASSOCIATION, INC. 141
AMERICAN CAVE CONSERVATION ASSOCIATION 141
AMERICAN CETACEAN SOCIETY 141
AMERICAN FARMLAND TRUST 142
AMERICAN FISHERIES SOCIETY, GREATER PORTLAND, OR CHAPTER 145
AMERICAN FISHERIES SOCIETY, PENNSYLVANIA CHAPTER 148
AMERICAN FISHERIES SOCIETY, VIRGINIA TECH CHAPTER 149
AMERICAN FOREST FOUNDATION 150
AMERICAN FORESTS (formerly American Forestry Association) 150
AMERICAN GEOGRAPHICAL SOCIETY 150
AMERICAN GROUND WATER TRUST 150
AMERICAN HIKING SOCIETY 150

KEYWORD INDEX - Environmental and Conservation Education 457

Keyword Index

AMERICAN NATURE STUDY SOCIETY ... 153
AMERICAN PIE (PUBLIC INFORMATION ON THE ENVIRONMENT) ... 153
AMERICAN RIVERS (formerly American Rivers Conservation Council) ... 154
AMERICAN SOCIETY FOR ENVIRONMENTAL HISTORY ... 154
AMERICAN WATER RESOURCES ASSOCIATION ... 156
ANGLERS FOR CLEAN WATER ... 157
APPALACHIAN MOUNTAIN CLUB ... 158
APPALACHIAN TRAIL CONFERENCE ... 158
ARCHBOLD BIOLOGICAL STATION ... 159
ARIZONA DEPARTMENT OF ENVIRONMENTAL QUALITY ... 42
ARIZONA GAME AND FISH DEPARTMENT ... 42
ARIZONA GEOLOGICAL SURVEY ... 42
ARKANSAS DEPARTMENT OF PARKS AND TOURISM ... 43
ARKANSAS ENVIRONMENTAL EDUCATION ASSOCIATION ... 160
ARLINGTON OUTDOOR EDUCATION ASSOCIATION, INC. ... 160
ASSOCIATION OF AVIAN VETERINARIANS ... 161
ASSOCIATION OF CONSERVATION ENGINEERS ... 161
ASSOCIATION OF CONSULTING FORESTERS OF AMERICA ... 161
ATLANTIC CENTER FOR THE ENVIRONMENT ... 162, 163
ATLANTIC STATES LEGAL FOUNDATION ... 163
AUDUBON INTERNATIONAL ... 163
AUDUBON NATURALIST SOCIETY OF THE CENTRAL ATLANTIC STATES ... 164
AUDUBON SOCIETY OF MISSOURI ... 164
AUDUBON SOCIETY OF PORTLAND ... 164
AUDUBON SOCIETY OF RHODE ISLAND ... 164
AUDUBON SOCIETY OF WESTERN PENNSYLVANIA ... 165
BAT CONSERVATION INTERNATIONAL ... 165
BERKSHIRE-LITCHFIELD ENVIRONMENTAL COUNCIL, INC. ... 165
BIG BEND NATURAL HISTORY ASSOCIATION ... 166
BILLFISH FOUNDATION ... 166
BOONE AND CROCKETT CLUB ... 167
BOTANICAL CLUB OF WISCONSIN ... 167
BOTANICAL SOCIETY OF WESTERN PENNSYLVANIA ... 167
BOUNTY INFORMATION SERVICE ... 167
BOY SCOUTS OF AMERICA ... 168
BRANDYWINE CONSERVANCY, INC. ... 168
BROOKS BIRD CLUB INC., THE ... 168
BROTHERHOOD OF THE JUNGLE COCK, INC., THE ... 168
CA DEPARTMENT OF EDUCATION, OFFICE OF ENVIRONMENTAL EDUCATION ... 45
CALIFORNIA NATIVE PLANT SOCIETY, THE ... 169
CALIFORNIA TRAPPERS ASSOCIATION ... 170
CAMP FIRE BOYS AND GIRLS ... 170
CAMP FIRE CONSERVATION FUND ... 171
CATSKILL CENTER FOR CONSERVATION AND DEVELOPMENT, INC., THE ... 174
CATSKILL FOREST ASSOCIATION ... 174
CENTER FOR ENVIRONMENTAL EDUCATION ... 174
CENTER FOR ENVIRONMENTAL INFORMATION ... 175
CENTER FOR ENVIRONMENTAL STUDY ... 175
CENTER FOR INTERNATIONAL ENVIRONMENTAL LAW (CIEL) ... 175
CENTER FOR MARINE CONSERVATION ... 176
CENTER FOR PLANT CONSERVATION ... 176
CENTER FOR RESOURCEFUL BUILDING TECHNOLOGY ... 176
CENTER FOR SCIENCE INFORMATION ... 176
CENTRO de INFORMACION, INVESTIGACION y EDUCACION SOCIAL (CIIES) ... 177
CHESAPEAKE BAY FOUNDATION, INC. ... 178
CHESAPEAKE BAY FOUNDATION, INC. (Maryland Office) ... 178
CHESAPEAKE BAY FOUNDATION, INC. (Virginia Office) ... 178
CHICAGO HERPETOLOGICAL SOCIETY ... 179
CHINA REGION LAKES ALLIANCE ... 179
CLEVELAND MUSEUM OF NATURAL HISTORY, THE ... 180
COALITION FOR EDUCATION IN THE OUTDOORS ... 181
COAST ALLIANCE ... 181
COASTAL SOCIETY, THE ... 182
COLORADO DEPARTMENT OF AGRICULTURE ... 50
COLORADO DEPARTMENT OF EDUCATION ... 50
COLORADO DEPARTMENT OF NATURAL RESOURCES ... 50
COLORADO STATE COOPERATIVE EXTENSION ... 51
COLORADO STATE FOREST SERVICE ... 51
COLORADO WILDLIFE HERITAGE FOUNDATION ... 183
COMMITTEE FOR THE NATIONAL INSTITUTE FOR THE ENVIRONMENT (CNIE) ... 183
CONCERN, INC. ... 184
CONNECTICUT AUDUBON SOCIETY, INC. ... 185
CONNECTICUT WATERFOWL ASSOCIATION, INC. ... 186
CONSERVATION DISTRICTS FOUNDATION INC. ... 187
CONSERVATION FUND, THE ... 187
CONSERVATION INTERNATIONAL ... 188
COOPERATIVE EXTENSION SERVICE (NORTH CAROLINA) ... 94
CORNELL LAB OF ORNITHOLOGY ... 189
COUNCIL FOR ENVIRONMENTAL EDUCATION ... 189, 243
COUSTEAU SOCIETY, INC., THE ... 190
DEEP-PORTAGE CONSERVATION RESERVE ... 191
DEFENDERS OF WILDLIFE ... 191
DELAWARE DEPARTMENT OF NATURAL RESOURCES AND ENVIRONMENTAL CONTROL ... 52
DELAWARE NATURE SOCIETY ... 192
DELAWARE SOLID WASTE AUTHORITY ... 53
DELAWARE STATE EXTENSION SERVICE ... 53
DELTA WATERFOWL FOUNDATION ... 192
DELTA WILDLIFE FOUNDATION ... 192
DEPARTMENT OF MARINE RESOURCES ... 71
DEPARTMENT OF PLANNING AND NATURAL RESOURCES ... 115
DEPARTMENT OF WILDLIFE CONSERVATION ... 98
DIVISION OF FORESTRY AND SOIL RESOURCES (GUAM) ... 58
DOGTOOTH GROUP ... 193
EAGLE NATURE FOUNDATION, LTD ... 197
EARTH DAY NEW YORK ... 197
EARTH FORCE ... 197
EARTH FOUNDATION ... 197
EARTH SHARE ... 197
EARTHWATCH INSTITUTE ... 199
ECOLOGICAL SOCIETY OF AMERICA, THE ... 199
ECOLOGY CENTER ... 199
ECOTOURISM SOCIETY, THE ... 199
EDUCATIONAL COMMUNICATIONS, INC. ... 200
ENERGY, MINERALS, AND NATURAL RESOURCES DEPARTMENT ... 88
ENVIRONMENT COUNCIL OF RHODE ISLAND ... 200
ENVIRONMENTAL AIR FORCE ... 201
ENVIRONMENTAL CAREER CENTER ... 201
ENVIRONMENTAL CENTER ... 60
ENVIRONMENTAL CONCERN, INC ... 201
ENVIRONMENTAL EDUCATION ASSOCIATION OF ILLINOIS (Iron Oaks Environmental Learning Center) ... 202
ENVIRONMENTAL EDUCATION ASSOCIATION OF INDIANA ... 202
ENVIRONMENTAL EDUCATION COUNCIL OF OHIO ... 203
ENVIRONMENTAL LAW INSTITUTE, THE ... 203
ENVIRONMENTAL RESOURCE CENTER (ERC) ... 204
ENVIROSOUTH, INC. ... 204
E-P EDUCATION SERVICES, INC. ... 196
EUROPEAN ASSOCIATION FOR AQUATIC MAMMALS ... 204
FAIRFAX AUDUBON SOCIETY ... 205
FEDERAL WILDLIFE OFFICER'S ASSOCIATION ... 205
FEDERATION OF ALBERTA NATURALIST ... 205
FEDERATION OF FLY FISHERS ... 205
FEDERATION OF WESTERN OUTDOOR CLUBS ... 206
FISH AND BOAT COMMISSION ... 103
FISHAMERICA FOUNDATION ... 206
FLORIDA AUDUBON SOCIETY ... 206
FLORIDA CONSERVATION FOUNDATION, INC. ... 207
FLORIDA NATIVE PLANT SOCIETY ... 207
FLORIDA ORNITHOLOGICAL SOCIETY ... 208
FLORIDA PANTHER PROJECT, INC., THE ... 208
FLORIDA SEA GRANT COLLEGE ... 55
FLORIDA SPORTSMEN'S CONSERVATION ASSOCIATION ... 208
FLORIDA STATE COOPERATIVE EXTENSION SERVICE ... 56
FLORIDA TRAIL ASSOCIATION, INC. ... 208
FOREST LANDOWNERS ASSOCIATION, INC. ... 209
FOREST SERVICE EMPLOYEES FOR ENVIRONMENTAL ETHICS (FSEEE) ... 209
FORESTRY COMMISSION (MISSISSIPPI) ... 79
FORESTRY COMMISSION (SOUTH CAROLINA) ... 107
FOSSIL RIM WILDLIFE CENTER ... 210
FOUNDATION FOR NORTH AMERICAN BIG GAME ... 210
FOUNDATION FOR NORTH AMERICAN WILD SHEEP ... 210
FRESHWATER FOUNDATION ... 211
FRIENDS OF THE RIVER ... 212
FUTURE FISHERMAN FOUNDATION ... 213
GALIANO CONSERVANCY ASSOCIATION ... 213
GAME AND FISH DEPARTMENT ... 125
GARDEN CLUB OF AMERICA, THE ... 213
GENERAL FEDERATION OF WOMEN'S CLUBS ... 213
GEORGE MIKSCH SUTTON AVIAN RESEARCH CENTER INC. ... 214
GEORGIA ENVIRONMENTAL COUNCIL, INC. ... 214
GEORGIA SEA GRANT COLLEGE PROGRAM ... 58
GIRL SCOUTS OF THE UNITED STATES OF AMERICA ... 215
GLOBAL ENVIRONMENTAL MANAGEMENT INITIATIVE (GEMI) ... 215
GREAT BEAR FOUNDATION ... 216
GREAT LAKES SPORT FISHING COUNCIL ... 216
GREAT SMOKY MOUNTAINS INSTITUTE AT TREMONT ... 217
GREEN (GLOBAL RIVERS ENVIRONMENTAL EDUCATION NETWORK) 218
GREEN MOUNTAIN CLUB INC., THE ... 218
GREEN SEAL ... 218
GROUNDWATER FOUNDATION, THE ... 219
HAWAII AUDUBON SOCIETY ... 219
HAWAII DEPARTMENT OF HEALTH ... 60
HAWAII NATURE CENTER ... 220
HAWK AND OWL TRUST, THE ... 220
HAWKWATCH INTERNATIONAL INC. ... 221
HEADLANDS INSTITUTE ... 221
HIGH DESERT MUSEUM, THE ... 221
HOLDEN ARBORETUM, THE ... 221
HOOSIER ENVIRONMENTAL COUNCIL ... 222
HUMBOLT FIELD RESEARCH INSTITUTE ... 223
HUMMINGBIRD SOCIETY, THE ... 223
IDAHO DEPARTMENT OF PARKS AND RECREATION ... 61

KEYWORD INDEX - Environmental and Conservation Education

IDAHO FISH AND GAME DEPARTMENT 61
IDAHO FISH AND WILDLIFE FOUNDATION 62
ILLINOIS ASSOCIATION OF CONSERVATION DISTRICTS 224
ILLINOIS DEPARTMENT OF NATURAL RESOURCES 63
ILLINOIS PRAIRIE PATH 225
INDIANA AUDUBON SOCIETY, INC. 226
INSTITUTE FOR EARTH EDUCATION, THE 227
INSTITUTE FOR ECOLOGICAL STUDIES 95
INSTITUTE OF ECOSYSTEM STUDIES 227
INTERFAITH COUNCIL FOR THE PROTECTION OF ANIMALS AND
 NATURE INC. (ICPAN) 227
INTERNATIONAL ASSOCIATION FOR ENVIRONMENTAL HYDROLOGY
 (IAEH) 228
INTERNATIONAL BICYCLE FUND 229
INTERNATIONAL CENTER FOR EARTH CONCERNS 229
INTERNATIONAL CENTER FOR GIBBON STUDIES 229
INTERNATIONAL CENTRE FOR CONSERVATION EDUCATION 229
INTERNATIONAL CRANE FOUNDATION 230
INTERNATIONAL EROSION CONTROL ASSOCIATION (IECA) 230
INTERNATIONAL HUNTER EDUCATION ASSOCIATION 231
INTERNATIONAL MARINE MAMMAL PROJECT, THE 231
INTERNATIONAL OCEANOGRAPHIC FOUNDATION 231
INTERNATIONAL SNOW LEOPARD TRUST 232
INTERNATIONAL SOCIETY FOR ENDANGERED CATS (ISEC) 233
INTERNATIONAL WILDERNESS LEADERSHIP (WILD) FOUNDATION ... 235
INTERNATIONAL WOLF CENTER (Educational Services) 236
IOWA ASSOCIATION OF NATURALISTS 237
IOWA NATIVE PLANT SOCIETY 237
IOWA TRAPPERS ASSOCIATION, INC. 238
ISLAND CONSERVATION EFFORT 239
IZAAK WALTON LEAGUE OF AMERICA ENDOWMENT 239
IZAAK WALTON LEAGUE OF AMERICA, INC., THE 240
J.N. (DING) DARLING FOUNDATION 241
KANSAS ASSOCIATION FOR CONSVERATION AND ENVIRONMENTAL
 EDUCATION 243
KANSAS DEPARTMENT OF AGRICULTURE 66
KANSAS FOREST SERVICE 67
KANSAS GEOLOGICAL SURVEY 67
KANSAS HERPETOLOGICAL SOCIETY 243
KANSAS ORNITHOLOGICAL SOCIETY 244
KANSAS STATE CONSERVATION COMMISSION 67
KEEP AMERICA BEAUTIFUL, INC. 244
KENTUCKY ASSOCIATION FOR ENVIRONMENTAL EDUCATION (KAEE)
 245
KENTUCKY DEPARTMENT OF AGRICULTURE 68
KENTUCKY DEPARTMENT OF FISH AND WILDLIFE RESOURCES 68
KEYSTONE CENTER, THE 245, 246
KIDS FOR SAVING EARTH WORLDWIDE 246
LADY BIRD JOHNSON WILDFLOWER CENTER (formerly the National
 Wildlflower Research Center) 246
LAKE SUPERIOR GREENS 246
LAND BETWEEN THE LAKES ASSOCIATION 247
LAND TRUST ALLIANCE, THE 247
LEAGUE OF WOMEN VOTERS OF THE U.S. 247
LEAGUE TO SAVE LAKE TAHOE 248
LEE COUNTY PARKS AND RECREATION SERVICES 56
LEGACY INTERNATIONAL 248
LIGHTHAWK 248
LOUISIANA DEPARTMENT OF AGRICULTURE 69, 70
LOUISIANA SEA GRANT COLLEGE PROGRAM 70
MAGIC 250
MAINE ASSOCIATION OF CONSERVATION COMMISSIONS (MACC) ... 250
MAINE AUDUBON SOCIETY 250
MAINE ENVIRONMENTAL EDUCATION ASSOCIATION, INC. 250
MAINE SEA GRANT PROGRAM 72
MARIN CONSERVATION LEAGUE 251
MARINE ENVIRONMENTAL RESEARCH INSTITUTE (MERI) 252
MARINE MAMMAL CENTER, THE 252
MARYLAND DEPARTMENT OF AGRICULTURE 73
MARYLAND FORESTS ASSOCIATION 252
MARYLAND ORNITHOLOGICAL SOCIETY, INC. 253
MARYLAND SEA GRANT COLLEGE 74
MASSACHUSETTS ASSOCIATION OF CONSERVATION COMMISSIONS
 (MACC) 253
MASSACHUSETTS COOPERATIVE FISH AND WILDLIFE RESEARCH UNIT
 (USDI) 75
MASSACHUSETTS ENVIRONMENTAL EDUCATION SOCIETY 253
MAX McGRAW WILDLIFE FOUNDATION 254
MICHIGAN AUDUBON SOCIETY 254
MICHIGAN DEPARTMENT OF ENVIRONMENTAL QUALITY 76
MICHIGAN LAND USE INSTITUTE 255
MID-ATLANTIC COUNCIL OF WATERSHED ASSOCIATIONS 256
MINNESOTA GROUND WATER ASSOCIATION 257
MINNESOTA HERPETOLOGICAL SOCIETY (James Ford Bell Museum of
 Natural History) 257
MINNESOTA NATIVE PLANT SOCIETY 257
MINNESOTA PARKS AND TRAILS COUNCIL 257
MINNESOTA WINGS SOCIETY, INC. 257
MISSISSIPPI NATIVE PLANT SOCIETY 258

MISSISSIPPI SOIL AND WATER CONSERVATION COMMISSION 80
MISSISSIPPI STATE EXTENSION SERVICES 80
MISSOURI PRAIRIE FOUNDATION 259
MONTANA DEPARTMENT OF FISH, WILDLIFE, AND PARKS 82
MOTE MARINE LABORATORY 261
MULE DEER FOUNDATION, THE 262
NATIONAL 4-H COUNCIL 262
NATIONAL ARBOR DAY FOUNDATION 262
NATIONAL ASSOCIATION FOR INTERPRETATION 262
NATIONAL ASSOCIATION OF BIOLOGY TEACHERS 262
NATIONAL ASSOCIATION OF CONSERVATION DISTRICTS 263
NATIONAL ASSOCIATION OF SERVICE AND CONSERVATION CORPS
 (NASCC) 264
NATIONAL ASSOCIATION OF STATE PARK DIRECTORS 264
NATIONAL ASSOCIATION OF UNIVERSITY FISHERIES AND WILDLIFE
 PROGRAMS 265
NATIONAL AVIARY IN PITTSBURGH 265
NATIONAL COALITION FOR MARINE CONSERVATION 266
NATIONAL FISH AND WILDLIFE FOUNDATION 267
NATIONAL FOREST FOUNDATION 268
NATIONAL GARDENING ASSOCIATION 268
NATIONAL GEOGRAPHIC SOCIETY 268
NATIONAL GROUND WATER ASSOCIATION, THE 269
NATIONAL HUNTERS ASSOCIATION, INC. 269
NATIONAL PARK FOUNDATION 269
NATIONAL RIFLE ASSOCIATION OF AMERICA 271
NATIONAL SCIENCE TEACHERS ASSOCIATION 271
NATIONAL SHOOTING SPORTS FOUNDATION, INC. 271
NATIONAL SPELEOLOGICAL SOCIETY, INC. 271
NATIONAL TREE TRUST 272
NATIONAL TRUST FOR HISTORIC PRESERVATION 272
NATIONAL WILDLIFE REHABILITATORS ASSOCIATION 275
NATURAL AND SCENIC RIVERS COMMISSION (ARKANSAS) 45
NATURAL SCIENCE FOR YOUTH FOUNDATION 278
NEBRASKA NATURAL RESOURCES COMMISSION 84
NEBRASKA STATE EXTENSION SERVICES 84
NEVIS HISTORICAL AND CONSERVATION SOCIETY 283
NEW ENGLAND WILD FLOWER SOCIETY, INC. 284
NEW HAMPSHIRE DEPARTMENT OF AGRICULTURE, MARKETS, AND
 FOOD 85
NEW HAMPSHIRE FISH AND GAME DEPARTMENT 86
NEW HAMPSHIRE LAKES ASSOCIATION 284
NEW HAMPSHIRE SEA GRANT PROGRAM 86
NEW JERSEY AUDUBON SOCIETY 285
NEW JERSEY CONSERVATION FOUNDATION 285
NEW YORK SEA GRANT 92
NEW YORK STATE COOPERATIVE EXTENSION 93
NEW YORK STATE OFFICE OF PARKS, RECREATION AND HISTORIC
 PRESERVATION 93
NEW YORK TURTLE AND TORTOISE SOCIETY 287
NORTH AMERICAN ASSOCIATION FOR ENVIRONMENTAL EDUCATION
 288
NORTH AMERICAN WOLF SOCIETY 289
NORTH CAROLINA COASTAL FEDERATION, INC. 290
NORTH CAROLINA FORESTRY ASSOCIATION 290
NORTH DAKOTA GAME AND FISH DEPARTMENT 95
NORTH DAKOTA STATE FOREST SERVICE 96
NORTH DAKOTA STATE SOIL CONSERVATION COMMITTEE 96
NORTHEAST SUSTAINABLE ENERGY ASSOCIATION 292
NORTHERN ALASKA ENVIRONMENTAL CENTER 292
NORTHERN VIRGINIA REGIONAL PARK AUTHORITY 117
NORTHWEST INTERPRETIVE ASSOCIATION 293
NOVA SCOTIA FORESTRY ASSOCIATION 293
OHIO ACADEMY OF SCIENCE, THE 294
OHIO AUDUBON COUNCIL, INC. 294
OHIO BIOLOGICAL SURVEY 295
OHIO COOPERATIVE FISH AND WILDLIFE RESEARCH UNIT (USDI) ... 96
OHIO ENVIRONMENTAL COUNCIL, INC. 295
OHIO ENVIRONMENTAL PROTECTION AGENCY 97
OKLAHOMA ACADEMY OF SCIENCE 295
OKLAHOMA STATE CONSERVATION COMMISSION 99
OKLAHOMA STATE EXTENSION SERVICES 99
OKLAHOMA WATER RESOURCES BOARD 99
OLYMPIC WILDLIFE RESCUE 297
OREGON COOPERATIVE FISH AND WILDLIFE RESEARCH UNIT (USDI)
 100
OREGON DEPARTMENT OF ENVIRONMENTAL QUALITY (DEQ) 101
OREGON PARKS AND RECREATION DEPARTMENT 101
OREGON SMALL WOODLANDS ASSOCIATION 298
ORNITHOLOGICAL COUNCIL 299
OUTDOOR WRITERS ASSOCIATION OF AMERICA INC. 299
OZARKS RESOURCE CENTER 300
PACIFIC NORTHWEST TRAIL ASSOCIATION 300
PACIFIC SEABIRD GROUP 300
PACIFIC WHALE FOUNDATION 301
PANOS INSTITUTE, THE 301
PENNSYLVANIA AUDUBON SOCIETY 301
PENNSYLVANIA DEPARTMENT OF AGRICULTURE 104

KEYWORD INDEX - Environmental and Humanitarian Education/Environmental Communication

Entry	Page
PENNSYLVANIA DEPARTMENT OF CONSERVATION AND NATURAL RESOURCES	105
PENNSYLVANIA FORESTRY ASSOCIATION, THE	302
PENNSYLVANIA RECREATION AND PARK SOCIETY, INC.	302
PENNSYLVANIA RESOURCES COUNCIL, INC., (formerly PA Roadside Council)	302
PHEASANTS FOREVER INC.	303
PHYSICIANS FOR SOCIAL RESPONSIBILITY	303
PINE BLUFF COOPERATIVE FISHERY RESEARCH PROJECT	45
POPULATION REFERENCE BUREAU INC.	305
POTOMAC APPALACHIAN TRAIL CLUB	305
PTARMIGANS, THE	306
PUBLIC LANDS FOUNDATION	307
PUERTO RICO ASSOCIATION OF SOIL AND WATER CONSERVATION DISTRICTS	307
PUERTO RICO CONSERVATION FOUNDATION, THE (PRCF	307
PUERTO RICO DEPARTMENT OF NATURAL AND ENVIRONMENTAL RESOURCES	105
PUERTO RICO SEA GRANT PROGRAM	105
PUERTO RICO STATE EXTENSION SERVICES	106
PUGET SOUNDKEEPER ALLIANCE	307
PURPLE MARTIN CONSERVATION ASSOCIATION	307
RACHEL CARSON COUNCIL INC. (formerly Rachel Carson Trust for the Living Environment Inc.)	308
RAINBOW PUSH COALITION	308
RAINFOREST ACTION NETWORK	308
RAINFOREST RELIEF	309
RAINFOREST TRUST INC., THE	309
RAPTOR CENTER, THE	309
RAPTOR EDUCATION FOUNDATION INC.	309
RAPTOR RESEARCH FOUNDATION, INC.	309
RARE CENTER FOR TROPICAL CONSERVATION	310
REEF RELIEF	310
RENEW AMERICA	310
RENEWABLE NATURAL RESOURCES FOUNDATION	310
RESOURCE RENEWAL INSTITUTE, THE	310
RHODE ISLAND STATE ASSOCIATION OF CONSERVATION DISTRICTS	311
RHODE ISLAND WILD PLANT SOCIETY	311
RINCON INSTITUTE, THE	312
TEXAS STATE SOIL AND WATER CONSERVATION BOARD	112
TEXAS WATER DEVELOPMENT BOARD	112
THE CROSBY ABORETUM, Mississippi State University	331
THORNE ECOLOGICAL INSTITUTE	331
THREE CIRCLES CENTER FOR MULTICULTURAL ENVIRONMENTAL EDUCATION	332
THRESHOLD INC.	332
TOGETHER FOUNDATION, THE	332
TREAD LIGHTLY! INC.	332
TREE PEOPLE	332
TRI-STATE BIRD RESCUE AND RESEARCH, INC.	333
TROUT UNLIMITED	333, 334, 335, 336, 337
TROUT UNLIMITED, PENNSYLVANIA COUNCIL	336
TRUST FOR WILDLIFE, INC.	338
TUG HILL TOMORROW, INC.	338
TURTLE CREEK WATERSHED ASSOCIATION, INC.	338
UNION OF CONCERNED SCIENTISTS	339
UNITED STATES COMMITTEE FOR THE UNITED NATIONS ENVIRONMENT PROGRAMME THE (U.S. and UNEP)	339
UNIVERSITY OF NEW HAMPSHIRE COOPERATIVE EXTENSION	86
UTAH B.A.S.S. CHAPTER FEDERATION	340
UTAH NATURE STUDY SOCIETY	340
UTAH STATE SOIL CONSERVATION COMMISSION	114
VERMONT AUDUBON COUNCIL	341
VERMONT B.A.S.S. CHAPTER FEDERATION	341
VERMONT DEPARTMENT OF AGRICULTURE, FOOD, AND MARKETS	115
VERMONT INSTITUTE OF NATURAL SCIENCE	341
VERMONT LAND TRUST	341
VERMONT NATURAL RESOURCES COUNCIL	341
VIRGIN ISLANDS CONSERVATION SOCIETY, INC.	342
VIRGINIA FORESTRY ASSOCIATION	342
VIRGINIA MUSEUM OF NATURAL HISTORY	118
VIRGINIA SEA GRANT PROGRAM	119
WASHINGTON B.A.S.S. CHAPTER FEDERATION	343
WASHINGTON FARM FORESTRY ASSOCIATION	344
WASHINGTON FOUNDATION FOR THE ENVIRONMENT	344
WASHINGTON STATE CONSERVATION COMMISSION	121
WASHINGTON STATE EXTENSION SERVICES	121
WASHINGTON STATE OFFICE OF ENVIRONMENTAL EDUCATION	122
WASHINGTON TOXICS COALITION	344
WASHINGTON TRAILS ASSOCIATION	344
WASHINGTON WILDLIFE FEDERATION	345
WATER ENVIRONMENT FEDERATION	345
WATER RESOURCES ASSOCIATION OF THE DELAWARE RIVER BASIN	345
WEST MICHIGAN ENVIRONMENTAL ACTION COUNCIL	346
WESTERN REGIONAL ENVIRONMENTAL EDUCATION COUNCIL	347
WHITETAILS UNLIMITED INC.	348
RIVER NETWORK	312
RIVERS COUNCIL OF WASHINGTON (formerly Northwest Rivers Council)	313
ROCKY MOUNTAIN ELK FOUNDATION	313
ROGER TORY PETERSON INSTITUTE	314
RUFFED GROUSE SOCIETY, THE	314
SAFARI CLUB INTERNATIONAL	314
SANIBEL-CAPTIVA CONSERVATION FOUNDATION, INC.	315
SAVANNAH RIVER ECOLOGY LABORATORY	107
SAVE SAN FRANCISCO BAY ASSOCIATION	315
SAVE THE DUNES COUNCIL	316
SAVE THE MANATEE CLUB	316
SAVE THE SOUND, INC.	316
SCENIC AMERICA	317
SEA SHEPHERD CONSERVATION SOCIETY	318
SIERRA CLUB FOUNDATION, THE	319
SOCIETY FOR CONSERVATION BIOLOGY	321
SOCIETY FOR ECOLOGICAL RESTORATION	321
SOCIETY FOR THE PROTECTION OF NEW HAMPSHIRE FORESTS	322
SOCIETY OF AMERICAN FORESTERS	298, 322, 344
SOCIETY OF WETLAND SCIENTISTS	322
SOIL AND WATER CONSERVATION SOCIETY (formerly Soil Conservation Society of America)	323
SOUND EXPERIENCE	323
SOUTH DAKOTA STATE EXTENSION SERVICES	109
SOUTHEASTERN COOPERATIVE WILDLIFE DISEASE STUDY	325
SOUTHWEST FLORIDA WATER MANAGEMENT DISTRICT (SWFMD)	56
STATE SOIL CONSERVATION COMMISSION (IDAHO)	62
STEAMBOATERS, THE	327
STOP	328
STRIPERS UNLIMITED INC.	328
STUDENT CONSERVATION ASSOCIATION, INC.	328
STUDENT PUGWASH USA	328
SUNCOAST SEABIRD SANCTUARY INC.	328
TALL TIMBERS RESEARCH INC.	329
TALLAHASSEE MUSEUM OF HISTORY AND NATURAL SCIENCE	329
TENNESSEE DEPARTMENT OF AGRICULTURE	110
TEXAS B.A.S.S. CHAPTER FEDERATION	330
TEXAS FORESTRY ASSOCIATION	331
TEXAS SEA GRANT PROGRAM	112
WILD CANINE SURVIVAL AND RESEARCH CENTER AND WOLF SANCTUARY	348
WILDERNESS EDUCATION ASSOCIATION	349
WILDFOWL TRUST OF NORTH AMERICA INC., THE	350
WILDLIFE ACTION, INC.	350
WILDLIFE CENTER OF VIRGINIA, THE	350
WILDLIFE DAMAGE REVIEW (WDR)	351
WILDLIFE EDUCATION PROGRAM AND DESIGN	351
WILDLIFE HABITAT COUNCIL	352
WILDLIFE INFORMATION CENTER, INC.	352
WILDLIFE PRESERVATION TRUST INTERNATIONAL, INC.	353
WILDLIFE SOCIETY, PENNSYLVANIA CHAPTER	356
WILDLIFE WAYSTATION	358
WINDSTAR FOUNDATION, THE	359
WISCONSIN ASSOCIATION FOR ENVIRONMENTAL EDUCATION, INC.	359
WISCONSIN CONSERVATION CORPS	123
WISCONSIN DEPARTMENT OF AGRICULTURE	123
WISCONSIN DEPARTMENT OF PUBLIC INSTRUCTION	124
WISCONSIN ENVIRONMENTAL EDUCATION BOARD (WEEB)	124
WISCONSIN PARK AND RECREATION ASSOCIATION	360
WISCONSIN SOCIETY FOR ORNITHOLOGY, INC., THE	360
WOLF EDUCATION AND RESEARCH CENTER	360
WOLF FUND, THE	360
WORLD CONSERVATION MONITORING CENTRE	361
WORLD FORESTRY CENTER	362
WORLD NATURE ASSOCIATION INC.	362
WORLD WOMEN IN THE DEFENSE OF THE ENVIRONMENT	363
WYOMING OUTDOOR COUNCIL	364
WYOMING STATE EXTENSION SERVICES	126
YELLOWSTONE GRIZZLY FOUNDATION (YGF)	364
YMCA EARTH SERVICE CORPS	365
YOUNG ENTOMOLOGISTS' SOCIETY INC.	365
ZERO POPULATION GROWTH INC.	365

Environmental and Humanitarian Education

Entry	Page
JANE GOODALL INSTITUTE, THE	242

Environmental Cleanup

Entry	Page
OREGON DEPARTMENT OF ENVIRONMENTAL QUALITY (DEQ)	101

Environmental Communication

Entry	Page
ENVIRONMENTAL MEDIA ASSOCIATION	204

Environmental Ethics

CALIFORNIA TRAPPERS ASSOCIATION	170
CENTER FOR ENVIRONMENTAL PHILOSOPHY	175
COALITION FOR EDUCATION IN THE OUTDOORS	181
COLORADO DEPARTMENT OF EDUCATION	50
NATIONAL WHISTLEBLOWER CENTER	273
NEWFOUNDLAND LABRADOR WILDLIFE FEDERATION	287
PUBLIC EMPLOYEES FOR ENVIRONMENTAL RESPONSIBILITY (PEER)	306, 307
SCIENTISTS CENTER FOR ANIMAL WELFARE	318
TEXAS SEA GRANT PROGRAM	112
UNITED NATIONS ENVIRONMENT PROGRAMME	339
WILD ONES - NATURAL LANDSCAPERS, LTD	349
WILDLIFE ACTION, INC.	350

Environmental Health

ALASKA DEPARTMENT OF ENVIRONMENTAL CONSERVATION	40
COLORADO ENVIRONMENTAL COALITION	182
NATIONAL ENVIRONMENTAL HEALTH ASSOCIATION	267

Environmental Justice

ALASKA CONSERVATION ALLIANCE	136
ALASKA CONSERVATION VOICE	137
AMERICAN PIE (PUBLIC INFORMATION ON THE ENVIRONMENT)	153
ATLANTIC STATES LEGAL FOUNDATION	163
CENTRO de INFORMACION, INVESTIGACION y EDUCACION SOCIAL (CIIES)	177
CHESAPEAKE BAY FOUNDATION, INC. (Maryland Office)	178
COMMUNITIES FOR A BETTER ENVIRONMENT	184
CONSERVATION FEDERATION OF MARYLAND/For A Rural Maryland (F.A.R.M.)	187
ECOLOGY CENTER	199
COOK INLET KEEPER	189
EARTHJUSTICE LEGAL DEFENSE FUND (formerly Sierra Club Legal Defense Fund, Inc.)	198
EARTHTRUST	199
ENDANGERED SPECIES COALITION	200
ENVIRONMENTAL CENTER	60
ENVIRONMENTAL DEFENSE CENTER, INC.	201
ENVIRONMENTAL LAW ALLIANCE WORLDWIDE (E-LAW)	203
ENVIRONMENTAL LAW INSTITUTE, THE	203
ENVIRONMENTAL LEAGUE OF MASSACHUSETTS (ELM)	203
ENVIRONMENTAL QUALITY COUNCIL	82
FISH AND WILDLIFE DIVISION/DEPARTMENT OF STATE POLICE	100
FOREST HISTORY SOCIETY, INC.	209
GOVERNOR OF SOUTH CAROLINA, JIM HODGES	107
HAWAII DEPARTMENT OF HEALTH	60
ILLINOIS ENVIRONMENTAL PROTECTION AGENCY	63
INTERNATIONAL ASSOCIATION OF NATURAL RESOURCE PILOTS	228
INTERNATIONAL COUNCIL OF ENVIRONMENTAL LAW	229
INTERNATIONAL MARINE MAMMAL PROJECT, THE	231
INTERNATIONAL MARITIME ORGANIZATION	231
KENTUCKY RESOURCES COUNCIL	245
LAND TRUST ALLIANCE, THE	247
LEGAL ENVIRONMENTAL ASSISTANCE FOUNDATION INC. (LEAF)	248
MANASOTA-88	251
MINERAL POLICY CENTER	256
MOUNTAIN LION FOUNDATION	261
NATIONAL FARMERS UNION	267
NATIONAL GRANGE, THE	269
NATIONAL WHISTLEBLOWER CENTER	273
NATURE SASKATCHEWAN	282
NEW HAMPSHIRE ASSOCIATION OF CONSERVATION COMMISSIONS	284
OKLAHOMA STATE BOARD OF AGRICULTURE	98
PINE BLUFF COOPERATIVE FISHERY RESEARCH PROJECT	45
PUGET SOUNDKEEPER ALLIANCE	307
SIERRA CLUB FOUNDATION, THE	319
SOCIETY OF AMERICAN FORESTERS	298, 322, 344
SOUTH CAROLINA DEPARTMENT OF HEALTH AND ENVIRONMENTAL CONTROL	108
SOUTHERN ENVIRONMENTAL LAW CENTER	325, 326
STEAMBOATERS, THE	327
TEXAS SEA GRANT PROGRAM	112
TRUSTEES FOR ALASKA	338
UNITED NATIONS ENVIRONMENT PROGRAMME	339
WASHINGTON FARM FORESTRY ASSOCIATION	344
WESTERN ENVIRONMENTAL LAW CENTER	346
WISCONSIN ASSOCIATION FOR ENVIRONMENTAL EDUCATION, INC.	359
WISCONSIN SOCIETY FOR ORNITHOLOGY, INC., THE	360
FEDERAL WILDLIFE OFFICER'S ASSOCIATION	205
GREAT LAKES UNITED	217
GREEN PARTY USA	218
LEGAL ENVIRONMENTAL ASSISTANCE FOUNDATION INC. (LEAF)	248
NATIONAL WHISTLEBLOWER CENTER	273
NEW HAMPSHIRE DEPARTMENT OF AGRICULTURE, MARKETS, AND FOOD	85
NEW YORK PUBLIC INTEREST RESEARCH GROUP (NYPIRG)	287
NORTH DAKOTA DEPARTMENT OF HEALTH	95
OHIO ENVIRONMENTAL COUNCIL, INC.	295
OREGON ENVIRONMENTAL COUNCIL	298
RIVER NETWORK	312
SOUTHWEST RESEARCH AND INFORMATION CENTER	326
STUDENT ENVIRONMENTAL ACTION COALITION (SEAC)	328
TENNESSEE ENVIRONMENTAL COUNCIL	330
URBAN HABITAT PROGRAM	340

Environmental Law

1000 FRIENDS OF FLORIDA	133
ADIRONDACK MOUNTAIN CLUB, INC., THE	134
AIR AND WASTE MANAGEMENT ASSOCIATION	135
AMERICAN CONSERVATION ASSOCIATION, INC.	141, 142
AMERICAN HORSE PROTECTION ASSOCIATION	151
AMERICAN PLANNING ASSOCIATION	154
AMERICAN SOCIETY FOR ENVIRONMENTAL HISTORY	154
ASSOCIATION OF MIDWEST FISH AND GAME LAW ENFORCEMENT OFFICERS	162
ATLANTIC STATES LEGAL FOUNDATION	163
BIODIVERSITY LEGAL FOUNDATION	166
CENTER FOR INTERNATIONAL ENVIRONMENTAL LAW (CIEL)	175
CIRCUMPOLAR CONSERVATION UNION	179
COMMUNITIES FOR A BETTER ENVIRONMENT	184
COMMUNITY RIGHTS COUNSEL	184
CONSERVATION AND RESEARCH FOUNDATION, INC., THE	186
CONSERVATION LAW FOUNDATION, INC. (CLF)	188

Environmental Legislation

VIRGINIA CONSERVATION NETWORK	342

Environmental Literacy

NORTH AMERICAN ASSOCIATION FOR ENVIRONMENTAL EDUCATION	288

Environmental Living

PENNSYLVANIA RESOURCES COUNCIL, INC., (formerly PA Roadside Council)	302

Environmental Planning

1000 FRIENDS OF FLORIDA	133
ADOPT-A-STREAM FOUNDATION, THE	134
ALASKA DEPARTMENT OF ENVIRONMENTAL CONSERVATION	40
AMERICAN BIRD CONSERVANCY	140
AMERICAN PLANNING ASSOCIATION	154
AUDUBON INTERNATIONAL	163
CALIFORNIA TRAPPERS ASSOCIATION	170
CENTER FOR WATERSHED PROTECTION	177
CHINA REGION LAKES ALLIANCE	179
COLUMBIA RIVER GORGE COMMISSION	119
COMMUNITY RIGHTS COUNSEL	184
COUNCIL ON ENVIRONMENTAL QUALITY (CONNECTICUT)	52
DELAWARE SOLID WASTE AUTHORITY	53
DEPARTMENT OF TRANSPORTATION (OREGON)	100
EARTHSCAN	198
FAIRFAX AUDUBON SOCIETY	205
FOSSIL FUELS POLICY ACTION INSTITUTE/ALLIANCE FOR A PAVING MORATORIUM	210
FRIENDS OF DISCOVERY PARK	211
GALIANO CONSERVANCY ASSOCIATION	213
INDIANA STATE GEOLOGICAL SURVEY	65
INTERNATIONAL ASSOCIATION OF NATURAL RESOURCE PILOTS	228
INTERNATIONAL SOCIETY FOR ECOLOGICAL ECONOMICS	233
KENTUCKY-TENNESSEE SOCIETY OF AMERICAN FORESTERS	245
LEGACY INTERNATIONAL	248
LIGHTHAWK	248
MAINE ASSOCIATION OF CONSERVATION COMMISSIONS (MACC)	250
MINNESOTA ENVIRONMENTAL QUALITY BOARD	78
MINNESOTA GROUND WATER ASSOCIATION	257

KEYWORD INDEX - Environmental Preservation/Environmental Protection

NATIONAL ASSOCIATION OF ENVIRONMENTAL PROFESSIONALS, THE (National Office) ... 263
NATIVE AMERICAN FISH AND WILDLIFE SOCIETY (NAFWS) ... 276
NATURAL AND SCENIC RIVERS COMMISSION (ARKANSAS) ... 45
NATURAL LAND INSTITUTE ... 277
NEVADA NATURAL HERITAGE PROGRAM ... 85
NEW HAMPSHIRE LAKES ASSOCIATION ... 284
NEW JERSEY CONSERVATION FOUNDATION ... 285
OFFICE OF ENERGY EFFICIENCY AND ENVIRONMENT ... 93
RESOURCE RENEWAL INSTITUTE, THE ... 310
SOUTH CAROLINA DEPARTMENT OF HEALTH AND ENVIRONMENTAL CONTROL ... 108
SOUTHWEST FLORIDA WATER MANAGEMENT DISTRICT (SWFWMD) . 56
STATE OF IDAHO, DIVISION OF ENVIRONMENTAL QUALITY ... 62
TEXAS SEA GRANT PROGRAM ... 112
TOGETHER FOUNDATION, THE ... 332
TREES FOR THE FUTURE, INC. ... 333
TUG HILL COMMISSION ... 94
UNITED NATIONS ENVIRONMENT PROGRAMME ... 339

Environmental Preservation

1000 FRIENDS OF FLORIDA ... 133
ADIRONDACK MOUNTAIN CLUB, INC., THE ... 134
ADOPT-A-STREAM FOUNDATION, THE ... 134
AGENCY OF NATURAL RESOURCES ... 114
ALBERTA WILDERNESS ASSOCIATION ... 137
AMERICAN BASS ASSOCIATION OF MARYLAND, THE ... 140
AMERICAN FEDERATION OF MINERALOGICAL SOCIETIES ... 142
AMERICAN FISHERIES SOCIETY, BONNEVILLE CHAPTER ... 145
AMERICAN FISHERIES SOCIETY, VIRGINIA TECH CHAPTER ... 149
AMERICAN FISHERIES SOCIETY, WISCONSIN CHAPTER ... 149
ARCHBOLD BIOLOGICAL STATION ... 159
ARKANSAS DEPARTMENT OF PARKS AND TOURISM ... 43
ASSOCIATION OF NEW JERSEY ENVIRONMENTAL COMMISSIONS ... 162
AUDUBON COUNCIL OF ILLINOIS ... 163
AUDUBON SOCIETY OF RHODE ISLAND ... 164
BERKSHIRE-LITCHFIELD ENVIRONMENTAL COUNCIL, INC. ... 165
BIRDLIFE INTERNATIONAL ... 166
CALIFORNIA NATIVE PLANT SOCIETY, THE ... 169
CALIFORNIA TRAPPERS ASSOCIATION ... 170
CALIFORNIA WATERFOWL ASSOCIATION ... 170
CALIFORNIANS FOR POPULATION STABILIZATION (CAPS) ... 170
CAVE RESEARCH FOUNDATION ... 174
CENTER FOR PLANT CONSERVATION ... 176
CENTER FOR RESOURCEFUL BUILDING TECHNOLOGY ... 176
CHARLES A. AND ANNE MORROW LINDBERGH FOUNDATION, THE ... 178
CONFEDERATED SALISH AND KOOTENAI TRIBES ... 185
DEFENDERS OF WILDLIFE ... 191
DELAWARE GREENWAYS, INC. ... 192
DEPARTMENT OF ENVIRONMENTAL PROTECTION (PENNSYLVANIA) 102
DRAGONFLY SOCIETY OF THE AMERICAS, THE ... 193
EARTH FOUNDATION ... 197
EARTH SHARE ... 197
ENERGY, MINERALS, AND NATURAL RESOURCES DEPARTMENT ... 88
ENVIRONMENTAL AIR FORCE ... 201
EUROPEAN CETACEAN SOCIETY ... 204
FAIRFAX AUDUBON SOCIETY ... 205
FEDERATION OF FLY FISHERS ... 205
FLORIDA EXOTIC PEST PLANT COUNCIL ... 207
FOREST TRUST ... 209
FOSSIL FUELS POLICY ACTION INSTITUTE/ALLIANCE FOR A PAVING MORATORIUM ... 210
GENERAL FEDERATION OF WOMEN'S CLUBS ... 213
GEORGE MIKSCH SUTTON AVIAN RESEARCH CENTER INC. ... 214
GEORGE WRIGHT SOCIETY, THE ... 214
GEORGIA COOPERATIVE FISH AND WILDLIFE RESEARCH UNIT (USDI) ... 57
GREEN (GLOBAL RIVERS ENVIRONMENTAL EDUCATION NETWORK) 218
HAWAII AUDUBON SOCIETY ... 219
HOOD CANAL LAND TRUST ... 222
IDAHO CONSERVATION LEAGUE ... 223
IDAHO DEPARTMENT OF PARKS AND RECREATION ... 61
ILLINOIS ENVIRONMENTAL PROTECTION AGENCY ... 63
ILLINOIS NATIVE PLANT SOCIETY ... 225
ILLINOIS NATURAL HERITAGE FOUNDATION ... 225
ILLINOIS PRAIRIE PATH ... 225
INSTITUTE FOR EARTH EDUCATION, THE ... 227
INTERAGENCY COMMITTEE FOR OUTDOOR RECREATION (IAC) ... 120
INTERNATIONAL SOCIETY FOR THE PRESERVATION OF THE TROPICAL RAINFOREST, THE ... 233
IOWA AUDUBON COUNCIL ... 237
IOWA NATIVE PLANT SOCIETY ... 237
IOWA TRAILS COUNCIL ... 238
KEEP AMERICA BEAUTIFUL, INC. ... 244
KEEP FLORIDA BEAUTIFUL, INC. ... 244
KIDS FOR SAVING EARTH WORLDWIDE ... 246
LAND TRUST ALLIANCE, THE ... 247
LEAGUE TO SAVE LAKE TAHOE ... 248
LEE COUNTY PARKS AND RECREATION SERVICES ... 56
LIGHTHAWK ... 248
MARIN CONSERVATION LEAGUE ... 251
MASSACHUSETTS ASSOCIATION OF CONSERVATION COMMISSIONS (MACC) ... 253
MAX McGRAW WILDLIFE FOUNDATION ... 254
MINNESOTA GROUND WATER ASSOCIATION ... 257
MINNESOTA NATIVE PLANT SOCIETY ... 257
MINNESOTA PARKS AND TRAILS COUNCIL ... 257
MISSOURI DEPARTMENT OF NATURAL RESOURCES ... 81
MISSOURI NATIVE PLANT SOCIETY ... 259
NATIONAL WILDLIFE REFUGE ASSOCIATION ... 275
NATURAL HERITAGE COMMISSION (ARKANSAS) ... 45
NATURAL LAND INSTITUTE ... 277
NATURE CONSERVANCY OF COLORADO, THE ... 279
NATURE CONSERVANCY, THE, IOWA CHAPTER ... 280
NATURE PRESERVES COMMISSION ... 63, 69
NEW HAMPSHIRE ASSOCIATION OF CONSERVATION COMMISSIONS ... 284
NEW JERSEY PINELANDS COMMISSION ... 88
NEW YORK STATE OFFICE OF PARKS, RECREATION AND HISTORIC PRESERVATION ... 93
NORTH CAROLINA RECREATION AND PARK SOCIETY, INC. ... 291
NORTH CASCADES CONSERVATION COUNCIL ... 291
NORTH DAKOTA GEOLOGICAL SURVEY ... 96
NORTHERN VIRGINIA REGIONAL PARK AUTHORITY ... 117
OLYMPIC PARK INSTITUTE ... 297
OPENLANDS PROJECT ... 297
OREGON NATURAL RESOURCES COUNCIL ... 298
OZARKS RESOURCE CENTER ... 300
PARKS AND RECREATION DEPARTMENT (NORTH DAKOTA) ... 96
PIEDMONT ENVIRONMENTAL COUNCIL ... 303
PRAIRIE CLUB, THE ... 305
PTARMIGANS, THE ... 306
RAPTOR EDUCATION FOUNDATION INC. ... 309
RARE CENTER FOR TROPICAL CONSERVATION ... 310
RHODE ISLAND WILD PLANT SOCIETY ... 311
SAVE THE SOUND, INC. ... 316
SCENIC HUDSON, INC. ... 317
SOUTH CAROLINA DEPARTMENT OF HEALTH AND ENVIRONMENTAL CONTROL ... 108
TEXAS SEA GRANT PROGRAM ... 112
TREAD LIGHTLY! INC. ... 332
TREES FOR THE FUTURE, INC. ... 333
VERMONT DEPARTMENT OF AGRICULTURE, FOOD, AND MARKETS . 115
WASHINGTON B.A.S.S. CHAPTER FEDERATION ... 343
WASHINGTON FOUNDATION FOR THE ENVIRONMENT ... 344
WASHINGTON WILDLIFE FEDERATION ... 345
WILD ONES - NATURAL LANDSCAPERS, LTD ... 349
WILDERNESS EDUCATION ASSOCIATION ... 349
WILDLIFE ACTION, INC. ... 350
WISCONSIN ASSOCIATION OF LAKES (WAL) ... 359
WISCONSIN DEPARTMENT OF AGRICULTURE (Land and Water Resources Bureau) ... 123
WISCONSIN PARK AND RECREATION ASSOCIATION ... 360
YMCA EARTH SERVICE CORPS ... 365

Environmental Protection

ADIRONDACK MOUNTAIN CLUB, INC., THE ... 134
ADOPT-A-STREAM FOUNDATION, THE ... 134
ALASKA CONSERVATION ALLIANCE ... 136
ALASKA CONSERVATION VOICE ... 137
ALASKA DEPARTMENT OF ENVIRONMENTAL CONSERVATION ... 40
ALLIANCE FOR THE CHESAPEAKE BAY ... 138
AMERICAN FISHERIES SOCIETY, PENNSYLVANIA CHAPTER ... 148
ANACOSTIA WATERSHED SOCIETY ... 157
ARIZONA DEPARTMENT OF ENVIRONMENTAL QUALITY ... 42
ARLINGTON OUTDOOR EDUCATION ASSOCIATION, INC. ... 160
ASSOCIATION OF NEW JERSEY ENVIRONMENTAL COMMISSIONS ... 162
AUDUBON SOCIETY OF PORTLAND ... 164
BRANDYWINE CONSERVANCY, INC. ... 168
CALIFORNIA TRAPPERS ASSOCIATION ... 170
CETACEAN SOCIETY INTERNATIONAL ... 177
CHESAPEAKE BAY FOUNDATION, INC. ... 178
CHESAPEAKE BAY FOUNDATION, INC. (Virginia Office) ... 178
COALITION FOR CLEAN AIR ... 181
CONNECTICUT AUDUBON SOCIETY, INC. ... 185
CONNECTICUT BOTANICAL SOCIETY ... 185
CONNECTICUT RIVER WATERSHED COUNCIL INC. ... 186
COUNCIL ON ENVIRONMENTAL QUALITY (CONNECTICUT) ... 52
DEFENDERS OF WILDLIFE ... 191
DELAWARE STATE EXTENSION SERVICE ... 53
DEPARTMENT OF ENVIRONMENT AND NATURAL RESOURCES (SOUTH DAKOTA) ... 109
DEPARTMENT OF ENVIRONMENTAL PROTECTION (MAINE0 ... 71
DEPARTMENT OF ENVIRONMENTAL QUALITY (ARKANSAS) ... 44

DEPARTMENT OF LAND AND NATURAL RESOURCES 59, 60
DEPARTMENT OF THE ENVIRONMENT 72
DESERT TORTOISE COUNCIL 193
FAIRFAX AUDUBON SOCIETY 205
FEDERAL WILDLIFE OFFICER'S ASSOCIATION 205
FLORIDA PUBLIC INTEREST RESEARCH GROUP (Florida PIRG) 208
FRIENDS OF THE EARTH 211
GEORGE MIKSCH SUTTON AVIAN RESEARCH CENTER INC. 214
GEORGE WRIGHT SOCIETY, THE 214
GEORGIA CONSERVANCY, INC., THE 214
GREAT LAKES UNITED 217
GREEN (GLOBAL RIVERS ENVIRONMENTAL EDUCATION NETWORK) 218
H. JOHN HEINZ III CENTER FOR SCIENCE, ECONOMICS, AND THE
  ENVIRONMENT 219
ILLINOIS NATIVE PLANT SOCIETY 225
INTERNATIONAL CENTER FOR EARTH CONCERNS 229
IOWA AUDUBON COUNCIL 237
IZAAK WALTON LEAGUE OF AMERICA, INC., THE 240
KENTUCKY RESOURCES COUNCIL 245
KIDS FOR SAVING EARTH WORLDWIDE 246
LEAGUE OF WOMEN VOTERS OF IOWA 247
LEE COUNTY PARKS AND RECREATION SERVICES 56
LEGAL ENVIRONMENTAL ASSISTANCE FOUNDATION INC. (LEAF) 248
LIGHTHAWK 248
MAINE ASSOCIATION OF CONSERVATION COMMISSIONS (MACC) 250
MASSACHUSETTS AUDUBON SOCIETY, INC. 253
MICHIGAN DEPARTMENT OF ENVIRONMENTAL QUALITY 76
MICHIGAN LAND USE INSTITUTE 255
MISSOURI NATIVE PLANT SOCIETY 259
MONTANA LAND RELIANCE 260
NATIONAL ASSOCIATION OF STATE DEPARTMENTS OF AGRICULTURE
  264
NATIONAL WILDLIFE REFUGE ASSOCIATION 275
NATIVE PLANT SOCIETY OF OREGON 276
NATURAL LAND INSTITUTE 277
NATURE CONSERVANCY OF COLORADO, THE 279
NEW HAMPSHIRE LAKES ASSOCIATION 284
NORTH CASCADES CONSERVATION COUNCIL 291
NORTHCOAST ENVIRONMENTAL CENTER 291
NORTHWEST RESOURCE INFORMATION CENTER 293
OKLAHOMA DEPARTMENT OF ENVIRONMENTAL QUALITY 98
OKLAHOMA NATIVE PLANT SOCIETY 296
OLYMPIC PARK INSTITUTE 297
OREGON NATURAL RESOURCES COUNCIL 298
PINE BLUFF COOPERATIVE FISHERY RESEARCH PROJECT 45
PREDATOR PROJECT 306
PUBLIC EMPLOYEES FOR ENVIRONMENTAL RESPONSIBILITY (PEER)
  .... 306, 307
RAINFOREST TRUST INC., THE 309
RAPTOR EDUCATION FOUNDATION INC. 309
RESOURCES FOR THE FUTURE 310
RIVER NETWORK 312
SOIL AND WATER CONSERVATION SOCIETY (formerly Soil Conservation
  Society of America) 323
ST. REGIS MOHAWK TRIBE 327
STATE OF IDAHO, DIVISION OF ENVIRONMENTAL QUALITY 62
TENNESSEE ENVIRONMENTAL COUNCIL 330
TURTLE CREEK WATERSHED ASSOCIATION, INC. 338
U.S. PUBLIC INTEREST RESEARCH GROUP 339
UNITED NATIONS ENVIRONMENT PROGRAMME 339
WASHINGTON FOUNDATION FOR THE ENVIRONMENT 344
WHALE AND DOLPHIN CONSERVATION SOCIETY 348
WHITE CLAY WATERSHED ASSOCIATION 348
WILDERNESS LAND TRUST, THE (Colorado Office) 349
WISCONSIN ASSOCIATION OF LAKES (WAL) 359
WISCONSIN PARK AND RECREATION ASSOCIATION 360
WORLD PAL (WORLD POPULATION ALLOCATION LIMITED INC.) 362

Erosion Control

MISSISSIPPI SOIL AND WATER CONSERVATION COMMISSION 80

Estuaries

AMERICAN OCEANS CAMPAIGN 153
NORTH CAROLINA COASTAL FEDERATION, INC. 290
NORTH CAROLINA SEA GRANT PROGRAM 95

Falconry

SOCIETY FOR THE PRESERVATION OF BIRDS OF PREY 322

Family Planning

AVSC INTERNATIONAL 165
PLANNED PARENTHOOD FEDERATION OF AMERICA INC. 304

Family Recreation

AMERICAN ASSOCIATION FOR LEISURE AND RECREATION (AALR) .. 139

Feedlots and Pollution

MINNESOTA CENTER FOR ENVIRONMENTAL ADVOCACY (MCEA) 256

Fieldwork

THORNE ECOLOGICAL INSTITUTE 331

Fire Prevention

DIVISION OF FORESTRY AND SOIL RESOURCES (GUAM) 58

Fish Wildlife Management

COLORADO COOPERATIVE FISH AND WILDLIFE RESEARCH UNIT
  (USDI) 50
WESTERN PACIFIC REGIONAL FISHERY MANAGEMENT COUNCIL 347

Fisheries

A.B. ENVIRONMENTAL EDUCATION CENTER 133
ADOPT-A-STREAM FOUNDATION, THE 134
AGENCY OF NATURAL RESOURCES 114
ALABAMA COOPERATIVE EXTENSION SYSTEM 39
ALABAMA COOPERATIVE FISH AND WILDLIFE RESEARCH UNIT (USDI)
  39
ALASKA CONSERVATION FOUNDATION 136
ALASKA COOPERATIVE FISH AND WILDLIFE RESEARCH UNIT 40
ALASKA DEPARTMENT OF FISH AND GAME 40
ALASKA SEA GRANT COLLEGE PROGRAM 41
ALLIANCE FOR THE CHESAPEAKE BAY 138
AMERICAN BASS ASSOCIATION OF MARYLAND, THE 140
AMERICAN FISHERIES SOCIETY 142, 144, 145, 146, 147, 148, 149, 283
AMERICAN FISHERIES SOCIETY, ALABAMA CHAPTER 144
AMERICAN FISHERIES SOCIETY, ALASKA CHAPTER 144
AMERICAN FISHERIES SOCIETY, ARIZONA-NEW MEXICO CHAPTER . 144
AMERICAN FISHERIES SOCIETY, ARKANSAS CHAPTER 144
AMERICAN FISHERIES SOCIETY, AUBURN UNIVERSITY STUDENT
  CHAPTER 145
AMERICAN FISHERIES SOCIETY, CALIFORNIA-NEVADA CHAPTER 145
AMERICAN FISHERIES SOCIETY, COLLEGE OF ENVIRONMENTAL
  SCIENCE AND FORESTRY CHAPTER 145
AMERICAN FISHERIES SOCIETY, COLORADO and WYOMING CHAPTER
  145
AMERICAN FISHERIES SOCIETY, FLORIDA CHAPTER 145
AMERICAN FISHERIES SOCIETY, GEORGIA CHAPTER 145
AMERICAN FISHERIES SOCIETY, HAWAII CHAPTER 146
AMERICAN FISHERIES SOCIETY, HUMBOLDT CHAPTER 146
AMERICAN FISHERIES SOCIETY, IDAHO CHAPTER 146
AMERICAN FISHERIES SOCIETY, ILLINOIS CHAPTER 146
AMERICAN FISHERIES SOCIETY, INDIANA CHAPTER 146
AMERICAN FISHERIES SOCIETY, IOWA CHAPTER 146
AMERICAN FISHERIES SOCIETY, KANSAS CHAPTER 146
AMERICAN FISHERIES SOCIETY, KENTUCKY CHAPTER 146
AMERICAN FISHERIES SOCIETY, LOUISIANA CHAPTER 146
AMERICAN FISHERIES SOCIETY, MICHIGAN CHAPTER 147
AMERICAN FISHERIES SOCIETY, MID-ATLANTIC CHAPTER 147
AMERICAN FISHERIES SOCIETY, MINNESOTA CHAPTER 147
AMERICAN FISHERIES SOCIETY, MISSISSIPPI CHAPTER 147
AMERICAN FISHERIES SOCIETY, MISSOURI CHAPTER 147
AMERICAN FISHERIES SOCIETY, NEW YORK CHAPTER 147
AMERICAN FISHERIES SOCIETY, NORTH CAROLINA CHAPTER 148
AMERICAN FISHERIES SOCIETY, OHIO CHAPTER 148
AMERICAN FISHERIES SOCIETY, OKLAHOMA CHAPTER 148
AMERICAN FISHERIES SOCIETY, OREGON CHAPTER 148
AMERICAN FISHERIES SOCIETY, POTOMAC CHAPTER 148
AMERICAN FISHERIES SOCIETY, SOUTHERN NEW ENGLAND CHAPTER
  149
AMERICAN FISHERIES SOCIETY, TEXAS A&M CHAPTER 149
AMERICAN FISHERIES SOCIETY, TIDEWATER CHAPTER 149
AMERICAN INSTITUTE OF FISHERY RESEARCH BIOLOGISTS 151
AMERICAN LEAGUE OF ANGLERS AND BOATERS 152

KEYWORD INDEX - Fisheries/Fisheries 463

Keyword Index

AMERICAN LITTORAL SOCIETY ... 152
AMERICAN OCEANS CAMPAIGN ... 153
ANGLERS FOR CLEAN WATER ... 157
ARKANSAS COOPERATIVE RESEARCH UNIT ... 43
ARLINGTON OUTDOOR EDUCATION ASSOCIATION, INC. ... 160
ASSOCIATION OF MIDWEST FISH AND GAME LAW ENFORCEMENT OFFICERS ... 162
AUDUBON SOCIETY OF RHODE ISLAND ... 164
BILLFISH FOUNDATION ... 166
BIODIVERSITY LEGAL FOUNDATION ... 166
BLACK BASS FOUNDATION ... 166
BROTHERHOOD OF THE JUNGLE COCK, INC., THE ... 168
CALIFORNIA SEA GRANT COLLEGE SYSTEM ... 46
CALIFORNIA TROUT, INC. ... 170
CALIFORNIA WILDLIFE FEDERATION ... 170
CANADIAN FEDERATION OF HUMANE SOCIETIES ... 172
CARIBBEAN CONSERVATION CORPORATION (Costa Rica Office) ... 173
CENTER FOR MARINE CONSERVATION ... 176
COASTAL CONSERVATION ASSOCIATION ... 181
COLORADO COOPERATIVE FISH AND WILDLIFE RESEARCH UNIT (USDI) ... 50
COLUMBIA BASIN FISH AND WILDLIFE AUTHORITY ... 183
COOPERATIVE EXTENSION SERVICE (NORTH CAROLINA) ... 94
COOPERATIVE EXTENSION SYSTEM (MASSACHUSETTS) ... 74
DEPARTMENT OF INLAND FISHERIES AND WILDLIFE ... 71
DEPARTMENT OF INTERIOR, U.S.G.S/B.R.D, SOUTH CAROLINA COOPERATIVE FISH AND WILDLIFE RESEARCH UNIT ... 107
DEPARTMENT OF LAND AND NATURAL RESOURCES ... 59, 60
DEPARTMENT OF MARINE RESOURCES ... 71
DESERT FISHES COUNCIL ... 193
ENVIRONMENTAL DEFENSE FUND, INC. ... 202
ENVIRONMENTAL ENTERPRISES ASSISTANCE FUND, INC. ... 203
FEDERATION OF FLY FISHERS ... 205
FISH AND BOAT COMMISSION ... 103
FISH AND WILDLIFE DIVISION/DEPARTMENT OF STATE POLICE ... 100
FISH AND WILDLIFE INFORMATION EXCHANGE ... 206
FISH AND WILDLIFE REFERENCE SERVICE ... 206
FLORIDA GAME AND FRESH WATER FISH COMMISSION ... 55
FLORIDA SEA GRANT COLLEGE ... 55
FLORIDA STATE COOPERATIVE EXTENSION SERVICE ... 56
FOOD AND AGRICULTURE ORGANIZATION OF THE UNITED NATIONS ... 209
FRIENDS OF THE SEA OTTER ... 212
GALIANO CONSERVANCY ASSOCIATION ... 213
GAME AND FISH DEPARTMENT ... 125
GEORGIA COOPERATIVE FISH AND WILDLIFE RESEARCH UNIT (USDI) ... 57
GREAT LAKES SPORT FISHING COUNCIL ... 216
GREAT LAKES UNITED ... 217
GREENPEACE, INC. ... 219
GULF OF MEXICO FISHERY MANAGEMENT COUNCIL ... 219
H. JOHN HEINZ III CENTER FOR SCIENCE, ECONOMICS, AND THE ENVIRONMENT ... 219
HAWAII COOPERATIVE FISHERY RESEARCH UNIT (USDI) ... 60
HUDSONIA LIMITED ... 222
HUNTSMAN MARINE SCIENCE CENTRE ... 223
IDAHO COOPERATIVE FISH AND WILDLIFE RESEARCH UNIT (USDI) ... 61
IDAHO FISH AND GAME DEPARTMENT ... 61
IDAHO FISH AND WILDLIFE FOUNDATION ... 62
INTERNATIONAL ASSOCIATION OF NATURAL RESOURCE PILOTS ... 228
INTERNATIONAL GAME FISH ASSOCIATION ... 231
INTERNATIONAL MARINE MAMMAL PROJECT, THE ... 231
INTERNATIONAL OCEANOGRAPHIC FOUNDATION ... 231
IOWA COOPERATIVE FISH AND WILDLIFE RESEARCH UNIT ... 65
IOWA DEPARTMENT OF NATURAL RESOURCES ... 65
ISLAND INSTITUTE, THE ... 239
IZAAK WALTON LEAGUE OF AMERICA ENDOWMENT ... 239
JACKSON HOLE CONSERVATION ALLIANCE ... 242
KANSAS DEPARTMENT OF WILDLIFE AND PARKS ... 67
KENTUCKY DEPARTMENT OF FISH AND WILDLIFE RESOURCES ... 68
LONG LIVE THE KINGS ... 249
LOWER MISSISSIPPI RIVER CONSERVATION COMMITTEE ... 249
MAINE ATLANTIC SALMON AUTHORITY (formerly Maine Atlantic Sea Run Salmon Commission) ... 71
MAINE COOPERATIVE FISH AND WILDLIFE RESEARCH UNIT (USDI) ... 72
MAINE SEA GRANT PROGRAM ... 72
MANOMET OBSERVATORY ... 251
MARINE LABORATORY (FLORIDA) ... 56
MARYLAND DEPARTMENT OF AGRICULTURE ... 73
MARYLAND DEPARTMENT OF NATURAL RESOURCES ... 73
MARYLAND SEA GRANT COLLEGE ... 74
MASSACHUSETTS COOPERATIVE FISH AND WILDLIFE RESEARCH UNIT (USDI) ... 75
MAX McGRAW WILDLIFE FOUNDATION ... 254
MICHIGAN DEPARTMENT OF NATURAL RESOURCES ... 76
MID-ATLANTIC FISHERY MANAGEMENT COUNCIL ... 256
MINNESOTA COOPERATIVE FISH AND WILDLIFE RESEARCH UNIT ... 77
MINNESOTA SEA GRANT COLLEGE PROGRAM ... 79
MISSISSIPPI COOPERATIVE FISH AND WILDLIFE RESEARCH UNIT (USDI) ... 79
MISSISSIPPI DEPARTMENT OF WILDLIFE, FISHERIES, AND PARKS ... 80
MISSISSIPPI INTERSTATE COOPERATIVE RESOURCE ASSOCIATION 258
MISSISSIPPI STATE EXTENSION SERVICES ... 80
MISSOURI COOPERATIVE FISH AND WILDLIFE RESEARCH UNIT (USDI) ... 81
MONTANA COOPERATIVE FISHERY RESEARCH UNIT (USDI) ... 82
MONTANA LAND RELIANCE ... 260
MOTE MARINE LABORATORY ... 261
NATIONAL ASSOCIATION OF UNIVERSITY FISHERIES AND WILDLIFE PROGRAMS ... 265
NATIONAL COALITION FOR MARINE CONSERVATION ... 266
NATIONAL FISH AND WILDLIFE FOUNDATION ... 267
NATIONAL MILITARY FISH AND WILDLIFE ASSOCIATION ... 269
NATIVE AMERICAN FISH AND WILDLIFE SOCIETY (NAFWS) ... 276
NATURAL RESOURCES COUNCIL OF AMERICA ... 278
NATURE CONSERVANCY OF COLORADO, THE ... 279
NEW HAMPSHIRE FISH AND GAME DEPARTMENT ... 86
NEW HAMPSHIRE SEA GRANT PROGRAM ... 86
NEW YORK STATE COOPERATIVE EXTENSION ... 93
NORTH AMERICAN FISHING CLUB ... 289
NORTH AMERICAN NATIVE FISHES ASSOCIATION ... 289
NORTH ATLANTIC SALMON CONSERVATION ORGANIZATION ... 289
NORTH CAROLINA BEACH BUGGY ASSOCIATION, INC. ... 290
NORTH CAROLINA SEA GRANT PROGRAM ... 95
NORTH CASCADES CONSERVATION COUNCIL ... 291
NORTH DAKOTA NATURAL SCIENCE SOCIETY ... 291
NORTHWEST ATLANTIC FISHERIES ORGANIZATION (NAFO) ... 292
NW ENERGY COALITION ... 294
OHIO COOPERATIVE FISH AND WILDLIFE RESEARCH UNIT (USDI) ... 96
OHIO SEA GRANT COLLEGE PROGRAM, F.T. STONE LABORATORY, AND GREAT LAKES AQUATIC ECOSYSTEM RESEARCH CONSORTIUM (GLAERC) ... 97
OKLAHOMA COOPERATIVE FISH AND WILDLIFE RESEARCH UNIT (USDI) ... 98
OLYMPIC PARK INSTITUTE ... 297
OREGON COOPERATIVE FISH AND WILDLIFE RESEARCH UNIT (USDI) ... 100
OREGON DEPARTMENT OF FORESTRY ... 101
OREGON SEA GRANT PROGRAM ... 101
OREGON TROUT, INC. ... 298
PACIFIC FISHERY MANAGEMENT COUNCIL ... 300
PACIFIC RIVERS COUNCIL ... 300
PENNSYLVANIA FEDERATION OF SPORTSMEN'S CLUBS ... 302
PINE BLUFF COOPERATIVE FISHERY RESEARCH PROJECT ... 45
PUERTO RICO DEPARTMENT OF NATURAL AND ENVIRONMENTAL RESOURCES ... 105
PUERTO RICO SEA GRANT PROGRAM ... 105
RESOURCES AGENCY, THE ... 47
RIVER ALLIANCE OF WISCONSIN ... 312
SCIENTISTS CENTER FOR ANIMAL WELFARE ... 318
SEA SHEPHERD CONSERVATION SOCIETY ... 318
SOUTH ATLANTIC FISHERY MANAGEMENT COUNCIL ... 323
SOUTH CAROLINA DEPARTMENT OF NATURAL RESOURCES ... 108
SOUTH CAROLINA SEA GRANT CONSORTIUM ... 108
SOUTH CAROLINA WILDLIFE FEDERATION ... 324
SOUTH DAKOTA COOPERATIVE FISH AND WILDLIFE RESEARCH UNIT (USDI) ... 109
SOUTH DAKOTA GAME, FISH, AND PARKS DEPARTMENT ... 109
SOUTH DAKOTA WILDLIFE FEDERATION ... 324
SOUTHEAST ALASKA CONSERVATION COUNCIL (SEACC) ... 324
SOUTHEASTERN ASSOCIATION OF FISH AND WILDLIFE AGENCIES .. 325
SOUTHEASTERN FISHES COUNCIL ... 325
STRIPERS UNLIMITED INC. ... 328
TENNESSEE B.A.S.S. CHAPTER FEDERATION ... 329
TENNESSEE CONSERVATION LEAGUE ... 330
TEXAS COOPERATIVE FISH AND WILDLIFE RESEARCH UNIT ... 111
TROUT UNLIMITED, OKLAHOMA COUNCIL ... 336
UPPER MISSISSIPPI RIVER CONSERVATION COMMITTEE ... 340
UTAH COOPERATIVE FISH AND WILDLIFE RESEARCH UNIT (USDI-USGS-BRD-CRU) ... 113
UTAH WILDLIFE FEDERATION ... 340
VIRGINIA COOPERATIVE FISH AND WILDLIFE RESEARCH UNIT (USDI) ... 117
VIRGINIA WILDLIFE FEDERATION ... 343, 346
WASHINGTON COOPERATIVE FISH AND WILDLIFE RESEARCH UNIT (USDI) ... 120
WASHINGTON SEA GRANT PROGRAM ... 121
WEST VIRGINIA COOPERATIVE FISH AND WILDLIFE RESEARCH UNIT ... 122
WESTERN PACIFIC REGIONAL FISHERY MANAGEMENT COUNCIL ... 347
WHALE AND DOLPHIN CONSERVATION SOCIETY ... 348
WILDLIFE FOREVER ... 351
WILDLIFE FOUNDATION OF FLORIDA, INC. ... 352
WILDLIFE HABITAT CANADA ... 352
WILDLIFE RESOURCES COMMISSION ... 95
WISCONSIN CONSERVATION CORPS ... 123
WISCONSIN COOPERATIVE FISHERY RESEARCH UNIT (USDI) ... 123
WISCONSIN SEA GRANT INSTITUTE ... 125
WISCONSIN WILDLIFE FEDERATION ... 360

WOODS HOLE OCEANOGRAPHIC INSITITUTION (WHOI) SEA GRANT PROGRAM 76
WYOMING COOPERATIVE FISH AND WILDLIFE RESEARCH UNIT (USDI) 126

Flood Control

RESOURCES AGENCY, THE 47

Flowers, Plants, and Trees

ABUNDANT LIFE SEED FOUNDATION 133
ADKINS ARBORETUM 134
AMERICA THE BEAUTIFUL FUND 138
AMERICAN ASSOCIATION OF BOTANICAL GARDENS AND ARBORETA, INC. 139
AMERICAN ASSOCIATION OF FIELD BOTANISTS 139
AMERICAN CHESTNUT FOUNDATION, THE 141
AUDUBON SOCIETY OF RHODE ISLAND 164
AUDUBON SOCIETY OF WESTERN PENNSYLVANIA 165
BIG BEND NATURAL HISTORY ASSOCIATION 166
BIOMASS USERS NETWORK 166
BOTANICAL CLUB OF WISCONSIN 167
BOTANICAL SOCIETY OF WESTERN PENNSYLVANIA 167
BROOKS BIRD CLUB INC., THE 168
CENTER FOR PLANT CONSERVATION 176
CONNECTICUT BOTANICAL SOCIETY 185
DELAWARE STATE EXTENSION SERVICE 53
DOGTOOTH GROUP 193
EARTHWATCH INSTITUTE 199
ELM RESEARCH INSTITUTE 200
ENVIRONMENTAL EDUCATION ASSOCIATION OF ILLINOIS (Iron Oaks Environmental Learning Center) 202
FLORIDA NATIVE PLANT SOCIETY 207
FOREST SERVICE (Texas) 111
GARDEN CLUB OF AMERICA, THE 213
HOLDEN ARBORETUM, THE 221
HUDSONIA LIMITED 222
ILLINOIS NATIVE PLANT SOCIETY 225
INDIANA AUDUBON SOCIETY, INC. 226
INDIANA NATIVE PLANT AND WILDFLOWER SOCIETY 226
INSTITUTE OF TROPICAL AGRICULTURE AND HUMAN RESOURCES ... 61
INTERNATIONAL PLANT PROPAGATION SOCIETY, INC., THE 232
IOWA NATIVE PLANT SOCIETY 237
IOWA NATURAL HERITAGE FOUNDATION 238
KANSAS WILDFLOWER SOCIETY 244
KIDS FOR SAVING EARTH WORLDWIDE 246
LADY BIRD JOHNSON WILDFLOWER CENTER (formerly the National Wildlflower Research Center) 246
MICHIGAN DEPARTMENT OF AGRICULTURE 76
MICHIGAN NATURAL AREAS COUNCIL 255
MICHIGAN NATURE ASSOCIATION 255
MISSISSIPPI NATIVE PLANT SOCIETY 258
MISSOURI NATIVE PLANT SOCIETY 259
NATIONAL ARBOR DAY FOUNDATION 262
NATIONAL AVIARY IN PITTSBURGH 265
NATIONAL BIRD-FEEDING SOCIETY 266
NATIONAL GARDENING ASSOCIATION 268
NATIVE PLANT SOCIETY OF NORTHEASTERN OHIO 276
NATURAL HISTORY SOCIETY OF MARYLAND, INC., THE 277
NATURE CONSERVANCY OF COLORADO, THE 279
NATURE SASKATCHEWAN 282
NEW HAMPSHIRE NATURAL HERITAGE INVENTORY 86
NEW YORK DEPARTMENT OF AGRICULTURE AND MARKETS 92
NORTH DAKOTA STATE FOREST SERVICE 96
NORTHERN VIRGINIA REGIONAL PARK AUTHORITY 117
OKLAHOMA BIOLOGICAL SURVEY 98
OKLAHOMA NATIVE PLANT SOCIETY 296
PENNSYLVANIA DEPARTMENT OF AGRICULTURE 104
PENNSYLVANIA RECREATION AND PARK SOCIETY, INC. 302
RHODE ISLAND STATE ASSOCIATION OF CONSERVATION DISTRICTS 311
STATE FORESTRY DIVISION (WYOMING) 126
TALL TIMBERS RESEARCH INC. 329
TREES FOR THE FUTURE, INC. 333
VIRGINIA FORESTRY ASSOCIATION 342
VIRGINIA NATIVE PLANT SOCIETY 343
WILD ONES - NATURAL LANDSCAPERS, LTD 349
WILDLIFE FOREVER 351
WYOMING NATIVE PLANT SOCIETY 364

Food Safety

GEORGIA DEPARTMENT OF AGRICULTURE 57
NATIONAL ENVIRONMENTAL HEALTH ASSOCIATION 267

Forest Management

ADIRONDACK MOUNTAIN CLUB, INC., THE 134
ALABAMA FORESTRY COMMISSION 39
ALASKA AUDUBON SOCIETY 136
DELAWARE STATE EXTENSION SERVICE 53
DIVISION OF FORESTRY AND SOIL RESOURCES (GUAM) 58
FLORIDA AUDUBON SOCIETY 206
FOREST SERVICE (Texas) 111
FRIENDS OF THE SAN JUANS 212
GALIANO CONSERVANCY ASSOCIATION 213
GEORGIA CONSERVANCY, INC., THE 214
HARDWOOD FOREST FOUNDATION 219
ILLINOIS WALNUT COUNCIL 225
INTERNATIONAL ASSOCIATION OF NATURAL RESOURCE PILOTS 228
INTERNATIONAL SOCIETY OF TROPICAL FORESTERS INC. 233
JACKSON HOLE CONSERVATION ALLIANCE 242
KANSAS FOREST SERVICE 67
LIGHTHAWK 248
LOUISIANA DEPARTMENT OF AGRICULTURE 69, 70
MANOMET OBSERVATORY 251
MISSOURI NATIVE PLANT SOCIETY 259
MONTANA LAND RELIANCE 260
MOUNT GRACE LAND CONSERVATION TRUST 261
NATIONAL FORESTRY ASSOCIATION 268
NEW YORK STATE COOPERATIVE EXTENSION 93
NEWFOUNDLAND LABRADOR WILDLIFE FEDERATION 287
NORTH CASCADES CONSERVATION COUNCIL 291
NORTHERN ALASKA ENVIRONMENTAL CENTER 292
NORTHWEST ECOSYSTEM ALLIANCE 293
PENNSYLVANIA DEPARTMENT OF CONSERVATION AND NATURAL RESOURCES 105
RESOURCES FOR THE FUTURE 310
SINAPU 319
SOUTHEAST ALASKA CONSERVATION COUNCIL (SEACC) 324
SOUTHEASTERN ASSOCIATION OF FISH AND WILDLIFE AGENCIES.. 325
SOUTHERN NEW ENGLAND FOREST CONSORTIUM, INC. 326
SOUTHWEST CENTER FOR BIOLOGICAL DIVERSITY 326
TENNESSEE CITIZENS FOR WILDERNESS PLANNING 329
TENNESSEE ENVIRONMENTAL COUNCIL 330
VIRGINIA NATIVE PLANT SOCIETY 343
WESTERN FORESTRY AND CONSERVATION ASSOCIATION 347
WILDLIFE HABITAT CANADA 352

Forest Stewardship

DIVISION OF FORESTRY AND SOIL RESOURCES (GUAM) 58

Forests and Forestry

ADIRONDACK NATURE CONSERVANCY/ADIRONDACK LAND TRUST, INC. 134
AGRICULTURAL EXTENSION SERVICE 110
ALABAMA COOPERATIVE EXTENSION SYSTEM 39
ALABAMA ENVIRONMENTAL COUNCIL 135
ALABAMA FORESTRY COMMISSION 39
ALASKA CONSERVATION FOUNDATION 136
ALASKA DEPARTMENT OF NATURAL RESOURCES 41
AMERICAN FOREST FOUNDATION 150
AMERICAN FORESTS (formerly American Forestry Association) 150
AMERICAN HIKING SOCIETY 150
AMERICAN LAND CONSERVANCY 151
AMERICAN LANDS (formerly Western Ancient Forest Campaign) 151
AMERICAN RESOURCES GROUP 154
AMERICAN WILDLANDS 156
ANCIENT FOREST INTERNATIONAL 157
ARKANSAS STATE EXTENSION SERVICES 44
ASSOCIATION OF CONSULTING FORESTERS OF AMERICA 161
BIOMASS USERS NETWORK 166
CALIFORNIA TROUT, INC. 170
CAMP FIRE CLUB OF AMERICA, THE 171
CATSKILL FOREST ASSOCIATION 174
CENTER FOR RESOURCEFUL BUILDING TECHNOLOGY 176
COLORADO FORESTRY ASSOCIATION 182
COLORADO STATE FOREST SERVICE 51
CONSERVATION INTERNATIONAL 188
COOPERATIVE EXTENSION SYSTEM (MASSACHUSETTS) 74
DEEP-PORTAGE CONSERVATION RESERVE 191
DELAWARE DEPARTMENT OF AGRICULTURE 52
DELAWARE FORESTRY ASSOCIATION 192

KEYWORD INDEX - Gap Analysis/Geology 465

Keyword Index

EARTHJUSTICE LEGAL DEFENSE FUND (formerly Sierra Club Legal Defense Fund, Inc.) ... 198
FEDERATION OF WESTERN OUTDOOR CLUBS ... 206
FLORIDA STATE COOPERATIVE EXTENSION SERVICE ... 56
FOOD AND AGRICULTURE ORGANIZATION OF THE UNITED NATIONS ... 209
FOREST HISTORY SOCIETY, INC. ... 209
FOREST LANDOWNERS ASSOCIATION, INC. ... 209
FOREST LANDOWNERS OF CALIFORNIA ... 209
FOREST SERVICE (Texas) ... 111
FOREST SERVICE EMPLOYEES FOR ENVIRONMENTAL ETHICS (FSEEE) ... 209
FOREST TRUST ... 209
FORESTRY COMMISSION (MISSISSIPPI) ... 79
FORESTRY COMMISSION (SOUTH CAROLINA) ... 107
FRIENDS OF THE BOUNDARY WATERS WILDERNESS ... 211
GEORGIA FORESTRY ASSOCIATION, INC. ... 215
GOVERNOR OF SOUTH CAROLINA, JIM HODGES ... 107
GREATER YELLOWSTONE COALITION ... 217
HAWAII SOCIETY OF AMERICAN FORESTERS ... 220
IDAHO FOREST OWNERS ASSOCIATION ... 224
ILLINOIS WOODLAND OWNERS AND USERS ASSOCIATION ... 225
INDIANA DEPARTMENT OF NATURAL RESOURCES ... 64
INDIANA FORESTRY AND WOODLAND OWNERS ASSOCIATION ... 226
INTERNATIONAL ASSOCIATION OF WILDLAND FIRE (formerly Fire Research Institute) ... 229
INTERNATIONAL PRIMATE PROTECTION LEAGUE ... 232
IOWA WOODLAND OWNERS ASSOCIATION ... 239
ISLAND INSTITUTE, THE ... 239
KANSAS FOREST SERVICE ... 67
LEAGUE OF WOMEN VOTERS OF WASHINGTON ... 248
LOUISIANA FORESTRY ASSOCIATION ... 249
MAINE AUDUBON SOCIETY ... 250
MARYLAND DEPARTMENT OF NATURAL RESOURCES ... 73
MARYLAND FORESTS ASSOCIATION ... 252
MASSACHUSETTS FORESTRY ASSOCIATION ... 253
MICHIGAN DEPARTMENT OF NATURAL RESOURCES ... 76
MICHIGAN FOREST ASSOCIATION ... 255
MICHIGAN STATE UNIVERSITY EXTENSION ... 77
MINNESOTA FORESTRY ASSOCIATION ... 257
MISSISSIPPI STATE EXTENSION SERVICES ... 80
MONTANA COOPERATIVE WILDLIFE RESEARCH UNIT (USGS/BRD) ... 82
MONTANA WILDERNESS ASSOCIATION ... 260
NATIONAL ARBOR DAY FOUNDATION ... 262
NATIONAL ASSOCIATION OF STATE FORESTERS ... 264
NATIONAL FOREST FOUNDATION ... 268
NATIONAL FORESTRY ASSOCIATION ... 268
NATIONAL TREE TRUST ... 272
NATIONAL WILD TURKEY FEDERATION, INC., THE ... 273
NATIONAL WOODLAND OWNERS ASSOCIATION ... 276
NATIVE AMERICAN FISH AND WILDLIFE SOCIETY (NAFWS) ... 276
NATURAL RESOURCES COUNCIL OF AMERICA ... 278
NEW HAMPSHIRE TIMBERLAND OWNERS ASSOCIATION ... 285
NEW JERSEY FORESTRY ASSOCIATION ... 286
NEW YORK FOREST OWNERS ASSOCIATION, INC. ... 287
NORTH CAROLINA FORESTRY ASSOCIATION ... 290
NORTH DAKOTA STATE FOREST SERVICE ... 96
NORTHCOAST ENVIRONMENTAL CENTER ... 291
NORTHWEST RENEWABLE RESOURCES CENTER ... 293
OHIO DEPARTMENT OF NATURAL RESOURCES ... 97
OHIO FORESTRY ASSOCIATION, INC., THE ... 295
OKLAHOMA STATE BOARD OF AGRICULTURE ... 98
OKLAHOMA STATE EXTENSION SERVICES ... 99
OREGON DEPARTMENT OF FORESTRY ... 101
OREGON SMALL WOODLANDS ASSOCIATION ... 298
PENNSYLVANIA FOREST STEWARDSHIP PROGRAM ... 105
PINCHOT INSTITUTE FOR CONSERVATION ... 303
PUBLIC EMPLOYEES FOR ENVIRONMENTAL RESPONSIBILITY (PEER) ... 306, 307
PUERTO RICO DEPARTMENT OF NATURAL AND ENVIRONMENTAL RESOURCES ... 105
RAINFOREST ACTION NETWORK ... 308
RAINFOREST ALLIANCE ... 309
RAINFOREST RELIEF ... 309
RHODE ISLAND B.A.S.S. CHAPTER FEDERATION ... 311
RUFFED GROUSE SOCIETY, THE ... 314
SAVE AMERICA'S FORESTS ... 315
SAVE-THE-REDWOODS LEAGUE ... 317
SMALL WOODLAND OWNERS ASSOCIATION OF MAINE, INC. ... 319
SOCIETY FOR THE PROTECTION OF NEW HAMPSHIRE FORESTS ... 322
SOCIETY OF AMERICAN FORESTERS ... 298, 322, 344
SOUTH CAROLINA B.A.S.S. CHAPTER FEDERATION ... 323
SOUTHERN ENVIRONMENTAL LAW CENTER ... 325, 326
STATE FORESTRY DIVISION (WYOMING) ... 126
TEXAS B.A.S.S. CHAPTER FEDERATION ... 330
TREE PEOPLE ... 332
TUG HILL TOMORROW, INC. ... 338
UNITED STATES TOURIST COUNCIL ... 339
UNIVERSITY OF NEW HAMPSHIRE COOPERATIVE EXTENSION ... 86
UTAH STATE EXTENSION SERVICES ... 114
VERMONT AUDUBON COUNCIL ... 341
VERMONT INSTITUTE OF NATURAL SCIENCE ... 341
VERMONT NATURAL RESOURCES COUNCIL ... 341
VERMONT STATE-WIDE ENVIRONMENTAL EDUCATION PROGRAMS (SWEEP) ... 341
WASHINGTON ENVIRONMENTAL COUNCIL ... 343
WASHINGTON STATE EXTENSION SERVICES ... 121
WEST VIRGINIA B.A.S.S. CHAPTER FEDERATION ... 346
WEST VIRGINIA STATE EXTENSION SERVICES ... 123
WILDERNESS SOCIETY, THE ... 349
WISCONSIN CONSERVATION CORPS ... 123
WISCONSIN DEPARTMENT OF NATURAL RESOURCES ... 124
WISCONSIN WATERFOWL ASSOCIATION, INC. ... 360
WORLD FORESTRY CENTER ... 362
WORLD RESOURCES INSTITUTE ... 362

Gap Analysis

IOWA COOPERATIVE FISH AND WILDLIFE RESEARCH UNIT ... 65

Gardening and Horticulture

ABUNDANT LIFE SEED FOUNDATION ... 133
ALABAMA COOPERATIVE EXTENSION SYSTEM ... 39
AMERICA THE BEAUTIFUL FUND ... 138
AMERICAN ASSOCIATION OF BOTANICAL GARDENS AND ARBORETA, INC. ... 139
ARKANSAS STATE EXTENSION SERVICES ... 44
BIG BEND NATURAL HISTORY ASSOCIATION ... 166
BIO-INTEGRAL RESOURCE CENTER ... 166
BOTANICAL SOCIETY OF WESTERN PENNSYLVANIA ... 167
COLORADO STATE COOPERATIVE EXTENSION ... 51
COMMUNITY ENVIRONMENTAL COUNCIL ... 184
DELAWARE STATE EXTENSION SERVICE ... 53
ECOLOGY CENTER ... 199
ENVIRONMENTAL CONCERN, INC. ... 201
GARDEN CLUB OF AMERICA, THE ... 213
HOLDEN ARBORETUM, THE ... 221
INSTITUTE OF TROPICAL AGRICULTURE AND HUMAN RESOURCES ... 61
MISSOURI NATIVE PLANT SOCIETY ... 259
NATIONAL COUNCIL OF STATE GARDEN CLUBS, INC. ... 266
NATIONAL FFA ORGANIZATION ... 267
NATIONAL GARDENING ASSOCIATION ... 268
NEW ENGLAND WILD FLOWER SOCIETY, INC. ... 284
NEW JERSEY STATE EXTENSION SERVICES ... 88
SMITHSONIAN INSTITUTION ... 320
SOUTH CAROLINA DEPARTMENT OF AGRICULTURE ... 107
TRUSTEES OF RESERVATIONS, THE ... 338
VIRGINIA FORESTRY ASSOCIATION ... 342
WESTERN PENNSYLVANIA CONSERVANCY ... 347
WILD ONES - NATURAL LANDSCAPERS, LTD ... 349
WINDSTAR FOUNDATION, THE ... 359
WYOMING NATIVE PLANT SOCIETY ... 364

Geographic Information Systems

MAINE COOPERATIVE FISH AND WILDLIFE RESEARCH UNIT (USDI) ... 72
OKLAHOMA BIOLOGICAL SURVEY ... 98

Geography

ASSOCIATION OF AMERICAN GEOGRAPHERS ... 161
KANSAS ACADEMY OF SCIENCE ... 242
LIGHTHAWK ... 248
MINNESOTA ORNITHOLOGISTS' UNION ... 257
NATIONAL GEOGRAPHIC SOCIETY ... 268
NEVADA BUREAU OF MINES AND GEOLOGY ... 84
POPULATION REFERENCE BUREAU INC. ... 305

Geology

AGENCY OF NATURAL RESOURCES ... 114
AMERICAN CAVE CONSERVATION ASSOCIATION ... 141
AMERICAN GEOLOGICAL INSTITUTE ... 150
AMERICAN GROUND WATER TRUST ... 150
AMERICAN MUSEUM OF NATURAL HISTORY ... 153
ARIZONA GEOLOGICAL SURVEY ... 42
BUREAU OF ECONOMIC GEOLOGY ... 111
BUREAU OF MINES AND GEOLOGY ... 82
CAVE RESEARCH FOUNDATION ... 174
CHIHUAHUAN DESERT RESEARCH INSTITUTE ... 179
DELAWARE GEOLOGICAL SURVEY ... 53
DEPARTMENT OF ENVIRONMENTAL PROTECTION (NEW JERSEY) ... 86

EARTHWATCH INSTITUTE 199
HUNTSMAN MARINE SCIENCE CENTRE 223
INDIANA STATE GEOLOGICAL SURVEY 65
IOWA DEPARTMENT OF NATURAL RESOURCES 65
KANSAS ACADEMY OF SCIENCE 242
KANSAS GEOLOGICAL SURVEY 67
LOUISIANA GEOLOGICAL SURVEY 70
MICHIGAN DEPARTMENT OF ENVIRONMENTAL QUALITY........ 76
MINNESOTA GEOLOGICAL SURVEY 78
MISSOURI DEPARTMENT OF NATURAL RESOURCES................ 81
NATIONAL GROUND WATER ASSOCIATION, THE 269
NATIONAL SPELEOLOGICAL SOCIETY, INC. 271
NEVADA BUREAU OF MINES AND GEOLOGY 84
NEW MEXICO BUREAU OF MINES AND MINERAL RESOURCES 89
NEW YORK GEOLOGICAL SURVEY AND STATE MUSEUM........ 92
NORTH DAKOTA GEOLOGICAL SURVEY 96
OKLAHOMA GEOLOGICAL SURVEY 98
PUERTO RICO SEA GRANT PROGRAM 105
STATE OFFICE OF CONSERVATION (LOUISIANA).................... 71
THE GLACIER INSTITUTE 331
VIRGINIA MUSEUM OF NATURAL HISTORY 118
WISCONSIN GEOLOGICAL AND NATURAL HISTORY SURVEY 125
WYOMING STATE GEOLOGICAL SURVEY 126

Grants

AMERICA THE BEAUTIFUL FUND.. 138
AMERICAN INSTITUTE OF BIOLOGICAL SCIENCES 151
AMERICAN WILDLIFE RESEARCH FOUNDATION, INC. 156
CENTER FOR THE STUDY OF TROPICAL BIRDS, INC. (Administrative
    Office) 177
DEPARTMENT OF ENVIRONMENT AND NATURAL RESOURCES (SOUTH
    DAKOTA).. 109
EARTHWATCH INSTITUTE 199
RAINFOREST ALLIANCE 309
RESOURCES AGENCY, THE... 47
WILD ONES - NATURAL LANDSCAPERS, LTD 349
WILSON ORNITHOLOGICAL SOCIETY...................................... 358
WORLD NATURE ASSOCIATION INC. 362

Grasslands

MONTANA COOPERATIVE WILDLIFE RESEARCH UNIT (USGS/BRD)..... 82

Great Plains

NORTH DAKOTA NATURAL SCIENCE SOCIETY...................... 291

Green Building

EARTH DAY NEW YORK 197

Green Certification

NATIONAL FORESTRY ASSOCIATION...................................... 268

Greenhouse Effect/Global Warming

AIR AND WASTE MANAGEMENT ASSOCIATION 135
AMERICAN ASSOCIATION FOR THE ADVANCEMENT OF SCIENCE..... 139
AMERICAN FORESTS (formerly American Forestry Association)............... 150
AMERICAN GEOGRAPHICAL SOCIETY 150
CENTER FOR ENVIRONMENTAL INFORMATION 175
CENTER FOR INTERNATIONAL ENVIRONMENTAL LAW (CIEL) 175
ENVIRONMENTAL AND ENERGY STUDY INSTITUTE (EESI) 201
GREENHOUSE ACTION 218
GREENPEACE, INC... 219
INTERNATIONAL INSTITUTE FOR ENERGY CONSERVATION 231
INTERNATIONAL MARITIME ORGANIZATION 231
INTERNATIONAL SOCIETY FOR THE PRESERVATION OF THE TROPICAL
    RAINFOREST, THE 233
MARINE SCIENCES RESEARCH CENTER (NEW YORK).............. 92
NORTH ATLANTIC SALMON CONSERVATION ORGANIZATION 289
NW ENERGY COALITION 294
OZONE ACTION 300
TREES FOR THE FUTURE, INC. 333
UNION OF CONCERNED SCIENTISTS 339
UNITED STATES COMMITTEE FOR THE UNITED NATIONS
    ENVIRONMENT PROGRAMME THE (U.S. and UNEP) 339
WINDSTAR FOUNDATION, THE 359
WORLD RESOURCES INSTITUTE 362

Greenways

MISSISSIPPI RIVER BASIN ALLIANCE 258

Ground Water Protection

MONTANA DEPARTMENT OF AGRICULTURE 82

Habitat Conservation

CENTRO de INFORMACION, INVESTIGACION y EDUCACION SOCIAL
    (CIIES).. 177
CONSERVATION TREATY SUPPORT FUND 188
VIRGINIA NATIVE PLANT SOCIETY.. 343

Harmful Algal Blooms

NORTH CAROLINA SEA GRANT PROGRAM 95

Hazardous Materials & Waste

MASSACHUSETTS HIGHWAY DEPARTMENT............................. 75

Health and Nutrition

AMERICA THE BEAUTIFUL FUND.. 138
AMERICAN CAMPING ASSOCIATION, INC. 141
ASSOCIATION OF STATE AND TERRITORIAL HEALTH OFFICIALS 162
AVSC INTERNATIONAL 165
CAMP FIRE BOYS AND GIRLS 170
CENTER FOR SCIENCE IN THE PUBLIC INTEREST 176
COLORADO STATE COOPERATIVE EXTENSION 51
DELAWARE STATE EXTENSION SERVICE 53
DESERT TORTOISE COUNCIL... 193
FOOD AND AGRICULTURE ORGANIZATION OF THE UNITED NATIONS
    209
HUMAN ECOLOGY ACTION LEAGUE INC. THE (HEAL) 222
INDIANA STATE DEPARTMENT OF HEALTH.............................. 64
INSTITUTE OF TROPICAL AGRICULTURE AND HUMAN RESOURCES... 61
KANSAS STATE DEPARTMENT OF HEALTH AND ENVIRONMENT 67
KEYSTONE CENTER, THE 245, 246
MAGIC 250
NATIONAL ASSOCIATION OF STATE DEPARTMENTS OF AGRICULTURE
    264
NATIONAL FARMERS UNION... 267
NORTH CAROLINA DEPARTMENT OF AGRICULTURE 94
PENNSYLVANIA FORESTRY ASSOCIATION, THE 302
PLANNED PARENTHOOD FEDERATION OF AMERICA INC..... 304
POPULATION ACTION INTERNATIONAL 304
PUERTO RICO STATE EXTENSION SERVICES 106
SCIENTISTS CENTER FOR ANIMAL WELFARE 318
SOUTHEASTERN COOPERATIVE WILDLIFE DISEASE STUDY.............. 325
TEXAS DEPARTMENT OF HEALTH 111
UNIVERSITY OF VERMONT EXTENSION.................................. 115
UTAH DEPARTMENT OF HEALTH 113
VERMONT DEPARTMENT OF HEALTH 115
WILDLIFE DISEASE ASSOCIATION 351
WORLD ASSOCIATION OF GIRL GUIDES AND GIRL SCOUTS (WAGGGS)
    361

Healthy Home

PENNSYLVANIA RESOURCES COUNCIL, INC., (formerly PA Roadside
    Council) 302

Highly Migratory Species

WESTERN PACIFIC REGIONAL FISHERY MANAGEMENT COUNCIL 347

Himalayan Range

HIMALAYAN WILDLIFE PROJECT.. 221

Historic Preservation

ALABAMA WATERFOWL ASSOCIATION, INC. (AWA) 135
AMERICA THE BEAUTIFUL FUND.. 138

KEYWORD INDEX - Hunting/International Conservation

AMERICAN LIVESTOCK BREEDS CONSERVANCY	152
APPALACHIAN TRAIL CONFERENCE	158
ARCHAEOLOGICAL CONSERVANCY	158
ARKANSAS DEPARTMENT OF PARKS AND TOURISM	43
CAVE RESEARCH FOUNDATION	174
DELAWARE GREENWAYS, INC.	192
DEPARTMENT OF PARKS AND RECREATION (GUAM)	58
DEPARTMENT OF TRANSPORTATION	27, 100, 106
ELM RESEARCH INSTITUTE	200
GEORGE WRIGHT SOCIETY, THE	214
INDIANA DEPARTMENT OF NATURAL RESOURCES	64
NATIONAL ASSOCIATION FOR INTERPRETATION	262
NATIONAL PARK FOUNDATION	269
NATIONAL PARK TRUST	270
NATIONAL TRUST FOR HISTORIC PRESERVATION	272
NEVIS HISTORICAL AND CONSERVATION SOCIETY	283
NEW YORK STATE OFFICE OF PARKS, RECREATION AND HISTORIC PRESERVATION	93
OFFICE OF STATE PARKS, DEPARTMENT OF CULTURE, RECREATION, AND TOURISM	71
OREGON PARKS AND RECREATION DEPARTMENT	101
PARKS AND RECREATION DEPARTMENT (NORTH DAKOTA)	96
RAINFOREST TRUST INC., THE	309
SMITHSONIAN INSTITUTION	320
SOUND EXPERIENCE	323
TALLAHASSEE MUSEUM OF HISTORY AND NATURAL SCIENCE	329
TRUSTEES OF RESERVATIONS, THE	338
TUG HILL COMMISSION	94
UNITED STATES TOURIST COUNCIL	339
WYOMING DEPARTMENT OF COMMERCE	126

Hunting

ALABAMA WATERFOWL ASSOCIATION, INC. (AWA)	135
ALASKA DEPARTMENT OF FISH AND GAME	40
ANIMAL PROTECTION INSTITUTE	157
ARCHERY MANUFACTURERS AND MERCHANTS ORGANIZATION (AMO)	159
BOONE AND CROCKETT CLUB	167
BOONE AND CROCKETT FOUNDATION	167
CALIFORNIA WATERFOWL ASSOCIATION	170
CALIFORNIA WILDLIFE FEDERATION	170
CAMP FIRE CLUB OF AMERICA, THE	171
COLORADO STATE COOPERATIVE EXTENSION	51
COLORADO TRAPPERS ASSOCIATION	183
DEPARTMENT OF FISH AND WILDLIFE (WASHINGTON)	119
DEPARTMENT OF INLAND FISHERIES AND WILDLIFE	71
DEPARTMENT OF INTERIOR, U.S.G.S/B.R.D, SOUTH CAROLINA COOPERATIVE FISH AND WILDLIFE RESEARCH UNIT	107
DEPARTMENT OF PUBLIC SAFETY	41
DEPARTMENT OF WILDLIFE CONSERVATION	98
DIVISION OF NATURAL RESOURCES	122
EVERGLADES COORDINATING COUNCIL (ECC)	204
FEDERAL CARTRIDGE COMPANY	205
FEDERAL WILDLIFE OFFICER'S ASSOCIATION	205
FISH AND WILDLIFE DIVISION/DEPARTMENT OF STATE POLICE	100
FLORIDA GAME AND FRESH WATER FISH COMMISSION	55
FOUNDATION FOR NORTH AMERICAN BIG GAME	210
FRIENDS OF ANIMALS INC.	211
GAME AND FISH DEPARTMENT	125
GAME COMMISSION	103
HOOD CANAL LAND TRUST	222
HUMANE SOCIETY OF THE UNITED STATES, THE	222
IDAHO FISH AND GAME DEPARTMENT	61
INTERNATIONAL ASSOCIATION OF NATURAL RESOURCE PILOTS	228
INTERNATIONAL HUNTER EDUCATION ASSOCIATION	231
INTERNATIONAL PROFESSIONAL HUNTERS' ASSOCIATION	232
IOWA DEPARTMENT OF NATURAL RESOURCES	65
IZAAK WALTON LEAGUE OF AMERICA ENDOWMENT	239
IZAAK WALTON LEAGUE OF AMERICA, INC., THE	240
KANSAS DEPARTMENT OF WILDLIFE AND PARKS	67
KANSAS STATE EXTENSION SERVICES	68
MAX McGRAW WILDLIFE FOUNDATION	254
MONTANA DEPARTMENT OF FISH, WILDLIFE, AND PARKS	82
MOUNTAIN LION FOUNDATION	261
MULE DEER FOUNDATION, THE	262
NATIONAL FIELD ARCHERY ASSOCIATION	267
NATIONAL HUNTERS ASSOCIATION, INC.	269
NATIONAL RIFLE ASSOCIATION OF AMERICA	271
NATIONAL SHOOTING SPORTS FOUNDATION, INC.	271
NATIONAL WILD TURKEY FEDERATION, INC., THE	273
NEW HAMPSHIRE FISH AND GAME DEPARTMENT	86
NORTH AMERICAN FALCONERS ASSOCIATION	288
NORTH AMERICAN GAMEBIRD ASSOCIATION, INC.	289
NORTH DAKOTA GAME AND FISH DEPARTMENT	95
NORTHEAST WILDLIFE ADMINISTRATORS ASSOCIATION	292
OREGON TROUT, INC.	298
PHEASANTS FOREVER INC.	303
QUEBEC WILDLIFE FEDERATION	308
ROCKY MOUNTAIN BIGHORN SOCIETY	313
ROCKY MOUNTAIN ELK FOUNDATION	313
SAFARI CLUB INTERNATIONAL	314
SOUTH CAROLINA DEPARTMENT OF NATURAL RESOURCES	108
STATE FISH AND WILDLIFE MANAGEMENT BOARD (NEW YORK)	93
TEXAS ORGANIZATION FOR ENDANGERED SPECIES	331
TROUT UNLIMITED, GUADELOUPE RIVER COUNCIL	334
WHALE AND DOLPHIN CONSERVATION SOCIETY	348
WHITETAILS UNLIMITED INC.	348
WILDLIFE FOREVER	351
WILDLIFE FOUNDATION OF FLORIDA, INC.	352
WILDLIFE LEGISLATIVE FUND OF AMERICA, THE, AND WILDLIFE CONSERVATION FUND OF AMERICA, THE	352
WILDLIFE RESOURCES AGENCY	110
WILDLIFE RESOURCES COMMISSION	95

Indigenous People

CIRCUMPOLAR CONSERVATION UNION	179

Inquiry Based Education

GREEN (GLOBAL RIVERS ENVIRONMENTAL EDUCATION NETWORK)	218

Insects and Butterflies

AMERICAN SOCIETY OF ZOOLOGISTS	156
AUDUBON SOCIETY OF RHODE ISLAND	164
AUDUBON SOCIETY OF WESTERN PENNSYLVANIA	165
BIO-INTEGRAL RESOURCE CENTER	166
DELAWARE STATE EXTENSION SERVICE	53
DRAGONFLY SOCIETY OF THE AMERICAS, THE	193
ENTOMOLOGICAL SOCIETY OF AMERICA	200
FISH AND WILDLIFE INFORMATION EXCHANGE	206
HAWAII NATURE CENTER	220
INDIANA AUDUBON SOCIETY, INC.	226
INSTITUTE OF TROPICAL AGRICULTURE AND HUMAN RESOURCES	61
MICHIGAN NATURE ASSOCIATION	255
NATIONAL COALITION AGAINST THE MISUSE OF PESTICIDES	266
NATURAL HISTORY SOCIETY OF MARYLAND, INC., THE	277
NATURE CONSERVANCY OF COLORADO, THE	279
NATURE SASKATCHEWAN	282
SMITHSONIAN INSTITUTION	320
STATE FORESTRY DIVISION (WYOMING)	126
WILD ONES - NATURAL LANDSCAPERS, LTD	349
XERCES SOCIETY, THE	364
YOUNG ENTOMOLOGISTS' SOCIETY INC.	365

International Conservation

AFRICAN WILDLIFE FOUNDATION	134
AFRICAN WILDLIFE NEWS SERVICE	135
AMERICAN ASSOCIATION OF ZOO KEEPERS, INC.	139
AMERICAN BIRD CONSERVANCY	140
AMERICAN SOCIETY OF MAMMALOGISTS	155
AMERICAN ZOO AND AQUARIUM ASSOCIATION (AZA)	157
ANCIENT FOREST INTERNATIONAL	157
ANIMAL WELFARE INSTITUTE	158
ANTARCTICA PROJECT	158
ASSOCIATION OF AVIAN VETERINARIANS	161
ATLANTIC CENTER FOR THE ENVIRONMENT	162, 163
BAT CONSERVATION INTERNATIONAL	165
BILLFISH FOUNDATION	166
BIRDLIFE INTERNATIONAL	166
CARIBBEAN CONSERVATION CORPORATION (Costa Rica Office)	173
CENTER FOR MARINE CONSERVATION	176
CENTER FOR THE STUDY OF TROPICAL BIRDS, INC. (Administrative Office)	177
CETACEAN SOCIETY INTERNATIONAL	177
CONSERVATION INTERNATIONAL	188
CONSERVATION TREATY SUPPORT FUND	188
CORAL REEF ALLIANCE, THE (CORAL)	189
DELTA WATERFOWL FOUNDATION	192
DUCKS UNLIMITED, INC. (Wetlands America Trust, Inc. Office)	196
EARTH FOUNDATION	197
EARTH ISLAND INSTITUTE	197
EARTHSTEWARDS NETWORK	198
EARTHTRUST	199
EARTHWATCH INSTITUTE	199
ECOTOURISM SOCIETY, THE	199
EDUCATIONAL COMMUNICATIONS, INC.	200
ENVIRONMENTAL AIR FORCE	201
ENVIRONMENTAL AND ENERGY STUDY INSTITUTE (EESI)	201
ENVIRONMENTAL DEFENSE FUND, INC.	202

ENVIRONMENTAL LAW ALLIANCE WORLDWIDE (E-LAW) 203
ENVIRONMENTAL LAW INSTITUTE, THE 203
EUROPARC FEDERATION 204
FEDERAL WILDLIFE OFFICER'S ASSOCIATION 205
FOSSIL RIM WILDLIFE CENTER 210
GAME CONSERVATION INTERNATIONAL (GAME COIN) 213
GEORGE MIKSCH SUTTON AVIAN RESEARCH CENTER INC. 214
GLOBAL ENVIRONMENTAL MANAGEMENT INITIATIVE (GEMI) 215
GREAT BEAR FOUNDATION 216
GREAT LAKES UNITED 217
HEADLANDS INSTITUTE 221
HUMMINGBIRD SOCIETY, THE 223
INSTITUTE FOR EARTH EDUCATION, THE 227
INTERFAITH COUNCIL FOR THE PROTECTION OF ANIMALS AND NATURE INC. (ICPAN) 227
INTERNATIONAL ASSOCIATION FOR ENVIRONMENTAL HYDROLOGY (IAEH) 228
INTERNATIONAL CENTRE FOR CONSERVATION EDUCATION 229
INTERNATIONAL COUNCIL OF ENVIRONMENTAL LAW 229
INTERNATIONAL CRANE FOUNDATION 230
INTERNATIONAL EROSION CONTROL ASSOCIATION (IECA) 230
INTERNATIONAL INSTITUTE FOR ENERGY CONSERVATION 231
INTERNATIONAL MARINE MAMMAL PROJECT, THE 231
INTERNATIONAL PRIMATE PROTECTION LEAGUE 232
INTERNATIONAL PROFESSIONAL HUNTERS' ASSOCIATION 232
INTERNATIONAL SNOW LEOPARD TRUST 232
INTERNATIONAL SOCIETY FOR ENDANGERED CATS (ISEC) 233
INTERNATIONAL SOCIETY OF TROPICAL FORESTERS INC. 233
INTERNATIONAL SONORAN DESERT ALLIANCE 234
INTERNATIONAL WILD WATERFOWL ASSOCIATION 235
INTERNATIONAL WILDERNESS LEADERSHIP (WILD) FOUNDATION ... 235
INTERNATIONAL WILDLIFE COALITION (IWC) AND THE WHALE ADOPTION PROJECT 235
INTERNATIONAL WOLF CENTER (Educational Services) 236
ISLAND RESOURCES FOUNDATION 239
KIDS FOR SAVING EARTH WORLDWIDE 246
NATIONAL WILDLIFE FEDERATION 273, 275
NATURE CONSERVANCY OF COLORADO, THE 279
NATURE CONSERVANCY, THE 279, 280, 281, 282
NORTH AMERICAN ASSOCIATION FOR ENVIRONMENTAL EDUCATION 288
NORTH AMERICAN COALITION ON RELIGION AND ECOLOGY (NACRE) 288
NORTH ATLANTIC SALMON CONSERVATION ORGANIZATION 289
NORTHWEST ATLANTIC FISHERIES ORGANIZATION (NAFO) 292
NORTHWEST RESOURCE INFORMATION CENTER 293
OCEAN VOICE INTERNATIONAL 294
PEREGRINE FUND, THE 303
RAINFOREST ACTION NETWORK 308
RAINFOREST ALLIANCE 309
RAINFOREST RELIEF 309
RENEWABLE NATURAL RESOURCES FOUNDATION 310
SEA SHEPHERD CONSERVATION SOCIETY 318
SIERRA CLUB 318, 319
SOCIETY FOR CONSERVATION BIOLOGY 321
SOCIETY FOR MARINE MAMMALOGY, THE 321
SOIL AND WATER CONSERVATION SOCIETY (formerly Soil Conservation Society of America) 323
THRESHOLD INC. 332
TREAD LIGHTLY! INC. 332
TREES FOR THE FUTURE, INC. 333
TRUST FOR WILDLIFE, INC. 338
UNITED NATIONS ENVIRONMENT PROGRAMME 339
UNITED STATES COMMITTEE FOR THE UNITED NATIONS ENVIRONMENT PROGRAMME THE (U.S. and UNEP) 339
UNITED STATES TOURIST COUNCIL 339
WESTERN HEMISPHERE SHOREBIRD RESERVE NETWORK (WHSRN) 347
WHALE AND DOLPHIN CONSERVATION SOCIETY 348
WILDLANDS PROJECT, THE 350
WILDLIFE CONSERVATION SOCIETY 350
WILDLIFE PRESERVATION TRUST INTERNATIONAL, INC. 353
WILSON ORNITHOLOGICAL SOCIETY 358
WORLD CONSERVATION MONITORING CENTRE 361
WORLD FORESTRY CENTER 362
WORLD WILDLIFE FUND 363
WORLD WOMEN IN THE DEFENSE OF THE ENVIRONMENT 363

International Trade and Environment

CENTER FOR INTERNATIONAL ENVIRONMENTAL LAW (CIEL) 175

International Wildlife

INTERNATIONAL OSPREY FOUNDATION INC., THE 232

Internships

AMERICAN ASSOCIATION OF BOTANICAL GARDENS AND ARBORETA, INC. 139
AMERICAN BASS ASSOCIATION OF WEST VIRGINIA, THE 140
AMERICAN CAMPING ASSOCIATION, INC. 141
ATLANTIC CENTER FOR THE ENVIRONMENT 162, 163
CADDO LAKE INSTITUTE, INC. 169
CENTER FOR ENVIRONMENTAL EDUCATION 174
CENTER FOR HEALTH, ENVIRONMENT, AND JUSTICE 175
CENTER FOR SCIENCE IN THE PUBLIC INTEREST 176
COMMUNITIES FOR A BETTER ENVIRONMENT 184
DEEP-PORTAGE CONSERVATION RESERVE 191
EARTH DAY NEW YORK 197
EARTHWATCH INSTITUTE 199
ECOLOGICAL SOCIETY OF AMERICA, THE 199
ECOLOGY CENTER 199
ENVIRONMENTAL CAREER CENTER 201
ENVIRONMENTAL CAREERS ORGANIZATION INC., THE 201
ENVIRONMENTAL RESOURCE CENTER (ERC) 204
FOSSIL RIM WILDLIFE CENTER 210
GREEN MOUNTAIN CLUB INC., THE 218
INSTITUTE FOR EARTH EDUCATION, THE 227
INTERNATIONAL MARINE MAMMAL PROJECT, THE 231
IOWA NATURAL HERITAGE FOUNDATION 238
MANOMET OBSERVATORY 251
MAX McGRAW WILDLIFE FOUNDATION 254
NATIONAL ASSOCIATION FOR INTERPRETATION 262
NATURE CONSERVANCY OF COLORADO, THE 279
NEW HAMPSHIRE FISH AND GAME DEPARTMENT 86
NORTHWEST ECOSYSTEM ALLIANCE 293
PACIFIC NORTHWEST TRAIL ASSOCIATION 300
PACIFIC WHALE FOUNDATION 301
PANOS INSTITUTE, THE 301
POPULATION INSTITUTE, THE 305
RAILS-TO-TRAILS CONSERVANCY 308
SOUTHEAST ALASKA CONSERVATION COUNCIL (SEACC) 324
SOUTHFACE ENERGY INSTITUTE 326
STUDENT CONSERVATION ASSOCIATION, INC. 328
THE GLACIER INSTITUTE 331
THORNE ECOLOGICAL INSTITUTE 331
THRESHOLD INC. 332
WILDERNESS EDUCATION ASSOCIATION 349

Interpretation

IOWA ASSOCIATION OF NATURALISTS 237

Interpretive Center

HAWAII NATURE CENTER 220

Islands

BARRIER ISLAND TRUST, INC. 165
FRIENDS OF THE SAN JUANS 212
GALIANO CONSERVANCY ASSOCIATION 213
HAWAII AUDUBON SOCIETY 219
HAWAII COOPERATIVE FISHERY RESEARCH UNIT (USDI) 60
HAWAII SOCIETY OF AMERICAN FORESTERS 220
ISLAND INSTITUTE, THE 239
ISLAND RESOURCES FOUNDATION 239
MAINE COAST HERITAGE TRUST 250
MICHIGAN NATURAL AREAS COUNCIL 255
PTARMIGANS, THE 306
PUERTO RICO SEA GRANT PROGRAM 105
SANIBEL-CAPTIVA CONSERVATION FOUNDATION, INC. 315
WESTERN PACIFIC REGIONAL FISHERY MANAGEMENT COUNCIL 347

Justice

THREE CIRCLES CENTER FOR MULTICULTURAL ENVIRONMENTAL EDUCATION 332

Lakes

ADIRONDACK PARK AGENCY 90
ADOPT-A-STREAM FOUNDATION, THE 134
AMERICAN SOCIETY OF LIMNOLOGY AND OCEANOGRAPHY 155
ASSOCIATION FOR THE PROTECTION OF THE ADIRONDACKS, THE . 160
ATLANTIC STATES LEGAL FOUNDATION 163
BLACK BASS FOUNDATION 166

KEYWORD INDEX - Land Conservation/Land Purchase 469

Keyword Index

CHINA REGION LAKES ALLIANCE 179
COMITE DESPERTAR CIDRENO 105
DEPARTMENT OF ENVIRONMENT AND NATURAL RESOURCES (SOUTH DAKOTA) 109
DEPARTMENT OF WATER RESOURCES (NEBRASKA) 83
FLORIDA AUDUBON SOCIETY 206
FLORIDA GAME AND FRESH WATER FISH COMMISSION 55
FLORIDA STATE COOPERATIVE EXTENSION SERVICE 56
FRESHWATER FOUNDATION 211
INDIANA DEPARTMENT OF NATURAL RESOURCES 64
INTERNATIONAL ASSOCIATION OF NATURAL RESOURCE PILOTS 228
IOWA DEPARTMENT OF NATURAL RESOURCES 65
KANSAS DEPARTMENT OF WILDLIFE AND PARKS 67
KANSAS WATER OFFICE 68
LAKE MICHIGAN FEDERATION 246
LAND BETWEEN THE LAKES ASSOCIATION 247
LEAGUE TO SAVE LAKE TAHOE 248
MICHIGAN DEPARTMENT OF ENVIRONMENTAL QUALITY 76
MINNESOTA BOARD OF WATER AND SOIL RESOURCES 77
MINNESOTA SEA GRANT COLLEGE PROGRAM 79
MONITOR INTERNATIONAL 259
MONO LAKE COMMITTEE 259
MUSKIES, INC. 262
NATIONAL BOATING FEDERATION 266
NEW HAMPSHIRE LAKES ASSOCIATION 284
NEWFOUNDLAND LABRADOR WILDLIFE FEDERATION 287
NORTH AMERICAN FISHING CLUB 289
NORTH AMERICAN LOON FUND 289
NORTH CASCADES CONSERVATION COUNCIL 291
OHIO ENVIRONMENTAL COUNCIL, INC. 295
OHIO SEA GRANT COLLEGE PROGRAM, F.T. STONE LABORATORY, AND GREAT LAKES AQUATIC ECOSYSTEM RESEARCH CONSORTIUM (GLAERC) 97
OKLAHOMA WATER RESOURCES BOARD 99
RESOURCES AGENCY, THE 47
SEAPLANE PILOTS ASSOCIATION 318
TAHOE REGIONAL PLANNING AGENCY 329
UNIVERSITY OF NEW HAMPSHIRE COOPERATIVE EXTENSION 86
WISCONSIN ASSOCIATION FOR ENVIRONMENTAL EDUCATION, INC. 359
WISCONSIN ASSOCIATION OF LAKES (WAL) 359
WISCONSIN COOPERATIVE FISHERY RESEARCH UNIT (USDI) 123
WISCONSIN SEA GRANT INSTITUTE 125

Land Conservation

LAND TRUST ALLIANCE, THE 247

Land Management

WASHINGTON WILDLIFE HERITAGE FOUNDATION (including Heritage Land Trust 345
WISCONSIN DEPARTMENT OF NATURAL RESOURCES 124

Land Preservation

1000 FRIENDS OF FLORIDA 133
ACRES LAND TRUST 133
ADIRONDACK MOUNTAIN CLUB, INC., THE 134
ADIRONDACK NATURE CONSERVANCY/ADIRONDACK LAND TRUST, INC. 134
ARLINGTON OUTDOOR EDUCATION ASSOCIATION, INC. 160
AUDUBON SOCIETY OF RHODE ISLAND 164
BARRIER ISLAND TRUST, INC. 165
CALIFORNIANS FOR POPULATION STABILIZATION (CAPS) 170
COMMUNITY RIGHTS COUNSEL 184
CONSERVATION FEDERATION OF MARYLAND/For A Rural Maryland (F.A.R.M.) 187
DEPARTMENT OF LAND AND NATURAL RESOURCES 59, 60
DESERT TORTOISE COUNCIL 193
EASTERN SHORE LAND CONSERVANCY 199
ECOLOGY CENTER 199
ENVIRONMENTAL AIR FORCE 201
ENVIRONMENTAL LEAGUE OF MASSACHUSETTS (ELM) 203
GALIANO CONSERVANCY ASSOCIATION 213
GRAND CANYON TRUST (Washington, DC Office) 216
IDAHO STATE DEPARTMENT OF AGRICULTURE 62
ILLINOIS ASSOCIATION OF CONSERVATION DISTRICTS 224
ILLINOIS AUDUBON SOCIETY 224
INTERTRIBAL BISON COOPERATIVE (ITBC) 236
IOWA NATURAL HERITAGE FOUNDATION 238
IOWA TRAILS COUNCIL 238
IZAAK WALTON LEAGUE OF AMERICA, INC., THE 240
JACKSON HOLE LAND TRUST 242
KANSAS WILDSCAPE FOUNDATION 244
KENTUCKY DEPARTMENT OF PARKS 68
KIDS FOR SAVING EARTH WORLDWIDE 246
LEE COUNTY PARKS AND RECREATION SERVICES 56
MAINE COAST HERITAGE TRUST 250
MASSACHUSETTS AUDUBON SOCIETY, INC. 253
MICHIGAN AUDUBON SOCIETY 254
MICHIGAN NATURE ASSOCIATION 255
MINNESOTA WINGS SOCIETY, INC. 257
MISSOURI PRAIRIE FOUNDATION 259
MONTANA LAND RELIANCE 260
MOUNTAIN LION FOUNDATION 261
NATIONAL PARKS AND CONSERVATION ASSOCIATION (NPCA) 270
NATIONAL WILDLIFE FEDERATION 273, 275
NATURAL AREAS ASSOCIATION 277
NATURAL LAND INSTITUTE 277
NATURE PRESERVES COMMISSION 63, 69
NATURE SASKATCHEWAN 282
NEW JERSEY AUDUBON SOCIETY 285
NEW JERSEY CONSERVATION FOUNDATION 285
NEW YORK-NEW JERSEY TRAIL CONFERENCE INC. 287
NORTH CASCADES CONSERVATION COUNCIL 291
OUTDOOR CIRCLE, THE 299
PARKS AND RECREATION DEPARTMENT (NORTH DAKOTA) 96
PENNSYLVANIA DEPARTMENT OF AGRICULTURE 104
PENNSYLVANIA DEPARTMENT OF CONSERVATION AND NATURAL RESOURCES 105
RAILS-TO-TRAILS CONSERVANCY 308
SAVE THE DUNES COUNCIL 316
SCENIC AMERICA 317
SCENIC HUDSON, INC. 317
SOUTHERN ENVIRONMENTAL LAW CENTER 325, 326
STATEWIDE PROGRAM OF ACTION TO CONSERVE OUR ENVIRONMENT (SPACE 327
TRUST FOR WILDLIFE, INC. 338
TRUSTEES OF RESERVATIONS, THE 338
TUG HILL TOMORROW, INC. 338
VERMONT INSTITUTE OF NATURAL SCIENCE 341
VIRGINIA OUTDOORS FOUNDATION 118
WASHINGTON WILDLIFE AND RECREATION COALITION 345
WESTERN PENNSYLVANIA CONSERVANCY 347
WILD ONES - NATURAL LANDSCAPERS, LTD 349
WILDERNESS LAND TRUST, THE (Colorado Office) 349
WISCONSIN DEPARTMENT OF AGRICULTURE (Land and Water Resources Bureau) 123
WORLD PARKS ENDOWMENT INC. 362
WYOMING DEPARTMENT OF COMMERCE 126
WYOMING STATE BOARD OF LAND COMMISSIONERS 126

Land Protection

CATSKILL CENTER FOR CONSERVATION AND DEVELOPMENT, INC., THE 174
LAND TRUST ALLIANCE, THE 247
NEW HAMPSHIRE DEPARTMENT OF AGRICULTURE, MARKETS, AND FOOD 85

Land Purchase

AMERICAN FARMLAND TRUST 142
AMERICAN LAND CONSERVANCY 151
AMERICAN RESOURCES GROUP 154
ANCIENT FOREST INTERNATIONAL 157
APPALACHIAN TRAIL CONFERENCE 158
ARCHAEOLOGICAL CONSERVANCY 158
CALIFORNIA TROUT, INC. 170
COLORADO WILDLIFE HERITAGE FOUNDATION 183
CONSERVATION FUND, THE 187
DESERT TORTOISE PRESERVE COMMITTEE, INC. 193
EARTH FOUNDATION 197
FLORIDA PANTHER PROJECT, INC., THE 208
GALIANO CONSERVANCY ASSOCIATION 213
INTERAGENCY COMMITTEE FOR OUTDOOR RECREATION (IAC) 120
IOWA DEPARTMENT OF NATURAL RESOURCES 65
IZAAK WALTON LEAGUE OF AMERICA, INC., THE 240
JACKSON HOLE LAND TRUST 242
LAND TRUST ALLIANCE, THE 247
MASSACHUSETTS ASSOCIATION OF CONSERVATION COMMISSIONS (MACC) 253
MICHIGAN NATURE ASSOCIATION 255
MINNESOTA PARKS AND TRAILS COUNCIL 257
MISSOURI PRAIRIE FOUNDATION 259
NATIONAL ASSOCIATION OF STATE OUTDOOR RECREATION LIAISON OFFICERS 264
NATIONAL ASSOCIATION OF STATE PARK DIRECTORS 264
NATIONAL PARK TRUST 270
NATURAL HERITAGE COMMISSION (ARKANSAS) 45
NATURAL LAND INSTITUTE 277
NATURE CONSERVANCY, THE 279, 280, 281, 282
NATURE CONSERVANCY, THE, IOWA CHAPTER 280

NEW JERSEY CONSERVATION FOUNDATION ... 285
OPENLANDS PROJECT ... 297
PIEDMONT ENVIRONMENTAL COUNCIL ... 303
PRAIRIE CLUB, THE ... 305
PUERTO RICO ASSOCIATION OF SOIL AND WATER CONSERVATION DISTRICTS ... 307
PUERTO RICO DEPARTMENT OF NATURAL AND ENVIRONMENTAL RESOURCES ... 105
RIVER NETWORK ... 312
ROCKY MOUNTAIN ELK FOUNDATION ... 313
SANIBEL-CAPTIVA CONSERVATION FOUNDATION, INC. ... 315
SAVE-THE-REDWOODS LEAGUE ... 317
SOCIETY FOR THE PROTECTION OF NEW HAMPSHIRE FORESTS ... 322
TRUST FOR PUBLIC LAND, THE ... 337
TURTLE CREEK WATERSHED ASSOCIATION, INC. ... 338
WASHINGTON WILDLIFE AND RECREATION COALITION ... 345
WASHINGTON WILDLIFE FEDERATION ... 345
WILDERNESS LAND TRUST, THE (Colorado Office) ... 349
WILDLIFE FOREVER ... 351
WORLD PARKS ENDOWMENT INC. ... 362

Land Use Planning

ADIRONDACK COUNCIL, THE ... 133
ADIRONDACK PARK AGENCY ... 90
ADOPT-A-STREAM FOUNDATION, THE ... 134
ALABAMA NATURAL HERITAGE PROGRAM ... 135
ALASKA DEPARTMENT OF NATURAL RESOURCES ... 41
AMERICAN CAVE CONSERVATION ASSOCIATION ... 141
AMERICAN FARMLAND TRUST ... 142
AMERICAN FISHERIES SOCIETY, WISCONSIN CHAPTER ... 149
AMERICAN GEOGRAPHICAL SOCIETY ... 150
AMERICAN HIKING SOCIETY ... 150
AMERICAN HORSE PROTECTION ASSOCIATION ... 151
AMERICAN PLANNING ASSOCIATION ... 154
AMERICAN SOCIETY OF LANDSCAPE ARCHITECTS ... 155
ARIZONA GEOLOGICAL SURVEY ... 42
ARIZONA LAND DEPARTMENT ... 42
ASSOCIATION FOR THE PROTECTION OF THE ADIRONDACKS, THE. 160
ASSOCIATION OF AMERICAN GEOGRAPHERS ... 161
AUDUBON INTERNATIONAL ... 163
CALIFORNIANS FOR POPULATION STABILIZATION (CAPS) ... 170
CENTER FOR WATERSHED PROTECTION ... 177
CHESAPEAKE BAY FOUNDATION, INC. (Maryland Office) ... 178
COAST ALLIANCE ... 181
COLORADO NATURAL HERITAGE PROGRAM ... 182
COLORADO STATE FOREST SERVICE ... 51
COLUMBIA RIVER GORGE COMMISSION ... 119
COMMUNITY ENVIRONMENTAL COUNCIL ... 184
COMMUNITY RIGHTS COUNSEL ... 184
CONFEDERATED SALISH AND KOOTENAI TRIBES ... 185
CONNECTICUT FUND FOR THE ENVIRONMENT ... 186
CONNECTICUT RIVER WATERSHED COUNCIL INC. ... 186
CONSERVATION FUND, THE ... 187
COUNCIL ON ENVIRONMENTAL QUALITY (CONNECTICUT) ... 52
DELAWARE ASSOCIATION OF CONSERVATION DISTRICTS ... 191
DELAWARE DEPARTMENT OF AGRICULTURE ... 52
DELAWARE STATE EXTENSION SERVICE ... 53
DESERT TORTOISE COUNCIL ... 193
ENVIRONMENTAL DEFENSE CENTER, INC. ... 201
ENVIRONMENTAL LEAGUE OF MASSACHUSETTS (ELM) ... 203
ENVIRONMENTAL QUALITY COUNCIL ... 82
E-P EDUCATION SERVICES, INC. ... 196
FLORIDA AUDUBON SOCIETY ... 206
FLORIDA DEFENDERS OF THE ENVIRONMENT, INC. (Home Office) ... 207
FLORIDA SPORTSMEN'S CONSERVATION ASSOCIATION ... 208
FOREST HISTORY SOCIETY, INC. ... 209
FOREST TRUST ... 209
FOSSIL FUELS POLICY ACTION INSTITUTE/ALLIANCE FOR A PAVING MORATORIUM ... 210
FRIENDS OF THE SAN JUANS ... 212
GALIANO CONSERVANCY ASSOCIATION ... 213
GEORGIA CONSERVANCY, INC., THE ... 214
GLOBAL CITIES PROJECT, THE ... 215
GRAND CANYON TRUST (Washington, DC Office) ... 216
IDAHO STATE DEPARTMENT OF AGRICULTURE ... 62
ILLINOIS DEPARTMENT OF AGRICULTURE ... 62
INTERAGENCY COMMITTEE FOR OUTDOOR RECREATION (IAC) ... 120
INTERNATIONAL ASSOCIATION FOR BEAR RESEARCH AND MANAGEMENT ... 228
INTERNATIONAL ASSOCIATION OF NATURAL RESOURCE PILOTS ... 228
INTERNATIONAL BICYCLE FUND ... 229
IOWA TRAILS COUNCIL ... 238
ISLAND RESOURCES FOUNDATION ... 239
IZAAK WALTON LEAGUE OF AMERICA, INC., THE ... 240
JACKSON HOLE CONSERVATION ALLIANCE ... 242
LAND TRUST ALLIANCE, THE ... 247
LEAGUE OF WOMEN VOTERS OF IOWA ... 247
LEAGUE TO SAVE LAKE TAHOE ... 248
LOWER MISSISSIPPI RIVER CONSERVATION COMMITTEE ... 249
MANOMET OBSERVATORY ... 251
MARIN CONSERVATION LEAGUE ... 251
MAX McGRAW WILDLIFE FOUNDATION ... 254
MICHIGAN ENVIRONMENTAL COUNCIL ... 255
MID-ATLANTIC COUNCIL OF WATERSHED ASSOCIATIONS ... 256
MINNESOTA BOARD OF WATER AND SOIL RESOURCES ... 77
MONTANA AUDUBON ... 260
MONTANA ENVIRONMENTAL INFORMATION CENTER ... 260
NATIONAL ASSOCIATION OF RECREATION RESOURCE PLANNERS .. 263
NATIONAL ASSOCIATION OF STATE PARK DIRECTORS ... 264
NATIONAL GRANGE, THE ... 269
NATIONAL MILITARY FISH AND WILDLIFE ASSOCIATION ... 269
NATIONAL TRUST FOR HISTORIC PRESERVATION ... 272
NATURAL LAND INSTITUTE ... 277
NEVADA BUREAU OF MINES AND GEOLOGY ... 84
NEW HAMPSHIRE ASSOCIATION OF CONSERVATION COMMISSIONS ... 284
NEW HAMPSHIRE LAKES ASSOCIATION ... 284
NEW JERSEY CONSERVATION FOUNDATION ... 285
NEW JERSEY ENVIRONMENTAL LOBBY ... 286
NEW JERSEY PINELANDS COMMISSION ... 88
NEW YORK GEOLOGICAL SURVEY AND STATE MUSEUM ... 92
NORTH CAROLINA COASTAL FEDERATION, INC. ... 290
NORTH CASCADES CONSERVATION COUNCIL ... 291
NORTH DAKOTA GEOLOGICAL SURVEY ... 96
NORTHWEST RENEWABLE RESOURCES CENTER ... 293
OFFICE OF ENERGY EFFICIENCY AND ENVIRONMENT ... 93
OKLAHOMA GEOLOGICAL SURVEY ... 98
OPENLANDS PROJECT ... 297
OREGON B.A.S.S. CHAPTER FEDERATION ... 297
OUTDOOR RECREATION COUNCIL OF BRITISH COLUMBIA ... 299
PUBLIC LANDS FOUNDATION ... 307
RENEWABLE NATURAL RESOURCES FOUNDATION ... 310
RESOURCES FOR THE FUTURE ... 310
RHODE ISLAND WILD PLANT SOCIETY ... 311
RIVER FEDERATION ... 312
SCENIC AMERICA ... 317
SIERRA CLUB FOUNDATION, THE ... 319
SOCIETY FOR RANGE MANAGEMENT ... 321
SONORAN INSTITUTE ... 323
SOUTH CAROLINA B.A.S.S. CHAPTER FEDERATION ... 323
SOUTHEAST ALASKA CONSERVATION COUNCIL (SEACC) ... 324
STATE WATER RESOURCES BOARD (RHODE ISLAND) ... 107
TAHOE REGIONAL PLANNING AGENCY ... 329
THRESHOLD INC. ... 332
TROUT UNLIMITED, PENNSYLVANIA COUNCIL ... 336
URBAN HABITAT PROGRAM ... 340
VIRGINIA B.A.S.S. CHAPTER FEDERATION ... 342
WEST MICHIGAN ENVIRONMENTAL ACTION COUNCIL ... 346
WISCONSIN ASSOCIATION OF LAKES (WAL) ... 359
WISCONSIN DEPARTMENT OF AGRICULTURE (Land and Water Resources Bureau) ... 123
WYOMING STATE GEOLOGICAL SURVEY ... 126

Landscape Analysis

UTAH COOPERATIVE FISH AND WILDLIFE RESEARCH UNIT (USDI-USGS-BRD-CRU) ... 113

Landscape Architecture

ADKINS ARBORETUM ... 134
AMERICAN SOCIETY OF LANDSCAPE ARCHITECTS ... 155
FRIENDS OF DISCOVERY PARK ... 211
INSTITUTE OF TROPICAL AGRICULTURE AND HUMAN RESOURCES ... 61
LADY BIRD JOHNSON WILDFLOWER CENTER (formerly the National Wildflower Research Center) ... 246
MISSISSIPPI NATIVE PLANT SOCIETY ... 258
SCENIC AMERICA ... 317
VIRGINIA NATIVE PLANT SOCIETY ... 343

Landscape Ecology

DEPARTMENT OF INTERIOR, U.S.G.S/B.R.D, SOUTH CAROLINA COOPERATIVE FISH AND WILDLIFE RESEARCH UNIT ... 107

Law Enforcement

FISH AND WILDLIFE DIVISION/DEPARTMENT OF STATE POLICE ... 100

KEYWORD INDEX - Legal Advocacy/Mining

Legal Advocacy

MINNESOTA CENTER FOR ENVIRONMENTAL ADVOCACY (MCEA) 256

Leisure

AMERICAN ASSOCIATION FOR LEISURE AND RECREATION (AALR) .. 139

Librarians/Information Professionals

NATURAL RESOURCES INFORMATION COUNCIL 278

Litter

PENNSYLVANIA RESOURCES COUNCIL, INC., (formerly PA Roadside Council) 302

Local Resource Conservation

COMMUNITY CONSERVATION CONSULTANTS/HOWLERS FOREVER, INC. 184

Mammals

A. E. HOWELL WILDLIFE CONSERVATION CENTER 133
AMERICAN HORSE PROTECTION ASSOCIATION 151
AMERICAN SOCIETY OF MAMMALOGISTS 155
AMERICAN SOCIETY OF ZOOLOGISTS 156
ANIMAL PROTECTION INSTITUTE 157
ANIMAL WELFARE INSTITUTE 158
AUDUBON SOCIETY OF WESTERN PENNSYLVANIA 165
BAT CONSERVATION INTERNATIONAL 165
BOUNTY INFORMATION SERVICE 167
CANADIAN COOPERATIVE WILDLIFE HEALTH CENTRE 171
DEPARTMENT OF PLANNING AND NATURAL RESOURCES 115
ELSA WILD ANIMAL APPEAL (Louisiana Chapter) 200
FEDERAL WILDLIFE OFFICER'S ASSOCIATION 205
FISH AND WILDLIFE INFORMATION EXCHANGE 206
FOUNDATION FOR NORTH AMERICAN BIG GAME 210
FRIENDS OF THE SEA OTTER 212
INTERNATIONAL MARINE MAMMAL PROJECT, THE 231
INTERNATIONAL PRIMATE PROTECTION LEAGUE 232
INTERNATIONAL WILDLIFE COALITION (IWC) AND THE WHALE ADOPTION PROJECT 235
INTERNATIONAL WOLF CENTER (Educational Services) 236
MASSACHUSETTS TRAPPER'S ASSOCIATION, INC. 254
MAX McGRAW WILDLIFE FOUNDATION 254
MICHIGAN NATURE ASSOCIATION 255
MOUNTAIN LION FOUNDATION 261
NATIONAL WILDLIFE REHABILITATORS ASSOCIATION 275
NATURAL HISTORY SOCIETY OF MARYLAND, INC., THE 277
NATURE SASKATCHEWAN 282
NEWFOUNDLAND LABRADOR WILDLIFE FEDERATION 287
OHIO COOPERATIVE FISH AND WILDLIFE RESEARCH UNIT (USDI) 96
PREDATOR PROJECT 306
SCIENTISTS CENTER FOR ANIMAL WELFARE 318
SMITHSONIAN INSTITUTION 320
SOCIETY FOR ANIMAL PROTECTIVE LEGISLATION 320
TALLAHASSEE MUSEUM OF HISTORY AND NATURAL SCIENCE 329
TRAFFIC USA 332
UTAH COOPERATIVE FISH AND WILDLIFE RESEARCH UNIT (USDI-USGS-BRD-CRU) 113
WELDER WILDLIFE FOUNDATION 345
WILDLIFE CENTER OF VIRGINIA, THE 350
WILDLIFE DAMAGE REVIEW (WDR) 351
WILDLIFE EDUCATION PROGRAM AND DESIGN 351
WILDLIFE FOREVER 351
WILDLIFE WAYSTATION 358
WORLD SOCIETY FOR THE PROTECTION OF ANIMALS (WSPA) 363
YELLOWSTONE GRIZZLY FOUNDATION (YGF) 364

Management Plans

WESTERN PACIFIC REGIONAL FISHERY MANAGEMENT COUNCIL 347

Manatees

MOTE MARINE LABORATORY 261

Mangrove Habitats

PUERTO RICO SEA GRANT PROGRAM 105

Mapping

OKLAHOMA GEOLOGICAL SURVEY 98

Marine Conservation

NATIONAL AUDUBON SOCIETY, LIVING OCEANS PROGRAM 265

Marine Mammals

ALASKA SEA GRANT COLLEGE PROGRAM 41
AMERICAN CETACEAN SOCIETY 141
AMERICAN SOCIETY OF MAMMALOGISTS 155
ANIMAL PROTECTION INSTITUTE 157
ANIMAL WELFARE INSTITUTE 158
CANADIAN FEDERATION OF HUMANE SOCIETIES 172
CASCADIA RESEARCH 174
CENTER FOR MARINE CONSERVATION 176
CETACEAN SOCIETY INTERNATIONAL 177
EARTH ISLAND INSTITUTE 197
EARTHTRUST 199
EUROPEAN ASSOCIATION FOR AQUATIC MAMMALS 204
EUROPEAN CETACEAN SOCIETY 204
FEDERAL WILDLIFE OFFICER'S ASSOCIATION 205
FRIENDS OF ANIMALS INC. 211
FRIENDS OF THE SAN JUANS 212
FUND FOR ANIMALS INC., THE 212
HUMANE SOCIETY OF THE UNITED STATES, THE 222
INTERNATIONAL ECOLOGY SOCIETY (IES) 230
INTERNATIONAL MARINE MAMMAL PROJECT, THE 231
INTERNATIONAL OCEANOGRAPHIC FOUNDATION 231
INTERNATIONAL WILDLIFE COALITION (IWC) AND THE WHALE ADOPTION PROJECT 235
MARINE ENVIRONMENTAL RESEARCH INSTITUTE (MERI) 252
MARINE MAMMAL CENTER, THE 252
MID-ATLANTIC FISHERY MANAGEMENT COUNCIL 256
NEW HAMPSHIRE SEA GRANT PROGRAM 86
PACIFIC WHALE FOUNDATION 301
PUERTO RICO SEA GRANT PROGRAM 105
SAVE THE MANATEE CLUB 316
SCIENTISTS CENTER FOR ANIMAL WELFARE 318
SEA SHEPHERD CONSERVATION SOCIETY 318
SMITHSONIAN INSTITUTION 320
SOCIETY FOR ANIMAL PROTECTIVE LEGISLATION 320
SOCIETY FOR MARINE MAMMALOGY, THE 321
WHALE AND DOLPHIN CONSERVATION SOCIETY 348
WORLD SOCIETY FOR THE PROTECTION OF ANIMALS (WSPA) 363

Marine Protected Areas

AMERICAN OCEANS CAMPAIGN 153
MARINE CONSERVATION BIOLOGY INSTITUTE 251

Mineral Resources

ARIZONA GEOLOGICAL SURVEY 42
INDIANA STATE GEOLOGICAL SURVEY 65
WYOMING STATE GEOLOGICAL SURVEY 126

Mining

ATLANTIC STATES LEGAL FOUNDATION 163
DEPARTMENT OF ENVIRONMENT AND NATURAL RESOURCES (SOUTH DAKOTA) 109
DESERT TORTOISE COUNCIL 193
MICHIGAN DEPARTMENT OF ENVIRONMENTAL QUALITY 76
MONTANA ENVIRONMENTAL INFORMATION CENTER 260
NORTH CASCADES CONSERVATION COUNCIL 291
NORTHERN PLAINS RESOURCE COUNCIL 292
RESOURCES FOR THE FUTURE 310
SOUTHWEST CENTER FOR BIOLOGICAL DIVERSITY 326
SOUTHWEST RESEARCH AND INFORMATION CENTER 326
WESTERN ENVIRONMENTAL LAW CENTER 346

Mountain Ecosystems

HAWK MOUNTAIN SANCTUARY ASSOCIATION 220

Museum

AMERICAN CAVE CONSERVATION ASSOCIATION 141

NAFTA Superhighway

FOSSIL FUELS POLICY ACTION INSTITUTE/ALLIANCE FOR A PAVING MORATORIUM 210

National Forests

SAVE AMERICA'S FORESTS 315

National Parks

GREAT SMOKY MOUNTAINS INSTITUTE AT TREMONT 217
HIMALAYAN WILDLIFE PROJECT 221
NATIONAL PARK FOUNDATION 269
NATIONAL PARKS AND CONSERVATION ASSOCIATION (NPCA) 270

Native Plants

AUDUBON SOCIETY OF WESTERN PENNSYLVANIA 165
LADY BIRD JOHNSON WILDFLOWER CENTER (formerly the National Wildlflower Research Center) 246
NATIVE PLANT SOCIETY OF OREGON 276

Natural Areas

ADIRONDACK MOUNTAIN CLUB, INC., THE 134
ALABAMA NATURAL HERITAGE PROGRAM 135
ARIZONA STATE PARKS BOARD 43
AUDUBON COUNCIL OF CONNECTICUT 163
BIG BEND NATURAL HISTORY ASSOCIATION 166
COLUMBIA RIVER GORGE COMMISSION 119
CONFERENCE OF NATIONAL PARK COOPERATING ASSOCIATIONS . 185
DELAWARE NATURE SOCIETY 192
DESERT FISHES COUNCIL 193
EASTERN SHORE LAND CONSERVANCY 199
FAIRFAX AUDUBON SOCIETY 205
FLORIDA EXOTIC PEST PLANT COUNCIL 207
FLORIDA NATIVE PLANT SOCIETY 207
FLORIDA TRAIL ASSOCIATION, INC. 208
GALIANO CONSERVANCY ASSOCIATION 213
HAWAII AUDUBON SOCIETY 219
IDAHO FISH AND WILDLIFE FOUNDATION 62
ILLINOIS NATIVE PLANT SOCIETY 225
INTERNATIONAL ASSOCIATION OF NATURAL RESOURCE PILOTS 228
IOWA DEPARTMENT OF NATURAL RESOURCES 65
IOWA NATURAL HERITAGE FOUNDATION 238
IZAAK WALTON LEAGUE OF AMERICA, INC., THE 240
LAND BETWEEN THE LAKES ASSOCIATION 247
MAINE COAST HERITAGE TRUST 250
MANOMET OBSERVATORY 251
MAX McGRAW WILDLIFE FOUNDATION 254
MICHIGAN NATURE ASSOCIATION 255
MISSOURI NATIVE PLANT SOCIETY 259
MONTANA LAND RELIANCE 260
NATURAL AREAS ASSOCIATION 277
NATURAL HERITAGE COMMISSION (ARKANSAS) 45
NATURAL LAND INSTITUTE 277
NATURE SASKATCHEWAN 282
NEW JERSEY CONSERVATION FOUNDATION 285
NEW YORK-NEW JERSEY TRAIL CONFERENCE INC. 287
NORTH CASCADES CONSERVATION COUNCIL 291
NORTHERN ALASKA ENVIRONMENTAL CENTER 292
OKLAHOMA NATIVE PLANT SOCIETY 296
OREGON NATURAL RESOURCES COUNCIL 298
OREGON PARKS AND RECREATION DEPARTMENT 101
OUTDOOR CIRCLE, THE 299
PARTNERS IN PARKS 301
PENNSYLVANIA DEPARTMENT OF CONSERVATION AND NATURAL RESOURCES 105
PUERTO RICO SEA GRANT PROGRAM 105
SOUTH CAROLINA DEPARTMENT OF NATURAL RESOURCES 108
SOUTHERN ENVIRONMENTAL LAW CENTER 325, 326
TALLAHASSEE MUSEUM OF HISTORY AND NATURAL SCIENCE 329
TENNESSEE CITIZENS FOR WILDERNESS PLANNING 329
TUG HILL TOMORROW, INC. 338
UTAH B.A.S.S. CHAPTER FEDERATION 340
VIRGINIA FORESTRY ASSOCIATION 342
VIRGINIA NATIVE PLANT SOCIETY 343
WASHINGTON TRAILS ASSOCIATION 344
WILD ONES - NATURAL LANDSCAPERS, LTD 349
WYOMING NATIVE PLANT SOCIETY 364

Natural History

ADIRONDACK MOUNTAIN CLUB, INC., THE 134
ALABAMA NATURAL HERITAGE PROGRAM 135
ALASKA NATURAL RESOURCE AND OUTDOOR EDUCATION ASSOCIATION 137
AMERICAN ASSOCIATION OF ZOO KEEPERS, INC. 139
AMERICAN BASS ASSOCIATION OF WEST VIRGINIA, THE 140
AMERICAN MUSEUM OF NATURAL HISTORY 153
AMERICAN NATURE STUDY SOCIETY 153
AMERICAN SOCIETY FOR ENVIRONMENTAL HISTORY 154
AUDUBON NATURALIST SOCIETY OF THE CENTRAL ATLANTIC STATES 164
AUDUBON SOCIETY OF MISSOURI 164
AUDUBON SOCIETY OF PORTLAND 164
AUDUBON SOCIETY OF WESTERN PENNSYLVANIA 165
CALIFORNIA ACADEMY OF SCIENCES 45, 169
CHIHUAHUAN DESERT RESEARCH INSTITUTE 179
CORNELL LAB OF ORNITHOLOGY 189
DELAWARE MUSEUM OF NATURAL HISTORY 192
ENVIRONMENT COUNCIL OF RHODE ISLAND 200
ENVIRONMENTAL RESOURCE CENTER (ERC) 204
ENVIROSOUTH, INC. 204
FEDERATION OF ALBERTA NATURALIST 205
FLORIDA ORNITHOLOGICAL SOCIETY 208
GREAT SMOKY MOUNTAINS INSTITUTE AT TREMONT 217
GREEN MOUNTAIN CLUB INC., THE 218
HAWAII NATURE CENTER 220
HEADLANDS INSTITUTE 221
HIGH DESERT MUSEUM, THE 221
HUMBOLT FIELD RESEARCH INSTITUTE 223
INTERNATIONAL WILDLIFE REHABILITATION COUNCIL (IWRC) 236
KANSAS ACADEMY OF SCIENCE 242
KANSAS HERPETOLOGICAL SOCIETY 243
MAINE AUDUBON SOCIETY 250
MAINE ENVIRONMENTAL EDUCATION ASSOCIATION, INC. 250
MARYLAND ORNITHOLOGICAL SOCIETY, INC. 253
MASSACHUSETTS AUDUBON SOCIETY, INC. 253
MICHIGAN NATURE ASSOCIATION 255
MISSISSIPPI NATIVE PLANT SOCIETY 258
MISSOURI NATIVE PLANT SOCIETY 259
NATIONAL ASSOCIATION FOR INTERPRETATION 262
NATIONAL GEOGRAPHIC SOCIETY 268
NATURAL HISTORY SOCIETY OF MARYLAND, INC., THE 277
NATURAL RESOURCES INFORMATION COUNCIL 278
NATURAL SCIENCE FOR YOUTH FOUNDATION 278
NATURE SASKATCHEWAN 282
NEW ENGLAND WILD FLOWER SOCIETY, INC. 284
NEW JERSEY AUDUBON SOCIETY 285
NEW MEXICO BUREAU OF MINES AND MINERAL RESOURCES 89
NORTH DAKOTA NATURAL SCIENCE SOCIETY 291
NORTHWEST INTERPRETIVE ASSOCIATION 293
OHIO BIOLOGICAL SURVEY 295
OKLAHOMA ACADEMY OF SCIENCE 295
PENNSYLVANIA AUDUBON SOCIETY 301
PENNSYLVANIA RESOURCES COUNCIL, INC., (formerly PA Roadside Council) 302
ROGER TORY PETERSON INSTITUTE 314
SMITHSONIAN INSTITUTION 320
SOCIETY FOR MARINE MAMMALOGY, THE 321
SOUTH DAKOTA B.A.S.S. CHAPTER FEDERATION 324
SOUTHEASTERN FISHES COUNCIL 325
TALLAHASSEE MUSEUM OF HISTORY AND NATURAL SCIENCE 329
THE GLACIER INSTITUTE 331
TRUST FOR WILDLIFE, INC. 338
VERMONT B.A.S.S. CHAPTER FEDERATION 341
WASHINGTON FARM FORESTRY ASSOCIATION 344
WILDLIFE EDUCATION PROGRAM AND DESIGN 351
WILSON ORNITHOLOGICAL SOCIETY 358
WISCONSIN GEOLOGICAL AND NATURAL HISTORY SURVEY 125
WORLD FORESTRY CENTER 362
WYOMING NATIVE PLANT SOCIETY 364

Natural Resource Conservation

CATSKILL CENTER FOR CONSERVATION AND DEVELOPMENT, INC., THE 174
KEYSTONE CENTER, THE 245, 246

KEYWORD INDEX - Natural Science/Nongame Wildlife 473

Keyword Index

Natural Science

NATURAL RESOURCES INFORMATION COUNCIL 278
THORNE ECOLOGICAL INSTITUTE 331

Natural Systems

SOUTHWEST FLORIDA WATER MANAGEMENT DISTRICT (SWFWMD) . 56

Nature Centers

IDAHO FISH AND WILDLIFE FOUNDATION 62

Nature Preservation

ADOPT-A-STREAM FOUNDATION, THE 134
ALABAMA NATURAL HERITAGE PROGRAM 135
ALASKA AUDUBON SOCIETY 136
ALBERTA WILDERNESS ASSOCIATION 137
AMERICAN FISHERIES SOCIETY, VIRGINIA TECH CHAPTER 149
BIG BEND NATURAL HISTORY ASSOCIATION 166
BIRDLIFE INTERNATIONAL 166
BOTANICAL CLUB OF WISCONSIN 167
BROOKS BIRD CLUB INC., THE 168
CALIFORNIA ACADEMY OF SCIENCES 45, 169
CALIFORNIA WILDLIFE DEFENDERS 170
CHESAPEAKE BAY FOUNDATION, INC. (Virginia Office) 178
COALITION FOR EDUCATION IN THE OUTDOORS 181
CONNECTICUT BOTANICAL SOCIETY 185
DEFENDERS OF WILDLIFE 191
DEPARTMENT OF PARKS AND RECREATION (GUAM) 58
DESERT TORTOISE COUNCIL 193
DOGTOOTH GROUP 193
EASTERN SHORE LAND CONSERVANCY 199
FEDERATION OF ALBERTA NATURALIST 205
GENERAL FEDERATION OF WOMEN'S CLUBS 213
GEORGE MIKSCH SUTTON AVIAN RESEARCH CENTER INC. 214
INDIANA NATIVE PLANT AND WILDFLOWER SOCIETY 226
INTERNATIONAL MARINE MAMMAL PROJECT, THE 231
IOWA NATURAL HERITAGE FOUNDATION 238
IOWA TRAILS COUNCIL 238
KIDS FOR SAVING EARTH WORLDWIDE 246
LEE COUNTY PARKS AND RECREATION SERVICES 56
MAX McGRAW WILDLIFE FOUNDATION 254
MICHIGAN NATURAL AREAS COUNCIL 255
MICHIGAN NATURE ASSOCIATION 255
MINNESOTA HERPETOLOGICAL SOCIETY (James Ford Bell Museum of Natural History) 257
MISSOURI NATIVE PLANT SOCIETY 259
MONTANA LAND RELIANCE 260
MOUNT GRACE LAND CONSERVATION TRUST 261
NATIONAL PARK FOUNDATION 269
NATURAL AREAS ASSOCIATION 277
NATURE PRESERVES COMMISSION 63, 69
NEVIS HISTORICAL AND CONSERVATION SOCIETY 283
NEW JERSEY CONSERVATION FOUNDATION 285
NORTH CASCADES CONSERVATION COUNCIL 291
NORTHWEST ECOSYSTEM ALLIANCE 293
OFFICE OF STATE PARKS, DEPARTMENT OF CULTURE, RECREATION, AND TOURISM 71
OHIO BIOLOGICAL SURVEY 295
OKLAHOMA TOURISM AND RECREATION DEPARTMENT 99
PARKS AND RECREATION DEPARTMENT (NORTH DAKOTA) 96
PARTNERS IN PARKS 301
RHODE ISLAND STATE ASSOCIATION OF CONSERVATION DISTRICTS 311
STATE PARKS AND RECREATION COMMISSION (WASHINGTON) 120
TRUST FOR WILDLIFE, INC 338
TRUSTEES OF RESERVATIONS, THE 338
UTAH B.A.S.S. CHAPTER FEDERATION 340
WASHINGTON WILDLIFE AND RECREATION COALITION 345
WHITE CLAY WATERSHED ASSOCIATION 348
WILD ONES - NATURAL LANDSCAPERS, LTD 349
WOLF EDUCATION AND RESEARCH CENTER 360
WORLD NATURE ASSOCIATION INC. 362
WYOMING DEPARTMENT OF COMMERCE 126
YOSEMITE RESTORATION TRUST 365

Nature Study

PENNSYLVANIA RESOURCES COUNCIL, INC., (formerly PA Roadside Council) 302
ROGER TORY PETERSON INSTITUTE 314

Navigation

MISSISSIPPI RIVER BASIN ALLIANCE 258

Networking

NORTH AMERICAN ASSOCIATION FOR ENVIRONMENTAL EDUCATION 288

Noise

MASSACHUSETTS HIGHWAY DEPARTMENT 75

Nongame Wildlife

ADIRONDACK MOUNTAIN CLUB, INC., THE 134
ADOPT-A-STREAM FOUNDATION, THE 134
AMERICAN SOCIETY OF MAMMALOGISTS 155
ANIMAL PROTECTION INSTITUTE 157
ARIZONA GAME AND FISH DEPARTMENT 42
ARIZONA STATE PARKS BOARD 43
AUDUBON INTERNATIONAL 163
BAT CONSERVATION INTERNATIONAL 165
BIODIVERSITY LEGAL FOUNDATION 166
CALIFORNIA WILDLIFE DEFENDERS 170
CANADIAN FEDERATION OF HUMANE SOCIETIES 172
CASCADIA RESEARCH 174
CENTER FOR THE STUDY OF TROPICAL BIRDS, INC. (Administative Office) 177
COLORADO COOPERATIVE FISH AND WILDLIFE RESEARCH UNIT (USDI) 50
CORNELL LAB OF ORNITHOLOGY 189
DEPARTMENT OF INTERIOR, U.S.G.S/B.R.D, SOUTH CAROLINA COOPERATIVE FISH AND WILDLIFE RESEARCH UNIT 107
DESERT TORTOISE PRESERVE COMMITTEE, INC. 193
DIVISION OF NATURAL RESOURCES 122
FAIRFAX AUDUBON SOCIETY 205
FEDERAL WILDLIFE OFFICER'S ASSOCIATION 205
FISH AND WILDLIFE INFORMATION EXCHANGE 206
FISH AND WILDLIFE REFERENCE SERVICE 206
FLORIDA ORNITHOLOGICAL SOCIETY 208
FLORIDA PANTHER PROJECT, INC., THE 208
FRIENDS OF DISCOVERY PARK 211
GAME AND FISH DEPARTMENT 125
GEORGE MIKSCH SUTTON AVIAN RESEARCH CENTER INC. 214
GOPHER TORTOISE COUNCIL 216
HAWAII AUDUBON SOCIETY 219
HAWK MOUNTAIN SANCTUARY ASSOCIATION 220
INTERNATIONAL ASSOCIATION OF NATURAL RESOURCE PILOTS 228
INTERNATIONAL OSPREY FOUNDATION INC., THE 232
KANSAS HERPETOLOGICAL SOCIETY 243
LOUISIANA AUDUBON COUNCIL 249
MANOMET OBSERVATORY 251
MAX McGRAW WILDLIFE FOUNDATION 254
MICHIGAN NATURE ASSOCIATION 255
MINNESOTA COOPERATIVE FISH AND WILDLIFE RESEARCH UNIT 77
MINNESOTA HERPETOLOGICAL SOCIETY (James Ford Bell Museum of Natural History) 257
MINNESOTA ORNITHOLOGISTS' UNION 257
MISSISSIPPI COOPERATIVE FISH AND WILDLIFE RESEARCH UNIT (USDI) 79
MONTANA COOPERATIVE WILDLIFE RESEARCH UNIT (USGS/BRD) 82
MOUNTAIN LION FOUNDATION 261
NATURAL AREAS ASSOCIATION 277
NEVADA NATURAL HERITAGE PROGRAM 85
NEW HAMPSHIRE FISH AND GAME DEPARTMENT 86
NEW YORK TURTLE AND TORTOISE SOCIETY 287
NEWFOUNDLAND LABRADOR WILDLIFE FEDERATION 287
NORTH AMERICAN LOON FUND 289
NORTH AMERICAN NATIVE FISHES ASSOCIATION 289
NORTH DAKOTA GAME AND FISH DEPARTMENT 95
NORTH DAKOTA NATURAL SCIENCE SOCIETY 291
NORTHEAST WILDLIFE ADMINISTRATORS ASSOCIATION 292
OHIO COOPERATIVE FISH AND WILDLIFE RESEARCH UNIT (USDI) 96
OKLAHOMA BIOLOGICAL SURVEY 98
OKLAHOMA COOPERATIVE FISH AND WILDLIFE RESEARCH UNIT (USDI) 98
OKLAHOMA TOURISM AND RECREATION DEPARTMENT 99
OREGON COOPERATIVE FISH AND WILDLIFE RESEARCH UNIT (USDI) 100
OREGON TROUT, INC. 298
PREDATOR PROJECT 306
PURPLE MARTIN CONSERVATION ASSOCIATION 307
RAPTOR RESEARCH FOUNDATION, INC. 309
SCIENTISTS CENTER FOR ANIMAL WELFARE 318

TALLAHASSEE MUSEUM OF HISTORY AND NATURAL SCIENCE......... 329
TENNESSEE CITIZENS FOR WILDERNESS PLANNING......................... 329
TRUMPETER SWAN SOCIETY, THE.. 337
UTAH B.A.S.S. CHAPTER FEDERATION.. 340
UTAH COOPERATIVE FISH AND WILDLIFE RESEARCH UNIT (USDI-USGS-BRD-CRU) 113
VERMONT AUDUBON COUNCIL.. 341
WEST VIRGINIA COOPERATIVE FISH AND WILDLIFE RESEARCH UNIT 122
WILD ONES - NATURAL LANDSCAPERS, LTD 349
WILDLIFE CENTER OF VIRGINIA, THE... 350
WILDLIFE FOREVER.. 351
WILDLIFE RESOURCES AGENCY 110
WILDLIFE RESOURCES COMMISSION 95
WILDLIFE SOCIETY, THE 357
WOLF EDUCATION AND RESEARCH CENTER............................... 360
WORLD SOCIETY FOR THE PROTECTION OF ANIMALS (WSPA) 363
WYOMING COOPERATIVE FISH AND WILDLIFE RESEARCH UNIT (USDI) 126

Nonpoint Source Pollution

MISSISSIPPI SOIL AND WATER CONSERVATION COMMISSION 80
NATIONAL WATER RESOURCES ASSOCIATION 272
OKLAHOMA STATE CONSERVATION COMMISSION 99

North Atlantic Salmon

NORTH ATLANTIC SALMON CONSERVATION ORGANIZATION 289

Nuclear Energy

SAFE ENERGY COMMUNICATION COUNCIL 315
UNION OF CONCERNED SCIENTISTS 339

Nuclear/Radiation

AGENCY OF NATURAL RESOURCES 114
CENTRAL STATES EDUCATION CENTER 177
CONSERVATION COUNCIL OF NORTH CAROLINA.......................... 187
GREEN PARTY USA.. 218
GREENPEACE, INC.. 219
INDIANA STATE DEPARTMENT OF HEALTH.................................... 64
MANASOTA-88... 251
NATIVE AMERICANS FOR A CLEAN ENVIRONMENT (NACE) 276
PHYSICIANS FOR SOCIAL RESPONSIBILITY 303
STUDENT PUGWASH USA 328
TEXAS DEPARTMENT OF HEALTH 111

Ocean Conservation

AMERICAN SOCIETY OF LIMNOLOGY AND OCEANOGRAPHY 155
NATIONAL AUDUBON SOCIETY, LIVING OCEANS PROGRAM 265
OREGON PARKS AND RECREATION DEPARTMENT 101

Oceanography

ALASKA SEA GRANT COLLEGE PROGRAM 41
FRIENDS OF THE SAN JUANS.. 212
GEORGIA SEA GRANT COLLEGE PROGRAM..................................... 58
HAWAII COOPERATIVE FISHERY RESEARCH UNIT (USDI) 60
HUNTSMAN MARINE SCIENCE CENTRE.. 223
INTERNATIONAL OCEANOGRAPHIC FOUNDATION 231
MAINE SEA GRANT PROGRAM 72
MARINE LABORATORY (FLORIDA) 56
MARINE SCIENCES RESEARCH CENTER (NEW YORK)........................ 92
MARINE TECHNOLOGY SOCIETY 252
MARYLAND SEA GRANT COLLEGE 74
NATIONAL GEOGRAPHIC SOCIETY 268
NEW HAMPSHIRE SEA GRANT PROGRAM....................................... 86
NORTH CAROLINA SEA GRANT PROGRAM 95
NORTHWEST ATLANTIC FISHERIES ORGANIZATION (NAFO) 292
OREGON SEA GRANT PROGRAM 101
PUERTO RICO SEA GRANT PROGRAM.. 105
RESOURCES AGENCY, THE... 47
SOUTH CAROLINA SEA GRANT CONSORTIUM 108
WASHINGTON SEA GRANT PROGRAM.. 121

WATER RESOURCES RESEARCH CENTER 61
WOODS HOLE OCEANOGRAPHIC INSITITUTION (WHOI) SEA GRANT PROGRAM 76

Open Space

ADIRONDACK COUNCIL, THE... 133
ADIRONDACK NATURE CONSERVANCY/ADIRONDACK LAND TRUST, INC. 134
ADOPT-A-STREAM FOUNDATION, THE 134
AMERICAN SOCIETY OF LANDSCAPE ARCHITECTS 155
ASSOCIATION OF NEW JERSEY ENVIRONMENTAL COMMISSIONS.... 162
AUDUBON SOCIETY OF RHODE ISLAND 164
CALIFORNIANS FOR POPULATION STABILIZATION (CAPS).............. 170
COMMUNITY RIGHTS COUNSEL... 184
CONNECTICUT AUDUBON SOCIETY, INC....................................... 185
EASTERN SHORE LAND CONSERVANCY.. 199
ENVIRONMENTAL LEAGUE OF MASSACHUSETTS (ELM) 203
GEORGIA CONSERVANCY, INC., THE 214
GLOBAL CITIES PROJECT, THE... 215
JACKSON HOLE CONSERVATION ALLIANCE 242
JACKSON HOLE LAND TRUST.. 242
MAINE COAST HERITAGE TRUST 250
MONTANA LAND RELIANCE... 260
MOUNT GRACE LAND CONSERVATION TRUST 261
NATIONAL ASSOCIATION OF RECREATION RESOURCE PLANNERS.. 263
NEW HAMPSHIRE LAKES ASSOCIATION 284
NEW JERSEY CONSERVATION FOUNDATION 285
NEW YORK-NEW JERSEY TRAIL CONFERENCE INC. 287
NORTH CAROLINA RECREATION AND PARK SOCIETY, INC............. 291
OUTDOOR CIRCLE, THE 299
ROCKY MOUNTAIN ELK FOUNDATION 313
SOUTHERN ENVIRONMENTAL LAW CENTER 325, 326
STATE PARKS AND RECREATION COMMISSION (WASHINGTON)........ 120
TRUST FOR PUBLIC LAND, THE... 337
TRUSTEES OF RESERVATIONS, THE 338
TUG HILL TOMORROW, INC. 338
VIRGINIA OUTDOORS FOUNDATION 118
WASHINGTON TRAILS ASSOCIATION 344

Open Spaces

INSTITUTE AND SCHOOL FOR ENVIRONMENT AND NATURAL RESOURCES, Univeristy of Wyoming (IENR and SENR)...................... 227

Outdoor Education

COALITION FOR EDUCATION IN THE OUTDOORS 181

Outdoor Ethics

IZAAK WALTON LEAGUE OF AMERICA, INC., THE............................... 240

Outdoor Recreation

AMERICAN ASSOCIATION FOR LEISURE AND RECREATION (AALR) .. 139
AMERICAN BASS ASSOCIATION OF WEST VIRGINIA, THE 140
AMERICAN BIRDING ASSOCIATION 141
AMERICAN CAMPING ASSOCIATION, INC. 141
AMERICAN CONSERVATION ASSOCIATION, INC. 141, 142
AMERICAN FISHERIES SOCIETY, VIRGINIA TECH CHAPTER 149
AMERICAN FORESTS (formerly American Forestry Association)............... 150
AMERICAN HIKING SOCIETY 150
AMERICAN LEAGUE OF ANGLERS AND BOATERS 152
AMERICAN NATURE STUDY SOCIETY 153
APPALACHIAN MOUNTAIN CLUB 158
APPALACHIAN TRAIL CONFERENCE 158
ARCHERY MANUFACTURERS AND MERCHANTS ORGANIZATION (AMO) 159
ARIZONA STATE PARKS BOARD 43
ARKANSAS DEPARTMENT OF PARKS AND TOURISM 43
ASSOCIATION OF CONSERVATION ENGINEERS 161
ASSOCIATION OF MIDWEST FISH AND GAME LAW ENFORCEMENT OFFICERS 162
AUDUBON SOCIETY OF PORTLAND... 164
BOY SCOUTS OF AMERICA 168
CALIFORNIA TROUT, INC... 170
CAMP FIRE BOYS AND GIRLS 170
COALITION FOR EDUCATION IN THE OUTDOORS 181
COLORADO DEPARTMENT OF NATURAL RESOURCES..................... 50
COLORADO STATE COOPERATIVE EXTENSION 51
COLUMBIA RIVER GORGE COMMISSION 119
CONFERENCE OF NATIONAL PARK COOPERATING ASSOCIATIONS . 185

KEYWORD INDEX - Overconsumption/Pesticides 475

Keyword Index

DEPARTMENT OF PARKS AND RECREATION (GUAM) 58
ECOTOURISM SOCIETY, THE 199
ENERGY, MINERALS, AND NATURAL RESOURCES DEPARTMENT 88
EVERGLADES COORDINATING COUNCIL (ECC) 204
FEDERATION OF WESTERN OUTDOOR CLUBS 206
FISH AND BOAT COMMISSION 103
FISHAMERICA FOUNDATION 206
FLORIDA GAME AND FRESH WATER FISH COMMISSION 55
FLORIDA SPORTSMEN'S CONSERVATION ASSOCIATION 208
FLORIDA TRAIL ASSOCIATION, INC. 208
FRIENDS OF ACADIA 211
FRIENDS OF THE RIVER 212
FUTURE FISHERMAN FOUNDATION 213
GIRL SCOUTS OF THE UNITED STATES OF AMERICA 215
GREEN MOUNTAIN CLUB INC., THE 218
IDAHO DEPARTMENT OF PARKS AND RECREATION 61
ILLINOIS PRAIRIE PATH 225
INDIANA DEPARTMENT OF NATURAL RESOURCES 64
INTERAGENCY COMMITTEE FOR OUTDOOR RECREATION (IAC) 120
INTERNATIONAL HUNTER EDUCATION ASSOCIATION 231
INTERNATIONAL OCEANOGRAPHIC FOUNDATION 231
IOWA NATURAL HERITAGE FOUNDATION 238
IOWA TRAILS COUNCIL 238
IOWA TRAPPERS ASSOCIATION, INC. 238
IZAAK WALTON LEAGUE OF AMERICA ENDOWMENT 239
KANSAS DEPARTMENT OF WILDLIFE AND PARKS 67
KENTUCKY DEPARTMENT OF PARKS 68
LEAGUE OF WOMEN VOTERS OF WASHINGTON 248
LEE COUNTY PARKS AND RECREATION SERVICES 56
LOUISIANA DEPARTMENT OF AGRICULTURE 69, 70
MICHIGAN DEPARTMENT OF NATURAL RESOURCES 76
MINNESOTA PARKS AND TRAILS COUNCIL 257
MISSISSIPPI DEPARTMENT OF WILDLIFE, FISHERIES, AND PARKS 80
MISSOURI DEPARTMENT OF NATURAL RESOURCES 81
MONTANA DEPARTMENT OF FISH, WILDLIFE, AND PARKS 82
MULE DEER FOUNDATION, THE 262
MUSKIES, INC. 262
NATIONAL ASSOCIATION OF RECREATION RESOURCE PLANNERS .. 263
NATIONAL ASSOCIATION OF STATE OUTDOOR RECREATION LIAISON OFFICERS 264
NATIONAL ASSOCIATION OF STATE PARK DIRECTORS 264
NATIONAL BOATING FEDERATION 266
NATIONAL FOREST FOUNDATION 268
NATIONAL PARK FOUNDATION 269
NATIONAL RIFLE ASSOCIATION OF AMERICA 271
NATIONAL SHOOTING SPORTS FOUNDATION, INC. 271
NATURAL SCIENCE FOR YOUTH FOUNDATION 278
NEW HAMPSHIRE LAKES ASSOCIATION 284
NEW YORK STATE OFFICE OF PARKS, RECREATION AND HISTORIC PRESERVATION 93
NEW YORK-NEW JERSEY TRAIL CONFERENCE INC. 287
NORTH CAROLINA BEACH BUGGY ASSOCIATION, INC. 290
NORTH CAROLINA RECREATION AND PARK SOCIETY, INC. 291
NORTH CASCADES CONSERVATION COUNCIL 291
NORTHERN VIRGINIA REGIONAL PARK AUTHORITY 117
NORTHWEST INTERPRETIVE ASSOCIATION 293
OFFICE OF STATE PARKS, DEPARTMENT OF CULTURE, RECREATION, AND TOURISM 71
OHIO DEPARTMENT OF NATURAL RESOURCES 97
OKLAHOMA TOURISM AND RECREATION DEPARTMENT 99
OLYMPIC WILDLIFE RESCUE 297
OREGON PARKS AND RECREATION DEPARTMENT 101
OUTDOOR RECREATION COUNCIL OF BRITISH COLUMBIA 299
OUTDOOR WRITERS ASSOCIATION OF AMERICA INC. 299
PACIFIC NORTHWEST TRAIL ASSOCIATION 300
PENNSYLVANIA AUDUBON SOCIETY 301
PENNSYLVANIA FORESTRY ASSOCIATION, THE 302
PENNSYLVANIA RESOURCES COUNCIL, INC., (formerly PA Roadside Council) 302
PIEDMONT ENVIRONMENTAL COUNCIL 303
PRAIRIE CLUB, THE 305
QUEBEC WILDLIFE FEDERATION 308
RAILS-TO-TRAILS CONSERVANCY 308
RESOURCES AGENCY, THE 47
RIVER FEDERATION 312
RIVERS COUNCIL OF WASHINGTON (formerly Northwest Rivers Council) 313
SAVE THE DUNES COUNCIL 316
SEAPLANE PILOTS ASSOCIATION 318
SOUND EXPERIENCE 323
SOUTH DAKOTA GAME, FISH, AND PARKS DEPARTMENT 109
SOUTHEAST ALASKA CONSERVATION COUNCIL (SEACC) 324
STATE FISH AND WILDLIFE MANAGEMENT BOARD (NEW YORK) 93
STATE MARINE BOARD (OREGON) 102
STATE PARKS AND RECREATION COMMISSION (WASHINGTON) 120
TEXAS ORGANIZATION FOR ENDANGERED SPECIES 331
TREAD LIGHTLY! INC. 332
TROUT UNLIMITED, GUADELOUPE RIVER COUNCIL 334
TRUST FOR PUBLIC LAND, THE 337
TUG HILL COMMISSION 94
UTAH WILDERNESS COALITION 340
VERMONT NATURAL RESOURCES COUNCIL 341
WASHINGTON NATIVE PLANT SOCIETY 344
WASHINGTON TOXICS COALITION 344
WASHINGTON TRAILS ASSOCIATION 344
WASHINGTON WILDLIFE HERITAGE FOUNDATION (including Heritage Land Trust 345
WILDERNESS EDUCATION ASSOCIATION 349
WILDLIFE ACTION, INC. 350
WILDLIFE FOREVER 351
WISCONSIN CONSERVATION CORPS 123
WISCONSIN DEPARTMENT OF NATURAL RESOURCES 124
WOLF EDUCATION AND RESEARCH CENTER 360
WYOMING DEPARTMENT OF COMMERCE 126
YOSEMITE RESTORATION TRUST 365
YOUNG ENTOMOLOGISTS' SOCIETY INC. 365

Overconsumption

RAINFOREST RELIEF 309

Ozone Depletion

OZONE ACTION 300

Pedestrian Environment

DEPARTMENT OF PUBLIC WORKS 53
FLORIDA TRAIL ASSOCIATION, INC. 208
INTERNATIONAL BICYCLE FUND 229
PACIFIC NORTHWEST TRAIL ASSOCIATION 300
PIEDMONT ENVIRONMENTAL COUNCIL 303

People of Color in the Environment

ATLANTIC STATES LEGAL FOUNDATION 163
CENTER FOR HEALTH, ENVIRONMENT, AND JUSTICE 175
ECOLOGY CENTER 199
ENVIRONMENTAL CAREER CENTER 201
ENVIRONMENTAL CAREERS ORGANIZATION INC., THE 201
INTERNATIONAL SONORAN DESERT ALLIANCE 234
MISSISSIPPI RIVER BASIN ALLIANCE 258
NATIONAL ASSOCIATION OF SERVICE AND CONSERVATION CORPS (NASCC) 264
STUDENT CONSERVATION ASSOCIATION, INC. 328
URBAN HABITAT PROGRAM 340

Pest Management

MONTANA DEPARTMENT OF AGRICULTURE 82

Pesticides

AMERICAN FISHERIES SOCIETY, WISCONSIN CHAPTER 149
AMERICAN PIE (PUBLIC INFORMATION ON THE ENVIRONMENT) 153
ARIZONA DEPARTMENT OF AGRICULTURE 41
BIO-INTEGRAL RESOURCE CENTER 166
CALIFORNIA ENVIRONMENTAL PROTECTION AGENCY 45
CENTER FOR SCIENCE IN THE PUBLIC INTEREST 176
COLORADO DEPARTMENT OF AGRICULTURE 50
COLORADO STATE COOPERATIVE EXTENSION 51
CONCERN, INC. 184
DELAWARE DEPARTMENT OF AGRICULTURE 52
DELAWARE STATE EXTENSION SERVICE 53
ECOLOGY CENTER 199
ENVIRONMENTAL LEAGUE OF MASSACHUSETTS (ELM) 203
E-P EDUCATION SERVICES, INC. 196
FEDERAL WILDLIFE OFFICER'S ASSOCIATION 205
FRIENDS OF THE EARTH 211
GALIANO CONSERVANCY ASSOCIATION 213
GEORGIA DEPARTMENT OF AGRICULTURE 57
HUMAN ECOLOGY ACTION LEAGUE INC. THE (HEAL) 222
IDAHO STATE DEPARTMENT OF AGRICULTURE 62
ILLINOIS DEPARTMENT OF AGRICULTURE 62
ILLINOIS ENVIRONMENTAL COUNCIL 224
ILLINOIS WALNUT COUNCIL 225
INSTITUTE OF TROPICAL AGRICULTURE AND HUMAN RESOURCES ... 61
IOWA ENVIRONMENTAL COUNCIL 237
KENTUCKY DEPARTMENT OF AGRICULTURE 68
LAKE SUPERIOR GREENS 246
LEGAL ENVIRONMENTAL ASSISTANCE FOUNDATION INC. (LEAF) 248
MANOMET OBSERVATORY 251

MARYLAND DEPARTMENT OF AGRICULTURE 73
MICHIGAN DEPARTMENT OF AGRICULTURE 76
MICHIGAN STATE UNIVERSITY EXTENSION 77
MINNESOTA CENTER FOR ENVIRONMENTAL ADVOCACY (MCEA) 256
MINNESOTA DEPARTMENT OF AGRICULTURE 77
MONTANA DEPARTMENT OF AGRICULTURE 82
NATIONAL 4-H COUNCIL 262
NATIONAL ASSOCIATION OF STATE DEPARTMENTS OF AGRICULTURE
 264
NATIONAL COALITION AGAINST THE MISUSE OF PESTICIDES 266
NEW JERSEY STATE EXTENSION SERVICES 88
NEW YORK DEPARTMENT OF AGRICULTURE AND MARKETS 92
NEW YORK PUBLIC INTEREST RESEARCH GROUP (NYPIRG) 287
NORTH CAROLINA DEPARTMENT OF AGRICULTURE 94
NORTH DAKOTA STATE SOIL CONSERVATION COMMITTEE 96
OKLAHOMA STATE BOARD OF AGRICULTURE 98
OREGON ENVIRONMENTAL COUNCIL 298
PENNSYLVANIA DEPARTMENT OF AGRICULTURE 104
PENNSYLVANIA RECREATION AND PARK SOCIETY, INC. 302
PHYSICIANS FOR SOCIAL RESPONSIBILITY 303
RACHEL CARSON COUNCIL INC. (formerly Rachel Carson Trust for the
 Living Environment Inc.) 308
RHODE ISLAND COOPERATIVE EXTENSION 106
SOUTH DAKOTA STATE EXTENSION SERVICES 109
VERMONT DEPARTMENT OF HEALTH 115
VIRGINIA DEPARTMENT OF AGRICULTURE AND CONSUMER SERVICES
 117
WASHINGTON DEPARTMENT OF AGRICULTURE 120
WEST VIRGINIA DEPARTMENT OF AGRICULTURE 122
WEST VIRGINIA STATE EXTENSION SERVICES 123
WESTERN ENVIRONMENTAL LAW CENTER 346
WILDLIFE DAMAGE REVIEW (WDR) 351
WISCONSIN DEPARTMENT OF AGRICULTURE 123

Planning Management

ALABAMA DEPARTMENT OF ECONOMIC AND COMMUNITY AFFAIRS,
 COASTAL PROGRAMS (ADECA) 39
AMERICAN PLANNING ASSOCIATION 154
AMERICAN WATER WORKS ASSOCIATION (AWWA) 156
COLORADO NATURAL HERITAGE PROGRAM 182
COMMUNITY RIGHTS COUNSEL 184
DEPARTMENT OF TRANSPORTATION 27, 100, 106
E-P EDUCATION SERVICES, INC. 196
GLOBAL ENVIRONMENTAL MANAGEMENT INITIATIVE (GEMI) 215
GUAM COASTAL MANAGEMENT PROGRAM 58
ISSAQUAH ALPS TRAILS CLUB (I.A.T.C.) 239
KANSAS WATER OFFICE 68
LEGACY INTERNATIONAL 248
NATIONAL ASSOCIATION OF RECREATION RESOURCE PLANNERS .. 263
NATIONAL ASSOCIATION OF STATE OUTDOOR RECREATION LIAISON
 OFFICERS 264
NEBRASKA NATURAL RESOURCES COMMISSION 84
NEW JERSEY PINELANDS COMMISSION 88
NEW YORK STATE COOPERATIVE EXTENSION 93
ORGANIZATION OF WILDLIFE PLANNERS 298
PINCHOT INSTITUTE FOR CONSERVATION 303
RIVER FEDERATION 312
SOUTHERN ENVIRONMENTAL LAW CENTER 325, 326
SOUTHERN NEW ENGLAND FOREST CONSORTIUM, INC. 326
STEAMBOATERS, THE 327
TENNESSEE ENVIRONMENTAL COUNCIL 330
TEXAS WATER DEVELOPMENT BOARD 112
TUG HILL COMMISSION 94
VERMONT AUDUBON COUNCIL 341
WATER RESOURCES DEPARTMENT 102

Plant Propagation

INTERNATIONAL PLANT PROPAGATION SOCIETY, INC., THE 232

Plants

CALIFORNIA NATIVE PLANT SOCIETY (CNDS) 169

Pollution Prevention

ALLIANCE FOR THE CHESAPEAKE BAY 138
AMERICAN OCEANS CAMPAIGN 153
AMERICAN WATER WORKS ASSOCIATION (AWWA) 156
ANACOSTIA WATERSHED SOCIETY 157
ARIZONA DEPARTMENT OF ENVIRONMENTAL QUALITY 42
ASSOCIATION OF NEW JERSEY ENVIRONMENTAL COMMISSIONS 162
ATLANTIC STATES LEGAL FOUNDATION 163

BRANDYWINE CONSERVANCY, INC. 168
CENTER FOR MARINE CONSERVATION 176
CENTRAL STATES EDUCATION CENTER 177
CENTRO de INFORMACION, INVESTIGACION y EDUCACION SOCIAL
 (CIIES) 177
CHINA REGION LAKES ALLIANCE 179
COALITION FOR CLEAN AIR 181
COLORADO DEPARTMENT OF EDUCATION 50
DEPARTMENT OF ENVIRONMENTAL PROTECTION (MAINE0) 71
DEPARTMENT OF THE ENVIRONMENT 72
ENVIRONMENTAL DEFENSE FUND, INC. 202
ENVIRONMENTAL ENTERPRISES ASSISTANCE FUND, INC. 203
GEORGIA CONSERVANCY, INC., THE 214
GLOBAL CITIES PROJECT, THE 215
GREAT LAKES UNITED 217
GREEN (GLOBAL RIVERS ENVIRONMENTAL EDUCATION NETWORK) 218
GROUNDWATER FOUNDATION, THE 219
INSTITUTE FOR CONSERVATION LEADERSHIP 227
INTERNATIONAL ASSOCIATION FOR ENVIRONMENTAL HYDROLOGY
 (IAEH) 228
IOWA TRAILS COUNCIL 238
KANSAS STATE DEPARTMENT OF HEALTH AND ENVIRONMENT 67
KIDS FOR SAVING EARTH WORLDWIDE 246
LAKE MICHIGAN FEDERATION 246
LEAGUE OF WOMEN VOTERS OF IOWA 247
LEGAL ENVIRONMENTAL ASSISTANCE FOUNDATION INC. (LEAF) 248
MICHIGAN DEPARTMENT OF ENVIRONMENTAL QUALITY 76
MICHIGAN ENVIRONMENTAL COUNCIL 255
NOVA SCOTIA FORESTRY ASSOCIATION 293
OHIO ENVIRONMENTAL COUNCIL, INC. 295
OKLAHOMA DEPARTMENT OF ENVIRONMENTAL QUALITY 98
OREGON ENVIRONMENTAL COUNCIL 298
PENNSYLVANIA RESOURCES COUNCIL, INC., (formerly PA Roadside
 Council) 302
STATE OFFICE OF CONSERVATION (LOUISIANA) 71
TENNESSEE DEPARTMENT OF AGRICULTURE 110
U.S. PUBLIC INTEREST RESEARCH GROUP 339
VIRGIN ISLANDS CONSERVATION SOCIETY, INC. 342
WISCONSIN ASSOCIATION OF LAKES (WAL) 359

Population Growth

ALLIANCE FOR THE CHESAPEAKE BAY 138
AMERICAN ASSOCIATION FOR THE ADVANCEMENT OF SCIENCE 139
AVSC INTERNATIONAL 165
CALIFORNIANS FOR POPULATION STABILIZATION (CAPS) 170
CARRYING CAPACITY NETWORK 174
CONSERVATION AND RESEARCH FOUNDATION, INC., THE 186
COUSTEAU SOCIETY, INC., THE 190
EARTHSCAN 198
EDUCATIONAL COMMUNICATIONS, INC. 200
FLORIDA AUDUBON SOCIETY 206
FOSSIL FUELS POLICY ACTION INSTITUTE/ALLIANCE FOR A PAVING
 MORATORIUM 210
GREENHOUSE ACTION 218
NORTHWEST ENVIRONMENT WATCH 293
PANOS INSTITUTE, THE 301
PLANNED PARENTHOOD FEDERATION OF AMERICA INC. 304
POPULATION ACTION INTERNATIONAL 304
POPULATION COMMUNICATIONS INTERNATIONAL 304
POPULATION INSTITUTE, THE 305
POPULATION REFERENCE BUREAU INC. 305
POPULATION-ENVIRONMENT BALANCE INC. 305
WILD EARTH 348
WORLD PAL (WORLD POPULATION ALLOCATION LIMITED INC.) 362
WORLDWATCH INSTITUTE 363
ZERO POPULATION GROWTH INC. 365

Prairies

BIODIVERSITY LEGAL FOUNDATION 166
GEORGE MIKSCH SUTTON AVIAN RESEARCH CENTER INC. 214
ILLINOIS NATIVE PLANT SOCIETY 225
INDIANA NATIVE PLANT AND WILDFLOWER SOCIETY 226
INTERTRIBAL BISON COOPERATIVE (ITBC) 236
IOWA NATIVE PLANT SOCIETY 237
IOWA NATURAL HERITAGE FOUNDATION 238
IOWA PRAIRIE NETWORK 238
KANSAS BIOLOGICAL SURVEY 66
KANSAS NATURAL RESOURCE COUNCIL 243
KANSAS WILDFLOWER SOCIETY 244
LAND BETWEEN THE LAKES ASSOCIATION 247
MICHIGAN NATURAL AREAS COUNCIL 255
MICHIGAN NATURE ASSOCIATION 255
MINNESOTA NATIVE PLANT SOCIETY 257
MISSOURI NATIVE PLANT SOCIETY 259
MISSOURI PRAIRIE FOUNDATION 259

NATIVE PLANT SOCIETY OF NORTHEASTERN OHIO 276
NATIVE PRAIRIES ASSOCIATION OF TEXAS.................................... 277
NORTH DAKOTA NATURAL SCIENCE SOCIETY................................. 291
OHIO COOPERATIVE FISH AND WILDLIFE RESEARCH UNIT (USDI)....... 96
OKLAHOMA NATIVE PLANT SOCIETY 296
PRAIRIE GROUSE TECHNICAL COUNCIL 306
PREDATOR PROJECT 306
SOCIETY FOR RANGE MANAGEMENT 321
SOCIETY OF TYMPANUCHUS CUPIDO PINNATUS LTD. 322
SOUTH DAKOTA COOPERATIVE FISH AND WILDLIFE RESEARCH UNIT (USDI) 109
VIRGINIA NATIVE PLANT SOCIETY... 343

Precision Farming

COLORADO STATE COOPERATIVE EXTENSION..................................... 51
CONSERVATION TECHNOLOGY INFORMATION CENTER..................... 188
DELAWARE STATE EXTENSION SERVICE 53
NATIONAL ASSOCIATION OF STATE DEPARTMENTS OF AGRICULTURE 264

Predators

ANIMAL PROTECTION INSTITUTE 157
BIODIVERSITY LEGAL FOUNDATION 166
CALIFORNIA TRAPPERS ASSOCIATION 170
CALIFORNIA WILDLIFE DEFENDERS... 170
COLORADO TRAPPERS ASSOCIATION 183
DEFENDERS OF WILDLIFE 191
FEDERAL WILDLIFE OFFICER'S ASSOCIATION 205
GEORGE MIKSCH SUTTON AVIAN RESEARCH CENTER INC. 214
KANSAS STATE EXTENSION SERVICES... 68
MOUNTAIN LION FOUNDATION 261
NORTHWEST ECOSYSTEM ALLIANCE 293
PREDATOR PROJECT 306
SINAPU 319
SOCIETY FOR THE PRESERVATION OF BIRDS OF PREY 322
UTAH COOPERATIVE FISH AND WILDLIFE RESEARCH UNIT (USDI-USGS-BRD-CRU) 113
WILD CANINE SURVIVAL AND RESEARCH CENTER AND WOLF SANCTUARY 348
WILDLIFE DAMAGE REVIEW (WDR)... 351
WOLF EDUCATION AND RESEARCH CENTER.................................... 360

Preservation

EAGLE NATURE FOUNDATION, LTD... 197

Preservation and Protection

OHIO COOPERATIVE FISH AND WILDLIFE RESEARCH UNIT (USDI)....... 96

Private Land Development

GREATER YELLOWSTONE COALITION.. 217

Professional Development

NORTH AMERICAN ASSOCIATION FOR ENVIRONMENTAL EDUCATION 288

Protecting Special Places

LAKE MICHIGAN FEDERATION.. 246

Public Farming

NATIONAL ASSOCIATION OF STATE DEPARTMENTS OF AGRICULTURE 264

Public Health Protection

ALASKA DEPARTMENT OF ENVIRONMENTAL CONSERVATION 40
AMERICAN OCEANS CAMPAIGN.. 153
AMERICAN WATER WORKS ASSOCIATION (AWWA)........................... 156
ASSOCIATION OF STATE AND TERRITORIAL HEALTH OFFICIALS 162
ATLANTIC STATES LEGAL FOUNDATION 163
DELAWARE SOLID WASTE AUTHORITY 53
DELAWARE STATE EXTENSION SERVICE 53
DEPARTMENT OF ENVIRONMENTAL PROTECTION (PENNSYLVANIA) 102
DEPARTMENT OF MARINE RESOURCES 71
FLORIDA STATE DEPARTMENT OF HEALTH.. 56
IDAHO STATE DEPARTMENT OF AGRICULTURE 62
INDIANA STATE DEPARTMENT OF HEALTH.. 64
INSTITUTE OF TROPICAL AGRICULTURE AND HUMAN RESOURCES... 61
KANSAS STATE DEPARTMENT OF HEALTH AND ENVIRONMENT 67
MICHIGAN DEPARTMENT OF PUBLIC HEALTH................................... 77
NORTH DAKOTA DEPARTMENT OF HEALTH 95
PENNSYLVANIA DEPARTMENT OF AGRICULTURE.............................. 104
SCIENTISTS CENTER FOR ANIMAL WELFARE 318
SOUTH CAROLINA DEPARTMENT OF HEALTH AND ENVIRONMENTAL CONTROL 108
STATE WATER RESOURCES BOARD (RHODE ISLAND) 107
TENNESSEE ENVIRONMENTAL COUNCIL.. 330
UTAH DEPARTMENT OF HEALTH... 113
WATER RESOURCES RESEARCH CENTER 61
WEST VIRGINIA DEPARTMENT OF AGRICULTURE 122
WORLD WOMEN IN THE DEFENSE OF THE ENVIRONMENT................ 363
ZERO POPULATION GROWTH INC. 365

Public Information

ARIZONA GEOLOGICAL SURVEY... 42

Public Lands

ADIRONDACK MOUNTAIN CLUB, INC., THE....................................... 134
ALASKA AUDUBON SOCIETY 136
ALASKA DEPARTMENT OF NATURAL RESOURCES 41
ALBERTA WILDERNESS ASSOCIATION 137
AMERICAN FEDERATION OF MINERALOGICAL SOCIETIES 142
AMERICAN FISHERIES SOCIETY, BONNEVILLE CHAPTER 145
AMERICAN FORESTS (formerly American Forestry Association)............... 150
AMERICAN HIKING SOCIETY 150
AMERICAN HORSE PROTECTION ASSOCIATION 151
AMERICAN LAND CONSERVANCY.. 151
AMERICAN LANDS (formerly Western Ancient Forest Campaign) 151
AMERICAN RESOURCES GROUP 154
AMERICAN SOCIETY FOR ENVIRONMENTAL HISTORY 154
AMERICAN SOCIETY OF LANDSCAPE ARCHITECTS 155
AMERICAN WILDLANDS 156
ANIMAL PROTECTION INSTITUTE 157
APPALACHIAN MOUNTAIN CLUB 158
ARIZONA LAND DEPARTMENT.. 42
ASSOCIATION FOR THE PROTECTION OF THE ADIRONDACKS, THE. 160
BIODIVERSITY LEGAL FOUNDATION 166
BOONE AND CROCKETT CLUB 167
CANADA-UNITED STATES ENVIRONMENTAL COUNCIL (United States Office) 171
CAVE RESEARCH FOUNDATION 174
COLORADO DEPARTMENT OF AGRICULTURE..................................... 50
COLORADO DEPARTMENT OF NATURAL RESOURCES........................ 50
COLORADO ENVIRONMENTAL COALITION 182
CONFERENCE OF NATIONAL PARK COOPERATING ASSOCIATIONS . 185
DESERT TORTOISE COUNCIL 193
EARTHJUSTICE LEGAL DEFENSE FUND (formerly Sierra Club Legal Defense Fund, Inc.).. 198
ECOLOGY CENTER 199
FEDERATION OF ALBERTA NATURALIST 205
FLORIDA AUDUBON SOCIETY 206
FLORIDA SPORTSMEN'S CONSERVATION ASSOCIATION 208
FOREST HISTORY SOCIETY, INC. 209
FOREST SERVICE (Texas) 111
FOREST SERVICE EMPLOYEES FOR ENVIRONMENTAL ETHICS (FSEEE) 209
FORESTRY COMMISSION (MISSISSIPPI) 79
FRIENDS OF ACADIA 211
GAME COMMISSION 103
GRAND CANYON TRUST (Washington, DC Office) 216
GREAT BEAR FOUNDATION 216
GREATER YELLOWSTONE COALITION... 217
HAWAII AUDUBON SOCIETY 219
IDAHO CONSERVATION LEAGUE 223
ILLINOIS PRAIRIE PATH 225
INTERAGENCY COMMITTEE FOR OUTDOOR RECREATION (IAC) 120
INTERNATIONAL ASSOCIATION FOR BEAR RESEARCH AND MANAGEMENT 228
IZAAK WALTON LEAGUE OF AMERICA, INC., THE.............................. 240
KANSAS DEPARTMENT OF WILDLIFE AND PARKS 67
KEEP AMERICA BEAUTIFUL, INC. 244
KENTUCKY DEPARTMENT OF PARKS 68
LAND BETWEEN THE LAKES ASSOCIATION 247
LEAGUE OF WOMEN VOTERS OF WASHINGTON 248
LEE COUNTY PARKS AND RECREATION SERVICES 56
MARIN CONSERVATION LEAGUE 251

MARYLAND DEPARTMENT OF NATURAL RESOURCES 73
MASSACHUSETTS ASSOCIATION OF CONSERVATION COMMISSIONS (MACC)... 253
MICHIGAN DEPARTMENT OF NATURAL RESOURCES 76
MINERAL POLICY CENTER 256
MINNESOTA PARKS AND TRAILS COUNCIL 257
MISSOURI DEPARTMENT OF NATURAL RESOURCES 81
MISSOURI NATIVE PLANT SOCIETY 259
MONTANA WILDERNESS ASSOCIATION 260
MOUNTAINEERS, THE (Conservation Division) 261
NATIONAL ASSOCIATION OF RECREATION RESOURCE PLANNERS .. 263
NATIONAL ASSOCIATION OF STATE DEPARTMENTS OF AGRICULTURE 264
NATIONAL ASSOCIATION OF STATE FORESTERS 264
NATIONAL ASSOCIATION OF STATE PARK DIRECTORS 264
NATIONAL FOREST FOUNDATION 268
NATIONAL GEOGRAPHIC SOCIETY 268
NATIONAL MILITARY FISH AND WILDLIFE ASSOCIATION 269
NATIONAL PARK FOUNDATION 269
NATIONAL PARK TRUST 270
NATIONAL PARKS AND CONSERVATION ASSOCIATION (NPCA) 270
NATIONAL TREE TRUST 272
NATIONAL WILD TURKEY FEDERATION, INC., THE 273
NATIONAL WILDLIFE REFUGE ASSOCIATION 275
NATURAL RESOURCES COUNCIL OF AMERICA 278
NEVADA BUREAU OF MINES AND GEOLOGY 84
NEW JERSEY CONSERVATION FOUNDATION 285
NORTH DAKOTA STATE FOREST SERVICE 96
NORTHCOAST ENVIRONMENTAL CENTER 291
NORTHERN ALASKA ENVIRONMENTAL CENTER 292
OFFICE OF STATE PARKS, DEPARTMENT OF CULTURE, RECREATION, AND TOURISM 71
OKLAHOMA NATIVE PLANT SOCIETY 296
OKLAHOMA TOURISM AND RECREATION DEPARTMENT 99
OREGON NATURAL RESOURCES COUNCIL 298
OUTDOOR CIRCLE, THE 299
PACIFIC NORTHWEST TRAIL ASSOCIATION 300
PACIFIC RIVERS COUNCIL 300
PARTNERS IN PARKS 301
PENNSYLVANIA FORESTRY ASSOCIATION, THE 302
PIEDMONT ENVIRONMENTAL COUNCIL 303
PINCHOT INSTITUTE FOR CONSERVATION 303
PREDATOR PROJECT 306
PUBLIC EMPLOYEES FOR ENVIRONMENTAL RESPONSIBILITY (PEER) 306, 307
PUBLIC LANDS FOUNDATION 307
QUEBEC WILDLIFE FEDERATION 308
SAVE AMERICA'S FORESTS 315
SAVE THE DUNES COUNCIL 316
SAVE-THE-REDWOODS LEAGUE 317
SIERRA CLUB 318, 319
SIERRA CLUB FOUNDATION, THE 319
SINAPU 319
SOCIETY FOR RANGE MANAGEMENT 321
SOCIETY OF AMERICAN FORESTERS 298, 322, 344
SONORAN INSTITUTE 323
SOUTHEAST ALASKA CONSERVATION COUNCIL (SEACC) 324
SOUTHERN ENVIRONMENTAL LAW CENTER 325, 326
SOUTHWEST CENTER FOR BIOLOGICAL DIVERSITY 326
STATE FISH AND WILDLIFE MANAGEMENT BOARD (NEW YORK) 93
STATE LANDS COMMISSION (CALIFORNIA) 50
STATE PARKS AND RECREATION COMMISSION (WASHINGTON) 120
STUDENT CONSERVATION ASSOCIATION, INC. 328
TENNESSEE CITIZENS FOR WILDERNESS PLANNING 329
TEXAS GENERAL LAND OFFICE 112
TREAD LIGHTLY! INC. 332
UTAH NATURE STUDY SOCIETY 340
UTAH STATE EXTENSION SERVICES 114
UTAH WILDERNESS COALITION 340
VIRGINIA NATIVE PLANT SOCIETY 343
WASHINGTON NATIVE PLANT SOCIETY 344
WASHINGTON TOXICS COALITION 344
WASHINGTON WILDLIFE AND RECREATION COALITION 345
WEST VIRGINIA B.A.S.S. CHAPTER FEDERATION 346
WILDERNESS SOCIETY, THE 349
WILDLIFE FOREVER 351
WISCONSIN LAND AND WATER CONSERVATION ASSOCIATION 359
WYOMING DEPARTMENT OF COMMERCE 126
WYOMING OUTDOOR COUNCIL 364
WYOMING STATE BOARD OF LAND COMMISSIONERS 126

Public Participation

PENNSYLVANIA CITIZENS ADVISORY COUNCIL TO DEPARTMENT OF ENVIRONMENTAL PROTECTION 301

Rainforests

ALASKA RAINFOREST CAMPAIGN 137
EARTH FOUNDATION 197
HAWAII NATURE CENTER 220

Raptors

A. E. HOWELL WILDLIFE CONSERVATION CENTER 133
ADOPT-A-STREAM FOUNDATION, THE 134
AUDUBON SOCIETY OF WESTERN PENNSYLVANIA 165
CENTER FOR THE STUDY OF TROPICAL BIRDS, INC. (Administrative Office) 177
CRAIGHEAD ENVIRONMENTAL RESEARCH INSTITUTE 190
FAIRFAX AUDUBON SOCIETY 205
FEDERAL WILDLIFE OFFICER'S ASSOCIATION 205
FLORIDA AUDUBON SOCIETY 206
GEORGE MIKSCH SUTTON AVIAN RESEARCH CENTER INC. 214
HAWK AND OWL TRUST, THE 220
HAWK MIGRATION ASSOCIATION OF NORTH AMERICA 220
HAWK MOUNTAIN SANCTUARY ASSOCIATION 220
HAWKWATCH INTERNATIONAL INC. 221
INTERNATIONAL OSPREY FOUNDATION INC., THE 232
KANSAS ORNITHOLOGICAL SOCIETY 244
NATIONAL AVIARY IN PITTSBURGH 265
NORTH AMERICAN FALCONERS ASSOCIATION 288
NORTHWEST ECOSYSTEM ALLIANCE 293
OREGON COOPERATIVE FISH AND WILDLIFE RESEARCH UNIT (USDI) 100
ORNITHOLOGICAL COUNCIL 299
PEREGRINE FUND, THE 303
RAPTOR CENTER, THE 309
RAPTOR EDUCATION FOUNDATION INC. 309
RAPTOR RESEARCH FOUNDATION, INC. 309
SOCIETY FOR THE PRESERVATION OF BIRDS OF PREY 322
SOUTH DAKOTA B.A.S.S. CHAPTER FEDERATION 324
VERMONT B.A.S.S. CHAPTER FEDERATION 341
WILDLIFE CENTER OF VIRGINIA, THE 350
WILDLIFE FOREVER 351
WILDLIFE INFORMATION CENTER, INC. 352
WILDLIFE WAYSTATION 358
WORLD BIRD SANCTUARY (formerly Raptor Rehabilitation and Propagation Project Inc. The) 361

Recreational Boating

STATE MARINE BOARD (OREGON) 102

Recycling

PENNSYLVANIA RESOURCES COUNCIL, INC., (formerly PA Roadside Council) 302

Reforestation

JANE GOODALL INSTITUTE, THE 242
TEXAS FORESTRY ASSOCIATION 331

Reintroduction

WILD CANINE SURVIVAL AND RESEARCH CENTER AND WOLF SANCTUARY 348

Remedial Action Plans

LAKE ERIE CLEAN-UP COMMITTEE, INC. 246

Renewable Resources

A.B. ENVIRONMENTAL EDUCATION CENTER 133
AGRICULTURAL EXTENSION SERVICE 110
ALABAMA FORESTRY COMMISSION 39
ALASKA DEPARTMENT OF FISH AND GAME 40
ALASKA DEPARTMENT OF NATURAL RESOURCES 41
AMERICAN FISHERIES SOCIETY 142, 144, 145, 146, 147, 148, 149, 283
AMERICAN FISHERIES SOCIETY, ALABAMA CHAPTER 144
AMERICAN FISHERIES SOCIETY, ALASKA CHAPTER 144
AMERICAN FISHERIES SOCIETY, ARIZONA-NEW MEXICO CHAPTER 144
AMERICAN FISHERIES SOCIETY, ARKANSAS CHAPTER 144
AMERICAN FISHERIES SOCIETY, AUBURN UNIVERSITY STUDENT CHAPTER 145
AMERICAN FISHERIES SOCIETY, CALIFORNIA-NEVADA CHAPTER ... 145

KEYWORD INDEX - Reproductive Rights/Reptiles and Amphibians

AMERICAN FISHERIES SOCIETY, COLLEGE OF ENVIRONMENTAL SCIENCE AND FORESTRY CHAPTER 145
AMERICAN FISHERIES SOCIETY, COLORADO and WYOMING CHAPTER 145
AMERICAN FISHERIES SOCIETY, FLORIDA CHAPTER 145
AMERICAN FISHERIES SOCIETY, GEORGIA CHAPTER 145
AMERICAN FISHERIES SOCIETY, HAWAII CHAPTER 146
AMERICAN FISHERIES SOCIETY, HUMBOLDT CHAPTER 146
AMERICAN FISHERIES SOCIETY, IDAHO CHAPTER 146
AMERICAN FISHERIES SOCIETY, ILLINOIS CHAPTER 146
AMERICAN FISHERIES SOCIETY, INDIANA CHAPTER 146
AMERICAN FISHERIES SOCIETY, IOWA CHAPTER 146
AMERICAN FISHERIES SOCIETY, KANSAS CHAPTER 146
AMERICAN FISHERIES SOCIETY, KENTUCKY CHAPTER 146
AMERICAN FISHERIES SOCIETY, LOUISIANA CHAPTER 146
AMERICAN FISHERIES SOCIETY, MICHIGAN CHAPTER 147
AMERICAN FISHERIES SOCIETY, MID-ATLANTIC CHAPTER 147
AMERICAN FISHERIES SOCIETY, MINNESOTA CHAPTER 147
AMERICAN FISHERIES SOCIETY, MISSISSIPPI CHAPTER 147
AMERICAN FISHERIES SOCIETY, NEW YORK CHAPTER 147
AMERICAN FISHERIES SOCIETY, NORTH CAROLINA CHAPTER 148
AMERICAN FISHERIES SOCIETY, OHIO CHAPTER 148
AMERICAN FISHERIES SOCIETY, OKLAHOMA CHAPTER 148
AMERICAN FISHERIES SOCIETY, OREGON CHAPTER 148
AMERICAN FISHERIES SOCIETY, POTOMAC CHAPTER 148
AMERICAN FISHERIES SOCIETY, SOUTHERN NEW ENGLAND CHAPTER 149
AMERICAN FISHERIES SOCIETY, TEXAS A&M CHAPTER 149
AMERICAN FISHERIES SOCIETY, TIDEWATER CHAPTER 149
AMERICAN FOREST FOUNDATION 150
AMERICAN INSTITUTE OF FISHERY RESEARCH BIOLOGISTS 151
AMERICAN RESOURCES GROUP 154
AMERICAN WATER RESOURCES ASSOCIATION 156
ARIZONA LAND DEPARTMENT 42
ARKANSAS STATE EXTENSION SERVICES 44
ASSOCIATION OF CONSULTING FORESTERS OF AMERICA 161
ASSOCIATION OF MIDWEST FISH AND GAME LAW ENFORCEMENT OFFICERS 162
ATLANTIC STATES LEGAL FOUNDATION 163
AUDUBON INTERNATIONAL 163
BOONE AND CROCKETT FOUNDATION 167
CALIFORNIA TRAPPERS ASSOCIATION 170
CANVASBACK SOCIETY 173
CARRYING CAPACITY NETWORK 174
CENTER FOR RESOURCEFUL BUILDING TECHNOLOGY 176
CHESAPEAKE BAY FOUNDATION, INC. (Maryland Office) 178
COLORADO STATE COOPERATIVE EXTENSION 51
CONFEDERATED SALISH AND KOOTENAI TRIBES 185
CONSERVATION AND RESEARCH FOUNDATION, INC., THE 186
COOPERATIVE EXTENSION SYSTEM (MASSACHUSETTS) 74
ECOLOGY CENTER 199
ENERGY, MINERALS, AND NATURAL RESOURCES DEPARTMENT 88
ENVIRONMENT COUNCIL OF RHODE ISLAND 200
ENVIRONMENTAL CONCERN, INC 201
ENVIRONMENTAL ENTERPRISES ASSISTANCE FUND, INC. 203
ENVIROSOUTH, INC. 204
FOREST LANDOWNERS ASSOCIATION, INC 209
FOREST SERVICE (Texas) 111
FORESTRY COMMISSION (MISSISSIPPI) 79
GEORGE MIKSCH SUTTON AVIAN RESEARCH CENTER INC. 214
GEORGIA CONSERVANCY, INC., THE 214
GEORGIA SEA GRANT COLLEGE PROGRAM 58
GREEN SEAL 218
GREENHOUSE ACTION 218
ILLINOIS DEPARTMENT OF AGRICULTURE 62
ILLINOIS WALNUT COUNCIL 225
INSTITUTE OF TROPICAL AGRICULTURE AND HUMAN RESOURCES 61
INTERNATIONAL SOCIETY OF TROPICAL FORESTERS INC. 233
KANSAS DEPARTMENT OF AGRICULTURE 66
KANSAS FOREST SERVICE 67
KEEP FLORIDA BEAUTIFUL, INC. 244
KENTUCKY-TENNESSEE SOCIETY OF AMERICAN FORESTERS 245
LOUISIANA DEPARTMENT OF AGRICULTURE 69, 70
LOUISIANA SEA GRANT COLLEGE PROGRAM 70
MARYLAND FORESTS ASSOCIATION 252
MICHIGAN WILDLIFE HABITAT FOUNDATION 255
NATIONAL 4-H COUNCIL 262
NATIONAL FARMERS UNION 267
NATIONAL FFA ORGANIZATION 267
NATIONAL FORESTRY ASSOCIATION 268
NATIONAL SHOOTING SPORTS FOUNDATION, INC. 271
NATIONAL TRAPPERS ASSOCIATION, INC. 271
NATIONAL TRUST FOR HISTORIC PRESERVATION 272
NEBRASKA STATE EXTENSION SERVICES 84
NEVEDA COOPERATIVE EXTENSION 85
NEW ENGLAND NATURAL RESOURCES CENTER 284
NEW HAMPSHIRE SEA GRANT PROGRAM 86
NEW JERSEY DEPARTMENT OF AGRICULTURE 87
NEW YORK STATE COOPERATIVE EXTENSION 93
NORTH AMERICAN COALITION ON RELIGION AND ECOLOGY (NACRE) 288
NORTH CAROLINA FORESTRY ASSOCIATION 290
NORTHWEST RENEWABLE RESOURCES CENTER 293
NW ENERGY COALITION 294
OFFICE OF ENERGY EFFICIENCY AND ENVIRONMENT 93
OHIO COOPERATIVE FISH AND WILDLIFE RESEARCH UNIT (USDI) 96
OHIO ENVIRONMENTAL COUNCIL, INC. 295
OLYMPIC WILDLIFE RESCUE 297
OREGON SMALL WOODLANDS ASSOCIATION 298
PACIFIC FISHERY MANAGEMENT COUNCIL 300
PENNSYLVANIA FEDERATION OF SPORTSMEN'S CLUBS 302
POPULATION ACTION INTERNATIONAL 304
PUBLIC LANDS FOUNDATION 307
QUEBEC WILDLIFE FEDERATION 308
RENEWABLE NATURAL RESOURCES FOUNDATION 310
RESOURCE RENEWAL INSTITUTE, THE 310
RESOURCES FOR THE FUTURE 310
SAFE ENERGY COMMUNICATION COUNCIL 315
SOCIETY FOR ECOLOGICAL RESTORATION 321
SOCIETY FOR RANGE MANAGEMENT 321
SOCIETY OF AMERICAN FORESTERS 298, 322, 344
SOIL AND WATER CONSERVATION SOCIETY (formerly Soil Conservation Society of America) 323
SOUTH CAROLINA ENERGY OFFICE 108
SOUTH CAROLINA WILDLIFE FEDERATION 324
SOUTH DAKOTA STATE EXTENSION SERVICES 109
SOUTH DAKOTA WILDLIFE FEDERATION 324
STATE FORESTRY DIVISION (WYOMING) 126
STATE SOIL CONSERVATION COMMISSION (IDAHO) 62
STATE WATER RESOURCES BOARD (RHODE ISLAND) 107
STUDENT CONSERVATION ASSOCIATION, INC. 328
TENNESSEE CONSERVATION LEAGUE 330
TEXAS STATE SOIL AND WATER CONSERVATION BOARD 112
TREES FOR THE FUTURE, INC. 333
TROUT UNLIMITED, OKLAHOMA COUNCIL 336
UNION OF CONCERNED SCIENTISTS 339
UTAH COOPERATIVE FISH AND WILDLIFE RESEARCH UNIT (USDI-USGS-BRD-CRU) 113
UTAH STATE EXTENSION SERVICES 114
UTAH STATE SOIL CONSERVATION COMMISSION 114
UTAH WILDLIFE FEDERATION 340
VIRGINIA SEA GRANT PROGRAM 119
VIRGINIA WILDLIFE FEDERATION 343, 346
WASHINGTON B.A.S.S. CHAPTER FEDERATION 343
WASHINGTON STATE CONSERVATION COMMISSION 121
WASHINGTON STATE EXTENSION SERVICES 121
WEST VIRGINIA STATE EXTENSION SERVICES 123
WILDLIFE SOCIETY, THE 357
WINDSTAR FOUNDATION, THE 359
WISCONSIN DEPARTMENT OF AGRICULTURE 123
WISCONSIN WILDLIFE FEDERATION 360
WORLD FORESTRY CENTER 362
WORLD RESOURCES INSTITUTE 362
WORLDWATCH INSTITUTE 363
WYOMING STATE BOARD OF LAND COMMISSIONERS 126
ZERO POPULATION GROWTH INC. 365

Reproductive Rights

PLANNED PARENTHOOD FEDERATION OF AMERICA INC. 304

Reptiles and Amphibians

ADOPT-A-STREAM FOUNDATION, THE 134
AMERICAN SOCIETY OF ICHTHYOLOGISTS AND HERPETOLOGISTS 155
AMERICAN SOCIETY OF ZOOLOGISTS 156
AUDUBON SOCIETY OF WESTERN PENNSYLVANIA 165
CALIFORNIA ACADEMY OF SCIENCES 45, 169
CANADIAN COOPERATIVE WILDLIFE HEALTH CENTRE 171
CARIBBEAN CONSERVATION CORPORATION (Costa Rica Office) 173
CHICAGO HERPETOLOGICAL SOCIETY 179
DESERT TORTOISE COUNCIL 193
FISH AND WILDLIFE INFORMATION EXCHANGE 206
FLORIDA COOPERATIVE FISH AND WILDLIFE RESEARCH UNIT (USDI) 54
GOPHER TORTOISE COUNCIL 216
KANSAS HERPETOLOGICAL SOCIETY 243
MICHIGAN NATURE ASSOCIATION 255
MINNESOTA HERPETOLOGICAL SOCIETY (James Ford Bell Museum of Natural History) 257
NATURAL HISTORY SOCIETY OF MARYLAND, INC., THE 277
NEW YORK TURTLE AND TORTOISE SOCIETY 287
NORTH CAROLINA HERPETOLOGICAL SOCIETY 290
NORTHWEST ECOSYSTEM ALLIANCE 293
SCIENTISTS CENTER FOR ANIMAL WELFARE 318
SMITHSONIAN INSTITUTION 320

Research

AMERICAN WILDLIFE RESEARCH FOUNDATION, INC.	156
ARCHBOLD BIOLOGICAL STATION	159
ARIZONA GEOLOGICAL SURVEY	42
ARKANSAS COOPERATIVE RESEARCH UNIT	43
ASSOCIATION OF FIELD ORNITHOLOGISTS	161
ATLANTIC SALMON FEDERATION	163
AUDUBON INTERNATIONAL	163
BAT CONSERVATION INTERNATIONAL	165
CALIFORNIA ACADEMY OF SCIENCES	45, 169
CANADIAN COOPERATIVE WILDLIFE HEALTH CENTRE	171
CENTER FOR THE STUDY OF TROPICAL BIRDS, INC. (Administrative Office)	177
CETACEAN SOCIETY INTERNATIONAL	177
CLEVELAND MUSEUM OF NATURAL HISTORY, THE	180
CRAIGHEAD WILDLIFE-WILDLANDS INSTITUTE	190
DELAWARE GEOLOGICAL SURVEY	53
DELAWARE MUSEUM OF NATURAL HISTORY	192
DELAWARE SOLID WASTE AUTHORITY	53
DEPARTMENT OF INTERIOR, U.S.G.S/B.R.D, SOUTH CAROLINA COOPERATIVE FISH AND WILDLIFE RESEARCH UNIT	107
DEPARTMENT OF TRANSPORTATION (OREGON)	100
EARTHWATCH INSTITUTE	199
ENVIRONMENTAL CENTER	60
ENVIRONMENTAL CONCERN, INC.	201
H. JOHN HEINZ III CENTER FOR SCIENCE, ECONOMICS, AND THE ENVIRONMENT	219
HUMMINGBIRD SOCIETY, THE	223
HUNTSMAN MARINE SCIENCE CENTRE	223
ILLINOIS WALNUT COUNCIL	225
INTERNATIONAL CENTER FOR GIBBON STUDIES	229
IOWA COOPERATIVE FISH AND WILDLIFE RESEARCH UNIT	65
ISLAND CONSERVATION EFFORT	239
LOUISIANA FORESTRY ASSOCIATION	249
MANOMET OBSERVATORY	251
MONTANA COOPERATIVE FISHERY RESEARCH UNIT (USDI)	82
NATIONAL BIRD-FEEDING SOCIETY	266
NEW HAMPSHIRE SEA GRANT PROGRAM	86
NEW YORK SEA GRANT	92
OHIO COOPERATIVE FISH AND WILDLIFE RESEARCH UNIT (USDI)	96
OHIO SEA GRANT COLLEGE PROGRAM, F.T. STONE LABORATORY, AND GREAT LAKES AQUATIC ECOSYSTEM RESEARCH CONSORTIUM (GLAERC)	97
OKLAHOMA ACADEMY OF SCIENCE	295
OKLAHOMA COOPERATIVE FISH AND WILDLIFE RESEARCH UNIT (USDI)	98
OUTDOOR RECREATION COUNCIL OF BRITISH COLUMBIA	299
PARTNERS IN PARKS	301
PINCHOT INSTITUTE FOR CONSERVATION	303
PINE BLUFF COOPERATIVE FISHERY RESEARCH PROJECT	45
PUERTO RICO CONSERVATION FOUNDATION, THE (PRCF)	307
RAILS-TO-TRAILS CONSERVANCY	308
RESPONSIVE MANAGEMENT	311
SAVE THE DUNES COUNCIL	316
SCIENTISTS CENTER FOR ANIMAL WELFARE	318
SOIL AND WATER CONSERVATION SOCIETY (formerly Soil Conservation Society of America)	323
UNIVERSITY OF VERMONT EXTENSION	115
VIRGINIA MUSEUM OF NATURAL HISTORY	118
WILD CANINE SURVIVAL AND RESEARCH CENTER AND WOLF SANCTUARY	348
WILDFOWL TRUST OF NORTH AMERICA INC., THE	350
WILSON ORNITHOLOGICAL SOCIETY	358
WOLF EDUCATION AND RESEARCH CENTER	360
WORLD NATURE ASSOCIATION INC.	362

Research Grants

CHARLES A. AND ANNE MORROW LINDBERGH FOUNDATION, THE	178

Resource Law Enforcement

DEPARTMENT OF PUBLIC SAFETY	41

Restoration

CHESAPEAKE BAY FOUNDATION, INC.	178
NATIVE PRAIRIES ASSOCIATION OF TEXAS	277

Riparian Restoration

SONORAN INSTITUTE	323

Rivers

ADIRONDACK PARK AGENCY	90
ADOPT-A-STREAM FOUNDATION, THE	134
ALLIANCE FOR THE CHESAPEAKE BAY	138
AMERICAN RIVERS (formerly American Rivers Conservation Council)	154
AMERICAN SOCIETY OF LIMNOLOGY AND OCEANOGRAPHY	155
AMERICAN WATER RESOURCES ASSOCIATION	156
ANACOSTIA WATERSHED SOCIETY	157
APPALACHIAN MOUNTAIN CLUB	158
BLACK BASS FOUNDATION	166
BORDER ECOLOGY PROJECT (BEP)	167
CHRISTINA CONSERVANCY, INC.	179
CONNECTICUT RIVER WATERSHED COUNCIL INC.	186
CONSERVATION COUNCIL OF NORTH CAROLINA	187
CRAIGHEAD ENVIRONMENTAL RESEARCH INSTITUTE	190
DEPARTMENT OF WATER RESOURCES (NEBRASKA)	83
DRAGONFLY SOCIETY OF THE AMERICAS, THE	193
ENVIRONMENTAL LEAGUE OF MASSACHUSETTS (ELM)	203
FLORIDA AUDUBON SOCIETY	206
FLORIDA DEFENDERS OF THE ENVIRONMENT, INC. (Home Office)	207
FRIENDS OF THE RIVER	212
GOVERNOR OF SOUTH CAROLINA, JIM HODGES	107
GREEN (GLOBAL RIVERS ENVIRONMENTAL EDUCATION NETWORK)	218
IDAHO DEPARTMENT OF PARKS AND RECREATION	61
INDIANA DEPARTMENT OF NATURAL RESOURCES	64
IOWA NATURAL HERITAGE FOUNDATION	238
IZAAK WALTON LEAGUE OF AMERICA, INC., THE	240
KANSAS NATURAL RESOURCE COUNCIL	243
KANSAS WATER OFFICE	68
LEAGUE OF WOMEN VOTERS OF WASHINGTON	248
LEGAL ENVIRONMENTAL ASSISTANCE FOUNDATION INC. (LEAF)	248
LONG LIVE THE KINGS	249
LOWER MISSISSIPPI RIVER CONSERVATION COMMITTEE	249
MAINE ATLANTIC SALMON AUTHORITY (formerly Maine Atlantic Sea Run Salmon Commission)	71
MID-ATLANTIC COUNCIL OF WATERSHED ASSOCIATIONS	256
MISSISSIPPI COOPERATIVE FISH AND WILDLIFE RESEARCH UNIT (USDI)	79
MISSISSIPPI INTERSTATE COOPERATIVE RESOURCE ASSOCIATION	258
MISSISSIPPI RIVER BASIN ALLIANCE	258
MISSOURI COOPERATIVE FISH AND WILDLIFE RESEARCH UNIT (USDI)	81
MONTANA COOPERATIVE FISHERY RESEARCH UNIT (USDI)	82
MONTANA LAND RELIANCE	260
MOUNTAINEERS, THE (Conservation Division)	261
NATIONAL BOATING FEDERATION	266
NATIONAL WATERWAYS CONFERENCE INC.	273
NATURAL AND SCENIC RIVERS COMMISSION (ARKANSAS)	45
NATURAL HERITAGE COMMISSION (ARKANSAS)	45
NEBRASKA NATURAL RESOURCES COMMISSION	84
NORTHERN ALASKA ENVIRONMENTAL CENTER	292
OKLAHOMA NATIVE PLANT SOCIETY	296
OKLAHOMA WATER RESOURCES BOARD	99
OREGON ENVIRONMENTAL COUNCIL	298
OREGON PARKS AND RECREATION DEPARTMENT	101
OUTDOOR RECREATION COUNCIL OF BRITISH COLUMBIA	299
PACIFIC RIVERS COUNCIL	300
PINE BLUFF COOPERATIVE FISHERY RESEARCH PROJECT	45
RESOURCES AGENCY, THE	47
RIVER ALLIANCE OF WISCONSIN	312
RIVER FEDERATION	312
RIVER NETWORK	312
RIVER OTTER ALLIANCE, THE	312
RIVERS COUNCIL OF WASHINGTON (formerly Northwest Rivers Council)	313
SCENIC HUDSON, INC.	317
SEAPLANE PILOTS ASSOCIATION	318
SOUTH DAKOTA COOPERATIVE FISH AND WILDLIFE RESEARCH UNIT (USDI)	109
SOUTHEAST ALASKA CONSERVATION COUNCIL (SEACC)	324
SOUTHEASTERN FISHES COUNCIL	325
SOUTHWEST FLORIDA WATER MANAGEMENT DISTRICT (SWFWMD)	56
TENNESSEE CITIZENS FOR WILDERNESS PLANNING	329
TEXAS B.A.S.S. CHAPTER FEDERATION	330
TEXAS WATER DEVELOPMENT BOARD	112
TROUT UNLIMITED	333, 334, 335, 336, 337
TURTLE CREEK WATERSHED ASSOCIATION, INC.	338
UPPER MISSISSIPPI RIVER CONSERVATION COMMITTEE	340
WATER RESOURCES ASSOCIATION OF THE DELAWARE RIVER BASIN	345
WATER RESOURCES DEPARTMENT	102
WEST VIRGINIA B.A.S.S. CHAPTER FEDERATION	346
WEST VIRGINIA COOPERATIVE FISH AND WILDLIFE RESEARCH UNIT	122
WISCONSIN COOPERATIVE FISHERY RESEARCH UNIT (USDI)	123

Road Construction

FOSSIL FUELS POLICY ACTION INSTITUTE/ALLIANCE FOR A PAVING MORATORIUM 210

Runoff

COAST ALLIANCE 181

Rural Development

ASSOCIATION OF NEW JERSEY ENVIRONMENTAL COMMISSIONS..... 162
CARIBBEAN NATURAL RESOURCES INSTITUTE...................................... 173
CATSKILL CENTER FOR CONSERVATION AND DEVELOPMENT, INC., THE 174
COLORADO STATE COOPERATIVE EXTENSION.. 51
FOOD AND AGRICULTURE ORGANIZATION OF THE UNITED NATIONS 209
FOREST TRUST 209
FORESTRY COMMISSION (SOUTH CAROLINA) 107
NATIONAL ASSOCIATION OF STATE DEPARTMENTS OF AGRICULTURE 264
NEW HAMPSHIRE DEPARTMENT OF AGRICULTURE, MARKETS, AND FOOD 85
OKLAHOMA NATIVE PLANT SOCIETY 296
OZARKS RESOURCE CENTER 300
TREES FOR THE FUTURE, INC. 333
TUG HILL COMMISSION 94
WISCONSIN DEPARTMENT OF AGRICULTURE (Land and Water Resources Bureau).. 123
YOSEMITE RESTORATION TRUST 365

Scholarships

BAT CONSERVATION INTERNATIONAL 165

Scholarships and Grants

AMERICAN GROUND WATER TRUST 150
ATLANTIC CENTER FOR THE ENVIRONMENT 162, 163
BOONE AND CROCKETT CLUB 167
CA DEPARTMENT OF EDUCATION, OFFICE OF ENVIRONMENTAL EDUCATION 45
CALIFORNIA TRAPPERS ASSOCIATION 170
CAMP FIRE CONSERVATION FUND 171
CAVE RESEARCH FOUNDATION 174
CENTER FOR HEALTH, ENVIRONMENT, AND JUSTICE 175
CHICAGO HERPETOLOGICAL SOCIETY 179
GAME CONSERVANCY U.S.A. (formerly American Friends of the Game Conservancy) 213
GARDEN CLUB OF AMERICA, THE 213
INTERNATIONAL WILD WATERFOWL ASSOCIATION 235
LOUISIANA FORESTRY ASSOCIATION.. 249
NATIONAL FIELD ARCHERY ASSOCIATION 267
NATIONAL WILD TURKEY FEDERATION, INC., THE.............................. 273
NEW YORK SEA GRANT 92
NORTH AMERICAN LOON FUND 289
TEXAS FORESTRY ASSOCIATION 331
WASHINGTON FARM FORESTRY ASSOCIATION.................................. 344
WELDER WILDLIFE FOUNDATION 345
WILDLIFE HABITAT CANADA 352
WILDLIFE PRESERVATION TRUST INTERNATIONAL, INC. 353
WISCONSIN ENVIRONMENTAL EDUCATION BOARD (WEEB) 124

Sea Grass

FLORIDA AUDUBON SOCIETY.. 206
FRIENDS OF THE SAN JUANS.. 212
NEW HAMPSHIRE SEA GRANT PROGRAM.. 86

Sea Turtles

MOTE MARINE LABORATORY 261

Seabed Disturbance

MARINE CONSERVATION BIOLOGY INSTITUTE 251

Seafood Technology

NORTH CAROLINA SEA GRANT PROGRAM 95

Social Justice

STUDENT ENVIRONMENTAL ACTION COALITION (SEAC).................... 328

Soil Conservation

BIOMASS USERS NETWORK.. 166
COMMITTEE ON AGRICULTURAL SUSTAINABILITY FOR DEVELOPING COUNTRIES 184
CONSERVATION DISTRICTS FOUNDATION INC. 187
DELAWARE ASSOCIATION OF CONSERVATION DISTRICTS 191
DELAWARE DEPARTMENT OF NATURAL RESOURCES AND ENVIRONMENTAL CONTROL 52
IDAHO STATE DEPARTMENT OF AGRICULTURE 62
ILLINOIS DEPARTMENT OF AGRICULTURE 62
ILLINOIS WALNUT COUNCIL.. 225
INDIANA DEPARTMENT OF NATURAL RESOURCES........................... 64
INTERNATIONAL EROSION CONTROL ASSOCIATION (IECA) 230
KANSAS STATE CONSERVATION COMMISSION 67
KENTUCKY DEPARTMENT OF AGRICULTURE.. 68
LEAGUE OF WOMEN VOTERS OF IOWA.. 247
MICHIGAN DEPARTMENT OF AGRICULTURE 76
MINNESOTA BOARD OF WATER AND SOIL RESOURCES 77
MISSISSIPPI SOIL AND WATER CONSERVATION COMMISSION 80
MONTANA DEPARTMENT OF NATURAL RESOURCES AND CONSERVATION.. 82
NATIONAL ARBOR DAY FOUNDATION 262
NATIONAL ASSOCIATION OF CONSERVATION DISTRICTS 263
NATIONAL ASSOCIATION OF STATE FORESTERS.................................. 264
NATIONAL FARMERS UNION.. 267
NATIONAL GRANGE, THE 269
NEBRASKA NATURAL RESOURCES COMMISSION 84
NEW HAMPSHIRE DEPARTMENT OF AGRICULTURE, MARKETS, AND FOOD 85
NEW JERSEY DEPARTMENT OF AGRICULTURE 87
NEW YORK DEPARTMENT OF AGRICULTURE AND MARKETS............... 92
NORTH CAROLINA DEPARTMENT OF AGRICULTURE 94
NORTH DAKOTA STATE SOIL CONSERVATION COMMITTEE................ 96
OHIO DEPARTMENT OF NATURAL RESOURCES 97
OKLAHOMA STATE CONSERVATION COMMISSION 99
PENNSYLVANIA DEPARTMENT OF AGRICULTURE.................................. 104
PUBLIC LANDS FOUNDATION 307
PUERTO RICO STATE EXTENSION SERVICES 106
SOIL AND WATER CONSERVATION SOCIETY (formerly Soil Conservation Society of America) 323
STATE SOIL AND WATER CONSERVATION COMMISSION (GEORGIA).. 58
STATE SOIL CONSERVATION COMMISSION (IDAHO)............................... 62
TENNESSEE DEPARTMENT OF AGRICULTURE 110
TEXAS STATE SOIL AND WATER CONSERVATION BOARD 112
UTAH STATE SOIL CONSERVATION COMMISSION................................ 114
VERMONT DEPARTMENT OF AGRICULTURE, FOOD, AND MARKETS. 115
VIRGIN ISLANDS CONSERVATION SOCIETY, INC. 342
WASHINGTON STATE CONSERVATION COMMISSION 121
WEST VIRGINIA DEPARTMENT OF AGRICULTURE 122
WISCONSIN DEPARTMENT OF AGRICULTURE (Land and Water Resources Bureau).. 123
WISCONSIN GEOLOGICAL AND NATURAL HISTORY SURVEY 125

Solar Energy

ENVIRONMENTAL ENTERPRISES ASSISTANCE FUND, INC. 203
FLORIDA CONSERVATION FOUNDATION, INC. 207
LEGAL ENVIRONMENTAL ASSISTANCE FOUNDATION INC. (LEAF)..... 248
NORTHEAST SUSTAINABLE ENERGY ASSOCIATION 292
NW ENERGY COALITION 294
SOUTH CAROLINA ENERGY OFFICE.. 108
UNION OF CONCERNED SCIENTISTS 339

Solid Waste

ALABAMA ENVIRONMENTAL COUNCIL 135
ALASKA HEALTH PROJECT 41
CHESAPEAKE BAY FOUNDATION, INC. (Pennsylvania Office) 178
CONSERVATION COUNCIL OF NORTH CAROLINA.................................. 187
DEPARTMENT OF ENVIRONMENT AND NATURAL RESOURCES (SOUTH DAKOTA).. 109
DEPARTMENT OF ENVIRONMENTAL QUALITY (ARKANSAS).................. 44
DEPARTMENT OF PUBLIC WORKS.. 53
ILLINOIS ENVIRONMENTAL COUNCIL 224
ISSAQUAH ALPS TRAILS CLUB (I.A.T.C.) 239
KANSAS STATE DEPARTMENT OF HEALTH AND ENVIRONMENT 67
MAINE ASSOCIATION OF CONSERVATION COMMISSIONS (MACC).... 250
MASSACHUSETTS HIGHWAY DEPARTMENT 75

MINERAL POLICY CENTER 256
NATIONAL ENVIRONMENTAL HEALTH ASSOCIATION 267
NEW HAMPSHIRE DEPARTMENT OF ENVIRONMENTAL SERVICES 86
OHIO ENVIRONMENTAL PROTECTION AGENCY 97
PENNSYLVANIA RECREATION AND PARK SOCIETY, INC. 302
SOUTH CAROLINA ENERGY OFFICE 108
WASHINGTON B.A.S.S. CHAPTER FEDERATION 343
WILDLIFE SOCIETY, PENNSYLVANIA CHAPTER 356
WISCONSIN DEPARTMENT OF NATURAL RESOURCES 124
WYOMING OUTDOOR COUNCIL 364

Solid Waste Management

AGENCY OF NATURAL RESOURCES 114
AIR AND WASTE MANAGEMENT ASSOCIATION 135
ALABAMA DEPARTMENT OF ENVIRONMENTAL MANAGEMENT 39
ALASKA DEPARTMENT OF ENVIRONMENTAL CONSERVATION 40
ARIZONA DEPARTMENT OF ENVIRONMENTAL QUALITY 42
ATLANTIC STATES LEGAL FOUNDATION 163
BORDER ECOLOGY PROJECT (BEP) 167
CALIFORNIA ENVIRONMENTAL PROTECTION AGENCY 45
CENTRAL STATES EDUCATION CENTER 177
COLORADO STATE COOPERATIVE EXTENSION 51
COMMUNITY ENVIRONMENTAL COUNCIL 184
CONCERN, INC. 184
CONNECTICUT PUBLIC INTEREST RESEARCH GROUP (ConnPIRG) ... 186
DELAWARE SOLID WASTE AUTHORITY 53
DEPARTMENT OF ENVIRONMENT AND NATURAL RESOURCES (SOUTH
  DAKOTA) 109
DEPARTMENT OF ENVIRONMENTAL PROTECTION (MAINE0 71
DEPARTMENT OF THE ENVIRONMENT 72
ENVIRONMENTAL EDUCATION ASSOCIATION OF ILLINOIS (Iron Oaks
  Environmental Learning Center) 202
ENVIROSOUTH, INC. 204
GENERAL FEDERATION OF WOMEN'S CLUBS 213
GLOBAL CITIES PROJECT, THE 215
HOOSIER ENVIRONMENTAL COUNCIL 222
IDAHO STATE DEPARTMENT OF AGRICULTURE 62
INFORM, INC. 226
IZAAK WALTON LEAGUE OF AMERICA, INC., THE 240
KEEP AMERICA BEAUTIFUL, INC. 244
KEEP FLORIDA BEAUTIFUL, INC. 244
LEAGUE OF WOMEN VOTERS OF IOWA 247
MARINE SCIENCES RESEARCH CENTER (NEW YORK) 92
MICHIGAN DEPARTMENT OF ENVIRONMENTAL QUALITY 76
MONTANA ENVIRONMENTAL INFORMATION CENTER 260
NATIONAL ASSOCIATION OF ENVIRONMENTAL PROFESSIONALS, THE
  (National Office) 263
NEW JERSEY STATE EXTENSION SERVICES 88
NEW YORK PUBLIC INTEREST RESEARCH GROUP (NYPIRG) 287
NEW YORK STATE COOPERATIVE EXTENSION 93
NEWFOUNDLAND LABRADOR WILDLIFE FEDERATION 287
NORTH DAKOTA DEPARTMENT OF HEALTH 95
NORTHERN PLAINS RESOURCE COUNCIL 292
OHIO ENVIRONMENTAL COUNCIL, INC. 295
OKLAHOMA DEPARTMENT OF ENVIRONMENTAL QUALITY 98
OREGON DEPARTMENT OF ENVIRONMENTAL QUALITY (DEQ) 101
SOUTH CAROLINA DEPARTMENT OF HEALTH AND ENVIRONMENTAL
  CONTROL 108
SOUTH DAKOTA ORNITHOLOGISTS' UNION 324
STOP 328
STUDENT ENVIRONMENTAL ACTION COALITION (SEAC) 328
TENNESSEE ENVIRONMENTAL COUNCIL 330
U.S. PUBLIC INTEREST RESEARCH GROUP 339
VIRGINIA DEPARTMENT OF ENVIRONMENTAL QUALITY 118
WASHINGTON STATE OFFICE OF ENVIRONMENTAL EDUCATION 122

Sport Fishing

ALASKA DEPARTMENT OF FISH AND GAME 40
AMERICAN BASS ASSOCIATION OF MARYLAND, THE 140
AMERICAN LEAGUE OF ANGLERS AND BOATERS 152
ARIZONA GAME AND FISH DEPARTMENT 42
BILLFISH FOUNDATION 166
BLACK BASS FOUNDATION 166
CALIFORNIA TROUT, INC. 170
CAMP FIRE CLUB OF AMERICA, THE 171
COASTAL CONSERVATION ASSOCIATION 181
DEPARTMENT OF FISH AND WILDLIFE (WASHINGTON) 119
DEPARTMENT OF INLAND FISHERIES AND WILDLIFE 71
DEPARTMENT OF INTERIOR, U.S.G.S/B.R.D, SOUTH CAROLINA
  COOPERATIVE FISH AND WILDLIFE RESEARCH UNIT 107
DEPARTMENT OF PUBLIC SAFETY 41
DEPARTMENT OF WILDLIFE CONSERVATION 98
DIVISION OF NATURAL RESOURCES 122
FEDERATION OF FLY FISHERS 205
FISH AND BOAT COMMISSION 103
FISH AND WILDLIFE INFORMATION EXCHANGE 206
FISHAMERICA FOUNDATION 206
FLORIDA GAME AND FRESH WATER FISH COMMISSION 55
FUTURE FISHERMAN FOUNDATION 213
GREAT LAKES SPORT FISHING COUNCIL 216
HOOD CANAL LAND TRUST 222
IDAHO FISH AND GAME DEPARTMENT 61
INTERNATIONAL GAME FISH ASSOCIATION 231
KANSAS DEPARTMENT OF WILDLIFE AND PARKS 67
MAINE ATLANTIC SALMON AUTHORITY (formerly Maine Atlantic Sea Run
  Salmon Commission) 71
MISSISSIPPI COOPERATIVE FISH AND WILDLIFE RESEARCH UNIT
  (USDI) 79
MISSISSIPPI INTERSTATE COOPERATIVE RESOURCE ASSOCIATION 258
MONTANA DEPARTMENT OF FISH, WILDLIFE, AND PARKS 82
MUSKIES, INC. 262
NATIONAL COALITION FOR MARINE CONSERVATION 266
NATIONAL FIELD ARCHERY ASSOCIATION 267
NEW HAMPSHIRE FISH AND GAME DEPARTMENT 86
NEW HAMPSHIRE SEA GRANT PROGRAM 86
NORTH AMERICAN FISHING CLUB 289
NORTH CAROLINA BEACH BUGGY ASSOCIATION, INC. 290
NORTH DAKOTA GAME AND FISH DEPARTMENT 95
OREGON TROUT, INC. 298
PACIFIC FISHERY MANAGEMENT COUNCIL 300
QUEBEC WILDLIFE FEDERATION 308
STRIPERS UNLIMITED INC. 328
UTAH COOPERATIVE FISH AND WILDLIFE RESEARCH UNIT (USDI-
  USGS-BRD-CRU) 113
WILDLIFE FOREVER 351
WILDLIFE FOUNDATION OF FLORIDA, INC. 352
WILDLIFE LEGISLATIVE FUND OF AMERICA, THE, AND WILDLIFE
  CONSERVATION FUND OF AMERICA, THE 352
WILDLIFE RESOURCES AGENCY 110
WISCONSIN COOPERATIVE FISHERY RESEARCH UNIT (USDI) 123

State Parks

PENNSYLVANIA DEPARTMENT OF CONSERVATION AND NATURAL
  RESOURCES 105

Stewardship

ENVIRONMENTAL EDUCATION COUNCIL OF OHIO 203
SONORAN INSTITUTE 323

Streams

AMERICAN SOCIETY OF LIMNOLOGY AND OCEANOGRAPHY 155
SAVE THE DUNES COUNCIL 316

Sustainability

IZAAK WALTON LEAGUE OF AMERICA, INC., THE 240
NATURAL RESOURCES INFORMATION COUNCIL 278
TEXAS FORESTRY ASSOCIATION 331

Sustainable Agriculture

PACIFIC RIVERS COUNCIL 300

Sustainable Buildings

NORTHEAST SUSTAINABLE ENERGY ASSOCIATION 292

Sustainable Development

ADIRONDACK COUNCIL, THE 133
ADIRONDACK NATURE CONSERVANCY/ADIRONDACK LAND TRUST,
  INC. 134
AFRICAN WILDLIFE FOUNDATION 134
AGRICULTURAL EXTENSION SERVICE 110
ALABAMA FORESTRY COMMISSION 39
ALASKA CONSERVATION ALLIANCE 136
ALASKA CONSERVATION VOICE 137
ALLIANCE FOR THE CHESAPEAKE BAY 138
AMERICAN GEOGRAPHICAL SOCIETY 150
AMERICAN LIVESTOCK BREEDS CONSERVANCY 152
ARIZONA LAND DEPARTMENT 42
ASSOCIATION FOR THE PROTECTION OF THE ADIRONDACKS, THE 160

ASSOCIATION OF NEW JERSEY ENVIRONMENTAL COMMISSIONS.... 162
ATLANTIC CENTER FOR THE ENVIRONMENT ... 162, 163
ATLANTIC STATES LEGAL FOUNDATION ... 163
AUDUBON INTERNATIONAL ... 163
AUDUBON NATURALIST SOCIETY OF THE CENTRAL ATLANTIC STATES ... 164
AUDUBON SOCIETY OF PORTLAND ... 164
BIOMASS USERS NETWORK ... 166
BOONE AND CROCKETT FOUNDATION ... 167
CAMPAIGN FOR A PROSPEROUS GEORGIA ... 171
CARIBBEAN NATURAL RESOURCES INSTITUTE ... 173
CARRYING CAPACITY NETWORK ... 174
CATSKILL CENTER FOR CONSERVATION AND DEVELOPMENT, INC., THE ... 174
CATSKILL FOREST ASSOCIATION ... 174
CENTER FOR RESOURCE ECONOMICS ... 176
CENTER FOR RESOURCEFUL BUILDING TECHNOLOGY ... 176
CHARLES A. AND ANNE MORROW LINDBERGH FOUNDATION, THE... 178
CIRCUMPOLAR CONSERVATION UNION ... 179
CLIMATE INSTITUTE ... 180
COASTAL SOCIETY, THE ... 182
COLORADO ENVIRONMENTAL COALITION ... 182
COLORADO STATE COOPERATIVE EXTENSION ... 51
COMMITTEE FOR THE NATIONAL INSTITUTE FOR THE ENVIRONMENT (CNIE) ... 183
COMMITTEE ON AGRICULTURAL SUSTAINABILITY FOR DEVELOPING COUNTRIES ... 184
COMMUNITY ENVIRONMENTAL COUNCIL ... 184
COMMUNITY RIGHTS COUNSEL ... 184
CONCERN, INC. ... 184
CONNECTICUT AUDUBON SOCIETY, INC. ... 185
CONSERVATION FEDERATION OF MARYLAND/For A Rural Maryland (F.A.R.M.) ... 187
COUSTEAU SOCIETY, INC., THE ... 190
DELAWARE GREENWAYS, INC. ... 192
DESERT FISHES COUNCIL ... 193
EARTH ISLAND INSTITUTE ... 197
EARTHSCAN ... 198
EARTHWATCH INSTITUTE ... 199
ECOTOURISM SOCIETY, THE ... 199
ENVIRONMENTAL ENTERPRISES ASSISTANCE FUND, INC. ... 203
ENVIRONMENTAL LAW INSTITUTE, THE ... 203
ENVIRONMENTAL LEAGUE OF MASSACHUSETTS (ELM) ... 203
FOREST TRUST ... 209
FOSSIL FUELS POLICY ACTION INSTITUTE/ALLIANCE FOR A PAVING MORATORIUM ... 210
FRIENDS OF THE SAN JUANS ... 212
GEORGIA SEA GRANT COLLEGE PROGRAM ... 58
GLOBAL CITIES PROJECT, THE ... 215
GLOBAL ENVIRONMENTAL MANAGEMENT INITIATIVE (GEMI) ... 215
GRAND CANYON TRUST (Washington, DC Office) ... 216
GREEN PARTY USA ... 218
GREEN SEAL ... 218
GUAM COASTAL MANAGEMENT PROGRAM ... 58
HAWAII SOCIETY OF AMERICAN FORESTERS ... 220
HEADLANDS INSTITUTE ... 221
ILLINOIS WALNUT COUNCIL ... 225
INTERFAITH COUNCIL FOR THE PROTECTION OF ANIMALS AND NATURE INC. (ICPAN) ... 227
INTERNATIONAL BICYCLE FUND ... 229
INTERNATIONAL CENTRE FOR CONSERVATION EDUCATION ... 229
INTERNATIONAL INSTITUTE FOR ENERGY CONSERVATION ... 231
INTERNATIONAL MARITIME ORGANIZATION ... 231
INTERNATIONAL SOCIETY FOR ECOLOGICAL ECONOMICS ... 233
INTERNATIONAL SONORAN DESERT ALLIANCE ... 234
INTERTRIBAL BISON COOPERATIVE (ITBC) ... 236
IOWA NATURAL HERITAGE FOUNDATION ... 238
KANSAS WATER OFFICE ... 68
LEGACY INTERNATIONAL ... 248
LOUISIANA SEA GRANT COLLEGE PROGRAM ... 70
MINNESOTA DEPARTMENT OF AGRICULTURE ... 77
MINNESOTA ENVIRONMENTAL QUALITY BOARD ... 78
MINNESOTA SEA GRANT COLLEGE PROGRAM ... 79
MONITOR INTERNATIONAL ... 259
MONO LAKE COMMITTEE ... 259
NATIONAL TRAPPERS ASSOCIATION, INC. ... 271
NATIONAL WILDLIFE FEDERATION ... 273, 275
NATURE CONSERVANCY, THE, IOWA CHAPTER ... 280
NEVIS HISTORICAL AND CONSERVATION SOCIETY ... 283
NEW HAMPSHIRE DEPARTMENT OF AGRICULTURE, MARKETS, AND FOOD ... 85
NEW HAMPSHIRE SEA GRANT PROGRAM ... 86
NEW JERSEY CONSERVATION FOUNDATION ... 285
NEW JERSEY ENVIRONMENTAL LOBBY ... 286
NORTHWEST ENVIRONMENT WATCH ... 293
NORTHWEST RENEWABLE RESOURCES CENTER ... 293
NORTHWEST RESOURCE INFORMATION CENTER ... 293
OHIO ENVIRONMENTAL COUNCIL, INC. ... 295
OZARKS RESOURCE CENTER ... 300
PANOS INSTITUTE, THE ... 301
POPULATION ACTION INTERNATIONAL ... 304
POPULATION REFERENCE BUREAU INC. ... 305
QUEBEC WILDLIFE FEDERATION ... 308
RAINBOW PUSH COALITION ... 308
RAINFOREST ALLIANCE ... 309
RESOURCE RENEWAL INSTITUTE, THE ... 310
RESOURCES FOR THE FUTURE ... 310
RETURNED PEACE CORPS VOLUNTEER FOR ENVIRONMENT AND DEVELOPMENT (RPCV-ED) ... 311
RHODE ISLAND WILD PLANT SOCIETY ... 311
RINCON INSTITUTE, THE ... 312
RIVER NETWORK ... 312
SAVE AMERICA'S FORESTS ... 315
SOCIETY FOR CONSERVATION BIOLOGY ... 321
SOIL AND WATER CONSERVATION SOCIETY (formerly Soil Conservation Society of America) ... 323
SONORAN INSTITUTE ... 323
SOUTH CAROLINA SEA GRANT CONSORTIUM ... 108
SOUTHEAST ALASKA CONSERVATION COUNCIL (SEACC) ... 324
SOUTHFACE ENERGY INSTITUTE ... 326
TENNESSEE ENVIRONMENTAL COUNCIL ... 330
TEXAS ORGANIZATION FOR ENDANGERED SPECIES ... 331
TOGETHER FOUNDATION, THE ... 332
UNION OF CONCERNED SCIENTISTS ... 339
UNIVERSITY OF VERMONT EXTENSION ... 115
UPPER MISSISSIPPI RIVER CONSERVATION COMMITTEE ... 340
UTAH STATE SOIL CONSERVATION COMMISSION ... 114
WASHINGTON SEA GRANT PROGRAM ... 121
WATER RESOURCES DEPARTMENT ... 102
WILDLIFE HABITAT COUNCIL ... 352
WILDLIFE SOCIETY, PENNSYLVANIA CHAPTER ... 356
WISCONSIN DEPARTMENT OF AGRICULTURE ... 123
WORLD ASSOCIATION OF GIRL GUIDES AND GIRL SCOUTS (WAGGGS) ... 361
WORLD PAL (WORLD POPULATION ALLOCATION LIMITED INC.) ... 362
WORLD RESOURCES INSTITUTE ... 362
WYOMING STATE EXTENSION SERVICES ... 126
ZERO POPULATION GROWTH INC. ... 365

Sustainable Ecosystems

ALASKA AUDUBON SOCIETY ... 136
ALASKA CONSERVATION FOUNDATION ... 136
AMERICAN INSTITUTE OF BIOLOGICAL SCIENCES ... 151
ATLANTIC STATES LEGAL FOUNDATION ... 163
BIODIVERSITY LEGAL FOUNDATION ... 166
BOONE AND CROCKETT FOUNDATION ... 167
CATSKILL FOREST ASSOCIATION ... 174
CENTER FOR MARINE CONSERVATION ... 176
CENTER FOR RESOURCE ECONOMICS ... 176
COLORADO STATE COOPERATIVE EXTENSION ... 51
COLORADO STATE FOREST SERVICE ... 51
COLORADO WILDLIFE HERITAGE FOUNDATION ... 183
COMMITTEE FOR THE NATIONAL INSTITUTE FOR THE ENVIRONMENT (CNIE) ... 183
COOPERATIVE EXTENSION SYSTEM (MASSACHUSETTS) ... 74
COUSTEAU SOCIETY, INC., THE ... 190
CRAIGHEAD WILDLIFE-WILDLANDS INSTITUTE ... 190
EARTHWATCH INSTITUTE ... 199
ECOLOGICAL SOCIETY OF AMERICA, THE ... 199
FOSSIL RIM WILDLIFE CENTER ... 210
FRIENDS OF DISCOVERY PARK ... 211
GUAM COASTAL MANAGEMENT PROGRAM ... 58
HAWAII COOPERATIVE FISHERY RESEARCH UNIT (USDI) ... 60
HUNTSMAN MARINE SCIENCE CENTRE ... 223
ILLINOIS ASSOCIATION OF CONSERVATION DISTRICTS ... 224
INDIANA NATIVE PLANT AND WILDFLOWER SOCIETY ... 226
INTERNATIONAL SNOW LEOPARD TRUST ... 232
INTERNATIONAL SOCIETY FOR ECOLOGICAL ECONOMICS ... 233
INTERNATIONAL SOCIETY OF TROPICAL FORESTERS INC. ... 233
IOWA COOPERATIVE FISH AND WILDLIFE RESEARCH UNIT ... 65
ISLAND INSTITUTE, THE ... 239
KANSAS BIOLOGICAL SURVEY ... 66
LOUISIANA DEPARTMENT OF AGRICULTURE ... 69, 70
LOWER MISSISSIPPI RIVER CONSERVATION COMMITTEE ... 249
MAGIC ... 250
MANASOTA-88 ... 251
MARYLAND FORESTS ASSOCIATION ... 252
MINNESOTA ENVIRONMENTAL QUALITY BOARD ... 78
MINNESOTA SEA GRANT COLLEGE PROGRAM ... 79
MONTANA WILDERNESS ASSOCIATION ... 260
NATURAL HERITAGE COMMISSION (ARKANSAS) ... 45
NEBRASKA STATE EXTENSION SERVICES ... 84
NEVEDA COOPERATIVE EXTENSION ... 85
NEW HAMPSHIRE SEA GRANT PROGRAM ... 86
NEW JERSEY CONSERVATION FOUNDATION ... 285
NEW JERSEY PINELANDS COMMISSION ... 88
NEW YORK STATE COOPERATIVE EXTENSION ... 93

NORTHERN ALASKA ENVIRONMENTAL CENTER.................................. 292
NORTHWEST ECOSYSTEM ALLIANCE 293
NORTHWEST RESOURCE INFORMATION CENTER 293
OHIO ENVIRONMENTAL COUNCIL, INC. 295
PENNSYLVANIA FOREST STEWARDSHIP PROGRAM........................ 105
PINCHOT INSTITUTE FOR CONSERVATION....................................... 303
RAINFOREST TRUST INC., THE 309
REEF RELIEF... 310
RESOURCE RENEWAL INSTITUTE, THE 310
RINCON INSTITUTE, THE 312
RIVERS COUNCIL OF WASHINGTON (formerly Northwest Rivers Council)
 313
SAVE AMERICA'S FORESTS 315
SOCIETY OF WETLAND SCIENTISTS 322
SOIL AND WATER CONSERVATION SOCIETY (formerly Soil Conservation
 Society of America) 323
SOUTH CAROLINA SEA GRANT CONSORTIUM 108
THE GLACIER INSTITUTE 331
WASHINGTON STATE EXTENSION SERVICES 121
WASHINGTON STATE OFFICE OF ENVIRONMENTAL EDUCATION...... 122
WATER RESOURCES DEPARTMENT 102
WESTERN HEMISPHERE SHOREBIRD RESERVE NETWORK (WHSRN)
 347
WESTERN PENNSYLVANIA CONSERVANCY 347
WILDERNESS SOCIETY, THE 349
WISCONSIN ASSOCIATION OF LAKES (WAL) 359

Sustainable Energy

NORTHEAST SUSTAINABLE ENERGY ASSOCIATION 292

Sustainable Resources

NATIONAL FORESTRY ASSOCIATION 268
NATURAL RESOURCES INFORMATION COUNCIL 278
SOCIETY FOR RANGE MANAGEMENT 321

Taiga

NORTHERN ALASKA ENVIRONMENTAL CENTER 292

Terrestrial Habitats

FISH AND WILDLIFE INFORMATION EXCHANGE 206
HAWAII NATURE CENTER.. 220
INTERNATIONAL ASSOCIATION OF WILDLAND FIRE (formerly Fire
 Research Institute) 229
MICHIGAN WILDLIFE HABITAT FOUNDATION 255
NEW HAMPSHIRE NATURAL HERITAGE INVENTORY 86
OKLAHOMA NATIVE PLANT SOCIETY 296
RHODE ISLAND STATE ASSOCIATION OF CONSERVATION DISTRICTS
 311
RINCON INSTITUTE, THE 312
SOUTH DAKOTA GAME, FISH, AND PARKS DEPARTMENT 109
UTAH COOPERATIVE FISH AND WILDLIFE RESEARCH UNIT (USDI-
 USGS-BRD-CRU) 113

Tourism

ECOTOURISM SOCIETY, THE.. 199

Toxic Reduction

MINNESOTA CENTER FOR ENVIRONMENTAL ADVOCACY (MCEA) 256

Toxic Substances

AGENCY OF NATURAL RESOURCES 114
ALLIANCE FOR THE CHESAPEAKE BAY 138
ARIZONA DEPARTMENT OF ENVIRONMENTAL QUALITY 42
BORDER ECOLOGY PROJECT (BEP) 167
CALIFORNIA ENVIRONMENTAL PROTECTION AGENCY 45
CENTER FOR HEALTH, ENVIRONMENT, AND JUSTICE 175
CENTRAL STATES EDUCATION CENTER 177
COMMUNITY ENVIRONMENTAL COUNCIL... 184
CONNECTICUT FUND FOR THE ENVIRONMENT 186
CONNECTICUT PUBLIC INTEREST RESEARCH GROUP (ConnPIRG)... 186
COOK INLET KEEPER.. 189
DEPARTMENT OF ENVIRONMENT AND NATURAL RESOURCES (SOUTH
 DAKOTA).. 109

ENVIRONMENTAL CAREERS ORGANIZATION INC., THE..................... 201
ENVIRONMENTAL LEAGUE OF MASSACHUSETTS (ELM) 203
FEDERAL WILDLIFE OFFICER'S ASSOCIATION 205
FLORIDA STATE DEPARTMENT OF HEALTH.. 56
GREAT LAKES UNITED.. 217
GREENPEACE, INC. 219
HUMAN ECOLOGY ACTION LEAGUE INC. THE (HEAL) 222
IDAHO STATE DEPARTMENT OF AGRICULTURE 62
ILLINOIS ENVIRONMENAL PROTECTION AGENCY 63
INDIANA STATE DEPARTMENT OF HEALTH 64
INFORM, INC. 226
KENTUCKY RESOURCES COUNCIL 245
LAKE SUPERIOR GREENS 246
MANASOTA-88.. 251
MICHIGAN DEPARTMENT OF ENVIRONMENTAL QUALITY 76
MINERAL POLICY CENTER 256
MONTANA ENVIRONMENTAL INFORMATION CENTER 260
NATIONAL ENVIRONMENTAL HEALTH ASSOCIATION 267
NEW MEXICO COOPERATIVE FISH AND WILDLIFE RESEARCH UNIT ... 89
NEW YORK PUBLIC INTEREST RESEARCH GROUP (NYPIRG) 287
OHIO ENVIRONMENTAL COUNCIL, INC. 295
PHYSICIANS FOR SOCIAL RESPONSIBILITY 303
RACHEL CARSON COUNCIL INC. (formerly Rachel Carson Trust for the
 Living Environment Inc.) 308
RAINBOW PUSH COALITION 308
SIERRA CLUB 318, 319
SOUTH CAROLINA DEPARTMENT OF HEALTH AND ENVIRONMENTAL
 CONTROL 108
STOP 328
STRIPERS UNLIMITED INC. 328
TENNESSEE ENVIRONMENTAL COUNCIL 330
TEXAS DEPARTMENT OF HEALTH 111
UTAH DEPARTMENT OF HEALTH 113
VERMONT DEPARTMENT OF HEALTH 115
WATER ENVIRONMENT FEDERATION 345
WESTERN ENVIRONMENTAL LAW CENTER 346
WILDLIFE DAMAGE REVIEW (WDR) 351
WILDLIFE SOCIETY, PENNSYLVANIA CHAPTER................................ 356
WYOMING OUTDOOR COUNCIL 364

Toxicology

CENTER FOR SCIENCE IN THE PUBLIC INTEREST 176
COLORADO DEPARTMENT OF AGRICULTURE.................................... 50
FLORIDA STATE DEPARTMENT OF HEALTH.. 56
INDIANA STATE DEPARTMENT OF HEALTH 64
MICHIGAN DEPARTMENT OF ENVIRONMENTAL QUALITY 76
MINNESOTA COOPERATIVE FISH AND WILDLIFE RESEARCH UNIT 77
NATIONAL COALITION AGAINST THE MISUSE OF PESTICIDES 266
OHIO SEA GRANT COLLEGE PROGRAM, F.T. STONE LABORATORY,
 AND GREAT LAKES AQUATIC ECOSYSTEM RESEARCH
 CONSORTIUM (GLAERC) 97
TEXAS DEPARTMENT OF HEALTH 111
UTAH DEPARTMENT OF HEALTH 113
VERMONT DEPARTMENT OF HEALTH 115
WASHINGTON COOPERATIVE FISH AND WILDLIFE RESEARCH UNIT
 (USDI) 120

Trail

ILLINOIS PRAIRIE PATH 225

Training

ALASKA HEALTH PROJECT 41
ALASKA NATURAL RESOURCE AND OUTDOOR EDUCATION
 ASSOCIATION 137
ASSOCIATION OF NEW JERSEY ENVIRONMENTAL COMMISSIONS..... 162
CARIBBEAN NATURAL RESOURCES INSTITUTE 173
CONFERENCE OF NATIONAL PARK COOPERATING ASSOCIATIONS . 185
CONSERVATION FUND, THE 187
ENVIRONMENTAL CAREER CENTER 201
GEORGIA FORESTRY ASSOCIATION, INC.. 215
HUNTSMAN MARINE SCIENCE CENTRE 223
INSTITUTE FOR CONSERVATION LEADERSHIP 227
INTERNATIONAL CENTER FOR GIBBON STUDIES 229
INTERNATIONAL HUNTER EDUCATION ASSOCIATION 231
IOWA WOMEN IN NATURAL RESOURCES 238
LOUISIANA FORESTRY ASSOCIATION... 249
MASSACHUSETTS ENVIRONMENTAL EDUCATION SOCIETY 253
MINNESOTA BOARD OF WATER AND SOIL RESOURCES 77
NATIONAL ASSOCIATION OF SERVICE AND CONSERVATION CORPS
 (NASCC) 264
NATIONAL WHISTLEBLOWER CENTER.. 273

KEYWORD INDEX - Transportation/Urban Environment

NORTH AMERICAN ASSOCIATION FOR ENVIRONMENTAL EDUCATION 288
OKLAHOMA ACADEMY OF SCIENCE 295
QUEBEC WILDLIFE FEDERATION 308
RESPONSIVE MANAGEMENT 311
SAFE ENERGY COMMUNICATION COUNCIL 315
SOIL AND WATER CONSERVATION SOCIETY (formerly Soil Conservation Society of America) 323
THREE CIRCLES CENTER FOR MULTICULTURAL ENVIRONMENTAL EDUCATION 332
WOLF EDUCATION AND RESEARCH CENTER 360
WORLD ASSOCIATION OF GIRL GUIDES AND GIRL SCOUTS (WAGGGS) 361

Transportation

AMERICAN COUNCIL FOR AN ENERGY-EFFICIENT ECONOMY 142
CHESAPEAKE BAY FOUNDATION, INC. (Pennsylvania Office) 178
CONSERVATION LAW FOUNDATION, INC. (CLF) 188
DELAWARE GREENWAYS, INC. 192
DEPARTMENT OF PUBLIC WORKS 53
DEPARTMENT OF TRANSPORTATION 27, 100, 106
DEPARTMENT OF TRANSPORTATION (OREGON) 100
DEPARTMENT OF TRANSPORTATION (RHODE ISLAND) 106
ENVIRONMENTAL AND ENERGY STUDY INSTITUTE (EESI) 201
ENVIRONMENTAL DEFENSE FUND, INC. 202
FOSSIL FUELS POLICY ACTION INSTITUTE/ALLIANCE FOR A PAVING MORATORIUM 210
FRIENDS OF THE EARTH 211
GEORGIA CONSERVANCY, INC., THE 214
GEORGIA FORESTRY ASSOCIATION, INC. 215
GLOBAL CITIES PROJECT, THE 215
ILLINOIS DEPARTMENT OF TRANSPORTATION 63
INFORM, INC. 226
INTERNATIONAL BICYCLE FUND 229
INTERNATIONAL INSTITUTE FOR ENERGY CONSERVATION 231
INTERNATIONAL MARITIME ORGANIZATION 231
IOWA TRAILS COUNCIL 238
MASSACHUSETTS HIGHWAY DEPARTMENT 75
NATIONAL GRANGE, THE 269
NEW JERSEY ENVIRONMENTAL LOBBY 286
NEW YORK PUBLIC INTEREST RESEARCH GROUP (NYPIRG 287
NORTHEAST SUSTAINABLE ENERGY ASSOCIATION 292
NORTHWEST ENVIRONMENT WATCH 293
OREGON B.A.S.S. CHAPTER FEDERATION 297
OREGON ENVIRONMENTAL COUNCIL 298
RESOURCES FOR THE FUTURE 310
SCENIC HUDSON, INC. 317
SOUTH CAROLINA B.A.S.S. CHAPTER FEDERATION 323
SOUTH CAROLINA ENERGY OFFICE 108
SOUTHERN ENVIRONMENTAL LAW CENTER 325, 326
STATE OFFICE OF CONSERVATION (LOUISIANA) 71
STOP 328
UNION OF CONCERNED SCIENTISTS 339
URBAN HABITAT PROGRAM 340
WASHINGTON TOXICS COALITION 344
YOSEMITE RESTORATION TRUST 365

Trapping

ANIMAL PROTECTION INSTITUTE 157
ANIMAL WELFARE INSTITUTE 158
BOUNTY INFORMATION SERVICE 167
CALIFORNIA TRAPPERS ASSOCIATION 170
CALIFORNIA WILDLIFE DEFENDERS 170
CANADIAN FEDERATION OF HUMANE SOCIETIES 172
COLORADO TRAPPERS ASSOCIATION 183
DEPARTMENT OF PUBLIC SAFETY 41
FRIENDS OF ANIMALS INC. 211
FUND FOR ANIMALS INC., THE 212
GAME COMMISSION 103
HUMANE SOCIETY OF THE UNITED STATES, THE 222
INTERNATIONAL ECOLOGY SOCIETY (IES) 230
IOWA TRAPPERS ASSOCIATION, INC. 238
KANSAS STATE EXTENSION SERVICES 68
MASSACHUSETTS TRAPPER'S ASSOCIATION, INC. 254
NATIONAL HUNTERS ASSOCIATION, INC. 269
NATIONAL TRAPPERS ASSOCIATION, INC. 271
NEW HAMPSHIRE FISH AND GAME DEPARTMENT 86
NEWFOUNDLAND LABRADOR WILDLIFE FEDERATION 287
NORTHWEST ECOSYSTEM ALLIANCE 293
RIVER OTTER ALLIANCE, THE 312
ROCKY MOUNTAIN BIGHORN SOCIETY 313
SOCIETY FOR ANIMAL PROTECTIVE LEGISLATION 320
WILDLIFE DAMAGE REVIEW (WDR) 351
WILDLIFE LEGISLATIVE FUND OF AMERICA, THE, AND WILDLIFE CONSERVATION FUND OF AMERICA, THE 352

Travel

ECOTOURISM SOCIETY, THE 199

Trees

LADY BIRD JOHNSON WILDFLOWER CENTER (formerly the National Wildlflower Research Center) 246

Trout

CALIFORNIA TROUT, INC. 170

Tundra

NORTHERN ALASKA ENVIRONMENTAL CENTER 292

Upstream Flood Prevention

OKLAHOMA STATE CONSERVATION COMMISSION 99

Urban and Rural Development

ROGER TORY PETERSON INSTITUTE 314

Urban Environment

ADOPT-A-STREAM FOUNDATION, THE 134
AMERICAN CONSERVATION ASSOCIATION, INC. 141, 142
AMERICAN FISHERIES SOCIETY, GREATER PORTLAND, OR CHAPTER 145
AMERICAN GEOGRAPHICAL SOCIETY 150
AMERICAN NATURE STUDY SOCIETY 153
AMERICAN PLANNING ASSOCIATION 154
AMERICAN SOCIETY OF LANDSCAPE ARCHITECTS 155
ASSOCIATION OF AMERICAN GEOGRAPHERS 161
ATLANTIC STATES LEGAL FOUNDATION 163
AUDUBON SOCIETY OF PORTLAND 164
BIO-INTEGRAL RESOURCE CENTER 166
CENTER FOR WATERSHED PROTECTION 177
COLORADO DEPARTMENT OF EDUCATION 50
COLORADO STATE COOPERATIVE EXTENSION 51
COMITE DESPERTAR CIDRENO 105
COMMUNITY RIGHTS COUNSEL 184
DELAWARE ASSOCIATION OF CONSERVATION DISTRICTS 191
DEPARTMENT OF PUBLIC WORKS 53
EARTH ISLAND INSTITUTE 197
EARTHSCAN 198
ELSA WILD ANIMAL APPEAL (Louisiana Chapter) 200
FOSSIL FUELS POLICY ACTION INSTITUTE/ALLIANCE FOR A PAVING MORATORIUM 210
GEORGIA CONSERVANCY, INC., THE 214
GIRL SCOUTS OF THE UNITED STATES OF AMERICA 215
HEADLANDS INSTITUTE 221
HUMAN ECOLOGY ACTION LEAGUE INC. THE (HEAL) 222
INTERNATIONAL PLANT PROPAGATION SOCIETY, INC., THE 232
MAGIC 250
MICHIGAN ENVIRONMENTAL COUNCIL 255
NATIONAL ASSOCIATION OF CONSERVATION DISTRICTS 263
NATIONAL ASSOCIATION OF SERVICE AND CONSERVATION CORPS (NASCC) 264
NATIONAL TRUST FOR HISTORIC PRESERVATION 272
NEW JERSEY CONSERVATION FOUNDATION 285
NEW JERSEY DEPARTMENT OF AGRICULTURE 87
NORTH AMERICAN ASSOCIATION FOR ENVIRONMENTAL EDUCATION 288
NORTH AMERICAN COALITION ON RELIGION AND ECOLOGY (NACRE) 288
OKLAHOMA STATE BOARD OF AGRICULTURE 98
OPENLANDS PROJECT 297
RAINBOW PUSH COALITION 308
RENEWABLE NATURAL RESOURCES FOUNDATION 310
SCENIC AMERICA 317
SIERRA CLUB FOUNDATION, THE 319
STATE SOIL AND WATER CONSERVATION COMMISSION (GEORGIA) .. 58
STOP 328
TREE PEOPLE 332
UNITED NATIONS ENVIRONMENT PROGRAMME 339
URBAN HABITAT PROGRAM 340
WESTERN PENNSYLVANIA CONSERVANCY 347
WORLD WILDLIFE FUND 363

YMCA EARTH SERVICE CORPS 365

Urban Forestry

ALABAMA FORESTRY COMMISSION 39
CLIMATE INSTITUTE 180
COLORADO STATE FOREST SERVICE 51
COOPERATIVE EXTENSION SYSTEM (MASSACHUSETTS) 74
DELAWARE DEPARTMENT OF AGRICULTURE 52
DIVISION OF FORESTRY AND SOIL RESOURCES (GUAM) 58
EARTHSTEWARDS NETWORK 198
ELM RESEARCH INSTITUTE 200
FOREST LANDOWNERS ASSOCIATION, INC. 209
FOREST SERVICE (Texas) 111
FORESTRY COMMISSION (MISSISSIPPI) 79
FORESTRY COMMISSION (SOUTH CAROLINA) 107
GLOBAL CITIES PROJECT, THE 215
INTERNATIONAL PLANT PROPAGATION SOCIETY, INC., THE 232
INTERNATIONAL SOCIETY OF TROPICAL FORESTERS INC. 233
KANSAS FOREST SERVICE 67
KENTUCKY-TENNESSEE SOCIETY OF AMERICAN FORESTERS 245
LOUISIANA DEPARTMENT OF AGRICULTURE 69, 70
NATIONAL ARBOR DAY FOUNDATION 262
NATIONAL ASSOCIATION OF STATE FORESTERS 264
NATIONAL TREE TRUST 272
NORTH DAKOTA STATE FOREST SERVICE 96
OKLAHOMA STATE EXTENSION SERVICES 99
OREGON DEPARTMENT OF FORESTRY 101
OUTDOOR CIRCLE, THE 299
SOUTHERN NEW ENGLAND FOREST CONSORTIUM, INC. 326
STATE FORESTRY DIVISION (WYOMING) 126
TREE PEOPLE 332
UNIVERSITY OF NEW HAMPSHIRE COOPERATIVE EXTENSION 86
VIRGINIA NATIVE PLANT SOCIETY 343
WASHINGTON NATIVE PLANT SOCIETY 344
YMCA EARTH SERVICE CORPS 365

Waste Management

PENNSYLVANIA RESOURCES COUNCIL, INC., (formerly PA Roadside Council) 302
WEST MICHIGAN ENVIRONMENTAL ACTION COUNCIL 346

Waste Resources

PENNSYLVANIA CITIZENS ADVISORY COUNCIL TO DEPARTMENT OF ENVIRONMENTAL PROTECTION 301

Water Conservation

CALIFORNIA TROUT, INC. 170
SOUTHWEST FLORIDA WATER MANAGEMENT DISTRICT (SWFWMD) . 56

Water Pollution

ALABAMA ENVIRONMENTAL COUNCIL 135
ALLIANCE FOR THE CHESAPEAKE BAY 138
AMERICAN FISHERIES SOCIETY 142, 144, 145, 146, 147, 148, 149, 283
AMERICAN GROUND WATER TRUST 150
AMERICAN OCEANS CAMPAIGN 153
ARIZONA DEPARTMENT OF ENVIRONMENTAL QUALITY 42
BROTHERHOOD OF THE JUNGLE COCK, INC., THE 168
CASCADIA RESEARCH 174
CENTER FOR MARINE CONSERVATION 176
CHINA REGION LAKES ALLIANCE 179
CLEAN OCEAN ACTION 180
COAST ALLIANCE 181
COASTAL SOCIETY, THE 182
COMMUNITIES FOR A BETTER ENVIRONMENT 184
CONNECTICUT FUND FOR THE ENVIRONMENT 186
CONNECTICUT RIVER WATERSHED COUNCIL INC. 186
CONSERVATION LAW FOUNDATION, INC. (CLF) 188
DEPARTMENT OF ENVIRONMENT AND NATURAL RESOURCES (SOUTH DAKOTA) 109
DEPARTMENT OF ENVIRONMENTAL QUALITY (ARKANSAS) 44
DEPARTMENT OF PUBLIC WORKS 53
DEPARTMENT OF THE ENVIRONMENT 72
ENVIRONMENTAL CAREERS ORGANIZATION INC., THE 201
ENVIRONMENTAL ENTERPRISES ASSISTANCE FUND, INC. 203
ENVIRONMENTAL LEAGUE OF MASSACHUSETTS (ELM) 203
FISHAMERICA FOUNDATION 206
FRESHWATER FOUNDATION 211
FRIENDS OF THE SEA OTTER 212
FUTURE FISHERMAN FOUNDATION 213
GREAT LAKES UNITED 217
GREEN (GLOBAL RIVERS ENVIRONMENTAL EDUCATION NETWORK)218
IDAHO CONSERVATION LEAGUE 223
IDAHO STATE DEPARTMENT OF AGRICULTURE 62
ILLINOIS ENVIRONMENTAL PROTECTION AGENCY 63
INTERNATIONAL ASSOCIATION FOR ENVIRONMENTAL HYDROLOGY (IAEH) 228
INTERNATIONAL EROSION CONTROL ASSOCIATION (IECA) 230
IOWA ENVIRONMENTAL COUNCIL 237
KANSAS GEOLOGICAL SURVEY 67
KANSAS STATE CONSERVATION COMMISSION 67
LAKE MICHIGAN FEDERATION 246
LEAGUE TO SAVE LAKE TAHOE 248
LEGAL ENVIRONMENTAL ASSISTANCE FOUNDATION INC. (LEAF) 248
MICHIGAN DEPARTMENT OF ENVIRONMENTAL QUALITY 76
MID-ATLANTIC COUNCIL OF WATERSHED ASSOCIATIONS 256
MINERAL POLICY CENTER 256
MINNESOTA DEPARTMENT OF AGRICULTURE 77
MINNESOTA SEA GRANT COLLEGE PROGRAM 79
MISSISSIPPI SOIL AND WATER CONSERVATION COMMISSION 80
NATIONAL ASSOCIATION OF CONSERVATION DISTRICTS 263
NATIONAL ASSOCIATION OF STATE DEPARTMENTS OF AGRICULTURE 264
NATIONAL BOATING FEDERATION 266
NATIONAL ENVIRONMENTAL HEALTH ASSOCIATION 267
NATIONAL GROUND WATER ASSOCIATION, THE 269
NATIONAL WATER RESOURCES ASSOCIATION 272
NEW HAMPSHIRE DEPARTMENT OF ENVIRONMENTAL SERVICES 86
NEW HAMPSHIRE SEA GRANT PROGRAM 86
NEW JERSEY DEPARTMENT OF AGRICULTURE 87
NORTH CAROLINA SEA GRANT PROGRAM 95
NORTH DAKOTA GEOLOGICAL SURVEY 96
OHIO ENVIRONMENTAL COUNCIL, INC. 295
OHIO ENVIRONMENTAL PROTECTION AGENCY 97
OHIO SEA GRANT COLLEGE PROGRAM, F.T. STONE LABORATORY, AND GREAT LAKES AQUATIC ECOSYSTEM RESEARCH CONSORTIUM (GLAERC) 97
OREGON ENVIRONMENTAL COUNCIL 298
PENNSYLVANIA RECREATION AND PARK SOCIETY, INC. 302
PUGET SOUNDKEEPER ALLIANCE 307
RACHEL CARSON COUNCIL INC. (formerly Rachel Carson Trust for the Living Environment Inc.) 308
RHODE ISLAND WILD PLANT SOCIETY 311
SAVE SAN FRANCISCO BAY ASSOCIATION 315
SAVE THE DUNES COUNCIL 316
SAVE THE HARBOR/SAVE THE BAY 316
SAVE THE SOUND, INC. 316
SOUTHEAST ALASKA CONSERVATION COUNCIL (SEACC) 324
SOUTHWEST RESEARCH AND INFORMATION CENTER 326
STOP 328
STRIPERS UNLIMITED INC. 328
TAHOE REGIONAL PLANNING AGENCY 329
TENNESSEE ENVIRONMENTAL COUNCIL 330
U.S. PUBLIC INTEREST RESEARCH GROUP 339
VERMONT DEPARTMENT OF AGRICULTURE, FOOD, AND MARKETS. 115
WATER RESOURCES ASSOCIATION OF THE DELAWARE RIVER BASIN 345
WHALE AND DOLPHIN CONSERVATION SOCIETY 348
WISCONSIN SEA GRANT INSTITUTE 125
WOODS HOLE OCEANOGRAPHIC INSITITUTION (WHOI) SEA GRANT PROGRAM 76

Water Pollution Management

A.B. ENVIRONMENTAL EDUCATION CENTER 133
ALABAMA DEPARTMENT OF ENVIRONMENTAL MANAGEMENT 39
ALASKA DEPARTMENT OF ENVIRONMENTAL CONSERVATION 40
AMERICAN FISHERIES SOCIETY, ALABAMA CHAPTER 144
AMERICAN FISHERIES SOCIETY, ALASKA CHAPTER 144
AMERICAN FISHERIES SOCIETY, ARIZONA-NEW MEXICO CHAPTER. 144
AMERICAN FISHERIES SOCIETY, ARKANSAS CHAPTER 144
AMERICAN FISHERIES SOCIETY, AUBURN UNIVERSITY STUDENT CHAPTER 145
AMERICAN FISHERIES SOCIETY, CALIFORNIA-NEVADA CHAPTER 145
AMERICAN FISHERIES SOCIETY, COLLEGE OF ENVIRONMENTAL SCIENCE AND FORESTRY CHAPTER 145
AMERICAN FISHERIES SOCIETY, COLORADO and WYOMING CHAPTER 145
AMERICAN FISHERIES SOCIETY, FLORIDA CHAPTER 145
AMERICAN FISHERIES SOCIETY, GEORGIA CHAPTER 145
AMERICAN FISHERIES SOCIETY, HAWAII CHAPTER 146
AMERICAN FISHERIES SOCIETY, HUMBOLDT CHAPTER 146
AMERICAN FISHERIES SOCIETY, IDAHO CHAPTER 146
AMERICAN FISHERIES SOCIETY, ILLINOIS CHAPTER 146
AMERICAN FISHERIES SOCIETY, INDIANA CHAPTER 146
AMERICAN FISHERIES SOCIETY, IOWA CHAPTER 146
AMERICAN FISHERIES SOCIETY, KANSAS CHAPTER 146

KEYWORD INDEX - Water Quality/Water Resources 487

Keyword Index

AMERICAN FISHERIES SOCIETY, KENTUCKY CHAPTER 146
AMERICAN FISHERIES SOCIETY, LOUISIANA CHAPTER 146
AMERICAN FISHERIES SOCIETY, MICHIGAN CHAPTER 147
AMERICAN FISHERIES SOCIETY, MID-ATLANTIC CHAPTER 147
AMERICAN FISHERIES SOCIETY, MINNESOTA CHAPTER 147
AMERICAN FISHERIES SOCIETY, MISSISSIPPI CHAPTER 147
AMERICAN FISHERIES SOCIETY, NEW YORK CHAPTER 147
AMERICAN FISHERIES SOCIETY, NORTH CAROLINA CHAPTER 148
AMERICAN FISHERIES SOCIETY, OKLAHOMA CHAPTER 148
AMERICAN FISHERIES SOCIETY, OREGON CHAPTER 148
AMERICAN FISHERIES SOCIETY, POTOMAC CHAPTER 148
AMERICAN FISHERIES SOCIETY, SOUTHERN NEW ENGLAND CHAPTER 149
AMERICAN FISHERIES SOCIETY, TEXAS A&M CHAPTER 149
AMERICAN FISHERIES SOCIETY, TIDEWATER CHAPTER 149
BORDER ECOLOGY PROJECT (BEP) 167
CALIFORNIA ENVIRONMENTAL PROTECTION AGENCY 45
CANVASBACK SOCIETY 173
CENTER FOR WATERSHED PROTECTION 177
CONNECTICUT PUBLIC INTEREST RESEARCH GROUP (ConnPIRG) ... 186
DELAWARE ASSOCIATION OF CONSERVATION DISTRICTS 191
DELAWARE DEPARTMENT OF NATURAL RESOURCES AND ENVIRONMENTAL CONTROL 52
EUROPEAN ASSOCIATION FOR AQUATIC MAMMALS 204
INTERNATIONAL MARITIME ORGANIZATION 231
KENTUCKY RESOURCES COUNCIL 245
LAKE ERIE CLEAN-UP COMMITTEE, INC. 246
MARINE SCIENCES RESEARCH CENTER (NEW YORK) 92
NATURAL AND SCENIC RIVERS COMMISSION (ARKANSAS) 45
OREGON DEPARTMENT OF ENVIRONMENTAL QUALITY (DEQ) 101
PENNSYLVANIA FEDERATION OF SPORTSMEN'S CLUBS 302
REEF RELIEF 310
RHODE ISLAND COOPERATIVE EXTENSION 106
SOUTH CAROLINA WILDLIFE FEDERATION 324
SOUTH DAKOTA WILDLIFE FEDERATION 324
SOUTHERN ENVIRONMENTAL LAW CENTER 325, 326
TENNESSEE CONSERVATION LEAGUE 330
TROUT UNLIMITED, OKLAHOMA COUNCIL 336
UTAH WILDLIFE FEDERATION 340
VIRGINIA WILDLIFE FEDERATION 343, 346
WASHINGTON STATE OFFICE OF ENVIRONMENTAL EDUCATION 122
WASHINGTON WILDLIFE FEDERATION 345
WATER ENVIRONMENT FEDERATION 345
WATER RESOURCES RESEARCH CENTER 61
WEST VIRGINIA B.A.S.S. CHAPTER FEDERATION 346
WISCONSIN ASSOCIATION FOR ENVIRONMENTAL EDUCATION, INC. 359
WISCONSIN WILDLIFE FEDERATION 360

Water Quality

ALASKA DEPARTMENT OF ENVIRONMENTAL CONSERVATION 40
ALLIANCE FOR THE CHESAPEAKE BAY 138
AMERICAN OCEANS CAMPAIGN 153
AMERICAN WATER WORKS ASSOCIATION (AWWA) 156
ARIZONA DEPARTMENT OF ENVIRONMENTAL QUALITY 42
ASSOCIATION OF NEW JERSEY ENVIRONMENTAL COMMISSIONS 162
AUDUBON INTERNATIONAL 163
AUDUBON NATURALIST SOCIETY OF THE CENTRAL ATLANTIC STATES 164
CHESAPEAKE BAY FOUNDATION, INC. (Virginia Office) 178
CHINA REGION LAKES ALLIANCE 179
COASTAL CONSERVATION ASSOCIATION 181
CONNECTICUT RIVER WATERSHED COUNCIL INC. 186
CONSERVATION TECHNOLOGY INFORMATION CENTER 188
COOK INLET KEEPER 189
DEPARTMENT OF ENVIRONMENT AND NATURAL RESOURCES (SOUTH DAKOTA) 109
DEPARTMENT OF ENVIRONMENTAL PROTECTION (MAINE0 71
ENVIRONMENTAL CENTER 60
ENVIRONMENTAL DEFENSE FUND, INC. 202
ENVIRONMENTAL LEAGUE OF MASSACHUSETTS (ELM) 203
ENVIRONMENTAL QUALITY COUNCIL 82
FLORIDA DEFENDERS OF THE ENVIRONMENT, INC. (Home Office) 207
FOREST SERVICE (Texas) 111
FRIENDS OF THE EARTH 211
GLOBAL CITIES PROJECT, THE 215
GREAT LAKES UNITED 217
GREEN (GLOBAL RIVERS ENVIRONMENTAL EDUCATION NETWORK) 218
GREEN PARTY USA 218
HOOSIER ENVIRONMENTAL COUNCIL 222
IDAHO STATE DEPARTMENT OF AGRICULTURE 62
INDIANA DEPARTMENT OF NATURAL RESOURCES 64
IOWA ENVIRONMENTAL COUNCIL 237
IZAAK WALTON LEAGUE OF AMERICA, INC., THE 240
KANSAS FOREST SERVICE 67
KANSAS STATE CONSERVATION COMMISSION 67
KANSAS STATE DEPARTMENT OF HEALTH AND ENVIRONMENT 67
LEAGUE OF WOMEN VOTERS OF IOWA 247
LOWER MISSISSIPPI RIVER CONSERVATION COMMITTEE 249
MASSACHUSETTS HIGHWAY DEPARTMENT 75
MINNESOTA BOARD OF WATER AND SOIL RESOURCES 77
MINNESOTA CENTER FOR ENVIRONMENTAL ADVOCACY (MCEA) 256
MISSISSIPPI RIVER BASIN ALLIANCE 258
MISSISSIPPI SOIL AND WATER CONSERVATION COMMISSION 80
MISSOURI AUDUBON COUNCIL 259
MONTANA ENVIRONMENTAL INFORMATION CENTER 260
NATIONAL ASSOCIATION OF STATE DEPARTMENTS OF AGRICULTURE 264
NATIONAL WILDLIFE FEDERATION 273, 275
NEW HAMPSHIRE LAKES ASSOCIATION 284
NEW JERSEY DEPARTMENT OF AGRICULTURE 87
NORTH CAROLINA COASTAL FEDERATION, INC. 290
NORTH CAROLINA SEA GRANT PROGRAM 95
NORTH DAKOTA DEPARTMENT OF HEALTH 95
NORTHERN ALASKA ENVIRONMENTAL CENTER 292
NORTHERN PLAINS RESOURCE COUNCIL 292
OHIO ENVIRONMENTAL COUNCIL, INC. 295
OKLAHOMA DEPARTMENT OF ENVIRONMENTAL QUALITY 98
OKLAHOMA WATER RESOURCES BOARD 99
OREGON B.A.S.S. CHAPTER FEDERATION 297
OREGON ENVIRONMENTAL COUNCIL 298
PUGET SOUNDKEEPER ALLIANCE 307
RIVER OTTER ALLIANCE, THE 312
SAVE THE HARBOR/SAVE THE BAY 316
SOCIETY FOR RANGE MANAGEMENT 321
SOIL AND WATER CONSERVATION SOCIETY (formerly Soil Conservation Society of America) 323
SOUTHEAST ALASKA CONSERVATION COUNCIL (SEACC) 324
SOUTHWEST FLORIDA WATER MANAGEMENT DISTRICT (SWFWMD) . 56
STATE MARINE BOARD (OREGON) 102
STATE OF IDAHO, DIVISION OF ENVIRONMENTAL QUALITY 62
STATE WATER RESOURCES BOARD (RHODE ISLAND) 107
TENNESSEE DEPARTMENT OF AGRICULTURE 110
TROUT UNLIMITED, PENNSYLVANIA COUNCIL 336
TURTLE CREEK WATERSHED ASSOCIATION, INC. 338
UPPER MISSISSIPPI RIVER CONSERVATION COMMITTEE 340
VIRGINIA B.A.S.S. CHAPTER FEDERATION 342
WESTERN ENVIRONMENTAL LAW CENTER 346
WHITE CLAY WATERSHED ASSOCIATION 348
WISCONSIN DEPARTMENT OF AGRICULTURE (Land and Water Resources Bureau) 123

Water Resources

AGENCY OF NATURAL RESOURCES 114
ALASKA CONSERVATION FOUNDATION 136
ALLIANCE FOR THE CHESAPEAKE BAY 138
AMERICAN BASS ASSOCIATION OF MARYLAND, THE 140
AMERICAN CAVE CONSERVATION ASSOCIATION 141
AMERICAN GROUND WATER TRUST 150
AMERICAN LEAGUE OF ANGLERS AND BOATERS 152
AMERICAN RIVERS (formerly American Rivers Conservation Council) 154
AMERICAN SOCIETY FOR ENVIRONMENTAL HISTORY 154
AMERICAN WATER RESOURCES ASSOCIATION 156
AMERICAN WATER WORKS ASSOCIATION (AWWA) 156
ANGLERS FOR CLEAN WATER 157
ARIZONA GEOLOGICAL SURVEY 42
ARIZONA LAND DEPARTMENT 42
ASSOCIATION OF AMERICAN GEOGRAPHERS 161
ASSOCIATION OF CONSERVATION ENGINEERS 161
ASSOCIATION OF NEW JERSEY ENVIRONMENTAL COMMISSIONS 162
BRANDYWINE CONSERVANCY, INC. 168
BUREAU OF ECONOMIC GEOLOGY 111
BUREAU OF MINES AND GEOLOGY 82
CALIFORNIA SEA GRANT COLLEGE SYSTEM 46
CALIFORNIA WATERFOWL ASSOCIATION 170
CANVASBACK SOCIETY 173
CENTRAL STATES EDUCATION CENTER 177
CHARLES A. AND ANNE MORROW LINDBERGH FOUNDATION, THE ... 178
CHINA REGION LAKES ALLIANCE 179
COASTAL CONSERVATION ASSOCIATION 181
COLORADO DEPARTMENT OF NATURAL RESOURCES 50
CONCERN, INC. 184
CONSERVATION DISTRICTS FOUNDATION INC. 187
CONSERVATION FUND, THE 187
COUSTEAU SOCIETY, INC., THE 190
DEEP-PORTAGE CONSERVATION RESERVE 191
DELAWARE GEOLOGICAL SURVEY 53
DEPARTMENT OF ENVIRONMENT AND NATURAL RESOURCES (SOUTH DAKOTA) 109
DEPARTMENT OF ENVIRONMENTAL PROTECTION (NEW JERSEY) 86
DEPARTMENT OF LAND AND NATURAL RESOURCES 59, 60
DEPARTMENT OF WATER RESOURCES (NEBRASKA) 83
DESERT FISHES COUNCIL 193
DUCKS UNLIMITED, INC. (Wetlands America Trust, Inc. Office) 196
EARTH SHARE 197

ENVIRONMENTAL AND ENERGY STUDY INSTITUTE (EESI) 201
ENVIRONMENTAL DEFENSE CENTER, INC. 201
ENVIRONMENTAL DEFENSE FUND, INC. 202
ENVIRONMENTAL LEAGUE OF MASSACHUSETTS (ELM) 203
ENVIRONMENTAL QUALITY COUNCIL 82
FISHAMERICA FOUNDATION 206
FLORIDA CONSERVATION FOUNDATION, INC. 207
FLORIDA DEFENDERS OF THE ENVIRONMENT, INC. (Home Office) 207
FRESHWATER FOUNDATION 211
FRIENDS OF THE RIVER 212
FUTURE FISHERMAN FOUNDATION 213
GEORGIA CONSERVANCY, INC., THE 214
GRAND CANYON TRUST (Washington, DC Office) 216
GREAT LAKES UNITED 217
GREEN (GLOBAL RIVERS ENVIRONMENTAL EDUCATION NETWORK) 218
GROUNDWATER FOUNDATION, THE 219
ILLINOIS ENVIRONMENTAL COUNCIL 224
INDIANA DEPARTMENT OF NATURAL RESOURCES 64
INTERNATIONAL ASSOCIATION FOR ENVIRONMENTAL HYDROLOGY (IAEH) 228
ISLAND RESOURCES FOUNDATION 239
IZAAK WALTON LEAGUE OF AMERICA, INC., THE 240
J.N. (DING) DARLING FOUNDATION 241
KANSAS DEPARTMENT OF AGRICULTURE 66
KANSAS FOREST SERVICE 67
KANSAS GEOLOGICAL SURVEY 67
KANSAS NATURAL RESOURCE COUNCIL 243
KANSAS STATE CONSERVATION COMMISSION 67
KANSAS STATE DEPARTMENT OF HEALTH AND ENVIRONMENT 67
KANSAS WATER OFFICE 68
LAKE ERIE CLEAN-UP COMMITTEE, INC. 246
LEAGUE OF WOMEN VOTERS OF THE U.S. 247
LONG LIVE THE KINGS 249
LOUISIANA GEOLOGICAL SURVEY 70
MAGIC 250
MAINE ASSOCIATION OF CONSERVATION COMMISSIONS (MACC) 250
MARINE TECHNOLOGY SOCIETY 252
MICHIGAN DEPARTMENT OF ENVIRONMENTAL QUALITY 76
MICHIGAN STATE UNIVERSITY EXTENSION 77
MID-ATLANTIC COUNCIL OF WATERSHED ASSOCIATIONS 256
MINNESOTA BOARD OF WATER AND SOIL RESOURCES 77
MINNESOTA ENVIRONMENTAL QUALITY BOARD 78
MINNESOTA GEOLOGICAL SURVEY 78
MINNESOTA SEA GRANT COLLEGE PROGRAM 79
MISSISSIPPI INTERSTATE COOPERATIVE RESOURCE ASSOCIATION 258
MISSISSIPPI SOIL AND WATER CONSERVATION COMMISSION 80
MONO LAKE COMMITTEE 259
MONTANA DEPARTMENT OF NATURAL RESOURCES AND CONSERVATION 82
MONTANA LAND RELIANCE 260
MUSKIES, INC 262
NATIONAL ASSOCIATION OF ENVIRONMENTAL PROFESSIONALS, THE (National Office) 263
NATIONAL ASSOCIATION OF STATE DEPARTMENTS OF AGRICULTURE 264
NATIONAL ASSOCIATION OF STATE FORESTERS 264
NATIONAL ENVIRONMENTAL HEALTH ASSOCIATION 267
NATIONAL GROUND WATER ASSOCIATION, THE 269
NATIONAL WATER RESOURCES ASSOCIATION 272
NATIONAL WATERWAYS CONFERENCE INC. 273
NATURAL AND SCENIC RIVERS COMMISSION (ARKANSAS) 45
NATURAL RESOURCES COUNCIL OF AMERICA 278
NEBRASKA NATURAL RESOURCES COMMISSION 84
NEVADA BUREAU OF MINES AND GEOLOGY 84
NEVEDA COOPERATIVE EXTENSION 85
NEW HAMPSHIRE ASSOCIATION OF CONSERVATION COMMISSIONS 284
NEW HAMPSHIRE DEPARTMENT OF AGRICULTURE, MARKETS, AND FOOD 85
NEW HAMPSHIRE DEPARTMENT OF ENVIRONMENTAL SERVICES 86
NEW JERSEY DEPARTMENT OF AGRICULTURE 87
NEW JERSEY PINELANDS COMMISSION 88
NEW MEXICO BUREAU OF MINES AND MINERAL RESOURCES 89
NEW YORK GEOLOGICAL SURVEY AND STATE MUSEUM 92
NEW YORK SEA GRANT 92
NEW YORK STATE COOPERATIVE EXTENSION 93
NORTHWEST RENEWABLE RESOURCES CENTER 293
OHIO DEPARTMENT OF NATURAL RESOURCES 97
OHIO ENVIRONMENTAL COUNCIL, INC. 295
OKLAHOMA GEOLOGICAL SURVEY 98
OKLAHOMA WATER RESOURCES BOARD 99
OREGON B.A.S.S. CHAPTER FEDERATION 297
PENNSYLVANIA CITIZENS ADVISORY COUNCIL TO DEPARTMENT OF ENVIRONMENTAL PROTECTION 301
PENNSYLVANIA FOREST STEWARDSHIP PROGRAM 105
POPULATION INSTITUTE, THE 305
PUBLIC EMPLOYEES FOR ENVIRONMENTAL RESPONSIBILITY (PEER) 306, 307
RESOURCES AGENCY, THE 47
RHODE ISLAND COOPERATIVE EXTENSION 106
RIVER FEDERATION 312
RIVERS COUNCIL OF WASHINGTON (formerly Northwest Rivers Council) 313
SAVE SAN FRANCISCO BAY ASSOCIATION 315
SAVE THE HARBOR/SAVE THE BAY 316
SEAPLANE PILOTS ASSOCIATION 318
SOCIETY FOR RANGE MANAGEMENT 321
SOCIETY OF WETLAND SCIENTISTS 322
SOUTH CAROLINA DEPARTMENT OF HEALTH AND ENVIRONMENTAL CONTROL 108
SOUTH DAKOTA ORNITHOLOGISTS' UNION 324
SOUTH DAKOTA STATE EXTENSION SERVICES 109
SOUTHWEST FLORIDA WATER MANAGEMENT DISTRICT (SWFWMD) . 56
STATE ENGINEER OFFICE/INTERSTATE STREAM COMMISSION 90
STATE FISH AND WILDLIFE MANAGEMENT BOARD (NEW YORK) 93
STATE SOIL AND WATER CONSERVATION COMMISSION (GEORGIA) .. 58
STATE SOIL CONSERVATION COMMISSION (IDAHO) 62
STATE WATER RESOURCES BOARD (RHODE ISLAND) 107
TENNESSEE CITIZENS FOR WILDERNESS PLANNING 329
TERRENE INSTITUTE, THE 330
TEXAS B.A.S.S. CHAPTER FEDERATION 330
TEXAS STATE SOIL AND WATER CONSERVATION BOARD 112
TEXAS WATER DEVELOPMENT BOARD 112
UNITED NATIONS ENVIRONMENT PROGRAMME 339
UPPER MISSISSIPPI RIVER CONSERVATION COMMITTEE 340
UTAH STATE EXTENSION SERVICES 114
VIRGINIA DEPARTMENT OF ENVIRONMENTAL QUALITY 118
WASHINGTON STATE CONSERVATION COMMISSION 121
WATER ENVIRONMENT FEDERATION 345
WATER RESOURCES ASSOCIATION OF THE DELAWARE RIVER BASIN 345
WATER RESOURCES DEPARTMENT 102
WATER RESOURCES RESEARCH CENTER 61
WEST MICHIGAN ENVIRONMENTAL ACTION COUNCIL 346
WEST VIRGINIA DEPARTMENT OF AGRICULTURE 122
WEST VIRGINIA STATE EXTENSION SERVICES 123
WILDLIFE SOCIETY, PENNSYLVANIA CHAPTER 356
WISCONSIN ASSOCIATION FOR ENVIRONMENTAL EDUCATION, INC. 359
WISCONSIN CONSERVATION CORPS 123
WISCONSIN DEPARTMENT OF AGRICULTURE (Land and Water Resources Bureau) 123
WISCONSIN DEPARTMENT OF NATURAL RESOURCES 124
WISCONSIN GEOLOGICAL AND NATURAL HISTORY SURVEY 125
WORLDWATCH INSTITUTE 363
WYOMING STATE EXTENSION SERVICES 126

Waterfowl

ALABAMA WATERFOWL ASSOCIATION, INC. (AWA) 135
AUDUBON SOCIETY OF WESTERN PENNSYLVANIA 165
CALIFORNIA WATERFOWL ASSOCIATION 170
CANVASBACK SOCIETY 173
CONNECTICUT WATERFOWL ASSOCIATION, INC. 186
DELTA WATERFOWL FOUNDATION 192
DUCKS UNLIMITED, INC. (Wetlands America Trust, Inc. Office) 196
HOOD CANAL LAND TRUST 222
HUNTSMAN MARINE SCIENCE CENTRE 223
INDIANA AUDUBON SOCIETY, INC. 226
INTERNATIONAL WILD WATERFOWL ASSOCIATION 235
IOWA DEPARTMENT OF NATURAL RESOURCES 65
J.N. (DING) DARLING FOUNDATION 241
LAKE ERIE CLEAN-UP COMMITTEE, INC. 246
MINNESOTA ORNITHOLOGISTS' UNION 257
MISSOURI COOPERATIVE FISH AND WILDLIFE RESEARCH UNIT (USDI) 81
MONTANA COOPERATIVE WILDLIFE RESEARCH UNIT (USGS/BRD) 82
NORTH AMERICAN GAMEBIRD ASSOCIATION, INC. 289
ORNITHOLOGICAL COUNCIL 299
QUEBEC WILDLIFE FEDERATION 308
SOUTH DAKOTA B.A.S.S. CHAPTER FEDERATION 324
SUNCOAST SEABIRD SANCTUARY INC. 328
TROUT UNLIMITED, GUADELOUPE RIVER COUNCIL 334
TRUMPETER SWAN SOCIETY, THE 337
WILDLIFE FOREVER 351
WISCONSIN SOCIETY FOR ORNITHOLOGY, INC., THE 360

Watersheds

ALLIANCE FOR THE CHESAPEAKE BAY 138
AMERICAN RIVERS (formerly American Rivers Conservation Council) 154
ANACOSTIA WATERSHED SOCIETY 157
ASSOCIATION OF NEW JERSEY ENVIRONMENTAL COMMISSIONS 162
CADDO LAKE INSTITUTE, INC. 169
CENTER FOR ENVIRONMENTAL STUDY 175
CENTER FOR MARINE CONSERVATION 176
CENTER FOR WATERSHED PROTECTION 177

KEYWORD INDEX - Wetlands/Wetlands

CHESAPEAKE BAY FOUNDATION, INC.	178
CHINA REGION LAKES ALLIANCE	179
CONNECTICUT RIVER WATERSHED COUNCIL INC.	186
CONSERVATION TECHNOLOGY INFORMATION CENTER	188
DEPARTMENT OF ENVIRONMENT AND NATURAL RESOURCES (SOUTH DAKOTA)	109
ENVIRONMENTAL DEFENSE FUND, INC.	202
ENVIRONMENTAL LEAGUE OF MASSACHUSETTS (ELM)	203
FLORIDA DEFENDERS OF THE ENVIRONMENT, INC. (Home Office)	207
FOSSIL FUELS POLICY ACTION INSTITUTE/ALLIANCE FOR A PAVING MORATORIUM	210
GREAT LAKES UNITED	217
GREEN (GLOBAL RIVERS ENVIRONMENTAL EDUCATION NETWORK)	218
IDAHO STATE DEPARTMENT OF AGRICULTURE	62
ILLINOIS WALNUT COUNCIL	225
IZAAK WALTON LEAGUE OF AMERICA, INC., THE	240
KANSAS STATE CONSERVATION COMMISSION	67
LAKE MICHIGAN FEDERATION	246
MARYLAND DEPARTMENT OF NATURAL RESOURCES	73
MINNESOTA BOARD OF WATER AND SOIL RESOURCES	77
MONTANA LAND RELIANCE	260
NATURAL LAND INSTITUTE	277
NEW HAMPSHIRE LAKES ASSOCIATION	284
NEW JERSEY CONSERVATION FOUNDATION	285
NEW JERSEY DEPARTMENT OF AGRICULTURE	87
NORTHCOAST ENVIRONMENTAL CENTER	291
NORTHWEST RESOURCE INFORMATION CENTER	293
OPENLANDS PROJECT	297
OREGON NATURAL RESOURCES COUNCIL	298
RESOURCES AGENCY, THE	47
RIVER ALLIANCE OF WISCONSIN	312
RIVER NETWORK	312
SAVE THE DUNES COUNCIL	316
SAVE THE HARBOR/SAVE THE BAY	316
SOCIETY FOR RANGE MANAGEMENT	321
SOIL AND WATER CONSERVATION SOCIETY (formerly Soil Conservation Society of America)	323
SOUTHEAST ALASKA CONSERVATION COUNCIL (SEACC)	324
SOUTHEASTERN FISHES COUNCIL	325
SOUTHWEST CENTER FOR BIOLOGICAL DIVERSITY	326
TENNESSEE CITIZENS FOR WILDERNESS PLANNING	329
TERRENE INSTITUTE, THE	330
THORNE ECOLOGICAL INSTITUTE	331
TROUT UNLIMITED, PENNSYLVANIA COUNCIL	336
TRUST FOR PUBLIC LAND, THE	337
VIRGINIA NATIVE PLANT SOCIETY	343
WHITE CLAY WATERSHED ASSOCIATION	348
WISCONSIN ASSOCIATION OF LAKES (WAL)	359
WISCONSIN DEPARTMENT OF AGRICULTURE (Land and Water Resources Bureau)	123

Wetlands

A. E. HOWELL WILDLIFE CONSERVATION CENTER	133
A.B. ENVIRONMENTAL EDUCATION CENTER	133
ACRES LAND TRUST	133
ADIRONDACK PARK AGENCY	90
ADKINS ARBORETUM	134
ALABAMA DEPARTMENT OF ENVIRONMENTAL MANAGEMENT	39
ALABAMA WATERFOWL ASSOCIATION, INC. (AWA)	135
ALASKA AUDUBON SOCIETY	136
ALASKA CONSERVATION ALLIANCE	136
ALASKA CONSERVATION VOICE	137
ALLIANCE FOR THE CHESAPEAKE BAY	138
AMERICAN FARMLAND TRUST	142
AMERICAN FISHERIES SOCIETY	142, 144, 145, 146, 147, 148, 149, 283
AMERICAN FISHERIES SOCIETY, ALABAMA CHAPTER	144
AMERICAN FISHERIES SOCIETY, ALASKA CHAPTER	144
AMERICAN FISHERIES SOCIETY, ARIZONA-NEW MEXICO CHAPTER	144
AMERICAN FISHERIES SOCIETY, ARKANSAS CHAPTER	144
AMERICAN FISHERIES SOCIETY, AUBURN UNIVERSITY STUDENT CHAPTER	145
AMERICAN FISHERIES SOCIETY, CALIFORNIA-NEVADA CHAPTER	145
AMERICAN FISHERIES SOCIETY, COLLEGE OF ENVIRONMENTAL SCIENCE AND FORESTRY CHAPTER	145
AMERICAN FISHERIES SOCIETY, COLORADO and WYOMING CHAPTER	145
AMERICAN FISHERIES SOCIETY, FLORIDA CHAPTER	145
AMERICAN FISHERIES SOCIETY, GEORGIA CHAPTER	145
AMERICAN FISHERIES SOCIETY, HAWAII CHAPTER	146
AMERICAN FISHERIES SOCIETY, HUMBOLDT CHAPTER	146
AMERICAN FISHERIES SOCIETY, IDAHO CHAPTER	146
AMERICAN FISHERIES SOCIETY, ILLINOIS CHAPTER	146
AMERICAN FISHERIES SOCIETY, INDIANA CHAPTER	146
AMERICAN FISHERIES SOCIETY, IOWA CHAPTER	146
AMERICAN FISHERIES SOCIETY, KANSAS CHAPTER	146
AMERICAN FISHERIES SOCIETY, KENTUCKY CHAPTER	146
AMERICAN FISHERIES SOCIETY, LOUISIANA CHAPTER	146
AMERICAN FISHERIES SOCIETY, MICHIGAN CHAPTER	147
AMERICAN FISHERIES SOCIETY, MID-ATLANTIC CHAPTER	147
AMERICAN FISHERIES SOCIETY, MINNESOTA CHAPTER	147
AMERICAN FISHERIES SOCIETY, MISSISSIPPI CHAPTER	147
AMERICAN FISHERIES SOCIETY, NEW YORK CHAPTER	147
AMERICAN FISHERIES SOCIETY, NORTH CAROLINA CHAPTER	148
AMERICAN FISHERIES SOCIETY, OHIO CHAPTER	148
AMERICAN FISHERIES SOCIETY, OKLAHOMA CHAPTER	148
AMERICAN FISHERIES SOCIETY, OREGON CHAPTER	148
AMERICAN FISHERIES SOCIETY, PENNSYLVANIA CHAPTER	148
AMERICAN FISHERIES SOCIETY, POTOMAC CHAPTER	148
AMERICAN FISHERIES SOCIETY, SOUTHERN NEW ENGLAND CHAPTER	149
AMERICAN FISHERIES SOCIETY, TEXAS A&M CHAPTER	149
AMERICAN FISHERIES SOCIETY, TIDEWATER CHAPTER	149
AMERICAN FISHERIES SOCIETY, WISCONSIN CHAPTER	149
AMERICAN LITTORAL SOCIETY	152
AMERICAN RIVERS (formerly American Rivers Conservation Council)	154
AMERICAN SOCIETY OF LIMNOLOGY AND OCEANOGRAPHY	155
AMERICAN WATER RESOURCES ASSOCIATION	156
AUDUBON COUNCIL OF ILLINOIS	163
AUDUBON SOCIETY OF PORTLAND	164
BRANDYWINE CONSERVANCY, INC.	168
CADDO LAKE INSTITUTE, INC.	169
CALIFORNIA NATIVE PLANT SOCIETY, THE	169
CALIFORNIA SEA GRANT COLLEGE SYSTEM	46
CALIFORNIA TRAPPERS ASSOCIATION	170
CALIFORNIA WATERFOWL ASSOCIATION	170
CANVASBACK SOCIETY	173
CENTER FOR RESOURCE ECONOMICS	176
COASTAL CONSERVATION ASSOCIATION	181
COASTAL SOCIETY, THE	182
COMMUNITY RIGHTS COUNSEL	184
CONNECTICUT BOTANICAL SOCIETY	185
CONNECTICUT RIVER WATERSHED COUNCIL INC.	186
CONNECTICUT WATERFOWL ASSOCIATION, INC.	186
CONSERVATION DISTRICTS FOUNDATION INC.	187
DELAWARE NATURE SOCIETY	192
DELTA WATERFOWL FOUNDATION	192
DELTA WILDLIFE FOUNDATION	192
DEPARTMENT OF INTERIOR, U.S.G.S/B.R.D, SOUTH CAROLINA COOPERATIVE FISH AND WILDLIFE RESEARCH UNIT	107
DRAGONFLY SOCIETY OF THE AMERICAS, THE	193
DUCKS UNLIMITED, INC. (Wetlands America Trust, Inc. Office)	196
ENVIRONMENTAL CONCERN, INC.	201
ENVIRONMENTAL DEFENSE FUND, INC.	202
ENVIRONMENTAL LAW INSTITUTE, THE	203
E-P EDUCATION SERVICES, INC.	196
EVERGLADES COORDINATING COUNCIL (ECC)	204
FLORIDA COOPERATIVE FISH AND WILDLIFE RESEARCH UNIT (USDI)	54
FORESTRY COMMISSION (SOUTH CAROLINA)	107
FRESHWATER FOUNDATION	211
FRIENDS OF DISCOVERY PARK	211
GEORGIA CONSERVANCY, INC., THE	214
GOVERNOR OF SOUTH CAROLINA, JIM HODGES	107
GREAT LAKES SPORT FISHING COUNCIL	216
GREAT LAKES UNITED	217
GREEN (GLOBAL RIVERS ENVIRONMENTAL EDUCATION NETWORK)	218
HAWAII NATURE CENTER	220
HUMBOLT FIELD RESEARCH INSTITUTE	223
ILLINOIS NATIVE PLANT SOCIETY	225
INSTITUTE FOR ECOLOGICAL STUDIES	95
INTERNATIONAL CRANE FOUNDATION	230
IOWA NATIVE PLANT SOCIETY	237
IOWA NATURAL HERITAGE FOUNDATION	238
ISSAQUAH ALPS TRAILS CLUB (I.A.T.C.)	239
KANSAS DEPARTMENT OF AGRICULTURE	66
KANSAS STATE CONSERVATION COMMISSION	67
KANSAS STATE EXTENSION SERVICES	68
KANSAS WILDSCAPE FOUNDATION	244
KENTUCKY DEPARTMENT OF AGRICULTURE	68
LAKE ERIE CLEAN-UP COMMITTEE, INC.	246
LEE COUNTY PARKS AND RECREATION SERVICES	56
LOUISIANA AUDUBON COUNCIL	249
LOUISIANA GEOLOGICAL SURVEY	70
LOUISIANA SEA GRANT COLLEGE PROGRAM	70
MASSACHUSETTS ASSOCIATION OF CONSERVATION COMMISSIONS (MACC)	253
MASSACHUSETTS HIGHWAY DEPARTMENT	75
MASSACHUSETTS TRAPPER'S ASSOCIATION, INC.	254
MICHIGAN NATURE ASSOCIATION	255
MICHIGAN WILDLIFE HABITAT FOUNDATION	255
MID-ATLANTIC FISHERY MANAGEMENT COUNCIL	256
MINNESOTA BOARD OF WATER AND SOIL RESOURCES	77
MISSISSIPPI DEPARTMENT OF WILDLIFE, FISHERIES, AND PARKS	80
MISSISSIPPI RIVER BASIN ALLIANCE	258
MISSOURI COOPERATIVE FISH AND WILDLIFE RESEARCH UNIT (USDI)	81
MISSOURI NATIVE PLANT SOCIETY	259
MONO LAKE COMMITTEE	259

MONTANA AUDUBON ... 260
MONTANA COOPERATIVE WILDLIFE RESEARCH UNIT (USGS/BRD) 82
MONTANA LAND RELIANCE ... 260
NATIONAL ASSOCIATION OF STATE DEPARTMENTS OF AGRICULTURE ... 264
NATIONAL COALITION FOR MARINE CONSERVATION ... 266
NATIONAL WATER RESOURCES ASSOCIATION ... 272
NATIONAL WILDLIFE FEDERATION ... 273, 275
NATIVE PLANT SOCIETY OF NORTHEASTERN OHIO ... 276
NEW HAMPSHIRE ASSOCIATION OF CONSERVATION COMMISSIONS ... 284
NEW HAMPSHIRE DEPARTMENT OF AGRICULTURE, MARKETS, AND FOOD ... 85
NEW HAMPSHIRE DEPARTMENT OF ENVIRONMENTAL SERVICES ... 86
NEW HAMPSHIRE SEA GRANT PROGRAM ... 86
NEW YORK STATE COOPERATIVE EXTENSION ... 93
NORTH AMERICAN CRANE WORKING GROUP ... 288
NORTH DAKOTA STATE SOIL CONSERVATION COMMITTEE ... 96
OHIO AUDUBON COUNCIL, INC. ... 294
OHIO ENVIRONMENTAL PROTECTION AGENCY ... 97
OKLAHOMA NATIVE PLANT SOCIETY ... 296
PENNSYLVANIA AUDUBON SOCIETY ... 301
PENNSYLVANIA FEDERATION OF SPORTSMEN'S CLUBS ... 302
PUERTO RICO ASSOCIATION OF SOIL AND WATER CONSERVATION DISTRICTS ... 307
RESOURCES AGENCY, THE ... 47
RHODE ISLAND COOPERATIVE EXTENSION ... 106
RIVER NETWORK ... 312
SANIBEL-CAPTIVA CONSERVATION FOUNDATION, INC. ... 315
SAVANNAH RIVER ECOLOGY LABORATORY ... 107
SAVE SAN FRANCISCO BAY ASSOCIATION ... 315
SAVE THE SOUND, INC. ... 316
SOCIETY FOR RANGE MANAGEMENT ... 321
SOCIETY OF WETLAND SCIENTISTS ... 322
SOIL AND WATER CONSERVATION SOCIETY (formerly Soil Conservation Society of America) ... 323
SOUTH CAROLINA B.A.S.S. CHAPTER FEDERATION ... 323
SOUTH CAROLINA DEPARTMENT OF AGRICULTURE ... 107
SOUTH CAROLINA DEPARTMENT OF HEALTH AND ENVIRONMENTAL CONTROL ... 108
SOUTH CAROLINA SEA GRANT CONSORTIUM ... 108
SOUTH CAROLINA WILDLIFE FEDERATION ... 324
SOUTH DAKOTA COOPERATIVE FISH AND WILDLIFE RESEARCH UNIT (USDI) ... 109
SOUTH DAKOTA WILDLIFE FEDERATION ... 324
SOUTHERN ENVIRONMENTAL LAW CENTER ... 325, 326
SOUTHWEST FLORIDA WATER MANAGEMENT DISTRICT (SWFWMD) . 56
STATE SOIL AND WATER CONSERVATION COMMISSION (GEORGIA).. 58
TAHOE REGIONAL PLANNING AGENCY ... 329
TENNESSEE CONSERVATION LEAGUE ... 330
TERRENE INSTITUTE, THE ... 330
THORNE ECOLOGICAL INSTITUTE ... 331
TROUT UNLIMITED, GUADELOUPE RIVER COUNCIL ... 334
TROUT UNLIMITED, OKLAHOMA COUNCIL ... 336
TRUMPETER SWAN SOCIETY, THE ... 337
U.S. PUBLIC INTEREST RESEARCH GROUP ... 339
UNITED STATES TOURIST COUNCIL ... 339
UTAH STATE EXTENSION SERVICES ... 114
UTAH WILDLIFE FEDERATION ... 340
VERMONT AUDUBON COUNCIL ... 341
VIRGINIA NATIVE PLANT SOCIETY ... 343
VIRGINIA SEA GRANT PROGRAM ... 119
VIRGINIA WILDLIFE FEDERATION ... 343, 346
WASHINGTON NATIVE PLANT SOCIETY ... 344
WASHINGTON SEA GRANT PROGRAM ... 121
WASHINGTON WILDLIFE FEDERATION ... 345
WATER RESOURCES ASSOCIATION OF THE DELAWARE RIVER BASIN ... 345
WESTERN HEMISPHERE SHOREBIRD RESERVE NETWORK (WHSRN) ... 347
WILDFOWL TRUST OF NORTH AMERICA INC., THE ... 350
WILDLIFE HABITAT CANADA ... 352
WISCONSIN ASSOCIATION OF LAKES (WAL) ... 359
WISCONSIN DEPARTMENT OF AGRICULTURE (Land and Water Resources Bureau) ... 123
WISCONSIN SOCIETY FOR ORNITHOLOGY, INC., THE ... 360
WISCONSIN WILDLIFE FEDERATION ... 360

Whales

INTERNATIONAL WILDLIFE COALITION (IWC) AND THE WHALE ADOPTION PROJECT ... 235
PACIFIC WHALE FOUNDATION ... 301

Whirling Disease

COLORADO COOPERATIVE FISH AND WILDLIFE RESEARCH UNIT (USDI) ... 50

Wild Cats

INTERNATIONAL SOCIETY FOR ENDANGERED CATS (ISEC) ... 233

Wilderness

ADIRONDACK MOUNTAIN CLUB, INC., THE ... 134
ALASKA CONSERVATION ALLIANCE ... 136
ALASKA CONSERVATION VOICE ... 137
ALBERTA WILDERNESS ASSOCIATION ... 137
AMERICAN FEDERATION OF MINERALOGICAL SOCIETIES ... 142
AMERICAN FISHERIES SOCIETY, BONNEVILLE CHAPTER ... 145
ANTARCTICA PROJECT ... 158
BERKSHIRE-LITCHFIELD ENVIRONMENTAL COUNCIL, INC. ... 165
CALIFORNIA TRAPPERS ASSOCIATION ... 170
CARRYING CAPACITY NETWORK ... 174
CENTER FOR ENVIRONMENTAL PHILOSOPHY ... 175
COLORADO ENVIRONMENTAL COALITION ... 182
DEFENDERS OF WILDLIFE ... 191
FOSSIL FUELS POLICY ACTION INSTITUTE/ALLIANCE FOR A PAVING MORATORIUM ... 210
FRIENDS OF THE BOUNDARY WATERS WILDERNESS ... 211
IDAHO CONSERVATION LEAGUE ... 223
INTERNATIONAL WILDERNESS LEADERSHIP (WILD) FOUNDATION ... 235
JACKSON HOLE CONSERVATION ALLIANCE ... 242
MICHIGAN NATURAL AREAS COUNCIL ... 255
MOUNTAINEERS, THE (Conservation Division) ... 261
NORTHCOAST ENVIRONMENTAL CENTER ... 291
NORTHERN ALASKA ENVIRONMENTAL CENTER ... 292
NORTHWEST INTERPRETIVE ASSOCIATION ... 293
OKLAHOMA NATIVE PLANT SOCIETY ... 296
OLYMPIC WILDLIFE RESCUE ... 297
OREGON NATURAL RESOURCES COUNCIL ... 298
OUTDOOR RECREATION COUNCIL OF BRITISH COLUMBIA ... 299
RIVER NETWORK ... 312
STUDENT ENVIRONMENTAL ACTION COALITION (SEAC) ... 328
TENNESSEE CITIZENS FOR WILDERNESS PLANNING ... 329
TEXAS B.A.S.S. CHAPTER FEDERATION ... 330
TRUST FOR PUBLIC LAND, THE ... 337
UTAH NATURE STUDY SOCIETY ... 340
UTAH WILDERNESS COALITION ... 340
WEST VIRGINIA B.A.S.S. CHAPTER FEDERATION ... 346
WILD EARTH ... 348
WILDERNESS EDUCATION ASSOCIATION ... 349
WILDERNESS LAND TRUST, THE (Colorado Office) ... 349
WILDERNESS SOCIETY, THE ... 349
WILDLANDS PROJECT, THE ... 350
YOSEMITE RESTORATION TRUST ... 365

Wildflowers

LADY BIRD JOHNSON WILDFLOWER CENTER (formerly the National Wildlflower Research Center) ... 246

Wildlands

ADIRONDACK MOUNTAIN CLUB, INC., THE ... 134
ALASKA AUDUBON SOCIETY ... 136
ALBERTA WILDERNESS ASSOCIATION ... 137
AMERICAN WILDLANDS ... 156
CALIFORNIA TRAPPERS ASSOCIATION ... 170
COALITION FOR EDUCATION IN THE OUTDOORS ... 181
FRIENDS OF THE BOUNDARY WATERS WILDERNESS ... 211
INTERNATIONAL ASSOCIATION OF WILDLAND FIRE (formerly Fire Research Institute) ... 229
IOWA NATURAL HERITAGE FOUNDATION ... 238
LAKE SUPERIOR GREENS ... 246
MISSOURI NATIVE PLANT SOCIETY ... 259
NATURAL AREAS ASSOCIATION ... 277
NORTHERN ALASKA ENVIRONMENTAL CENTER ... 292
OREGON NATURAL RESOURCES COUNCIL ... 298
SINAPU ... 319
WILD EARTH ... 348
WILDLANDS PROJECT, THE ... 350
WYOMING NATIVE PLANT SOCIETY ... 364

Wildlands Management

ADIRONDACK MOUNTAIN CLUB, INC., THE 134

Wildlife and Wildlife Habitat

ADIRONDACK COUNCIL, THE 133
ADKINS ARBORETUM 134
AFRICAN WILDLIFE FOUNDATION 134
AFRICAN WILDLIFE NEWS SERVICE 135
ALABAMA COOPERATIVE FISH AND WILDLIFE RESEARCH UNIT (USDI) 39
ALABAMA WATERFOWL ASSOCIATION, INC. (AWA) 135
ALASKA AUDUBON SOCIETY 136
ALASKA CONSERVATION FOUNDATION 136
ALASKA COOPERATIVE FISH AND WILDLIFE RESEARCH UNIT 40
ALASKA DEPARTMENT OF FISH AND GAME 40
ALBERTA WILDERNESS ASSOCIATION 137
AMERICAN BIRDING ASSOCIATION 141
AMERICAN CETACEAN SOCIETY 141
AMERICAN CHESTNUT FOUNDATION, THE 141
AMERICAN FISHERIES SOCIETY, GREATER PORTLAND, OR CHAPTER 145
AMERICAN FISHERIES SOCIETY, PENNSYLVANIA CHAPTER 148
AMERICAN WILDLANDS 156
ANIMAL PROTECTION INSTITUTE 157
ARCHERY MANUFACTURERS AND MERCHANTS ORGANIZATION (AMO) 159
ARIZONA GAME AND FISH DEPARTMENT 42
ARKANSAS STATE EXTENSION SERVICES 44
ASSOCIATION OF CONSERVATION ENGINEERS 161
ASSOCIATION OF CONSULTING FORESTERS OF AMERICA 161
ATLANTIC SALMON FEDERATION 163
AUDUBON COUNCIL OF ILLINOIS 163
AUDUBON INTERNATIONAL 163
AUDUBON SOCIETY OF MISSOURI 164
AUDUBON SOCIETY OF WESTERN PENNSYLVANIA 165
BAT CONSERVATION INTERNATIONAL 165
BIODIVERSITY LEGAL FOUNDATION 166
BIRDLIFE INTERNATIONAL 166
BOONE AND CROCKETT CLUB 167
BOONE AND CROCKETT FOUNDATION 167
BOUNTY INFORMATION SERVICE 167
BROOKS BIRD CLUB INC., THE 168
CADDO LAKE INSTITUTE, INC. 169
CALIFORNIA TRAPPERS ASSOCIATION 170
CALIFORNIA WILDLIFE DEFENDERS 170
CALIFORNIA WILDLIFE FEDERATION 170
CAMP FIRE CLUB OF AMERICA, THE 171
CAMP FIRE CONSERVATION FUND 171
CANADA-UNITED STATES ENVIRONMENTAL COUNCIL (United States Office) 171
CANADIAN FEDERATION OF HUMANE SOCIETIES 172
CARIBBEAN CONSERVATION CORPORATION (Costa Rica Office) 173
CENTER FOR ENVIRONMENTAL STUDY 175
CENTER FOR THE STUDY OF TROPICAL BIRDS, INC. (Administative Office) 177
CHARLES A. AND ANNE MORROW LINDBERGH FOUNDATION, THE... 178
CHESAPEAKE WILDLIFE HERITAGE (CWH) 179
COLORADO DEPARTMENT OF EDUCATION 50
COLORADO ENVIRONMENTAL COALITION 182
COLORADO WILDLIFE HERITAGE FOUNDATION 183
COLUMBIA BASIN FISH AND WILDLIFE AUTHORITY 183
COLUMBIA RIVER GORGE COMMISSION 119
COMMITTEE FOR THE NATIONAL INSTITUTE FOR THE ENVIRONMENT (CNIE) 183
CONNECTICUT AUDUBON SOCIETY, INC. 185
CONNECTICUT WATERFOWL ASSOCIATION, INC. 186
CONSERVATION AND RESEARCH FOUNDATION, INC., THE 186
CRAIGHEAD ENVIRONMENTAL RESEARCH INSTITUTE 190
DEEP-PORTAGE CONSERVATION RESERVE 191
DEFENDERS OF WILDLIFE 191
DELTA WILDLIFE FOUNDATION 192
DEPARTMENT OF FISH AND WILDLIFE (WASHINGTON) 119
DEPARTMENT OF INLAND FISHERIES AND WILDLIFE 71
DEPARTMENT OF INTERIOR, U.S.G.S/B.R.D, SOUTH CAROLINA COOPERATIVE FISH AND WILDLIFE RESEARCH UNIT 107
DESERT TORTOISE COUNCIL 193
DESERT TORTOISE PRESERVE COMMITTEE, INC. 193
DUCKS UNLIMITED, INC. (Wetlands America Trust, Inc. Office) 196
EARTH SHARE 197
EARTHJUSTICE LEGAL DEFENSE FUND (formerly Sierra Club Legal Defense Fund, Inc.) 198
EARTHTRUST 199
ECOLOGICAL SOCIETY OF AMERICA, THE 199
ECOLOGY CENTER 199
EDUCATIONAL COMMUNICATIONS, INC. 200
ENVIRONMENT COUNCIL OF RHODE ISLAND 200
ENVIRONMENTAL AIR FORCE 201
ENVIRONMENTAL DEFENSE CENTER, INC. 201
ENVIRONMENTAL EDUCATION ASSOCIATION OF ILLINOIS (Iron Oaks Environmental Learning Center) 202
EVERGLADES COORDINATING COUNCIL (ECC) 204
FAIRFAX AUDUBON SOCIETY 205
FEDERATION OF NEW YORK STATE BIRD CLUBS, INC. 205
FEDERATION OF WESTERN OUTDOOR CLUBS 206
FISH AND WILDLIFE DIVISION/DEPARTMENT OF STATE POLICE 100
FISH AND WILDLIFE INFORMATION EXCHANGE 206
FISH AND WILDLIFE REFERENCE SERVICE 206
FLORIDA AUDUBON SOCIETY 206
FLORIDA CONSERVATION FOUNDATION, INC. 207
FLORIDA DEFENDERS OF THE ENVIRONMENT, INC. (Home Office) 207
FLORIDA GAME AND FRESH WATER FISH COMMISSION 55
FLORIDA PANTHER PROJECT, INC., THE 208
FLORIDA SPORTSMEN'S CONSERVATION ASSOCIATION 208
FOREST SERVICE EMPLOYEES FOR ENVIRONMENTAL ETHICS (FSEEE) 209
FOUNDATION FOR NORTH AMERICAN BIG GAME 210
FOUNDATION FOR NORTH AMERICAN WILD SHEEP 210
FRIENDS OF ANIMALS INC. 211
FUND FOR ANIMALS INC., THE 212
GAME AND FISH DEPARTMENT 125
GAME COMMISSION 103
GAME CONSERVANCY U.S.A. (formerly American Friends of the Game Conservancy) 213
GAME CONSERVATION INTERNATIONAL (GAME COIN) 213
GEORGIA COOPERATIVE FISH AND WILDLIFE RESEARCH UNIT (USDI) 57
GOPHER TORTOISE COUNCIL 216
GREAT BEAR FOUNDATION 216
GREATER YELLOWSTONE COALITION 217
HAWAII AUDUBON SOCIETY 219
HAWK AND OWL TRUST, THE 220
HAWKWATCH INTERNATIONAL INC. 221
HIGH DESERT MUSEUM, THE 221
HOOD CANAL LAND TRUST 222
HUMANE SOCIETY OF THE UNITED STATES, THE 222
IDAHO COOPERATIVE FISH AND WILDLIFE RESEARCH UNIT (USDI) 61
IDAHO FISH AND WILDLIFE FOUNDATION 62
ILLINOIS AUDUBON SOCIETY 224
ILLINOIS ENVIRONMENTAL COUNCIL 224
ILLINOIS PRAIRIE PATH 225
ILLINOIS WALNUT COUNCIL 225
INSTITUTE FOR ECOLOGICAL STUDIES 95
INTERFAITH COUNCIL FOR THE PROTECTION OF ANIMALS AND NATURE INC. (ICPAN) 227
INTERNATIONAL ECOLOGY SOCIETY (IES) 230
INTERNATIONAL MARINE MAMMAL PROJECT, THE 231
INTERNATIONAL PROFESSIONAL HUNTERS' ASSOCIATION 232
INTERNATIONAL SOCIETY FOR ENDANGERED CATS (ISEC) 233
INTERNATIONAL WILD WATERFOWL ASSOCIATION 235
INTERNATIONAL WILDLIFE COALITION (IWC) AND THE WHALE ADOPTION PROJECT 235
INTERNATIONAL WILDLIFE REHABILITATION COUNCIL (IWRC) 236
INTERNATIONAL WOLF CENTER (Educational Services) 236
INTERTRIBAL BISON COOPERATIVE (ITBC) 236
IOWA AUDUBON COUNCIL 237
IOWA COOPERATIVE FISH AND WILDLIFE RESEARCH UNIT 65
IOWA NATURAL HERITAGE FOUNDATION 238
IOWA TRAPPERS ASSOCIATION, INC. 238
J.N. (DING) DARLING FOUNDATION 241
JACKSON HOLE CONSERVATION ALLIANCE 242
JACKSON HOLE LAND TRUST 242
JANE GOODALL INSTITUTE, THE 242
KANSAS ORNITHOLOGICAL SOCIETY 244
KANSAS STATE EXTENSION SERVICES 68
KANSAS WILDSCAPE FOUNDATION 244
KENTUCKY DEPARTMENT OF FISH AND WILDLIFE RESOURCES 68
LEAGUE OF WOMEN VOTERS OF WASHINGTON 248
LEE COUNTY PARKS AND RECREATION SERVICES 56
LOUISIANA AUDUBON COUNCIL 249
LOUISIANA FORESTRY ASSOCIATION 249
MAGIC 250
MAINE COOPERATIVE FISH AND WILDLIFE RESEARCH UNIT (USDI) 72
MARYLAND ORNITHOLOGICAL SOCIETY, INC. 253
MASSACHUSETTS COOPERATIVE FISH AND WILDLIFE RESEARCH UNIT (USDI) 75
MASSACHUSETTS TRAPPER'S ASSOCIATION, INC. 254
MICHIGAN NATURE ASSOCIATION 255
MICHIGAN WILDLIFE HABITAT FOUNDATION 255
MINNESOTA COOPERATIVE FISH AND WILDLIFE RESEARCH UNIT 77
MINNESOTA WINGS SOCIETY, INC. 257
MISSISSIPPI STATE EXTENSION SERVICES 80
MISSOURI COOPERATIVE FISH AND WILDLIFE RESEARCH UNIT (USDI) 81
MONTANA DEPARTMENT OF FISH, WILDLIFE, AND PARKS 82
MONTANA LAND RELIANCE 260
MONTANA WILDERNESS ASSOCIATION 260
MOUNTAIN LION FOUNDATION 261
MOUNTAINEERS, THE (Conservation Division) 261

MULE DEER FOUNDATION, THE 262
NATIONAL 4-H COUNCIL 262
NATIONAL ASSOCIATION OF UNIVERSITY FISHERIES AND WILDLIFE
  PROGRAMS 265
NATIONAL AVIARY IN PITTSBURGH 265
NATIONAL FISH AND WILDLIFE FOUNDATION 267
NATIONAL FOREST FOUNDATION 268
NATIONAL MILITARY FISH AND WILDLIFE ASSOCIATION 269
NATIONAL PARK TRUST 270
NATIONAL RIFLE ASSOCIATION OF AMERICA 271
NATIONAL SHOOTING SPORTS FOUNDATION, INC. 271
NATIONAL TRAPPERS ASSOCIATION, INC. 271
NATIONAL WILDLIFE REFUGE ASSOCIATION 275
NATIONAL WILDLIFE REHABILITATORS ASSOCIATION 275
NATURAL RESOURCES COUNCIL OF AMERICA 278
NATURE CONSERVANCY, THE 279, 280, 281, 282
NEBRASKA STATE EXTENSION SERVICES 84
NEW MEXICO COOPERATIVE FISH AND WILDLIFE RESEARCH UNIT ... 89
NEWFOUNDLAND LABRADOR WILDLIFE FEDERATION 287
NORTH AMERICAN CRANE WORKING GROUP 288
NORTH AMERICAN GAMEBIRD ASSOCIATION, INC. 289
NORTH AMERICAN LOON FUND 289
NORTH AMERICAN WOLF SOCIETY 289
NORTH DAKOTA NATURAL SCIENCE SOCIETY 291
NORTHEAST WILDLIFE ADMINISTRATORS ASSOCIATION 292
NORTHWEST ECOSYSTEM ALLIANCE 293
OHIO AUDUBON COUNCIL, INC. 294
OKLAHOMA ACADEMY OF SCIENCE 295
OKLAHOMA BIOLOGICAL SURVEY 98
OKLAHOMA COOPERATIVE FISH AND WILDLIFE RESEARCH UNIT
  (USDI) 98
OLYMPIC WILDLIFE RESCUE 297
OREGON COOPERATIVE FISH AND WILDLIFE RESEARCH UNIT (USDI)
  100
OREGON TROUT, INC. 298
OUTDOOR WRITERS ASSOCIATION OF AMERICA INC. 299
PACIFIC SEABIRD GROUP 300
PENNSYLVANIA AUDUBON SOCIETY 301
PENNSYLVANIA FOREST STEWARDSHIP PROGRAM 105
PENNSYLVANIA RESOURCES COUNCIL, INC., (formerly PA Roadside
  Council) 302
PHEASANTS FOREVER INC. 303
PRAIRIE CLUB, THE 305
PRAIRIE GROUSE TECHNICAL COUNCIL 306
PREDATOR PROJECT 306
PTARMIGANS, THE 306
QUAIL UNLIMITED, INC. 307
QUEBEC WILDLIFE FEDERATION 308
RAINFOREST TRUST INC., THE 309
RAPTOR RESEARCH FOUNDATION, INC. 309
ROCKY MOUNTAIN BIGHORN SOCIETY 313
ROCKY MOUNTAIN ELK FOUNDATION 313
RUFFED GROUSE SOCIETY, THE 314
SAFARI CLUB INTERNATIONAL 314
SANIBEL-CAPTIVA CONSERVATION FOUNDATION, INC. 315
SAVANNAH RIVER ECOLOGY LABORATORY 107
SAVE SAN FRANCISCO BAY ASSOCIATION 315
SAVE THE MANATEE CLUB 316
SINAPU 319
SOCIETY FOR ANIMAL PROTECTIVE LEGISLATION 320
SOCIETY FOR THE PROTECTION OF NEW HAMPSHIRE FORESTS 322
SOCIETY OF TYMPANUCHUS CUPIDO PINNATUS LTD. 322
SOIL AND WATER CONSERVATION SOCIETY (formerly Soil Conservation
  Society of America) 323
SOUTH CAROLINA B.A.S.S. CHAPTER FEDERATION 323
SOUTH DAKOTA GAME, FISH, AND PARKS DEPARTMENT 109
SOUTHEASTERN ASSOCIATION OF FISH AND WILDLIFE AGENCIES .. 325
STATE FISH AND WILDLIFE MANAGEMENT BOARD (NEW YORK) 93
TALL TIMBERS RESEARCH INC. 329
TEXAS ORGANIZATION FOR ENDANGERED SPECIES 331
THE GLACIER INSTITUTE 331
THORNE ECOLOGICAL INSTITUTE 331
THRESHOLD INC. 332
TROUT UNLIMITED, GUADELOUPE RIVER COUNCIL 334
TRUMPETER SWAN SOCIETY, THE 337
TRUST FOR WILDLIFE, INC. 338
TURTLE CREEK WATERSHED ASSOCIATION, INC. 338
UNIVERSITY OF NEW HAMPSHIRE COOPERATIVE EXTENSION 86
UTAH B.A.S.S. CHAPTER FEDERATION 340
UTAH COOPERATIVE FISH AND WILDLIFE RESEARCH UNIT (USDI-
  USGS-BRD-CRU) 113
VIRGINIA COOPERATIVE FISH AND WILDLIFE RESEARCH UNIT (USDI)
  117
WASHINGTON COOPERATIVE FISH AND WILDLIFE RESEARCH UNIT
  (USDI) 120
WASHINGTON FARM FORESTRY ASSOCIATION 344
WASHINGTON STATE OFFICE OF ENVIRONMENTAL EDUCATION 122
WASHINGTON TRAILS ASSOCIATION 344
WASHINGTON WILDLIFE AND RECREATION COALITION 345
WASHINGTON WILDLIFE HERITAGE FOUNDATION (including Heritage
  Land Trust 345
WELDER WILDLIFE FOUNDATION 345
WEST VIRGINIA COOPERATIVE FISH AND WILDLIFE RESEARCH UNIT
  122
WESTERN ENVIRONMENTAL LAW CENTER 346
WHALE AND DOLPHIN CONSERVATION SOCIETY 348
WHITETAILS UNLIMITED INC. 348
WILDFOWL TRUST OF NORTH AMERICA INC., THE 350
WILDLIFE CENTER OF VIRGINIA, THE 350
WILDLIFE CONSERVATION SOCIETY 350
WILDLIFE EDUCATION PROGRAM AND DESIGN 351
WILDLIFE FOUNDATION OF FLORIDA, INC. 352
WILDLIFE HABITAT CANADA 352
WILDLIFE HABITAT COUNCIL 352
WILDLIFE INFORMATION CENTER, INC. 352
WILDLIFE LEGISLATIVE FUND OF AMERICA, THE, AND WILDLIFE
  CONSERVATION FUND OF AMERICA, THE 352
WILDLIFE PRESERVATION TRUST INTERNATIONAL, INC. ... 353
WILDLIFE RESOURCES COMMISSION 95
WILDLIFE SOCIETY, THE 357
WILSON ORNITHOLOGICAL SOCIETY 358
WISCONSIN SOCIETY FOR ORNITHOLOGY, INC., THE 360
WOLF FUND, THE 360
WORLD CONSERVATION MONITORING CENTRE 361
WORLD WILDLIFE FUND 363
WYOMING COOPERATIVE FISH AND WILDLIFE RESEARCH UNIT (USDI)
  126
WYOMING OUTDOOR COUNCIL 364
YELLOWSTONE GRIZZLY FOUNDATION (YGF) 364

Wildlife Disease

CANADIAN COOPERATIVE WILDLIFE HEALTH CENTRE 171
FOUNDATION FOR NORTH AMERICAN WILD SHEEP 210
GAME CONSERVANCY U.S.A. (formerly American Friends of the Game
  Conservancy) 213
INTERNATIONAL WILDLIFE REHABILITATION COUNCIL (IWRC) 236
MARINE MAMMAL CENTER, THE 252
OREGON COOPERATIVE FISH AND WILDLIFE RESEARCH UNIT (USDI)
  100
SOUTHEASTERN COOPERATIVE WILDLIFE DISEASE STUDY 325
TRI-STATE BIRD RESCUE AND RESEARCH, INC. 333
WILDLIFE CENTER OF VIRGINIA, THE 350
WILDLIFE DISEASE ASSOCIATION 351

Wildlife Management

AFRICAN WILDLIFE NEWS SERVICE 135
ALABAMA COOPERATIVE EXTENSION SYSTEM 39
ALABAMA COOPERATIVE FISH AND WILDLIFE RESEARCH UNIT (USDI)
  39
ALASKA COOPERATIVE FISH AND WILDLIFE RESEARCH UNIT 40
AMERICAN ASSOCIATION OF ZOO KEEPERS, INC. 139
AMERICAN HORSE PROTECTION ASSOCIATION 151
AMERICAN ZOO AND AQUARIUM ASSOCIATION (AZA) 157
ARCHERY MANUFACTURERS AND MERCHANTS ORGANIZATION (AMO)
  159
ARIZONA GAME AND FISH DEPARTMENT 42
ARKANSAS COOPERATIVE RESEARCH UNIT 43
ASSOCIATION OF CONSULTING FORESTERS OF AMERICA 161
ASSOCIATION OF MIDWEST FISH AND GAME LAW ENFORCEMENT
  OFFICERS 162
ATLANTIC SALMON FEDERATION 163
AUDUBON SOCIETY OF RHODE ISLAND 164
BOUNTY INFORMATION SERVICE 167
CALIFORNIA WILDLIFE DEFENDERS 170
CAMP FIRE CLUB OF AMERICA, THE 171
CAMP FIRE CONSERVATION FUND 171
CANADA-UNITED STATES ENVIRONMENTAL COUNCIL (United States
  Office) 171
CANADIAN FEDERATION OF HUMANE SOCIETIES 172
CENTER FOR MARINE CONSERVATION 176
CENTER FOR THE STUDY OF TROPICAL BIRDS, INC. (Administrative
  Office) 177
COLORADO DEPARTMENT OF NATURAL RESOURCES 50
COLORADO TRAPPERS ASSOCIATION 183
CONFEDERATED SALISH AND KOOTENAI TRIBES 185
CONNECTICUT WATERFOWL ASSOCIATION, INC. 186
CONSERVATION DISTRICTS FOUNDATION INC. 187
COOPERATIVE EXTENSION SERVICE (NORTH CAROLINA) 94
DELAWARE DEPARTMENT OF NATURAL RESOURCES AND
  ENVIRONMENTAL CONTROL 52
DEPARTMENT OF INTERIOR, U.S.G.S/B.R.D, SOUTH CAROLINA
  COOPERATIVE FISH AND WILDLIFE RESEARCH UNIT 107
DEPARTMENT OF LAND AND NATURAL RESOURCES 59, 60
DEPARTMENT OF PUBLIC SAFETY 41

DESERT TORTOISE PRESERVE COMMITTEE, INC. 193
DIVISION OF NATURAL RESOURCES 122
EARTHWATCH INSTITUTE 199
EUROPEAN CETACEAN SOCIETY 204
EVERGLADES COORDINATING COUNCIL (ECC) 204
FEDERAL CARTRIDGE COMPANY 205
FISH AND WILDLIFE INFORMATION EXCHANGE 206
FISH AND WILDLIFE REFERENCE SERVICE 206
FLORIDA GAME AND FRESH WATER FISH COMMISSION 55
FLORIDA STATE COOPERATIVE EXTENSION SERVICE 56
FOUNDATION FOR NORTH AMERICAN BIG GAME 210
FOUNDATION FOR NORTH AMERICAN WILD SHEEP 210
GAME COMMISSION 103
GAME CONSERVANCY U.S.A. (formerly American Friends of the Game Conservancy) 213
GAME CONSERVATION INTERNATIONAL (GAME COIN) 213
GEORGIA COOPERATIVE FISH AND WILDLIFE RESEARCH UNIT (USDI) 57
GOPHER TORTOISE COUNCIL 216
GREATER YELLOWSTONE COALITION 217
IDAHO FISH AND GAME DEPARTMENT 61
INDIANA DEPARTMENT OF NATURAL RESOURCES 64
INTERNATIONAL ASSOCIATION FOR BEAR RESEARCH AND MANAGEMENT 228
INTERNATIONAL CENTER FOR GIBBON STUDIES 229
INTERNATIONAL ECOLOGY SOCIETY (IES) 230
INTERNATIONAL HUNTER EDUCATION ASSOCIATION 231
INTERNATIONAL OSPREY FOUNDATION INC., THE 232
INTERNATIONAL PROFESSIONAL HUNTERS' ASSOCIATION 232
INTERNATIONAL WOLF CENTER (Educational Services) 236
IOWA DEPARTMENT OF NATURAL RESOURCES 65
IOWA TRAPPERS ASSOCIATION, INC. 238
IZAAK WALTON LEAGUE OF AMERICA, INC., THE 240
KANSAS STATE EXTENSION SERVICES 68
MAINE COOPERATIVE FISH AND WILDLIFE RESEARCH UNIT (USDI) 72
MARYLAND DEPARTMENT OF NATURAL RESOURCES 73
MASSACHUSETTS COOPERATIVE FISH AND WILDLIFE RESEARCH UNIT (USDI) 75
MASSACHUSETTS TRAPPER'S ASSOCIATION, INC. 254
MICHIGAN DEPARTMENT OF NATURAL RESOURCES 76
MICHIGAN STATE UNIVERSITY EXTENSION 77
MINNESOTA SEA GRANT COLLEGE PROGRAM 79
MINNESOTA WINGS SOCIETY, INC. 257
MISSISSIPPI DEPARTMENT OF WILDLIFE, FISHERIES, AND PARKS 80
MISSISSIPPI STATE EXTENSION SERVICES 80
MOUNTAIN LION FOUNDATION 261
MULE DEER FOUNDATION, THE 262
MUSKIES, INC. 262
NATIONAL TRAPPERS ASSOCIATION, INC. 271
NATIONAL WILD TURKEY FEDERATION, INC., THE 273
NATIVE AMERICAN FISH AND WILDLIFE SOCIETY (NAFWS) 276
NEW HAMPSHIRE FISH AND GAME DEPARTMENT 86
NEW YORK STATE COOPERATIVE EXTENSION 93
NORTH AMERICAN GAMEBIRD ASSOCIATION, INC. 289
NORTH AMERICAN WOLF SOCIETY 289
NORTH DAKOTA GAME AND FISH DEPARTMENT 95
NORTHEAST WILDLIFE ADMINISTRATORS ASSOCIATION 292
OHIO DEPARTMENT OF NATURAL RESOURCES 97
OKLAHOMA STATE EXTENSION SERVICES 99
OREGON COOPERATIVE FISH AND WILDLIFE RESEARCH UNIT (USDI) 100
PEREGRINE FUND, THE 303
PRAIRIE GROUSE TECHNICAL COUNCIL 306
PREDATOR PROJECT 306
PURPLE MARTIN CONSERVATION ASSOCIATION 307
QUEBEC WILDLIFE FEDERATION 308
ROCKY MOUNTAIN BIGHORN SOCIETY 313
RUFFED GROUSE SOCIETY, THE 314
SINAPU 319
SOCIETY FOR ECOLOGICAL RESTORATION 321
SOCIETY FOR MARINE MAMMALOGY, THE 321
SOCIETY FOR THE PROTECTION OF NEW HAMPSHIRE FORESTS 322
SOCIETY OF TYMPANUCHUS CUPIDO PINNATUS LTD. 322
SOUTH CAROLINA DEPARTMENT OF NATURAL RESOURCES 108
SOUTHEASTERN ASSOCIATION OF FISH AND WILDLIFE AGENCIES 325
SOUTHEASTERN COOPERATIVE WILDLIFE DISEASE STUDY 325
STATE FORESTRY DIVISION (WYOMING) 126
TALL TIMBERS RESEARCH INC. 329
TEXAS ORGANIZATION FOR ENDANGERED SPECIES 331
TRAFFIC USA 332
UTAH NATURE STUDY SOCIETY 340
VERMONT NATURAL RESOURCES COUNCIL 341
VIRGINIA COOPERATIVE FISH AND WILDLIFE RESEARCH UNIT (USDI) 117
WASHINGTON TRAILS ASSOCIATION 344
WELDER WILDLIFE FOUNDATION 345
WESTERN HEMISPHERE SHOREBIRD RESERVE NETWORK (WHSRN) 347
WHITETAILS UNLIMITED INC. 348
WILDLIFE CONSERVATION SOCIETY 350
WILDLIFE DAMAGE REVIEW (WDR) 351
WILDLIFE FOUNDATION OF FLORIDA, INC. 352
WILDLIFE HABITAT COUNCIL 352
WILDLIFE LEGISLATIVE FUND OF AMERICA, THE, AND WILDLIFE CONSERVATION FUND OF AMERICA, THE 352
WILDLIFE MANAGEMENT INSTITUTE 352
WILDLIFE RESOURCES AGENCY 110
WILDLIFE RESOURCES COMMISSION 95
WILDLIFE SOCIETY, THE 357
WOLF FUND, THE 360
WYOMING COOPERATIVE FISH AND WILDLIFE RESEARCH UNIT (USDI) 126
WYOMING STATE EXTENSION SERVICES 126
YELLOWSTONE GRIZZLY FOUNDATION (YGF) 364

Wildlife Rehabilitation

A. E. HOWELL WILDLIFE CONSERVATION CENTER 133
ASSOCIATION OF AVIAN VETERINARIANS 161
AUDUBON SOCIETY OF PORTLAND 164
CALIFORNIA WILDLIFE DEFENDERS 170
COLUMBIA BASIN FISH AND WILDLIFE AUTHORITY 183
ELSA WILD ANIMAL APPEAL (Louisiana Chapter) 200
FOUNDATION FOR NORTH AMERICAN WILD SHEEP 210
FUND FOR ANIMALS INC., THE 212
GAME CONSERVANCY U.S.A. (formerly American Friends of the Game Conservancy) 213
INTERNATIONAL PRIMATE PROTECTION LEAGUE 232
INTERNATIONAL WILDLIFE REHABILITATION COUNCIL (IWRC) 236
MARINE MAMMAL CENTER, THE 252
NATIONAL WILDLIFE REHABILITATORS ASSOCIATION 275
NATURAL SCIENCE FOR YOUTH FOUNDATION 278
NEW YORK TURTLE AND TORTOISE SOCIETY 287
RAPTOR CENTER, THE 309
RIVER OTTER ALLIANCE, THE 312
ROCKY MOUNTAIN BIGHORN SOCIETY 313
SUNCOAST SEABIRD SANCTUARY INC. 328
TRI-STATE BIRD RESCUE AND RESEARCH, INC. 333
TROUT UNLIMITED, PENNSYLVANIA COUNCIL 336
TRUST FOR WILDLIFE, INC. 338
WILDLIFE CENTER OF VIRGINIA, THE 350
WILDLIFE WAYSTATION 358
WOLF FUND, THE 360
WORLD SOCIETY FOR THE PROTECTION OF ANIMALS (WSPA) 363

Wildlife Research

JANE GOODALL INSTITUTE, THE 242

Wolves

DEFENDERS OF WILDLIFE 191

Women in the Environment

CENTER FOR HEALTH, ENVIRONMENT, AND JUSTICE 175
ECOLOGY CENTER 199
GIRL SCOUTS OF THE UNITED STATES OF AMERICA 215
IOWA WOMEN IN NATURAL RESOURCES 238
WILDLIFE FOREVER 351
WORLD ASSOCIATION OF GIRL GUIDES AND GIRL SCOUTS (WAGGGS) 361
WORLD WOMEN IN THE DEFENSE OF THE ENVIRONMENT 363

Youth Organizations

AMERICAN BASS ASSOCIATION OF MARYLAND, THE 140
AMERICAN CAMPING ASSOCIATION, INC. 141
AMERICAN FISHERIES SOCIETY, VIRGINIA TECH CHAPTER 149
AMERICAN NATURE STUDY SOCIETY 153
ARCHERY MANUFACTURERS AND MERCHANTS ORGANIZATION (AMO) 159
BLACK BASS FOUNDATION 166
BOY SCOUTS OF AMERICA 168
BROTHERHOOD OF THE JUNGLE COCK, INC., THE 168
CADDO LAKE INSTITUTE, INC. 169
CENTER FOR ENVIRONMENTAL EDUCATION 174
CENTER FOR ENVIRONMENTAL STUDY 175
COOPERATIVE EXTENSION SERVICE (NORTH CAROLINA) 94
EARTH FORCE 197
EARTHSTEWARDS NETWORK 198
ENVIRONMENTAL EDUCATION COUNCIL OF OHIO 203
GIRL SCOUTS OF THE UNITED STATES OF AMERICA 215

KANSAS STATE EXTENSION SERVICES 68
KANSAS WILDSCAPE FOUNDATION 244
KIDS FOR SAVING EARTH WORLDWIDE 246
LEGACY INTERNATIONAL.. 248
NATIONAL 4-H COUNCIL 262
NATIONAL ASSOCIATION OF SERVICE AND CONSERVATION CORPS
    (NASCC)... 264
NATIONAL FFA ORGANIZATION... 267
NATIONAL FIELD ARCHERY ASSOCIATION 267
NATIONAL GARDENING ASSOCIATION... 268
NATIONAL HUNTERS ASSOCIATION, INC.. 269
NATIONAL RIFLE ASSOCIATION OF AMERICA...................................... 271
NATURAL SCIENCE FOR YOUTH FOUNDATION 278
NEW JERSEY STATE EXTENSION SERVICES 88
NORTH CAROLINA RECREATION AND PARK SOCIETY, INC................ 291
OHIO ACADEMY OF SCIENCE, THE.. 294
PENNSYLVANIA FORESTRY ASSOCIATION, THE 302
PUERTO RICO STATE EXTENSION SERVICES 106
SOUND EXPERIENCE... 323
STUDENT CONSERVATION ASSOCIATION, INC. 328
STUDENT ENVIRONMENTAL ACTION COALITION (SEAC).................... 328
TREE PEOPLE 332
TRUST FOR WILDLIFE, INC... 338
UNIVERSITY OF VERMONT EXTENSION... 115
WASHINGTON NATIVE PLANT SOCIETY... 344
WILDLIFE ACTION, INC.. 350
WORLD ASSOCIATION OF GIRL GUIDES AND GIRL SCOUTS (WAGGGS)
    361
YMCA EARTH SERVICE CORPS.. 365
YOUNG ENTOMOLOGISTS' SOCIETY INC.. 365

Zoological Parks

AMERICAN ZOO AND AQUARIUM ASSOCIATION (AZA) 157
EUROPEAN ASSOCIATION FOR AQUATIC MAMMALS 204
TALLAHASSEE MUSEUM OF HISTORY AND NATURAL SCIENCE......... 329
WILDLIFE CONSERVATION SOCIETY... 350

Zoology

AMERICAN ASSOCIATION OF ZOO KEEPERS, INC. 139
AMERICAN INSTITUTE OF BIOLOGICAL SCIENCES 151
AMERICAN MUSEUM OF NATURAL HISTORY 153
AMERICAN SOCIETY OF ICHTHYOLOGISTS AND HERPETOLOGISTS. 155
AMERICAN SOCIETY OF ZOOLOGISTS.. 156
CHICAGO HERPETOLOGICAL SOCIETY 179
DESERT FISHES COUNCIL 193
EARTHWATCH INSTITUTE 199
ENTOMOLOGICAL SOCIETY OF AMERICA 200
INTERNATIONAL CENTER FOR GIBBON STUDIES 229
MONTANA NATURAL HERITAGE PROGRAM 83
NATIONAL ASSOCIATION OF BIOLOGY TEACHERS 262
NATIONAL AVIARY IN PITTSBURGH... 265
NEW YORK TURTLE AND TORTOISE SOCIETY 287
OKLAHOMA BIOLOGICAL SURVEY 98
PACIFIC SEABIRD GROUP... 300
TALLAHASSEE MUSEUM OF HISTORY AND NATURAL SCIENCE......... 329
WASHINGTON NATURAL HERITAGE PROGRAM 121
WILSON ORNITHOLOGICAL SOCIETY.. 358
YOUNG ENTOMOLOGISTS' SOCIETY INC.. 365

STAFF NAME INDEX

A

AASHEIM, RON..........82
AASNESS, PERRY..........77
ABAJIAN, PAUL..........390
ABAWI, FAROUQ G...........59
ABBEY, ROBERT..........24
ABBOY, JIM..........314
ABE, ELAINE T...........60
ABEL, MIKE..........126
ABELE, LAWRENCE G...........372
ABENT, ROB..........76
ABER, JOHN..........381
ABERNETHY, VIRGINIA..........174, 305
ABLER, RONALD F...........161
ABRAHAM, FRED..........195
ABRAHAM, RONALD..........97
ABRAMS, SHELDON..........152
ABRAMSON, SUSAN..........171
ABSHER, CURTIS..........69
ABZUG, BELLA..........361
ACEVEDO, MIGUEL..........390
ACFALLE, JOSEPH L.M...........58
ACHITOFF, PAUL..........198
ACK, BRAD..........216
ACKELSON, MARK..........237, 308
ACKELSON, MARK C...........238
ACKER, FREDERICK G...........254
ACKER, RANDY..........121
ACORD, BOBBY R...........29
ACUNA, GENE..........111
ADAIR, JANICE..........40
ADAIR, SUE..........205
ADAMS, BETSY..........15
ADAMS, BILL..........122
ADAMS, CINDY..........136, 301
ADAMS, CLARKE E...........357
ADAMS, GILBERT..........167
ADAMS, JOHN H...........278
ADAMS, KAY..........263
ADAMS, PAMELA A...........52
ADAMS, RON..........209
ADAMS, SANDRA..........349
ADAMS, STAN..........264
ADAMS, STANFORD M...........94
ADAMS, STEVE..........86
ADAMS, TIM..........107
ADAMS, VIVIAN..........221
ADAMS, WENDY..........137
ADAMSON, LARRY..........129
ADAMSON, TERRENCE B...........268
ADAMS-WILEY, MARY..........156
ADCOX, LAURIE..........263
ADDIS, JAMES T...........124
ADELHARDT, LAURIE J...........73
ADELMAN, DAVID..........327
ADELMAN, IRA R...........379
ADELMANN, GERALD W...........297
ADELMANN, PEGGY..........78
ADHIKARI, AMBIKA..........234
ADLER, BILL..........184
ADRIAN, BILL..........351
AFTON, ALAN D...........69
AGBABIAN, MIHRAN S...........370
AGLE, JIM..........94
AGLI, JIM..........138
AGNEESSENS, JEANNE..........241
AGRISS, TERRY..........91
AGUDLO, JAMIE..........17
AGUILAR, ALEX..........321
AGUILERA-CALZADILLA, E. JOSE..........309
AGUSTIN, RAYMOND SAN..........300
AHERN, CATHERINE A...........154
AHERN, JOHN..........296
AHKEAH, ROBERT..........159
AHMED, A. KARIM..........184
AHNER, LEWIS A., JR...........266
AIKEN, PATRICIA..........333
AILES, JOHN..........122
AITON, REID..........170
AKERS, JOHN..........68
AKEY, STEVEN..........27
AKISHINO, PRINCE..........363
ALBERICI, THERESA..........103
ALBERTS, BRUCE M...........271
ALBERTS, JAMES J...........372
ALBO, LIA..........212
ALBRECHT, JEAN..........379
ALBRIGHT, JOHN..........163
ALBRIGHT, LARRY..........179
ALBRIGHT, MADELINE..........16
ALBRIGHT, MEL..........142
ALBRINK, ANNE..........326
ALBRO, DEAN..........106
ALDEN, ROBIN..........71
ALDERSON, JAMES..........277
ALDRICH, ALYSSA..........31
ALDRICH, DORRIE..........28
ALDRICH, WINTHROP J...........93
ALESII, BRUNO..........188
ALEXANDER, BEN..........323
ALEXANDER, CHARLES..........297
ALEXANDER, EDWARD J...........183
ALEXANDER, GERALD..........68
ALEXANDER, GLEN..........264
ALEXANDER, H. LLOYD, JR...........53
ALEXANDER, LaVERNE..........215
ALEXANDER, LLOYD..........66
ALEXANDER, MAURICE M...........156
ALEXANDER, PETER A...........252
ALEXANDER, VERA..........366
ALEY, TOM..........141
ALIE, RONALD..........86, 292
ALIPIO, MEL..........230
ALIRE, CAMILA..........370
ALKIRE, BILL..........119
ALLAN, J. COLIN..........113
ALLAN, J. DAVID..........154
ALLARD, G...........37
ALLARD, JOHN B., II..........49
ALLEE, A. LEE..........70
ALLEE, BRIAN J...........183
ALLEN, ALAN..........330
ALLEN, ARTHUR S...........375
ALLEN, BETTY..........283
ALLEN, BILL..........195
ALLEN, CHRISTOPHER..........103
ALLEN, CRAIG R...........107
ALLEN, DARCY..........216
ALLEN, DAVID B...........26
ALLEN, DENNIS M...........388
ALLEN, GERALD..........368
ALLEN, J. FRED..........57
ALLEN, JEFF..........298
ALLEN, JERRY W...........308
ALLEN, JOHN H...........223
ALLEN, LISA G...........81
ALLEN, MARTYE..........246
ALLEN, MELODY..........364
ALLEN, TOM..........24
ALLEN, W...........192
ALLEN, W. DALE..........338
ALLEN, WILLIAM L...........268
ALLER, CHUCK..........54
ALLERY, VIRGINIA P...........273
ALLEY, JAMIE..........127
ALLGOOD, DAVID..........181
ALLHANDS, LAURA..........180
ALLISON, CHRIS..........90
ALLISON, DAVID L...........143
ALLISON, K. L...........100
ALLISON, M. LEE..........114
ALLISON, SHARON W...........304
ALLMAN, DENNIS..........306
ALPAUGH, LES..........87
ALTADONNA, LEIGH..........301
ALTENSTADTER, SHELLEY..........34
ALTER, HARVEY..........339
ALTER, THEODORE R...........105
ALTIERI, DIANNE..........315
ALTMAN, ELLIE..........134
ALTWINE, BOB..........283
AMACK, REX..........83
AMANTIA, ANNE MARIE B...........304
AMARATUNGA, T...........293
AMBROSETTI, RON..........388
AMBROSINO, MARGIE..........309
AMES, DAVE..........91
AMES, OAKES..........201
AMIOTTE, SUE..........283
AMON, LAWRENCE J...........274, 275
AMONTREE, TOM..........29
AMOR, ADLAI..........219
AMORY, CLEVELAND..........212
AMTMANN, LINDSEY..........345
ANABLE, MICHAEL E...........42
ANASTOR, DENNY..........314
ANAYA, SCOTT..........136
ANDELMAN, SANDY..........321
ANDELT, WILLIAM F...........51
ANDERS, KRISTIE..........315
ANDERSEN, DAVID E...........77
ANDERSON, ALETA..........133
ANDERSON, BOB..........20, 347
ANDERSON, BROOK D...........14
ANDERSON, BRUCE..........288
ANDERSON, BRUCE H...........208
ANDERSON, CAROLYN..........232
ANDERSON, CHEL..........211
ANDERSON, D. C...........362
ANDERSON, D. LARRY..........114
ANDERSON, DAVE L...........100
ANDERSON, DAVID..........36, 75, 370
ANDERSON, DAVID E..........379
ANDERSON, DAVID R...........50
ANDERSON, DONALD C...........97
ANDERSON, DONALD K...........103
ANDERSON, ERIC..........393
ANDERSON, FLETCHER..........269
ANDERSON, GLEN..........182
ANDERSON, GREG..........199
ANDERSON, GREGORY J...........151
ANDERSON, JAMES..........193
ANDERSON, JAMES S...........360
ANDERSON, JOHN..........344
ANDERSON, JOHN M...........223
ANDERSON, JOHN W...........231, 297
ANDERSON, JOHN W., II..........231
ANDERSON, JON W...........115
ANDERSON, KARL..........285
ANDERSON, KEN..........109
ANDERSON, LEE G...........256
ANDERSON, M. G...........194
ANDERSON, MARGOT..........30
ANDERSON, MARY..........323
ANDERSON, MIKE..........355
ANDERSON, PAUL..........236
ANDERSON, R. C...........386
ANDERSON, RENAE..........31
ANDERSON, ROBERT..........19
ANDERSON, ROBERT D...........58
ANDERSON, ROLF..........218
ANDERSON, STANLEY H...........126
ANDERSON, STEVE..........209
ANDERSON, STEVEN H...........393
ANDERSON, SUSAN..........138
ANDERSON, THOMAS C...........75
ANDERSON, THOMAS R...........316
ANDERSON, WILLIAM A., JR...........244
ANDERTON, KATE..........317
ANDO, RODOLFO L...........58
ANDRADE, WILLIAM..........254
ANDREA, RICHARD..........208
ANDREAS, TERRY L...........377
ANDREN, ANDERS W...........125
ANDREWS, ADOLPHUS, JR...........248
ANDREWS, BILL..........45
ANDREWS, EMILIE M...........52
ANDREWS, JOHN..........94
ANDREWS, MICHAEL..........279
ANDREWS, OAKLEY V...........173
ANGEL, ELSA M...........212
ANGELL, JOHN M...........14
ANGELL, TONY..........122
ANGELLE, PEDRO..........70
ANGERMEIER, PAUL L...........117
ANGERS, JEFF..........181
ANGLE, RICHARD W., JR...........308
ANGLE-FRANZINE, MARY A...........317
ANGVIK, JANE..........41
ANNELLI, JOSEPH..........30
ANTHONY, CARL..........340
ANTHONY, CRAIG E...........49
ANTHONY, MARK..........96
ANTHONY, ROBERT G...........100, 357, 386
ANTHONY, VERNICE DAVIS..........77
ANTISTA, JAMES V...........55
ANTWI, KWABENA..........204
ANUNSEN, CATHY SUE..........212
APA, TONY..........354
APGAR, DESIGNEE BILL..........15
APODACA, TED..........90
APP, LEON E...........118
APPEL, BRAD VAN..........189
APPEL, MADELEINE..........317
APPELGATE, JAMES E...........381
APPELGATE, LINDA D...........237
APPLEGATE, MICHAEL..........17
APSLEY, BRUCE..........333
APSLEY, DAVE..........20
ARAMAKI, CHUCK..........322
ARAMBURU, AL..........48
ARCHER, HUGH N...........69
ARCHER, HUGH V...........102
ARCHER, KATHY..........341
ARCHER, WILLIAM R...........112
ARCHEY, WARREN..........264
ARCHIBALD, GEORGE..........230
ARCHULETA, RICHARD..........236
AREEN, JUDITH..........371
ARENA, CHRISTINE..........333
ARENDT, RANDALL G...........277
ARGANBRIGHT, DONALD G...........367
ARGO, GENE..........244
ARGOW, KEITH A...........154, 268
ARMAS, LUPE..........27
ARMITAGE, BRIAN J...........295
ARMOUR, HARRIS A., III..........329
ARMOUR, KARYN..........132
ARMSTRONG, BOB..........23
ARMSTRONG, JAMES..........392
ARMSTRONG, SHERI-LYNN..........279
ARMY, THOMAS J...........32
ARNETT, ED..........356
ARNOLD, CATHERINE..........54
ARNOLD, STEPHEN D...........373
ARNOLDI, JOAN M...........30
ARNST, JAMES E...........111
ARONICA, LOUIS..........253
ARONOFF, MARCIA..........202
ARREOLA, DIANE..........18
ARRINGTON, BOB..........120
ARRINGTON, DAVID..........16
ARRINGTON, NANCY..........343
ARRIOLA, VINCENT P...........58
ARSENAULT, GEORGE..........131
ARSENAULT, WILLIAM..........298
ARSMAN, TOM..........385
ARTERO, ANTHONY..........59
ARTERO, VICTOR T...........59
ARTHUR, BILL..........319
ARTHUR, GREGG..........125
ARTHUR, SHEILA..........306
ARTLEY, DON..........83
ASBELL, G. FRED..........304
ASBURY, DONNA..........190
ASH, BETTY..........80
ASH, CAROL..........279
ASHCROFT, MARY..........341
ASHE, DANIEL M...........26
ASHEY, MIKE..........55
ASHLEY, KEN..........182
ASHLEY, LATRELLE..........80
ASHLEY, LATTELLE..........80
ASHMEADE-HAWKINS, BRETT EVELYN..........309
ASHMEADE-HAWKINS, MARK EVELYN..........309
ASKINS, RENEE..........360
ASKINS, ROBERT A...........370
ASLIN, RAYMOND G...........67
ASMUSSEN, DENNIS..........78
ASNER, EDWARD..........233
ASPER, EDWARD..........235
ASPERODITES, PHILIP N...........71
ATCHISON, ROBERT L...........67
ATEN, CAROL..........270
ATERNO, KATHLEEN..........180
ATKIN, JOHN..........316
ATKINSON, NANCY..........31
ATKINSON, SAMUEL F...........390
ATKINSON, THOMAS..........85
ATWOOD, JOHN..........134
ATWOOD, TIM..........267
AUCOIN, DENNIS..........249
AUCOIN, HAROLD..........130
AUER, BOB..........83
AUFDERHEIDE, NADIA..........221
AUGULIS, RICHARD P...........13
AUGUST, PETER V...........388
AUGUSTINE, ED..........231
AUGUSTINE, GENE..........17
AUGUSTINE, JOHN..........276
AUGUSTINE, MICHAEL E...........347
AUIRKE, KELLY..........308
AUNAN, LAURI..........344
AURAND, DARWIN..........102
AUSTEN, DOUGLAS J...........143
AUSTIN, ALICE..........255
AUSTIN, BARBARA..........90
AUSTIN, BILL..........353
AUSTIN, BOB..........75
AUSTIN, JANE..........291
AUSTIN, JIM..........31
AUSTIN, KATHY..........262
AUSTIN, TERRY..........268
AVALOS, EDWARD..........89
AVARY, KATHERINE LEE..........123
AVENI, VIRGINIA..........295
AVERY, DAVID L...........64
AVERY, JIMMY L...........70
AXLINE, MICHAEL..........203, 346
AXLINE, MICHAEL D...........386
AXON, JAMES..........68
AYCOCK, MARLYN..........30
AYER, CLAIRE..........341
AYER, DAVID..........310
AYER, DONALD B...........154
AYERS, JOSEPH..........373
AYLSWORTH, LINDA..........236
AYLWARD, KEVIN..........128
AYMOND, HAROLD J...........375
AYRES, ED..........363
AYRES, HENRY F., JR...........171

B

BAAS, JOHN M...........357
BABBITT, BRUCE..........9, 23, 269
BABCOCK, KENNETH..........196
BABIN, DANIEL J...........70
BABIN, EDWARD..........304
BACH, CATHERINE..........378
BACH, MARYANNE..........25
BACHERT, DEL..........383
BACHMAN, PETER H...........256
BACINSKI, PETE..........285
BACKUS, PETER..........312
BACON, BOB..........108

496 **STAFF NAME INDEX**

Staff Name Index

BACON, LAWRENCE R. 153
BACONE, JOHN 64
BACQUET, CHARLES, III 36
BADAKY, ANN 27
BADAL, ROBERT 52
BADGER, RUTHE 124
BADRUDDIN, ABU 389
BAER, RICHARD A. 382
BAERTSCHE, STEPHEN R. 97
BAETGE, JIM 329
BAGENT, JACK L. 70
BAGGOTT, ERIN E. 124
BAGLEY, CHUCK 121
BAGLEY, LAUREN 205
BAGNALL, CLAIRE 198
BAHE, AL 109
BAICICH, PAUL 141
BAILEY, DICK 102
BAILEY, ED 202
BAILEY, JAMES 21
BAILEY, JOHN 271
BAILEY, LONNIE 258
BAILEY, RICHARD 59
BAILEY, ROBERT 129
BAILEY, VICKY A. 14
BAILIFF, MEGAN 121
BAILIFF, MEGAN D. 182
BAIN, MARK B. 92
BAINES, PRESCOTT S. 108
BAIR, SALLY 104
BAIRD, CAROL 169
BAIRD, DENNIS 224
BAIRD, ROBERT 346
BAIRD, RONALD C. 13
BAIRD, STEPHEN W. 297
BAIRD, WARREN 226
BAITON, WILLIAM 226
BAKAMJIAN, LYNN 165
BAKER, ANNETTE 356
BAKER, BRUCE 325
BAKER, BRUCE J. 124
BAKER, D. JAMES 12
BAKER, DALE 92
BAKER, DAYTON 265
BAKER, ELAINE 229
BAKER, J. 8
BAKER, JOHN R. 204
BAKER, KEN 127
BAKER, ROBERT J. 155
BAKER, TOM 68
BAKER, VIC R. 367
BAKER, WILLIAM C. 178
BAKKER, JOE 55
BALAAM, ROBERT J. 87
BALD, GEORGE 85
BALDA, WILLIAM 354
BALDES, RICHARD J. 273
BALDOCK, JAMES 273
BALDWIN, DICK 101
BALDWIN, LORI 363
BALDWIN, MARK 314
BALE, CHARLES 68
BALENOVIC, IVAN 172
BALFOUR, DAVID 75
BALFREY, WILLO 261
BALL, ALLAN 71
BALL, GREG 345
BALL, I. J. 82
BALL, JEAN M. 135
BALL, LINDSAY A. 100
BALL, LOUISE M. 384
BALLANTINE, SUE 323
BALLANTYNE, CHRIS 319
BALLANTYNE, J. 386
BALLANTYNE, JOE 132
BALLARD, JOE N. 21
BALLASH, BETSEY L. 170
BALLENTIN, EVERETTE 226
BALLENTINE, JANE 157
BALLENTINI, NICOLE 342
BALSILLIE, DAVID 131
BALTON, DAVID A. 16
BALTZ, DON 147
BAMBERY, CAROL 76
BAMBRICK, DALE 119
BAMMEL, GENE 392
BAN, HIDEYUKI 180
BANCROFT, THOMAS 349
BANDEL, DONALD 23
BANDY, JOHN 63
BANE, SANDRA O. 350
BANGART, RICHARD L. 35
BANGERT, SUZANNE 124
BANKER, HARRY J. 183
BANKER, MARK E. 314
BANKERS, GARY 297, 361
BANKES, NIGEL 171
BANKS, JOHN 72
BANNER, ROGER E. 114
BANTA, JOHN 90
BANYOTS, JERRY 177
BANZHAF, WILLIAM H. 322
BAPST, RICHARD 302
BARAJAS, GRACIELA 234
BARBARO, HENRY 76
BARBEE, ROBERT 25
BARBER, EDNA 20
BARBER, GERALD R. 273, 275
BARBER, HARRY A. 358
BARBER, PATRICIA S. 53
BARBER, PHYLLIS 237
BARBER, SYD 132
BARCINAS, JEFF 59
BARCLAY, JOHN S. 52
BARCLAY, LESLIE 286
BARD, JOHN F. 244
BARDSLEY, MARC 291
BARFIELD, RODNEY 95
BARGER, DON 270
BARISH, RICHARD 286
BARKER, BOB 140
BARKER, DAVID READ 259
BARKER, I. 171
BARKER, RICHARD F. 87
BARKER, ROY 16
BARKLEY, BILL 127
BARKMAN, ROBERT 253
BARKOW, LEE 24
BARLAT, ROGERS 381
BARLOW, MICHELE 364
BARLOW, MIKE 297
BARLOW, RICHARD J. 52
BARLOW, ROGER 80
BARLOW, VIRGINIA 342
BARLUFFE, ROSANE 309
BARNA, DAVID 25
BARNARD, GEOFFREY S. 216
BARNARD, STAN 125
BARNARD, WILLIAM H. 220
BARNES, A. JAMES 374
BARNES, ALLEN 169
BARNES, DONALD G. 10
BARNES, JIM 158
BARNES, JUDY 357
BARNES, MISTIANNA H. 68
BARNES, PETRA 30
BARNES, THOMAS G. 69
BARNETT, AUDREY 140
BARNETT, CLAIRE L. 160
BARNETT, EMILY 293
BARNETT, MARK 277
BARNETT, TIMOTHY L. 134
BARNETT, ZRNIE 54
BARNETTE, JAMES 5
BARNEY, JEFF 224
BARNHART, GERRY 91
BARON, ROBERT 235
BARONE, GEORGE J., JR. 52
BARR, DAVID N. 158
BARR, MARI 24
BARRAM, DAVID 34
BARRE, DAVID 219
BARRESI, JAMES 71, 87
BARRET, MORLEY 127
BARRETO, JOSI L. 189
BARRETT, GARY 151
BARRETT, LONICE C. 57
BARRETT, MICHAEL 362
BARRETT, WILLIAM O. 167
BARRETT-HEFFINGTON, JULIE 246
BARRICKLOW, DEANNA 226
BARRICLOW-ARVIN, SUSANNA 226
BARRINGTON, GENE 334
BARRITT, DAVID 231
BARRON, DAVID 205
BARRON, EDWIN H. 111
BARRON, PAT 203
BARROW, WILLIE T. 308
BARRY, DONALD J. 23
BARRY, JOHANNAH 157
BARRY, ROBERT 18
BARRY, WILLIAM N. 223
BARSAMILAN, LORETTA 46
BARSCH, RAYMOND E. 48
BARSHAW, DIANA 374
BARSHIELD, ROBERT 91
BARSTOW, ROBBINS 178
BARTH, CHRIS 331
BARTH, DON 298
BARTH, ERIK J. 117
BARTHOLOMEW, CHARLES L. 387
BARTLEY, JULIE 333
BARTNICKI, PENNY 357
BARTO, JOHN, ESQ. 327
BARTOLOME, JAMES W. 369
BARTON, BOB 173
BARTON, RICK 73
BARTON, SANDY 114
BARTON, STEPHEN 62
BARTON, THOMAS 64
BARTSCH, ERIC 118
BARTTER, KATE 97
BARZEN, JEB 230
BASDEN, THOMAS J. 123
BASILI, GIANFRANCO 206
BASMAN, CEM 262
BASS, EDWARD P. 363
BASS, LEE M. 112
BASSETT, DONALD A. 314
BASSETT, KAREN 246
BASTIAN, BLAIR 128
BATEMAN, HUGH 70
BATES, BOB 19
BATES, DAVID R. 168
BATES, MIKE 44
BATES, NORMAN 110
BATES, RICK 132
BATES, ROBERT M. 68
BATES, SCOTT 21
BATES, TERRIE 56
BATKER, CAROL A. 95
BATORY, JOAN 302
BATT, AL 257
BATT, BRUCE 195
BATT, PHILIP E. 61
BATTEY, JAMES F. 391
BATZLI, GEORGE O. 373
BAUCHMAN, ANN 83
BAUER, JEFFREY 385
BAUER, TOM 27
BAUGH, DONALD R. 178
BAUGHMAN, JOHN 125, 346
BAUGHMAN, MELVIN J. 79
BAUM, BOB 24
BAUM, KENT 26
BAUMANN, J. MICHAEL 313
BAUMANN, MIKE 210
BAUMGARTNER, DAVID M. 121
BAUST, JOHN 55
BAXTER, PATRICIA J. 286
BAY, CRANDALL 368
BAY, MICHAEL 296
BAYDACK, RICHARD 376
BAYER, ROBIN 250
BAYES, MARK 140
BAYLES, DAVID 300
BAYLESS, STEVE R. 195
BAYLIFF, WILLIAM H. 8
BAYNES, A. SIDNEY 95
BAZZELL, DARRELL L. 124
BEACH, ARTHUR B. 35
BEACH, GARY 125
BEACH, GARY G. 126
BEAL, CAROL 36
BEAL, KENNETH 142
BEALS, ED 376
BEAMER, JOHN 66
BEAN, HAROLD 54
BEAN, LARRY 66
BEANE, JEFF 290
BEANE, MARJORIE 363
BEAR, DINAH 10
BEARD, DANIEL 265
BEARD, MOLLY 284
BEARD, RON 72
BEARY, KRISTIN 193
BEARZI, JAMES 90
BEASLEY, DAVID B. 383
BEASLEY, R. SCOTT 389
BEASON, ROBERT C. 359
BEATTIE, JAMES T. 106
BEATTY, ROBERT 163
BEAUCHAMMP, DAVID A. 390
BEAUCHAMP, DAVID 113
BEAUDETTE, PAUL 200
BEAUMONT, LUCIEN 131
BEAVAN, JIM 73
BECH, REBECCA 29
BECHARD, MARC J. 309
BECHTEL, JOHN H., III 271
BECK, JIM A. 366
BECK, LOUIS A. 49
BECK, MIKE 164
BECK, MILTON 17
BECK, RAY 83
BECK, ROBERT 334
BECK, TREY 182
BECKEMEYER, ROY 244
BECKER, CARL 277
BECKER, DALE 355
BECKER, DENNIS 295
BECKER, JOHN 242
BECKER, KENNETH 115
BECKER, LAWRENCE R. 115
BECKER, NANCY 225
BECKER, PHIL 218
BECKER, RONALD E. 70
BECKER, S. WILLIAM 327
BECKMAN, DAVE 132
BECKWITH, ERNEST E. 52
BECKWITH, JANE 298
BECKWITH, WENDY, II 154
BEDNARZ, ROBERT 266
BEECHER, BOB 131
BEECHER, WILLIAM M. 35
BEELMAN, JOYCE 20
BEEMER, JAMES 23, 269
BEESON, M. GAULT, JR. 350
BEGGS, GAIL 131
BEGIN, PAUL 132
BEHLEN, THOMAS 8
BEHLEN, TOM 97
BEHLING, MARY C. 123
BEINECKE, JOHN B. 220
BEISSINGER, STEVEN 153
BELCHER, L. 100
BELFIT, SCOTT 20
BELGER, MONTE 27
BELISLE, BRAD 185
BELK, PERDITA 31
BELL, BOB 170
BELL, CHRISTINE 360
BELL, DICK 363
BELL, ELIZABETH 257
BELL, HUBERT 35
BELL, LARRY 89
BELL, LINDA 169
BELL, MIKE 89
BELL, NANCY 187, 188
BELL, STU 165
BELL, WILLIAM 250
BELLAFIORE, VINCENT J. 373
BELLER, MELANIE 23
BELLINGER, JOHN 21
BELLIVEAU, MICHAEL 184
BELLON, JIM 17
BELOTE, MONTE 157
BELOW, THEODORE H. 208
BELSON, JERRY 25
BELZ, JOHN 196
BEMELMANS, MADELEINE 320
BEMIS, JILL A. 277
BENDER, BOB 68
BENDER, DAVE 62
BENDER, MARY 104
BENDER, NORMAN 52
BENDICK, ROBERT 280
BENEDETTO, DEBRA 254
BENEDICT, LES 327
BENEDICT, MARK A. 187
BENEDICT, PHILIP R. 115
BENEFIELD, GARY 136
BENEKE, JOHN 45
BENEKE, PATRICIA 23
BENFORADO, JAY 10
BENGTSON, PETE 261
BENJAMIN, SHARON K. 256
BENNET, DEBBY 134
BENNETT, ALBERT F. 156
BENNETT, BETSY 94
BENNETT, C. THOMAS 228
BENNETT, C. TOM 68, 325
BENNETT, CHUCK 44
BENNETT, COLIN 343
BENNETT, D. W. 152
BENNETT, DERY 180, 181
BENNETT, EARL H. 62
BENNETT, JAMES P. 167
BENNETT, JIM 95, 192
BENNETT, JOEL 191
BENNETT, KAREN 86
BENNETT, ROBERT 4, 75
BENNETT, SHAUN 261
BENNETT, TONY 323
BENNETT, WILLIAM 237
BENNETT, WILLIAM J. 49
BENOIT, MARY ANN 353
BENSON, CAMERON 201
BENSON, CARL 159
BENSON, DELWIN E. 51
BENSON, HAROLD W. 275
BENSON, LAURA 157
BENSON, RALPH W. 337
BENSON, ROBERT A. 385
BENSON, SERENA 350
BENSON, SUSAN 72
BENSON, THOMAS 76
BENSON, WILLIAM F. 14
BENT, MITCH 337
BENTLEY, STELLA 366
BENTLEY, WILLIAM R. 383
BENTON, DAVID 40
BENTON, JO A. 134
BENTON, MICHELLE 120
BEREN, PETER 318
BERENDSEN, PIETER 67, 243
BERG, DAVID 313
BERG, GEORGE VAN DEN 313
BERG, JUDITH 312
BERG, KARLYN ATKINSON 351
BERG, NORMAN A. 323
BERG, THOMAS 96, 97
BERGEN, PETER 90
BERGEN, ROGER 199
BERGER, ALAN 157
BERGER, JOEL 380
BERGER, PAULA A. 257
BERGER, WOLFGANG 370
BERGERON, ROBERT 36
BERGERSEN, ERIC P. 50
BERGEY, HANS 311, 326
BERGGREN, ELIZABETH 211
BERGMAN, HAROLD 227
BERINGER, PETER 72
BERKOWITZ, ALAN R. 227
BERKOWITZ, FRANCINE 320
BERND-COHEN, TINA 182
BERNER, ROBERT 251
BERNHARD, MARY 339
BERNHEIMER, R. A. 48

STAFF NAME INDEX 497

BERNSTEIN, CAROL 355
BERNSTEIN, JOHN 73
BERNSTEIN, NEIL 236
BERNSTEIN, PAMELA 197
BEROVITS, ANNETTE 351
BERRY, CHARLES R. 389
BERRY, CHARLES R., JR. 109
BERRY, JIM 314
BERRY, JOHN 23
BERRY, RICHARD 100
BERRYHILL, DON 55
BERRYMAN, JACK H. 228, 242
BERRYMAN, WILLIAM 83
BERTHELSEN, PETER S. 303
BERTHIAUME, BOB 282
BERTHIAUME, LUC 131
BERTRAND, BILL 340
BERTRAND, GERARD A. 253
BESKÉ, ALAN 288
BEST, CONSTANCE 247
BEST, PETER B. 321
BEST, STEPHEN 235
BEST, TROY L. 155
BETHELL, HELEN D. 253
BETIT, ROD 113
BETSILL, CARL 356
BETSOLD, ROBERT J. 28
BETTAS, GEORGE A. 167
BETTINGER, MARK 319
BETTS, LYNN 31
BEVACQUA, FRANK 8
BEVAN, D. 9
BEVERLIN, JERRY 63
BEVERLY, JOHN 302
BEVERSDORF, CHERYL A. 162
BEYER, DEAN E., JR. 355
BEYERLE, J. MICHAEL 101
BEZANSON, CHAR 257
BEZANSON, JANICE 331
BHUMBLA, D. K. 123
BIAGGI, ROBERTO E. 307
BIAGGNE, RUSS 224
BIANCHI, STEPHANIE 34
BIBEAULT, LUCIEN 311
BIBELRIETHER, HANS 204
BIBLER, BART 56
BICKFORD, JAMES 69
BICKNELL, WILLIAM B. 356
BIDDLE, JOEL 310
BIDER, BILL 67
BIDWELL, DENNIS 142
BIECHELE, DOUG 196
BIEKER, CHIRS 31
BIENEMAN, GRETCHEN L. 171
BIFERA, FRANK 90
BILBREY, ELLEN 43
BILBY, ROBERT E. 144
BILDSTEIN, KEITH L. 309
BILLIG, PRISCILLA P. 59
BILLING, VESTA C. 71
BILODEAU, GILBERT M. 71
BILSKI, NANINE 138
BINGAMAN, BOB 340
BINGAMAN, LARRY 316
BINGHAM, DEREK 362
BINGHAM, W. RICHARD 169
BINGMAN, BOB 318
BINKLEY, C. S. 368
BINNEY, GEORGE A. 332
BIRCH, CLARE J. 131
BIRCHER, NANCY 127
BIRCHFIELD, SUSAN 99
BIRD, MARY LYNNE 150
BIRD, PAUL E. 35
BIRDSALL, JOHN 303
BIRELY, LINDA E. 144
BIRES, FRAN 227
BISBEE, BILL 276
BISBEE, G. DANA 86
BISCHOFF, DONALD C. 28
BISHOP, GERALD 274
BISHOP, JOE 334
BISHOP, PARVIN L. 168
BISHOP, RICHARD 66
BISHOP, SARAH G. 301
BISSELL, JAMES 180
BISSET, DOUGLAS 135
BISSON, ALAIN 308
BISSON, HENRI 24
BISSONETTE, JOHN A. 113, 390
BIVANS, WAYNE 313
BIVENS, SANDY 200
BIVINGS, ALBERT E. 23
BIXBY, DONALD 152
BJERKE, JOHN 164
BJORNN, THEODORE C. 61
BLACK, DIANE 136
BLACK, SUSAN 75
BLACKBURN, WILBERT 32
BLACKLOCK, NADINE 257
BLACKMON, BOB 44, 367
BLACKMORE, E. 129
BLACKWELDER, BRENT 211
BLACKWELL, JACK A. 33
BLACKWELL, JOHN 362
BLACKWELL, LINDA 108
BLADES, MICHAEL 310
BLAHA, KATHY 337
BLAHNA, DALE 114
BLAIR, AARON 308
BLAIR, BOWEN 337
BLAIS, CLAUDETTE 132
BLAKE, J. 64, 129
BLAKE, ROBERT O. 184
BLAKE, WILLIAM M. 352
BLAKELY, DON 314
BLAKEMAN, PETER 85
BLAKESLEE, GEORGE M. 372
BLANCHARD, KATHLEEN A. 162
BLANCHARD, MARY JOSIE 25
BLANCHFIELD, JEFFRY 49
BLANCO, FRANSISCO JAVIER 189
BLANKENAU, DONALD G. 83
BLANKENSHIP, TERRY L. 346
BLANTON, NANCY 121
BLAUG, ELISABETH 10
BLAUVELT, MARK 336
BLAUWKAMP, TERRY 314
BLAZER, ARTHUR 276
BLEDSOE, PAUL 24
BLEDSOE, SUSAN M. 214
BLEED, ANN SALOMON 83
BLEIER, W. J. 384
BLESSINGTON, JACQUE 139
BLEVINS, B. B. 46
BLEVNS, B. B. 48
BLEW, RAYMOND L., JR. 285
BLICK, LARRY 31
BLILEY, THOMAS 5
BLINN, CHARLES R. 79
BLISS, JIM 182
BLISS, PATTY 136
BLOCH, BARBARA 47
BLOCK, RANCE 313
BLOCKSTEIN, DAVID E. 299
BLOOD, MARCUS 18
BLOOM, FLOYD E. 139
BLOOMBERG, AL 121
BLOOME, PETER 101
BLOOMER, LAWRENCE J. 107
BLOT, KIM T. 92
BLOUIN, GLEN 172
BLOYD, BARRY 99
BLUE, KAREN 187
BLUEMLE, JOHN P. 96
BLUM, PETE 64
BLUM, UDO 383
BLUMBERG, FRED 111
BLUMENFELD, JOSH 139
BLUMSTEIN, CARL 142
BLUNDO, JOHN 76
BOATWRIGHT, MIKE 68
BOBARAKIS, STEPHEN 91
BOBBITT, VAN M. 121
BOBZIEN, STEVEN 357
BODDICKER, MAJ. L. 183
BODE, JEFFREY JON 293
BODIN, MARK 328
BOE, JANET 355
BOEHM, DAVID 386
BOEHMER, PEGGY 162
BOEHMKE, JOHN 25
BOER, ARNOLD H. 128
BOERBOOM, JIM 78
BOERGERS, DAVID P. 14
BOERSMA, P. DEE 321
BOESCH, DONALD F. 377
BOEZI, LOUIS J. 12
BOGAN, SANDRA 206
BOGAR, DEBRA A. 263
BOGARD, CAROL 254
BOGER, BRUCE A. 35
BOGGESS, WILLIAM P., II 213
BOGGUS, TOM G. 111
BOGNER, TERRY 224
BOHAM, RUSSEL 368
BOHLE, JR., EDWARD R. 240
BOHLEN, E. U. 176
BOHMFALK, ERWIN 350
BOICE, L. PETER 13
BOKMA, ROBERT 29
BOKUNIEWICZ, H. J. 92
BOLDUC, HERVE 131
BOLEN, KENNETH R. 84
BOLEN, PATRICK 159
BOLGER, DAVID A. 28
BOLIVER, BRUCE 387
BOLLE, ROBERT L. 8
BOLLINGER, DON 344
BOLLINGER, TRENT 171
BOLTON, BERNIE 237
BOLTON, HANNIBAL 26, 143
BOND, ROB 134
BONDRUP-NIELS, SOREN 384
BONER, REX 187
BONGOLAN, DIXIE 301
BONILLA, HILDA 307
BONINE, JOHN 203
BONNEY, RICK 189
BONSER, MIKE 239
BONTADELLI, PETE 48
BOOKS, DAVE 82
BOONE, KATHY 315
BOONE, ROBERT E. 157
BOPP, DENNY 82
BORD, JEFF 360
BORD, ROGER 360
BORDELON, MIKE 101
BORDEN, DAVID V.D. 7
BORDOGNA, JOSEPH 34
BOREMAN, JOHN G. 377
BOREN, ANN F. 191
BOREN, JON 90
BOREN, MIKE 166
BORJA, MELVIN B. 59
BORN, STEPHEN 333
BORNEMAN, JANET 329
BORNER, MARKUS 211
BORRE, LISA 259
BORUFF, CHET 62
BOSH, JONI 157
BOSMAN, CORRIE 137
BOSSERT, TERRY R. 102
BOST, LARRY 165
BOST, RON 209
BOSTIC, JAMES E., JR. 214
BOSTICK, WILLIAM G., JR. 352
BOSWORTH, DALE 33
BOSWORTH, ROBERT 40
BOSWORTH, ROBERT W. 322
BOTELER, FRANK 120
BOTELER, FRANKLIN E. 61
BOTH, MEL 216
BOTTI, MARY 236
BOTTMAN, ROBERT P. 121
BOTTOMLEY, TIMOTHY 18
BOTTORFF, JIM 358
BOTTS, DEWEY 94, 95
BOTZLER, R. 351
BOUCHARD, GEORGE D. 128
BOUCHARD, J. ROBERT 196
BOULDEN, R. 37
BOULON, RALF H., JR. 115
BOULTON, MARK N. 229
BOURQUE, HERB 31
BOURQUE, PETER M. 71
BOURQUE, WAYNE 299
BOUTIN, TOM 41
BOVWER, EDWARD J. 376
BOWDEN, B. 272
BOWDEN, SHIRLEY 191
BOWER, GWEN 104
BOWERS, JANET L. 156
BOWERS, JEFFREY S. 122
BOWIE, D. 37
BOWIE, DAVID 333
BOWLER, TOM 237
BOWLES, IAN 188
BOWLES, JOHN 168
BOWMAN, MARGARET 154
BOWMAN, MARLENE 72
BOWMAN, PHIL 70
BOWMAN, STEVEN G. 117
BOWYER, JOHN S., JR. 86
BOYCE, MARK S. 358
BOYCE, TIMOTHY C. 40
BOYD, AVIS E. 328
BOYD, KEN 41, 42
BOYD, KENNETH 20
BOYD, ROBERT 221
BOYD, SUSAN 185
BOYD, TERRY 39
BOYD, WADE 347
BOYDSTUN, L. B. 48
BOYER, DOROTHY 349
BOYER, TOM 120
BOYKIE, TERRY 263
BOYKIN, BILL 107
BOYKIN, ESTHER 198
BOYKIN, LYNN 273
BOYLE, E. MICHAEL 347
BOYLE, HARVEY 128
BOYLE, STEWART 231
BOYLES, JOHN L. 355
BOYLES, ROBERT 182
BOYLES, ROBERT L. 295
BOYLESTON, LARRY 107
BOYUM, BILL 121
BOZEK, MICHAEL A. 123
BOZEK, NANCY C. 276
BRABANDER, JERRY 356
BRACE, ROBERT J. 361
BRACKETT, DAVID 36, 234
BRACKETT, SUSAN A. 256
BRADBERY, TERRY 116
BRADBURY, BETSY 268
BRADBURY, MICHAEL 356
BRADLE, TIM 263
BRADLEY, BILL 85
BRADLEY, DARBY 341
BRADLEY, HARRY 200
BRADLEY, RUTH S. 222
BRADSHAW, LINDA 161
BRADSTREET, MICHAEL 166
BRADWISCH, WILLIMA A. 145
BRADY, PEG 74
BRAGG, WILLIAM F. 352
BRAIBANTI, RALPH 16
BRAINERD, LYMAN B., JR. 165
BRAMBLE, BARBARA J. 274
BRAME, DICK 181
BRANAN, JOHNNY 58
BRANCH, CHARLES T. 79
BRANDLE, JAMES 380
BRANDON, HEATHER 361
BRANDRUP, MIKE 66
BRANDT, MIKE 262
BRANDWEIN, PAUL F. 304
BRANHAM, MIKE 232
BRANNAN, MARK 27
BRANNON, EDGAR B. 303
BRANTLY, ROBERT M. 325, 352
BRASWELL, ALLEN 20
BRASWELL, ALVIN 290
BRATSCH, GENE 178
BRAUS, JUDY 288
BRAXTON, LOWELL 113
BRAY, PAUL M. 160
BRAY, SHIRLEY 137
BRAZELTON, DON 65
BRAZIL, DIRK 119
BRAZIL, J. 129
BRDICKA, BARBARA 97
BREAKELL, JOHN 185
BREATHITT, LINDA K. 14
BREAU, KASHA 185
BREAUSSEAU, JERILYN 198
BREAZEALE, DANIEL P., SR. 107
BRECHER, ALAN M. 201
BRECKENRIDGE, RICHARD 224
BRECKENRIDGE, ROY M 62
BREEDY, JIM 228
BREEN, BARRY N. 11
BREESE, LYNN 298
BREEZE, ROGER 32
BREITE, DENNIS V. 361
BREITMEYER, RICHARD 47
BREMER, LINDA M. 352
BREMICKER, TIM 78
BREMIER, WALTER D. 368
BRENDEN, TRAVIS O. 149
BRENDLER, THOMAS 210
BRENNAN, LEONARD A. 329
BRENNEMAN, CLOYD E. 301
BRENNEMAN, RUSSELL 186
BRENNEMAN, RUSSELL L. 284
BRESHEARS, ALLEN W. 81
BRESSOR, JAMES E. 114
BRESTRUD, CRAIG 210
BREUTING, ROBERT G., Ph.D. 246
BREWER, WAYNE 91
BREWSTER, ALAN 363
BREZONIK, PATRICK 379
BRICE, WILLIAM 78
BRIDGES, ROCK 195
BRIDI, JEFFREY S. 103
BRIENICH, ANNA 302
BRIENZO, GARY 262
BRIGGS, GEORGE 139
BRIGGS, MARK 312, 323
BRIGGS, ROGER 46
BRIGGS, XAVIER de-SOUZA 15
BRIGHT, FAY 331
BRIKER, RICHARD W. 366
BRININSTOOL, BILL 89
BRINKLEY, DAVID G. 118
BRINKLEY, JESSIE 270
BRISCOE, ROBBIE B. 81
BRISKEY, LISA M. 350
BRISTOL, PETER 221
BRISTOL, TIM 325
BRISTOW, BRIAN T. 148
BRITT, BRUCE 208
BRITT, PEGGY 77
BRITTELL, DAVE 119
BRITTINGHAM, MARGARET 105
BRO, KENNETH M. 392
BROBRCK, ROD 298
BROCK, BARBARA GEYER 313
BROCK, GREG 55
BROCK, JENNY 208
BROCK, JOHN A. 214
BROCK, RICHARD E. 59
BROCK, ROBERT H., JR. 383
BROCKBANK, DOTTI 113
BROCKMAN, MATT 111
BROCKMANN, JANE 151
BRODA, JANICE 207
BRODDRICK, RYAN 48
BRODERICK, BRIAN 75
BRODERICK, STEPHEN 52
BRODERICK, THOMAS F. 75
BRODIE, PAM 318
BRODIE, W. B. 293
BRODY, ANNIE 197
BROGGI, JILL 266
BROGIE, MARK 283
BROHMAN, MARK 83
BROKAW, HOWARD P. 140
BROMLEY, PETER T. 94
BROOKRESON, BILL 120
BROOKS, BOB 193
BROOKS, CHRISTOPHER L. 108
BROOKS, CONNIE 113

Staff Name Index

STAFF NAME INDEX

BROOKS, IRENE B. ...103
BROOKS, JAMES ...71
BROOKS, JERRY ...55
BROOKS, KEVIN ...40
BROOKS, LILA ...170
BROOKS, MICHAEL J. ...194
BROOKS, R. J. ...386
BROOKS, WILLIAM ...107
BROOKS, WILLIAM T. ...26
BROSMAN, KEN ...226
BROTHERS, DAN ...39
BROTHERTON, TOM ...51
BROUGHTON, WILLIAM C. ...121
BROUHA, PAUL ...32, 152
BROUN, RICHARD ...15
BROUSSARD, AMY ...112
BROWDER, HAL C. ...365
BROWER, DAVID R. ...197
BROWN, A. GILSON ...138
BROWN, ANITA ...30
BROWN, ART ...120
BROWN, ARTHUR R., JR. ...87, 285
BROWN, BETH ...238
BROWN, BOB ...111, 246, 367, 389
BROWN, CARL ...273
BROWN, CAROL ...10, 100
BROWN, CHARLES, JR. ...273
BROWN, CRAIG L. ...50
BROWN, DANNY R. ...117
BROWN, DIANE V. ...105
BROWN, DON ...67
BROWN, DONALD ...314
BROWN, DONALD P. ...211
BROWN, DORI ...160
BROWN, FRANK ...68
BROWN, GARY ...125
BROWN, GEORGE W. ...386
BROWN, GREGORY N. ...391
BROWN, HUGH J. ...373
BROWN, JAMES E. ...101
BROWN, JEANETTE L. ...10
BROWN, JESSICA ...162
BROWN, JOE D. ...80
BROWN, JOHN W. ...59
BROWN, JUNE G. ...14
BROWN, KAREN ...37
BROWN, KAREN J. ...357
BROWN, KARL G. ...105
BROWN, KAY ...136, 137
BROWN, KIRK ...63
BROWN, LAWRENCE C. ...151
BROWN, LEE ...204
BROWN, LESTER R. ...363
BROWN, LINFIELD C. ...377
BROWN, MARVIN ...264
BROWN, MARVIN D. ...81
BROWN, MARY ...237
BROWN, MICHELE ...40
BROWN, NATE ...26
BROWN, OTIS ...231
BROWN, OTIS B. ...372
BROWN, PATRICK W. ...373
BROWN, PERRY J. ...380
BROWN, PETER G. ...195
BROWN, QUINCALEE ...345
BROWN, RANDALL L. ...49
BROWN, RICHARD ...313, 314
BROWN, ROBERT D. ...358
BROWN, RONALD A. ...80
BROWN, SCOTT ...89
BROWN, STEPHANIE ...172
BROWN, STEVE ...93
BROWN, THOMAS ...91
BROWN, TIM ...217, 246
BROWN, TOM ...55, 313
BROWN, TOMMY L. ...93, 382
BROWN, TORREY C. ...350
BROWN, VALERIE ...338
BROWN, WENDY ...288
BROWN, WHITNEY E. ...177
BROWNE, BROOKS ...203
BROWNELL, WILLIAM ...270
BROWNER, CAROL ...10
BROWNFIELD, RAY ...188
BROWNING, DAVE ...198
BROZ, GORDON ...76
BRUBAKER, CAROLE CASTO ...64
BRUBAKER, DAVID ...218
BRUCE, ANN ...329
BRUCE, GERON ...40
BRUCE, JAMES R. ...323
BRUCE, KATHRYN ...36
BRUCKER, THOMAS H. ...291
BRUCKNER, CHARLES ...104
BRUELL, HARRY ...264
BRUENE, DAN ...237
BRUENING, GLEN ...90
BRUFFY, ROBERT ...15
BRUMBACH, JOE ...101
BRUMM, JERRY ...306
BRUNER, CLARK ...39
BRUNINGA, KRISTIN RIPPETO ...331
BRUNNER, JUDY ...121
BRUNNER, THOMAS ...179
BRUNS, DALE A. ...387

BRUNSON, MARTIN W. ...81
BRUS, KEITH ...303
BRUSENDORFF, ANNE CHRISTINE ...7
BRUSH, GRACE S. ...376
BRUSH, PETER N. ...13
BRUST, PATRICIA ...349
BRYAN, CHARLES F. ...69, 375
BRYAN, RORKE B. ...386
BRYAN, SUSAN MILES ...261
BRYANT, ART ...240
BRYANT, DANA ...55
BRYANT, DAVID ...58
BRYANT, DOUGLAS E. ...108
BRYANT, FRED C. ...390
BRYANT, HAROLD ...31
BRYANT, LARRY ...179
BRYANT, MAGALEN O. ...267
BRYANT, MASON D. ...144
BRYANT, SHERMAN ...225
BRYCE, PHILIP A. ...85
BRYNE, DONALD H. ...118
BRYSON, CAROLYN ...226
BRYSON, JOHN C. ...256
BUCCINI, J. ...37
BUCHANAN, GALE A. ...58
BUCHANAN, ROGER ...367
BUCHANAN, STUART ...91
BUCHANAN, WADE ...51
BUCHER, H. WILLIAM ...165
BUCHERT, BEVERLY ...387
BUCHNER, JAY ...337
BUCHNER, KATHY ...334
BUCK, MICHAEL G. ...60
BUCKELEW, A. R., JR. ...168
BUCKLEY, BILL ...360
BUCKLEY, ROBERT G. ...112
BUCKLIN, ANN ...86
BUCKMAN, ARTHUR ...17
BUDD, BOB ...321
BUDD, WILLIAM ...392
BUDNEY, GREGORY ...189
BUDNIK, STEVE ...262
BUDZIK, MICHAEL ...97
BUECHLER, DENNIS ...183
BUECKEN, DONNA VAN ...349
BUEHLER, DAVID ...357
BUFFETT, JIMMY ...316
BUFFINGTON, JOHN D. ...26
BUHLER, ANDY ...168
BUHLER, MARILYN ...168
BUISCH, WILLIAM W. ...30
BUISING, CHARISSE ...280
BULGER, PAUL ...257
BULL, JULIANNA F. ...96
BULLARD, JAMES ...168
BULLOCK, JIMMY ...258
BULLOCK, MIKE ...55
BULLOCK, STEVE ...190
BULLOCK, THOMAS F. ...286
BULMAN, JIM ...66
BUMA, GERRIT ...357
BUNDY, SUSAN ...106
BUNDY, WILLIAM F. ...106
BUNN, RICHARD ...269
BUNNING, BONNIE ...121
BUNTING, BRUCE W. ...363
BUNURI, TARIQ J. ...234
BURACK, TOM ...164
BURCH, RICHARD E. ...195
BURCH, TOMMY ...331
BURCHARD, CHRISTI ...261
BURCHELL, L. CHARLES ...379
BURCHFIELD, JAMES ...380
BURDEN, ALLEN ...28
BURDETTE, JOHN ...346
BURDICK, LALOR ...284
BURDICK, NEAL ...134
BUREAU, SANDRA ...90
BUREK, TOM ...136
BURGDORF, JAYNA ...112
BURGER, ALAN ...300
BURGER, BILL ...353
BURGER, CARL ...142
BURGER, J. ...368
BURGESS, DAVID ...387
BURGESS, HARRIET ...151
BURGESS, VAN ...113
BURGETT, MEG ...136
BURGEYNE, GEORGE E., JUR. ...76
BURGSTRUM, SUE ...238
BURHENNE, W. E. ...229
BURHENNE-GUILMIN, FRANCOISE ...234
BURKE, ALBERTA ...170
BURKE, DAVID ...73
BURKE, J. AUSTIN ...25
BURKE, MARK ...276
BURKE, MARK A. ...361
BURKE, PATRICIA M. ...78
BURKE, PATTY ...78
BURKE, RON ...224
BURKE, STEVEN F. ...289, 351
BURKE, TIMOTHY ...134
BURKERT, RONALD P. ...314
BURKHALTER, PAUL ...57
BURKHART, HAROLD E. ...391

BURKHART, JIM ...140
BURKS, DENNIS ...44
BURKS, JEFFREY S. ...113
BURKS, JOCKO ...344
BURKS, MARGARET ...252
BURLINGTON, D. BRUCE ...14
BURMAN, HOWARD R. ...214
BURMASTER, RAY ...170
BURNETT, GARY ...277
BURNETT, GROVE ...346
BURNETT, STEVE ...171
BURNEY, DARYL ...258
BURNHAM, KENNETH P. ...50
BURNHAM, LAURIE ...176
BURNHAM, WILLIAM ...303
BURNHAM, WILLIAM A. ...303
BURNLEY, BEN R. ...195
BURNS, DENVER P. ...33
BURNS, HERBERT ...76
BURNS, JAMES W. ...47
BURNS, KATHRYN ...272
BURNS, STEPHEN G. ...35
BURNS, WILLIAM ...20
BURPEE, ROBERT ...13
BURRESON, E. M. ...391
BURTON, JIM ...42
BURTON, JOHN V. ...44
BURTON, MIKE ...195
BURTON, NELSON ...240
BURTON, ROBERT ...20
BURTT, EDWARD H., JR. ...358
BURTT, TONY ...231
BURWELL, DAVID ...308
BUSCH, RICK ...116
BUSCH, STEPHEN D. ...192
BUSE, JOHN ...201
BUSH, CHARLES ...68
BUSH, DONNA ...348
BUSHEY, THOMAS ...115
BUSHWAY, RODNEY ...376
BUSHY, TOM ...115
BUSSERT, ELLEN ...98
BUSTY, F. E. ...114
BUTAMINA, KABUIKA ...385
BUTCHER, GREGORY S. ...141
BUTELHO, KIM ...164
BUTLER, C. ...129
BUTLER, LUVENIA ...110
BUTLER, PAUL J. ...310
BUTLER, PEGGY ...344
BUTLER, SYDNEY J. ...157
BUTLER, TOM ...348
BUTTERFIELD, BRUCE ...268
BUTTFIELD, CARY ...253
BUTTON, KAREN ...136
BUTTS, G. GREG ...43
BUZICKY, GREG ...78
BYERS, C. RANDALL ...167
BYERS, KURT ...41
BYFORD, JIM ...389
BYFORD, RON ...90
BYKER, GAYLEN J. ...314
BYRNE, CHRIS ...212
BYRNE, LESLIE ...14
BYRNE, ROBERT L. ...353
BYRUM, LARRY ...98

C

CABASSO, ISRAEL ...383
CABLE, TED T. ...374
CABOT JR., CHARLES ...188
CABUSAO, DOMINGO S. ...59
CACCESE, ALBERT E. ...93
CACKETTE, TOM ...46
CADE, TOM J. ...303
CADUTO, MARIE LEVESQUE ...341
CAESAR, PETULA ...307
CAFAZZO, VEDA M. ...295
CAGNONI, TODD ...225
CAHILL, JOHN P. ...91
CAHILL, M. ...129
CAHOON, DONALD ...322
CAIN, ALAN G. ...41
CAIN, RICHARD ...80
CAIRNS, JOHN, JR. ...391
CALAMBOKIDIS, JOHN ...91
CALDWELL, COLLEEN A. ...89, 144
CALFEE, ALAN ...254
CALHOUN, CHARLES ...25
CALHOUN, JACK ...284
CALHOUN, JEAN A. ...42
CALKINS, JOHN ...159
CALKINS, WILLIAM ...24
CALLAHAN, DEB ...247
CALLAHAN, JOHN J. ...14
CALLAN, LEONARD J. ...35
CALLAWAY, DIANE ...139
CALLENDER, JIM ...170
CALLENDER, WILLIAM A. ...248
CALLICOTT, J. BAIRD ...175, 233
CALQUHOUN, BARBARA ...119
CALSSLE, BETH ...292

CALVERLEY, BRETT ...194
CALVERT, WILLIAM ...19
CALVIN, DAVID J. ...362
CALVO, PATRICK ...300
CAMENZIND, FRANZ J. ...242
CAMERON, BARRY ...384
CAMERON, BOB ...128
CAMERON, DON ...267
CAMHI, MERRY ...265
CAMP, JUDITH ...246
CAMP, PAUL J. ...26
CAMP, SAMUEL ...60
CAMPA, HENRY, III ...355
CAMPBELL, BRAD ...10
CAMPBELL, CARL ...69
CAMPBELL, DANIEL D. ...34
CAMPBELL, ERICK ...189
CAMPBELL, FAITH T. ...188
CAMPBELL, JAMES ...255
CAMPBELL, JOHN ...299
CAMPBELL, LEE ...182
CAMPBELL, LINDA ...331, 357
CAMPBELL, MARILYN F. ...224
CAMPBELL, R. E. ...99
CAMPBELL, TREVOR ...56
CAMPEN, DONALD O., JR. ...118
CAMPION, TOM ...293
CANCILLA, JODEANE ...250
CANDEE, ROGER ...166
CANHAM, CHARLES D. ...227
CANNALEY, PAUL ...174
CANNON, ED ...290
CANNON, MONA ...319
CANNON, SHELTON M. ...14
CANNON, STUART M. ...23
CANNON, SUE ...99
CANNY, M. ...8
CANTER, BRAM D.E., ESQ ...207
CANTON, STEVE ...288
CANTOR, RAY ...86
CANTRELL, SHAWN ...212
CANTU, NORMA V. ...13
CANTU, REYNALDO ...234
CANZANO, PASQUALE S. ...53
CAPITO, CHARLES P. ...122
CAPLINGER, KEN ...122
CAPORALE, WALTER ...230
CAPOTOSTO, PAUL ...186
CAPPELLI, MARTIN A. ...106
CAPUTO, GUY P. ...35
CARACO, NINA M. ...227
CARDAMONE, JEREMIAH J., ESQ ...345
CARETTE, JACQUES ...38
CAREY, HENRY H. ...210
CAREY, JOHN ...12
CAREY, ROBERT L. ...357
CARGILE, R.L. ...43
CARIS, BARRY ...165
CARISON, STEVEN A. ...368
CARL, A.B. ...338
CARLEY, WAYNE W. ...263
CARLIN, DAVE ...28
CARLINE, ROBERT F. ...104, 142, 387
CARLOUGH, YOLA ...210
CARLSON, BETH ...136, 137
CARLSON, CATHY ...275
CARLSON, CHUCK ...260
CARLSON, DAVID ...50
CARLSON, FRED ...87
CARLSON, HERB ...305
CARLSON, JAN ...97
CARLSON, MIKE ...136
CARLSON, STEPHAN ...79
CARLSTROM, TERRY ...25
CARLTON, GARY ...46
CARLTON, GINNY ...359
CARLTON, JASPER ...166
CARLY, KEITH ...170
CARMAN, SAM ...202
CARMICHAEL, TIM ...181
CARMICHAEL, WILLIAM D. ...301
CARNEVALE, ELLEN ...305
CARNEY, JAMES ...83
CARNEY, JAN K. ...115
CARON, DIANE ...88
CAROTHERS, LESLIE ...185
CARPENTER, BETSY ...88
CARPENTER, JESSE A. ...311
CARPENTER, LEN ...353
CARPENTER, LEN H. ...358
CARPENTER, TAMMY L. ...141
CARPER, THOMAS R. ...7
CARR, ARCHIE, III ...351
CARR, BRUCE ...157
CARR, CAROLYN ...318
CARR, DAVID ...173
CARR, TIMOTHY ...67
CARRE, PETER J. ...239
CARRIER, MIKE ...66
CARRIER, NORMAN D. ...131
CARRIERRE, MURDOCH ...132
CARRIGAN, WADE ...290
CARRILLO, PAUL ...48
CARROLL, AUSTIN ...247
CARROLL, JAMES L. ...273

STAFF NAME INDEX 499

CARROLL, JOHN ... 342
CARROLL, ROBERT ... 295
CARROW, CYNTHIA ... 347
CARSALAD, H. ... 209
CARSON, C. DEAN ... 107
CARSON, CHARLES G., III ... 352
CARSON, EVERETT B. ... 278
CARSON, GENE ... 159
CARSON, JACK ... 99
CARSON, PAUL E. ... 314
CARTEE, LARRY D. ... 299
CARTER, ALLEN ... 44
CARTER, ALLEN D. ... 285
CARTER, BILLY ... 80
CARTER, CURT ... 202
CARTER, DAVID ... 267
CARTER, DOUGLAS ... 312
CARTER, ED ... 110
CARTER, JAMES A. ... 76
CARTER, JAMES R. ... 193
CARTER, JIM ... 336
CARTER, JIMMY ... 136
CARTER, LARRY ... 226
CARTER, THOMAS ... 240
CARTER, WILFRED M. ... 163
CARTIN, ANITA ... 287
CARTLIDGE, ROBERT ... 296
CARTWRIGHT, ALLEN W., JR. ... 73
CARY, DAN ... 56
CASADA, JIM ... 299
CASADEVALL, THOMAS ... 24
CASADEVALL, THOMAS J. ... 26
CASE, BOYD ... 38
CASE, DELBERT W. ... 196
CASE, DUANE ... 256
CASE, JAMES C. ... 126
CASE, LARRY D. ... 267
CASE, MARSHAL T. ... 338
CASE, RONALD M ... 380
CASELLA, SAM ... 154
CASEY, CHARLIE ... 212
CASEY, P. JEFFREY ... 34
CASHDAN, LISA ... 337
CASRER, JOHN ... 87
CASSADA, DAWN L. ... 51
CASSAT, RICHARD ... 44
CASSELMAN, JOHN ... 143
CASSELMAN, TRACY ... 356
CASSIDY, THOMAS J, JR. ... 154
CASSTEVENS, KAY L. ... 13
CASTANO, JUANITA ... 235
CASTANZDA, KENIA ... 234
CASTLE, CHRIS BARNEY ... 215
CASTLES, TOM ... 260
CASTLETON, CARL ... 29
CASTRO, BERNADETTE ... 93
CATANESE, CAROL ... 348
CATES, GEORGE L. ... 272
CATES, ROBERT D. ... 49
CATLIN, RONALD ... 109
CATO, JAMES C. ... 55
CATON, PATTI ... 388
CATTANY, RONALD W. ... 50
CATTON, JON ... 218
CAUTHEN, STEPHEN M. ... 40
CAVALLO, SHARON ... 261
CAVANAUGH-GRANT, DEBORAH ... 224
CAVERLY, TIM ... 72
Caves, H.A. ... 98
CAWTHON, DON ... 389
CAZA, CAROLINE ... 352
CECCHINI, DAN, JR. ... 289
CECCHINI, EVELEEN ... 341
CECCHINI, SUE ... 289
CECERE, AL LOUIS ... 268
CECIL, JARVIS B. ... 347
CECIL, MARIA W. ... 191
CELEBREZZE, ANTHONY J., III ... 295
CELLARIUS, RICHARD, JR. ... 319
CENARRUSA, PETE T. ... 61
CERAMI, EMMA ... 80
CERSKI, JOE ... 301
CERTO, RICK ... 29
CERVOSKI, ANDREA ... 358
CESSNA, STELLA ... 80
CESTERO, BARB ... 323
CHABOT, WARNER ... 176
CHACKO, A. JIM ... 376
CHAFEE, JOHN H. ... 3, 6
CHAFFIN, CHRIS ... 160, 271
CHAIKOVSKY, HELEN ... 203
CHALLINOR, DAVID ... 135
CHALMERS-WATSON, NICOLA ... 362
CHAMBERLAIN, DENISE K. ... 102
CHAMBERLAIN, LEE ... 204
CHAMBERLAIN, WILLIAM ... 287
CHAMBLEE, CARY D. ... 108
CHAMPBELL, LESLIE ... 72
CHAMPEAU, RANDY ... 393
CHAMUT, PAT ... 36
CHAN, STELLA ... 199
CHAN, SUSAN ... 139
CHANCELLOR, RICHARD ... 125
CHANDA, DAVID ... 87
CHANDLER, C. RAY ... 161
CHANDLER, HARRY ... 342
CHANDLER, MIKE ... 44
CHANDLER, WILLIAM J. ... 270
CHANEY, ED ... 293
CHANG, DAVID ... 382
CHANG, MINGTEH ... 389
CHANNEL, DAVID ... 364
CHANTRY, CHRISTINE ... 263
CHAPCO, WILLIAM ... 388
CHAPIN, CHARLES E. ... 89
CHAPIN, JIM ... 209
CHAPLIN, ANGELA ... 342
CHAPMAN, BOB C. ... 44
CHAPMAN, DANA ... 323
CHAPMAN, DEB ... 202
CHAPMAN, SANDRA ... 372
CHAPPELL, GORDON ... 343
CHAPPELL, JOHN ... 247
CHARLAND, DAVE ... 205
CHARLES, ... 64
CHARLES, LALORA ... 326
CHASAN, REBECCA ... 151
CHASE, JAYNI ... 175
CHASE, KENNETH S. ... 196
CHASE, ROBERT F. ... 267
CHATEAUNEUF, RUSSELL J. ... 106
CHATWOOD, CAROL ... 297
CHAVE, EDITH H. ... 220
CHAVERS, JIMMY ... 18
CHAVEZ, CARL ... 49
CHAZIN, DANIEL ... 287
CHEATER, MARK ... 279
CHEKAY, D. A. ... 194
CHENG, PEG ... 293
CHENOWETH, RICHARD ... 306
CHENOWITH, MIKE ... 240
CHEPEL, LEONARD I. ... 292
CHEREL, DONNA ... 279
CHERRY, AL ... 233
CHERRY, JOHN ... 55
CHESEMORE, RONALD G. ... 14
CHESKY, DAVID ... 230
CHESNEY, NORMA ... 214
CHICKERING, PERI ... 331
CHILD, DENNIS ... 370
CHILD, WILLIAM ... 63
CHILDRESS, DON ... 66, 82
CHILDS, STARLING W. ... 165
CHINCHILLI, JOLENE ... 178, 302
CHING, PATRICK ... 19
CHINLUND, DEDE ... 323
CHINN, JIM ... 306
CHIPMAN, RICHARD B. ... 356
CHIPPING, DAVID ... 169
CHIPPONERI, L. LUCINDA ... 49
CHISM, JOHN E. ... 245
CHISOLM, CHARLES H. ... 79
CHOA, TERESITA ... 361
CHOKSI, KASHYAP ... 262
CHORNESKY, LIZ ... 279
CHREST, HELEN ... 138
CHRISTENBURY, EDWARD S. ... 36
CHRISTENSEN, ALAN ... 313
CHRISTENSEN, BILL ... 313
CHRISTENSEN, DALE ... 100
CHRISTENSEN, DOUG ... 223
CHRISTENSEN, JAMES ... 113
CHRISTENSEN, JIM ... 236
CHRISTENSEN, MARY ... 164
CHRISTENSEN, NORMAN L. ... 383
CHRISTENSEN, STAN ... 297
CHRISTENSEN, TOM ... 291
CHRISTENSEN, WALTER A. ... 29
CHRISTENSON, JAMES A. ... 43
CHRISTIAN, QUENTINE ... 138
CHRISTIAN, RICHARD T. ... 148
CHRISTIAN, TIM ... 313
CHRISTIANSON, JAY ... 113
CHRISTIE, RHIAN ... 355
CHRISTISEN, D. M. ... 259
CHRISTMAN, RUSSELL F. ... 384
CHUDLEIGH, TED ... 131
CHURA, MARK R. ... 53
CHYTILO, MARC ... 201
CICHRA, CHARLES ... 56
CIELO, ANGEL ... 29
CILEK, JEFFREY R. ... 303
CINFIO, RALPH ... 313
CISAR, ELIZABETH J. ... 187
CISNEROS, ELLA ... 332
CITSAY, MARK ... 257
CITTA, JR., JOE ... 283
CLAEYS, THOMAS ... 96
CLAFLIN, THOMAS ... 393
CLAIR, FRANK ST. ... 82
CLAMEN, MURRAY ... 8
CLANCEY, PAT ... 260
CLAPPER, CHARLES ... 25
CLAPPER, RUSSELL W. ... 275
CLARK, BETH ... 158
CLARK, BRUCE ... 63
CLARK, CAMERON D. ... 131
CLARK, CHRISTOPHER ... 189
CLARK, DEBBIE L. ... 14
CLARK, EDWARD E., JR. ... 350
CLARK, EDWARD, JR. ... 273
CLARK, JAMIE R. ... 26
CLARK, JAMIE RAPPAPORT ... 24, 26
CLARK, JERRY ... 267
CLARK, JOHN ... 170
CLARK, JON ... 184
CLARK, MARTHA ... 252
CLARK, MIKE ... 218, 300
CLARK, NANCY ... 43, 206
CLARK, PEGGY ... 209
CLARK, RAY ... 10
CLARK, ROBERT ... 269
CLARK, ROBERT O. ... 366
CLARK, ROGER ... 56
CLARK, ROSS ... 375
CLARK, SANDY ... 81
CLARK, SHARON ... 77
CLARK, SUSAN ... 341
CLARK, TOM ... 257
CLARKE, CHARLES C. ... 11
CLARKE, H. A. ... 37
CLARKE, KATHLEEN ... 113
CLARKE, LORETTA ... 128
CLARKE, MARION L. ... 55, 56
CLARKE, NANCY ... 206
CLARKSON, DAN ... 313
CLARTEN, PAUL V. ... 314
CLASBY, BOB ... 40
CLATTERBUCK, WAYNE K. ... 245
CLAUSSEN, JULIE E. ... 146
CLAY, BOB ... 194
CLAY, BRUCE ... 63
CLAY, L. ... 173
CLAY, WILLIAM H. ... 29
CLAYPOOLE, DALE ... 46
CLAYTON, CHARLES ... 241
CLAYTON, CHUCK ... 324
CLAYTON, PAT ... 205
CLAYTOR, P.E., RICHARD A. ... 177
CLEAR, JAMES J. ... 15
CLEARY, FRANCES ... 287
CLEARY, MICHAEL ... 196
CLEARY, PAT ... 245
CLEAVER, JERRY ... 16
CLEGG, MICHAEL T. ... 47
CLEM, FIONA ... 94
CLEM, JOHN C. ... 228
CLEMENT, STEPHANIE M. ... 211
CLEMMER, GLENN ... 84, 85
CLEVELAND, THEODORE G. ... 390
CLEVER, ROBERT E. ... 332
CLEWELL, RICHARD ... 21
CLIBURN, J. W. ... 379
CLIFFORD, RICHARD K. ... 52
CLINCH, BUD ... 83
CLINE, DAVE ... 246
CLINE, JOHN R. ... 259
CLINE, MIKE ... 250
CLINE, TIM ... 365
CLOSE, MELVIN D. ... 84
CLOSSON, LARRY ... 63
CLOTWORTHY, CHRISTOPHER ... 311
CLOUGH, RICH ... 82
CLOUTIER, TERRY ... 314
CLUGSTON, RICHARD M. ... 222
CLUSEN, CHARLES ... 142
CLUTTER, DAVID ... 277
COAD, JOSEPHINE B. ... 59
COAN, GENE ... 318
COATES, PHILIP G. ... 75
COATS, J. D. ... 297
COATS, ROBERT ... 226
COBB, ALTON B. ... 80
COBB, DAVID T. ... 95
COBB, JAMES C. ... 68
COBB, JANET S. ... 365
COBB, THOMAS L. ... 160
COBLE, DANIEL W. ... 123, 393
COBOURN, JOHN ... 85
COBURN, THOMAS ... 383
COCCHIARELLA, VICKI ... 82
COCHRAN, DONALD K. ... 74
COCHRAN, J. KIRK ... 92
COCHRAN, LARRY ... 343
COCHRAN, PHIL ... 345
COCHRAN, STEVE ... 202
COCHRANE, CHARLES S. ... 278
COCKRELL, DAVID ... 349
COCKRELL, FREEDY ... 206
CODY, MARTIN L. ... 369
COEN, ROSS ... 292
COFFEY, DAN J. ... 40
COFFEY, KAREN ... 285
COFFIN, SHARON ... 132
COFFMAN, CHARLES C. ... 122
COHEN, DAVE ... 159
COHEN, EDWARD ... 24
COHEN, ELANA ... 248
COHEN, NEVIN ... 226
COHEN, WILLIAM ... 13
COHEN, WILLIAM M. ... 15
COKINOS, CHRIS ... 243
COLADARCI, KELLY ... 242
COLANGELO, PETER A. ... 103
COLBERT, K. ... 129
COLBURN, KENNETH A. ... 86
COLBURN, WILLIAM ... 311
COLBY, RICHARD ... 381
COLE, CATHY ... 212
COLE, DONALD ... 23
COLE, JONATHAN J. ... 227
COLE, LESLIE ... 69
COLE, MARILYN ... 139
COLE, MOLLY, ... 379
COLE, PRESTON ... 262
COLE, RICHARD A. ... 382
COLE, ROGER H. ... 156
COLE, TOM ... 20, 220
COLEMAN, BOB ... 20
COLEMAN, CATHERINE ... 23
COLEMAN, ELIZABETH B. ... 70
COLEMAN, JOHN ... 48, 338
COLEMAN, MARK S. ... 98
COLEMAN, RONNY J. ... 49
COLEMAN, RUTH ... 198
COLEMAN, STEPHEN A. ... 69
COLEMAN, STEVE ... 69
COLEMAN, TOM ... 20
COLES, DICK ... 348
COLES, SHEILA ... 348
COLETTE, MARTINE ... 358
COLEY, R. W. ... 194
COLGROVE, GARY S. ... 30
COLLIER, CAROL ... 102
COLLIER, CAROL R. ... 7
COLLINS, CARRIE ... 154
COLLINS, EDMOND B. ... 123
COLLINS, KAREN ... 49
COLLINS, KEITH ... 29
COLLINS, LEROY, III ... 165
COLLINS, MARK ... 361
COLLINS, NANCY ... 235
COLLINS, PATRICK ... 29
COLLINS, RALPH ... 69
COLLINS, RESEE ... 206
COLLINS, RICHARD W. ... 72
COLLINS, ROBERT ... 279
COLLINS, SAMUEL J. ... 35
COLLISON, DEBBIE ... 179
COLLOPY, MICHAEL W. ... 386
COLOMA-AGARAN, GILBERT S. ... 60
COLOMBO, ROBERT ... 145
COLON, AILEEN ... 34
COLTON, ELDON L. ... 238
COLTON, JOHN H. ... 252
COLVIN, BILL ... 79
COLVIN, GORDON ... 91
COLVIN, WILLIAM ... 196
COLWELL, KEITH ... 130
COLWELL, MARK ... 368
COLWELL, RITA ... 34, 139
COLWELL, STEPHEN ... 189
COMBS, TERRY ... 183
COMEAU, ROXANNE ... 172
COMPTON, DONNA C. ... 337
COMPTON, JIM ... 312
COMPTON, STEVEN C. ... 268
CONANT, BRUCE ... 337
CONDA, JUDY ... 208
CONDER, GRACE M. ... 215
CONDON, BABS ... 213
CONDON, MARK ... 250
CONE, JOSEPH ... 101
CONGEL, FRANK ... 35
CONGLETON, JAMES L. ... 61
CONKEY, ALICE ... 270
CONKLE, TAMMY ... 269
CONKLIN, ED ... 54, 55
CONKLING, PHILIP W. ... 239
CONLEY, JAN ... 217, 246
CONLEY, JERRY M. ... 81
CONLEY, RON ... 57
CONNELL, JIM ... 132
CONNELL, KATHLEEN ... 50
CONNELLY, B. A. ... 130
CONNELLY, KENNETH L. ... 168
CONNELLY, PETER ... 128
CONNER, MARK C. ... 179
CONNOLLY, JAMES ... 157
CONNOLLY, MATTHEW B., JR. ... 196
CONNOR, ELEANOR ... 385
CONNORS, RHEA ... 293
CONOVER, MARION ... 66, 258
CONOVER, MICHAEL ... 390
CONRAD, ANN ... 211
CONRAD, CAROLYN ... 168
CONRAD, MARIANNE ... 285
CONRAD, W. BROCK ... 108
CONROY, DONALD B. ... 288
CONROY, MICHAEL J. ... 57
CONSOLVO, CHARLES W. ... 239
CONSTANTZ, GEORGE ... 312
CONTI, FRANK ... 49
CONVERSE, KATHY ... 351
CONWAY, KEVIN ... 113
CONWAY, MICHAEL D. ... 103
CONWAY, MIKE ... 40
CONWAY, WILLIAM ... 351
COOCH, EDWARD W., JR. ... 179
COOGAN, MIKE ... 294
COOK, ALISON ... 312
COOK, CAROLYN RIDGEWAY ... 391
COOK, DEAN ... 134
COOK, DIANE M. ... 231

Staff Name Index

500 **STAFF NAME INDEX**

Staff Name Index

COOK, DON 128
COOK, EDWARD H. 99
COOK, ERNEST 337
COOK, FELIX W. 25
COOK, GLENN 254
COOK, HARRY N. 273
COOK, JIM D. 347
COOK, JOHN 2, 25
COOK, JOHN R., JR. 201
COOK, MICHAEL B. 12
COOK, MICHAEL L. 165
COOK, RICHARD 164
COOK, ROBERT 351
COOK, ROBERT L. 112
COOK, SUSAN 121
COOK, WAYNE E. 10
COOK, WM. RON 29
COOKE, GILBERT 368
COOKE, GREGG 11
COOKE, MARGARET R. 76
COOKENDORFER, PAUL 327
COOKSEY, JAMES L. 111
COOKSEY, SARAH 53
COOL, DONALD A. 35
COOL, K. L. 76
COOLEY, DON 39
COOLEY, MIKE 249
COON, JOHN 300
COONROD, BRUCE 109
COONS, JANICE 373
COOPER, CARDELL 15
COOPER, GORDON 287
COOPER, JACK 221
COOPER, JOHN 109
COOPER, KATHY 172
COOPER, KEVIN 353
COOPER, L. FRANK 335
COOPER, RICK 121
COOPER, RITA 120
COOPER, TOBY 261
COOPERMAN, HOWARD 33
COPASS, LUCY 248
COPE, OLIVER B. 151
COPELAND, KATHY 56
COPONY, JAMES A. 116
COPPELMAN, PETER D. 15
COPPING, ANDREA 121
COPPINGER, PAUL L. 14
CORAN, LAURIE 352
CORBIN, JOHN S. 60
CORBIN, LEROY C. 104
CORDES, JOHN F., JR. 35
CORDIVIOLA, STEVEN J. 68
CORDOVA, ROBERT 182
COREIL, PAUL D. 70
CORESON, RICHARD 100
CORKRAN, DON K. 165
CORLETT, WILLIAM S. 302
CORNELIUS, MICHAEL 17
CORNELIUS, STEVE 323
CORNELL, JILL 287
CORNELL, RONALD C. 295
CORNETT, BRUCE 295
CORNUS, H. P. 293
CORNWALL, G. 37
CORR, WILLIAM 14
CORRAL, THAIS 361
CORRELL, DAVID L. 320
CORSO, MICHAEL 292
CORVEN, JIM 347
CORWIN, WICKHAM 196
CORY, WALLACE N. 62
COSTA, CATHERINE A. 285
COSTANZA, ROBERT 233
COSTELLO, JOHN T. 64
COTE, DIANA 40
COTE, LAWRENCE S. 123
COTNOIR, LILIANE 217
COTSWORTH, ELIZABETH 11
COTTER, B. PAUL, JR. 35
COTTINGHAM, KALEEN 120
COTTLE, CURT 107
COTTRELL, KIRBY 63
COTTRELL, MARIE 19
COUCH, JOHN 344
COUFAL, JAMES E. 322
COUGHLIN, PAUL F. 357
COUINS, VANNESSA 165
COULOMBE, MARY 303
COULON, CHRISTINA 31
COULTER, JANE 32
COULTER, L. L. 141
COUMBE, LOUISE 180
COUNTS, TOM U. 353
COURSON, BUD 70
COURTEMANCHE, GERRY 297
COURTER, J. CARLTON, III 117
COURTNEY, DEBORAH 118
COURTNEY, DENZIL 140
COURTNEY, ELIZABETH 341
COURTNEY, F. G. 184
COURTNEY, WILL 249
COURVILLE, MARY L. 348
COUSINS, WALTER B. 323
COUSTEAU, FRANCINE 190
COUSTON, TOM 216
COWAN, JOHN 140
COWART, VICKI 50
COWELL, SKIP 219
COWEN, RAYMOND, III 91
COWIN, TIMOTHY H. 93
COWPERTHWAITE, JAMES M. 183
COX, GREGORY 254
COX, J. ROBERT 318
COX, LINDA J. 118
COX, LIZ 258
COX, MICHAEL 276
COXE, TRUDY 74
COZENS, TOBY 142
CRABB, A. CHARLES 47
CRABB, DAN 55
CRADDOCK, J. HILL 141
CRADICK, AMY 87
CRAFT, JEREMY 55
CRAFT, ROBERT D. 117
CRAGO, TRACEY I. 76
CRAIG, CHARLES 100
CRAIG, CLIFFORD B. 114
CRAIG, JON 98
CRAIG, RAY 101
CRAIGHEAD, CHARLES S. 190
CRAIGHEAD, DEREK J. 190
CRAIGHEAD, FRANK C., JR. 190
CRAIGHEAD, FRANK L. 190
CRAIGHEAD, JOHN J. 190
CRAM, ROBERT 327
CRAMER, JOYCE W. 305
CRANDALL, DERRICK 152
CRANDALL, DERRICK A. 154
CRANE, DALE 270
CRANE, FRED 237
CRANE, KELLY 126
CRANE, NEIL 250
CRANE, TED 49
CRANER, LORI 287
CRANFORD, GERALD F. 35
CRAPA, JOSEPH R. 10
CRAVEN, BILL 243
CRAVEN, SCOTT 125
CRAVES, JULIE 254
CRAWFORD, BOB 54
CRAWFORD, BRUCE 119
CRAWFORD, PHILLIP E. 121
CRAWFORD, RICHARD 95
CRAWFORD, RICHARD D. 384
CRAWFORD, WALTER C., JR. 361
CRAWFORD, WM. H. 98
CRAWFORTH, TERRY 84
CRAWFORTH, TERRY R. 85
CREECH, DENNIS 326
CREIGHTON, ALBERT, JR. 338
CREIGHTON, JOHN W., JR. 168
CRENSHAW, LARRY 135
CRENSHAW, TERESA 52
CRESSEL, MARY 30
CRICK, MERIBETH 136
CRICKENBERGER, ROGER 94
CRIER, TIMBER 285
CRINER, GEORGE 376
CRISELL, ROB 158
CRISPIN, SUSAN 83
CRISS, ANNE 275
CRIST, LARRY 115
CRISTINI, ANGELA 152
CROKE, L. 129
CROMBIE, GEORGE 75
CRONENBERGER, VIRGINIA 168
CRONIN, JOHN A. 203
CRONIN, LESLIE 164
CRONK, EDYE 327
CROOKS, JOAN 344
CROONQUIST, DAVE 162
CROSMAN, SHIRL 210
CROSS, BILLY JOE 195
CROSS, BOB 46
CROSS, DIANA 25
CROSS, GERALD H. 119
CROSSMAN, MARIAN 165, 301
CROUCH, BARTH V. 303
CROUCH, ROGER 136
CROUCH, SHERRY 42, 299
CROUSE, RICHARD J. 150
CROW, RICK 17
CROWELL, CHUCK 267
CROWELL, CRAVEN 36
CRUDELE, JULIE 219
CRUEA, DARRELL 109
CRUM, ED 337
CRUSER, HOLLY 343
CRUZ, ELISABETH T. 59
CRUZ, FRANK 59
CRUZ, JOAQUIN Q. 59
CUBBAGE, FREDERICK W. 384
CUBBAGE, JAMES 174
CUELLAR, YVONNE 232
CULLEN, J. B. 85
CULLINEY, JOHN 59
CULLUM, SHERMAN D. 45
CULLY, JACK F., JR. 66, 374
CULP, PETE 24
CULP, WES 121
CULPEPPER, JAMES L. 70
CULTER, RAY 279
CUMBERLEDGE, CARROLL 346
CUMBIE, RICHARD H. 40
CUMMING, HAROLD G. 385
CUMMINGS, B. J. 307
CUMMINGS, BOB 250
CUMMINGS, DIANNE 159
CUMMINGS, J. GLEN 128
CUMMINGS, LORI 344
CUMMINGS, ROBERT 363
CUMMINGS, THERESA 63
CUMMINS, DAVID G. 181
CUMMINS, GARY 25
CUMMINS, JAMES D. 8
CUMMINS, JAMES L., JR. 193
CUNNIFF, SHANNON 24
CUNNINGHAM, DON 83
CUNNINGHAM, GARY 29
CUNNINGHAM, JAMES A. 265
CUNNINGHAM, RICHARD N. 86
CUNNINGHAM, WILLIAM 156
CUOMO, ANDREW M. 15
CURAN, DAVID 336
CURL, SAM E. 99
CURLEY, ROSEMARY 131
CURNEW, K. 129
CURNOW, RICHARD D. 29
CURRAN, WILLIAM J. 90
CURRIE, PATRICIA 233
CURTIS, HENRY Q. 248
CURTIS, MARC 258
CURTIS, PAUL 93
CURTISS, BILL 198
CURTNER, KATHRYN A. 124
CURTNER, TOM R. 44
CUSHING, CAROL 297
CUSHING, COLBERT 288
CUSHMAN, ROBERT M. 14
CUSTER, ADRIE 30
CUSTODIO, NARCISO G., P.E. 59
CUTLER, RUTH 186
CWYNAR, THOMAS J. 81
CYPHER, BRIAN 357
CYPHERT, MARIE 241
CYR, KAREN D. 35
CZINSKI, BEN 378

D

DAAR, SHEILA 166
DABBS, KARL 157
DAGGERHART, RENEE 108
DAGGETT, SUSAN 198
DAHL, ANN 165
DAHLMAN, DOUGLAS 200
DAIGLE, J.J. 193
DAILEY, FRED L. 96
DALE, BOB 209
DALE, BOLEYN 343
DALE, DICK 351
DALEY LAURSEN, STEVEN B. 79
DALEY, JAMES G. 356
DALEY, RICHARD 139
DALEY, WILLIAM M. 12
DALEYLAURSEN, STEVEN B. 379
DALMAS, THELMA 343
DALMIDA-SMITH, BEULAH 115
DALPRA, CURTIS 8
DALTON, BERNADETTE 229
DALTON, CAROL ANN 171
DALTON, MORRIS 315
DALTON, RICHARD 87
DALY, JOHN 120
DAMIAN, FRANCIS P. 59
D'AMICO, JOSEPH S. 41
DAMRON, JACK 19
DAMRON, JOHN E. 201
DANCHUCK, WILLIAM 165
DANDO, MURIEL A. 222
DANDOY, SUZANNE E. 118
DANELLO, MARY ANN 14
DANET, ROBERT 116
D'ANGELO, ROBERT 103
DANIEL, DAVID E. 373
DANIEL, GLENDA 297
DANIEL, W. B. 122
DANIELL, ROBERT 69
DANIELS, HARRY V. 94
DANIELS, KEVIN 181
DANIELS, MICHAEL B. 44
DANIELS, ROBERT A. 81
DANIELS, SAM 150
DANSON, TED 153
DANVIR, RICK E. 113
DANZIG, RICHARD 27
DAOU, ADAMA 234
DAOUST, PIERRE-YVES 171
DARROW, ROBERT, M.D. 342
DARROW, STEVE 341
DARTLAND, DIANA 55
DASHER, DOUG 20
DASTRUP, B. CURTIS 113
DATES, HAROLD F. 151
DAUBENDIEK, BERTHA 255
DAUDI, SABINA 203
DAUGHERTY, M. SUE 267
DAUGHTRY, DAVE 42
DAUKAS, JIMMY 142
DAVID MCLARN 172
DAVID, BARBARA 186
DAVID, KIRK 224
DAVID, PETE 354
DAVID, ROBERT 266
DAVIDSEN, DONALD R. 92
DAVIDSON, AL 183
DAVIDSON, CHARLES F. 187
DAVIDSON, DENNIS 87
DAVIDSON, ED 206
DAVIDSON, JASON 85
DAVIDSON, MARION 286
DAVIDSON, SUSAN 267
DAVIES, BRIAN D. 230
DAVIES, J. CLARENCE, III 311
DAVIES, KATE 191
DAVIES, PETER 363
DAVIES, RICHARD W. 43
DAVIES, SUSAN 288
DAVIES, TUDOR T. 12
DAVIS, AL 42
DAVIS, BOB 195
DAVIS, CAMERON 246
DAVIS, CAROLYN D. 73
DAVIS, CHARLES A. 277
DAVIS, CLARK M. 9
DAVIS, DONALD R., 367
DAVIS, GARY S. 289
DAVIS, GRAY 45, 50
DAVIS, HOWARD 284
DAVIS, J. BRADLEY 297
DAVIS, JERRY 353
DAVIS, JERRY D. 136
DAVIS, JOHN 64
DAVIS, JOHN C. 67
DAVIS, JOHN F. 39
DAVIS, MARILYN 114
DAVIS, MARILYN A. 124
DAVIS, MIKI 171
DAVIS, PAUL 110, 200
DAVIS, PAUL EVAN 110
DAVIS, RAYMOND E. 116
DAVIS, ROBERT L., JR. 271
DAVIS, ROGER L. 99
DAVIS, SARA H. 158
DAVIS, SPENCER 209
DAVIS, WILLIAM E. 69, 359
DAVIS, WILLIAM R. 288
DAVIS-HAMILTON, S. 348
DAVISON, DAVE 133
DAVIT, CAROL 259
DAWS, RUSSELL 329
DAWSON, JAMES 266
DAY, BETTY 182
DAY, GUS 169
DAY, JENNIFER 8
DAY, M. H. 169
DAY, MARK 10
DAY, RICHARD 274
DAY, ROBERT D. 310
DE DARDEL, CLAES 234
DE GHETALDI, EVELYN BALLARD 133
de la ROCHA, ROSAMELIA 15
DE LA TORRE, DONNA 34
de la TORRE, REBECCA 31
DEAN, ANTHONY T. 297
DEAN, ELLEN A. 369
DEAN, ROB 128
DEAN, ROSE 212
DEAN, TOMMY 308
DEANE, JAMES G. 171, 191
DEANGELIS, MARIE 368
DEARBORN, RONALD K. 41
DEASON, WAYNE O. 25
DEATHERAGE, KAREN 137
DEATON, LINDA 329
DEATON, ROGER 107
DEBON, RICHARD 284
DeBONIS, JEFF 307
DeBRES, KAREN 242
DeBRUIN, RODNEY H. 126
DeCECCO, STEVE 125
DECKER, BOB 20, 261
DECKER, DANIEL J. 357
DECKER, STEVE 82
DECOOK, JOHN 319
DEDRICK, ALAN 32
DEEB, DAN 273
DEFERRARI, GINA 332
DEFOLLIART, LINDA 292
DeGARMO, GLEN 19
DEGEN, PAULA 185
DEGRAAF, RICHARD M. 377
deGRAFFENREID, JEFF 135
DEGROSKY, MIKE 229
DeGROVE, JOHN 133
DEHART, DOUG 100
DeHART, H. GRANT 73

STAFF NAME INDEX 501

DeHART, MICHELE 183
DEHAVEN, RON 29
DEHAYES, DONALD H. 391
DEIGER, GARY E 103
DEISNER, VICKI LEE 295
DeKING, DAVID L 284
DEL GIUDICE, PAULA 273
DELANEY, DENISE 246
DELANEY, EDWARD L. 350
DELANEY, KEVIN 40
DELANEY, RICHARD F. 378
DeLEERS, JR., LAWRENCE N. 322
DELFAY, ROBERT T. 271
D'ELIA, CHRISTOPHER F. 74
DELISLE, JENNIFER 355
DELLER, NANCY 48
DELMATIER, CHARMAINE REFSDAL 364
DELOACH, JAMIE 55
DeLUISE, FRANK 26
DELUSSA, BRUCE 381
DEMARTINO, JOSEPH 195
DeMASTER, DOUGLAS P. 321
DeMATTEO, JENELL 323
DEMETERIO, ERLINDA 59
DEMETRESCU, JEFF 232
DEMIDOVICH, BILL 97
DEMPSEY, BERNARD S. 192
DENISON, JIM 298
DENKER, TERRY 67
DENKERS, STEPHEN G. 196
DENLEY, GEORGE T. 30
DENMAN, SCOTT 315
DENNERLEIN, BUCKY 351
DENNERLEIN, CATHERINE 136
DENNERLEIN, CHIP 270
DENNIS, ANN 169
DENNIS, JANE 360
DENNIS, MIKE 279
DENNY, ARTHUR, JR. 236
DENNY, GUY 97
deNOYELLES, FRANK 66
DENPON, JOAN E 46
DENTE, CHUCK R. 356
DENTON, DAN 195
DENVER, JOHN 359
DENWORTH, JOANNE R. 302
DePERRY, GERALD 7
DEPINTO, JOHN A. 373
DePOLO, MICHAEL 255
DEPPNER, DAVE 333
DEPPNER, REMEDIOS G. 333
DEPUIT, EDWARD J. 392
DERASARY, RANI 232
DERDERIAN, JAMES 5
DERENDINGER, MICHAEL 228
DERKROAK, G. VON 386
DERKSEN, ARTHUR J. 147
DEROSA, SHERI D. 76
DERR, CHARLES W., JR. 141
DERR, FREDERICK M. 261
DERR, REX 120
DERTY, CHANTAL 230
DERUITER, DARLA S. 349
DESARO, JIM 223
DESCHENES, JOE 20, 23
DeSMIT, RON 137
DESOTO, ROB 51
D'ESPOSITO, STEPHEN 256
DESSECKER, DAN 314
DESSUREAULT, MICHEL 387
DeSTEFANO, STEPHEN 41
DETER, ROSS 48
DEUSCHL, DENNIS E. 28
DEUTSCHER, ARLENE 31
DEUVALL, DALE 336
DEVANEY, EARL E. 11
DEVANEY, LAUREL 137
DeVAUGHN, STEVEN 34
DEVAUL, GERALD A. 168
DEVEREAUX, AL 54
DeVERTER, DEBRA 48
DEVICK, WILLIAM 60
DEVILLARS, JOHN P. 11
DEVINE, ALICE 66
DEVINE, M. D. 388
DEVINE, RITA 287
DEVINE, ROBIN 18
DEVITT, R. J. 331
DEVOE, M. RICHARD 108
DeVRIES, DENNIS 260
DEW, ALOMA 69
DEWALD, SANDRA 315
DeWALLE, WENDY VAN 238
DEWEES, CHRISTOPHER 46
DEWELL, DAN 12
DEWEY, JESSICA W. 358
DEWEY, ROBERT 191
DEWHURST, DAVID 112
DEWITT, LAURENCE B. 93
DEXTER, DAVID 181
DEYRUP, NANCY 159
DHONDT, ANDRE 189
DIA, LATAWNYA 31
DIAGE, PETER H. 369
DIAMANTE, JOHN 332
DIAMOND, A W. 381
DIANA, JAMES S. 378
DIANICH, MIKE 306
DIAZ, DONNA 42
DIBATTISTA, CARMINE N. 52
DIBBLEE, RANDALL 131
DIBLASI, PHILIP 174
DiCAMILLO, JODI 271
DICKENSON, DAN 338
DICKERSON, BILL 94
DICKERSON, DENNIS 46
DICKERSON, MARIA 340
DICKIE, KATIE 111
DICKLE, JOHN R. 240
DICKSON, ANDREW 363
DICKSON, JAMES G. 273
DICKSON, JAN 175, 390
DICKSON, KENNETH L 390
DICKSON, LANA 89
DIDRICKSON, BETSY 230
DIERKER, KARL 75
DIERKES, FRED 356
DIERSING, VIC 23
DiFAZIO, FAYE E. 116
DIGIULO, RICHARD T. 383
DILLARD, JIM 110
DILLER, LOWELL 353
DILLER, TOM 307
DILLINGHAM, HUGH J., III 352
DILLION, C. I., III 391
DILTZ, DOTTY 54
DILWORTH, TIM 381
DIMASE, JOSEPH D. 164
DIMONTI, ANNE 164
DINGER, JAMES S. 69
DINKINS, GERRY 325
DINTAMAN, RAY C., JR. 74
DIOUF, JACQUES 209
DiPASQUALE, NICHOLAS 52
DiPIETRO, BARBARA 135
DIPOLVERE, EDWARD 285
DIPPEL, DONNIE 111
DIPPEL, JOSEPH J. 52
DIRINGER, ELLIOT 10
DIRUS, GRETA J. 35
DISHNER, O. GENE 117
DISTEFANO, JAMES J. 86
DITTMAR, ARTHUR 255
DITTMER, BOB 188, 315
DITTO, ROSE M. 213
DIX, DAVID 176, 259
DIXON, BRIAN 365
DIXON, DAVID 176
DIXON, DORIS 212
DIXON, JOHN R. 342
DOAK, GARY 75
DOAN, DOUG 129
DOBBERPUHL, JUNE 167
DOBOLEK, ROBERTA A. 42
DOBROWOLSKI, JAMES P. 390
DOCHERTY, MOLLY 72
DODD, JAMES F., III 196
DODGION, LEWIS H. 84
DODSON, ERIC 163
DODSON, RONALD G. 163
DOGGETT, MARJORIE 232
DOHERTY, CATE 316
DOHERTY, JAMES 351
DOHERTY, JONATHAN 119
DOHERTY, JOSEPH M. 118
DOHM, LAUREL L. 355
DOHM, SUZANNE 287
DOLAN, ALAN 294
DOLAN, JoANN 287
DOLAN, JOHN 259
DOLAN, PETER 165
DOLD, JENNIFER 344
DOLENCE, ROBERT C. 102
DOLINER, J. D. 203
DOLLIVER, SHARON 58
DOLLOFF, C. ANDREW 391
DOMBECK, MIKE 32
DOMBROSKI, MARK 208
DOMINGUEZ, ANNETTE 112
DOMINGUEZ, R. 293
DOMINITZ, SID 291
DOMINQUEZ, LARRY 89
DOMURAT, RON 181
DONAGHUE, LINDA R. 33
DONAHOE, JEFFERY M. 8, 26
DONAHUE, JEFF 133
DONALD, DENNIS 279
DONALDSON, PETER 305
DONALDSON, WALT 113
DONAU, ALFRED S. 314
DONAUER, KATHLEEN 282
DONCASTER, ANNE 236
DONELIN, DAN 374
DONHEFFNER, PAUL E. 102
DONLON, JEANNE 87
DONNA, DAVID 258
DONNAN, EDMUND A., JR. 242
DONNELLEY, THOMAS, II 63
DONNELLY, GERARD T. 139
DONNELLY, JOHN 115
DONNELLY, KEVIN 53
DONNELLY, LLOYD J. 35
DONNELLY, PAULA 163
DONNELLY, T.W. 193
DONNELLY, THOMAS F. 272
DONOHUE, GAVIN 91
DONOHUE, TERRY 63
DONOHUE, THOMAS N. 339
DOOLEY, MARLEN 86
DOOLIN, PATRICIA K. 244
DOOLITTLE, WARREN T. 233
DOOM, CHUCK 324
DORAN, JEFF 207
DORAN, TERRY 120
DORE, CLIRE 72
DORFMAN, MARK 206
DORNFELD, SUSAN 164
DOROFF, SUE 312
DORRANCE, SAMUEL 176
DORRELL, TONY 262
DORSEY, CHRIS 196
DORSEY, MAURICE W. 54
DOSCH, JEANNE 276
DOSCHER, PAUL A. 322
DOSS, JIM 295
DOTT, DON S. 69
DOTT, DONALD S., JR. 69
DOUBLEDAY, BILL 36
DOUGAL, EDWARD 389
DOUGHERTY, CYNTHIA C. 12
DOUGLAS, DONALD J. 192
DOUGLAS, JAMES 83
DOUGLAS, JEAN WALLACE 138
DOUGLAS, LARRY 130
DOUGLAS, LINDA 208
DOUGLAS, MICHAEL E. 155
DOUGLAS, PETER 47
DOUGLAS, TILLMAN 326
DOUGLASS, GUS R. 122
DOW, BOB 18
DOW, JOCELYN 361
DOWLER, BERNARD F. 122
DOWN, SERENA 325
DOWNEY, LAURA 243
DOWNEY, MORTIMER L. 27
DOWNING, DARLENE 174
DOWNS, JOAN 351
DOWSE, MARCY 78
DOXTATER, GARY 64
DOYLE, BECKY 62
DOYLE, BRIAN 86
DOYLE, CASSIE 127
DOYLE, FRANCES 19
DOYLE, PAT 173
DOYLE, ROBERT 390
DOYLE, WAYNE 67
DRAGHI, PAUL 371
DRAGICEVICH, RODNEY 254
DRAHOVZAL, JAMES 68
DRAKE, DEBBIE 47
DRAPER, ERIN 265
DRAPER, WAYNE 37
DRAPER, WILLIAM H., JR. 304
DRASSAL, CHRIS 257
DRAUGHON, DAVID 110
DRAWE, D. LYNN 346
DREESEN, ALAN D. 111
DREHER, KARL J. 61
DREIBAND, SUSAN 26
DREIMAN, JOHN 226
DRENNAN, KATHLEEN 160
DREW, MIMI 54, 55
DREW, RICHARD 55
DREYER, GLENN D. 370
DRIGGERS, DONALD 13
DRISH, MARY ANN 65
DROBNEY, RONALD D. 81
DROTTAR, PETER 17
DRUCKENMILLER, HOWARD S. 124
DRUDING, BARBARA 333
DRUMMOND, KAREN 271
DRURY, BROOKE 261
DRYDEN, RON 210
DU FAULT, ARTHUR 264
DUBICK, DENISE 348
DUBOIS, FRANK A. 89
DUBORD, DANIEL J. 179
DuBROCK, CALVIN W. 104
DUCKLOW, H. W. 391
DUDA, MARK DAMIAN 311
DUDLEY, NICK 220
DUDLEY, SALLY 162
DUENO, JOSE A. 307
DUERR, NAOMI 84
DUESTERHAUS, RICHARD L. 310
DUFAULT, ARTHUR W. 113
DUFF, DON 333
DUFF, JAMES H. 168
DUFFORD, WICK 344
DUFFY, AMY 107
DUFFY, CLARK 68, 243
DUFFY, GREG 325
DUFFY, GREG D. 98
DUFFY, KIM 224
DUFFY, WALTER 368
DUFFY, WALTER G. 45
DUGAN, PATRICK 234
DUGGAN, JOSEPH J. 303
DUIKER, PETER M. 385
DUJACK, STEPHEN R. 203
DUKE, ROBIN CHANDLER 304
DUKEMINIER, CLARICE 292
DULL, JACK 55
DUMELIE, MIKE 132
DUNAGAN, ROB 166, 179
DUNBAR, LYNN 158
DUNCAN, CHARLES D. 161
DUNCAN, JUDY 98
DUNCAN, PETER 91
DUNCAN, ROBERT W. 116
DUNKERLEY, MIKE 301
DUNKLE, RICHARD 32
DUNKLE, S.W. 193
DUNKS, JIMMY 195
DUNLAP, JOHN D., III 46
DUNLAP, THOMAS R. 209
DUNMYER, JAMES W. 73
DUNN, ALLEN 108, 388
DUNN, CHRIS 20
DUNN, CINDY ADAMS 301
DUNN, DIANNA K. 365
DUNN, FRANK 130
DUNN, GARY A. 365
DUNN, LOREN 344
DUNN, MIKE 29
DUNN, ROBERT G. 256
DUNNAM, SYLVIA 208
DUNNE, PETER 285
DUNNIGAN, JOHN H. 7
DUNNING, CHERY L. 18
DUNSTAN, FRANK 91
DUNSTAN, THOMAS C. 373
DUNTON, KIRSTEN 186
DUNWELL, FRAN 91
DuPAUL, WILLIAM 119
DUPAUL, WILLIAM D. 391
DuPREE, GALE 283
DUPREE, THOMAS 106
DUPUIS, JOSEPH E. 185
DUPUY, CHARLES 249
DUQUESNAY, LEMERCIER 309
DURAN, DAVID 90
DURAND, LEILANI 220
DURANT, JOHN 377
DURHAM, DARYL 273
DURHAM, DAVID F. 174
DURHAM, FLOYD 44
DURHAM, PATRICK 276
DURKIN, ELIZABETH 305
DURNING, ALAN 293
DUROCHER, PHIL 112
DUROCHER, PHILIP P. 143
DURRELL, GERALD M. 353
DURRETT, JAMES F., III 214
DURST, DOUGLAS 197
DURYEA, MARY L 56
DUTRUMBLE, DANNY 164
DUTTEN, DIANA 310
DUTTENHEFNER, KATHY 96
DUTTON, MARK 20
DUVALL, CHUCK 140
DUYVEJONCK, JON 340
DYE, PAUL 235
DYER, A. ALLEN 370
DYER, POLLY 297
DYKES, JOHN 67
DYKSTRA, BETTY 314
DYNE, RANDY VAN 294
DZIUBEK, DAN 387

E

EADDY, DONALD 94
EADIE, DIANE 284
EAGAN, LLOYD L. 124
EAGLE, KEMPER E. 343
EAGLE, TIM 110
EAMES, CLIFF 136
EARHART, JOHN E. 310
EARLE, PAMELA 270
EARLEY, LARRY S. 95
EASTER, BECKY 170
EASTERSON, BRAD 154
EASTERSON, TONI BENNETT 153
EASTON, CHUCK 286
EATHERLY, CHARLES R. 43
EATON, AMY 260
EATON, PAM 340
EATON, PAMELA 349
EAV, BOV B 33
EBENSTEINER, RICHARD J. 230
EBERLE, BRUCE 335
EBERSBACH, PAUL 17
EBERT, SUSAN 112
EBNETER, STEWART D. 35
ECCLES, STEPHEN 140
ECH, EDWIN 380
ECHEVERRIA, JOHN 157
ECHOLS, ALEX 267
ECHOLS, LOUIE S. 121
ECK, ROBERT 82
ECKBERG, CHARLES 184

Staff Name Index

502 STAFF NAME INDEX

ECKELBARGER, KEVIN 72
ECKER, MICHAEL E. 191
ECKERT, AL 44
ECKERT, ROBERT T. 381
EDELBROCK, JERRY 251
EDELMAN, JIM 341
EDER, LOUIS S. 81
EDER, TIM 274
EDGAR, CECILIA F. 95
EDGE, DANIEL 101
EDGE, W. DANIEL 357
EDGELL, ROBERT L. 192
EDGERTON, WAYNE 78
EDMINSTER, CARL 367
EDMONDS, ROBERT LEE 86
EDMONDSON, JIM 170
EDSON, DAVID 154
EDSON, DEAN 282
EDSON, JACK D. 276
EDTABROOK, NORMAN B. 252
EDWARD, ROB 319
EDWARDS, ALLEN 209
EDWARDS, BERT T. 305
EDWARDS, CHIQUITA 227
EDWARDS, GARY B. 26
EDWARDS, GEORGE 95
EDWARDS, GORDON 194
EDWARDS, JOHN 3, 121
EDWARDS, MARK 57
EDWARDS, ROBERT L. 55
EDWARDS, THOMAS C., JR. 390
EDWARDS, WILLIAM C. 304
EDWARDS,, THOMAS C., JR. 113
EFLIN, JAMES 373
EGAR, D. 37
EGBERT, ALLAN L. 55, 352
EGE, FREDERICK 335
EGER, REBECCA 251
EGGERS, GORDON 225, 277
EGGERT, PAUL 29
EHLERS, ANGELA 324
EHLERT, CHARLES 291
EHM, WILLIAM 65
EHRENREICH, DIXIE L. 372
EHRESMAN, MARLENE 238
EHRET, PAUL 64
EHRHARDT, BARBARA J. 374
EHRHARDT, JANE 151
EHRLICH, PAUL R. 365, 369
EICHBAUM, WILLIAM M. 363
EIDT, DAN 130
EIKEN, DOUGLAS K. 81
EISENBARTH, JOHN 336
EISENBERG, JOHN M. 14
EISING, JUDY 206
EISNER, THOMAS 364
EITNIEAR, JACK CLINTON 177
EK, ALAN 379
EKDAHL, JAMES 76
EKEY, ROBERT 349
ELAM, DAYTON 330
ELAM, ROBERT 15
ELBOW, GARY 266
ELCOCK, DEVORATH 342
ELDEN, RICHARD 66
ELDER, AL 29
ELDER, DON 312
ELDER, JOHN 254
ELDERS, CONNIE 243
ELDRENKAMP, PAUL 292
ELDRIDGE, BILL 80
ELDRIDGE, CHARLES L. 239
ELFNER, LYNN EDWARD 294
ELKINS, ELIZABETH A. 383
ELLEDGE, SHANNON 19
ELLIKER, ROBERT 241
ELLIOT, HERSCHEL 387
ELLIOTT, BOOK 166
ELLIOTT, CATHERINE 72
ELLIOTT, JAMES 76
ELLIOTT, JONI 285
ELLIOTT, MARILYN 39
ELLIOTT, RICH 49
ELLIS, CINDY 168
ELLIS, FLORIDA 214
ELLIS, JANET 260
ELLIS, TOM 94
ELOWE, KENNETH D. 71
ELROD, LEWIS 142
ELROD, SCOTT M. 254
ELS, DAVID E. 268
ELSBREE, MARK 188
ELSER, ALLEN 114
ELSING, HENRY 324
ELTON, JOSEPH 118
ELY, CRAIG 100
ELZERMAN, ALAN W. 388
EMERSON, DAVID L. 164
EMERTON, DAN 217
EMERY, BOB 355
EMERY, MARILYN 187
EMMANUELE, KURT A. 139
EMMETT, KATHRYN 129
EMO, KYRA 306
EMORY, WILLIAM H. 322
EMPSON, G. RAYMOND 244
ENGBERG, KRISTEN 219
ENGEL, JAY 333
ENGELMAN, ROBERT 304
ENGELMANN, EB 100
ENGELSMA, FRANS J. 204
ENGH, DOUG 159
ENGLE, CAROLE R. 44
ENGLE, DAVID M. 385
ENNS, BOB 128
ENO, AMOS S. 267
ENO, JACKSON F. 303
ENTZ, MICHAEL 296
EPIFANIO, JOHN M. 143
EPLIN, JIM 306
EPPERSON, DEBORAH 216
EPSTEIN, SARAH G. 305
ERARD, ISABELLE 190
ERB, JAMES E. 103
ERDMANN, RICHARD L. 188
ERICH, SUE 376
ERICKSON, DONNA 378
ERICKSON, GARY 195
ERICKSON, GERRY RING 191
ERICKSON, KIM 98
ERICKSON, RON 132
ERICKSON, TERESA 292
ERICSSON, SALLY 10
ERIKSON, JAMES 27
ERNST, HARLEY 51
ERNST, JOHN 78, 134
ERNST, MARION V. 361
ERNSTER, JOHN 78
ERSKINE, ANDREA L. 71
ERTMER, SUSAN 197
ERTTER, ROBERT S. 274
ERVEY, EARL F. 285
ERVIN, DAVID E. 221
ESCARCEGA, FERNANDO 112
ESCOE, WAYNE 57
ESDEN, JIM 391
ESHBAUGH, DAVE 164
ESPINOSA, JUDITH 273
ESPOSITO, GERARD L. 53
ESPY, JAMES J. 247, 250
ESPY, JAMES J., JR. 250
ESSON, JOHN 19, 201
ESTABROOK, E. PENN 71
ESTELL, GRANT 376
ESTILL, ELIZABETH 33
ETGEN, ROBERT J. 199
ETHRIDGE, TOM 215
EUBANK, BOB 343
EULER, D. 385
EUSTON, SUSANNA MACKENZIE 215
EVANS, BROCK 200, 206
EVANS, DAVID L. 12, 13
EVANS, GAIL 154
EVANS, JEFF 211
EVANS, JOSEPH R. 308
EVANS, KEVIN 285
EVANS, LEMUEL A. 252
EVANS, MARSHA JOHNSON 215
EVANS, PETER 204
EVANS, RICK 43
EVANS, THOMAS W. 343
EVANS, WALLACE 104
EVENSON, KIRK 333
EVERAGE, CYNTHIA 197
EVERETT, MIKE 62
EVERITT, BOB 119
EVERTS, TODD 82
EWBANK, THOMAS A. 226
EWERT, D. MERRILL 93
EWING, AL 40
EWING, JOHN 115
EWING, PATRICIA 363
EWING, ROBERT 25
EWING, ROBERT J. 25
EXTER, RANDEE 13
EZELL, ANDREW W. 81

F

FABER, PHYLLIS 169
FABER, SCOTT 154
FABIAN, NELSON E. 267
FABIAN, TERRY R. 102
FACCIANI, STEVE 125
FAGAN, J. RICHARD 104
FAGO, DON 149
FAHEY, JOHN M., JR. 268
FAHEY, MICHAEL, JR. 276
FAHEY, TIMOTHY J. 382
FAIRBANK, BOB 258
FAIRCLOTH, BUD 192
FAIRFIELD, CAROL PRICE 321
FAIRLEIGH, LARRY 120
FAKUNDINY, ROBERT H. 92
FALBO, JEAN A. 369
FALCO, CARL 95
FALCONER, ALLAN 390
FALENDER, ANDREW J. 158
FALK, DONALD A. 321
FALKENHEINER, DORIS 249
FALKNER, BOB 344
FALSTROM, KEN 201
FALTEISEK, JAN 257
FALWELL, JEROME C. 246
FANCY, CLAIR 54
FANDREM, JIM 170
FARBER, LAURIE 227
FARIAS, ENRIQUE G. 45
FARLAND, WILLIAM H. 11
FARLEY, TIM 48
FARMER, DON 159
FARNSWORTH, LARRY 376
FARR, CLARENCE 61
FARRAR, ROY 360
FARRAR, SALLY 360
FARRELL, DOLORES 48
FARRELL, J. PAT 378
FARRELL, THOMAS 138
FARREN, RICHARD 208
FARREY, PATRICE 252
FARRIS, ALLEN 66
FARRIS, BILL 66
FARRIS, VERA KING 382
FARRISH, KENNETH 389
FARRO, ANTHONY J. 87
FARWELL, FRANCIS C. 275
FAST, DON 127
FAST, SARAH 323
FATZ, RAYMOND J. 19
FAUROT-DANIELS, ELLEN 212
FAUSKE, GLENDA 96
FAUST, RALPH 47
FAUST, RICHARD 211
FAUTH, JOHN L. 383
FAUTH, LAURA 308
FAVORITE, ROGER 305
FEAVEL, YVONNE 359
FE-BORNSTEIN, MARC 205
FEDEWA, DENNIS 76
FEDORKO, NICK, III 123
FEDUCCIA, DONALD P. 70
FEE, EVERETT J. 155
FEGELY, BETTY LOU 299
FEIERABEND, J. SCOTT 274
FEINBERG, WILLIAM 180
FELDMAN, JAY 197, 266
FELDMAN, MARCUS W. 369
FELDMAN, RICHARD D. 64
FELDT, GLORIA 304
FELLOWS, EDRISE 283
FELLOWS, LARRY D. 42
FELSKE, BEVERLY 299
FELT, STEVE 225
FENN, DENNIS B. 26
FENNELLY, KATHERINE 79
FENNESSY, FRANCIS M. 124
FENSTEMACHER, RON 220
FENTY, GREG 282
FENWICK, GEORGE H. 140
FERAL, PRISCILLA 211
FERENCE, LARRY 271
FERGUSON, JAMES 95
FERGUSON, JOE 40
FERGUSON, JOHN L. 43
FERGUSON, TIM 358
FERMUND, WAYNE 380
FERNALD, E. A. 372
FERNANDEZ, IVAN 376
FERNANDEZ, NOE 112
FERNANDEZ, NURIA 28
FERNANDEZ, PETER 29
FERNANDEZ-VANCLEUS, JOHN 106
FERNDON, ELINOR 215
FERNHOLM, BO 8
FERRANTE, GRETCHEN 285
FERRE, ANTONIO LUIS 189
FERRELL, BLAINE 245
FERRELL, STEVE 42
FERRELL, YVONNE 61, 264
FERRING, REID 390
FERRIS, CRAIG 195
FERRIS, DONALD 240
FERRIS, ROBERT M. 191
FERRIS, SHIRLEY 51
FERRULO, MARK 208
FERRY, MILES 113, 114
FERTIG, WALTER 364
FESSENDEN, JOSEPH E. 71
FESTER, JAMES 106
FETTEROLF, CARLOS 143
FEWIN, ROBERT F. 111
FEWLESS, DENNIS 95
FICKES, TED 182
FICKIES, ROBERT H. 92
FIELD, DAVID B. 158, 376
FIELD, REBECCA 75, 377
FIELDER, JOHN 349
FIELDER, NICK 110
FIELDS, JAMES D. 122
FIELDS, JIM 192
FIELDS, ROBERT C. 275
FIELDS, TIMOTHY, JR. 11
FIES, MICHAEL L. 358
FIGUEROA, FRANK 34
FIJALKOWSKI, DENNIS 255
FILIATRAULT, PATRICK 308
FILION, BERNARD 194
FILIPEK, STEPHEN 143
FILLMORE, RUSS 160
FINCH, JAMIE 34
FINCH, JOHN 290
FINCK, ELMER 291, 354
FINDEN, JEFFERY S. 303
FINDEN, JEFFREY S. 303
FINDLAY, STUART E.G. 227
FINERTY, MARTIN J., JR. 252
FINGERHUT, BERT 349
FINGERMAN, MILTON 156, 375
FINLEY, DAVID A. 125
FINN, SUSAN 230
FINNERTY, MAUREEN 25
FINNEY, DANA 21
FINNEY, GEORGE 36
FINNEY, KEN 184
FINSER, JACK 124
FIRKINS, JIM 88
FISCHER, BURNELL 64
FISCHER, DUF 157
FISCHER, EDWARD 338
FISCHER, HANK 191
FISCHER, JOHN 212
FISCHER, R. MONTGOMERY 274
FISH, STEVEN O. 52
FISHER, BERT 173
FISHER, JANET L. 122
FISHER, JONATHAN 274
FISHER, LYNDAL 18
FISHER, RANDY 10
FISHER, ROBROY 193
FISHER, THOMAS W. 240
FISHER, WAYNE 128
FISHER, WILLIAM L. 98
FISHMAN, JAMES 265
FISK, ANDREW 72
FISKE, KEN 224
FITCH, LARRY 114
FITE, EDWARD D., III 312
FITTERER, LINDA 302
FITTS, DANIEL T. 90
FITZGERALD, ANNE 52
FITZGERALD, BEN 343
FITZGERALD, BRIAN T. 158
FITZGERALD, MARTHA 178
FITZGERALD, SUSAN 354
FITZGERALD, TOM 245
FITZGIBBON, TREVOR 345
FITZPATRICK, JIM 309
FITZPATRICK, JOHN 153, 189
FITZPATRICK, NEAL 164
FITZPATRICK, SCOTT 164
FITZSIMMONS, KEVIN 43
FITZSIMMONS, TOM 119
FITZSIMONS, JOSEPH B.C. 331
FLANDERS, P. HOWARD 114
FLANIGAN, FRANCES 138
FLATTERY, TOM 63
FLAVIN, CHRISTOPHER 363
FLAVIN, THOMAS M. 297
FLECKENSTEIN, LEONARD J. 11
FLEMING, EMILY J. 122
FLEMING, GENE 49
FLEMING, HOWARD 187
FLEMING, MARY 299
FLESKES, CAROL 119
FLETCHER, KATHY 261, 318, 344
FLETCHER, MADYLYN 388
FLETCHER, RICH 262
FLETCHER, RODERICK 102
FLICK, GEORGE J., JR. 119
FLICKER, JOHN 265
FLICKINGER, STEPHEN 370
FLINT, JIM 268
FLINT, PETER H. 192
FLINT, ROBERT B., JR. 319
FLOOD, DAVID JAY 221
FLOOD, JAMES 196
FLORA, JOHN J. 227
FLORY, RONALD K. 102
FLOWERS, R.B. 193
FLOYD, BARRY 195
FLOYD, DON 262
FLOYD, THELMA 32
FLOYD, TIMOTHY 364
FLOYD, VERONICA 152
FLUHARTY, MARLENE 319
FOGEL, GARY 179
FOGERTY, DANIEL J. 64
FOLEY, ARTHUR P. 158
FOLEY, DANA 278
FOLEY, GARY J., Ph.D. 11
FOLEY, KATHY 56
FOLGER, JEFFREY 185
FONDREN, WALTER W., III 181
FONG, D. 128
FONSECA, GUSTAVO 188
FONTAINE, BEN 152
FONTAINE, COLETTE 128
FONTENOT, BENNIE 70

Staff Name Index

STAFF NAME INDEX 503

FOOS, ANNABELLE 385
FOOTE, EDWARD T., II 231
FOOTE, KAREN 70
FOOTE, RAY 317
FOOTE-SMITH, CHRISTY 75
FORBES, G. J. 381
FORBES, JOHN RIPLEY 278
FORBES, PETER 337
FORCE, JO ELLEN 373
FORCIER, LAWRENCE K. 115
FORD, ARTHUR 26
FORD, BILL 181
FORD, BRITT J. 271
FORD, CHARLES 20
FORD, CINDY 243
FORD, CYNTHIA 244
FORD, ELLEN 361
FORD, MIKE 313
FORD, RICHARD 377
FORD, THOMAS P. 103
FORD, TIM 54, 206
FORD, TOM 206
FORDHAM, WAYNE 16
FORDICE, D. KIRK 7
FOREMAN, DAVE 318, 348, 350
FORER, LYLE 104
FOREST, BEN 180
FORESTELL, PAUL H. 301
FORGEY, WILLIAM W. 349
FORKAN, PATRICIA 222
FORNOS, WERNER 305
FORREST, CHRIS 272
FORREST, ROSEMARY 107
FORREST, STEVE 306
FORSGREN, HARV 32
FORSGREN, TED 181
FORSING, JOHN 13
FORSYTHE, STEVE 26
FORTUNA, ROGER A. 34
FORTUNE, JAMES 352
FOSBURGH, WHIT 333
FOSTER, BARBARA 69
FOSTER, BILL 43
FOSTER, BOB 334
FOSTER, DAVID E. 44
FOSTER, DAVID G. 141
FOSTER, KENT 223
FOSTER, NANCY CARTER 16
FOSTER, NANCY, Ph.D. 12
FOSTER, PHILLIPS 362
FOTI, TOM 45
FOULKE, SCOTT 336
FOUNTAIN, BOB 135
FOUNTAIN, MICHAEL 389
FOURKILLER, NORMA 276
FOUST, ALLEN 287
FOUST, BRADY 392
FOUT, EVE D. 303
FOWLER, BILL 334
FOWLER, JAMES F. 70
FOWLER, JERRY 29
FOWLER, JOHN 34
FOWLER, R. B. 194
FOWLER, RON 109
FOWLER, TIM 254
FOX, ANNE C. 61
FOX, DOUG 376
FOX, EFFIE 343
FOX, H. JAMES 297
FOX, HOWARD 198
FOX, J. CHARLES 72
FOX, JEANNE M. 11
FOX, JENNIFER 164
FOX, JIM 120
FOX, JOHN C. 231
FOX, JONHATHAN C. 12
FOX, MARVIN 359
FOX, MIKE 236
FOX, RICHARD 287
FOX, RON 110
FOX, SHERRY 344
FOX, SUSAN 301
FOX, TOM 168
FOX-PRZEWORSKI, JOANNE 339
FOY, DOUGLAS 197
FOY, DOUGLAS I. 188
FOY, MIKE 358
FRALEY, GEORGE 296
FRAME, BRUCE C. 28
FRAMPTON, GEORGE T., JR. 10
FRAMSTEAD, PAUL 262
FRANCE, JEAN 276
FRANCE, SUSAN A. 83
FRANCIS, JAMES T. 146
FRANCIS, JOE 83
FRANCIS, MICHAEL 349
FRANCIS, ROBERT T., II 34
FRANCIS, RONALD G. 187, 263
FRANCK, SCOTT 287
FRANCKO, DAVID A. 385
FRANK, ANNETTE R. 227
FRANK, BARBARA 40
FRANK, BOBBI 364
FRANK, DAVID 13
FRANK, HAROLD 77
FRANK, JEFF 245
FRANK, MICHAEL 338
FRANK, REBECCA L. 183
FRANKLIN, THOMAS M. 358
FRANTZ, PETER J. 63
FRANZI, ANITA 251
FRASER, CELESTE 266
FRASER, KAREL 9
FRASIER, GARY 322
FRASIER, JOHN E. 348
FRASIER, STAN 261
FRATE, GINO DEL 353
FRATICELLI, BECKY 31
FRAWLEY, BRIAN 354
FRAYER, W E. 378
FRAZEE, JOAN 344
FRAZIER, GERALD W. 161
FREDERICK, DAVID 40
FREDERICKS, TODD 75
FREDIN, TRACY 379
FREDRIKSSON, KURT 40
FREE, STUART L. 156
FREEDBERG, JEAN 318
FREEDGOOD, JULIA 142
FREEDMAN, DAVID 57
FREEL, MAETON 353
FREELAND, AL 20
FREEMAN, BRENDA 113
FREEMAN, CHARLES 99
FREEMAN, CHRIS 85
FREEMAN, CRAIG C. 244
FREEMAN, HELEN 232
FREEMAN, MARY C. 325
FREEMAN, ROBIN 342
FREEMAN, WRAY 107
FREER, VALERIE M. 205
FREESE, ED 237
FREHNER, SYLVIA 38
FREILICH, LARRY 319
FRENCH, DWIGHT 102
FRENCH, HOLLY 314
FRENCH, JIM 120
FRENCH, JUDITH 97
FRENCH, MARILYN 364
FRENCH, STEVEN P. 364
FRETZ, THOMAS A. 74
FREUDENBERG, KIT 62
FREWLING, JOHN 102
FREY, LOIS 115
FREY, PAUL D. 70
FREYER, MARY ANNE 208
FREZIERS, JOHN 182
FRI, ROBERT 219, 320
FRICK, LINDA 91
FRICK, STEVEN W. 195
FRIDGEN, CYNTHIA 378
FRIDGEN, JOSEPH D. 378
FRIEDE, JOHN 138
FRIEDMAN, IRMIE 372
FRIEDMAN, MITCH 293
FRIEDMAN, ROBERT 219
FRIEDMAN, SIEGLINDE 135
FRIESEN, GREGG 244
FRIESEN, JOE 42
FRIESENG, TRACEY 304
FRINK, JOHN 333
FRISCHKORN, CARL 122
FRISTOE, BRAD 20
FRITA, JOHN 46
FRITTS, JOHN 267
FRITZ, ANN 96
FRITZ, BETSY 142
FRITZ, GARY 83
FRITZELL, ERIC 101
FRITZELL, ERIK 265
FRITZELL, ERIK K. 386
FRIZZELL, BRUCE 27
FROCHLICH, DAVID 256
FROEHLICH, GENICE 353
FROHMAN, GARY 206
FROILAND, THOMAS 378
FROMAN, SANDRA S. 271
FROME, MICHELE 258
FRONT, ALAN 337
FROST, CECIL 94
FROST, DAN 304
FROST, PETER 275
FROTHINGHAM, ERIC 327
FRUCI, DICK 284
FRUMKIES, JOAN 287
FRY, JOHN 303, 343
FRY, TOM 24
FRYE, CLAYTON W., JR. 242
FRYE, E. O. 239
FRYE, GRANVILLE H. 30
FRYE, JACK E. 118
FRYE, MEL 94
FRYE, WILLIAM H. 49
FUENTES, LORRAE 169
FUENTES, PEDRO J. 307
FUHRMAN, RUSSEL 21
FUJIOKA, ROGER 60
FUJIOKA, ROGER S. 61
FULBRIGHT, DENNIS 141
FULCHER, SANDY 237
FULFORD, LOY 110
FULGENZI, JIM 63
FULGHAM, KEN 368
FULGHAM, TOM 196
FULLER, DAVID 356
FULLER, JAMES 83
FULLER, JOE 112
FULLER, KATHRYN S. 363
FULLER, MANLEY F. 208
FULLER, STEPHEN 206
FULLWOOD, CHARLES R. 94, 95
FULLWOOD,, CHARLES R., JR. 94
FULMER, CAROL 107
FULMER, TOM 117
FULTON, DAVID C. 77
FULTON, SCOTT C. 10
FUNCHES, JESSE L. 35
FUNK, TIM 221
FUNK, WILLIAM 330
FURNESS, GEORGE A., JR. 188
FURTADO, JOE 169
FUTRELL, J. WILLIAM 203
FUTTER, ELLEN V. 153

G

GABELHOUSE, DON, JR. 83
GABRIEL, NANCY 268
GABRIELE, LARRY 125
GADAWSKI, TED 194
GADBERY, EARL 158
GADD, COLLEEN 183
GADE, MARY A. 63
GADZIK, CHUCK 72
GAFFNEY, SUSAN 15
GAGE, ROBERT 44
GAGE, SARAH 344
GAGNON, ALAIN 308
GAGNON, MANON 308
GAGNON, RONALD 106
GAHERTY, KEN 336
GAHL, JOHN 62, 347
GAILOR, ALLEN K. 68
GAINER, CARL E. 122
GAINES, GARY 82
GAINES, SALLY 259
GAJIGAS, MARIA M. 106
GALANTI, GERI-ANN 229
GALAT, DAVID L. 81
GALDA, BEATA 82
GALE, JULIE 216
GALES, LAWRENCE A. 98
GALIN, DAVID 251
GALINDO, TEDDY MERCADO 105
GALIZIOLLI, STEVE 159
GALL, BONNIE 296
GALL, DAVID 133
GALLAGHER, ANDY 122
GALLAGHER, DAWN 72
GALLAGHER, FRANK 87
GALLAGHER, JOHN J., JR. 87
GALLAGHER, TIM 189
GALLAGHER, WILLIAM J. 220
GALLAY, PAUL 91
GALLIK, KENNETH 268
GALLO, FRANK DAL 50
GALLOWAY, BOB 131
GALVIN, DENIS 25
GAMBELL, R. 8
GAMEZ, RODRIGO 37
GAMILL, STEWART, III 331
GAMON, JOHN 121
GANGLOFF, DEBORAH 150
GANN, GEORGE 321
GANSAUER, DIANE 183
GANSBERG, BILL 120
GANSELL, STUART I. 103
GANSKE, TED 137
GANTZ, RICHARD 64
GANZLIN, BILL K. 379
GARAVELLI, RON 80
GARBISCH, EDGAR W. 201
GARBISCH, JOANNA L. 201
GARBY, CRAIG 327
GARCES, GRACE OMEGA 59
GARCIA, ANDRES 307
GARCIA, BENITO 90
GARCIA, EUGENE 13
GARCIA, JUANITA 105
GARCIA, JUDY 170
GARCIA, SANTANA 47
GARCIA, TERRY D. 12
GARCIA-FANTE, ANITA 49
GARDILL, WALTER 167
GARDINER, DAVID M. 11
GARDNER, CHARLES 94
GARDNER, DAN, Ph.D. 196
GARDNER, LORI 322
GARDNER, PAUL 158
GARIBALDI, LOUIS 351
GARLAND, BILL 20
GARLAND, BROOKS 110
GARLAND, KATHLEEN 88
GARNER, JAMES W. 116
GARNER, SUE 330
GARNER, WILLIAM B. 39
GARNHAM, DALE 251
GARNHAM, DARLENE 251
GARRETT, ELIZABETH A. 259
GARRETT, GARY 193
GARRISON, JAMES 313
GARRISON, JOHN R. 152
GARRISON, LYNN 68
GARRISON, R.W. 193
GARRISON, SAMUEL 87
GARTSIDE, MICHAEL 177
GARVEY, JANE 27
GASKILL, PAUL 383
GASKINS, DARIUS W., JR. 311
GASPERI, ENRICO 342
GASTON, JANE W. 134
GATCHELL, JOHN 261
GATES, BILL 20
GATES, BRYAN 168
GATES, KEITH 58
GATES, PHIL 333
GATES, RICK 101
GATEWOOD, STEVE 350
GATJE, PETER 305
GATTLE, THOMAS, JR. 70
GAUDET, DIANE 131
GAUDET, JENNIFER 218
GAUDETTE, ROBERT P. 73
GAULDIN, MICHAEL 23
GAUME, NORMAN 90
GAUNT, CAROL 296
GAUTHIER, CLAUDE 308
GAUVIN, CHARLES F. 333
GAW, HERSHEL 20
GAY, CHARLES W. 114
GAY, GEORGE 115
GAYMAN, BEN 322
GEALT, MICHAEL A. 387
GEARAN, MARK 36
GEARING, JANE 309
GEATZ, RON 279
GEBALLE, GORDON 186
GEBHARDT, ALLEN S. 110
GEBHARDT, BRUCE 289
GEBHARDT, KARL 294
GECHAS, LEE 163
GEER, BILL 313
GEER, WILLIAM H. 313
GEHRKE, CRAIG 349
GEIGER, RAYMOND K. 54
GEIGER, SHARON 222
GEIGER, TOM 344
GELABERT, PEDRO A. 105
GELBARD, ALENE 305
GELFAND, JULIE 171, 173
GELL, ROBERT L. 223
GELLER, HOWARD 142
GELLER, MICHAEL D. 381
GENETTI, ALBERT J., JR. 21
GENNINGS, MIKE 57
GENNRICH, RUTH 243
GENTRY, GEORGE D. 161
GENTZ, EDWARD J. 350
GEORGE, CLINTON 115
GEORGE, DEBORAH 127
GEORGE, FELICIA 64
GEORGE, LOU 314
GEORGE, PAUL 120
GEORGE, SARAH B. 155
GEORGE, SUSAN 191
GERARD, JENNIE 338
GERBER, JOHN E. 179
GERBER, JOHN M. 74
GERBER, LEAH 321
GERBRACHT, JIM 354
GERHARD, LEE C. 67
GERHARDT, JOHN 50
GERINGER, JIM 125, 126
GERL, JANET 348
GERL, PETER J. 348
GERL, WILLIAM E., JR. 348
GERREIN, DAVID 69
GERRITS, ROGER 32
GERSON, JEFF 347
GERSON, LESLIE 16
GERTEISEN, DON 55
GESKE, JOEL 237
GESKE, NANCY 237
GESNER, SUSAN 172
GFELLER, WARREN 244
GHAI, DHARAM 38
GHOLZ, HENRY L. 372
GIBBONS, JERRY 252
GIBBONS, ROBERT M. 29
GIBBONS, WHIT 107
GIBBS, LOIS MARIE 175
GIBBS, TREY 214
GIBSON, DAVID H. 160
GIBSON, MARGE 236
GIBSON, RICK 101
GIERSON, LESLIE 322
GIESECKE, JOHN H. 274
GIESEN, KENNETH 306
GIESFELDT, MARK F. 124
GIESSMAN, NORBERT D. 81
GIFFHORN, KENWOOD 102
GIFFORD, GERALD F. 380

Staff Name Index

504 STAFF NAME INDEX

GIGUERE, SUZANNE ... 131
GILBERT, ALPHONSE H. ... 391
GILBERT, BRIAN ... 130, 276
GILBERT, CAROLINE ... 212
GILBERT, DAVID E. ... 101
GILBERT, JAMES R. ... 376
GILCHREST, NORMAN ... 139
GILCHRIST, DOOLEY ... 232
GILCHRIST, DUNCAN ... 210
GILDER, GIL ... 39
GILES, WARREN ... 241
GILFORD, ROBERT J. ... 103
GILL, DEBORAH ... 287
GILL, FRANK ... 153, 265
GILL, GARY ... 60
GILL, JOSEPH P. ... 73
GILL, SANDRA H. ... 268
GILLEPSIE, JAMES ... 363
GILLESPIE, BRIAN ... 128
GILLESPIE, FRANCIS P. ... 35
GILLESPIE, JAMES ... 65
GILLET, F. WARRINGTON, JR. ... 213
GILLETTE, AMY ... 224
GILLEY, SUSAN ... 310
GILLIGAN, PAT ... 313
GILLILAND, KIM ... 40
GILLILAND, MARRY ... 282
GILLILAND, ROBERT L. ... 114
GILLIS, JIM L., JR. ... 57
GILLIS, RONNIE ... 294
GILLS, ROY ... 329
GILMAN, BENJAMIN A. ... 3, 5
GILMORE, BRUCE ... 74
GILMORE, GEORGE ... 252
GILMORE, R. GRANT ... 145
GILMORE, THOMAS J. ... 285
GILSDORF, MICHAEL ... 30
GILSON, JAMES ... 44
GILWORTH, RON ... 286
GIMELLO, RICHARD ... 87
GINGERY, GARY L. ... 82
GINGOLD, JAN ... 312
GINSBERG, JOSHUA ... 351
GINSBURG, ALAN L. ... 13
GIOVANNITTI, ERNEST F. ... 102
GIPSON, CHESTER ... 30
GIPSON, PHILIP S. ... 66, 374
GIRTON, DON ... 245
GISH, STACEY ... 68
GLASER, LUIS ... 231
GLASS, GARY B. ... 127
GLASS, JAMES H. ... 352
GLASS, JOHN D. ... 41
GLASS, ROBERT H. ... 289
GLASSCOCK, SELMA N. ... 346
GLAZE, WILLIAM H. ... 384
GLEASON, JIM ... 196
GLEIBER, JOHN ... 321
GLICKMAN, DAN ... 28
GLIDDEN, CLIFFORD ... 49
GLIDDEN, TIM ... 278
GLISSMAN, INGE ... 232
GLOCK, JAMES W. ... 300
GLODEN, TERESA ... 76
GLOVER, ALLAN ... 194
GLOVER, RONALD L. ... 81
GLOWKA, ARTHUR ... 316
GLUECK, TOM ... 20
GLYNN, THOMAS P. ... 15
GNAM, ROSEMARIE ... 239
GOBER, PATRICIA ... 161
GODDARD, CHRIS ... 7
GODDARD, KEN ... 27
GODFREY, MARY ... 74
GODISH, DR. JOHN PICHTELL, DR. FRED SIEWERT, THAD ... 373
GODISH, THAD ... 373
GODSHALK, GORDON ... 379
GOELZ, PETER ... 34
GOERGEN, GLENN N. ... 322
GOERL, VINCETTE ... 32
GOETZ, RAY ... 95
GOFF, BENNY ... 258
GOFF, GARY R. ... 93
GOING, TONY ... 285
GOLBERG, JUDY ... 248
GOLBY, DAVID ... 68
GOLD, LORETTA ... 254
GOLD, PAULA W. ... 188
GOLDEN, JENNIFER ... 329
GOLDEN, OLIVIA ... 14
GOLDEN, RAYMOND L. ... 275
GOLDEN, WILLIAM T. ... 139
GOLDENTYER, ELIZABETH ... 29
GOLDMAN, CAROLINE TAYLOR ... 187
GOLDMAN, LYNN R. ... 11
GOLDMAN, PATTI ... 198
GOLDSTEIN, ALFRED ... 261
GOLDSWORTHY, PATRICK D. ... 291
GOLDZBAND, LAWRENCE ... 48
GOLLEDGE, REGINALD G. ... 161
GOLLY, WAYNE ... 79
GOLVER, EDWARD N. ... 167
GOMES, JAMES R. ... 203
GOMES, W. R. ... 47
GONELLA, VICTOR ... 170
GONZALES, GABRIEL ... 18
GONZALES, JUDE ... 89
GONZALES, SANTIAGO ... 89
GONZALES, TOM ... 273
GONZALEZ, I. MILEY ... 32
GONZALEZ, MANUEL ... 234
GONZALEZ, MILEY ... 28
GONZOLEZ, MARIA LOURDES ... 37
GOOD, ALICIA M. ... 106
GOOD, KAREN ... 102
GOODE, ANN E. ... 10
GOODE, RALPH ... 185
GOODENOUGH, ERIC ... 195
GOODHEART, JAMES R. ... 303
GOODHEART, JIM ... 255
GOODING, RICHARD A. ... 167
GOODLING, BILL ... 5
GOODMAN, ALBERT ... 345
GOODMAN, DAVID ... 370
GOODMAN, JIM ... 68
GOODMAN, NANCY ... 203
GOODMAN, SHERRI W. ... 13
GOODNIGHT, BILL ... 224
GOODPASTER, GARY ... 196
GOODSON, RALPH ... 215
GOODWIN, ANDREW ... 44
GOODWIN, DANIEL ... 320
GOODWIN, GARY ... 194
GOODWIN, MELVIN ... 219
GOODWIN, RICHARD H., SR. ... 186
GOOHART, JIM ... 44
GORDON, BRUCE ... 249
GORDON, CLAY ... 19
GORDON, GAYLE ... 24
GORDON, GERALD ... 340
GORDON, GUY ... 76
GORDON, KATHY ... 25
GORDON, KEN ... 10
GORDON, ROBERT ... 94
GORDON, RUE E. ... 274
GORDON, THEODORE ... 193
GORE, BOB ... 120
GORE, RON ... 39
GORMAN, KEVIN ... 298
GORMAN, ROBERT F. ... 41
GOROSPE, KATHY ... 12
GORSEN, MAUREEN ... 47
GOSE, ROBERT L. ... 177
GOSLINER, MICHAEL L. ... 8
GOSSELIN, ANDRE ... 387
GOSSWEILER, WILLIAM ... 20
GOSTOMSKI, TED ... 392
GOSWAMI, D. YOGI ... 372
GOTHARD, TIM ... 136
GOTSCH, JERRY ... 174
GOTT, EDWIN H., JR. ... 314
GOTT-JANZEN, GEORGEEN ... 299
GOUDY, BILL ... 314
GOUGEON, THOMAS A. ... 279
GOUGH, KASSANDRA ... 48
GOUGH, MARY ... 226
GOULD, JOHN E. ... 150
GOULD, LINDA ... 192
GOULD, MARK ... 388
GOULD, RICK ... 229
GOURLAY, JIM ... 163
GOVER, CHARLES H. ... 123
GOVER, CHUCK ... 123
GOVER, KEVIN ... 23, 24
GOVONI, JEFF ... 143
GRABB, ROBERT W. ... 117
GRABOWICZ, GREGORY J. ... 103
GRACE, JAMES ... 105
GRADY, SUE ... 124
GRAEBNER, JEAN ... 164
GRAEF, HENRY ... 305
GRAF, WILLIAM L. ... 161
GRAFF, DELANO R. ... 103
GRAFF, WALTER ... 158
GRAFTON, WILLIAM ... 123
GRAHAM, ALAN R. ... 128
GRAHAM, BOB ... 1, 100
GRAHAM, C. ... 37
GRAHAM, CHRISTOPHER L. ... 255
GRAHAM, DANIEL J. ... 130
GRAHAM, GEORGE G. ... 108
GRAHAM, JAMES A. ... 94
GRAHAM, PAT ... 311
GRAHAM, PATRICK ... 228
GRAHAM, PATRICK J. ... 82
GRAHAM, RON ... 110
GRAHAME, DIDY ... 362
GRAHAME, IAIN ... 362
GRAHM, GARY ... 112
GRAMS, DENNIS D. ... 11
GRAND, JAMES B. ... 39
GRANDY, JOHN W. ... 223
GRANN, DOUGLAS H. ... 351
GRANOFF, MICHAEL D. ... 339
GRANOSKI, CHARLES M., JR. ... 151
GRANQUIST, DEBORAH ... 341
GRANSKOU, MARY ... 173
GRANT, ANDREW H., II ... 342
GRANT, GARY ... 205
GRANT, JAMES E., JR. ... 44
GRANT, MALCOLM J. ... 106
GRANT, R. ALEXANDER ... 14
GRANT, WILLIAM ... 240
GRASSI, ANTHONY P. ... 154
GRASSO, TOM ... 178
GRAVES, DON ... 69
GRAVES, DONALD H. ... 375
GRAVES, J. E. ... 391
GRAVES, JIMMY ... 80
GRAVES, LEON C. ... 115
GRAVES, RANDY L. ... 195
GRAVES, SAM BRUCE, SR. ... 259
GRAY, BRIAN T. ... 194
GRAY, DAVID ... 331
GRAY, DON ... 201
GRAY, GERALD J. ... 150
GRAY, JAN ... 323
GRAY, MARY McPHAIL ... 51
GRAY, PAMELA A. ... 188
GRAY, PAUL ... 85
GRAY, RICHARD ... 211, 382
GRAY, TERRENCE ... 106
GRAYBEAL, JAMES ... 53
GRAYBILL,, J. CARL, JR. ... 103
GREATHEAD, R. SCOTT ... 142
GREELEY, MAUREEN L. ... 361
GREEN, BUTCH ... 140
GREEN, CHAMPE ... 99
GREEN, CHAMPE B ... 356
GREEN, DANA ... 17
GREEN, DANIEL ... 217
GREEN, EMILY ... 217
GREEN, EMORY ... 93
GREEN, GEORGE ... 112, 234
GREEN, GREG ... 101
GREEN, KIRBY ... 54
GREEN, KIRBY, III ... 54
GREEN, LANE ... 329
GREEN, LEAH ... 198
GREEN, ORVILLE ... 62
GREEN, RANDY ... 6, 340
GREENBERG, ART ... 31
GREENE, BETSY ... 248
GREENE, DALE ... 215
GREENE, GEORGE ... 234
GREENE, JEFF ... 39
GREENE, JOSEPH A. ... 103
GREENE, STEVE ... 272
GREENE, THOMAS ... 292
GREENE, WADE ... 247
GREENFIELD, TONY ... 168
GREENHALGH, RANDY ... 340
GREENLEE, JACK ... 20
GREENLEE, JASON ... 229
GREENSHIELDS, BRUCE ... 30
GREENSTEIN, JOEL G. ... 26
GREENWOOD, CARY ... 101
GREENWOOD, M. R. ... 139
GREENWOOD, STEVE ... 101
GREER, JIM ... 100, 346
GREEVES, JOHN T. ... 35
GREGG, BILL ... 26
GREGG, FRANK ... 323
GREGG, GEORGE ... 104
GREGG, PETE ... 92
GREGORY, ALBERT ... 55
GREGORY, GARY ... 50
GREGORY, JAMES D. ... 384
GREGORY, JOHN ... 110
GREGORY, LAURA ... 260
GREGORY, TOMMY ... 80
GREIFER, JOHN ... 29
GRESE, ROBERT ... 255
GRESHAM, W. W., JR. ... 193
GRESSMANN, MICHAEL ... 172
GREVE, WILLIAM F., JR. ... 309
GRIBBLE, ROBERT ... 345
GRIEBLING, RICHARD ... 51
GRIES, DANIEL ... 360
GRIEVE, VIKKI ... 354
GRIFFEL, ROBERT ... 62
GRIFFEN, PHILIP ... 92
GRIFFIN, DIANE F. ... 131
GRIFFIN, JOHN R. ... 73
GRIFFIN, JUNE ... 343
GRIFFIN, STAN ... 333, 334
GRIFFIN-JONES, MARY MURRAY ... 133
GRIFFITH, BRAD ... 40
GRIFFITH, GARY A. ... 223
GRIFFITH, LEON ... 64
GRIFFITH, RICK ... 269
GRIFFITH, ROBERT D. ... 302
GRIFFITHS, DON ... 299
GRIGGS, JAMES H. ... 39
GRIGSBY, STEVE ... 243
GRILLEY, DORIAN ... 257
GRILLOT, CHRIS ... 238
GRIMES, BRIAN K. ... 35
GRIMES, ROY ... 68, 354
GRIMES, STANELY ... 284
GRIMM, ERIC ... 56
GRIMM, NANCY ... 366
GRIMMETT, HAROLD K. ... 45
GRINDAL, BRUCE T. ... 372
GRIP, KJCU ... 7
GRISHAW, LETITIA J. ... 15
GRIZZARD, KENT ... 79
GRIZZLE, JOHN M. ... 366
GROFFMAN, PETER M. ... 227
GRONOWSKI, ROBERT ... 84
GROSBOLL, CAROLYN T. ... 63
GROSBOLL, CAROLYN TAFT ... 63
GROSS, DAVID W. ... 93, 382
GROSS, JOEL ... 15
GROSS, JOHN ... 224
GROSS, KAY ... 199
GROSSI, RALPH E. ... 142
GROSSWILER, ED ... 364
GROSVENOR, GILBERT M. ... 268
GROTON, JIMMY ... 329
GROVER, TONY ... 119
GROVES, EARL ... 273
GROVES, PAM ... 292
GRUBER, ALAN ... 158
GRUBINGER, VERN ... 115
GRUE, CHRISTIAN E. ... 120
GRUENBERG, PHIL ... 46
GRUENEBAUM, JANE ... 248
GRUMBACH, ANTONIA M. ... 242
GRUMBINE, DENNIS ... 104
GRUNDMAN, KELLY ... 141
GRUSNICK, RICHARD ... 39
GRUSPE, OSCAR V. ... 333
GRUTHOFF, BRUCE ... 195
GRYDER, R. J. ... 41
GRYNIEWSKI, JAMES ... 77
GUARINO, JENNIFER ... 341
GUDAUSKAS, HERTA ... 251
GUDES, SCOTT B. ... 12
GUENSLER, DARRELL ... 47
GUENTER, HERB ... 42
GUENTHER, JOHN ... 78
GUERRI, ELMER A. ... 162
GUEST, DAVID G. ... 198
GUILFOYLE, JOAN ... 160
GUILIANO, WILLIAM ... 387
GUION, ANN F. ... 185
GUISE, DENNIS T. ... 103
GUISINGER, ALLEN W. ... 273, 275
GUITJENS, JOHN C. ... 380
GULLESTAD, P. ... 293
GULLIFORD, JAMES B. ... 65
GULLIVER, R. ... 129
GUMMEY, CHARLES F., JR. ... 192
GUNDERSON, JAMES D. ... 362
GUNDERSON, JEFFREY ... 79
GUNN, ROBERTA M. ... 307
GUNN, SUE ... 349
GUNTER, JOHN E. ... 379
GUNTON, RUSSELL ... 104
GUPTA, GIAN ... 377
GURITZ, DAVE ... 202
GUTIERREZ, FRANKLIN J. ... 58
GUTOWSKI, CAROLYN M. ... 288
GUY, CHRISTOPHER ... 146
GUY, CHRISTOPHER S. ... 66, 374
GUYMON, JIM ... 114
GUZMAN, LOUANN C. ... 58
GUZMAN, ROSA N. ... 105
GUZZARDI, JOSEPH ... 170
GUZZO, DOROTHY P. ... 87
GWYN, THOMAS W. ... 365
GWYNNE, JOHN ... 351

H

HAAS, WAYNE T. ... 61
HABERMAN, BOB ... 343
HABERWAVY, STEVE ... 318
HACK, DON ... 20
HACKLEY, PATRICK D. ... 285
HADAN, ASHOK C. ... 35
HADDAD, KEN ... 55
HADDOCK, JAMES D. ... 133
HADI, DIANE ... 55
HADLEY, JAMES ... 81
HADLEY, KATHY ... 261
HAERING, HANS PETER ... 363
HAFFNER, MARLENE ... 15
HAGAN, MARK ... 17, 269
HAGAN, PAUL ... 224
HAGELE, F. JOHN ... 197
HAGEMEYER, RICHARD H. ... 13
HAGEN, JOHN F. ... 42
HAGEN, VONNY ... 78
HAGENER, JEFF ... 83
HAGENIERS, MARILYN ... 242
HAGENSTEIN, PERRY ... 284
HAGGIE, MICHAEL ROBIN ... 179
HAGLEY, CYNTHIA ... 79
HAHN, LESLIE E. ... 278
HAHN, MARIANNE ... 163
HAHN, MARTHA G. ... 24
HAIR, JAY D. ... 274, 359
HAIRE, MICHAEL ... 73
HAJOST, SCOTT A. ... 235
HAKES, JAY E. ... 14

Staff Name Index

STAFF NAME INDEX

HALBERT, SUSAN ... 332
HALES, DAVID ... 16
HALEY, WENDELL P. ... 239
HALFHILL, MICHELE ... 122, 203
HALFORD, DOUGLAS ... 354
HALFPENNY, GEOFF ... 192
HALL, ALAN ... 57
HALL, BARBARA ... 220
HALL, BEN ... 247
HALL, CATHY ... 187
HALL, DAVE ... 303
HALL, DOUG ... 279, 354
HALL, GEORGE A. ... 253
HALL, J. MICHAEL ... 13
HALL, JAMES ... 34
HALL, JEANNE ... 56
HALL, JIM ... 86
HALL, JOHN ... 80, 114
HALL, KEN ... 168
HALL, LINNEA ... 357
HALL, PATRICIA ... 309
HALL, PINKY ... 54
HALL, RICHARD ... 113
HALL, ROBERT E. ... 135
HALL, STEPHEN ... 106
HALL, STEVE ... 195, 231
HALL, TRACEY ... 164
HALLAM, ROBERT ... 230
HALL-ARBER, MADELEINE ... 144
HALLET, DIANA L. ... 81
HALLETT, JEAN ... 212
HALLIBURTON, BOBBY J. ... 268
HALLINAN, JACQUELINE ... 346
HALLOCK, STEPHANIE ... 101
HALLOWELL, SAMUEL H., JR. ... 164
HALLUM, ALAN ... 57
HALLWARD, CLARE ... 178
HALMAN, EDWARD L. ... 35
HALSTEAD, PETE ... 226
HALVERSON, BARBARA ... 239
HALVORSON, CHRISTINE ... 138
HALVORSON, WILLIAM ... 321, 367
HAM, MICHAEL L. ... 58
HAM, SUSAN M. ... 58
HAMANN, RICHARD, ESQ. ... 207
HAMBLEY, MARK ... 16
HAMBURG, MARGARET ... 14
HAMDY, FAROUK ... 29
HAMILTON, BRUCE ... 318
HAMILTON, CHRIS ... 250
HAMILTON, JOAN ... 318
HAMILTON, JOHN ... 258
HAMILTON, JOHN M. ... 64
HAMILTON, LANSIN R. ... 257
HAMILTON, LARRY E. ... 24
HAMILTON, LISA ... 343
HAMILTON, MILTON H., JR. ... 109
HAMILTON, RICHARD B. ... 95
HAMILTON, SAM ... 27
HAMILTON, STANLEY F. ... 61
HAMILTON, THOMAS E. ... 33
HAMLET, SHELBY P. ... 213
HAMLIN, PETE ... 66
HAMM, B. ... 273
HAMMAKER, JOHN L. ... 278
HAMMEL, PAT ... 295
HAMMER, R. DAVID ... 380
HAMMERSCHMIDT, RON ... 67
HAMMON, JOSEPH ... 335
HAMMOND, BRAD ... 63
HAMMOND, JERRY ... 96
HAMMOND, K. R. ... 174
HAMMOND, STEPHEN ... 91
HANCE, ROBERT ... 78
HANCOCK, DON ... 326
HANCOCK, J. ... 129
HAND, EDWARD F. ... 311
HANDLEY, BARBARA ... 220
HANDLEY, JOSEPH ... 129
HANDLEY, VIRGINIA ... 212
HANEBERG, WILLIAM C. ... 89
HANES, KIKU A. ... 187
HANES, KIKU H. ... 187
HANEY, ALAN ... 393
HANEY, DONALD C. ... 68
HANKINS, JOSEPH A. ... 187
HANKINSON, JOHN H., JR. ... 11
HANLEY, DONALD P. ... 121
HANNA, CAROLYN ... 392
HANNA, GLENDA ... 137
HANNA, ROBERT B. ... 383
HANNAH, JUDITH ... 370
HANNON, BRUCE M. ... 177
HANOUSEK, RICHARD O. ... 303
HANSCH, SUSAN ... 47
HANSEL, JOHN P. ... 200
HANSELKA, C. WAYNE ... 110
HANSELL, TYLER ... 102
HANSEN, DAVE ... 130
HANSEN, DAVID ... 238
HANSEN, DOUG ... 109
HANSEN, ED ... 139
HANSEN, KATY ... 311
HANSEN, KELLY ... 158
HANSEN, PAUL ... 240, 380
HANSEN, SUSAN TAYLOR ... 138

HANSER, MARIEANNE ... 260
HANSON, DARRELL ... 237
HANSON, HARLEY ... 196
HANSON, JAMES ... 74
HANSON, JESSE ... 96
HANSON, MARCIA ... 261
HANSON, MARTIN ... 258
HANSON, MICHAEL T. ... 353
HANSON, NELS ... 344
HANUS, ANN ... 101
HARCOMBE, PAULA A. ... 389
HARDER, DWIGHT ... 42
HARDIE, DAVID ... 242
HARDING, BEN ... 269
HARDING, ROBIN ... 283
HARDING, RUSSELL J. ... 76
HARDISKY, TOM ... 356
HARDY, FRED ... 250
HARDY, JOE ... 80
HARDY, PAM ... 221
HARDY, STUART ... 339
HARDY, YVAN ... 38
HARELSON, THOMAS L. ... 124
HARFORD, CARLTON ... 238
HARGRAVE, NANCY G. ... 151
HARGROVE, EUGENE C. ... 175, 390
HARKIN, TOM ... 2, 6
HARLAND, JIM ... 113
HARLOW, HENRY J. ... 393
HARLOW, TRUDY ... 26
HARLOWE, ANNA ... 200
HARM, MINDY ... 223
HARMON, BOB ... 110
HARMON, DAVID ... 214
HARMON, LARRY ... 195
HARNACK, RONALD D. ... 77
HARNER, GREG ... 47
HARPER, CRAIG ... 110
HARPER, HERBERT ... 110
HARPER, JAKE ... 135
HARPER, SALLYANNE ... 10
HARRELL, REGINAL M. ... 144
HARRIMAN, BETTIE R. ... 360
HARRINGTON, GEORGE C. ... 284
HARRINGTON, H. MICHAEL ... 61
HARRINGTON, RALPH ... 214
HARRINGTON, RUBE ... 30
HARRINGTON, STEVEN A. ... 210
HARRIS, B. L. ... 111
HARRIS, BETTY H. ... 190
HARRIS, BILL ... 313
HARRIS, C. COLEMAN ... 267
HARRIS, CRAIG K. ... 143
HARRIS, DONNY ... 44
HARRIS, DOUGLAS ... 268
HARRIS, DUANE ... 57
HARRIS, EARL ... 57
HARRIS, ELIZABETH ... 255
HARRIS, ELLEN STERN ... 190
HARRIS, FRED ... 95
HARRIS, H. J. ... 392
HARRIS, HERBERT S., JR. ... 277
HARRIS, JACK H. ... 259
HARRIS, JAMES ... 230
HARRIS, JIM ... 120
HARRIS, KATE ... 292
HARRIS, MARY C. ... 273, 275
HARRIS, MIKE ... 57
HARRIS, PAT ... 259
HARRIS, RAY ... 288
HARRIS, RAY E. ... 126
HARRIS, RAYMOND ... 250
HARRIS, RHONDA ... 345
HARRIS, ROD ... 127
HARRIS, SHIRLEY ... 307
HARRIS, WILL ... 72
HARRISON, CHARLES W. ... 107
HARRISON, CRAIG S. ... 140
HARRISON, DAVID B. ... 87
HARRISON, JAMES M. ... 9
HARRISON, JEREMY ... 361
HARRISON, JOHN T. ... 60, 220
HARRISON, LYNN ... 54
HARRISON, MARK ... 99
HARRISON, ROBERT ... 209
HARRISON, ROSS ... 65
HARRISON, TED ... 337
HARRISON, TOM ... 132
HARRISON, VERNA E. ... 73
HARRISON, WILLIAM E. ... 67
HARRISON, WILLIAM F. ... 88
HARRISTON, PEYTON T., JR. ... 36
HARROD, LEIGH ... 257
HARSCH, J. WILLIAM ... 164
HARSHAW, HOWARD L. ... 104
HART, DONNA ... 236
HART, LARRY G. ... 116
HART, MARJORIE L. ... 317
HART, RAY ... 49
HART, T. MIKE ... 42
HARTE, EDWARD H. ... 142
HARTER, ROBERT ... 381
HARTFIELD, LIBBY ... 80
HARTIG, BENJAMIN C. ... 323
HARTLE, WILLIAM E. ... 103
HARTLEY, MITSCHKA J. ... 355

HARTMAN, BRAD ... 55
HARTMAN, HERB ... 72
HARTMAN, MARCIA ... 298
HARTMAN, SCOTT ... 272
HARTMAN, STEVE ... 169
HARTMAN, WILLIAM E. ... 245
HARTNETT, DAVID C. ... 374
HARTWELL, DAVID ... 247
HARTWIG, WILLIAM F. ... 26
HARUN, KEVIN ... 136
HARVEY, ALYNN D. ... 253
HARVEY, DAVE ... 132
HARVEY, HOLGER H. ... 192
HARVEY, JAMES T. ... 321
HARVEY, M. ... 8
HARVEY, M. J. ... 389
HARVEY, MARK ... 155
HARVEY, ROSE ... 337
HARVEY, TOM ... 112
HARWOOD, TERRY ... 138
HASAY, RED ... 160
HASELTINE, SUSAN ... 26
HASEMAN, LEO ... 78
HASENYAGER, ROBERT ... 113
HASHIMOTO, ANDREW ... 100
HASLETT, BILLYE ... 21
HASSEL, HARRY S. ... 13
HASSELL, JOHN ... 99
HASSETT, JOHN ... 383
HASSLER, CURT ... 392
HASTEY, EDWARD L. ... 24
HATAKEYAMA, HISAKO ... 363
HATCH, CHARLES R. ... 372
HATCH, ELLIS ... 86
HATCH, WHITNEY ... 154
HATCHER, BOB ... 110
HATCHER, RICHARD ... 98
HATFIELD, NINA ROSE ... 24
HATT, ROYD ... 289
HAUB, CARL ... 305
HAUGE, THOMAS M. ... 124
HAUGH, JOSEPH S. ... 118
HAUGHIAN, PHIL ... 231
HAUGLAND, GARY ... 287
HAUN, LES ... 110
HAUPTMAN, MIKE ... 261
HAUSEL, W. DAN ... 127
HAUSER, CARL E. ... 81
HAUSER, RON ... 259
HAUSRATH, ALAN ... 224
HAVE, JIM/DONNA ... 164
HAVENS, JIM ... 164
HAVILAND, JIM ... 260
HAWKES, JANET ... 153
HAWKEY, DAVID J. ... 348
HAWKINS, H. ROSS ... 223
HAWKINS, JOHN ... 251
HAWKINS, JOYCE ... 30
HAWKINS, RICHARD ... 43, 367
HAWKINS, SEAN ... 212
HAWKINS, T. EVELYN ... 309
HAWKS, RICHARD ... 383
HAWLEY, CLIFF ... 90
HAWLEY, JOYCE ... 169
HAWLEY, KYLE ... 223
HAWLEY, SUSAN ... 270
HAWTHORNE, DON ... 99
HAWTHORNE, JOSETTA ... 190, 347
HAYAKAWA, MITSUTOSHI ... 179
HAYASHI, DENNIS W. ... 14
HAYASHI, STUART ... 20
HAYDEN, ELIZABETH A. ... 35
HAYDEN, MICHAEL ... 247
HAYDEN, MIKE ... 156, 213
HAYDEN, WORTH ... 128
HAYES, DANIEL B. ... 147
HAYES, DANIEL C. ... 241
HAYES, HELEN ... 246
HAYES, IRENE ... 254
HAYES, JOHNNY H. ... 36
HAYES, LARK ... 325
HAYES, LISA ... 159
HAYES, SAMUEL E., JR. ... 104
HAYES, TOM ... 254
HAYHURST, PAGE ... 391
HAYNE, JAMES L. ... 331
HAYNES, JANE ... 294
HAYNES, JIM ... 110
HAYNING, JOHN E. ... 155
HAYWOOD, CARLTON ... 8
HAYWOOD, MARY JOY ... 167
HAZARD, NANCY ... 292
HAZELL, ED ... 206
HAZELWOOD, SUSAN ... 164
HAZEN, DALE ... 315
HAZLEWOOD, PETER T. ... 310
HEAD, CHUCK ... 110
HEAD, DOUG ... 207
HEAD, SHAWN ... 358
HEALEY, BURKE ... 99
HEALEY, M. ... 368
HEALY, JONATHAN ... 75
HEALY, ROBERT G. ... 384
HEAPS, CHIP ... 195
HEARN, J. L. ... 73
HEATH JR., RALPH T. ... 328

HEATH, HELEN B. ... 328
HEATH, RICHARD ... 112
HEATHCOTE, ISOBEL ... 172
HEATON, LOUIS, III ... 70
HEATON, RAYMOND V. ... 113
HEATWOLE, CHARLES A. ... 382
HEATWOLE, HAROLD F. ... 384
HEBBLETHWAITE, JOHN ... 188
HEBER, SHARON ... 56
HEBERT, GEORGES ... 328
HECHINGER, DEBORAH S. ... 363
HECKER, VINCE ... 307
HECKERT, MARK ... 236
HECKLY, SUSAN ... 236
HEDDEN, BILL ... 216
HEDGE, ROGER ... 226
HEDRICH, ANNE ... 278
HEELAN, CYNTHIA ... 370
HEFFERAN, COLIEN ... 32
HEGEMAN, INGEBORG ... 253
HEGWOOD, RON K. ... 168
HEHR, JOHN ... 334
HEIDE, CHERYL ... 78
HEIDENREICH, BILL ... 237
HEIDER, WILLIAM A. ... 266
HEIDINGER, ROY C ... 373
HEIDORN, RANKY ... 63
HEIKEN, DOUG ... 298
HEIKES, DAVID ... 44
HEIL, GERALD ... 78
HEILIG, DAN ... 364
HEILIGMANN, RANDALL B. ... 97
HEIMERMANN, DALE ... 77
HEIMLICH, JOE E. ... 98
HEIN, DAVE ... 260
HEIN, LISA ... 238
HEINEKAMP, NEIL ... 160
HEINEMANN, GENE ... 277
HEINZE-LACEY, BEVERLY ... 275
HEISSEL, DAN ... 65
HEISTAD, ERLING ... 186
HEISTER, CARLA ... 390
HEITSCHMIDT, RODNEY K. ... 321
HEITSERBERG, JON ... 356
HELFRICH, LOUIS A. ... 119
HELFRICH, PHILIP ... 61
HELINSKI, RONALD R. ... 353
HELL, DAVID ... 55
HELLEM, STEVEN B. ... 215
HELLER, VICTOR J. ... 55
HELLMAN, RICHARD A. ... 339
HELMER, WILLIAM ... 92
HELMS, JESSE ... 3, 6
HELMS, JOHN ... 324
HELSLEY, CHARLES ... 59
HEMENWAY, JOHN ... 342
HEMERICKS, GARY ... 81
HEMESATH, LISA ... 239
HEMMER, DENNIS ... 125
HEMMING, JIM ... 189
HEMOND, JOHN A. ... 250
HEMPEL, FRED J. ... 28
HEMPSTEAD, MABEL S. ... 311
HENDEE, JOHN ... 235
HENDEE, JOHN C. ... 373
HENDERSON, BRIAN ... 19
HENDERSON, CLAY ... 206
HENDERSON, CLIFF ... 127
HENDERSON, DAVID ... 286
HENDERSON, FRED ... 173
HENDERSON, JOAN ... 99
HENDERSON, K. R. ... 68
HENDERSON, KARLA ... 291
HENDERSON, PATRICK M. ... 245
HENDERSON, SCOTT ... 43
HENDERSON, WILLIAM M. ... 10
HENDREN, DIANE ... 63
HENDRICKS, CAROL ... 299
HENDRICKS, DONALD R. ... 191
HENDRICKS, ELAINE G. ... 191
HENDRICKS, MICHAEL L. ... 148
HENDRICKS, SCOTT ... 214
HENDRICKSON, DEAN ... 155
HENDRIX, STEPHEN ... 374
HENERT, MARTIN M. ... 124
HENGTES, ROBERT ... 81
HENKE, SCOTT ... 357
HENLEY, R. PAGE, JR. ... 213
HENNE, PAUL W. ... 26
HENNE-KERR, JACKIE ... 355
HENNEY, JANE ... 15
HENNINGS, RONALD ... 125
HENRY, DALE ... 195
HENRY, GENE M. ... 195
HENRY, MARK ... 302
HENRY, ROBERT D. ... 53
HENRY, STEVE ... 89
HENRY, THEODORE B. ... 145
HENSCHEL, KIRA ... 180
HENSEL, DAVE ... 64
HENSHAW, BLAIN ... 130
HENSINGER, KURT THELEN ... 76
HENSLER, RONALD ... 393
HENSLEY, DEMPSLY ... 391
HENSLEY, DOUG ... 68

506
STAFF NAME INDEX

HENSLEY, JOHN 33
HENSON, RICHARD 383
HENZEL, TIM 360
HEPHNER, TRACY SEIDMAN 90
HERB, WILLIAM 20
HERBERT, CURTIS L., JR. 14
HERBST, DAVID L. 64
HEREFORD, SCOTT 288
HERGENRADER, GARY 84, 264
HERGLOTZ, KEVIN 47
HERMAN, ALEXIS M. 15
HERMAN, KENNETH 274
HERMAN, LYNN 53
HERMAN, STEVEN A. 11
HERR, CHRISTIAN R. 104
HERRGESELL, PERRY 48
HERRICK, THERESA 367
HERRICKS, ROSETTA M. 9
HERRING, HARTWELL 217
HERRING, JENNIFER 351
HERSCHLER, MICHAEL 294
HERSHEY, DON 102
HERSHEY, ROGER W. 319
HERSHNER, C. H., JR. 391
HERTZ, ANNABELL 363
HERTZEL, ANTHONY 257
HERWIG, MARK 303
HERZBERG, MARK 286
HESLA, CHRIS 324
HESS, DAVID E. 103
HESS, GENE K. 192
HESS, RICHARD 104
HESS, THOMAS, JR. 355
HESS, TIM 114
HESSELINK, FRITZ 234
HESSER, KAREN L. 302
HESSION, JACK 318
HESTBECK, JAY B. 75
HESTON, CHARLTON 271
HETTINGER, EDWARD 233
HEUMANN, JUDITH 13
HEWETT, DIANNA 360
HEWLETT, ELIZABETH 74
HEYMAN, IRA MICHAEL 320
HEYNEMAN, SUSAN 260
HHULL-SEIG, CAROLYN 321
HIATT, KEMP 249
HIBBARD, DON 60
HIBBARD, JOHN E. 186
HICKEN, BARRY 131
HICKEY, DAN 268
HICKS, BILLY G. 110
HICKS, GWYN 150
HICKS, JOHN 91
HIERONYMOUS, ALAN 231
HIGBY, SUE 341
HIGGINS, KENNETH F. 109
HIGGS, CHARLES E. 124
HIGGS, ERIC 321
HIGHSMITH, R. TOD 360
HIGHT, ROBERT C. 50
HIGHTOWER, MIKE 112
HILDEBRAND, CINDY 238
HILDEBRAND, DEAN C. 95
HILDEBRANDT, DON 359
HILDRETH, HORACE A., JR. 239
HILER, EDWARD A. 111
HILGENDORF, MARAN BRAINARD 186
HILL, BARBARA 356
HILL, BARRY 23
HILL, CARLTON LEE 118
HILL, DAVE 52
HILL, ISABEL 107
HILL, JAMES R., II 307
HILL, JOHN R. 65
HILL, LAWRENCE W. 322
HILL, LOREN 165
HILL, MEREDITH L. 102
HILL, MURRAY 130
HILL, TESSA 246
HILL, THOMAS D. 111
HILL, THOMAS K. 110
HILLARD, ANNE 31
HILLBERRY, GARY 34
HILLER, JOE 126
HILLHOUSE, JAMES D. 336
HILLMAN, BOB 62
HILLMAN, CONRAD N. 195
HILLS, DAVIE 318
HILLY, JAMES 327
HILTON, J. RICHARD 322
HILTON, JAREL 135
HILTON, KEN 345
HILTON, LAWRIE 251
HIMLAN, ED 253
HINCHEY, DON 343
HINDS, JUDITH 304
HINELSLY, PHILLIP 39
HINES, JAMES 75
HINEY, JIM 112
HINKLEY, BILL 55
HINMAN, KEN 266
HINSHAW, JEFFREY M. 94
HINTON, RANDY 91
HIPPENSTEEL, PETER A. 64
HIPPLER, MELISSA 307
HIRAI, LAWRENCE 20
HIRAIWA, GAISHI 216
HIRNER, DEIRDRE 187
HIRNING, KATHLEEN M. 14
HIRREL, SUZANNE SMITH 44, 160
HIRSCH, DAVE 356
HIRSCH, JUDE 384
HIRSH, HEIDI 17
HIRSHFIELD, MICHAEL 178
HIRST, ERIC 329
HIRTH, DAVID H. 391
HISEY, GLENN E. 304
HITCHCOCK, LOREN 44
HITCHCOCK, RAY 78
HITCHINGHAM, RICHARD 255
HITZ, RUSSELL 360
HJERTAAS, DALE 282
HJORT, H. W. 209
HLUCHY, MICHELE M. 382
HOACHLANDER, SHAYNE 356
HOAGLAND, ROY 157, 178
HOARE, JOHN 351
HOBBS, ALMA 32
HOBBS, GAIL 266
HOBSON, CYNTHIA 48
HOBSON, DAVID C. 117
HOBSON, WILLIAM 337
HOBSTETTER, PETE 228
HOCHHALTER, SCOTT 96
HOCHMAN, PATRICIA 186
HOCHMUTH, JAY C. 124
HOCK, WINAND K. 105
HOCKER, JEAN W. 247
HOCOG, ESTANISLAO 300
HOCUTT, CHARLES 377
HODANBOSI, ROBERT 97
HODDER, JAN 300
HODGDON, HARRY E. 357
HODGES, CATHLEEN 354
HODGES, ELOISE 338
HODGES, M. WAYNE 35
HODGES, MIKE 238
HODGES, THERESA 67
HODGSON, CHRIS 131
HODGSON, ERNEST 384
HODSDON, JOHN 284
HODSON, RONALD G. 94, 95
HOECKER, JAMES 14
HOEDT, JEFF 97
HOEFER, PHIL 51
HOFER, DOUG 109
HOFF, DENA 292
HOFFBUHR, JACK W. 156
HOFFMAN, BOB 18
HOFFMAN, HENRY 338
HOFFMAN, JUDIE 247
HOFFMAN, JULIE 345
HOFFMAN, LANTZ A. 103
HOFFMAN, MICHAEL R. 81
HOFFMAN, NANCY 213
HOFFMAN, NINA 268
HOFFMAN, ROBERT C. 312
HOFFMAN, STEPHEN 221
HOFFMAN, STEVEN M. 256
HOFMAN, ROBERT J. 8
HOGAN, KATHLEEN 227
HOGG, JOHN T. 190
HOHMAN, TOM 64
HOHMANN, STEPHEN 69
HOHN, BONNIE 343
HOKIT, JIM 183
HOLAHAN, GARY M. 35
HOLBROOK, TODD 57
HOLDEN, NELDA 324
HOLDER, GLENN 131
HOLDING, OLIVIA 290
HOLENSTEIN, JULIAN 217
HOLFORD, MATT 335
HOLLABAUGH, PAUL 226
HOLLAND, BRUCE 17
HOLLAND, CLAIRE 136
HOLLAND, DAVID 26
HOLLAND, MAURICE J. 386
HOLLATZ, DONALD 333
HOLLE, DEBORAH 331
HOLLERN, MICHAEL 221
HOLLEY, ROBERT D. 328
HOLLINGSWORTH, CAROL 31
HOLLINS, ROSALIND 70
HOLLIS, M. CLAYTON, JR. 244
HOLLIS, SUE 259
HOLLOWAY, THOMAS 186
HOLLUMS, DON 50
HOLMAN, BILL 94
HOLMAN, BLAIR 347
HOLMER, STEVE 152
HOLMES, CHARLES A. 135
HOLMES, JERRY 249
HOLMES, JOHN R. 46
HOLMES, MARK 297
HOLMES, MARTY 313
HOLMES, PATTI 186
HOLMES, ROBERT 19
HOLMES, ROGER 78, 228, 268
HOLMWOOD, JOSEPH 43
HOLPERIN, JIM 333
HOLSINGER, SHAWN 19
HOLST, GLENDA 137
HOLST, STAN 250
HOLSTON, SHARON SMITH 14
HOLT, DENNIS 39
HOLT, JAN 361
HOLTCAMP, RONALD 333
HOLZ, BERNIE 125
HOMAN, THOMAS R. 122
HOMANN, RICH 51
HOMER, PEGGY 331
HOMULAS, PETER 36
HONNOLD, DOUGLAS L. 198
HOOD, LAMARTING 387
HOOD, LAURA 191
HOOD, WAYNE J. 140
HOOGENBOOM, HUGO 304
HOOPER, BILL 170
HOOPER, JON 368
HOOT, LYNNE 252
HOOTEN, CHARLES R. 122
HOOTMAN, LARRY 126
HOOVEN, LYNN 57
HOPKINS, LEWIS D. 373
HOPKINS, LORAH 256
HOPKINS, SUZANNE B. 252
HOPKINS, THOMAS L. 116, 118
HOPPE, RICHARD T. 355
HOPPER, DENNIS 58
HOPPER, GEORGE M. 110, 389
HOPPER, HILARY LAMBERT 150
HOPPER, STEVE 259
HOPPIE, ROBERT W. 61
HOPPLE, RICHARD V. 154
HORAN, JAMES 120
HORIUCHI, CINDY 50
HORN, CHARLES 39
HORN, CHARLES E. 118
HORN, FLOYD P. 32
HORN, STEVE 1, 47
HORN, THOMAS F. 162
HORN, WILLIAM P. 352
HORNBACK, JOHN E. 69
HORNE, PETER 86
HORNER, WESLEY R. 168
HORRIGAN, JIM 318
HORTON, ALISON 255
HORTON, BECKY 160
HORTON, DICK 270
HORTON, JESSE 20
HORTON, P. M. 108
HORTON, PAUL 83
HORVATH, BILL 263
HORWICH, ROB 184
HORZEPA, GEORGE 87
HOSHINO, MAKOTO 363
HOSKING, WILLIAM 40, 80
HOSKINS, JOHN D. 81
HOSKINS, MARILYN W. 233
HOSKINS, ZACHARY 240
HOSKISSON, WAYNE 340
HOTALING, LESLIE 53
HOUCK, OLIVER A. 375
HOUGH-GOLDSTEIN, JUDITH A. 371
HOUGHLAND, PAUL, JR. 219
HOUGHTON, JOHN 163
HOURCLE, LAURENT R. 371
HOUSER, ANDREW 126, 130
HOUSER, RON 137
HOUSKA, THOMAS E., II 53
HOUSTON, EDWARD 391
HOUSTOUN, DOMINIQUE M. 148
HOVER, JEROLD 67
HOVIS, JULIE 354
HOVORKA, DUANE 283
HOWARD, ALICE 27
HOWARD, BRUCE S. 317
HOWARD, DENNIS 99
HOWARD, LARRY L. 30
HOWARD, PRESTON 94
HOWARD, RICHARD P. 362
HOWARD, THAD 290
HOWARD, THEODORE E. 381
HOWARD, WILLIAM W. 352
HOWE, HENRY F. 184
HOWE, KAREN 323
HOWE, PAUL 342
HOWE, PAUL R. 342
HOWE, RICHARD 338
HOWE, ROBERT 393
HOWE, SANDY 206
HOWELL, ARTHUR E., JR. 133
HOWELL, CALVIN 283
HOWELL, DOROTHY 133
HOWELL, LIZ 364
HOWELL, LYNN 31
HOWELL, RALPH 80
HOWERY, LARRY 43
HOWIE, JOHN SHARP 193
HOWLAND, WILLIAM G. 218
HOWMAN, KEITH 362
HOWREY, MYRA 248
HOYLE, JOHN C. 35
HOYLE, JOYCE 110
HOYT, JOHN A. 227
HRENO, JOHN R. 172
HUBBARD, GRAYDON 279
HUBBARD, JAMES 150
HUBBARD, JAMES E. 51
HUBBARD, RICHARD 75
HUBBART, LORI 169
HUBBELL, CHARLOTTE 237
HUBBELL, STEPHEN P. 184
HUBBS, CLARK 151
HUBER, ERIC 198
HUBER, JOY 313
HUBER, MICHAEL 152
HUBER, PHIL 19
HUBERT, JAMES 196
HUBERT, WAYNE A. 126
HUDDLESTON, ROBERT 240
HUDKINS, CORDIE 122
HUDON, MARC 217
HUDSON, CAMPBELL, III 186
HUDSON, CHARLES E. 337
HUDSON, DON 251
HUDSON, JOYCE 166
HUDSON, MICHAEL KEITH 353
HUDSON, MIKE 20
HUDSON, NOAH 341
HUDSON, STEWART 242
HUEBLE, TOM 324
HUEBNER, ELAYNE 55
HUEBNER, MARTIN 206
HUELMAN, PATRICK 79
HUEY, KIM 243
HUFF, JANE 164
HUFFAKER, STEVE 62
HUFFMAN, ALAN 258
HUFFMAN, JAMES 386
HUFFMAN, RANDY 122
HUFFORD, RONALD H. 331
HUFFSTATLER, MARLA 258
HUGHES, BRIAN 56
HUGHES, CLAUDE 152
HUGHES, DANIEL C., JR. 192
HUGHES, DEBBIE 286
HUGHES, GARY R. 76
HUGHES, JOHN A. 53
HUGHES, LANCE 276
HUGHES, MARK 198
HUGHES, WALT 48
HUGLER, EDWARD 15
HUGO, NANCY 343
HUGOSON, GENE 77
HUGUNIN, MARC 257
HULL, DONALD A. 100
HULL, HADLAI A. 187
HULL, JAMES B. 111
HULL, KENT 345
HULL, RICHARD 311
HULSE, CHARLES A. 392
HULSEY, BRETT 319
HULTIN, JERRY MACARTHUR 27
HUMISTON, GLENDA 169
HUMPHREY, G. W. 311
HUMPHREY, GILBERT W. 352
HUMPHREY, LOUISE 329
HUMPHREY, STEPHEN R. 321
HUMPHREYS, DAVID J. 154
HUMPHREYS, JAY 56
HUMPHRIES, REBECCA 76
HUMPHRIES, WILLIAM C., JR. 161
HUMRICKHOUSE, SCOTT 124
HUNSAKER, J. E. 100
HUNST, JIM 77
HUNT, DUTSON 90
HUNT, FRAN 349
HUNT, GARY 94
HUNT, HUGH 132
HUNT, JOEL 255
HUNT, JOHN D. 373
HUNT, JOHN DIXON 387
HUNT, KAYE 324
HUNT, SUZELLE 157
HUNTER, BRUCE 390
HUNTER, DAVID B. 175
HUNTER, DICK 130
HUNTER, JIM 269
HUNTER, RHONDA 127
HUNTER, RICHARD G. 56
HUNTER, TIM 19
HUNTER, TOM 7
HUNTINGTON, GEOFF 102
HUNTINGTON, JENNIFER 158
HUNTINGTON, JIM 244
HUNTLEY, EDWARD F. 49
HUNTZINGER, TOM 66
HUNYADI, BILL 313
HUPPERT, GEORGE 393
HURD, ELMER 24
HURD, G. DAVID 280
HURLEY, FREDERICK B., JR 71
HURST, HAROLD 110
HURT, ROBIN 232
HURWICH, EVELYN M. 179
HURWITZ, JOSEPH 261
HUSE, BRIAN 270

Staff Name Index

STAFF NAME INDEX 507

HUSSAIN, MOHAMMED ZAKIR ... 234
HUSSEMAN, TERRY ... 119
HUSSEY, SHARON WOODS ... 215
HUSSMANN, WILLIAM H. ... 74
HUTCHEON, RICHARD J. ... 13
HUTCHESON, DONALD W. ... 68
HUTCHINGS, JAMES ... 158
HUTCHINS, MICHAEL ... 157
HUTCHINS, SAMUEL ... 115
HUTCHISON, BUCK ... 183
HUTCHISON, FRED ... 158
HUTCHISON, LYNNE ... 158
HUTCHISON, THEODORE ... 238
HUTTLINGER, RETTA ... 268
HUTTON, GALE ... 83
HYDE, ARNOUT, JR. ... 122
HYGNSTROM, SCOTT E. ... 84
HYLAND, JOSEPH M. ... 195

I

IANNOTTI, JOHN ... 90
IFJU, GEZA ... 391
IHRKE, CHARLES ... 392
IMAMURA, K. ... 9
IMBERGAMO, BILL ... 264
IMBRECHT, CHARLES R. ... 48
IMLAY, MARC ... 253
IMLAY, MARK ... 20
IMMERGUT, MEL M. ... 166
IMPALLOMENI, VICTORIA ... 310
INCERPI, ANGELO ... 114
INGLE, DON ... 255
INGMAN, DAN ... 120
INGRAHAM, RUTH ANN ... 226
INGRAM, JULIETTE ... 268
INGRAM, TERRENCE N. ... 197
INMAN, ROGER ... 56
INTEMANN, LESLIE ... 189
INTINO, FRANK A. ... 51
IOANNIDES, GERRY ... 97
IONNO, SANDRA ... 328
IRBY, LYNN R. ... 380
IRELAND, JOHN ... 168
IRELAND, KATE ... 329, 352
IRVIN, TOMMY ... 57
IRVIN, WILLIAM ROBERT ... 176
IRVING, MARTIN ... 129
IRWIN, ELISE R. ... 39
IRWIN, FRANCISCA ... 134
IRWIN, JOE R. ... 314
IRWIN, MARILYN ... 237
IRWIN, PAUL ... 229
IRWIN, PAUL G. ... 222, 227, 363
IRWIN, RODNEY H. ... 74
ISAAC, ROBERT A. ... 58
ISAACSON, M. ... 368
ISELY, J. JEFFREY ... 107
ISER, DARYL ... 313
ISLAM, ANWARUL ... 234
ISO-AHOLA, S. ... 377
ISOM, NOELYN ... 83
ISON, JEANNE JAHNIGEN ... 9
ISRAEL, NELLIE ... 292
ITCHMONEY, ROBERT ... 87
ITURREGUI, MIGUEL ... 307
ITZKOFF, DONALD M. ... 28
IURI, MARIA GRAZIA ... 234
IVANKO, JOHN ... 288
IVERSON, DAVE ... 209
IVERSON, PAUL J. ... 84
IVES, SUSAN ... 337
IVEY, OLIN M. ... 215
IZMIRIAN, RICHARD ... 205

J

JABLOW, JUDY ... 10
JACAMO, DALE DE ... 50
JACANGELO, DOMINIC ... 93
JACK, MARY L. ... 163
JACKSON BIRD, W. L. ... 96
JACKSON, ARVA ... 190
JACKSON, BEN D. ... 58
JACKSON, CHARLES N. ... 322
JACKSON, JEFFERY J. ... 58
JACKSON, JEROME A. ... 161
JACKSON, JESSE L. ... 308
JACKSON, JOHN ... 217
JACKSON, KATHRYN J. ... 36
JACKSON, KEN ... 69
JACKSON, LOIS ... 31
JACKSON, MARION T. ... 373
JACKSON, PATTI ... 342
JACKSON, R. MARK ... 355
JACKSON, ROBERT ... 336
JACKSON, SCOTT D. ... 74
JACKSON, SHIRLEY ANN ... 35
JACKSON, SUSAN M. ... 8
JACKY, STEVE ... 101
JACOBI, JOHN ... 112
JACOBS, BERNICE ... 152
JACOBS, CANDACE ... 120
JACOBS, LYNDA ... 206
JACOBS, MARK ... 79
JACOBS, ROBERT T. ... 33
JACOBSEN, JUDITH E. ... 365
JACOBSON, K. N. ... 114
JACOBSON, MICHAEL F. ... 176
JACOBSON, MICHAEL G. ... 56
JACQUOT, RAYMOND G. ... 241
JAGNANDAN, SALLY ... 65, 66
JAGNOW, DAVID ... 271
JAHN, LARRY A ... 373
JAHN, LAWRENCE ... 342
JAHNKE, MARLENE ... 229
JAHNS, BRENDA ... 50
JAKUBIAK, JOYCE ... 77
JAMERSON, NANCY ... 116
JAMES, ANN ... 388
JAMES, CAROL ... 173
JAMES, FRANCES C. ... 151
JAMES, M. R. ... 304
JAMISON, DAPHNE W. ... 342
JAMISON, KATHLEEN ... 52
JANECKA, RICK ... 89
JANES, STEWART ... 386
JANEWAY, KATHERINE ... 364
JANIK, PHIL ... 32
JANN, BEATRICE ... 204
JANOPAUL, MONA ... 333
JANOWSKI, JOHN P. ... 192
JANSEN, RUUD ... 234
JANSSEN, LEN ... 327
JANTUAH, F. A. ... 204
JAQUET, NEIL ... 183
JARANOWSKI, MARTIN ... 162
JARRED, ADA ... 375
JARRETT, JEFFREY D. ... 103
JARRETT, THOMAS W. ... 122
JARVI, CHRIS ... 270
JARVIS, R. ... 129
JAUHOLA, CHRISTINE ... 24
JAYEWARDENE, HIRAN ... 236
JAYNE, JERRY ... 224
JEAN, DENYS ... 131
JEAN, YVES ... 173
JEANS, RICK ... 296
JEFF, GLORIA J. ... 28
JEFFORDS, JAMES ... 6
JEFFRIES, KEVIN ... 245
JELINSKI, DAVID ... 123
JENGO, JUDY ... 87
JENKINS, CAROLYN JEFFERSON ... 248
JENKINS, JAMES H., JR. ... 70
JENKINS, NEAL ... 348
JENKINS, OLIVIA ... 39
JENKINS, RONALD S. ... 116
JENKS, BRETT ... 310
JENNE, ALAN ... 356
JENNER, JUDY ... 158
JENNINGS, CECIL A. ... 57
JENNINGS, WILLIAM R. ... 107
JENNY, J. PETER ... 303
JENSEN, DEBORAH ... 279
JENSEN, JIM ... 260
JENSEN, JOHN W. ... 366
JENSEN, JON M. ... 353
JENSEN, MAX ... 113
JENSEN, MIA ... 242
JENSEN, SHARON ... 47
JEPPSON, PHIL ... 62
JERNIGAN, ALEX ... 181
JESERNIG, JIM ... 120
JESS, J. MICHAEL ... 83
JESSE, DICK ... 107
JESSUP, DAVID ... 351
JESSUP, WILLIAM ... 316
JESTER, DOUGLAS ... 76
JEWETT, FREEBORN ... 158
JEWETT, FREEBORN G., JR. ... 308
JEWETT, JOAN ... 27
JEWETT, MIKE ... 102
JEWETT, TONY ... 261
JEZOWSKI, TERRENCE W. ... 165
JINDRA, TOM ... 205
JOAQUIN, JOSEPH ... 234
JOCK, KEN ... 327
JOHANNES, CLINT ... 282
JOHANSEN, PAUL ... 346
JOHANSEN, PAUL R. ... 122
JOHN, CHACKO J. ... 70
JOHNDROWN, WAYNE ... 20
JOHNS, DAVID ... 6, 350
JOHNS, PAUL ... 357
JOHNSEN, ARTHUR M. ... 299
JOHNSON, ARNOLD W. ... 49
JOHNSON, BERN ... 203
JOHNSON, BERNARD ... 114
JOHNSON, BILL ... 177
JOHNSON, BRUCE ... 227
JOHNSON, BUSTER ... 330
JOHNSON, CHARLES ... 115
JOHNSON, CHARLES R. ... 392
JOHNSON, CHRISTINE M. ... 28
JOHNSON, COY ... 196
JOHNSON, DALE ... 380
JOHNSON, DAVID ... 6
JOHNSON, DENNY ... 240
JOHNSON, DEREK ... 205
JOHNSON, DONNA ... 274
JOHNSON, EARL ... 83
JOHNSON, EDWARD R. ... 99
JOHNSON, EILEEN MORGAN ... 273, 275
JOHNSON, ELAINE ... 78, 355
JOHNSON, ERIC ... 120
JOHNSON, ERIC A. ... 268
JOHNSON, FRED ... 271
JOHNSON, GARY R. ... 79
JOHNSON, GEORGE E. ... 230
JOHNSON, GERALD ... 18
JOHNSON, HAROLD L. ... 205
JOHNSON, HOWARD ... 205
JOHNSON, HUEY D. ... 310
JOHNSON, JAMES E. ... 43, 119
JOHNSON, JAMES R. ... 109
JOHNSON, JIM ... 276
JOHNSON, JODIE ... 331
JOHNSON, JOE ... 177
JOHNSON, JUDY ... 120
JOHNSON, KATHLIN R. ... 49
JOHNSON, KENDALL ... 321, 373
JOHNSON, KENNETH S. ... 98
JOHNSON, LADY BIRD ... 246
JOHNSON, LARRY ... 82
JOHNSON, LAURA ... 279
JOHNSON, LAURA ECKERT ... 120
JOHNSON, LEE ... 185
JOHNSON, LEONARD R. ... 372
JOHNSON, LESLIE ... 348
JOHNSON, LLORAN ... 313
JOHNSON, MARK ... 314
JOHNSON, MARSHA ... 215, 240
JOHNSON, MICHAEL ... 367
JOHNSON, NOLTON ... 57
JOHNSON, PAT ... 262
JOHNSON, PATRICIA S. ... 109
JOHNSON, PAULETTE ... 387
JOHNSON, RALPH ... 205
JOHNSON, REX ... 279
JOHNSON, RICHARD H. ... 203
JOHNSON, RICHARD S. ... 196
JOHNSON, RICK ... 187, 223
JOHNSON, ROBERT ... 337
JOHNSON, ROBERT J. ... 352
JOHNSON, ROGER ... 95
JOHNSON, RON ... 154
JOHNSON, RON J. ... 84
JOHNSON, RUSSELL ... 302, 348
JOHNSON, SAM ... 3, 101, 279
JOHNSON, SARA E. ... 312
JOHNSON, STANLEY ... 230
JOHNSON, STANLEY S. ... 117
JOHNSON, STEVE ... 351
JOHNSON, TRUDYE MORGAN ... 74
JOHNSON, TULLIE HOYLE ... 173
JOHNSON, TWIG ... 363
JOHNSON, VARRI ... 168
JOHNSON, VICTOR ... 248
JOHNSON, WALTER ... 270
JOHNSON, WARREN ... 24
JOHNSON, WES ... 336
JOHNSTAD, KRISTIN ... 365
JOHNSTON, GERALD G. ... 45
JOHNSTON, JIM ... 62
JOHNSTON, JOHN ... 122
JOHNSTON, LEE ... 130
JOHNSTON, TRACY ... 313
JOHNSTON, WALLACE ... 330
JOLLIFFE, LANE ... 62
JOLLY, BILL ... 120, 344
JOLLY, WILLIAM C. ... 120
JONASSON, HARLEY ... 128
JONES, A. JOSE ... 371
JONES, ALAN ... 330
JONES, BARRY ... 130
JONES, BOB ... 140
JONES, BOBBY ... 166
JONES, BRENDA A. ... 268
JONES, C. CLARK ... 119
JONES, CAROL ... 15
JONES, CHRISTA ... 225
JONES, CINDA ... 268
JONES, CLIFFORD L. ... 220
JONES, CLIVE G. ... 227
JONES, DALE A. ... 356
JONES, DAVID ... 94
JONES, DENA ... 157
JONES, DONNA ... 300
JONES, DOUG ... 55, 195
JONES, GWILYM S. ... 373
JONES, JACK ... 379
JONES, JAMES ... 122
JONES, JANE ... 45
JONES, JEFF ... 201
JONES, JIM ... 86
JONES, JOHN F. ... 151
JONES, JOHN PAUL, III ... 161
JONES, KEN ... 49
JONES, KENT ... 113
JONES, LAIRD ... 40
JONES, LLOYD ... 129
JONES, LYDIA C. ... 222
JONES, MARSHALL ... 26
JONES, MICHAEL ... 225
JONES, MIKE ... 329
JONES, PETER ... 176
JONES, PHIL ... 247
JONES, PHYLLIS ... 205
JONES, RICHARD G. ... 243
JONES, RICHARD W. ... 126
JONES, ROBERT ... 19, 23
JONES, ROGER ... 359
JONES, SAMUEL ... 253
JONES, SANDRA ... 243
JONES, SHARON ... 269
JONES, SHELDON R. ... 42
JONES, SONJA B. ... 14
JONES, STEPHEN B. ... 39
JONES, TAMMY ... 263
JONES, W. ALLEN ... 192
JONES, WENDY M. ... 204
JONES-LEVITZ, BETH ... 232
JONKEL, CHARLES ... 216
JONTZ, JIM ... 151
JOOSS, JUDY ... 359
JORDAN, CARL ... 243
JORDAN, DERRIL B. ... 23
JORDAN, EDWARD L. ... 35
JORDAN, III, WILLIAM R. ... 321
JORDAN, JUDY ... 296
JORDAN, KEITH C. ... 131
JORDAN, ROBERT ... 196
JORDAN, ROBERT R. ... 53
JORGENSEN, ED ... 283
JORGENSEN, ERIC ... 198
JORGENSEN, NEAL A. ... 393
JORGENSON, JOHN ... 353
JOSEPH, JAMES ... 8
JOSEPH, JIM ... 87
JOSLIN, PAUL ... 137
JOSLIN, ROBERT ... 32
JOST, DANA N. ... 284
JOY, JAMES A., III ... 108
JUBINSKY, GREG ... 207
JUDD, H. LEE ... 211
JUDGE, NANCY ... 361
JUDYCKI, DENNIS C. ... 28
JUDZIEWICZ, EMMET J. ... 167
JULIAN, RICHARD ... 185
JULICH, TINA ... 296
JUNGMAN, GREG ... 313
JURIS, RONALD ... 121
JURZYKOWSKI, M. CHRISTINE ... 210
JUSO, ED M. ... 209
JUST, R. E. ... 377

K

KABRAJI, ABAN MARKER ... 235
KADLEC, JOHN ... 390
KADUCK, JENNIFER ... 57
KAELKE, MICHELLE ... 325
KAHN, BERND ... 372
KAHN, MOHAMID ... 54
KAHRS, ROBERT F. ... 30
KAILING, ALEX F. ... 360
KAINER, KAREN ... 387
KAISER, KIM ... 286
KAKABADSE, SRA YOLANDA N. ... 234
KAKABADSE, YOLANDA N. ... 234
KAKAKHEL, SHAFQAT ... 339
KAKFWI, STEPHEN ... 129
KALINOWSKI, LIZ ... 73
KALLAN, STEVE ... 349
KAM, ALAN ... 59
KAM, WENDELL W.S. ... 60
KAMALPOUR, HAMID ... 17
KAMBESIS, PATRICIA ... 174
KAMENS, RICHARD ... 384
KAMMERER, GEORGE ... 170
KAMMEYER, FRANCINE ... 47
KAMP, DICK ... 167
KAMP, MARTY ... 296
KAMPRATH, EUGENE J. ... 384
KANAREK, HAROLD ... 73
KANDLE, JAY ... 285
KANE, ANTHONY R. ... 27
KANE, ELYSE ... 119
KANE, PATRICIA ... 285
KANE, RICHARD ... 285
KANE, WILLIAM F. ... 35
KANGAS, P ... 377
KANGAS, P. ... 377
KANIA, GARY ... 267
KANIHO, DANIEL ... 219
KAPINGA, MARGARET ... 251
KAPLAN, LORI ... 64
KAPPE, KARL ... 113
KAPPNER, AGUSTA ... 13
KAPSNER, PATRICK ... 336
KAPUR, NAMRITA ... 203
KAPUSCINSKI, ANNE ... 79
KARAS, CHRISTINE ... 25
KARIMI, HAMID ... 53
KARLSTROM, ERNEST ... 293
KARPAN, KATHERINE ... 24
KARPAN, KATHY ... 25

Staff Name Index

508

STAFF NAME INDEX

Staff Name Index

KARPINSKI, GENE 186, 339
KARPOWICZ, ZBIGNIEW 234
KARR, BOB L. 379
KARR, CRAIG L. 124, 264
KARSON, JEFFREY A. 383
KASABACH, HAIG 87
KASHIWADA, STEPHEN L. 49
KASSEL, JOHN 114
KASTER, GARY 295
KASTL, MIKE 99
KATERERE, YEMI 234, 365
KATERERE, YEMI M. 233
KATONA, STEVEN 376
KATSOUROS, MARY HOPE 219
KATULA, RAYMOND S. 289
KATZ, DANIEL 362
KATZ, DANIEL R. 309
KATZ, LARRY 314
KAUFFMAN, JOHN T. 138
KAUFFMAN, REAH JANISE 363
KAUFMAN, GREGORY D. 301
KAUFMAN, IRA 248
KAUFMAN, KENN 141
KAUFMAN, NANCY 27
KAUFMANN, MILTON M. 259
KAUL, N. G. 91
KAVALOK, TONY 313
KAVITS, PHILIP B. 274
KAVOURAS, LOU 56
KAWAMATSU, KIYOSHI 216
KAWAMURA, MITSUGU 363
KAYE, JORDAN 59
KAYES, TERRENCE B. 84
KAYS, JONATHAN 74
KEA, PHIL 57
KEAGLE, BOB 93
KEARNEY, STEVE 128
KEATHLEY, DANIEL E. 378
KEATING, TIM 309
KEATON, JACK 228
KECK, ROB 273
KEEFE, MARY LOUISE 143
KEEGAN, JOHN 140
KEELER, CARL R. 240
KEELS, VALERIE 256
KEENE, W. JAMES 290
KEENER, LEE 368
KEESE, STEPHEN 305
KEIR, JAMES R. 358
KEIRY, BILL 109
KEISER, TERRY D. 295
KEITH, ALLAN R. 141
KEITH, BILL 118
KEITH, ROBBIE 171
KEITH, ROBERT 218
KEITHLEY, C. A. 374
KELBER, MIM 361
KELIHER, PAT 181
KELLAR, BRYAN 43
KELLEHER, DANIEL L. 88
KELLER, C. LAWRENCE 285
KELLER, CHARLES E. 226
KELLER, CRAIG 34
KELLER, J. TIMOTHY 374
KELLER, JANET 106
KELLER, JAY 365
KELLER, SCOTT 287
KELLER, SUE 41
KELLEY, BRENDA 227
KELLEY, CHARLES D. 39
KELLEY, ERIC DAMIAN 154
KELLEY, PAT 94
KELLOGG, BOB 98
KELLOGG, CYNTHIA 286
KELLSEY, DONNA 132
KELLY, ALLAN L. 298
KELLY, ALLEN L. 298
KELLY, CHARLES J., JR. 178
KELLY, EAMON A. 34
KELLY, J. MICHAEL 374
KELLY, JACK 89
KELLY, JOHN J., JR. 12
KELLY, KATHY 250
KELLY, KEITH 30
KELLY, LINDA 17
KELLY, NATHAN (90
KELLY, PADGETT 389
KELLY, RAYMOND W. 33
KELLY, RICHARD 343
KELLY, THOMAS E. 11
KELSCH, STEVEN 384
KELSCH, TOM 267
KELSEY, DARMIN 152
KELSEY, HARRY 286
KELSEY, HARVEY M., JR. 160
KELTON, KEITH 40
KEMPER, STEVE 84
KENALL, ROBERT 142
KENDALL, ANDREW 164
KENDALL, HENRY 339
KENDALL, KATE 228
KENDALL, ROBERT 142
KENDROT, STEVE 191
KENITZ, ALICE 283
KENNAMER, JAMES EALR, Ph.D. 273
KENNAY, JILL 225
KENNEDY, BARBARA 381
KENNEDY, DAVID N. 49
KENNEDY, FRANCES H. 187
KENNEDY, GEORGE 200
KENNEDY, HARRY E., III 284
KENNEDY, JAMES C. 196
KENNEDY, JAMES H. 390
KENNEDY, JIM 129
KENNEDY, JODY 182
KENNELLY, JOHN J. 366
KENNINGTON, JOHN 296
KENNOY, WILLIAM H. 36
KENNY, MICHAEL P. 46
KENRICH, JOHN 130
KENT, AL 286
KENT, FRED 197
KENT, ROBERT 92
KENT, SHERMAN T. 185
KENYON, SHARMAN 368
KEOUGH, DOROTHY 19
KEOUGH, JANET 322
KEPPY, KAROL 188
KERAMIDA, VASILIKI 9
KERN, CAROLE 238
KERN, PENNY 133
KERNS, JUNIOR 21
KERR, BOB 57
KERR, DOUG 306
KERR, LORALEE 77
KERR, NANCY 366
KERR, THOMAS J. 350
KERSAVAGE, CAROL 299
KERTON, ALLAN 255
KERTULLA, JAY 41
KESEL, GEORGE F. 347
KESSEN, ANN 257
KESSLER, ED 290
KETCHAM, PAUL 164
KETCHUM, JUNE 296
KEULARTS, JOZEF 115
KEY, MARY P. 98
KEY, TOMMY 215
KEYS, ELLEN G. 214
KEYSER, EMMETT 109
KHANNA, DAVINDER 270
KHARE, PRAD 345
KIBLER, MANDY 107
KIDD, CLAREN 98
KIDD, SUSAN 272
KIDWELL, BIRTRUN, JR. 240, 241
KIEFER, JOHN D. 68
KIERNAN, MICHAEL 7
KIESER, WALTER F. 365
KIFER, ALLEN 104
KIFF, LLOYD F. 303
KIK, DAVE 245
KIKEL, DAVID A. 301
KILBOURNE, JAMES 15
KILBURN, MARC 44
KILDALL, ROBERT E. 211
KILEY, MICHAEL 64
KILGORE, MISSY L. 329
KILGUSS, KATE 316
KILLHAM, AMY 219
KILLIAN, BERNARD P. 63
KILLIAN, H. STEVEN 44
KILLISHEK, MARTHA 360
KILPATRICK, BARBARA 178
KIMBALL, CLYDE W. 70
KIMBALL, GORDON 263
KIMBALL, JOHN 113
KIMBALL, KENNETH 158
KIMBALL, SUZETTE 26
KIMBALL, THOMAS L. 274
KIMBLE, CHRISTY 296
KIMBLE, MELINDA L. 16
KIME, P. L. 325
KIMMEL, J. TIMOTHY 288
KIMMEL, WILLIAM 386
KIMMETT, D. 37
KINCAID, DAN 276
KINCANNON, LINN 223
KINDERFATHER, KATHY 138
KINDINGER, PAUL 188
KINDLER, RANDY 330
KINDLER, ROGER A. 223
KINDRACHUK, ROBERT 194
KING, ALBERT D. 128
KING, BARNETT 135
KING, BARRY 342
KING, CLYNT 217
KING, CURTIS 110
KING, DIANA 220
KING, FREDERICK J. 167
KING, GERALD 45
KING, JAMES 180, 195
KING, JUSTIN 355
KING, KENNETH V., JR. 222
KING, LARRY 53
KING, MARYDE 160
KING, NICELMA J. 47
KING, PAUL 135
KING, ROBERT 20
KING, SCOTT 245
KING, TERI 283
KING, WARREN 341
KINGFISHER, PAME 276
KINGSLEY, ERIC W. 285
KINNEY, STEPHANIE 16
KINSCH, MICHELLE 345
KINSELLA, JOHN S. 30
KIRCHHOFF, RICHARD W. 264
KIRCHOFF, MATT 136
KIRK, JOHN 109
KIRKLAND, GORDON L., JR. 155
KIRKLEY, ANN 107
KIRKPATRICK, MARTHA 71
KIRKPATRICK, TERRY 121
KIRN, DON J. 210
KIRSCH, EILEEN 189
KIRSCH, KATYA 325
KIRSCH, PETER 155
KIRSCHENMANN, THOMAS R. 303
KIRSHNER, LYN 188
KIRTLEY, J. ROSS 99
KIRWIN, DENNIS L. 273
KISEDA, JOHN 56
KISNER, BRENDA 306
KISSINGER, WILL 82
KITCHENS, WILEY M. 54
KITTS, JAMES R. 79
KIVIAT, ERIK 222
KIVIRIST, LISA 288
KLAAS, ERWIN 374
KLAAS, ERWIN E. 65
KLAASSEN, HAROLD E. 374
KLABUNDE, CHARLES 329
KLEIN, BILL 314
KLEIN, GEORGE D. 88
KLEIN, HANK 135
KLEIN, MARY 182
KLEIN, MICHAEL 308
KLEIN, RICK 157
KLEINAU, ZIGGY 217
KLEINE, DOUGLAS M. 323
KLEISS, BARBARA 323
KLEMARCZYK, RONALD 284
KLIMEK, JENNIFER 137
KLINE, LAWRENCE 272
KLING, JEANNE M. 241
KLINGER, PAMELA 20
KLINGHAMMER, ERICH 289
KLINGMAN, BRUCE 347
KLINK, JOHN C. 385
KLOCKE, ROBERT A. 152
KLPFENSTEIN, NORM 31
KNAPP, JILL 237
KNAPP, MALCOLM R. 35
KNAPP, MARY F. 28
KNAPP, WILLIAM 26
KNATTERUD, NEIL 95
KNEIPP, SARA 169
KNERR, ANTHONY D. 173
KNICKERBOCKER, DENNIS 255
KNIGHT, CAREY T. 148
KNIGHT, CHARLES 147
KNIGHT, DAVID 176
KNIGHT, ELAINE 108
KNIGHT, FRED K. 195
KNIGHT, JIM 83, 94
KNIGHTON, LINDA 353
KNIPLING, E. B. 32
KNIPLINS, EDWARD 32
KNOBBE, EDWARD T. 385
KNOBLOCH, KEVIN 158
KNOCHE, LARRY 67
KNOLL, RALPH 72
KNOOP, JEFF 294
KNOTHE, KEN 386
KNOTTS, DAVID M. 231
KNOTTS, HOWARD 276
KNOUF, KEN 21
KNOWLES, CAROL 63
KNOWLES, KATHY 53
KNOWLES, TOMMY 112
KNOX, JOHN A. 197
KNOX, ROBERT J. 11
KNUFFKE, DARRELL 349
KNUTH, BARBARA 382
KNUTSON, OWEN 256
KOBERSTEIN, INGRID 211
KOCH, DON 66
KOCH, LOUISA 13
KOCH, MINDY 76
KOCH, STELLA 157
KOCHERT, MICHAEL N. 309
KOCHEVAR, RICHARD 89
KOCIOLEK, PATRICK 169
KOECHLIN, MANFRED 217
KOEHLER, BART 325
KOEHLER, MICKEY 226
KOEHLER, ROBERT P. 309
KOENEKE, MARY ALICE 205
KOENIG, LARRY 62
KOENIG, ROBERT 226
KOENIG, STANLEY W. 254
KOENIG, WALTER 189
KOEPPER, ROBERT C. 383
KOEPSEL, KIRK 319
KOERNER, BETTE 261
KOERTH, RICHARD 67
KOESTER, KEVIN 223
KOFFLER, RAY 241
KOFMEL, PHYLLIS 294
KOFORD, ROLF R. 65
KOGON, D. 308
KOHL, BARRY 249
KOHL, JOHN 359
KOHLENBERG, A. MAX 164
KOHN, BARBARA 153
KOHN, STEPHEN M. 273
KOHONEN, TAPANI 7
KOHRING, MARGARET A. 187
KOJIS, BARBARA 116
KOK, C. K. 100
KOLANKIEWICZ, LEON 174
KOLB, C. HAVEN 277
KOLBE, ED 101
KOLBENSCHLAG, PETE 182
KOLL, LAURENCE F. 257
KOLLINS, WILLIAM J. 15
KOMMEDAHL, THOR 257
KONDO, ED 38
KONIGSBERG, JAN 136
KONIGSMARK, KEN 239
KONOP, DANE 13
KONSIS, KEN 224, 225
KOONG, KELVIN 101
KOONS, JEFF 371
KOONS, ROBERT 313
KOONTZ, DOROTHY 294
KOOP, WAYNE C. 18
KOOPMAN, ROBERT 32
KOPECKY, MARY JO 124
KOPF, VIRGIL E. 116
KOPP, RICK 375
KORBONITS, ROBERT 104
KORDEK, WALT 122
KORDELL, NORM 78
KORNEGAY, DOCK 291
KOSS, BILL 120
KOSS, CHRISTOPHER D. 241
KOSTAKOW-KAMPE, RITVA 7
KOSTMAYER, PETER H. 365
KOTCHMAN, LARRY 96
KOTEFF, STEVE 189
KOUDA, MICHEL 234
KOUKOL, DAVID 283
KOURLIS, THOMAS A. 50
KOVALICK, WALTER W., JR. 12
KOVEN, ANNE 297
KOVEN, JOAN F. 252
KOWALSKI, JANET 40
KOYL, GREG 127
KRAFT, MICHAEL 392
KRAFT, PAUL 129
KRAHN, GORDY 238
KRAMER, DAN 227
KRAMER, DONALD E. 41
KRAMER, JERRY 153
KRAMER, JOE 67, 268
KRAMER, JONATHAN G. 74
KRAMER, LARRY E. 195
KRAMER, R. J. 230
KRAMER, RANDAL A. 383
KRAMER, STUART 132
KRAMPER, VINCE 84
KRANTZBERG, JOAN 131
KRAPF, KRISTEN L. 310
KRASNY, MARIANNE E. 93, 382
KRAUSE, TOM 272
KREAG, GLENN 79
KREAMER, DAVID 380
KREBS, WILLIAM A. 327
KREGER, MICHAEL 362
KREIDER, KALEE 219
KREIDER, KARIN 309
KREIFELS, CINDY 219
KREIL, RANDY 96
KREITZ, VON 332
KREMER, JOHN 224, 242
KREMER, ROXANNE 233
KREMSER, ULRICH 7
KREPPS, BOB 260
KRESEK, RAY 154
KRESS, EMILY 64
KRESS, STEPHEN 265
KRICHER, JOHN C. 359
KRIEGER, WAYNE 101
KRILL, ROBERT M. 124
KRIPOWITCZ, ROBERT S. 13
KRIS, MARY ELLEN 91
KRISHNA, CHANDRU 310
KROENING, NANCY 206
KROHN, WILLIAM B. 72, 376
KROLL, JAMES C. 389
KRONBERG, SCOTT 109
KRONRAD, GARY D. 389
KRONSBERG, JONATHON 196
KROP, LINDA 201
KROPF, MARTHA 169
KROSHUS, JAMES 315
KRUCKENBERG, LARRY 125, 346
KRUEGER, CHARLES C. 382

STAFF NAME INDEX 509

KRUEGER, WILLIAM 78, 386
KRUG, KELLY 47
KRUIDENIER, BILL 233
KRULISCH, LEE 318
KRULL, JOHN N. 378
KRUMPERMAN, CHRIS 185
KRUPNICK, ALAN 311
KRUPOVAGE, JOHN 19
KRUPP, FRED 202
KRUSE, KARL 317
KRUSE, KIPP C. 373
KRUZAN, JOHN C. 195
KRUZANSKY, CHARLES 201
KUEHL, S. A. 391
KUEHN, ROBERT R. 375
KUESTER, ED 55
KUHLMANN, MICHAEL W. 58
KUHN, ROGER 83
KUHN, STAN 65, 66
KUHNS, MIKE 114
KULETZ, KATHY 300
KULHAVY, DAVID 389
KULL, ROBERT, JR. 16
KULLBERG, JOHN F. 320
KUMABE, ELIZABETH 59
KUMMEL, JOHN C. 40
KUMMERFELDT, PETER 313
KUMPE, MARY A. 133
KUNKEL, CLAIR 100
KUNKEL, JAMES W. 67
KUNKEL, PETER 185
KUNKEL, TOM 91
KUNKLE, DAN R. 352
KURTZ, JAMES A. 124
KURTZ, SANDI 330
KURTZMAN, SCOTT 302
KUSER, JOHN 381
KUSHLAN, JAMES 153
KUSSY, EDWARD V.A. 28
KUTTEL, MIKE 119
KUWABARA, JEFF 59
KWAK, THOMAS J. 43
KWETZ, BARBARA 75
KYANKA, GEORGE H. 383
KYLE, ELVA 279

L

LaBARR, MARK 167
LABEDZ, TOM 283
LABIE, SYLVIA 55
LABONDE, JERRY 161
LABORDE, SARA 119
LABOSKY, PETER 387
LABRECQUE, JEAN 206
LACAVE, GERALDINE 204
LACK, JOE PAUL, JR. 286
LACKEY, JOANNA 89
LACROIX, CAROLE ANN 193
LACY, GARY 269
LACY, JAMES 245
LaFAYETTE, RUBY 282
LAFLAMME, BRIAN 17
LAFLAMME, YVON 308
LAFRAMBOISE, ROY 96
LAFRANCH, TIM 49
LAFRENIERE, NORMAND 38
LAHSHER, CARL W. 16
LAI, CHUN K. 233
LAIRD, JIMMY 80
LAIST, DAVID W. 8
LAITE, MURRAY 301
LAKE, BARRY 110, 329
LALLY, MIKE 150
LALO, JULIE 347
LAM, JULIA 268
LAMB, BILL 24
LAMB, GENE 263
LAMB, GEORGE R. 171, 242
LAMB, ROBERT L. 24
LAMBERSON, TOM 83
LAMBERT, DONALD 253
LAMBERT, WILLIAM 79
LAMBERTSON, RONALD E. 27
LAMBORN, ALAN 370
LAMMERS, OWEN 232
LAMONT, GIL 157
LAMONTAGNE, MICHEL 37
LAMSON, SUSAN 271
LANCASTER, BRIAN 252
LANCE, ALAN G. 61
LANCE, LINDA 10
LANCERO, ROSALIE A. 59
LANCTOT, RANDY P. 249
LAND, EDWARD J., JR. 271
LANDAU, MATHEW 381
LANDEN, LAURA 200
LANDHERR, LARRY 79
LANDIS, WAYNE 392
LANDRENEAU, DWIGHT 71
LANDRUM, NEY C. 264
LANE, JOE 42
LANE, PETER 227
LANE, S. R. 100
LANG, CHUCK 298
LANG, MAC 231
LANGE, MARY DAILY 247
LANGE, ROBERT 26
LANGE, TED 292
LANGFORD, DAVID K. 331
LANGFORD, GEORGE R. 329
LANGFORD, LYNDA 132
LANGLOIS, C. 37
LANGSTAFF, MAXIM 133
LANGSTON, JAY 273
LANING, BRENT 66
LANPHEAR, KATHLEEN 106
LANT, CHRISTOPHER 156
LANZA, GUY R. 377
LANZA, LAURA 200
LaPATRA, SCOTT 143
LaPAZ, LOURDES 231
LAPERRIERE, JACQUELINE D. 40
LAPHAM, BURKS 185
LAPIERRE, WAYNE R., JR. 271
LaPOINTE, BRIAN 310
LAPPIN, BERT 348
LAPPIN, DAWN Y. 348
LaPRADE, YVON 308
LARKINS, JOHN T. 35
LARMER, JEFF 156
LAROCCO, PAT 241
LARSEN, MIKE 324
LARSON, GARY E. 29
LARSON, J. S. 100
LARSON, JACK 291
LARSON, JANET 162
LARSON, LOREN R., II 161
LARSON, LYNN 42
LARSON, PETER 78
LARSON, ROBERT P. 303
LARSON, STAN 291
LaRUE, ED 193
LASH, JONATHAN 363
LASHER, DOUGLAS N. 195
LASITER, FRANK 169
LASMANIS, RAYMOND 121
LASSILA, KATHRIN 278
LASSOIE, JAMES P. 93, 382
LATER, MONTE 61
LATHAN, JOANNE 218
LATKA, BECKY 283
LATTIMER, DICK 159
LATTIS, RICHARD 351
LAU, JOLENE 31
LAUB, HEATHER 276
LAUBER, DARRELL 257
LAUER, PEGGY 310
LAUGHLIN, KEITH 10
LAUN, H. CHARLES 167
LAUNDS, JOHN 279
LAURIN, NICHOLAS 173
LAUSTALOT, TOM 170
LAUTMAN, KAY 138
LAVALLIER, KAREN 272
LAVERTY, KENT 224
LAVERTY, LYLE 33
LaVINE, KRISTEN 355
LAVKULICH, L. M. 368
LAVODNY, CHERYL 30
LAVOIE, GERALD 308
LAWAETZ, HANS 342
LAWALL, LINA ANN 196
LAWHERN, TIM 231
LAWING, JACQUIE 15
LAWLER, JIM 78
LAWLER, MARY ANN 24
LAWLEY, ROBERT 63
LAWLOR, TIMOTHY 368
LAWRENCE, CHARLES S., III 134
LAWRENCE, KARIN 323
LAWRENCE, LOUISE 73
LAWS, BRENT 195
LAWSON, CAROL 141
LAWSON, JAY 125
LAWSON, MARVIN A. 117
LAWSON, SHIRLEY 269
LAWTHERS, MARTY 218
LAWTON, SAMUEL T., JR. 297
LAX-EDISON, DONNA 197
LAXTON, WILLIAM 10
LAYER, MARILYN W. 342
LAYHER, WILLIAM G. 45
LAYZER, JAMES B. 110, 389
LAZENBY, WILLIAM R. 57
LEA, GEORGE D. 307
LEACH, FRANKLIN R. 295
LEACH, LARRY 254
LEADER, RICHARD 277
LEAHY, JAMES 186
LEAMAN, BRUCE M. 8
LEAPE, JAMES P. 363
LEAPER, ERIC 269
LEARY, JOHN 345
LEAVERS, DOUG 299
LEAVITT, DALE F. 76
LEAVITT, MARCY 90
LeBARRON, SANDY 90
LeBLANC, CECILE 358
LeBOUBON, D. 129
LEBOURVEAU, H. 194
LeCAVALIER, JOHN 203
LECHLIDER, GEORGE 252
LECHNER, LARRY 132
LECKIE, FRED D. 116
LECOUNT, ALBERT 385
LEDBETTER, BROWNIE 361
LEDDY, LINDA E. 251
LEDGERWOD, RAY 263
LEDGERWOOD, RAY 100
LeDOUX, AL 68
LEE, AMY FREEMAN 222
LEE, CHARLES 206, 354
LEE, CHARLES D. 68
LEE, CRAIG 337
LEE, DOROTHY 323
LEE, JASON 145
LEE, KAI N. 378
LEE, MERCEDES 265
LEE, NELSON 337
LEECH, MICHAEL 231
LEEK, NANCY McINNIS 130
LEEMAN, WAYNE 128
LEES, MARY ELLEN 254
LEETE, JEANETTE 257
LEFEBVRE, RICHARD 90
LeFEVRE, R. JAMES 304
LEFF, DAVID K. 52
LeGATE, SHARI 361
LEGG, MICHAEL 389
LEGGETT, DONNA 273
LEHMBERG, VERNE 205
LEHOLM, ARLEN G. 77
LEIB, JONATHAN 266
LEIGHTON, F. A. 171
LEIN, GREGORY M. 144
LEINBACH, PHIL 346
LEINER-MALANGA, SALLY 211
LEITMAN, STEVE 207
LeJEUNE, CYRIL 69
LEKENS, RICHARD 64
LEKWA, STEVE 65
LeMASTER, DENNIS 303
LEMASTER, DENNIS C. 374
LeMAY, BILL 88
LEMCHE, E. 9
LEMKE, DAVID 331
LEMMERMAN, JAMES 257
LEMMERT, BRUCE A. 358
LEMMON, CAROL 185
LEMOINE, STEVE 140
LEMONS, PEGGY 259
LENHART, CYNTHIA 140
LENHART, CYNTHIA R. 220
LENHART, DAVID 389
LENNON, GEORGE D. 32
LENON, HERBERT L. 378
LENSINK, CALVIN 275
LENZINI, PAUL A. 228
LEONARD, CHRIS 18
LEONARD, DOROTHY L. 74
LEONARD, GERALD 176
LEONARD, NANCY 102
LEONARD, TOM 346
LEOPOLD, DON 277
LEPRIEUR, GERRY 129
LeQUIRE, ROGER W. 95
LERE, MARK E. 147
LERNER, JOEL A. 75
LEROHL, MEL I. 366
LERUD, LARS 389
LESHY, JOHN D. 24
LESINO, ROBERT C. 26
LESLIE, DAVID M., JR. 98, 356, 385
LESSER, CHARLES A. 53
LETELLIER, SYLVIE 38
LEUTHOLD, PAUL 360
LeVAKE, BARBARA 50
LeVASSEUR, DOUG 288
LEVIN, ARNOLD E. 35
LEVINE, MEGAN LESSER 93
LEVINE, STEPHEN 377
LEVITT, JOSEPH A. 15
LEVKOVITZ, THEA 345
LEVY, CHERI 176
LEVY, RON 20
LEWELLAN, GAIL 78
LEWIN, JULIE 212
LEWIS, A. 368
LEWIS, ANN 157
LEWIS, CEDRICK 342
LEWIS, DARRELL L. 21
LEWIS, DONALD 370
LEWIS, GEORGE W. 58
LEWIS, HUNTER 363
LEWIS, JEFF 79, 90
LEWIS, JIM 54
LEWIS, KATE 75
LEWIS, LARRY S. 214
LEWIS, LESLIE 200
LEWIS, PETER G. 150
LEWIS, ROBERT 32
LEWIS, STACIE 209
LEWIS, SYLVIA 154
LEWIS, VIOLA O. 73
LEWIS, W. BRUCE 194
LEWIS, WILLIAM M., JR. 155
LI, HIRAM W. 100
LIBONATI, MARGARET, M.D. 352
LIBURDI, MARY COLLEEN 163
LICHTMAN, PAMELA 242
LICK, ROLAND 204
LIDDLE, ANDY 90
LIDHOLM, ELAINE J. 117
LIEB, MARILYN M. 247
LIEBERMAN, DAVID A. 231
LIEBERMAN, IRENE 31
LIEBERMAN, JAMES 35
LIECHTI, PAUL M. 66
LIECHTY, THORN 260
LIEDTKE, CLIFF 101
LIEPMANN, SUZANNA 341
LIFFMANN, MICHAEL M. 70
LIFT, JIM 199
LIGGETT, SHARON A. 329
LIGHTLY, I. CLAYTON 252
LIGON, DAVID 99
LIKENS, GENE E. 227
LILE, DARIES 51
LILES, F. GRAHAM, JR. 58
LILIEN, JACK 378
LILLARD, DAVID 150
LILLEBO, TIM 298
LILLEY, MIKE 286
LIME, DAVIE W. 379
LIMING, ROBERT G. 107
LIMTIACO, DAVID T. 58
LINAM, LEE ANN 331
LINCER, JEFFREY L. 357
LINCICOME, KAY 305
LINCK, MADELEINE 337
LINDAHL, DEBORAH 183
LINDAHL, LASSE 376
LINDBERGH, REEVE 178
LINDBLAD, ERICK 315
LINDEKUGEL, BUCK 325
LINDER, DON 296
LINDER, SANDRA 169
LINDGREN, RICHARD 172
LINDHEIM, LEONARD C. 34
LINDQUIST, DAN 65
LINDSAY, DENTON 324
LINDSAY, DONALD 232
LINDSEY, JENNIFER 242
LINDSEY, S. MARK 28
LINDSEY, SUE 348
LINDSTROM, BILL 337
LINDVALL, MARK 355
LINE, LES 338
LINEHAN, JOHN J. 35
LING, BILLY 258
LINGLE, GARY R. 288
LINGLEBACH, JENEPHER 341
LINK, PHILIP S. 13
LINKHART, DAVID 295
LINKOUS, FRANK A. 117
LINNERTZ, JAMES 291
LINSENBIGLER, MICHAEL 30
LINSTRAND, LEN 209
LINTNER, MARLI 164
LINTON, GORDON J. 28
LINTOTT, LLOYD 251
LINZEY, ALICIA V. 155
LINZEY, FRED G. 126
LIPKIS, ANDY 332
LIPKIS, KATIE 332
LIPPE, PAMELA 197
LIPPHARDT, GEORGIA 50
LIPPOLD, BOB 163
LIPTON, DOUG 74
LISA, GWEN 17
LISS, CATHY 158
LITTLE, EDWARD T. 169
LITTLE, IRENE 35
LITZER, TAMMY 273
LIVERETT, JAMES 64
LIVERETT, JIM 64
LIVERMORE, MICHAEL 287
LIVESAY, DAKOTA 314
LIVINGSTON, GIL 341
LIVINGSTON, ROBERT J. 372
LIVINGSTON, WILLIAM 376
LLEWELLYN, SIMON 37
LLEWELLYZ, JANET 55
LLEWELYN, MICHAEL 101
LLOYD, HERB 245
LLOYD, JAMES W. 178
LLOYD-JONES, DONALD 150
LLOYD-O'CONNOR, SHARON 248
LOANE, AIN 7
LOCANDRO, ROGER 88
LOCHHEAD, JAMES S. 50
LOCKARD, FRANK R. 195
LOCKETT, PETER J. 128
LOCKWOOD, DAVID R. 303
LOCKWOOD, JEFFREY 309
LOCKYER, CHRISTINA 204
LOEB, B. 317
LOEB, MICHAEL 319
LOEB, STANFORD 374
LOEHRLEIN, MYRNA 247
LOESCH, MARTIN 345

Staff Name Index

STAFF NAME INDEX

LOEWEN, JAMES ... 19
LOFTIN, KELLY ... 44
LOGAN, EDWARD W. ... 33
LOGAN, ROBERT W. ... 69
LOGGINS, TOMMY ... 57, 58
LOHAUS, PAUL H. ... 35
LOHNES, ROBIN C. ... 151
LOHR, EDWARD R., SR. ... 140
LOHRER, FRED ... 159, 208
LOHRER, FRED E. ... 208
LOISELLE, BETTE ... 229
LOKEN, STEVE ... 176
LOKKESMOE, KENT ... 78
LOMENZO, SUE ... 349
LONG, ALAN J. ... 56
LONG, EILEEN ... 392
LONG, FRANKLIN, JR ... 301
LONG, J. ROBERT ... 261
LONG, JACK ... 95
LONG, JAMES ... 213
LONG, KEITH R. ... 374
LONG, MICHAEL B. ... 50
LONG, MIKE C. ... 54
LONG, SHANNON ... 256
LONG, STEPHEN ... 342
LONG, STEWART ... 368
LONG, WILLIAM ... 260
LONGANECKER, DAVID ... 13
LONGEST, HENRY L., II ... 11
LONGINI, ROSE ... 213
LONG-THOMPSON, JILL ... 28
LOOCK, HARRY VAN ... 207
LOOMIS, MIKE ... 290
LOOS, PETER ... 277
LOPEZ, ARTHUR ... 28
LOPEZ, DONALD T. ... 90
LOPEZ, RAPHAEL ... 34
LOPEZ, VOLTAIRE ... 307
LOPEZZO, THOMAS ... 333
LOPOUKHINE, NIK ... 321
LORD, LINDA ... 207
LORENZ, JEROME ... 265
LORENZ, JOYCE ... 315
LORRAIN, JANICE ... 300
LOSCUTOFF, WILLIAM V. ... 46
LOSORDO, THOMAS M. ... 94
LOTTINSM, HELEN ... 221
LOTZE, JOERG-HENNER ... 223
LOUCKS, WILLIAM L. ... 67
LOUI, RAE M. ... 59, 60
LOUKO, KEN ... 334
LOVAGLIO, RONALD B. ... 72
LOVE, DAVID W. ... 89
LOVE, DUNCAN ... 205
LOVEJOY, THOMAS E. ... 353
LOVELADY, GREGORY W. ... 120
LOVELAND, DAVID ... 232
LOVELESS, DAVID ... 68
LOVETT, GARY M. ... 227
LOW, ERIC ... 250
LOWE, GEORGE ... 218
LOWE, LORI ... 160
LOWE, WILLIAM R. ... 235
LOWEY, JACQUELINE ... 25
LOWNES, PHIL ... 116
LOWREY, JEFFIFER ... 283
LOWRY, KATHY ... 251
LUBBEN, CALVIN D. ... 252
LUBER, GAYE ... 247
LUCAS, CLINTON ... 346
LUCAS, DON ... 297
LUCAS, HAROLD ... 15
LUCAS, STEVEN ... 64
LUCAS, TERRI ... 19
LUCCKINO, MIKE ... 205
LUCE, DAVID ... 139
LUCKEY, AMY ... 203
LUCZKOVICH, JOSEPH J. ... 149
LUDDER, DAVID ... 248
LUDKE, J. LARRY ... 26
LUDWIG, DANEIL R. ... 276
LUDWIG, JOHN ... 195
LUECKE, CHRIS ... 390
LUESHEN, WILLETTA ... 227
LUFTIG, STEPHEN D. ... 11
LUGAR, RICHARD ... 6
LUJAN, ANTONIO ... 286
LUKAS, DEBBIE ... 210
LUKASCYK, JOSEPH ... 197
LUKASIK, LYNDA ... 217
LUKENS, BILL ... 224
LUKENS, RONALD R. ... 7
LUKENS, SCOTT ... 164
LUKOWSKI, PAUL ... 19
LUM, CALVIN W.S. ... 60
LUMPKIN, RUSS ... 273
LUND, BEN ... 278
LUND, LANNY J. ... 369
LUND, TY ... 127
LUNDBERG, JAN ... 210
LUNDBERG, ROBERT ... 207
LUNDIN, CLIFFORD R. ... 285
LUNDSTROM, DARNELL ... 96
LUPARDUS, APRIL ... 136
LUSCHER, KATHY ... 312

LUTTRELL, ALLEN ... 69
LUTZ, CHARLES G. ... 70
LUTZ, JUDY ... 213
LUVEN, DAVID VAN ... 86
LYLES, ETTA ... 73
LYMAN, R. J. ... 75
LYMAN, ROBERT M. ... 126
LYMN, NADINE ... 199
LYNCH, ALISA ... 166
LYNCH, GEORGE ... 247
LYNCH, KATHY ... 170
LYNCH, KENNETH ... 91
LYNCH, LARRY ... 343
LYNCH, ROBERT ... 50
LYNE, RANDY ... 150
LYNN, FRANCES, ... 384
LYON, DALE ... 293
LYON, DAVID ... 238
LYON, DR. PAUL CHANDLER ... 373
LYON, JAMES S. ... 274
LYON, JONATHAN ... 184
LYON, TIMOTHY F. ... 373
LYONS, CATHY ... 161
LYONS, CHARLES ... 376
LYONS, JAMES ... 28
LYONS, JOHANNA ... 318
LYONS, MIKE ... 314
LYTLE, TOM ... 313

M

MAAS, RICHARD P. ... 384
MacARTOR, JUNE ... 192
MACASKILL, KEN ... 130
MacAULAY, ED. ... 130
MacAULEY, DON ... 132
MACBETH, ERIC J. ... 9
MacCALLUM, WAYNE F. ... 74
MacCASKEY, MICHAEL ... 268
MacCOLL, KIM, JR. ... 298
MACDERMOTT, FRANCES ... 198
MACDONALD, BONNIE ... 279
MACDONALD, CHARLES ... 254
MacDONALD, JULIE ... 47
MacDONALD, LARRY ... 250
MacDONALD, LAURIE ... 191
MacDONALD, WILLIAM ... 141
MacDOUGALL, GERALD ... 131
MacDUFF, BARBARA ... 306
MACFARLANE, BILL ... 289
MacGREGOR, BARBARA ... 238
MacGREGOR, FORREST ... 141
MacGREGOR, MOLLY ... 312
MACHLIS, GARY ... 372
MACHOL, BEN ... 59
MACIEJEWSKI, PAUL ... 336
MacINTYRE, DONALD D. ... 83
MacINTYRE, JAMES ... 332
MacIVER, DONALD ... 253
MACK, WAYNE ... 108
MACKAY, JEAN ... 163
MacKAY, ROSEMARY J. ... 288
MacKENZIE, A. ... 37
MACKIERNAN, GAIL B. ... 74
MACKINLAY, DON ... 143
MACKLEY, JAMES ... 29
MACLAUCHLAN, DONALD E. ... 228
MacLEAN, JIM ... 131
MACLEAN, JOHN ... 313
MACPEACK, MALCOLM ... 389
MacPHEE, NANCY ... 56
MacRAVEY, RICHARD D. ... 183
MACRORY, BOB ... 39
MACY, JIM ... 81
MACY, SYDNEY S. ... 188
MADDEN, KEVIN P. ... 14
MADDEN, MURDAUGH ... 363
MADDEN, ROY ... 27
MADDEN, WILLIAM B. ... 112
MADDOX, LORI ... 346
MADDOX, TERRY ... 217
MADDY, DEBORAH ... 102
MADDY, JAMES D. ... 269
MADEMA, DAVID B. ... 314
MADEWELL, TERRY ... 19
MADIGAN, PATRICIA ... 97
MADISON, ELIZABETH M. ... 187
MADL, DONALD C. ... 103
MADRID, TITO ... 90
MADRONE, ROSE ... 157
MADSEN, ARLAN ... 164
MADSEN, SARAH ... 356
MADY, JAMES ... 257
MAECHTLE, KATHY ... 360
MAGAGNA, JIM ... 126
MAGGIORE, PETER ... 90
MAGID, MARILYN ... 280
MAGNUSSEN, STEPHEN ... 24
MAGUIRE, MEG ... 317
MAHADEVAN, KUMAR ... 261
MAHER, CONNIE ... 157
MAHER, RON ... 194
MAHLER, ROY ... 159

MAHON, JIM ... 217
MAHONEY, RONALD ... 61
MAHONEY, S. ... 129
MAHOOD, ROBERT K. ... 323
MAI, PHUONG ... 333
MAINELLA, FRAN ... 54, 55
MAINELLA, FRAN P. ... 264
MAJERES, JOHN D. ... 324
MAJKUT, STEPHEN ... 106
MAJOR, MARLA ... 211
MAJOT, JULIETTE ... 232
MAK, KING ... 18
MAKAREVICH, PAUL, JR. ... 196
MAKI, JON ... 375
MAKKONEN, HANNU ... 383
MAKRIS, JAMES L ... 11
MALCOLMSON, PATRICIA E. ... 131
MALDONADO, WALTER ... 340
MALECHEK, JOHN C. ... 390
MALECKI, RICHARD A. ... 92
MALEK-WILEY, DARRYL ... 258
MALER, TRACIE ... 205
MALICK, BUCK ... 9
MALLET, JERRY ... 61
MALLETT, ROBERT L. ... 12
MALLEY, ANNE MARIE ... 169
MALLISON, PETE ... 54, 55
MALLON, TIM ... 208
MALLORY, BILL ... 163
MALLOY, TIMON ... 197
MALM, RICHARD L. ... 342
MALMBERG, PAUL ... 120
MALONE, THOMAS C. ... 155, 376
MALONE, WILLIAM ... 56
MALONEY, RICK ... 99
MALOUF, ROBERT E. ... 101
MALSAWMA, ZUALI ... 305
MALSCH, MARTIN G. ... 35
MALTBY, EDWARD ... 234
MALUIA, PHILO F. ... 235
MAMANE, P. M. ... 235
MANACKE, NANCY ... 97
MANES, ROB ... 67
MANFREDO, MICHAEL ... 370
MANGINO, SUZANNE ... 268
MANHART, EDWARD W. ... 103
MANICH, DAVID ROZ ... 64
MANION, ANDREA ... 319
MANION, BRUCE ... 38
MANION, THOMAS A. ... 392
MANKIN, CHARLES J. ... 98
MANKO, JOSEPH M. ... 302
MANLEY, DONALD J. ... 195
MANLY, CHARLIE ... 237
MANN MACDONALD, JEAN ... 212
MANN, DAVE ... 343
MANN, DEBORA ... 258
MANN, JUDY ... 202
MANNAUSA, LEONARD ... 246
MANNER, MARK ... 200
MANNING, AL ... 239
MANNING, BRENT ... 63
MANNING, ED ... 259
MANNING, GLORIA ... 32
MANNING, HARVEY ... 239
MANNING, JAY ... 119
MANNO, JACK ... 217
MANSFIELD, TERRY ... 49
MANSIUS, DON ... 72
MANSON, CONNIE ... 121
MANSPEAKER, BARBARA ... 139
MANTELL, MICHAEL A. ... 47
MANTHEY, REBECCA ... 179
MANTLER, CHARLES ... 267
MANTRAS, CARLOS ... 307
MANUEL, HILDA ... 24
MANUEL, HILDA A. ... 24
MANUS, ANDREW T. ... 53
MAPLE, JOHN ... 269
MAPLE, TERRY ... 157
MARACCHINI, JERRY ... 89
MARCUM, LARRY ... 110
MARCUS, ANDREW ... 291
MARCUS, FELICIA A. ... 11
MARCUS, NANCY H. ... 56
MAREK, KRISTINA S. ... 99
MARET, JOSEPH ... 44
MARGALIT, JEFFREY ... 34
MARGOLIS, KEN ... 312
MARHEINE, BRUCE ... 195
MARINO, JIM ... 253
MARINO, MICHAEL ... 138
MARINOSKE, STAN ... 132
MARK, RICHARD F. ... 292
MARKEE, W. D. ... 100
MARKELL, VICTORIA ... 304
MARKEN, WILLIAM R. ... 248
MARKER, NANCY ... 53
MARKHAM, BARBARA ... 56
MARKS, EUGENIA S. ... 164
MARKS, ISAAC N. ... 74
MARKS, KATHLEEN ... 99
MARLER, E. ... 59
MARLOWE, NANCY ... 10

MAROON, JOSEPH ... 178
MARQUARD, ROBERT ... 221
MARQUEZ, ANGEL B. ... 59
MARQUIS, MICHAEL ... 29
MARR, KATHRYN ... 73
MARRA, SANDRA ... 305
MARROCCO, FREDERICK A. ... 102
MARROQUIN, RAUL ... 23
MARS, ADRIENNE ... 363
MARS, VIRGINIA C. ... 353
MARSH, AMY ... 292
MARSH, DONNIE ... 177
MARSH, ELAINE ... 217
MARSH, LANGDON ... 101
MARSH, MINA ... 45
MARSHALL, GREGORY A. ... 87
MARSHALL, JOHN ... 329
MARSHALL, KENNETH ... 327
MARSHALL, MICHAEL ... 113
MARSHALL, TOM ... 206
MARSTON, RICHARD A. ... 161
MARTEL, ANDRE ... 131, 132
MARTEL, GARY F. ... 116
MARTENS, CHRISTOPHER ... 384
MARTENS, LAUREN ... 182
MARTENS, TOM ... 230, 261
MARTI, MONTE ... 343
MARTIAN, THOMAS T. ... 35
MARTIN, A. JEFF ... 125
MARTIN, ARTHUR ... 246
MARTIN, BRUCE ... 82
MARTIN, GALE ... 80, 258
MARTIN, JACK W. ... 15
MARTIN, JAMES ... 326
MARTIN, JAMES D. ... 39
MARTIN, JERRY ... 46
MARTIN, JOHN ... 20
MARTIN, JOHN Q. ... 34
MARTIN, JR, W. TOM ... 270
MARTIN, KEITH W. ... 296
MARTIN, RAY ... 302
MARTIN, ROSS ... 113
MARTIN, STEVE ... 237
MARTIN, THOMAS ... 153
MARTIN, THOMAS D. ... 197
MARTIN, THOMAS E. ... 82
MARTIN, TOM D. ... 197
MARTIN, VANCE G. ... 235
MARTINE, TOM ... 273
MARTINEAU, DANIEL ... 171
MARTINELLI, DEBRA K. ... 124
MARTINEZ, ARTHUR C. ... 191
MARTINEZ, CAMERON ... 276
MARTINEZ, ELUID L. ... 24
MARTINEZ, ELVID L. ... 24
MARTINEZ, FRANK ... 159
MARTINEZ, NEFTALI GARCIA ... 177
MARTINEZ, RICARDO ... 28
MARTINEZ, TOBY ... 88
MARTINEZ, WILDA ... 32
MARTINKO, ED ... 374
MARTINKO, EDWARD ... 66
MARUTANI, MARI ... 59
MARVINNEY, ROBERT ... 72
MARX, GRAHAM A. ... 213
MARXER, DALE ... 260
MARYNOWSKI, SUSAN ... 173
MASAKI, CARL T. ... 60
MASICA, SUE ... 25
MASON, GWEN ... 24
MASON, LAWRENCE N. ... 188
MASON, TIMOTHY A. ... 191
MASOUREDIS, LINUS ... 48
MASSE, RICHARD ... 17
MASSEY, JOSEPH G. ... 379
MASSEY, WILLIAM L. ... 14
MASSICOT, PAUL ... 73
MASSMAN, CAROLE ... 83
MASSO, TOM ... 77
MASSUCCI, STEPHANIE ... 92
MAST, GARY ... 263
MASTENBROOK, BRIAN G. ... 355
MASTERS, A. ... 129
MASTERS, RON ... 99
MASTERS, SANDY ... 269
MASTERSON, LYNN ... 383
MASTERSON, MARK ... 156
MASTERSON, NANCY ... 150
MATA, ERIC ... 37
MATAAC, CELSO ... 333
MATEO, NICOLAS ... 37
MATHENY, CHARLES ... 247
MATHER, CHARLES M. ... 295
MATHER, JOHN R. ... 150
MATHER, MARTHA F. ... 75
MATHER, RICHARD P. ... 103
MATHER, SANDRA ... 266
MATHERNE, CHARLES ... 70
MATHEWS, BOB ... 67
MATHEWS, KATE ... 191
MATHEWS, LAURIE ... 50
MATHEWS, NANCY ... 277
MATHEWS, ROBIN ... 392
MATHEWS-AMOS, AMY ... 251
MATHIAS, WARREN ... 104

STAFF NAME INDEX

MATHIS, DONALD ... 371
MATHIS, MAXINE ... 263
MATHIS, RANDALL ... 44
MATHIS, SUZANNE ... 270
MATHUR, BHARAT ... 63
MATHURIN, DORIS A. ... 164
MATOWANYIKA, JOSEPH Z. ... 365
MATSUO, PAUL T. ... 60
MATSUURA, RENEE ... 113
MATTESON, SUMNER ... 360
MATTHEW, EARL ... 331
MATTHEW, LAURIE ... 170
MATTHEWS, BRUCE ... 76
MATTHEWS, DOUG ... 129
MATTHEWS, GEORGE C. ... 231
MATTHEWS, GEORGE G. ... 352
MATTHEWS, KATHLEEN S. ... 389
MATTHEWS, MICHAEL J. ... 356
MATTICE, JACK S. ... 92
MATTISON, ANDREA ... 249
MATTISON, DONALD R. ... 387
MATTISON, JIM ... 127
MATTSON, LESLIE ... 242
MATUSZEWSKI, MARK ... 69
MATYAS, JAIME ... 274
MATZ, MIKE ... 326, 340
MAUERMANN, SUE ... 119
MAUGHAN, O. EUGENE ... 41, 367
MAUGHAN, RALPH ... 224
MAULDIN, ALFRED C. ... 145
MAULSON, TOM ... 7
MAURER, GLENN E. ... 102
MAURER, JAMIE ... 162
MAURIES, JIM ... 336
MAURO, FLO ... 79
MAURO, FLORENCE ... 153, 304
MAUTZ, WILLIAM ... 86
MAVNEY, STEVE ... 330
MAW, IAN ... 381
MAXFIELD, LONNIE ... 210
MAXWELL, COLIN ... 173
MAXWELL, FRANK ... 283
MAY, DALE ... 52, 356
MAY, DALE W. ... 52
MAY, HENRY ... 78
MAY, JEANINE ... 31
MAY, JOHN D. ... 123
MAYBANK, BLAKE ... 141
MAYER, ERIC ... 222
MAYER, MIKE ... 227
MAYEUX, L. J. ... 196
MAYFIELD, PAUL ... 159
MAYMI, CARMEN R. ... 24
MAYNARD, C. CHARLES ... 54
MAYNARD, CAROLINE P. ... 173
MAYNES, FRANK E. ... 10
MAYO, MARDA ... 157
MAZAMBANI, DAVID ... 166
MAZGAJ, BOB ... 195
MAZIK, ROBERT A., SR. ... 338
MAZMANIAN, DANIEL A. ... 378
MAZUMDER, ASIT ... 155
MAZUR, DOUG ... 132
McADAM, STEVE ... 49
McAFEE, ROBERT ... 160
McALLISTER, DARRELL ... 66
McALLISTER, DON E. ... 294
McALONEY, KEITH ... 194
McATEER, J. DAVITT ... 15
McBRIDE, GREGORY B. ... 28
McBRIDE, SUSAN C. ... 146
McBURNEY, MARY ... 338
McCABE, GREG ... 191
McCABE, JANET ... 64
McCABE, JOHN J. ... 150
McCABE, MICHAEL ... 11
McCABE, RICHARD E. ... 353
McCAIN, JOHN ... 1, 6
McCALL, JERRY C. ... 13
McCALL, VIRGINIA ... 206
McCALLUM, BETH ... 353
McCANDLESS, GARY ... 161
McCANDLESS, JUDITH ... 69
McCARDLE, EUGENE ... 171
McCARTER, KATHERINE S. ... 199
McCARTHY, JOHN ... 223
McCARTHY, LAURA ... 210
McCARTY, COLLEEN ... 215
McCASLIN, GARY ... 90
McCLAIN, J. ... 147
McCLAIN, RUSS ... 161
McCLAREN, MITCHEL ... 367
McCLELLAND, STEVEN W. ... 123
McCLELLAND, WILLIAM ... 94
McCLELLAND-DICTSON, NIKKOAL ... 147
McCLENDON, MONTY ... 25
McCLENNEY, AYODELE ... 16
McCLOSKEY, J. MICHAEL ... 256
McCLOSKEY, MICHAEL ... 318
McCLOY, TOM ... 87
McCLURE, BETH ... 107
McCLURE, GLENNA ... 83
McCOLLOUGH, MARK ... 355
McCOLLUM, JERRY ... 215
McCOMB, WILLIAM C. ... 377
McCONKEY, PAM ... 120
McCONNAUGHAY, K. ... 373
McCONNELL, CHESTER A. ... 353
McCONNELL, CORDREE ... 76
McCONNELL, JAMES ... 59
McCORMACK, ALAN ... 263
McCORMICK, DALE ... 176
McCORMICK, SEAN ... 335
McCORMICK, STEVE ... 280
McCORTY, GENE ... 112
McCOWAN, ROD ... 13
McCOWN, JOHN ... 319
McCOY, JOHN P., JR. ... 299
McCOY, SANDY ... 169
McCRACKEN, JAMES ... 19
McCRACKEN, JEFFREY S. ... 25
McCRAY, KEVIN ... 269
McCREA, EDWARD J. ... 288
McCRIMMON, DONALD A. ... 378
McCUE, CATHRYN ... 325
McCULLOUGH, F. ALBERT, III ... 201
McCULLOUGH, FRED ... 168
McCULLOUGH, KAREN ... 159
McCULLY, PATRICK ... 232
McCURDY, KEVIN ... 19
McCURDY, MARY ... 269
McCUTCHEON, GLORIA L. ... 124
McCYNSKI, PAUL ... 277
McDANIEL, CAROL ... 288
McDANNOLD, DORI ... 136
McDERMOTT, JAMES F. ... 34
McDEVITT, WAYNE ... 94
McDONALD, JOE ... 79
McDONALD, JOHN ... 297
McDONALD, JULIE ... 365
McDONALD, MARY V. ... 153
McDONALD, MICHAEL ... 79
McDONALD, MOIRA ... 267
McDONALD, NORRIS ... 174
McDONALD, ROBERT B. ... 54
McDONALD, SANDRA F. ... 222
McDOUGLE, JANICE ... 33
McDOWELL, DAVID ... 234
McDOWELL, JUDITH E. ... 76
McDOWELL, ROBERT ... 228
McDOWELL, ROBERT L. ... 87
McDOWELL, WILLIAM ... 381
McEUEN, ARCHIE ... 209
McFADDEN, CHARLES ... 391
McFADDEN, JACK ... 130
McFADDEN, MIKE ... 354
McFALL, DON ... 63
McFARLAND, ROBERT J. ... 44
McFATE, R. BRUCE ... 302
McFERRIN, JOHN ... 346
McGARLAND, ALBERT M. ... 11
McGAUGHEY, LARRY ... 316
McGEHEE, ROSS ... 80
McGEORGE, LESLIE ... 87
McGEOUGH, RICK ... 66
McGHEE, STEVE ... 308
McGILL, WILLIAM ... 65
McGILVRAY, LAURIE ... 182
McGINN, JOSEPH ... 75
McGINNES, MARC ... 201
McGINNIS, JIM ... 42
McGLAUFLIN, KATHY ... 150, 190, 347
McGLENN, JOHN ... 345
McGLENN, RONNI ... 241
McGLYNN, DIANE ... 301
McGOVERN, MICHAEL ... 31
McGOWAN, KEVIN ... 189
McGRANE, PAT ... 31
McGRATH, CHRIS ... 356
McGRATH, DAVID B. ... 308
McGRATH, M. ... 129
McGRAW, CHRISTY ... 136
McGREAL, SHIRLEY ... 232
McGREGOR, BONNIE ... 26
McGREGOR, CATHY ... 127
McGREGOR, GREGOR I. ... 253
McGUE, CHRISTIE L. ... 14
McGUIGAN, DAVE ... 109
McGUIRE, A. DAVID ... 40
McGUIRE, ROBERT ... 260
McGUIRE, STEVE ... 260
McGUIRE, TERRY W. ... 46
McGUIRE, WALTER ... 215
McGURRIN, JOSEPH ... 333
McHENRY, MARJORIE ... 269
McHENRY, THOMAS J. P. ... 353
McHUGH, JOHN ... 3, 131
McHUGH, MARTIN J. ... 87
McHUGH, MARY-MARGARET ... 138
McINERNEY, JAN ... 260
McINNIS, MARTHA ... 204
McINTOSH, ALAN ... 391
McINTOSH, ALAN W. ... 391
McINTOSH, W. CHAD ... 76
McINTOSH, WINSOME ... 191, 247
McINTYRE, GARY ... 225, 277
McINTYRE, JIM ... 132
McINTYRE, ROBERT W. ... 337
McIVOR, CAROLE C. ... 41
McKAY, TIM ... 291
McKEAG, MICHAEL ... 276
McKEATING, GERALD ... 37
McKEE, DES ... 131
McKEE, DRISCOLL ... 213
McKEE, KATHY ... 237
McKEE, LARRY ... 98
McKEEHAN, BRENDA ... 263
McKEEL, DALE ... 317
McKENNA, MIKE ... 95
McKENNEY, DENNIS D. ... 327
McKENZIE, MARY ... 52
McKEON, JOSEPH F. ... 144
McKEW, JOHN ... 351
McKIBBEN, CAREY ... 225
McKINLEY, CRAIG R. ... 94
McKINNEY, DAVID ... 110
McKINNEY, KIM ... 348
McKINNEY, LARRY ... 112
McKNELLY, PHIL ... 94
McKNIGHT, BETTY ... 153
McKNIGHT, DIANE M. ... 155
McLAIN, GLADYS ... 321
McLAIN, PAT ... 121
McLANDRESS, ROBERT ... 170
McLANE, SUSAN ... 164
McLARN ... 172
McLAUD, LARRY ... 223
McLAUGHLIN, EDWARD ... 72
McLAUGHLIN, WAYNE ... 120
McLAURY, ELDON ... 360
McLAVEY, ROBERT G. ... 50
McLEAD, MARY ... 16
McLEAN, BOB ... 66
McLEAN, WALLACE ... 114
McLELLAN, ANNE ... 38
McLELLAN, BRUCE ... 228
McLELLAN, JIM ... 258
McLENAGHAN, THERESA ... 172
McLENNAN, DAN ... 142
McLEOD, ANDREW H. ... 106
McLEOD, CHARLES ... 248
McLEOD, DAVID ... 94
McLEOD, JAMES ... 323
McLEOD, RICHARD ... 85
McLOSKEY, JEAN C. ... 38
McMAHAN, VICTOR ... 154
McMAHON, EDWARD T. ... 187
McMAHON, KIMBERLY A. ... 213
McMAHON, THOMAS ... 380
McMAHON, TOM ... 170
McMANUS, BRIAN ... 83
McMANUS, ROGER E. ... 176
McMINN, JOHN ... 334
McMULLEN, BRAD ... 307
McMULLEN, ROBERT ... 152
McMURRAY, DENNIS ... 63
McMURRAY, JOHN ... 181
McNAMARA, CAROLE J. ... 265
McNAMARA, DANIEL, JR. ... 187
McNAMARA, ED ... 298
McNAMARA, TIMOTHY ... 20
McNANEY, RICK ... 29
McNEELY, JEFFREY A. ... 234
McNEELY, LORI ... 332
McNEIL, EDWARD ... 134
McNEIL, RICHARD J. ... 382
McNICHOL, LAURA ... 263
McNICHOLL, MARTIN K. ... 168
McNULTY, TIM ... 297
McOUAT, MARC ... 137
McPHERSON, RONALD D. ... 13
McQUEEN, CYRUS ... 390
McQUEEN, MIKE ... 187
McQUILKIN, GEOFFREY ... 259
McQUILKIN, WILLIAM ... 206
McQUILLAN, RICHARD ... 231
McQUINN, MARY ANN ... 30
McQUIVEY, ROBERT ... 85
McSHANE, JOAN ... 271
McSHANE, LISA ... 172
McSHARRY, JOSEPH ... 277
McSWEEN, PAUL E., III ... 331
McSWEENEY, KEVIN ... 393
McTAOISH, BLAIR ... 128
McVAY, LAURA ... 238
McVETY, PAM ... 54
McWHITE, RICHARD ... 269
McWHITE, RICK ... 17
MEACHAM, BRYAN ... 113
MEAD, ROBERT ... 120
MEADE, GLADYS ... 181
MEADE, JAMES W. ... 142
MEADOWS, WILLIAM H., III ... 349
MEALEY, STEPHEN P. ... 61
MECH, L. DAVID ... 236
MECHLER, JOHN ... 314
MEDLIN-HENSCHEL, KIRA ... 217
MEDWID, WALTER M. ... 236
MEEHAN, PAT ... 48
MEEHAN, ROSA ... 351
MEEK, LANCE ... 296
MEEK, ROYCE ... 296
MEEKS, STEPHANIE ... 279
MEFFE, GARY ... 321
MEGASON, PATRICIA J. ... 49
MEHLHAFF, LARRY ... 319
MEHMEL, GRETCHEN ... 355
MEIER, DAVID J. ... 124
MEIER, JIM ... 298
MEIKLE, DOUG ... 383
MEIKLE, DOUGLAS B. ... 385
MEIKLEJOHN, BRAD ... 187
MEIKLEJOHN, DOUGLAS ... 286
MEILLEUR, BRIEN A. ... 176
MEINEN, BOB ... 101
MEISTER, JACK ... 52
Melcher, Duane ... 300
MELCHER, STEVE ... 153
MELIVS, THOMAS O. ... 26
MELLGREN, TIM ... 176
MELLON, DIANNE ... 165
MELLON, S. PROSSER ... 314
MELLOTT, JOHN ... 100
MELONE, RUTH SPARKS ... 247
MELTON, MICHAEL R. ... 99
MENDENHALL, BARBARA ... 280
MENDEZ, KENNETH ... 333
MENEDEZ, BIANCA ... 305
MENGAK, MICHAEL ... 391
MENGAK, MICHAEL T. ... 358
MENKE, ROBERT ... 90
MENSINGER, JOANNE ... 239
MENZEL, BRUCE W. ... 265, 374
MENZIES, R.A.L. ... 317
MERAL, GERALD H. ... 304
MERCADO, TEDDY ... 105, 106
MERCER, DR. LINDA ... 71
MERCER, MALCOLM ... 234
MERCER, MARK ... 255
MERCHANT, DAVID M. ... 164
MERCHANT, HENRY ... 371
MEREDITH, DENISE ... 24
MERKER, BJORN ... 229
MERLINI, LAURAINE ... 215
MERRELL, WILLIAM J. ... 219
MERRIAM, ANNE ... 253
MERRIAM, DAN ... 243
MERRIFIELD, BOB ... 111
MERRIFIELD, ROBERT G. ... 367, 389
MERRIMAN, TIM ... 262
MERRIMIAN, ALEX ... 311
MERRITT, CLIFTON ... 156
MERRITT, JOYCE S. ... 139
MERRITT, REGNA ... 298
MERSKY, RONALD L. ... 387
MERTENS, TOM ... 248
MESAROS, KEN ... 82
MESCHIEVITZ, JESSIE ... 9
MESLOW, E. CHARLES ... 353
MESNER, NANCY ... 114
MESS, WALTER L. ... 117
MESSER, SUSAN ... 305
MESSERLE, KERRY L. ... 103
MESSERSMITH, DONALD ... 362
MESSICS, DAVE ... 313
MESSINGER, LUKE E. ... 191
MESSMER, TERRY A. ... 114
METCALF, MARY ... 318
METHIER, RON ... 57
METHOD, TIMOTHY ... 64
METHVEN, ANDREW ... 373
METTER, JEFF ... 253
METZ, LORRAINE ... 128
METZGER, ED ... 140
METZGER, KATHERINE ... 284
MEUSCHKE, DON ... 19, 269
MEYER, BILL ... 94
MEYER, CATHY ... 202
MEYER, CHARLOTTE ... 176
MEYER, CHRIS ... 287
MEYER, FRED ... 270
MEYER, GEORGE E. ... 124
MEYER, GERALD F. ... 14
MEYER, JEFF ... 150
MEYER, STEVEN R. ... 121
MEYERS, LEE ... 57
MEYERS, RANDALL ... 308
MEYERS, ROGER ... 20
MEYERS, STEPHEN ... 115
MEYRELES, KAREN ... 48
MEZAINIS, VALDIS ... 32
MIANO, MICHAEL P. ... 122
MICHAEL, ED ... 217
MICHAEL, TOM ... 346
MICHAELS, ARTHUR J. ... 103
MICHAELS, GAIL ... 326
MICHAELS, KEITH ... 44
MICHAELSON, STANLEY M. ... 81
MICHEL, MARK ... 158
MICHEL, SHARON L. ... 124
MICHELI, RON ... 126
MICHLIN, LEE ... 46
MICHNY, FRANK ... 25
MICKA, RICHARD G. ... 246
MIDDAUGH, DANIEL ... 41
MIDDAUGH, JIM ... 298
MIDDLETON, FREDERICK S., III ... 325
MIELKE, ART ... 291
MIGHETTO, LISA ... 154
MIGLARESE, JOHN V. ... 108
MIHALO, MARK ... 316
MIHALYE, SUE ... 217
MIKICS, DENISE ... 87
MIKKELSEN, JAMES ... 21

512 STAFF NAME INDEX

MIKOL, GERALD 91
MILANESE, SYLVIA 15
MILANO, STEVE 244
MILBURN, CINDY 231
MILES, DENNY 298
MILES, JOHN 89
MILES, RALPH 113
MILES, ROBERT L. 228
MILHOAN, JAMES L. 35
MILIUS, PAULINE H. 15
MILLARD, KEN 213
MILLER, A. WILLIAM, II 268
MILLER, ALLAN 386, 387
MILLER, ALLEN H. 125
MILLER, AMY 240
MILLER, BARBARA 185
MILLER, BEN 357
MILLER, BETHANY 120
MILLER, BRIAN K. 65
MILLER, BRUCE J. 59
MILLER, C.W. 182
MILLER, CAROLYN 30
MILLER, CHARLIE 215
MILLER, CHRIS 342
MILLER, CHRISTOPHER G. 303
MILLER, CLAIRE 296
MILLER, CRAIG 48, 191
MILLER, DAMIEN 313
MILLER, DARREN A. 355
MILLER, DAVID 181, 224
MILLER, DAVID E. 122
MILLER, DAVID R. 52
MILLER, DELMER 240
MILLER, DENNIS J. 179
MILLER, ED 99
MILLER, EDWIN L. 385
MILLER, ERICA A., DVM 276
MILLER, FRED 97
MILLER, GELNN 106
MILLER, GLENN 380
MILLER, GORDON 38
MILLER, HENRY 15
MILLER, HOWARD 193
MILLER, HUBERT J. 35
MILLER, JACQUELIN N. 60
MILLER, JAMES E. 357
MILLER, JANE 226
MILLER, JERRY 64, 226
MILLER, JOHN 20
MILLER, KARIN E. 252
MILLER, KITTY 284
MILLER, MARVIN 183
MILLER, MIKE 67
MILLER, MONIQUE 348
MILLER, PAMELA K. 189
MILLER, PAUL 338
MILLER, RANDALL 80
MILLER, ROBERT 233, 393
MILLER, ROSS H. 59
MILLER, S. FRANCES 64
MILLER, SARAH 172
Miller, Shawn 334
MILLER, STEVEN W. 124
MILLER, TODD 181, 290
MILLER, WILLIAM R., III 330
MILLIMAN, JOHN D. 391
MILLING, MARCUS E. 150
MILLION, PHIL 26
MILLS, BOB 208
MILLS, EDWARD L. 382
MILLS, MARQUESA 156
MILLS, ROBERT H. 71
MILLS, THOMAS J. 33
MILLS, W. L., JR. 374
MILLS, WAYNE A. 178
MILMORE, DOLOLRES 187
MILNER, KELSEY 380
MILTON, FLOYD T. 79
MILTON, JOHN P. 332
MIMS, ROBERT D. 195
MIMS, SUSAN 39
MINCEY, JOHN 217
MINER, EDNA 242
MINER, KIRK W. 242
MINER, PAUL F. 47
MINGES, DAVID A. 73
MINOR, DOUG 292
MINOR, MARIE F. 343
MINTON, DWIGHT 218
MINTON, R. VERNON 39
MIOFF, STEPHANIE 302
MIRAGLIA, FRANK 35
MIRANDA, L. E. 80
MIRANDE, CLAIRE 230
MIRELSON, ROBERT N. 21
MISHKIN, STEPHEN R. 135
MISSELDINE, CAROL K. 255
MITCHELL, ANDREW 199
MITCHELL, ANNE 172, 232
MITCHELL, BRAD 75
MITCHELL, CHARLES 271, 329
MITCHELL, DEAN L. 358
MITCHELL, DENNIS 135
MITCHELL, DON R. 159
MITCHELL, FRANK S. 86
MITCHELL, FRED 77
MITCHELL, GARY R. 67
MITCHELL, JOHN HANSON 253
MITCHELL, KIMBERLY A. 203
MITCHELL, LARRY 267
MITCHELL, PETER 127
MITCHELL, RALPH 19
MITCHELL, RICK 55
MITCHELL, ROBERT 216
MITCHELL, ROBERT C. 103, 104
MITCHELL, ROBIN 207
MITCHELL, STACY 31
MITCHELL, VASTINE 290
MITCHELSON, WILLIAM D. 266
MITHCHELL, PAIGE 31
MITRONOVAS, WALTER 92
MITSCH, WILLIAM 323
MITTEN, SUE 132
MITTERMEIER, RUSSELL 188
MITTON, LINDA R. 162
MITZEL, DAVID 333
MIYASAKI, EVERAND 168
MLECOCH, COLLEEN 78
MMAHFOOD, STEPHEN M. 81
MOATS, L. R. 194
MOBERLY, STANLEY A. 273
MOBLEY, JULIA PECK 44
MOBLEY, MIKE 110
MOCK, GEORGE B. 161
MODISETTE, CHRISTOPHER 326
MOE, RICHARD 272
MOEHLE, CARM 334
MOEHLE, MARK 296
MOEN, AARON N. 382
MOFFITT, CHRISTINE M. 142
MOFFITT, DONNA 94
MOFFOT, JANE-KERIN 163
MOGER, EDWIN J. 55
MOHAI, PAUL 378
MOLINA, SUKI 223
MOLINARES, ALEXIS 189
MOLINI, WILLIE 84
MOLITORIS, JOLENE M. 28
MOLL, RUSSEL 77
MOLL, RUSSELL A. 155
MOLLER, PETER G. 370
MOLTZ, LARRY 111
MOLVRAY, MIA 98
MOMBOURQUETTE, JOHN 130
MONAGHAN, THOMAS A. 81
MONCUR, JAMES E.T. 61
MONIZ, GARY 60
MONK, JOHN 249
MONOSTORY, LES 241
MONROE, BILL 299
MONROE, MARTHA C. 56
MONSON, JOHN 285
MONTAGUE, DEADERICK C. 325
MONTALBANO, FRANK, III 55
MONTGOMERY, STEVE 244
MONTGOMERY, STEVEN L. 273
MONZON, RICK 297
MOOBERRY, DAVID D. 333
MOOD, JUDY GILSON 315
MOODY, BLAIR 298
MOODY, DAVE 358
MOODY, DAVID W. 310
MOODY, HOWARD H. 271
MOODY, J. WILLIAM 97
MOODY, JOAN 191
MOODY, MICHAEL W. 71
MOOERS, STEFFI 248
MOON, MARILYN 239
MOON, THOMAS 386
MOORE, ANDREW 264
MOORE, BARBARA 13
MOORE, BARRY K. 104
MOORE, DAVID F. 286
MOORE, ENOCH S. 103
MOORE, GEORGE S., JR. 27
MOORE, GREG 269
MOORE, HEATHER 207
MOORE, J. 37
MOORE, JEAN 222
MOORE, JENNIFER 36
MOORE, JERRY N. 221
MOORE, JOCELYN 215
MOORE, JOE 56
MOORE, JOHN R. 333
MOORE, JULIA A. 34
MOORE, MONTGOMERY 114
MOORE, PAUL 327
MOORE, PETER B. 285
MOORE, RANDY 263
MOORE, RICHARD 164
MOORE, ROBERT 177
MOORE, RONALD 20
MOORE, STEVE 108
MOORE, TERRENCE D. 88
MOORE, VIRGIL K. 62
MOORE, WILLIAM 391
MOOREHOUSE, DAVID 25
MOORHEAD, ALEXANDER 116
MOORING, JEAN 225
MOORING, PAUL 225
MOOTNICK, ALAN 229
MOOTY, JOHN J. 355
MOPPERT, KYLE 205
MOQUIN, GABRIEL F. 51
MOQUIN, RICHARD 86
MORAN, CHARLES A. 226
MORAN, DAVE 256
MORAN, MARC 91
MORAN, MARK 17
MORAST, DANIEL 235
MORAVCIK, PHILIP S. 61
MORDEN, CLIFFORD 220
MORDICA, JAMES 79
MOREHOUSE, DOUG 331
MOREHOUSE, W. BRADLEY 185
MORENO, MARIO 13
MORETTI, MILES 114
MOREY, GLENN B. 78
MORGAN, ANN 24
MORGAN, DON R. 210
MORGAN, DONALD ACE 304
MORGAN, E. PHILIP 374
MORGAN, ELLEN B. 80
MORGAN, ERIKA 71
MORGAN, EVELYN 245
MORGAN, GIL 215
MORGAN, JOHN M. 158
MORGAN, MAX G. 113
MORGAN, MICHAEL D. 393
MORGAN, PAMELA 19
MORGAN, PHILLIP 9
MORGAN, PHILLIP S. 275
MORGAN, RICK 297
MORGAN, ROBERT L. 113
MORGAN, ROY 157
MORGAN, WALDO 111
MORGENWECK, RALPH 27
MORGESTER, JAMES J. 46
MORI, ART 248
MORI, BETTY N. 214
MORIARTY, MARVIN E. 26
MORIGEAU, SAM 185
MORIN, NANCY 139
MORING, JOHN R. 72
MORITZ, THOMAS D. 45, 169
MORKILL, ANNE 353
MORREIRA, MARICA A. 106
MORRELL, L. ROSS 55
MORRILL, VALERIE 21
MORRILL, WILLIAM F. 166
MORRIS, BILL M. 35
MORRIS, CROCKETT 342
MORRIS, DON 18
MORRIS, ED 44
MORRIS, EDWARD W., JR. 28
MORRIS, FREDERICK E. 188
MORRIS, GEORGE F. 213
MORRIS, HILLIARD 225
MORRIS, JIM 97
MORRIS, JOHN 94
MORRIS, JOSEPH E. 146
MORRIS, LARRY 46
MORRIS, LAWRENCE B. 162
MORRIS, LISA 97
MORRIS, MERVIN G. 169
MORRISON, DAVID L. 35
MORRISON, JAMES 168
MORRISON, LARRY R. 259
MORRISON, MERRIE 140
MORRISON, RON 129
MORRISON, TOM 72
MORRISON, VENNING 323
MORRISON, WILLIAM V. 50
MORRISSEY, ROBIN 44
MORRISSEY, WILLIAM 78
MORRITT, CLIFTON 156
MORRONE, MICHELE 97
MORROS, PETER G. 84
MORROW, DAVE 113
MORROW, PARTICE A. 379
MORROW, PATRICK 21
MORSE, CHARLIE 232
MORSE, COY 99
MORSE, HERBERT 327
MORTENSEN, CHARLES O. 373
MORTENSEN, RAY 333
MORTON, DAVID 377
MORTON, ROBERT M. 354
MOSEL, MIKE 282
MOSER, DON 320
MOSER, LYNN 133
MOSES, AMOS 99
MOSES, JOHN LEE 271
MOSHER, JIM 240
MOSHER, PETER N. 72
MOSLEY, CAROLYN 10
MOSS, DEWITT 272
MOSS, GEORGE 353
MOSS, KAREN 226
MOSS, RICHARD 343
MOSTELLER, DALE 291
MOTAVALLI, PETER 59
MOTE, WILLIAM R. 261
MOTT, DAVE 82
MOTTERSHAW, RICHARD 63
MOTYKA, CONRAD 114
MOULTON, NORM 250
MOUNT, DANA K. 95
MOUNT, PAUL 50
MOUNTAIN, BRUCE 238
MOUNTAIN, DENNIS 290
MOURAD, TERESA M. 203
MOURADJIAN, LARRY 106
MOURADJIAN, MELANIE 106
MOUTON, EDMOND, LDWF 355
MOWRY, KENNETH 104
MOYER, BRUCE 102
MOYER, STEVEN N. 333
MOYER, TERRY L. 354
MOYER, WILLIAM F. 53
MOYER-ANGUS, MARIA 197
MOYO, SAM 365
MOZER, DAVID 229
MTELITS, MICHAEL D. 16
MUCKENFUSS, ED 107
MUDD, EDWARD W., JR. 166
MUELDENER, KARL 67
MUELLER, MIKE 313
MUESSIG, KARL 87
MUETER, FRANZ 292
MUHLSTOCK, BESS 306
MUHWEEZI, ALEX 235
MUISE, LEO 130
MULALA, SALLY LINDA 235
MULDOON, JOE 132
MULDOON, PATRICK 175
MULDOON, PAUL 172
MULFORD, JON K. 349
MULHOLLAND, DAVID 306
MULIERI, BONNIE 73
MULKEY, MARCIA E. 11
MULLANE, NEIL 101
MULLEN, BOB 100
MULLER, CARL 104
MULLER, MARK 217
MULLIGAN, SHAWN 331
MULLIGAN, TIM 368
MULLINS, ART 346
MULLINS, GARY W. 385
MULRANE, TONI E. 96
MULVIHILL, JOHN 313
MUMMA, JOHN 51, 346
MUMMA, TRACY 176
MUND, NAT 187
MUNDY, ROY, JR 9
MUNGARI, ROBERT 92
MUNGER, MARK 304
MUNOZ, MANNY 55
MUNOZ, MIGUEL 106
MUNOZ, PAT 312
MUNRO, KAREN 345
MUNSON, RICHARD H. 221
MUNSON, ROBERT W. 313, 352
MURARO, JOAN 63
MURAWSKI, ANTHONY B. 103
MURDOCH, TOM 134
MURKOWSI, FRANK 6
MURPHY, BARBARA 317
MURPHY, BRIAN R. 391
MURPHY, CHARLIE 365
MURPHY, COLLEEN 260
MURPHY, DOUGLAS 174
MURPHY, ED 300
MURPHY, EDWARD C. 366
MURPHY, HOY 122
MURPHY, JAMES 19
MURPHY, KIRK 313
MURPHY, MARGARET H. 147
MURPHY, MIKE 66
MURPHY, PATRICIA M. 43
MURPHY, REG 269
MURPHY, RICKY 290
MURRAY, ALAN 44
MURRAY, ANN P. 330
MURRAY, BENNIE 21
MURRAY, DOUGLAS 338
MURRAY, JOHN A. 348
MURRAY, KEN 293
MURRAY, NANCY A. 151
MURRAY, NORMAN 219
MURRAY, PETER 230
MURRAY, RICHARD 74, 292
MURRAY, WILLIAM 168
MURRAY, WILLIAM E. 213
MURRELL, K. D. 32
MURRIETA, JOANQUIN 323
MURRINER, EDWARD 276, 361
MURZIN, RICHARD 131
MUSGRAVE, RUTH S. 177
MUSIL, ROBERT K. 303
MUTSIGWA, J. K. 365
MYERS, ED 249
MYERS, GARY T. 110
MYERS, GORDON 95
MYERS, JAN 226
MYERS, KATE 151
MYERS, LARRY 49
MYERS, MARVIN 19
MYERS, NETTIE H. 109

Staff Name Index

STAFF NAME INDEX

N

NAAB, WALTER ... 276
NABORS, JOHNSIE ... 27
NABORS, LEILA ... 135
NADARAJAH, RAMINI ... 172
NADEL, STEVE ... 142
NAEGEL, ANNETTE S. ... 239
NAFTZGER, ROY E. ... 231
NAGATA, RALSTON H. ... 60
NAGY, LEWIS, JR. ... 93
NAIL, ANNE ... 159
NAJJAR, STEPHEN ... 19
NAKAMOTO, GUY ... 248
NAKANO, JIM ... 102
NAKATANI, JAMES ... 60
NANCE, JIM ... 110
NANEE, LARRY ... 44
NANIA, JEFF ... 360
NANNINI, EDWARD N. ... 210
NARDOZZI, CHARLIE ... 268
NARGANG, RONALD ... 78
NASH, CHARLES ... 267
NASH, CLAUDE ... 80
NASH, HENRY ... 55
NASON, ROCHELLE ... 248
NASSAR, RON ... 249
NASSER, AHMED ... 42
NATES, LARRY E. ... 323
NATIONS, JAMES ... 188
NATTIER, JAMES ... 150
NAUGHTON, NELL ... 158
NAVARRE, A. EDWARD ... 74
NAVO, KIRK ... 354
NAYDOL, ALLAN ... 19
NAZE, KEVIN ... 348
NAZIR, MUHAMMAD ... 128
NAZZARO, ANDREW A. ... 378
NDIAYE, ABDOULAYE ... 235
NDINGA, ASSITOU ... 235
NEAL, MARY ... 29
NEAVE, DAVID J. ... 352
NEELY, DAN ... 233
NEELY, ROBERT K. ... 378
NEENAN, TOM F. ... 238
NEGRI, SHARON ... 306
NEHRIG, R. EDWIN ... 104
NEIGHBOR, BRUCE ... 198
NELLIS, DAVID ... 115
NELSEN, BETTY JO ... 124
NELSON, BARRY N. ... 315
NELSON, COURTLAND ... 113
NELSON, COURTLAND C. ... 264
NELSON, CURTIS ... 334
NELSON, D. JAMES ... 303
NELSON, DAVID ... 324
NELSON, DENNIS ... 347
NELSON, EDWARD N. ... 295
NELSON, GARLAND ... 57
NELSON, GARTH ... 282
NELSON, GAYLORD ... 349
NELSON, JAY ... 40
NELSON, JEFFREY ... 196
NELSON, JIM ... 376
NELSON, JOHN I., JR. ... 86
NELSON, JON ... 211
NELSON, KAREN ... 78
NELSON, KIMBERLY ... 102
NELSON, KIRK ... 83
NELSON, LARRY ... 78, 108
NELSON, LORI ... 270
NELSON, MICHAEL J. ... 73
NELSON, MIKE ... 164
NELSON, PATT ... 296
NELSON, ROBERT R. ... 261
NELSON, RON ... 102
NELSON, TARA S. ... 164
NELSON, THOMAS ... 354
NELTNER, THOMAS ... 63
NEMSICK, KATHY ... 180
NERAASEN, T. G. ... 194
NERRIE, BRIAN L. ... 119
NERVIG, ROBERT M. ... 30
NESBITT, STEPHEN A. ... 288
NESBITT, WILLIAM HAROLD ... 210
NESBITT, WM. HAROLD ... 228
NESSI, DOM ... 24
NESZPAUL, SUSAN ... 347
NETTLES, VICTOR F. ... 325
NEU, TIM ... 18
NEUBACHER, DON ... 251
NEUMAN, JANET ... 101
NEVELS, DON ... 79
NEVENDORF, KLAUS ... 100
NEVES, RICHARD J. ... 117, 391
NEVILLE, JOSEPH ... 302
NEWBERRY, ERIC ... 329
NEWBOLD, JOHN ... 290
NEWBOLD, JOHN P. ... 290
NEWBOLD, MARGARET ... 384
NEWBOLD, SHARON ... 290
NEWBROUGH, STACEY SNYDER ... 237
NEWCOMER, RICHARD ... 305
NEWELL, LEONARD ... 220
NEWHOUSE, DAVID ... 160
NEWLAND, LEO ... 390
NEWMAN, ARNOLD ... 233
NEWMAN, CHRISTIAN ... 216
NEWMAN, CONSTANCE BERRY ... 320
NEWMAN, DEBBIE SCOTT ... 224
NEWMAN, MARK ... 99
NEWMAN, SHAWN ... 297
NEWMAN, THEODORE ... 163
NEWTON, CARLTON M. ... 391
NEWTON, STEVE ... 209
NICHOLAS, WENDY ... 272
NICHOLS, GEORGE D. ... 259
NICHOLS, JAMES ... 28
NICHOLS, LACY ... 53
NICHOLS, MARVIN ... 15
NICHOLS, NANCY ... 262
NICHOLS, RON ... 31
NICHOLS, WILLIAM ... 71
NICHOLSON, AL ... 62
NICHOLSON, BETH ... 316
NICHOLSON, RICHARD S. ... 139
NICKAS, GEORGE ... 350
NICKENS, EDDIE ... 291
NICKERSON, DON ... 314
NICKERSON, NORMA ... 380
NICKUM, DAVID ... 333
NICOLESCU, JERRY ... 62
NICOLICH, JANE ... 288
NICOLL, JILL ... 269
NIEBAUGER, PETER ... 24
NIEDBALA, PETER C. ... 195
NIELAND, JENNIFER ... 360
NIELSEN, CRAIG A. ... 73
NIELSEN, LARRY A. ... 387
NIEMELA, VIC ... 37
NIESWIADOMY, MIKE ... 390
NIGHTINGALE, STUART L. ... 14
NIKIDES, HARRY ... 64
NIKIDES, HARRY S. ... 64
NILAND, GARY F. ... 102
NILES, LARRY ... 87
NIMKIN, DAVID ... 221
NIMRY, BASIL ... 65, 66
NISHI, YUJI ... 179
NISHIDA, JANE T. ... 72
NIX, DAN ... 48
NIX, T. LARRY ... 214
NIXON, PHILIP ... 289
NOAH, JIM ... 259
NOAKE, D. ... 386
NOBISS, LIONEL ... 251
NOBLE, RICHARD L. ... 384
NOECHEL, PAUL ... 140
NOEL, JOAN ... 245
NOEM, ROLLIE ... 109
NOERENBERG, CHANDLER ... 344
NOKA, RANDY ... 276
NOLAN, PAT ... 213
NOLAND, STEWART ... 299
NOLD, CARL R. ... 76
NOLT, BEN ... 104
NOLTE, DAVID ... 334
NOLTE, RICHARD H. ... 150
NOMSEN, DAVID E. ... 303
NOONAN, PATRICK F. ... 187
NORBRIGA, DAVID ... 219
NORDEN, ARNOLD ... 277
NORDSTROM, CARL R. ... 87
NORLAND, ERIC ... 98
NORMAN, BILL ... 383
NORMAN, GAYLE ... 31
NORMAN, PHILIP E. ... 355
NORRENA, ED ... 37
NORRIE, KENNETH D. ... 61
NORRIS, BARRY ... 102
NORRIS, JENNY ... 136
NORRIS, LANCE ... 314
NORRIS, SHARON ... 31
NORRY, PATRICIA G. ... 35
NORSE, ELLIOTT A. ... 251
NORTH, DOUG ... 313
NORTHCUTT, BEN ... 230
NORTHROP, KATHY ... 297
NORTON, JAMES ... 335
NORTON, JEANNE ... 241
NORTON, STEPHEN ... 376
NORTON, W. W. ... 349
NORWOOD, EARL D., JR. ... 195
NOVAK, CHRISTINA ... 103
NOVAK, CHRISTOPHER A. ... 330
NOVAK, MICHAEL ... 385
NOVINGER, GARY D. ... 81
NOVOTNY, LAWRENCE ... 324
NOWAK, MATT ... 20
NOWASAD, ROBERT ... 315
NSANJAMA, HENRI ... 363
NUGENT, JACK ... 196
NUMATA, MAKOTO ... 282
NUNCI, HELEN ... 307
NUNLEY, JOHN F., III ... 125
NUNNARI, BARBARA ... 214
NUQUIST, ANDREW ... 218
NYAHAY, RICHARD ... 92
NYMARK, DENNIS ... 208

O

O'DAY, JODI R. ... 187
OAKES, CHERYL ... 209
OAKES, JOY ... 157
OATES, FRANCES HAMILTON ... 223
OATES, WILLIAM E. ... 111
OBARA, LINDA ... 289
OBER, RICHARD ... 322
OBIAS, VIRGILIO L. ... 59
O'BISO, PATTY ... 315
OBR, JOE ... 66
O'BRIEN, CHRISTINE ... 221
O'BRIEN, DONAL C., JR. ... 52, 265
O'BRIEN, DONALD C., JR. ... 163
O'BRIEN, ERIC ... 270
O'BRIEN, G. PATRICK ... 42
O'BRIEN, KEVIN ... 205
O'BRIEN, PHILIP J. ... 86
O'BRIEN, RINDY ... 349
O'BRIEN, W. JOHN ... 374
O'CONNOR, ANTHONY ... 36
O'CONNOR, CARL ... 125
O'CONNOR, DAVID J. ... 10
O'CONNOR, J. DENNIS ... 320
O'CONNOR, JOE ... 128
O'CONNOR, MATTHEW B. ... 303
O'CONNOR, MICHAEL ... 21
ODATO, GENE ... 105
ODELL, DANIEL K. ... 321
ODELL, THOMAS ... 185
ODOM, BOB ... 70
ODOM, PERRY ... 54
O'DONNELL, CATHY ... 185
OELSCHLAEGER, MAX ... 175
OELSHAEGER, MAX ... 390
O'FALLON, SHANNON ... 137
OFFIELD, PAXSON H. ... 303
OFFNER, ELLEN ... 304
OFFUTT, SUSAN ... 30
OGAN, CHESTER ... 353
O'GARA, ANITA ... 238
OGBURN, STEW ... 48
OGDEN, KEITH ... 262
OGDEN, MARK ... 225
OGE, MARGO T. ... 11
OGILVIE, KEN ... 304
OGLESBY, GENE ... 283
OGLESBY, RON ... 46
O'GORMAN, DENIS ... 127
O'GRADY, RICHARD ... 151
OGUNLEYE, BISI ... 361
OH, MARTY ... 113
O'HARA, FREDERICK M., JR. ... 175
O'HARA, JAMES A. ... 14
O'HARA, STEPHEN J. ... 208
OHMART, TOM ... 42
OHMSTEDE, WILL ... 181
OKECHUKWU, ALEXANDER ... 193
OKOH, ROBERT M. ... 377
OKUN, MELVA ... 384
OKUTOMI, KIYOSHI ... 282
OLAH, OTTO ... 129
O'LAUGLIN, JAY ... 373
OLDHAM, HAP ... 38
OLDHAM, THOMAS E. ... 149
OLDROYD, RICHARD ... 341
OLDS, JERRY ... 113
O'LEARY, NORMA ... 185
OLENA, HELEN ... 102
OLIVE, FRANK ... 348
OLIVER, JOHN C. ... 105
OLIVER, JOHN E. ... 373
OLIVER, KESHA A. ... 201
OLIVER, MARK L. ... 144
OLIVER, TERRY KRAFT ... 231
OLIVIER, W. S. ... 325
OLIVIERI, ALISON ... 304
OLIVIERI, SILVIO ... 188
OLIVIERO, MELANIE BETH ... 301
OLIVOLO, BETTY ... 347
OLKOWSKI, HELGA ... 166
OLKOWSKI, WILLIAM ... 166
OLMEDA, RAFAEL ... 106
OLMSTEAD, DON ... 10
OLMSTEAD, WILLIAM J. ... 35
OLMSTED, CHARLES ... 183
OLMSTED, ED ... 182
OLSEN, ARNOLD ... 82
OLSEN, GENE ... 65
OLSEN, GEORGE ... 260
OLSEN, GLENN H. ... 161
OLSEN, JILL ... 196
OLSEN, LARRY ... 77
OLSON, DAN ... 125
OLSON, ELLIOTT ... 333, 335
OLSON, GLENN E. ... 265
OLSON, JEFF ... 349
OLSON, LAYTON ... 305
OLSON, LEONARD ... 112
OLSON, RICH ... 126
OLSON, ROGER O. ... 73
OLSON, W. KENT ... 211
OLTMANN, JULIE E. ... 48
OMANS, JIM ... 27

O (cont.)

O'NEIL, WILLIAM A. ... 231
O'NEILL, CHARLES ... 226
O'NEILL, JAMES ... 53
O'NEILL, MARY ... 78
O'NEILL, RICHARD P. ... 14
O'NEILL, SHEILA ... 316
ONIZUICA, ERIC W. ... 60
ONSTAD, CHARLES ... 32
OPLER, PAUL ... 364
OPPELT, TIMOTHY ... 11
OPPEN, BILL ... 132
OPPENHEIMER, JOHN R. ... 382
ORAM, JOHN ... 182
ORASIN, CHARLES J. ... 191
ORAZE, MICHAEL J. ... 29
ORBACH, MICHAEL K. ... 182, 383
ORCUTT-BAILEY, ANNE M. ... 59
O'REGAN, FRED ... 230
ORENDORFF, BEA ... 276
ORENSTEIN, RONALD ... 236
O'RIORDAN, JON ... 127
ORLANDI, ROBIN ... 310
OROSZ, SUSAN E. ... 161
ORR, DAVID ... 385
ORT, JON F. ... 94
ORTON, MARY ... 154
OSBORN, BRENDA K. ... 314
OSBORN, FREDERICK, III ... 317
OSBORN, JOHN ... 345
OSBORN, NIC ... 165
OSBORN, OZZIE ... 224
OSBORNE, NA'TAKI ... 171
OSBORNE, PATRICK ... 229
OSBURN, BENNIE ... 47
OSBURN, GERALD ... 104
OSBURN, GERALD T. ... 104
OSHIMA, YASUYUKI ... 242
OSKAY, CLARE ... 226
OSMAN, JOSEPH ... 103
OSTBY, FREDERICK P. ... 13
OSTER, WALTER G. ... 172
OSTERBAUER, RON ... 309
OSTERMANN, THOMAS W. ... 126
OSTERVICH, JOSEPH A. ... 167
OSTFELD, RICHARD S. ... 227
OSTROM, AARON ... 343
O'SULLIVAN, PATRICK ... 372
OSWALD, BRIAN ... 389
OTEY, KIRK ... 336
OTHBERG, KURT L. ... 62
OTIS, DAVID L. ... 107
O'TOOLE, MICHAEL ... 91
OTTE, CHUCK ... 244
OTTE, RONALD L. ... 41
OTTENBREIT, RODNEY J. ... 25
OTTER, RICHARD C. ... 317
OTTINGER, MARY ANN ... 156
OTTINGER, RICHARD L. ... 201
OTTO, LORRIE ... 180
OTTO, RALPH ... 32
OTTUM, MARGARET ... 390
OUTLAW, BRENDA ... 290
OVERCASH, JESSE L. ... 358
OWEN, DANA ... 325
OWEN, HAROLD ... 291
OWEN, JAMES E. ... 49
OWEN, JON ... 345
OWEN, LUTHER ... 20
OWENDOFS, JAMES M. ... 13
OWENS, GLENDA ... 23
OWENS, JIM ... 343
OWENS, STEVE ... 68
OWENSBY, CLENTON ... 374
OWINGS, MARGARET ... 212
OWINGS, RAYMOND ... 28
OWNBY, JAMES D. ... 385
OWUSU, F. A. ... 204
OWUSU, JOHN KWADWO ... 204
OXENHANDLER, SALLY ... 81
OXFORD, RICHARD B. ... 42
OXLEY, FLO ... 246
OXLEY, MARY J. ... 96
OZENBERGER, JIM ... 364

P

PABLO, MICHAEL T. ... 185
PACE, MICHAEL L. ... 227
PACHAL, DIANNE ... 137
PACHECO, PEGGY FANTOZZI ... 253
PACKARD, HEATH G. ... 275
PADALINO, JOHN ... 304
PADDA, DARSHAN S. ... 115
PADOR, MILA P. ... 59
PADOVAN, LYNNE ... 225
PAGAC, GERALD ... 64
PAGANO, PENNY ... 138
PAGE, BERTHA ... 331
PAGE, LARRY M. ... 155
PAGE, PETER ... 87
PAGE, SAM ... 275
PAGE, STACY ... 305
PAGEL, MARTHA O. ... 102
PAHL, BARBARA ... 272

514

STAFF NAME INDEX

Staff Name Index

PAIGE, DAN ... 81
PAIGE, STEVE ... 67
PAINTER, DOUGLAS ... 271
PAIS, DAVID ... 207
PALAZZO, JOSE TRUDA, JR. ... 235
PALIN, BRUCE ... 63
PALMASSE, CANUTE ... 114
PALMER, CHARLES ... 112
PALMER, CHRISTOPHER ... 273, 275
PALMER, GEORGE ... 296
PALMER, JEFFREY ... 324
PALMER, JERRY ... 27
PALMER, LANGDON ... 285
PALMER, MOLLIE ... 54
PALMER, WILLIAM H. ... 345
PALOLA, ERIC ... 274
PALUMBO, NANCY ... 93
PAMPUSH, GEOFF ... 298
PANDOLFI, FRANCIS ... 32
PANIO, JOHN, JR. ... 231
PAPERIELLO, CARL J. ... 35
PAPPAS, PETER ... 385
PAQUETTE, CHUCK ... 157, 197
PAQUIN, EMERY ... 129
PARADIS, RICHARD ... 327
PARADIS-BRANT, LAURIE ... 185
PARDUE, DAN ... 226
PARENT, DAVID ... 257
PARENT, TOM ... 72
PARENTEAU, AL ... 132
PARENTEAU, PATRICK ... 391
PARISH, WILL ... 248
PARK, JAMES ... 63
PARKER, ACE ... 209
PARKER, BRAIN ... 205
PARKER, BUCK ... 198
PARKER, DAVID C. ... 161
PARKER, EDWARD ... 292
PARKER, EDWARD C. ... 52
PARKER, FORD H. ... 133
PARKER, GRANT ... 313
PARKER, JOHN ... 90, 338
PARKER, MARY BETH ... 215
PARKER, NICK C. ... 111
PARKER, RANDY ... 113
PARKER, RON ... 90
PARKER, WARREN K. ... 210
PARKER, ZOANN ... 104
PARKHURST, JAMES A. ... 119
PARKS, STEVE ... 240
PARMENTER, FRED ... 335
PARMER, ALYCE ... 55
PARMER, DELARIE ... 19
PARONE, LARRY G. ... 331
PARR, LINDA ... 205
PARR, MIKE ... 140
PARRISH, DONALD L. ... 391
PARRISH, JAMES D. ... 60, 372
PARRY, CHRISTIANE ... 47
PARSONS, KATHARINE C. ... 251
PARSONS, M. ... 129
PARSONS, RICHARD ... 314
PARSONS, SCOTT ... 36
PARUPIA, IQBAL ... 319
PASHLEY, DAVID ... 140
PASQUARELLO, THOMAS ... 383
PASQUIER, ROGER ... 362
PASQUIER, ROGER F. ... 310
PASSACANTANDO, JOHN ... 300
PATAKI, GEORGE E. ... 7
PATE, DENNIS ... 323
PATE, PRESTON ... 94
PATEL, DHUN B. ... 87
PATINO, REYNALDO ... 111
PATRICK, LISA P. ... 214
PATRICK, STEVE ... 110
PATTEN, DUNCAN ... 322
PATTEN, SUSAN ... 361
PATTERSEN, DANIEL ... 193
PATTERSON, BILL ... 286
PATTERSON, GARY ... 381
PATTERSON, GREGG ... 44
PATTERSON, NANCI ... 198
PATTERSON, RICH ... 225
PATTERSON, RICK ... 271
PATTERSON, ROGER G. ... 25
PATTON, BOB ... 209
PATTON, DAN ... 112
PATTON, DAVID R. ... 366
PATTON, DOROTHY E. ... 11
PATTON, JAMES L. ... 70
PATTON, MARK ... 98
PATTON, SARA ... 294
PAUL, DENNIS F. ... 391
PAUL, ELLEN ... 299
PAUL, LINDA M.B. ... 220
PAUL, PAT ... 31
PAUL, TERI L. ... 359
PAULIN, DONALD J. ... 65
PAULSON, JR, HENRY M. ... 303
PAWELL, JUDY ... 66
PAXSON, DON ... 243
PAYNE, ADAM ... 359
PAYNE, JACK ... 196
PAYNE, LARRY ... 32
PAYZANT, THOMAS ... 13
PAZZISH, DEBBIE ... 54
PEABODY, TIMOTHY ... 71
PEACOCK, PATRICIA ... 353
PEAK, WAYNE ... 370
PEARCE, RON ... 27
PEARCE, TIM ... 192
PEARIGEN, MIKE ... 330
PEARL, MARY C. ... 353
PEARLMAN, NANCY ... 200
PEARSE, JOHN S. ... 169
PEARSON, JAMES ... 30
PEARSON, WILLIAM D. ... 375
PEASE, JAMES ... 354
PEASE, JAMES L. ... 66
PECHMANN, JOHN E. ... 95
PECHURA, CONSTANCE ... 328
PECK, W. RALPH ... 82
PEDDERSON, RON ... 165
PEDDICORD, CAROL J. ... 353
PEDERSEN, AMANDA ... 15
PEDERSEN, CRAIG D. ... 112
PEDERSEN, JIM ... 306
PEDERSEN, JORDAN ... 113
PEDERSON, CHARLES L. ... 373
PEDROTTI, DANIEL A. ... 167
PEEBLES, ROBERT K. ... 167
PEEBLES, ROGER W. ... 228
PEEK, MOTTELL D. ... 171
PEEL, ELLEN ... 166
PEELER, MARIA ... 120
PEET, MAITLAND ... 297
PEIRNO, THERESA ... 73
PEKINS, PETER ... 381
PELLEGRINO, ROBERT R. ... 52
PELLERIN, JOANNA ... 85
PELSUE, NEIL ... 115
PELZ, JOYCE ... 294
PELZMAN, RON ... 49
PENDEXTER, KARLA ... 242
PENGRA, BRUCE ... 324
PENN, JULIE ... 325
PENNAZ, STEVE ... 289
PENNER, FRANK ... 251
PENNINGTON, STEPHEN ... 66
PENNY, DALE ... 328
PENTZ, LINDA ... 315
PEPPER, TERRY ... 191
PERCIASEPE, ROBERT ... 10
PERCIVAL, DEAN ... 253
PERCIVAL, H. FRANKLIN ... 54
PERCY, W. A., II ... 193
PEREZ-GIBSON, MICHAEL ... 120
PERKEY, ARLYN ... 268
PERKINS, ANJEANETTE ... 239
PERKINS, CRAIG ... 332
PERKINS, MITCH ... 108
PERKO, DANIEL J. ... 126
PERKS, ROB ... 307
PERL, DIANE M. ... 322
PERNAS, ANTONIO J. ... 207
PEROCK, WAYNE ... 84
PERRIN, WILLIAM F. ... 321
PERRY, EARL ... 269
PERRY, FRED ... 185
PERRY, JOHN ... 285
PERRY, LEE ... 71
PERRY, LEE E. ... 71
PERRY, RALPH ... 181
PERRY, RANDALL ... 58
PERRY, RICK ... 111
PERRY, STEPHEN G. ... 86
PERSCHEL, ROBERT ... 349
PERSINGER, CHARLES ... 323
PERSSON, CAROL V. ... 138
PERSSON, VERNON H. ... 49
PESACHOWITZ, ALVIN M. ... 10
PESANELLI, ANTHONY ... 185
PETE, MARY ... 40
PETERMAN, LARRY ... 82
PETERS, EDWARD ... 169, 380
PETERS, JOHN R. ... 302
PETERSEN, HARLAN D. ... 79
PETERSEN, MARK ... 59
PETERSEN, WAYNE R. ... 141
PETERSEN-KEYS, PATRICIA ... 239
PETERSON, ARLENE ... 348
PETERSON, ARTHUR ... 116
PETERSON, CHARLES ... 354
PETERSON, EDWARD ... 169
PETERSON, GAYLE ... 256
PETERSON, GORDON ... 241
PETERSON, JACK E. ... 42
PETERSON, JAMES ... 266
PETERSON, JEFF ... 224
PETERSON, JOHN W. ... 273
PETERSON, JUDY ... 341
PETERSON, L. EARL ... 54
PETERSON, MARK ... 270
PETERSON, R. MAX ... 228
PETERSON, ROLF ... 236
PETERSON, SCOTT ... 356
PETERSON, THOM ... 346
PETRICHENKO, PAUL ... 30
PETRITZ, DAVID C. ... 65
PETRON, STEPHEN E. ... 273
PETRONGOLO, TONY ... 87
PETROSKEY, DALE A. ... 268
PETRUCCI, BRYAN ... 142
PETSONK, ANNIE ... 202
PETTIT, WALT ... 46
PETTIT, WILLIAM ... 285
PETTUS, VICKI ... 69
PETZING, KIM ... 202
PEUKAN, MATT ... 141
PEYTON, BERNIE ... 228
PFAENDER, FREDERIC ... 384
PFANNMULLER, LEE ... 78
PFEIFFER, DAN ... 343
PFEIFFER, PETER W. ... 68
PFERRMAN, GARY ... 327
PFISTER, ROBERT ... 380
PFUND, ROSE T. ... 59
PHARES, DONALD P. ... 122
PHELPS, JOHN E. ... 373
PHELPS, ROBERT ... 43
PHENNEGER, SHARON ... 142
PHILIP, CRAIG E. ... 273
PHILLIPS, ADRIAN ... 234
PHILLIPS, BLAINE T. ... 192
PHILLIPS, BRAD ... 358
PHILLIPS, DAVE ... 132
PHILLIPS, DAVID ... 197, 231
PHILLIPS, DWAIN ... 31
PHILLIPS, JAMES EDDIE ... 99
PHILLIPS, JOHN ... 75
PHILLIPS, JOHN C. ... 165
PHILLIPS, PASCHAL ... 245
PHILLIPS, PATRICIA A. ... 79
PHILLIPS, PAULA ... 136, 137
PHILLIPS, RICHARD ... 114
PHILLIPS, WILSON H., JR. ... 271
PHILP, JAMES F. ... 72
PIASECKI, BRUCE W. ... 382
PICHTEL, JOHN R. ... 373
PICKENS, MARY ANNE ... 276
PICKERD, HOWARD C. ... 126
PICKERING, RAY ... 104
PICKETT, FRANK ... 355
PICKETT, SCOTT ... 221
PICKETT, STEWARD T.A. ... 227
PIERCE, BERT E. ... 122
PIERCE, BETH ... 181
PIERCE, CLAY L. ... 65
PIERCE, DON ... 63
PIERCE, JACQUELYN ... 213
PIERCE, JIM ... 180
PIERCE, MARC ... 196
PIERCE, PHILLIP ... 23
PIERCE, RICHARD ... 319
PIERCE, RICHARD B. ... 196
PIERCE, ROBERT A., II ... 82
PIERCE, URBAN ... 72
PIERCE, VIRGINIA ... 333
PIERGROSSI, MONICA ... 182
PIERINI, ELIZABETH ... 248
PIERPONT, EDITH K. ... 286
PIERSON, AL ... 24
PIERSON, GEORGE H. ... 286
PIERSON, TERRY ... 232
PIETERSE, DI ... 232
PIETRAFESA, LEONARD J. ... 384
PIETSON, WILLIAM ... 96
PIKE, DOUG ... 181
PIKE, JENNIFER ... 158
PIKE, JOHN ... 86
PIKE, STEPHEN J. ... 118
PILCHER, THOMAS ... 17
PILE, WELLS ... 164
PILKINGTON, ALAN R. ... 191
PILS, CHARLES M. ... 124
PIMLOTT, DOROTHY ... 237
PINCETL, STEPHANIE ... 184
PINDAR, GEORGINE ... 278
PINKELMAN, JAMES ... 28
PINNIX, CLEVE ... 120
PIOTROW, PHYLLIS T. ... 304
PIOTROWSKI, GENE ... 73
PIPER, GRETHELYN ... 342
PIPKEN, JAMES ... 24
PIPPIN, JOHN ... 298
PIRAINO, NANCY ... 359
PIRET, FERN V. ... 74
PIRNER, STEVE ... 109
PISANI, DONALD J. ... 154
PISTER, EDWIN P. ... 193
PITCOCK, ANGELA ... 110
PITELKA, LOUIS F. ... 376, 377
PITTMAN, JANNIE ... 174
PITTMAN, WILLIAM ... 19
PITTMAN-EVANS, BRAD ... 28
PITTS, ALEXANDRA ... 26
PITTS, DON ... 17, 269
PIVA, ALFIO ... 37
PIZZUTO, ERNEST ... 284
PLAGEMAN, TIM ... 356
PLANTE, PATRICK ... 194
PLATT, DAVID ... 239
PLATT, DOROTHY K. ... 340
PLATT, DWIGHT ... 244
PLATT, DWIGHT R. ... 244
PLATTS, H. GREGORY ... 268
PLEMONS, J. M. ... 58
PLETCHEN, KATHY L. ... 392
PLETSCHER, DANIEL H. ... 380
PLITT, PAT ... 276
PLOCH, MANDY ... 349
PLOCKELMAN, CYNTHIA ... 56
PLUMB, JOHN A. ... 366
PLUMB, SYLVIA ... 218
POCIUS, E. WAYNE ... 210
PODOLSKY, W. J. ... 128
PODRABSKY, GAYLE ... 211
POHLAD, BOB R. ... 391
POHLMAN, TERESA ... 16
POINDEXTER, DAVID O. ... 305
POIRIER, LUC ... 131
POKRAS, MARTHA ... 276
POLAR, TOM ... 354
POLASEK, JOSEPH P. ... 124
POLI, MARISA J. ... 316
POLISCHUK,, WASYL J., JR. ... 103
POLITINO, TONY ... 122
POLLACK, AMY E. ... 165
POLLARD, BEN ... 99
POLLES, SAM ... 80
POLLI, RUDOLPH ... 115
POLLOCK, GLENN ... 238
POLLOCK, LEONA ... 282
POLTAK, RONALD F. ... 9
POMERANCE, RAFE ... 16
POMEROY, PAUL W. ... 35
POMEROY, WALTER L. ... 138
POND, ROBERT B. ... 328
PONGRATZ, EVA ... 204
PONTTI, MICHAEL R. ... 222
POOLE, ANNE ... 286
POOLE, JOHN ... 39
POOLE, KERRY ... 128
POOLE, SAMUEL ... 56
POOLE, WILLIAM J., JR. ... 271
POOR, HEIDI M. ... 307
POPE, CARL ... 318
POPE, DAVID L. ... 66
POPE, ELLEN ... 322
POPHAM, JAMES ... 18
POPKIN, RODGER ... 141
PORATH, WAYNE R. ... 81
PORTER, MARY JANE ... 14
PORTER, SANDRA ... 55
PORTER, WILLIAM F. ... 383
PORTERFIELD, RANDY ... 314
PORTERFIELD, RICHARD ... 150
PORTNER, LINDA E. ... 35
PORTNEY, PAUL R. ... 311
POST, DIANA M. ... 308
POST, ROGER A. ... 353
POTASH, LAURA ... 344
POTTER, BRUCE G. ... 239
POTTER, DAVE ... 376
POTTER, ROBERT G. ... 49
POTTER, THOMAS D. ... 13
POTTER, WILLIAM GRAY ... 58
POTTIE, JAMES ... 21
POTTINGER, LORI ... 232
POTUCEK, DOROTHY ... 316
POULSEN, DOROTHY ... 260
POWELL, ANN ... 338
POWELL, ANNE ... 155
POWELL, BARBARA JEAN ... 205
POWELL, CHRISTOPHER ... 149
POWELL, DAVE ... 137
POWELL, JIMMIE ... 6
POWELL, LOUCHES, JR. ... 163
POWELL, PETER ... 322
POWELL, ROYDEN ... 73
POWELL, STEVE ... 73
POWELL, SUSAN ... 131
POWER, DONNA ... 197
POWERS, BRAD ... 73
POWERS, JOHN ... 182
POWERS, ROY, JR. ... 141
POWERS, TOM ... 48
POYNTER, KEN Q. ... 276
POZDENA, RANDY ... 298
PRANIS, EVE ... 268
PRATHER, KERRY W. ... 146
PRATT, JAMES R. ... 386
PRATT, JEROME J. ... 348
PRCHAL, DOUG ... 96
PREBBLE, DEBBIE ... 55
PRECARIO, PETE ... 294
PRENDERGAST, GREGORY ... 76
PRESCOTT, HEIDI ... 212
PRESNAL, DANNY ... 111
PREUSS, PETER W. ... 11
PREZANT, R. S. ... 379
PRICE, HARRY F. ... 122
PRICE, HUGH C. ... 257
PRICE, JEFF ... 140
PRICE, JIM ... 161, 319
PRICE, JONATHAN G. ... 84
PRICE, MARK STANLEY ... 134
PRICE, SCOTT ... 308
PRICE, WILLIAM E. ... 118

STAFF NAME INDEX 515

PRICKETT, WILLIAM 192
PRIME, MEREDITH 134
PRINCE, BERNADINE 142
PRINDLE, FRED 256
PRINGLE, PAT 297
PRITCHARD, CHUCK 169
PRITCHARD, MARY LOU 283
PRITCHARD, PAUL C. 270
PRITCHARD, PETER 178
PRITCHETT, BRYAN 273
PRITCHETT, REBECCA 136
PROBASCO, IRENE 294
PROBST, MARIAN 212
PROESCHOLDT, KEVIN 211
PROHASKA, JANE 279
PROPST, LUTHER 312, 323
PROSSER, KATHY 246
PROUSE, C. GORDON 128
PROUTY, JORDAN S. 289
PROUTY, SALLY 97
PROVOST, DAN 254
PRUIT, PHILIP 18
PRUITT, WILLIAM A. 117
PRYOR, EMILIE M. 310
PTACEK, PATRICK 84
PTAK, THOMAS J. 28
PTOLEMY, JUANITA 148
PUFFINBERGER, CHARLES W. 73
PUGH, ELIZABETH B. 317
PUGH, LARRY 313
PUGH, SUZANNE 30
PULFORD-EARLE, CURTIS RUSSELL 309
PUPPE, GARY 291
PURNELL, TIL 316
PURSER, PAUL 296
PURSGLOVE, SAMUEL R. 314
PUTNAM, HUGH, JR. 254
PUTNAM, JEFFREY 285
PUTZ, ROBERT E. 187
PYLE, LIZBETH A. 161
PYLE, PHILIP E., JR. 168

Q

QUACKENBUSH, EVERETT 93
QUACKENBUSH, MARY 293
QUAKENBUSH, LORI 40
QUALLEY, GEORGE 49
QUANSTROM, WALLY 246
QUARLES, LYNN 29
QUARLES, WILLIAM 166
QUARTERMAN, CYNTHIA 24
QUAYLE, FREDERICK M. 118
QUAYLE, MOURA 368
QUERBES, BETTY-LANE 152
QUIGLEY, KRISTEN 345
QUIGLEY, MIKE 64
QUILL, STEPHEN F. 314
QUIMBY, BILL 314
QUINK, THOMAS 75, 253
QUINLIVAN, JUDY 344
QUINN, CATHERINE 340
QUINN, RANDY 21
QUINN, ROBERT 94
QUIRK, BILL 20
QUIRK, THOMAS F. 171
QUIROLO, CRAIG 310
QUIROLO, DEEVON 310
QUISENBERRY, BILL 80
QURESHI, ATA 181
QUY, LAURENCE 251

R

RABB, HARRIET S. 14
RABBON, PETER D. 50
RABENI, CHARLES 379
RABENI, CHARLES F. 81
RACE, SAMUEL R. 87
RACHLIN, J. W. 151
RADER, JOHN B. 122
RADER, MIKE 244
RADOSEVICH, STEVEN R. 386
RAEL, WILFRED 326
RAFFAELE, HERBERT A. 26
RAFLE, PETER 333
RAGANTESI, DAVE 313
RAGLIN, KENNETH A. 35
RAHMAN, ANIS UR 221
RAINEY, C. TOM 352
RAINEY, JOHN S. 273, 275
RAINFORD, SYLVIA 31
RAINS, GLORIA 251
RAINS, MICHAEL T. 33
RAINWATER, BILL 159
RAISBECK, LIZ 312
RAIT, KEN 298
RAKESTRAW, DARIEL 191
RAKOW, SALLY 48
RAKOW, STEVE 271
RALEY, CATHERINE 358
RALSTON, ART 237
RALSTON, PATRICK R. 64
RALSTON, PETER 239
RAMAKKA, JAMES 355
RAMIN, ROBERT 157
RAMIREZ, CONSTANCE 23
RAMIREZ, SAUL 15
RAMOS, KATHERINE 149
RAMSAY, RICHARD E. 238
RAMSAY, SCOTT 72
RAMSEY, CHARLES 107
RAMSEY, O. J. 222
RAMUS, JOSEPH S. 383
RANDALL, ROBERT 338
RANDLES, RICHARD K. 91
RANDOLPH, ANITA 81
RANDOLPH, LANNY 283
RANDOLPH, THERON G. 222
RANDS, TIM 197
RANK, CINDY 346
RANKEL, GARY L. 24
RANKIN, BOBBY J. 382
RANNEY, SALLY A. 156
RANNEY, VICTORIA POST 63
RANSEL, KATHERINE 154
RANSOM, MICHEL D. 374
RAO, P. S. 56
RAO, S. T. 91
RAPIER, KENNY 68
RAPPA, PETER J. 59
RAPPAPORT, BRET 349
RASCHKE, BOB 263
RASH, J. E. 248
RASKER, RAY 323
RASMUSSEN, DEAN 282
RASMUSSEN, G. ALLEN 114
RASMUSSEN, JAMES L. 13
RASMUSSEN, JERRY L. 258
RASMUSSEN, MATT 209
RASOR, LORI 298, 344
RASOR, LORI D. 224, 298, 344
RATCLIFF, D. C. 111
RATCLIFFE, JERE B. 168
RATHBUN, DENNIS K. 35
RATLIFF, FRED 313
RATNASWAMY, MARY 355
RAUPP, M. J. 377
RAUSCHER, KEN 76
RAUSSER, GORDON C. 47
RAWLINS, CHIP 364
RAWLINS, WAYNE 100
RAWLS, MEG 290
RAWSON, MAC, JR. 58
RAY, ARTHUR W. 72
RAY, HURLON 45
RAY, SAMMY 151
RAYBURN, RICHARD G. 49
RAYMOND, JANIS 130
RAYSBROOK, CHARLES F. 48
REA, PHILLIP S. 384
READ, CHARLOTTE J. 316
READE, JUDITH G. 385
REAGLE, GEORGE L. 28
REAGOR, KAREN P. 245
REAKA, MARJORIE L. 156
REAMES, CLARK 20
REAMES, SPENCER E. 294
REAVIS, RICHARD E. 84
REBACH, STEVE 377
REBACK, RICHARD 24
RECHT, PHILIP R. 28
RECKHOW, KENNETH H. 383
RECORD, RICHARD 71
REDDEN, DAVID N. 317
REDDING, AL 135
REDDING, BILL 258, 319
REDDING, BILL, S 258
REDDING, JOHN H. 214
REDDING, RUSSELL C. 104
REDIG, PATRICK T. 309
REDMAN, DANIELL E. 277
REDMAN, DONNELL E. 277
REDMOND, CHARLES 366
REDMOND, CHARLES L. 366
REDMOND, DENNIS 225
REEB, MARY LOU 125
REED, A. SCOTT 102
REED, ANDREA 212
REED, BILL 286, 346
REED, CAROL 286
REED, CHARLES J. 52
REED, DANNY 68
REED, DONALD P. 70
REED, FRANK 164
REED, HOLLY 332
REED, MARCY 329
REED, MARY 286
REED, NATHANIEL P. 133
REED, TIM 306
REED, WENDY G. 333
REED-SMITH, JAN 139
REES, SANDY 120
REESE, ART 125
REESE, HUDSON 342
REESE, KERRY PAUL 354
REESE, PEG 31
REES-WEBBE, ROBIN 220
REEVES, BILL 110, 258
REEVES, JO LYN 273
REEVES, JOHN B. 108
REEVES, REGGIE 110
REEVES, WILLIAM B. 205
REFFALT, BILL 349
REGAN, DIANE 40
REGAN, RON 114, 292
REGELIN, WAYNE 40
REGENSTEIN, LEWIS G. 227
REGISTER, RICHARD 210
REGISTER, WAYNE 330
REGN, ANN 310
REGO, PAUL 356
REHARD, JAMES 82
REHEIS, HAROLD 57
REICE, SETH R. 384
REICHARDT, WILLIAM A. 221
REICHELT, CYNTHIA 209
REICHER, DAN W. 14
REID, C.P. PATRICK 367
REID, KENNETH D. 156
REID, SHARON 159
REID, TIMOTHY W. 240
REIFEL, GEORGE C. 194, 240
REIFSNIDER, BETSY 212
REIFSNYDER, DANIEL A. 16
REIFSTECK, SHAWN 189
REILLY, PATRICK 28
REILLY, ROBIN 129
REILLY, WILLIAM K. 142
REINERS, GARY B. 280
REINERTSON, KENNETH 16
REINHARDT, BRUCE 17
REISER, HILDY 18
REISING-JONES, CATHERINE 160
REITAN, JULIA 319
REITER, AL 296
REITER, LAWERNCE W., Ph.D. 11
REITSMA, JAN 75
REMMICK, RONALD 145
REMPEL, RON 48
REMUS, JR., KURT W. 322
REMUS, LAUREL 91
RENARD, YVES 173
RENEAU, JACK 167
RENNER, ROBERT C. 156
RENNER, TRACY 364
RENNICK, KYME 97
RENO, JANET 15
RENSCH, W. AUGUSTUS 381
RENWICK, RITA 224
RESHETNIAK, PETER 309
RESS, PAULA 299
RESSMEYER, JOHN 99
REUTER, DON 94
REUTTER, JEFFREY M. 97
REWERTS, MILAN A. 51
REYES, CARMEN 142, 242
REYES, LUIS A. 35
REYNOLDS, BETSY 293
REYNOLDS, CHRIS 46
REYNOLDS, DEBBIE 309
REYNOLDS, JAMES B. 40, 366
REYNOLDS, JAMES R. 29
REYNOLDS, JIM 62
REYNOLDS, JOHN 25
REYNOLDS, JOHN E., III 321
REYNOLDS, MARY 236
RHOADES, DIANA 137
RHOADES, RUSSELL F. 42
RHOADS, JOHN 73
RHODE, ARLYNE 267
RHODEA, TOM 249
RHODES, ED 342
RHODES, HOWARD 54
RHODES, LISA 76
RHORER, SKIP 70
RHOTON, JOHN 300
RHYNER, CHARLES 392
RICART, JUAN L. 307
RICCI, HUGH H. 84
RICE, ARTHUR R. 384
RICE, CHUCK 291
RICE, DAVID K. 85, 160
RICE, JAMES A. 94
RICE, JIM 254
RICE, JOE DAVID 43
RICE, MARY 325
RICE, MARY E. 320
RICE, RONALD L. 34
RICE, RUDY 263
RICH, JAMES 68, 194
RICH, TOM 99
RICHARDS, DOUGLAS P. 379
RICHARDS, HARRY E. 104
RICHARDS, KARYN B. 90
RICHARDS, KEVIN R. 81
RICHARDS, LYNDA 259
RICHARDS, LYRA 283
RICHARDS, NORM 131
RICHARDS, STACEY A. 102
RICHARDSON, BILL 13
RICHARDSON, CHERYL 136
RICHARDSON, DAVID 127
RICHARDSON, DON 159
RICHARDSON, JAMES 194
RICHARDSON, JOAN 284
RICHARDSON, JUDITH 185
RICHARDSON, KERMIT W. 269
RICHARDSON, LAURA 92
RICHARDSON, LINDA R. 222
RICHARDSON, MICHAEL 203
RICHARDSON, NANCY 163
RICHARDSON, ROBERT A. 318
RICHARDSON, RUSTY 350
RICHARDSON, STEVEN 24
RICHARDSON, TIM 246
RICHBOURG, JOE 107
RICHMOND, ALAN 18
RICHMOND, MILO E. 92, 382
RICHTER, DANIEL D. 383
RICKARDS, WILLIAM L. 119
RICKER, KAREN T. 97
RICKMAN, DEE 83
RIDER, DANIEL R. 252
RIDER, PAUL E., SR. 236
RIDGLEY, HEIDI 191
RIDINGTON, JILLIAN 213
RIDLEY, TAZ 210, 314
RIEFF, SUSAN 274
RIEHM, JOHN P. 372
RIEKE, BETSY 370
RIEPE, DONALD 152
RIGBY, WILLIAM 340
RIGDON, SAM T. 214
RIGSBY, ALEX 297
RIGTRUP, HOWARD 113
RIKE, KAY 108
RILEY, BARB 130
RILEY, DAN 262
RILEY, DANNY 55
RILEY, DAVID T. 196
RILEY, JOHN 206
RILEY, LARRY 42
RILEY, LEWIS R. 73
RILEY, MICHAEL E. 238
RILEY, RICHARD W. 13
RILEY, TERRY Z. 353
RILEY, TOM L., JR. 44
RILEY, VINCE 307
RILEY, WILSON 305
RILLERO, ANNE 301
RIMMER, CHRISTOPHER 341
RIMMER, DAVID 181
RINEER, ROBERT 253
RING, BETTINA K. 116
RING, GINETTE 267
RING, ROBERT L. 244
RINGELSPAUGH, KEITH 328
RINGGENBERG, KEITH 170
RINGLEMAN, JIM 196
RINGLER, NEIL H. 383
RINGLING, ROCK 260
RINGO, JEROME C. 273
RIORDAN, CRAIG 376
RIORDAN, J. 37
RIPLEY, ARLENE 288
RIPLEY, BARBARA G. 114
RIPLEY, BOB 110
RIPLEY, J. DOUGLAS 16
RIPLEY, J. JOY 172
RIS, HOWARD, JR. 339
RISDON, KARLA 285
RISK, PAUL H. 389
RISKA, MIKE 192
RISNES, PHILLIP 324
RISSLER, RICHARD L. 30
RISTIC, HENRY 34
RISTOW, MARK 326
RITCHIE, LEAH COX 77
RITTENOUR, CHARLES W., JR. 40, 135
RITTER, MARK 165
RIVALIN, ROLAND E. 194
RIVERA, DENNIS 308
RIVERO, ELIEZER COLON 105
RIVERS, CAITLIN 261
RIZZIO, TONY 20
ROACH, GREG 130
ROACH, RON 129
ROBAK, E. W. 381
ROBAK, SYD 128
ROBBINS, BONNIE 232
ROBBINS, CHANDLER S. 253
ROBBINS, CHRIS 332
ROBBINS, J. R. 271
ROBBINS, JOE 140
ROBBINS, MICHELLE 150
ROBEL, ROBERT J. 374
ROBERG, REX R. 44
ROBERSON, DONNIS 80
ROBERTS, ADAM 158
ROBERTS, CHRISTOPHER M. 7
ROBERTS, JACKIE PRINCE 202
ROBERTS, JOANNE 345
ROBERTS, KENNETH J. 71
ROBERTS, KITTY 25
ROBERTS, M. H. 391
ROBERTS, RALPH 172
ROBERTS, ROBY 377
ROBERTS, WILLIAM 202
ROBERTSON, ANNA 236

Staff Name Index

ROBERTSON, BILL 249
ROBERTSON, CHARLOTTE 222
ROBERTSON, DAVID K. 381
ROBERTSON, GEORGE, JR. 135
ROBERTSON, GORDON C. 122
ROBERTSON, HOPE E. 286
ROBERTSON, JAMES 125
ROBERTSON, JENNIFER B. 270
ROBERTSON, JIM 112, 236
ROBERTSON, JOHN M. 76
ROBERTSON, KEN 338
ROBERTSON, PETER D. 10
ROBERTSON, SUE 39
ROBERTUS, JOHN 46
ROBICHAUD, JACQUE 36
ROBINETTE, H. RANDALL 379
ROBINETTE, RANDALL 81
ROBINS, TODD 307
ROBINSON, BILL 44
ROBINSON, BINA 230
ROBINSON, HOWARD 160
ROBINSON, JILL 230
ROBINSON, JOHN 351
ROBINSON, JOHN M. 250
ROBINSON, KAYNE B. 271
ROBINSON, MARY 333
ROBINSON, MICHAEL 159, 320
ROBINSON, MURIEL 164
ROBINSON, NICHOLAS 234
ROBINSON, SCOTT 273
ROBINSON, SHARON 13
ROBINSON, STEVE 295
ROBINSON, THOMAS E. 23
ROBINSON, TOM 121, 216
ROBISON, LEWELLYN 34
ROBISON, ROD 223
ROBSON, DIANA BIZECKI 282
ROBY, DANIEL D. 100
ROBY, ROBERT 324
ROBY, TIM 76
ROCK, LESLIE 358
ROCKEFELLER, DAVID, JR. 136
ROCKEFELLER, LAURANCE 142
ROCKEFELLER, LAURANCE S. 142, 242
ROCKEFELLER, WINTHROP P. 166
ROCKEY, SARAH 32
ROCKWELL, NANCY 101
ROCQUE, ARTHUR J., JR 52
RODD, THOMAS 240
RODEFELD, NELS 98
RODEN, ROBERT W. 124
RODENBURG, FRANCES 172
RODENHAUSER, KARL 91
RODGERS, A. J. 294
RODGERS, JOHN 388
RODGERS, KIRK 209
RODGERS, THOMAS F. 166
RODIN, A. 293
RODRIGUES, DAVID A. 164
RODRIGUEZ, CARLOS MARIO 37
RODRIGUEZ, DAN 19
RODRIGUEZ, KATJA 294
RODRIGUEZ, MIGDALIA 307
RODRIGUEZ, PEDRO 106
ROEKEL, DENNIS VAN 267
ROEMER, PETER 156
ROER, KATHLEEN 77
ROGERS, BILL 183
ROGERS, DON 57
ROGERS, FRANK 80
ROGERS, JOHN G., JR. 26
ROGERS, KATRINA 216
ROGERS, KENNETH C. 35
ROGERS, MARIHELEN 267
ROGERS, MIKE, SR. 314
ROGERS, MITCHELL J. 195
ROGERS, NANCY 186
ROGERS, SAM 90
ROGERS, WILL 338
ROGLER, DONNA K. 174
ROHALL, RONALD 301
ROHRBACK, DONALD H. 355
ROHY, DAVID A. 48
ROJAS, ESTHER 307
ROJAS, SONIA 37
ROLFE, GARY L. 373
ROLFE, KEVIN 137
ROLFSMEYER, CHUCK 359
ROM, BECKY 211
ROMANIUK, NESTOR 173
ROMANO, GREGORY 87
ROMANO, JEFFREY 319
ROMANO, KATHIE 352
ROMINGER, RICHARD 29
ROMMEL, FRED 104
ROMO, JOHN 304
RONK, THOMAS P. 81
RONNING, KATHLEEN 221
ROONEY, PETER M. 45
ROSE, BEN 218
ROSE, CHRIS 338
ROSE, GERALD 78
ROSE, MARCI L. 310
ROSE, PAT 55
ROSEN, MARTIN J. 337
ROSEN, RUDY 314
ROSENBERG, ANDREW A. 12
ROSENKRANCE, LESTER 24
ROSENOW, JOHN 262
ROSENTHAL, LYNN 391
ROSEWATER, ANN 14
ROSS, CARL 315
ROSS, DAVID 141
ROSS, DENWOOD F. 35
ROSS, GALE 72
ROSS, GEORGE 130
ROSS, GERALD E. 81
ROSS, LAWRENCE 203
ROSS, STEPHEN T. 379
ROSSE, VERNE L. 84
ROSSI, C. E. 35
ROSSI, JIM 182
ROSSITER, WILLIAM W. 178
ROSS-SHANNON, BRUCE 225
ROSS-SHANNON, BRYCE 277
ROSTER, TOM 66
ROSTVET, ROGER 95
ROSWAL, GLENN 138
ROTENBERRY, JOHN T. 189
ROTH, FRANK A., II 44
ROTH, ROBERT 97
ROTH, ROLAND R. 181
ROTHBART, HERBERT L. 32
ROTHBART, PAUL 186
ROTHE, ANN L. 338
ROTHMAN, HAL 209
ROTHMAN, HAL K. 155
ROTMAN, ART 174
ROUNDS, JOHN 298
ROUNDTREE, LINWOOD 34
ROUSSEL, JOHN 70
ROUSSOPOULOS, PETER J. 33
ROUTTEN, BARBARA 201
ROVNER, MARK J. 363
ROWAN, FRAN 138
ROWAN, JOSEPH F. 195
ROWDABAUGH, KIRK 42
ROWLAND, NATHAN 18
ROWLEY, CRAIG 261
ROWNTREE, LESTER 369
ROY, KRISHNA K. 176
ROYAL, BRIAN 194
ROYCE, BOB 62
ROYCE, CRAIG 101
RUATOR, RAUL A. 210
RUBENSTEIN, PAUL D. 21
RUBER, ERNEST 373
RUBIN, BARRY M. 374
RUBIN, ROBERT E. 33
RUBINGH, JIM 50
RUBINOFF, IRA 320
RUBINOFF, ROBERTA 320
RUCH, JEFF 307
RUCH, JEFFREY 307
RUCKEL, TONY 318
RUDDELL, JOHN 55
RUDDELL, JOHN M. 54
RUDE, MARY 56
RUDNYCKYI, DAR 179
RUDY, CAROL 227
RUE, FRANK 40
RUECKERT, RON 124
RUEFF, MATHEW 64
RUFF, MARGARET 296
RUFF, ROBERT L. 125
RUGG, ROBIN 332
RUGG, TOM 269
RUGGLES, BOB 132
RUGO, FRED 335
RUHL, B. SUZI 248
RUMERY, ALICE 282
RUMKE, MICHAEL 214
RUMP, JACK 50
RUNDLETT, MIKE 119
RUNDQUIST, ERIC 243
RUNGE, RUSSELL 259
RUNNING, STEVEN 380
RUNNING-GRASS 332
RUSCH, DONALD H. 123
RUSHING, BETTIE 24
RUSSELL, CLAYTON 392
RUSSELL, DIANNE 227
RUSSELL, KEITH C. 173
RUSSELL, LIANE B. 330
RUSSELL, ROBERT C. 240
RUST, MARIE 25
RUTH, HARRY 298
RUTH, TERRY 20
RUTHERFORD, JAY 114
RUTLEDGE, WALLACE 101
RUTTER, CAROLYN 105
RUTTLE, JACK 268
RUYLE, GEORGE 43, 367
RYAN, BARBARA 26
RYAN, HUGH 264
RYAN, J. HUGH 107
RYAN, JOHN 293
RYAN, PAT 257
RYAN, W. S. 10
RYDELL, MICHELE 151
RYDER, LONNIE 54
RYDGREN, ANN 191
RYEL, KEN 98
RYEL, RICHARD 199

S

SAAVEDRA, PAUL 90
SABEAN, BARRY C. 130
SABELLA, SUSAN 219
SABININA, JOHN 335
SABLAN, JOSEPH G. 58
SACKETT, BRUCE 83
SACKS, KATHLEEN 318
SADLER, LYNN 261
SADZEWICZ, JOHN 97
SAER, ANNE 247
SAFINA, CARL 265
SAGE, SAMUEL H. 163
SAGER, BILL 187
SAGER, PAUL 392
SAGOFF, MARK 233
SAGSVEEN, MURRAY 95
SAILOR, BYRON 255
SAINSBURY, JACK 100
SAKOFS, MITCHELL 349
SAKUMA, TOMOKO 303
SALARI, AHMAD 113
SALAS, JESUS T. 59
SALAZAR, RODOLFO 233
SALBER, LEE 196
SALDANA, LYDIA 112
SALEH, FARIDA 390
SALES, MARIE 79
SALISBURY, JENNIFER 88, 89
SALKIN, CHARLES 53
SALKIN, CHARLES A. 264
SALLEE, DAN 340
SALLEY, MARK 20
SALMON, TERRELL P. 47
SALVAGGIO, JAMES M. 102
SALWASSER, HAL 33
SAMA, JEFFREY 91
SAMMET, LISA 391
SAMMON, ROBERT 263
SAMPLE, V. ALARIC 303
SAMPLES, PETER O. 327
SAMPLINER, TOM 276
SAMPSON, CAROL L. 14
SAMPSON, WALTER 40
SAMS, M. PAUL 107
SAMUEL, DAVE 392
SAMUEL, JOSEPH 342
SAMUELS, WILLIAM 208
SANBORN, CLINT 315
SANBORN, PETER 344
SANCHEZ, FRANK 286
SANCHEZ-ARINO, TONY 232
SAND, MAURE 96
SANDALOW, DAVID 10
SANDBERG, JULIE 120
SANDER, KEVIN 262
SANDERS, DAVID G. 28
SANDERS, DWIGHT E. 50
SANDERS, GREGORY L. 116
SANDERS, REED 68, 353
SANDERS, ROD 79
SANDERS, WILLIAM H., III 11
SANDERSON, LESLIE 263
SANDERSON, REED 353
SANDERSON, RICHARD E. 11
SANDHEINRICH, MARK B. 393
SANDIFER, PAUL A. 7, 108
SANDLER, CRAIG D. 271
SANDMEIER, TERRY 313
SANDO, ROD 78
SANDO, RODNEY W. 78
SANDOVAL, ANDREW 89
SANDS, DAVID 283
SANDT, JOSH 74
SANFORD, CAROLYN 165
SANFORD, WHITTY 186
SANGER, DAVE 347
SANGUINETTI, GINA 384
SANSOM, ANDREW 112
SANT, ROGER W. 363
SANT, VICKI 304
SANTACROCE, LISA 185
SANTA-CRUZ, LISA 332
SANTANGINI, JOHN 55
SANTASANIA, CARMEN 301
SANTORO, ANTHONY, 388
SARABI, BRIGETTE 312
SARGENT, ROGER 254
SARGENT, TOM 248
SARJEANT, BILL 282
SARKO, ANATOLE 383
SARRO, JAMES V. 50
SARTAR, MARGARET 18
SARTY, JIM 130
SASAKI, TOM 134
SASLAW, LARRY 357
SATHER, DAWN 253
SATOU, KARLA 322
SATRE, SONNY 66
SATTERLEE, FRANCIS 228
SAUER, KLARA 317
SAUER, KLARA B. 317
SAUER, RICHARD 262
SAUNDERS, DAVID K. 243
SAUNDERS, JOHN L. 81
SAUNDERS, LINDA 247
SAUNDERS, LLOYD 21
SAUNDERS, NORM 253
SAUNDERS, PATTI 136, 137
SAUNDERS, STUART 135
SAUNDERS, STUART T., JR. 134
SAUNDRY, PETER D. 184
SAVERY, JOE 330
SAVILLE, DAVE 346
SAVIOE, BRANDT 70
SAVITT, CHARLES 176
SAVITZ, JACQUELINE 181
SAVITZKY, ALAN H. 155
SAWHILL, JOHN 219
SAWHILL, JOHN C. 135, 279
SAYRE, DAN 176
SAYRE, JOHN A. 249
SAZAKI, MARE 193
SCALET, CHARLES G. 265, 389
SCALET, GINGER 324
SCALF, ANNA MARIE 238
SCALICE, JOHN A. 36
SCALPONE, JAN 180
SCAMEHORN, EILEEN 254
SCANLON, EDWARD H. 183
SCANLON, JOHN 36
SCARBRO, MAXINE S. 213
SCARDAC, TONY 214
SCARTH, JONATHAN 192
SCELZA, BROOKE 77
SCHACKER, B. 37
SCHADEWALD, PAUL 95
SCHAEFER, JOYCE 213
SCHAEFER, LARRY 196
SCHAEFER, MICHAEL 196
SCHAEFER, RICK 361
SCHAFER, JACQUELINE E. 48
SCHAFFER, CORLISS 300
SCHAFFER, ERIC V. 11
SCHAFFER, REBECCA F. 14
SCHALCH, NANCY 292
SCHALLER, GEORGE 351
SCHALLERT, RUSSELL C. 322
SCHASSER, JAMES 268
SCHASSLER, STEVE 91
SCHATZ, DANIEL 107
SCHAUER, RON 357
SCHECHTER, CLAUDIA 269
SCHECKEDANZ, JERRY G. 90
SCHEIBELHUT, BECKY 273
SCHEIBLE, MICHAEL 46
SCHELBLE, RAY 340
SCHELVAN, LANCE 313
SCHEMAN, CAROL 14
SCHENCK, ERIC W. 355
SCHENCK, JOHN 20
SCHENDEL, BEVERLY 276
SCHENK, WILLIAM 25
SCHERER, MATT 66
SCHERKENBACH, TIMOTHY K. 78
SCHERR, JACOB 301
SCHICK, ART 344
SCHICKEDANZ, JERRY G. 90
SCHIFF, DAVID T. 351
SCHIFFER, LOIS J. 15
SCHIFFERLE, PATRICIA 248
SCHILLER, FRED 208
SCHIMMING, BRIAN A. 123
SCHINKTEN, JEFFREY B. 348
SCHISLER, JOHN 132
SCHISLER, LEE C., JR. 164
SCHLENDER, JAMES H. 7
SCHLENK, CORNELIA G. 92
SCHLESINGER, PATRICIA 284
SCHLEUNING, ALEXANDER J., II 213
SCHLICKEISEN, RODGER 191
SCHLOSS, ALICE 222
SCHLOSS, JEFFREY 86
SCHMECKPEPER, ERIC J. 245
SCHMIDLIN, KENT 125
SCHMIDLIN, THOMAS W. 294
SCHMIDT, BOB 162
SCHMIDT, EDITH 58
SCHMIDT, ELLEN 225
SCHMIDT, GENE 225
SCHMIDT, JOHN L. 195
SCHMIDT, JOHN V. 295
SCHMIDT, LOU 333
SCHMIDT, PAUL 26
SCHMIDT, ROBERT 114
SCHMIDT, ROBERT E. 289
SCHMIDT, W. JOHN 50
SCHMIDT, WALTER 55
SCHMIDTKE, DANITA 128
SCHMIT, LARA 323
SCHMIT, MICHAEL W. 103
SCHMITT, EDWARD C. 362

STAFF NAME INDEX 517

SCHMITT, JOHN 63
SCHMITTEN, ROLLAND A. 12
SCHNEEMAN, BARBARA O. 47
SCHNEIDER, COLLEEN 237
SCHNEIDER, JOHN 256
SCHNEIDER, KEITH 255
SCHNEIDER, NEAL W. 124
SCHNEIDER, PAT 180, 279
SCHNEIDER, REBECCA L. 93
SCHNELL, GARY D. 98
SCHNELL, ROBERT 245
SCHOCH, DEBORAH 341
SCHOCK, ANDREW 275
SCHOEN, JOHN W. 136
SCHOENE, KEITH 364
SCHOENFELDER, JACK 179
SCHOFIELD, DAVE 159
SCHOLES, PETER 345
SCHOLL, STEVE 47
SCHOLLENBERG, SHIRLEY 136
SCHOLLEY, SUSAN 329
SCHONING, JIM 46
SCHOOLMASTER, ANDY 390
SCHOONMAKER, PETER R. 348
SCHRAM, GUS, III 181
SCHRAMM, HAROLD L., JR. 80
SCHRAUFNAGEL, JOHN 246
SCHRECK, CARL B. 100, 386
SCHREGARDUS, DONALD 97
SCHREUDER, JACK 128
SCHROEDER, DAVID B. 371
SCHROEDER, LARRY 374
SCHROEDER, LELAND 383
SCHROEDER, RICHARD T. 254
SCHROM, DAVID 250
SCHUBERT, PAUL 36
SCHUECK, THOMAS 44
SCHUELER, THOMAS R. 177
SCHUERCH, KATE 187
SCHUERG, ALVIN 111
SCHUL, LANCE 313
SCHULER, RICHARD 208
SCHULLER, REID 277
SCHULTE, GERRY G. 144
SCHULTZ, BOB 141
SCHULTZ, CAROLINE 166, 173
SCHULTZ, CHARLES 334
SCHULTZ, CLIFFORD J. 196
SCHULTZ, HAROLD 364
SCHULTZ, JANET T. 28
SCHULTZ, WILLIAM D. 104
SCHULTZE, GORDON 285
SCHUMACHER, AUGUST 28
SCHUMACHER, MARTHA 191
SCHUMACHER, MILTON 311
SCHUTTE, TED 210
SCHUURMANS, ROBERT 109
SCHVARTZ, GARY 240
SCHWAAB, ERIC C. 74
SCHWALBE, CHARLES 29
SCHWAMBERGER, FRANK 15
SCHWARTZ, CHERRY 240
SCHWARTZ, JIM 126
SCHWARTZ, JOHN D. 77
SCHWARTZ, SUZANNE 112
SCHWARTZMAN, ANDREW 315
SCHWARZ, FREDERICK A., JR. 278
SCHWEICH, PAULA J. 135
SCHWEIGER, LARRY J. 347
SCHWEITZER, SARAH 354
SCHWERD, WILLIAM M. 156
SCHWERGART, JOE 56
SCHWETZ, BERNARD A. 14
SCHWINDT, FRANK 95
SCHWOLERT, PHIL 51
SCIASCA, JAMES 356
SCOGGIN JR., L. J. 159
SCOLES, STEVE 97
SCORBY, R. D. 100
SCOTT, RUSSELL, JR. 183
SCOTT, BOB 127
SCOTT, BRENT 319
SCOTT, DON 131
SCOTT, DOUGLAS 212
SCOTT, J. MICHAEL 61, 189, 372
SCOTT, JERRY 261
SCOTT, LORNE 132
SCOTT, MIKE 392
SCOTT, ROBERT R. 324
SCOTT, STEVE 107
SCOTT, SUE 163
SCROGGINS, RONALD M. 35
SCUDDAY, JAMES F. 179
SCULLY, R. TUCKER 16
SEABORN, ERIC 20
SEACREST, SUSAN 219
SEAGER, JOHN 365
SEALE, ROBERT L. 35
SEALES, FRANK, JR. 28
SEAMAN, WILLIAM 55
SEARLE, COLGATE 388
SEASE, DEBBIE 319
SEASE, STEPHEN B. 114
SEBERT, D. 273
SEBERT, DAN A. 99
SEBESTA, DAWN 221
SEBREN, RAY 44
SECKLER, THOMAS 87
SEDAM, STEPHEN 265
SEDGWICK, WALTER C. 329
SEDGWICK-POLING, SUSAN 361
SEDINGER, JAMES S. 366
SEE, MARIANNE 40
SEED, PETER 257
SEEDORF, DON 247
SEEKINS, RODDY 112
SEELEY, ROD R. 372
SEELY, CLARK 101
SEGEBRECHT, LINDA 218
SEGELKE, MIKE 159
SEGER, JAMES L. 300
SEGERSON, LUCY 139
SEIBEL, JOHN 359
SEIBERT, TOM 84
SEIF, JAMES M. 102
SEIKI, KATSUO 216
SEIP, WILLIAM F. 277
SEITZ, JOHN S. 11
SEKERAK, CAROLYN 354
SEKSCIENSKI, STEVE 20
SEKUL, GEORGE 7
SELBIG, WILLIAM 124
SELBY, SUSAN 283
SELF, JAMES M. 105
SELF, PEYTON 193
SELIGMANN, PETER 188
SELL, ROBIN 354
SELLARS, RICHARD W. 214
SELLERS, H. WILLIAM 168
SELLERS, JUDITH 279
SELLERS, STEPHEN 64
SELVA, STEVEN 376
SELVIDGE, MAGGIE 245
SELZ, KATHLEEN 264
SELZER, LAWRENCE A. 188
SEMENCHUK, GLEN 205
SENN, MIKE 42
SEPTON, GREGORY 322
SEPULVEDA, JOSE 177
SEPULVEDA, MARIA 305
SERCHUK, ADAM 377
SEREY, REN 74
SERIE, PATRICIA 344
SEROLD, BRYAN 111
SERYNEK, THOMAS 316
SETSER, JIM 57
SETTERGREN, CARL 380
SETTINA, NITA 73
SEVIER, HELEN 157, 165
SEWARD, ROY E. 117
SEWELL, RUSSELL W. 303
SEXSTON, TERRY 27
SEXTON, BARBARA A. 103
SEXTON, KAREN 185
SEXTON, ROBERT T. 352
SEYDEL, ERICKA 64
SEYMOUR, CARL 287
SHACKLETON, M. 368
SHADE, HARMON 273
SHAFER, THOMAS 20
SHAFFER, EL 113
SHAFFER, MARK 191
SHAFFER, VERNON K. 103
SHALALA, DONNA 14
SHALLENBERGER, ROBERT 26
SHAMROCK, CINDY 49
SHAND, VALERIE J. 328
SHANK, FRED R. 14
SHANKLIN, DONNA R. 44
SHANKS, BERN 183
SHANKS, BERNARD 119
SHANNON, JOHN T. 44
SHANTORA, V. 37
SHAO, LAWRENCE C. 35
SHAPIRO, DOUGLAS Y. 378
SHARBAUGH, RICHARD 104
SHARIK, TERRY 390
SHARP, DAWN 244
SHARP, DEBBIE 99
SHARP, GREGORY 338
SHARP, JANE 187
SHARP, WARREN 305
SHARPE, SEAN 173
SHARPLESS, JANANNE 48
SHATTUCK, WILLIAM 109
SHAVELSON, BOB 189
SHAVER, C. MACK 317
SHAVER, PAT 321
SHAVER, STEPHEN 389
SHAW, BARBARA L. 175
SHAW, FRANK 131
SHAW, GEORGE T. 188
SHAW, JAMES H. 385
SHAW, JONATHAN 139
SHAW, LARRY 78
SHAW, R. LEWIS 108
SHAW, SUSAN D. 252
SHAW, VICTORIA A. 265
SHAW, WILLIAM W. 367
SHAWYER, COLIN 220
SHEA, ALLEN K. 124
SHEA, ERNEST 187
SHEA, ERNEST C. 263
SHEA, PATRICK 24
SHEA, RUTH 218
SHEA, RUTH E. 337
SHEAFFER, C. BRUCE 25
SHEALY, RICHARD 148
SHEAVLEY, SEBA 176
SHEAY, RON 286
SHEDLOCK, MARLO 137
SHEEHAN, FRANCIS 91
SHEERAN, LORI 229
SHEESLEY, DAN 29
SHEFFER, GARY 90, 91
SHEFFIELD, JIM 83
SHELBURNE, JENNIFER 133
SHELBY, CLIFF 299
SHELBY, JAMES 154
SHELBY, JOYCE 204
SHELBY, LUKE 89
SHELDON, DAVID 75
SHELDON, FRED 153
SHELDON, KARIN P. 256
SHELDON, NOEL K. 150
SHELL, JIM 44
SHELLEY, THOMAS 286
SHELLMAN, DWIGHT 169
SHELTON, A. J. 58
SHELTON, DWIGHT 226
SHELTON, JO-ANN 369
SHELTON, KIRSTEN 137
SHELTON, L. ROBERT 28
SHEPARD, BILL 252
SHEPARD, JOHN 323
SHEPARD, MELVIN 290
SHEPHERD, WILLIAM M. 45
SHEPPARD, JACK 74
SHERBURNE, FREDA 306
SHERBY, LOUISE 382
SHERIDAN, NEIL W. 186
SHERMAN, BRUCE A. 52
SHERMAN, C. WENDY 16
SHERMAN, DOUGLAS 46
SHERMAN, ROBERT 215
SHERMAN, THOMAS L. 352
SHERMAN-DIXON, EVITA 311
SHEROAN, DONALD 20
SHERON, BRIAN 35
SHERRATT, DENNIS 132
SHERRILL, G. R. 198
SHERRIN, TISH 133
SHERRINGTON, PETER 137
SHERROD, C. LEE 331
SHERROD, STEVE K. 98, 214
SHESTAKOVA, IRINA 9
SHETLER, STANWYN 343
SHICK, J. MALCOLM 376
SHIEK, ABDUL 20
SHIEL, VINCENT W. 352
SHIELDS, ANNE 23
SHIELDS, DAVID D. 168
SHIELDS, ELIZABETH B. 187
SHIELDS, GERALD F. 366
SHIELDS, JEFF 294
SHIER, CARL 173
SHIMALLA, THOMAS 304
SHIMBERG, STEVEN 274
SHIMBERG, STEVEN J. 274
SHINGLETON, MICHAEL V. 122
SHINN, ROBERT C., JR. 87
SHIPMAN, CLYDE 53
SHIPP, CAROL 87
SHIRE, MIKE 195
SHIREY, RUTH I. 266
SHIRLEY, ELAINE 152
SHIRLEY, KAREN 364
SHIRRELL, JIM 44
SHISHIDO, DOREEN K. 60
SHIVELY, JOHN 41
SHOESMITH, MERLIN 128
SHON, FREDERICK J. 35
SHOR, WILLISTON 289
SHORMA, GARY 125
SHOUN, GARY 50
SHOWALTER, RONALD G. 118
SHRINER, ERNIE 213
SHROPSHIRE, TOMMY 80, 299
SHROUFE, DUANE L. 42
SHUFFIELD, BOB 20
SHULTZ, MICHAEL 178
SHULTZ, PAUL T. 174
SHUPE, TODD F. 70
SHUPP, BRUCE 157, 165
SHUSTER, BUD 3, 5
SHUTT, BARRY 104
SHWAYDER, PATTI 51
SHY, MARILYN 254
SIAR, CHARLES 240
SIBLEY, JOHN A., III 214
SIBLEY, MARGARET 25
SICKING, JOE 283
SIDDIQUI, ISI 29, 47
SIDELL, BRUCE 72, 376
SIEG, TERENCE Y. 325
SIEGRIST, GARY 254
SIEMBIEDA, WILLIAM 368
SIENER, JOSEPH 64
SIEVERS, DONALD 354
SIEWERT, RACHEL 36
SIGG, JAKE 169
SIGMAN, WILLIAM 226
SIGMON, NEAL 267
SIKORSKI, JERRY 292
SILBERSTEIN, JANE 392
SILVA, ERALD 90
SILVA, MARY H. 15
SILVA, RALPH 75
SILVER, DAN 119
SILVER, JONATHAN 150
SILVER, ROBIN 326
SILVERMAN, BARRY 371
SILVERMAN-GENT, LISA 251
SILVESTER, ROBERT 358
SILVEY, PATRICIA 15
SILVY, NOVA 357
SIM, LEE H. 113
SIMCOX, DAVID E. 368
SIMINO, LARRY 115
SIMMONS, DON 120
SIMMONS, JOHN F. 103
SIMMONS, RODERICK HOYT 253
SIMMS, HERMAN L. 28
SIMMS, WILLIAM 169
SIMON, DAVID 270
SIMON, JAMES F. 15
SIMON, LAURA 212
SIMONDS, KITTY M. 347
SIMONS, BOB 207
SIMONSEN, CHARLIE 33
SIMPSON, ANDY 342
SIMPSON, ANN 216
SIMPSON, BILL 233
SIMPSON, HAROLD 51
SIMPSON, JOHN 64
SIMPSON, LARRY B. 7
SIMPSON, MICHAEL 196
SIMPSON, NANCY 63
SIMPSON, ROBERT 150
SIMPSON, TOMMY 350
SIMS, ROBERT B. 269
SIMS, RONALD CHARLES 390
SIMS, SUE 46
SINAY, KEN 261
SINCLAIR, ELLERY W. 165
SINCLAIR, MARK 114
SINGER, HAROLD 46
SINGER, JOHN 376
SINGER, PHILIP C. 384
SINGERMAN, PHILLIP A. 12
SINGH, PREM 59
SINGH, SUSAN 311
SINGHAUS, BARBARA 304
SINGHURST, JASON 331
SIRCH, JAMES 185
SIRY, JOE 207
SISSON, WALT 154
SITKO, BRUCE 313
SITZMAN, LARRY 84
SIVER, PETER A. 370
SIX, LAWRENCE D. 300
SKALICKY, JIRI 37
SKEELE, TOM 306
SKILLMAN, ROBERT A. 146
SKINNER, PETER 92
SKINNER, RICHARD 72
SKOLFIELD, MELISSA 14
SKOUSEN, JEFFREY G. 123
SKOVRON, DAVID 134
SKRYPEK, JACK 78
SKULBERG, PER KRISTIAN 221
SLAFER, ANNA 310
SLATER, CARL A. 168
SLATER, JOE 254
SLATER, RODNEY 27
SLATTERLY, MARK 65, 66
SLAYTON, MIKE 56
SLEDD, CHARLES A. 116
SLEDGE, JAMES L., JR. 79
SLETTELAND, TRYG 300
SLIFER, JAMES C. 63
SLITER, J. THOMAS 6
SLOAN, DAVID 103
SLOAN, MARY MARGARET 150
SLOCUM, ROBERT W., JR. 290
SLOMAN, RICHARD D. 174
SLUSHER, JOHN P. 82
SLUTZ, JIM 64
SMALL, CHRISTINE 191, 216
SMALL, DAVID 52
SMALL, EUGENE L. 197
SMALL, PARKS 216
SMALLIDGE, PETER J. 93
SMALLWOOD, CLAY 207
SMALLWOOD, JOHN A. 358
SMALLWOOD, LOU 45
SMARDON, RICHARD C. 383
SMART, MILES 163
SMART, ROBERT 128
SMILEY, MARC 298
SMITH and FRANCESCA CUTHBERT, DAVID 379
SMITH, ALISON 91
SMITH, ALLEN 349

Staff Name Index

Name	Page
SMITH, ALLYN D.	47
SMITH, ALSON M.	348
SMITH, ANDREW	31
SMITH, ARTHUR	131
SMITH, B. F.	122
SMITH, BILL	130
SMITH, BILLY RAY	68
SMITH, BOB	5
SMITH, BRADLEY F.	392
SMITH, BRUCE	119
SMITH, C. HOLMES	227
SMITH, C. MANNING	266
SMITH, CARL J.	123
SMITH, CHARLES	343
SMITH, CHARLES R.	382
SMITH, CHRISTINA	82
SMITH, CLYDE, JR.	173
SMITH, CONNIE G.	98
SMITH, D. V.	269
SMITH, DAN	6
SMITH, DANIEL B.	108
SMITH, DANIEL C.	150
SMITH, DAVID A.	9
SMITH, DAVID N.	36
SMITH, DIANE	111
SMITH, DONALD	326
SMITH, DONALD H.	52
SMITH, DOUGLAS W.	14
SMITH, DUANE A.	99
SMITH, ED	85
SMITH, ELAINE	343
SMITH, ELEANOR	163
SMITH, ERNEST H.	111
SMITH, FAYE M.	269
SMITH, FRANCIS	337
SMITH, GEORGE A.	327
SMITH, GLORIA	201
SMITH, GREG	97
SMITH, GUY, IV	165
SMITH, H. DUANE	155
SMITH, HENRY H.	391
SMITH, HENRY W.	108
SMITH, J. READ	263
SMITH, JACK	306
SMITH, JACKIE	207
SMITH, JANE A.	81
SMITH, JEFF	164
SMITH, JIM	262
SMITH, JOAN	30
SMITH, JOHN	94, 111
SMITH, JOHN C.	160
SMITH, JOHN EARL	330
SMITH, JOHN W.	81
SMITH, JON	333
SMITH, JOSEPH	15
SMITH, KAREN L.	42
SMITH, KATHY	120
SMITH, KELLY	76
SMITH, KEN	90
SMITH, KENT	48
SMITH, KEVIN	208
SMITH, LAMAR	43, 322
SMITH, LARRY C.	239, 346
SMITH, LAURA J.	164
SMITH, LAVERNE	26
SMITH, LAWRENCE	251
SMITH, LAWRENCE R.	118
SMITH, LAWRENCE S.	275
SMITH, LES	231
SMITH, LORA	216
SMITH, MARK	57, 87
SMITH, MARSHALL	13
SMITH, MARY GRACE	44
SMITH, McCLAIN	255
SMITH, MICHAEL	107
SMITH, MITCHELL	165
SMITH, NANCY	25
SMITH, NEVIN	54, 55
SMITH, P. GREGORY	322
SMITH, PARKER	252
SMITH, PEG	141
SMITH, POLLY	315
SMITH, R. DAVID	93
SMITH, RAY	333
SMITH, RIC	335
SMITH, RICHARD T.	53
SMITH, ROB	319
SMITH, ROBERT	247
SMITH, ROBERT L.	52
SMITH, ROGER	19
SMITH, ROSEALMA	211
SMITH, SARAH	285
SMITH, SCOTT	160, 269
SMITH, STACEY	338
SMITH, STEWART J.	171
SMITH, THOMAS L.	118
SMITH, TOM	18
SMITH, TURNER, JR.	203
SMITH, WAYNE	296
SMITH, WAYNE H.	372
SMITH, WILLIAM H.	124
SMITH, WINSTON D.	155
SMITH, ZANE G., JR.	150
SMITH-WALTERS, CINDI	389
SMOAK, CAMERON	57
SMOLKO, JOHN	110
SMULIAN, ROBERT D.	214
SMULLEN, SCOTT	12
SMYRL, PETER J.	277
SNAPE, WILLIAM J., III	191
SNEATH, WILLIS A.	104
SNEED, PAUL	367
SNIDER, PAT	182
SNIFFEN, JAMES	339
SNODGRASS, JERRY	224
SNODGRASS, SARA JO	111
SNOOK, JOHN	168
SNYDER, ELLEN	86
SNYDER, JAMES P.	102
SNYDER, KATHARINE	15
SNYDER, KEITH A.	103
SNYDER, STEVE	108
SO, FRANK	154, 283
SOARES, FRANK	283
SOBECK, EILEEN	15
SOBEL, DAVID	175
SOBEL, JACK	176
SOBEL, KELLI	76
SOBREVILLA, CLAUDIA	188
SOCHASKY, LEE	10
SOEST, SALLY W.	297
SOHN, ARNIE	66
SOHN, HOWARD	101
SOKOLOW, JERRY	133
SOLANO, PATRICK J.	103
SOLBERG, TRYGVE A.	124
SOLDWEDEL, ROBERT	87
SOLES, ROGER E.	16
SOLIVA, BELMINA I.	58
SOLLMAN, DAVID	272
SOLOMON, GERALD	5
SOLOMON, KENNETH E.	303
SOLOMON, MARK	223
SOLOW, STEVEN	15
SOMACH, STUART	212
SOMERS, ANN BERRY	290
SOMMER, GEORGE	340
SOMMERS, LARRY	268
SOMONOVIC, SLOBODAN	376
SONDERMAN, DEBRA E.	24
SONDERMEYER, GARY	86
SONIAT, LYLE M.	70
SONNTAG, DOUG	314
SOOTS, ROBERT F., JR.	21
SOPER, L.	129
SOPER, NANCY	88
SORENSEN, ANN	142
SORENSEN, SHIRLEY	208
SORENSEN, STEVEN	244
SOSEBEE, RONALD E.	321
SOSNOWSKI, SUSNA	107
SOTO, KEN	36
SOTO, TOM	259
SOUBA, FRED, JR.	333
SOUKUP, MICHAEL	25
SOULE, MICHAEL	350
SOUTHWICK, DAVID L.	78
SOVAS, GREGORY	91
SOWARD, LARRY	111
SOWERS, RAYMON	109
SOWERS, RAYMOND A.	109
SOYKA, SHERI SYKES	288
SPACIE, ANNE	374
SPAGNOLE, JAMES	46
SPAIDE, ROBERT	29
SPALDING, H. CURTIS	316
SPALDING, THOMAS W.	42
SPALINK, DAN	240
SPALT, ALLEN	266
SPALTHOFF, YVONNE	200
SPAN, KRISTIN	364
SPANGENBERG, N. EARL	156
SPANGLER, CONRAD T., III	117
SPANGLER, KATHY	270
SPARKMAN, CHRIS	80
SPARKS, JAMES	273
SPARKS, JULIE HOLMES	65
SPARROWE, ROLLIN D.	353
SPAULDING, JACK	162
SPEAKER, BOB	21
SPEAKES, LeLAND, JR.	210
SPEAR, BOB	154
SPEAR, MICHAEL J.	26
SPEARS, JAMES D.	40
SPECTOR, PAUL	153
SPECTOR, PAUL C.	221
SPEEDY, LOREE	167
SPEICH, STEVEN M.	300
SPEICHER, DARRYL K.	164
SPEIS, THEMIS P.	35
SPELKE, LEE	253
SPELL, LESTER, JR.	80
SPELLER, S. DEBROAH	144
SPENCE, AMY	327
SPENCE, BETTY	157
SPENCE, TALBERT	265
SPENCER, JIM	44
SPENCER, JOHN W.	28
SPENCER, RANDY	355
SPERLING, LARRY	124
SPEYER, ALEXANDER C., III	347
SPICER, BRADLEY E.	70
SPICKLER, DONALD	252
SPIGARELLI, STEVEN A.	379
SPILDE, ERIC	333
SPINO, G. DOMENIC	338
SPINOSA, SALVATOR	114
SPITZER, STEVE	179
SPIVAK, RANDI	151
SPIVY-WEBER, FRANCIS	259
SPOCK, NICHOLS, MD.	103
SPONENBERG, PHILLIP	152
SPONSLER, MIKE	64
SPOON, ED	205
SPOONER, CHARLIE	327
SPOORES, CRAIG	271
SPRAGUE, ANN	358
SPRAGUE, LYNN	33
SPRANGER, MICHAEL S.	121
SPRATLING, BOYD	85
SPRECHER, KAREN MALOY	23
SPRING, LYNELLE	127
SPRINGER, GARY	298
SPRINGER, KIM	242
SPRINGER, MICHAEL L.	35
SPRUANCE, HALSEY	168
SPRYNCZYNATYK, DAVID A.	96
SPURGIN, PAT	119
SPURLOCK, THAD	70
SQUIER, ANNE	119
SRONCE, KEVIN	63
ST. JOHN, JOHN JUDITY	32
ST.GERMAIN, EILEEN	211
STAAKE, JEFF	81
STAATS, LEWIS J.	382
STACEY, B.	37
STACEY, DONNIE L.	195
STACHECKI, CHESTER J.	53
STACKHOUSE, STEVE	67
STADLER, G. MARK	71
STAEBLER, REBECCA N.	322
STAFFORD, SUSAN	370
STAGGS, MICHAEL D.	124
STAHL, ANDY	209
STAHL, JANE	52
STALCUP, STEVE	224
STALEY, DOROTHY	31
STALLING, DICK	375
STALLINGS, E. F.	316
STANGEL, PETER W.	267
STANGELL, JULIE	298
STANIFORD, RICHARD B.	369
STANKEWICH, HENRY G.	104
STANKEY, GEORGE H.	386
STANKIEWICZ, STEVE	66
STANLEY, DERREK	173
STANLEY, ELAINE G.	11
STANLEY, PATRICIA M.	244
STANLEY, ROYA	66
STANSELL, KENNETH B.	26
STANT, JEFF	222
STANT, JEFFREY	222
STANTON, NANCY	393
STANTON, ROBERT G.	24, 25, 269
STAPANIAN, MARTIN	385
STAPAUIDU, MARTIN	96
STAPER, GEORGE	32
STAPLES-BORTNER, SANDRA	357
STAPLETON, JOHN	69
STAPLETON, MICHAEL	387
STAPP, WILLIAM	218
STARK, MARION	212
STARK, ROBERT M.	348
STARKE, BO	136
STARKEY, EDWARD E.	386
STARKWEATHER, JEAN	251
STARLING, D. ALLEN	195
STARNER, ROSS E.	104
STARR, JAMES D.	116
STARR, PATRICK	302
STARRS, PAUL	150
STARTZELL, DAVID N.	158
STAUFFER, JAMES L.	238
STAUFFER, JAY R., JR.	387
STAUNTON, NICKY	343
STAUTON, EDWARD P.	185
STEARNS, FRANK	105
STEEBY, JAMES A.	80
STEELE, JIM	48, 73
STEELE, PHILIP H.	379
STEELE, ROBERT L.	190
STEEN, DALE	115
STEENSTRA, NORM	346
STEFFEN, CHUCK	354
STEFFES, LAUREL J.	124
STEGMIER, ROBERT	240
STEGNER, ED	187
STEHSEL, DONALD L.	170
STEIGER, GRETCHEN	174
STEIMLE, FRANK	152
STEIN, KALMAN	197
STEIN, ROLAND	67
STEINBACH, DONNY W.	111
STEINBACH, TOM	158
STEINDLER, MARTIN J.	35
STEINER, KIM C.	387
STEINER, MARY	299
STEINER, ROLAND C.	8
STEINMAUS, MARY	311
STEINWAND, TERRY	95
STENMETZ, JOHN C.	65
STENSTROM, MICHAEL K.	369
STEPHENS, KYLE	113
STEPHENS, RONALD.	391
STEPHENSON, CHARLES	174
STEPHENSON, JOHN	357
STEPHENSON, JULIE	313
STEPHENSON, ROBERT	30
STERLING, PAMELA P	11
STERMAN, DAVID	91
STERN, LOREN	120
STERNER, ROBERT	379
STESSMAN, NEAL	25
STEVENS, CHRISTINE	158, 320
STEVENS, DAVID	114, 341
STEVENS, GRETCHEN	222
STEVENS, MARY	291
STEVENS, MARY P.	80
STEVENS, ROGER L.	320
STEVENS, RON	212
STEVENS, TED	1, 6
STEVENS, WILLIAM	205
STEVENSON, BARBARA	173
STEVENSON, FRED	205
STEVENSON, JOHN	129
STEVENSON, KATE	25
STEVENSON, MICHAEL M.	325
STEVENSON, NANCY	119
STEVENSON, STEPHANIE	16
STEVENSON, TOD	89
STEWARD, DENNIS W.	81
STEWART, ALLAN	131
STEWART, CONNIE	291
STEWART, DEAN W.	81
STEWART, DOUG	129
STEWART, GARLAND	334
STEWART, GARY	194
STEWART, GEORGE	152
STEWART, HARRY T.	86
STEWART, MAXINE	51
STEWART, RONALD	32
STICKNEY, ROBERT R.	112
STILES, DAVID A.	384
STILES, LYNN	381
STINE, JEFFREY	154
STIRLILNG, ED	225
STIRLING, EDWIN W.	277
STIRLING, IAN	321
STITH, E. MELODEE	24
STITZHAL, DAVID	344
STOCKDALE, JUDITH M.	201
STOCKER, MAX	143
STOCKLEY, CAROL	134
STOCKWELL, SALLY	289
STOECKEL, JOSEPH	367
STOETZEL, MANYA	200
STOFFLE, CARLA J.	367
STOFLET, ROGER	21
STOGNER, JOSEPH D.	391
STOIBER, CARLTON R.	35
STOKES, ALLAN	66
STOKES, BARBARA KAUFFMAN	178
STOKES, DONALD	266
STOKES, HANK	98
STOKES, JOHN C.	88
STOKES, JUDY	86, 160
STOKES, JULIA S.	93
STOKES, ROBERT	87
STOKES, RODNEY	76
STOLGITIS, JOHN	106
STOLTZ, JIM	306
STONE, ALAN T.	376
STONE, ALEXANDER	152
STONE, ANDREW W.	150
STONE, CHARLIE	101
STONE, DENNIS	290
STONE, LEE	277
STONE, M. BRIAN	114
STONE, MIKE	125
STONE, NATHAN M.	44
STONE, SHERIDAN	20
STONECIPHER, HARLAND	98
STOPLMAN, PAUL M.	11
STOREY, RICHARD D.	263
STORM, GERALD L.	104
STORMO, JACK	27
STORRS, NORMAN	85
STORY, RICK	352
STOSSEL, ROBERT, JR.	208
STOTT, WILLIAM	350
STOUDER, DEANA	385
STOUFFER, LARISSA	188
STOUT, GENE	20
STOUT, REBECCA J.	44
STOVER, SUSAN	261
STOWE, JOE C.	345
STRAHL, STUART	265
STRAILEY, ROBERT	103
STRAIT, DONALD S.	186
STRASKRABA, MILAN	37

STAFF NAME INDEX 519

STRATHE, STERLING 359
STRATMAN, OMAR 136
STRATTON, JIM 41
STRAUGHAN, BAIRD 227
STRAUGHAN, THOMAS 101
STRAUSE, HOWARD 260
STRAWN, SHEILA 296
STRAYER, BOB 305
STRAYER, DAVID L. 227
STREEGER, ROBERT G. 196
STREET, KATHRYN 348
STREETER, TRACY D. 67
STREICH, JOHN 98
STREIFEL, DENNIS 127
STREIT, TED 122
STRICKLER, JOHN 243
STRICKLER, RICHARD 102
STRIEGLER, THOMAS L. 26
STRINGER, JEFF 69
STROBEL, MARK 257
STROEDER, CELINA 129
STROHM, ROBERT D. 274
STROM, STEVEN 381
STROMSTAD, RONALD A. 196
STRONG, DAVID 302
STRONG, HANK 247
STRONG, TED 7
STROUBE, ROBERT B. 118
STROUD, CHRIS 348
STROUP, EDDIE 290
STROUP, RAY 314
STRUBLE, DAVE 72
STRUBLE, ROBERT, JR. 256
STRUHS, DAVID 75
STUART, DAVID W. 372
STUART, DON 343
STUART, KRIS 200
STUBBENDIECK, JAMES 380
STUCHLIK-EDWARDS, SUSAN 52
STUCKEY, RONALD L. 294
STUCKY, DONALD J. 373
STUCKY, NORMAN P. 81
STUDER, MARIE 199
STUDLEY, JANNIENNE S. 13
STUDT, JOHN 21
STUDY, WILLIAMS S., JR. 209
STUMBOUGH, GRANT 126
STUMP, JEFF 47
STUMVOLL, RANDALL 93
STUNTZNER, RONALD E. 161
STURDY, JERRY 20
STURGEON, WALTER B., JR. 235
STURGES, DAVID 286
STURGES, WILTON 372
STURGESS, MELINDA 98
STURLA, KIMBERLY 212
STURM, CHARLES 180
STURM, ROBERT 6
STURM, RUSSELL 231
STURMER, JERRY 184
STURTEVANT, BOB 51
STUSHNOFF, BRIAN G. 190
STUTZMAN, ROGER 223
STUWE, BRUCE 345
SU, CHIN 17
SUBLETT, ROSS 351
SUBLETTE, DICK 55
SUCKLING, KIERAN 326
SUECK, PATRICIA 301
SULLIVAN, ALFRED D. 379
SULLIVAN, BETH 247
SULLIVAN, CHARLES 91
SULLIVAN, DANIEL F. 383
SULLIVAN, EDWARD O. 71
SULLIVAN, JAMES J. 46
SULLIVAN, JEREMIAH J. 34
SULLIVAN, JOHN H. 156
SULLIVAN, KEVIN J. 75
SULLIVAN, KRISTI 356
SULLIVAN, LARRY 43
SULLIVAN, MICHAEL 78
SULLIVAN, MICHELE 52
SULLIVAN, MONICA 248
SULLIVAN, RICK 175
SULLIVAN, TIM 356
SULLIVAN, TIMOTHY 258
SULTON, MAUREEN 187
SUMMERS, JIM 346
SUMMERS, LAWRENCE H. 33
SUMMERS, WILLIAM J. 17
SUNDERLAND, LARRY 164
SUNLEY, WILLIAM T. 63
SURKIN, ELLIOT 338
SUTCLIFFE, DAN 356
SUTCLIFFE, SCOTT 189
SUTHERLAND, DAVID M. 188
SUTTLES, RON 98
SUTTON, KEITH 44
SUTTON, ROBERT 106
SUTTON, SCOTT T. 171
SVARRE, K. L. 209
SVEDARSKY, DANIEL, ... 379
SVEDARSKY, W. DANIEL 357
SVEIKAUSKAS, GEDDY 174
SVENSEN, GENE 19
SWACINA, LINDA 29
SWAIN, HILARY 159
SWAN, CHRISTOPHER 377
SWANEY, JIM 294
SWANSON, D. 293
SWANSON, DAVE 356
SWANSON, DAVID 324
SWANSON, GERRY 36
SWANSON, KYLE 238
SWANSON, MERV 132
SWANSON, PAUL F. 103
SWANSON, ROBERT 311
SWANSON, SHERMAN 85
SWARTZ, PAUL O. 10
SWARTZ, STEVEN L. 321
SWATFIGURE, RON 119
SWAYNE, CHERYL 67
SWEDBURG, RANDY 139
SWEENEY, JOHN R. 108, 388
SWEET, MELINDA M. 244
SWEETMAN, SARAH 315
SWENARCHUK, MICHELLE 172
SWENGEL, SCOTT 230
SWENSON, GUY A. 289
SWENSON, LELAND H. 267
SWENSON, PAUL 78
SWENSON, SMOKEY 262
SWIFT, BYRON 362
SWIFT, CAMM C. 145
SWINGLE, WAYNE E. 219
SWITKES, GLEN 232
SWOPE, MARJORY 85
SWOPE, MARJORY M. 284
SYKES, JACK C. 118
SYLVESTER, SUSAN L. 124
SZCZYTKO, STAN 393
SZOJKA-PARNELL, ANIKO 323
SZYMANSKI, EDWARD S. 106

T

TABATA, RAYMOND S. 59
TABER, ANDREW 351
TABOR, LANCE 122
TABORSKY, THERESEA 387
TAE, MICHELE 223
TAFF, STEVEN 79
TAFT, JOHN 229
TAHTINEN, SHARON 66
TAILLON, ANDRE 131
TAIT, LYN 127
TAIT, SANDRA 251
TAITANO, CONCHITA S.N. 59
TAK, JETTY 230
TAKAGI, JINZABURO 180
TAKASUGI, PATRICK A. 62
TAKETA, KELVIN 279
TALBOT, MARTHA H. 308
TALBOTT, SCOTT 125
TALLEY, JOHN H. 53
TALLMAN, DAN 324
TALSMA, ART 313
TALUTO, SUSAN 90
TAMARU, CLYDE 59
TAMAYOSE, JOY 354
TANAKA, ROBERT T. 29
TANNER, GREGG 85
TAPIA, ALVARO ARAGON 177
TAPPERO, DENICE 342
TAR, NANCY 254
TARBURTON
, JOHN F., JR. 52
TARIM, SONER 149
TARKINGTON, KEN 110
TARNOPOL, JOE 20
TARPLEY, RICHARD 53
TARPLIN, RICHARD 14
TATARIAN, TRISH 357
TATE, DAVID 225
TATE, MICHAEL J. 121
TATES, DENNIS 18
TATUM, REID 110
TAUBERT, BRUCE 42
TAVARES, AIMEE 200
TAYER, JEFF 119
TAYLOR, ALFRED H., JR. 142
TAYLOR, ANNE 94
TAYLOR, BARBARA 222
TAYLOR, BARBARA S. 122
TAYLOR, BILL 163
TAYLOR, CHARLES 246, 385
TAYLOR, CONSTANCE E.S. 295
TAYLOR, DAISAN 21
TAYLOR, DAVID 334
TAYLOR, G. DONALD 71
TAYLOR, GARY J. 228
TAYLOR, J. BLAKE 64
TAYLOR, J. MARVIN 161
TAYLOR, JAMES M. 35
TAYLOR, JANICE 192
TAYLOR, JANICE E. 271
TAYLOR, JEFFREY H. 85
TAYLOR, JO 361
TAYLOR, JOHN 57
TAYLOR, JOHN I. 154
TAYLOR, KENT 110
TAYLOR, M. 37
TAYLOR, MICHAEL R. 15
TAYLOR, PRICEY 290
TAYLOR, ROBERT 98
TAYLOR, STEPHEN H. 85, 86
TAYLOR, SYLVIA M. 255
TAYLOR, TAMMY 188
TAYLOR, THOMAS N. 374
TAYLOR, TIM 203
TAYLOR, TOM 217
TAYLOR, WALTER K. 208
TAYLOR, WILLIAM 378
TAYLOR, WILLIAM W. 77, 142
TAYLOR, WILLIE 24
TAYLOR-ROGERS, SARAH J. 74
TAZIK, DAVE 269
TEACHEY, GLENN 273
TEAL, JOHN M. 188
TEBO, MICHAEL 311
TEETERS, NELSON 226
TEFFEAU, K. MARC 134
TEIG, DONALD 20
TEILLON, H. BRENTON 114
TEMPERO, JAMES 338
TEMPLE, RYAN S. 210
TEMPLETON, ALAN R. 380
TEMPLETON, BILLY R. 271
TEMPLETON, DAVID 109
TENEYCK, ELIZABETH Q. 35
TENNENBAUM, CELIA 265
TENNEY, PAMELA 42
TENNISON, HARRY 213
TENORE, KENNETH R. 376
TERBORGH, JOHN W. 383
TERRELL, MICHAEL 10
TERRELL, SANDRA 390
TERRY, LYNN 46
TESKE, RICHARD H. 14
TESKEY, ROBERT O. 372
TESSLER, ALLAN 242
TESTU, JOSEPH K. 222
TESTU, VIRGINIA M. 222
THACHER, THOMAS D., II 134
THACKSTON, EDWARD L. 389
THADANI, ASHOK C. 35
THADEN, GERALD 324
THAIN, DAVID 84
THALER, DENNIS 364
THAYER, PAUL 50
THE RIGHT HONORABLE THE EARL OF SHAFTESBURY, ... 220
THEISS, NANCY 68
THELEN, MICHELLE 258
THEOBALD, NORMAN 237
THERKELSEN, ROBERT L. 48
THEURER, MIKE 67
THEUT, JODY 180
THIBAULT, ROGER E. 385
THIBEAULT, GERALD 46
THIBEDEAU, RICHARD 75
THIEDE, GERALD 76
THIEL, CHRISTINE 84
THIELE, JOHN, JR. 202
THIELE, TIM 194
THIERET, JOHN W. 245
THIERMANN, ALEX B. 29
THIEROIT, RICHARD T. 49
THIESSEN, LARRY 251
THILSTED, JOHN 89
THIVIERGE, BRUCE E. 140
THOELECKE, TIMOTHY N. 254
THOEMKE, KRIS 274
THOMANN, JUDY DIOUS 64
THOMAS, CHRISTING 393
THOMAS, DAN 216
THOMAS, DIANE C. 222
THOMAS, DONNA 169
THOMAS, EDWARD L. 28
THOMAS, EMY 342
THOMAS, EVAN 126, 130
THOMAS, GARY 160
THOMAS, J. TOL 193
THOMAS, JACK WARD 380
THOMAS, JAMES B., JR. 13
THOMAS, JOEL T. 359
THOMAS, JUDY ISACOFF 166
THOMAS, MARSHAL 215
THOMAS, MAXINE S. 273
THOMAS, PAUL 115
THOMAS, SANDY 292
THOMAS, TIMOTHY P. 358
THOMAS, V. G. 386
THOMASHOW, CINDY 175
THOMASHOW, MITCHELL 381
THOMASON, BILL 80
THOMAS-SLAYTER, BARBARA P. 377
THOMLISON, BRYAN 218
THOMPSON, BOB 119
THOMPSON, BRUCE C. 89
THOMPSON, CHRISTINE 324
THOMPSON, CINDY 39
THOMPSON, CLYDE 32
THOMPSON, CRAIG 364
THOMPSON, DIANE 65
THOMPSON, DIANNE E. 14
THOMPSON, DONALD W. 196
THOMPSON, DONNA 139
THOMPSON, DOUG 238
THOMPSON, EDWARD, JR. 142
THOMPSON, F. E. 80
THOMPSON, HUGH L., JR. 35
THOMPSON, JACK 39
THOMPSON, JOHN 224
THOMPSON, JOHN D. 254, 354
THOMPSON, JUDY 171
THOMPSON, LARRY 206, 248
THOMPSON, M. PETE 375
THOMPSON, MARK 69
THOMPSON, MAX C. 244
THOMPSON, NINA 81
THOMPSON, RICHARD E. 112
THOMPSON, STEPHEN E. 338
THOMPSON, STEVE 360
THOMPSON, STEVEN A. 98
THOMPSON, TERRIE H. 367
THOMPSON, THOMAS 292
THOMSEN, JORGEN 188
THOMSON, DAVID 173
THOMSON, ROBB 86
THORN, COLIN E. 373
THORNBURGH, TOM 329
THORNDIKE, DAN 102
THORNE, OAKLEIGH, II 331
THORNTON, BILL 130
THOROUGHGOOD, CAROLYN 53
THORP, LYNN 219
THORPE, DORIS 164
THORPE, KENNETH 306
THORSON, GARY 126
THORVIG, LISA J. 78
THRASHER, BARBARA SUE 343
THRAUS, MIKE 99
THRONSON, HOWARD 121
THRUNE, ELAINE M. 275
THURGOOD, BEN A. 340
THURM, KEVIN 14
THURMAN, STEVE 20
THURMOND, JIMMIE V., III 331
THURSTON, ANCYL 319
THUYER, DAN 207
TIBBETTS, DAVID 157
TICE, DAVID A. 154
TICE, R. DEAN 270
TICHENOR, CAREY 68
TICHY, TED 285
TIDEMAN, LARRY J. 109
TIELL, JENNIFER 97
TIERNAN, JOSEPH A. 138
TIERNEY, TIMOTHY 134
TIERNEY, VANYLA S. 302
TIESLER, TOM 110
TIGHE, DENNIS 261
TIGNER, TIMOTHY C. 116
TILESTON, JULES 41
TILESTON, PEG 136
TILLEY, FOREST 209
TILLSON, JOHN 80
TILT, WHITNEY C. 267
TIMKO, JOHN F. 42
TIMM-DRYDEN, DIANA 222
TIMMEL, BERTHA M. 245
TIMMERMAN, JAMES A. 108
TIMMERMAN, JAMES A., JR. 108
TIMMINS, SHERRY 66
TIMMONS, TOM J. 375
TINDAL, D. LESLIE 107
TINDALL, BARRY 270
TINSLEY, JOHN, III 174
TINSLEY, NIKKI I. 10
TINSLEY, RICHARD 348
TIPPETT, RUSSELL K. 385
TIPTON, W. HORD 24
TISCHLER, BONNI G. 33
TITUS, ELIZABETH C. 328
TITUS, RUSSELL R. 81
TIXIER, SUSAN 182
TJADEN, BOB 74
TOBIN, DAVID 275
TOBIN, RICHARD 259
TODD, CLYDE M. 249
TODD, IAN 9
TODD, LAURA 356
TOEPFER, KAREN 243
TOEPFER, KLAUS 339
TOEWS, DON 132
TOKUE, MICHIAKI 287
TOLBERT, VIRGINIA R. 288
TOLING, ANNA 143
TOLLIVER, JIM 155
TOM, GARRY 225
TOMAN, MICHAEL 311
TOMASSON, DAVID 128
TOMB, SPENCER 273
TOMERA, PATSY 283
TOMPKINS, DAVID L. 107
TON, SHEILA 51
TONER, KEN 129
TONKIN, PATRICIA 362
TONNING, STEPHEN 196
TONSO, STEVE 196
TONSOR, STEPHEN J. 387

Staff Name Index

520 STAFF NAME INDEX

TOOHEY, MARY M. ... 120
TOOHEY, MICHAEL J. ... 273
TOOLE, ROBERT ... 263
TOOR, WILL ... 370
TOOTHAKER, JAMES S. ... 102
TOPHAM, GORDON ... 113
TOPLISEK, TIMOTHY R. ... 21
TOPPING, JANE ... 206
TOPPING, JOHN C., JR. ... 181
TOPPING, STEVEN ... 128
TORELL, DAVE ... 313
TORGERSON, OLIVER A. ... 81
TORIDIS, THEODORE ... 371
TORLEY, CORAL ... 241
TORNOW, THOMAS R. ... 357
TORRANCE, MIKE ... 353
TORRENCE, JIM ... 293
TORRES, ALFONSO ... 30
TORRES, GLORIA M. ... 106
TORSBERG, ROBERT ... 197
TOSSETT, WES ... 291
TOTH, RICHARD E. ... 390
TOTMAN, LORI A. ... 191
TOUGAARD, O. ... 9
TOW, KENNETH R. ... 65
TOWLE, EDWARD L. ... 239
TOWLE, EVERETT ... 319
TOWLE, JUDITH A. ... 239
TOWNS, ELEANOR S. ... 33
TOWNSEND, BOB ... 115
TOWNSEND, C. VINCENT ... 266
TOWNSEND, LAIRD ... 199
TOWNSHEND, R. J. ... 377
TRAINER, DANIEL O. ... 348
TRAISI, CHUCK ... 212
TRAMMONTANO, RONALD ... 92
TRANTHAM, KATHI ... 300
TRASK, R. ... 129
TRAUGOTT, TIMOTHY A. ... 80
TRAVELSTEAD, JACK G. ... 117
TRAVER, TIM ... 341
TRAVERS, WILLIAM D. ... 35
TRAVIS, WILL ... 49
TRAVOUS, KENNETH E. ... 43, 264
TREANOR, ROBERT R. ... 49
TREFRY, STU ... 121
TREGONING, JOSEPH E. ... 123
TREMAYNE, ERNEST ... 277
TREMBLAY, JEAN-PIERRE ... 308
TREMBLAY, MARC J. ... 311
TREMBLAY, MICHELE L. ... 285
TREMBLE, ELAINE ... 31
TRENOWETH, ROY W. ... 84
TRENT, STEVEN J. ... 34
TRENT, TRACEY ... 62
TRESS, WILL ... 253
TRETIAK, WES ... 251
TREVETT, DAVID H. ... 195
TRIESTE, MARION ... 319
TRIFF, MICHAEL ... 338
TRIMBLE, BILLY ... 334
TRIMBLE, BOB ... 225
TRINE, CHERYL ... 153
TRIPP, JAMES T. ... 202
TRIPP, JIM ... 197
TROJE, FRAN ... 261
TROTTER, ROBERT ... 33
TROXELL, PAM ... 392
TROY, DICK ... 49
TROYCHAK, MARY ... 364
TROYER, THOMAS A. ... 256
TROYNA, LAVONNE ... 65
TRUBY, BILL ... 57
TRUDEAU, MAURICE ... 107
TRUE, TODD ... 198
TRUEBLOOD, JACK ... 62
TRUESDELL, CHARMANE ... 253
TRUITT, BRUCE A. ... 221
TRUJILLO, TOM ... 89
TRULAND, MARY W. ... 178
TRULAND, ROBERT W. ... 178
TRUMPER, KATHERINE ... 129
TRYON, CRAIG ... 94
TRYON, LEEANNE ... 344
TSCHANZ, ERIC ... 139
TSOSIE, CARL A. ... 236
TSOSIE, MARY ANN ... 326
TUBBS, NANCY JO ... 236
TUCK, AL ... 80
TUCKER, DANA ... 276
TUCKER, DON ... 362
TUCKER, JUDY ... 182
TUCKER, RICHARD THOMPSON ... 254
TUCKER, ROBERT ... 72
TUCKER, THURMAN ... 258
TUDOR, BOB ... 86
TUFTS, ROBERT ... 49
TUGAEFF, BARBARA ... 157
TUGNED, TOM ... 97
TUKAHIRWA, ELDAD ... 235
TULANG, MIKE ... 219
TULIUS, MARY ... 113
TULL, J F. ... 372
TULL, MICHAEL ... 273
TULLI, C. GEORGE, JR. ... 118
TULLOCH, DAVE ... 132
TULLY, WILLIAM P. ... 383
TULOU, CHRISTOPHE A.G. ... 52
TUMINSKI, RONALD ... 86
TUNBERG, GAIL ... 356
TUNGESVICK, KEVIN ... 226
TUOHY, MARY BETH ... 63
TUPPER, DOUG ... 127
TURLINGTON, JEFF ... 290
TURNBOW, ROBERT ... 20
TURNBULL, WILLIAM G. ... 194
TURNER, AL, JR. ... 384
TURNER, CLINTON V. ... 54
TURNER, DANIEL C. ... 222
TURNER, DEE ... 243
TURNER, JOHN ... 247
TURNER, JOHN F. ... 187
TURNER, RICHARD B. ... 146
TURNER, ROBERT ... 356
TURNER, RONALD ... 50
TURNER, RONALD J. ... 82
TURNER, TIM ... 272
TURNER, TOM ... 198
TURNER, WAYNE ... 330
TURNEY, JOHN ... 285
TURNEY, THOMAS C. ... 90
TURNIPSEED, R. MICHAEL ... 84
TURNPENNY, COLLIN ... 131
TURPIN, DICK ... 83
TURRINI, TONY ... 274
TUSSENBROOK, LEE VAN ... 119
TUTEN, JOHN C., JR. ... 353
TUTHILL, ED ... 93
TUTTLE, CRAWFORD M. ... 45
TUTTLE, MERLIN D. ... 165
TUTTLE, SUZANNE ... 277
TUYN, PETER VAN ... 338
TWEDT, GREG ... 239
TWISS, JOHN R., JR. ... 8, 328
TYDINGS, JOSEPH D. ... 304
TYER, ED ... 231
TYLER, BOB ... 80
TYLER, DARRYL ... 52
TYLER, DUDE ... 260
TYLER, HARRY R., JR. ... 277
TYLER, JACK D. ... 296
TYLER, N. ... 111
TYLER, WILLIAM E. ... 164
TYMCHUK, LEE ... 137
TYRL, RONALD J. ... 295
TYSON, TISH ... 205
TYZBIR, ROBERT ... 115

U

UBOH, CORNELIUS E. ... 104
UCELLI, LORETTA M. ... 10
UCHIDA, DEAN ... 60
UDALL, STEWART ... 262
UECKER, CHERYL ... 348
UERZ, JEFFERY A. ... 116
UGARENKO, LEN ... 228
UHER, JEROME ... 270
UHLENHUTH, KAREN ... 259
UHMANN, TANYS ... 355
ULLENSVANG, LEON P. ... 361
ULMAN, SUZANNE ... 170
ULRICH, ANN R. ... 339
ULRICH, DAVID A. ... 11
ULTEE, CASPER J. ... 185
UMANSKY, DAVID ... 320
UMBANHOWAR, CHARLES ... 257
UMBER, HAROLD ... 96
UMHOFER, PETER ... 10
UNDERHILL, TODD ... 206
UNDERWOOD, CRAIG ... 135
UNDERWOOD, H. BRIAN ... 383
UNDERWOOD, JOANNA D. ... 226
UNDERWOOD, PETER ... 130
UNGER, DANIEL ... 389
UNKENHOLZ, DENNIS ... 109
UNSWORTH, MICHAEL H. ... 386
UPGREN, TED ... 95
UPHAM, MARY LOU ... 311
URBAN, DICK ... 330
URBAN, RIC ... 139
URQUHART, THOMAS A. ... 250
URRUTIA, AL ... 17
URSIC, MARGOT ... 193
USINGER-LESQUEREUX, JANET ... 85
UYEHARA, LETITIA N. ... 60
UZZELL, JAMES ... 125

V

VACEK, HENRY S. ... 91
VAIL, NITA ... 47
VAIL, VIRGINIA ... 55
VALANTINE, DIANE ... 298
VALDEZ, ANA GLENA ... 37
VALDEZ, LORI ... 31
VALDEZ-PIZZINI, MANUEL ... 106
VALENCIC, CYNTHIA ... 248
VALENTINE, AL ... 227
VALENTINE, BRADLEY E. ... 358
VALENTINE, GARY ... 331
VALENTINE, LUISE ... 137
VALENTINETTI, RICHARD A. ... 114
VALLEE, JUDITH ... 316
VALLENDER, LEONARD J. ... 171
VALLES, CYNTHIA PORTALATIN ... 31
VAN ABBEMG, JIM ... 287
VAN AKEN, ALAN G. ... 58
VAN ATTA, SUSAN ... 184
VAN DER ZEL, D. W. ... 325
VAN DYKE, JOHN F. ... 255
VAN GILDER, GAIL L. ... 192
VAN HUSEN, CARL ... 319
VAN LOCKWOOD, PETER ... 180
VAN MATRE, STEVE ... 227
VAN PUTTEN, MARK ... 273, 275
VAN ROEKEL, JOEL ... 237
VAN ROSSUM, MAYA ... 152
VANALLER, ROBERT T. ... 79
VanBLARICOM, GLENN R. ... 120
VANBUSKIRK,, MAX A., JR. ... 104
VANCE, LAWRENCE ... 97
VANCE, MARIAN ... 317
VANCE, TAMARA ... 118
VANDEL, GEORGE ... 66, 109, 268
VANDERMARK, PETER ... 318
VANDERSTEEN, CHARLES A. ... 249
VANG, ALFRED H. ... 108
VANICEK, C. DAVID ... 368
VANLOPIK, JACK R. ... 70
VANN, ALLEN ... 56
VANNICE, DEREK ... 233
VANNICE, ENRIQUE LAHMANN ... 235
VANNICE, MICHAEL SWEATMAN ... 235
VanZYLL de JONG, M. ... 129
VARGAS, EMILIO ... 106
VARLAMOFF, SUSAN ... 214
VARNELL, KATHLEEN B. ... 57
VARNES, BARBARA ... 292
VARNEY, ROBERT ... 86
VARNEY, ROBERT W. ... 86
VARRONE, JOHN ... 33
VASQUEZ, PRISCILLA ... 279
VASUKI, N. C. ... 53
VATTIMO, BRIAN R. ... 93
VAUGHAN, ANGUS M. ... 256
VAUGHAN, HERBERT ... 338
VAUGHAN, MICHAEL R. ... 117
VAUGHN, CARYN C. ... 98
VAUGHN, DENISE ... 300
VAUGHN, JAMES ... 64
VAUX, HENRY J., JR. ... 47
VEAL, C. DAVID ... 40, 80
VEDDER, AMY ... 351
VEGA, DIANA ... 234
VEGA, ROGER R. ... 62
VEHRS, KRISTIN ... 157
VEILLON, EDGAR F. ... 249
VEITH, GILMAN D., Ph.D. ... 11
VENEMAN, ANN M. ... 47
VENSKUS, JILL ... 163
VENTURACCI, EDDIE ... 85
VENTURINI, PETER D. ... 46
VER CAUTEREN, KURT ... 355
VERANTH, JOHN ... 340
VERARDO, DENZIL ... 49
VERDOLIVA, FRAN ... 91
VERMAAK, COENRAAD ... 232
VERMILLION, NORMA ... 343
VERPLOEG, ALAN J. ... 126
VESPE, FRANK ... 317
VESSELL, C. RANDALL ... 380
VEST, GARY ... 13
VETTER, WAYNE E. ... 86
VEVERKA, MARY JO ... 15
VEZZANI, MAX ... 51
VEZZANT, MAX ... 51
VIBERT, JOAN ... 243
VICE, DAVID ... 64
VICENTE, RALPH ... 166
VICK, CHRIS ... 348
VICKERMAN, SARA ... 191
VICKERS, KYLE ... 81
VICORY, ALAN H., JR. ... 9
VICTOR, PETER, ... 386
VICTOR, ROBERT ... 178
VIDRINE, WINTON ... 70
VIEHWEG, JILL ... 224
VIETOR, JEAN ... 226
VIETS, PAT ... 12
VIGOTSKY, TIMOTHY G. ... 24
VIGUE, CHARLES ... 371
VILCHES, MARIA ... 177
VILELLA, FRANCISCO J. ... 80
VILJOEN, C. ... 325
VILLAFANE, AWILDA ... 34
VINCE, SUSAN ... 207
VINCE, SUSAN, ESQ. ... 207
VINCENT, FREDERICK J. ... 106
VINCENT, HOWARD K. ... 303
VINCENT, MATT ... 157
VINCENT, RANDALL ... 225
VINCENT, RANDY G. ... 277
VINCENT, WILLIAM J. ... 138
VINES, SUSAN TURNER-LOWE ... 271
VINES, TERRY L. ... 270
VINEY, ANGELA ... 324
VINEYARD, JERRY D. ... 249
VINEYARD, MICHAEL G. ... 244
VINING, LEN ... 314
VINT, MARY ... 312, 323
VIOLA, BETH A. ... 10
VIRDEN, TERRY ... 24
VIRDER, TERRY ... 24
VIRGIN, RANDY ... 136
VIRGINIA, ROSS A. ... 381
VIRTS, HENRY A. ... 73
VISNOSKY, MARTY ... 217
VISSERS, BERT ... 130
VITELLO, CHRISTOPHER ... 147
VLADECK, BRUCE C. ... 14
VODAK, MARK C. ... 88
VOELTZ, BARBARA ... 83, 278
VOGEL, BEA ... 260
VOGEL, DAVID ... 54
VOGEL, HARRY ... 164
VOGEL, RICHARD M. ... 377
VOGELMANN, H. W. ... 186
VOGT, ALBERT R. ... 379
VOGT, CARL E. ... 79
VOIGHT, DAVID ... 339
VOIGHTS, BRUCE ... 237
VOLESKY, MIKE ... 260
VOLK, JOHN ... 52
VOLK, MICHAEL ... 318
VOLPE, STEPHEN ... 106
VON ARB, SANDRA ... 353
VON EHWEGAN, TODD ... 237
VON FINGER, KEVIN ... 20
VON FURSTENBERG, EGON ... 309
VON RUEDEN, GERALD ... 18
VONDRACEK, BRUCE ... 147
VONDRACEK, BRUCE C. ... 77
VONNAHME, DON ... 63
VOORHIS, KEN ... 217
VORAC, TOM ... 20
VORE, JOHN ... 355
VORONTSOVA, MASHA ... 230
VOSS, HANS ... 255
VRANCART, RON ... 131
VREELAND, JUSTIN ... 353
VROOM, JEFF ... 293
VULK, JAN ... 323

W

WAADE, LINDA ... 181
WAAK, PATRICIA ... 265
WAAS, PETE ... 23
WADDEL, IAN G. ... 127
WADDELL, JAMES ... 157
WADDILL, CHRISTINE ... 56
WADE, JAMES ... 74
WADE, JEPTHA H. ... 251
WADE, JERRY & EDGE ... 164
WADSWORTH, FRANK H. ... 233
WADSWORTH, HENRY A. ... 65
WAESCH, TORSTEN ... 229
WAGENER, KARL J. ... 52
WAGGONER, LYNDA ... 347
WAGNER, BARBARA ... 341
WAGNER, CURTIS J., JR. ... 14
WAGNER, DAWN ... 18
WAGNER, DON ... 287
WAGNER, FREDERICH H. ... 390
WAGNER, JR., SIDNEY ... 241
WAGNER, PHILIP ... 64
WAGNER, PHILLIP ... 195
WAGNER, ROBERT ... 142, 301
WAGNER, STEVE ... 299
WAGNER, TONY ... 225
WAGNER, WILLIAM R. ... 175
WAHL, MARY ... 101
WAINWRIGHT, JANET ... 345
WAINWRIGHT, NANCY ... 351
WAITE, G. THOMAS, III ... 222
WAKEMAN, NANCY ... 315
WALDMAN, DOUG ... 202
WALDO, JAMES C. ... 293
WALDO, THOMAS S. ... 198
WALDON, CAROLYN ... 274
WALDON, JEFFERSON L. ... 206
WALDORF, ILENE ... 298
WALES, ROBERT W. ... 379
WALKE, TED R. ... 103
WALKER, ALICE ... 157
WALKER, BILL ... 7
WALKER, BRUCE ... 328
WALKER, CASSIE ... 232
WALKER, DARRELL ... 364
WALKER, DON ... 68
WALKER, DOUGLAS C. ... 277
WALKER, HIRAM J. ... 28
WALKER, JAMES B. ... 158

Staff Name Index

STAFF NAME INDEX 521

WALKER, JIM 80, 127
WALKER, KYLE 100
WALKER, LEE 116
WALKER, MARK 85
WALKER, MARY S. 289
WALKER, MASON 21
WALKER, NATHALIE 198
WALKER, RANDY 170, 251
WALKER, RICHARD E. 133
WALKER, RICHARD L.H. 194
WALKER, STEPHEN 368
WALKER, TERI 216
WALKER, WILLIAM W. 79
WALKER-GAYLE, C. 297
WALKINGSTICK, TAMARA L. 44
WALL, DIANA 370
WALL, GEORGE 59
WALL, JULIUS F. 194
WALL, W. VIRGIL, JR. 324
WALLA, WALTER J. 69
WALLACE, ALICE 223
WALLACE, BILL 121
WALLACE, BOB 247
WALLACE, CHARLES R. 376
WALLACE, DON 47
WALLACE, KATHLEEN 78
WALLACE, ROBERT B. 304
WALLENSTEIN, PAM 239
WALLER, DAVID 57, 228
WALLER, WILLIAM T. 390
WALLIN, PHIL 312
WALLIS, CLIFF 137, 173
WALLIS, PHILIP S. 277
WALLUS, ROBERT 149
WALPER, FRANK 244
WALRATH, GARY 82
WALSBERG, GLENN E. 189
WALSH, BILL 219
WALSH, BOB 25
WALSH, DICK 134
WALSH, EDWARD J., JR. 212
WALSH, JOHN 363
WALSH, KATHLEEN 46
WALSH, KEVIN 76
WALSH, LINDY 312
WALSH, NOREEN 356
WALSH, PAT 269
WALSH, PATRICK 125
WALSH, STEPHEN J. 325
WALSH, WILLIAM 28
WALSH-McGEHEE, MARTHA 239
WALTER, GEORGE 223
WALTER, HARTMUT S. 369
WALTER, HELEN 343
WALTER, JAMES A. 21
WALTERS, DIANE 232
WALTERS, TOM 238
WALTHER, CECILIA 355
WALTMAN, JIM 349
WALTON, BECKY J. 108
WALTON, JOHN 109
WALTON, LYNN 58
WALTZ, DON 48
WALTZ, ROBERT 64
WALVOORD, THOMAS 152
WALZ, STEPHEN A. 117
WAMPLER, GLEN 20
WAMPLER, STEVE 20
WANKEL, EDWARD F. 93
WARBURTON, GORDON 228
WARBURTON, GORDON S. 356
WARD, BETTYE 305
WARD, BILL 243
WARD, BOB 20, 110
WARD, C. H. 389
WARD, HAROLD R. 388
WARD, J. KEVIN 112
WARD, MILTON H. 168
WARD, ROBERT L. 284
WARD, SYLVIA 292
WARD, VIVIANLEE 263
WARD, WESLEY 338
WARDWELL, BOB 20
WARE, JAMES L. 196
WARE, NINA 348
WARING, LINDA 120
WARLAND, ROBERT 91
WARMAN, TIM 142
WARNER, BARRY L. 104
WARNER, GLENN 52
WARNER, JAKE 315
WARNER, JAMES 78
WARNER, JOSEPH S. 227
WARNER, LIZ 31
WARNER, ROBERT 329
WARR, JAMES W. 39
WARREN, BOB 27
WARREN, CHARLES L. 183
WARREN, DAVID 98, 160
WARREN, JR., MELVIN L. 325
WARREN, L. J. 194
WARREN, MAGGIE 230
WARREN, MELVIN L., JR. 155
WARREN, PHILIP D. 195
WARREN, ROBERT J. 357
WARREN, SCOTT R. 370
WARREN, WAYNE 97
WARREN, WESLEY 10
WARSKOW, BILL 43
WARTENBERG, CHARLES 236
WARWICK, JOHN J. 156
WASCOM, KATHY 249
WASHINGTON, VAL 201
WASLEY, BILL 32
WASSERMAN, PAMELA 365
WASSON, THOMAS 299
WASTE, STEPHEN M. 143
WATERLAND, LUTHER 260
WATERS, DORIS H. 154
WATERS, MIKE 291
WATKINS, ERIC 19
WATKINS, JOYCE 31
WATKINS, SHIRLEY 28
WATSON, ALEXANDER 279
WATSON, CAROLYN 73
WATSON, DENNIS 68
WATSON, GARY 233
WATSON, JAY 349
WATSON, JIM 327
WATSON, JOEL 360
WATSON, MICKEY 54, 55
WATSON, NORMA H. 202
WATSON, PAUL 318
WATSON, RAY ANN 49
WATT, DORIS J. 359
WATT, THEISEN 236
WATTERS, EUGENE 295
WATTON, DAVE 131
WATTS, ARDEAN 221
WATTS, DAVID L. 80
WATTS, DEBRA 183
WAUGH, GARY W. 33
WAUGH, NATALIE 274, 275
WAYLAND, ROBERT H., III 12
WEATHERS, KATHLEEN C. 227
WEAVER, BONNIE 371
WEAVER, BURTON D., JR. 69
WEAVER, DENNIS 113
WEAVER, G. H. 375
WEAVER, J. STEPHEN 84
WEAVER, REG 267
WEAVER, SCOTT C. 328
WEBB, CONNIE 383
WEBB, DONALD W. 288
WEBB, MARK R. 161
WEBB, ROBERT 248
WEBB, ROBERT C. 68
WEBBER, JOE 34
WEBBER, PETER 75
WEBER, BARBARA 32
WEBER, KEN 164
WEBER, MARY 305
WEBER, MIKE 229
WEBER, ROBERT C. 133
WEBER, SUSAN N. 49
WEBER, TERRANCE 257
WEBER, WILLIAM 351
WEBER, WILLIAM D. 240
WEBSTER, BILLY 13
WEBSTER, JANICE 378
WEBSTER, WILLIAM B., III 192
WECKERLY, SUE 261
WEDDERBURN, LESLIE 56
WEDDLE, GORDON K. 244
WEDDLE, TOM 72
WEDEN, DONALD R. 315
WEDGE, MARGARET 244
WEEKES, STEVE 223
WEEKS, BILL 279
WEEKS, HARMON, JR. 354
WEEKS, HAROLD J. 148
WEERTS, BURT 57
WEFER, FRED L. 271
WEFLEN, KATHLEEN 78
WEGE, PETER M. 175
WEGWART, GORDON 78
WEHRI, TOM 169
WEIDENHAFT, RAY A. 126
WEIDLER, MARK E. 90
WEIKERT, BILL 311
WEIL, MICHAEL 392
WEILBURG, BURKLEY C. 164
WEILER, BILL 227
WEILER, JEFF 185
WEILER, SUSAN C. 155
WEIN, HOWARD 302
WEINBERG, CARL 377
WEINGARDEN, KAREN 255
WEINSTEIN, KENNETH 28
WEINSTOCK, LAWRENCE G. 11
WEIR, DAVID 308
WEIS, JANICE 386
WEISE, LYNDA M. 124
WEISER, BRENDA 263
WEISMILLER, R. A. 377
WEISS, ZEZE 138
WEISSMAN, ARTHUR 218
WEISZ, SAM 190
WEITZ, FRED 280
WELCH, ALISON 129
WELCH, BARBARA 251
WELCH, LINDA 97
WELCH, PATRICIA 371
WELCH, SUSAN 89
WELCH, THOMANS 81
WELD, CHRISTOPHER M. 266
WELDON, DANIEL M. 209
WELDON, I. DEWAYNE 111
WELLER, CANDACE 207
WELLER, GENE 85
WELLING, CURTIS 134
WELLS, J. DENNIS 42
WELLS, JAMES W. 46
WELLS, RANDALL S. 321
WELLS, ROGER 308
WELLS, SUE 266
WELLS, THOMAS 87
WELLS, WESLEY 57
WELLS, WILLIAM, III 256
WELSCH, DAVID 111
WELSH, DONALD S. 102
WELSH, JIM 71
WELSH, LES 249
WELTER, JOHN 337
WELTON, RICHARD 181
WELTY, CLAIRE 387
WENDELL, DOUGLAS J. 302
WENDELL, E. W. 168
WENGER, KARL F. 322
WENTWORTH, JIM 354
WENTWORTH, RAND 337
WENTZ, MARILYN 267
WENTZ, W. ALAN 196
WENZLICK, JOHN 335
WERMUS, SUSAN 342
WERNER, CAROL 201
WERTHMAN, IONE 282
WESLEY, CARLOS 189
WESLEY, DAVID 313
WESSEL, PAUL C. 350
WESSELS, THOMAS 381
WESSON, JIM 117
WEST, B. KENNETH 269
WEST, CHARLES F. 285
WEST, DAN 97
WEST, GARY 89
WEST, JANE NOLL 337
WEST, MARY BETH 16
WEST, RICHARD 128, 286
WEST, RICHARD F. 286
WEST, RICHARD L. 208
WEST, ROBERT 80
WEST, ROY 169
WEST, STANFORD 339
WEST, W. E., JR. 111
WEST, WILLIAM R. 240
WESTBROOK, CHRISTOPHER 383
WESTENBERGER, JANE 150
WESTERHOLT, DUANE 83
WESTFALL, GREGORY 156
WESTHOFF, D. S. 377
WESTIN, CLARENCE 191
WESTLUND, MARK 308
WESTNEY, MIKE 207
WESTON, JUDY J. 107
WESTRA, LAURA 233
WESTWOOD, RICHARD 128
WESTWORTH, FRANK W. 317
WETHERELL, JODEEN 316
WETHERELL, VIRGINIA B. 54
WETTER, LES 194
WETZEL, WAYNE 83
WEXLER, MARK 274
WEYMOUTH, GEORGE A. 168
WEYRICK, RICHARD 381
WHALEY, ROSS S. 383
WHARTON, TOM 299
WHATE, RICH 217
WHEALEY, LOIS 294
WHEATLEY, HENRY U. 239
WHEATON, CHRIS 100
WHEATON, FRED 377
WHEATON, JIM 212
WHEELER, DAN 110
WHEELER, DOUGLAS P. 47
WHEELER, GERALD F. 271
WHEELER, MARC 325
WHEELER-BARTOL, ANN 298
WHELAN, GARY E. 143
WHELAN, TENSIE 157
WHIDDEN, ARDEN 130
WHIFFEN, NORMAN 328
WHINNERY, ELLIE 116
WHIPKEY, BOB 276
WHIPPEN, WILLIAM 255
WHIPPLE, CRAIG 114
WHIPPLE, GLEN 126
WHISENHUNT, TIM 159
WHITAKER, GENE 263
WHITCOMB, MARYANN 13
WHITCOMB, ROGER 114
WHITE, BARBARA 32
WHITE, BEATRICE E. 330
WHITE, BEN 158
WHITE, BILL 44
WHITE, CAROL 327
WHITE, CHARLES R. 49
WHITE, DARYL W. 24
WHITE, DAVID 92, 357, 375
WHITE, DAVID C. 30
WHITE, DAVID J. 207
WHITE, DONALD 199
WHITE, HOWARD S. 240
WHITE, J. PHELPS, III 90
WHITE, JEAN 340
WHITE, JERALD 157
WHITE, JESSE L., JR. 7
WHITE, JIM 19, 192
WHITE, JOHN R. 40
WHITE, MARGY 25
WHITE, NORM 341
WHITE, PATRICK J. 353
WHITE, RHETT 94
WHITE, ROBERT G. 82, 380
WHITE, RON 314
WHITE, RONALD 152
WHITE, RONALD J. 89
WHITE, STEPHEN B. 375
WHITEHEAD, CLIFTON J. 110
WHITEHEAD, DAVID 357
WHITEHEAD, S. C. 9
WHITEHURST, DAVID K. 116
WHITFIELD, BRUCE 290
WHITING, R. MONTAGUE 389
WHITMAN, CHRISTINE TODD 7
WHITMAN, F. BRUCE 103
WHITNEY, JACK 342
WHITNEY, MARCIA 242
WHITNEY, STEVE 349
WHITSON, BOB 111, 367, 389
WHITTEKIEND, J. C. 322
WHITTEMORE, DON 67
WHITTEMORE, RAY 196
WHITTEN, R. 129
WHITWORTH, MICHAEL 89
WHORISKEY, FREDERICK 163
WIANT, HARRY V., JR. 322
WICH, KENNETH 268
WICHERS, BILL 125
WIDELL, CHERILYN E. 49
WIDEN, JEFF 182
WIEBERS, DAVID O. 223
WIECKING, DAVID K. 118
WIECKO, GREG 59
WIEDENFELD, DAVID 153
WIEDOW, GALE 139
WIEGAND, CHUCK 364
WIEGER, BILL 249
WIEGERS, GEORGE 333
WIEGMAN, PAUL G. 347
WIELAND, RONALD 258
WIERSMA, BRUCE 376
WIESSNER, ANDY 349
WIEST, JENNIFER 253
WIGLEY, P. B. 84
WILAND, LAURENCE 392
WILCOCKS, AL 132
WILCOX, BILL 51
WILCOX, PAMELA B. 84
WILCOX, THOMAS F. 149
WILCOXSON, CATHERINE 263
WILDEMAN, JOHN 92
WILDER, GEORGE 276
WILDES, EMERSON 311
WILDIE, JOHN 19
WILDS, DOUGLAS K. 331
WILDY, WAYNE 225
WILES, CHARLES 240
WILHELMI, DEBRA 120
WILKE, RICHARD 393
WILKENSON, RIP 270
WILKER, VERN 256
WILKIN, NANCY 127
WILKINS, CHRISTINE 266
WILKINS, JANE 217
WILKINSON, BOB 197
WILKINSON, HAROLD 322
WILKINSON, JIM 165
WILKINSON, JOE 238
WILKINSON, MINDY 220
WILKINSON, TERRY 55
WILKOFF, LESLIE 264
WILLARD, PATRICK 330
WILLARD, STEVE 20
WILLEKE, GENE E. 385
WILLEMSEN, ALAN M. 213
WILLER, CHUCK 151
WILLEY, KATHLEEN 42
WILLIAMS, ANGELA 321
WILLIAMS, BRUCE 69
WILLIAMS, BRUCE A. 210
WILLIAMS, CARNEN S. 302
WILLIAMS, CECILIA 90
WILLIAMS, CHARLES W. 78
WILLIAMS, CINDY 146
WILLIAMS, DARRYL 134
WILLIAMS, DEBORAH 15
WILLIAMS, DOUG 195
WILLIAMS, ERIC 85
WILLIAMS, FRANKLIN 290
WILLIAMS, GARY 262
WILLIAMS, GENE S. 324
WILLIAMS, HANS M. 389
WILLIAMS, J. D. 61

Staff Name Index

STAFF NAME INDEX

WILLIAMS, J. DAVID ... 324
WILLIAMS, JIM ... 257, 288
WILLIAMS, JOHN ... 72
WILLIAMS, K. H. ... 28
WILLIAMS, KENNY ... 196
WILLIAMS, LORI ... 176
WILLIAMS, MARY ... 55
WILLIAMS, MYRA ... 54, 55
WILLIAMS, PHIL ... 232
WILLIAMS, ROBERT ... 158
WILLIAMS, ROBERT W. ... 33
WILLIAMS, ROSE ... 227
WILLIAMS, ROY L. ... 168
WILLIAMS, STEVE ... 100
WILLIAMS, STEVEN A. ... 67
WILLIAMS, SYBIL ... 253
WILLIAMS, TERRI E. M. ... 321
WILLIAMS, TIM ... 302
WILLIAMS, WAYNE ... 383
WILLIAMSON, CAROL ... 243
WILLIAMSON, DAYLE E. ... 84
WILLIAMSON, DONALD E. ... 162
WILLIAMSON, JERRY ... 20
WILLIAMSON, JOHN E. ... 391
WILLIAMSON, LONNIE L. ... 353
WILLIAMSON, MARY JANE ... 228
WILLIAMSON, MAURICE ... 344
WILLIAMSON, ROBERT L. ... 29
WILLIAMSON, SCOT J. ... 353
WILLICH, MIKE ... 131
WILLICK, MIKE ... 130
WILLIFORD, E. JOHN ... 39
WILLINGHAM, JOE ... 169
WILLIS, ELIZABETH ... 272
WILLIS, JACK ... 334
WILLIS, JULIE ... 18
WILLIS, MICHELE ... 97
WILLIS, PAT ... 343
WILLMOTT, JOHN ... 55
WILLSEY, BILL R. ... 194, 196
WILMORE, SANDRA ... 316
WILSHIRE, HOWARD ... 306
WILSON, ANA CRISTINA ... 323
WILSON, BILLY ... 296
WILSON, CHARLES L. ... 139
WILSON, CYNTHIA ... 158
WILSON, EDWARD M. ... 32
WILSON, G. RICHARD ... 113
WILSON, GARY ... 177
WILSON, GEORGE A. ... 303
WILSON, JACK A. ... 69
WILSON, JAMES R. ... 215
WILSON, JIM ... 190
WILSON, JOE ... 34
WILSON, JOHN ... 260
WILSON, JOHN CHARLES ... 329
WILSON, JOHN H. ... 202
WILSON, JONATHAN SINCLAIR ... 198
WILSON, JOSEPH W. ... 245
WILSON, KARMIN ... 238
WILSON, LARRY ... 44, 64
WILSON, LARRY J. ... 65
WILSON, LEONARD ... 341
WILSON, LYNN C. ... 161
WILSON, MICHAEL D. ... 60
WILSON, MIKE ... 199
WILSON, NORMA ... 299
WILSON, P. G. ... 209
WILSON, PATRICIA ... 272
WILSON, PAUL ... 206
WILSON, PAUL L. ... 241
WILSON, RICHARD A. ... 49
WILSON, RICHARD D. ... 10
WILSON, SALLY ... 230
WILSON, STEPHEN R. ... 44
WILSON, STEVE N. ... 44
WILSON, SUSAN M. ... 103, 302
WILSON, TED ... 326
WILSON, TERRY ... 177
WILTSE, MILTON ... 41
WILTSHIRE, BOB ... 205
WIMMER, KENT ... 208
WINCHCOMBE, RAYMOND J. ... 227
WINDISH, DOROTHY C. ... 53
WINDSOR, DONALD A. ... 205
WINDSOR, M.L. ... 289
WINDUS, WALTER ... 318
WINEGRAD, GERALD ... 140
WINER, ARTHUR M. ... 369
WINGERTER, LORI ... 218
WINGET, CARL ... 38
WINGO, W. BRUCE ... 118
WINKEL, ROB ... 87
WINKEL-DEIN, MARGARET ... 78
WINKLEMAN, DANA L. ... 98
WINKLER, KARL P. ... 49
WINN, CHESTER M. ... 49
WINN, RON ... 205
WINOKUR, ROBERT S. ... 12

WINOKUR, ROBERT S., JR. ... 12
WINSOR, DEANE ... 93
WINSTEAD, JOE E. ... 375
WINSTEIN, MARK ... 315
WINSTON, ELEANOR ... 257
WINSTON, JUDY ... 118
WINTER, MICHAEL ... 28
WINTER, WAYNE ... 109
WINTERFELD, DELBERT ... 263
WINTERON, GUY ... 130
WINTERS, OWEN D. ... 278
WINTERS, S. JEFF ... 263
WINTHROP, FREDERIC ... 338
WIPPERMAN, THOMAS A. ... 266
WIRTH, BARRY ... 25
WISE, DAVID ... 81
WISE, W. M. ... 92
WISEMAN SNIDER, PAT ... 159
WISEMAN, EARL ... 36
WISEMAN, LAURENCE D. ... 150
WISHART, RICK ... 194
WISNIEWSKI, JOSEPH ... 359
WITMER, PAMELA A. ... 103
WITT, BRAD ... 101
WITT, DOUR ... 136
WITT, LARRY ... 83
WITT, PETER A. ... 111, 367, 389
WITT, STEVEN C. ... 176
WITTE, JEFF M. ... 89
WITTER, KAREN ... 63
WITTKAMP, TOM ... 18
WITTMAN, STEPHEN ... 125
WITTY, RICHARD ... 292
WIYGUL, ROBERT ... 198
WIZNER, ANDY ... 186
WOBESER, G. A. ... 171
WODDER, REBECCA R. ... 154
WOEHR, JAMES R. ... 353
WOGAN, TERRI ... 213
WOHL, JIM ... 194
WOLCOTT, JAMES E. ... 21
WOLF, ANNETT ... 153
WOLF, CHRISTINE ... 212
WOLF, DAVE ... 302
WOLF, HAZEL ... 206
WOLF, MICHAEL ... 103
WOLF, THOMAS ... 336
WOLF-ARMSTRONG, MARK ... 308
WOLFE, GARY J., Ph.D. ... 313
WOLFE, SHELDON ... 252
WOLFSON, JANE L. ... 382
WOLINSKI, JEFFREY A. ... 277
WOLMAN, M. GORDON ... 376
WONG, ALBERT W.C. ... 59
WONG, KATHLEEN ... 365
WONG, LYLE ... 60
WONKLE, JILL ... 56
WOO, ROY ... 101
WOOD, BARRY E. ... 196
WOOD, BOB ... 173
WOOD, DIANE W. ... 363
WOOD, DOUGLAS ... 220
WOOD, JIM ... 160
WOOD, LARRY F. ... 54
WOOD, MARY ... 346
WOOD, MEGAN EPLER ... 199
WOOD, PETRA BOHALL ... 122
WOOD, RANDOLPH ... 83
WOOD, ROBERT D. ... 357
WOOD, ROYCE ... 210
WOOD, WENDELL ... 298
WOODBURY, PAUL ... 195
WOODFIELD, GRANT ... 134
WOODFIN, BILL ... 325
WOODFIN, WILLIAM L., JR. ... 116
WOODFORD, EILEEN ... 270
WOODFORK, LARRY D. ... 123
WOODLEY, JOHN PAUL, JR. ... 116
WOODRING, STEPHEN ... 335
WOODS, BILL AND ERIN ... 344
WOODS, MARY ANNE ... 23
WOODS, SUSANNE ... 244
WOODS, TERRY K. ... 141
WOODSUM, HAROLD E., JR. ... 250
WOODWARD, DAVE ... 110
WOODWARD, JOHN ... 249
WOODWARD, SUE ... 296, 365
WOODWELL, DAVITT ... 302
WOODWORTH, NEIL ... 134
WOOLAWAY, CHRISTINE ... 59
WOOLBRIGHT, LAWRENCE ... 163
WOOLEY, BOB ... 128
WOOLEY, JAMES B., JR. ... 303
WOOLF, ALAN ... 373
WOOLLEY, TED ... 113
WOOLSEY, SUZANNE H. ... 271
WOOTEN, CURTIS ... 195
WOOTEN, JEAN W. ... 379
WOOTEN, MICHAEL C. ... 366

WOOTTON, SUSAN ... 214
WORD, DAVID ... 57
WORKMAN, DAVE ... 121
WORKMAN, RANDALL ... 59
WORLEY, IAN A. ... 391
WORSTER, JENNI ... 97
WORTHEN, MIKE ... 29
WOTEKI, CATHY ... 28
WOTT, JOHN A. ... 232
WOUTERS, WAYNE ... 36
WRANGLER, EVELYNNE ... 172
WRAY, PAT ... 100
WRAY, PAUL H. ... 66
WRAZEN, JOHN ... 390
WRIGHT, ALVIN ... 108
WRIGHT, ANGUS ... 368
WRIGHT, BISHOP ... 208
WRIGHT, BOSLEY ... 169
WRIGHT, CHUCK ... 23
WRIGHT, G. TOD ... 194
WRIGHT, KATHERINE R. ... 118
WRIGHT, L. DONELSON ... 391
WRIGHT, LLOYD D. ... 385
WRIGHT, R. GERALD ... 61
WRIGHT, R. MICHAEL ... 134
WRIGHT, SCOTT M. ... 139
WRONA, NANCY C. ... 42
WROTH, KINVIN L. ... 391
WUEBKER, PETE ... 351
WUERCH, H. VICTOR ... 59
WUOLO, RAY ... 257
WURSTER, SCOTT C. ... 331
WURTZ, DON ... 13
WUTHNOW, DONA ... 345
WYANT, DAN ... 76
WYATT, ROBERT ... 357
WYATT, RODNEY ... 53
WYDRA, ROBERT J., JR. ... 187
WYK, TJISKA VAN ... 198
WYKLE, KENNETH R. ... 27
WYKOFF, RANDOLPH ... 15
WYLDE, JOHN ... 248
WYLIE, THOMAS C. ... 103
WYNN, G. ... 368
WYNN, ROBERT ... 47
WYPYSZINSKI, ALEX ... 88
WYSE, JAMES P. ... 286
WYSS, HANSJORG ... 326
WYSS, JOHN ... 29

Y

YACKULIC, CORRIE ... 346
YAGER, JILL ... 385
YAGER, MARY ... 262
YAICH, SCOTT C. ... 44
YAMAKAWA, DAVID ... 133
YAMAMURA, TSUNETOSHI ... 179
YAMANAKA, MARILOU B. ... 59
YAMASE, KAZUHIRO ... 242
YANDALA, DEBORAH ... 203
YANK, ANDREA J. ... 278
YANKE, RONALD C. ... 303
YAPLE, CHARLES H. ... 181
YAROSEWICK, STANLEY J. ... 381
YARROW, GREG ... 108
YATES, A. J. ... 47
YATES, GRAEM ... 266
YATSKIEVYCH, GEORGE ... 259
YEADON, GEOFFREY ... 206
YEATES, J. WILLIAM ... 261
YEE, LANE ... 47
YEE, PETRA ... 232
YELLOWTAIL, WILLIAM P., JR. ... 11
YELVERTON, JOHN R. ... 58
YERGER, DALE ... 191
YERKS, LINDA ... 225
YESARATNE, SHIRANEE ... 234
YODER, SUSAN ... 47
YORK, SHERRIE ... 309
YORKS, J. WAYNE ... 104
YOSHIDA, TOMIO ... 363
YOSHINAGA, ALVIN ... 220
YOUELL, CAROL ... 186
YOUK, DENNIS ... 243
YOUNG, ANDERSON B. ... 383
YOUNG, BILL ... 1, 5
YOUNG, BOBBY R. ... 111
YOUNG, COLIN ... 137
YOUNG, DAVID ... 254
YOUNG, DON ... 1, 4
YOUNG, DON A. ... 194
YOUNG, FRANK ... 346
YOUNG, H. VANCE ... 87
YOUNG, JAMES A. ... 103
YOUNG, JIM ... 47, 126, 130, 249, 319
YOUNG, JOHN A. ... 81

YOUNG, KIRA ... 311
YOUNG, LARRY ... 340
YOUNG, NORMAN C. ... 61
YOUNG, RICHARD E. ... 303
YOUNG, RON ... 232
YOUNG, THOMAS A. ... 68
YOUNGBERG, GARTH ... 221
YOUNGER, LISA ... 328
YOUNGERS, CHARLIE ... 207
YOUNGREN, JIM ... 249
YOUNGSON, JIM ... 47
YOUNKER, GORDON ... 340
YOUNKIN, DAVE ... 228
YOUNKMAN, DAVID ... 153
YOUNT, ROBERT E. ... 42
YOUSEY, THOMAS J., III ... 338
YOW, DAVID LEE ... 148
YUDELMAN, MONTAGUE ... 305
YUILL, THOMAS M. ... 393
YURKOW, RUSSELL ... 131

Z

ZABEL, CYNTHIA ... 353
ZABEL, RICHARD ... 347
ZABER, JOHN ... 391
ZABOR, BILL ... 333
ZACKHEIM, HUGH ... 312
ZADER, WILLIAM T. ... 190
ZAELKE, DURWOOD J. ... 175
ZALE, ALEXANDER ... 82
ZALE, ALEXANDER V. ... 143
ZALESKY, PHIL ... 291
ZALESKY, PHILIP ... 297
ZAMORA, NATALIA ... 37
ZARILLO, KIM ... 207
ZARNOWITZ, JILL ... 100
ZATE, DANIEL ... 189
ZAW-MON, MERRYLIN ... 73
ZEGEL, WILLIAM C. ... 135
ZEHLER, RAY ... 241
ZEITLER, KAREN ... 192
ZEKOR, DAN ... 299
ZELAZNY, JOHN ... 337
ZELAZNY, JULIAN ... 164
ZEMEK, SUSAN ... 120
ZENCEY, MATTHEW ... 137
ZENICH, HAROLD, Ph.D. ... 11
ZENN, RICK ... 362
ZEPATOS, THALIA A. ... 312
ZEPP, ANDREW ... 247
ZERINGUE, OSWALD ... 36
ZEVIN, SUSAN ... 12
ZEZULAK, DAVE ... 49
ZIARNO, GERARD ... 141
ZICHELLA, CARL ... 319
ZIDEK, JIRI ... 89
ZIEHM, ROBERT ... 252
ZIELINSKI, ELAINE ... 24
ZIELINSKI, SALLY A. ... 253
ZIEMER, ROBERT R. ... 368
ZIERENBERG, NANCY ... 351
ZIFFER, KAREN ... 188
ZIGROSSI, NORMAN A. ... 36
ZILANOV, V. ... 9
ZILUCA, PAUL G. ... 118
ZIMMERMAN, GERALD R. ... 48
ZIMMERMAN, H. NEIL ... 287
ZIMMERMAN, HERBERT M. ... 124
ZIMMERMAN, JAY ... 18
ZIMMERMAN, RICHARD ... 123
ZIMMERMAN, ROY P. ... 35
ZIMMERMANN, ALBERT W. ... 289
ZINN, JAN ... 302
ZIPF, CINDY ... 180
ZIPPERER, WAYNE ... 383
ZIRKLE, ERNEST ... 87
ZODER, KATHERINE ... 193
ZOELLNER, CRAIG ... 237
ZOON, KATHRYN C. ... 14
ZOPF, RICHARD ... 174
ZORN, C. KURT ... 374
ZUKOWSKY, RON ... 132
ZUPP, RICHARD ... 256
ZURAWSKI, RON ... 110
ZUSCHLAG, NANCY ... 51
ZUURING, HANS R. ... 380
ZWANK, PHILLIP J. ... 390
ZWETTLER, KATHLEEN ... 125
ZWICK, DAVID ... 180
ZWICK, SUSAN MADER ... 130
ZWOLINSKI, MALCOM J. ... 367
ZYGMUT, ED ... 302

GEOGRAPHIC INDEX

CANADA
  GOVERNMENT ORGANIZATIONS
    INTERNATIONAL WHALING COMMISSION 8
    DEPARTMENT OF CANADIAN HERITAGE 36
    ENVIRONMENTAL PROTECTION SERVICE 37

ALBERTA
  GOVERNMENT ORGANIZATIONS
    ENVIRONMENTAL CONSERVATION SERVICE 36
    ENVIRONMENTAL CONSERVATION SERVICE 36
    ENVIRONMENTAL CONSERVATION SERVICE 37
  NON-GOVERNMENTAL ORGANIZATIONS
    ALBERTA FISH AND GAME ASSOCIATION, THE 137
    ALBERTA TRAPPERS ASSOCIATION 137
    ALBERTA WILDERNESS ASSOCIATION 137
    AMERICAN FISHERIES SOCIETY, MID-CANADA CHAPTER 147
    ARCTIC INSTITUTE OF NORTH AMERICA 159
    ASSOCIATION FOR FISH AND WILDLIFE ENFORCEMENT TRAINING 160
    DUCKS UNLIMITED (Alberta, Canada) 194
    FEDERATION OF ALBERTA NATURALIST 205
    HERITAGE INTERPRETATION INTERNATIONAL 221
    WILDLIFE SOCIETY, ALBERTA CHAPTER 353
  STATE GOVERNMENT ORGANIZATIONS
    ALBERTA DEPARTMENT OF ENVIRONMENTAL PROTECTION 127
      Communications Division 127
      Corporate Management Service 127
      Environmental Service 127
      Land and Forest Service 127
      Natural Resources Service 127

BRITISH COLUMBIA
  GOVERNMENT ORGANIZATIONS
    NORTH PACIFIC ANADROMOUS FISH COMMISSION 9
    PACIFIC SALMON COMMISSION 9
    ENVIRONMENTAL CONSERVATION SERVICE 36
    ENVIRONMENTAL CONSERVATION SERVICE 36
    ENVIRONMENTAL CONSERVATION SERVICE 37
  NON-GOVERNMENTAL ORGANIZATIONS
    AMERICAN FISHERIES SOCIETY, NORTH PACIFIC INTERNATIONAL CHAPTER 148
    BRITISH COLUMBIA FIELD ORNITHOLOGISTS 168
    BRITISH COLUMBIA WATERFOWL SOCIETY, THE 168
    CRESTON VALLEY WILDLIFE MANAGEMENT AUTHORITY 190
    GALIANO CONSERVANCY ASSOCIATION 213
    IZAAK WALTON LEAGUE OF AMERICA, INC., THE
      California Division 240
    OUTDOOR RECREATION COUNCIL OF BRITISH COLUMBIA 299
    SEA SHEPHERD CONSERVATION SOCIETY
      Canada Office 319
  STATE GOVERNMENT ORGANIZATIONS
    MINISTRY OF ENVIRONMENT, LANDS, AND PARKS 127
    MINISTRY OF FISHERIES 127
    MINISTRY OF SMALL BUSINESS TOURISM AND CULTURE 127

EDINBURGH
  NON-GOVERNMENTAL ORGANIZATIONS
    NORTH ATLANTIC SALMON CONSERVATION ORGANIZATION 289

MANITOBA
  NON-GOVERNMENTAL ORGANIZATIONS
    AMERICAN FISHERIES SOCIETY
      Canadian Aquatic Resources Section 143
    DELTA WATERFOWL FOUNDATION 192
    DUCKS UNLIMITED (Manitoba, Canada) 194
    MANITOBA NATURALISTS SOCIETY 251
    MANITOBA WILDLIFE FEDERATION 251
    WILDLIFE SOCIETY, MANITOBA CHAPTER 355
  STATE GOVERNMENT ORGANIZATIONS
    DEPARTMENT OF INDUSTRY, TRADE AND TOURISM 128
    MANITOBA DEPARTMENT OF NATURAL RESOURCES 128
      Central Region 128
      Eastern Region 128
      Northeastern Region 128
      Northwestern Region 128
      Western Region 128

NEW BRUNSWICK
  GOVERNMENT ORGANIZATIONS
    ST. CROIX INTERNATIONAL WATERWAY COMMISSION (Canadian Office) 10
    ENVIRONMENTAL CONSERVATION SERVICE 36
    ENVIRONMENTAL CONSERVATION SERVICE 36
    ENVIRONMENTAL CONSERVATION SERVICE 37
  NON-GOVERNMENTAL ORGANIZATIONS
    ATLANTIC SALMON FEDERATION 163
    HUNTSMAN MARINE SCIENCE CENTRE 223
    NEW BRUNSWICK WILDLIFE FEDERATION 284
  STATE GOVERNMENT ORGANIZATIONS
    NEW BRUNSWICK DEPARTMENT OF NATURAL RESOURCES AND ENERGY 128

NEWFOUNDLAND
  NON-GOVERNMENTAL ORGANIZATIONS
    NEWFOUNDLAND LABRADOR WILDLIFE FEDERATION 287
  STATE GOVERNMENT ORGANIZATIONS
    NEWFOUNDLAND DEPARTMENT OF FOREST RESOURCES AND AGRIFOODS 128
      Ecosystem Health Division 128
      Inland Fish and Wildlife Division 129
      Legislation and Compliance Division 129
      Regional Offices 129

NOVA SCOTIA
  NON-GOVERNMENTAL ORGANIZATIONS
    DUCKS UNLIMITED (Nova Scotia, Canada) 194
    NORTHWEST ATLANTIC FISHERIES ORGANIZATION (NAFO) 292
    NOVA SCOTIA FORESTRY ASSOCIATION 293
    NOVA SCOTIA WILDLIFE FEDERATION 293
  STATE GOVERNMENT ORGANIZATIONS
    DEPARTMENT OF FISHERIES AND AQUACULTURE 129
    DEPARTMENT OF NATURAL RESOURCES 130
    NEW MEXICO DEPARTMENT OF NATURAL RESOURCES
      Corporate Service Unit 130
      Land Services Division 130
      Regional Services 130
      Renewable Resources 130

ONTARIO
  GOVERNMENT ORGANIZATIONS
    INTERNATIONAL JOINT COMMISSION (Canada Office) .. 8
    INTERNATIONAL JOINT COMMISSION (Great Lakes Regional Office) 8
    DEPARTMENT OF FISHERIES AND OCEANS 36
    ENVIRONMENTAL CONSERVATION SERVICE 36
    ENVIRONMENTAL CONSERVATION SERVICE 36
    ENVIRONMENTAL PROTECTION SERVICE 37
    ENVIRONMENTAL CONSERVATION SERVICE 37
    NATURAL RESOURCES CANADA, CANADIAN FOREST SERVICE 37
  NON-GOVERNMENTAL ORGANIZATIONS
    AMERICAN FISHERIES SOCIETY
      Southern Ontario Chapter 144
    AMERICAN FISHERIES SOCIETY, NORTHWESTERN ONTARIO CHAPTER 148
    BIRDLIFE INTERNATIONAL 166
    CANADIAN ARCTIC RESOURCES COMMITTEE, INC. 171
    CANADIAN ENVIRONMENTAL LAW ASSOCIATION 172
    CANADIAN FEDERATION OF HUMANE SOCIETIES 172
    CANADIAN FORESTRY ASSOCIATION 172
    CANADIAN INSTITUTE FOR ENVIRONMENTAL LAW AND POLICY (CIELAP) 172
    CANADIAN INSTITUTE OF FORESTRY/INSTITUT FORESTIER DU CANADA 172
    CANADIAN NATIONAL SPORTSMEN'S SHOWS 172
    CANADIAN NATURE FEDERATION 172
    CANADIAN PARKS AND WILDERNESS SOCIETY 173
    CANADIAN SOCIETY OF ENVIRONMENTAL BIOLOGISTS 173

GEOGRAPHIC INDEX

CANADIAN WILDLIFE FEDERATION 173
DOGTOOTH GROUP 193
DUCKS UNLIMITED (Ontario, Canada) 194
FEDERATION OF ONTARIO NATURALISTS 206
INTERNATIONAL SOCIETY FOR ENVIRONMENTAL ETHICS
.... 233
INTERPRETATION CANADA 236
JACK MINER MIGRATORY BIRD FOUNDATION, INC. 242
NATURE CONSERVANCY OF CANADA, THE 279
OCEAN VOICE INTERNATIONAL 294
ONTARIO FEDERATION OF ANGLERS AND HUNTERS,
INC., THE 297
ONTARIO FORESTRY ASSOCIATION 297
POLLUTION PROBE FOUNDATION 304
SIERRA CLUB
   Canada Office 318
WILDLIFE HABITAT CANADA 352
STATE GOVERNMENT ORGANIZATIONS
MINISTRY OF NATURAL RESOURCES
   Algonquin Forestry Authority 130
   Corporate Services Division 130
   Field Services Division 130
   Fish and Wildlife Branch 130
   Natural Resource Management Division 130
   Northeast Region 131
   Northwest Region 131
   Ontario 131
   Science and Information Resources Division 131
   South Central Region 131
NIAGARA ESCARPMENT COMMISSION 131

PRINCE EDWARD ISLAND
STATE GOVERNMENT ORGANIZATIONS
DEPARTMENT OF ENVIRONMENTAL RESOURCES
(PRINCE EDWARD ISLAND) 131

QUEBEC
GOVERNMENT ORGANIZATIONS
ENVIRONMENTAL CONSERVATION SERVICE 36
ENVIRONMENTAL CONSERVATION SERVICE 36
ENVIRONMENTAL PROTECTION SERVICE 37
ENVIRONMENTAL CONSERVATION SERVICE 37
NON-GOVERNMENTAL ORGANIZATIONS
ATLANTIC CENTER FOR THE ENVIRONMENT (QLF Canada
Office) 163
DUCKS UNLIMITED (Quebec, Canada) 194
GREAT LAKES UNITED (Montreal Office) 217
INTERNATIONAL UNION FOR CONSERVATION OF
NATURE AND NATURAL RESOURCES (IUCN) THE
WORLD CONSERVATION UNION
Outposted Centre Canada 234
PROVINCE OF QUEBEC SOCIETY FOR THE PROTECTION
OF BIRDS, INC. 306
QUEBEC WILDLIFE FEDERATION 308
STOP 328
STATE GOVERNMENT ORGANIZATIONS
DEPARTMENT OF ENVIRONMENT AND WILDLIFE
(QUEBEC) 131

SASKATCHEWAN
NON-GOVERNMENTAL ORGANIZATIONS
CANADIAN COOPERATIVE WILDLIFE HEALTH CENTRE 171
DUCKS UNLIMITED (Saskatchewan Operation, Canada) .. 194
NATURE SASKATCHEWAN 282
SASKATCHEWAN WILDLIFE FEDERATION 315
STATE GOVERNMENT ORGANIZATIONS
SASKATCHEWAN ENVIRONMENT AND RESOURCE
MANAGEMENT 132
   Corporate Services 132
   East Boreal 132
   Enforcement and Compliance Branch 132
   Fire Management and Forest Protection Branch 132
   Grassland 132
   Operations 132
   Parkland 132
   Policy and Assessment 132
   Programs 132
   Shield 132
   West Boreal 132

YUKON TERRITORY
NON-GOVERNMENTAL ORGANIZATIONS
YUKON FISH AND GAME ASSOCIATION 365
STATE GOVERNMENT ORGANIZATIONS
DEPARTMENT OF RENEWABLE RESOURCES 132

UNITED STATES
GOVERNMENT ORGANIZATIONS
ENVIRONMENTAL PROTECTION AGENCY 10
DEPARTMENT OF THE AIR FORCE
   MAJOR AIR COMMANDS 16
DEPARTMENT OF THE AIR FORCE
   MAJOR U.S. INSTALLATIONS 17
DEPARTMENT OF THE NAVY
   U.S. MARINE CORPS 27
U.S. DEPARTMENT OF AGRICULTURE
   ANIMAL AND PLANT HEALTH INSPECTION SERVICE .. 29

ALABAMA
GOVERNMENT ORGANIZATIONS
TENNESSEE VALLEY AUTHORITY 36
DEPARTMENT OF THE ARMY
   U.S. ARMY CORPS OF ENGINEERS 21
NON-GOVERNMENTAL ORGANIZATIONS
ALABAMA ASSOCIATION OF SOIL AND WATER
CONSERVATION DISTRICTS 135
ALABAMA B.A.S.S. CHAPTER FEDERATION 135
ALABAMA ENVIRONMENTAL COUNCIL 135
ALABAMA NATURAL HERITAGE PROGRAM 135
ALABAMA WATERFOWL ASSOCIATION, INC. (AWA) ... 135
ALABAMA WILDLIFE FEDERATION 136
AMERICAN FISHERIES SOCIETY, ALABAMA CHAPTER 144
AMERICAN FISHERIES SOCIETY, AUBURN UNIVERSITY
STUDENT CHAPTER 145
ANGLERS FOR CLEAN WATER 157
BASS ANGLERS SPORTSMAN SOCIETY (B.A.S.S, INC.) 165
ENVIROSOUTH, INC. 204
NATIONAL SPELEOLOGICAL SOCIETY, INC. 271
NATURE CONSERVANCY, THE, ALABAMA CHAPTER ... 280
SIERRA CLUB
   Southeast Office 279
TROUT UNLIMITED, RIVERSIDE COUNCIL 336
TROUT UNLIMITED, SHADES VALLEY COUNCIL 336
WILDLIFE SOCIETY, ALABAMA CHAPTER 353
STATE GOVERNMENT ORGANIZATIONS
ALABAMA COOPERATIVE EXTENSION SYSTEM 39
ALABAMA COOPERATIVE FISH AND WILDLIFE RESEARCH
UNIT (USDI) 39
ALABAMA DEPARTMENT OF AGRICULTURE AND
INDUSTRIES 39
ALABAMA DEPARTMENT OF CONSERVATION AND
NATURAL RESOURCES 39
ALABAMA DEPARTMENT OF ECONOMIC AND
COMMUNITY AFFAIRS, COASTAL PROGRAMS (ADECA)
.... 39
ALABAMA DEPARTMENT OF ENVIRONMENTAL
MANAGEMENT 39
ALABAMA FORESTRY COMMISSION 39
ALABAMA SEA GRANT PROGRAM 40
ALABAMA SOIL AND WATER CONSERVATION
COMMITTEE 40
GOVERNOR OF ALABAMA, DONALD SIEGELMAN 39

ALASKA
GOVERNMENT ORGANIZATIONS
DEPARTMENT OF THE ARMY
   U.S. ARMY CORPS OF ENGINEERS 21
DEPARTMENT OF THE INTERIOR
   UNITED STATES FISH AND WILDLIFE SERVICE 26
U.S. DEPARTMENT OF AGRICULTURE
   UNITED STATES FOREST SERVICE 32
NON-GOVERNMENTAL ORGANIZATIONS
ALASKA ASSOCIATION OF SOIL AND WATER
CONSERVATION DISTRICTS 136
ALASKA AUDUBON SOCIETY 136
ALASKA CENTER FOR THE ENVIRONMENT 136
ALASKA CONSERVATION ALLIANCE 136
ALASKA CONSERVATION FOUNDATION 136
ALASKA CONSERVATION VOICE 137

GEOGRAPHIC INDEX

ALASKA NATURAL RESOURCE AND OUTDOOR
EDUCATION ASSOCIATION 137
ALASKA RAINFOREST CAMPAIGN 137
ALASKA WILDLIFE ALLIANCE, THE 137
AMERICAN FISHERIES SOCIETY, ALASKA CHAPTER... 144
COOK INLET KEEPER 189
EARTHJUSTICE LEGAL DEFENSE FUND (formerly Sierra
Club Legal Defense Fund, Inc.)
Southeast Alaska Office 198
IZAAK WALTON LEAGUE OF AMERICA, INC., THE
Alaska Division 240
KODIAK BROWN BEAR TRUST 246
NATIONAL PARKS AND CONSERVATION ASSOCIATION
(NPCA)
Alaska Regional Office 270
NATIONAL WILDLIFE FEDERATION
Alaska Project Office (AK, HI) 274
NATURE CONSERVANCY, THE, ALASKA CHAPTER 280
NORTHERN ALASKA ENVIRONMENTAL CENTER 292
SIERRA CLUB
Alaska Office 318
SOUTHEAST ALASKA CONSERVATION COUNCIL (SEACC)
.... 324
TROUT UNLIMITED, ALASKA COUNCIL 334
TRUSTEES FOR ALASKA 338
WILDLIFE FEDERATION OF ALASKA 351
WILDLIFE SOCIETY, ALASKA CHAPTER 353
STATE GOVERNMENT ORGANIZATIONS
ALASKA COOPERATIVE FISH AND WILDLIFE RESEARCH
UNIT 40
ALASKA DEPARTMENT OF ENVIRONMENTAL
CONSERVATION 40
ALASKA DEPARTMENT OF FISH AND GAME 40
ALASKA DEPARTMENT OF NATURAL RESOURCES 41
ALASKA HEALTH PROJECT 41
ALASKA SEA GRANT COLLEGE PROGRAM 41
ALASKA STATE EXTENSION SERVICES 41
DEPARTMENT OF PUBLIC SAFETY 41
Division of Fish and Wildlife Protection 41
GOVERNOR OF ALASKA, TONY KNOWLES 40

AMERICAN SAMOA
STATE GOVERNMENT ORGANIZATIONS
AMERICAN SAMOA DEPARTMENT OF AGRICULTURE ... 41
GOVERNOR OF AMERICAN SAMOA, TAUESE P.F. SUNIA
.... 41

ARIZONA
NON-GOVERNMENTAL ORGANIZATIONS
AMERICAN FISHERIES SOCIETY, ARIZONA-NEW MEXICO
CHAPTER 144
ARIZONA ASSOCIATION OF CONSERVATION DISTRICTS
.... 159
ARIZONA B.A.S.S. CHAPTER FEDERATION 159
ARIZONA WILDLIFE FEDERATION 159
BORDER ECOLOGY PROJECT (BEP) 167
GRAND CANYON TRUST 216
INTERNATIONAL SONORAN DESERT ALLIANCE 234
NATIONAL ASSOCIATION OF STATE PARK DIRECTORS
.... 264
NATURE CONSERVANCY, THE, ARIZONA CHAPTER 280
RINCON INSTITUTE, THE 312
SAFARI CLUB INTERNATIONAL 314
SIERRA CLUB
Southwest Office 319
SONORAN INSTITUTE 323
SOUTHWEST CENTER FOR BIOLOGICAL DIVERSITY... 326
THRESHOLD INC. 332
TROUT UNLIMITED, ARIZONA COUNCIL 334
WILDLANDS PROJECT, THE 350
WILDLIFE DAMAGE REVIEW (WDR) 351
WILDLIFE SOCIETY, ARIZONA CHAPTER 353
STATE GOVERNMENT ORGANIZATIONS
ARIZONA COOPERATIVE FISH AND WILDLIFE RESEARCH
UNIT (USDI) 41
ARIZONA DEPARTMENT OF AGRICULTURE 41
Animal Services Division 42
Environmental Services Division 42
Integrated Pest Management (IPM) 42
Plant Services Division 42
ARIZONA DEPARTMENT OF ENVIRONMENTAL QUALITY 42
ARIZONA GAME AND FISH DEPARTMENT 42
ARIZONA GEOLOGICAL SURVEY 42
ARIZONA LAND DEPARTMENT 42
ARIZONA STATE EXTENSION SERVICES 43
ARIZONA STATE PARKS BOARD 43
GOVERNOR OF ARIZONA, JANE DEE HULL 41

ARKANSAS
GOVERNMENT ORGANIZATIONS
DEPARTMENT OF THE ARMY
U.S. ARMY CORPS OF ENGINEERS 21
NON-GOVERNMENTAL ORGANIZATIONS
AMERICAN FISHERIES SOCIETY, ARKANSAS CHAPTER
.... 144
ARKANSAS ASSOCIATION OF CONSERVATION
DISTRICTS 159
ARKANSAS B.A.S.S. CHAPTER FEDERATION 159
ARKANSAS ENVIRONMENTAL EDUCATION ASSOCIATION
.... 160
ARKANSAS WILDLIFE FEDERATION 160
NATURE CONSERVANCY, THE, ARKANSAS CHAPTER 280
OZARK SOCIETY, THE 299
TROUT UNLIMITED, ARKANSAS COUNCIL 334
WILDLIFE SOCIETY, ARKANSAS CHAPTER 353
STATE GOVERNMENT ORGANIZATIONS
ARKANSAS COOPERATIVE RESEARCH UNIT 43
ARKANSAS DEPARTMENT OF PARKS AND TOURISM 43
ARKANSAS GAME AND FISH COMMISSION 43
ARKANSAS STATE EXTENSION SERVICES 44
DEPARTMENT OF ENVIRONMENTAL QUALITY
(ARKANSAS) 44
FORESTRY COMMISSION (ARKANSAS) 44
GOVERNOR OF ARKANSAS, MIKE HUCKABEE 43
NATURAL AND SCENIC RIVERS COMMISSION
(ARKANSAS) 45
NATURAL HERITAGE COMMISSION (ARKANSAS) 45
PINE BLUFF COOPERATIVE FISHERY RESEARCH
PROJECT 45
STATE PLANT BOARD (ARKANSAS) 45

CALIFORNIA
GOVERNMENT ORGANIZATIONS
INTER-AMERICAN TROPICAL TUNA COMMISSION 8
ENVIRONMENTAL PROTECTION AGENCY 10
DEPARTMENT OF THE ARMY
U.S. ARMY CORPS OF ENGINEERS 21
DEPARTMENT OF THE INTERIOR
BUREAU OF RECLAMATION 24
UNITED STATES FISH AND WILDLIFE SERVICE 26
U.S. DEPARTMENT OF AGRICULTURE
ANIMAL AND PLANT HEALTH INSPECTION SERVICE.. 29
RESEARCH EDUCATION AND ECONOMICS 32
UNITED STATES FOREST SERVICE 32
U.S. TREASURY DEPARTMENT
U.S. CUSTOMS SERVICE 33
NON-GOVERNMENTAL ORGANIZATIONS
ACTION FOR NATURE, INC. 133
AMERICAN CETACEAN SOCIETY 141
AMERICAN FISHERIES SOCIETY, CALIFORNIA-NEVADA
CHAPTER 145
AMERICAN FISHERIES SOCIETY, HUMBOLDT CHAPTER
.... 146
AMERICAN LAND CONSERVANCY 151
AMERICAN OCEANS CAMPAIGN 153
AMERICAN SOCIETY OF ZOOLOGISTS 156
ANCIENT FOREST INTERNATIONAL 157
ANIMAL PROTECTION INSTITUTE 157
BIO-INTEGRAL RESOURCE CENTER 166
CALIFORNIA ACADEMY OF SCIENCES 45,
CALIFORNIA ASSOCIATION OF RESOURCE
CONSERVATION DISTRICTS 169
CALIFORNIA B.A.S.S. CHAPTER FEDERATION 169
CALIFORNIA NATIVE PLANT SOCIETY (CNDS) 169
CALIFORNIA NATIVE PLANT SOCIETY, THE 169
CALIFORNIA TRAPPERS ASSOCIATION 170
CALIFORNIA TROUT, INC. 170
CALIFORNIA WATERFOWL ASSOCIATION 170

CALIFORNIA WILDLIFE DEFENDERS 170
CALIFORNIA WILDLIFE FEDERATION............................ 170
CALIFORNIANS FOR POPULATION STABILIZATION (CAPS)
.... 170
CENTER FOR SCIENCE INFORMATION 176
COALITION FOR CLEAN AIR 181
COMMUNITIES FOR A BETTER ENVIRONMENT 184
COMMUNITY ENVIRONMENTAL COUNCIL..................... 184
COOPER ORNITHOLOGICAL SOCIETY 189
CORAL REEF ALLIANCE, THE (CORAL)........................ 189
COUNCIL FOR PLANNING AND CONSERVATION 190
DESERT FISHES COUNCIL.. 193
DESERT TORTOISE COUNCIL 193
DESERT TORTOISE PRESERVE COMMITTEE, INC. 193
EARTH ISLAND INSTITUTE.. 197
EARTHJUSTICE LEGAL DEFENSE FUND (formerly Sierra
  Club Legal Defense Fund, Inc.) 198
ECOLOGY CENTER 199
EDUCATIONAL COMMUNICATIONS, INC....................... 200
ENVIRONMENTAL DEFENSE CENTER, INC. 201
ENVIRONMENTAL DEFENSE FUND, INC.
  West Coast Office 202
ENVIRONMENTAL MEDIA ASSOCIATION 204
FOREST LANDOWNERS OF CALIFORNIA 209
FOSSIL FUELS POLICY ACTION INSTITUTE/ALLIANCE
  FOR A PAVING MORATORIUM 210
FRIENDS OF THE RIVER 212
FRIENDS OF THE SEA OTTER 212
GLOBAL CITIES PROJECT, THE.................................... 215
HEADLANDS INSTITUTE.. 221
INTERNATIONAL ASSOCIATION FOR BEAR RESEARCH
  AND MANAGEMENT 228
INTERNATIONAL CENTER FOR EARTH CONCERNS..... 229
INTERNATIONAL CENTER FOR GIBBON STUDIES........ 229
INTERNATIONAL MARINE MAMMAL PROJECT, THE 231
INTERNATIONAL RIVERS NETWORK 232
INTERNATIONAL SOCIETY FOR THE PRESERVATION OF
  THE TROPICAL RAINFOREST, THE 233
INTERNATIONAL WILDERNESS LEADERSHIP (WILD)
  FOUNDATION 235
INTERNATIONAL WILDLIFE REHABILITATION COUNCIL
  (IWRC) 236
LEAGUE TO SAVE LAKE TAHOE 248
LIGHTHAWK 248
MAGIC 250
MARIN CONSERVATION LEAGUE.................................. 251
MARINE MAMMAL CENTER, THE.................................. 252
MONO LAKE COMMITTEE 259
MOUNT SHASTA AREA AUDUBON SOCIETY 261
MOUNTAIN LION FOUNDATION 261
NATIONAL FIELD ARCHERY ASSOCIATION 267
NATIONAL PARKS AND CONSERVATION ASSOCIATION
  (NPCA)
  Pacific Regional Office 270
NATIONAL TRUST FOR HISTORIC PRESERVATION
  Western
 2
  72
NATURAL RESOURCES DEFENSE COUNCIL, INC.
  Los Angeles, California Office 278
  San Francisco, California Office 278
NATURE CONSERVANCY, THE, CALIFORNIA CHAPTER280
NORTHCOAST ENVIRONMENTAL CENTER 291
PLANNING AND CONSERVATION LEAGUE................... 304
RAINFOREST ACTION NETWORK................................. 308
RESOURCE RENEWAL INSTITUTE, THE 310
SAVE SAN FRANCISCO BAY ASSOCIATION 315
SAVE-THE-REDWOODS LEAGUE 317
SEA SHEPHERD CONSERVATION SOCIETY.................. 318
  USA Office 318
SIERRA CLUB... 318
  Southern California/Nevada Branch 319
SIERRA CLUB FOUNDATION, THE................................ 319
SOCIETY FOR MARINE MAMMALOGY, THE................... 321
SOCIETY FOR THE PRESERVATION OF BIRDS OF PREY
  322
STANFORD ENVIRONMENTAL LAW SOCIETY 327

THREE CIRCLES CENTER FOR MULTICULTURAL
  ENVIRONMENTAL EDUCATION................................... 332
TREE PEOPLE.. 332
TROUT UNLIMITED, CALIFORNIA COUNCIL................... 334
TRUST FOR PUBLIC LAND, THE 337
URBAN HABITAT PROGRAM 340
WILDLIFE SOCIETY, CALIFORNIA CENTRAL COAST
  CHAPTER 353
WILDLIFE SOCIETY, CALIFORNIA NORTH COAST
  CHAPTER 353
WILDLIFE SOCIETY, SACRAMENTO-SHASTA CHAPTER356
WILDLIFE SOCIETY, SAN FRANCISCO BAY AREA
  CHAPTER 357
WILDLIFE SOCIETY, SAN JOAQUIN VALLEY CHAPTER 357
WILDLIFE SOCIETY, SOUTHERN CALIFORNIA CHAPTER
  357
WILDLIFE WAYSTATION.. 358
WORLD PHEASANT ASSOCIATION OF U.S.A. INC......... 362
YOSEMITE RESTORATION TRUST 365
STATE GOVERNMENT ORGANIZATIONS
CA DEPARTMENT OF EDUCATION, OFFICE OF
  ENVIRONMENTAL EDUCATION..................................... 45
CALIFORNIA ACADEMY OF SCIENCES
  California Academy of Sciences Library 45
CALIFORNIA COOPERATIVE FISHERY RESEARCH UNIT
  (USGS).. 45
CALIFORNIA ENVIRONMENTAL PROTECTION AGENCY. 45
  California Air Resources Board 46
  Department of Pesticide Regulation 46
  Department of Toxic Substances Control 46
  Integrated Waste Management Board, IWMB................... 46
  Office of Environmental Health Hazard Assessment......... 46
  Water Resources Control Board...................................... 46
CALIFORNIA SEA GRANT COLLEGE SYSTEM 46
CALIFORNIA STATE EXTENSION SERVICES 47
DEPARTMENT OF FOOD AND AGRICULTURE
  (CALIFORNIA)... 47
GOVERNOR OF CALIFORNIA, GRAY DAVIS..................... 45
RESOURCES AGENCY, THE 47
  California Coastal Commission.. 47
  California Coastal Conservancy 47
  California Conservation Corps... 48
  California Energy Commission 48
  California Water Commission 48
  Colorado River Board of California 48
  Department of Boating and Waterways 48
                                    Department of Conservation
 48
  Department of Fish and Game 48
  Department of Forestry and Fire Protection 49
  Department of Parks and Recreation............................... 49
  Department of Water Resources 49
  Fish and Game Commission 49
  Native American Heritage Commission 49
  San Francisco Bay Conservation and Development
  Commission 49
  State Reclamation Board 49
  Wildlife Conservation Board 50
STATE LANDS COMMISSION (CALIFORNIA) 50
COLORADO
GOVERNMENT ORGANIZATIONS
ENVIRONMENTAL PROTECTION AGENCY.................... 10
DEPARTMENT OF THE AIR FORCE
  MAJOR AIR COMMANDS 16
DEPARTMENT OF THE INTERIOR
  BUREAU OF LAND MANAGEMENT................................ 24
  BUREAU OF RECLAMATION.. 24
  UNITED STATES FISH AND WILDLIFE SERVICE 26
U.S. DEPARTMENT OF AGRICULTURE
  RESEARCH EDUCATION AND ECONOMICS................. 32
  UNITED STATES FOREST SERVICE 32
NON-GOVERNMENTAL ORGANIZATIONS
AMERICAN BIRDING ASSOCIATION 141
AMERICAN HUMANE ASSOCIATION.............................. 151
AMERICAN WATER WORKS ASSOCIATION (AWWA)..... 156
AMERICAN WILDLANDS 156

GEOGRAPHIC INDEX

ASSOCIATION OF MIDWEST FISH AND GAME LAW ENFORCEMENT OFFICERS.................................. 162
BIODIVERSITY LEGAL FOUNDATION 166
CADDO LAKE INSTITUTE, INC... 169
COLORADO ASSOCIATION OF SOIL CONSERVATION DISTRICTS.. 182
COLORADO B.A.S.S. CHAPTER FEDERATION............... 182
COLORADO ENVIRONMENTAL COALITION 182
COLORADO FORESTRY ASSOCIATION 182
COLORADO NATURAL HERITAGE PROGRAM............... 182
COLORADO TRAPPERS ASSOCIATION 183
COLORADO WATER CONGRESS 183
COLORADO WILDLIFE FEDERATION 183
COLORADO WILDLIFE HERITAGE FOUNDATION 183
EARTHJUSTICE LEGAL DEFENSE FUND (formerly Sierra Club Legal Defense Fund, Inc.)
   Rocky Mountain Office 198
EARTHLAW 198
ENVIRONMENTAL DEFENSE FUND, INC.
   Rocky Mountain Office 202
INTERNATIONAL EROSION CONTROL ASSOCIATION (IECA)... 230
INTERNATIONAL HUNTER EDUCATION ASSOCIATION 231
IZAAK WALTON LEAGUE OF AMERICA, INC., THE
   Colorado Division 240
KEYSTONE CENTER, THE... 245
LIGHTHAWK
   Rocky Mountain Field Office.. 249
NATIONAL ASSOCIATION FOR INTERPRETATION 262
NATIONAL ENVIRONMENTAL HEALTH ASSOCIATION .. 267
NATIONAL FARMERS UNION 267
NATIONAL ORGANIZATION FOR RIVERS (NORS) 269
NATIONAL PARKS AND CONSERVATION ASSOCIATION (NPCA)
   Rocky Mountain Regional Office 270
NATIONAL TRUST FOR HISTORIC PRESERVATION
   Mountains and Plains 272
NATIONAL WILDLIFE FEDERATION
   Rocky Mountain Natural Resource Center (AZ, CO, NM, UT) 274
NATIVE AMERICAN FISH AND WILDLIFE SOCIETY (NAFWS) 276
NATURE CONSERVANCY OF COLORADO, THE 279
NATURE CONSERVANCY, THE
   Western Region Office 279
NATURE CONSERVANCY, THE, COLORADO CHAPTER 280
NORTH AMERICAN WOLF SOCIETY 289
RAPTOR EDUCATION FOUNDATION INC. 309
RIVER OTTER ALLIANCE, THE... 312
ROCKY MOUNTAIN BIGHORN SOCIETY 313
SINAPU.. 319
SOCIETY FOR RANGE MANAGEMENT 321
THORNE ECOLOGICAL INSTITUTE................................... 331
TROUT UNLIMITED, COLORADO COUNCIL..................... 334
WILDERNESS EDUCATION ASSOCIATION..................... 349
WILDERNESS LAND TRUST, THE (Colorado Office)........ 349
WILDLIFE SOCIETY, COLORADO CHAPTER 354
WINDSTAR FOUNDATION, THE 359
YELLOWSTONE GRIZZLY FOUNDATION (YGF) 364

STATE GOVERNMENT ORGANIZATIONS
COLORADO COOPERATIVE FISH AND WILDLIFE RESEARCH UNIT (USDI)... 50
COLORADO DEPARTMENT OF AGRICULTURE 50
COLORADO DEPARTMENT OF EDUCATION..................... 50
COLORADO DEPARTMENT OF NATURAL RESOURCES. 50
   Colorado Geologic Survey 50
   Division of Minerals and Geology 50
   Division of Parks and Outdoor Recreation 50
   Division of Water Resources 51
   Division of Wildlife.. 51
   Oil and Gas Conservation Commission 51
   Soil Conservation Board... 51
   State Board of Land 51
   Water Conservation Board 51
COLORADO DEPARTMENT OF PUBLIC HEALTH AND ENVIRONMENT 51
COLORADO STATE COOPERATIVE EXTENSION............. 51
COLORADO STATE FOREST SERVICE 51
GOVERNOR OF COLORADO, BILL OWENS...................... 50

CONNECTICUT
NON-GOVERNMENTAL ORGANIZATIONS
AMERICAN BASS ASSOCIATION OF CONNECTICUT, THE 140
AMERICAN FISHERIES SOCIETY
   Northeastern Division.. 144
AMERICAN PIE (PUBLIC INFORMATION ON THE ENVIRONMENT) 153
AUDUBON COUNCIL OF CONNECTICUT......................... 163
BERKSHIRE-LITCHFIELD ENVIRONMENTAL COUNCIL, INC... 165
CETACEAN SOCIETY INTERNATIONAL............................ 177
CONNECTICUT ASSOCIATION OF SOIL AND WATER CONSERVATION DISTRICTS, INC. 185
CONNECTICUT AUDUBON SOCIETY, INC. 185
CONNECTICUT B.A.S.S. CHAPTER FEDERATION 185
CONNECTICUT BOTANICAL SOCIETY.............................. 185
CONNECTICUT FOREST AND PARK ASSOCIATION...... 186
CONNECTICUT FUND FOR THE ENVIRONMENT 186
CONNECTICUT PUBLIC INTEREST RESEARCH GROUP (ConnPIRG) 186
CONNECTICUT WATERFOWL ASSOCIATION, INC. 186
E-P EDUCATION SERVICES, INC. 196
FRIENDS OF ANIMALS INC.. 211
KEEP AMERICA BEAUTIFUL, INC....................................... 244
NATIONAL SHOOTING SPORTS FOUNDATION, INC...... 271
NATURE CONSERVANCY, THE, CONNECTICUT CHAPTER 280
SAVE THE SOUND, INC... 316
TROUT UNLIMITED, CONNECTICUT COUNCIL 334
WILDLIFE SOCIETY, NEW ENGLAND CHAPTER 356

STATE GOVERNMENT ORGANIZATIONS
CONNECTICUT DEPARTMENT OF AGRICULTURE........... 51
COUNCIL ON ENVIRONMENTAL QUALITY (CONNECTICUT) 52
DEPARTMENT OF ENVIRONMENTAL PROTECTION (CONNECTICUT) 52
GOVERNOR OF CONNECTICUT, JOHN G. ROWLAND..... 51
UNIVERSITY OF CONNECTICUT COOPERATIVE EXTENSION.. 52

DELAWARE
GOVERNMENT ORGANIZATIONS
DEPARTMENT OF THE INTERIOR
   UNITED STATES FISH AND WILDLIFE SERVICE 26

NON-GOVERNMENTAL ORGANIZATIONS
CHRISTINA CONSERVANCY, INC. 179
COALITION FOR NATURAL STREAM VALLEYS, INC...... 181
DELAWARE ASSOCIATION OF CONSERVATION DISTRICTS.. 191
DELAWARE AUDUBON SOCIETY....................................... 191
DELAWARE B.A.S.S. CHAPTER FEDERATION 191
DELAWARE FORESTRY ASSOCIATION............................ 192
DELAWARE GREENWAYS, INC.. 192
DELAWARE MUSEUM OF NATURAL HISTORY 192
DELAWARE NATURE SOCIETY.. 192
DELAWARE WILD LANDS, INC. 192
DELMARVA ORNITHOLOGICAL SOCIETY 192
HUMMINGBIRD SOCIETY, THE 223
MID-ATLANTIC FISHERY MANAGEMENT COUNCIL....... 256
NATURE CONSERVANCY, THE, DELAWARE CHAPTER 280
SAVE WETLANDS AND BAYS... 316
TRI-STATE BIRD RESCUE AND RESEARCH, INC........... 333
TROUT UNLIMITED, DELAWARE STATE COUNCIL........ 334

STATE GOVERNMENT ORGANIZATIONS
DELAWARE DEPARTMENT OF AGRICULTURE................. 52
DELAWARE DEPARTMENT OF NATURAL RESOURCES AND ENVIRONMENTAL CONTROL................................ 52
   Division of Air and Waste Management............................ 52
   Division of Fish and Wildlife.. 53
   Division of Parks and Recreation....................................... 53
   Division of Water Resources 53
DELAWARE DEPARTMENT OF NATURAL RESOURCES AND ENVIRONMENTAL CONTROL
   Division of Soil and Water Conservation............................ 53
DELAWARE GEOLOGICAL SURVEY 53
DELAWARE SEA GRANT PROGRAM 53

DELAWARE SOLID WASTE AUTHORITY 53
DELAWARE STATE EXTENSION SERVICE 53
GOVERNOR OF DELAWARE, THOMAS R. CARPER 52
DISTRICT OF COLUMBIA
GOVERNMENT ORGANIZATIONS
HOUSE COMMITTEE ON RESOURCES 4
HOUSE COMMITTEE ON AGRICULTURE 4
HOUSE COMMITTEE ON APPROPRIATIONS 5
HOUSE COMMITTEE ON COMMERCE 5
HOUSE COMMITTEE ON EDUCATION AND THE
   WORKFORCE 5
HOUSE COMMITTEE ON INTERNATIONAL RELATIONS 5
HOUSE COMMITTEE ON RULES 5
HOUSE COMMITTEE ON TRANSPORTATION AND
   INFRASTRUCTURE 5
SENATE COMMITTEE ON AGRICULTURE, NUTRITION,
   AND FORESTRY 5
SENATE COMMITTEE ON APPROPRIATIONS 6
SENATE COMMITTEE ON COMMERCE SCIENCE AND
   TRANSPORTATION 6
SENATE COMMITTEE ON ENERGY AND NATURAL
   RESOURCES 6
SENATE COMMITTEE ON ENVIRONMENT AND PUBLIC
   WORKS 6
SENATE COMMITTEE ON FOREIGN RELATIONS 6
SENATE COMMITTEE ON LABOR AND HUMAN
   RESOURCES 6
APPALACHIAN REGIONAL COMMISSION 7
ATLANTIC STATES MARINE FISHERIES COMMISSION . 7
INTERNATIONAL JOINT COMMISSION (Headquarters) ... 8
MIGRATORY BIRD CONSERVATION COMMISSION 8
COUNCIL ON ENVIRONMENTAL QUALITY 10
ENVIRONMENTAL PROTECTION AGENCY 10
ADVISORY COUNCIL ON HISTORIC PRESERVATION .. 34
GENERAL SERVICES ADMINISTRATION 34
NATIONAL TRANSPORTATION SAFETY BOARD 34
NUCLEAR REGULATORY COMMISSION 34
PEACE CORPS OF THE UNITED STATES 35
COUNCIL ON ENVIRONMENTAL QUALITY 52
DEPARTMENT OF COMMERCE 12
   ECONOMIC DEVELOPMENT ADMINISTRATION 12
   NATIONAL OCEANIC AND ATMOSPHERIC
      ADMINISTRATION 12
DEPARTMENT OF DEFENSE 13
DEPARTMENT OF EDUCATION 13
DEPARTMENT OF ENERGY 13
   FEDERAL ENERGY REGULATORY COMMISSION 14
DEPARTMENT OF HEALTH AND HUMAN SERVICES 14
DEPARTMENT OF HOUSING AND URBAN DEVELOPMENT
   15
DEPARTMENT OF JUSTICE 15
DEPARTMENT OF LABOR 15
   JOB CORPS 15
DEPARTMENT OF STATE 16
   BUREAU OF OCEANS AND INTERNATIONAL
      ENVIRONMENTAL AND SCIENTIFIC AFFAIRS 16
   UNITED STATES MAN AND THE BIOSPHERE PROGRAM
      (U.S. MAB) 16
DEPARTMENT OF THE AIR FORCE 16
   MAJOR AIR COMMANDS 16
DEPARTMENT OF THE ARMY 19
   U.S. ARMY CORPS OF ENGINEERS 21
DEPARTMENT OF THE ARMY CONSERVATION DIVISION
   ASSISTANT CHIEF OF STAFF FOR INSTALLATION
      MANAGEMENT 23
DEPARTMENT OF THE INTERIOR 23
   BUREAU OF INDIAN AFFAIRS 24
   BUREAU OF LAND MANAGEMENT 24
   BUREAU OF RECLAMATION 24
   NATIONAL PARK SERVICE 25
   OFFICE OF SURFACE MINING RECLAMATION AND
      ENFORCEMENT 25
   UNITED STATES FISH AND WILDLIFE SERVICE 26
DEPARTMENT OF THE NAVY 27
   U.S. MARINE CORPS 27
DEPARTMENT OF TRANSPORTATION 27
   FEDERAL AVIATION ADMINISTRATION 27
   FEDERAL HIGHWAY ADMINISTRATION 27
   FEDERAL RAILROAD ADMINISTRATION 28
   FEDERAL TRANSIT ADMINISTRATION 28
   NATIONAL HIGHWAY TRAFFIC SAFETY
      ADMINISTRATION 28
   SAINT LAWRENCE SEAWAY DEVELOPMENT
      CORPORATION 28
   U.S. COAST GUARD 28
U.S. DEPARTMENT OF AGRICULTURE 28
   ANIMAL AND PLANT HEALTH INSPECTION SERVICE .. 29
   ECONOMIC RESEARCH SERVICE 30
   NATURAL RESOURCES CONSERVATION SERVICE
      (formerly Soil Conservation Service) 30
   RESEARCH EDUCATION AND ECONOMICS 32
   UNITED STATES FOREST SERVICE 32
U.S. TREASURY DEPARTMENT 33
   U.S. CUSTOMS SERVICE 33
NON-GOVERNMENTAL ORGANIZATIONS
AFRICAN WILDLIFE FOUNDATION 134
AMERICA THE BEAUTIFUL FUND 138
AMERICAN ASSOCIATION FOR THE ADVANCEMENT OF
   SCIENCE 139
AMERICAN BIRD CONSERVANCY 140
AMERICAN CONSERVATION ASSOCIATION, INC. 141
AMERICAN COUNCIL FOR AN ENERGY-EFFICIENT
   ECONOMY 142
AMERICAN FARMLAND TRUST 142
AMERICAN FISHERIES SOCIETY
   Fisheries Law Section 143
AMERICAN FISHERIES SOCIETY, POTOMAC CHAPTER 148
AMERICAN FOREST FOUNDATION 150
AMERICAN FORESTS (formerly American Forestry
   Association) 150
AMERICAN HORSE PROTECTION ASSOCIATION 151
AMERICAN INSTITUTE OF BIOLOGICAL SCIENCES 151
AMERICAN LANDS (formerly Western Ancient Forest
   Campaign) 151
AMERICAN LEAGUE OF ANGLERS AND BOATERS 152
AMERICAN OCEANS CAMPAIGN (Washington DC Office) 153
AMERICAN ORNITHOLOGISTS' UNION 153
AMERICAN PLANNING ASSOCIATION 154
AMERICAN RECREATION COALITION 154
AMERICAN RIVERS (formerly American Rivers Conservation
   Council) 154
AMERICAN SOCIETY OF LANDSCAPE ARCHITECTS 155
AMERICANS FOR THE ENVIRONMENT 157
ANIMAL WELFARE INSTITUTE 158
ANTARCTICA PROJECT 158
ASSOCIATION OF AMERICAN GEOGRAPHERS 161
ASSOCIATION OF STATE AND TERRITORIAL HEALTH
   OFFICIALS 162
CANADA-UNITED STATES ENVIRONMENTAL COUNCIL
   (United States Office) 171
CARRYING CAPACITY NETWORK 174
CENTER FOR ENVIRONMENT 174
CENTER FOR INTERNATIONAL ENVIRONMENTAL LAW
   (CIEL) 175
CENTER FOR MARINE CONSERVATION 176
CENTER FOR RESOURCE ECONOMICS 176
CENTER FOR SCIENCE IN THE PUBLIC INTEREST 176
CIRCUMPOLAR CONSERVATION UNION 179
CLEAN WATER ACTION 180
CLEAN WATER FUND 180
CLEAN WATER NETWORK, THE 180
CLIMATE INSTITUTE 180
COAST ALLIANCE 181
COMMITTEE FOR THE NATIONAL INSTITUTE FOR THE
   ENVIRONMENT (CNIE) 183
COMMITTEE ON AGRICULTURAL SUSTAINABILITY FOR
   DEVELOPING COUNTRIES 184
COMMUNITY RIGHTS COUNSEL 184
CONCERN, INC. 184
CONSERVATION INTERNATIONAL 188
DEFENDERS OF WILDLIFE 191
DISTRICT OF COLUMBIA SOIL AND WATER
   CONSERVATION DISTRICT 193
EARTH SHARE 197

GEOGRAPHIC INDEX

EARTHJUSTICE LEGAL DEFENSE FUND (formerly Sierra Club Legal Defense Fund, Inc.)
  Washington, DC Office 198
ECOLOGICAL SOCIETY OF AMERICA, THE 199
ENDANGERED SPECIES COALITION 200
ENVIRONMENTAL AND ENERGY STUDY INSTITUTE (EESI) 201
ENVIRONMENTAL DEFENSE FUND, INC.
  Capital Office 202
ENVIRONMENTAL LAW INSTITUTE, THE 203
FRIENDS OF THE EARTH 211
GENERAL FEDERATION OF WOMEN'S CLUBS 213
GLOBAL ENVIRONMENTAL MANAGEMENT INITIATIVE (GEMI) 215
GRAND CANYON TRUST (Washington, DC Office) 216
GREEN SEAL 218
GREENPEACE, INC. 219
H. JOHN HEINZ III CENTER FOR SCIENCE, ECONOMICS, AND THE ENVIRONMENT 219
HUMANE SOCIETY OF THE UNITED STATES, THE 222
INTERNATIONAL ASSOCIATION OF FISH AND WILDLIFE AGENCIES 228
INTERNATIONAL INSTITUTE FOR ENERGY CONSERVATION 231
INTERNATIONAL UNION FOR CONSERVATION OF NATURE AND NATURAL RESOURCES (IUCN) THE WORLD CONSERVATION UNION
  Outposted Office 235
  U.S. Office, Washington, DC 235
ISLAND RESOURCES FOUNDATION 239
  Washington, DC Office 239
KEYSTONE CENTER, THE (Washington, D.C. Office) 246
LAND TRUST ALLIANCE, THE 247
LEAGUE OF CONSERVATION VOTERS 247
LEAGUE OF WOMEN VOTERS OF THE U.S. 247
MARINE TECHNOLOGY SOCIETY 252
MINERAL POLICY CENTER 256
NATIONAL ASSOCIATION OF CONSERVATION DISTRICTS 263
NATIONAL ASSOCIATION OF ENVIRONMENTAL PROFESSIONALS, THE (National Office) 263
NATIONAL ASSOCIATION OF SERVICE AND CONSERVATION CORPS (NASCC) 264
NATIONAL ASSOCIATION OF STATE DEPARTMENTS OF AGRICULTURE 264
NATIONAL ASSOCIATION OF STATE FORESTERS 264
NATIONAL AUDUBON SOCIETY
  Washington, D.C. Office 265
NATIONAL COALITION AGAINST THE MISUSE OF PESTICIDES 266
NATIONAL EDUCATION ASSOCIATION 267
NATIONAL FISH AND WILDLIFE FOUNDATION 267
NATIONAL FOREST FOUNDATION 268
NATIONAL GEOGRAPHIC SOCIETY 268
NATIONAL GRANGE, THE 269
NATIONAL PARK FOUNDATION 269
NATIONAL PARK TRUST 270
NATIONAL PARKS AND CONSERVATION ASSOCIATION (NPCA) 270
NATIONAL RESEARCH COUNCIL 271
NATIONAL TREE TRUST 272
NATIONAL TRUST FOR HISTORIC PRESERVATION 272
NATIONAL WATERWAYS CONFERENCE INC. 273
NATIONAL WHISTLEBLOWER CENTER 273
NATIONAL WILDLIFE FEDERATION
  Office of Federal and International Affairs 274
NATIONAL WILDLIFE REFUGE ASSOCIATION 275
NATURAL RESOURCES COUNCIL OF AMERICA 278
NATURAL RESOURCES DEFENSE COUNCIL, INC.
  Washington, D.C. Office 278
NORTH AMERICAN ASSOCIATION FOR ENVIRONMENTAL EDUCATION 288
NORTH AMERICAN COALITION ON RELIGION AND ECOLOGY (NACRE) 288
ORNITHOLOGICAL COUNCIL 299
OZONE ACTION 300
PANOS INSTITUTE, THE 301
PARTNERS IN PARKS 301
PHYSICIANS FOR SOCIAL RESPONSIBILITY 303
PINCHOT INSTITUTE FOR CONSERVATION 303
POPULATION ACTION INTERNATIONAL 304
POPULATION INSTITUTE, THE 305
POPULATION REFERENCE BUREAU INC. 305
POPULATION-ENVIRONMENT BALANCE INC. 305
PUBLIC EMPLOYEES FOR ENVIRONMENTAL RESPONSIBILITY (PEER) 306
RAILS-TO-TRAILS CONSERVANCY 308
RAINBOW PUSH COALITION 308
RENEW AMERICA 310
RESOURCES FOR THE FUTURE 310
RIVER NETWORK
  Eastern Office 312
SAFE ENERGY COMMUNICATION COUNCIL 315
SAVE AMERICA'S FORESTS 315
SCENIC AMERICA 317
SIERRA CLUB
  Washington, DC Office 332
SMITHSONIAN INSTITUTION 320
  National Museum of Natural History 320
  National Zoological Park 320
  Office of Fellowships and Grants 320
  Office of International Relations 320
  Smithsonian Press/Smithsonian Productions 320
SOCIETY FOR ANIMAL PROTECTIVE LEGISLATION 320
SOUTHERN UTAH WILDERNESS ALLIANCE (Washington, DC Office) 326
STUDENT PUGWASH USA 328
TRAFFIC USA 332
TROUT UNLIMITED, NATIONAL CAPITAL COUNCIL 335
U.S. PUBLIC INTEREST RESEARCH GROUP 339
UNITED STATES CHAMBER OF COMMERCE 339
UNITED STATES COMMITTEE FOR THE UNITED NATIONS ENVIRONMENT PROGRAMME THE (U.S. and UNEP). 339
UNITED STATES TOURIST COUNCIL 339
WILDERNESS SOCIETY, THE 349
WILDLIFE LEGISLATIVE FUND OF AMERICA, THE, AND WILDLIFE CONSERVATION FUND OF AMERICA, THE
  Washington, D.C.National Affairs Office 352
WILDLIFE MANAGEMENT INSTITUTE 352
WILDLIFE SOCIETY, NATIONAL CAPITAL CHAPTER 355
WORLD RESOURCES INSTITUTE 362
WORLD WILDLIFE FUND 363
WORLD WOMEN IN THE DEFENSE OF THE ENVIRONMENT 363
WORLDWATCH INSTITUTE 363
ZERO POPULATION GROWTH INC. 365

STATE GOVERNMENT ORGANIZATIONS
DEPARTMENT OF HEALTH, Environmental Health Administration, (District of Columbia) 53
DEPARTMENT OF PUBLIC WORKS 53
DISTRICT OF COLUMBIA STATE EXTENSION SERVICES 54

FLORIDA
GOVERNMENT ORGANIZATIONS
DEPARTMENT OF THE AIR FORCE 16
  MAJOR AIR COMMANDS 16
DEPARTMENT OF THE ARMY
  U.S. ARMY CORPS OF ENGINEERS 21
U.S. TREASURY DEPARTMENT
  U.S CUSTOMS SERVICE 33

NON-GOVERNMENTAL ORGANIZATIONS
1000 FRIENDS OF FLORIDA 133
AMERICAN FISHERIES SOCIETY, FLORIDA CHAPTER . 145
AMERICAN LITTORAL SOCIETY (Coral Reef Conservation Center Office) 152
ARCHBOLD BIOLOGICAL STATION 159
ARCHERY MANUFACTURERS AND MERCHANTS ORGANIZATION (AMO) 159
ASSOCIATION OF AVIAN VETERINARIANS 161
BARRIER ISLAND TRUST, INC. 165
BILLFISH FOUNDATION 166
CARIBBEAN CONSERVATION CORPORATION 173
CONSERVANCY OF SOUTHWEST FLORIDA, THE 186
EARTHJUSTICE LEGAL DEFENSE FUND (formerly Sierra Club Legal Defense Fund, Inc.)
  Florida Office 187

EVERGLADES COORDINATING COUNCIL (ECC) 204
FLORIDA ASSOCIATION OF SOIL AND WATER
    CONSERVATION DISTRICTS 206
FLORIDA AUDUBON SOCIETY 206
FLORIDA B.A.S.S. CHAPTER FEDERATION 207
FLORIDA CONSERVATION FOUNDATION, INC. 207
FLORIDA DEFENDERS OF THE ENVIRONMENT, INC.
    (Home Office) 207
FLORIDA EXOTIC PEST PLANT COUNCIL 207
FLORIDA FORESTRY ASSOCIATION 207
FLORIDA NATIVE PLANT SOCIETY 207
FLORIDA ORNITHOLOGICAL SOCIETY 208
FLORIDA PANTHER PROJECT, INC., THE 208
FLORIDA PUBLIC INTEREST RESEARCH GROUP (Florida
    PIRG) 208
FLORIDA SPORTSMEN'S CONSERVATION ASSOCIATION
    208
FLORIDA TRAIL ASSOCIATION, INC. 208
FLORIDA WILDLIFE FEDERATION 208
GAME CONSERVANCY U.S.A. (formerly American Friends of
    the Game Conservancy) 213
GOPHER TORTOISE COUNCIL 216
GULF OF MEXICO FISHERY MANAGEMENT COUNCIL .. 219
INTERNATIONAL GAME FISH ASSOCIATION 231
INTERNATIONAL OCEANOGRAPHIC FOUNDATION 231
INTERNATIONAL OSPREY FOUNDATION INC., THE 232
ISLAND CONSERVATION EFFORT 239
IZAAK WALTON LEAGUE OF AMERICA, INC., THE
    Florida Division 240
J.N. (DING) DARLING FOUNDATION 241
KEEP FLORIDA BEAUTIFUL, INC. 244
LEGAL ENVIRONMENTAL ASSISTANCE FOUNDATION INC.
    (LEAF) 248
MANASOTA-88 251
MOTE MARINE LABORATORY 261
NATIONAL AUDUBON SOCIETY
    Everglades Campaign Office 265
    Tavernier Science Center 265
NATIONAL WILDLIFE FEDERATION
    Everglades Project Office 274
NATURE CONSERVANCY, THE, FLORIDA CHAPTER 280
RAINFOREST TRUST INC., THE 309
REEF RELIEF 310
SANIBEL-CAPTIVA CONSERVATION FOUNDATION, INC.
    315
SAVE THE MANATEE CLUB 316
SMITHSONIAN INSTITUTION
    Smithsonian Marine Station at Link Port 320
    Smithsonian Tropical Research Institute 320
SOUTHEASTERN FISHES COUNCIL 325
SUNCOAST SEABIRD SANCTUARY INC. 328
TALL TIMBERS RESEARCH INC. 329
TALLAHASSEE MUSEUM OF HISTORY AND NATURAL
    SCIENCE 329
TROUT UNLIMITED, NORTH FLORIDA COUNCIL 336
TROUT UNLIMITED, SOUTH FLORIDA CHAPTER 336
WILDLIFE FOUNDATION OF FLORIDA, INC. 352
WILDLIFE SOCIETY, FLORIDA CHAPTER 354
STATE GOVERNMENT ORGANIZATIONS
FLORIDA COOPERATIVE FISH AND WILDLIFE RESEARCH
    UNIT (USDI) 54
FLORIDA DEPARTMENT OF AGRICULTURE AND
    CONSUMER SERVICES 54
    Division of Forestry 54
    Office of Agricultural Water Policy 54
    Soil and Water Conservation Board 54
FLORIDA DEPARTMENT OF ENVIRONMENTAL
    PROTECTION 54
    Air Resources Management Division 54
    Beaches and Shores Division 54
    Ecosytem Management Division 54
    Environmental Resource Permitting Division 55
    Law Enforcement Division 55
    Legislative and Cabinet Affairs Division 55
    Marine Resource Division 55
    Recreation and Parks division 55
    State Lands Division 55

Waste Management Division 55
    Water Facilities Division 55
FLORIDA GAME AND FRESH WATER FISH COMMISSION
    55
FLORIDA SEA GRANT COLLEGE 55
FLORIDA STATE COOPERATIVE EXTENSION SERVICE . 56
FLORIDA STATE DEPARTMENT OF HEALTH 56
GOVERNOR OF FLORIDA, JEB BUSH 54
LEE COUNTY PARKS AND RECREATION SERVICES 56
MARINE LABORATORY (FLORIDA) 56
SOUTH FLORIDA WATER MANAGEMENT DISTRICT 56
SOUTHWEST FLORIDA WATER MANAGEMENT DISTRICT
    (SWFWMD) 56
GEORGIA
GOVERNMENT ORGANIZATIONS
ENVIRONMENTAL PROTECTION AGENCY 10
DEPARTMENT OF THE AIR FORCE
    MAJOR AIR COMMANDS 16
DEPARTMENT OF THE ARMY
    U.S. ARMY CORPS OF ENGINEERS 21
    U.S. ARMY FORCES COMMAND 23
DEPARTMENT OF THE INTERIOR
    UNITED STATES FISH AND WILDLIFE SERVICE 26
U.S. DEPARTMENT OF AGRICULTURE
    RESEARCH EDUCATION AND ECONOMICS 32
    UNITED STATES FOREST SERVICE 32
NON-GOVERNMENTAL ORGANIZATIONS
AMERICAN FISHERIES SOCIETY, GEORGIA CHAPTER 145
CAMPAIGN FOR A PROSPEROUS GEORGIA 171
FOREST LANDOWNERS ASSOCIATION, INC. 209
FOREST OWNERS ASSOCIATION (GEORGIA) 209
GEORGIA ASSOCIATION OF CONSERVATION DISTRICT
    SUPERVISORS 214
GEORGIA B.A.S.S. CHAPTER FEDERATION 214
GEORGIA CONSERVANCY, INC., THE 214
GEORGIA ENVIRONMENTAL COUNCIL, INC. 214
GEORGIA ENVIRONMENTAL ORGANIZATION, INC (GEO)
    215
GEORGIA FORESTRY ASSOCIATION, INC. 215
GEORGIA TRAPPERS ASSOCIATION 215
GEORGIA WILDLIFE FEDERATION 215
HUMAN ECOLOGY ACTION LEAGUE INC. THE (HEAL) .. 222
INTERFAITH COUNCIL FOR THE PROTECTION OF
    ANIMALS AND NATURE INC. (ICPAN) 227
NATIONAL WILDLIFE FEDERATION
    Southeastern Natural Resource Center (AL, FL, GA, NC,
    SC, TN, VI) 275
NATURAL SCIENCE FOR YOUTH FOUNDATION 278
SOUTHEASTERN COOPERATIVE WILDLIFE DISEASE
    STUDY 325
SOUTHFACE ENERGY INSTITUTE 326
TROUT UNLIMITED, GEORGIA COUNCIL 334
WILDLIFE SOCIETY, GEORGIA CHAPTER 354
STATE GOVERNMENT ORGANIZATIONS
GEORGIA COOPERATIVE FISH AND WILDLIFE RESEARCH
    UNIT (USDI) 57
GEORGIA DEPARTMENT OF AGRICULTURE 57
    Consumers Services Library 57
GEORGIA DEPARTMENT OF EDUCATION 57
GEORGIA DEPARTMENT OF NATURAL RESOURCES 57
    Coastal Resources Division 57
    Environmental Protection Division 57
    Historic Preservation Division 57
    Parks, Recreation and Historic Sites Division 57
    Pollution Prevention Assistance Division 57
    Program Support Division 57
    Wildlife Resources Division 57
GEORGIA FORESTRY COMMISSION 57
GEORGIA SEA GRANT COLLEGE PROGRAM 58
GEORGIA STATE EXTENSION SERVICES 58
GOVERNOR OF GEORGIA, ROY BARNES 57
STATE SOIL AND WATER CONSERVATION COMMISSION
    (GEORGIA) 58
GUAM
NON-GOVERNMENTAL ORGANIZATIONS
PACIFIC BASIN ASSOCIATION OF SOIL AND WATER
    CONSERVATION DISTRICTS 300

GEOGRAPHIC INDEX

STATE GOVERNMENT ORGANIZATIONS
DEPARTMENT OF PARKS AND RECREATION (GUAM).... 58
DIVISION OF FORESTRY AND SOIL RESOURCES (GUAM) 58
    GOVERNOR OF GUAM, CARL T.C. GUTIERREZ............. 58
    GUAM COASTAL MANAGEMENT PROGRAM 58
    GUAM DEPARTMENT OF AGRICULTURE......................... 58
        Division of Aquatic and Wildlife Resources 58
    GUAM ENVIRONMENTAL PROTECTION AGENCY 59
    GUAM EXTENSION SERVICE 59
    GUAM SEA GRANT PROGRAM 59

HAWAII
GOVERNMENT ORGANIZATIONS
DEPARTMENT OF THE AIR FORCE
    MAJOR AIR COMMANDS 16
DEPARTMENT OF THE ARMY
    U.S. ARMY CORPS OF ENGINEERS.............................. 21
NON-GOVERNMENTAL ORGANIZATIONS
AMERICAN FISHERIES SOCIETY, HAWAII CHAPTER.... 146
CONSERVATION COUNCIL FOR HAWAII........................ 187
EARTHJUSTICE LEGAL DEFENSE FUND (formerly Sierra
    Club Legal Defense Fund, Inc.)
    Hawaii Office.. 198
EARTHTRUST 199
HAWAII ASSOCIATION OF CONSERVATION DISTRICTS 219
HAWAII AUDUBON SOCIETY.. 219
HAWAII NATURE CENTER... 220
HAWAII SOCIETY OF AMERICAN FORESTERS.............. 220
HAWAIIAN BOTANICAL SOCIETY....................................... 220
LIFE OF THE LAND 248
NATURE CONSERVANCY, THE
    Pacific Office.. 279
NATURE CONSERVANCY, THE, ASIA/PACIFIC PROGRAM
.... 280
NATURE CONSERVANCY, THE, HAWAII CHAPTER........ 280
OUTDOOR CIRCLE, THE 299
PACIFIC WHALE FOUNDATION.. 301
WESTERN PACIFIC REGIONAL FISHERY MANAGEMENT
    COUNCIL 347
WILDLIFE SOCIETY, HAWAII CHAPTER........................... 354
STATE GOVERNMENT ORGANIZATIONS
DEPARTMENT OF LAND AND NATURAL RESOURCES
    Division of Boating and Ocean Recreation (DOBOR......... 59
    Division of Water Resource Management,......................... 59
DEPARTMENT OF LAND AND NATURAL RESOURCES
    (HAWAII) 60
    Division of Aquatic Resources... 60
    Division of Conservation and Resources Enforcement...... 60
    Division of Forestry and Wildlife 60
    Division of Historic Preservation 60
    Division of State Parks 60
    Land Division 60
ENVIRONMENTAL CENTER... 60
GOVERNOR OF HAWAII, BENJAMIN CAYETANO............. 59
HAWAII COOPERATIVE FISHERY RESEARCH UNIT (USDI)
.... 60
HAWAII DEPARTMENT OF AGRICULTURE....................... 60
HAWAII DEPARTMENT OF HEALTH 60
INSTITUTE OF MARINE BIOLOGY...................................... 60
INSTITUTE OF TROPICAL AGRICULTURE AND HUMAN
    RESOURCES 61
WATER RESOURCES RESEARCH CENTER..................... 61

IDAHO
GOVERNMENT ORGANIZATIONS
DEPARTMENT OF THE INTERIOR
    BUREAU OF LAND MANAGEMENT................................ 24
    BUREAU OF RECLAMATION.. 24
NON-GOVERNMENTAL ORGANIZATIONS
AMERICAN FISHERIES SOCIETY
    Fish Health Section 143
AMERICAN FISHERIES SOCIETY, IDAHO CHAPTER 146
ENVIRONMENTAL RESOURCE CENTER (ERC) 204
IDAHO ASSOCIATION OF SOIL CONSERVATION
    DISTRICTS... 223
IDAHO B.A.S.S. CHAPTER FEDERATION......................... 223
IDAHO CONSERVATION LEAGUE 223
IDAHO ENVIRONMENTAL COUNCIL 223

IDAHO FOREST OWNERS ASSOCIATION 224
IDAHO WILDLIFE FEDERATION 224
NATURE CONSERVANCY, THE, IDAHO CHAPTER 280
NORTHWEST RESOURCE INFORMATION CENTER 293
PEREGRINE FUND, THE... 303
RAPTOR RESEARCH FOUNDATION, INC. 309
TROUT UNLIMITED, IDAHO COUNCIL.............................. 334
WILDLIFE SOCIETY, IDAHO CHAPTER 354
WOLF EDUCATION AND RESEARCH CENTER 360
STATE GOVERNMENT ORGANIZATIONS
DEPARTMENT OF LANDS (IDAHO) 61
DEPARTMENT OF WATER RESOURCES (IDAHO) 61
GOVERNOR OF IDAHO, DIRK KEMPTHORNE 61
IDAHO COOPERATIVE EXTENSION.................................... 61
IDAHO COOPERATIVE FISH AND WILDLIFE RESEARCH
    UNIT (USDI) 61
IDAHO DEPARTMENT OF PARKS AND RECREATION 61
IDAHO FISH AND GAME DEPARTMENT 61
IDAHO FISH AND WILDLIFE FOUNDATION....................... 62
IDAHO GEOLOGICAL SURVEY.. 62
IDAHO STATE DEPARTMENT OF AGRICULTURE 62
STATE OF IDAHO, DIVISION OF ENVIRONMENTAL
    QUALITY 62
STATE SOIL CONSERVATION COMMISSION (IDAHO)..... 62

ILLINOIS
GOVERNMENT ORGANIZATIONS
ENVIRONMENTAL PROTECTION AGENCY.................... 10
DEPARTMENT OF THE AIR FORCE
    MAJOR AIR COMMANDS 16
DEPARTMENT OF THE ARMY
    HQ ARMY MATERIAL COMMAND, INSTALLATIONS AND
        SERVICES ACTIVITY 20
    U.S. ARMY CONSTRUCTION ENGINEERING RESEARCH
        LABORATORIES CERL 21
    U.S. ARMY CORPS OF ENGINEERS............................. 21
U.S. DEPARTMENT OF AGRICULTURE
    RESEARCH EDUCATION AND ECONOMICS................ 32
U.S. TREASURY DEPARTMENT
    U.S. CUSTOMS SERVICE.. 33
NON-GOVERNMENTAL ORGANIZATIONS
AMERICAN FISHERIES SOCIETY
    North Central Division 143
AMERICAN FISHERIES SOCIETY, ILLINOIS CHAPTER.. 146
ASSOCIATION OF CONSERVATION ENGINEERS 161
AUDUBON COUNCIL OF ILLINOIS.................................... 163
CENTRAL STATES EDUCATION CENTER 177
CHICAGO HERPETOLOGICAL SOCIETY 179
EAGLE NATURE FOUNDATION, LTD. 197
EAST CENTRAL ILLINOIS FUR TAKERS 199
ENVIRONMENTAL EDUCATION ASSOCIATION OF ILLINOIS
    (Iron Oaks Environmental Learning Center).................. 202
GREAT LAKES SPORT FISHING COUNCIL 216
ILLINOIS ASSOCIATION OF CONSERVATION DISTRICTS
.... 224
ILLINOIS ASSOCIATION OF SOIL AND WATER
    CONSERVATION DISTRICTS 224
ILLINOIS AUDUBON SOCIETY... 224
ILLINOIS B.A.S.S. CHAPTER FEDERATION 224
ILLINOIS ENVIRONMENTAL COUNCIL 224
ILLINOIS NATIVE PLANT SOCIETY 225
ILLINOIS NATURAL HERITAGE FOUNDATION................ 225
ILLINOIS PRAIRIE PATH 225
ILLINOIS WALNUT COUNCIL 225
ILLINOIS WOODLAND OWNERS AND USERS
    ASSOCIATION 225
INTERNATIONAL SOCIETY OF ARBORICULTURE 233
IZAAK WALTON LEAGUE OF AMERICA, INC., THE
    Illinois Division 240
LAKE MICHIGAN FEDERATION 246
MAX McGRAW WILDLIFE FOUNDATION.......................... 254
NATIONAL BIRD-FEEDING SOCIETY 266
NATIONAL TRAPPERS ASSOCIATION, INC. 271
NATIONAL TRUST FOR HISTORIC PRESERVATION
    Midwest Office 279
NATURAL LAND INSTITUTE 277
NATURE CONSERVANCY, THE, ILLINOIS CHAPTER..... 280
OPENLANDS PROJECT 297

PRAIRIE CLUB, THE 305
TROUT UNLIMITED, ILLINOIS COUNCIL 334
UPPER MISSISSIPPI RIVER CONSERVATION COMMITTEE
 340
WILDLIFE SOCIETY, ILLINOIS CHAPTER........................ 354
WINCHESTER NILO FARMS 359
STATE GOVERNMENT ORGANIZATIONS
GOVERNOR OF ILLINOIS, GEORGE RYAN..................... 62
ILLINOIS DEPARTMENT OF AGRICULTURE..................... 62
 Soil and Water Conservation Districts Advisory Board...... 63
ILLINOIS DEPARTMENT OF NATURAL RESOURCES....... 63
ILLINOIS DEPARTMENT OF TRANSPORTATION.............. 63
ILLINOIS ENVIRONMENTAL PROTECTION AGENCY 63
NATURE PRESERVES COMMISSION 63

INDIANA
NON-GOVERNMENTAL ORGANIZATIONS
ACRES LAND TRUST... 133
AMERICAN CAMPING ASSOCIATION, INC..................... 141
AMERICAN FISHERIES SOCIETY, INDIANA CHAPTER .. 146
CONSERVATION TECHNOLOGY INFORMATION CENTER
 188
ENVIRONMENTAL EDUCATION ASSOCIATION OF INDIANA
 202
HOOSIER ENVIRONMENTAL COUNCIL 222
INDIANA ASSOCIATION OF SOIL AND WATER
 CONSERVATION DISTRICTS, INC. 225
INDIANA AUDUBON SOCIETY, INC. 226
INDIANA B.A.S.S. CHAPTER FEDERATION.................... 226
INDIANA FORESTRY AND WOODLAND OWNERS
 ASSOCIATION 226
INDIANA NATIVE PLANT AND WILDFLOWER SOCIETY . 226
INDIANA STATE TRAPPERS ASSOCIATION, INC. 226
INDIANA WILDLIFE FEDERATION 226
IZAAK WALTON LEAGUE OF AMERICA, INC., THE
 Indiana Division 240
NATURE CONSERVANCY, THE, INDIANA CHAPTER 280
NORTH AMERICAN WILDLIFE PARK FOUNDATION, INC.
 289
SAVE THE DUNES COUNCIL... 316
 Save the Dunes Conservation Fund 316
WILDLIFE SOCIETY, INDIANA CHAPTER........................ 354
STATE GOVERNMENT ORGANIZATIONS
GOVERNOR OF INDIANA, FRANK O'BANNON................. 63
INDIANA DEPARTMENT OF ENVIRONMENTAL
 MANAGEMENT 63
INDIANA DEPARTMENT OF NATURAL RESOURCES....... 64
 Division of Soil Conservation.. 64
INDIANA STATE DEPARTMENT OF HEALTH 64
INDIANA STATE GEOLOGICAL SURVEY 65
PURDUE UNIVERSITY EXTENSION SERVICES................ 65

IOWA
NON-GOVERNMENTAL ORGANIZATIONS
AMERICAN FISHERIES SOCIETY, IOWA CHAPTER........ 146
INDIAN CREEK NATURE CENTER.................................. 225
IOWA ACADEMY OF SCIENCE 236
IOWA ASSOCIATION OF NATURALISTS.......................... 237
IOWA ASSOCIATION OF SOIL AND WATER
 CONSERVATION DISTRICT COMMISSIONERS 237
IOWA AUDUBON COUNCIL.. 237
IOWA B.A.S.S. CHAPTER FEDERATION 237
IOWA CONSERVATION EDUCATION COUNCIL, INC...... 237
IOWA ENVIRONMENTAL COUNCIL 237
IOWA NATIVE PLANT SOCIETY 237
IOWA NATURAL HERITAGE FOUNDATION..................... 238
IOWA TRAILS COUNCIL... 238
IOWA TRAPPERS ASSOCIATION, INC. 238
IOWA WILDLIFE FEDERATION 238
IOWA WILDLIFE REHABILITATORS ASSOCIATION........ 238
IOWA WOMEN IN NATURAL RESOURCES 238
IOWA WOODLAND OWNERS ASSOCIATION................. 239
IZAAK WALTON LEAGUE OF AMERICA ENDOWMENT .. 239
IZAAK WALTON LEAGUE OF AMERICA, INC., THE
 Iowa Division... 240
LEAGUE OF WOMEN VOTERS OF IOWA........................ 247
MACBRIDE RAPTOR PROJECT....................................... 249
MISSISSIPPI INTERSTATE COOPERATIVE RESOURCE
 ASSOCIATION 258

NATIONAL ASSOCIATION OF UNIVERSITY FISHERIES
 AND WILDLIFE PROGRAMS 265
NATURE CONSERVANCY, THE, IOWA CHAPTER 280
RETURNED PEACE CORPS VOLUNTEER FOR
 ENVIRONMENT AND DEVELOPMENT (RPCV-ED)...... 311
SOIL AND WATER CONSERVATION SOCIETY (formerly Soil
 Conservation Society of America) 323
WILDLIFE SOCIETY, IOWA CHAPTER............................. 354
STATE GOVERNMENT ORGANIZATIONS
GOVERNOR OF IOWA, TOM VILSACK 65
IOWA ASSOCIATION OF COUNTY CONSERVATION
 BOARDS 65
IOWA COOPERATIVE FISH AND WILDLIFE RESEARCH
 UNIT 65
IOWA DEPARTMENT OF AGRICULTURE AND LAND
 STEWARDSHIP
 Bureau of Field Services 65
 Bureau of Financial Incentive Program............................. 65
 Bureau of Mines and Minerals... 65
 Bureau of Water Resources 65
 Division of Soil Conservation... 65
IOWA DEPARTMENT OF NATURAL RESOURCES............ 65
 Administrative Services Division....................................... 65
 Cooperative North American Shotgunning Education
 Program 66
 Energy and Geological Resources Division 66
 Environmental Protection Division 65
 Fish and Wildlife Division 66
 Forests and Forestry Division 66
 Parks 66
 Waste Management Division 66
IOWA STATE EXTENSION SERVICES.............................. 66

KANSAS
GOVERNMENT ORGANIZATIONS
ENVIRONMENTAL PROTECTION AGENCY..................... 10
NON-GOVERNMENTAL ORGANIZATIONS
AMERICAN ASSOCIATION OF ZOO KEEPERS, INC. 139
AMERICAN FISHERIES SOCIETY, KANSAS CHAPTER .. 146
GRASSLAND HERITAGE FOUNDATION.......................... 216
HOLLY SOCIETY OF AMERICA, INC................................ 222
KANSAS ACADEMY OF SCIENCE 242
KANSAS ADVISORY COUNCIL FOR ENVIRONMENTAL
 EDUCATION... 243
KANSAS ASSOCIATION FOR CONSVERATION AND
 ENVIRONMENTAL EDUCATION.................................... 243
KANSAS ASSOCIATION OF CONSERVATION DISTRICTS
 243
KANSAS AUDUBON COUNCIL... 243
KANSAS B.A.S.S. CHAPTER FEDERATION..................... 243
KANSAS HERPETOLOGICAL SOCIETY.......................... 243
KANSAS NATURAL RESOURCE COUNCIL 243
KANSAS ORNITHOLOGICAL SOCIETY 244
KANSAS WILDFLOWER SOCIETY 244
KANSAS WILDLIFE FEDERATION 244
KANSAS WILDSCAPE FOUNDATION 244
NATIONAL FLYWAY COUNCIL
 Central Flyway Office.. 268
NATURE CONSERVANCY, THE, KANSAS CHAPTER 281
NORTH AMERICAN BENTHOLOGICAL SOCIETY 288
NORTH AMERICAN FALCONERS ASSOCIATION 288
NORTH DAKOTA NATURAL SCIENCE SOCIETY 291
SOCIETY OF WETLAND SCIENTISTS 322
WILDLIFE DISEASE ASSOCIATION................................. 351
WILDLIFE SOCIETY, KANSAS CHAPTER........................ 354
STATE GOVERNMENT ORGANIZATIONS
GOVERNOR OF KANSAS, BILL GRAVES 66
KANSAS BIOLOGICAL SURVEY 66
KANSAS COOPERATIVE FISH AND WILDLIFE RESEARCH
 UNIT 66
KANSAS DEPARTMENT OF AGRICULTURE 66
KANSAS DEPARTMENT OF WILDLIFE AND PARKS......... 67
 Operations Office 67
 Region 1 67
 Region 2 67
 Region 3 67
 Region 4 67

GEOGRAPHIC INDEX

KANSAS DEPARTMENT OF WILDLIFE AND PARKS, Region 5 67
KANSAS FOREST SERVICE 67
KANSAS GEOLOGICAL SURVEY 67
KANSAS STATE CONSERVATION COMMISSION 67
KANSAS STATE DEPARTMENT OF HEALTH AND ENVIRONMENT 67
KANSAS STATE EXTENSION SERVICES 68
KANSAS WATER OFFICE 68

KENTUCKY
GOVERNMENT ORGANIZATIONS
DEPARTMENT OF THE ARMY
  U.S. ARMY CORPS OF ENGINEERS 21
NON-GOVERNMENTAL ORGANIZATIONS
AMERICAN BASS ASSOCIATION OF KENTUCKY, THE .. 140
AMERICAN CAVE CONSERVATION ASSOCIATION 141
AMERICAN FISHERIES SOCIETY, KENTUCKY CHAPTER 146
CAVE RESEARCH FOUNDATION 174
KENTUCKY ACADEMY OF SCIENCE 244
KENTUCKY ASSOCIATION FOR ENVIRONMENTAL EDUCATION (KAEE) 245
KENTUCKY ASSOCIATION OF CONSERVATION DISTRICTS 245
KENTUCKY AUDUBON COUNCIL 245
KENTUCKY B.A.S.S. CHAPTER FEDERATION 245
KENTUCKY RESOURCES COUNCIL 245
KENTUCKY WOODLAND OWNERS ASSOCIATION 245
KENTUCKY-TENNESSEE SOCIETY OF AMERICAN FORESTERS 245
LAND BETWEEN THE LAKES ASSOCIATION 247
LEAGUE OF KENTUCKY SPORTSMEN, INC. 247
NATURE CONSERVANCY, THE, KENTUCKY CHAPTER 281
SCENIC AMERICA
  Scenic Kentucky 317
SOUTHEASTERN ASSOCIATION OF FISH AND WILDLIFE AGENCIES 325
TROUT UNLIMITED, KENTUCKY COUNCIL 335
WILDLIFE SOCIETY, KENTUCKY CHAPTER 354
STATE GOVERNMENT ORGANIZATIONS
GOVERNOR OF KENTUCKY, PAUL E. PATTON 68
KENTUCKY DEPARTMENT OF AGRICULTURE 68
KENTUCKY DEPARTMENT OF FISH AND WILDLIFE RESOURCES 68
KENTUCKY DEPARTMENT OF PARKS 68
KENTUCKY GEOLOGICAL SURVEY 68
KENTUCKY SOIL AND WATER CONSERVATION COMMISSION 69
KENTUCKY STATE EXTENSION SERVICES 69
KENTUCKY STATE NATURE PRESERVES COMMISSION 69
NATURAL RESOURCES AND ENVIRONMENTAL PROTECTION CABINET 69
  Department for Environmental Protection 69
  Department for Natural Resources 69
  Department for Surface Mining Reclamation and Enforcement 69
  Environmental Quality Commission 69
  Nature Preserves Commission 69

LOUISIANA
GOVERNMENT ORGANIZATIONS
DEPARTMENT OF THE ARMY
  U.S. ARMY CORPS OF ENGINEERS 21
U.S. TREASURY DEPARTMENT
  U.S. CUSTOMS SERVICE 33
NON-GOVERNMENTAL ORGANIZATIONS
AMERICAN FISHERIES SOCIETY, LOUISIANA CHAPTER 146
AMERICAN LUNG ASSOCIATION OF LOUISIANA, INC. ... 152
EARTHJUSTICE LEGAL DEFENSE FUND (formerly Sierra Club Legal Defense Fund, Inc.)
  Louisiana Office 198
ELSA WILD ANIMAL APPEAL (Louisiana Chapter) 200
LOUISIANA ASSOCIATION OF CONSERVATION DISTRICTS 249
LOUISIANA AUDUBON COUNCIL 249
LOUISIANA B.A.S.S. CHAPTER FEDERATION 249
LOUISIANA FORESTRY ASSOCIATION 249
LOUISIANA WILDLIFE FEDERATION, INC. 249
NATURE CONSERVANCY, THE, LOUISIANA CHAPTER . 281
WHOOPING CRANE CONSERVATION ASSOCIATION INC. 348
WILDLIFE SOCIETY, LOUISIANA CHAPTER 355
STATE GOVERNMENT ORGANIZATIONS
GOVERNOR OF LOUISIANA, M. J. FOSTER, JR. 69
LOUISIANA COOPERATIVE FISH AND WILDLIFE RESEARCH UNIT (USDI) 69
LOUISIANA DEPARTMENT OF AGRICULTURE
  Office of Forestry 69
LOUISIANA DEPARTMENT OF AGRICULTURE AND FORESTRY 70
LOUISIANA DEPARTMENT OF WILDLIFE AND FISHERIES 70
LOUISIANA GEOLOGICAL SURVEY 70
LOUISIANA SEA GRANT COLLEGE PROGRAM 70
LOUISIANA STATE EXTENSION SERVICES 70
OFFICE OF STATE PARKS, DEPARTMENT OF CULTURE, RECREATION, AND TOURISM 71
STATE OFFICE OF CONSERVATION (LOUISIANA) 71

MAINE
GOVERNMENT ORGANIZATIONS
ST. CROIX INTERNATIONAL WATERWAY COMMISSION 10
ST. CROIX INTERNATIONAL WATERWAY COMMISSION 10
NON-GOVERNMENTAL ORGANIZATIONS
A. E. HOWELL WILDLIFE CONSERVATION CENTER 133
AMERICAN BASS ASSOCIATION OF MAINE, THE 140
ASSOCIATION OF FIELD ORNITHOLOGISTS 161
CHINA REGION LAKES ALLIANCE 179
CONSERVATION LAW FOUNDATION, INC. (CLF) (Maine Office) 188
FRIENDS OF ACADIA 211
HUMBOLT FIELD RESEARCH INSTITUTE 223
ISLAND INSTITUTE, THE 239
MAINE ASSOCIATION OF CONSERVATION COMMISSIONS (MACC) 250
MAINE ASSOCIATION OF CONSERVATION DISTRICTS 250
MAINE AUDUBON SOCIETY 250
MAINE B.A.S.S. CHAPTER FEDERATION 250
MAINE COAST HERITAGE TRUST 250
MAINE ENVIRONMENTAL EDUCATION ASSOCIATION, INC. 250
NATURAL RESOURCES COUNCIL OF MAINE 278
NATURE CONSERVANCY, THE, MAINE CHAPTER 281
SMALL WOODLAND OWNERS ASSOCIATION OF MAINE, INC. 319
TROUT UNLIMITED, MAINE COUNCIL 335
WILDLIFE SOCIETY, MAINE CHAPTER 355
STATE GOVERNMENT ORGANIZATIONS
DEPARTMENT OF ENVIRONMENTAL PROTECTION (MAINE0 71
DEPARTMENT OF INLAND FISHERIES AND WILDLIFE 71
DEPARTMENT OF MARINE RESOURCES 71
GOVERNOR OF MAINE, ANGUS S. KING, JR. 71
MAINE ATLANTIC SALMON AUTHORITY (formerly Maine Atlantic Sea Run Salmon Commission) 71
MAINE COOPERATIVE FISH AND WILDLIFE RESEARCH UNIT (USDI) 72
MAINE DEPARTMENT OF AGRICULTURE, FOOD, AND RURAL RESOURCES 72
MAINE DEPARTMENT OF CONSERVATION 72
  Land Use Regulatin Commission 72
  Maine Forest Service 72
  Natural Resource Information & Mapping 72
MAINE DEPARTMENT OF CONSERVATION Bureau of Parks and Lands) 72
MAINE SEA GRANT PROGRAM 72
UNIVERSITY OF MAINE COOPERATIVE EXTENSION 72

MARYLAND
GOVERNMENT ORGANIZATIONS
INTERSTATE COMMISSION ON THE POTOMAC RIVER BASIN 8
MARINE MAMMAL COMMISSION 8
DEPARTMENT OF COMMERCE

NATIONAL OCEANIC AND ATMOSPHERIC
ADMINISTRATION... 12
DEPARTMENT OF HEALTH AND HUMAN SERVICES
FOOD AND DRUG ADMINISTRATION........................... 14
DEPARTMENT OF THE AIR FORCE
MAJOR AIR COMMANDS 16
DEPARTMENT OF THE ARMY
U.S. ARMY CORPS OF ENGINEERS..................................... 21
U.S. DEPARTMENT OF AGRICULTURE
ANIMAL AND PLANT HEALTH INSPECTION SERVICE.. 29
RESEARCH EDUCATION AND ECONOMICS................. 32
NON-GOVERNMENTAL ORGANIZATIONS
ADKINS ARBORETUM... 134
ALLIANCE FOR THE CHESAPEAKE BAY
Balitmore Office 138
AMERICAN BASS ASSOCIATION OF MARYLAND, THE.. 140
AMERICAN FISHERIES SOCIETY 142
Estuaries Section... 143
Southern Division.. 144
AMERICAN HIKING SOCIETY 150
AMERICAN ZOO AND AQUARIUM ASSOCIATION (AZA) 157
ANACOSTIA WATERSHED SOCIETY 157
AUDUBON NATURALIST SOCIETY OF THE CENTRAL
ATLANTIC STATES.. 164
BROTHERHOOD OF THE JUNGLE COCK, INC., THE 168
CENTER FOR WATERSHED PROTECTION 177
CHESAPEAKE BAY FOUNDATION, INC. 178
CHESAPEAKE BAY FOUNDATION, INC. (Maryland Office)
.... 178
CHESAPEAKE FARMS 179
CHESAPEAKE WILDLIFE HERITAGE (CWH).................... 179
CONFERENCE OF NATIONAL PARK COOPERATING
ASSOCIATIONS 185
CONSERVATION FEDERATION OF MARYLAND/For A Rural
Maryland (F.A.R.M.)... 187
CONSERVATION TREATY SUPPORT FUND 188
EASTERN SHORE LAND CONSERVANCY 199
ENTOMOLOGICAL SOCIETY OF AMERICA..................... 200
ENVIRONMENTAL CONCERN, INC. 201
FISH AND WILDLIFE REFERENCE SERVICE 206
HENRY A. WALLACE INSTITUTE FOR ALTERNATIVE
AGRICULTURE (HAWIAA) 221
INSTITUTE FOR CONSERVATION LEADERSHIP............ 227
INTERNATIONAL SOCIETY FOR ECOLOGICAL
ECONOMICS... 233
INTERNATIONAL SOCIETY OF TROPICAL FORESTERS
INC.. 233
IZAAK WALTON LEAGUE OF AMERICA, INC., THE 240
Maryland Division... 240
JANE GOODALL INSTITUTE, THE 242
MARYLAND ASSOCIATION OF CONSERVATION
DISTRICTS.. 252
MARYLAND B.A.S.S. CHAPTER FEDERATION 252
MARYLAND FORESTS ASSOCIATION 252
MARYLAND NATIVE PLANT SOCIETY 252
MARYLAND ORNITHOLOGICAL SOCIETY, INC. 253
MONITOR INTERNATIONAL.. 259
NATIONAL 4-H COUNCIL 262
NATIONAL BOATING FEDERATION 266
NATIONAL MILITARY FISH AND WILDLIFE ASSOCIATION
.... 269
NATURAL HISTORY SOCIETY OF MARYLAND, INC., THE
.... 277
NATURE CONSERVANCY, THE, MARYLAND/D.C.
CHAPTER 281
RACHEL CARSON COUNCIL INC. (formerly Rachel Carson
Trust for the Living Environment Inc.) 308
RENEWABLE NATURAL RESOURCES FOUNDATION.... 310
RIVER FEDERATION... 312
SCIENTISTS CENTER FOR ANIMAL WELFARE 318
SEAPLANE PILOTS ASSOCIATION 318
SOCIETY OF AMERICAN FORESTERS 322
TREES FOR THE FUTURE, INC. 333
TROUT UNLIMITED, MARYLAND COUNCIL (Mid-Atlantic)335
WILDFOWL TRUST OF NORTH AMERICA INC., THE...... 350
WILDLIFE HABITAT COUNCIL 352
WILDLIFE SOCIETY, MARYLAND-DELAWARE CHAPTER
.... 355
WILDLIFE SOCIETY, THE.. 357
WORLD NATURE ASSOCIATION INC.............................. 362
STATE GOVERNMENT ORGANIZATIONS
DEPARTMENT OF THE ENVIRONMENT 72
GOVERNOR OF MARYLAND, PARRIS N. GLENDENING .. 72
MARYLAND DEPARTMENT OF AGRICULTURE............... 73
Agricultural Commission... 73
State Soil Conservation Committee 73
MARYLAND DEPARTMENT OF NATURAL RESOURCES.. 73
Chesapeake Bay and Watershed Programs 73
Management Services 73
Public Lands Division 73
Resource Management Services..................................... 74
MARYLAND SEA GRANT COLLEGE 74
MARYLAND STATE EXTENSION SERVICES................... 74
MARYLAND-NATIONAL CAPITAL PARK AND PLANNING
COMMISSION.. 74

MASSACHUSETTS
GOVERNMENT ORGANIZATIONS
NEW ENGLAND INTERSTATE WATER POLLUTION
CONTROL COMMISSION.. 9
DEPARTMENT OF THE ARMY
U.S. ARMY CORPS OF ENGINEERS............................... 21
DEPARTMENT OF THE INTERIOR
UNITED STATES FISH AND WILDLIFE SERVICE 26
U.S. TREASURY DEPARTMENT
U.S. CUSTOMS SERVICE.. 33
NON-GOVERNMENTAL ORGANIZATIONS
AMERICAN BASS ASSOCIATION OF MASSACHUSETTS,
THE 140
AMERICAN FISHERIES SOCIETY
Physiology Section... 144
Socioeconomics Section.. 144
APPALACHIAN MOUNTAIN CLUB..................................... 158
ATLANTIC CENTER FOR THE ENVIRONMENT............... 162
CONNECTICUT RIVER WATERSHED COUNCIL INC. 186
CONSERVATION LAW FOUNDATION, INC. (CLF)........... 188
EARTHWATCH INSTITUTE 199
ENVIRONMENTAL CAREERS ORGANIZATION INC., THE
.... 201
ENVIRONMENTAL DEFENSE FUND, INC.
Alliance for Environmental In Innovation......................... 202
ENVIRONMENTAL LEAGUE OF MASSACHUSETTS (ELM)
.... 203
INTERNATIONAL FUND FOR ANIMAL WELFARE 230
INTERNATIONAL WILDLIFE COALITION (IWC) AND THE
WHALE ADOPTION PROJECT 235
MANOMET OBSERVATORY.. 251
MASSACHUSETTS ASSOCIATION OF CONSERVATION
COMMISSIONS (MACC) 253
MASSACHUSETTS ASSOCIATION OF CONSERVATION
DISTRICTS.. 253
MASSACHUSETTS AUDUBON SOCIETY, INC. 253
MASSACHUSETTS B.A.S.S. CHAPTER FEDERATION.... 253
MASSACHUSETTS ENVIRONMENTAL EDUCATION
SOCIETY... 253
MASSACHUSETTS FORESTRY ASSOCIATION 253
MASSACHUSETTS TRAPPER'S ASSOCIATION, INC...... 254
MOUNT GRACE LAND CONSERVATION TRUST 261
NATIONAL PARKS AND CONSERVATION ASSOCIATION
(NPCA)
Northeast Regional Office 270
NATIONAL TRUST FOR HISTORIC PRESERVATION
Northeast Office 272
NATURE CONSERVANCY, THE
Eastern Office 279
NATURE CONSERVANCY, THE, MASSACHUSETTS
CHAPTER 281
NEW ENGLAND ASSOCIATION OF ENVIRONMENTAL
BIOLOGISTS (NEAEB)... 284
NEW ENGLAND NATURAL RESOURCES CENTER 284
NEW ENGLAND WILD FLOWER SOCIETY, INC. 284
NORTHEAST SUSTAINABLE ENERGY ASSOCIATION ... 292
SAVE THE HARBOR/SAVE THE BAY............................... 316
STRIPERS UNLIMITED INC... 328

GEOGRAPHIC INDEX

TROUT UNLIMITED, MASSACHUSETTS/RHODE ISLAND COUNCIL 335
TRUSTEES OF RESERVATIONS, THE 338
UNION OF CONCERNED SCIENTISTS 339
WESTERN HEMISPHERE SHOREBIRD RESERVE NETWORK (WHSRN) 347
WORLD SOCIETY FOR THE PROTECTION OF ANIMALS (WSPA) 363

STATE GOVERNMENT ORGANIZATIONS
COOPERATIVE EXTENSION SYSTEM (MASSACHUSETTS) 74
EXECUTIVE OFFICE OF ENVIRONMENTAL AFFAIRS
   Division of Fisheries and Wildlife 74
EXECUTIVE OFFICE OF ENVIRONMENTAL AFFAIRS (MASSACHUSETTS) 74
   Animal Health 75
   Bureau of Land Use 75
   Bureau of Markets 75
   Bureau of Pesticides 75
   Department of Environmental Management 75
   Department of Environmental Protection 75
   Department of Fisheries, Wildlife, and Environmental Law Enforcement 75
   Department of Food and Agriculture 75
   Division of Agricultural Development 75
   Division of Regulatory Services 75
   Division of Wetlands and Waterways, ... 75
   Metropolitan District Commission, ... 75
   Watershed Division 75
GOVERNOR OF MASSACHUSETTS, ARGEO PAUL CELLUCCI 74
MASSACHUSETTS COOPERATIVE FISH AND WILDLIFE RESEARCH UNIT (USDI) 75
MASSACHUSETTS HIGHWAY DEPARTMENT 75
WOODS HOLE OCEANOGRAPHIC INSITITUTION (WHOI) SEA GRANT PROGRAM 76

MICHIGAN
GOVERNMENT ORGANIZATIONS
GREAT LAKES FISHERY COMMISSION 7
DEPARTMENT OF THE ARMY
   U.S. ARMY CORPS OF ENGINEERS 21
NON-GOVERNMENTAL ORGANIZATIONS
AMERICAN FISHERIES SOCIETY
   Computer User Section 143
   Fisheries History Section 143
   International Fisheries Section 143
AMERICAN FISHERIES SOCIETY, MICHIGAN CHAPTER 147
CENTER FOR ENVIRONMENTAL STUDY 175
GEORGE WRIGHT SOCIETY, THE 214
GREEN (GLOBAL RIVERS ENVIRONMENTAL EDUCATION NETWORK) 218
IZAAK WALTON LEAGUE OF AMERICA, INC., THE
   Michigan Division 240
LAKE ERIE CLEAN-UP COMMITTEE, INC. 246
MICHIGAN ASSOCIATION OF CONSERVATION DISTRICTS 254
MICHIGAN AUDUBON SOCIETY 254
MICHIGAN B.A.S.S. CHAPTER FEDERATION 254
MICHIGAN ENVIRONMENTAL COUNCIL 255
MICHIGAN FOREST ASSOCIATION 255
MICHIGAN LAND USE INSTITUTE 255
MICHIGAN NATURAL AREAS COUNCIL 255
MICHIGAN NATURE ASSOCIATION 255
MICHIGAN UNITED CONSERVATION CLUBS, INC. 255
MICHIGAN WILDLIFE HABITAT FOUNDATION 255
NATIONAL WILDLIFE FEDERATION
   Great Lakes Natural Resource Center (IL, IN, MI, OH, WI) 274
NATURE CONSERVANCY, THE, MICHIGAN CHAPTER .. 281
SAFARI CLUB INTERNATIONAL
   Michigan Office 314
SCENIC AMERICA
   Scenic Michigan 317
TROUT UNLIMITED, MICHIGAN COUNCIL 335
WEST MICHIGAN ENVIRONMENTAL ACTION COUNCIL 346
WILDLIFE SOCIETY, MICHIGAN CHAPTER 355
YOUNG ENTOMOLOGISTS' SOCIETY INC. 365

STATE GOVERNMENT ORGANIZATIONS
GOVERNOR OF MICHIGAN, JOHN ENGLER 76
MICHIGAN DEPARTMENT OF AGRICULTURE 76
MICHIGAN DEPARTMENT OF ENVIRONMENTAL QUALITY 76
MICHIGAN DEPARTMENT OF NATURAL RESOURCES 76
MICHIGAN DEPARTMENT OF PUBLIC HEALTH 77
MICHIGAN SEA GRANT COLLEGE PROGRAM 77
MICHIGAN STATE UNIVERSITY EXTENSION 77

MINNESOTA
GOVERNMENT ORGANIZATIONS
DEPARTMENT OF THE ARMY
   U.S. ARMY CORPS OF ENGINEERS 21
DEPARTMENT OF THE INTERIOR
   UNITED STATES FISH AND WILDLIFE SERVICE 26
U.S. DEPARTMENT OF AGRICULTURE
   UNITED STATES FOREST SERVICE 32
NON-GOVERNMENTAL ORGANIZATIONS
AMERICAN FISHERIES SOCIETY, MINNESOTA CHAPTER 147
CHARLES A. AND ANNE MORROW LINDBERGH FOUNDATION, THE 178
DEEP-PORTAGE CONSERVATION RESERVE 191
FEDERAL CARTRIDGE COMPANY 205
FRESHWATER FOUNDATION 211
FRIENDS OF THE BOUNDARY WATERS WILDERNESS 211
INTERNATIONAL ECOLOGY SOCIETY (IES) 230
INTERNATIONAL WOLF CENTER (Administrative Offices) 236
INTERNATIONAL WOLF CENTER (Educational Services) 236
IZAAK WALTON LEAGUE OF AMERICA, INC., THE
   Minnesota Division 240
KIDS FOR SAVING EARTH WORLDWIDE 246
MINNESOTA ASSOCIATION OF SOIL AND WATER CONSERVATION DISTRICTS 256
MINNESOTA B.A.S.S. CHAPTER FEDERATION 256
MINNESOTA CENTER FOR ENVIRONMENTAL ADVOCACY (MCEA) 256
MINNESOTA CONSERVATION FEDERATION 256
MINNESOTA FORESTRY ASSOCIATION 257
MINNESOTA GROUND WATER ASSOCIATION 257
MINNESOTA HERPETOLOGICAL SOCIETY (James Ford Bell Museum of Natural History) 257
MINNESOTA NATIVE PLANT SOCIETY 257
MINNESOTA ORNITHOLOGISTS' UNION 257
MINNESOTA PARKS AND TRAILS COUNCIL 257
MINNESOTA WILDLIFE HERITAGE FOUNDATION, INC. .. 257
MINNESOTA WINGS SOCIETY, INC. 257
MISSISSIPPI RIVER BASIN ALLIANCE 258
NATIONAL FLYWAY COUNCIL
   Mississippi Flyway Office 268
NATIONAL PARKS AND CONSERVATION ASSOCIATION (NPCA)
   Heartland Regional Office 270
NATIONAL WILDLIFE REHABILITATORS ASSOCIATION 275
NATURE CONSERVANCY, THE
   Midwest Office 279
NATURE CONSERVANCY, THE, MINNESOTA CHAPTER 281
NORTH AMERICAN FISHING CLUB 289
PHEASANTS FOREVER INC. 303
POPE AND YOUNG CLUB 304
RAPTOR CENTER, THE 309
TROUT UNLIMITED, MINNESOTA COUNCIL 335
TRUMPETER SWAN SOCIETY, THE 337
WILDLIFE EDUCATION PROGRAM AND DESIGN 351
WILDLIFE FOREVER 351
WILDLIFE SOCIETY, MINNESOTA CHAPTER 355

STATE GOVERNMENT ORGANIZATIONS
GOVERNOR OF MINNESOTA, JESSE VENTURA 77
MINNESOTA BOARD OF WATER AND SOIL RESOURCES 77
MINNESOTA COOPERATIVE FISH AND WILDLIFE RESEARCH UNIT 77
MINNESOTA DEPARTMENT OF AGRICULTURE 77
MINNESOTA DEPARTMENT OF NATURAL RESOURCES 78
MINNESOTA ENVIRONMENTAL QUALITY BOARD 78
MINNESOTA GEOLOGICAL SURVEY 78
MINNESOTA POLLUTION CONTROL AGENCY 78

Brainerd, MN.. 78
Detroit Lakes, MN 79
Duluth, MN.. 79
Marshall, MN... 79
Rochester, MN.. 79
MINNESOTA SEA GRANT COLLEGE PROGRAM.............. 79
MINNESOTA STATE EXTENSION SERVICES 79

MISSISSIPPI
GOVERNMENT ORGANIZATIONS
GULF STATES MARINE FISHERIES COMMISSION......... 7
DEPARTMENT OF THE ARMY
    U.S. ARMY CORPS OF ENGINEERS............................ 21
U.S. DEPARTMENT OF AGRICULTURE
    RESEARCH EDUCATION AND ECONOMICS................. 32
NON-GOVERNMENTAL ORGANIZATIONS
AMERICAN FISHERIES SOCIETY, MISSISSIPPI CHAPTER
    147
DELTA WILDLIFE FOUNDATION..................................... 192
DUCKS UNLIMITED, INC. (South Mississippi and South
    Central Flyways) 196
LOWER MISSISSIPPI RIVER CONSERVATION COMMITTEE
    249
MISSISSIPPI ASSOCIATION OF CONSERVATION
    DISTRICTS, INC... 258
MISSISSIPPI B.A.S.S. CHAPTER FEDERATION 258
MISSISSIPPI NATIVE PLANT SOCIETY 258
MISSISSIPPI WILDLIFE FEDERATION............................. 258
NATURE CONSERVANCY, THE, MISSISSIPPI CHAPTER281
THE CROSBY ABORETUM, Mississippi State University .. 331
WILDLIFE SOCIETY, MISSISSIPPI CHAPTER 355
STATE GOVERNMENT ORGANIZATIONS
DEPARTMENT OF ENVIRONMENTAL QUALITY
    (MISSISSIPPI) 79
    Office of Land and Water Resources............................... 79
FORESTRY COMMISSION (MISSISSIPPI) 79
GOVERNOR OF MISSISSIPPI, KIRK FORDICE 79
GULF COAST RESEARCH LABORATORY........................ 79
MISSISSIPPI COOPERATIVE FISH AND WILDLIFE
    RESEARCH UNIT (USDI)... 79
MISSISSIPPI DEPARTMENT OF AGRICULTURE AND
    COMMERCE 80
MISSISSIPPI DEPARTMENT OF WILDLIFE, FISHERIES,
    AND PARKS 80
MISSISSIPPI SEA GRANT PROGRAM 80
MISSISSIPPI SOIL AND WATER CONSERVATION
    COMMISSION 80
MISSISSIPPI STATE DEPARTMENT OF HEALTH.............. 80
MISSISSIPPI STATE EXTENSION SERVICES 80

MISSOURI
GOVERNMENT ORGANIZATIONS
DEPARTMENT OF THE ARMY
    U.S. ARMY CORPS OF ENGINEERS............................ 21
NON-GOVERNMENTAL ORGANIZATIONS
AMERICAN FISHERIES SOCIETY, MISSOURI CHAPTER 147
AUDUBON SOCIETY OF MISSOURI 164
BOUNTY INFORMATION SERVICE................................... 167
CAMP FIRE BOYS AND GIRLS 170
CENTER FOR PLANT CONSERVATION 176
CONSERVATION FEDERATION OF MISSOURI............... 187
INTERNATIONAL CENTER FOR TROPICAL ECOLOGY .. 229
MISSOURI ASSOCIATION OF SOIL AND WATER
    CONSERVATION DISTRICTS...................................... 259
MISSOURI AUDUBON COUNCIL 259
MISSOURI B.A.S.S. CHAPTER FEDERATION.................. 259
MISSOURI NATIVE PLANT SOCIETY............................... 259
MISSOURI PRAIRIE FOUNDATION 259
NATIONAL COUNCIL OF STATE GARDEN CLUBS, INC.. 266
NATURE CONSERVANCY, THE, MISSOURI CHAPTER .. 281
OZARKS RESOURCE CENTER.. 300
SCENIC AMERICA
    Scenic Missouri.. 317
TROUT UNLIMITED, MISSOURI COUNCIL 335
WILD CANINE SURVIVAL AND RESEARCH CENTER AND
    WOLF SANCTUARY.. 348
WILDLIFE SOCIETY, MISSOURI CHAPTER..................... 355
WORLD BIRD SANCTUARY (formerly Raptor Rehabilitation
    and Propagation Project Inc. The) 361

STATE GOVERNMENT ORGANIZATIONS
GOVERNOR OF MISSOURI, MEL CARNAHAN.................. 81
MISSOURI COOPERATIVE FISH AND WILDLIFE
    RESEARCH UNIT (USDI)... 81
MISSOURI DEPARTMENT OF AGRICULTURE 81
MISSOURI DEPARTMENT OF CONSERVATION 81
    Fisheries Division.. 81
    Forestry Division... 81
    Protection Division.. 81
    Wildlife Division... 81
MISSOURI DEPARTMENT OF NATURAL RESOURCES.... 81
MISSOURI STATE EXTENSION SERVICES....................... 82

MONTANA
GOVERNMENT ORGANIZATIONS
DEPARTMENT OF THE INTERIOR
    BUREAU OF RECLAMATION... 24
U.S. DEPARTMENT OF AGRICULTURE
    UNITED STATES FOREST SERVICE 32
NON-GOVERNMENTAL ORGANIZATIONS
AMERICAN FISHERIES SOCIETY
    Education Section 143
AMERICAN FISHERIES SOCIETY, MONTANA CHAPTER147
BOONE AND CROCKETT CLUB....................................... 167
BOONE AND CROCKETT FOUNDATION......................... 167
CENTER FOR RESOURCEFUL BUILDING TECHNOLOGY
    176
CONFEDERATED SALISH AND KOOTENAI TRIBES........ 185
CRAIGHEAD WILDLIFE-WILDLANDS INSTITUTE............ 190
EARTHJUSTICE LEGAL DEFENSE FUND (formerly Sierra
    Club Legal Defense Fund, Inc.)
    Montana Office 198
FEDERATION OF FLY FISHERS 205
GREAT BEAR FOUNDATION 216
GREATER YELLOWSTONE COALITION........................... 217
MONTANA ASSOCIATION OF CONSERVATION DISTRICTS
    260
MONTANA AUDUBON 260
MONTANA B.A.S.S. CHAPTER FEDERATION 260
MONTANA ENVIRONMENTAL INFORMATION CENTER. 260
MONTANA FOREST OWNERS ASSOCIATION................ 260
MONTANA LAND RELIANCE 260
MONTANA LAND RELIANCE (Eastern Office) 260
MONTANA WILDERNESS ASSOCIATION........................ 260
MONTANA WILDLIFE FEDERATION 261
NATIONAL WILDLIFE FEDERATION
    Northern Rockies Natural Resource Center (ID, MT, WY)274
NATURE CONSERVANCY, THE, MONTANA CHAPTER.. 281
NORTHERN PLAINS RESOURCE COUNCIL 292
PREDATOR PROJECT 306
RIVER NETWORK
    Northern Rockes Office
        Riverlands Conservancy Field Office 312
ROCKY MOUNTAIN ELK FOUNDATION 313
    Intermountain Region Office.. 313
    North-Central Region Office 313
    Northeast Region Office 313
    Northwest Region Office 313
    Pacific Southwest Region Office..................................... 313
    South-Central Region Office... 314
    Southeast Region Office 314
THE GLACIER INSTITUTE 331
TROUT UNLIMITED, MONTANA COUNCIL 335
WILDERNESS WATCH 350
WILDLIFE SOCIETY, MONTANA CHAPTER..................... 355
STATE GOVERNMENT ORGANIZATIONS
BUREAU OF MINES AND GEOLOGY................................ 82
ENVIRONMENTAL QUALITY COUNCIL 82
GOVERNOR OF MONTANA, MARC RACICOT.................. 82
MONTANA COOPERATIVE FISHERY RESEARCH UNIT
    (USDI) 82
MONTANA COOPERATIVE WILDLIFE RESEARCH UNIT
    (USGS/BRD).. 82
MONTANA DEPARTMENT OF AGRICULTURE.................. 82
MONTANA DEPARTMENT OF FISH, WILDLIFE, AND PARKS
    82
MONTANA DEPARTMENT OF NATURAL RESOURCES AND
    CONSERVATION 82

GEOGRAPHIC INDEX

MONTANA NATURAL HERITAGE PROGRAM.................... 83
MONTANA STATE EXTENSION SERVICES...................... 83

NEBRASKA

GOVERNMENT ORGANIZATIONS
DEPARTMENT OF THE ARMY
   U.S. ARMY CORPS OF ENGINEERS............................. 21

NON-GOVERNMENTAL ORGANIZATIONS
ASSOCIATION OF GREAT LAKES OUTDOOR WRITERS 162
GROUNDWATER FOUNDATION, THE 219
INLAND BIRD BANDING ASSOCIATION 227
IOWA PRAIRIE NETWORK.. 238
IZAAK WALTON LEAGUE OF AMERICA, INC., THE
   Nebraska Division 240
NATIONAL ARBOR DAY FOUNDATION 262
NATURE CONSERVANCY, THE, NEBRASKA CHAPTER 281
NEBRASKA ASSOCIATION OF NATURAL RESOURCE
   DISTRICTS... 282
NEBRASKA AUDUBON COUNCIL 282
NEBRASKA B.A.S.S. CHAPTER FEDERATION................ 283
NEBRASKA CHAPTER OF THE AMERICAN FISHERIES
   SOCIETY 283
NEBRASKA ORNITHOLOGISTS' UNION, INC. (University of
   Nebraska State Museum)... 283
NEBRASKA WILDLIFE FEDERATION, INC. 283
NORTH AMERICAN CRANE WORKING GROUP 288
WILDLIFE SOCIETY, NEBRASKA CHAPTER 355

STATE GOVERNMENT ORGANIZATIONS
DEPARTMENT OF ENVIRONMENTAL QUALITY
   (NEBRASKA)... 83
DEPARTMENT OF WATER RESOURCES (NEBRASKA) ... 83
GAME AND PARKS COMMISSION..................................... 83
   Game and Parks Commission 83
GAME AND PARKS COMMISSION-NEBRASKA
   AK-Sar-Ben Aquarium... 84
GOVERNOR OF NEBRASKA, MIKE JOHANNS................... 83
NEBRASKA DEPARTMENT OF AGRICULTURE 84
NEBRASKA GEOLOGICAL SURVEY................................... 84
NEBRASKA NATURAL RESOURCES COMMISSION.......... 84
NEBRASKA STATE EXTENSION SERVICES 84

NEVADA

GOVERNMENT ORGANIZATIONS
DEPARTMENT OF THE INTERIOR
   BUREAU OF RECLAMATION.. 24

NON-GOVERNMENTAL ORGANIZATIONS
MULE DEER FOUNDATION, THE...................................... 262
NATURE CONSERVANCY, THE, NEVADA CHAPTER...... 281
NEVADA ASSOCIATION OF CONSERVATION DISTRICTS
.... 283
NEVADA WILDLIFE FEDERATION 283
TAHOE REGIONAL PLANNING AGENCY 329
TROUT UNLIMITED, NEVADA COUNCIL 335
WILD HORSE ORGANIZED ASSISTANCE, INC. (WHOA) 348
WILDLIFE SOCIETY, NEVADA CHAPTER........................ 355

STATE GOVERNMENT ORGANIZATIONS
DIVISION OF AGRICULTURE... 84
GOVERNOR OF NEVADA, KENNY GUINN 84
NEVADA BUREAU OF MINES AND GEOLOGY................. 84
NEVADA DEPARTMENT OF CONSERVATION AND
   NATURAL RESOURCES.. 84
   State Conservation Commission 85
NEVADA DIVISION OF WILDLIFE...................................... 85
NEVADA NATURAL HERITAGE PROGRAM...................... 85
NEVEDA COOPERATIVE EXTENSION 85

NEW HAMPSHIRE

GOVERNMENT ORGANIZATIONS
NORTHEASTERN FOREST FIRE PROTECTION
   COMMISSION... 9
DEPARTMENT OF THE ARMY
   U.S. ARMY CORPS OF ENGINEERS............................. 21

NON-GOVERNMENTAL ORGANIZATIONS
AMERICAN BASS ASSOCIATION OF NEW HAMPSHIRE,
   THE 140
AMERICAN FISHERIES SOCIETY, ATLANTIC
   INTERNATIONAL CHAPTER....................................... 144
AMERICAN GROUND WATER TRUST 150
ASSOCIATION FOR CONSERVATION INFORMATION, INC.
.... 160
AUDUBON SOCIETY OF NEW HAMPSHIRE..................... 164
DUCKS UNLIMITED, INC. (North Atlantic Flyway and Ohio)
.... 196
ELM RESEARCH INSTITUTE 200
NATURE CONSERVANCY, THE, NEW HAMPSHIRE
   CHAPTER 281
NEW HAMPSHIRE ASSOCIATION OF CONSERVATION
   COMMISSIONS... 284
NEW HAMPSHIRE ASSOCIATION OF CONSERVATION
   DISTRICTS... 284
NEW HAMPSHIRE B.A.S.S. CHAPTER FEDERATION..... 284
NEW HAMPSHIRE LAKES ASSOCIATION 284
NEW HAMPSHIRE TIMBERLAND OWNERS ASSOCIATION
.... 285
NEW HAMPSHIRE WILDLIFE FEDERATION.................... 285
NORTH AMERICAN LOON FUND..................................... 289
SEACOAST ANTI-POLLUTION LEAGUE 318
SOCIETY FOR THE PROTECTION OF NEW HAMPSHIRE
   FORESTS.. 322
STATEWIDE PROGRAM OF ACTION TO CONSERVE OUR
   ENVIRONMENT (SPACE 327
STUDENT CONSERVATION ASSOCIATION, INC. 328
TROUT UNLIMITED, NEW HAMPSHIRE COUNCIL.......... 335

STATE GOVERNMENT ORGANIZATIONS
COUNCIL ON RESOURCES AND DEVELOPMENT 85
DEPARTMENT OF RESOURCES AND ECONOMIC
   DEVELOPMENT... 85
GOVERNOR OF NEW HAMPSHIRE, JEANNE SHAHEEN.. 85
NEW HAMPSHIRE DEPARTMENT OF AGRICULTURE,
   MARKETS, AND FOOD.. 85
   State Conservation Committee....................................... 85
NEW HAMPSHIRE DEPARTMENT OF ENVIRONMENTAL
   SERVICES 86
NEW HAMPSHIRE FISH AND GAME DEPARTMENT......... 86
NEW HAMPSHIRE NATURAL HERITAGE INVENTORY..... 86
NEW HAMPSHIRE SEA GRANT PROGRAM 86
UNIVERSITY OF NEW HAMPSHIRE COOPERATIVE
   EXTENSION... 86

NEW JERSEY

GOVERNMENT ORGANIZATIONS
DELAWARE RIVER BASIN COMMISSION......................... 7

NON-GOVERNMENTAL ORGANIZATIONS
AMERICAN BASS ASSOCIATION OF NEW JERSEY, THE
.... 140
AMERICAN FISHERIES SOCIETY, MID-ATLANTIC
   CHAPTER 147
AMERICAN LITTORAL SOCIETY..................................... 152
ASSOCIATION OF NEW JERSEY ENVIRONMENTAL
   COMMISSIONS... 162
BIOMASS USERS NETWORK 166
CLEAN OCEAN ACTION.. 180
COMMITTEE FOR NATIONAL ARBOR DAY..................... 183
DUCKS UNLIMITED, INC. (Meadowlands Office) 196
NATURE CONSERVANCY, THE, NEW JERSEY CHAPTER
.... 281
NEW JERSEY AGRICULTURAL SOCIETY 285
NEW JERSEY ASSOCIATION OF CONSERVATION
   DISTRICTS... 285
NEW JERSEY AUDUBON SOCIETY................................. 285
NEW JERSEY B.A.S.S. CHAPTER FEDERATION 285
NEW JERSEY CONSERVATION FOUNDATION 285
NEW JERSEY ENVIRONMENTAL LOBBY....................... 286
NEW JERSEY FORESTRY ASSOCIATION....................... 286
NORTHEAST ASSOCIATION OF FISH AND WILDLIFE
   RESOURCE AGENCIES.. 291
TROUT UNLIMITED, NEW JERSEY COUNCIL................. 335
WILDLIFE SOCIETY, NEW JERSEY CHAPTER 356

STATE GOVERNMENT ORGANIZATIONS
DEPARTMENT OF ENVIRONMENTAL PROTECTION (NEW
   JERSEY) 86
   Division of Fish, Game, and Wildlife 87
   Division of Parks and Forestry... 87
   Division of Publicly Funded Site Remediation................... 87
   Division of Solid and Hazardous Waste 87
   Geological Survey... 87
   Green Acres and Recreation Program............................. 87
GOVERNOR OF NEW JERSEY, CHRISTINE T. WHITMAN 86

NEW JERSEY DEPARTMENT OF AGRICULTURE............. 87
   State Soil and Conservation Committee 87
NEW JERSEY PINELANDS COMMISSION...................... 88
NEW JERSEY SEA GRANT PROGRAM 88
NEW JERSEY STATE EXTENSION SERVICES 88

NEW MEXICO

GOVERNMENT ORGANIZATIONS
DEPARTMENT OF THE AIR FORCE 16
DEPARTMENT OF THE ARMY
   U.S. ARMY CORPS OF ENGINEERS............................. 21
DEPARTMENT OF THE INTERIOR
   UNITED STATES FISH AND WILDLIFE SERVICE 26
U.S. DEPARTMENT OF AGRICULTURE
   UNITED STATES FOREST SERVICE 32

NON-GOVERNMENTAL ORGANIZATIONS
AMERICAN FISHERIES SOCIETY, NEW MEXICO STATE
   UNIVERSITY STUDENT CHAPTER 147
ARCHAEOLOGICAL CONSERVANCY.............................. 158
CENTER FOR WILDLIFE LAW.. 177
FOREST TRUST 209
NATIONAL PARKS AND CONSERVATION ASSOCIATION
(NPCA)
   Southwest Regional Office 270
NATURE CONSERVANCY, THE, NEW MEXICO CHAPTER
.... 281
NEW MEXICO ASSOCIATION OF CONSERVATION
   DISTRICTS.. 286
NEW MEXICO BASS CHAPTER FEDERATION................ 286
NEW MEXICO ENVIRONMENTAL LAW CENTER 286
NEW MEXICO WILDLIFE FEDERATION........................... 286
SOUTHWEST RESEARCH AND INFORMATION CENTER 326
WILDLIFE SOCIETY, NEW MEXICO CHAPTER 356

STATE GOVERNMENT ORGANIZATIONS
ENERGY, MINERALS, AND NATURAL RESOURCES
   DEPARTMENT 88
      Administrative Services Division... 88
      Energy Conservation and Management Division 88
      Forestry and Resources Conservation Division 88
      Mining and Minerals Division... 88
      Oil Conservation Division 88
      State Parks and Recreation Division 88
GOVERNOR OF NEW MEXICO, GARY JOHNSON 88
NEW MEXICO BUREAU OF MINES AND MINERAL
   RESOURCES... 89
      Geological Information Center Library 89
NEW MEXICO COOPERATIVE FISH AND WILDLIFE
   RESEARCH UNIT.. 89
NEW MEXICO DEPARTMENT OF AGRICULTURE 89
NEW MEXICO DEPARTMENT OF GAME AND FISH.......... 89
      Albuquerque NM Office.. 89
      Las Cruces NM Office 89
      Raton NM Office 89
      Roswell NM Office 89
NEW MEXICO ENVIRONMENT DEPARTMENT 89
NEW MEXICO SOIL AND WATER CONSERVATION
   COMMISSION 90
NEW MEXICO STATE EXTENSION SERVICES 90
STATE ENGINEER OFFICE/INTERSTATE STREAM
   COMMISSION 90

NEW YORK

GOVERNMENT ORGANIZATIONS
ENVIRONMENTAL PROTECTION AGENCY..................... 10
DEPARTMENT OF THE ARMY
   U.S. ARMY CORPS OF ENGINEERS............................. 21
   U.S. MILITARY ACADEMY 23
U.S. DEPARTMENT OF AGRICULTURE
   ANIMAL AND PLANT HEALTH INSPECTION SERVICE.. 29
U.S. TREASURY DEPARTMENT
   U.S. CUSTOMS SERVICE... 33

NON-GOVERNMENTAL ORGANIZATIONS
ADIRONDACK COUNCIL, THE 133
ADIRONDACK MOUNTAIN CLUB, INC., THE 134
ADIRONDACK NATURE CONSERVANCY/ADIRONDACK
   LAND TRUST, INC. 134
AMERICAN CONSERVATION ASSOCIATION, INC. (New
   York Office).. 142
AMERICAN FISHERIES SOCIETY, COLLEGE OF
   ENVIRONMENTAL SCIENCE AND FORESTRY CHAPTER
.... 145
AMERICAN FISHERIES SOCIETY, NEW YORK CHAPTER
.... 147
AMERICAN GEOGRAPHICAL SOCIETY 150
AMERICAN LITTORAL SOCIETY (New York Office) 152
AMERICAN LUNG ASSOCIATION 152
AMERICAN MUSEUM OF NATURAL HISTORY............... 153
AMERICAN WILDLIFE RESEARCH FOUNDATION, INC. .. 156
ASSOCIATION FOR THE PROTECTION OF THE
   ADIRONDACKS, THE.. 160
ATLANTIC STATES LEGAL FOUNDATION 163
AUDUBON INTERNATIONAL... 163
AVSC INTERNATIONAL 165
CAMP FIRE CLUB OF AMERICA, THE 171
CAMP FIRE CONSERVATION FUND 171
CATSKILL CENTER FOR CONSERVATION AND
   DEVELOPMENT, INC., THE 174
CATSKILL FOREST ASSOCIATION 174
CENTER FOR ENVIRONMENTAL EDUCATION............... 174
CENTER FOR ENVIRONMENTAL INFORMATION........... 175
COALITION FOR EDUCATION IN THE OUTDOORS........ 181
CORNELL LAB OF ORNITHOLOGY 189
COUSTEAU SOCIETY, INC., THE (New York Office) 190
DRAGONFLY SOCIETY OF THE AMERICAS, THE 193
EARTH DAY NEW YORK... 197
ENVIRONMENTAL ADVOCATES 201
ENVIRONMENTAL DEFENSE FUND, INC. 202
FEDERATION OF NEW YORK STATE BIRD CLUBS, INC.205
FUND FOR ANIMALS INC., THE 212
GARDEN CLUB OF AMERICA, THE 213
GIRL SCOUTS OF THE UNITED STATES OF AMERICA.. 215
GREAT LAKES UNITED.. 217
GREEN PARTY USA 218
HUDSONIA LIMITED 222
INFORM, INC. 226
INSTITUTE OF ECOSYSTEM STUDIES 227
IZAAK WALTON LEAGUE OF AMERICA, INC., THE
   New York Division 241
JACKSON HOLE PRESERVE, INC. 242
MARINE ENVIRONMENTAL RESEARCH INSTITUTE (MERI)
.... 252
NATIONAL AUDUBON SOCIETY..................................... 265
   Project Puffin 265
   Scully Science Center 265
NATIONAL AUDUBON SOCIETY, LIVING OCEANS
   PROGRAM 265
NATIONAL FLYWAY COUNCIL
   Atlantic Flyway Office... 268
NATURAL RESOURCES DEFENSE COUNCIL, INC......... 278
NATURE CONSERVACNY, THE, NEW YORK EASTER
   CHAPTER 279
NATURE CONSERVANCY, THE
   New York Region Office... 279
NATURE CONSERVANCY, THE, NEW YORK ADIRONDACK
   CHAPTER 281
NATURE CONSERVANCY, THE, NEW YORK
   CENTRAL/WESTERN CHAPTER................................. 281
NATURE CONSERVANCY, THE, NEW YORK LONG ISLAND
   CHAPTER 281
NATURE CONSERVANCY, THE, NEW YORK LOWER
   HUDSON CHAPTER 281
NATURE CONSERVANCY, THE, NEW YORK SOUTH
   FORK/SHELTER ISLAND CHAPTER 281
NEW YORK ASSOCIATION OF CONSERVATION
   DISTRICTS, INC. 286
NEW YORK B.A.S.S. CHAPTER FEDERATION................ 287
NEW YORK FOREST OWNERS ASSOCIATION, INC....... 287
NEW YORK PUBLIC INTEREST RESEARCH GROUP
   (NYPIRG.. 287
NEW YORK TURTLE AND TORTOISE SOCIETY 287
NEW YORK-NEW JERSEY TRAIL CONFERENCE INC. ... 287
PLANNED PARENTHOOD FEDERATION OF AMERICA INC.
.... 304
POPULATION COMMUNICATIONS INTERNATIONAL 304
RAINFOREST ALLIANCE... 309

GEOGRAPHIC INDEX

RAINFOREST RELIEF 309
ROGER TORY PETERSON INSTITUTE 314
SAVE THE SOUND, INC. (GARVIES POINT MUSEUM) ... 316
SCENIC HUDSON, INC. 317
SIERRA CLUB
   Northeast Office 319
ST. REGIS MOHAWK TRIBE 327
TROUT UNLIMITED, NEW YORK COUNCIL..................... 335
TUG HILL TOMORROW, INC. 338
UNITED NATIONS ENVIRONMENT PROGRAMME (North America Regional Office) 339
WILDLIFE CONSERVATION SOCIETY 350
WILDLIFE SOCIETY, NEW YORK CHAPTER 356
WORLD PAL (WORLD POPULATION ALLOCATION LIMITED INC.) 362
WORLD PARKS ENDOWMENT INC. 362

STATE GOVERNMENT ORGANIZATIONS
ADIRONDACK PARK AGENCY 90
DEPARTMENT OF ENVIRONMENTAL CONSERVATION (NEW YORK) 90
   Divisin of Environmental Permits 91
   Division of Air Resources 91
   Division of Environmental Enforcement 91
   Division of Environmental Remediation 91
   Division of Fish, Wildlife and Marine Resources 91
   Division of Forest Protection & Fire Management 91
   Division of in Mineral Resources 91
   Division of Information Services 91
   Division of Lands and Forests 91
   Division of Law Enforcement 91
   Division of Legal Affairs 91
   Division of Management and Budget 91
   Division of Operations 91
   Division of Public Affairs and Education 91
   Division of Solid & Hazardous Materials 91
   Division of Transportation Services 91
   Division of Water 91
   Press Office 91
   Regional Directors 91
ENVIRONMENTAL PROTECTION BUREAU 91
GOVERNOR OF NEW YORK, GEORGE E. PATAKI 90
MARINE SCIENCES RESEARCH CENTER (NEW YORK) .. 92
NEW YORK COOPERATIVE FISH AND WILDLIFE RESEARCH UNIT 92
NEW YORK DEPARTMENT OF AGRICULTURE AND MARKETS 92
   State Soil and Water Conservation Committee 92
NEW YORK DEPARTMENT OF HEALTH 92
NEW YORK GEOLOGICAL SURVEY AND STATE MUSEUM 92
NEW YORK SEA GRANT 92
NEW YORK STATE COOPERATIVE EXTENSION 93
NEW YORK STATE OFFICE OF PARKS, RECREATION AND HISTORIC PRESERVATION 93
OFFICE OF ENERGY EFFICIENCY AND ENVIRONMENT . 93
STATE FISH AND WILDLIFE MANAGEMENT BOARD (NEW YORK) 93
   Region 3 93
   Region 4
   Region 5 93
   Region 6 93
   Region 7 94
   Region 8 94
   Region 9 94
TUG HILL COMMISSION 94

NORTH CAROLINA
GOVERNMENT ORGANIZATIONS
DEPARTMENT OF THE ARMY
   U.S. ARMY CORPS OF ENGINEERS 21
U.S. DEPARTMENT OF AGRICULTURE
   UNITED STATES FOREST SERVICE 32

NON-GOVERNMENTAL ORGANIZATIONS
AMERICAN FISHERIES SOCIETY
   Early Life History 143
AMERICAN FISHERIES SOCIETY, NORTH CAROLINA CHAPTER 148
AMERICAN LIVESTOCK BREEDS CONSERVANCY 152
AMERICAN SOCIETY FOR ENVIRONMENTAL HISTORY 154
CAROLINA BIRD CLUB, INC. 173
CONSERVATION COUNCIL OF NORTH CAROLINA 187
ENVIRONMENTAL DEFENSE FUND, INC.
   North Carolina Office 202
FOREST HISTORY SOCIETY, INC. 209
NATIONAL HUNTERS ASSOCIATION, INC. 269
NATURE CONSERVANCY, THE
   Southeast Office 279
NATURE CONSERVANCY, THE, NORTH CAROLINA CHAPTER 281
NORTH CAROLINA ASSOCIATION OF SOIL AND WATER CONSERVATION DISTRICTS 290
NORTH CAROLINA B.A.S.S. CHAPTER FEDERATION 290
NORTH CAROLINA BEACH BUGGY ASSOCIATION, INC. 290
NORTH CAROLINA COASTAL FEDERATION, INC. 290
NORTH CAROLINA FORESTRY ASSOCIATION 290
NORTH CAROLINA HERPETOLOGICAL SOCIETY 290
NORTH CAROLINA RECREATION AND PARK SOCIETY, INC. 291
NORTH CAROLINA WILDLIFE FEDERATION 291
PROFESSIONAL BOWHUNTERS SOCIETY 306
SCENIC AMERICA
   Scenic North Carolina 317
SOUTHERN ENVIRONMENTAL LAW CENTER (North Carolina Office) 326
TROUT UNLIMITED, NORTH CAROLINA COUNCIL 336
WILDLIFE SOCIETY, NORTH CAROLINA CHAPTER 356

STATE GOVERNMENT ORGANIZATIONS
COOPERATIVE EXTENSION SERVICE (NORTH CAROLINA) 94
GOVERNOR OF NORTH CAROLINA, JAMES B. HUNT, JR. 94
NORTH CAROLINA DEPARTMENT OF ENVIRONMENT AND NATURAL RESOURCES 94
NORTH CAROLINA COOPERATIVE FISH AND WILDLIFE RESEARCH UNIT (USDI) 94
NORTH CAROLINA DEPARTMENT OF AGRICULTURE 94
NORTH CAROLINA DEPARTMENT OF ENVIRONMENT AND NATURAL RESOURCES
   State Soil and Water Conservation Commission 95
NORTH CAROLINA SEA GRANT PROGRAM 95
WILDLIFE RESOURCES COMMISSION 95

NORTH DAKOTA
NON-GOVERNMENTAL ORGANIZATIONS
AMERICAN FISHERIES SOCIETY, DAKOTA CHAPTER .. 145
DUCKS UNLIMITED, INC. (Central Flyway Office) 196
MUSKIES, INC. 262
NATURE CONSERVANCY, THE, NORTH DAKOTA CHAPTER 281
NORTH DAKOTA ASSOCIATION OF SOIL CONSERVATION DISTRICTS 291
NORTH DAKOTA WILDLIFE FEDERATION, INC. 291
WILDLIFE SOCIETY, NORTH DAKOTA CHAPTER 356

STATE GOVERNMENT ORGANIZATIONS
GOVERNOR OF NORTH DAKOTA, EDWARD T. SCHAFFER 95
INSTITUTE FOR ECOLOGICAL STUDIES 95
NORTH DAKOTA DEPARTMENT OF AGRICULTURE 95
NORTH DAKOTA DEPARTMENT OF HEALTH 95
NORTH DAKOTA GAME AND FISH DEPARTMENT 95
NORTH DAKOTA GEOLOGICAL SURVEY 96
NORTH DAKOTA STATE EXTENSION SERVICE 96
NORTH DAKOTA STATE FOREST SERVICE 96
NORTH DAKOTA STATE SOIL CONSERVATION COMMITTEE 96
NORTH DAKOTA WATER COMMISSION 96
PARKS AND RECREATION DEPARTMENT (NORTH DAKOTA) 96

OHIO
GOVERNMENT ORGANIZATIONS
OHIO RIVER VALLEY WATER SANITATION COMMISSION 9
DEPARTMENT OF THE AIR FORCE
   MAJOR AIR COMMANDS 16
DEPARTMENT OF THE ARMY
   U.S. ARMY CORPS OF ENGINEERS 21

NON-GOVERNMENTAL ORGANIZATIONS
  AMERICAN FISHERIES SOCIETY
    Water Quality Section 144
  AMERICAN FISHERIES SOCIETY, OHIO CHAPTER........ 148
  CANVASBACK SOCIETY.. 173
  CENTRAL OHIO ANGLERS AND HUNTERS CLUB.......... 177
  CLEVELAND MUSEUM OF NATURAL HISTORY, THE 180
  DAWES ARBORETUM, THE.. 191
  ENVIRONMENTAL EDUCATION COUNCIL OF OHIO 203
  HOLDEN ARBORETUM, THE 221
  INTERNATIONAL SOCIETY FOR ENDANGERED CATS
    (ISEC)... 233
  INTERNATIONAL WILD WATERFOWL ASSOCIATION 235
  IZAAK WALTON LEAGUE OF AMERICA, INC., THE
    Ohio Division... 241
  LEAGUE OF OHIO SPORTSMEN 247
  NATIONAL AUDUBON SOCIETY
    Great Lakes, IL, IN, KY, MI, MN, OH, WI...................... 265
  NATIONAL GROUND WATER ASSOCIATION, THE 269
  NATIVE PLANT SOCIETY OF NORTHEASTERN OHIO ... 276
  NATURE CONSERVANCY, THE, OHO CHAPTER 281
  NORTH AMERICAN ASSOCIATION FOR ENVIRONMENTAL
    EDUCATION (Membership and Publications Office)....... 288
  OHIO ACADEMY OF SCIENCE, THE................................ 294
  OHIO ALLIANCE FOR THE ENVIRONMENT 294
  OHIO AUDUBON COUNCIL, INC. 294
  OHIO B.A.S.S. CHAPTER FEDERATION.......................... 295
  OHIO BIOLOGICAL SURVEY.. 295
  OHIO ENVIRONMENTAL COUNCIL, INC. 295
  OHIO FEDERATION OF SOIL AND WATER
    CONSERVATION DISTRICTS.. 295
  OHIO FORESTRY ASSOCIATION, INC., THE 295
  SCENIC AMERICA
    Scenic Ohio 317
  TROUT UNLIMITED, OHIO COUNCIL................................ 336
  WILDLIFE LEGISLATIVE FUND OF AMERICA, THE, AND
    WILDLIFE CONSERVATION FUND OF AMERICA, THE 352
  WILDLIFE SOCIETY, OHIO CHAPTER 356
  WILSON ORNITHOLOGICAL SOCIETY............................ 358
STATE GOVERNMENT ORGANIZATIONS
  ENVIRONMENTAL REVIEW APPEALS COMMISSION....... 96
  GOVERNOR OF OHIO, ROBERT TAFT.............................. 96
  OHIO COOPERATIVE FISH AND WILDLIFE RESEARCH
    UNIT (USDI) 96
  OHIO DEPARTMENT OF AGRICULTURE 96
  OHIO DEPARTMENT OF NATURAL RESOURCES 97
  OHIO ENVIRONMENTAL PROTECTION AGENCY............. 97
  OHIO STATE EXTENSION SERVICES 97

OKLAHOMA
GOVERNMENT ORGANIZATIONS
  DEPARTMENT OF THE ARMY
    U.S. ARMY CORPS OF ENGINEERS............................... 21
NON-GOVERNMENTAL ORGANIZATIONS
  AMERICAN FEDERATION OF MINERALOGICAL SOCIETIES
    142
  AMERICAN FISHERIES SOCIETY
    Fisheries Management Section 143
  AMERICAN FISHERIES SOCIETY, OKLAHOMA CHAPTER
    148
  GEORGE MIKSCH SUTTON AVIAN RESEARCH CENTER
    INC. 214
  NATIVE AMERICANS FOR A CLEAN ENVIRONMENT
    (NACE) 276
  NATURE CONSERVANCY, THE, OKLAHOMA CHAPTER 281
  OKLAHOMA ACADEMY OF SCIENCE............................... 295
  OKLAHOMA ASSOCIATION OF CONSERVATION
    DISTRICTS... 296
  OKLAHOMA AUDUBON COUNCIL 296
  OKLAHOMA B.A.S.S. CHAPTER FEDERATION 296
  OKLAHOMA NATIVE PLANT SOCIETY 296
  OKLAHOMA ORNITHOLOGICAL SOCIETY...................... 296
  OKLAHOMA WILDLIFE FEDERATION............................... 296
  OKLAHOMA WOODLAND OWNERS ASSOCIATION 296
  TROUT UNLIMITED, OKLAHOMA COUNCIL..................... 336
  WILDLIFE SOCIETY, OKLAHOMA CHAPTER 356
STATE GOVERNMENT ORGANIZATIONS
  DEPARTMENT OF WILDLIFE CONSERVATION 98
  GOVERNOR OF OKLAHOMA, FRANK KEATING 98
  OKLAHOMA BIOLOGICAL SURVEY................................... 98
  OKLAHOMA COOPERATIVE FISH AND WILDLIFE
    RESEARCH UNIT (USDI) 98
  OKLAHOMA DEPARTMENT OF ENVIRONMENTAL QUALITY
    98
  OKLAHOMA GEOLOGICAL SURVEY 98
  OKLAHOMA STATE BOARD OF AGRICULTURE............... 98
  OKLAHOMA STATE CONSERVATION COMMISSION 99
  OKLAHOMA STATE EXTENSION SERVICES 99
  OKLAHOMA TOURISM AND RECREATION DEPARTMENT
    99
  OKLAHOMA WATER RESOURCES BOARD 99

OREGON
GOVERNMENT ORGANIZATIONS
  COLUMBIA RIVER INTER-TRIBAL FISH COMMISSION ... 7
  PACIFIC STATES MARINE FISHERIES COMMISSION .. 10
  DEPARTMENT OF THE ARMY
    U.S. ARMY CORPS OF ENGINEERS............................... 21
  DEPARTMENT OF THE INTERIOR
    UNITED STATES FISH AND WILDLIFE SERVICE 26
  U.S. DEPARTMENT OF AGRICULTURE
    UNITED STATES FOREST SERVICE 32
NON-GOVERNMENTAL ORGANIZATIONS
  AMERICAN FISHERIES SOCIETY
    Equal Opportunities Section 143
    Marine Fisheries Section... 143
  AMERICAN FISHERIES SOCIETY, GREATER PORTLAND,
    OR CHAPTER 145
  AMERICAN FISHERIES SOCIETY, OREGON CHAPTER. 148
  AUDUBON SOCIETY OF PORTLAND 164
  COLUMBIA BASIN FISH AND WILDLIFE AUTHORITY 183
  ENVIRONMENTAL EDUCATION PROJECT (John Inskeep
    Environmental Learning Center)..................................... 203
  ENVIRONMENTAL LAW ALLIANCE WORLDWIDE (E-LAW)
    203
  FOREST SERVICE EMPLOYEES FOR ENVIRONMENTAL
    ETHICS (FSEEE).. 209
  HIGH DESERT MUSEUM, THE.. 221
  IZAAK WALTON LEAGUE OF AMERICA, INC., THE
    Oregon Divison.. 241
  NATIONAL WILDLIFE FEDERATION
    Western Natural Resource Center (CA, NV, OR, WA) 275
  NATIVE PLANT SOCIETY OF OREGON............................ 276
  NATURAL AREAS ASSOCIATION 277
  NATURE CONSERVANCY, THE, OREGON CHAPTER.... 281
  OREGON ASSOCIATION OF CONSERVATION DISTRICTS
    297
  OREGON B.A.S.S. CHAPTER FEDERATION 297
  OREGON ENVIRONMENTAL COUNCIL........................... 298
  OREGON NATURAL RESOURCES COUNCIL................. 298
  OREGON SMALL WOODLANDS ASSOCIATION 298
  OREGON SOCIETY OF AMERICAN FORESTERS........... 298
  OREGON TROUT, INC. 298
  OREGON WILDLIFE HERITAGE FOUNDATION............... 298
  PACIFIC FISHERY MANAGEMENT COUNCIL.................. 300
  PACIFIC RIVERS COUNCIL 300
  PUBLIC EMPLOYEES FOR ENVIRONMENTAL
    RESPONSIBILITY (PEER) (West Coast Office) 307
  RIVER NETWORK 312
  STEAMBOATERS, THE 327
  TROUT UNLIMITED, OREGON COUNCIL 336
  WASHINGTON SOCIETY OF AMERICAN FORESTERS .. 344
  WESTERN ENVIRONMENTAL LAW CENTER................... 346
  WESTERN FORESTRY AND CONSERVATION
    ASSOCIATION 347
  WILDERNESS LAND TRUST, THE (Oregon Office) 349
  WILDLIFE SOCIETY, OREGON CHAPTER....................... 356
  WORLD FORESTRY CENTER... 362
  XERCES SOCIETY, THE 364
STATE GOVERNMENT ORGANIZATIONS
  DEPARTMENT OF FISH AND WILDLIFE (OREGON) 100
  DEPARTMENT OF GEOLOGY AND MINERAL INDUSTRIES
    100
  DEPARTMENT OF TRANSPORTATION (OREGON) 100
  FISH AND WILDLIFE DIVISION/DEPARTMENT OF STATE
    POLICE 100

GEOGRAPHIC INDEX

GOVERNOR OF OREGON, JOHN A. KITZHABER 100
OREGON COOPERATIVE FISH AND WILDLIFE RESEARCH UNIT (USDI) 100
OREGON COOPERATIVE FISH AND WILDLIFE RESEARCH UNIT (USDI) 100
OREGON DEPARTMENT OF AGRICULTURE 100
OREGON DEPARTMENT OF ENVIRONMENTAL QUALITY (DEQ) 101
OREGON DEPARTMENT OF FORESTRY 101
OREGON PARKS AND RECREATION DEPARTMENT 101
OREGON SEA GRANT PROGRAM 101
OREGON STATE EXTENSION SERVICES 101
STATE MARINE BOARD (OREGON) 102
WATER RESOURCES DEPARTMENT 102
    Water Resources Commission 102

PENNSYLVANIA
GOVERNMENT ORGANIZATIONS
SUSQUEHANNA RIVER BASIN COMMISSION 10
ENVIRONMENTAL PROTECTION AGENCY 10
DEPARTMENT OF THE ARMY
    U.S. ARMY CORPS OF ENGINEERS 21
U.S. DEPARTMENT OF AGRICULTURE
    RESEARCH EDUCATION AND ECONOMICS 32
    UNITED STATES FOREST SERVICE 32

NON-GOVERNMENTAL ORGANIZATIONS
AIR AND WASTE MANAGEMENT ASSOCIATION 135
ALLIANCE FOR THE CHESAPEAKE BAY
    Harrisburg Office 138
AMERICAN ASSOCIATION OF BOTANICAL GARDENS AND ARBORETA, INC. 139
AMERICAN CANAL SOCIETY, INC. 141
AMERICAN FISHERIES SOCIETY
    Bioengineering Section 142
AMERICAN FISHERIES SOCIETY, PENNSYLVANIA CHAPTER 148
AMERICAN LITTORAL SOCIETY (Delaware Riverkeeper Crossin) 152
AMERICAN NATURE STUDY SOCIETY 153
AUDUBON SOCIETY OF WESTERN PENNSYLVANIA 165
BOTANICAL SOCIETY OF WESTERN PENNSYLVANIA .. 167
BRANDYWINE CONSERVANCY, INC. 168
CHESAPEAKE BAY FOUNDATION, INC. (Pennsylvania Office) 178
ENVIRONMENTAL AIR FORCE 201
HAWK MIGRATION ASSOCIATION OF NORTH AMERICA 220
HAWK MOUNTAIN SANCTUARY ASSOCIATION 220
IZAAK WALTON LEAGUE OF AMERICA, INC., THE
    Pennsylvania Division 241
MID-ATLANTIC COUNCIL OF WATERSHED ASSOCIATIONS 256
NATIONAL AVIARY IN PITTSBURGH 265
NATIONAL COUNCIL FOR GEOGRAPHIC EDUCATION .. 266
NATIONAL TRUST FOR HISTORIC PRESERVATION
    Mid Atlantic 272
NATURAL LANDS TRUST, INC. 277
NATURE CONSERVANCY, THE, PENNSYLVANIA CHAPTER 281
NORTH AMERICAN NATIVE FISHES ASSOCIATION 289
NORTHEAST CONSERVATION LAW ENFORCEMENT CHIEFS' ASSOCIATION (CLECA) 292
NORTHEAST WILDLIFE ADMINISTRATORS ASSOCIATION 292
OUTDOOR WRITERS ASSOCIATION OF AMERICA INC. 299
PENNSYLVANIA ASSOCIATION OF CONSERVATION DISTRICT DIRECTORS, INC. 301
PENNSYLVANIA AUDUBON SOCIETY 301
PENNSYLVANIA B.A.S.S. CHAPTER FEDERATION, INC. 301
PENNSYLVANIA CITIZENS ADVISORY COUNCIL TO DEPARTMENT OF ENVIRONMENTAL PROTECTION .. 301
PENNSYLVANIA ENVIRONMENTAL COUNCIL, INC. (PEC) 302
PENNSYLVANIA FEDERATION OF SPORTSMEN'S CLUBS 302
PENNSYLVANIA FORESTRY ASSOCIATION, THE 302
PENNSYLVANIA RECREATION AND PARK SOCIETY, INC. 302
PENNSYLVANIA RESOURCES COUNCIL, INC., (formerly PA Roadside Council) 302
POCONO ENVIRONMENTAL EDUCATION CENTER 304
PURPLE MARTIN CONSERVATION ASSOCIATION 307
RARE CENTER FOR TROPICAL CONSERVATION 310
RUFFED GROUSE SOCIETY, THE 314
STUDENT ENVIRONMENTAL ACTION COALITION (SEAC) 328
TROUT UNLIMITED, PENNSYLVANIA COUNCIL 336
TURTLE CREEK WATERSHED ASSOCIATION, INC. 338
WATER RESOURCES ASSOCIATION OF THE DELAWARE RIVER BASIN 345
WESTERN PENNSYLVANIA CONSERVANCY 347
WHITE CLAY WATERSHED ASSOCIATION 348
WILDLANDS CONSERVANCY 350
WILDLIFE INFORMATION CENTER, INC. 352
WILDLIFE PRESERVATION TRUST INTERNATIONAL, INC. 353
WILDLIFE SOCIETY, PENNSYLVANIA CHAPTER 356

STATE GOVERNMENT ORGANIZATIONS
DEPARTMENT OF ENVIRONMENTAL PROTECTION (PENNSYLVANIA) 102
    Citizens Advisory Council to DEP 103
FISH AND BOAT COMMISSION 103
    Region 1 Northwest 103
    Region 2 Southwest 103
    Region 3 Northeast 103
    Region IV Southeast 103
    Region V North Central 103
    Region VI South Central 103
GAME COMMISSION 103
GOVERNOR OF PENNSYLVANIA, TOM RIDGE 102
PENNSYLVANIA COOPERATIVE FISH AND WILDLIFE RESEARCH UNIT 104
PENNSYLVANIA DEPARTMENT OF AGRICULTURE 104
    Region I 104
    Region II 104
    Region III 104
    Region IV 104
    Region V 104
    Region VI 105
    Region VII 105
    State Conservation Commission 105
PENNSYLVANIA DEPARTMENT OF CONSERVATION AND NATURAL RESOURCES 105
PENNSYLVANIA FOREST STEWARDSHIP PROGRAM .. 105
PENNSYLVANIA STATE EXTENSION SERVICES 105

PUERTO RICO
NON-GOVERNMENTAL ORGANIZATIONS
CENTRO de INFORMACION, INVESTIGACION y EDUCACION SOCIAL (CIIES) 177
CONSERVATION TRUST OF PUERTO RICO 189
PUERTO RICO ASSOCIATION OF SOIL AND WATER CONSERVATION DISTRICTS 307
PUERTO RICO CONSERVATION FOUNDATION, THE (PRCF 307

STATE GOVERNMENT ORGANIZATIONS
COMITE DESPERTAR CIDRENO 105
GOVERNOR OF PUERTO RICO, PEDRO J. ROSSELLO. 105
PUERTO RICO DEPARTMENT OF AGRICULTURE 105
PUERTO RICO DEPARTMENT OF NATURAL AND ENVIRONMENTAL RESOURCES 105
PUERTO RICO SEA GRANT PROGRAM 105
PUERTO RICO STATE EXTENSION SERVICES 106
SOIL CONSERVATION COMMITTEE OF PUERTO RICO 106

RHODE ISLAND
NON-GOVERNMENTAL ORGANIZATIONS
AMERICAN FISHERIES SOCIETY, SOUTHERN NEW ENGLAND CHAPTER 149
AUDUBON SOCIETY OF RHODE ISLAND 164
ENVIRONMENT COUNCIL OF RHODE ISLAND 200
NATURE CONSERVANCY, THE, RHODE ISLAND CHAPTER 281
RHODE ISLAND B.A.S.S. CHAPTER FEDERATION 311
RHODE ISLAND FOREST CONSERVATORS ASSOCIATION 311

RHODE ISLAND STATE ASSOCIATION OF
  CONSERVATION DISTRICTS.. 311
RHODE ISLAND WILD PLANT SOCIETY......................... 311
SAVE THE BAY, INC... 316
SOUTHERN NEW ENGLAND FOREST CONSORTIUM, INC.
  326
TROUT UNLIMITED, RHODE ISLAND COUNCIL
  (Narragansett).. 336
STATE GOVERNMENT ORGANIZATIONS
DEPARTMENT OF ENVIRONMENTAL MANAGEMENT
  (RHODE ISLAND).. 106
DEPARTMENT OF TRANSPORTATION (RHODE ISLAND)
  106
GOVERNOR OF RHODE ISLAND, LINCOLN ALMOND.... 106
RHODE ISLAND COOPERATIVE EXTENSION................. 106
RHODE ISLAND STATE CONSERVATION COMMITTEE . 107
STATE WATER RESOURCES BOARD (RHODE ISLAND) 107

SOUTH CAROLINA
GOVERNMENT ORGANIZATIONS
DEPARTMENT OF THE ARMY
  U.S. ARMY CORPS OF ENGINEERS.............................. 21
NON-GOVERNMENTAL ORGANIZATIONS
AMERICAN FISHERIES SOCIETY, SOUTH CAROLINA
  CHAPTER... 148
BLACK BASS FOUNDATION 166
DUCKS UNLIMITED, INC. (Low Country Initiative)............. 196
DUCKS UNLIMITED, INC. (South Atlantic Flyway)............. 196
GULF AND CARIBBEAN FISHERIES INSTITUTE............... 219
INTERNATIONAL PRIMATE PROTECTION LEAGUE....... 232
NATIONAL ASSOCIATION OF RECREATION RESOURCE
  PLANNERS 263
NATIONAL TRUST FOR HISTORIC PRESERVATION
  Southern Office 272
NATIONAL WILD TURKEY FEDERATION, INC., THE....... 273
NATURE CONSERVANCY, THE, SOUTH CAROLINA
  CHAPTER 282
NORTH AMERICAN GAMEBIRD ASSOCIATION, INC. 289
QUAIL UNLIMITED, INC.. 307
SOUTH ATLANTIC FISHERY MANAGEMENT COUNCIL . 323
SOUTH CAROLINA ASSOCIATION OF CONSERVATION
  DISTRICTS 323
SOUTH CAROLINA B.A.S.S. CHAPTER FEDERATION.... 323
SOUTH CAROLINA FORESTRY ASSOCIATION 324
SOUTH CAROLINA WILDLIFE FEDERATION................... 324
TROUT UNLIMITED, SOUTH CAROLINA COUNCIL.......... 336
WILDLIFE ACTION, INC.. 350
WILDLIFE SOCIETY, SOUTH CAROLINA CHAPTER 357
STATE GOVERNMENT ORGANIZATIONS
DEPARTMENT OF PARKS, RECREATION, AND TOURISM
  107
FORESTRY COMMISSION (SOUTH CAROLINA)............. 107
GOVERNOR OF SOUTH CAROLINA, JIM HODGES 107
SAVANNAH RIVER ECOLOGY LABORATORY 107
SOUTH CAROLINA DEPARTMENT OF AGRICULTURE .. 107
SOUTH CAROLINA DEPARTMENT OF HEALTH AND
  ENVIRONMENTAL CONTROL 108
  Office of Ocean and Coastal Resource Management
    (OCRM) 108
SOUTH CAROLINA DEPARTMENT OF NATURAL
  RESOURCES 108
SOUTH CAROLINA ENERGY OFFICE 108
SOUTH CAROLINA SEA GRANT CONSORTIUM 108
SOUTH CAROLINA STATE EXTENSION SERVICES 108

SOUTH DAKOTA
NON-GOVERNMENTAL ORGANIZATIONS
INTERTRIBAL BISON COOPERATIVE (ITBC).................. 236
IZAAK WALTON LEAGUE OF AMERICA, INC., THE
  South Dakota Division 241
NATIONAL FLYWAY COUNCIL 268
NATURE CONSERVANCY, THE, SOUTH DAKOTA
  CHAPTER 282
SOUTH DAKOTA ASSOCIATION OF CONSERVATION
  DISTRICTS... 324
SOUTH DAKOTA B.A.S.S. CHAPTER FEDERATION 324
SOUTH DAKOTA ORNITHOLOGISTS' UNION 324
SOUTH DAKOTA RESOURCES COALITION.................... 324
SOUTH DAKOTA WILDLIFE FEDERATION 324
WILDLIFE SOCIETY, SOUTH DAKOTA CHAPTER........... 357
STATE GOVERNMENT ORGANIZATIONS
BOARD OF MINERALS AND ENVIRONMENT.................. 109
DEPARTMENT OF ENVIRONMENT AND NATURAL
  RESOURCES (SOUTH DAKOTA) 109
GOVERNOR OF SOUTH DAKOTA, WILLIAM J. JANKLOW
  109
SOUTH DAKOTA COOPERATIVE FISH AND WILDLIFE
  RESEARCH UNIT (USDI) 109
SOUTH DAKOTA DEPARTMENT OF AGRICULTURE...... 109
  Division of Resource Conservation and Forestry 109
  State Conservation Commission 109
SOUTH DAKOTA GAME, FISH, AND PARKS DEPARTMENT
  109
SOUTH DAKOTA STATE EXTENSION SERVICES........... 109

TENNESSEE
GOVERNMENT ORGANIZATIONS
TENNESSEE VALLEY AUTHORITY................................ 36
DEPARTMENT OF ENERGY
  CARBON DIOXIDE INFORMATION ANALYSIS CENTER 14
DEPARTMENT OF THE ARMY
  U.S. ARMY CORPS OF ENGINEERS.............................. 21
NON-GOVERNMENTAL ORGANIZATIONS
AMERICAN ASSOCIATION OF FIELD BOTANISTS 139
AMERICAN FISHERIES SOCIETY, TENNESSEE CHAPTER
  149
BASS RESEARCH FOUNDATION 165
DUCKS UNLIMITED, INC. 194
DUCKS UNLIMITED, INC. (Wetlands America Trust, Inc.
  Office).. 196
ENVIRONMENTAL ACTION FUND (EAF) 200
GREAT SMOKY MOUNTAINS INSTITUTE AT TREMONT 217
HARDWOOD FOREST FOUNDATION.............................. 219
NATIONAL FOUNDATION TO PROTECT AMERICA'S
  EAGLES (Save The Eagle) 268
NATIONAL PARKS AND CONSERVATION ASSOCIATION
  (NPCA)
  Southeast Regional Office... 270
NATURE CONSERVANCY, THE, TENNESSEE CHAPTER
  282
TENNESSEE ASSOCIATION OF CONSERVATION
  DISTRICTS... 329
TENNESSEE B.A.S.S. CHAPTER FEDERATION.............. 329
TENNESSEE CITIZENS FOR WILDERNESS PLANNING . 329
TENNESSEE CONSERVATION LEAGUE......................... 330
TENNESSEE ENVIRONMENTAL COUNCIL 330
TENNESSEE FORESTRY ASSOCIATION 330
TENNESSEE WOODLAND OWNERS ASSOCIATION...... 330
TROUT UNLIMITED, TENNESSEE COUNCIL................... 336
WILDLIFE SOCIETY, TENNESSEE CHAPTER 357
STATE GOVERNMENT ORGANIZATIONS
DEPARTMENT OF ENVIRONMENT AND CONSERVATION
  (TENNESSEE)... 109
GOVERNOR OF TENNESSEE, DON SUNDQUIST........... 109
TENNESSEE COOPERATIVE FISHERY RESEARCH UNIT
  (USDI) 110
TENNESSEE DEPARTMENT OF AGRICULTURE 110
  State Soil Conservation Committee.............................. 110
TENNESSEE STATE EXTENSION SERVICES 110
WILDLIFE RESOURCES AGENCY 110

TEXAS
GOVERNMENT ORGANIZATIONS
ENVIRONMENTAL PROTECTION AGENCY.................... 10
DEPARTMENT OF THE AIR FORCE 16
  MAJOR AIR COMMANDS 16
DEPARTMENT OF THE ARMY
  U.S. ARMY CORPS OF ENGINEERS.............................. 21
U.S. DEPARTMENT OF AGRICULTURE
  ANIMAL AND PLANT HEALTH INSPECTION SERVICE.. 29
  RESEARCH EDUCATION AND ECONOMICS................. 32
U.S. TREASURY DEPARTMENT
  U.S. CUSTOMS SERVICE.. 33
NON-GOVERNMENTAL ORGANIZATIONS
AMERICAN FISHERIES SOCIETY
  Fish Culture Section.. 143
  Fisheries Administrators Section 143

GEOGRAPHIC INDEX

AMERICAN FISHERIES SOCIETY, TEXAS A&M CHAPTER 149
AMERICAN FISHERIES SOCIETY, TEXAS CHAPTER 149
AMERICAN INSTITUTE OF FISHERY RESEARCH BIOLOGISTS 151
AMERICAN SOCIETY OF ICHTHYOLOGISTS AND HERPETOLOGISTS 155
AMERICAN SOCIETY OF MAMMALOGISTS 155
BAT CONSERVATION INTERNATIONAL 165
BIG BEND NATURAL HISTORY ASSOCIATION 166
BOY SCOUTS OF AMERICA 168
CENTER FOR ENVIRONMENTAL PHILOSOPHY 175
CENTER FOR THE STUDY OF TROPICAL BIRDS, INC. (Administative Office) 177
CHIHUAHUAN DESERT RESEARCH INSTITUTE 179
COASTAL CONSERVATION ASSOCIATION 181
CONSERVATION DISTRICTS FOUNDATION INC. 187
COUNCIL FOR ENVIRONMENTAL EDUCATION 189
EARTH FOUNDATION 197
ENVIRONMENTAL DEFENSE FUND, INC.
   Texas Office 202
FOSSIL RIM WILDLIFE CENTER 210
GAME CONSERVATION INTERNATIONAL (GAME COIN) 213
INTERNATIONAL ASSOCIATION FOR ENVIRONMENTAL HYDROLOGY (IAEH) 228
INTERNATIONAL PROFESSIONAL HUNTERS' ASSOCIATION 232
LADY BIRD JOHNSON WILDFLOWER CENTER (formerly the National Wildflower Research Center) 246
NATIONAL ASSOCIATION OF CONSERVATION DISTRICTS (League City Office) 263
NATIONAL TRUST FOR HISTORIC PRESERVATION
   Texas and New Mexico Offices 272
NATIONAL WILDLIFE FEDERATION
   Gulf States Natural Resource Center (AR, LA, MS, TX) .. 274
NATIVE PLANT SOCIETY OF TEXAS 276
NATIVE PRAIRIES ASSOCIATION OF TEXAS 277
NATURE CONSERVANCY, THE, TEXAS CHAPTER 282
PRAIRIE GROUSE TECHNICAL COUNCIL 306
SCENIC AMERICA
   Scenic Texas 317
SIERRA CLUB
   Texas Office 319
TEXAS ASSOCIATION OF SOIL AND WATER CONSERVATION DISTRICTS 330
TEXAS B.A.S.S. CHAPTER FEDERATION 330
TEXAS COMMITTEE ON NATURAL RESOURCES 331
TEXAS FORESTRY ASSOCIATION 331
TEXAS ORGANIZATION FOR ENDANGERED SPECIES . 331
TEXAS WILDLIFE ASSOCIATION 331
TROUT UNLIMITED, GUADELOUPE RIVER COUNCIL 334
WELDER WILDLIFE FOUNDATION 345
WESTERN REGIONAL ENVIRONMENTAL EDUCATION COUNCIL 347
WETLAND HABITAT ALLIANCE OF TEXAS 347
WILDLIFE SOCIETY, TEXAS CHAPTER 357

STATE GOVERNMENT ORGANIZATIONS
AGRICULTURAL EXTENSION SERVICE 110
BUREAU OF ECONOMIC GEOLOGY 111
FOREST SERVICE (Texas) 111
GOVERNOR OF TEXAS, GEORGE W. BUSH 110
GUADALUPE-BLANCO RIVER AUTHORITY 111
TEXAS COOPERATIVE FISH AND WILDLIFE RESEARCH UNIT 111
TEXAS DEPARTMENT OF AGRICULTURE 111
TEXAS DEPARTMENT OF HEALTH 111
TEXAS GENERAL LAND OFFICE 112
TEXAS PARKS AND WILDLIFE DEPARTMENT 112
TEXAS SEA GRANT PROGRAM 112
TEXAS STATE SOIL AND WATER CONSERVATION BOARD 112
TEXAS WATER DEVELOPMENT BOARD 112

UTAH
GOVERNMENT ORGANIZATIONS
UPPER COLORADO RIVER COMMISSION 10
DEPARTMENT OF THE INTERIOR
   BUREAU OF RECLAMATION 24
U.S. DEPARTMENT OF AGRICULTURE
   UNITED STATES FOREST SERVICE 32

NON-GOVERNMENTAL ORGANIZATIONS
AMERICAN FISHERIES SOCIETY
   Introduced Fish Section 143
AMERICAN FISHERIES SOCIETY, BONNEVILLE CHAPTER 145
GRAND CANYON TRUST (Utah Office) 216
HAWKWATCH INTERNATIONAL INC. 221
JACK H. BERRYMAN INSTITUTE FOR WILDLIFE DAMAGE MANAGEMENT 242
NATURAL RESOURCES INFORMATION COUNCIL 278
NATURE CONSERVANCY, THE, UTAH CHAPTER 282
SOUTHERN UTAH WILDERNESS ALLIANCE (Moab Office) 326
SOUTHERN UTAH WILDERNESS ALLIANCE (St. George Office) 326
SOUTHERN UTAH WILDERNESS ALLIANCE (SUWA) 326
TREAD LIGHTLY! INC. 332
TROUT UNLIMITED, UTAH COUNCIL 336
UTAH ASSOCIATION OF SOIL CONSERVATION DISTRICTS 340
UTAH B.A.S.S. CHAPTER FEDERATION 340
UTAH NATURE STUDY SOCIETY 340
UTAH WILDERNESS COALITION 340
UTAH WILDLIFE FEDERATION 340
UTAH WOODLAND OWNERS COUNCIL 341
WILDLIFE SOCIETY, UTAH CHAPTER 358

STATE GOVERNMENT ORGANIZATIONS
GOVERNOR OF UTAH, MIKE LEAVITT 113
UTAH COOPERATIVE FISH AND WILDLIFE RESEARCH UNIT (USDI-USGS-BRD-CRU) 113
UTAH DEPARTMENT OF AGRICULTURE 113
UTAH DEPARTMENT OF HEALTH 113
UTAH STATE DEPARTMENT OF NATURAL RESOURCES 113
   Division of Forestry, Fire and State Lands 113
   Division of Oil, Gas and Mining 113
   Division of Parks and Recreation 113
   Division of Water Rights 113
   Division of Wildlife Resources 113
   Office of Energy and Resource Planning 113
   Regional Supervisors 113
   State Soil Conservation Committee 114
UTAH STATE DEPARTMENT OF NATURAL RESOURCES, Division of Water Resources 114
UTAH STATE EXTENSION SERVICES 114
UTAH STATE SOIL CONSERVATION COMMISSION 114

VERMONT
NON-GOVERNMENTAL ORGANIZATIONS
AMERICAN CHESTNUT FOUNDATION, THE 141
ATLANTIC CENTER FOR THE ENVIRONMENT (New England Office) 162
BLUEBIRDS ACROSS VERMONT PROJECT 167
CONSERVATION AND RESEARCH FOUNDATION, INC., THE 186
CONSERVATION LAW FOUNDATION, INC. (CLF) (Vermont Office) 188
ECOTOURISM SOCIETY, THE 199
GREEN MOUNTAIN AUDUBON SOCIETY 218
GREEN MOUNTAIN CLUB INC., THE 218
MERCK FOREST AND FARMLAND CENTER, INC. 254
NATIONAL GARDENING ASSOCIATION 268
NATIONAL WILDLIFE FEDERATION
   Northeast Natural Resource Center (CT, MA, ME, NH, NY, RI, VT) 274
NATURE CONSERVANCY, THE, VERMONT CHAPTER .. 282
TOGETHER FOUNDATION, THE 332
TROUT UNLIMITED, VERMONT COUNCIL 337
TRUST FOR WILDLIFE, INC. 338
VERMONT ASSOCIATION OF CONSERVATION DISTRICTS 341
VERMONT AUDUBON COUNCIL 341
VERMONT B.A.S.S. CHAPTER FEDERATION 341
VERMONT INSTITUTE OF NATURAL SCIENCE 341
VERMONT LAND TRUST 341
VERMONT NATURAL RESOURCES COUNCIL 341

VERMONT STATE-WIDE ENVIRONMENTAL EDUCATION
  PROGRAMS (SWEEP) 341
VERMONT WOODLANDS ASSOCIATION 342
WILD EARTH 348
STATE GOVERNMENT ORGANIZATIONS
AGENCY OF NATURAL RESOURCES 114
  Department of Environmental Conservation 114
  Department of Fish and Wildlife 114
  Department of Forests, Parks, and Recreation 114
  Environmental Board 115
  Vermont Geological Survey 115
GOVERNOR OF VERMONT, HOWARD DEAN 114
UNIVERSITY OF VERMONT EXTENSION 115
  Publications Office 115
VERMONT DEPARTMENT OF AGRICULTURE, FOOD, AND
  MARKETS 115
  Natural Resources Conservation Council 115
  State Conservation Commission 115
VERMONT DEPARTMENT OF HEALTH 115

VIRGIN ISLANDS
NON-GOVERNMENTAL ORGANIZATIONS
NATURE CONSERVANCY, THE, VIRGIN ISLANDS
  CHAPTER 282
VIRGIN ISLANDS CONSERVATION DISTRICT 342
VIRGIN ISLANDS CONSERVATION SOCIETY, INC. 342
STATE GOVERNMENT ORGANIZATIONS
COOPERATIVE EXTENSION SERVICE (VIRGIN ISLANDS)
  115
DEPARTMENT OF PLANNING AND NATURAL RESOURCES
  115
  Division of Fish and Wildlife 116
GOVERNOR OF THE VIRGIN ISLANDS, ROY L.
  SCHNEIDER 115
VIRGIN ISLANDS SOIL AND WATER CONSERVATION
  DIVISION 116

VIRGINIA
GOVERNMENT ORGANIZATIONS
NORTH AMERICAN WETLANDS CONSERVATION
  COUNCIL 9
NATIONAL SCIENCE FOUNDATION 34
DEPARTMENT OF LABOR
  MINE SAFETY AND HEALTH ADMINISTRATION 15
DEPARTMENT OF THE AIR FORCE
  MAJOR AIR COMMANDS 16
DEPARTMENT OF THE ARMY
  ARMY TRAINING AND DOCTRINE COMMAND 19
  HEADQUARTERS, U.S. ARMY TRAINING AND
    DOCTRINE COMMAND 19
  U.S. ARMY CORPS OF ENGINEERS 21
DEPARTMENT OF THE INTERIOR
  U.S. GEOLOGICAL SURVEY 25
  U.S. GEOLOGICAL SURVEY BIOLOGICAL RESOURCES
    DIVISION 26
NON-GOVERNMENTAL ORGANIZATIONS
ALLIANCE FOR THE CHESAPEAKE BAY 138
  CRIS Office 138
AMERICAN ALLIANCE FOR HEALTH PHYSICAL
  EDUCATION AND RECREATION AND DANCE 138
AMERICAN ASSOCIATION FOR LEISURE AND
  RECREATION (AALR) 139
AMERICAN BASS ASSOCIATION, INC. 140
AMERICAN FISHERIES SOCIETY
  Genetics Section 143
  Native People Fisheries Section 143
AMERICAN FISHERIES SOCIETY, TIDEWATER CHAPTER
  149
AMERICAN FISHERIES SOCIETY, VIRGINIA CHAPTER . 149
AMERICAN FISHERIES SOCIETY, VIRGINIA TECH
  CHAPTER 149
AMERICAN GEOLOGICAL INSTITUTE 150
AMERICAN RESOURCES GROUP 154
AMERICAN SPORTFISHING ASSOCIATION 156
AMERICAN WATER RESOURCES ASSOCIATION 156
ARLINGTON OUTDOOR EDUCATION ASSOCIATION, INC.
  160
ASSOCIATION OF CONSULTING FORESTERS OF
  AMERICA 161
CENTER FOR HEALTH, ENVIRONMENT, AND JUSTICE 175
CHELONIA INSTITUTE 178
CHESAPEAKE BAY FOUNDATION, INC. (Virginia Office). 178
COASTAL SOCIETY, THE 182
CONSERVATION FUND, THE 187
COUSTEAU SOCIETY, INC., THE 190
EARTH FORCE 197
ENVIRONMENTAL CAREER CENTER 201
ENVIRONMENTAL ENTERPRISES ASSISTANCE FUND,
  INC. 203
FAIRFAX AUDUBON SOCIETY 205
FISH AND WILDLIFE INFORMATION EXCHANGE 206
FISHAMERICA FOUNDATION 206
FOUNDATION FOR NORTH AMERICAN BIG GAME 210
FUTURE FISHERMAN FOUNDATION 213
INTERNATIONAL ASSOCIATION OF NATURAL RESOURCE
  PILOTS 228
IZAAK WALTON LEAGUE OF AMERICA, INC., THE
  Virginia Division 241
LEGACY INTERNATIONAL 248
NATIONAL ASSOCIATION OF BIOLOGY TEACHERS 262
NATIONAL COALITION FOR MARINE CONSERVATION . 266
NATIONAL FFA ORGANIZATION 267
NATIONAL FORESTRY ASSOCIATION 268
NATIONAL RECREATION AND PARK ASSOCIATION 270
NATIONAL RIFLE ASSOCIATION OF AMERICA 271
NATIONAL SCIENCE TEACHERS ASSOCIATION 271
NATIONAL WATER RESOURCES ASSOCIATION 272
NATIONAL WATERSHED COALITION 272
NATIONAL WILDLIFE FEDERATION 273
NATIONAL WILDLIFE FEDERATION ENDOWMENT, INC. 275
NATIONAL WILDLIFE PRODUCTIONS, INC. 275
NATIONAL WOODLAND OWNERS ASSOCIATION 276
NATURE CONSERVANCY, THE 279
NATURE CONSERVANCY, THE, LATIN AMERICA AND
  CARRIBBEAN DIVISION 281
NATURE CONSERVANCY, THE, VIRGINIA CHAPTER 282
PIEDMONT ENVIRONMENTAL COUNCIL 303
POTOMAC APPALACHIAN TRAIL CLUB 305
PUBLIC LANDS FOUNDATION 307
RESOURCE-USE EDUCATION COUNCIL 310
RESPONSIVE MANAGEMENT 311
SAFARI CLUB INTERNATIONAL
  Washington, DC Office 315
SOUTHERN ENVIRONMENTAL LAW CENTER 325
TERRENE INSTITUTE, THE 330
TROUT UNLIMITED 333
TROUT UNLIMITED, VIRGINIA COUNCIL 337
VIRGINIA ASSOCIATION OF CONSERVATION DISTRICTS
  342
VIRGINIA B.A.S.S. CHAPTER FEDERATION 342
VIRGINIA CONSERVATION NETWORK 342
VIRGINIA FORESTRY ASSOCIATION 342
VIRGINIA NATIVE PLANT SOCIETY 343
VIRGINIA SOCIETY OF ORNITHOLOGY 343
VIRGINIA WILDLIFE FEDERATION 343
WATER ENVIRONMENT FEDERATION 345
WILDLIFE CENTER OF VIRGINIA, THE 350
WILDLIFE SOCIETY, VIRGINIA CHAPTER 358
STATE GOVERNMENT ORGANIZATIONS
DEPARTMENT OF FORESTRY 116
DEPARTMENT OF GAME AND INLAND FISHERIES 116
  Region I 116
  Region II 116
  Region III 116
  Region IV 116
  Region V 116
DEPARTMENT OF MINES, MINERALS AND ENERGY 116
  Division of Energy 117
  Division of Gas and Oil 117
  Division of Mined Land Reclamation 117
  Division of Mineral Mining 117
  Division of Mineral Resources 117
DEPARTMENT OF MINES, MINERALS, AND ENERGY
  Division of Mines 117
GOVERNOR OF VIRGINIA, JAMES S. GILMORE II 116
MARINE RESOURCES COMMISSION (VIRGINIA) 117

GEOGRAPHIC INDEX

NORTHERN VIRGINIA REGIONAL PARK AUTHORITY ... 117
VIRGINIA COOPERATIVE FISH AND WILDLIFE RESEARCH
   UNIT (USDI) 117
VIRGINIA DEPARTMENT OF AGRICULTURE AND
   CONSUMER SERVICES 117
VIRGINIA DEPARTMENT OF CONSERVATION AND
   RECREATION 117
   Board of Conservation and Recreation 118
   Breaks Interstate Park Commission 118
   Chippokes Plantation Farm Foundation 118
   Conservation and Development of Public Beaches Board 118
   Division of Administration 118
   Division of Dam Safety 118
   Division of Natural Heritage 118
   Division of Planning and Recreation Resources 118
   Division of Soil and Water Conservation 118
   Division of State Parks 118
   Virginia Cave Board 118
   Virginia Soil and Water Conservation Board 118
VIRGINIA DEPARTMENT OF ENVIRONMENTAL QUALITY
   118
VIRGINIA DEPARTMENT OF HEALTH 118
VIRGINIA MUSEUM OF NATURAL HISTORY 118
VIRGINIA OUTDOORS FOUNDATION 118
VIRGINIA SEA GRANT PROGRAM 119
VIRGINIA STATE EXTENSION SERVICES 119

WASHINGTON
GOVERNMENT ORGANIZATIONS
INTERNATIONAL PACIFIC HALIBUT COMMISSION 8
ENVIRONMENTAL PROTECTION AGENCY 10
DEPARTMENT OF THE ARMY
   U.S. ARMY CORPS OF ENGINEERS 21

NON-GOVERNMENTAL ORGANIZATIONS
ABUNDANT LIFE SEED FOUNDATION 133
ADOPT-A-STREAM FOUNDATION, THE 134
AFRICAN WILDLIFE NEWS SERVICE 135
AMERICAN FISHERIES SOCIETY
   Western Division 144
AMERICAN SOCIETY OF LIMNOLOGY AND
   OCEANOGRAPHY 155
CASCADIA RESEARCH 174
EARTHJUSTICE LEGAL DEFENSE FUND (formerly Sierra
   Club Legal Defense Fund, Inc.)
   Seattle, Washington Office 198
EARTHSTEWARDS NETWORK 198
ENVIRONMENTAL EDUCATION ASSOCIATION OF
   WASHINGTON 203
FEDERATION OF WESTERN OUTDOOR CLUBS 206
FRIENDS OF DISCOVERY PARK 211
FRIENDS OF THE EARTH
   Northwest Regional Office (WA, OR, ID) 212
FRIENDS OF THE SAN JUANS 212
GREENHOUSE ACTION 218
HOOD CANAL LAND TRUST 222
INTERNATIONAL ASSOCIATION OF WILDLAND FIRE
   (formerly Fire Research Institute) 229
INTERNATIONAL BICYCLE FUND 229
INTERNATIONAL PLANT PROPAGATION SOCIETY, INC.,
   THE 232
INTERNATIONAL SNOW LEOPARD TRUST 232
ISSAQUAH ALPS TRAILS CLUB (I.A.T.C.) 239
IZAAK WALTON LEAGUE OF AMERICA, INC., THE
   Washington Division 241
LEAGUE OF WOMEN VOTERS OF WASHINGTON 248
LIGHTHAWK
   Northwest Field Office 249
LONG LIVE THE KINGS 249
MARINE CONSERVATION BIOLOGY INSTITUTE 251
MOUNTAINEERS, THE (Conservation Division) 261
NATURE CONSERVANCY, THE, WASHINGTONG CHAPTER
   282
NORTH CASCADES CONSERVATION COUNCIL 291
NORTHWEST ECOSYSTEM ALLIANCE 293
NORTHWEST ENVIRONMENT WATCH 293
NORTHWEST INTERPRETIVE ASSOCIATION 293
NORTHWEST RENEWABLE RESOURCES CENTER 293
NW ENERGY COALITION 294
OLYMPIC PARK ASSOCIATES 296
OLYMPIC PARK INSTITUTE 297
OLYMPIC WILDLIFE RESCUE 297
PACIFIC NORTHWEST TRAIL ASSOCIATION 300
PACIFIC SEABIRD GROUP 300
PTARMIGANS, THE 306
PUGET SOUNDKEEPER ALLIANCE 307
RIVERS COUNCIL OF WASHINGTON (formerly Northwest
   Rivers Council) 313
SAN JUAN PRESERVATION TRUST, THE 315
SIERRA CLUB
   Northwest Office 319
SOCIETY FOR CONSERVATION BIOLOGY 321
SOUND EXPERIENCE 323
TEENS FOR RECREATION AND ENVIRONMENTAL
   CONSERVATION (TREC) 329
TROUT UNLIMITED, WASHINGTON COUNCIL 337
WASHINGTON ASSOCIATION OF CONSERVATION
   DISTRICTS 343
WASHINGTON B.A.S.S. CHAPTER FEDERATION 343
WASHINGTON ENVIRONMENTAL COUNCIL 343
WASHINGTON FARM FORESTRY ASSOCIATION 344
WASHINGTON FOUNDATION FOR THE ENVIRONMENT 344
WASHINGTON NATIVE PLANT SOCIETY 344
WASHINGTON RECREATION AND PARK ASSOCIATION 344
WASHINGTON TOXICS COALITION 344
WASHINGTON TRAILS ASSOCIATION 344
WASHINGTON WILDERNESS COALITION 345
WASHINGTON WILDLIFE AND RECREATION COALITION
   345
WASHINGTON WILDLIFE FEDERATION 345
WASHINGTON WILDLIFE HERITAGE FOUNDATION
   (including Heritage Land Trust 345
WILDLIFE SOCIETY, WASHINGTON CHAPTER 358
WOLF HAVEN INTERNATIONAL 361
YMCA EARTH SERVICE CORPS 365

STATE GOVERNMENT ORGANIZATIONS
COLUMBIA RIVER GORGE COMMISSION 119
DEPARTMENT OF ECOLOGY 119
   Central Regional Office 119
   Eastern Regional Office 119
   Northwest Regional Office 119
   Southwest Regional Office 119
DEPARTMENT OF FISH AND WILDLIFE (WASHINGTON) 119
GOVERNOR OF WASHINGTON, GARY LOCKE 119
INTERAGENCY COMMITTEE FOR OUTDOOR
   RECREATION (IAC) 120
STATE PARKS AND RECREATION COMMISSION
   (WASHINGTON) 120
   Eastern Region 120
   Northwest Region 120
   Puget Sound Region 120
   Southwest Region 120
WASHINGTON COOPERATIVE FISH AND WILDLIFE
   RESEARCH UNIT (USDI) 120
WASHINGTON DEPARTMENT OF AGRICULTURE   120
WASHINGTON DEPARTMENT OF NATURAL RESOURCES
   120
   Central Region 121
   Northeast Region 121
   Northwest Region 121
   Olympic Region 121
   South Puget Sound Region 121
   Southeast Region 121
   Southwest Region 121
WASHINGTON NATURAL HERITAGE PROGRAM 121
WASHINGTON SEA GRANT PROGRAM 121
WASHINGTON STATE CONSERVATION COMMISSION . 121
WASHINGTON STATE EXTENSION SERVICES 121
WASHINGTON STATE OFFICE OF ENVIRONMENTAL
   EDUCATION 122

WEST VIRGINIA
GOVERNMENT ORGANIZATIONS
DEPARTMENT OF THE ARMY
   U.S. ARMY CORPS OF ENGINEERS 21

NON-GOVERNMENTAL ORGANIZATIONS
A.B. ENVIRONMENTAL EDUCATION CENTER 133

AMERICAN BASS ASSOCIATION OF WEST VIRGINIA, THE 140
AMERICAN FISHERIES SOCIETY, WEST VIRGINIA CHAPTER 149
APPALACHIAN TRAIL CONFERENCE 158
BROOKS BIRD CLUB INC., THE 168
INSTITUTE FOR EARTH EDUCATION, THE 227
IZAAK WALTON LEAGUE OF AMERICA, INC., THE
  West Virginia Division 241
NATURE CONSERVANCY, THE, WEST VIRGINIA CHAPTER 282
ORGANIZATION OF WILDLIFE PLANNERS 298
TROUT UNLIMITED, WEST VIRGINIA COUNCIL 337
WEST VIRGINIA ASSOCIATION OF CONSERVATION DISTRICT SUPERVISORS ASSOCIATION, INC. 346
WEST VIRGINIA B.A.S.S. CHAPTER FEDERATION 346
WEST VIRGINIA HIGHLANDS CONSERVANCY 346
WEST VIRGINIA WILDLIFE FEDERATION, INC. 346
WILDLIFE SOCIETY, WEST VIRGINIA CHAPTER 358
WOODLAND OWNERS ASSOCIATION OF WEST VIRGINIA 361

STATE GOVERNMENT ORGANIZATIONS
DIVISION OF NATURAL RESOURCES 122
GOVERNOR OF WEST VIRGINIA, CECIL UNDERWOOD 122
WEST VIRGINIA BUREAU OF ENVIRONMENT 122
WEST VIRGINIA COOPERATIVE FISH AND WILDLIFE RESEARCH UNIT 122
WEST VIRGINIA DEPARTMENT OF AGRICULTURE 122
  West Virginia State Soil Conservation Committee 122
WEST VIRGINIA GEOLOGICAL AND ECONOMIC SURVEY 123
WEST VIRGINIA STATE EXTENSION SERVICES 123

WISCONSIN
GOVERNMENT ORGANIZATIONS
GREAT LAKES INDIAN FISH AND WILDLIFE COMMISSION 7
MINNESOTA-WISCONSIN BOUNDARY AREA COMMISSION 9
U.S. DEPARTMENT OF AGRICULTURE
UNITED STATES FOREST SERVICE 32

NON-GOVERNMENTAL ORGANIZATIONS
AMERICAN FISHERIES SOCIETY, WISCONSIN CHAPTER 149
BOTANICAL CLUB OF WISCONSIN 167
CITIZENS NATURAL RESOURCES ASSOCIATION OF WISCONSIN, INC. 180
COMMUNITY CONSERVATION CONSULTANTS/HOWLERS FOREVER, INC. 184
FEDERAL WILDLIFE OFFICER'S ASSOCIATION 205
INTERNATIONAL CRANE FOUNDATION 230
IZAAK WALTON LEAGUE OF AMERICA, INC., THE
  Wisconsin Division 241
LAKE SUPERIOR GREENS 246
NATIONAL ASSOCIATION OF STATE OUTDOOR RECREATION LIAISON OFFICERS 264
NATIONAL WOODLAND OWNERS ASSOCIATION (FORMERLY WISCONSIN WOODLAND OWNERS ASSOCIATION) 276
NATURE CONSERVANCY, THE, WISCONSIN CHAPTER 282
NORTH AMERICAN BLUEBIRD SOCIETY 288
RIVER ALLIANCE OF WISCONSIN 312
SIERRA CLUB
  Midwest Office 319
SOCIETY FOR ECOLOGICAL RESTORATION 321
SOCIETY OF TYMPANUCHUS CUPIDO PINNATUS LTD. 322
TREES FOR TOMORROW, INC., NATURAL RESOURCES EDUCATION CENTER 333
TROUT UNLIMITED, WISCONSIN COUNCIL 337
WHITETAILS UNLIMITED INC. 348
WILD ONES - NATURAL LANDSCAPERS, LTD 349
WILDLIFE SOCIETY, WISCONSIN CHAPTER 358
WISCONSIN ASSOCIATION FOR ENVIRONMENTAL EDUCATION, INC. 359
WISCONSIN ASSOCIATION OF LAKES (WAL) 359
WISCONSIN B.A.S.S. CHAPTER FEDERATION 359
WISCONSIN LAND AND WATER CONSERVATION ASSOCIATION 359
WISCONSIN PARK AND RECREATION ASSOCIATION .. 360
WISCONSIN SOCIETY FOR ORNITHOLOGY, INC., THE. 360
WISCONSIN WATERFOWL ASSOCIATION, INC. 360
WISCONSIN WILDLIFE FEDERATION 360

STATE GOVERNMENT ORGANIZATIONS
GOVERNOR OF WISCONSIN, TOMMY G. THOMPSON .. 123
WISCONSIN CONSERVATION CORPS 123
WISCONSIN COOPERATIVE FISHERY RESEARCH UNIT (USDI) 123
WISCONSIN COOPERATIVE WILDLIFE RESEARCH UNIT (USDI) 123
WISCONSIN DEPARTMENT OF AGRICULTURE 123
WISCONSIN DEPARTMENT OF AGRICULTURE (Land and Water Resources Bureau) 123
WISCONSIN DEPARTMENT OF NATURAL RESOURCES 124
WISCONSIN DEPARTMENT OF PUBLIC INSTRUCTION. 124
WISCONSIN ENVIRONMENTAL EDUCATION BOARD (WEEB) 124
WISCONSIN GEOLOGICAL AND NATURAL HISTORY SURVEY 125
WISCONSIN SEA GRANT INSTITUTE 125
WISCONSIN STATE EXTENSION SERVICES 125

WYOMING
NON-GOVERNMENTAL ORGANIZATIONS
AMERICAN FISHERIES SOCIETY, COLORADO and WYOMING CHAPTER 145
CRAIGHEAD ENVIRONMENTAL RESEARCH INSTITUTE 190
FOUNDATION FOR NORTH AMERICAN WILD SHEEP ... 210
INSTITUTE AND SCHOOL FOR ENVIRONMENT AND NATURAL RESOURCES, Univeristy of Wyoming (IENR and SENR) 227
IZAAK WALTON LEAGUE OF AMERICA, INC., THE
  Wyoming Divisoin 241
JACKSON HOLE CONSERVATION ALLIANCE 242
JACKSON HOLE LAND TRUST 242
NATURE CONSERVANCY, THE, WYOMING CHAPTER .. 282
POWDER RIVER BASIN RESOURCE COUNCIL 305
SIERRA CLUB
  Northern Plains 319
TROUT UNLIMITED, WYOMING COUNCIL 337
WESTERN ASSOCIATION OF FISH AND WILDLIFE AGENCIES 346
WILDLIFE SOCIETY, WYOMING CHAPTER 358
WOLF FUND, THE 360
WYOMING ASSOCIATION OF CONSERVATION DISTRICTS 364
WYOMING B.A.S.S. CHAPTER FEDERATION 364
WYOMING NATIVE PLANT SOCIETY 364
WYOMING OUTDOOR COUNCIL 364
WYOMING WILDLIFE FEDERATION 364

STATE GOVERNMENT ORGANIZATIONS
DEPARTMENT OF COMMERCE 125
ENVIRONMENTAL QUALITY DEPARTMENT 125
GAME AND FISH DEPARTMENT 125
GOVERNOR OF WYOMING, JIM GERINGER 125
INDUSTRIAL SITING DIVISION/DEPARTMENT OF ENVIRONMENTAL QUALITY 126
STATE FORESTRY DIVISION (WYOMING) 126
WYOMING COOPERATIVE FISH AND WILDLIFE RESEARCH UNIT (USDI) 126
WYOMING DEPARTMENT OF AGRICULTURE 126
WYOMING DEPARTMENT OF COMMERCE
  Division of State Parks and Historic Sites 126
WYOMING STATE BOARD OF LAND COMMISSIONERS 126
WYOMING STATE EXTENSION SERVICES 126
WYOMING STATE GEOLOGICAL SURVEY 126

New Organization Information:

Please use this form to submit a request to list your organization in the 2000 *Conservation Directory*, or make a suggestion of an organization you feel should be included in the directory to the editorial staff.

Information submitted on photocopies of this form will be accepted.

PLEASE TYPE OR PRINT CLEARLY

❏ **Request for Listing** ❏ **Suggested New Organization**

Organization Name: _____

Address: Street _____

        City _____ **State** _____ **Zip** _____

Email: _____ **WWW:** _____

Phone Number: _____ **Fax Number:** _____

Contact Person: _____

✶ **SUBMISSIONS CAN BE MADE ONLINE AT www.nwf.org/pubs/consdir/**

Further information will be sent to each organization.

Please Mail Form To: NATIONAL WILDLIFE FEDERATION®
                      ATTN: RUE GORDON
                      8925 LEESBURG PIKE
                      VIENNA, VA 22184
                      Phone: (703) 790-4402; Fax: (703)790-4468
                      Email: gordon@nwf.org

UPDATE YOUR LISTING:

Information submitted on photocopies of this form will be accepted.

PLEASE TYPE OR PRINT CLEARLY

Organization Name: _____

Address: Street _____

        City _____ **State** _____ **Zip** _____

Email: _____ **WWW:** _____

Phone Number: _____ **Fax Number:** _____

Current Page as found in the 1999 Directory _____

Changes to your description:

_____

_____

_____

_____

Add Contact Person: _____

Remove Contact Person: _____

Please give us a contact name for the person we can obtain updates from.

Name _____ **Phone** _____

Further updating materials will be sent to all organizations listed in the 1999 *Conservation Directory* when updating begins for the 2000 *Conservation Directory*.

Please Mail Form To: NATIONAL WILDLIFE FEDERATION®
                      ATTN: RUE GORDON
                      8925 LEESBURG PIKE
                      VIENNA, VA 22184
                      Phone: (703) 790-4402; Fax: (703)790-4468
                      Email: gordon@nwf.org

NOTES

NATIONAL WILDLIFE FEDERATION®
8925 Leesburg Pike Vienna, Virginia 22184-0001

http://www.nwf.org/nwf

NOTES

NATIONAL WILDLIFE FEDERATION®
8925 Leesburg Pike Vienna, Virginia 22184-0001

http://www.nwf.org/nwf

NOTES

NATIONAL WILDLIFE FEDERATION®
8925 Leesburg Pike Vienna, Virginia 22184-0001

http://www.nwf.org/nwf

NOTES

NATIONAL WILDLIFE FEDERATION®
8925 Leesburg Pike Vienna, Virginia 22184-0001

http://www.nwf.org/nwf